International Maritime Dictionary

An encyclopedic dictionary of useful maritime terms and phrases, together with equivalents in French and German.

RENÉ de KERCHOVE

SECOND EDITION

VAN NOSTRAND REINHOLD COMPANY
New York

TO
MY WIFE

Copyright © 1961, 1948 by Van Nostrand Reinhold Company Inc.
Library of Congress Catalog Card Number 83-3564
ISBN 0-442-02062-7

All rights reserved. No part of this work covered by the copyright hereon may be reproduced or used in any form or by any means — graphic, electronic, or mechanical, including photocopying, recording, taping, or information storage and retrieval systems — without written permission of the publisher.

Printed in the United States of America

Published by Van Nostrand Reinhold Company Inc.
135 West 50th Street
New York, New York 10020

Van Nostrand Reinhold Company Limited
Molly Millars Lane
Wokingham, Berkshire RG11 2PY England

Van Nostrand Reinhold
480 La Trobe Street
Melbourne, Victoria 3000, Australia

Macmillan of Canada
Division of Canada Publishing Corporation
164 Commander Boulevard
Agincourt, Ontario M1S 3C7 Canada

16 15 14 13 12 11 10 9 8 7 6 5 4 3 2

Library of Congress Cataloging in Publication Data

Kerchove, René de, baron
   International maritime dictionary.

  Includes bibliographical references and index.
  1. Naval art and science — Dictionaries. 2. Dictionaries, Polyglot. I. Title.
V24.K33   1983   623.8'03   83-3564
ISBN 0-442-02062-7

PREFACE TO THE SECOND EDITION

In the 15 years that have elapsed since the publication of the first edition, many new terms have come into use in marine transportation and related fields. Some of them denote new methods and devices which scientific progress has brought to navigation, marine meteorology and naval architecture. Other new terms stem from changes in construction and equipment, navigational aids, as well as in marine insurance practices and many related topics.

In the preparation of this edition the policy has been to select from the compiler's extensive files the more important of these terms, especially those which are coming into widespread use. At the same time, many terms have been added which were not included in the first edition, and which are clearly within the scope of this book. A considerable number of these new entries were suggested by users of the first edition. It is to be hoped that this second edition will continue to enjoy a similar measure of cooperation.

PREFACE TO THE FIRST EDITION

This volume is a handy book of reference placed at the disposal of all who are interested professionally or otherwise in marine transportation and allied subjects. It includes words and definitions related to seamanship, commercial shipping, maritime and international law, ship construction and equipment, naval architecture, marine insurance and average, navigation, oceanography and marine meteorology, methods and gear used in commercial fisheries, navigational appliances and nautical instruments, shipbuilding materials, boatbuilding, yachting, and whaling.

Few, if any, maritime dictionaries in the English language have been published during the second quarter of this century. On the other hand, there is hardly any recent book on shipping, shipbuilding, yachting, naval architecture, and similar subjects, which does not include a glossary of terms. This fact seems to prove that definitions of the various terms contained in the text are considered essential. The aim of the compiler has been to build up a comprehensive work which would cover the terms scattered in these various glossaries and to introduce a considerable amount of new material in this ever-expanding field.

A unique feature of the work is the description of the salient characteristics of native or local craft from all parts of the world. This particular field has been woefully neglected in earlier books.

At the request of the United States Government, large sections of this material were placed at its disposal during the war. The designation, identity, and description of native craft in our far-flung theatres of operation proved valuable.

The inclusion of French and German equivalents has been deemed necessary in view of the fact that, in the technical as well as in the commercial and legal fields, the multiplicity of languages used by the shipping and seafaring communities is much greater than in any other profession. The war period during which all contacts with Europe were severed has unfortunately prevented me from completing this task as thoroughly as I should have wished.

Where the subject matter tends to interlock considerably with neighboring branches of science and practice I have endeavored to adhere to the nautical side of the boundary. I would like to point out to the users of this book that all matters solely concerned with the Navy war vessels, and naval affairs in general, have been purposely omitted.

Deep-sea commercial fishing with its methods and gear has been given an important place, contrary to what has been the custom in earlier works. Terms related to marine power plants have been kept to a strict minimum, as their terminology is in most instances similar to that of stationary power plants on land.

Owing to the disappearance of deep-sea sailing vessels, the number of definitions related to this branch of nautical knowledge has been reduced in order to make room for basic terms on welding, telecommunications, radio navigation, and other subjects which have lately found expanding applications in the shipping field.

Although great care has been exercised to ensure the accuracy of information, and in spite of conscientious proofreading, some errors may have been overlooked. I will be grateful to have these called to my attention.

R. de K.

New York, N. Y.
April, 1947

ACKNOWLEDGMENTS

I would like to thank the following publishers and organizations for their generous assistance during the period when this volume was being compiled.

The Lawyers Co-operative Publishing Company, Rochester, N. Y.
American Journal of International Law, Washington, D. C.
Prentice-Hall Inc., New York City.
Houghton Mifflin Company, Boston, Mass.
Simmons-Boardman Publishing Corporation, New York City.
Shipbuilding and Shipping Record, London.
The Rudder, New York City.
McGraw-Hill Book Company, Inc., New York City.
Marine Engineering and Shipping Review, New York.
Welin Davit and Boat, Perth Amboy, N. J.
Yachting Inc., New York.
American Bureau of Shipping, New York.
Society of Naval Architects and Marine Engineers, New York.
Hyde Windlass Company, Bath, Maine.
D. Appleton-Century Company, Inc., New York.
Encyclopaedia Britannica, Chicago, Ill.
Journal of Commerce and Shipping Telegraph, Liverpool, England.

In the compilation of this book help has been given at various times by many people. Although the number of those who have cooperated is too large to permit recording all their names here, I should like to list the following men to whom I am particularly grateful.

Mr. William Cogswell, Secretary, Grace Line, New York.
Captain William J. Meyer, New York.
Mr. George G. Sharp, Naval Architect, New York.
Mr. E. L. Stewart, Marine Design Department, Standard Oil Company of New Jersey.
Mr. Frank A. Taylor, Curator of Engineering, U. S. National Museum, Washington, D. C.
Mr. John Lyman (U.S.N.R.), Hydrographic Office, Washington, D. C.
Mr. James Hornell, St. Leonards on Sea.
Mr. Frank G. G. Carr, Assistant Librarian of the House of Lords, London.
Vice-Admiral J. D. Nares (retired), International Hydrographic Bureau, Monaco.
Captain M. Adam, French Navy, Brest.
Mr. E. G. Barillon, Ingénieur Général du Génie Maritime, Paris.
Mr. P. V. H. Weems, Annapolis, Md.
Professor Littauer, Naval Academy, Annapolis, Md.

A

A. International code of signals burgee vertically divided, white at the hoist, blue at the fly. When hoisted singly indicates that the vessel is undergoing speed trials. When used as a signal between tug and tow it means "Towing hawser is fast."

A#1. A symbol or registry mark issued by Lloyd's Register of shipping to indicate that the quality of equipment of a vessel classed with this register is of first rate. Also used colloquially in a general sense to imply first class or first rate.

AA. ALWAYS AFLOAT (*chartering*).

A.A.R. AGAINST ALL RISKS (*marine insurance*).

A.B. ABLE BODIED, placed after a seaman's name on ship's papers.
See **Able Seaman.**

A.H. AFTER HATCH.

ALT. ALTITUDE.

A.P. AVERAGE PAYABLE (*marine insurance*).

A. P. ADDITIONAL PREMIUM (*marine insurance*).

A. R. ALL RISKS (*marine insurance*).

A/S. ALONGSIDE.

A/T. AMERICAN TERMS (*grain trade*).

AAK. A bargelike, flat-bottom sailing craft from the Netherlands used for transportation and fishing.

The most noticeable feature is the construction of the bow. There is no stem; the bottom planking or plating forms a flat surface which curves up longitudinally to the level of the deck or gunwale. The smaller units are sloop-rigged and the larger (*Aakschip*) ketch-rigged. All are fitted with leeboards. The small *Lemmer Aak*, which originates from the river Lemmer, is used for pleasure or fishing. It is rigged like a *Boeijer* and engages in the herring fisheries with fixed nets or lines.

AALBOOT. A Dutch sailing boat, of the same type as the *Botter*, employed in eel fisheries with a stationary bag net (*Ankerkuil*) of conical shape, about 90 ft. long.

It is built with low foredeck, raised afterdeck and fish well, about 13 ft. long, amidships. Most of these boats are nowadays built of steel. The rig consists of a collapsible pole mast stepped in a tabernacle with gaffmainsail, foresail, and jib. Length 45 to 49 ft. Breadth 14.4 to 15 ft. Depth 6.5 to 7.2 ft.

ABACK. A sail is said to be aback when the wind presses on it in such a way as to impede the forward motion of the vessel or to force it astern.
Fr: *Coiffé; Masqué;* Ger: *Back Legen.*
See **To Brace Aback, Taken Aback.**

ABAFT. Astern of toward the stern. At the rear of, with reference to a ship or any part of it. Opposite to *forward of*.
Fr: *Sur l'arrière de;* Ger: *Hintenaus.*

ABAFT THE BEAM. Behind a horizontal line drawn through the middle of a ship at right angles to the keel.
Fr: *Sur l'arrière du travers;* Ger: *Achterlich von dwars.*

ABANDONMENT. Insurance term used to indicate that the damage suffered by a vessel is such as to constitute a constructive total loss, and that the assured may abandon the subject matter to the underwriters and claim for a total loss even though the insured property is recoverable and/or being repaired.
Fr: *Abandon; Délaissement;* Ger: *Ausgebung; Abandon; Abandonierung.*
See **Notice of Abandonment.**

ABANDONMENT CLAUSE. A marine insurance clause that states the conditions under which the owners of a vessel are allowed to abandon the ship to the underwriters. It generally refers to abandonment in the event of capture, seizure, detention, or blockade.
Fr: *Clause d'Abandon;* Ger: *Abandonklausel.*

ABEAM. In a direction 90 degrees from the ship's head. Opposite the waist of the ship.
Fr: *Par le travers;* Ger: *Quer Ab; Dwars Ab.*

ABLE SEAMAN. One who performs all regular and emergency duties required in the deck department of a ship; stands watch at bow of vessel or in crow's nest for possible obstructions; takes depth soundings; transmits information to navigating bridge by voice or telephone; steers vessel as directed, using either a wheel on the bridge or emergency steering apparatus at the stern; breaks out, rigs, overhauls, and stows cargo-handling gear and running gear; overhauls lifeboats and lifeboat gear and lowers and raises lifeboats; makes minor repairs to deck and deck equipment; washes decks; chips paint and paints wood or metal fixtures; splices wire rope and cordage; stows and removes cargo from hold; knows the various knots and how to worm parcel, serve and seize. He must be able to hold up his end of the job when it comes to climbing and working in places where both armhold and foothold are difficult.

The Seaman's Act of March 4th, 1915, requires that on American merchant marine vessels operating on the high seas able bodied seamen must be 18 years old or more and must have had three years' previous service on deck at sea or on the Great Lakes on vessels of 100 gross tons or over. On merchant vessels of 500 tons gross or under operating in sheltered waters (bays and sounds) and which do not carry passengers, any deck hand who is 18 years of age or over and has had at least 12 months of service either at sea and in connecting waters or on the Great Lakes, may be rated as able seaman. Every American able seaman must hold a certificate issued by the government. When working aboard vessels carrying liquid cargo he must hold a tankerman's certificate.

In Great Britain the term able-bodied seaman has been recently superseded in Board of Trade regulations by "efficient deck hand."

Fr: *Matelot;* Ger: *Vollmatrose.*

U. S. Coast Guard, Manual for Lifeboatmen and Able Seamen (revised), Washington, 1945.

ABOARD. In or on a ship or other floating vessel. On the deck or in the hold of a ship. Sometimes called on board.

Fr: *A Bord;* Ger: *An Bord.*

ABOVE DECK GIRDER. A horizontal girder built on the outside of a hatch coaming and running fore and aft between hatchways. It is connected with brackets and bulb angles to the deck beams. Also called hatch stiffener.

Ger: *Überdeckträger.*

ABOX. The position of the head yards when they are braced aback, the after sails remaining full.

Fr: *Contre brassé devant;* Ger: *Mit Vorsegel Back Gebrasst.*

ABREAST. Lying or moving side by side. Used to indicate the situation of a vessel in regard to another object: lying so that the object is on a line with the beam.

Fr: *Par le travers;* Ger: *Dwars Ab.*

ABSENCE FLAG. A small, square, blue flag hoisted at the starboard spreader of a yacht to signify that the owner is not on board. It is kept flying until his return. At night it is often replaced by a blue light hoisted in the same place.

Ger: *Entfernungsflagge.*

ABSOLUTE CONTRABAND. A term applied in international law to articles manufactured and primarily or ordinarily used for military purposes in time of war.

Fr: *Contrebande Absolue;* Ger: *Absolute Konterbande.*

ABURTON. A method of stowage of casks or other cargo in which the goods are placed athwartship instead of in a fore-and-aft direction.

Fr: *Arrime en Travers.*

ACCELERATION. A change in the rate of motion of any body. In navigation applied to heavenly bodies. The acceleration of the moon is the increase of the mean motion caused by a slow change in the eccentricity of the terrestrial orbit.

Fr: *Accélération;* Ger: *Beschleunigung.*

ACCIDENT BOAT. A term which applies in passenger vessels to a ship's boat kept permanently swung outboard and ready to be launched at shortest notice in the event of anyone falling overboard. A special crew is told off to man it at the signal "man overboard." This boat as a rule is smaller and lighter than the ordinary lifeboat. Typical dimensions: 22 ft. by 7 ft. by 3 ft. Sometimes called emergency boat or sea boat.

ACCOMMODATION. Rooms and living quarters for persons on board a vessel.

Fr: *Emménagements;* Ger: *Wohnraum.*

See **Crew's Accommodation, Passenger Accommodation.**

ACCOMMODATION BERTH (G. B.). A berth alongside a pier or quay regularly reserved by a shipping line with fixed sailing dates, and subject to long term agreement with harbor authorities.

ACCOMMODATION LADDER. A term applied to a portable flight of steps suspended over the side of a vessel from a gangway to a point near the water, providing an easy means of access from a small boat. Accommodation ladders are usually supplied with two platforms, one at each end. Sometimes called gangway ladder.

Fr: *Echelle de Coupée;* Ger: *Fallreepstreppe.*

ACCRUES. See **False Meshes**.

ACHROMATIC. A term applied to optical lenses in which aberration and colors dependent thereon are partially corrected.
Fr: *Achromatique;* Ger: *Akromatisch.*

ACLINIC LINE. See **Magnetic Equator**.

A-COCKBILL. See **Cockbill**.

ACORN. A small ornamental piece of wood of conical or globular shape above the masthead vane to prevent the latter from being blown off.
Fr: *Girouette;* Ger: *Flügelspill; Eichel.*

ACOUSTIC SOUNDING. Also called echo sounding. The principle of acoustic sounding consists in indirect evaluation of depth by means of the time taken by a sound wave to travel over this depth. It is based, therefore, on the precise knowledge of the speed of propagation of sound through sea water, which averages 4,900 ft. per second. In order to obtain a sounding a submarine sound wave or group of waves is produced. The departing wave acts first on the microphonic transmitter, then after being reflected by the bottom, the returning wave or echo acts on the arrival microphonic receiver. The first microphone starts the time measurement. The second stops it. The distance traveled by the wave is deduced from the interval of time, taking the velocity of the wave through the water to be constant. The use of special apparatus of high precision has made possible the measurement of extremely brief intervals of time with sufficient accuracy for navigational purposes. The depth is automatically shown on a luminous scale or on a recording sheet.
Fr: *Sondage Acoustique;* Ger: *Schallotung.*
Hutchings, "Echo Sounding Equipment for Ships," Institution of Engineers and Shipbuilders in Scotland. *Transactions,* vol. 79 (1935-36): International Hydrographic Bureau (Special Publications), *Hydrographic Review* (Monaco), vols. 2 and 3 (1925); vol. 7 (1930); vol. 8 (1931); vol. 10 (1933); vol. 14 (1937); vol. 16 (1939).

ACT OF GOD. An expression used in bills of lading meaning any cause which proceeds from the violence of nature, or that kind of force of the elements which human ability could not have foreseen or prevented.
The expression Act of God is not synonymous with *force majeure* but it includes every loss by *force majeure* in which human agency by act or negligence has had no part, and which cannot be foreseen. In charter parties and bills of lading the result of an act of God ranks first among the risks from liability for which shipowners exclude themselves.
Fr: *Force Majeure; Fait de Dieu;* Ger: *Höhere Gewalt; Elementarereignisse.*

ACT OF WAR. A term employed in various meanings. It has no distinctive technical significance in international law, but wherever used it refers to the employment of force.
Fr: *Act de Guerre; Fait de Guerre;* **Ger:** *Gewaltakte.*

ACTUAL TOTAL LOSS. A ship is considered an actual loss when damaged to such an extent as to be unrepairable, or if the labor or materials required to carry out the necessary repairs are not procurable.
Fr: *Perte Totale Réelle;* Ger: *Absoluter Total Verlust.*

ADDRESS COMMISSION. A commission paid by the vessel at the port of discharge to the ship's agents or to the charterers.
Fr: *Commission d'Adresse;* Ger: *Adresskommission.*

ADEWU. West African dugout canoe from Togo with long pointed ends and pronounced sheer, employed in the coastal fisheries.

ADIRAPATAM BOAT. An Indian balance-board fishing canoe about 37 ft. long, used for fishing in muddy shallow waters. It is steered by a pair of quarter steering boards instead of a fixed rudder. The length of the balance board is about 34 ft.

ADJACENT ZONE. Expression used in international law to denote waters beyond the limit of the territorial sea, where rights have been asserted by a great many states for specific functions or interests, such as customs enforcement, security, fishing and so on. Also called: Contiguous zone.

ADJUSTABLE BLADE. In a built-up propeller, a blade that can be rotated through a small angle, thereby altering the pitch, as is occasionally found necessary in practice after a vessel is in service.
Fr: *Aile à Pas réglable;* Ger: *Verstellbarer Flügel.*

ADJUSTABLE PITCH PROPELLER. A built-up propeller with provision to adjust the pitch plus or minus a few inches.
Fr: *Hélice à pas réglable;* Ger: *Verstellpropeller.*

ADJUSTER. An expert specially employed

in cases of general average to ascertain and state the amount or percentage that each of the parties interested must pay in order to make up for the loss sustained by some for the general good. Also called average adjuster, average stater, average taker.

Fr: *Dispacheur;* Ger: *Dispacheur.*

ADJUSTING WEDGE. One of the wooden wedges used in launching to raise a vessel up and onto the cradle from the keel blocks. Oak or ash is generally used for these wedges. They are somewhat longer than the width of the ways. The taper is from ⅜ to ¾ in. to the foot. The width about 4 in. Sometimes called launching wedge.

Fr: *Languette;* Ger: *Stapelkeil; Schlagkeil.*

ADMIRAL. 1. A naval officer of flag rank. **2.** The skipper of a North Sea fishing boat who gives the sailing directions and the signals for shooting or hauling the gear to a fleet of 50 to 60 trawlers working together. **3.** A large wooden fid about 40 inches long, formerly used to open the eyes of hemp rigging.

ADMIRALTY. The system of jurisprudence relating to and growing out of the jurisdiction and practice of the admiralty courts. The body of law that concerns maritime cases both civil and criminal.
Benedict, E. C., *The Law of American Admiralty,* New York, 1940; Mayers, E., *Admiralty Law and Practice in Canada,* London, 1928; Roscoe, E. S., *Admiralty Jurisdiction and Practice,* London, 1931.

ADMIRALTY COEFFICIENT. A coefficient used in preliminary estimations of the power required in a new design to attain the desired speed. It is represented by the formula:

$$C = \frac{D^{\frac{2}{3}} \times V^3}{ihp}$$

where D is the displacement in tons, V the speed in knots, ihp the indicated horsepower. A single value of the coefficient, although reasonably satisfactory throughout the normal speed range of generally similar ships, is not applicable to ships of varying type. Also called admiralty constant.

Fr: *Coefficient de l'Amirauté;* Ger: *Admiralitätskoeffizient.*

The accuracy of the approximation and the reliability of the method depend wholly on the similarity between ships and propellers under comparison. It is based on the assumptions that the propulsive efficiency is constant, and that the whole resistance of the ship follows the law of surface friction resistance.

"Circular C and the Admiralty Constant," *Marine Engineer and Motorship Builder* (London), vol. 48 (August, 1925).

ADMIRALTY COURT. A term applied to a court that has cognizance of all maritime cases whether of civil or criminal nature, such as collisions, contracts for seamen's wages, actions to recover possession of a ship, damages and injuries to shipping, salvage, pilotage and towage cases, charter parties and bills of lading, bottomry, respondentia, jettison, maritime contributions and average, damages and trespasses taking place on the high seas, actions to recover necessities supplied to a ship, or the furnishing of materials and repairs. These courts exist in England and the United States.

Fr: *Cour d'Amirauté;* Ger: *Seeamt.*

In England it forms a branch of the Probate, Divorce and Admiralty Division of the High Court of Justice, the judge being appointed by the Crown as one of the judges of the High Court. The English Court of Admiralty is twofold, the Instance Court and the Prize Court. The civil jurisdiction of the Instance Court extends generally to such contracts as are made upon the sea, and are founded in maritime service or consideration.

In the United States, admiralty jurisdiction is vested in the district courts, subject to revision by the Circuit Court of Appeals and the Supreme Court of the United States.

ADMIRALTY DROITS (G.B.). Proceeds from the sale of enemy ships seized in port or captured by noncommissioned vessels, or from wrecks and derelicts.

ADMIRALTY FLAG. A British sea flag used by the Lords of the Admiralty when afloat. It is a plain red flag with a clear yellow anchor in the center.

ADMIRALTY JURISDICTION. Admiralty and maritime jurisdiction extends to all things done upon and relating to the sea; to transactions relating to commerce and navigation, to damages and injuries upon the sea, and to all maritime contracts, torts, and injuries. The term "maritime contracts" includes among other things charter parties, affreightment marine hypothecations, contracts for maritime services in the building, repairing, supplying, navigating, and salvaging of ships.

Fr: *Juridiction Maritime;* Ger: *Seegerichtsbarkeit.*

In U. S. A. the admiralty jurisdiction given to the courts by the Constitution extends over all public navigable waters, without regard to their being influenced by the tide. In other countries it extends only to everything done on the water below the low water mark.

ADMIRALTY LAW. See **Admiralty.**

ADMIRALTY PUMP. A direct-acting simplex or duplex pump with the piston and plunger on a vertical rod.

ADRIFT. Floating at random; not fastened by any kind of moorings; at the mercy of winds and currents; loose from normal anchorage. A vessel is said to be adrift when she breaks away from her moorings, warps, and so on.

Fr: *En Dérive;* Ger: *Treibend.*

AD VALOREM DUTY. A customs duty which is a percentage made upon the value of goods.

Fr: *Droit ad Valorem;* Ger: *Wertzolle.*

AD VALOREM FREIGHT. Bill of lading freight charged on goods of very high value at so much per cent on the declared value of the goods.

Fr: *Fret ad Valorem;* Ger: *Wert Fracht.*

ADVANCE. The distance a vessel continues to travel on a course before responding to a change of helm. The distance that the ship has advanced in a direction parallel to the original course measured from the point where the helm was put over.

See **Transfer.**

ADVANCE FREIGHT. Freight taken from shippers to cover ship's disbursement during loading. The sum advanced is shown on the bills of lading and is insured by the shippers.

Fr: *Avance de Fret;* Ger: *Frachtvorschuss.*

ADVANCE MONEY. Funds advanced by a shipmaster to seamen during the voyage at any port where the vessel may load or deliver cargo. The amount so advanced is limited by law and usually represents one-half of the wages earned and remaining due.

Fr: *Avance;* Ger: *Handgeld.*

ADVANCE NOTE (G.B.). A draft upon the owner or agent of a vessel given by the master to a seaman on signing the articles of agreement. Advance notes are as a rule for a month's wages and, as they are payable three days after the sailing of the ship, they enable the vessel's seamen to leave some provision for their relatives ashore. This practice is illegal in the United States.

Ger: *Vorschussanweisung; Heuernota.*

ADVANCE SAIL. See **Advance Staysail.**

ADVANCE STAYSAIL. A light weather four-sided staysail set above the main staysail in staysail-rigged schooner yachts. It is hoisted to the mainmast truck with its head running at a steep angle or parallel to the headstay to a point on the foremast.

The luff runs down the foremast to which it is attached either by slides on a track on the after side or by hanks to a strong tricing stay. The clew to the sail comes aft to a point abreast the mainmast and sheets to the taffrail or deck. It is said to be highly efficient and a beautifully setting windward driving sail. It was invented by Starling Burgess and first used in 1925 on the schooner *Advance.* According to their shape these sails are known as short hoist advance, heavy advance, wide advance, or balloon main topmast staysail.

ADVECTION FOG. A fog formed by a body of relatively warm and humid air moving over a relatively cold surface. The great majority of sea fogs are advection fogs.

ADZE. A hand tool similar to an ax, but with a thin, arching blade, having its edge in a plane at right angles to the handle. It is used by shipwrights for rough and fine trimming of planks and timbers lying horizontally, and in working about drydocks. The user ordinarily straddles the work and swings the adze down between his legs in the cutting stroke.

Fr: *Herminette;* Ger: *Deichsel.*

AEROFOIL PROPELLER. A propeller designed in accord with aerodynamic principles based on the circulation theory instead of as a true screw. The blades, instead of being of true geometrical form, are of a streamlined airfoil section with blunt or rounded leading edge and thin following edge. The face pitch decreases toward the hub and the arched driving face of the blades has its maximum ordinate at about $\frac{1}{3}$ the cord from the leading edge. The margin of efficiency of the aerofoil propeller over the true screw is about 10 to 12%.

Allan J. F., *"Aerofoil Sections and Their Adoption in Propeller Design,"* North East Coast Institution of Engineers and Shipbuilders, Newcastle upon Tyne, *Transactions,* vol. 54 (1938).

AERIAL. See **Antenna.**

AERIAL WIRE. A transmission wire having one end attached to the connector of a midship-log boom and the other to the log clock mounted on the wing of the navigation bridge.

AEROLITE. A meteoric stone that falls on the earth's surface from beyond the atmosphere.

Fr: *Aérolite;* Ger: *Luftstein; Aerolith.*

AFFIRMATIVE FLAG. Letter "C" of the International Code of Signals used as a single letter signal. Means "Yes."

Fr: *Pavillon Affirmatif;* Ger: *Bejahungsflagge.*

AFFREIGHTMENT. A contract of affreightment is one with a shipowner to hire his ship or part of it for the carriage of goods. Such a contract generally takes the form of a charter party or a bill of lading. In French law, the terms freighting and affreighting have different usages. The owner of a ship is called the freighter (*fréteur*); he is the lessor. The merchant is called the affreighter (*affréteur*); he is the hirer.

Fr: *Affrètement;* Ger: *Befrachtung.*
Scrutton, T. E., *The Contract of Affreightment,* London, 1933.

AFJORDBAAT. Generic name for Norwegian open boats of the type originating from the Afjord district and distinguished from each other by the number of oars used. The *femboring* is a 10-oared boat; the *firing*, 8-oared; the *seksring*, 6-oared; and the *faering*, 4-oared. Length 19.5 to 52 ft.

AFLOAT. In a floating condition; the converse of aground.

Fr: *A flot;* Ger: *Flott; Schwimmend.*

AFT. In, near, or toward the stern of a vessel.

Fr: *A l'arrière; Derrière;* Ger: *Hinten.*
See **Abaft, Fore and Aft.**

AFTERBODY. That part of a vessel that is abaft the greatest transverse section. The portion of the hull abaft amidships. It consists of the run and the portion of the parallel body abaft amidships.

Ger: *Hinterschiff.*

AFTER BREAST ROPE. A breast rope running out from the afterend of the ship across the counter, or nearly so.

Fr: *Traversier Arrière;* Ger: *Hintere Dwarsfeste.*

AFTER COMPASS. An emergency steering compass which forms part of the statutory equipment of seagoing vessels of the merchant marine. It is placed aft on the center line of the ship either in the steering engine room or on the poop deck.

Ger: *Achterdeckskompass.*

AFTERDECK. Part of a deck extending abaft the midship portion of a vessel.

Ger: *Hinterdeck.*

AFTERGUARD. 1. Term formerly used by seamen berthed in the forecastle or fore deckhouse to designate the master, officers, and in a general sense all those who were quartered amidships and in the afterpart of the ship.

2. In a yacht, the owner and his guests.

AFTERHOODS. The whole of the afterends of the planking rabbeted into the sternpost.

Fr: *Barbes de l'Arrière;* Ger: *Hintere Plankenenden.*

AFTERLEECH. The aftermost or lee margin of a fore-and-aft sail.

Fr: *Chûte au Point;* Ger: *Das Aussenliek; Achterliek.*

AFTER MAST. The mast nearest the stern. In a one or two mast vessel (except in ketches and yawls) it is the mainmast. On a three mast vessel it is the mizzen mast; on a four mast vessel the jigger mast; on a five mast vessel the spanker mast; on a six mast vessel the driver mast and on a seven mast vessel the pusher mast. The designation of masts in schooners where there are more than two masts is the same as in a ship or barque.

Fr: *Mât Arrière;* Ger: *Achtermast.*

AFTERNOON WATCH. The watch from noon till 4 P.M. The nautical day begins at noon.

Ger: *Nachmittagswache.*

AFTER PEAK. The space between the aftermost transverse watertight bulkhead and the stern frame. It is frequently used as a trimming tank, or as a freshwater tank.

Fr: *Coqueron Arrière;* Ger: *Hinterpiek.*

AFTER PEAK BULKHEAD. The aftermost transverse watertight bulkhead, installed to isolate possible leakage in the stern, which can result from a variety of causes, among them being corrosion or damage in the stern tube, shell leaks caused by propeller vibration, loose rivets and the like. Also called stuffing box bulkhead.

Fr: *Cloison de Presse étoupe;* Ger: *Stopfbuchsenschott.*

AFTER PERPENDICULAR. A vertical line through the intersection of the load water line with the after side of the rudder post.

Fr: *Perpendiculaire Arrière;* Ger: *Hintere Perpendikel; Hinteres Lot.*
See **Forward Perpendicular.**

AFTERRAKE (U. S.). That part of the stern that overhangs the keel.

AFTER SAILS. The sails that belong to the main and mizzen masts in three-masted vessels, and that keep the ship to windward. All canvas on the main mast of a brig.
Fr: *Phares de l'Arrière;* Ger: *Achtersegel; Hintergeschirr.*

AFTERSPRING. A hawser or line that leads aft from a point in the ship to a point on shore, checking a vessel from going ahead. Such lines are generally used in mooring or docking. The after bow spring, after waist spring, and after quarter spring make fast on board at points in the bow, waist, and quarter, respectively.
Fr: *Garde Montante de l'Arrière; Amarre de Poste Arrière;* Ger: *Heckspring.*

AFTER TIMBERS. A series of radiating cant frames abaft the fashion-pieces and below the wing transom, stepped partly on the deadwood and partly on the stepping pieces bolted to the sides of the inner sternpost.
Fr: *Arcasse;* Ger: *Heck.*

AFTER YARDS. Term used to denote collectively all yards other than those on the foremast.

AGE. The interval between the time of new and full moon and the time of the next spring high water.
Fr: *Age;* Ger: *Alter.*

AGE OF TIDE. The interval between the transit of the moon at which a tide originates and the appearance of the tide itself. Sometimes called retard of tide.

AGALE.
See **Alemania.**

AGENCY FEE. A fee charged to the ship by the ship's agent or shipowner, representing payment for services while the ship was in port. Sometimes called attendance fee.
Fr: *Frais d'Agence;* Ger: *Vertretergebühren.*

AGETAGURI-AMI-BUNE. Japanese fishing sampan of Aomori district (Northern Japan). Length 36 ft. Breadth 7.2 ft. Depth 2.85 ft. Crew 9.
One of the features of the hull is that there are 3 projecting beams on the starboard side and only 2 on the port side. None of these beams extends across the vessel as usual in this type of craft. The boat is rigged with one mast that sets a square sail of about 390 sq. ft. area.

AGETON'S NAVIGATIONAL METHOD. A method devised to reduce the amount of labor and time of computation in solving the astronomical triangle. It consists of a set of conveniently arranged tables arranged primarily for computation of altitudes and azimuths from the dead reckoning position. U. S. Hydrographic Office, Publication 211, Washington.

AGGEBOOT. Small open boat about 7 ft. long, 3 ft. breadth at stern, 1 ft. at bows, used for shrimping on the German North Sea coast.

AGONIC LINE. A line joining points on the earth's surface where there is no magnetic variation.
Ger: *Agonische Linie.*

AGOWU. A West African dugout canoe from Togo, hewn out of a palm tree trunk.

AGREED VALUE CLAUSE. A bill of lading clause which limits the responsibility of the carrier to a named sum per package or per shipping unit.
Fr: *Clause Valeur Agréée;* Ger: *Abschätzungsklausel.*

AGROUND. When a vessel rests on something solid other than the blocks in a drydock or slipway she is said to be aground. A vessel "takes the ground" when the tide leaves it aground for want of sufficient depth of water, a fairly frequent occurrence in open docks.
Fr: *Echoué;* Ger: *Am Grund; Festsitzen.*

AGULHAS CURRENT. A branch of the South Indian equatorial current that flows down through the Mozambique Channel along the eastern coast of Africa, and upon arriving off the Agulhas bank is deflected south and farther to the east. A strong current that attains sometimes a speed of 4½ knots.

AGWALLA. Asiatic seaman serving as fireman under Lascar agreement.

AHEAD. In a direction or position pointing forward. Forward of the bow.
Fr: *En Avant;* Ger: *Voraus.*

AHEAD REACH. The distance traveled by a mechanically propelled ship proceeding at full power from the time of reversal of the engines until the ship is brought to a dead stop.
Ger: *Vorwärts Reiche.*

AHEAD STEERING TEST. A seatrail test carried out with the vessel steaming ahead at full designed power. The rudder is moved (1) from amidships to hard left (2) from hard left to hard right (3) from hard right to hard left (4) from hard left to amidships or vice versa; the rudder being held in each hard over position for approximately ten seconds. In large vessels equipped with two steering engines the test is repeated for each engine.

AHIMA. African dugout canoe used in the fisheries of the Gold Coast. It varies much in size: the smaller type, 10 to 12 ft. long and 2 or 3 ft. broad, is called *ahima*; a larger type, some 30 ft. long by 6 ft. beam, is called *anlese*. All larger canoes have weatherboards in the bow consisting of planks raised 2 ft. or more, to keep out the water.

The natives venture far out to sea in these canoes, using a large rectangular mat sail spread by a bamboo sprit. There is a single mast, to the head of which the sail is either hoisted by means of a small line run through the mast or, more frequently, made fast with a seizing. Such a sail is worked by means of a sheet and a brace on the sprit. Another kind of square-shaped sail is used by fishermen without true mast, but held up by 2 or 3 poles.

AHLIMA. A very small West African dugout canoe from Togo, of the same type as the *adewu*.

AHOY. An exclamation to attract the attention of persons at a distance when hailing a vessel or boat.

Fr: *Ohé; Ho;* Ger: *Ahoi; Ho.*

AHULL. A sailing ship under bare poles with helm lashed alee, letting the vessel take up her own position. Also called hulling.

Fr: *A la Cape Sèche;* Ger: *Vor Top und Takel.*

AID TO NAVIGATION. A charted mark to assist navigators, such as buoys, beacons, lights, radio beacons, and the like. Generally, any information published for the assistance of mariners.

Fr: *Aide de Navigation.*

AIR-COOLED CARGO. Cargo cooled by the air blast system in which trunks are laid in the holds and decks through which cold air is blown all around and through the cargo. The trunks are fitted with small sliding doors that can be opened or closed during the voyage, according to which part of the hold requires more or less cold air.

AIR COURSE. Air spaces from 4 to 6 in. wide, running fore and aft in the sides of a wooden ship to provide for a circulation of air between the frames, ceiling, and planking. Their purpose is to prevent decay in the timbers.

Fr: *Virure d'Aération;* Ger: *Luftgang.*

AIR FUNNEL. An empty space formed by the omission of a timber in the upper works to admit fresh air into a ship's hold and convey the foul air out.

AIR HAMMER. A mechanical hammer operated by compressed air that acts on a small piston and delivers a succession of rapid blows. Pneumatic riveting hammers are usually designed to size according to stroke. They vary from 4 to 9 in. The two most popular sizes for shipbuilding are the 5- and 6-in. stroke. By fitting the pneumatic hammer with an appropriate tool, it can be used for chipping, or caulking. Also called pneumatic hammer, pneumatic riveter.

Fr: *Marteau à Air Comprimé;* Ger: *Presslufthammer.*

AIR HOLE. One of the air passages provided in the upper part of the floor plates and longitudinals of a double bottom so that when the water rises above the lightening holes the air contained in the tank may still have ample means of escape and nowhere check the rise of water and the complete filling of the tank.

Fr: *Trou d'Air;* Ger: *Luftloch.*

AIR PIPE. A pipe running from a fuel oil tank, or a ballast tank or other water space, to the upper deck to prevent the formation of air locks when the liquid is pumped in, or inversely. Air pipes are fitted at the outboard corners of each tank and at the opposite end to that at which the filling pipe is placed. In tanks that may be pumped up, the upper end is made permanently open and fitted with a gooseneck.

Fr: *Tuyau d'Air;* Ger: *Luftrohr.*

AIR RESISTANCE. That part of a ship's resistance to motion that is due to the resistance of the air to the above-water portion of the ship moving through it. Sometimes called wind resistance. With superstructures of ordinary type, the air resistance is approximately 2½ per cent of the water resistance, when the ship moves through still air. A head wind equal to the ship's speed will increase this figure to 10 per cent.

Fr: *Résistance à l'air;* Ger: *Luftwiderstand.*

Hughes, G., "The Effect of Wind on Ship Performance," I.N.A., London, *Transactions*, vol. 75 (1933); Stevens, E. A., "Wind Resistance," *Jour.* A.S.N.E., vol. 48 (1936); Hughes, G., "Air Resistance of Ship's Hulls," Institute of Engineers and Shipbuilders in Scotland, *Transactions*, vol. 83 (1939).

AIR SCOOP.
See **Wind Catcher.**

AIR STRAKE. The uppermost strake of ceiling in a wooden hull. It is put on just below the sheer clamp with a narrow opening between the top of the strake and the bottom of the sheer clamp for air circulation.
Fr: *Virure d'Aération;* Ger: *Luftgang.*

AIR WINCH. A type of winch used on small motor craft. It is driven by low-pressure air supplied by a separate oil engine installed in the engine room and coupled to an air compressor. This delivers air to a container connected to the winches or winch by ordinary piping.
Fr: *Treuil à Air Comprimé;* Ger: *Press Luftantrieb Winde; Druckluftgetriebene Winde.*

AIYEBU. A single-outrigger dugout canoe from the D'Entrecasteaux Islands (British New Guinea) with long, pointed, solid ends. It is mostly propelled by paddles, but when a favorable wind is blowing, a temporary mast with a long rectangular sail of interwoven coconut leaves is set in the bow of the canoe. This canoe will hold 2 to 8 persons.

AKAALA. Single-outrigger Australian dugout canoe of the Walmbaria natives from Flinders Island (North Queensland) with sharp bow, rounded forefoot, and shelflike projection at the stern. Length over-all 16 to 19 ft. Breadth 16 to 22 in.
The outrigger float is connected to the hull by 6 pairs of double sticks that pierce the washstrakes. It is 12 ft. long and lashed at a distance of 2 ft. from the canoe.

ĀKONA. A double canoe used for local transportation at Port Moresby (British New Guinea). It is composed of two dugouts called *asi,* with a platform.

ALA. Small single outrigger dugout canoe about 12 ft. long, 17 in. deep, of the Lorabada tribe of Papua (British New Guinea).

ALAMANA KAIGHI. Open rowing boat with pointed stern employed with a seine net in the fisheries of the Sea of Marmara and the Black Sea. The larger craft have a length of about 40 ft. with a tonnage of 6½ tons and are propelled by 12 oars double banked. The smaller boats are about 30 ft. in length, with a capacity of 4 tons, and pull 8 oars.

ALAMANATA. A Bulgarian fishing boat decked at stern, usually propelled by oars. A small sail is set with fair wind. Approximate length 45 ft. Employed in the coastal mackerel fisheries.

ALEE. On or toward the sheltered side of a ship. Away from the wind. Also called to leeward.

Fr: *Sous le Vent;* Ger: *Leewärts.*

ALEMIA. A single-outrigger Australian dugout canoe of the Mutumui natives from Barrow Point (North Queensland). Similar to the *tuppal.* Sometimes called *agale.*

ALGAE. Flowerless marine plants, either one-celled, or primitive multicelled types, found chiefly as seaweeds, but also growing in rivers, marshes, and so on. They are grouped by color as blue-green, green, brown, red, and yellow-green.
Fr: *Algue;* Ger: *Algen.*

The first four are usually attached plants, the last is characteristically a floating form. They do not exhibit a true root, leaf, or stem such as higher types of plant life possess. The Red Sea owes its name to a floating form of blue-green alga that has a secondary red pigment, and is responsible for the red color sometimes seen in the surface waters. A typical green alga is Ulva (sea lettuce). The "kelp beds" are made up of brown algae, as is the gulfweed, Sargassum. The red algae are typified by sea moss, Polysiphonia, and the coral alga, Lithothamnion.

ALHETA. An open boat used for trading between the islands of San Miguel and Santa Maria in the Azores. The rig is composed of three masts with lateen sails, the mainmast being foremost. Some of these boats occasionally carry a jib or headsail. The crew includes 8 men and 2 boys. Length about 60 ft. Breadth 8½ to 10 ft.

ALIA. A double-hulled seagoing canoe of Tongan design used by the natives of Samoa. The two canoes are held together by a platform.

ALIDADE. That part of a transit or theodolite consisting of the telescope, standards, upper plate, and the attached levels and verniers.

ALIEN TONNAGE TAX. A federal tax of 50 cents per net ton imposed upon vessels of American registry on which an alien is an officer, unless such an alien fills a vacancy below the rank of master during a foreign voyage or a voyage between Atlantic and Pacific U. S. ports.

ALIGNMENT. Arrangement of lights or objects in one straight line.
Fr: *Alignement;* Ger: *Leitung.*

ALIS-ALIS. A type of fishing *proa* used in eastern Java. The hull is planked and built with a keel. The ends are terminated by flat surfaces Y- or T-shaped and decorated with bright colored paintings. It is similar in hull form to the trading *jangolan,* but smaller. The rig consists of two masts with triangular shaped sails.

ALIST. Said of a ship in a transversely inclined position, having a list, keeled over.
Fr: *Gîté*.

ALLEYWAY. A narrow corridor in passengers' or crews' accommodations. Sometimes called passageway.
Fr: *Coursive*; Ger: *Verkehrsgang*.

ALL FOURS MOORINGS. A method of mooring in which the ship is held with 4 riding chains from bows and quarters. Sometimes called four arms moorings.
Fr: *Corps Mort à Quatre Itagues*; Ger: *Vierkant Vertauung*.

ALLISION. The striking of a moving vessel against one that is stationary.

ALLOTMENT. A portion, usually not exceeding one-half, of a seaman's wages made payable to a relative or other designated person, or to a bank for his account.

ALLOTMENT NOTE. An order for payment of a portion, not exceeding one-half, of a seaman's wages to a relative.
Fr: *Note de Délégation*; Ger: *Anweisung*.

ALLOWANCE. A fixed scale expressed in seconds per mile and used in yacht racing to equalize some assumed difference in "size," as determined by an empirical formula, such as the former "Thames measurement rule," the former "Seawanhaka rule," or the present-day "International rule" and "Universal rule." Sometimes called time allowance.
Fr: *Allégeance*; Ger: *Rabatt*.

ALL RISKS. A term loosely used in marine insurance. It means all the risks printed or written in the policy as distinct from "all risks from whatsoever nature." It is often used synonymously with the term "with average" to distinguish it from an insurance on F.P.A. terms.
Fr: *Tous Risques*.

ALL TIME SAVED. The chartering expression "All time saved both ends" is used in connection with dispatch money. It means that time (lay days) for loading and discharging is reversible and usable at either end, dispatch money or demurrage being settled at port of discharge.

ALL TOLD. Expression used in charter parties with reference to deadweight capacity. It means that the capacity mentioned in the charter represents the ship's total carrying capacity including bunkers, water, provisions, dunnage, stores and spare parts.

ALMANAC, NAUTICAL. An annual publication containing the astronomical ephemeris for calculating a ship's position from observations of the celestial bodies.
Fr: *Ephémérides Nautiques*; Ger: *Nautisches Jahrbuch*.

Nautical almanacs are issued by the leading maritime nations. The Hydrographic Office (U. S.) publishes two editions, a complete edition for the use of astronomers, hydrographers, and others engaged in calculations of great precision, and another edition conveniently arranged for the use of aviators and others using rapid methods of navigation. Various private almanacs are issued containing additional information regarding coastal lights, buoyage, instruments, tables, and so on, of value to the mariner.

ALOFT. On or to a higher part of a ship, as the rigging, generally with reference to the deck. Overhead.
Fr: *En Haut*; Ger: *Oben*.

ALONGSIDE.
See Free Alongside.

ALONGSIDE DATE (G.B.). The date when a vessel will be ready to receive export cargo.

ALTAR STEP. One of the stepped courses provided in the upper part of the side walls of a drydock, used for supporting the wale shores.
Fr: *Gradin*; Ger: *Galerie*; *Stufenweg*.

ALTERNATING AND FLASHING LIGHT. An alternating light with short flashes followed by a longer period of darkness.
Fr: *Feu alternatif clignotant*; Ger: *Wechselfeuer mit Blinken*.

ALTERNATING FIXED AND FLASHING LIGHT. Alternating light with steady, relatively dim light, varied at intervals by a brighter flash.
Fr: *Feu alternatif fixe à éclat*; Ger: *Fest und Blitz Wechselfeuer*.

ALTERNATING FIXED AND GROUP FLASHING LIGHT. Alternating light with steady and relatively light followed by a group of flashes at regular intervals.
Fr: *Feu alternatif fixe à éclats groupés*; Ger: *Fest und Grupperblitz Wechselfeuer*.

ALTERNATING GROUP FLASHING LIGHT. Alternating light with several flashes in quick succession followed by a dark period.
Fr: *Feu alternatif à éclats groupés*; Ger: *Wechselfeuer mit Gruppblinken*.

ALTERNATING GROUP OCCULTING LIGHT. Colored light with short periods of darkness in groups followed by steady light.

Fr: *Feu alternatife à occultations groupées;* Ger: *Gruppen unterbrochenes Wechselfeuer.*

ALTERNATING OCCULTING LIGHT. Alternating light with, at regular intervals, a sudden and total eclipse, the duration of darkness being always less than or equal to that of the light.

Fr: *Feu alternatif à occultations;* Ger: *Wechselfeuer.*

ALTERNATING LIGHT. With reference to aids to navigation, the term alternating added to the character of a light indicates that during the system of changes there is an alteration in the color of the light. When used alone the word alternating refers to a fixed light whose color alters at regular intervals.

Fr: *Feu Alternatif;* Ger: *Wechselfeuer.*

ALTITUDE. Arc of a circle of altitude contained between a celestial body and the horizon.

Fr: *Hauteur;* Ger: *Höhe.*

See **Apparent Altitude, Circles of Altitude, Circles of Equal Altitude, Double Altitude, Equal Altitude, Ex-Meridian Altitude, Meridian Altitude, Observed Altitude, Parallel Altitude, Simultaneous Altitudes, True Altitudes.**

ALTITUDE AZIMUTH. A navigational method used for obtaining the bearing of a heavenly body by solving the astronomical triangle for the angle at the zenith, or azimuth.

Ger: *Hohenazimut.*

ALTOCUMULUS. A cloud formation of white or grayish fleecy cloudlets, usually rounded, and partly shaded. They are often found in flocks or rows, frequently so crowded that the cloudlets join in the central portion. The average altitude is 13,000 ft.

ALTOSTRATUS. A dense gray cloud formation usually sheetlike in form, but at times thin enough so that the sun and moon can be seen faintly shining through. Occasionally this type occurs as a compact, dull grayish mass. The average altitude is 15,000 ft.

ALUMINUM. A light-weight, silver-white, nonferrous metal that forms alloys of exceptional strength/weight ratio. It is highly resistant to atmospheric corrosion, but is very susceptible to corrosion in the presence of salt water.

See **Aluminum Foil.**

Fr: *Aluminium;* Ger: *Aluminium.*

Aluminum Alloys in Marine Construction, Shipbuilder and Marine Engine Builder, Newcastle upon Tyne, vol. 46 (March, 1939); Lamb, J., Aluminum in Shipbuilding, Shipbuilding and Shipping Record (London), vol. 53, (May, 1939); Taylor, G. O., Aluminum and Its Alloys in Marine Construction, Metal Industry (London), vol. 62 (March-April, 1943).

Aluminum alloys usually contain more than 90 per cent aluminum, the remainder being copper, manganese, and magnesium, or magnesium, silicon, and chromium. Such alloys in sheets and extended sections have been used occasionally for the construction of ship's lifeboats, and small craft. In merchant ship construction partition bulkheads, cabin linings, deckhouses, scuttles, port lights, window and skylight frames, and ventilation trunking have been made of aluminum alloys.

Aluminum alloys can be wrought, forged, cast and worked. With proper heat treatment full strength can be developed in the stronger alloys. However, they are difficult to weld, in comparison with other construction metals, and do not solder easily.

ALUMINUM BRONZE. An alloy which consists of copper with about 9% aluminum, and up to 5% iron and nickel. Used for the manufacture of moderate size propellers, and also for die-cast propellers of small craft. It is particularly resistant to cavitation and erosion as well as to the more normal types of corrosion.

Fr: *Bronze d'aluminum;* Ger: *Aluminum Metall.*

ALUMINUM FOIL. Thin sheets of aluminum rolled to a thickness of 0.00028 in. and used in refrigerated storage and cargo spaces as insulating material.

Ger: *Aluminium Folien.*

Its insulating properties result from the fact that the surfaces of the aluminum reflect radiant heat, and that the thin sections of the foil conduct very little heat directly.

When installed in crumpled form it is, for all practical purposes, without weight; a cubic foot weighs but 3 oz., as compared with 10 lbs. for cork board. It has the added advantage of being both fire- and vermin-proof.

ALUMINUM PAINT. A covering used for metal and wood. It is very rust-resistant and possesses excellent covering power. The pigment is composed of aluminum bronze powder or paste, made up of tiny flat flakes of pure aluminum.

Fr: *Peinture Aluminium;* Ger: *Aluminium Farbe.*

A very hard-drying spar varnish or a synthetic resin varnish is used as a vehicle. About 2 lbs. of powder to the gallon of vehicle is considered sufficient. On iron or steel a primer of rust-inhibitive paint such as red lead is first applied and followed with 2 coats of aluminum paint. It is largely used for ventilators, davits, standards, railing, and so on. In holds and companionways, where light is at a premium, the high reflectivity of aluminum paint has led to its use in these parts of the ship.

On wood, aluminum paint can be used both as a primer and as a finishing coat. As a primer it is particularly effective, since it seals the wood, keeping moisture entirely out.

Aluminum Paint, Marine Engineering and Shipping Age (New York), vol. 40, January, 1935.

ALVARENGA. A name applied to a boat or lighter used along the coast of Pernambuco and Bahia (Brazil) to transport goods between ship and shore. It is sometimes rigged with a small mast and sail. Length 32 to 60 ft. Capacity 20 to 120 tons. In the province of Rio it is known by the name of *saveiro.*

ALWAYS AFLOAT. A chartering term by which is meant that there must be sufficient depth of water, so that the vessel can lie afloat on her laden draft at all times of the tide at the berth, anchorage or dock where she is to load or discharge. It is generally held that there is no breach of contract if the vessel can only get to and from the assigned berth at certain times of the tides.

Fr: *Toujours à flot;* Ger: *Immer flott.*

AMA-BUNE. A Japanese open seine boat used in conjunction with the *uomi-bune* and the *onaka-bune* for working scare cord net.

AMBERGRIS. A biliary secretion having ambrein as its principal constituent, arising in the intestines of the sperm whale. It occurs in lumps weighing from a few ounces to 100 lbs. It may be found in the animal, floating in the sea, or washed up on the shore. Specific gravity between 0.78 and 0.92; melting point ranging from 60° to 65° C. It is extensively used in the preparation of perfumes.

Fr: *Ambregris;* Ger: *Bernstein.*

Stevenson, C. H., *Aquatic Products in Arts and Industry,* Washington, 1902.

AMERICAN BUREAU LENGTH. Ship's length as used for classification purposes and determined according to rules of American Bureau of Shipping. Same as Lloyd's Length. It is the distance in feet on the estimated summer loadline, from the fore side of the rudder or sternpost.

AMERICAN BUREAU OF SHIPPING. A classification society and register of shipping founded in New York City in 1862 under the name of American Shipmaster's Association. In 1898 the name was changed to American Bureau of Shipping. Until the beginning of the First World War its activities were largely confined to American-built coasting vessels. In 1916 it was united with the Great Lakes Register. Under the provisions of the United States Load-Line Acts of 1929 and 1935 it has the authority to assign load lines.

Symbols: ✠ **A.1.** is assigned to vessels built under special supervision of the bureau's surveyors to the requirements of the rules for any trade in any part of the world at the appropriate minimum freeboard.

✠ signifies that the vessel has not been built under supervision of the bureau.

E. This letter placed after the classification symbol signifies that the equipment of the vessel is in compliance with the requirements.

✠ **AMS.** indicates that the machinery and boilers have been built under the society's survey.

"**With freeboard,**" after the symbol ✠ **A.1.,** indicates that the vessel has been built under survey to modified scantlings for a particular freeboard which is assigned by the society.

Luckenbach, J. L., "The American Bureau of Shipping," Society of Naval Architects and Marine Engineers, *Historical Transactions* (New York, 1945).

AMERICAN CLAUSE. A clause contained in marine insurance policies when the insured has two insurances upon the same interest, in the same property, and for the same risk.

Under this clause the underwriters become liable according to the order of date of their policies, and the insured can recover from the second underwriter only where the amount of the first policy is insufficient to pay the loss. This clause is limited in its operation solely to cases of double insurance.

AMERICAN INSTITUTE OF MARINE UNDERWRITERS. Organization founded in New York in 1898 whose membership includes ocean marine insurance firms established in U. S. A. and foreign underwriting companies admitted to do marine insurance transactions in U. S. A. The Institute does not write insurance, its functions being those of advice and information. It has four standing committees, one on admissions, one on forms and clauses, one on legislation and one on relations with carriers.

AMERICAN VESSEL. A term which includes all documented vessels, also any undocumented vessel owned, chartered by or made available to the United States Government, or any department or agency thereof. The term also applies to any American owned tug, barge or other watercraft (documented or undocumented) used in essential water transportation or in the fishing trade or industry.

AMERICAN WHIPPING. A whipping put on the end or middle of a rope, and in which the ends are first reef knotted together instead of being cut off close to the whipping.

AMERICAN WHITEWOOD. A general name for various hardwoods, which includes tulip wood, basswood, canary wood. These woods are light and fairly tough. They are free from knots, easily worked, and bend well when steamed. They are very open grained and porous but are made durable by dosing with an oil filling.

AMIDSHIPS. Generally speaking, the word amidships means in the middle portion of a vessel. The point of intersection of two lines, one drawn from stem to stern, the other across the beam (or widest part) is the actual midships. By extension, amidships is also employed to locate any object or part of the ship lying in the line of the keel.

Fr: *Au Milieu du Navire;* Ger: *Mittschiffs.*
See **Midship Section.**

AMPHIDROMIC POINT. Point on a tidal chart where the cotidal lines meet.
Fr: *Point Amphidromique;* Ger: *Amphidromien.*

AMPLITUDE. The angle at the zenith between the prime vertical and the vertical circle passing through the body observed.
Fr: *Amplitude;* Ger: *Amplitude.*
See **Tidal Amplitude.**

AMPLITUDE OF PITCH. The extent, measured in degrees, of a ship's angular motion about a transverse axis through her center of gravity.
Fr: *Amplitude du tangage;* Ger: *Stampfamplitude.*

AMPLITUDE OF ROLL. The extent (in degrees) of transverse oscillations of a ship about its longitudinal axis in a seaway.
Fr: *Amplitude du roulis;* Ger: *Rollamplitude.*

ANABATIC WIND. The converse of katabatic wind. A daytime local wind caused by the warming up of the atmosphere in low ground that causes convectional currents of air to rise up the slopes of the surrounding high lands.

ANAN. Name given by the Yahgan Indians of Tierra del Fuego to a bark canoe with pointed ends. Sometimes called *en-anan.*

The *anan* was made of large slabs of bark of the evergreen beech, sewed together with thin strips of whalebone and supported by numerous ribs made of split wintersbark (*Drimys winteri*), held in place by gunwales that were sewed to the edge of the bark shell. The slender tips of bow and stern were tied by a braided grass rope. The seams were calked with seaweed. There were usually five thwarts. These canoes usually lasted not more than 6 months. They were propelled by 2 or 4 paddles. Their dimensions varied greatly, the length ranging from 13 to 25 ft., and the breadth from 2.3 to 4 ft. With a fair wind a temporary mast with square sail is rigged. Since about 1900, the Yahgan Indians have replaced their bark canoes by dugouts.

ANCHOR. A heavy forging or casting comprising a shank with large shackle or ring at one end and two arms with palms at the other, so shaped as to grip the sea bottom, and by means of a cable or rope hold a vessel, boat, or any other floating structure in a desired position regardless of wind and current.

Fr: *Ancre;* Ger: *Anker.*
See **Back Anchor, Bower Anchor, Best Bower Anchor, Close-stowing Anchor, Double Fluke, Fisherman's Anchor, Kedge Anchor, Mooring Anchor, Mushroom Anchor, Sea Anchor, Sheet Anchor, Shifting-Stock Anchor, Stem Anchor, Stocked Anchor, Stockless Anchor, Stream Anchor.**

The safety of a vessel at anchor depending entirely on its ground tackle, every effort is made to give the different parts of an anchor the most suitable shape conducive to good holding power on the sea bottom.

The principal points of excellence in an anchor are: holding power under various conditions, strength, quick holding, quick tripping, freedom from fouling, facility of stowing and of fishing, facility of sweeping, and facility of transport in or by boats. Slight differences in design make a considerable difference in the holding power of anchors.

The center of gravity of any type of anchor should be located as near as possible to a line perpendicular to the shank passing through the bills when the anchor is placed on the ground in order to have the maximum pressure or weight on this part. But at the same time, to prevent any toppling over when the anchor is lying on inclined or uneven ground, it is necessary that the center of gravity should be kept near the head. It is customary, for this reason, when designing anchors of admiralty pattern, to place the center of gravity at about 0.42 of the total length of the anchor. With stockless anchors, because of the great weight of the head and the absence of stock, the center of gravity is located very near the axis around which the flukes swing and, therefore, beyond the vertical line passing through the bills. The weight and pull on the cable prevent any tipping over. The dimensions of anchors are in proportion to the total volume of the ship and the scantlings of the different parts are arrived at by empirical deductions after testing.

The weight of anchors is determined by the section of the cable, the diameter of which is determined by the ship's displacement. Anchors used by sailing vessels are heavier than those of mechanically propelled vessels of the same displacement on account of windage.
British Standard Institution, Standard No. 3006, *Anchors*, London, 1924; Leahy and Farrin, "Determining Anchor Holding Power from Model Tests," Society of Naval Architects and Marine Engineers, *Transactions*, vol. 43 (1935); Nielly, R., *Ancres, Chaînes et Aussières*, Paris, 1913; Raclot, "*Note sur les ancres*," Bureau Veritas, *Bulletin Technique*, Paris, vol. 7 (1925); Tillmann, M., *Anker und Ankerketten im Seeschiffbetrieb*, Düsseldorf, 1912.

ANCHORAGE. A place where a ship anchors or may anchor. An area set apart for anchored vessels in a harbor.

Fr: *Mouillage;* Ger: *Ankerplatz.*

A suitable place for anchoring is sheltered from wind and sea, does not interfere with harbor traffic, and has a sea bottom that gives good holding to anchors. The anchorage space alloted to a vessel should include a circle with a radius equal to the combined length of anchor cable and ship. A depth of 7 to 8 fathoms at low water is usually considered sufficient for ordinary requirements.

ANCHORAGE BUOY.
See **Mooring Buoy.**

ANCHORAGE PERMIT (U. S.). A permit issued by the U. S. Coast Guard to small pleasure and commercial craft in certain federal anchorages where heavy concentration exists. The permit is valid for one year and specifies the type of mooring and tackle to be used such as weight and number of anchors, distance at which anchors must be placed apart, type and color of anchor buoy.

ANCHOR AND CHAIN CERTIFICATE. A document issued by a classification society or a government agency, if the vessel is not classed, which states that the anchors and chain cables of the ship mentioned in the certificate comply with the society's requirements as regards numbers, weights, and sizes, and that they have satisfactorily passed the required tests and inspection. The surveyor's number and initials and the month and year of test are indicated on the certificate and stamped on each anchor and on one link in each shot of chain.

Ger: *Ankerzertifikat.*

ANCHOR AND CHAIN CLAUSE. A clause sometimes included in marine policies that states that underwriters are free from costs of recovering anchors and cables broken by stress of weather while the vessel is afloat.

ANCHOR BALL (U. S.). A visual signal displayed by vessels sailing on inland waters, the Great Lakes and western rivers of the United States, when moored or anchored in a fairway or channel where traffic is liable to congestion or confusion. It consists of a black ball or shape not less than 2 ft. in diameter shown in the forward part of the vessel where it can best be observed.

ANCHOR BAR. A wooden hand spike used for prying an anchor off the billboard.

Fr: *Anspec;* Ger: *Handspake.*

ANCHOR BED. A sloping support or platform located on the forecastle on which a stocked anchor is stowed and secured when at sea. It usually extends a little over the side so as to throw the anchor clear when let go. Sometimes called billboard.

Ger: *Schweinsrücken.*

ANCHOR BELLS. Signals made with the ship's bell on the forecastle as the anchor is being hove in, to keep the bridge informed as to how much of the cable is still out, by striking the bell once for every shackle (15 fathoms) out. When the anchor is aweight the bell is struck rapidly for two or three seconds.

ANCHOR BLADE. The back of the palm of an anchor.
Fr: *Patte d'ancre;* Ger: *Ankerschaufel.*

ANCHOR BY THE STERN. To have the cable brought in through a stern pipe so that when the anchor is let go from the bow the vessel will ride by the stern. Some ships have a stern anchor and cable for this purpose.
Fr: *Mouiller de l'arrière.*

ANCHOR CABLE. A heavy chain used for holding a vessel at anchor. Sometimes called chain cable. Chain cables are usually composed of lengths or shots of 15 fathoms each, connected by shackles. The length of cables varies from 60 fathoms in small vessels to 330 fathoms in the largest. A swivel is inserted at a distance of three or four links from the anchor to prevent twisting. The size of the chain is determined by the diameter of the bar of which the links are made.
Fr: *Cable-Chaîne;* Ger: *Ankerkette; Ankertau.*

Chain cables are generally hand forged and welded, although in 1924, cast steel chain was adopted by the United States Navy. Subsequently, it has also been approved by classification societies. In these chains the studs are cast with the links, the length of each link usually being about 6 diameters of the iron of which it is made and the breadth about 3½ or 4 diameters. The purpose of the stud is to prevent the link from extending unduly when under strain. The strength of stud link chains may be taken as 1.6 to 1.8 times that of the iron from which they are made, and about 50 per cent greater than the corresponding size of unstudded link chain.

Wrought-iron chain cables with diameters up to about 2¾ in. can be manufactured by hand. For larger sizes, owing to the difficulty of obtaining satisfactory welds by hand, steam forging hammers are employed. In manufacturing chain cables the bars are cut to the required length of link at an angle for forming the welds, and after being heated are bent by machinery to the form of a link and welded by smiths, each link being inserted in the previous one before welding. The links are usually welded at the crown, although a side weld is also used by some makers. Electrical resistance welding has in recent years been applied to the manufacture of chain cables and links fabricated in this manner have been approved by classification societies. Comparative tests of different types of chain cables to determine their ultimate strength have given the following results, for chain of 1-in. diameter:

Ultimate strength: Wrought-iron Chain: 65,000 lbs. Cast-steel Chain: 100,000 lbs. Die-lock Chain: 145,000 lbs.

Coburn, F. G., *"Power Forging of Chain Cables,"* Society of Naval Architects and Marine Engineers, *Transactions,* vol. 24, New York, 1916; *"The Manufacture and Testing of Cast Steel Chain Cables,"* American Society of Naval Engineers, *Journal,* vol. 30 (1918); Otterson, J. E., *"Notes on Chain Cables,"* Society of Naval Architects and Marine Engineers, *Transactions,* vol. 21, New York, 1913; Scott-Glover, T., *"Welding Applied to Stud Link Chain Cables,"* Institution of Engineers and Shipbuilders in Scotland, *Transactions,* Glasgow, vol. 86, 1943; Vermeersch, P., *"Procédés récents de la fabrication des chaînes a haute resistance,"* *Le Génie Civil,* nos. 21 and 22 (November, 1930).

ANCHOR CAPSTAN. A power-driven capstan of small height in which the drum or barrel is replaced by a cable holder. Sometimes called dwarf capstan, capstan windlass, vertical windlass.
Fr: *Cabestan de Mouillage; Cabestan à barbotin;* Ger: *Ankerspill.*

The driving spindle passes down to a lower deck where it is geared to a steam or electric motor. A warping head is sometimes provided above the wildcat. It is generally used as a substitute to the windlass in large high-speed vessels on account of its compactness and strength. The cable holder is equipped with an individual mechanism similar to that used on a windlass. The shaft is keyed at its lower end to a driving worm wheel. Cable holders are not provided with pawling arrangements or with other means for hand operation. Band brakes are fitted.

ANCHOR CHAIN.
See Anchor Cable.

ANCHOR CRANE. A small pivoting crane placed on the center line forward of the windlass, used for hoisting a stock anchor on deck after it has been hove above water. Anchor cranes have replaced cat davits and fish davits formerly used.
Fr: *Grue de Capon;* Ger: *Ankerkran.*

A tackle suspended from the end of the crane is hooked into an eye fixed on the shank at the center of gravity of the anchor. Anchor cranes or davits are little used nowadays except for handling the spare bower.

ANCHOR DAVIT. A davit formerly used for anchor work such as catting and fishing the anchor. In modern vessels anchor davits are no longer used, the anchor being either pulled up in the hawse pipe or lifted on deck by the anchor crane.
Fr: *Bossoir d'Ancre;* Ger: *Ankerdavit.*

ANCHOR DECK. A term applied to the top of a small forecastle used principally for stowing the anchors or anchor handling gear.
  Fr: *Teugue;* Ger: *Ankerdeck.*
ANCHOR DUES. Dues paid by a ship for anchoring in certain ports and harbors and using the quays, landing stages, and so on.
  Fr: *Droits d'Ancrage;* Ger: *Ankergeld.*
ANCHORED. The condition of a vessel held to the ground by one or more anchors.
  Fr: *Au mouillage;* Ger: *Vor Anker legen; Verankert.*
ANCHOR GEAR. Applies to anchors, chains, windlass, controller, hawse and chain pipes, devil's claws, hawse and chain pipe covers, chain locker fittings, anchor beds, anchor davits and cranes with tackle.
  Fr: *Apparaux de mouillage;* Ger: *Ankergerschirr.*
ANCHOR HOY.
  See Mooring Lighter.
ANCHOR ICE. A term applied to submerged ice attached to the sea bottom at depths up to 60 or 70 feet or more, and irrespective of the nature of its formation.
  Fr: *Glace d'ancre;* Ger: *Ankereis Grundeis.*
ANCHORING BERTH. Space in a roadstead or river with sufficient depth of water and room for a vessel to lie at anchor.
  Fr: *Poste de mouillage;* Ger: *Ankerplatz.*
ANCHOR LIGHT.
  See Riding Light.
ANCHOR LINE. Line carried on small craft for anchoring.
ANCHOR LINING. Sheathing fastened to the bows of a vessel to prevent injury to the planking by the bill of a stock anchor when fished or hauled up. Sometimes called bow doubling. (Obsolete.)
  Ger: *Ankerfütterung.*
ANCHOR PLATE. The metal resting place for the inboard fluke of a stocked anchor when the latter is fished. Sometimes called anchor bed.
ANCHOR POCKET. A recess in the bow plating large enough to admit the head of a stockless anchor so that there is no projection outside of the shell plating.
  Fr: *Logement d'Ancre;* Ger: *Versenkte Ankerkluse; Ankertasche.*
ANCHOR RING. The ring bolted to the upper end of the shank, to which the chain is shackled.
  Fr: *Cigale, Organeau;* Ger: *Ankerring.*
ANCHOR RAFT. A raft for carrying out a heavy anchor in an emergency. It is constructed on three spars lashed together in triangular form. Empty drums, barrels or tanks are secured to the spars to augment buoyancy.
ANCHOR SHACKLE. A heavy shackle made of wrought iron, cast steel or unwelded forged steel by which the anchor is con-

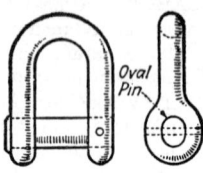
Anchor Shackle

nected to its cable. It is fastened to the shank by a round pin secured with a forelock. Also called jew's harp.
  Fr: *Manille d'Étalingure; Main d'Ancre;* Ger: *Ankerschakel.*
The forelock pin of the shackle is kept from coming out by being made a little short so there will be no projection that might be injured when the cable is running out. Lead pellets are driven in at either end to fill up the holes in the shackle, which are made with a groove or score; thus as the pellets are driven in, they expand or dovetail and keep the small pin in place.
ANCHOR SHANK. The main piece of an anchor having the arms at one end and the anchor shackle at the other.
  Fr: *Verge;* Ger: *Ankerschaft.*
ANCHOR SHOE. A flat block of hard wood, convex on the back and scored out on the flat side to take the bill of the anchor to prevent damage to the vessel's planking when the anchor is raised or lowered. Also, a broad triangular piece of wood sometimes fastened to the fluke of an anchor to increase its holding in soft ground.
  Fr: *Savate;* Ger: *Ankerschuh.*
ANCHOR STATIONS. The allotted places of the crew when a ship is coming to anchor, or when the anchor is being hove up.
  Fr: *Postes de Mouillage;* Ger: *Anker Station.*
ANCHOR STOCK FASHION. Arrangement of timber which bears a resemblance to the shape of a wooden anchorstock. It may be described as a piece of timber which fits into both connecting members exactly as one half of a scarph on one member fits into the other member. It is

used instead of scarphs for working out pieces of planksheer, rails, and similar parts from timbers of limited width.
Ger: *Ankerstock Form Replankung.*

ANCHOR TACKLE. A strong gun tackle with upper block fastened to the fore trestletrees. Used in small sailing vessels for getting the anchor over the rail.
Fr: *Candelette;* Ger: *Anker Talje.*

ANCHOR (to). To cast anchor, to come to anchor, to lie or ride at anchor. To ride with 2 anchors in a line ahead, the cables being nearly parallel to each other.
Fr: *Mouiller;* Ger: *Vor Anker gehen; Ankern; Zu Anker gehen.*

ANCHOR TRIPPER. A device for casting loose a ship's anchor.
Fr: *Mouilleur;* Ger: *Ankerschlipper.*
See **Tumbler.**

ANCHOR WATCH. A small number of men kept on duty when a ship is riding at anchor, to be in readiness to perform any duty that may be required, such as to let go a second anchor, veer out or take in cable, or man a boat.
Fr: *Quart de Rade;* Ger: *Anker Wache.*

Although international regulations make no provision for an anchor watch it is nevertheless the duty of every vessel to keep an anchor watch on deck where it is able not only to know that the anchor lights are burning but also to watch for approaching vessels and use whatever means may be required to notify an approaching vessel of its presence if the anchor lights give insufficient notice. The sufficiency of the watch must depend upon the circumstances of the case: a stricter watch being required when and where the danger from passing vessels is greater.

ANCHOR WITH A SPRING. To attach an after hawser to the anchor ring before letting go, so that when the anchor is down and an equal strain brought upon the cable and the hawser, the vessel will ride to a bridle presenting her broadside to the wind or tide, whichever prevails.
Fr: *S'embosser;* Ger: *Ankern mit einem Spring.*

ANEMOMETER. An instrument used for measuring the velocity of atmospheric currents.
Fr: *Anemomètre;* Ger: *Windmesser.*

There are two types for marine use: (a) the cup or Robinson's anemometer, consisting of four hemispherical cups attached to the ends of a metal cross which rotates under the force of the wind. The velocity is indicated by the revolutions of a vertical shaft geared to an indicator. (b) The pressure or Dine's anemometer, consists essentially of a Pitot tube head connected to a manometer; the wind exerts a pressure on one limb and a suction on the other, the combined effect being recorded on a chart.

ANEROID BAROMETER. An instrument which indicates the pressure of the atmosphere. It consists of a thin, circular, metallic chamber, partially exhausted of air, and hermetically sealed, hence very susceptible to the slightest changes in external pressure.
Fr: *Baromètre Anéroide;* Ger: *Aneroid-barometer.*

The center of one of the circular walls is connected to a pointer by an arrangement of levers and springs, which has the effect of greatly magnifying its movements. This pointer traverses a graduated dial, and can be set to any desired pressure reading by means of a screw at the back of the instrument. The advantages of the aneroid are its convenient size, facility of transport, and the rapidity with which it shows any change of atmospheric pressure. It is, however, less accurate than the mercurial barometer.

ANGA. A single-outrigger dugout canoe with low freeboard from northern New Britain (Bismarck Archipelago). The hull is painted at bow and stern with designs representing fishes, leaves, eyes, human tongues, and other figures.

ANGANIA. Double-outrigger Australian dugout canoe of the Gudang people from northern Cape York Peninsula. The hull length ranges from 15 to 30 ft. The ends are produced into flat shelflike projections. The outrigger is made of two booms that pass over the gunwales and a float of light wood fastened across them at each end.

ANGARY.
See **Right of Angary.**

ANGELKAHN. Keel-built fishing boat with pointed stern and clinker planking, used chiefly on the coast of East Prussia for the capture of eels and perch. These boats are rigged with one pole mast and tall squaresail. A center board is fitted and there is a fish well just abaft the mast. The after-end is decked. Fishermen usually use them to fish in pairs with a dragnet, and they are said to be fast under sail. Length 33 to 40 ft. Breadth 8 to 10 ft. Depth 3.3 ft. Draft about 1.9 to 2.4 ft. Height of mast about 42 ft.

ANGEL'S FOOTSTOOL. Colloquial term used in clipper ship days to denote any light sail above the skysails. Also called heaven disturber or star shifter.

ANGELSICKE.
See **Sicke.**

ANGGE. A very crude dugout canoe with single outrigger from Lepers' Island (New Hebrides). The bow is shaped like a flattened shelf. Sometimes called *ango*.

ANGLE. An angle bar.
Fr: *Cornière;* Ger: *Winkel.*
See **Backing Angle, Bearding Angle, Bulb Angle, Conversion Angle, Danger Angle, Drift Angle, Hour Angle, Staple Angle, Upsetting Angle.**

ANGLE BAR. A rolled or wrought bar of iron or steel with its cross section in the form of a right angle having equal or unequal flanges. Also called angle iron. In ship work it is used for frames, bulkhead stiffeners, and for the attachment of one plate or bar to another. Its size is rated by the lengths of the flanges and weight per foot run or its thickness.
Fr: *Cornière;* Ger: *Winkeleisen; Winkelprofil.*
The toe of each flange is its free edge. The heel is where the flanges join to form a right angle. The inside of the right angle is the fillet. The whole inner surface is known as the bosom.

ANGLE-BAR STRAP.
See **Bosom piece.**

ANGLE COLLAR. Smithed angle bar fitted where continuous structural parts, such as keelsons, stringers, and frames, penetrate watertight plating, bulkheads or tank top, permitting efficient calking around the joist and insuring watertightness. Sometimes called staple angle or stapling.
Fr: *Cornière d'étanchéité;* Ger: *Winkelkropf; Winkelkragen.*

ANGLE LUG.
See **Clip.**

ANGLE OF DIP. The angle which a magnetic needle makes with the horizontal. Also called: Angle of inclination.
Fr: *Angle d'indinaison Magnétique;* Ger: *Neigungswinkel.*

ANGLE OF ENTRANCE. The angle formed by the center line of the ship and the tangent to the designed waterline at the forward perpendicular.
Fr: *Angle d'Acuité;* Ger: *Zuschärfungswinkel.*

ANGLE OF HEEL. The angle of transverse inclination measured from the vertical when a vessel heels over. Sometimes called heeling angle or list.

Fr: *Angle de Gîte;* Ger: *Krangungswinkel.*

ANGLE OF REPOSE. The maximum angle at which grain, coal, or other products loaded in bulk will retain their form or remain in a heap. The angle of repose for grain is 25 to 35°; for coal 30 to 45°; for ore 30 to 50°.
Ger: *Böschungswinkel; Liegewinkel.*

ANGLE OF RUN. The inclination of the stern at the load waterline to the ship's plane of symmetry. Owing to the double curvature of the shell plating in that region, it is difficult to measure this angle with precision.

ANGLE SEXTANT. A special form of sextant used on board surveying vessels for measuring horizontal or shore angles.

ANGULAR DISTORTION. A term used in welding technique to denote distortion of structural members caused by heating, when stresses are set up at right angles to the neutral axis of the base metal.
Fr: *Distortion angulaire;* Ger: *Eckig Verformung.*

ANGULATED SAIL, MITERED SAIL. A jib-headed sail in which the head cloths run in a different direction from those of the foot. They both join in a diagonal known as the miter or last. The sail is sometimes called mitered sail.

The principle of the angulated method is so to place the cloths that there is no knuckle, by winding the warp threads so that they are all equally acted upon by the strain from the sheet. Angulated sails are made with less cloth, as they do not require so much round on the fore leech. The angulated jib lasts longer and requires less trimming of sheets than does the vertical-cut jib, the strain of which is from the clew to the stay, thus forming a bag in the upper and lower parts of the sail.

ANNIE OAKLEY. In yachting parlance, a parachute spinnaker pierced with small holes to let out dead air.

ANOA. A dugout canoe of the Goajira Indians on the Atlantic Coast of Northern Colombia.

ANSWER. A vessel is said to answer her helm when she moves in obedience to a movement of the rudder.
Fr: *Obéir à; Répondre;* Ger: *Beantworten.*

ANSWERING PENNANT. A pennant of the International Code of Signals, striped red and white vertically, flown when answering a signal. Sometimes called answering

pendant.
> Fr: *Flamme du Code;* Ger: *Signalbuchwimpel; Antwortwimpel.*

ANTENNA. In radio: the conductor or system of conductors for radiating or receiving electric waves. Also called aerial. On merchant ships it consists usually of a horizontal wire supported by the masts and a vertical wire joined to the horizontal portion at one end (inverted L aerial) or at the center (T aerial). The material for antennas affording the best compromise electrically and mechanically is silicon-bronze copper-weld steel wire.
> Fr: *Antenne;* Ger: *Antenne.*

ANTHELION. A mock sun appearing at a point in the sky opposite to and at the same altitude as the sun. It is believed to be produced by the reflection of sunlight from ice crystals.

ANTICORROSIVE PAINT. A bottom composition applied to the underwater body of steel ships before the anti-fouling paint, as a protection against corrosion of shell plating. Its composition generally includes grain alcohol, gum shellac, turpentine, pine tar, oil, zinc oxide and zinc dust. One hundred weight of this paint covers about 3,150 sq. ft.
> Fr: *Peinture Anticorrosive;* Ger: *Rostschutzanstrich; Antikorrosivekomposition.*

Adamson, N. E., "Technology of Ship Bottom Paints," U. S. Navy Department, Bureau of Construction and Repair, Bulletin No. 10, 1936.

ANTI-CYCLONE. An atmosphere system in which the wind circulates round an area of high pressure, clockwise in the North Hemisphere and counter-clockwise in the South Hemisphere. The winds are usually moderate to light, and fine weather prevails.
> Fr: *Anticyclone;* Ger: *Antizyklone Hoch.*

ANTICYCLONIC WIND. A wind circulation about an area of high atmospheric pressure.

ANTIFOULING PAINT. A composition that, like the copper sheathing on wooden vessels, is proof against the attachment of seaweed, barnacles, bryozoa, annelids, hydroids and other marine growths on underwater shell plating of steel vessels. Also called antifouling composition.
> Fr: *Peinture Antifouling;* Ger: *Anwuchsverhindernde Farbe; Fäulnissichere Farbe; Antifoulingkomposition; Antifäulnisfarbe.*

The antifouling properties of these compositions are obtained by the use of a poisonous ingredient such as mercuric oxide in paints for steel ships, and copper oxide in paints for wooden ships. The latter composition is often called "copper paint." Mercuric arsenate, mercuric phenate, mercuric oleate, cuprous cyanide, zinc cyanide, and zinc stearate are also used as poisonous ingredients by some manufacturers. The antifouling paints, at best, lose their protective properties after some months, hence vessels' bottoms have to be repainted at regular intervals, the length of which depends on the particular seas navigated, whether warm tropical seas favorable to marine growths or comparatively cool seas. Antifouling coatings contain instead of oil a volatile spirit such as naphtha, benzine, turpentine, or bisulphide of carbon, in which resins or gums are dissolved and, in addition, to give color and body, a pigment such as red oxide. Recently plastic coatings have been developed which promise greatly improved protection through a longer period. Adamson, N. E., *Technology of Ship Bottom Paint and Its Importance to Commercial and Naval Activities,* Washington, 1937; Kelly, "Fouling and Anti-Fouling," *Nautical Magazine,* Glasgow, vol. 126 (1931); Skeens, H. C., "Painting Ship Surfaces," *Paint Manufacture,* London, vol. 7, nos. 5 and 10 (1937).

ANTIPODEAN DAY. The day gained in crossing the meridian of 180° when sailing westward.

ANTI-ROLLING TANKS. A system for damping the rolling motions of a ship among waves by means of tanks or water chambers so disposed that the water content in the tanks is made to circulate from one side of the ship to the other. Also called water chambers.
> Fr: *Caisses Anti Roulis;* Ger: *Schlingertanks.*

The effect in reducing rolling is based on the timing of the motion of the water in the chambers in relation to the motion of the ship and is proportional to the moment of transference. The most recent developments of this system are due to Dr. Frahm, whose anti-rolling tank is designed to have a definite period and definite moment of transference. It is composed of U-shaped reservoirs in which, by proportioning the sectional area of the vertical arms to the sectional area of the horizontal arm, the period of the contained water can be lengthened or shortened to a suitable value according to the ship's own period of roll. In the Frahm tanks there is an air duct connecting the tops of the vertical arms. In this air duct there is a valve that can be closed so that the air may be imprisoned and the water prevented from oscillating in the tanks, thus putting them out of action. These tanks are most effective when their own period is less than that of the ship by about 70 per cent for large ships. The main advantage of the system lies in its simplicity and low cost. But it is relatively inefficient in damping the roll when compared with the gyro stabilizer, and its behavior is somewhat erratic when the sea is not of regular trochoidal pattern, which is frequently the case in a seaway.

ANTI-TRADE WINDS. Upper atmospheric currents at an altitude of 6000 ft. or more found in the trade wind regions and flowing from the equatorial regions towards the poles.

Fr: *Contre-Alisés;* Ger: *Gegenpassat.*

ANVIL CIRRUS. A cirrus cloud with anvil-shaped top as a result of the convection currents penetrating to high levels where the cloud particles become frozen and are carried away by strong upper winds. Also called: False cirrus.

Fr: *Faux Cirrus;* Ger: *Ambos Cirruswolke.*

AO-TSENG. Chinese dip-net fishing boat from Swatow (Kwangtung Province). The net is hung from the end of a pole that projects from the bows. Length 25 ft. Breadth 8½ ft.

AP. A single-outrigger dugout from Sawi Bay (Nicobar Islands) of same type as the *due.* The high stem and stern are ornamented with carvings.

APEAK. 1. In a vertical position or nearly so. Pointing upwards. In an up-and-down direction. An anchor is said to be apeak and a ship to be hove apeak when the cable and ship are brought, by tightening of the former, as nearly into a perpendicular line with the anchor as possible without breaking it from the ground.

Fr: *A Pic;* Ger: *Auf und Nieder.*

2. The position of yards when topped by opposite lifts. A yard or gaff or boom is apeak or topped when it hangs obliquely to the mast.

Fr: *Apiqué;* Ger: *Kaien.*

3. The position of oars when their blades are held obliquely upward, as in a boat with an awning, while the crew are awaiting the order to "give way."

Fr: *Apiqué.*

APHELION. The point in the orbit of a celestial body farthest from the sun.

Fr: *Aphélie;* Ger: *Aphelium; Sonnenferne.*

APOFO. A West African craft employed in the sea fisheries of the Ivory Coast.

The body of the canoe is a broad doubleended dugout with longitudinal curvature of the bottom and no sheer at gunwales. Each end terminates in a flat, elongated shelf. Viewed in cross section the hull presents a bottom with sharp dead rise and pronounced tumble home of the sides above waterline. There are no thwarts. The sides are tied together by transverse rattan lashings running from one gunwale to the other. These lashings are placed one, at each end and two, in the central part. The beam length ratio is about 4. The boats have one mast without stays or shrouds that carries a rectangular shaped sail. Two poles or sprits cross the sail diagonally from head to foot.

APOGEE. The position of a heavenly body when farthest from the earth.

Fr: *Apogée;* Ger: *Apogaum.*

APPAREL and TACKLE. The appurtenances or equipment of a ship such as sails, rigging, anchors, boats, and other gear in general. The expression apparel and tackle is met only in shipping documents, such as charter parties.

Fr: *Apparaux et Agrès;* Ger: *Gerät und Tackelage; Seil und Treil.*

APPARENT ALTITUDE. The arc of a circle of altitude contained between a celestial body and the sensible horizon, or the observed altitude corrected for index error (if any) and dip.

Fr: *Hauteur Apparente;* Ger: *Scheinbare Höhe.*

APPARENT HORIZON. The boundary circle in which the heavens and earth appear to meet. It is the primitive circle in one of the systems of co-ordinates for defining points of the celestial concave relative to the position of an observer on the earth's surface. Sometimes called visible horizon.

Fr: *Horizon Apparent;* Ger: *Sichtbarer Horizont; Seehorizont; Kimm.*

APPARENT NOON. The instant of the transit of the true sun over the upper branch of the observers' meridian.

Fr: *Midi vrai;* Ger: *Scheinbarer Mittag.*

APPARENT PLACE. The point on the celestial sphere to which a celestial body is referred by an observer stationed on the earth's surface.

Fr: *Lieu Apparent;* Ger: *Scheinbarer Ort.*

APPARENT SLIP. The difference between the speed of the stream projected by the propeller and the speed of the ship, in relation to a fixed point in the water, clear of the wake.

Fr: *Recul Apparent;* Ger: *Scheinbarer Slip.*

APPARENT SUN. The real sun as it appears to an observer on the earth. The apparent sun does not appear to move uniformly since its motion varies with its distance from the earth. For the purpose of time measurement, therefore, astronomers invented the Mean Sun.

Fr: *Soleil Apparent;* **Ger**: *Scheinbare Sonne.*

See **Mean Sun.**

APPARENT TIME. Time based upon the true position of the sun as distinguished from mean time, which is measured by a fictitious sun moving at a uniform rate. Its noon is the time when the sun crosses the meridian.

Fr: *Heure Solaire Vraie;* Ger: *Scheinbare Zeit.*

APPARENT WIND. The variation from the true wind caused by a vessel's speed. The wind felt by an observer on a moving vessel. It is the resultant of the actual motion of the wind and a motion equal and opposite to that of the ship.

Fr: *Vent Apparent;* Ger: *Scheinbarer Wind; Gefühlter Wind.*

APPENDAGE. A general term for any part projecting from the underwater portion of the hull, such as shaft bossings, bar keel, bilge keel, rudder, propeller struts, skeg, propeller hub.

Fr: *Appendice;* Ger: *Anbau.*

APPLE STERN. A stern with very pronounced rounding of buttocks, as found on some Dutch sailing craft. A stern with convex profile.

APPRAISER. Representative of a marine insurance company who is expert in the appraisal of damaged goods. Sometimes called surveyor.

APPRENTICE (G. B.). A youth bound by a writing, called indenture, to serve under the master of a vessel for a certain period, generally 4 years. The term apprentice refers usually to boys who are less than 18 years of age.

Fr: *Pilotin;* Ger: *Jungmann.*

APPROACH SIGNAL. A term used to define one of the port signals as used by a vessel nearing a harbor. They include cautionary signals such as: **1.** port closed or entrance obstructed; **2.** bar and entrance signals; **3.** local current signals; **4.** local pilot and harbor entrance lights.

Fr: *Signal d'approche;* Ger: *Ansegelungssignal.*

APPROPRIATED BERTH. A berth assigned under lease for the continuous use of a shipping firm having a line of ships running regularly to and from the port.

Fr: *Poste Reservé;* Ger: *Fester Liegeplatz.*

APPROPRIATED GOODS. Goods that are surplus at the completion of a vessel's discharge and which are handed over by the ship to the consignee in lieu of the goods short when the bill of lading was presented.

APPURTENANCES. All the tackle and furniture necessary to the proper operation of a vessel for the purposes for which it was designed. The term appurtenances in admiralty law has a wider meaning than furniture. Some articles are universally regarded as appurtenances, whereas others are appurtenances only by usage in respect to the particular occupation in which the vessel is at the time engaged.

APRON. 1. A sheet of netting stretching from the bottom of the heart upward to the pot in a pound net.

2. The portion of a wharf, pier, or quay lying between the waterfront edge and the shed. The portion of a wharf carried on piles beyond the solid fill.

Fr: *Radier;* Ger: *Docksohle.*

3. A curved piece of timber fayed on the after side of the stem from the head down to the deadwood. It provides the necessary surface for securing the hood ends of the planking and strengthens the stem.

Fr: *Contre-Étrave;* Ger: *Innensteven; Binnenvorsteven.*

See **Bunt Apron, Landing Apron.**

APRON PLATE See **Bow Chock Plate.**

ARAGOSTAI; GOLETA ARAGOSTARA. Italian carrier engaged in the transportation of live lobsters between Sardinia and Continental harbors. Its hull is keel built with overhanging clipper stem and elliptical stern. It has two decks and is fitted with a fishwell amidships of sufficient capacity to accommodate about 6,000 lbs. of live lobsters. It is rigged as a two masted fore-and-aft schooner with three headsails. Length 69 to 96 ft. Breadth 18 to 21 ft. Depth 7.2 to 8.9 ft. Gross tonnage 52 to 91. Crew 5 to 6. Some boats are equipped with auxiliary engines of 40 to 90 hp.

ARBITRATION CLAUSE. A charter party clause that states that all disputes under the charter shall be referred to arbitration. Not enforceable in the United States.

Fr: *Clause d'Arbitrage;* Ger: *Schiedsgericht Klausel.*

ARC. See **Limb.**

ARCFORM VESSEL. A recent type of construction adopted for cargo vessels in which the sharp bilge is entirely dispensed with. In order to fine the bilge without reducing displacement or filling the ends, the comparatively normal form is retained by replacing the area lost at the lower waterlines by an equivalent area at the upper ones, with the requisite increase in breadth in the region of the load waterline. The Arcform hull has an appreciable reduction in immersed midship girth, and in addition, owing to the easy bilge, the lower lines promote a better flow to the propeller, giving improved propulsive efficiency. The result of model experiments and voyage performances of Arcform vessels has proved that this type is economical for cargo carriers. Isherwood, Sir J. W., "The Arcform Ship," North East Coast Institution of Engineers and Shipbuilders, Newcastle upon Tyne, *Transactions,* vol. 51 (1933–34).

ARCH. An elliptical molding sprung over the cove at the lower part of the taffrail. (Obsolete.)

See **Propeller Arch.**

ARCH BOARD. A decorated frame across a ship's stern outside of the planking. It is sunk at the lower part of the taffrail and frames the stern windows. Also called Cove (obsolete).

Fr: *Couronnement;* Ger: *Heckbord.*

ARCHED SQUALL. A violent squall, so called because it rises with a black cloudy arch. These squalls are mostly encountered in the eastern seas.

Fr: *Grain Arqué;* Ger: *Gewitterbö.*

ARCH FRAMING. A patented system of framing especially adapted for vessels of the self trimming type. Up to the molded depth the normal hull construction is unaltered. At this position, instead of the usual deck with bridge superstructure, a transverse arch construction is applied. The deck is practically at bridge deck height and is continuous fore and aft, unbroken by wells.

Fr: *Construction en Arc;* Ger: *Gewölbe Bauart.*

Not only is it claimed that the transverse

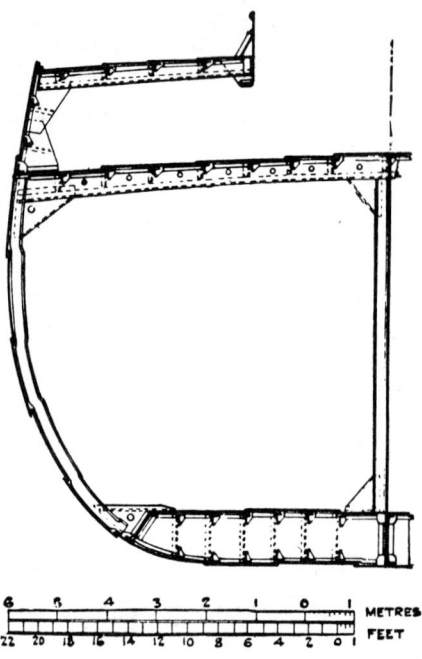

Arcform Vessel

section is particularly advantageous to self trimming, since it provides a deeper hold free from all obstructions, but the inverse sheer, which is one of the essential features of the system, favorably affects the vessel's longitudinal strength. The arch-form of deck also provides an increased reserve of buoyancy which is said to improve the seagoing qualities and makes the vessel easier to trim on a level keel. The forecastle and poop are sheered in the usual way. The inventors of this system of construction claim a reduction of 18% in the weight of steel as compared to a cargo ship built on the ordinary transverse principle.

Ballard, M., *"The Arch Principle of Ship Construction,"* Institution of Engineers and Shipbuilders in Scotland, *Transactions,* vol. 29, Glasgow, 1922–23.

ARCH KNEE. A crooked timber fitted between the propeller post and the rudder post and forming the upper face of the propeller aperture in a wooden vessel.

Fr: *Sommier;* Ger: *Bogenstück.*

ARC OF VISIBILITY. The portion of a circle, defined by limiting bearings if necessary, throughout which a light is visible from seaward.

Fr: *Secteur de Visibilité;* Ger: *Sichtbarkeit Bogen.*

ARCTIC CIRCLE. The parallel of 66° 32' north latitude, which forms the southern margin of the Arctic zone and is at a distance from the North Pole equal to the obliquity of the ecliptic. The same circle in the southern hemisphere is called Antarctic Circle and forms the northern limit of the Antarctic zone.

Fr: *Cercle Polaire Arctique;* Ger: *Nördlicher Polarkreis.*

ARCTIC CURRENT. An Atlantic Ocean current, that sets out of Davis Strait, flows southward down the coasts of Labrador and Newfoundland, passing along the eastern shoulder of the Grand Banks to its southern confines and to a variable extent beyond, according to the season, where it encounters the Gulf Stream. It brings with it the ice that is frequently encountered off Newfoundland in certain seasons.

ARCTIC FRONT. The line of discontinuity between very cold air flowing directly from the Arctic regions, and polar maritime air that has moved away from its source region and been warmed through contact with the ocean surface.

Fr: *Front Polaire;* Ger: *Polar Front.*

ARCTIC SMOKE. A sea fog consisting of ice crystals formed during the passage of air over water that is warmer than the air. It has been observed both in the Arctic and Antarctic regions as well as in some of the Norwegian fjords.

ARDENCY. The tendency of a ship under sail to fly into the wind (sometimes called griping), particularly when sailing with the wind abeam or on the quarter. This is attributed to the center of lateral resistance being forward of the center of effort. The converse of ardency is slackness or leewardliness. Ardency is influenced by the increase of pressure on the lee bow, shape of the bow, length of middle body, amount of heel, and strength of wind.

Fr: *Ardent;* Ger: *Luvgierigkeit.*

ARM. 1. The elbow at the lower end of the shank of an anchor, which terminates in the flukes.

Fr: *Bras;* Ger: *Ankerarm.*

2. A narrow portion of the sea projecting from the main body.

Fr: *Bras de Mer;* Ger: *Meeresarm.*

See **Index Arm, Righting Arm, Rudder Arm, Upsetting Arm.**

ARM CLEAT. A cleat with one arm or horn. Sometimes called horn cleat.

Fr: *Taquet à Une Oreille;* Ger: *Hornklampe.*

ARMED MAST. A wooden mast made of two single timbers fastened to each other.

ARMED MERCHANTMAN. See **Private Armed Vessel.**

ARMING. Tallow or other substance placed in the cup-shaped recess of a sounding lead before it is cast so that some sand or mud or whatever the sea-bottom is composed of adheres to the lead and thus may be examined. If the bottom is clean and rocky this fact may also be detected by the effect on the arming or by indentations on the lead itself. These would be bright if cut by sharp rock.

Fr: *Garniture de Plomb de Sonde;* Ger: *Lotspeise.*

ARMORED ROPE. Wire rope made of 6 strands with center hemp core, and a flat wire wound around the periphery of each strand. Chiefly used in salvage, or similar work.

ARMORING. A term that refers to each of the outer walls of netting in a trammel net.

Fr: *Aumée;* Ger: *Ledderung.*

AR-NOH. A Siberian canoe made of drift bark on wooden frames and used by the Samoyedes of Kolguev Island. Two bilge keels are fitted, but there is no center keel. Length about 9 ft. Breadth 3½ ft.

AROSUTAHU. Name given by the Arawak Indians of Guiana to a *corial* or dugout canoe fitted with a wash strake.

ARREST. The temporary detention of a ship with a view to its ultimate release when the purpose of the arrest has been fulfilled, as distinguished from capture.

Fr: *Détention; Mise à la Chaine;* Ger: *Anhaltung; Arrest.*

The arrest of a ship at law is a step in a legal process which may either be a measure taken against a claim, or a measure in execution of a judgment. In the first case (provisional arrest) the shipowner may be fully solvent when certain claims are made against his vessel. When security within the jurisdiction is given, the vessel is immediately released.

ARRET DE PRINCE. The right of a belligerent to detain neutral vessels which are in its ports to prevent their carrying news of some military event which would be valuable to the enemy. The loss caused to the owners of the detained vessels is made good by the belligerent who detains them.

Fr: *Arrêt de Prince;* *Arrêt de Puissance;* Ger: *Verfügung von hoher Hand.*

ARRIVED SHIP. A chartering expression the meaning of which depends on the terms of the charter party. If a ship is ordered to a named berth, or wharf, it is not an arrived ship until it reaches that point.

Where a vessel is chartered to a dock within a port, it is an arrived ship when it arrives within that dock, even if no loading or discharging berth is available. Similarly if ordered to a specified river it is an arrived ship when it is in that river although no berth may be available. Lay days commence as soon as the vessel is an arrived ship.

ARSE. The bottom part of a block, opposite the end through which the fall is rove. Also called breech.

Fr: *Cul;* Ger: *Blockherd.*

ARTICLES OF AGREEMENT. The document containing all particulars relating to the terms of agreement between the master of the vessel and the crew. Sometimes called ship's articles, shipping articles.

Fr: *Rôle d'Équipage;* Ger: *Musterrolle.*

It contains the nature, description and capacity of all members of the crew, the amount of wages each one is to receive, the scale of provisions to be served; any regulations as to fines, lawful punishments for misconduct, etc. In Great Britain articles of agreement of foreign-going vessels are executed in the presence of a Board of Trade Marine Superintendent; in the United States, before a Shipping Commissioner or Collector of Customs. International Labor Office, "Seamen," *Studies and Reports,* Series P, no. 1, Geneva (1926); International Labor Office, "Hours of Work on Board Ships," *Studies and Reports,* Series P, no. 3, Geneva (1929).

See **Average Agreement, Running Agreement, Salvage Agreement.**

ARTIFICIAL HARBOR. A harbor where the desirable shelter from wind and sea has been obtained artificially by the building of moles, piers, breakwaters and jetties. Also applied to harbors created by sinking concrete barges, vessels and the like to form a temporary sheltered anchorage.

Fr: *Port Artificiel;* Ger: *Künstlicher Hafen.*

ARUT. A plank-built trading canoe from Southeast Borneo with rising curved stem piece and a thatched roof. The stern is broad and square.

ARUT TAMBANGAN. A canoe similar to the *arut* but smaller and used as a ferry.

ASCENSIONAL DIFFERENCE. An arc of the equinoctial intercepted between the horizon and the hour circle of the object at rising and setting.

Fr: *Différence d'Ascension Droite;* Ger: *Aufsteigungs Unterschied.*

ASH. A tough wood with great elasticity much used in boat building for frames, carlines, gunwales, and occasionally for stems. Oars, boat hooks, and capstan bars are usually those of white ash. It is also used for accommodation ladders, wooden gratings, and Jacob's ladders. When seasoned it weighs about 44 lb. 1 cu. ft. It is very pliable when soaked or steamed.

Fr: *Frêne;* Ger: *Esche.*

ASH BUCKET. A steel bucket about 15 in. in diameter, with a depth of 22½ in., used for hoisting ashes from the fireroom of coal-burning vessels to the upper deck where they are dumped in the ash chute.

Fr: *Seau à Escarbilles;* Ger: *Ascheimer; Aschekübel.*

ASH CHUTE. A steel chute either portable or built into the vessel's side, by which ashes are dumped overboard from a coal-burning vessel. Ash chutes are generally formed of castings at the ship's side and side casing, joined by lengths of fabricated plates with welded seams and flanges.

Fr: *Manche à Escarbilles;* Ger: *Aschenauslauf; Ascheschutte.*

ASH EJECTOR. A device by which furnace ashes are forced overboard by hydraulic pressure from coal-burning vessels. In some systems the ashes are ejected through openings above the waterline in the side plating, in other designs through the ship's bottom.

Fr: *Escarbilleur Hydraulique; Escarbilleur;* Ger: *Ascheejektor; Ascheauswerfer.*

ASH HOIST. A steam, electric, or pneumatic hoist by which ash buckets are raised from the stokehold platform to a point sufficiently high above water level to be tipped into the ash chute (coal-burning ships).

Fr: *Treuil à Escarbilles;* Ger: *Ascheheisswinde.*

ASHORE. On the shore. On land. The converse of at sea.

Fr: *A terre;* Ger: *Aus Land.*

ASH WHIP. A fall and block used on steamers for hoisting ashes from stokehold to ash chute.

ASI.
See **Ahona.**

ASPHALT CEMENT. A bituminous composition of the nature of bituminous enamel, used for coating the bottoms of chain lockers and other spaces subject to vibration and where Portland cement would be apt to crack or suffer damage.

ASSESSOR, NAUTICAL. In Great Britain a man of nautical skill and experience who assists the judge in an admiralty action in determining points of fact and probability, but who has no voice in the judgment. Where the court is assisted by nautical assessors, the evidence of other experts on question of nautical science or skill is usually rejected.

Fr: *Conseiller Nautique;* Ger: *Nautischer Beisitzer.*

ASSIGNMENT CLAUSE. A clause incorporated in a marine insurance policy permitting the person in whose name the insurance has been effected to transfer his interest in the policy to another person. The assignment is usually made by endorsement and delivery.

ASSISTANT ENGINEER. A duly certified or licensed engineer who takes charge of an engine-room watch. In Great Britain called watch engineer.

Fr: *Mécanicien chef de quart;* Ger: *Wachhabender Maschinist.*

ASTAY. In line with a stay. The anchor is astay when, in heaving in, the direction of the cable forms an acute angle with the water's edge.

Fr: *A pic;* Ger: *Stagweise.*

ASTERN. Toward the stern. An object or vessel that is abaft another object or vessel. In nautical language the word behind is never used.

Fr: *Sur l'arrière;* Ger: *Achteraus.*

See **Fall Astern, Go Astern, Right Astern.**

ASTERN STEERING TEST. A test carried out during sea trials with engines running at full speed astern. The rudder is moved from hard left to hard right in a similar manner as in the ahead steering test. This test is particularly designed to have steering gear and rudder tried under the most exacting conditions likely to be met in service.

ASTEROID. A small planet or planetoid circulating around the sun between the orbits of Mars and Jupiter.

ASTROLABE. An ancient astronomical instrument for measuring altitudes of celestial bodies.

ASTRONOMICAL DAY. The solar day reckoned from noon to noon, so called because of its former use in astronomical calculations.

Fr: *Jour Astronomique;* Ger: *Astronomischer Tag; Sterntag.*

ASTRONOMICAL TIME. The time formerly used for astronomical observations. It was reckoned from noon (0 hours) of one day through 24 hours, that is, to the following noon. It was 12 hours behind civil time.

Fr: *Heure Astronomique;* Ger: *Astronomische Zeit.*

Up to the close of the year 1924, astronomical time was in general use in nautical almanacs. Beginning with the year 1925, the American Ephemeric and Nautical Almanac and similar publications of other countries abandoned the old astronomical time and adopted Greenwich civil time for the data given in the tables.

ASTRONOMICAL TRIANGLE. A spherical triangle on the celestial sphere whose vertices are the pole, the zenith and the observed celestial body. One side is the polar distance of the celestial body, another the zenith distance, and the third the co-latitude of the observer.

Fr: *Triangle de Position;* Ger: *Astronomisches Grunddreieck; Poldreieck.*

AT ANCHOR. A vessel is "at anchor" in accordance with international rules of the road (A) when her anchor is down and holds. (B) when she is held by something equivalent to her anchor, such as a mooring buoy or similar moorings. A vessel made fast to the shore, i.e., to a bank, quay, pier, floating pontoon, is not "at anchor."

Fr: *Au mouillage; Mouillé;* Ger: *Verankert; Vor Anker biegend.*

AT AND FROM. Expression used in marine insurance policies meaning that the insurance attaches as soon as the goods are laden on the vessel "at" a port, continuing until the vessel sails, at which time the word "from" takes effect.

ATHWART HAWSE. Expression used in connection with a ship's position across the bow of another ship at anchor.

Fr: *En travers de la touée.*

ATHWARTSHIPS. At right angles to the fore-and-aft line of a vessel.

Fr: *En travers;* Ger: *Querschiffs.*

ATLUKWODIYAK. A dugout canoe about 30 to 33 ft. long and 5 ft. beam employed in the cod and halibut fisheries by the Makah and Clallam Indians from Cape Flattery and Juan de Fuca Strait. It has a gracefully curving bow, blunt straight stern, and flat bottom. It is manned by a crew of 4 or 5. The Clyoquot and Nittinat people of southern Vancouver use the same type of craft.

ATOLL. A ring-shaped coral reef, often carrying low sand islands, enclosing a body of water, usually called a lagoon.

Fr: *Atoll;* Ger: *Atoll.*

ATRIP. 1. A sail is atrip when it is hoisted to the cap, sheeted home, and ready for trimming.

Ger: *Aufgehisst.*

2. A yard is atrip when it is swayed up ready to have the stops cut for crossing.

3. A mast is atrip when the fid is out and the spar ready for lowering.

4. An anchor is atrip when it is just drawn from the ground and hanging perpendicularly. Also called aweigh.

Fr: *Dérapé;* Ger: *Los; Gelichtet.*

ATRY. The condition of a sailing craft when it is lying to under storm trysail. Sometimes called trying.

Fr: *A la cape;* Ger: *Beiliegen.*

AT SEA. 1. Said of a vessel that has left its moorings or berth in complete readiness for sea although it may still be within the confines of a port (*marine insurance term*).

2. Out on the ocean, away on a voyage, out of sight of land.

ATTESTATION CLAUSE. A marine insurance clause certifying that the policy has been signed by a duly authorized person of the insurance company, thereby formally binding the contract.

AUGMENTATION. The apparent increase in the semidiameter of the moon as it approaches the zenith.

AUGMENTATION OF SEMIDIAMETER. A correction applied to the apparent semidiameter when a celestial object is in the zenith of the observer.

AUSTRALIA CURRENT. A branch of the South Equatorial current of the Pacific Ocean, which branches off the latter in the neighborhood of the Fiji Islands and flows in a South-West direction until it reaches the East Coast of the Australian Continent where it takes a southerly direction.

Fr: *Courant d'Australie;* Ger: *Australstrom.*

AUTO-ALARM. Radio-electrical apparatus connected to the ship's wireless set for the reception of auto-alarm signals. Power supply is from the ship's main 115- or 230-volt Direct Current.

Fr: *Appareil Auto Alarme;* Ger: *Autoalarmapparat; Automatischer Notruf.*

The device comprises two principal units; namely, a fixed timed radio receiver and selector and a junction box. The radio receiver is designed to accept signals of 500 kilocycles, plus or minus 12½ kilocycles, so that, in the event that the transmitter on the ship in distress is not exactly on frequency some tolerance is possible. After the radio signal is amplified and rectified by the radio receiver, it actuates a small high-speed relay, which in turn initiates vacuum tube timing circuits in the selector. The function of these timing circuits is to accept dashes having a duration somewhere between 3½ and 4½ seconds and spaces between 1/10 and 1½ seconds. If the incoming signals fall within these timing tolerances, after passing through the selector circuits, the signals actuate a stepping relay that advances one position for each correctly timed dash and space. After the receipt of 4 such signals the stepping relay has advanced to its final position where it controls a bell-ringing relay that locks in and causes bells to ring on the bridge, in the radio room, and in the radio operator's cabin.

The chief purpose of the auto-alarm receiver is to relieve merchant ships of certain categories of the obligation of keeping a continuous radio watch, which would necessitate a larger staff of operators or watchers. According to the regulations laid down by the International Convention for the Safety of Life at Sea (1929), this apparatus is compulsory for all passenger and cargo vessels with a gross tonnage of 1600 tons or more, whenever a continuous watch is not kept.

U. S. Federal Communications Commission, *Ship Radiotelegraph Safety Rules,* Washington, 1937.

AUTO-ALARM SIGNAL. A radio signal based on international conventions that permits automatic reception of a distress call at times when the radio operator of a vessel is not on duty. The signal consists of a series of dashes and spaces, each dash having a duration of 4 seconds, with an interval of 1 second between dashes.

Fr: *Signal Auto-Alarme;* Ger: *Automatischer Notruf.*

U. S. Federal Communications Commission, *Ship Radiotelegraph Safety Rules,* Washington, 1937.

AUTO FERRY. A vehicular ferry used for the transportation of automobiles and trucks.

AUXILIARY. A naval vessel with the primary function of service to the fleet, as opposed to combatant ships, which are designed to fight offensively. Some of the more important auxiliary vessels are: the oilers, gasoline tankers, repair ships (including destroyer tenders, submarine tenders, aircraft tenders), supply ships, store ships, ammunition ships, tugs, rescue vessels, and so on.

AUTOMATIC FOG GUN. Automatic sound signal in which a mixture of air and acetylene gas is exploded at regular intervals in a gun chamber. The admission of air and acetylene is controlled by an automatic gas valve and the charge is fired by a spark. The explosions continue without any attention from the time the apparatus is started until it is shut off by the attendant.

AUTOMATIC STEERER.
See Gyropilot.

AUTOMATIC SOUND BUOY. A buoy, either bell or whistle, the sonic apparatus of which is actuated by the motion of waves.

Fr: *Bouée Sonore Automatique;* Ger: *Automatische Heulboje; Automatische Heultonne.*

AUTOMATIC STEERING. A method of steering ships wherein the human element is entirely replaced by automatic means, which apply to the rudder a deflection proportional to the deviation of the ship from the prescribed course. Up to now the gyropilot is the only apparatus which has proved successful for the automatic steering of merchant vessels.

Fr: *Gouverne Automatique;* Ger: *Selbststeuerung.*

The advantages of automatic over hand-controlled steering lie in greater actual and effective distance covered by the ship for the same fuel consumption, with less wear and tear on the steering gear. These advantages must, however, be balanced against the extra initial cost of the gyropilot, and the cost of its upkeep.

Clifford, F. S., "Principles and Practice of Automatic Steering, Institute of Marine Engineers, London, *Transactions,* vol. 38 (1926); Leechman, G., *The Theory and Practice of Steering,* Glasgow, 1927; Parker, M., "The Steering of Ships," Institute of Marine Engineers, London, *Transactions,* 1925; Williams, H. G., "Steering of Ships," North East Coast Institution of Engineers and Shipbuilders, Newcastle upon Tyne, *Transactions,* vol. 48, 1927-28.

AUTOMATIC TIDE GAUGE. An instrument that registers automatically the rise and fall of tides. In some instruments the registration is accomplished by the printing of the heights at regular intervals; in others by a continuous graph in which the height of the tide is represented by the ordinates of the curve and the corresponding time by the abscissae.

Fr: *Marégraphe;* Ger: *Selbstzeichnender Pegel.*

AUTOMATIC VENTILATING SIDE LIGHT. A side light in which there is an air passage which, although normally open, is closed automatically by a buoyant float when submerged by waves or when the ship rolls.

AUTOMATIC WELDING. A method or process of electric welding with equipment that automatically controls the entire welding operation. It is adapted to flat work. Also called machine welding.

Fr: *Soudure Automatique;* Ger: *Automatische Schweissung.*

The feeding of the filler metal into the weld and the movement of the arc along the seam is accomplished automatically. The electrode consists of a continuous copper-coated bare wire, and the slag or flux is introduced separately into the welding zone

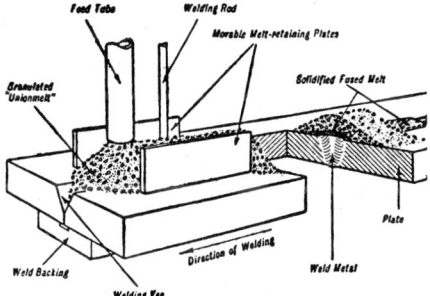

in the form of a powder and not in the form of a coating round the electrode. The carriage that carries the apparatus is driven by a built-in electric motor. It has a speed which varies according to thickness of material and may attain as much as 72 in. per minute. "Unionmelt" is a patented process of this type.

Newell, E. F. and Sillifant, R. R., Modern Developments in Manual and Automatic Arc Welding in Ship Construction, Institute of Welding, *Transactions,* vol. 6 (London, 1943).

AUTONOMOUS PORT. A port controlled by a local independent body, usually appointive in part and elective in part, representing the several interests: governmental, municipal, shipping and trading, which are principally concerned in its proper administration.

Fr: *Port Autonome;* Ger: *Selbstregieren der Hafen.*

It is a type of port trust. Systems of autonomous ports vary with the special laws under which they are authorized in various countries. There are no autonomous ports in U. S. A. London, Liverpool, Havre, Bordeaux, Genoa and Venice are among the most important ones.

AUTUMNAL EQUINOX. The time when the sun crosses the celestial equator in autumn, about September 22. The point in the heavens where this intersection lies.

Fr: *Équinoxe d'Automne;* Ger: *Herbst Aquinoctium.*

AUXILIARIES.

See **Auxiliary Machinery.**

AUXILIARY MACHINERY. A term applied collectively to all machinery and apparatus forming the nonpropulsive equipment of a vessel. Generally called auxiliaries.

Fr: *Appareils auxiliaires; Auxiliaires de bord;* Ger: *Schiffshilfsmaschinen.*

See **Deck Auxiliaries, Engineroom Auxiliaries, Hull Auxiliaries.**

AUXILIARY POWERED VESSEL. A vessel fitted with both sail and machinery for propulsive purposes. The term is not restricted to any particular rig or type of machinery, nor is there a limit to the power installed, below which a vessel is a sailer and above which it is considered as a mechanically propelled vessel.

Fr: *Navire à Moteur Auxiliaire;* Ger: *Hilfsbetriebenes Schiff; Motorsegler.*

The engines of auxiliary propelled vessels are usually of low power and chiefly intended to save the cost of tugs when entering or leaving harbor or to make headway when becalmed, and also to increase the safety of the vessel. Auxiliary power has many points in its favor for sailing vessels engaged in small coasting, and for fishing smacks. In recent years internal-combustion engines have largely superseded steam engines for auxiliary powered vessels and in many cases have made the employment of such vessels remunerative. For cruising yachts the auxiliary engine is usually designed to give sufficient power to drive the boat at a speed corresponding to a speed-length ratio of not less than 0.8.

Blom, C., The Future of Sailing Vessels Fitted with Auxiliary Motors, Institution of Naval Architects, *Transactions,* vol. 69 (London, 1927); Liljegreen, Coal, Oil, or Wind, Institution of Engineers and Shipbuilders in Scotland, *Transactions,* vol. 64 (Glasgow, 1920).

AUXILIARY RUDDER HEAD. A false rudder head situated forward of the main rudder head and connected to it by a yoke and parallel bars. This system is adopted when the width of the ship is insufficient to allow an ordinary tiller to be fitted at the extreme afterend of the vessel.

Fr: *Fausse Mèche;* Ger: *Blinde Ruderschaft.*

AUXILIARY VESSEL. A term applied generally to all merchant ships and pleasure craft whether belligerent or neutral used for the transportation of enlisted men, munitions of war, fuel, provisions, water or any other kind of naval supplies; also those which are designed as repair ships or charged with the carrying of dispatches or the transmission of information, specifically if said vessels are obliged to carry out the sailing orders given them directly or indirectly by a belligerent fleet.

A merchantman which transfers, by its own act, to war vessels the fuels which it has aboard either as cargo or bunkers is considered as auxiliary vessel to the war fleet to which delivery has been made.

In the Treaty for the limitation of Naval Armaments of 1936, an Auxiliary Vessel is defined as follows: A naval surface vessel with standard displacement of more than 100 tons, which is normally employed on Fleet duties or as troop transport, or in some other way than as a fighting ship and which is not specifically built as a fighting ship. (U. S. Treaty Series, No. 919)

Fr: *Navire Auxiliaire; Batiment Auxiliare.*

Ger: *Hilfsschiff; Hilfsbeischiff.*

See **Fleet Train.**

AVAST. An order to stop, to cease hauling.

Fr: *Tiens bon;* Ger: *Festhieven.*

AVERAGE. The term used in maritime commerce to signify damages or expenses resulting from the perils of navigation in a marine adventure. It also implies partial, as distinguished from total, loss. In this term is also included the contribution or adjustment made by merchants for goods that have been lost or thrown overboard. In an insurance including the term "free of all average" (F.A.A.) no claim for deterioration or partial loss is recoverable, it being in effect an insurance against total loss only.

Fr: *Avarie;* Ger: *Haverei; Havarie.*

AWNING SIDE STOPS. The small lines used for hauling the edge of an awning out to the ridge rope.
Fr: *Amarrages de Tente;* Ger: *Sonnensegel Seite Bindseln.*

AWNING STANCHION. Upright pillar placed at the ship's side or erected on the midships line for spreading an awning. Stanchions for awnings may be of forged iron or tubing. Their upper part is suitably formed to support the ends of the cross rafters and take the fore-and-aft ridge lines.
Fr: *Montant de Tente;* Ger: *Sonnensegelstutz.*

AWNING STOPS. Short rope ends or robands spliced into the ridge of an awning to tie it up when furled.
Fr: *Hanet de Tente;* Ger: *Sonnensegel Bindseln.*

AWNING STRETCHER. One of the wooden beams that run from ridgepole to awning stanchion for spreading an awning.
Fr: *Arbalétrier;* Ger: *Sonnensegel Querlatte.*

AXIALLY INCREASING PITCH. A propeller blade with a greater pitch at the following edge than at the leading edge has an axially increasing pitch.
Fr: *Pas Croissant Axial;* Ger: *Axial Variable Steigung.*

AYE-AYE. The orthodox reply to an order, signifying that it will be executed.

AZIMUTH. The angle formed at the zenith by the meridian of the observer and the vertical circle passing through a heavenly body. It is measured clockwise, starting from the north point, from 0 to 360°.
Fr: *Azimut;* Ger: *Azimut.*
See **Altitude Azimuth.**

AZIMUTH CIRCLE. 1. The vertical circle that passes through a celestial body or terrestrial object.
Fr: *Cercle Azimutal;* Ger: *Azimutkreis.*
2. Navigational instrument used in conjunction with a compass for taking azimuths (bearings) of celestial objects. Also called bearing finder. It consists essentially of a graduated circle that fits accurately over the compass bowl and is provided with sight vanes and a reflecting prism.
Fr: *Cercle de Relèvement;* Ger: *Kompassalhidadenkreis.*

AZIMUTH COMPASS. A compass with a card divided into degrees and with vertical sights. It is specially used for taking bearings. On board a ship, the compass is mounted on a stand in a commanding position so that an observer can sweep the horizon. It is fitted with sight vanes, shades, and reflectors. The standard compass used is the azimuth compass.
Fr: *Compas de Relèvement; Compas Azimutal;* Ger: *Azimut Kompass; Peilkompass.*

AZIMUTH DIAGRAM. A graphical method used in celestial navigation for obtaining the true azimuth of a heavenly body.

AZIMUTH MIRROR. A navigational instrument consisting of a ring made of nonmagnetic metal which fits over the top of a compass bowl and is used at sea for taking bearings of terrestrial or celestial objects. Sometimes called azimuth circle.
Fr: *Miroir Azimutal;* Ger: *Kompassdiopter.*

It carries two sighting vanes for taking bearing of terrestrial objects. One of these vanes has a peep-sight and the other, immediately opposite to it, has a vertical sighting wire mounted in an open frame.

The observer turns the instrument around its vertical axis until the object comes on the extension of the line from the observer's eye through the peep-sight to the sighting wire. At the bottom of the wire frame is a reflecting prism so installed that it reflects the view of the compass card directly below the wire to the vision of the observer, enabling him to read the compass bearing while keeping the object lined up with the sighting vanes.

For bearings of the sun, use is made of two vanes at right angles to the sighting vanes. One of these vanes consists of a tilting mirror which can be adjusted to reflect the rays of the sun to a slit in the vane housing diametrically opposite. This housing contains a 45 degree prism which turns the ray of sunlight downward on the edge of the compass card.

AZIMUTH TABLES. Navigational tables that give the successive bearings of a celestial body at given intervals, generally 4 or 10 minutes, for local apparent or civil time. They are mostly used in compensating magnetic compasses.
U. S. Hydrographic Office, Publications H. O. 71 and H. O. 120, Washington, D. C.

B

B. Burgee of the international code of signals of plain red color which, when flown by itself, indicates that the ship is taking in or discharging explosives.

B.C. BRITISH CORPORATION.
B/D. BAR DRAFT (*charter parties*).
b.d.i. BOTH DAYS INCLUSIVE (*marine insurance*).
B/H. 1. BORDEAUX/HAMBURG RANGE OF PORTS. 2. BILL OF HEALTH.
B/L. BILL OF LADING.
B.M. 1. BOARD MEASURE. 2. METACENTRIC RADIUS.
b/t. BERTH TERMS (*chartering*).
B.V. BUREAU VERITAS.

BABANASI. A small single-outrigger dugout canoe from the D'Entrecasteaux Islands (British New Guinea) that will hold 1 or at most 2 persons and used mainly for fishing.

BACK. 1. The forward side of a propeller blade. The after side is called *face*.
  Fr: *Face Antérieure;* Ger: *Vorderfläche.*
  2. Small line fastened on the hook of a cat block or fish block by which it is swung and hooked to the anchor. Also called backrope.
  Fr: *Queue;* Ger: *Steert.*
  3. The upper part of a trawl net next to the mouth at center. The square is the central portion of the net that overhangs the ground in front of and above the ground rope in trawling. Also called upper leaf, upper blade.
  See **Cat Back, Fish Back, Jamb Back.**

BACK (to). 1. To haul sails over to windward. In square-rigged vessels this is done only on special occasions, when it is called "laying the sails aback."
  Fr: *Masquer;* Ger: *Backholen.*
  2. To carry out a small anchor, as the stream or kedge anchor, ahead of the heavier one by which the ship usually rides, in order to support the latter and prevent it from loosening or dragging.
  Fr: *Empenneler;* Ger: *Verkatten.*
  3. To reverse the engines of a vessel so that the ship may be stopped or made to go astern.
  Fr: *Renverser;* Ger: *Zurückschlagen.*

BACK ANCHOR. A small anchor, such as the stream or kedge anchor, carried out ahead of a large one, such as a bower, in order to support it and prevent it from loosening or coming home in bad ground.
  Fr: *Ancre d'Empennelle;* Ger: *Kattanker.*

BACK AND FILL. To work a sailing vessel in a narrow channel to windward with a weather tide when there is no room for tacking, by alternately backing and filling the sails so as to make the ship shoot from one side of the channel to the other while being carried on by the tide.
  Fr: *Dériver Vent dessus Vent dedans;* Ger: *Backen und Füllen.*

BACK AROUND. When the wind changes direction in a counterclockwise manner it is said to back around, as for instance from northeast to northwest by way of north, in the Northern Hemisphere.
  Ger: *Aufkrimpen.*

BACK BAR, BACKING BAR.
  See **Backing Angle.**

BACKBOARD. A board placed across the stern sheets of a rowboat to support the backs of the occupants.
  Fr: *Dossier;* Ger: *Lehnbrett.*

BACKBONE. A rope stitched to the back of an awning and running fore and aft along the middle line. The crowfoot, by which the awning is triced up, is spliced to the backbone.
  Fr: *Fune;* Ger: *Befestigungstau; Strecktau.*

BACK CLOTH. A triangular piece of canvas fastened to the jackstay of a yard in the middle to facilitate stowing the bunt of a large square sail (obsolete).

BACKED NOTE (G.B.). A note countersigned by a shipping firm's representative authorizing the receiving clerk (ship's clerk) to accept delivery of the goods specified in the note.
  Fr: *Bon de Livraison;* Ger: *Abgestempelter Verladungsschein; Kaiempfangschein.*

BACKER. A broad piece of sennit nailed around a yardarm inside the sheave and fitted with an eye or thimble. The head earing is rove through it.
  Ger: *Taustropp.*

BACKER UP.
  See **Holder.**

BACK FREIGHT. Freight charged to a shipper when a vessel cannot deliver her cargo at intended destination and has to return to the loading port with it. Also

30

remuneration for and expenses incurred in getting cargo transhipped and reshipped owing to such cargo being forbidden at the port of destination.

BACKHANDED ROPE. Rope made by twisting each strand right-handed, or in the same direction as the yarns, and laying the strands together left-handed.

BACKING ANGLE. A short length of angle bar placed at the back along the standing flanges of two angle bars abutting and used as a connection. Also called back piece, backing bar, back bar.
Ger: *Winkellaschenprofil.*

BACKING-OUT PUNCH. A heavy punch used with a maul for driving out a rivet already in place, after its head has been removed by drilling, chipping, or burning.
See **Driving Punch, Nail Punch, Rove Punch.**

BACKING RUN. A light bead of weld metal deposited on the root side of a butt weld. Also called sealing run.
Fr: *Reprise à l'Envers.*

BACKING STRIP. Term used by welders to denote a strip of metal, asbestos, carbon, etc., temporarily fastened to the back side of a plate to keep the molten metal from falling through a grooved butt joint that is being welded.

BACKING WIND. A wind that works round against the hands of a clock or against the sun.
Fr: *Recul;* Ger: *Krimpender Wind; Aufkrimpender Wind.*

BACK PIECE. One of the vertical pieces on the after side of the main piece, in a wooden rudder. Also called rudder back piece.
Ger: *Hacke; Ruderhacke.*

BACK POST. The main vertical post in a stern frame upon which the rudder is hung and on which the rudder gudgeons are fixed. Also called rudder post.
Fr: *Etambot Arrière;* Ger: *Hintersteven; Rudersteven.*

BACK PRESSURE. In a reciprocating steam engine, the pressure against the piston during the return stroke, the amount of this pressure being measured in pounds per square inch above a vacuum.

BACK RABBET LINE. The apex of the angle formed by the rabbet in a rabbeted joint. Also called middle line.
Fr: *Fond de Rablure;* Ger: *Innenkante der Spundung.*

BACKROPE. 1. A small rope attached to the hook of a cat block or fish block to facilitate hooking it in the anchor ring.
Fr: *Queue;* Ger: *Steert.*
2. A rope leaded at regular intervals for keeping drift nets in a vertical position after they have been shot. Also called footrope, sole-rope, back, leadline, lower taut.
Fr: *Souillardure.*

BACK SHORE. One or two shores placed on the outside of each ground way at the lower end of the ship resting against a heavy cleat bolted to the ways to assist in keeping the ground ways from moving in a fore-and-aft direction during launching operations.
Fr: *Arc Boutant de Billot; Arc Boutant de Chantier;* Ger: *Aufklotzung Stütze.*

BACKSHORE. The portion of the shore covered by water during exceptional storms. The reverse of foreshore.

BACK SIGHT. The altitude of a heavenly body taken backward or with reference to a point on the horizon directly opposite to that used ordinarily. The angle so measured is subtracted from 180 degrees to obtain the altitude.

BACKSPLICE. A way of preventing a rope's end from unlaying, used instead of a whipping. The rope is first crowned. Then each strand is tucked over and under against the lay, halving the strands before the last tuck.
Fr: *Cul de porc;* Ger: *Schauermannsknoten.*

BACKSTAYS. Ropes forming part of the standing rigging. They stretch from mastheads (except with lower masts) and tend aft from the masts. Their lower ends are fastened on each side of the ship to the chain plates. They serve to support the masts against forward pull and are named according to the mast they support.
Fr: *Galhauban;* Ger: *Pardune.*
See **Breast Backstay, Preventer Backstay, Shifting Backstay, Traveling Backstay.**

BACKSTAYSAIL-RIG. A modified jibheaded ketch rig in which the usual mizzen mast is replaced by a stump mast. A backstay bolted to the horn timber runs through the top of the stump mast to the mainmast head. On this stay a jibheaded sail, called backstaysail, is carried. It has a conventional boom sheeted in the usual way.

BACKSTAY STOOL. Planking or light plating projecting from the sides of sailing craft, to which the ends of backstays are made fast. They serve the same purpose as the channels for the shrouds.
 Ger: *Unterschlag der Pardunen.*
BACK-STRAPPED. Said of a vessel under sail with fair wind but unable to stem the current.
BACKWARD DIP.
 See **Tipping.**
BACKWARD LETTER.
 See **Letter of Indemnity.**
BACKWARD SHIP. A vessel due to load sometime ahead.
BACKWASH. Water thrown aft by motion of a ship's propeller or paddle wheels.
 Fr: *Remous;* Ger: *Schraubenstrom.*
BACK WATER. To back oars, or to back water, means to drive a boat backward by pushing the oars in the direction contrary to that employed in ordinary rowing.
 Fr: *Scier; Nager à culer;* Ger: *Streichen.*
BACKWEIGHT METHOD. A method used in working light cargo using a swinging derrick, the inboard guy of which is led through a block at the head of a stationary derrick at the opposite side of the hatch. To this guy, at a suitable height, is hung a weight called "deadman" or "backweight," and the outboard guy is rove as a runner, the hauling part of which is brought to a winch and hauls the derrick against the weight of the backweight. When the motor is reversed, the weight of the backweight hauls the swinging derrick back into position.
BACK-WINDING. A term used in yacht racing by which is meant the turning or diverting of a current of air by the sails of one boat so as to affect adversely a competing boat.
BADAN. Small Arab sailing vessel from the Gulf of Oman, with a straight vertical or a knee stem, sharp stern with false sternpost made of thin planking and narrow drop rudder with tackle controls. There is no deck. The hull is constructed of teak planking with jackwood topstrakes. It has no center-line keel. There are two grounding keels which have a slight up-curve at the ends. The rig consists of a pole mast without rake and a settee sail. Also called *bedeni* or *badani* in local dialects. Other varieties of this type are called *badan safai* and *badan seyad.*

BADRA. Australian double-outrigger dugout canoe used for fishing and turtle hunting by the natives of Lower Batavia river on the Gulf of Carpentaria. Also called *partara.*
 The hull is shaped with an elliptical projecting ledge at each end. That at the bow is the longest and forms a sort of platform on which the hunter stands when on the lookout for turtles. The two outrigger booms are fixed to the body of the canoe by means of lashings passed through holes drilled in the gunwale. Their ends are fastened to the float by sets of pegs. A central staging is occasionally rigged. This is built up of two poles parallel with the sides of the canoe made fast to both booms and smaller pieces closely laid upon them transversely.
BADGE, QUARTER. Round shaped piece of hardwood fitted as a protection to the transom and plank endings in a square-sterned rowboat. It is fastened to the fashion-piece, gunwale, and rubber.
 Ger: *Blinde Hecktasche; Tasche.*
 In former times it was a carved ornament near the stern of those vessels that had no quarter galleries. It was shaped to carry the sides of the transom out in a neat curve, thereby relieving the square boxlike appearance the transom would otherwise have had.
BAD WEATHER. Term which, as used in charter parties, is generally held to mean not only weather during which cargo could not by any possibility be loaded or discharged, but also weather that is not reasonably fit and proper for working cargo; weather in which it is not reasonably safe to attempt loading or unloading with the appliances at hand, such as lighters; or weather unfit for loading or unloading by reason of the state of the sea as well as that of the atmosphere.
BAFFLING WIND. Wind frequently shifting and light airs.
 Fr: *Brises Folles;* Ger: *Umlaufender Wind.*
BAG (to). Sails are said to bag when setting too full with slack canvas and taut leeches.
 Fr: *Faire le Sac;* Ger: *Bauchen.*
BAG CARGO. General term for all kinds of merchandise carried in bags. Sometimes called bagged cargo.
 Fr: *Chargement en Sacs;* Ger: *Sackladung; Sackgut.*
BAGGAGE. Such articles of personal convenience or necessity as are usually carried by passengers for their personal use. It includes whatever the passenger takes with him for his personal use or convenience, either with reference to the immediate neces-

sities or the ultimate purpose of the journey.
Fr: *Baggage;* Ger: *Reisegepäck.*
BAGGAGE DECLARATION (U. S.).
Customs form filled out by each passenger when landing to obtain immediate clearance for accompanying baggage. All dutiable articles are to be mentioned in this declaration, which is sworn before a customs officer.
BAGGAGE FOREMAN. One in charge of all baggage porters on the pier or quay.
BAGGAGE LIEN. The lien that the owner or master of a vessel has on the baggage that a passenger carries with him, for all unpaid charges for transportation that the passenger incurs during the journey.
BAGGAGE MASTER. A member of the purser's department who has charge of all passengers' luggage stowed in the ship's hold or baggage room.
Fr: *Maître Baggagiste;* Ger: *Gepäckmeister.*
BAGGAGE ROOM. A compartment reserved for the storing of passengers' luggage and so located as to be of easy access from passengers' quarters.
Fr: *Soute à Bagages;* Ger: *Gepäckraum.*
BAGGAGE SUFFERANCE (G. B.).
See **Baggage Declaration.**
BAGGER. A machine that automatically places bulk material in bags for purposes of transportation.
BAGHLA. Lateen-rigged Arab trading vessel found in the Red Sea, South Coast of Arabia, West Coast of India, Persian Gulf and Gulf of Oman. It takes its name from the Arabic word *baghl,* a mule, and is the largest cargo carrier of Arab design, with a tonnage varying from 150 to 400 tons. Also called *baggala.* Length overall, 100 to 140 ft. Breadth 20 to 28 ft. Depth 11½ to 18 ft.

The hull is built with long raking grab bow and transom stern, the latter often elaborately carved and provided with quarter projections. The stem head terminates in the form of a grooved bollard with short peg on the top. The deck extends fore and aft, with a poop deck aft. The rudder head passes through a rudder trunk to the poop deck. It is controlled by a tiller with steering chains led to the barrel of a steering wheel. The rig consists of two or three masts with settee sails made of coarse canvas. The *baghla* in recent years is being gradually replaced by the *ghanja.*
BAG LANYARD. Small line leading through grommets at the top of a sea bag, used for closing it.
BAG NET. A name for all the nets, fixed or moving, in which the fish are received into a pocket: trawl nets, shrimp nets, stow nets, filter nets, hoop nets, seines.
Fr: *Filet à Poche;* Ger: *Sacknetz.*
BAGPIPE. To bagpipe the mizzen is to lay it aback by bringing the sheet to the weather mizzen rigging.
Fr: *Border au Vent;* Ger: *Backlegen.*
BAG ROPE. A strong line that runs from the rigging to the bulwarks in a trawler and prevents the net swinging too far in when the gear is hauled aboard after a tow.
Fr: *Retenue.*
BAGUIO. A tropical wind of hurricane force in the Philippine Islands area and China Sea that generally occurs at the time of change of monsoons.
BAG WRINKLE. Chafing gear wound round and round a stay or topping lift to prevent a sail from chafing against a stay or a topping lift. It is made of old rope ends that extend in bunches of 12 in. long and spaced about 6 to 10 ft. apart. Also called baggy wrinkle.
Fr: *Paillet d'Étai.*
BAHTRAY.
See **Oko.**
BAIDAR.
See **Bidarrah.**
BAILING PIECE. A section of a purse seine or net extending about 10 or 12 fathoms along the center of the cork line and having about the same depth as length.
BAILLIE ROD. An apparatus used for deep sea soundings. It consists of a metal tube about two feet in length with rounded conical top through which passes a movable steel rod. The lower end of the tube screws on and off, and contains a double flap valve to retain the bottom specimen.
BAIT. Any substance thrown into the water or placed on a hook to allure fish to swallow the hook and thereby be caught. The baits used for cod fishing vary according to the time of the year. Herring, mackerel, capelan, clams, and squid are mostly used.
Fr: *Boëtte;* Ger: *Köder.*
See **Ground Bait, Gurry Bait.**
BAIT BOARD. A board about 6 in. wide and 4 ft. long placed across the center of a fishing dory, the two ends fitting into a slot at each gunwale, to hold bait in readiness to be put quickly on hooks. It has small strips of wood tacked on top to keep bait from sliding off, and a half-round hole 2 in. deep and 3 in. wide on the after side, to

BAIT BOAT—BALANCE LUG

keep the fish from sliding around while being unhooked.

BAIT BOAT. See **Striker Boat**.

BAIT SEINE. A seine net about 600 ft. long and 20 to 40 ft. deep which forms part of the equipment of tuna boats. Used for taking anchovies or sardines to be kept alive in the bait tanks, and for catching mackerel which are chopped to bits to feed the bait fish until the latter are thrown back into the sea as "chum" to attract the tuna.

BAKA WAGA. A single-outrigger dugout canoe from N-iw-a (Aniwa) Island, New Hebrides. A boxlike superstructure is sewed on the underbody.

BALANCE BOARD. A heavy plank laid athwart the gunwales of small sailing craft so that one end projects outboard. By loading the projecting section on the weather side, with one or more crewmen, an efficient counterpoise is obtained.

Fr: *Balancier;* Ger: *Ausbalancierungsbrett.*

BALANCE CANOE. A canoe fitted with a transverse plank or pole laid athwart the gunwale. This is equivalent to an outrigger boom, but without the float. Balance canoes are found in South India.

Fr: *Pirogue à Balancier;* Ger: *Kanu mit Balancier Stange.*

BALANCED FRAME. See **Square Frame**.

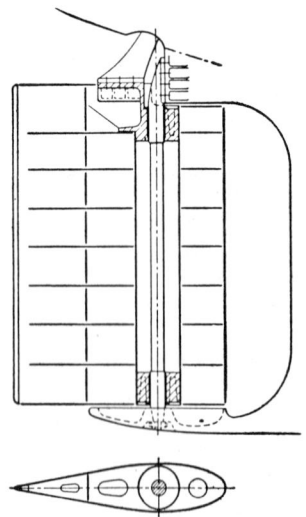

Balanced Streamlined Rudder

BALANCED RUDDER. A rudder in which part of the blade surface, generally from 12 per cent to 20 per cent, is forward of the axis so that the water pressure on this portion counterbalances that on the after part. Also called equipoise rudder.

Fr: *Gouvernail Compensé;* Ger: *Balance Ruder; Schwebe Ruder.*

Its advantage over an unbalanced rudder is that the torque required to change the rudder angle is reduced; consequently less power is needed in the steering engine. If the area forward of the axis exceeds 20 per cent to 25 per cent of total area, there may be difficulty in bringing the rudder back amidships.

BALANCE JIB. Term used by Chesapeake Bay boatmen to denote a clubfooted jib set flying used on sloop-rigged crabbing skiffs. The fore end of the club extends beyond the bowsprit; hence its name. Also called stick-out jib.

BALANCELLE. See **Bilancella**.

BALANCE LUG. A lugsail with boom. About one-fifth to one-sixth of the area of the sail is on the foreside of the mast. A small tack tackle is made fast to the boom a little on the after side of the mast and when hoisted the sail is tacked down by the

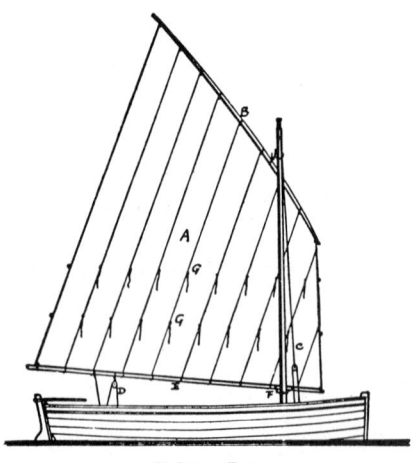

Balance Lug

A. Balance lugsail
B. Lug yard
C. Halyards
D. Sheet
E. Boom
F. Parral on Boom
G. Reef Points

tackle. When going about, the yard is dipped, the boom remaining on the same side of the mast on both tacks. Also called French lug.

Fr: *Voile de Lougre Bomée;* Ger: *Balance Luggersegel.*

BALANCE RATIO. The ratio, in a balanced rudder, of the blade area situated forward of the rudder stock to that of the area abaft.

Fr: *Rapport de Compensation;* Ger: *Waage Verhältnis.*

BALANCE REEF. A reef in the spanker or fore-and-aft gaff mainsail which runs diagonally from the leech cringle of the close reef to the throat of the sail. It is the closest reef and makes the sail triangular or nearly so, the peak standing up like the letter "A" on the boom. The term is frequently applied to the (horizontal) close reef, particularly on board fore-and-aft-rigged vessels.

Fr: *Ris Diagonal;* Ger: *Balancereff.*

BALANCE REEF BAND. A reef band that crosses a spanker or trysail from the throat to the clew diagonally making it nearly triangular, used in heavy weather.

Fr: *Bande de ris Diagonal;* Ger: *Balancereffband.*

BALANCING BAND.
See **Gravity Band.**

BALANCING CLAMP.
See **Gravity Band.**

BALANCING RING. A ring fitted to the balancing band on the shank of a stocked anchor for fishing the anchor with a crane.

BALANDRA. 1. A Philippine sailing dugout with planked sides and double outriggers used for the transport of fish and fishery products on the Visayan Sea. It is rigged with one mast, a sprit mainsail with boom, and a jib-headed foresail that tacks down to the stem.

2. A Peruvian boat used for transportation between the mainland and the Lobos Islands. The hull is square-sterned and decked. The rig consists of a gaff mainsail and two headsails. Length 25 to 30 ft. Breadth 7 to 10 ft. Depth 3½ to 6 ft. Capacity 10 to 14 tons.

BALANDRITA. A sloop-rigged fishing boat of Pacasmayo (Peru), smaller than the *balandra* but otherwise similar.

BALCH LINE. In a trawl net, a Manila rope about 1¼ in. in circumference, to which the foot of the net is hung. It is seized to the footrope by short pieces of rope or marline called "settings" spaced about 1 ft. apart on the wings and about half that distance in the middle or bosom. Also called bolsh line, auxiliary footrope.

Fr: *Ralingue de Ventre;* Ger: *Bulschleine.*

BALDHEAD CUTTER. A sailing cutter with short pole mast and no topsail above the mainsail.

BALDHEADED. A term used in connection with various rigs and usually denoting that some of the regular spars and sails are temporarily or permanently absent. When used in connection with a square-rigged ship it denotes that no sails are set above the topgallants. In a schooner that no topmasts are rigged. Also called bald.

BALDHEADED SCHOONER. Name given in North America to a type of schooner that carries no topmast and is usually fitted with an auxiliary motor.

Fr: *Goëlette à phares abaissés.*

BALDIE. A long-line herring boat built on the Moray Firth (G.B.). The length of keel is from 38 to 40 ft. and the stern is of the cruiser type. It is propelled by motor but carries steadying sails. Length over-all 20 to 80 ft., with 2½ to 3 beams to length. Also called Newhaven yawl.

The sailing baldie or Newhaven yawl is still used for small-line fishing over the whole of the east coast of Scotland. In Banffshire it is often called a skiff. The hull is carvel-built with almost vertical stem and sternpost. It is decked forward. The rig consists of a lofty dipping lug with 4 rows of reef points hoisted on a tall mast stepped far forward, and tacked down to stemhead. Some of the larger boats carry a jib and a standing-lug mizzen.

BALE. A package of soft or nonrigid material, usually more or less rectangular in form, compressed and warped with burlap or other fibrous material secured by wire, straps, rope, or other fastening.

Fr: *Balle;* Ger: *Ballen.*

BALE (to). To remove water from an open boat by means of a baler. Also, to bail.

Fr: *Vider; Écoper;* Ger: *Ausschöpfen; Ausösen.*

BALE CAPACITY. The capacity of a ship's cargo spaces in cubic feet measured to the inside of cargo battens, to tank top ceiling, and to underside of beams. Ten per cent of the bale capacity is usually deducted to obtain the effective capacity for general cargo. Also called bale measure, bale cubic.

Fr: *Capacité Volumétrique en Balles;* Ger: *Ballenladung Inhalt.*

BALE CARGO. Generic term for various manufactured goods wrapped in burlap or similar material for oversea transportation. Some raw materials such as cotton and wool

are also made up in bale form. Also called baled goods.
Fr: *Chargement en Balles;* Ger: *Ballenladung.*

BALEIRA. A whaling boat used on the coasts of Brazil (province of Bahia), very lightly built and fast under sail and oar. The rig consists of a small mast placed well aft to leave the fore end clear, and a lugsail. Length 40 to 60 ft. Breadth, ¼ to ⅕ of the length.

BALE MEASURE.
See **Bale Capacity.**

BALER. Any small utensil used for removing water from an open boat. Also called scoop, skeet.
Fr: *Écope;* Ger: *Ösfass.*

BALE SLING. A single strop or rope, the ends of which have been short-spliced so as to form a continuous piece. It is doubled and passed around a bale or bag, the two ends meeting at the top, where one end is slipped through the other. The hook of the hoisting block is passed into the loop.
Fr: *Élingue Double;* Ger: *Doppelte Schlinge.*

BALIKDJI KAIGHI. A small Turkish boat used for trammel and line fishing. It has the usual rising at ends typical in these waters. Length 23 to 30 ft.

BALL. Day signal about 2 feet in diameter used on coastal stations for making distance signals in combination with a drum and a cone. It is used on board ship (1) by vessels not under command, (2) by vessels engaged in laying or picking up submarine cables, (in conjunction with a diamond), (3) by vessels anchored, (4) by vessels aground, (5) by wreck marking vessels. Also called "globe" when used as a topmark.
Fr: *Ballon;* Ger: *Ball - Signallball.*

BALLAHOU. A two-masted, fore-and-aft rigged trading schooner from Bermuda and the West Indies.
The hull is built with plumb bow, sharp dead rise, little sheer, a short, full transom, and a good deal of rake to the sternpost. The rig consists of a foremast nearly vertical and a mainmast with sharp rake aft. The sails are narrow and tall. There is no boom on the foresail, which overlaps the mainsail. The fore gaff has little peak, while the main gaff is peaked up to an extremely sharp angle.

BALLAM; BELEM; VALLAM. In India the word is used to designate a large dugout canoe found on the Malabar coast and generally used in the hook and line fisheries.
The Arabs have copied the design in planked boats of larger dimensions capable of carrying mast and sail and have retained for this enlarged and improved vessel the Indian name of its prototype.
The Red Sea *belem* from Shukra (near Aden) is conspicuous by its long raking stem. It is rigged with one mast and a settee sail. Some *belem* are decked aft.

BALLAST (in). A ship is said to be in ballast when it carries no cargo, but only ballast. A yacht, in marine parlance, is always considered in ballast.
Fr: *Sur Lest;* Ger: *In Ballast.*

BALLAST. Heavy material placed low in ships used to maintain proper stability, trim, or draft.
Fr: *Lest;* Ger: *Ballast.*
See **Boom Ballast, Permanent Ballast, Shifting Ballast, Water Ballast.**

BALLAST KEEL. A keel used in sailing craft to increase resistance to heeling when under sail by inducing a low center of gravity which in turn increases the righting arms. Also called metal keel.
Ger: *Bleikiel.*
It is bolted to the wooden or steel framing of the hull. Its weight may vary from 30 per cent to 40 per cent of the displacement for cruising yachts and from 50 per cent to 65 per cent for racing yachts. It is usually made of cast lead or cast iron and in some boats is of intricate shape requiring great accuracy in design and manufacture. Lead is always used in racing yachts, and elsewhere if cost is not of first importance.

BALLAST LINE. A system of piping, usually wrought iron, solid-drawn, or lapwelded steel, installed in the ship's hold for filling and emptying ballast, peak, and deep tanks.
Fr: *Tuyautage de Ballast;* Ger: *Ballastleitung; Ballasteinrichtung.*

BALLAST PORT. An opening used for the handling of sand or rubble ballast.
Fr: *Sabord de Lestage;* Ger: *Ballastpforte.*

BALLAST PUMP. A pump used for filling and emptying the ballast tanks. It has by-passes so that it can serve the bilge drainage, sanitary and fire systems either alone or in conjunction with the other pumps.
Fr: *Pompe des Ballasts;* Ger: *Ballastpumpe.*

BALLAST SUCTION PIPE. A ballast pipe for filling or draining any of the water

spaces. Also called ballast suction.
Fr: *Tuyau de Ballast;* Ger: *Ballastrohr.*
In the main ballast tanks the usual practice is to fit a center line and wing suctions in each tank. In the ends of the vessel where there is a good rise of floor center line suctions only are provided. Ballast suctions usually run within the double bottom, passing through manholes or lightening holes in floors and held in position by clips. In some vessels they are led outside along the tank top, each one passing down as required.

BALLAST TANK. A double-bottom, peak, or deep tank for the carriage of water ballast.
Ger: *Ballastwassertank.*

BALLISTIC ERROR. In a gyro compass, the error induced by any change in speed or direction that may cause a small amount of mercury, in the mercury ballistic, to flow from one container to the other. This may cause oscillation of the gyro-axle to overshoot its resting position.
Fr: *Déviation balistique;* Ger: *Ballistisch-esfehler.*

BALL LIGHTNING. A phenomenon which occurs during thunderstorms in circumstances which vary considerably. The discharge of electricity takes the form of globes of fire generally between 10 and 20 centimeters in diameter. Sometimes they occur after a brilliant flash of ordinary lightning, at other times when there has been no flash at all. Also called Globular lightning.
Fr: *Éclair en boule;* Ger: *Kugelblitz.*

BALLOON FORESAIL. A large jib-headed sail carried in lieu of the working forestaysail. In yachts it is generally cut on the diagonal with cloths perpendicular to the foot and leech. Also called balloon forestaysail.

Fr: *Trinquette Ballon;* Ger: *Ballon-kluver.*

BALLOON JIB. A large, triangular racing sail of light canvas between the topmast head and the bowsprit head. The spinnaker is sometimes carried forward as a balloon jib in racing. Also called ballooner.
Fr: *Foc Ballon;* Ger: *Ballonkluver; Jager.*

The balloon jib is set flying and carried only with a free wind. On a broad reach the balloon jib is considered by some as more effective than the Genoa jib owing to its greater area. It is usually sheeted to the main boom by means of a snatch block through which the sheet is rove and led inboard.

BALLOON JIB TOPSAIL. A yacht sail made of light canvas, set on the jib topsail stay, and sheeting to the quarter of the vessel. When this sail is set, it generally takes the place of all other headsails.
Fr: *Clin Foc Ballon;* Ger: *Ballon Flieger; Ballonkluver Topsegel.*

BALLOON SAIL. A general term used for light racing and cruising sails found on yachts, such as balloon jib, balloon topsail and foresail, shadow sail, and water sail.
Fr: *Ballon;* Ger: *Ballonsegel.*

BALLOON STAYSAIL. A racing sail of recent origin set in conjunction with a parachute spinnaker. It is hanked on a special stay attached to the mast about 60% of its height above deck and terminating on deck at the weather rail about 2 ft. from the stemhead. It overlaps the mast like a Genoa jib and is made of the lightest sailcloth.
Ger: *Ballonstagsegel.*

BALLOON TOPSAIL. A racing gaff topsail of quadrilateral shape cut with more belly and having a longer yard than the yard topsail. The outer part of the foot is secured to a small club and extends beyond the peak of the gaff. It is very large in comparison with the other topsails.
Fr: *Flèche Ballon;* Ger: *Ballon Topsegel.*

BALLOT. A small bale, weighing usually from 70 to 120 lbs.

BALL PLUG. An automatic boat plug used on self-bailing lifeboats.
It consists of a cagelike fixture with a soft rubber ball fitted over the drain hole in the bottom of the boat. When the boat is afloat the water pressure forces the ball against its seat and prevents any ingress of water through the drain hole. When the boat is hoisted out of the water the ball drops down into the cage thereby opening the drain hole and allowing any water in the boat to drain out.

BALOK. A Malay trading craft from the Lesser Sunda Islands. It is lug-rigged with one or two masts. It has a peculiar slightly outrigged platform at the stern. Length 30 ft. Breadth 6 ft.

BALONG. A sailing craft used for fishing by the Milanau people of Sarawak (North Borneo). The hull consists of a dugout base with planked sides and square-shaped end pieces projecting in the form of narrow horizontal platforms. It is rigged with two masts and dipping lugsails. Length 30 to 40 ft.

BALSA. 1. A raft found on the West Coast of South America, made of 5, 7, or 9 large beams of balsa wood up to 60 ft. long, arranged side by side with the longest placed in the center.

These logs are firmly held together by crossbars, lashings, and stout planking near the ends. The *balsa* generally carries one large sail hoisted to a pair of shears formed by two poles crossed and lashed together at the top. It is steered by means of two broad planks which project, one at each end, through a slit a few inches wide by 1 or 2 ft. long. These planks may be drawn up or thrust down to the depth of 10 or 12 ft. By judiciously raising or lowering one or both of these planks the raft may not only be steered but also tacked or worn. Small fishing *balsas* found in the northerly ports of Peru are usually unrigged. They are propelled by means of one or two broad plank oars that the fishermen thrust straight down into the water at the stern and use as levers against the ends of the logs.

2. The term *balsa* is also applied to grass boats of various shape made of bundles of rushes, reeds, and so on and used by natives on rivers or lakes in Nevada, Peru, Mexico, and Senegambia.

BALSA WOOD. An extremely buoyant wood, lighter than cork, utilized for lifebuoy fittings, lifebuoys, and life rafts, also in the manufacture of plywood for the construction of small craft. The average weight per cubic foot is 7 to 8 lbs.

Muhlenbruch, C. W., "Mechanical Properties of Balsa Wood," American Society for Testing Materials, *Proceedings*, vol. 37 (1937).

BALTCON. Code name of the Baltic and International Maritime Conference coal charter, 1921.

BALTIC AND INTERNATIONAL MARITIME CONFERENCE. A conference founded in 1905 under the name of Baltic and White Sea Conference by a group of shipowners from various countries interested in the coal and timber trades to and from the Baltic and the White Sea.

By 1930 it had grown to an international conference of shipowners and shipbrokers representing twenty-one maritime nations and controlling over 9,900,000 tons with a view to defending shipowners and protecting their interests. It brought into being and general use many standard forms of charter parties such as the Baltime, Baltcon, Gencon, and so on, which are used all over the world.

BALTIC BOW. A term used to denote a type of bow or stem found on icebreakers and vessels that have to force their way through ice. It recedes sharply just below the waterline, its purpose being to allow the fore part of the vessel to ride over the surface of the ice and crush it by its weight. Emerson, I. A., "Effect of Shape of Bow on Ship Resistance," Institution of Naval Architects, London, *Transactions*, vol. 79 (1937).

BALTIME. Code name of the Baltic and International Maritime Conference standard form of time charter.

BALTIMORE BERTH GRAIN CHARTER. A standard charter party form by which steamers are to be loaded with grain according to berth terms, and with customary berth dispatch. Charterers occasionally take an option to ship cargo other than grain on payment of any expenses over and above what grain would cost. This form, which was adopted in 1913, is known by the letter "C."

BALTIMORE CLIPPER. A name formerly given in the U. S. A. to a sharp-built schooner or brig-rigged vessel with a tonnage from 90 to 200 tons. The masts were given a great amount of rake in order to preserve a proper balance of sail; the hull had great dead rise and cutaway ends. Length 35 to 120 ft. on deck. The type is now obsolete.

Chapelle, H. I., *The Baltimore Clipper*, Salem, Mass., 1930.

BALTWOOD. Code name for a Standard Charter relating to timber cargoes from Baltic ports. This charter which came into operation in 1926 replaces the "Scanfin" and "Ruspruss" forms.

BALUK. Open rowboat pulling 6 oars used for the transportation of people and stores around Constantinople. The oarsmen stand when rowing. Length 40 ft. Breadth 8 ft., 2 in. Depth 4.3 ft.

BAMBOO SPAR. A spar made of bamboo stalks, used for small sailing yachts up to about 3 tons. These spars are very tough but since they have a tendency to split, they are usually served with tarred marline between joints, and small air holes are drilled in them.

BANAWA. A plank-built trading craft from Macassar similar to the *paduakan*. It has two quarter rudders, one or two masts and bowsprit. It is mostly used for transportation of cattle. Also called *benau*.

BANCA. Generic term for dugouts or built-up craft with square ends from the Philippines, which are larger than the *baroto* and *panagatan*. Length 16 to 23 ft. Breadth about 2 ft., 4 in. Depth 2 ft.
There are several types of *bancas*, known locally as *chinchorroan, sapiawan, dinapalang*. All are of similar build, with bow and stern turned up in overhanging fashion. Transverse stability is obtained by fastening outside, a little above the waterline, two large bamboo spars that extend fore and aft. *Bancas* are propelled by oars or paddles.

BAND. A strip of canvas from ⅓ to ½ the breadth of a cloth, sewed on to prevent sails from splitting.
See **Belly Band, Boom Band, Breast Band, Derrick Band, Foot Band, Futtock Band, Girt Band, Gooseneck Band, Gravity Band, Hound Band, Mast Band, Reef Band, Balance Reef Band, Rudder Band, Spider Band, Skeg Band, Sling Band, Stem Band, Truss Band.**

BANDING. A strip of canvas sewed over the tabling of a sail at head, luff, foot, and leech, from the clew up above the reef cringles. Also called strengthening piece.
Fr: *Galon.*

BANDONG. 1. A Malay sailing boat built of merawan wood and generally used for transporting firewood and charcoal between the Rhio Islands and Singapore. The *bandong* is lug-rigged with one or two masts. Average capacity 4.8 to 9½ tons. Length 54 ft. Breadth 13 ft. Depth 6 ft.
2. In Western Borneo, a river canoe with outboard platforms for poling.
3. A planked canoe with sharp ends, propelled by paddles, used by Kalaka fishermen (Sea Dyaks) of Borneo. Length 30 ft. Breadth 3½ ft. Depth 3 ft.

BANG-CHOON. An open sail and rowing seine-boat found near Singapore and Hainan Island (southern China). The hull is round-bottomed with rockered keel. A false keel of half-round section extends over about ⅔ of the total length. Length 37 ft., 3 in. Breadth 4 ft., 9 in. Depth 2 ft. (molded).
The planking, made of seriah wood, is carvel-laid. Plank edges are fastened with diagonally driven nails. The frames are natural crooks of penaga wood. The flattened stem has a pronounced rake. Sharp stern with portable decking. The rig consists of two short masts with peculiarly shaped spritsails, long in the head and with small leech. The foremast is stepped near the stem, the mainmast at half length or thereabouts. The luff of the foresail extends forward of mast and tacks down to the stem.

BANGKO. A paddle and sailing outrigger canoe from the Moluccas (Ternate) used for the transportation of persons between the islands. The hull is built on the same lines as the *orembai*. It has a small thatched roof shelter amidships. Also called *prao bangko, prao kaguna*.

BANK. 1. A plateau of any material over which the depth of water is relatively small but sufficient for safe navigation (6 to 100 fathoms) and on which there is no island or archipelago projecting above the surface of the water. It may act as a support for any secondary formation such as shoals or reefs, which are dangerous to navigation.
Fr: *Banc;* Ger: *Anhöhe; Bank.*
2. A shallow area consisting of shifting forms of silt, sand, mud, gravel, and so forth. Used only with a qualifying word, as "sandbank," "gravel bank," and so on.
Fr: *Banc;* Ger: *Bank.*
3. The side of a river channel, especially that part that usually rises above the water level. The two banks of a river are called right and left as seen when looking downstream.
Fr: *Berge;* Ger: *Deich; Gestade.*

BANK (to). To bank a fire, i.e., to cover it with ashes, and use other means—as closing the dampers and pit doors—to make it burn low and at the same time prevent its becoming extinguished.
Fr: *Couvrir;* Ger: *Aufbanken; Aufschütten.*

BANKED FIRES. Coal fires in marine boilers are banked to suppress combustion. Banking is accomplished by covering the hot bed of coals with ashes or green coal. Sufficient heat is given off to supply small steam demands and the banked fire may be readily stirred up to full intensity.
Fr: *Feux Couverts;* Ger: *Aufgebanktes Feuer.*

BANKEROHAN. A Philippine dugout of the *baroto* type used in the Visayan region to ferry passengers and goods across streams. It is heavily built with comparatively flat bottom, wide beam, and double outriggers. Another variety of *bankerohan*, of wider beam with thicker bottom and sides, is used for transportation of goods only; it has no outriggers.

BANKSKOITE. See **Bankskuta.**

BANKSKUTA. Generic name for Swedish deep-sea craft, with a tonnage ranging from 30 to 70 tons burden, formerly employed in the North Sea bank fisheries with hook and line. Similar Norwegian craft are called *bankskoite*. *Bankskuta:* Length over-all 51.4 to 63 ft. Length, keel, to 42 ft. Breadth 18.4 to 26.8 ft. Depth 7 to 13.3 ft. (molded). *Bankskoite:* Length over-all 60 ft. Length, keel, 34 ft. Breadth 21 ft. Depth 8 ft. (hold).

The ends are full and rounded above water but hollowed out a great deal below the load line, giving a very sharp rise of floors near the keel. There is a raked and slightly curved stem, sharp-raking stern, and flush deck; moderate sheer with raised bulwarks at fore end. The vessels are ketch-rigged with pole masts and running bowsprit. There are two headsails. The mainsail has no boom. The topsails on both masts are jack-yarders with long head and yard.

BANTING. A trading *prao* from Northern Java and Achin (Sumatra), with short and broad hull and inward curved stem. The upper works extend outboard at the stern, forming a base for a small house or shelter. It is rigged with two or three masts and has two quarter rudders. Length 90 ft. Breadth 27 ft. Depth 7 ft. Capacity 28 tons.

BAR. 1. A bank or shoal usually at the mouth of a river obstructing the entrance or rendering it difficult. Bars are formed of large quantities of alluvial matter eroded from the land and deposited at or near the river mouth. This alluvial deposit brought down from upstream forms obstructions to littoral drift and collects material carried in suspension by the sea.

Fr: *Barre;* Ger: *Barre; Hafenbarre.*

2. Section; shape. A general term embracing all forms of rolled steel bars such as angles, tees, channels, I beams, and bulb bars as distinguished from plates. Also called section, shape.

Fr: *Profilé;* Ger: *Profil; Profileisen.*
American Marine Standards Committee, Pamphlet No. 85, *Rolled Steel Shapes for Shipbuilding*, Washington, 1932.

BARANGAY; BARANGAYAN. A planked boat with sharp stern and double outriggers, found on the North Coast of Mindanao Island (Cagayan district), propelled by oars and sails and rigged with two masts. A raised platform of bamboo is provided for handling the sails.

BARBARICCIO. See **Cabanella.**

BAR BOUND. Said of a vessel detained inside or outside a harbor by the condition of the sea on the bar.

BAR BUOY. A buoy indicating the location of a bar at the mouth of a river or harbor.

Fr: *Bouée de Barre;* Ger: *Barretonne.*

BARCA. A type of open boat chiefly propelled by oars and occasionally setting a small sail, found in the Gulf of Venice and Bay of Trieste. Length 32½ ft. Breadth 6 ft., 4 in. Inside depth 1 ft., 8 in. Also called *barchetta.*

The hull is flat-bottomed with rounded stem and sharp rounded stern. There is a cuddy deck at each end. These boats are engaged in trawling, manned by a crew of 20; for sardine and other fisheries the crew is reduced to 4 or 6 hands.

BARCACA. Sailing barge found in the provinces of Rio Grande do Norte, Parahyba, Pernambuco, Alagoas, and Sergipe (Brazil). It is rigged with two or three masts and gaff sails; no headsails. Length 70 ft. Breadth 13 ft. Depth 4 ft., 3 in. Tonnage 45.

These craft are built with flat bottom, walled sides, square transom stern with outboard rudder, and are keelless. They are chiefly engaged in the transportation of sugar and cotton along the coast.

BARCA CAPACIOTA.

See **Capaciota.**

BARCA CARLOFORTINA. Decked sailing boats originating from Carloforte in Sardinia, chiefly used for lobstering and provided with a small fish well that can accommodate from 22 to 44 lbs. of live lobsters. Length 23.8 ft. Breadth 8.2 ft. Depth (inside) 2.3 ft.

The hull is double-ended with vertical stem and sharp stern. The well is located abaft the mast. The rig, of Spanish type, consists of a short mast raking forward, with lateen mainsail and short jibboom with one headsail. Some boats are fitted with an auxiliary motor, forward of the mast and with the propeller shaft running through the top of the well.

BARCA DA PORTAS. An open boat employed in the tunny fisheries off the coast of Portugal, with sharp stern and rising stem and sternpost. It is used for closing the aperture of the large tunny nets; hence its name. On one side of the boat a platform extending from bow to stern is built to enable the crew to handle the fish, which are of considerable size. The rig consists of a spritsail.

BARCA DA TESTA. A strongly built rowing and sailing boat employed in the Portuguese fisheries. The stem and sternpost are fitted with a projecting piece or cathead for handling the nets. It is rigged with a settee sail.

BARCA DE JABEGA. See Jabega.

BARCA DE PARELLA. See Pareja.

BARCA DI GRADO. Double-ended open boat originating in Grado and employed in the local fisheries of the Gulf of Trieste and Friulian coast. Length 32.4 ft. Breadth 6.2 ft. Depth 1.6 ft.

The hull is flat-bottomed, without keel, with convex-curved stem and round stern. There is a cuddy aft, which extends approximately over ⅓ of the boat's length. One portable mast is stepped forward through a thwart, with balanced lugsail.

BARCA FIOCINARA. See Barca.

BARCA I CONZU. See Cuzzulara.

BARCA I SARDI. See Sardara.

BARCA POZZOLANA. Open fishing boat found in Neapolitan waters and chiefly employed in the setting of trammels and other fixed nets. It is built with clipper stem and sharp stern, and rigged with one portable mast, lateen mainsail, and jib. Length 30.3 ft. Breadth 8.1 ft. Draft 1.9 ft.

BARCARECCIO. Term used to denote collectively the fleet of open craft employed in Italy for working the *tonnara* or fixed tunny net. The following boats are included in the *barcareccio: vascello, caporais, palischermo, bastardo, musciara, musciaretta, rimorchio, coalanitto.*

BARCA TRASURALLEVA. Three-masted, lateen-rigged fishing boat from the Balearic Islands, with high projecting stemhead. It has a large mainsail, small foresail, and large jib. The foremast and mainmast have a forward rake; the jigger mast is upright.

BARCHETTA. See Barca.

BARCO. A small sailing coaster from the province of Bahia (Brazil). Length 36 to 72 ft. Tonnage 20 to 120.

BARCO DE BUARCOS. A Portuguese open fishing boat originating in the fishing port of Buarcos and rigged with two masts and lateen sails, having small cuddy decks at the ends. The mainmast is stepped at half length and has a forward rake of about 30 degrees. The aftermast or mizzen is smaller and has only 20 degrees of rake.

BARCO DE CAMINHA. An open boat with raked stem from the estuary of the river of Minho (Portugal) used for inshore fishing. Length 16.4 ft. Breadth 6.3 ft. Depth 2.3 ft.

BARCO DO MINHO. Row boat from the Minho river with long, graceful raking stem and round stern. Extreme length 27 ft.; length 13 ft. Breadth 5 ft., 3 in. Inside depth 1 ft. The keel and framing are of oak with planking of pine or chestnut.

BARCO ILHAVO. A Portuguese flat-floored open boat with very high curved stem and stern. The fore part is decked over and used as a cuddy. This type of boat is chiefly engaged during the winter months in the capture of sardines between Cape Roca and Cape Espichel. It is also used in different parts of the coast to fish with a net called *chinchorro*. It resembles the *varinho*. A mast is stepped amidships and sets a lateen, but this type of boat is more usually propelled by oars.

BARCO MOLICEIRO. The *barco moliceiro* and *barco saleiro* are very similar craft used on the saline marshes of the Aveiro (Portugal). *Barco saleiro:* Length 60 ft. Breadth 8½ to 9 ft. Capacity 18 to 20 tons. Sail area 344 sq. ft. *Barco moliceiro:* Length 36 to 47.8 ft. Breadth 7.8 to 8.1 ft. Depth 2.3 to 2.7 ft. Capacity 2 to 2½ tons.

The shallow hull, built without keel, with tall and gracefully curved stem and sternpost, and peculiarly shaped rudder fitted with a yoke. The fore part is decked. The boats are propelled by sail and oars. The rig consists of a slender mast about 30 ft. long without shrouds and a standing lug. The luff of the sail is extended by two bowlines with bridles, one at the foot, the other near the head. The latter leads to the stemhead. There are two lines of reef points near the head. A second mast placed forward is occasionally rigged on the *barco moliceiro*. The *barco moliceiro* is chiefly used for collecting and transporting sea grass and weeds (*molico*), the *barco saleiro* for salt.

BARCO POVEIRO. A Portuguese open boat similar to the *lancha poveira* but of smaller size and used for inshore fishing. It originated in the Portuguese village Povoa de Varzim, from which locality it derives its name. It is built of locally grown pine wood, except the keel. The rig consists of a mast stepped well forward and with slight forward rake, on which sets a lateen sail tacked down to the stemhead. Oars numbering 4 are used in calm weather. The *barco de poveiro* is called *sardinheira* when engaged in sardine fisheries.

See **Povera**.

BARCO SALEIRO.
See Barco Moliceiro.

BAR DRAFT. The amount of water over a bar measured at low water.

BAREBOAT CHARTER
See Demise Charter.

BARE ELECTRODE. In arc welding a metal electrode not provided with a flux covering.
Fr: *Electrode Nue;* Ger: *Blanke Elektrode; Nackte Elektrode.*

BAREUX. Name given locally in the District of Boulogne (France) to a type of fishing boat, about 30 ft. in length, employed during the summer as a liner and in the winter as a herring drifter.

When lining, the *bareux* are cutter-rigged. But owing to the necessity of having a lowering mast when fishing with drift nets they change over to lug rig during winter months. Two main mast steps are provided for the different rigs and the cut of the gaff mainsail is such as to permit its use as a lug mainsail when drifting. Another peculiarity of these boats is the small hatch placed forward of the helmsman's cockpit. The fisherman tending the hand lines in heavy weather stands waist-deep in this hatch to avoid being washed overboard. During the winter months this aperture is planked over and caulked to make a flush deck for drift-net fishing. The name *bareux* is given to these boats because their catch is chiefly made up of bass (*bar* in French). The hull is carvel-built with bent frames; some have a transom stern, others a counter.

BARGE. 1. A term applied to a flag officer's boat, in naval usage, or to an elegantly fitted boat, or craft of ceremony, propelled by oars or mechanically, and reserved for the use of high officials when transported in state. In a legal sense a barge is usually held to be a boat or vessel and hence within the letter of the laws relating to such craft.
Fr: *Canot d'apparat;* Ger: *Galaboot.*

2. Also *lighter.* A general name given to flat-bottomed rigged or unrigged craft of full body and heavy construction (built of wood, iron, steel, or concrete), specially adapted for the transportation of bulky freight such as coal or lumber, sand, stone, and so on. Some types trade solely on rivers and canals but a great number are built and equipped for short-distance coastwise traffic.
Fr: *Chaland;* Ger: *Leichter; Prahm; Kahn; Schute.*
See **Coasting Barge, Dumb Barge, Dummy Barge, Dump Barge, Hopper Barge, New York Sailing Barge, Oil Separating Barge, Schooner Barge, Solent Barge, Twin-End Barge, Tank Barge, Thames Sailing Barge.**

BARGEE. One who manages a barge. One of the crew on a barge. Also called bargeman.
Fr: *Batelier; Gabarier;* Ger: *Leichterschiffer; Leichterführer.*

BARGE YACHT. Very shallow-draft sailing yacht with flat bottom, wall sides, and sharp chine, in which lateral resistance is obtained from leeboards in order to minimize leeway under sail.

BARGING PORT. A port or harbor where the method of distribution of import and export goods is chiefly by barges, in contradistinction to a cartage port, where carted traffic is prevalent. Sometimes called barge port.

BARING-AN. A dugout used by the Philippine natives on Samar Island for fishing with a shore seine called *baring.* It is similar to the *sapiao-an* and is used for transporting the net and the catch.

BARINO. A boat decked at both ends and with peculiar rising stem, found at the mouth of the Tagus and used for transport. It is rowed or sailed and carries a lugsail or a lateen. Length 60 ft. Breadth 12 ft. Depth 4 ft.

BARK. Strictly, a three-masted bark.
Fr: *Barque;* Ger: *Bark.*
See **Five-Masted Bark, Four-Masted Bark, Jackass Bark, Three-Masted Bark.**

BARK CANOE. A canoe in which the skin is made of bark fastened to a light framing. In some types the single sheet of bark is used for the outer skin. In others, two or more sheets are placed either longitudinally or transversely from gunwale.
Fr: *Pirogue en écorce;* Ger: *Rindenboot.*

The single-sheet canoes may be classified as two different species distinguished by the way in which they are finished at the ends. In some the ends are tied together, in others they are laced or sewed, and in others the ends are blocked with clay. In single-sheet canoes the length does not exceed 12 to 14 feet and may be as small as 5 feet. The best bark canoes are made of three pieces. Those made of two or one piece have a tendency to buckle or bulge in the center. In the Indian canoes of North America the ribs are made of split and skinned roots of jack-pine or cedar with the flat side against the bark.

BAR KEEL. A keel projecting below the bottom of the vessel and made of long bars forged from scrap iron or scrap steel or rolled from open hearth steel ingots, to which the flanged garboard plates are riveted. Nowadays this type of keel is used only in the construction of small vessels such as yachts, fishing craft, coasters. Also called hanging keel.

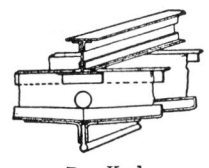

Fr: *Quille massive;* Ger: *Massiver Kiel; Balkenkiel.*

BARKENTINE. A three-masted vessel square-rigged on the foremast and fore-and-aft rigged on the main and mizzen. The fidded topgallant mast and square fore-course, the absence of the trysail abaft the foremast, and of the forestaysail are the main features that distinguish the barkentine rig from the square topsail schooner rig. Three-masted barkentines were first built about 1850, four-masters about 1880, and five-masters not until 1918. Also called *Barquentine, Barkantine.*

Fr: *Trois-Mâts Goëlette;* Ger: *Dreimastschoner.*

BARKING. The action of putting on sails or nets a protective mixture consisting of yellow ocher, tallow, cutch, and oak bark. The mixture is boiled and applied still boiling with long-handled brushes, first on one side, then on the other.

Fr: *Tannage;* Ger: *Abrinden.*

BARKINO. A small, lightly built open boat with square stern, propelled by sail or oars, used by fishermen on the lagoon of Ortebello (Tuscany). The rig consists of one short mast placed near the stem with a triangular sail laced to the mast.

BARK RIG. A rig adopted for three-, four-, and five-masted vessels in which the after mast is fore-and-aft-rigged, the other masts having square yards.

Fr: *Gréement de Barque;* Ger: *Barktakelung.*

BARLING SPAR. A round stick or piece of timber with a length of 28 to 30 ft. and a girth at the butt of 4 to 5 hands, suitable for spar making.

BARNACLE. A small, primitive marine animal with a calcareous shell, which in its adult form lives attached directly by its base to some foreign object, such as a ship's hull, wharf piles, and the like.

Its distribution is worldwide; however, only certain species are found over wide areas or in different localities. The young animal is free-swimming for as long as 2 or 3 months, then it attaches itself to a suitable surface and takes up permanent abode. Thereupon it commences to secrete the shell, which grows both in diameter and height as the animal matures. After it has formed this shell house, toxic ship-bottom paints will not affect it.

Although immersion in fresh water for 48 hours will kill the animal, its shell will remain attached to a ship's bottom until removed by scraping.

The barnacle is a persistent and troublesome source of fouling on ship's bottoms.

Wilson, D. P., *Life of the Shore and Shallow Sea,* London, 1937.

BAROGRAM. The record of atmospheric pressure traced on the drum sheet of a barograph.

Fr: *Barogramme;* Ger: *Barogramm.*

BAROGRAPH. An aneroid barometer fitted with a lever which bears a pen, recording upon a revolving drum variations of atmospheric pressure.

Fr: *Barographe; Baromètre enregistreur;* Ger: *Barograph.*

BAROMETER. An instrument for measuring atmospheric pressure.

Fr: *Baromètre;* Ger: *Barometer.*

See **Aneroid Barometer, Marine Barometer, Mercurial Barometer.**

BARONG. An open craft used for fishing in coastal waters of Western Borneo. It is rowed or sailed. The rig consists of one mast that is placed forward of amidships and that carries a square sail. The sail is controlled by vangs from the yardarms and sheets from below. The steering is done by twin rudders or a long oar. Also called *prao-tukan.* Length 31 ft. Breadth 9 ft., 6 in. Depth 3 ft., 8 in.

BAROTO. A double-outrigger dugout canoe from the Philippine Islands. The fore end turns up gradually from the waterline, forming a sweeping curve. The stern is similarly shaped but shorter. The smallest one-man canoe has a length of about 13 ft. with a breadth of 1 ft. 4 in. and a depth of 1 ft. 7 in. The largest craft, which carry up to 10 persons vary in length from 30 to 40 ft. and in breadth from 3 to 4 ft. It is rigged with a square or triangular sail. Used in fishing and transportation in Visayan province.

BAR PILOT. Pilots who confine their operations to the navigation of vessels across the bar of a river or at the entrance to a channel or harbor.

Fr: *Pilote de Barre;* Ger: *Barrelotse.*

BAR PORT. A harbor that can be entered only when the tide rises sufficiently to permit passage of vessels over a bar.

Fr: *Port à Barre;* Ger: *Barrehafen.*

BARQUET. A small open boat from the French Mediterranean shores similar to the *bette* but without washboards.

BARRA. Australian dugout canoe from Melville Island (Northern Territory). The hull is sharp at both ends with vertical cutwater and round bottom. There is no difference in shape between bow and stern, both narrowing in a similar way and sheered up at the ends. Length 15 ft. Breadth 2 ft. Depth at ends 2 ft. 6 in.

When the log is hewed out, a slab about six inches in width and two in thickness is left running across from side to side, about a third of the length from one end. This

Barkentine

BARQUETA. Name given in various parts of Portugal to a flat-bottomed rowboat similar to the *bateira.*

BARQUETTE. Small boat, found on the French Mediterranean coast, with rounded stem rising well above the gunwale. The sternpost has an inboard curve. These boats are either open, half-decked, or fully decked with relatively high washboards that curve inboard. The lateen rig is generally used. Length 16 ft. 5 in. Breadth 6 ft. Depth 2 ft. 10 in.

BARQUILLA. A small Spanish rowboat with sharp stern. It has one mast and lateen sail.

BARQUINHA. Small open boat with raking stem and transom stern resembling the *batel* but smaller and fitted with a small well for keeping fish alive. Used on the Tagus river.

slab has a hole in the center through which the mast is passed to be stepped into a block at the bottom of the canoe.

BARRATRY. An unlawful or fraudulent act, or very gross and culpable negligence, by the master or mariners of a vessel in violation of their duty as such, directly prejudicial to the owner or cargo, and without his consent. Smuggling, trading with an enemy, casting away the ship, and plundering or destroying cargo are considered barratry.

Fr: *Baraterie;* Ger: *Baratterie; Betrügerei.*

BARREL. 1. The drum roller or cylinder of a crane, winch, or capstan about which the rope or chain winds. In a steering apparatus the barrel is the cylinder on which the tiller ropes or chains are wound.

Fr: *Tambour;* Ger: *Trommel.*

2. A measure used in the British fish trade. It varies in size and contents according to the fish under consideration. A barrel of cured herrings contains between 900 and 1000 fish and weighs 2 6/7 cwt. A barrel of red herrings contains 160 fish. A barrel of fresh herrings contains 660 fish.

3. A measure of fuel oil, used in oil-burning, steam, and Diesel-driven ships. In the trade 1 barrel of petroleum oil, unrefined, is equal to 42 gallons.

See **Capstan Barrel, Irish Barrel**.

BARREL BULK. A unit used in freight measurement equivalent to 5 cu. ft.

BARREL CARGO. Generic term for liquid or dry goods stowed in barrels, casks, hogsheads, pipes, puncheons, or other containers in a vessel's hold.

Fr: *Chargement en Barils;* Ger: *Fassladung.*

BARREL HOOKS.
See **Can Hook**.

BARREL MAN. Member of the crew in a sealing vessel stationed in a barrel slung at the top of the highest mast. This position, being of great importance, is generally occupied either by the captain himself or his first officer, armed with a powerful telescope on the lookout for any indications that may point the way to seals.

BARREL SLING. A sling made of a short length of rope with a cant hook at each end for grasping the staves of a cask. A sling made from a length of rope with an eye spliced on one end and 2 half hitches on the other. Also called butt sling, claws, clip hooks.

Fr: *Patte à futaille;* Ger: *Fass Lange.*

BARRIER. The edge of great polar glaciers that enter the sea but remain attached to the land.

Fr: *Barrière de Glace.*

BARRIER ICE. Floating ice which has broken off from the outer margin of the Arctic or Antarctic ice sheet. Also called Shelf ice.

Fr: *Glace de banquise;* Ger: *Barriereis.*

BARRIER REEF. Name given to reefs separated from the adjacent coast by a channel or lagoon, commonly from 20 to 40 fathoms in depth, as distinct from fringing reefs, which are closely attached to the shore.

Fr: *Barrière de Récifs;* Ger: *Barrierenriff; Dammriff.*

BAR SIGNAL. A signal made at a river entrance where it is necessary to cross a bar when entering a harbor.

Fr: *Signal de Barre;* Ger: *Barresignal.*

BAR STEM. The bow framing that forms the apex of the intersection of the sides of a ship forward. It is practically a vertical continuation of the bar keel and is made of a steel casting or forging in one or more pieces. Also called stem post, stem.

Fr: *Etrave;* Ger: *Vorsteven; Vordersteven.*

BARU. 1. Large plank-built canoe from the island of Malaita (Solomon group). Length 42 ft. Breadth 5 ft. 3 in. Depth 3 ft. 3 in.

2. A plank-built canoe of the same type as the *mon*. It is found in Ndai Island (Gower Island), southeastern Solomon Islands. The smaller boats of this type are called *beroko*.

BAR WEIR. A fish weir located beside a sandbar where the bar is left bare at low tide, thus serving as part of the enclosure.

BASE LINE. A line formed by the intersection of the central fore-and-aft vertical plane of the ship with a horizontal plane passing inside or outside the keel amidships. It is from this line that all heights to points on the ship's hull are measured.

Fr: *Ligne d'Eau Zéro;* Ger: *Bodenlinie.*

BASE PLATE.
See **Bed Plate**.

BASIN. 1. A depression in the sea bottom, of a roughly round outline.

Fr: *Bassin;* Ger: *Bassin.*

2. An enclosed area of water surrounded by quay walls constructed to provide means for the transfer of cargoes from ship to quay, warehouses, and other storage places or to river craft lying alongside and vice versa. The term dock should, strictly speaking, be applied only to wet docks closed by gates. It is, however, commonly and popularly employed in a wider sense.

Fr: *Darse;* Ger: *Dock; Hafenbecken.*

See **Building Basin, Fitting-out Basin, Half-Tide Basin, Model Basin, Open Basin, Scouring Basin, Tidal Basin, Turning Basin, Wet Basin**.

BASKET. A day signal shown at sea by draggers and trawlers, and also by vessels fishing with gill nets or lines, except trolling lines. When the lines or gill nets extend from the vessel more than 500 feet horizontally, the basket is shown in conjunction with a cone, apex upwards.

Fr: *Panier;* Ger: *Korb.*

BASKET BOAT. A boat in which the outer shell is made of basket work and rendered watertight by the application of some plastic coating.

In French Indo-China and Tonkin, basket boats were largely used by natives as late as 1928 and many are found plying on the rivers and canals. They are pushed along by means of long bamboo poles. The frame consists of laths of split bamboo, twisted together. The interstices of the basket work are caulked with a mixture of cattle dung and coconut oil. Most basket boats are 6 ft. long, 4 ft. wide, and about 10 in. deep, but the largest are said to carry up to 20 tons. Both ends are elliptical and sheered up. The gunwale is bordered with bamboo stems and above the gunwale four or more beams, according to the size of the craft, are lashed. The outer skin is checkwork basketry, while the inner side is of twilled weaving.

The *guffas* or basket boats used for transport and fishing in Irak, carry up to 12 and 16 tons and are propelled by paddles. The shell of these is made of pomegranate branches interwoven with a layer of straw and palm branches by means of palm fiber rope. The outside is covered with liquid bitumen. In South America the basket boat is represented by the widely distributed *pelota*, made of a woven framework covered with skin and usually circular, sometimes triangular or rectangular. Basket boats are represented in Europe by the *coracles* used on Welsh and Irish rivers for salmon fishing. In India, Tibet and China, they are also in use, but these have a covering of hide. The East Indian saucer-shaped basket boat used on the Bowami river is locally called *parachal* and is made by covering a light frame of split rattan with oilcloth. Its diameter is 2 ft. 10½ in.

BASS ROPE. Coarse rope made of the fibers of some species of rushes (*Juncus loevis*).

BAST. The inner bark of certain trees. It is ususally shipped in bales. Also called bass, raffia.

BASTARDO. Open rowboat about 33 ft. long employed in the Italian tuna fisheries with the *tonnara* net. Four to 6 of these craft are needed for each *tonnara*. They are stationed on each side of the end chamber (*camera della morte*) in line with the *palischermo* boats.

BASTARD PITCH. A mixture of colophony, black pitch, and tar boiled down, forming a liquid substance.

See **Pitch**.

BAST ROPE. Cordage made of the fibers of the inner bark of the lime tree or linden. King, A., "Mechanical Properties of Philippine Bast-fiber Ropes," *Philippine Journal of Science*, vol 14 (1919).

BAT. The hammered-up end of a rivet.

See **Baty**.

BATE. A term employed in the chilled-meat trade which represents an allowance of weight on account of the cover or wrapper in which the meat is brought from the country of origin.

See **Bating**.

BATEAU. Term used in North America to designate various types of small craft. Sometimes called batteau. In the Northern United States and Canada the *bateau* is a double-ended flat-bottomed, rowing boat having raked bow and stern, flaring sides, strong sheer and rockered bottom. These boats are much used by lumbermen on the rivers. Length 30 ft. Breadth 6 ft. Depth 1 ft. 2 in.

On the Chesapeake Bay a bateau is the same as a skipjack, differing from it only by the fact that the bateau is half decked with cuddy and cockpit. Length 27 ft. 7 in. Breadth 8 ft. 9 in. Depth 2 ft. 2 in. This type has long head, square stern, and centerboard.

A bateau is also a small half-decked, V-bottom, centerboard crab fishing boat with cat yawl rig. Length 21 ft. Breadth 8 ft. 4 in. Depth 2 ft.

In some localities a scow is called a bateau.

See **Shoalwater Oyster Bateau**.

BATEAU BOEUF. Native sailing trawler on the Mediterranean Coast of France, employed only for pair-fishing, each boat towing one trawl warp. Length on deck 52 ft. Breadth 16 ft. Depth 5 ft. 3 in.

The length of these boats varies from 50 to 55 ft. They are decked and have a moderately raked sternpost with pointed stern. Their rig is very similar to that of the *tartane* although the mast is shorter and there is no topmast. There is no gear for reefing the mainsail. In strong winds the latter is taken off and replaced by a smaller triangular sail bent to a suitable spar. There is no standing rigging.

BATEIRA. Small flat-bottom open rowing and sailing boat from Portugal. The *bateira caçadeira* has a high curved stem with forward cuddy and pointed stern. The rig consists of a short mast and lateen sail.

BATEL. The Portuguese *batel* is a large double-ended open boat chiefly used for the transportation of the catch in the coastal sardine fisheries. It differs from the *lancha* only by its smaller size. The name *batel* is also given to a class of small single-masted sailing trawlers with high bows and round stern from the fishing ports of Barreiro, Seial, and Setubal. They are lateen-rigged and set a jib. The *batel* from Peniche is a double-ended open boat with wash strakes. Length 34.4 ft. Breadth 10.3 ft. Depth 4 ft. Capacity 7 tons. It sets a small lateen sail and is often seen around the Burling and Farallones Islands. The *batel* used for river fishing is built with raking stem and pointed stern.

The Spanish *batel* as employed in the coastal fisheries of Guipuzcoa and Vizcaya is a much smaller boat with a length ranging from 15 to 20 ft., 3 thwarts and rigged with 1 mast and lugsail.

See Batelao.

BATELAO. A small coaster of the Persian Gulf and West Coast of India, with a chub figurehead, used in the offshore pearl fisheries of Muscat and neighboring ports. Also called *batel*, *batil*. Length over-all, 48 to 66 ft. Beam 9.5 to 16 ft. Depth 4 ft. to 7 ft.

The larger boats are decked over for a short length forward and aft. The stern is sharp with vertical sternpost. They are rigged with two masts, the foremast, or main mast, with a forward rake and the mizzen upright. The smaller boats have one mast only. All carry settee sails. The foresail tacks down to a long spar the heel of which is fastened to the mast. Tonnage from 30 to 100.

BATELLAZZO. A boat employed in the lagoon fisheries of the Gulf of Venice. Length 30 to 40 ft. Tonnage 1 to 3. Crew 3 to 4. Also called *barderella*.

BATELO. A small dhow used on the East African coast. About 30 tons. Length 51 ft. Beam 10 ft. Depth 4½ ft.

BATHYCURRENT. Ocean current flowing at a considerable depth below the sea surface without disturbing the latter.

BATHYMETRIC CHART. A chart, mainly used for hydrographic surveying, on which the contour of the sea bottom is represented by continuous depth curves instead of by individual soundings. By this method many more soundings can be shown than on ordinary charts. This makes navigation on soundings more accurate, particularly when an automatic sounding device, such as the fathometer, is used.

Fr: *Carte Bathymétrique;* Ger: *Tiefenkarte.*

BATHYMETRY. The art or science of measuring sea depths.

BATHYTHERMOGRAPH. An instrument for recording the temperature of the sea at various depths, which can be operated while underway.

BATIL. See Batelao.

BATING. The process in net making of reducing the number of meshes in a piece of netting that is not of rectangular shape. It is made by including two bights of the previous round in the knot to complete a mesh. It is also known as doubling, stowing, stealing, taking in, shrinking, narrowing.

Fr: *Rapetissure;* Ger: *Abnehmen.*

BATINGS. Upper part of a trawl net between the square and the cod end.

Fr: *Bas de Dos;* Ger: *Hinternetz.*

BATTANA.
See Battello.

BATTEAU.
See Bateau.

BATTELA. An open Indian coastal craft trading between Cambay and Bombay. Length over-all 88 ft. Breadth 20 ft. Depth 8 ft.

The hull with long raking stem and transom stern is crudely built, the frames being rough logs of jungle wood. At the ends the planking is built up about 2 ft. higher than amidships. Wooden uprights are fitted in the covering board in the waist and to these a matting washboard is secured by lashings. *Battelas* are rigged with two masts, settee sails, and a light running bowsprit with one jib. The masts have a slight forward rake. The mainmast is stepped amidships and the mizzen is at the forward part of the crew space. A small jigger mast is occasionally seen on the larger boats. They range in size from 40 to 100 tons.

BATTELLINA. Small, open flat-bottom boat with straight raking stem and round stern used on the Istrian and Dalmatian coasts for inshore fishing with small nets or hooks and lines. In some localities (Barcola, Monfalcone) the *battellina* has a transom stern. It is decked forward and has two thwarts. Also called *passera*. One small mast is stepped through the after thwarts and carries a balanced lugsail. Length 14 to 17½ ft. Breadth 4.7 to 5.5 ft. Depth 1.5 to 1.9 ft. Tonnage 0.7 to 1.4.

BATTELLO. A fishing boat from the Upper Adriatic and Gulf of Trieste decked fore and aft, and used for the capture of sardines in the lagoons. Length 23 to 32 ft. Breadth 6 to 8 ft. Depth (inside) 2.5 to

3.1 ft. Capacity 2.5 to 7 tons. Also called *battana, battelluccio.*

There are two hatches, one at half length the other just abaft the mainmast, and small bulwarks about 10 in. high. The stem is sharp and the stern round. The rig consists of two masts with boomed lugsails; the foresail is very small in comparison with the mainsail. The foremast is unshipped when sailing close hauled and a jib-headed sail is set between mainmast and stem head.

BATTEN. 1. A thin strip of clear white pine, used in fairing the ship's lines in the mold loft.

2. A thin straight strip of wood used as an auxiliary for reference or measurement: (1) in erecting structures, during the vessel's building, (2) in setting up a drydock to receive a ship.

3. Name given in the timber trade to pieces of soft wood, 6, 7 or 8 in. wide; 2, 2½, 3, and 4 in. thick; 5 to 30 ft. long.

Fr: *Volige;* Ger: *Leiste.*

See **Cargo Batten, Hammock Batten, Hatch Batten, Keel Batten, Mold Loft Batten, Reefing Batten, Rigging Batten, Sail Batten, Sheering Batten.**

BATTEN DOWN. To cover up and fasten down. Usually said of hatches when they are covered up with tarpaulins, which are fastened down with hatch battens.

Fr: *Condamner;* Ger: *Verschalken; Schalken.*

BATTENED SAIL. A sail on which battens or splines of wood are fitted, usually in pockets, perpendicularly to the leech to keep it flat, to assist in reefing, and to prevent any flicker at the outer or after leech. They are usually fitted to mainsails of small yachts, sailing canoes, and all small sails made of duck or other light material, but not to the sails of larger yachts.

Fr: *Voile Lattée;* Ger: *Spreizlattende Segel.*

BATTENING BAR (BATTEN BAR).
See **Hatch Batten.**

BATTENING IRON.
See **Cleat.**

BATTERING RAM. A general name for various types of rams used during the process of removing support from under a vessel during preparations for launching the ship.

Fr: *Bélier; Billard;* Ger: *Handramme; Schlagbalken.*

BATTLEDORE. A projecting piece fitted on a riding bitt to separate the two parts of the chain cable when taking a turn (obsolete).

Fr: *Paille de Bitte;* Ger: *Betingshörner.*

BATWING SAIL. A sail used on racing canoes and small pleasure craft in which a greater effective area is secured by extending the after edge with wooden battens encased in several pockets that run across the sail radially from the mast.

Ger: *Fledermaussegel; Hammer Keulensegel.*

These long battens that extend from the leech to the luff give the sail a uniform arching and produce a somewhat rigid surface. They also admit of a change in the arching at will as demanded by the circumstances: the greater the tension under which the battens are inserted and made fast in the pockets, the greater the arching of the sail. In a light breeze thin and flexible battens may be used, while in a stiff breeze a set of less pliable ones is used. Its proponents claim that batwing sail is cheaper and will last longer than the ordinary one.

BATY. A roughly hewn dugout canoe used for fishing and transportation by the natives of the Kamchatka Peninsula in sheltered waters and for crossing rivers. It is a narrow and heavy craft hollowed out like a trough, with rounded bow and squarish stern. It is manned by 4 hands, 2 forward and 1 aft, using long poles. Its average length is about 40 ft. For heavy loads 2 boats are lashed together and a platform built across. It is called *bat* or *baty* by the Russians and *elle-ut* by the Koryak.

BAWLEY. A shallow draft broad-beamed boat employed in the whitebait, sprat, whelk, and shrimp fisheries around the Thames and Medway estuaries. The hull is wholly decked and carvel-planked with vertical stem, raked sternpost, square transom stern, and outboard rudder. These boats are cutter-rigged with short lower mast, long topmast, and very long gaff giving a nearly perpendicular leech to the mainsail. The latter has no boom and the sheet travels on a horse. A jib topsail is often carried. Length overall 32 to 37 ft. Breadth 11 to 11.5 ft. Draft 4 to 5 ft. Displacement 14.2 tons. Sail area 875 sq. ft.

Blake, W. M., "A Harwich Bawley," *Yachting,* New York, vol. 50 (October, 1931).

BAY. 1. The expanse of water between two capes or headlands. A comparatively slight indentation in the coastline, as distinguished from a gulf, loch, firth, and so on. The limit of maritime jurisdiction (called seaward limit) of a bay or estuary the entrance to which does not exceed 10 nautical miles in width is a line drawn across the entrance. Where the entrance exceeds 10 nautical miles in width, the seaward limit is a line drawn across the bay or estuary where the width first narrows to 10 nautical miles.

Fr: *Baie;* Ger: *Bucht; Bai; Meerbusen.*

2. Term used by shipyard welders to denote the space between any transverse bulkhead and the nearest web frame in the berth or between one web frame and the next. The bay is a subdivision of the berth.

BAYAMO. Violent squall blowing from the land on the south coast of Cuba, and especially from the Bight of Bayamo. It is accompanied by thunder and lightning, and generally terminates with rain.

BAY CRAFT (U. S.). A name sometimes given to vessels or boats traversing only bays and canals to reach their destination.

BAY ICE. Young ice which first forms on the sea in autumn and of sufficient thickness to prevent navigation. Also called gulf ice.

Fr: *Glace de Baie.*

BEACH. The margin of land exposed to tidal action. The tract of land between high- and low-water mark. Sometimes called strand.

Fr: *Plage; Estran;* Ger: *Strand; Ufer.*

BEACH (to). To run or to haul a ship or boat upon a beach, for the purpose of cleaning or repairing its bottom, to prevent its sinking in deep water, and so on.

Fr: *Échouer;* Ger: *Auf den Strand setzen.*

BEACH BOAT. 1. A general term covering small rowboats used on open beaches and designed for ease of launching and hauling up. Such a boat has little depth of keel and is flat-floored, to float off more easily when launched and not to strain when landing, as a sharp bottom boat does. For use on steep beaches the bottom of the boat can be made somewhat sharper than that it would be for use on a flat sandy beach. Beach boats usually have no iron band on the keel since this would cause them to drag heavily in launching and hauling up. Instead, one or two side keels or shoes are frequently fitted.

Ger: *Strandboot.*

2. Term used on the coast of Maine (U. S. A.) to denote a small open boat, cat-rigged with main spritsail. The hull is clinker built with pointed stern and curved stem. It is mostly employed in the general fisheries of eastern Maine. The name "beach boat" is derived from Moose-abec Beach (Jonesport), where this type is supposed to have originally been built. Length 15 ft. Beam 4¾ ft.

BEACHCOMBER. A term applied in the fishing industry to any person who obtains his living by gathering the products or refuse of the beach.

BEACH GEAR (U. S.). A term applied to a type of standardized gear carried by salvage vessels or tugs sent out to assist a stranded vessel. A standard set of beach gear includes a 4 ton anchor, 2 or 3 one hundred fathoms lengths of extra flexible 1⅝ inch steel wire, a 20-fathom shot of 2¼ inch chain cable, fairlead blocks, plate shackles, carpenter's wire, rope stoppers, a heavy 4-sheave purchase with ⅝ inch diameter wire rope fall. An ordinary salvage ship carries four sets of gear which are considered sufficient for the majority of strandings.

BEACH SEINE. A dragnet of small depth and variable length shot in shallow water and dragged ashore.

Fr: *Senne droite;* Ger: *Zeise; Zugwade; Wadenets.*

When hauled onto the shore care is taken that the lead line always touches the bottom. A line is generally attached to each end of the net. One end of the net is made fast ashore and the other is laid out from a small boat forming a semicircle with its diameter parallel to the shore. The meshing ranges from ¼ inch up to 6 in. being small in the main body of the net and large in the wings. The larger seines of this type have a length of 2500 yds.

BEACH SKIFF.

See **Scow.**

BEACON. A conspicuous mark used as a guide to mariners or in surveying work, either a landmark, erected on an eminence near the shore, or a mark moored or driven into the bottom in shoal water. In many instances beacons are tall masonry structures built on headlands for recognition purposes. All beacons have some distinguishing mark: those on land are generally painted some distinctive color; while those on sandbanks, and so on, are surmounted by a topmark (globe, diamond, triangle, and so on). Sandbank beacons are very often steel masts sunk into the sand.

Fr: *Amer; Balise;* Ger: *Bake.*

See **Circular Radio Beacon, Directional Radio Beacon, Fixed Beacon,**

Floating Beacon, Radio Beacon, Rotating Radio Beacon.

BEACONAGE. 1. A system of beacons.

Fr: *Balisage;* Ger: *Bebakung; Betonnung.*

2. A fee charged against vessels for the maintenance of buoys and beacons.

Fr: *Droits de Balise;* Ger: *Bakengelder.*

BEACONBOAT. A sort of small lightship without keeper, sometimes used in lieu of a lightship for economy's sake. The source of light is usually liquified acetylene or oil gas. The light is turned on at sunset and off at sunrise by means of a clockwork mechanism. Also called gas boat.

BEACON SIGNAL. A wireless signal consisting of a characteristic combination of letters transmitted in Morse code continuously at a speed of about 15 words per minute at stated intervals. During fog there is a 1-minute transmission every 4 minutes; in clear weather, 1 every half hour. Also called radio beacon signal.

BEAD. A globule of metal deposited in oxyacetylene or electric welding during a single pass of the welding rod.

Fr: *Cordon;* Ger: *Schweissnaht.*

BEADING. A hardwood half round used on small wooden craft to cover the joint at the sides between the decking and the sheer strake. When canvas-covered decks are used it also covers the edge of the canvas. Sometimes called cover bead.

Fr: *Liston;* Ger: *Leiste.*

BEAD WELD.

See **Light Closing Weld.**

BEAK. A sort of curved false stem projecting ahead of the true stem. It is still found on lateen-rigged craft and boats in the Mediterranean; also in the Chesapeake bugeye.

Fr: *Éperon;* Ger: *Gallionsknie; Gallion; Tulle.*

BEAM. 1. The width of a ship. Also called breadth.

Beam is one of the principal factors governing a vessel's transverse stability, and therefore her behavior in a seaway. It also has an important influence upon her resistance. Experience has proved that it is advantageous from the standpoint of economical propulsion to use as large a beam as is practical and consistent with satisfactory stability qualities, in conjunction with finer ends than was once the practice while maintaining the required displacement.

Average length to breadth ratios for merchant vessels:

Fast passenger vessels .. 9.0 to 9.8
Intermediate vessels 8
Cargo vessels .... 7.1 to 8
Tugs .... about 5
Sailing vessels .... 6.3 to 7.2
Coasters .... 5 to 6.3

Fr: *Bau; Largeur;* Ger: *Breite.*

2. A transverse structural member of the ship's framing. Beams as joists support the deck against pressures that may be sustained from cargo or from masses of water falling thereon in heavy weather. As ties and struts they support and hold at fixed distance the vessel's sides and check racking tendencies in the transverse section.

Fr: *Barrot;* Ger: *Balken.*

See **Boat Beam, Box Beam, Brake Beam, Breast Beam, Bridle Beam, Built Beam, Cant Beam, Deck Beam, Grub Beam, Half Beam, Hatch Beam, Hatch-end Beam, Hold Beam, Ice Beam, Panting Beam, Sponsor Beam, Spur Beam, Tie Beam, Towing Beam, Transom Beam.**

BEAM BRACKET.

See **Beam Knee.**

BEAM CHOCK. Blocks of timber used in wooden vessels under the beams. They are attached to frame timbers and beams by iron hanging knees.

Fr: *Taquet de Barrot;* Ger: *Querbalken.*

BEAM END. The extremity of a beam where it joins the ship's side.

Ger: *Balkenkopf.*

BEAM-ENDS. A vessel is on her beam-ends when listed to an angle where her beams are almost vertical, and her righting power insufficient to return her to the upright. The cause may be shifting ballast or cargo; or unsymmetrical flooding. In sailing craft the cause may be a sudden squall or heavy seas.

Fr: *Engagé;* Ger: *Zum kentern liegen.*

BEAM ENGINE. An old type of steam engine utilizing a beam. The connecting rod from the piston is connected to one end of the beam, while the "Pitman" from the crank is connected to the other end. The beam is pivoted at its center. This type of engine may still be seen on some ferry boats in the United States.

Fr: *Machine à Balancier;* Ger: *Balanziermaschine.*

BEAM FILLING. Cargo stowed between the beams of a vessel. Small cargo particularly suited for filling space between beams and immediately under deck.

Fr: *Remplissage sous barrots;* Ger: *Vollstauung der Deckbalken.*

BEAM KNEE—BEAM TRAWL

BEAM KNEE. In ship construction, connections used in tying transverse beams to the frames, making the ship more rigid at deck corners, and reinforcing the frames. A

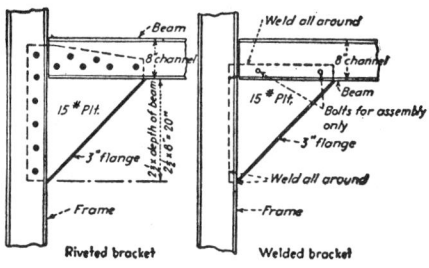

Beam Knee. (*Courtesy McGraw-Hill Book Company, N. Y.*)

beam bracket may be (1) a riveted or welded triangular plate, flanged at its free edge; (2) a short angle welded across the joint, with the small corner opening filled with a filler piece; or (3) made by splitting the beam, turning the lower arm down and welding it to act as a brace. Sometimes called beam bracket, or bracket knee.
Fr: *Gousset de barrot;* Ger: *Balkenknie.*
See **Bracket**.

BEAM MOLD. A pattern showing the curvature or camber of the beams of a vessel, and the length of each beam.
Fr: *Gabarit de barrot;* Ger: *Balkenmallung.*
See **Beam**.

BEAM SEA. Sea that strikes the vessel in a direction perpendicular or nearly so to the line of the keel. Beam seas are parallel to the fore-and-aft center line of the ship.
Fr: *Mer de travers;* Ger: *Dwarsseegang.*

BEAM SHOE. One of the steel fittings riveted or welded inside the hatch coaming to support the end of a hatch beam. Sometimes called beam socket.
Fr: *Support de Barrot Mobile;* **Ger**: *Schiebebalken-Lager.*

BEAM SOCKET.
See **Beam Shoe**.

BEAM TRANSMITTER.
See **Beacon Signal**.

BEAM TRAWL. A triangular purse-shaped net with the mouth extended by a horizontal wooden beam and raised about 3 ft. from the ground by means of 2 iron frames or heads, one at each end. The beam is fastened at each end to the top of an iron frame shaped like an irregular stirrup, which is fitted to it at right angles by a square socket

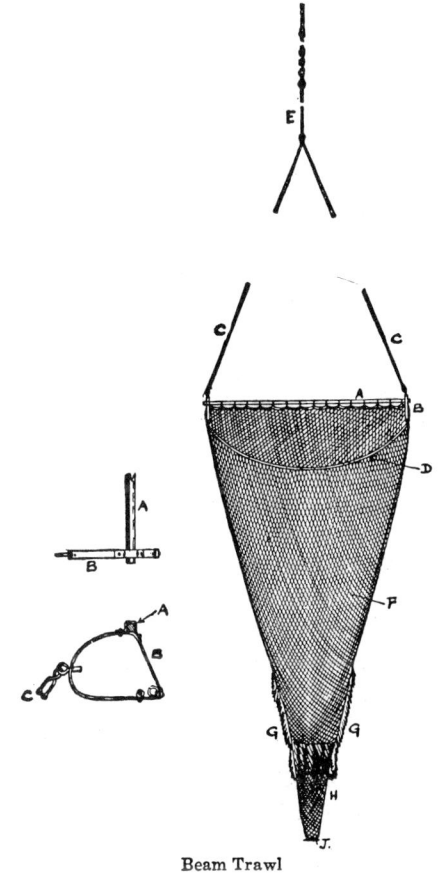

Beam Trawl
A. Beam
B. Trawl head
C. Bridle rope and shackle
D. Foot rope
E. Warp
F. Belly
G. Rubbing Pieces
H. Cod end
J. Cod end tie

at the top. The upper part of the net only is fastened to the beam, the under portion dragging on the ground.
Fr: *Chalut à Perche;* Ger: *Baumschleppnetz; Baumkurre.*

The beam trawl is towed by means of a single warp fastened to a bridle or span and attached to the trawl heads. Beam trawls are used only by small trawlers, or sailing smacks. A full size beam trawl is from 40 to 50 ft. along the beam and about 100 ft. in length.

The otter trawl, requiring a constant steady strain to keep it fishing properly, is unsuitable for a sailing trawler, which is dependent on the vagaries of the wind. If the vessel loses headway the boards may fall flat, thereby closing the mouth of the

BEAM WIND—BECATE

net, while the mouth of the beam trawl is always open irrespective of the vessel's speed. Collins, J. W., *The Beam Trawl Fishery of Great Britain*, U. S. Bureau of Fisheries, Bulletin, Washington, D. C., 1887.

BEAM WIND. A wind blowing in a direction at right angles with the keel or nearly so.
 Fr: *Vent de Travers;* Ger: *Seitenwind.*

BEAR. A square block of wood weighted with iron and faced with a sand stone. It is dragged to and fro on wooden decks for scouring purposes.

BEAR (to). 1. To lie in a certain direction from a designated origin, and measured from a specified reference point or direction.
 2. To move or tend to move in a certain direction or manner.
 See **True Bearing, Relative Bearing.**

BEAR AWAY. To put the helm up and run off to leeward. To turn a ship's head away from the wind. Sometimes called to bear up.
 Fr: *Laisser Arriver;* Ger: *Abhalten.*

BEARDING. Also called bearding line, stepping point. **1.** The line of intersection of the keel, deadwood stem and sternpost of a ship, with the outer surface of the frame timbers.
 2. The diminution of the edge or surface of a piece of timber from a given line, as in the stem or deadwood of a ship.
 3. The line of intersection of the outside plating with the stem and sternpost.
  Fr: *Courbe de dégraissement;* Ger: *Behauen.*

BEARDING ANGLE. Angle bar connecting stem and keel plate.

BEAR DOWN. In a boat under sail, to put the helm down and turn toward the direction of the wind. To approach from windward a ship or any other object. To run toward.
 Fr: *Laisser Porter;* Ger: *Zusteuern.*

BEARING. The direction or point of the compass in which an object is seen, or the direction of one object from another, with reference to (1) the nearest cardinal point of the compass, or (2) true north, measuring clockwise.
 Fr: *Relèvement;* Ger: *Peilung.*
 See **Compass Bearing, Cross Bearing, Four-Point Bearing, Magnetic Bearing, Reciprocal Bearing, Relative Bearing, True Bearing.**

BEARING FINDER.
 See **Azimuth Circle.**

BEARING LINE.
 See **Bearing.**

BEARING SIGNAL. A signal of the international code made with a group of three numeral pennants preceded by the letter "X," the three figures indicating degrees.
 See **Bearing.**

BEAR IN WITH. To steer for. To run or tend toward.
 Fr: *Gouverner sur; Mettre le cap sur;* Ger: *Zuhalten.*

BEAR OFF. 1. To push or breast off a wharf or ship's side. Also to shove off.
 Fr: *Déborder;* Ger: *Abstossen.*
 2. To bear off the land. To steer away from; the reverse of: to bear in with.
 Fr: *Porter au Large;* Ger: *Abfahren; Abhalten.*

BEAT. To make progress against the wind (and therefore close-hauled) by a zigzag course with the wind first on one bow and then on the other.
 Fr: *Louvoyer;* Ger: *Lavieren; Kreuzen.*
 See **Brading.**

BEAUFORT SCALE. A numerical scale rating winds according to ascending velocity, as follows:

Beaufort Number	State of Air	Velocity in knots
0.	Calm	0– 1
1.	Light airs	1– 3
2.	Slight breeze	4– 6
3.	Gentle breeze	7–10
4.	Moderate breeze	11–16
5.	Fresh breeze	17–21
6.	Strong breeze	22–27
7.	Moderate gale (high wind)	28–33
8.	Fresh gale	34–40
9.	Strong gale	41–47
10.	Whole gale	48–55
11.	Storm	56–65
12.	Hurricane	Above 65

 Fr: *Échelle de Beaufort;* Ger: *Beaufort Skala.*

BECALMED. 1. Said of a sailing vessel unable to make progress owing to lack of wind.
 Fr: *Encalminé;* Ger: *In Windstille.*
 2. The condition of a sail or vessel cut off from wind by other sails or another vessel.
 Fr: *Déventé;* Ger: *Bekalmen.*

BECATE. One of the short loops inserted at regular intervals in the ground rope of a trawl line to provide a fastening for the ganging (a corruption of "Becket"—U. S.).

BÊCHE DE MER. A species of large sea slug or sea cucumber. When dried it is used for food in the Far East. Also called trepang.

BECK. A tub, especially as in *fore-line beck*, a term formerly used by British whalemen to denote a shallow tub in the center of a whaleboat in which the first hundred fathoms of the whale line were flaked down.

BECKET. 1. Also becket bridle. A short piece of rope with a knot at one end and an eye at the other, or an eye at both ends. It is used for temporarily confining ropes or small spars.

Fr: *Chambrière;* Ger: *Knebelstropp.*

2. A handle made of a rope grommet or ring. The rope handle of a wooden deck bucket.

Fr: *Manchette;* Ger: *Schlinge.*

3. A rope grommet or metal eye at the bottom of a block for securing the standing end of a fall. In metal blocks the becket and shell are cast in one piece.

Fr: *Ringot;* Ger: *Hundsfot; Blockauge.*

4. A piece of Manila line about 1 ft. long, by which each ganging is fastened to the ground line in halibut-trawl gear.

5. Also sling cleat. A wooden cleat or hook fastened on the fore or main rigging for the tacks and sheets to lie in when not in use.

Fr: *Taquet de Suspension.*

See Bunt Jigger Becket, **Reefing Becket,** Steering Wheel Becket Yard Becket.

BECKET BEND.
See Double Sheet **Bend.**

BECKET BLOCK. A block in which the strap extends below the shell and is provided with a rope grommet or metal eye (becket) to attach the end of a rope.

Fr: *Poulie à Ringot.*

BECKET BRIDLE.
See Becket.

BECKET ROWLOCK. A rowlock formed of a rope grommet secured over a tholepin.

BECUE. To becue an anchor or grapnel means to bend the end of the warp to the crown instead of to the ring, stopping the bight with rope yarn to the anchor ring. If the anchor is jammed in the bottom, a heavy heave on the cable will part the stop at the ring, and the whole heaving strain is then brought on the crown. The anchor is then whipped out of its holding easily. This method is employed by fishermen working over rocky bottom. Also called Scowing or Crowning.

BED.
See **Mock.**

BEDA. A native cargo carrier on the east coast of the Malay Peninsula rigged with one mast and large lugsail. These boats are also propelled by oars. They vary much in shape, size, and build.

BEDENI. An Arab dhow used in the Oman and Mahra coasting trade. The hull has straight lines, no sheer, and high sternpost. The larger boats are rigged with two upright masts. The smaller have one mast. An intricate system of ropes and beams is used for steering, as in the *zaruk.*

See **Badan.**

BEDPLATE. Also called base plate, sole plate. **1.** A foundation framework for a marine steam engine, consisting of longitudinal and cross girders of cast steel, secured to the engine keelsons, which are built up with the ship's hull. The engine frame columns, and main bearings land on the bedplate. Base plates for propelling engines of merchant ships are made of cast iron, cast steel or welded plate girders. They have either a flat or a dropped bottom.

2. A similar boxlike foundation on a deck, supporting an auxiliary engine.

Fr: *Bâti; Plaque de Fondation;* Ger: *Maschinengrundplatte.*

BEDROOM STEWARD. In a ship carrying passengers, one who is in charge of a set of staterooms or cabins, makes up beds and keeps them in order. He attends to the occupants and serves meals in the rooms when called upon to do so. Sometimes called cabin steward.

Fr: *Garçon de Cabine;* Ger: *Kammersteward.*

BEDUANG. A plank-built trading boat with double outriggers from Madura and North Eastern Java. It has the same hull form with forked ends as the *alis-alis* and is rigged with two masts. The foremast stepped in the bows is short and fixed. The mainmast is made up of a portable pole or strut which supports the yard of the lateen-shaped sail. The dimensions of these craft vary widely; the length of the largest ranging from 46 to 52 ft., while the smallest are only about 16½ ft. long. Also called *peduang* or *prahu peduang.*

BEE.
See Blocks.

BEE BLOCKS. Pieces of wood on each side of the bowsprit through which the forestays are rove. Also called bowsprit bees.

Fr: *Violons;* Ger: *Violinen.*

BEETLE.
See Reeming Beetle.

BEFORE THE BEAM—BELL BOOK

BEFORE THE BEAM. In a direction which lies forward of a line drawn at right angles to the keel at the midship section of the ship.

Fr: *Sur l'avant du travers;* Ger: *Vorderlicher als dwars.*

BEFORE THE MAST. An expression formerly used to describe the station of seamen who had their accommodation in the forecastle, as distinguished from officers who were berthed aft. Thus a man before the mast meant a common sailor and not an officer. In modern vessels these conditions are altered, since part of the crew is frequently berthed in the after part of the vessel, with the officers amidships.

Ger: *Vor dem Mast.*

BEFORE THE WIND. Said of a sailing craft running directly with the wind, that is, when the wind comes over the stern and the yards are or would be braced square across.

Fr: *Vent Arrière;* Ger: *Mit dem Winde.* See **Running Free.**

BELAN. A plank-built paddling canoe from the Moluccas with high upturning stem and stern pieces. Used for transportation and racing in sheltered waters on Banda Islands, Tanimbar, and Kei Islands. Average length 50 to 60 ft.

BELAT. A strong wind from N to NNW encountered on the south coast of Arabia between December and March.

BELAY. To take one or more "S" turns with a rope around a cleat or belaying pin, without tying it in a knot. Also, to cancel an order.

Fr: *Tourner; Amarrer;* Ger: *Belegen.*

BELAYING CLEAT. A piece of wood or metal with single or double horns used for belaying ropes.

Fr: *Taquet de Tournage;* Ger: *Belegklampe.*

American Marine Standards Committee, *Cleats for Ships,* Pamphlet 76, Washington, D. C., 1931.

BELAYING PIN. A short bar of iron, brass, or wood used for belaying ropes of the running rigging.

Fr: *Cabillot de Tournage;* Ger: *Belegnagel.*

Belaying pins vary in length from 10 to 18 in. and in diameter from 1½ to 3¼ in. They are put through holes in rails called pinrails or fiferails, according to their position out at the ship's side, or inboard and partly surrounding a mast. They are prevented from falling out of the rail by a shoulder a little above the middle of their length. They are also used on boat davits for belaying boat falls.

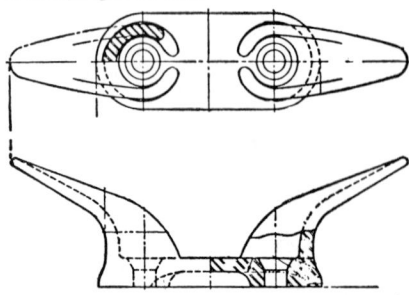

Belaying Cleat. (*American Marine Standard.*)

BELAYING PIN RACK. A framing of wood or iron fitted with belaying pins. Sometimes called pin rack.

Fr: *Ratelier de Manoeuvre;* Ger: *Nagelbank.*

BELEM.
See **Ballam.**

BELFAST RIG (G. B.). Term applied to full-rigged ships with double fore and main topgallants and a single topgallant sail on the mizzen. They were built by Harland and Wolff at Belfast and had uncommonly great rake to all three masts.

BELFRY. The ornamental frame in which a ship's bell is hung.

Fr: *Beffroi;* Ger: *Glockenstahl; Glockengalgen.*

BELL. A bell and clapper of the usual shape used aboard ship as a means of announcing time at regular intervals, as a signal when the ship is anchored in a fog, or as an alarm in emergencies. Sometimes called ship's bell, fog bell.

Fr: *Cloche de Bord;* Ger: *Schiffsglocke.* See **Submarine Bell.**

The efficiency of a bell used as a sound signal is of low value. A bell of 8 in. diameter can be heard in normal weather at a distance not greater than about 2000 ft. A ship's bell should be placed at about 6 ft. above deck and in an exposed position where the sound waves can travel without hindrance. The minimum size for a ship's bell to be used for signaling is not less than 8 in., according to British and United States regulations.

BELL BOOK. A book usually kept by a junior officer, in which are entered the speeds, directions and times of engine movements as they are relayed to the engine room while the ship is maneuvering.

BELL BUOY. A buoy surmounted by a bell that is rung either by the action of the waves or by carbonic acid gas. There is frequently no clapper. Iron balls rolling about on a plate under the bell's mouth strike against the inner surface of the bell.

Fr: *Bouée à Cloche;* Ger: *Glockenboje; Glockentonne.*

BELLMAN. One who assists a diver, pearl fisherman or sponger to dress in diving suit and helmet, examines air and communication lines; supplies tools or other equipment before the diver enters the water; receives instructions from person under water, such as pulling in or letting out the life line. Also called diver helper, diver tender, liftline man.

BELL-MOUTH VENTILATOR. A ventilator that terminates on a weather deck in the form of a 90° elbow with an enlarged bell-shaped opening, in order to obtain an increased supply of air when facing the wind. Sometimes called cowl ventilator.

Fr: *Manche à Air à Pavillon;* Ger: *Glockenförmiger Lüfter.*

BELL PURCHASE. A tackle consisting of 4 single blocks, 2 fixed and 2 movable, with one bight of the fall fixed to one of the movable blocks.

BELL ROPE. A hand rope attached to the clapper of a bell.

Ger: *Steert.*

BELL WHISTLE. A whistle in which air or steam is forced into a bell-shaped casting fitted on a central spindle. It emits a note of lower pitch than the organ whistle, and its sound carries farther. It is adjusted by screwing the bell up or down the central spindle. Sometimes called dome whistle.

Fr: *Sifflet à Cloche;* Ger: *Glockenpfeife.*

BELLY. 1. The part of a sail that bulges out under the pressure of wind. The amount of belly in a sail varies directly with the amount of curve of the foot. It is obtained by cutting the foot in a curve, and increases the efficiency of a sail in light winds.

Fr: *Sac; Ballon;* Ger: *Bauch.*

2. Also lower blade; ground. The lower portion of a trawl net, immediately beneath the batings, and of similar size and shape.

Fr: *Ventre;* Ger: *Bauchstück.*

3. The inside or hollow of curved timber, the outside of which is called the back.

See **False Bellies.**

BELLY BAND. A strengthening band of canvas sewed across a square sail below the lower reef band. It is called middle band when half way between the reef and the foot of the sail.

Fr: *Renfort de Remplissage;* Ger: *Bauchband.*

BELLY GUY. A rope that supports the middle part of a derrick.

Ger: *Mittelgei.*

BELLY LINE. Strong line used in large otter trawls to strengthen the quarter and after portion of the net. Belly lines run from the quarters of the ground rope, back along a diagonal line of meshes to the lace hood along which they run back to the cod end. Sometimes called rip line, rib line.

Ger: *Mittelgei; Rebenleine.*

BELLY ROBBER (U. S.). Slang term for chief steward.

BELLY STAY. A rope applied from above half-mast down when a mast requires extra support.

BELLY STRAP. A rope slung around an open boat to which the hanging pendant is attached when the boat is carrying out an anchor. Sometimes called belly sling.

BELT GRIPE. One of two pieces of sword matting used for securing a boat hung at davits, against the strongback. The upper ends of the gripes are secured to the davit heads, and the lower ends to a lashing for setting up the gripes, made fast at the deck edge midway between the davit sockets.

Fr: *Sangle d'Embarcation;* Ger: *Bootsbrok; Brokmatte.*

BELTING.

See **Guard Rail.**

BENA. A plank-built canoe from Guadalcanal (Solomon Islands) with single outrigger. The stern piece rises from the top strake. There is a quadrangular board at the stem in front of the fore washboards.

BENAU.

See **Banawa.**

BENCH HOOK. A long curved hook with a swivel and lanyard attached to a sailmaker's bench so that the canvas can be pulled taut as the sewing progresses. Sometimes called sail hook.

Fr: *Crochet d'établi.*

BENCH MARK. A mark affixed to a permanent object in tidal observations to provide a datum level. The standard bench mark of the U. S. Coast and Geodetic survey consists of a brass disc about three inches in diameter with a shank about two and a half inches long for insertion into a building or other support.

Fr: *Repère de marée;* Ger: *Pegelfestpunkt.*

BEND (to). 1. To fasten by means of a bend or knot. A general term for fastening anything as to bend one rope to another, the anchor to its cable, and so on.

Fr: *Frapper; Faire Ajut;* Ger: *Anstecken.*

2. To bend a sail is to make it fast to its proper yard, gaff, or stay ready for setting.

Fr: *Enverguer;* Ger: *Anschlagen.*

3. A method of fastening one rope to another or to a ring, loop, and so on, by passing the rope through a loop and fastening it back around its own end.

Fr: *Ajut; Étalingure; Noeud;* Ger: *Stek; Stich; Knoten.*

BENDING BLOCK. See **Bending Floor.**

BENDING FLOOR. A latticed flooring or platform consisting of heavy cast iron blocks or large iron plates laid together and secured, about 4 to 6 in. thick perforated with closely spaced holes about 1½ in. square and 4 to 5 in. center to center. These holes are used to secure dogs and wedges that pin down the angle frames after they are heated in a furnace, for bending and beveling them to the required shape. Also called bending slab, bending table, bending block, furnace slab, leveling block, bending platform.

Fr: *Plaque à cintrer;* Ger: *Richtplatte.*

BENDING FURNACE. A long fluelike furnace of reverberatory type situated at one end of the bending slabs and fired either by gas, coal, or oil, used for heating the frame bars. Also called angle furnace, plate furnace.

Fr: *Four à réchauffer;* Ger: *Spantglühofen.*

BENDING JACKSTAY. 1. One of a set of ropes, iron rods, or strips of wood attached to a mast, yard or gaff to which the head of a sail is bent (made fast). 2. A rod or rope running up and down the forward side of a mast on which a square yard travels. 3. The term is also applied to the outer or boundary rope of a netting or awning running through the heads of awning stanchions, to which the awning is stretched. Sometimes called just jackstay.

Fr: *Filière d'Envergure;* Ger: *Jackstag; Auschlag Jackstag.*

BENDING MOMENT. The moment at any given point of the ship's structure (if the ship is considered as a beam or girder) that tends to produce hogging or sagging. It is the sum of the products of the forces acting to produce bending and the perpendicular distances from the lines of action of these forces to the point under consideration. The maximum bending moment is frequently expressed as a ratio of the product of the ship's length and displacement.

Fr: *Moment Fléchissant;* Ger: *Biegemoment; Biegungsmoment.*

See **Hog, Sag.**

BENDING SHACKLE. A shackle placed with the bowed end aft, and connecting the chain cable to the anchor shackle. It is somewhat larger than the connecting shackles and differs in the method of securing the bolt. It is always placed with crown aft. Sometimes called end shackle.

Fr: *Cigale; Organeau;* Ger: *Verbindungschackel.*

BENDING TABLE. See **Bending Floor.**

BENDS. 1. A form of compressed-air sickness common among deep-sea divers. It is felt in the elbows, shoulders, or knees and varies from extreme pain to a dull ache. It occurs during the diver's ascent or even after he has reached the surface. It is due to the transition from a higher to a lower atmospheric pressure, and is caused by the liberation of nitrogen bubbles, which block the blood vessels.

It is relieved by recompression, which may be applied by sending the diver down under water again or by submitting him to increased air pressure in a recompression chamber. Sometimes called caisson disease.

2. The seizings put on a clinch.

BENEAPED. Said of a vessel that is left aground by the spring tides so that she cannot be floated until the next spring tide. Sometimes called neaped.

Ger: *Benept.*

BENT FRAME. A wooden frame to which the desired curvature has been given by bending it after it has been steamed for a certain length of time. Bent frames are lighter for the same strength than sawed frames. They are used for small sailing craft up to about 30 to 40 ft. waterline length. Sometimes called steamed frame.

Fr: *Membrure Ployée; Membrure Etuvée;* Ger: *Eingebogener Spant.*

Frames over 4 sq. in. in sectional area cannot be bent readily. The steaming time is about an hour per inch of thickness. Motor boats up to 40 ft. in length are satisfactorily built on steamed frames. The usual woods for bent frames are American rock elm, ash, white oak, hackmatack. Steamed frames are occasionally laminated in parts by sawing them down on the flat. The two positions where this is done to advantage are in the knuckle of the counter and in the hard turn of the garboards.

BENTINCK. A triangular course (sail), so named after its inventor, Captain Bentinck.

BENTINCK BOOM. In small square-rigged vessels, a boom stretched at the foot of a square foresail. It was used particularly by whaling vessels sailing in ice, when it was necessary to see ahead clearly. Fitted to the spar was a bridle, to the middle of which a tackle was shackled. The lower block of the tackle was shackled to an eyebolt in the deck amidships. This formed the foresheet. From each end of the boom a rope led through a block halfway out the bowsprit and back to the rail. These ropes acted as braces. To furl the sail the spar was hoisted up under the foreyard and the sail was stowed like an upper topsail.

Ger: *Baumfock Baum.*

BENT IRON. A wood caulking tool with blade bent sidewise so that it can be driven into an angle that could not be reached with the common iron. It is used for the garboard planking along the keel in wooden shipbuilding.

BENT KNEE. A type of wooden knee used in boatbuilding consisting of steamed square stock bent over a mold and fitted cold. A through-fastened throat block is fitted at the back of the knee.

BENZON TERM. A term used in the measurement of racing yachts. It represents the difference in feet between the measurement of the girth of the yacht's hull taken round the skin surface and the girth at the same place measured with a string pulled taut. This measurement is taken at 6/10 the distance from the fore end of the water line. It was evolved by A. Benzon, a Danish yachtsman.

Fr: *Terme de Benzon;* Ger: *Benzon Grenze.*

BERG.

See **Iceberg.**

BERGY BITS. Term used in Polar terminology to denote medium-size pieces of ice detached and rounded on the top which may originate either from a glacier or from disrupted hummocky ice.

Fr: *Blocs mamelonnés;* Ger: *Eisstücke.*

BERM. The nearly horizontal formation or embankment along a beach caused by deposit of material under the influence of waves.

BERMAT. A type of boat found in tidal waters on the west coast of the Malay Peninsula. It is fitted with a small, roughly-made gallery aft and is steered with a paddle. The rig consists of one mast with a square-headed dipping lugsail. Sometimes called *gelmat.*

BERMUDA CUTTER. A sailing cutter in which the gaff mainsail is replaced by a jib-headed or Marconi mainsail.

Fr: *Cotre Bermudien;* Ger: *Hochgetakelter Kutter.*

BERMUDA RIG. A fore-and-aft rig adopted for small craft and especially for racing and cruising yachts, in which the gaff and jib topsails are replaced by a lofty leg-of-mutton sail. The luff runs on a mast-track and the sail sets with single halyards fastened to a headboard made of wood with brass facings. Sometimes called Marconi rig, jib-headed rig.

Fr: *Gréement Bermudien; Gréement Marconi;* Ger: *Hochtakelung; Focktakelung.*

The Bermuda rig requires a taller mast than gaff-rigged craft (about 20 per cent longer) and usually stayed with two sets of spreaders. The foot of the sail is shorter than with the gaff rig, as modern aerodynamics have shown that the height-width ratio of a sail plan has a great effect on its efficiency and that the best height for a sail is theoretically greater than practical considerations of mast-staying and handling will allow. Shrouds that in ordinary rigs leave the mast in a body at the hounds are distributed at the salient points of stress and compression and the tension is adjusted exactly and maintained by rigging screws. Stretch in the wire being equalized and the mast kept straight, virtually all the strain is taken off the deck, and rubber pads are often used instead of mast wedges. The ratio of hoist to foot in Bermuda rigs varies between 2.5 to 1 for small yachts and 1.5 to 1 for larger ones. Bermuda sails are more efficient than gaff sails when sailing close-hauled, owing to the fact that in a gaff sail the head falls to leeward on account of the weight of the gaff, while with a triangular sail a more uniform surface is obtained. Also the boom is shorter and consequently easier to handle. As against the above advantage it is claimed that triangular sails are apt to split being almost always "cross cut" and, if made of heavier canvas they are ineffective in light weather. Also there is heavy wear in reefing, which shortens the life of these sails.

Gray, A., *Marconi Rigging,* New York, 1932.

BERMUDA SAIL.
See **Bermuda Rig.**

BERMUDA SCHOONER. A schooner-rigged vessel in which the gaff sails are replaced by Bermuda or Marconi sails.

Fr: *Goëlette Bermudienne;* Ger: *Hochtakeltschuner.*

BERMUDA SLOOP. A sloop-rigged sailing craft formerly used for trading and racing in the Bermuda Islands. It was particularly adapted to the local weather and waters, which permitted the use of a large rig and put a premium on windward ability. Also called Bermudian, mudian, mugian sloop. Length over-all 23 ft. 10 in. to 37 ft. 4 in. Breadth 8 ft. 2 in. to 11 ft. 6 in. Draft 4 ft. 6 in. to 6 ft. 3 in.

The hull was relatively short, with good beam and great draft aft, having a cutaway forefoot and square stern. It carried a large amount of ballast. Besides a long main boom and short jibboom it had a long raking mast stepped just over the forefoot, usually unsupported by shrouds or stays. The loose foot jib-headed mainsail was hoisted to a height of twice and sometimes three times the length of keel. The only other sail besides a small foresail or jib, was a peculiarly shaped topsail with sprit, which was set over the mainsail when running free in fine weather. In some boats the main halyards were fastened to a headboard, in others to a very short gaff. Bermuda sloops were considered the fastest sailing craft in the world for working to windward in smooth water. The type is now extinct.

BERMUDIAN. A term, in yachting parlance, applied indiscriminately to the original Bermuda rig, to the leg-of-mutton sail on a pole mast, and to the same sail set on a gunter yard.

BERO. Outrigger dugout canoe from Timor Island with wash strake made of wood or palm leafs. It is rigged with a tripod mast and a rectangular sail in which the drop is less than half the length of mast. Also called *prao bero, berok.*

BEROKO.
See **Baru.**

BERONGABOY. Single outrigger Australian dugout canoe of the Koko-Baltja tribe from Weary Bay (Queensland). The body is round-bottomed with pronounced tumble home at the sides. Average length, 21 ft.

BERTH. 1. The shelf-like space allotted to a passenger or member of the crew as a sleeping place.

Fr: *Couchette;* Ger: *Koje.*

2. Term used by shipyard welders to denote a portion of the hull between two transverse bulkheads. Its length in the midship portion of the hull is roughly between nine and twelve frame spaces. Each berth is subdivided into two sections, the division line being at the level of the bilge or closing strake.

3. Sea room. Space kept or to be kept for safety or convenience between a vessel under sail and other vessels on the shore, rocks, and so on, used especially in the phrase "to give a wide berth," which means to keep well away from.

4. The place assigned to a vessel in port when anchored or lying alongside a pier, a quay, a wharf, and so on, where it can load or discharge.

Fr: *Poste;* Ger: *Liegeplatz; Kaiplatz.*

See **Appropriated Berth, Building Berth, Dredged Berth, Foul Berth, Loading Berth, Mud Berth, On the Berth, Pipe Berth, Swinging Berth, Transom.**

BERTHAGE. 1. The space alongside a wharf or quay for the reception of shipping.

2. Also berthing dues or berth charges. A term occasionally applied to the charges assessed against a ship for the use of a berth alongside a wharf or quay when there is no loading or unloading of cargo, the vessel being tied up for repairs, supplies, etc. The word "berthage" is frequently used in place of "dockage."

Fr: *Droits de quai; Droits de stationnement;* Ger: *Raumgebühr; Dockgebühr.*

BERTH CARGO. Cargo that consists mainly of commodities that line vessels carry to fill up surplus capacity when it is not found possible to get the more profitable high-class liner cargo. It is usually taken at less than the regular line rate of freight.

BERTH CHARGE. The cost of a berth, or the use of a quay by a vessel while loading or discharging. It is a port charge, not a "due" on cargo. Sometimes called tariff charge or dockage.

Fr: *Droit de Stationnement;* Ger: *Standgeld.*

BERTH CHARTER. A form of charter which implies that the ship has not been hired for the transportation of a full definite cargo; the charterer expecting to be able to do so places the vessel on the berth, i.e., he holds it in the loading port and invites shippers to book cargo space.

BERTH CLAUSE. A charter party clause that provides that the vessel is to take its turn for loading or discharging. This prevents the lay days from beginning until the vessel reaches a berth. Sometimes called turn berth clause.
Ger: *Rote Klausel; Berth Klausel.*
BERTHING. The outside planking above the sheer strake.
BERTHING DUES.
See Berthage, Dockage.
BERTHING MASTER. One who under the authority of the harbor master has charge of the berthing and mooring of ships and supervises all operations connected therewith.
BERTHING RAIL. A railing on each side of the knee timbers for the safety of the men when they were out in the head (obsolete).
BERTHING SIGNAL. A harbor signal to indicate the berth assigned to an arriving vessel. Flags, shapes, and lights are used for these signals.
Fr: *Signal de Poste;* Ger: *Liegeplatzsignal.*
BERTH NOTE. A form of contract used on the Danube which frees the chartering broker from liability for freight and demurrage while giving him the right to engage cargo for a ship at a profit.
BERTHON BOAT. A folding boat sometimes used as lifeboat on small craft.
BERTH OWNER (G. B.). Term applied in England to an owner who offers his ships as common carriers to transport goods for all and sundry in a particular trade. Sometimes called berth shipowner.
BERTH RATES. The rates of freight charged by regular lines of shipping. Berth rates apply almost universally to partial cargoes. Also called Berth Freights.
Ger: *Platzfrachten.*
BERTH TERMS. A chartering expression meaning that the vessel is to be loaded as fast as it can take in as customary at port of loading, and to be discharged as fast as it can deliver at the port of discharge.
BERTH TRAFFIC. The business of transporting goods by sea using vessels that are put on the berth for a particular voyage without regular date of sailing, the latter being decided upon when sufficient cargo has been obtained.
BESE. A Javanese sea-going sailing barge employed in coastal waters between Semarang and Sidayu. Also a plank-built fishing boat of the Mayang type from the northern coast of middle Java.
BESET. The situation of a vessel when closely surrounded by ice and unable to move.
Fr: *Bloqué;* Ger: *Eingeengt.*
BEST BOWER ANCHOR. An anchor about the same size as the bowers, carried in addition to them. Not being intended for immediate use, it is generally securely lashed in place. It is a spare anchor and usually 15 per cent heavier than the other two bowers. Some large vessels carry two spare bowers. Sometimes called spare anchor.
Fr: *Ancre de réserve;* Ger: *Reserve Anker.*
BETIL. A double-ended Arab dhow with elaborately decorated bows and stern used for pearling in the Gulf of Persia. Probably extinct.
BETTE. A Mediterranean rowing and sailing boat originating from the western shores of Provence around Martigues and Sète. The hull is very similar in form to a dory, with flat bottom, hard chine, and straight flaring sides. Stem and sternpost have a pronounced rake, the former making an angle of about 112°, the latter about 110° to 115°.

In former days the maximum length was about 23 ft. but since the beginning of this century it has been reduced to about 21 ft. for the largest and 10 ft. for the smallest type. A wash strake is fitted to boats that have a length of 17½ ft. or more. It is comparatively high (10 in.) amidships, gradually decreasing toward the ends, where it finishes flush with the gunwale. Up to a length of 19 ft., the sides are composed of 3 planks, and above this length, 4 strakes are used. The rig consists of a lateen mainsail and a jib with tack fastened to the raised stemhead. The length of mast is 3 ft. 4 in. less than the keel length—the sail area varies from 1.7 to 2.6 of the area of circumscribed parallelogram to the boat's bottom plane. For a 13½ ft. boat, this is equivalent to about 90 sq. ft., increasing to 300 sq. ft. for a 21-ft. boat.

BETWEEN WIND AND WATER. That part of a ship's side or bottom that is frequently brought above the water by the rolling of the vessel or by variation in immersion due to travel in a seaway.
Ger: *Zwischen Wind und Wasser.*

BEVEL. 1. The angle contained by two adjacent sides of any structural member when more or less than 90°; as distinguished from square.
Fr: *Équerrage*; Ger: *Schmiegung*.
2. The angle contained by the two flanges of a frame bar.
See **Close Bevel, Frame Bevel, Standing Bevel.**

BEVEL BOARD. A wooden board upon which are drawn the bevels applying to some part of the ship's structure such as the frames and given to the shipwrights in the yard for ready reference.
Fr: *Planchette d'équerrage*; Ger: *Schmiegebrett*.

BEVELER. A hand lever with a jaw at one end employed by furnace men for opening the flanges of angle bars or channels and to give them the required bevel in smithing the frame bars. Also called beveling lever, weeze bar (U. S.).
Fr: *Levier à Griffe*; Ger: *Handbieger*.

BHANDARY. Member of an Asiatic crew who cooks for lascars and is especially qualified in the preparation of rice and East Indian dishes.

BHUR. A seagoing barge from the Ganges estuary (Bengal) with pointed ends, used for transportation of jute and timber. It is thatched all over except for a small space forward. Capacity 50 to 100 tons.

BIABINA. Large plank-built canoe of Ysabel Island (Solomon Islands). These canoes will hold as many as 50 paddlers, who sit 2 abreast on thwarts that rest on 2 longitudinal poles lashed to the frames.

BIBBS. Fitted pieces of timber bolted to the hounds of a mast with their edges level with the hounds and giving additional support to the trestletrees. The bibbs strengthen the mast in that part where it is most liable to strain and injury.
Fr: *Faux Élongis*; Ger: *Hummer*.

BIBBY TANDEM CABINS. An arrangement of cabin adopted on passenger vessels by which each cabin has access to the ship's side and is provided with its own natural light. Separate doors from each cabin to the passage are also provided.

BIDAR. 1. A paddling dugout canoe (also called *sampan bidar*) with single wash strake from Palembang (Sumatra) used for the transport of persons from ship to shore on open roadsteads. Smaller type: Length 12 to 25 ft. Breadth 4 to 6 ft. Larger craft with a length of 40 ft. and a breadth of 9 ft. are occasionally seen.
2. In the Rhio Archipelago there is another type of seagoing *bidar* rigged with one mast and very similar to the *julung-julung*.
3. On the Malay Peninsula the *bidar* is a rowboat with beak head. Length 24 ft. Beam 4 ft. Depth 2 ft. Capacity about 2½ tons. It is manned by a crew of 3.

BIDARKA. Sharp-ended, round-bottomed, keelless skin boat used by the Eskimos of northwest Alaska (Aleutian Islands). Sometimes called *paitalik*. The *bidarka* differs from the *kayak* of the eastern coast by its comparatively blunt bow with a hole at the extremity for attaching the painter, and its short and almost vertical stern. It is propelled by double-bladed paddles. The top of the *bidarka* is entirely covered or decked except for the manholes. Both two-hole and three-hole *bidarkas* are used by the Aleuts. Two-hole *bidarka*: Length 19 ft. 6 in. Beam 30 in. Depth 21 in.
The three-hole *bidarka* is little used for fishing, being a boat designed chiefly for cruising or for carrying white traders about the country. Length over-all 23 ft. 7 in. Beam 36 in. Depth from top of manhole rim 19 in.
Average dimensions of one-hole *bidarka*: 14 by 2 by 1.4 ft.

BIDARRAH. Russian name used in the Sea of Okhotskh, Bering Sea, Aleutian, and Kodiak Islands to denote the umiak skin boat. Also called *baidar, baidarrah*.

BIDEFORD POLACKER. A two-masted English sailing coaster that originated from Bideford (Devonshire) and was rigged as a polacca on the foremast. The last of these vessels was lost in 1930 and the type is now extinct. Length 51 to 74 ft. Breadth 15 to 18.6 ft. Hold depth 7.6 to 12.6 ft.
The hull, of rounded lines and massive proportions, was built with knee bow and square stern. It had bluff bows, round bottom, and good sheer, and was decked from stem to stern with one cargo hatch between the masts.
The rig consisted of a bowsprit with long running jibboom and two headsails. The foremast was a heavy short pole spar with square foresail and single topsail. There were no foot ropes to the topsail yard; the sail was stowed by the men standing on the foreyard foot ropes. The foresail was rigged with a Bentinck boom, with loose-footed gaff mainsail and yard topsail. There were two staysails between the masts. Studding

sails were used in light winds. These vessels carried sweeps for use in narrow waters.

BIDUK. Double outrigger planked canoe found in the Strait of Sunda and Achin (Sumatra), with forked stem and stern; used for transportation of goods. It is rigged with 1 or 2 masts and a quadrilateral sail made of leaves and a sort of bowsprit with headsail. Capacity 5 to 9 tons. Also called *bido*.

BIFURCATION BUOY. A buoy placed at the outer end of a middle ground, that is to say at the end nearest to the entrance of a harbor, river, or estuary when coming from seaward.

Fr: *Bouée de Bifurcation;* Ger: *Spaltungstonne.*

BIGELOW BOOM. A very light and flexible boom invented by Commodore Paul Bigelow of Bellport, N. Y. Along each side of the boom there is a wire stay and a strut with 3 notches in it. It is possible by pulling the stay into each one of the notches to give some lateral curvature to the boom according to the force of the wind.

BIGHT. 1. The bend or loop in a rope. The double part when it is folded. In knotting, that part of the rope between the end and the standing part.

Fr: *Double; Balant;* Ger: *Doppelpart.*

2. A slightly receding bay or recess in a seacoast between comparatively distant headlands. Long and gradual bend of a coastline.

Fr: *Anse;* Ger: *Bucht.*

BIGHTED SAIL. A sail that has each cloth between the seams folded and sewed once, twice, or three times, in parallel direction to the seam. The sail is then described as single-, double-, or treble-bighted. The object of bighting is to prevent the sagging of the canvas between the seams and to equalize the stretching of the whole surface of the sail. The extra weight of canvas resulting from these folds is compensated by the better setting of the sail and a smoother surface. This process was used only for racing sails and has practically been abandoned since crosscut sails have come into vogue.

BIGLET. The bight of a cargo sling through which the rove or long end is passed.
See **Bite.**

BILANCELLA. A fishing or coasting vessel resembling the *tartana* but of smaller tonnage. It works a net called *bilancia;* hence its name. A similar French vessel is called *balancelle;* Spanish, *balancela*. It originated in Naples but is found all along the west coast of Italy, Southern France, and Spain, with different rigs however. The Italian *bilancella* has one mast without rake and carries a lateen or settee mainsail and a jib set flying; it is a small edition of the *tartana*. The Spanish *balancela* has a short mainmast raking forward and a small jigger mast with high peaked lateen sail. One headsail. There are two grounding keels to haul the vessel on the beach. Rounded stern, curving inboard. The average dimensions of the *balancela* are: Length 40 to 60 ft. Breadth 11 ft. 6 in. to 15 ft. 8 in. Depth 4 to 4.9 ft. Sail area of larger type —3250 sq. ft.

Bilancella

In the island of Elba the *bilancella* is known as *laccone*. The *bilancella peschereccia* of the Ligurian coast as described by Admiral Paris (*Souvenirs de Marine*) has a straight stem and slightly raking stern post with sharp stern, and differs very much in hull design from the Spanish boats. The deck has little camber and there are no grounding keels. Typical dimensions: Trading *bilancella* from Liguria: Length 65.6 ft. Breadth 14.2 ft. Depth 6.5 ft. Fishing *bilancella* from Puglia: Length 39.3 ft. Breadth 13.1 ft. Depth 3.9 ft. Fishing *bilancella* from Campania: Length 30.6 ft. Breadth 7.4 ft. Depth 2.4 ft.

BILGE. 1. The lower internal part of the hull, adjacent to the keelson, where the bilge water collects. In vessels with a double bottom, the triangular channel or waterway formed by the tank margin plate and the curvature of the outside shell. It runs fore and aft and is subdivided into sections by the ship's transverse bulkheads.

Fr: *Bouchain;* Ger: *Kimm.*

2. Generally, any space in the lower part of a ship's hold where waste water collects and in which bilge suctions are placed for pumping out.

Fr: *Fonds;* Ger: *Bilge; Kielraum.*

See **Blow the Bilges, Easy Bilge, Sharp Bilge, Turn of Bilge.**

BILGE AND CANTLINE. A term applied to a method of stowing barrels in a ship, the bilges of the upper tier of which fit into the cantlines of the lower tier at the quarters. This system economizes spaces and insures stability.

BILGE BLOCK. One of a row of wooden blocks similar to keel blocks used for supporting the bilges of a ship on the stocks or in a dry dock. Also called Bilge Cribbing.

Fr: *Tin Latéral;* Ger: *Kimmklotz; Kimmstapel.*

BILGE BOARD. A board projecting from each bilge and housed in a case or trunk when not used.

Ger: *Kimmschwert.*

Bilge boards are fitted to flat-bottomed, shallow-draft racing boats known in the United States as bilge-board scows. They are designed so that they will be vertical when the scow is sailing at the desired angle of heel. Bilge boards are more effective in resisting lateral pressure than centerboards, since they are nearly vertical when the boat heels, and thus present a surface normal to the direction of pressure. The result is that the area of each bilge board may be made less than the necessary area of a centerboard for the same hull, and frictional resistance is diminished.

BILGE BOARD SCOW. Punt-shaped, smooth water, racing boat of minimum draft with square or rounded bow, very flat floors, a firm bilge, and parallel sections throughout. Also called inland lake scow. Bilge boards are fitted instead of a centerboard. The windward board is housed in its trunk when sailing close-hauled. These scows are sloop-rigged. They are claimed to be the fastest boats for their size. Speeds of 16 mi. and over have been recorded when reaching in a strong breeze.

The idea of this design is to obtain a great increase of waterline length, combined with a marked decrease in beam when heeled under sail. This feature is combined with very light displacement and big sail area and the use of the weight of the crew as shifting ballast. Some of the largest scows are fin keelers.

Ger: *Kimmschwertyacht.*

BILGE BRACKET. A bracket connecting the inner bottom or tank top to the frames at the bilges. Sometimes called tank-side bracket, tank-side knee, wing bracket.

BILGE CEILING. Inside planking fitted at the turn of the bilge.

Fr: *Vaigres de bouchain;* Ger: *Kimmwegerung.*

BILGE DIAGONAL. 1. A diagonal in the body plan whose plane is normal to the vessel's surface at the turn of bilge.

2. A straight line in the body plan, extending from the intersection of the load line with the center longitudinal plane to the intersection of the "rise of floor" line with the half breadth line.

Fr: *Lisse des Bouchains;* Ger: *Kimmsente; Flursente.*

BILGE FREE. A method of stowing barrels and casks so that they are supported by chocks or beds placed under the quarters, leaving the center or "bilge" off the floor of the hold.

BILGE HAT.

See **Drain.**

BILGE INJECTION. A line from the circulating pumps of a marine engine room to the bilge. By means of this connection, water from the bilge may be pumped overboard through the surface condenser of the power plant, thus providing an additional means of pumping out a flooded engine room. A non return or check valve must be provided on the injection line to prevent flooding of the ship by mistake.

Fr: *Aspiration Principale aux Bouchains;* Ger: *Hauptbilgerohr.*

BILGE INJECTION VALVE.

See **Injection.**

BILGE KEEL. A fin fitted to the hull on each side of a ship at the turn of the bilge to reduce rolling.

Fr: *Quille de Roulis;* Ger: *Schlingerkiel; Kimmkiel.*

It usually consists of a bulb plate running fore and aft attached to the shell by angle bars although it may be a built up V-section, wood-filled. The length varies from 30 to 40 per cent of the ship's length. Tank experiments have shown that the increase in propulsive resistance of a vessel on an even keel due to the fitting of bilge keels may amount to about 4 per cent, and that this is increased by at least 2 per cent under average conditions of trim when the vessel is pitching even to a slight extent.

BILGE KEELSON. 1. A fore-and-aft girder placed across the frames at the turn of the bilge in an open-bottom vessel. In vessels built with a double bottom the margin plate acts as a bilge keelson.

Fr: *Carlingue de Bouchain;* Ger: *Kimmkielschwein; Kimmstringer.*

2. Also bilge log, bilge plank. One of several timbers extending fore and aft inside the bilge of a wooden hull, to strengthen the frame.

Fr: *Serre d'Empatture;* Ger: *Binnenkimm; Kimmweger.*

BILGE LINE. The system of piping ex-

BILGE LOG—BILGE WELL

tending fore and aft for the removal of water that collects in the bilges of a vessel, resulting from sweating of the hull or other causes, and from tank top and watertight flats. In cargo vessels, it usually includes a main suction line between engine and boiler rooms and an auxiliary suction line running fore and aft with branches to different compartments.

Fr: *Tuyautage de cale;* Ger: *Bilgeleitung; Lenzleitung.*

BILGE LOG. One of the logs of the bilge ways that supports the hull when launching.

See **Bilge Keelson.**

BILGE MAIN. Section of the bilge system between the bilge pump and the bilge suction chest.

Fr: *Collecteur principal de Cale;* Ger: *Hauptbilgeleitung.*

BILGE PLANKS. Strengthening planks of the inner or outer skin at turn of bilge.

Fr: *Bordages de Bouchain;* Ger: *Kimmplanken.*

BILGE PLATING. The bottom plating covering the outside of the frames in the bilge of a vessel.

Fr: *Bordé de Bouchains;* Ger: *Kimmbeplattung.*

BILGE PUMP. A pump used aboard ship to remove accumulations of water in the vessel's hold and other compartments and discharge it overboard. Bilge pumps are often geared to and from part of the main engines when these are of the reciprocating type. When fitted with the necessary connections to the bilge system, sanitary, ballast, and general service pumps are usually considered as independent bilge pumps.

Fr: *Pompe de Cale;* Ger: *Lenz Pumpe; Bilgepumpe.*

Spanner, E. F., Bilge Pumping in Relation to Safety At Sea, Institute of Marine Engineers, London. *Transactions,* vol. 44, February, 1932.

BILGE RAIL. A fore-and-aft piece of wood scored out at intervals, or a metal rod fitted outside the planking of a lifeboat above the turn of bilge to provide a handhold for persons struggling in the water should the boat capsize.

Ger: *Kimmreling.*

BILGE SHORE. Short, heavy timbers used in addition to the bilge blocks as supports for a vessel at or near the turn of bilge when the ship is being built or is dry-docked.

Fr: *Accore latérale; Accore de Bouchain;* Ger: *Kimmstütze.*

BILGE STRAKE. Longitudinal course of planking or plating situated at the turn of bilge.

Fr: *Virure de Bouchain;* Ger: *Kimmgang.*

BILGE SUCTION. The arrangement of piping, and so on, in connection with a pump for expelling water that has accumulated in the bilges.

Fr: *Aspiration aux Bouchains;* Ger: *Kimmsaugung.*

BILGE SUCTION PIPE. One of a system of drain pipes placed on each side at the afterend of each of the holds or compartments. They may be led over the tank-side gutters or they may pass through lightening holes in the bracket plates.

Fr: *Tuyau de Cale;* Ger: *Bilgerohr.*

BILGE WATER. The water that collects in the bilges of a vessel, which generally becomes foul and noxious.

Fr: *Vidange de Cale;* Ger: *Bilgenwasser; Kielraumwasser.*

BILGE WELL. A partial depth well for the purpose of collecting bilge water which may find its way to the tank top, especially in vessels where the latter extends horizontally to the ship's sides. Sometimes called drainage well, pocket well.

Fr: *Puisard;* Ger: *Brunnen.*

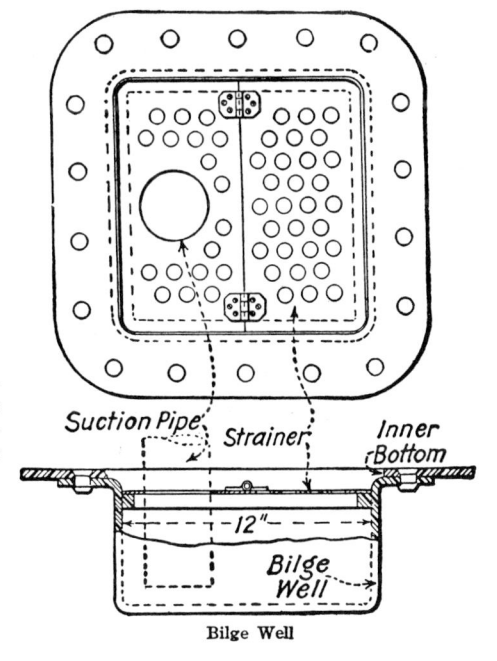

Bilge Well

These wells are located at the afterend of each compartment. In order to maintain the efficiency of the double bottom they do not extend closer than 18 inches to the shell plating. The tank-top plating is perforated in way of the wells, thus providing a preliminary straining of the water before it reaches the suction strainers on the bilge pipes.

BILIBILI. Single outrigger dugout canoe from Espiritu Santo Island (New Hebrides). The bow and stern are carved and bear on the upper side a flat surface which serves as a seat. The breadth is such that two men can sit side by side. In the central part there is a movable platform that consists of transverse boards held in position on both sides by a long pole.

BILL. 1. The point that forms the extremity of the flukes of an anchor. Sometimes called Pea.

Fr: *Bec;* Ger: *Ankerspitze.*

2. Any of the various certificates, lists, or documents—always specifically identified, as bill of health, bill of lading, and so on.

See **Boat Stations Bill, Fire Bill, Portage Bill, Station Bill, Victualing Bill.**

BILLBOARD.
See **Anchor Bed.**

BILLETHEAD. A term used when there is no figurehead and the termination of the head is formed by a fiddle-shaped scroll turning aft or inwardlike, as distinguished from scrollhead. Sometimes called fiddlehead.

Ger: *Galionskrulle; Einwärts gebogene Krulle.*

BILL OF ENTRY. The paper or declaration that the merchant hands to the customs entry clerk. A written account of goods entered at the customhouse, whether imported or intended for export.

Fr: *Déclaration en Douane;* Ger: *Zolleinfuhrschein; Zolldeklaration.*

BILL OF HEALTH. A certificate given to the master of a vessel by the customs authorities in a home port or by the consul in a foreign port, describing the general health or sanitary conditions of the port from which the vessel sails. Sometimes called certificate of pratique, certificate of health.

Fr: *Patente de Santé;* Ger: *Gesundheitspass; Sanitätspass.*

See **Clean Bill of Health, Foul Bill of Health, Suspected Bill of Health.**

BILL OF LADING. A document by which the master of a ship acknowledges having received in good order and condition (or the reverse) certain specified goods consigned to him by some particular shipper, and binds himself to deliver them in similar condition —unless the perils of the sea, fire, or enemies prevent him—to the consignees of the shipper at the point of destination on their paying him the stipulated freight.

Fr: *Connaissement;* Ger: *Konnossement; Frachtbrief.*

See **Blank Bill of Lading, Clean Bill of Lading, Export Bill of Lading, Liner Bill of Lading, Omnibus Bill of Lading, Order Bill of Lading, Received for Shipment Bill of Lading, Shipped Bill of Lading, Ship's Bill of Lading, Straight Bill of Lading, Through Bill of Lading.**

The forms of bill of lading, like the forms of charter parties, vary considerably, special provisions being often inserted to meet special cases. It is the usual practice to prepare three copies of bill of lading. One is retained by the master, another by the consignor, and the third is forwarded to the consignee.

Carver, T. G., *Law Relating to the Carriage of Goods by Sea,* London, 1938; Scrutton, T. E., *Charter Parties and Bills of Lading,* London, 1939; Thompson, G. M., *Law Relating to Bills of Lading,* London, 1925.

BILL OF SALE. The universal instrument of transfer of ships in the usage of all maritime nations. It is the customary document by which the ownership of vessels is evidenced. Under international maritime law a bill of sale is necessary to pass title to a ship.

Fr: *Acte de Vente;* Ger: *Kaufbrief.*

BILL OF SIGHT (G. B.). A form used in connection with the customs entry of goods when an importer is unable to complete the normal form. It enables packages to be opened in the presence of a customs official. When this is done, the sight is said to be "perfected."

Ger: *Zollerlaubnisschein.*

BILL OF STORE (G. B.). A license permitting duty free reimportation of British goods that have been exported from the United Kingdom within five years of the date of original exportation.

BILL OF STORES (U. S.). A license granted by the customs authorities to merchant ships by which they are allowed to carry stores and provisions for the voyage duty free.

BILL OF SUFFERANCE. A customs permit or license granted to shipping firms engaged in the coasting trade by which dutiable goods are allowed to be loaded and landed without paying customs duty provided they are handled at a sufferance wharf.

BILLY BOY. A seagoing sailing barge from the east coast of England, formerly used for inland as well as for coastal navigation. The hull was flat-bottomed with rounded ends and carried leeboards. These craft were sloop- or ketch-rigged with square topsail and running bowsprit. Now extinct.

BILO.
See **Bilus.**

BILOLANG. A double outrigger sailing canoe from Macassar with flat bottom and vertically rising stem piece, rigged with one mast and a triangular or quadrilateral spritsail. It is used for fishing or transportation. In the traders there is a roofed shelter built over the outrigger booms and extending slightly outboard on each side. When the triangular sail is used it is set with point downward. Also called *balolang, biroang.*

BILUS. A double outrigger dugout canoe with wash strake made of bark and used for interinsular trading and fishing by the people of Visayas (Philippine Islands). Also called *bilo*. It is rigged with one mast, a sprit mainsail with boom, and a jib-headed foresail. It is essentially an enlarged *sibidsibiran* and is fast under sail.

BINABINA. Plank-built seagoing canoe without outrigger of the Solomon Islands. The fore end terminates with a high, curved stem. It is handled by 10 paddlers and a steersman. Length 22 ft. Breadth 2 ft. 3 in.

BINDER.
See **Slip.**

BINDING. A wrought-iron ring around a lower deadeye.

BINDING STRAKE. 1. One of the thick deck planks running just outside the line of hatches, in a wooden vessel, and jogged down over the beams and ledges. Also called bolt strake. 2. The uppermost but two of the strakes of planking in carvel-built open boats. It is one of the first put on with the garboard strake. 3. A strake of planking having greater strength or thickness than the other strakes.

Fr: *Virure de Liaison;* Ger: *Verbindungsgang.*

BINGKUNG. Open plank-built fishing craft from Western Java of approximately the same tonnage as the *mayang*. It is distinguished from the latter by the absence of the curved blade-shaped pieces rising at bow and stern. In some localities the name *tjondong* is used instead of *bingkung*. Length 39 ft. Breadth 9.8 ft.

The *bingkung-soto* is a smaller variety of the same type employed in the line and net fisheries of the Cheribon Residency.

BINNACLE. The stand on which the compass bowl is supported. The body of the binnacle is usually built of hard, well-seasoned wood, or is a nonmagnetic metal pedestal. The upper part consists of a protective brass cover or hood.

Fr: *Habitacle;* Ger: *Kompasshaus; Kompassständer.*

See **Compensating Binnacle.**

BINNACLE COVER. A dome-shaped appliance made of brass that fits down over the top of the binnacle protecting the compass. Sometimes called binnacle hood.

Fr: *Capot d'Habitacle;* Ger: *Kompasshause; Kompassbezug; Kompasskappe.*

It contains lamps (oil or electric) to illuminate the compass card at night, and has a glass plate at the rear side through which the helmsman can see the compass and thus ascertain the direction of the ship's head. Binnacles for gyroscopic compasses are smaller and flatter and have electric light near the lubber point only.

BINNACLE LIGHT. Oil or electric lamp fitted in the binnacle cover for illuminating the compass card.

Fr: *Lampe d'habitacle;* Ger: *Nachthauslampe.*

BINOCULARS. A telescopic instrument for the use of both eyes at once, having two tubes, each furnished with lenses. Binoculars collect as much light as the object glasses permit from a larger area of the field than a telescope but with lesser magnification. They provide an aid to vision that, if not of the high power of the telescope, is a much closer approach to the natural manner of viewing objects.

Fr: *Jumelles;* Ger: *Doppelglas.*

BIPOD MAST. A patent shroudless mast consisting of two transversely inclined welded steel supports of elliptical section which meet at the trestle trees. The goosenecks for cargo derricks are attached at the foot of these supports. The topping lift blocks are installed on the trestle tree arms on both sides, and vertically above the position of the goosenecks. The pivoting of the derrick booms is no longer interfered with by shrouds and the derricks can be swivelled around as far as the goosenecks will allow. When used for heavy lifts the bipod mast is stayed in a fore and aft direction as would a·mast of standard construction. The two legs or supports can be used for the ventilation of cargo spaces below. When compared to the ordinary construction of derrick posts, there is a substantial saving in weight.

Fr: *Mât bipode;* Ger: *Zweibein Mast.*

BIRCH. A moderately hard wood. Two kinds are used in ship construction, the black and the yellow. The black is the most durable and is preferred by shipbuilders for keels, floor timbers, garboard and bottom planking. Weight per cu. ft. (seasoned) about 45 lbs.

Fr: *Bouleau;* Ger: *Birkenholz.*

BIROANG.
See **Bilolang.**

BISHOP'S RING. A dull reddish-brown ring which is seen at certain periods round the sun on a clear day. It was first observed after the great eruption of Krakatoa in 1883, and remained visible until 1886. It was due to the minute particles shot out by the eruption and remaining in the atmosphere at great heights. It was seen again after the Mount Pelee (Martinique) eruption in 1902.

Fr: *Anneau de Bishop.*

BISQUINE. A small lug-rigged French fishing boat with two or three masts. Its rig is similar to that of the *chaloupe;* its tonnage varies from 30 to 40. The foremast is placed right in the eyes. There is a bowsprit with large jib. Each mast carries a lugsail and lug topsail. Average dimensions of a *bisquine* from Granville: Length over-all 40 ft. Breadth 11 ft. Depth 7 ft. 10 in. The *bisquine* differs from the *chaloupe* by the cut of the foresail, which is much smaller and peaked higher. The mainsail is a dipping lug. A small jigger is occasionally set.

BITE. The short end of a rope sling through which the long end or rove is passed before it is hooked to the cargo whip.

BITT. A strong post of wood or iron for belaying, fastening, and working ropes, cables, mooring lines, and so on. Bitts are usually in pairs, named according to their uses. Although also called bollard, the latter term is more generally applied to a cast-iron or timber post fixed on a pier or quay for securing mooring lines.

Fr: *Bitte; Bollard;* Ger: *Poller, Beting.*

See **Bowsprit Bitt, Carrick Bitts, Cross Bitt, Mooring Bitts, Pawl Bitt, Riding Bitts, Small Bitts, Towing Bitts, Windlass Bitts.**

BITT (to). To take a rope around the bitts in order to fasten it or to put a check on the rope paying out.

Fr: *Prendre un tour de bitte;* Ger: *Betingschlag nehmen; Um die Beting schlagen.*

See **Double Bitt (to).**

BITT BRACKET. A strong bracket placed on the fore or after part of bitts in order to reinforce them.

Fr: *Taquet de Bitte;* Ger: *Betingstützplatte.*

BITTER END. The inboard end of the anchor cable. It is usually rove through a ring at the bottom of the chain locker and brought up and made fast to a beam or other accessible place by a sliphook or lashing, which admits of easy slipping if required.

Fr: *Étalingure de Puits;* Ger: *Hintere Betingschlag.*

BITT PIN. A large steel pin fitted across a bitt to prevent the cable or rope from jumping off while being veered or eased off.

Fr: *Paille de Bitte;* Ger: *Betingstange.*

BITT STANDARD. Inverted knees placed above deck and bolted to the fore part of cable bitts, riding bitts and bowsprit bitts. Sometimes called Samson knee.

Fr: *Montant de Bittes;* Ger: *Betingsknie.*

BITUMASTIC.
See **Bituminous Enamel.**

BITUMEN CARRIER. A tank vessel specially designed for the transportation of bitumen in bulk. Special heating coils are installed in the tanks for raising the temperature of the cargo to about 270° F., in order to keep the highly viscous bitumen in a manageable condition for loading and unloading. Also called Asphalt carrier, Bitumen tanker. There are two longitudinal bulkheads, but only the center compartments which are much wider than usual are used for cargo. The wing tanks are used for ballast.

BITUMINOUS ENAMEL. A composition employed to protect the inaccessible surfaces of internal structural parts of steel ships against corrosion. Sometimes called bitumastic enamel.

Fr: *Enduit au Bitumastic;* Ger: *Bitumastik Emailleanstrich.*

This protection against corrosion requires two materials, the priming solution and the enamel proper. The enamel consists of a homogeneous mixture composed largely of asphalt and containing other ingredients such as rosin, Portland cement, slaked lime, petroleum, the amount of mineral matter varying between 15 per cent and 40 per cent by weight. The primer consists of a similar bituminous mixture containing no added mineral matter and thinned with a solvent to a satisfactory brushing consistency. The steel surfaces are first primed, and when the primer has dried to a slightly tacky state, it is ready for the application of the enamel. The enamel is melted and heated to a temperature not exceeding 375° F. and then mopped on quickly, since it sets and hardens very rapidly. Bituminous enamels are mostly used in coal bunkers, ballast tanks, bilges, chain lockers, and other inaccessible places.

BLACK CEDAR. An excellent wood for boats and canoes up to about 50 ft. in length. It is exceedingly light, very tough, and pliable, and has excellent durability. Its weight is about 27 lbs. per cu. ft. when seasoned.

BLACKING. A mixture of two-thirds pine tar and one-third coal tar, formerly applied to hemp standing rigging as a preservative.

Fr: *Galipot*; Ger: *Lappfalbe*.

BLACK PINE. A hardwood used largely in the United States of America for planking of small boats. Also called cyprus pine.

Fr: *Pin Noir*; Ger: *Schwartzfichte*.

BLACK SEA BERTH TERMS. A form of contract under which a steamer is chartered to load on the berth a full cargo of grain or seeds, but charterers have the option of shipping general cargo under specified conditions.

BLACK SEA MOORING. A mooring line which consists of 180 ft. of 10-in. Manila with one end spliced to a 60-ft. length of 1¾-in. wire rope, with a 5-ft. eye splice in the end of the wire.

BLACK STRAKE. A term formerly applied to a broad strake of planking that was parallel to and worked upon the upper edge of the wales. It derived its name from being paved with pitch and was the boundary for the painting of the topsides.

Fr: *Fourrure de Préceinte*; Ger: *Breitegang*.

BLACKWALL HITCH. A hitch used for fastening the hook of a tackle to a rope. It consists of a half hitch made across the back of the hook in such a way that the standing part jams the loose end across the body of the hook.

Fr: *La Gueule de Loup*; *Noeud de bec d'oiseau*; Ger: *Einfacher Hakenschlag*.

BLADE AREA. The actual area of the surface of the driving face of the propeller blade.

Fr: *Surface des Ailes*; Ger: *Flügelfläche*.

Average total blade area:
For 4-bladed propellers,
 35–45 per cent of disc area
For 3-bladed propellers,
 27–33 per cent of disc area
For 2-bladed propellers,
 20–25 per cent of disc area

BLANDONGAN. A very small East Indian outrigger canoe of *jukung* type from Madura, with forked ends and wash strakes. The rig consists of one mast with rectangular sail. Abaft the mast there is a small platform for the crew. In the Besuki District (Java) the *blandongan* is more of the *sampan* type and sets a triangular sail.

BLANK BILL OF LADING. A bill of lading in which the name of receivers or consignees is not mentioned, the goods being delivered to bearer.

Fr: *Connaissement au Porteur*; Ger: *Blanko Konnossement*.

BLANKET. A yachting term which applies to two boats sailing on parallel courses when one gets to windward of the other thereby taking wind away from the latter's sails. It is used as a weapon of contest in yacht racing.

BLANKET NET (U. S.). An impounding net suspended by one end from an outrigger in a boat and pulled in from the bottom by a line drawn from the deck.

BLANKET PIECE (U. S.). A whaling term. A piece of blubber 12 to 15 ft. long and 5 to 6 ft. wide.

BLAST. The sound made by blowing an instrument such as a whistle (steam or compressed air), a siren, or a fog horn.

Fr: *Son*; Ger: *Ton*.

See **Long Blast, Short Blast.**

BLATIK. Local name given to the *prao mayang* in Pulo Kembang (Madura Strait). Also called *praun blatik*.

BLAZER. A small Dutch fishing boat found mostly around Texel Island, resembling the *botter* but larger. It is provided with a fish well. The curved stemhead has less tumble home, and the stern is fuller than that of the *boeier*. *Blazers* when built with a *boier* stern are known as *blazerboier*. They work with a small trawl, and a number of them have been fitted with auxiliary engines.

BLEEDER.
See **Bleeder Plug.**

BLEEDER COCK.
See **Plug, Sea Plug, Sea Valve.**

BLEEDING. Breaking down grain from bags to bulk to permit more economical stowage in a vessel's hold.

BLEKINGSEKA. A Swedish open fishing boat common on the coasts of the province of Blekinge. Single mast with sprit mainsail and jib-headed foresail. Round stern with long overhang. Length over-all 26½ to 29½ ft. Breadth 11½ to 13 ft.

BLIND BUCKLER. A solid buckler used to close the opening of the hawse pipe when the cable is unbent. It is put on after a plug, called hawse plug, has been placed in the hawse pipe.
Fr: *Tape d'Écubier; Mantelet Plein;* Ger: *Klusenpfropfen.*

BLIND HATCH. A hatch opening in a 'tween-deck over which extends the unbroken expanse of the deck above.

BLIND HOLE. The converse of "fair hole."
Fr: *Trou Borgne;* Ger: *Blindes Loch.*

BLIND LEAD. A term used in polar waters denoting a *lead* closed at one end thus preventing a vessel from proceeding any further.

BLIND ROLLERS. Relatively heavy and often dangerous ocean swell caused by water in motion meeting lesser depth as it passes over shoals or approaches land.
Fr: *Vagues de Fond.*

BLINK. A glow on the horizon caused by the reflection of sunlight from the surface of an ice pack or floating mass of ice or from land covered with snow. Sometimes called ice blink.
Ger: *Eisblink.*

BLINKER. A lamp or set of lamps connected with a telegraph key for signaling by Morse code.
See **Morse Signaling Lamp.**

BLINKER LIGHT.
See **Morse Signaling Lamp.**

BLISTER. Additional outer skin which extends on each side of the hull over the parallel middle body near the waterline. It improves transverse stability when the vessel is in the spent condition. Blisters which communicate with the open sea, are fitted on some ships as an anti-rolling device, and replace anti-rolling tanks built within the hull.
Fr: *Soufflage;* Ger: *Anschwellung.*

BLISTERS. Raised projections on the surface of steel plates caused by bubbles of gas getting under the outer layer of metal during manufacture. Can also be caused by the non-expulsion of cinder or sand in the original rolling process.
Fr: *Soufflures;* Ger: *Blasen.*

BLIZZARD. A high wind accompanied by a great cold and drifting or falling snow.
Ger: *Schneesturm.*

BLOATER. An ungutted herring lightly salted and smoked, intended for immediate consumption. It is first kept in salt for 12 to 18 hours, then placed on a spit and afterward smoked at a comparatively high temperature for a period that varies from 2½ to 6 days.

BLOCK. A mechanical contrivance consisting of one or more grooved pulleys mounted in a casing or shell fitted with a hook, eye, or strap by which it may be attached.
Fr: *Poulie;* Ger: *Block.*

Blocks are used for transmitting power or changing the direction of motion by means of a rope or chain passing around the movable pulleys. They are single, double, treble, or fourfold according to the number of sheaves or pulleys. They receive different names according to their shape, purpose, or mode of application. Many of the blocks used on board ship are named after the ropes or chains rove through them. Blocks for marine use must be of substantial construction. The general practice is to use steel blocks with wire ropes and wood blocks with fiber ropes. They are made with a great variety of shackles, hooks, jaws, eyes, eyebolts, etc., to meet the particular requirements of the service intended. Steel block sizes are usually given in inches according to diameter of sheave and wooden block sizes according to length of shell.

BLOCKADE. A measure of war by which the forces of one belligerent obstruct communication with the shore or ports in the possession of the other. To be effective and binding it must be known and must be maintained by a force sufficient to render ingress or egress from the port or coastal area really and apparently dangerous. It is not necessary that the place should be invested by land as well as by sea. Penalty for breach of blockade is capture and condemnation.
Fr: *Blocus;* Ger: *Blockade.*

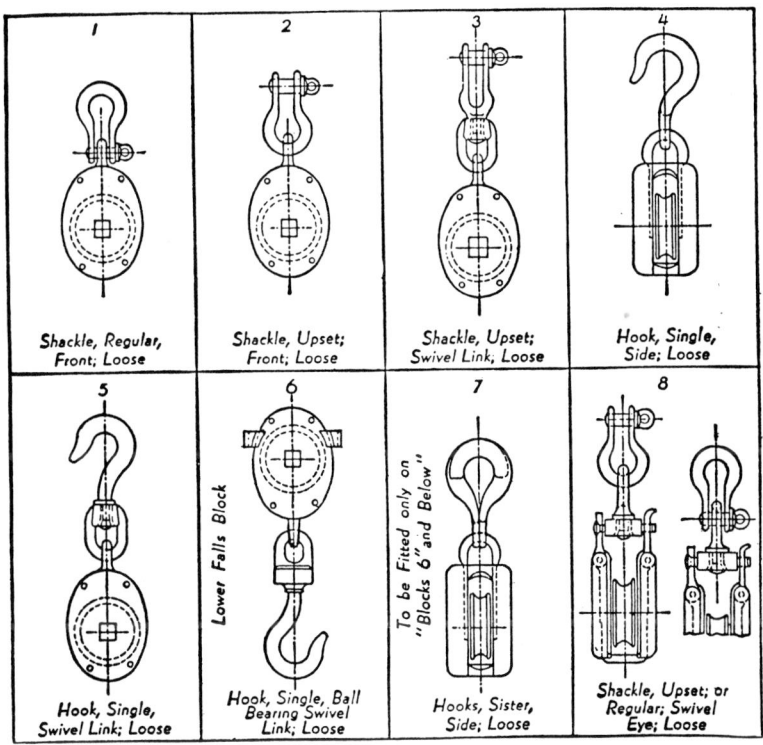

Blocks

1. Shackle, Regular, Front; Loose
2. Shackle, Upset; Front; Loose
3. Shackle, Upset; Swivel Link, Loose
4. Hook, Single, Side; Loose
5. Hook, Single, Swivel Link; Loose
6. Hook, Single, Ball Bearing Swivel Link; Loose
7. Hooks, Sister, Side; Loose
8. Shackle, Upset; or Regular; Swivel Eye; Loose

See Commercial Blockade, Military Blockade, Pacific Blockade.

BLOCK AND BLOCK. See Two Blocks.

BLOCK COEFFICIENT. The ratio of the immersed volume of a ship to the product of the waterline length, breadth, and draft.

Fr: *Coefficient de Remplissage;* Ger: *Deplacementskoeffizient; Völligkeitsgrad der Verdrängung; Deplacements Völligkeitsgrad.*

Passenger vessels	0.50 to 0.65
Cargo carriers and tankers	0.65 to 0.78
Barges	0.78 to 0.90
Tugs	0.56 to 0.60
Yachts	0.35 to 0.55

Lovett, W. J., "Proportions and Block Coefficients of Merchant Steamers," Institution of Naval Architects, London, *Transactions,* vol. 64 (1922); Lovett, "Maximum Block Coefficients and the Economic Disadvantage of Full Form," Society of Naval Architects and Marine Engineers, New York, *Transactions,* vol. 34 (1926).

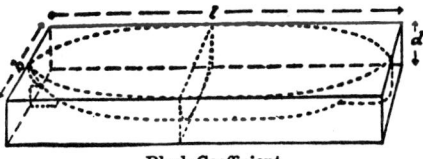

BLOCKING. A collective name for the wooden shores and blocks placed under a vessel's keel and bilges when on a building berth or in drydock. Also called cribbing, making up.

Fr: *Attinage; Billotage; Empilage;* Ger: *Aufklotzung; Stapelung.*

BLOCKING OFF. The operation of wedging cargo tightly in a ship's hold, not completely filled, so that it will not shift in heavy weather.

BLOCK ISLAND BOAT. A two-masted,

BLOCK MAST—BLOCK SPAN 70

Blocks

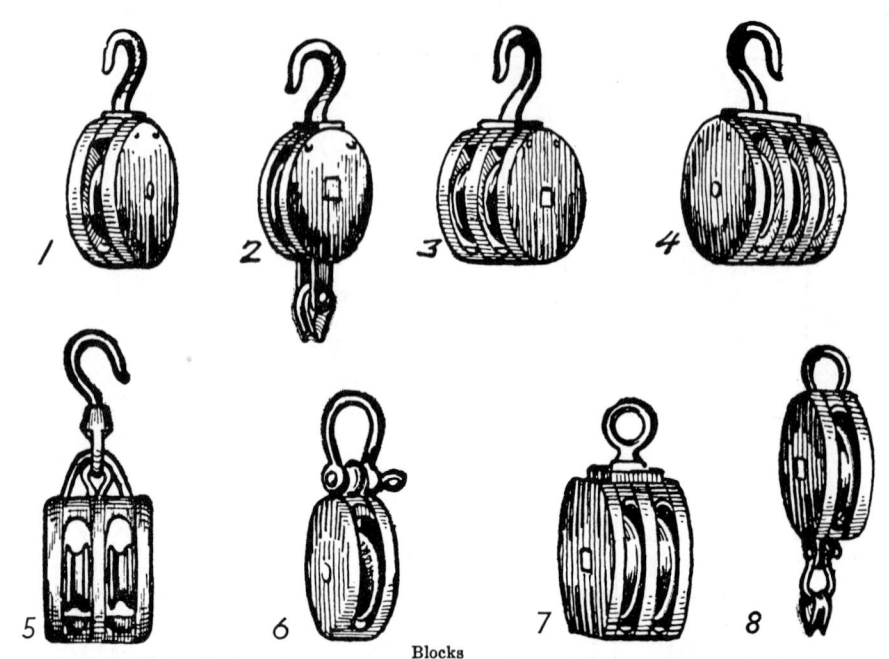

1. Single block with fixed hook
2. Single block, fixed hook and thimble
3. Double block and hook
4. Treble block and fixed hook
5. Double block with loose swivel hook
6. Single block with side shackle
7. Double block with swivel eye
8. Single block with bow and becket

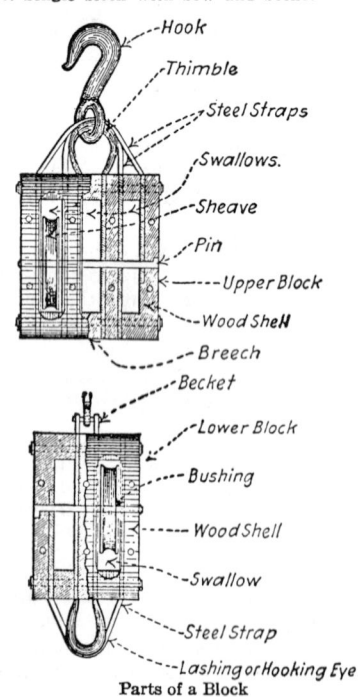

fore-and-aft-rigged keel boat with a length from 20 to 40 ft., sharp bow and stern, long straight keel with drag, and lap-strake planking, used for fishing about Block Island (Rhode Island). The rig consists of two masts and sails with short gaffs almost leg-of-mutton shape. The foremast is up in the bows. There is no standing rigging. The foresail has no boom and no headsails are carried. The type is now obsolete.

BLOCK MAST. A short mast square at the head as used with lateen-rigged vessels. In the square of the masthead, sheaves for the halyards are fixed.
Fr: *Mât de Calcet.*

BLOCK MODEL. A ship's model in which the hull is cut from a single block of wood. A full model of a ship in one piece. Also called solid block model.
Ger: *Blockmodell.*

BLOCK-OUT MOLD. A template used for outlining the approximate size of a steel plate to be furnaced.

BLOCK SPAN. A light wire span stretching between the two lower purchase blocks of lifeboat falls to prevent twisting while they are rounded up.

Parts of a Block

Hook
Thimble
Steel Straps
Swallows
Sheave
Pin
Upper Block
Wood Shell
Breech
Becket
Lower Block
Bushing
Wood Shell
Swallow
Steel Strap
Lashing or Hooking Eye

BLOOD MONEY. Fee given by a shipmaster to a crimp or a boarding-house keeper for the procurement of seamen.

BLOWER. A mechanical fan, usually of a rotary type, used to supply air in large quantities at low pressure. The air is used (1) for ventilation of living quarters; (2) for forced draft of boilers.

Fr: *Ventilateur;* Ger: *Gebläse.*

BLOW THE BILGES. 1. Said of a ship when the water in its bilges, as a result of violent rolling, is forced up through the crevices in the ceiling planks and comes into contact with the cargo. The expression is used chiefly in respect to vessels without a double bottom.

See **Bilge.**

2. Said of a barrel when it swells, usually at the middle.

BLUBBER. The fat of whales and other Cetacea, from which oil is obtained.

Fr: *Couenne;* Ger: *Walfischspeck.*

The blubber lies under the skin and over the muscles. The quantity yielded by a large whale varies from 40 to 50 cwt. It is the most profitable portion of a whale. Its thickness may vary from an inch to a foot. It is a hard, strong, and tough substance, forming a real skin but not firmly attached to the body except at the head and tail. Its thickness and quality depend on the species of whale and on the individual. The color is yellow or creamy.

BLUBBER GAFF. Short-handled hook used on whaling vessels for dragging blubber about the decks.

BLUBBER GUY. A heavy rope stretched from the lower main masthead to the lower foremast head in a whaling vessel, to which the speck falls were attached for flensing (obsolete).

BLUBBER HOOK. A large iron hook suspended from the cutting tackle for stripping blubber from a whale.

BLUBBER TOGGLE. A hardwood pin several feet long and about 6 in. in diameter, formerly used on whaling vessels for hoisting blubber. It was buttoned through a strop in the blanket piece which fastened to the cutting tackle.

BLUEBACK. A British nautical chart so called from the fact that it is backed with a blue material. These charts are published privately, as distinguished from the admiralty charts issued by the Hydrographic Department of the Admiralty. They are drawn to a smaller scale and embrace a larger area than the admiralty chart, and are mostly used by coasters, fishermen, and yachtsmen.

Luymes, J., "The Blueback," *Hydrographic Review,* Monaco, vol. 8 (1931).

BLUE ENSIGN. A national flag of Great Britain flown by ships belonging to colonial services of the state, also by vessels under government charter. All merchant vessels whose masters are officers of the Royal Naval Reserve and that are manned by a crew in which ten men at least belong to the Naval Reserve are allowed to fly the blue ensign.

BLUE LIGHT. A pyrotechnical light used for signaling at sea. It burns for a period of ½ to 1 minute and shows a bright bluish-white light. It is frequently used by pilot vessels to call the attention of passing vessels.

Ger: *Blaufeuer; Blaulicht.*

BLUENOSE. A nickname given by seamen to British North American sailing vessels and their crews. Properly applied, this name should cover Nova Scotia ships only and not those of the New Brunswick and Quebec provinces.

BLUE PETER. A blue signal flag with white square in the center, hoisted on the foremast by merchant vessels to indicate that the vessel is ready to sail.

Fr: *Pavillon de Départ;* Ger: *Blauer Peter; Fahrtflagge.*

BLUE PIGEON. Seamen's slang term for a sounding lead.

BLUE POLE. The pole of a magnet which, according to convention, is painted blue and indicates the south-seeking end.

Fr: *Pôle bleu;* Ger: *Blauer Pol.*

BLUFF. Cliff or headland with an almost perpendicular face.

Fr: *Bluff;* Ger: *Bluff.*

BLUNT BOLT. A bolt driven into a plank and timber as a partial or extra security. It is not driven right through the timber and is therefore often referred to as a short-driven bolt. Also called dump bolt.

Fr: *Cheville à Bout Perdu;* Ger: *Stumpfbolzen.*

BOARD. 1. A plank, timber, partition, or the like, specifically identified as to function.

See **Back Board, Bait Board, Bevel Board, Bilge Board,** etc.

2. In the operation of sailing craft: to bring hard down the tacks and sheets, especially those of the courses, so that the ship may sail as close as possible to the wind.

BOARD FOOT. A unit of measurement used in the American timber trade. One board foot is the equivalent of a piece of wood 1 ft. x 1 ft. x 1 in., or 144 cu. in. One thousand board feet is called a mille. It is equal to 83⅓ cu. ft. Twelve board feet equal 1 cu. ft.

BOARDING. Hailing and entering a vessel officially in order to examine her papers and her cargo or to ascertain the sanitary conditions of the crew and passengers on entering a harbor. Boarding is usually performed by the harbor medical officer and is compulsory for all vessels coming from the high seas. Government vessels, pilot vessels, small fishing vessels, and in general craft that remain close to the shore are not boarded when coming into a harbor.

Fr: *Arraisonnement;* Ger: *Entern.*

BOARDING CLERK. The employee of a shipping firm whose duty it is to communicate with ships on their arrival in port.

Ger: *Waterclerk.*

BOARDING INSPECTOR (U. S.). A customs officer who boards vessels arriving from foreign ports, examines the ship's papers, certifies the cargo manifest, seals or otherwise secures the hatches and openings until permit for unlading is received and a discharging officer assigned to the vessel. The duties of boarding inspector are frequently performed by discharging inspectors Also called boarding officer.

BOARDING KNIFE. A swordlike knife mounted on a straight handle, used by whalemen to sever the blanket pieces.

BOARDING STATION. A place where vessels entering harbor "bring to" to permit boarding by the customs officers.

BOARD OF TRADE. A government department in Great Britain which has to a large extent the supervision over all matters connected with commerce and industry. It is subdivided into five departments, called harbour, marine, commercial, labour and statistics, and railway departments.

The Marine Department regulates the survey of passenger steamers, examination of masters and mates, shipping offices for engagement and discharge of seamen and generally all questions relating to ships and their crews, including load line regulations, the detention of unseaworthy ships and inquiries into wrecks.

The Harbour Department has charge of foreshores belonging to the crown, the protection of navigable harbors and channels. It controls the provisional orders under the Pier and Harbour Acts and Pilotage Acts; also, the settlement of bylaws made by harbor authorities; the lighthouse funds of lighthouse authorities of the United Kingdom. Wrecks, salvage and quarantine regulations are also dealt with by this department.

The Finance Department deals with the financial side of all branches of the Board of Trade among which are the accounts of harbors, lighthouses, mercantile marine offices, and merchant seamen's funds, and also consular accounts for disabled seamen abroad, seamen's savings banks, and money orders.

BOAT. A small open craft propelled by oars, sails, or some form of engine. This term is also applied to larger vessels built to navigate rivers and inland waters, and sometimes to seagoing vessels, but, in such case it is mostly used as part of a compound word or expression as for instance: steamboat, ferryboat, cargo boat, fishing boat.

Fr: *Embarcation; Bateau; Canot;* Ger: *Boot; Fahrzeug.*

BOAT (to). To boat the oars, i.e., to take them out of the rowlocks and place them fore and aft on the thwarts.

Fr: *Embarquer;* Ger: *Einnehmen.*

BOATAGE. The service and charge against the ship for taking mooring lines ashore with rowboats when the ship is being berthed. Also called boat hire, boatman charge.

Fr: *Lamanage;* Ger: *Bootsbeihilfe.*

BOAT AWNING. An awning stretched over a boat in order to protect the occupants in hot climates.

Fr: *Tendelet;* Ger: *Bootszelt.*

See **Canopy.**

BOAT BEACON. A combined beacon and light erected on a ship-shaped structure. Typical dimensions: Length 55 feet, Breadth 22, Depth molded 11 feet.

See **Lightboat.**

BOAT BOOM.

See **Boat Spar, Riding Boom.**

BOATBUILDER. One who builds vessels or craft without a deck or but partially decked and propelled partly by sails and partly by oars, or wholly by oars. Also called boatwright.

Fr: *Constructeur d'Embarcations;* Ger: *Bootsbauer.*

The distinction between a boatbuilder and a shipbuilder is not of marked character and cannot be sharply defined. The builder of wooden boats must be experienced in the details of construction of all types of carvel,

BOAT CHOCK—BOAT CRUTCH

clinker- and diagonal-built or canvas-covered boats, pleasure or lifeboats, canoes, small yachts. He should be skilled in the use of carpenter's, boatbuilder's and joiner's tools, and familiar with the properties of all kinds of wood used in boatbuilding. The builder of steel boats is one who builds, fits up, and repairs all kinds of steel boats, pontoons, and floats. He must be a skilled sheet-metal worker capable of working all gauges of steel up to and including 10 gauge. He must be

fits into the binnacle. Inside the binnacle is an arrangement for locking the gimbal ring and compass bowl to prevent their swinging when carried by hand from place to place.

Fr: *Compas d'Embarcation;* Ger: *Bootskompass.*

BOAT COVER. A cover made of number 6 to 9 canvas spread over a ship's boat when not in use as a protection against rain

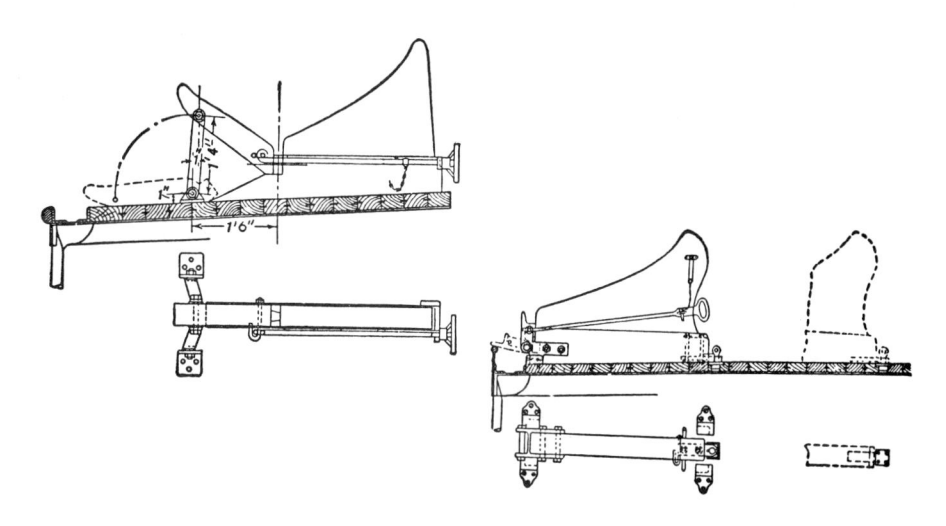

Boat Chock

able to work from drawings and templates, set forms, bend frames, lay decks, and line up a boat.

BOAT CHOCK. One of the wooden block or padded metal forms placed athwartships conforming to the shape of the outside contour of a boat and used as stowage rests. One of the cradles in which a ship's boat rests when it is on the deck. The chocks are usually placed at quarter length from the boat's stem and stern post.

Fr: *Chantier d'Embarcation;* Ger: *Bootsklampe.*

BOAT COMPASS. A liquid compass specially designed for use in small craft and open boats. The card is marked in points, half points, and quarter points. The compass bowl is fitted by means of a gimbal ring into a small portable binnacle made of wood and brass and provided with a handle at the top. A paraffin candle or electric lamp

and spray.

Fr: *Etui d'Embarcation;* Ger: *Bootkleid.*

It is supported in the middle by a ridgepole or strongback, which may or may not be stayed transversely to the gunwale on each side. There are 5 or 6 three-cornered lugs on each side, which allow the cover to be stretched taut by lengths of point line passed under the keel. This method is preferred to that of securing the sides with a lacing around studs or lacing buttons fastened below the gunwale.

BOAT CRADLE.

See **Boat Chock.**

BOAT CROTCH. A forked upright in a whaleboat on the starboard gunwale forward, to hold the "live irons." Called mik in British Greenland fishery (obsolete).

BOAT CRUTCH. A substitute for rowlocks in single-banked boats. Boat crutches are made of metal, more or less fork-shaped, and are shipped in the gunwale for the oars to work in. They are fastened to the gunwale with lanyards.

Fr: *Tolet à Fourche;* Ger: *Rojegabel; Rudergabel.*
See Boat Chock.

BOAT DAVIT. One of a pair of projecting steel girders on the sides or stern of a vessel used for suspending, lowering, and hoisting a ship's boats.

Fr: *Bossoir d'Embarcation;* Ger: *Bootsdavit.*

The length of a davit is in proportion to the required outreach. Its diameter is based on the weight it has to support and its height above the uppermost point of support. Metallic davits are made of wrought iron, wrought steel, or cast steel.
British Standards Institution, Standard 3009, *Boat Davits and Stowage,* London, 1928.

BOAT DECK. Uppermost deck, of light construction, on which lifeboats and other life saving appliances are stowed. It is also used as a promenade space on passenger vessels.

Fr: *Pont des Embarcations;* Ger: *Bootdeck.*

BOAT DRAIN. A fitting with a small hole in the bottom of a ship's boat for draining it when it is hoisted out of the water.

Fr: *Nable;* Ger: *Wasserablassloch.*

BOAT DRILL. Exercise practiced by the crew in swinging out, lowering, and handling ship's lifeboats.

Fr: *Manoeuvre des Embarcations; Exercice d'Embarcations;* Ger: *Bootsmanöver; Bootsübung.*

BOAT DRILL SIGNAL. Six or more short blasts followed by one long blast of the ship's whistle, supplemented by the same signal on the general alarm bells. Also called boat stations signal. For dismissal from boat stations: three short blasts of the whistle.

BOAT FALL. The ropes by which a ship's boats are lowered or hoisted. Also called boat tackle fall, davit fall.

Fr: *Garant de Bossoir;* Ger: *Bootstaljenläufer.*

Boat falls are made of Manila on small and medium-sized vessels. Wire rope is preferable if several boats are to be lowered from one set of davits, as hemp rope is difficult to manage with high-sided vessels. Even if nontoppling blocks are used, fiber ropes have a tendency to wind themselves in a six-strand cable as soon as the boat is water-borne and the weight has been taken off the blocks. Thereafter it is almost impossible to get the bottom blocks up again.

BOAT GRIPE. One of the two lashings used at sea to secure a boat hanging in the davits against the strongback. Boat gripes are made of several thicknesses of canvas, matting, or sennit. They cross diagonally on the outside of the boat and are provided with lanyards or monkeytail slips for letting go. Also called belt gripe.

Fr: *Sangle d'Embarcation;* Ger: *Bootsbrok.*

BOAT HANDLING SIGNALS. Whistle signals used when handling life boats at sea. One short blast to lower boats. Two short blasts to stop lowering boats.

BOAT HARBOR. A sheltered water area in a harbor provided with moorings, floats and buoys for small boats, yachts, and so on. Also called boat haven, marina.

BOAT-HEADER (U. S.). 1. The officer who stands in the stern sheets of a whaleboat and manipulates the steering oar and "heads" the boat toward the whale. Called headsman in Great Britain (obsolete).

2. A fisherman in charge of a small boat in the cod and halibut fisheries (dory) that puts off from a larger vessel. There are usually two men in each boat, one to fish and one to stun, hook and help hauling the fish aboard.

BOAT HOOK. An iron hook with a straight prong at its hinder part, fixed to a long pole. By its help a boat is either pulled to, or pushed from, any place, or is capable of holding on to another object. Also called pole hook.

Fr: *Gaffe;* Ger: *Bootshaken.*

BOATILA.
See **Doni.**

BOATING. The art or practice of rowing or sailing small boats.

Fr: *Canotage;* Ger: *Bootfahren.*

BOAT KEG. A small wooden cask large at the base with bunghole and bung. Formerly used in small boats to carry drinking water.

Fr: *Baril de Galère;* Ger: *Ankerfässchen.*

BOAT LACING. Three strand dressed hemp line used principally as lacing for boat covers and awnings. Size is determined by weight which varies from 4 ounces to 4 pounds per 30 fathom bank. It is manufactured in fourteen different sizes.

BOAT LAMP. Lifeboat oil lamp showing an all round white light and fitted with a receiver of sufficient capacity to burn for eight hours. It is constructed of nonmagnetic material and uses colza oil.

Fr: *Fanal d'embarcation;* Ger: *Bootslanterne.*

BOAT LASHING. A device for securing a ship's boat to its chocks. It usually consists at the upper end of a short length of chain with a flat hook, which fits over the gunwale. Under this hook there is a pelican-hook for quick release. The lower end of the gripe is secured by a lashing to an eyebolt or a ring in the deck.

Fr: *Saisine d'Embarcation;* Ger: *Klausurring; Bootskrabber.*

See **Gripe.**

BOAT LINE. A line for small boats to hang to when they come alongside a ship.

BOATMAN. One who with the help of a small rowboat assists ships in and out of dock, and when necessary, from berth to berth by moving bow and stern lines to wherever they are required. The term also includes men who work on rivers as longshoremen and unlicensed pilots on coastal craft that are not required to employ a licensed pilot.

Fr: *Canotier; Lamaneur;* Ger: *Jollenführer; Bootbeihilfer.*

BOATMAN CHARGE.
See **Boatage.**

BOAT NAIL. A nail made of soft and ductile galvanized iron or copper, with large oval or round head and rectangular section tapering to a blunt or chisel point, capable of being effectively clinched.

Fr: *Clou d'Embarcation;* Ger: *Bootsnagel.*

Nails used in boatbuilding may be either driven dead, or driven through, with the point clinched over, or riveted over roves, the latter method being used only with copper nails. Boat nails are of various lengths, generally from 3 in. to 10 in. long, rose-headed, and square at the point. Copper boat nails are of the cut or wire variety. The cut nail has a thicker and larger head and is of tapered shape. The wire nail has a round and parallel shaft.

BOAT PAINTER. A rope attached to the stem ringbolt of a small boat, used for securing it. A short piece of rope secured in the bow of a boat, used for towing or making fast.

Fr: *Bosse d'Embarcation;* Ger: *Fangleine.*

BOAT PLUG. Small tapering plug made of cork or soft pine wood or metal screw plug, used for stopping up the drain hole in the bottom of a boat.

Fr: *Tapon; Bouchon de Nable;* Ger: *Bootspflock; Bootspfropfen.*

BOAT-PROPELLER GEAR. A manually operated mechanism designed for screw propulsion of open boats. Also called hand-operated propeller.

It is claimed to be specially adapted to ship's lifeboats as occupants not used to rowing, such as passengers, are able to assist in operating a boat as soon as it is afloat. This gear consists of a series of hinged levers on each side of the boat. The levers are placed between the thwarts. Their lower ends are connected by a fore-and-aft rod. Each one of the rods connects with a crank disk fitted to a thwartship shaft. On this thwartship shaft is a gear wheel geared to a fore-and-aft shaft carrying the screw propeller. A reversing gear consisting of a ratchet wheel keyed to the thwartship shaft and two oppositely arranged pawls allows the propeller to revolve in the required direction.

BOAT RATIONS. Statutory food rations kept in each lifeboat throughout the voyage while the ship is at sea. They are packed in watertight containers suitably labelled and stowed in watertight tanks.

Fr: *Rations d'embarcations;* Ger: *Rettungsboot Rationen.*

BOAT RIVET. A type of fastening used by boatbuilders, usually a copper cut nail riveted over a copper burr (rove) after the latter is driven with a hollow punch, and the projecting portion of the nail is cut off about 1/8 in. above the surface of the burr.

BOAT ROPE. A line with one end made fast on the fore deck near the pilot ladder. The loose end is thrown to any boat which wishes to come alongside.

Fr: *Faux bras;* Ger: *Fangleine.*

BOAT SCREW. A type of fastening used by boatbuilders.

Fr: *Vis à Bois;* Ger: *Bootsschraube.*

Boat screws are either of hot-dipped galvanized iron or of nonferrous material such as bronze, Everdur, or stainless steel. They are used when the frames are of the web type and of such depth that a copper rivet would not pass through unless it were very long. They also secure hood ends of planking to the stem and sternpost.

BOAT'S CREW. The company of seamen who man a rowboat. It includes the coxswain, oarsmen, and bowman. According to the International Convention for Safety of Life at Sea the crews of lifeboats on passenger vessels must include a certain number of certified boatmen.

Fr: *Armement;* Ger: *Bootsmannschaft.*

BOAT SIGNALS. Emergency sound signals made with the ship's whistle when handling life boats. Lower boats: 1 short blast. Stop lowering boats: 2 short blasts. Dismissal from boat stations: 3 short blasts. Swing out boats: 4 short blasts. Man emergency boat: one long and one short blast.

BOAT SKATE. One of the vertical hardwood fenders fitted to the inboard side of a ship's lifeboat to facilitate launching from the high side of a listed vessel. They extend from the gunwale to well under the turn of bilge and are so designed as to be easily detachable after the boat is afloat.

Fr: *Patin d'Embarcation.*

BOAT BEAM. Framing placed at a certain height above deck for a boat to rest upon. Usually a heavy fore and after is located appropriately below and parallel to the boat's keel. This baulk bears transverse members which carry the boat chocks upon which the boat rests. Also called boat skid.

Fr: *Barres de Théorie;* Ger: *Barringsbalken; Bootsgalgen.*

BOAT SKID. One of the heavy vertical planks sometimes fitted to the outside plating abreast of the davits and extending from the boat-deck to the load line to keep the boat clear of any projecting part by which it might be damaged when it is being lowered or hoisted.

See **Boat Beam.**

BOAT SLING. A sling of rope or chain used for hoisting or lowering a boat. There is one forward and one aft. The forward sling has one end secured to a ringbolt in the stem and the other to a link plate fastened to the keel. The after sling is similarly secured to the sternpost and keel.

Fr: *Patte d'Embarcation;* Ger: *Bootstropp; Zurrbroken.*

BOAT SPADE. A short-handled spade carried in a whaleboat and used for cutting a hole when attaching a line to a dead whale before towing (obsolete).

BOAT SPAR. The fore-and-aft spar used with round bar davits to secure for steadying a boat when it is swung out. It is provided with puddings for fending. Also called boat boom, rolling spar, griping spar, strongback, pudding boom, pudding bag spar.

Ger: *Zurrbaum.*

BOAT STAND. Cast-iron column for supporting lifeboat chocks in an elevated position to permit a better passage or more space at the sides on the boat deck. There are usually two boat stands for each boat.

Fr: *Support d'Embarcation;* Ger: *Bootsständer.*

BOAT STATIONS. The allotted place of each person when the lifeboats are being lowered.

Fr: *Postes d'Embarcations;* Ger: *Bootsstation.*

BOAT STATIONS BILL. A posted list showing to which lifeboat each member of the crew and passenger has to report in the event of an emergency.

Fr: *Rôle d'Appel aux Postes d'Embarcations;* Ger: *Bootsrolle.*

BOAT STEERER. In a whaleboat the man who pulls the harpoon oar, darts the iron into the whale, and then steers while the boat-header lances the mammal (obsolete).

BOATSWAIN. A petty officer on board ship who has immediate charge of all deck hands.

Fr: *Maître d'Équipage;* Ger: *Bootsmann.*
See **Boatswain's Whistle.**

The boatswain must be a thorough seaman and know how all work upon rigging and general upkeep of the vessel should be carried out. He also has under his care: boats, anchors, cables, cordage, cargo gear, and deck stores. On large vessels the boatswain is assisted in his duties by one or more boatswain's mates.

The more exclusive function of the boatswain is the superintendence and control that he exercises over the men. He summons the crew to their duties, assists, with his mates, in the necessary business of the ship, and relieves the watch when its time expires. His calls on the crew are made by a whistle of peculiar shape.

BOATSWAIN'S CALL.
See **Boatswain's Whistle.**

BOATSWAIN'S CHAIR. An oak board about ¾ or ⅞ in. thick and 24 in. long with four holes, one at each corner. It has two pieces of line about 6 ft. long formed into loops with ends passed through the holes in the board and spliced on the under side and is hoisted aloft by a whip. It is used for sending a man aloft where foothold is not obtainable, as when painting or doing rigging work.

Fr: *Chaise de Gabier; Chaise de Mâture;* Ger: *Bootsmannstuhl.*

BOATSWAIN'S LOCKER. A small compartment in which are kept tools and small stuff for repairing and making up rigging or cargo gear.

Fr: *Magasin du Maître d'Équipage;* Ger: *Bootsmannsvorratskammer; Bootsmannshellegat.*

BOATSWAIN'S MATE. A petty officer acting as an assistant to the boatswain.

Fr: *Second Maître d'Équipage;* Ger: *Bootsmannsmaat.*

BOATSWAIN'S WHISTLE. A small silver pipe of peculiar shape used by the boatswain and his mate to attract attention of the crew by emitting various strains or shrills, each of them signifying a specific purpose. Also named boatswain's call.

Fr: *Sifflet de Manoeuvre;* Ger: *Bootsmannspfeife.*

McCarthy, S., The Boatswain's Call, U. S. Naval Institute, *Proceedings,* vol. 39, no. 147, Annapolis, 1913.

BOAT TACKLE. A purchase of two blocks doubled or trebled and a length of rope, used for hoisting or lowering ship's boats.

Fr: *Palan d'Embarcation;* Ger: *Bootstalje.*

Lower blocks are fitted with a swivel and long link for hooking on to the boat, and if they are not of the nontoppling type an iron outrigger about 2 ft. long is riveted to the top. To this outrigger a length of wire running between the two blocks prevents the falls from twisting when the boat reaches the water and the blocks are unhooked.

BOAT WINCH. An electric winch placed on the boat deck of large passenger vessels for handling lifeboats. Also called boat hoist.

Fr: *Treuil de Bossoir;* Ger: *Bootswinde.*

In some instances there are no drums and the boat winch consists of two vertical or horizontal gypsyheads around which the boat falls are taken. Where large boats with single-wire falls are used the winch is equipped with drums around which the falls remain permanently wound. Boat winches of this type are supplied with two independent brakes for lowering. The main brake is so arranged that it must always return to its "on" position as soon as it ceases to be held by hand in the "off" position.

BOBAO. A small paddling canoe from Tonga Islands with single outrigger. It is the counterpart of the Samoan *pao-pao.* Also called *boobao.*

The canoe has a dugout hull, with rounded bottom and tumble-home sides. The hull ranges in size from 10 to 15 ft. with a molded breadth at gunwale of 8 to 9 in., increasing at bilge to 12 to 16 in., and a depth of 12 to 15 in. The outrigger consists of two straight booms projecting 5 to 7 ft. outboard attached usually to a cylindrical float by two U-shaped flexible withies. These are in some canoes replaced by two small uprights that cross one another above the boom.

BOBBIN. Large heavy wooden rollers fastened to the footrope of a trawl net when fishing over rough ground. They vary in diameter from 6 to 26 in. Each roller has an iron bush through the center and through this the wire rope that forms the core of the ground rope is rove.

Fr: *Diabolo.*

Bobbins are known as rolling bobbins, setting bobbins, or bead bobbins. The rolling bobbins are placed at the center or bosom of the ground rope. They are from 16 to 26 in. in diameter and 6 to 7 in. thick. The rolling bobbins are interspaced with one or two setting bobbins, according to rig. These do not revolve, their purpose being to keep the rolling bobbins apart and to serve as a means of attaching the ground rope to the fishing line of the trawl. The setting bobbins are about 9 in. in diameter, having a groove cut around their circumference for the wire to the fishing line. The bead bobbins are carried at the wings of the ground rope. They are about 6 in. in diameter and also free to revolve about the wire.

A steel bobbin patented and known as the "Ross" rolling bobbin is occasionally used on the center of the ground rope. It is a steel sphere of about a 20-in. diameter. These bobbins are said to last longer than the wooden ones and to be more effective in enabling the ground rope to ride over obstacles on the sea bottom.

BOBBIN SHAFT. A short length of shafting occasionally fitted near the afterend of the tunnel to facilitate withdrawal of the propeller shaft for inspection.

BOBSTAY. A rope, chain, or iron rod that extends from bowsprit end to stem and counteracts the lifting strain of the forestay.

Fr: *Sous Barbe;* Ger: *Wasserstag.*

In craft rigged with a reefing bowsprit, as the outboard length of the spar varies the bobstay is set up with a tackle. A gun tackle is used and hooked into the end of the bobstay and the lower eye of the cranse iron. The fall comes inboard and is fastened to a cleat at the bowsprit bitts.

In large sailing ships when three bobstays are fitted they are called inner bobstay, middle bobstay, cap bobstay. When there are two, inner bobstay and cap bobstay.

BOBSTAY PIECE. A piece of compass timber fitted and bolted to the back of the figurehead and to its supporting piece or knee-of-the-head. Also called lace piece, lacing.

Fr: *Courbe de Capucine;* Ger: *Gallionschegg.*

BOBSTAY PLATE. A metal fitting bolted to the bobstay piece, through which the lower end of bobstay is attached to the stem.

Fr: *Piton de Sous Barbe.*

BOBSTAY TRICE—BOILER EFFICIENCY

BOBSTAY TRICE. A line used in small craft to pull up the bobstay so that it will not chafe against the cable while the boat is at anchor.

BOCK. An open boat with small deck or cuddy forward engaged in beam trawl fishing or lining in the district of Locquivy (Brittany). Length 33 ft. Breadth 10 ft. Depth 11 ft.

The rig consists of a pole mast with gaff mainsail, jackyard topsail, foresail, and jib. Larger types are found in Locquivy and Port Even. These are chiefly engaged in lobstering off the Irish and English south coasts where they are usually known as "French crabbers." Their maximum length attains 53 ft. They have comparatively great beam and deep draft and are very efficient under sail. Most of them have recently been supplied with auxiliary motors.

BODDEN-BOOT. A small open boat used in the inshore herring fisheries on shoals named Bodden off the Pomeranian Coast (Baltic), around the Island of Rügen, Greifswald, and so on.

The hull is built with keel, square stern, clinker planking. There are two thwarts. The rig consists of a tall foresail that tacks down to stemhead, and has four lines or reef points. The boom mainsail is gaff-headed with loose foot and 4 reef bands. It is cut very long in the head, as is customary in these waters.

BODY OIL. 1. Ordinary whale oil from the blubber, as distinguished from head oil.

2. The term also refers to oil obtained from the bodies of any fat fish, for instance, mackerel and herring. Used as tanning oil.

BODY PLAN. An end view showing curves of the sides of the ship's transverse frame lines. Frame lines forward of the midship section are shown on the right of the center line, while those aft of the midship section are on the left of the center line.

Fr: *Vertical;* Ger: *Spannriss; Seitenriss.*

BOEIJER. A small Dutch sloop fitted with leeboards. Also called *Boeier. Boeijers* vary in length from 26 to 65 ft.

It has very rounded bows, the planking or plating meeting the stem at right angles. The stem projects slightly underwater. The bow and stern are almost identical. The leeboards especially in the smaller types are unusually broad and almost fan-shaped. The mast is stepped in a tabernacle and placed well aft. The bottom is flat but the bilges are rounded like those of a flat-floored dinghy. A bowsprit is usually carried.

BOEUF.

See **Bateau Boeuf.**

BOG. A local name given on the South Coast of England (Hastings) to a small decked fishing boat used for beam trawling. These boats are lug-rigged with two masts. The stern is indifferently of lute or elliptical shape. Length over-all 23 ft. Length of keel 18 ft. Breadth 9.5 ft. Depth of hold 3.8 ft.

BOGGIN LINE. A length of chain and a wire pendant shackled on each side of the rudder horn. Their purpose is to retain control of the rudder and facilitate steering in case of accident to the steering gear. Also called rudder pendant.

Fr: *Sauvegarde;* Ger: *Sorgleine.*

BOILER CAPACITY. The maximum number of boiler horsepower that can be generated in a boiler. In marine practice the capacity is usually based on 10 sq. ft. of heating surface per horsepower.

BOILER CASING. The partition enclosing the space above the boiler room in the way of the boiler hatch.

Fr: *Encaissement des Chaudières;* Ger: *Kesselumbau; Schornsteinumbau; Kesselmantel.*

The boiler casing forms a trunk of sufficient size for the installation and removal of boilers and affords the necessary space to accommodate the smokestack and ventilator cowls that lead to the boiler room. The top of the casing extends well above the weather deck if the ship has no superstructure, and is carried through the superstructure if there is one. The length and the width of the boiler casing depend on the position and the diameter of the smoke pipe. The width also varies with the space required for the boiler uptakes.

BOILER CHOCK. A vertical bracket fixed to the tank top or floor, the upper corner of which overlaps the face of the boiler. Also called collision chock.

Fr: *Taquet de Choc;* Ger: *Kesselstopper.*

One chock is placed at the end of each boiler to guard against the forward motion of the boiler in the event of an end-on collision. Collision chocks are also useful in preventing the gradual fore-and-aft movement of the boiler due to long and continued expansion and contraction.

BOILER EFFICIENCY. The ratio of the heat actually transmitted to the water in the boiler to the total heat developed by the combustion of the fuel.

Fr: *Rendement des Appareils Évaporatoires;* Ger: *Kesselwirkungsgrad.*

Boiler efficiency is determined by the quantity of feed water fed to the boiler, amount of fuel burned, steam pressure in the boiler and temperature of feed water.

Efficiency of Scotch boiler...68 to 77 per cent
Efficiency of water-tube
    boiler (large tubes).......63 to 84 per cent

BOILER FOUNDATION. Modern express-type marine boilers are secured in place by saddles and supports. The saddles, formed of plates and shapes joined by welding, are shaped to fit the under side of the water drums, and are welded to an inverted T structure. The saddles land on supports built up as pedestals, secured to the ship's structure by welding or riveting.

BOILER HATCH. A hatch around smokestacks and uptakes, fitted over the boiler room. It is usually made large enough to provide for the installation or removal of boilers.
    Fr: *Panneau des Chaufferies;* Ger: *Kesselluke.*

BOILER HORSEPOWER. One boiler horsepower is conventionally taken as being equal to an evaporation of 34.5 lbs. of water per hour from and at 212° F.

BOILERMAKER. One engaged in the construction, assembly, or repair of boilers. Some of the largest and fastest merchant vessels carry an unlicensed man as boilermaker, to whom are assigned boiler-repair duties.
    Fr: *Chaudronnier.*

BOILER ROOM. Compartment in which the ship's boilers are located.
    Fr: *Compartiment Chaudières;* Ger: *Kesselraum.*

BOILERS. Steam generating units used aboard ship to provide steam for propulsion, by reciprocating engines or turbines, or for auxiliary purposes, such as heating, or for both.
    See **Fire-tube Boiler, Water-tube Boiler.**
Boilers are classified by relative location of combustion spaces and water spaces, as (1) fire-tube boilers, (2) water-tube boilers; and also by methods of circulation of water: (1) natural circulation; (2) forced circulation; (3) forced recirculation.
The boiler must provide for combustion of fuel, transfer of heat from fuel to water, circulation of water, and circulation of steam.
The boiler consists of: (1) a furnace; (2) the boiler proper, a closed pressure vessel containing originally the water from which the steam is generated; (3) the uptakes; (4) internal piping and external connections for water supply; (5) internal piping and external connections for drawing off steam; (6) appliances and fittings for control of operation, and for safeguard against damage.

BOILER STOOL. One of the cradles formed by vertical plating and angles, on which a cylindrical boiler rests. The upper edge is curved to the radius of the boiler shell. Their number for each boiler varies from 2 to 4 according to size. Also called boiler bearer, boiler foundation.
    Fr: *Berceau de Chaudière;* Ger: *Kesselstuhl.*

BOKA. A small dugout canoe from Aru Islands (Banda Sea) with or without outriggers.

BOKKA-YOKO. Single-sheet bark canoe of the Raminyeri tribe from Encounter Bay in South Australia.

BOKURA. A small open boat from the Maldive Islands that looks rather like half a walnut shell and that may carry 2 or 3 people. It is used as a ferry in sheltered waters.

BOLD BOW. A bow in which the waterlines at stem form a comparatively obtuse angle. Also called bluff bow, rounded bow, broad bow, full bow.
    Fr: *Avant Plein;* Ger: *Breiter Bug; Voller Bug.*

BOLD HAWSE. A ship is said to have a bold hawse when the hawse holes are high above water.

BOLD SHORE. A steep coast line which vessels may approach closely without danger of grounding.
    Fr: *Côte Accore;* Ger: *Steilküste.*

BOLIO. A built-up canoe from the Ganges estuary (Bengal). It has a length of 6 to 10 beams with greatest breadth amidships and from stem to stern almost follows the true curve of a circle. It is similar to the *panshi* but larger. Also called *boleah, baulia, bhaolia.*

BOLL. A half-decked fishing boat found at the mouth of the river Ems and in the Zuider Zee, about 28 ft. in length and 9 ft. beam with flat bottom and leeboards. It is fore-and-aft-rigged with one mast, gaff mainsail, topsail, and jib foresail.

BOLLARD. See **Bitt, Loggerhead.**

BOLLARD. Single or double cast steel posts secured to a wharf or pier and used for mooring vessels by means of lines extending from the vessel and fastened to the post. Double-post bollards are raked at an angle of about 60 degrees from each other. Also called *Checking Bollard, Warping Bollard.*
    Fr: *Bollard;* Ger: *Landpoller; Verholpoller.*
American Marine Standards Committee

BOLLARD CLEAT—BOLT

Standards P no. 1 and no. 4, Bollards and Cleats for Docks, Washington, D. C., 1931.

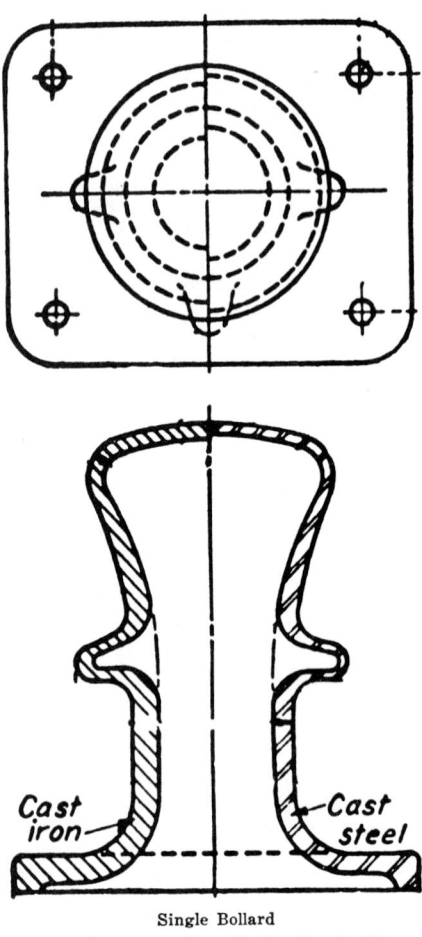

Single Bollard
Bollards. (*American Marine Standards*)

BOLLARD CLEAT. A combined bollard and cleat secured to a wharf or pier and used for warping or mooring vessels.

BOLLARD TIMBER.
See **Knighthead**.

BOLO. A double-ended dugout canoe of round cross section from the Duala coastal tribes of the Cameroons. These craft vary in size, the largest being propelled by a crew of 24 paddlers. The bow and stern are square and flat at gunwale level.

The *bolo-bu-nene* of the Batanga people is a large sailing dugout fitted with wash strake and used for traveling along the coast and in some instances venturing as far as the Island of Fernando-Po. Coasting trips from **Kribi** to **Duala** are frequently made with these craft.

BOLSH.
See **Balch Line**.

BOLSTER. A general term for various pieces of timber fixed in different positions to prevent chafing between ropes and other parts of the rigging.

Fr: *Coussin*; Ger: *Kissen; Polster*.

See **Hawse Bolster, Rowlock Bolster**.

1. A piece of softwood covered with tarred canvas placed on the trestletrees and against the mast for the collars of the shrouds to rest upon.

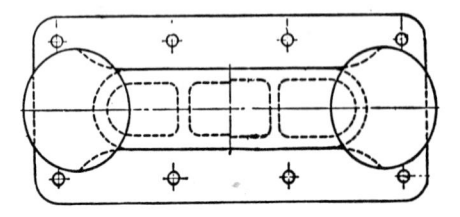

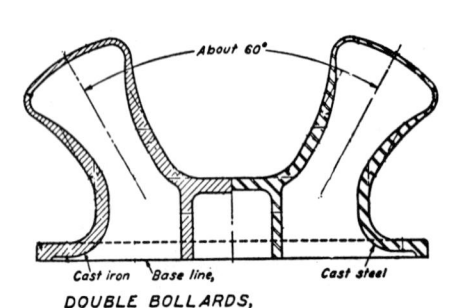

DOUBLE BOLLARDS.
Bollards. (*American Marine Standards*)

2. Block of wood fitted on the side of a mast to fill up the angle between top of trestletree and masthead to prevent the rigging being cut against the outer edge of the trestletree.

BOLSTER PLATE (U. S.). A doubling plate adjoining the hawse hole to protect the bow plating from the chafing of the anchor cable.

BOLT. 1. Bolts, as used in the building of wooden vessels or boats, are stout metal pins secured by riveting for holding permanently fast together different parts of the framing. They are made of copper, yellow metal or galvanized iron.

Fr: *Cheville*; Ger: *Bolzen*.

Copper or yellow metal bolts when used are principally employed for the underwater surface of the outside planking, as are treenails. Bolts of various shapes and design are also used on deck for several purposes in connection with the rigging. Such are hookbolts and eyebolts. Yellow metal and especially copper bolts are very extensible and therefore liable to stretch under heavy strain. An iron bolt will stand more strain and yet recover its form by virtue of its elasticity.

A bolt varies in dimensions according to material and locality where made:

See **Blunt Bolt, Carriage Bolt, Chain Bolt, Clinch Bolt, Deck Bolt, Dog Bolt, Drain Bolt, Drift Bolt, Eyebolt, Forelock Bolt, Holding Down Bolt, Hookbolt, In-and-Out Bolt, Lag Bolt, Rag Bolt, Ring Bolt, Rod Bolt, Screw Bolt, Set Bolt, Shackle Bolt, Square Bolt, Stud Bolt, Throat Bolt, Toggle Bolt, Wring Bolt.**

2. A roll of canvas of definite length and width as supplied by manufacturers to the trade.

Fr: *Pièce;* Ger: *Beutel.*

Material	Width of Bolt (in Inches)	Length of Bolt (in Yards)	
Unbleached or Ship Flax	24	40–42	[Great Britain]
Unbleached or Ship Flax	22	90	[U. S. A.]
Unbleached or Ship Flax	22½	65	[France]
Unbleached or Ship Flax	24	38¼	[Germany]
Half or Full Bleached Flax	24	42	
Half or Full Bleached Flax	15–18	100	
American Cotton	24	42	
American Cotton	15–18	100	
Egyptian Cotton	15–18	100	
Tarpaulin Canvas	36	100	

BOLTED SECTIONAL DOCK. A type of floating dock usually built in three sections of approximately equal lengths, the two end sections being stepped to form landings when carrying out a self-docking operation.

BOLTER. A shipyard worker who places the bolts and does all the "laying-up" of structural members before or in advance of the reamers and riveters. When unbolted holes have been reamed the bolters change the bolts and clean out any burrs or chips between plates. The bolter foreman is assisted by quartermen bolters and leadingmen bolters. Also called bolter up.

Fr: *Charpentier en Fer.*

BOLTER-UP.

See **Plater.**

BOLTING. 1. In wooden shipbuilding the operation by which the various timbers and planking of a wooden ship are fastened; bolts, spikes, and treenails being used.

Fr: *Chevillage;* Ger: *Verbolzung.*

2. The fitting and securing of plating and framing by nuts and screw bolts before riveting.

Fr: *Montage;* Ger: *Montage.*

BOLT ROPE. Hawser-laid hemp or wire cordage sewed on the edges of sails to strengthen them, to which all the gear used in clewing up is attached. Also called roping.

Fr: *La Ralingue;* Ger: *Liek.*

Each bolt rope takes its name from its position on the sail, that is, luff rope, leech rope, foot rope. When made of fiber rope it is obtained by careful selection and preparation of the fibers and it has a soft lay. It is a better wearing rope than the ordinary grade. Nowadays in trading vessels and yachts bolt ropes are frequently made of flexible wire. In cruising yachts white hemp or wire rope is used. Fishing boats use tarred hemp bolt rope with extra soft lay 1½ to 4 in. in circumference for purse lines. Three-Stranded Manila bolt rope 5 in. or more in circumference is used for towing hawsers.

BOLT ROPE NEEDLE. A curved sail needle used for sewing Manila bolt rope around sails, awnings, and so on. Also called Lolly needle, roping needle, short spur needle.

Fr: *Aiguille à Ralinguer;* Ger: *Lieknadel.*

BOM. A Dutch fishing craft formerly found in Scheveningen-Katwyk and Noordwyk, with beam equal to about half its length and with bow and stern almost alike. It was strongly built to be beached on the sands and to withstand the heavy pounding when lying half-afloat. Bommen are no longer built. Tonnage ranged from 25 to 100. Crew 2 to 10.

BOMBARDA. A twomasted flat-bottomed Italian coaster with a capacity of 80 to 150 tons. The mainmast, made of a single spar, is stepped at midlength

Bombarda

and carries square sails. The mizzen, placed very far aft, carries a driver and gaff topsail. Two headsails set on the bowsprit.

BONDED STORES. Ship's stores which can be delivered under special arrangements direct from a bonded warehouse to the vessel without payment of the customs duties.

Fr: *Approvisionnements non Dédouanés;* Ger: *Unverzollte Vorräte.*

BONDED VALUE—BONNET

BONDED VALUE. Refers to the gross market value of merchandise of a character usually sold "in bond" as distinguished from "duty paid" value. The term is used in marine insurance reports on cargo surveys.
  Fr: *Valeur en Douane; Valeur non Dédouanée;* Ger: *Unverzollte Wert.*

BONDED VALUE CLAUSE. A marine policy clause whereby the underwriter agrees to adjust claims for particular average, that is, partial loss on goods, on the basis of the gross value on arrival at destination *less duty*; instead of following the usual practice of *including duty.*

BONDED WAREHOUSE. A public or privately owned warehouse where dutiable goods are stored pending payment of duty or removal under bond. The storage and delivery of goods are under the supervision of customs officers and if the warehouse is privately owned the keeper has to enter into a bond as indemnity in respect of the goods deposited, which may not be delivered without a release from the customs.
  Fr: *Entrepôt de Douane;* Ger: *Zolllager; Zollspeicher.*

BONDING. Operation performed on tankers to prevent electrical discharges caused by a difference of potential between ship and shore when loading or unloading. It consists in connecting a shore grounded cable to a single pole switch on board ship before connecting the ship to shore cargo hoses.

BOND NOTE. A customs form required before dutiable goods can be removed or transported from a bonded warehouse. Sometimes called customs warrant.
  Fr: *Acquit à Caution;* Ger: *Zollbegleitschein; Zollauslieferschein.*

BONE. The white foam at the stem caused by a vessel's motion through the water.

BONGO. A square-ended Ecuadorian dugout canoe rigged with mast and sail. The hull is built with a top strake of great depth and thickness, made of balsa wood, which through its buoyancy acts as an outrigger when the canoe heels over. Its length varies from 32 to 39 ft. The *pongo* of the Maracaibo lagoon and adjacent rivers (Venezuela) is a large flat-bottom dugout with a capacity of several tons.

BONITERA. A Spanish half-decked centerboard boat with high raking stem piece, sharp or transom stern and five thwarts, employed for trolling bonito and tuna on the Cantabrian coast. Also called *lancha bonitera.* It is rigged with two masts and lugsails. The small foremast has no rake and the much taller mainmast rakes aft. This type of boat has been mostly replaced by small steam launches called *lanchillas de vapor.* Length 54.6 ft. Breadth 12.4 ft. Depth 5.6 ft.

BONITOLERA. Small Spanish open boat used for near-shore trolling on the Cantabrian Coast. It is rigged with one mast and lateen sail.

BONJEAN CURVE. Curve of areas of transverse sections versus draft and of moments of transverse areas above the base line versus draft. Bonjean curves enable the naval architect to obtain the displacement of a vessel at any desired trim.

These curves are also used in launching calculations to determine successive values of the force of buoyancy acting upon the immersed portion of the ship as it gradually becomes waterborne.

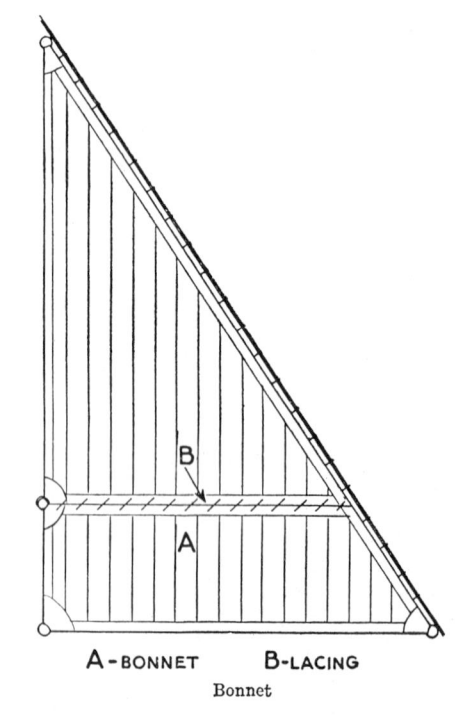

A - BONNET   B - LACING
Bonnet

BONNET. 1. A portable wood or metal protecting hood placed over the engines (petrol) in an open boat.
  Fr: *Capot;* Ger: *Haube.*

2. An additional strip of canvas made to

fasten with latchings to the foot of a fore-and-aft sail to increase its area and gather more wind. Also called studsail.

Fr: *Bonette Maillée*; Ger: *Bonnet*.

Bonnets are used in small lug-rigged craft to avoid the weight of a bag of canvas when the sail is reefed. They are in shape exactly similar to the foot of the sail they are intended for. They have a head tabling 2½ inches broad, on which a line of 12-thread stuff named keel line is sewed in bights to form the latchings. By casting the lacing adrift the bonnet is easily detached from the foot of the sail. When used with jibs the bonnet is usually one third the depth of the sail it belongs to. Cruising yachts occasionally have a bonnet laced to the foot of the small spinnaker. When used at the foot of a boom mainsail it is called a water sail.

BOOBY HATCH. An access hatch leading from a weather deck into the accommodation. A small hatchway, used for obtaining access inside the vessel without removing the main hatches.

This term also refers to a small portable companion, the framework of which is lashed to the deck when in use. Sometimes called companion hatch.

Fr: *Panneau de Descente*; Ger: *Kajütenluke*; *Schiebeluke*.

BOOK. Term used by whalemen to denote slices of blubber as cut on the mincing horse before being pitched into the try pots. The blubber was left adhering to a rind like the leaves of a book; hence its name. Also called Bible.

See **Cargo Book, Continuous Discharge Book, Molding Book, Prayer Book, Scrap Log Book, Ship's Log Book, Strake Book.**

BOOKING CLERK. An official in a shipping office who performs the duties pertaining to the sale and assignment of passenger accommodations.

BOOM. 1. A general name given to a projecting spar or pole that provides an outreach for extending the foot of sails, or mooring boats, handling cargo, bearing a ship away from a quay wall, and so on.

Fr: *Bôme*; *Gui*; *Tangon*; Ger: *Baum*; *Spiere*; *Ausleger*.

See **Awning Boom, Bentinck Boom, Bigelow Boom, Boat Boom, Cargo Boom, Fish Boom, Fore Boom, Hatch Boom, Jacky Boom, Jibboom, Flying Jibboom, Jumbo Boom, Lattice Boom, Martingale Boom, Park Avenue Boom, Placery Boom, Rid-**

ing Boom, Ringtail Boom, Sail Boom, Studding Sail Boom, Sounding Boom, Spinnaker Boom, Swinging Boom, Yard Boom.

2. A two-masted lateen-rigged vessel employed for trading on the coasts of Arabia and East Africa, and for pearling in the Persian Gulf. It originated in Koweit. Also called *bum*. Length over-all 36 to 110 ft. Breadth 18 to 23 ft. Depth 8 to 12 ft.

The straight stem piece projects forward for a considerable distance and is built out into a sort of planked bowsprit. The top is rounded but undecorated. The sharp sternpost is similar to that of the *Dhangi*, having a strong rake and heavily built. The

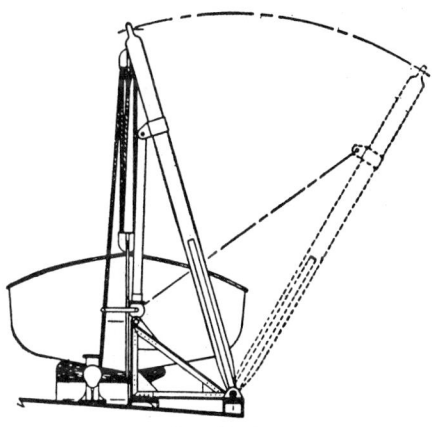

Boom Davit

deck extends from stem to stern with raised afterdeck. The steering is done by a wheel connected to the rudder by a system of yoke lines leading from the quarters. The mainsail is a lateen and the mizzen a small settee. The mainsail tacks down bowsprit fashion to a long spar, the heel of which is lashed to the mast.

BOOM BALLAST. A system of ballasting formerly used by sailing ships when in harbor. One or more booms were slung over the side and secured to the vessel by chain lashings. When no longer required they were disconnected and floated away. Thus this method avoided taking aboard and discharging several hundred tons of ballast.

BOOM BAND. A metal band at the after-end of a sail boom. It is made in two parts held together on the boom by bolts and nuts and fitted with an extra half band for holding the sheet-block hook.

BOOM CHOCK. A wooden chock secured to the top of the boom gallows and hollowed out to receive and hold the head of a cargo boom when lowered. It is fitted with a clamp or with lashing eyes to hold the boom in place. Also called boom cradle, boom rest.

Fr: *Support de Gui*; Ger: *Baumkrücke*.

BOOM CLEAT. A flat piece of wood perforated with holes and projecting on each side of a sail boom at the afterend. The reef pendants are passed through the holes and tied down when the sail is reefed. Also called reefing cleat.

Fr: *Violon de Ris*; Ger: *Reffklampe; Schmierklampe*.

BOOM CRUTCH. A portable fitting for resting the main boom of small fore-and-aft-rigged craft when in port. A stanchion to support the lowered end of a cargo boom at sea. Also called boom rest, cradle or derrick support.

BOOM GUY. A rope or tackle used for steadying the spanker boom when it is running free. Sometimes called lazy guy.

Fr: *Retenue de Gui*; Ger: *Bullentau*.

BOOM HORSE. 1. An iron bar fastened on the top of a boom at the afterend, serving as a clew outhaul.

2. An iron bar with semicircular curvature made into the band at the afterend of a boom for the sheet block to travel on. Also called boom traveler.

BOOM IRON. Iron band and fitting placed at the yardarm, through which a studding sail boom is run in and out. Sometimes called withe.

Fr: *Blin de Bonnette*; Ger: *Baumbügel; Spierenbügelring*.

BOOM JIGGER TACKLE. A small double and single block-tackle used for rigging studding-sail booms in and out on a lower yard. Also called Boom Jigger (obsolete).

Fr: *Cartahu de Bout Dehors*; Ger: *Leesegel Spierentalje*.

BOOMKIN.
See **Bumkin**.

BOOM MAINSAIL. A fore-and-aft or gaff mainsail in which the foot is extended by a boom. The mainsail of a cutter, sloop, schooner, and so on.

Fr: *Grand-voile Bômée*.

BOOM OFF. To keep a vessel berthed at a pier or quay some distance away from the apron by means of heavy logs or booms.

Ger: *Abbaumen*.

BOOMS. 1. Term formerly used to denote the space in a vessel's waist used for stowing boats and spare spars. The space between the fore and mainmast in which the boom boats were stowed.

2. The spare spars of a sailing vessel.

Fr: *Drôme*.

BOOM SADDLE. A collar or bracket on a lower mast, upon which the jaws of a boom rest when there is no gooseneck. Also called boom crutch.

Fr: *Support de Gui*; Ger: *Gabel; Baumkrücke*.

BOOM SPAR. A round stick or piece of timber with a length of 20 to 25 ft. and a girth at the butt of 3 to 4 hands (12 to 16 in.) suitable for spar making.

Fr: *Matereau*.

BOOM TABLE. A steel structure built up around a mast from the deck or an outrigger attached to a mast to support the heel bearings of cargo booms. It provides working clearances when a number of booms are used with one mast.

BOOM TACKLE. A tackle that leads forward of the boom when a vessel under sail is running before the wind.

Fr: *Palan de Retenue de Gui*; Ger: *Baumtalje*.

BOOM TRAVELER.
See **Boom Horse**.

BOOMY. A name given in Great Britain to a coastal sailing barge rigged with a gaff and boom mainsail and mizzen.

BOOT.
See **Mast Coat**.

BOOT IRON. A wood caulking tool with long, sharp blade, used for getting the oakum into places not easily reached by the ordinary caulking irons, such as corners and very short or very narrow seams. Formerly used for heavy work.

BOOT TOPPING. The surface of the outside plating between light and load lines.

Boot Iron

BOOT-TOPPING PAINT. A special paint applied to the outer shell plating between light and load waterlines, over the anticorrosive coating.

It is required for the reason that antifouling paints are short-lived when alternately wet and dry, and also because ordinary topside paint does not resist the erosive action of the waves.

Fr: *Peinture de Flottaison;* Ger: *Wassergangsfarbe; Boottopfarbe.*

BORA. A cold northeasterly wind, occasionally of hurricane strength, experienced on the coasts of Albania and Dalmatia. It lasts over periods that vary from one day to well over a week and occurs generally when there is a considerable difference in temperature between the mountain range and sea level.

BORE. 1. The generation of a tidal wave of unusual height that moves with considerable rapidity, caused in certain narrowing estuaries by the flood-tide water being temporarily held back by the water flowing down the river.

Fr: *Mascaret;* Ger: *Springflut.*

2. One, two, or three successive waves of great height and violence at flood tide moving up an estuary or river. Also called eagre, pororoca.

Fr: *Mascaret;* Ger: *Gezeitenbrandung; Sprungwelle; Flutwelle; Bore.*

Krey, H., "Die Flutwelle in Flussmündungen und Meeresbuchten," *Versuchsanstalt für Wasserbau und Schiffbau, Mitteilungen,* Heft 3, Berlin, 1926.

BORING. Pressing a ship through small ice or young ice under sail or power.

BOROTANG. Single outrigger Micronesian dugout canoe from Palau Islands. It is similar to the *kotraol* except for the hull, which is heavier and deeper. This canoe is employed for the transportation of heavy cargo.

BOSHUM BOAT. Local name for a shallow-draft, open boat used for fishing in sheltered waters on the Eastern Hampshire Coast (England). It is rigged with a single lugsail cut very narrow and unusually high in the hoist, which sets on a mast stepped well forward.

BOSOM. 1. The middle part of the curve formed by the foot rope of a trawl net. The section of the net between the wing connections.

2. The inside of an angle bar.

BOSOM BAR.
See **Bosom Piece.**

BOSOM KNEE. A horizontal wooden knee occasionally called lap-knee placed on the forward side of a beam. A similar knee placed on the after side of the beam is called a lodging knee, lodger knee, or lodge knee.

Fr: *Courbe Horizontale;* Ger: *Schlafendes Knie.*

BOSOM PIECE. A short piece of angle bar used as a butt strap or connecting piece for the ends of two angle bars. It is fitted inside the flanges of the bars it joins. Sometimes called bosom bar or bosom plate.

Fr: *Cornière Couvre-Joint;* Ger: *Stosswinkel; Winkellasche.*

BOSS. The center piece of a magnetic compass card, supported by the pivot. Also called cap. In dry card compasses it is usually made of aluminum in the form of a cone fitted at the apex with a polished stone (sapphire, ruby, or beryl). In liquid compasses it consists of a float or air vessel that provides the necessary buoyancy to the card.

Fr: *Disque; Chape;* Ger: *Hütchen; Kompasshütchen.*

See **Pintle Boss, Propeller Boss, Stern Boss.**

BOSS FRAME. One of the frames that curves out around the stern tube.

Fr: *Lunette d'Étambot;* Ger: *Nussspant.*

BOSSING. The swelled portion of the shank of a stock anchor through which a hole is bored for the stock to go through.

Fr: *Culasse.*

See **Shell Bossing.**

BOSS PLATE. A furnaced plate fitted around the bossing of the propeller frame where the shaft emerges from the hull.

Fr: *Tôle de Bossage;* Ger: *Nussplatte.*

BOSTON CUTTER.
See **Irish Boat.**

BOSTON SMACK. A cutter-rigged sailing boat used in the coastal fisheries between the Wash and the Humber River on the east coast of England. There are two classes: the larger, with a length ranging from 40 to 60 ft., is decked fore and aft. The smaller, with an average length of 30 ft., is half-decked. Both types are built with straight stem, low overhanging counter stern, and low bulwarks.

BOTARGO. A kind of food made from mullet roe.

BOTE. A generic term used in Spain and Portugal to denote all small open rowboats, corresponding to the word "boat" in English.

In southern Portugal, however, this term is applied to a decked boat with lateen sail and oars, generally used in the coastal fisheries. Length 28.8 ft. Breadth 10.1 ft. Depth 3.2 ft. It carries a crew of 5 to 7 hands.

BOTENG PAMUNUAKAN. A Philippine paddling or rowing dugout from Panay and Negros Islands hewn out of a *lau-an* trunk and modeled after a modern rowboat, with vertical stem and transom stern.

It has a rudder which swings on pintles. It is chiefly used for working fish traps and seines, where it has been found more handy than the long and slender *banca*, besides having a capacity about twice as large as a *banca* of equal length. It is sometimes rigged with a small sail or fitted with a motor and used for towing *bancas* or other small craft.

BOTTER. A flat-bottom, half-decked, sloop-rigged Dutch vessel from 30 to 50 ft. long. Capacity 3 to 9 tons. Also called *botaak, botschuit.* Length 40 ft. Breadth 13 ft. Depth 4 ft. Draft about 2.3 ft.

The *botter* differs from the *boier* by its high bows with overhanging stem, ending in a raised pointed stemhead, and its low, round stern with narrow quarters. Half deck forward. Fish well amidships. Long and narrow leeboards. The flat bottom runs into a chine at the bilge. The mast has no shrouds. A running bowsprit with jib is occasionally seen. The mainsail has a short curved gaff and loose foot. A single halyard is used for hoisting the gaff. The *botter* is considered the best seaboat among Dutch craft. It is extensively used for fishing and shrimping in the Zuider Zee and North Sea. Its design makes for riding out heavy weather with dry decks.

BOTTLE PAPER. A printed form supplied by the U. S. Hydrographic Office on which the latitude, longitude, and date are entered by the captain of a vessel when at sea. It is placed in a sealed bottle and thrown overboard. The date and place of its ultimate recovery furnish information concerning the speed and direction of ocean currents.

Ger: *Flaschenfindezettel.*

BOTTLE RIGGING SCREW. A turnbuckle with a single screw and a swivel at the end opposite to the screw. Sometimes called pipe turnbuckle, sleeve turnbuckle. Used to connect the ends of bobstays to the stem. The screw is enclosed in a tube as a protection against corrosion.

Fr: *Ridoir à Fourreau; Ridoir à Lanterne.*

BOTTOM. 1. The portion of a vessel's structure between keel and lower turn of bilge.

Fr: *Petit fond;* Ger: *Boden.*

See **Foul Bottom, Water Bottom, Copper Bottom, Flat Bottom, Inner Bottom, Single Bottom, Double Bottom.**

2. The term bottom is also applied in a general sense to the whole of the ship's surface below the waterline.

3. In bottomry it is used with reference to the ship as a whole.

BOTTOM BOARDS. Portable flooring fitted on the bottom of an open boat to protect the framing and fastenings of plank landings.

Fr: *Payol;* Ger: *Fussboden; Rennlatten.*

BOTTOM COMPOSITION. A general name for anticorrosive and antifouling paints such as used on ship's bottoms. Bottom compositions on steel ships prevent corrosion and fouling. This has led to the general practice of painting the bottom with two kinds of paint over the priming coat.

Fr: *Peinture de Carène; Peinture Sous-Marine;* Ger: *Schiffsbodenfarbe.*

See **Anticorrosive Paint, Antifouling Paint.**

BOTTOM LINE. A general name for fishing lines used for catching fish near the bottom from a stationary boat or from the land. Also called ground line. Such lines generally have metal or wooden spreaders.

Fr: *Palangre; Ligne de Fond;* Ger: *Grundleine.*

BOTTOM LOG. A generic term for various types of patent logs in which the apparatus is fitted directly to the ship's bottom plating, in contradistinction to the towed log, in which a rotator is attached to the end of a line. The continuous record of the speed through the water and the distance run are measured either in pressure units (pitometer log) or in units of rotation (impeller-type log).

Hoppe, H., "Ship's Speed Meters," Institution of Engineers and Shipbuilders in Scotland, *Transactions,* vol. 81 (1937-38).

BOTTOM PINTLE. The lowest pintle of a rudder. It usually supports the weight of the rudder and, to lessen friction, has a conical hemispherical bearing surface. Also called heel pintle, bearing pintle.

Fr: *Aiguillot Inférieur;* Ger: **Unterer Fingerling;** *Tragfingerling.*

BOTTOM PLANKING. The part of the planking which extends from the diminishing planking to the garboard planking.

Fr: *Bordé de Point;* Ger: *Bodenbeplankung.*

BOTTOM PLATING. Shell plating extending across the bottom or flat of the ship on both sides of the keel. The term is occasionally applied to the whole plating situated below the waterline.

Fr: *Bordé des Fonds;* Ger: *Bodenbeplattung.*

BOTTOMRY. A monetary loan in cases of necessity on the security of the *ship and cargo* conjointly, the sums so advanced being repayable to the lender a certain number of days after the arrival of the vessel. Also called bottomry loan, gross adventure. If the vessel is lost before arrival at destination, the lender loses his money, as it is payable only on condition that the vessel arrives. Bottomry is seldom resorted to nowadays.

Fr: *Prêt à la Grosse; Contrat de Grosse; Prêt à Retour de Voyage;* Ger: *Bodmerei.*

BOTTOMRY BOND. A document under seal by which a shipmaster binds himself in a penalty to repay a sum borrowed and advanced for the necessities of the ship; the vessel freight and cargo being made liable for the repayment of same provided the ship arrives safely at its destination. No bottomry bond is valid unless the money borrowed is absolutely essential in order that the ship may be put in such a state that it can prosecute its voyage and there is no possibility of obtaining money by any other means.

Fr: *Contrat de Grosse Aventure;* Ger: *Bodmereibrief.*

BOTTOMRY LIEN. The maritime lien created by a bottomry bond upon a ship, its freight, and its cargo, which may be enforced if the vessel arrives safely at the port of destination. A bottomry lien is inferior in rank to a seamen's lien, to a lien for master's wages, to a lien for general average claim, to a lien for freight, to a materialman's lien.

Fr: *Privilège du Prêteur à la Grosse;* Ger: *Bodmereipfandrecht.*

BOTTOM STRAKE. Any strake of plating or planking on the bottom of a ship between garboard and bilge strakes.

Fr: *Virure de Fond;* Ger: *Bodengang.*

BOTTOM WINGS. The lower parts of the trawl net opening. They are fixed in front to the ground rope, at the sides to the square and top wings, and behind to the head of the belly. Their length is that of the square and upper wings combined.

Fr: *Grande Aile;* Ger: *Unternetzflügel.*

BOUDARKA. An open boat used in the fisheries of the Astrakhan region (Russia). Also called baudarka. The boudarka is generally about 20 ft. long and 5 ft. wide, lightly built with narrow, pointed, flat bottom; round bilge, flaring sides, and long sharp ends. It has a good sheer, strongly raking stem and sternpost with very narrow V-shaped stern. It is rigged with one mast, stepped a little forward of amidships, which carries a lug or spritsail.

BOUGUER'S HALO. A halo surrounding a point in the sky diametrically opposite the sun. Called also Ulloa's ring, or white rainbow.

BOULICHE. A beach boat of Spanish type used in the fisheries of Algeria. The beamy hull is built with shallow center keel and two grounding keels. Length 23 to 26 ft.

BOULTER BOAT. Local name given on the south coast of England to small fishing boat very similar to the Plymouth hooker but larger and working with long lines

BOULTERS. A term used by fishermen from Devon and Cornwall, to denote "great lines" with 500 to 2000 hooks.

BOUND. A term which refers to the destination or condition of a vessel.

Fr: *Faire route pour;* Ger: *Bestimmt.*

See **Fogbound, Homeward Bound, Icebound, Ironbound, Outward Bound, Tide-Bound, Wind-Bound.**

BOUNDARY ANGLE BAR. 1. Angle bar forming the boundary connection of a transverse bulkhead with the shell plating. Also called boundary bar, bounding bar.

Fr: *Cornière Cadre;* Ger: *Begrenzungswinkel.*

2. Generally, a bar connecting the edges of a bulkhead to the shell, decks, tank top, or another bulkhead.

BOUND FOR GUAM. Idiomatic phrase which means in nautical slang: bound for no specific place.

BOUNDARY PLANK. One of the planks, generally made of teak or other hardwood, worked in a deck around deck erections, houses, casings, hatch coamings, masts, ventilators and so on, where the wood decking comes in direct contact with metal and is likely to absorb rust, or allow leakage and corrosion.

Fr: *Pièce de Bordure;* Ger: *Randplanke.*

BOUNTY. Reward paid by a government to the crew of a warship for the capture, sinking, or destruction of enemy vessels. Also called prize bounty, head money.

Ger: *Prisengeld.*

In the United States prize bounties have been abolished by law. In Great Britain the Naval Prize Act provides that the officers and men of such British warships as were actually present at the taking or destroying of an enemy armed ship are entitled to have distributed among them as prize bounty a sum calculated at the rate of five pounds sterling for each person on board the enemy ship at the beginning of the engagement.

BOVO. A Sicilian coasting vessel of comparatively large capacity with an average tonnage ranging from 25 to 40. Length 40 to 60 ft. Breadth 13 to 18 ft. Depth 6 to 7 ft. Draft 5 to 6 ft. Also called *pareggia*.

Bovo

The rig consists of a mainmast without rake stepped slightly forward of amidships, a low bowsprit nearly horizontal, several headsails, and a small jigger mast with gaff or lateen sail. The raking stem is very much like that of the *tartana*. The stern is square or round. The deck has a pronounced round of beam and is nearly at the same height at ends as amidships.

BOW. 1. The forward part or head of a vessel, more particularly above waterline, beginning where the sides trend inward and terminating where they close or unite in the stem. Also, the forepart of a vessel forward of the greatest transverse section.

Fr: *Avant;* Ger: *Bug.*
See Baltic Bow, Bold Bow, Bulbous Bow, Clipper Bow, Flare Out Bow, Lean Bow, Pram Bow, Ram Bow, Spoon Bow, Straight Bow.

2. The afteredge of the rudder blade. Also called bow piece.

BOW ASSEMBLY (U. S.). A prefabricated unit built on the assembling ways and transported bodily to the building ship. In moderate size vessels it comprises collision bulkhead, forward portions of upper and second decks, stores, flat and chain locker, center line swash bulkhead; all of which are pre-assembled with the stem, forepeak framing, shell plating and hawse pipes. In large vessels the bow assembly is divided into two sub-assembly sections.

Fr: *Tronçon de l'avant;* Ger: *Vorschiff Bausektion.*

BOW BOX (U. S.). A sunken cuddy board in the bows of a whaleboat where the forward end of the whale line was coiled. In Great Britain called foregoer kid.

BOW BREAST. A breast line from forward to keep the bow in the dock or quay; always used in mooring or docking.

Fr: *Traversier Avant;* Ger: *Bug Dwarstau.*

BOW CHOCK. A fair-lead placed near the bows of the vessel.

Fr: *Chaumard Avant;* Ger: *Bugaufklotzung; Bugklampe; Buglippe.*

BOW CHOCK PLATE. One of the plates fastened on each side of the stemhead and extending a short distance aft for housing the bow chocks, or bow mooring pipes; also for assisting in keeping the forecastle dry. Also called spirketting plate, apron plate.

Fr: *Fargue;* Ger: *Bugaufklotzungplatte; Nasenblech.*

BOW DOUBLING. A thick sheathing secured on each bow of a wooden vessel to

BOWER; BOWER ANCHOR. One of the anchors carried on each bow and designated as port bower and starboard bower. They are the main anchors by which a ship rides. Two of them are always in readiness for immediate use, one being shackled to the port and the other to the starboard cable.

Fr: *Ancre de Bossoir;* Ger: *Buganker.*

BOW FAST.
See Bow Rope.

BOW FENDER. A large fender made of matting thrummed and stuffed with old rope, fastened to the stem or harbor tugs to permit pushing directly against the side of ships. Also called pudding fender.

Ger: *Bugfender.*

BOW KNOT. A reef knot finished with the bights of the ropes which are being joined together instead of with the bare ends.

BOWL. One of a set of small buoys attached at intervals to the balch or buoy rope of a drift net. Also called pallet, buff, pellet (G. B.).

Fr: *Quart à Poche; Tanvez; Demi;* Ger: *Netzboje; Brail.*

Bowls are made of different shape according to local practice of fishermen. They are usually colored distinctively to indicate their position in the fleet or fitted at half or quarter of the fleet with a staff carrying a small flag.

BOW LIGHTHOUSE. A steel structure in the form of a small tower located on each side of the forecastle, formerly used for housing the sidelights. Also called side-light castle.

Fr: *Tourelle de Fanaux;* Ger: *Leuchtturm.*

BOWLINE. 1. A rope attached to the leech of a sail by a bridle and leading forward. Its purpose is to steady the weather leech and thus make the ship sail nearer the wind.

Fr: *Bouline;* Ger: *Bulin; Bulien; Buleine.* See **French Bowline, Running Bowline, Spanish Bowline, Spar Bowline.**
2. See **Bow Rope.**

BOWLINE BEND. A bend made from the bowline knot and used for bending two lines together.
Fr: *Noeud de Bouline;* Ger: *Pfahlstek.*

BOWLINE BRIDLE. The span on the leech of a sail to which the bowline is attached. Short ropes connecting the leech of a square sail with the bowline.
Fr: *Branche de Bouline;* Ger: *Bulienspriet.*

BOWLINE CRINGLE. Eyelets worked in the leech of a square sail for the purpose of securing a bowline bridle.
Fr: *Patte de Bouline;* Ger: *Bulinenlagel.*

BOWLINE KNOT. A knot made by an involution of the end and a bight upon the standing part of a rope. It does not slip or jam and can be cast loose instantly, as the tension is released. Also called *Bowline Hitch,* which is the seaman's regular term for making a loop at the end or bight of a rope.
Fr: *Noeud de Chaise simple;* Ger: *Pfahlstek.*

BOWMAN. 1. The oarsman who sits nearest to the bow of a boat. The hand in a boat's crew who rows the foremost oar and handles the boat hook when coming alongside. Sometimes called **bow oar.**
Fr: *Brigadier;* Ger: *Bugriem; Bugmann.*

2. In a whaleboat, the second oar next to the harpooner. The bow oar sees that all whalecraft is clear and attends the wants first of the boat steerer and then of the boat header.

BOW PAINTER. A rope fastened to a mooring ring at the stem of a rowboat, as distinguished from the stern fast attached to the sternpost ringbolt.
Fr: *Bosse de lof; Bosse Avant;* Ger: *Bugleine.*

BOW PIECE. A term applied to the curved piece forming the after edge of the blade of a wooden rudder.
Ger: *Ruderschegg.*

BOW PLATING. Shell plates in the bow of a vessel.
Fr: *Bordé de l'Avant;* Ger: *Bugbeplattung.*

BOW POINTER. One of the thick pieces of timber shaped in the form of knees and placed directly across the stem to strengthen the forepart and unite the bows on each side. Also called **forehook.**
Fr: *Guirlande d'Étrave;* Ger: *Bugbefestigung; Bugband.*

BOW PORT. Opening formerly provided close to the stem of ships regularly engaged in the timber trade, to allow long logs to be loaded or discharged endwise. Occasionally there was one provided for the 'tween-decks and another for the hold. Also called **raft port, lumber port.**
Fr: *Sabord d'Étrave;* Ger: *Bugpforte.*

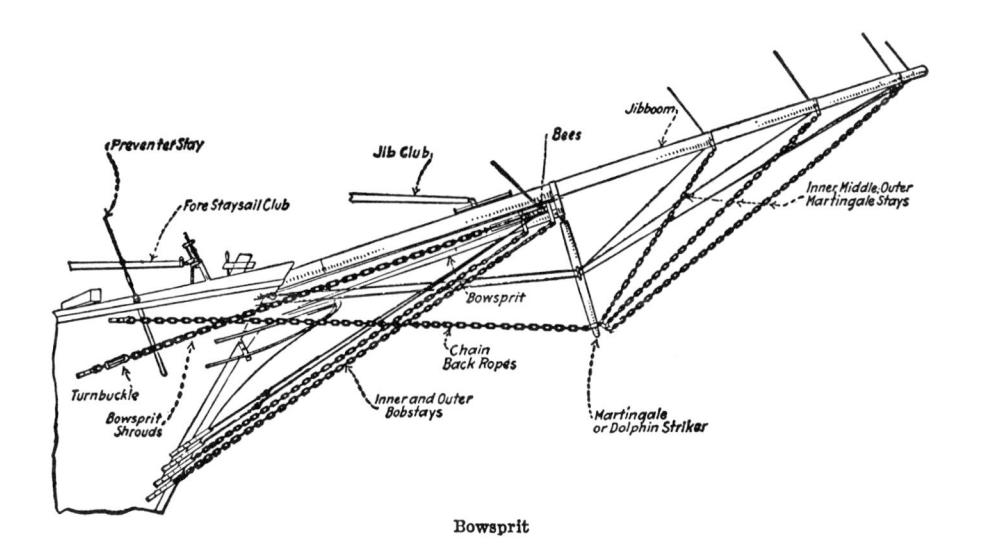

Bowsprit

BOW ROPE. A mooring or docking line led forward through a bow chock and making an angle of less than 45 deg. with the fore-and-aft line of the vessel. Also called bow line, bow fast.
    Fr: *Amarre de Bout;* Ger: *Vordere Verholleine.*

BOW RUDDER. A rudder fitted in special vessels such as cross-channel boats, ferryboats, drifters, in order that their steering qualities may be maintained, when going astern. Also called auxiliary rudder. This type of rudder is placed immediately abaft the stem bar and so formed as to maintain the fairness of the vessel's bow lines.
    Fr: *Gouvernail Avant;* Ger: *Bugruder.*

refueling seaplanes.

BOWSPRIT. A spar which projects forward from the stem of a sailing boat or vessel. Its purpose is to extend the head sails, thereby counteracting the effect of the after sails and keeping the sail plan balanced. It is also one of the main supports of the foremast, which is fastened to it by stays.
    Fr: *Beaupré;* Ger: *Bugspriet.*
    See **Horn Bowsprit, Running Bowsprit, Standing Bowsprit, Bowsprit Cap.**

In ordinary trading vessels the bowsprit rises at an angle of about 20 to 30 deg. from the horizon. It is secured in place by heavy framing at the heel or inboard end, just

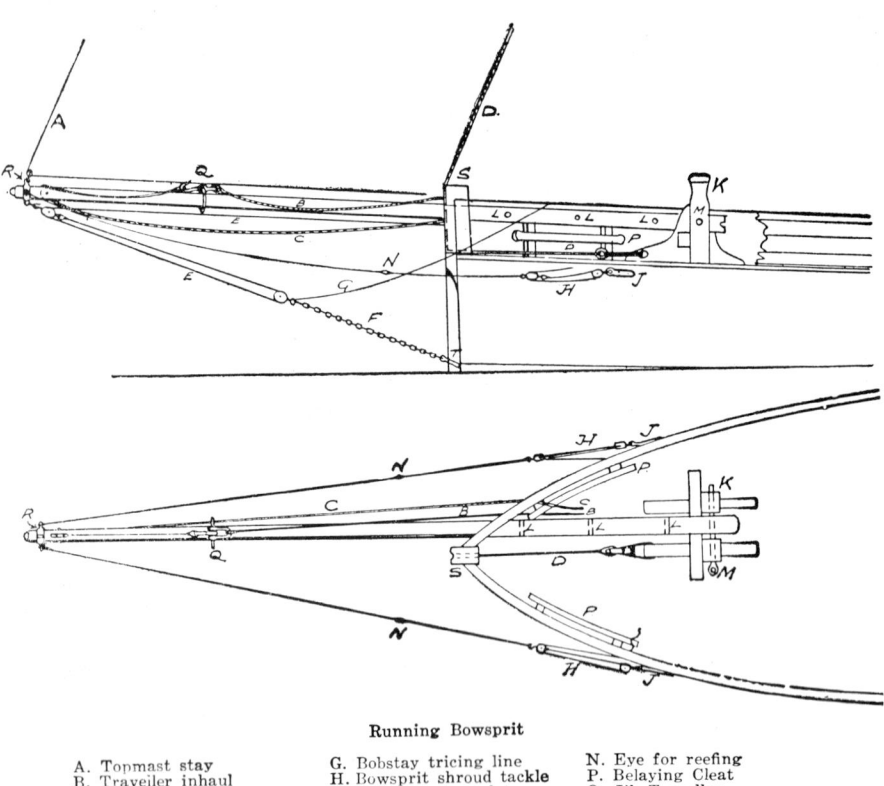

Running Bowsprit

A. Topmast stay
B. Traveller inhaul
C. Jib Traveller outhaul
D. Forestay
E. Bobstay tackle
F. Chain Bobstay
G. Bobstay tricing line
H. Bowsprit shroud tackle
J. Bowsprit stay plate
K. Bitts
L. Fid Holes
M. Bowsprit fid
N. Eye for reefing
P. Belaying Cleat
Q. Jib Traveller
R. Cranse iron
S. Stem head
T. Bobstay plate

BOWSE. To haul with a tackle, usually downward.
    Fr: *Palanquer;* Ger: *Auftaljen.*

BOWSER BOATS (U. S.). A small boat fitted with tanks containing gasoline for inside the bows, by iron straps or lashings called "Gammoning," which hold it down to the stem, and outside the ship by the bobstay. The outer end is the head, the inner one the heel. The inboard portion is named housing.

BOWSPRIT BED. Pieces of wood fitted around the bowsprit where it rests above the stem to secure and prevent it from moving sideways. By extension, that part of the stem and knightheads between which the bowsprit lies. Also called bowsprit pillow, bowsprit chocks.
Fr: *Coussin de Beaupré;* Ger: *Bugsprietbett; Bugsprietbettung.*

BOWSPRIT BITT. One of the strong upright timbers secured to the beams below deck and serving as bowsprit step. A crosspiece prevents the bowsprit from slipping in or canting up. Called also bowsprit heel bitt, Samson post.
Fr: *Bittes de Beaupré;* Ger: *Bugspriet Beting.*

BOWSPRIT CAP. The cap on the outer end of the bowsprit through which the jibboom traverses.
Fr: *Chouque de Beaupré;* Ger: *Bugspriet Eselshaupt.*

BOWSPRIT CHOCK.
See Bowsprit Bed.

BOWSPRIT HORSE. One of the ridgeropes which extend from the bowsprit cap to the knightheads (obsolete).
Fr: *Filière de Beaupré;* Ger: *Laufstag; Klimmstag.*

BOWSPRIT PILLOW.
See Bowsprit Bed.

BOWSPRIT SHROUD. One of the ropes or chains giving lateral support to the bowsprit. The outer end is fastened to the bowsprit cap or band and the inboard end to the bow plating or planking.
Fr: *Hauban de Beaupré;* Ger: *Bugstag.*

BOWSPRIT SHROUD PLATE. The fittings by which the bowsprit shrouds are attached to the hull on each side of the bow.

BOW STOPPER.
See Controller.

BOW STROP. A loop or strop passed through a hole in the stem of a small boat and to which the painter is attached. Also called bow strap.

BOW WAVE. The wave set up by the bows of a vessel moving through the water. Also called wave of displacement.
Fr: *Vague d'Étrave;* Ger: *Bugwelle.*

Bow waves may give some indication of the efficiency of the hull form generating them. The height and resistance due to bow waves can be modified by modifying bow sections at and below waterline, and by exercising care in the design of the form in this region. On the other hand, bow waves may be the result of some constructional feature which is creating a disturbance which adds little resistance to the vessel in its progress.

BOX. 1. The space between the backboard and the sternpost of a rowboat, where the coxswain sits.

2. A unit of measure for selling fresh fish by weight, used by North Sea fishermen, in Grimsby, on the east coast of England. A box of round fish contains approximately 112 lbs., a box of flat fish 140 lbs.

BOX BEAM. A hollow beam of rectangular section made of riveted or welded plates and shapes.
Fr: *Barrot en Caisson;* Ger: *Kastenbalken.*
See **Box Girder.**

BOX DOCK. A simple form of double-walled floating dock in which the two walls and the bottom pontoon are one permanent structure. It is not self-docking and for this reason is principally made in small sizes and where there is a large dock adjacent on which it can be docked when necessary.

It is the simplest form and earliest type of floating dock. It is still in use mainly for small docks and constitutes a convenient means of dealing with small craft. As the structure is not divided into several sections as is the case in pontoon docks it has greater longitudinal strength than other types of floating docks. Fr: *Box Dock;* Ger: *Einfache Sektionsdock.*

BOX GIRDER. A hollow steel girder of rectangular cross section, made of riveted or welded plates and angles.
Fr: *Support en Caisson;* Ger: *Kastenträger.*

BOX GUNWALE. The upper part of the sides in an open boat when a capping is worked over the top edge of the planking, the frame heads, and the inwale.

BOX HAULING. A method of bringing a ship, when close-hauled around upon the other tack by throwing the head sails aback, if it refuses to tack and there is no room to wear.
Fr: *Virer lof pour lof en culant;* Ger: *Backhalsen.*

BOX-HEARTED TIMBER. Timber sawed in such a manner that the heart of the tree is inside through the whole length. It refers more particularly to long pieces, such as keels and sawed spars.

BOX HOOK. Sharp pointed hook with short shank and thick wooden handle set at right angles to the shank. Used by stevedores to up-end boxes and bales, for a hand hold or for adjusting a sling underneath. It is shorter and heavier than the cotton hook.

BOXING. 1. In wooden shipbuilding, any projecting wood forming a rabbet such as the boxing of the knightheads; the center counter timber.

2. A piece of hardwood connecting frame timbers (futtocks).

3. The scarf joint which unites the stem bar with the fore end of the keel.

Fr: *Écart du brion;* Ger: *Stevens Laschung.*

BOXING FLEET (G. B.). A fleet composed of a number of North Sea trawlers congregated in one place and fishing under the guidance of a so-called "admiral" or leader who forwards the daily catch by carrier. The term "boxing fleet" arises from the fact that the fish are packed in wooden boxes, in contradistinction to the "single boaters" who use baskets.

BOX KEEL.
See **Duct Keel.**

BOX KEELSON. A heavy type of keelson consisting of riveted plates and angles forming a hollow girder of rectangular section. Now practically obsolete, on account of the danger of corrosion troubles within.

Fr: *Carlingue en Caisson;* Ger: *Kastenkielschwein.*

BOX LINE. The line coiled in the bow box of a whaleboat. Also called box warp.

BOX OFF. To back the headsails or haul the headsheets aweather so as to pay off the ship's head if it has approached too near the wind in consequence of bad steering or of a sudden shift of wind.

Fr: *Contre-Brasser Devant;* Ger: *Afbrassen.*

BOX SCARF. A scarf made by cutting out one half of the thickness of each timber without taper ends. This scarf is used for ordinary rough work not requiring much strength. Also called half-and-half lap scarf.

Fr: *Écart à mi-bois;* Ger: *Büchsenlaschung.*

BOX THE COMPASS. To name the 32 points of the compass in proper sequence from the north through east, south, and west back to north.

BOX WARP.
See **Box Line.**

BOY. A youngster serving on a merchant or fishing vessel in order to acquire the necessary training to become a sailor. British regulations do not allow boys under 13 years of age to go to sea. They cannot be employed in the engine room or stokehold.

BRACE. One of the ropes by which the horizontal motion of yards is controlled. Braces for lighter yards are usually formed of a single rope fastened to the yardarm. Those for heavier ones consist of a pendant with block through which the brace reeves. Fore and main braces lead aft. Mizzen braces lead forward to the mainmast.

Fr: *Bras;* Ger: *Brasse.*

BRACE (to). To swing or turn around the yards of a ship by means of the braces.

Fr: *Brasser;* Ger: *Brassen.*

BRACE ABACK. To trim the yards of a ship in such a manner that the wind strikes the sails from their forward side.

Fr: *Contre-brasser; Brasser à culer;* Ger: *Backbrassen.*

BRACE ABOUT. To brace the yards in a contrary direction as when tacking.

Fr: *Changer;* Ger: *Rundbrassen; Herumbrassen.*

BRACE BUMKIN. A short and heavy outrigger projecting from each quarter in square-rigged vessels to which the main brace, main lower topsail and main upper topsail brace blocks are shackled. It is hinged on the ship's side so that when the vessel is in port it can be brought to a fore-and-aft direction.

Fr: *Arc-boutant de brasseyage; Pistolet de Bras;* Ger: *Grossbrassknie; Brassbaum; Brassarm.*

BRACE IN. To bring the yards more nearly athwartships. A square-rigged vessel is said to be braced in when it is running free.

Fr: *Fermer;* Ger: *Beibrassen; Zurückbrassen.*

BRACE PENDANT. A length of rope or chain into which the brace block is spliced at one end, the other being fastened to the yardarm.

Fr: *Pantoire de Bras;* Ger: *Brasschenkel.*

BRACERA. See **Brazzera.**

BRACE SHARP. To cause the yards to have the smallest possible angle with the keel.

Fr: *Brasser en Pointe;* Ger: *Scharfbrassen.*

BRACE UP. To bring the yards nearer to a fore-and-aft direction by hauling on the lee braces.

Fr: *Brasser sous le Vent; Ouvrir;* Ger: *Anbrassen.*

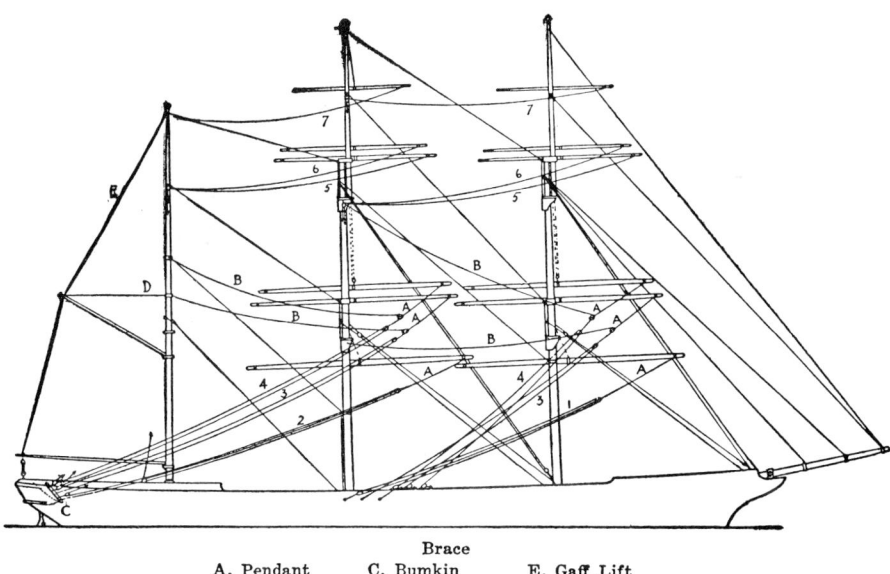

	Brace	
A. Pendant	C. Bumkin	E. Gaff Lift
B. Runner	D. Span	
1. Fore Brace	3. Lower Topsail Brace	6. Upper Topgallant Brace
2. Main Brace	4. Upper Topsail Brace	7. Royal Brace
	5. Lower Topgallant Brace	

BRACE WINCH. A hand winch used on large sailing vessels for trimming lower and topsail yards.

Fr: *Treuil de Brasseyage;* Ger: *Brassenwinde.*

The brace winch consists of a steel frame with three horizontal shafts. Each shaft is fitted with two grooved drums of conical shape. The braces (port and starboard) of each yard have their ends fastened to one set of drums. The rotation of the drums, which is effected by crank handles with suitable spur gearing, hauls in one brace and simultaneously unwinds the corresponding brace on the other side so that there is practically no slack during the operation.

BRACKET. A steel plate, usually of triangular shape, and commonly with a reinforcing flange, used to stiffen or tie beam angles to bulkheads, frames to longitudinals, or any two structural parts which meet at an angle, in order to strengthen the joint against flexure. A bracket differs from a gusset in that it meets at least one of the surfaces to which it is attached, angularly, being secured thereto by a riveted flange or a piece of angle bar. The two terms are, however, used interchangeably. Also called knee plate.

Fr: *Mouchoir; Gousset;* Ger: *Stützplatte; Knieblech.*

See Beam Knee, Bilge Bracket, Bitt Bracket, Tripping Bracket.

BRACKET FLOOR.
See Skeleton Floor.

BRACKET FRAME. A frame in which the frame bar, the reverse bar, and the longitudinals are connected by bracket plates leaving a portion of the frame bar and reverse bar midway between two adjacent longitudinals, unconnected.

Ger: *Kimmstütze.*

BRACKETLESS ISHERWOOD FRAMING. A system of longitudinal framing developed by Sir J. Isherwood in 1925, in which brackets fitted for the purpose of connecting the longitudinals at bulkheads are entirely eliminated.

Fr: *Construction Isherwood Sans Goussets;* Ger: *Isherwood Knieblechfreie Bauart.*

In order to provide compensation for the omission of brackets, the relative position of transverse members has been modified by placing them nearer the bulkheads. Continuity of longitudinal strength is maintained by fitting liners to the shell plates at the bulkheads where the longitudinals are cut. This system is claimed to be economical in weight and cost of construction, and to reduce broken stowage.

Isherwood, Sir J. W., *The Bracketless System,* Institution of Engineers and Shipbuilders in Scotland, *Transactions,* vol. 69, Glasgow, 1926.

BRACKISH. A term applied to a mixture of fresh water and sea salt.

Fr: *Saumâtre;* Ger: *Brack; Brackwasser.*

BRAD. A particular kind of nail without head or shoulder on the shank. Used where the nails are driven entirely into the wood.

Fr: *Pointe;* Ger: *Spiekernagel.*

BRADDENKAHN.

See **Keitelkahn.**

BRADING. To make a net by hand. Also known as beating and weaving.

Fr: *Maillage;* Ger: *Schlagen.*

BRAGAGNA. Crudely built open boat from Chioggia (Adriatic), rigged with 2 or 3 masts, lugsails, and bowsprit. It is used for trawling in the Venetian lagoons with a *paranzella* net. Length 29 to 36 ft. Tonnage 10 to 12. Crew 2 to 4.

BRAGOZZO. Shallow-draft sailing trawler from the Adriatic originating from Chioggia near Venice. It is sometimes called *trabaccolo da Pesca* although in design and construction it differs considerably from the *trabaccolo.* Called *schiletto* in the district of Ancona. Length 28 to 46 ft. Breadth 7.7 to 12.5 ft. Depth 2.7 to 4 ft.

The hull is round and bluff at both ends with sheer line rising sharply forward, flat bottom, no keel, curved stem and sternpost with tumble home. The rudder is of large area extending considerably below the bottom and so arranged that it can be lifted by means of a tackle which has its upper block fastened to the mainmast. The *bragozzo* is decked fore and aft with the exception of a small space just abaft the mainmast, which serves as cockpit for the helmsman.

The rig consists of two pole masts, fore and mainmast, with balanced lugsails and a jibboom with a single jib. The foremast is short and rakes forward. The mainmast has no rake. Particulars of sail plan for a Bragozzo with a length of 40 ft., mainmast 29.5 ft., foremast 19 ft., jibboom 11.5 ft., mainsail area 441 sq. ft., foresail area 215 sq. ft., jib 54 sq. ft.

BRAIL. 1. Running gear by which loose-footed gaff sails such as spankers, trysails, and so on, are gathered into the mast for furling. They are middled and stoppered to the afterleech, with a hauling part on each side reeving through a block fastened on the mast at a point corresponding to that one at which they are stopped to the leech. They are known as foot brail, middle brail, and peak brail according to their position.

Fr: *Cargue;* Ger: *Geitau.*

See **Throat Brail.**

2. A short heavy stick about 18 in. long fastened at each extremity of the wings in a *lampara* or round haul net.

BRAILER. A dip net about 4 ft. in diameter and 4 ft. deep with a long handle, used for transferring the catch of a purse seine or other similar gear from the net to the boat's hold.

It is attached to the hook of the derrick fall with 3 ropes of equal length fastened around the top of the net. The fish are released through a hole in the bottom of the net, which has several 1½-in. rings fastened around the edges. A chain is run through the rings and pulled tight, closing the hole. When the chain is slackened the weight of the fish opens the hole allowing the fish to drop out.

BRAILING FALL. A wire fall with Manila tail used with a brail net when transferring the catch of a seine to the boat. It is rove through a single block fastened to the derrick head or to a pennant running from the mast to a suitable point. The tail end is taken to the winch gipsy. Also called jilson snorter.

BRAIL LINE. 1. A line fastened to the bottom of a purse seine by which the lead line is lifted to the cork line. It passes through metal rings attached to the side or up-and-down line. Also called breast purse line.

2. A line rove through a series of rings at the bottom of a dip net or brailer which can be pursed while filling and opened at the bottom for dumping its contents.

BRAIL UP. To haul in by means of brails.

Fr: *Carguer.*

BRAKE BEAM. One of the handles by which a pump windlass is worked.

Fr: *Bringuebale;* Ger: *Spillhebel.*

BRANCH. A nautical term in the United States for a warrant or commission authorizing the holder thereof to pilot vessels in certain waters.

BRANCH PILOT (U. S.). A licensed navigator who is familiar with taking charge of a ship and taking it into or out of port at the particular place where he is engaged in the business.

BRASH ICE. A collection of small fragments and rounded nodules of ice frozen together, and through which a ship can easily force its way. Also called brash.

Fr: *Bourguignon.*

BRASHNESS. The tendency of timber to break without a splintering fracture. A sign of decay.

BRASS. Generic term for various non-ferrous alloys of copper and zinc to which small percentages of other metals such as manganese, nickel, lead, and tin are added to give special properties. Castings of ordinary commercial brass have a tensile strength of 20,000 lbs. per sq. in. Forgings have a tensile strength of 40,000 lbs. Brass castings are used for deck plates and caps, drain plugs, name letters, number plates, scupper pipes, skylight hinges and so on.

Fr: *Laiton;* Ger: *Messing.*

BRAVE WEST WINDS. The boisterous westerly winds blowing over the ocean between latitudes 40° and 50°.

Ger: *Braver Westwind.*

BRAZIL CURRENT. The portion of the South Equatorial current that turns south along the coast of Brazil and flows as far as the Rio de la Plata, where it turns eastward to mingle with the general easterly drift of the Southern Ocean.

BRAZZERA. Small fishing boat of the southern Adriatic. The hull is built with keel, decked at ends, curved stem, sharp stern, flat bottom, bold sheer forward. The rig consists of a portable mast, dipping lugsail, and jib with short bowsprit. Length 30 to 40 ft. Also called *bracera.*

BREACHING.

See Uptake.

BREAD AND BUTTER MODEL. A model constructed of a number of horizontal layers cut from a single plank and glued together. The outline of each layer is ascertained from deck plan drawings and accurately traced on a plank, which is cut to shape before being glued. The glued planks are then trimmed to the faired hull form, templates made up from the body plan being used.

BREADTH.

See Beam.

BREAK. 1. The point at which a deck erection or superstructure such as poop, forecastle, or bridge house is discontinued; thus the break of the forecastle is the after-end of the forecastle; and the break of the poop the forward end of the poop.

2. For tonnage measurement purposes a break is defined as the space above the line of the upper deck when the deck is cut off and continued by another at a higher level. The height of the break being the distance from the underside of the upper deck to the underside of the break deck.

Fr: *Décrochement;* Ger: *Zerbrechung.*

BREAK. To break a flag, that is, to hoist it to the masthead or other position in the rigging, rolled up in a bundle and secured with a slippery hitch or bow knot and to set it flying of a sudden by giving a pull on the halyards downhaul which contains the slip knot.

Fr: *Déferler;* Ger: *Losbrechen.*

BREAKAGE. 1. The room or space lost in stowing cargo, that is, the unavoidable space between packages. Breakage constitutes the difference between measurement and stowage. Also called broken stowage.

Fr: *Vide; Grenier; Garniture; Vide d'Arrimage.*

2. An allowance made for loss because of destruction of merchandise.

3. A term in bills of lading that refers only to breakage of goods caused by unavoidable circumstances or by act of God, without any negligence on the part of the shipowner or his servants.

Fr: *Casse; Bris;* Ger: *Bruch.*

BREAK BULK. To destroy the entirety of a ship's cargo considered as a unit by opening the hatches and commencing to unload.

Fr: *Entrer en déchargement;* Ger: *Lastbrechen.*

BREAK BULKHEAD. A transverse bulkhead at the end of a superstructure such as bridge house or forecastle.

Fr: *Fronteau;* Ger: *Frontschott.*

BREAKDOWN CLAUSE. A clause found in charters that provides that in the event of loss of time due to insufficiency of the crew, want of stores or provisions, engine breakdown or any other damage or cause that constitutes an obstacle to the proper working of the ship for more than 24 working hours, the hire shall cease until the vessel is put back into an efficient working condition. Also called off hire clause.

Ger: *Breakdown Klausel.*

BREAKDOWN LIGHT.

See Not under Command Light.

BREAKER. 1. One of several waves breaking into foam against the shore, a sandbank, or a reef near the surface.

Fr: *Brisants;* Ger: *Brechsee; Sturzsee; Brandungswellen.*

2. A small cask or barrel used in a ship's lifeboat for drinking water. Capacity one quart of water for each person. Also called barricoe.

Fr: *Baril de Galère;* Ger: *Bootsfass.*

BREAK GROUND. To release the anchor from the bottom. Sometimes called to break out.

Fr: *Déraper;* Ger: *Ausbrechen.*

BREAKING SIGHTS. Operation performed at the launch of a vessel to ascertain by means of sights conveniently located the amount of hog or sag (if any) sustained by the hull during launching. The sights are checked before and after the vessel is waterborne.

BREAK LEAVE. To remain away from a ship after the time specified for returning has expired.

Ger: *Urlaub; Überschreiten.*

BREAK OUT. A term used by stevedores to denote the act of conveying goods stowed in a ship's hold from the place occupied to the square immediately under the hatchway.

Fr: *Désarrimage;* Ger: *Auseisung.*

See **Break Ground.**

BREAK SHEER. Said of a ship at anchor when forced the wrong way by wind or current and thus not lying well for keeping the cables clear of each other or keeping clear of the anchor.

Fr: *Embrader sur l'Ancre.*

BREAKUP CLAUSE. A hull clause inserted in marine insurance policies when the vessel becomes a total loss. It states that in ascertaining whether the vessel is a constructive total loss or an actual total loss, the insured value is to be taken as the repaired value, and nothing in respect of the damaged or breakup value of the vessel shall be taken into account.

BREAKWATER. 1. A small athwartship or V-shaped coaming abaft the hawse holes on the forecastle, acting as a protection against the seas shipped over the bows and preventing the water entering through the hawse pipes from rushing aft by diverting it to the ship's sides. Also called manger.

Fr: *Brise-Lames;* Ger: *Brechwasser.*

2. Any structure or contrivance such as a mole, mound, wall or sunken hulk serving to break the force of the waves and protect a harbor or anything exposed to the force of waves.

Fr: *Jetée;* Ger: *Wellenbrecher.*

BREAM. 1. To clear a wooden ship's bottom of shells, seaweed, ooze, barnacles, etc., by applying to it kindled furze, reeds, oil-soaked oakum or light combustibles so as to soften the pitch and loosen adherent matters which are afterwards easily scraped and brushed off. Also called sweal, grave, charring.

2. To clean the barnacles, paint, and so on from a ship's bottom by use of a blow-torch.

Fr: *Flamber;* Ger: *Brennen; Abflammen.*

BREAST BACKSTAY. An extra support to a topmast consisting of a rope extending from topmast head on the weather side to the channels forward of the standing backstays.

Ger: *Seitenpardune.*

BREAST BAND. A band of canvas or a rope passed around the body of the man who heaves the hand lead, to prevent his falling overboard.

Fr: *Sangle de Sondeur;* Ger: *Brustleine.*

BREAST BEAM. 1. A beam at the break of a quarterdeck poop or forecastle.

Fr: *Barrot de Fronteau;* Ger: *Frontbalken.*

2. The transverse beam nearest to midships, on the forecastle deck or poop.

BREAST FAST.

See **Breast Rope.**

BREASTHOOK. 1. A triangular gusset plate fitted between the decks or deck stringers just abaft the stem, for the purpose of strengthening the bow framing.

2. Inside timber or iron fitting bent to a V shape and fastened horizontally at the fore end of the ship between the decks to unite the bows and strengthen the forepart of the structure. Also known as forehook, bow pointer or breast knee.

Fr: *Guirlande;* Ger: *Bugband; Deckband.*

BREAST LINE. In a seine net: a vertical continuation of the lead and cork lines at the ends of the net. Also called up-and-down line. Its purpose is to prevent the weight of the lead line from tearing the netting and to take the towing strain on the net.

See **Breast Rope.**

BREAST OFF. To moor a vessel some distance from a quay or wharf, say 15 to 20 ft., in order to allow lighters and so on, to work between ship and quay. The vessel is held in position by long heavy timbers called breasting-off spars.

BREAST PLATE—BRIDGE PIECE

BREAST PLATE. A small, horizontal plate connecting the bow chock plates of the stem, breasthook fashion.

BREAST RAIL. The railing running athwartship on the bridge afterend of the forecastle, fore end of the poop or quarterdeck (obsolete).

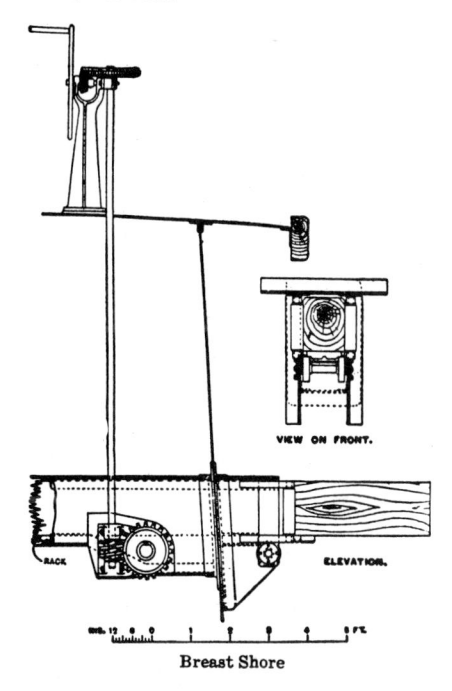

Breast Shore

BREAST ROPE. A mooring or docking line leading at an angle of about 90 deg. with the fore-and-aft line of the vessel. Also called Breast fast.

Fr: *Amarre Traversière; Traversier;* Ger: *Dwarsfeste.*

BREAST SHORE. One of a line of props or shores, braced nearly horizontal against an altar, supporting transversely a ship in dry dock at the level of her load waterline. Also called wale shore, side shore. In modern dry docks where large ships are docked, breast shores are frequently made of telescopic lattice girders, which can be moved in and out electrically and which are geared together across the deck.

Fr: *Clef d'accorage;* Ger: *Dwarsstütze.*

BREAST STROKE. A stroke in which the oarsmen of a single-banked boat push the loom of the oar well forward beyond their bodies.

BREASTWORK. An athwartship railing such as found at the break of the poop or forecastle (obsolete).

BREECH. 1. The outer angle of a knee timber as distinguished from the inner angle or throat.

2. The end of a block farthest from the hook or eye.

Fr: *Cul;* Ger: *Herd.*

BREECHES BUOY. A lifebuoy used in connection with a rocket apparatus or lyle gun, by means of which the person to be rescued from a stranded vessel is brought to the shore. A pair of canvas breeches is attached to the lower part of the buoy.

Fr: *Bouée à Culotte;* Ger: *Hosenboje.*

BREEZE. A current of air less than a wind. In sailors' parlance the word "breeze" often refers to a strong wind, but generally speaking it is a movement of air of no particular strength.

Fr: *Brise;* Ger: *Brise.*

See Fresh Breeze, Gentle Breeze, Land Breeze, Light Breeze, Mackerel Breeze, Moderate Breeze, Strong Breeze, Topgallant Breeze.

BRICKFIELDER. A hot northerly wind blowing over the south coast of the Australian continent during the summer months.

BRIDGE; BRIDGE DECK. A partial deck extending from side to side of a vessel over a comparatively short length amidships, forming the top of a bridge house or partial superstructure.

Fr: *Pont du Château;* Ger: *Brückendeck.*

See Captain's Bridge, Long Bridge, Monkey Bridge, Navigating Bridge, Short Bridge, Warping Bridge.

BRIDGE HOUSE. An erection amidships above the main deck the top of which forms the bridge deck. It affords a favorable position for living quarters and provides a raised platform for navigating purposes and protection for engine and boiler room openings.

Fr: *Château;* Ger: *Brückenbau; Brückenhaus.*

BRIDGEMASTER. A member of the crew of a seal-hunting vessel who is stationed on the bridge and transmits reports from the scunner to the captain or officer directing the course of the vessel.

BRIDGE PIECE. The upper part of the stern frame forming an arch over the propeller aperture. It bridges the rudder post and propeller post. Also called arch.

Fr: *Sommier;* Ger: *Bogenstück.*

BRIDLE. A span of chain or rope with both ends secured. The hauling power is applied to the bight or middle portion.
Fr: *Patte d'Oie;* Ger: *Hahnepot; Sprut.*
See **Becket Bridle, Bowline Bridle, Cargo Bridle, Dandy Bridle, Mooring Bridle, Towing Bridle, Trawl Bridle.**

BRIDLE BEAM. A hatch beam or a fore and after fitted across a hatchway. Also called strongback.

BRIDLE LINE. One of the small lines, or loops, by which the rings are fastened along the lead lines in a purse seine. Each line is made of 15-thread Manila and is 14 to 16 ft. long.

BRIG. A two-masted square-rigged vessel. It is the smallest seagoing vessel completely square-rigged and has a tonnage ranging from 200 to 350, length 90 to 100 ft., breadth 24 to 30 ft. and depth of hold 12 to 18 ft.

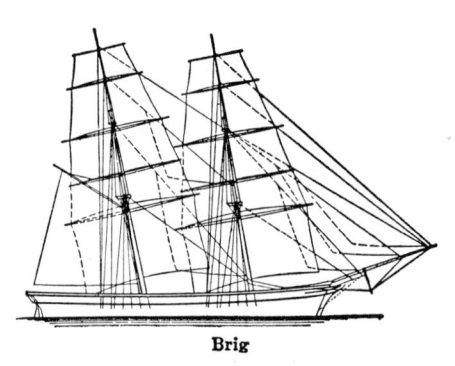

Brig

The disappearance of this rig is due to the superior handiness of fore-and-aft sails for weatherly work and the necessity for reducing crews in order to compete with mechanically propelled vessels.
Fr: *Brick;* Ger: *Brigg.*
See **Cutter Brig, Four-Masted Brig, Jackass Brig, Schooner Brig.**

BRIGANTINE. 1. A brig without a square mainsail, for example, a vessel that carries all the square sails of a brig on both the fore- and mainmasts with the exception of the main course.
2. The term "brigantine" nowadays more usually refers to a two-masted vessel with square rig on the foremast and fore-and-aft rig (no top) on the mainmast.
Fr: *Brigantin;* Ger: *Schonerbrigg.*

BRIG RIG.
See **Brig.**

BRIGHTWORK. 1. A term used to describe all brass that is kept polished.
2. Sometimes used in boatman's parlance to denote any items such as varnished topsides, deckhouses, spar, or trim, that are finished in natural wood showing the grain of the material.

BRINE.
See **Refrigerator System Brine.**

BRING. To attach a cable to the capstan or a rope to a winch.
Fr: *Garnir;* Ger: *Legen.*

BRING BY THE LEE. To incline so rapidly to leeward of the course that the vessel's lee side is unexpectedly brought to windward.
Fr: *Masquer sous le vent;* Ger: *Unter den Wind bringen.*

BRING TO. 1. To cause a ship to come to a standstill, or to keep a ship stationary by making one sail act against another.
2. Also, to heave another vessel with a blank shot.
Fr: *Mettre en Panne;* Ger: *Abbringen; Beilegen.*

BRING UP. To come to a standstill, with an anchor, or by fouling an obstacle or by striking the sea bottom.
Fr: *Faire Tête;* Ger: *Aufbringen.*

BRISTOL BAY GILL NET BOAT. A sailboat used in the salmon fisheries of Alaska. These craft are from 28 to 30 ft. long with a beam of 8 to 9 ft., double-ended with short deck at bow and stern and waterways at sides. They are divided into several compartments. The two shackles of nets, each 75 fathoms long, are carried in the stern compartment. In the forward compartment bedding, provisions, an oil stove, water and provisions are stowed. Amidships there is a centerboard trunk with fish boxes on each side. When down, the centerboard projects about 2 ft. below the bottom. The cat rig with boomed spritsail is most frequently seen.

BRITCONT. Code name for British Chamber of Shipping General Home Trade Charter (1928). Used only in trades where there is no special chamber of shipping charter.

BRITISH CORPORATION. A British classification society founded in 1890 by leading Clydeside and West of Scotland shipowners, engineers and shipbuilders, and officially appointed under the Merchant Shipping Acts for the assignment of freeboards on behalf of the Board of Trade.

Symbols used in the register:

B.S.* Indicates that the vessel is classed British Standard, the highest class obtainable, and has been built under survey. The same letters without the star indicate that the vessel has not been surveyed during construction. When ships are built for a particular trade, the particulars of this trade or service are inserted in brackets after the symbol B.S.

M.B.S.* Signifies that the machinery and boilers are classed British Standard and have been built under survey. The star is omitted when the engines and boilers are classed but not built under special survey.

A black horizontal line through the symbol indicates that the class has been withdrawn for noncompliance with the rules. The symbol inserted between brackets denotes that the class has been withdrawn at the owner's request.

BROACH TO. Said of a vessel under sail when running with the wind on the quarter. The ship's head comes up suddenly toward the wind in consequence of a sea striking the stern or through bad steering. A frequent cause of dismasting or loss of spars.

Fr: *Lancer dans le Vent; Faire un Lan;*
Ger: *Anbrechen; Schnell aufluven.*

BROADAX. An ax with broad blade and long handle used by boatbuilders for hewing timber. The handle is offset to clear the user's hand which is nearest the bit when cutting through timber.

Fr: *Doloir;* Ger: *Breitbeil.*

BROAD HATCHET. A small broadax used by boatbuilders to hew the edges of narrow timber.

BROAD PENNANT. Oblong swallow-tailed pennant with the fly about twice as long as the hoist. Its edges may be parallel or taper to two tips.

Fr: *Flamme de Commandement;* Ger: *Commodoreständer; Breitwimpel.*

BROAD REACH. Said of a sail boat when sailing with the wind a little free but still forward of the beam.

Fr: *Courir Grand Largue.*

BROADSEAMING. A term used in sailmaking to denote the shortening of the edges of a sail by gradually widening the seam or lap of the cloths where they are sewed together from the middle toward the edges. The roach is obtained by broadseaming.

Fr: *Couture Forcée.*

BROAD STRAKE. One of the three strakes of planking next to the garboard strake, which gradually diminish in thickness until they are as thick as the bottom planking.

Fr: *Ribord;* Ger: *Nebenkielgang.*

BROGAN. Small Chesapeake Bay centerboard boat of bugeye type about 40 ft. long, half-decked, with two masts and leg-of-mutton sails. Used for oyster tonging.

BROKEN-BACKED. Descriptive of the condition of a ship when, from faulty construction or from grounding, its structure is distorted, causing both ends to droop. Also called hogged.

Fr: *Arqué;* Ger: *Katzenrücken; Kielbruch; Katzenbuckel.*

BROKEN STOWAGE. A timber-trade term for pieces of timber 6 to 8 ft. long used to fill up space room in a vessel's hold. Such pieces pay freight at only two-thirds of the standard rate and are sometimes called "ends." Bills of lading and charter parties often contain the clause "Ends exceeding 3% to pay full freight."

Fr: *Bois d'Arrimage;* Ger: *Staulucken; Stauhols.*

See Breakage.

BROKEN WATER. An area of small waves and eddies occurring in what otherwise is a calm sea. Waves breaking on and near shallows, or by the contention of currents in a narrow channel.

Fr: *Clapotis.*

BROKERAGE. The fee or commission charged for transacting business as a broker.

Fr: *Courtage;* Ger: *Befrachtungsgebühr; Kourtage; Maklergebühr.*

BROKERAGE CLAUSE. A charter party clause which states the rate of brokerage to be paid.

Fr: *Clause de Courtage;* Ger: *Courtage Klausel.*

BROKER'S ORDER (G. B.). An authority for certain goods to be shipped from craft.

Ger: *Verladungsanweisung.*

BROKER'S RETURN (G. B.). A list sent by the wharfinger to the freight brokers showing all the goods that have been placed on board a vessel.

Ger: *Ladungsverzeichnis.*

BRONZE. A generic name for nonferrous alloys with copper and tin as the principal elements, to which zinc is added to soften them and assist in making sound castings, and lead as a softening element to improve the machining qualities. Other metals are sometimes introduced for special purposes.

Fr: *Bronze;* Ger: *Bronze.*
See **Manganese Bronze, Phosphor Bronze, Tobin Bronze.**

Bronze castings are used in shipbuilding for stern tube bushings, shaft and rudder stock liners, propeller nut caps, wedges on watertight doors, bitts, chocks, cleats and fairleads of small craft, sea connections and manifolds, and hardware of all sorts when strength and resistance to corrosion are essential.

Rolled or drawn bronze is used for wire rope.

BRONZE ROPE. Wire rope made of phosphor bronze (92 per cent copper, 8 per cent tin, 0.1 to 0.2 per cent phosphorus). Owing to its relatively low strength and its large amount of stretch under tension, it is little used on merchant ships except for gear near magnetic compasses, or for radio antennas. In small craft tiller ropes are frequently made of extra flexible bronze rope of 6 x 6 x 7 construction with cotton core in each strand and hemp central core.

BROUGHT BY THE LEE. 1. The situation of a vessel going free when it has fallen off so much as to bring the wind around its stern and the sails are taken aback on the other side.

Fr: *Empanner.*

2. An expression used when a vessel under sail is running and the wind changes from one quarter to the other.

BROW. 1. A small curved or flanged plate fitted to the shell plating over an airport to prevent water trickling down the ship's side from entering the airport when open. Also called eyebrow.

Fr: *Cil.*

2. A runway with wooden cleats to facilitate entry and exit between ship and shore. It is usually fitted with rollers at the shore end to allow for the movement of the vessel. Also called gangplank.

Fr: *Planche de Débarquement; Planche à Terre;* Ger: *Landungssteg; Laufplanke.*

3. A plate forming a riser on the sides of a 'tween-deck hatch coaming. It enables the stevedores to truck cargo on the hatch covers so that it can be hoisted from the square of the hatchway. Also called brow plate.

BROW LANDING. A platform consisting of a wooden grating hinged to the side of a ship at deck level to support the inboard end of a brow.

BROW TRUCK. The truck or rollers upon which the shore end of a brow rests.

BRUKUTAN. A Javanese trading *prao* with keel and pointed incurving stem and stern pieces. It has a planked deck and a small deckhouse amidships, through which the mast is stepped.

BRUSSELS CONVENTION. An international convention for the unification of rules governing bills of lading, as passed by the International Diplomatic Conference held in Brussels in October, 1922. The convention was an improvement on the Hague Rules 1921, and so far as Great Britain is concerned its findings have been given legal effect by the Carriage of Goods by Sea Act, 1924.

BUBONIC PLAGUE. An epidemic disease of high mortality. Also called plague. According to the International Sanitary Convention 1926, a ship is considered as plague-infected when it has a case of human plague on board, or if a case of human plague breaks out more than six days after embarkation, or if plague-infected rats are found on board. The ship is regarded as suspect if a case of human plague breaks out on board in the first six days after embarkation or if investigations regarding rats have shown the existence of an unusual mortality among them without determining the cause thereof. A ship is regarded as healthy notwithstanding its having come from an infected port, if there has been no human or rat plague on board either at the time of departure or during the voyage, and if there is none on arrival, and investigation regarding rats does not show the existence of an unusual mortality.

Fr: *Peste;* Ger: *Pest.*

BUCKET DREDGE. A dredging machine which has as its main feature a continuous chain of buckets running around a rigid frame called the ladder extending down from the hull of the dredge to the bottom of the water. Also called ladder dredge, elevator dredge.

Fr: *Drague à Godets;* Ger: *Eimerbagger.*

The buckets run empty down the underside of the ladder, dig into the material as they turn around the end, and return full along the top of the ladder. On reaching the top each bucket as it turns over discharges its contents into a chute which conveys the elevated material to the vessel's own hopper or to a barge. The revolving members of each end of the ladder are called tumblers and the top tumbler drives the bucket chain.

BUCKET LANYARD. A small line attached to the handle of a bucket used

for drawing water over the ship's side.
Ger: *Halteleine.*

BUCKLE CORK. In a mackerel net: a cork float placed at the end of the cork rope and bearing the initials of the owner for identification purposes.

BUCKLER. A general term applied to various devices designed to prevent the entry of water through hawse pipes, chain pipes, and the like.

BUCK UP. To hold a rivet-head tight against the members being joined, while the rivet is being driven. This is done with a "holder-on," driven by an air hammer, and ensures a tight joint.

BUFFALO (U. S.). The bulwarks extending above the forecastle deck on each side of the stem in the extreme bow.

BUFFALO RAIL (U. S.). A low wooden rail on the forecastle of schooners.

BUGEYE. A canoe-shaped centerboard boat from Chesapeake Bay with long bullethead stem fitted with headrails and trail boards, and sharp stern finished off in the manner of a miniature pink stern. Stem and sternpost have a pronounced rake. Average dimensions: Length on deck 54 ft. Breadth 14 ft. Draft 3 ft., without board.

Up to about 40 ft. in length the hull was built of 3 or 4 logs, one forming the keel and garboards and the others shaped from the solid wood to the desired model on the outside and hollowed out on the inside to form the bilges and topsides. There were only one or two seams on each side where the side logs were fastened to the keel log with driftbolts. The larger craft had only one log which formed the keel and garboards. Above this the boat was planked and framed in the ordinary way. In late years bugeyes have been planked and framed right through. Some have been built with round stern. The rig consists of two raking pole masts (main and mizzen) with leg-of-mutton sails. The foremast is stepped well forward, the mainmast just aft of amidships. The bowsprit is short and hogged down on the long head.

The largest bugeyes, which have a length ranging from 70 to 80 ft., are used as market boats, the others as oyster fishermen. Brewington, M. V., *Chesapeake Bay Bugeyes*, Newport News (Va.), 1941.

BUILDER'S CERTIFICATE. A document issued by the commissioner of navigation and forwarded by the shipbuilders to the owners, setting forth such details as are necessary to specifically identify a newly completed vessel. This certificate, accompanied by a classification certificate and a declaration of ownership, is handed over to the authorities by whom the registry is effected. It permits a vessel to proceed from the shipyard for her trials or to another port to get fuel, provisions and equipment. It is used without making the regular inspection and the customhouse clearance certificate is not required. Also called carpenter's certificate.

Fr: *Certificat de Construction;* Ger: *Beilbrief.*

BUILDER'S MODEL. A half model of the hull, built layer fashion, generally of dark and light wood alternately. Used in shipyards to show off the lines in a design. Stillman, C. K., The Development of the Builder's Half Hull Model in America. Marine Historical Association, Mystic, Conn. *Publications,* vol. 1, no. 7, 1933.

BUILDERS' OLD MEASUREMENT. A tonnage rule formerly used by shipbuilders for estimating the size of ships, based upon 40 cu. ft. as the equivalent of one ton, instead of 100 cu. ft. as in the New Measurement Rule. Tonnage under the Old Measurement was arrived at by the following formula:

$$\frac{(L - 3/5B \times B \times \frac{1}{2}B)}{94}$$

Dimensions in feet. L = Length. B = Breadth.

Fr: *Jauge Ancienne;* Ger: *Alte Vermessungs Methode.*

This rule was promulgated in 1773 and continued to be in force until about 1854. With its heavy tax on beam and no depth factor it produced a narrow and deep type of ship, wet and dangerous, slow under canvas. It seriously menaced the prosperity of the shipping industry at the time.

It was essentially a rule of thumb, based upon the length and breadth of a ship, in which it was erroneously estimated that the depth was as a rule equal to half the breadth.

The term "Carpenter's Measurement" referred to any of the length × breadth × depth/factor systems of determining tonnage, whereas "Builders' Old Measurement" referred more particularly to the old British formula as given above.

BUILDER'S POLICY. A policy that covers risks incidental to the construction or building of vessels. It generally extends from the time of laying of keel until the vessel is handed over to her owners. Also called construction policy.

Ger: *Baurisiko Police.*

BUILDER'S TRIAL. A trial sometimes given by the builders to a new vessel before conducting acceptance trials. It is generally an abbreviated version of the contract acceptance trial.

BUILDING BASIN. A basin in which ships are built. In construction and layout it is similar to the graving dock, being provided with dock gates and pumping plant for the admission of the quantity of water necessary to float the vessel and permit it to be towed out to the fitting-out basin. Also called building dock, shipbuilding dry dock.

Fr: *Bassin de Construction;* Ger: *Baudock.*

The ships are built on horizontal keel blocks, which is advantageous in making it possible to plumb and level structural assemblies as they are erected, after being brought out from the workshops and bays. This system also eliminates the process of launching and the difficulties and uncertainties associated with it, including the construction of launching cradles and launching ways. In some instances recessed galleries are provided on each side of the basin. They are used as storage space and for the performance of such operations as assembly of fittings, pipe threading, and so on.

Newell, W. S., "Todd Bath Basin Type Shipyard," *Marine Engineering,* New York, vol. 48 (October, 1943); Newell, "Shipyard Uses Basins," *Engineering News Record,* vol. 129 (August, 1942).

BUILDING BERTH. See **Slipway.**

BUILT BEAM. A beam formed of several sections riveted together. Also called built-up beam.

Fr: *Barrot d'Assemblage;* Ger: *Gebauter Balken.*

BUILT BLOCK. A block having its shell made of several pieces of wood or iron riveted or bolted together. Also called made block.

Fr: *Poulie d'Assemblage;* Ger: *Zusammengesetzter Block.*

BUILT FRAME. A frame in which the section is made of two bars riveted together, as distinguished from a solid frame. Owing to the developments in steel-rolling facilities this type of frame has been almost entirely superseded by bulb-angle or channel-type sections.

Fr: *Membrure Composite; Membrure d'Assemblage;* Ger: *Gebauter Spant.*

BUILT PILLAR. A pillar formed of plates and sections riveted together. Also called built-up stanchion. Today pipe stanchions made of seamless drawn or welded steel pipe have generally replaced built pillars.

Fr: *Épontille d'Assemblage;* Ger: *Profilstahlstütze.*

BUILT RUDDER FRAME. The framing of a rudder in which the arms are separate forgings or castings, these being shrunk on to and keyed to the rudderstock. Also called built-up rudder frame.

Fr: *Cadre d'Assemblage;* Ger: *Gebauter Ruderrahmen.*

BUILT SPAR. A spar composed of several pieces of wood glued together, either solid or hollowed out at the center. Also called built-up spar. Such spars are of less proportional diameter and therefore lighter than solid spars.

Fr: *Espar d'Assemblage;* Ger: *Gebaute Rundholz.*

BUILT-UP MODEL. The replica of a ship in which every structural part of the hull, frames, planks, beams, etc., is formed and fastened in place separately. Also called built model.

Davis, C. G., The Built Up Ship Model (Salem, Mass.), 1933.

BUILT-UP PROPELLER. A propeller made with separate blades. The root of each blade carries a circular flange, which fits into a corresponding recess in the boss. This

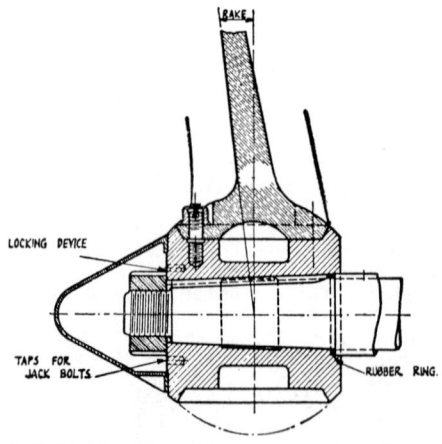

Built-Up Propeller. (*Courtesy American Bureau of Shipping*)

serves to secure the blade to the boss by stud bolts. The holes in the flanges are usually made slightly oblong, thus allowing for a slight change in the pitch by turning

the flange.
> Fr: *Hélice à Ailes rapportées;* Ger: *Schraube mit aufgesetzten Flügeln.*

BULB ANGLE. An angle bar with unequal flanges. It differs from ordinary angles in having a bulb or rib at the toe of the longest flange. Sometimes called bulb bar.
> Fr: *Cornière à Boudin;* Ger: *Wulstwinkel; Winkelbulb.*

BULB BAR.
See **Bulb Angle.**

BULB IRON.
See **Bulb Plate.**

BULB KEEL. A keel with outside ballast used in small racing craft. It is made of a vertical plate with a lead or cast iron streamlined protuberance attached to the lower edge.
> Fr: *Bulb; Quille à bulbe;* Ger: *Wulstkiel.*

BULBOUS BOW. A design of bow in which the forward frames are swelled out at the forefoot into a bulbous formation, which prevents the ship dipping too easily and in the case of long hulls assists the steering. It is credited with a higher propulsion efficiency as long as it is completely submerged, but is liable to damage if it breaks to the surface in rough weather. Also called club foot.
> Fr: *Avant à Bulbe;* Ger: *Wulstbug.*

The idea in designing a bulbous bow is to fine the waterline as much as possible, to make the flare vertical at waterline and to put the displacement removed from the vicinity of the waterline beneath the surface in the form of a bulb. It is, in theory, diametrically opposite to the Maier form. The greatest gain of this type of bow is obtained in vessels with a speed-length ratio of about 1.

Wigley, W. C. S., "The Theory of the Bulbous Bow and its Practical Application," North East Coast Institution of Engineers and Shipbuilders, Newcastle upon Tyne, *Transactions,* vol. 52 (1935-36).

BULB PLATE. A rolled plate with a bulb or swell on one edge. Used for beams, bilge keels, stringers. Generally superseded by bulb angle and Tee bulb bars. Also called bulb iron.
> Fr: *Fer à Boudin;* Ger: *Wulstplatte; Flachbulb; Flachwulstprofileisen.*

BULB TEE.
See **Tee Bar.**

BULCON. Code name of the Bulgarian Berth Contract, 1911: a grain charter party.

BULIONA. Single outrigger dugout canoe of the Balad people from northern New Caledonia.

BULK CARGO. Usually a homogeneous cargo stowed in bulk, that is to say, loose in the hold and not enclosed in any container such as boxes, bales, bags, casks, and so on. Also called bulk freight. Bulk cargo may be composed of (1) free flowing articles such as oil, grain, coal, ore, and so on, which can be pumped or run through a chute or handled by dumping; (2) articles that require mechanical handling such as coke, bricks, pig iron, lumber, steel beams, and so on.
> Fr: *Chargement en Vrac;* Ger: *Schuttladung; Bulkladung; Gleichartige Ladung.*

Hardy, A. C., *Bulk Cargoes* (London), 1926.

BULKHEAD. A name given to any vertical partition, whether fore and aft or athwartships, which separates different compartments or spaces from one another.
> Fr: *Cloison;* Ger: *Schott.*

See **Centerline Bulkhead, Collision Bulkhead, Corrugated Bulkhead, End Bulkhead, Fireproof Bulkhead, Grain Bulkhead, Joiner Bulkhead, Recessed Bulkhead, Screen Bulkhead, Structural Bulkhead, Wash Bulkhead, Watertight Bulkhead.**

BULKHEAD COAMING. A term applied to a strake of plating running across the top and bottom of poop, bridge, and forecastle bulkheads. It is thicker than the remaining plating.
> Fr: *Hiloire de Fronteau;* Ger: *Schottsulle.*

BULKHEAD DECK. The uppermost continuous deck to which all transverse watertight bulkheads are carried. It is made watertight in order to prevent any compartment accidentally open to the sea from flooding the adjacent one.
> Fr: *Pont de Cloisonnement;* Ger: *Schottendeck.*

BULKHEAD LINER. A liner fitted in the space between the boundary bar of a watertight bulkhead and the outer strake of shell plating. It is wider than the flange of the bar in order to compensate for the weakness in the outside plating due to the close spacing of rivets necessary to ensure watertightness.
> Fr: *Cale de Compensation;* Ger: *Fullplatte; Schottfullblech; Schottfullstück.*

Bulkhead

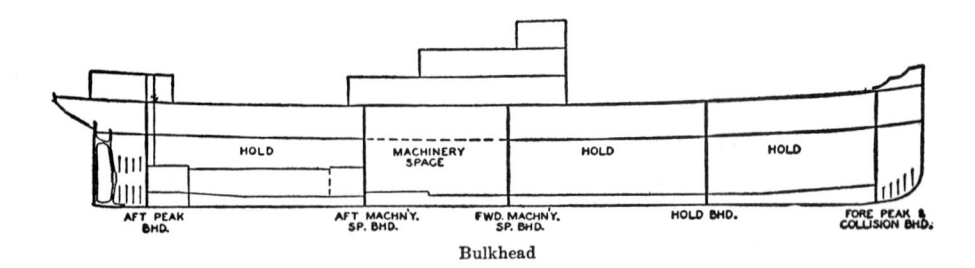

BULKHEAD SLUICE. An opening cut in a bulkhead just above the tank top connecting angle, fitted with a valve that may be operated from the deck above.

BULKHEAD STIFFENER. Bars of rolled section, angles, bulb angles, or channels, welded or riveted vertically on one side of a bulkhead to strengthen it. The scantlings of stiffeners are regulated according to the water pressure to which the bulkhead may be subjected. Stiffeners are fitted with brackets or lug attachment at both ends.

Fr: *Montant de Cloison;* Ger: *Schott Versteifungsprofil.*

BULLDOSER; BULLDOZER. A hydraulic portable machine used in shipyards for bending heavy shapes such as frames and beams. It is mounted on rollers so that it may be moved over the bending slab. A loose pin which fits the holes in the bending slab serves as an abutment for the machine.

Fr: *Presse à Cintrer;* Ger: *Spantbieger.*

BULL EARING. 1. An earing for hauling out the edge of an awning.

Fr: *Raban de Tente.*

2. An earing fastened to the yard instead of to the sail.

BULLET BLOCK. A single-sheave egg-shaped wooden block with rope strap used for jib sheets. Its shape helped to prevent it from catching in other gear as it was dragged across the headstays when going about.

BULLEY NET (U. S.). A net used in Key West (Florida) for catching spiny lobster and crawfish from a boat.

BULL GEAR. In a turbine-driven ship equipped with single reduction gears, a large, low-speed gear mounted on the forward, or inboard, end of the main shaft.

BULLHEAD RIVET. A rivet with inverted conical point which fits smooth with the surface. Also called countersunk rivet or countersunk-head rivet. Used below the water-line on shell plating to provide a smooth finish, and minimum resistance to the ship's motion through the water. Bullhead rivets are also used for staples, and bulkhead boundary bars where the heads may require caulking.

Countersunk Bullhead Rivet

Fr: *Rivet à Tête fraisée;* Ger: *Senkkopf Niete; Versenkte Niete.*

BULLJOWLER. The space used in a fishing lugger from Mount's Bay (England) for the stowage of nets and gear.

BULLOCK BLOCK. A large iron gin block fitted under the topmast crosstrees to take the topsail tie.

BULL RAIL. A heavy timber on the apron of a wooden pier.

BULL ROPE. 1. A line leading through a bull's-eye at the end of the bowsprit to a mooring buoy. Used in small craft to prevent the buoy from striking against the bows. In a general sense the term refers to any rope used to prevent some object or part from chafing or grinding against another.

2. A rope used in cargo holds by stevedores when goods have to be dragged from the ends or wings of a hold to the hatch square, to prevent the cargo fall from rasping on the underside of hatch coaming and to secure a better horizontal pull.

Ger: *Beiholer.*

3. A rope formerly used on square-rigged vessels to secure the upper yardarm of a topgallant or royal yard when sent down from aloft. It was rove through a bull's-eye fastened to the forward shroud of the lower rigging.

Ger: *Aufholer.*
See **Draw Rope.**
BULL'S EYE. 1. A round piece of thick glass, convex on one side, inserted into a weather-exposed door, skylight cover, or scuttle hatch for the purpose of admitting light. Also called fixed light.
Fr: *Verre Mort;* Ger: *Bullauge.*
2. A round or oval wooden block without sheave. It has a groove around for the strop and a hole for the lead of a rope.
See **Eye.**
BULL'S-EYE SQUALL. A squall occurring off the coasts of South Africa. It is characterized by the appearance of a small isolated cloud which marks the vortex of the atmospheric disturbance.
BULL THE BUOY. Said of a vessel or small boat whose sides bump repeatedly against a buoy.
BULLWHANGER. A short length of plaited rope, with an eye worked in the end, nailed to the back of a lower yard to prevent the earing from slipping under the yard.
BUL-VUL. A single outrigger dugout canoe from Lavongai Island (New Hanover), Bismarck Archipelago. Both ends of the hull have small carvings. The motive usually chosen is a bird's head. The dimensions of the larger canoes are: length 40.3 ft., breadth 1.7 ft., depth 2.3 ft.
BULWARK NETTING. Network made of ratline stuff or wire line seized in diamond shape and stretched between open railing stanchions on passenger decks.
Fr: *Filets de Pavois;* Ger: *Reling Netzwerk.*
BULWARK RAIL. Bulb-angle or other special section, by which the upper edge of the bulwark plating is stiffened.
Fr: *Lisse de Pavois;* Ger: *Schanzkleid Reling; Relingsleiste; Relingsprofileisen.*
BULWARKS. 1. The raised woodwork or plating running along each side of the vessel above the weather deck helping to keep the decks dry, and serving also as a fence against losing deck cargo or men overboard.
2. The upper section of the frames and side plating, which extends above and around the upper deck.
Fr: *Pavois;* Ger: *Schanzkleid; Verschanzung.*
See **Pigsty Bulwarks, Topgallant Bulwarks.**

BULWARK STANCHION. 1. In wooden hulls the upper part of top timbers extending above the plank sheer and supporting the bulwark planking.
2. In steel vessels a brace set at an angle from the deck to a bulwark plate to strengthen and support it. The heel is secured to the waterway angle bar while the upper end is bent inboard for the support of the rail. A horizontal arm called a spur is provided midway. Also called bulwark stay or bulwark brace.
Fr: *Allonge de Revers; Jambette de Pavois;* Ger: *Schanzkleidstütze.*
BULWARK STAY.
See **Bulwark Stanchion.**
BUM.
See **Boom.**
BUM BOAT. A small open rowboat employed in carrying supplies for sale to vessels in a harbor.
Ger: *Bumboot.*
BUMKIN. A short outrigger projecting from each bow and used for extending the foretack or weather clew of a square foresail (obsolete). Also called boomkin.
Fr: *Minot; Boute-Lof; Porte Lof; Pistolet d'Amure;* Ger: *Butluv.*
BUMKIN SHROUD. Strong ropes, iron stays or chains that hold the bumkins in position. Also called bumkin braces.
BUMP.
See **Fair in Place.**
BUMPER (U. S.). A shipyard blacksmith who operates with a heavy maul and does the shaping of furnaced plates; also fairing in place of shell plates in repair jobs and other similar work, called bumping.
BUNDER BOAT. Open sailing boat about 30 ft. long with 2½ ft. draft, rigged with a lateen sail, used by licensed watermen on Bombay Harbor.
BUNG.
See **Plug.**
BUNGAY. A small sailing coaster of Central America, schooner-rigged, with two headsails. Trades between Belize and North Honduras.
BUNK; COT-BED. 1. A raised recess or compartment enclosed on three sides, used as sleeping berth in ships.
2. A semiportable sleeping berth accommodating two or three men, each above the other, on a pipe berth. The pipe berths hinge and stow vertically when not in use The word is used in contradistinction to

"hammock." A bunk is fixed, a hammock slung.

Fr: *Couchette;* Ger: *Koje.*

BUNK BOARD. 1. A vertical wooden board placed on the side of a sleeping bunk nearest to the ship's side in steel vessels to protect the occupant from sweat or condensation. Bunk boards are compulsory in crew spaces, according to regulations.

2. A portable wooden board fitted along the open side of a bunk to keep the occupant from being thrown out on the deck when the ship rolls heavily.

Fr: *Planche à Roulis.*

BUNKER. 1. A compartment for storing fuel below decks.

Fr: *Soute;* Ger: *Bunker.*

See **Cross Bunker, Hold Bunker, Permanent Bunker, Pocket Bunker, Side Bunker, Spare Bunker, Temporary Bunker, 'Tween-deck Bunker.**

2. To load coal or fuel into a vessel's bunker for its own use as distinguished from loading it as cargo. The meaning of the term is usually limited to the conveyance of the fuel over the ship's sides. Handling and trimming of solid fuel form separate services.

Fr: *Souter;* Ger: *Bunkern.*

BUNKER CLAUSE. A charter party clause stating that charterers are to take over and pay for bunkers on delivery of vessel and owners are to take over and pay for bunkers on redelivery at current price of respective ports. This clause usually states the maximum and minimum number of bunkers there are to be on board on delivery and redelivery of vessel.

Ger: *Bunkerklausel.*

BUNKER RING. Cast-iron ring cover, fitted flush with the deck where coal bunkers are loaded through circular deck scuttles.

Fr: *Bouchon de Soute;* Ger: *Bunker Deckel.*

BUNKER SCUTTLE. A circular opening in a deck consisting of a cast-iron rim riveted to the deck. Its upper edge is flush with the deck planking or plating. Into this rim fits a portable cast-iron cover whose upper surface is grooved to prevent slipping. Also called coal scuttle, flush scuttle, deck scuttle.

Fr: *Trou à Charbon;* Ger: *Kohlenloch; Bunkerschuttloch; Kohlenbunkerloch.*

BUNKER STAY. A horizontal tie piece between bunker bulkhead and ship's side.

Fr: *Entretoise de Soute;* Ger: *Bunkerstütze; Bunkeranker.*

BUNT. 1. Part of a seine consisting of a square of 400 to 500 meshes in the center of the net made of heavy twine and bearing practically the whole weight of the catch when the seine is pursed.

2. In a trawl net, the portion of the wings nearest to the quarters.

3. The bag, pouch, or middle part of a sail that serves to catch the wind and keep it. In furled sail the bunt is the middle gathering which is tossed up on the center of the yard. Also called belly.

Fr: *Fond;* Ger: *Bauch; Buk.*

See **High Bunt, Low Bunt.**

BUNT APRON. Strengthening pieces sewed in the middle of a square sail to take the chafe of the mast and top. Also called mast lining.

Fr: *Renfort de Chapeau.*

BUNT GASKET. A gasket fastened to the bending jackstay at the middle of the yard for securing the bunt of a large square sail (whole topsail or course). It is made of wove matting 2 or 3 lengths wide, with the two legs crossed and an eye in each end, or of a triangular piece of canvas fastened by its base to the jackstay and with an eye at the point where the bunt jigger is clapped on.

Fr: *Couillard;* Ger: *Bauchbeschlag; Bauchseising; Bukbandsel.*

BUNTING. A fabric made of long staple coarse English wool in an open and plain weave having two-ply warp and single weft. It dyes with brilliant effects and is used for making flags. It is usually supplied in bolts of 40 yds. with a width of 18 in. and a weight of about 5¼ lbs.

Fr: *Etamine;* Ger: *Flaggentuch.*

BUNT JIGGER. A purchase formerly used for rousing up the bunt when furling a whole topsail. Also called top jigger, bunt whip. A bunt whip was used for lighter sails.

Fr: *Palan d'Hune; Chapeau;* Ger: *Bauchaufholer.*

BUNT JIGGER BECKET. A rope, span, or bridle placed in the middle of a yard to haul up and stow the bunt of a sail. Also called bunt slab line, bunt apron lanyard.

Fr: *Couillard;* Ger: *Bauchstropp.*

BUNTLINE. One of the lines hauling the foot of a sail above and forward of the yard for convenience in furling. Buntlines are rove through blocks at the masthead or the

top rim, lead down forward, and toggle to the foot of the sail some distance outside the midship line on each side.
Fr: *Cargue-Fond;* Ger: *Buggording; Bauchgording.*

BUNTLINE CLOTH. The lining sewed up a sail in the direction of a buntline to prevent it from being chafed.
Fr: *Bande de Cargue Fond;* Ger: *Bauchgordinglapp; Bukslapp.*

BUNTLINE HITCH. A hitch formerly used for bending buntlines to the foot of a square sail. Consists of a clove hitch tied around its own standing part in the opposite way, to which two half hitches are taken.

BUNTLINE SPAN. A piece of rope with a cringle for a buntline to reeve through.
Fr: *Patte de Cargue Fond;* Ger: *Buggording Spann.*

BUNTLINE TOGGLE. A toggle seized to the footrope of a sail, to which the buntline is attached by an eye.
Fr: *Cabillot de Cargue Fond;* Ger: *Bauchgordingknebel.*

BUNT LIZARD. A piece of rope having two legs with a thimble spliced to the end of each and made fast to the topsail tie. The buntlines reeve through the thimbles, which act as fair-leaders.
Fr: *Guide de Cargue Fond;* Ger: *Bauchgordingbrille.*

BUOY. A floating object employed as an aid to mariners to mark the navigable limits of channels, their fairways, sunken dangers, isolated rocks, mined or torpedo grounds, telegraph cables, and the like. An *anchor buoy,* made fast by a line to the anchor, is used to mark the position of a ship's anchor after letting it go. *Mooring buoys* are used for securing a ship in lieu of anchoring. They vary in size and construction from a log of wood to the large steel mooring buoys used for ocean liners.
Fr: *Bouée;* Ger: *Boje; Tonne.*

BUOYAGE. 1. The fee paid by a vessel for the use of mooring buoys. Sometimes called buoy hire.
Fr: *Droits d'Amarrage.*

2. The provision of buoys and beacons for the guidance of mariners along the coast and into harbors, rivers, and so on. Also called coast marking.
Fr: *Balisage;* Ger: *Betonnung; Betonnungssystem.*

The French term "balisage" includes beacons and buoys, while the English word "buoyage" refers only to buoys. Two systems of buoyage are in use:

(a) The lateral system, which lends itself more particularly to the marking of well-defined channels, and which indicates the location of dangers in relation to the route to be followed by navigators in their vicinity.

(b) The cardinal system, which lends itself more particularly to the marking of shoals, and which indicates the direction of the mark from the danger. This direction is defined by characteristics appropriate to the nearest point of the true compass.

Buoyage includes all fixed or floating marks other than lightships and lighthouses, serving to indicate either natural dangers or the lateral limits of navigable channels or accidental obstacles such as wrecks. Great Britain, Foreign Office, *International Agreement for a Uniform System of Maritime Buoyage,* Miscellaneous 8, London, 1937; International Hydrographic Bureau, Monaco, *Buoyage and Buoy Lighting Systems of the World,* U. S. Hydrographic Office, Washington, 1926.

BUOYANCY. The resultant of upward forces, exerted by a liquid upon a floating body equal to the weight of water displaced by this body.
Fr: *Flottabilité;* Ger: *Schwimmfähigkeit; Auftriebskraft; Schwimmkraft.*
See **Center of Buoyancy, Reserve Buoyancy.**

BUOYANCY TANK. One of the metal or wooden watertight cases fitted inside a lifeboat to provide increased buoyancy and prevent the boat from sinking if filled with water. Such tanks are made of wood, copper, or galvanized sheet steel. Also called boat tank, air case, air tank.
Fr: *Caisson à Air;* Ger: *Bootstank; Luftkasten.*

The required buoyancy may be given by placing the tanks along the sides, or by having end tanks at bow and stern, or by using a combination of both systems. When tanks are made of wood they are of the built-in type, one or two layers of planking being used. In British foreign-going vessels wooden air cases are not allowed, copper or yellow brass being the only materials permitted.

BUOYANT APPARATUS. A general term for deck seats, deck chairs, life rafts, life floats and other similar objects found on passenger vessels that have sufficient buoyancy to assist survivors of a sinking vessel to keep afloat.
Fr: *Flotteur;* Ger: *Schwimmgerät.*

The buoyancy is ascertained by dividing by 32 the number of pounds of iron that an apparatus is capable of supporting in fresh water. The result gives the number of persons it is capable of supporting. The buoyant apparatus must have a line becketed around the outside, and must be of such size, strength, and weight as to be handled without mechanical appliances and thrown overboard, without damage, from the deck where it has been stowed.

BUOY DUES. Port charges assessed against the ship for the maintenance of channel buoys.

Fr: *Droits de Balisage;* Ger: *Bakengeld.*

BUOY MOORINGS. Permanent moorings in which the mooring cable is carried up to the water surface and supported by a large mooring buoy. The ship is secured to the buoy by a hawser or by its own cable.

Fr: *Corps Mort à Coffre;* Ger: *Festmachertonne.*

BUOY LINE. 1. Generic term for a line connecting a surface buoy and submerged fishing gear.

2. A name given by fishermen to each of the small ropes about 2 or 3 fathoms long connecting the back or top or cork rope of a drift net to buoys, dans, or pallets. Also called buoy rope.

Fr: *Badingue;* Ger: *Bojereep.*

BUOY ROPE BEND.
See **Fisherman's Bend.**

BUOY SLING. A sling used for keeping a buoy riding upright; rope fittings about a wooden buoy to which the buoy rope is so attached that the buoy will ride upright.

Fr: *Patte de Bouée;* Ger: *Bojestropp.*

BUQUE. An open boat used for inshore fishing on the coasts of Portugal. It has a curved stem with raised headpiece and round stern. Rig, single mast with lateen sail. Used as a tender to the *galeao* for seining.

BUR.
See **Roove.**

BURDEN. The number of tons of lading which a ship is able to carry in addition to the weight of her hull and equipment. Sometimes called burthen. It is equal to the difference between the displacement when light and the displacement when loaded. In Great Britain the term "tons burthen" is understood in practice, and always construed to mean the net registered tonnage of a vessel.

Fr: *Portée Utile;* Ger: *Tragfähigkeit; Tragkraft; Ladefähigkeit.*

BURDENED VESSEL. The vessel which according to the rules of the road for two approaching vessels should keep out of the way of the other one.

BURDWOOD'S TABLES. Azimuth tables for the sun in general use in the British merchant service. The azimuth is given for each 4 minutes of time or at 2 minute intervals when changing rapidly. Minutes of arc are expressed by tenths of degrees. Similar tables in the U. S. are called "Rev Azimuth Tables."

BUREAU OF LIGHTHOUSES (U.S.). A Federal agency under the Department of Commerce, created in 1910, to replace the Lighthouse Board. It was placed under the authority of the Commissioner of Lighthouses and was responsible for the construction, operation and upkeep of land structures and floating equipment on the United States Coast, and the Great Lakes. The service outside Washington was divided into 19 districts, each under the charge of a lighthouse inspector. In 1938 the Bureau of Lighthouses was transferred to the Treasury Department and placed under the U. S. Coast Guard.

BUREAU VERITAS. French classification society and register of shipping established in 1828 and officially appointed for the assignment of freeboard in France and in Great Britain.

Symbols:

✺ ① 3/3 L.1.1. indicates the highest class for steel vessels. The encircled "I" expresses the first division, of which there are three. The division is determined by the scantlings of the hull. The two rings denote that the ship is divided into a sufficient number of watertight compartments to enable her to remain afloat in smooth water with any two open to the sea. A single circle has the same meaning but refers to one compartment instead of two.

The sign "3/3" indicates the condition of hull and machinery, of which "3/3" is the best. Other signs such as "5/6" indicate a lower standard.

The letter "L" indicates that the vessel is classed for unrestricted ocean trading. Other letters for limited or restricted ocean trading are "G" for great coasting trade, "P" for small coasting trade, "M" for Mediterranean or channel trade, "A" for Atlantic trade.

The first figure of the symbol "1.1" indicates that the structural wooden parts of the hull (decks, ceilings, etc.) are entirely satisfactory. The second figure has the same significance in respect to the vessel's equipment and includes masts, spars, rigging, anchors, and cables. The numbers vary from "1.1" to "3.3" according to standard obtained.

The letters "P.R." indicate that the vessel has been strengthened for ice; the letters "A and C.P." that anchors and cables have been tested in accordance with the Society's rules.

A diamond enclosing the character denotes that the ship is a passenger vessel which has complied with the regulations of the International Convention for Safety of Life at Sea.

The character of a sailing ship enclosed within a square shows that the subdivision is so arranged that each mast is located in a separate watertight compartment.

The class of wooden vessels is indicated by a number (in heavy type), which precedes the character of the vessel. This number varies from 16 to 3 and indicates the division in which the vessel has been classed, which is determined according to method of construction and scantlings. When two numbers precede the character of the vessel the first one indicates the division and the second the duration in years assigned to the character. For instance, 12–10 signifies that the vessel belongs to the 12 years division and is classed for 10 years.

The other symbols are the same as for steel vessels.

BURGEE. A swallow-tailed flag used as a distinguishing pennant by yachts and merchant vessels. In merchant vessels it often bears the name of the vessel. On yachts it usually bears the insignia of the owner's club. There are two burgees in the International Code of Signals: Letters "A" and "B." The relative dimensions of a burgee are usually one-half the length at heading and one-fourth at swallow tail.

Fr: *Guidon;* Ger: *Doppelständer; Splitflagge.*

See **Club Burgee.**

BURGOO. Seamen's slang for porridge.

BURLAP. A light kind of sacking manufactured of jute and used for making bags, separation cloths, and so on.

Fr: *Toile de Jute;* Ger: *Grobe Leinwand; Sackleinwand.*

BURNED OUT CONDITION.
See **Spent.**

BURNER. A term generally applied to the entire assembly of apparatus, mounted on the front of an oil-burning marine boiler, which delivers fuel oil, and air for combustion of the oil, to the furnace. The major parts of the burner assembly are the atomizer, the air register, and the valves and fittings required for connecting the atomizer to the fuel oil line and for controlling the flow of oil to the atomizer.

Fr: *Brûleur;* Ger: *Oelbrenner.*

BURNING TORCH.
See **Flame Cutter.**

BURN-OFF PLATE. A device used for releasing a vessel when launched. It consists of a steel plate attached to the forward end of each sliding way and is also secured to the ground ways. The plate is burned off with acetylene torches when the ship is to be released. Also called sole plate.

BURR EDGE. The rough uneven edge of a punched or burned hole, or plate.

BURTON. A small tackle formed by two blocks with a hook block in the bight of the running part. Generally used for setting up or tightening the rigging or to shift weights, or for other various purposes.

Fr: *Palan de Hune; Palan de Dimanche;* Ger: *Klappläufer.*

See **Double Spanish Burton, Single Burton, Spanish Burton, Top Burton.**

BURTON FALL.
See **Yard Whip.**

BURTONING.
See **Burton System.**

BURTON MAN. One of a stevedore gang who stands on deck and throws the hook of the hatch fall around the burton fall in the so-called "Burton system" of handling cargo.

BURTON PENDANT. A long rope with a loop which goes over a topmast head with an eye spliced at each end. The loop is not in the middle of the rope so that one leg is long and the other short. It is used for lifting heavy weights.

Fr: *Pantoire de Candelette;* Ger: *Marsstange Hänger.*

BURTON SYSTEM. A method of loading or unloading cargo which is similar to the double-whip or split-fall system (see "Whip"). Also called Burtoning.

The two systems differ in that in the "Burton System" the draft after being lifted from the pier or barge is *not* landed on deck before being lowered through the hatchway. A man called the "Burton man" is stationed on deck and throws the hook of the *hatch whip* around the *yard whip* while the draft is being lifted from the pier, the two falls being thus united. Just before the draft is about to be lowered through the hatchway the burton man releases the hook of the yard whip and throws it back to the pier for another draft. When unloading the movements are reversed.

BURTON TACKLE (U. S.). A method of

handling cargo with ship's gear, in which the process of lifting and slewing the drafts is effected with two derricks held in a fixed position, and two whips. The ends of the whips are fastened (married) to a single cargo hook. One derrick, called hatch boom, extends over the hatchway and plumbs it. The other, called yard boom, is swung outboard over the edge of the pier or over a lighter lying alongside.

When unloading, the draft, after being lifted clear of the ship's hold by the hatch whip, is swung clear of the ship's side and lowered by the yard whip while the other whip is slackened.

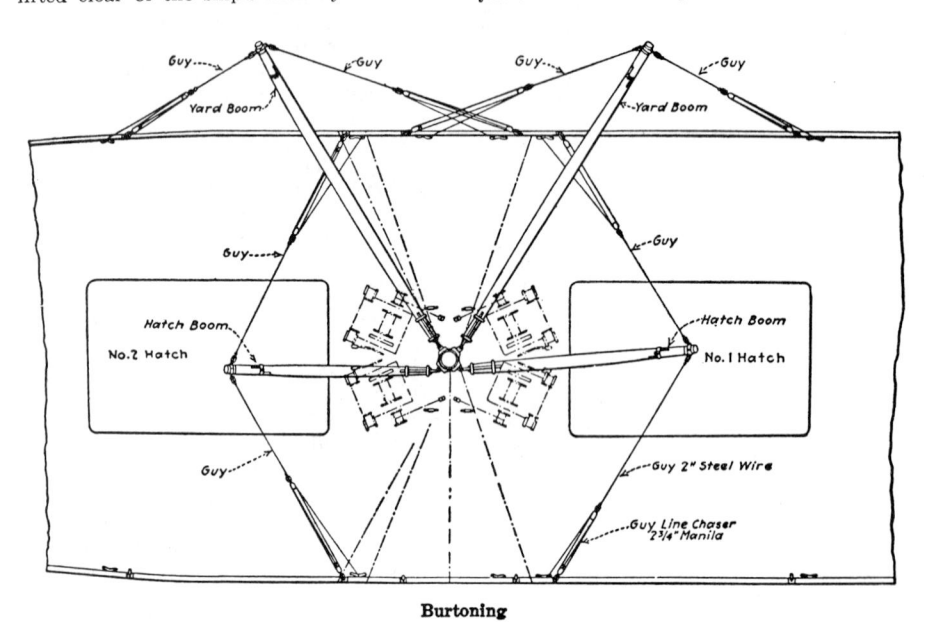

BURY. See **Housing**.

BUSH. A square-shouldered piece of metal fitted in the center of the sheave of a block and forming the bearing for the pin. Also called bushing, coak, bouching.

Fr: *Dé*; Ger: *Hülse; Busch.*

BUSHEL (G. B.). A fish measure used in Great Britain. The equivalent of ½ cwt. of sprats.

BUSO. A small double-ended open boat used as a tender to larger fishing craft in Spain; also as ship's boat.

BUSS. A two-masted schooner-rigged vessel from 50 to 70 tons burthen, carrying two houses or sheds one at each end, and formerly employed in the herring fisheries of the North Sea. Now extinct.

BUSTER. Heavy squall lasting from one to three hours observed on the south and southeast coasts of Australia. The direction of the wind is from south to southeast. Also called southerly buster.

BUTT. 1. The end of two planks or plates which exactly meet endwise. Also called end joint. In wooden shipbuilding both ends are calked. In riveted steel ships butts are joggled, lapped, or strapped for riveting, and caulked afterwards. In welded construction, butt joints are usually V'd or J'd out before welding; no calking is necessary.

2. A cross joint or a longitudinal part.

Fr: *About;* Ger: *Stoss.*

BUTT BLOCK. A piece of wood which serves as a backing to the butts of outside planking. Also called back strap. The minimum thickness of back straps should be equal to that of the planking.

Ger: *Plankenstoss.*

BUTT CALKING. The calking of a butt joint of steel plates; the edge of each plate near the joint is split, usually with an air-driven chisel, and the two edges forced together with a calking tool, usually driven

Burtoning

by an air hammer. This is done to obtain a watertight joint.

Fr: *Matage d'About;* Ger: *Stossverstemmung.*

BUTT CHOCK. Angular piece of wood tree nailed to the heads and heels of frame timbers at their abutments to act as a lap to the joint and make up the deficiency at the inner angle.

Fr: *Cale d'Empatture;* Ger: *Stosskolben.*

BUTTER BOX (G. B.). Name formerly given to brig-rigged trading vessels of bluff form, from London, Bristol and other English ports (obsolete).

BUTTER RIG. A topsail schooner rig, in which a topgallant sail was set flying over double topsails. Butter-rigged schooners were used in the nineteenth century for carrying dairy products on the east coast of England and were so called to distinguish them from schooners carrying a standing fore-topgallant yard.

BUTTERWORTH TANK CLEANING SYSTEM. A device for cleaning and gas-freeing oil tanks by means of high-pressure jets of hot water. The apparatus consists essentially of double opposed nozzles which rotate slowly about their horizontal and vertical axes, projecting two streams of hot water at a pressure of about 175 lb. per sq. in., against all inside surfaces of the deck, bulkheads and shell plating. The combination of heat and velocity result in removing thoroughly oil and oil-soaked scale even on surfaces that are not directly exposed to the streams.

BUTTING. The placing of two planks or plates end to end. Also called abutment.

Fr: *Aboutement;* Ger: *Stossung.*

BUTT JOINT. A term applied where the connection between two parts is made by bringing their ends or edges together and fastening them with a strap which overlaps both pieces. Sometimes called flush joint. Butt connections can also be made by welding, in which case a strap is not necessary.

Fr: *Joint à Franc-Bord;* Ger: *Stossverbindung.*

BUTTJOLLE.
See **Jolle.**

BUTTOCK. 1. The intersection of the molded surface of a ship's hull with a vertical plane at a given distance from the center longitudinal plane of the ship and parallel to it. Buttocks are shown in the profile drawing of the ship's lines. **2.** The rounded overhanging portion of the lower stern in front of the rudder, merging underneath into the run.

Fr: *Fesses;* Ger: *Bilien.*

BUTTOCK LINES. The lines representing the traces of vertical sections parallel to the vessel's longitudinal center plane. They are called bow lines when in the forebody, and buttock lines when in the afterbody. Bow and buttock lines are spaced at convenient equal intervals from the ship's center line to the outside edge on the midship section. Thus, a two-foot buttock indicates two lines two feet outboard from the center line on both port and starboard sides.

Fr: *Sections longitudinales;* Ger: *Schnitte; Sentenriss.*

BUTTOCK STAFF. The upper timbers forming the framing of the rounded part of a vessel's stern.

BUTTON. A leather stop fitted to the loom of an oar to prevent it from slipping outboard. It consists usually of a collar made up of two thicknesses of sole leather, nailed on. Buttons are seldom fitted to sea oars except those used on pleasure craft.

BUTT PLATE. A short plate extending from frame to frame in composite ships, placed under the butts of two planks of the same strake so as to stiffen the butt.

Fr: *Tôle d'About;* Ger: *Stossplatte.*

BUTT RIVETING. The edges of two plates brought one against the other and riveted to a covering plate or strap, embracing the two.

Fr: *Rivetage à Franc Bord;* Ger: *Stossblechvernietung; Stossvernietung.*

BUTT STRAP. Strip of plating which connects the plates of a butt joint.

Fr: *Couvre-Joint;* Ger: *Laschblech; Stossblech.*

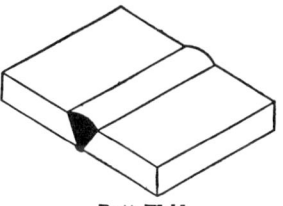

Butt Weld

BUTT WELD. The welding of a butt joint.

Fr: *Soudure à Franc-Bord; Soudure bout à bout;* Ger: *Stumpfschweissung; Stossschweissung.*

BUY BOAT (U. S.). Generic term for

boats operated by fish dealers who buy the catch on the fishing grounds from other craft.

BUYS BALLOT'S LAW. A natural law discovered by the Dutch professor, Buys Ballot, and which is of considerable value to seamen. It states that if an observer stands facing the wind, the center of low atmospheric pressure will be from 8 to 12 points on the observer's right hand in the Northern Hemisphere, and on his left hand in the Southern Hemisphere.

BUZZO. Sicilian sail- and rowboat engaging in the net-and-line fisheries at Trapani and adjacent waters. It is an open boat with flat bottom. The sides have a great amount of flare. Rig, one portable mast with lateen sail. The mast is always unstepped when fishing, sailing being only resorted to when leaving or making port. Average dimensions: Length 29 to 36 ft. Breadth 9.8 to 12 ft. Depth 3.9 to 4.9 ft. Crew 4 to 10.

In Cefalu, on the north coast of Sicily, the *buzzo* is a smaller boat with a length ranging from 10 to 13 ft. and a crew of 3 or 4 hands.

BY THE HEAD. 1. To go by the head, to sink head foremost. Said of a foundering ship.

Fr: *Par l'Avant;* Ger: *Vorlastig.*

2. The state of a ship which by her lading or through some other cause draws more water forward than aft.

Fr: *Sur Tête;* Ger: *Kopflastig.*

BY THE RUN. To let go a rope altogether when lowering instead of keeping a turn on a cleat or belaying pin.

Fr: *Filer en grand; Filer en bande.*

BY THE STERN (G. B.). The state of a ship which by her lading or build has an excess of draft aft as compared to forward. In the United States called drag.

Fr: *Sur Cul;* Ger: *Achterlastig.*

BY THE WIND. Sailing as nearly to the direction of the wind as the ship will lie with her sails full. In sailing-ship parlance, within six points of the wind. Also called on the wind, on a wind, upon a wind.

Fr: *Au Plus Près;* Ger: *Beim Winde.*

See **Before the Wind, Between Wind and Water, Down the Wind, In the Wind, Off the Wind, To the Wind, Under the Wind.**

C

C and E COMMISSION AND EXCHANGE.
CC. CIVIL COMMOTION.
C.E. CENTRE OF EFFORT (*naval architecture*).
C. I. CONSULAR INVOICE.
C.F.O. COAST FOR ORDERS or CALLING FOR ORDERS (*chartering*).
C.I.F. COSTS INSURANCE AND FREIGHT. It means that the goods are to be provided by the seller, all necessary charges and freight and insurance having been paid.
Fr: *Cout; Assurance; Fret;* Ger: *Kosten; Versicherung; Fracht.*
C.I.F. and C and I COSTS INSURANCE AND FREIGHT AND COMMISSION AND INTEREST. The banks charge the shippers interest from the time that the draft is negotiated until the remittance arrives at place of shipment.
C.I.F.L.T. COST INSURANCE AND FREIGHT LONDON TERMS.
C/L CRAFT LOSS (*insurance*).
C.L.R. CENTER OF LATERAL RESISTANCE (*naval architecture*).
co-L CO-LATITUDE (*navigation*).
CONT. (B.H.) Bordeaux-Hamburg range of continental ports (*chartering*).
CONT. H.H. Le Havre-Hamburg range of continental ports (*chartering*).
C.P. CHARTER PARTY.
C/P CUSTOM OF THE PORT (*grain trade*).
C.P.D. CHARTERER PAYS DUES.
C/T CONFERENCE TERMS.
C.T.L. CONSTRUCTIVE TOTAL LOSS (*insurance*).
C.T.L.O. CONSTRUCTIVE TOTAL LOSS ONLY.

C-1 VESSEL. A single-screw cargo vessel of United States Maritime Commission standardized design, propelled by geared turbine or Diesel engines. There are two classes in this category: one of the full scantling type; the other of the shelter-deck type.

	C-1 Full Scantling Type	C-1 Shelter-Deck Type
Length over-all..	416 ft.	413 ft.
Length Betw. Perp.	395 ft.	390 ft.
Breadth molded..	60 ft.	60 ft.
Depth molded ...	37 ft. 6 in.	37 ft. 6 in.
Draft	27 ft. 6 in.	23 ft. 6 in.
Deadweight capacity	9,000 tons	7,400 tons
Bale capacity ...	450,146 cu. ft.	451,288 cu. ft.
Cargo capacity..	7,285 tons	6,240 tons
Displacement ...	12,875 tons	11,100 tons
Gross tonnage ..	6,750	5,000
Shaft horse-power	4,000	4,000
Speed	14 knots	14 knots
Crew	43	43
Passengers......	8	8

Marine Engineering and Shipping Review, New York, vol. 44 (August, 1939).

C-2 VESSEL. A single-screw shelter-deck vessel of United States Maritime Commission standard type with Diesel motor or geared turbine propulsion.

Length over-all	459 ft.
Length Betw. Perp..	435 ft.
Beam molded	63 ft.
Depth molded	40 ft. 6 in.
Draft loaded	25 ft. 10½ in.
Displacement loaded	13,900 tons
Tonnage gross	6,240 tons (7,169)
Tonnage net	3,730 tons (4,328)
Deadweight capacity	9,073 tons (7,618)
Grain capacity	595,890 cu. ft. (638,881)
Bale capacity	548,730 cu. ft. (562,849)
Shaft horsepower ...	6,000
Service speed	15½ knots
Crew	41
Passengers	12

Marine Engineering and Shipping Review, New York, vol. 43 (April, 1938).

C-3 VESSEL. A standard merchant vessel of United States Maritime Commission design. The hull is of the shelter-deck type with raking stem and cruiser stern. Single-screw propulsion is provided, with geared turbines or Diesel engines. There are two types of C-3 vessels; one is exclusively a cargo carrier, and the other a combination cargo and passenger vessel. With the exception of the elimination of passenger quarters requiring one deck less in the midship superstructure, the cargo type is essentially the same as the combination passenger and cargo vessel.

	C-3 Cargo Ship	C-3 Passenger and Cargo Ship
Length over-all..	492 ft.	492 ft.
Length Betw. Perp.	465 ft.	465 ft.
Breadth molded .	69 ft. 6 in.	69 ft. 6 in.
Depth molded ..	42 ft. 6 in.	42 ft. 6 in.
Draft loaded	28 ft. 6 in.	27 ft. 3 in.
Displacement ...	17,615 tons	17,600 tons
Deadweight capacity	11,920 tons	10,725 tons
Cargo capacity..	9,918 tons	9,763 tons
Bale capacity ...	730,541 cu. ft.	655,000 cu. ft.
Shaft horsepower	8,500	8,500
Speed (service).	16½ knots	16½ knots
Passengers	12	52 to 111
Crew	43	76
Gross tonnage ..	7.773	....

Marine Engineering and Shipping Review, New York, vol. 44 (January, 1939); vol. 45 (July, 1940).

CAB (G. B.). Covered-in shelter of each end of the navigation bridge.

See **Wing Shelter.**

CABALLITO. A native raft of the Peruvian coast made of reed bundles lashed together. The smallest type is made of two bundles, securely bound with ropes and with tapering ends curving upwards. At a distance of about one-fifth of the length from the stern the inner and upper reeds of each bundle terminate squarely to form the forward end of a pit, where the fish are kept. The pit, which is about a foot deep at its forward end, rises gradually to the top of the *caballito* near the stern.

The fisherman sits astride just forward of the pit with his legs hanging in the water, or resting on the side of the boat. A paddle made of a plain split of bamboo is used for propelling the *caballito*. It is claimed to be a wonderful craft in heavy weather for riding breakers and is at the same time a thoroughly practical fishing boat when manned by an experienced native. The larger *caballitos* have a length of about 15 ft.

CABANELLA. Small open boat about 16 ft. long used by the fishing master during the capture of tuna in Italian coastal waters with a *tonnara* net. It is called *musciaretta* in Sicily and *barbariccio* in Sardinia.

CABIN. 1. An apartment or small room in a ship for the use of officers or passengers.
2. In naval vessels, the captain's quarters.

Fr: *Cabine;* Ger: *Kajüte; Schiffskammer.*

See **Inside Cabin, Outside Cabin, Trunk Cabin, Bibby Tandem Cabin.**

CABIN DE LUXE. A special suite of apartments consisting of sitting room, sleeping room and bathroom found on high-class passenger vessels.

Fr: *Cabine de Luxe;* Ger: *Luxuskabine.*

CABIN LINER. A vessel with all modern standards of speed and comfort in which only one class of cabin passengers is carried instead of first and second class. The cabin class accommodation is similar to that of the second class in the three-class express liner. These vessels usually carry some cargo and may or may not have accommodation for third-class passengers. Also called cabin ship.

CABIN PASSENGER. Any passenger on board ship entitled to the use of a cabin or part of it, as distinguished from steerage passengers, who are usually accommodated in common quarters.

Fr: *Passager de Cabine;* Ger: *Kajütenfahrgast.*

The term "cabin passenger," in accordance with the British Board of Trade regulations, is applied to all passengers to whom a clear superficial space of 36 sq. ft. is allotted for the exclusive use of each adult; who are messed throughout the voyage at the same table as the master or first officer of the ship, and whose fare or passage is at least 25 pounds per adult for the entire passage, or 65 shillings for every 1,000 miles of the length of the voyage. Each cabin passenger must be in possession of a duly signed contract ticket in the form prescribed.

U. S. Passenger Act of 1882 provides that the space allotted to the exclusive use of each cabin passenger be not less than 36 clear, superficial ft. of deck space.

CABIN SHIP.
See **Liner.**

CABIN TOP. A built-on structure extending from abaft the mast to the cockpit, in small craft, leaving waterways on each side. Its purpose is to provide head room below deck. It may have a skylight on top and ports in the sides. Also called coach roof, trunk cabin.

CABIN TRUNK.
See **Cabin Top.**

CABLE. 1. A heavy fiber or wire rope or a chain. The term is most frequently used, in its nautical sense, to indicate the means by which a ship is connected with her anchor.

Fr: *Câble;* Ger: *Kabel.*

2. Heavy cordage from 10 to 30 in. in circumference made of three plain- or hawser-laid ropes twisted together left-handed.

Fr: *Câble;* Ger: *Kabeltau.*

3. A cable length, a traditional unit of nautical measure derived from the length of a ship's cable in former days, but bearing no relation to the length of a present day ship's anchor cable.

Fr: *Encâblure;* Ger: *Kabellänge.*

Authorities differ as to the length of a cable. In the British and German Navies one cable is equal to one-tenth of a nautical mile or 608 feet (185 meters). In the United States Navy one cable length is 120 fathoms or 720 ft. (219 meters). In the French Navy and in Spain since the adoption of the metric system one cable length is 200 meters (656 feet); in Portugal, 258 meters (846 feet); in Holland, 225 meters (738 feet); and in Russia, 183 meters (600 feet).

CABLE BUOY. 1. A small metal or wooden buoy made fast to the anchor by means of a rope and used to mark the position of the anchor so that, should the riding chain part or the anchor become foul, its location is still indicated by the buoy, and it may be easily recovered. Also called anchor buoy.

Fr: *Bouée d'Orin;* Ger: *Ankerboje.*

2. A small buoy, used with some types of permanent moorings. It is of no greater size than required to support a light chain attached to the mooring-cable pendant. This small chain is used for hauling the upper end of the ground chain aboard, where it is secured to the ship's cable.

Fr: *Bouée de Corps Mort;* Ger: *Vertauboje.*

CABLE CHOCK. An oval casting with horn-shaped projections extending partly over a recess, in the throat of which a cable or hawser is run. It is used for changing or maintaining the direction of a rope or chain so that it is delivered fairly to bollards, bitts, or a drum. It is designed to avoid wear and tear by friction. Chocks are placed in the forward and after ends of a ship, and sometimes along its side. Also called fairleader or warping chock.

Fr: *Chaumard de Déhalage;* Ger: *Verholklampe; Leitklampe.*

See **Bow Chock, Closed Chock, Open Chock, Roller Chock, Rowser Chock, Stern Chock.**

American Marine Standards Committee, Standard 60, *Chocks for Ships,* Washington, 1929.

CABLE CLENCH; CABLE CLINCH. 1. A half hitch stopped to its own part. Formerly used for fastening a rope cable to the anchor ring.

Fr: *Noeud d'Étalingure;* Ger: *Ankerstich.*

2. A forging secured to the ship's structure at the bottom of each chain locker to which the bitter end of a chain cable is fastened. A chain slip is secured to the bolt of the end link, the slip being triced up in the chain locker so that the cable may be slipped if required. Also called clench plate, cable holdfast.

Fr: *Étalingure d'Ancre;* Ger: *Kettenständer.*

CABLE FLAGS. Small numerical flags shown on the forecastle when cables are being worked, to indicate to the bridge how much cable is out.

CABLE HOLDER.
See **Wildcat.**

CABLE JACK. A handspike fitted with a fulcrum and a stand. Used for lifting heavy chain cables to enable slip hooks to be passed underneath.

CABLE-LAID ROPE. A term formerly exclusively applied to a rope consisting of nine strands, made by laying three plain ropes together left-handed. It is now used to denote three, or sometimes four, plain-laid, three-stranded ropes twisted together in the opposite direction to the twists in the several ropes. It is also known as water-laid rope.

Fr: *Cordage Commis en Grelin; Grelin;* Ger: *Kabelschlag Tauwerk; Kabeltrosse.*

This mode of formation is adopted principally for ropes much exposed to the action of water even though their thickness may not be very great. Cable-laid rope is harder and more compact than other kinds, but the additional twist given to cable-laid rope in laying it up makes it about 30 per cent weaker than plain-laid rope.

CABLE LIFTER.
See **Wildcat.**

CABLE MARKINGS. Marks consisting of turns of seizing wire around the studs of cable links to indicate the length of cable out of the chain locker. At the end of the first length (15 fathoms) from the anchor there is one turn of wire on the stud of the *first* studded link abaft the connecting shackle. At the end of the second length (30 fathoms) *two* turns on the *second* link and so on at each length. In U.S.A. the wire marked links are painted white so they may be more easily noted when the cable is running out.

Ger: *Ankerkette Marken.*

CABLE MOLDING. A molding carved in the form of a rope and formerly used as a decoration on a vessel's stern.

Ger: *Schiffstauverzierung.*

CABLE SHIP. A vessel usually owned by a cable company or the postal authorities, and employed for the laying down, maintenance and repairs of submarine telegraph cables. These ships must carry fuel, water, and provisions for long periods at sea as the cable repair may take a long time. Also called cable vessel, cable layer (U. S.).

Fr: *Navire Câblier;* Ger: *Kabelschiff.*

It is not possible to carry out cable work in bad weather and it frequently happens that the ship has to stand on her buoys if a blow comes up in the middle of operations. Experience has shown that reciprocating engines of the compound or triple expansion type give the best results, for this form of power is the most suitable for cable service, which requires long periods of grappling at a speed of about one knot.

The auxiliary load of a cable ship is a high one, and a comprehensive installation of special machinery is provided. Cable machinery must be capable of lifting weights up to about 20 tons from extreme depths. The most important auxiliary is the special machinery for picking up and paying out cables, including the bow and stern sheaves, over which the cable can run off, leading up to the machines and overboard. There is also the "turning-over" gear for moving cables from one tank to another, and various types of sounding apparatus. In some cable vessels the business of picking up and paying out is done by one combined engine. The paying-out gear, situated at the stern, usually consists of a large drum around which the cable passes several times in order to enable it to get a good grip. The drum is mounted on a shaft carrying brakes, controlled by automatic straps.

Paying-out gear is also fitted with a prime mover to enable it to haul cable on board again if necessary or to pull it out of the tank where the cable is of insufficient weight to lay out by its own accord. The picking-up gear, located in the bows, is usually duplicated, having one drum for the port and one for the starboard side. The two parts can be worked separately, each having its own drive. It is usual in cable-ship practice to adopt a clipper type of stem, because this permits the bow sheaves to be well clear of the hull structure, and renders the building of a platform forward of the stem unnecessary.

Long lengths of cable are carried and stored in cylindrical tanks. There are two general methods of arranging the tanks. Either two or three are placed forward of the machinery space and the remaining one aft of the machinery space.

CABLE'S LENGTH. See **Cable**.

CABLE STOPPER. Stopper provided for relieving the strain on the cable holders or riding bitts, when a vessel is riding to anchor, also for holding the cable while shifting the anchor chain, or making up for mooring. Sometimes called chain stopper.

Fr: *Stoppeur;* Ger: *Patentstopper; Kettenkneifer.*

CABLET. A cable-laid rope of less than 10 in. in circumference.

Fr: *Cablot.*

CABLE TANK. A large cylindrical tank made of light plating and used in cable vessels for stowing telegraph cables.

Fr: *Puits à Cables;* Ger: *Kabeltank.*

On large cable ships the tanks sometimes have an inner concentric tank for the stowage of cables of smaller diameter. The space at the sides of the tanks is used as a coal or oil bunker. Circular hatches are provided over the tanks. The cable is coiled on a gently tapering steel cone built from the base of the tank and fitted with a special arrangement known as crinoline to prevent the cable from kinking as it runs overboard. The interior of the cone is generally used for the storage of fresh water.

CABLE VESSEL. See **Cable Ship**.

CABOOSE. Term formerly applied to the cook room or kitchen when placed on deck. It is sometimes used to denote a portable cast-iron stove used in coasting vessels for cooking on deck.

See **Galley**.

CACHALOTE. A Spanish open fishing boat from Lequeito in the province of Vizcaya of a type between the *bonitera* and the *trainera*. In Ondarroa it is called *mirinaque*. It is of lighter construction than the *bonitera,* in order to be easier to handle with oars, but heavier than the *trainera*. In size it ranges from 7 to 13 tons. Dimensions of a 10-ton boat: length 42.1 ft.; breadth 9.2 ft.; depth 3.6 ft.

CADET OFFICER. A subjunior officer in the United States Merchant Marine; a student officer who gives the other officers such assistance as they may call upon him to give. He must have had at least two years experience in the deck department.

United States Maritime Commission, Regulations Governing Appointments as Cadet Officers in the Merchant Marine of the United States, Washington, 1939.

Fr: *Elève Officier.*

CAGE ANTENNA. A group of parallel wires arranged in the form of a cylinder, connected together, and used as an antenna.

Fr: *Antenne-Prisme.*

CAIQUE. 1. A small Turkish coaster; single-masted with sprit mainsail, square topsail, forestaysail, and one or more jibs. It is built with long bow, low waist, round bilge and high stern. The waist is generally protected by a portable canvas strake, which is removed in light weather.

2. A small, graceful, canoe-like craft

used as a rowboat on the Bosporus. It is fast but cranky. The oars have their looms enlarged into round masses to counterbalance the outboard weight. The average length of the boat varies from 40 to 50 ft., although some attain up to 66 ft. with a length to breadth ratio of about 5 to 1.

3. An open boat, occasionally named *camin*, originating from Yport and Etretat (Normandy), which has nothing in common with the lightly built Turkish craft of the same name. The *caique* from Normandy is peculiarly rigged and heavily built and was originally designed as a beach boat. Length of large boats 24½ ft. Breadth 9½ ft. Depth 5 ft. Small ones with a length of 17 to 20 ft. have two masts.

The hull is short and the lines enable these boats to spread a considerable amount of canvas. The mainmast is one and a half times the boat's length and sets a large standing lug with topsail. The lug foresail is tacked down to a small outrigger or bumkin, which has a negative steeve, that is, points toward the water surface. This sail can be used only when the sea is comparatively smooth. In a breeze the mainmast is lowered in a crutch placed on the part quarter. The foretack is then fastened to the stemhead and the sheet is taken aft. A small lug jigger assists in balancing the sail plan. There is no standing rigging with the exception of the mainstay. None of the boats are decked, but a loose planking is fitted over the beams.

4. Also *cahique*, a Portuguese fishing boat found on the coast of Algarve, Setubal, and as far north as Lisbon. Dimensions vary greatly but typical dimensions are: Length 48.5 ft. Breadth 12.7 ft. Depth 4.2 ft. Draft 3.3 ft. The internal capacity is usually between 15 and 25 cu. m.

It is rigged with two masts and settee sails. The mainmast rakes forward and the mizzenmast aft. It is decked fore and aft and has three hatches, bluff bows, and high sheer. These boats sail as far south as Larache (Morocco) and are employed in deep sea fishing.

CAISSON. 1. A device used for repairing outside damage to the hull at or below the waterline while the vessel is afloat. Also called cofferdam.

Fr: *Suçon;* Ger: *Schwalbennester.*

It consists of a strong wooden box with the top and one side open. The edges at the open side are shaped to the form of the vessel from a pattern made by a diver. They are covered with a thick padding of canvas and oakum. The box is manœuvred so as to bring the padded edges against the ship's side and the open top a foot or so above the water. The water is then pumped out and the external water pressure holds the caisson tight against the ship. Workmen can then enter the interior of the box and repair the ship's hull.

2. A steel structure used for closing the entrance of wet docks, dry docks, and locks. Also called floating caisson. Caissons are built with buoyancy chambers and ballast tanks so that by means of valves and a pump or ejector the weight of the contained water ballast can be varied at will for floating or sinking the caisson.

Fr: *Bateau-Porte;* Ger: *Schleusenschiff; Torschiff; Schleusenponton.*

See **Rolling Caisson.**

CALAO. A large, open sailing and rowing boat of heavy construction fitted with numerous thwarts (12) and used in Southern Portugal for working inshore stationary nets (*almadreva*) in the tunny and sardine fisheries. It is occasionally rigged with a lug or lateen sail. It has no sheer, a rounded stem of peculiar design, and pointed stern. *Calaos* are frequently used to carry nets and gear between fishing grounds and shore.

CALASHEE WATCH. A term of contempt for a slack watch.

CALDERETA. A hot sharp mountain wind of the northern coastal area of Venezuela.

CALDRON. A small deep or basin on the sea-bottom of more or less circular, elliptical, or oval form.

Fr: *Gouffre;* Ger: *Kessel.*

CALF. (1) A portion of a berg breaking away from the berg and rising to the surface of the water. (2) The young of a marine mammal. (3) A small island lying near a large one.

CALIFORNIA CURRENT. A current that flows south-southeasterly, following the trend of the western coast of North America. It originates in the drift from the Kuroshiwo in approximate latitude 50° north and terminates in the North Equatorial Current.

CALINEIRA. A small *lancha* from the Algarve Province used for fishing with a small dragnet named *chavega*.

CALK; CAULK. In nautical slang, to sleep when on duty.

CALKER; CAULKER. A shipyard hand who secures the water and oil tightness of the joints of a ship's structure by burring or driving up the edges of plates or angles along the riveted seams.

Fr: *Mateur;* Ger: *Stemmarbeiter.*

CALKER'S BOX; CAULKER'S BOX. Small wooden box containing oakum and used as a bench when calking wood decks.

Fr: *Selle de Calfat;* Ger: *Kalfaterfutte; Kalfaterkiste; Wergfass*

CALKING; CAULKING. 1. Burring or driving up the edges of iron or steel plates and sections along riveted seams to make them watertight.

Fr: *Matage;* Ger: *Verstemmen.*

Burtner, E., Oil and Watertight Joints in Ship's Hulls, *Marine Engineering,* New York, vol. 23, July, 1918.

2. Forcing a quantity of calking material into the seams of the planks in a ship's decks or sides to make them watertight.

Fr: *Calfatage;* Ger: *Kalfatern.*

See **Butt Calking, Lap Calking, Calking Chisel.**

After the material is driven hard, hot melted pitch or marine glue is poured into the groove to keep water from reaching it. In general practice $7/8$ in. planking is the minimum thickness that can be made watertight by the use of calking oakum. Calking cotton and cotton wicking are used for thinner planking. Planking and decking of $1/2$ in. or less is usually calked with cotton wicking (lampwicking). Light seams backed with battens can be calked with plastic material put in with a putty knife.

CALKING CHISEL; CAULKING CHISEL. A chisel used for calking the seams of riveted joints.

Fr: *Matoir;* Ger: *Stemmeisen.*

CALKING COTTON; CAULKING COTTON. Material used for calking the seams of wooden boats with planking up to $1\frac{1}{2}$ in. in thickness, instead of oakum. The seams are subsequently puttied.

Fr: *Coton à Calfater;* Ger: *Kalfater Baumwolle.*

CALKING EDGE; CAULKING EDGE. The edge which is accessible for calking. In shell and deck plating it is the outside or sight edge.

Fr: *Côté Matage;* Ger: *Stemmkante; Stemmseite.*

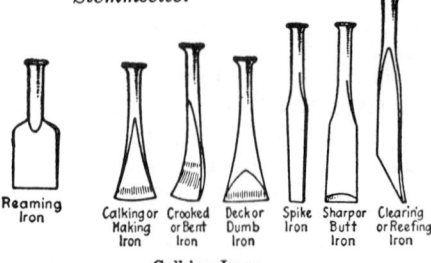

Reaming Iron | Calking or Making Iron | Crooked or Bent Iron | Deck or Dumb Iron | Spike Iron | Sharpor Butt Iron | Clearing or Reefing Iron

Calking Irons

CALKING IRON; CAULKING IRON. A general term for the various chisels used in calking wooden ships.

Fr: *Ciseau de Calfat; Fer de Calfat;* Ger: *Kalfateisen.*

CALKING MALLET; CAULKING MALLET. A mallet or beetle for driving calking irons. A long head and short-handled wood mallet with metal hoops used by calkers for striking a reaming, opening, calking, or horsing iron. The handle is comparatively short and wedge-shaped at the hammerhead, so that it may be quickly shipped or unshipped at will.

Fr: *Maillet de Calfat;* Ger: *Kalfater Hammer; Stemmknüppel.*

CALKING SIDE; CAULKING SIDE. That side of riveted watertight plating from which the butts and seams are calked.

CALKING WELD; CAULKING WELD. A light, continuous weld, used where strength is not important; where the seam is to be watertight, oiltight, or gastight. The weld should be so executed that no leakage is visible under a water, oil or air pressure of 25 lb. per square inch. Also called sealing bead.

CALKING WHEEL; CAULKING WHEEL. A device used for calking the seams of light planking under $5/8$ in. in thickness with a single strand of wicking.

CALK SEAM; CAULK SEAM. A slightly beveled joint formed by two timbers or planks that are to be calked. The amount of bevel given is about one-sixteenth of an inch for each inch depth of seam.

CALL. To make a short stop in a harbor, etc.

Fr: *Faire Escale;* Ger: *Anlaufen.*

CALLAO ROPE (U. S.). A mooring device used by lighters when working cargo alongside a vessel anchored in an open roadstead. It consists of a 15-ft. length of fiber cordage about 12 inches diameter with a wire pendant at each end.

CALLING FOR ORDERS. A situation which arises when a vessel leaves her final loading port before actual discharging ports within a certain range are named. It gives the vessel her right to break her voyage and collect orders as to discharging ports. This situation seldom occurs since wireless messages can be sent while vessel is at sea.

CALLING THE SOUNDINGS. The announcement made in a loud voice by the leadsman, who gives the depth of water when heaving the hand lead.

Fr: *Chanter la Sonde;* Ger: *Loten ausrufen.*

In calling the soundings the following phraseology is used:

If on an exact fathom which has a distinctive mark, "by the *mark* two" (or three, five, seven, etc.).

If on an exact fathom which has no identifying mark, "by the *deep* four" (or six, eleven, eighteen, etc.).

If between fathoms, to the nearest quarter, as, "and a quarter six" or "a quarter less five."

CALL SIGNAL. Radio signal used to identify a particular radio station.

Fr: *Indicatif d'appel;* Ger: *Anrufzeichen.*

CALM. The state or condition of the atmosphere when there is no wind.

Fr: *Calme;* Ger: *Windstille.*

CALUP. A small, open fishing boat found in the district of Pauillac and the Estuary of the River Gironde (France). Length 16½ ft. Breadth 5 ft. Depth 1 ft. 8 in.

CALVING. The breaking away of a mass of ice from a berg or glacier.

Fr: *Vélage.*

CAMBER. The roundup or convexity of a ship's deck beams, the form of which is a segment of a circle or part of a parabola. Also called crop, round of beam, crown of beam.

Fr: *Bouge;* Ger: *Balkenbucht.*

The standard camber for beams of weather decks, measured as total rise, varies from 1/50 to 1/48 of the ship's beam amidships. It is measured at the center line of the ship at greatest molded-breadth, and is the distance from the chord to the top of the arch.

CAMBERED WAYS. Standing ways having a declivity in the form of a camber, which gradually gets greater toward water end. The effect of this during the launching is to shorten the time that the forward poppets are under strain owing to increase of acceleration when the stern is waterborne.

Fr: *Voie de Lancement à Profil Courbe;* Ger: *Kreisförmige Ablaufbahn.*

CAMEL. 1. A heavy fender float used for keeping a vessel off a wharf or quay, usually consisting of four square logs bolted together.

2. A buoyant device consisting of a hollow steel cylinder or a pontoon of shipshape form used in salvage work. Also called lifting pontoon.

Fr: *Chameau; Ponton de Relevage;* Ger: *Kamel; Hebeleichter; Hebezylinder; Hebeprahm.*

After being well secured to the wreck the camel is pumped out, its buoyancy giving it the required lifting power. A central well is usually provided, through which the lifting cables or chains are taken to the winches. The lifting capacity of these craft ranges from 50 to 250 tons.

During the First World War, Messrs. Vickers, Armstrong built an apparatus for this purpose, consisting of very large waterproofed canvas bags interconnected by a tube made of the same material. The lifting power was obtained by filling them with compressed air supplied by a salvage vessel

CANAL PORT. A port similar to a river port, the difference being that the waterway is entirely artificial.

CANARIES CURRENT. A southwesterly flowing current off the northwest coast of Africa.

CAN BUOY. A truncated buoy with flat top.

Fr: *Bouée en cône renversé;* Ger: *Stumpfe Tonne.*

CANCELING DATE. A stated date after which, if a vessel is not ready to load, the intending charterers have the option of canceling the charter. The passing of the canceling date leaves the owner's obligation unimpaired unless the charterer releases him.

Fr: *Date de Résiliation;* Ger: *Widerrufsdatum.*

CANCELLATION CLAUSE; CANCELING CLAUSE. A clause in a charter party whereby the charterer reserves the right to cancel the charter if the ship fails to arrive on a specified day at a named port, ready to load.

Fr: *Clause d'Annullation;* Ger: *Cancelling Klausel.*

CANDLE POWER. A unit of luminous intensity used in a light-list to designate the power of the light. Most maritime countries have adopted since 1909 the international candle (equal to one decimal candle).

Fr: *Bougie;* Ger: *Normalkerze.*

CAN HOOKS. A contrivance for slinging a cask by the ends of the staves. Also called chine hooks. It is composed of a piece of rope or chain with a flat hook at each end, the tackle or fall being hooked in the middle of the bight. The rope or chain is sometimes replaced by two rods fastened to a center ring.

Fr: *Patte à Futaille;* Ger: *Klammenhaken.*

CANNED GOODS. An expression covering all canned or tinned meats, fish, fruits, jams, and so on, usually shipped in cases.

Fr: *Conserves en Boîtes;* Ger: *Konserven.*

CANNED WILLIE (U. S.). Slang term for canned corned beef.

CANOA. 1. An open sailing boat found on the coast of Brazil, rigged with two or three short masts and lateen sails. Length 23 to 72 ft. Breadth 2 ft. 2 in. to 4 ft. Depth 16 to 28 in. The mainmast has a slight forward rake. The other masts are vertical. The hull is built with long overhangs at bow and stern. The smaller boats of this type with sharper sections are also known under the name of *batelao.*

2. A small fishing boat from Southern Portugal also used for transporting the catch of other boats. There are several types of *canoas,* known locally as *canoa de Picada, Enviada,* or *Andaina.*

The hulls are built with straight stem and transom or sharp stern. The larger boats of this class are decked fore and aft. The smaller ones are half decked or open and remain near the shore. The rig in most types is composed of a single mast with lateen sail. Some of the open boats carry a spritsail. There are no headsails.

The boats used by deep-sea fishermen of Belem, Cezimbra and Setubal known as *canoas* are similar in design to the open *catraio* boat, but of larger tonnage.

3. A dugout with planked sides used by fishermen on the coast of Peru and made of Ecuadorian hardwood. It is 40 ft. or more in length and very seaworthy when well manned.

CANOE. 1. A term applied in America and Europe to small craft of long and narrow proportions, short at both ends, propelled by double paddles or sails and used for racing, traveling, exploring, and as pleasure boats.

Fr: *Canoe; Canadienne;* Ger: *Kanu; Kanadier.*

Modern canoes may be classed, according to the relative proportion of their paddling and sailing qualities, into five groups:

a. Paddling canoe propelled solely by paddle.

b. Sailable paddling canoe, in which the sail is used as an auxiliary. Flat floor, ends well rounded, little sheer. Length 14 ft. Breadth 27 in.

c. Sailing, cruising and paddling canoe in which both qualities are about equal, as in most cruising canoes. Flat floor, sternpost nearly upright, keel of 2 to 3 in. or centerboard. Length 14 ft. Breadth 30 in.

d. Paddlable sailing canoe, built mainly for sailing, the paddle being auxiliary.

e. Sailing canoe. This is a larger type accommodating a crew of 2 or 3 and occasionally using oars as auxiliaries. Metal centerboard. Length 15 ft. Breadth 33 in.

Miller, W. H., *Canoeing, Sailing and Motor Boating,* London, 1928; Nessmuk, *Wood Craft,* London, 1895; Stephens, *Canoe and Boat Building,* New York, 1891; Tiller, A., *Kanubau und Segeln,* Berlin, 1919.

2. A general name for a light boat of primitive design, open from end to end and used for transport and fishing by maritime populations in different parts of the world.

Fr: *Pirogue;* Ger: *Kanu; Paddelboot; Piroge.*

See **Balance Canoe, Bark Canoe, Canvas Canoe, Double Canoe, Double Outrigger Canoe, Dugout Canoe, Outrigger Canoe.**

Canoes are either solid built, hewn out of a tree as the dugout, or made with an outer shell of planks, skins, bark or canvas, strengthened by a light framing. The sizes of canoes vary in different countries according to the use to which they are put, and the size of the timber or other material available, but as a rule they are nowadays seldom more than 30 ft. in length, and proportionally narrow compared with the length. They are propelled by single or double paddles held in the hand without a fixed fulcrum, the crew facing forward.

Canoes may be classified as follows:
a. Dugout canoes.
b. Plank-built canoes.
c. Bark canoes.
d. Skin boats or canoes.
e. Canvas boats or skiffs.

There are also double canoes and outrigger canoes of two types, the single outrigger and the double outrigger.

Haddon-Hornell, *Canoes of Oceania,* Bernice P. Bishop Museum, Special Publications 27–29, Honolulu (1936–38); Paris, E. F., *Essai sur la construction navale des peuples extra européens,* Paris; Suder, H., *Vom Einbaum und Floss zum Schiff,* Institut für Meereskunde Veröffentlichungen, Neue Folge, Heft 7, Berlin (1930).

CANOE FRAME. A term used in wooden boatbuilding to denote a thin wide frame bent on the flat. It is mostly used in hulls requiring very sharp bends in the frames.

CANOE STERN. A sharp stern with overhang built much in the same manner as the spoon or overhung bow. It gives increased deck space and makes it easier to obtain flat buttocks than does the ordinary sharp stern. Generally speaking it is conducive to good balance in sailing-craft hulls.

Fr: *Arrière de Canoe;* Ger: *Kanu Heck; Wikinger Heck.*

CANOE YACHT. Term used to denote a sailing yacht with canoe stern.

CANOE YAWL. Small yawl-rigged cruising yacht 20 to 30 ft. B. P. length with a beam of 6 to 10 ft., a canoe-shaped stern, and rounded stem. The headsails include either a single foresail, which sets on a wood roller, or a jib and forestaysail.

Fr: *Yawl Canoe;* Ger: *Kanu Yawl.*

CANOPY; CANOPY COVER. A canvas hood secured to uprights shipped in the gunwale of an open boat as a protection against the weather. A light awning over the stern sheets of a boat.

Fr: *Tendelet;* Ger: *Bootszelt.*

CANT BEAM. One of the deck beams extending radially abaft the transom beam at the stern of a vessel.

Fr: *Barrot Dévoyé;* Ger: *Gillungsbalken.*

CANT BODY. That part of a vessel's hull near the ends where the sides of the frames are not square to the line of the keel but are inclined aft in the forebody and *forward* in the afterbody.

CANT FRAME. A frame that does not stand normal to the longitudinal vertical middle plane, but is slanted so as to be nearly normal to the outer plating. Also

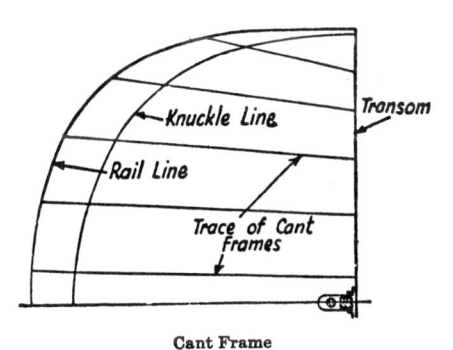

Cant Frame

called cant. In steel ships cant frames are used only to support the overhang of the stern or counter abaft the transom frame. The heels of these frames butt on the transom floor and their heads are bracketed to the cant beams. In wooden hulls forward cants are swung in a forward direction; aftercants are swung aft.

Fr: *Couple Dévoyé;* Ger: *Kantspant; Balanzierspant; Gillungspant.*

CANTILEVER FRAMING. A system of framing used in single-deck vessels of the self-trimming type. The frames are cut several feet below deck and bracketed to other angle bars. These bend inward diagonally to the base of a fore-and-aft girder, which is continuous underneath the deck, except in way of hatchways, where it projects above the deck to form the coamings.

Fr: *Construction à Cantilever;* Ger: *Cantilever-Bauart System.*

The topside vertical frames are of smaller section and are bracketed at the knuckles of the main frames. The triangular space at topsides is arranged for water ballast. The great strength developed by this framework makes hold pillars unnecessary.

CANTING PIECE.

See **Tripping Palm.**

CANTLINE. A stowage term to denote the space or groove between two fore-and-aft tiers of casks stowed side by side.

CANT PIECE. Term used by whalemen to denote a rectangular piece of blubber about 2 ft. wide and 30 to 40 ft. in length, according to the size of the animal.

CANT PURCHASE.

See **Cutting Tackle.**

CANT SPAR. A round stick or piece of timber with a length or 33 to 35 ft. and a girth at the butt of 5 to 6 hands (20 to 24 in.) for spar making.

CANT TIMBER. One of the frame timbers in the cant bodies. Cant timbers have their planes inclined to the sheer or canted, but perpendicular to the half-breadth plan.

Fr: *Couple Dévoyé;* Ger: *Kantspant.*

CANVAS. A double-warp, single-weft fabric made of hemp, flax, or cotton fibers, used for making sails, awnings, covers, tarpaulins, etc. Also called sailcloth.

Fr: *Toile à Voile;* Ger: *Segeltuch.*

See **Cotton Canvas, Flax Canvas, Multiple-Ply Canvas, Single-Ply Canvas, Storm Canvas, Twisted-Thread Canvas, Working Canvas.**

Canvas is classified in different numbers according to its strength. The numbers vary according to the material used; and also with the custom of different countries where manufactured. In Great Britain there are 16 different numbers ranging from 0000 to 12, numbers 1 to 8 being mostly used. In the United States the numbers vary from 0 to 12. In France they vary from 0 to 8, the lowest figure indicating, in each case, the strongest fabric. Canvas is supplied in bolts, which have different measurements in each country (see *Bolt*). Canvas is also designated by weight, in which case the lineal yard of 28½ in. width is taken as unit.

CANVAS BUCKET. A bucket with a diameter of about 3½ inches and a depth of 11 inches made of No. 4 canvas. The rim is a mast hoop and the bottom a wood disc. It is mostly used on merchant ships for taking sea water samples for determining temperature.

Fr: *Seau en toile;* Ger: *Segeltuchputze; Schlagputze.*

CANVAS BOAT. A small boat in which the framing is made of wood and the outer skin of canvas or sailcloth. Canvas boats have been successfully employed as fishing or pleasure boats. Staunch and able craft have been built on this system. Canvas hulls are best suited for long narrow boats and therefore are particularly well adapted to canoe building.

See **Collapsible Boat.**

CANVAS CANOE. Canvas canoes are made over a solid mold. The ribs or frames, made of white cedar and about 2 to 3 in. in width, ¼ or ⅜ in. thick, are placed on the mold. On the top thin cedar strips, usually ⅛ in. thick, are placed. The ribs are fastened to gunwales and hardwood stems at each end. Over all a piece of canvas filled with a preparation and given several coats of paint and varnish is stretched tightly. The canvas canoe construction is identical with that of the birch bark, after which it is patterned. It has, however, the advantage of an even, smooth surface, of greater rigidity and faster lines.

Field, P. B., *Canvas Canoes*, New York, 1887; Webb, F., *Manual of the Canvas Canoe*, New York, 1898.

CANVAS FENDER. A bag of canvas stuffed with oakum.

Fr: *Ballon en Toile à Voile;* Ger: *Segeltuchfender.*

CANVAS SLING. A sling made of No. 1 canvas roped with 3-in. Manila and provided with hooking bridles. Used for slinging bag flour, coffee, and very light and small case goods.

Fr: *Elingue limandée;* Ger: *Seil mit doppelter Schlinge.*

CANYON. A furrow cutting across the continental shelf. Such furrows are numerous, and their size and character vary greatly. They have been termed, variously, submarine canyons, valleys, mock valleys, and gulleys.

Sverdrup, Johnson, and Fleming, *The Oceans*, New York, 1942.

See **Continental Shelf.**

CAORLINA. Double-ended open boat with fine lines and curved stem used for fishing in the Venetian lagoons (Caorle and Burano). Length 29 to 36 ft. Breadth 4.5 ft. Depth 2.2 ft. Tonnage 1 to 2. Crew 2 to 8.

CAP. The center piece or fitting in a compass card, supported by the pivot. The part which bears against the pivot has a polished beryl, sapphire or agate stone setting.

Fr: *Chape;* Ger: *Hütchen.*

Bray, J. R., *Pivots and Caps in Compasses*, London (1917).

CAPACITY PLAN. A general plan or inboard profile which gives all data relating to the capacity of cargo spaces, tanks, bunkers, storerooms and the location of the center of gravity of each of these spaces.

Ger: *Stauungsplan.*

The capacity of cargo spaces, other than tanks, is generally given in cubic feet for bale cargo and bulk cargo. The capacity of the tanks may be given in cubic feet, gallons, barrels, tons or a combination of these.

CAP BLOCK. 1. One of the square pieces of hardwood, laid upon the blocks on which a ship is built, to receive the keel.

Fr: *Faux-Tin;* Ger: *Passtück.*

2. A soft wood block, about 6 in. thick, placed upon the hardwood keel blocks set up for dry-docking a vessel. They accommodate such irregularities of the keel as rivet heads and butt straps, and are easily and cheaply renewed.

CAPE. A promontory facing the open water.

Fr: *Cap;* Ger: *Vorgebirge; Kap.*

See **Umbrella.**

CAPE ANN OAR (U. S.). An oar with square loom used by Gloucester fishermen.

CAPE COD HEAD. A sort of hinged hood made of sheet metal and fitted on top of the galley smokestack.

CAPE HORN CURRENT. A branch of the Antarctic easterly drift in the vicinity of Cape Horn and Falkland Islands.

CAPEL. An end connection for wire rope made with a metal cap instead of an eye splice. It is frequently used with wires of such construction that they cannot be spliced such as the 1×19 wire.

See **Rope socket.**

CAPELIN SEINE. Seine used in Nova Scotia, New Brunswick, Labrador, and Newfoundland fisheries. It is from 20 to 75 fathoms long and 2 to 8 fathoms deep. The mesh is graduated from ¾ in. in the bunt to 2 in. on the end of arms.

CAPE ROSEWAY WHERRY. Open rowboat employed in the lobster and inshore fisheries of Penobscot Bay, Maine.

The hull has a sharp bow, round bilge; narrow, flat bottom, and very narrow heart-shaped transom stern. Its length ranges from 12 to 18 ft. It is entirely open and seldom provided with sails.

CAPE STIFF. A slang term by which the crews of sailing ships denoted Cape Horn.

CAP JIB. Name occasionally given to a jib which has its stay fastened to an eye in the bowsprit cap.

CAP LOG. A horizontal timber on a quay or pier, bolted to the vertical timbers or secured to the masonry to receive the impact of vessels lying along side. Also called Cap Wale.

CAPORAIS. A bargelike open craft similar to the *vascello* and also employed in the tunny fisheries in Italian coastal waters. Also called *Mesciara da Rais*. Length 49.2 ft. Breadth 13.1 ft. Depth 2.9 ft.

CAP SCUTTLE. A small hatchway with rabbeted coamings and headledges, closed by a cap or lid made to fit over the outside of the coamings.

Ger: *Spund; Kistluke.*

CAP SHORE. A supporting spar placed under the forepart of a wooden mast cap. Its purpose was to support the cap when it had the weight of the bunt of the topsail yard on it. It is not required with iron caps as these are supported by a knee on each side and are stronger in themselves. Also called cap stanchion.

Fr: *Chandelle de Chouque;* Ger: *Eselstütze.*

CAPSIZE. To turn over; to upset. The capsizing of a ship is caused by the elevation of the center of gravity above the metacenter, thus creating an unstable equilibrium.

Fr: *Chavirer;* Ger: *Kentern; Kopseisen.* See **Metacenter.**

CAPSTAN. A machine used on board ship when mechanical power is required for raising anchor, hoisting yards, lifting heavy weights, or any other similar work.

Fr: *Cabestan;* Ger: *Gangspill.*

See **Anchor Capstan, Crank Capstan, Drift Capstan, Geared Capstan, Gipsy Capstan, Steam Capstan.**

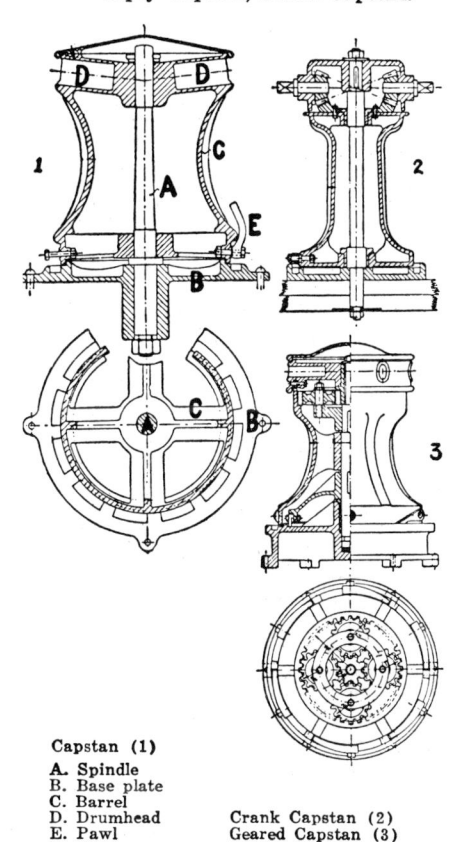

Capstan (1)
A. Spindle
B. Base plate
C. Barrel
D. Drumhead
E. Pawl

Crank Capstan (2)
Geared Capstan (3)

A capstan consists primarily of a cast-steel barrel of circular form mounted on a vertical spindle, with largest diameter at top and bottom and smallest in the middle, to allow the rope around it to surge up or down as the number of turns is increased. The barrel is fixed to the spindle by keys. At the top of the capstan, or drumhead, recesses are provided for shipping the capstan bars if it is to be operated by hand. To prevent the capstan walking back when it is operated by hand, pawls are fitted to the lower edge.

CAPSTAN BAR. A lever by which a capstan is worked when operated by hand. The bars are generally made of ash and fitted at the inner end with cast-steel shoes which fit into the recesses (pigeon holes) of the capstan head. Their length varies from 5 to 6½ ft.

Fr: *Barre de Cabestan;* Ger: *Spillspake.*

CAPSTAN KNOT. An application of the figure-of-eight knot. It is unreliable except for temporary purposes or very light work.

CAP STAY. A stay which runs from the cap of one mast to the cap of another. Also called triatic stay.

Fr: *Etai de Chouque;* Ger: *Genickstag.*

CAPTAIN'S BRIDGE. A bridge or platform situated under the flying or navigating bridge. In many ships the master's accommodation is located here. Also called upper bridge.

CAPTAIN'S ENTRY (G. B.). A provisional entry passed by the captain of a ship, when it is desirable to discharge the whole cargo at some particular place or in cases where the merchant has omitted to pass the prime entry within the prescribed time.

Fr: *Déclaration du Capitaine.*

CAPTAIN'S ENTRY CHARGES. Charges incurred by the ship for the landing and storage of goods when the consignee fails to take delivery as fast as the ship can deliver or may require, according to the bill of lading terms.

CAPTURE. The act or hostile operation whereby a belligerent warship compels a vessel to conform to her will and obey her orders after the right of visit and search have been concluded.

Fr: *Capture; Prise;* Ger: *Aufbringung; Kapern; Prise.*

The sending of a prize crew on board is not essential to constitute a capture. In contradistinction to visit and search, which is only of a temporary character, capture is effected with the object of bringing the seized property before the prize court for adjudication. Enemy vessels are captured for the purpose of appropriating them in the exercise of the right of a belligerent to confiscate all enemy property found on the open sea, or in the territorial waters of the enemy. Neutral merchant vessels are captured for the purpose of confiscating vessel or cargo, or both, as punishment for certain special acts, the punishment being pronounced by a prize court. Capture is deemed lawful when effected by an enemy or belligerent ship properly commissioned in accordance with international law. The right of capture at sea belongs by virtue of international law to every sovereign state in time of war.

Garner, J. W., *Capture at Sea,* London, 1927; Loreburn, *Prize Law During the World War,* London, 1927; Richmond, *Imperial Defense and Capture at Sea in War,* London, 1932.

CAR. A wooden box for the temporary storage of live fish. Also called fish car, fish box.

Fr: *Vivier.*

It has open seams or numerous small holes to permit the free circulation of water. The buoyancy of the wood keeps it at the surface of the water, though with little more than the upper side exposed. Fish cars are usually moored to wharves or stakes, or anchored in shallow water near shore.

CARBON ELECTRODE. An electrode made of carbon, used in the carbon arc-welding process.

Fr: *Electrode en Charbon;* Ger: *Kohle Electróde.*

CARDINAL POINT. One of the four principal points of the compass—north, south, east, west.

Fr: *Point Cardinal;* Ger: *Kardinalpunkt.*

CAREEN. To cause a ship to lie over on one side for the purpose of examining the underwater body on the opposite side, and of calking, repairing, cleaning, paying with pitch, or breaming it. Careening nowadays is resorted to only by small vessels such as fishing craft, and so on. The number of drydocks and marine railways available in most harbors has contributed toward this change. Also called heave down.

Fr: *Caréner; Abattre en Carène;* Ger: *Kielholen.*

CAREENING TACKLE. A tackle led from masthead to some external point when a vessel is in drydock to prevent it from falling over in the event of an accident to the bilge blocks or shores, or for careening a small vessel on a hard at low water to facilitate scrubbing and painting the bottom. Also called masthead tackle.

Fr: *Caliorne d'Abattage;* Ger: *Kielholtalje.*

CAR FLOAT. A harbor craft. A large decked barge or scow fitted with tracks and used for ferrying railroad cars over short distances.

CARGO. The lading or freight of a merchant vessel. The goods, merchandise, or whatever is conveyed in a ship for payment of freight. A general term for all merchandise carried on board a trading vessel.

Fr: *Cargaison; Chargement;* Ger: *Ladung; Frachtgut.*

See Air-Cooled Cargo, Bag Cargo, Bale Cargo, Barrel Cargo, Berth Cargo, Distress Cargo, Residue Cargo.

CARGO BATTEN. One of the planks fitted to the inboard side of frames in the hold or cargo spaces of a steel vessel in order to keep the cargo away from the shell plating, and avoid all contact with metallic surfaces. These battens are usually about 6 by 1½ in., running fore and aft and bolted to the frames about 1 ft. apart. Also called hold sparring, hold batten, sparring batten.

Fr: *Latte de Vaigrage;* Ger: *Wegerungslatte.*

CARGO BLOCK. A term which applies in general to all single- or multiple-sheaved metal blocks used on board ship for cargo lifting purposes. It includes topping lift, derrick-head, and heel or lead blocks.

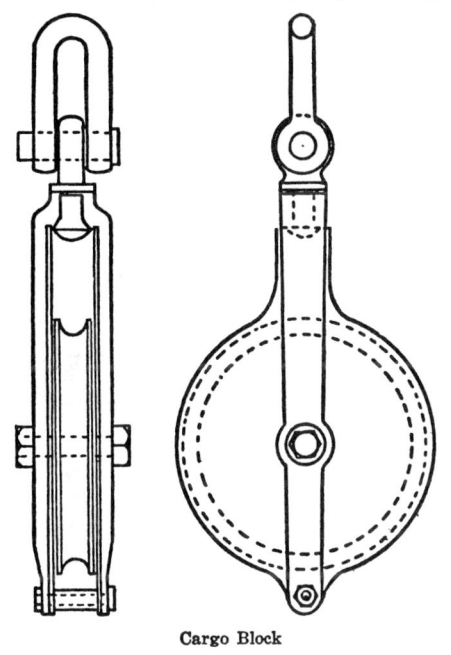

Fr: *Poulie de Mât de Charge;* Ger: *Ladeblock.*

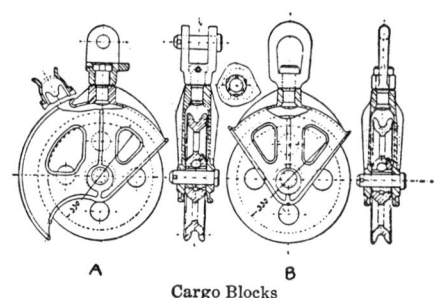

Cargo Block

Cargo Blocks
A. Lead block / Heel block
B. Head Block

The requirements of cargo blocks are subject to statutory regulations in most maritime countries. The blocks are usually designed with a minimum safety factor of five. Sheaves are made of cast metal and provided with efficient means of lubrication (grease or graphite); hooks, eyes, beckets, shackles of wrought iron or mild steel. For side plates and cheeks mild or cast steel, wrought iron or malleable cast iron are generally used.

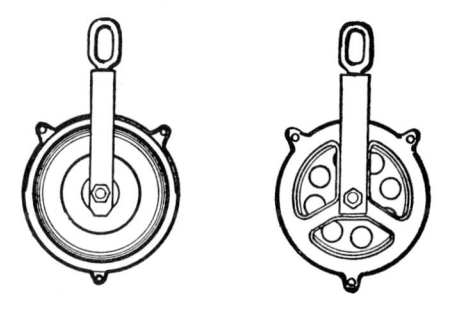

Cargo Blocks

For every block or group of blocks a test certificate is supplied by the manufacturers, and the safe working load in tons is marked on each block.

CARGO BOAT. See **Freighter.**

CARGO BOOK. A book made up by the ship's purser or chief officer from the tally sheets. It lists the vessel's cargo laden in each hold by marks and numbers, consigned to each port.

Ger: *Ladebuch.*

CARGO BOOM. See **Derrick.**

CARGO BRIDLE. A bridle consisting of four legs of equal length, one end of each spliced to an iron ring, the other end into the eye of a hook. Such bridles are used to lift wooden trays, cargo nets, and so on.

CARGO CHUTE. An inclined wooden trough used for handling goods between ship and shore.

Fr: *Glissière;* Ger: *Ladeschlitten.*

CARGO CLUSTER. Electric lighting apparatus used on deck or under deck when working cargo at night. Also called cargo reflector. It consists essentially of a circular enamelled reflector 14 to 20 in. in diameter fitted with 5 to 8 lamp holders and a wire guard to protect the lamps.

Ger: *Sonnenbrenner.*

CARGO DEADWEIGHT.
See **Net Capacity.**

CARGO DOOR. A door fitted in the ship's side for closing a cargo port.
Fr: *Porte de Chargement;* Ger: *Ladepforte.*
See **Cargo Port.**
This term is also applied to a door fitted in an upper bulkhead for access from one hold into the next one. Cargo doors are usually secured by strongbacks fitted inside, spun yarn or rubber packing being used at the joints to obtain watertightness.

CARGO FALL. Rope rove through the cargo and lead blocks of a derrick, leading to winch drum and used for working cargo in and out of a ship, usually made of specially soft woven brand 3½-in. Manila rope or of 2½-in. flexible steel wire of 6x16, or 6x19 construction. Also called cargo runner.
Fr: *Garant de Mât de Charge;* Ger: *Ladeläufer; Dirkläufer; Lastseil; Ladejolle.*

CARGO GEAR. General term applied to all gear located in the vicinity of cargo hatches and used for loading and discharging. It includes winches, cargo booms and their fittings, i.e., spans (topping lifts), heel and head blocks, guys, cargo runners.
Fr: *Apparaux de manutention;* Ger: *Ladegeschirr.*

CARGO HATCH. A general term applied to any deck opening leading to the cargo holds.
Fr: *Panneau de Déchargement;* Ger: *Ladeluke.*
The length of cargo hatches in ordinary cargo carriers varies from 28 to 34 ft. but in small coasting vessels single hatches up to 40 ft. length are found. The width of cargo hatches may be taken on an average as 40 per cent of the molded breadth of the ship.
Buchanan, J. G., "Hatchways," Institution of Naval Architects (London), *Transactions,* vol. 79 (1937); Buchsbaum, G., "Ladeluken und Stabilität," Schiffbautechnische Gesellschaft, *Jahrbuch,* vol. 39 (1938).

CARGO HOIST.
See **Whip.**

CARGO HOOK. Hook fastened at the end of a cargo whip for loading and landing cargo.
Fr: *Crochet de Mât de Charge;* Ger: *Ladehaken; Lasthaken; Losshaken.*
British Standards Institution, Standard no. 482, *Crane and Sling Hooks,* 1933.

CARGO JACK. A screw jack used by stevedores where cargo is to be forced into small spaces or the stowage factor is to be reduced; especially in the case of bale goods such as cotton and wool.

CARGO LIEN. A lien which may exist on account of salvage, demurrage, general average or other maritime service. Also called lien on cargo.
Fr: *Privilège sur le chargement;* Ger: *Ladungspfandrecht.*
It is not, properly speaking, a maritime lien although it is invoked principally in behalf of the vessel or her owners on account of the freight and other charges due for the service of carrying the goods.

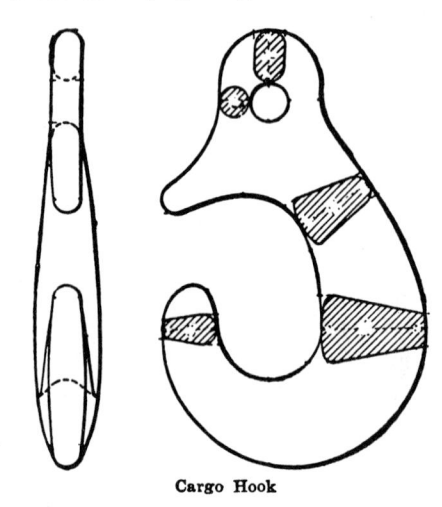

Cargo Hook

CARGO LIGHT.
See **Cargo Cluster.**

CARGO LINER. A vessel which carries cargo exclusively and operates with sister

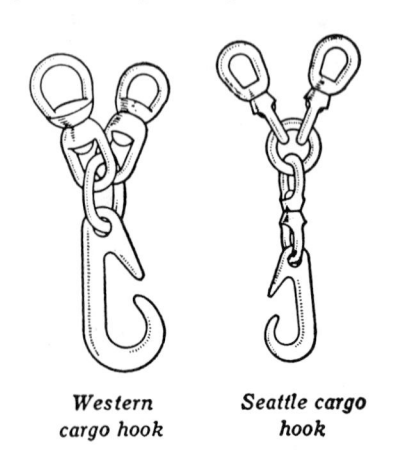

Western cargo hook

Seattle cargo hook

CARGO LIST—CARGO PUMP

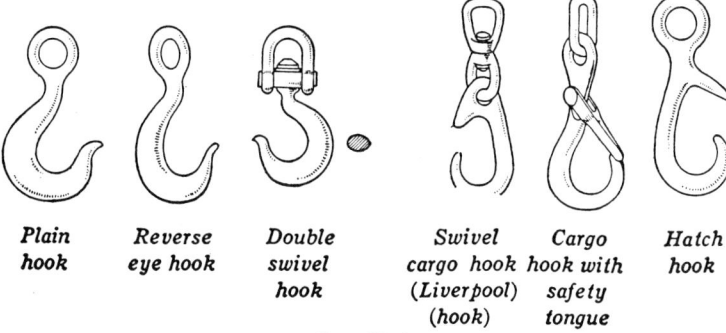

| Plain hook | Reverse eye hook | Double swivel hook | Swivel cargo hook (Liverpool) (hook) | Cargo hook with safety tongue | Hatch hook |

Cargo Hooks

ships over a definite route on fixed schedules. These vessels are adapted to the carriage of the many different kinds of freight and are frequently built for the particular trade in which they engage, for example, silk liners.

Fr: *Navire de Charge Régulier;* Ger: *Linienfrachtschiff.*

Cripps, L. H., "The Economics of Cargo Liners," Institution of Naval Architects (London), *Transactions,* vol. 72 (1930).

CARGO LIST. A record of the goods accepted for loading on one vessel. With this list and the capacity drawing of the ship loading plans are worked out with the stevedores.

CARGO MAST (U. S.). One of a series of strong, vertical girders erected near the edge of a pier or against the outer surface of the pier-shed to facilitate loading and discharging of vessels moored alongside.

The height of the masts is generally about 60 to 80 ft. above low-water level and they are connected at the top by a horizontal beam. Holes in the beam are spaced at intervals of 2 or 3 ft. for attaching stirrups and cargo blocks. A fall or whip passes through each block, one end leading to an electric winch on the pier. The other end is married or joined to one of the ship's cargo falls for burtoning.

CARGO MAT. A mat used as an extra protection for some kinds of cargo over dunnage wood and woven from various fibrous materials.

Fr: *Matte; Toile de Fardage;* Ger: *Ladungsmatte; Garniermatte.*

CARGO NET. A square net of varying size made of Manila, wire rope, or chain and used for slinging case goods or small package freight. The mesh is from 5½ to 7 in. square. When of square shape these nets are made in sizes 8 ft. x 8 ft. 9 in. or 10 ft. sq. The chains used vary from ¼ in. to ⅜ in. Also called net sling.

Fr: *Filet d'Elingue;* Ger: *Ladungnetz; Netzschlinge.*

CARGO PLAN. A plan giving the quantities and description of the various items composing a ship's cargo also their disposition in the vessel, after the loading is completed. Also called stowage plan.

Fr: *Plan d'Arrimage;* Ger: *Ladungsplan.*

The principal purpose of this document is to enable the agents at various ports of call to make the necessary arrangements in advance for the expeditious discharge and disposal of the cargo. If the information given on this plan is correctly stated, an accurate estimate of the amount of time for unloading in each port can be made. The cargo plan also gives information respecting the disposal of weights throughout the vessel, which is essential from the point of view of trim and stability.

CARGO PORT. An opening in the ship's side especially provided for loading or discharging cargo in 'tween-decks. Also called side port.

Fr: *Sabord de Chargement;* Ger: *Ladepforte.*

Side ports where package freight is handled make possible the speeding of a ship's departure beyond the capacity of ships having hatchways only. However cargo ports, if not maintained in satisfactory watertight condition, may be a source of grave danger.

CARGO PUMP. Pump used on a tank vessel for handling the discharge of cargo at the termination of the loaded passage and the discharging or transfer of ballast on the light or unloaded passage. Located at the bottom of the pump room, these pumps are usually of the common duplex type, which carries the steam almost to the full length of the stroke.

CARGO RICE. A mixture of rough rice and paddy in about 75–25 proportion. The purpose of mixing paddy with rough rice is to prevent the grain lying too close together and to ensure air circulation through the cargo during transportation.

CARGO SHEET. A list prepared by the wharfinger to enable the shipowner's office staff to check the bills of lading before signing them.

CARGO SHEET CLERK (U. S.). One who superintends the loading or unloading of a vessel and is responsible for correct delivery of the cargo. In Great Britain called ship's clerk. All tallymen are under his supervision. He receives a copy of the dock receipts and tally sheets which furnish the basic information for making the ship's manifest.

Ger: *Verladungskommis; Expedient.*

CARGO SKID. A wooden platform placed between a wharf and the ship's bulwarks on which cargo is dragged to the deck and swung over the square of the hatch.

Ger: *Ladeschlitten.*

See **Single Fall and Skid Method.**

CARGO SPACES. All spaces used for the stowage of dry cargo or tanks for liquid cargo.

Fr: *Locaux à marchandises;* Ger: *Laderaume.*

CARGO SUPERINTENDENT (G. B.). An executive appointed by shipowners to direct all matters relating to cargo loaded or discharged while a ship is in port. He is assisted on board by a ship's clerk.

CARGO UNDERWRITER. One who insures cargoes.

Fr: *Assureur sur Facultés;* Ger: *Ladung Assekuradeur.*

CARGO WHIP. A rope or chain used in connection with a derrick for handling cargo. One end is provided with a heavy hook. The other end is rove through the derrick block and taken to the winch. Also called cargo hoist, cargo rope.

Fr: *Filin de Hissage; Garant de Mât de Charge; Cartahu de Mât de Charge;* Ger: *Lastseil; Ladeseil; Windenläufer.*

CARGO WINCH. A steam or electric winch used for handling cargo from a quay, a pier, or a lighter to the ship's hold and vice versa. Two-ton drafts on a single whip is the average maximum load for general cargo. For medium heavy lifts of 5 to 10 tons a two-part purchase is used, with double-geared winches in low gear for the heavier loads. Thirty tons is usually the limit for heavy lifts on ordinary cargo vessels. Special gear with multiple purchase up to seven parts and compound geared winches is provided for such cargo.

Fr: *Treuil à Marchandises;* Ger: *Ladewinde.*

Morton, L. T., Ship's Cargo Handling Gear, North East Coast Institution of Engineers and Shipbuilders, Newcastle upon Tyne, *Transactions,* vol. 57 (1940–44).

CARGO-WORTHY. A term sometimes applied to a vessel internally adapted for the transportation of some particular kind of cargo.

CARLING. A short fore-and-aft timber or steel girder placed under a deck to stiffen it, used in way of mooring bitts, winches, windlasses, hatchways, masts, and so on. It may run continuously under the deck beams or intercostally. Also called carline, header.

Fr: *Entremise; Elongis;* Ger: *Rippe; Schlingen.*

See **Hatch Carling, Mast Carling.**

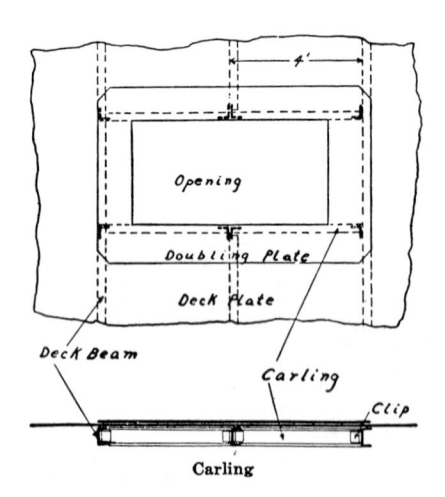

Carling

CARLING KNEE. A horizontal knee that fills the angle between a carling or ledge and a deck beam.

Fr: *Courbe d'Entremise;* Ger: *Scheerstock.*

CAROCHOS. A small open boat similar

CARPENTER—CARVEL PLANKING

to the *bareira* originating from the Estremadura (Portugal).

CARPENTER. See **Ship's Carpenter.**

CARPENTER'S MATE. A petty officer acting as assistant to a ship's carpenter.

Fr: *Second Charpentier;* Ger: *Zimmermann's Maat.*

CARPENTER'S STOPPER. A patent wire rope stopper used for salvage work. It is designed for temporarily holding a rope which is under heavy strain without causing damage to the strands. It consists of a metal box made in two longitudinal halves joined with a hinge. Internally one side of the box is parallel with, and the other inclined to, the lead of the rope. A wedge piece slides in against the inclined side. When the rope is inserted the lid is shut and, immediately any pull comes on the rope, the wedge piece is drawn hard into the block and jams the rope.

CARRIAGE BOLT. A galvanized steel or bronze bolt with crowned head used in fastening keel timbers when these are too small to drift or where there is danger of splitting. A short portion of the shank, directly under the head, is square to prevent turning when the nut is set up.

CARRICK BEND. A kind of knot formed on a bight by putting the end o a rope over its standing part, and then passing it. The carrick bend and double carrick bend are mostly used in bending hawsers together. Also called Sailor's Knot or Anchor Bend.

Fr: *Noeud de Vache;* Ger: *Kreuzknoten; Heling.*

CARRICK BITTS. Upright pieces of timber supporting the ends of a wooden windlass barrel. Also called carrick heads, windlass bitts.

Fr: *Petites Bittes de Guindeau;* Ger: *Bratspillbeting; Spillbeting.*

CARRICK HEADS. See **Carrick Bitts.**

CARRIER. The owner or charterer of a vessel who enters into a contract of carriage with a shipper.

Fr: *Transporteur;* Ger: *Frachtführer.*

See **Common Carrier, Nonconference Carrier, Ore Carrier, Timber Carrier.**

CARRIER'S RISKS. In marine insurance the risks of loss or damage to goods arising in the course of their loading, handling, stowage, carriage, custody, care and discharge by the shipowner and his servants.

CARRY AWAY. To give way, break, part, or wash overboard. Used to describe an accident to spars, sails, cargo, or any fixtures.

Fr: *Perdre; Rompre;* Ger: *Abbrechen.*

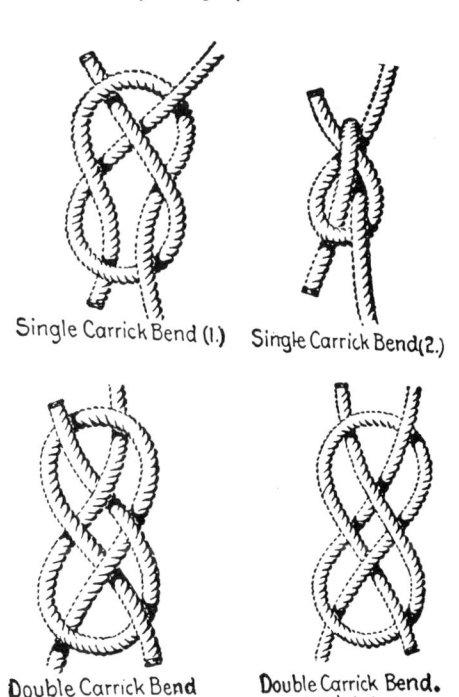

Single Carrick Bend (1.)   Single Carrick Bend (2.)

Double Carrick Bend   Double Carrick Bend. (2nd Method)

Carrick Bend

CARTEL SHIP. A commissioned vessel sailing under a flag of truce employed in the exchange of prisoners of war pursuant to an agreement or in the carriage by sea of proposals from one belligerent to the other.

It is generally supplied with a pass or safe conduct granted by the commissary of prisoners residing in the country of the enemy, or by the naval authorities of the belligerent state. Cartel ships are immune from capture both in transporting prisoners to their national port and in returning from that service. The usual practice for a cartel ship sailing between two countries at war with each other is to fly the colors of both belligerents.

Fr: *Navire Parlementaire;* Ger: *Parlamentarschiff.*

CARVEL PLANKING. A system of planking in which the outside planking of a vessel or boat is flush: the edges meeting and giving the shell a smooth surface instead of overlapping as in the clinker system. The lines for carvel-built boats are laid down on a floor—just as in the building of large vessels—molds made, and bevelings taken for the timbers.

Fr: *Bordé à franc-bord;* Ger: *Krawel Beplankung.*
See **Clinker Built.**

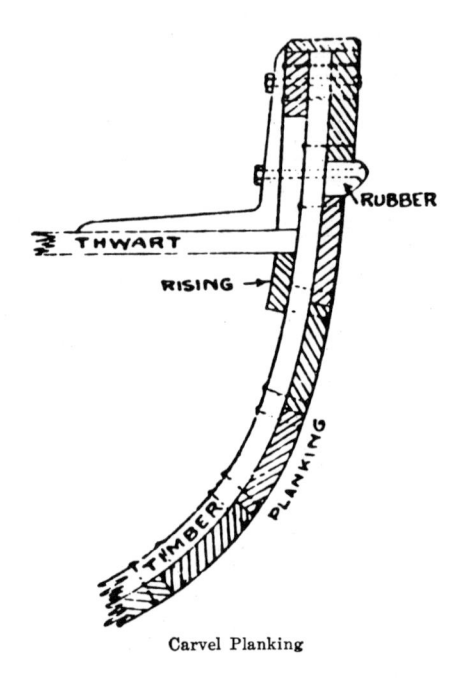

Carvel Planking

CARVING NOTE. A document handed by the British authorities to one applying for the registration of a vessel. It requires the intended gross tonnage and the registered number to be endorsed by the registrar of shipping and is an application to have these cut or "carved" in the main beam of the vessel.

CASCO. Sailing scow used in Manila Bay, Pasig River, and Laguna de Bay for conveying goods from ship to shore and up river. Length 42.6 ft. Breadth 6.5 ft. Depth 3.4 ft.

The hull is strengthened with 3 or 4 heavy crossbeams projecting outboard and fastened at their ends to bamboo splits which form an outside platform running fore and aft. The side and bottom planking are connected with heavy wooden knees. The *casco* is propelled by paddles or sails. The rig consists of fore and mainmast with Chinese lugsails.

CASE. Term used by whalemen to denote a cavity in front of and above the skull of sperm whales. It forms a receptacle for spermaceti.

CASE-BUCKET. An implement used by whalemen for bailing spermaceti from the case. It has a round or pointed base and is forced down into the case with a beam and tackle.

CASEIN GLUE. A glue consisting of casein, soda, silica, lime and other mineral matter, used for plywood work, for built-up spars, and so on.

CASE OIL. A term applied to cargo consisting of various kinds of petroleum products, chiefly gasoline, kerosene and benzine, which are commonly shipped in metal containers packed in wooden boxes or cases. Also called packed petroleum.

CASING. 1. A covering made of light plating and installed around or about any part or object as a protection.

2. In marine engineering, the covering of any piece of machinery, such as boiler casing, engine casing, turbine casing, valve casing. Lagging on pipes is also considered a form of casing.

Fr: *Encaissement;* Ger: *Umbau.*
See **Boiler Casing, Machinery Casing.**

CASK BUOY. A wooden or metal buoy having the shape of a cask.
Fr: *Bouée-Tonne;* Ger: *Fasstonne.*

CAST. The act of heaving of the lead into the sea to ascertain the depth of water.
Fr: *Sonder;* Ger: *Lotwerfen; Loten.*

CAST. 1. To throw a vessel to port or starboard when getting underway by the use of headsails or rudder for stern way, or by a spring line to a kedge.
Fr: *Abattre; Faire abattre;* Ger: *Wenden.*

2. The term is also variously used, as, to cast anchor, and so on.

CAST AWAY. To commit a wilful act that causes a vessel to perish, to be lost, or to make it necessary to abandon her.

CASTAWAY. One belonging to a wrecked vessel.
Fr: *Naufragé;* Ger: *Schiffbrüchige.*

CASTING. A drawing or plan used in sailmaking. It indicates the shape and length of each individual cloth in a sail. Also called cutting plan.

CASTINGS. In shipbuilding practice a term which refers collectively to stems, stern frames, rudder frames, stern tubes, skegs, propeller struts, bitts, chocks, mooring pipes, hawse pipes, chain pipes, and other hull fittings made of cast steel or cast iron.

Fr: *Pièces de Moulage;* Ger: *Gussstücke.*
Frear, H. P , "Manufacture of Heavy Steel Castings for Ships," Society of Naval Architects and Marine Engineers (New York), *Transactions,* vol. 31 (1923).

CAST LOOSE. To let go, as a rope or line.

CAST NET. A circular net varying in diameter from 12 to 15 ft. It is thrown in such a way as to fall flat upon the water and, dropping rapidly to the bottom, incloses any fish that may happen to be beneath it.

Fr: *Epervier;* Ger: *Wurfnetz; Wurfgarn.*
It has lead balls around the edge and a long rope attached to the center. When the rope is hauled on, the lead balls at the edge come together at the bottom, so that the net is pursed up when drawn from the water and the fish are found therein as in a pocket.

CAST OFF. 1. To throw off. To let go. To unfurl.

Fr: *Larguer;* Ger: *Loswerfen.*

2. Part of the service performed by line runners when mooring and unmooring vessels. It consists of releasing the mooring lines holding the vessel from the bollards or mooring cleats on the pier.

Fr: *Larguer les Amarres;* Ger: *Festmacheleinen losmachen.*

CAST STEEL CHAIN. Anchor chain made by pouring molten steel into molds. Half the links required for a shot are completed and laid out, a space being left between adjacent links which is about equal to what the space between them will be when they have been joined to form a chain. Interlocking molds are placed between each pair of complete links and the casting material is poured in. When the molds are removed a shot of chain remains, the studs having been cast as an integral part of each link. The material used is a chrome-nickel steel with approximately 0.35% carbon; 0.80% manganese; 1.5% nickel and 0.6% chromium. The heat treatment for sizes greater than 1½ inch is as follows: heating to 1650 degrees F.—cooling in the furnace to 1550 degrees; quenching in cold water; tempering at 1100 degrees.

Fr: *Châine d'acier moulé;* Ger: *Stahlguss Ketten.*

CAST-STEEL ROPE. Rope made from crucible-steel wires. It is used for standing rigging and derrick guys and when so employed should be galvanized. The tensile strength ranges from 155,000 to 190,000 pounds per sq. in. Also called crucible-steel rope.

Fr: *Filin en Acier Fondu;* Ger: *Gusstahldraht Tauwerk.*

CAT. Open, clinker-built fishing boat from the South Coast of England resembling the Deal lugger.

It differed from the Deal boats, being somewhat smaller and having no foredeck. Amidships there was a small portable shelter called a caboose. The rig consisted of two masts. The foremast stepped in a tabernacle in the bows carried a large dipping lugsail with several rows of reef points. The mizzenmast was upright and stepped against the transom. Type now extinct.

CAT (to). To heave the ring of a stocked anchor to the cat head.

Fr: *Caponner;* Ger: *Anker Katten.*

CATAMARAN. 1. A generic name for various native-built sailing rafts made of bamboo, balsa, or mahogany logs tied together in various ways, found in East Indies, Formosa, Solomon Islands, Ceylon, Brazil, in which localities they are used chiefly for inshore fishing.

See **Konga, Kola Maram, Jangada, Tek Pai, Balsa, Singhalese Catamaran, Vizagapatam Catamaran.**

2. A name applied to double- or treble-hulled craft used in Europe and the United States for pleasure and racing.

The hulls of pontoons are tied together by diagonal braces and beams which provide the necessary standing room for handling. Catamarans are among the fastest sailing craft afloat. Various catamarans about 30 ft. long and with a sail area of 1,000 sq. ft. are known to have exceeded the speed of 20 knots. Sails are carried without any ballast to counteract the heeling effect of the wind. Against this they are slow in stays, and prone to nose-dive or blow over endwise. To minimize this tendency, the center of effort has to be kept low. Catamarans sail faster on the wind than before it. In their design the greatest difficulty is to avoid the severe stresses which are set up in the joints connecting the pontoons. In the three-hulled craft, the stresses and twist can be taken squarely, since the system lends itself to stronger and simpler bracing than the two-hulled one.

CAT-BACK. A small line bent on to the cat hook to turn the hook as required when catting the anchor.

Fr: *Queue de Capon;* Ger: *Kattblocksteert.*

CAT BLOCK. A large double or treble to which the cat hook is attached, and em-

CATBOAT—CAT RIG

ployed to bring the anchor up to the cathead.
Fr: *Poulie de Capon;* Ger: *Kattblock.*

CATBOAT. A centerboard sailing boat originating in design from New York and afterward developed into a working boat employed by fishermen off Cape Cod. Characterized by its single sail (it carries no jib) and its small length to breadth ratio. The hull is decked and has a large cockpit. The freeboard forward is exceptionally high, a 28-ft. boat having 5 ft. of freeboard at the stem. The breadth is usually just short of half the waterline length. The size of the catboat varies from 10 to 32 ft. on the load waterline. Also called Una boat. Typical dimensions and other particulars: Length over-all 23 ft. 4 in. Sail area 650 sq. ft. Length waterline 22 ft. 6½ in. Ballast 2,500 lbs. Breadth 11 ft. Draught (board up) 2 ft. 4 in. Freeboard at stem 4 ft. 4 in. Draught (board down) 6 ft. 6 in. Least freeboard 1 ft. 9 in.

The great power of these boats is derived from an almost excessive initial stability, the ability to carry sail being obtained chiefly from their breadth, while the ballast they carry is used primarily to give the necessary weight for overcoming the shock of head seas. Stones and large pebbles form the favorite ballast and are placed in the middle third of the boat, well winged out. The mast is a very stout stick stepped in the eyes of the boat and unsupported, there being no shrouds. The entire running rigging consists of two halyards, two lazy jacks, a single topping lift (usually rigged with a gun tackle), and a sheet.
Chapelle, H. I., *American Sailing Craft,* New York, 1936.

CATCH A CRAB. To fail to extricate an oar from the water at the end of the stroke.

CATCH FAKE. An unseemly doubling in a badly coiled rope.
Fr: *Faux Plet;* Ger: *Fang der Bucht.*

CATCH RATLINE.
See **Sheer Ratline.**

CAT DAVIT. A davit from which the catfall in old-fashioned vessels was rigged, used for lifting the stock end of the anchor.
Fr: *Bossoir de Capon;* Ger: *Kattdavit.*

CATENARY. The curve assumed by a chain or rope hanging freely between two points of support.

CAT FALL. The rope hauled upon when the cat block is secured to the anchor in hoisting it to the cathead.
Fr: *Garant de Capon;* Ger: *Kattläufer.*

CATHEAD. A beam of wood or metal projection over each bow, having sufficient outreach to support a stocked anchor clear of the ship's side either before letting go or previously to stowing on board. There is an eye underneath and a thumb cleat on the side to take the catting chain—one or two sheaves are fitted on the outboard end for the catfall. In former days the end of the cathead was carved to represent the head of a cat; hence its name.
Fr: *Bossoir de Capon;* Ger: *Kranbalken.*

CATHEAD KNEE. A wooden knee by which the cathead is strengthened outboard from underneath.

CATHEAD STOPPER. A small short-link chain by which a bower anchor with stock is held fast when it has been catted. Also called cat stopper, ring stopper.
Fr: *Bosse de Bout;* Ger: *Porteurleine der Kattstopper.*

CAT HOLE. One of the apertures in the ship's quarters for passing hawsers, springs, or mooring lines.
Fr: *Écubier d'embossage;* Ger: *Heckkluse; Hinterkluse.*

CAT HOOK. A large hook fitted to the strap of a cat block, used for hooking the anchor ring when catting or hoisting a stocked anchor, to lift it to the cat head. Also called catting hook.
Fr: *Crochet de Capon;* Ger: *Katthaken.*

CAT PENDANT. A wire pendant fitted with a heart thimble and link at each end, used for placing the anchor on the anchor bed. One end is rove through the lower and upper blocks of the cat davit and hooked or shackled to the gravity band on the anchor—the other end being brought to the capstan.
Fr: *Pantoire de Capon;* Ger: *Kattschenkel.*

CAT PURCHASE.
See **Cat Tackle.**

CATRAIO. Large open fishing boat of the Estremadura coast (Portugal). The rig consists of a large triangular foresail with short bowsprit; a sprit mainsail and a very small sprit mizzen sheeted to a long outrigger. Length 56 ft. Breadth 15 ft. Also called *bote de Catraiar.*

CAT RIG. A rig used for small boats consisting of one large sail hoisted in a peculiar manner. Also called Forbes cat rig.
Fr: *Gréement de Cat boat;* Ger: *Cat Takelung.*

The mast is stepped very far forward and a yard considerably longer than the mast runs along it carrying the head of the sail, combining both the mainsail and topsail of other rigs. The foot of the sail is of considerable length, requiring a boom extending several feet over the stern. A single stay running from masthead to stemhead forms the only standing rigging.

CAT SCHOONER. A two-mast fore-and-aft schooner rig without head sails, formerly used in New England as an inshore fishing craft.

CAT'S PAW. 1. The ruffled surface of the water caused by a flaw during light airs. A light air perceived at a distance in a calm, by the impressions made on the surface of the sea, which it sweeps very gently, and then passes away, being equally partial and transitory. Sometimes called a cool.

Fr: *Risée;* Ger: *Kuhlte; Leichtes Lüftchen.*

2. A particular twist in the bight of a rope by which two eyes are formed. The hook of a tackle can be passed through these for hoisting purposes.

Fr: *Gueule de Raie; Patte de Chat;* Ger: *Katzenpfote.*

CAT TACKLE. The tackle formerly used in hoisting an anchor. It includes the cat block, the catfall, and the sheaves in the cat head. Sometimes called cat purchase.

Fr: *Palan de Capon;* Ger: *Katt Takel.*

CATTAIL. Name formerly given to the inner part of the cat head which lapped under one of the forecastle beams.

CATTING CHAIN. A small chain by which a stocked anchor is suspended to the cathead after it has been transferred from its stowed position and is ready to let go. The chain is attached to an eye under the cathead, rove through the anchor ring, up over the thumb cleat on the side of the cathead, the end being brought inboard and secured to a cleat.

Fr: *Bosse de Bout; Chaîne de capon;* Ger: *Porteurleinkette.*

CATTING LINK. A special link with broad palm secured to the end of a catting pendant.

Fr: *Maille de Capon;* Ger: *Kattglied.*

CATTING SHACKLE. A special flat screw shackle used for shackling the anchor to the catting pendant, the bolt of the shackle resting in the broad palm of the catting link.

Fr: *Manille de Capon;* Ger: *Kattschakel.*

CATTLE FITTINGS. A general name for the various fittings and arrangements provided for on the decks of vessels where livestock is carried. They include breast boards, division boards, footlocks, rump boards, throughs, and footboards.

Ger: *Viehverschläge.*

U. S. Department of Agriculture, Bureau of Animal Industry, Order no. 132, Regulations governing the inspection, handling and safe transport of animals carried by ocean steamers, Washington, 1906; British Board of Trade, Sea Transport Department, "Specifications for Fitting Ships for the Transport of Horses and Mules," London, 1925.

CATTLEMAN. One of the men on board a cattle vessel who feeds and attends to the cattle during the voyage. Also called cattle attendant.

Fr: *Convoyeur de Bétail ·* Ger: *Viehwärter; Viehtreiber.*

Cattlemen are usually supplied and paid by the shipper. They sign the ship's articles. The charter party in many instances includes a provision enabling the shipowner to recover all expenses incurred in respect of these men, including repatriation expenses. The number of cattle attendants is specified by statutory regulations. On American ships one attendant is required for each 50 head

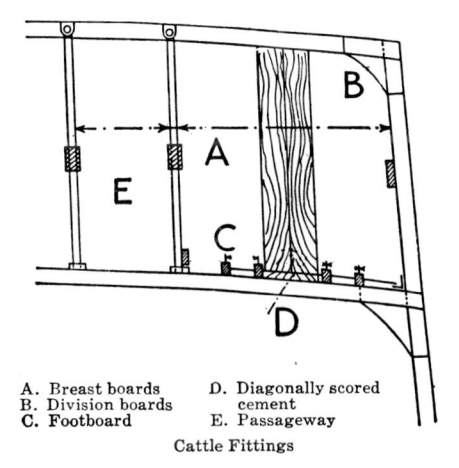

A. Breast boards
B. Division boards
C. Footboard
D. Diagonally scored cement
E. Passageway

Cattle Fittings

of cattle; for sheep and goats, one attendant for each 150 head in winter and each 200 head in summer voyages.

CATTLESHIP. A vessel fitted for the transportation of livestock on upper decks in open or covered spaces. Horses, asses, mules, cattle, sheep are generally carried on cattleships. Regulations regarding the construction of pens or stalls, ventilation, light, allowable deck space are enforced by the principal maritime nations for the conveyance of these animals.

Fr: *Transport à Bestiaux;* Ger: *Viehtransportschiff.*

See **Cattle Fittings**.

CATTLE VESSEL.
See **Cattleship**.

CATWALK.
See **Fore-and-Aft Bridge**.

CAT YAWL. A yawl with the mainmast stepped close to the stem and the after one halfway out on the counter. In this rig there is no bowsprit or headsail. Also adopted for large catboats over 30 ft. long.

Fr: *Cat Yawl;* Ger: *Cat Yawl.*

See **Jolly Boat**.

CAUF (G. B.). A rowboat about 10 ft. long shaped like half a walnut shell, with narrow transom stern. It was carried by Yorkshire cobles for long lining.

CAULKING COMPOUND. A caulking material for making watertight the seams between strakes of planking. It is a rubber compound of polysulfide polymers in which the vulcanizing accelerator is added just before use. No preliminary caulking with oakum or cotton wick is necessary, but a somewhat different level has to be cut in the wood. It has better initial flexing properties than marine glue, and good stability under wide temperature changes.

CAUTIONARY SIGNAL. A signal by means of which a vessel approaching a harbor communicates its character to port authorities or other interested parties. The signal usually consists of a single flag from the International Code.

Fr: *Signal d'Avertissement;* Ger: *Warnungssignal.*

CAVIL; CAVEL. A large wooden pin of square cross-section fitted in a pin rail and formerly used on sailing vessels for belaying the larger ropes (obsolete).

Fr: *Fileux;* Ger: *Belegklampe; Warpklampe.*

CAVILING DAYS. A chartering term used in the working of coal trade charter parties, to denote one of the days on which pitmen arrange to change their places of work in the mines and on which no work is done.

CAVITATION. A phenomenon occurring under certain conditions during the rotation of a screw propeller, wherein air cavities are formed in contact with the propeller blades, reducing its thrust, and thereby reducing propulsive efficiency.

Fr: *Cavitation;* Ger: *Kavitation; Hohlraumbildung.*

Among the remedies for cavitation are (1) increased blade area; (2) increased propeller immersion; (3) slower speed of rotation. Technically, cavitation results from the separation of the streamline flow from the surface of the propeller blade due to insufficient pressure gradient in the fluid. Eggert, E. F., *Propeller Cavitation,* Society of Naval Architects and Marine Engineers, vol. 40 (1932); Kell, C. O., "Propeller Cavitation Studies," Institute of Naval Architects, *Transactions,* 1934; Smith, L. P., "Cavitation on Marine Propellers," American Society of Mechanical Engineers, *Transactions,* 1937.

CAY. A low insular bank of sand, coral, and so on, awash or drying at low water. Also called **key**.

Fr: *Cay.*

CAYUCO. A dugout canoe with sharp ends used by the Arowak Indians for transportation in the coastal waters of Northern Colombia westward of Riohacha. Its length ranges from 25 to 46 ft. with a breadth of 4 to 8 ft. It is rigged with a mast and spritsail, and is steered nowadays with rudder and tiller.

CEILING. In meteorology the height of the cloud base above the earth's surface.

Fr: *Plafond.*

CEILING. A term applied to the inside planking of a vessel. Also called **foot waling**. In wooden ships the ceiling or inner planking is necessary for the structural strength of the hull. In steel vessels it is fitted as a flooring for the cargo to rest upon.

Fr: *Vaigrage;* Ger: *Wegerung; Bodenwegerung.*

See **Close Ceiling, Diagonal Ceiling, Floor Ceiling, Spar Ceiling**.

CEILING HATCH. An opening in the hold ceiling fitted with a cover which can be removed when the cargo is out. These hatches provide access to the sides and bottom inside the ship for cleaning and repairs.

Fr: *Panneau de Vaigrage;* Ger: *Wegerungsluke.*

CEILING PLANK. One of the timbers forming the ceiling of a vessel.

Fr: *Vaigre;* Ger: *Garnierplanke.*

CELESTIAL EQUATOR.
See **Equinoctial**.

CELESTIAL MERIDIAN. The great circle of the celestial sphere, which passes

through the poles and the zenith of the place of observation.
Fr: *Cercle de Déclinaison;* Ger: *Himmelsmeridian.*

CELESTIAL NAVIGATION. The methods of determining the ship's position at sea by astronomical observation of the sun, moon, stars, and planets.
Fr: *Navigation Astronomique;* Ger: *Astronomische Navigation.*

CELESTIAL POLE. One of the two opposite points of the celestial sphere where it is pierced by the earth's axis.
Fr: *Pôle Céleste;* Ger: *Himmelspol; Weltpol.*

CELESTIAL SPHERE. An imaginary surface in which the different heavenly bodies are interspersed in space at various distances from the earth, in their positions relative to the earth's center. Also called celestial concave.
Fr: *Sphère Céleste;* Ger: *Himmelskugel.*

CELLULAR DOUBLE BOTTOM. A double bottom subdivided into a great number of small compartments or cells bounded by the floors in a fore-and-aft direction and transversely by intercostal girder plates. The cells are arranged in separate groups or compartments enclosed by the center vertical girder, watertight floors and the margin plate.
Fr: *Double Fond Cellulaire;* Ger: *Zellartiger Doppelboden.*

CELO-NAVIGATION.
See **Nautical Astronomy.**

CEMENCO. Code name for British Chamber of Shipping Charter Party relating to cement cargoes for all ports in Great Britain and Ireland and on the continent between Brest and the River Elbe.

CEMENT BOX. Emergency device to stop leakage in the shell plating. It consists of a wooden framework with sides about six inches high and sufficiently large to cover the damaged area. The plating and rivets at the seat of leakage having been scaled and cleaned with caustic, and the various leaks temporarily stopped by placing a small quantity of dry cement over each, the frame is placed in position. The cement, mixed with fresh water containing a quantity of common soda in solution is then poured and molded into shape.

CEMENT WASH. A wash made of two-thirds Portland Cement and one-third fire clay mixed with fresh water, used in steel hulls as a protective coating against corrosion in double-bottom compartments and tanks containing fresh water. It has no elasticity and loosens easily from metallic surfaces when dry. Bituminous and other compositions have nowadays largely replaced cement wash for such spaces.
Fr: *Lait de Ciment;* Ger: *Zementmilch.*

CENTERBOARD. A movable fin or sliding keel made of wood or metal, pivoting in a fore-and-aft slot at the forward lower corner. Its purpose is to increase the area of lateral resistance when a sailing boat is working to windward, and to prevent excessive leeway. It is raised or lowered by means of a pendant let into the afteredge. It is used mostly in small sailing boats and yachts whose draft is less than about one-third of the breadth. Also called drop keel, center plate, pivoting centerboard.
Fr: *Dérive;* Ger: *Mittelschwert; Binnenschwert.*

CENTERBOARD CASE.
See **Trunk.**

CENTERBOARD PENDANT. The rope by which a centerboard is pulled up or lowered.
Fr: *Pendeur de Dérive;* Ger: *Schwertschenkel.*

CENTERBOARD TRUNK. The watertight casing or slot inside which a centerboard is housed when raised. Also called centerboard case.
Fr: *Puits de Dérive;* Ger: *Schwertkasten.*

It is built with a vertical headledge or headblock at each end and is limited at its bottom by fore-and-aft logs or pocketpieces. The sides are strengthened by vertical frames and knees.

CENTERBOARD WELL.
See **Trunk.**

CENTER GIRDER. The continuous fore-and-aft middle-line member of any ship that is built with a double bottom. Also called vertical keel. It consists of the center keel plate with top and bottom angles and the connecting angles at sides for the floors. It is limited at its bottom by the flat keel plate sometimes known as the "outer keel" and at its top by the center strake of the inner bottom sometimes known as the "inner keel."
Fr: *Support Central;* Ger: *Mittelträger; Mittelkielplatte.*
See **Center Keelson.**

CENTERING CHAIN. A light chain which carries a red and white disc or similar signal used in conjunction with range sights, when dry-docking a vessel, for centering her over the keel blocks.

CENTER KEELSON. A longitudinal girder on the center line of the bottom framing. Also called center through plate, vertical center keelson, middle line keelson. In double-bottomed vessels it is termed center girder or vertical keel and is usually continuous.

Fr: *Carlingue Centrale;* Ger: *Mittelkielschwein.*

CENTER LINE. In naval architecture it refers to a line of symmetry between the port and starboard sides of any vertical section or any horizontal section. It appears as a straight line in the half breadth and body plans. All half breadths are taken from this line.

Fr: *Axe Longitudinal;* Ger: *Mittschiffslinie.*

CENTER LINE BULKHEAD. A longitudinal bulkhead extending between hatchways on the ship's center line. Centerline bulkheads are mostly found on grain carriers, where they take the place of shifting boards.

Fr: *Cloison Axiale;* Ger: *Mittellängsschott.*

CENTER OF BUOYANCY. A point through which passes the resultant of all upward forces by which a ship floating freely in still water is supported. Also called center of immersed bulk. In vessels of ordinary form it is found that the distance of the center of buoyancy below the load waterline varies from 8/20 to 9/20 of the mean draft to top of keel.

Fr: *Centre de Carène;* Ger: *Verdrängungsschwerpunkt; Formschwerpunkt; Deplacementschwerpunkt.*

CENTER OF EFFORT. The point at which the resultant of wind on the total surface of the sails may be conceived to act. Also called center of pressure.

Fr: *Point Vélique;* Ger: *Segelschwerpunkt.*

There is usually no allowance made for variation in wind pressure over the sails and the center of effort is assumed to be the common center of area of the whole sail plan. It is also defined as a point in a sail where the pressure of the wind on all parts of the sail *forward* of this point is equal to the pressure of the wind on all parts of the ship *abaft* this point. In order to insure weatherliness the center of effort should be abaft the center of lateral resistance of the boat's immersed hull, but in well-designed boats the center of pressure is slightly *forward* of a line passing through the center of lateral resistance.

CENTER OF FLOATATION. The geometric center of gravity, or center of area of the water plane at which a vessel floats. A vessel pitches, or rotates (about a transverse horizontal axis) through this point, when actuated by an external force.

See **Buoyancy.**

CENTER OF GRAVITY. The point at which the combined weight of all the various items which make up a vessel's total weight may be considered as concentrated.

Fr: *Centre de Gravité;* Ger: *Systemschwerpunkt; Gewichtsschwerpunkt.*

CENTER OF LATERAL RESISTANCE. The point through which the resultant of resistance of the ship's immersed hull to lateral motion is passing. The center of lateral resistance is ordinarily assumed to be coincident with, or near, the center of gravity of the central immersed longitudinal plane.

Fr: *Centre de Dérive;* Ger: *Schwerpunkt des Treibungwiderstands; Lateralschwerpunkt.*

CENTER PLANK.

See **Sailing Thwart.**

CENTER-PLATE RUDDER. A rudder composed of one heavy plate held to the rudderstock or main piece by arms projecting therefrom on either side. Also called single-plate rudder, flat-plate rudder.

Fr: *Gouvernail à Tôle simple;* Ger: *Plattenruder; Einplattiges Ruder.*

CENTIPEDE. A strong rope or strip of oak running the length of the bowsprit and jibboom on each side, with short stops of sennit at intervals, used in stowing jibs.

CENTRIFUGAL PUMP. A pump consisting of a shaft to which vanes are attached and which rotates in a circular casing. Water is sucked into the casing near the center or rotating shaft and is impelled outward along the vanes by centrifugal force. It escapes through a discharge pipe at the circumference of the casing.

Fr: *Pompe Centrifuge;* Ger: *Centrifugal Pumpe.*

Centrifugal pumps are suitable for low and medium heads and medium to large capacities. They are particularly adapted to high speeds but are not economical for small capacities and high heads.

CENTROCON. Code name for standard charter party used for shipments of wheat, maize, rye, linseed, rape seed in bags or bulk.

CENTUM CLAUSE. A charter party clause the underlying principle of which is to fix a definite percentage to cover war risks insurance premium, any difference above it being paid by the time charterers and any difference between the percentage and a lower premium being refunded by owners to time charterers.

CERTIFICATE OF DISCHARGE. A written testimony given to a seaman on completion of his shipping agreement. Also called discharge ticket.

Fr: *Certificat de Débarquement;* Ger: *Entlassungsschein.*

It is signed by the master and countersigned by the seaman in the presence of a shipping commissioner or superintendent. It gives the name and official number of the ship, port of registry, tonnage, description of voyage, name of seaman, place and date of birth, character, capacity, date of entry, date of discharge and port of discharge.

CERTIFICATE OF DISINFECTION. A written record of the details relating to the disinfection of a vessel or part thereof, issued by the port sanitary authorities to the captain or agents for the information of subsequent ports.

It gives particulars of the portion of the vessel dealt with, the disinfectant used and, if gas is employed, the mean strength of delivery and exhaust. It is made out at the master's request and is not compulsory.

CERTIFICATE OF IDENTIFICATION. A certificate issued by the Bureau of Marine Inspection and Navigation to every seaman upon a merchant vessel of the United States of the burden of 100 gross tons or more. It contains the signature of the bearer and a statement of his nationality, age, personal description, photograph, thumbprint and home address. Also called seaman's passport.

CERTIFICATE OF ORIGIN. 1. A document signed by a consular officer of the port of shipment of goods. It entitles the consignee to get the goods imported at the port of discharge under certain privileged conditions.

2. A certificate issued by the chamber of commerce certifying the origin of goods destined to be exported.

Fr: *Certificat d'Origine;* Ger: *Ursprungsattest.*

CERTIFICATE OF OWNERSHIP. The document attesting to the oath of ownership required before a vessel can be registered, enrolled, or licensed. The oath is taken before the collector of customs. Also called owner's oath for license.

Fr: *Acte de Propriété;* Ger: *Eigentumszertifikat.*

CERTIFICATE OF PROTECTION (U. S.). A certificate granted by the United States government to a foreign-built undocumented yacht, purchased by a citizen of the United States and entitling the vessel to legal protection as property of an American citizen.

CERTIFICATE OF RECORD (U. S.). A certificate granted by the customs to a vessel built in the United States, but belonging wholly or in part to an alien, and never before documented.

CERTIFICATE OF REGISTRY. A document issued by the government establishing the nationality and ownership of a vessel and entitling her to the benefits and privileges appertaining to all vessels of the nation to which she belongs. It contains such particulars as are usually descriptive of the identity of the vessel. Also called ship's register.

Fr: *Acte de Nationalisation;* Ger: *Schiffszertifikat.*

CERTIFICATE OF SEA STORES (U. S.). A certificate issued by the customs authorities on the arrival of a vessel from a foreign port, covering stores placed under seal by the customs officers.

CERTIFICATE OF SURVEY. A certificate furnished by the port authorities as to the external condition of goods when the latter were discharged from a vessel.

Fr: *Certificat de Visite;* Ger: *Besichtigungsprotokoll; Besichtigungsschein.*

CERTIFIED MANIFEST. A ship's manifest certified by a consular officer to meet certain requirements of a country as to the importation of goods.

CERTIFIED VESSEL (U. S.). A vessel built in a foreign country and owned by American citizens. Such a vessel carries a "sea letter" as register.

CESSER CLAUSE. A clause contained in charter parties by which the charterer's liability under the charter party is to cease on shipment of the cargo, the shipowner taking a lien on the cargo for freight, dead freight, demurrage in discharging, and average. Also called limitation of liability clause.

Fr: *Cesser Clause;* Ger: *Cesser Klausel.*

CHAFING—CHAIN BARREL STEERING GEAR

CHAFING. The action of being fretted and worn by rubbing; applies to ropes, parts of the ship's structure, cargo, and so on.

Fr: *Ragage;* Ger: *Schamfielung.*

CHAFING BATTEN. A wooden batten fastened to the standing rigging to avoid wear by friction.

Fr: *Latte de ragage;* Ger: *Schamfilungslatte.*

CHAFING CHAIN. Short length of chain led through a towing chock to prevent chafing of a towline in the chock.

CHAFING GEAR. Various devices such as mats, battens, strips of leather, canvas, baggy-wrinkle, worming, parcelling, roundings and service of all kinds in the rigging to prevent injury by chafing.

CHAFING MAT. A mat-like binding wound around a hawser or rope or laid under the end of a plank or spar, to prevent chafing or wear.

Fr: *Paillet de Portage;* Ger: *Schamfielungsmatte.*

CHAFING PIECE. 1. Additional piece of canvas sewed on to a sail or awning in places where the canvas is particularly apt to be chafed.

Fr: *Placard;* Ger: *Lappung; Schamfielungslapp.*

2. A piece of plating fitted over such parts of the hull as are subject to rapid wear by chafing, as for example the lower edges of hatch coamings, the deck plating under the anchor cables, and so on. Also called chafing plate.

Fr: *Tôle de ragage;* Ger: *Schamfielungsplatte.*

3. A wooden batten fastened in the rigging to prevent chafing. Also called chafing board.

Fr: *Latte de ragage;* Ger: *Schamfielungsbrett.*

CHAIN BARREL STEERING GEAR. A steering gear in which the power is conveyed to the tiller by means of chains and rods. Also called rod and chain steering gear.

Fr: *Appareil à gouverner à Drosses;* Ger: *Reepleitungs Rudermaschine.*

The turning or motive power, if any, is usually steam in this type of gear. The steering engine is placed amidships and is controlled from the bridge by means of shafting. The link between the engine and the rudder is composed as far as possible of straight rods, but where a change of direction is

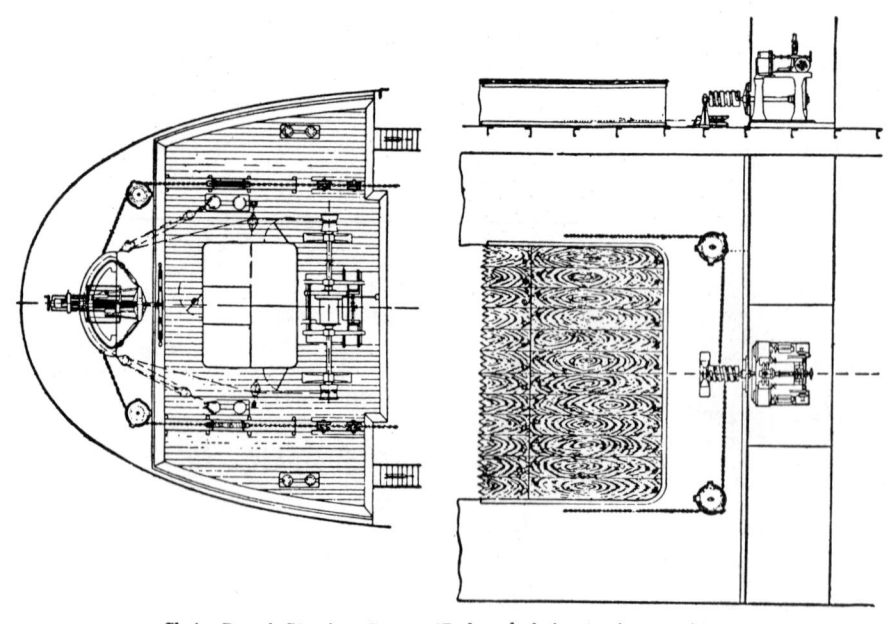

Chain Barrel Steering Gear. (Rod and chain steering gear)

necessary the rods are connected by lengths of chain passing around suitably placed fairlead pulleys. It is a very common form of steering gear for small cargo vessels.

CHAIN BOAT.
See **Mooring Lighter**.

CHAIN BOLT. One of the bolts which passes through the toe links and secures the chains to the ship's side planking.
Fr: *Cheville de Cadène;* Ger: *Puttingsbolzen.*

CHAIN CHECK STOPPER. A chain stopper used for controlling a wire when it is being paid or run out. It is rove around the wire through a deck bolt, one end of the chain being secured and the other tailed with a jigger. By tending the jigger the wire can be kept under control.

CHAIN DRAGS.
See **Drag**.

CHAIN GIRTH. The girth measured from deck to deck under and around the keel with string tape or chain pulled taut.
Fr: *Chaine;* Ger: *Kettenumfang.*

CHAIN GRAB.
See **Wildcat**.

CHAIN HOIST. A lifting apparatus which consists of a combination of an endless chain, two or more blocks and certain gears for the application of power, usually applied by a secondary hauling chain of endless construction transmitting the handpower to the upper block. Used in the engine room for lifting heavy machinery parts and in dry dock for lifting rudders, propellers and so on.
Fr: *Palan à chaînes;* Ger: *Ketten Aufzug.*

CHAIN HOOK. A handled hook 18 to 36 in. long used for handling the chain cables about the deck or in the chain locker.
Ger: *Kettenhaken.*

CHAIN INTERMITTENT WELDING. A welding technique in which corresponding increments of a double fillet joint are directly opposite each other.
Fr: *Soudure en Chaîne;* Ger: *Kettenschweissung; Gleichmässig Unterbrochenes Schweissung.*

CHAIN LEGS. A double chain sling consisting of two lengths of chain attached to one ring and provided with a hook at each free end. Also called "chain fours."

CHAIN LOCKER. A compartment located forward, under the windlass, in which the anchor cables are stowed. It is usually subdivided inside by a longitudinal bulkhead pipe fitted on each side of the vessel directly under the windlass to lead the anchor chains to the chain locker. Also called deck pipe, navel pipe, spill pipe, spurling gate. At the top end of each pipe a portable cover of galvanized plating with opening for the passage of the chain is provided. The bottom ends in the chain locker are fitted with a heavy half-round chafing ring.
Fr: *Ecubier de Pont;* Ger: *Deckkluse.*

CHAIN PLATE. One of the strips of plating secured to the side of a ship, to which the lower deadeye or the lower end of a shroud or backstay is fastened. Also called chain.
Fr: *Cadène;* Ger: *Puttingeisen; Rüsteisen.*

CHAIN RIVETING. Rows of rivets placed in parallel lines both in the longitudinal and transverse directions. Used generally where two, or more, rows of rivets are required in the butts and seams of plating.
Fr: *Rivetage en Chaine;* Ger: *Kettennietung.*

CHAIN SLING. A length of short link chain used for working cargo and generally provided with a ring at one end and a hook at the other, or two lengths of chain attached to a ring with a hook at their free ends. The double branch chain sling consists of two chains about 12 ft. long with hook on one end and a single ring coupling for both at the other.
Fr: *Elingue en Chaîne;* Ger: *Kettenschlinge.*

Chain slings for bag and jute cargo are usually made of ⅝-in. chain 24 ft. long. For general cargo ¾-in. chain 20 ft. long. For handling rails, pipes, steel joists, and so on, ⅝-in. chain 10 ft. long. For heavy lift up to 5 tons 1-in. chain with a length of 15 ft.
British Standards Institution, London, Standard 781, *Wrought Iron Chain Slings,* 1938.

CHAIN SPLICE. A splice used for securing a rope to a chain.

CHAIN STOPPER.
See **Controller**.

CHAIN TILLER. A tiller which is acted upon by ropes or chains leading to a drum. The motion of the drum is obtained by a handwheel or steering engine.
Fr: *Barre à Drosses.*

CHALEU. A single outrigger dugout canoe from central New Ireland (Bismarck Archipelago). The blunt-ended bow terminates in an elongated shelf which bends slightly downward.

CHALOUPE. Name given on the French Atlantic coast from Bayonne to Brest to a type of fishing boat which derived from the former *chasse-marée*. The type is probably extinct now.

It is rigged with two masts, standing lugsails, and one headsail. In very light winds topsails are set and a jigger mast with small lug stepped aft. The hull is built with sharp stern, decked fore and aft with small cockpit for the helmsman. The foresail is sheeted well aft overlapping the mainsail, and has 4 rows of reef points. Length 47.2 ft. Breadth 16.7 ft. Depth 7.0 ft.

CHALUPA. Name given on the coast of Peru to a small decked fishing boat of Mediterranean origin with sharp stern and broad beam. A centrally placed mast on which a spritsail and jib are set forms the rig.

CHAMFER. To bevel the edge of a plate.

Fr: *Chanfreiner;* Ger: *Schmiegen.*

CHANGE OF TIDE. The substitution of one condition of tide (rising or falling) for another (falling or rising) or of one direction of flow of tide to another.

Fr: *Renverse de la Marée;* Ger: *Umsetzen des Stromes.*

CHANNEL. 1. The deeper part of a river, estuary, and so on. That part of a body of water of sufficient depth to be used for navigation. Also called approach.

Fr: *Chenal;* Ger: *Fahrrinne; Fahrwasserkanal.*

2. Also chain wale. Flat ledges of wood or steel projecting outboard from the ship's sides and forming outriggers for the shrouds. In modern vessels and small craft the channels have disappeared, shroud plates being secured to the gunwale or sheer strake.

Fr: *Porte-Haubans;* Ger: *Ruste.*

3. Also channel bar. A rolled bar having a cross section shaped like a U, often used for frames, beams, bulkhead stiffeners, and stanchions. It is made of two flanges and a web.

Fr: *Fer U;* Ger: *U Profil; Rinneneisen.*

CHANNEL BUOY. One of a set of buoys indicating the limits and direction of a navigational channel. In most maritime countries all buoys on one side of the channel are painted in one color, those on the opposite side in another color. They are also numbered consecutively, starting from the seaward end of the channel.

Fr: *Bouée de Chenal;* Ger: *Fahrwassertonne.*

CHANNEL MONEY (G. B.). Money which a seaman on a British ship can claim at the time when he lawfully leaves the ship at the end of the voyage, or of his engagement. The amount is either two pounds sterling or one-quarter the balance of wages due, whichever is the least. The balance must be paid to the seaman within 48 hours of arrival.

CHANNEL NAVIGATION. That which is required when a ship has to be navigated in narrow channels with dangers on both sides, and in rivers and their approaches.

CHANNEL WALES. Three or four thick strakes of planking worked between the upper and lower deck ports for the purpose of strengthening the topsides (obsolete).

CHANTEY.

See **Shanty.** Also called Chanty.

CHAPELING; CHAPELING SHIP. Said of a ship under sail taken aback in a light breeze and made to recover on the same tack by the helm alone, without bracing the yards, and causing her to make a complete circle until she arrives at her original position.

Fr: *Faire Chapelle.*

CHARACTERISTIC. Nature or composition of the beam of light exhibited by a navigational mark such as a lighthouse, lightship or lightbuoy.

Fr: *Caractéristique;* Ger: *Charakteristik.*

CHARANGUERO. A Spanish decked sailing vessel employed in the small coasting trade on the coast of Andalucia and the Guadalquivir estuary. It is lateen-rigged with two masts. The foremast is stepped near the bow; the mizzen is very short and located near the stern. There is a bowsprit with one headsail.

CHARGES CLAUSE. A charter party clause which regulates who is to pay harbor tolls, wharfage, dues and duties on cargo, pilotage, towage, and so on.

CHARIGMA. A single-outrigger dugout canoe from the Andaman Islands similar to the *gilyanga* but larger.

CHARLIE NOBLE. A colloquial term applied to the hood of the galley smoke pipe. Sometimes used to denote the entire smoke pipe including hood.

CHARR (to).
See **Bream (to).**

CHART.
See **Nautical Chart.**

CHART BLOCK. The reproduction of a small portion of a nautical chart published in *Notices to Mariners* or equivalent pamphlets. It gives the corrections to apply or cancels existing matter on the chart. It is usually pasted to the chart for which it is issued.

CHART DATUM. The plane of reference to which all data as to depths on charts are referred.
Fr: *Zéro des Cartes;* Ger: *Kartennull.*
See **Nautical Chart.**

On American charts the level of *mean* low water at ordinary spring tides is adopted for the Atlantic coast and the level of *lower* low water for the Pacific coast. Admiralty charts founded on foreign surveys use the datum of the original authority. In countries of the European continent, excluding France and Spain, mean low water at ordinary spring tides is used. In France and Spain charts are datumed on lowest low water possible.
Warburg, H. D., "Coordination of Chart Datums," *Hydrographic Review* (Monaco), vol. 2 (May, 1925).

CHARTED VISIBILITY. The visibility of coastal lights as given on charts and in light lists. Charted visibilities are calculated for an assumed height of eye of 15 ft. above sea level.

CHARTER.
See **Charter Party.**

CHARTER COMMISSION. The compensation paid by a shipowner or operator to a broker for the chartering of a vessel.
Fr: *Commission d'Affrètement;* Ger: *Befrachtungskommission.*

It is usually inserted as a clause in the charter party and is calculated as a percentage on the gross freight, the figure depending on the size of the vessel, the nature of services required by the owner of the vessel, the custom of the port, and other similar contingencies.

CHARTERED FREIGHT. Term by which freight is known when payment is made for the cargo space of an entire vessel or a part thereof under a charter party agreement.
Ger: *Chartergeld.*

CHARTERER. The person to whom is given the use of the whole of the carrying capacity (earning space) of a ship for the transportation of goods or passengers to a stated port or for a specified time. The remuneration and conditions of the contract are contained in the charter or charter party.
Fr: *Affréteur;* Ger: *Befrachter; Charterer.*

CHARTERING BROKER. A person or firm engaged in the business of finding charters for ships or tonnage for the requirements of merchants. Also called chartering agent.
Fr: *Courtier d'Affrètement;* Ger: *Befrachtungsmakler.*

All negotiations for tonnage and the fixing thereof are carried out by the chartering broker, who is presumed to be acquainted with the accommodations at ports and the size of vessel that can safely get into these ports; also the approximate charges and usual dispatch. He has a thorough knowledge of the clauses contained in the charter parties relating to the particular trade he is interested in. The ordinary course is for the document signed by the parties to be kept by the broker, who gives out certified copies of it as may be required. The broker receives a commission from the shipowner on the agreed or estimated freight.

CHARTER MONEY. The sum charged for the hiring of a vessel in its entirety.

CHARTER PARTY. An agreement by which a shipowner agrees to place an entire ship, or a part of it, at the disposal of a merchant or other person, for the conveyance of goods, binding the shipowner to transport them to a particular place, for a sum of money which the merchant undertakes to pay as freight for their carriage. Sometimes called charter.
Fr: *Charte Partie;* Ger: *Charterpartei; Frachtvertrag; Charter.*

Charters are either time, voyage, or demise. A charter party forms the basic shipping paper or agreement between the charterer and the shipowner or his agent. It is usually a lengthy document containing detailed clauses as to the tonnage, capacity, and condition of the vessel, the course it is to pursue, loading and discharging ports, ports of call, methods of loading and discharging, signature of bills of lading, employment of stevedores, free time within which vessel shall be loaded and the demurrage per day payable thereafter, liability and insurance, commission and freight brokerage due to the ship broker, and the rate of compensation.

Jenkins, E., *Chartering,* London, 1929; MacMurray & Cree, *Charter Parties of the World,* London, 1935; Poor, W., *American Law of Charter Parties,* New York, 1920; Scrutton, T. E., *Contracts of Affreightment,* London, 1925.

CHARTER RATES. The tariff currently

applied for chartering tonnage in a particular trade. Charter rates are usually based upon the weight or measurement ton or other specific unit of the particular trade in which the vessel engages. Under time charters the payment to the owner is generally based upon the deadweight capacity of the vessel if it is a cargo carrier, and upon the gross register tonnage if it is a passenger vessel.

Fr: *Taux d'Affrètement;* Ger: *Chartersatz.*

CHART HOUSE.
See **Chart Room.**

CHART ROOM. A room on or near the bridge provided with the necessary fittings and furniture for the handling and stowage of charts and where the chronometers are placed. Also called chart house.

Fr: *Chambre des Cartes; Kiosque de Veille;* Ger: *Navigationszimmer; Kartenhaus; Kartenzimmer.*

CHASSE MAREE. A three-masted French lugger from Britanny, formerly employed in the fisheries and small coasting trade. Now extinct.

See **Lougre.**

CHAVEGA. A seine boat from the South Coast of Portugal (Algarve Province) employed in the sardine fisheries with a net of the same name. Also called *Xavega.* Length 31.9 ft. Breadth 8.2 ft. Depth 2.3 ft.

It has a peculiar long pointed stem which rises considerably above water level; sharp stern with curved stern post. There is no rudder; a long sweep is used for steering. The afterpart is decked and there are ten or more thwarts for the rowers.

CHEBACCO BOAT. A pink-stern fishing boat originating from Chebacco (now Essex) Mass., much used until about 1820 for inshore fishing in New England.

CHECK. A small split running parallel to the grain in a piece of timber, usually caused by strains produced during seasoning.

CHECK (to). 1. To slack off slowly; to stop a vessel's way gradually by a line fastened to some fixed object or an anchor on the bottom.

2. To ease off a rope a little, especially with a view to reducing the tension.

3. To stop or regulate the motion, as of a cable when it is running out too violently or too fast.

Fr: *Choquer;* Ger: *Fieren; Abstoppen; Schrecken.*

CHECKER (U. S.). One of the portable wood divisions or planks that form the sides of the fish pounds on the deck of a fishing vessel. In Great Britain called pound board.

Ger: *Bohle; Fischschotten.*

See **Tallyman.**

CHECKERED PLATE. A plate used as flooring, marked with raised diamond checkers or squares to provide good footing. Used in engine and fire rooms. Also called diamond decking.

Fr: *Tôle à Empreintes;* Ger: *Riffelplatte.*

CHECK HELM. The helm applied when a ship is brought back on her course, to prevent her going beyond the proper course and to stop the swing as the ship's head approaches this course. Also called meeting rudder.

CHECKING BOLLARD. A bollard used ashore for warping ships through dock entrances; the friction afforded by several turns of rope being utilized for checking the vessel's way. They are not fitted with whelps or lips but the head is usually of bulbous shape. Also called warping bollard, or deadhead.

Fr: *Bollard;* Ger: *Verholpoller; Landpoller.*

American Marine Standards Committee, Pamphlet 77, *Bollards and Cleats for Docks,* Washington, 1931.

CHECK RING.
See **Stern Tube End Plate.**

CHECK ROPE. A term applied to a rope used in checking the way of a vessel when docking or warping. A hawser having one end fastened to a dock and the other end turned around a bitt so that it may be slackened or held taut.

Fr: *Retenue;* Ger: *Schricktau.*

CHECK STOPPER. One of a series of ropes used when launching a vessel. They are fastened to an anchor or to a coil of heavy chain, and designed to part in turn as the cable runs out serving as a check to the natural velocity of the ship's motion.

Fr: *Bosse Cassante;* Ger: *Murbe Stopper.*

See **Drag.**

CHEEK. 1. One of the faces or projecting parts on each side of a masthead, and of suitable shape to sustain the trestletrees upon which the framing of the top together with the topmast rests. Also called mast cheek or shoulder. When made of steel they are known as "cheek-plates" and are riveted on each side of the mast. They are made of thick plating about 50 per cent heavier than the mast. The upper edge is stiffened by a large angle bar and the forward edge by a half-round molding or small angle. The term "cheek" is used when referring to a lower mast only; for other masts the term "hound" is used.

Fr: *Jottereau;* Ger: *Mastbacke.*

2. One of the two sides or framing of a block.

Fr: *Joue;* Ger: *Backe; Blockbacke.*

CHEEK BLOCK. 1. One of the small pieces of wood fastened to the sides of a mast to take the loops of shrouds, also to the front and back to take the loops of stays. When used with wire rigging they are metal surfaced to prevent damage through chafing.

Fr: *Martyr;* Ger: *Sattel.*

2. A half shell covering a sheave on the side of a mast or spar. Used on gaffs and booms.

Fr: *Joue de vache;* Ger: *Scheibenklampe; Schildpatt.*

CHEEK KNEE. One of the side knee-pieces by which the cutwater is secured to the bows of the ship.

Fr: *Jottereau;* Ger: *Schliessknie.*

See **Head Cheeks.**

CHEEKPIECE. A strengthening piece of oval section fitted to the upper portion of the rudder of an open boat and carried down below the upper pintle.

Fr: *Joue de Safran.*

CHEEK PLATE.

See **Cheek.**

CHEESEMAN'S RIG.

See **Butter Rig.**

CHELINGA. An open surf boat of the Coromandel Coast with square body amidships and sharp ends. The planking is sewed with coconut fibre and has a thickness of about 2 in. There are no frames. These boats are mainly used to carry passengers and goods from ship to shore through the breakers. Length 35 to 40 ft. Breadth 10 ft. Depth 7 ft. Also called *salangu.*

CHEMPLONG. Large East Indian paddling canoe from Sumatra, now believed extinct. Length 60 ft. Breadth 5 ft. Depth 2 ft. 3 in. Capacity about 2¼ tons. Crew 12.

CHEN-KOO. An open fishing boat from Swatow (China) with a length of 29 ft. and breadth of 10 ft.

CHEQUERED BUOY. A harbor or channel buoy painted with broad parallel lines of sharply contrasting colors.

Fr: *Bouée peinte par bandes;* Ger: *Gestreifte Tonne.*

CHESSTREE. Piece of wood with one or several sheaves, bolted to the topsides through which the tack of a course was rove and extended to windward (obsolete).

Fr: *Porte Lof;* Ger: *Halsklampe.*

CHESTNUT. A soft coarse-grained wood with good lasting qualities. A certain percentage of chestnut may be used in the framing of wooden hulls without loss of class, although for fastenings it does not possess the strength or holding power of other hardwoods used in ship construction.

Fr: *Châtaigner;* Ger: *Kastanienholz.*

CHIEF CABIN PASSENGER (G. B.). A term occasionally used to denote a first class passenger.

CHIEF CLERK. 1. A member of the crew belonging to the purser's department and entrusted with clerical duties.

2. In the United States the executive in a shipping organization who supervises the receiving, delivery, and timekeeping departments and who is, generally speaking, in charge of all clerical forces.

CHIEF ENGINEER. The senior engineer officer, responsible for the satisfactory working and upkeep of the main and auxiliary machinery and boiler plant on board ship.

Fr: *Chef Mécanicien;* Ger: *Leitender Ingenieur; Leitender Maschinist; Obermaschinist.*

CHIEF OFFICER. The officer next in rank to the master on board a merchant vessel. The one upon whom the command of the vessel would fall in the event of death or disability of the captain. Also called first-mate, chief mate, mate.

Fr: *Second;* Ger: *Ober Offizier.*

On vessels carrying three licensed officers the chief officer usually stands the morning and evening watches. In the larger passenger vessels it is the practice to assign an additional watch-keeping officer to relieve the chief officer of his watch-standing duties. Since the chief officer is second in command he is the master's direct representative. All officers are under his orders in matters pertaining to operation and maintenance of the vessel, except in so far as such matters are the direct responsibility of the chief engineer or chief steward.

CHIEF STEWARD. One who has full control of the steward's department on board ship. He has charge of and is responsible for the discipline of all hands belonging to his department. On passenger vessels he is responsible for the comfort and service of all passengers. He obtains and regulates the issue of all provisions and stores which are

to last him through the voyage. He is in charge of the inspection and proper storage of provisions.
Fr: *Premier maître d'Hôtel;* Ger: *Proviantmeister; Obersteward.*

CHILL BOX. A refrigerated room on board ship maintained at a temperature above freezing. This room is used for thawing thoroughly frozen food and for keeping fresh foods for short periods of time.
Fr: *Chambre de décongélation.*

CHILLED CARGO. A name given to cargo cooled through a mild process of refrigeration whereby only a thin outside layer of the product is cooled, the temperature ranging from 29° to 42° F.
Fr: *Cargaison Refroidie; Cargaison Réfrigérée;* Ger: *Kühlgut; Gekühlte Ladung.*

CHIME WHISTLE. A whistle or set of whistles emitting several harmonious notes musically tuned to obtain a greater volume of sound.
Fr: *Sifflet Harmonique;* Ger: *Harmonische Pfeife; Zweiklangpfeife.*

CHINCHORRO. 1. A small open boat used in the Spanish and Portuguese fisheries for working a seine also called *chinchorro*. In Spain the larger type of *pareja* carries on board a small *chinchorro* boat which is put over the side and used as a tender when the vessel reaches the fishing grounds. The *chinchorro* is mostly dependent on oars for propulsion although larger units are seen with one short mast and lateen sail. Length 18 to 29 ft. Breadth 4.1 to 6.5 ft. Depth 1.4 to 1.9 ft.

2. In the merchant marine the smallest ship's boat, equivalent to the dinghy.

CHINCHORROHAN. A canoelike boat of the Philippines belonging to the *banca* type and sometimes fitted with outriggers. It has from 10 to 14 thwarts. The paddles are long-handled with narrow oblong blades. It is used for fishing with the *chinchorro* net, and often sets an auxiliary sail.

CHINE. 1. The line of intersection between the sides and the bottom of a flat or V-bottom hull.
See **Chine Piece.**

2. In a wooden ship the thick part of a waterway projecting above the deck and hollowed out on the inboard edge to form a watercourse. Also called chine.
Fr: *Serre-Gouttière;* Ger: *Wassergang.*

CHINEDKULAN. A plank-built rowing canoe from Botel Tobago Island with high rising stern and stem, similar to the *tatara* but much larger. It has accommodation for 10 rowers (seated) and a helmsman (standing) with a long steering oar. Length 24.6 ft. Breadth amidships 2.4 ft. Height of ends 7 ft. Depth amidships 2.4 ft.

The 4 strakes of planking are strengthened by 2 frames or ribs placed symmetrically about one-third of the boat's length from each end, fastened with rattan lashings to the comb cleats of the planks. Additional strengthening is supplied by 5 horizontal cross members, which besides acting as supports for the thwarts supply lateral thrust to the sides of the boat.

Similar craft are constructed by the Bataans of the Northern Philippines.

CHINE AND CHINE. A method of stowing casks when placed end to end.

CHINE PIECE. A longitudinal piece which runs from stem to stern where the side and bottom frames join in a V-bottom boat. Also called chine log.
Fr: *Lisse d'angle;* Ger: *Kimmweger.*

CHINESE LUG. A balanced lugsail extended by battens as found on Chinese junks and similar craft. Each batten is fitted with a sheet, all these sheets terminating in one or two hauling parts which are led through an outrigger from the stern to give sufficient drift to haul out the sail as flat as a board and with the upper part remaining very much at the same angle as the lower.
Fr: *Voile de Jonque;* Ger: *Chinesisches Luggersegel.*

CHING. A generic name given to small boats used for fishing with hand lines for red snapper, in the Gulf of Mexico. It covers any craft from a registered vessel of less than 20 tons to a small motorboat.

The *chings* are usually similar in type to fishing schooners but smaller. Some are of nondescript type and rig ranging from double-ended sponge boats to designs with bluff bows and flat or slightly rounded sterns. They work in a radius of 30 to 150 miles from port. Crew 3 to 7 hands.

CHINSE. To calk temporarily by forcing oakum or cotton into the seams of a small boat with a chisel or the point of a knife. To calk lightly where the planks will not stand heavy blows.
Fr: *Boucher;* Ger: *Verstopfen.*

CHINSING IRON. A calker's tool for chinsing.
Fr: *Ciseau à boucher;* Ger: *Stopfeisen.*

CHIPPER; CHIPPER AND CALKER.

Chinese Lug

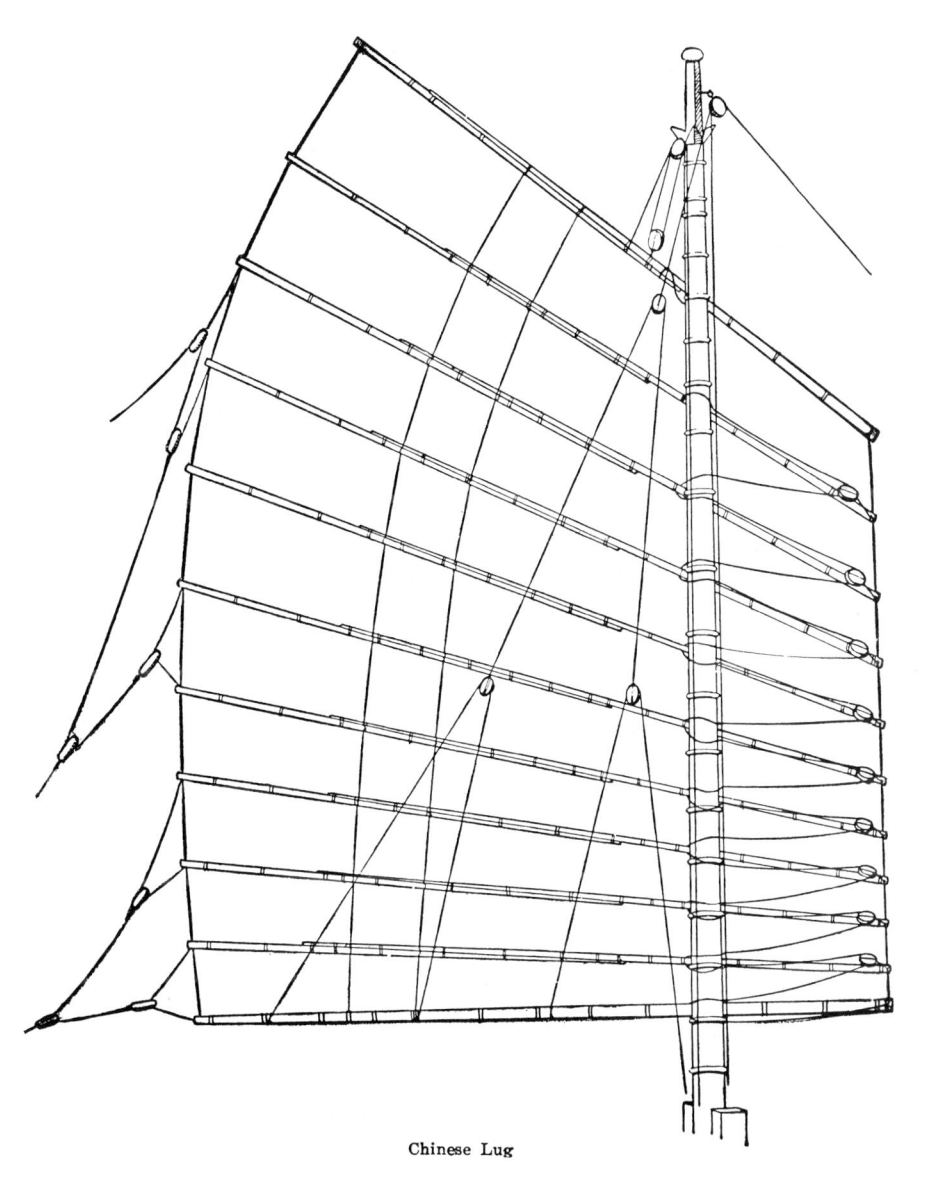

A shipyard worker who trims, cuts, and prepares the edges of various structural parts for calking, welding, fitting, or finishing purposes. He operates an air-driven chipping hammer. He is frequently referred to as chipper and calker because he also calks, using the same air-hammer with calking chisels.

Fr: *Ragréeur;* Ger: *Splitter; Behauer.*

CHIPPING HAMMER. 1. Small hammer with sharp peen and face set at right angles to each other, used on board ship for chipping and scaling of metallic surfaces. It is made from high-grade tool steel with cutting edges, approximately 1⅛ in., hardened, tempered and ground. Also called scaling hammer, or boiler pick.

Fr: *Marteau à Piquer;* Ger: *Rosthammer.*

2. An air-driven hammer equipped with variously shaped chisel-like tools, for vee-ing out, gouging, rounding off, cutting, and dressing steel-plate edges.

CHIPS. Colloquial name given by seamen to a ship's carpenter.

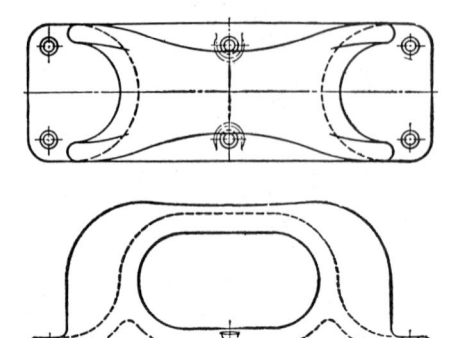

Plain Closed Chock. (*American Marine Standard*)

CHOCK. 1. A shaped block of wood used to prevent anything from shifting when a vessel rolls. The term is also applied to blocks of wood used as connecting or reinforcing pieces or as filling pieces. Sometimes termed bolster.

See **Boat Chock, Boom Chock, Bowsprit Chock, Cross Chock, Dowsing Chock, Filling Chock, Floor Head Chock, Rolling Chock, Rudder Chock, Shell Chock, Shifting Chock.**

2. A heavy wooden or metal fitting secured on a deck or on a dock, having jaws through which line or cable passes, and for which it serves as a fair-lead.

Fr: *Coussin; Cale;* Ger: *Aufklotzung.*

CHOCK (to). In stowing goods, to secure them with dunnage or otherwise so that there will be no displacement through the motion of the vessel when at sea. Also called chock off, block off.

Ger: *Abstauen.*

CHOCKABLOCK.
See **Two Blocks.**

CHOCK PIN. A slender oak pin passing through the chocks of a whaleboat to keep the whale line from jumping.

CHOCOLATE GALE. Colloquial expression used for denoting a brisk northwest wind in the West Indies.

CHOKE. To thrust the hauling part of a tackle close to the block, under the other parts, thus jamming the hauling part and keeping the tackle from rendering.

Fr: *Faire Mordre.*

CHOLERA. An infectious disease prevailing epidemically. According to the International Sanitary Convention of 1926 any vessel shall be regarded as *infected* by cholera if there is a case on board or if there has been a case during the five days previous to the arrival of the ship in port. A ship shall be regarded as *suspected* if there was a case of cholera at the time of departure or during the voyage but no fresh case previous to arrival. Although a ship may be arriving from an infected port, it shall be considered *healthy* if there was no case of cholera either at the time of departure, during the voyage, or on arrival.

Fr: *Choléra;* Ger: *Cholera.*

CHOPPY SEA; CHOPPING SEA. Tumbling waves dashing against each other with a short and quick motion. Also called cockling sea.

Fr: *Mer Courte;* Ger: *Kabbelige See.*

CHOTE. An open boat with raking stem from Chittagong and the Hooghly estuary (Bengal). The hull is of V cross section. When properly ballasted it is said to be a good sea boat.

CHRONOMETER.
See **Marine Chronometer.**

CHRONOMETER BOX. A wooden or metallic box placed at one end of the chart room table, where the ship's chronometers are accommodated. Also called chronometer cabinet.

It is divided into three compartments each of which is lined at the sides and bottom with portable felt cushions to prevent any movement or vibration of the chronometers. A hinged glass-paneled cover is fitted over each compartment.

CHRONOMETER CORRECTION. Chronometer error with the sign reversed,

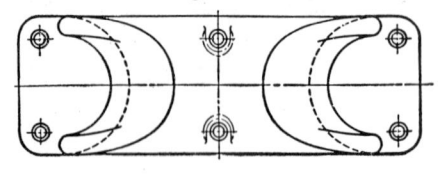

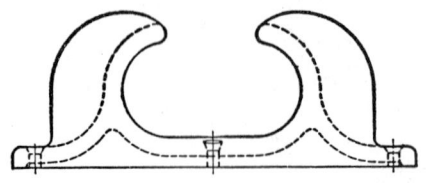

Plain Open Chock. (*American Marine Standard*)

so that when applied to the chronometer reading the corresponding Greenwich civil is obtained.

CHRONOMETER ERROR. The accumulated loss or gain from Greenwich civil time resulting from the daily rate of a chronometer. The error is positive if the chronometer is fast, otherwise negative. Also called Chronometer Correction.

CHRONOMETER RATE. The difference between two errors of the chronometer divided by the time elapsed between the finding of those two errors.

Fr: *Marche Chronométrique;* Ger: *Chronometergang.*

CHRONOMETER RECORD BOOK. A book kept by the navigating officer in which are recorded the daily readings of the ship's chronometers and corresponding temperatures. It enables the navigator to ascertain their rate at different temperatures and also detect any irregularity should it occur in one of them.

Fr: *Journal des Montres;* Ger: *Chronometerjournal.*

CHRONOMETRIC DISTANCE. The difference in time between and meridians of two places.

CHUBASCO. Violent squall on the West Coast of Mexico.

CHUM.
See Ground Bait.

CHUM BOAT.
See Striker Boat.

CHUMMER. One of the crew in a fishing boat whose duty it is to scatter bait on the surface of the sea to attract a school of fish during fishing operations.

CHURNING. Term used by seamen to describe the agitation on the surface of the water caused by the action of the propeller.

CIPHERING. Rebetting the edges of planks or boards to half-thickness in order to maintain tightness of seams in case of shrinkage of the wood. This procedure is adopted for hold ceilings, bulwarks, deckhouse sides.

CIRCLE "C" METHOD. A method used by naval architects for computing the power and speed of cargo ships. Its name is derived from the fact that the computation makes use of a coefficient which is designated by the symbol (C).

The formula is:

$$(C) = \frac{427.1 \times \text{Effective Horsepower}}{\text{Displacement } 2/3 \times \text{Speed } 3}$$

This method assumes that the resistance is practically all frictional and that the power varies as the cube of the speed.

CIRCLE COEFFICIENTS. Coefficients based on Froude's notation and employed in Great Britain for estimating speed, resistance, and hull form in the design of vessels. Also called circle constants. They apply to ships and models of all sizes and afford an easy and quick method of comparison of forms as regards shape and the relation of their speed and power to dimensions. (C) is a resistance constant. It is strictly a characteristic of the hull and is usually plotted against one of the functions of speed. (K) and (P) are speed constants used for recording resistance data and, with the admiralty coefficient, for estimating power requirements. (M) is a length constant. (S) a skin resistance constant.

CIRCLES OF ALTITUDE. One of the great circles on the celestial sphere perpendicular to the observer's horizon, hence passing through his zenith and nadir. They are so called because altitudes of heavenly bodies are measured along them.

Fr: *Vertical;* Ger: *Höhenkreis; Vertikal.*

CIRCLE OF DECLINATION. One of the great circles of the celestial sphere perpendicular to the equinoctial; so called because the declination of heavenly bodies is measured upon them. Also called hour circle.

Fr: *Cercle de Déclinaison;* Ger: *Stundenkreis.*

CIRCLE OF EQUAL ALTITUDE. A circle on the earth's surface from every point of which a given heavenly body has the same observed altitude at any given time.

Ger: *Gleicher Höhenkreis.*

CIRCLE OF LATITUDE. 1. Any one of the great circles of the celestial sphere perpendicular to the plane of the ecliptic.

2. A meridian on the terrestrial sphere along which latitude is measured.

Fr: *Cercle de Latitude; Parallèle de Latitude;* Ger: *Breitenparallel.*

CIRCLE OF LONGITUDE. 1. A small circle of the celestial sphere parallel to the plane of the ecliptic.

2. A parallel of latitude on the terrestrial sphere along which longitude is measured.

Fr: *Cercle Méridien.*

CIRCLE OF RIGHT ASCENSION. A great circle passing through the poles of the celestial sphere.

CIRCLE OF VISIBILITY. The circle of visibility of a light is the distance at

which a light is visible when the height of the observer's eye is 15 feet above sea level.
Fr: *Circle de Visibilité;* Ger: *Sichtbarkeits Kreis.*

CIRCULAR-HEADED SKYLIGHT. A rectangular skylight in which the ends are vertical and the upper part semicircular. The sides are used as seats.

CIRCULAR RADIOBEACON. A radiobeacon the signal from which is radiated with equal intensity in all directions.
Fr: *Radiophare à Rayonnement Circulaire;* Ger: *Rundfunksender; Kreisfunkbake.*
See **Radio Beacon.**

CIRCUMPOLAR. A term applied in nautical astronomy to a heavenly body when it has two meridian passages; one above and one below the elevated pole.
Fr: *Circumpolaire;* Ger: *Zirkumpolar.*

CIRCUMZENITHAL ARC. A halo phenomenon with most vivid coloring. It is observed in the same azimuth as the sun, but at a higher altitude, and is usually a comparative short arc convex to the sun.

CIRRO-CUMULUS. A type of cloud formed of small globular masses or white flakes without shadows, or showing very slight shadows, arranged in groups and often in lines. Cirro-cumulus clouds develop from cirro-stratus. Either cirro-cumulus or altocumulus clouds, when arranged in regular waves covering the sky, but showing blue sky in the gaps, produce a "mackerel sky." The average altitude of cirro-cumulus clouds is 24,000 feet.

CIRRO-STRATUS. A thin whitish sheet of clouds sometimes covering the sky completely and giving it merely a milky appearance (when it is called cirro-nebula, or cirrus haze), at other times presenting more or less distinctly a fibrous formation like a tangled web. Halos around the sun or moon are often caused by cirro-stratus clouds. The average altitude of this cloud is 29,000 feet.

CIRRUS. Detached fibrous variety of cloud of delicate appearance, often of featherlike structure, and generally whitish.
See **False Cirrus, Cirro-Cumulus, Cirro-Stratus.**

In shape cirrus clouds are isolated tufts, threads spreading out like feathers, straight or curved filaments terminating in tufts, or thin filaments in a blue sky. They are sometimes arranged in parallel belts which cross a portion of the sky in a great circle. The three cirrus types, cirrus, cirro-cumulus, and cirro-stratus, are always composed of minute ice crystals, while other clouds are composed of water droplets. The average altitude of cirrus clouds is 31,000 feet.

CIVIL DAY. A mean solar day commencing at midnight. Also called calendar day.
Fr: *Jour Civil;* Ger: *Bürgerlicher Tag.*

CIVIL SALVAGE. Salvage strictly speaking consists in the preservation of life or property from some of the dangers of the sea, but the term is more often used to denote the money compensation or reward made by the owner of a ship or cargo for services rendered by persons other than the ship's company in preserving ship and cargo from wreck, fire, or capture at sea.

Fr: *Sauvetage;* Ger: *Bergung; Bettung; Bergeleistung.*

Salvage services are distinguished from towage chiefly by the fact that they are afforded in imminent peril and danger to ships and their cargoes in distress, these being extricated and relieved from the peril and danger and brought to a place of safety. The same term is also applied to the salvor's service and the salvor's reward.
Carver, *Law Relating to the Carriage of Goods by Sea,* London, 1925; Kennedy, A. R., *Treatise on the Law of Civil Salvage,* London, 1936; Raynor, C. D., "Civil Salvage," Insurance Institute of London, *Jour.,* vol. 30 (1937).

CIVIL TIME. Time reckoned by the motion of the mean sun with respect to the specified geographical location. Sometimes called civil mean time. The civil day begins at the instant of transit of the mean sun over the lower branch of meridian, that is, it runs from midnight to midnight.

Fr: *Heure Civile;* Ger: *Bürgerliche Zeit.*

CLACK BOX.
See **Storm Valve.**

CLAMP. 1. A heavy strake of timber fastened to the inside face of the frame timbers under and supporting the shelves. Also called sheer clamp, clamp strake.

In small craft, where shelves are often dispensed with the clamp is secured directly to the beams. In other craft the shelves are secured to the inside face of the clamp with their top flush with the top edge of the clamp.

Fr: *Serre-Bauquière;* Ger: *Stossweger; Unterbalkweger.*

2. See **Fish Front.**

3. A one-cheeked block, the spar to which it is fastened forming the other cheek. Also called cheek block.

Fr: *Galoche;* *Joue de Vache;* **Ger:** *Scheibeklampe.*

4. In a sextant, a screw carried by the index bar for holding it against the limb. Also called clamping screw.

Fr: *Vis de Pression;* Ger: *Klemmschraube.*

CLAMP STRAKE.
See **Clamp.**

CLAP ON. 1. To clap on to a rope means "to catch hold in order to haul upon it."
2. To clap on a stopper or a tackle means to put on a stopper or a tackle.
3. To clap on canvas means to make more sail.

CLAPPER.
See **Tongue.**

CLASS. Class when referring to vessels of commerce means the character assigned to a vessel by a classification society, depending on the design of the vessel, the quality of materials employed, the scantlings of the various structural members, and the outfit and equipment, all of which should be up to the standard specified by the society's rules. To ensure that the condition and seaworthiness of classed vessels are maintained they are examined periodically and upon the result of such survey depends the continuance of the class.

Fr: *Cote;* Ger: *Klasse.*

See **Handicap Class, Open Design Class, Open Class, Restricted Class.**

CLASSIFICATION. The assigning of characters to merchant ships according to certain rules established by a classification society. All classification rules have for their object the attainment and maintenance of a determined standard of structural efficiency based on the assumption that vessels receive ordinary seamanlike treatment in the course of their employment.

Fr: *Classification;* Ger: *Klassifikation.*

See **Society.**

Classification societies' rules are not absolutely rigid in every detail, as the progress of shipbuilding methods and materials makes it necessary that a certain amount of latitude be allowed. They represent the minimum standards which the society considers necessary for a particular type of vessel. In classed vessels the materials and the actual building are under the supervision of the society's surveyors. Inspectors are sent to the steel works; every frame, plate, or other structural part is checked or stamped. The propelling plant, i.e., engines, boilers, and so on, is also under their observation.

At the completion of the building and after trials at sea, classification certificates are issued and handed to the owners.

Cornish, H. J., "The Classification of Merchant Shipping," Institution of Naval Architects (London), *Transactions,* vol. 47 (1905); Lucas, T., *Classification Rules,* Society of Naval Architects and Marine Engineers (New York), vol. 8 (1900); MacAllister, C. A., "Relation of Classification to Safety of Ships," *Marine Review* (New York), vol. 58 (October, 1928); Thearle, S. J. P., "The Classification of Merchant Shipping," *Watt Anniversary Lecture for 1914,* Greenock, 1914.

CLASSIFICATION CERTIFICATE. A document issued by the classification society or register for which the vessel has been surveyed stating that the ship has been found to comply with the rules of the society. It also mentions the class granted to the vessel and the conditions which have to be complied with if the class is to be maintained.

Fr: *Certificat de Classification;* Ger: *Klassifikations Zertifikat; Klassenzertifikat.*

Surveys, repairs and any alterations to the hull or machinery of the vessel are mentioned on the certificate and must bear the visa of the society's surveyor under whose inspection the work has been carried out. Two certificates are issued to mechanically propelled vessels, one for the hull and another for the engines and/or boilers.

CLASSIFICATION CLAUSE. A marine insurance clause designating various standards of classification according to the principal registers of shipping, commonly used by underwriters as a basis of quotation on cargo where the actual carrying vessels are not yet determined.

Fr: *Clause de Classification;* Ger: *Klassifikation Klausel.*

CLASSIFICATION SOCIETY. A private organization which has as its purpose the supervision of vessels during their construction and afterward, in respect to their seaworthiness and upkeep, and the placing of vessels in grades or "classes" according to the society's rules for each particular type of vessel.

It is not compulsory by law that a shipowner have his vessel built according to the rules of any classification society; but in practice, the difficulty in securing satisfactory rates of insurance for an unclassed vessel makes it a commercial obligation.

The principal classification societies are: Lloyd's Register, London; American Bureau of Shipping, New York; Bureau Veritas, Paris; British Corporation, Glasgow; Germanischer Lloyd, Berlin; Norske Veritas, Oslo; Registro Italiano, Rome; Japanese Marine Corporation (Teikoku Kaiji Kyokai), Tokyo.

CLASS RACING. A term used to denote yacht racing by linear rating measurement or tonnage, when either the first yacht to finish is the winner, or the vessel saving its time by a fixed scale of time allowance in proportion to the rating of the yacht and the length of the course.

See **Handicap Racing.**

CLASS RATES (U. S.). Rates of freight which apply to goods moving intermittently or in small quantities.

CLAW OFF. To beat or turn to windward from a lee shore.

Fr: *S'élever;* Ger: *Abkreuzen; Aufkreuzen.*

CLEADING. The wooden casings at the sides of a lifeboat, behind which the buoyancy tanks are fitted.

Ger: *Bekleidung.*

CLEAN. 1. Shipping documents such as bill of health, bill of lading, mate's receipt, and so on, are termed "clean" when no mention of any damage or imperfection appears. When any clause detrimental to shippers or any restriction is inserted the documents become "dirty" or "foul."

Fr: *Net;* Ger: *Rein.*

2. Free from danger as an anchorage, a coast, a harbor, as opposed to "foul."

3. A term generally used to express the acuteness or sharpness of a ship's body.

CLEAN BILL OF HEALTH. A clean bill of health means that the ship sailed at a time when no infectious disease was supposed to exist at the port of departure.

Fr: *Patente de Santé Nette;* Ger: *Reiner Gesundheitspass.*

CLEAN BILL OF LADING. A bill of lading which states that the goods have been shipped in good order and condition without any qualifications or remarks.

Fr: *Connaissement Net;* Ger: *Reines Konnossement.*

CLEAN CHARTER. A charter party which is supposed to be free from all commission and agency fees, and to make the freight payable without the deduction of any discount.

Fr: *Charte Partie Nette;* Ger: *Reine Charterpartie.*

CLEAN FULL. Refers to sails when they are kept drawing steadily. Synonymous to rap full.

Fr: *Bon plein;* Ger: *Gut Voll.*

CLEAN RUN. Refers to a fine-lined afterbody which causes little disturbance of the water when the ship is in motion. The converse of full run.

CLEAR. State of the atmosphere when free from mist, haze, rain or snow, the air being transparent so that distant objects can be distinctly seen.

Fr: *Clair;* Ger: *Klar.*

CLEARANCE. The act of clearing a ship entered at the customhouse.

Fr: *Acquit de Douane; Expedition en Douane;* Ger: *Klarierung; Ausklarierung; Einklarierung.*

CLEARANCE CERTIFICATE. A document issued by the customs authorities to the master of a vessel sailing for a foreign port when all legal requirements have been fulfilled, thereby authorizing the ship to leave port. Also called clearance or Cocket Card.

Fr: *Congé; Passeport;* Ger: *Klarierungsattest; Klarierungspapier.*

CLEARANCE INWARD. A customhouse certificate showing the quantity of dutiable goods still remaining on a ship after the cargo has been discharged and before taking on board any outgoing cargo.

Fr: *Expédition à l'Entrée;* Ger: *Einklarierungsattest.*

CLEARANCE LABEL (G. B.). A document similar to a clearance certificate, issued by the British customs authorities. It is affixed to the victualing bill and constitutes the authority for the vessel to proceed.

CLEARANCE NOTE (G. B.). A document issued by the customs authorities in British ports when a vessel is cleared inward after discharging her cargo. It states among other things the quantities of dutiable goods, such as ship's stores, left on the vessel under seal. The ship may then begin to load outgoing cargo.

CLEARANCE OUTWARD. A document in the nature of a certificate given by the customs authorities to an outward-bound vessel in which it is stated that the master has entered and cleared his ship according to law and regulations of the port, paid all dues and charges, and is authorized to depart.

Fr: *Expédition de Sortie;* Ger: *Ausklarierungsattest.*

CLEAR BERTH. The waterplane area within the radius of an anchored vessel's swing at the turn of the tide, comprising her over-all length, plus the scope of cable to which she is riding and a suitable allowance for the fall of the tide. For two or more vessels at anchor to have clear berths it must be impossible for either to come in contact under any condition of wind and tide. Also called swinging berth.

Fr: *Poste d'Évitage;* Ger: *Ankerplatz; Schwairaum.*

CLEAR DAYS. A specified number of days reckoned exclusively of the first and last days.

Fr: *Jours Francs;* Ger: *Klare Tage.*

CLEAR HAWSE. To disentangle the anchor cables when they are twisted. Also called to open hawse.

Fr: *Dégager les Chaînes; Dépasser les tours de Chaîne;* Ger: *Ankerketten klarieren.*

CLEAR HAWSE PENDANT. A short length of open link chain or wire used in clearing hawse or when using a mooring swivel. One end is fitted with a slip hook and the other with a shackle to which a long tail or wire rope is spliced.

Fr: *Faux-bras à dépasser les tours de chaîne; Itague d'Affourchage;* Ger: *Kettenschenkel.*

CLEAR HAWSE SLIP. A cable stopper fitted with a slip hook at one end and a roller shackle at the other for reeving a hawser through.

CLEARING BEARING. A bearing of some conspicuous object which leads clear of a danger laid off from it.

CLEARING LINE. A line drawn through two conspicuous objects, such as two lighthouses, by which vessels are to steer to clear some danger.

Fr: *Alignement;* Ger: *Richtungslinie.*

CLEARING MARKS. Two marks showing on a chart a straight line through which a vessel runs clear of certain dangers or will lead her into a channel or deep water.

Fr: *Amers de Sécurité;* Ger: *Klarierung Marke.*

CLEAR SKY. A cloudless sky. In meteorological parlance a day of clear sky is one on which the average cloudiness at the hours of observation is less than two-tenths of the sky.

Fr: *Ciel pur;* Ger: *Wolkenloser Himmel.*

CLEAR VIEW SCREEN. A device which affords a clear area in a bridge or wheel house window in foul weather, for an aid to navigation. It consists of a polished glass disk about 11 in. in diameter, supported on its center by a bearing and actuated by an electric motor. The motor operates at such a speed that the rotating glass disk throws off rain, spray, snow, and so on, and tends to remain in a state of transparency under any weather condition. Also called clear vision screen wiper.

CLEAT. 1. A short transverse piece of wood nailed to a sloping gangway to give sure footing.

Fr: *Tasseau; Latte de Pied;* Ger: *Fusslatte.*

2. A wedge fastened to a ship's side to catch the shores in a launching cradle or dry dock.

Fr: *Le Taquet;* Ger: *Klampe.*

See **Belaying Cleat.**

CLERK. Any member of the crew assigned clerical duties.

Fr: *Commis;* Ger: *Schreiber.*

CLEW. One of the two lower corners of a square sail. In all triangular sails and in four-sided sails where the head is not parallel to the foot the after lower corner is the clew. Also called clue.

Fr: *Point;* Ger: *Schothorn.*

See **Hammock Clew, Spanish Clews, Spectacle Clew, Weather Clew.**

CLEW (to). 1. To haul a square sail up to a yard previous to furling by means of the clew lines or clew garnets; also, to haul up the clew of a fore-and-aft sail. The term "clew up" is used when the clews are run up to the yard, as of a course or lower topsail.

2. To "clew down" means to haul on the clew lines, slack away on the halyards, and force the yard down.

Fr: *Carguer;* Ger: *Aufgeien.*

CLEW CRINGLE. A loop or eye formed in the boltrope at the clew of a sail. The rope cringle is nowadays superseded by the clew iron or clew ring.

Fr: *Patte de Point d'Écoute;* Ger: *Schothornlagel.*

CLEW IRON.

See **Spectacle Clew.**

CLEW JIGGER. A light tackle formerly used for clewing up whole or single topsails and courses forward and above the yard.

CLEW LINE. One of the ropes by which the clews of a square sail are hauled up to the yard. They lead from the clews to the yard arm and down on deck. Also called clew rope.

Fr: *Cargue Point*; Ger: *Geitau*.

For topsails and courses the clew lines are double and reeve through a block at the clew, the standing part being clinched on the yardarm. Clew lines or clew ropes are also fitted to trysails or spankers with a fixed gaff for hauling the clew up to the jaws of the gaff, and on the gaff topsails for hauling the clew up to the head. Clew lines and clew garnets fulfill the same function but the latter term is applied only to the lines used for a course.

CLEW PATCH. A strengthening patch on the lower corners of a square sail or the after lower corner of a fore-and-aft sail.

Fr: *Renfort de Point*; Ger: *Schothornlappen*.

CLEW RING. An iron ring, placed at each clew of a square sail, into which three thimbles are inserted, two for splicing to each boltrope and the third for the clew-line block strap.

Ger: *Schothornring*.

CLEW ROPE. A rope leading from the clew of a gaff sail to the jaws of the gaff; used for tricing up the clew.

CLEW TRAVELER. An iron ring fastened to the clew of a gaff sail and made to travel on the boom end to haul out the clew.

Fr: *Rocambeau d'Écoute*; Ger: *Ausholring*.

CLICK.
See **Pawl**.

CLIFF. Land projecting nearly vertically from the water or from the surrounding land.

Fr: *Falaise*; Ger: *Klippe*.

CLINCH. A method mostly used for tying a heavy rope to a ring or cringle when the rope is too large for easy knotting. The turns are held together with seizings. Clinches are also tied in buntlines and leechlines.

Fr: *Etalingure*; Ger: *Stich*.

See **Inside Clinch, Outside Clinch**.

CLINCH (to). To burr the end of a bolt or the point of a nail upon a ring or washer by beating it with a hammer. This is done to prevent its drawing after it has been driven through the parts to be assembled. Also called clench.

Fr: *River sur Virole*; Ger: *Klinken*.

CLINCH BOLT. A long through fastening, used by wooden ship- and boatbuilders, having its end riveted over a washer or clinch ring. It is usually made of galvanized iron, or copper, and is used for fastening scarfed joints, stems, deadwoods, keelsons, stringers, clamps, and knees.

Fr: *Cheville à Virole*; Ger: *Nietbolzen; Klinkbolzen*.

CLINCH NAIL. Generic term for nails made of malleable metal such as copper, wrought iron, and so on, which after being driven through from the outside are bent over on the inside of the frame. Clinch-nails used for boat building are usually cut nails made of copper. Wire nails are also used.

Fr: *Clou à river*; Ger: *Stauchnagel*.

CLINCH RING. A kind of round washer made of galvanized wrought iron, or of bronze, with a hole in the center, over which the head of a bolt is clinched. Also called clench ring.

Fr: *Virole*; Ger: *Klinkring*.

CLINKER-BUILT. Said of a boat constructed with clinker planking. Also called clincher built.

Fr: *Construction à Clins*; Ger: *Klinkerbauart*.

See **Carvel-Planking, Clinker Planking**.

Clinker-built boats are constructed upon temporary transverse molds fastened at their proper station on the keel. Floors, futtocks, and hooks are put in after the planking is completed, and fastened to the latter by outside-driven nails clinched on burrs. The clinker method is used for comparatively small craft. It is preferred for boats which have to be beached frequently.

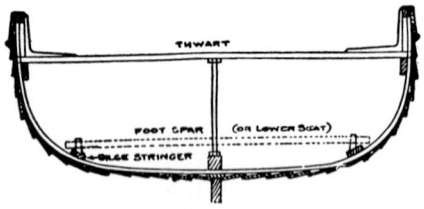

Clinker Planking

CLINKER PLANKING. A method of planking used for small craft in which the lower edge of each strake overlaps the upper edge of the strake next below. Also called clench planking, clinch planking, lap planking, lapstrake planking.

See **Clinker-Built**.

Fr: *Bordé à clins*; Ger: *Klinker Beplankung; Klinkerbauart*.

Each strake is fastened to the next below

it by nails driven from the outside, and clinched inside, through the landings or overlaps. Toward the ends a gradually deepening rabbet is taken out of each edge at the landings, so that the projection of each strake beyond the next below it gradually diminishes, and they all fit flush with each other into the rabbets of the stem and stern post. It is a light form of construction, strong and flexible, and therefore extensively used for dinghies, ship's lifeboats, and so on.

CLINKER PLATING. A system in which strakes are fitted overlapping like the slates of a roof.

Fr: *Bordé à Simples Clins;* Ger: *Klinkerplattung.*

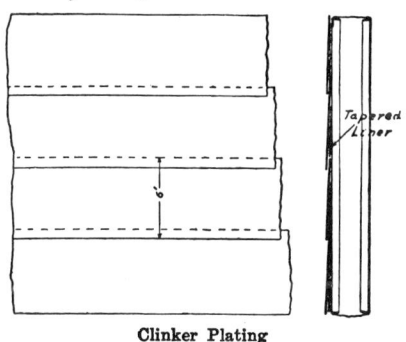

Clinker Plating

CLINOMETER. An instrument which indicates the angle of roll or pitch of a vessel. It may consist of a pendulum reading against a graduated arc, or of a bubble in a curved, graduated, liquid-filled glass tube.

Fr: *Clinomètre;* Ger: *Krängungspendel.*

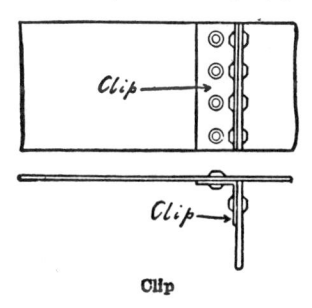

Clip

CLIP. A short piece of angle iron used in shipbuilding to connect various parts of the structure such as floor or bracket plates to vertical keel or longitudinals. Clips may be welded or riveted. Also called lug, angle clip, lug piece, angle lug.

Fr: *Taquet;* Ger: *Lugwinkel.*

See **Floor Clip, Margin Clip.**

CLIP HOOK. Two hooks or one hook in two parts, each forming a mousing for the other, and suspended from the same link or eye. Much used about a ship's rigging. A pair of hooks provided with a slip ring which, when in position, holds them together. Also called clasp hook, clove hook, sister hooks, sister clip, match hooks.

Fr: *Croc à Ciseaux;* Ger: *Doppelhaken.*

CLIPPER. A word of American origin derived from the phrase "to move at a fast clip." It first appeared in American literature about 1812 and is frequently applied nowadays to any fast vessel regardless of type.

Fr: *Clipper;* Ger: *Klipper.*

See **Tea Clipper.**

CLIPPER BOW. Bow in which the stem forms a concave curve which projects outboard above the waterline. Also called fiddle bow, cutwater bow, knee bow, overhanging bow.

Fr: *Avant à Guibre;* Ger: *Klippersteven; Uberhängender Bug.*

CLIPPER SHIP. A type of fast, square-rigged vessel used chiefly in the California, Australia and China tea trades from 1843 until the opening of the Suez Canal in 1869. Also called clipper. Clipper ships formed the highest development ever attained in wooden sailing-ship construction. The hulls were built exclusively of wood until about 1863 when the first composite-built tea clippers were brought out. The stem was carried out forward in a curved line to extreme limit, thereby lengthening the bow above water. The general drawing out and sharpening of the forebody brought the greatest breadth further aft than was usual with former types of sailing vessels. Fining out of the afterbody by rounding up the ends of the main transom was also one of the innovations adopted for clipper-built hulls.

Fr: *Clipper;* Ger: *Klipperschiff; Klipper.*

See **Baltimore Clipper, Fruit Clipper.**

British built tea clippers differed from their American contemporaries by having considerably less sheer and freeboard with lower bulwarks and smaller breadth. They were fast in moderate and light winds while the American built vessels were at their best in strong breezes. Their greater breadth in proportion to length increased their power to carry sail. This, as well as their longer and sharper ends, enabled the American vessels to be driven harder in strong winds. Clippers were usually barks or full-rigged ships. In the early days of the clipper ship era (1841–55) schooner and brig-rigged clippers were employed in the opium trade between India and China. Their tonnage varied from 90 to 300. The tonnage of the square-rigged vessels varied widely. The "Chrysolite," measuring 471 tons, is believed to be the smallest on record. The well-known "Republic," with a tonnage of 3,357, was by far the largest ever built.

The term "steam clipper" was occasionally used about 1855 to denote the first iron-built sailing ships fitted with auxiliary engine, trading from the British Isles to Australia.

The name "medium clipper" has been given in the United States to a type of clipper ship which succeeded about the year 1855, the so-called "extreme clipper." Medium clippers were not so sharp and did not carry as heavy spars or so much canvas as the older ships, but their deadweight carrying capacity was greater, and they could be handled with a smaller crew.

Cutler, C. C., *Greyhounds of the Sea*, New York, 1930; Clark, *The Clipper Ship Era*, New York, 1911; Lubbock, B., *China Clippers*, Glasgow, 1916; Lubbock, B., *Colonial Clippers*, Glasgow, 19?; Longridge, C., *The Cutty Sark*, London, 1933; Howe, *American Clipper Ships*, Salem, 1926.

CLOSE BEVEL. Beveling in which the flanges of a frame form an acute angle. Also called under bevel, shut bevel.

Fr: *Équerrage en maigre;* Ger: *Schmiegung unter dem Winkel.*

CLOSE CEILING. Ceiling in which the planking is fitted edge to edge. In vessels with double bottom close ceiling is usually laid from the margin plate to the upper part of the bilge, though in many ships it is laid only over the bilges and under the hatchways.

Fr: *Vaigrage Plein;* Ger: *Feste Wegerung.*

CLOSED BRIDGE HOUSE. A bridge house totally enclosed by bulkheads at forward and afterends.

CLOSED CHOCK. A chock closed across the top. An oval-shaped casting through which hawsers or lines are passed, having no opening at the top. Also called rowser chock.

Fr: *Chaumard Fermé;* Ger: *Geschlossene Klampe.*

CLOSED-IN BRIDGE. A navigating bridge where the wheelhouse forms the midship part, its fore-side being a shelter common to both.

CLOSED-IN SPACES. Term used in the measurement of ships for tonnage. It refers to the spaces above the upper deck protected from the weather and having no openings in the sides, deck, or ends sufficiently large to entitle these spaces to exemption as open spaces.

Fr: *Espaces Clos;* Ger: *Eingeschlossene Räume.*

CLOSED STOKEHOLD. A fire room in which an artificial air pressure is maintained by forcing air with blowers. All openings are closed and air locks are fitted for access purposes. In the closed-ashpit system the boiler room is open and the air is admitted to the furnaces by valves in the furnace fronts. Also called closed fireroom.

Fr: *Tirage en Vase clos;* Ger: *Geschlossener Heizraum.*

CLOSE-HAULED. The trim of a vessel's sails when it endeavors to make progress in the nearest direction possible toward that point of the compass from which the wind blows. Also called on a wind, by the wind.

Fr: *Au plus près;* Ger: *Am Wind; Scharf beim Wind.*

To come within the meaning of the "rules of the road," as to close-hauled vessels, it is not necessary that the vessel be sailed as near the wind as it will lie, but only as near as it can be sailed considering the type of vessel, the sea, and the wind, and make the best progress to windward.

It has been held by the courts that a ship sailing full and by and being kept a good full is close-hauled. With baffling winds, a vessel has been held close-hauled when sailing from half a point to two points free; but under ordinary circumstances a vessel has been held not close-hauled where it has the wind two points free. A schooner within about four points off the wind has been held close-hauled.

CLOSE HAULED VESSEL. One sailing as practical to the wind.

Fr: *Navire au plus près;* Ger: *Beidemwinder.*

CLOSE-LINK CHAIN. Chain in which the links are so short relative to their width that studs cannot be fitted. Also called short-link chain. It is used on board ship for bowsprit shrouds, cargo slings, topping lifts, funnel guys, steering leads, and so on. Up to 5/8 in. in diameter short-link chain is used as anchor cable for small yachts, and so on.

Fr: *Chaîne à Mailles Serrées;* Ger: *Kurzgliedrige Kette.*

CLOSE PACK. Ice pack composed of floes, mostly in contact, and completely checking navigation.

CLOSE REACH. An expression used in connection with a boat sailing just a point or two off close-hauled, with sheets almost flat.

CLOSE STOWING ANCHOR. A stocked anchor in which the plane of the blades when stowed is the same as that of the stock.

CLOSE UP. A flag or group of flags is said to be close up or "two-blocked" when it is hoisted to the full extent of the halyards. Sometimes called two-blocked.

CLOSING DATE. Expression used in the sailing schedules of regular liners to announce the latest date for delivery of goods for shipment by a particular vessel.

Fr: *Date de cloture;* Ger: *Schluss Datum.*

CLOSING STRAKE. Term used by shipyard welders to denote the bilge strake of shell plating, which is the last one to go on in a welded hull.

CLOTH. One of the breadths of canvas sewed together to make a sail. The width of a sail is denoted by the number of cloths it contains. For yachts and other small vessels cloth widths of 14 to 20 in. are generally used. The standard width for deep-sea trading vessels in 22 in. Cloths of gaff-headed sails run vertically or horizontally to the afterleech, the latter system being preferred for racing craft in order to reduce air friction caused by vertical seams. Vertical cloths give more strength to reef points as these can be placed in each seam where the sail is twice as strong. They are always used in sails for trading and fishing vessels.

See **Back Cloth, Buntline Cloth, Goring Cloth, Hammer Cloth, Lining Cloth, Mast Cloth, Slack Cloth, Square Cloths, Weather Cloth.**

Fr: *Laize;* Ger: *Kleid.*

CLOTHES STOPS. Small lanyards fastened to clothing to hang by when washed.

CLOUD. A visible assemblage of particles of water or ice formed by the condensation of vapour in the air.

Fr: *Nuage;* Ger: *Wolke.*

See **Noctilucent Cloud, Scarf Cloud.**

There are ten main types of clouds which may be grouped as follows:

High Clouds: Cirrus, Cirro-stratus, Cirro-cumulus.

Intermediate Clouds: Alto-stratus, Alto-cumulus.

Low Clouds: Strato-cumulus, Nimbo-stratus, Cumulus, Cumulo-nimbus, Stratus. British Admiralty, Hydrographic Department, *Naval Meteorological Service Cloud Atlas,* London, 1924; Clarke, G. A., *Clouds,* London, 1926; U. S. Hydrographic Office, Publication 112, *Illustrative Cloud Forms for the Guidance of Observers,* Washington, 1897.

CLOUDINESS. Amount of sky covered by clouds. Usually expressed by a scale of tenths of sky covered.

Fr: *Nebulosité;* Ger: *Bewölkung.*

CLOUDLESS. Said of the skies when without a cloud.

Fr: *Sans nuages;* Ger: *Wolkenlos.*

CLOUD SCALE. Numerical scale used in weather observations, "0" indicating a clear sky and "10" a completely overcast one.

Fr: *Echelle de nébulosité;* Ger: *Wölken Skala.*

CLOUT NAIL. A flat-headed nail (flat circular head) with section of body partly round and partly square.

Fr: *Clou à Tête Etampée;* Ger: *Plattnagel.*

Clove Hitch

CLOVE HITCH. A knot consisting of two half hitches in opposite directions put round the object to which it is desired to make fast. Used for fastening a rope to a spar or for securing ratlines to the shrouds, also to tie the first row of meshes to the head rope of a net.

Fr: *Demi-Clef à Capeler;* Ger: *Webeleinsteck.*

CLUB. A small spar laced to the foot of a gaff-topsail, thus allowing the clew to be extended beyond the peak of the gaff.

Fr: *Bôme; Balestron;* Ger: *Schottraa; Fussraa.*

A club differs from a boom in that while the boom goes the full length of the sail, the club extends only part way along the foot. The term jackyard is only used in connection with a gaff-topsail.

CLUBBING. 1. Drifting down a current with an anchor dragging out. Vessels drifting in this manner generally have a spring from the quarter to the ring of the anchor, by which they can be sprung broadside to the current.

Fr: *Dériver sur son Ancre;* Ger: *Vor schleppenden Anker treiben.*

2. Putting the bight of a rope over some object.

CLUB BURGEE. A burgee which bears the insignia of a yacht club. It is flown at masthead by single-masted yachts, at mainmast head on yawls and ketches, at foremast head on schooners and mechanically propelled yachts, and at bow staff on motor cruisers and launches.

Fr: *Guidon de Club;* Ger: *Clubflagge.*

CLUB FOOT. 1. A form of forefoot in which displacement or volume is placed near the keel and close to the forward perpendicular as in the bulbous bow.

2. (U. S.). The flattened, broadened after-end of the stem, formed of a plate or casting flattened out where it adjoins the plate keel and closed gradually to where it is welded to the solid stem bar.

CLUB HAUL (to). 1. An evolution resorted to by a sailing vessel in heavy weather on a lee shore, in which the vessel is cast on the opposite tack by the use of a line from a kedge anchor leading to the lee quarter.

Fr: *Faire croupiat;* Ger: *Klubholen.*

2. A method of insuring that a mechanically propelled vessel at anchor swings in the desired direction at tide turn. A wire is led from the quarter which will apply the purchase in the required direction, the chain cable being veered slightly at the same time.

CLUB LINK.
See **Harp Shape Shackle.**

CLUB TERMS. Special terms and warranties of various mutual protection and indemnity insurance clubs.

CLUB TOPSAIL. A triangular gaff-topsail in which the upper part of the luff is laced to a light spar called club, extending above the truck. A similar but shorter club extends the foot of the sail beyond the gaff.

Fr: *Flèche Bômé;* Ger: *Schottraatoppsegel.*

CLUE.
See **Clew.**

CLUMP BLOCK. Small, short, and thick working block with a solid rounded shell and wide, squat sheaves and swallows. It takes a rope half its own circumference in thickness.

Fr: *Moque à réa; Moque à rouet;* Ger: *Klumpblock.*

CLUMSY CLEAT.
See **Thigh Thwart.**

CLUTCH WINCH. A winch in which the drum and gear wheel are keyed fast to the shaft, as distinguished from the cone friction winch in which the drum is fitted loose on the shaft.

CLYDE LUG (G. B.). A standing lugsail carried to a great height by a long and heavy yard. The sheet travels on a horse fastened to the transom of the boat.

COACH ROOF.
See **Cabin Top.**

COACHWHIPPING. Ornamental covering made up from line, nettles or other suitable decorative material, and used for stanchions, bell ropes and similar fittings, also a fancy whipping on the pointed end of a man-rope.

Fr: *Queue de rat;* Ger: *Kutscherpeitschen.*

COAK. A small piece of hardwood used as an additional security in scarfing two pieces of timber.

Fr: *Dé;* Ger: *Stosszapfen; Holzpflock; Zylinderzapfen.*

COAKED SCARF. A locked scarf which has a certain number of coaks laid in the surfaces of the joint, by which the resistance to sliding and the holding of bolts is increased.

Fr: *Ecart à Dés;* Ger: *Zapfenlaschung.*

COAKING. The placing of pieces of hardwood, either round or square, in the edges or faying surfaces of pieces of wood which are to be scarfed to prevent their working or sliding over each other.

Fr: *Assemblage à Dé;* Ger: *Schakwerk.*

COALANNITO. Small open boat rowed by one man, stationed over the entrance of the end chamber (*camera della morte*) in order to observe the movements of the fish. It is used by Italian fishermen in the tuna fisheries with stationary nets. Also called *barca di guardia.*

COAL CAPACITY. The capacity of a ship's cargo spaces measured to the underside of beams or deck longitudinals and 3 in. from the frame-bar heel at the vessel's sides.

COAL CHUTE. Tubular structures about 20 in. in diameter fabricated of steel plate, extending from an upper deck to a bunker, where bunker coal is tipped through coaling scuttles. Also called coaling shoot.

Fr: *Manche à Charbon;* Ger: *Kohlenschutte; Kohlenstürze; Bunkerschutte; Kohlenschacht.*

COAL CHUTE COVER. A cast-iron shutter at deck level of a coal-chute opening.

Fr: *Tape de Conduit à Charbon;* Ger: *Kohlenschuttedeckel.*

COAL DOOR. A horizontal or vertical sliding door fitted to a bunker bulkhead. Also called bunker door.

Fr: *Porte de Charbonnage;* Ger: *Bunkertür.*

COAL FIRING. The process or method by which coal is used as fuel in the boiler furnaces for the production of steam:

Fr: *Chauffe au Charbon;* Ger: *Kohlenfeuerung.*

COAL HATCH. A small hatchway in an upper deck or twin deck used for bunkering. Also called coaling hatchway.

Fr: *Trou à Charbon;* Ger: *Kohlenluke.*

COAL HOIST. A steam or electric hoist of small power used for handling coal in bags or baskets when bunkering. Also called coal winch.

Fr: *Treuil de charbonnage;* Ger: *Kohlenwinde.*

The winch is worked with two gipsy heads each taking a Manila whip. Coal hoists are placed either on coaling barges or on board ship. In the latter case they can also be used as boat hoists in an emergency. The average weight of coal baskets is from 336 to 360 lb.

COAL HOLE. A name given to coaling hatchways of long and narrow shape, on the lower decks. They have no coamings and the beams are not cut. They are closed when necessary by wooden hatch covers.

Fr: *Trou à Charbon;* Ger: *Bunkergat.*

COAL HULK. A hulk used for coal storage.

Fr: *Ponton à Charbon;* Ger: *Kohlenhulk.*

COALING PORT. A square opening cut in the side plating in way of the bunkers, used for coaling passenger vessels. Also called coal port.

Fr: *Sabord de Soute; Porte de Charbonnage;* Ger: *Kohlenpforte.*

COALING TRUNK. A steel casing built under a coaling hatchway in order that the coal may pass down the bunkers without inconvenience in the upper 'tween deck and cargo or passenger space.

Fr: *Tambour de Soute;* Ger: *Bunkerschacht.*

COALING WHIP. A type of gear used on steamers when taking coal on board with bags or baskets. It consists of a tightly stretched wire which spans the hatchway and to which one or several gins are fastened. A single fall is rove through each gin.

Ger: *Kohlenwippe.*

COAL PASSER. Member of a ship's crew on a coal-burning steamer who shovels or wheels coal from the bunkers to locations within convenient reach of firemen; moves or trims coal within bunkers to prevent its being shifted by the motion of the ship; cleans boiler pits of ashes and disposes of ashes overboard.

COALTARP. Code name for British Chamber of Shipping Charter Party for coal tar, pitch in bulk, and pulpwood from the east and west coasts of England, Scotland and from Belgian, Dutch, and German ports, also the Atlantic coast of America to ports between the River Elbe and the near-Mediterranean ports.

COAMING. The raised borders about the edge of hatches and scuttles for preventing water on deck from running below.

Fr: *Hiloire; Surbau;* Ger: *Lükensüll; Süll.*

See **Hatch Coaming, Ventilator Coaming.**

COAMING BAR. Angle bar connecting hatch, deckhouse coamings, or other raised structural work with the deck. Also called foundation bar.

Fr: *Cornière d'Hiloire;* Ger: *Sullwinkel.*

COAMING CHOCK. One of the pieces fitted in the deck at each corner of wooden hatch coamings.

Fr: *Coussin d'Hiloire.*

COAMING STAY. A bar or plate set up at an angle from deck to coaming stiffener. It is welded or fastened with slips at both ends.

Fr: *Jambette d'Hiloire;* Ger: *Luksullstutz.*

COAMING STIFFENER. Horizontal bulb angle bar fitted to the coamings of weatherdeck hatchways, and to which the hatch cleats are fixed.

Fr: *Renfort d'hiloire;* Ger: *Süllversteifungsprofil.*

COARSE RIPPER. Expression used by North American fishermen to denote a school of large mackerel moving fast as distinguished from the expression "fine ripper," which denotes a small school of mackerel of uncertain or small size.

COAST. The part of the land next to the sea. This term includes natural appendages of the territory which rise out of the water, although they may not be of sufficient firmness to be inhabited or fortified. Shoals perpetually covered with water are not included under the term "coast." "Coast" is the term used with reference to the land, while "shore" is the term used with reference to the sea.

Fr: *Côte;* Ger: *Küste.*
See **Open Coast.**

COASTAL CURRENT. A current which flows approximately parallel to the shore. It may be tidal, transient, or wind-driven.

Fr: *Courant côtier;* Ger: *Kustenstrom.*

ing consists of a diagonally laid double skin of teak or mahogany, experience having demonstrated that a wooden boat of this construction will stand far more punishment than a steel boat, whether on a sandy or a rocky shore. The boat is divided internally by several transverse and longitudinal watertight steel bulkheads.

Coastal lifeboats are flush-decked and have one or two cabins, one forward and one aft of the machinery compartment. Some are purely power vessels, having only small sails for steadying purposes: others have sails and a centerboard, and may be considered as sailing boats.

They are of the self-righting or non-self-

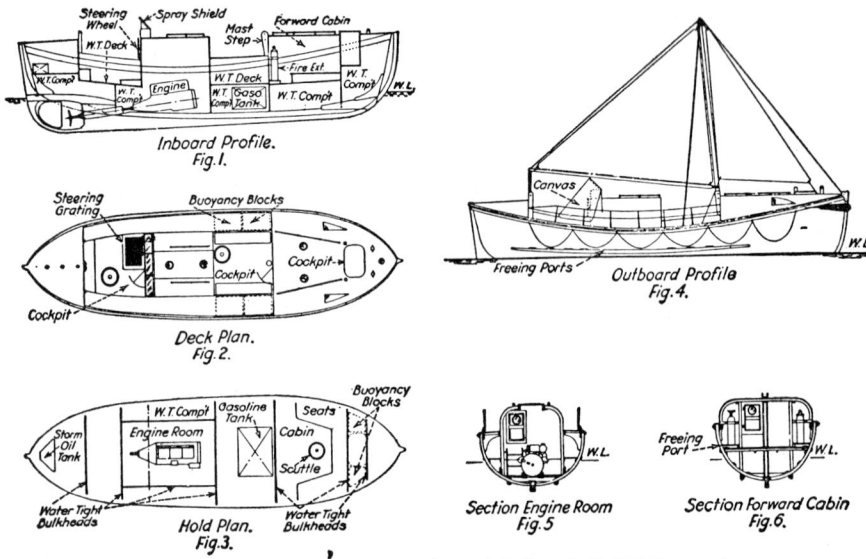

36'-8" Motor Lifeboat, Type "TR"- Self- Bailing, Self - Righting
Coastal Lifeboat

COASTAL LIFEBOAT. A lifeboat permanently stationed ashore at some suitable point of the coast, designed to assist vessels in distress.

Fr: *Canot de Savetage de Côte;* Ger: *Küstenrettungsboot.*

This type of lifeboat is designed to be unsinkable even if its sides are stove-in. This is attained by several means; the first one being to fit every available space, whether above or below deck, with air cases. Secondly, large tubes are fitted from the deck down through the bottom of the boat. Any water that comes on board finds its way out through these tubes, the buoyancy of the boat causing it to rise and to relieve herself of the water in this way. The plank-

righting types. The former, if upset, will right itself, as it is unstable in the upside down position, owing to the high watertight air boxes which characterize its construction. The non self-righting type comprises rowing and sailing boats. They are broader than the self-righting ones and have a very large initial stability, and an excellent range of stability. The non self-righting, or ordinary boat, is almost un-capsizable. Her very high stability is secured by water taken on board as ballast when she is floated. The required quantity is floated into a large but low-sided tank suitably subdivided so that the whole bulk of water cannot shift.

Barnett, J. R., *Modern Motor Lifeboats of the Royal National Lifeboat Institution,* London, 1933; Pyszka, A., "Rettungsboote an den Deutschen Küsten," *Verein Deutscher Ingenieure Zeitschrift,* vol. 81 (June. 1937).

COASTAL NAVIGATION. That part of a sea passage in which the navigator has the load in sight on one side of his course and the open sea on the other.

Fr: *Navigation côtière; Bornage;* Ger: *Küstenfahrt.*

COASTAL PACK. Name given to the ice pack when it is attached to the shore.

COASTAL RADIO STATION. A radio station installed ashore or in coastal waters for issuing radio navigational aids to ships. It includes radio direction finding stations, radio beacons, radio warning stations.

Fr: *Poste radiotélégraphique de terre;* Ger: *Küstenfunkstelle.*

COASTAL SIGNALS. A name given to signals that are of general significance for several ports or a certain section of the coast of any country. They include some particular tide signals, lifesaving, distress, assistance or warning signals.

Fr: *Signal Côtier;* Ger: *Küstensignal.*

COAST AND GEODETIC SURVEY (U. S.). A government bureau of the Department of Commerce, charged among other things with the survey of the Atlantic, Gulf, and Pacific coasts of the United States including Alaska and all other coasts under the jurisdiction of the United States. Its work includes deep-sea soundings, temperature, and current observations along the said coasts; and the magnetic observations. It issues the notices to mariners; tide tables; nautical charts, and coast pilots.

COASTCON. Code name for the 1920 coal charter on the British coasts.

COASTER. A vessel specially designed, equipped, manned and licensed to engage regularly in the coasting trade, whether plying coastwise or making short sea passages within certain specified geographical limits.

Fr: *Caboteur;* Ger: *Küstenfahrer.*

Dugdale, E. W., "Coaster Development during the past fifty years," North East Coast Institution of Engineers and Shipbuilders, (Newcastle upon Tyne), *Transactions,* vol. 51 (1935); Rogers, C. H. D., "Modern Motor Coasters of Restricted Draft," North East Coast Institution of Engineers and Shipbuilders, *Transactions,* vol. 54 (1938).

COAST GUARD. A force, usually naval in character, maintained in some countries to suppress smuggling or to afford assistance to vessels in distress or wrecked, and to perform other duties incidental to a seaboard, such as signaling, and so on.

Fr: *Guarde Côte;* Ger: *Küstenwächter.*

In France, although there is no coast guard service in the sense of that maintained by Great Britain and the United States, a number of semaphore stations are established and manned by long service men from the navy, called *guetteurs sémaphoriques.*

Smith, D. H. and Powell, F. W., *The Coast Guard,* Institute for Government Research, Service Monograph of the U. S. Government 51, Washington, 1929.

COASTING BARGE. A barge so built and equipped that it can be reasonably expected to ride out the ordinary perils of the sea and which, in fact, does go to sea even though it may not have any means of self propulsion. Also called seagoing barge.

Fr: *Chaland de mer;* Ger: *Seeleichter.*

COASTING LEAD. A sounding lead with sinker weighing from 25 to 50 lb., and about 18 in. long for sounding in depths of 20 to 60 fathoms.

Ger: *Mittellot.*

COASTING LIGHTS. A general term for all lights which lead the navigator from one point to another along the coast.

Fr: *Feux de Côte;* Ger: *Küstenfeuer.*

COASTING TRADE. A term applied in a general sense to the trade carried on between ports of the same country as distinguished from that carried on with foreign ports. Also called intercoastal navigation. According to the laws of some maritime nations, the term is also applied to the trade carried within the geographical limits of the foreign trade.

Fr: *Cabotage;* Ger: *Mittlererfahrt; Küstenfahrt.*

Vessels engaged in this trade are subject to different laws and regulations from overseas traders, and their masters must keep their books showing that their cargoes come strictly within the definition of coasting trade. The term "coasting trade" occasionally includes the trade between the mother country and its colonies. As used in commercial treaties, it includes sea trade between any two ports of the same country, whether on the same coast or on different coasts, provided always that the different coasts are, all of them, the coasts of one and the same country, as a political and geographical unit.

League of Nations, Committee on Ports and Navigation Publication, "The meaning attached to the term *Coasting Trade* in various countries," Geneva, 1931; Robinson, M. A., "British Coasting Trade," Institute of Transport (London), *Jour.,* vol. 18, no. 7 (1937).

COASTING VESSEL.
See **Coaster.**

COAST PILOT. (1) One who conducts vessels along a coast.
Fr: *Pilote côtier;* Ger: *Küstenlotse.*
(2) A nautical book giving detailed description of coastal waters with instructions as to navigating them. Also called **Sailing Directions.**
Fr: *Pilote côtier;* Ger: *Uferanweisung.*

COAST SURVEY FLAG (U. S.). A blue flag with large white circle upon which a triangle in red is superimposed. Flown by craft of the U. S. Coast and Geodetic Survey Bureau.

COAST WAITER (G. B.). Officer of the Customs who superintends the landing or loading of goods of coastal shipping.
Ger: *Küstenzollwachter.*
See **Landwaiter.**

COASTWISE VOYAGE (U. S.). A voyage on which a vessel in the usual course of employment proceeds from one port or place in the U. S. or her possessions to another port or place in the U. S. or her possessions and passes outside the line dividing inland waters from the high seas (customs regulations).

COAT. A piece of tarred or painted canvas or leather worked around a mast and mast hole, rudder casing, pump, and so on, where it passes through a weather deck to keep the water from dripping below. Its upper edge is held in place by a tightly fitting grommet and its lower end is secured to the deck (wood) on a ring of sheet lead. Also called apron.
Fr: *Braie;* Ger: *Kragen.*
See **Mast Coat, Rudder Coat.**

COBLE. A clinker-built open boat used by fishermen on the northeast coast of England, with high, flaring bows, deep forefoot, a very raking round or square stern, and a rudder projecting a considerable distance below it. Instead of having a keel, the coble is built on a ram plank, which extends from the stem, where its section is vertical, to the stern, where it is flat with a slight upward curve to stand the shocks of beaching stern first. For the same reason there are also two skids extending one on each side of the bottom from amidships to the stern. The rig usually adopted is a standing or dipping lugsail. Length 28 ft. Breadth 5 ft. 5 in. Depth 2 ft. 3 in.
See **Salmon Coble.**

COBLE OAR. An oar used by the coble boats, of the northeast coast of England.
These oars are made of two separate parts, the loom of the oar being a square or flat-sided piece. The blade and the loom are usually joined by two iron bands, which secure and hold the two parts firmly together. The flat part of the loom rests on the gunwale and the oar cannot be feathered. An iron ring is attached to the oar at its proper equipoise. This ring fits loosely over an iron thole pin so that the oar cannot go adrift when trailing.

COCKBILL. Having the end or ends cocked up, as an anchor when suspended from the cathead ready for letting go.
Fr: *Faire Peneau;* Ger: *Vor den Krahn Fieren.*

COCKBILL (to). To cockbill the yards; to top them by one lift to an angle with the deck. A symbol of mourning.
Fr: *Mettre en Pantenne; Apiquer;* Ger: *Auftoppen.*
In a full-rigged ship the yards are topped up on one side on the fore- and mizzenmasts and on the opposite side on the mainmast. The most appropriate time for cockbilling yards is daylight. Dark is the proper time for squaring them in again. The spanker gaff should be lowered well down.

COCKET CARD.
See **Clearance Certificate.**

COCKLER; COCKLER GALLEY. An open, shallow-draft, sailing boat, originating from Leigh and used for raking cockles on the Thames Estuary. It had the same rig as the bawley and was fitted with a centerboard. Length 28 ft. Breadth 9 ft. Depth 2½ ft. The sailing craft have in recent years been replaced by larger motorboats decked at ends.

COCKPIT. A well or sunken space in the afterdeck of a small boat for the use of the helmsman and crew. It is generally surrounded by a coaming not less than 6 in. in height and has seating accommodation around the stern and sides. It is separated from the cabin by a low bulkhead to keep out the water. Also called steering well.
Fr: *Cockpit;* Ger: *Cockpit.*
See **Self-Draining Cockpit.**

COCKSCOMB. A notched cleat on the yardarm to facilitate hauling out the reef earings.
Fr: *Taquet de Bout de Vergue;* Ger: *Stossklampe.*

COD. That part of the tack of a revolving storm in which the center has reached its most westerly point and begins to move eastwards.

CODE BOOK. International signal book which gives all instructions for making up phraseology of messages used at sea between vessels of different nationalities. Editions of the book are printed in English, French, German, Italian, Japanese, Norwegian and Spanish.

Fr: *Code de signaux;* Ger: *Signalbuch.*

CODE FLAG. 1. One of the alphabet flags of the international code of signals.

Fr: *Pavillon du Code;* Ger: *Signalbuchflagge.*

2. Red and white vertically-striped pennant of the international code of signals. Also called answering pennant.

Fr: *Flamme du Code;* Ger: *Signalbuchwimpel.*

COD END. The extreme end of a trawl net about 10 ft. long, which acts as general receptacle for the various fishes which enter the net. It is closed by a draw rope. Also called pocket, purse, bag, fish bag.

Fr: *Cul;* Ger: *Steert.*

COD-END LINE. Short line passed through the last meshes of the cod-end in a trawl net and knotted. After the cod-end is hoisted inboard, the cod line is untied and the fish falls on deck. Also called cod-end rope, cod line, drawline.

Fr: *Raban de cul;* Ger: *Codleine.*

COD LINE. 1. Three pounds twelve or eighteen-thread stuff made of white hemp or cotton. Used for hammock clews, for catching codfish, and so on.

Fr: *Ligne à Morue; Ligne à Dorys;* Ger: *Dorsch Schnur.*

2. Name given by Grimsby fishermen to a line with one end fastened to the beam of a trawl net, and the other to the cod-end. In other localities it is termed poke line, poop line.

Fr: *Parpaillot;* Ger: *Pokleine; Cotleine.*

CODLING. A young cod. The market value of these is about one half or less that of large codfish.

Fr: *Anon;* Ger: *Sprag.*

COD LIVER OIL. The oil obtained from livers of codfish.

Fr: *Huile de foie de Morue;* Ger: *Lebertran.*

In former days the livers were thrown into a tub and left there until through decomposition the oil floated on the surface because of its specific weight and was then collected. It is now obtained by steam heating the livers of captured fish immediately after they have been cleaned and the gallbladder has been removed.

There are three grades of cod liver oil on the market: the pale or shore oil; the pale brown or straight oil, which contains about 3.75 per cent fatty acids; the dark brown or banks oil, which contains from 11 to 29 per cent fatty acids.

COFFERDAM. 1. The empty space between two bulkheads separating two adjacent compartments. It is designed to isolate the two compartments from each other, to prevent the liquid contents of one compartment from entering the other in the event of the failure of the partitions of one to retain their tightness. In oil tankers cargo spaces are always isolated from the rest of the ship by cofferdams fitted at both ends. Up to 5 cofferdams, besides the pump room, are found on large oil tankers.

Fr: *Cofferdam;* Ger: *Kofferdamm.*

2. See Caisson.

COFFIN PLATE. A shell plate used on the propeller bossing of a twin-screw vessel. It is an inverted boss plate and is so named on account of its shape.

COG.

See Dowel.

COGGING. A process used in boatbuilding for strengthening a joint at faying surfaces.

Fr: *Assemblage à Dé;* Ger: *Schakwerk.*

It consists of sinking shallow holes, which come opposite to each other in the abutting faces of the two parts and making hardwood cogs or keys which, when they are brought together, will fill both holes. It relieves the bolts or fastenings of shearing stresses. It is of the nature of a dowel but is not bored right through.

COIL. A quantity of rope made up into a series of rings lying close one above the other. Rope is sold by the coil, which contains 200 fathoms standard length. Rope in 100-fathom lengths is called half-coils.

Fr: *Glène;* Ger: *Tauwerkrolle.*

In Great Britain the length of coils varies as follows: Hawser-laid rope, 90 or 120 fathoms; shroud-laid rope, 106 fathoms; cable-laid rope, 100 fathoms; cotton rope, 60 fathoms.

COIL (to). To lay a rope down in circular turns. If the rope is laid up right-handed it is coiled from left to right and vice versa if laid up left-handed.

Fr: *Lover;* Ger: *Aufschiessen.*

COIRO. African dugout canoe from the Ivory Coast employed in the sea fisheries and on the lagoon of Alladian. There are no thwarts; the sides are held together with

Cold front cloud. (Official U.S. Navy photograph.)

palm-fiber lashings. It is similar to the *enieni,* and always made of very light timber.

COIR ROPE. Rope made from the fibrous husks of the coconut (*cocos nucifera*) and having about one-third to one-fourth the breaking strength of Manila rope. It is sufficiently buoyant to float on the surface of the water. It is usually a three-stranded right-hand rope. It is often wrongly called "grass rope" or "bass rope."

Fr: *Bastin;* Cordage en Pitte; **Ger:** *Basttau; Grasleine; Grastau.*

Coir rope is about one-third the weight of hemp of equal size. It is used as kedge warp, mooring spring, or towing hawser. It is very resistant to salt water but soon rots in fresh water. Coir is employed in lieu of oakum in the South Seas for calking native-built boats. Native Indian sailing barks of about 300 tons gross are still using coir rope for the whole of their running rigging. It is a local product made in Jaffna.

Coir rope, owing to its great elasticity, is frequently used for towing, as well as for moorings by ships lying in a port where a swell is liable to run. It is usually made up in short lengths with a thimble and wire (or chain) strap at one end and is used in conjunction with Manila or wire moorings.

COL. A neck of low pressure between two anticyclones.

COLATITUDE. The complement of the latitude of a heavenly body or the difference between the latitude and ninety degrees.

Fr: *Co-Latitude;* **Ger:** *Breitenkomplement.*

COLD FRONT. The discontinuity at the forward edge of an advancing cold air mass which is displacing warmer air in its path.

Fr: *Front froid;* **Ger:** *Kaltfront.*

COLD WALL. A current of cold water from the Arctic Ocean which flows in a southwesterly direction close inside the Gulf Stream.

COLIN-ARCHER FORM. Applies to a particular design of water lines for small sailing craft such as pilot boats, fisherman, cruising yachts and so on. It was based on the 'wave form' theory in which fore and after body curves are given a trochoidal shape corresponding to that of the oscillating deep sea wave. This design was promoted by a Norwegian naval architect named Colin-Archer, in the seventies, and has been most extensively adopted ever since by Scandinavian builders of small craft.

Colin-Archer, "The Wave Principle Applied to the Longitudinal Desposition of Immersed Volume," Transactions, Institution of Naval Architects, London, 1878.

COLLAPSIBLE BILGE BLOCK. One of a series of building blocks which can be lowered without being removed so as to transfer the weight of the hull to the cradle just before launching.

See **Sand Jack.**

COLLAPSIBLE BOAT. A boat built of a number of canvas members, each of them consisting of a framework of wood forming part of the frame of the contour of the boat when in place and having two layers of specially prepared canvas stretched over them. Also called folding boat, Berthon boat, falt boat. When the boat is not in use, the frames with their canvas covers fold up together very much like the leaves of a book, the leaves being the canvas-covered frames, which are attached to the keel, stem, and sternpost. The thwarts, bottom boards, and other inside fittings are made in halves and hinged in the center so that they fold up inside the boat when the latter is stowed. The length varies from 7 to 28 ft.

Fr: *Berthon;* **Ger:** *Berthon Boot; Klappboot.*

The oars and other appurtenances are carried between the sides of the boat. Collapsible boats are usually made on the whaleboat or double-bowed system. The canvas employed in their construction is especially strong and it is claimed that the two skins employed for the framing act as air tanks making them virtually insubmersible. Since it is impracticable to protect canvas and similar textiles from insects and other vermin, the use of this type of boat on merchant vessels has been abandoned.

COLLAPSIBLE DAVIT. A davit with its heel hinged to the deck, arranged to lie flat when not in use, in order to free the deck from obstructions.

Fr: *Bossoir Rabattable;* **Ger:** *Klappdavit.*

COLLAPSIBLE MAST. A mast hinged near the deck so as to lie horizontally or nearly so. Also called strike mast, lowering mast, knuckle mast. It is used by small craft which have to pass under bridges and by fishing boats working with drift nets in order to reduce leeway. The tabernacle is located entirely above deck except when the heel goes below deck.

Fr: *Mât basculant;* **Ger:** *Klappbarer Mast.*

COLLAR. 1. The eye or loop at the end of a stay or shroud which goes over the masthead.
Fr: *Collier;* Ger: *Auge.*
See **Angle Collar, Davit Collar, Mast Collar, Plate Collar.**
2. A strap or grommet in which is seized a heart or deadeye.

COLLAR KNOT.
See **Masthead Knot.**

COLLIER. 1. A vessel specially designed for the carriage of coal cargoes.
Fr: *Navire Charbonnier;* Ger: *Kohlenschiff.*
2. The term collier is also loosely applied to any vessel regularly employed in the coal trade whether specially built for the purpose or not.
Owing to the difficulty of trimming this type of vessel on a level keel when loaded with a cargo of homogeneous density, colliers are frequently built with a raised quarter deck and with machinery aft, thus avoiding the construction of shaft tunnels and increasing the capacity of after holds. Wide self-trimming hatches are provided so that the holds can be filled sufficiently to sink the vessel to her load line without hand trimming.
Mitchell, E. H., "Special Features in the Design and Loading of Self-Trimming Colliers," Institution of Naval Architects (London), *Transactions,* vol. 81 (1939); Swan, J., "Diagrams and Data Pertaining to Various Coal Carrying Vessels," *Marine Engineering and Shipping Review,* vol. 42, no. 5 (1937).

COLLIER'S PATCH. The application of a thick coat of tar over worn out parts of a sail.

COLLIERY GUARANTEE. A form of contract between charterer and colliery used in British ports.
It is obtained from the colliery, which is to supply the cargo and load the ship on terms in accordance with the colliery guarantee. There is usually a clause in all coal charters which provides that the ship shall be loaded according to colliery guarantee terms.

COLLIERY TURN. A loading turn which as distinguished from the regular turn is regulated by the output of the colliery. The vessel is only berthed when her particular consignment is ready and not when a berth is vacant according to order of arrival.

COLLIMATION ERROR. Error in a sextant due to the lack of parallelism between the line of sight of the telescope and plane of the instrument.
Fr: *Erreur de Collimation;* Ger: *Kollimationsfehler.*

COLLISION. The act of ships or vessels striking together. In marine insurance it is immaterial whether the vessel collided with is engaged in the performance of a voyage or is in a state of wreck. But collision with stationary objects, such as piers, landing stages, and dock gates is not included among the risks covered under the term collision.
Fr: *Abordage;* Ger: *Kollision; Zusammenstoss.*
In a collision resulting from fortuitous circumstances which no human foresight could have prevented, all useful precautions having been taken to avoid this misfortune, and no ship having infringed any collision regulation, both parties bear their own damages. In a collision which results from want of due diligence or skill on one or both sides, or an infringement of the regulations for preventing collisions at sea, where both ships are to blame, the damage done to ships and cargoes is estimated and divided between the ships in proportion to the negligence or improper navigation of each vessel, unless it is impossible to establish different degrees of fault, when the liability is apportioned equally.
Camps, H. E. J., "Ship Collisions," North East Coast Institution of Engineers and Shipbuilders (Newcastle upon Tyne), *Transactions,* vol. 51 (1934-35); Marsden, *Collisions at Sea,* London, 1934; Roscoe, E. S.,

Measure of Damages in Actions of Maritime Collision, London, 1930.

COLLISION BULKHEAD. The foremost transverse watertight bulkhead extending from the bottom to the freeboard or bulkhead deck. The principal object of this bulkhead is to keep water out of the forward hold in case of collision and to confine the damage to the forward section of the vessel.

Fr: *Cloison d'Abordage;* Ger: *Kollisionsschott.*

COLLISION CLAUSE. A marine insurance clause usually incorporated in the insurance on hulls in addition to the ordinary marine risks. Underwriters agree to pay their proportion of three-fourths of the damage done by the insured vessel to another vessel up to, but not exceeding, the value stated in the policy. Also called running down clause.

Fr: *Clause d'Abordage;* Ger: *Kollisionsklausel; Kollision pro rata Klausel.*

Under another form of the clause the underwriters agree to pay the total damage for which the owner is liable, up to the insured value of the vessel insured. Shipowners liability for collision under British Law is limited by statute.

COLLISION COURSE. A course which may result in collision. Two ships whose courses are converging are on a collision course when the bearings between them remain constant.

COLLISION DRILL. Exercise in closing all watertight doors in a minimum length of time as would be necessary in the event of damage below the waterline. Also called watertight door test.

Fr: *Manœuvre des Portes Étanches;* Ger: *Schottenmanöver.*

COLLISION MAT. A mat used for stopping temporarily the inrush of water through an accidental opening in the hull below the waterline.

Fr: *Paillet d'Abordage;* Ger: *Lecksegel; Kollisionsmatte; Lecktuch.*

A collision mat is made of two thicknesses of the heaviest canvas with hemp roping worked round the sides, a thimble at each corner and two cringles on each side for fastening the lowering lines, bottom lines, and chains. One side of the mat, the ship side, is thrummed with 3-in. rope yarns worked close together. The size usually ranges from 6 to 15 ft. square.

COLLOIDAL FUEL. A liquid fuel composed of approximately 68 per cent fuel oil, 30 per cent powdered coal and up to 2 per cent fixateur, itself 70 per cent combustible.

Fr: *Combustible Colloidal.*

The powdered coal is held in chemical combination or suspension with the fuel oil and is kept from settling by the action of the fixateur. It will not foul a screen of 16 meshes to the inch. The flashpoint of colloidal fuel depends on the kind of oil used and tends to be slightly higher than the straight oil. Its calorific value per cu. ft. is equal to that of the straight oil used.

COLONIAL TRADE. Sea-borne commerce between ports of a number of geographic entities separated by stretches of open sea but under a single sovereignty.

COLOR OF THE SEA. The color of the sea, observed ashore or on board a ship, varies from a deep blue to an intense green, and in certain circumstances is brown or brown-red. Blue is typical of open oceans, green is common in coastal areas, brown or "red" water is observed in coastal regions only.

Ger: *Meereswasserfarbe.*

The blue color is attributed to the scattering of light against the water molecules themselves, or against suspended minute particles smaller than the shortest visible wave lengths. The transition to green may be due to a yellow substance which is a metabolic product related to the minute vegetation floating in the sea. For an explanation of the "red" color sometimes observed see **Algae.**

Sverdrup, Johnson, Fleming, *The Oceans,* New York, 1942.

COLORS. The distinguishing flag shown by a vessel to denote what nation she belongs to.

Fr: *Couleurs;* Ger: *Nationalflagge; Fahne.*

See **Ensign, False Colors.**

COLURES. The two great circles passing through the celestial poles dividing the ecliptic into four equal parts, and marking the seasons of the year. The circle of celestial latitude whose longitude is zero is the colure of the equinoxes; and that whose longitude is 90° is the colure of the solstices.

Fr: *Colures;* Ger: *Koluren.*

COMB. A wooden form used by riggers in weaving mats, gaskets, and so on.

COMB CLEAT. A semicircular piece of wood bolted on by its circumference, having a hole to receive a grommet or to pass a rope end through.

Fr: *Pomme Gougée;* Ger: *Kamm.*

COMBINATION BUOY. Generic term which refers to any buoy in which light

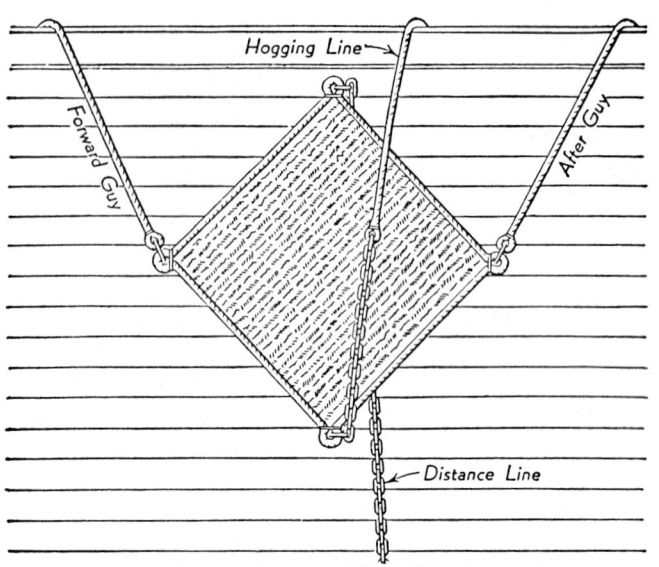

Fig. 1.—MAT ON DECK, READY TO GO OVER

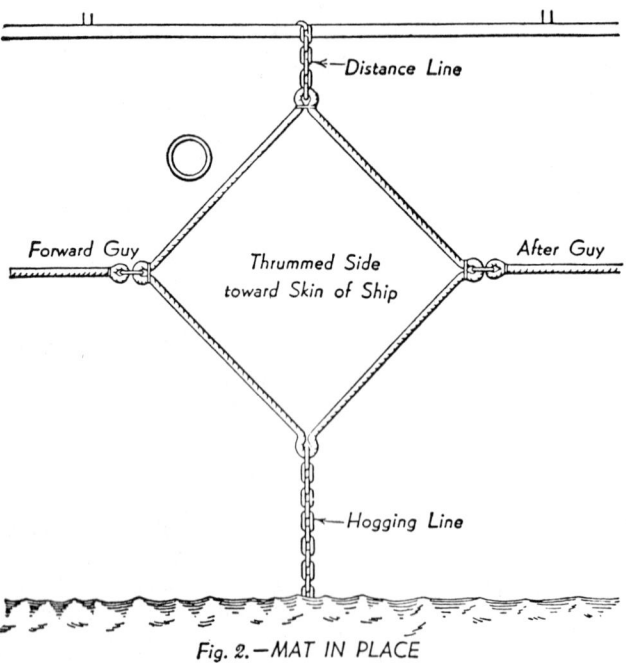

Fig. 2.—MAT IN PLACE

Collision Mat

and sound signals are combined, as for instance, a lighted bell buoy or a lighted whistle buoy.

COMBINATION DRIVE. A system of ship propulsion in which a reciprocating engine attached to a propeller exhausts into a low-pressure turbine also driving a propeller. In the usual arrangement there are two reciprocating engines, either compound or triple, which exhaust into a low-pressure turbine on a center screw. Manœuvering is done with the reciprocating engines only. This combination gives better economy than either the reciprocating engine or the direct-acting turbine. With the advent of reliable turbine reduction gears this type of drive is no longer in use.

COMBINATION FRAMING. A combined longitudinal and transverse system of framing in which the decks and bottom are longitudinallly framed while the sides are supported by transverse frames.

Fr: *Construction Mixte;* Ger: *Kombiniertes Spantensystem.*

COMBINATION LIGHT. A running light carried by steam or motor vessels of less than 40 tons gross. Also called Combination Lantern. It is so built as to show simultaneously a green and a red light from dead ahead to two points abaft the beam on the starboard and port sides respectively.

Under U. S. inland and pilot rules all motor boats less than twenty-six feet in length are required to exhibit a combination lantern in the fore part of the boat not lower than the white light aft.

Fr: *Fanal Combiné;* Ger: *Doppelfarbige Laterne.*

COME ABOUT.
See **Tack (to).**

COME ALONG (U. S.). Term used by shipyard erectors. Applies to a device consisting of two angle lugs tack-welded on two shell or deck plates to be assembled. A long screw bolt passes through holes in the lugs. By heaving on the nut the plates are made to approach each other slowly and accurately until the exact clearance for welding is obtained.

COME HOME. Said of an anchor when it fails to hold, or of any object that is being hauled upon when it begins to move.

Fr: *Draguer;* Ger: *Durchgehen.*

COME ROUND. To turn toward the wind; to luff or bring the ship's head nearer to the wind. Also called come to.

Fr: *Venir au Lof;* Ger: *Anluven.*

COME TO. When anchoring: a ship is said to have "come to" when her way is stopped, and she is riding by her anchor and cable.

COME UP. To come forward on a rope and slacken it.

Ger: *Auffieren.*

COME UP BEHIND! Signal given by a hand who has to belay the fall of a tackle which is being hauled upon so that all hands may release the fall thus enabling him to catch a turn round the belaying pin.

COMMANDER. A heavy beetle or wooden mallet used by sailmakers and riggers for beating down the eyes of rigging, and so on.

Fr: *Maillet à Épisser;* Ger: *Muskeule.*

COMMERCIAL BLOCKADE. A naval operation conducted in time of war with the object of closing the ports of the enemy against foreign commerce. At the commencement of such a blockade a delay is usually granted by international committee to permit neutral vessels in enemy ports to sail.

Fr: *Blocus Commercial;* Ger: *Handelsblockade.*

COMMERCIAL SPEED.
See **Service Speed.**

COMMODITY RATES (U. S.). Rates of freight applied individually to articles which move regularly and in large quantities such as steel, cement, petroleum goods, grain, and so on.

COMMODORE. 1. Name given by courtesy to the senior captain of a line of passenger vessels.

2. A flag officer of the United States Navy ranking below rear admiral, but above captain.

3. The president of a yacht club.

Fr: *Commodore;* Ger: *Kommodor.*

COMMON CARRIER; COMMON CARRIER BY WATER. A person or firm that carries on the business of transporting for hire goods and/or passengers by land or water. The term is applicable to steamboat companies, owners, and masters of vessels of all kinds engaged in the business of marine transportation.

The question whether a "tramp" owner is a common carrier or not is one of some doubt in the law courts.

Fr: *Transporteur en Commun;* Ger: *Samtfrachtführer.*

COMMON LAW LIEN. A lien depending upon possession of the thing. Liens on ves-

sels exist at common law for construction and repairs. A shipmaster has by common law a lien on goods for charges incurred in carrying them; on general average contributions; on expenses incurred in protecting and preserving the goods carried on his ship.
Fr: *Privilège de Droit Commun;* Ger: *Gemeinpfandrecht.*

COMMON LINK. In an anchor cable the standard or normal link of which the cable is made. In the interest of uniformity the so-called "commercial link" which has a length of six times the diameter of the iron from which it is made has been adopted in the merchant marine of most nations for the common links of anchor cables.
Fr: *Maille Ordinaire; Maille Courante;* Ger: *Gewöhnliches Glied; Gewöhnliche Schake.*

COMPANION.
See **Companionway.**

COMPANION HATCH; COMPANION HATCHWAY. A small hatch giving access to accommodation below and over which a companion is built.
Fr: *Panneau de Descente;* Ger: *Kajütenluke.*

COMPANION LADDER.
See **Companionway.**

COMPANIONWAY. 1. Steps leading from a companion hatchway to a cabin or saloon below deck. Also called companion ladder.
Fr: *Descente; Echelle de descente;* Ger: *Niedergang; Niedergangstreppe.*

2. A steel or wooden hood with doors built over a small hatchway on a weather deck, house top or cockpit, for covering and making weathertight an entrance to the deck below. The top is sometimes sloped but in most cases it is circular and fitted with a sliding cover. Also called companion.
Fr: *Capot de Descente;* Ger: *Niedergangskappe; Lukenkappe.*

COMPARTMENTATION.
See **Subdivision.**

COMPARTMENT STANDARD. The number of watertight compartments in a vessel which may be flooded up to the margin line without causing the vessel to sink.
Ger: *Vorschriftmässig Abteilung.*

COMPASS.
See **Mariner's Compass.**

COMPASS ADJUSTER. A shore expert who specializes in the adjustment of magnetic compasses by swinging the ship after they have been placed on board.
Ger: *Kompassprüfer; Kompass Adjustierer.*

COMPASS ADJUSTMENT. The process of placing magnets and iron masses (correctors) near the magnetic needle so as to neutralize the effect of magnetism existing or induced in the ship's hull and fittings, with the purpose of correcting the error so caused and bringing the compass needle to point as nearly as possible to the magnetic north. It is based on the general principle that the effect of iron and steel of the ship, acting at various distances, can be balanced by magnets and soft iron placed close to the compass. Also called Compensation.
Fr: *Régulation du compas;* Ger: *Kompassregulierung; Kompensierung des Kompass.*

Gillie, J. C., *Navigator's Handbook on Modern Compass Adjusting,* London, 1943; Heck and Parker, *Compensation of the Magnetic Compass,* Washington, 1923; Kielhorn, L. V., *Treatise on Compass Compensation,* New York, 1942.

COMPASS BEARING. A bearing stated as a compass direction and expressed as a compass course, that is, in degrees and fractions of a degree.
Fr: *Relèvement au compas; Cap au compas;* Ger: *Kompasspeilung.*

COMPASS BOWL. A hemispherical brass or copper receptacle covered by a glass plate in which the compass card is mounted. Also called compass chamber.
Fr: *Cuvette;* Ger: *Kompassbüchse; Kompasskessel; Kompassgehaüse.*

The bowl is suspended by two concentric brass rings, called gimbals, with knife-edge bearings set at right angle which take the motion of the vessel, and has a lead weight at the bottom to keep it in a level position when the vessel rolls and pitches. The bowl is fitted in the center with a brass pivot tipped with osmium-iridium alloy, which although very hard can be sharply pointed and does not corrode.

COMPASS BRIDGE.
See **Compass Platform.**

COMPASS CARD. The circular card attached to the needles of a magnetic compass. Its circumference is divided according to two systems of notation. In one system the readings are given in degrees from 0 to 90 and from N and S to E and W. It is known as the quadrantal system. In the second system, now generally adopted, the readings are by degrees from 0 (N) right around the card (clockwise) to 359. The use of points has been almost entirely abandoned except on small craft and open boat compasses. There are two principal types of cards for magnetic compasses, the dry and the liquid compass cards.

Fr: *Rose;* Ger: *Kompassrose; Windrose.*

The Kelvin (Thomson) compass card may be regarded as the standard for the *dry type* of compass. It consists of a strong paper card with the central parts cut away and its outer edge stiffened by a thin aluminum ring. The pivot is fitted with an iridium point upon which rests a small aluminum cap (boss) fitted with a polished sapphire bearing worked to the form of an open cone. Radiating from this boss are 32 silk threads whose outer ends are made fast to the inner edge of the card. These threads sustain the

to the card. The card is of a curved annular type, the outer ring being convex on the upper and inner side.

COMPASS CHAMBER. The upper part of the binnacle within which the compass bowl is suspended. It is provided with "V" shaped bearing upon which the gimbal ring is suspended.

Ger: *Kompassgehause.*

COMPASS CORRECTIONS. The corrections which must be applied to the indications of the instrument to obtain the reading that would be given if the North point of the compass card corresponded to the north point of the horizon. See: **Compass Error.**

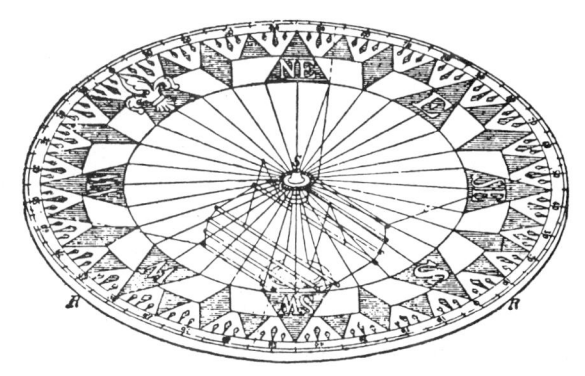

Kelvin Compass Card

weight of the suspended card and their elasticity tends to decrease the shocks due to the vessel's motion. Eight small magnetic needles 2 to 3½ in. long are secured to two parallel silk threads and are slung from the aluminum rim of the card by other silk threads which pass through eyes in the ends of the outer pair of needles. The lightness of the Kelvin card, which weighs about 190 grains as compared with 1,600 grains for an ordinary 10-in. dry card, greatly reduces the friction between the cap and pivot and adds considerably to the life of both.

The *liquid compass* card is fitted in the center with a light brass float or air vessel, the buoyancy of which is so calculated in relation to the specific gravity of the fluid as to take most of the weight off the pivot. In a 7½-in. card the pressure on the pivot is between 60 and 90 grains at 60° F.; the weight of the card in the air being 3,000 grains. The magnet system of a liquid compass card consists of 2 or 4 bundles of steel wires sealed in little copper tubes secured

Fr: *Corrections du compas;* Ger: *Kompass Verbesserungen.*

COMPASS COURSE. The course which refers to the magnetic compass by which the ship is steered. The angle between the compass north or south and the fore-and-aft line of the ship. Also called compass heading.

Fr: *Route au Compas;* Ger: *Kompasskurs.*

COMPASS COVER. A loose fitting canvas cover placed over a binnacle when not in use as a protection against rain, spray and so on.

Fr: *Etui d'habitacle;* Ger: *Kompassbezug.*

COMPASS ERROR. The angle between the direction of the compass needle and the true meridian, due to the combined effect of the variation and deviation.

Fr: *Erreur du Compas;* Ger: *Kompassfehler; Fehlweisung.*

See **Deviation, Magnetic Declination.**

Standard books on navigation describe the methods generally used for determining the compass error as follows:
  a. By reciprocal bearings requiring a station ashore.
  b. By bearings of the sun.
  c. By ranges ashore, requiring that the magnetic bearing of the range be known.
  d. By a distant object on land.
  e. By comparison with a gyrocompass which has a known error.

COMPASS FLAT.
 See **Compass Platform.**

round view of the horizon, and is used for taking bearings. Also called compass bridge, monkey bridge, compass flat.
 Ger: *Peildeck.*

COMPASS POLE. A pole made of wood or nonmagnetic metal from the top of which hangs a compass.
 Ger: *Kompasssäule.*

COMPASS READING GLASS. Semicircular magnifying glass fitted to a steering compass to facilitate observation of slight changes in ship's heading.

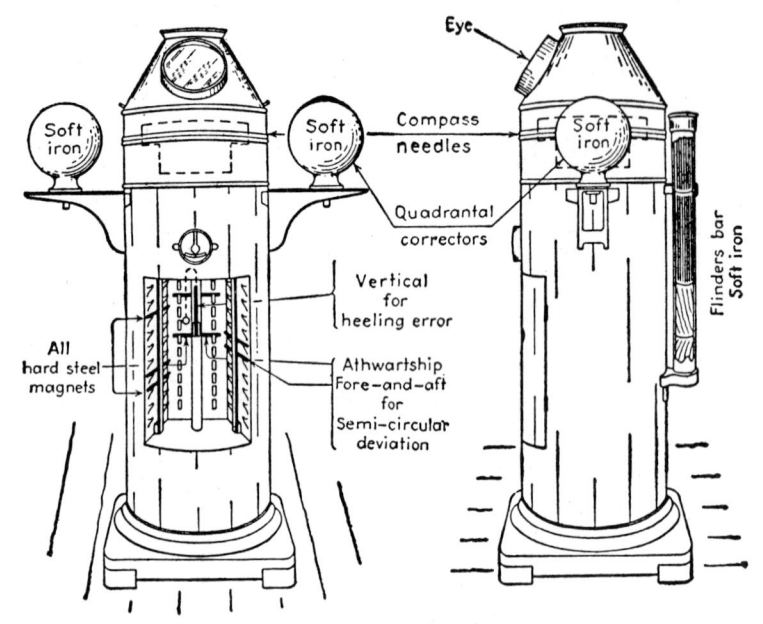

Compensating Binnacle

COMPASS PIVOT. The pivot which stands in the center of the bowl in a magnetic compass and on which the boss of the compass card bears. In dry-card compasses the pivot is made of brass and tipped with osmium-iridium alloy sharply pointed, which is extremely hard and does not corrode. In liquid compasses the pivot is made of hard bronze.
 Fr: *Pivot de Boussole;* Ger: *Kompasspinne.*

COMPASS PLATFORM. A platform formed by the top of the wheelhouse and chartroom on which the standard (magnetic) compass is located. It gives a nearly all-

COMPASS ROSE. An outer and two inner graduated circles engraved on a nautical chart, used for laying off courses or bearings. The outer circle represents a true compass graduated from 000° true North to 360° measured clockwise. The inner circles are magnetic compasses, and include the effect of variation in the given locality.
 See **Card.**
 Fr: *La Rose du Compas;* Ger: *Die Kompassrose.*

COMPASS TIMBER. A name given to curved or arched timbers used in wooden ship construction. The term is restricted to timber bent or curved in its growth to the

extent of more than five inches in a length of twelve feet.
Fr: *Bois Courbant;* Ger: *Krummholz.*

COMPENSATED COMPASS. A magnetic compass compensated for deviation by means of magnet bars placed in a compensated binnacle.
Fr: *Boussole compensée;* Ger: *Kompensierter Kompass.*

COMPENSATING BINNACLE. A binnacle containing groups of magnets placed below the compass so that their combined effect is that of a single magnet whose axis is intersected at its middle point by the vertical line through the compass center.
Fr: *Habitacle à Compensateurs;* Ger: *Kompensierendes Kompasshaus.*

The different magnets are disposed as follows: (a) in a magnet chamber immediately below the compass; (b) on a pair of arms projecting horizontally and supporting the two compensating globes; (c) on a central tube located in the vertical axis of the binnacle; (d) on an outside tube which houses the Flinder's bar.

COMPENSATING COILS. A group of electric wire coils placed around a magnetic compass for correcting errors while the degaussing system is in operation.

COMPENSATING MAGNET.
See **Compensator.**

COMPENSATION.
See **Adjustment.**

COMPENSATOR. A piece of soft iron or bar magnet to compensate or neutralize the effect of the iron of a ship on the compass needle. Also called magnetic compensator, compensating magnet.
Fr: *Aimant Compensateur;* Ger: *Kompensationsmagnet.*

COMPLEMENT. The number of crew employed upon a vessel for its safe navigation.

COMPLETE SUPERSTRUCTURE VESSEL. A vessel in which the upper or freeboard deck is covered from stem to stern by a continuous superstructure deck.
Fr: *Navire à Superstructure continue;* Ger: *Schiff mit vollem Aufbau; Durchlaufendes Aufbauschiff.*

The freeboard is calculated and marked from the superstructure deck and the class will be marked "With freeboard." If a tonnage opening is provided in the superstructure deck, the vessel is still regarded as a complete superstructure vessel for classification purposes, but the freeboard is calculated from the second deck, which then becomes the freeboard deck.

COMPOSITE BOILER. 1. A cylindrical fire-tube marine boiler in which the main feature is the substitution of a dry-back common combustion chamber for the usual wet-type divided combustion chamber. A series of tubes forming a water wall within the combustion chamber is provided and maintain rapid circulation in the boiler.
Fr: *Chaudière à Circulation Accélérée.*
2. Auxiliary steam boiler placed on the exhaust line of an internal combustion engine, in which steam can be raised either by the exhaust gases or by separate oil burners when the main engines are at standstill.

COMPOSITE CONSTRUCTION. 1. The composite system of shipbuilding, in which the hull is built of iron, with the exception of the shell which is made of wood. It was introduced between the years 1860 and 1870 when the China tea trade was conducted with large sailing vessels and a quick run home was so important that the cleanliness of bottom provided by copper sheathing was thought essential. Not many vessels were built on this plan, for although those built proved strong and durable, the advantage of immunity from fouling was an insufficient offset to their great cost, and heavy weight of the hull. For these reasons, the composite system of construction is practically obsolete in ordinary merchant ship construction. For yachts and other special vessels it is still employed, being particularly suitable for large racing yachts in which the hull is subjected to heavy stress owing to the enormous sail area.
Fr: *Construction Composite;* Ger: *Kompositbau.*

The advantage of this form of construction over all-wood construction is that for any given tonnage, more internal space is available for cargo or accommodation, in consequence of the small scantlings of frames compared with wooden frames. In composite hulls the frames must be closely spaced (not more than 18 in. apart) on account of the calking, there being nothing to calk against like the back of wooden frames. The planking is fastened to the frames by bolts, set up on the frames with nuts. The holes in the frames are punched or drilled, and after the plank is fitted to the frames and temporarily secured, the plank is bored to receive the head of the bolt and its stem. The bolt is luted with white lead, and with a thread of oakum under its shoulder. It is punched in through the plank and framed and set up with a nut. A plug, also luted with white lead, is driven over the head of the bolt to fill the hole in the plank. The butts of the planks do not meet on the frame but between the frames and are secured by steel straps. Composite construction is also adopted for speed boats, which are now mostly built with wooden shell, and steel or light alloy framing and with inside planking of cedar.

The term "semi-composite" is used when referring to craft built of wood with the exception of alternate frames and floors which are steel. There is also a steel girder running about 10 ft. fore and aft under the heel of each mast. This system is frequently employed for building small yachts.

2. A system of construction for steel hulls in which transverse framing is adopted for the sides of the vessel and longitudinal framing for the outer bottom, inner bottom, and decks.

Fr: *Construction Mixte.*

COMPOSITE SAILING. A combination of *great circle* and *parallel sailing.* This course is adopted by the navigator when he finds that the great circle track leads him into high latitudes where ice or bad weather is likely to be encountered. He therefore decides on one parallel of latitude as the highest to which he can sail in safety. The shortest route then consists of a portion of that parallel and the arcs of two great circles tangential to it, one of which intersects the point of departure and the other the destination.

COMPOUND DREDGE. A dredge comprising two or more types of dredging appliances, as for instance a suction-hopper dredge.

Fr: *Drague mixte.*

COMPOUND GEARED WINCH. A cargo winch which has a double set of gear reductions with a clutch to connect one or the other reduction. The high gear ratio is used to handle the normal drafts while heavy lifts are handled on the low gear ratio.

COMPRADORA. A Brazilian dugout canoe found in the coastal waters of Bahia and chiefly used as a carry-away boat meeting the other fishing boats out at sea and bringing their catch to the nearest market. Length over-all 28 ft. Beam 4 ft. Depth 2 ft.

The hull is flat-bottomed with scoop-shaped bow; rounded sides with considerable tumble home; flat V-shaped stern with long overhang. It is fitted with two thwarts: one in the bow and the other amidships, through which the masts are stepped. Both masts have a pronounced forward rake and each carries a lateen sail. There is no rudder, a paddle being used for steering.

COMPRESSOR. A device for holding the chain cable. It consists of a curved lever fitted to the underside of a deck and pivoted at one end, so as to allow the curve to sweep over the lower orifice of the deck pipe. A small tackle is hooked to the free end of the lever. When the compressor is "bowsed-to" the chain cable is jammed between it and the deck pipe.

Fr: *Étrangloir;* Ger: *Kneifstopper; Zwischendeckstopper.*

Ships used to ride by the compressor, the cable holder being used only for checking the cable running out. When a ship had been given the necessary cable, the cable holder was eased up and the compressor "bowsed-to." Improvements in the design of windlasses have rendered the fitting of compressors unnecessary nowadays.

COMPULSORY PILOT. A pilot who in observance with the laws and regulations of local authorities must be taken on board to direct the vessel through specified waters.

Fr: *Pilote Obligatoire;* Ger: *Zwangslotse; Pflichtlotse.*

COMPULSORY PILOTAGE. The compulsory employment of a pilot on all ships or on certain classes of ships, prescribed in many localities, for the safety of navigation.

Fr: *Pilotage Obligatoire;* Ger: *Lotsenzwang.*

According to the law of most countries, a pilot whose employment is compulsory is to be regarded not as controlling the navigation but simply as an adviser of the master, who remains responsible for all loss and damage resulting from the negligent navigation of his ship.

The following classes of vessels are usually exempted from compulsory pilotage: war vessels, yachts, fishing vessels, ferryboats, tugs, dredges, sludge vessels, barges or other similar craft, ships of less than 50 tons (gross tonnage).

CONCLUDING LINE. A line hitched to every step down the middle of a rope ladder.

Ger: *Mitteltau.*

CONDEMNATION. Confiscation of a vessel or her cargo, or both, as decreed by a prize court of the belligerent.

Fr: *Confiscation;* Ger: *Kondemnation.*

CONDENSER. A device in which exhaust steam is received from the main engines, turbines, or auxiliary machinery and converted into water, which is thereby regained for further use in the boiler feed system instead of being irretrievably lost. The usual type of condenser comprises a shell, enclosing a nest of tubes. Exhaust steam flows around the tubes, and sea water flows through them, absorbing heat from the steam, which condenses as it cools.

The four principal factors governing the design of condensers for high powered steam propulsion plants are: (1) High rate of heat transfer from exhaust steam to circulating water; (2) low pressure differential between the exhaust steam inlet and the connection of the air-ejector suction; (3) low differential between temperature of exhaust steam entering and condensate leaving the condenser; (4) maximum protection of condenser components from erosion and corrosion.

CONDITIONAL CONTRABAND. A term applied in international law to articles which may be and are used for purposes of war and peace according to circumstances.

Fr: *Contrebande Conditionnelle*; Ger: *Relative Konterbande*.

CONFERENCE. The organization through which several shipping lines administer their agreements in order to fix passenger and/or freight rates, sailings, and other matters of mutual interest relating to particular routes or parts. Also called shipping ring.

Fr: *Conférence*; Ger: *Konferenz*.

A conference may be merely a gentlemen's agreement, calling only for occasional meetings of the interested managers to discuss questions of administration, forms of bills of lading, sailing dates, methods of receiving and delivering cargo, and so on. In other cases, the agreement is based upon a firm and binding contract, which is executed in writing, signed, sealed and includes penalties on any of the signatories who may violate its terms.

See **Baltic and International Maritime Conference.**

Boyd, W., "Agreements and Conferences in Their Relation to Ocean Rates," American Academy of Political and Social Science (Philadelphia) *Annals*, vol. 55 (1914); Gottheil, P., "Historical Development of Steamship Agreements and Conferences in the American Foreign Trade," American Academy of Political and Social Science (Philadelphia) *Annals*, vol. 55 (1914); Gregg, E. S., *Rate Procedure of Steamship Conferences*, U. S. Bureau of Foreign and Domestic Commerce, Trade Information Bulletin 221, Washington, 1924; Stevens, W. H. S., The Administration and Enforcement of Steamship Conferences and Agreements, American Academy of Political and Social Science (Philadelphia) *Annals*, vol. 55 (1914).

CONFUSED SEA. Maximum state of sea disturbance. Douglas Scale no. 9.

Fr: *Mer Confuse*; Ger: *Durcheinanderlaufende See*.

CONICAL BUOY. A buoy which has a pointed upper part.

Fr: *Bouée Sphéro-conique*; Ger: *Spitzetonne*.

CONJUNCTION. The position of two celestial bodies when they are in the same longitude.

Fr: *Conjonction*; Ger: *Konjunktion*.

CONN. To direct the helmsman as to the movements of the helm, especially when navigating in narrow channels or heavy traffic.

CONSIGNEE. The person to whom goods are consigned as stated on the bills of lading.

Fr: *Consignataire de Marchandises*; Ger: *Empfänger*.

CONSIGNOR. The person named in a bill of lading as the one from whom the goods have been received for shipment.

Fr: *Expéditeur*; *Chargeur*; Ger: *Absender*; *Versender*.

CONSOL. A long range radio navigational aid consisting essentially of a medium frequency radio transmitter with special directional aerial system produced by three aerials in a line, evenly spaced at a distance of the order of three times the wave length of the transmitter. The signals can be received by a normal communication receiver. Ranges over the sea of 1,000 miles by day and 1,200 miles by night may normally be expected. Consol provides in many instances a crude determination of position on the order of a poor astronomical observation, during periods sometimes long prior to landfall. It is not usable within 25 miles of the transmitter and not sufficiently accurate for making landfalls. Consol stations are in existence at Bushmills (Great Britain), Stavanger (Norway), Ploneis (France), Lugo (Spain) and Sevilla (Spain).

CONSTANT DEVIATION. A deviation which appears in a magnetic compass when the vessel's soft iron is not symmetrically arranged on each side of the fore-and-aft center plane, or when the compass is not on the midship fore-and-aft line. It is small in amount and does not alter with a change in latitude.

See **Deviation.**

CONSTRUCTION DIFFERENTIAL SUBSIDY (U. S.). A subsidy granted by the Federal Government to a domestic shipbuilder to compensate for the excess cost of a newly built vessel over the estimated cost if the same vessel was constructed under similar plans and specifications in a foreign shipbuilding center.

CONSTRUCTION SUBSIDY. Grants made by a government to national shipyards as a protection against foreign competition and to foster shipbuilding enterprise. These grants are usually calculated on gross tonnage for the hull and on weight or horsepower for propelling machinery. Also called construction bounty.

Fr: *Prime à la Construction;* Ger: *Schiffbauprämie.*

CONSTRUCTIVE TOTAL LOSS. Constructive total loss arises when the character of the loss is such that the insured has reasonable grounds for giving up the voyage altogether, that is if the adventure is destroyed altogether, although the goods themselves be not lost.

Ger: *Konstruktiver Totalverlust.*

To establish such a loss it must be shown that a shipowner of ordinary prudence and uninsured would not have gone to the expense of raising and repairing the vessel, because its market value when raised and repaired would probably be less than the cost of restoration.

CONSUL. An official commissioned in the diplomatic service of a government to hold office and to represent it at a particular place in a foreign country. The consul is charged with the supervision of all shipping sailing under the flag of the appointing state which enters the port where he resides. He controls and legalizes ship's papers, inspects them on arrival and departure, and settles disputes between the master and crew or passengers. He assists sailors in distress; undertakes the repatriation of shipwrecked crews and passengers and attests marine protests and surveys.

Fr: *Consul;* Ger: *Konsul.*

Busch, E., Die Stellung des Deutschen Konsuls im Schiffahrstverkehr, Berlin, 1913; U. S. Consular Bureau, *Digest of Consular Regulations Relating to Vessels and Seamen,* Washington, 1921.

CONSULAGE. Fees charged by a consul for some of the duties of his office.

Fr: *Frais Consulaires.*

CONSULAR INVOICE. An invoice prepared on a special form obtained from a consul and vise-ed (sighted and signed) by him to secure the admission of goods in certain foreign countries. Four or more copies are usually needed and fees are payable to the consul who certifies the documents. The purpose of these invoices is to prevent an understatement of values with a consequent avoidance of the full payment of import duties.

Fr: *Facture Consulaire;* Ger: *Konsular Warenrechnung; Konsulatsfaktur.*

CONSULAR PASSENGER. A passenger, usually a destitute seaman, placed on board ship by the consul in a foreign port and whose passage is paid for by the government on arrival at a home port.

CONSUMPTION ENTRY. Entry at customs by the consignee for imported merchandise. When the entry is filed the classification and values stated are compared with the description and values in the invoice and the proper amount of duties estimated.

CONTACT CLAUSE. A clause frequently found in marine hull policies under which liners are insured. This clause provides that notwithstanding the "free of particular average" warranty, claims arising from contact with any substance (ice included), other than water, shall be paid.

CONTINENT. A term used in shipping parlance to describe the range of ports between Bordeaux and Hamburg, both inclusive.

CONTINENTAL SHELF. The slightly submerged plain that forms a border to most of the continents. It varies in width from about 10 to 100 mi. and slopes more or less gently from the edge of the land to a specified depth usually 100 fathoms (though in some cases as much as 300 fathoms). It then ends abruptly, and there is a steep slope to the ocean depths.

Fr: *Plateau Continental;* Ger: *Kontinental Schelff.*

CONTINENTAL SLOPE. The declivity from the off-shore border of the continental shelf to oceanic depths. It is characterized by a marked increase in slope.

CONTINENTAL TERRACE. The zone around the continents, extending from low-water line to the base of the continental slope.

CONTINUATION CLAUSE. A marine insurance clause found in practically all time policies which provides that if at the end of the period of insurance the ship is at sea, the insurance may be extended until her arrival at some port, subject to previous notice to the underwriters. Also called **expiration clause.**

Fr: *Clause de Prolongation de Risque;* Ger: *Verlängerungsklausel.*

CONTINUOUS DISCHARGE BOOK. A document issued by the maritime authorities to seamen when they sign on at the beginning of a voyage and retained by the men when they sign off as a record of their service during that period. Each book carries a photograph and description of its owner with a blank for the date of his shipment and discharge, and the proper record of his conduct and efficiency.

Fr: *Livret de marin.*

CONTINUOUS FLOOR. A floor plate extending in one length from center line to bilge passing through or over longitudinal and inner bottom framing. The converse of intercostal floor.

Fr: *Varangue Continue;* Ger: *Durchlaufende Bodenwrange.*

CONTINUOUS VOYAGE. A term used in international maritime law which refers to the transportation of contraband goods destined ultimately to an enemy port, although apparently consigned to a neutral port, from which they are transhipped to their final destination. Under this doctrine the two voyages are considered as one, and the seizure of the cargo by blockading vessels is justified.

Baty, T., *Prize Law and Continuous Voyage,* London, 1914; Gantenbein, J. W., *The Doctrine of Continuous Voyage,* Portland (Oregon), 1929.

CONTINUOUS WELD. A fusion weld extending along the entire length of the joint, as distinguished from intermittent weld, and tack weld.

Fr: *Soudure Continue;* Ger: *Durchlaufende Schweissung.*

CONTLINE. The space between the strands of a rope. It is filled with the worming when a rope is served.

CONTRABAND. Prohibited or dutiable goods smuggled into a country.

Fr: *Contrebande;* Ger: *Konterbande.*

See **Absolute Contraband, Conditional Contraband, War Contraband.**

CONTRABAND TRADE. 1. In time of war, the supplying of a belligerent with contraband of war.

2. In time of peace, the smuggling of goods the importation or exportation of which is forbidden.

Fr: *Commerce de Contrebande;* Ger: *Schleichhandel.*

CONTRACT LIEN. A lien on charges specifically mentioned in the charter party or bill of lading and agreed upon by contract between the shipowners and the charterers or shippers.

Ger: *Vertragspfandrecht.*

These charges usually include dead freight, demurrage, damages for detention, advance freight, charter party freight, all moneys due to the shipowners under the provisions of the bill of lading.

CONTRACT SERVICE. A term generally used in connection with postal services, colonial services, or, in a general way, shipping services required in the public interest of a country, and for which agreements are entered into between a shipowner or a shipping corporation and a government. It might include transportation by sea of mails, government personnel or goods, troops and their equipment, or the maintenance of regular shipping services with colonies.

Fr: *Service Contractuel.*

CONTRACT STEVEDORE. An individual or firm who undertakes to load or discharge vessels on the basis of specific agreement. International Labor Office, Geneva, Twelfth Session, "Protection Against Accidents of Workers Engaged in Loading or Unloading Ships," 1928.

CONTRA PROPELLER. A contrivance designed to increase the propeller efficiency. It consists of vertical and horizontal stationary blades attached to the rudderpost when adapted to a centerline propeller, or forward of each propeller in case of a multiple-screw vessel.

Fr: *Contre Hélice;* Ger: *Gegenschraube; Kontrapropeller.*

The design of the contra propeller is based on the following theory: The ordinary screw propeller when revolving sets a large volume of water rotating and this absorbs a considerable amount of power which is lost as far as the propulsion of the vessel is concerned. The function of the contra propeller is to change the rotary motion of the propeller jet and guide it in a straight rearward stream. In thus being deflected this mass of water gives back to the vessel a large part of the energy, which otherwise would be lost, by reacting on the contra propeller blades, imparting thereby additional forward thrust in the direction of the ship's motion.

It is claimed that by fitting this contrivance to the rudderpost an increase of about 7 per cent in power is obtained in practice.

Overgaard, O., "Combined Streamline Rudder and Guide Vanes.—Latest Developments of Contra-Propellers," Society of Naval

Architects and Marine Engineers, *Transactions*, 1925.

CONTRA-GUIDE RUDDER. A double-plate streamlined rudder in which the blade is offset in opposite directions, at the level of the propeller hub, in such a manner that each propeller blade in passing by the rudder throws its stream of water against the offset face of the rudder. This deflection of the propeller jet into a straight fore-and-aft direction increases the useful thrust in the direction of motion of the vessel.

Ger: *Leitflächenruder; Contraruder.*

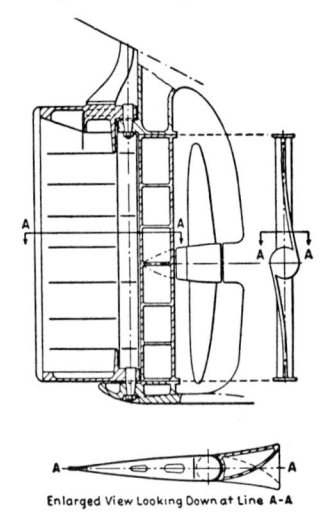

Contra-Guide Rudder

CONTRA-SOLEM. Expression used in meteorology and oceanography to denote motion influenced by Coriolis force in an anti-clockwise direction in the Northern hemisphere and clockwise direction in the Southern hemisphere.

CONTRIBUTORY VALUE. In a general average statement the arrived value of property saved from loss or destruction by a general average act, on which is based the proportional contribution of the various interests to the expenses or sacrifice made for the common safety of all.

Fr: *Valeur Contributive;* Ger: *Beitragspflichtiger Wert.*

CONTROLLER. A device secured to the deck near the hawsepipe for taking the strain of the anchor cable off the windlass; also as a safety to prevent the anchor cable from running out accidentally while getting the anchor up. Also called bow stopper, cable stopper, riding chock, chain stopper.

Fr: *Chemin de Fer; Stoppeur;* Ger: *Kontroller; Deckstopper; Klusenstopper.*

See **Lever Controller, Screw Controller.**

CONTROLLING DEPTH. In chart work, the least depth available for navigation. It controls the draft of vessels using the area.

Fr: *Profondeur Vérifiée.*

CONTROL STATIONS. One of the spaces in which main navigating equipment, radio room, fire recording equipment, emergency generator is located.

Fr: *Postes de Sécurité;* Ger: *Kontrolle Stelle.*

CONTWOOD. Code name for a Baltic and International Maritime Conference Charter Party applicable to shipment of sawed wood from the Baltic to Continental ports. It is worded in such a way that it can also be applied in other directions where no standard charter parties exist.

CONVECTION. 1. Name given to the physical process embodying the ascent and descent of air, resulting from differences of density and changes in pressure and temperature.

2. The descent of heavy air to replace the rising light air.

CONVERGENCY. In wireless radio direction finding, allowances made for the varying meridional expansion or contraction as the bearing line crosses toward the equator or one of the poles.

CONVERSION ANGLE. The difference between the rhumb-line course and the great-circle course and vice versa when one course is converted to the other on a Mercator chart. The modified conversion angle is the correction applied to a great-circle tangential course to convert it to the chord of a great-circle course.

CONVERTED TIMBER. Timber cut for different purposes and classified as thickstuff, planks, boards, carlings, and scantlings.

Fr: *Bois Débité;* Ger: *Zersägtes Holz.*

CONVOY. 1. A fleet or group of merchant vessels assembled for passage together and escorted by one or more warships as protection against the attacks of enemy airplanes, surface vessels or submarines. In peace time convoys of merchant vessels are occasionally formed under special circumstances, as for instance navigation through heavy ice, in which case the escorting vessel is an icebreaker.

Neutral merchant vessels under convoy of a vessel of war of their own nationality are deemed to be exempt from visit or search by belligerent warships. The acceptance by a neutral vessel of the convoy of a belligerent warship is an illegal act and affords ground for condemnation if the vessel is captured by the other belligerent.

Fr: *Convoi;* Ger: *Konvoy; Flottengeleit.* Great Britain, Parliamentary Papers, Miscellaneous 13, 1918; Lederle, Die Konvoyierung Neutraler Handelschiffe, Berlin, 1917.

2. Naval force appointed by a government to sail with and protect a group of merchantmen during a passage. Also called escort.

Fr: *Escorte;* Ger: *Geleitschiffe; Eskorte.*

3. The act of escorting a fleet of trading vessels in war time.

Fr: *Convoyage;* Ger: *Konvoyierung.*

COOLER ROOM. On air-cooled fruit carriers a compartment where brine pipes and cooler fans are located and from which air ducts lead to the refrigerated cargo spaces. There are usually two or more cooler rooms on each such vessel.

COOPER. A dock worker who takes care of repairs or reconditioning to damaged packages or cases. In theory this refers to both inward and outward goods but actually it applies only to incoming cargo as the damage-cargo clerk does not accept any damaged outgoing cargo. It is the shipper's obligation to put it in shipping condition.

COOPERAGE. A charge made by the carrier and paid on delivery of the goods to the consignee for putting hoops on casks; also for reconditioning damaged packages or cases which have been insecurely or unsafely packed to stand ordinary travel.

COPING. Turning the ends of iron lodging knees so that they may hook into the beams.

COPPER-BOTTOMED. Said of a wooden vessel having the underwater part of the hull sheathed with copper as a protection against the growth of fouling organisms and to prevent the ravages of teredo and other borers. Also called copper-sheathed.

Fr: *Doublé en cuivre;* Ger: *Kupferbodig; Kupferhaut.*

COPPER-FASTENED. Said of a wooden ship whose planking below the loadline is fastened with copper or bronze instead of iron or steel bolts.

Fr: *Chevillé en Cuivre;* Ger: *Kupferfestverbolzung; Kupferfest.*

The object of having all metal work in the bottom made of copper is that the vessel may afterwards be copper-sheathed without danger of the sheathing corroding the heads of bolts by galvanic action, as occurs when copper and iron are in contact with sea water.

COPPERING HAMMER. A boatbuilder's hammer with large flat face and curved peen ending in a claw.

COPPER PAINT. An antifouling composition used on wooden hulls.

Copper paints are usually compounded so that they remain soft in the water, being frequently applied just before the vessel is launched. Thus the copper salts which poison the borers are more active and they catch and kill many minute organisms which can grow only on a hard surface.

Copper-bronze bottom paints are harder and smoother than ordinary copper coatings.

COQUETA. Portuguese two-masted sailing boat with lateen mainsail and gaff-headed mizzen.

CORACLE. A small paddle boat made by covering a lathe framing with oilcloth or calico waterproofed outside with a coating of pitch and tar. Length, over-all, 3 ft. 10 in. to 5 ft. 8½ in. Breadth 3 ft. to 3 ft. 4½ in. Depth 11 in. to 1 ft. 3½ in. Weight 18 to 50 lb.

The skeleton frame is made of 6 or 7 laths arranged in a fore-and-aft direction interwoven with a varying number of laths worked at right angles to the former. Around the bent-up ends of these 2 sets of frames 3 rows of withies are plaited or woven to keep the laths in place and to form a strengthening gunwale.

Coracles are still used on rivers and marshes in Wales and Ireland, also for salmon fishing on the Severn.

CORALLINA. Decked sailing boat used for gathering coral on the west coast of the Italian Peninsula and the south coast of Sicily, Sardinia, Tunisia. The tonnage varies from 10 to 24. The most common type has a length of 42 to 45 ft. Breadth 10.6 to 13 ft. Depth 3.7 ft. Capacity 14 to 16 tons.

These boats usually work in fleets numbering about 20, with a specially constructed dredging apparatus called *ingegno,* in which the coral plants become entangled and are then hoisted to the surface. The boats are double-ended, keel-built with flat floor, moderate sheer, round bilge, carvel planking, and deep rudder. The older boats had a straight vertical stem. Recent craft have an overhanging curved stem. The crew's accommodation is aft and the cabin forward. The rig consists of one mast with lateen mainsail and jib set flying.

CORD SEAM. A sailmaker's seam in

which the edges are brought together as in the round seam, but slightly rolled in on the cloth and stitched to it. From 3 to 4 stitches are taken per inch.

Fr: *Couture piquée et rabattue;* Ger: *Papennaht.*

CORE. The heart strand of a rope around which the other strands are laid.

Fr: *Âme;* Ger: *Seele.*

CORIAL. A one piece dugout canoe with pointed ends used on the coastal waters and estuaries of Venezuela and the Guianas. Also called *curiara, guajibaca, luampo.*

The width, depth, and angle of slope of the extremities vary in different areas. The largest boats have a length of about 49 ft. with a breadth of 4.9 to 6.5 ft. and are occasionally rigged with a short mast and square sail made from the stem of palm leaves.

CORINTHIAN. A yachting term used to denote a person who follows the sea but not as a means of livelihood; especially one who does not accept remuneration for services in handling or serving on a yacht. The object of this term is to distinguish amateurs from professionals.

CORK FENDER. Netting made of rope yarn filled with cork shavings.

Fr: *Ballon de Défense;* Ger: *Korkfender.*

CORK LINE.
See **Headline.**

CORK-LIGHT TRIM. An expression used to denote the condition of a vessel which has been stripped of all gear and movable objects previous to heaving down or during salvage operations.

CORK PAINT. A special paint containing granules of cork, which are applied upon the paint coating. Used for interior surfaces in living quarters, storerooms, and so on, that are directly exposed to chilling by conduction through metal from the action of wind or water, or where sweating would occur as a result of the opposite extremes in temperature. The coat next to the priming paint must of necessity be a thick coat of an adhesive nature to which the cork will adhere well. The cork grains should be able to pass through a No. 8 sieve but must be large enough to be held on a No. 12 sieve.

Fr: *Peinture au liège;* Ger: *Korkfarbe.*

CORNER BOAT.
See **Skipjack.**

CORONA. A series of colored rings around the sun or moon, produced by diffraction of the light by droplets of water suspended in the atmosphere. It is distinguished from a halo, which is due to refraction, by the fact that the sequence of the colors is reversed, the red of the halo being inside; that of the corona outside.

Fr: *Couronne;* Ger: *Ring; Korona.*

CORONAZO. Strong southerly wind of the west coast of Mexico.

CORRECTED ESTABLISHMENT. The average lunitidal interval for a lunar month. The mean of high water intervals for all stages of the tide at a certain place. Also called mean establishment.

Ger: *Verbesserte Hafenzeit.*

CORRECTED TIME. The time taken by a sailing yacht to cover a course with its time allowance deducted therefrom.

Fr: *Temps Corrigé;* Ger: *Verbesserte Zeit.*

CORRECTION FOR RUN. Allowance applied to a ship's position plotted on a chart which brings it foreward in accordance with vessel's course and speed to any time required.

CORRECTIONS FOR SHEER. Numerical correction applied to freeboard calculation for excess or deficiency or sheer line above or below standard sheer curve.

Fr: *Correction de tonture;* Ger: *Sprungkorrektur.*

CORRECTION OF ENDS. Term used in naval architecture to denote corrections used when applying the trapezoidal rule to ship calculations if the contour of the ship's form is such as to lead clearly to an error when the rule is applied directly.

Fr: *Corrections d'Aboutissement.*

CORRESPONDING SPEEDS. Speeds which bear the same relation to each other as that of the square roots of linear dimensions of the ships involved. This presupposes the existence of geometrical similitude between the ship's underwater form so that the wave formations resulting are similar. Used in speed and power calculations by naval architects.

Fr: *Vitesses Correspondantes;* Ger: *Korrespondierende Geschwindigkeiten.*

CORROSION. Deterioration of metals due to oxidation or rusting. On iron and steel it is chiefly due to the action of carbonic acid contained in water and humid air. It is aggravated by the salts present in sea water. Protection against corrosion usually involves a protective coating which keeps oxygen away from the metal surface.

Fr: *Corrosion;* Ger: *Korrosion.*
Duke, O., Corrosion of Tankers and Marine Equipment, American Petroleum Institute, *Bull.,* vol. 9, no. 7 (1938); Furer, J. A., "Care and Protection Against Corrosion of Ships, Hulls and Fittings," American Society of Naval Engineers, *Jour.,* vol. 38 (1926); Montgomerie and Lewis, "Corrosion in Hulls of Merchant Vessels," Institution of Engineers and Shipbuilders in Scotland, *Transactions,* vol. 75 (1931–1932); Skinner, H. E., "Notes on Ship Corrosion," Institution of Naval Architects (London), *Transactions,* vol. 81 (1939).

CORRUGATED BULKHEAD. A steel bulkhead constructed of riveted or welded panels of dished or pressed form. In such bulkheads the corrugations are vertical. The purpose of this design is to provide a stronger bulkhead with minimum expenditure of weight and material. It has been successfully used in tanker construction. Also called fluted bulkhead.

Fr: *Cloison Ondulée;* Ger: *Gewellter Schott.*

CORRUGATED PLATE. A plate rolled into parallel furrows or ridges.

Fr: *Tôle Ondulée;* Ger: *Gewellte Platte.*

CORRUGATED VESSEL. A patent type of ship in which two horizontal projections or corrugations in the shell plating are arranged between load waterline and the upper turn of bilge with a view to economy of power in propulsion.

Fr: *Navire à Flancs Ondulés;* Ger: *Schiff mit gewellter Aussenhaut.*

It is claimed that the effect of these corrugations in a moving ship is to retard the formation of waves arising from the vertical motion of water after contact with the immerser surface and to increase the horizontal velocity of flow between the bows and quarters, thus preventing the bow waves from attaining their full amplitude and, as a result, to reduce the eddy, and wave making resistance. There are no side stringers. The carrying capacity is increased by 3½ to 4 per cent.
Hayer and Telfer, Propulsive Performance of the Corrugated Ship, Marine Engineering (New York), vol. 29 (May, 1924).

COSINE-HAVERSINE FORMULA. A trigonometrical formula used in solving the astronomical triangle when the zenith distance is desired in establishing a Sumner line by the Marcq St. Hilaire or intercept method.

COST AND FREIGHT. A price which covers the cost of the goods, delivery f.o.b., and the freight charges to agreed port, but not marine insurance.

Fr: *Coût et Frêt;* Ger: *Kosten und Fracht.*

COST INSURANCE AND FREIGHT. A price which includes in addition to the cost and freight charge, the cost of taking out appropriate marine insurance.

Fr: *Coût Assurance et Frêt;* Ger: *Kosten Versicherung und Fracht.*

Under a C.I.F. contract it is the duty of the buyer to take delivery and pay costs of discharge, lighterage, and landing at port of discharge, in accordance with the bill of lading clauses; paying also any import duties, customs, and wharfage charges.
Goitein, H., *The Law as to C.I.F. Contracts,* London, 1924.

COSTON LIGHT. A slow-burning pyrotechnic light invented by B. F. Coston in 1840 and used for signaling at sea. It consists of a combination of chemicals made to change suddenly and distinctly from one color to another. Three colors are used: white, red and blue, which by suitable arrangements of sequence allow thirteen signals to be made. Also called Coston signal.

Fr: *Feu Coston;* Ger: *Costonsches Kunstfeuer.*

COSTON SIGNAL.
See **Coston Light.**

COT. A ship's bed made of canvas stretched on a wooden frame and swung like a hammock.

Fr: *Cadre;* Ger: *Schwingbett.*

COTIDAL CHART. A chart of the ocean showing cotidal lines or lines which connect the places at which the tidal waves arrive simultaneously.

Fr: *Carte Cotidale;* Ger: *Flutstundenlinie Karte.*

Marmer, H. A., "On Cotidal Maps," *Geographical Review* (New York), January, 1928.

COTIDAL LINES. Lines on a chart joining points at which water takes place simultaneously; lines showing the successive positions of the crest of the tidal wave.

Fr: *Lignes cotidales;* Ger: *Linien gleicher Hochwasserzeiten.*

COTTON CANVAS. Sailcloth manufactured from the raw fibers of cotton. Called also cotton duck, duck, drill.

Fr: *Toile de Coton;* Ger: *Baumwollstoff; Yachttuch; Schiertuch.*

It is not as strong as flax and will not

wear as long, but keeps its shape better and consequently is always used for racing sails. Cotton canvas is divided primarily into American and Egyptian; the former is cheaper than Egyptian, but is inferior to it in quality. A range of 30 or more different weights and qualities are manufactured in widths of 15 to 18 in. and bolts of about 100 yd.—24 in.-width in bolts of 42 yd. Egyptian canvas is made of long staple fibers of light coffee color instead of the pure white characteristic of American canvas. Heavy cotton canvas is still used by Indian trading vessels and other smaller craft of similar origin.

COTTON CLOUDS. Clouds of the fracto-nimbus type which appear beneath a cirrus veil and are frequently the forerunners of a tropical cyclone.

COTTON HOOK (U. S.). A sharp pointed hook with short handle used by longshoremen for stowing bales of cotton.

COTTON ROPE. Light, flexible, inexpensive rope of good appearance made from cotton fibers and used for reef points, lacings, man ropes, braided log lines and deep sea lead lines, dinghy fenders, sheets or warps on yachts and small sailing boats. It is not satisfactory for halyards, as it stretches.

Fr: *Cordage en Coton;* Ger: *Baumwolltau.*

Cotton rope is more flexible than hemp when dry but is apt to get hard and stiff when wet. It is not as strong as Manila. It is usually made in sizes ranging from a 5/16-in. to ¾-in. circumference with a minimum breaking strength of 130 to 500 lb.

COTTON TWINE. Twine used for making nets. Also called netting twine.

Fr: *Fil de Pêche;* Ger: *Netzgarn.*

Cotton twines are of two main kinds, beating cotton (in which the fibers are only lightly twisted together), which is used for drift nets and is laid right-handed, and salmon or seine twine, in which the fibers are twisted up rightly and laid left-handed, and, therefore, "laid coarse." Seine twine is used for trawls, seines, longlines, and snoods.

Twisted cord made of three yarns is used for nets when great strength is desired. Its thickness varies with the kind of net which is to be made.

Trawl twine is usually two-, three-, or four-thread stuff. It is dry, tarred, or copperoleated.

COTTON WICKING. A calking material used for lightly built open boats. It is stranded into strings of 1/16 to ⅛ in. Ger: *Dochtwieke.*

COUNTER. Term applied to that portion of the ship's stern between the knuckle and the waterline. The underside of the stern overhang abaft the rudder. Also known as fantail.

Fr: *Voûte;* Ger: *Gillung.*

COUNTER BRACE. To brace the yards in contrary directions on the different masts. Also called brace by.

Fr: *Contre-Brasser;* Ger: *Gegenbrassen.* See **Brace.**

COUNTER RAIL. The ornamental rails across the stern into which the counter finished (obsolete).

COUNTERSINKER. A shipyard worker who bevels the holes in steel plates or shapes which have been previously drilled or punched, in order that the head of the rivet may be made flush with the plate and that the shank of the rivet when driven may be thickened.

COUNTERSINKING. The operation of cutting the sides of a drilled or punched hole into the shape of the frustrum of a cone. This shape provides a shoulder for the rivet and allows a flush surface to be maintained. The angle of countersink varies from about 60° in the smaller size holes to 37° in the larger ones.

Fr: *Fraisage;* Ger: *Versenkung.*

COUNTER STERN. A form of stern in which the upper works extend abaft the rudderpost, forming a continuation of the lines of the hull. Also called overhanging stern.

Fr: *Arrière à Voûte;* Ger: *Gillungsheck.*

COUNTER TIMBER. The inclined framing in a square-sterned wooden vessel which projects aft from the wing transom and forms the counter.

Fr: *Jambette de Voûte; Quenouillette;* Ger: *Gillungholz.*

COUPON (U. S.). As used in shipbuilding and engineering, a specimen piece of metal used for testing purposes. Coupons of ship steel, boiler-steel, forgings, castings, welds, and so on, must be tested and found to satisfy minimum requirements specified by classification societies rules or government regulations before acceptance. Also called Test bar.

Fr: *Barrette d'Essai;* Ger: *Probestück.*

COUREAU, COURALIN, COUREAULEUR. 1. Small sailing trawler similar to the *filadière* and used around La Rochelle and the Island of Oleron in the Bay of Biscay for fishing in the narrows called Coureaux, from which the name originates. Tonnage about 4.

2. The word "Coureau" was used to denote a type of seagoing sailing barge with a tonnage ranging from 25 to 75, employed in the coasting trade between Rochefort and La Rochelle. Length 97.2 ft. Breadth 20.5 ft. Depth 6.1 ft. Capacity 160 tons.

COURSE. 1. A sail bent to one of the lower yards of a square rigged vessel. The foresail is the forecourse, the mainsail the main course, and the crossjack the mizzen course.

COURSE MADE GOOD. That course which a vessel makes good over the ground, after allowing for the effect of currents, tidal streams, and leeway caused by wind and sea.

Fr: *Route Corrigée;* Ger: *Segelkurs.*

COURSE RECORDING MACHINE. An electrical instrument by which the courses and distances steamed are recorded on a moving strip of paper, which is generally of sufficient length to last for a period of thirty days. Also called course recorder.

Fr: *Traceur de Route;* Ger: *Kursschreiber.*

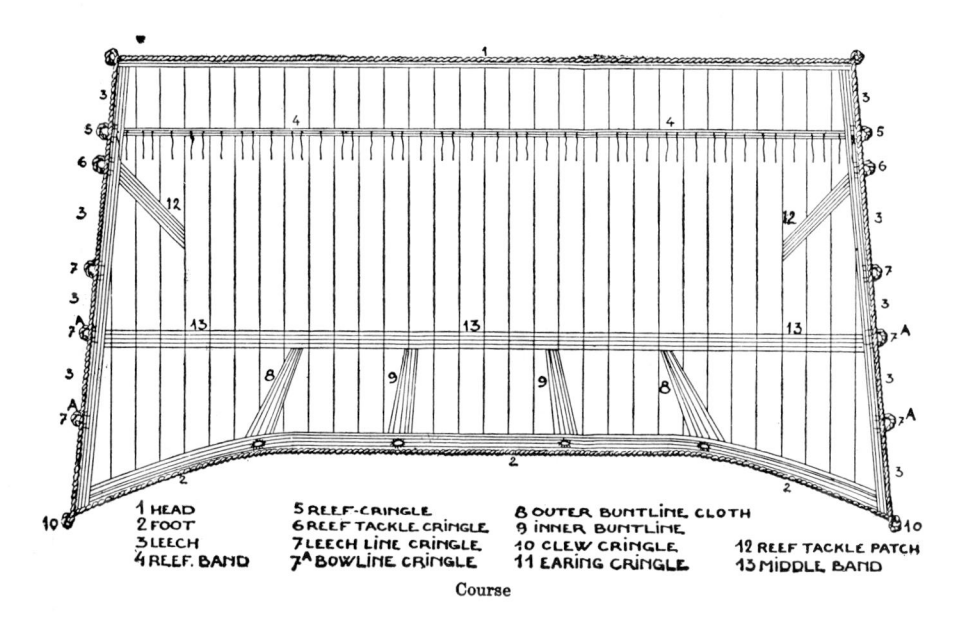

1 HEAD
2 FOOT
3 LEECH
4 REEF BAND
5 REEF-CRINGLE
6 REEF TACKLE CRINGLE
7 LEECH LINE CRINGLE
7A BOWLINE CRINGLE
8 OUTER BUNTLINE CLOTH
9 INNER BUNTLINE
10 CLEW CRINGLE
11 EARING CRINGLE
12 REEF TACKLE PATCH
13 MIDDLE BAND

Course

Fr: *Basse Voile;* Ger: *Untersegel.*

2. The direction in which a ship is steered in making her way from point to point during a voyage. The point of the compass on which a ship sails. Also called track. Courses are measured from the north clockwise in degrees to the fore-and-aft line of the vessel.

Fr: *Route;* Ger: *Kurs.*

See **Compass Course, Magnetic Course, True Course.**

COURSE CORRECTOR. An instrument of the Pelorus type for determining compass deviations.

It consists of:
(a) An iron-faced chart board on which the chart is laid.
(b) A controller operating in conjunction with the master gyrocompass and electrical log controlling the direction in which the plotter moves and the distance which it travels over the chart.
(c) A magnetically operated plotter, having two pairs of electromagnets which are alternately attracted to the iron face of the chart board.

COURSE SIGNAL. A signal from the international code composed of a group of

three numeral pennants denoting degrees from 000 to 359, measured clockwise It is preceded by an appropriate group from the code.
Ger: *Kompass Signal.*

COVE. 1. A recess in a coastline smaller than a creek and usually affording anchorage and shelter to smaller craft.
Fr: *Anse;* Ger: *Bucht; Kleine Bucht; Kove.*
2. A concave moulding; the arch moulding sunk at the lower part of the taffrail (obsolete).
Ger: *Kehlung; Wölbung.*

COVERED ELECTRODE. A metal electrode provided with a flux covering applied externally by painting, dipping, wrapping, or other method. Also called coated electrode. The flux covering vaporizes at the tip when the arc is struck, and the vapor protects the arc and the puddle of molten metal resulting, thus providing a steady arc and a clean, unoxidized weld.
Fr: *Electrode Enrobée;* Ger: *Bekleidete Elektrode; Umhüllte Elektrode.*

COVERING BOARD.
See **Plank Sheer.**

COVERING NOTE. In marine insurance, a note issued by the broker to the insured after the original "slip" has been initialed for the total sum required. It sets out the abbreviated details of the slip in more explicit form and gives the names of the underwriters with whom the insurance has been effected. It has no legal force until the policy has been issued, and is binding in honor only. Also called cover note.
Ger: *Versicherungsauszug.*

COVERING STRAKES. Narrow strips of plating used for covering the butt joints of shell plates in the flush plating system.

COWES KETCH. A sailing barge used for local transportation in Southampton water and the Solent. Also called Solent barge. In hull form it greatly resembles the Humber keel, except that it has fined ends. It is decked for about two-thirds of its length. The rig is that of a ketch without mizzen topsail. There is a short bowsprit nearly horizontal. In the most recent steel-built craft the pointed stern has been changed into a vertical transom stern.

COW HITCH. A knot by which the ends of rigging lanyards are secured. It consists of two half hitches in which the ends come out parallel and in the same direction. Also called lanyard hitch, deadeye hitch.
Fr: *Noeud de Ride; Noeud de Soldat;* Ger: *Taljereepsknoten.*

COWL. The bell or hood-shaped top of a ventilator pipe on a weather deck making an angle of 90° with the pipe or duct, and having an enlarged opening to obtain increased air supply when facing the wind and to increase the velocity of air down the ventilator pipe. The smaller cowls are trimmed by hand, while the larger ones are fitted with turning gear, roller bearings being provided to reduce friction. Also called ventilator cowl.
Fr: *Guérite; Capuchon;* Ger: *Luftermündung; Lufterkopf.*

COWL COVER. A protective canvas cover fitted over a ventilator cowl to prevent spray finding its way down the ventilator when switched back to wind.

COW'S TAIL. The frayed end of a rope.

COXCOMB. A piece of wood bolted to the yardarm. It has notches on the upper side and keeps the turns of the reef earing from slipping inward.

COXCOMBING (COCKSCOMBING). Ornamental covering made with small stuff tied in consecutive half hitches. Used for covering hand-rails, rings or any round objects subject to wear and hard usage. It is made in various styles using from one to six strands.
Ger: *Hahnenkamm.*

COXSWAIN. The person who has charge of a boat and its crew in the absence of officers. In double-banked boats he steers; but in single-banked boats he pulls the stroke oar, the rudder being usually fitted with a yoke and steered by an officer. In naval boats, the coxswain is the rating who steers the boat. Also cockswain.
Fr: *Patron d'Embarcation;* Ger: *Bootführer; Bootsteurer.*

COXSWAIN'S BOX. In a rowboat the space between the backboard and the stern.

CRAB. A small capstan fixed in a frame and made portable so that it may be used for different purposes.
Ger: *Winde.*

CRAB (to). To drift sidewise or to leewards.
Ger: *Dwars Wegtreiben.*
See **Catch a Crab.**

CRABBER'S EYE KNOT. A running eye

or loop knot with extra friction. If made correctly it seldom slips. Also called cross running knot.

CRAB BOAT. General term for fishing craft used in lobstering, crabbing, whelking, etc. Also called crabber.

Ger: *Krabbenfischer.*

CRAB CLAW SAIL. A heart-shaped sail pointing downward with semi-circle cut away from the head. It is made of strips of matting 12 to 20 ft. long and 12 to 15 in. wide. It is used by natives from Papua in their canoes. Each side of the sail is fastened to a spar with a knot at its lower end to prevent slipping of the lashing.

CRAB WINCH. A term applied to a small hand winch.

Fr: *Petit Treuil; Treuil à bras;* Ger: *Kruppelwinde.*

Morton, L. T., "Ship's Cargo Handling Gear," North East Coast Institution of Engineers and Shipbuilders (Newcastle upon Tyne), *Transactions,* vol. 57 (1940–41).

CRACKERHASH. Sailor's dish consisting of pieces of salt pork mixed with biscuits and then baked.

CRADLE. 1. The framework of wood or steel on which a vessel is placed while being hauled up on a marine railway.

Fr: *Ber;* Ger: *Schlitte.*

See **Launching Cradle.**

2. A form of plates and angles on which a furnaced plate is shaped when owing to its contour a press or bending rolls cannot be used. Also called mocking-up mold.

3. A bracket which holds a standing yard out from the mast. Also called truss.

4. See **Boat Chock.**

5. See **Boom Crutch.**

CRADLE PLATE. In a launching cradle, a plate passing from the heads of the fore poppets on one side right under the vessel and up to the poppet heads on the other side. It is riveted on both sides to the shelf and its supporting angles. Packing is introduced between the cradle plate and the hull. Also called swing plate, banjo, saddle strap.

Ger: *Sattelplatte.*

CRAFT. A term in marine parlance applied to every kind of vessel but more especially to small vessels when referred to collectively. For marine insurance purposes a craft is any barge, lighter, river trader or any other boat or vessel employed in carrying, shipping, or discharging the goods insured.

Fr: *Bateau;* Ger: *Fahrzeug.*

See **Bay Craft, Davit Craft, Dumb Craft, Entry Craft, Sailing Craft, Water Craft, Yard Craft.**

CRAFT CLAUSE (G. B.). A marine insurance cargo clause covering goods and merchandise while in transit by craft, raft, or lighter to and from the vessel. Each craft, raft, or lighter is usually deemed as a separate risk and the insured is not to be prejudiced by any agreement exempting lightermen from liability. In the United States called risk of boats clause.

Fr: *Clause de risques d'Allèges;* Ger: *Leichtfahrzeugklausel.*

CRAN. A unit of measure used on the east coast of Scotland for selling herring by the bulk:

1 cran of fresh fish is the equivalent of 45 gal.

1 cran of salted fish is the equivalent of 37½ gal.

CRANAGE. A charge made for hire of shore cranes in loading, unloading or repairing vessels.

Fr: *Frais de Grue;* Ger: *Krangeld, Krangebühren.*

The rates quoted for crane hire are dependent upon a number of factors such as type of crane (steam, hydraulic, electric); location (wet basin or graving dock); lifting capacity; purpose (cargo, stores, equipment); weight lifted (charged per lift or per ton); time (hourly or daily rate, or both); extras (slings, transportation of crane, overtime and so on). When cranes are used for other than heavy lifts or bulk materials, it is usually at the port operator's option and to facilitate his operations. In such instances, cranage is a part of the handling, loading or unloading charge. When a terminal crane is used in a direct transfer it becomes part of the service of loading and unloading or discharging vessels. As this is part of the stevedoring service, it is paid for by the ship and the cranage is usually on the hourly basis.

CRANE LINE. A line to keep a lee backstay from chafing against the yards when braced sharp up.

CRANE RIGGER. A shipworker who handles the heavy pieces such as girders, beams, plates, boilers, castings, forgings, and so on, which are to be transported by cranes in a shipyard. He signals the crane for operation, and directs it to desired location. Also called craneman.

CRANG.

See **Kreng.**

CRANK. Said of a vessel when it lacks sufficient initial stability and consequently is easily inclined by any external force such as the wind or sea. Also called cranky.

Fr: *Instable;* Ger: *Rank.*

See **Loll.**

CRANK CAPSTAN. A type of capstan used on small vessels where available deck space is not sufficient for the men to walk around and in which the bars are replaced by two cranks. It is either single- or double-acting.

Fr: *Cabestan à Manivelles;* Ger: *Gangspill mit Handkurbelantrieb.*

CRANK SHAFT. A shaft turned by cranks which changes reciprocating motion into circular motion, as in steam engines and internal combustion engines.

Fr: *Arbre à manivelles; Arbre Coudé;* Ger: *Kurbelwelle.*

CRANSE. An iron hoop or band, with eyes, fitted to bowsprit end, masthead, or the end of any other spar and to which shrouds, stays, blocks, and so on, are shackled. Also called cranse iron, crance iron.

Fr: *Collier à Pitons;* Ger: *Nockring.*

CRATER. The pool of molten metal at the arc of an electric weld. The terminus of a weld, designated on a plan.

CRAVAT. A shield plate shaped like the frustrum of a cone and attached to the top of the inner smokestack to protect the space between outer and inner smokestack against rain and spray. Also called cap.

CREASING. In net making the process by which the number of meshes of a sloping piece of netting is *increased.* Local synonyms, letting out, rising, making, hitching, half knees. The converse of bating.

Ger: *Zunehmen.*

CREASING STICK. A wooden or metal tool split at one end and used by sailmakers for creasing seams in canvas.

CREEK. A narrow sheltered inlet; narrower and extending farther into land than a cove and tidal throughout its whole length.

Fr: *Crique;* Ger: *Kleine Bucht; Wyk.*

CREEL.

See **Lobster Trap.**

CREST. A narrow rise of more or less irregular longitudinal profile which constitutes the top of an elevation of the sea bottom.

Fr: *Crête;* Ger: *Kamm.*

CREW. The company of seamen or seafaring men who man a ship, vessel, or boat. In a broad sense it includes all the officers and men on board a ship who are on the articles. In a more restricted sense it is applied to the men only, to the exclusion of officers. Also called ship's crew.

Fr: *Equipage;* Ger: *Besatzung; Mannschaft; Schiffsmannschaft; Schiffsbesatzung.*

See **Boat's Crew, Nucleus Crew, Prize Crew, Runner Crew.**

CREW LIST. A list, forming part of the ship's papers, which contains the names and nationality of every member of the crew, the capacity, in which each seaman is to serve, the amount of wages each seaman is to receive. It forms an appendix to the articles of agreement.

Fr: *Rôle d'Equipage;* Ger: *Mannschaftliste.*

CREW'S ACCOMMODATION. Spaces on board ship occupied by the ship's company and deducted as such from the gross tonnage. Also called crew space, crew's quarters.

Fr: *Poste d'Équipage;* Ger: *Besatzungsraum; Logis; Mannschaftraum.*

In every maritime country the minimum cubic space and deck area allowed for each seaman is regulated by law.

Table of minimum crew space capacity for each seaman:

	Cu. ft.	*Sq. ft.*
Great Britain	120.0	15.0
Great Britain (Lascars)	72.0	12.0
U. S. A.	120.0	16.3
France	123.5	16.14
Germany	106 to 123	16.14

Church, J. E., "Crew Accommodations in Merchant Ships," Institute of Marine Engineers (London), *Transactions,* 1943; Steinwerz, H., "Die Unterbringung von Mannschaften auf Deutschen Seeschiffen," Schiffbautechnische Gesellschaft, *Jahrbuch,* vol. 39 (1938); Watts, E. H., "Design of Living Quarters in Tramp Ships," Institution of Naval Architects (London), *Transactions,* vol. 87 (1945).

CREW'S CUSTOMS DECLARATION. A list of all articles acquired abroad by officers and members of the crew, except such articles as are exclusively for use on the voyage. It is appended to the list of sea stores and gives the name of officer or member of the crew, the description of the article and the cost or value. Articles which are not to be landed are placed under seal.

CRIBBING.

See **Blocking.**

CRIBBING RAM. A battering ram used for knocking the collapsible cribbing from under a vessel before launching. It is about 12 ft. long and is handled with five ropes by ten men.

CRIMP.
See **Joggle.**

CRINGLE. Loop grommet or eye formed in the boltrope of a sail at the clew, leech, tack, throat, or head. It consists of a strand of rope formed into a circular eye, and worked around a thimble. With wire boltropes the cringle is usually an iron ring or a spectacle.

Fr: *Patte*; Ger: *Lagel; Legel.*

See **Bowline Cringle, Clew Cringle, Head Cringle, Luff Cringle, Reef Cringle, Tack Cringle.**

CRINGLE FID. A large cone with flat base of 4 to 6 in. in diameter and a length of 30 to 40 in. It is made of hickory wood and used in splicing large hawsers. Also called standing fid or monument.

CRINOLINE. In cable vessels, a framework resembling a crinoline in structure, fitted in each cable tank to prevent the telegraph cable from kinking while it is paid out.

Fr: *Crinoline*; Ger: *Krinoline; Schutzring.*

CRITERION OF SERVICE.
See **Criterion of Service Numeral.**

CRITERION OF SERVICE NUMERAL. A numeral which indicates the degree to which a ship departs from the *primarily cargo* type of vessel and approaches the *primarily passenger type.* It is used to obtain the factor of subdivision in accordance with the rules contained in the 1929 International Conference for Safety of Life at Sea.

The criterion of service numeral is based on the relative volume of passenger and crew spaces, the number of passengers, and the relative volume of machinery space below the margin line.

Fr: *Critérium de Service*; Ger: *Verwendungszwecknummer.*

CRITICAL DOCKING DRAFT. A draft of water at which a ship loses her initial stability when being dry-docked.

CRITICAL SPEED. The number of revolutions of the engines when synchronization occurs between the periods of vibration of the hull and those caused by the inertia of the reciprocating parts of engines.

Fr: *Vitesse Critique*; Ger: *Kritische Geschwindigkeit.*

CROATAN SOUND BOAT. A sailing and rowing boat used in the gill-net shad fishery of Croatan Sound and adjacent waters in North Carolina. It is a carvel-built, open, centerboard craft of the sloop type with long sharp bow, rising floor, fine run, raking V-shaped stern and good sheer. It is rigged with a single mast sprit mainsail and jib, the latter tacking down to the stemhead. Length over-all 23 ft. 6 in. Beam 7 ft. Depth from top of gunwale to keel 2 ft. 6 in.

CROOK. General term for hardwood branches (oak) used for boatbuilding of all thicknesses from 4 in. upward grown to almost every conceivable curve, from a sharply acute angle out of which breast hooks can be cut, to right-angled knees for fastening deck beams to frames, or thwarts to a boat's sides, and to the widely obtuse-angled crooks that are needed for stems, aprons, floors, stern knees, and so on.

Fr: *Courbe*; Ger: *Knieholz; Gabelholz.*

The smallest crooks are those used in open boats for thwart knees. These are usually from 4 to 6 in. in diameter. Large crooks for stems of yachts and fishing boats may be as much as 24 in. in diameter. When ready for use they are sawed to flitches of the thickness that is needed and the template laid on them to mark the exact shape required to be cut out.

CROOKED IRON. A general term for various wood caulker's tools in which the working end of the tool is not in the same plane as the handle. Crooked dumb irons, caulking irons and making irons are used for caulking in close corners, alongside hatch coamings or ventilators and so on.

CROP.
See **Camber.**

CROPPING. A term used in ship repairing; applies to the cutting away of some wasted or damaged structural part of the hull to let in a new piece.

CROSS. To hoist from the deck and put in place on a mast, such as a yard on a square-rigged vessel.

Fr: *Croiser*; Ger: *Kreuzen.*

CROSS BEARINGS. The bearings of two or more objects crossing each other at the position of the observer. Used for plotting a ship's position on a chart when near a coast.

Fr: *Relèvements Croisés*; Ger: *Kreuzpeilung.*

CROSS BITT. Horizontal piece of wood or iron which crosses the bitts on the forward or after side. When made of wood, a hardwood piece is fitted to take the wear. Also called bolster piece, crosspiece.

Fr: *Traversin de Bitte;* Ger: *Betingsbalken.*

CROSS BUNKER. Bunker formed by partitioning off forward of stokehold bulkhead, a portion of the hold right across the ship.

Fr: *Soute Transversale;* Ger: *Querbunker.*

CROSS CHANNEL VESSEL. Term used in European waters to denote a type of fast seagoing vessel with a gross tonnage ranging between 1,900 and 4,200, and a speed of 18 to 24 knots engaged largely if not entirely in the transportation of passengers and mail on short sea trips between railroad terminals in Great Britain and those on the Continent, Ireland, and the Channel Islands. Also called cross channel packet.

Fr: *Paquebot de Manche;* Ger: *Kanalschiff.*

Cross Channel vessels are in most instances owned by railroad companies. Their length and draft are limited by the terminal facilities, narrow harbor entrances and tortuous channels which have to be navigated at all periods of the tide.

Denny, M. E., "Presidential Address," Institute of Marine Engineers (London) *Transactions,* vol. 47, part 8 (September, 1935); Gregson, "Propelling Machinery for Cross Channel Packets," Institution of Mechanical Engineers (London), *Transactions,* vol. 147 (1942); Tripp, G. W., Developments in Cross-Channel Packets, Engineer, London, vol. 160, August, 1935.

CROSS CHOCK. Pieces of timber fayed across the deadwood to make good the deficiency of the lower heels of the futtocks.

Fr: *Billot; Clef;* Ger: *Stosskalben.*

CROSS CURVES OF STABILITY. A series of curves in which the righting lever of transverse stability is plotted for a number of constant angles of inclination on an abscissa of displacement or a curve connecting displacement and value of righting lever of stability for any constant angle of inclination but varying draft.

CROSSCUT SAIL. A sail in which the seams run across the sail at right angles to the leech.

This type of cut is mostly used for mainsails of racing and cruising yachts. The seams run the same way as the flow of air off the sail and theoretically do not cause the friction that the seams of a vertically-cut sail would set up. This cut is also considered preferable for a gaffsail with laced foot where the greatest strain occurs between foot and head. Crosscut sails are not as strong as, nor do they stand the hard usage of, the usual vertical-cut sail. The crosscut is especially advantageous for headsails, where the canvas next to the luff is constantly stretching and likely to pull the sail out of shape.

CROSS GORE. The length measured across a gaffsail from the nock or height of gaff on the mast to the clew.

CROSS-GRAIN. Cross-grain, or grain-cut, timber is that which is cut athwart the grain when the latter does not partake of the shape required.

Fr: *Contre-fil;* Ger: *Gegen die Maserung.*

CROSS HANDLE. A cleat placed on the handle of a sweep or steering oar to facilitate grasping.

Fr: *Menille;* Ger: *Griffklampe.*

CROSS HAWSE.
See **Cross in the Hawse.**

CROSSING SHIP. According to the rules of the road a ship is crossing another whenever the lines of their courses if prolonged intersect. A vessel coming up with another from any direction less than two points abaft the beam is a crossing ship. Also called crossing vessel.

CROSS IN THE HAWSE. A term expressing the condition arising when a ship moored with two anchors swings through 180°, one cable lying across the other. Also called cross hawse.

Fr: *Croix dans les Chaînes;* Ger: *Kreuzzeitige Ketten.*

CROSSJACK. The square sail extending below the lowest yard on the mizzenmast of a full-rigged ship.

Fr: *Voile Barrée;* Ger: *Kreuzsegel; Bagiensegel.*

CROSSJACK YARD. The lower yard on the mizzenmast.

Fr: *Vergue Barrée; Vergue Sèche;* Ger: *Bagien Raa.*

CROSS LEECH. One of the two ropes which run diagonally from the head cringles of a main course to the middle of the foot and to which the midship tack is shackled.

CROSS LOG. One of the heavy transverse timbers making up the floor of a building slip, and upon which the keel blocks and groundways are laid. Also called **Stage plank.**

Fr: *Traversin de cale;* Ger: *Querstück der Ablaufbahn.*

CROSSOVER LINE. In oil tank vessels a section of the cargo system which actually crosses over from one main pipe line to the corresponding one on the other side of the ship. In each pump room there are two crossover lines and on deck two or more others.
Fr: *Traverse;* Drain *Traversier.*

CROSSPIECE. A bar or timber connecting two knightheads or two bitts.
Fr: *Traversin;* Ger: *Betingbalken.*

CROSS PLANKING. A system of bottom planking employed in the construction of small craft with flat or V bottom. The bottom planks are laid at right angles to the fore-and-aft centerline of the hull.

CROSS POINTING. Tapering a rope's end by cutting away the inner yarns and braiding the outer yarns.

CROSS RAFTER. A sloping beam supporting a deck awning. The upper end rests on the ridge spar while the other end is supported by an awning stanchion. Also called awning spar.
Fr: *Arbalétrier;* Ger: *Dachsparrenholz.*

CROSS SEA. A confused irregular sea often running contrary to the wind. It is frequently caused by the shifting wind of a cyclonic storm, or in a strait where wind and tide are in conflicting directions.
Fr: *Mer Contraire;* Ger: *Kreuzsee.*

CROSS SEIZING. A seizing used for binding two ropes crossing each other at right angles. Also for battens or to secure mast hoops. Also called right angle seizing.
Fr: *Amarrage Croisé;* Ger: *Kreuzbindsel.*

CROSS SPALL. A horizontal timber used for temporarily bracing a frame during construction, until the deck beams are in place.
Fr: *Planche d'Ouverture; Lisse d'Ouverture;* Ger: *Spreizlatte.*

CROSS SPRINGS. A collective term for the forward and after-spring ropes by which a vessel is secured to a pier or quay, the two lines crossing each other.

CROSS SWELL. A movement of the ocean similar to a cross sea except that it undulates without breaking violently.
Fr: *Houle Battée;* Ger: *Kreuzende Dünung.*

CROSS TACKLE. A small tackle used for swifting in (i.e., bringing closer together) the shrouds. Also called swifting tackle. It is set horizontally below the top of a mast. Now obsolete.
Fr: *Pantoquière;* Ger: *Schwichttalje.*

CROSS TIMBER. Piece of timber bolted athwartships to the windlass bitts for taking turns with the cable or belaying ropes to.
Fr: *Traversin;* Ger: *Dwarsholz.*

CROSSTREES. Wood or steel spreader with slot at each end over which the mast-head shrouds are led in fore and aft rigged craft.
Fr: *Barres de Flèche;* Ger: *Dwarssaling.*

CROSS WHISTLE (to). To answer another vessel's sound signal with one of a different meaning as for instance when one blast of the whistle is answered by two blasts.

CROTCH ISLAND PINKIE. Local name given around Yarmouth (Maine) to a Hampden boat built with sharp stern. Now obsolete.
See **Hampden Boat.**

CROWD. 1. To make an extra spread (of sail) in order to increase the speed of a ship. Also called drive.
2. To carry a press of sail in order to avoid stranding or some imminent danger.
Fr: *Forcer;* Ger: *Pressen.*

CROWFOOT. 1. A single block through which is rove a piece of wire fitted with clip hooks at each end. A third leg is spliced into the arse of the block. It is used for supporting the middle part of an awning.
2. A combination of small lines rove through an euphroe and secured to the backbone of an awning.
Fr: *Araignée;* Ger: *Hahnepoot.*

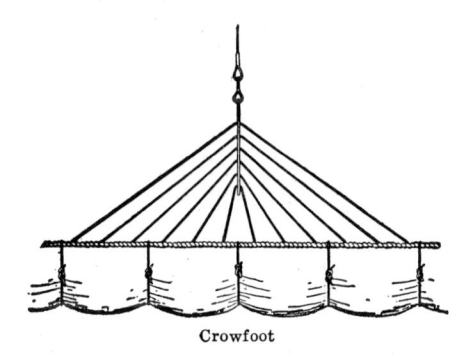

Crowfoot

CROWFOOT HALYARDS. The halyards used for suspending the crowfoot of an awning.
Fr: *Drisse d'Araignée;* Ger: *Spinnkopf.*

CROWN. 1. That part of a stock anchor where the shank and the arms join. Also called head.

2. In stockless anchors it is the part between the arms where they pivot on the shank. A hole is provided through which the shank is passed when the anchor is assembled.

Fr: *Croisée;* Ger: *Ankerkreuz.*

3. The top part of a block, opposite to the breech. Also called throat.

Fr: *Collet;* Ger: *Tauraumende.*

4. See **Crown Knot.**

CROWNING.
See **Becuing.**

CROWN KNOT. A knot by which the strands of a rope's end are back spliced in order to prevent unraveling. Also called crown. It is never used alone but always as part of other knots.

Fr: *Tête d'Alouette;* Ger: *Kreuzknoten.*

CROWN OF BEAM.
See **Camber.**

CROW'S NEST. A lookout station placed on the foremast. It is usually cylindrical in form for convenience and protection of the lookout man. The height of a crow's nest varies from 3 ft. 6 in. to 4 ft. 6 in. It is placed either below the masthead light or above the hounds, depending on the height of the mast.

Fr: *Nid de Pie;* Ger: *Krähennest; Ausguck; Mastkorb.*

CRUCIFORM BOLLARD. Small bollard bolted to the ship's deck or to a boat davit and used for checking the falls when lowering a lifeboat.

Fr: *Croisillon;* Ger: *Kreuzpoller.*

CRUISER.
See **Cruising Yacht.**

CRUISER STERN. A form of stern in which the underwater surface near the stern is broad and nearly flat, ending in a knuckle at load waterline level. Above this knuckle the surface is of approximately conical shape, this conical surface being inclined upward, and inward that is, with tumble home. The horizontal sections of this part are sometimes elliptical and sometimes ogival.

Fr: *Arrière de Croiseur;* Ger: *Kreuzerheck.*

The advantages of the cruiser stern may be summed up as follows: for an over-all length this stern gives the maximum mean immersed length, with resulting decrease in power and consequently machinery weight necessary for a given speed, varying with the size of the ship, being greater in smaller ships, as well as increase in stability and deck room, and better protection to screws in harbor. A conical cruiser stern has greater buoyancy and depth than one of the counter type and is of better form to resist pooping in a following sea. Cruiser sterns of very

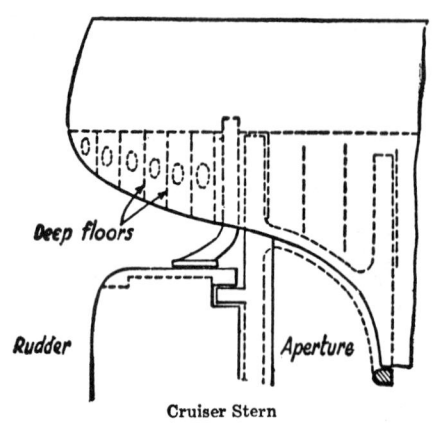

Cruiser Stern

full shape are frequently fitted to single screw vessels with the result that the excessive buoyancy aft compared with the small amount forward creates an unbalanced couple, thereby causing the fore end of the ship to dip deeper into head seas than would be the case if the forward and the after wedges of immersion were equal or nearly so. The propeller efficiency is generally less than in ships with countersterns, where the waterlines are finer and the streamlines closing in have less vertical component in their motion.

Baker, G. S., Design of Stern of Single Screw Ships, Liverpool Engineering Society, *Transactions,* vol. 52, 1931.

CRUISING CLUB RULE. A yacht measurement rule used in North America in long-distance races. As applied to cruising yachts it is intended to develop a fast, able, ocean racer; and also to enable cruising auxiliaries, existing before the rule was developed, to race on a reasonable handicap basis. As well as providing a formula for measuring hulls and sail areas, it makes due allowance for the theoretical difference of speed of various rigs; limits the light sails used, and makes allowances for different types of propellers, and so on.

CRUISING RADIUS. The maximum distance a ship can travel at a given speed without refueling. Also called steaming range.

Fr: *Distance Franchissable; Rayon d'Action;* Ger: *Fahrstreckenaktionsradius.*

CRUISING YACHT. Yacht chiefly designed to cruise for long distances on open waters. Also called cruiser. The essential qualities of a good cruiser are seaworthiness, ease of handling, comfort, roominess for a long voyage and all-round ability to take whatever comes. There is no definition of what constitutes, strictly speaking, a cruising yacht, as distinguished from a racer, and the descriptive terms used are only relative. Speed in a cruising yacht is desirable but only in conjunction with the qualities aforementioned.

From the designing standpoint, a cruising yacht should have a fair amount of underwater body, a firm bilge, and good freeboard.
Fr: *Yacht de Croisière; Cruiser;* Ger: *Kreuzeryacht; Tourenyacht.*

CRUPPER CHAIN.
See Heel Chain.

CRUSHING STRIPS. A device used for lessening the pressure exerted on the forepoppets of a launching cradle during launching operations when the stern of the vessel begins to lift as it becomes buoyant.

It consists of a series of white pine strips arranged across the sliding ways under the poppets in such a manner that they will bear the normal launching load but will crush when the ship pivots and thereby redistribute the load over a larger portion of the forward end of the sliding.

CRUTCH. 1. A stanchion of wood or iron with forked upper end to receive and support a spar, mast, yard, boom or derrick when not in use.
Fr: *Chandelier; Support;* Ger: *Krücke.*
See Boat Crutch, Boom Crutch, Steering Crutch.

2. A compass timber or knee fitted in the stern of the ship with the arms running forward across the timbers of the stern. Also called stern pointer.
Fr: *Guirlande Arrière;* Ger: *Heckband; Hinterpiekband.*

CUBIC.
See Cubic Capacity.

CUBIC CAPACITY. The inside measurement of the ship's cargo compartments taken in cubic feet in order to ascertain what amount of measurement goods can be carried. Also called measurement capacity. It is given in grain and bale measurements.
Fr: *Capacité Volumétrique;* Ger: *Kubisher Inhalt.*

CUBIC MEASUREMENT. A general term which refers to all cargo not carried on a deadweight basis (rate of freight). Cubic measurement is generally calculated at 40 cu. ft. to the ton. It is obtained by reducing all measurements (height, length, breadth) to the same denomination, e.g., feet, inches, meters, etc. The cubic units in a package, box, case and so on being the product of the three dimensions.
Fr: *Cubage;* Ger: *Raumbedarf.*

CUBIC NUMBER. A numeral used by naval architects for preliminary calculations in a new design. It is 1/100 of the product of length, breadth and depth. The usual procedure is to relate weight of structure, cost, or bulk to this number and, when a new project comes forward, to work from the ratios of vessels of similar type. The ratios obtained by its use can be reduced to practically constant figures over a considerable range of dimensions.

CUCKOLD'S NECK, CUCKOLD'S KNOT. A hitch by which a rope is secured to a spar. The two parts of the rope cross each other and are seized together. It is similar to a throat seizing except that cross turns are taken.
Fr: *Barbouquet;* Ger: *Tauschleife.*

CUDDY. A cabin or cook room at forward or afterend in a lighter, barge, or other small craft. A locker in a small open boat. Also a wooden platform situated in the stern of a boat upon which a drift net is coiled.
Fr: *Tille;* Ger: *Plicht.*

CUDDY BOARD. A short decking over the bow or stern of a whaleboat.

CULLER. A name given in the fish trade to a person appointed by fish merchants to sort the fish according to size and quality. On an oyster boat one who separates or picks out small oysters from the large.

CULLING BOARD (U. S.). A wide board laid across a tong boat amidships, on which the culler, armed with a short stick, separates the salable from the undersized oysters, shells, and other debris.

CULMINATION. The greatest and least altitudes of a celestial body when crossing the meridian.
Fr: *Culmination;* Ger: *Kulmination.*

CULTCH. Local term used in England to denote old shells and other substances spread over the oyster grounds by dredgermen to receive the spat which adheres to it in the spawning season. Also culch.
Ger: *Austernbrut.*

CUMPIT. A planked open boat from Mindanao, Philippine Islands, larger than the *vinta* and without outriggers. It is rigged with one mast and a square sail. Each boat has a distinctive mark on its sail indicating the village to which it belongs. *Cumpits* have a high freeboard and are said to be good sea boats. Also called *auang-cumpit*.

CUMULATIVE HOURS. An expression included in coal charters under which the owners are required to give the charterers several days' notice of the actual day on which the vessel will be at the loading port. Also called accumulative hours.

Should the vessel arrive after its expected date of readiness, although not missing its canceling date, charterers are allowed so many extra hours for loading and these hours accumulate according to the number of hours the vessel was late. In practice cumulative hours do not usually exceed 36.

CUMULO-NIMBUS. A heavy mass of cloud rising in the form of mountains, turrets, or anvils, generally surmounted by a sheet or screen of fibrous appearance (*false cirrus*), and having at its base a nimbus-type cloud. Also called thunder cloud, shower cloud.

From the base local showers of rain, snow, or hail usually fall, and frequently a thunderstorm develops.

CUMULUS. Thick clouds, of which the upper surface is dome-shaped, exhibiting rounded protuberances, while the base is horizontal, snowy white at the top, growing darker at the base. Also called wool pack clouds.

Fr: *Cumulus;* Ger: *Cumulus; Haufenwolke.*

See **Cumulo-Nimbus, Fracto-Cumulus.**

The average altitude of the base is 4,000 feet, and the top towers to an average altitude of 10,000 feet. A flat type of cumulus without protuberances is called cumulus humulis or fair weather cumulus. Towering cumulus of cauliflower-like appearance that when observed increases in size is called cumulus congestus, and may develop into cumulo-nimbus.

CUNNER. A log canoe from the lower Chesapeake Bay (U. S.) used for fishing and oyster tonging. Sometimes called kinoo. It is also referred to as Virginia log canoe to differentiate it from the Maryland log canoe. The hull of Virginia craft has a harder bilge and better stability than the Maryland log canoe. They are rigged with one mast, jib-headed mainsail, and one headsail. Length, over-all, 34 ft. 7 in. Breadth 7 ft. 10 in.

The Maryland type has two masts and cat-yawl rig. It carries a larger sail area than the Virginia boats, and hiking boards are used to increase the stability when sailing by the wind. Length 27 ft. 6 in. Breadth 5 ft. 3 in. Depth 2 ft. 9 in.

CUNNINGHAM REEF. A system of roller reef for square topsails in which the sail is reefed by rolling it upon the yard, which is made to revolve.

Fr: *Ris Cunningham;* Ger: *Cunningham Patent Reff.*

In reefing the sail it is the weight of the yard which causes it to revolve. It is applied by rolled-up bands or ropes on the yard, one end being fixed to the yard, or by the action of an endless chain, representing the topsail tie within which the yard is suspended. One end of the chain is fixed, and when the other is slacked or hauled upon, the sail is rolled up or unrolled on the principle of a parbuckle. A valvular cloth, which works up and down with the yard, closes the aperture required in the center of the sail to enable it to pass the fittings on the yard. A spar extends from lift to lift abaft the yard, to prevent chafe against the lee rigging.

CUP. A fitting of cast iron in which the spindle of a capstan works.

CUPRO NICKEL. A non-ferrous alloy consisting of 70 per cent copper and 30 per cent nickel. Used in ship construction for condenser tubes and, in some instances, for pipe lines handling sea water, and sea chests.

CUP SHAKE. Clefts which follow the annual rings in timber. Also called ring shake. It results from the pulling apart of the annual rings, and may be caused by the effect of wind or shrinkage of the heartwood.

CURING. A series of operations by which the preservation of the flesh of fish is insured through salting, drying, pickling or smoking.

Fr: *Marinage;* Ger: *Einpökeln.*

See **Smoke Curing.**

Duthrie, R. J., *The Art of Fish Curing*, Aberdeen, 1911.

CURRAGH. A primitive type of canvas boat found in the bays of the west coast of Ireland. The ribs or framing are made of wooden hoops and the shell of tarred canvas laid in horizontal strips. The larger types vary in length from 16 to 18 ft. with a breadth of 2½ to 3 ft. They are manned by a crew of 4, each one using a pair of oars. Their build is extremely light and each boat can be carried ashore by one man.

Curraghs are used for fishing with hook and line. They should not be confused with the *coracle*. The latter is a river craft and is always propelled by paddle.

Hornell, J., *British Coracles and Irish Curraghs*, London, 1938.

CURRENT. The movement of water in a horizontal direction. Ocean currents can be classified as: (1) periodic currents, due to the effect of the tides; (2) seasonal currents, due to seasonal winds; and (3) permanent flowing currents. Ocean currents are often also divided into drift currents and stream currents; the first are broad, shallow, slow-moving; the latter are narrow, deep and fast-moving and gain their unusual velocity and depth from constriction in a strait.

Marmer, H. A., *The Sea*, New York, 1930.

Fr: *Courant;* Ger: *Strömung.*

CURRENT CHART. A chart on which all tidal current data are graphically depicted. There is usually a set of 12 charts, each giving the direction and velocity of the current for each hour of the tide and presenting a comprehensive view of the tidal current movement in a particular area.

Ger: *Stromkarte.*

CURRENT SAILING. A method of sailing used for correcting the discrepancy between dead reckoning and true position due to the effect of a current of known set and drift. It consists essentially of determining the necessary alteration in the vessel's course to compensate for the effect of the current.

CURTAIN PLATE. A fore-and-aft vertical plate which connects the outboard ends of beams of a deck supported at ship's sides by stanchions or open framework.

Fr: *Bandeau;* Ger: *Fächerplatte.*

CURVE OF BUOYANCY. A curve used in calculations for longitudinal strength of ships and based upon the principle that the upward pressure on a floating body is equal to the weight of the water displaced by that body. It is constructed with the ship's length as a base and with ordinates representing the upward force of buoyancy for each point in the ship's length. Also called curve of centers of buoyancy.

Fr: *Courbe des Centres de Carène;* Ger: *Formschwerpunktkurve.*

See **Bonjean's Curves.**

CURVE OF CENTER OF GRAVITY OF WATER PLANE. A curve indicating the longitudinal position of the center of gravity of the hull's water plane for any and all drafts. In changing trim, a vessel rotates about a transverse axis through the center of gravity of the water plane.

Fr: *Courbe des centres de Gravité de flottaison;* Ger: *Kurve der Schwimmflächen Schwerpunkte.*

CURVE OF FLOTATION. The envelope of all the possible waterlines of a ship when inclined transversely at constant displacement. It is the locus of the projections of the centers of flotation at each waterline.

CURVE OF LOADS. A curve used in calculations for longitudinal strength of ships, in which ordinates are equal to differences between the weights and the buoyancy per foot run of a ship, plotted along the length. It represents the resultant of the vertical forces of weight and buoyancy at each point.

Fr: *Courbe des Charges;* Ger: *Belastungskurve.*

CURVE OF LONGITUDINAL CENTERS OF BUOYANCY. A curve plotted to show the variation in value of the distance of the vessel's center of buoyancy from a given base line (generally half-length) measured in a fore-and-aft direction and corresponding to variations in draft and displacement.

Fr: *Courbe des Centres de Carène en Longueur;* Ger: *Langsschiff Formschwerpunktkurve.*

CURVE OF RESISTANCE. A curve showing graphically the resistance of a ship or model to towing as obtained by experiments in a model basin. The model is run at various speeds and its resistance is shown for each speed. These resistances are plotted as ordinates with the speed as abscissae and the points thus obtained are joined by a curve.

Fr: *Courbe de Résistance;* Ger: *Widerstandkurve.*

CURVE OF RIGHTING ARMS.

See **Curve of Statical Stability.**

CURVE OF SECTIONAL AREAS. A curve whose ordinates are areas of cross sections up to a given waterline corresponding to each point in the length. Read to a suitable scale, these ordinates represent the buoyancy per unit of length.

Fr: *Courbe des Aires de Couples;* Ger: *Spantarealkurve.*

CURVE OF STABILITY.

See **Stability Curve.**

CURVE OF STATICAL STABILITY. A curve showing the righting arm (or lever),

GZ, at all angles of inclination, for a ship at a specified displacement. Also called curve of righting arms. From such a curve the stability characteristics can be derived. By multiplying the righting arm at a given angle of heel by the ship's displacement, the restoring moment can be obtained.

Fr: *Courbe des Couples de Redressement;*
Ger: *Stabilitätsmomentkurve; Kurve der Hebelarme.*

See **Righting Lever, Stability.**

CURVE OF TONS PER INCH IMMERSION. A curve showing the additional displacement corresponding to an increase of one inch deeper immersion at any given waterline.

Ger: *Tons per Zoll Eintauchungkurve.*

CURVE OF TRANSVERSE METACENTERS. A curve showing the height of the transverse metacenter above base line corresponding to any given displacement.

Fr: *Courbe des Métacentres;* Ger: *Kurve der Breiten Metazentren.*

CURVE OF VERTICAL CENTERS OF BUOYANCY. The projection on the plane of inclination of the locus of the center of buoyancy for varying inclinations with constant displacement.

Fr: *Courbe des Centres de Carène en Hauteur;* Ger: *Vertikale Formschwerpunktkurve.*

CURVE OF WATER-PLANE AREAS. A curve indicating the area of water plane corresponding to any draft.

Fr: *Courbe des aires de flottaison;* Ger: *Skala der Wasserlinienfläche; Schwimmflächenskala.*

CURVE OF WEIGHTS. A curve showing the actual weight of the vessel and its contents for each unit of length. The converse of the curve of buoyancy.

Fr: *Courbe des Poids;* Ger: *Gewichtskurve.*

CUSTOMARY AVERAGE. A term used to mean that the franchise to be applied, in the event of claims for particular average, shall be that which is customary to the insured interests. Also called average accustomed.

Ger: *Havarie nach Seegebrauch.*

CUSTOMARY DEDUCTIONS. Trade allowances which are taken into account by an insurer when adjusting a loss. For example, in the event of damage to a vessel, allowances are made for old material replaced by new.

Fr: *Déductions d'usage;* Ger: *Gebräuchlicher Nachlass; Gebräuchlicher Abzug.*

CUSTOMARY DISPATCH. A chartering term which relates to the loading and discharging of vessels and is generally understood to mean due diligence according to lawful, reasonable and well-known custom of the port involved. It has also been held that these words do not relate to the average or usual conditions surrounding such a loading or discharging, but are to be read and understood in relation to the circumstances, ordinary or extraordinary, which exist at the time of the operations. Continuous customary dispatch stipulates for the omission of usual part-day stoppages.

Ger: *Gewöhnliche Beförderung.*

CUSTOM OF LLOYD'S (G. B.). An expression used by average adjusters which relates to some particular point on which the law is doubtful, or not yet defined, but about which, for practical convenience, it is necessary that there should be some uniform rule. By the term is understood the customs of English adjusting whether affecting general or particular average.

CUSTOM OF THE PORT. A usage which by common consent and uniform practice has become the law of the place or of the subject matter to which it relates.

Fr: *Usages du Port;* Ger: *Gewohnheitsrecht; Gebräuche der Hafen.*

The practice or habit in regard to discharge, storage, or loading of goods at a port, for example whether shipowner, dock authority, railway company, or consignee shall pay for labor on board a vessel, for the handling of goods on a dock. The "prevailing custom of the port" though nowhere fully chronicled is a potent factor in deciding contentious cases by law.

CUSTOMS APPRAISER. A customs officer responsible for the examination and appraisal of all imported merchandise and for furnishing to the collector of customs all information necessary for the assessment of duty on such merchandise in accordance with the terms of the tariff act.

CUSTOMS AUTHORITIES. The government officials to whom are entrusted the collection of taxes, duties, or tolls imposed by law on imported or exported merchandise.

Fr: *Autorités Douanières;* Ger: *Zollbehörde.*

CUSTOMS BILLS OF ENTRY. In Great

Britain refers to lists issued daily by the Customs Administration, giving the names of ships arriving at the principal British ports with an abstract of their cargo. Another similar list consists of a daily record of the exports, imports, and movements of shipping at the ports concerned.

CUSTOMS BOND. 1. The security required by the customs authorities for dutiable goods on which duty has not been paid. Such goods are said to be "in bond" or "under bond."

Fr: *Acquit à Caution;* Ger: *Zollbürgschein.*

2. A fine paid by an importer for failure to comply with the customs regulations.

CUSTOMS BROKER. An agent who attends to the entrance and clearance of vessels and goods through the customs house. In most countries the customs broker has a license granted by the customs authorities. Also called customhouse broker.

Fr: *Agent en Douane;* Ger: *Zollmakler; Zolldeklarant.*

CUSTOMS DUTY. Taxes imposed by a government upon the importation or exportation of certain goods or commodities. They are levied as a means of revenue for the country.

Fr: *Douane; Droits de Douane;* Ger: *Zoll.*

CUSTOMS GUARD (U. S.), CUSTOMS OFFICER. A customs officer appointed to guard merchandise in customs custody and to prevent the illegal or irregular landing or delivery of imported goods. In Great Britain called water guard.

Fr: *Douanier;* Ger: *Zollbeamter.*

Customs guards keep watch over the vessel, vehicles, stores, or pier to which assigned. They are authorized to stop and search any person or vehicle leaving a vessel or pier to which they are assigned and to open and examine packages in the possession of such persons. They have authority to arrest any person detected in the act of smuggling.

CUSTOMS PATROL INSPECTOR. A customs officer who patrols the border, seacoast, or harbor for the purpose of detecting and preventing smuggling and other frauds against the revenue laws. He also cooperates with the various federal agencies in enforcing the various federal laws which are particularly applicable to conditions in the assigned territory.

CUSTOMS WARRANT. A document issued by the customs authorizing a warehouse keeper to release certain dutiable goods from a bonded warehouse. Also called bond note.

Fr: *Warrant;* Ger: *Zollauslieferschein.*

CUSTOMS WATERS. The waters on which the customs authorities are or may be enabled or permitted to board, search, examine, or seize a vessel, or otherwise enforce upon it the laws of the country. These waters always extend beyond the limits of territorial waters.

Fr: *Zone douanière maritime;* Ger: *Seezollgebiet.*

CUTAWAY FOREFOOT. 1. A forefoot so shaped that the intersection of stem and keel lines form an obtuse angle.

2. The term is also used to denote a form of forefoot in which the fore end of the keel is raised above the horizontal for a certain distance aft of the stem. Also called raised forefoot.

Fr: *Brion Rogné;* Ger: *Runder Stevenlauf.*

CUTCH. A dry extract from the wood of *Acaia Catechu* of India and Burma or from the mangrove of Borneo used as tanning or barking material for the preservation of nets. Also called *Catechu.*

Fr: *Cachou;* Ger: *Ketchu.*

CUT SPAR. A spar cut from a baulk.

Fr: *Espar Débité;* Ger: *Behauenes Rundholz.*

CUT SPLICE. Two rope ends spliced so as to form a slit. Used in standing rigging for pendants, jib guys, breast backstays.

CUTTER. 1. A one-mast rig with gaff mainsail, stay foresail, jib and topsail, running or reefing bowsprit, and long housing topmast. The mainsail is generally loose footed, the jib and gaff topsail are set flying, the latter sometimes on a yard.

Fr: *Côtre;* Ger: *Kutter; Kutterzeug.*

In former days cutters carried also a large square sail with topsail above, but these are now obsolete. The rig is suitable for boats of any size and for small vessels up to 60–80 tons. Beyond this tonnage the ketch or schooner rig is considered preferable as being lighter and capable of easier handling in a seaway. The mast is usually stepped at a distance of about two-fifths of waterline length abaft the fore perpendicular in craft with straight stem and one-third in those with overhanging stem. The sail area is approximately divided as follows: mainsail 0.5 of total area; foresail 0.2 to 0.25; and jib 0.2 to 0.35 of mainsail area.

The terms "cutter" and "sloop" are often confused in common parlance.

2. A ship's rowing and sailing **boat of 16 to 34 ft.** length, square-sterned, used **as a** general utility boat and pulled with double-banked oars. Usually rigged with standing lug and foresail.

Fr: *Canot de Service;* Ger: *Kutter.*
See **Baldhead Cutter, Bermuda Cutter, Boston Cutter, Tortola Cutter.**

CUTTER-GIG. A ship's boat of intermediate type between the cutter and the gig. It is pulled single-banked with **4 or 6** oars. Its length ranges from 20 to 23 ft.

CUTTER RIG.
See **Cutter.**

CUTTER STAY FASHION. A method of turning in a deadeye in a hemp shroud, and so called because it was originally used for the forestay of cutters. The end part of the stay or shroud is taken around the standing part and stopped back to its own part. This method was occasionally used for lower rigging although it is not so strong as the ordinary way.

CUTTER STROKE. A navy rowing stroke, being a short quick sweep of the oar as used in a double-banked boat. Also called short stroke.

Fr: *Nage Courte;* Ger: *Kutterschlag.*

CUTTING. Part of an open railing that is made portable and can be removed for admittance of a gangway or the top of the accommodation ladder.

Fr: *Coupée.*

CUTTING BLOCK. A hardwood block used by sailmakers as a foundation when cutting a hole in sailcloth with a punch.

CUTTING-DOWN LINE. 1. A curved line forming the upper side of the floor timbers amidships and continuing to the stem and stern over the deadwoods, representing the curve on which the keelson lies.

Fr: *Lisse de Dessus de Quille;* Ger: *Verbindungskurve.*

2. The line that forms the upper part of the knee of the head, above the cheeks.

CUTTING IN.
See **Flensing.**

CUTTING-IN TACKLE (U. S.). A purchase used on whaling vessels for hoisting the blubber when flensing a whale lying alongside. In Great Britain called cant purchase, speck tackle. In American whalers the upper block was made fast to the main lower masthead. In British Greenland vessels the upper block was fastened to a rope stretched between the fore- and mainmast heads called blubber guy.

CUTTING IRON. A wood caulking iron used for removing threads or oakum. It has a tapered section so as to clear itself when being driven along the seam. Also called rave iron, Jerry iron, reefing iron, raising iron.

Fr: *Fer taillant;* Ger: *Schneide Eisen.*

CUTTING MACHINE. A more or less portable device utilizing an oxyacetylene cutting torch mounted on a carriage, which runs on a track, used for cutting steel plates in straight lines or special shapes. The degree of automatic control is adjustable.

CUTTING SPADE. A wide, flat, long-handled, chisel-shaped implement for cutting blubber. Specifically, one used on the cutting stage, as distinguished from one used on deck, the latter being called a deck spade.

CUTTING STAGE. A kind of platform suspended over the side of a whaling vessel upon which the men stood while flensing a whale lying alongside. (Now obsolete.)

The fore-and-aft stage was made of a single plank about 12 in. wide and varied in length on different ships.

The outrigger stage was a three-plank stage boomed out some 10 ft. over the dead whale and provided with a rope lashed to iron stanchions from 3 to 3½ ft. high, forming a railing for the safety of the cutters.

The outer corners were held in place by watch tackles, one hooked to a strop in the main rigging, the other to a stanchion forward of the gangway. The inner ends were supported by lanyards.

CUTTING TORCH. An oxyacetylene torch fitted with a tip which has a central passage through which a controllable flow of oxygen passes. It is used for rapid cutting of steel plates to required shape. Such torches can be used as hand tools, or in a cutting machine.

Fr: *Chalumeau de découpage;* **Ger:** *Schneidbrenner.*

CUTWATER. A term used in modern parlance to denote the forward edge of the stem, at or near the waterline. Also called false stem. In wooden ships it referred to a timber of the knees of the head fayed to the stem above the gripe.

Fr: *Taillemer; Gorgère;* Ger: *Brustholz; Greep.*

CUZZULARA. Double-ended eight-oared open boat from the east coast of Sicily, employed in the hook-and-line fisheries. Also known as *barca i conzu.* Length 33 ft. Breadth 7.4 ft. Depth 2.3 ft.

It is keel-built with tall stemhead (palummedda) rising about 5 ft. above the gunwale and with the forepart of the stem prolonged by a beakhead (sperone) said to be of Greek origin. The whole forward structure is decorated in bright-colored designs.

CYCLOIDAL PROPULSION. A system of marine propulsion in which the propeller consists of a horizontal disc bearing a number of blades rotatable about their longitudinal axes. Because of the high gear tooth pressure and cavitation these propellers, in the present state of mechanical development, are considered unsuitable for speeds greater than 20 knots and only used for intermittent operation service in coastal or harbor craft (ferries, etc.) Maneuverability is greatly superior to the screw propeller drive with rudder.

Fr: *Propulsion cycloidale;* Ger: *Cykloide Antrieb.*

CYCLONE. A term usually referring to a revolving storm in the North Indian Ocean, Bay of Bengal, Arabian Sea, South Indian Ocean.

Fr: *Cyclone;* Ger: *Zyklon.*

See **Cyclonic Wind, Lunar Cyclone, Secondary Cyclone.**

CYCLONIC DEPRESSION. A term which applies generally to extra-tropical revolving storms which are larger in area and not so violent as tropical cyclones.

Ger: *Cyclonartig Depression.*

CYCLONIC WIND. A wind circulation about an area of low atmospheric pressure. In the Northern Hemisphere the circulation is anticlockwise, while in the Southern Hemisphere it is clockwise.

CYLINDRICAL BUOY. A buoy having the form of a cylinder with flat top. A buoy showing a flat top above water. Also called can buoy.

Fr: *Bouée Plate;* Ger: *Stumpfe Tonne.*

CYPRESS. A wood from southern U. S. used extensively for small-boat and yacht construction. Along the coast of the Gulf of Mexico the wood is generally called red cypress; farther north, yellow cypress, and in the extreme northern range, white cypress. It is soft, durable, and bends easily, but has the disadvantage of soaking up water very readily and for this reason must be kept well covered with paint. Used for floor and frame timbers, aprons, deadwood hooks and pointers, and for natural-grown knees. In small-boat construction it is used for planking, painted cabin trunks and canvas-covered decks. Average weight per cu. ft. 41 lbs. when seasoned.

Fr: *Cyprès;* Ger: *Cypresse.*

D

D. Flag of the international code of signals showing 3 horizontal stripes; yellow, blue and yellow. When hoisted singly, means: "Keep clear. Am maneuvering with difficulty."

D.A. VESSEL MUST BE DISCHARGED AFLOAT (chartering).

D.B. and B. DEALS, BOARDS AND BATTENS (timber trade).

D.B. DEALS AND BATTENS (timber trade).

D.C. DEVIATION CLAUSE (chartering).

Dec. DECLINATION.

Dep. DEPARTURE.

Dev. DEVIATION.

D. F. DEAD FREIGHT.

Diff. DIFFERENCE.

D. L. DIFFERENCE OF LATITUDE.

D. L. (or D.). DIFFERENCE OF LONGITUDE.

D. L. O. DISPATCH, LOADING ONLY.

D. P. DIRECT PORT.

D. R. DEAD RECKONING.

D. W. DOCK WARRANT.

D.W. DEADWEIGHT.

d.w.c. DEADWEIGHT CAPACITY.

D. SHACKLE. A shackle in which the screwed pin has an eye on the head. Also called eye screw shackle.
  Fr: *Manille en D.*

DAB.
  See **Dob.**

DABCHICK (G. B.). A very small racing sailboat.

DAFFINS.
  See **Norsals.**

DAGGER. 1. Diagonal timber or steel plate by which launching poppets are held together and braced longitudinally. Also called dagger piece or cross piece.
  2. Any structural member that is diagonal in position.

DAGGER BOARD. A sliding keel formed by a board or plate which moves in a vertical plane, sliding up and down in a narrow trunk and not pivoted as a centerboard. It is used in small fishing and pleasure craft. The dagger board is completely withdrawn when not in use.
  Ger: *Kurzes Schwert.*

DAGGER KNEE. A knee placed obliquely or diagonally. A knee which has its arms brought up aslant or nearly so to the under side of the beam adjoining. Dagger knees were chiefly used in connection with lower deck beams in order to preserve as much stowage as possible in the hold.
  Fr: *Courbe Diagonale; Courbe Oblique;*
  Ger: *Diagonalknie.*

DAGGER PLANK. The plank by which the heads of launching poppets are tied together.

DAGO STROKE. A colloquial expression used to denote a method of rowing in which oarsmen take a long stroke and then pause before taking the next stroke.

DAILY RATE. The daily variation, or change in error, of a chronometer in 24 hours. It is determined by noting the error on several days, and dividing the total change in error by the number of days elapsed between the first and last observations.
  Fr: *Marche Diurne;* Ger: *Täglicher Gang.*

DAILY SUPPLY TANK. A fresh-water tank placed on top of machinery casing, or in some other elevated position, which provides by gravitation the supply of fresh water for cooking and drinking. Also called daily service tank.
  Ger: *Tagestank.*
  See **Gravity Tank.**

DALAMA. Double outrigger, paddling and sailing dugout canoe from Mindanao and Sulu Archipelago (Philippine Islands). It is rigged with a tripod mast and sets a quadrilateral fore-and-aft sail.

DALCA. Planked open boat found along the coast of Chili between Chiloe Archipelago and Cape Horn. Length 14 to 26 ft. Breadth 3½ to 4 ft. Depth 3 to 3½ ft. (Now extinct.)

DALIAN-MAOUNASSI. A Turkish fishing boat built on similar lines to those of the *salapooria* lighter. It is used for handling set nets.

DAMAGE CARGO CLERK (U. S.). A clerk who has charge of all damaged cargo and who consolidates all damaged cargo reports received from receiving clerks, hatch checkers, and coopers.

DAMAGE CERTIFICATE. A document issued by dock authorities when goods are landed from a ship in a damaged condition stating the cause and extent of damage.
  Fr: *Certificat d'Avaries;* Ger: *Schadenzertifikat.*

DAMAGE REPAIRS. Repairs which

result from damage caused by heavy weather, collision, grounding, and, generally speaking, perils of the sea as distinguished from those caused by the normal wear and tear of the vessel, which are usually known as voyage repairs.

Fr: *Réparations d'Avaries;* Ger: *Beschädigungsreparaturen.*

Adam, J. L., "Notes on Damage to Ships," Institute of Engineers and Shipbuilders in Scotland, *Transactions,* vol. 72 (1928–29); King, J. F., *Heavy Weather Damage,* North East Coast Institution of Engineers and Shipbuilders, Newcastle upon Tyne (1934–35).

DAMAGE REPORT. A document issued at the conclusion of a damage survey by one of the parties interested.

Fr: *Rapport d'Avarie;* Ger: *Schadenbericht.*

DAMAGES FOR DETENTION. A chartering term which applies to damages for delay (of the vessel) contrary to the terms of the charter party, even when the lay days are not exceeded or where no demurrage is stated, or where demurrage is stipulated for a limited period. It is to be distinguished from demurrage which is compensation at a stipulated rate for exceeding lay days.

DAMAGE SURVEY. A survey held by representatives of the owners, and underwriters, and, if the vessel is classed, the classification society's surveyor, in order to ascertain the extent of damage sustained and to take the necessary steps to restore the vessel to its former condition.

Fr: *Expertise d'Avarie;* Ger: *Havarie Besichtigung; Schadenbesichtigung.*

DAMLOG. A double outrigger canoe from Visayas (Philippine Islands) similar to the *baroto* and rigged with one mast.

DAMPER. A damper is a device inserted in the uptakes or stack of the boiler to control the flow of flue gases up the stack. Dampers are also installed in air ducts leading to the boiler furnace to control the incoming air. In both cases the eventual effect of the damper is to act as a control in the combustion process.

Fr: *Papillon;* Ger: *Dampfklappe.*

DAN. A small buoy made of wood or cork squares strapped together by iron bands, or inflated sheepskin, supporting a stout pole, which bears a flag by day and a lamp by night. Also called dan buoy.

Fr: *Boque;* Ger: *Breil.*

The dan is used by fishermen to mark the position of deep sea lines or as a center about which a steam trawler is worked. It is usually secured with a messenger rope attached to a weight or anchor resting on the bottom. It is also used for the support of drift nets. One of them is placed at the end of four nets, the space in between being supplied with bowls or pellets.

DANDY. 1. A hybrid type of boat, between a smack and a lugger. It is rigged with a loose-footed gaff mainsail, and a standing lug mizzen sheeted to a boom.

2. A fore-and-aft rig adopted by small coasters or fishing vessels with a main and mizzen or jigger mast. When the mizzen is about half the size of the mainsail it is usually known as a *ketch.* With a smaller mizzen about one-quarter of the area of the mainsail it is called a *yawl.* In yachting parlance, however, the term "ketch" refers to a vessel with the mizzen mast stepped forward of the rudderhead, and "yawl" indicates that the mizzen mast is stepped abaft the rudderhead.

Fr: *Côtre à Tapecul;* Ger: *Anderthalbmaster.*

See **Ketch, Yawl.**

3. According to some writers the term "dandy" is applied to a two-masted rig with triangular mizzen (or jigger) and boomless mainsail.

4. A sail carried at or near the stern in small craft. It may be a lugsail, gaff sail, or triangular sail. Also called mizzen, jigger.

Fr: *Tapecul;* Ger: *Treiber.*

DANDY BRIDLE. In a beam trawl a rope having a piece of chain at its lower end, made fast permanently to that end of the beam which comes aft when taken on board. One end is shackled to the trawl head or to the end of the beam; the other end is secured to the trawl warp just above where the bridles shackle on. It is used as an aid in heaving up and securing the afterend of the beam to the stern of the vessel.

DANDY LINE. A small fishing line used in Scotland for catching herring among shoals. It consists of two wires similar to knitting pins and about 2 ft. long. These wires are crossed and have, attached to each end, a snood about 6 in. long with a small hook. The line is lowered without bait 12 to 14 fathoms below the surface at sunset.

DANDYFUNK. A sailor's dish consisting of sea biscuits pounded up in a canvas bag and mixed with water into a paste to which was added molasses. (Obsolete.)

DANDY RIG. A rig which is almost identical with the yawl rig. The principal difference is in the mizzen, which in the dandy rig is jib-headed and sets without yard or gaff.

DANDY WINCH. 1. A term used by British fishermen to denote a small geared hand winch situated abreast of the mizzenmast and supported between a bitt head and the vessel's rail. Also called dandy wink. It was used on sailing trawlers to heave up the afterend of the trawl beam by means of the dandy bridle.
See **Bridle**.
2. A small steam capstan used by sailing trawlers to bring in the trawl. Also called dandy.

DANFORTH ANCHOR. A stockless anchor with long thin, flat and sharp pointed flukes and in which the stock (also called anti-rolling rod) passes through the crown.
It is claimed that this anchor has about three times the holding power of a stocked anchor of ordinary design and around ten times that of a stockless anchor of the conventional type. On account of its great holding power and light weight it has been found especially valuable as a stern anchor in landing craft for use in retracting them from a beach.

DANGER ANGLE. In coastal navigation, a horizontal angle between two fixed objects on shore lying approximately at the same distance on either side of a danger to be cleared, outside of which it is considered safe for the ship to pass. It may also be the vertical angle subtended by a lighthouse or other prominent object on shore, the height of which is known, at a safe distance from the obstruction to be cleared. The navigator sets this angle on his sextant and knows that as long as the observed angle does not exceed that shown on his sextant, the danger will be safely cleared.
Fr: *Cercle de Distance; Segment Capable;* Ger: *Gefährlicher Winkel.*

DANGER BUOY, MARK BUOY. 1. A general term for any kind of buoy made of a small cask, piece of wood, or a spar, or built of steel plates, used as a signal. It is generally moored with a sinker or clump rather than with an anchor.
2. A buoy marking a danger to navigation, such as a shoal spot.

In the United States, danger buoys are horizontally striped with red and black; in British and French waters, with black and white.
Fr: *Bouée d'Avertissement;* Ger: *Warnungsboje.*
See **Wreck Buoy**.

DANGEROUS CARGO. A general term which includes goods liable to cause damage to the vessel or to endanger human life as well as those which are a source of danger to other cargo.
Fr: *Marchandises Dangereuses;* Ger: *Gefährliche Güter.*

Regulations are issued in different countries as to which goods come under this heading and as to the conditions of their shipment. Passenger and emigrant vessels are in most countries forbidden to carry dangerous goods.
Aeby, J., *Dangerous Goods,* Antwerp, 1938; Barr, H. K., *Stowage and Dangerous Cargo,* New York, 1918; British Board of Trade, *Memorandum Relating to the Carriage of Dangerous Goods and Explosives in Ships,* London, 1931; *Regulations Governing the Transportation of Explosives and Other Dangerous Articles on Board Vessels,* U. S. Bureau of Marine Inspection and Navigation, Washington, 1941.

DANGEROUS QUADRANT. That half of the front of a revolving storm that is on the side of the recurvature of the path. The danger lies in the possibility of the vessel being carried into the most violent area of the storm, or to a point over which the vortex will pass.
Fr: *Secteur Dangereux;* Ger: *Gefährlicher Viertelkreis.*

DANGEROUS SEMICIRCLE. The semicircle of a cyclonic storm track in which the direction of the wind, as it blows around the center, is combined with the speed of translation of the cyclone along its track. In the Northern Hemisphere it is the right-hand side of the storm track.
Fr: *Demi cercle Dangereux;* Ger: *Gefährliches Viertel.*

DANGEROUS WRECK. A wreck submerged in less than 10 fathoms of water.

DANGERS OF NAVIGATION. A term ordinarily construed as equivalent in meaning to dangers or perils of the sea, and restricted in meaning to dangers of an inevitable character.

DANGERS OF ROADS. A phrase which when used in connection with marine transportation refers to dangers incident to roads or roadsteads where vessels ride at anchor. It is an expected peril in bills of lading and charter parties.

DANGERS OF THE SEAS. A phrase used in charter parties and bills of lading which may be interpreted to mean dangers that arise upon the sea, or it may mean only those which arise directly and exclusively from that element of which that is the efficient cause. In either sense it includes only losses arising from extraordinary conditions beyond the control of human skill and prudence. The phrase "Dangers of the Seas" has frequently been construed as equivalent to "Perils of the Sea."
Fr: *Fortune de mer;* Ger: *Seegefahre.*

DANGHI.
See **Dhanghi.**

DANGLES. A series of iron rings joined together by festoons of chain, through which the ground rope of a beam or otter trawl is rove.
Fr: *Trouvillaise.*

DANISH FISHING PRAM. A clinker-built keelboat used in cod fisheries with trawl lines within a radius of about 20 mi. from the coast. Length 16 ft. Beam 5 ft. 8 in. Depth 2 ft. 2 in. Height of mast above gunwale 13 ft. 3 in. Mast step 6 ft. 4 in. from stem. Length of topsail pole 18 ft. (Typical.)
The pram has a long flaring overhanging bow with a narrow V-shaped end; straight raking stem with deep forefoot; round rising floor; flaring sides and deep skeg aft; square stern with straight raking sternpost and square-heeled rudder. It is decked at ends, with washboards along the sides, the open space being oval in shape and about two-thirds the boat's length. It is sloop-rigged with sprit mainsail and jib set flying from stemhead. In light winds a jib-headed topsail is set on a long pole, the sheet reeving through the upper end of the sprit, and a second jib is sometimes set on a reefing bowsprit.

DAN LENO. Term used by British trawlermen to denote the wooden spreaders fastened at the trawl mouth when using the so-called "French gear" or "French trawl," in which the otter boards are carried some distance ahead of the net (15 to 30 fathoms). The Dan Lenos are 4 x 4 in. or **5 x 5** in. sections, 3 to 5 ft. in length.
Fr: *Guindineau.*
Some trawlers have a pair of small otter doors called Dan Leno boards in place of Dan Leno posts, typical dimensions being 4 ft. x 3 ft. x 2 in.

DAN LENO BOARD.
See **Dan Leno.**

DAN LINE. A special kind of rope consisting of right-handed three-strand stuff. It is used by fishermen for fastening a dan buoy to the lines or in steam trawling to a small anchor. Also called dan tow.
Fr: *Badingue;* Ger: *Breiltau.*

DAN TOW.
See **Dan Line.**

DANUBE RUDDER.
See **Salmon Tail.**

DAP. The groove or notch cut in the outside of frame timbers to receive or hold steel strappings.

DAPANG. A double outrigger canoe of the Samal Moros (Philippine Islands) similar to the *vinta.* The hull is a dugout with sides raised by wash strakes sewed on with coir yarns. The ends are bifid (bifurcated) and fitted with the characteristic splashboard.

DASHER BLOCK.
See **Jewel Block.**

DATE LINE. The date line or "date of calendar line" is a modification of the 180° meridian, which by international agreement is drawn so as to include islands of any one group on the same side of the line. Also called international date line. When crossing this line on a westerly course the date must be advanced one day, and conversely when on an easterly course the date is retarded one day.
Fr: *Ligne antiméridienne;* Ger: *Datumgrenze.*

DATURA-ODI. See **Odi.**

DAVIT. A name given to small derricks of various designs used for hoisting boats, anchors, and ladders, for handling stores, and so on. Round davits are made of forged ingot steel bent to shape. Nowadays they are frequently made of steel tubing, or built-up welded shapes.
See **Anchor Davit, Boat Davit, Cat Davit, Collapsible Davit, Fish Davit, Gravity Davit, Hatch Davit, Hose Davit, Mechanical Davit, Quadrant Davit, Radial Davit, Round Bar Davit, Stern Davit.**

DAVIT BEARING.
See **Davit Collar.**

DAVIT BOLLARDS. Small bollards used

for checking boat falls when lowering ship's lifeboats.

According to British Board of Trade instructions for lifesaving appliances, the provision of davit bollards is compulsory when boats exceed 20 ft. in length; double-headed bollards are specified for boats from 20 to 25 ft.; for larger boats bollards of

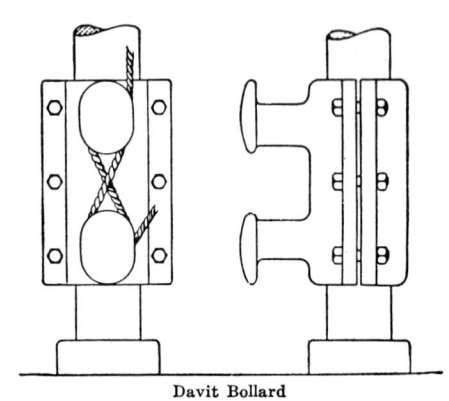

Davit Bollard

cruciform type attached to the deck are required.

DAVIT BUST.
See **Davit Collar.**

DAVIT CLEAT. A cleat secured to a boat or davit for belaying boat falls. Horn cleats are allowed on ship's lifeboat davits only when the length of boat does not exceed 20 ft.

Fr: *Cabillot de Bossoir;* Ger: *Davit Klampe.*

DAVIT COLLAR. A fitting which holds a round bar davit in position and serves as a side bearing. Also called davit keeper, davit ring, davit cranse.

Fr: *Collier de Bossoir;* Ger: *Davit Halslager.*

DAVIT CRAFT. General term used for denoting collectively the service- or lifeboats carried on davits by large vessels.

Fr: *Canots de Bossoir; Drôme;* Ger: *Seitenboote.*

DAVIT CRANSE.
See **Davit Collar.**

DAVIT GUY. A light rope secured to the outer eye on the side of each davit and set taut on the rail by a lanyard in order to keep the davits at right angles to the keel.

Fr: *Retenue de Bossoir; Bras de Bossoir;* Ger: *Davitgeie; Davitbrasse.*

DAVIT HEAD. That part of the top of a davit where the upper block of the boatfalls is attached. In round bar davits it is swelled and spherical with a hole in the center for an eyebolt.

Fr: *Tête de Bossoir;* Ger: *Davitkopf.*

DAVIT KEEPER.
See **Davit Collar.**

DAVIT PEDESTAL. A cast-iron or steel stand bolted to the deck, used for housing and supporting the foot or a round bar davit.

Fr: *Fontaine de Bossoir;* Ger: *Davitlagerbock.*

DAVIT RING.
See **Davit Collar.**

DAVIT SOCKET. A small casting into which the heel of a round bar pivoting davit is stepped.

Fr: *Crapaudine de Bossoir;* Ger: *Davitspur.*

DAVIT SPAN. A line connecting two davit heads so that when one davit is turned around the other follows.

Fr: *Entremise de Bossoir;* Ger: *Davitständer.*

DAVIT SPREADER (U. S.). A steel plate fitting with two eyes at the head of a round bar davit. The davit guy is shackled to one eye and the davit span to the other. In Great Britain called spectacle plate.

Fr: *Piton de Bossoir;* Ger: *Davitaugplatte.*

DAVIT STAND. A casting in the form of a hollow column for housing the heel of a

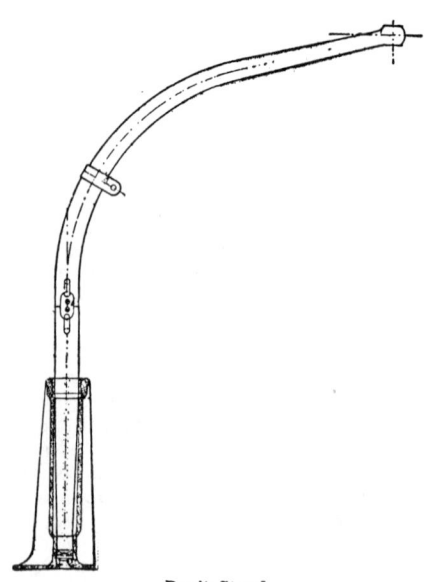

Davit Stand

round bar davit. It combines both davit keeper and davit socket in one.

Fr: *Fontaine de Bossoir;* Ger: *Davitständer.*

DAY AND NIGHT TELESCOPE. A refracting telescope for general use at sea. Its power varies from 12 to 25. Also called ship's telescope.

DAY-BEACON RANGE. Two day-beacons located some distance apart on a specific true bearing. When marking channels they are colored and numbered in the same manner as channel buoys.

DAY GAINED.
See **Day Lost.**

DAY LOST. The day dropped by a vessel traveling west when crossing the 180° meridian. The converse is day gained, when a vessel is traveling east and a day is added to the calendar as the vessel crosses the 180° meridian.

See **Date Line.**

DAYMARK. An unlighted aid to navigation such as a buoy or beacon visible only by daylight. Also **Day shape.**

Fr: *Marque de jour;* Ger: *Tagesmark.*

DAY OF ENTRY. The day or date at which the master of a seagoing vessel has deposited the ship's papers at the customhouse in order to obtain the licenses to land goods.

Fr: *Date de Déclaration;* Ger: *Einklarierungtag.*

DAYS OF GRACE. 1. The period specified in a declaration of blockade during which neutral vessels in the blockaded port are allowed to leave the port.
2. The period at the outbreak of hostilities during which a belligerent ship in an enemy port is allowed to depart freely.

Fr: *Jours de Grâce;* Ger: *Respekttage.*

DAY'S RUN. The distance sailed by a ship during the 24 hours of a nautical day.

Fr: *Chemin Parcouru;* Ger: *Durchgesegelte Strecke.*

DAY'S WORK. The work of computation required in navigating a ship for every 24 hours.

Fr: *Point d'Arrivée;* Ger: *Etmal.*

Bowditch, "American Practical Navigator," H. O. 9, U. S. Hydrographic Office, Washington, 1944.

DAZZLE PAINTING. A method of painting a ship's external surfaces so that all characteristic forms of the ship are broken up by masses of strongly contrasted density.

An observer in another vessel or submarine then has difficulty in identifying the type of vessel and in estimating its course, speed and distance away.

Wilkinson, N., "The Dazzle Painting of Ships," Royal Society of Arts (London), *Jour.,* vol. 68 (March 12, 1920).

DEAD BEAT COMPASS. A magnetic liquid compass so constructed that the card reaches its position with little or no oscillation.

It was evolved by Messrs. Henry Hughes & Son (London) 1920. In it the diameter of the card is much reduced and its weight, which is about 115 grains, is the minimum compatible with practical construction. The

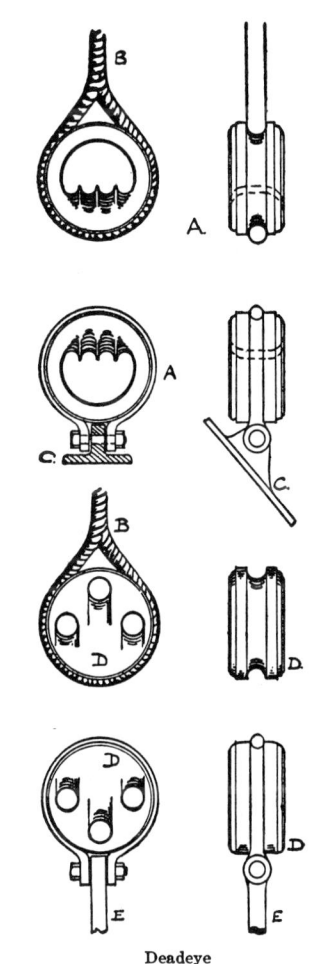

Deadeye

A. Shroud Collar   **D.** Deadeye
B. Shroud   **E.** Chain Plate
C. Shroud Plate

wide space between the sides of the bowl and the edge of the compass card prevents the needle from being affected by eddies which may be induced in the liquid by the motion of the ship. The magnets, which are only 2½ in. long for a 10-in. card, are made of cobalt. A special system of damping filaments, coupled with a method of suspending the compass in the binnacle by means of plungers and shock-absorbing material, makes the whole instrument resistant to the effects of vibration, rolling, pitching, or turning.

Fr: *Compas Amorti.*

DEADEYE. A stout disk of hard wood, strapped with rope or iron, through which holes (usually 3) are pierced for the reception of lanyards. They are used as blocks to connect shrouds and chain plates.

Fr: *Cap de Mouton;* Ger: *Jungfer; Jungfernblock.*

There is a groove in the circumference in which the strap, in the lower deadeye, and the bight of the shroud in the upper deadeye, lies. Lower deadeyes have a metal strap with the ends bolted to the upper part of a shank holding them to the body of the ship.

DEAD FLAT.
See **Square Body.**

DEAD FREIGHT. Claim exacted for nonfulfillment of a charter. Dead freight is charged on cargo space unoccupied or weight short-shipped.

Fr: *Faux Fret;* Ger: *Fehlfracht; Fautfracht.*

DEADHEAD. 1. A rough block of wood used as anchor buoy.

2. In the United States a term which refers to a passenger not paying for or working his passage, as for instance a passenger traveling on a pass, etc.

See **Bollard.**

DEAD HORSE. A ceremony carried out by the crews of British sailing ships when they had been at sea four weeks. By that time they had worked off their advance note and had begun to earn something for the end of the voyage. A framework vaguely resembling a horse and stuffed with shavings and oakum was hoisted to the foreyard arm, set alight, and cut adrift.

DEADLIGHT. 1. A heavy round glass or bull's eye inserted in a door or skylight to give light inside.

Fr: *Verre Mort;* Ger: *Bullauge.*

2. A round plate of brass or steel, working on a hinge, and screwing down upon a sidelight, serving to protect the glass port light in heavy weather. Also called port lid.

Fr: *Contre Hublot;* Ger: *Blende; Laden.*

DEAD LOAD.
See **Useful Load.**

DEADMAN. A single rope used for pulling inboard a swinging derrick after the draft has been lowered over the ship's side.

DEAD MEN.
See **Irish Pennants.**

DEAD NETTING. A piece of netting of rectangular shape without accrues or batings.

DEAD RECKONING. 1. The process by which the position of a vessel at any moment is found by applying to the last well-determined position the run that has been made since, using for this purpose the ship's course and the distance indicated by log.

Fr: *L'estime;* Ger: *Logrechnung; Gissung.*

Positions by dead reckoning are less accurate than those determined by observation of celestial bodies or bearings of terrestrial objects, since their correctness depends upon the accuracy of the estimation of the run. The course made good by the ship may differ from that which is believed being made good, by reason of imperfect steering, improper allowance for compass error, leeway (caused by the wind) and also the effects of unknown currents; the estimated distance over the ground may be in error on account of inaccurate logging and unknown currents. Nevertheless, the dead reckoning is an invaluable aid to the navigator, and affords the only available means (except radio direction finding), of determining the location of a vessel at sea during periods, which may last for several days, when the weather is such as to render astronomical observations impossible.

2. The position of a ship found by dead

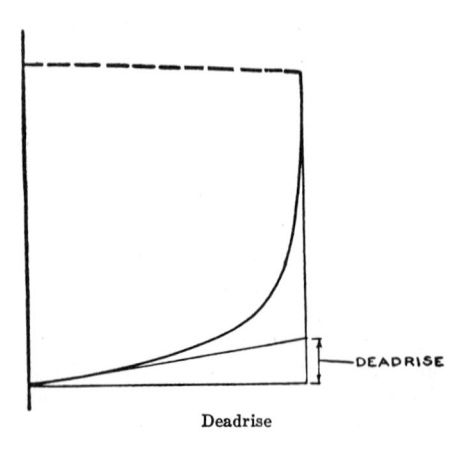

Deadrise

reckoning. Also called dead reckoning position.
Fr: *Point Estimé;* Ger: *Gegisstes Besteck; Gegisstes Schiffsort.*

DEADRISE. A line on the body plan showing the angle that the midship frame makes with the horizontal plane at keel. It is expressed by the number of inches rising above the base line at half breadth. Also called rise of floor, rise of bottom.
Fr: *Relevé de Varangues;* Ger: *Aufkimmung.*

DEADRISE BOAT. See "V" Bottom Boat.

DEAD ROPE. A rope or line for hauling purposes with no block to assist the work.
Fr: *Brin Simple.*

DEAD WATER. That water which is drawn along with the vessel at her waterline, especially aft. Vessels with round buttocks have little or no dead water.
Fr: *Eau Morte; Carène Liquide;* Ger: *Totwasser; Kielwasser.*

DEADWEIGHT. See Deadweight Capacity, Net Capacity, Useful Deadweight.

DEADWEIGHT CAPACITY. The vessel's lifting capacity, or the number of tons of 2,240 lb. that a vessel will lift when loaded in salt water to her summer freeboard marks. Also called deadweight tonnage.
Fr: *Port en Lourd;* Ger: *Tragfähigkeit; Gesamtzuladung; Ladevermögen.*

Deadweignt capacity includes: crew and effects; passengers and luggage; provisions and stores; fresh water in storage tanks, service tanks, and piping; furniture, bedding, napery, cooking utensils and apparatus, crockery, plate, and cutlery; mails and specie; parcels; cargo; coal in bunkers and on fire grates; oil fuel in tanks and piping; salt water ballast; spare gear; bilge water; and ashes. In English-speaking countries, it is expressed in long tons of 2,240 lbs. In countries which have the metric system metric tons of 2,204 lbs. are used.

Hurst, O., "Deadweight of Cargo Ships," *Shipbuilding and Shipping Record* (London), vol. 49, no. 1 (January, 1937).

DEADWEIGHT CARGO. Any cargo with a stowage factor of 40 or less; that is, which measures less than 40 cu. ft. to the ton.
Fr: *Marchandises Lourdes;* Ger: *Schwergut; Gewichtsbelastung.*

DEADWEIGHT CARGO FACTOR. A constant which, if multiplied by the registered tonnage, gives as a result the approximate deadweight cargo which the vessel can carry on her designed draft.

DEADWEIGHT EFFICIENCY. The ratio of deadweight capacity to designed displacement.

DEADWEIGHT RATIO. The ratio of useful load capacity in tons to displacement at load draft. Also called deadweight displacement coefficient.

Average Values of Deadweight Ratios

North Atlantic express, passenger, and mail vessel.......... 0.20 to 0.27
Intermediate vessel .... 0.40 to 0.51
Cargo vessels 2,000 to 16,500 tons displacement .... 0.69 to 0.73
Oil tankers 1,900 to 15,000 tons displacement .... 0.58 to 0.73
Coasting vessels 450 to 2,000 tons displacement .... 0.45 to 0.63
Sailing vessels .... 0.65 to 0.75

DEADWEIGHT SCALE. A scale on which are plotted the deadweight capacities corresponding to the various drafts of water between light and loaded displacements. Also called Displacement Scale.
Fr: *Echelle de Déplacement;* Ger: *Lastenmasstab.*

DEADWOOD. 1. In wooden ships the solid timbering built forward and abaft the square frames and upon which the heels of the cant timbers are stepped. It is bolted to keel and sternpost aft and to keel and stem forward. Also called rising wood.
2. In steel ships with cruiser or transom stern, the structure between the keel line and the sternpost.
Fr: *Massif;* Ger: *Füllhölzer; Aufklotzung.*

DEADWORKS. That part of a vessel's hull which is above water when it is laden. Also called upper-works.
Fr: *Accastillage; Oeuvres Mortes;* Ger: *Oberbau; Oberwerk.*

DEAERATOR. An apparatus, operated at a pressure above atmospheric, for the removal of oxygen and soluble gases from boiler feed water to prevent corrosion.

DEAL. A plank or board of soft wood (pine or fir) from 2 to 4 in. thick, over 7 in. in width, and of various lengths exceeding 6 ft. The standard size is 2½ in. thick, 11 in. broad and 12 ft. long. When under 6 ft. long it is called dead-end.
Ger: *Diele; Tannenbrett.*

1 Petrograd Standard *deal* is 1 piece of 3" x 11" x 6'.
120 of these make one Standard.
1 Swedish Standard *deal* is 1 piece 3" x 11" x 14'.

1 Norwegian Standard *deal* is 1 piece 3" x 9" x 12'.

DEAL GALLEY. A long, clinker-built, 4-oared, pulling and sailing boat with very fine lines, originating from Deal on the southeast coast of England. The stern ended in a small transom. It was rigged with a mast stepped amidships and a tall, narrow, dipping lug tied to the yard by knittles. The tack hooked to the weather gunwale. There were two rows of reef points. Length 27 to 30 ft. Breadth 4.7 to 5 ft. (Average.)

In going about, instead of dipping, one sail was lowered and another sail hoisted on the other side of the mast. It was mostly used for attending to vessels anchored in the Downs; also for transferring pilots from vessels going up the Thames Estuary. The type is now extinct.

DEBACLE. The breaking of the ice in the spring which generally lasts from 2 to 6 weeks. The term is chiefly used in connection with the great rivers of Russia, Siberia, and the North American continent.

Fr: *Debâcle;* Ger: *Eisbruch.*

DECCA RADIO SYSTEM. A British radio system for determining a ship's position at sea. It is based on the *phase* difference between the waves received from two transmitting stations and the receiving station on board ship, in contradistinction to the Loran, in which time difference is used.

DECK. A principal component of the ship's structure, consisting of a planked or plated surface, approximately horizontal, extending between the ship's sides, and resting upon a tier of deck beams. A deck serves as a working surface, or flooring, and also as a divisional structure which subdivides the ship. The uppermost complete deck forms a weathertight, and usually watertight, covering. Decks also form parts of the ship girders; that is, they contribute to the structural strength and rigidity of the hull.

Fr: *Pont;* Ger: *Deck.*

See After Deck, Anchor Deck, Awning Deck, Boat Deck, Bridge Deck, Broken Deck, Bulkhead Deck, Embarkation Deck, Fidley Deck, Flush Deck, Raised Foredeck, Forecastle Deck, Freeboard Deck, Half Deck, Harbor Deck, Hurricane Deck, Laid Deck, Lower Deck, Lowest Passenger Deck, Passenger Deck, Main Deck, Orlop Deck, Platform Deck, Poop Deck, Portable Deck, Promenade Deck, Quarter Deck, Raised Quarter Deck, Saloon Deck, Shade Deck, Shelter Deck, Spar Deck, Splined Deck, Straight Deck, Strength Deck, Sun Deck, Superstructure Deck, Tonnage Deck, Trunk Deck, Turret Deck, Turtle Deck, 'Tween Deck, Upper Deck, Watertight Deck, Weather Deck, Weathertight Deck, Well Deck.

DECK AUXILIARIES. All machinery located on the upper decks used for working the vessel and handling the cargo. This includes capstans, windlass, winches, steering gear. Also called deck machinery.

Fr: *Auxiliaires de Pont;* Ger: *Deckhilfsmaschinen.*

Cambers, "Ship's Deck Auxiliaries," North East Coast Institution of Engineers and Shipbuilders (Newcastle upon Tyne), *Transactions,* vol. 55 (1939); Frohwein, P. H., *Deck Machinery,* Scranton, Penna., 1933; Jahn, G., "Die Gebräuchlichsten Deckshilfsmaschinen in Konstruktion und Praxis," *Schiffbau,* vol. 36 (1935), 4, 5, 6, 7, 9, 11; vol. 37 (1936), 1, 2; Morton, L. T. "Ship's Deck Machinery," Liverpool Engineering Society, *Transactions,* vol. 57 (1936).

DECK BEAM. A thwartship member of a vessel's structure which supports deck plating and which acts as a strut or tie connecting the vessel's sides. The beams of the upper deck may be considered as the horizontal continuation of the side frames, and, in conjunction with the deck, they contribute to the ship girder.

Fr: *Barrot de Pont;* Ger: *Deckbalken.*

DECK BOLT. A flat head bolt with square neck, used principally for securing deck planking to steel deck plating or deck beams. Deck bolts are fitted with a grommet soaked in white lead, under the head, and also under the washer at the point. The head plug is bedded in white lead.

Ger: *Deckbolzen; Deckschraube; Deckholzschraube.*

In modern practice, the deck bolts consist of threaded studs, arc-welded to the deck. This obviates the necessity for holes in the plating, which affect inherent tightness. The deck planks are drilled to suit the studs, laid in place, and bolted down by applying nuts to the threaded ends of the studs.

DECK BUCKET. Bucket made of teakwood and brass hoops, with rope bail (handle), and ship's name painted on one side. Usually stowed in a rack on the navigating bridge. The bail is commonly made of a 3-stranded rope finished off with a

Matthew Walker knot at each end. Leather washers are provided between the bucket ear and the knot.

DECK CADET (U. S.). A youngster employed in the deck department of American subsidized mail steamers in accordance with the United States navigation laws which provide that each vessel of this category must carry one American-born boy under 21 years of age for each 1,000 register tons and for each majority fraction thereof. The boys employed in the engine room are called engineer cadets.

DECK CARGO. All goods carried on the exposed decks of a vessel. Also called deck load. This term does not refer to cargo carried in covered-in deck spaces such as bridges, poops, and so on.

Fr: *Pontée;* Ger: *Deckladung; Decklast; Deckgüter.*

Deck cargoes may be mentioned under three headings:
1. Those that are carried on deck because they are dangerous, such as acids and other similar liquids, or highly inflammable goods such as celluloid scraps and varnishes.
2. Those that are carried on deck because of their size and shape.
3. Those that are carried on deck because the vessel is full underdeck but not down to the loadline. This category covers cargoes such as timber, and so on. The expression "deck cargo" according to the 1906 British Merchant Shipping Act means cargo carried in any uncovered space not included in the cubical contents forming the ship's registered tonnage. When timber cargoes are considered, the expression "deck cargo" refers to deals, battens, or other wooden goods of any description where the height exceeds 3 ft. above the deck.

According to Suez Canal tonnage measurement rules, deck cargo is not included in the measurement. The British measurement rules include deck loads for harbor and other dues.

Great Britain, "Merchant Shipping Advisory Committee Report on the Carriage of Timber Deck Cargoes," London, 1926.

DECK CLEAT. A heavy cleat made of cast steel and primarily used on barges and and other harbor craft for fastening mooring lines. Similar cleats are also installed on wharves and piers. Also called mooring cleat.

Fr: *Taquet de Pont; Taquet d'Amarrage;* Ger: *Deckklampe.*

DECK COLLAR. The bolster which forms the top flange of a hawse pipe. Also called **deck flange**.

Fr: *Collerette de pont;* Ger: *Deckflansch.*

DECK COVERING. See **Decking**.
DECK CRANE. A revolving steam, hydraulic, or electric jib crane fitted on deck as a substitute for ordinary winches.

Fr: *Grue de Bord;* Ger: *Deckkran; Bordkran.*

Wundram, O., "Neuere Bordhebezeuge," *Werft-Reederei-Hafen,* vol. 17, no. 20 (1936).

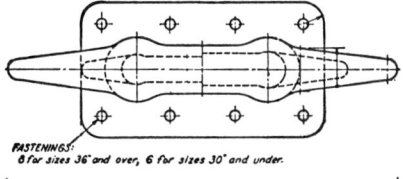

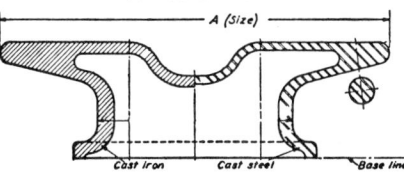

Deck Cleat. (*American Marine Standard*)

DECK CREW. See **Shore Gang**.
DECK DOWEL. See **Plug**.
DECK DRAIN. A through fitting in the deck of a compartment or on a deck space subject to wetting down, connected through drainage piping to the ship's drainage system. Deck drains are usually equipped with strainers, and may be fitted with screw-down valves.

Fr: *Dalot;* Ger: *Speigat.*
See **Scupper**.

DECKED LIFEBOAT. A lifeboat in which the buoyancy is obtained by a watertight subdivision of the hull and *not* by the addition of air tanks. Also called pontoon lifeboat.

Fr: *Canot de Sauvetage Ponté;* Ger: *Gedecktes Rettungsboot.*

The occupants are accommodated above the deck which is flush, or with a well, according to different types. Non-return drain valves are fitted below deck. The shell is constructed of double planking or of metal. The bulwarks are fixed or collapsible.

DECK ENGINEER. An unlicensed petty officer responsible for keeping deck auxiliary machinery such as mooring capstans and cargo winches, windlass, steering engine and other similar mechanical equipment in good operating condition. When no plumber is carried in the ship's complement, he also repairs defects or damage in domestic or sanitary plumbing systems.

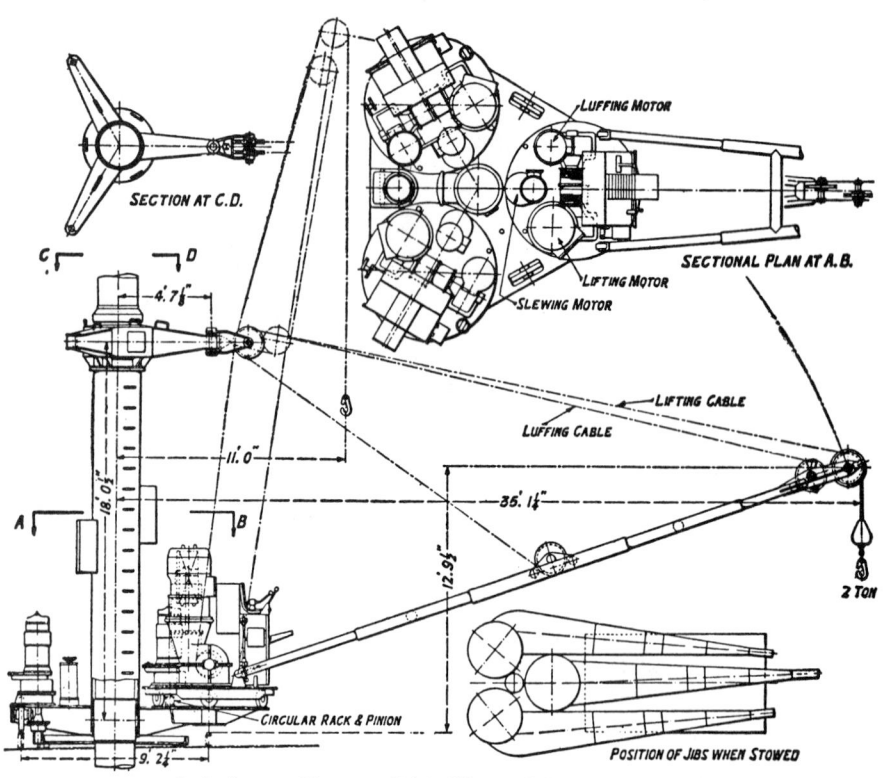

Deck Crane. (*Courtesy Shipbuilding and Shipping Record.*)

DECK ERECTION. An erection on the upper deck extending to the vessel's sides and involving an upward extension of the shell plating. Forecastle, bridge and poop are the usual deck erections of merchant ships.

Fr: *Superstructure;* Ger: *Aufbau.*

DECK GANG. The force of longshoremen stationed on the deck of a vessel when loading or discharging cargo. It includes boom riggers, winchmen, hatch tenders, sidemen, drum-end men and the slingmen on the wharf apron. Also called deck crew.

Ger: *Schauerleute.*

DECK GIRDER. A continuous girder running in a fore-and-aft direction on the underside of deck beams and situated in line with a row of stanchions to distribute their supporting effect to all beams. It also applies to a continuous range of intercostal plates and bars running fore and aft between the beams.

Fr: *Entremise sous Barrots;* Ger: *Deckträger.*

DECK HAND. A seaman from the deck department. In Great Britain the term applies also to one of the crew of a fishing boat.

Ger: *Decksmann.*

DECK HAND-LINER. Fishing craft in which hand lines are worked from the deck of the vessel.

DECK HAND-LINING. A method in which hand-lining is carried on from the deck of a vessel as distinguished from that carried on from an open boat. It is occasionally referred to as dry hand-lining.

DECK HEIGHT. The vertical distance between the molded lines of two adjacent decks. In cargo vessels it usually varies from 7 ft. 6 in. to 9 ft. In passenger accommodation it varies with the standard of comfort desired but seldom falls below 8 ft. 6 in. at sides, 10 ft. to 10 ft. 6 in. being more usual;

while in way of public rooms it is generally 11 to 14 ft. or even more for decorative reasons.

Fr: *Hauteur d'entrepont;* Ger: *Deckshöhe.*

DECK HOOK. 1. In wooden vessels a solid block of wood or natural knee which terminates the framing of a wooden deck at the stem. It is bolted to the stem, apron, and to the clamps against which it rests.

Fr: *Tablette;* Ger: *Deckband; Deckwrange.*

2. In steel shipbuilding a triangular-shaped plate fitted forward at the extreme end of a deck or deck stringer to strengthen the connection between side-plating stem and deck plating.

Fr: *Tablette;* Ger: *Deckband.*

DECK HORSE. An iron bar placed athwartships on deck, on which a thimble, ring, or traveler carrying the lower sheet-block of a fore-and-aft sail may travel from side to side when tacking, and so on. Also called leefange.

Fr: *Vire-Lof;* Ger: *Leitwagen.*

DECKHOUSE. A light superstructure built on an upper or a weather deck, which does not extend over the full breadth of the vessel.

Fr: *Rouf;* Ger: *Deckhaus.*

Three forms of construction are used for deckhouses in merchant vessels: all steel, composite, or all wood. The latter form is usually adopted for small houses such as combined wheel and chart house.

DECKHOUSE FORECASTLE. A deckhouse around or near the foremast which, in sailing ships, was used for the accommodation of the crew.

DECKING. A general term for various compositions and materials used as substitutes for wooden planking to cover steel decks not exposed to weather, excessive moisture or heat. In living quarters decks are usually so covered with the object of providing surfaces easily kept clean and sanitary. All decking material should be non-absorbent, incombustible, provide a good foothold and be bad conductor of heat. Bituminous and magnesia cement deck sheeting are mostly used. Also called deck covering, deck sheathing, deck composition.

Fr: *Revêtement de Pont;* Ger: *Decksbelag.*

Selby, G. W., Magnesite Composition Decking, International Marine Engineering, vol. 23 (April, 1918); Swanson, E., Deck Coverings for Modern Ships, Marine Engineering, vol. 47 (July, 1942); Thayer, H. H., Pocket Book of Ship Materials, pp. 142-171 (New York, 1924); Thompson and Spanner, "Modern Developments of Asphaltic Flooring for Use on Board Ship," Institution of Marine Engineers (London), *Transactions,* vol. 44 (1932).

DECK IRON. A wood calking tool with broad, straight edge. It has a thick blade and very little taper, and is used for widening narrow seams. Also called dumb iron.

Fr: *Guignette.*

DECK LADDER. A wood or metal ladder for outside access, fitted with handrails and stanchions.

Fr: *Echelle de Pont;* Ger: *Decktreppe.*

DECK LIGHT. A heavy prismatic glass inserted in a deck.

Fr: *Verre de Pont;* Ger: *Deckglass.*

DECK LINE. A line drawn through the intersection of the molded line of deck beams and the molded line of frames. It is approximately the intersection of the lower surface of the deck stringer plate with the inner surface of the shell plating.

Fr: *Ligne de Pont;* Ger: *Decklinie.*

DECK LINE AT CENTER. A line in the sheer plan formed by the intersection of the deck at top of beams with the central longitudinal plane.

Fr: *Livet Milieu;* Ger: *Mittschiffsdecklinie.*

DECK LINE AT SIDE. A line showing the fore-and-aft curvature of the upper deck at side in the sheer plan, and the excess of freeboard at bow and stern over that amidships. In the body plan the deck line is represented by the curve passing through the intersection of the deck heights with the side of the ship.

Fr: *Livet en Abord;* Ger: *Seitendecklinie.*

DECK LOAD.
See **Cargo.**

DECK LOG. Also called Captain's Log, scrap log book, rough log book. A full nautical record of a ship's voyage, written up at the end of each watch by the officer of the watch. The principal entries are: Courses steered, distance run on each course, compass variation and deviation allowed on each course, leeway, conditions of sea, weather, sky, barometer readings at regular intervals, temperatures of air and water, position of ship at noon each day by dead reckoning and by observation, apparent set and drift of current, course and distance made good each day from noon to noon, difference of longitude made each day for the correction of ship's time, distance at which principal headlands were passed, sounding of bilges and tanks, keeping of lookouts, sounding of fog signals, and any unusual happening: fire, collision, stranding, and the like.

Fr: *Journal de Mer; Casernet; Carnet de Passerelle;* Ger: *Brückenbuch; Decknotizen; Tagebuchkladde.*

DECK LONGITUDINAL. In a longitudinally framed hull the closely spaced stiffeners which run fore and aft below the decks, and are riveted or welded to the deck plates.

Fr: *Membrure Longitudinale de Pont;* Ger: *Deckslangsspant.*

DECK NAIL. A cut nail of rectangular section tapering to a chisel point with raised head—used in wooden ship construction for deck, outer and ceiling planking. Also called rose nail, square boat spike.

Fr: *Clou à Bordage;* Ger: *Decksnagel.*

See **Spike**.

DECK OFFICER. As distinguished from engineer officer, refers to all officers who assist the master in navigating the vessel when at sea, and supervise the working of cargo when in port.

Fr: *Officier de Pont;* Ger: *Deckoffizier.*

DECK OUTFIT. A collective term which includes towing lines, hawsers, warps, heaving lines, awnings, weather cloths and curtains, canvas covers, fire extinguishers and axes, life buoys and preservers, ship's bells, clocks, navigating outfit, carpenter and boatswain's outfits, fire and deck wash-hose nozzles, spare cordage, deck department paints, medicine chests and medical supplies.

Fr: *Inventaire de Pont;* Ger: *Decksinventar.*

DECK PAINT. A special paint used on steel decks exposed to weather, which dries rapidly, forming a hard water-resisting wear-resisting coating.

Fr: *Peinture de Pont;* Ger: *Deckanstrich.*

DECK PASSENGER. A term relating to a class of passengers for which no accommodation or quarters are provided except for a certain amount of superficial deck space in the 'tween-decks. Also called unberthed passenger.

Fr: *Passager de Pont; Passager sans installation de couchette;* Ger: *Deckspassagier; Decksfahrgast.*

See **Pilgrim**.

DECK PILLAR. A pillar extending between two decks. Also called stanchion.

Fr: *Epontille d'entrepont;* Ger: *Deckstütze.*

DECK PIPE. A tubular cast iron or steel fitting providing for the passage of the anchor cable from the windlass to the chain locker. A portable cover of galvanized metal is provided for closing each deck pipe at deck level when the vessel is at sea. The bottom end of the deck pipes are strengthened by a heavy half round chafing ring. Also called chain pipe, spurling gate, spill pipe, navel pipe.

Fr: *Ecubier de Pont;* Ger: *Deckkluse.*

DECK PLANKING. A collective name for the planks of a deck.

Fr: *Bordé de Pont;* Ger: *Deckbeplankung.*

Deck planking can be laid in several ways:
1. With tapered planks sheered to the curvature of the plan.
2. With planks laid in straight parallel lengths.
3. In parallel planks sheered to the curvature of the sides and abutting against a king plank.

Preferred woods for deck planking are teak and fir.

DECK PLATE. A small brass fitting set in flush with the deck, forming the upper extremity of an air or sounding pipe. The designation of the tank to which the pipe leads is engraved on each deck plate.

Fr: *Nable de Pont;* Ger: *Decks Verschraubung.*

DECK PLATING. The plating forming the covering of a deck, considered collectively.

Fr: *Bordé de Pont;* Ger: *Deckbeplattung.*

DECK POND. Flat portable wood divisions about 18 to 27 in. deep held in place by steel sockets attached to the deck of a trawler. Also called deck pounds or checkers (U. S.).

Fr: *Dalle;* Ger: *Hürde; Hocke; Pfandstall.*

Deck ponds are found in the forward well in front of the winch and utilized for sorting fish after the cod end of the trawl net has been emptied on deck and before placing them below to be packed into boxes for stowage in the hold.

DECK SCOW. A bargelike craft for harbor use, on which the cargo is carried above deck.

Fr: *Chatte;* Ger: *Gedeckter Leichter.*

DECK SEAMANSHIP. That branch of seamanship embracing the practical side from the simplest rudiments of marlinespike seamanship up to navigation as opposed to engineering. It includes small-boat handling, ground tackle, steering, heaving the lead, signaling, and the like.

DECK SHEATHING. See **Decking.**

DECK SPADE. A short-handled cutting spade used on deck of a whaling vessel.

DECK STEWARD. One who looks after the comfort and convenience of passengers on the upper or promenade deck. He attends to the supply and placing of deck chairs and rugs. He serves meals on deck when called upon to do so.

Fr: *Garçon de Pont;* **Deck steward;** Ger: *Decksteward.*

DECK STOPPER. A stopper for securing the anchor cable forward of the windlass. It consists of a pelican hook and turnbuckle inserted into a short length of chain, and secured to an eye plate on the deck. In small craft it is made of a piece of rope with stopper know or an iron toggle with lanyard.

Fr: *Bosse de mouillage; Bosse à bouton;* Ger: *Stopper.*

DECK STOPS. Rudder stops fastened to the deck in way of the tiller or quadrant, designed to limit the sweep to an angle of about 35 degrees.

Fr: *Butoirs de Barre;* Ger: *Ruderausschlag.*

DECK STORES. The spare gear and consumable stores provided for the upkeep and safe working of the ship and her cargo gear. Rope, blocks, paint, canvas are among the principal items. Also called **boatswain's stores.**

Fr: *Approvisionnements de Pont;* Ger: *Deckvorräte.*

These items vary according to trade and type of vessel but the following are generally found on all ships: tackles, spare blocks, cargo gins, snatch blocks, wood fenders, cork fenders, marlinespikes, hand spikes, crowbars, chain hooks, chain slings, screw shackles, ballast shovels, scrapers, chipping hammers, painter's falls and planks, boatswain's chairs, pilot ladders, holystones, deck scrubbers, squeegees, brooms, paint brushes and pots, canvas, sewing palms and needles, rope, twine, spunyarn, marline, seizing wire, heaving lines.

DECK STRAKE. One of the rows of planks or plates that constitute the outside or upper surface of a deck. Midship strakes are designed by letter "M" and numbered from the stern. Side strakes are denoted by letter P for port, and S for starboard strakes, followed by a number.

Fr: *Virure de pont;* Ger: *Deckgang.*

DECK STRINGER. Outer deck plate having its outboard edge attached to the shell plating or to the inside of the framing by the stringer bar. Also called **stringer plate.**

Fr: *Tôle gouttière;* Ger: *Decksstringer.*

DECK STRONGBACK. A thin plank let into the deck beams along the center line of the deck on which the king plank is secured.

DECK TACKLE. A heavy purchase, usually twofold, used in handling ground tackle, mooring ship, and generally for heavy work about the decks.

Fr: *Caliorne;* Ger: *Decktalje.*

DECK TRANSOM. A timber extending across the stern at the after extremity of the deck, on which the ends of the deck planks rest in a square-sterned vessel.

Fr: *Barre de Pont;* Ger: *Deckworp.*

DECK WATCH. A timekeeper of superior construction used for taking sights, time signals, timing a ship over a measured mile and other occasions when it is necessary to have an accurate timekeeper in such location where chronometers cannot be directly observed. Also called **hack watch, pocket watch, stop watch, comparing watch.**

Fr: *Montre d'Habitacle.*

These watches are used as subsidiaries to the chronometers and, as they can be relied on to maintain good time over brief periods, they make it unnecessary to expose or remove the chronometers from their cases. Deck watches are usually provided with a large second hand designed to start or stop as required by the user.

DECK WATCHMAN. A watchman who patrols the decks of a ship, while it is tied to a dock, to prevent illegal trespass and to protect the ship's equipment and cargo from theft and damage by fire.

DECLARATION OF LONDON, 1909. An international declaration on principles of naval warfare signed in London on February 26, 1909. It was meant to serve a twofold purpose: (1) to supply the law on disputed questions to be applied by the judges of the International Prize Court; and (2) to express in clear, precise language the agreement which the powers participating in the conference had reached upon certain principles of maritime warfare.

The Declaration of London never became binding by ratification upon any of the powers represented.

DECLARATION OF PARIS. An international agreement signed in 1856 by accredited representatives of all recognized maritime powers with the exception of the United States, Spain, Mexico, and Venezuela. It contains the following clauses:
1. Privateering is, and remains, abolished.
2. The neutral flag covers enemy goods with the exception of contraband of war.
3. Neutral goods with the exception of contraband of war are not liable to capture under enemy's flag.
4. Blockades, in order to be binding, must be effective; that is to say, maintained by a force really sufficient to prevent access to the coasts by the enemy.

Fr: *Déclaration de Paris;* Ger: *Pariser Erklärung; Pariser Berechtsdeklaration.*

Smith, H. A., "The Declaration of Paris in Modern War," *Law Quarterly Review* (London), vol. 55 (1939), pp. 237–49. U. S. Naval War College, International Law Situations, Washington, 1909.

DECLINATION. The angular distance of a heavenly body from the celestial equator measured on the hour circle passing through this body. It is reckoned north or south of the equinoctial.

Fr: *Déclinaison;* Ger: *Deklination; Abweichung.*

See **Circle of Declination, Magnetic Declination, Parallel of Declination.**

DECLINATION COMPASS. An instrument consisting of a compass combined with a telescope by which the magnetic declination of any place may be measured when its astronomical meridian is known.

Fr: *Compas de Déclinaison;* Ger: *Deklination Busole.*

DECLINATIONAL INEQUALITIES. The variations of tidal heights and intervals that are caused by the varying declinations of the sun and moon.

Ger: *Deklinationsungleichheit.*

DECLIVITY BOARD. A device used by shipwrights and shipfitters in conjunction with a carpenter's level for plumbing vertical members running athwartships and for leveling horizontal members in the fore-and-aft direction of a ship on the building ways. It takes into account the declivity of the ways.

DEDUCTED SPACE. Term used in tonnage rules to denote the enclosed parts of a ship which are subtracted from the gross tonnage to arrive at the net tonnage.

Fr: *Espace Déduit;* Ger: *Ausgeschlossener Raum.*

DEDUCTIBLE SPACES. In tonnage measurement applies to such spaces which form part of the gross tonnage, and are not adaptable to the carrying of cargo. The basic spaces forming such miscellaneous deductions comprise berthing spaces for officers and crew; galleys and bakeries; latrines and washrooms; engineer's office; wireless rooms; hospital spaces; dispensaries; master's quarters; spaces for steering gear; anchor gear; chain lockers; lamp rooms; boatswain's locker; chart room; donkey boiler; sail room. The deduction for propelling power is based on the proportion that the sum of the actual volumes of the engine room and other spaces assigned to propelling machinery bears to the gross tonnage of the vessel. In screw-propelled vessels a total deduction of 32% of the gross tonnage is permitted for propelling power, provided the actual volume of the propelling machinery lies between 13 and 20% of the gross tonnage.

Fr: *Espaces deductibles;* Ger: *Abzüge vom Bruttoraumgehalt.*

DEEP. 1. The distance in fathoms between two successive marks on a lead line. The word is used in announcing soundings when the depth is greater than the mark under water and less than the one above it.

2. The deepest part of a depression in the sea bottom. Oceanographic deeps are secondary and smaller bounded areas within the great ocean basins whose depth exceed 16,000 to 20,000 ft.

Fr: *Fosse;* Ger: *Tiefe.*

DEEP FLOOR. A term applied to any of the floors in the forward and afterends of a vessel. These floors are much deeper than in the main body.

Fr: *Haute Varangue;* Ger: *Hohe Bodenwrange.*

DEEP FOREFOOT. A forefoot formed by the intersection of a vertical stem and horizontal keel meeting at an angle of about 90 degrees.

Fr: *Brion Droit.*

DEEP FRAME. A frame which is about 50 per cent deeper than an ordinary frame.

Fr: *Membrure Renforcée;* Ger: *Hoher Spant.*

DEEP FRAMING. A system of framing in which the athwartship scantlings of each frame are sufficiently increased to dispense with hold beams or plate frames, thereby securing clear holds well adapted for the carriage of self-trimming cargoes shipped in bulk.

Fr: *Construction à Membrures Renforcées;* Ger: *Hohe Spannung.*

DEEPING. A light cotton net about 30 to 35 yd. long and 10 to 13 yd. deep. These nets are bent end to end in a long row called a "fleet" or train of nets, a fleet of large herring drifters being as much as 3½ mi. long.

Fr: *Alèze;* Ger: *Ansatzstück.*

The first net nearest the boat is called "puppy": at the end of the next four nets is a dan or buoy with a pole carrying a small flag. The mesh of the deepings vary in size according to the specie and size of fish to be captured. The buoyancy of the upper part of the net is obtained by means of cork floats fastened about 3 ft. apart. Mackerel nets are usually from 90 to 100 ft. in length with meshing of 9/16 of an inch to 12/16 of an inch. The cable runs under the net.

DEEPS. In a hand lead line the fathoms at 1, 4, 6, 8, 9, 11, 12, 14, 16, 18, 19, which are not marked on the line.

See **Deep.**

DEEP-SEA LEAD. A sounding lead with sinker weighing from 75 to 120 lb. and used for depths of from 60 to 200 fathoms.

Fr: *Grande Sonde;* Ger: *Tieflot.*

DEEP-SEA LEAD LINE. A ⅛- or ½-in. 9- or 18-thread, cable-laid line of white hemp used with a deep-sea lead. It is from 120 to 150 fathoms long and used with a lead weighing from 28 to 30 lb.

Fr: *Ligne de Grande Sonde;* Ger: *Tieflotleine.*

The deep-sea lead line is marked in the same way as a hand lead line up to 20 fathoms, then, with 1 knot at 25 fathoms, 3 knots at 30 fathoms, 1 knot at 35 fathoms, 4 knots at 40 and so on to 95. Then at 100 fathoms a piece of bunting, at 105 one knot, at 110 a piece of leather, at 115 one knot, at 120 two knots, and so on as in the first 100 fathoms.

DEEP-SEA SEINE. A Danish seine used in offshore waters as distinguished from the shore seine used along the coastline. It has a spread of about 25 fathoms and is made of fine cotton twine. It is used in depths of 30 fathoms or less and where the tides are moderate. It has long wings like an ordinary seine and a pocket in the center.

One of the great advantages of the seine over the trawl is that the light net creeps along quietly making much less disturbance than the otter board and chain ground rope. Also, the fish come on board unharmed instead of dead and often mangled, and the small fry can be shoveled back into the sea.

DEEP-SEA THERMOMETER. A thermometer for ascertaining the temperature of the sea at any depth. The instrument is automatically reversed at any given depth and the temperature is recorded by the mercury column broken at the moment of reversal.

DEEP STOWAGE. Stowage of cargo in a hold where there is no 'tween-deck to break the depth. Bulk cargoes and some bagged or barrel goods are stowed in this manner.

DEEP TANK. Portions of a vessel's hold partitioned off and specially constructed to carry water ballast and also arranged to carry dry cargo eventually.

Fr: *Cale à Eau;* Ger: *Hochtank; Tieftank.*

The usual plan is to have deep tanks at either or both ends of the engine and boiler space, extending from side to side of the vessel, but they are occasionally fitted in the wings only. The purpose of deep tanks is to provide additional ballast without unduly lowering the center of gravity in large modern cargo vessels of bluff form, where double bottoms do not afford the necessary amount of ballast. They are bounded at each end by reinforced watertight bulkheads, and at the top by a watertight steel deck or flat. They usually run from the tank top up to or above the lower deck.

DEFERRED REBATE. An instrument used to enforce conference agreements. It allows the shipper periodically a certain percentage return on the amounts paid out to shipping companies, provided he has during the time covered, limited his patronage to conference lines.

Fr: *Rabais Différé; Rabais de Fidélité;* Ger: *Zurückgestellter Rabatt.*

Barber, H., "Deferred Rebate Systems," American Academy of Political and Social Science (Philadelphia), *Annals,* vol. 55 (September, 1914); Deckinger, M., *Die Rechtliche Behandlung des Rabattversprechens,* Kiel (Universität), 1915; Great Britain, *Imperial Shipping Committee. Report on the Deferred Rebate System,* London, 1923.

DEFICIENCY CLAUSE. A clause used in the grain trade by which it is agreed that freight is paid on delivered weight at port of discharge.

Ger: *Deficiency Klausel.*

DEFLECTOR. An instrument used by compass adjusters to measure the directive force acting on the compass needle without reference to celestial or terrestrial objects.

Fr: *Déflecteur de Boussole;* Ger: *Kompassdeflektor.*

The deflector in most common use was invented by Lord Kelvin and consists of a pair of permanent magnets (unlike poles together) working on a hinge at the top, the magnets being in an upright position. The lower ends are closed or separated by means of a tangent screw, thus increasing or decreasing their magnetic power. A pin in the center of the deflector fits into the cavity in the center of the glass cover of the compass, and this enables the deflector to be turned about at will in the same manner as an azimuth mirror. The measure of the force acting on the compass needle is read from the scales on the instrument and tangent screw head.

DEGAUSSING. Equipping a ship with a "degaussing" cable as a protection against magnetic mines. The cable is arranged around the hull and fed with a current of the correct value to neutralize the magnetic effect of the hull.

Fr: *Dégaussage;* Ger: *Entmagnetisierung.*

DE HORSEY RIG. A rig used for ship's boats in the British Navy. It consists of a triangular or jib-headed foresail and gaff mainsail. The latter is loose-footed and has the lower half of its luff laced to the mast and the upper part fitted with hoops. Two brails are used for clewing up against the mast.

DELAWARE STURGEON SKIFF. Local name given by fishermen engaged in the gill-net, sturgeon fishery of the Delaware River and Bay to a large open gilling skiff. Length on keel, 25 ft. Beam 8 ft. Capacity 5 tons. It is larger than the shad skiff, but of similar design.

DELIVERY CLAUSE. An expression used in charter parties. Sometimes called disposal clause. This clause, also known as commencement of hire, stipulates the time, date, and place at which the vessel is being placed at the charterer's disposal.

Fr: *Clause de Livraison;* Ger: *Delivery Klausel; Ablieferungsklausel.*

DELIVERY CLERK (U. S.). An assistant to the wharf superintendent entrusted with the receipt and disposition of cargo discharged from vessels. It is the duty of this clerk to make up a delivery book and to obtain signatures for all cargo delivered. He is assisted by dock checkers in tallying cargo deliveries.

DELIVERY ORDER. 1. An order issued by the owner of goods, requesting the superintendent of a dock, warehouse or wharf, to deliver goods to a person or persons specified or to bearer. Also called landing order.

Fr: *Bon de Livraison;* Ger: *Lieferschein; Lieferungsauftrag.*

2. A written order issued by the ship's agent whereby the captain is authorized to deliver goods to the person designated in the order.

Fr: *Ordre de Livraison;* Ger: *Ablieferungsschein; Teilkonnossement.*

DELTA. The tract of land at the mouth of a river formed by deposit and silt.

Fr: *Delta;* Ger: *Delta.*

DEMERSAL FISH. Fishes that live at the bottom of the sea. Cod, ling, haddock, plaice, halibut, sole, turbot, brill are among the better known demersal fishes.

DEMISE CHARTER. A charter in which the bare ship is chartered without crew; the charterer, for a stipulated sum, taking over the vessel with a minimum of restrictions. Also called bare-pole charter, bare-hull charter, bare-boat charter.

Fr: *Affretement Coque-Nue;* Ger: *Mietvertrag.*

A demise charter is an agreement by which the charterer becomes for the time being practically the owner of the hired vessel. He appoints the captain, engages the crew and pays their wages. He provisions and equips the ship and becomes liable for all running charges. He pays all disbursements and keeps hull and machinery in efficient repair. Usually, the actual owner makes no restrictions as to the trading limits or cargoes to be carried. The principal obligations of a demise charterer are to pay the owners an agreed sum in the event that the vessel is lost and to redeliver her in the same condition as when chartered, ordinary wear and tear excluded.

DEMURRAGE. 1. Detention of a vessel by the freighter, charterer or receivers of the cargo in loading or unloading beyond the "lay-days" allowed in the charter party. A vessel so detained is said to be on demurrage.

Fr: *Surestarie;* Ger: *Überliegezeit.*

2. A fixed sum, per day or per hour, agreed to be paid for the detention of a vessel under charter at the expiration of lay-days. It is an extended freight to the ship in compensation for earnings it is compelled to lose. In calculating demurrage the usual practice is to count all days after the

expiration of lay-days, including Sundays and holidays.
Fr: *Surestarie;* Ger: *Liegegeld.*
Mittag, R., Das Liegegeld, Hamburg, 1935; Stephens, Law Relating to Demurrage, London.

DEMURRAGE CLAUSE. A charter party clause which relates to the number of days the vessel is to remain on demurrage after lay-days have expired.

DEMURRAGE DAYS. The days a vessel under charter is detained beyond the lay-days. A fixed number of demurrage days is usually provided for in the charter party. If the vessel is detained beyond this number, damages for detention will be recoverable by the owners.
Fr: *Jours de Surestaries;* Ger: *Uberliegetage.*

DEMURRAGE LIEN. The lien which the shipowner has on money due for the detention of the vessel by the charterers in loading or unloading beyond the time provided for in the charter party.

The English doctrine is that no such lien exists unless so stipulated in the charter party and included in the bill of lading. In American courts it is held that such lien exists and is enforceable in admiralty regardless of the existence or nonexistence of an express stipulation for a lien or even for demurrage.

A contract giving the vessel a lien for demurrage is valid at either the port of loading or the port of discharge.

DENGUE. A small open boat employed in the sardine fisheries on the coast of Cantabria (Spain).

DENNY-BROWN STABILIZER. An installation to reduce the rolling of ships at sea. It consists of two fins, one on each side of the ship projecting from the hull at about the turn of the bilge as near midships as possible. The fins are so controlled that as the ship rolls the forward velocity of the ship causes the water to exert an upward pressure on the fin on the descending side of the ship, and a downward force on the ascending side, thus providing a definite righting couple. The tilt of the fins is decided by the action of the ship operating on electrically driven gyroscopes, which through electric and hydraulic relays, operate the maneuvering gear of the fins. The fins are withdrawn into recesses in the hull when not in use. Hydraulic machinery is employed for tilting the fins and retracting them inside the hull. Wallace, W., "Experiences in the Stabilisation of Ships," Transactions, Institution of Engineers and Shipbuilders, Scotland, vol. 98, 1955.

DENSE FOG. A term applied in international meteorological practice to a fog where the limit of visibility ranges between 25 and 50 yards.
Fr: *Brouillard intense;* Ger: *Undurchsichtiger Nebel.*

DEPARTURE. 1. The distance a vessel makes good east or west. It is measured along a parallel of latitude and is always expressed in miles.
Fr: *Chemin Est-Ouest;* Ger: *Abweitung.*

2. Also point of departure. The point or position from which the reckoning of a voyage is commenced. It is usually established by bearing and distance from a lighthouse or prominent landmark.
Fr: *Point de Partance;* Ger: *Abfahrtsort; Abfahrtspunkt.*

3. The point or time at which a vessel arrives outside the administrative limits of the port.

DEPOSITING DOCK. A combination consisting of a single-sided floating dock attached by hinged booms to a floating outrigger and a number of grids built up of piles of masonry along the foreshore. The pontoon or platform of the dock instead of being a continuous caisson is divided into separate fingers each attached to the wall of the deck. When a vessel has been raised on the dock, the whole floating structure with the vessel on it is warped in between the stationary fingers of the grid. The dock is then lowered, the vessel remaining deposited high and dry on the grid. The dock is then withdrawn, ready to pick up and deposit other vessels if required.
Ger: *Absetzdock; Fingerdock.*

DEPOT TUG (G. B.). Small harbor tug used for barge handling, breaking craft out of barge roads, mooring up vessels, and so on.

DEPTH. The vertical distance measured at the middle of the vessel's length from top of keel or top of ceiling to top of upper deck at sides, or amidships. The designed depth depends on the draft and freeboard required.
Fr: *Creux;* Ger: *Tiefe.*
See **Controlling Depth, Freeboard Depth, Molded Depth, Registered Depth.**

DEPTH GAUGE. 1. Also called hydrobarometer. A general name for any form of instrument used for the measurement of depths indicated by sounding tubes in sea soundings.

2. An instrument for determining the depth of water by means of the pressure the latter exerts.

DEPTH OF HOLD. The vertical distance between the top of floor at center or double bottom at side and the top of main deck beam at the vessel's center line amidships.

Fr: *Creux de cale;* Ger: *Raumtiefe.*

DEPTH ON SILL. The depth of water over the entrance sill of a dock or dry dock.

Fr: *Profondeur sur radier;* Ger: *Drempel Tiefe.*

DEPTH RECORDER.
See **Echo Sounder.**

DERATIZATION. An operation performed with a view to destruction of rats on board ship, carried out with the ship loaded or after discharging the cargo. Various poisons are used: phosphorus, arsenic and strychnine, as well as such gases as sulphur dioxide.

Fr: *Dératisation;* Ger: *Entrattung.*

See **Ratproofing.**

All the poisons mentioned kill rats but the dead bodies are liable to decompose and result in stench. Steam has also been used with success in lieu of fumigation by one the above mentioned gases. Rats are considered the worst of all vermin on board ship as they damage cargo and are plague carriers.

Clark, P. W., "The Ratproofing of new ships," Society of Naval Architects and Marine Engineers (New York), *Transactions,* vol. 47 (1939); Grubbs and Holsendorf, *The Ratproofing of Vessels,* U. S. Public Health Service, Report 93, Washington, 1931; Randier, P. G. F., *Dératisation et désinsectisation des navires par la chloropicrine,* Rennes, 1926; *Ship Rats and Plague,* U. S. Public Health Service, Report 182, Washington, 1914.

DERATIZATION CERTIFICATE. The International Sanitary Convention of Paris, 1926, requires that all vessels excepting certain coasting vessels shall be furnished with a deratization certificate or a deratization exemption certificate, which will remain valid for six months. Also called fumigation certificate.

Fr: *Certificat de Dératisation;* Ger: *Entrattungsschein.*

DERELICT. 1. Goods or any other commodity abandoned or relinquished by its owner, specifically a vessel abandoned at sea. A ship is derelict either by consent, compulsion, or stress of weather.

2. Personal property abandoned or thrown away at sea by the owner in such a manner as to indicate that he intends to make no further claim thereto.

Fr: *Épave;* Ger: *Wrackgut.*

See **Quasi Derelict.**

It is generally admitted that to constitute derelict in maritime law, in respect of salvage, it is necessary that the thing is found deserted or abandoned upon the seas whether it arose from accident or necessity or voluntary dereliction. The abandonment by the crew must be final without hope of recovery or intention to return.

Services in rescuing a derelict are salvage services.

DERMAJU. A plank-built fishing craft with straight stem originating from Indramaju in Western Java.

DERRICK. A form of crane consisting of a boom and mast with a whip and tackle connected to a deck winch, for raising and lowering weights, the boom capable of being topped up by means of lifts. The heel of the boom rests either on deck or on the foot of the mast. The word "derrick" can be applied to any swinging boom plumbing a hatch, supported by a topping lift and controlled sideways by guys or vangs. Such a boom is used for loading and discharging cargo and is called a cargo boom.

Fr: *Mât de Charge;* Ger: *Ladebaum.*

See **Burton System, Heavy Derrick, Hydraulic Derrick, Lattice Derrick, Slewing Derrick, Tubular Derrick, Weldless Derrick.**

Cargo booms are made of wooden spars, lattice girder, or steel tubing. For lifts of 3 to 5 tons, tubular steel booms have superseded pitch pine derricks formerly used. The number of cargo booms depends on the size of hatches and methods adopted for handling the cargo. When separate cargo booms are employed for hoisting and slewing, four are generally rigged on each side of the mast. The outreach of cargo booms, when swung out over the side at right angles to the vessel's center line, varies from 8 ft. in small coasters to 12 to 18 ft. in average-sized vessels. The cargo hook in working position covers about two-thirds the length of hatchway with a derrick inclination of 35° to 45° from the horizontal.

American Marine Standards Committee, Standard 49, *Cargo Boom Fittings,* Washington, 1928; Standard 50, *Cargo Boom Fittings.* Washington, 1930.

DERRICK BAND. Steel band fitted at the head of a cargo boom or derrick with lugs for topping-lift blocks, port and starboard guy pendants, and cargo blocks.

Fr: *Cercle de Mât de Charge;* Ger: *Ladebaum Löschringband; Nockband.*

DERRICK CAP PIECE. A steel casting fitted over the head of a tubular cargo boom and to which the cargo block, topping lift, and guy pendants are shackled. It replaces the derrick band. Also called **Derrick head fitting.**

Fr: *Ferrure de tête;* Ger: *Nockbeschlag.* See cut under "Derrick."

DERRICK GUY. Guy fastened at the head of a cargo derrick for trimming or steadying. It generally consists of a wire pendant with rope tackle. Also called boom guy.

Fr: *Retenue de Mât de Charge;* Ger: *Ladebaumgeie.*

DERRICK HEAD. The upper extremity of a derrick where the topping lift, cargo block and guy pendants are secured.

Fr: *Tête de corne; Tête de mât de charge;* Ger: *Baumnock.*

DERRICK HEAD BLOCK. Block attached to a derrick head through which the cargo runner reeves.

Fr: *Poulie de charge;* Ger: *Ladeblock.*

DERRICK HEEL BLOCK. A single sheaved steel block attached at the foot of a cargo boom for leading the cargo runner to the winch. Also called **lead block.**

Fr: *Poulie de pied de corne;* Ger: *Leitblock.*

DERRICK LIGHTER. A harbor lighter fitted with hoisting apparatus and able to handle its own cargo without the assistance of ship's winches and tackle. A self propelled harbor lighter; also called Steam lighter.

DERRICK POST (U. S.).
See **Samson Post (G. B.).**

DERRICK STOOL. A small platform built at a height of about 8½ ft. above deck around a mast where more than two derricks are required on each side of the mast or where it is desired to set winches parallel to the center line of the ship. It is bracketed to the mast or supported by stanchions or sometimes plated over and used as a deck locker. Also called derrick table, mast table, boom table.

Fr: *Tablette de Mât de Charge; Support de Mât de Charge;* Ger: *Ladebaumkonsole; Ladebaumstuhl.*

DESERTION. Absence without leave of a member of the crew or failing to join a ship in due time after signing an agreement to

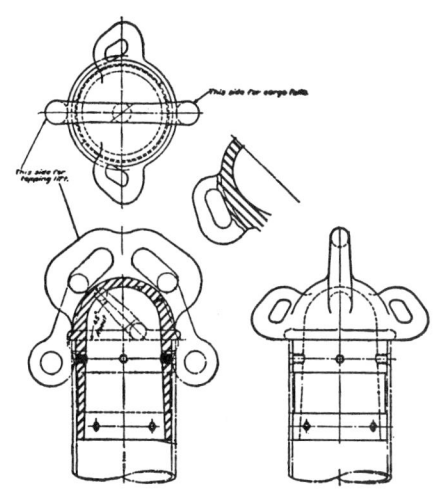

Derrick Head fittings

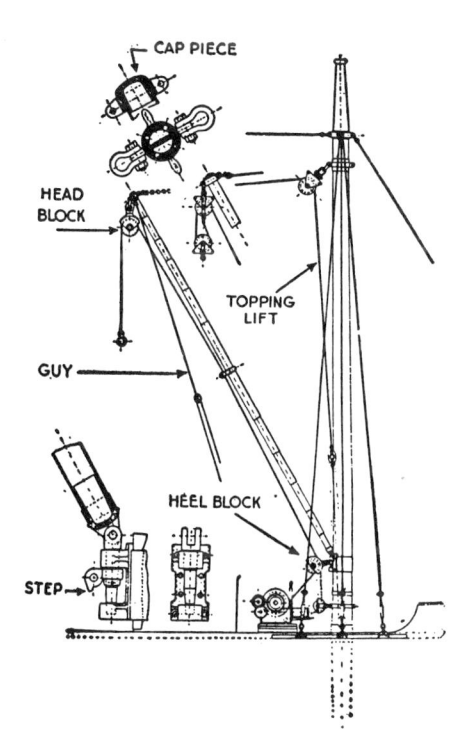

Derrick (Cargo Boom)

proceed to sea.

Fr: *Désertion;* Ger: *Desertion.*

DESIGNED DISPLACEMENT. The displacement of a vessel when floating at her designed draft.

DETACHABLE LINK. A special link for anchor chains by means of which "U" shaped connecting shackles can be dispensed with. It consists of a "C" shaped forging with collar-like projections and two coupling plates. The latter slot over the collar-like projections thereby filling the gap in the "C" forging. The stud of the link forms part of the coupling plates and fits into a pocket in the closed side of the "C" piece. The coupling plates are held together by a tapered steel pin locked at its larger end by a lead plug. A hand hammer and punch are used for opening or closing the link.

Fr: *Maille amovible; Maille demontable;* Ger: *Abnehmbares Glied.*

DETACHED KEEL AND KEELSON. An arrangement occasionally adopted in vessels without double bottom, the keelson being above the floors and **not in contact** with the keel.

DETACHING APPARATUS.
See **Releasing Gear.**

DEVELOPED AREA. The developed area of a propeller blade is the actual area of the blade surface irrespective of its shape. The developed area of the propeller is the sum of the developed areas of its blades.

Fr: *Surface développée;* Ger: *Abgewickelte Fläche.*

DEVELOPER.
See **Loftsman.**

DEVIATION. 1. Deviation may be defined as a departure without justification and under no necessity from the proper and usual course of an agreed voyage, whereby the character and the incidents of such voyage are altered.

The true objection to a deviation is not the increase of the risk, it is that the party contracting has voluntarily substituted another voyage for that which has been insured. The most serious consequences of this deviation are its effects on the insurance covering ship and cargo, for it amounts to a change of the risk. The benefit of the charter party exceptions are forfeited and the insurance is lost.

If it is made out that the departure is justified, it will not have the effect of a deviation. The master has always an implied permission to do what is necessary for the preservation of the vessel and the lives of those on board. It is not a deviation to put into a port to obtain provisions, to get repairs required for the safety of the ship, to replace officers or crew who have been lost during the voyage and without whom it is unsafe to proceed. Sickness or stress of weather may excuse deviation even when falling short of absolute necessity, and lastly deviation is always allowable for the purpose of saving life.

Fr: *Déroutement;* Ger: *Abweichung vom Kurse.*

2. The amount by which a ship's magnetic compass needle points to one side or the other of magnetic north. It is east or plus if the compass points east of magnetic north and west or minus, if it points west of the magnetic north. Deviation is caused by the ship's changed magnetic field, which changes with every change of heading.

Fr: *Déviation;* Ger: *Deviation.*

See **Constant Deviation, Quadrantal Deviation, Semicircular Deviation.**

Brown, C. H., *Deviation and the Deviascope,* Glasgow, 1928.

DEVIATION CLAUSE. A charter party clause enabling the ship to call at places other than the port of discharge.

Fr: *Clause de Déroutement;* Ger: *Abweichungsklausel; Deviationsklausel.*

See **Deviation.**

DEVIATION TABLE. An arrangement in tabular form of the deviation of the magnetic needle for each point of the compass.

Fr: *Table de Déviation;* Ger: *Steuertafel; Deviationstabelle.*

DEVIL. 1. The seam in a wooden deck which bounds the waterway. It is so-called from its difficulty of access in calking.

2. A seam in the planking of a wooden ship on or below the waterline.

See **Devil's Claw, Sneak Box.**

DEVIL'S CLAW. A very strong split-hook made to grasp a link of a chain cable and used as a stopper. Also called screw stopper. The usual practice in the merchant service is to have one claw, with turnbuckle for each cable, attached by an eye to the forward end of the windlass bed plate.

DEVIL'S COFFIN.
See **Sneak Box.**

DGHAISA.
See **Draissa.**

DHANGI. An Indian trading vessel similar in rig to the Arab *baghla.* These vessels are double-ended and decked fore and aft with poop. Tonnage 50 to 200. Length over-all 69.4 ft. Length of keel 47.2 ft. Breadth 22.7 ft. Depth 10.4 ft. (Typical.)

Two peculiar projecting pieces of wood extend forward beyond the stemhead in line with the gunwale. Most dhangis have two masts with a slight forward rake. The mainmast is secured at deck level to a spar on foreside. The *dhangi* differs from the *baghla* chiefly by its sharp raked stern with poop.

DHONI. See **Doney.**

DHOW. A generic term applied to all the Arabic lateen-rigged, grab-built vessels of the Indian Ocean. Also called dau. The main features are a long overhang forward, a great beam and rise of floor, and a marked raking transom stern. They are fast, able, seagoing vessels. The shell plating is generally worked in two thicknesses. Length 85 ft. Breadth 20 ft. 9 in. Depth 11 ft. 6 in. (Average.)

Fr: *Boutre;* Ger: *Dau.*

According to Hornell the term "dhow" is not recognized or used by the Arabs themselves, who use "baghla" for the larger and "sambuk" for the smaller vessels of this type. The true dhow is the dau of Zanzibar: a small open boat used specially for the transport of firewood. It is a local synonym for the *sambuk*, a boat of quite small size with sharp stern.

The *dhow* has a long raking stem running steeply to the point of greatest draft, which is situated well forward, whence the keel slopes up toward aft. This places the center of buoyancy far forward and prevents the bows from being thrown off either by the impact of an oncoming sea or the initial pressure of a squall when sailing on the wind. Many of them are sheathed on 2½-in. plank bottom with 1-in. board, with a preparation of chunam and oil called "galgal" between. This makes the vessel very durable and deters the inroads of teredos. Outside the sheathing there is a coat of the same material as that between the sheathing and planking.

DIAGONAL. Reference planes used on the lines plan to define the longitudinal molded form of the hull through the turn of the bilge and just above and below it. These planes run diagonally downward from the centerline plane normal to the molded-hull surface.

Fr: *Lisse Oblique; Ligne d'Arêtes;* Ger: *Sentebene.*

See **Bilge Diagonal.**

DIAGONAL AND LONGITUDINAL PLANKING. A system of double-skin planking in which the inner skin is laid at an angle and lightly fastened to the keel gunwale and stringers. The outer is laid longitudinally as in carvel planking, with a canvas or cotton fabric between. In this system the ribs or frames are dispensed with, the plank being laid on stringers. It results in a very strong hull with great elastic strength.

DIAGONAL BRACE. Iron straps or plates with a thickness of from ¾ to 1½ in. and a width of 3 to 6 in., used for tying the frame timbers of a wooden hull to each other and extending diagonally from within a short distance of the keelson to the topsides. Also called diagonal truss.

Fr: *Bande Diagonale;* Ger: *Diagonalband; Diagonalschiene.*

DIAGONAL BULKHEAD. A diagonally planked wooden bulkhead made up with two cross layers of planking at an angle of 45°. Two thicknesses of tarred felt are laid between the courses of planking.

Fr: *Cloison en bordages Croisés;* Ger: *Diagonalgebauter Schott.*

DIAGONAL CEILING. A method of inside planking used on wooden hulls where the planks are laid diagonally between the bilges and the deck in order to increase the longitudinal strength of the whole structure.

Fr: *Vaigrage Diagonal;* Ger: *Diagonalwegerung.*

DIAGONAL-CUT SAIL. A general term for various sails in which the cloths above the "last" or miter run at right angles to the leech and perpendicular to the foot below the last. The sail is cut out in two sections, a head section and a foot section. These sections meet and are joined at the last or miter, which is the seam made by joining the two sections, and should bisect the angle of the clew.

Sails made in this fashion are fitted with a wire luff rope. They keep their shape well as any tendency to bagginess is counteracted by the method of construction. Jibs, forestaysails, gaff-topsails, and Genoa jibs are usually cut diagonally, as are "loose-foot" Bermuda mainsails.

DIAGONAL FRAMING. A system of (steel) side framing where the frames are run in a diagonal direction, supported by relatively wide spaced web frames; the bottom and decks being framed as in the ordinary transverse system.

Fr: *Membrures diagonales;* Ger: *Diagonale Bespannung.*

DIAGONAL JIB. A jib cut in two sections, and jointed by a diagonal seam from the clew to the stay.

DIAGONAL LINES. Straight lines extending from the longitudinal middle-line plane to the frame sections of the body plan. Sometimes called diagonals. They are represented by curved lines on the half breadth and sheer plans.

Fr: *Sections Obliques;* *Lisses Planes;* Ger: *Senten im Spantenriss.*

DIAGONAL PILLAR. A hold pillar placed at a considerable athwartships angle so as to leave the bottom of the hold quite clear under a hatchway. Used in small coasting vessels. Called also diagonal stanchion.

Fr: *Epontille Diagonale;* Ger: *Querlaufende Stütze.*

DIAGONAL PLANKING. A method of planking in which the shell of a wooden vessel or boat is formed by two layers of planks crossing each other at right angles and making an angle of 45° with the transverse frames. This system of planking is adopted for the sturdiest motorboats or pulling boats, known as double-skin boats.

Fr: *Construction à Bordages Croisés;* Ger: *Diagonalbauart.*

DIAGONAL STRAPPING. In wooden shipbuilding a method of bracing to improve the longitudinal strength of the hull, consisting of flat wrought iron bars arranged in lattice form and fitted diagonally inside the frame timbers, from beams to bilges. Also called diagonal bracing or diagonal trussing.

Fr: *Bandes Diagonales;* Ger: *Diagonalschiene.*

DIAGONAL TIE PLATE. In sailing vessels, strips of plating laid diagonally from side to side under a wooden deck. They are riveted to the beams and butt-strapped to the stringer plates and longitudinal tie plates. They are designed as strengthening against the racking stresses transmitted to the deck by the masts.

Fr: *Bande Diagonale;* Ger: *Diagonalschienen.*

DIAMOND BEACON. Beacon with diamond-shaped topmark or daymark used in the French and British buoyage systems to denote the outer end of a middle ground which may be passed on either side.

Fr: *Amer à Voyant biconique;* Ger: *Diamantbake.*

DIAMOND-HANGING MESH. Meshes hung at an angle of 45° to the head and foot of a net. The meshes of most nets hang diamond-wise.

DIAMOND KNOT. An ornamental knot used for manropes and footropes where it is necessary to provide a good hold for the hands or feet. Also called footrope knot, single diamond knot.

Fr: *Pomme d'Etrier;* *Noeud de Hauban* (*Anglais*); *Noeud de Tireveille Simple;* Ger: *Fallreepsknoten; Diamantknoten.*

DIAMOND PLATE. A strap of conventional diamond shape uniting and strengthening parts of framing which cross each other in the same place.

Fr: *Mouchoir en Losange;* Ger: *Diamantplatte.*

DIAMOND RIG. A term applied to the standing rigging of a Bermuda or Marconi mast in which the upper shrouds, instead of leading to the chain plates, are returned to the mast, where they fasten just above the lower spreaders. It is usual with this arrangement to have the lower shrouds made of heavier wire.

DIAMOND SHROUD. A shroud as used on racing and cruising yachts which instead of leading down to the deck runs over the cross-trees and fastens to another point on the mast.

DIAPER PLATE.
See **Horseshoe Plate.**

DIAPHONE. A compressed-air sound-signal apparatus used by coastal stations in foggy weather and emitting a low powerful note, each blast terminating with a sharp descending note termed "grunt."

The diaphone consists of a cylinder with slits cut in its walls, and a hollow piston with similar corresponding slits which slides in it. Compressed air forces this piston up and down rapidly, at each movement releasing a puff of air through the slits. This results in a very arresting and penetrating sound, which gives in a conical horn or trumpet a note of about 180 vibrations per second.

DIAPHRAGM. A web plate with flange angles placed between two other structural members to stiffen them laterally.

DIAPHRAGM HORN. A foghorn in which sound is produced by means of a disk diaphragm vibrated by compressed air, steam or, electricity. Duplex or triplex units of different pitch produce a chime signal.

DIAPHRAGM PLATE. A dividing plate or partition, which in part-awning or raised-quarter deck vessels fulfills the functions of a division and connection between the ends of the awning deck and the quarter deck.

Fr: *Tôle Diaphragme;* Ger: *Trennungsplatte.*

DICKY (G. B.). A small seat fitted in some square sterned rowboats in the angle made by the gunwale and transom, on which the coxswain sits when the boat is under oars. Also called **Quarter seat.**

DIE-LOCK CHAIN. A modern type of anchor chain in which each link is made of two separate sections: a male and a female section. The male section has a number of

See **Anchor Cable.**

DIESEL-ELECTRIC DRIVE. The Diesel-electric propulsion system comprises one or several Diesel engines driving direct-current shunt-wound generators or alternators, which supply electrical power to the propelling motor or motors coupled to the propeller shaft. The generators and motors are separately excited from smaller generators known as exciters, which are directly connected to the generator shafts and driven by the same engines that drive the generators.

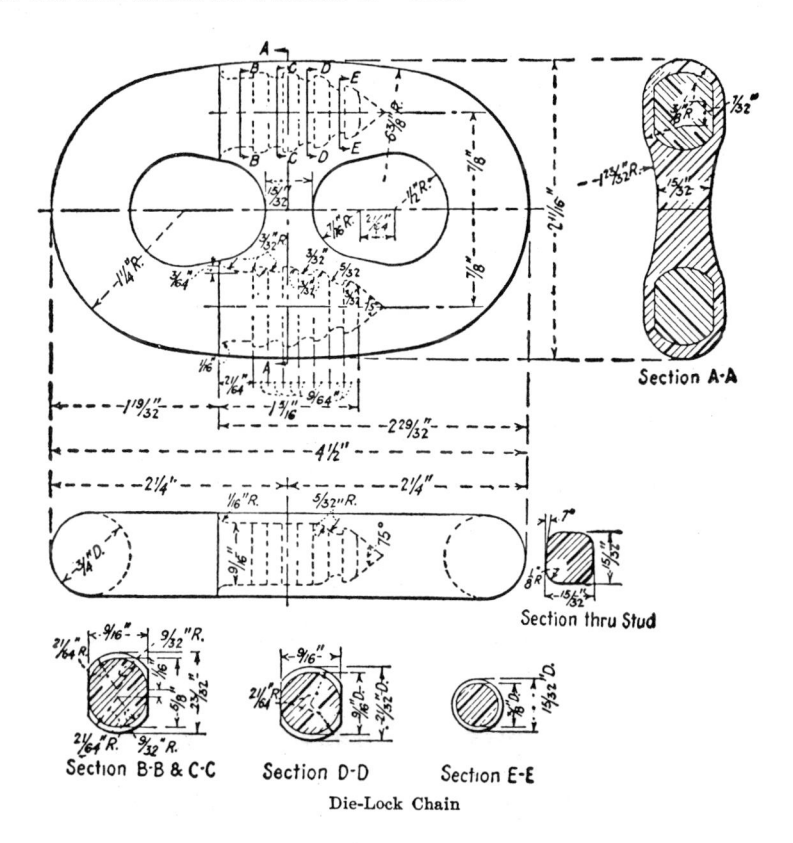

Die-Lock Chain

shoulders and, during manufacture, holes are punched in the female section. The male section is inserted cold, and the heated female section is swaged down on the male section.

Tests have shown that this mechanical lock is stronger than the full section at the quarters of the links, and that such chain is stronger than wrought-iron or cast-steel chain of equal size.

Fr: *Propulsion Diesel-Electrique;* Ger: *Motor Elektrischer Antrieb.*

The system lends itself with extreme readiness to remote or bridge control and regulation for any speed from zero to maximum in either direction. The Diesel engines operate at constant speed and in only one direction of rotation irrespective of the speed or direction of rotation of the propeller.

Diesel-electric propulsion has a particularly useful field for those craft in which the power needed for the auxiliaries is high when compared to the total output as is the case with refrigerated vessels, fruit carriers, oil tankers, dredgers. Tugboats operating in restricted waters such as harbors, bays, and rivers, offers an important field for Diesel-electric drive, the pilot house control providing a precision of operation which no other direct form of propulsion can approximate.

DIESEL ENGINE. An oil engine working on the following principle: air is drawn into a cylinder and compressed to a pressure sufficiently high to raise the temperature so as to insure auto ignition of oil fuel injected into the cylinder at the end of compression at a graduated rate. The working pressure in the cylinder does not rise above the compression pressure. After combustion is complete, the gases expand adiabatically to the end of the stroke. The gases are then exhausted and the cycle starts again.

Fr: *Moteur Diesel;* Ger: *Verbrennungsmotor; Brennkraftmaschine.*

The over-all thermal efficiency of internal combustion engines is about 35-37 per cent of the energy of the fuel in a useful form at the shaft of the engine. The mechanical efficiency of the latest types varies from 75 to 83 per cent.

Diesel engines are advantageous in that the plant requires a relatively small space, can be operated by a small number of men, has small loss in stand-by condition, gives good astern power and efficiency as compared with backing turbines, and provides long cruising range per ton of fuel. However, the requirements for overhaul and maintenance, as well as replacement parts, are considerable. The fuel is more expensive than that used in boilers, and the engines cannot be operated efficiently at low power or extreme full power for lengthy periods.

Hawkes, C. J., Development of the Heavy Oil Engine for Ship Propulsion, North East Coast Institution of Engineers and Shipbuilders (Newcastle upon Tyne), *Transactions,* vol. 52 (1935-36); Hunter-Keller-Stromberg, "Diesel Engines for Cargo Ships," Institution of Engineers and Shipbuilders in Scotland, *Transactions,* vol. 82 (1938-39).

DIESEL-HYDRAULIC WINCH. A cargo winch in which the necessary power is supplied by a Diesel-driven hydraulic pump placed in the engine room. This system is mainly confined to small coasting vessels equipped with two winches, where the same pump also supplies power to the windlass and capstan, as these auxiliaries and the winches are not required to be in service simultaneously.

DIESEL OIL. A term which refers specifically to petroleum distillate of 20 to 30 degrees Baumé on which the majority of Diesel-engined ships operate. Some of the large marine Diesel engines are operated on bunker "C" oil of 10 to 18 degrees Baumé with the oil heated to the flash point. Also called gas oil.

Fr: *Huile de Moteur;* Ger: *Dieselöl.*

Stanley Robinson, R., *Diesel Engine Fuels, Marine Engineer,* London, vol. 49, March-April-May, 1926; American Society for Testing Materials, Diesel Fuel Specifications (New York, 1939).

DIFFERENTIAL BLOCK. A chain hoist block with two or more sheaves of different diameters.

Fr: *Poulie différentielle;* Ger: *Differentialflaschenzug.*

DIFFERENCE OF LATITUDE. The angular distance between the latitudes of two places measured on a meridian.

Fr: *Différence en Latitude;* Ger: *Breitenunterschied.*

DIFFERENCE OF LONGITUDE. The difference of longitude of two places on the earth's surface is the arc of the equator included between their meridians, or the corresponding angle at the pole.

Fr: *Différence de Longitude;* Ger: *Längenunterschied.*

DIHENGE. A one-man dugout canoe sharp at both ends and of round cross section made of light native wood, used by the Batanga people of the Cameroons. Length 10 to 13 ft. Breadth 9 in. to 1.6 ft. The paddler sits on a sort of transverse bulkhead placed amidships. It is used by the fishermen of Kribi and, although very unstable, crosses the bar daily.

DIMENSIONS. The measurements which define the hull of a vessel, consisting of: the length over-all, length between perpendiculars, molded breadth, molded depth, and, for merchant vessels, the registered length, registered breadth, and registered depth. Sometimes called principal dimensions.

DIMINISHING PLANK.

See **Diminishing Strakes.**

DIMINISHING STRAKES. Planking worked under the wales and thinning progressively to correspond with the thickness of the bottom planking. This term also applies to the broad strakes between garboard and bottom planking where the strakes have the same thickness. Also called diminishing stuff.

Fr: *Bordé de Diminution;* Ger: *Verjüngungsplanken.*

DINAPALANG. A flat-bottomed dugout of the Philippine Islands shaped like the *sapiaoan* but with stern and stem rounded instead of triangular. It is propelled by oars and steered by means of a rudder with tiller. There are thwarts for ten oarsmen. It is mostly used for fishing but also as general utility boat along the coasts.

DINGHY. 1. A small rowboat with transom stern, single-banked with 2 or 4 oars, used as an extra boat on merchant vessels. It is usually the smallest ship's boat. Also called dingey, cockboat.

2. A small open boat used as tender and lifeboat in a yacht. Rig: one portable mast and spritsail.

Fr: *Youyou;* Ger: *Beiboot; Dingi.*

3. A decked boat, short and beamy, used for the transportation of passengers and goods in sheltered waters around the Indian peninsula. Also called dengi. It carries the whole of its load above deck. Indian dinghys are made in all sizes, from the small one-man craft 25 to 30 ft. in length and about ½ ton burden used as a ferry on the rivers of Bengal, to the large cargo carriers from Karachi used as lighters.

See **Pram Dinghy, Sponge Dinghy, Stem Dinghy.**

DIOPTRIC LIGHT. A coastal light in which the light from the burner is concentrated into parallel beams by means of refracting lenses and prisms.

Fr: *Feu Dioptrique;* Ger: *Dioptrisches Feuer.*

DIOPTRIC TELESCOPE. A refracting telescope.

DIP. 1. A correction to be applied to the observed altitude of a celestial body owing to the depression of the observer's horizon and due to the curvature of the earth's surface. Also called depression. The apparent dip is the angle between the observer's visible and sensible horizons, but the element of refraction has to be taken into consideration in order to arrive at the true dip.

Fr: *Dépression;* Ger: *Kimmtiefe; Depression.*

See **Magnetic Dip.**

2. The pronounced downward movement of the bows during the launch of a vessel when the fore poppets have passed beyond the ends of the ground ways. Also called dipping, lifting. It occurs at the moment when the buoyancy provided by the

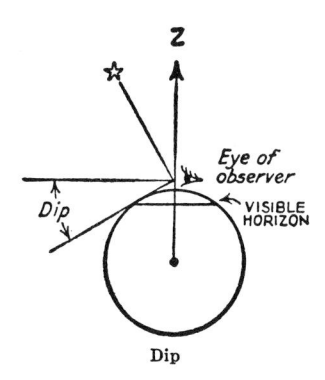

immersed portion of the hull is larger than the weight of the fore end as it leaves the ground ways.

Fr: *Salut;* Ger: *Jumpen.*

DIP. Downward inclination of a magnetic needle.

Fr: *Inclinaison;* Ger: *Neigung; Inklination.*

See **Magnetic dip.**

DIP (to). 1. To lower and then raise again the ensign as a mark of courtesy to passing vessel.

Fr: *Faire Marquer;* Ger: *Dippen.*

2. A heavenly body is said to dip after it has crossed the meridian.

3. To lower and shift on the opposite side of the mast the yard of a lugsail when tacking. Hence, the name "dipping lug."

Fr: *Gambeyer;* Ger: *Dippen.*

DIP (at the). A flag is said to be "at the dip" when hoisted about half the length (height) of the halyards.

Fr: *à Mi-Drisse;* Ger: *Halbstock.*

DIP CHART. A chart showing the dip or angle which the magnetic needle makes with the plane of the horizon in various geographical positions on the surface of the earth.

U. S. Hydrographic Office, Washington, Chart, H.O. 1700.

Fr: *Carte d'inclinaison magnétique;* Ger: *Inklinationskarte.*

DIP CIRCLE.

See **Dipping Compass.**

DIP NET. A net used for transferring the catch of a deep-sea seine after it has been brought alongside. It is operated either entirely by hand or partly by hand and partly by power. Also called scoop, brailer.

Fr: *Epuisette;* Ger: *Streichnetz.*

DIPPER. Colloquial name given by navigators to the constellation "Ursa Major."

DIPPER DREDGE. A dredge fitted with excavating machinery similar in its construction to the ordinary steam shovel except that the platform carrying the machinery consists of a barge instead of a car.

Fr: *Drague à Pelle;* Ger: *Schaufelbagger; Löffelbagger.*

The principal features are the bucket, the arm to which it is attached, and the boom which supports and guides the arm. The boom is mounted on a turntable so that dredging can be undertaken around a wide arc.

DIPPING.
See **Pivoting.**

DIPPING COMPASS. An instrument which consists of a magnetic needle suspended between centers, a vertical graduated circle whose center coincides with the axis of the needle, and a graduated horizontal circle. It is used to measure the angle of dip or inclination of the magnetic needle. Also called dip compass, inclination compass, dip circle.

Fr: *Compas d'Inclinaison;* Ger: *Inklination Bussole; Neigungskompass.*

DIPPING LINE. One of the small lines fastened to the heel of the yard of a dipping lugsail to swing the yard on the other side of the mast when tacking.

DIPPING LUG. A lugsail with the halyards bent at a point about two-fifths of the length of the yard from its forward end.

Fr: *Voile de Lougre Volante; Voile à Bourcet Gambeyant;* Ger: *Dippende Luggersegel; Lose Luggersegel.*

The tack hooks well forward of the mast, there being generally an eyebolt on either bow for this purpose. The sail is set to leeward of the mast. When going about, the yard has to be dipped each time to the new lee side of the mast. Although one of the finest drawing sails, it is little used, on account of its unhandiness in making tacks.

DIPPING NEEDLE. A magnetic needle hanging on a horizontal axis and capable of moving only in a vertical plane. It indicates the angle which the line of magnetic force makes with the horizon. Also called inclination needle.

Fr: *Aiguille d'Inclinaison;* Ger: *Inklinationsnadel.*

See **Dipping Compass.**

DIP ROPE. A length of open-link chain or wire used with a clear-hawse pendant. Also called hawse rope. The outer end is fitted with a shackle large enough to engage a link of the anchor cable and the inner end with a long tail of Manila rope.

Fr: *Itague d'Affourchage.*

DIPSEY. The float of a fishing line. Also called cork buoy.

Fr: *Flotte;* Ger: *Korkschwimmer.*

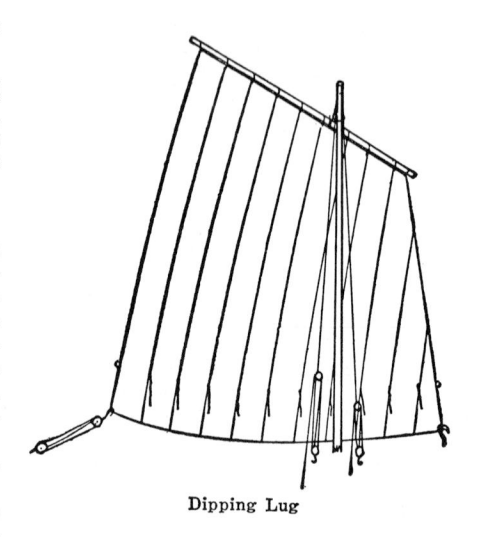

Dipping Lug

DIPSEY LEAD.
See **Deep sea lead.**

DIRECT-ACTING PUMP. A type of reciprocating pump in which the plunger of the water end is driven directly by the rod which carries the piston of the steam end, in contradistinction to the indirect-acting pump, in which the plunger of the water end is driven by a beam or linkage which is connected to and actuated by the steam piston rod of a separate reciprocating engine. An indirect-acting pump sometimes driven by a crank, is rotated by a turbine or motor.

DIRECT BILL OF LADING. A bill of lading which covers shipments between direct ports of loading and discharge of the vessel concerned.

Fr: *Connaissement en droiture.*

DIRECT CONNECTED STEERING GEAR. A hand or power steering gear in which the necessary power is applied to the tiller without any intermediary transmissions such as chains, rods, or shafting.

Fr: *Appareil à Gouverner à Commande Directe;* Ger: *Rudermaschine mit direktem Antrieb.*

DIRECT DRIVE. A propulsion system in which the propeller shafting is directly connected to the main engines and turns at the same number of revolutions as the prime mover. Direct drive in modern practice is used only with reciprocating engines.

Fr: *Transmission Directe;* Ger: *Direkter Antrieb.*

DIRECTIONAL RADIO BEACON. A wireless station which emits a beam of waves in one or several definite directions or sectors. Also called beam transmitter or a directional wireless beam transmitter.

Fr: *Radiophare Directionnel; radiophare à faisceau tournant;* Ger: *Gerichtete Funkbake.*

A direction-finding receiver (direction finder or radio compass) is *not* necessary as signals of this kind are confined to narrow *beams,* and distinguished by different Morse letters.

DIRECTION FINDER.
See **Radio Compass.**

DIRT MONEY. A term in usage in the grain trade. Also called **dust allowance.**

Refers to the handling of dusty grain, which, when discharged with pneumatic elevator, suffocates the men in the hold if worked fast and hides the ship in a cloud of dust.

DIRTY BALLAST. Applies to the washings of tanks in which crude oil, diesel oil, or the heavier grades of gas oil have been carried.

DIRTY SHIP. Refers to oil tankers which have been carrying unrefined products, such as crude oil, lubricating oil, fuel oil, which necessitates cleaning of tanks and piping before a cargo of *clean* oil, i.e., gasoline or diesel can be taken.

Ger: *Schmutzige Schiff.*

DISABLED. Said of a vessel injured or impaired in such a manner as to be incapable of proceeding on her voyage.

Fr: *En Avarie;* Ger: *Dienstunfähig.*

DISBURSEMENT CLAUSE. A marine insurance clause which limits the amount of subsidiary insurances which a shipowner may place on policy proof of interest (P.P.I.) conditions to a percentage of the insured value, of the policy on hull and machinery.

DISBURSEMENT INSURANCE. Part of the hull insurance placed by a shipowner on his vessel in an amount over and above the valuation agreed upon in the full form policy.

Fr: *Assurance débours;* Ger: *Ausgabe Versicherung.*

DISBURSEMENTS. 1. Payments made by the master or by the ship's agents on behalf of the owners. They include customs fees, bunkers, stores, and sundry expenses during a vessel's stay in port. The largest items which may come under this heading are the cost of loading or discharging, and cash advances made by the agents to the master for crew's wages, and ship repairs, if any.

Fr: *Mises dehors;* Ger: *Auslagen.*

2. A compendious term used in marine insurance policies to describe any interest which is outside the ordinary interests of hull, machinery, cargo, and freight.

Fr: *Frais d'Armement;* Ger: *Schiffsbedürfnissgelder.*

The term refers in general to moneys expended by the owners incidental and preparatory to, or in connection with, the continuance or the performance of a voyage, including fuel, provisions and stores for passengers and crew, port charges, etc.

DISBURSEMENTS WARRANTY. A marine insurance clause (hull) which governs the insurances on other than specific interests at risk which the shipowner is permitted to effect. It places a limit, usually 25% of insured value of hull, on the extent to which the owners may insure freight for time on chartered, on board or not on board, terms.

A warranty included in hull policies, by which the owners of the vessel are limited regarding the amount of disbursement insurance they may effect on "Policy proof of interest" or "Full interest admitted" terms.

DISC AREA. The area of the circle described and enclosed by the tips of propeller blades.

Fr: *Aire du disque;* Ger: *Kreisfläche; Schraubendiskfläche.*

DISC-AREA RATIO. The ratio of developed area to disc area of a screw propeller.

Fr: *Coefficient d'Aire;* Ger: *Kreisflächenverhältnis des Schraubendisks.*

See **Developed Area, Disc Area.**

DISCHARGE. A formal document given to seamen when they are leaving a vessel released from duty. Also called discharge ticket.

Fr: *Certificat de Débarquement;* Ger: *Entlassungsschein.*
See **Scale Discharge.**

DISCHARGE (to). 1. To take the cargo out of a vessel. To unload.
Fr: *Décharger;* Ger: *Löschen.*
The operation of getting the cargo out of a ship is the business of the shipowner as part of his contract of carriage. Landing is the business of the receiver of the cargo or his agent, and is at his cost. Although discharging and landing is usually one continuous operation it is generally accepted in practice that discharging ceases when the goods are out of reach of the ship's tackle.
2. To release from duty or service any member of the crew.
Fr: *Débarquer;* Ger: *Abmustern.*

DISCHARGE OVERSIDE.
See **Overside delivery.**

DISCHARGING BERTH. The space or place allotted to a vessel in port for unloading cargo.
Fr: *Poste de Déchargement;* Ger: *Löschplatz.*

DISCRIMINATION. Differential treatment imposed by a government upon foreign vessels or goods; generally under one of the following forms; by payment of harbor dues in gold currency instead of the current paper money; by rebates in customs duties on goods carried by national vessels; by arbitrary valuations for customs purposes.
Fr: *Privilège;* Ger: *Unterscheidung.*

DISC SHEAVE. A solid sheave of wood or metal, that is, one without spokes.
Fr: *Réa Plein;* Ger: *Massige Scheibe.*

DISEMBARKATION. The act of landing from a ship. This term refers particularly to passengers or cattle that walk ashore.
Fr: *Débarquement;* Ger: *Ausschiffung.*

DISEMBOGUE. To pass out of the mouth of a river, gulf, bay.
Fr: *Débouquer;* Ger: *Hinausfahren.*

DISENGAGING GEAR. Apparatus for use in conjunction with the tackles or falls by which a lifeboat is lowered from the deck of a vessel. It consists of a hand-controlled gear located within reach of the person in charge of the boat. By applying a hand force of from 15 to 30 lb. on a lever or line both ends of the boat are simultaneously released from the falls. Also called releasing gear, disengaging apparatus, detaching apparatus.

Fr: *Appareil de Décrochage;* Ger: *Detachierapparat; Boot Slipvorrichtung.*
American Marine Standards Committee, Standard 58, *Lifeboat Disengaging Apparatus,* Washington, 1929.

DISHED PLATE. A plate of U shape, in cross section, as used for connecting the stem and sternpost to the keel.
Fr: *Tôle Emboutie;* Ger: *Gepresste Platte.*

DISMASTED. Said of a vessel with mast or masts carried away by the force of the wind, stranding, collision, and so on.
Fr: *Démâté;* Ger: *Entmastet.*

DISPATCH. (1) A term used to designate the total time allowed by charterparty for the loading and discharging of a vessel. (2) A ship construction term used to denote a conveniently sized form or drawing which illustrates or completely describes a single job, and which specifies in detail the materials required to accomplish the work. There are three types of dispatches: Fabrication, Subassembly and Installation. The first two are for shop and craft fabrication work. The installation dispatch specifies and distributes the work on the ships.
Fr: *Jours de Planche;* Ger: *Chartermässige Liegezeit.*

DISPATCH DAYS. Days saved in the loading or discharge of a vessel within the time (laydays) allowed under the charterparty. Also **Despatch days.**
Fr: *Jours de rachat de planche;* Ger: *Beförderungstage.*

DISPLACEMENT. The number of tons of water displaced by a vessel afloat (1 ton = 2240 lb.). The sum of light weight and dead weight is equal to the displacement.
Fr: *Déplacement;* Ger: *Wasserverdrängung.*
See **Load Displacement, Light Displacement, Volume of Displacement.**
In accordance with Archimedes' principle, displacement and weight are equivalent quantities for floating bodies so that the displacement of a vessel is not only the weight of the water she displaces at a given draft but also the weight of vessel and contents at that draft.

DISPLACEMENT COEFFICIENT. The product of the two-thirds power of the displacement and the cube of the speed, divided by the indicated horsepower.
See **Admiralty Coefficient.**

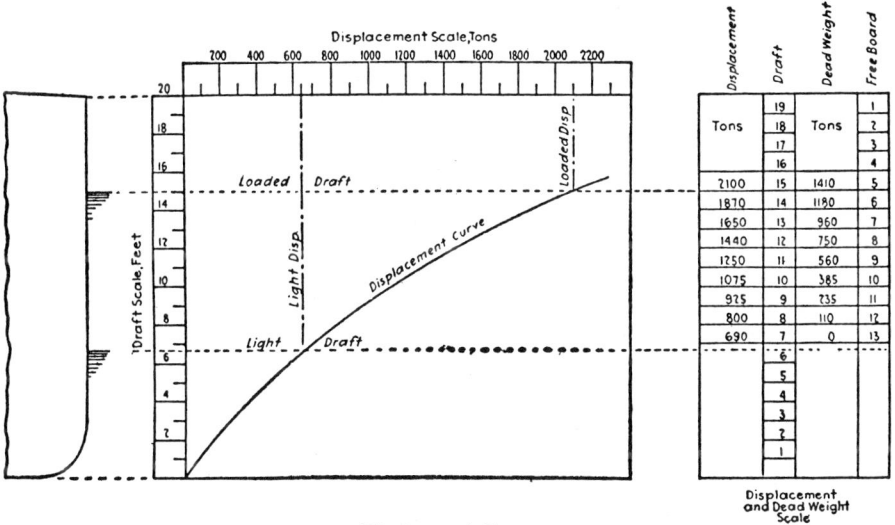

DISPLACEMENT CURVE. A curve showing to a suitable scale the displacement of a vessel in fresh or salt water at any specified draft, the displacement being expressed in tons of 2,240 lb. Also called curve of displacement.
Fr: *Courbe de Déplacements;* Ger: *Verdrängungskurve; Deplacementskurve; Tragfähigkeitsskala; Deplacementsskala.*

DISPLACEMENT LENGTH. 1. The length used in displacement calculations.
2. Length measured from specially located perpendiculars near one or both ends of yachts and vessels of unusual design when length as measured by the usual methods

DISPLACEMENT SCALE. A scale showing the displacement at varying drafts and the number of tons required to put the ship down one inch at each of the various drafts.
Fr: *Echelle de déplacements;* Ger: *Deplacementsskala; Verdrangungsskala.*

DISPLACEMENT TON. The unit of displacement. That volume of the fluid in which the ship may be afloat that weighs 2,240 lb. In salt water it measures 35 cu. ft.
Fr: *Tonne de Déplacement;* Ger: *Deplacementstonne.*

DISPLACEMENT TONNAGE. See Displacement.

Displacement Curve

would not constitute a good average index of the underwater form. It is sometimes measured from the foreside of the screw aperture.

DISPLACEMENT-LENGTH COEFFICIENT. The displacement-length coefficient is the ratio of a vessel's displacement in tons to 1/100 of its length in feet cubed. It is essentially a criterion of the amount of displacement established upon a given length.
Ger: *Verdrängungslänge-Koeffizient.*
Displacement-Length Coefficient for Typical Merchant Vessels:
  Fast passenger ships ... 65 to 115
  Intermediate vessels ... 100 to 170
  General cargo carriers .. 140 to 250
  Small cargo vessels .... 200 to 250

DISTANCE FREIGHT. Freight proportionate to the mileage of the voyage actually performed. Distance freight is not recognized by common law in the United States and Great Britain. It is recognized in German, Italian, and Spanish law.
Fr: *Fret de Distance; Fret proportionnel;* Ger: *Distanzfracht; Besegelte Fracht.*

DISTANCE LINE. One of the lines fastened to the upper corners of a collision mat, by which it is lowered to the desired location. Also called lowering line, guy line.

DISTANCE MADE GOOD. The length in nautical miles of the rhumb line joining two places.

Fr: *Route parcourue;* Ger: *General Distanz; Gesamt Distanz.*

DISTANT CONTROL GEAR.
See **Follow-up Gear.**

DISTILLING CONDENSER. In a distilling plant, a device for condensing to fresh water the steam produced in the evaporator by heating brine (sea water). It utilizes a continuous flow of sea water as a coolant.

DISTILLING PLANT. An installation for producing fresh water from sea water. Normally it consists of an evaporator and distilling condenser, with associated pumps, piping, gauges, valves, and auxiliary equipment.
See **Evaporator.**

DISTRESS. A term used when a ship requires immediate assistance from unlooked for damage or danger, such as important breakdown, lack of food, or any accident.
Fr: *Détresse;* Ger: *Seenot.*

DISTRESS CARGO. A term sometimes used to denote cargo shipped at higher than current rate of freight when the shipper is compelled to forward at once in order to satisfy the terms of his sales contract.

DISTRESS FLAG. Any flag displayed as a signal of distress. When the national flag is so used, it is generally displayed upside down or hoisted at half-mast.
Fr: *Pavillon de Secours;* Ger: *Notflagge.*

DISTRESS FREQUENCY. The radio frequency alloted to distress calls by international agreement. For ships at sea and aircraft it is 500 kilocycles.
Fr: *Onde de sauvegarde;* Ger: *Not Periodenzahl; Not Frequenz.*

DISTRESS GUN. A gun fired every minute as a distress signal by a vessel in imminent danger.
Fr: *Canon de Détresse;* Ger: *Notschutz.*

DISTRESS LIGHT. A self-igniting red light capable of burning and giving forth a brilliant flame of not less than 500 candle power for at least 2 minutes. Under the International Conference for Safety of Life at Sea, every lifeboat equipment must include 12 distress lights in a watertight metal container.
Fr: *Feu Pyrotechnique;* Ger: *Notsignal Feuer.*

DISTRESS SIGNAL. An urgent signal meaning that help is needed. The distress signal by international code is a two-flag signal beginning with letter "N." "N A" means aground; "N M" means am on fire, etc. Signals of distress are of various kinds; hoisting the national flag halfmast or upside down, firing guns or rockets, showing blue lights, sending by wireless the letters "S.O.S."
Fr: *Signal de Détresse;* Ger: *Notsignal.*

DISTRIBUTION BOX. A cast-metal box, fitted with a number of valves, into which a number of pipes, connected to pumps and tanks or compartments, are led. For bilge and ballast systems separate valve chests are usually provided for the forward and afterholds. They are so arranged that one pump can be made to draw from any one of the compartments connected with it. Also called valve chest, manifold.
Fr: *Boîte de Distribution;* Ger: *Gruppenventilkasten; Schieberkasten; Wechselventilkasten.*

DITTY BAG. A bag about 14 in. high and 7 in. in diameter made of light duck canvas with eyelet holes around the hem, containing a sailmaker's palm, sail needles, twine, marline and a marlinespike. It forms part of the standard equipment for ship's lifeboats.
Ger: *Kravsack.*

DIURNAL ACCELERATION. Excess of the apparent motion of the stars to that of the sun.
Fr: *Acceleration Diurne;* Ger: *Taglicke Beschleunigung.*

DIURNAL ARC. The apparent arc described by a celestial body from its rising to its setting.
Fr: *Cercle diurne;* Ger: *Tagbogen.*

DIURNAL CIRCLE. One of the circles of the celestial sphere on which a heavenly body appears to move daily across the sky from east to west, rising in the east and setting in the west.
Fr: *Cercle Diurne;* Ger: *Abweichungsparallel.*

DIURNAL INEQUALITY. The difference in height of the two high waters or of the two low waters of each day. The difference changes with the declination of the moon and to a lesser extent with the declination of the sun.
Fr: *Inégalité Diurne;* Ger: *Tägliche Ungleichheit.*

DIURNAL MOTION. The motion of celestial bodies performed in, or occupying, one day.

Fr: *Mouvement diurne;* Ger: *Tagliche Drehung.*

DIURNAL PARALLAX. See Parallax.

DIURNAL RANGE. The difference between mean higher high water and mean lower low water, in those places where the tide is chiefly diurnal.
Fr: *Amplitude Diurne;* Ger: *Tägliche Tidenhub.*

DIURNAL TIDE. Tide occuring once daily. Tide having one high water in a tidal day.
Fr: *Marée diurne;* Ger: *Eintatige Gezeit.*

DIURNAL WIND. Refers to local sea breeze by day and land breeze by night.

DIVER. One skilled in the practice of diving, equipped with either a helmet or headpiece (shallow-water diving), or a diving suit (deep-sea diving).
Fr: *Scaphandrier;* Ger: *Taucher.*
Shallow-water diving with helmet alone is practicable in depths up to 40 ft. Deep-sea divers have worked for short periods in depths of more than 300 ft.
Davis, R. H., Deep Diving and Submarine Operations, London, 1935.

DIVERGING WAVES. A system of waves at the bow and stern caused by the motion of a ship through the water, the crests of which slope aft. Their creation requires part of the ship's propulsive power and results in "wave-making resistance," a component of the ship's total resistance to propulsion.
Fr: *Vagues Divergentes;* Ger: *Divergierende Wellen.*

DIVIDED UPTAKES. An installation in which the boiler uptakes are removed from the center line of the ship and are led to port and starboard in the shape of two narrow ducts, which divide under the passenger decks, lead up at the wings of the promenade deck, and converge in the base of each smoke pipe at boat-deck level.
Fr: *Conduits de Fumée Lateraux;* Ger: *Verteilte Rauchfangführung.*
The purpose of this installation is to give a free, uninterrupted passage along the ship's center line, available for public rooms. The loss of longitudinal strength entailed by cutting twin apertures at the wings of steel decks, is made up by suitable structural compensation.

DIVING SUIT. A hermetically sealed dress with necessary appliances for diving and working under water. Also called diving dress, diving gear.
The suit itself is made of solid sheet rubber between inner and outer layers of twill. It has a collar of thick vulcanized rubber, which fits a corselet, pierced with holes for the reception of corselet studs. The corselet itself is made of tinned copper and has a metal band around its outer edge with projecting studs.
The helmet is also of tinned copper. Inlet and outlet valves of the non-return type are provided. The outlet valve can be adjusted by the diver so as to regulate the pressure in the helmet, which is kept slightly higher than that of the surrounding water. The helmet is fastened to the corselet by means of a segmental ring which fits into a corresponding ring on the corselet. Three windows of glass ½ in. thick are fitted on the sides and front of the helmet.
The diver also wears a weighted belt, fitted with lead weights, and heavy shoes, also weighted with lead, to assist him in maintaining an erect position while working below the surface.
An air hose made of canvas, steel wire, and rubber with an inside diameter of ⅝ in. supplies air to the helmet from an air pump or air bottles. A breast rope brought up under the diver's right arm and secured to the corselet with a lanyard serves for signaling and as a safety device. A telephone, now fitted to all diving suits, is of great value and plays an important part in salvage operations.
Davis, R. H., *Diving Manual,* London, 1935; U. S. Navy, *Diving Manual,* Washington.

DOAI. See Duc.

DOATY (G. B.). Said of the condition of timber when stained with yellow and black spots.

DOB. Small East Indian outrigger dugout canoe from Aru Islands (Banda Sea) similar to the *boka.* Also called dab.

DOBBYING. Seamen's term for washing clothes.

DOBLE. A centerboard boat from the Medway estuary, employed in drift-net or beam-trawl fisheries and rigged with single mast, boomed spritsail and jib-headed foresail, set flying and tacked down to the stemhead. It is decked at ends with waterways running fore and aft and a sharp stern. A fish well is built amidships through which the center plate moves. Length 12 ft. Breadth 4.3 ft. Depth 1.5 ft. (Average.)

DO-BUNE. A Japanese boat employed in the local herring and salmon fisheries. It is similar to the *samba-bune* but smaller and pulls 8 oars. Length over-all 16 ft. 8 in. Breadth 4 ft. 5 in. (Typical.)

DOCK. Artificial basin provided with suitable installations for loading or unloading close to the sea where vessels can lie afloat. The space may communicate freely with the stream or harbor, or the entrance to it may be closed by gates or a lock. Dock gates are usually employed when the rise and fall of the tide exceeds 10 to 12 ft.
    Fr: *Bassin;* Ger: *Hafenbecken.*

DOCK (to). To take, bring, or receive a ship into dock.
    Fr: *Entrer au Bassin;* Ger: *Docken.*

DOCKAGE. A charge or due levied against a vessel in cases where, in addition to harborage, the vessel makes use of the dock accommodation of a port for the purpose of taking in or discharging cargo. Also called quayage, berthing dues, dock tonnage dues.
    Fr: *Droits de Quai; Droits de Bassin;* Ger: *Dockgeld; Kaikosten; Kaigeld; Kaiabgaben.*

Dockage may be additional to the harbor tonnage dues or the former may cover the latter. Dockage charges are assessed in some ports on the gross tonnage, in others on the net tonnage, and in still others on the vessel's length. In most ports ships lying second out are not charged for dockage.
See **Penalty Dockage.**

DOCKAGE PERIOD. The period of time during which the stand of the tide and current will permit the gates of a wet dock to remain open and vessels to enter or leave the dock.

DOCK BOSS (U. S.). One in charge of all checkers employed on a dock or pier. Assists the receiving clerk, delivery clerk and stevedores and informs the harbor master where loaded lighters should be placed. Instructs checkers where to place cargo received from trucks.

DOCK DUES. See **Dockage.**

DOCKER. A laborer employed for loading and discharging vessels in the docks. Also called longshoreman.
    Fr: *Docker; Débardeur;* Ger: *Dockarbeiter; Kaiarbeiter; Hafenarbeiter.*

DOCK FLOOR. The bottom of a dry dock. It usually has a slight fall from back to front and from center to sides to facilitate drainage.
    Fr: *Radier;* Ger: *Sohle.*

DOCKING. The operation or charge made for assisting a vessel into a dock.
    Fr: *Entrée au Bassin;* Ger: *Docken.*

DOCKING BRIDGE. A raised transverse platform extending from side to side at the stern and used by the officer attending to the after mooring lines, when bringing the ship alongside a wharf, dock or pier. Also **Warping bridge.**
    Fr: *Passerelle de manoeuvre;* Ger: *Achterbrücke.*

DOCKING CLAUSE. A marine insurance clause by which the insured vessel is permitted to dock, undock, change docks and go into drydock as often as may be necessary during the currency of the policy.

DOCKING KEEL.
See **Grounding keel.**

DOCKING PLAN. A plan used by those in charge of a dry dock to determine the blocking required for a particular vessel prior to entering the dock. It consists of a longitudinal section with transverse bulkheads, engine and boiler spaces, and sea connections indicated. At various points cross sections are shown giving form of bottom, rise of floors, and fineness of ends. For ships with considerable shape, tables of offsets are included to facilitate setting bilge blocks and cribbings and blocking under docking keels. In the case of tank vessels with riveted hull, the plan shows the position of keel butts and the extent thereof.

DOCKING PLUG. A screwed set pin of from 7/8 to 1¼-in. diameter made of brass and fitted in the garboard strake of the shell plating at the bottom of each compartment to drain the water which remains in the ballast tanks when the vessel is in dry dock. Also called drain plug, bottom plug, bleeder plug, drain bolt, bleed cock.
    Fr: *Nable; Bouchon de Nable;* Ger: *Bodenventilstöpsel; Pflock; Aussenhautpflock.*

DOCKING TELEGRAPH. An apparatus forming a communication between the bridge and stern for signaling special orders while warping the ship in and out of dock. It is usually combined with an engine direction telltale, the dial of which indicates the speed and direction in which the engines are working.
    Fr: *Transmetteur d'Ordres Arrière;* Ger: *Docktelegraph.*

DOCKING WINCH. A ship's winch. See **Warping winch.**

DOCK LINE (U. S.). A line established by legislative authority along the shores of a navigable waterway, out to which riparian owners have the privilege of filling in and building.

DOCKMAN. See **Wharfman.**

DOCKMASTER. 1. An official subordinate to the harbormaster responsible for supervising the locking in or out of vessels or craft at the dock gates, directing the movements and berthing of ships using any dock under his control. Also called berthing officer. He is assisted by piermaster.

Fr: *Officier de Port;* Ger: *Dockmeister.*

2. An official responsible for the correct setting of blocks and drydocking of ships.

DOCK MOORINGS. Moorings in a wet dock used by vessels waiting for loading or discharging berths to become vacant, or also by vessels under repair or awaiting dry docking.

DOCK PASS (G. B.). 1. A document issued by the dock authorities before a vessel leaves the dock. It is a voucher that the dock dues have been paid.

2. A pass to be given up at the entrance to a pier or dock as authorization that goods are allowed to leave the premises. Also called truckman's pass.

Fr: *Permis d'Enlèvement.*

3. Pass issued by the Bureau of Customs, authorizing the bearer to board incoming vessels after such vessels have been inspected by quarantine authorities.

DOCK RECEIPT. A receipt issued by a shipping firm when goods are delivered at the wharf before shipment. Also called receiving note. It is later exchanged for the bill of lading.

Fr: *Reçu Provisoire;* Ger: *Ablieferungschein; Kaiempfangschein; Ubernahmeschein.*

DOCK RENT. Charge for storage of goods on a dock quay or pier. Also called **Dock charges.**

Ger: *Dockgeld.*

DOCK SHEET (U. S.). A document on which all information regarding a particular shipment of goods, such as tallying, weighing and measuring, is indicated previous to the issuance of the bill of lading. Dock sheets and tally sheets constitute the original records for the wharf department.

DOCKSIDE CRANE. A crane located on a pier or quay for transferring general cargo to and from seagoing vessels. It is erected on the roof of shed or on a gantry on the quay. The gantry may be portal or half portal. The usual capacity of dockside cranes varies from ½ to 5 tons with a radius of 25 to 90 feet.

Fr: *Grue de Quai;* Ger: *Kaikran.*

DOCK SIGNAL. Any of the signals applying to a closed basin or wet dock constituting a subdivision of a port.

Fr: *Signal de Port;* Ger: *Docksignal.*

DOCK SILL. The platform or flooring at the entrance of a dry dock. The timber or foundation against which the gates of a dock or lock shut. The depth of water which will float a vessel in or out is measured from the sill to the surface. Also called apron.

Fr: *Seuil;* Ger: *Dockhaupt; Drempel.*

DOCK SUPERINTENDENT (G. B.). A person responsible for the supervision of operations at the dockside or pier, including the discharge of vessels, the housing and delivery of goods, the dispatch of outgoing cargo and all routine work in the process of cargo handling between ship and shore. In the United States called wharf superintendent. Sometimes called traffic manager.

DOCK TONNAGE DUES.

See **Dockage.**

DOCK TRIALS. A four to six hour trial of the main engines at or near the highest revolutions it is practically possible to maintain with the vessel moored alongside the dock or fitting-out basin. After the trials the engines are opened up for examination. The steering gear and windlass are also tested at dock trials. The usual test for the steering gear includes continuous operation for at least two hours during which the rudder is moved from hard over to hard over, using alternately the wheelhouse steering wheel and any of the other steering station apparatus. The windlass is operated, raising and lowering each anchor, running out as much chain as the depth of dock permits.

Fr: *Essais au point fixe.*

DOCK TUG. A tug whose duty it is to shift a more or less large inert mass from berth to berth in still water. This duty is occasionally performed by the simple process of "butting," or pushing broadside on the ship to be moved.

Fr: *Remorqueur de Bassin;* Ger: *Dockschlepper.*

DOCK UP (G. B.). A bargeman's term, meaning to clew up part of a sail for the benefit of the helmsman.

DOCK WARRANT (G. B.). A negotiable instrument issued by the dock owners to the owner of goods imported and warehoused in the docks, as a recognition of his title to the goods, upon the production of the bill of lading. Also called warehouse receipt.

Fr: *Warrant; Récépissé-Warrant;* Ger: *Warenschein; Lagerpfandschein; Waren Lagerschein.*

DOCK WINCH. A portable or stationary winch installed on a pier or dock, used in transferring cargo between ship and shore.

DOCUMENT (to) (U. S.). To provide a vessel with the necessary papers required by law to establish ownership and nationality. In Great Britain called to register.

See **Certificate of Registry.**

According to the navigation laws of the United States, vessels engaged in foreign trade are given a certificate of registry. Coasting and fishing vessels if over 20 tons gross have a certificate of enrollment, and those with a tonnage ranging from 5 to 20 a license. Pleasure vessels of 16 tons or more sail under a license.

DODDLE NET. A dip net used by fishermen in the North Sea to dip fish out of a beam trawl when an unusually large catch has been made. Called also diddle-net.

DODGER. Canvas screens fitted at corners of the flying bridge to protect navigating officers from spray, wind, rain, and generally bad weather. Teak shelters are frequently constructed in their stead.

Fr: *Cagnard;* Ger: *Schutzkleid.*

DOG. 1. A handle used on hinged watertight doors to force the door frame against its gasket. It can be operated from both sides of the door. Also called snib. In Great Britain called clip.

Fr: *Tourniquet;* Ger: *Handhebel.*

2. A short iron bar with sharpened ends bent at right angles and pointed. The ends are driven into the built-up wooden keel blocks at the bottom of a dry dock to secure them together and to prevent them from floating. Also called dog iron.

Fr: *Crampe;* Ger: *Klammer.*

3. An iron implement used by shipwrights with a fang at one end and at the other an eye in which a rope may be fastened. It is used to haul objects. Another common form has a fang at each end.

Fr: *Renard;* Ger: *Balkhaken; Teufelsklaue.*

4. A piece of steel rod bent to somewhat less than a right angle, used for clamping down shapes or plates on the bending floor or slab when they are taken out of the furnace. Also called slab dog.

Fr: *Valet;* Ger: *Eisenbügel.*

See **Manhole Dog, Mooring Dog.**

DOG-BITCH THIMBLE. A contrivance by which the topsail sheet block was prevented from making a half turn in the clew, as often happened when the block was secured there.

DOGBODY. A transom-sterned New England boat, with cat schooner rig, much used until about 1820 for inshore fishing. It was gradually replaced by the pinky.

DOG BOLT. A bolt used in connection with a dog for holding a manhole cover, hatch cover, or inspection door in place.

Ger: *Klammerbolzen.*

See **Drop Bolt.**

DOG CURTAIN. A flap on a canvas binnacle cover which permits viewing the compass card.

DOGGER. A small vessel of about 150 tons formerly employed in the North Sea cod and herring fisheries. It was generally rigged with a main- and mizzenmast and resembled a ketch or galliot in hull form. (Now extinct.)

DOGGING. To whip together adjoining strands of a (fiber) rope after they have been unlaid and halved, a procedure adopted when putting an eye splice in a mooring line.

DOG IRON.

See **Dog.**

DOG'S EAR. One of the irregular-shaped corners of an awning formed by the openings to accommodate the masts and stays which pass through it.

DOGSHORE. Short timbers used for holding temporarily a small- or medium-sized vessel about to be launched, while keel blocks and shores are removed and until actual release takes place. Also called dagger. They consist of diagonal timbers, one on each side of the ways, abutting against projections (dog cleats) on the standing and on the sliding ways. Under each dogshore there is a small block or trigger. To release the vessel the triggers are removed and the dogshores knocked down by a falling weight.

Fr: *Clef de Berceau; Clef de Lancement;* Ger: *Schlittenständer.*

DOG-STOPPER. A stopper put on to enable the men to bitt the cable or to relieve the strain on the windlass. These stoppers are usually made of chain except in small craft, where a piece of rope is used with a stopper knot or an iron toggle and lanyard for lashing to the cable.

Fr: *Barbarasse;* Ger: *Kettenstopper.*

DOGU. A single outrigger dugout canoe from Palau Islands (Micronesia) similar in design to the *kotraol*. It is used for transportation between the islands of Peliliu and Ngeaur; also for fishing. The hull is strongly built for rough work.

DOG VANE. A light vane to show the direction of the wind, generally placed in the mizzen or aftershrouds. It is made of bunting in the shape of a conical bag or with a cork and feathers.

Fr: *Penon;* Ger: *Verkicker.*

DOG WATCH. One of the two two-hour watches between 4 and 8 P.M. The dog watches permit a shift in the order of the watch every 24 hours so that the same men will not have the same watch every night.

Fr: *Petit Quart;* Ger: *Plattfuss.*

DOLDRUMS. A belt of calms and light airs lying between the trade winds of the Northern and Southern Hemispheres. At the winter solstice its average northern limit is in five degrees north of latitude in the months about the summer solstice, 12 degrees north. The southern limit lies nearly always to the north of the equator, varying between 1 and 3 degrees north latitude.

Fr: *Calmes Equatoriaux; Pot au Noir;* Ger: *Stiller Gürtel; Doldrums; Aquatorialkalmen.*

DOLLIE. A small wrought-iron bollard about 6½ in. high fixed on the coping stone along the edge of a dock wall, used for the mooring lines of barges and other harbor craft.

DOLLOP. A sea that leaps over the bulwark rail and breaks on deck.

DOLLY. 1. A tool used by riveters which takes the place of the holding-on hammer used for hand-riveting. Also called dolly bar, hobby.

Fr: *Tas;* Ger: *Nietstöckchen; Gegenhalter.*

The spring dolly bar is made of a piece of 3-in. pipe about 12 in. long having at one end an ordinary cast-steel handle, while at the other there is a bushing through which a set screw holds the cup or snap. Inside the pipe there is a piece of round iron about 6 in. long backed by a spiral spring.

2. A tool used to turn or hold angles, tees, or similar bars in position while they are tack-welded, riveted, or fitted to other objects. It is provided with a plate head, slotted in two directions.

DOLPHIN. 1. A spar or block of wood made fast to an anchor, having a ringbolt at each end through which a hawser can be rove. Used for small craft to ride by.

2. A series of pudding fenders extending around an open boat just below the gunwale.

Fr: *Bourrelet;* Ger: *Taukranz.*

See **Fender.**

3. A mooring post or buffer placed at the entrance of a dock, alongside a wharf or in the middle of a stream. In the first and second instances it is used as a buffer. In the third it is used as a mooring post by vessels which discharge their cargoes without going alongside a dock or wharf. Each dolphin is generally composed of a series of heavy piles contiguous to each other. They are arranged in a circle, brought together and capped over the top.

Fr: *Duc d'Albe;* Ger: *Dukdalben.*

DOLPHIN-STRIKER. A short wood or iron spar which hangs down from the bowsprit cap to spread the martingale stays. Also called martingale boom. The boom usually ends in a spear on the lower end and is therefore known as dolphin-striker.

Fr: *Arc-Boutant de Martingale;* Ger: *Stampfstock.*

DOME. An isolated elevation of the sea bottom rising steeply but not coming within 100 fathoms of the surface.

Fr: *Dôme;* Ger: *Kuppel.*

DOMESTIC VOYAGE (U. S.). A voyage performed by a vessel engaged in the coasting trade on the northern, northeastern, and northwestern frontiers of the United States or any other coastwise trade, or in the intercoastal trade.

DONDEI. Generic term for dugout canoes from Minahassa and the Sangir-Talaud group (North Celebes). There are several varieties called *dondei blotto, dondei kalebat* and *dondei tumbilung*. The larger craft have double outriggers and are rigged with a mast and oblong rectangular sail. The smallest, used only in sheltered waters, have no outriggers.

DONEGAL YAWL.

See **Dronthiem.**

DONEY. A coaster from the east coast of India and Ceylon. Also called *doni, dhoni*. Length 70 to 100 ft. Breadth 20 to 21 ft. Depth 12 to 14 ft. The craft has a keel-less flat bottom. The fore- and afterbody are similar in form. The loaded draft is about 9 ft. The rig consists of one, two or three masts with lateen or gaff sails. Headsails are carried on a bowsprit with huge jibboom.

These vessels trade from Madras to Ceylon and the Gulf of Mannar.
See **Jaffna Doni, Kalla Doni, Shoe Doni.**

DONKEY BOILER. A small vertical or horizontal fire-tube boiler supplying steam to auxiliaries and heating plant in port when the fires are drawn from main boilers.
Fr: *Chaudière Auxiliaire;* Ger: *Hilfskessel; Donkeykessel.*

DONKEY ENGINE. A small reciprocating steam engine found in large sailing vessels, used for several subsidiary purposes such as working the windlass, hoisting sails, pumping water, handling cargo.
Fr: *Petit Cheval;* Ger: *Kleine Winde; Donkey.*

DONKEYMAN (G. B.). This term refers to the man in charge of a donkey boiler. (Except in American vessels.)
Fr: *Alimenteur;* Ger: *Donkeymann.*
See **Donkey Boiler.**

DONKEY PUMP. An additional steam pump which can be employed when the main engines are not working and which is so connected to the piping system that it can be used for feeding the donkey boiler, washing decks, removing water from the bilges, and also as fire pump. Also called Pony pump.
Fr: *Petit Cheval;* Ger: *Donkeypumpe.*

DONKEY'S BREAKFAST. In nautical slang, a straw mattress.

DONKEY TOPSAIL. A four-sided gaff-topsail the head of which is laced to a light spar named topsail yard extending beyond the masthead. Frequently used on small boats and hoisted above a balance lugsail. There may or may not be a jackyard in addition. Also called yard topsail, square-headed topsail, jack topsail, lug topsail.
Fr: *Flèche Carré;* Ger: *Raatoppsegel; Vierkanttoppsegel.*

DOOB. A two-mast, fore-and-aft schooner-rigged coasting vessel from the northern Black Sea. It is keel-built with round bilges, raking stem, bluff bow, and transom stern with outboard rudder. Length 99.5 ft. Breadth 32.6 ft. (Typical.)

DORMANT MESHES. The meshes between the norsels in a wall-pattern net.

DORNA. A Spanish fishing boat from Galicia with an over-all length of about 19½ ft. and 13 ft. at keel. It is decked forward. The afterpart is divided into two compartments; one for stowing nets and the other for the catch.

DORY. A small flat-bottomed open rowboat of American origin, chiefly used by fishermen for setting their trawl lines. Dories are often built with removable thwarts so that they can be nested or stowed within one another when not in use. Some fishing vessels carry as many as 20 of these boats on deck. They are lightly built so as to be easily lifted by the rope beckets fastened at bow and stern. Length over-all 19 ft. 3 in. Length of bottom 15 ft. Depth 28 in. Width at bottom 35 in. Width at gunwales 4 ft. 9 in. Weight 260 lb. Draft, light, 3½ in.; with 1,200 lb. 5 in.; with 1 ton, 14 in. Freeboard at 14 in. draft, 15 in. (Typical.)
Fr: *Doris;* Ger: *Dory.*
See **Dugout Dory.**

The dory is always rated according to the length of bottom, which varies from 15 to 18½ ft. in the New England type. The stem is straight or slightly rounded and the flat stern is of almost triangular shape pointing downward so that both ends are nearly sharp below water. The bottom is made of 3 or 4 planks of ⅞-in. pine with frames of 1-in. white oak and natural crook knees. The frames are not butted but extend almost across the entire bottom planking, and are cross-fastened together. The side planking, of white pine, is about ⅝ in. thick, in 3 wide strakes. Dories are sometimes rigged with a small spritsail.

Large sailing dories up to 40 ft. long were formerly used in the shore fisheries and were generally rigged with two masts and broad leg of-mutton sails, the forward one being the largest. These boats had a centerboard and though the bottom was flat, as in the bank dory, the sides were molded with some round or curve in section. They have been replaced by motorboats. Modified sailing dories of this type are still built for pleasure purposes.

DORY GAFF. An iron hook with a wooden handle for securing heavy fish, such as halibut, cod, haddock, and lifting them into a boat, generally a dory. Some have a thick and heavy handle made of hardwood so that it can also be used as a club to stun the fish. The hook is sometimes barbed like a fish hook.
Fr: *Gaffe; Gaffeau; Gaffion;* Ger: *Knocke.*

DORY HAND-LINER. Term used to denote fishing craft in which hand-lining is carried out from dories. New England dory hand-liners carry 12 to 14 dories of 13 ft. length.

DORY HAND-LINING. A method of hand-lining carried out from dories, one or two men going out in each dory. Two or three lines are operated by each man, the

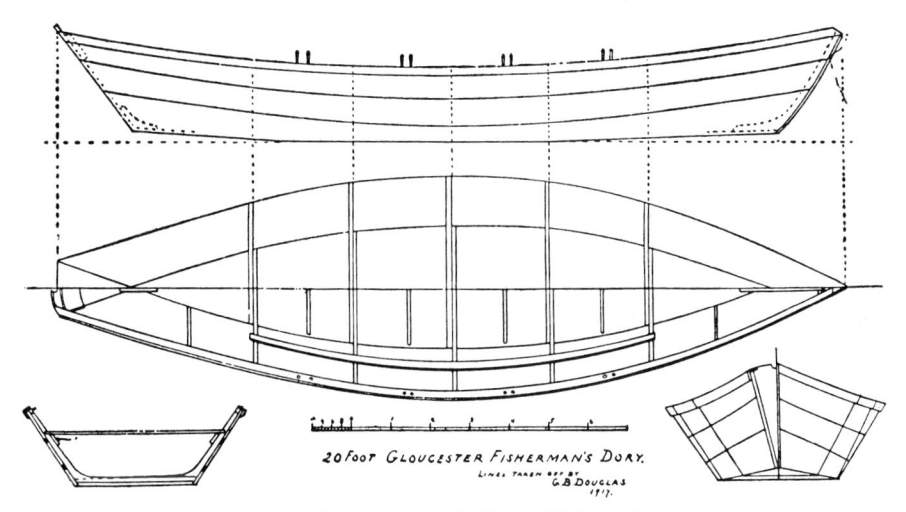

Dory. *(Courtesy The Rudder Publishing Co.)*

number being regulated by the depth of water, strength of tide, etc. It is carried in depths usually not exceeding 45 fathoms and, more generally, in depths ranging between 3 and 18 fathoms.

DORY KNIFE. A knife with a 5½-in. pointed blade used by the dorymen in the cod and halibut line fishery.

DORY ROLLER. Appliance fitted to dories engaged in the trawl-line fisheries. It consists of a wooden roller attached to the gunwale 3 or 4 feet from the stem. Its object is to aid in hauling the trawl lines which pass over it.

DORY TACKLE. A whip purchase with two single blocks used by trawl-line fishing vessels for hoisting or lowering their dories. On some craft the purchases are fastened to the fore and main rigging; on others the forward tackle is fastened to the after main shroud and the after one to the main boom topping lift. Still others have both tackles fastened to the crosstrees.

DORY TRAWLER. See **Liner 3**.

DOUBLE. 1. To sail round or pass beyond (a cape) so that the point of land separates the ship from her former position.

Fr: *Doubler;* Ger: *Dublieren.*

2. To cover a wooden ship with extra planking either internally or externally when through age or otherwise its planking joints have loosened.

Fr: *Doubler;* Ger: *Verdoppeln.*

DOUBLE ALTITUDE. A method used for establishing the position of a ship at sea, in which two altitudes of a celestial body are observed, with an interval of time between them. On applying the ship's run during the interval to the two position lines so obtained, the position of the ship is determined, but not accurately.

Fr: *Double Hauteur;* Ger: *Höhe mit Zwischenzeit.*

DOUBLE AND SINGLE FASTENING. A method of fastening outside planking to frames in which each plank has one wood and one metal fastening in every alternate frame and two wood and two metal fastenings in the other frames. Also called alternate fastening.

DOUBLE AWNING. In ships sailing through tropical waters double awnings are frequently spread. The second awning runs parallel to and above the first, about a foot higher.

DOUBLE BANK. 1. Of a rope: to clap men on both sides of it. 2. Of an oar: to set two men pulling one oar.

DOUBLE-BANKED. Said of a rowboat in which two opposite oars are pulled by rowers seated on the same thwart. Sailing launches, barges and cutters are double-banked.

Fr: *Armé en Couple;* Ger: *Doppelruderig.*

DOUBLE-BITT. To pass a mooring line

or cable around another bitt besides its own; also to give it more turns around the bitts than usual so that it will be more securely fastened.

Fr: *Doubler le tour de bitte;* Ger: *Betingschlag verdoppeln.*

DOUBLE BLACKWALL HITCH. A more secure form of blackwall hitch. Also called stunner hitch.

Fr: *Gueule de loup Double;* Ger: *Doppelter Hakenschlag; Doppelter Hollander.*

DOUBLE BLAST. A phonetic signal given by vessels under way when meeting and which means "I am directing my course to port."

DOUBLE BLOCK. A block having two sheaves.

Fr: *Poulie double;* Ger: *Zweischeibiger Block.*

DOUBLE BOLLARD. Bollard with two columns or posts extending upward from a common base.

Fr: *Bittes doubles;* Ger: *Doppelpoller.*
See cut p. 75.

DOUBLE BOTTOM. General term for all watertight spaces contained between the outside bottom plating, the tank top, and the margin plates. Also called water bottom. It extends transversely from bilge to bilge and longitudinally from forepeak to afterpeak tanks. The double bottom is subdivided into a number of compartments called "tanks," which may contain water ballast, oil fuel, boiler-feed water or drinking water according to requirements.

Fr: *Double Fond;* Ger: *Doppelboden.*
Adam, J. L., "Construction and Maintenance of Double Bottoms," Institution of Engineers and Shipbuilders in Scotland, *Transactions,* vol. 65 (1922).

DOUBLE-BOWED. Said of a vessel or boat when both extremities are built alike so that it is able to move in one direction or the opposite with equal facility and without being turned round. Also called double-ended.

Fr: *Amphidrôme;* Ger: *Doppelender.*

DOUBLE CANOE. A double-hulled craft consisting of two canoes of different sizes united by crossbeams or booms, on which a platform is constructed. The space between them varies from 4 to 7 ft. The mast and sail are fitted to the larger of the two canoes or hull. The fore-and-aft ends of the two boats forming the double canoe are usually decked over. While single canoes rarely exceed 30 ft. in length, the length of the double canoes ranges from 60 to 70 ft. with a breadth of 4 to 5 ft. amidships.

Fr: *Pirogue à Deux Corps;* Ger: *Doppelboot; Doppelkanu.*

Seagoing double canoes are still found in the Cook Islands (Polynesia) and in the southeast part of New Guinea (Melanesia). Double canoes are fairly common on rivers in Asia, where they are used as ferry boats.

DOUBLE CARD. A compass card graduated in degrees and quarter points. The degrees are on the periphery and the points just inside. It is the most generally used card on merchant vessels, yachts, fishermen, motorboats, etc.

DOUBLE CHAIN SLING. A chain sling used for handling short pipes and similar materials. The chains are passed around the draft one close to each end. Each hook is then caught around the standing part of the chain to which it is attached.

Fr: *Elingue en chaîne, double;* Ger: *Doppel Hakenkette.*

See **Chain sling.**

DOUBLE-CLEWED JIB. A jib with double sheets forming a combination of jib and flying jib; used on racing craft. The lower sheet hauls just abaft the mast, the upper one hauling right aft on to the taffrail. It is sometimes fitted with a club. The head of the sail reaches near the masthead. Called also quadrilateral jib, Greta Garbo.

Fr: *Foc à Double Écoutes.*

It is claimed that in this type of jib the air currents are speeded up on lee side of forestaysail and mainsail. It was first used by the yacht "Vigilant" in the America Cup Race of 1893.

DOUBLE-COMPOUND ENGINE. A reciprocating steam engine having 4 cylinders, 2 high-pressure and 2 low-pressure, working on a shaft having 4 cranks. The high-pressure cylinders work on the inner cranks and the low-pressure cylinders work on the outer cranks. The high-pressure cranks are set at right angles to each other and each low-pressure crank is set at 180° to the adjacent high-pressure crank, which makes it possible for the engine to start from any position without special starting gear.

DOUBLE CROWN. To finish the end of a rope by following the parts of the single crown a second time with the ends of the strands. Also called double crown knot.

Fr: *Tête d'Alouette Double;* Ger: *Türkischer Knoten.*

DOUBLE CURVED PLATE. A furnaced plate with transverse curvature in the fore and aft directions.
  Fr: *Tôle à double courbure;* Ger: *Doppelt gekrümmte Platte.*

DOUBLE DIAGONAL PLANKING. A system of planking used for small boats in which the inside and outside strakes run at an angle of 45 degrees the keel, each in the opposite direction.
  Fr: *Construction à doubles bordages croisés;* Ger: *Doppeldiagonal Beplankung.*

DOUBLE DIAMOND KNOT. A knot used at the upper end of a side or hand rope as an ornamental stopper knot.
  Fr: *Double Noeud de Hauban (Anglais);* *Double Noeud de Tireveille;* Ger: *Englischer Fallreepsknoten.*

DOUBLE-DORY FISHING. Expression used on the Atlantic Coast of the United States and Canada by trawl-line fishermen when each dory carries two men, as distinguished from single-dory fishing with one man to a dory.
  Double-dory fishing is the method used when fishing on the banks for fish that are to be dressed and salted on board the vessel. The other method of fishing, commonly known as shore fishing or fresh fishing, is used when a vessel is to be out only a short time and the fish, dressed and iced, is brought in fresh.

DOUBLE ENDED BOILER. A cylindrical fire-tube boiler with two sets of furnaces opening from either end of a shell of double length. It is equivalent to a pair of single-ended boilers placed back to back with back heads removed and shells joined.
  Fr: *Chaudière à double façade;* Ger: *Zweienderkessel; Doppelenderkessel.*

DOUBLE ENDER. (1) A boat built with sharp stern having nearly same lines as the bow. (2) See **Double bowed.**

DOUBLE-EXPANSION ENGINE. A reciprocating steam engine in which steam is supplied directly to the first or high pressure cylinder, where the first expansion takes place. Thence it exhausts into a cylinder of larger diameter, a low-pressure cylinder, in which it expands once more, after which it exhausts into the condenser. Also called compound engine

DOUBLE FASTENING. The fastening of planks in such a way that each strake of planking has two fastenings driven into each frame.
  Fr: *Chevillage Double;* Ger: *Doppelte Befestigung; Doppelte Verbolzung.*

DOUBLE FLUKED ANCHOR. An anchor with arms hinged or pivoted at the crown and so designed that both palms bite in the ground simultaneously.
  Fr: *Ancre articuleé;* Ger: *Anker mitbeweglichen armen.*

DOUBLE FORE-AND-AFT PLANKING. Outside planking laid in two layers, the seams of the inside planks corresponding to the centers of the outside planks and the whole, fastened together, making the skin practically one piece of wood. Thick paint or varnish is smeared between the two thicknesses. In small hulls the inner skin is covered with muslin or some other fabric laid in paint. The combined thickness of the two planks is slightly less than the normal thickness of single planking as the double planking offers greater resistance to longitudinal stresses.
  Double planking is of great advantage in sailing boats and powerboats on account of its strength. No calking is necessary. The chief objections to it are its cost, which is about 75 per cent higher than single planking, and the difficulty of repairing in the event of severe damage.

DOUBLE FUTTOCK. Timbers in the cant bodies extending from the deadwood to the run of the second futtock.
  Fr: *Allonge Double;* Ger: *Doppelte Auflanger.*

DOUBLE GAFF RIG. A combination of sails used on the aftermast of the large bark-rigged trading vessels. Two gaffs were fitted so that canvas on the mizzen or jigger mast could be shortened down with a minimum of labor when necessary while in light winds it provided plenty of sail area.
  Lyman, J., Double Gaff Rigs, The American Neptune, vol. 6, no. 1 (January, 1946).

DOUBLE LARK'S HEAD. A knot serving the same purpose as a lark's head but more secure.

DOUBLE LUFF TACKLE. A purchase composed of a treble and a double block, with the standing part fastened to the double block and the hauling part at the treble block.

DOUBLE-OUTRIGGER CANOE. A canoe with a float on each side, which is held out at a certain distance by a certain number of spars varying from 2 to 5, known as outrigger booms.

Fr: *Pirogue à Deux Balanciers;* Ger: *Doppel-Ausleger Kanu.*

According to Dr. Haddon, the double-outrigger with two booms occurs in craft in East Africa and Madagascar, and in the great majority of smaller Indonesian craft in New Guinea, and the Malay Archipelago. A double-outrigger with four booms is found on Waigu and neighboring islets, and with four or more booms, as far as Cape d'Urville. In Geelvink Bay the double-outrigger canoe predominates in the western part, and the single-outrigger in the eastern. The double-outrigger canoe is entirely absent from Oceania, except in the Nissan Islands. Double-outrigger canoes are also found in Torres Straights and North Queensland.

DOUBLE PADDLE. Paddle which has a blade at each end, used alternately on each side of canoe. Its length varies according to the beam of the canoe and is usually from 7 to 9½ ft.

Fr: *Pagaye-Double;* Ger: *Doppelpaddel.*

The double paddle is derived from the Eskimo type. Double paddles over 7 ft. long are usually cut in two and jointed by two brass tubes of different diameters, the smaller fitting tightly inside the larger. The object of this is for convenience of stowage when not in use and also to allow feathering when paddling against the wind. To feather, the blades are turned at right angles to each other so that the blade in the air will present only its edge to the wind.

DOUBLE PURCHASE. A tackle consisting of two single-sheaved blocks, the standing part being fastened to one of them.

Fr: *Palan à Deux Poulies simples;* Ger: *Doppelte Talje.*

DOUBLE SHEET BEND. A bend used for bending ropes together when they are not too large. The end of the bending line is passed *twice* around the standing line, and through its own part, giving added security. Also called double bend, double becket bend.

Fr: *Noeud d'écoute double;* Ger: *Doppelter Schotenstek.*

DOUBLE SPANISH BURTON. A tackle rove with one double and two single blocks. One of the single blocks is fastened to the hauling part of the double block.

Fr: *Bredindin Double;* Ger: *Wientakel.*

DOUBLE SPANKER.
See **Double Gaff Rig.**

DOUBLE-SPAN MOORINGS. A type of mooring similar to the span mooring but in which each end of the ground chain is fastened to a span with two anchors.

DOUBLE SPRIT.
See **Wishbone.**

DOUBLE TIDE. A double-headed tide, that is, a high water consisting of two maxima of nearly same height, separated by a relatively small depression; or a low water consisting of two minima, separated by a relatively small elevation. Also called agger. On the south coast of England the term "gulder" refers to double low water.

DOUBLE TOPSAILS. A rig in which the single topsail, as formerly carried on square-rigged vessels, is divided horizontally into two sails for ease and convenience of handling. In this rig an additional yard is carried, called the lower topsail yard, which is slung on the cap of the lower mast instead of being hoisted and lowered as in the single-topsail arrangement. The lower topsail has approximately the same area as a single topsail when close-reefed so that letting go the topsail halyards at once reduces the sail to a close reef, the clews of the upper topsail being lashed to the lower topsail yardarms. Moreover, the sails are of better dimensions for handling with small crews.

Fr: *Double Huniers;* Ger: *Doppelte Marssegel.*

The clipper ship "Great Republic," built in 1853, was one of the first vessels in the United States to have double topsails. British ships had them about 1865 and began rigging their vessels with double topgallants in the early seventies.

DOUBLE VEE WELD. A butt weld with fusion faces beveled from both surfaces so as to form two V-shaped welds.

Fr: *Soudure en "X";* Ger: *"X" Schweissung.*

DOUBLE WALL AND CROWN KNOT. A double wall knot with double crown. It is used for the end of manropes, stoppers, gangway stanchion lines, and so on.

Fr: *Cul de Porc double et tête d'Alouette;* Ger: *Doppelter Fallreepsknoten.*

DOUBLE WALL KNOT. Made from a wall knot and used as a stopper to prevent a rope from unreeving. It is formed by allowing each strand again to follow its lead as given in a single wall knot. Also called stopper knot.

Fr: *Cul de Porc Double;* Ger: *Doppelter Schauermannsknoten.*

DOUBLE-WAY LAUNCHING. A method

of end launching in which a track consisting of two standing ways spaced about one-third of the vessel's breadth is built under the ship, and for some distance out under water. Sliding ways are placed on the track and upon these a cradle is built supporting the vessel to be launched. By wedging up the cradle the weight of the ship is transferred to the ways, which allows the keel-blocks and building blocks to be removed. The launching grease placed between the standing and sliding ways decreases frictional resistance, after which the inclination of the ways is sufficient when combined with the force of gravity to move the vessel when the cradle is released. Also called two-way launching.

Fr: *Lancement sur Flancs;* *Lancement sur Double Coulisse;* Ger: *Stapellauf mit Seitenschlitten.*

DOUBLE WHARFAGE (U. S.). Double the amount of the usual charge for the use of a wharf, recoverable by law when a vessel leaves without paying wharfage.

DOUBLE WHIP. A purchase comprising two single blocks, one movable and the other fixed, the standing part made fast to the movable block. It increases the power fivefold. Also called double purchase, gun tackle.

Fr: *Cartahu Double;* Ger: *Doppelte Steertalje; Doppeltes Jollentau.*

DOUBLE-WHIP SYSTEM. A method of working cargo in which two booms and two winches are employed, one boom extending over the hatchway, the other over the pier or lighter lying alongside. In loading, the draft is taken from the pier by the fall of the outboard boom. It is landed on deck where the cargo hook is released and thrown back on the pier. The second or hatch fall is then hooked to the draft, which is lifted clear of the hatch coaming and lowered into the hold. In discharging, the movements are reversed. Also called split-fall system.

DOUBLING. 1. The doubled edge or skirt of a sail.

Fr: *Renfort; Placard;* Ger: *Lappung.*

2. A second thickness of planking or plating covering a surface, particularly part of a deck or outside shell of a vessel. A covering of wood applied to the underwater parts of iron or steel vessels to prevent corrosion and to inhibit fouling of the bottom.

Fr: *Doublage; Soufflage;* Ger: *Doppelhaut.*

3. The part of a mast included between trestletrees and cap, or that part where the heel of an upper mast overlaps the lower one.

Fr: *Ton;* Ger: *Doppelung.*

See **Bow Doubling.**

A. Cap
B. Peak Halliards Block
C. Throat Halliards Block
D. Bolster
E. Topping Lift
F. Runner Pendant
G. Jib Halliards
H. Mast Rope
I. Fid
J. Crosstrees
K. Yoke
L. Mast Cheek
M. Fore Stay
N. Lower Mast
O. Topmast

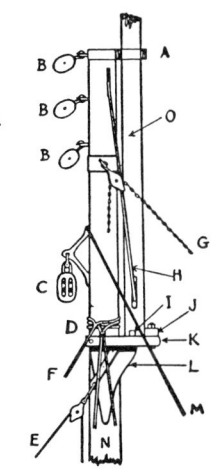

Doubling

DORY SKIFF. Open boat of dory type with transom stern. Length 10 to 15 ft.

DOUBLING PLATE. An additional plate fitted inside or outside of another as a reinforcement or where excessive wear is expected.

Fr: *Tôle Doublante;* Ger: *Doppelungsplatte.*

DOUBLING PREVENTER CLAMP. A clamp consisting of a flat plate which lies athwartship on the top of a masthead and is held down by two stout rods. Its function is to hold the heel of the topmast or topgallant mast and the head of the mast next below together at the doublings.

DOUGLAS FIR. A wood of tough and elastic nature which can be used for all woodwork in a wooden hull, with the exception of rudder stock and treenails. Also used for decking and joiner work on steel ships. It is suitable for solid spars, as it can be obtained in long lengths clear of knots. Weight when seasoned 30 to 35 lbs. per cu. ft. Also called Oregon pine.

Fr: *Pin d'Oregon;* Ger: *Oregon Fichtenholz.*

DOUGLAS SCALE. A scale for denoting the condition of waves and swell recommended for international use at the International Meteorological Conference of Copenhagen in 1929.

State of Sea	Swell
0 Calm	0 No swell
1 Smooth	1 Low swell (short or average length)
2 Slight	2 Low swell (long)
3 Moderate	3 Moderate swell (short)
4 Rough	4 Moderate swell (average length)
5 Very rough	5 Moderate swell (long)
6 High	6 Heavy swell (short)
7 Very high	7 Heavy swell (average length)
8 Precipitous	8 Heavy swell (long)
9 Confused	9 Confused swell

DOUSE. 1. To strike, take in or lower in haste, as a sail or a mast. **2.** To slacken suddenly as a rope.

DOVETAIL PLATE. Small plates of gun metal let in the heel of a wooden sternpost and keel, on each side, to bind them together. The top fastenings are in the post; the bottom fastenings in the keel. Similar plates are used for joining stem and gripe. Also called fishtail plate.

Fr: *Etrier;* Ger: *Schwalbenschwanzplatte; Stevenbeschlag.*

DOWEL. A cylindrical piece of hardwood of suitable diameter and length, used for additional security in joining two pieces of timber together to prevent them from slipping. Also called cog, coak.

Fr: *Dé; Clef;* Ger: *Nuss; Dubel; Zylinderzapfen.*

See **Deck Dowel.**

DOWN. A mound, hill, or ridge or drifted sand heaped up by the wind on the seacoast. Also called dune.

Fr: *Dunes;* Ger: *Sanddüne.*

DOWNCAST VENTILATOR. A ventilator by which fresh air is taken to the different compartments of the ship when natural ventilation is adopted.

Fr: *Manche d'Aspiration;* Ger: *Saugelüfter; Einziehender Lüfter.*

DOWN EASTER. A type of sailing ship which was built in New England shipyards after 1869 for the American intercoastal trade. They were fast ships although of fuller lines and better carrying capacity than the clippers. All but the last ones were built of timber. They were mostly full-rigged ships. The earlier ones carried passengers. Although built for the California grain trade, a number of them during the late nineties were engaged in the Hawaiian sugar trade from Honolulu to East Coast ports.

Lubbock, B., *The Down Easters,* Boston, 1929.

DOWNHAUL. A rope by which a sail is hauled down when it may not be trusted to come down by its own weight.

Fr: *Halebas;* Ger: *Niederholer.*

Downhauls are named after the sail they serve. A staysail or jib downhaul is secured to the head cringle of the sail, and leads then through the hanks and a leading block to the deck. A spanker or trysail downhaul is made fast to the upper aftercorner of the sail, and leads thence through a block at the jaws of the gaff to the deck. A gafftopsail downhaul (and clew line) is made fast to the clew and leads thence through a block at the head to the deck.

DOWN THE WIND. The reverse of in or by the wind: that is to say, in the same direction the wind is blowing. Along the course of the wind.

Ger: *Mit dem Winde.*

DOWNSTREAM. In the direction in which the current is flowing.

Ger: *Stromabwärts.*

DOWNTON PUMP. A hand pump, which is also a force pump, worked by cranks on each side of the pump chamber. It is arranged to draw from all compartments and from the sea, and to discharge either overboard or to the fire main. When the suction lift exceeds 24 ft., an extension piece is fitted above the pump chamber so that the latter may be within 24 ft. of the rose box.

Fr: *Pompe Downton;* Ger: **Downton Pumpe.**

DOWSING CHOCK. A piece of timber fayed across the apron and lapped in the knightheads, or inside planking above the upper deck. Also dousing chock.

Fr: *Guirlande d'Ecubiers;* Ger: *Klusenband.*

DOWELING. A method of coaking using round pieces of hardwood instead of oblong pieces, one-half of the dowels being let into each of the faying surfaces.

Fr: *Assemblàge à Dé;* Ger: *Verdubeln; Verzapfen.*

DRABLER, DRABBLER. A small additional sail laced to the foot of a bonnet on the square sail of a sloop or schooner or to a jib to give it more drop.

Fr: *Bonnette de Sous Gui;* Ger: *Unterbonnett.*

DRAFT. 1. A sailmaker's term denoting the parabolic curve given to a fore-and-aft sail by roaching. Draft is considered advantageous when sailing in light airs, but flat

sails are said to be better with stronger winds.
Fr: *Rond;* Ger: *Rundung.*
2. See **Sling.**
3. Also draught. The depth of water which a ship requires to float freely. The depth of a vessel below the waterline, measured vertically to the lowest part of the hull, propellers or other reference points.
Fr: *Le Tirant d'Eau;* Ger: *Tiefgang.*
See **Bar Draft, Critical Docking Draft, Extreme Draft, Light Draft, Loaded Draft, Mean Draft, Molded Draft.**

In ship design draft is relatively inexpensive from the weight standpoint as compared with length or beam. Larger draft involves increase in the depth of the strength girder, which in turn makes for a lowering of the longitudinal stresses in the ship's structure. Maximum draft means maximum beam and reasonable coefficients of form and reasonable value of useful load. It is, however, important to bear in mind the fact that harbors to which vessels drawing more than 25 to 26 ft. have ready access are comparatively limited in number.

DRAFT GAUGE. An instrument consisting of a hydrostatic gauge placed in the ship forward or aft in a convenient position against the ship's side below the level of the light load-line, fitted with a sea cock. After calibration, the rise and fall of mercury or water in the gauge indicates the ship's draft. Also called draft indicator, internal draft gauge.
Fr: *Indicateur de Tirant d'Eau;* Ger: *Tiefgangsanzeiger.*

DRAFT MARKS. Also draught marks. External marks either cut into each side of the stem and sternpost, or formed of cast-metal figures attached by screws, so that the ship's draft can be ascertained from without.
Fr: *Echelle de Tirants d'Eau; Piétage;* Ger: *Tiefgangsmarken; Tiefgangsskala; Ahming.*

The height of the figures or letters must not be less than 6 in., and they are painted a contrasting color for visibility. The bottom of any draft figure is placed in coincidence with the waterline that the draft figure is intended to indicate. Draft marks are usually only single numerals corresponding to the right-hand or unit's digit of the number representing the draft.

DRAG. The force which acts on the immersed surface of a rudder blade in a direction perpendicular to the ship's motion when the rudder is put over.
Ger: *Ruderdruckkomponente.*

DRAG (to). To drag anchor. To draw or trail it along the bottom when it will not hold.
Fr: *Chasser;* Ger: *Vor Anker treiben.*

DRAG. One of the components of the force which acts on the rudder in a direction perpendicular to that of the ship's travel.

DRAG BOAT.
See **Dragging.**

DRAG CHAINS. Chains used in the launching of ships where the breadth of river or water area is limited, and it is desired to restrict the movement of the vessel as it enters the water. It consists of several groups of chains coiled and resting in heaps on the bottom of the shipway. One end of each heap is connected by a wire to an eye plate riveted or welded to the ship's shell plating. Each group comes into play gradually so as to make the tendency to arrest the vessel's motion progressive.
Fr: *Chaînes de Retenue;* Ger: *Bremsketten.*

DRAGGER. A generic term used on the Atlantic Coast of the United States to denote small otter trawlers of various types and sizes, which engage in the shore fisheries, usually within 50 miles of the coast line. They are nowadays all motor-propelled and equipped with trawl winches geared to the main engines. They usually work their trawl from the starboard side. The smallest boats are about 40 ft. long and carry a crew of 3. The largest, which are 90 ft. long and manned by 8 men, are occasionally able to fish offshore.

DRAGGING (U. S.). 1. Term used by New England fishermen to mean working with gill nets set from the bow of a boat instead of anchoring the nets and leaving them unattended overnight. The vessels are called drag-boats.
See **Drifting.**
2. See **Trawling.**

DRAG LINK. A name given to the connecting rods by which the motion of the dummy rudderhead is transmitted to the rudder crosshead.
Fr: *Tireveille;* Ger: *Ruderlenkstange.*
See **Dummy Crosshead.**

DRAG SEINE. A seine worked from a small boat in shallow waters. The wings are attached to spars.

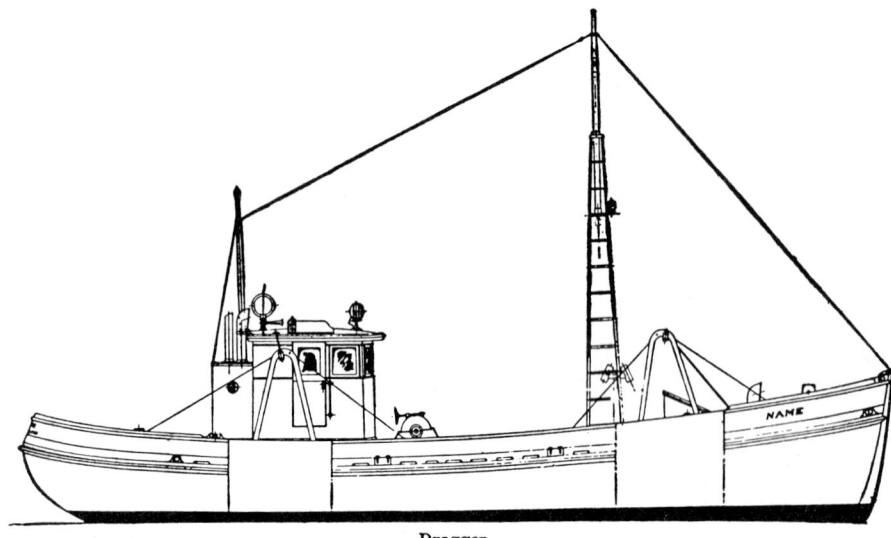

Dragger

DRAG SURFACE. The forward surface of a propeller blade. It is usually rounded to insure sufficient thickness and to give the necessary strength to the blade. Also called back.
Fr: *Face Antérieure;* Ger: *Vorderfläche.*
DRAI. A bark canoe used by the Olltscha and Goldi tribes of lower Amur River. It is comparatively deep and narrow and usually decked over with bark for a short distance at each end. Length 18½ ft. Breadth 2½ ft. Depth 11 in. (Typical.)
DRAINAGE PUMP.
See **Stripping Pump.**
DRAIN BOLT.
See **Docking Plug.**
DRAIN HAT.
See **Drain Pot.**
DRAIN HOLE. 1. A small hole from 1 to 2¼ in. in diameter, pierced in the garboard strake of the shell plating and located in the afterpart of each double-bottom tank, hold, or pump well. It is fitted with a brass screwed plug and when the ship is in dry dock is used for removing all water which the pumps have been unable to clear. Also called bleeder hole.
Fr: *Nable;* Ger: *Bodenventil; Wasserablassloch.*
See **Drain Bolt, Docking Plug.**
2. One of the small holes or slits about 1 in. deep punched through the floor plate and frame bar of a ballast tank, just above the concrete ballast. Its function is to assist drainage. Also called drain slit, drainage hole.
Fr: *Anguiller;* Ger: *Spülloch; Wasserlaufloch.*
DRAIN POT. One of the small receptacles, shaped like an inverted top hat and about twice that size; fitted to the tank top for the purpose of freeing hold spaces of water without detriment to the completeness of the watertight inner bottom. Drain pots are fitted in vessels where the tank top is carried right out to the shell without forming a gutterway. Also called drain hat, hat box, bilge hat.
Fr: *Puisard;* Ger: *Saugnapf.*
DRAISSA. A rowboat used in Malta for harbor work. It has a small deck at each end. A high stem which looks like the blade of a scimitar rises well above the gunwale. Above the gunwale is a portable wash strake formed of several panels. Also called *dghaisa.*
DRAISSA-TAL-PASS. A two-mast sprit-rigged boat decked at ends, used for transportation of goods between the Island of Gozo and Malta. The hull is built with high stem, typical in these waters, and deep wash strake on each side. Also called *dghaisa-tal-pass,* Gozo boat. Length 36 ft. Breadth 12 ft. Depth 3.5 ft. (Typical.)
DRAW. 1. To sink to a specified depth in floating. A ship draws so many feet of

water, according to the depth of her immersed body.
Fr: *Caler;* Ger: *Ziehen.*
See **Draft.**
2. A term applied when the wind pressure on a sail puts a strain on the sheet. A sail is said to draw when properly trimmed and filled with wind.
Fr: *Porter;* Ger: *Tragen.*

DRAWBACK. Money refunded by the customs upon the re-exportation of import goods on which duty had been levied. The goods may be re-exported either in the same or in a different form from which they were imported. The claim or drawback entry must be presented to the customs before the goods are shipped.
Fr: *Décharge d'Exportation;* Ger: *Zollvergütung; Rückzoll; Export Bonifikation.*

DRAW BUCKET. A small bucket with sides made of heavy canvas and wooden bottom. The top and bottom rims are strengthened by rope grommets. The bail is spliced to the top grommet and is provided with an eye for fastening the bucket rope. Used for taking sea water temperatures.

DRAWING SPLICE. A splice for joining two heavy fiber ropes together. It is formed by unlaying several fathoms on each end, then placing them together and forming a short splice, then leaving about one fathom of each strand and reducing the remainder of each by cutting away some of the yarns to taper them; then the end of each strand is neatly pointed and laid along taut in the lines of the rope and secured by quarter, middle, and end seizings. It is termed a drawing splice because it can easily be taken apart.

DRAWING STRING. A rope which runs along the leech of gaff-foresails, mainsails and jibs, being spliced into the head cringle and leading down through the space in the tabling between the bolt rope and the sewing of the seam. It then leads out through an eyelet hole at the clew and on the mainsail leads through a small lead block and makes fast on the boom. On the foresail and boom it makes fast in the clew cringle. It is used to strengthen the leech and prevent that part of the sail from flapping when the leech is too slackly roped or when the body of the sail has shrunk through dampness.

DRAW ROPE. A running line around the cod end of a trawl net by which it is hove aboard. The slip knot at the extreme end when cast off opens the cod end and allows the fish to fall on deck. Also called bull rope, cod line, cod-end rope, G string.
Fr: *Raban de Sac;* Ger: *Reihleine; Cotleine.*

DREADING. A chartering term which means that at loading port the charterers are given the option of shipping general cargo, charterers paying all expenses over and above a bulk cargo at loading port: freight to be equivalent to what it would be with a full bulk cargo. Also called dreadage.

DREADING AT BOTH ENDS. Same as above when applying to the port of discharge as well as to loading port.

DREDGE, DREDGER. A vessel or floating structure equipped with excavating machinery, employed in deepening channels and harbors, and removing submarine obstructions such as shoals and bars. The hull of dredgers is of ship-shape or pontoon-shape. The former is usually used for self-propelled, seagoing dredges, while the latter is used only for the stationary non-propelled craft.

The rule that dredges engaged in work in furtherance of navigation are *vessels* within the meaning of maritime law is sustained by an overwhelming weight of authority.
Fr: *Drague;* Ger: *Bagger.*

See **Bucket Dredge, Compound Dredge, Dipper Dredge, Grab Dredge, Hopper Dredge, Oyster Dredge, Suction Dredge.**

Dekker, P. M., *Dredges and Dredging Appliances,* London, 1927; Paulman-Blaum, *Die Bagger,* Berlin, 1923; Prelini, C., *Dredges and Dredging,* London, 1911; Shankland, E. C., *Dredging of Harbours and Rivers,* London, 1931.

DREDGED BERTH. A berth alongside a wharf or dock or in a tidal river, which has been dredged to a sufficient depth to enable vessels to remain afloat at all states of the tide.
Fr: *Souille; Fosse;* Ger: *Vertiefung.*

DREENINGS.
See **Slumgullion.**

DREEVER. A local type of herring boat from Kinsale County, Ireland.

DREISONSTOK NAVIGATIONAL METHOD (H. O. 208). A method devised by Captain Dreisonstok of the United

States Navy, used for solving the astronomical triangle rapidly. It provides a quick and easy solution for determining: (1) a line of position; (2) the compass error; (3) meridian altitude; (4) reduction to the meridian; (5) identification of an unknown star; (6) great circle course and distance. The solution is applicable to any celestial body regardless of its position or the latitude of the observer. The method should not be used for altitudes above 75 degrees. U. S. Hydrographic Office, Washington, Publication 208.

DRESSED FULL. Said of a ship when, in addition to the national flag aft and on the main masthead, signal flags and pennants are used to decorate the ship and are strung on a taut line.

Fr: *Grand Pavois;* Ger: **Grosse Flaggengala.**

DRESSED FULL WITH UP AND DOWN FLAGS. Sailing merchant vessels frequently dressed ship by arranging the lines of flags on each mast from the masthead to the water following the extremities of the yardarms on each side.

Fr: *Grand Pavois Transversal;* Ger: *Ausflaggen über Masttoppen und Raanocken.*

DRESSED RAINBOW FASHION. To full-dress ship all the flags of the International Code of Signals are hoisted. On naval vessels the naval signal code flags are hoisted as well. Normally, these flags are arranged in a line from the stem up along the line of the stays, then between mastheads, down to the stern. In addition the national colors are hoisted at masthead, and the jack forward. In sailing vessels the flags were arranged in a line from the water's edge by means of weighted lines at bow and stern.

Fr: *Grand Pavois Longitudinal; Grand Pavois à l'Anglaise.*

DRESSED WITH MASTHEAD FLAGS. Dressing ship in its simplest form, which consists of having the national colors at the mastheads and at the peak or head of spanker gaff or color staff and hoisting the jack on its own staff in the bow.

Fr: *Petit Pavois;* Ger: *Kleine Flaggengala; Toppflaggen.*

DRESS GANG. A team of men employed in the deep-sea fisheries for dressing the fish on deck immediately after its capture. In the cod fisheries it is usually made up of a throater, a header, a splitter, and a skinner.

DRESSING LINE. Lines leading from the stem over the topmasts and down to the stern of a ship, to which flags are attached for dressing ship.

Fr: *Cartahu de Pavois;* Ger: *Flaggejolltau.*

DRESS SHIP. To ornament a ship with flags. It is usually carried out on national holidays, on the occasion of some particular celebration, in honor of some distinguished person, or as a mark of courtesy towards foreign nation when its own ships are dressed. Should the dressing be a courtesy to a foreign government the colors of that nation are hoisted at the mainmast head. No national colors are used in dressing a ship except at masthead. In steamships the house flag is generally flown on the mainmast and the national flag on the foremast.

Fr: *Pavoiser;* Ger: *Ausflaggen.*

DRIED FISH. Dried fish are usually first salt-cured, although sometimes they are dried directly. Many different processes are in use for drying fish but that most generally used is as follows: after being cleaned and split the fishes are salted either with dry salt or in brine vats, where they remain until ready for market. They are then dried in the sun, care being taken to prevent overlong exposure to strong sunlight.

Fr: *Poisson Séché;* Ger: *Getrockneter Fisch.*

DRIFT. 1. The speed at which a current runs.

Fr: *Dérive du Courant; Force d'un Courant;* Ger: *Driftstromung; Driftfahrt; Stromversetzung; Abdrift.*

2. The length of a rope from a point where it is made fast whether stretching to another point or fastening, remaining loose or coiled as an extra length, or running from the standing block to the running block of a tackle. The distance that a tackle will reach from its fixed point.

3. The difference in diameter between the size of a bolt or treenail and the hole into which it is to be driven. Also that between the circumference of a mast hoop and the circumference of the mast on which it is to slide.

Fr: *Hale;* Ger: *Drift.*

4. A place where the sheer of the upper works is raised and the rails or the sides of a superstructure are cut off and ended with a scroll, as for instance at the break of a raised deck or in small craft at the break of a cabin trunk. Also called drift piece.

Fr: *Rabattue;* Ger: *Unterbrochener Gang.*

5. A smooth tapered pin for stretching rivet-holes that are not fair and bringing them into alignment. Also called drift pin.

Fr: *Broche;* Ger: *Lochraumer; Dorn.*

6. A long punch used for backing out other bolts.

Fr: *Repoussoir;* Ger: *Durchschlag.*

7. The distance that rivet holes are out of line.

8. See **Driftbolt.**

DRIFT ANGLE. The angle between a tangent to the circular path of the center of gravity of a vessel when turning under the influence of the rudder, and the central longitudinal line of the vessel.

Fr: *Angle de Dérive;* Ger: *Derivationswinkel.*

DRIFT BOAT. Generally a boat for fishing with drift nets. Also called drifter, drift fisher.

See **Herring Drifter, Logger.**

DRIFTBOLT. A type of fastening used in boatbuilding. It has a washer or clench ring and upset head on the exposed end, and is slightly pointed on the other. Also called drift.

Ger: *Spannagel.*

Driftbolts are always driven obliquely (canted) to the seam they fasten and are used on keels, deadwoods, rudders, centerboards and similar places where there is ample wood and clinch bolts cannot be used or are unnecessary.

They are made of galvanized wrought iron or steel rod, cut to the required length with a hacksaw. The point is then tapered on an anvil, cold, with a hammer.

DRIFT BOTTLE. A sealed bottle put overboard at a fixed position for the purpose of ascertaining the general drift of ocean currents.

Fr: *Bouteille Flottante;* Ger: *Treibflasche; Flaschenpost.*

DRIFT CAPSTAN. A steam capstan used for hauling in the gear on fishing vessels, where deck space is limited. It consists of a central tube or shaft secured to the deck on a base plate and carrying the engine bedplate on the top. The central tube, steam and exhaust pipes and engine are fixed, while the capstan barrel connected by suitable gearing revolves around this tube. Differential gear is used for speed reduction as required and handgear is provided in case of breakdown or lack of steam. This type of capstan provides clear deck space all around the apparatus and the machinery is clear of running rigging and ropes.

DRIFT CURRENT. A slow-moving ocean current. Term especially applied to the continuations of the Gulf Stream as it branches on leaving the American Continent to proceed across the Atlantic Ocean, and also to continuations of the Kuroshiwo as it crosses the Pacific Ocean.

Fr: *Courant de Dérive;* Ger: *Triftströmung; Driftströmung.*

DRIFT HOOP.

See **Mast Hoop.**

DRIFT ICE. Loose, very open pack, or unattached pieces of floating ice where water preponderates over ice. Such ice is navigable with ease. Also called sailing ice.

Fr: *Glace Dérivante;* Ger: *Treibeis.*

DRIFTING. The process of enlarging punch holes and removing burrs with a tapered steel tool (drift). A drift is also used to drive out rivets.

See **Drift-Net Fishing.**

DRIFT LEAD. A heavy (80 lb.) lead used when a vessel is riding at anchor to a heavy wind, sea or current, to indicate whether the anchor is holding or dragging. Such indications are given by observing the direction of the line leading from the ship to the lead, which is on the bottom.

DRIFT LINE. Fishing line used for the capture of pollack and conger. It is a single-hook line without sinker, which is allowed to drift out from an anchored boat.

DRIFT-LINE FISHING. A method of hand-lining in which leads are placed at regular intervals as sinkers, usually two fathoms apart. Drift lines are occasionally used entirely without leads at the stern of a boat and sometimes with a cork float.

Fr: *Pêche aux Lignes Courantes;* Ger: *Schleppleine Fischerei; Treibangel Fischerei.*

DRIFT NET. A general term for all gill nets which are not fixed to the bottom but are attached to a boat or a series of buoys, and are allowed to drift with the tide or wind between the surface and the bottom of the sea. The fish swimming in shoals or schools strike against the nets and are entangled by their gills in the meshes. The drift net is essentially a completely sub-

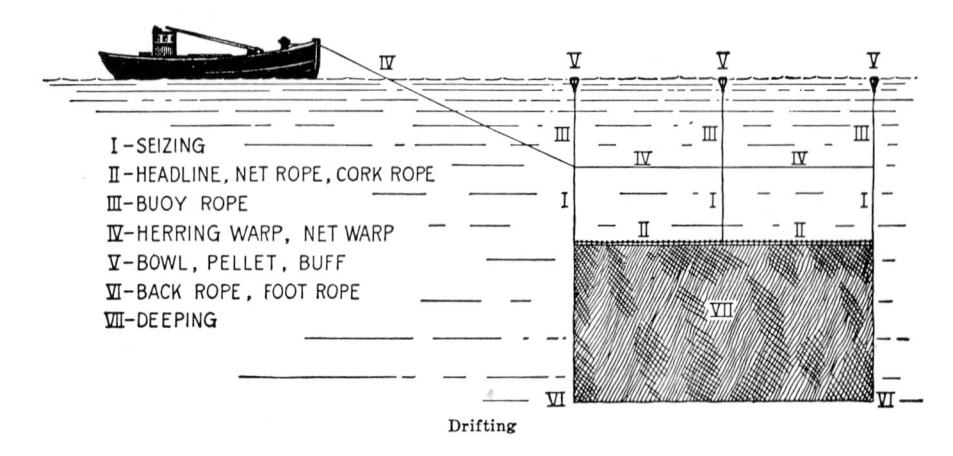

I—SEIZING
II—HEADLINE, NET ROPE, CORK ROPE
III—BUOY ROPE
IV—HERRING WARP, NET WARP
V—BOWL, PELLET, BUFF
VI—BACK ROPE, FOOT ROPE
VII—DEEPING

Drifting

merged curtain of netting one end of which is attached to a boat called a drifter.

Fr: *Filet Dérivant;* Ger: *Treibnetz; Schwimmnetz.*

The size of the meshes vary according to the specie of fish which has to be captured. The average number of *meshes* to the yard may be taken as follows:

Large herring nets....29–35 meshes
Small   "   " 36   "
Mackerel nets 25–39   "
Pilchard   " 36–38   "
Sprat   " 62–66   "

The majority of gill nets are used for the capture of pelagic fish such as the herring, pilchard, mackerel, and sprat. They are either fished for on, or sunk beneath the water surface. The larger fleets of drift nets, such as pilchard herring and mackerel nets, are usually worked with warps since the headlines alone would not be sufficient to stand the strain.

DRIFT-NET FISHING. A method of fishing with nets not drawn through the water but allowed to drift or drive with the tide, in a more or less perpendicular position. Also called drifting, dragging.

Fr: *Pêche aux Filets Dérivants;* Ger: *Treibnetzfischerei.*

When fishing, sailing drifters take up a position stern-on to the tide, steamboats drift with stem to windward. The nets are always laid out over the bow, connected up in line, and carried by the tide until they form one long line, one end of which is attached to the boat. The position of the nets is indicated by the line of bladder floats. The fish swim against the nets, push their heads through and then, owing to their gills opening, find that they cannot withdraw their heads and in this way are caught in large numbers.

DRIFT PIECE. One of the curved pieces of timber connecting the plank-sheen to the gunwale. (obsolete.)

DRIFT PIN.
See **Drift.**

DRIFT RAIL. The rails of the poop-deck, quarter deck and forecastle which ended with a scroll at the break. (Obsolete.)

Fr: *Lisse de Rabattue;* Ger: *Zerbrochene Gangreling.*

DRIFT SAIL. A sail attached to a hawser, thrown overboard, and veered ahead so as to act as a drag or sea anchor and keep the ship's head to the sea in heavy weather.

DRIFT SEINE. A small, North Sea seine, in which the ends are kept apart by a floating spar or by small otter boards. The bag is valved by a funnel of netting. When in use it drifts with the tide or current.

DRILL. The act of training the ship's company in some particular duty by repeated exercises. The date, time, and other particulars of each drill are entered in the log book.

Fr: *Manoeuvre; Exercice;* Ger: *Übung; Rollenmanöver.*

See **Boat Drill, Collision Drill, Fire Drill.**

DRILLER. A shipyard worker who operates a portable power-driven drill, breast drill, or ratchet drill. Also called reamer, and in Great Britain, rimer. His duties are to drill holes where it is not convenient or possible to punch or drill before erection. Drillers also ream out, countersink, and tap

rivet holes wherever necessary.
Fr: *Perceur;* Ger: *Bohrer.*

DRIP PAN.
See **Save All.**

DRIVE. A term used in marine practice to designate the means or system by which the power generated in the prime mover is transmitted to the main or propeller shafting.
See **Direct Drive, Electric Drive, Geared Drive.**

DRIVE (to). To be moved to leeward by the force of the wind without control of the vessel's motion.
Fr: *Être Drossé; Être Dépalé;* Ger: *Abtreiben.*

DRIVE BOAT.
See **Striker Boat.**

DRIVER. The fifth mast from forward on a six-masted schooner. The fore-and-aft sail set abaft the spanker mast.
Ger: *Besanmast; Besan.*

DRIVEUR. A flat-bottom centerboard sailing boat of from 3 to 5 tons used for collecting spat on the natural mussel beds in the Bay of Biscay near La Rochelle.

DRIVING MALLET.
See **Setting Maul.**

DRIVING PUNCH. A heavy type of roove punch with which timber and plank fastenings within arm's reach can be rooved and clenched by one man. Also called heavy punch.
See **Backing-out Punch, Nail Punch, Rove Punch.**

DRIVING SAIL. A general term for all sails in which the vertical component due to the pressure of wind acts in a downward direction. Gaff sails, for instance, have a downward or depressing component.

DRIVING SHORE. A contrivance used when launching a small vessel to initiate her motion down the ways. It consists of a heavy timber abutting diagonally against the stem, under which wedges are driven with sledges or with a battering ram in an effort to raise the ship's head.
Fr: *Arc-Boutant de Chasse;* Ger: *Schlagständer.*

DRIVKVASE. A Danish shallow-draft boat employed in the eel fisheries of the Little Belt. The design corresponds to the "Quase" (see reference). It has curved stem and sternpost, low floor, round bilge, full lines at bow and stern. The ends are decked and there are wide washboards along the sides, thus leaving an oblong space amidships in which is the well. Length over-all 24 ft. Beam 8 ft. 3 in. Depth 2 ft. 9 in. Length of open space 7 ft. 9 in. Width 4 ft. 6 in. (Typical.)

The *drivkvase* is rigged with two pole masts, a mainmast stepped about one-third the boat's length from the stem; a mizzenmast close to the stern; and a standing bowsprit. It carries two headsails, loose-footed gaff-mainsail and standing-lug mizzen with boom. The mizzen is sheeted to an outrigger, which also serves to fasten one of the warps of the dragnet with which these boats work. The other warp is fastened at bowsprit end. The leeboards are lowered or raised with chains attached to the mainmast.

DRIZZLE. Very fine rain similar to mist.
Fr: *Bruine; Crachin;* Ger: *Sprühregen; Staubregen.*

DROGHER. A seagoing sailing barge from Trinidad Island, used for local trading in the Gulf of Paria between Port of Spain, San Fernando, La Brea and to some extent across to Venezuela. The over-all length runs up to about 60 ft. Save for a deck forward they are open. Their rig consists of one mast with a sort of split lugsail. They are manned by a crew of 3 or 4.

DROGUE.
See **Drag.**

DROITS OF ADMIRALTY (G. B.). The perquisites which were attached in former days to the Office of the Admiralty of England. They are nowadays paid into the Exchequer for public use. Of these perquisites the most important is the right to the property of enemy vessels seized on the breaking out of hostilities. Droits of Admiralty also include all unclaimed wreck, flotsam, jetsam, ligan and derelict which are now dealt with by the receiver of wrecks for the district.

DRONTHIEM. A double-ended yawl of Norwegian origin used on the coast of Donegal (Ireland), between Fair Head, and County Sligo. Also known as Greencastle or Donegal "Yawl." Some are open, others built up forward with a half-deck, clipper bows, and a counter aft to give more deck space. The largest boats have a keel length of 28 ft. and a beam of 8 ft. 6 in.

They are fitted with three mast-steps and can be rigged either as schooners or with one mast with standing lug and jib. The lugsail is occasionally replaced by a spritsail. They are not handy under sail except off the wind, being poor in stays, and thus largely depend on oars. Their ends are very fine and sharp with a quick rise of floors. Deal is used for planking ½ in. in thickness and clincher built. The oars are 14 ft. long with a narrow 4-in. blade. They are usually hauled up on the beach on their return home. The original boats were built in Norway (Trontheim) with a view of being sold on arrival. They measured 24 ft. on keel with 6 ft. beam.

DROP (to). To drop astern: to pass or move toward the stern: to let another vessel pass ahead either by slackening the speed of the vessel that is passed or because of the higher speed of the vessel passing.

Fr: *Tomber;* Ger: *Aussacken.*

DROP. The depth of a square sail from head to foot in the middle, this word being applied to the courses only. The word "hoist" is used for the other square sails. It is also occasionally used for "depth."

Fr: *Chute;* Ger: *Tiefe.*

DROP BOLT. A bolt used to secure a hatch or airport cover. It is characterized by an eye at one end, through which passes a staple securing the bolt permanently to the fixed structure. The other end is threaded, and fits a slotted pad in the hatch, or cover which is secured by means of a nut. Also called dog bolt.

Ger: *Klammerbolzen.*

DROP KEEL. A device used in shallow-draft sailing craft for the purpose of preventing the boat or vessel from sagging to leeward when sailing with the wind abeam or when beating to windward. It consists of a piece of plank or a plate, which drops through a case and slot in the hull, reaching some distance below the bottom. Also called sliding keel.

DROPPING MOOR. A method of mooring in which the vessel first brings up on one anchor (the weather or upstream anchor) and then drops back past the chosen middling berth and lets go the second anchor, subsequently hauling back to the chosen position between the two anchors.

DROP RUDDER. A narrow, deep rudder which extends well below the keel. It is mostly found in small sailing craft built with flat bottom, its purpose being to augment the area of lateral resistance and reduce leeway when working to windward.

DROP STRAKE. A strake of outside plating which terminates at some distance from the stem or stern frame and abuts against a stealer plate, merging two strakes into one where the termination occurs. Also called goring strake.

Fr: *Virure en Pointe;* Ger: *Auslaufendergang; Splissgang; Verlorener Gang.*

See **Stealer.**

DROSS. Refuse or skimmings especially metallurgical. Usually shipped in pigs or slabs.

DRUM. A figure or shape resembling a drum, used in making distance signals, in combination with a ball and cone.

Fr: *Cylindre;* Ger: *Zylinder.*

DRUM-END MAN. One of the deck hands in a gang of stevedores who operates a whip over the drum end of a winch.

DRUMHEAD. A circular portion of a capstan head designed to take the ends of the capstan bars. Also called trundlehead.

Fr: *Chapeau;* Ger: *Gangspillkopf.*

DRUM HOOK. One of a pair of cant hooks which run loose on a wire strap attached to a hoisting ring. By the use of a group of these hooks several drums can be hoisted in one draft.

DRUXEY. A state of decay in timber with white spongy veins.

Fr: *Grisette;* Ger: *Wurmstichig.*

DRY. Said of a vessel when it ships little water on deck in heavy weather.

DRY COMPASS. A term applied to a magnetic compass in which the weight of the card is entirely borne by the pivot as distinguished from the liquid compass in which the card is almost floating and supported by the liquid contained in the bowl. Also called dry-card magnetic compass. In small seagoing craft the dry-card compass is practically useless owing to the quick and violent motion of the bowl.

Fr: *Compas à Rose Sèche;* Ger: *Trockenkompass.*

DRY DOCK. An enclosed basin into which a ship is taken for underwater cleaning and repairing. It is fitted with watertight entrance gates which when closed permit the dock to be pumped dry. In modern dry docks the gates opening in the middle and hinged at sides have been replaced by a caisson or pontoon that fits closely into the entrance. The caisson is flooded and sunk in place, and can be pumped out, floated and warped away from the dock entrance to permit passage of vessels. Also called graving dock, graving dry dock.

Fr: *Cale Sèche; Forme de Radoub;* Ger: *Trockendock.*

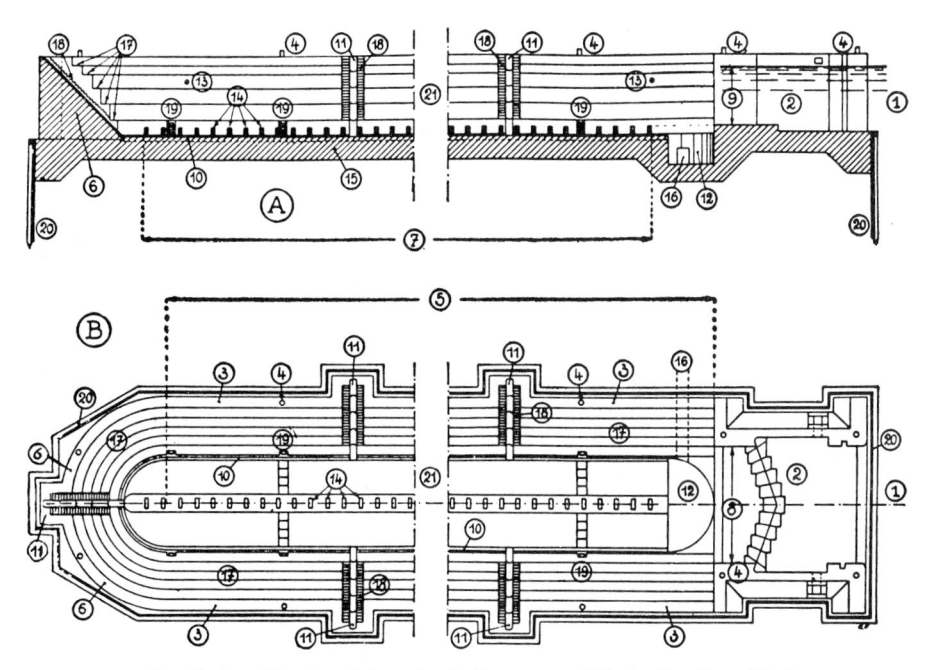

Dry Dock. (*Courtesy International Congresses of Navigation Committee*)

A. Longitudinal Section of a Dry Dock or Graving Dock
B. Plan of a Dry Dock or Graving Dock
1. Basin or Harbour
2. Entrance gate
3. Side wall
4. Bollard
5. Working or available length, *usable length*
6. Head Wall (semicircular)
7. Length over keel blocks
8. Width at entrance gate
9. Depth of water on sill
10. Side gutters for drainage
11. Slide
12. Rudder pit
13. Mooring ring
14. Keel block
15. Floor of dry dock
16. Culvert leading to sump of pumps
17. Altars or steps
18. Steps
19. Ladder
20. Sheet pile cut off or curtain
21. Interior of dry dock

DRY DOCK DUES. Charges levied by the port authority for the use of a dry dock. The usual basis of assessment is the gross tonnage of the vessel.
 Fr: *Frais de cale sèche;* Ger: *Trockendock-Abgabe.*
DRY FOG. A haze due to the presence of dust, held in suspension in the atmosphere.
DRY HARBOR. A minor harbor which is dry or nearly so at low water. Also called stranding harbor. Vessels using it must take the ground.
 Fr: *Port d'Échouage;* Ger: *Strandhafen.*
DRY ROT. A decay affecting seasoned timber, caused by various fungi. It penetrates the timber, destroying it. Damp, unventilated spaces are most favorable to the development of dry rot.
 Fr: *Carie Sèche;* Ger: *Trockenfäule.*

Ramsbottom, J., Dry-Rot in Ships, Essex Naturalist, vol. 25 (1937).
DRY TANK. Part of a ship's double bottom, situated under the boilers, in which no water is carried. This prevents any possible effect of corrosion brought about by the combined action of dampness and heat.
 Fr: *Ballast Sec;* Ger: *Lufttank.*
DRY WEIR. A weir set on flats where the tide ebbs and leaves it dry at low water, when the fish can be taken out.
DUAL VALUATION. A method used in valuation of ships for insurance purposes whereby it is possible for owners to reduce the cost of the cover. With this method one valuation is agreed for the purpose of average claims and another, and lower valuation, is settled for the purpose of total loss claims.

Ger: *Doppelwertbestimmung.*

This system gives effect to the idea that the value of a ship which is getting on in years should normally have been steadily written down and the sum which she represents to her owner, in the event of total loss, should, therefore, be very different from her original cost. On the other hand, the expense of repairing an aged vessel in the event of an accident may be expected to be at least as heavy as, if not greater than, the cost of repairing a new ship, while in cases of strandings or disablement the expense incurred in salvage is similar. So in order to cover the cost of all the claims for damage an underwriter needs a reasonably large value for average claims, making practicable a moderate rate of premium, as an alternative to a low value on which a high rate of premium would be required. The same considerations do not affect the values agreed upon for total loss claims.

DUAL VALUATION CLAUSE. A hull clause contained in marine insurance policies. Its purpose is to give one value, a low one, for total loss settlements; and a second one, a higher one, for partial loss and damage claims.

It is based on the theory that when the value of tonnage is low and underwriters' premiums reduced, repair costs do not follow this level. On the other hand, if insurance is effected on a value higher than current market price the shipowners receive an inadequate return for their money in the event of total loss.

By charging a *total loss only* premium on the lower value, and *a partial damage premium on the higher value, a fair average for both parties is maintained.

DUBBING. To cut off and smooth with an adze scraper or plane. The term is also used when referring to any work performed with an adze. To dub a vessel bright is to remove the outer surface of the planking with an adze or plane.

Fr: *Dressage;* Ger: *Abschlichten.*

DUCK. See **Cotton Canvas.**

DUCT KEEL. A keel built of plates and angles in box form extending in the fore part of vessels built with a double bottom. It has the same height as the floors. The internal space is clear of transverse stiffening. It is used to house ballast and other piping leading forward, which otherwise would have to run through the cargo holds.

The box girder keel has also been introduced lately in oil tankers with engines and boiler rooms aft. It forms a pipe alley in the upper central portion and is of sufficient size to work in for piping repairs.

Fr: *Quille en Caisson;* Ger: *Tunnelkiel; Kastenkiel; Kastenförmiges Kiel.*

Spanner, E. F., The Duct Keel, Marine Engineer (London), vol. 56, no. 672 (September, 1933).

Transverse Section

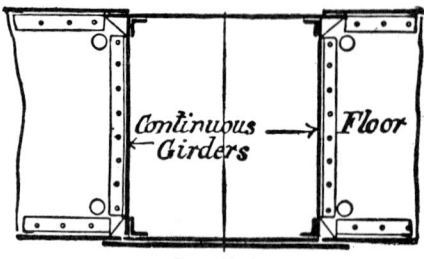

Duct Keel

DUE. Single outrigger canoe from Nicobar Islands which varies in length from 8 to 50 ft. Also called *doai.* The largest is built in the central and southern groups. The smallest at Car Nicobar.

All but the smallest canoes are rigged according to size with from 1 to 4 short bamboo masts, each supported by 4 widespread shrouds of rattan. On these are set lateen-shaped sails with a short tack, made of cotton or pandamus leaves. The masts are stepped on the thwarts, never on the bottom of the canoe.

The stem of these canoes is carried high in a graceful curve and terminates in a long drawn out ornament adorned with a stiff flag at the apex.

DUGOUT.

See **Dugout Canoe.**

DUGOUT CANOE. A canoe formed of a single tree trunk hollowed out by hewing or burning and rounded off on the outside. Sometimes called dugout, or log canoe.

Fr: *Pirogue;* Ger: *Einbaum.*

Large dugouts are often given greater freeboard by the addition of one or two strakes of planking on each side with a solid end piece at bow and stern. Such canoes are found throughout the world, being constructed by people of widely diverse origin for navigation of rivers and inland as well as coastal waters.

Nooteboom, C., De Boomstamkano in Indonesie Leiden (1932).

DUGOUT DORY. A sailing boat from British Honduras used for trolling around the cays. The hull is a dugout made of mahogany or cedar, with stem and sternpiece fastened to the ends. The rudder is fitted with a yoke. The length ranges from 15 to 28 ft. over-all but the smaller size is most commonly seen. The rig consists of one mast with club footed foresail and gunter mainsail. These boats are heavily ballasted with pig iron.

DUMB BARGE. A barge which has no means of self-propulsion in the way of sails or engine power and which has to be towed or is allowed to drift under the influence of the tide or current. Recent law cases in England have ruled dumb barges out of the admiralty jurisdiction. American admiralty courts have considered cases involving dumb craft which for many purposes are "vessels." Also called nonpropelled barge, dumb scow.

Fr: *Chaland non propulsé;* Ger: *Schute.* Stephens, E. O., Thames Dumb Barges, Institution of Naval Architects, *Transactions,* vol. 87 (London, 1945).

DUMB BRACE.
See **Dumb Chalder.**

DUMB COMPASS.
See **Pelorus.**

DUMB CHALDER. A metal cleat or block bolted to the afterside of a wooden sternpost for the end of a rudder pintle to rest upon. It assists the rudder braces by preventing the whole weight of the rudder from resting on them. Also called saucer, or dumb brace.

Fr: *Fausse Penture;* Ger: *Ruderträger.*

DUMB CRAFT. Generic name for various types of floating structures not capable of self-propulsion or of steering or of making signals. In maritime law such craft are for many purposes "vessels" and their owners are vessel owners.

DUMB IRON. A type of calking iron used in wood boatbuilding, for opening up and straightening the seams in new work, preliminary to working in the cotton and/or oakum threads.

See **Deck Iron, Calking Iron, Making Iron, Spike Iron, Reefing Iron, Reeling Hook.**

DUMB SHEAVE. 1. A groove in the heel of a spar for a rope to lie in, which acts in lieu of a revolving sheave. **2.** A block without sheave, through which a rope reeves.

Fr: *Encornail;* Ger: *Tote Scheibe.*

DUMMY.
See **Pontoon.**

DUMMY BARGE (G. B.). A floating raft or pontoon used for breasting ships off quays and for the reception of goods.

DUMMY CROSSHEAD. The crosshead fitted over a dummy rudderhead, and connected to the crosshead proper by drag links, when the afterend of the ship, abreast of the rudder, is too narrow to allow of a tiller being fitted to the rudder stock direct.

Fr: *Traverse de Fausse Mèche;* Ger: *Blinder Kreuzkopf.*

See **Drag Link.**

DUMMY FUNNEL. An extra funnel not used as an outlet for smoke, sometimes fitted in passenger vessels on esthetic grounds of symmetry, balance of outline, or suggestion of power. Dummy funnels have been used for various purposes such as: storeroom, engine-room ventilation, housing of emergency lighting set, motor silencers of large dimensions, and so on.

Fr: *Fausse Cheminée;* Ger: *Blinder Schornstein.*

DUMMY GANTLINE. A gantline made of old rope, to which the working gantline is married. It is left rove through the block when the working gantline is not in use and acts as a messenger.

Fr: *Faux-Cartahu.*

DUMP BARGE. Barge used for harbor works and constructed so that by giving it a list the contents are dumped from the deck on to the desired spot. Also called self-dumping barge.

Fr: *Chaland Basculeur.*

DUMP FASTENING. A metal fastening which does not go quite through both pieces of timber, so that only one end is visible. It is usually made of a small round bolt with solid head and of the same thickness throughout. Also called dump.

Fr: *Chevillage à Bout Perdu;* Ger: *Stumpfverbolzung.*

DUMPING BOARDS. Planking or ceiling laid on the tank top underneath the hatch openings to protect the inner bottom plating. Also called dumping planks.

DUMP-SCOW. A non-propelled harbor craft utilized for the transportation and disposal of excavated material, dredgings, garbage, ashes, etc. Usually built with a hopper bottom by means of which the load may be dumped when the doors are opened. Also called garbage scow.

DUNDA. A flat-bottom boat or barge which plies the Indus River from Mithancote to the sea. It is rigged with one mast and square sail and has a capacity of 5 to 7 tons. Also called *dundi*.

DUNGARVAN BOAT. Name given by Boston (Mass.) fishermen to a cutter-rigged craft which is said to have resembled the Galway hooker from Ireland. These boats had a reasonably sharp, rounding bow, square stern with outboard rudder. They were deep in proportion to their length, with a wide stem and deep keel, and they were excellent sea boats. The forward part was decked over, thus forming a cuddy where the crew ate and slept. There was a cockpit aft with a seat around it. The midship part was partially covered on each side. In the bottom there was the ballast, on top of which the fish and gear were stowed. The bowsprit was adjustable and two jibs were carried, one being set on a stay, the lower end of which fastens to the stem. In other respects these boats did not differ materially from ordinary sloops.

In spring, summer, and fall the boats were employed in the cunner, haddock, and other fisheries for the Boston market. In autumn most of them engaged in the herring fishery with gill nets at Cape Ann and other points in Massachusetts Bay. (Now extinct.)

DUNNAGE. A term applied to loose wood or other material used in a ship's hold for the protection of cargo.

Fr: *Bois d'Arrimage; Bois de Fardage;*
Ger: *Garnierholz; Stauholz; Garnierung.*

See **Ship Dunnage, Side Dunnage.**

Dunnaging serves the following purposes according to the nature of the cargo carried:

1. To protect it from contact with water from the bilges, or leakage from other cargo, from the ship's side, or from the double bottom tank.

2. To protect it from contact with moisture or sweat which condenses on the ship's sides, frames, bulkheads, stringers, brackets, and so on, and falls down on the cement caps, from where it finds its way into the bilges.

3. To provide air passages for the heated, moisture-laden air to travel to the sides and bulkheads along which it ascends toward the uptakes.

4. To prevent chafing as well as to chock-off and secure cargo by filling in broken stowage, i.e., spaces which cannot be filled with cargo.

DUNNAGE CHARGES. The cost of purchasing and installing dunnage materials in the holds and 'tween-decks of a vessel before and during loading operations.

DUPLEX STRAINER. A type of strainer ordinarily used in fuel or lubricating oil lines, so constructed that the flow can be diverted from one of two chambers to the other. This permits the removal of either strainer basket for cleaning without interruption of service.

DUTCHMAN. A steel filling-in piece or wedge, occasionally used in riveting where it is difficult to have the faying surfaces of two parts properly drawn together. Also called shim liner.

Fr: *Lardon;* Ger: *Füllstück.*

See **Graving Piece.**

DUTCHMAN'S LOG. A method of finding the speed of a ship at a given moment when out of sight of land. Two observation stations, one forward and one aft, are selected on the upper deck. The horizontal distance between the stations is accurately measured and at each station a fixed open sight is set up. Each station is connected by buzzer to a control position. Floats of suitable shape and size are catapulted from forward as far as possible on the bow. At the moment the float passes the line of sight, the observer at each station presses his buzzer, both times being noted accurately at the control position. The distance between the observation stations, divided by the elapsed time between observations is equal to ship's speed.

DWARF SKYLIGHT. A small, low skylight with single pitched top projecting from the side of a deckhouse and used for lighting passageways and cabins below. Also called "lean-to" skylight.

of the same float, gives the speed in feet per second, which can be translated into knots. About five floats are required for each set of observations.

DYNAMICAL STABILITY. The dynamical stability of a vessel at any angle of heel is the work which has been done in inclining it from the upright to that angle. It is measured in foot tons. A knowledge of dynamical stability is essential in the design of sailing craft as a guide in fixing the area and distribution of sails.

Fr: *Stabilité Dynamique;* Ger: *Dynamische Stabilität.*

E

E. Flag of the international code of signals divided horizontally in blue and red. When flown by itself indicating, "I am directing my course to starboard."
EbN. EAST BY NORTH.
E.b.S. EAST BY SOUTH.
E.H.P. EFFECTIVE HORSEPOWER.
emb EMBARGO.
ENE EASTNORTHEAST.
ESE EASTSOUTHEAST.
Eq.T. EQUATION OF TIME.
E.P. ESTIMATED POSITION.
EAPOIE.*
See **Eloha**.
EARING, EARRING. A short piece of rope secured to a cringle for hauling out the cringle of a sail or awning to its proper yard, gaff, boom, or stanchion when bending or reefing. Earings are named after the part of the sail which they secure; for example, head earing, nock earing, tack earing, clew earing, reef earing.
Fr: *Empointure;* Ger: *Nockbindsel.*
See **Bull Earing, Head Earing, Luff Earing, Reef Earing**.
EASE. 1. To ease the helm: to reduce the amount of helm when it is hard over. When sailing against a head sea this includes easing the weather helm, and luffing to meet the sea bow-on and at the same time deaden the ship's headway so that the ship and sea meet less violently.
Fr: *Redresser;* Ger: *Aufkommen.*
2. To ease a line: to slacken it gently when taut.
Fr: *Mollir;* Ger: *Lose geben.*
EASING OUT LINE (U. S.). A line used in conjunction with a dip rope for easing out a chain cable which has been unshackled. Also called hook rope.
EAST INDIAMAN.
See **Indiaman**.
EASTING. The distance, expressed in nautical miles, a ship makes good in an easterly direction. It is equal to departure when sailing on a true east course. The converse is westing.
EASTING DOWN. An expression used by sailing ship crews to denote the eastward run from the Cape of Good Hope to Australia.
EASY BILGE. A bilge with easy curve, found in hulls designed with large rise of floor. Also called slack bilge.

Fr: *Bouchain à grand rayon.*
EASY SAIL. A vessel is said to be "under easy sail" when having such canvas spread as will not cause laboring or straining.
EATING. A term used in sailmaking to denote the length of the gore which overlaps the creasing of a seam.
Fr: *Embu.*
EAT TO WINDWARD. To make progress to windward when sailing close-hauled.
Fr: *Manger au Vent;* Ger: *Luv abschneisen.*
EBB. The reflux or falling tide. The return of tidewater toward the sea. The term EBB is used only on marine charts when the stream turns within an hour of the corresponding high and low water. Also called ebb tide, ebb stream, ebb current.
Fr: *Jusant; Courant de Jusant;* Ger: *Ebbstrom; Ebbströmung.*
EBB-TIDE GATE. One of the gates at the *inner* entrance of a tidal dock or lock chamber.
Fr: *Porte d'Èbe;* Ger: *Ebbetor.*
EBOLONGO. A dugout canoe of the coastal Duala tribe in the Cameroons, with clipper-shaped bow. For a short distance at each end the bottom is shaped in the form of a keel.
ECCENTRIC ERROR. The error in a sextant arising from the great difficulty in placing the center of motion given to the index bar exactly in the center of the arc, or from the contraction or expansion of the metal. Also called centering error.
Ger: *Exzentrizitätsfehler.*
ECHO RANGING. The determination of direction and distance of underwater objects from a vessel, by observing the echoes of underwater sound.
Fr: *Détection sous-marine;* Ger: *Unterwasserschal Apparat.*
ECHO SOUNDER. An apparatus for measuring the depth of water by means of vibrations sent out from the vessel. In measuring of depths by echo methods a ship emits an underwater sound impulse which travels outward through the sea at uniform speed. On reaching the ocean bed, part of the sound impulse is reflected and returns to the ship in the form of an echo, where its arrival is registered by hydrophones. The transmitter and hydrophone

are mounted on the bottom of the ship, the hull acting as a nonrigid reflector and imparting directional properties to the combination, experience having proved that there is a marked concentration of energy along the axis of the transmitter. When a vessel is on soundings the depth can be determined by the angle of reflection formed between the line of sound and that of the echo. But in general practice the time interval occupied by the sound in traveling is utilized. This is divided by two and multiplied by the velocity of sound in salt water, which averages 4,900 ft. per second. Also called echo depth finder, fathometer, acoustic sounder.

Fr: *Sondeur Acoustique;* Ger: *Akustisches Lot;* *Echolot.*

ECHO SOUNDING.
See **Acoustic Sounding.**

ECLIPTIC. That great circle on the celestial sphere which the sun appears to describe in one year, around the earth from east to west, in consequence of the revolution of the earth in its orbit around the sun. The ecliptic is divided into twelve parts called "signs," each containing 30°. It is inclined at an angle of 23° — 27' to the equinoctial. This angle is known as the obliquity of the ecliptic.

Fr: *Écliptique;* Ger: *Ekliptik.*

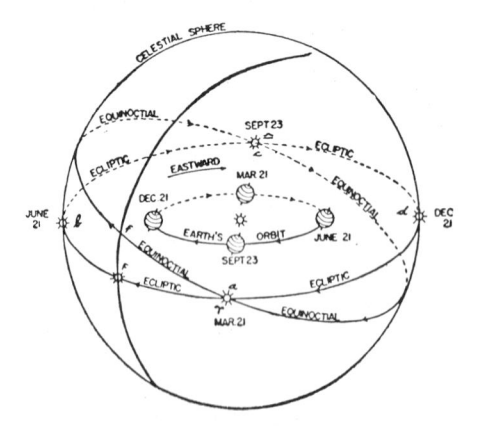

ECLIPTIC
a. Vernal Equinox.
   (First Point of Aries).
c. Autumnal Equinox.
   (First Point of Libra).
d. Winter Solstice.
b. Summer Solstice.
F.f. Sun's declination (North).
a.f. Sun's right ascension.

ECONOMIC SPEED. The speed at which one ton of cargo can be carried at lowest cost. Two conflicting considerations enter into the determination of the economic speed of ships, owing to the fact that the burden of the "capital" charges entering into the cost of transport, such as expenditure on crew, is reduced the more quickly the voyage is performed; whereas the expenditure on fuel increases the more speedy the transport. Another factor affecting the economic speed is the extent to which the shipper is interested in having his goods transported with minimum delay. Therefore the problem cannot be viewed on the assumption that every ton of cargo is of the same value as every other ton; the *value* and not merely the *weight* of the goods should enter into the reckoning of the economic speed. Low-valued bulk-cargoes, such as coal-ores, and so on, should be differentiated from high-valued general or refrigerated cargoes.

Fr: *Vitesse Économique;* Ger: *Ökonomische Geschwindigkeit.*

EDDY WIND. An air current which is beaten back, or returns from a sail, bluff, hill, or anything which impedes its passage.

Fr: *Revolin;* Ger: *Fallwind.*

EDGE. The thin border of a steel plate, by which its thickness is measured.

Fr: *Can;* Ger: *Rand.*

See **Burr Edge, Calking Edge, Flanged Edge, Following Edge, Landing Edge, Leading Edge, Sight Edge.**

EDGE SCARF. A scarf in which the depth is measured across the wide face or side of the timber. Also called vertical scarf.

Fr: *Écart long; Écart à Sifflet.*

EDGE STRIP.
See **Seam Strap.**

EDHOW.
See **Mtepe.**

EFFECTIVE HORSEPOWER. The power required to tow the bare hull through still water. By bare hull is meant the hull without appendages, such as propellers, shaft supports, rudder. For a given hull form, E.H.P. varies according to the displacement and speed. Also called tow-rope horsepower.

Fr: *Puissance Effective; Puissance de Remorquage;* Ger: *Schlepp-Pferdestärke; Effective Pferdestärke.*

EGER. A Danish open boat, from the island of Bornholm, employed in the herring fisheries. It is wide and deep with clinker planking, sharp stern, straight raking stem and sternpost. The rig consists of sprit

Echo Sounder

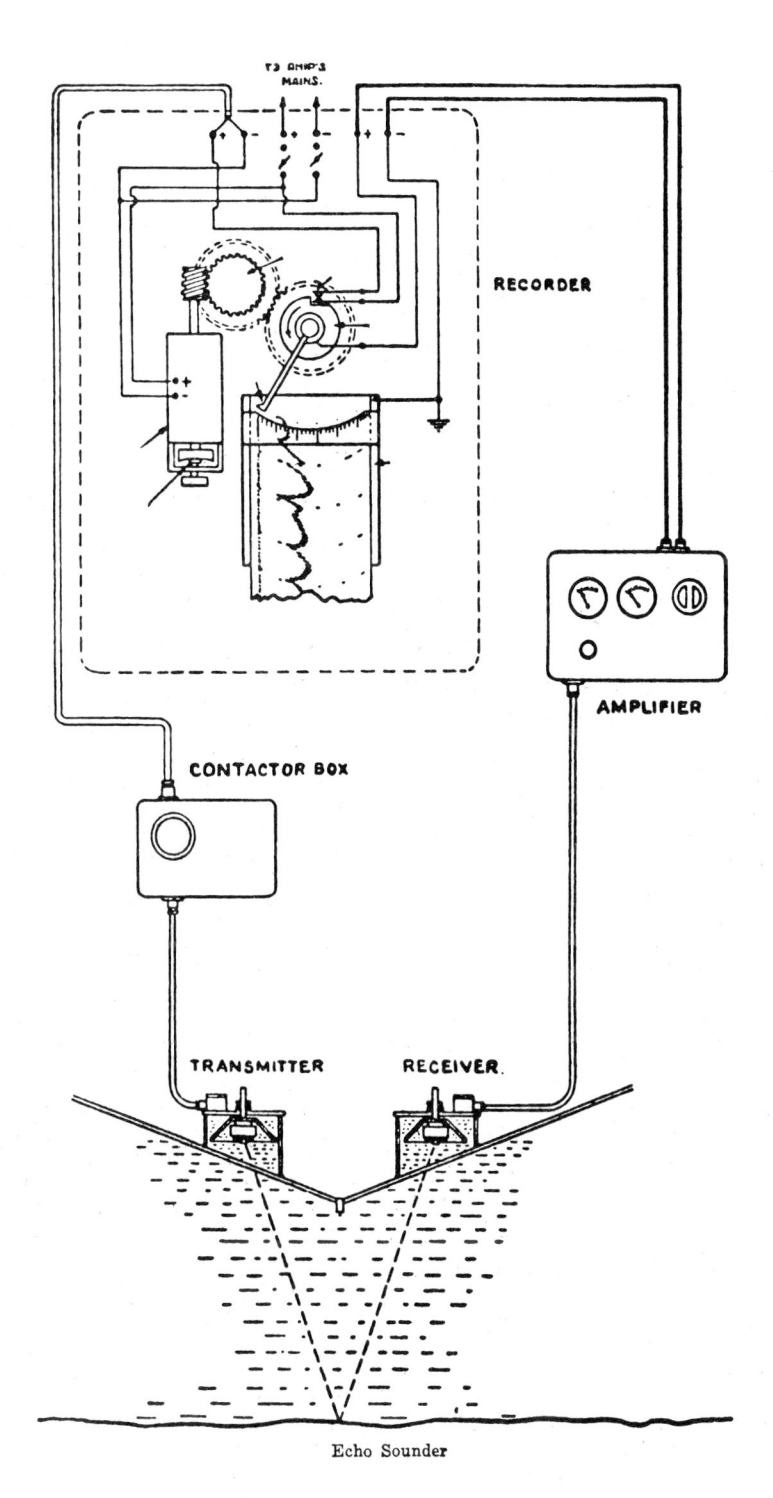

mainsail and mizzen, topsail, and jib. Length 22 ft. 9 in. Breadth 8 ft. Depth 3 ft. 5 in. (Average.)

EIGHT-MAN BOAT. A heavy, double-ended clinker-built boat used by fishermen in the Faroe Islands. The rig consists of a dipping lugsail. When sailing close to the wind the mast is stepped nearly amidships. With a fair wind it is stepped further forward and a mizzen spritsail is set aft. Length over-all 27 ft. Keel 16 ft. 5 in. Breadth 6.3 ft. Depth aft 4 ft. The boat is equipped with 8 heavy 12-ft. oars.

EIKERISSEREN. A Turkish coasting vessel fuller and broader than the Tshektirme, rigged with one mast, sprit mainsail, square foresail, two headsails. The mainsail has two rows of reef points which run parallel to the luff.

EIKING. 1. The process or act of making good the deficiency in the length of any piece by scarphing or butting another piece, as at the end of deck hooks, cheeks or knees.

2. A name given to the arms of breast hooks, deck hooks, or crutches when made up of several pieces.

E-KUO. Single outrigger paddling canoe from Nauru Island (Micronesia). The hull consists of a narrow channeled keel piece extending the whole length of the canoe and of sides formed of two wide strakes closed in at each end by two semisolid endpieces. A curved projection shaped in the form of a horn rises at each end. Length 17.6 ft. Breadth 2.1 ft. Depth 1.3 ft.

ELAPSED TIME. In yacht racing, the actual sailing time of a yacht over a course, any time allowance being disregarded.

Fr: *Temps écoulé;* Ger: *Gesegelte Zeit.*

ELASTIC QUADRANT. See Spring Tiller.

ELBOW IN THE HAWSE. The twist formed in the cables of a ship with two anchors down after swinging through an arc of 360 degrees.

Fr: *Tour dans les Chaînes;* Ger: *Kabelschlag.*

ELECTRIC ARC WELDING. A method of fusion welding which includes two main processes: "carbon-arc" welding and "metal (or metallic)-arc" welding. In the *carbon-arc* welding the filling metal is supplied by a separate filler rod. This filler rod is completely outside the electrical circuit, whereas in *metal-arc* welding the filler rod is actually used as one of the poles from which or to which the arc is struck. Metal-arc welding is the process in most common use today in the marine engineering and shipbuilding industries.

Fr: *Soudure à l'Arc;* Ger: *Lichtbogen Schweissung.*

See **Fusion Welding, Electrode.**

Arnott, D., *Examples of Arc Welded Ship Construction,* Society of Naval Architects and Marine Engineers, New York, 1934; Faerman, W. L., *Electric Welding Installation and Organization in Shipyards,* Institution of Naval Architects (London), *Transactions,* vol. 79 (1937); Hunter, N. M., *Shipbuilding by Welding,* North East Coast Institution of Engineers and Shipbuilders (Newcastle upon Tyne), *Transactions,* vol. 52 (1935–36); Lincoln, J. F., Arc Welding Foundation, *Arc Welding in Design, Manufacture and Construction,* 1939; Rossell, H. E., *Riveting and Arc Welding in Ship Construction,* New York, 1934.

ELECTRIC DRIVE. The system of propulsion in which the prime mover generates electric energy used to drive an electric motor which in turn drives the propeller. Also called electric propulsion. The electric drive with turbo generators was first applied about 1911–12, but it was not until 1927 that large passenger ships were fitted with this type of machinery.

Fr: *Propulsion Électrique;* Ger: *Elektrischer Antrieb.*

Among the advantages claimed for electrically driven ships are the following:

1. The disabling of one or more of the prime movers, turbines or Diesel engines, does not vitally impair the operation of the ship since they are not directly connected to the line of shafting.
2. The flexibility in regard to the location of the machinery assists greatly in the distribution of weights.
3. The location of the propelling motors aft avoids long shafts.
4. Each pair of propulsion motors can be placed in a separate watertight compartment.
5. 100 per cent of power is available for astern running.

In its present stage of development electric propulsion suffers from several disabilities:

1. The percentage loss of 5 to 10 in the transformation of mechanical to electrical energy.
2. The greater initial cost when compared with other mechanical forms of propulsion.
3. The greater weight per horsepower than the direct connected power plants.
4. The greater floor space occupied.

Electric drive is used with both turbines and Diesel engines as prime movers. Particular advantages which make it suitable for harbor and other special craft include flexibility of operation and control, ease of direct control from pilot house, and the freedom allowed in selection of the location of component parts (except main motors). The disadvantages of weight, extra additional cost, and transmission losses are largely compensated for by the greater efficiency of single direction turbines.

On the basis of a geared turbine installation weighing 1.00 units for specified power, electric installation weights and fuel expenditures for the same power are as follows:

Installation	Weight	Fuel Consumption
Geared turbine	1.00	1.00
Diesel-electric	1.74	.90
Turbo-electric	1.31	1.32

Berg, E., "Electric Propulsion of Ships," North East Coast Institution of Engineers and Shipbuilders (Newcastle upon Tyne), *Transactions*, vol. 43 (1926); Robinson, S. M., *Electric Ship Propulsion*, New York, 1922; Woolnough, W. H., "Electrical Propulsion for Small Vessels," Institution of Engineers and Shipbuilders in Scotland (Glasgow), *Transactions*, vol. 74 (1931).

ELECTRIC LOG. A general term for patent screw logs of different types in which a make-and-break attachment closes an electric circuit every 1/10 of a mile, transmitting the record of the rotator electrically from the taffrail register to a dial on the navigating bridge.

Fr: *Loch Électrique;* Ger: *Elektrischer Log.*

ELECTRIC STEERING GEAR. A type of steering gear entirely controlled by electric power. The movements of the rudderhead are obtained either by a single motor supplied with current from the ship's mains, or by a so-called four-unit system, in which the driving motor derives its current from a combination of motor, generator and small exciter. Also called all-electric steering gear.

There is no telemotor control between wheel house and steering compartment in the all-electric gear. In the single-motor system rudder head control is obtained by means of magnetically operated contactors. In the four-unit system the steering wheel controls a generator field by means of two rheostats: one in the wheel house, the other in the steering compartment.

Fr: *Appareil à Gouverner Électrique;* Ger: *Elektrischer Steuerapparat.*

See **Screw Steering Gear, Steam Steering Gear, Electro-hydraulic Steering Gear.**

As formerly constructed, electric steering gear consisted of an electric motor driving a right or left hand screw, as in the steam engine in steam steering gear. The screw was part of a standard screw steering gear. The motor was activated by a controller at a remote station, such as the bridge, or pilothouse. With the controller in neutral, the motor was at rest; throwing the controller handle in either direction caused the motor to rotate in an appropriate direction, moving the rudder. As long as the controller was off neutral, the rudder continued to move. There was no "follow-up" feature. When the control switch was returned to neutral, the motor armature was decelerated and stopped by dynamic braking action. Magnetic brakes held the motor at rest.

Electro-hydraulic steering gear has superseded electric steering gear for naval and merchant marine applications.

ELECTRIC TELEGRAPH. An electrically operated ship's telegraph in which the connection between transmitter and receiver consists of a single cable. Both transmitter and receiver are identical in construction and contain a small electric motor with current taken from the ship's lighting main. There are in each one two balance resistance banks with a number of tappings corresponding with the orders to be transmitted and acknowledged. When the operating handle of the transmitter is moved to give a new order, contact is made with a different tapping and a potential difference is set up across the field of the motor in the receiver, which causes the motor armature to rotate. This rotation moves the contact of the receiving pointer to a tapping corresponding to that of the lever on the transmitter and, when this is reached, the potential difference is reduced to zero and the motor stops. The movement of the operating handle on the transmitter causes a warning bell or buzzer on the transmitter to sound and also a bell on the receiver. The sound continues at both stations until the receipt of the order is acknowledged by the engineer at the receiver.

Fr: *Transmetteur d'Ordres Électrique;* Ger: *Elektrischer Telegraph.*

ELECTRIC TELEMOTOR. An electrical controller between the steering wheel and steering engine. There are 14 points of contact on the contact disc: 7 on each side of midship, which correspond to rudder angles of 3-6-9-14-24-34 and 44 degrees. In this apparatus a pedestal with controller hand is usually fitted instead of a steering wheel.

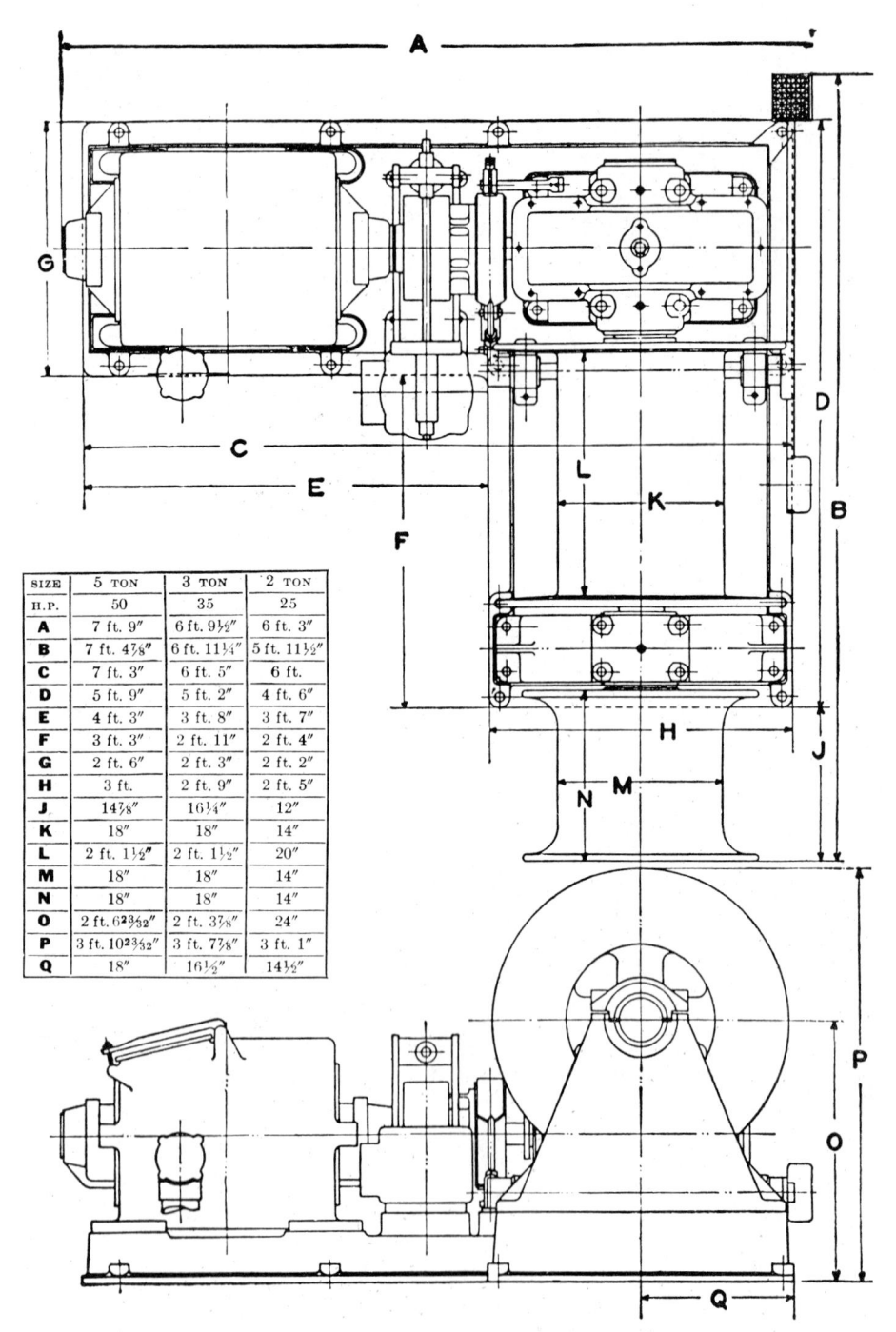

SIZE	5 TON	3 TON	2 TON
H.P.	50	35	25
A	7 ft. 9"	6 ft. 9½"	6 ft. 3"
B	7 ft. 4⅞"	6 ft. 11¼"	5 ft. 11½"
C	7 ft. 3"	6 ft. 5"	6 ft.
D	5 ft. 9"	5 ft. 2"	4 ft. 6"
E	4 ft. 3"	3 ft. 8"	3 ft. 7"
F	3 ft. 3"	2 ft. 11"	2 ft. 4"
G	2 ft. 6"	2 ft. 3"	2 ft. 2"
H	3 ft.	2 ft. 9"	2 ft. 5"
J	14⅞"	16¼"	12"
K	18"	18"	14"
L	2 ft. 1½"	2 ft. 1½"	20"
M	18"	18"	14"
N	18"	18"	14"
O	2 ft. 6$\tfrac{23}{32}$"	2 ft. 3⅞"	24"
P	3 ft. 10$\tfrac{23}{32}$"	3 ft. 7⅞"	3 ft. 1"
Q	18"	16½"	14½"

Electric Cargo Winch. (*Courtesy Hyde Windlass Company*)

256

ELECTRIC WINCH. A deck winch driven by electric power. Ship's electric winches are made in a number of different types, the difference between them being either in the system of gearing from motor to barrel, in the type of drive adopted for the motor, or in the current used. The mechanical parts of electric winches are either spur-geared or worm-geared. The former are provided with a mechanical-change speed gear as on steam winches. Spur-geared winches are frequently adopted for cargo vessels on account of their low first cost and simplicity.

In the worm-geared type the necessary speed change is carried out electrically and automatically. Worm-geared winches are usually adopted for passenger and high-class cargo vessels because of their quiet operating characteristics, although they are more expensive in first cost than the spur-geared type.

Fr: *Treuil électrique;* Ger: *Elektrische Ladewinde.*

The winch is usually fitted with three separate brakes: (a) a foot brake for lowering and light speed control; (b) a magnetic brake for holding the load automatically in the "off" position of the controller; (c) a centrifugal brake for limiting lowering speeds to a safe figure.

ELECTRODE. As used in electric arc welding, a rod of metal, either bare or covered, or of carbon through which current is conveyed between electrode holder and arc. In metal-arc welding, the base metal of the electrode is deposited in molten form in the crater of the arc, and solidifies to form the weld metal making up the joint. In carbon-arc welding a filler rod is used for this purpose.

Fr: *Électrode;* Ger: *Elektrode.*

See **Bare Electrode, Carbon Electrode, Covered Electrode, Metal Electrode.**

ELECTRO-HYDRAULIC STEERING GEAR. A steering gear which utilizes a hydraulic transmission. It consists of an electric motor driving a variable delivery pump, delivering oil under pressure alternately to either of two cylinders or to opposite ends of two double-acting cylinders. Variations in delivery of oil actuate two rams in the cylinders, and the rams, acting directly through a pivoted crosshead, move the tiller. This system is now considered to be more rugged and reliable than steam-steering gear and much more economical in running costs. Upkeep is at a minimum, and follow-up of steering-wheel movements is rapid and accurate. The steering wheel is usually connected to this type of steering gear through a self-synchronous transmission. Also called Hydro-Electric steering gear.

Fr: *Appareil à gouverner Hydro-Électrique;* Ger: *Elektrisch-Hydraulisch Steuervorrichtung.*

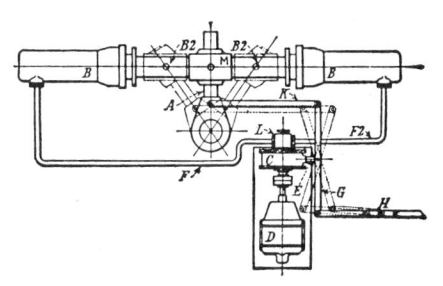

Electro-Hydraulic Steering Gear.
(*Courtesy American Engineering Co.*)

A. Tiller
B. Hydraulic Cylinders
B2 Rams
D. Variable Delivery pump
E. Pump control spindle
F. Cylinder Hydraulic piping
G. Floating lever
H. Telemotor connection
K. Tiller connection
L. By-pass valve
M. Rapson slide

ELECTRO-HYDRAULIC WINCH. A winch in which an electric motor running at constant speed and in one direction is coupled directly to the pump portion of a hydraulic transmission gear. This pump delivers oil to the motor portions of the hydraulic machine which drives through spur or worm gearing the main shaft to which the barrel and warping ends are keyed. The control is obtained by means of a hand wheel or lever which varies the amount of oil delivered to the hydraulic motor and also changes the direction of delivery as required.

Fr: *Treuil Hydro-Électrique;* Ger: *Elektrisch-Hydraulische Ladewinde.*

See **Hydraulic Transmission.**

ELECTROLYTIC ACTION. The wastage which takes place between two different metals in contact when immersed in sea water. Also known as electrolysis.

Fr: *Electrolyse;* Ger: *Elektrolyse.*

ELECTRO-MAGNETIC CLUTCH. A friction clutch in which an electromagnet is used to apply pressure between the friction surfaces. Should not be confused with electro-magnetic slip coupling.

ELECTRO-MAGNETIC COUPLING. A type of flexible coupling used between high-speed Diesel engines and mechanical reduction gears to prevent the transmission of torsional vibrations from engine crankshaft to the gear, and to permit two or more Diesel engines to be simply and flexibly coupled through helical gearing to the propeller shaft. The coupling is made up of two rotating cylindrical electromagnets, one within the other, separated by an air gap, one magnet being mounted on the engine shaft, the other on the gear shaft. Also called electro-magnetic slip coupling.

 Fr: *Transmission électro-magnétique;*
 Ger: *Elektromagnetische Kupplung.*

Leggett, W. D., Geared Diesel Marine Applications, Society of Naval Architects and Marine Engineers, New York, *Transactions*, vol. 47, 1939; Metz, *Electro-Magnetic Slip Couplings*, Inst. of Marine Engineers, London, 1937.

ELEPHANTA. A south or southeasterly wind of gale force which blows along the coast of Malabar during the months of September and October.

ELEVATED COMPASS. General term for different types of magnetic compasses placed in an elevated position so as to be beyond the influence of the ship's iron, such as the masthead compass, the pole compass.

ELEVATED POLE. The elevated pole of an observer is the pole of his hemisphere and is always above the horizon.

 Ger: *Erhöhte Pole.*

ELEVATOR. An appliance specially designed for the discharge by electric or pneumatic power, of bulk grain direct from a vessel's hold into store or waiting craft or railway trucks. Also called grain elevator.

 Fr: *Élévateur à grain;* Ger: *Getreideheber.*

There are two types of elevators, the bucket and the pneumatic. The bucket elevator consists essentially of an endless chain of buckets following an elliptical path, set vertically. In the pneumatic elevator a vacuum is created in a receiving chamber by means of an exhauster or pump, thus causing an inrush of air and grain. The grain having reached the receiving chamber is discharged therefrom through a special kind of valve. The capacity of pneumatic elevators ranges between 100 and 200 tons of grain per hour. Their main advantage over the bucket type is that they require no manual feeding.

ELLIOTT EYE. An eye worked over a thimble in the end of a cable or hawser.

ELLIPTICAL LIFE RAFT. A life raft consisting of a cylinder of elliptical shape. This cylinder is made of either compartmented copper tubing covered with cork and canvas or of balsa wood covered with canvas. The elliptical body carries a net which, when passengers are on the raft, sinks about 3½ ft. A wooden platform is usually attached to the net to give a more comfortable footing. The smallest size of this type of raft, which weighs only 40 lb., can be launched overboard by one man and can support 5 persons.

ELLIPTICAL STERN. A form of stern with short counter in which the upper part above the knuckle is approximately an elliptical cone enlarging upward from the knuckle, the surfaces below being a continuation of the forms of the ship's bottom. Also called round stern. This type of stern is common in merchant ships. In tugboats the plating above the knuckle is vertical or has tumble home.

 Fr: *Arrière Rond;* Ger: *Elliptisches Heck; Rundheck; Rundgatt.*

ELM. A wood used for keels, keelsons, transoms, deadwood, rails, wales, and in some boats for the lower planking. It is difficult to preserve when used as planks for small craft unless well seasoned and constantly protected. Particularly suited to all parts likely to be bumped or damaged in work boats. Holds nails strongly but has a tendency to warp and split. Weight: 35 lb. per cu. ft.

 Fr: *Orme;* Ger: *Ulmenholz.*

See Rock Elm, Wych Elm.

ELOA. A double-outrigger dugout canoe from the Island of Engano on the western coast of Sumatra. The sides are raised with a wash strake. The stem and sternpieces are ornamented with carvings and birds or other decorations. Also called *enana, eapoie.*

EMBACLE. Heaping up of ice following on a renewed freezing.

 Fr: *Embâcle;* Ger: *Eisgang.*

EMBARGO. A stoppage or seizure of a ship or merchandise by sovereign authority. Specifically, a restraint or prohibition imposed by the authorities of a country on merchant vessels or other ships to prevent their leaving its ports. It is, in its nature and policy, a temporary measure. The embargo is sometimes applied on the ships

or goods of the power ordering it; sometimes on foreign vessels or property and used as a means of coercing a settlement of difficulties that have not yet culminated in war or in preparation for impending war. The former is called "civil" or pacific embargo; the latter "hostile" embargo.
Fr: *Embargo;* Ger: *Hafensperre.*

EMBARKATION. The act of going or placing on board a vessel or boat.
Fr: *Embarquement;* Ger: *Einschiffung.*

EMBARKATION DECK. The upper deck where the necessary arrangements have been made for the embarkation of passengers and crew in the lifeboats.
Fr: *Pont d'Embarquement;* Ger: *Einbootungsdeck.*

EMBARKATION NOTICE. A memorandum sent by a shipping line a few days before sailing date to prospective passengers. It gives detailed directions as to place and hour of embarkation and instructions regarding the labeling and other arrangements for the dispatch of baggage.

EMBAYMENT. An extension of a trough or basin in the sea bottom stretching toward the continent, relatively wide.
Fr: *Golfe;* Ger: *Bucht.*

EMBUN. A one-piece single-outrigger dugout canoe without wash strakes from the coast of New Ireland (Bismarck Archipelago).

EMERGENCY ASTERN TEST. A sea-trial test during which, with the vessel running full ahead, the engines are reversed to full astern. The head reach from the time the first signal is given until the ship is stopped is measured by dropping boxes over the side and clocked. Time required to stop shaft and to work up to full astern revolutions is recorded in engine room.

EMERGENCY BATTERY. Electric storage battery of "lead-acid" or "nickel-alkaline" type installed in a special room, or in special deck boxes, for the operation of the emergency lighting and power system. The capacity of the battery must be sufficient to operate the system for at least twelve hours. On vessels where the batteries are operated in conjunction with a Diesel emergency generating set, the capacity of the battery must be sufficient to operate the emergency lighting for a minimum of one-and-a-half hours. When the battery provides the only power supply for signalling, communication, or alarm system, it should be of sufficient capacity to operate the equipment connected thereto for at least one week.
Fr: *Batterie de Secours;* Ger: *Notbatterie.*

EMERGENCY BOAT. A lifeboat rigged in such a manner as to be ready for instant lowering away. Generally found on passenger vessels. Also called **ready lifeboat, accident boat.**

EMERGENCY LIGHTING SET. A self-contained electric generator station placed as high up as possible in the ship and driven by some form of oil engine. It must be capable of operating the safety lighting system in different parts of the ship, and of providing for the illumination of lifeboats in process of or immediately after being launched.
The International Convention for Safety of Life at Sea (1929) makes it compulsory for all passenger vessels engaged in international voyages to have an emergency lighting set. Also called emergency generator system.
Fr: *Poste Électrogène de Secours;* Ger: *Notbeleuchtungszentrale.*

EMERGENCY RECEIVER. Radio receiver capable of being energized solely by the ship's emergency power supply.
Fr: *Récepteur de sécurité;* Ger: *Not Empfanger.*

EMERGENCY SQUAD. A group of specially selected and trained men from all departments on a passenger vessel, capable of handling any emergency that might occur. Their number usually varies from 6 to 24 men depending on the size of the crew. They are placed under the direct control of the chief officer.
Fr: *Equipe de Secours;* Ger: *Notfall Gruppe.*

EMERGENCY STEERING GEAR TEST. A test carried out during sea trials with vessel under way at 50% of maximum ahead speed. The rudder is moved about from hard left to hard right in a similar manner as in the ahead steering test and held in each position to emergency steering is recorded as well as time required for each rudder movement.
Fr: *Essai d'appareil à gouverner de secours;* Ger: *Probe der Notsteuerapparat.*

EMERGENCY TILLER. 1. A tiller used as a spare fitting in addition to the quadrant or yoke when there is a breakdown in the steering engine or gear by which the vessel is normally steered. Also called relieving tiller. Arrangements are provided for attachment of the relieving tackles to the emergency tiller.

2. A tiller composed of two bars placed in the same plane and working in a dummy rudderhead.

Fr: *Barre de Rechange; Barre de Secours; Barre de Fortune;* Ger: *Reservepinne.*

EMIGRANT SHIP. According to British law the expression "emigrant ship" means every ship, British or foreign, which carries on any voyage from the United Kingdom to any port out of Europe and not within the Mediterranean more than 50 steerage passengers or a greater number of steerage passengers than in the proportion of one statute adult to every 20 tons of the registered tonnage in a mechanically propelled vessel. The definition includes a ship, which, having proceeded from a port outside the British Isles, takes on board at any port in the British Isles such a number of steerage passengers as would, either with or without the steerage passengers already on board, constitute her an emigrant ship.

Fr: *Navire à Émigrants;* Ger: *Auswanderungsschiff.*

EMPLOYMENT CLAUSE. Clause contained in time charters by which the captain, although appointed by the owners, is placed under the orders and direction of the charterers as regards employment, agency, or other similar arrangements. He has to follow their instructions on all matters related to the loading and discharging of cargo.

Fr: *Clause d'Emploi;* Ger: *Employmentklausel.*

ENANA. See **Eloa.**

ENCLOSED SPACE TONNAGE. A term applied to the measurement tonnage equal to the area of enclosed spaces above the upper deck multiplied by the height of the spaces, divided by one hundred. The following are exempted from enclosed space tonnage: machinery spaces, wheelhouse, spaces for preparing food, condenser rooms, lavatories and bathrooms, skylights, companion ways and booby hatches.

END BULKHEAD. A transverse bulkhead forming the termination of a superstructure such as forecastle, bridge house, or poop.

Fr: *Cloison d'Extrémité;* Ger: *Endschott; Frontschott.*

END COAMING. The athwartship coaming of a hatchway. Also called head ledge.

Fr: *Hiloire Transversale;* Ger: *Quersulle.*

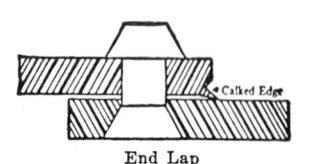

End Lap

END LAP. The joint between two plates where the butts overlap. Also called butt lap.

Fr: *Recouvrement d'Abouts;* Ger: *Stossüberlappung.*

END LAUNCHING. The launching of a vessel stern first, the building berth forming an angle with the waterfront which may vary from 90 to about 10 degrees.

Fr: *Lancement en Long;* Ger: *Längsablauf.*

END LINK. In an anchor cable an unstudded link with parallel sides. It is fitted on each side of the joining shackles. The extreme length of the end link varies from 6.6 to 6.75 times the diameter of the iron of which the common links are made. Also called open link. Relative dimensions of end link and common link for a 2 in. cable:

	Diameter	Length	Extreme Width
Common link	2.0 in.	12.0 to 12.3 in.	7.2 in.
End link	2.4 in.	13.2 to 13.5 in.	8.0 in.

Fr: *Maille de bout; Maille d'Extrémité;* Ger: *Verbindungsglied; Endglied.*

END-ON-BARREL STEERING GEAR. A power steering gear of the rod and chain type with two chain barrels (port and starboard) located athwart ships at either side of the engine room casing.

Ger: *Querschiffs Steuerwelle Rudermaschine.*

ENDROL. A generic name for single-outrigger dugout canoes of the Admiralty Islands (Bismarck Archipelago). The smaller ones are dugouts with rounded sides; the larger craft are provided with one or two wash strakes. A platform is built on the outrigger side and another on the offside. The mast is stepped in a thick cup-like projection on the offside and propped up by a curved shore resting on one of the outrigger booms. The mat sail is rectangular and is slung obliquely between two spars. Some of the largest canoes have two masts. Length 39 ft. Breadth 1½ ft. Depth at center 1 ft. 4 in.

END TANK. One of the buoyancy tanks of triangular shape provided at each end of a lifeboat.
>Fr: *Caisson d'Extrémité;* Ger: *Endluftkasten.*

ENGINE BED.
>See **Engine Foundation.**

ENGINE EFFICIENCY. Engine efficiency may be defined as the ratio of the power which reaches the propeller compared with that actually developed at the crankshaft of a reciprocating engine or the rotor of a turbine.
>Fr: *Rendement des Appareils Moteurs;* Ger: *Maschinen-Wirkungsgrad.*

ENGINEER SURVEYOR. A surveyor who specializes in the supervision of marine engines and boilers.
>Fr: *Expert Mécanicien;* Ger: *Maschinenbesichtiger.*

ENGINE FOUNDATION. A built-up, box-like tabular structure of plates and bars, formerly riveted, and nowadays frequently welded, which acts as a support for the main engine(s), and distributes the load of the engines' weight to the framing and plating of the hull. Also called engine seating, engine frame, engine bed.
>Fr: *Carlingage de Machines;* Ger: *Maschinenfundament.*

Ordinarily the engine foundation is made up of two massive box girders, one on each side of the engine centerline. Each of these consists of two fore-and-aft bearer plates connected by a heavy cover plate, with internal cross diaphragms and external brackets.

ENGINE FRAME.
>See **Engine Foundation.**

ENGINE HATCH. A hatch fitted over the engine room. It is usually provided with a large skylight having hinged covers which can be operated from below.
>Fr: *Panneau des Machines;* Ger: *Maschinenluke.*

ENGINE MAINTENANCE MAN (U. S.). An unlicensed member of the crew who assists the chief engineer and other engineer personnel of a ship in repairing and maintaining propulsive, auxiliary, generating and other engines and mechanical equipment. Performs the watch tasks of oiler or fireman as required.

ENGINE ROOM. A compartment in a ship where the main propulsion machinery is located. Also called machinery space.
>Fr: *Chambre des Machines;* Ger: *Maschinenraum.*

ENGINE-ROOM AUXILIARIES. All machinery in the engine and boiler rooms which assists in the working of the propelling plant, among which are feed pumps, feed heaters, ash ejectors, fan engines, distillers, evaporators, lubricating-oil pumps, steering engines, and so on.
>Fr: *Auxiliaires de Machine;* Ger: *Maschinenraumhilfsmaschinen.*

ENGINE ROOM LOG. A book in which are entered by the engineer officers all particulars relating to the operation of the propelling and auxiliary machinery. It forms a tabulated summary of the performance of the engines and boilers. Also called engineer's log book.
The usual entries are as follows:

DAILY:	The supply, consumption and remainder of fuel in bunkers.
EVERY HOUR:	The boiler pressure.
	The temperature in engine and boiler rooms.
	The condenser vacuum.
	The number of revolutions per minute.
EVERY WATCH:	The salinity of boiler water.
	The temperature of engine room.
	The temperature of stern tube water.
	The temperature of boiler feed water.
	The temperature of sea water.

>Fr: *Journal de la Machine;* Ger: *Maschinentagebuch; Maschinenjournal.*

ENGINE ROOM STORES. A general term for the various consumable stores necessary for the working and upkeep of the engines and boilers on board ship.
>Fr: *Approvisionnements Machines;* Ger: *Maschinenvorräte.*

ENGINE SEATING.
>See **Engine Foundation.**

ENGINE TELEGRAPH. A device for transmitting and receiving orders mechanically or electrically, between two stations in a ship, ordinarily the navigating bridge or pilot house, and the engine room. Sometimes called engine order telegraph.

Fr: *Transmetteur d'Ordres aux Machines;* Ger: *Maschinentelegraph.*

See **Electric Telegraph.**

The engine order telegraph incorporates (1) a transmitter for sending an order relating to engine speed and direction, (2) a receiver which indicates the transmitted order, (3) a repeat-back which is in effect a reverse transmitter-receiver for acknowledgment of orders, and (4) a bell or gong at each station which rings when the transmitter or repeat-back handle is moved.

On cargo vessels and small craft engine telegraphs are of a simple wire-and-chain type; in high class passenger vessels it is more usual to find electric telegraphs of the self-synchronous or step-by-step follow-up type.

ENGLISH POT.

See **Creel.**

ENIENI. African dugout canoe used for fishing on the lagoon of Appollonien (Ivory Coast). Length 13 to 16 ft. Breadth 1.6 to 1.9 ft. It is propelled by paddles and sets a square sail spread by two diagonally placed poles stepped at about one-third the length from the stern.

ENLARGED LINK. In an anchor cable: a stud link with rounded sides connected on one end to an end link and on the other to a common link. Its length varies from 6.5 to 6.6 times the diameter of the iron of which the common links are made. Relative dimensions of enlarged link and common link for a 2 in. cable:

	Diameter	Length	Extreme Width
Common link	2 in.	12 to 12.3 in.	7.2 in.
Enlarged link	2.2 in.	13 to 13.2 in.	8.0 in.

Fr: *Grande Maille;* Ger: *Grosses Glied; Grosse Schake.*

ENROLLMENT (U. S.). The document issued by the United States government to vessels of 20 tons burden or more engaging solely in domestic or coasting trade or fisheries, as distinguished from the Register, which is confined to vessels engaging in foreign trade.

ENSIGN. The flag carried by a ship as insignia of her nationality. The ensign is hoisted on a pole or staff over the taffrail. In sailing vessels at peak of gaff. If the aftermost sail is a Bermuda or Marconi sail the ensign is displayed at a point on the leech that would be the peak of an ordinary gaff sail. At anchor it is displayed at a staff on the taffrail to starboard of the boom if the latter extends beyond the taffrail. In port it flies between 8 A.M. and sunset: at sea only when saluting or meeting strangers. Turned upside down it is a signal of distress; half-hoisted a sign of mourning.

Fr: *Pavillon National;* Ger: *Nationalflagge.*

See **Blue Ensign, Yacht Ensign.**

International law has no uniform rules regulating the conditions under which vessels are entitled to fly the flag of a particular nation. Each individual state fixes its own conditions of registration and there is no uniformity in respect to them. All that international law has prescribed is that the maritime state which authorizes a vessel to use its flag must provide this vessel with the proper documents or papers and thereupon exercise in respect to the vessel the degree of jurisdiction permitted by law.

ENTABLATURE. An overhead table or frame sustained by columns between which and the base plate the cylinders and working parts of an inverted reciprocating engine are carried.

Fr: *Entablature;* Ger: *Oberrahmen.*

ENTER. 1. To deposit a ship's papers at the custom in order to obtain license to land goods.

Fr: *Entrer en douane;* Ger: *Einführen.*

2. To furnish to customs officers an itemized list of goods brought in from a foreign port to obtain clearance.

Fr: *Déclarer en douane;* Ger: *Deklarieren; Klarieren.*

3. To come or go into a harbor, a dock, etc.

Fr: *Entrer;* Ger: *Einlaufen; Einkommen.*

ENTERING AND LEAVING SIGNALS. A general term for port signals, such as right of way, dredger and fairway obstruction, quarantine examination, customs and immigration examination.

Fr: *Signaux d'Entrée et de Sortie de Port;* Ger: *Einfahrtsignal; Abfahrtsignal.*

ENTER INWARDS. To report a ship or her cargo at the custom house on arrival in port.

Fr: *Déclarer à l'entrée;* Ger: *Einklarieren.*

ENTER OUTWARDS. To report a ship or her cargo at the custom house before beginning to load.

Fr: *Déclarer à la sortie;* Ger: *Ausklarieren.*

ENTRANCE. 1. The immersed part of the hull forward of the parallel body or, if the latter is nil, forward of the cross section of greatest area.

Fr: *Façons de l'avant;* Ger: *Zuschärfung.*
2. In dock engineering the term "entrance" or "gate entrance" usually implies an entrance closed by a single pair of gates or caisson as distinguished from a lock which has two pairs of gates or caissons. Also called gate entrance.
See **Angle of Entrance, Length of Entrance.**
ENTRANCE LOCK. A lock situated between the tidewater of a harbor or river and an enclosed basin when their levels vary. It has two pairs of double gates by which vessels can pass either way at all times of the tide. Also called tide lock, guard lock.
Fr: *Sas;* Ger: *Schleusenkammer.*
ENTREPOT TRADE. A term sometimes applied to the re-export trade of a country.
ENTRY. 1. The formalities required by the customs laws to be made for the landing or discharge of goods from an importing ship within 24 hours of arrival.
2. A declaration to be delivered to the customs authorities to obtain clearance of a vessel or of imported goods.
Fr: *Déclaration en Douane;* Ger: *Klarierung; Zolldeklaration.*
ENTRY CRAFT. Any craft (barge, lighter, and so on) specially hired by the master of a vessel to receive the cargo when the consignee fails in his obligation to take delivery of same according to bill of lading terms.
ENTRY DECLARATION.
See **Quarantine.**
ENTRY INWARDS. The report of a newly arrived vessel, which must be made to the customs before it can commence discharging. It consists of a general declaration of the ship's cargo, dutiable stores, and so on, signed by the master. Besides the report the master must deliver at the customhouse offices the following documents: certificate of pratique; ship's letter, declaration and information regarding wreckage, derelict vessels, ice and other dangers to navigation; details of casualties if any.
Fr: *Déclaration à l'Entrée; Entrée en Douane;* Ger: *Einfuhrdeklaration; Eingangsdeklaration.*
ENTRY OUTWARD. A report lodged at the customhouse by every vessel about to load cargo for export. Details of the vessel, nationality, master's name, destination, number of crew, load-line details, port of loading, last voyage, where lying, name and address of brokers, and date of entry inwards, have to be stated.
Fr: *Déclaration à la Sortie; Déclaration de Sortie;* Ger: *Ausfuhrdeklaration..*
ENVIADA. Name given on the south coast of Portugal to a craft employed as "fish carrier" from ship to shore or from port to port. It is called *andaina* or *canoa da Picada* on the coast of Algarve. In Spain the *enviada* is a small decked boat from 3 to 5 tons used as a carrier for the *pareja.*
EPOCH. The time, expressed in days and decimals of a day, elapsed between the error of a chronometer on one date and the error on another date.
EQUAL ALTITUDES. Observations of a heavenly body when at the same altitude both east and west of the meridian.
Fr: *Hauteurs Égales;* Ger: *Korrespondierende Höhen.*
EQUAL-ANGLE BAR. Angle bar, which has both flanges of the same width.
Fr: *Cornière à ailes égales;* Ger: *Gleichschenkeliger Winkel.*
EQUATION OF TIME. The difference between apparent time, determined by the meridian passage of the real sun, and mean time determined by the meridian passage of the mean sun.
Fr: *Equation du Temps;* Ger: *Zeitgleichung.*
EQUATORIAL COUNTER CURRENT. An Easterly flowing stream in the Atlantic and Pacific Oceans between the North equatorial current, and the South equatorial current.
Fr: *Contre-courant équatorial;* Ger: *Äquatoriale Gegenströmung.*
EQUATORIAL CURRENT. One of the Westerly ocean currents near the equator. There are two equatorial currents in the Atlantic, and two in the Pacific, named respectively North equatorial current and South equatorial current.
Fr: *Courant équatorial;* Ger: *Äquatorialstrom.*
EQUATORIAL TIDE. One of the tides which occur near the time when the moon is over the equator. At this time the tendency of the moon to produce a diurnal inequality is at a minimum.
EQUINOCTIAL. A great circle in the celestial sphere which has its plane perpendicular to the axis of the heavens. Every point of it is equidistant from the north

and south celestial poles. Also called celestial equator.
Fr: *Equinoctial;* Ger: *Äquinoktial; Himmelsäquator.*

EQUINOCTIAL COLURE. The great circle of the celestial sphere which passes through the equinoctial points of the ecliptic. Also called **zero hour circle.**
Fr: *Colure equinoctial;* Ger: *Aquinoktiale Kolure.*

EQUINOCTIAL POINTS. The two points where the ecliptic intersects the equinoctial. They are known as the vernal equinoctial point and autumnal equinoctial point, but are also called "first point of aries" and "first point of libra" from the constellations within which they lie.
Fr: *Points Equinoxiaux;* Ger: *Äquinoktialpunkte; Nachtgleichenpunkte.*

EQUINOCTIAL TIDE. Tides during the equinoxes when the rise and fall reach their maximum owing to the relative position of the earth, moon, and sun.
Fr: *Grande Marée;* Ger: *Äquinoktialtide.*

EQUINOX.
See **Equinoctial Points.**

EQUIPMENT. In relation to a ship, this term includes tackle apparel, furniture, provisions, stores or any other gear that is used in or about a ship for the purpose of fitting or adapting it for the sea or for the service intended. Equipment includes anchors, cables, boats, life saving appliances, nautical instruments, signal lights, and so on. It does not include donkey engines, pumps, windlass, steering engine and other similar machinery. The expression *"outfit and equipment"* may be defined as including all portable articles necessary or appropriate for the navigation, operation, or maintenance of a vessel, which are not permanently incorporated in or permanently attached to the hull or propelling machinery.
Ger: *Ausrüstung.*

EQUIPMENT NUMERAL, EQUIPMENT NUMBER. The numeral under which are tabulated the requirements of the classification society under which the vessel is built as regards anchors, cables, tow ropes, warping and mooring lines.
Fr: *Nombre d'Équipement;* Ger: *Ausrüstungsnummer.*

EQUIPMENT SUBSIDY. A subsidy paid to shipowners and calculated on the number of days that a vessel is in commission. Also called equipment bounty.
Fr: *Compensation d'Armement;* Ger: *Betriebszuschuss.*

EQUIVALENT GIRDER. A diagrammatic representation of the disposition of that material, in cross section, which contributes to the longitudinal strength of the hull. Such a diagram shows the distribution of material in relation to the neutral axis, which is ordinarily near the designed waterline. When any of the structural members have not the same strength in tension and compression, or when they are regarded as contributing to one and not to the other, or, when allowance is made for rivet holes in tension but not in compression, then two separate girders must be considered, one when the ship is hogging and one when sagging.
Ger: *Äquivalenter Träger.*
King, J. F., "Girders in Ships," North East Coast Institution of Engineers and Shipbuilders (Newcastle upon Tyne), *Transactions,* 1924-25.

ERECTION. The process of taking to the way, hoisting into place, fitting together and bolting up the various components of the ship's hull previous to riveting or welding. These include preassembled sections, pillars, stanchions, frames and the like.
Fr: *Montage;* Ger: *Montage.*
See **Pre-Erection.**

ERECTOR (U. S.). Shipyard worker who puts together and secures fabricated parts to form the ship's structure.

ERROR IN NAVIGATION. Expression used in bills of lading and charter parties, which includes failure to lay off the correct course; failure to allow correctly for tides and currents; incorrect application of compass error; mathematical errors in working out sights; incorrect identification of lighthouses, marks and buoys; incorrect interpretation of rules of the road at sea.
Failure to put into a port of refuge; putting to sea in the face of bad weather reports; standing due to negligence; failure to have a lookout.
Fr: *Faute Nautique.*

ESCAPE. Small supplementary opening provided in the wings of a deck above a bunker or over a hold where bulk cargo is loaded. It is used for trimming purposes so that there are no vacant spaces left at sides.
Fr: *Échappée;* Ger: *Notausgang.*
See **Tunnel Escape.**

Midship Section of Ship A

Equivalent girder B

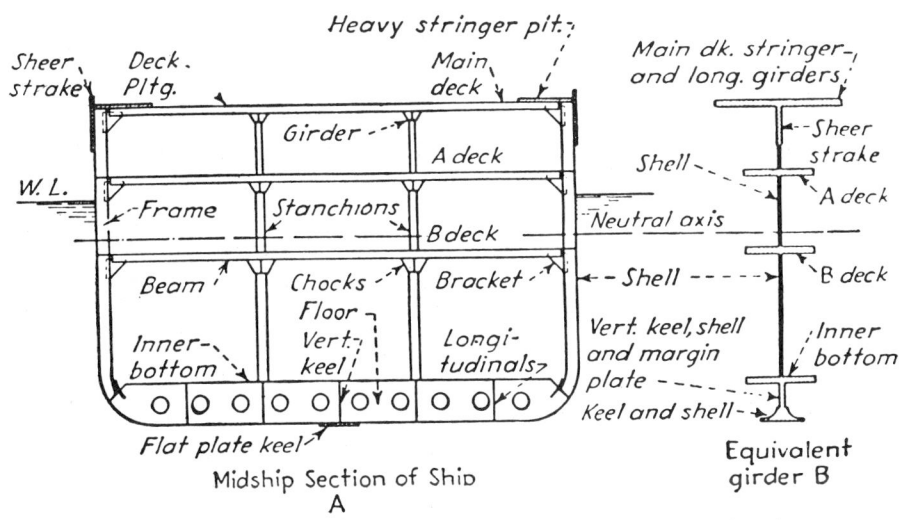

Equivalent Girder. (*From Baker, E., Steel Shipbuilding, by permission of McGraw-Hill Book Company, N. Y.*)

ESCAPE HATCH. 1. A small hatch about two feet square in the clear cut in a 'tween-deck or weather deck for the safe exit of men engaged in trimming or stowing coal or grain.

2. In general, any hatch installed with the primary purpose of permitting personnel to escape from a compartment when ordinary methods of egress are blocked.

Fr: *Panneau d'échappée*; Ger: *Sicherheitsluke*.

ESCAPE TRUNK. Emergency exit from the lower part of the vessel to the weather deck usually located at the afterend of the shaft tunnel.

Fr: *Échappée*; Ger: *Ausgangschacht*; *Notausgang*.

ESCUTCHEON.
See **Arch Board**.

ESTUARY. 1. An arm of the sea. **2.** The tidal compartments of a river subject to tidal influence extending as far as the limit of palpable tidal action. **3.** The coastal section of a river which is to a greater or lesser extent invaded by the sea and subject to tidal phenomena.

Fr: *Estuaire*; Ger: *Flussmündung*.

ESTUARY HARBOR. A harbor formed by the lower tidal compartment of a river.

Fr: *Port en Rivière*; Ger: *Mündungshafen*; *Stromhafen*.

ESTIMATED POSITION. A position established by applying current to a dead-reckoning position. Applies also to a fix made by taking radio bearings.

Fr: *Point Corrigé*; Ger: *Verbessertes Besteck*.

ÉTADIER. Small fishing boat originating from the districts of St. Valéry sur Somme and Etretat (Normandy) used for inshore fishing. Its name is derived from a net with which these boats work and which is known as *étade*. Some of the boats are decked, others open. Length 20 to 26 ft. Breadth 10 to 11½ ft. Depth 4 ft. 4 in. to 5 ft. Crew 8 to 12. (Typical.)

The boats from Etretat are clinker-built and open, while those from St. Valéry have carvel planking and are decked. They carry washboards 20 to 30 centimeters high. The bows are bluff. The rig consists of a lug mainsail, a bowsprit and jib, and a three-cornered jigger laced to the mast and with the sheet extended by a long outrigger. The jigger mast is stepped off the centerline to give free motion to the tiller. The loose footed mainsail is sheeted with a tackle to a horse extending right across the boat at a height of about 4 to 5 ft. above deck.

ETEA. A very small single-outrigger dugout canoe from San Cristobal (Solomon Islands), about 13 ft. long and 19 in. wide. The outrigger is a fan palm branch deprived of its leaves.

ETESIAN WINDS. Northerly winds blowing in summer over the eastern Mediterranean.

Fr: *Vent Étésien*; Ger: *Etesischer Wind*.

EUPHROE. A hardwood batten or brass fitting pierced with a number of holes through which the small lines of a crowfoot are rove. It is used for holding the top part of an awning in place.

Fr: *Hernier;* Ger: *Spinnekopp.*

EUROCLYDON.
See **Levanter.**

EVAPORATOR. A heat-transfer device in the distilling plant, which utilizes steam (usually auxiliary exhaust steam) to heat sea water. The resulting vapor is condensed in the distilling condenser to fresh water, to be used for boiler feed and general ship's use.

Fr: *Bouilleur Évaporateur;* Ger: *Destillierapparat; Frischwassererzeuger; Verdampfer.*

See **Distilling Plant, Distilling Condenser.**

Evaporators are generally grouped in two classes, the submerged-tube type, in which tubes or coils carrying steam are immersed in the brine, and the film type, in which tubes or coils carrying steam are sprayed with the brine. In both types, the brine is pumped successively to evaporator units operating in a declining pressure and temperature range as the brine becomes more concentrated.

EVEN KEEL. A vessel is said to be on even keel when her draft is the same at bow and stern.

Fr: *Sans Différence;* Ger: *Gleichlastig.*

EVER. A type of craft originating from the Elbe Estuary engaged in small coasting or fishing. Also called *Ewer.* The tonnage ranges between 6 and 98 but the wooden trading *Ever* is usually between 40 and 60 tons in size. The hull is flat-bottomed with ample sheer forward, square stern, and outside rudder. It is broader and has less sheer than the *Jacht.* Leeboards are fitted.

See **Fischer Ever, Kutter Ever.**

Seagoing boats of this type are ketch-rigged with the mainmast at nearly half length and small mizzen stepped way aft. The sail plan is composed of three headsails on standing bowsprit, a gaff mainsail with boom, gaff topsail and small mizzen.

EVERKAHN. A ketch-rigged seagoing lighter with hull of design similar to that of the *Ever* but having the same arrangement of hatchways as the *Kahn.* Also called *Besahn-ever.* Tonnage 44 to 55. Length 56 ft. Breadth 17½ ft. Depth 6 ft. 9 in. Draft 5 ft. 8 in. (Average.)

EVER GALEASS. Small coaster of the *Ewer* type but more seaworthy than the ordinary *Ewer.* It is ketch-rigged with main and mizzen topmasts, standing bowsprit, square foresail set flying, and jib topsail. The hull is built with keel, and leeboards are dispensed with. Tonnage 40 to 95.

EX. When prefixed to the name of a ship it means "Out of" and indicates the particular vessel from which goods were landed or taken out. When used to identify a vessel, it is prefixed to the vessel's former name or names and is usually in parenthesis following the name that the vessel bears at the time.

EXCEPTED PERILS. Term used in a Charter Party or Bill of Lading to denote those perils which are excepted in the contract, provided that such perils could not have been avoided by reasonable care and diligence on the part of the shipowners, or carriers and his servants. For the consequences resulting solely from the occurrence of these perils the shipowner, charterer or carrier are not liable. Excepted perils include: acts of God; public enemies; pirates; robbers; thieves (whether on board or not); barratry of master and mariners; arrest and restraints of princes, rulers and peoples; strikes, lock-outs or stoppage of labor; leakage; ullage; spiles; jettison; injurious effects of other goods; fire; perils of boilers; steam or steam machinery and consequences of defects therein, or damages thereto; detention by ice: breakdown of steamer; latent defect; risk of craft; risk of storage afloat or ashore; collision; detention by railways; Force Majeure; accidents; improper opening of valves; errors of judgment by master.

EXCEPTED PERILS CLAUSE. A clause, contained in charter parties and bills of lading which states that ship and carrier are exempted from responsibility for any loss, damage or delay in loading or discharging arising or resulting from acts of God, public enemies, restraint of princes, rulers and people, pirates, fires, strikes, perils of the sea and generally speaking all accidents beyond control. Also called exception clause, exceptional clause.

Fr: *Clause d'Exonération;* Ger: *Freizeichnungklausel; Befreiungsklausel.*

EXCESS CLAUSE. A marine insurance hull clause which states that in case the claims under the collision clause cannot be recovered in full by the shipowner, by reason of the difference between the insured value and the sound value of the vessel, the underwriters will pay such proportion of the excess as the sum insured bears to the difference between the vessel's sound and insured values.

Ger: *Kollision's Exzedentenklausel.*

EXCESS OF HATCHWAY. A term used in tonnage measurement to denote the space in hatchways or within the coamings over and above one-half per cent of the gross tonnage. It is added to the gross tonnage by the admeasurers.

Fr: *Excédent d'Ecoutilles;* Ger: *Übermass in Luken.*

According to British and Suez Canal measurement rules hatchways are exempted from measurement to a maximum of one-half per cent of the gross tonnage of the ship, the excess being added to the gross tonnage. Panama Canal rules provide a deduction of one-half of one per cent of the tonnage of hatchways.

EXCLUDED PORTS. In time charters: the ports where charterers are not allowed to take the vessel for some particular reason such as those where fever or pestilence are prevalent, or where hostilities are being carried on; also icebound ports, etc.

Fr: *Ports exdus;* Ger: *Aussgeschlossene Hafen.*

EX-DOCK. Refers to merchandise sold from ship's side not including carting.

EXEMPTED SPACE. Term used in tonnage measurement to mean open spaces in permanent erections such as poops, bridges, forecastles, when they are not fitted with doors or other permanently attached means of closing them. They are not included in the gross tonnage.

Fr: *Espace Exempté;* Ger: *Nicht eingemessener Raum.*

EXEMPT PILOT. A term used in Great Britain in connection with pilots who conduct ships which are exempted from the compulsion to carry a pilot either because their masters hold a pilotage certificate or because they are under certain tonnage. These ships take an exempt pilot as a precaution.

EXFOLIATION. The gradual wasting away of copper sheathing of (wooden) ships in sea water.

Fr: *Exfoliation;* Ger: *Abblätterung.*

EXHAUST TURBINE. A geared turbine connected to the shaft of a reciprocating engine through an elastic or hydraulic coupling and in which the remaining energy in the steam leaving the low-pressure cylinder is utilized before exhausting into the condenser. The turbine is by-passed when the reciprocating engines are working astern, by a change-over valve which opens the passage of steam to the condenser and releases the oil pressure on the hydraulic coupling. The exhaust turbine system is considered suitable for powers ranging from 400 to 6,000 hp.

Fr: *Turbine d'Évacuation; Turbine d'Échappement;* Ger: *Abdampfturbine.*

Experience has demonstrated that the addition of an exhaust turbine of the Bauer-Wach type has increased the revolutions of the reciprocating engines by 10 per cent, which is equivalent to an increase in power of 25 to 30 per cent with the same steam consumption, at normal speeds.

Torsion meter measurements show that the use of an exhaust turbine in conjunction with reciprocating engines materially decreases the unevenness of the turning movement produced by the reciprocator when working alone, and has a fly-wheel effect which tends to reduce the racing of the propeller in heavy weather. Exhaust turbines or main shafting have been fitted to a large number of recently built vessels as well as to existing vessels when improvements in steaming performances were desired.

EXHAUST VENTILATION. A system of mechanical ventilation in which vitiated air in a ship's compartment is removed by fans, while fresh air is supplied through natural ventilators. This system finds application to lavatory accommodation, third-class passengers' and crew's accommodation, storerooms, and occasionally to domestic departments. In this system the blowers are connected with the uptake air shafts.

Fr: *Ventilation par Suction;* Ger: *Ausstromlüftung.*

EXHAUST VENTILATOR. Ventilator used as an exhaust in mechanical ventilation.

Fr: *Manche d'Évacuation;* Ger: *Drucklüfter; Windsauger.*

EX-MERIDIAN ALTITUDE. The observation of a celestial body taken to ascertain the latitude shortly before or after it has crossed the meridian. Navigators employ this method particularly when the object to be observed has been or is likely to be obscured by clouds at its meridian

passage. By applying a tabulated correction to the observed altitude, the latitude can be found accurately under favorable conditions when the hour angle is not too large.
Fr: *Hauteur Circumméridienne;* Ger: *Nebenmeridianhöhe; Zirkummeridianhöhe.*

EX-MERIDIAN LATITUDE. Latitude obtained by the observation of a celestial body shortly before or shortly after it has crossed the meridian.
Fr: *Latitude Ex-Méridienne; Latitude Circumméridienne;* Ger: *Nebenmeridianbreite; Aussenmeridianbreite.*

EXPANSION CHAMBER. A self-adjusting chamber of corrugated metal by means of which the bowl of a liquid compass is kept constantly full without the appearance of air bubbles or the development of undue pressure caused by the change in volume of the liquid due to changes of temperature.
Ger: *Ausdehnungstaum.*

EXPANSION HATCH. A term applied to hatches with high coamings fitted on oil tankers for the purpose of allowing space for the expansion of oil due to changes in temperature.
Fr: *Coffre d'Expansion;* Ger: *Expansionsluke; Expansionsschacht.*

EXPANSION JOINT. 1. A sliding joint in the superstructure or deck plating, installed to permit linear movement fore-and-aft between the adjacent connected sections when the ship hogs and sags, in order to obviate the development of destructive stresses.
Fr: *Joint Glissant;* Ger: *Expansionsfalt.*
2. A simple joint in steam piping to obviate distortion due to expansion and contraction over wide ranges of temperature variation.

EXPANSION TRUNK. 1. The upper portion of a cargo tank in an oil tanker, forming a comparatively small trunk above the main tank with which it is permanently in communication. These trunks serve to relieve pressure in the main tanks in the event of expansion of their contents due to changes in temperature, at the same time keeping the lower tanks full in order to avoid strains on the bulkheads and deck and loss of stability due to the motion of a liquid cargo with a large free surface, which would occur if the main tanks were not kept completely full.

Fr: *Coffre d'Expansion;* Ger: *Expansionsschacht.*
2. Trunkways which extend a short distance down from the hatches into oil tanker compartments.

EXPORT BILL OF LADING. A term used in the United States to denote bills of lading made for goods or merchandise destined to foreign countries as distinguished from bills of lading for domestic merchandise.

EXPORT DUTY. Customs duty required by law to be paid on the exportation of certain goods.
Fr: *Droit de Sortie;* Ger: *Ausfuhrzoll.*

EXPORTER'S INVOICE. A private invoice which accurately lists all the packages being shipped, their numbers, weight, measurement, description, and cost. It also contains the name of the vessel on which the goods are being shipped, their destination, and marks of the consignee.
Fr: *Facture d'Expédition;* Ger: *Ausfuhr Warenrechnung.*

EXPRESS LINER. A term which refers to a type of passenger vessel of very high speed and standard of luxury, in which three classes of passengers are carried. There is no space available for ordinary cargo. It carries only mail and small quantities of high-grade cargo, generally referred to as express matter, which can be handled quickly and pays special rates.
Christie, J. D., "Liner Development During Past Fifty Years," North East Coast Institution of Engineers and Shipbuilders (Newcastle upon Tyne), *Transactions,* vol. 51 (1934–35); de Vito, E., "Atlantic Liners," Institution of Naval Architects (London), *Transactions,* vol. 71 (1929).

EXPRESS WARRANTY. A warranty which must be included in or written on the insurance policy, or must be contained in some document incorporated, by reference, into the policy.
Fr: *Garantie Expresse;* Ger: *Ausdrückliche Garantie.*

EX-QUAY. Conditions of a contract for the purchase of goods in which the goods are discharged from the ship at seller's cost.
Fr: *Franco Quai.*

EX-SHIP. Conditions of sale for goods under which the purchaser is responsible for taking delivery of the goods at the ship's side. Also called "free overside."
Fr: *Bord à Bord;* Ger: *Ab Schiff.*

EXTENSION CLERK (U. S.). An assistant to the receiving clerk. He extends the three dimensions, length, width, and height into cubic or volume of each and every package received and loaded into the vessel.

EXTRA FLEXIBLE WIRE ROPE. A 6-strand wire rope with 7 hemp cores, the wires of each strand being wrapped around a core. It is the most flexible type of wire rope and is used for towing hawsers, mooring lines, warps, running rigging, where great flexibility or elasticity are required. Generally made in 6 x 12, 6 x 24, 6 x 30 construction. Also called running rope.

EXTRA-MASTER. In Great Britain the recipient of a certificate delivered by the Board of Trade to master mariners who have been through a special course of studies and examination. It is officially recognized but not officially demanded.

EXTRA RISKS. The risks which are occasionally added to an ordinary marine insurance policy such as war risk, theft and pilferage, and the like. The terms of such additional cover are usually typewritten on the policy or incorporated therein by the adhesion of printed slips.

EXTRATERRITORIALITY. The operation of the laws of a State or Country beyond or outside of its physical boundaries. A ship on the high seas is subject to the laws of the country whose flag she bears. It is a jurisdiction over the persons and property of its citizens. In foreign ports or in territorial waters the privilege of freedom from local territorial jurisdiction based on the theory that a vessel is a floating portion of the country whose flag she flies has nowadays been rejected by most maritime nations. Although in actual practice all questions affecting the ship's internal discipline and legal relations are left to the authorities of the flag State, a merchant vessel in foreign ports must observe the laws of police and security of the country in which the vessel finds itself. Merchant ships in foreign waters cannot provide refuge for persons fleeing from the local authorities or for political refugees. The authorities of the port enjoy the power to arrest such persons.

Fr: *Exterritorialité;* Ger: *Exterritorialitat.* Charteris, "The Legal Position of Merchantmen in Foreign Ports." *British Year Book of International Law,* 1920/21; Tremlett-Fell, E., "Jurisdiction over Foreign Private Merchant Vessels and Seamen." *Johns Hopkins* *University Studies in Historical and Political Science,* Series 40, No. 3, Baltimore, 1922.

EXTREME BREADTH. The maximum breadth of a ship measured outside plating, planking, fenders, beading or any other permanent attachment to the hull.

Fr: *Largeur au fort;* Ger: *Breite über Alles.*

EXTREME DRAFT. The vertical distance from the designed waterline to the lowest projecting portion of the vessel at any point in a vessel's length. Also called keel draft.

Fr: *Tirant d'Eau Maximum;* Ger: *Grosster Tiefgang.*

EXTREME LENGTH. Also *length overall.* **1.** The length measured between the forward and after extremities of the hull, or the dimensions required to contain the ship in a lock or dry dock.

2. The length measured from a perpendicular to the base line and tangent to the most forward projection of the stem, to a line perpendicular to the base line and tangent to the afterend of the stern.

Fr: *Longueur Hors-Tout;* Ger: *Grösste Länge; Länge über alles.*

EYE. 1. The loop in a shroud or stay which goes over the masthead.

Fr: *Oeil;* Ger: *Auge.*

2. The hole at the end of the shank through which the anchor ring or anchor shackle is inserted. Also called anchor eye.

Fr: *Oeil;* Ger: *Ankerauge.*

3. A nautical expression indicating the direction from which the wind blows. In a tropical cyclone the eye is the central calm area.

Fr: *Lit.*

EYE BLOCK. A rope-strapped block with a thimble seized in the strap.

EYEBOLT. A bolt with an eye at one end.

Fr: *Piton à oeil;* Ger: *Augenbolzen.*

EYELET. Also eyelet hole, lacing hole. **1.** Small holes worked in a sail with palm and needle, and through which the reef points are run for half their length, then sewed to the eyelet hole.

2. The holes for the robands to go through in bending a sail. They are usually worked buttonhole fashion and strengthened by small metal rings or grommets made of several thicknesses of twine.

3. One of the small holes along the edge of an awning through which the lacing is rove.

Fr: *Oeil de Pie; Oeillet de Transfilage;* Ger: *Gatchen; Reffgatt; Schnurloch; Segelösen.*

EYE PLATE. A plate or casting with an eye normal to its surface and formed solid with the plate. Also called pad eye, lug pad.

Fr: *Piton à Plaque;* Ger: *Augplatte.*

EYES. That part of a ship's bows near the hawse holes.

Fr: *Avant;* Ger: *Vorschiff.*

See **Bull's Eye, Elliott Eye, Flemish Eye. Lacing Eyes, Pad Eye, Ropemaker's Eye, Rudder Eye.**

EYE SPLICE. A loop spliced in the end of a rope. It is more frequently used than any other splice.

Fr: *Épissure à Oeil;* Ger: *Augsplissung.*

EYE TACKLE. A tackle with an eye on each block.

F

F. International code of signals flag showing red diamond on white ground. Indicates when flown singly: "I am disabled. Communicate with me."

F. Freeboard mark which indicates the fresh water load line in summer.

f.a.c. FAST AS CAN (loading or discharging).

F.A.A. FREE OF ALL AVERAGE (insurance).

F.A.S. FREE ALONGSIDE SHIP.

Fath. FATHOM.

F.C. and S. FREE OF CAPTURE AND SEIZURE (insurance).

F.C. and S. and R. and C.C. FREE OF CAPTURE, SEIZURE, RIOTS AND CIVIL COMMOTIONS (insurance).

F. and D. FREIGHT AND DEMURRAGE.

f.d. FREE DISCHARGE or FREE DISPATCH.

F.f.a. FREE FROM ALONGSIDE.

F.G.A. FOREIGN GENERAL AVERAGE.

F.G.A. FREE OF GENERAL AVERAGE (insurance).

f.h. FOREHATCH.

F. I. A. FULL INTEREST ADMITTED (marine insurance).

f.i.b. FREE INTO BUNKERS or FREE INTO BARGE (coal trade).

F.I.O. FREE IN AND OUT (chartering).

F.O. FOR ORDERS.

F.o.q. FREE ON QUAY.

f.o.r.t. FULL OUT RYE TERMS (grain trade).

f.o.s. FREE ON STEAMER.

F.O.W. FIRST OPEN WATER.

F.P. FLOATING POLICY (insurance).

F.P.A. FREE OF PARTICULAR AVERAGE.

F.P.A.A.C. FREE OF PARTICULAR AVERAGE, AMERICAN CONDITIONS. (See *Average*.)

F.P.A.E.C. FREE OF PARTICULAR AVERAGE, ENGLISH CONDITIONS. (see *Average*.)

F. P. I. L. FULL PREMIUM IF LOST (marine insurance).

F/R. FREIGHT RELEASE. (see *Release*.)

F.t. FULL TERMS.

f.w.d. FRESH WATER DAMAGE.

No F. C. and S. FREE OF CAPTURE AND SEIZURE CLAUSE DELETED (insurance).

F.C. and S. CLAUSE. An abbreviation for "free of capture and seizure" clause, by which war risks are excluded from a marine policy and can only be covered by special agreement. The full clause reads:

"Warranted free of capture, seizure, arrest, restraint or detainment, and the consequences thereof, or of any attempt thereof (Piracy excepted) and also from all consequences of hostilities or war-like operations whether before or after declaration of war."

Fr: *Clause Franc de Capture et Saisie;*
Ger: *Frei von Prise und Besitz Klausel.*

F.I.O. CHARTER. The "free in and out" charter is made on the basis that the charterer is liable for all the usual costs of ship management, with the exception of the costs of loading and discharging cargo, and of putting the vessel into dock, which are paid for by the owners. The shipowner provides the vessel and the crew.

F.K. FRAMING (FOSTER KING FRAMING). A transverse system of framing adopted for tank vessels which embodies deep keelsons and stringers carried between the bulkheads and strongly bracketed to them.

FABRICATE. Shipbuilding term which refers collectively to the various processes used in a shipyard to form the component parts of a steel hull. The principal of these processes are: bending of plates and shapes, shearing, planing, punching, drilling, reaming, countersinking, flanging, forging, welding, cutting or burning, joggling, furnacing, chamfering, scarphing, riveting, milling.

FABRICATED STERN FRAME. A stern frame fabricated with riveted or welded mild steel plates.

Fr: *Etambot en tôles façonnées;* Ger: *Walzblechhintersteven.*

The sole piece is made a continuation of the after keel plate. The lower part of the body post is made of bent plate, butt-welded to the top edge of the sole plate as well as continuing down inside the sole plate to the bottom and welded. The forward edges of the body post are curved forward toward the bottom to give a longer weld to the upper edges of the sole plate. Webs are welded into the sole plate for connection to the center keel and floors. The part above the boss, made in similar manner to the rest, runs from the boss over the screw aperture, with webs for the attachment of floor plates of the afterframes, and a central web where necessary. The propeller boss is simply a thick ring of cast steel, to which the upper and lower parts of the body post are welded, with vertical reinforcing webs above and below the boss casting. The rudder post is similarly of bent plate, butt-welded to the top of the sole plate and continued down to the bottom; the upper open side of the sole plate is closed by a plate welded to the afteredge of the body post and fore edge of the rudderpost. The gudgeons are of cast steel; the lowest one being welded into the afterend of the sole plate; the intermediate ones being welded into the open part of the rudderpost, and the space between them closed by a welded-in plate.

Carter, N., Substitution of Fabricated Structures for Stern Castings, The Shipbuilder and Marine Engine Builder, (Newcastle upon Tyne), vol. 48, April, 1941.

FABRICATED VESSEL. A vessel built by pre-assembly or prefabrication methods whereby large structural sections of the hull weighing approximately from 20 to 70 tons are riveted or welded in fabricating shops or bays situated near the building slip and then transported bodily by cranes on to the slip where they are assembled with other sections similarly constructed.

Ger: *Fabriksmässig gebautes Schiff.*

Except as to details which may be modified to provide for ease of fabrication, the fabricated ship does not differ essentially in structure or form from any other ship assembled on the building slip. The sections most usually prefabricated are double bottom, structural bulkheads, bow, stern, deckhouses.

FACE. The after surface of a propeller blade, which acts on the water to drive the vessel forward. Also called driving face, thrust surface, driving surface.

Fr: *Face poussante;* Ger: *Druckfläche.*

FACE BAR. A stiffening angle bar fitted along the inner edge of a web frame, stringer, or bracket.

FACE PIECES. The pieces of wood wrought on the forepart of the knee of the head.

Fr: *Remplissage de la Guibre;* Ger: *Galionsfullstuck; Galionsauslage.*

FACE PLATE. 1. A plate fitted perpendicularly to the web and fastened to the flanges at one end of a frame, stiffener, or girder, to compensate for the continuous plating attached to the flanges at the other edge.

Fr: *Bandeau;* Ger: *Facherplatte.*

2. In welded construction, a narrow plate fitted to the free edge of a flat bar stiffener, perpendicular to it, to lend rigidity. By extension, the term is loosely applied to any such plate welded to the free edge of a structural component to stiffen it.

FACING. The superposition of one piece of timber upon another in order to give it additional strength or finish.

Fr: *Placage.*

FACTOR OF SUBDIVISION. A factor which multiplied by the floodable length gives the maximum permissible length of any compartment. Also called permissible factor. The value of this factor depends on the length of the ship, and for a given length varies according to the nature of the service for which the ship is intended, as established by the International Convention for the Safety of Life at Sea, 1929.

Fr: *Facteur de Cloisonnement;* Ger: *Abteilungsfaktor.*

See **Floodable Length.**

"Subdivision of Ships," in *Principles of Naval Architecture,* Russell and Chapman, New York, 1939.

FACTORY VESSEL. A general term for different types of vessels used in the fishing industry, equipped with suitable plant to transform or prepare the catch as a marketable product without assistance from shore.

Fr: *Bâtiment-Usine;* Ger: *Fischverarbeitungsschiff; Fabrikschiff.*

The plant on board factory vessels is arranged to utilize the catch to the utmost advantage. Some fish are fit only for conversion into cattle, pig, or poultry food; others are valuable for their oil content (menhaden). Others still, such as cod and shark, have livers which provide valuable medicinal oil. Some, such as salmon, crabs, and so on, are tinned or canned on board, and finally, fishes like halibut are placed in cold storage for sale at any convenient market. The tonnage of factory vessels varies according to the species of fish to be caught and the plant necessary for their transformation. The largest are the whale-oil factory vessels with a tonnage of about 20,000.

Factory vessels have served with profit as tenders to smaller fleets of fishing boats in the Greenland halibut and Japanese crab fisheries.

Fiedler, R. H., "The factory ship," American Fisheries Society, vol. LXVI, Washington (1936).

FAIR. To return to its original form a plate or angle which has been bent out of shape. In welded ship construction, it is frequently necessary to fair bulkheads and decks after they have been welded, to remove dimples, humps, and hollows resulting from the heat of welding and stresses caused by it.

Fr: *Redresser;* Ger: *Glätten; Zurichten.*

FAIR HOLES. Holes in two or more pieces of metal to be riveted together which show a clear unobstructed passage through, as distinguished from blind or unfair holes which do not coincide.

Fr: *Trous rectifiés;* Ger: *Richtige Nietlöcher.*

FAIRING. A correcting process performed in laying down the ship's lines in the mold loft, to insure the regularity or evenness of the water lines, bow and buttock lines when transferring to full size the sheer drawing on the mold loft floor.

Fr: *Balancement des Formes;* Ger: *Ausstraken.*

FAIRING RIBBAND. A type of ribband consisting of a flat steel bar of suitable cross section, used in the vicinity of welded seams of decks, bulkheads and light shell plating, for the purpose of reducing buckling during welding.

FAIRING STRONGBACK. A strongback made of two flat bars bolted together, and ashers between them as spacers. A bolt with nut is welded to the center of the indentation and by tightening the nut the center of the hollow comes part way into place. By hammering around the periphery of the hollow the strain on the plate is relieved and the surface of the plate remains smooth and fair. The fairing strongback is used by ship-repairers for pulling out small bumps in shell or deck plates. For deep sharp indentations a hole, slightly larger than the bolt, is drilled through the plate and countersunk on the convex side.

FAIR IN PLACE. A term used in ship repairing by which is meant the restoring to original shape of any part of the ship's structure not damaged seriously enough to necessitate actual removal from the ship for repair. In the United States also called to bump.

Fr: *Redresser sur Place.*

FAIR ISLE SKIFF. A boat used in Fair Isle, Shetland Islands, for line fishing for skate or coalfish. Pointed bow and stern, very flat midship section, and marked sheer fore and aft. Single mast stepped amidships and square sail. Length over-all 22 ft. Keel 15.5 ft. Breadth 5.7 ft. Depth 3 ft.

FAIRLEADER. 1. A strip of board with holes in it for running rigging to pass through. 2. Any ringbolt, eye, or loop which guides a rope in the required direction.

A short length of wood with holes bored in it, or a block or thimble of wood or metal suitably placed to lead ropes to their proper places. Also called lead.

Fr: *Conduit; Rateau;* Ger: *Wegweiser Klotje; Wegweiserbrett.*

See **Warping Chock.**

FAIRWATER. 1. A conical-shaped cap fitted over the locknut at the afterend of the propeller shaft to prevent an abrupt change in the streamlines. Also called fairwater cone, propeller cap, fairwater cap.

Fr: *Chapeau;* Ger: *Konische Kappe; Schraubenkonus.*

2. Any casting or plate affixed to the hull with a view to maintaining smooth streamline flow of water. Plating fitted about the ends of shaft tubes or struts to prevent a sharp change in the direction of streamlines.

FAIRWATER CAP.
See **Fairwater.**

FAIRWATER CONE.
See **Fairwater.**

FAIRWATER SLEEVES. Sleeves of steel plate, or composition, in the shape of a truncated cone, fabricated in halves, and secured to the end of the strut bearing and stern-tube bearing, to promote streamline flow and reduce resistance to progress through the water in multiple screw vessels.

See **Fairwater.**

FAIRWAY. That part of a river, harbor, and so on, where the main navigable channel for vessels of larger size lies. The usual course followed by vessels entering or leaving harbor. Also called ship channel. The word "fairway" has been generally interpreted to include any navigable water on which vessels of commerce habitually move, and, therefore, embraces the water inside channel buoys where light-draft vessels frequently navigate and not merely the ship channel itself.

Fr: *Passe;* Ger: *Fahrwasser.*

FAIRWAY BUOY. A buoy marking the fairway in a channel. They are painted in black and white or red and white vertical stripes. Also called mid-channel buoys.

Fr: *Bouée de Direction; Bouée de Mi-Chenal;* Ger: *Ansteuerungstonne; Mittelfahrwassertonne.*

FAIR WIND. A general term for the wind when favorable to a ship's course. "Fair" is more comprehensive than "large" since it includes about 16 points.

Fr: *Bon Vent;* Ger: *Günstiger Wind.*

FAKATORA. An East Indian planked-up

FAKE—FALL TUB

boat with double outriggers from Galela Bay (Moluccas) used for trading to Ternate and Batjan, also in the local fisheries. The hull is built with a keel about 3½ in. deep running the whole length. There are 7 strakes of planking on each side of the keel. Each strake has a row of projecting perforated lugs over which the frames are fitted and tied thereto by cord lashings made from black palm fiber. A cabin or shelter is built on strong thwarts projecting a few inches outboard. A bamboo framework affords stowage for light gear above the cabin roof. Length 24 ft. Breadth 5 ft. Depth 25 in. (Typical.)

The rig consists of a tripod bamboo mast. A tabernacle is provided at the fore end of the cabin. The twin legs are about the length of the cabin. The unpaired leg is stepped halfway between the cabin and the stem. The sail is of oblong quadrilateral shape made of cotton or matting with yard and boom. To carry the yard a Y-shaped peg is inserted into the top end of one of the paired mast legs.

FAKE. One of the circles or windings of a rope as it lies in a coil. One complete circle of a rope is a fake. A number of such turns makes a tier, and several tiers superimposed, a coil.

Fr: *Plet; Glène;* Ger: *Bucht.*
See **Catch Fake, Figure-Eight Fake, Flemish Fake, French Fake, Long Fake.**

FALBAT. Open seal-hunting boat originating from the districts of Norrbotten and Vesterbotten in the northern part of the Gulf of Bothnia. Norbotten boats: Length 28 ft. Breadth of 8 ft. Depth of 2 ft. 8 in. Vesterbotten boats: Length about 34 ft.

The hull is built with a swim bow, sharp stern, short and deep keel shod with iron, and a very raking sternpost. The planking is clinker-laid with detachable washboards above the gunwale. The rig consists of a square sail carried on a slender mast without step. The stay is made secure by an arrangement which allows it to be cast loose instantly, and the mast lowered on the arrival of a squall. The largest boats carry a small sprit mizzen. Each boat carries 2 small tenders of same type and build in which 2 men take place when hunting.

FALBOOT. A type of folding boat consisting of a framework of wood over which is stretched a skin of rubberized material. It is manufactured as a single seater or as a two seater. Owing to the great width of the beam and to the fact that the center of gravity is below the waterline, it has a considerable transverse stability. A single seater weighs about 45 lbs. being about 14 feet in length and 2½ feet in width. It can be loaded with safety up to about 500 lbs. The average two seater weighs about 60 lbs. being about 17 feet long and about 3 feet wide with a carrying capacity of about 700 lbs. The draft ranges from 3 to 4 inches of water. Also known under the trade name of "FOLBOT."

FALCA. Name given in British and Dutch Guiana to a *corial* fitted with washboards running from stem to stern on each side.

FALL. 1. The entire length of rope in a tackle. The end secured to the block is called the standing part, the opposite end the hauling part.

2. In hoisting machinery, the part of the rope to which power is applied; one end being rove through the derrick block and the other carried to the wind.

Fr: *Garant;* Ger: *Laufer; Seil.*
See **Boat Fall, Brailing Fall, Burton Fall, Cargo Fall, Catfall, Married Fall, Rapid Transit Fall, Speck Fall, Split Fall, Topping Lift Fall, Up and Down Fall.**

FALL ASTERN. To be outdistanced by another vessel. Also called to drop astern.

Fr: *Perdre;* Ger: *Achteraussacken.*

FALL BLOCK. The block of a purchase to which the hauling part of the fall first leads.

FALL BOOM.
See **Hatch Boom.**

FALL COVER. Canvas cover fitted over boat falls of vessels trading in Northern waters to prevent snow lodging in between the parts of the fall where it is likely to freeze solid and thus render the tackle useless.

FALLING TIDE. The actual falling of the tide from high water to the next low water.

Fr: *Marée descendante; Reflux; Perdant;* Ger: *Ebbe.*

FALL IN WITH. To meet, as one ship which meets another at sea.

FALL OFF. To deviate from the course to which the head of the ship was previously directed. To drop away from the wind, in contradistinction to "coming to."

Fr: *Abattre;* Ger: *Abfallen.*

FALL TUB. Framework tub placed near the davits into which the boatfalls are coiled.

FALSE BELLIES. See Rubbing Pieces.

FALSE CIRRUS. The cirrus formed on the top of Cumulo-Nimbus, which often becomes detached.

FALSE COLORS. A "ruse de guerre" recognized by international law which consists of showing a neutral or enemy ensign. The use of false colors by merchant vessels in time of war to avoid capture or destruction is a well-established custom in the history of maritime warfare and is not contrary to international law. It is, however, generally admitted that this ruse should be resorted to only when the vessel is in imminent danger and should be restricted to that period.

FALSE KEEL. SHOE. A wooden keel composed of elm plank or thick stuff fastened lightly under the main keel to protect it in case of grounding. If the ship should strike the ground the false keel is designed to give away, thus saving the main keel.

Fr: *Fausse Quille;* Ger: *Loskiel.*

FALSE MESHES. A name given to the loops inserted in any given row of meshes by which the number of meshes is increased in that part of the net. Sometimes called accrues, quarterings, stowing meshes. It is also known as "creasing." An extra mesh added in a net to increase its size.

Ger: *Einhängemasche.*

FALSE POST. A piece of timber affixed to the afterside of the main post (sternpost) to make good a deficiency in size.

Fr: *Faux-Etambot;* Ger: *Loser Hintersteven.*

FALSE RAIL. A timber fayed down upon the rail of the head in a wooden ship to strengthen it. Also called spray board. It formed the seat of ease at the afterend next to the bow. (Obsolete.)

FALSE STEM. Scarfed timbers fayed to the forepart of the stem in a wooden ship, extending from the gripe upward.

Fr: *Taillemer;* Ger: *Aussensteven; Schegg.*

FALSE TACK. To shoot up in the wind and fill off on the same tack again: a trick sometimes practised in yacht racing when two vessels are working close-hauled together.

FALSTERBAT. A Danish decked fishing boat from the island of Falster with keel, straight stem, square stern and slightly raked sternpost. It is cutter-rigged with pole mast, loose-footed gaff mainsail, two headsails, and yard topsail. Length over-all 48 ft. Length of keel 39 ft. Breadth amidships 13 ft.

FALT BOAT.
See Collapsible Boat.

FANCY LINE. A line running through a block fastened under the gaff at the jaws and used as a downhaul. A line for overhauling the lee topping lift.

Fr: *Halebas de Corne;* Ger: *Gaffel Niederholer.*

FANNING.
See Ghosting.

FANTAIL (U. S.). The overhanging stern section of vessels which have round or elliptical after endings, from waterline to uppermost decks which extend well abaft the after perpendicular.

FANTAIL GRATING (U. S.). A wooden grating fitted at the after end of tugboats, trawlers, and similar craft. It prevents lines and gear from fouling the tiller and is used as a platform for the stowage of hawsers and mooring lines.

FANTAIL STERN. A type of yacht stern in which the shell planking or plating sweeps up to a sharp point to join the deck planking forming a very elongated counter with great overhang. This type of stern has been almost entirely abandoned in recent years. It is likely to pound in rough weather and creates eddy resistances at any but relatively low speeds.

FAOTASI. A native craft of the Samoan Islands, being a cross between the Polynesian War canoe, now extinct, and the New Bedford whaleboat. They are built of 0.5-in. carvel planking with seam battens; an extra heavy keelson is fitted to prevent hogging and sagging. They are used for the transportation of natives and market produce. Being light and easily handled they are well suited for surf work. Length over-all 56 ft. 6 in. to 67 ft. Height, bow, 3 ft. 5 in. to 3 ft. 6 in. Height, midships, 2 ft. 3 in. to 2 ft. 5 in. Beam 4 ft. 9 in. Height, stern, 3 ft. 4 in. The largest are manned by a crew of 36 oarsmen.

FARELLA. A small fishing boat from Malta. Also called *ferilla*. The rig consists of a single spritsail which hoists on a short stout mast placed right in the head of the boat. The heel of the sprit instead of resting in a snotter attached to the mast is stepped in one of the sockets cut in the upper surface of an arched deck thwart placed a foot or so abaft the mast, and moved from one to another as is best suited to the strength and direction of the wind. The sheer and round of beam are considerable. A small hatchway is pierced in the deck nearly amidships. Length 14 to 26 ft. Breadth 6½ to 8.3 ft. Molded depth 3 ft. 3 in. (Typical.)

FAREWELL WHISTLE. Three prolonged blasts on the ship's whistle as a salute or farewell when leaving port. If meant for another ship, the latter should return the courtesy by blowing also three times. The first ship then gives a short blast in acknowledgment.

Ger: *Abfahrt Pfeifesignal.*

FASHIONED PLATE. A shaped plate which can be worked into the desired shape without furnacing.

Fr: *Tôle Façonnée;* Ger: *Formplatte.*

Fashioned plates are worked in the underwater part of the hull at any point where a streamlined effect or an otherwise flat projection is desired.

FASHION PIECE. One of the timbers fashioning the afterpart of a square-sterned ship below the wing transom, terminating at the tuck and forming the shape of the stern. Also called fashion timber. It is rabbeted to the sternpost and wing transom.

Fr: *Estain;* Ger: *Randsomholz.*

FASHION PLATE STEM. A stem fabricated from mild steel plates. Also called plated stem, soft nose stem. The plates are bent cold into a U form, to sections taken from the mold loft, by a knife tool under a hydraulic press, or from the plate furnace in convenient lengths and riveted or welded into the lower part of the stem to which the vertical center keel can be riveted or welded. Transverse webs are fitted for connection to the forepeak floors and at the height of the decks and stringers; also at intermediate points to secure rigidity. The lower extremity of the stem is lap-welded or riveted to the forward butt of the foremost keel plate, or flush-butted with an internal buttstrap. The leading hooding ends of the bow plates lap inside the stem and are thus protected from the erosive action of the water.

Fr: *Etrave en Tôles façonnées;* Ger: *Walzblechvorsteven; Formplatte Vorsteven.*

FASHION TIMBER. See Fashion Piece.

FAST. A rope or chain by which a vessel is secured to a wharf, pier, quay, etc. It is named according to its position: bow fast, head fast, breast fast, quarter fast, or stern fast. Also called mooring line.

Fr: *Amarre de Poste;* Ger: *Festmachetau.*

See Bow Fast, Breast Fast, Head Fast, Quarter Fast, Shore Fast, Stern Fast.

FAST BOAT. Expression formerly used by whalemen which signifies that the whaleboat actually engaged in the capture was fast to the whale by means of harpoon and line, in contradistinction to a loose boat, or one which had not succeeded in striking a whale.

FASTENING. A general term applied to nails, spikes, bolts, screws, and treenails used for connecting the various structural parts of a wooden hull.

Fr: *Chevillage;* Ger: *Verbolzung; Nagelbefestigung.*

See Double Fastening, Double and Single Fastening, Dump Fastening, Inside Fastening, Outside Fastening, Single Fastening, Spike Fastening, Through Fastening.

The number of fastenings to be driven is as a rule regulated by the width of the plank, and the diameter by its thickness and the material of which the fastening is made. In boatbuilding five varieties of fastenings are used: riveted nails, clinched nails, screws, bolts, drifts.

FAST ICE. A floe extending from the land and fast to it. Called also land floe, shore floe, ice foot.

FATA MORGANA. The multiple mirage observed in the Straits of Messina. It is a phenomenon of narrow waters and is peculiar because there is much distortion and repetition of images. It is a combination of land mirage (inferior mirage) and sea mirage (superior mirage) and abnormal refraction.

It has been observed in other localities in Italy under the names of "Mutate" and "Lavandaja."

FATHOM. A nautical measure equal to 6 ft. used for measuring cordage, anchor chains, lead lines, also depth of water at sea.

Fr: *Brasse;* Ger: *Faden.*

FATHOM LINE. A line drawn on a nautical chart through all positions which have the same depth at mean low water springs. It indicates the contour of the sea bottom. Also called isobath.

Fr: *Ligne des Sondes; Isobathe;* Ger: *Lotungslinie; Tiefenlinie.*

FATHOMETER. See **Echo Sounder.**

FAY. To unite two planks or plates closely, in such a manner as to bring the meeting surfaces into intimate contact.

FAYING SURFACE. The meeting surfaces of two pieces of wood or metal as they lie against each other when bolted or riveted together.

Fr: *Faces de Placage;* Ger: *Zusammenzufügende Fläche; Dichtungsfläche.*

FEATHER. The curve in the blade of an oar. Oars for working in open waters are usually without feather; but in smooth water oars it is almost invariable.

FEATHERING PADDLE WHEEL. A paddle wheel in which the floats are mechanically and automatically placed and maintained in their true position for maximum efficiency. Throughout the immersion the floats act solely to accelerate a stream of water in the proper direction for propulsion. They are hung on pins and are swung in such a way that they enter and leave the water nearly in an edgewise direction.

Fr: *Roue à Aubes Articulées;* Ger: *Bewegliches Schaufelrad.*

There are two types of feathering wheels. In one, sometimes called the English or European type, the feathering of the floats is effected by their levers being connected to, and revolving about, a pin fixed to the sponson beam of the paddle box set eccentrically to the paddle shift axis. In the second, or American type, an eccentric is fitted to the outer end of the shaft main bearing of such a diameter as to permit of feathering sufficiently and clearing the bearing and its base.

The working parts of the feathering gear usually have the pins cased with bronze and the holes in which they fit are bushed with lignum vitae. Feathering wheels for equivalent power are of much smaller diameter than those with radial floats and are run at a much higher number of revolutions. They are particularly adapted to ships operating under varying conditions of draft.

Bragg, E. M., "Feathering Paddle Wheels," Society of Naval Architects and Marine Engineers (New York), *Transactions,* vol. 24 (1916).

FEATHERING SCREW PROPELLER. See **Reversible Propeller.**

FEATHERING STROKE. A stroke in which the blade of the oar is turned horizontally immediately after it leaves the water and kept so until it has been brought forward and is ready to be dipped again.

FEAZINGS. The unlaid or ragged end of a rope.

FEEDER. A sort of grain reservoir consisting of a boarded or plated trunkway built around a hatchway between two decks. It is filled with grain which falls automatically and fills any vacant spaces that may form in a lower hold, thus providing against the settling of the grain when the latter is loaded in bulk.

Fr: *Feeder;* Ger: *Feeder.*

FEELER. A very thin flat knifelike steel blade with wooden handle, used for testing the seams of riveted work to determine whether the faying surfaces have been properly drawn together. Also called Feeler knife.

FELUCA. A lateen-rigged trading craft of Italy. A similar craft in France is known as *felouque,* in Spain as *falua,* in Portugal as *fallua.* They are the most northern lateen-rigged craft found in European waters. The largest boats are decked fore and aft but the average are decked only at the ends or from stem to foremast. The hull is keel-built with straight stem and transom stern. The rig consists of two short masts of the same length. There are no headsails. The sails are furled by clewing up at the foot. They are never reefed. Length 49.4 ft. Breadth 13.8 ft. Depth 6.2 ft. Sail area 1,056 sq. ft. Deadweight 12 tons. (Typical.)

Feluca

FEMBORING. A type of sailing and rowing boat used for fishing in the northern districts of Norway. It is clinker-built and rigged with one mast and square sail. It pulls 10 short blade oars. Length 36 ft. Breadth 8 ft. Depth 2 ft. amidships.

FEMBORSEKOR. Name given in South Sweden (Blekinge) to a small open boat used in the cod and flounder fisheries. It is rigged with sprit mainsail and jib-headed foresail. Length 13 to 16 ft. Breadth 6½ ft. Crew 2 to 3. (Typical.)

FEMKJEPING. A Norwegian open boat from the Nordfjord. Also called *foringsbaat.* It pulls 5 pairs of oars and is used for fishing in the fjords.

See **Nordfjordbaat.**

FENDER. Term applied to various devices, fixed or portable, serving to cushion the shocks and protect the shell plating when a vessel comes in contact with a quay wall, or the like, or another vessel. Also called bumper.

Fr: *Défense;* Ger: *Fender.*

See Bow Fender, Canvas Fender, Cork Fender, Guard Rail, Grommet Fender, Mat Fender, Permanent Fender, Pile Fender, Pudding Fender, Rod Fender, Rope Fender, Spar Fender.

FENDER SPAR. A floating spar used for fending off a moored vessel from a quay wall or pier.

See Camel.

FENLAND PUNT. Flat-bottomed double-ended boat in which the sides meet the bottom in a sharp chine. The stem and sternpost project below the bottom, with a view to preventing the punt from grounding hard and fast.

See Farella. **FERILLA.**

FERRYBOAT. A vessel in which passengers and goods are conveyed over narrow waters.

Fr: *Bac; Ferryboat; Transbordeur;* Ger: *Fahrboot; Verkehrsboot; Fähre.*

See Passenger Ferry, Train Ferry, Auto Ferry.

Johnson, E., Ferryboats, Society of Naval and Marine Engineers, *Historical Transactions* (New York, 1945).

FERRY BRIDGE. A floating or hanging structure, hinged or movable, fastened to a wharf, to facilitate passing on or off a ferryboat. Also called floating bridge.

FERRY RACK. A structure of piles and fenders to receive and guide a ferryboat into its slip.

FETCH. 1. The distance from the weather shore where the formation of waves (breakers) commences.

2. The extent of a bay or gulf from point to point.

FETCH (to). To make a desired point particularly when there is an adverse condition of wind or tide to be reckoned with. Also called to reach.

Fr: *Gagner; Atteindre;* Ger: *Erreichen.*

FETCH HEADWAY. To gather motion ahead, said of a vessel.

Fr: *Prendre de l'Erre;* Ger: *Fahrt bekommen; Steuer bekommen.*

FETCH STERNWAY. To gather motion astern, said of a vessel.

Fr: *Faire Marche Arrière.*

FETCH WAY (to). Said of any object on board ship which moves from its assigned place when this motion results from pitching or rolling.

Ger: *Herschütteln.*

FIBER CLAD ROPE. A combination wire and fiber rope in which each strand is completely enclosed in a continuous marline or hemp covering and twisted around a hemp core. Also called marline-clad rope.

Fr: *Cordage Mixte;* Ger: *Bekleidetes Stahltauwerk; Hanfdrahttauwerk.*

The number of strands is 4, 5, or 6, and the number of wires in a strand varies from 7 to 19. The marline covering prevents friction between the strands when the rope is in use. It affords a protection against moisture and keeps from the wire any abrasive and destructive foreign matter. Fiber-clad rope weighs about 30 per cent less than Manila rope of the same strength. It is used for ship's running rigging, boat falls, halyards, topping lifts, cargo hoists, and so on.

FIBERGLAS. Insulating material used for refrigerating purposes and as heat and sound insulation. It is made of extremely fine glass fibers, matted and pressed into boards. The glass fibers conduct heat poorly, and they enclose minute air or void spaces which add to the total insulating value. Fiberglas is incombustible and is not subject to corrosion. See Mineral Wool.

FIBER ROPE. General term for cordage made of vegetable fibers such as hemp, Manila, flax, cotton, coir, sisal, in contradistinction to wire rope.

Fr: *Cordage en Fibre;* Ger: *Fasertauwerk.*

Fiber rope may be either white or tarred. A yarn or thread is first made up of a number of fibers twisted together, then the strand is made up of two or more yarns twisted together in the opposite direction. The rope is formed of three or more strands twisted together in the opposite direction to that in which the strands are twisted. Incorporating a considerable amount of twist increases the friction and consolidates the fibers.

FID. A square, wedge-shaped bar of wood or iron used to support a housing topmast or topgallant mast by inserting it through the fid hole in the heel of the mast. The ends of the fid resting on the trestletrees take the weight of the mast and maintain it in place. The fid is also used in small craft to keep a running bowsprit in place. Also called mast fid.

Fr: *Clef;* Ger: *Schlossholz.*

See **Cant Fid, Cringle Fid, Preventer Fid, Splicing Fid.**

FIDDED TOPMAST. A topmast stepped forward of the lower masthead. Also called housing topmast. Its weight is supported by a fid which, passing through a fid hole, rests upon the trestletrees. It permits the mast to be struck or housed if desired.

Fr: *Mât à Clef;* Ger: *Stange mit eingesetztem Schlossholz.*

FIDDLE. A contrivance made of small cords passed through wooden bridges or frames, used in heavy weather to prevent dishes, cups and other objects from rolling off a table. Also called rack.

Fr: *Violons;* Ger: *Schlingerborden.*

FIDDLE BLOCK.
See **Long Tackle Block.**

FIDDLE HEAD. A substitute for the traditional figurehead in the form of a scroll. It is generally called fiddle head when the scroll turns outward (evolute) and billet head when it turns inward (involute).

Fr: *Guibre à Volute;* Ger: *Einwarts gebogenes Krullgallion.*

FID HOLE. A rectangular hole in the heel of a top mast, through which the fid passes.

Fr: *Trou de clef de mât;* Ger: *Schlossholzgat.*

FIDLEY. An opening or trunkway immediately above a fireroom, having great width, through which the boiler uptakes, lower stack, and fireroom ventilators are led. At the top deck or just above it is decked over with light plating. Small hatchways with grating covers are provided.

Fr: *Encaissement; Aération de Chaufferie;* Ger: *Oberheizraum; Schornsteinumbau.*

FIDLEY DECK. A raised platform over the engine and boiler rooms, more particularly around the stack.

FIDLEY GRATING. Steel gratings fitted over the boiler room hatches. Also called stokehold grating.

Ger: *Oberheizraum Grating.*

FIDLEY HATCH. A small hatchway in the fidley deck around the smokestack and uptakes. It is generally closed by a steel grating.

Fr: *Panneau d'Aération;* Ger: *Schornsteinluke.*

FIELD ICE. Ice formed in fields or large flat areas in polar waters, of such extent that its limits cannot be seen from the masthead. Also called ice field. Field ice is a hindrance to navigation, but can be negotiated by ships especially fitted.

Fr: *Champs de Glace;* Ger: *Feldeis.*

FIFE RAIL. A rail arranged in a semicircle at the foot of a mast, provided with holes for belaying pins.

Fr: *Le Ratelier de Mât;* Ger: *Die Nagelbank.*

FIFIE. A fishing vessel from the east coast of Scotland used as herring drifter. These boats are very fine-bodied with a hollow section (Block coefficient 0.23) and very fast under sail. They are lug-rigged. Length over-all 56 to 72 ft. Beam 18 to 21 ft. Draft 6.2 to 7 ft. Displacement 47 to 72 tons.

Fifies are decked fore and aft. The planking, which was formerly clinker-laid, is now carvel-built. Bilge keels are fitted. There is a large hatchway just forward of the mizzenmast where the nets are stowed. The stern and sternpost have no rake, and there is no slope in the keel.

FIGHTING SHIP. 1. A vessel used on a particular run by an owner or charterer in order to exclude or prevent competition by driving another vessel or line out of the same trade.

2. A vessel placed "on the berth" by conference lines at a time when a non-conference vessel is booking cargo as a means to crush non-conference competition and for the purpose of bidding the rates down to a wholly unremunerative level.

FIGURE-EIGHT FAKE. A method of coiling rope in which the turns form a series of overlapping figure-eights advancing about one or two diameters of the rope at each turn.

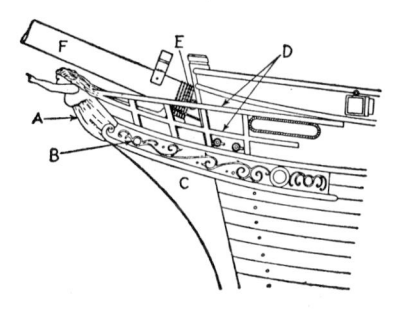

FIGUREHEAD
A. Figurehead   D. Head Rail
B. Trail Board   E. Gammoning
C. Cutwater   F. Bowsprit

FIGURE-EIGHT KNOT. A knot forming

a large knob, used to prevent ropes from unreeving or fraying, and used at ends of falls. This knot will not jam in the sheave. Sometimes called German knot, Flemish knot.

Fr: *Noeud d'Arrêt;* Ger: *Achterstick.*

FIGUREHEAD. An ornamental figure such as a statue or bust placed on the projecting part of the head of a ship with a curved stem, over the cutwater and immediately under the bowsprit.

Fr: *Figure d'Étrave;* Ger: *Galionsfigur; Galionsbild; Bugfigur.*

FILADIÈRE. A flat-floored, shallow-draft sailing boat used for fishing on the lower reaches of the river Gironde. The boat is decked forward and has a sharp stern. The ends have a pronounced sheer. It is rigged with a tall mast stepped close to the stem and carries a large standing lug. Many of these boats are used as racing craft and are said to be very fast under sail. Length 20 ft. Breadth 8 ft. 4 in. Depth 3 ft. (Average.)

Larger, full-decked boats of the same type are found around the Island of Oleron. They measure about 4 tons and are called *couralin.*

FILL. To trim the sails so that the wind will catch them full.

Fr: *Faire Servir;* Ger: *Füllen; Vollbrassen.*

FILL AND STAND ON. To proceed on the course after having been brought up in the wind or hove to. Also called to fill away.

FILLER METAL. Metal added to a fusion weld by use of a filler rod. Sometimes called deposit metal.

Fr: *Métal d'Apport;* Ger: *Schweissmaterial.*

FILLER. A piece of wood used in wood shipbuilding to make up a deficiency in any part of the structure. Also called filling chock.

Fr: *Remplissage;* Ger: *Füllstück.*

See **Dutchman.**

FILLET. Term used in the fish trade to denote the clear boneless meat of a fish. Also called fish fillet. It is obtained by cutting the flesh from the sides, thus producing two boneless strips of clear meat. This eliminates the bones, head and waste, and effects a great saving in transportation costs. The filleting of fish was developed in 1922 in Boston (Mass.) and is chiefly adopted for haddock fillets.

FILLET WELD. A type of weld generally used for joining the surfaces of two structural parts meeting at right angles. It is approximately triangular in cross section and is laid down externally to the parts joined. The parts joined are sometimes notched, V'd or J'd in way of the weld to increase strength.

Fr: *Soudure d'Angle; Soudre à Clin;* Ger: *Kehlschweissung; Kehlnaht.*

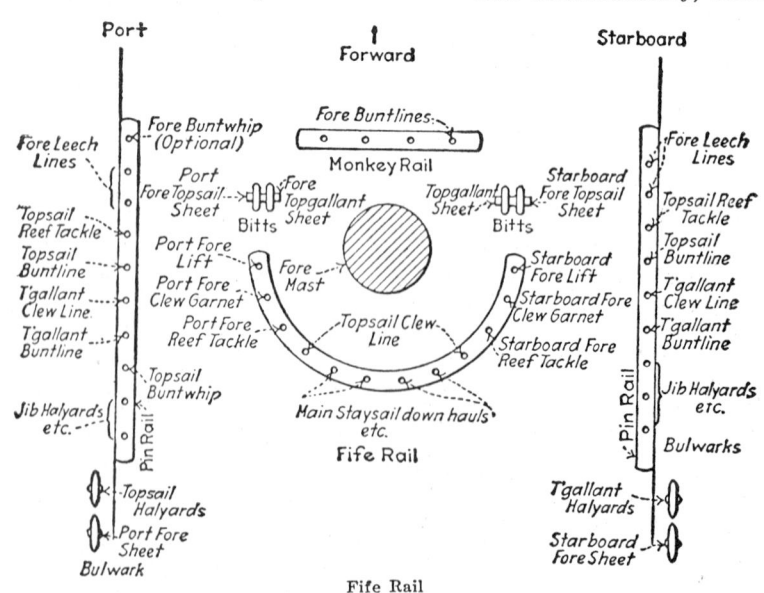

Fife Rail

FILLING.
See **Weft, Beam Filling, Filling Frame.**

FILLING CHOCK. Timber filling worked in the triangular space between the bobstay piece, the gammoning piece, and the stem.
Fr: *Remplissage;* Ger: *Füllstück.*

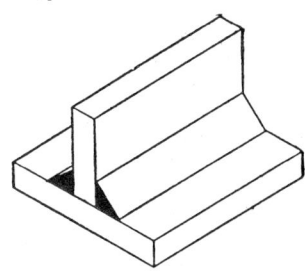

Fillet Weld

FILLING FRAMES. Pieces of timber placed in the space between the frames wherever special solidity is required, and which extend from the keel to about the turn of bilge. Also called fillings. In wooden vessels of small or moderate size filling frames are often omitted.
Fr: *Couple de Remplissage;* Ger: *Füllholz; Fullspant.*

FILLING-IN BOARDS. Narrow pieces of planking used for filling in when the gap which occurs between the outer deck plank and the margin plank is not the same on each side of the deck.
Fr: *Remplissage;* Ger: *Füllhölzer; Auslage.*

FILLING PIECE. See **Liner.**

FILLINGS. Pieces of hardwood between the shank and the loom of an oar or scull, called upper and under fillings according to their position.
Fr: *Remplissage;* Ger: *Kamm.*

FILLING TIMBER.
See **Filling Frames.**

FILLING TRANSOM. In a wooden vessel with square stern one of the transoms placed between the wing and deck transoms or between two deck transoms.
Fr: *Remplissage d'Arcasse;* Ger: *Füllhölzer der Deckworp.*

FILUKA. See **Taka.**

FINAL COURSE. The last course steered before arriving at the final position when sailing on a great circle track.
Ger: *Endkurs.*

FINAL DIAMETER. 1. With reference to a ship's turning circle, the perpendicular distance between the tangent to the curve at the point where the ship has swung through 180° and that where it has swung through 360°.
Fr: *Diamètre de Giration;* Ger: *Drehkreisdurchmesser.*
2. The diameter of the circle formed by the path of a vessel with the helm kept hard over.

FINAL LANDING. The day on which the entire consignment of goods as shown on the bill of lading has been landed from the ship.

FINAL PORT. The last port of destination. The last port of the intended voyage. The term is not restricted to the final port of discharge of the outward cargo.
Ger: *Umschlaghafen.*

FINAL PORT OF DESTINATION.
See **Final Port.**

FINAL SAILING. Applies to a ship, ready in every respect to proceed on the contemplated voyage and without intention to return, as soon as she is beyond the limits of the port construed in a commercial sense and irrespective of the legal or fiscal limits of the port.

FIN CHAIN. A short chain strapped around the small of one of the flippers. It was used for the first blanket when cutting in a right whale.

FIN KEEL. A deep short keel in the form of a fin with ballast on the lower edge, used by racing yachts. Its object is twofold, first to increase the area of immersed lateral plane, thus improving windward sailing, and second, to provide outside ballast at the greatest possible distance from the center of gravity in order to increase transverse stability under sail. The first fin keel was designed by G. N. Herreshoff in 1891.
Fr: *Fin Keel; Bulb;* Ger: *Flossenkiel; Wulstkiel.*

FIORD. See **Fjord.**

FIR. A pinaceous tree sometimes used for keels of small boats because it is obtainable in large timbers and long lengths. Its weight is about 37 lbs. per cubic foot. Also used for ship's spars and bottom planking.
Fr: *Sapin;* Ger: *Kiefernholz.*

FIRE ALARM SIGNAL. A continuous rapid ringing of the ship's bell for a period of not less than ten seconds supplemented by the continuous ringing of the general alarm bells for not less than ten seconds. For dismissal from fire alarm stations the general alarm bells are sounded three times, supplemented by three short blasts of the whistle.

FIRE AND BILGE PUMP. A general service pump with independent sea suction and overboard delivery. It is used for keeping the bilges free of water, washing decks, and as an auxiliary fire pump. It is more or less constantly in operation at sea.

FIRE BILL. A posted list of the stations allotted to officers and men in case of fire. Also called fire stations bill.
> Fr: *Rôle d'appel aux Postes d'Incendie;* Ger: *Brandrolle; Feuerrolle.*

FIRE BOAT. A harbor craft fitted with fire pumps and other fire-fighting apparatus for assisting vessels and protecting warehouses, piers, and so on, against damage by fire. Sometimes called fire float.
> Fr: *Bateau-Pompe;* Ger: *Feuerlöschboot; Spritzen Prahm.*

FIRE BULKHEAD. According to the International Convention for Safety of Life at Sea of 1929, a fireproof bulkhead is one capable of resisting, intact, for one hour, a fire having a temperature of about 1500°F. Fireproof bulkheads on passenger vessels should be fitted at intervals not exceeding 131 ft. Also called fire-proof bulkhead, fire-resisting bulkhead.
> Fr: *Cloison d'Incendie; Cloison Coupe-Feu;* Ger: *Feuerschott; Rauchschott.*

FIRE DETECTOR. General term for various patented apparatuses and systems providing means for locating and reporting automatically by visible and audible means to a distant position (bridge or chartroom) an abnormal rise in temperature or the presence of smoke in any compartment of the ship.

Three basic types are used:
1. The electric system, in which thermostats operating by heat close an electric circuit, which in turn starts an alarm bell and light on the indicating apparatus.
2. The pneumatic-tube system, using thermostats composed of copper tubing containing air, the expansion of which produces visible and audible signals.
3. The smoke-pipe system, in which the presence of fire is indicated visually and by the sense of smell by smoke drawn through small pipes by a constant running exhaust fan.

Under the rules of the International Convention for Safety of Life at Sea of 1929, this equipment is compulsory in passenger spaces and in certain non-patrollable parts of passenger vessels.
> Fr: *Détecteur d'Incendie; Avertisseur automatique d'Incendie;* Ger: *Automatischer Feuermelder; Selbsttätiger Feuermelder.*

FIRE DRILL. Exercise practiced by the crew when called to fire stations in order to insure that fire pumps and all other fire fighting equipment is in order and effectively handled.
> Fr: *Exercice d'Incendie; Manoeuvre d'Incendie;* Ger: *Feuerübung; Feuerlöschmanöver.*

FIRE HOSE. A rubber-lined cotton or linen hose about 2½ in. diameter used on board ship for fire fighting. Fire hoses are usually coiled and stowed on racks with nozzles near each fire plug.
> Fr: *Manche à Incendie;* Ger: *Feuerschlauch.*

FIREMAN.
See Stoker.

FIREMAN SERANG. A member of a lascar crew who acts as leading fireman, but supervises Asiatic firemen and coal trimmers only.

FIREMEN'S QUARTERS. The compartment(s) allotted to firemen, stokers, and trimmers as living space.
> Fr: *Poste des Chauffeurs;* Ger: *Heizerlogis.*

FIRE POINT. The temperature at which a fuel oil, if ignited, will continue to burn.
> Fr: *Point d'Inflammabilité;* Ger: *Brennpunkt.*

See **Flash Point.**

FIREPROOF PAINT. A protective coat applied on board ship to inside woodwork, with the object of making it temporarily fireproof and to steel structures to retard paint combustion. Also called fire-resistant paint. These paints are selected for such parts as electric cable moldings, fire-resisting bulkheads, and so on. They are made of pigments which when attacked by flames do not support combustion but leave behind an incombustible skin.
> Fr: *Peinture Ignifuge;* Ger: *Feuerfeste Farbe.*

FIRE PUMP. A centrifugal or reciprocating pump that supplies sea water to all fire hose connections. In small vessels the donkey pump serves as a fire pump. Large ships have an independent fire pump which may also be used as general service pump. According to government or classification rules every mechanically propelled vessel must have at least one steam or motor pump especially arranged for fire purposes and connected to a fire main extending fore and aft along the upper deck gutter or bulwarks, supplied with nozzles at intervals of about 50 ft. for the attachment of flexible hose. Hand fire pumps must be of such size that one stroke of the piston displaces 100 cu. in. or more.

Fr: *Pompe à Incendie;* Ger: *Feuerlöschpumpe.*
See **Bilge Pump.**

FIREROOM.
See **Stokehole.**

FIRE STATIONS. The allotted place of each member of the ship's company or each passenger in the event of fire alarm.

Fr: *Postes d'Incendie;* Ger: *Feuerlösch Station.*

FIRE-TUBE BOILER. A marine boiler in which combustion gases are led to the uptakes through large tubes around which water circulates. Sometimes called Scotch boiler.

Fr: *Chaudière à Tubes de Fumée; Chaudière Ignitubulaire;* Ger: *Flammrohrkessel; Zylinderkessel; Heizröhrenkessel.*

It consists of a cylindrical shell with internal circular furnaces. When coal fuel is used, grate bars subdivide the furnaces in two parts, the lower part forming the ash pit. The combustion gases pass through a combustion chamber in the back of the boiler and from there return through tubes to the front end, smoke box, and uptake. The larger types are made double-ended with common or separate combustion chambers.

In recent years, water-tube boilers have largely superseded fire-tube boilers, specially for reasons of efficiency and economical operation.

FIRE WARP. A warp run out to a buoy by a vessel handling dangerous goods alongside a pier or quay so that it can be moved away rapidly in the event of fire.

FIRING. 1. A Norwegian open boat which pulls 4 pairs of oars, used in fisheries of the Afjord. A similar type of boat employed in the Nordfjord fisheries is called *firroing.*
See **Nordfjordbaat.**

2. A term which refers to the operation of a steam boiler so as to maintain the required head of steam. In modern usage it usually includes the maintenance of steam pressure and temperature, the care of the fires, the care of all firing appurtenances such as burners, etc., as well as the preparation of the fuel for firing.

Fr: *Chauffe;* Ger: *Feuerung.*
See **Coal Firing, Oil Firing.**

FIRING JIB. Apparatus employed on light vessels for firing explosive fog signals. It consists of a 2-in. tube about 20 ft. long, supported by a swivel clamp and rigged out over the ship's side at an angle of about 30 degrees to the vertical. A T head is fitted to the outboard end of the jib and from each end of this head projects a pair of wire clips from which the *tonite* cartridges are suspended by means of their detonator wires. Insulated cables are carried from the T head down through the tube to the fog signalman's shelter where the cartridges are exploded by pressing an electric contactmaker.

FIRST ASSISTANT ENGINEER. On U. S. merchant ships the engineer officer next in command to the chief engineer; customarily in charge of the 4 to 8 engine room watches. On merchant ships of Great Britain and France the engineer of equivalent rank is called second engineer.

Fr: *Second Mécanicien;* Ger: *Erster Maschinen Assistent.*

FIRST DOG WATCH. The dog watch from 4 to 6 P.M.

FIRST FUTTOCK. Futtock bolted to a floor and extending across the keel. Also called lower futtock, ground futtock, navel timber, navel futtock.

Fr: *Première Allonge; Genou; Demie Varangue;* Ger: *Sitzer.*

FIRST OPEN WATER. Chartering term used in connection with ice-bound ports, by which the owner of the vessel instead of stating a specific day of readiness to load in the charter, places himself under obligation to present his vessel at the first opportunity to enter the port free from ice obstruction.

FIRST POINT OF ARIES. The equinoctial point formed by the intersection of the ecliptic with the celestial equator as the sun passes from south to north declination, on or about March 21. Also called vernal equinox.

FIRST POINT OF CANCER. One of the two points of the ecliptic when the sun is at its greatest distance from the equinoctial. It is the commencement of the sign of the ecliptic of same name. Also

called **summer solstitial point**.
>Fr: *Point solsticial d'été;* Ger: *Wendepunkte des Krebses; Sommer Solstitialpunkt.*

FIRST POINT OF CAPRICORN. One of the two points on the ecliptic when the sun is at its greatest distance from the equinoctial and enters Capricorn. Also called **winter solstitial point**.
>Fr: *Point solsticial d'hiver;* Ger: *Wendepunkte des Steinbocks; Winter solstitialpunkt; Wintersonnenwende.*

FIRST POINT OF LIBRA. The equinoctial point formed by the intersection of the ecliptic with the celestial equator as the sun passes from north to south declination, on or about September 21. Also called autumnal equinox.

FIRST WATCH. A four-hour watch from 8 P.M. till midnight.
>Fr: *Premier Quart;* Ger: *Erste Wache.*

FIRTH. A long arm of the sea practically land-locked.
>Fr: *Firth.*

FISCHER EVER. Small *ever* employed in deep sea fisheries and usually provided with a fish well. It has finer lines than the trading *ever* and very high forward sheer. A centerboard is fitted in some boats instead of the leeboards. The stem has a pronounced rake, the bottom is built without keel, and the stern is very narrow. The average tonnage is about 30 gross. The smaller boats have one pole mast with gaff mainsail and two headsails. The larger boats are ketch-rigged. Length 49 to 61 ft. Breadth 17.7 to 20.3 ft. Depth 5.5 to 7.3 ft. Length of well 18.6 to 21 ft.

FISCHERKAHN. A term embracing various fishing craft of the same type found in the Kurische Haff (East Prussia), among which are the *Keitelkahn, Kurrenkahn, Bräddenkahn,* and *Netzkahn.* The names vary according to type of fishing gear used.

FISH. A tapering batten of hard wood bound to a yard or other spar to strengthen it.
>Fr: *Jumelle;* Ger: *Schalung.*

FISH (to). 1. To hoist the flukes of an anchor toward the top of the bow after catting in in order to stow it.
>Fr: *Traverser;* Ger: *Fischen; Pentern.*

See **Catting**.

2. The action of strengthening or joining two parts by means of external attachment. On a spar fishing is done by lashing smaller pieces of wood sawed lengthwise and hollowed out, around the affected part.
>Fr: *Jumeler;* Ger: *Fischen.*

FISHBACK. A line from the back of the fish hook used to assist in hooking it to the anchor arm.
>Fr: *Queue de Traversière;* Ger: *Fischblocksteert.*

FISH BLOCK. A heavy double or treble block fitted with a large hook and sometimes with a short length of chain. Used for fishing the anchor.
>Fr: *Poulie de Traversière;* Ger: *Fischblock.*

FISH BOOM. A boom formerly used to extend the (anchor) fish tackle over the bow. It was pivoted in a gooseneck on the forward side of the foremast. (Obsolete.)
>Fr: *Arc-Boutant de Traversière;* Ger: *Ankeraufwindebaum.*

FISH CARRIER. A small vessel employed as tender to fishing fleets for the purpose of collecting and conveying ashore the catch of the boats. Also called carry away boat. In the Canadian maritime provinces and on the western and southern coasts of Newfoundland the so-called carrying smack is a boat used for transportation of lobsters from the small local ports to the shipping ports or to the pounds.
>Fr: *Chasseur;* Ger: *Jäger.*

Most of the North Sea fish carriers have no appliances for the preservation of fish, which is handed over from open boats in ordinary ice boxes. The position of the fleet is broadcast daily at stated times in order to direct the carriers.

A small, open boat, 18 ft. by 2.5 ft. is generally used for conveying fish from trawler to carrier. It is clinker-built and fitted with 84 cu. ft. of air cases, arranged at bow and stern and under the midship thwart. About 18 cu. ft. of cork is placed between the thwart knees.

FISH DAVIT. An iron davit used in conjunction with a cat davit for raising the fluke end of a stocked anchor and placing it on the bill-board.
>Fr: *Bossoir de Traversière;* Ger: *Fischdavit.*

FISHERMAN BOSS. A fisherman who directs the captain on a fishing vessel relative to the location of fishing grounds, the time for fishing operations, the speed at which the boat should run and so on.
>Fr: *Maître de pêche.*

FISHERMAN'S ANCHOR. Small anchor with long shank used by fishermen when working with ground lines in order to fasten the gear to the sea bottom. The weight of these anchors varies according to local conditions. In the North Sea halibut, cod, and haddock fisheries a 28-lb. anchor is used.

FISHERMAN'S BEND. A bend used for securing a rope to a buoy or a hawser to a kedge anchor, also for bending halyards to yards on small sailing craft. It is formed by taking a round turn with the end coming under the standing part, under both turns and tucked over and under the turns. The greater the pull on the halyards, the more tightly the parts of the bend are jammed against the spar. Also called anchor bend, studding sail halyard bend.

Fr: *Noeud d'orin;* Ger: *Fischerstek; Fischerknoten.*

FISHERMAN'S EYE KNOT. An application of the fisherman's knot. Used for making a loop in a piece of gut.

Fr: *Noeud sur le Pouce;* Ger: *Fischerknoten.*

FISHERMAN'S FENDER. A term applied to a fender made of several turns of old hawser served over with smaller rope.

FISHERMAN'S STAYSAIL. A sail set flying between the foremast and mainmast in small trading and fishing schooners. It is square on the luff and has two sets of halyards. One set leading through a block at the fore lower masthead and the other at mainmast head. It also has a tack and sheet to trim it down. It is roped on head luff and clew and made from a lighter cloth than the working sails. It is primarily a fair weather sail set with the wind abeam or abaft the beam.

FISHERY. **1.** A place or equipment installed on a certain spot for the capture of fish or other sea products.

Fr: *Pêcherie;* Ger: *Fischfang; Fischerei.*

2. The right to take fish at a certain place or in particular waters.

Fr: *Droit de Pêche;* Ger: *Fischereigebiet.*

See **Several Fishery.**

FISHERY HARBOR. A harbor specially planned for the convenience of fishing boats and equipped with all the necessary appliances for the speedy handling of fish.

Fr: *Port de Pêche;* Ger: *Fischereihafen.*

FISH FRONT. A strengthening slab placed on the front of a made mast to protect it from chafing when striking or sending up a topmast, and so on. Also called clamp. (Obsolete.)

Fr: *Jumelle de Frottement;* Ger: *Schale; Schalstück.*

FISH HOLD. The main hold of a fishing vessel, specially designed and fitted for the carriage of fish. Fish holds are usually fitted with vertical divisions having portable wooden shelves. The fish are mixed with ice and placed on the shelves.

Fr: *Cale à Poisson;* Ger: *Fischraum.*

In some vessels the fish hold is insulated by layers of compressed cork or other insulating material, on boundary surfaces. The lining is made of white pine coated with protective composition. In recently built American trawlers sheets of 22 to 24 gauge thickness, made of Monel metal, have been used as lining. A galvanized iron backing and wooden corner pieces are employed to fasten the sheets.

FISH HOOK. 1. A large iron hook attached to the fish pendant or to the lower block of the fish tackle and used for hooking the arm of the anchor so as to fish it.

Fr: *Crochet de Traversière;* Ger: *Penterhaken; Fischhaken.*

2. Barbed instrument of varying size and form for catching fish.

Fr: *Hameçon;* Ger: *Angel; Fischangel.*

Fish hooks are made of straight wires of proper length flattened at one end. The barb is formed by a single blow with a chisel. The point having been sharpened, the proper curve or twist is given to the hook. The soft iron wire is then case-hardened to give it the required stiffness and elasticity, by immersion in hot animal oil. The hooks are subsequently brightened by friction and tempered. Deep-sea fishermen use the Kirby Bent or Ordinary Bent types of hooks, which are manufactured in 14 different sizes.

FISHING BOAT. Any vessel of any size and in whatever way propelled, which is, for the time being, employed in sea-fishing, or in the sea-fishing service for profit. It has also been defined in international conventions as any vessel or boat employed in the capture of sea fish or for the treatment of sea fish or any boat or vessel used partly or wholly for the purpose of transport of sea fish.

Fr: *Bateau de Pêche; Embarcation de Pêche;* Ger: *Fischerboot; Fischereifahrzeug.*

FISHING GROUNDS. Areas of the sea in which fishing is normally or frequently carried on.

Fr: *Fonds de Pêche;* Ger: *Fischgrund.*

FISHING LINE. 1. General term for cordage, similar to white line, of which the

FISHING NET—FISH TACKLE

various gears used in the hook and line fishery are made.

Fr: *Ligne de Pêche; Corde;* Ger: *Schnürleine; Angelschnur.*

See **White Line.**

2. A rope on a trawl net for fastening the bobbins to the bosom.

Ger: *Fischleine.*

FISHING NET. An open-work fabric forming meshes of suitable size and used for the capture of fish.

Fr: *Filet;* Ger: *Netz.*

Nets are made either by hand or machinery. Ordinary simple rectangular pieces of netting as found in drift nets can be made by machinery. Shaped nets (trawls, and so on) can be made only by hand. The principal substances used for the manufacture of nets are: Manila from the fibers of the *Mussa textilis*; cotton from the down attached to the seeds of *Gossypom*; hemp from the fiber of the hemp plant, *Cannabis sativa*, the most usual being Russian or Italian; sunn hemp from the plant *Crotalaria juncea*, which is chiefly used in India; flax, from the fiber of the flax plant, *Linum usitatissimum*. The numerous forms of fishing nets are named according to the manner in which they are used and the way in which the fish are captured.

Augur, C. H., *Fish Nets, Their Construction and the Application of Various Forms in American Fisheries*, U. S. Bureau of Fisheries, Bul., vol. 13, Washington, 1893.

FISHING STORES. A term occasionally used to denote hooks, gaffs, nippers, and knives as used by boats in the fishing trade.

FISHING TRADE. Trade connected with the capture and conveyance of sea products.

Fr: *Navigation à la Pêche;* Ger: *Fischereifahrt.*

FISH JIG. A weighted line or steel rod with several fish hooks set back to back, to which a small hand line is fastened. Also called dolphin striker, fish-line jigger. It is thrown overboard in a shoal of fish and jerked suddenly upward, so that one or more fish are usually caught on the hooks. The use of this appliance is generally forbidden by law as being very destructive.

Fr: *Faux;* Ger: *Fischstachel.*

FISH MEAL. The offal of fish or fish scrap specially treated to be used as food for animals. The chief difference between the methods of manufacture of fish scrap for fertilizer and for meal is that the latter must be prepared from perfectly fresh raw material carefully dried without scorching.

Fr: *Tourteau de Poisson;* Ger: *Fischmehl.*

Two grades of fish meal are found on the market: first, the white meal made from nonfatty or white-fleshed fish such as cod, halibut, plaice, hake, pollack, etc., and secondly, the dark meal made from fish containing a high percentage of oil, such as herring, sardine, mackerel, pilchard, menhaden, shad, salmon. Fish meal is used as animal food by cattle breeders and poultry growers.

Le Clerc, J. A., *The Fish Meal Industry*, U. S. Bureau of Foreign and Domestic Commerce, Trade Information Bull. 538, Washington, 1928.

FISH OIL. A name given to various kinds of oil obtained from different species of fish. The most important fish oils are menhaden, herring, sardine and sprat-salmon. These oils find usage in numerous industries, in human and animal nutrition, and as actual food products.

Fr: *Huile de Poisson;* Ger: *Fischöl.*

Brocklesby, H. N., *The Chemistry and Technology of Marine Animal Oils*, Ottawa, 1941; Chastenet, *Les Huiles d'Animaux Marins*, Paris, 1925.

FISH PENDANT. A stout rope or chain having a thimble on one end and the fish hook on the other. It is attached to the lower block of the fish tackle and leads through a sheave in the fish boom. (Obsolete.)

Ger: *Fischreep.*

FISH POUND. A fixed fish trap of the barrier type. Also called weir. It generally consists of a stone wall built across the mouth of a creek and of such height that it can be covered only at high spring tides. At one point there is an opening which can be closed, thus retaining any fish that made their way into the creek on flood tide. When the opening is closed the water can pass through a grating in the door and when the creek is dry the fish are collected.

Fr: *Parc; Ecluse; Gord;* Ger: *Fischteich.*

See **Deck Pound, Ice Pound.**

FISH SPEAR. A spear with 3 to 5 barbed prongs used for the capture of some species of fishes, such as bonitos.

Fr: *Foëne;* Ger: *Elger.*

FISH TACKLE. 1. The purchase hooked to the cod end of a trawl net for lifting it aboard after each drag.

2. A heavy two- or threefold purchase formerly used for hoisting the anchor up to the bow. It hooks at the head of the fish davit and to the balancing link on the anchor shank or to the arm of the anchor.

A Spanish burton is used nowadays on small craft.
Fr: *Traversière; Palan de Traversière;* Ger: *Fischtakel.*

FISH TACKLE PENDANT. A pendant with an eye spliced into its upper end to go over the fore topmast head. The lower end has a spliced eye with thimble into which a two- or threefold block purchase for lifting the anchor can be hooked.
Fr: *Pantoire de Traversière;* Ger: *Fischreep; Fischtakel Hänger.*

FISH TRAP.
See **Pound Net.**

FISH WELL. A compartment in the bottom of a fishing vessel for keeping fish alive from the time they are caught until the boat reaches port. Also called wet well.
Fr: *Vivier;* Ger: *Bün.*
The fish well is limited fore and aft by two watertight bulkheads. A platform called well deck and extending athwartships from side to side at waterline level forms the top of the compartment. A four-sided, watertight funnel or trunk, extending upward to the main deck, is built amidships and used for introducing the fish into the well. A constant circulation of sea water is kept up within the compartment through a number of small holes pierced in the outside planking or plating.

FITTED PINTLE. A pintle fitted as a separate part to the rudderarm. Usually tapered, and hove up tight in tapered snug holes by a nut on the upper end.
Fr: *Aiguillot Rapporté;* Ger: *Angebrachter Fingerling; Eingefügter Fingerling.*

FITTER UP.
See **Shipfitter.**

FITTING-OUT BASIN. An area of water near a shipyard used for berthing ships afloat while completing the installation of machinery, upper works of hull, gear, and so on, after launching.
Fr: *Bassin d'armement;* Ger: *Ausrüstung-Dock; Ausrüstung-Bassin.*

FITTINGS. As used in marine insurance this term covers the permanent fittings of a vessel including those required for the particular trade in which she is engaged, the provisions for the crew and the fuel and engine-room stores.

FIVE-MASTED BARK. A vessel rigged with square sails on 4 masts and fore-and-aft sails on the aftermast. The question of naming 5 masts has never been satisfactorily settled, but the most generally adopted nomenclature is fore, main, mizzen, jigger, and spanker or after jigger.
Fr: *Cinq-mâts barque;* Ger: *Fünfmastbarke.*
Only six trading vessels were rigged as 5-masted barks, their tonnage ranging from 3,800 to 5,600 gross. They were said to be difficult to handle under sail, it being necessary to wear ship when going about. Most of them lacked stability and were noted as tender ships. Auxiliary steam or internal-combustion engines were installed in several of these vessels and they were all supplied with deep tanks or double bottom for ballasting purposes. The largest 5-master bark was the "France" (1912). She had a sail area of 70,000 sq. ft. and a loaded displacement of 10,730 tons.

FIVE-MASTED TOPSAIL SCHOONER. A rig adopted after the First World War for a few trading vessels with auxiliary power, among which were the "Carl Vinnen," the "Suzanne Vinnen," the "Adolf Vinnen" of Bremen. These vessels are square-rigged with double topsails and single topgallants on the first and third masts. They carry on each lower yard a square sail, which brails up to the mast. It is worked by inhauls and outhauls and is bent to the underside of the yard by clips or travelers sliding on a jackstay. Also called schooner bark.

FIX. A term denoting the determination of a ship's position by observations of celestial or terrestrial objects, or by a combination of both. This term is used only when the position so obtained is not open to doubt.
Fr: *Point;* Ger: *Besteck.*
See **Running Fix.**

FIX. A vessel is termed "fixed" when definite arrangements regarding a charter or hire have been completed, or a rate of freight has been agreed upon.
Fr: *Fixer; Arrêter;* Ger: *Bestimmen.*

FIX (to). To secure a cargo for a ship.
Ger: *Bestimmen.*

FIXED AND FLASHING LIGHT. A fixed coastal light varied at regular intervals by a single flash of greater brilliancy. The flash may or may not be preceded and followed by an eclipse.
Fr: *Feu Fixe à Éclats;* Ger: *Festes- und Blinkfeuer; Festes Feuer mit Blinker.*

FIXED AND GROUP FLASHING LIGHT. A fixed light displayed from a lighthouse and varied at regular intervals by a group of two or more flashes of rela-

tively greater brilliancy. The group may or may not be preceded and followed by an eclipse.
Fr: *Feu Fixe à Éclats Groupés;* Ger: *Festfeuer mit Blink-Gruppen.*

FIXED BEACON. A beacon attached rigidly to the sea bottom or to the ground as distinct from a floating beacon. Also called tower beacon.
Fr: *Balise Fixe;* Ger: *Stehende Bake.*

FIXED LIGHT. A coastal light in which the illuminating apparatus gives a continuous light of uniform intensity.
Fr: *Feu Fixe;* Ger: *Festfeuer.*

FIXED NET. A general name for all kind of stationary nets used for the capture of inshore fish or fish which enters rivers. They are temporarily or permanently moored to the beach or at the bottom of the sea in contradistinction to movable nets, which are allowed to drift or are dragged through the water.
Fr: *Filet Fixe;* Ger: *Stellnetz; Stehendes Netz; Setznetz.*

FIXED SIDE LIGHT. Ship's side light or airport in which the lense frame or glass holder is not hinged and therefore cannot be opened. This type is used for providing light only, and is generally located near the waterline. Also called nonopening side scuttle.
Fr: *Hublot Fixe;* Ger: *Festes Seitenfenster.*
American Marine Standards Committee, Standard no. 3, Fixed Lights for Ships, Washington, 1927.

FJORD, FIORD. A long narrow arm of the sea between high lands.

FLAG. A piece of bunting or similar material of various shapes and colors displayed from a staff or halyard to indicate nationality or to make visual signals. The vertical measurement of a flag is called hoist, height or depth. Its length is called fly.
Fr: *Pavillon;* Ger: *Flagge.*
Gordon, W., *Book of Flags*, London, 1933; Irving, J., *Manual of Flag Etiquette*, London, 1931; Mead, H. P., *Sea Flags*, Glasgow, 1938.

FLAG CHEST. A chest or locker fitted in the wheel house. Also called flag locker, signal chest. It is built with internal division plates placed vertically and horizontally so as to form 28 square pigeon holes. Each of the holes has a name plate stamped with the name of the code flag.
Fr: *Coffre à Pavillons;* Ger: *Flaggenkasten.*

FLAG CLAUSE. A bill of lading clause which provides that the carrier's liability is to be determined by the laws of the country specified in the document.

FLAG CLIP. Small elliptical brass fitting opening at its side by which signal flags can be quickly bent together or to signal halliards. A swivel is incorporated to prevent turns in the halliards.
Fr: *Mousqueton;* Ger: *Flaggenschakel.*

FLAG DISCRIMINATION. Preferential treatment in the matter of charges or facilities accorded to the ships of some particular nation.
Fr: *Privilège de Pavillon;* Ger: *Flaggenzuschlag.*
Berglund, A., "Discriminatory Duties on Imports in American Bottoms," American Academy of Political and Social Science (Philadelphia), *Annals*, vol. 94 (1921); Maxwell, L. W., *Discriminating Duties and the American Merchant Marine*, London, 1926.

FLAG DROGUE. A whaling implement consisting of a flag rigidly fastened by its pole to a small piece of plank. The latter is loaded with lead to retain the flag in a vertical position. It is fastened to a captured whale with a harpoon and line. Its purpose is to impede the flight of a wounded whale or to waif a dead whale. Also called waif drug.

FLAG LOFT. A shop where flags are made.
Fr: *Pavillonnerie;* Ger: *Flaggenwerkstatt.*

FLAG OFFICER. Naval officer with the rank of Commodore or above. So called because he is entitled to fly his personal flag which indicates his rank.
Fr: *Officier Général;* Ger: *Flagg-Offizier.*

FLAG SALUTE. The act of running down temporarily the ensign as an act of courtesy between two ships passing each other or between ship and shore. It is effected by slowly lowering the ensign to what is termed the dip position, that is to say two-thirds of the distance it has been hoisted whether at the staff or at the peak. The ensign is kept in that position until the salute has been answered and then slowly re-hoisted.
Fr: *Salut du Pavillon;* Ger: *Flaggengruss; Schiffsgruss.*

FLAGSTAFF. A pole on which a flag is hoisted and displayed.

Fr: *Hampe de Pavillon; Bâton de Pavillon; Mât de Pavillon;* Ger: *Flaggenstock; Flaggenpol; Flaggenstange.*

FLAGSTAFF SOCKET. A bronze socket into which the flagstaff is stepped. It is usually provided with a hasp which fits in the hand rail above. Also called flagpole socket.

Ger: *Flaggstockhülsen.*

FLAG SURTAX. A percentual surcharge levied by a nation on goods brought in on ships sailing under a foreign flag.

Fr: *Surtaxe de Pavillon;* Ger: *Flaggenzoll; Flaggenzuschlag.*

FLAG TOGGLE. Small wooden toggle about 1½ inch long, spliced to a flag line or connection to another when flag clips are not used.

Fr: *Cabillot;* Ger: *Flaggen Knebel.*

FLAKE. 1. A flat layer of a coiled rope.

2. Also a small stage hung over a vessel's side for workmen to stand on while calking, etc.

FLAM.

See Flare.

FLAMBARD. A two-masted fishing boat of 3 to 4 tons formerly used on the coast of Normandy for trawling or lining. Length 20 to 26 ft. Breadth 7 ft. 7 in. to 8 ft. 8 in. Depth 3 ft. 4 in. to 4 ft. (Typical.)

The rig is composed of a lug foresail, a gaff mainsail with boom, and a yard topsail. Boats with this rig were found from the Seine Estuary as far south as La Rochelle. In the Bay of Granville near St. Malo, the *flambard* rig with topsail on both masts was used by small open boats about 21 ft. in length at waterline, and 7 ft. 8 in. beam. The name of *flambard* was also given in former days to large fishing luggers from Dieppe and Treport which had the same rig as the *chasse-marée.*

FLAMBOY (G. B.). A flare-up light made of a kerosene torch and used as a warning light.

FLAME CUTTER. The apparatus used for flame cutting of metals. Also called burning torch. It consists of two cylinders, one containing oxygen, the other acetylene or hydrogen, usually the former. A hose leads from each cylinder to a single torch operated by hand. The gas or preheater flame raises the temperature of the steel to a point where it is rapidly oxidized. The blast of oxygen causes the oxidation, blowing the oxide through the steel and forming a "cut."

FLAME CUTTING. A process of cutting steel, based on rapid oxidation by means of a blast of oxygen accompanied by gas preheater, both emitted simultaneously by a torch fitted with a cutting tip. Also called Burning.

FLAME GOUGING. Use of a special oxyacetylene cutting torch to gouge out V-shaped or U-shaped grooves in steel plate, or to remove undesirable welds. It is a more rapid substitute for chipping with a pneumatically driven chisel.

FLAME SAFETY LAMP. A lamp used for testing the oxygen content in various compartments, such as oil tanks, fuel tanks, water tanks, and the like, before sending men in these spaces. Safety lamps form part of the regulation equipment aboard passenger vessels.

Fr: *Lampe de Sureté;* Ger: *Sicherheitslampe.*

FLANGE. 1. The turned edge of a plate, shape, girder or section which acts to resist a bending moment.

Fr: *Bord Tombé;* Ger: *Flansch.*

2. One of the two projecting parts of a structural shape or bar.

Fr: *Aile;* Ger: *Schenkel.*

3. An annular ring provided at the end of one pipe as a means of connection to another pipe also carrying a similar ring. Two pipes joined by flanges are said to have a "flanged joint." Flanges are provided with bolt holes and come in standard sizes or in pairs for matching purposes. They are usually welded or screwed to the pipe itself.

Fr: *Bride;* Ger: *Rohrflansch.*

FLANGED EDGE. The edge of a plate bent an angle of 90 degrees for a width of a few inches.

Fr: *Bord Tombé;* Ger: *Geflanschte Kante.*

FLANGED KNEE. A plate knee having the diagonal edge flanged to increase stiffness.

Fr: *Gousset à Bord Tombé;* Ger: *Geflanschtes Knieblech.*

FLANGED PLATE. Any plate bent in a more or less angular form. Also a plate having one or more of its edges bent through an angle of 90°. The flange serves as a substitute for an angle iron, and prevents buckling of the plate under compressive load.

Fr: *Tôle à Bord Tombé;* Ger: *Geflanschte Platte.*

FLANGE-TURNER (U. S.). A shipyard worker employed in the structural shop. His duties involve the processes of shaping and forming such as rolling, flanging, joggling, and straightening of structural plates.

FLANGING. Cold bending of the edge of a metal plate in a special machine. Applied in ship construction to floors, deck girders, tank margin plates, deck stringer plates, bulkhead stiffeners, bracket plates, to dispense with connecting angles or to stiffen the free edge.

Ger: *Flanschen.*

FLAPPER. A short tongue of netting, 40 to 50 meshes at the top, 20 to 22 at the bottom, inserted between the batings and the belly near the cod end of a trawl and fastened only to the top. It is easily lifted by incoming fish but tends to prevent their escape. Also called trap.

Fr: *Tambour;* Ger: *Netzklappe; Flabber.*

FLARE. Term used in naval architecture to denote the spreading outward from the waterline to the rail of the ship's sides at the bow. The word flam refers more specifically to the upper section of the flare.

Fr: *Dévers;* Ger: *Ausbauchung.*

FLARE OUT BOW. Bows in which the sides spread out transversally from the central longitudinal plane at upper waterlines.

Fr: *Avant à dévers;* Ger: *Springender Bug.*

FLARE UP.
See **Flare Up Light.**

FLARE UP LIGHT. A temporary and intermittent light shown at intervals by small craft such as pilot boats and fishing boats to call the attention of other vessels. Also called flare up. It sometimes consists of a can filled with paraffin in which a plug of tow is dipped and then lit.

Fr: *Torche; Flare Up;* Ger: *Flackerlicht; Flackfeuer; Blusfeuer.*

FLASHING LIGHT. A light displayed from a lighthouse in which the luminous rays are instantaneously eclipsed and again as suddenly revealed to view by the vertical movement of opaque cylinders in front of the reflectors, the duration of light being always less than that of darkness.

Fr: *Feu à Éclats;* Ger: *Blinkfeuer.*

FLASH POINT. The temperature at which a fuel oil begins to give off explosive vapors. A fuel may or may not continue to burn at the flash point and in fact the flash point and the fire point of the same fuel oil seldom coincide.

Fr: *Point d'Eclair;* Ger: *Entflammungspunkt.*
See **Fire Point.**

FLAT. 1. A generally level area, frequently left bare by the falling tide.

Fr: *Sèche;* Ger: *Untiefe.*

2. A small partial lower deck built without camber.

Fr: *Plateforme;* Ger: *Plattform.*
See **Platform Deck, Watertight Flat.**

3. A barge or lighter. The term flat is generally used in Great Britain for any lighter longer than a canal boat, the local distinction being that any flat not propelled by steam is a barge, although it may be a "sailing flat."

4. Structural steel section of varying length and thickness and up to 6 in. in width used in ship construction for liners, butt straps, seam straps, and so on. Also called flat bar.

Fr: *Plat; Fer Plat;* Ger: *Flacheisen.*

FLAT BOTTOM. A ship so constructed that the lower edge of the floors is horizontal or nearly so.

Fr: *Fond plat;* Ger: *Flacher Boden.*

FLATCHIE. Heavily built open boat from the Orkney Islands. It is rigged with one or two masts and spritsails or standing lugs with or without boom.

FLAT FISH. A name applied to a large group of fishes which have the body much compressed. Both eyes are on one side of the head, the blind side colorless. They usually live at the bottom of the sea and hide in the sand. The best known species are the plaice, halibut, turbot, sole, brill, witch, flounder, dabs.

Fr: *Poisson Plat;* Ger: *Plattfisch.*

FLAT-GRAIN PLANK. A method of sawing planks in which the log is sawn longitudinally without regard to the medullary rays. The planks cut near the outer edges contain a large proportion of sap.

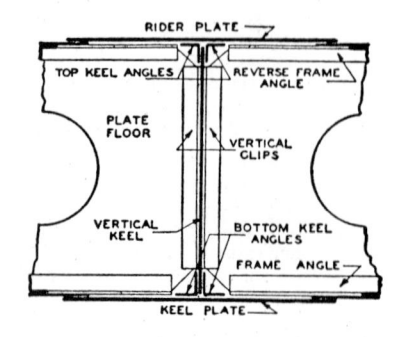

FLAT KEEL. The heavy central bottom strake of shell plating to which the bottom angles of the center girder or vertical keel are riveted or to which the bottom of the vertical keel is welded. Also called plate keel.

Fr: *Quille Plate;* Ger: *Flachkiel.*

When great strength is required the flat plate keel consists of two plates riveted together with the butts staggered. Flat plate keels have superseded bar keels in commercial vessels with the exception of small craft such as tugs, sailing coasters, and the like.

FLATMEN. Term used in Lancashire and Cheshire for the men employed in steering and navigating flats. Also called lightermen, bargemen.

FLATNER. A small sailing boat found on Bridgewater Bay (Somerset, G. B.) and resembling a Newfoundland dory. It is double-ended with big sheer forward and aft, and thwartship rocker. A centerboard is fitted. These boats are built in two sizes known as the "foreboater" and "bay-boat," the former having slightly more freeboard. Foreboater: Length over-all 19 ft. 6 in. Beam at floor 3 ft. 10 in. Beam at gunwale 5 ft. 6 in. Depth amidships (gunwale to bottom) 1 ft. 9 in. Depth at bow 22 in. Draft 4 in. The rig consists of a spritsail and a small jib. Flatners are rowed or sailed. The rudder reaches well below the bottom of the boat, giving more grip. The bottom is flat and dished up towards the ends.

FLAT OF BOTTOM. That portion of a ship's bottom without rise between keel and bilge, or having a rise without curvature.

Fr: *Petit fond;* Ger: *Flach.*

FLAT PLATE KEELSON. Horizontal plate laid on top of the floors and riveted to them and to the vertical keel plate.

FLATS. A level place on an arm of the sea over which the water stands or flows. A place more or less under water and not navigable by ordinary vessels on account of the shallowness of the water.

Ger: *Watte.*

FLAT SAWING. The manner of sawing timber in a direction tangential to the annual rings.

FLAT SCARF. A scarf where the depth reads across the edge or narrow face of the timber. It has its surfaces opposite to the sides, such as keelson and keel scarfs.

Fr: *Écart Plat;* Ger: *Glattes Lasch.*

FLAT SEAM. A seam used for tabling two overlapping cloths together. The stitches run obliquely to the seam, forming a zigzag which allows the cloth to stretch without tearing away.

Fr: *Couture à point broché;* Ger: *Flache Naht.*

FLAT SEIZING. A lashing for securing two ropes together or two parts of the same rope to make an eye. It has only one layer of turns and is only a light seizing. It differs from the round seizing by having cross turns taken over the first layer of turns and no riding turns.

Fr: *Amarrage Plat;* Ger: *Plattbindsel.*

FLAT SHOAL. A shoal on which the waves of the sea may break but which does not uncover.

Fr: *Basse; Batture;* Ger: *Watt.*

FLAT SENNIT. Plain plaiting made with any number of strands, odd or even. Usually 5 to 7 strands. Also called common sennit, English sennit.

Fr: *Tresse Plate;* Ger: *Platting.*

FLAT SHORE. A low flat stretch of land immediately bordering on the sea.

Fr: *Côte basse;* Ger: *Flachküste.*

FLAT STERN. A form of stern in which the upper and aftermost part of the counter is flattened in a plane perpendicular to the longitudinal axis of the ship as distinguished from the elliptical or round stern. Also called square transom stern.

Fr: *Arrière Carré;* Ger: *Plattes Heck; Plattgatt.*

FLATTEN IN. To draw the clew or sheet of a sail toward the middle of the ship. It gives greater turning power to the vessel.

Fr: *Border Plat.*

FLAT WELD. A weld made on a surface lying horizontally or at an angle not more than 45° to the horizontal, the weld being made from the upper or top side of the parts jointed. Also called downhand weld, underhand weld.

Fr: *Soudure à Plat.*

FLAX CANVAS. Sailcloth made of flax fibers obtained from the stem of the plant *Linum usitatissimum.* It has from 14 to 18 two-fold warp threads per inch and from 12 to 36 weft threads (called shots) per inch. The usual widths are 15, 18, 24, 30, and 36 in. Flax canvas is undesirable for yacht sails. It is loose in texture and elastic in substance but its wearing qualities are superior to cotton and it is therefore generally used by merchant vessels.

Fr: *Toile de Lin;* Ger: *Flachs Segeltuch; Flachsstoff.*

The threads of flax canvas are single in the weft and double in the warp. Trysails and storm jibs of yachts are generally made of flax canvas. Trading and fishing vessels have their sails made of brown flax, also known as ship flax, which is an unbleached grayish-drab sailcloth, of the cheapest quality. It is made up in a 24-in. width in bolts of approximately 42 yd. Half-bleached flax is of finer texture than brown flax and is grayish white. The fibers are of a longer staple. Full-bleached flax is woven from the best long fibers and is pure white.

FLAX ROPE. Cordage made of flax fiber and confined to the use of signal halyards, log lines, shot lines, fishing lines, sewing twine, and so on, on merchant vessels.

Fr: *Cordage en Lin;* Ger: *Flachsstauwerk.*

Flax ropes have recently come into fashion for yachting, especially in racing craft. The strength and endurance of flax is superior to the best hemp. It is considered as the highest quality line made because of its light weight for a given strength and its weather-resisting properties.

FLEET. 1. A collection of ships, either war or merchant.

2. The totality of drift nets shot by one vessel. The number of nets composing a fleet varies according to the tonnage of the vessel or local regulation and may attain 300 to 400 for the largest types, extending over a distance of 4 to 5 miles.

Fr: *Tessure;* Ger: *Fleet; Netzfleet.*

See **Boxing Fleet.**

FLEET (to). 1. To free or loosen the blocks of a tackle when they have been drawn together.

Fr: *Reprendre;* Ger: *Ablagen.*

2. To come up a rope so as to haul to more advantage.

Ger: *Verfahren.*

FLEETER. Smaller type of North Sea steam fishing vessel which, as its name implies, works in company with other boats of similar type.

Fleeters are supplied with sufficient bunkers to last from 6 to 8 weeks, during which time they remain on the fishing grounds and periodically deliver their catches to a carrier. They work together in fleets of 50 to 60 boats. All these vessels will trawl, as directed by an *admiral*, in proximity to a mark boat, whose position is known to the owners from day to day. The fish is daily fetched to market by fast carriers.

Two, or sometimes three, admirals accompany each fleet for three weeks in succession. The admiral gives the direction of sailing to the fleet and the signals for shooting or hauling trawls. Each fleet uses a mark boat, which anchors or shifts position at the order of the admiral.

Wood, W., *The Fleeters,* London, 1935.

FLEET TRAIN. A term which describes collectively fleet tankers, ammunition ships, cargo ships, store ships, repair ships, sea-going tugs, and so on, employed to maintain, repair, and supply war ships and enabling a naval force to remain at sea for considerable periods. It is also referred to in naval parlance as service force.

FLEMISH DOWN. A method of coiling rope on deck in which the ends of each succeeding flake are pushed slightly under the preceding one.

FLEMISH EYE. An eye splice used for the collar of a stay. This splice is useful when the strain is such as to tend to spread the two parts apart. Also used for making a small eye at the end of a pointed rope. Also called selvage eye.

Fr: *Oeil à la Flamande;* Ger: *Flämisches Auge.*

FLEMISH FAKE. A fake or coil of rope in which the separate turns are concentric and lie flat on the deck, without riding over each other.

Fr: *Glène Plate.*

FLEMISH HORSE. A short additional footrope at the end of a yard for the use of the yardarm man who has to sit straddling the yardarm and who passes the reef earing. It has an eye spliced at each end, one end goes over the eyebolt in the yardarm and the other is seized to the yard a few feet inside the lift. (Obsolete.)

Fr: *Faux-Marchepied; Marchepied de Bout de Vergue;* Ger: *Nockpferd.*

FLENSING (G. B.). The act of removing the oleaginous blanket from a whale before the operation of trying out. This was formerly done with the whale lying alongside. It is now performed on the flensing deck of the whale factory vessel or the slipway of the shore whaling station. In the United States called flinching, cutting in.

Fr: *Dépecer;* Ger: *Flensen.*

FLETTNER ROTORSHIP. A vessel propelled by wind action on Flettner rotors, which are large, vertical, hollow cylinders, rotated at slow speed by low-power electric motors. Beam winds acting on the rotors cause a resultant forward impelling force, due to the "magnus effect," or cross-wind effect. These ships were found practical, but incapable of competing economically with steam vessels.

Flettner's sailless ship explained, *Power*, New York, vol. 60, no. 27 (December, 1924).

FLETTNER RUDDER. A German patent rudder which consists of a partially balanced main rudder, at the trailing edge of which a small auxiliary rudder is attached. The auxiliary rudder is steered by hand or by a small steering engine and, when oblique to the lines of flow, exerts a force which turns the main rudder and holds it at any desired angle.

FLEXIBLE ROPE. A type of wire rope consisting of a large number of wires of comparatively small diameter with one or several hemp cores. It is used for standing and running rigging, mooring and towing lines, wheel ropes, etc. Its strength is less than other wire rope of equal diameter and its stretch is higher. The constructions mostly used for flexible ropes are 6 x 19 and 6 x 12 with center hemp core and hemp center in each strand. Also called hoisting rope.

Ger: *Biegsames Drahtseil.*

FLICKERING LIGHT. A flashing light in which the light increases and decreases irregularly in intensity.

Fr: *Feu scintillant;* Ger: *Flackernd Feuer.*

FLIGHT. A sharp rise in some outside part of the hull such as rail or counter.

FLINCHING.
See **Flensing.**

FLINDERS BAR. A soft iron bar placed in the fore-and-aft center vertical plane, on the foreside of the binnacle when the north point of the compass is drawn toward the stern by the vertical soft iron, and on the afterside when the north point is drawn in the contrary direction. Its purpose is to compensate for part of the semicircular error. It consists of a round bar 3 in. in diameter and of whatever length (6 to 24 in.) is found proper for the actual position of the compass of any particular ship.

Fr: *Barre de Flinders;* Ger: *Flindersstange.*

FLITCH. 1. Term used in the New England halibut fisheries to denote the thick layer of boneless flesh on each side of the backbone, removed when dressing the fish.

2. A slab or piece of timber sawed from the outer part of a log.

FLITCH TIMBER. One of several timbers fastened side by side in a wooden ship to form a compound frame having a natural bend, and occasionally used at the turn of the bilge, to increase stiffness of the framing.

FLOAT. 1. A scow-shaped floating platform with a deck used in a harbor for bringing goods alongside or for taking them away. Although not capable of making signals or of steering or of self-propulsion, floats are, for many purposes, considered vessels and as such come under admiralty jurisdiction.

See **Car Float.**

2. Any buoyant object attached to nets or fishing lines to keep them at the required depth or to prevent them from sinking. They are made of wood, aluminum, cork, or glass spheres.

Fr: *Flotte;* Ger: *Schwimmklotz.*

See **Car Float, Life Float, Seine Float.**

Glass balls are necessary for nets which are set in deep water (60 fathoms) as it has been found that cork floats are apt to lose their buoyancy owing to the pressure which at these depths forces the water into the pores of the cork. Heavy aluminum balls and tubes have lately come into use for deep-water trawling, replacing the glass balls which do not stand up well under continuous pressure.

FLOATING BEACON. A beacon used in offshore hydrographic and surveying work, generally moored with three backed grapnels. Also called water signal. It is composed of the barrel, the ballast tube, and the top-mark, the latter consisting of a mast fitted at the head with intercrossed pieces of wood arranged in two rectangular planes and secured at their periphery with steel wire.

Fr: *Balise Flottante;* Ger: *Treibbake.*

Floating beacons are used in the course of coastal hydrographic operations when it is found necessary to extend the soundings outside the limit of visibility of the signals erected on land. These beacons should be very buoyant and capable of resisting a rough sea during several consecutive months of immersion.

FLOATING BREAKWATER. A contrivance consisting of a series of square frames of timber connected by mooring chains or cables attached to anchors or stone blocks in such a manner as to form a basin within which vessels riding at anchor may be protected from the violence of the waves.

FLOATING CLAUSE. A charter party clause providing that a vessel shall be directed to proceed only to a port or berth where it can safely lay afloat at all times. Sometimes called berth clause.
  Fr: *Clause "toujours à Flot"*; Ger: *Berth Klausel.*

FLOATING CRANE. A portable crane mounted on a scow or pontoon and used for harbor work where heavy lifts are required. On smaller types the lifting apparatus consists of a jib crane, on the larger ones of a hammerhead crane. The lifting capacity of floating cranes varies from 12 to 350 tons.
  Fr: *Ponton-Grue*; Ger: *Schwimmender Kran.*

FLOATING DOCK. A dock which generally consists of a bottom pontoon on which a ship may be lifted out of the water and two side walls to give stability to the bottom pontoon. Also called pontoon dock.
  Fr: *Dock Flottant*; Ger: *Schwimmdock.*
  The dock is lowered by admitting water to proper compartments and is raised with the ship in place by pumping out the water. The pumps and engines are usually placed in one of the side pontoons.

FLOATING ELEVATOR. Elevator machinery erected on a floating structure and generally used for transferring grain from attendant barges to the holds of ships, or vice versa. When not permanently moored but capable of navigating from place to place, although used only in one harbor, floating elevators are considered ships or vessels and come within Admiralty jurisdiction.
  Fr: *Elévateur flottant*; Ger: *Schwimmend Getreideheber.*

FLOATING GANTRY. A double cantilever gantry crane of large capacity and high lift, installed on a barge or pontoon. It allows a load to be raised from a dock or ship and deposited on the deck of the pontoon or vice versa.
  Fr: *Ponton grue à portique*; Ger: *Schwimmende Portalkran.*

FLOATING LIGHT. Light attached to a lifebuoy for use when anyone falls overboard at night.
  Ger: *Wasserlicht.*

FLOATING POLICY. A policy which describes the insurance in general terms and leaves the name of the ship or ships and other particulars to be defined by subsequent declaration which may be made by endorsement on the policy or in other customary manner. Also called declaration policy, running policy.
  Fr: *Police Flottante*; Ger: *Laufende Police; Generalpolice.*

FLOATING POWER. The sum of the utilized and reserve buoyancy of a vessel, or the displacement of the completely watertight portion of the vessel when entirely submerged. The utilized buoyancy is that required to support the weight of the vessel.
  Ger: *Schwimmkraft.*

FLOATING REDUCTION SHIP. A vessel provided with plant used in processing whales or fish.
  See **Factory Vessel.**

FLOATING SHEERLEGS.
  See **Sheer Hulk.**

FLOATING STAGE. A raft-like wooden structure used by seamen and ship repairers for working alongside. Also float stage (U. S.).
  Fr: *Ras*; Ger: *Kalfatfloss.*

FLOAT LINE. 1. Trolling line carried from the middle part of the pole.
  2. The line on the top of a net to which the floats are attached.

FLOATMAN (U. S.). One who has charge of a car float.

FLOE. An area of ice, other than fast ice, whose limits are within sight, as distinct from an ice field. Also called sea floe.
  Fr: *Banquise Flottante*; Ger: *Schwimmendes Eisfeld.*

FLOE BERG. In ice nomenclature: refers to large masses of sea ice broken off from ancient floes of great thickness when they are forced upon the shore and presenting the appearance of small icebergs.
  Ger: *Eisschollenberg.*

FLOE ICE. Floe ice consists of drift ice frozen into small fields, a floe carrying the meaning of a small field. An area of ice other than fast ice whose limits are within sight. Light floes are between 1 and 2 ft. in thickness. Floes thicker than this are known as heavy floes. Prevents navigation.
  Fr: *Fragments plats de Banquise flottante*; Ger: *Scholleneis.*

FLONDRIER. A small open fishing boat of about 3 tons found on the coast of Calvados (France). These boats work chiefly with trammel nets for catching flat fish. Length 21 ft. Breadth 6 ft. 8 in. Draft 3 ft. (Typical.) Cutter rig.

FLOOD. The inflow of the tide as opposed to ebb. The period during which the tidal current is flowing toward the land. In tidal terminology the term "flood" is used only when the stream turns within an hour of the corresponding high and low water. Also called flood stream.
    Fr: *Flot; Courant de Flot; Flux;* Ger: *Flutstrom; Flut.*
    See **Windward Flood.**

FLOOD (to). To fill a compartment below the waterline with water admitted from the sea in case of fire or danger of explosion.
    Fr: *Noyer;* Ger: *Fluten.*

FLOODABLE LENGTH. The maximum fraction of a ship's total length at any given point which can be flooded without the ship being submerged beyond the margin line. It applies only to passenger vessels conforming to the 1929 International Convention for Safety of Life at Sea.
    Fr: *Longueur Envahissable;* Ger: *Flutbare Länge.*
    See **Margin Line.**

FLOODABLE LENGTH CURVE. A curve drawn upon the profile of a ship. At each point the ordinate equals the maximum portion of the length of the ship that can be flooded without submerging the vessel beyond the margin line. Sometimes called flooding length curve.
    Fr: *Courbe des Longueurs Envahissables;* Ger: *Kurve der flutbaren Länge.*

FLOOD CURRENT. The movement of a tidal current toward the shore or up a tidal stream.
    Fr: *Courant de Flot;* Ger: *Flutströmung.*

FLOOD TIDE GATE. One of the gates at the outer entrance of a tidal dock or lock chamber.
    Fr: *Porte de Flot;* Ger: *Fluttor.*

FLOOR. A structural member in the bottom of a ship, usually at every frame, and running athwartships from bilge to bilge. Also called floor plate. The inner flanges or webs of the frame bars are riveted to the lower edge of the floor and the reverse bars riveted to the top.
    Fr: *Varangue;* Ger: *Bodenwrange; Bodenstück.*
    See **Bending Floor, Bracket Floor, Continuous Floor, Deep Floor, Dock Floor, Grill Floor, Intercostal Floor, Partial Floor, Plank Floor, Rise of Floor, Rising Floor, Shallow Floor, Skeleton Floor, Solid Floor, Transom Floor, Watertight Floor.**

Floors are generally cut in the way of the vertical keels. In the way of side keelsons they are continuous in some ships and intercostal in others. In vessels of small tonnage which do not have a double bottom, floors are usually made of a single plate from bilge to bilge. The purpose of floors is to strengthen and stiffen the ship's bottom structure.

FLOOR CEILING. That part of the hold ceiling which extends from the thick strakes to the keelson in a wooden vessel. Planking fitted on the top of the floors or tank top in the cargo holds.
    Fr: *Vaigres de Fond;* Ger: *Flachwegerung; Bodenwegerung.*

FLOOR CLIP. Angle clip used to connect the longitudinals and brackets to the floors. Also called floor lug.

FLOOR HEADS. 1. The extreme end of a floor plate at the junction of frame and reverse angle bars.
    Fr: *Extrémité de Varangue; Tête de Varangue;* Ger: *Oberende einer Bodenwrange.*
    2. The outer end of a floor timber. Also called the rung head.

FLOORHEAD CHOCK. A piece of wood shaped to form a scarf joint at the abutment of floor and futtock in a wooden ship.
    Fr: *Cale d'Empatture;* Ger: *Stosskalben.*

FLOORING OFF. Term used by stevedores to denote the stowing of the lower tier of cargo in the hold of a ship. It is also applied to the dunnaging of cargo between tiers.

FLOOR PLATE. 1. In a solid floor: the transverse vertical plate or plates which extend between the tank top and bottom plating. In single bottom vessels: the plating between reverse bar and frame bar.
    Fr: *Tôle varangue;* Ger: *Bodenwrangenblech.*
    2. Checkered plate of small size which forms a raised platform above the tank top in stokehold and engine room.
    Fr: *Tôle de parquet;* Ger: *Flurplatte.*

FLOOR RIBBAND. A ribband supporting the outer ends of floor timbers while the frames are being erected.

Fr: *Lisse des Façons;* Ger: *Flursente.*

FLOOR TIMBER. Cross timbers uniting the heels of two futtocks and crossing the keel. The timbers fixed athwart the keel and upon which the framing is erected.

Fr: *Varangue;* Ger: *Bauchstück; Bodenwrange.*

FLOTSAM. When cargo is jettisoned, that which floats is termed flotsam. Also a name for the goods which float upon the sea when cast overboard for the safety of the ship or after vessel has foundered.

Fr: *Épaves Flottantes;* Ger: *Treibgut; Seetriftige Güter.*

FLOWING. The condition of a sheet when eased off.

Fr: *Filé.*

FLOWING SHEETS. Sheets eased up or slackened off when sailing free.

Fr: *Ecoutes filées;* Ger: *Raumschoten.*

FLUKE.

See **Palm.**

FLUKE CHAIN. Chain strap put around the "small" or root of the tail and by which the whale was held alongside. It led to a deck pipe forward of the forerigging.

FLUKE SPADE. A name applied by whalemen to the boat spade when it is used as an offensive weapon for "hamstringing" a whale. It carries a light line by which it is recovered. (Obsolete.)

FLURRY. Whalemen's term to denote the dying actions of a Cetacean after it has been harpooned.

FLUSH DECK. A term applied to an upper deck which has no poop, bridge, or forecastle erection extending from side to side of the vessel.

Fr: *Pont Ras; Pont Plat;* Ger: *Glattdeck.*

FLUE GAS SYSTEM. A safety device used when discharging cargo on oil tankers. It consists of a system by which the combustion gases emerging from the smokestack are piped through filters and coolers in the engine room and passed on at 2 or 3 pounds pressure to each tank as it is being discharged of its contents. This gas being mainly carbon dioxide would extinguish any flame in case of fire. At the same time it creates a constant low pressure heat over the cargo as the oil level lowers in discharging.

Ger: *Rauchgassystem.*

FLUSH DECK VESSEL. A vessel which has no side-to-side erections such as bridge, forecastle or poop, above the freeboard or weather deck, only lightly built casings and skylights being fitted over the engine and boiler room openings.

Fr: *Navire à Pont Ras;* Ger: *Glattdeckschiff.*

Freeboard rules have the effect of discouraging the construction of this type of vessel with the result that excepting small craft, such as trawlers and coasting vessels, there are very few seagoing ships of flush deck type. A large sheer of the weather deck is of great importance in these vessels as it increases reserve buoyancy at ends and assists the ship to weather heavy head or following seas.

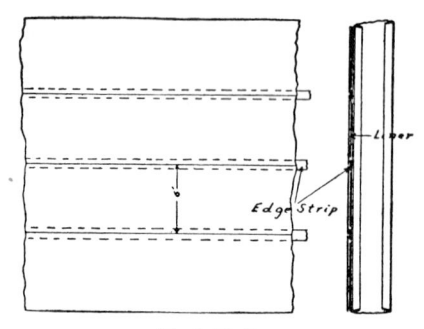

Flush Plating

FLUSH PLATING. A system of plating in which the different strakes fit against one another edge to edge, forming a smooth surface on one side. The edges and butts are connected by edge strips and butt straps on the inside.

Fr: *Bordé à Franc Bord;* Ger: *Glattbeplattung.*

FLUXGATE COMPASS. A compass which consists of several symmetrical solenoids arranged usually as an equilateral triangle through which alternating current is passed that is affected by the earth's magnetic field so that the varying current through the solenoids may be made to give a reading on a dial which can be translated into points or degrees of a compass card.

The fluxgate compass is maintained in the same horizontal plane by means of a gyroscope and its readings are taken on distant dials at convenient places in the ship.

FLY. The length of a flag measured from the staff to the extreme end that flutters in the wind.

Fr: *Battant;* Ger: *Länge.*

See **Vane.**

FLY BACK. The upper block of topsail halyards.

FLY BLOCK. 1. A block whose position shifts to suit the working of the tackle with which it is connected.
Fr: *Poulie volante;* Ger: *Oberer Fallblock.*
2. In a Spanish burton or similar purchase: the moving block in which the hauling part of the fall works.

FLY-BY-NIGHT. A square sail set flying sometimes carried by small cutter- or schooner-rigged craft when running before the wind.
Fr: *Fortune.*

FLYING (SET FLYING). A general term which refers in most instances to a sail which is so rigged that it can be sent aloft and set from the deck. Studding sails were in this category. A jib or staysail may be set flying upon its own luff, without the aid of a stay. The foot of the jib hauls out on the boom, and the luff is stretched taut by the halyards.

FLYING BRIDGE. 1. A term applied in the latter half of the 19th century to a series of gangways which connected the poop of sailing vessels with the forecastle head making use of the deck houses on the way. These gangways were carried on portable stanchions at the level of deck house roofs. They were made of wood and had a width of 30 to 36 inches.
Ger: *Laufbrucke.*
2. Narrow platform located on top of the navigation bridge, where the standard compass is fitted.
Fr: *Passerelle haute.*

FLYING FORESAIL. A square foresail set flying on small fore-and-aft rigged-vessels.
Fr: *Fortune;* Ger: *Breitfock.*

FLYING GUYS. The rigging by which the flying jibboom is stayed sideways.
Fr: *Haubans de Clin-Foc;* Ger: *Aussenkluverbackstage.*

FLYING JIB. The sail set on the fore topgallant royal stay in square-rigged vessels. It is used in light winds and has its tack fastened to the flying jibboom end.
Fr: *Clin-Foc;* Ger: *Vor-Bramstagsegel; Aussenkluver.*

FLYING JIBBOOM. A light spar running out beyond the jibboom. It lies alongside of the jibboom for half its length, being secured to it by a lashing, and by a heel clamp to the bowsprit cap. It passes through a whyte at the boom end. Nowadays it is made of one piece with the jibboom.
Fr: *Bayonnette de Clin-Foc; Bâton de Clin-foc;* Ger: *Aussenkluverbaum; Jägerstock; Jägerbaum.*

FLYING KITES. A general term for various sails formerly carried in light winds above the skysails. The term was occasionally used for topgallant and royal studding sails. In yachting parlance, it applies to spinnakers, club topsails, balloon sails, bonnets and similar racing sails.
See **Moonsail; Star Gazer; Curse of the Gods; Sky Gazer.**

FLYING LIGHT. Said of a vessel unloaded and floating with her designed load line well out of the water.

FLYING NIGHTINGALE. Standing rigging extending from the flying jibboom end to the dolphin striker.
Fr: *Martingale de Clin-foc;* Ger: *Aussenkluver Stampfstag; Aussenkluverdomper.*

FLYING MOOR. To moor under sail using the headway of the vessel to run out double the desired length of chain on the first anchor, then backing and letting go the second anchor, heaving in half the amount of cable on the first anchor. This is generally practiced in a tideway in such manner that a ship rides to one anchor during the ebb and to the other during the flood.

FLYING PROA.
See **Popo.**

FLYING SAIL. A sail which sets flying, that is, which is not bent to a yard, mast or gaff but is set from the deck as the jib of a cutter.

FLYING SKYSAIL. A skysail that is stowed with the royal. The yard has neither lifts nor braces, and the clews are secured to the royal yardarms.

FLYING SOUNDER. A name applied to any deep-sea sounding machine with which soundings can be taken without stopping the ship.
Fr: *Machine à Sonder; Sondeur;* Ger: *Tieflotungsapparat.*

FLYING START. A term used in yachting parlance to denote a method of starting a race in which the signals are given while the competitors are already in motion instead of an alternative method in which the boats are waiting at the starting line with their sails down and moored by their sterns to a hawser.

In the flying start as now generally used an imaginary line is taken between two marks at right angles to the course the racing boats must take to reach the first marker boat. Two guns are fired exactly five minutes apart, and the competitors are required to keep behind the line until after the second gun is fired, the object being to cross the line with good way on as soon as possible after the second gun, requiring good judgment, as in the event that the boat is over the line too soon it must go back and recross it.

FLYING STUDDING SAIL. A studding sail set flying between the masts.

FLY MESHING. A method used for sloping the edge of a net which is not of rectangular shape. It is largely used for the wings of the otter trawl which taper rapidly towards the lower end of the opening.

FLY NET. A drift net in which the foot of the net has a simple raw selvage with little or no strengthening as distinguished from the so-called "foot rope" nets in which there is a strengthening of light rope along the foot of the net.

FOALSFOOT. A tool used in shipyards to cut out part of a hole in a plate to be riveted when unfair, thus making the hole neither round, square, nor oval. Also called hole cutter.

FOAM. Generic term applied to a chemical fire extinguishing medium. The oxygen supply is cut off by throwing a blanket of soupy foam over the fire. It is the most effective means used on board ship for the extinction of petroleum fires.

The chemicals necessary to produce this foam are carried in tanks of various size and may either be piped to the various compartments or the containers may be moved about the ship and the foam directed through a rubber hose.

Fr: *Mousse;* Ger: *Schaum.*

FOG. Anything which obscures the clearness of the atmosphere, but specifically in meteorology the obscuration caused by the minute globules of water floating in the air. The formation of sea fog is generally caused by a warm moist wind passing over relatively cold water; or occasionally by a cold wind passing over warm water.

Fr: *Brouillard;* Ger: *Nebel.*

See **Advection Fog, Dry Fog, Mock Fog, Radiation Fog.**

Barlow, E. W., "Fog at Sea," *The Marine Observer* (London), vol. 6 (March–June, 1930).

FOG BELL. A bell used as fog signal at certain land stations, lighthouses, and by light vessels. At most stations it is operated mechanically.

Fr: *Cloche de Brume;* Ger: *Nebelglocke.*

FOGBOUND. Said of a vessel unable to proceed on account of fog.

Fr: *Arrêté par la brume;* Ger: *Vom Nebel gehindert.*

FOG BOW. A white rainbow caused by extremely small raindrops or by fog. To be visible, the observer must either be near the cloud or in the fog. Also called "Ulloa's Ring."

Ger: *Nebelbogen.*

FOG EYE. A spot of sunlight showing through fog.

FOG GONG. A sound signal apparatus used as a substitute for a bell on board small seagoing vessels.

Fr: *Gong de brume;* Ger: *Nebelgong.*

FOG GUN. A fog signal consisting of a gun fired at regular intervals.

Fr: *Canon de Brume;* Ger: *Nebelgeschütz.*

FOGGY. State of the atmosphere characterized by fog.

Fr: *Brumeux;* Ger: *Nebelig.*

FOGHORN. A horn or trumpet blown by hand, steam, or air; for use at sea and in coastal stations during foggy weather. For small sea-going vessels the "plunger" type of foghorn is rarely acceptable, the mouth-blown horn never. The rotary and crank-bellows types are the most efficient. In order to comply with the regulations for preventing collisions at sea, a fog horn must be constructed in such a way as to be able to give either long or short blasts.

Fr: *Cornet de Brume;* Ger: *Nebelhorn.*

FOG PATCH. A small area of fog.

Fr: *Bouchon de brume;* Ger: *Nebelschwaden.*

FOG SIGNAL. Generic term for sound and wireless signals employed aboard ship and on shore stations in fog, mist, falling snow or heavy rainstorms. Fog signals may be classified as follows: 1. Sound signals transmitted through the atmosphere by sirens, whistles, diaphones, nautophones, bells, gongs, guns and detonating rockets. 2. Submarine signals such as submarine bells and oscillators. 3. Wireless signals from radio beacons.

Fr: *Signal de Brume;* Ger: *Nebelsignal.*

FOG SPAR.
See **Position Buoy.**

FOLDING ANCHOR. A small anchor having stock and flukes so designed that when not in use they can be folded against the shank for convenience in stowing. Also called **Portable Anchor.**
Fr: *Ancre Articulée;* Ger: *Klappbareanker.*

FOLLOWING EDGE. When a propeller rotates, the blades cut through the water in the ship stream. The leading edge of each blade enters the undisturbed water first; the following edge trails.
Fr: *Arête de Sortie; Bord de Sortie;* Ger: *Austretende Flügelkante.*

FOLLOWING SEA. One running in the direction of the ship's course.
Fr: *Mer de l'Arrière;* Ger: *Fortlaufende See.*

FOLLOW-UP GEAR. Any device which insures that a "slave," or repeater, at a remote station follows exactly the motion, linear or angular displacement of a master, or control, at a control station. Such installations are common in modern steering gear. Follow-up gear may be mechanical, employing levers, gears, differentials, etc., pneumatic or hydraulic, as in the telemotor; or electrical, as in the self-synchronous and step-by-step systems.
Fr: *Appareil de commande à Distance;* Ger: *Fernsteuerapparat.*

FOLLYER.
See **Volyer.**

FONTINHEIRA. A flat-bottom open boat with transom stern used in the lobster fisheries on the coast of Ericeira (Portugal). It is rigged with one mast and lateen sail and pulls 4 oars.

FOOT. 1. The lower edge of a sail.
2. The side of a fore-and-aft sail extending between tack and clew.
Fr: *Fond; Bordure;* Ger: *Fussliek; Unterliek.*
See **Board Foot, Club Foot, Crow Foot.**

FOOTBAND. A strengthening band of canvas along the foot of a square sail on the afterside.

FOOTBOARD.
See **Stretcher.**

FOOTLING. Fore-and-aft strips of wood fitted in the bottom of an open boat. They differ from bottom boards by being secured to the frames or floors, whereas the bottom boards are portable. Also called foot waling.

FOOTLOCKS. Ledges of wood fixed to the decks of cattle-carrying vessels to prevent the animals from slipping and falling in heavy water.

FOOT OUTHAUL. A line for hauling out the clew of a boom sail. It is rove through a sheave at the boom end.
Ger: *Lagerausholer; Schothornwipper.*

FOOTRAILS. Moldings on a ship's stern.
Ger: *Heckverzierung.*

FOOT ROPE. 1. Pieces of served wire rope extending under a yard from the middle to the yardarm, supported by stirrups, upon which the men stand when reefing or furling a sail. Footropes are also found beneath the overhang of the spanker boom of a schooner and under the bowsprit and jibboom. They are named according to the spar to which they are fastened.
Fr: *Marchepied;* Ger: *Pferd; Fusspferd.*
2. The boltrope along the foot of a sail.
Fr: *Ralingue de Fond;* Ger: *Fussliek.*

FOOT SPAR. Athwartship pieces of wood placed at the bottom of a rowboat, fastened to the bilge stringers or cleats, against which the oarsmen place their feet. Also called stretcher.
Fr: *Marchepied de Nage;* Ger: *Fusslatte; Stemmbretter.*

FORBES LOG. A patent log of the submerged screw type which indicates the vessel's speed at any moment and records the distance traveled at the same time. It consists essentially of a bronze tube fitted vertically through the bottom plating near the point about which the vessel pivots in turning. Water passing through two openings in the tube acts to rotate a small helical rotator in the tube at a speed dependent upon the speed of the vessel through the water. The rotator's motion is transferred by a spindle to a magneto in which a small current is thus generated. The voltage of this current is registered on voltmeters which are calibrated to read directly in knots. Rotation is also transferred to a small commutator which electrically operates a distance recorded located adjacent to the speed indicator.
Fr: *Log Forbes;* Ger: *Forbes Logge.*

FORBES RIG. A rig invented by Captain R. B. Forbes, and used for the first time on the topsail schooner "Midas" in 1841. In this rig the topmast is fidded abaft the lower masthead, and the lower topsail yard hoisted on the lower masthead from the eyes of the lower rigging to the cap. The lower topsail has two reefs with reef tackles, buntlines and clew lines, as in the single topsail rig. The upper topsail hoists on the topmast and has the same gear as the lower topsail. Occasionally one finds the topmast fidded forward of the lower masthead, in which case the lower topsail yard hoists on the doubling of the topmast. This rig was considered an improvement upon the single topsail rig but was eventually superseded by Howes' rig which is the double topsail rig of today.

FORCED-CIRCULATION BOILER. A boiler in which the water is circulated by a pump additional to the feed pump. This pump has a suction in a collecting drum or some low point of the boiler and forces the water successively through various parts of the heating surfaces. The unevaporated water collects at this pump's suction and is recirculated.

Fr: *Chaudière à Circulation forcée;* Ger: *Zwanglaufkessel.*

Forced-circulation boilers are characterized by high generating capacity for their size and weight, and by their ability to raise steam very quickly from a cold boiler. The Velox, La Mont, Benson, and Loeffler boilers are of this type.

FORCED DRAFT. Artificial means for increasing the rate of combustion in a boiler by creating an excess of air pressure under the fuel. Also called mechanical draft. The two systems most commonly adopted in marine practice are the closed stokehold and the closed ashpits.

Fr: *Tirage Forcé;* Ger: *Forcierter Zug; Künstlicher Zug.*

FORE. A term used chiefly in words denoting some parts of a ship's framing, equipment, or machinery which lies near the stem or in that direction, in contradistinction to aft, also parts connected with the foremast.

Fr: *Avant;* Ger: *Vorn.*

FORE AND AFT. From stem to stern; lengthwise; placed or directed parallel to the vessel's keel.

Fr: *En Long; Longitudinal;* Ger: *Längsschiffs.*

FORE AND AFT BRIDGE. A series of connecting gangways between the forward and after bridges or between a bridge house and a forecastle deck or poop deck. It is commonly found on tankers, where such an installation is desirable on account of the slippery condition of the upper deck. Sometimes called "monkey bridge." Also called connecting bridge, flying bridge, catwalk.

Fr: *Passavant;* Ger: *Verbindungsbrücke; Laufbrücke; Überlauf.*

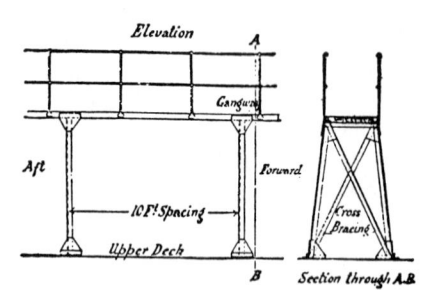

Fore and Aft Bridge

FORE AND AFT CORRECTORS. The small round bar magnets placed in a fore and aft direction within the binnacle for correcting coefficient "B" of the semicircular error.

Fr: *Barreaux aimantes longitudinaux;* Ger: *Langsschiffsmagnete.*

FORE AND AFTER. A longitudinal steel or wooden hatch girder which supports the hatch covers when the latter are disposed athwartships.

Fr: *Galiote;* Ger: *Längsbalken; Scherstock.*

FORE-AND-AFT MOORINGS. Moorings in which the ship is secured fore and aft by 2 or 4 riding chains. Also called bow and stern moorings. These moorings are used in harbors and rivers where there is not sufficient room available for swinging. Stationary vessels which remain in harbor for an indefinite period frequently moor to fore-and-aft moorings.

Fr: *Embossage;* Ger: *Bug und Heck Vertauung.*

FORE-AND-AFT RIG. General term for all rigs in which the sails extend from the centerline to the lee side of the ship or boat, and are set on stays, gaffs, booms, sprits, lateen yards, lugyards. In fore-and-aft-rigged vessels the center of effort of the sails should be far enough from the ship's head to give the vessel a natural tendency to luff.

Fr: *Gréement Aurique; Gréement à Voiles en Pointe;* Ger: *Schraatsegel Takelung.*

In trades where there is much windward work the fore-and-aft rig allows the vessel to approach nearer to the wind than the square rig, as the sails can be trimmed more nearly in a line with the keel. On the other hand, it is less efficient when sailing free, when the sails do not draw well; booms may get damaged when gybing, and this may endanger the whole rigging. It is for the above reasons, that the barkentine, schooner-brig, or other mixed rigs are often preferred to the purely fore-and-aft rig.
Morris, E. P., *The Fore-and-Aft Rig in America*, New Haven (Conn.), 1929.

FORE-AND-AFT SAIL. Sails which pivot at their forward edge and are bent to travelers, sliding up and down stays, railways, or hoops when bent on a mast or spar. When furled they are either lowered or pulled in and brailed to the mast.
Fr: *Voile Aurique;* Ger: *Schratsegel.*

FORE-AND-AFT TACKLE. Any kind of tackle used in the line of the keel. A watch tackle used for stretching the backbone of an awning.

FOREBOATER. See **Flatner.**
FOREBODY. See **Body.**
FOREBOOM. The boom of a gaff-foresail.
Fr: *Bôme de Misaine-Goëlette;* Ger: *Schonersegelbaum.*

FORE CABIN PASSENGER (G. B.). A term synonymous with second class passenger.

FORECASTLE. 1. A short superstructure or erection situated over the bows. It affords additional buoyancy and increases the lifting power at the fore end of the ship. The inside space is generally used for the crew's accommodation.
2. A forward living compartment for the crew.
Fr: *Le Gaillard;* Ger: *Back.*
See **Deckhouse Forecastle, Long Forecastle, Monkey Forecastle, Short Forecastle, Sunk Forecastle, Topgallant Forecastle.**

FORECASTLE CARD (U. S.). An exact copy of the shipping articles with the signatures omitted. It is signed and stamped by the shipping commissioner and posted in the crew's quarters.

FORECASTLE DECK. A term applied to a deck extending from the stem over a forecastle.
Fr: *Pont du Gaillard;* Ger: *Backdeck.*
FORECASTLE RAIL. Bars or pipes extending between stanchions around the forecastle.
Fr: *Rambarde de Gaillard;* Ger: *Backreling.*

FOREFOOT. 1. A term applied to the intersection of the curved portion of the stem with the keel. The forward end of a vessel's stem which is stepped on the keel.
Fr: *Brion;* Ger: *Stevenlauf.*
2. The compass or sharpness of a ship's lateral plane at stem and under water. Also called gripe.
See **Cutaway Forefoot, Steep Forefoot.**

FOREFOOT KNEE. A vertical knee placed at the forward end of the keel to connect it with the stem or the apron. Also called stem knee.
Fr: *Marsouin;* Ger: *Stevenknie; Beitknie.*

FOREFOOT PLATE. A furnaced shell plate riveted or welded to the curved portion of the stem and keel. The frame portion is curved both transversely and longitudinally, and the flange is curved to suit the rounded forefoot.

FOREGANGER. See **Foregoer.**
FOREGIRT. See **Spar Bowline.**
FOREGOER. A line, used for whaling, about 40 to 50 fathoms in length. Also called foreline, foreganger. It is made of finest Italian hemp 4-in. stuff and is attached to the harpoon shank by means of a ring. The other end is spliced to a 5-in. whale line 120 fathoms long. The foreline is coiled down on a table in front of and under the gun.
Fr: *Harpoire;* Ger: *Vorläufer.*

FOREHAND. To take the strain by hand on a piece of gear near the moving block so that it may be belayed.

FORE HOODS. The forward ends of the outside planking rabbeted into the stem.
Fr: *Barbes de l'Avant;* Ger: *Vordere Plankenenden.*

FOREHOOK. See **Bow Pointer.**
FOREIGN GENERAL AVERAGE. A marine insurance term which indicates that the adjustment of general average losses may be according to foreign law.

FOREIGN GENERAL AVERAGE CLAUSE. A marine insurance policy clause which states that general average is payable according to foreign statement or per York-Antwerp rule, if in accordance with the contract of affreightment. By "foreign statement" is meant that general average losses are computed and adjusted according to the law of the port of discharge or the port of destination; or, if the voyage is broken up and abandoned, the port where the adventure is actually terminated.

FOREIGN-GOING VESSEL. A vessel engaged in foreign trade, that is, outside the limits of the home and coasting trades, assigned by the laws and regulations of the flag under which the vessel sails.

Fr: *Navire Long Courrier;* Ger: *Langefahrt Schiff.*

FOREIGN TRADE. As used in shipping refers to all transportation by merchant ships between countries other than that under whose flag a vessel is registered.

Fr: *Navigation au Long Cours;* Ger: *Lange Fahrt.*

FOREIGN VOYAGE. In legal parlance refers to a voyage within the limits of foreign jurisdiction.

FORELOCK. A round or flat wedge of iron used to maintain a bolt in place. It passes through a mortise hole at the end of the bolt.

Fr: *Goupille; Clavette;* Ger: *Splint.*

FORELOCK BOLT. A bolt having in one end a slot into which a key or cotter pin may be inserted to prevent the bolt being withdrawn.

Fr: *Cheville à Goupille;* Ger: *Splintbolzen.*

FOREMAN SHIP CARPENTER.
See **Shipwright.**

FOREMAN STEVEDORE. The person in charge of a stevedore gang. Also called dock boss in the United States.

Fr: *Chef Arrimeur;* Ger: *Stauervize; Stauerbaas.*

FOREMAST. The mast before the main mast.

Fr: *Mât de misaine;* Ger: *Fockmast; Vormast.*

FORENOON WATCH. A name given to the watch from 8 A.M. till noon.

Fr: *Quart du Matin;* Ger: *Vormittagswache.*

FOREPEAK. The space between the collision bulkhead and the stem. When made watertight it is used as a trimming or fresh-water tank.

Fr: *Coqueron Avant;* Ger: *Vorpiek.*

FORERAKE. The forward inclination of the stem, masts, etc., beyond a perpendicular.

Fr: *Elancement;* Ger: *Ausfall.*

FORE REACH. If two ships are sailing together close-hauled and one draws ahead of the other ship the former is said to forereach on the latter.

Fr: *Gagner;* Ger: *Totsegeln.*

FORE REACHING. Making a wide sweep in turning so as to gain headway from the impetus acquired, instead of turning short.

FORE RIGGING. The standing and running rigging of the foremast.

Fr: *Gréement de misaine;* Ger: *Focktakelage.*

FORE RUNNER. A piece of cloth tied on a hand long line about 90 ft. from the long chip to mark the limit of the stray line.

Fr: *Houache;* Ger: *Vorlaufer.*
See **Foregoer.**

FORERUNNERS. Low-amplitude, long period swell not detectable by eye, and arriving before the main body of waves from a storm.

FORESAIL. 1. A triangular sail hanked to the forestay on a cutter, yawl or ketch. The foremost sail of a sloop. Also called stay foresail.

Fr: *Trinquette;* Ger: *Fock Stagsegel; Stagfock.*

2. The sail bent to the foreyard in a square-rigged vessel. Also called fore course.

Fr: *Misaine;* Ger: *Fock; Focksegel.*

See **Balloon Foresail, Flying Foresail, Gaff Foresail, Lug Foresail, Monkey Foresail, Reaching Foresail, Stay Foresail, Tow Foresail.**

FORE SHEET HORSE. An iron span set athwartships at the middle of the deck under the after end of the fore boom on a schooner. A similar span upon which the forestaysail sheet block travels when the latter sail is club-footed. Also called forehorse.

Fr: *Vire-Lof de Trinquette;* Ger: *Leuwagen.*

FORE SHEET IRON (G. B.). Small iron bumkin which projects outside a small open boat for about 5 to 7 in. to which the tack of the lug mainsail hooks. Used on fishing luggers of East Cornwall.

FORE SHEETS. A small platform in the bow of an open boat. Also called headsheets.

Fr: *Caillebotis avant;* Ger: *Vorderboot.*

FORESHORE. That part of the seashore which lies between the crest of the berm and ordinarily low-water mark and which is ordinarily traversed by the uprush and backwash of the waves as the tides rise and fall.
Fr: *Estran;* Ger: *Vorland; Seeufer.*

FORE STAYSAIL. A jib-shaped sail set from the forestay. It is sometimes fitted with a boom named forestaysail club. Also called stay foresail. The word "Jumbo" refers generally to the forestaysail of a fore-and-after.
Fr: *Trinquette; Tourmentin;* Ger: *Stagfock.*

FORE STEAMING LIGHT. The white navigation light carried by power-driven vessels on or before the foremast. Also called **Fore masthead light.**
See **Range Light.**

FORE-TOPMAST STAYSAIL. A jib which sets on the fore-topmast stay next to the forestaysail. Also called standing jib.
Fr: *Petit Foc;* Ger: *Vor-Stangestagsegel.*

FORETURN. A term used in fiber rope-making to denote the twist in each strand, as distinguished from the twist in the rope called "afterturn."
Fr: *Toronnage.*

FORGINGS. Generic term for large solid structural steel parts used in hull construction, such as stem, sternpost, propeller struts, rudder stock, tiller. Most forgings are nowadays replaced by castings.
Fr: *Pièces de Forge;* Ger: *Schmiedestücke.*

FORK. The place where a stay is divided into two parts so as to embrace the mast.

FORMED ROPE. A term sometimes applied to wire rope made of 6 strands of 19 wires each and hemp core. In larger sizes it is used for standing rigging. It is the usual make of rope for otter trawl warps.

FORM STABILITY. The stability given by calculation of the vessel's molded volume of displacement under various conditions of trim and draft.
Fr: *Stabilité des formes;* Ger: *Formstabilität.*

FORWARD. At or in the direction of the bow. Also the fore part of a ship.
Fr: *Devant; Alavant;* Ger: *Voraus; Vorderschiff.*

FORWARD BREAST ROPE. A breast rope which runs out from the forepart of the ship across the stem or nearly so.
Fr: *Traversier Avant;* Ger: *Vordere Dwarsfeste.*
See **Breast Rope.**

FORWARDING AGENT. One who receives goods for transportation, delivers them to the carrier, and performs various services for the shipper. Also called freight forwarder. He is neither a consignor nor a carrier and is not paid for the transportation.
Fr: *Commissionnaire Expéditeur;* Ger: *Spediteur.*

Forwarding agents quote freight rates from inland localities or seaports to foreign seaports or inland points. They supervise the handling of shipments while in the hands of rail and ocean carriers; advise concerning insurance rates and the form of marine insurance for any particular shipment; furnish advice on customs requirements of foreign countries, weights, packing and marking; receive goods consigned to them, book space on ships, arrange for the delivery to steamer, which includes cartage, lighterage and storage, where necessary. They take out the necessary shipping papers such as consular invoices, export customs clearances, bills of lading; assemble the documents in proper form for banking purposes and dispose of them in accordance with the terms of sales and instructions from the shipper. They also arrange for collection of invoice amount at destination if required. They assemble small packages or shipments and send them in bulk or with other shipments all on one bill of lading at reduced pro rata charges. Freight forwarders in large ports or commercial centers usually specialize either on shipments to particular countries or handle mainly the shipments of certain industries. Others act as manufacturer's agents.

Gregg, E. S., *Freight Forwarding in the United States and Abroad,* U. S. Bureau of Foreign and Domestic Commerce, Trade Information Bulletin 310, Washington, 1925.

FORWARD BOW SPRING. A mooring line which leads forward of the bow breast rope.
Fr: *Gardemontante de l'avant;* Ger: *Bug Vorleine.*

FORWARD LEECH.
See **Luff.**

FORWARD PERPENDICULAR. A vertical line through the intersection of the load waterline with the fore side of the stem.
Fr: *Perpendiculaire Avant;* Ger: *Vorderer Perpendikel; Vorderes Lot.*

FORWARD SPRING. A line or hawser extending from well forward in the ship to a point on shore abreast of the ship's stern. It acts to check a vessel's forward motion. Also called bow spring.
  Fr: *Garde Montante de l'avant; Amarre de Poste Avant;* Ger: *Bugspring.*

FOTHER. To stop a leak at sea. To haul over a leak a sail, a tarpaulin, or a bag made of old canvas and filled with pulled rope yarns. (Obsolete.) Also called fodder. Ger: *Füttern.*
  See **Collision Mat.**

FOUL. A word generally used in opposition to "clear," implying entangled, embarrassed, or contrary. An anchor is said to be foul when the cable is entangled.
  Fr: *Engagé;* Ger: *Faul; Unklar.*

FOUL. To impede as by collision or entanglement.
  Ger: *Anfahren; Verwickeln.*

FOUL ANCHOR. Anchor with the slack of its cable twisted round the stock or one of the flukes. The symbol of Admiralty.
  Fr: *Ancre engagée;* Ger: *Unklar Anker.*

FOUL BERTH. A berth or anchorage in a roadstead or harbor of such a nature that the vessel when occupying it cannot swing without fouling another ship, or an object ashore, or grounding. According to the "custom of seamen" it is generally admitted that a vessel anchoring too near another ship and giving her a foul berth is responsible for any damage that might occur as the result of the two ships colliding.
  Fr: *Mauvais Évitage;* Ger: *Schlechter Schwairaum.*

FOUL BILL OF HEALTH. A foul bill of health or the absence of a clean bill of health imports that the place of departure was infected when the vessel left.
  Fr: *Patente de Santé Brute;* **Ger:** *Unreiner Gesundheitspass.*

FOUL BOTTOM. 1. Uneven, hard, rocky sea bottom offering poor holding for anchors. A bottom where rocks or wrecks endanger the safety of vessels.
  Fr: *Mauvais Fond;* Ger: *Fauler Grund.*
  2. Said of a ship's bottom which through a prolonged period of immersion in sea water has a growth of weeds and barnacles on its surface.
  Fr: *Carène Sale;* Ger: *Fauler Boden.*

FOULED BY THE FLUKES. Said of an anchor when the cable has taken a turn around the upper fluke.
  Fr: *Surpatté;* Ger: *Armunklar.*

FOULED BY THE STOCK. An anchor is fouled by the stock when slack cable is entangled around the stock.
  Fr: *Surjalé;* Ger: *Stockunklar.*

FOUL GROUND. An area of water where the sea bottom does not provide good holding for the anchors.
  Fr: *Fond de mauvaise tenue;* Ger: *Schlechter Ankergrund.*
  See **Foul Bottom.**

FOUL HAWSE. A ship is said to have a foul hawse if her hawse is neither open nor clear; that is, when the chains are entangled or twisted together by the swinging around of the ship.
  Fr: *Tours dans les Chaînes;* Ger: *Unklare Ketten.*

FOULING. A generic term for the mass of organisms, animal and vegetable, which becomes attached to the underwater surfaces of a ship's hull while it is waterborne.
  Fr: *Salissure;* Ger: *Anwuchs.*
  These growths comprise several main groups of organisms, chiefly annelido, barnacles, molluscs, and certain sea grasses. Fouling results in a serious reduction in speed, and requires the expenditure of additional fuel on a given run between ports. Bengough and Shepheard, "The Corrosion and Fouling of Ships," Institution of Naval Architects (London), *Transactions,* vol. 85 (1943); Visscher, J. P., *Nature and Extent of Fouling of Ship's Bottoms,* U. S. Bureau of Fisheries, Bull., vol. 43, Washington (1929).

FOUNDATION PLATE. A fore-and-aft horizontal plate fitted on top of floors, upon which the center keelson rests.
  Fr: *Sole;* Ger: *Fundamentplatte.*

FOUNDER. To fill and sink at sea. To be overwhelmed by the sea in deep water.
  Fr: *Sombrer; Couler;* Ger: *Überschwemmung; Untergehen; Sinken; Wegsinken.*

FOURAREEN. An open boat from the Shetland Islands used mostly for pulling but occasionally rigged with a square sail or standing lug with or without a boom. Also called fourern. The stem and stern are raked. It pulls 4 oars and is in design a small edition of the sixern.

FOUR ARM MOORING. A permanent mooring consisting of a buoy with single riding chain or pendant attached to four ground chains with anchors forming an angle of 90 degrees with each other. Also called Leg mooring.

Fr: *Corps mort à quatre branches;* Ger: *Vier arm Vertauböje.*

FOURFOLD BLOCK. A block with 4 sheaves.
Fr: *Poulie quadruple;* Ger: *Vierscheibiger Block.*

FOURFOLD PURCHASE. A tackle consisting of 2 blocks with 4 sheaves in each, the standing part being fast to either one of the blocks.
Fr: *Caliorne à Quatre Réas; Appareil;* Ger: *Vierscheibiger Gien.*

FOUR-MASTED BARK.
See Shipentine.

FOUR-MASTED BRIG. A name which has occasionally been given in United States to four-masted sailing craft which were square-rigged on the 2 forward masts and fore-and-aft rigged on the 2 other masts.

FOUR-POINT BEARING, BOW AND BEAM BEARING. The simplest and most commonly used method of determining the distance off a terrestrial object when coasting. The object is observed when it is four points (45°) on the bow and again when it is abeam, the time and patent log reading being noted at each observation. The distance of the ship runs in the interval is the distance off when abeam.
Fr: *Relèvement des quatre quarts;* Ger: *Doppelpeilung.*

FOX. 1. A strand formed by twisting several rope yarns together.
2. Two yarns hand-twisted against their lay and rubbed with tarred canvas. Used for seizings or to weave a mat or paunch.
Fr: *Commande; Tresse;* Ger: *Füchsel; Nitzel; Füchsjes.*
See Spanish Fox.

FOX TAILING (U. S.). Boatbuilding term applied to the process of splitting the point of a treenail and setting an oak wedge in it before entering it in its hole. When driven home the wedge is forced into the treenail by the bottom of the hole. Also called Blind wedging.

FOY (G. B.). Whalemen's term for the meeting of captains and mates in the cabin of a whaler at sea. Also called mollie, gam. (Obsolete.)

FOY BOAT. A clench-built, open boat with a length of about 15 ft. and a breadth of 4 ft. 6 in., used on the river Tyne and its estuary for assisting vessels when warping into dock or berth. It is a deep-heeled boat of light construction with narrow transom stern, two thwarts, and bow and stern boards. The rig consists of a single dipping lug on a 10-ft. mast raking at about 20° and held by a hoop on the forethwart.
Until recent years the Foy boats used to meet vessels a considerable distance offshore. They are now very rarely sailed and for river work they are pulled with an oar from each thwart or sculled from the stern.

FRACTO-CUMULUS. Low-lying clouds constantly changing in shape, resembling cumulus clouds as if torn by a strong wind. They are generally seen when the sky clears up after a long spell of rain.

FRACTO-NIMBUS. A nimbus cloud breaking into detached fragments.

FRAME. One of the transverse girders forming the ribs of the hull and extending from the keel to the highest continuous deck. The term "frame" when used in a general sense includes a combination of three parts: frame bar, reverse bar, and floor plate. The frames act as stiffeners holding the outside plating or planking in shape and maintaining the transverse form of the ship.
Fr: *Couple; Membrure;* Ger: *Spant.*

FRAME AREAS. The areas of the transverse sections of the immersed body at each joint of intersection of the designed water plane with the center longitudinal plane. Also called Area of Sections.
Fr: *Aires des Couples;* Ger: *Spantflächen; Spantenskala.*

FRAME BAR. Angle bar riveted to the lower edge of the floor plate and to the shell plating, as distinguished from the reverse bar.
Fr: *Cornière Membrure;* Ger: *Spantwinkel.*
See Reverse Bar.

FRAME BEVEL. The angle at which the two flanges or surfaces of a frame meet, when not at right angles, owing to the inward slant of the vessel's sides toward the bow and stern.
Fr: *Equerrage des Couples;* Ger: *Spantschmiegung.*

FRAME, IN. A vessel is said to be in frames when all the frames are erected and regulated in place on the building slip before the outside plating or planking is put on.
Fr: *En Membrures;* Ger: *In Spanten stehen.*

FRAME LINER. A liner of the same

width as the flange of a framebar and extending between the edges of adjacent inside strakes of shell plating. It fills the space between the frame bar and the outer strake. Also called frame slip, packing piece.

Fr: *Cale Sous Membrure;* Ger: *Spant Hinterlagstück; Spantfüllstreif.*

FRAME LINES. The intersection of the molded surface of the hull with vertical transverse planes perpendicular to the center line. Also called frame stations.

Fr: *Couples de Tracé;* Ger: *Spantlinien; Spantenriss.*

Frame lines get their name from the fact that the ship's frames or ribs are made to this shape and are installed transversely in the ship, except in longitudinally framed vessels. They are shown in the body plan of the lines drawing. Frame lines are usually numbered progressively from the forward end to the afterend of the ship.

FRAME MODULUS. The ratio $\dfrac{I}{Y}$ of the midship frame below the lowest tier of beams. "I" being the moment of inertia in inch units of the frame girder about its neutral axis, and "Y" the distance in inches from the neutral axis to the most distant part of the frame girder.

Ger: *Spantmodul.*

FRAME MOLD. The template for a frame, giving the outside shape or contour from the keel upward.

Fr: *Gabarit de Membrure;* Ger: *Spantmallung.*

FRAME SPACING. The distance between heel and heel of consecutive frames, the amount of which is usually in accordance with classification societies' rules. Also called timber and space, berth and space.

Fr: *Maille; Écartement des Membrures;* Ger: *Spantentfernung; Inholz und Fach.*

In wooden ships it is the distance between the molding edge of one timber and the molding edge of the one next to it. In these vessels the frames are spaced very close together and occasionally adjusted to each other. In steel ships the average distance varies from about 20 in. in a 100-ft. vessel to about 32 in. in a 600-ft. vessel. In large warships, 4-ft. frame spacing is common.

FRAME SQUAD. A squad of shipyard laborers consisting usually of 5 or 6 platers assisted by a number of helpers, to whom is entrusted the work of making the frames, i.e., bending, beveling, marking and punching of rivet holes. In the U. S. the term frame squad is restricted to a crew of workmen who assemble and erect the frames.

FRAME TIMBER. In wooden ship construction, one of the ribs or transverse members which extend up on each side of the keel and support the outside planking and the ceiling. Also called bend.

Fr: *Membrure; Couple;* Ger: *Inholz; Spantholz.*

A wooden frame is formed of several curved pieces of timber. The lower piece is the floor timber or ground futtock, which extends across the keel. The next piece is the first futtock, the lower part of which laps on one side of the floor, with the upper part lapping on one side of the second futtock, the lower end of the latter butting against the upper end of the floor timber. The successive pieces are called third, fourth . . . etc., futtocks and the last one, top timber. The various pieces are throughbolted to each other across the central joint, thus forming a complete frame.

FRAMING NUMERAL.

See **Transverse Numeral.**

FRAMING PLAN. A diagrammatic plan showing the distribution and type of construction of the frames.

FRAMING RIBBAND. A timber ribband for holding transverse frames in position when erected on the building berth. It usually extends from forepeak to afterpeak bulkheads. Held in place by stage poles (outriggers) vertical supports, and spur shores.

Fr: *Fleuriau; Lisse de Construction;* Ger: *Sente.*

FRANCHISE. A percentage of the insured value on the hull or cargo which the underwriters expressly agree not to cover. The object of franchise is to avoid unnecessary trouble over small claims, and allows the underwriter to offer lower rates than would otherwise rule. This percentage is generally 3 per cent in English policies and 5 per cent in American policies.

Fr: *Franchise;* Ger: *Franchise.*

FRANCHISE CLAUSE. A hull clause in a marine insurance policy which states that the underwriters will not pay claims falling under particular average when the loss is under 3 per cent of the insured value, but nevertheless when the vessel shall have been stranded, sunk or on fire, or in collision with another ship or vessel, underwriters shall pay the damage occasioned thereby, and the expense of sighting the bottom after stranding shall be paid if reasonably

incurred, even if no damage be found.
Fr: *Clause de Franchise;* Ger: *Franchise Klausel.*

FRANKLIN LIFEBUOY (U. S.). Ring-shape copper lifebuoy equipped with a calcium carbide self-ignited light. A luminous buoy.

FRAP. To bind tightly by passing ropes around. The act of crossing and drawing together the parts of a tackle or other combination of ropes to increase tension.
Fr: *Genoper; Brider;* Ger: *Zusammenzeisen.*

FRAPPING TURNS. A number of crossing turns in a lashing to tighten and secure the round turns.
Fr: *Bridure.*

FRAZIL ICE. Ice which forms on a ship's sides in very cold weather in rapidly flowing rivers. The movement of the water prevents the ice crystals from forming a solid sheet of ice.

FREE. A ship is running free when it is not obliged to brace its yards sharp up. The converse of close-hauled.
Fr: *Largue;* Ger: *Raumer Wind.*
See **Going Free.**

FREE (to). To bale or pump water out of a boat or a ship.
Fr: *Étancher;* Ger: *Lenzpumpen; Lenzen.*
See **Bilge Free.**

FREE ALONGSIDE. Trade term which implies that the goods should be placed by the shipper within reach of the ship's tackle in a condition fit for shipment. The exact meaning of the word "alongside" is often determined by the custom of the port, but is generally a pure question of fact.
Fr: *Sous Palan;* Ger: *Frei aus Schiff.*

FREEBOARD. The vertical distance measured on the vessel's side amidships from the load water line to the upper side of the freeboard deck or a point corresponding to it.
Fr: *Franc Bord;* Ger: *Freibord.*
See **Load Water Line, Freeboard Deck.**
The qualification *"with freeboard"* indicates that on account of structural limitations a vessel has a freeboard in excess of the statutory minimum; i.e., that she is not allowed to load as deeply as vessels having the maximum draft permitted by the dimensions. This excess of freeboard, which is quite common in new construction, will vary depending on the purpose and trade for which the vessel is designed.
Bruhn, J., "Freeboard and Strength of Ships," Institution of Naval Architects (London), *Transactions,* 1920; U. S. Bureau of Marine Inspection and Navigation. Regulations for the establishment of load lines, Washington, 1936.

FREEBOARD DECK. The uppermost complete deck having permanent means of closing all openings in its weather portions. In flush-deck ships and ships with detached superstructures it is the upper deck. In complete superstructure-deck ships, it is the deck below the superstructure deck.
Fr: *Pont de Franc Bord;* Ger: *Freiborddeck.*

FREEBOARD DEPTH. Term used in freeboard regulations to denote the depth measured from the top of the keel at midlength to the point of intersection of the top surface of the stringer plate of the freeboard deck and the outside of the vessel at side.
Fr: *Creux de Franc Bord;* Ger: *Freibordhöhe.*

FREEBOARD LENGTH. Length used or freeboard assignment in accordance with the International Loadline Convention of 1930. It is measured on the summer load waterline from the fore side of the stem to the afterside of the rudderpost. If no rudderpost is fitted then the length is taken to the axis of the rudderstock.

FREEBOARD MARKS. The disc, lines and letters on a ship's sides indicating the maximum permissible load line in accordance with the international load line convention (1930).
Fr: *Marques de franc-bord;* Ger: *Freibordmarke.*
See **Load Waterline.**

FREEBOARD RATIO. The freeboard to the lowest point of the margin line divided by the draft amidships to top of keel.

FREEBOARD ZONES. Geographical limits adopted by the International Load Line Convention in 1930 by which the oceans have been marked off into different zones: summer, winter, and tropical, for the determination of freeboard. During these periods the respective seasonal load lines on ship's sides become the statutory load lines.
Fr: *Zône de Franc Bord;* Ger: *Freibord Zone.*
British Board of Trade, "Load Line," *Explanatory Notes on the Chart of Zones and Seasonal Areas,* London, 1932.

FREE DISPATCH. A chartering expression denoting that there is no indemnity payable for time gained in loading or discharging.

Fr: *Sans Bonification pour Temps Gagné;* Ger: *Frei von Beschleunigungsgebühr.*

FREEDOM OF THE SEAS. The rule of the law of nations by which the open sea is not under the sovereignty of any state whatever. It involves freedom of navigation for vessels of all nations, whether men-of-war, public vessels, or merchant vessels. No rights whatever of salute exist between vessels meeting on the open sea.

Fr: *Liberté des Mers;* Ger: *Meeresfreiheit.*

Baty, T., "The Free Sea," *American Journal of International Law,* vol. 35 (1941); Crecraft, E. W., *Freedom of the Seas,* New York, 1935; Hays, A. G., "What Is Meant by the Freedom of the Seas," *American Journal of International Law,* vol. 12 (1918); Ryan, J. W., *Freedom of the Seas and International Law,* New York, 1941.

FREE HARBOR. A chartering term: an alternative form of C.I.F. contract, mostly used in the Bombay trade. Under this clause the shipper is liable for all risks and charges until the goods reach their port of destination.

FREE IN AND OUT. A chartering term by which is meant that the owner who charters his ship is responsible for all the usual costs of ship management with the exception of loading and discharging cargo and of putting the vessel in dry dock if required to do so by the charterer.

Fr: *Franco Chargement et Déchargement;* Ger: *Frei ein und aus.*

FREEING PORT. A rectangular or oval opening in the bulwarks, close to the deck and fitted with a flap cover which opens outward to allow water shipped on deck to run freely overboard. Also called freeing scuttle, wash port, bulwark port, clearing port.

Fr: *Sabord de Décharge;* Ger: *Wasserpforte; Klusenpforte.*

FREE LIGHTERAGE. Harbor lighterage service performed by a railroad system as part of its service included in the freight rate, between railhead and any part of the port.

FREE OF ADDRESS. A chartering clause which means that no address charges shall be made on the freight at the port of discharge.

FREE OF AVERAGE. A term used in marine insurance policies by which the insurer is exempted from all average charges. The subject matter is insured against total loss only. Sometimes called free of general and particular average.

Fr: *Franc d'Avaries;* Ger: *Frei von Havarie; Frei von Beschädigung.*

FREE OF PARTICULAR AVERAGE AMERICAN CONDITIONS. A marine insurance clause as distinguished from free of particular average English conditions.

In the American conditions the clause reads: "free of P.A. unless caused by stranding, sinking, burning, or collision with another vessel." In the English conditions it reads: "free of P.A. unless the vessel or craft be stranded, sunk, burnt, or in collision."

There is a difference between the two clauses owing to the legal construction placed by the courts upon the wording used.

FREE OF TURN. A chartering term by which a steamer's time will commence to count for loading or discharging from her arrival, whether there is a berth available or not.

Ger: *Frei von Torn; Frei von Reihenfolge.*

FREE ON BOARD. A mercantile expression used in sale contracts which denotes that the goods have to be delivered by the shippers on board the vessel at a particular place, free of all charges.

Fr: *Franco Bord;* Ger: *Frei an Bord.*

Gibb, A. D., *Sale of Goods on C. I. F. and F. O. B. Terms,* London, 1924.

FREE OVERBOARD. A term by which the buyer is to supply craft to take delivery of goods from the vessel. The seller's responsibility ceases as soon as the goods leave the vessel's slings.

Fr: *Sous Palan;* Ger: *Frei über Bord.*

FREE PILOTAGE. The converse of compulsory pilotage. Pilotage is said to be free and compulsory when free for certain classes of vessels and compulsory for others.

Fr: *Pilotage Libre.*

FREE PORT. A term applied to ports, or zones within ports, in which vessels can load or unload and where commercial or even manufacturing businesses may be carried on without payment of import or export duties.

It is only when goods pass from the free area into the hinterland for consumption that import duty is payable. The object of free ports is to facilitate traffic by reshipment to other countries The bonded warehouse system effects the same ends as free ports, but is not so simple and speedy. There are no free ports in England, United States or France. In Europe, until 1939, Copenhagen, Danzig and Hamburg were free ports, also Hong Kong, Singapore, and Penang in the Far East.

Fr: *Port Franc;* Ger: *Freihafen.*

FREE REACHING. Sailing with the wind on the quarter.

Fr: *Courir grand largue;* Ger: *Mit Backstagwind Segeln.*

FREE SHIP. A ship of a nation which is neutral during a war.

FREE STEM (G. B.). A chartering term denoting that a vessel can secure a loading berth immediately on arrival in port instead of being placed on a stemming list for loading in rotation.

FREE SURFACE. Any body of liquid in a ship which has an unconfined upper surface, free to remain parallel to the horizontal as the ship rolls and pitches, is said to have a free surface. Free surface always has a deleterious effect on transverse stability, which varies as the cube of the breadth of the free surface, parallel to the ship's beam. Also called loose water.

FREE TANK. A tankerman's term to denote a partially filled tank.

FREE TIME. Chartering term which denotes the duration of time between the moment that the notice of readiness has been handed to the charterers and the beginning of lay days.

FREE WIND. A wind blowing at such an angle with the keel of a vessel that it is practically a quartering wind or one which blows over the quarter of the ship.

Fr: *Vent Largue;* Ger: *Achterlicher Wind; Raumer Wind.*

FREEZER (U. S.). One who is in charge of the care and operation of refrigerating equipment on board ship.

FREE ZONE. A maritime zone, limited in extent, which differs from adjacent territory in being exempt from the customs regulations affecting goods destined for re-export. It consists of an isolated, inclosed, and policed area in or adjacent to a port of entry, furnished with the necessary facilities for loading, unloading, supplying fuel and ship's stores and for storage and reshipment of goods.

Fr: *Zône Franche;* Ger: *Freigebiet.*

See **Free Port.**

As regards customs duties there is, in this reserved area, freedom and immunity. Goods may be landed, stored, mixed, blended, repacked, manufactured and reshipped without the payment of duty and without intervention by customs officials.

FREIGHT. The price paid to a shipowner for the transportation of goods or merchandise by sea from one specific port to another. The word freight is also used to denote goods which are in the process of being transported from one place to another. The term freight is strictly applicable to the carriage of goods only, and not to the carriage of passengers, although in modern times it has been used in an extended sense so as to be applied to all rewards or compensation paid for the use of a ship.

Fr: *Fret;* Ger: *Fracht; Frachtgeld.*

See **Advance Freight, Back Freight, Cargo, Chartered Freight, Dead Freight, Distance Freight, Full Freight, Gross Freight, Guaranteed Freight, Lump Freight, Over Freight, Time Freight.**

Ordinary freight is usually quoted W/M, which means that the shipowner reserves the right to charge per ton *weight* or per ton *measurement* according to which may be more advantageous to him. Practically all shipping companies classify goods under four divisions with a "special" class in addition, Class 1 being a high or low rate according to the nature or composition of the goods. The unit of freight may be defined as the weight or measurement on which the freight rate is calculated for a particular commodity.

The use of specific units other than weight/measurement, for quoting freight rates, is mainly confined to those trades in which standardized bags, cases, bales, or other commercial units have been widely adopted by shippers. Grain rates are usually quoted per bushel or per quarter; flour per bag or barrel; coffee per bag; case oil per case; lumber per measurement feet; live animals per head; rates on gold bullion or coin are mostly quoted in terms of a percentage of the commodity's value.

Giese, K., *Das Seefrachttarifwesen,* Berlin, 1919; Merchant, E. O., "Rate Making in Domestic Water Transportation," American Academy of Political and Social Science (Philadelphia), *Annals,* vol. 55 (1914); Sanderson, A. E., *Ocean Freight Rates in United*

States Foreign Trade, U. S. Bureau of Foreign and Domestic Commerce Trade Information Bulletin 434, Washington, 1926; Sanderson, A. E., *Control of Ocean Freight Rates in Foreign Trade*, U. S. Bureau of Foreign and Domestic Commerce Trade Promotion Series 185, Washington, 1938; Zuellig, S., *Die Seefrachten 1920-1938*, Zurich, 1942.

FREIGHTAGE. The total capacity of a ship available for the carriage of cargo. When expressed as a weight it is the cubic capacity divided by the density of the cargo, that is, the number of cubic feet it occupies to the ton.

FREIGHT BROKER. One who brings together a shipper and a carrier to negotiate the terms and conditions of freight contracts. He is paid by the carrier on the basis of freight collected or paid.

Fr: *Courtier d'Affrètement;* Ger: *Schiffsmieter.*

FREIGHT CLAUSE.
See **Hire and Payment Clause.**

FREIGHT CLERK.
See **Shipping Clerk.**

FREIGHT COLLISION CLAUSE (G. B.). A marine insurance clause which provides for recovery in respect of sums paid, by way of collision damages, solely in respect of freight.

FREIGHT DEPARTMENT. The department in a shipping organization where freight rates are made, bills of lading and freight contracts, whipping permits, delivery orders and shipping instructions issued and, in general, all the traffic functions of a shipping line are performed.

Fr: *Departement du fret;* Ger: *Frachtabteilung.*

FREIGHTER. 1. A freight- or cargo-carrying vessel. Also called a cargo boat.

Fr: *Cargo; Navire de charge;* Ger: *Frachtschiff.*

2. The person for whom the owner of a ship agrees to carry goods or to whom is given the use of the whole or part of the cargo space of the ship for the transportation of goods or passengers on a specified voyage or for a specified time for which a specified price called freight is paid to the owner for the carriage of the goods or the use of the ship.

Fr: *Affréteur; Chargeur;* Ger: *Befrachter; Ablader.*

See **Shipper, Charterer.**

FREIGHT FORWARD. A term which denotes that under the transportation agreement freight is payable by the consignee at port of destination. The opposite of "freight prepaid."

FREIGHT FORWARDER. A person or firm who acts on behalf of a shipper or exporter and attends to all the necessary details of shipping, insuring and documenting of goods. He takes delivery at the port or point of shipment. His services include: customs export clearance, booking of freight space, preparation of bills of lading, making out dock receipts, taking care of cartage or lighterage, making up consular invoices and all certificates which shipment may require.

Fr: *Expéditeur;* Ger: *Spediteur.*

FREIGHT IN FULL. A chartering expression denoting that port charges, pilotages, consulages, light dues, trimming and lighterage at discharging port are paid by shipowners.

FREIGHTING VOYAGE. A voyage made solely for the transportation of goods on freight as distinguished from a trading voyage during which buying and selling of goods is carried out on account of owners or shippers.

FREIGHT INSURANCE. Insurance taken on the compensating for the use of a ship or the carriage of merchandise. It is taken on the usual and reasonable freight as could be obtained at the port of departure for the voyage. Passage money unless specified is not usually covered by freight insurance. The insurable value is the gross amount of the freight at the risk of the assured, plus the charges of insurance.

Fr: *Assurance fret;* Ger: *Frachtgeld Versicherung.*

FREIGHT NOTE (G. B.). Statement drawn up by a broker or a shipping firm showing the amount of freight due, with weights and measurements of cargo. Also called freight account, freight bill.

Fr: *Décompte de Fret;* Ger: *Frachtrechnung; Frachtanweisung.*

FREIGHT PENDING. The amount which the charterer of a ship has agreed to pay to the owners for the prolonged use of the vessel after the time limited by the charter. It extends to passage money and to freight prepaid at the port of departure.

FREIGHT RATE. The charge made for the transportation of freight.

Fr: *Taux de Fret; Cours du Fret;* Ger: *Frachtraten; Frachtsatz.*

FREIGHT RELEASE. 1. An authorization issued by a shipping company to the superintendent of a dock, or by the chief officer of a vessel to a specified person or persons, when the delivery of the cargo is made in other than bill of lading quantities. Also called release.

Fr: *Bon de Livraison;* Ger: *Freistellungsschein.*

2. A document issued by the carriers representative at the port of destination and handed to the consignee of goods after the freight account has been settled. It gives authority to the captain of the vessel carrying the goods or to other authorized persons to deliver the goods to the holder of the freight release. This procedure is used when goods are shipped under "freight forward" conditions.

Fr: *Laisser Suivre;* Ger: *Auslieferungsschein.*

FREIGHT SHIP. In British Admiralty regulations this term refers to any merchant ship in which accommodation or space is engaged by the government for the conveyance of personnel, horses, or mules, or for the carriage of stores, the ship not being exclusively at the disposal of the government as would be true of a transport.

FREIGHT TON. A unit of volume or weight used for quoting freight rates, in which 40 cu. ft. or 2,240 lbs. are taken as the equivalent of one ton. Also called stevedore ton. The measurement or weight is generally at ship's option. For freight purposes the term ton may also be applied to a number of hundredweights to be the equivalent of 1 ton and varying according to the goods.

Fr: *Tonneau d'Affrètement; Tonneau de Mer;* Ger: *Masstonne; Frachttonne.*

FREIGHT TONNAGE. Measure of the total cubic capacity of a vessel which is available for the carriage of cargo and usually expressed in tons of 40 cu. ft. measurement.

Fr: *Capacité Utile;* Ger: *Nutztragfähigkeit.*

See **Cubic Capacity.**

FRENCH BOWLINE. A nonslipping hitch forming a double loop. Generally used when sending a man over the side or on any job in a dangerous location, where he will need the use of both hands. One of the loops is used as a seat and the other fits under his armpits with the knot at his breast. Also called double bowline, bowline on the bight.

Fr: *Noeud de Chaise Double;* Ger: *Doppelter Pfahlstich.*

FRENCH FAKE. A peculiar mode of coiling a rope by running it backward and forward in parallel bends so that it may run readily and freely. It is often adopted for rocket lines or in other similar instances where great expedition in uncoiling is necessary. The long fake is similar to the French fake except for the fact that the turns lead from the end instead of the side as in the French fake.

Fr: *Glène Filante;* Ger: *Französische Bucht.*

FRENCH REEF. A method of reefing square sails in which a jack rope and toggles fastened to the jackstay are used instead of reef points. In the days of whole topsails the usual practice was to have the first and second reef bands with jack ropes and the third and fourth reef bands with reef points.

Fr: *Ris à Filière.*

FRENCH SENNIT. A variety of flat sennit in which an odd number of nettles are regularly and evenly woven one under and then over the others in succession. It is more open than the flat sennit, but similarly made.

FRENCH SHROUD KNOT. A shroud knot in which the three strands of one end are walled over those of the opposite end.

Fr: *Noeud de Hauban Simple;* Ger: *Französischer Knoten.*

FREON. Trade name for dichlorodifluoromethane, an odorless, non-toxic and very stable refrigerant based on the structure of carbon tetrachloride. It has become the standard refrigerant in merchant-ship installations and is used in systems employing reciprocating compressors.

FRESH BREEZE. A wind with a velocity of 17 to 21 nautical miles per hour and an average pressure of 1.31 lb. per square foot. Beaufort's scale No. 5.

Fr: *Bonne Brise;* Ger: *Frische Brise.*

FRESH WATER MARK. Loadline mark indicating on ship's side minimum permissible freeboard when the ship is floating in fresh water having a density of 1000 ounces or 62½ pounds per cubic foot.

Fr: *Marque de franc-bord en eau douce;* Ger: *Susswassermarke.*

FRESH WATER PUMP. A pump arranged to draw water from the ship's fresh-water tanks. In modern installations it maintains automatically the pressure on the fresh-water system. It is controlled by a pressure governor and discharges to the system through a reserve pressure tank.

Fr: *Pompe à Eau Douce;* Ger: *Frischwasserpumpe.*

FRESHEN. To shift the position of a rope or chain exposed to friction. To freshen hawse means to veer a little chain in order to bring the chafe of the hawsepipe in another place.

Fr: *Rafraîchir;* Ger: *Auffieren.*

FRESHENING WIND. A wind which grows more brisk or strong.

Fr: *Vent Fraichissant;* Ger: *Auffrischender Wind.*

FRESHET. A flood or overflowing of a river by reason of heavy rains, melted snow, and so on.

Fr: *Crue;* Ger: *Oberwasser.*

FRESH GALE. A continuous wind moving with a velocity between 34 and 40 nautical miles per hour. Force 8: Beaufort's scale.

Fr: *Petit Coup de Vent;* Ger: *Stürmischer Wind.*

FRESHWATER STAY (U. S.). Term occasionally used on fore-and-aft schooners to denote a stay leading from the foretopmast truck to the lower masthead of the mast next abaft it.

FRICTIONAL BELT. A term used in hydrodynamics to denote a comparatively thin layer of water around the hull of a ship in motion. It moves in the same direction as the ship and with velocity diminishing to nil at the outer fringe of the belt.

FRICTIONAL COEFFICIENT. A coefficient used in model basin work denoting the resistance of unit area of surface in liquid of unit density and at unit velocity.

Fr: *Coefficient de Frottement;* Ger: *Reibungswert.*

Taylor, D. W., Method for Estimating Ship Frictional Coefficients, Society of Naval Architects and Marine Engineers (New York), *Transactions,* vol. 41 (1933).

FRICTIONAL GEARED WINCH. A cargo winch with a cone friction drum fitted loose on its shaft. A conical flange fits into a corresponding cone on the gear wheel, the latter being keyed fast to the shaft. The cones of the drum and gear wheel are forced into contact by means of a *spiral* operated by a hand lever, the resulting friction providing the driving force. A spring operates and releases the drum when the lever is thrown out. A powerful adjustable strap brake operated by a foot lever prevents the drum from being overhauled by the load when the cones are thrown out of contact. Also called cone friction winch, winding winch, elevator winch.

Fr: *Treuil à Embrayage à Friction;* Ger: *Friktionswinde.*

This type of winch is used for fast, light loads. Double-barreled friction winches are occasionally found in ships where there is lack of deck space for two winches at one hatch. The hoisting can be done on each drum simultaneously or independently; the drums being independent of each other.

FRICTIONAL WAKE. Wake due to the frictional drag of the hull through the water.

FRIENDSHIP SLOOP. Sloop-rigged centerboard boat found along the coast of Maine (U. S.), used for lobstering and general fishing. It is also known as Muscongus Bay Boat. This type was mostly built at the village of Friendship, from which its name is derived. The over-all length ranged from 24 to 40 ft. These boats are easily distinguished by their strong sheer, elliptical transom, clipper bow, and high freeboard forward. Length over-all 28 ft. 6 in. Breadth 9 ft. 5 in. Draft 5 ft. 4 in. (Typical.)

Chapelle, H. I., "The Friendship Sloop," *Yachting* (New York), vol. 53 (July, 1932).

FRONT. A term used in meteorology to denote the line of separation between cold and warm air.

Fr: *Front;* Ger: *Front.*

FRONTIER VESSEL (U. S.). Any enrolled or licensed vessel engaged in the foreign and coasting trades on the northern, northeastern, and northwestern frontiers of the United States.

FRONT LIGHT. The lower of two range lights. The light nearest to the observer when on the range.

Fr: *Feu antérieur;* Ger: *Unterfeuer.*

FRONT SHACKLE. A shackle which stands so that its edge or side is in line with the sheave opening of the block to which it is fastened.

FROUDE'S LAW OF COMPARISON. A law enunciated by the British Scientist,

William Froude, and used in Naval architecture for the computation of residuary resistance. It establishes that the residuary resistances of similar ships at corresponding speeds vary directly with their displacement.

Fr: *Loi de Froude;* Ger: *Froudesches Gesetz.*

FROZEN CARGO. A cargo which is hard frozen before shipment and kept so during the voyage. The carrying temperature for this class of cargo is generally from 10° to 18° F. Beef, mutton, pigs, veal, offal, butter, rabbits, and poultry are among the frozen cargoes generally carried.

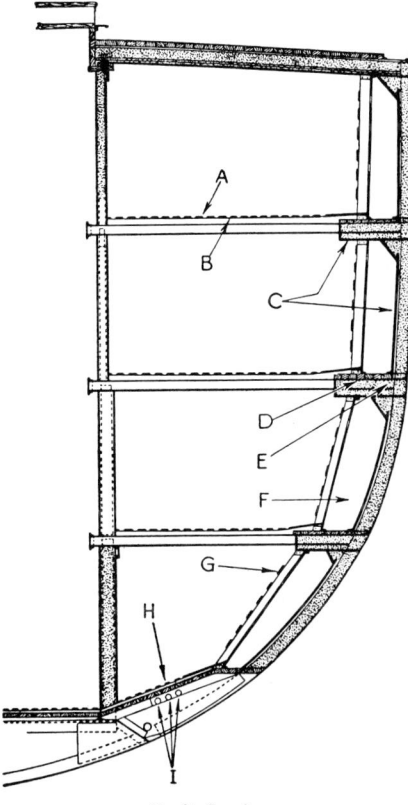

Fruit Carrier
A. Sparred Grating
B. Grounds
C. Tongued and Grooved Lining
D. Waterproof Paper
E. Granulated Cork
F. Air Trunk
G. Boarding with openings
H. Portable Ceiling
I. Bilge and Ballast systems

Fr: *Marchandises Congelées;* Ger: *Gefrierladung.*

FRUIT CARRIER. A refrigerated vessel designed for the carriage of fruit. Also called fruit ship.

Fr: *Transport de Fruits;* Ger: *Fruchttransportschiff.*

There are comparatively few vessels of the purely fruit-carrying type, owing to the fact that with cargoes of such low density as fruit it is often found difficult to load such vessels down to their load-line marks, and it is often preferable from a commercial standpoint to build ships which carry fruit in the 'tween-decks and general or other cargo in the holds.

The banana carrier, however, is an exception to this rule and there are a number of these vessels which have their entire cargo space insulated for the transport of fruit. Refrigeration is usually obtained by forced-air circulation, the air being cooled by passing over a battery of brine coils and forced by a fan through the fruit, after which it returns to the battery for recoiling. Bananas are carried in bunches stored in bins or in bulk at a carrying temperature of about 55°.

Fruit carriers are high-speed vessels, their service speed ranging between 14 and 16 knots. The largest have a gross tonnage of about 6,000. Accommodation for a limited number of passengers is usually provided. The hull is built with several 'tween-decks to avoid damage to the cargo by crushing, and to facilitate air circulation.

Kidd and West, The Problems of Apple Transport Overseas, (Great Britain) Ministry of Agriculture, Scientific and Industrial Research Department, Special Report no. 20 (London, 1924); Owen, H. P., "Ocean Carriage of Fresh Fruit," British Cold Storage and Ice Association, *Transactions,* vol. 22, no. 2 (1925-26).

FRUIT CLIPPER. Name given about 1845 to fast small schooners which traded between Great Britain and the Mediterranean in raisins, figs, currants, and so on.

FRUIT FITTINGS. Wooden bins installed in banana carriers to separate the cargo and prevent its settling. Each bin is about 10 ft. square and made up of wooden uprights with slots into which portable battens are fitted to form the sides. At the bottom there are portable gratings about 3 in. deep.

FRUSTRATION. The phrase "frustration of the adventure" as used in charter parties implies a delay due to circumstances for which neither the shipowner nor the charterer nor shipper is responsible, and not contemplated when the contract of affreightment was made. It entitles either party to treat that contract as at an end if the delay is so long as to make it unreasonable to insist on either going on with the adventure. The question of the length of the delay so as to become unreasonable is a matter of fact, all the circumstances of the case being taken into account.

Fr: *Frustration;* Ger: *Verhinderung.*

FRUSTRATION CLAUSE. A clause framed in a marine insurance policy preventing the assured from claiming a total loss in the event of his shipment being prevented from completing the voyage, owing to the outbreak of war.

Fr: *Clause d'Échec de l'Aventure;* Ger: *Verhinderungsklausel.*

FUEL COEFFICIENT. A coefficient used for comparing ship performances and stated as follows:

$$\frac{D^{\frac{2}{3}} \times V^3}{F}$$

where $D=$ displacement in tons
$V=$ speed in knots
$F=$ fuel consumption, in tons per day

Fr: *Coefficient de Consommation.*

FUEL OIL. A name given to the heaviest grades of residual fuel used in marine oil-burning boilers. Also called boiler oil. It consists of the residue of certain crude oils after the lighter fractions, such as benzine, kerosene, gas-oils, and lubricating oils, have been removed by distillation. At a temperature of about 100° F. it flows freely and is easily handled by pumps.

Fr: *Mazout;* Ger: *Heizöl; Brennöl; Masut.*

Fuel oil varies in specific gravity from about 0.880 to 0.995 at 68° F., according to the base origin. The chemical composition is about 86 per cent carbon, 12 per cent hydrogen, 1½ per cent oxygen and ½ per cent sulfur. Its flash point should not be less than 150° F. Viscosity not greater than 40 Engler at 70° F. It should not contain more than 1 per cent of water or sediment, and its sulfur content should not be over 1.5 per cent. The advantages of fuel oil as compared with coal may be summarized as follows: high evaporative power per unit weight; ease of handling; perfect control of combustion to suit different requirements of service; cleanliness; reduction in number of firemen; availability; no ashes; greater thermal efficiency.

FUEL OIL CERTIFICATE (U. S.). A certificate issued by government authorities to a new vessel permitting the use of fuel oil in her boilers.

FUEL OIL HEATER. An apparatus which uses high pressure auxiliary steam to heat fuel oil to the proper temperature for efficient combustion by the burners in the boilers. It is installed between the fuel oil service pump and the burners.

FUEL SHIP. See **Tanker.**

FUEL TANK. Oiltight compartment, designed to carry liquid fuel for the vessel's consumption.

Fr: *Soute à Combustible Liquide;* Ger: *Heizöltank.*

FUKANAWA. Japanese fishing sampan chiefly employed for capturing sharks with nets. There the two types: one from the Yamaguchi district, the other from the Oita district in the Island of Kyushu. Both are rigged with two masts. Yamaguchi boats: Length 32 ft. Breadth 8 ft. Depth 2.6 ft. Crew 4. Oita boats: Length 35 ft. Breadth 8.5 ft. Depth 3.3 ft. Draft 1.8 ft. Crew 16. Displacement 5.6 tons.

FULL. The state of the sails when the wind fills them so as to carry the vessel ahead.

Fr: *Plein;* Ger: *Voll.*

See **Clean Full.**

FULL AND BY. Said of a sailing vessel when all sails are drawing full and the course steered is as close to the wind as possible.

Fr: *Près et Plein;* Ger: *Voll und Bei.*

FULL AND CHANGE. An expression used to denote the times when the greatest tidal effect is produced. These occur at the period of full moon and at the period of change, or new moon. Also known as Establishment of the port.

FULL AND DOWN. Expression used for denoting the condition of a loaded vessel when the cargo is of such nature as to fill all available spaces in her holds and 'tween-decks and at the same time of sufficient weight to bring her down to her designed load line.

FULL CARGO. Full cargoes are those in which the registered net tonnage of the vessel is exceeded by cargo of one description, for example, rice, raw sugar, and so on.

Fr: *Chargement Complet; Plein Chargement;* Ger: *Volle Ladung.*

FULL-ENDED. A vessel is said to be full-ended when the extremities of the waterlines at load-line level are strongly convex and the ends of the curve of sectional areas are full, indicating that displacement is carried well forward and aft, toward the ends of the vessel. The opposite of hollow-ended.

FULLER. A metal calking tool used for laying up the metal in way of a beveled calking edge and around liners, in order to provide a better bearing surface for the splitter. When slightly bent near the end it is called "bent fuller" as distinguished from the "straight fuller."

FULL FILLET WELD. A fillet weld in which the sides of the triangular weld cross section are at least equal to the full thickness of the plate edge.
  Fr: *Soudure d'Angle Renforcée;* Ger: *Volle Kehlschweissung; Volle Kehlnaht.*

FULL FREIGHT. The total freight as stipulated in the charter party or bill of lading.
  Fr: *Plein Fret;* Ger: *Volle Fracht.*

FULL HERRING. English name for herring with fully developed roe or milt which has not spawned. Also called prime herring. The trade term "large full" refers to a brand of salted fish 11½ in. long or more (600 to 650 in a barrel), the term "full" when 10¼ in. long (700 per barrel), "mat full" when not less than 9¼ in. long (900 to 1,000 per barrel).
  Fr: *Hareng gai;* Ger: *Vollhering.*

FULL-RIGGED SHIP. The term full-rigged ship as descriptive of a particular rig denotes a vessel with a bowsprit and three masts, each of which carries square sails. Also called square-rigged ship. The names of sails on each of the masts from the deck upward are as follows: The courses (foresail, mainsail, cross jack), lower topsails, upper topsails, lower topgallant sails, upper topgallant sails, royals, skysails. The mizzenmast carries a gaff sail named spanker or driver. This rig has been carried occasionally by vessels of very small tonnage as for instance the "E. Richardson," built in 1873, which registered 301 tons gross. The last steel-built trading vessels of this rig had a tonnage which varied between 1,200 and 2,900 gross.
  Fr: *Trois-mâts carré;* Ger: *Vollschiff; Vollgetakeltes Schiff.*

FULL RUDDER. The maximum angle to which the rudder may be moved.

FULL-SCANTLING VESSEL. The position of the load line on seagoing vessels depends on the strength of the hull, provided that a reasonable margin of buoyancy is left. It is, therefore, unnecessary to increase the scantlings of a vessel when this margin has been reached as freeboard cannot be reduced beyond this point. A full-scantling vessel is one in which the scantlings correspond to the above mentioned margin of buoyancy and in which full strength of the ship's structure is maintained up to the uppermost continuous deck. Classification societies require, according to the depth of the vessel, that 1, 2, or 3 full decks should be provided for, if the vessel is to be accepted as a full-scantling vessel.
  Fr: *Navire à Échantillons Pleins;* Ger: *Volldeckschiff; Volldecker.*

The expression "three-decked ship" was some years ago used for full-scantling vessel. In present practice, equivalent strengthening of beams has led to the suppression of lower decks, and cargo ships of any size are built with only one continuous deck if cargoes of great density are to be carried. This type of vessel is specially adapted for heavy deadweight trade where goods of great density are carried such as ores, coals, machinery, rails, the full-scantling vessel having a great deadweight carrying power with the minimum internal volume of capacity.

FUMIGATION. The disinfection of various compartments in a vessel by filling them with a gaseous agent such as hydrocyanic acid gas or sulfur dioxide in order to destroy rats, mice, mosquitoes, fleas, lice and all insect pests which act as germ carriers.
  Fr: *Fumigation;* Ger: *Schiffsräucherung.*

Fumigation with sulfur is performed by igniting a certain quantity of sulfur in the space to be fumigated. With this method at least 24 hr. are required; viz: 12 hr. for preparing the materials and fumigating and 12 hr. after opening up, for the gas to disperse.

Fumigation by carbon monoxide, sodium cyanide, or potassium cyanide has a much greater penetrating as well as toxic power. The exposure is, therefore, greatly reduced, 2 hr. being usually sufficient for empty holds and accommodation generally. The gas, however, is of a most deadly nature and scrupulous precautions must be taken by those in charge of operations. American

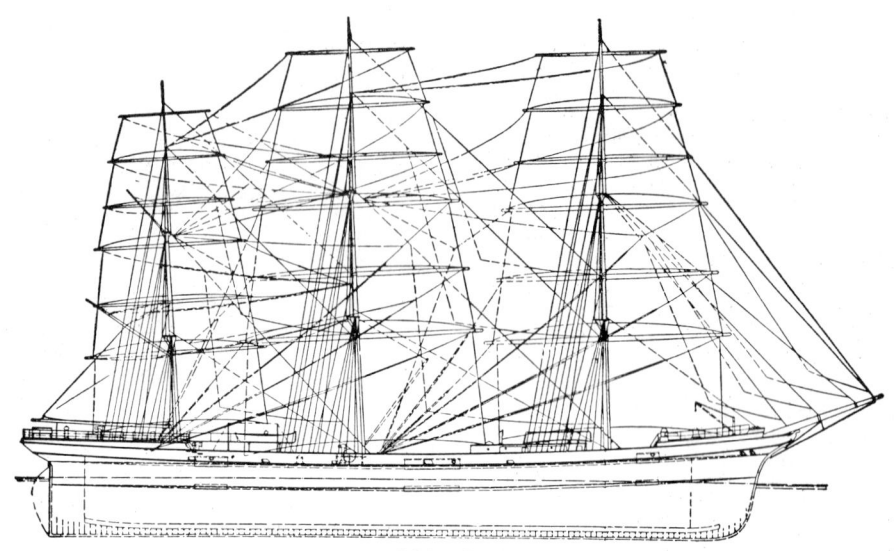

Full-Rigged Ship

regulations (1922) require that all vessels bringing passengers into the United States or trading to that country from foreign ports must be fumigated every six months. Great Britain, Health Ministry, Memorandum on the Fumigation of Ships with Hydrogen Cyanide, London, 1928; U. S. Public Health Service, *Ship Fumigation*, Public Health Reports, vol. 37, no. 44 (November, 1922); U. S. Public Health Service, *Ventilation of Ships after Fumigation with Poisonous Gases*, Washington, 1923.

FUNE. General term for Japanese flat-bottomed fishing sampan. Sometimes called *bune, buney*. The hull, built of heavy planking without frames, is of prismatic section. The deck is formed of small portable panels as usual in this type of boat. The rig consists of one or more masts; each of which carries a square sail. The sails are made of vertical cloths loosely laced together with sheets leading aft from the foot of each cloth. When not in use these boats are run stern first on to the beach and pulled up.

FUNNEL. See **Stack**.

FUNNEL MARKS. The distinctive signs, letters, and so on, painted as identification marks of vessels' ownership.

Ger: *Schornsteinabzeichen*.

Talbot Booth, E. C., House Flags and Funnels of British and Foreign Shipping Companies (London, 1936).

FUNNEL PAINT. A special paint very resistant to high temperatures, usually made of zinc oxide, white lead, litharge, and dammar varnish thinned with kerosene, and with a substantial amount of dryer added. Another mixture also used consists of white lead, silica, litharge, boiled linseed oil, and mineral spirits. This mixture is tinted to the desired shade.

Fr: *Peinture Pour Cheminée;* Ger: *Schornsteinfarbe*.

FUNNEL SHROUD

See **Smokestack Guy**

FUNNY. A light, clinker-built rowboat, long and narrow, used for racing in smooth waters, and from 20 to 30 ft. in length. It seats only one person and is equipped with outriggers for the oarlocks. It is pointed at bow and stern and open throughout. For a length of 30 ft. its breadth varies from 24 to 30 in. It is rowed with a pair of sculls.

FURL. To roll up a sail to its yard, boom, mast, or stay, and fasten it with a gasket to secure it snugly. Also called to take in.

Fr: *Serrer; Rabanter;* Ger: *Festmachen; Beschlagen; Bergen; Unterschlagen*.

FURLING IN A BODY. A particular method of furling a square sail, practiced only when in port. Also called harbor furl, harbor stow. It is performed by gathering all loose canvas in the center of the yard; thereby making the yard appear much thinner and lighter than when the sail is furled in the usual manner. Canvas covers were used to keep the sail dry and clean.

FURLING IN THE BUNT. The usual manner of furling a square sail when at sea, by which loose canvas is spread over the yard as picked up.

FURLING LINE. 1. A small line secured to the mast of a boat and used for furling a fore-and-aft sail. **2.** A small line used to bind a fore-and-aft-sail to a gaff or boom after it is furled. Short independent lengths of rope used for this purpose are called stops. When used for square sails they are known as gaskets.

Fr: *Chambrière;* Ger: *Beschlagleine.*

FURNACED PLATE. A plate heated and fashioned to the desired shape, and usually curved in its three dimensions. A furnaced plate can also be described as a plate which cannot be developed and therefore must be heated in order to mold it into shape. It is usual to begin the work on a flanging press and finish it in the furnace. Boss plates, soft nose plates, forefoot plates, Oxter plates, and some tank-top margin plates are usually furnaced.

Fr: *Tôle Chaudronnée; Tôle façonnée à chaud;* Ger: *Feuerplatte.*

FURNACE MAN. A shipyard worker who heats, handles, and bevels frame bars, and fashion plates when they come out of the bar or plate furnace. Also called frame turner.

FURNACE SLAB. See **Bending Floor.**

FURNITURE. Term used in marine insurance policies to denote collectively all the fittings or things in the nature of fixtures which, although not actually affixed to the ship, are provided by the shipowner for use on the ship, and are reasonably necessary to the navigation of the ship or to carry properly the kind of cargo ordinarily transported by such a ship. Also called outfits.

FURRING. 1. Double planking of a ship's sides; also called doubling.

Fr: *Soufflage;* Ger: *Spikerhaut.*

2. Strips of timber or metal or boards fastened to frames, brackets, beams, and the like, to bring their faces to the required level or shape for attachment of sheathing, ceiling, or flooring in living quarters.

FURROW. A fissure of the sea bottom which penetrates into a continental or insular shelf in a direction more or less perpendicular to the coast line.

Fr: *Sillon;* Ger: *Furche.*

FUSION WELDING. Generic term for various processes of welding metals in the molten state without the application of mechanical pressure or blows. The weld is produced in a fluid state with or without the addition of a weld metal having physical properties closely comparable with those of the parent metal. It includes gas blowpipe, electric arc, atomic hydrogen, and thermit welding.

Fr: *Soudure par Fusion; Soudure Autogèné;* Ger: *Schmelzschweissung.*

"Marine Code for Welding and Gas Cutting," *American Welding Society Journal,* vol. 14 (February, 1935).

FUTTOCK. In wooden shipbuilding a name given to the curved pieces of timber which compose the frame timbers. They are named according to their location: first futtock, second futtock, and so on.

Fr: *Allonge;* Ger: *Auflanger.*

See **Double Futtock, First Futtock.**

FUTTOCK BAND.
See **Futtock Hoop.**

FUTTOCK CHAINS.
See **Futtock Plate.**

FUTTOCK HOOP. The band or hoop around a lower mast, having a number of eyebolts to which the lower extremity of the topmast futtock shrouds fasten. Also called futtock band, spider band, futtock wye.

Fr: *Cercle de Trélingage;* Ger: *Putting Band; Putting Ring.*

FUTTOCK PLANK.
See **Limber Strake.**

FUTTOCK PLATE. One of the chain plates secured to the side rims of a mast top, with a deadeye in the upper part to which the topmast rigging is set up in the same way as the chain plates of the lower rigging. There is an eye in the lower end into which the futtock shrouds hooks. Also called futtock chain.

Fr: *Latte de Hune;* Ger: *Puttingsschiene.*

FUTTOCK SHROUDS. Short shrouds made of iron rods which extend from the lower futtock chain plates to the futtock band fitted around the mast below. Their function is to hold down the top rims to the lower mast and so resist the upward pull of the topmast shrouds.

Fr: *Gambes de Revers;* Ger: *Puttings-wanten.*

FUTTOCK STAFF. A length of wood or iron covered with canvas or leather seized across the topmast rigging like a sheer pole.

Fr: *Quenouillette;* Ger: *Schwichtungslatte.*

FYKE NET. An arrangement built on the same principle as a pound net but different in construction. It consists of a leader ending between the extended arms of a net which is nothing more than an ordinary set net.

Smith, H. M., *Fyke Nets and Fyke Net Fisheries,* U. S. Fish Commission, Bull., vol. 12 (1892).

G

G. A flag of the international code of signals showing a series of six yellow and blue vertical bars of equal width. Hoisted signifies: "I require a pilot."

G/A GENERAL AVERAGE.
G/A Con. GENERAL AVERAGE CONTRIBUTION.
G/A Dep. GENERAL AVERAGE DEPOSIT.
G. A. and S. GENERAL AVERAGE AND SALVAGE (marine insurance).
G.A.T. GREENWICH APPARENT TIME.
G.C.T. GREENWICH CIVIL TIME.
G.F. GOVERNMENT FORM (chartering).
G.H.A. GREENWICH HOUR ANGLE.
G.L. GERMANISCHER LLOYD.
G.M. TRANSVERSE METACENTRIC HEIGHT.
G.M.T. GREENWICH MEAN TIME.
G.S.T. GREENWICH SIDEREAL TIME.

GAB ROPE. A line clinched to the foot of a jib to assist in furling.

GADGET (U. S.). Slang term applied by seamen to anything whose name is unknown to them or also to denote makeshift contrivances on board ship. Also called gilguy (U. S.), gilhickey (U. S.), hootnany (U. S.), gimmick, gismo (U. S. Navy).

GAETA. A half-decked sailing and rowing boat from the Istrian and Dalmatian coasts employed in the sardine fisheries with seines and drift nets. The hull is keel-built with slightly curved stem, vertical sternpost and sharp stern. Stemhead and sternpost rise about 1.6 ft. above the gunwale. Length 16 to 26 ft. Breadth 6.5 to 8 ft. Depth 4.9 to 6.5 ft. Carrying capacity 2 to 6 tons. Crew 3 to 5. (Average.)

The deck extends for about one-eighth of the boat's length from the stem. The frames are of oak; the carvel planking of pine. There is a small hatchway on the foredeck. The rig consists of one vertical mast stepped at about ⅓ length from the stem, and a settee or balanced lugsail. One headsail.

GAFF. A spar for extending the head of a fore-and-aft quadrilateral sail, as the mainsail of a sloop or the spanker of a ship.
Fr: *Corne;* Ger: *Gaffel.*
See **Monkey Gaff, Railway Gaff, Running Gaff, Spanker Gaff, Standing Gaff, Wishbone Gaff.**

GAFF-FORESAIL. The gaff sail which sets abaft the lower foremast of a schooner.
Fr: *Misaine-Goëlette;* Ger: *Schonersegel.*

GAFF SAIL. A four-sided fore-and-aft sail extended by two spars, a gaff and a boom, which has its forward side or luff pivoting about a mast to which it is attached by hoops or slides. Gaff sails are laced, loose-footed, or boomless. In the first instance, the foot is either laced or stop-

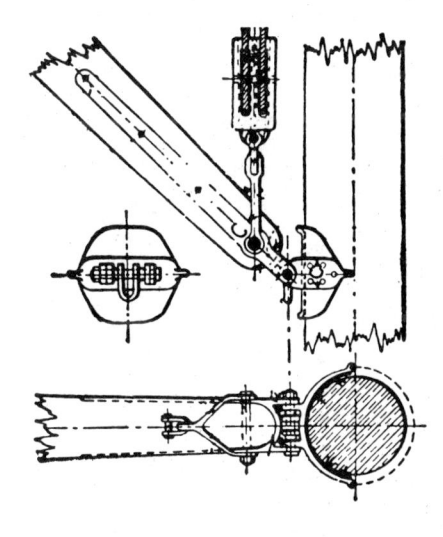

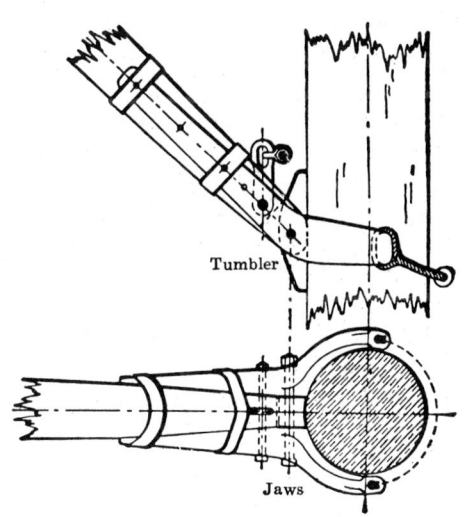

Gaff

319

pered to a wooden jackstay on top of boom from tack to clew, or extended by a boom-track with slides. In loose-footed gaff sails,

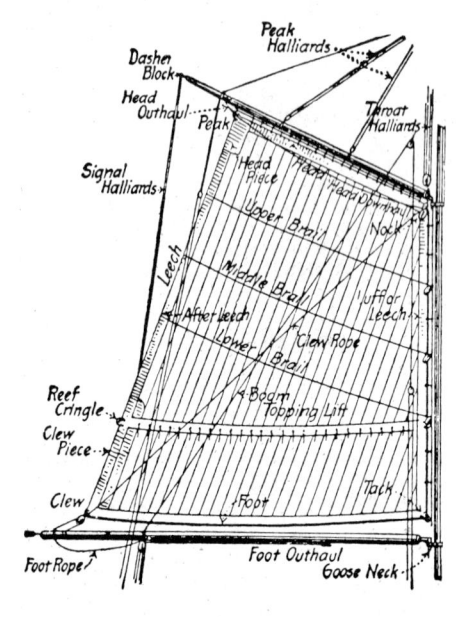

Gaff Sail

only the tack and clew are secured to the boom. The bunt of the foot is left free to take up a curve under the pressure of wind. These sails are cut with a round in the foot amounting to 2 or 3 per cent of length, and are considered more efficient for cruising than the other types, but the boom must be heavier and the sail made of stouter material. Boomless gaff sails are not suited for yacht or deep-sea work; however, they are used on small coasters, and fishing boats on account of the ease with which they may be partially brailed up. Vangs are required on the gaff.

Fr: *Voile à Corne;* Ger: *Gaffelsegel.*

On merchant vessels the cloths of a gaff sail run parallel to the leech. On racing yachts they are generally of the cross-cut type with narrow cloths, perpendicular to the leech, and instead of reef points the sail is pierced with one or more lines of holes fitted with brass eyelets through which a lacing is passed when reefing. Several methods are used for extending the head of the sail. With a hoisting gaff it is fastened to the spar either by a continuous lacing with half hitch at each turn round the gaff or by separate stops. With a stand-ing gaff a track with slides is fitted on the under side of the spar and the sail is taken in with brails. The luff of a gaff sail is usually from two-thirds to four-fifths the length of the foot, the length of the head between three-fifths and two-thirds that of the foot. The amount of peak for the gaff depends upon the proportions of hoist and foot. An angle of 35 degrees with the topmast is considered an average. Generally speaking a low sail with long boom should have a high peak while a tall sail with short boom should be cut with a flat head.

GAFF SLIDE. Metal slide which runs on the track of a standing gaff to extend or take in the head of a gaff sail.

Fr: *Griffe de corne;* Ger: *Gaffel Gleiter.*

GAFF TOPGALLANT SAIL. A fore-and-aft sail which was set on the jigger mast of four-masted barks; above the monkey or upper gaff of a split jigger.

GAFF-TOPSAIL. A fore-and-aft sail set above a gaff with sheet led to the gaff end. Also called fore-and-aft topsail, standing gaff-topsail.

Fr: *Flèche;* Ger: *Toppsegel; Dreikant-toppsegel.*

The sail is hoisted by means of a halyard passing through a sheave or block attached near the topmast head. The foot stretches along the gaff. The angle between the mast and the leech should be from 45 to 50 degrees. The luff should be kept straight and close to the mast. A single or double leader is used for this purpose, or a track similar to that used for a Bermuda mainsail.

GAFF-TOPSAIL HALYARDS. One of the halyards rove through a sheave on the mast and bent to the yard or head cringle of a gaff-topsail.

Fr: *Drisse de Flèche;* Ger: *Gaffeltopp-segelfall.*

GAFF-TOPSAIL YARD. A small yard to which the head of a gaff-topsail is bent.

Fr: *Vergue de Flèche;* Ger: *Gaffeltop-segelraa.*

GAFF TRYSAIL. A quadrilateral-shaped boomless storm sail, the head of which is laced to a small gaff. The latter should be about half the length of the spar carried in ordinary weather. There is one reef. Gaff trysails set better and have more driving power than the thimble-headed sails of same area.

Fr: *Goëlette de Cape; Artimon;* Ger: *Gaffel Treisegel.*

GAGALI. A small, brig-rigged, Turkish coasting vessel from the Black Sea with inboard curving stem, V-shaped transom stern and outboard rudder. The construction of the transom, planked vertically and with sternpost outside the planking, is one of the distinguishing features of this type of vessel. The flush deck runs fore-and-aft with one main hatch amidships and two scuttle hatches, one at each end. Washcloths held by wooden stanchions are provided amidships to protect the deck load from spray. Length 40 to 78 ft. Depth 6.5 to 10.6 ft. Breadth 12.7 to 20 ft. Draft 5.9 to 9.5 ft.

GAINING RATE. The daily change of error when a chronometer is running too fast.

Fr: *Avance Diurne;* Ger: *Täglicher Gewinn.*

GAL. West African dugout canoe employed by the Uolof people in the fisheries of the coast of Senegal, with long pointed ends, round bottom, and keel line curving up toward bow and stern. A decking covers the ends. The central space is surrounded by a wash strake connected at the fore- and afterend by a transverse board or breakwater. These planks are attached by seizings to the underbody. Length 10 to 30 ft. Breadth 2 to 4 ft. Also called *lotkio.*

The timber from which the boats are hewn is obtained from the forests near Rufisque. Sail, oar, and paddle are used for propulsion. At Dakar and adjoining region the paddles are spoon-shaped. At St. Louis (Guet n. Dar.) short oars are used and rowers stand up facing the bow. The rig consists of a bamboo mast stepped nearly amidships, which sets a large spritsail with boom.

GALAWA. A dugout canoe with double outriggers from Zanzibar with a wash strake pegged on the sides. These canoes are mostly built in the Comoro Islands and brought to the mainland by dhows. They are rigged with a mast and settee sail. When under sail a rudder is used for steering. Length 17 ft. Breadth 2 ft. 6 in. (Average.) Also *ngalawa.*

GALAY.
See **Panco.**

GALE. A wind between a strong breeze and a storm. A continuous wind blowing in degrees of a moderate, fresh, strong, or whole gale and varying in velocity from 28 to 55 nautical miles an hour.

See **Chocolate Gale, Fresh Gale, Moderate Gale, Strong Gale, Whole Gale.**

GALEAO. An inshore boat used on the coasts of Portugal for drift-net fishing and rigged with a short mast raking forward, setting a lateen sail with very short luff. It is decked fore and aft. The stem is straight with raised stem head. Length 52 to 66 ft. Breadth 10 to 13.2 ft. Depth inside 3 to 5 ft.

GALEASS, GALEAS. A small sailing coaster from the German coasts of the Baltic, similar in hull form to the *jagt* but larger. It is used in Norway as fish carrier and in the seal fishery in polar waters. The hull is built with straight stem and transom stern. Length 50 to 70 ft. Breadth 15 to 24 ft. Depth 5 to 11½ ft. Tonnage from 40 to 200. (Average.)

The fore-and-aft rig comprises a mainmast and short mizzen, the latter being little more than a jigger and answering the same purpose. There are three headsails. A square yard with flying foresail is rigged under the mast hounds inside of the forestay.

GALEASSEWER. German sailing coaster with *ewer* hullform and Galeass rig.

GALELA CANOE. A planked canoe of the double-outrigger variety found in the Moluccas and used for trading and fishing throughout the islands. A fairly roomy cabin is provided. Length 24 ft. Beam 5 ft. Depth 25 in. The keel is 3½ in. deep, running the whole length.

The planking is made up of 7 strakes on each side of the keel. Each strake has a row of perforated lugs and these are made to coincide vertically with those above and below in adjoining strakes. The frames are fitted over the vertical rows of projecting cleats and tied thereto by cord made from black palm fiber.

GALEON. A Spanish sailing boat used for small coasting and sardine fishing on the coasts of Galicia and Pontevedra. It is lugrigged with two masts. The galeon is decked aft, and has a sharp stern. When used in the sardine fisheries it carries a crew of 18 to 20 hands. Length 50 ft. Breadth 23½ ft. molded. Depth 3 ft. 4 in. (Average.)

GALEONETE. A Portuguese fishing boat of same type and rig as the *galeao* but smaller. The mast has no rake.

GALIOT. A flat-bottom, seagoing sailing barge, with good sheer used in the small coasting trade of Germany, the Scandinavian countries, and the northern waters of Holland. The type was much in favor during the second half of the nineteenth century and was considered a better sailer than the kuff. It has gradually been replaced by small, two-masted fore-and-aft schooners and more recently by motor coasters.

Fr: *Galiote;* Ger: *Galiot.*

The wooden galiot was keel-built with overhanging clipper stem, and a round stern with vertical sternpost and outboard rudder. Leeboards or a steel centerboard were generally fitted. The rig consisted of a mainmast which carried a square foresail set flying with square topsail or raffee above. The gaff mainsail had a boom and gaff-topsail. A standing bowsprit with three or four headsails completed the mainmast gear. The mizzenmast was rigged like that of an ordinary ketch with gaff mizzen and gaff-topsail. The latest were built in 1934. Length 57.4 to 72 ft. Breadth 16.4 to 20.5 ft. Hold depth: 5.7 to 7.4 ft. Gross tonnage 37 to 72. (Average.)

The modernized galiot as constructed in German yards after World War I is a shallow-draft steel-built auxiliary sailing craft with flat plate keel and leeboards, specially adapted for the transportation of bulk cargoes up rivers and canals and on short sea voyages. Grounding keels are fitted enabling the vessel to be aground safely if necessary at low tide. The overhanging stem is similar to that in wooden hulls. The stern is elliptical with counter and rudder port. The rig has been simplified to a square flying foresail and no (square) topsail on the mainmast. The mizzen is bald-headed. Length 93.1 ft. Breadth 22.1 ft. Depth molded, 7.8 ft. Draft 6.7 ft. Deadweight capacity 195 tons. Tonnage, gross, 139; net, 98. Motor 40 hp. Sail area 3,660 sq. ft. (Typical.)

GALLERIES. Balconies over the stern of ships with access from the stern windows. (Obsolete.)

See **Quarter Galleries.**

GALLEY. 1. A ship's kitchen or cookhouse. In modern deep-sea cargo vessels the galley equipment generally includes an oil- or coal-fired cooking range, 1 or 2 steam-jacketed boilers, supplementary steam oven and occasionally an electrically-heated baker's oven.

Fr: *Cuisine;* Ger: *Kochhaus; Kombuse.*

Barry, D. J., "Passenger Ship Galleys and Pantries," *Marine Engineering and Shipping Age,* vol. 38, no. 3 (March, 1933).

2. A clinker-built, open ship's boat, formerly used by war vessels. Its length ranged from 28 to 36 ft. and it was pulled by a crew of 10 to 12 men. It could be sailed or rowed. The term galley describes the form of the boat. It is larger than the gig.

See **Cockler Galley, Deal Galley, Trawl Galley.**

GALLEY PUNT. An English, clinker-built, open sailing and rowing boat formerly used to tend on windbound ships anchored in the Downs off Dover, carrying off stores, landing pilots, and so on.

There were two classes. The larger ones from 27 to 30 ft. long with a beam rather less than ¼ of the length.

The second class were between 21 and 23 ft. long and were locally known as "two-handed punts," because two men could work them. They had one thwart less than the first class and larger stern sheets.

All galley punts were rigged with one mast stepped at half length, on which was set a square-headed dipping lugsail. Now extinct.

GALLEY RANGE. A coal, oil, or electric stove installed in the galley to cook food.

GALLEY STROKE. A style of rowing in which the men rise to their feet as they advance the oar and fall back as they finish the stroke. It was formerly used in galleys.

GALLOWS. 1. Two or more transverse frames rising above deck amidships to support spare spars, boats, and oars.

Fr: *Support;* Ger: *Galgenstreber.*

2. Strong framework (also called boom gallows, derrick gallows) consisting of a transverse beam known as gallow-top, supported by two uprights called gallow stanchions or gallow bitts, on which are rested cargo derricks or sail boom when not in use.

Fr: *Support de Bôme;* Ger: *Baumgalgen.*

See **Skid Beams.**

GALOFARO. A whirlpool in the Strait of Messina, at one time called "charybdis."

GALU. Single-outrigger Melanesian dug-out canoe of the Uvea people from Wallis Island (Loyalty Islands).

GALVANIC ACTION. The corrosive action on metals, produced by a galvanic current. Owing to its dissolved salts, sea water promotes a galvanic current between dissimilar metals.

Fr: *Effet Galvanique;* Ger: *Galvanische Wirkung.*

GALVANIZING. Application of a zinc coating to the outer surface of iron or steel structural members, fastenings, fittings, and the like, to provide resistance to corrosion. The zinc coating can be applied by hot dip process galvanizing, electrogalvanizing, or sherardizing.

Fr: *Zingage; Galvanisation;* Ger: *Verzinkung.*

Humann, P., "Das Metallspritzverfahren im Schiffbau," *Werft, Reederei, Hafen,* vol. 16, no. 3 (1935); Thayer, H. H., "Zinc Coatings for Shipbuilding Purposes," *Marine Engineering* (New York), vol. 28 (1923).

GALVETA. A small trading vessel from the west coast of India rigged with two masts and settee sails. No headsails. The hull is built with long raking stem and round stern with galleries as in ancient vessels. Length over-all 77 ft. Length of keel 44 ft. Breadth 20 ft. Depth 13 ft. Tonnage 11 to 110. (Typical.)

GALWAY HOOKER. An Irish baldhead cutter-rigged craft with two headsails, found in Galway and on the Connemara coast, and used in small coasting and inter-island trades. The length varies from 30 to 40 ft. with a deadweight capacity of 7 to 25 tons. These boats are decked at ends and have a raked transom stern and pronounced tumble home of sides amidships. The stem is longer and narrower than usual for such a boat. The planking is carvel-built. The mast is not stepped through the deck, but held by an iron strap to the main beam.

GAMMING. A whaleman's term for the visits paid by crews to one another at sea. (Obsolete.)

GAMMONING. The lashings of rope or chain which secure the bowsprit to the stem piece and are passed backward and forward in the form of an X over the bowsprit. In later days the rope or chain has been replaced by an iron band set up with nuts and screws. Also called gammon iron.

Fr: *Liure de Beaupré;* Ger: *Bugsprietsurring; Bugsprietwuhling.*

GAMMONING FASHION. A term applied to a lashing in which the turns cross after the manner of the gammoning. (Obsolete.)

GAMMONING FISH. A batten of wood on the top of the bowsprit over which the turns of chain or rope forming the gammoning are passed.

Fr: *Taquet de Liure;* Ger: *Wuhlings Verschalung.*

GAMMONING HOLE. A hole in the knee of the head through which the gammoning is rove. Also called **gammoning scuttle.**

Fr: *Trou de liure;* Ger: *Wuhlingsgat.*

GAMMONING SCUTTLE.
See **Gammoning Hole.**

GAMMON IRON.
See **Gammoning.**

GAMMON KNEE. A knee timber bolted to the stem just below the bowsprit. Also called gammoning piece.

Fr: *Courbe d'Éperon;* Ger: *Gallionsknie.*

GAMMON PLATE. An iron plate bolted to the stem for securing the gammon shackles.

Fr: *Tôle de Liure;* Ger: *Bugspriet; Surringplatte.*

GANGBOARD. The center part or plank of the decked ends in an open boat. It is made of the same material and scantlings as the thwarts.

Ger: *Laufplanke.*
See **Gangway.**

GANG CASK. A small cask which is between a breaker and a barrel in size.

GANGER. A steel-wire pendant fitted with an eye in each end and a shackle at one end. It is used when laying out a heavy anchor with an open boat and permits the operations of unshackling the cable and shackling on the hawser to be performed after the anchor is submerged under the boat. This term is also applied to one or more lengths of small chain fastened temporarily to a sheet anchor or spare anchor and brought into the hawse hole or just outside when bending or unbending the anchor to its cable.

Ger: *Vorlauf.*

GANG HOUR (U. S.). A unit of labor time used by longshoremen.

GANGING.
See **Snood.**

GANGPLANK.
See **Brow.**

GANGWAY. 1. A narrow, portable platform used as a passage by persons entering or leaving a vessel moored alongside a quay or pier. It has a minimum width of 22 in. and is fenced on each side to a height of about 2 ft. 9 in. by means of a railing or taut ropes or chains. Also called gangboard, gangplank.

Fr: *Passerelle de Débarquement;* Ger: *Laufplanke; Landgang; Gangplanke.*

2. A command requiring all hearers to make way, or stand aside, to permit the passage of a senior, or of a working party.

3. A passage into or out of a ship in the shape of movable portions of bulwarks or railing on the weather deck; also doors in the side plating. Also called port gangway.

Fr: *Coupée;* Ger: *Fallreep.*
See **Accommodation Ladder.**

GANGWAY PORT. An opening in the

ship's side or a hinged portion of the bulwarks for the purpose of providing access for people or to facilitate the handling of cargo. Also called entrance port or gangway door.

> Fr: *Coupée; Sabord de Coupée; Porte de Coupée;* Ger: *Fallreepspforte; Eingangspforte.*

They are usually made of plating with cast steel framing and a beading all around which bears on rubber strips. Screwed clamping devices are used around the outer edge of the door frame with strongbacks to support the body of the door.

GANJA.
See **Ghanja.**

GANTLINE. A whip purchase consisting of a rope passing through a single block on the head of a mast, top of a smokepipe, and so on, to hoist up rigging, staging, flags, sending aloft gear or men having to do some work aloft. Usually made of 2-in. Manila rope from 10 fathoms upward in length. Also called girtline, girt-line.

> Fr: *Cartahu;* Ger: *Jolltau; Jollentau; Jolle.*

See **Dummy Gantline.**

GARAGAR. A single-outrigger paddling and sailing canoe from the Marshall Islands used within the lagoons for inshore fishing. The hull is made of a round-bottomed dugout underbody, two end pieces of equal size and shape, and a wash strake on each side.

GARBAGE CHUTE. A chute hung over the ship's side or built into the ship, through which garbage is thrown overboard. Also called slop chute.

> Fr: *Manche à Saletés; Manche à Ordures;* Ger: *Schundauslauf; Ausguss; Abfallschutte.*

GARBAGE SCOW.
See **Dump Scow.**

GARBLING. A term used by customs and dock officials which may be defined as the process of separating the inferior or damaged portions of a commodity from the sound parts to avoid payment of duty on the former. This term is often used in connection with spices or tobacco.

GARBO.
See **Double-Clewed Jib.**

GARBOARD.
See **Strake.**

GARBOARD PLANKING. Strakes of planking varying in number from 2 to 6, of increased thickness and nearest to the keel.

> Fr: *Bordés de Galbord; Galbord;* Ger: *Kielgang Beplankung.*

GARBOARD STRAKE. The first range of planks laid on a ship's bottom next to the keel. The strake of plating next to the keel. Also called sand strake.

> Fr: *Virure de Galbord;* Ger: *Kielgang; Sandstrak.*

GARDENING UP.
See **Tomahawking.**

GARLAND. A grommet or ring of rope lashed to a spar when hoisting it. A collar of rope wound around the head of a mast to keep the shrouds from chafing.

> Fr: *Grosse Erse;* Ger: *Taukragen.*

GARNET. 1. Name formerly given to ropes fastened to the clews of a course and used for hauling them up to the yard. Also called clew garnet.

> Ger: *Garnat.*

2. A purchase formerly used for taking cargo in or out in merchant ships. It was fixed to the mainstay.

GARNSICKE.
See **Sicke.**

GAROUPEIRA. Small fishing boat found on the coast of Brazil between Bahia and Rio de Janeiro and employed in the fisheries off the Abrolhos Islands. These boats are built with sharp stern and fully decked. The run is fine and the bows fairly full. They have a raked sternpost. They are rigged with two masts and a bowsprit. The mainmast carries a lateen. The mizzen is a triangular sail known as *burriquete* and its sheet is fastened to a deck horse. Some of these boats, when rigged with a lug mainsail instead of a lateen are called *perne* in the province of Bahia.

GARVEY. Open boat with flat-bottom, and scow-shaped hull used on the bays and sounds of the New Jersey and Delaware (U. S.) coasts. They are propelled by motor, sails, or oars and are used for transportation by oystermen and clam diggers. Some are punt-shaped and those fitted for sailing have a centerboard. Their length ranges from 12 to 30 ft. over-all, the beam being about one-quarter of the length. Cat or sloop rig with sprit or gaff mainsail.

GARVIE HERRING.
See **Sprat.**

GAS BUOY. A lighted buoy used for marking important channels, to afford safe entrance and exit by night. Gas buoys are provided with a reservoir of compressed illuminating gas which may last for several months according to the size of the buoy and degree of compression.

Fr: *Bouée à Gaz;* Ger: *Gasboje.*

GAS CERTIFICATE. A certificate issued by a port chemist or other certified chemist after taking samples of the air contained in the tanks of an oil carrier after the cargo has been pumped out. Also called gas-free certificate. It is endorsed with one of the following notations: (1) safe for men, (2) not safe for fire, (3) safe for men and fire, (4) not safe. In practice, a compartment is considered safe if the air in all the lower pockets of the tank tests under 0.2 per cent hydrocarbon content.

Fr: *Certificat de Dégazage;* Ger: *Entgasungsattest.*

GAS DEVOURER (G. B.). An apparatus used in oil tankers for clearing gas from a tank after the cargo has been discharged. It works in conjunction with a steam ejector bolted to the discharge end of the cargo pipe system on deck, a steam connection being made with a deck steampipe. The ejector causes a powerful flow of air through the pipeline in the tank, which vaporizes the fluid left in the tank around the suction. This system insures that the cargo pipelines are free from gas and oil, as well as the tank.

Fr: *Ejecteur de Dégazage;* Ger: *Gastrennungsapparat.*

GAS FREEING. The procedure or method employed in oil tankers by which cargo tanks are cleared of dangerous or explosive gases, after the oil has been pumped out, in order to prevent fires and injury to persons and property when these tanks are cleaned or undergo repairs. A gas-free certificate is issued after the air is tested for hydrocarbon vapor.

Fr: *Dégazage;* Ger: *Entgasung.*

GASKET. 1. Small line, canvas strap, or plaited stuff employed to secure a sail to a yard boom or gaff when furled. When used on yards they are called bunt gaskets, quarter gaskets, or yardarm gaskets, according to their location. Also called sail tier.

Fr: *Garcette; Raban;* Ger: *Beschlagseising; Seising.*

See **Bunt Gasket, Harbor Gasket, Sea Gasket.**

2. A collar or liner installed between two faying structural surfaces or pipe flanges to prevent leakage.

Fr: *Joint;* Ger: *Dichtung.*

3. A rubber strip against which the knife edge of a watertight door or scuttle cover bears. A similar strip against which a watertight hatch lands.

GAS STORAGE. In refrigerated ships a process by which the cargo is carried in gas-tight spaces where the composition of the atmosphere as well as the temperature is controlled. This system permits the transportation of chilled cargo on long voyages and makes hard freezing, with temperature control only, unnecessary.

GAS WELDING. A fusion welding process wherein the welding heat is obtained from a gas flame, the temperature of the flame being sufficient to reduce the parts to such a plastic condition that on cooling they are joined securely together. The oxyacetylene flame is the one used in the most common form of gas welding today.

Fr: *Soudure au Chalumeau;* Ger: *Gasschweissung.*

GATHERING LINE. See **Lazy Jack.**

GA-TWAAT. A Koryak skin boat of the Sea of Okhotsk constructed after the type of the Aleut and Eskimo umiak and consisting of a wooden framing covered with seal or walrus skin. As compared with the Eskimo skin boat it has several peculiarities of form and construction of the frame. In proportion to its length it is very wide, and at both ends of the frame bows are tied to the gunwale, giving both stem and stern a semicircular shape. The keel or central timber is made of a single timber bent upward in the direction of the bow after the fashion of a sledge runner. The stemhead terminates in a fork which serves as a lead for the harpoon line. This fork is sometimes made of a separate piece with a human face carved on it. There are 4 or 5 thwarts tied with thongs to the gunwales. At the bow and the stern there is a semicircular platform. The after one serves as a seat for the steersman while the forward one is the seat of the harpooner. The maximum width is nearer the stern. It is propelled by 8 to 10 oarsmen. Length 29.5 ft. Breadth 8.2 ft. (Typical.)

A rectangular sail made of dressed reindeer skins sewed together is used with fair winds. It sets on a tripod mast made of 3 long poles tied together at one end with a thong which passes through drill holes. The head of the sail is sewed to a yard which is slung from the top of the tripod by means of a stout thong. The tripod is set up in the middle of the boat by tying both ends of two of the poles to the ribs on one side of the boat, while the third pole is fastened on the other side of the boat.

GATE. A door closing the entrance of a lock or basin.
Fr: *Porte;* Ger: *Tor; Schleusentor.*
See **Tide Gate, Flood Tide Gate, Ebb Tide Gate.**

GATE (U. S.). A hinged, semicircular, metal band attached to a thwart in an open boat, to help stay a mast.
See **Mast Hasp.**

GATE VALVE. A type of valve in which the closure is effected by the linear motion of a wedge-shaped unit called the gate.

GAUGE. 1. The position of a vessel relatively to another. The vessel to windward is said to have the weather gauge. The vessel to leeward has the lee gauge.

2. A measuring device, such as a steam gauge, which indicates steam pressure; or a draft gauge, which indicates draft of water.
See **Automatic Tide Gauge, Bourdon Gauge, Depth Gauge, Staff Gauge, Tide Gauge.**

GAUSSIN ERROR. A temporary component of deviation caused by magnetism introduced by the earth's magnetic field in soft iron during a period in which the vessel lies in one direction after a sharp change of course.
Fr: *Erreur de Gaussin;* Ger: *Gaussische Fehler.*

GEARED TURBINE. A turbine installation with some form of gearing between the engine and the propeller shafting in order that each of them may run at its most economical number of revolutions. The nature of the steam turbine requires high speed for high efficiency, while the screw propeller must operate at a comparatively low speed to obtain a high propulsive efficiency. The power is transmitted from the turbine to the propeller shaft through one or more pinions on the turbine shaft meshing with a gear wheel (bull gear) on the main shafting. Double helical gearing has superseded the ordinary straight-tooth spur gearing which was originally used. The efficiency of the reduction gear is estimated at 98 per cent.
Fr: *Turbine à Engrenages;* Ger: *Turbine mit Zahnradübersetzung.*

Geared turbines have been adopted with success for almost every type of merchant craft from the cargo vessel to the fastest and largest liners, and in most steam-driven naval vessels. Two distinct types of geared turbines are now in use: the single-geared turbine, in which the speed reduction is carried in one stage, and the double-geared turbine, in which two stages are adopted. Single gears are especially suited to ships with a high propeller speed and where steam conditions are favorable to low turbine speeds. The most powerful geared turbine plants in the merchant marine are of the single geared type.

GAY-BAO. A three-masted sailing craft from the Gulf of Tong-King (Indo-China). The hull is double-ended with rounded forefoot and considerable overhang at ends. The flat keel consists of a heavy plank. The under water part of the hull is made of woven bamboo strips coated with a waterproof mixture of resin, lime and wood oil. The purpose of this system of construction is to prevent the damage on wooden planking caused by teredo worms which abound in these waters. Internally the hull is divided by several transverse bulkheads. There is a pronounced tumble home of the planked topsides and the beam ends project about one foot outboard on each side. The rig consists of two or three masts with battened lugsails for the larger craft and plain lugsails for the smaller which navigate in sheltered waters. Length 40 to 70 ft. Breadth 9 to 14 ft. Depth 5½ to 10 ft. Draft 3 to 6½ ft.

GAY-DIANG. An Annamese coasting and fishing vessel with raking stem and sharp stern. It is a combination of a junk-like hull with lateen rig. Three masts are carried, the after one being the tallest. The foremast is stepped on the stem and the middle mast is placed halfway between the other two. The shrouds, made of rattan, are fastened to curved chain plates. The drop of the mainsail exceeds the ship's length. Length 50 ft. Breadth 15 ft. Depth 7 ft. 6 in. molded.

GAY-RO. A small fishing boat used in the estuaries of Indo-China. It is fitted at the bows with shears for working large rectangular dip net. Length 6½ to 10 ft. Breadth 1.6 ft. Also called *gay-ta.*

GAY-YU. Open fishing boat from the Gulf of Tong-King (Indo-China), with flat bottom and flattened, cross-planked, rising bow and stern. There are no frames. The hull is formed of broad strakes of planking pegged and fastened together with coir lashings.

Seam battens are fitted inside. There is a thatched-roof cabin amidships. A deep centerline rudder is used for steering and acts as centerboard when the boat is being sailed. A balance pole weighed with stones is rigged on the weather side, taking the place of an outrigger. The rig consists of two masts with boomed lugsails. A third sail is set in light winds when fishing. The foremast, stepped in the bows, is much smaller than the mainmast. These boats are generally working with a drag net in the Bay of Tourane. The warps are fastened to two booms, rigged out one at each end of the boat, which drifts with the wind broadside on. Length 47 ft. Breadth 7.9 ft. Depth 3.9 ft. (Typical.)

GBANKE. A one-man fishing dugout canoe from the Susu people of French Guinea (West Africa).

GEAR. The ropes, blocks, tackles, and the like, of any particular spar, sail, and so on, spoken of collectively. It is also a term of very general application which signifies arrangements of machinery for working pumps, rudder, anchors, cargo, and so on.

Fr: *Appareil; Garniture;* Ger: *Geschirr; Vorrichtung; Gerät.*

See **Boat-Propeller Gear, Chain Barrel Steering Gear, Direct Connected Steering Gear, Disengaging Gear, Electric Steering Gear, Emergency Steering Gear, Indirect Connected Steering Gear, Married Gear, Pneumatic Steering Gear, Roller Gear, Skylight Gear, Steering Gear.**

GEARED CAPSTAN. A hand capstan in which an increase of power is obtained by means of a system of planet gearing fitted inside the head which is independent of the barrel. By reversing the rotation of the head the power is increased threefold. Also called power capstan, double purchase capstan, double-acting capstan.

Fr: *Cabestan à double Effet;* Ger: *Zahnrad Gangspill; Gangspill mit Radübersetzung.*

GEARED DIESEL ENGINES. A type of propelling machinery in which two or four medium-speed Diesel motors drive the main shafting through single reduction gearing and electric slip, or hydraulic couplings.

The advantages claimed for this system as compared with direct Diesel drive are smaller engine room, lighter weight, lower cost of running and upkeep, economy of fuel, lower center of gravity of machinery. The first ships of this type built just after World War I, were equipped with surplus submarine motors.

Fr: *Moteur à transmission par engrenages;* Ger: *Verbrennungsmotor mit Zahnradgetriebe.*

Bruce, D., *Geared Diesel Machinery,* Institute of Marine Engineers, London, *Transactions,* vol. 56 (1944).

GEARED DOOR. A watertight door fitted with rack and pinion gearing through which it can be operated from above the bulkhead deck. Also called geared bulkhead door.

Fr: *Porte à Fermeture à Distance;* Ger: *Handschliessvorrichtungstür.*

GEARED DRIVE. The system in which a high-speed prime mover such as a turbine operates the driven member, for example, a propeller through a system of reduction gears to reduce the speed at which the driven member operates.

Fr: *Transmission par engrenages réducteurs;* Ger: *Zahnradgetrieb.*

See **Electric Drive.**

GEBO. A double paddling canoe of Milne Bay, British New Guinea, made by fastening together two *waona* canoes with cross poles. A platform is laid over the poles. The steering is done with an ordinary paddle.

GEE RADIO-SYSTEM. A British patent radio system similar to Loran, for determining ships' positions at sea.

GEHAZI. A Zanzibar boat of Arab design similar to the *sambuk.* The stem is slightly curved but has no overhang as in the *sambuk.* There is a deck aft. It is rigged with one vertical or slightly raked mast and an Arab lateen which tacks down to the outer end of a light bowsprit. These boats trade locally between Zanzibar, Pemba, and the mainland; also to Madagascar and occasionally Aden. Also called *jehazi.*

GENCON. Code name for the Uniform General Charter of the Baltic and International Maritime Conference.

GENERAL AVERAGE. A general contribution of money paid by all parties concerned in a marine adventure in direct proportion to their several interests when a voluntary and deliberate sacrifice has been made of one or more of the parties' goods in time of peril with a view to saving the remainder of the property.

Fr: *Avarie Commune;* Ger: *Grosse Haverei.*

GENERAL AVERAGE FACT. Any extraordinary sacrifice or expenditure voluntarily and reasonably made or incurred in time of peril for the purpose of preserving the property imperiled in the common adventure.

GENERAL AVERAGE CONTRIBUTION. A deposit made by the insured which represents the proportional share of general average losses. Also the proportionate contribution toward the cost incurred by all interests involved in general average losses. Also called general average deposit.

Fr: *Contribution d'Avarie;* Ger: *Havereibeiträge; Havereivergütung.*

It is made by the consignees of goods to the shipowners and is intended as a security for the payment of general average contribution when finally ascertained to be due from the particular shipment on which it is made. General average deposit is taken as an additional security to that of the average bond and not as a substitute for the latter.

GENERAL AVERAGE LOSS. Expenses incurred by the insured for the common safety or preservation of the subject matter insured. General average losses include: general average contributions, salvage charges, particular charges.

GENERAL CARGO. A cargo composed of miscellaneous goods carried in units or small quantities which vary in weight, size, condition, nature, and class. Commodities for which no rates of freight are specifically named but usually well above the average. Also called package freight (U. S.).

Fr: *Marchandises Diverses;* Ger: *Gemischte Ladung; Stückgutladung.*

GENERAL CARGO RATES. Rates of freight established on some routes on all articles which are not included in the commodity rates.

GENERAL INFERENCE. A description of the general pressure distribution in the atmosphere and changes of pressure in progress, together with a statement of the type of weather likely to be expected.

Fr: *Prévision du type de temps;* Ger: *Allgemeine Wetterlage.*

GENERAL SHIP (U. S.). A ship in which the owners engage separately with a number of shippers, unconnected with each other, for the transportation of their respective goods to the place of the vessel's destination. The opposite of a chartered ship.

GENOA JIB. A triangular headsail setting on the fore topmast stay by hanks and used in cruising and racing craft, when reaching. Also called reaching jib. It overlaps the mainsail for about one-third to one-half its width.

Fr: *Foc de Près; Foc de Gênes.*

It is claimed that its efficiency is due to the increase of the draft funnel on the lee side of the mainsail thereby increasing the power of that sail. Developed by the Swedish yachtsman, Sven Salén, in 1927, it was first used in a regatta at Genoa; hence its name. It has practically superseded the balloon jib.

GENTLE BREEZE. A wind with a velocity of 7 to 10 nautical mi. per hour. Mean pressure .28 lb. per square foot. Beaufort's scale No. 3.

Fr: *Petite Brise;* Ger: *Leichte Brise.*

GEOCENTRIC. Concentric with the earth as distinguished from heliocentric, which means concentric with the sun. The geocentric place of an object is its position referred to the celestial sphere, having the center of the earth for center. It supposes the observer to be at the center of the earth.

Fr: *Géocentrique;* Ger: *Geozentrisch.*

GEOCENTRIC LATITUDE. The angle subtended at the center of the earth between the plane of the equator and that radius of the earth which passes through the place. It is determined by applying to the geographic latitude a correction known as the reduction of latitude.

Fr: *Latitude Géocentrique;* Ger: *Geozentrische Breite.*

GEOGRAPHICAL LATITUDE. The angle which the perpendicular to the earth's surface at the place of observation makes with the plane of the equator. Also called **Normal latitude** or **True latitude.**

Fr: *Latitude géographique; Latitude Terrestre;* Ger: *Geographische Breite.*

GEOGRAPHICAL MILE. One minute of longitude at the equator or 6,087.1 feet.

Fr: *Mille géographique;* Ger: *Seemeile; Geographische Meile.*

GEOGRAPHICAL SIGNAL. A four letter signal from the international code, having letter "A" as the upper flag in the group.

Fr: *Signal géographique;* Ger: *Geographisches Signal.*

GEOGRAPHIC RANGE.
See **Luminous Range.**

GEO-NAVIGATION. The methods of determining a ship's position from relation to objects on the earth as opposed to celo-navigation, which depends upon observation of celestial objects. It includes piloting, navigation by dead reckoning, and use of radio bearings of known points.

GEORDIE. A name formerly given to the collier brigs trading between Newcastle, Blyth, Tynemouth, Shields, and Sunderland to London. They were ships of about 200 tons built with very full section, apple-bowed and square-sterned. Some were built without sheer. They were generally rigged with single topsails and topgallants, royals being the exception rather than the rule. After 1852 they were replaced by steam colliers.

GERMANISCHER LLOYD. German classification society established in 1867. Vessels classed for restricted trade limits have the following letters added to their general character: letter "K" indicates great coasting trade; letter "k" small coasting trade, and letter "E" that the hull has been strengthened for ice. Letter "O" indicates that the class has expired or has been withdrawn; the month and year being shown thereunder in the register book.

GHANJA. An Arab craft of the Persian Gulf with incurved raking stem and a high stern, with a short counter, under which hangs a boat, and 2 or 3 masts. It is commonly employed by Arab traders throughout the Arabian Sea and along the East African coast as far south as Zanzibar. Is derived from the Indian *kotia* of which it is the Arab counterpart. Also called *gunja*. Length over-all 70 to 100 ft. Breadth 18 to 24 ft. Depth 8½ to 11 ft. Tonnage 70 to 200. (Typical.)

These boats are fully decked and have a raised quarter-deck aft. They are very seaworthy. The usual rig consists of a large lateen sail hoisted on the raking mainmast with a smaller sail on a vertical mizzenmast. The largest *ghanjas* carry a third mast or jigger.

GHATIRA. Arabian coasting vessel from the Red Sea and Persian Gulf similar in hull form to the *sambuk* but much smaller and open except for a small raised deck aft. It is rigged with one mast and a settee sail. Length over-all 39.6 ft. Length at waterline 36.3 ft. Breadth 11.6 ft. Depth moulded 4.9 ft. Draft 4 ft. (Typical.) Also called Khatira.

GHOBUN. A single-outrigger dugout canoe from Astrolabe Bay (British New Guinea) with long horizontal, pointed, solid ends, one wash strake on each side and high decorated breakwaters. The smaller *ghobun* are rigged with a single mast stepped in the hull. The larger have two divergent masts amidships. The sails are rectangular with yard and boom.

GHOSTING. Said of a vessel under sail making headway although there appears to be no wind. Also called fanning.

GIBBER. Name given in the New England hook-and-line fisheries to the member of a dressing gang who opens the fish, takes out the gills and entrails and then throws it into a barrel of water to soak the blood off. His hands are protected by mittens.

GIBBOUS. A term which refers to the shape of the moon when between half and full. The planets Mercury, Venus and Mars present a similar appearance at times.
Fr: *Gibbeux;* Ger: *Buckelig.*

GIG. 1. A light, clinker-built ship's boat with narrow square stern, adapted either for rowing or sailing. Its length varies from 18 to 30 ft., and it is rowed single-banked with 4, 6, or 8 oars. The gig is built with lighter scantlings than the cutter and has more sheer at ends. Its length to breadth ratio is about 5 as compared with 3.7 for a cutter of same length. It was usually set aside for the master's or commanding officer's use.
Fr: *Yole;* Ger: *Gigboot.*
See **Cutter-Gig, Racing Gig, St. Ives Gig.**
2. See **Fish Jig.**

GIFT ROPE.
See **Guest Rope.**

GIG STROKE. A long sweeping stroke pulled with long oars in a single-banked boat. The stroke is followed by a 2-second pause after the blade leaves the water, then the oar is swung forward and immediately dipped.
Fr: *Nage de Parade; Nage de Baleinière;* Ger: *Gigschlag.*

GIG TACKLE. A term used by whalemen to denote one of the small fore-and-aft-tackles for securing whaleboats to the davits.

GILGUY.
See **Gadget.**

GILHICKEY. See **Gadget**.

GILL NET. A general name for fixed or drift nets in which the fish are caught by becoming entangled in the netting. The size of mesh is such as to allow the passage of the head of the fish but not the body: the fish is thus caught by the gills. Gill nets can be divided into two main classes, the set nets or fixed gill nets and the drift nets.

Fr: *Filet Maillant;* Ger: *Wandnetz.*

GILSON. Name given by fishermen to a wire tackle for hauling inboard the cod end of an otter trawl. For heavy bags a stronger purchase called fish tackle is used. Also called jilson.

GILYANGA. A single-outrigger dugout canoe from the Andaman Islands, used for the capture of turtles. The hull is crudely built without sheer, and with rounded ends. The bow is prolonged horizontally to form a shelf with an overhang of about 4 ft. to give the crew a footing when spearing fish. At the stern a corresponding but much reduced projection is also present. Length 28 ft. Breadth 3 ft. Depth 3 ft. (Typical.)

GIMBALS. A system of rings or hoops pivoted one within the other and arranged to maintain any object suspended in their center with about 3 degrees of freedom. This permits the suspended object to seek a horizontal position and remain in it regardless of the ship's motion. Various accessories on board ship, such as compasses, barometers, cabin lamps, chronometers, are suspended on gimbals.

Fr: *Cardan;* Ger: *Doppelring; Kardanring.*

GIN. See **Gin Block**.

GIN BLOCK; GIN; WHIP GIN. Iron block with single pulley sheave of large diameter fitted in a skeleton frame. Used on derrick heads and spans in conjunction with a whip for handling cargo.

Fr: *Chape;* Ger: *Laderad; Lossrad.*

GIN TACKLE. A purchase consisting of a double and a treble block, the standing part of the fall being fast to the double block. It increases the power five fold.

Fr: *Caliorne de Braguet;* Ger: *Hebezeug.*

GINGERBREAD; GINGERBREAD-WORK. Carved decorations or moldings of a ship's head, stern, and quarters. Also called garnish.

GINGER ROLLS. Term used by whalemen to denote the plaited folds or furrows of the throat and breast of the humpback, finback, and sulfur bottom whales.

Gin

GIPSY. A small, spool-shaped auxiliary drum with filleted flanges at each end fitted outside the main framing of a cargo winch, windlass or mooring winch for handling topping lifts, vangs, and for general utility work in mooring and other similar operations. Also called gipsy head, nigger head, warping end, whipping drum, winch head. Some are provided with whelps, others have a smooth machine-finished surface. The inboard end is given a larger flange than the outboard end so that the rope cannot wind itself axially along the head in the manner of a screw thread but is forced to slide axially, the larger flange giving rise to wedging action when the loaded part of rope nestles into the fillet.

Fr: *Poupée;* Ger: *Spillkopf; Trossenspillkopf; Verholspillkopf.*

GIPSY CAPSTAN. A capstan operated by steam or electricity where no provision is made for hand operating and no cable holder is fitted. Also called warping capstan.

Fr: *Cabestan de Touage;* Ger: *Verholspill.*

GIRT. The situation of a ship moored so taut by her cables as to be prevented from swinging to wind or tide. The ship thus held endeavors to swing but her side bears upon

one or the other of the cables, which catches her on her keel and interrupts her in the act of traversing.
Fr: *Embossé*; Ger: *Steif vertaut*.

GIRT BAND. A strip of canvas worked across the middle portion of a sail to provide additional strength. Also called belly band.

GIRTH. A ship's measurement taken from gunwale to gunwale around the bottom on any frame line. It was formerly used for determining the scantlings of vessels and is still used as a factor in yacht measurement rules.
Fr: *Périmètre*; Ger: *Umfang*.
See **Chain Girth, Skin Girth**.

GIRTH RULE.
See **Linear Rating**.

GIRTH STATION A factor used in yacht measurement formulas. The forward and after girth stations are located where the chain girths taken vertically from covering board to covering board are respectively one-half and three-quarters the greatest beam. The purpose of this factor is to tax overhangs.

GIRTH STICK. In ship construction a strip of wood of square cross section for "lifting" a shell plate. The spacing of rivet holes in each frame is marked on it. Its purpose is to check the spacing of the frame rivet holes as laid out from the template.

GIRTLINE.
See **Gantline**.

GIVE WAY. To leave the way clear. To make room for. (Rules of the Road).
Fr: *S'écarter*; Ger: *Weichen*.

GIVE WAY VESSEL. Any vessel which, according to articles 17-19-20 and 24 of the rules of the road at sea, must keep out of the way of an approaching vessel so as to avoid risk of collision. Also called burdened vessel.
See **Burdened Vessel**.

GLACIER BERG. An iceberg carved from the glaciers, usually much crevassed and with broken strata.

GLASSES.
See **Binoculars**.

GLATIK.
See **Blatik**.

GLAZING. A process which consists in dipping frozen fish in tanks of water that are in a room where the temperature is about 20° F. On removing the fish from the water they are at once coated with ice. Repeated dippings add to the thickness of the icy coating.

GLOACHOAG. Name given to a fishing boat of the west coast of Ireland, similar in design and rig, but slightly larger than the *pookhaun*. Used in the herring fisheries. Also called *glotoga*.

GLOBE BUOY. A buoy with topmark in the shape of a globe placed at the end of a staff. Also called staff and globe buoy.
Fr: *Bouée à Voyant Sphérique*; Ger: *Kugelbakentonne*.

GLOBE LANTERN. A ship's lantern with globular-shaped glass, visible all around the horizon, such as used for anchor lights, not-under-command lights, cable vessel's lights, pilot vessel's light.
Fr: *Verrine*; Ger: *Kugellaterne*.

GLORY HOLE. A term applied in nautical slang to a lazaret or to the steward's sleeping quarters aft in the 'tween-decks; also, to the firemen's quarters on a steamer.

GLORY HOLE STEWARD. On passenger vessels one who keeps the stewards' quarters clean and in order.

GLUT. A becket or piece of rope with a thimble, sewed or spliced in the center near the head of a square sail, into which the bunt whip or bunt jigger was hooked when hauling up the bunt for furling. Whole topsails frequently had three gluts; two abaft for furling and one forward for a midship-buntline used in taking in the last reef.
Ger: *Bauchstropp*.

GLUT HERRING. An American herring-like fish closely related to the alewife.
Fr: *Hareng d'Été*; Ger: *Ameris Hering*.

GNOMONIC CHART. A chart or map which presents a portion of the world with all great circles shown as straight lines radiating from a particular point. It is produced by projecting a spherical chart of the world on to a plane which touches the globe at one point.
Fr: *Carte Gnomonique*; Ger: *Gnomonische Karte*.

GNOMONIC PROJECTION. A system of projection used for nautical charts, based upon a system in which the plane of projection is tangent to the earth at some given point. The eye of the spectator is situated at the center of the sphere. There, being in the plane of every great circle simultaneously, the eye will see all such circles projected as straight lines where the visual rays passing through these circles

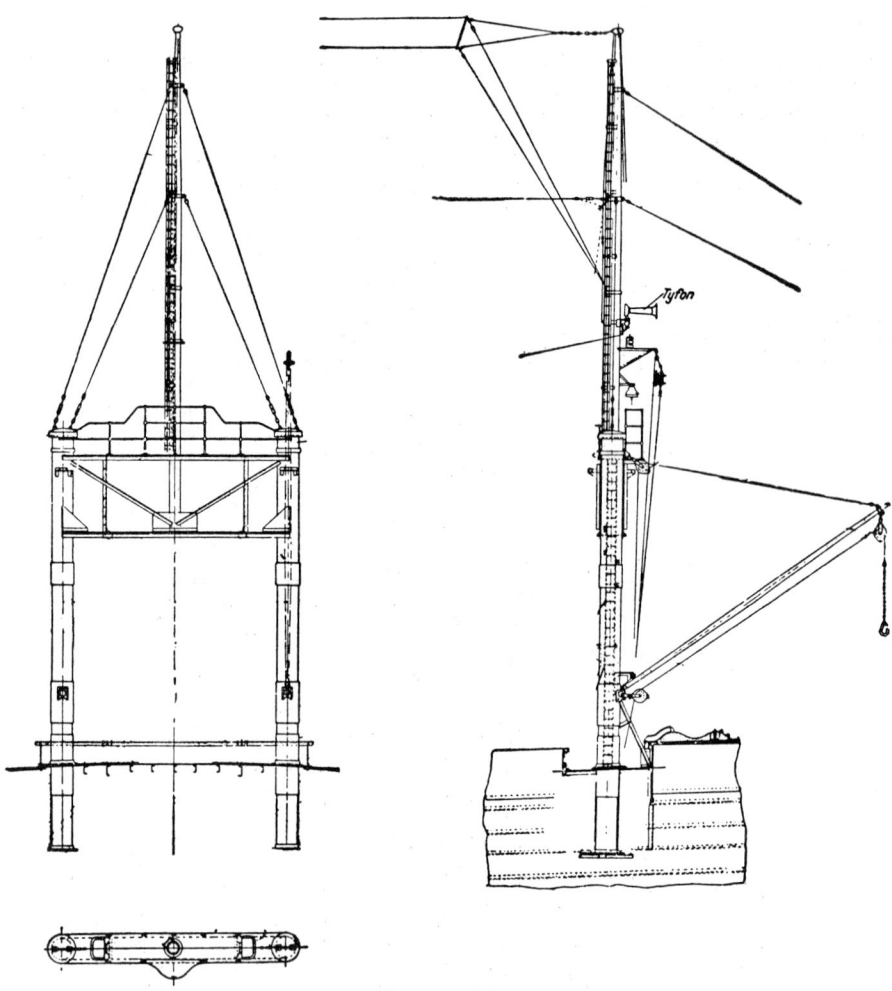

GOA—GOAL-POST MAST 332

Goal Post Mast

intersect the plane of projection.
Fr: *Projection Gnomonique;* Ger: *Gnomonische Projektion.*
See **Mercator's Projection, Polyconic Projection.**

Gnomonic projection charts are not used for navigational purposes except in the polar regions where the Mercator projection cannot be made use of. Their use is generally limited to the finding of the course and distance at any time in great-circle sailing.

GOA. Polynesian plank-built canoe of the same type as the *mon* from Alu (Shortland Islands) in the northwestern Solomon Islands. Its length ranges from 40 to 50 ft.

with a beam of 3½ to 4 ft. The smaller craft are called *goa*, the larger *muro*.

GO ABOUT. To go on or to the opposite tack.
Fr: *Virer de bord;* Ger: *Wenden; Überstag gehen.*

GOAL-POST MAST. A type of mast introduced in 1890 by British shipbuilders, which consists of two vertical steel posts placed athwartships at a certain distance from the centerline. A transverse girder connects the upper ends of the two posts and a wooden pole or topmast placed amidships on the girder is used for carrying the masthead light, or for signaling purposes. This arrangement permits the use of shorter derricks and is especially useful where cargo has to be handled from alongside. Also called pair masts.

Fr: *Mât à Portique;* Ger: *Doppelmasten.*

GO ASTERN. To move sternward.

Fr: *Culer;* Ger: *Rückwärtsgehen.*

GOB LINE. One of two ropes which fit over the dolphin striker with a cuckoo's neck, the ends setting up the bows. It is frequently replaced by a chain. Also called gob rope, martingale backrope.

Fr: *Moustache;* Ger: *Achter-Geie.*

GOB STICK. A stout oak club about 2 to 4 ft. long used by Newfoundland dorymen in the halibut fisheries to stun the large fish so that they can be gaffed and hauled into the dory with safety. It is also used in the cod fisheries to unhook the fish from the hook by running it down the throat of the fish until it fills the shank of the hook, and then with a quick push and haul clearing the hook.

GODOWN. A slang term used in Far Eastern ports to denote a warehouse or storehouse.

GOGUET. Small open boat used for inshore fishing in the Baie de Seine, Normandy. It is chiefly engaged in the capture of mussels and occasionally for fish with small lines. In some localities (Barfleur, Saint Vaast, Saint Marcouf) these boats are called *plate*, but should not be confused with the *platte*, also found at the estuary of the River Seine. The *goguet* is mostly propelled by oars and has no standing rig. Length 13½ ft. Breadth 5 ft.

GOING FREE. Sailing with the sheets eased and the wind on or abaft the beam. Also called running free or running large.

Fr: *Courir Largue;* Ger: *Raumschotts segeln.*

See **Free.**

GOLD-DUSTER. Open boat formerly used by Humber watermen for boarding ships coming into the river and taking ropes ashore when going into dock. The hull was clinker-built with plumb stem, sharp stern, very small sheer. The rig included two portable masts with spritsails. Length 18 ft. Breadth 6½ ft. (Typical.) Now extinct.

GOLO. Small West African dugout. Also called *goro*. Called kru canoe by Europeans.

Its elegant hull, most carefully fashioned and finished, is hewed from the light and buoyant wood of the cotton tree and thinned down to the thickness of about half an inch. Each end is finely tapered, ending in a slightly swollen extremity. There is a well-marked sheer forward; a slight one aft. The afterend is decked over for a distance of 2 to 2½ ft. and at its forward margin it is finished off by a low breakwater consisting of a vertical board about 4 in. high placed transversely. There are neither ribs nor thwarts. Their place is taken by a number of thin cylindrical wooden struts with bluntly pointed ends to prevent the slender sides from becoming distorted. Length overall 18 to 20 ft. Beam 14 to 15 in. Depth 11 to 12 in. (Average.) It is employed for hand-lining in coastal waters.

GONDEL.

See **Grundel.**

GONG BUOY. A buoy similar in construction to a bell buoy but sounding a distinctive note because of the use of sets of gongs, each of which has a different tone.

GONIOMETER.

See **Radio Compass.**

GOOD FULL. When applied to sails, means that in a ship sailing close to the wind, the sails are all drawing and well filled.

Fr: *Bon plein;* Ger: *Gut voll.*

GOODS. Term which in marine insurance means goods in the nature of merchandise and does not include personal effects or provisions and stores for ship's use. The term "goods" as used in charter parties and bills of lading includes wares, merchandise, and articles of every kind whatsoever except live animals and cargo which by contract is carried on deck.

Fr: *Marchandises;* Ger: *Güter.*

See **Canned Goods, Cloth Goods, Kentledge Goods, Measurement Goods, Wet Goods.**

GOOSENECK. 1. A fitting which secures the hinged end of a gaff, boom, or derrick to the mast. It allows the spar to be topped or lowered or to be trained laterally. Also called Pacific iron (U. S.).

For the smallest spars it consists simply of a hook-shaped piece which fits into an eyebolt.

The cargo derrick gooseneck is a steel casting or forging riveted to the mast, having an upper and lower horizontal palm. These palms have bushed bearings for taking a vertical spindle or swiveling pin on which the derrick is trained. This vertical pin in turn forms the bearing for a

horizontal pin about which the derrick is topped or lowered. The heel fitting of the derrick is formed with double jaws which carry the horizontal pin.
> Fr: *Vit de Mulet;* Ger: *Schwanenhals; Spürzapfen; Gänsehals.*

2. A bight made in the standing part of a rope when tying a bowline knot.

GOOSENECK BAND. Forging securing a gooseneck to the mast. Sockets with belaying pins are usually fitted on this band.
> Fr: *Cercle de Vit de Mulet;* Ger: *Schwanenhalsband.*

GOOSENECK SCRAPER. Iron scraper about 12 inches long, with one end bent over at right angles to the handle and sharpened. Generally used on board ship for scraping pitch from the seams of a deck.

GOOSEWINGED. Said of a sail when the clew of a course or topsail is hauled (triced) up and lashed to the yard.

GORE. A term used to denote the angles cut slopewise at one or both ends of the cloth in sailmaking, so as to widen the sail or give the required sweep to the foot or leech.
> Fr: *Coupe; Pointe de Laize;* Ger: *Gillung.*

See **Cross Gore.**

Square mainsails, cross jacks, and square topsails are gored in the leeches. Square foresails have straight leeches. Jibs are gored on luff and foot. The gores are named head gores, leech gores, or foot gores according to their location.

GORING. That part of the skirt of a square sail where it actually widens from the upper part of head toward the foot.
> Ger: *Ausschnitt.*

GORING CLOTH. Pieces of canvas cut on the bias and added to the breadth of a sail.
> Fr: *Laize de Pointe;* Ger: *Schragen.*

GOUGE SPADE. A half-round spade used by whalemen to cut holes in blubber for reeving chains or ropes or embedding hooks.

GOURSE. Gulf of Genoa sailing and rowing boat of Italian origin (*guscio*) with sharp stern, upright stem and sternpost, little sheer, and no tumble home at sides. Compared with the Marseilles *barquette* it has more depth and is not fitted with washboards. Length 19 ft. Breadth 6½ ft. Depth 2 ft. 3 in. (Average.)

There is no particular rig for this type of boat. Some of them set a lateen, others a lugsail, and those used as pleasure craft are decked and rigged with a sliding gunter or a gaff sail.

GOZZETTO. A Sicilian open fishing boat with one mast and lateen sail employed in local fisheries. Also called *vuzziteddu.* The stemhead rises about 3.2 ft. above the gunwale; the sternpost about 1.2 ft. Length 14.7 ft. Breadth 4.9 ft.

GOZZO. Small double-ended open sailing and rowboat employed in various inshore fisheries of the Italian peninsula. Sometimes called *guzzo.* Size and dimensions vary in different localities. The *gozzo* from the Ligurian coast has the fore end decked over for a short length, and is fitted with 2 or 3 thwarts. The stemhead and sternpost rise considerably above the gunwale. The former rakes aft; the latter forward. It is rigged with one portable mast and lateen sail.

GRAB BUCKET. A device for handling bulk cargoes; also used for dredging. It consists essentially of two steel scoops hinged at one point and so arranged that they are open when lowered into the material to be excavated, and automatically close as soon as the lifting tension is applied. Also called clamshell bucket, grapple bucket, grab.
> Fr: *Benne Preneuse;* Ger: *Greifeimer.*

GRAB DREDGE. A steel floating structure fitted with one or more grab cranes. Also called grapple dredge.
> Fr: *Drague à Benne Preneuse;* Ger: *Greifbagger.*

The grab itself is made in two parts, each of curved steel plates, which by suitable mechanism controlled by the driver can be open or shut at will. With the jaws open the grab is allowed to fall heavily and bury itself in the river or harbor bottom. The jaws are then closed; the grab is raised and discharged into a barge or a hopper by opening the jaws again. The capacity of grabs lies usually between 60 and 120 cu. ft.

Grab dredges are particularly useful for maintaining docks, harbors and rivers free of silt. The self-propelled type with hopper is most frequently adopted, although in some localities grab cranes are fitted on a dumb barge and discharged into ordinary hopper barges.

GRAB ROD. One of the small horizontal rods riveted to a bulkhead, to a hatch coaming, or to a mast to form a ladder.
> Fr: *Main de Fer;* Ger: *Rundeisengriffe.*

GRAB ROPE. A line secured waist high above a boat boom or gangplank for steadying oneself. Also called hand rope.

GRADUATED MERIDIANS. The two meridans, marked in degrees and minutes, which form the boundary of a nautical chart on the right and left. Latitude is measured on these meridians, also distance between two places.
Fr: *Echelle des milles;* Ger: *Graduiertes Meridiane.*

GRADUATED PARALLELS. The two parallels which bound a nautical chart at top and bottom. Longitude is measured on these parallels.
Ger: *Gradegeteilte Parallele.*

GRAFT. To cover a ringbolt, block strop, or any similar object, with a weaving of small cord or rope yarns.
Fr: *Garnir; Fourrer;* Ger: *Überweben.*

GRAIN. 1. A term variously defined in different countries. In the U. S. the term grain is applied collectively to unhusked or threshed seeds or fruits of various food plants, specifically the cereal grasses, although in commercial usage also to flax, peas and sugar cane seed. According to the British Merchant Shipping Act it is used to denote corn, rice, paddy, pulse, peas, beans, seeds, and other species of plants, such as oats, nuts or nut kernels. In Canada the term includes corn, wheat, rye, barley, peas, and other grain except oats. In Australia, underwriters' regulations define grain as wheat, barley, oats, peas and cargoes of like nature.

Grain was formerly carried mostly in bags. Lately, however, the bulk trade has very much increased, as it was found that it is more convenient and economical to carry grain in bulk, owing to modern discharging appliances, such as elevators. Freight rates on grain are expressed in cents per bushel of 60 lb.
Fr: *Céréales;* Ger: *Korn; Getreide.*
See **Heavy Grain, Light Grain.**
Board of Underwriters of New York, Rules for Loading Grain, New York, 1929; Port Warden of Montreal, Regulations for the Loading and Carriage of Grain Cargoes; Australian Navigation Act 1912–20, Grain Loading Regulations, Canberra.
2. The direction of the fibers in wood.
Fr: *Fil;* Ger: *Maserung.*
See **Cross Grain.**

GRAIN BULKHEAD. A grain-tight partition fitted longitudinally in the lower hold of a vessel which carries grain in bulk. It extends from tank top to lower deck.

Fr: *Bardis;* Ger: *Getreideschott; Kornschott.*

GRAIN CAPACITY. The capacity of a ship's cargo spaces in cubic feet measured to outside of frames, top of ceiling, and top of beams, including hatchways. Also called grain cubic.
Fr: *Capacité Volumétrique en Céréales;* Ger: *Korn kubisher Inhalt; Getreide kubisher Inhalt.*

GRAIN CARGO CERTIFICATE. A document issued to vessels carrying grain cargoes in bulk. It certifies that all the precautions and conditions laid down by the competent authorities for the safety of such vessels have been complied with. In U. S. ports this is usually issued by a surveyor appointed by the New York Board of Underwriters.
Ger: *Getreide Ladungsattest.*

GRAIN FITTINGS. The system of feeders and shifting boards installed in the holds of vessels which carry grain in bulk as a precaution against any shifting of the cargo while at sea.
Fr: *Bardis;* Ger: *Getreide Beschlag.*

GRAIN-LADEN SHIP. A ship carrying an amount of grain of more than one-third of the registered tonnage of the vessel. This third is computed at the rate of 100 cu. ft. for each register ton, where the grain is reckoned in measures of capacity. Where the grain is reckoned in measures of weight, it is computed at the rate of two tons weight for each ton of registered tonnage.

GRAINS. A two-tined barbed spear in which each prong is about 3 in. long. It fits on the end of a pole 15 ft. or more in length. Used in Florida for the capture of crawfish.

GRAPNEL. An implement having four prongs or hooks radiating from a common shank, the shank at the other end being fitted with a ring. It is used as an anchor for small boats up to about 3 tons displacement or for recovering objects dropped overboard. The ends of the prongs are usually flattened in order to give better holding power. Also called grappling hook.
Fr: *Grappin;* Ger: *Dreganker; Greifer; Dragger.*

GRATED HATCH. A wood or steel openwork cover used for closing a hatchway while still providing ventilation for underdeck spaces. Also a hatchway so covered.
Fr: *Panneau Grillagé;* Ger: *Lukengrating.*

GRATING. Open lattice work of wood or metal so arranged to form a flush surface admitting light and air. Wooden gratings are used for such purposes as drainage, platforms, open bilge covers, door steps, and so on.

Fr: *Caillebotis;* Ger: *Gitter; Grating; Lattengitter.*

See **Fantail Grating, Fidley Grating, Skylight Grating, Steel Grating.**

GRATING COVER. A circular cast-iron cover designed as a grating and fitted at deck level over a coal chute to provide ventilation to a bunker.

Fr: *Tape Ajourée;* Ger: *Grating Deckel.*

GRATING PLATFORM. Steel gratings suitably arranged in engine rooms and stokeholds at different heights with communicating ladders for access to the different parts of engines and boilers.

GRAVE.
See **Bream.**

GRAVING DOCK. A drydock in which ships are repaired, as opposed to a building dock, in which ships are built.

See **Drydock.**

GRAVING. 1. Scraping, cleaning, painting, or tarring the underwater body. (Obsolete.)

Fr: *Radoubage;* Ger: *Reinigung.*

2. A form of patching wooden ships or boats in which a knot or other defect found in a timber is repaired without affecting its strength. The damaged spot is cut out with a chisel, payed with luting, hot pitch, or marine glue, and a square or rectangular block is driven into the cavity.

GRAVING PIECE. A small piece of wood inserted in a larger one to fill a cavity left when a decayed or damaged portion is removed. Both pieces should be of the same wood, the grain should be parallel, and an adhesive such as casein glue should usually be used. Also called chock, dutchman.

Fr: *Romaillet;* Ger: *Spund.*

GRAVITY BAND. A band with shackle fitted on the shank of a stocked anchor near the center of gravity. It is fitted on anchors designed to be stowed on a billboard and lifted by an anchor davit or crane. Also called balancing band, balancing clamp.

Ger: *Kattschakel; Schwebering; Transportschakel.*

GRAVITY DAVIT. A system of davits in which each boat is supported by a pair of cradles with rollers, which, on being released, move under the action of gravity, along an inclined trackway, composed of two channels with their open sides facing each other, to the outboard position. At the end of the travel the davits rotate along a horizontal axis and the boat can then be lowered to the surface of the water.

Fr: *Bossoir Automatique;* Ger: *Schwerkraftdavit.*

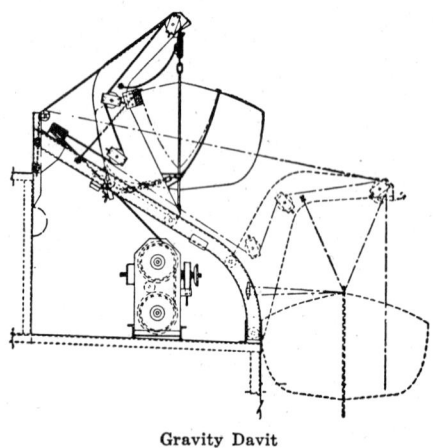

Gravity Davit

The trackways upon which the cradles move are inclined at an angle of 35° to the horizontal. The upper end of the cradle is curved outboard and from this the boat block is suspended. Single-wire ropes are used as falls and led to a winch on deck. This type of davit is particularly suitable for lifeboats of large size and it has the advantage of keeping the boat deck free for the use of passengers.

GRAVITY TANK. A tank, located high in the ship, into which fresh water is pumped periodically from low storage tanks. The ship's fresh water piping system is fed from the gravity tank, from which the water flows under gravity head.

GRE. Australian tied-bark canoe employed for fishing and transportation by the coastal Gippsland tribes of Victoria. The smallest craft are about 7½ ft. in length and carry 2 people; the largest are 18 ft. long and carry 5 or 6. Also called *yuro.*

GREASE IRON. One of several flat pieces of steel about ⅝ in. thick and 3 in. wide placed across the ground ways and spaced about 20 ft. apart to prevent the cradle from resting on the launching grease before the weight of the ship is transferred from the keel blocks and shores to the launching ways. Also called separator.

GREASER. Unlicensed member of the engine room staff who oils and greases bearings and moving parts of main engines, auxiliaries and electric motors aboard ship; makes regular rounds of machinery and supplies proper grade of oil and grease usually according to a predetermined schedule. Also called oiler.

Fr: *Graisseur;* Ger: *Schmierer; Lagerhälter.*

GREAT CIRCLE. The great circles of a sphere are those whose planes pass through the center of that sphere.

Fr: *Grand Cercle;* Ger: *Hauptkreis.*

GREAT CIRCLE CHART. A chart on which the earth's surface is projected on a plane tangent to the earth's surface by rays from the earth's center. It is used particularly for finding course and distance by great circle sailing and usually covers some particular area of the ocean frequently navigated. The point of tangency is not at the pole, but is chosen for each chart to give the least distortion for the whole area covered.

See **Gnomonic Chart.**

GREAT CIRCLE SAILING. The art of conducting a ship from one point to another by the shortest possible route, namely, along the arc of a great circle. As the great circle, with the exception of the meridians and the equator, intersects each meridian at a different angle, in order to steer along it a ship would have to be continually altering her course. In practice this is not possible, and the mariner therefore selects a number of points on the great circle track a short distance apart and sails on the rhumb lines connecting them

Fr: *Navigation Orthodromique; Navigation par Arc de Grand Cercle;* Ger: *Segeln im grössten Kreise.*

See **Rhumb Line.**

Berkeley, L. M., *Great-Circle Sailing,* New York, 1926.

GREAT CIRCLE TRACK. A track intersecting each meridian at a varying angle in great circle sailing.

Fr: *Route par arc de grand cercle;* Ger: *Grosskreiskurs.*

GREAT LINES. A term used by North Sea fishermen to denote a type of long lines fitted with large hooks and long, widely-spread snoods. Chiefly used for cod, conger, skate, dog fish, and halibut. The great lines are left down for longer intervals than the small lines. The number of hooks may vary from 1000 to 5500. The snoods are corked so as to lift them off the bottom and prevent their being robbed by small creatures. Also called overs, trot lines. Up to fourteen miles of lines may be shot by a single vessel. They are hauled in by a motor or steam driven line hauler.

Fr: *Grandes Cordes;* Ger: *Langleinen.*

GREAT LINING. Fishing carried on with great lines over the deeper banks of the ocean. Hand-lining in depths of over 60 fathoms.

Fr: *Pêche aux Grandes Cordes;* Ger: *Grundangelfischerei; Langleinenfischerei.*

GREENCASTLE YAWL.

See **Dronthiem.**

GREEN FISH. Trade name for cod, hake, haddock, herring when unsalted.

Ger: *Ungetrockneter Fisch.*

GREEN FLASH. A meteorological phenomenon associated with the moment sunrise or sunset occurs, and the small segment of the upper part of its disc momentarily turns a vivid green or bluish green. This phenomenon only lasts a fraction of a second. Also called **Green ray.**

Fr: *Rayon vert;* Ger: *Grüne Strahl.*

GREENHEART. A hard and strong wood originating from Guiana, highly resistant to the attacks of marine borers. It is useful in shipbuilding for all purposes where great strength and durability are required, as in rudder stocks. Weight when seasoned 51 to 62 lb. per cu. ft.

Fr: *Greenheart;* Ger: *Greenheart.*

GREEN SEA. A mass of water shipped on a vessel's deck, so considerable as to present a greenish appearance. An unbroken wave.

Fr: *Baleine;* Ger: *Grundliche Sturzsee.*

GREENWICH CIVIL TIME (U. S.). Mean solar time in which the day commences at midnight on the meridian of Greenwich. Mean time counted from Greenwich mean midnight. Also called Greenwich mean time (G. B.), universal time.

Fr: *Temps moyen de Greenwich;* Ger: *Mittlere Greenwich Zeit.*

GREENWICH HOUR ANGLE. The Greenwich hour angle of a celestial body is the angle at the pole between the meridian of Greenwich and the hour circle of the body.

Fr: *Angle Horaire de Greenwich;* Ger: *Greenwicher Stundenwinkel.*

GREENWICH MEAN TIME. See **Greenwich Civil Time.**

GREENWICH TIME OF SIDEREAL NOON. The mean solar time at Greenwich when the first point of Aries is on the local meridian.

Fr: *Temps Sidéral de Greenwich;* Ger: *Greenwich Sternzeit.*

GREGALE. Name given by the Maltese people to a strong northeasterly wind which blows in the Ionian Sea and neighboring parts of central Mediterranean mainly during the winter.

GRETA GARBO. See **Double-Clewed Jib.**

GRIBBLE. A species of shipworm (*Limnoria terebrans*) much smaller than the *Teredo navalis*. It bores its way to and fro in the wood and is, therefore, easily detected. Very destructive to submerged timber.

Fr: *Limnorie;* Ger: *Bohrassel.*

GRIDIRON. An open framework of parallel beams or girders for supporting a ship in a tidal dock, which dries out at low water, permitting bottom examination and repairs to be carried out during a period which varies according to the range of tides. Also called careening grid.

Fr: *Gril de Carénage; Banc de Carénage;* Ger: *Balkenrost; Kielbank; Trockengrating.*

GRILL FLOORING. See **Grating.**

GRIN. A vessel is said to grin when her bows dive into the sea and come up streaming with water.

GRIP. That part of an oar gripped by the hands when rowing. Also called handle, grasp.

Fr: *Poignée;* Ger: *Rudergriff; Riemengriff.*

GRIP. To hold; said of an anchor when the flukes get embedded in the ground.

Fr: *Crocher;* Ger: *Greifen; Halten.*

GRIPE. 1. The area about the junction of stem and keel. Also called forefoot.

2. A curved piece of timber which joins the keel of a wooden ship to the cutwater. It is bolted to the fore side of the stem under the cutwater and is sometimes further secured by two horseshoe-shaped copper straps.

Fr: *Brion;* Ger: *Unterlauf; Vorlauf.*

3. One of the metal fastenings for securing a ship's boat in its stowage or cradle.

Fr: *Saisine;* Ger: *Bootskrabber.*

4. One of the bands made of canvas, matting or sennit fitted with thimbles in the ends and passed from davit head over and under a boat when secured for sea. They cross diagonally outside of the boat and are provided with lanyard or monkey tail slips for letting go.

Fr: *Sangle;* Ger: *Bootsbrok.*

GRIPE (to). A vessel gripes when it tends to come up into the wind while sailing close-hauled.

Fr: *Être Ardent;* Ger: *Luvgierig sein.* See **Ardency.**

GRIPE IN. To secure a boat for sea by use of gripes.

GRIPE IRON. See **Horseshoe.**

GRIPE LASHING. A lashing spliced to the legs of the gripes and secured either to the davit head or the strongback.

GRIPE PIECE. See **Gripe.**

GRIPE PLATE. See **Horseshoe.**

GROIN. A structure projecting from shore and designed to break the current and thereby check erosion and build out the shore by a deposit of new material.

Fr: *Epi;* Ger: *Buhne.*

GROMMET. 1. Also *grummet* or grummet ring. A ring of hemp, wire, or rope made from a single strand by laying it up three times around its own part.

Fr: *Erseau;* Ger: *Taukranz; Grummetstropp.*

2. A small eyelet in a sail through which a stop or roband is passed. Also a metal eyelet, frequently made of two parts, punched together and fitted in the edge of a sail, awning, or hammock.

Fr: *Oeuillet;* Ger: *Gattlagel.*

3. A thread of oakum dipped in white lead and wound around a deck bolt to make it watertight.

Fr: *Cravate;* Ger: *Hanfzopf.*

GROMMET FENDER. A portable fender consisting of rope grommets grafted or covered with rope yarns.

Fr: *Erseau de Défense;* Ger: *Taukranzfender.*

GROMMET RING. See **Grommet.**

GROOMSPORT YAWL. An open boat of Norwegian origin from Belfast Lough (Northern Ireland) with rounded stem and sharp stern. The smaller craft are rigged with one mast and dipping lug. The larger boats with over 20 ft. keel have two masts, the shorter one stepped forward. Both sails have their foot extended by a boom.

GROOVED-BUTT CALKING TOOL. A tool used for flush nonwatertight calking where appearance is a consideration.

GROSS-FORM CHARTER. A voyage charter by which the owner pays for all regular expenses incident to the voyage from the time the ship is berthed until the cargo is discharged.

Ger: *Brutto Charter.*

Not only are the operating expenses, subsistence, stores, and supplies for deck and engine, as well as fuel, paid by the owners, but also port charges, towage, pilotage, wharfage, stevedoring, and all ordinary expenses that arise from the regular prosecution of the voyage, or that are incident to the loading and discharging of cargo. Contingent costs such as demurrage, lighterage and extra expenses for working cargo on Sundays and holidays are in addition to the charter rate and borne by the charterers. The gross form charter is the one by which the owner assumes the greater obligations. Trip charters are usually of the gross-form type.

GROSS FREIGHT. 1. Freight money without any allowance for navigation charges or dues, cost of fuel, and so on.

2. The sum payable to the shipowner for freight without deducting the expenses of earning the freight.

3. The sum payable to the shipowner with the premiums of insurance and commissions.

Fr: *Fret Brut;* Ger: *Bruttofracht.*

GROSS TON. A unit of capacity of 100 cu. ft. (2.83 cu. meters) used for ascertaining the legal or register tonnage of vessels. Also called register ton, vessel ton.

Fr: *Tonne de Jauge;* Ger: *Registertonne.*

GROSS TONNAGE. The gross tonnage or gross register tonnage of a vessel consists of its total measured cubic contents expressed in units of 100 cu. ft. or 2.83 cu. m. The actual cubical contents of any space is measured in accordance with prescribed methods and formulas as originated by Moorsom, which are incorporated in the measurement rules of the leading maritime countries.

Fr: *Tonnage Brut; Jauge Brute;* Ger: *Brutto-Tonnengehalt; Bruttoraumgehalt; Grosstonnage.*

The lack of uniformity in gross tonnage for vessels of various nations results not only from the various methods of measurement employed, but also from differences as to the number of spaces which are excluded from measurement. Since some spaces are excluded from measurement it follows that, in practice, the gross tonnage of a vessel does not represent its entire enclosed cubical capacity.

GROUND. To run ashore. To strike the bottom through ignorance, violence, or accident.

Fr: *Échouer; Se mettre au plein;* Ger: *An Grund geraten; Auflaufen.*

GROUNDAGE. 1. A port charge or harbor due exacted for permission to anchor.

2. A fee charged by port authorities for allowing a ship to remain in port.

GROUND BAIT. Bait thrown overboard to attract fish. Also called toll bait in the United States. It is usually made of slivers of fish passed through a bait mill and ground up into a mush. Water is added to it before it is used, and when in this condition it also is termed chum or stosh.

GROUND CHAIN. Heavy chain used with permanent moorings and connecting the various legs or bridles. In single mooring there is no ground chain, the vessel being made fast to the riding chain.

Fr: *Chaîne de Fond;* Ger: *Muringketten.*

GROUND-GLASS SOUNDING TUBE.
See **Sounding.**

GROUNDING. See **Ground.**

GROUNDING CLAUSE. A hull clause in marine insurance policies which states that grounding in certain rivers, canals, and bars is not to be deemed a stranding.

GROUNDING KEEL. Grounding keels are composed of doubling strips of plate or built-up girders, or of elm logs secured between two angle bars fitted to the bottom of the vessel at a distance from the centerline corresponding to the position of the docking keel blocks when a vessel is in dry dock. Their purpose is to distribute the pressure on the bottom of the ship when it is in dry dock, and thus to obviate undue strain. Their under side is in the same horizontal plane as the center keel, so that they serve as additional support.

Fr: *Quille d'Échouage;* Ger: *Scheuerkiel.*

GROUND LINE.
See **Long Line.**

GROUND LOG. A form of log used for showing the direction and speed of a vessel over the ground in shoal water. It

GROUND ROPE—GROW 340

consists of an ordinary log line with a hand lead of 7 to 9 lb. substituted for the log chip. When used, the lead remains fixed at the bottom and the line shows the path and speed of the ship and the effect of any current which may exist.

Fr: *Loch de Fond;* Ger: *Grundlog.*

GROUND ROPE. A heavy wire or Manila rope attached to the lower edge of the mouth of a trawl net with the object of preventing the escape of the fish underneath the net. Also called **footrope**.

Fr: *Bourrelet;* Ger: *Grundtau.*

When trawling on rough ground the footrope is furnished with wooden rollers called bobbins. In large trawl nets it has a center core of wire covered by old netting and this is rounded with old Manila. When complete it measures about 10 in. in circumference.

Fr: *Apparaux de Mouillage;* Ger: *Ankergeschirr; Grundgeschirr; Grundtakelung.*

GROUND WARP. A Manila and wire rope 25 to 50 fathoms in length which runs between the ends of the wings and the otter boards in a French-rigged **trawl** net.

Fr: *Bras.*

GROUND-WAYS. Timbers made fast to the ground, extending fore and aft under the hull on each side of the keel to form a broad surface track on which a ship is end-launched. Ground-ways for a side launching are much the same.

Fr: *Coulisse de Lancement;* Ger: *Ablaufbahn.*

GROUP ALTERNATING LIGHT. A continuous coastal light with colors alternating in groups.

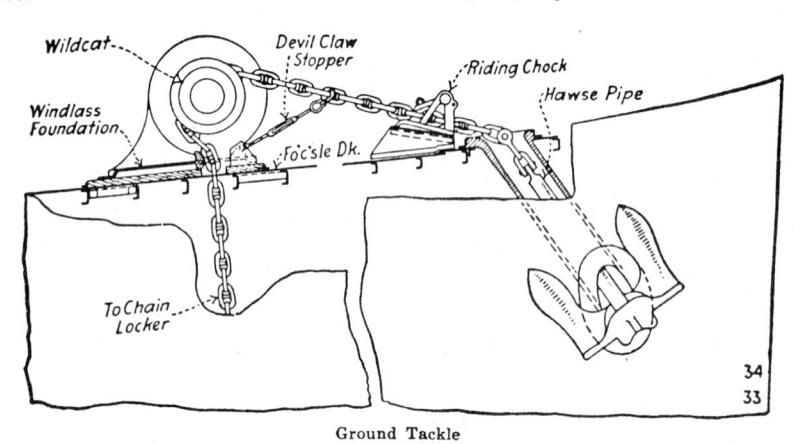

Ground Tackle

GROUNDS. Pieces of wood laid transversely, at each frame, over the inner bottom plating and to which the ceiling planking is fastened. Grounds are not fastened to the inner bottom but laid in a mixture of tar and cement while the mixture is wet. As it hardens it firmly secures them. Also called **ceiling beams**.

Fr: *Lambourdes;* Ger: *Blindhölzer.*

GROUND SWELL. A sudden swell preceding a gale, which rises along shore, often in fine weather and when the sea beyond it is calm. A swell remaining after a gale.

Fr: *Houle de fond;* Ger: *Grunddünung.*

GROUND TACKLE. A general term for the anchors, cables, warps, springs, and so on, used for securing a vessel at anchor.

Fr: *Feu à changement de coloration par groupes;* Ger: *Wechselfeuer mit Gruppen.*

GROUP FLASHING LIGHT. A light showing at regular intervals a group of two or more flashes.

Fr: *Feu à Éclats Groupés;* Ger: *Gruppenblinkfeuer.*

GROUP OCCULTING LIGHT. A steady light with, at regular intervals, a group of two or more sudden eclipses.

Fr: *Feu à Occultations Groupées;* Ger: *Unterbrochenes Feuer mit Gruppenunterbrechung.*

GROW. An anchor cable is said to **grow** in the direction in which it is lying.

Fr: *Appel;* Ger: *Weise.*
See **Tend.**

GROWLER. A low-lying mass of floe ice which is not easily seen by approaching vessels owing to its dark indigo color. It is therefore a menace to shipping. It is usually caused by the capsizing and disintegration of an iceberg.
Fr: *Grondeur.*

GROWN FRAME. A natural crooked piece of wood used for the framing of small craft. Grown frames are preferred to sawed or bent frames when the molding is in excess of the siding.
Fr: *Membrure de Brin;* Ger: *Gewachsener Spant.*

GROWN SPAR. A solid spar obtained from a natural tree of suitable diameter as distinguished from a spar cut from a balk.
Fr: *Espar en bois de Brin;* Ger: *Erwachsenes Rundholz.*

GRUB BEAM. A curved timber which forms the contour of a round stern when made of a single laminated frame instead of several short pieces.

GRUNDEL. A Dutch boat of the same type as the *punter,* with the difference that the stern is built with a transom. Also called *gondel.* It is used for fishing or transportation on inland waters and rarely ventures out to sea. Length 46.5 ft. Breadth 12.4 ft. (typical.)

"G" STRING. See **Draw Rope.**

GUAJIBACA. Name given by the Guarani (Warrau) Indians of Venezuela and Guiana to the *corial.*
See **Corial.**

GUARANTEED FREIGHT (U. S.). Freight payable even if the goods are not delivered according to the terms of the contract, if such failure results from causes beyond the control of the shipowner.

GUARANTEE ENGINEER. A marine engineer on a new vessel appointed by the engine builders and paid by the owners. His duty is to control and verify on their behalf the smooth working of the whole plant during a certain period after the ship has left the builders' yard.
Fr: *Mécanicien de Garantie;* Ger: *Garantie-Maschinist.*

GUARD CHAIN. Short-link galvanized iron chain used with portable stanchions around hatchway openings, accommodation ladders, etc.

GUARDING. The strengthening border about 5 to 10 meshes deep on the sides of each lint in a drift net.
Fr: *Waretaille;* Ger: *Randmaschen.*

GUARD RAIL (G. B.). 1. The uppermost of a series of rails around an upper deck to prevent people from falling overboard. It is made of wood and must be at a minimum height of 3 ft. 6 in. from the deck. Also called accommodation rail.
Fr: *Rambarde;* Ger: *Handleiste.*
2. A fore-and-aft timber bolted to the ship's side at deck level, serving as a fender. (In Great Britain called belting.) A similar timber carried along the sides just above the waterline is called bilge guard rail.
Fr: *Ceinture;* Ger: *Reibholz; Scheuerleiste.*

GUARD ROPE. A light rope at the head, foot, and sides of a drift or gill net.
Fr: *Vactait.*

GUDGEON. One of the several lugs projecting from the after side of the stern or rudderpost to support the rudder. Also called rudder brace, rudder lug, rudder snug. Each gudgeon is bored out to receive the corresponding pintle fastened to the forepart of the rudder, which thus turns as upon hinges. Gudgeons are cast with, forged on, bolted, or welded to the sternpost.
Fr: *Fémelot;* Ger: *Ruderöse.*

GUESS-WARP. 1. A line or hawser carried in a small boat from a ship to a buoy, anchor, or the shore in order to warp the vessel towards it. Also called guest-warp. A portion of the hawser is coiled in the boat to insure reaching the desired point. It is from the necessity of judging the distance by the eye that it is called "guess-warp."
Fr: *Faux-Bras Élongé en Créance;* Ger: *Jageleine; Vertauleine.*
2. A line from forward, rove through a thimble at the outer end of a boat boom, rigged by naval vessels in harbor, to which the ship's boats and visiting boats may secure. A toggle is fitted through the line abaft the thimble.

GUEST FLAG. A yacht flag displayed in place of the absence flag when the owner is not on board and the boat is being used by guests. It is a blue rectangular flag with a diagonal white bar.
Fr: *Pavillon d'Invités;* Ger: *Gastflagge.*

GUEST ROPE. 1. A line to assist the towline either to steady the tow or to lengthen the towline or act as a preventer.
2. The grab rope that runs alongside to

assist boats coming to the gangway. It leads from forward through a bull's eye on to the boat boom. **3.** A stout rope slung outside a vessel fore and aft to give a hold for boats, lighters, barges to ride by when alongside. This term is also applied by some to any rope used to attach a boat astern of a vessel.

Fr: *Faux-Bras de Tangon;* Ger: *Bootstau.*
Also **Grab Rope, Boat Line, Gift Rope.**

GUFFA.
See **Basket Boat.**

GUILALO. A shallow-draft open boat used in the small coasting trade around the Philippine Islands. Also called *jilalo*. It is sharp at both ends. The hull has fine lines at both ends with pronounced flare. Length 65 ft. Breadth 10 ft. Draft 2½ to 3 ft. (Average.)

These boats are rigged with two masts. The tallest or mainmast is placed just forward of amidships. The shrouds are fastened to spars acting as outriggers. The foremast is much shorter than the main and placed right forward. Oars with circular blades are used for propulsion when becalmed.

GUINEA CURRENT. An easterly flowing current in the Gulf of Guinea.
Buchanan, J. Y., The Guinea and Equatorial Currents, Geographical Journal (London) (March, 1896).

GUL. Melanesian dugout canoe with double outrigger from Mabuiag Island (Torres Straits). Also called *nar*.

The hull is built with round bottom, each end sloping up to a blunt point. A wash strake extends from bow to stern and is closed at both ends by a breakwater. It is fastened to the body of the canoe with sennit lashing and split bamboo is placed over the seam. Diagonally crossed struts are inserted in the hollow of the hull to keep the sides apart. Length 30 to 60 ft.

The outrigger consists of two booms placed about 6 ft. apart and projecting about 10 to 12 ft. on each side. It was formerly rigged with large oblong plaited mats, which were kept rigid by being skewered on each side to a bamboo pole. Two sails were generally used and there was no mast. These have nowadays been replaced by European fore-and-aft sails with mast.

GULBA. A dugout canoe used by the Goldi people of the Lower Amur River (Siberia). It is hewed from a hammagda tree, and is deeper, narrower, and thicker than the Otonga canoe. Termed *moma* by the Oroki people.

GULF PORTS. In chartering applies to the Gulf of Mexico, Port Arthur or Galveston to Tampa inclusive.

GULF STREAM. A warm current of the North Atlantic Ocean originating in the westward equatorial current and deflected northward by the South American coast into the Gulf of Mexico, whence it follows approximately the North American coast as far as Nantucket Island and is then deflected more eastward. In the Gulf of Mexico its velocity attains over 4 nautical miles per hour but in the North Atlantic it is reduced to between 10 and 15 miles per day.

GULLER. A special bit used by boatbuilders to make a slight countersink in planks to receive the fastenings.

GULLY. A term used in oceanography to denote the relatively narrow extension of a *trough* or *basin* of the sea bottom stretching towards the continent.

Fr: *Chenal;* Ger: *Rinne.*

GUNDALOW. Name applied in some parts of New England to scows or barges used in gathering marsh hay, or for lightering. One type of gundalow is a sailing barge, and was used on the Piscataqua River, New Hampshire, for river trade between Portsmouth and Dover. The hull was built of logs hewn and bolted together somewhat like a Chesapeake log canoe. Its form was similar to that of the bilge-board racing scow. The midsection had a flat bottom, quick round bilge, and sharply flared top fittings. The bow and stem were shaped like the ends of a teaspoon, the bow being the sharper. Length over-all 69 ft. 10 in. Breadth 19 ft. Depth 4 ft. 5 in. (in hold amidships). Capacity 60 tons. (Typical.)

The boats had but one leeboard, and were rigged with a stump mast forward and a lateen sail fitted with a counter weight to aid in handling when going under bridges. There was a small cabin aft and a long hatch amidships. An outboard rudder was used for steering. The wheel was abaft the cabin trunk.

GUNG.
See **Fleet.**

GUN HARPOON. A weapon used on a whale catcher, measuring 5 to 6 ft. in length and 3½ in. in diameter and weighing about 100 lb. The shank, or part which enters the gun, is perforated throughout its length by an elongated slit so as to allow the shackle connecting the harpoon with the line to remain outside the mouth of the gun when the shank is inserted in the barrel.

A hollow cast-iron cap filled with blasting powder may be screwed to the tip of the harpoon, forming its point. A time fuse discharges the bomb inside the body of the whale, 3 to 5 seconds after the harpoon has left the muzzle of the gun. It has four 10-in. prongs hinged to the spearhead, which open out at an angle of 45° when the line tightens after the harpoon has struck.

Ger: *Geschützharpune.*

GUN METAL. A non ferrous alloy used in shipbuilding. It is of value for bronze castings where strength and resistance to corrosion at ordinary temperatures are required. It contains 88 per cent copper, 10 per cent tin, and 2 per cent zinc. It is used for stern-tube bushings, shaft liners, gear wheels, pad eyes and ringbolts.

Fr: *Laiton Rouge;* Ger: *Geschützbronze.*

GUNNING. A process used in steel shipbuilding to secure watertightness by filling the space between faying surfaces with red lead paste forced under high pressure with a putty gun. Gunning is usually resorted to only when other, more certain methods of procuring tightness, as calking or welding, have been found impracticable.

GUNNY. Gunnies are bags of standard size made from jute. The word "gunny" covers all kinds of jute goods such as Hessian and rough sacking.

GUN PORT DOOR. A door in the ship's side plating used for various purposes according to its location. In passenger vessels it is generally used for gangways as a means of access to the ship or also for ventilation purposes at sea.

Fr: *Porte de coupée;* Ger: *Landgangtur.*

See **Cargo Door.**

GUNSTOCKING. A broad deck plank of teak cut to a curve on one side and notched on the other to fit the ends of the deck planks at bow and stern where the deck narrows in a curve.

GUN TACKLE. A tackle composed of a fall and two single blocks.

Fr: *Palan à Deux Poulies Simples;* Ger: *Doppelte einscheibige Talje.*

GUNTER IRON. One of the two fittings by which a gunter-yard is secured to its mast, the lower one being at the throat of the sail and the upper one between the throat and masthead. Both are fitted with a locking pin for taking the spar down when not in use.

Fr: *Blin;* Ger: *Gleitring.*

GUNTER LUG. A sort of standing lug, very high in the peak, with the yard nearly vertical. The yard is kept to the mast by jaws or some similar device at the lower end and further up is hooked to a traveler as an ordinary standing lug. The yard does not stand quite parallel with the mats as does that of a true gunter. The term "gunter lug" is a misnomer as the sail is neither a true sliding gunter nor a true lug. Gaff lug would be a better term as the alteration is really the fitting of gaff jaws and halyards on a lug yard and sail but the effect is much more that of a true gunter than of a gaff sail, as in the latter the gaff sags to leeward while the so-called gunter lug does not. It is one of the best rigs for small racing boats but the gaff sail is far superior in larger craft as the long yard of the gunter becomes unmanageable.

Fr: *Houari;* Ger: *Houarisegel.*

See **Lugsail.**

GUNTER RIG. A small boat rig in which the sail, called gunter, is extended by a yard secured to a short mast by two iron travelers known as gunter irons, which make the yard stand nearly parallel to the mast and well above it. Also called sliding rig.

Fr: *Gréement Houari;* Ger: *Houari Takelung; Gleitzeug.*

The yard is hoisted by a single halyard rove through a sheave hole at masthead. A variation of this rig consists of fitting the lower end of the yard with jaws and a parrel rope and setting the sail with two halyards, peak and throat. The peak halyard is bent to a mast traveler, which hooks into a span. In this rig yard and boom are generally of the same length. It was a popular rig for open dinghies, sailing canoes and half-deck racing boats until the advent of the Bermuda rig.

GUNTER YARD. A light spar used for setting a gunter sail. It slides abaft the mast, to which it is connected by means of two fittings called gunter irons, one fixed to the lower end of the yard and one higher up. A variation of the rig is now prevalent in which the lower end of the yard is fitted with jaws.

Fr: *Vergue de Houari;* Ger: *Schieberahe.*

GUNWALE. 1. The upper edge of a vessel's or boat's side.

2. An imaginary line formed by the intersection of the shell plating with the weather-deck stringer plate. In wooden hulls the line of intersection of the plank sheer with the topmost side plank.

Fr: *Lisse de Plat-Bord;* Ger: *Dollbaum.*
See **Box Gunwale, Open Gunwale.**

GUNWALE BAR. Angle bar connecting the sheer strake to the upper or weather-deck stringer plate.

Fr: *Cornière Gouttière;* Ger: *Schandeckelwinkel; Stringerwinkel.*

GUNWALE CAPPING. A top piece in open boats where the gunwale is away from the sheer strake by the amount of the rib thickness (Box gunwale).

GUNWALE RAIL. Hand rail running along the gunwale in a lifeboat to provide facility of access into the boat from the water. Also called jackstay.

GUNWALE TANK.
See **Topside Tank.**

GURDY.
See **Line Roller, Trawl Roller.**

GURRY (U. S.). The refuse after cleaning or dressing fish, consisting of heads and viscera. Called offal in Great Britain. It is thrown overboard or in some cases sold for reducing.
See **Bait.**

GURRY BAIT. Name given by Atlantic Banks fishermen to cod, haddock, or hake cut into strips 5 or 6 in. in length and about 2 in. wide and used as bait in the halibut fisheries. Also called gurry.

GURRY FISH. See **School Fish.**

GURRY PEN (U. S.). Oblong bin about 3 ft. deep fastened with lashings to the deck of a vessel engaged in the hook-and-line fisheries and used for stowing salt bait (gurry) during fishing operations.

GUSCIO. See **Gourse.**

GUSSET. 1. A triangular or square plate lying in a horizontal or slightly inclined plane used for reinforcing the connection between the margin plate, tank-side bracket, and frame. In some vessels a continuous fore-and-aft tie plate is used instead to avoid fitting numerous small gussets. Also called gusset plate.

2. A tie plate, used for fastening beams, frames, stanchions and the like to other structural members.

Fr: *Gousset;* Ger: *Fächerplatte.*

GUSSET PLATE. See **Gusset.**

GUST. A sudden increase in the velocity of the wind of short duration. It is often experienced near mountainous coasts. Gusts are probably due to a turbulent or eddy motion arising from the friction offered by the ground to the flow of the current of air.

Fr: *Rafale Fougue;* Ger: *Windstoss.*

GUT. A narrow passage or contracted strait connecting two bodies of water.

Fr: *Goulet;* Ger: *Fahrrinne.*

GUTTER. Member of the crew of a cod-fishing vessel who belongs to the splitting or dressing gang, who opens the bellies of the fish, removes the livers for oil, and tears out the viscera.

Fr: *Éhochteur.*

GUY. 1. A rope or whip supporting or steadying a spar in a horizontal or inclined plane such as a bowsprit, a davit, a cargo boom and so on. 2. A slack rope extending between two masts and carrying a block or tackle is also occasionally called "guy." 3. A rope used to steady an object when hoisted or lowered.

Fr: *Retenue;* Ger: *Geie.*

See **Belly Guy, Blubber Guy, Boom Guy, Davit Guy, Derrick Guy, Flying Guys, Jib Guy, Jumper Guy, Steam Guy.**

GUY SPAN. A cargo rig used for handling long pieces of cargo, such as steel rails and lumber. Also called steam schooner guy (U. S.). It consists of a gun tackle. One block is shackled to the head band of each derrick, the hauling part of the tackle leading along the derrick down to the deck, being made fast to a cleat on the mast.

GUZZO. Open fishing boat of the Adriatic originating from the Gulf of Trieste, employed in strand fisheries. The hull is built with keel, rounded stem and sternpost, sharp stern. It has a cuddy at each end and three thwarts. The rig consists of a portable mast with sprit or lateen sail. Length 14.7 to 16 ft. Breadth 4.9 ft. Depth (inside) 1.9 ft.

See **Gozzo.**

GUZZONO. Half-decked Italian sailing boat employed in the local fisheries of the Ligurian coast. It is of the same type and rig as the *leudo rivano* but smaller and carries no jib.

GYASSA. A two- or three-mast, lateen-rigged, seagoing barge of Arab build from the Nile delta, employed in the local coasting trade of the Gulf of Suez, northern Red Sea, and eastern Mediterranean, for transporting cargoes of coal and rice. Also called *gaiassa.*

The hull is wall-sided, with high bow decked at a steep angle right up to the stemhead, and transom stern with large rudder. The flat bottom is fitted with a short length of keel forward as well as aft, which runs gradually into the hull amidships: the purpose of which is for protection when grounding, as well as for giving more grip in the water. The fore- and mainsail are lateen and set outside the rigging. The mizzen is a settee sail with yard slung inside the rigging.

GYBE. When sailing free, to put the helm over so as to bring the boom on the opposite side.

To cause fore-and-aft sails to swing over from one side to the other when running at high speed by electrical power. A dial mechanically connected with the discs has the points and diagram of the mariner's compass marked on its face and from it is indicated the ship's true course. Secondary or repeating dials are electrically connected to indicate the course at other stations on board. These are called gyro-repeaters. The directive force of a gyro-compass is maximum at the equator and nil at the poles.

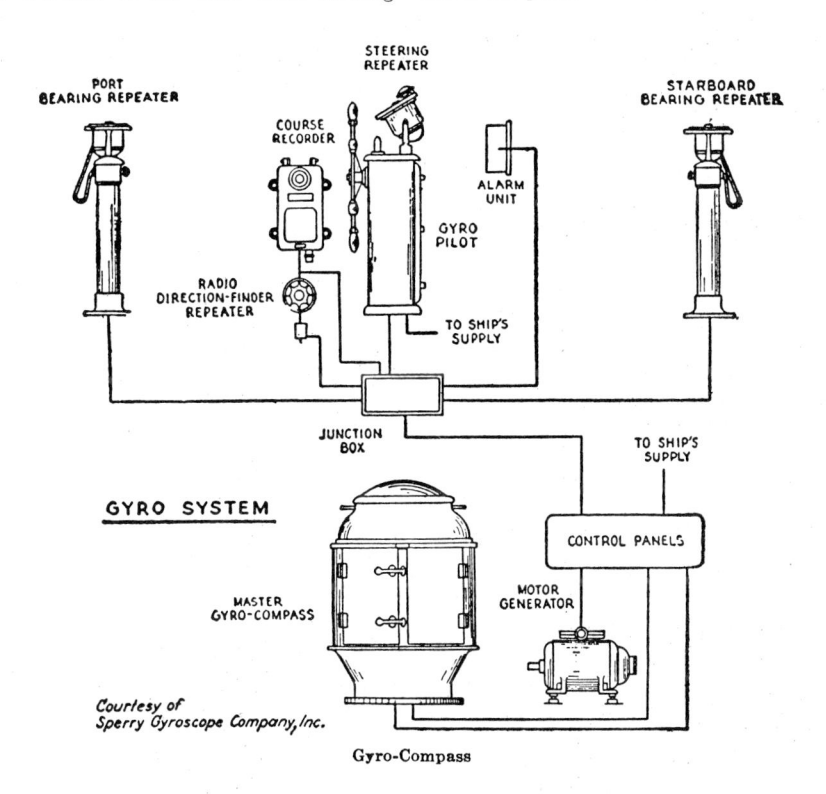

Courtesy of Sperry Gyroscope Company, Inc.

Gyro-Compass

free, through the wind getting on the lee side of the sails. Also jibe. The opposite of tacking.

Fr: *Coiffer;* Ger: *Giepen; Durchkaien.*

GYPSY.

See **Gipsy.**

GYRO COMPASS. An instrument receiving its directive force from a gyroscope operated by electric motors. Its directive action is based on the mechanical laws governing the dynamics of rotating bodies. It consists essentially of a heavy disc mounted in gimbals with a free suspension and driven

Fr: *Compas Gyroscopique;* Ger: *Kreisel-kompass.*

See **Compass.**

Rawlings, *The Theory of the Gyrocompass* (London, 1929); Sperry Gyroscope Company, *Gyro Compass and Gyro Pilot Manual* (New York, 1944).

GYRO-MAGNETIC COMPASS. A compass which combines the characteristics of a gyroscope and a magnetic compass in such a manner as to provide gyro-stabilized magnetic indications devoid of oscillation, lag and swing, despite any motion of the vessel in a seaway. It consists of a magnetic compass placed at any location where deviations errors are minimum, and connected to a gyro unit and two compass repeaters. It is mainly designed for small craft such as fishing vessels, sea-going tugs and yachts.

GYRO-PILOT. An automatic steering apparatus connected to the repeater of a gyro-compass, designed to hold a vessel on the desired course without helmsman. Also called automatic steerer, iron quartermaster.

Fr: *Auto Gouvernail;* Ger: *Selbststeuer.*

The ordinary action of the helmsman is obtained in this apparatus by the repeater-compass motor, which drives a contact-making arrangement. In the repeater the slightest sheer of the vessel off her course generates a flow of current, which actuates a relay. The relay starts a motor, which drives the steering wheel through a sprocket chain. A clutch permits the gyro-pilot to be thrown out of gear whenever it is desired. Desired alterations in the vessel's course are introduced through a small handwheel placed on the repeater compass. Each complete revolution of this wheel corresponds to a change of 10 degrees in the course steered. In case of emergency or breakdown the gyro-pilot can be instantaneously thrown out of gear and the ship steered by the ordinary hand gear.

GYROSCOPIC STABILIZER. A heavy electrically driven gyroscope with a weight of about 1 per cent of the ship's displacement, designed to reduce the amount of rolling.

Fr: *Stabilisateur Gyroscopique;* Ger: *Schiffskreisel.*

The stabilizer consists of a main stabilizing gyro with vertical spinning axle so mounted that it can be precessed in the horizontal plane by means of a circular rack engaging with the pinions of the precession motor. It is capable of opposing the roll-producing couples by a series of equal and opposite couples with practically no lag between the roll-producing couple and the opposing stabilizing couple. Its advantages over other systems is high roll-quenching efficiency when working within its roll-quenching range. Its drawbacks are high initial cost and comparatively large net weight of equipment.

Chalmers, T. W., *The Automatic Stabilization of Ships,* London, 1931.

H

H. Flag of the international code of signals divided vertically in two: white at the hoist; red at the fly; When hoisted simply indicates "I have a pilot on board."

H. MERIDIAN ALTITUDE (nautical astronomy).
h. ALTITUDE (nautical astronomy).
H.A. HOUR ANGLE (nautical astromony).
H/A or D. HAVRE-ANTWERP OR DUNKIRK range of ports in (grain trade).
h/c HELD COVERED (marine insurance).
H.D. HOURLY DIFFERENCE (nautical astronomy).
H.E. HEIGHT OF EYE (nautical astronomy).
H/H. HAVRE-HAMBURG range of ports in (grain trade).
H. and M. HULL AND MACHINERY OR MATERIALS (marine insurance).
H.O. HYDROGRAPHIC OFFICE. All charts and books issued by this office are identified by the letters H.O. preceding the serial number of the publication.
H.P. HORIZONTAL PARALLAX.
H.W. HIGH WATER.
H.W.F. and C. HIGH WATER FULL AND CHANGE.
H.W.O.S.T. HIGH WATER ORDINARY SPRING TIDES.

HAAF.
See Sixern, Sexaern.

HACK CHRONOMETER. A chronometer which fails on test to meet the exacting requirements of a standard chronometer, but which is sufficiently accurate to warrant no further adjustment or additional test. If there are three chronometers, the third or least reliable is frequently a hack chronometer. It is used for comparison purposes.

HACKMATACK. A tough and durable wood used in boat building in the form of knees or crooks. It is very suitable for stems, keels and breast-hooks of small boats. Also called tamarack, American larch.
Fr: *Mélèze d'Amérique*; Ger: *Hackmatack*.

HACK WATCH. A deck watch used when taken sights. It is compared with the ship's chronometers immediately before and after every observation.
Fr: *Computeur; Montre d'habitade*; Ger: *Beobachtungs Uhr; Handuhr*.

HACUA. Name given by the Yahgan Indians to their summer canoe, made of bark and similar to the *anan*.

HADDOCK LINE. A 2-lb. white line used for catching haddock and whiting. The total number of hooks in a set varies between 1,000 and 4,000. Also called small line.
Fr: *Ligne à Cabillaud; Petites Cordes*; Ger: *Schellfischschnur*.

HAGUE CONVENTION (1907). A series of 13 agreements drawn up by the delegates of 44 countries at the second international peace conference held at the Hague in 1907. It included:
1. A convention relative to the status of enemy merchant ships at the outbreak of hostilities.
2. A convention relative to the conversion of merchant ships into warships.
3. A convention relative to certain restrictions with regard to the exercise of the right of capture in naval war.
4. A convention relative to the creation of an international prize court.
American Journal of International Law, vol. 2 (1908).

HAGUE RULES (1921). Rules defining the risks to be assumed by sea carriers under bills of lading adopted by the International Law Association at the Hague Conference in 1921. A code defining the respective rights and liabilities of shipowners and shippers in the carriage of goods by sea. These rules were voluntarily drawn up at an International Conference of Shipowners, Traders, Underwriters, Bankers, etc., held at The Hague in 1921 and adopted by the International Law Association.
Fr: *Règles de la Haye*; Ger: *Haager Regeln*.
See York-Antwerp Rules, Warsaw-Oxford Rules.
Cole, S. D., *The Hague Rules Explained*, London, 1927.

HAIL. 1. A ship is said to hail from the port where it is registered, and to which it therefore properly belongs.
Fr: *Avoir Son Port d'Attache*; Ger: *Stammen*.
2. To call out, to address a boat or vessel, as, "Ahoy!"
Fr: *Héler; Arraisonner*; Ger: *Preien; Anpreien*.

HAILING STATION. 1. A station at

HAIR BRACKET—HALF-FLOOR TIMBER

the entrance of a lock where dockmasters advise pilots or shipmasters of vessels entering the lock of the number of the berth allocated to the ship. It is usually equipped with a loud speaker.

2. A station or post ashore from which inward ships are hailed to ascertain their last port of call and outward ships their destination.

HAIR BRACKET. An ornamental scroll terminating one of the rails of the head just below the figure head.

HAJER. A general term for Danish seine boats built in different sizes from 15 to 25 tons. Also called *Hai*. They are deep and broad decked fore and aft, with transom stern and carvel planking. They are cutter-rigged and fitted with an auxiliary engine of from 35 to 40 hp. Length 41.2 ft. Breadth 13.7 ft. (Typical.)

HAKAS. Polynesian single-outrigger dugout canoe from Alu (Shortland Island), northwestern Solomon Islands. The long sharp pointed bow has a little carving on the under surface, while the stern has a diamond-shaped protuberance. There is a deep wash strake. The outrigger apparatus is at a distance of about one-third of the canoe's length from the bow rather than at mid length. It is rigged with mast and sail.

The smaller boats, which are used only in sheltered waters, are from 16 to 18 ft. long, and so narrow that the occupant sits on a board placed on the gunwale with only his feet and legs inside the canoe.

HALF-AND-HALF LAP SCARF. A scarf made by cutting one-half of the thickness of each of two timbers, which are lapped and securely bolted or spiked together. This scarf is used for ordinary rough work, not requiring much strength.

See **Scarf**.

HALF BEAM. A deck beam extending only part way across the hull and cut off at a hatchway or other deck opening, as distinguished from a through beam, which runs from side to side. Also called short beam.

Fr: *Barrotin; Demi-bau;* Ger: *Kurzbalken.*

HALF BLOCK MODEL. A solid wooden model showing in outboard profile half of the hull form of a ship. Also called Half model.

Fr: *Modèle demi-bloc;* Ger: *Halbmodell.*

HALF BOARD. The action of a sailboat which luffs up into the wind until the headway has nearly ceased, and is then made to pay off on the same tack. Also called pilot's luff.

HALF-BREADTH PLAN. A plan or top view of half of a ship divided longitudinally, showing the waterlines, bow and buttock lines, and diagonal lines of construction.

Fr: *Plan Horizontal;* Ger: *Wasserlinienriss; Wasserpassriss; Grundriss.*

HALF-BREADTHS. Ordinates perpendicular to a vertical longitudinal plane dividing a vessel into two symmetrical halves. One-half the molded beam.

HALF BUCKLER. A hawse buckler shipped when the cables are bent and made with a score to fit the cable. Half bucklers are put on after filling the hawsehole with shakings around the cable. Also called riding buckler.

Fr: *Demi-Tape d'Écubier;* Ger: *Halber Klusendeckel.*

HALF-CROWN SEIZING. A seizing for securing together two ropes which cross each other, used when the stress on each rope is unequal.

Fr: *Amarrage en Étrive.*

HALF DECK. In sailing ship parlance the term refers to a deck-house located abaft the mainmast where the carpenter, sailmaker and apprentices had their quarters. It was connected overhead to the poop by a fixed gangway with heavy teak railing.

Fr: *Faux Tillac;* Ger: *Halbdeck.*

HALF-DECKED BOAT. A boat having a deck extending only over the fore part of the hull. Also a boat decked at ends with narrow deck or waterway on each side within the gunwales, the purpose of the deck being to render it safer under sail when listing over in a breeze. The term does not apply, however, to a small boat with both stern sheets and foresheets covered in, although the space decked over may measure exactly half the superficial area. If, on the other hand, only one plank is run around inside and covered into even a small forepeak or cuddy the boat is considered half-decked.

Fr: *Bateau mi-ponté;* Ger: *Halbgedecktes Boot.*

HALF-FLOOR TIMBER. In a wooden vessel, one of the timbers of the frame. Its head abuts against the heel of the second futtock. Its heel is bolted to the keel. Half of its length is bolted to the cross timber and the other half to the first futtock.

Fr: *Genou de Fond; Fausse Varangue; Demie Varangue;* Ger: *Halbbodenwrange.*

HALF FRAME. See **Half Timber.**

HALF HITCH. A hitch formed by passing the end of a rope around the standing part and bringing it up through the bight. It is seldom used alone.

Fr: *Demi Clef;* Ger: *Halberschlag; Halber Stek.*

Half Hitch

HALF HITCH AND TIMBER HITCH. A bend used for towing spars or for hoisting a light spar on end. Also called timber and half hitch. The half hitch is taken first, and the timber hitch formed afterward with the end.

Fr: *Noeud de Bois et Barbouquet; Noeud de Bois et Demi-Clef;* Ger: *Halberschlag mit Balkenstek.*

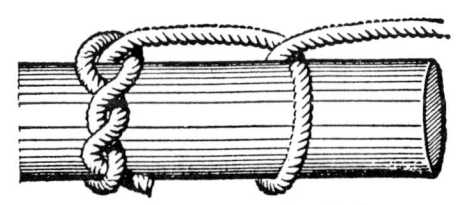

Half Hitch and Timber Hitch

HALF MAST. A flag is half-masted when hoisted some distance below the truck of a mast or flagstaff or below the peak of a gaff. Used as a distress signal or as a mark of respect for the dead.

Fr: *A mi-drisse en berne;* Ger: *Halbmast.*

HALF-MAST HOOP. A leather-bound, iron half-hoop used on small sailing craft, in conjunction with a rope bridle seized into an eyelet on the sail. A snap hook is fitted at one end of the bridle for hitching to the iron half-hoop.

HALF-MILE RULE. An expression which refers to the practice of making the necessary audible signals when vessels are half a mile from and approaching each other in such a manner that a risk of collision is present.

HALF PILOTAGE. Compensation for services tendered by a pilot and refused.

HALF POINT. A subdivision of the compass card equal to 5 degrees and 37 minutes of the circle.

Fr: *Demi-quart;* Ger: *Halbstrick.*

HALF PORT. One of two shutters, upper and lower, which close a porthole.

Fr: *Mantelet Brisé;* Ger: *Halbe Stückpfortenklappe.*

HALF-RATER. A term formerly used to denote a class of racing sailboats with a waterline length of 15 ft. They were so called because they rated one-half under the English rule of racing measurement used in 1895. They carried a jib and mainsail.

HALF-ROUND IRON. A rolled steel shape used in shipbuilding for stiffening casings, for moldings, and for hatch coamings. In section it is semicircular, or a segment of a circle. Also called convex iron, bead iron, coping.

Fr: *Fer Demi-Rond;* Ger: *Halbrund-Profileisen.*

HALF SHEAVE. A device used at the masthead of a small boat or elsewhere, to lessen the friction of a rope. Also called dead sheave.

Fr: *Encornail;* Ger: *Halbscheibe.*

HALF TIDE. Condition of the tide halfway between highest and lowest water.

Fr: *Mi-Marée;* Ger: *Mitte der Gezeit.*

HALF-TIDE BASIN. Half-tide basins are virtually locks on a very large scale. They differ from locks only in their irregular shape and great size. The gates of half-tide basins are kept open for several hours after high water so that belated vessels can enter as long as there is sufficient depth of water over the outer sill. Vessels may remain in the half-tide dock until the ensuing flood tide. If it is desirable to establish immediate communications with the inner harbor, it is kept open by admitting water into the half-tide basin from some external supply.

Fr: *Bassin de Mi-Marée;* Ger: *Halbtidehafen; Halbtidebecken.*

HALF TIMBER. 1. In wooden vessels, the short frame timbers in the cant bodies which correspond to the lower futtocks in the square body. 2. A frame set square with the center line of the ship but *not* crossing the keel. Also called half-frame.
Fr: *Demi-Membrure;* Ger: *Sitzer.*
See **Futtock.**

HALF TOPSAIL. Term formerly applied to a sail that set with a gaff above the square sail of a cutter. (Obsolete.)

HALIBUT BROOM. A disgorger used by halibut fishermen. It is made of oak with one end flattened and sharpened.

HALIBUT GAFF. A handled hook with sharp point, used by New England dorymen for gaffing fish after they have been captured.
Ger: *Ketshaken.*

HALIBUT LINE. A 3-lb. white line used for catching halibut.
Fr: *Ligne a Flétan;* Ger: *Heilbuttschnur; Buttleine.*

HALO. An extensive luminous ring around the sun or moon. It results from the refraction of light in ice crystals, which compose the highest cirrus clouds. Halos may be colored.
Fr: *Halo;* Ger: *Hof; Halo.*

HALVED DOOR. A door built in two independent sections, one above the other, so that the upper half may be open while the lower half is closed. These doors are frequently used for access to galleys and pantries, as well as ship's offices. The lower compartment is often fitted with a ledge to form a serving counter. Also called dutch door, barn door.
Fr: *Porte Coupée;* Ger: *Halbtür.*

HALYARD. A rope or purchase used for hoisting or lowering yards, spars, or sails on their respective masts or stays. The power of the purchase is suited to the weight of the sail or yard. Topsail halyards are the heaviest. Also *halliard.*
Fr: *Drisse;* Ger: *Fall.*
See Crowfoot Halyards, Gaff-Topsail Halyards, Lazy Halyards, Peak Halyards, Signal Halyards, Throat Halyards, Trip Halyards.

HALYARD BEND, HALLIARD BEND. A bend used for fastening temporarily the halyards in a small sailing boat. Also called slip bend, slippery hitch, jamming hitch. A turn is taken around a thwart, a loop is passed underneath this turn so that the knot can be cast off at any time.
Fr: *Noeud de Drisse;* Ger: *Fallstek.*

HALYARD RACK. A wooden framework in which the running part of a halyard is kept coiled so that it may always be clear for running.
Fr: *Baille à Drisse;* Ger: *Fallbalje.*

HALYARD TACKLE. Tackle fastened to the tye, by means of which a yard is hoisted or lowered. Also called halyard purchase.
Fr: *Caliorne de Drisse;* Ger: *Fallgien.*

HAMBROLINE. Small stuff used for seizings. Also called hamber. Three-yarn, right-handed, untarred hemp cord tightly laid, which runs about 92 ft. to the pound. It is of approximately the same size and yardage as roundline but with opposite twist. It is used in small craft as lacing for attaching sails to yards, gaffs, and so on.
Fr: *Quarantenier;* Ger: *Bindselleine.*

HAMMOCK. A kind of hanging bed about 3 ft. wide and 6 ft. long made of canvas. It has a number of cords at each end called clews, which are brought together and secured to an iron ring hung on a hook attached to a fitted deck beam at each end. Hammock battens or spreaders are usually at each end of the hammock to keep it open.
Fr: *Hamac;* Ger: *Hängematte.*

HAMMOCK BATTEN. A strip of wood used to extend the ends of a hammock and keep them spread out. Also called spreader.
Fr: *Bastet de Hamac;* Ger: *Hängematte-Latte.*

HAMMOCK CLEW. The combination of nettles by which a hammock is suspended.
Fr: *Araignée de Hamac;* Ger: *Hängematte Hahnenpot.*

HAMMOCK CLOTH. A tarpaulin spread over hammocks or over the openings in hammock nettings.
Fr: *Toile à Hamac;* Ger: *Hängematte-körpertuch.*

HAMMOCK GIRTLINE. Line or lines on which scrubbed hammocks are stopped to dry.
Fr: *Ceinture de Hamac;* Ger: *Hängemattejolle.*

HAMMOCK NETTINGS. Spaces in naval vessels in which hammocks are stowed daily after they are lashed. (Obsolete.)

HAMMOCK STOP. Lanyard at each end of a hammock, by which it is slung.
Fr: *Hanet d'Araignée de Hamac;* Ger: *Hängemattensteert.*

HAMPDEN BOAT. A small half-decked centerboard fishing boat from Casco Bay, Maine (U. S.). The hull is square-sterned with raking transom. There is a good deal of drag to the keel and considerable hollow in the after sections. The bow is high, straight and somewhat wall-sided. A few boats have been built with overhanging counter and rounded stem. In recent years the model has been modified at the stern for the installation of a motor. Length 17 to 27 ft. Breadth 6 ft. 9 in. to 8 ft. Depth 1 ft. 9 in. to 2 ft. 9 in.

Sailing craft are now obsolete. The rig formerly in use consisted of two spritsails, some of the larger boats 24 to 27 ft. long had a short bowsprit and carried a jib. They were fast under sail and very weatherly.

HAMPER. Equipment comprising a part of the outfitting of a vessel, especially spars, rigging, and so on, located above deck. This equipment though ordinarily indispensable, can, under some circumstances, become a source of danger and inconvenience. Also called top hamper.

HAND. To furl, as a sail.
Fr: *Serrer;* Ger: *Beschlagen.*

HAND DECK-PUMP. A lift pump worked by a hand lever pivoted to a portable standard which is shipped in a socket in the deck. Also called handy billy. Its discharge overflows on deck. Its suction leads to the bilges.
Fr: *Pompe à Balancier;* Ger: *Deckhandpumpe.*

HANDELKVASE. A fish carrier used in the Danish flounder fisheries around Skagen and northern Jutland. It is a welled-boat, which buys directly from the fishermen at sea and carries the fish alive to Copenhagen, where the catch is sold on board to fishmongers. It is ketch- or schooner-rigged. Length 40 to 60 ft. Breadth 12 to 16 ft. Depth 6 to 8 ft. The capacity of the well ranges from 2,000 to 6,000 flounders weighing on an average 88 lb. to a 100 fish.

HAND FLAG. A smally rectangular flag with staff, used for making signals by hand, using the semaphore alphabet.
Fr: *Panneau;* Ger: *Winkflagge.*

HAND GRAB. A metal bar fastened to a bulkhead or elsewhere to provide a hand hold for steadying a person when a ship rolls or pitches in a seaway.

HAND HOLE. A small hole in plating, to permit access by hand for cleaning or inspection, usually covered by a bolted plate when not in use. Such holes are found in boilers, and other engineering equipment of like nature.

HANDICAP. The distinction between sailing yachts of unequal size competing in the same race, established on a basis of tonnage or other characteristics, in order to obtain a more equal contest among competitors. The handicap may appear either in the measurement rules or in the time allowances determined for each boat before starting.
Fr: *Handicap;* Ger: *Handikap.*

HANDICAP CLASS. A class assigned for racing to a yacht which has become too old or is out-built for speed in her regular class, although still sufficiently efficient to race. In handicap classes time allowance is assigned on an arbitrary basis by an official handicapper, or is figured in percentage of elapsed time. In some of the more informal races handicaps are given at the start; that is, the slowest boat starts first and the fastest last. The first to finish is the winner.
Fr: *Série Handicap;* Ger: *Handikapklasse; Ausgleichklasse.*

HANDICAP RACING. A form of yacht racing in which each vessel has a handicap decided according to its merits: type, rig, displacement, and so forth.
Ger: *Ausgleichrennen.*
See **Racing Number, Class Racing.**

HANDINESS. The maneuvering qualities of a vessel under sail or power.
Fr: *Manoeuvrabilité;* Ger: *Manövrierfähigkeit.*

HANDKAHN. Small open sail and rowboat with V-stern found on the Frisches Haff (East Prussia).

HANDLE. That part of an oar, of smaller diameter than the loom, gripped by the hand. Also called grip, grasp.
Fr: *Poignée;* Ger: *Griff.*

HAND LEAD. A sounding lead with a sinker weighing from 5 to 14 lb., used in depths of 20 fathoms or less.
Fr: *Petite Sonde;* Ger: *Handlot.*

HAND LEAD LINE. A hemp or braided cotton line $5/8$ to $1\frac{1}{8}$ inch circumference and 25 to 30 fathoms in length, bent to a hand lead. Hand-lead lines are marked as follows: At 2 fathoms from the lead: two strips of leather; at 3 fathoms from the lead: three strips of leather; at 5 fathoms from the lead: a white rag (linen-duck or bunting); at 7 fathoms from the lead: a red

HAND LINE—HAND MAST

woolen rag; at 10 fathoms from the lead: a piece of leather with hole; at 13 fathoms from the lead: a blue rag (flannel or serge); at 15 fathoms from the lead: a piece of white bunting; at 17 fathoms from the lead: a red woolen rag; at 20 fathoms from the lead: two knots on a bit of line.

The fathoms at 1–4–6–8–9–11–12–14–16–18–19 are not marked and are called "deeps."

Fr: *Ligne de Petite Sonde;* Ger: *Handlotleine.*

HAND LINE. A fishing line which is continuously attended to by the fisherman either working from the deck of his vessel or from a dory, instead of being anchored

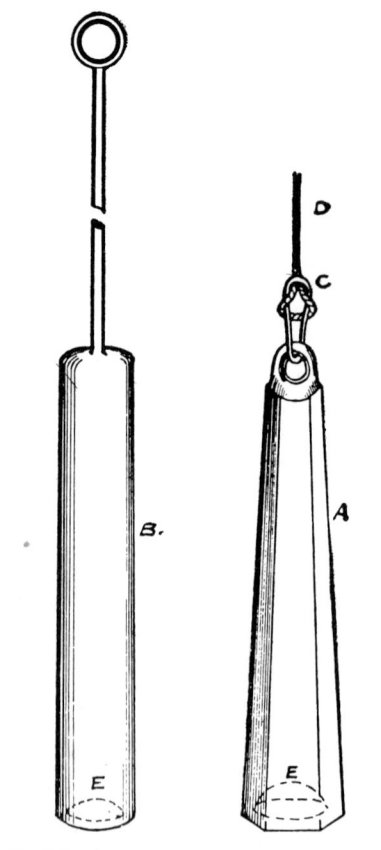

A. Hand Lead
B. Sinker used with patent sounding machine
C. Iron ring for eye of lead line
D. Lead line eye
E. Cavity for arming

and buoyed like the long line or trawl line. Also called whiffing line, ripper line.

Fr: *Ligne à Main;* Ger: *Handleine; Schnurleine; Handangelleine.*

A hand line is made of special hard-laid untarred cotton twine. It is fitted with a spreader to which are attached four snoods, and is weighted with lead. The hooks are fastened at the ends of the snoods.

HANDLING CHARGES. The charges levied against the goods for moving them to and from reach of ship's tackle and the place of rest on wharves, piers, quays, sheds, warehouses. It includes stacking, tiering, breaking out, elevating, and trimming of merchandise on wharves or in sheds and warehouses.

Fr: *Frais de Manutention;* Ger: *Umschlagspesen.*

HAND-LINING. A method of lining in which the line is held by the fisherman and drawn as soon as the pull of the fish on the line is felt. Also called hand-line fishery. It is employed with the boat at anchor or in motion. Fishing at anchor or moored is subdivided into ground fishing and drift-line fishing.

Fr: *Pêche aux Lignes à Main; Pêche aux Petites Cordes;* Ger: *Handleinefischerei; Handschnurfischerei.*

HAND LOG. A primitive device for measuring a vessel's speed through the water. Also called chip log, ship log, common log. It makes use of a line knotted at every 47 ft. 3 in., and a 28-second sandglass. A weighted piece of wood named the log chip, shaped to the sector of a circle, is attached to the end of the log line and trails astern. The number of knots which go overboard in the wake of the log chip while the 28-second glass is running out is equal to, or is taken as being equal to, the speed of the ship in nautical miles per hour.

Fr: *Loch à Touret;* Ger: *Handlog.*

A 90-ft. length of "stray line" is provided between the log chip and the zero point from which the counting of the log begins. This stray-line portion is intended to carry the log chip clear of the influence of the ship's wake. This form of log is fairly satisfactory for speeds up to about 10 knots and is still used in sailing craft. It has been almost completely supplanted by the patent or taffrail log and by automatic devices such as the pitometer log in mechanically propelled vessels.

HAND MAST. A round stick suitable for mast-making, with a girth at butt of not less than 24 in. (six hands) and not more than 70 in. Round sticks with a smaller girth are called spars.

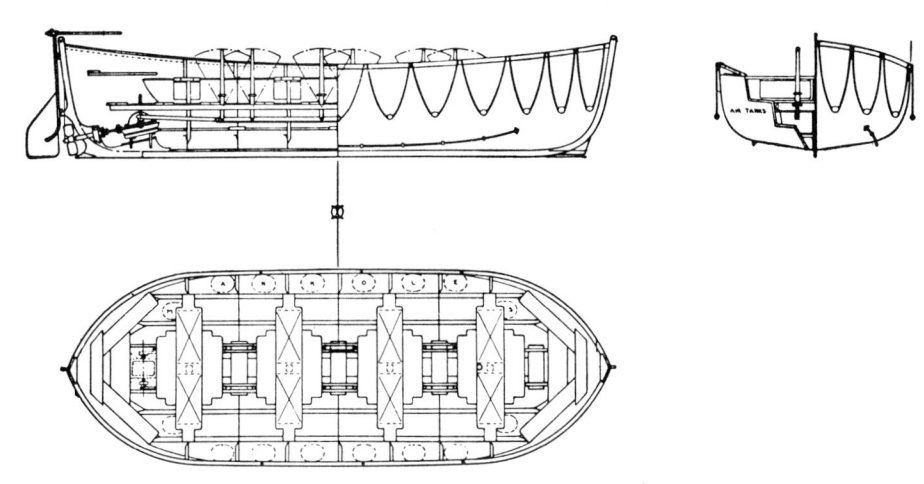

Hand Propeller Metallic Lifeboat With Built-In Air Tanks
(Courtesy Welin Davit and Boat Corporation)

HAND-OPERATED PROPELLER.
See **Boat Propeller Gear.**

HAND OVER HAND. The act of hauling rapidly upon a rope by the men passing their hands alternately one before the other, or one above the other if they are hoisting.
Fr: *Main Sur Main;* Ger: *Hand über Hand.*

HAND PUMP. Hand pumps used on shipboard are worked by cranks or by a lever: they are placed on the upper deck and owing to their high suction are difficult to operate. In mechanically propelled vessels they are used only for emergency purposes or to empty small compartments such as fore- or after peak tanks.
Fr: *Pompe à Bras;* Ger: *Handpumpe.*

HAND RAIL. A rail fitted along the sides of a ladder, also on the top of open railing or bulwark plating of passenger decks. It is made of teakwood about 4 to 8 in. in width or of steel tubing.
Fr: *Main Courante; Rambarde;* Ger: *Handlauf; Handleiste.*
American Marine Standards Committee, Standard 86, *Hand-Rail and Shelf-Rail Fittings,* Washington, 1932.

HAND RIVETING. Riveting performed by two men, each striking alternate blows to hammer the point of the rivet into the required shape.
Fr: *Rivetage à la Main;* Ger: *Handnietung.*

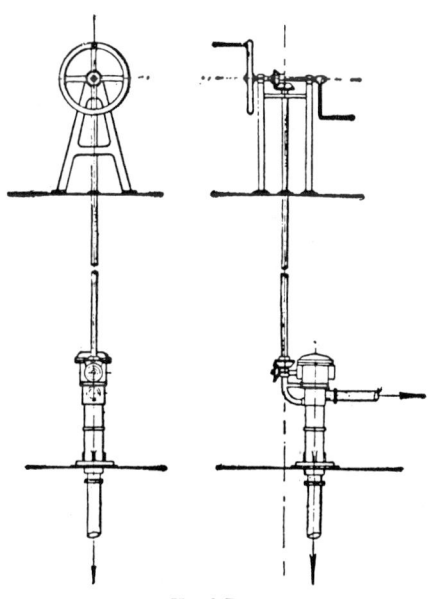

Hand Pump

The weight of hand-riveting hammers varies from 3½ to 5½ lb.; according to the size of rivets. It is generally agreed that hand riveting ceases to be satisfactory when the diameter of rivets exceeds ⅞ in. Hand riveting has been almost entirely supplanted by pneumatic riveting in modern ship construction.

HANDSOMELY. Gradually or carefully,

as when slacking or easing a rope on which there is a strain.
Fr: *A la Demande.*

HANDSPIKE. A bar used as a lever for various purposes, as in moving weights, heaving about a windlass, and so forth. It also refers to a short spike used for splicing and tucking in short ends of wire to finish off a splice.
Fr: *Anspec;* Ger: *Handspake.*

HAND-STEERING GEAR. A steering gear in which the motion of the rudder is imparted by a hand-driven steering wheel of large diameter either directly connected to the rudderhead or through steering chains. Also called hand-power steering gear. In ordinary trading vessels a hand-steering gear is usually provided for use in an emergency in the event of failure of the power-steering gear.
Fr: *Appareil à gouverner à Bras;* Ger: *Handbetriebene Steuermaschine.*

HAND SWAB. A small swab, without handle, made of canvas threads.
Fr: *Faubert;* Ger: *Dweil.*

HAND TILLER. A tiller which, in small boats, consists of a piece of timber inserted in the rudderhead. Also called boat tiller.
Fr: *Barre Franche.*

HANDY BILLY.
See **Hand Deck Pump, Watch Tackle.**

HANDY VESSEL. Applies to vessels which according to the trade they are usually engaged in, can on account of their size, capacity and draft go to practically all ports without restrictions.

HANG.
See **Sny.**

HANGING CLAMP. Iron fitting that can be fixed to various parts of a ship to hang stages to, or the like. Also called C clamp.

HANGING COMPASS. A compass suspended face downwards. A ship's compass arranged for observation from below the card. Sometimes called a tell-tale compass. Also called overhead compass, inverted compass.
Fr: *Compass Renversé;* Ger: *Hängekompass; Kajütskompass.*

HANGING KNEE. Wooden knee having one leg fastened against the upright side or the under side of a beam and the other leg against the ship's side. The need for hanging knees is obviated by installing stronger shelves and clamps.
Fr: *Courbe Verticale;* Ger: *Hängeknie.*

HANGING STAGE. A plank hung by each end over the ship's side for men to sit on while chipping, painting, or doing any other work.
Ger: *Stellage.*

HANK. 1. A small coil of line, yarn, or cord.
Fr: *Manoque;* Ger: *Strähn; Strang; Knäuel.*

2. A fitting of wood, gun metal, or iron seized to the luff of a sail, which is made to run on a stay. It is by the means of hanks that the sail is so secured that it will travel up and down the stay with its luff held close to it. Metal hanks are used with wire stays and wooden ones with hemp or Manila. Mast rings are sometimes called hanks.
Fr: *Bague d'Envergure;* Ger: *Stagreiter; Sauger; Lagel.*

HARBOR. Any place which affords good anchorage and a fairly safe station for ships, or in which ships can be sheltered by the land from wind and sea. Also called haven. It is not necessary that it be landlocked or absolutely safe for ships. It is enough that it affords a reasonably safe place of retreat from wind and storms. A place where ships are brought for commercial purposes to load and unload goods and passengers.

The term "harbor" strictly speaking applies only to the area of water with the works necessary for its formation, protection, and maintenance, such as breakwaters, jetties, and so on. A port is made up of a harbor plus the freight and passenger structures such as docks, wharves, quays, and so forth, with their equipment.
Fr: *Port;* Ger: *Hafen.*
Brysson-Cunningham, *Dock Engineering,* London, 1922.

HARBOR AUTHORITY. In Great Britain, applies to all persons or bodies of persons corporate or unincorporate, who are proprietors of, or entrusted with the duty or invested with the power of constructing, improving, managing, maintaining or lighting, a harbor.
Fr: *Autorites Portuairés;* Ger: *Hafenbehörde.*

HARBOR CHARTER (U. S.). An oral contract for the hiring of a harbor craft, the terms of which may be largely customary.

HARBOR COMMISSION. A duly authorized and appointed body of persons to whom is entrusted the management and operation of a commercial harbor.

HARBOR DECK. A term applied to the side deck lying close to the waterline in a turret-deck vessel. It is formed by the inboard curvature of the side plating between the trunk and the sides of the vessel.

Fr: *Pont de Refuge;* Ger: *Hafendeck.*

HARBOR DUES. Various local charges against all seagoing vessels entering a harbor, to cover maintenance of channel depths, anchorage grounds, buoys, lights and generally all maintenance and administration expenses. Also called harbormaster's fees, harbor fees. Harbor dues include tonnage dues, light dues, buoy dues, anchorage dues. Fishing boats, tugs, lighters, and other harbor craft are usually exempted.

Fr: *Frais de Navigation; Péages; Droits de Navigation;* Ger: *Hafenmeistergebühren; Befahrungsabgaben.*

Anderson, J., "The Assessment of Harbour and Other Dues for Merchant Ships," Institution of Engineers and Shipbuilders in Scotland, *Transactions.* vol. 65 (1922); Ritherdon, R., *Dues and Port Charges on Shipping Throughout the World,* New York, 1920; U. S. War Department, Corps of Engineers, Miscellaneous Series 1, *Port and Terminal Charges at United States Seaports,* Washington, 1942.

HARBOR GASKET. A gasket made of plaited stuff or strips of canvas for use when a vessel is in port and sails are furled in a body. The yardarm and quarter gaskets are passed square. The bunt gaskets cross each other.

Fr: *Tresse Plate;* Ger: *Hafenbeschlagseising.*

HARBOR LAUNCH. A launch used in harbors for various purposes, such as a tender to vessels calling, also for carrying people between ship and shore, for lifesaving, for carrying quarantine officers, and so on. Also called general service launch. These boats are usually decked forward, the cabin occupying the after space.

Fr: *Vedette;* Ger: *Hafenbarkasse.*

HARBOR LINE. A line along the shore of a navigable waterway, established by legislative authority, out to which the owners of the upland have the privilege of filling in and building.

HARBOR MANAGER (G. B.). The chief executive of a port authority. Also called port director, harbor board president (U. S.).

HARBORMASTER. 1. An officer who has charge of mooring and berthing of ships and of enforcing the regulations respecting a harbor. He is usually a State official with extensive authority. He has power to regulate the times of landing and the unloading and loading of vessels, to make room for such as need to be immediately accommodated; to collect harbor fees; and to enforce obedience to his lawful orders.

Fr: *Capitaine de Port;* Ger: *Hafenkapitän.*

2. Refers to a dock employee designated by the head stevedore to shift lighters or other craft alongside the dock and hatches. He is responsible for placing all floating cargo where and when needed.

HARBOR OF REFUGE. A harbor provided as a temporary refuge on a stormy coast for the convenience of passing shipping. Also called port of refuge. It may or may not be part of a shipping port.

Fr: *Port de Refuge;* Ger: *Nothafen; Zufluchtshafen.*

HARBOR SIGNALS. A general term for local signals, such as pilot and quarantine signals, tidal signals, traffic signals, and any other local signal used for the working of a port. Also called port signals.

Fr: *Signaux de Port;* Ger: *Hafensignale.*

HARBOR STOW. See **Furl.**

HARBOR TUG. A small tug used for various duties in a harbor, roadstead, or estuary, such as towing barges and lighters, docking, undocking, helping ships up to moorings, and turning them when leaving moorings. Also called craft tug, barge tug.

Fr: *Remorqueur de Port;* Ger: *Hafenschlepper.*

In many ports a design of tug has been developed which best meets the local requirements of each harbor. Hardly two harbors are alike in the exact type of vessel that is employed.

Courtney, R. C. W., "Harbor Tug Design," *Marine Engineer* (London), vol. 58 (April, 1935).

HARD. 1. To the full extent; therefore, to put the helm hard over; to put it as far as it will go in the direction indicated, that is, port or starboard.

Fr: *Toute;* Ger: *Hart.*

2. A sloping stone roadway or jetty at the water's edge for convenience in landing and putting out.

A firm foreshore used for beaching boats.

HARD AND FAST. Said of a vessel when

firmly aground on the rocks, a shoal, or a beach.
Fr: *Bien pris;* Ger: *Hoch und Trocken.*
HARDENING UP. Operation performed in riveting work to provide a harder set on a rivet point. It is accomplished by coming back with the hammer and finishing it off after it has cooled somewhat.
Fr: *Rebattage.*
HARD FISH. A term applied to cod, ling, haddock, and so on, when salted and dried.
Ger: *Getrockneter Stockfisch.*
HARD HERRING. Name given in England to a highly cured herring prepared for foreign consumption. The fish are salted in brine for 2 days and then smoked for a period of 2 to 3 weeks. The red herring may be defined as a round herring heavily salted and smoked for a long time. It is exported to Italy and other Mediterranean countries and can be kept for months in dry condition.
Ger: *Bückling.*
HARD LAY. In cordage, an angle of lay greater than the standard lay. It reduces the breaking strain and flexibility of the rope but produces more compactness and resistance to the absorption of moisture. Also called short lay.
HARD PATCH. A riveted patch made watertight by calking.
Fr: *Placard maté;* Ger: *Genieteter Flick.*
See **Soft Patch.**
HARDWOOD. Timber converted from slow-growing trees, which bear leaves, as distinguished from the needles of the softwooded conifers. Hardwoods mostly used for ship- and boatbuilding include elm, ash, oak, teak, mahogany, beech, hackmatack, American whitewood.
Fr: *Bois dur;* Ger: *Hartholz; Laubholz.*
See **Wood.**
U. S. Bureau of Standards, Commercial Standard, C.S. 60–36, *Hardwood Dimension Lumber,* Washington, 1936.
HARING SCHUYT. A Dutch herring boat, similar in design and rig to the *schokker* but of smaller tonnage and with less freeboard.
HARMATTAN. A periodical easterly wind from northeast to east-northeast which prevails on the west coast of Africa generally in December, January, and February, between 30° of latitude and the equator.
Fr: *Harmattan;* Ger: *Harmattan.*
HARMONIC ANALYSIS. A mathematical process used for tidal predictions by which the observed tide at any place is resolved into a number of simple constituent tides.
It is based on the relative positions of the earth, sun, and moon and their ever changing relative distances, all of which exert an effect on the tidal undulation. Their mutual attraction results in a composite wave, the reduction of which into constituent simple waves, and their recombination according to the distances and positions of the sun, earth, and moon, are obtained by this method.
Schureman, P., *Manual of Harmonic Analysis and Prediction of Tides,* U. S. Coast and Geodetic Survey, Special Publication 98, Washington, D. C., 1924.
HARMONIC CONSTANTS. Tidal constants which consist of the amplitudes and epochs of the harmonic constituents.
Fr: *Constantes Harmoniques;* Ger: *Harmonische Konstante.*
See **Harmonic Analysis.**
HARMONIC CONSTITUENT. One of the harmonic elements in a mathematical expression for tide-producing force and in corresponding formulas for the tide itself.
Fr: *Composante Harmonique;* Ger: *Harmonische Komponent.*
HARNESS CASK. A cask kept on deck, in which brine is soaked from salt beef preparatory to cooking. It is usually partitioned and the beef stays one week in each of the two sections.
Fr: *Baille à Salaisons;* Ger: *Rationsfass.*
HARNESS HITCH. A hitch used for fastening a man to a bowline. It enables a loop to be quickly made in a rope, the ends of which are not free.
Fr: *Gueule de Raie;* Ger: *Notstek.*
HARPINS. The continuation of the ribbands at the forward and after ends of a ship under construction and so fastened to keep the cant frames in original position until the outside planking or plating is worked. Also called harpings. Harpins are trimmed to required shape, while ribbands are made of straight timber and bent if necessary.
Fr: *Lisses d'exécution;* Ger: *Bugsente; Hecksente.*
HARPOON. A missile weapon for capturing marine mammals and large fish, consisting essentially of a barbed head and a shank to which a long cord is attached. Also called hand harpoon.
Fr: *Harpon;* Ger: *Harpune.*
See **Gun Harpoon.**
HARPOONEER. One who harpoons a

whale. Also *harponier*. The word harpooner is not used by whalemen.

HARPOON LOG. A patent screw log in which the indicating dials and wheel work are enclosed in a cylindrical case of the same diameter as the body of the rotator or fan, forming with it a compact machine which is towed astern. This type of log has to be hauled aboard for each reading and for this reason has been generally superseded by the taffrail log.

HARPOON OAR. The forward oar in a whaling boat, which was pulled by the harponeer in approaching a whale. (Obsolete.)

HARP-SHAPE SHACKLE. A lyre-shaped shackle used for joining the chain cable to the anchor, so shaped that another cable may be fastened in addition to the ordinary chain. It is not used with stockless anchors. Also called harp shackle, Jews' harp, club link.
 Fr: *Manille à Violon; Main d'Ancre;*
 Ger: *Ankerschakel.*

HARTFORD SHACKLE. A special shackle for securing chain cable to a buoy.

HASP. A hinged metal strap at the stemhead of a sloop, fastened by a forelock in order to secure the bowsprit down.
 Fr: *Moraillon; Blin;* Ger: *Haspe; Klampe.*
 See **Mast Hasp.**

HASTINGS PUNT. Local name given on the south coast of England to an open fishing boat used for inshore trawling. The hull is round-bottomed with lute stern and clinker planking. Except for a small cuddy at the fore end they are undecked. The rig is that of a two-masted lugger with short mizzenmast, and small jib, which sets on a reeving bowsprit. Length over-all 17 ft. Length on keel 15 ft. Breadth 7.5 ft. Depth 2.2 ft. (Typical.)

HAT BOX. See **Drain.**

HATCH. An opening, generally rectangular, in a ship's deck affording access into the compartment below. Also *hatchway.*
 Fr: *Panneau; Écoutille;* Ger: *Luke.*
 Burn, W. S., "Hatchways," Institution of Naval Architects (London), *Transactions,* vol. 79 (1937).

HATCH BAR. Wooden beams or steel bars laid across the top of a cargo hatchway, over the tarpaulins, to prevent the latter from surging. Hatch bars are bolted down at each end. Also called hatch clamping beam.
 Ger: *Lukeneisen; Längsriegel.*

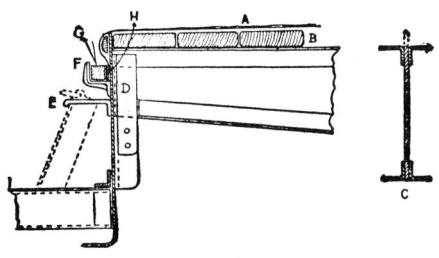

Hatch
A. Tarpaulin
B. Hatch Covers
C. Hatch Beam—Hatch Web—Strong Back
D. Beam Socket—Beam Shoe—Hatch Beam Carrier
E. Coaming Stiffener
F. Coaming cleat—Batten cleat—Hatch batten clip
G. Battening Wedge—Hatch Wedge
H. Battening Iron—Hatch Batten
I. Deck

HATCH BATTEN. A flat iron bar used for securing the edges of the tarpaulin against the hatch coamings. The batten and edge of the tarpaulin are kept in place by the hatch and cleats and wedges. Also called battening bar, hatch bar, battening iron.
 Fr: *Barre d'Écoutille;* Ger: *Schalklatte; Persenningleiste; Schalkleiste; Lukenschalk.*

HATCH BATTEN CLIP.
See **Hatch Cleat.**

HATCH BEAM. A portable transverse beam placed across a cargo hatchway, that acts as a bearer to support the hatch covers. The ends fit into sockets riveted to the inside face of hatch coamings. Also called hatchway beam, hatch web, bridle beam.
 Fr: *Barrot Mobile;* Ger: *Schiebebalken; Scherstock.*

HATCH BOAT (U. S.). A small half-decked fishing vessel having one or more wells closed by hatches, for live fish.

HATCH BOOM. A boom which plumbs a cargo hatch and is used in connection with a yard boom. Also called hatch derrick.

HATCH CARLING. A fore-and-aft girder at the side of a hatchway, running under the coamings, to which the partial or half deck beams are connected.
 Fr: *Hiloire Renversée;* Ger: *Lukenrippe; Lukenschlinge.*

HATCH CARRIER. A steel fitting riveted to the inner surface of the hatch coaming to support the end of a fore-and-after or hatch beam (crossbeam). Also called hatch socket, beam socket, hatch beam shoe.

Fr: *Support de Barrot Mobile;* *Support de Galiote;* Ger: *Schiebebalkenlager.*

HATCH CHECKER (U. S.). A checker or tallyman who records the marks and numbers of packages loaded into a specific hold or 'tween-deck and informs the plan clerk as to location. Plan clerk and hatch checkers work together for the purpose of establishing exact stowage of all cargo loaded.

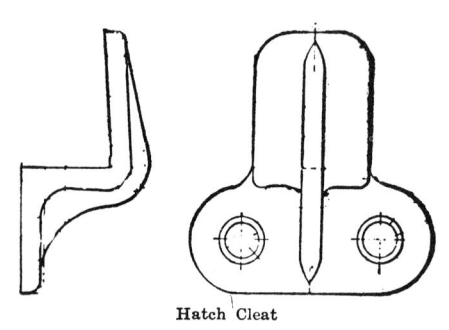

Hatch Cleat

HATCH CLEAT. One of the clips attached to the outside of the cargo hatch coamings for holding hatch battens and edges of tarpaulin covers. Also called hatch batten clip, batten cleat.

Fr: *Taquet d'Hiloire;* Ger: *Schalkklampe; Schalkklampenwinkel.*

As laid down by international convention, hatch cleats are to have a minimum width of 2½ in. They should be spaced at intervals of not more than 24 in. from center to center and end cleats should not be more than 6 in. from hatch corners.

HATCH COAMING. The vertical plating built around a hatchway to prevent water from getting below, to serve as framework for the strongbacks, hatch covers, and so on, and to secure the tarpaulins. Its purpose is also to stiffen the edges of the hatch openings thereby restoring the strength lost to the deck by cutting these openings.

Fr: *Hiloire; Surbau;* Ger: *Luksulle.*

HATCH COVER. A wooden cover or metallic shutter fitted over a hatchway to prevent the ingress of water into the ship's hold. Also called hatchway cover.

Fr: *Panneau d'Écoutille;* Ger: *Lukendeckel.*

There are many types available and these may be classified as follows: (1) ordinary wood covers with or without metal reinforcements at ends; (2) small metal covers of various designs and of the same size and battening arrangements as the wood covers; (3) large steel hinged covers of same dimensions as the hatchway and generally so constructed that hatch beams can be dispensed with. In this type no tarpaulins are provided, soft packing being used to make a watertight joint with the hatch coamings. Wood covers are usually made of white pine or spruce planks in sections which can be handled by the crew. Pitch pine covers with ends protected by steel bands or closed end shoes are frequently found in better class ships. Double-plank covers are strengthened by a vertical galvanized center plate between the planks.

"Fermeture des panneaux de chargement," Bureau Veritas (Paris), *Bulletin Technique,* March, 1937; Schwarz, F., "Die Lukenverschlüsse und Sicherheit der Schiffe," Schiffbautechnische Gesellschaft, *Jahrbuch,* vol. 28 (1927).

HATCH DAVIT. A small portable davit overhanging a hatch, used for loading or unloading light weights, stores, provisions, by means of a whip, the block of which is hooked into an eye in the upper end of the davit.

Fr: *Bossoir d'Écoutille;* Ger: *Lukendavit.*

HATCH DERRICK. A derrick or cargo boom worked in conjunction with a yard derrick. It lifts the draft from the vessel's hold until it gets above deck whence it is taken over by the yard derrick and swung over the ship's side.

Fr: *Mât de charge d'en dedans;* Ger: *Lukenbaum.*

HATCH-END BEAM. A strong beam fitted at the end of a hatchway to compensate for the reduction in structural strength caused by the opening in the deck.

Fr: *Barrot d'extrémité de Panneau;* Ger: *Lukenendbalken.*

HATCH END PROTECTION. A metal fitting which protects the ends of wooden hatch covers. It is either an open end-band or a closed end-shoe.

HATCHET. A small ax with a short handle designed to be used with one hand. It forms part of the regulation outfit for ship's lifeboats.

Fr: *Hachot;* Ger: *Kappbeil.*

HATCH FOREMAN. One of the longshoremen who supervises the dock, deck and hold gangs of a specific hatch to see that cargo is efficiently handled and stowed in the designated part of the ship. Hatch foremen receive their instructions from the ship foreman.

HATCH GRATING. Wooden grating placed over a hatching in lieu of a solid hatch cover to ensure ventilation between decks. Also called **grating hatch**.
  Fr: *Caillebolis de panneau;* Ger: *Lukengrating.*

HATCH-HOURS. A unit of labor time which represents the total number of hours worked at all hatches of the ship in loading or discharging cargo.

HATCH-LOCKING BAR. A flat iron bar laid across the top of a hatchway and secured at one end by a padlock, so that there may be no unauthorized entry into the ship's cargo spaces. When a hatch is bonded the custom seal is placed on the bolt of the locking bars.
  Ger: *Lukenriegel; Lukenbügel.*

HATCHMAN.
  See **Hatch Tender.**

HATCH MAST (U. S.). Applies to a mast located near a hatchway and rigged for handling cargo only.

HATCH MOLDING. A solid or hollow bar of half-round section fitted at the top of hatch coamings to protect the tarpaulin from damage by chafing against the sharp edges of the coaming plates.

HATCH-REST BAR. An angle bar of special rolled section or a Zee bar running along the upper edge of the hatch-coaming plates and forming a ledge for the ends of the hatch covers to rest on. Also called **ledge bar, hatch-rest section, hatch bearer, hatch-ledge bar, hatch zee.**

Hatch Rest Bar

  Fr: *Cornière d'Appui de Panneau;* Ger: *Lukenprofileisen.*

HATCH RING. One of the iron rings at each end of hatch covers, used for lifting the covers or put them in place.
  Fr: *Boucle de Panneau;* Ger: *Ringartiger Lukendeckelgriff.*

HATCH SOCKET. See **Carrier.**

HATCH SPEED. The speed of transfer of cargo between the ship's hold and the apron of the pier or quay. At U. S. ports it is usually given per stevedore gang per hour. In other ports in tons per hour.

HATCH STANCHION. One of the portable stanchions fitted around the hatch opening of a lower deck as a protection against people falling below by accident.

  Fr: *Chandelier d'Écoutille;* Ger: *Lukenstütze.*

HATCH STOPPER. A strong rope fastened on the hatch coaming to assist the hatch coaming as a partial compensation for the opening in the deck plating. Also called **hatch-side girder.** It transmits the load or part thereof from the half beams to the hatch-end beams.
  Fr: *Hiloire Renversée;* Ger: *Lukenlängsträger.*

HATCH TACKLE. A tackle suspended over a hatch for handling cargo or stores. Also called **hatch whip.**
  Ger: *Lukentalje.*

HATCH TENDER. One of the men belonging to a deck gang of longshoremen. He is stationed at the hatchway opening, gives the necessary signals to the winchman, supervises the raising and lowering of sling-loads, and attends to the falls when necessary. Also called **hatchman, hatchminder, hatch signal man.**

HATCH TENT. A tarpaulin or canvas awning spread over an open hatchway during heavy rain while loading or unloading. Also called **rain cloth** or **rain awning.**
  Fr: *Taud;* Ger: *Regenzelt; Regensegel.*

HATCHWAY.
  See **Hatch.**

HATCH WEB.
  See **Beam.**

HATCH WEDGE. 1. A triangular piece of hardwood used for securing the hatch battens and thus holding the tarpaulins in place. The wedge is driven hard between the cleat and the batten and is made of wood having good swelling capacities when wetted.
  2. In hinged, dogged hatches, wedge-shaped forgings fitted to the hatch frame, upon which the hatch dogs bear when set up.
  Fr: *Coin d'Écoutille;* Ger: *Lukenschalkkeil.*

HATCH WHIP. A cargo whip used with a boom or derrick over a hatchway to lower or raise the cargo from the ship's hold. Also called **up-and-down fall.**
  Fr: *Cartahu d'en dedans.*

HATTA-AMI-BUNE. Japanese fishing sampan from Kumamoto working with nets. It is rigged with one or two masts. Sails made of Matsuemon native cotton cloth. Length over-all 42 ft. Breadth 10.0 ft. Depth

3.9 ft. Draft 2.5 ft. Displacement 12.8 tons. (Typical.)
HATTAKUCHI-BUNE. Small Japanese circle-net fishing sampan from Kumamoto. Length over-all 30 ft. Breadth 8 ft. Depth 2.6 ft. (Typical.) It is rigged with two masts. The sails are made of a kind of cotton drill called *ayamomen*.
HATTATE-BUNE. Small Japanese fishing sampan from Kumamoto, rigged with two masts. Length over-all 28 ft. Breadth 7.5 ft. Depth 2.3 ft.
HAUL. A single draft of a net or the fish caught by hauling a net once.
Ger: *Stelle; Fischzug.*
HAUL (to). 1. To move a vessel in a harbor from one pier or quay to another, or across a river. Also called to shift.
Fr: *Déhaler;* Ger: *Werpen.*
2. The changing of the direction of the wind toward the ship's head. The opposite of "to veer."
3. To alter a ship's course, change the direction of sailing, move on a new course.
Fr: *Changer;* Ger: *Drehen.*
4. To pull on a rope, in a general sense. It is more particularly applied when pulling upon a single rope without the assistance of blocks or other mechanical contrivance. The particular nature of the pull is usually indicated by the word used with "haul," as "haul up," "haul in," and so on.
Fr: *Haler;* Ger: *Holen; Ziehen.*
HAUL AROUND. Sailing ship term to denote the action of bracing around simultaneously all the yards of a mast when going about ship.
Fr: *Changer;* Ger: *Rundbrassen.*
HAUL BLOCK. A steel block slung under a cargo derrick, to give a fair lead to the cargo whip from the cargo block down to the winch drum. Also called lead block.
Fr: *Poulie Basse;* Ger: *Fussblock; Leitblock.*
HAUL DOWN. The opposite of hoisting.
Fr: *Amener;* Ger: *Niederholen.*
HAUL FORWARD. When the direction of the wind changes it is said to haul forward if it finally blows from a direction nearer to the ship's head. Also called to draw ahead.
Fr: *Refuser;* Ger: *Vorwärtsdrehen; Schrallen.*
HAUL IN. 1. To pull or bowse at a single rope.
Fr: *Haler;* Ger: *Einholen.*
2. To haul in with, means to change the course of a ship so as to approach an object.

Fr: *Rallier;* Ger: *Nähern.*
HAULING LINE. 1. A small line, of ¼-in. diameter or larger made of 3-strand, tarred hemp Manila, secured to a hawser and thrown to an approaching vessel or a dock by means of which a heavier line is hauled ashore. Also called heaving line. A small sandbag containing about 1½ lb. of sand is occasionally attached to one end of the line.
Fr: *Ligne d'Attrape; Lance Amarre;* **Ger:** *Wurfleine.*
2. A small line lowered to the deck from aloft to be bent on to such small articles as are used for work going on in the rigging, as a maul, a marline spike, and the like.
Fr: *Va et Vient;* Ger: *Jolle.*
3. Twine used to seize the selvage of a net to the fish-net rope.
HAULING OFF BUOY. A harbor buoy placed in midstream or in the middle of a dock and to which a vessel makes fast when moving away from her berth.
Fr: *Bouée de déhalage;* Ger: *Verholboje.*
HAULING PART. The free end of a fall, which is laid hold of in hauling.
Fr: *Courant;* Ger: *Anholpart.*
HAULING WIND. A wind that changes around the compass in the direction of the movements of clock hands or with the sun. Also called veering wind. When the wind changes its direction toward the bow of the ship it is said to haul (U. S.).
Fr: *Virement du Vent;* Ger: *Umspringender Wind; Ausschiessender Wind.*
HAUL OFF. To alter the course of a ship so as to get further away from an object.
Fr: *S'élever;* Ger: *Entfernen.*
HAUL ROUND. A change in the direction of the wind from east to west by way of the south, or in a clockwise direction. Also called to haul around.
Fr: *Sauter;* Ger: *Umspringen; Drehen.*
HAUL TAUT. To take in the slack, to tighten up.
Fr: *Embraquer; Appuyer;* Ger: *Los Einholen.*
HAUL UP. A sailing vessel is said to haul up when it comes or is brought nearer to the wind, or nearer its course if it has been sailing to leeward of it.
Fr: *Loffer;* Ger: *Aufgeien; Anluven.*
HAUL-UP LINE. In the otter trawl fisheries, a line with one end fastened to the splitting strop and the other to a becket in the center of the head rope where it is readily accessible as the net comes up to

the surface. By hauling on this line the splitting strop is raised above water and the fish tackle can be hooked preparatory to getting the cod end aboard.

HAVANA DOCK. A floating dock in which the side walls are given the full depth of the structure. The floor pontoons are bolted to the walls with fish plate joints. The end pontoons are shaped to bow and stern lines to improve their navigability. It is so named because the first dock constructed on this principle was located in Havana.

Ger: *Havannadock*.

HAVERSINE. A contraction of "half-versed sine." The versed sine of an angle is the difference between the cosine and unity, and is written "versine." The use of haversines is peculiar to the nautical profession; navigational tables contain the natural haversines and also the logarithmic haversines for all angles.
Goodwin, H. B., "The Haversine in Nautical Astronomy," U. S. Naval Institute *Proceedings*, vol. 36 (1910), p. 735.

HAWSE. 1. That part of the bow where the hawsepipes are located. **2.** The space between the ship's head and the anchors. The area of water which extends from the ship itself when anchored to the point on the water surface directly above the anchor. **3.** The situation of the cables before the ship's stem when moored with two anchors, out from forward, one on the starboard and the other on the port bow.

Fr: *Touée*.

See Athwart Hawse, Bold Hawse, Clear Hawse, Cross in the Hawse, Elbow in the Hawse, Foul Hawse, Open Hawse, Round Turn in the Hawse, Hawse-Full

HAWSE BAG.
See Jackass.

HAWSE BLOCK. A wooden plug which fits into a hawsepipe to prevent the entrance of sea water. Also called hawse plug.

Fr: *Tampon d'écubier*; Ger: *Klusedeckel*.

HAWSE BOLSTER. 1. In a steel vessel, one of the bossings at each end of a hawsepipe to ease the cable over the edges and prevent undue abrasive action of the chain. **2.** A rounded piece of hardwood sheathed with iron and fitted around the hawseholes of a wooden vessel as a protection against chafing by the cable. Also called bolster.

Fr: *Coussin d'écubier*; Ger: *Klusebacke, Klusenpolster*.

HAWSE BUCKLER. Iron plate shutter over a hawsepipe, used to confine the hawse plug and prevent the inrush of sea water. Also called hawse flap.

Fr: *Mantelet d'écubier*; Ger: *Klusendeckel*.

HAWSE-FALLEN. To ride hawse-fallen is to be anchored with the water coming in at the hawseholes carrying everything before it.

HAWSE-FULL. A vessel at anchor is said to be riding hawse-full or to be hawsing when lying uneasy and pitching heavily.

HAWSEHOLE. One of the cylindrical holes in the bows of a vessel on each side of the stem, into which the hawsepipes are fitted.

Fr: *Écubier*; Ger: *Kluseloch*.

HAWSE HOOK. The breasthook over the hawseholes.

Ger: *Klusenband*.

HAWSEPIECE. In a wooden vessel one of the cant frames standing next to the knightheads and fitted close together so as to form a solid mass of timber for the passage of the hawseholes. Also called hawse timber.

Fr: *Allonge d'écubier*; Ger: *Klusholz*.

HAWSEPIPE. A cylindrical or elliptical pipe made of cast steel or iron, situated

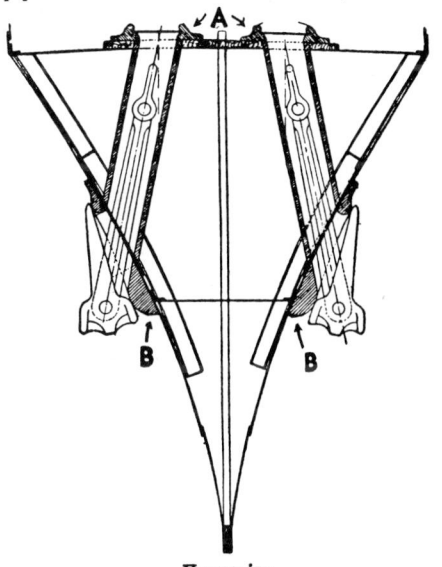

Hawsepipe
A. Deck Flange B. Shell Flange

near the stem, through which the anchor cable runs.
  Fr: *Manchon d'écubier; Écubier de Mouillage;* Ger: *Ankerkluse; Klusenrohr.*

According to the type of anchor the hawsepipe may be formed by a heavy rim for the passage of the cable, or by a casting which forms a lining for the hawsehole proper and prevents the cable from tearing the bow plating. In ships carrying their anchors stowed (stockless anchors) in the hawsepipes the latter are made with an inside diameter of 10 to 14 times the nominal chain size so that the pin in the bending shackle will be accessible. Heavy rounded flanges or bolsters are provided to bear against the bow plating and deck.

HAWSER. Fiber rope 5 to 24 in. in circumference used for towing or working the ship. It may be plain-laid or hawser-laid (left-handed).
  Fr: *Aussière;* Ger: *Trosse; Kabeltau.*

When plain-laid it is usually called towline. A wire towline or warping hawser is generally made with 6 strands and 37 wires to each strand. It has no hemp core in the strands, but has a hemp center core. Circumference 1 to 8¾ in.

HAWSER BEND. A method of joining two hawsers which must reeve through a small opening. Also called reeving line bend. It occupies less space than the carrick bend. It is made by taking a half hitch with each end around the other hawser, and seizing the ends.
  Fr: *Noeud d'Étalingure;* Ger: *Kabelstek; Trossenstek.*

HAWSER-LAID ROPE. A rope in which 3 right-handed strands are laid up left-hand. Manila hawser-laid ropes are manufactured in sizes ranging from ⅝ in. to 15 in. in circumference; hemp from ½ to 16 in.
  Fr: *Cordage commis en Aussière; Aussière en Trois;* Ger: *Trossenschlag Tauwerk.*

Hawser-laid ropes do not require a heart because the angles formed by the union of the 3 strands are so obtuse that the pressure of the operation of closing causes the strands to fill up the central space completely. Nowadays the terms "hawser-laid" and "cable-laid" are applied indiscriminately to 9-stranded and 3-stranded rope.

HAWSER PORT. See **Mooring Pipe.**

HAWSER REEL. A heavy reel for the stowage of hawsers when not in use. In its simplest form it consists of a cylindrical drum on which the hawser is wound. At each end a disc-shaped guard is fitted to keep the hawser in place. Hawser reels are generally mounted on frames with a brake by which the paying out of the rope can be controlled.
  Fr: *Touret à Aussière;* Ger: *Trossenwinde.*

HAWSE ROPE. See **Dip Rope.**

HAWSER RUDDER. A kind of jury rudder consisting of a length of hawser run out over the stern of the vessel, with guys from its extreme end leading to each quarter of the ship. By hauling in and slacking away the guys the ship may be roughly steered.

HAWSER THIMBLE. A large galvanized thimble with wide score for splicing into the ends of heavy wire mooring ropes. It ranges in size, measured by width at the widest part, from 5½ in. to 11 in.
  Fr: *Cosse d'Aussière;* Ger: *Trosskauschen.*

HAWSE TIMBER. See **Hawsepiece.**

HAWSING IRON. Wood calking tool with long iron handle attached. Also called horsing iron, horse iron. It is held by one man and driven in the seams by another with a horsing beetle. It is driven into the seams after the oakum has been set with a light iron to drive it home. It may be sharp like the reaming iron or it may have a square edge like the calking iron. Used only in heavy work.
  Fr: *Pataras Travaillant;* Ger: *Klameieisen.*

HAZE. Minute droplets of water suspended in the air, producing in the aggregate an opaqueness of the atmosphere. Also called water haze. A grayish vapor less dense than a fog.
  Fr: *Brumasse;* Ger: *Dunst.*

HAZY. State of the atmosphere when obscured by haze.
  Fr: *Brumeux;* Ger: *Hasiges Wetter; Dunstig.*

HE. Single-outrigger dugout canoe from Lifu (Chabrol) Island, Loyalty Islands.

HEAD. 1. In net-making, the end at which a net is started as opposed to the foot, the end at which it is finished. Also called selvage, headmasting, ringmasting, twine meshing.

2. The upper side of a square sail. The upper side of a quadrilateral fore-and-aft sail.
  Fr: *Tétière; Envergure;* Ger: *Rahliek; Oberliek.*

3. The upper part of a triangular fore-and-aft sail, such as a jib or staysail, where the halyards are made fast.

Fr: *Point de Drisse;* Ger: *Kopf.*
4. The upper end of any object such as a mast, a spar, a frame, a rudder, and so on.
Fr: *Tête;* Ger: *Kopf.*
5. The whole forepart of a ship including the bows.
Fr: *Avant;* Ger: *Vorderteil; Bug.*
HEAD FOR. To have the ship's head pointing toward a certain object or destination.
Fr: *Faire Cap Sur;* Ger: *Liegen.*
HEADBOARD. A small piece of boarding grooved around its edge to receive the end of the bolt rope, fastened at the head of a jib or Bermuda sail. The sail's upper thimble is seized to it.
Ger: *Kopfbrett.*
See **Trail Board.**
HEAD CHEEK. One of the outside knees worked above and below the hawsepipes in the angle formed by the planking and stem. They were ornamented and formed the basis of the head, connecting the whole structure of the bows to which they were bolted. Also called cheek knee. (Obsolete.)
Fr: *Dauphin;* Ger: *Schlussknie; Schliessknie.*
HEAD CRINGLE. The loop worked into the upper corners of a square sail, the upper and after corner (peak) of a quadrilateral fore-and-aft sail, or the head of a triangular sail.
Fr: *Patte d'Empointure;* Ger: *Kopflagel.*
HEAD EARING. One of the ropes which secure the two upper cringles of a square sail to the yardarms by alternate passings of the line through the head cringles and around the spar.
Fr: *Raban d'Empointure;* Ger: *Nockbindsel.*
HEADER. 1. A name given on Newfoundland cod fishing vessels to the man who cuts open the fish, tears out the entrails, and breaks off the head of fish before passing them on to the gutter or splitter.
Fr: *Etêteur;* Ger: *Kopfabschneider.*
2. One who supervises a small group of longshoremen. Also called straw boss.
See **Carling.**
HEAD FOREMAN. See **Ship Foreman.**
HEAD HOLE. One of the eyelets in the tablings of a sail through which the rovings are thrust.
Fr: *Oeillet de Tétière;* Ger: *Gatchen.*
HEADING. The direction in which a ship actually points or heads at any particular moment. It is the angle between the meridian and the ship's keel, and is expressed in the same manner as the course.
Fr: *Cap;* Ger: *Richtung.*
HEADLAND. A precipitous cape or promontory.
Fr: *Promontoire;* Ger: *Landzunge.*
HEADLAND LIGHT. A lighthouse located on a cape or promontory and chiefly used for coastal navigation. These lights are as a rule less powerful than landfall lights.
HEADLEDGE. The athwartship coamings at the forward and afterends of a hatchway. Also called end coaming.
Fr: *Hiloire Transversale;* Ger: *Quersull; Querlukensull.*
HEADLIGHT. A white light carried on the foremast of a power-driven vessel when under way.
Fr: *Feu de tête de mât;* Ger: *Topplaterne.*
HEADLINE. The corked line of a fish net which gives the net the necessary buoyancy to hang perpendicularly by its own weight. It is generally made of two parallel ropes with their lay in opposite directions to prevent kinking. Also called net rope, cork rope, float line, top rope, cork line, upper taut, top back and flue.
Fr: *Fincelle;* Ger: *Sperreep; Speerreep.*
HEAD MONEY.
See **Bounty.**
HEAD NETTING. An ornamental netting formerly used in merchant ships instead of the planking fayed to the headrails.
Ger: *Seitennetz des Galions.*
HEAD ON. With the head of the ship directly toward or in a right line with some object, or the sea or wind.
Fr: *Droit Devant;* Ger: *Genau von Vorn.*
HEAD OUTHAUL. The line by which the head of a standing gaffsail is hauled out. It is rove through a sheave at end of gaff and block at mast.
Fr: *Hale dehors de pic;* Ger: *Gaffelausholer.*
HEAD PUMP. A hand pump taking water through a sea cock placed forward of the collision bulkhead in the forepeak.
Ger: *Bugpumpe.*
HEADRAIL. One of the rails at the ship's head extending from the back of the figurehead to the bow. Also called rail of the head.
Fr: *Lisse d'Éperon;* Ger: *Galionsreling; Galionsleiste.*

HEADREACH. 1. The headway made by a sailing vessel lying atry or trying under very reduced canvas as distinguished from the drift, dead to leeward, made by a vessel when lying ahull.

2. The distance to windward made by a vessel while tacking.

HEADREACHING. A condition of sail trim intermediate between heaving to and turning or beating to windward, when it is desired to make headway, although the circumstances prevent carrying on, running, or turning, in the ordinary manner. When the weather and sea conditions call for heaving to, if there is land to keep clear of to leeward, or if for any other reason an almost entirely leeward drift is not permissible, then the vessel is kept headreaching. That is to say, it is given such amount of sail, so trimmed, and such helm, as to keep it going ahead without forcing it and risking dismasting. Generally, when heaving to a vessel is trying to make as little headway as possible, and when headreaching, as much headway and as little leeway as possible.

HEADROPE. 1. A rope forming the upper edge of the opening in a trawl net, to which the square and wings are marled. Each end is fastened to the top of an otter board. Glass floats or other devices are sometimes fitted along this rope to give more buoyancy and ensure that the mouth of the trawl keeps open. A third otter board is sometimes used for this purpose.

Fr: *Raban de Dos;* Corde de Dos; Ger: *Kopftau.*

2. The rope to which the head of a quadrilateral sail is sewed. The boltrope at the head of a sail.

Fr: *Ralingue d'Envergure;* Ger: *Rahliek; Anschlagliek.*

3. A rope which supports or stays the head of a mast.

HEADSAILS. Generic term for all sails which may be set on the bowsprit, jibboom, and flying jibboom, or forward of the foremost mast. The term is sometimes extended to include the sails set on the foremast.

Fr: *Voiles de l'Avant;* Ger: *Vorsegel.*

HEAD SEA. A sea in which the waves oppose a ship's course, so that the ship must rise over or cut through each. Their effect depends upon their height, form, and speed; sometimes they are steep, quick and irregular, so that a ship is caught by a second before it has recovered from the first.

Fr: *Mer Debout;* Ger: *Gegensee.*

HEADSMAN.
See **Boat Header.**

HEAD SPADE. A long and round-shanked cutting spade used by whalemen for separating the case from the junk, and the latter from the white horse.

HEAD SPRING (FORWARD SPRING). A mooring spring which leads aft (from the ship). Large vessels are frequently moored alongside with two head springs named "Fore head spring" and "After head spring."

Fr: *Garde montante;* Ger: *Bug Achterleine.*

HEADSTAY. In small craft with pole masts such as sailing yachts, the foremast stay which runs from truck to stemhead or bowsprit end. It is commonly known as topmast stay when a fidded topmast is carried.

Fr: *Etai de Flèche;* Ger: *Stengevorstag.*

HEAD STEVEDORE (U. S.). One who hires and supervises all longshoremen for a particular ship and dock; is in charge of all loading and unloading.

HEADSTICK. A short round stick about 15 in. long, to which the head of a triangular sail such as spinnaker or jib, set flying, is fastened before being sewed on. It prevents the head of these sails from twisting, as they are very likely to, because their luff is not confined to a stay.

Fr: *Bâton de Foc;* Ger: *Kluverholz.*

HEAD STRAP. A whaleman's name for a chain sling used in hoisting the case and junk.

HEAD SWELL. Swell advancing directly against or in opposition to the course of the vessel.

Fr: *Houle de l'avant;* Ger: *Gegendunung.*

HEAD TENON. A square tenon which terminates the head of a wooden mast and fits into the cap.

Fr: *Tenon de Chouque;* Ger: *Kopfzapfen.*

HEAD TIMBER. One of the vertical timbers on each side of the knees of the head, resting on the cheek and shoring up the rails of the head.

HEADWAY. A vessel's motion forward or ahead.

Fr: *Erre en Avant;* Ger: *Fahrt.*

HEAD WIND. A breeze blowing from the direction of the ship's intended course. Also

called foul wind.
Fr: *Vent Debout;* Ger: *Gegenwind.*
See **Scant Wind.**

HEAD YARDS. The yards on the foremast of a full-rigged ship.
Fr: *Phare de Misaine;* Ger: *Vortopp.*

HEALTH OFFICER. A medical officer belonging to the harbor authorities' staff and in charge of medical inspection of incoming vessels according to international quarantine regulation. Also called port medical officer. All medical marine operations such as isolation of crew, fumigation, deratization and preventive measures concerning the transmission of epidemic diseases are under his supervision.
Fr: *Officier de Santé;* Ger: *Hafenarzt; Quarantänearzt.*

HEART. 1. A slack twisted strand which forms the core of a shroud-laid rope. A fiber rope running through the center of a hemp or wire rope.
Fr: *Ame;* Ger: *Herz; Seele.*
2. Heart-shaped part of a pound net placed at the end of the leader to direct fish into the pot.
Fr: *Chambre;* Ger: *Fangkammer.*
3. A circular or heart-shaped wooden block used as a deadeye. It is made with 1 large hole in the center for the turns of the rope instead of having 3 separate holes like an ordinary deadeye and a groove around its circumference. Used with hemp rigging for stays and bowsprit shrouds.
Fr: *Moque;* Ger: *Stagblock; Doodshoft.*

HEART SHAKE. Clefts which occur in timber that has been felled after maturity. The butt end of the log is usually first affected and the defect may continue for some distance during seasoning. Heart shakes cross the pith and widen out as they approach it.

HEART-SHAPED THIMBLE. Thimble made of galvanized iron for general use. These thimbles are made with split end or solid end. The latter are much stronger and generally adopted in sailmaking for head and tack thimbles with luff wires. Heart-shaped thimbles range in size from ¾ in. to 5 in. Also called pear-shaped thimble.
Fr: *Cosse en Poire;* Ger: *Eierkauschen; Spitzkauschen; Herzkauschen.*

HEATER. One who heats the rivets for the riveter, using either coke, coal, gas, or oil furnaces. Also called rivet heater. He must be able to determine when the rivet is heated to the proper temperature.
Fr: *Chauffeur de Rivets;* Ger: *Nietenwärmer.*

HEATING COILS. On all ships, the fuel-oil tanks are provided with heating coils located in the bottom of the tank near the exit valve. These coils are used to lower the viscosity of the oil when the ship is steaming through cold waters in order to permit easy pumping of the fuel. Such coils are also located in cargo-fuel tanks.
Fr: *Serpentin de réchauffage;* Ger: **Heizrohrleitung.**

HEATING TONGS. Tongs used by riveters to take a rivet from the fire.

HEAVE. The vertical rise and fall of the waves or sea.
Fr: *Levée;* Ger: *Gieren.*

HEAVE (to). To pull on a rope or cable with mechanical aid, as distinguished from hauling by hand.
Fr: *Virer;* Ger: *Hieven; Werfen; Lichten.*

HEAVE AROUND. To cause the drum of a capstan, or the barrel of a winch or windlass to revolve.

HEAVE DOWN.
See **To Careen.**

HEAVE PAWL. The order to turn the (hand) capstan or windlass till the pawl drops in or falls against the stopper.
Fr: *Virer au Linguet;* Ger: *Pallhieven; Pallwinden.*

HEAVER. 1. A smooth round wooden staff, generally from 2 to 3 feet long, used for twisting or heaving tight a rope or strap.
Fr: *Trésillon;* Ger: *Drehknüppel.*
2. A shore laborer employed about docks or piers to handle goods to and from vessels. The word is usually employed in conjunction with the class of merchandise handled, as, coal heaver.
3. A sailmaker's tool consisting of a fluted tapering metal pin fitted with a handle at right angles to the pin as on an auger. Also called stitch mallet.
Fr: *Épinglette.*
4. A long rocker arm used in connection with a pump brake windlass, giving the necessary leverage to turn the windlass barrel. Also called windlass heaver.
Fr: *Bringueballe;* Ger: *Hebebaum.*

HEAVE SHORT. To heave the anchor cable until the vessel is nearly over her

HEAVE THE LEAD—HEAVY CARGO

anchor or until the cable is at an angle of about 45 degrees with but little more chain out than the depth of water.

Fr: *Virer à Pic;* Ger: *Kurzhieven.*

HEAVE THE LEAD. To take soundings with the hand lead.

Fr: *Sonder;* Ger: *Lotwerfen.*

HEAVE THE LOG. To determine the ship's speed by the log line and glass. The order to throw the log chip overboard.

Fr: *Filer le loch;* Ger: *Logwerfen; Loggen.*

HEAVE TIGHT. To pull or haul anything tight. Also to heave taut.

Fr: *Raidir;* Ger: *Steifhieven.*

motion brings the cable on board and raises the anchor to the hawsepipe.

Fr: *Lever l'Ancre;* Ger: *Anker hieven; Anker lichten.*

HEAVING. The vertical motion given to the ship as a whole, especially noticeable when broadside-on to the waves.

Fr: *Levée;* Ger: *Aufsteigende Bewegung.*

HEAVING BOARD. A board of hardwood about 10 in. long and 1 in. thick with a hole in the middle and one in each corner in a diagonal line with the center hole, all of different diameter. It is used by sailmakers for working bolt rope out prepara-

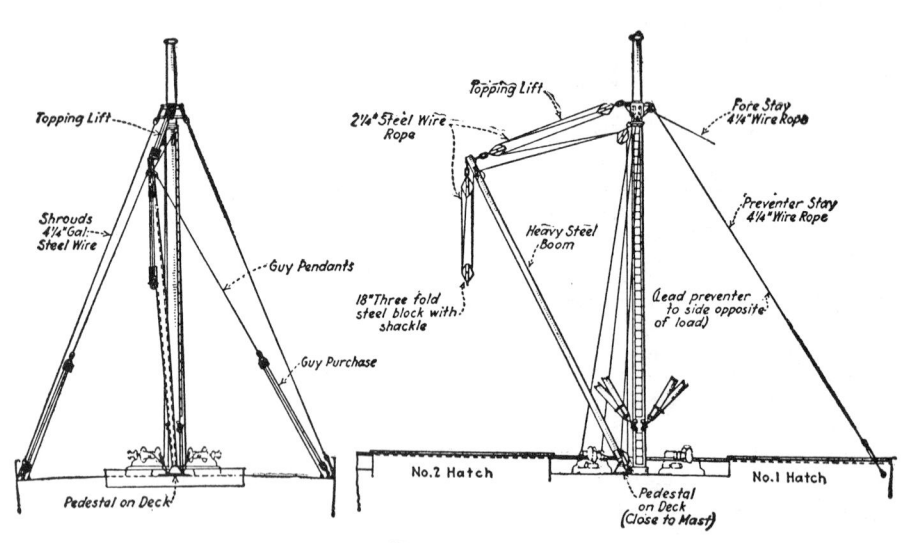

Heavy Derrick

HEAVE TO. To put a sailing vessel in the position of lying-to, by putting the helm down or hauling in the weather braces or both, to cause the wind to act on the forward surface of the sails or to cause the sails to counteract each other. Thereby the vessel's way is checked or the vessel is held with no way on. Also called to heave aback, to bring to. The term "heave to" is often applied to the act of laying a vessel to.

Fr: *Mettre en Panne;* Ger: *Beilegen.*

HEAVE UP. To hoist or raise.

Fr: *Hisser;* Ger: *Aufhieven.*

HEAVE UP ANCHOR. To raise the anchor from the bottom by taking the cable to a capstan or windlass, which by its rotary

tory to sewing it on the sail, in order to make the needle work under the strands more easily.

HEAVING LINE.

See **Hauling Line.**

HEAVING LINE KNOT. A knot used to weigh the end of a heaving line so that it will carry when thrown against the wind. It is used as an alternative to a monkey's fist.

HEAVING LINE BEND. A method of bending a very small line to a large rope. Used in bending a heaving line to a hawser.

HEAVY CARGO. Goods which bring a ship down to its loaded draft marks without

completely filling the space available for cargo. The dividing line between heavy and light cargo varies according to type of ship (full scantling or shelterdeck type) number of tweendecks, bale space and deadweight available for cargo.
 Fr: *Marchandises lourdes;* Ger: *Schwergut.*
 See **Light Cargo.**

HEAVY DERRICK. A steel derrick usually rigged abaft the foremast on the centerline of the ship for handling heavy weights. Also called jumbo boom. It is sometimes stepped on the deck in which case the heel is provided with a ball and socket joint. More recently the practice has been to have the pivoting eye, to which the forked end of the derrick is attached, forged into one with a heavy base plate recessed into a cast steel deck plate.

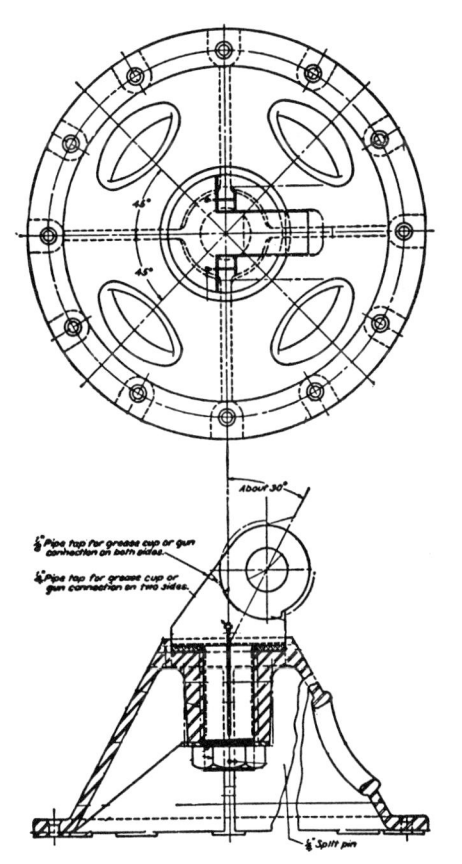

Heavy Derrick Step. (*American Marine Standard*)

Another method consists of a vertical pin, or spigot, cast in one with a base plate of cast steel. On this spigot rotates a heavy band, and on this band is forged a heavy eye which carries the forked end of the derrick.
 Fr: *Mât de charge pour poids lourds;* Ger: *Schwergutbaum.*

Handling heavy loads on board ship. Liverpool Journal of Commerce, Shipbuilding and Engineering Edition (July 16, 1942).

HEAVY FLOE. In ice terminology, applies to floe ice thicker than two feet.

HEAVY GRAIN. Wheat, maize, and rye, which stow more closely than barley or oats, which are termed "light grain."
 Ger: *Schwergetreide.*

HEAVY ICE. Accumulation of ice fragments of considerable thickness, difficult to get through.
 Fr: *Glace Épaisse.*

HEAVY LIFT. Said of a package exceeding limit set, which is usually 2,000 lb. beyond which a heavy-lift charge is added to the freight rate on each ton weight or fraction thereof for handling. In the uniform North Atlantic bill of lading clauses (1937) any single piece or package exceeding 4,430 lb. in weight is made to pay an extra charge for loading or discharging.
 Fr: *Poids Lourd;* Ger: *Schwergut.*

HEAVY LIFT SHIP. A sea-going vessel specially designed and equipped for transportation and handling consignments of rolling stock: locomotives, tenders, railway-coaches, and small craft such as tugs, lightships, hopper barges, or similar heavy units, either on deck or below. The machinery is aft leaving the midship portion of the hull for the stowage of units of considerable length. The main hatch may attain 100 feet in length with derrick of 200 tons capacity. The tonnage ranges from 2400 to 7900 tons gross.

HEAVY SEA. A sea in which the waves run high. A wave moving with great force.
 Fr: *Forte Mer;* Ger: *Schwerer Seegang; Hochgehender Seegang.*

HEEL. 1. The transverse inclination of a vessel due to the action of the waves, the wind, a greater weight upon one side, etc., usually transitory. When of a more or less permanent nature it is termed "list."
 Fr: *Bande; Gîte;* Ger: *Krangung.*

2. The lower end of a mast, derrick, or pillar. **3.** The inboard end of a bowsprit or jibboom. **4.** The lower end of any part of a ship's structure, i.e., frame, stem, etc.

Fr: *Pied Emplanture;* Ger: *Fuss.*

HEEL CHAIN. Short length of pudding chain supporting the heel of a topmast. It leads from one side of the lower-mast head under the topmast and up on the other side of the lower-mast head. Also a similar chain passing round the bowsprit cap around the heel of the jibboom. Also called Crupper chain. (Obsolete.)

Fr: *Liure de Bâton de Foc;* Ger: *Domperkette.*

HEELING. The square or octagonal part of a wooden topmast or topgallant mast through which the fid hole is cut.

Fr: *Caisse;* Ger: *Vierkant.*

See **Inclining Experiment.**

HEELING ADJUSTER. An instrument used for the compensation of the heeling error in magnetic compasses when the vessel is at rest. It consists of a dip needle having a weight which can be shifted in position. A scale is provided for showing the various distances of the weight from the point of suspension of the needle.

After having been set up and leveled ashore, the heeling adjuster is placed in the binnacle, with the compass removed, setting it in the magnetic meridian, which after other compensations should correspond to compass North. The vertical heeling magnet is then moved up and down until the needle of the adjuster is horizontal. The magnet is then secured in this position.

HEELING CORRECTOR. In a compensating binnacle, a cylindrical magnet placed in a hollow brass tube in the vertical axis of the binnacle. The magnet is fitted with a hook at each end and held at the proper height by a chain which passes over a roller at the top of the tube and is secured to a cleat or a drum in the magnet chamber.

Fr: *Aimant Correcteur de Bande;* Ger: *Krangungsmagnet.*

HEELING ERROR. The influence or error in a magnetic compass resulting from permanent and induced magnetism when a ship has a list to port or starboard. Also called heeling deviation. It is due to the fact that all horizontal iron in the vessel's structure tends to assume a quasi-vertical position when the ship heels, and in doing so receives magnetism by induction from the earth. As a rule heeling error is greatest on north and south courses and least on east and west courses.

Fr: *Déviation due à la Bande;* Ger: *Krangungsfehler.*

HEELING MAGNET.
See **Heeling Corrector.**

HEELING MOMENT.
See **Upsetting Moment.**

HEELING TANK. Side ballast tanks provided in an ice breaker in the midship section of the hull, in order to produce forcible rolling of the ship after a prolonged stay in icebound regions when the hull becomes frozen on all sides, and thus to break the ship loose.

Fr: *Caisse d'Inclinaison;* Ger: *Krangungstank.*

HEEL LASHING. A lashing securing the inner end of a boom when it is rigged out.

Fr: *Aiguillette de Bout-Dehors;* Ger: *Fusslaschung.*

HEEL PIECE. Angle bar about 3 ft. long serving as a connecting piece for the ends of two bars at their abutment. The flanges of the heelpiece are reversed from those of the bars it connects. Also called frame buttstrap, heel bar.

Ger: *Fusslaschung.*

HEEL ROPE. A rope applied to the heel of any object, particularly that which is rove through a sheave at the heel of a wooden jibboom or bowsprit for the purpose of running it out, or in the heel of a topmast for lowering, and so forth.

Fr: *Guinderesse;* Ger: *Stänge Windreep.*

HEEL-TAPPER. Local name formerly given to a small fore-and-aft type of inshore fishing schooner from New England. The hull was square-sterned with short full bows and run and knee stem. Now extinct.

HEEL TENON. The projecting part at the foot of a wooden lower mast which fits into the mortise of the mast step.

Fr: *Tenon d'Emplanture;* Ger: *Fusszapfen.*

HEIGHT. The height of tide is the vertical distance at any moment between water level and chart datum.

Fr: *Hauteur;* Ger: *Höhe der Gezeit.*

HEIGHT OF HIGH WATER. The height of the water above the chart datum at the moment of high water.

Fr: *Hauteur de la pleine mer;* Ger: *Hochwasserstand.*

HEIGHT OF LOW WATER. The height of the water measured above the chart datum at the moment of low water.

Fr: *Hauteur de la basse mer;* Ger: *Niedriger Wasserstand.*

HEIGHTS. A term used when representing geometrically the outer form of a vessel, and denoting one of the ordinates measured vertically from the horizontal plane intersecting the base line.

HELIACAL. A star rises heliacally when it first becomes visible in the morning after having been hidden in the sun's rays. It sets heliacally when it is first lost in the evening twilight owing to the sun's proximity.

Fr: *Héliaque;* Ger: *Heliatisch.*

HELIOCENTRIC. Concentric with the sun. The heliocentric place of a heavenly body is its position referred to a celestial sphere concentric with the sun.

Fr: *Héliocentrique;* Ger: *Heliozentrisch.*

HELM. The helm proper is the tiller, but the term is often used to mean the rudder and the gear for turning it. The word "helm" describes the whole of the steering apparatus in the form of rudder, tiller, chains, engine, wheel, telemotor, and so on.

Fr: *Barre;* Ger: *Ruder; Steuer; Helm.*

See **Check Helm, Lee Helm, Weather Helm.**

HELM DOWN. In sailing craft: an order to place or push the tiller on the lee side.

Fr: *Barre en Dessous;* Ger: *Ruder in Lee.*

HELM INDICATOR. Electrically operated apparatus designed with the object of indicating continuously the angle of the ship's rudder on the navigating bridge or any other desired position. In some systems the apparatus is operated by an electric battery (Siemens Indicator), in others through a small synchronous converter connected to the ship's current. Also called rudder telltale, rudder angle indicator.

Fr: *Répétiteur d'Angle de Barre;* Ger: *Ruderzeiger.*

HELM ORDERS. At the International Conference on Shipping held in London in 1928 agreement was arrived at to adopt the naval terms "left" and "right" when giving orders to the man at the wheel instead of the terms "port" and "starboard" as then universally used in the merchant marine.

The recommendations made by the Conference were as follows:

1. That the order given to the man at the wheel should indicate the direction in which the ship's head should turn.
2. That this practice should be uniform throughout the world.
3. That the words "port" and "starboard" or their ordinary national equivalents should no longer be used in giving helm orders.
4. That the words "left" and "right" or their ordinary equivalents should be adopted. Also called steering orders.

Fr: *Commandements à la Barre;* Ger: *Ruderkommando.*

These recommendations were made compulsory by legislation in the U. S. in 1936, in Great Britain in 1931, and in France in 1934.

The apparent anomaly which existed in helm orders when the words "port" and "starboard" were used dates back to the days when the order "port" means "port the tiller," the rudder and the ship's head going to starboard, and vice versa.

HELM PORT. An aperture through which the rudderstock passes into the hull of a vessel. Also called rudder port. It is a round opening at the top of the rudder casing or trunk and is fitted with a stuffing box to prevent the influx of sea water.

Fr: *Jaumière; Louve;* Ger: *Ruder Kopfloch; Hennegat.*

HELM PORT TRANSOM. A timber to strengthen the helm port.

HELMSMAN. An able-bodied seaman performing duties appropriate to quartermaster but not rated as such. In passenger vessels and cargo liners quartermasters are usually employed as helmsmen. Also called steersman, wheelman.

Fr: *Homme de Barre; Barreur;* Ger: *Rudersmann; Rudergast; Steuermann; Rudergänger.*

HELM UP. An order, given in sailing craft, to push the tiller to the weather side.

Fr: *Barre au Vent;* Ger: *Ruder nach Luv.*

HEMP. A plant of the genus *Cannabis*. The fibers of *Cannabis* are the hemp of commerce but the products from many totally different plants are often included under the general name of "hemp." In some cases the fiber is obtained from the stem while in others it comes from the leaf.

Fr: *Chanvre;* Ger: *Hanf.*

See **Italian Hemp, Manila Hemp, Mauritius Hemp, Russian Hemp, Sisal Hemp, Sunn Hemp.**

HEMP ROPE. A rope made of the fibers of the hemp plant, *Cannabis sativa.* The fibers are made into yarns, the yarns into strands, and three or more strands twisted together to form a rope. Hemp rope where exposed to weather requires tarring, as otherwise it decays rapidly. When untarred it is called white rope. Its breaking strength is about three quarters that of Manila.

Fr: *Cordage en Chanvre;* Ger: *Hanftauwerk.*

Italian, Russian, and American hemp are the most common varieties, but there are also phormium hemp from New Zealand, sunn hemp from the East Indies, Mauritius hemp, and sisal hemp, which are occasionally used. The last two are usually mixed with Manila hemp. Sisal hemp does not stand salt water well. In the roping of sails hemp rope is used almost exclusively; it is also used for runing rigging and shroud lanyards as well as for "small stuff": ratline, roundline, houseline, marline, etc.

HENEQUEN. See **Sisal Rope.**

HEN FRIGATE. An expression formerly used by American whalemen to denote a ship in which the captain was accompanied by his wife on the voyage.

HENGST. A Dutch fishing boat with pointed stem and round stern. The *hengst* has many points in common with the *hoogaar,* but the straight stem is shorter than in the latter and has a steeper angle of rake. The wash strake does not become so narrow at the stem or sternpost. The rig is the same as that of the *hoogaar.* It is employed in the salmon fisheries, also for shrimping and oystering.

HERMAPHRODITE SCHOONER. A topsail schooner in which the gaff-foresail is replaced by main staysails. An uncommon rig, used in England around 1850.

HERRING BOAT. General term for various types of boats used in the herring fisheries.

Fr: *Harenguier;* Ger: *Heringsboot.*

HERRING-BONE PLANKING. A method of cross planking used in boatbuilding and in which the bottom planks are set at an angle to the center line, sloping aft from keel line to bilge.

HERRING BONING. A method of sewing up rents in a sail with small cross stitches, by which the seam is kept flat.

Fr: *Videlle;* Ger: *Fischgrätenverband.*

HERRING COT. An open centerboard fishing boat from Wexford county on the southeast coast of Ireland. The hull is sharp at both ends with raking stem and flat bottom. There is a short length of keel at bow and stern, and a bilge or grounding keel extending some distance on each side amidships. The centerboard is about 5 ft. deep. The rig consists of three masts with spritsails. Length, over-all, 30 ft. Breadth 7 to 8 ft. (Now extinct.)

HERRING-DRIFTER. A wooden or steel single-screw vessel used in the herring, mackerel and sprat fishery on the east coasts of England and Scotland.

Fr: *Dériveur;* Ger: *Treibnetzfischer.*

The type is virtually a small edition of the trawler or dragger, with a similar profile and arrangement, except that the trawl winch is replaced by a powered capstan located forward for hauling in the nets. Also called *driver.*

It is rigged with two masts: main and mizzen. The mainmast is stepped in a tabernacle and lowered when the vessel is riding to her nets. In British North Sea herring drifters the catch is brought daily to land by the vessels themselves. The fishery is always prosecuted at night and seldom at a greater distance than 30 miles from the coast. The fish-hold is divided into several compartments with vertical partitions. Salt is carried in some of these divisions so that if the catch is too small to be worthwhile taking to harbor at once it may be slightly salted on board and landed later.

A number of new types fitted with motors instead of steam engines have been introduced recently with the aim of attaining greater economy.

Dimensions: Length between perpendiculars 86 ft. Breadth 18.6 ft. Depth 9½ ft. Draft, forward, 5.2 ft. Aft, 10.7 ft. Displacement 185 tons. Indicated horsepower 215 (typical).

Edward and Todd, Steam Drifters, Institution of Engineers and Shipbuilders in Scotland, *Transactions,* vol. 82 (1938-39); Smith, R. M., Design and Construction of Small Craft, London (1924).

HERRING-TRAWL. Trawl net used in waters where it has been found that at certain periods herring take to the bottom. The dimensions of the various parts are the same as in ordinary trawl except that the cod end is longer and that the meshes of the cod end, belly, and batings are all of same size. The speed of towing is greater, reaching 3½ knots. Special devices are used for lifting the headrope.

Heuer

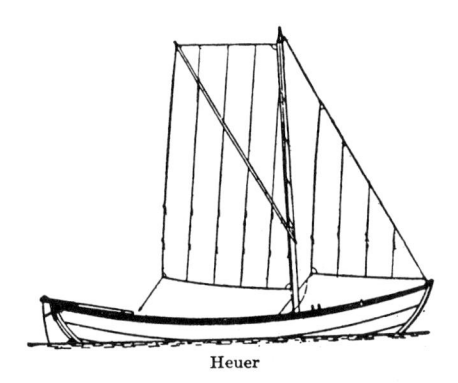

HERRING-WARP. The heavy rope by which one end of a fleet of drift nets is attached to the drifter. Also called bush rope, messenger, fleet rope. It generally consists of a five-strand tarred Manila rope 3½ or 3¾ in. in diameter, in joined lengths of 120 fathoms.

Fr: *Aussière;* Ger: *Fischreep.*

HEUER, HEUERBOOT. A half-decked, double-ended beach boat used for inshore fishing on the coasts of Mecklenburg and Western Pomerania. A centerboard is provided and there is a small fish well just aft of the centerboard trunk. The rig consists of a portable mast with sprit mainsail and jib foresail. A low-powered motor is usually fitted nowadays. Length over-all 22 ft. Breadth 4.7 ft. Depth 4.7 ft. (Average.)

HEWN TIMBER. Timber squared for measurement.

Fr: *Bois Equarri;* Ger: *Behauenes Holz.*

HIGH AND DRY. The situation of a ship which is aground so as to be seen dry upon the strand when the tide ebbs from her.

Fr: *Echoué à Sec;* Ger: *Hoch und trocken.*

HIGH BUNT. A term denoting that a great amount of canvas is stowed in the center of a yard when the sail is furled.

HIGH ELASTIC LIMIT STEEL. Mild steel with an elastic limit of 16 to 17 tons per square inch; tensile strength 30 to 35 tons; elongation not less than 20 per cent on 8-in. gauge. Cost about 25 per cent higher than ordinary mild steel. When it replaces mild steel, the reduction of about 10 per cent in scantlings gives a corresponding increase of deadweight capacity.

Barr, Martin and Wall, "High Elastic Limit Steel and Its General Applications," Institution of Naval Architects (London), *Transactions,* 1924; Service, T. M., "High Elastic Limit Steel for Shipbuilding and Marine Engineering Purposes," Institution of Engineers and Shipbuilders in Scotland, *Transactions,* vol. 70 (1926-27); Trask, E. P., "The Use of High Elastic Steel in Ship Construction," Society of Naval Architects and Marine Engineers (New York), *Transactions,* vol. 51 (1943).

HIGHER HIGH WATER. The terms "higher high water" or "first high water," "lower high water" or "second high water"; "higher low water," or "first low water"; "lower low water" or "second low water"; are used when referring to harbors where there are two tides in the same day showing differences in height, due to the presence of considerable diurnal inequality. The expression "higher high water" denotes the higher of two high waters of a tidal day, and "higher low water" the higher of the two low waters of a tidal day.

Fr: *Pleine Mer Supérieure;* Ger: *Höheres Hochwasser.*

HIGH INJECTION VALVE. An injection valve fitted on the ship's side well above the main injection valve, to avoid trouble experienced in shallow waters and rivers by sand, or other solid matter being drawn into the circulating pump through the main injection.

Fr: *Soupape auxiliaire de prise d'eau;* Ger: *Oberinjektionsventil.*

HIGH SEA. A sea with wave heights of 15 to 24 ft.; No. 6 Beaufort Scale.

Fr: *Mer Grosse;* Ger: *Hohe See.*

HIGH SEAS. The term high seas, in municipal and international law, denotes all that continuous body of salt water in the world that is navigable in its character and that lies outside territorial waters and

Herring Drifter

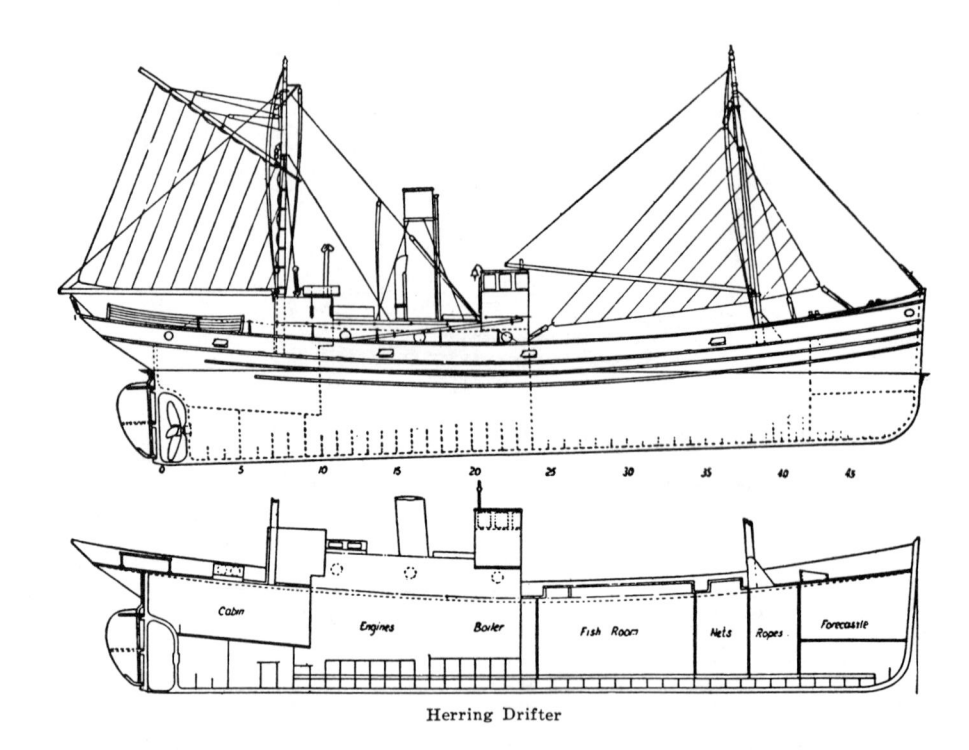

maritime belts of the various countries. Also called open sea.

Fr: *Haute Mer;* Ger: *Hohe See.*

Percy, *Maritime Trade in War,* Yale, 1930.

HIGH TENSILE STEEL. Steel with a tensile strength of from 34 to 38 tons per square inch and an elongation of not less than 20 per cent, used particularly in topside strength members, strength deck, and sheer strake. In the use of this material rivet holes are drilled, not punched. In the building of several well-known vessels ("Mauretania," "Bremen," "Monarch of Bermuda") the use of high tensile steel permitted reductions in thickness of strength members to be made varying from 10 to 12 per cent, with a corresponding saving in weight.

Fr: *Acier à haute Résistance;* Ger: *Hochwertiger Stahl.*

Bennett, W., *Special Quality Steels for Shipbuilding,* Society of Naval Architects and Marine Engineers, *Transactions,* New York, 1931, vol. 39.

HIGH TIDE.
See **High Water.**

HIGH WATER. The maximum height reached by a rising tide. The height may be due solely to the periodic tidal forces or it may have superimposed upon it the effects of prevailing meteorological conditions.

Fr: *Pleine Mer;* Ger: *Hochwasser.*

HIGH WATER FULL AND CHANGE. The average high-water lunitidal interval on the days of new or full moon. As on those days the moon's transit occurs approximately at noon or midnight, the high water full and change is then approximately the time of high water.

Fr: *Pleine Mer de Syzygie;* Ger: *Syzygiales Hochwasser.*

HIGH-WATER MARK. The intersection of the plane of mean high water with the shore. Also called high-water line.

Fr: *Laisse de Haute Mer;* Ger: *Flutmarke; Flutlinie.*

HIGH-WATER STAND. The interval of time at high water during which the level of the water does not vary noticeably.

Fr: *Etale de Pleine Mer;* Ger: *Stillstand des Hochwassers.*

HIGH WIND. A strong wind of force 10. A heavy gale.
Fr: *Grand vent;* Ger: *Starker Wind.*

HINGED BULKHEAD DOOR. A watertight door of rectangular shape with rounded corners. The hinges are ovalized to obtain better contact between door and bulkhead. Snibs are fitted so as to make the door readily workable from either side of the bulkhead. The watertightness is obtained by means of a strip of rubber attached to the bulkhead, this strip being compressed against the edge of an angle bar riveted around the door frame.
Fr: *Porte à Charnières;* Ger: *Klapptür; Hängetür.*
See **Watertight Door.**

HINGED WATERTIGHT DOOR. A watertight door closed by catches or dogs mounted on both sides of the bulkhead frame or on the door, which by engaging with wedge pieces pull the door home against the bulkhead. Watertightness is attained by fitting a rubber strip all around the door.
Fr: *Porte etanche à charnières;* Ger: *Wasserdichte Klapptür.*

HIPPED SKYLIGHT. A skylight which, unlike the ordinary pitched skylight, has no solid ends by which light is obstructed.

HIPPING. A term denoting the work of increasing the breadth of a wooden hull about the waterline by backing each frame with timber and planking over.

HIP TANK. A design of cellular double-bottom tanks, in which the inner bottom rises from the center toward the sides.

HIRE AND PAYMENT CLAUSE. Charter party clause stating the agreed amount to be paid for the hire of the vessel and when and how it is to be paid. Also called freight clause.

HITCH. A temporary knot by which a rope is fastened to another object, either directly or around it.
Fr: *Clef; Noeud; Amarrage;* Ger: *Stek; Schlag; Stich.*

HOBBLING PILOT. A pilot who has the necessary nautical knowledge of local waters but no license. He is usually located at small ports which are unable to afford the services of a licensed pilot. Also called hobbler.
Fr: *Pratique; Lamaneur;* Ger: *Wildlotse; Treidler.*

HOBBY. See **Dolly.**

HODDY. The strengthening border about 5 or 10 meshes deep of each lint in a fleet of drift nets. It includes the heading at the top, the reining at the foot and the guarding at sides. The meshes which constitute the hoddy are made of double or stronger material. Also called board.

HODY. Generic name for various Indian open fishing boats from Bombay and adjacent waters rigged with one mast and lateen sail. The stem is curved and the sternpost slightly raked. Length 22 to 40 ft. Breadth 4¼ to 8 ft.

HOG. 1. Condition of a vessel wherein the buoyancy is more than the weight over approximately the midship half-length with less buoyancy than weight at both ends, so that the tendency of the vessel is to arch up or "hog" amidships. Such a condition results in a bending moment, which stresses the top members of the vessel in tension, the bottom members in compression. The stresses are termed hogging stresses.
Fr: *Arc;* Ger: *Aufbucht.*
See **Sag.**
Cornbrooks, T. M., "Data on Hog and Sag of Merchant Vessels," Society of Naval Architects and Marine Engineers (New York), *Transactions,* vol. 23 (1915).
2. A brushlike frame of timber, hauled along a ship's bottom under water to clean it. (Obsolete.)
Fr: *Goret;* Ger: *Farke.*
3. See **Hog Piece.**

HOG BOAT. An English offshore fishing boat, 8 to 12 tons burden, from the Sussex coast, with wide beam, flat floors, and stout bilge pieces for convenience in launching and hauling up on the beaches. The hull was clinker-built and fully decked. In the early part of the nineteenth century the rig consisted of two spritsails, a foresail, and a jib. Later, when used for drifting, the boats were lug-rigged. About 1880 the rig was altered again and reduced to one mast on which a high peaked gaff sail without boom was set in addition to the two headsails and running bowsprit. This rig was used until the hog boats vanished, about 1890.

HOGGING LINE. One of the lines attached to the lower corners of a collision mat. They pass under the keel and are used in working the mat over the injured part. Also called bottom line, keel hauling line.
Fr: *Passeresse de Paillet.*

HOGGING MOMENT. The moment, usually expressed in foot-tons, at any given point along the ship's length, of the forces which tend to cause a vessel to hog. These moments are usually plotted in a curve of bending moments.
    Fr: *Moment fléchissant d'Arc;* Ger: *Aufbuchtungsmoment.*
    See **Hog, Longitudinal Strength.**

HOGGY.
    See **Hog Boat.**

HOG PIECE. A fore-and-aft piece of timber bolted to the top of the keel in small boats to provide a good landing edge for the garboard strakes and a solid foundation for calking. The keel is left square in section and has no rabbet cut in. Also called **rabbet plank, lay board, keel batten, hog stave.**
    Fr: *Chapeau;* Ger: *Innenkiel.*

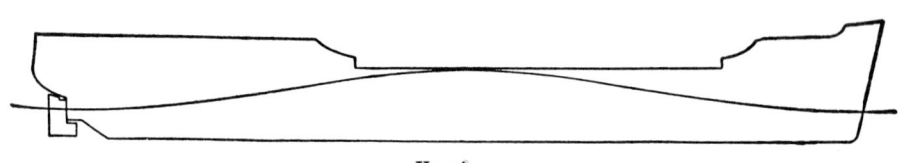

Hogging

HOGSHEAD HOOKS.
    See **Can Hooks.**

HOG STAVE.
    See **Hog Piece.**

HOIST. 1. The quantity of cargo taken in or out of a ship in one sling or heave. Also called draft.
    Fr: *Elinguée;* Ger: *Aufzug.*
    2. The midship depth or vertical distance from head to foot of all square sails, except courses. The depth of a course is called drop. The fore edge of a staysail, or jib.
    Fr: *Chute;* Ger: *Heiss.*

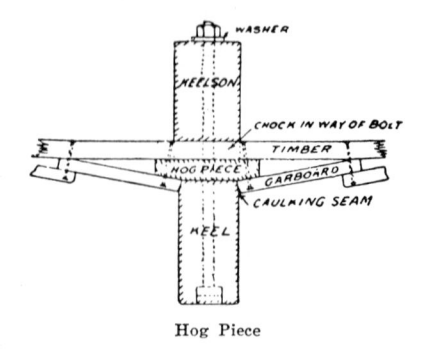

Hog Piece

3. The vertical height of a flag as opposed to the fly. The side of a flag to which the halyards are bent.
    Fr: *Guindant;* Ger: *Tiefe.*
    4. A number of flags fastened together for hoisting as a signal. Also called flag hoist.

HOIST (to). To raise or lift, especially by means of a rope, block, or tackle.
    Fr: *Hisser;* Ger: *Heissen.*

HOISTING POLE. A light spar by which the head of a club topsail is extended above the masthead.
    Fr: *Vergue de Flèche;* Ger: *Topsegel Kopfraa.*

HOISTING ROPE. Term frequently applied to a six-stranded wire rope with nineteen wires in each strand, and a central hemp core.
    See **Special Flexible Hoisting Rope.**

HOISTING SPEED. The speed at which the designed load can be handled with deck machinery, such as winches, windlass capstans, and so on, working at full load.
    Fr: *Vitesse de Hissage;* Ger: *Hebegeschwindigkeit; Seilgeschwindigkeit.*

HOLD. 1. A general name for the spaces below deck, designated for the stowage of cargo. More particularly those spaces between the lowest deck and bottom of the ship or tank-top, if there is a double bottom.
    2. On a warship, the space below the lowest platform.
    Fr: *Cale;* Ger: *Raum; Unterraum; Laderaum.*
    See **Fish-Hold, Insulated Hold, Lower Hold.**

HOLD BATTEN CLEAT. One of the small lugs welded or riveted to the frames in cargo spaces, by which the sparring battens are held in place. Also called **hold batten clip, sparring cleat.**
    Fr: *Taquet de Vaigre;* Ger: *Wegerungshalter.*

HOLD BEAM. One of the beams, installed in a hold, similar to a deck beam. They have no plating or planking on them except at sides where a stringer plate is fitted. The object of this arrangement, now seldom adopted, was to assist the transverse frames by providing additional support for the ship's sides between the upper deck and the floors.
Fr: *Barre Sèche;* Ger: *Raumbalken.*

HOLD BEAM FRAMING. In the hold beam system the required supporting effect to the sides lost by the suppression of an imaginary or theoretical lower deck is provided by retaining the stringer plate and hold beam every fifth frame, and making both extra strong. No longer in general use.
Fr: *Construction à Barres Sèches;* Ger: *Raumbalkenspannung.*

HOLD BUNKER. A bunker located below the lower deck.
Fr: *Soute de Cale;* Ger: *Raumbunker.*

HOLD CREW. The longshoremen who work in a ship's hold or 'tween-deck when loading or unloading. They work in two groups, one on the port side, the other on the starboard side. Each group has four men.

HOLDING-DOWN BOLT. A term applied to bolts used for securing any object to its foundation, for example, a deck winch. Also called anchor bolt.
Fr: *Boulon de Fixation;* Ger: *Fundamentbolzen.*

HOLDING GROUND. A term used in describing an anchorage area; called "good" or "foul" according to whether or not the material of which the bottom is composed will prevent a ship's anchor from dragging. Clay is considered the best, then mud, then sand.
Fr: *Fond de Bonne Tenue;* Ger: *Ankergrund.*

HOLDING-UP HAMMER. A heavy hammer held against the head of a rivet to supply inertia while it is being hammered up. Some holding-up hammers are provided with a long shaft suspended at mid-length from a hookbolt. The worker pulls down the end of the shaft thus applying an upward pressure on the rivet head. Also called holder on.
Fr: *Abattage;* Ger: *Vorhalter; Nietstempel.*

HOLD LADDER. A steel ladder extending between two decks and giving access to the cargo spaces below the upper deck. It is usually composed of steel rungs fitted between two round pillars. Also called hatch ladder.
Fr: *Échelle de Cale;* Ger: *Raumleiter; Stützenleiter.*

HOLD MAN. One of a gang of stevedores or longshoremen who works in the holds and 'tween-decks of a vessel.
Fr: *Calier;* Ger: *Schauermann.*

HOLD ON. To keep all one has when pulling on a rope. To stop or cease pulling.
Fr: *Tenir bon;* Ger: *Stoppen; Beibleiben; Halten; Festhalten.*

HOLD STANCHION. A stanchion which extends from the inner bottom or top of floors to the lowest tier of deck beams. Also called hold pillar.
Fr: *Épontille de Cale;* Ger: *Raumstütze.*

HOLD STRINGER. Fore-and-aft girders of varying section, worked on the vessel's side above the turn of bilge, to increase the longitudinal strength of the hull and prevent fore-and-aft movement of the frames.
Fr: *Serre de Cale;* Ger: *Raumstringer.*

HOLD WATER. 1. To check the progress of a rowboat by immersing the oars with the blades vertical and keeping them stationary.
Fr: *Étaler sur les avirons;* Ger: *Wasser halten.*
2. A command to this effect given to a boat's crew.
Fr: *Avirons dans l'eau;* Ger: *Haltwasser.*

HOLE CUTTER.
See **Foalsfoot.**

HOLIDAY. 1. A day of exemption from labor or work. In chartering, the term refers to holidays at the port where the ship is lying and not to those observed by the ship. Ship's holidays are counted as working days if the crew are ready to work and if there is no holiday on shore.
Fr: *Jour Férié;* Ger: *Festtag.*
2. Any part or space left bare or uncovered when paying, painting, blacking, or tarring.

HOLLOW MAST. A wooden mast of hollow section. Owing to the fact that the required amount of wood in a hollow mast is considerably less than that of a solid mast with equivalent strength, the weight aloft is considerably reduced and this type of mast is in general use for racing and cruising yachts. In the wake of spreaders and points of attachment of shrouds and stays, solid blocks of wood are inserted. The after side is straight, all the tapering being cared for by the forward side. It is made solid from the heel to a point above the partners. Bolsters and cheek blocks are built on the outside, unless metal tangs are fitted to take the rigging. Also called hollow-built mast.

Fr: *Mât Creux;* Ger: *Hohlmast.*

HOLLOW PILLAR. A pillar of round section, usually composed of steel plates riveted or welded together. Also called tubular pillar, or pipe stanchion.

Fr: *Épontille Creuse;* Ger: *Hohle Stütze.*

HOLLOW QUOIN. The vertical concave recess formed in the wall in which the heel of a dock or lock gate turns.

HOLLOW SEA. A condition usually occurring where there is shoaling water or a current setting against the waves. The line from crest to trough makes a sharp angle, and consequently the sea is very dangerous to smaller craft.

Fr: *Mer Creuse;* Ger: *Hohle See.*

HOLLOWS OF RESISTANCE. Portions of the curves of resistance plotted on a speed base which show a sagging tendency as compared with other portions of the curve.

Fr: *Creux de la Courbe de Résistance.*

HOLLOW SPAR. A spar of round, square, oval or pear-shaped cross section composed of comparatively thick layers of wood glued together. The thickness of the shell is, on an average, about 20 per cent of the outside diameter. Also called built spar.

Fr: *Espar Creux;* Ger: *Hohlrundholz.*

The first hollow spars were made by splitting a solid stick, hollowing the center and gluing the two halves. In a later process the spar is produced by cutting a board in the direction of the grain, wetting it on one side, heating it on the other, and bending the board on the heated side. Hollow spars are of greater proportional diameter than solid spars, but the great saving in weight is of considerable advantage in cruising as well as in racing yachts. They are made of very even grained wood, free from knots, such as Virginia or Canadian spruce, basswood, yellow pine, and so on, with casein glue as a binder.

HOLLOW WAYS. Launching ways where the standing ways are built with a groove, and the sliding ways with a projection that fits into this groove, thereby keeping the vessel's motion straight while being launched. It eliminates the use of ribbands.

HOLMES LIGHT. A tin canister containing calcium phosphide, attached to a float. To the bottom of the tin a tube with perforated end is fastened. At the top of the tin is a cone, the apex of which is cut off before the light is used. When the Holmes Light is thrown into the sea, water enters below the light, spontaneously inflammable phosphine escapes above, and burns with a brilliant flame and much white smoke. The action of sea water on calcium phosphide generates the phosphine gas.

This principle is also employed in the Franklin life buoy, which was in general use in the United States Navy prior to World War II.

Fr: *Feu Pyrotechnique Holmes;* Ger: *Holmeslicht.*

See **Light**.

HOLYSTONE. A soft white sandstone used with loose sand and water for scrubbing wooden decks.

Fr: *Pierre à briquer;* Ger: *Scheuerstein.*

HOMARDIER. A decked sailing boat used by French lobstermen, usually fitted with a fish-well in which the catch is kept alive. The smaller type of lobster boat as found on the coasts of Brittany has a length of 20 to 33 ft., tonnage 12 to 22, with cutter rig. The larger type is ketch-rigged and generally fitted with an auxiliary engine. Length over-all 72 ft. Keel 48 ft. Tonnage 89. Capacity of well (water) 40 tons. Length of well about one third of waterline length. Sail area: mainsail 180 sq. m., main topsail 55, foresail 50, jib 110, mizzen 50, mizzen topsail 20, total, 465 sq. m. (Average.) The largest *homardiers* are 90 ft. long, with a displacement of 110 tons.

HOME. A term describing the ultimate position of an object on board ship. An anchor for instance is said to be home when hove up hard in the hawse pipe. When used in relation to gear or rigging the word means: as far as it will go. Square sails are sheeted home when the clews are extended as far as possible towards the yardarms.

Fr: *À poste.*

HOME PORT. 1. (U. S.) According to an Act of Congress approved on June 26th, 1884 the home port marked upon the stern is either the port where the vessel is registered or enrolled, or the place in the same district where the vessel was built, or where one or more of the owners reside.

2. The terminal port of a vessel; not neces-

sarily the port of registry. The port from which a ship operates. The home port of a seaman is the port at which he signed on or the port in his own country at which he signs off.

HOME TRADE. A term applied in Great Britain to the trade carried on within the following limits: all ports of the United Kingdom and Irish Free State, the Channel Islands, the ports on the continent of Europe between the River Elbe and Brest, inclusive. In the United States of America the expression "intercoastal trade" refers to traffic to noncontiguous territories or dependencies (Atlantic to Pacific).

Fr: *Grand Cabotage;* Ger: *Kleine Fahrt.*

HOMEWARD BOUND. Said of a vessel returning to the country or port to which it belongs.

Ger: *Auf der Rückreise begriffen.*

HONOR POLICY. See **Wager Policy.**

HOOD. See **Hood End, Afterhoods, Fore Hoods.**

2. A covering for a companion hatch, skylight, scuttle, etc.

Fr: *Capot;* Ger: *Kappe.*

See **Binnacle Hood, Spray Hood.**

3. A piece of tarred or painted canvas used for covering the eyes of hemp rigging to prevent damage by water.

HOOD END. The end of a plank which fits into the rabbet of the stem or sternpost. Also called hooding end or hood.

Fr: *Barbe;* Ger: *Plankenenden.*

See **Afterhoods, Fore Hoods.**

HOOGAARS. A Dutch fishing boat with shovel bows, long straight stem set at an angle of about 45° and low narrow stern. The bottom is quite flat with chines. The greatest beam is abreast of the mast. The upper strake of planking has a pronounced tumble home and is bound by a large rubbing strake. Its greatest depth is amidships; it narrows toward the stem and sternpost. The leeboards are long and narrow and lie on the sloping top strake. *Hoogaars* from Aarnemuiden are sprit-rigged but elsewhere they are rigged with gaff-mainsail and staysail. These boats are chiefly employed in mussel and shrimp fishing in the estuaries of the Maas and Scheldt Rivers. Length over-all 42.5 ft. Breadth 14.5 ft. Depth 5 ft. (typical.)

HOOK AND BUTT. A method of scarfing planks by laying the butts over each other in such manner that they resist tensile strain to part them.

Fr: *Écart Double;* Ger: *Hakenlaschung.*

HOOK BLOCK. A block with a hook, the latter being either fixed, swiveled, or loose. It is called a front hook block when the fixed hook points out in the same plane as the sheave. It is termed a side hook block if the hook points out in a direction perpendicular to the sheave.

Fr: *Poulie à Croc;* Ger: *Hakenblock.*

HOOK BOLT. A bolt having one end in the form of a hook.

Fr: *Cheville à Croc;* Ger: *Hakenbolzen.*

HOOKER. A general name for fishing vessels which use lines and hooks rather than nets. It does not indicate any particular rig, build or type. Also called liner.

Fr: *Cordier;* Ger: *Angelleinfahrzeug; Angelfahrzeug.*

HOOK-HOLE DAMAGE. Damage caused to goods by careless use of hooks in stowing and breaking out cargo.

HOOK IRON. An implement used by fishermen for disgorging hooks from fish or for killing them. It is made of three-quarter-inch (19 m/m) iron, 13 to 16 in. long, with a knob at one end, and with the opposite end flattened and split so as to fit over the bend of a hook.

HOOK ROPE. A rope with a hook. A wire or hemp rope from 10 to 15 fathoms long with an iron hook at the end, used in clearing hawse.

Fr: *Filin à Croc;* Ger: *Hakentau.*

HOOK SCARF. A locked scarf made by cutting a nib and a hook taper on each of two timbers. Used on keels, stems, keelsons, and miscellaneous heavy work.

Fr: *Écart à Trait de Jupiter;* Ger: *Hakenlaschung.*

HOOK TACKLE. A tackle with a hook on each block.

HOOP NET. A baited trap consisting of a conical bag with rigid circular mouth. It is baited and set on the bottom and periodically hauled suddenly to the surface. Dabs, prawns, and lobsters are taken with these nets.

Fr: *Verveux; Balance;* Ger: *Garnreuse; Plumper; Glippen.*

HOORI. An Indian cargo carrier which follows closely the lines of the Western-designed schooners and brigs. It is a keeled boat with either round or square stern sometimes rigged as a fore-and-aft two-masted schooner but generally with brigantine or brig rig. They are built all around the Bay of Bengal and as far west as the Laccadive Islands, Moulmein, Akyab, Chittagong, Cochin and Calicut, and occasionally in Andaman, Maldive and Laccadive Islands. These vessels are usually well-found and well manned and carry deadweight cargoes up to 500 tons.

HOOTNANY.
See **Gadget**.

HOPPER BARGE. A steel or wooden barge of very full midship section employed in harbors and used for the disposal of mud, gravel, sand, etc., taken from a dredger and then conveyed to a dumping ground where the cargo is discharged through the bottom. Also called dump scow.
> Fr: *Chaland à Clapets; Porteur de Déblais;* Ger: *Baggerschute; Baggerprahm; Klappschute; Klappenprahm.*

The central part of the barge is transversely divided into a number of hoppers, each consisting of a box with steeply inclined sides. The bottom is made up of a number of heavy hinged doors, two for each hopper, which open outward and are supported and worked by chains led to a central girder. The doors are usually actuated by steam winches or hydraulic rams. The side compartments are left empty to provide buoyancy. The majority of hopper barges now in use are the self-propelled type with a capacity between 600 and 2,000 tons.

Smith, Munro R., *The Design and Construction of Small Craft,* London, 1924.

HOPPER DREDGE. A dredge so designed that the spoil is received into a specially formed hold or hopper in the hull of the vessel. When the hold is full, the vessel proceeds to sea or any convenient spot to dump its load.
> Fr: *Drague Porteuse;* Ger: *Hopperbagger.*

HORI. A dugout employed as ship's boat by Arab seagoing craft, also for inshore fishing. The bottom part is a dugout with a wash strake added to each side. When used for fishing, a short mast with lateen sail is added. Maximum length about 18 feet.

HORIZON GLASS. The silvered mirror or speculum attached to the frame of a sextant, the upper half of which is left clear, permitting the horizon to be seen directly through it. The image of the sun or star is seen by reflection from the index mirror of the sextant in the lowered or silvered part. Also called horizon mirror.
> Fr: *Petit Miroir;* Ger: *Kleiner Spiegel.*

See **Index Glass**.

HORIZON SHADE. One of the pivoted colored glasses which can be swung before the horizon mirror of a sextant to regulate the intensity of light.
> Fr: *Bonnette de Petit Miroir;* Ger: *Blendglas.*

HORIZONTAL INDUCTION. Horizontal component of the transient magnetism induced in the soft iron of a ship.
> Fr: *Induction horizontale;* Ger: *Horizontalinduktion.*

HORIZONTAL INTENSITY CHART. A chart showing the horizontal component of the earth's total magnetic force as it affects the compass needle in various geographical positions on the surface of the earth. U. S. Hydrographic Office, Washington, Chat. H.O. n° 1701.
> Fr: *Carte d'intensité d'aimantation;* Ger: *Horizontale Intensitat Karte.*

HORIZONTAL PARALLAX. The particular value of the diurnal parallax when the celestial body appears in the observer's horizon.
> Fr: *Parallaxe Horizontale;* Ger: *Horizontale Verschub.*

HORIZONTAL SLIDING DOOR. A watertight-bulkhead door so designed that it can be moved horizontally for opening and closing. It is fitted with shafting and bevel hand gear so that it can be operated from above the bulkhead deck. These doors are usually power-operated from a central control station located on the navigating bridge.
> Fr: *Porte à coufissement horizontal;* Ger: *Wagerechte Schiebetur.*

HORN. 1. One of the side pieces which form the jaw of a gaff or boom.
> Fr: *Joue;* Ger: *Backe.*

2. One of the outer ends of crosstrees. Also one of the horizontal arms of a cleat.
> Fr: *Oreille;* Ger: *Arm.*

3. That part of a fog signal apparatus which distributes and amplifies the sound emitted therefrom.
> Fr: *Trompette; Pavillon;* Ger: *Schalltrichter.*

See **Cheek**.

HORN BOWSPRIT. A bowsprit of reduced length without jibboom as fitted on modern trading vessels. Its length being

considerably shorter than that of a bowsprit and jibboom combined, the total area of headsails is reduced and only three jibs are set instead of the customary four. This is counterbalanced by stepping the foremast further forward.
Ger: *Hornbugspriet.*

HORN CLEAT. See **Arm Cleat.**

HORNING. The setting of the frames and bulkheads of a vessel square to the keel after the proper inclination to the vertical due to the declivity of the ways has been given.
Fr: *Balancement.*

HORN TIMBER. A centerline timber which forms the backbone of the stern overhang abaft the sternpost. It is fastened to the top of the sternpost by a mortise and tenon, or, if wide enough, it passes around on both sides of the deadwood.
Fr: *Allonge de Voûte Fourchette;* Ger: *Mittelheckspant.*

HORSE. 1. A bar of iron or a rope on which some part of the rigging is made to travel. A rope for a sail to travel on.
Fr: *Mât de Corde;* Ger: *Leiter.*
2. An iron rod between the fife rail stanchions to which the lead blocks are secured.
3. One of the frame molds used in connection with the process of mocking up. See **Mocking Up.**

HORSE LATITUDES. Zones of high atmospheric pressure on the northern or southern limit of the trade winds, where calms and variable winds prevail. The conditions are unlike those in the doldrums in that the air is fresh and clear, and calms are not of long duration.
Fr: *Zone des Calmes tropicaux;* Ger: *Rossbreiten.*

HORSEMAN. One of the crew of a herring drifter whose special duty it is to put on and cast off buoys and seizings when shooting or hauling in the nets.

HORSEPIECE. Whaling term. A piece of blubber about 2 ft. long and six in. wide, cut from a blanket piece.

HORSESHOE CLAMP. A strap of iron or gun metal shaped like a horseshoe and let into the stem and gripe on opposite sides. These straps are bolted through together and serve to strengthen the connection between stem and keel in a wooden hull. Also called gripe plate, horseshoe plate, gripe iron.

Fr: *Etrier;* Ger: *Verbindungsklammer.*

HORSESHOE LIFEBUOY. A lifebuoy shaped like a horseshoe, so that the user can enter it with facility. It is fitted at one extremity with a line about 2 ft. long, to enable the user to secure himself in the buoy.
Fr: *Bouée en Fer à Cheval;* Ger: *Hufeisenförmiger Rettungsring.*

HORSESHOE PLATE. A small plate fitted on the counter where the rudderstock enters the trunk. When made in one piece it has the shape of a horseshoe; hence its name. It is frequently made of two pieces completely surrounding the stock and bolted to the shell plate so as to permit removal. Also called plate collar or apron plate.

HORSESHOE SPLICE. A splice in which two ends of a short piece of rope are sidespliced into the bight of another rope so that when the latter is pulled taut the splice will stand out distinct, with some resemblance to a horseshoe. Also called span splice.
Fr: *Epissure en Greffe;* Ger: *Hufeisensplissung; Buchtsplissung.*

HORSESHOE THRUST BEARING. A type of thrust bearing having a number of collars forged on the shaft. Also called horseshoe thrust block. The bearing is provided with a number of separate horseshoe-shaped pieces which fit over two threaded rods, one on each side of the bearing.
Fr: *Butée à Collets Mobiles;* Ger: *Kammdrucklager; Kammlager.*
Each shoe has lugs which bear against nuts on the side rods, thereby permitting individual adjustment of each shoe, as well as the removal of any shoe and its replacement by a spare one at sea. The shoes are usually of cast steel lined with white metal for the bearing surface. Lubrication is forced, or the collars may run in a bath of oil.

HORSE UP. To harden down the oakum of the seams in heavy wooden planking with a horsing iron. Also called to horse.
Fr: *Rabattre; Patarasser;* Ger: *Klameien.*

HORSING. Undesirable practice resorted to during a steel calking operation when the faying surfaces make a bad contact, one man holding the calking tool and another striking it with a long-shafted hammer.

HOSE. A flexible tube or pipe.
Fr: *Manche;* Ger: *Schlauch.*
See **Fire Hose, Oil Hose, Scupper Hose.**

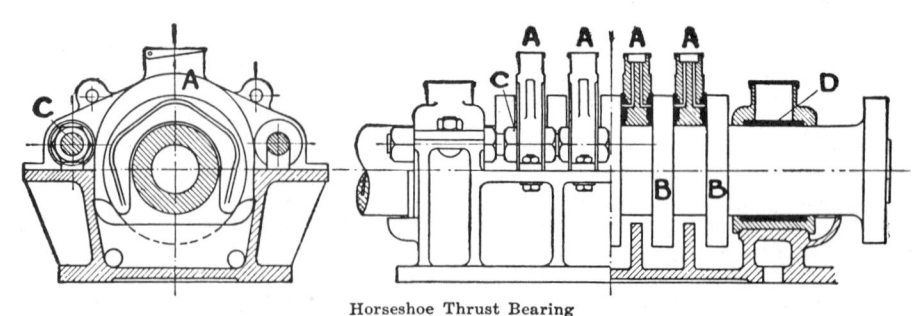

Horseshoe Thrust Bearing
A. Horseshoe—Thrust Block Shoes   B. Thrust Collar   C. Adjusting Nut   D. Thrust Bearing

American Marine Standards Committee, Standard 7, *Kinds and Sizes of Hose for Ship Equipment*, Washington, 1927.

HOSE DAVIT. A round bar davit used on tank vessel for handling oil hose. It is rigged with two wire rope guys and a Manila fall rove through a pair of 9-in. double-sheaved wooden blocks.

HOSE TESTING. A method of testing the watertightness of riveted joints in new work, by playing along the joint a strong jet of water from a hose, under a pressure of about 30 lb. per sq. in. If no water is forced through the joint it is assumed to be watertight.

Fr: *Essai à la Lance;* Ger: *Spritzenprobe.*

HOSPITAL. According to U. S. regulations all merchant vessels making voyages of more than three days duration between ports and which carry a crew of 12 or more seamen are compelled to have a hospital provided with at least one bunk for every 12 men carried, with a maximum of 6 bunks.

On British ships a hospital is compulsory with a crew of 12 men or more except when the vessel is engaged in coasting trade or when the trip does not exceed three days and nights at sea.

Fr: *Hopital;* Ger: *Krankenraum.*

Payne, G. E. B., Survey of Hospital Accommodation on Merchant Ships, The Shipbuilder (Newcastle upon Tyne), vol. 50 (May, 1943).

HOSPITAL SHIP. A vessel constructed, equipped, and assigned specially and solely for the transportation of wounded, sick, and shipwrecked. Hospital ships must be respected and are exempt from capture. According to The Hague Convention of 1907, hospital ships are divided into three classes:

1. Military hospital ships which are governernment vessels equipped and manned by the belligerents. They are not on the same footing as men-of-war during their stay in port.

2. Private hospital ships equipped at the cost of private individuals or officially-recognized relief societies of the belligerent states. They are given an official commission and a special certificate by their government.

3. Neutral hospital ships equipped wholly or in part at the cost of private individuals or recognized relief societies of neutral states, with the previous consent of their own government and with the authorization of the belligerent.

Fr: *Navire Hopital;* Ger: *Lazarettschiff; Hospitalschiff.*

All hospital ships must afford relief and assistance to the wounded, sick, and shipwrecked of both belligerents. Their names must be communicated to the belligerents at the commencement of or during hostilities and in any case before they are employed. Military hospital ships are painted white outside with horizontal band of green about 1½ meters in width. The other two classes have a horizontal band of red of similar width. This special painting must be made sufficiently plain by night. All hospital ships fly the white flag with a red cross, and if belonging to a neutral fly at the mainmasts the national flag of the controlling belligerent.

HOTCHPOTCH (U. S.). Term used in admiralty practice to signify the collection of all items of damage to both ships which have been injured in a collision after it has been admitted that both contributed to the loss. It is then the practice to divide the loss between the two ships.

HOT SPOTS. Term used by shipfitters to denote tack welds made at regular intervals to hold deck or shell plates temporarily in their relative position after erection for later welding.

HOUND BAND. A band fitted around the upper part of a mast to provide attachment for the shrouds.

HOUNDING. That portion of a lower mast between the hounds and the deck. That portion of a topmast or any upper mast from the cap upward to the hounds above. The hounded length of a pole mast is measured from deck to pole.

Fr: *Guindant.*

HOUNDS. The projections at side of a masthead serving as supports for the trestletrees. That part of a mast where the head commences and upon which the trestletrees rest. Also called mast hounds, shoulder.

Fr: *Jottereaux; Noix;* Ger: *Mastbacke; Schulter.*

HOUR ANGLE. The spherical angle at the elevated pole, intercepted between the meridian of a place and the hour circle passing through a celestial body is called the hour angle of the body.

Fr: *Angle Horaire;* Ger: *Stundenwinkel; Zeitwinkel.*

HOUR CIRCLE. One of the great circles of the celestial sphere passing through the poles. They are formed by projecting the meridians of longitude on the earth to the celestial sphere. Also called circle of declination.

Fr: *Cercle Horaire;* Ger: *Stundenkreis.*

HOURI. A name given to a lug-rigged boat of the French *chasse-marée* type, in which the foresail tack is fastened to a chesstree. Probably extinct.

HOUSE. 1. To stow or secure in a safe place. Said of a topmast when, after swaying and taking out the fid, it is lowered and secured to the lower mast without taking off the rigging.

Fr: *Caler;* Ger: *Bergen.*

2. Said of an anchor when it is hard up in the hawse pipe.

3. An awning is housed by hauling the stops down and securing them to the rail.

HOUSEBOAT. A boat fitted with permanent or temporary living quarters for use in sheltered waters. In the Far East these craft are very common and are generally propelled by oars or sweeps. In Western countries houseboats are most frequently used as pleasure boats for inland travel.

Fr: *House Boat;* Ger: *Wohnschiff; Hausboot.*

Hunt, Houseboats and Houseboating (New York, 1905).

HOUSE COAMING. The horizontal strake of plating forming the boundary at top and bottom of a deckhouse.

Fr: *Bandeau;* Ger: *Deckhaus Sullplatte.*

HOUSE FLAG. A distinguishing flag of a shipping firm. The flag of the house to which a ship belongs. It is flown from the mainmast.

Fr: *Pavillon de Compagnie;* Ger: *Reedereiflagge; Hausflagge; Kontorflagge.*

Baker, Carver and Morrell, House Flags of the Principal Owners and Operators of American Vessels of the Port of New York, New York, 1921; Talbot Booth, E. C., House Flags and Funnels of British and Foreign Shipping Companies, London, 1936; Wedge, F. J. N., Brown's Flags and Funnels of British and Foreign Steamship Companies, Glasgow, 1934.

HOUSELINE. A three-thread tarred hemp cord spun from left to right and laid from right to left, a little stouter than marline and running about 160 ft. to the pound. It is superior to spun yarn and smaller than roundline. Used for the same purposes as marline.

Fr: *Lusin;* Ger: *Husing.*

HOUSING. The housing of a mast is that portion measured from top of deck at mast hole to bottom of step socket. The housing of a bowsprit is the inboard length from face of stem to heel. Also called bury. (U. S.)

Fr: *Logement; Portant;* Ger: *Masthausung.*

HOUSING ANCHOR.
See **Stockless Anchor.**

HOUSING LINE. A line near the deck to which the edge of an awning is secured when housed.

Fr: *Ligne de Revers.*

HOUSING STOPPER. A short piece of chain with turnbuckle and pelican hook at one end and a shackle at the other. The afterend is shackled to an eyeplate in the deck and the forward end is hooked to the anchor chain. The chain part is sometimes done away with. Used for drawing the anchor close up into the hawsepipe and relieving the strain on the cable holder when at sea. Also called screw stopper.

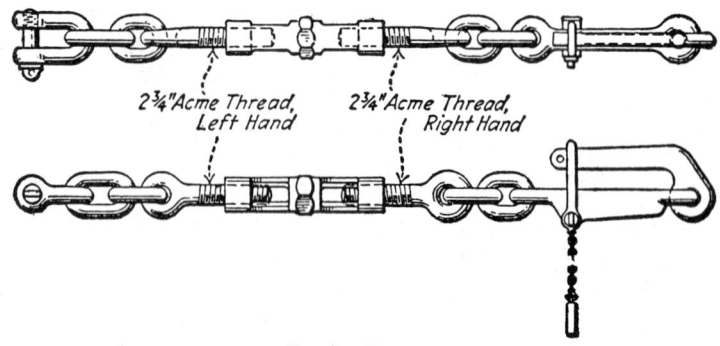

Housing Stopper

Fr: *Bosse à Ridoir; Saisine à Ridoir*; Ger: *Kettenklau*.

HOVERING VESSEL (U. S.). Any vessel found or kept off the coast within or without the customs waters if, from the history, conduct, character or location of the vessel, it is reasonable to believe that such vessel is used or may be used to introduce merchandise into the country in violation of the customs laws.

HOY. Formerly a seagoing sailing barge used as a tender to larger vessels or for carrying stores, water, etc. to ships in bays and roads, also for the conveyance of passengers and luggage along the seacoast. It was usually sloop-rigged, and in Holland, ketch-rigged. Nowadays, this term is used to denote a heavily built unrigged barge or scow, for transportation in harbors of heavy or bulky articles, such as mooring anchors, ammunition, etc.

Fr: *Heu*; Ger: *Lastboot*.

See **Anchor Hoy**.

HSIAO-TUI-SHUAN. A Chinese fishing junk from Chusan Archipelago (Hangchow Bay) about 24 ft. long. These boats work in pairs with a drag net and are of the same type as the *ta-tui-shuan*.

HSIE-HAI-SHUAN. A small three-mast, coasting junk from Taku, seldom exceeding 70 ft. in length. It trades between Tientsin, Chefoo, and smaller ports on the southern shores of the Gulf of Pechili, carrying chiefly fish paste, seaweed, and dried, salted fish as cargo.

HU. Single outrigger dugout canoe of the Iai people from Wallis Island in the Loyalty group.

HUER. A lookout man posted on an elevation near the sea, who by concerted signals directs fishermen when a shoal of fish is in sight.

HUFFLER (G. B.). A mud pilot. One who pilots barges and other small craft through the arches of a river.

HUG. 1. To hug the wind: to keep the ship as close to the wind as possible.

Fr: *Serrer*; Ger: *Dicht am Winde halten*.

2. To hug the land: to sail along as close as possible to a weather shore.

Fr: *Serrer la Côte*; Ger: *Dicht am Lande halten*.

HULK. Generally, an unrigged hull condemned as unfit for the risks of the sea and used as a floating depot in a harbor or roadstead.

Fr: *Ponton*; Ger: *Speicherschiff; Hulk*.

See **Coal Hulk, Sheer Hulk**.

HULL. The body of a vessel exclusive of masts, yards, sails, rigging, machinery and equipment.

Fr: *Coque; Corps*; Ger: *Rumpf; Schiffsrumpf; Schiffskörper; Schiffskasko*.

HULL-APPENDAGE RATIO. The ratio of resistance of naked hull to hull with the appendages. Appendage resistance in percentage of naked hull resistance varies from 5 to 7 in single-screw and 10 to 19 in twin-screw ships. Also called hull-appendage factor, hull factor.

HULL AUXILIARIES. A general term used for denoting all the auxiliaries which do not appertain to the main propelling machinery. Under this heading are included deck auxiliaries for working the ship and cargo, the lighting and refrigerating plant, pumps for handling liquid cargoes, ballast and bilge pumps.

Fr: *Auxiliares de coque;* Ger: *Schiffshilfsmaschinen.*

Achenbach, A., *Schiffshilfsmaschinen,* Berlin, 1922; Seward, H. L., Marine Engineering, vol. 2, chapter viii, New York (1944).

HULL BALANCE. In sailing craft, the effect of shape of the hull form coupled with the distribution of weights on sailing qualities. With proper hull balance, when the boat is heeled, the hull goes down neither by the stern nor by the head and has no excessive tendency to sail in a circle (which would require checking by excessive helm).

Fr: *Équilibre de Résistance.*

To secure this balance there should be virtually no shift of the center of buoyancy when the boat heels to a normal sailing angle. The fore-and-aft bodies should balance in their respective length and sections. The rig should be suited to and balance with the hull. The centers of effort, of buoyancy, and of lateral resistance should be in correct relation to each other.

HULL DOWN. Said of a vessel when it is so far from the observer that the hull is invisible owing to the convexity of the earth's surface, while the masts and stack are still seen. The opposite of "hull up."

Ger: *Rumpf unter der Kimm.*

HULL EFFICIENCY. In propeller design, the ratio of net work or horsepower required to draw a ship at a given speed when towed without propeller, to that required to drive the same hull at the same speed through the water by its propeller. It may also be defined as:

$$\frac{1 \text{ minus thrust deduction coefficient}}{1 \text{ minus wake fraction}}$$

Fr: *Rendement de Carène;* Ger: *Schiffsformgütegrad.*

HULL FACTOR.
See Hull-Appendage Ratio.

HULL GIRDER. The girder formed by the hull considered in its entirety as a box girder resisting hogging and sagging stresses. The calculations relating to the hull girder are used for determining the sizes and effective combination of the component parts of a ship's structure so that it has sufficient strength to resist the various stresses to which it is subjected under working conditions. Ordinarily only the continuous longitudinal members are considered as contributing to the hull girder.

HULL POLICY. A marine insurance policy in which the subject matter insured includes the hull proper with materials, outfits and equipment, cabin fittings, machinery, boilers, fuel, engine stores, deck stores and provisions for the officers and crew, and if a vessel is engaged in a special trade the ordinary fittings requisite for the trade.

Fr: *Police sur Corps;* Ger: *Kasko Police.*

HULL UNDERWRITER. The person with whom the ship's hull, machinery, apparel, and tackle is insured.

Fr: *Assureur sur Corps;* Ger: *Kaskoversicherer.*

HUMBOLDT CURRENT. A cold current flowing northward and northwestward off the west coast of South America. It forms a part of the circulatory system of the South Pacific Ocean and in the vicinity of Cape Blanco turns westward and joins the south equatorial current. The name "Corriente del Peru" was adopted by a resolution of the Ibero-American Oceanographic Conference at its Madrid-Malaga meeting in 1935. Also called Peruvian Current.

Schott, G., Der Peru Strom, *Annalen der Hydrographie,* vol. LIX, nos. 5-6-7, Berlin, 1931.

HUMMOCK. An elevation in field or floe ice caused by two or more bodies of ice being pressed together. Hummocky ice is formed by the edges of ice floes meeting in strong breezes, by which they are pushed up and formed into pyramids.

Fr: *Hummock;* Ger: *Eishocker.*

HUMMOCKING. Process of pressure formation of ice.

Ger: *Eishügel.*

HUMMOCKY ICE. Elevations in field or floe ice caused by bodies of ice pressed together with the edges pushed up and forming pyramids named hummocks. Impedes navigation.

Fr: *Glace Moutonnée.*

HUNDRED. A British unit of measure for the sale of fish by numbers. In Cornwall a hundred of pilchards contains 120 fish, a hundred of mackerels contains 124 fish. In the herring trade a "long hundred" contains 132 fish and is the equivalent of 33 warps.

HUNG-JOU-SHUAN. Chinese fishing boat from Swatow (Kwang-Tung Province). Employed for dredging cockles from the sea bottom with a net. Length 28 ft. Beam 8 ft. (Typical.)

HUNG-TU-SHUAN. A North China junk from the Gulf of Pechili with pram-like bows. Also called Pechili junk. The sides have an abrupt round or tumble home, similar to that found in a turret deck vessel. It is divided internally by a considerable number of transverse watertight bulkheads (14 for a waterline length of 113 ft.). The bottom is flat. The deck has a pronounced camber. The five masts are placed as follows: the foremast right in the eyes outside the bulwarks on the port side; the two mainmasts on the center line; the large mizzen is just forward and to the portside of the rudder well. The small mizzen or quarter mast is against the bulwarks on the port side. Length over-all 115 ft. Length waterline 113 ft. Breadth moulded 32 ft. Breadth at deck level 23 ft. Loaded draft 9 ft. Light draft 4 ft. Displacement loaded 608 tons. Displacement light 229 tons. (Typical.) The largest are 180 ft. in length and 30 ft. beam at deck level.

The sails have a straight leech and luff, and are lofty and narrow, with very little peak to the yard. They are made of two layers of heavy cotton canvas stitched together and tanned, strengthened vertically with ropes and stiffened horizontally with the usual battens. A staysail is often set between the forward mainmast and the mainmast. These junks trade mostly between Antung (Manchuria), Newchang, Tsingtao, Chefoo, and Shanghai.

Waters, D. W., The Pechili Trader, Mariners' Mirror, London, vol. 25, January, 1939.

HURDY GURDY. A contrivance used by dorymen off the Newfoundland bank fisheries when hauling in their trawls in deep water (150 to 200 fathoms). Also called gurdy. It consists of a roller and crank handle fixed temporarily on the gunwale of the dory, near the bows.

HURRICANE. A name given to revolving storms which occur in the North Atlantic (West Indies), South Pacific, Indian Ocean, and China Seas, Beaufort Scale force 12. It is usually called "typhoon" in China Seas and "cyclone" in Arabian Sea, Bay of Bengal, and South Indian Ocean.

Fr: *Ouragan;* Ger: *Orkan.*

Hennessy, J., Hurricanes of the West Indies and North Atlantic, *The Marine Observer,* vol. 9, no. 103, London, 1932.

HURRICANE DECK. An upper deck of light scantlings above the superstructures. Used as promenade deck on passenger vessels.

Ger: *Hurrikandeck.*

HURRICANE LANTERN. A lantern so made that its flame is undisturbed by violent winds. Also called tornado lantern.

HUT-CHOCK (U. S.). In a ship under construction, a chock of wood with notch to receive the end of a shore for holding a frame timber in position after it has been erected.

HVALERBAAT. A decked sailing boat from Southern Norway used in Oslofjord and adjacent waters for fishing and also as pilotboat. It is built with rounded ends and clinker planking and has a length ranging between 31 and 36 ft. The rig consists of a short mast with sprit mainsail and stay foresail which tack down to stemhead.

HVASSING. An open boat from Bohuslan (Sweden) used for setting trawl lines for a larger parent ship called *bankskuta*. It is also employed in the coastal fisheries for haddock. Sometimes called Kak. Length over-all 21 ft. 7 in. Breadth 8 ft. 4 in. Depth 3½ ft. (Typical.)

The hull is built with raking stem, rising floor, well-shaped run and V-shaped transom stern. It has a moderate sheer with quick rise at the bow and is provided with three thwarts and a stern seat. The rig consists of a sprit mainsail and jib with bowsprit. Oars 12 ft. 2 in. in length are used when there is no wind.

HYDRAULIC POWER TRANSMITTER. A device or machine in which power is transmitted by the kinetic energy of a liquid discharged by an impeller on a primary shaft against the vanes of a turbine runner on a secondary shaft. Also called hydraulic coupling, hydraulic clutch.

Fr: *Transmission Hydro-Mécanique;* Ger: *Hydraulischer Transformator.*

It is used in conjunction with geared Diesel marine drive and installed between engines and reduction gear. It is also used with exhaust turbines.

Its object is to protect engine and gears from damage due to sudden shock loads, such as piston seizure or fouled propeller. In the case of multi-engine drive with geared Diesels it also permits its disconnecting a single engine for repairs or operation at reduced power.

HYDRAULIC DERRICK. A derrick which carries a hydraulic ram with pulleys, chains and the necessary mechanism for lifting, slewing and lowering slings of cargo. Power is supplied by an accumulator located in the engine room.

Fr: *Mât de charge hydraulique;* Ger: *Hydraulischer Ladebaum.*

HYDRAULIC RIVETER. A device which drives rivets by hydraulic pressure only. Also called riveting ram or bull riveter. The pressure on the rivets may attain up to 160 tons. Portable machines are used in shipyards, but large stationary rams are generally used for production riveting in fabricating shops.

Fr: *Riveteuse Hydraulique;* Ger: *Hydraulische Nietpresse.*

Hydraulic riveting is considered greatly superior in strength and reliability to any other form of riveting, where rivets of large diameter are used. The proportion of hydraulic riveting does seldom exceed 25 per cent of total number of rivets in vessels of ordinary construction. Keel plates, double bottoms, intercostals, frames, and part of the shell plating in large vessels are pressure-riveted.

HYDRAULIC STEERING GEAR. A type of steering gear widely used in naval vessels and modern merchant ships, in which a modified hydraulic transmission is used to actuate rams working in cylinders. These rams, or hydraulic plungers, are coupled to the rudder yoke. The cylinders in which the rams move are supplied with oil by a hydraulic pump, the flow of oil being controlled from the steering station by a telemotor or self-synchronous transmission.

Fr: *Appareil à Gouverner Hydraulique;* Ger: *Hydraulische Steuermaschine.*

The advantages of this type of steering gear lie in the low consumption of power, ready response to wheel movements with little lag, and small deck space and head room requirements in the steering-gear room, as well as light weight, and flexibility in arrangement of components.

HYDRAULIC TRANSFORMER. A hydro-mechanical system of geared drive for ahead or astern motion, developed in Germany by Föttinger for the purpose of reducing the speed of the prime mover, turbine, or Diesel engine down to the desired speed of the propeller shafting, the whole apparatus being contained in a single casing. Sometimes called hydraulic transmitter, Föttinger transformer. It consists essentially of a water turbine wheel mounted on the main shaft and a centrifugal pump mounted on the turbine (or Diesel) shaft. Water is delivered by the pump to the turbine wheel and from the motor it passes to a tank and thence to the inlet of the pump. The ratio of reduction is determined by the design of the turbine and pump. Reversing is accomplished by a separate water circuit with another water turbine on the main shaft, a valve directing the water to either the ahead or astern turbine as required.

Fr: *Transmission Hydro-Mécanique; Transformateur Föttinger;* Ger: *Hydraulischer Transformator; Föttinger Transformator.*

The system has never been used to any great extent on commercial vessels, as geared reduction sets were found to be lighter and less expensive. Various installations were made on German vessels, the largest one being on the twin-screw passenger vessel "Tirpitz," with 10,000 shaft horsepower on each shaft.

Föttinger, H., "Recent Development of the Hydraulic Transformer," Institution of Naval Architects (London), *Transactions,* vol. 56 (1914).

HYDROCONIC HULL CONSTRUCTION. A method of ship construction based on the use of developable surfaces throughout, these being a combination of conical and cylindrical surfaces. This method is claimed to reduce labor costs by about 35%. It has been adopted for hulls of harbor craft.

HYDROFOIL. A hull supported clear of the water surface, while under way by the dynamic lift of underwater wings (hydrofoils). For certain speed-length ratios the hydrofoil offers a substantial reduction in resistance and a marked improvement in seakeeping capability over displacement craft.

Fr: *Hydro-glisseur;* Ger: *Tragflugelboot.*

HYDROFOIL RUDDER.
See **Streamline Rudder.**

HYDROGRAPHER. One who studies and practices the science of hydrography. Often applied to the one in charge of a hydrographic department.

Fr: *Ingénieur Hydrographe;* Ger: *Hydrograph; Seekartenzeichner.*

HYDROGRAPHIC OFFICE (U. S.). An office of the Navy Department which was established in 1866.

The Hydrographic Office exists for the improvement of the means for navigating safely the vessels of the United States Navy and of the Merchant Marine, by providing accurate and inexpensive nautical charts, sailing directions, navigational books, and manuals of instruction for the use of all vessels of the United States, and for the benefit and use of navigators generally.

Fr: *Service Hydrographique;* Ger: **Hydrographisches Amt.**
Weber, G. A., *The Hydrographic Office,* Baltimore (Md.), 1926.

HYDROGRAPHIC SURVEY. The science and process of determining the contour of coasts, harbors, entrances of rivers, the position and distances of objects on the shore line, of islands, rocks, shoals, pinnacles, the depth of water over certain areas, and of obtaining particulars as to the nature of the sea bottom, the purpose of which is the production of charts for use in navigation. Also called nautical survey, marine survey.

Fr: *Levé Hydrographique;* Ger: **Hydrographische Vermessung.**

Nautical surveys vary in character according to the nature of the work, its importance to navigation, and the time available. The scale upon which the surveys are usually plotted range from ½ in. to 2 or 3 in. to the sea mile in coast surveys for the ordinary purposes of navigation, according to the requirements. For detailed surveys of harbors and anchorages a scale from 6 to 12 in. is usually adopted, but in special cases, scales as large as 60 in. to the mile are occasionally used.

Robinson, J. L., *Elements of Marine Surveying,* London, 1904.

HYDROGRAPHIC SURVEYOR. An officer serving under the head of the Hydrographic Service, who specializes in marine surveys, chart making, etc. Also called hydrographic engineer.

Fr: *Ingénieur Hydrographe;* Ger: **Hydrograph.**

HYDROGRAPHY. The science which treats of the waters of the globe.

Fr: *Hydrographie;* Ger: *Hydrographie.*

See **Nautical Hydrography.**

HYDROMETER. An instrument for measuring the specific gravity of liquids. It is used on board ship to find the density of the water in which the vessel floats and is based on the principle that floating bodies displace a quantity of liquid equal to their own weight. It consists of a glass tube expanded at its lower end into a large bulb filled with small shot or mercury. The tube contains a scale graduated from 0 at the top to 40 at the lower end. The usual **hydrometer reading in sea water of the** Atlantic Ocean is about 25; meaning that there are 25 ounces to a cubic foot.

Fr: *Hydromètre;* Ger: *Aräometer.*

HYDROPHONE. A multiple contact microphone in a watertight case, specially designed to be effective in receiving submarine signals emitted by an oscillator, as well as their echoes.

Fr: *Hydrophone;* Ger: *Schallempfänger.*

HYDROPLANE. A racing boat whose propeller acts in or against the water and which has one or more breaks in the longitudinal continuity of the immersed surface, thus forming more than one lifting surface against the water.

Fr: *Hydroplane; Hydroglisseur;* Ger: *Gleitboot; Stufenboot.*

See **Multistep Hydroplane, Single Step Hydroplane.**

Streeter, J., *How to Build Flying Boat Hulls,* London, 1936.

HYDROSTATIC TEST. A pressure test applied to a compartment or tank by filling it with water in order to verify the tightness or strength or both. The pressure varies according to classification society requirements.

Fr: *Essai hydrostatique;* Ger: *Wasserprobe.*

HYGROGRAPH. An automatically recording instrument for measuring relative humidity based on the property of human hair increasing its length with increase of relative humidity and vice versa.

Fr: *Hygromètre Enregistreur;* Ger: *Selbstregistrierender Hygrometer.*

HYGROMETER. An instrument for measuring the state of humidity of the air. It consists of two thermometers placed side by side in a wooden screen. One of the bulbs is covered with muslin which is kept continually moist by means of a strand of cotton wick, one end of which is immersed in a reservoir of fresh water. The difference between the two readings is an indication of the relative humidity of the atmosphere.

Fr: *Hygromètre;* Ger: *Hygrometer.*

HYSTERESIS. A term applied to the small amount of magnetism remaining in soft iron after the magnetic field has been removed due to the fact that the so-called soft iron is never theoretically pure. Also called Gaussian error.

Fr: *Erreur de Gaussin;* Ger: *Verzögerung.*

I

I. Flag of the international code of signals showing black disc on yellow ground, indicating when hoisted singly: "I am directing my course to port."

I.B. 1. INNER BOTTOM. 2. IN BOARD.

I.C. INDEX CORRECTION (sextant).

I.E. INDEX ERROR (sextant).

I.T.M. INCH TRIM MOMENT.

I.S. INDIAN SUMMER (freeboard marks).

I/V. INCREASED VALUE (marine insurance).

IBABURA. A balanced canoe employed in the minor coasting trade between ports of western Colombia, Buenaventura, Tumaco, Choco bay, etc. Also called *imbabura*. A dugout forms the basis of the hull. On this there are superimposed, according to size, 1, 2, or 3 outward flaring strakes of planking. These strakes are secured inside by a number of ribs spaced widely apart. The stern, narrow and transom shaped, is built of short boards connecting the afterends of the side strakes. The *ibabura* is sloop-rigged and steered with an oar inserted through a hole in the transom. Length: 30 to 40 ft. A balance log is lashed outboard on each side.

I. BAR. A rolled steel bar of I section. Also called I beam.

ICE BEAM. One of the beams running from load waterline downward, often fitted in wooden whaling or sealing vessels for strengthening the hull transversely against the pressure of closing ice.

ICEBERG. A large floating mass of ice detached from a glacier at sea level. The movement of the glacier downward causes it to protrude into the sea, by which it is in part supported until the weight becomes so great that more or less of it breaks off. The portion so detached from the glacier floats about, driven by winds and currents.

Fr: *Iceberg;* Ger: *Eisberg.*

See **Floe Berg, Glacier Berg, Tabular Berg.**

"Icebergs and Their Location in Navigation," *Engineering* (London), vol. 93 (June 7, 1912).

ICE BLINK. A glow on the horizon caused by the reflection of sunlight from the surface of an ice pack or floating mass of ice or from land covered with snow. Also called ice sky.

Fr: *Clarté des Glaces;* Ger: *Eisblink.*

ICEBOUND. A term meaning that a vessel is surrounded by ice and prevented from proceeding on her voyage.

Fr: *Bloqué par les Glaces;* Ger: *Eingeeist.*

ICEBOX. 1. An arrangement provided in icebreakers on the shell plating in way of the afterend of the engine room to provide the necessary supply of sea water for circulation. It consists of a rectangular well formed in the bottom shell plating and carried up to the required level in the engine room. Its top portion is supplied with valves drawing water from the outside. A system of steam pipe is led from the boilers to melt away any ice formation in the box.

Fr: *Caisse de Déglaçage.*

2. One of the insulated boxes with refrigerating apparatus placed in a pantry or other rooms where perishable stores for daily use are placed.

Fr: *Glacière;* Ger: *Kühlschrank.*

ICEBREAKER. A vessel used for keeping open a navigable passage through ice. Icebreakers are heavily built to stand the shock of ramming the ice or of running up on it at the bow and breaking it by virtue of their weight. They are often fitted with a bow screw placed under overhanging bows. The midship section is wedge-shaped so that if the vessel is squeezed between two converging masses of ice it will, by its shape, tend to rise. In order to strengthen the hull a belt about 6 ft. deep named "ice belt" is fitted along the water line. The plating of this belt is of extra thickness and is worked perfectly flush with inboard butt straps, to reduce friction with the ice.

Fr: *Brise-Glace;* Ger: *Eisbrecher.*

Two different methods are used to attack the ice. In the first the vessel is designed to ram and cut through the ice like a wedge. The best results with this method are obtained in broken up and floating ice with openings between the separate ice fields. Vessels using this method have a straight stem and no forward propeller.

When the second method is resorted to, the icebreaker is built with a spoon bow and round bow sections, which arrangement causes the fore part of the vessel to ride up on the ice and crush it by its weight. This procedure attains its maximum efficiency in compact, uniform ice fields, heaped-up

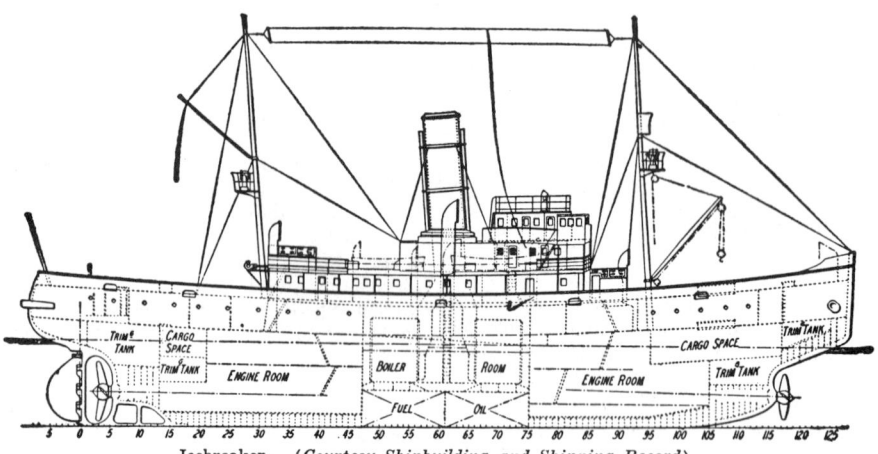

Icebreaker. (*Courtesy Shipbuilding and Shipping Record*)

blocks of ice or pack ice. Recently designed icebreakers represent a compromise enabling them to employ both methods of ice attack. The forward screw is used when the vessel is going ahead, to suck the water from under the ice, driving it aft under the ship's hull, thus creating a vacuum under the ice. The ice being deprived of its original support is thus more easily broken by the weight of the vessel. When moving astern, the forward screw drives the water away from the ice and washes the broken ice asunder.

Goulajeff, J., "Ice Breakers," *Shipbuilder and Marine Engine Builder*, vol. 42 (March, 1935); Schroeder, H., "Eisbrecher," *Verein Deutscher Ingenieure Zeitschrift*, vol. 83, no. 5 (1939).

ICE BULLETIN. Wireless message broadcasted by Radio Argentia in Newfoundland twice daily at 0118 hour and 1318 Greenwich time. It gives all information regarding the location and movements of ice in the North Atlantic.

Fr: *Bulletin d'information des glaces.*

ICE CHART. A monthly chart of the Western North Atlantic with indicated tracks and route notices.

ICE CLAUSE. A clause used in the construction of charter parties, by which, in the event that ice prevents a vessel from entering its port of discharge, the ship is at liberty, after agreement with the receivers, to proceed to the nearest accessible port to deliver the cargo at the customary rate of discharge and conditions of the substituted port.

Fr: *Clause de Glaces;* Ger: *Eisklausel.*

ICE CLIFF. A cliff of ice covered by earth and vegetation as found along the coasts of Greenland.

Fr: *Falaise de glace;* Ger: *Eisklippe.*

ICE CODE. An international code used by shipping interests to report on ice conditions in any particular area. It was first introduced in 1930 in the Baltic and was later extended to other seas by international agreement.

0.................No ice
1.................Slush or young ice
2.................Fast ice
3.................Drift ice
4.................Packed slush or strips of hummocked ice
5.................Open lead near shore
6.................Heavy fast ice
7.................Heavy drift ice
8.................Hummocked ice
9.................Ice jamming

ICE DRAG. Large iron hook used in polar navigation. It is planted in the ice ahead of the vessel and used as a kedge in warping her along. Also **ice anchor** or for mooring.

Ger: *Eisdraggen.*

ICE DRIFT.
See Drift Ice.

ICE EDGE. The boundary between pack ice and the open sea; the position of which depends on wind and tides. Its position varies considerably from month to month.

Fr: *Rebord des glaces;* Ger: *Eiskante.*

ICE FIELD. A sheet of sea ice extending over a considerable area. It is of such extent that its termination cannot be seen from the crow's nest.
Fr: *Champ de Glace;* Ger: *Eisfeld.*

ICE FOOT. Ice step attached to the shore, unmoved by tides, and remaining after the fast ice has moved away.
Fr: *Lisière des glaces;* Ger: *Eisfuss.*

ICE FREE. Said of a harbor, river, estuary and so on, when navigation is not impeded by ice.
Fr: *Libre de glace;* Ger: *Eisfrei.*

ICE ISLAND. A term occasionally applied to a very large tabular iceberg.

ICE KNEE. One of the angular blocks of wood filling the space forward by the stem and the bow planks in a wooden whaling vessel as a strengthening against the pressure of the ice. They decrease in thickness until they are incorporated with the common ceiling below the forechains.

ICE NIP. Two ice fields meeting.

ICE OBSERVATION SERVICE. International service conducted by U. S. Coast Guard in the North Atlantic Ocean in addition to the Ice Patrol Service, and carried out by long range aircraft based at the U. S. Naval Station of Argentia (Newfoundland).

ICE PACK. Generic term for any area of pack ice, however small. Also called pack.
Fr: *Pack;* Ger: *Pack.*
See **Close Pack, Coastal Pack, Open Pack.**

ICE PATROL. The International Ice Patrol was started in April, 1912, after the loss of the S.S. "Titanic," by the United States Government, to maintain a patrol to the north of the Atlantic steamship routes in order to give notice by wireless to vessels of the southward course of the ice, and of zones made dangerous thereby. The object of the patrol is to locate icebergs and field ice nearest to the transatlantic steamship lanes. The natural lines governing formation and movements of ice in the North Atlantic are nowadays determined to the extent of permitting approximate forecasts similar to meteorological forecasts. Having located the ice, the patrol vessel on duty sends daily radiograms at 6 P.M. (75th Meridian time) to vessels, using 600 meters wave length. In these messages are given the description of the ice, that is, field or berg, the date, time latitude and longitude, and any other data useful to shipping.
Fr: *Service de Surveillance des Glaces;* Ger: *Eismeldedienst; Eispatrouille.*

The ice season usually lasts three months, April, May and June. Three vessels of the United States Coast Guard service are detailed each year to maintain the patrol during that season. Two of these are Coast Guard cutters of about 2,000 tons based at Halifax. The third vessel, of about 220 tons, is used for collecting oceanographic data. This information is used in establishing current charts showing the direction and velocity of ice-bearing currents.
International Ice Observation and Ice Patrol Service in the North Atlantic, Annual Reports 1913 to 1941, U. S. Coast Guard Bulletin, Washington, 1913–1941.

ICE PATROL VESSEL. A government vessel operated by the U. S. Coast Guard Service and engaged in the observation of iceberg movements in the vicinity of the Grand Banks of Newfoundland.
Fr: *Navire patrouilleur des glaces;* Ger: *Eiswachschiff.*

ICE PLANK. A sort of navigating bridge extending across the deck of a polar vessel from one side to the other. Also called **Spike plank.**

ICE POUND. A section of a fishing vessel's hold, used to stow ice. It is usually forward of the fish room. A door provides convenient access from the ice pound to the fish room.
See **Deck Pound, Fish Pound.**

ICE ROOM. An insulated space below deck in fishing vessels where crushed ice used in preserving the catch is kept. It is usually located in the fore end of the fish room.
Ger: *Eisbunker; Eisraum.*

ICE SKY.
See **Ice Blink.**

ICE STRENGTHENING. An increase in the scantlings of frames, plating, and riveting in the fore part of the hull to reinforce it for navigation in ice. This strengthening extends horizontally for about three-fifths of the ship's length from the stem and vertically from 1 to 3 ft. above load line and 3 or 4 ft. below light-waterline.
Ger: *Eisverstärkung; Eisdoppelung; Eisgürtel.*

IDAWANG. A small East Indian canoe without outriggers, used in the local fisheries of Aru Islands (Banda Sea). Also called *inang*.

IDLER. A member of the crew whose time at sea is not divided into watches and who normally works during the day and is off duty at night; such is usually the case for the following ratings: boatswain, carpenter, sailmaker, storekeeper, lamp trimmer, donkeyman. Also called day worker.
Ger: *Freiwächter*.

IDOKI. A generic term for various types of canoes in the Papuan Gulf (British New Guinea). The small *idoki* canoes are single-outrigger dugouts with pointed ends and about 21 ft. long. The larger type consists of double canoes, or multiple canoes of 4 or 5 hulls from 12 to 30 ft. long. Multiple canoes are called *kakau*.

IJON-IJON. A plank-built native craft from eastern Java used mostly for transportation of persons and goods. Some of these boats are occasionally employed in the fisheries.

IMMERSION SCALE (U. S.). A scale showing the number of tons required to immerse or put down a vessel at its various drafts. Also called draft scale.
Fr: *Echelle de tirants d'eau;* Ger: *Tiefgangskala*.
See **Displacement curve.**

IMMIGRATION OFFICER. A government official charged with the duty of enforcing the immigration laws in relation to all persons disembarking from vessels in a seaport.
Fr: *Inspecteur de l'immigration;* Ger: *Einwanderungskommissär*.

IMPERIAL COASTING TRADE (G. B.). A term which refers to sea-borne trade between the British Isles and the colonies and dominions, as well as between the British Isles themselves.

IMPLIED WARRANTY. A warranty such as seaworthiness of vessel, and the legality of the trade in which the vessel is engaged. It is one which, from custom or usage, is implied without being necessarily mentioned in the policy.
Fr: *Garantie Implicite;* Ger: *Unbedeutliche Garantie*.

IMPORT DUTY. Customs duty required by law to be paid on the importation of certain goods.
Fr: *Droit d'Entrée;* Ger: *Einfuhrzoll*.

IMPROPER NAVIGATION. As used in marine insurance the term "improper navigation" means the doing of something improper with the ship or part of the ship in the course of the voyage. It may be the result of some structural defect in the vessel or from its gear being out of order, as well as from the negligence of those on board. It also applies to the act of navigating a vessel when it is not in a fit condition to be navigated with safety to itself, its cargo, or its passengers.
Fr: *Navigation Fautive;* Ger: *Fehlerhafte Navigation*.

IMPULSE TURBINE. A turbine in which the escaping steam from a fixed nozzle strikes against the blades of a revolving wheel, forcing it to rotate.
Fr: *Turbine a action;* Ger: *Aktionsturbine*.

IN-AND-OUT BOLT. A bolt which goes clear through the parts it connects, such as bolts in knees, riders, and so on, which are driven through the ship's sides or athwartships. Also called through bolt.
Fr: *Cheville à travers bois;* Ger: *Durchbolzen*.

IN AND OUT PLATING (U. S.). A system of plating in which the inner strakes fay to the frames or beams and the outer strakes are distant therefrom by the thickness of the inner strakes. Inner and outer strakes alternate. Also called sunken and raised plating (G. B.).
Fr: *Bordé à Double Clins;* Ger: *An und abliegende Plattung*.

INANG.
See **Idawang.**

INBOARD. Toward the fore-and-aft centerline of the ship. Inside the deck edge or shell plating, as opposed to outboard.

INBOARD CARGO. The lading within the hold of a ship in distinction from freight such as horses, cattle, or any deck cargo.

In and Out Plating

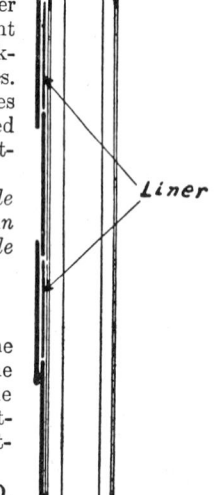

INBOARD PROFILE. A plan representing a longitudinal section through the center of the ship, showing deck heights, transverse bulkheads, and assignment of space located on the center plane or between the center and shell on the far side.

Fr: *Coupe Longitudinale*; Ger: *Längsschiffsplan*; *Längsschnitt*.

INBOARD PROFILE PLAN.
See **Profile**.

INBOUND FREIGHT. Cargo carried by a homeward bound ship. Also called return freight.

Fr: *Fret de Retour*; Ger: *Rückfracht*.

INCHMAREE CLAUSE. A clause usually inserted in hull policies by which the underwriter agrees to cover loss or damage to hull and machinery of the vessel through any latent defect. Its name originates from the test case fought by British underwriters in the House of Lords in 1887 when the steamer "Inchmaree" incurred damage as a result of the negligence of engineers. It was decided that such damage was not a peril of the seas and was not, therefore, covered by the marine policy.

INCH MAST. A square stick or piece of timber suitable for making a mast or spar. Inch masts are classed according to the number of inches at the side.

INCLINING EXPERIMENT. An experiment carried out on board ship to ascertain the transverse metacentric height or distance between the metacenter and the center of gravity. The procedure consists in moving a known weight a known distance from one side of the deck to the other, which causes the ship's center of gravity to move out a small distance toward the side to which the weight has been moved. The angle of heel caused by shifting the weight is ascertained by a long plumb line, which may be suspended from the upper deck and extend to the tank top. The horizontal shift of the center of gravity and the angle of heel are respectively one side and one angle of a right triangle, of which the metacentric height is another side. With one angle and one side known, the metacentric height which forms the other side of the triangle is found by a very simple trigonometric calculation. This experiment indicates the transverse metacentric height only for the condition of loading of the ship at the time of the experiment.

Fr: *Essai de Stabilité*; Ger: *Krangungsversuch*.

Hovgaard, W., "Inclining Experiments with Ships of Small or Negative Stability," Institution of Naval Architects (London), *Transactions*, vol. 68 (1926); Tawresey, J. G., "The Inclining Experiment," Society of Naval Architects and Marine Engineers (New York), *Transactions*, vol. 36 (1928).

INCLINOMETER.
See **Dip Circle**.

INCREASING PITCH. A propeller in which the pitch of blades increases from the leading edge to the trailing edge either radially or axially.

Fr: *Pas Croissant*; Ger: *Wachsende Steigung*; *Variable Steigung*.

INCREMENT OF ROLL. The amount of growth or increase in rolling until the maximum is reached

INDENTURES (G. B.). The articles or conditions of agreement between shipowner and apprentice in the British merchant marine.

INDEPENDENT PIECE.
See **Stem Piece**.

INDEX ARM. See **Index Bar**.

INDEX BAR. The movable arm of a sextant which swings across the frame and the graduated arc. Also called index arm. It carries the vernier and tangent screw at its lower end.

Fr: *Alidade*; Ger: *Zeigerarm*; *Alhidade*.

INDEX ERROR. An error in the angle indicated by a sextant, resulting from the index and horizon glasses not being parallel to one another when the pointer on the vernier indicates zero on the arc. Also called perpendicularity error.

Fr: *Erreur Instrumentale*; *Erreur d'Index*; Ger: *Instrumentalfehler*; *Indexfehler*.

INDEX GLASS. In a sextant, the mirror mounted on the upper end of the index bar, perpendicular to the plane of the limb. Also called index mirror.

Fr: *Grand Miroir*; Ger: *Grosser Spiegel*.

INDEX SHADE. On a sextant, one of the colored glasses mounted on a pivot and fitted to the index glass for regulating the light of the sun or reducing its glare, to permit accurate observation.

Fr: *Bonnette de Grand Miroir*; Ger: *Blendglas*; *Verdunklungsglas*.

INDIAMAN. A term occasionally applied to any ship in the East Indian trade, but in strict parlance one of the large sailing ships formerly owned by the East India Company for that trade. Also called East Indiaman.

Chatterton, E. K., *The Old East Indiamen*, London, 1933.

INDIAN HEADER (U. S.). A New England fishermen's term for a type of schooner built with round stem instead of the usual plumb stem. The first boats were given Indian names. (Obsolete.)

INDIAN JOLLY BOAT. A single-masted lateen-rigged sailing boat from Bombay and Karachi. The Bombay boat has a straight stem and is of lighter build than the Karachi boat. The latter has a curved stem and is larger and heavier. Both types have a square stern and are provided with loose-fitted decking from the stem to the third thwart. This covering acts as a deck from which the sail is worked; the space below is used as a cuddy for the crew. The mast is stepped in the center of the boat and has a considerable fore rake. A jib is occasionally set.

INDICATED HORSEPOWER. The power delivered by the pistons of a reciprocating engine. It is calculated from the areas of the indicator diagrams.

Fr: *Puissance Indiquée;* Ger: *Indizierte Pferdestärke.*

INDICATOR DIAGRAM. A diagram which records the varying pressures in the cylinder of a reciprocating engine during a complete revolution of the shaft, or double stroke of the piston. Also called indicator card. The diagram is recorded by means of a device called an indicator, which embodies a drum rotated by the movement of the engine crankshaft. Upon the drum, a stylus moves, actuated by pressure inside the engine cylinder. From the indicator diagram, the mean effective pressure throughout the stroke can be calculated, and thus, if the bore, stroke, and speed in revolutions per minute of the engine are known, the indicated horsepower can be derived.

Fr: *Diagramme d'Indicateur;* Ger: *Indikatordiagramm.*

INDIRECT ACTING PUMP. A pump which is driven by means of a beam or linkage, connected to and motivated by the piston rod of a detached steam reciprocating engine.

Fr: *Pompe attelée.*

INDIRECT CONNECTED STEERING GEAR. A steering gear in which the turning power is conveyed to the rudderstock by means of shafting, chains, ropes, or other leads. The chains or ropes are passed around a drum actuated by a steam engine provided with a controlling valve and valve gear connected to the steering wheel. Not in general use for modern ships of large or moderate size.

Fr: *Appareil à Gouverner à Commande Indirecte;* Ger: *Rudermaschine mit indirektem Antrieb.*

INDUCED DRAFT. A system of forced draft which consists of the application of large blowers designed to draw the hot combustion gases out of the boiler uptakes, and discharge them into the funnel.

Fr: *Tirage induit;* Ger: *Saugzug.*

INDUCED MAGNETISM. In dealing with steel ships the term refers to the earth's magnetic force induced in the iron or steel of the hull. Induced magnetism is the source of all magnetic disturbances of the compass needle.

Fr: *Magnetisme Induit;* Ger: *Inducierter Magnetismus.*

INFECTION, THEORY OF. A doctrine adopted by the United States, Great Britain, and Japan, according to which innocent goods seized on a neutral vessel and found on the same vessel as contraband goods are considered contaminated and therefore of infectious nature and liable to confiscation.

INFERIOR TRANSIT. The crossing of the meridian at the lower altitude by a celestial body whose declination is of the same name as, and of less altitude than that of the observer.

Fr: *Passage inférieur;* Ger: *Untere Kulmination.*

See **Superior Transit.**

INFERIOR MERIDIAN. That part of a meridian which lies below the horizon. Also called **Lower branch of the meridian.**

Fr: *Méridien Inférieur;* Ger: *Unteren Meridian.*

INFLAMMABLE CARGO. Inflammable cargoes include any article which is liable to spontaneous combustion, and volatile liquids emitting inflammable vapors.

Fr: *Marchandises Inflammables;* Ger: *Feuergefährliche Ladung.*

INFORMING GUN. The firing of a blank shot by a warship or commissioned vessel that wishes to exercise the right of search, as a signal to a merchantman for the latter to stop and lay to. Also called affirming gun.

Fr: *Coup de Semonce;* Ger: *Warnungsschuss.*

The requirement that the affirming gun

shall be fired is common in European continental practice but is not obligatory according to British and American views. It is customary for the war vessel to fly her colors when the gun is fired.

INHAUL, INHAULER. 1. A line or rope employed for bringing a spar or other inboard object. Usually called brail.

2. A line by which the head of a standing gaffsail is taken in or a running bowsprit hauled inboard.

Fr: *Hale à Bord;* Ger: *Einholer; Näherholer.*

INHERENT VICE. The natural tendency of some particular goods to waste or become damaged, as, for instance, spontaneous heating of copra or hemp, black rot in apples, disease of livestock, fermentation of liquids, and the like. Shipowners and underwriters usually decline responsibility for such a risk.

Fr: *Vice Propre;* Ger: *Originalfehler; Innerer Verderb.*

INITIAL COURSE. The first course steered when sailing on a great circle track.
Ger: *Anfangskurs.*

INITIAL STABILITY. The resistance offered by a ship to inclination from the upright position. It is measured by the metacentric height.

Fr: *Stabilité Initiale;* Ger: *Anfangsstabilität.*

See **Metacentric Height.**

INLAND RULES. The rules of the road enacted by Congress, governing the navigation of inland waters of the United States.
See **Rules of the Road.**

INLAND WATERS (U. S.). As used in marine insurance this term denotes canals, lakes, streams, rivers, watercourses, inlets, bays and arms of the sea between projections of land. When no specific line is prescribed, the dividing line at all buoyed entrances from seaward to bays, sounds, rivers or other estuaries is a line approximately parallel with the general trend of the shore, drawn through the outermost buoy or other navigational aid of any system of buoyage. The inland waters of a state are those inside its marginal sea as well as the waters within its land territory.

Fr: *Eaux Intérieures;* Ger: *Binnengewässer.*

INLET. A narrow opening by which a body of water penetrates into the land.
Fr: *Goulet;* Ger: *Einfahrt.*

INNER BOTTOM. See **Tank Top.**

INNER HARBOR. A harbor protected by piers or minor breakwaters, generally provided with tidal quays at which vessels berth.

Fr: *Arrière Port;* Ger: *Binnenhafen.*

INNER JIB. The headsail which is next forward to the forestaysail on large sailing vessels. This term is also applied to a sail set between the fore-topmast staysail and the outer jib.

Fr: *Petit Foc;* Ger: *Binnenkluver.*

INNER KEEL. The inner plate of a double, flat plate keel.

Fr: *Tôle Quille Intérieure;* Ger: *Innenkiel.*

INNER POST. A piece of timber brought on and fayed to the fore side of the main sternpost for the purpose of seating transoms upon it.

Fr: *Contre-Etambot;* Ger: *Binnen Hintersteven.*

INNER RABBET LINE. The upper or inside trace of the groove which forms the rabbet. The line of intersection of the plating and the stem or sternpost. Also called bearding line.

Fr: *Trait Intérieure de Rablure;* Ger: *Innere Spundungslinie.*

INNER STRAKE. A strake of plating in direct contact with the frames or beams.

Fr: *Virure de Placage;* Ger: *Anliegender Gang.*

INNER WATERWAY. One of the inner or inboard strakes of waterway planking. Also called thin waterway. They are about 1 or 1½ in. thicker than the remainder of the deck and are sunk between the beams and ledges to bring their upper surfaces level with the adjacent planking.

Fr: *Serre-Gouttière;* Ger: *Inneres Leibholz; Nebenwassergang; Innerer Wassergang.*

IN OARS. An order to lay the oars in the boat when lying on the oars or when the oars have been tossed or trailed. Also called boat the oars.

Fr: *Rentrez;* Ger: *Einriemen.*

INRIGGER. A boat which has her rowlocks on the gunwale, as distinguished from an outrigger, which has these extended on arms.

INSHORE FISH. Species of fish found within a short distance from the shores. These embrace a great variety of small size and find their harbor and shelter among rocks and stones, seaweed, eel grass, and so on. They can be taken from beaches, rocks, and wharves, or by small boats near the shore. They are among those most frequently taken in weirs, pounds, and fykes. The scup, sea bass, whiting, red snapper, pompano, mullet belong to this group.

INSHORE FISHERIES. Fisheries along the seashore carried on by small open boats and other craft usually within territorial waters. They include the catching of shrimp, lobsters, crabs, prawns; the breeding and fattening of oysters; the gathering of cockles and mussels, and so on. Also called coast fisheries.

Fr: *Pêche Côtière; Petite Pêche;* Ger: *Küstenfischerei.*

INSHORE NAVIGATION. Navigation carried out at a comparatively short distance from the coastline.

Fr: *Bornage;* Ger: *Nahfahrt.*

INSIDE CABIN. A cabin separated from the ship's side by another room or space.

Fr: *Cabine Intérieure;* Ger: *Innenkammer.*

INSIDE CLINCH. A clinch with the end bent close round the standing part till it forms a circle and a half and making a running eye when seized. Also called inner clinch.

Fr: *Noeud de Bouline Double;* Ger: *Innerer Klinsch; Binnenstich.*

INSIDE FASTENING. A name given to fastenings or bolts driven from inside the vessel.

Ger: *Binnenbefestigung.*

IN SQUARE KNEE. A knee in which the arm and body form an acute angle. Also called close-bevel knee.

IN STAYS. 1. Said of a vessel under sail heading into the wind with all sails shaking.

2. The position of a vessel under sail during the act of going about from one tack to the other.

Fr: *Vent Devant;* Ger: *In der Wendung liegen.*

See **Tack.**

INSTITUTE CARGO CLAUSES. A set of clauses adopted by the Institute of London Underwriters which provide an extension of the ordinary marine policies and are very often included in policies on goods.

Fr: *Clauses sur Facultés de l'Institut.*

INSTITUTE TIME CLAUSES. The institute time clauses (hull and cargo) represent an aggregate of amendments to, and graftings upon the original form of Lloyds policy of marine insurance. From time to time these clauses are altered or added to by the London Institute of Marine Underwriters.

INSTITUTE WARRANTIES. Warranty clauses usually defined and included in insurance policies according to the rules of the Institute of London Underwriters.

Fr: *Garanties de l'Institut de Londres.*

Dean and King Page, *The Institute Warranties* (Liverpool, 1935).

INSULAR SHELF. Area of sea bottom around an island which extends from the line of permanent immersion to the point where there is a marked or steep descent towards ocean depths.

Fr: *Socle insulaire;* Ger: *Inselschelf.*

INSULATED HOLD. Space for the carriage of frozen, chilled, or cooled cargoes where all exposed steelwork is covered with a thick layer of nonconducting material such as charcoal, granulated or slab cork, mineral wool, fibrous glass, and so on.

Fr: *Cale frigorifique;* Ger: *Kühlraum; Ladekühlraum.*

When brine is used as a cooling medium it is circulated through coils or grids of piping fixed under the deck and on the sides of each compartment. In cold air plants the cooling medium is circulated through wooden ducts or trunkways provided with suitable openings at intervals. The average loss in capacity of a hold due to insulation ranges from 17 per cent for large holds to 22 per cent for small holds and 'tween-deck spaces.

Balfour, R., Construction and insulation of holds of vessels engaged in the carriage of refrigerated cargoes, Fourth International Congress of Refrigeration, Proceedings, London, 1924.

INSULATION. The nonconducting material used for lining compartments or spaces on board ship which are intended for the transportation of refrigerated cargo. Cork, in granulated or block form, silicate of cotton (also called slagwood), and charcoal were generally used. Mineral wool and fibrous glass have recently come into use.

Fr: *Isolement; Isolation;* Ger: *Isolierung.*

The insulating material is kept in position by double thicknesses of tongued and grooved sheeting with one or two layers

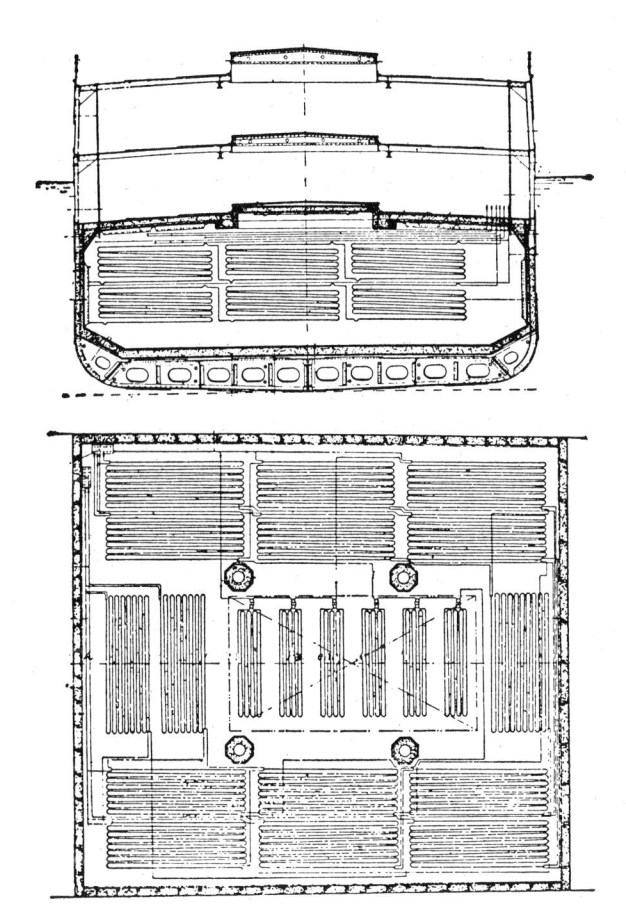

Insulated Hold. (*Cross Section Plan*)

of waterproof paper interposed between.

The insulation of fruit-carrying spaces is effected by a double belt of insulation. An air trunk is formed in between. The air is driven around this trunk and admitted to the hold through small ports at the sides.

Buchanan, R. M., Insulation and Fittings of Refrigerated Spaces on Shipboard, Association of Engineering and Shipbuilding Draughtsmen (London, 1930).

INSURANCE.
See **Marine Insurance**.

INSURANCE BROKER. An agent or middleman between the insured and the underwriter to effect insurance policies on ships, freights, cargo or any of them. Also called policy broker. The insurance broker sees to the adjustment and settling of losses where they occur.

Fr: *Courtier d'Assurance;* Ger: *Versicherungsmakler.*

INSURANCE CERTIFICATE. 1. A certificate issued by the insurer or his accredited agent when a shipment is made against an open or floating policy, the holder being entitled to the protection afforded under this policy.

2. A preliminary document issued by the brokers to certify to the insured that an insurance as described has been effected with the named underwriters and that the policy will be delivered as soon as it is ready.

Fr: *Certificat d'Assurance;* Ger: *Versicherungszertifikat; Versicherungsschein.*

INSURANCE CLAUSE. A marine insurance cargo clause which states that the underwriters are not liable for any loss, detriment, or damage to any goods which are capable of being covered by insurance by the shippers. Also called parasite clause.

Fr: *Clause de Risques Assurables;* Ger: *Assekuranzklausel; Parasite Klausel.*

INTERACTION. See Suction.

INTERCARDINAL POINT. One of the four points of the compass midway between the cardinal points: northeast, southeast, southwest, northwest. Also called semicardinal point.

Fr: *Point Intercardinal.*

INTERCEPT. The difference between the observed and calculated zenith distance of a heavenly body.

Fr: *Point Intercardinal;* Ger: *Zwischenkardinal Strich.*

INTERCEPT METHOD. A method of obtaining a position line at sea which involves calculating a heavenly body's zenith distance on the assumption that the dead reckoning is correct. Also called Marcq St. Hilaire method. The true zenith distance is then found by observation, and the difference, called the intercept, is applied either toward or away from the observed body along the azimuth line according to whether the true zenith distance is less or greater than that calculated.

Of late, short methods of calculating intercepts, such as Dreisonstok, Ageton, and H. O. 214, have supplanted the earlier cosine-haversine application of this method. Sommerville, *The St. Hilaire Method in Practice*, Glasgow, 1929; Uttmark, F. E., *The Marcq St. Hilaire Method*, New York, 1919.

INTERCOASTAL. Refers to seaborne trade or navigation between domestic ports situated on noncontiguous sea coasts.

INTERCOASTAL SHIPPING ACT (1933). An act passed by Congress in 1933 which provides that every common carrier by water in intercoastal trade shall file with the United States Maritime Commission and keep open to public inspection schedules showing all the rates of freight, fares, and charges for or in connection with transportation between intercoastal points on its own route.

INTERCOSTAL. A general term used for denoting longitudinal parts of the hull's structure which on account of obstructions cannot be worked continuous, and must be cut in comparatively short lengths between transverse structural members.

Fr: *Intercostal;* Ger: *Interkostal.*

INTERCOSTAL FLOOR. A floor composed of a range of small plates fitted between continuous side girders and securely clipped to them.

Fr: *Varangue Intercostale;* Ger: *Durchschnittene Bodenwrange.*

INTERCOSTAL KEELSON. A keelson built up of a series of intercostal plates between the floors.

Fr: *Carlingue Intercostale;* Ger: *Zwischenplatten Kielschwein.*

INTERCOSTAL PLATE. Any longitudinal plate extending between two transverse members of the ship's structure and landing upon each of them.

Fr: *Tôle Intercostale;* Ger: *Zwischenplatte; Interkostale Platte.*

INTEREST POLICY. One whereby definite or definable interests are insured in contradistinction to the wager policy.

Fr: *Police avec Intérêt;* Ger: *Anteil-Police.*

INTERMEDIATE FRAME. A frame in the double bottom which has no floor plate, in ships with floor plates fitted only to alternate frames. Also called skeleton frame.

Fr: *Membrure Intermédiaire;* Ger: *Zwischenspant.*

INTERMEDIATE LINK. A stud link, fitted between the end link and the common link in the anchor cable. Its diameter is 1.1 times the nominal diameter of the common link.

Fr: *Maille de Renfort; Grande Maille;* Ger: *Grosses Glied.*

INTERMEDIATE PORT. A port at which a vessel stops for loading and discharging cargo between the port of departure and the final port of destination.

Fr: *Port Intermédiaire;* Ger: *Zwischenhafen.*

INTERMEDIATE SHAFT. One of the lengths of main drive shafts between the thrust bearing and the propeller shafts. Also called line shaft, tunnel shaft. They are usually connected to each other by flanged couplings.

Fr: *Arbre Intermédiaire;* Ger: *Laufwelle.*

INTERMEDIATE VESSEL. The term "intermediate" applied to ocean-going vessels embraces a variety of ships which generally carry larger quantities of cargo and fewer passengers than the ocean-going passenger liner, the exact quantities of each being variable. Intermediate vessels usually run on routes where speed is not the main requirement and where cargo as well as passengers make their running a paying proposition, also where the number of passengers available does not justify the running of purely passenger lines.

Fr: *Paquebot Mixte;* Ger: *Fracht- und Fahrgastschiff.*

The term is applied to vessels of lower class than the express boats and scheduled to perform a given voyage in somewhat longer time. Freight rates by intermediate boats are generally less than by the faster boats and hence they tend to attract non-urgent or comparatively low-value cargo.

INTERMITTENT LIGHT. A lighthouse showing successively periods of light and of darkness of equal duration.

Fr: *Feu isophase; Feu intermittent;* Ger: *Unterbrochenes Feuer.*

INTERMITTENT QUICK FLASHING LIGHT. A coastal light in which the duration of quick flashes is interrupted by eclipses equal to the duration of the flashes.

Fr: *Feu scintillant intermittent;* Ger: *Unterbrochenes Funkelfeuer.*

INTERMITTENT WELDING. A series of short fusion welds laid down in uniformly spaced segments called increments.

Fr: *Soudures Alternées;* Ger: *Unterbrochene Schweissung.*

INTERNAL COMBUSTION ENGINE. Generic name for reciprocating engines in which the power for driving the pistons is provided either by electric ignition of a mixture of volatile gas and air compressed to a moderate pressure (gasoline engines); or by the slow combustion of oil injected into a charge of air compressed above ignition point (oil engines). Gasoline engines are used for the propulsion of small craft, oil engines for trading vessels of any size as well as for small boats.

Fr: *Moteur à Combustion Interne;* Ger: *Verbrennungsmotor.*

INTERNAL-STRAPPED BLOCK. A built-up wooden block in which a wrought-iron or steel strap is fitted in the shell. When there are several sheaves there is a strap on each side of every sheave. The pin works on the strap instead of the shell as is true of rope-strapped block. These blocks are measured in circumference from crown to tail, around the score. Also called internal-bound block.

Fr: *Poulie Havraise;* Ger: *Block mit innenliegendem Beschlag; Block mit Beschlag im Gehäuse.*

INTERNATIONAL CODE OF SIGNALS. A signal book printed in the language of all maritime nations, assigning arbitrary meanings to different arrangements of flags or displays of lights which are thus intelligible to all possessing the book. It consists of 26 square flags, ten numeral pendants, one answering pendant, and three substituters or repeaters. *One*-flag signals are urgent or very common signals. *Two*-flag signals are mostly distress and maneuvering signals. *Three*-flag signals are for points of the compass, relative bearings, standard times, verbs, punctuation, also general code and decode signals. *Four*-flags are used for geographical signals, names of ships, bearings. *Five*-flag signals are those relating to time and position. *Six*-flag signals are used when necessary to indicate north or south or east or west in latitude and longitude signals. *Seven*-flags are for longitude signals containing one hundred degrees or more.

Fr: *Code International de Signaux;* Ger: *Internationales Signalbuch.*

INTERNATIONAL (1929) CONVENTION FOR THE SAFETY OF LIFE AT SEA. An international convention which embodies the recommendations made by the International Maritime Conference held in London in 1929 to determine by international agreement uniform standards regarding the safety of human life at sea. The purpose of the conference was to make vessels thoroughly efficient as regards construction, subdivision and devices to assist navigation, and, in the event of accident, to make life saving appliances efficient and suitable to meet all reasonable demands.

The provisions of the convention apply to all passengers' vessels and in some instances to cargo vessels of 1,600 tons gross or over. A similar conference had been held in 1914 and had recommended certain rules and standards some of which were embodied in the national laws of different countries. No international standards, however, came into existence after this first conference. The rules of the second convention of 1929 have been ratified and enforced by the governments of the following countries: Argentina, Australia, Belgium, Brazil, Bulgaria, Canada, China, Denmark, Egypt, Estonia, Finland, France, Great Britain, India, Ireland, Italy, Japan, Netherlands,

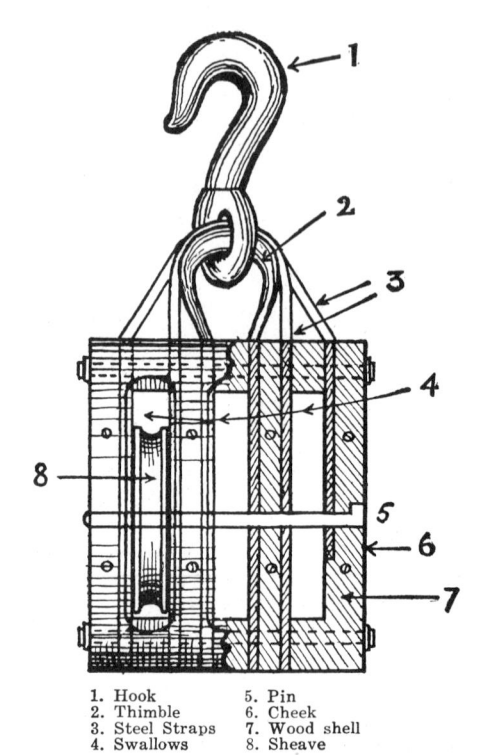

1. Hook	5. Pin
2. Thimble	6. Cheek
3. Steel Straps	7. Wood shell
4. Swallows	8. Sheave

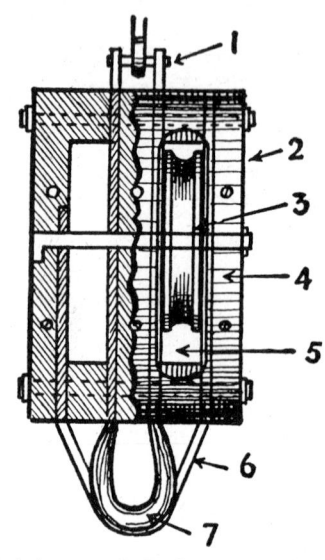 1. Becket	5. Swallow
2. Cheek	6. Steel Strap
3. Bushing	7. Lashing or Hooking Eye
4. Wood Shell	

Internal-Strapped Block

New Zealand, Norway, Panama, Poland, Portugal, Russia, Sweden, and the United States.

Rock, G. H. and Tawresey, J. G., "The International Conference of 1929 and the New Convention for Safety of Life at Sea," Society of Naval Architects and Marine Engineers (New York), *Transactions*, vol. 37 (1929); U. S. State Department, Treaty Series 910, *International Maritime Conference for Safety of Life at Sea*, Washington, 1937.

INTERNATIONAL HYDROGRAPHIC BUREAU. A scientific institution founded in 1921 and consisting of representatives of twenty-two nations organized for the purpose of coordinating the hydrographic work of the participating governments. Its principal aims are the introduction of uniformity in conventional signs and methods related to the production of nautical charts, lighting and buoyage of coasts, sailing directions, regulations for navigation and allied subjects. It has permanent headquarters in the principality of Monaco. Its publications consist of a periodical *The Hydrographic Review*, annual reports, and special pamphlets on technical subjects. The participating nations in 1939 were: Argentina, Australia, Brazil, Chile, China, Denmark, Egypt, France, Great Britain, Greece, Italy, Japan, the Netherlands, Norway, Peru, Poland, Portugal, Siam, Spain, Sweden, and the United States.

INTERNATIONAL LOAD LINE CERTIFICATE. A document issued by a government or a duly appointed person or organization such as a classification society, stating the minimum freeboard granted to any particular vessel and giving the position of the load-line disc on the ship's side. Since 1932, international load-line certificates have been issued in accordance with the provisions of the International Load-Line Convention, 1930. Load-line certificates are valid for a period of five years subject to certain intermediate inspections of the ship. They are issued to every ship with a tonnage of 150 tons gross or above engaged in international voyages, with the exception of yachts, ships solely engaged in fishing, and ships not carrying cargo or passengers.

Fr: *Certificat International de Franc-Bord;* Ger: *Internationales Freibordzertifikat.*

INTERNATIONAL MARITIME COMMITTEE. An organization, founded in 1905, composed of international lawyers designated by different countries to promote uniformity in relation to certain questions of maritime law, such as collision, salvage, maritime liens, limitation of shipowners' liabilities, and so on.

INTERNATIONAL MARITIME LAW. The system of rules which civilized states acknowledge between them and which relates to the affairs and business of the sea, to ships, their crews and to marine conveyance of persons and property. Also called international law of the sea. International maritime law is divided into public and private international maritime law. The former consists of the rules adopted for the settlement of questions relating directly to sovereign states, the latter of those adopted for settling litigations between subjects belonging to different nations.

Garner, J. W., *International Law and the World War*, London, 1920; Hall, W. E., *Treatise on International Law*, London, 1925; Oppenheim, L. F. L., *International Law*, London, 1935; Pearce Higgins and Colombos, *The International Law of the Sea*, London, 1943.

INTERNATIONAL RADIO SILENCE. Three minute periods of radio silence on the frequency of 500 kilocycles (distress frequency) commencing 15 and 45 minutes after each hour during which all ship's radio stations listen on that frequency for distress signals.

Fr: *Régime silence international;* Ger: *Internationales Funkstille.*

INTERNATIONAL RULE. A yacht measurement rule adopted since 1906 by international agreement among European nations. It is expressed as follows:

$$\text{Rating} = \frac{L + 2d + \sqrt{S.A.} - F}{2.37}$$

L = length, d = difference in feet between skin girth and chain girth, $S.A.$ = sail area, F = freeboard.

This rule has lately been used in various classes of racing craft in America. In general this rule follows the universal rule but technically it is supposed to be a little more modern and to produce a somewhat faster boat. Like the universal rule each boat is designed specially to come within the rating called for for each particular class. The international rule takes care of the 6 metre, 8 metre, 12 metre, etc., boats.

Fr: *Règle de jauge Internationale;* Ger: *Internationale Messformel.*

INTERNATIONAL RULES. The rules of the road established by agreement between maritime nations, governing the navigation of the high seas.

See **Rules of the Road.**

INTERNATIONAL VOYAGE. A voyage from any country to which the 1929 International Convention for Safety of Life at Sea applies to a port outside such country or vice versa. Colonies, overseas territory, or territory under mandate are for this purpose regarded as separate countries.

INTERNATIONAL WATERWAY. All parts of a waterway which in its course naturally navigable to and from the sea separates or traverses different countries.

INTERNATIONAL WEATHER CODE. A code used for the transmission of ship weather reports at sea. It consists of five figure groups; a ship report usually having four such groups in addition to the vessel's name. The first group tells the day of the week; the octant of the earth's surface and the latitude. The second tells the longitude and Greenwich mean time. The third gives the wind direction and force, and the weather. The fourth gives the barometric pressure in millibars; the visibility in miles and the temperature in degrees Fahrenheit.

Fr: *Code Météorologique International;* Ger: *Internationales Wetterschlüssel.*

INTERTROPICAL FRONT. The boundary between the trade wind systems of the Northern and Southern hemispheres. See **Doldrums.**

IN THE WIND. 1. A ship is in the wind of another when it is directly to windward of it.

2. A ship itself is in the wind when it is pointing up and has its sails either shaking or aback, or is so close to the wind as to have the wind spilled from the sails.

Fr: *Dans le Vent; En Ralingue;* Ger: *In den Wind.*

INVERSION. Used to denote inversion of temperature gradient. The expression is used in meteorology to denote a condition where temperature of the atmosphere increases with height contrary to the normal condition where the reverse is the case.

INVERTED-V-BOTTOM BOAT. See **Sea Sled.**

INVERTING TELESCOPE. A bell-shaped telescope of relatively high power used with a sextant. The arrangements of the lenses is such that the objects seen through it appear inverted. This telescope is provided with two eye pieces, one of which is of higher magnifying power than the other. Each of them is fitted with cross wires at its focus in order to define the line of collimation.

Fr: *Lunette Astronomique*; Ger: *Gestirn Teleskop.*

INWALE. A piece of timber fastened inside the frame or timbers of an open boat and extending along the top strake of planking. It answers the purpose of the clamp used in decked boats.

Fr: *Lisse Verticale*; Ger: *Dollbord; Wagerung.*

INWARD CHARGES. General term for charges incurred by a vessel or her cargo when entering a port.

Fr: *Frais à l'Entrée*; Ger: *Einfuhrkosten.*

INWARD CLEARANCE CERTIFICATE. When a ship arrives at a port it is the duty of the master to report at the customhouse to give the necessary particulars as to the cargo and crew. There are then certain dues to be paid; and as soon as these have been settled permission is given for the ship to be unloaded. When unloading is completed and the ship has been searched by the customhouse authorities to ascertain that there are no dutiable nor prohibited articles on board, an inward clearance certificate is delivered. Also called entry certificate.

Fr: *Expédition d'Entrée; Déclaration à l'Entrée; Entrée en Douane*; Ger: *Einklarierungs Attest.*

INWARD MANIFEST. A manifest handed by the master to the customs authorities on arrival of the vessel in a port. Stores and provisions which have to be declared are mentioned on this manifest.

Fr: *Manifeste d'Entrée*; Ger: *Einfuhrmanifest.*

IRISH BARREL. In the fish trade, a container in which fresh mackerel are packed for shipment. It is a watertight wooden barrel having a capacity of 150 lb. of fish, 45 lb. of ice, and enough sea water to float the fish. The buoyancy given by the water prevents the fish from being bruised excessively in transit.

IRISH BOAT. A type of New England fishing boat built in Boston in the sixties. Also called Boston cutter. It was similar in rig to the Galway Hooker. The hull had more dead rise and sharper lines. The stem was nearly vertical. The stern was finished off with a heart-shaped transom, also set nearly upright. Now extinct.

See **Dungarvan Boat.**

IRISH MOSS. A variety of brown seaweed or kelp found along the Irish and New England coasts.

IRISH PENNANT, DEAD MEN. Rope yarns hanging about the rigging; loose reef points or gaskets flying about; fag ends of ropes, any untidy loose end of line which should be stowed or tucked in.

IRISH SEA STERN. A type of stern common in Irish Sea trading ketches and schooners, particularly those built in Lancashire. Also called Lancashire Stern. It is well rounded, and finished to an almost vertical sternpost. There is no transom or counter, but the bulwarks are carried right around in a bold sweep and splayed outward so as to surround the rudderhead.

IRISH SPLICE. Turns hove in the lay of a ratline to shorten it to the required length.

IRON. The name commonly applied by whalemen to a harpoon. Live irons were the first and second harpoons which rested ready to hand in the crotch of the whaleboat. Loose irons were those without lines attached. (Obsolete.)

IRON BARK. A strong, heavy hardwood, also called Australian blue gum, extensively used on the Pacific coast of the U. S. for stems, sternposts, rudderposts and keel shoes of fishing vessels. Also of value for fenders, wearing strips and similar service for which white oak is used on the east coast. Weighs about 70 lb. per cu. ft. when seasoned.

Fr: *Bois de Fer*; Ger: *Eisenholz.*

IRON BOUND. Said of a rocky coast without anchorage.

Ger: *Felsige Küste.*

IRON QUARTERMASTER. See **Gyropilot.**

IRON ROPE. Wire rope formerly in common use on board ship. It has nowadays been replaced by steel rope with higher strength and better wearing qualities. It is more pliable and softer than steel rope. Average tensile strength 80,000 pounds per square inch.

IRONS, IN. 1. A vessel under sail is in irons when up in the wind and unable to pay off on either tack.
2. This term also refers to a ship unable to turn freely, such as a tugboat with tow rope secured right aft.

optic chart through places having the same barometric tendency.

ISHERWOOD FRAMING. A system of framing in which the ordinary closely spaced transverse frames and beams are disposed longitudinally, the transverse strength being maintained by heavy web frames spaced 10 to 12 ft. apart. Also called longitudinal framing. Longitudinals are usually fitted in continuous lengths between transverse bulkheads, at which they are cut and bracketed, the web frames or transverses being notched to pass them.

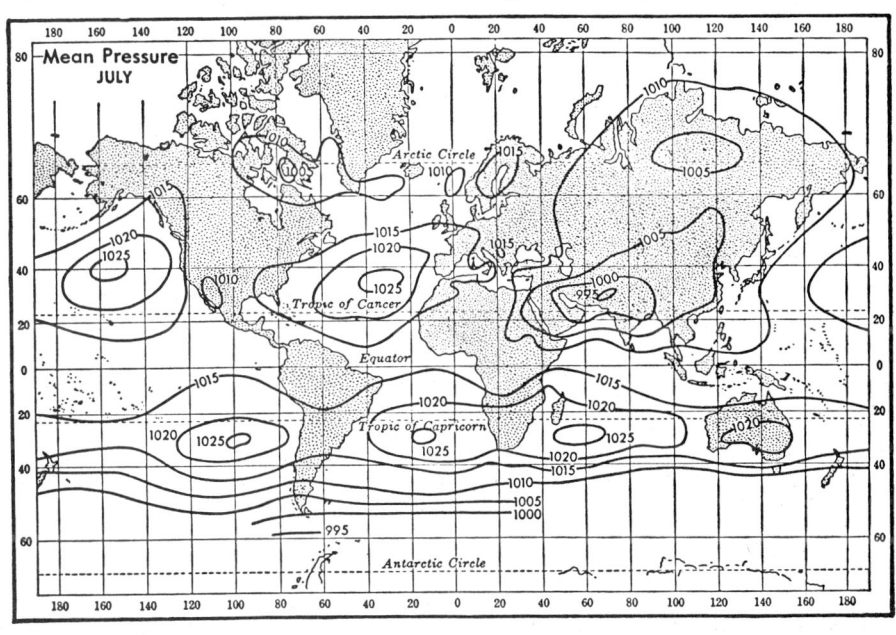

Isobaric Chart

IRON-SICK. The condition of a wooden hull in which the iron fastenings are loose. Also called nail sickness. It is due to corrosion of the metal by gallic acid contained in the timber and also to the reaction of the oxidized metal on the wood, which results in enlarged rotten holes discolored with rust.
Ger: *Schadhaftes Eisenwerk.*

IRON-STRAPPED BLOCK. A wooden block with an outside strap made of wrought iron. Also called ironbound block.
Fr: *Poulie Ferrée;* Ger: *Block mit Eisenbeschlag.*

ISALLOBARS. A term applied in meteorology to lines or curves drawn on a syn-

Fr: *Construction Isherwood;* Ger: *Isherwood Bauart; Langsspantenbauart.*
Isherwood, J. W., "A New System of Ship Construction," Institution of Naval Architects (London), *Transactions,* 1908.

ISINGLASS. A gelatin made from the dried swimming bladders of sturgeon and other fishes.

ISLE OF SHOALS BOAT. A double-ended half-decked sailing boat from Ipswich Bay (Massachusetts) also locally known as *shay.* The hull was built with straight keel with some drag to it, straight slightly raking stem, sharply raked sternpost, moderate sheer, clinker planking. These boats were rigged like the Hampden boats or with gaff sails in the same arrangement. Length 22 ft. Breadth 7 ft. Depth 3 ft. (Typical.) Type now obsolete.

ISOBAR. A line on a chart connecting places on the earth at which the barometric pressure is the same at a given time or on the average for a given period. Also called isobaric line.

Fr: *Isobare;* Ger: *Isobare.*

ISOBARIC CHART. A chart showing lines joining all places having equal barometric pressure.

Fr: *Carte Isobarique;* Ger: *Isobarische Karte.*

ISOBATH.
See **Fathom Line.**

ISOCLINAL CHART. A chart on which show the lines of equal magnetic dip or inclination on the earth's surface.

Ger: *Isoklinenkarte.*

ISOCLINAL LINE, ISOCLINAL. Curves drawn through all points where the magnetic needle makes the same angles with the horizon. The line of no dip is called magnetic equator.

Fr: *Ligne Isocline;* Ger: *Isoklinische Linie.*

ISODYNAMIC LINE. Isodynamic lines are those of equal magnetic intensity or horizontal force on the needle.

Fr: *Ligne Isodynamique;* Ger: *Isodynamische Linie.*

ISOGONIC LINE. Lines passing through all points where the magnetic needle is deflected from the geographical meridian by the same amount.

Fr: *Ligne Isogone;* Ger: *Isogonische Linie.*

ISOHALINES. Lines of equal salinity of sea water.

ISOTHERM. A line on a chart connecting places on the earth at which the mean temperature is the same.

Fr: *Isotherme;* Ger: *Isotherme.*

ISTHMUS. A narrow neck of land which joins a peninsula to its continent, or two islands together.

Fr: *Isthme;* Ger: *Isthmus.*

ITALIAN HEMP. A fiber of great length from the plant *Cannabis sativa,* grown in the province of Piedmont. The finest quality of hemp is obtained from it.

ITCHEN PUNT. A small cutter-rigged boat used by fishermen and pilots in Southampton water and the Solent. Also called Itchen ferry. It is built with straight transom stern, iron keel, carvel planking, forward deck and has a large cockpit with waterways and coaming. The rig consists of a gaff and boom mainsail with jack-yard gaff-topsail, foresail, and occasionally a jib. For fishing the punts are worked with two sails only. The foresail sets on a short bumkin. When a jib is used the bowsprit is made fast alongside the bumkin. Length over-all 27 ft. 9 in. Beam 7 ft. 10 in. Depth 3 ft. 9 in. (Typical.)

J

J. Flag of the international code of signals showing three equal horizontal divisions: two blue and one white.

See **Semaphore Flag**.

J. and W.O. JETTISON AND WASHING OVERBOARD.

JABEGA. A Spanish open seine-boat propelled by oars and employed for working a beach seine, called *jabega*, three boats being employed with each net. Its name is derived from *jabeque*, the Spanish word for *xebec*, of which it is a diminutive. There are several local types of *jabega* boats. Those seen around Malaga are fitted with a beakhead forward and curved stem and sternpost rising about 2½ ft. above the gunwale. Oars and fishing buoys can be stowed between them when not in use, leaving the inside of the boat clear for handling the net. The tonnage of these boats ranges from 2½ to 5.

The *jabega* boat is double-ended and steered with a long sweep. In the Malaga type of boat the steering oar rests outboard on a small bumkin called *espaldilla*.

The *jabega* from Conil (Cadiz) has four thwarts and a tall stemhead, but no rising sternpost. In another type the side planking is raised amidships for a short length and the thwarts are placed in the afterpart of the boat, leaving the midships and fore port clear for stowing the net, and so on.

In the Balearic Islands the same type of boat is called *laud*.

JACHT. 1. A cutter-rigged sailing coaster from the east coast of Schleswig-Holstein formerly employed in the small coasting trade between Baltic ports. The hull was carvel-built with sharp floors, deep keel, rounded stem, and transom stern with outboard rudder. The rig consisted of a pole mast and narrow headed loose-footed gaff-mainsail, jackyard topsail, jib-headed foresail and two jibs. The bowsprit was standing or running, with jibboom, and in some instances a dolphin striker. Now probably extinct.

2. A North Sea cutter-rigged fishing boat originating from East Frisia. The hull is bluff-bowed with full buttocks and fitted with leeboards. The mainsail has a short head with small gaff and long foot. It is chiefly employed in the fisheries over the shoals of Frisian coastal waters.

JACK. 1. A flag showing the canton or union of the national ensign without the fly. It is hoisted on a jack staff at the bowsprit cap when in port. It is also used as a signal for a pilot when shown at the fore. In vessels without bowsprit the jack staff is placed above the stemhead.

Fr: *Pavillon de Beaupré*; Ger: *Bugflagge*.

See **Yellow Jack**.

2. A schooner-rigged vessel from 10 to 25 tons, used in Newfoundland fisheries. It is generally full and clumsy, with little overhang at the counter, and carries a mainsail, a foresail and a jib, and occasionally a small mainstaysail.

3. An athwartship bar of iron fitted at the topgallant masthead, to give spread to the royal shrouds.

Fr: *Barres de Perroquet*.

4. A device for lifting heavy equipment or for applying great pressure at a desired point. Jacks may work either on a screw or a hydraulic principle but in all cases are designed to lift heavy weights by the application of a small force over a long period of time.

Fr: *Vérin*; Ger: *Hebeschraube*; *Hebemaschine*.

See **Cable Jack, Cargo Jack, Lazy Jack, Sand Jack**.

JACKASS. 1. A conical canvas stopper stuffed with tarred oakum and fitted where hawseholes lead under the forecastle. Also called hawse bag. It is pulled into the pipe with big end outboard, and hove tight by means of a rope tail. Jackasses are a most effective method of making hawseholes watertight in ships using stocked anchors.

Fr: *Sac d'Ecubier*; Ger: *Klussack*.

2. Heavy, roughly built boat used in Newfoundland.

JACKASS BARK. 1. A three-masted vessel, square-rigged on the foremast, setting square topsails and topgallant sails over a gaff-mainsail, and fore-and-aft rigged on the mizzen. Also called jigger bark, hermaphrodite bark.

2. A four-masted vessel, square-rigged on fore and main masts and gaff-rigged on the mizzen and jigger masts.

3. Any other sailing vessel with three or more masts carrying combinations of square and gaff sails, not otherwise named.

According to some, a jackass bark has fidded topgallant masts but no tops, and carries courses on fore and main, while a three-mast topsail schooner has "schooner" topmasts minus the fidded topgallant masts, and sets her courses flying.

JACKASS BRIG. Name formerly given by American seamen to a brig-rigged vessel which did not set a square mainsail, and had a fore topmast and fore-topgallant mast made of one spar. The term has also been applied to brigantines used in the Labrador seal fishery from 1850 to 1880. They carried yards on the mainmast in the summer time, when engaged in the fishery, in order to have the advantage of two square-rigged masts when working among ice floes. In the winter the yards were sent down and they sailed as "half brigs."

JACKASS GUNTER. A variation of the gunter rig in which the upper mast iron is replaced by a wire span with traveler and upper halyard. Also called bastard gunter.

JACKASS RIG. Generic term applied to any rig which differs in some point from the main type to which it belongs.

See **Jackass Bark, Jackass Brig.**

JACK CROSS-TREES. Single iron cross-trees at head of a topgallant mast for spreading the royal shrouds. This term also refers in fore-and-aft rigged vessels to hinged cross-trees which enable the topmast to be lowered, as is usually done in topsail barges and some other small craft.

Fr: *Croisette; Barres de Perroquet;* Ger: *Querstange.*

See **Cross-trees.**

JACKING ENGINE. An auxiliary steam engine or electric motor fitted to the drive shaft in a main propulsion plant, to permit moving the main engine or turbine. It is used when the engines must be turned over in port, to permit repairs, adjustment and inspection. Also called turning engine.

Fr: *Vireur;* Ger: *Drehvorrichtung.*

JACKKNIFE. A seaman's horn- or wood-handled clasp knife with a shackle for attaching a lanyard. The blade is about 3 in. in length and has a sheep-foot point.

JACK LADDER. A ladder with wooden steps and rope sides.

JACKLINE.

See **Reefing Jackstay.**

JACK PIN. One of a set of belaying pins fitted across the shrouds.

Fr: *Cabillot de Ratelier;* Ger: *Belegnagel.*

JACK ROD. A length of metal rod or small pipe supported at frequent intervals by welded or riveted eyebolts on the ship's structure, to which the awnings, weather cloths, canvas covers, and the like, are secured with seizings. Also called jackstay.

Fr: *Filière d'Envergure;* Ger: *Jackstag.*

JACK ROPE. 1. The rope lacing which bends the foot of a sail to a boom.

Fr: *Transfilage;* Ger: *Lissung; Reihleine.*

2. A line rove through the grommets of a reef band for reefing with the use of a toggle on the jackstay.

Fr: *Filière de Ris;* Ger: *Reffleine.*

3. A wire rope by which the foot of a fore-and-aft sail is secured to its boom. It runs fore and aft through eyebolts screwed in on the top of the boom and through small thimbles sewed on the boltrope at the foot of the sail at every seam.

4. See **Lacing.**

JACK STAFF. Small flagstaff on which merchant vessels hoist a company's house flag and warships the union jack. It is placed on the stemhead or, if a bowsprit is carried, on the bowsprit cap. The jack is never flown while the vessel is under way.

Fr: *Bâton de Pavillon de Beaupré;* Ger: *Göschstock.*

JACKSTAY. A stay used on racing and cruising yachts to counteract the strain produced by the thrust of a gaff on the mast. It runs from masthead over a short strut placed at the height of the gaff jaws when the sail is hoisted, down to the deck, where it is spliced around the mast beneath a cleat. A turnbuckle is usually fitted just above the lower splice.

Fr: *Contre-Étai;* Ger: *Jackstag.*

See **Awning Jackstay, Bending Jackstay, Jack Rod, Reefing Jackstay.**

JACKYARD. A light spar laced to the head of a square-cut gaff topsail. It is carried acockbill, the highest end raking toward the stern. Also called jenny yard.

Fr: *Vergue de Flèche;* Ger: *Gaffeltoppsegel Raa.*

JACKYARDER.

See **Jackyard Topsail.**

JACKYARD TOPSAIL. A square-cut gaff-topsail in which the head is bent to a small spar which sets at an angle after the fashion of a lugsail. The foot is loose and does not project beyond the gaff end. Also called jackyarder or lug topsail.

Fr: *Flèche Carré; Flèche à Vergue;* Ger: *Raa Toppsegel.*

JACKY BOOM. A term used by fishermen to denote a short boom laced on the afterpart of the foot of a lug mizzen. To the middle of this spar the sheet is bent and led through a block on the outer end of the mizzen outrigger.

JACKY TOPSAIL (G. B.). A gaff topsail with long yard extending nearly vertically above the mast head. It is smaller than the jigger topsail and has no jigger yard at the clew. Also called **Jubilee topsail.**

JACOB'S LADDER. A ship's ladder consisting of rope or chain sides with wood or metal rungs regularly spaced. One end is usually fitted with sister hooks or a shackle for hooking on.

Fr: *Echelle de Revers;* Ger: *Jakobsleiter.*

JAEGT. A Norwegian coasting vessel employed in the transportation of dried cod, cod roe, cod liver oil, etc., from the Nordland fishing stations to Bergen and other coastal ports where these products are gathered for export. It is single-masted and very broad and bluff. Length over-all 60 ft. Beam 38 ft. Breadth at stern 14 ft. 7½ in. Molded depth 12 ft. Depth of keel 18 in. Length of portable deck 32 ft. 3 in. Length of mast above deck 57 ft. 3 in. Length of mainyard 37 ft. 6 in. Topsail yard 27 ft. (Typical.)

The curved stem piece rises vertically 8 or 9 ft. above deck. The square stern is excessively full, with little or no run. The center part of the vessel is not decked; portable boards are used to protect the cargo. A rowboat is carried on two strong stern davits made of wood and projecting outboard about 3 ft. 9 in. The hull is built with clinker planking and treenail fastenings. The rig consists of a pole mast stepped almost in the center and nearly upright, with four shrouds and two backstays on each side. There are two stays fastening to the stem. A tall square mainsail with three or four bonnets, a square topsail, and a jib form the sail plan.

JAFFNA DONI. A small Indian coasting vessel of about 150 tons built in northern Ceylon and rigged as a two-masted fore-and-aft schooner with enormously developed bowsprit on which as many as five headsails are set. In Hindu ships the hull is built with raked stem with inwardly curved ornamented stemhead. The Moslem ships have a plain stemhead. There is a short deck at each end terminated by a high transverse breakwater. The waist is covered by a thatched roof of palm leaves. Length between perpendicular 100 ft. Breadth 21 ft. 2 in. Depth (molded) 14 ft. Tons 144.

JAGGERY. A very dirty damp sugar obtained from the sap of various palm trees.

JAGOHAN. A Javanese trading craft similar to the *penjaleng.*

JAGT. A small coasting vessel employed in Norway for the transportation of salted fish and various other purposes, including the seal fisheries. In hull form it resembles the *jaegt,* although it is considered in Norway as an improvement on the latter, with its sharp bow, raking transom, fore-and-aft deck, and carvel planking. Length over-all 61 ft. 8 in. Beam 17½ ft. Depth 8 ft. 4 in. (Typical.)

Its rig is totally different, being essentially fore and aft, with gaff and boom mainsail, gaff-topsail, and 3 or 4 headsails. The mast is stepped about two-fifths of the vessel's length from the bow. A square sail, set flying, is carried in addition. The average tonnage is about 40.

JAKE. A name given in the Canadian Maritime Provinces to a two-mast fore-and-aft schooner with transom stern.

JALAK. A two-masted trading vessel from the east coast of the Malay Peninsula, built of *giam* wood and of same rig as the *penjajap.* It is known as *payang* at Trengganu. Length 72 ft. Breadth 12 ft. Depth 9 ft. Capacity 5 tons.

JALBA. A small craft from Hodeida (Red Sea) with curved stem like a *sambuk* but with less overhang and a high raking stern. Also called *jalbuti.* The rig consists of one mast with lateen sail. Arab ship's boat slung from the stern.

JALOR. Generic name given to different types of native craft from the East Indies, of which there are many varieties. Sometimes called *jalur.*

On the east coast of Sumatra (Indragiri and Palembang) the name refers to a flat-bottomed small dugout. Some are so small that they can barely carry one man. In western Sumatra, the *jalor* is an outrigger canoe of the largest type made up of a dugout with planked sides. It is rigged with two or even three masts and has a very long, roofed shelter, which extends beyond the stern and terminates in a sort of transom.

JAMB BACK. See **Jam Hammer.**

JAMB CLEAT. A wooden or steel cleat used when launching a vessel. Also called launching cleat. It is secured to the ship in such a manner that it will catch the head of a shore.

Fr: *Taquet de Lancement.*

JAM CLEAT. A deck cleat with horns of unequal length. When belaying a rope the hauling part is pulled across under the long horn where it jams between the horn and the deck.

JAM HAMMER. A special type of pneumatic holding-on hammer used in heavy riveting, and for double-gunning rivets (driving from both ends). It is adapted to use in cramped quarters. Also called jam riveter or jamb back.

    Fr: *Tas Pneumatique;* Ger: *Pneumatischer Gegenhalter.*

JAMIE GREEN. See **Jimmy Green.**

JAMMED. A ship under sail is jammed in the wind when she is squeezed close up into it so as to lay half her upper canvas aback. A rope is jammed when it will not haul over a sheave.

    Ger: *Bekneigen; Lebendig halten.*

JANGADA. A sort of catamaran consisting of 4 or 5 logs of balsa wood pinned together with wooden pegs and rigged with a light mast which carries a triangular sail. *Jangadas* range in length from 20 to 26 ft., with a breadth of from 6 to 8 ft. They are used for fishing on the northeast coast of Brazil. Steering is effected by means of a deep broad-bladed rudder, which is inserted into the weather of two oblique slots between the logs aft. This rudder and a deep wooden dagger centerboard give the necessary lateral resistance. As the pressure of the rudder is likely to force the after logs apart these are bound together with a form of Spanish windlass.

When the boat is being sailed, the foot of the sail is kept constantly wet. There are no less than five different steps for the heel of the mast according to the direction of the wind. The sail is kept constantly laced to the mast and when it is to be taken in the boom is unshipped and the sail wrapped around the mast. A single shifting backstay is the only rigging apart from the sheet, which is a single part.

Jangadas work as far as 30 to 40 miles offshore. They are very fast, reaching along at 10 knots. The crew consists of 3 or 4 men. When the boat is being beached, the rudder and centerboard are unshipped, and, with the sail set, the boat shoots right up on the beach. It is then run higher on rollers. As its buoyancy depends entirely on the logs, which readily absorb water, it is necessary to run it ashore after every trip to allow the logs to dry.

JANGOLAN. East Indian coaster from eastern Java and Madura Island, also occasionally used by fishermen as a carrier. The hull is plank-built and of the same type as the *alisalis*. The bow has the form of a wedge-shaped transom. A sort of permanent decking is provided and runs fore and aft. The beam ends project outside the planking. The rig is the same as in the *sekong* with bowsprit, short foremast stepped near the bow, and lateen mainsail without mast. A thatched roofing of bamboo mats protects the cargo from rain and sun.

JANSEN CLAUSE. A marine insurance clause intended to relieve an underwriter for the first 3 per cent of any claim in the event of a particular average on ship, although stranded, sunk, or burnt, owners agreeing to remain uninsured for this 3 per cent.

JAPAN CURRENT.
See **Kuroshiwo.**

JAPAN STREAM.
See **Kuroshiwo.**

JASON CLAUSE. A clause included by shipowners in the bills of lading to protect themselves against the consequences of damage through unseaworthiness, latent defects, negligence, and so on, for which the shipowners are not responsible, the consignees, cargo owners, or shippers agreeing to contribute in the event of general average arising from any of these causes. It is so termed because the validity of this clause was admitted in court after eight years of litigation in connection with cargo carried by the steamer "Jason."

JATEN. A very small dugout canoe from southern Java and Madura, with double outriggers and rigged with a bamboo mast and triangular shaped sail. Also called prao jaten. It has no wash strake and the ends are sharp and flat. The crew consists of 1 or 2 hands. These craft are used for fishing and venture out in open waters at comparatively long distances from shore. Double-bladed paddles are used when moving against head-winds.

JAW. The fore end of a gaff which half encircles the mast, the prongs of which are called cheeks or horns. It is also called throat.

    Fr: *Mâchoire;* Ger: *Klaue; Gaffelschuh.*

JAW PARREL.
See **Jaw Rope.**

JAW ROPE. A rope passed through and

across the jaws of a gaff to hold it against the mast. It is generally threaded through wooden beads or trucks to prevent jamming.

Fr: *Racage;* Ger: *Racktau; Klaurack.*

JAW STRAP. A whaleman's name for a chain sling used for hoisting the jaw of a whale when cutting in. (Obsolete.)

JEEP. Small single screw coaster with a capacity of about 2800 tons dead weight, employed in the short sea trades, principally in the Baltic.

JEGONG. A small dugout canoe of the same type as the *jaten,* used in the fisheries of southern Java. This term is also used to denote a large plank-built fishing craft from western Java.

JEHAZI.
See *Gehazi.*

JEITERA. A Spanish fishing boat from the province of Galicia used for working a drift net called *jeito* in the Sardine and Anchovy fisheries. The interior of the boat is divided into five compartments: the first one near the stem is used for ropes, the second (*trilla*) for the crew's accommodation, the next one (*cadeira*) is used for nets, and the aftermost one (*pana*) for the catch. The hull is built with sharp stern, pronounced sheer forward and is steered with a long oar (no rudder). Length 19.7 ft. Breadth 8.1 ft. Depth 2.6 ft. (Typical.) The rig consists of a single lugsail or lateen with mast stepped in the bows. Also called jaitera.

JELOTONG. An inferior gutta-percha obtained by tapping the jelotong tree.

JENNY YARD. Name given on the east coast of England to a jackyard.

JEQUE. An open fishing boat from the Azore Islands with fine entrance and run. It has the reputation of being a very good sea boat with excellent sailing qualities. The rig consists of 1 or 2 masts with lateen sails. Some boats carry a headsail. The frames are of cedar and the planking is iron-fastened. Length 30 ft. Breadth 5½ ft.

JERKING (G. B.). A colloquial term used for denoting the search of a ship by a custom's officer called jerker to ascertain if there are any unentered goods concealed.

Fr: *Visite de Douane;* Ger: *Zollbeamten Untersuchung.*

JERK NOTE. A permit issued by the collector of customs to the master of a vessel authorizing him to receive on board goods for his outward cargo, after the whole of the inward cargo has been discharged and no unentered goods have been found.

JET PROPULSION. A system of propulsion for water craft in which a jet of water is pumped astern causing the ship to move forward due to the equal and opposite reaction set up by the astern force of the jet. The system is still in the experimental stage for marine use. Also called hydraulic propulsion.

Fr: *Propulsion hydraulique;* Ger: *Hydromotor Antrieb.*

Barnaby, S. W., Institution of Civil Engineers (London), *Proceedings,* vol. 77 (1884); Anon., "The Hydraulic Propulsion of Ships," *Engineer* (London), vol. 131 (February, 1921); Rabbeno, "Allgemeine Betrachtung über Strahlpropeller," *Werft-Reederei-Hafen,* vol. 10 (December, 1929).

JETSAM. 1. Cargo which after being jettisoned remains under water. Goods which when cast out from a ship by way of jettison sink. **2.** Goods jettisoned for the preservation of the ship and cargo.

Fr: *Épave rejetées;* Ger: *Seewurf; Angeschwemmtes Strandgut; Strandtriftige Güter.*

See **Flotsam, Lagan, Wreck.**

JETTISON. The act of throwing goods overboard to lighten a ship or improve stability in stress of weather or in other cases of necessity or emergency. Any jettison of goods for the purpose of saving the whole adventure is a general average loss except in the case of deck cargo. This exception, however, does not apply when deck cargo is carried in accordance with the recognized custom of the trade.

Fr: *Jet à la Mer;* Ger: *Seewerfen; Über Bord werfen.*

JETTY. An engineering structure projecting into the water, of the nature of a pier, dike, embankment, constructed of timber, earth, stone or a combination thereof. By means of jetties at the mouth of a river and at the entrance to a tidal harbor, the channel may be narrowed and the current concentrated so as to increase the depth of water over the entrance bar. The term "jetty" is also applied to a narrow projecting wharf in Great Britain, but not in the United States.

Fr: *Jetée;* Ger: *Hafendamm; Leitdamm.*

JEWEL BLOCK. A small single block placed at the end of a signal yard, of a spanker or a monkey gaff for reeving ensign or signal halyards.

Jews' Harp

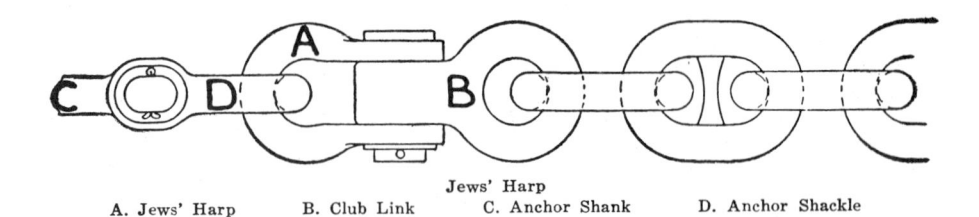

A. Jews' Harp   B. Club Link   C. Anchor Shank   D. Anchor Shackle

Fr: *Poulie de bout de Vergue;* Ger: *Flaggleineblock.*

JEWS' HARP.
See **Harp-Shape Shackle**.

JIB. A triangular sail extended upon a stay between the bowsprit or jibboom and the

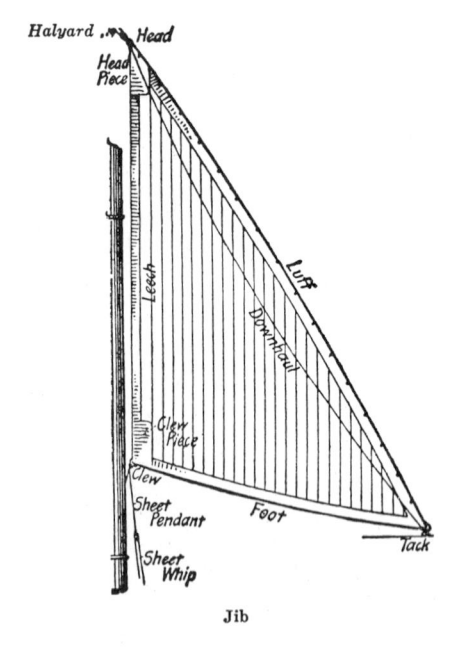

Jib

foremast. It is usual, except in very small vessels, to carry 3 or 4 jibs named, from inboard, fore-topmast staysail, inner jib, outer jib, flying jib. Among headsails, jibs are the most powerful sails for casting or turning the ship's head, being at the greatest distance from the vessel's center of effort. They are usually cut on the diagonal plan with the cloths perpendicular to the foot and leech. The luff rope is made of wire or fiber rope.

Fr: *Foc;* Ger: *Kluver; Kluverfock.*
Dyce, W. C., *Treatise on Jibs,* 1876.

JIB AND MAINSAIL RIG. A sloop rig without topmast. Also called **pole masted sloop.**

JIBBOOM. An extension of the bowsprit. A wooden spar arranged to unship by drawing inboard through the bowsprit cap. In modern sailing vessels the jibboom has been done away with, since the adoption of spike-bowsprits, in which the jibboom and bowsprit are combined into one steel spar.
Fr: *Bâton de foc;* Ger: *Kluverbaum.*

JIBBOOM SADDLE. A chock of wood on top of the bowsprit inside the rigging, in which the heel of the jibboom is fixed and held steady.
Fr: *Coussin de bout-dehors;* Ger: *Sattel des Kluverbaums.*

JIB CAT (U. S.). A cat-rigged boat with bowsprit and a jib which spreads from bowsprit end to masthead. The extreme forward position of the mast distinguishes the Jib-Cat from the ordinary sloop.

JIBE. To shift suddenly and with force from one side to the other. Said of fore-and-aft sails when through bad steering or some other unexpected cause, the wind being aft or on the quarter, the sails fill suddenly on the opposite side. When sailing free, to put the helm over so as to bring the boom on the opposite side. Also gybe.
Fr: *Trélucher;* Ger: *Giepen.*
See **Tack**.

JIB GUY. One of the ropes or chains staying a jibboom sidewise. Also called jibboom guy. They lead from the outboard end of the spar to the bows of the vessel where they set up. In former days their support was improved by outriggers extending from the bowsprit cap, called whiskers or spritsail gaffs.

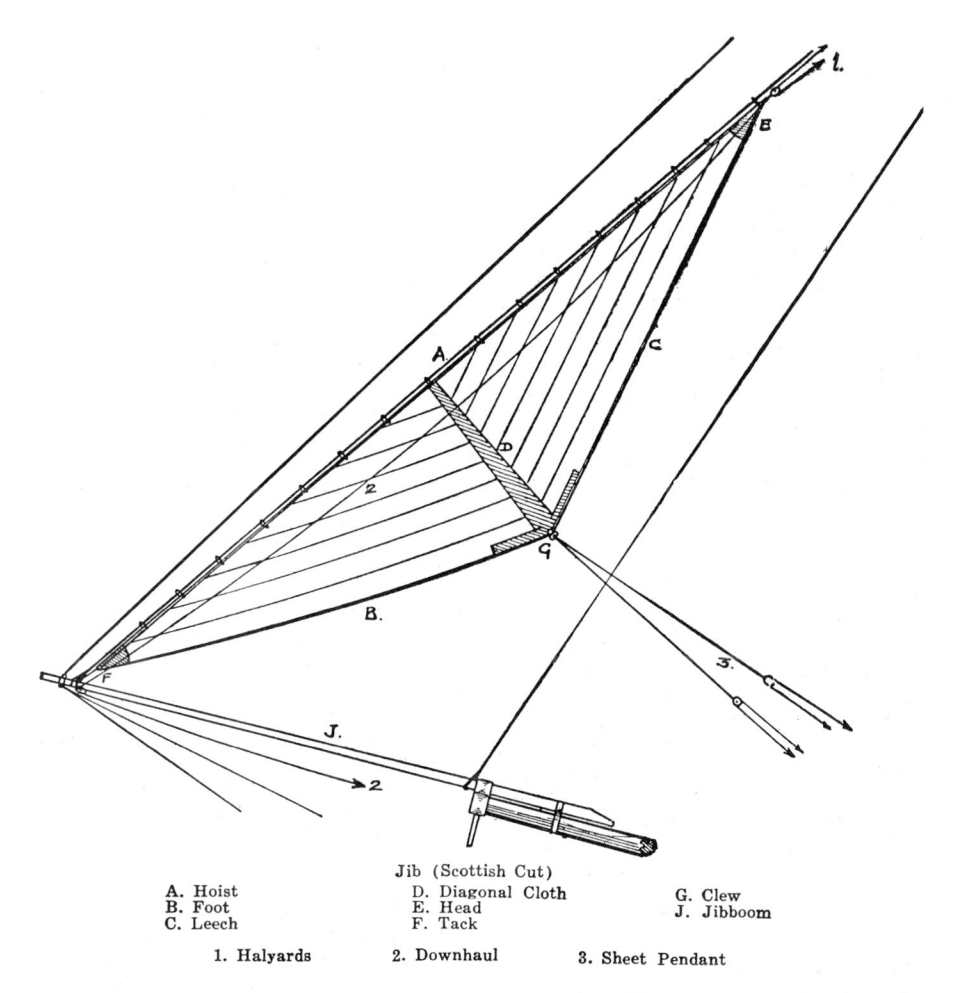

Jib (Scottish Cut)
A. Hoist   D. Diagonal Cloth   G. Clew
B. Foot   E. Head   J. Jibboom
C. Leech   F. Tack
1. Halyards   2. Downhaul   3. Sheet Pendant

Fr: *Hauban de Foc;* Ger: *Kluverbackstag.*

JIBHEAD. An iron fitting fastened to the head of a jib, used to shorten a sail by cutting off the point, after it has stretched too much by wear.

Ger: *Kluverkopfstück.*

JIB-HEADED SAIL. A general term for all sails of triangular shape such as jibs, staysails, Bermuda sails.

Fr: *Voile Triangulaire;* Ger: *Dreieckiges Segel.*

JIB-HEADED TOPSAIL. A fore-and-aft topsail of triangular shape which sets above a gaff or spritsail. Its head draws up to the topmast head. Its luff is kept to the mast by hoops, by a lacing, or by one or two jackstay leaders. There are no reef points, the sail being completely furled in rough weather or replaced by a smaller one. It is commonly set on a topmast, but occasionally on a long-headed pole mast.

Fr: *Flèche Pointu;* Ger: *Dreikanttoppsegel.*

JIB-HEADER. A gaff-topsail shaped like a jib.

JIB NETTING. A triangular netting rigged under the jibboom to give men footing against falling overboard while loosing or furling headsails.

Fr: *Filet de Beaupré;* Ger: *Kluverbaumnetz.*

JIB-O-JIB. Also jib topsail. **1.** A small three-cornered sail, occasionally found in trading vessels which sets outside and above other headsails. A sixth jib set as a jib topsail on the fore royal or fore-topgallant stay in square-rigged vessels.

Fr: *Foc en l'Air;* Ger: *Kluver Toppsegel.*

2. A triangular headsail running on the topmast stay in fore-and-aft rigged boats, and set above the other headsails, with its tack well above the jibboom instead of being fastened to it.

Fr: *Clin Foc; Foc en l'Air;* Ger: *Flieger.*

JIB TRAVELER. A large iron ring to which the tack of a jib is made fast. The ring goes around the bowsprit and runs in and out, by means of an outhaul and inhaul. Also called tack ring.

Fr: *Rocambeau de Foc;* Ger: *Kluver Leiter.*

JIB TRICING LINE. A small line let into the miter in the middle of a jib. It is led forward to a small block on the jib luff, down to another block at the jib tack, and then aft. This line acts as a lazy jack gathering forward the bunt of the sail. In practice a double-ended line is rigged, passing on both sides of the sail, both falls being trimmed at the same time.

Fr: *Cargue de Foc;* Ger: *Kluver Aufholer.*

JIG. 1. A small tackle composed of a double and a single block or two single blocks. The upper block is fastened permanently or temporarily to the end of a topping lift, halyard, runner, and so on, or to its purchase, the lower block to an eyeplate or some fixed object on deck. Also called jigger.

Fr: *Palan d'Etarque; Etarquoir;* Ger: *Strecker; Handtalje.*

2. A flattened and slightly curved piece of white bone or bright metal bearing at one end one or more hooks, and attached to a line by the other end, with a swivel in between. When trolled or drawn through the water its form causes it to spin round. It attracts the fish by its motion and brightness. Also called jig hook.

Fr: *Cuiller;* Ger: *Rollangel; Angelköder.*

See **Fish Jig, Squid Jig.**

JIG BOAT. A wooden open boat with clipper stem and canoe stern used in the mackerel fisheries of California. Its length ranges between 20 and 35 ft. It is propelled by a motor and has no rig.

JIGGER. 1. A small gaff or jib-headed sail set on a jigger mast at the stern of small craft. In yachts its presence constitutes the yawl rig.

Fr: *Tapecul;* Ger: *Besahn; Besan; Besansegel; Beilieger.*

See **Boom Jigger, Bunt Jigger, Clew Jigger, Split Jigger, Stick Up.**

2. The gaff sail on the fourth mast of a five- or six-masted schooner.

3. The gaff sail on the jigger mast of a four-masted bark, sometimes rigged with two gaffs.

4. The course on the aftermost mast of a square-rigged four-masted ship.

Fr: *Voile Barrée; Artimon;* Ger: *Jigger; Besan.*

5. In the Pacific Coast salmon fisheries, a hook-shaped extension on each side of the heart of a pound net. It helps lead the fish in the required direction.

See **Jig.**

JIGGER BUMKIN. Portable spar overhanging the stern. At its outer end there is a block through which the sheet of the jigger or mizzen is led. Used on yawl-rigged craft.

Fr: *Bout-Dehors de Tapecul;* Ger: *Treiberbaum.*

JIGGER MAST. 1. The aftermost mast of a four- or five-masted bark. The fourth mast of a five- or six-masted schooner.

Fr: *Mât d'Artimon;* Ger: *Jiggermast; Kreuzmast.*

2. A small mast stepped abaft or forward of the rudderhead in small craft and used for setting a jigger. It is the mizzenmast of a yawl, dandy, or ketch.

Fr: *Mât de Tapecul;* Ger: *Besahnmast; Jagermast.*

JIGGER TACKLE.

See **Watch Tackle.**

JIGGING. 1. Taking short pulls at a tackle fall.

2. Catching fish with a jig.

3. Collective name for sails set above the moonrakers. Also known as "God above all" sails. (Obsolete.)

JILALO.

See **Guilalo.**

JILSON.

See **Gilson.**

JIMMY GREEN. A fore-and-aft four-sided sail which sets along the bowsprit and jibboom under the headsails. Also called Jamie Green. It was formerly used by clipper ships. Its upper side was hanked to a rope traveler extending from jibboom end to cathead. It was sheeted down to the lower end of the martingale boom and the foot or after side was flattened or eased off by means of a pendant from the fore rigging and a whip to the forecastle head. The sail was made of No. 4 canvas and cut as a topgallant stunsail but with more depth.

JINGLE BELL (U. S.). A bell located in the engine room and by which signals for full steam ahead or astern are transmitted from the bridge. It is used in connection with a gong which gives signals for other movements.

JINNY YARD (G. B.). A small spar or club attached to the foot of the mizzen in fishing luggers from East Cornwall. It extends about a quarter of the length. The sheet is made fast by a hook through a strap seized on the spar.

JO. Dugout canoe with single outrigger from Jamma Island (Dutch New Guinea) with blunt bow and backward curved figurehead. A platform extending outboard on each side is attached to the outrigger booms. In the smaller boats the upper part of the stem is carved in the form of a human head. The outrigger is carried on the port side.

JOG.
See **Lip.**

JOGGED FRAME. In boat building, a type of wooden frame with notches corresponding to each strake of planking. It is used only with lap-strake planking, for the purpose of giving additional support and stronger connection between framing and planking in craft used for landing on rough beaches.

JOGGING. 1. Fishermen's term to denote suspension of fishing operations during heavy weather; also the abatement of stormy rough seas. **2.** A term descriptive of the slow, heavy motion of a vessel when she is hove to, close-hauled under some sail and with her helm lashed down.

JOGGLE. A setting back of part of a plate or bar to obtain a flush surface where other parts cross, or to enable it to fit around a projection as a butt strap. Also called crimp.
Fr: *Juglinage; Épaulement;* Ger: *Joggelung.*

JOGGLED FRAME. A frame in which offsets are worked in way of laps of the shell plating, thus dispensing with the necessity of fitting liners.

Fr: *Membrure Épaulée;* Ger: *Gejoggeltes Spant.*

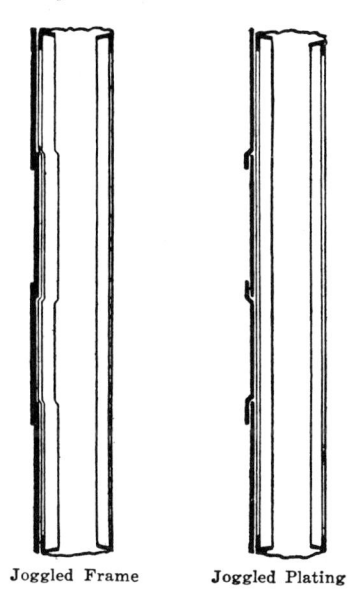

Joggled Frame   Joggled Plating

JOGGLED PLATING. A system of plating in which the edges of plates are joggled thus dispensing with liners.
Fr: *Bordé à Clins Épaulés;* Ger: *Gejoggelte Plattung.*

JOGGLE SHACKLE. A long, slightly bent, shackle used for hauling the cable round the bow when mooring, or to hang off a cable.
Fr: *Manille d'Affourchage;* Ger: *Vertauung Schackel.*

JOGGLING MACHINE. A power machine employed in shipbuilding yards to form a joggled edge on a plate, or in joggling a bar. Also called joggler.
Fr: *Presse à Jugliner;* Ger: *Joggelpresse.*

JOHNSON'S METHOD. Navigational method for determining a ship's position at sea by two successive altitudes of the sun, or by simultaneous altitude of two celestial bodies with a difference of azimuth of at least two points.

JOHORAN. A plank-built fishing prao with short stem piece from Krawang (Java).

JOINER. A shipyard worker who makes the woodwork necessary for the completion of a ship or boat such as wooden deckhouses, bridge shelters, steering wheel, skylights, flag lockers, guard rails, steering gear

JOINER BULKHEAD—JULUNG　　　　　　　　　　　　　　　　　　　**412**

covers, deck ladders, also interior work such as insulation of refrigerated holds, berths, cabinets, closets, shelves and so on. He does not perform carpentry of a heavy or rough character. Also called ship joiner.

　Fr: *Menuisier de marine;* Ger: *Schiffstischler.*

JOINER BULKHEAD. Wood or light metal bulkhead such as those used in cabins, offices, and storerooms, and which do not actually contribute to the structural strength of the ship proper.

　Fr: *Cloison d'Emménagements.*

JOINER DOOR. A door made of wood, sheet metal, or metal-covered wood, used wherever air- and watertightness are not required.

JOINER SHACKLE. A common bow shackle by which the lengths or shots of anchor cable are joined. The pin is oval, its greatest diameter being in the direction of the strain. The ends are flush with the lugs. Joiner shackles are always fitted with crown or bowed-end leading forward.

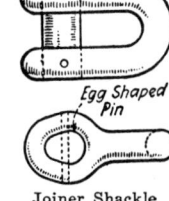

The forelock pin or small pin is kept from coming out by being made a little short so as not to show any projection which might be damaged when the cable is running out. Lead pellets are driven in at either end to fill up the holes in the shackle, which are made with a groove or score, so that as the pellets are driven they expand or dovetail, keeping the small pin in its place. The pin is of oval or egg shape cross section. Also called *connecting shackle.*

Egg Shaped Pin

Joiner Shackle

　Fr: *Manille de Jonction; Manille d'Ajust;* Ger: *Verbindungsschackel.*

JOINT OWNER. One of the owners of a ship or ships belonging to two or more persons.

　Fr: *Co-Armateur;* Ger: *Mitreeder; Parteireeder.*

JOINT PIECE. A small piece of plate used for various purposes, principally as a butt strap.

　Fr: *Bande;* Ger: *Verbindungsplatte.*

JOLLE. A term applied in Germany to a flat-bottom sailing boat of the same type as the *ewer,* with rounded rising stem, transom stern, and outboard rudder. The length in the older type was from 15 to 16 ft. on keel. It has gradually been increased to 27 or 28 ft. over-all. *Jollen* were formerly half-decked but now have a full deck. They carry one mast and are fore-and-aft rigged. The *Buttjolle* is used in the halibut fisheries. In Sweden the term *jolle* is used indifferently for yawl or dinghy. It is also used in Denmark and Norway. The German *Jolle* from the west coast of Schleswig-Holstein is a small coaster from 7 to 21 tons with sharp stern and cutter rig, chiefly employed in transportation of farm produce.

　See **Luhe-Jolle.**

JOLLY BOAT. 1. A small unballasted sloop-rigged sailing boat with centerboard, used for racing in sheltered waters. It is larger than the sailing dinghy, but its over-all length does not exceed 18 ft.

　Ger: *Jolle.*

2. A lightly built ship's boat with sharp stern, rowed with 4 or 6 oars. In trading schooners it was usually carried at the stern.

　Fr: *Yole;* Ger: *Jollboot.*

JOLLY JUMPERS. A collective name given to the sails which were set above the moonrakers in clipper ships. Also called *flying kites.*

JOLLY ROGER. A pirate's flag, carrying the skull and crossbones. (Obsolete.)

JUBILEE RIG (G. B.). Term which refers to the rig of British square-rigged vessels with stump topgallant masts, that is, setting nothing above topgallant sails. So-called because it was introduced in Queen Victoria's Jubilee year.

JUKUNG. A generic term used to denote various types of native craft of the Malay Archipelago in which the hull consists either of a simple dugout or of a dugout base with sides raised by planks. Also called *jungkung, dyukun.* The craft which do not have raised sides are generally used for transportation or fishing in sheltered waters or, in some cases, as tenders to the larger seagoing fishing boats when setting or hauling in their nets. When working at sea the smaller *jukung* are provided with single or double outriggers. The larger types of *jukung* are employed in the offshore fisheries or also for the conveyance of goods along the coast.

The word "jukung" is usually followed by a descriptive term which indicates a particular form of hull or the usage to which the boat is put. When used alone, as for instance on the east and south coasts of Java, the word "jukung" denotes the smallest type of one-man or two-man dugout.

JULUNG. A large trading *prao* from eastern Madura resembling in type the *paduakan* from Macassar. It has a portable decking of bamboo splits. This name is also applied in Madura to a small *jukung* with outriggers in which the stern is shaped like the tail of a fish named *julung*.

See **Prao Julung-Julung**.

JUMBO (U. S.). 1. The forestaysail on fore-and-aft-rigged vessels.

2. A triangular sail which sets, point downward, on the foreyard of a square-rigged vessel or a topsail schooner in place of the regular foresail. It has no sheets or tack and the point near the deck is pivoted by a short club or by a clew iron set up with a single rope or tackle at the foot of the foremast.

JUMBO BOOM. The spar laced to the afterpart of the foot of a forestaysail in fore-and-aft rigged vessels. Also called forestaysail club (U. S.).

See **Derrick, Heavy Derrick**.

JUMPER. A preventer rope made fast in such a way as to prevent a yard, mast, or boom from giving way in an upward direction.

See **Whisker Jumper**.

JUMPER GUY. One of the ropes for staying down the ends of the bowsprit whiskers. They are spliced around and around each end of the whiskers outside the jib guys, and led down to a roller sheave or gin block close to the stem, not far above water and thence up through a fair-lead in the knightheads, to the forecastle.

JUMPER STAY. 1. Generic term for any stay set up in heavy weather to prevent a yard from jumping.

2. A name given to an extra stay which leads from the lower mastheads to the side of the vessel where it is set up with a tackle. Also called spring stay, preventer stay.

Fr: *Faux Étai*; Ger: *Springstag*.

3. A term sometimes applied to the wire running from the funnel to the foremast, to which signal halyards are secured.

4. In fore-and-aft-rigged sailing yachts, a short stay which runs from masthead over a short strut to a point just below the head of jib stay. It increases the rigidity of the top part of the mast and counteracts the downpull of the mainsail.

Fr: *Faux Étai*; Ger: *Jumpstag*.

JUMPER STAY COMPASS. A compass suspended from a jumper stay of a ship with an arrangement for locking the card and then lowering it to the deck. The compass being suspended above the vessel's deck is less affected by the ship's magnetism.

JUMPER STAY SPREADER. A short spreader fitted on the forward side of the mast in fore-and-aft rigged racing and cruising yachts, over which the jumper stay or jackstay runs. Also called jumper stay strut, jackstay strut.

JUMP SHIP. To leave ship without proper authority. To desert.

JUNCTION BUOY. A buoy placed at the inner end of a middle ground.

Fr: *Bouée de Jonction*; Ger: *Kreuztonne*.

JUNK. 1. Old or condemned cable and cordage used when untwisted for making points, foxes, gaskets, swabs, mats, spunyarn, nettle stuff, lacings, seizings; and when picked into fibers used for making oakum for calking.

Fr: *Vieux Filin*; Ger: *Zerhacktes Tauwerk*.

2. Term used by whalemen to denote a thick, elastic mass which occupies the fore part of the head of a sperm whale, immediately under the case. It is about equally composed of white horse and oily matter, both oil and spermaceti.

3. A name applied collectively in the Western hemisphere to all large, native-built, seagoing Chinese luggers, with high poop and overhanging bow. The underwater body has fine lines, but the frequent absence of keel in the junk does not permit it to work well to windward. A deep rudder lowered down the trunk when at sea extends well beneath the ship. The sails are balanced-lugs extended and stiffened by battens. The pole masts number from two to five. In the large 5-mast trading junks from northern China they are placed as follows: the bowmast is stepped right forward either inboard or outboard of the port bulwark; the foremast and mainmast are in the centerline; the mizzenmast is stepped right aft offset to port of the centerline and a short distance forward of the mizzen there is a small quartermast stepped against the port bulwark. None are stepped vertically, some having a forward rake, others a rake aft.

Fr: *Jonque*; Ger: *Dschunke*.

Donnelly, I. A., *Chinese Junks*, Shanghai, 1924.

JURY. Term used in connection with any temporary or makeshift fitting, structure, rig, gear, sail, and so on, used in an emer-

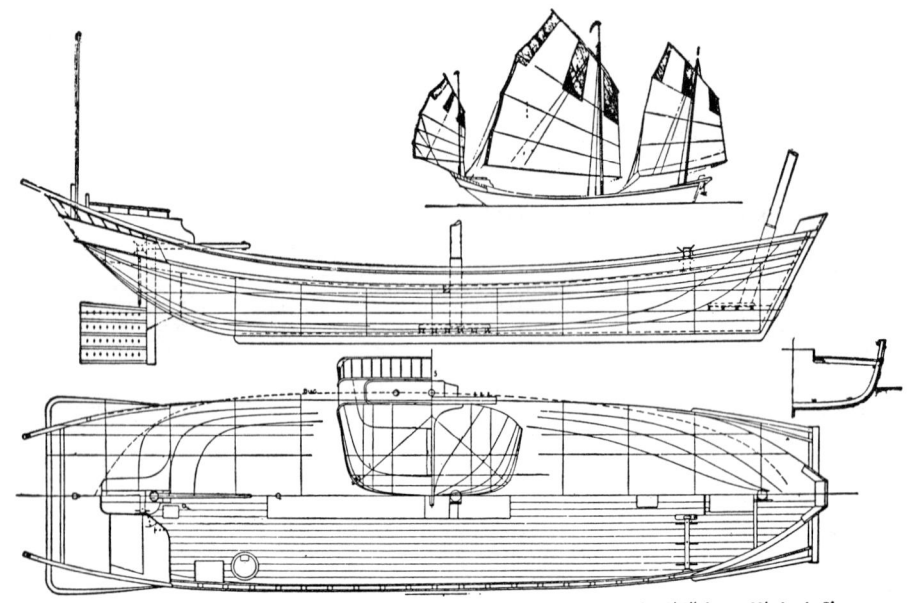

Junk. (*Courtesy* "*Yachting*" *N. Y.*)
Length, w. l., 92' 6"; beam, 28'; depth, 7'.

gency to work a vessel or boat to the nearest port.

Fr: *de Fortune;* Ger: *Not.*

JURY MAST. A term applied to any mast temporarily erected to take the place of one that has been carried away or cut away to relieve pressure in a storm. Also, applied to a temporary mast erected in a new vessel before rigging.

Fr: *Mât de Fortune;* Ger: *Notmast.*

JURY RIG. A temporary or makeshift rig or part thereof set up by the ship's crew to take the place of that which has been lost or carried away.

Fr: *Gréement de Fortune;* Ger: *Nottakelage.*

JURY RUDDER. A temporary rudder rigged in an emergency for supplying a vessel with the means of steering when an accident has befallen the rudder.

Fr: *Gouvernail de Fortune;* Ger: *Notruder.*

JURY SAIL. A sail which is temporarily set on a jury spar aboard a vessel which has been dismasted, to bring her to port.

Fr: *Voile de Fortune;* Ger: *Notsegel.*

JUTE ROPE. Jute is used for cheap ropes but has no strength when used alone. Mixed with hemp it makes a useful rope. It is also used as heart or core for four-stranded fiber ropes and wire ropes.

K

K. Letter denoted by the international code flag showing two equal vertical divisions: yellow on the hoist and blue on the fly. As a single letter signal it means: "Stop your vessel instantly."

KABA. East Indian outrigger canoe from Flores (Lesser Sunda Islands). Average length 26 ft. Breadth 3.2 ft.

KABANG. A fishing canoe used by the Selung people of the Mergui Archipelago (Indian Ocean). Also called *kebang*. The hull is made of a dugout basis with forked stem and round stern. The sides are built up a foot or more with pieces of palm stem strongly tied together and calked with palm hemp. The boat is partly decked with split bamboo. Length 23 to 32 ft. Breadth 4 to 4½ ft. Depth 3.2 ft. (Typical.)

A portable mast held by two shrouds and a backstay with lugsail made of palm leaves plaited together is used with fair winds. At other times the boat is propelled by two roughly fashioned oars. One oarsman stands in the bow, the other at the stern—somewhat as a Venetian gondola is manned. When sailing, a quarter rudder is used.

KAEP. A Micronesian single-outrigger dugout canoe from Palau Islands. The hull is wedge-shaped in cross section, with pronounced convexity (rocker) of the fore-and-aft bottom line. In hewing out the hull a wide ledge is left projecting horizontally inward on each side of the opening, forming a narrow waterway. A thick, roughly triangular piece forming a short deck is fitted at each extremity of the hull. In addition to the two outrigger booms a number of equidistant thwart bars cross the hull. A boarded platform is fitted between the outrigger booms. The sail is of the Oceanic lateen type with apex set downward. The mast is stepped in a chock just over the windward gunwale. Length 33 ft. Breadth 14 in. Depth 25 in. (Average.)

KAHN. A flat-bottomed seagoing barge without keel, very beamy amidships and narrow aft, with rounded stem and flat stern. The deck construction presents several peculiarities. The planking is clinker-laid, and the two end hatches are of triangular shape. The *Kahn* originates from the lower Weser and may vary in size from 8 to 125 tons. The largest are ketch-rigged with square sail set flying. The smaller are cutter-rigged. All carry leeboards.

KAIRYOO KAWASAKI. Modernized Japanese fishing sampan from Hokkaido Island, schooner-rigged with a gaff-foresail, large staysail, and gaff mainsail. No headsails. A centerboard is fitted amidships. Length over-all 36.5 ft., waterline 33 ft. Breadth 8.1 ft. Depth 2.4 ft. Sail area 618 sq. ft. Oars 6. Crew 6.

KAK.
See **Hvassing**.

KAKAP JERAM. A Malay open fishing boat of the Selangor coast. The hull is built of Meranti wood with figurehead on stem and ornamental sternpost. A wash strake made of split bamboo strips and palm leaves is held in position by lashing to knees brought up from the boat's frames. It is steered by a long paddle rudder. Forward an athwartship balk is used for winding the cable and bitting it. The rig consists of a pole mast with battened sail. Length 13 ft. Breadth 7 ft. Depth 3 ft. Freeboard 1 ft. Crew 3. Length of mast 23 ft. (Typical.)

KALAMBA. A large one- or two-masted trading prao with double outriggers, from Nias and Mentawei Islands (West Sumatra). The hull is built from a dugout, and has planked sides. The sails are of palm leaves. Also called *kalabba*.

KALAUNG. A small, schooner-rigged sailing vessel from Mindanao, Philippine Islands, of the same type as the *panco* but slightly larger. Also called *auang kalaung*.

KALIPOULO. A fishing dugout with single outrigger from the Trobriand Islands (British New Guinea). It it a large canoe with pointed ends, which are usually carved. The hollowed-out portion is flanked by a wash strake on each side and by transverse carved and painted breakwaters.

KALLA DONI. Large, heavy Indian balance-board boat from Point Calimere (Palk Strait) employed in traffic with North Ceylon. Also called *boatila manche*. The hull is of clumsy build with rounded stem, transom stern, and carvel planking. There is a low-decked poop aft. The outboard rudder, instead of being hung on the transom in the usual fashion, is fastened to a sort of fin built of thick planks, strengthened with battens extending about 4 ft. abaft the transom. The rig consists of three masts with square-headed lugsails. The very short foremast has a pronounced forward rake and is stepped just abaft the bows. The mizzenmast is stepped near the foreside of the poop at a short distance from the mainmasts. These two have little or no rake. The outrigger is of the so-called balance-board type. It consists of a heavy plank laid athwart the gunwales and projects only a few feet on each side of the hull.

KAMCHATKA CURRENT. A branch of the Kuroshiwo current which separates from it in 40° north latitude near longitude 146° or 147° E., flowing to the northeast in the direction of the Aleutian Islands at about 18 miles a day.

KAMIA. A single-outrigger canoe of the Austral Islands (Polynesia). Also called *yaka*.

KANDA BACHE KAIK. A Turkish type of fishing boat with a length ranging from 42 to 45 ft.

KANU. Single-outrigger dugout canoe of the Manongoes people from southeastern New Caledonia.

KAPOK. The silky fibers investing the seed pods of the kapok tree (*Ceiba pentandra*), found chiefly in Java. Kapok is very buoyant and will carry about 25 times its own weight in fresh water, while cork carries only 6 times its weight. On account of its great buoyancy and freedom from waterlogging it is employed to a large extent in the manufacture of lifebuoys, lifebelts, seat covers, and other lifesaving appliances.
Coburn, F. C., "Kapok for Life Preservers," *Engineering Magazine*, vol. 48 (December, 1914); Court, A. B., "Kapok," U. S. Naval Institute *Proceedings*, vol. 43, no. 167 (1917).

KAPPBAULK. In the timber trade, round pieces of timber about 18 ft. in length and 11 in. in diameter at the small end.

KARABEL. A sailing ship of the Sea of Azov and Black Sea, with low freeboard and immense beam, but well-shaped ends. It is usually schooner-rigged, the sails having the square peak peculiar to Russian craft.

KARAVETA.
  See **Oanga**.

KARBASS. A double-ended boat from the Gulf of Archangel (White Sea) used for transportation and also for hunting sea mammals during the summer months. Also called *karbatz*. The hull is built with curving stem and sternpost and bluff ends. Some of the boats navigating on rivers and estuaries are built with plumb stem and transom stern. The seagoing *karbass* is rigged with one mast stepped at a distance of about one-third length from the stem, on which a spritsail is set. The river *karbass* has two masts both sprit-rigged. The foremast is stepped very close to the stem. Length 40 ft. Breadth 8 ft. Depth 5 ft. (Typical.)

KAREKET. An East Indian outrigger canoe from Madura used in the trawl-line fisheries. Also called *panting kareket*.

KAT. A single-outrigger dugout canoe without wash strakes or end pieces, from LeMaire Islands (British New Guinea). Also called *kiata*. The rig consists of an elongated, oblong-shaped sail made of coconut palm leaves, with yard and boom. The sail is narrower at the head than at the foot. Length of canoe 24 ft.

KATABATIC WIND. A wind caused by downward currents of air and peculiar to mountainous districts and high coastline. It may strike the sea with great violence and spread along the surface.
  Fr: *Vent catabatique;* Ger: *Katabatisch Wind.*

KATSUO TSURA. Japanese Bonito fishing boat found in the districts of Kagoshima, Kochi, Shizuoka, Wakayama, Chiba, and Kumano. Also called katsuo bune. They fish with lines and wooden hooks. The hull is built on the model of the Japanese sampan with flat bottom, fine, long-drawn-out lines forward, deep rudder, square stern and sides, outboard projecting beams to support the yulohs, spare spars, and bamboo fishing rods. The deck is formed of portable panels. All boats are provided with bait compartment or tank. They are said to be able sea boats and to sail fast when running free. The rig varies according to localities from one to three masts, all setting square sails made of Japanese cotton cloth.

The Kagoshima district boats have two masts, fore and main. The foremast stepped right in the bows has no rake. Approximate length 23 ft. The mainmast has a pronounced rake aft and is stepped well abaft amidships. Approximate length 39 ft. Boats from the Kochi district have three masts, fore, main, and mizzen. The latter is stepped abaft amidships. The Shizuoka district boats have three masts, of which the mainmast is the aftermost. A crutch is fitted next to the rudder for supporting the spar when lowered. Approximate length of masts 22 ft., 24 ft., 35 ft. In the Wakayama district the boats have one mast about 30 ft. in length. Boats from the Chiba district have three masts with moderate rake aft, the mainmast being the aftermast as in Shizuoka district. The other two are stepped at a short distance from each other right in the bows of the vessel. The mainmast can be lowered on a crutch.

PARTICULARS OF KATSUO BOATS

District	Lgth. in ft.	Brdth. in ft.	Depth in ft.	Draft in ft.	Sail Area sq. ft.	Displacement tons
Kagoshima	50.0	10.6	4.4	2.4	965	15.2
Kochi	43.0	9.3	3.5	2.5	...	...
Shizuoka	40.0	8.3	3.6	..	850	...
Wakayama	41.5	7.5	2.8	..	300	...
Chiba	36.5	7.3	3.3	2.6	890	...
Kumano	50.0	6.5	2.4	8.7	...	...

KATSURANAWA-BUNE. Japanese one-mast seining sampan from Hiroshima district employed with the scare-cord seine. Length 29.4 ft. Breadth 7.3 ft. Depth 2.7 ft. Displacement 3.6 tons.

KATTU. A sailing coaster from Burma rigged with two masts and lateen sails. Its capacity is about 1,000 baskets of unhusked rice (9,000 gallons).

KAUA. A single-outrigger dugout canoe from Koaru, Gulf of Papua, of which there are two types. The smaller boats are only about 12 ft. long, and have bow and stern similar with toothlike carvings underneath. The larger canoes, which are used for fishing with a seine, are 40 ft. or more in length and have elaborate carvings at ends. The outrigger float is in the form of a small dugout.

KAURI PINE. A New Zealand wood used for deck, shell planking, and cabin fittings. Its weight is from 33 to 35 lb. per cubic foot. It has superseded yellow pine for deck planking and should be well seasoned before use. Kauri pine is also resistant to teredo attack.

Fr: *Cèdre de Virginie;* Ger: *Kauri; Virginisches Cedernholz.*

KAVINEHE NENGAU. A single outrigger canoe from Tanna Island (New Hebrides) of same underbody as the nengau and with a box-like superstructure built above the dugout. Battens are fitted over the seams to make them watertight.

KAWASAKI. Japanese fishing sampan found off the island of Hokkaido and in the Akita district, employed in the trawl-line cod fisheries. As there are no harbors in the region where these fisheries are located, the boats are strongly built and flat bottomed, to enable them to put out from open shores, and land through a high breaking surf. The rig consists of one portable mast stepped abaft the center of the boat, on which is set a loose-footed square sail made of a very thin kind of sedge matting (a sort of grass cloth). The cloths which hang vertically are not sewed, but are laced together. Hokkaido boats: Length over-all 41 ft. 10½ in. Breadth 10 ft. Depth 3 ft. 6½ in. Sail area 357 sq. ft. Akita boats: Length over-all 35 ft. Breadth 7.4 ft. Depth 2.3 ft. Sail area 345 sq. ft. Crew 13.

KAYAK. A skin canoe consisting of a wooden framing covered with skins, usually of the crested or bearded seal variety. The kayak is still in use over a great extent of the Arctic regions, from east Greenland westward across Arctic America, and along some 800 miles of Asiatic coast both westward and southward from the Bering Straits. One-man kayak: Length 17 ft. 8 in. Breadth 1 ft. 6 in. Depth 1 ft. 6 in. Draft 9 in. Weight 35 lb. Manhole 16 × 15 in. Frames, 1 in. × 12/16 in. Paddle 6 ft. 3 in. long. Blades made of two pieces which overlap for a distance of about 2 ft.

The frames are made of single pieces of wood cut to desired thicknesses with an adze, steam bent and fastened to longitudinals with seizings made of sealskin strips and to the keel with wooden or bone pegs. The thickness of the keel piece seldom exceeds one inch.

When the frame is finished, it is covered with sealskin, sewed with sinew thread, using a waterproof stitch. This is done by passing the needle through only half the thickness of the skin at each stitch, therefore when the thread is pulled tight there is no stitching visible on the outside of the skin. When the covering is finished the whole kayak is given several coats of blubber to preserve the skins, and to fill up any small holes left in the seams. The frame of the circular opening for the occupant is supplied with small pegs, about ⅜ to ¾ in. long, all around its circumference. Each peg corresponds to an eyelet in the skin which forms the decking. By this means the tension of the skins which are still soft while building the boat can be adjusted to obtain a perfect fit. When the skins dry after the boat is completed, they shrink, and any slack which could not be avoided when sewing the pieces together is thus taken up. The double-bladed paddle is made as short as possible, with a protective covering of whalebone or narwhal ivory along both edges and at the ends of the blades, which are very thick.

In the Eskimo kayak the framing is made of whalebone ribs. Prow and stern are made of walrus teeth. It is completely decked, the covering being laced about the paddler, who sits in the opening amidships.

KEAMA. A single-outrigger dugout canoe with two wash strakes on each side secured by paired knees lashed at intervals. Also called *waga*. It is used by natives of d'Entrecasteaux Islands (British New Guinea) for traveling over long distances. The ends of the wash strakes are closed by carved breakwaters. The rig consists of a short stout mast with a prong near its head, supported by stays. The sail is of triangular oceanic elongated design and is made of sago palm leaves.

KECKLING. Chafing gear consisting of old rope. Used for covering a hemp cable to protect it from chafe. Rope wound round the long ends left in splicing the eye in a rope cable, the ends having been wormed into the lays of the cable.

Fr: *Fourrure;* Ger: *Schladding.*

KEDAH CANOE. A small boat used for fishing in the northwest Malay states. The lower part of the hull is hollowed out of a tree trunk. The ends are cut to shape with stem and stern pieces worked in. Upper planking strakes are built on ribs, carvel fashion. The rig consists of one mast with boomed lugsail made of woven matting and shrouds made of rattan.

KEDGE ANCHOR. A light anchor used for kedging a ship from place to place. That is, the anchor is carried out to a distance from the ship, and dropped. The ship is then pulled to it by means of capstans or winches. It is the smallest anchor on board.

Fr: *Ancre à Jet;* Ger: *Wurfanker; Warpanker.*

See **Anchor.**

KEDGING. Moving a ship by means of small anchors and hawsers.

Fr: *Touer;* Ger: *Warpen.*

KEEL. 1. The main center-line structural member, running fore and aft along the bottom of a ship, sometimes referred to as the backbone. It is composed either of long bars scarfed at their ends, or in larger ships of heavy plates connected by riveting or welding. In wooden vessels it is composed of pieces of timber as long as can be obtained, scarfed together at their ends.

Fr: *Quille;* Ger: *Kiel.*

2. A rabbet is cut on each side to receive the edge of garboard planks.

See **Center Girder, Flat Keel, Keelson.**

3. A barge-like craft found on the lower reaches of the Humber River which bears the distinction of being the only single-masted craft in the British Isles with square rig. The double-ended hull is flat-bottomed, decked at bow and stern and with narrow waterways on either side of the hatch. The stem projects above deck. The sternpost is cut off flush with the deck to allow the tiller to work over it. The craft is carvel-planked. It has leeboards, which are raised and lowered by wires from the afterends, led to geared crab winches on either quarter. The mast, stepped in a tabernacle, is located a little forward of amidships. The sail plan consists of a square mainsail with two reef bands and square topsail. A pair of shrouds on each side and a strong forestay form the only standing rigging. Length 58 ft. to 62.5 ft. Breadth 14½ ft. to 15.5 ft. Depth 8 ft. Draft 5 ft. to 7 ft. Deadweight capacity 70 to 100 tons.

4. A unit of weight formerly used in the coal trade of the east coast of England. It represented the quantity of coal carried in a "Keel" (barge) or 8 Newcastle chaldrons or 21 tons 4 hundredweights (21.54 metric tons).

KEELAGE. A duty or toll charged for permitting a ship to enter and anchor in a port or harbor.

KEEL BATTEN. See **Hog Piece.**

KEEL BENDER. A heavy duty power press used for flanging heavy plates, such as in forming the beveled flanges of a dished flat keel.

KEEL BLOCK. One of a series of short timbers on which the keel of a vessel rests while it is being built or repaired and which afford access to work beneath. Also called middle block.

Fr: *Tin de Construction;* Ger: *Stapelklotz; Kielklotz; Kielpalle; Kielstapel; Stapelblock.*

These blocks are placed over the cross logs and are built up to a height above ground of 3½ to 4 ft. The declivity of the keelblocks and the height of the foremost block is determined in conjunction with the declivity of the launching ways. They are spaced about 4 ft. apart from bow to stern, allowing easy access to the work. Keel blocks are also used in dry docks to afford a uniform and level support for a ship's keel. The simplest form is made of timber throughout, with hardwood base and softwood cap. The various parts are united by straps or staples. Cast-iron keel blocks consist of three castings with a soft wooden capping piece. Concrete blocks of similar construction are now in common use.

KEEL BOAT. Local name for a small, decked motor boat built of wood and used for inshore fishing on the east coast of England (Yorkshire). It has a small wheelhouse aft and a collapsible mast stepped at the fore end of the fish hold. Average length 48 ft. Crew 5.

KEEL CONDENSER. A surface condensing apparatus fitted to steam launches and similar craft. It consists of a fore and aft copper tube attached outside of the keel. The exhaust steam is drawn through the tube by the air pump, condensation taking place by contact with the surfaces kept cool by the surrounding sea water.

KEELER. In the New England hook-and-line mackerel fisheries, a shoal square box of wood about 2 by 3 ft. square into which the fish are thrown after being split. Also called gib-keeler.

KEEL LINE. The line of the fore-and-aft member running along the center line of the ship at its lowest part.

Fr: *Ligne de Quille;* Ger: *Kiellinie.*

KEEL RAIL. A steel grab rod fitted on the bottom of a lifeboat to provide a hand hold for persons struggling in the water should the boat be capsized. Also called **bilge rail.**

Fr: *Tringle de quille;* Ger: *Kimmreling.*

KEEL SIDING. The depth or vertical measurement of a keel as opposed to the "molding" or athwartship's width.

Fr: *Droit de quille;* Ger: *Kielhöhe.*

KEEL SLAB. A heavy reinforcing side bar riveted on each side of a hanging keel.

Ger: *Kielschiene.*

KEELSON. A fore-and-aft center line girder extending from stem to sternpost and located either above or between the floor plates in order to prevent tripping or fore-and-aft movement, also giving longitudinal strength to the hull and distributing any local thrust over a wide area. The term keelson is generally used in connection with single bottom vessels. The same member in a vessel with a double bottom is usually given the name of center girder or vertical keel.

Fr: *Carlingue;* Ger: *Kielschwein; Binnenkiel.*

See Bilge Keelson, Box Keelson, Center Keelson, Detached Keel and Keelson, Flat Plate Keelson, Intercostal Keelson, Rider Keelson, Side Keelson, Sister Keelson, Through Plate Center Keelson.

KEELSON BOARD. Applies in boatbuilding to a length of wood secured to the upper part of the hog piece, and extending from the fore deadwood for about two-thirds of the length of the boat. Sockets are cut in it to receive the mast step and the heels of the thwart pillars. The inboard edges of the floorboards are secured to it.

KEELSON LUG. One of the short lengths of angle bar connecting a keelson to a floor plate.

KEELSON TIMBER. Timber fitted to, and laid upon, the middle of the floor timbers and bolted through floors and keel for binding and strengthening the lower part of the hull. The molding of a keelson is its depth, and the siding, its breadth.

Fr: *Carlingue;* Ger: *Kielschwein.*

KEEL STOP. A small metal fitting on the keel of a ship's boat, at the afterend. It acts as a stop in locating the boat in a fore-and-aft position when stowing the boat on the chocks.

KEEL-TRACK RAM. A battering ram used for knocking out keel blocks. Made of an oak timber about 14 ft. long, with ropes to accommodate fourteen men.

KEEPER PLATE. A small piece of plate used as a locking device. Also called locking plate.

Fr: *Frein;* Ger: *Umschlagblech.*

KEG BUOY. A buoy used by fishermen to mark the position of trawl lines. It consists of a small watertight keg with a capacity of a little over a quarter of a barrel. Through the keg runs a flagpole tightly wedged to prevent leakage and strongly fastened by stout lines to prevent its coming out. To this the flag is fastened above and the buoy line below.

Ger: *Fasstonne.*

KEITELKAHN. Small flat-bottomed open fishing boat of the Kurische Haff (East Prussia). Also called *Kurrenkahn, Braddenkahn.* The hull is built with flat stem, apple stern, and carvel planking. Two leeboards are fitted. There is a small cuddy at each end. The mainmast is stepped on the foreside of a heavy thwart amidships. It is rigged with a mainmast 33 to 40 ft. long and a small foremast about 16 ft. long stepped in the bows and setting a spritsail. The mainsail is either a sprit or boomless gaffsail. A small square extra sail is occasionally hung from the main sprit. Length 30 to 36 ft. Breadth 8 to 10 ft. Draft 3 ft. 3 in. (Average.) The name varies according to the gear used.

KELP. A common term for seaweed which consists of different species of *Fucus*. In a more restricted sense the term "kelp" is confined to the produce of seaweed when burned.

Fr: *Algues; Varech;* Ger: *Seegras; Kelp.* Tressiger, *Marine Products of Commerce,* New York, 1923.

KENCHING. A method of salting in which fish, either split or round, are piled in layers in the hold of a ship or on the floor of a warehouse, each layer being covered in turn with a layer of salt.

Fr: *Saler en Vert;* Ger: *Gefassung.*

KENTER SHACKLE. A shackle in two parts with fitted stud used in connecting shots of chain cable. The stud is kept in place with a steel pin which runs diagonally through the stud and both parts of the shackle. The kenter shackle ensures smoother working in the whelps of the wildcat, thus eliminating the tendency of the cable to jump.

Fr: *Maille démontable;* Ger: *Kenter-Bauart Schakel.*

KENTLEDGE. Pig iron or metal scrap used as ballast.

KENTLEDGE GOODS. A term sometimes applied to heavy goods stowed in the lower holds and contributing to the stability of the vessel.

KENT PURCHASE. A tackle formerly used by whalers to cant or turn the whale when it was lying alongside during flensing operation. (Obsolete.)

KERRY CANOE. A canvas rowboat used in Ireland in the Dingle and Ballyferriter districts for long-line fishing. The hull is built with 1½-in. fir stringers spaced 5¼ and 1½ in. × ½ in. elm ribs also spaced 5¼-in. centers. There is an upper and lower gunwale 3 in. × 1¼ in. framed with small stanchions between. The outer skin is made of No. 4 canvas, tarred.

These boats are claimed to be very seaworthy. Their buoyancy, high stern, and flaring bows make them very dry. With the wind abeam a small leeboard is hung over the lee quarter, which keeps the boat from blowing up into the wind. They row 2 or 4 men, generally sculling with little straight paddles about 2 in. wide, hung on tholepins.

KETCH. A fore-and-aft rig with two masts, the main- and mizzenmasts each carrying a gaff-headed or jib-headed sail. It differs from the two-masted schooner in that the larger mast and sail stand foremost, and the smaller or mizzenmast and sail aftermost, whereas in the schooner the reverse is true. The headsails of the ketch are the forestaysail and jib.

Fr: *Ketch;* Ger: *Ketsch; Anderthalbmaster; Besankutter.*

See **Cowes Ketch, Main Trysail Ketch, Schooner Ketch.**

It is an old form of rig and is specially suitable for coastal navigation, as the largest sail is all inboard and the sail plan well balanced under almost any condition. It is chiefly used by small trading or fishing vessels such as the *galiot, galeass, ewer, logger* and by yachts. The mizzenmast is stepped forward of the sternpost or rudderhead.

KETCH RIG. See **Ketch.**

KEVEL. Large wooden cleats fastened to the bulwark stanchions, and to which ropes are belayed. Also called cavil. (Obsolete.)

Fr: *Fileux;* Ger: *Kreuzklampe.*

KEWO-U. A canoe employed for coastal transport in the lagoons of Trobriand Islands. It is a simple dugout with one outrigger.

KEY. 1. A slightly tapered piece of wood to drive into scarfs, to wedge deck planks, or to join any pieces of wood tightly to each other.

Fr: *Clef;* Ger: *Keil.*

2. A wedge, pin, or long thin bar of metal used to lock two parts of a machine or structure into the desired relative position.

See **Cay.**

KEYING RING. A lead ring driven around the forelock pin of an anchor shackle as a locking device.

KEY MODEL. A model of a vessel formed by different layers of board fastened together by keys and screws.

KEY SCARF. A locked scarf made by cutting slots for one or more keys through the joint at the center. The pieces are lapped and bolted, and the key driven tight.

Fr: *Ecart à Clef;* Ger: *Keillaschung.*

KHASABA.

See **Baghla.**

KIALU. A plank-built canoe made of rough, native hewn slabs, used by the Alakaluf Indians of eastern Magellan Strait. The bottom board is bent upward at the ends and forms the stem and stern, which protrude above the sides. The latter are composed of two strakes lashed to each other and to the bottom board. The planks are drawn together with the bast of Cypress or a runner plant (*Campsidium*) and are made watertight with moss and fat. Small sticks stretching from gunwale to gunwale form the thwarts. Oars made of two pieces are used for propulsion. Each boat carries three long pulling oars and a short steering oar.

KIBBLINGS. Term used in the vicinity of Newfoundland to denote the parts of fish which are used for bait.

KICKER (G. B.). Small lug mizzen which sheets on an outrigger. Used on fishing luggers of east Cornwall.

KICKING STRAP. Whaleman's term for a rope across the top of the clumsy cleat and fastened at each end, under which the whale line was led. It prevented the whale line from sweeping aft if it should jump from the chocks. (Obsolete.)

KID. 1. A box or pen made of wood, built on the deck of fishing craft to receive fish as they are taken on board. Also called deck pond.

2. A shallow tub or pan in which a seaman's food was served. Also called mess kid.

Fr: *Gamelle*.

KID BOARD. Board used by dory fishermen at each end of the dory to keep the catch from sliding into the standing room while fishing. The forward kid board is fitted upright under a thwart and the after one under the bait board.

KILLER.
See Gob-Stick.

KILLER BOAT.
See Whale Catcher.

KILLER CLUB. A short round stick used by fishermen to club halibut on the snout and stun them before taking them into the dory. Also called gob stick.

KILLICK. 1. A stone with a rope attached to it, used as an anchor by small boats.

2. A small anchor for a boat.

Fr: *Crapaud*; Ger: *Kleiner Bootsanker; Muringstein*.

Nance, R. Morton, "Killicks," *Cambridge Antiquarian Society Proceedings*, vol. 23, 1922.

KILLICK HITCH. A timber hitch and half hitch drawn around a boulder or large stone, which acts as an anchor for small boats, set nets, lobster pots, and so on.

KING BRIDGE. A truss extending athwartship between the heads of a goalpost mast.

KING PLANK. A hardwood deck plank located on the center line, and serving as abutment in the "swept" method of laying deck planking.

Ger: *Fischung; Fischplanke*.

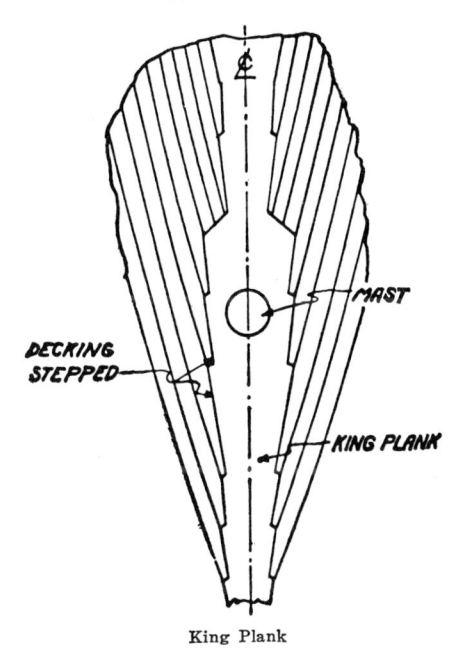

King Plank

KING POST. 1. A short heavy mast which serves to support a boom.

2. The centerline pillars in a ship's hold.
See Samson Post.

KINGSBURY THRUST BEARING. A single collar thrust bearing used for main engines in lieu of a horseshoe thrust bearing. It depends for its performance upon the load-carrying characteristics of wedge-shaped films of oil, which form automatically under load between the rotating elements, and the segments of the stationary element. A similar bearing called Mitchell thrust bearing is patented in Great Britain.

See Horseshoe Thrust Bearing.

Gibson, J. H., The Mitchell thrust block, Liverpool Engineering Society, *Transactions*, vol. 38 (1917); Smith, W. W., The Kingsbury Thrust Bearing, American Society of Naval Engineers *Journal*, vol. 24, 1912.

KING SPOKE. The upper spoke of a hand steering wheel which is up when the rudder is amidships. Also called up-and-down spoke. It is usually indicated by some special mark, such as a turk's-head.

KINGSTON VALVE. A conical valve opening outward and so arranged that the pressure of the sea forces the valve on its seat or closes it. Such valves are generally used in ballast tanks of submarines, as sea connections.

KINK. A sharp bend which disturbs the lay of a rope, generally due to an excess of twist.

Fr: *Coque;* Ger: *Kink; Schleife.*

KINOO. See **Cunner.**

KINU. See **Goaq.**

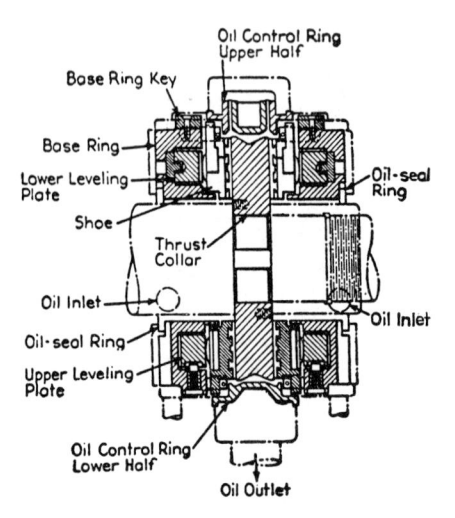

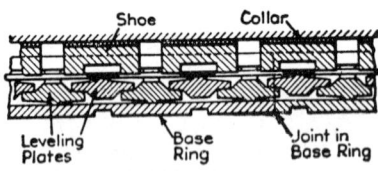

Kingsbury Thrust Bearing

KIPPER. A herring which, after having been split and gutted, is slightly salted and then smoked for about 12 hours before being packed. Fires of oak turnings and sawdust are used for the smoking. Also called kippered herring.

Ger: *Bückling; Räucherhering; Fleckhering.*

KIRAP. East Indian double outrigger dugout canoe with forked ends, used in the coastal fisheries of Sangi and Talund Islands (Celebes).

KIRJIME. A sharp-ended, decked vessel used for local trading and fishing on the southwest coast of the Caspian Sea. It has a straight, raking stem and sternpost, flaring sides, flat bottom and pronounced sheer at ends. Length 15 to 28 ft.

The hull is built of lime-tree wood, walnut, and oak. It has a flush deck with low bulwarks, and one hatch amidships. The rig consists of a single pole mast stepped about two fifths of the vessel's length from the stem, supported by four shrouds on each side. On this is set a large square sail.

KIRKEBAAT.

See **Sekskeiping.**

KIRK'S ANALYSIS. A method used for calculating the resistance of a hull through the water and thus the power required for any particular speed. It is based on the calculation of the approximate wetted surface of the hull, and allowing a certain factor of horsepower per hundred sq. feet of wetted surface for the type of hull considered. The horsepower is arrived at by multiplying the wetted surface divided by 100 into the rate for that type of hull. Having the rate for one speed, that for other speeds can be determined on the basis that power increases as the cube of the speed.

Fr: *Formule de Kirk;* Ger: *Kirksche Widerstandsformel.*

KIT. A unit of weight used in the fish trade on the east coast of England. One kit weighs about 168 lb. The equivalent of 12 stone trawl fish.

KITCHEN RUDDER. A patent steering and reversing device for small craft. It consists of twin metal blades, both spade-shaped, which normally form a circular aperture abaft the screw propeller. To reverse, the two blades are turned in opposite directions so as to form a cup behind the propeller. The propeller wake is diverted in this cup and ejected in a forward direction. The braking effect is high and instances are recorded of launches fitted with this gear being brought to rest in their own length from full speed.

KITE DRAG. A sea anchor consisting of two or more spars lashed together at their center. A chain is passed around the outer ends forming the periphery. To this chain is laced a baggy canvas shaped to the frame. A bridle leads from the spars to which a towing hawser is made fast. A tripping line is bent to the end of one of the spars to capsize the whole contrivance when hauling aboard.

Fr: *Ancre flottante;* Ger: *Dragg Anker.*

KITES. In general, the highest and lightest sails in square-rigged vessels set above royals, such as skysails, moonsails, stargazers; also royal and topgallant studding sails. Sometimes called flying kites, jolly jumpers. In yachting parlance Genoa jibs, spinnakers and other similar sails are termed "kites."

KIYI. A scrubbing brush (U. S. Navy).

KJEKS. A Norwegian rowboat from Nordland of the same type as the *femboring,* but of smaller size. It has a length of about 18 ft. and pulls two pairs of oars. It is used for hand-line fishing in coastal waters.

KLEWE. A dugout with planked sides and double outriggers from Achin (Sumatra), used for small coasting trade between Singkei, Sibolga and Padang. The ends are forked. Capacity 5 to 10 tons.

KLIPFISK. Scandinavian trade name given to codfish cured by the process of spreading the fish on the rocks after it has been split and salted as distinguished from "stockfisk" which is hung up round to dry.

KLITJIRAN. Small Javanese dugout canoe without washboards, of the *jakung* type, employed in the Pekalongan district for fishing on the strand and river estuaries with lines and small nets.

KNEE. 1. A plate, usually of triangular shape, provided for the purpose of rigidly connecting intersecting structural members. Also called plate bracket, plate knee. Chiefly used in shipbuilding for attaching beam ends to frames, frames to margin plate, deck girders to beams or to bulkheads, and so on.

Fr: *Gousset;* Ger: *Knieblech.*

2. A natural grown timber with two arms at right angle or nearly so; also a heavy wrought iron bar similarly shaped. They are used in wooden shipbuilding to connect different beams and timbers and are named from the position in which they are placed.

Fr: *Courbe;* Ger: *Knie.*

See **Bosom Knee, Dagger Knee, Lodging Knee.**

KNEE OF THE HEAD. Projecting timbers fastened to the stem and specially designed for relieving the upward strain caused by the foremast rigging on the bowsprit. Also called head knee.

Fr: *Éperon; Guibre;* Ger: *Gallion.*

A stem so constructed is known as a clipper stem, in contradistinction to a straight stem. Its forepart should form a handsome serpentine line or inflexed curve. The principal pieces of which it is composed are called main piece and lacing.

KNIFE-EDGE LINER (G. B.). Small wedge-shaped liner used to make-up a tight joint in the event of deficient workmanship, such as in the case of a badly beveled angle bar where the toe has pulled up tight and the heel is off. It is neither required nor permitted in high-class work. Sometimes called shim liner (U. S.), razor-edge liner (U. S.).

KNIFE LANYARD. Small braided or plaited cord attached to the shackle of a jackknife. The other end is worn around the seaman's neck to prevent the knife from falling from aloft.

KNIGHTHEAD. The first timbers on either side of the stem. Also called apostle. They form the sides of the seat or bed for the reception of the bowsprit, the top of the stem itself forming the actual resting place. Knightheads are either placed fore and aft or canted, according to whether the vessel is full or very sharp at the bow. These timbers are rarely seen in small craft.

Fr: *Apôtre;* Ger: *Ohrholz; Judasohr.*

KNIGHTHEAD FRAME. A frame situated a short distance from the stem in steel sailing vessels and connected to a small triangular bulkhead with round aperture for the bowsprit to pass through.

Ger: *Ohrholzspant.*

KNIGHTS. A name given to small bitts placed behind a mast, with several sheaves in the head, through which running rigging is rove.

KNITTLE. Small line made of rope yarns twisted together, used for seizings or for hammock clews.

Fr: *Hanet;* Ger: *Knüttel.*

KNOCKABOUT. 1. A sailing yacht of simple sloop rig consisting of jib and mainsail. The stay sets up on the stemhead. Knockabouts were usually keel boats though some were centerboarders and could be handled very quickly. The original knockabout rig was intended for small craft but it has developed and is now, with some modifications, used on boats of comparatively large size, 40 to 100 ft.

2. In the United States the word "knockabout" is also applied in a general sense to sailing craft without bowsprits; thus a fish-

ing schooner so rigged is referred to as a "knockabout" or "knockabout schooner."

KNOCKABOUT RIG. A style of rig evolved about 1900 with the object of abolishing the bowsprit in small craft. The jib is bent on a stay which sets up on the stemhead. It is chiefly used for yachts and fishing schooners. This rig became popular in the New England cod fishing fleet between 1905 and 1910.

KNOCKED-DOWN. The situation of a vessel listed over by wind to such an extent that it does not recover.

KNOLL. An elevation of the sea bottom with small ground area and steep slope, generally surrounded by navigable water.

Fr: *Dôme; Mamelon;* Ger: *Kuppe; Anhöhe.*

KNOT. 1. A unit of speed. The term "knot" means velocity in nautical miles per hour whether of a vessel or a current. It is the measurement of a section of a (chip) log line usually 47 ft. and 3 in. long.

Fr: *Noeud;* Ger: *Knoten.*

See **Chip Log.**

2. An interlacement of parts of a rope by twisting the ends about each other and then drawing tight the loops thus formed for the purpose of fastening them together or to another object or to prevent slipping. In a general sense the term "knot" embraces the words "bend" and "hitch." In a more restricted sense knot may be defined as a method of forming a knob, a loop or a noose in a rope. In practice the three terms "knot," "bend," and "hitch" are rather loosely used. Aldridge, A. F., *Knots,* New York, 1918; Ashley, C. W., *Book of Knots,* New York, 1944; Cahoon, K. E., *Practical Knots and Splices,* Annapolis, 1942; Day, C. L., *Sailors' Knots,* London, 1934; Graumont and Hensel, *Encyclopedia of Knots,* New York, 1940; Renner, C., *Knoten spleissen, etc.,* Berlin, 1933; Spencer, C. L., *Knots, Splices and Fancy Work,* Glasgow, 1934.

KNOTTED SHEEPSHANK. A variety of sheepshank (of which there are several forms) which does not loosen if the rope is slackened.

KNUCKLE. The angle formed by the shell plating at the intersection of the counter and the upper part of the stern at or just below the deck.

Fr: *Coude;* Ger: *Knick.*

KNUCKLE LINE. Line formed by the abrupt change in direction of plating, frames, or other structural part of a ship. The term is specifically used when referring to the line at the apex of the angle dividing the upper and lower part of the counter in vessels with elliptical stern. It also refers to the angle formed in some ships by the forecastle shell plating with the strakes below. There is also a knuckle line in the margin plate of the double bottom where it is flanged to meet the tank top.

Ger: *Knicklinie.*

KNUCKLE MOLDING. Ornamental strip of wood or steel of half-round cross section, fitted over the knuckle line at the stern.

Fr: *Liston de la Voûte;* Ger: *Unterheckleiste.*

KNUCKLE STRAKE. The range of planking at the stern where the ship's side takes a sharp angle upward near the taffrail.

Ger. *Knickgang.*

KNUCKLE TIMBER. One of the top timbers in the forward and afterbody whose heads stand nearly perpendicular, or with a slight tumble home.

Fr: *Allonge Coudée;* Ger: *Ohrspant.*

KNUCKLING. Contraction on butt or tee welded plating resulting from shrinkage of the weld across the top as it cools.

KOA. Single-outrigger dugout canoe of the Wailu and Kanala people from eastern New Caledonia. Also called *kwa, ktuin.*

KOE. Single-outrigger seagoing dugout canoe of the Nengone people of Mare Island, Loyalty Group. Similar to the *niu.*

KOILA WALLA. Asiatic member of engineer's department serving as coal trimmer under lascar agreement.

KOKAR SKOT. Finnish open sailing boat employed in the herring fisheries from the Island of Kokar in the Aland Archipelago. Also called *skeite.* It is clinker-built with raking curved stem and square stern. It has three thwarts and is ceiled inside. The rigging consists of two masts with loose-footed sprit foresail and boomed sprit mainsail. A small jib tacks to the stemhead. The sails are bent to hoops on the masts. Length over-all 25 ft. 4 in. Beam 9 ft. 2 in. Depth 2 ft. 8 in. Stem to foremast 3 ft. 4 in. (Typical.)

KOKU. The standard lumber measurement employed by the Japanese, which equals 10 cu. ft. or 120 board ft.

KOLEK. A generic name given in the East Indies and Malaya to various craft which differ from each other in size, hull form, and rig. Sometimes called *kolik, kule,* *sampan.* The smallest is the *kolek pulo* or island canoe from Malaya. It is a plank-built boat about 7 ft. long, 2½ ft. broad with turned up ends in the form of a bow. It draws about one foot of water and is worked by one man with a double-bladed paddle. A small mast and gaff are used for setting sail in fair wind. It is employed for fishing with hook and line.

The *kule* from Achin (Sumatra) is a trading craft with two quarter rudders and rigged with two masts and lugsails. Its capacity ranges from 20 to 40 tons.

The *kolek tetap* from western Java is a prao of the *mayang* type and has no outriggers.

The *kolek kelibat* from the Malay Peninsula is a plank-built craft with upturned ends. Its length ranges from 13 to 17 ft. Its breadth from 2½ to 3½ ft. It is steered by a rudder with yoke lines and propelled by three large paddles. It has a small sail with gaff like the *kolek pulo.*

The *kolek mantang, kolek selat,* and *kolek tambang* are used for transportation and fisheries between the islands of Rhio Archipelago.

The *kolek pukat,* a craft of the *mayang* type, is employed in the mackerel fisheries of Bantam (Eastern Java) with a *pukat* net. Rigged with one mast with boomed lateen, quarter rudder.

The *kolek-pengayer* from the Malay peninsula, east coast of Johore, is built with long keel, rounded forefoot, and carvel planking fastened to heavy grown frames, spaced about 3 ft. apart, and extending nearly up to the gunwale. The frames are connected by a single stringer on each side. There is only one thwart through which the mast is stepped. The stern and stempost are usually tall and decorated. The *kolek pengayer* is entirely open and unballasted. It holds a good wind but is somewhat slow in stays. It is lug-rigged with one or two masts according to size. In one-masted boats the tack belays to the mast thus forming a standing lug. The larger boats set two dipping lugs of Malay type. Length 23 ft. Breadth 4 ft. Depth 2 ft. Capacity 20 picul (1.2 tons). Length of mast 24 ft. Freeboard 1 ft. (Average.)

KOLEKAN. 1. A half-decked two-masted sailing craft originating from Madura and employed for inter-island trading between Java, Borneo and the southern Malay Peninsula. The keel-built double-ended hull is made of teak wood. It has no frames, the sides are held together by cross beams with ends projecting through the outer planking. Amidships there is a thatched roof of about 25 ft. length made of woven matting. Two quarter-rudders are used for steering. The rig consists of two short masts of rectangular section. A triangular sail with bamboo yard and boom is set on each mast; the foresail has about half the area of the mainsail. Length 55 ft., breadth 13 ft., depth 5 ft. It is handled by a crew of 6.
Blake, W. M., The Madura Prau, *Yachting,* New York, vol. 45 (January, 1929).

2. A small plank-built fishing craft from eastern Java of the mayang type. Also called sampan kolekan.

KOLE-KOLE. An East Indian plank-built canoe from Amboina (Moluccas) similar to the *orembai* but fitted with double outrigger.

KOLEKSTOCK. An open fishing skiff from Dalaro and its neighborhood in the coastal archipelago of Stockholm. It has a sharp bow, rounded stem, round bilge, and raking square stern. It is built with keel and clinker planking. The rig consists of a square sail setting on a mast which stands about one-third the boat's length measured from stemhead. Length over-all 20 ft. Breadth 6 ft. 4 in. Depth 23¾ in. (Typical.)

KONTING. A local Javanese name for *mayang.*

KOO-YUK. Australian single-sheet bark canoe with tied ends, of the Warrimee tribe from Port Stephens in New South Wales.

KOP. A double outrigger canoe from Nissan (Solomon Islands). It is a narrow dugout with both ends pointed. The opening is so constricted that a man must sit with one leg placed in front of the other. The bow has a squared shelf. Holes are bored in the gunwales for the two outrigger booms.

KOREA. Single-outrigger dugout canoe from Point Nekete, eastern New Caledonia. Also called *pote.*

KORT NOZZLE. A cylindrical shaped, plate built, casing fitted around propellers of shallow draft units to increase efficiency by allowing a larger disc diameter.
Fr: *Tuyère Kort;* Ger: *Kort Düse.*

KOSTER BOAT. A small double-ended fishing boat originating from Koster Island (Sweden) with a length ranging from 20 to 35 ft. The hull is built with clinker planking round stem, powerful bilges and large beam. These boats are sloop-rigged with boomless mainsail, one headsail, no bowsprit. The sail area for the largest boats is approximately 1,100 sq. ft. A large number of koster boats have been transformed into cruising yachts.

KOTIA. Indian trading vessel originating from Cutch. The hull is built with long curving stem, square stern, elaborately carved, and high poop with stern windows. The rudderhead runs through the counter. The rig consists of two masts with forward rake, which carry settee sails. The mainmast is stepped at half length and the mizzen a little abaft the break of the poop. The mainsail tacks down to a spar which projects just outside the stemhead. There are no headsails.

KOTIK.
See **Potik**.

KOTRAOL. A single-outrigger canoe from the Palau Islands (Carolines), employed for light transport and for fishing. It is generally propelled by paddles but a mast and sail are rigged with fair wind. The hull is extremely narrow for its length. There are 6 thwart bars used as seats for the paddlers; each projects outboard on the outrigger side to a distance equal to about half the width of the hull. In fishing canoes these outboard sections are used for stowing rods, spears, and other gear.

KOTSCHMARA. Russian boat from the White Sea used in the local coasting trade and in the fisheries. Also called *kochmara*. It is of the same type and rig as the *lodia* and has a carrying capacity of about 10 tons.

KO-TSENG-SHUAN. A fishing junk from Anping (Formosa) built of a species of cedar called "nan mu" or of camphor wood. These junks are decked. The fore hatch is always kept closed. When fishing the main hatch is open and the catch is thrown into it. The rig consists of one mast. When hired for the transportation of goods an additional short mast is stepped in the bows. The crew numbers four. Length 35 to 42 ft. Breadth 8 to 12 ft.

KOVA. An East Indian built up canoe with double outriggers from Timor Archipelago similar to the *gepung*. It is propelled by paddles or by a small spritsail. Length 14½ to 16 ft. Breadth 1.6 ft. Depth 1.8 ft. (Average.)

KRENG. Whaling term used in the Greenland fishery to denote the stripped carcass of a whale. Also called *crang*.

KROMAN. An East Indian trading and fishing craft from Madura and adjacent islands of same type as the *peduang*, but smaller. A portable deck is provided. Length 37.7 ft. Breadth 10.2 ft. Depth 3.3 ft. (Typical.)

KRU CANOE. A dugout used in Sierra Leone (W. Africa) for inshore fishing with lines. They are specially numerous in the coastal fishery of the peninsula. The Kru canoe is usually cut from the trunk of the cotton tree and is hollowed out to a very thin shell. Each end is finely tapered, ending in a slightly swollen knob, giving a good grip when the canoe has to be hauled ashore. The afterend, for a distance of about 2 ft., is decked in, with a small transverse breakwater at the fore end.

KUBA. Single-outrigger dugout canoe with a length ranging from 32 to 65 ft., and used for transportation by the Nakanai people of New Britain (Bismarck Archipelago). The ends form a flat shelf which is especially long and narrow at the bow. Also called *a-kuba*.

KUBBOOT. Small open sailing craft formerly used for line fishing on the southern waters of the Zuider Zee. The flat-bottom hull is similar to that of the *schouw* with carvel planking on bottom and broad strakes of clinker work at sides. The rig consists of a jib-headed mainsail with boom and a foresail tacked down to stemhead. The mast is stepped right in the bows. Length at waterline 16 ft. Breadth (extreme) 6 ft.

KUDASTRE. A Philippine sailing coaster from the Western Visayan Islands constructed on the same lines as the *parao* but of heavier build. It is fitted with double outriggers. The rig includes two pole masts and bowsprit. The mainsail and foresail have a gaff and boom. The gaffs are held to the masts by a rope sling or snotter as no jaws are provided.

KUFF. A small sailing coaster of Dutch origin formerly engaged in short sea voyages in the Baltic and North seas. Also called *koff, kofschip*. It was chiefly by the form of its hull that it differed from other craft. The bow and stern were very full and round and the sheer was greater aft than forward. Some of these vessels were built with keel and round bilges; others were built with flat bottom and carried leeboards. The side planking of the upper works was strengthened with heavy wales extending all around. Although the *kuff* was usually ketch-rigged some of the larger boats had the topsail-schooner or the bark rig. The last *kuffs* were built in the nineties and it is believed that this type of craft is now extinct. Ketch rig: Length 55 to 77 ft. Breadth 13 to 19 ft. Hold depth 4.9 to 8.1 ft. Tonnage 40 to 90 gross. (Average.) Topsail schooners: Length 62 to 91 ft. Breadth 14 to 22 ft. Hold depth 6.5 to 11.4 ft. (Average.)

The schooner-rigged *kuffs* were known as *schonerkuffs*.

KUKLTAI. Dugout canoe of the Alakaluf Indians of western Magellan Strait, which has taken place of the bark canoe. Also called *je-kukltai*. Some of these craft are said to be very large often holding 20 to 30 persons. One end of these canoes is cut off square. The sides are often raised by a wash strake.

KULBIA. Australian three-piece sewed-bark canoe of the Byellee and Kukubura tribes from Keppel Bay and Curtis Island (Queensland).

KULLA.
See **Oruwa**.

KUNDARA. Small trading vessel from the Laccadive Islands employed for carrying produce to the mainland ports of Mangalore, Calicut, and Telicherry. The hull is similar to that of the Indian *pattimar*. The overhanging bow ends in a curious upright stem piece. The poop is large and has stern galleries built out aft and on the quarters. The planking is sewed with coir yarn. The rig consists of one mast with lateen sail. A small lateen mizzen is sometimes added.

KUNDUL. Australian bark canoe of the Moondjan tribes from Moreton and Stradbroke Islands (Queensland). It is made of a single sheet from 12 to 20 ft. long, and has pointed ends. The gunwale is strengthened by a long withe of wattle. To keep the sides apart the smaller canoes have a cross stick at center. In the larger craft there is one stick at each end. The big canoes carry as many as ten people and all are propelled by poles about 10 ft. long. These poles are used alternately on one side and on the other according to the course steered and without touching the bottom.

KUNGKI. A West African dugout used by the Susu people of French Guinea. The canoe is round-bottomed and rockered fore and aft with pointed ends and no sheer. The bow is finished off with a high up-curved end piece terminated with a knob. The stern piece of similar design projects outboard horizontally. Paddles only are used for propulsion.

KURRIDJA. Australian one-piece tied-bark canoe of the Yuin tribe from Jervis Bay (New South Wales).

KUTTER. Ketch-rigged decked sailing craft with fish well used by the Germans in the North Sea and Baltic trawl fisheries. Also called *Fischereikutter*. There were formerly two types called locally *Plattekutter* and *Scharfkutter;* the former built with flat bottom and the other with round bottom. The flat-bottom wooden hull has been gradually superseded by the steel-built round-bottom boat in which an auxiliary engine has been fitted. Length 59.2 ft. Breadth 19 ft. Depth 7.9 ft. Length of fish well 20.4 ft. (Typical.)

KUTTER EVER. Cutter-rigged boat with general hull design of the Ever and provided with centerboard. Used for fishing in the North Sea and off the mouth of the Elbe River.

KVASE.
See **Quatze**.

KVASSAR, KVASSE. A cutter-rigged boat with well, used in the Swedish flatfish fisheries in the Kattegat. The type originates from Rää. These boats have a tonnage ranging from 5 to 10 tons burden. They are rigged with boom mainsail, jib-headed gaff-topsail, foresail, and jib set flying on a running bowsprit.

KWAK. A Dutch sailing boat employed in the fisheries of the Zuider Zee and estuary of the river Ij. It works with two drag nets towed simultaneously one on each side of the boat. The hull is the same as in the *botter* and is rigged with one mast, gaff mainsail, two headsails, and a square foresail set flying.

KWAN. Single-outrigger dugout canoe of the Wameni people of southwestern New Caledonia.

L

L. Letter denoted by the international code flag showing two yellow and two black squares. When flown as a single letter signal it means: "Stop, I have something important to communicate."

L.A.N. LOCAL APPARENT NOON.
L. (or lat.) LATITUDE.
L.A.T. LOCAL APPARENT TIME.
L.B.P. LENGTH BETWEEN PERPENDICULARS.
L.C. LONDON CLAUSE (chartering).
L.C.T. LOCAL CIVIL TIME.
L.D. LOAD DRAFT.
ldg. LOADING.
L.H.A.R. LONDON-HAMBURG-ANTWERP-ROTTERDAM (port range).
Lkg. and Bkg. LEAKAGE AND BREAKAGE.
L.M.C. LLOYD'S MACHINERY CERTIFICATE.
L.M.T. LOCAL MEAN TIME.
Lo. (or long.) LONGITUDE.
L.O.A. LENGTH OVER-ALL.
L.R. LLOYD'S REGISTER.
L.S.T. LOCAL SIDEREAL TIME.
l.t. LONG TON.
Lun.Int. LUNITIDAL INTERVAL.
L.W. LOW WATER.
L.W.L. LOAD WATER LINE.
L.W.O.S.T. LOW WATER ORDINARY SPRING TIDE.
L. Freeboard mark indicating the load line applicable to all seasons and zones for vessels specially constructed for the transportation of complete cargoes of timber.
L.F. Freeboard mark indicating the fresh water load line of vessels specially constructed for the carriage of complete cargoes of timber.
L.S. Freeboard mark. Indicates the load line in summer for vessels carrying a timber deck cargo.
L.T. Freeboard mark. Indicates the load line in tropical zones for vessels carrying a timber deck cargo.
L.W. Freeboard mark. Indicates the load line in winter for vessels carrying a timber deck cargo.

LABEL CLAUSE. A marine insurance cargo clause which clears the underwriters' liability in insurances effected upon bottled goods when the labels on the bottles have been damaged.

LABEL PLATE. One of the small metal or plastic plates embossed or engraved and fitted above the entrance of various rooms or compartments, also near valves or other equipment, to identify and indicate use. Also called index or name plate.

Fr: *Plaque Indicatrice;* Ger: *Zeigeplatte.*

LABOR (to). The act of a ship pitching and rolling heavily in a turbulent sea, in such a manner as to bring dangerous strain upon the hull, propelling machinery, masts, or rigging.

Fr: *Fatiguer;* Ger: *Arbeiten.*

LABRADOR CURRENT. A current setting out of Davis Strait, flowing southward down the coasts of Labrador and Newfoundland, passing along the eastern shoulder of the Grand Bank to its southern confines and to a variable extent beyond, according to the season. In the region between the 41st and 42nd parallels of latitude it encounters the Gulf Stream drift and turns to the eastward, paralleling the Gulf Stream waters toward the northward and eastward. It brings with it the ice so frequently met at certain seasons off Newfoundland. Also called Arctic current.

LACE. To draw together with a lacing passed through eyelet holes such as an awning, a bonnet, and so on.

Fr: *Mailler;* Ger: *Schnüren.*

LACE HOODS. The line along which the top and bottom parts of a trawl net are laced together.

LACE PIECE. See Lacing.

LACHSANGELBOOT. The *Lachsangelboot* or salmon liner is used for line fishing in East Prussia. The hull is built with keel, clinker planking, strongly raked stem, and sternpost. Leeboards are provided. The sail plan includes a lowering mast with sprit mainsail and jib foresail. Length of keel 22 to 32½ ft. Length over-all 25 to 36 ft. Breadth amidships 7½ to 8 ft. Draft 1 to 2½ ft. (Average.)

LACING. A knee timber fayed to the back of the figurehead and knee of the head and bolted to them. Also called lace piece.

Fr: *Courbe de Capucine;* Ger: *Gallionsschegg.*

See Lacing Line.

LACING EYES. A ring or eye of metal secured to the edge of a sail, awning, and so on, used to retain the lacing which holds

the sail to the boom, gaff, or yard.
 Fr: *Oeilleton;* Ger: *Schnürlöcher.*
LACING HOLE.
 See **Eyelet.**
LACING LINE. Also lacing. **1.** Rope or cord by which a jib-headed sail is loosely confined to a stay so that it can be hoisted or lowered.
 2. Line or rope used to lash the head or foot of a fore-and-aft sail to a gaff, yard, or boom.
 3. A rope or cord rove through eyelet holes along the edge of a sail or awning to secure the two edges together temporarily.
 Fr: *Transfilage;* Ger: *Lissung; Reihleine; Lissleine; Schnürleine.*
LADDER. A metal, wooden, or rope stairway.
 See **Sea Ladder, Accommodation Ladder.**
LADDERWAY. An opening in a deck for passage of passengers or crew up or down to another deck.
 Fr: *Panneau de Descente;* Ger: *Niedergangsluke.*
LAGAN. Any goods or other articles cast overboard from a sinking vessel and buoyed so as to be subsequently recovered. Also called ligan, logan.
 Ger: *Versenktes Gut; Wrackgut.*
LAG BOLT. A type of fastening occasionally used in wooden boatbuilding. Also called lag screw. It consists of a screw with a wood-screw thread, either cone point or gimlet point, made of galvanized steel, bronze or alloy, with a square or hexagonal head.
LAGGING. The periodic retardation in time of the occurrence of high and low water due to changes in the relative positions of the moon and sun. The tide lags from neaps to springs, the lunitidal interval being more than the average over this period.
 Fr: *Perdant; Déchet;* Ger: *Gezeitverspätung.*
LAGOON. A body of shallow water bordering on the sea but usually separated from it by a ridge of sand dunes, a sand spit or an atoll.
 Fr: *Lagune;* Ger: *Lagune.*
LAID DECK. A wooden deck with narrow planks laid parallel to the curvature of the covering board, as distinguished from a "straight" deck.
 Fr: *Pont à Bordages Courbes.*
 See **Swept Planking.**

LAID ROPE. A term applied to wire rope made of 6 strands of 7 wires each. Used for standing rigging.
LAKAMPIARA. A canoe used among the islands and bays of northern Madagascar. Its length is about 26 ft., and double outriggers project about 5 ft. on either side. The sail is spread by means of two sprits stepped into holes which run along the center line. When going before the wind, the sprits are placed in the holes which are nearest together; when close-hauled, those which are farthest apart.
 The hull consists of a tree trunk hewn out, with a plank (washboard) on either side.
LAKANA. Generic term for dugout canoes from the east coast of Madagascar, mostly used by the Betsimisaraka people for fishing in the lagoons and sheltered coastal waters. Two types are found: the largest, with a length ranging from 26 to 32 ft., has pointed ends finished off by an upward curve cut off square at apex. The smaller type has less freeboard and is more primitive in design. The ends are flattened out and terminate in the form of a beak. All craft are hewed out of a species of hardwood, *Calophyllum inophyllum.* There are no outriggers.
LAKANDRAO. Single-outrigger dugout canoe from the northwest coast of Madagascar. The bow is fashioned into a small, curved up spur, V-shaped at apex. It is rigged with a square shaped sail similar to that used in the *lakampiara* and held up by two poles.
LAKANFIAR. Single-outrigger dugout canoe from the west coast of Madagascar used by the natives for the capture of sea turtles. One of its distinguishing features is the fore end piece, which is fashioned into a horn-shaped inward curving projection, and a flattened distal portion, which projects horizontally beyond the body of the canoe. It is secured to the hull by hardwood pins. Great importance is attached by native fishermen to this end piece, which is supposed to have magic powers and is regularly smeared with blood of the captured animals. The body of the dugout is round in cross section, with concave cutwater and rounded forefoot. It has no sheer at gunwale. It is hewed out of a soft and light wood. The length ranges from 23 to 26 ft. The rig consists of a square sail supported by two poles. There is no mast.

LAKANJILO. A single-outrigger dugout canoe used for transportation on the northwest coast of Madagascar. The body of these craft is wedge-shaped in cross section and one of its distinguishing features is the shape of the bow, which has a small curved up spur cut square at apex and of triangular cross section. Length 33 ft. Breadth 3.3 ft. (Average.) The rig consists of an Arab lateen or settee sail made of matting with area of from 53 to 107 sq. ft. The tall mast is stepped near the bow and passes through a thwart, to which it is securely lashed. There is one shroud on each side, which fastens to the forward outrigger boom. A backstay is fastened amidships to the after outrigger boom.

LAKATOI. A New Guinea compound canoe formed of several dugouts lashed together side by side, covered with a roughly made superstructure used as deck. It is really a highly specialized raft. One or two rattan sails of shieldlike or crab-claw shape are carried and bent to light curved spars pointing downward: the point forming the tack, and the biggest area being nearest to the masthead.

LAMBDA. The name of the Greek letter λ. It is used in navigation as a symbol to denote the relationship between the mean directive force or magnetic compass needle and the directive force it would have if the disturbing elements caused by the ship's magnetism were removed and the needle responded solely to terrestrial magnetism.

LAMBUT. 1. An East Indian trading prao from Madura and Bali Islands.
2. In eastern Java, a small native boat equipped with European cutter rig and rudder.

LAMINATED TIMBER. A material recently used in wooden boatbuilding for structural parts of practically any desired length, width, or thickness, such as keel, stem, frames and so on. It is composed of relatively thick laminae of wood (about 1 in.) perfectly surfaced and glued together under pressure with cold-setting urea glue which is not affected by salt water and other factors of exposure. It is claimed that full length keels, with stem turned out by lamination in a single prefabricated unit without joints, provide over four times the strength of the usual construction with scarfs and bolts.

LAMPARA. A net of Italian origin used for encircling and impounding schools of fishes in open water. Also called round-haul net. It is made of cotton and consists of three parts: two wings of coarse mesh and a central bag of finer mesh. The upper edge is held at the surface of the water by a light line strung with cork floats and the lower edge is held by a heavily weighted lead line. Lampara used in the mackerel fisheries: Length 175 to 200 fathoms. Depth in the bag 20 to 35 fathoms. Meshing, wings 14 to 16 in., throat 2 to 4 in., bag ¾ to 1 in. (Average.)

Scofield, N. B., The Lampara Net, California Fish and Game Commission, vol. 10, no. 2 (1922).

LAMPARA BOAT. Double-ended boat used in the sardine and mackerel fisheries on the coast of California and working with a ring net. Some of the boats have no hold and carry the whole catch on deck. Others have a small hold capable of taking up to 12 tons. One mast with derrick is stepped amidships and there are no sails. The pilot house forward of the mast, and a power winch with 2 gypsy heads are located amidships. Each boat carries a skiff to which one end of the net is attached.

Boats capable of carrying over 20 tons usually work for the canneries. Smaller ones are market boats. Length 35 to 60 ft. Breadth 9 to 14 ft. Depth 3 to 5 ft. Net tonnage 5 to 14. Engines (Diesel) 15 to 50 hp. Deadweight capacity 7 to 50 tons. Crew 3 to 8.

LAMPARO. Mediterranean seine boat from the coast of Algeria. The hull is double-ended, keel-built with straight stem projecting 19 to 23 in. above the gunwale. The Italian-built boats have the stemhead cut off horizontally and capped by a small half-round molding slightly longer than the stem. The Spanish boats have more beam and the stemhead has an oval-shaped molding. Both types are decked forward with waterways extending over three-quarters of the length. The rig, which consisted of a lateen mainsail and jib, is nowadays frequently abandoned and replaced by a motor.

LAMP BOARD.
See Sidelight Screen.

LAMP BRACKET. A bracketed small shelf on foremast or mainmast upon which an electric navigation light is permanently fixed. Masthead lamp stand.

LAMP LOCKER. See **Lamp Room.**

LAMP CAGE. Light metal framework in which running lights or anchor lights are run up with halliards.

LAMP ROOM. In merchantmen, a small room, usually located in the forepart of the ship on the upper deck where the oil-burning lanterns and navigation lights are stored. Also called lamp locker.
 Fr: *Lampisterie;* Ger: *Lampenraum; Lampenkammer.*
 It is provided with steel tanks for kerosene, binnacle oil, lubricating oil, and clean waste oil for deck use. United States regulations provide that this space must be wholly lined with metal and fitted with a steampipe for fire-fighting purposes.

LAMP TRIMMER. A seaman or junior petty officer in charge of all lamps on board and responsible to the boatswain for keeping them in working order.
 Fr: *Lampiste;* Ger: *Lampenputzer.*

LANCASHIRE NOBBY. A sailing trawler found between the River Dee and Whitehaven. The hull is full-bodied aft as far as the rudderpost, which gives ample buoyancy to the stern. It is designed with low freeboard aft to facilitate handling of the trawl gear. It has a curved stem, narrow counter, and raked sternpost. The planking is carvel-built. There is a long narrow cockpit which extends forward almost as far as the mast. Nobbies can be beached easily. Rubbing strakes are fitted at the bilges to protect the planking.
 The boats are all cutter-rigged with pole mast. The jib sets on a long jibboom. The mainsail has three rows of reef points. A jack-yard topsail sets above the gaff. In the last years all nobbies have been fitted with motors of 8 to 18 hp. according to size. The sail plan has been cut down and jib and jibboom are seldom seen.

LANCETTA. Shallow-draft open sailboat from the east coast of the Italian peninsula employed in the local fisheries with a beam trawl. The hull is of the same type as the *bragozzo* but much smaller: tonnage 2 to 5. The rig consists of a balance lugsail and jib. A number of these hail from San Benedetto del Tronto where they work at a distance of 3 to 5 miles from the coast.

LANCHA. 1. Generic term used in the Iberian peninsula to denote a variety of small open boats propelled by sails and oars. When used as a ship's boat the *lancha* corresponds to the *launch* or *pinnace* formerly found on merchant and war vessels, with seven or eight thwarts and rigged with two masts and lugsails. It is always larger than the *bote* or boat.

The *lancha de Pesca* employed in the various fisheries of Spain varies in size, build and rig according to localities. The *lancha* of the Cantabrian coast used in the sardine fisheries with seines is rigged with two masts and lugsails.

In Portugal the term *lancha* refers to several types of boats, which differ considerably from each other. Some are built with transom stern, others with sharp stern. They are rigged with one or two masts and lateen, settee, or lugsails. Others are only rowboats. Length from 38.7 to 58.8 ft. Breadth 11.4 to 13.4 ft. Depth 4.6 to 5.1 ft.

The *lancha da Armacoes* (Peniche) is a rowboat of full lines and sharp stern, with four thwarts. The afterpart is used for stowing nets and gear. It is employed in the tuna and sardine fisheries with fixed nets.

2. Seagoing sailboat used for trading on the coast of Brazil (Bahia State), the cargo usually consisting of cocoa beans. These craft are decked fore and aft. The stern is round with a projecting upper stern piece. The larger type is rigged with three masts and has no bowsprit or headsails. The mainsail and mizzen are loose-footed gaffsails. The foremost carries a square foresail with long hoist. It is tacked down to the stem. There is a smaller type of *lancha* rigged with two masts and single mast step. The foremast is perpendicular and sets a square sail. The mainmast has a pronounced rake aft and sets a loose-footed gaffsail. The foresail luff is held to windward by a spar bowline.

LANCHA CALERA. A sail- and rowboat from Vizcaya and Guipuzcoa in northern Spain, employed in the hook and line fisheries. These boats work usually in fleets at a distance ranging from 15 to 20 miles from the shore. Length 47.7 ft. Breadth 9.8 ft. Depth 3.9 ft. Displacement 8 tons. Length of foremast 36 ft. Mainmast 42 ft. Length of foreyard 28 ft. Main yard 30 ft. Foresail 120 sq. ft. Mainsail 200 sq. ft. Crew 21 when long- or hand-lining, 8 when trolling. (Typical.)

The hull is built with keel, vertical stem, and sharp stern. A deep rudder extends from 3½ to 4 ft. below the keel line, in addition to which a centerboard is fitted amidships.

The planking has strakes about 4½ in. in width, and is made of oak or walnut below the waterline and of Norway pine above. Galvanized-iron fastenings. Some boats are open, others half-decked. The rig consists of two masts with lugsails. The foremast, about 6 ft. shorter than the mainmast, is stepped near the bow, the mainmast amidships. The oars are 16 ft. long and pulled double-banked.

LANCHA CAMINHA. A fishing boat from northern Portugal. Length (keel) 32 ft. Breadth 11 ft. Depth of hold 3 ft. 8 in. (Average.) There is a small deck amidships about 6 ft. in length known as "tilha." The hull is built of local pine wood. The rig consists of one mast with lugsail.

LANCHANG. 1. A coasting vessel of the Malay Peninsula rigged with two or three forward-raking masts stepped in tabernacles, square-headed dipping lugsails on the fore- and mainmast, and a small gaff mizzen. A bowsprit and two headsails are set forward. The hull is carvel-built with clipper stem, over which a fore gallery is built for the ground tackle. This also serves as a bumkin for spreading the tack of the foresail.

A deck cabin and stern gallery are added over the straight sternpost. Two quarter rudders are used for steering.

2. An East Indian fishing craft from Achin (northern Sumatra), keel-built, with sharp ends and propelled by oars. Employed as a seine boat. Also called pukat.

3. This name is also used in Malay language to denote a trading prao decked fore and aft and rigged with one mast and bowsprit.

LANCHANG TOARU. A Malay trading vessel from Bandar rigged with two pole masts and gaff sails. The hull is short and beamy with raking stem, sharp stern, centerline rudder with tiller; bow and stern galleries. It has a thatch-roofed shelter just abaft the mainmast over the hatchway.

LAND BLINK. A glare in the sky similar to ice blink but produced by ice-covered land.

LAND BOARD (U. S.). Planks placed alongside a hatchway when loading or discharging cargo with a single whip, to protect the wooden deck.

LAND BREEZE. A breeze that blows from the land at night because heat is radiated more rapidly from the land than from the sea. The opposite of sea breeze.

Fr: *Brise de Terre;* Ger: *Landwind.*

See **Sea Breeze.**

LANDED TERMS. Signifies that the price or rate of transportation includes lighterage (if any), dock dues, and charges incurred in landing goods at destination port.

Fr: *Franco Déchargement;* Ger: *Franko Löschung.*

LANDFALL. An approach or a coming to land, also the land so approached or reached. The land first sighted at the end of a sea voyage.

Fr: *Atterrage;* Ger: *Ausdünung; Landkennung.*

LANDFALL MARK. General term applied to a lightship or buoy with tall superstructure used to indicate the seaward approach to a harbor or estuary. The name is frequently displayed conspicuously on these marks.

LAND ICE. General term for field or floe ice which has not been detached from the shore since the winter.

LANDING. 1. The amount by which two plates overlap each other at their edge connection. Also called seam lap. The extent to which the joints of riveted plates pass over one another in the direction of their length.

Fr: *Recouvrement des Cans;* Ger: *Längsnaht.*

2. The distance between the center of a rivet hole and the edge of a bar or plate.

See **Shell Landings.**

LANDING APRON. A steel bridge for the adjustment of level between the deck of a ferryboat and the shore. It is hinged on the abutment at the shore end and has its outboard end suspended by cables or chains which are attached to a cross girder of the apron and to two pivoted balance beams, the rear ends of which carry counterweights to balance the weight of the apron.

LANDING CARD. A card issued in some ports to all passengers just before debarkation. In most instances these cards are numbered and correspond to figures indicated on the passenger list or manifest.

Fr: *Carte de Débarquement;* Ger: *Ausschiffungskarte.*

LANDING CHARGES. A general term applied to the initial charges for landing import goods. It covers such items as receiving the goods from a vessel lying alongside the dock or from barges or lighters, also wharfage and delivery from the dock to land conveyance or to warehouse, shed, and so on.

Fr: *Frais de mise à Terre;* Ger: *Landungskosten; Landungsgebühren.*

LANDING CLERK. The representative of a shipping line who boards incoming passenger vessels before they reach the disembarkation pier and gives the passengers information regarding railroad travel, immigration and customs formalities, hotels, and so on.

LANDING EDGE. The edge of a plate over which another plate laps, visible from inside the shell or under a deck, tank top, and the like. Also called molded edge, sheet line. The opposite of sight edge.

Ger: *Nahtstreifen.*

See **Sight Edge.**

LANDING ORDER.

See **Delivery Order.**

LANDING RATE (G. B.). Term used to describe the initial payments or charge made on goods for the operation of landing and warehousing or delivering goods from a ship in dock.

LANDING STAGE. A floating platform, usually anchored at the end of a wharf or pier, for the landing or embarking of passengers and goods.

Fr: *Appontement;* Ger: *Landungsbrücke; Ponton Landung; Schwimmende Landung; Anlandebrücke.*

LANDING STRAKE. 1. The upper strake but one in a rowboat, between the sheer strake and the binding strake. **2.** The two upper strakes of planking in a small boat.

LAND LANE. Opening through an ice floe, leading towards the shore.

LANDLOCKED. Surrounded by land, said of harbors and anchorages.

LANDMARK. Any conspicuous object ashore that serves as a guide to navigation.

Fr: *Amer;* Ger: *Landmarke.*

LANE. One of the recognized shipping tracks crossing an ocean or sea. Also called shipping lane.

Fr: *Route de Navigation;* Ger: *Fahrtrouten; Dampferwege.*

LANG LAY ROPE. A type of wire rope in which the individual wires are twisted in the same direction as the strands which make up the rope.

Fr: *Cablage Lang;* Ger: *Lang Seil.*

LANGOUSTIER.

See **Lobster Boat.**

LANTERN KEG. A small keg containing a lantern, candles, flint and steel, matches, tobacco and hard bread, which formed part of a whale boat's equipment to be used in an emergency. (Obsolete.)

LANYARD. A rope reeving through the deadeyes, used for setting up the rigging. Lanyards are made of four-strand hard-laid tarred hemp or Manila 2 to 4½ in. in circumference, or of fine steel wire. In most vessels nowadays turnbuckles are used with wire rigging in lieu of lanyards.

Fr: *Ride;* Ger: *Taljereep.*

See **Bag Lanyard, Bucket Lanyard, Knife Lanyard, Whistle Lanyard.**

LANYARD HITCH. A hitch formerly used in making fast the hauling part of a lanyard running through the deadeyes.

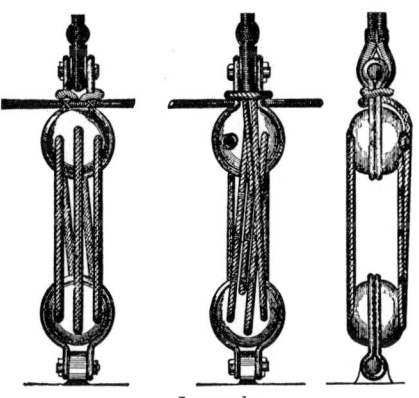

Lanyards

LANYARD STOPPER. A short length of rope or wire with a large knot (stopper knot) or toggle at one end, and with a rope lanyard of a smaller sized rope. The other end of the stopper has a large hook or shackle. The latter secures into an eyebolt in the deck, and the lanyard is wound about the cable and stopper while the knot keeps it from slipping. This stopper is used for temporarily holding mooring ropes when they have been hauled taut. They are stoppered off before the rope or wire is taken off the gypsy head preparatory to being put on the bitts. Also called deck stopper.

Fr: *Bosse à Bouton;* Ger: *Taustopper.*

LANYARD STUFF. Four-strand tarred Russian hemp rope ¾ to 1 in. in diameter used for lanyards and miscellaneous purposes on board ship.

Fr: *Filin à Rides;* Ger: *Taljereepgut.*

LANYARD THIMBLE. Galvanized-iron triangular thimble used in shrouds to enable

several turns to be taken with the lanyard. The turns not riding on each other allow tight reeving more easily than if a heart-shaped thimble is used. These thimbles range in size from 1 to 2½ in.
  Fr: *Cosse à Ride;* Ger: *Taljereepkauschen.*

LAOUTELLO. Sicilian fishing boat very broad amidships and narrow in the stern. It has the same rig as the *schifazzo* with the mast raking forward. Length 20 to 33 ft. Burden 3 to 5 tons.

LAP. 1. The distance that one piece of material is laid over another in a lapped joint. Also called lapping.
  2. The overlaying of plank or plate edges in clinker work.
  Fr: *Recouvrement;* Ger: *Überlapp.*

LAPATAGANAN. Dugout canoe of the Yahgan Indians from the eastern stretches of the Strait of Magellan, which has taken the place of the *anan* or bark canoe. It has short, rounded ends and is fitted with a broad wash strake on each side. Length 16.5 ft. (Approximate.)

LAP CALKING. The calking of a lap joint. Also called edge calking. In this process one plate edge is either planed or chipped and then split and forced down against the other plate to provide a tight joint.

LAPIL. A generic name for single-outrigger dugout canoes of Aitape district in British New Guinea. Also called *epil.* The small canoes are from 16 to 19 ft. long and 1 ft. wide. The larger, 39 to 50 ft. long, 2.5 to 2.6 ft. wide carrying 1 to 2 tons. The wash strakes are higher amidships and support a raised platform with a crate at each end. The mast of the larger canoes is a slender sapling 26 to 29 ft. high. The oblong sail is from 17 to 24 ft. high by 4.9 to 7.3 ft. broad with yard and boom.

LAPIS. A bargelike craft of shallow draft propelled by oars and used for the transportation of goods on the rivers and sheltered waters of the Philippine Islands. Also called *tapague.*

LAPPED JOINT. A joint in which one part overlaps the other, thus avoiding the use of a strap.
  Fr: *Joint à Clin; Joint à Recouvrement;* Ger: *Überlappung.*
  See **Lap.**

LAP RIVETING. The riveting of two plates which have their edges overlapping each other.
  Fr: *Rivetage à Clins;* Ger: *Überlappungsnietung.*

LAPSTRAKE. A term applied to boats built on the clinker system, in which the strakes are overlapping. The top strake laps over the outside of the strake below.

LAPSTRAKE PLANKING.
  See **Clinker Planking.**

LARCH. A wood which, if of first class quality, is often used for planking wooden craft. When used for clinker construction it is as durable as oak. Unless well over one inch in thickness it is not as good as other woods for planking, especially in the case of carvel-built boats. A large number of fishing boats are larch-built on oak frames. Seasoned larch weighs about 37 lb. per cubic foot. Light skiffs built entirely of this wood are very satisfactory. Larch roots make good knees.
  Fr: *Mélèze;* Ger: *Larche.*

LARGE. To sail large: to run with the sheets well eased off when the wind is fair, so that the sails receive the full effect of the wind. Going large: sailing with the wind on the quarter or from some point abaft the beam. To *sail large* is equivalent to *sail free.*
  Fr: *Largue;* Ger: *Raum.*

LARK'S HEAD. A bend used for fastening a line to a ring when the same tension is exerted on both standing parts.
  Fr: *Tête d'Alouette.*

LASH. A line used by English drifters which connects the warp of a drift net fished on the surface at the junction of adjacent lints. Also called strop.

LASH (to). To secure by binding closely with a rope or small stuff.
  Fr: *Aiguilleter; Amarrer; Saisir;* Ger: *Laschen; Seefest zurren.*

LASHING. A general term given to any rope or small stuff used for binding or making fast one thing to another, such as an eye to a spar, a spar to another, and so on.
  Fr: *Saisine; Amarrage; Aiguillette;* Ger: *Laschung; Sorrung; Zurrung.*
  See **Heel Lashing, Packing Lashing, Parrel Lashing, Rose Lashing, Sheer Head Lashing, Span Lashing, Stage Lashing.**

LASHING EYES. Eyes formed in two parts such as in the strap of a block, or in the fork of a stay, and connected by a lashing. The loops in the ends of two ropes through which the lashing is passed securing them together.

Fr: *Oeil de Fourche d'Étai*; Ger: *Bandselauge*.

LASHING POST. An upright on the upper deck to which lashings for deck cargo are fastened.

LASHING RING PAD. A pad eye with loose ring attached, located along the bulwarks and hatch coamings for securing deck cargo.

LASHING SHACKLE. A shackle especially large in the bow and wider at the jaws than ordinary shackles. It is fitted to the heavier classes of double and treble blocks, to permit of their taking a Manila or wire rope lashing.

LASH RAIL. Strong wooden rail bolted inside of the bulwarks and to which casks or other deck gear can be lashed.

LASKETS. Loops of small cord in the head rope of a bonnet for lacing the latter. Also called latchings. The center loop or lasket serves as a key to the rest and prevents them from unreeving. It is called latching key. Latchings are usually 6 in. long and 6 in. apart except the two middle ones, which are 18 in. long to fasten off with.

Fr: *Bride*; Ger: *Lissleine*.

LASSE. A small rowing boat with shallow draft made in the district of Oleron and near La Rochelle (France). It is used by oystermen to transport their gear on the beds and collect the oysters or mussels. The *lasse* has a length of about 13 ft. with good beam and flat bottom which rises forward and gives ample sheer to the boat. The stern is broad and square. A single thwart is fitted amidships. No sail is carried.

LAST. 1. A measure formerly used on the east coast of Scotland and England for the sale of herring by numbers. It averaged 13,200 herrings with an approximate weight of 30 cwt. The last is no longer in use, fish being now sold by the cran. A last is the equivalent of ten crans. A last of codfish is 12 barrels, each barrel containing about 50 fish.

Fr: *Last*; Ger: *Last*; *Schiffslast*.

2. The seam which bisects the clew angle in Scottish and miter or diagonally cut sails. Also called diagonal miter seam.

LATEEN RIG. A rig of Arab origin but later adopted and used in the Mediterranean, Red Sea, and Persian Gulf, by fishing and coasting craft. It is well suited to smooth water and light winds, but is perilous in heavy seas and strong winds on account of the lofty sail peaks and the difficulty of reefing them satisfactorily. The masts are short and stand perpendicular, or with a forward rake. Lateen-rigged boats are usually fast under sail, particularly when close-hauled. The lateen rig is heavy and requires a large crew when compared with the usual fore-and-aft rig, but it allows the vessel to carry a large spread of canvas without a great transverse inclination. It is especially dangerous if the vessel is taken aback. The shrouds are set up as runners in order that they may be shifted when the vessel goes about.

Fr: *Gréement à Antenne*; Ger: *Lateinische Takelung*.

This mode of rigging does not present so great a surface of sail in relation to the heeling moment as the lug; but possesses advantages in light winds, when close-hauled. When sailing before the wind, and in a rough sea, it is the most disadvantageous of all rigs; and when by the wind, it is more liable to be taken aback than the common lug.

Vence, J., *Bateaux à Voilure Latine*, Paris, 1892.

LATEEN SAIL. A triangular sail extended by a long tapering yard slung at about one-quarter the distance from the lower end, which is brought down at the tack, causing the yard to stand at an angle of 45° or more. It is commonly found in the Mediterranean and eastern seas.

Fr: *Voile à Antenne*; *Voile Latine*; Ger: *Lateinsegel*.

Bouyer, L., Les Voiles Latines, Le Yacht, vol. 1 (Paris, April–August, 1878).

LATEEN YARD. A long tapering yard swung at an angle of about 45° from the horizontal by halyards and attached to the mast at a point approximately one-third or two-fifths of its length. It is made of two grown spars as nearly as possible of the proper size, and fished or scarfed together.

Fr: *Antenne*; Ger: *Lateinraa*; *Lateinischeraa*.

LATERAL PLANE. The underwater profile of a boat. The surface of immersed longitudinal plane which varies according to underwater form of hull and rig. The method of comparison for different hulls is by its ratio to immersed midsection area. For yachts 4.0–6.0 is an average figure.

Fr: *Plan de Dérive*; Ger: *Lateralplan*.

LATERAL RESISTANCE. The resistance which a vessel offers to a lateral motion of translation through the water. Lateral resistance is of special importance in sailing craft, and it is for the purpose of increasing it that projecting keels, centerboards and leeboards are fitted.
>Fr: *Résistance à la Dérive;* Ger: *Treibungswiderstand; Seitlicher Widerstand; Lateralwiderstand.*

LATITUDE. The latitude of a place is its angular distance north or south of the equator. It is measured by the arc of the meridian intercepted between the equator and the place in question, or by the angle subtended by this arc at the center of the earth.
>Fr: *Latitude;* Ger: *Breite.*

See **Colatitude, Ex-Meridian Latitude, Horse Latitudes, Middle Latitude.**

LATITUDE BY DEAD RECKONING. The latitude deduced from the compass course and logged distance sailed since the last fix. Also called latitude by account.
>Fr: *Latitude par l'Estime;* Ger: *Loggebreite.*

LATITUDE BY OBSERVATION. The latitude obtained by observations of celestial bodies, or by bearings of terrestrial objects.
>Fr: *Latitude observée;* Ger: *Beobachtete Breite.*

LATITUDE CONSTANT. A combination of the several values used in the computation of latitude by meridian altitude, in order to obtain a constant to which simple addition or subtraction of observed altitude gives the latitude. Also called **Meridian Altitude Constant.**
>Fr: *Constante de Latitude;* Ger: *Breitenkonstante.*

LATITUDE ERROR. The small angle in a gyroscopic compass, at which the gyro axis settles from the meridian. It varies with the latitude; from zero at the equator this error increases to 2.9 degrees at 60 degrees North or South latitude. It is Easterly in North latitudes and Westerly in South latitudes.
>Fr: *Erreur de Latitude;* Ger: *Breitenfehler; Fahrtfehler.*

LATITUDE FACTOR. Term used to denote the change in latitude from a given point in a Sumner line brought about by a change of one minute in longitude.
See **Sumner Line.**

LATITUDE FROM. The latitude of the place sailed from taken as the point of departure.
>Fr: *Latitude de départ;* Ger: *Verlassene Breite.*

LATITUDE SCALE. Unit marked at the side of a chart which represents one degree of latitude of a particular part of the terrestrial globe.
>Fr: *Echelle des latitudes;* Ger: *Breitenskala.*

LATTICE BOOM. A cargo derrick made up of riveted structural steel shapes or lattice work, used for lifting heavy weights, usually 20 tons and more. Also called lattice derrick.
>Fr: *Mât de Charge en Treillis;* Ger: *Gitterladebaum.*

LATTICE MAST. Steel mast constructed of riveted structural steel shapes or lattice work.
>Fr: *Mât en Treillis;* Ger: *Gittermast.*

LAUD. Small sailing craft employed for trading or fishing in the western Mediterranean. The hull is built with a hanging keel and, in the case of the smallest units, with two grounding keels for beaching. It has a convex curved stem with projecting sternhead. A canoe stern is usual on small fishing boats. A round stern with overhang on the others. The larger boats are decked fore and aft, the smaller only at ends with broad waterways running along each side of the open hold amidships. The rig consists of one, two, or three masts according to tonnage and use. The small boats employed in the dragnet fisheries (*falucho de Pareja*) have one lateen mainsail with or without headsail. Larger craft used mainly for transportation are rigged with two masts; the mizzenmast is stepped well aft and has no rake. The sail is either a standing lateen or a spritsail and is sheeted to a long bumkin. The largest type has three masts with lateen sails on all masts or with a sprit mizzen. All two- and three-mast boats carry a long jibboom with one headsail. The fore- and mainmasts have a pronounced forerake. Maximum carrying capacity 100 tons. Fishing *laud* or *falucho*: Length 31.7 ft. Breadth 8.5 ft. (Typical.) Two-mast *laud* or *falucho*: Length between perpendiculars 59 **ft.** Breadth 16.4 ft. Depth 6.9 ft. (Typical.)

LAUNCH. 1. A large, heavy and beamy ship's boat with flat floors and rather shallow draft, formerly used and designed for carry-

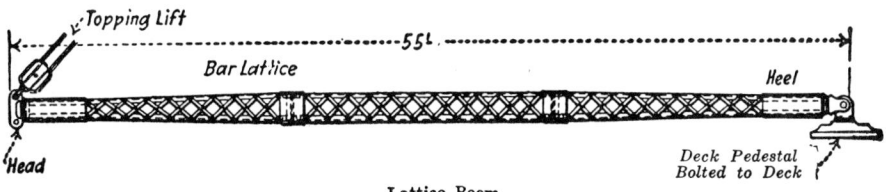

Lattice Boom

ing stores and men. (Obsolete.)

Fr: *Grand Canot;* Ger: *Ruderbarkasse.*

See **Long Boat, Harbor Launch, Towing Launch, Motor Launch.**

2. Small open or half-decked boat with mechanical propulsion, usually employed commercially for various purposes in harbors, estuaries, rivers and occasionally for making short trips in coastal waters. Launches are sometimes carried on deck by ocean steamers and put in the water for towing native craft with freight over bars and shoals when it is not possible for the vessels themselves to come alongside the wharves.

See **Harbor Launch, Sardine Launch, Towing Launch.**

LAUNCHING. The sliding of a ship by the action of its own weight into the water down inclined launch ways prepared for the purpose. The practice of launching varies according to local conditions. There are four representative methods most generally adopted, i.e., single-way launching, two-way launching, side launching, and end launching.

Fr: *Lancement;* Ger: *Stapellauf; Ablauf.*

See **Double-way Launching, End Launching, Launching Cradle, Side Launching, Single-way Launching.**

During the building of a ship the structure is supported by blocks and shores. These are removed just before launching, the weight being transferred to a cradle which slides on the standing ways toward the water. Large wedges are forced home between the top of the sliding ways and the hull of the ship so that when the bilge blocks and shores supporting the structure are withdrawn the weight is borne by the sliding ways.

Hillhouse and Riddlesworth, "On Launching," Institution of Naval Architects (London), *Transactions,* 1917; Keith, H. H. W., "Launching," in *Principles of Naval Architecture, vol. I,* Society of Naval Architects and Marine Engineers, New York, 1939; Lesley, E. P., *Launching Practice on the Pacific Coast,* Society of Naval Architects and Marine Engineers, New York, 1905; Robinson, R. H. M., *Launching Practice on the Atlantic Coast,* Society of Naval Architects and Marine Engineers, New York, 1904.

LAUNCHING CLAUSE. An insurance clause in a builder's policy which defines and limits the risks accepted by the underwriters at the launch of a vessel.

LAUNCHING CRADLE. A frame placed under a vessel to support it on the ways until it is waterborne. It slides down the timbers called standing ways. The upper part consists of making-up or filling pieces formed of cross wedge-shaped blocks of balk timbers neatly fitted to the shell plating. The sliding ways form the lower part of the cradle. Very commonly the forward part and afterpart are disconnected amidships so as to facilitate their recovery after the vessel is waterborne.

Fr: *Berceau de Lancement; Ber;* Ger: *Wiege; Ablaufgerüst.*

The cradle is built underneath the vessel after the standing ways have been laid and extends over a distance of 0.6 to 0.8 of the ship's length. When two sliding ways are adopted the weight of the cradle represents about 6 to 8 per cent of the vessel's displacement. In single-way launching this weight is reduced to about 1 to 1.5 per cent.

LAUNCHING CURVES. A set of curves and lines used in launching calculations to determine the tendency of the vessel to tip and the amount of pressure on the fore poppets as the ship travels down the ways. They include: (1) The curve of moment of hull weight about the ends of ways. This curve begins after the center of gravity has passed the way ends and is a constantly increasing moment expressed as a straight line. (2) The curve of buoyancy which begins when the keel enters the water. (3) The curve of moment of buoyancy about the ends of ways. (4) The moment of hull weight about the fore poppets. It is expressed as a straight line, being the product of the launching weight and the distance of center of gravity from the fore poppets. (5) The curve of moment of buoyancy about the fore poppets.

Fr: *Courbes de Lancement;* Ger: *Stapellaufkurven.*

Wilson, F., Composite Launching Curves, *Marine Engineering,* vol. 47, February, 1942.

LAUNCHING DRAGS. Piles of chain or steel plates attached to a vessel to be launched by cables or wire ropes for the purpose of decreasing its velocity as it enters the water. They are of such length that they become taut when the vessel nears the launchway ends. Thereafter the tow drags over the surface of the ground and thus creates a resistance which slows and ultimately stops the vessel. The weight of drags is usually proportionate to the weight of the vessel and declivity of ways. Also called chain drags.

Fr: *Bosses Cassantes;* Ger: *Schleppketten.*

LAUNCHING GREASE. A lubricant applied between the sliding and ground ways in order to lessen friction between sliding surfaces when launching a vessel. Patent greases are now in use, but tallow or stearine or a mixture of both has been commonly employed. It must be sufficiently viscous to resist being squeezed out when the weight is brought on the cradle. Soft soap, train oil, and colza oil with tallow are also used.

Fr: *Lubréfiant de Lancement;* Ger: *Ablaufschmiere.*

The composition is chosen by experience as suitable for the locality and the time of year the launch is to take place. A different make-up will be required in the summer to that which proves suitable for a winter launch. Compositions also vary if the launching weight per square foot of surface on the ways is light or heavy.

King Salter, J. J., *Experiments on Tallows Used for Launching Ships,* Institution of Naval Architects (London), *Transactions,* 1921.

LAUNCHING PAWL.
See **Launching Trigger.**

LAUNCHING POPPET. The upright timbers erected on each side at the forward and afterends of the sliding ways to support the extremities of the ship when launching. The lower ends rest on the sliding ways and the upper ends abut against brackets riveted to the hull. In very large ships the fore poppets are occasionally made in the form of trunnion bearings. In twin-screw ships the afterpoppets are built as struts under the shaft bossings.

Fr: *Colombier;* Ger: *Schlittenstütze.*

See **Fore Poppet, After Poppet.**

LAUNCHING RIBBAND. Strips of oak or hardwood which run the whole length of the standing ways in order to prevent the sliding ways from spreading outward.

Fr: *Joue de Guidage;* Ger: *Führungsleiste.*

LAUNCHING TRIGGER. A device used for releasing a ship when launched. It holds the ship on the ways just before the launch

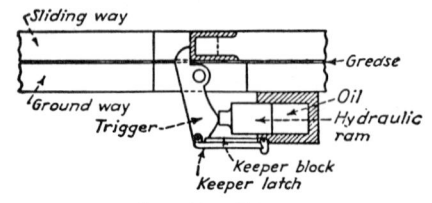

Launching Trigger

when keel and bilge blocks have been knocked down. Also called launching pawl, trigger dog.

Fr: *Clef de Lancement; Vérin de Retenue; Verrou Hydraulique;* Ger: *Stopphebel.*

Two types are used: mechanical and hydraulic. The mechanical trigger is made up of an arrangement of timbers and a spur shore, the release of which is effected by cutting a rope lashing with an axe. The hydraulic trigger which is generally used for launching large vessels, consists of a ram cylinder, the piston of which bears against the lower end of a heavy pawl pivoted in the ground ways. The upper end of the pawl is forced by the pressure in the cylinder against a steel shoe placed in the sliding ways. To release the pawl a cock is opened which lets the water out of the cylinder.

Robin Howell, H. B., Launching Triggers, North East Coast Institution of Engineers and Shipbuilders, *Transactions,* vol. 61, Newcastle on Tyne, 1945.

LAUNCHING WAYS. The inclined structure, generally of timber, by means of which a vessel slides down from the building slip into the water. There are two sets of launching ways: the standing or fixed ways and the sliding or bilge ways.

Fr: *Voie de Lancement; Chemin de Glissement;* Ger: *Schlagbetten; Ablaufbahn.*

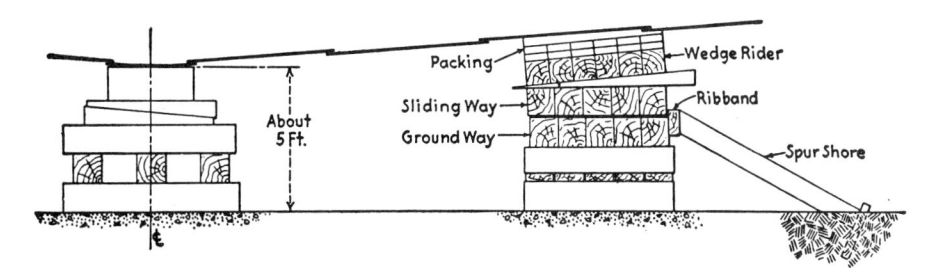

Launching Ways. (*Courtesy Society of Naval Architects and Marine Engineers, N. Y.*)

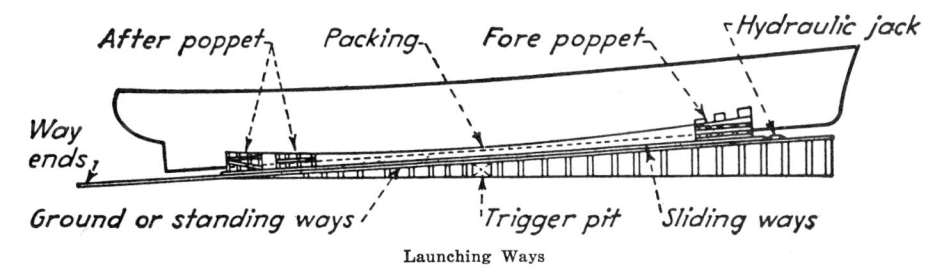

Launching Ways

LAWAK. A small fishing dugout of *jukung* type from western Java. It is without outriggers. Also called *lawakan, lelawak*.

LAW DIVISION CLERK (U. S.). A representative of the law division of the customhouse who opens and examines the contents of packages refused by the consignee or his representative.

LAW OF ARCHIMEDES. Hydrostatical principle discovered by Archimedes, which states that if a body be immersed in a fluid the body will experience an upward force equal, to the weight of the fluid displaced by the body.

Fr: *Loi d'Archimede;* Ger: *Archimedisches Prinzip.*

LAW OF MARQUE. The law of nations governing the seizure of property of a hostile nation on the high seas.

LAW OF THE FLAG. The law which determines the conditions under which a ship is entitled to the nationality whose flag she flies. Also called law of ship's flag. It is also the national law which governs all juridical relations of a private nature concerning a ship. It is the law of the port where the ship is registered or of the State to which the ship belongs by nationality. The *Lex Rei Sitae* which generally governs the usucapion of other kinds of property on land is replaced, with regard to ships, by the law of the flag.

Fr: *Loi du Pavillon;* Ger: *Flaggenrecht.*

See **Flag.**

League of Nations (Publication), *National Laws Governing the Granting of the Right to Fly a Merchant Flag*, Geneva, 1931; Mueller, R., *Das Flaggenrecht von Schiffen und Luftfahrzeugen*, Hamburg, 1926; Rienow, R., *The Test of the Nationality of a Merchant Vessel*, New York, 1937.

LAW OF STORMS. The theory of motion of the winds within a storm area and the progressive movements of storms. It is based on the supposition that the air currents within the limits of the storm disc move in nearly concentric circles around a center of low pressure; from right to left or against the hands of a watch in the Northern Hemisphere; and from left to right, or with the hands of a watch in the Southern Hemisphere; so that when facing the wind, the center lies on the right hand in the Northern and on the left hand in the Southern Hemisphere.

Ger: *Windgesetze.*

Creswell, M., Notes on the history and development of the law of storms, *The Marine Observer*, vol. 9, nos. 101-102-103, London, 1932.

LAWS OF MECHANICAL SIMILITUDE. The laws used in naval architecture for the computation of power and resistance of similar ships or ships having (1) the same geometrical form; (2) all corresponding dimensions in the same ratio; (3) all weights similarly distributed and varying as the third power of their linear ratio.

Fr: *Lois de Similitude;* Ger: *Ähnlichkeitsgesetze.*

LAWS OF OLERON. The earliest known laws that governed practice upon the high seas. Also called Rules of Oleron. The Laws of Oleron date from the fourteenth century and were based on a collection of sea customs from the Near East. A record of these was made for the maritime court of the Island of Oleron (Bay of Biscay) in order that they might serve as a code among mariners of the western seas.

LAY. 1. The direction in which the different strands of a rope are twisted, also the amount of twist. The twisting or turning of the several component parts or strands forming a rope. The twist in the strands is designated as the foreturn and that in the rope itself as the afterturn. In a well-laid rope these turns balance each other, the opposite turns acting against each other to keep the strands together. The strength of a rope depends to some extent upon the amount of twist or lay in it. The softer the lay, the stronger the rope, but the poorer the wearing qualities. A rope is soft, medium, common, plain-, or hard-laid.

Angle of Lay for Various Ropes

	Manila	Hemp
Hawser-laid rope	39°	42°
Shroud-laid rope	40°	45½°
Cable-laid rope	37°	39°
Cable-laid rope, strands	31°	31°
Boltrope		36°
Spunyarn		28°

Fr: *Toronnage; Commettage; Cablage;* Ger: *Schlag.*

See **Hard Lay, Right-hand Lay, Soft Lay, Unkinkable Lay.**

2. The share in the proceeds of the catch due each member of the crew in fishing vessels.

LAY (to). 1. Used in the sense of to go or to come, when giving orders to the crew as: lay forward, lay aft, lay aloft, and so on.

Ger: *Legen.*

2. To direct the course of a vessel.

3. To lay a rope: to twist the strands together.

Fr: *Commettre; Cabler;* Ger: *Schlagen.*

LAY ALOFT. Order given to the men to go up in the rigging; the opposite is "lay down from aloft."

Fr: *Montez;* Ger: *Aufentern!*

LAYAN. An East Indian double-outrigger sailing canoe from Achin (northern Sumatra) of same type as the *lelayan;* the latter is employed for transportation of goods and passengers while the *layan* is used for fishing only. The mast carries a rectangular sail made of palm leaves. A headsail is sometimes set on a small bowsprit.

LAY BOARD.
See **Hog Piece.**

LAY BY. A portion of a river or maritime canal widened and provided with rows of piles or dolphins to which a vessel can tie up to allow another ship proceeding in the opposite direction to pass.

Fr: *Gare;* Ger: *Liegeplatz.*

LAY BY (to). To bring a vessel almost to a standstill. To come to a stationary position with the ship's head toward the wind. Also called to lie, to lay.

LAY DAYS. The time allowed to the master of a vessel for loading or unloading. In the absence of any custom to the contrary, Sundays are not computed in the calculation of lay days. According to a mass of legal decisions, fractional parts of a lay day do not count as fractions but as whole days. Lay days do not begin to count until a vessel has been reported at the customhouse and notice served upon the charterer.

Fr: *Jours de Planche; Staries;* Ger: *Liegezeit; Liegetage.*

LAY-DAY STATEMENT. Document made out by the master of a vessel in port, in which are given day by day all particulars regarding loading or discharging times, stoppages, times for trimming cargo, and so on, in order that the owners may be provided with all facts necessary for the computation of lay days, demurrage and dispatch. It is signed by the master and the charterers.

LAYER OUT (U. S.). A shipyard worker who indicates on the plates and shapes the operations necessary for fabrication such as shearing, planing, punching, bending, flanging, beveling, and so on. Also called liner off (G. B.). The layer out has usually the same qualifications as the shipfitter but his work is confined to laying out in the shop, whereas the shipfitter does his work largely on the ship (G. B.).

See **Laying Out.**

LAYING OFF. Striking on the mold loft floor the lines of the hull in full size. Also called laying down, lofting. From these lines together with certain additional ones that are used in those parts of the ship where extreme curvature occurs, the expanded dimensions as well as the shape of every item entering into the ship's structure may be obtained, and a wood, paper, or metal template can be made up showing all the details of the fabrication of each part.

Fr: *Tracé à la Salle;* Ger: *Schnürbodenarbeit; Abschnüren.*

Atwood, E. L., *A Text Book of Laying Off,* London, 1938; Halliburton, A. C., *Mold Loft Work,* Scranton (Pa.), 1940.

LAYING OUT. Placing the necessary indications on plates and bars for shearing, planing, punching, beveling, bending, rolling, and so on, from templates made in the mold loft or taken from the hull.

LAYING UP. A term used in connection with riveting work. It refers to the driving in of the rivet by means of blows of a heavy holding-on hammer on the rivet head so as to expand the rivet's diameter and bring it into close contact with the work of filling the hole before clenching the point.

LAY-IN THE OARS. To unship the oars and place them in the boat.

Fr: *Rentrer les Avirons;* Ger: *Riemen einlegen.*

LAY OFF. To remain stationary outside a harbor.

LAY ON THE OARS. 1. To cease rowing and keep the oars parallel with the water surface.

2. An order to a pulling boat's crew to stop pulling and to hold their oars with the blades horizontal and the oars at right angles to the keel of the boat.

Fr: *Armez les Avirons;* Ger: *Riemen Platt!*

LAY OUT. 1. To lay out on the oars means to pull with more force.

Fr: *Souquer sur les Avirons;* Ger: *Auslegen.*

2. To lay out a warp or mooring line, that is, to carry it in a boat to a distance from the ship to which one end is attached.

Fr: *Élonger;* Ger: *Ausfahren; Ausbringen.*

LAY UP. To tie a vessel up, dismantle or unrig her for a prolonged period of unemployment.

Fr: *Désarmer;* Ger: *Auflegen; Abrüsten.*

LAZARETTE. 1. The space above the after peak between decks used as storeroom for provisions in some vessels. A small 'tween-decks storeroom.

Fr: *Cambuse;* Ger: *Lazarett.*

2. An isolation hospital for patients with contagious diseases from vessels in quarantine.

Fr: *Lazaret;* Ger: *Lazarett; Quarantäneanstalt.*

LAZY GUY. Running rigging to steady a boom in a seaway. A light tackle or rope rigged to prevent a boom from swinging around.

LAZY HALYARD. A halyard consisting of a light line taking the place of, and rove in the same manner as the halyard proper, which can then be unbent and coiled away.

LAZY JACK. One of the lines rove through thimbles seized on to the boom topping lifts and looped under the boom. Also called lazy line, jack, gathering line. When the sail is lowered they prevent the folds of canvas from falling on deck.

Ger: *Fangleine.*

LAZY LINE.

See **Lazy Jack.**

LAZY PAINTER. A hemp line about five fathoms in length, used for tying up a small boat when in still water. Also called harbor painter. The inboard end is shackled into the stem ring.

LAZY TACK. A running bight put on the tack of a fore-and-aft topsail set flying, and around a stay to keep the sail from blowing away while it is hoisted.

LEACH LINE.

See **Leech Line.**

LEAD. 1. In sailing craft, the distance between the center of effort and the center of lateral resistance. It is usually expressed as a fraction of the waterline length and varies widely with the type of boat. The center of effort is generally forward of the center of lateral resistance.

Average Values of Lead

Square-rigged trading vessels........ 0.067
Fore-and-aft rigged vessels 0.039
Cruising yachts 0.030
Racing scows .... 0 to 0.15

Ger: *Voreilung.*

2. A term used in polar regions to denote a narrow channel or lane of water between fields or floes of ice.
3. The direction of a strand in a knot. The direction of a rope.

LEAD. 1. A heavy malleable metal used in shipbuilding for stern tubes of small wooden vessels; also formerly as lining in rudder trunks, hawsepipes, sea valves and other apertures through the planking and ceiling of wooden hulls. In sailing yachts it is used for keels and ballast.

Fr: *Plomb;* Ger: *Blei.*

2. A device for obtaining soundings. Also called sounding lead. It usually consists of a lead sinker of nearly cylindrical or prismatic shape having a length of five or six times its diameter. The lower and larger end has a cup-shaped recess, and there is a hole in the other end for the lead line. The recess in the bottom is for the arming, which usually consists of tallow to pick up a sample of the sea bottom. Sounding leads are of different sizes and are named according to their weight and use. For soundings greater than 20 fathoms sounding machines are now generally used.

Fr: *Sonde; Plombe de Sonde;* Ger: *Lot; Lotblei.*

See **Casting Lead, Deep-Sea Lead, Drift Lead, Hand Lead.**

LEAD BLOCK. Small wooden snatch block with tail, used when heaving the hand lead.

Fr: *Poulie de Ligne de Sonde;* Ger: *Lotblock.*

LEADER. A fence for leading fish into a pound net, fyke net, or weir. The leader usually runs out in a straight line from the shore and consists of a stonewall, a fence of laths or brush or a vertical net stretched on poles.

Fr: *Guideau;* Ger: *Leitwehr; Leitgarn.*

See **Tricing Stay.**

LEADER CABLE. A submerged electric cable, through which an alternating current capable of transmitting code signals is sent. Also called piloting cable. The shipboard receivers consist of two coils; one hung over each side of the vessel, and each connected to a telephone receiver. When the vessel is to one side of the cable, a loud signal is heard in the nearer receiver and a weak one on the other. The vessel is maneuvered until the audibility of the signal produced in both receivers is the same, at which time, it will be directly over the cable.

Fr: *Cable Guide;* Ger: *Leitkabel; Lotsenkabel.*

It has been found by experience that vessels could pick up the cable at a distance of about 1,200 yards and then follow it up without the assistance of any other navigational aids. The leader cable is particularly helpful in case of fog or thick weather to enable vessels to proceed up a channel at the entrance of a harbor. British Admiralty, Signal Department, *Technical Notes on the Leader Cable System,* London, 1921; Hanson, E. C., *The Audio-Piloting Cable System,* Washington, 1920.

LEADING BLOCK. A general name for any block used in altering the direction of pull on a rope. Also called lead block. A single block used to provide a fair lead for running gear.

Fr: *Poulie de Retour;* Ger: *Leitblock; Führungsblock.*

LEADING EDGE. The lower edge of a propeller blade when the blade is in a horizontal position and moving downward. With outward-turning screws, for a right-hand propeller it lies on the starboard side and for a left-hand, to port. It can also be defined as the edge of the blade which first meets the water when a ship is moving ahead.

Fr: *Arête d'Entrée; Bord d'Entrée;* Ger: *Eintretende Flügelkante.*

LEADING FIREMAN. In Great Britain the foreman of a watch in the stokehold of a steamer. Also called leading hand. He is responsible for the maintenance of the working pressure in the boilers. In smaller ships this duty falls on the watchkeeping engineer.

Fr: *Chef de Chauffe;* Ger: *Oberfeuermeister.*

LEADING LIGHTS.
See **Range Lights.**

LEADING LINE. A line drawn on a chart through two leading marks. The names of the marks and their true bearing from seaward, when in transit are generally written along the line.

Fr: *Ligne de Relèvement;* Ger: *Leitlinie.*

LEADING MARKS. A name given in chart work to two conspicuous objects which, if kept in line, will lead a vessel into a channel or deep water, or clear of certain dangers.

Fr: *Amers de Direction;* Ger: *Leitmarke.*

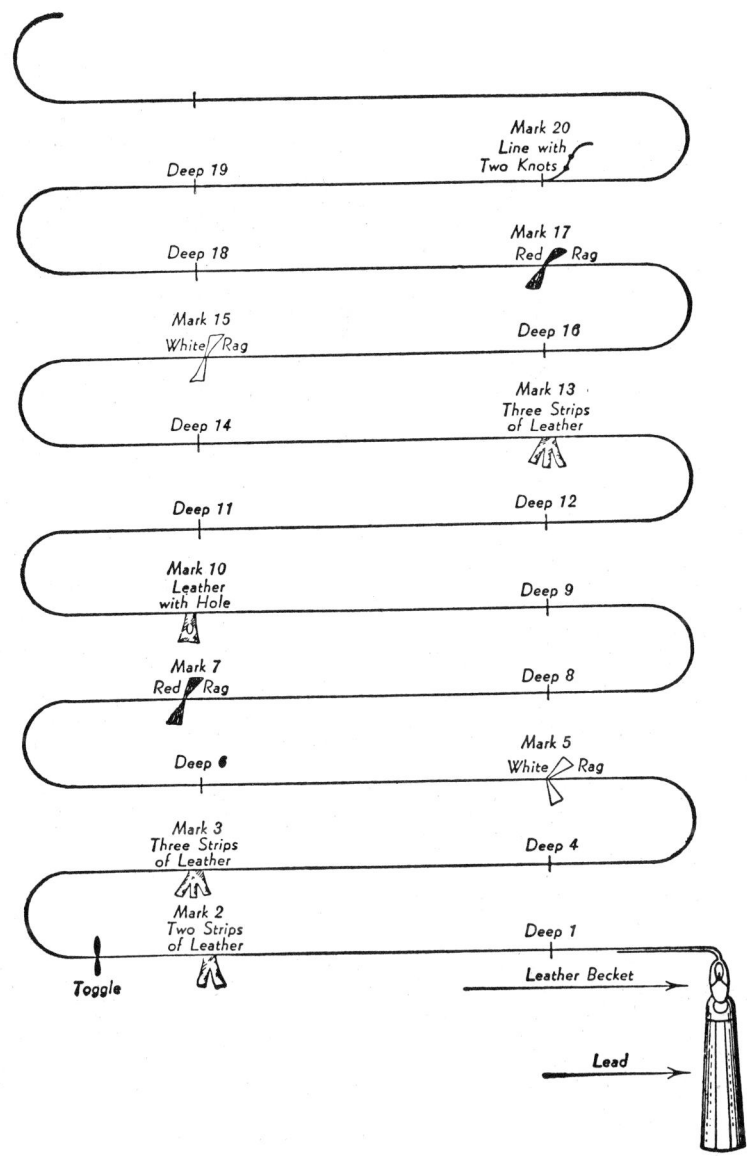

Lead Line

LEADING PART. The hauling part of a fall, which is led through a snatch block.
Fr: *Retour;* Ger: *Laufender Teil.*
LEADING WIND. A wind abeam or quartering, more particularly a free or fair wind in contradistinction to a scant wind.
Fr: *Vent Portant;* Ger: *Raumwind.*

LEAD LINE. A line attached to a deep sea or drift lead, used for ascertaining the depth of water when taking soundings by hand. If a sounding machine is employed the line is replaced by a sounding wire. Lead lines are made of cotton, flax, or hemp, and are braided or left-laid. The size varies according to the weight of the lead. They must be smooth, flexible, and have a polished surface. The line adopted by the American Marine Standards Committee is made of cotton cord braided over a heart of phosphor bronze wire cord.

Fr: *Ligne de Sonde;* Ger: *Lotleine.*

In the United States lead lines are designated by a number which expresses the diameter in thirty-seconds of an inch. The lead line is attached to the sinker either by passing it through the eye of the lead, knotting the line and securing the loose end by seizing or, if the size of the eye permits, by making a long loop at the end of the line which can be rove through the eye and passed over the head of the lead.

LEADS. The parts of the fall in a tackle between the two blocks.

LEADSMAN. One who takes soundings with a hand lead; generally from a sounding platform or in the chains. Sometimes called chainsman.

Fr: *Sondeur;* Ger: *Lotgast.*

LEADSMAN'S GRIPE.
See **Breast Band.**

LEADSMAN'S PLATFORM. A small wooden platform about two feet square projecting over the ship's side and used when taking a cast with a hand lead. Sometimes called chainsman's platform. It is hinged to the ship's side so that it can be lashed up to the side railing when not in use. In merchant vessels there is one platform on each side, under or forward of the bridge. In large passenger vessels two similar platforms are sometimes fitted aft near the docking bridge.

Fr: *Plateforme de Sonde;* Ger: *Lotgast Plattform; Lothpodest.*

LEAGUE. A measure of length used in estimating sea distances. Its length varies among different nations. In Great Britain, France, United States, and Spain, the league has a recognized length of 6,075 yards (5,554.9 meters).

Fr: *Lieue Marine;* Ger: *Lige.*

LEAKAGE. A term used in bills of lading to apply not only to the leaking of liquids from their casks or other containers but also to the loss attendant upon breaking alone, such as for instance the breakage of glass cases stowed in a cargo. Leakage is considered as normal when it does not exceed 3 per cent for liquids in metal containers and 5 per cent for those in casks, barrels, and so on.

Fr: *Coulage;* Ger: *Leckage; Leckverlust.*

LEAN. The flesh of the whale as distinguished from the blubber or fat.

LEAN BOW. Narrow bow. The opposite of bluff bow. A bow with hollow sections.

Fr: *Avant fin;* Ger: *Scharfer Bug.*

LEANING. Removal of the pieces of flesh and muscle which adhere to the inside of the blubber of a whale.

LEBECHE. A warm and dry southwesterly wind on the southeast coast of Spain.

LEDGE. 1. A shelf-like projection or a ridge of rocks under water near the shore.

Fr: *Ceinture Rocheuse;* Ger: *Felsenreihe.*

2. In wooden ships one of the pieces of the deck frame running athwartships lying between the beams and let into the carlings and knees.

Fr: *Hiloire Transversale;* Ger: *Rippe.*

See **Head-Ledge.**

LEE. Of or pertaining to the part or side toward which the wind blows, or which is sheltered from the wind, as opposed to weather.

Fr: *Sous le Vent;* Ger: *Lee.*

See **Brought by the Lee.**

LEE ANCHOR. 1. When riding at a single anchor, applies to that anchor which has not been dropped.

2. When tow bowers are down, it applies to the anchor at which the ship is not riding.

3. The anchor on the lee bow.

Fr: *Ancre sons de vent;* Ger: *Leeanker.*

LEEBOARD. A plate or frame of planks lowered over the lee side of a shallow-draft boat with flat bottom. It lessens the leeway when the boat is sailing close-hauled, by giving increased lateral resistance. There is one leeboard on each side. Leeboards are fan-shaped or flat, and are fixed to the hull by an adjustable bolt locked by a cotter pin.

Fr: *Dérive Latérale;* Ger: *Seitenschweert; Leebord.*

The length should be about twice the depth of the boat but in some boats it is longer. According to some it should be about one-fifth the length of the boat, and, at its broadest part, two-thirds its own length, at its narrowest part, one-third its own length. A well-designed leeboard may be about one-quarter less in area compared with a centerboard of equal efficiency, owing to the fact that it is nearly vertical when the boat is inclined to its normal sailing angle, whereas the centerboard inclines to the angle into which the boat heels.

LEECH. The side of a square sail, or the afteredge of a fore-and-aft sail. Also called skirt when referring to square sails.
Fr: *Chûte;* Ger: *Seitenliek.*
See **After Leech, Forward Leech, Mast Leech.**

LEECH LINE. A line made fast at about the middle of the leech of a sail and passing right up through a block on the yards to pull the leech up to the yard. Also called leach line.
Fr: *Cargue Bouline;* Ger: *Nockgording.*

LEECH ROPE. The boltrope running along the leech of a sail, that is, along the after edge of fore-and-aft sails or the sides of square sails.
Fr: *Ralingue de Chûte;* Ger: *Stehliek.*

LEEFANGE.
See **Deck Horse.**

LEE HELM. A sailing craft is said to carry lee helm when the helm has to be kept alee to counteract slackness and keep it on its course.

LEE SHORE. The shore that lies under a vessel's lee.
Fr: *Terre sous le Vent;* Ger: *Legerwall.*

LEE SIDE. The side of a ship which is farther from the wind.
Fr: *Bord sous le Vent;* Ger: *Leeseite.*

LEE TACK. The tack of a course on the lee side which is left slack when a ship is sailing close-hauled.
Fr: *Amure de Revers.*
See **Tack.**

LEE TIDE. A tide running in the same direction as the wind.
Fr: *Marée Portant sous le Vent.*

LEEWARD. Situated on the side turned away from the wind as opposed to windward. Toward the lee.
Fr: *Sous le Vent:* Ger: *Leewärts.*

LEEWARDLINESS.
See **Slackness.**

LEEWARD TIDE. A tide running in the same direction that the wind blows.
Ger: *Nach Lee setzend Ström.*

LEEWAY. The lateral movement of a ship to leeward of her course, estimated from the angle formed between the line of the ship's keel and the line which the ship actually describes through the water, as shown by her wake. Also called drift.
Fr: *Dérive;* Ger: *Abtrijt; Leeweg.*

LEFT-HANDED ROPE. A fiber rope in which the yarns and strands are twisted in the same direction (right-handed) and laid up left-handed. Left-handed rope is considered more pliable and less liable to kink than plain laid rope. Also called backhanded or left-laid.
Fr: *Cordage commis à Gauche;* Ger: *Linksgeschlagenes Tauwerk.*

LEFT-HAND LAY. A lay in which the turn has been made in a clockwise direction.

LEFT-HAND PROPELLER. A propeller in which the rotation of the blades is from right to left with the ship moving ahead and the observer facing forward.
Fr: *Hélice à Pas à Gauche;* Ger: *Linksgehender Propeller; Linksgängiger Propeller.*

LEG. 1. One of the shores used by small craft for keeping the boat upright at low tide.
Fr: *Béquille;* Ger: *Strebe.*
2. A name given to a prolongation, about 16 ft. in length, of the headrope and ground rope in large otter trawls in order to allow weeds and other clogging matter to pass between the hind end of the otter board and the front end of the wing, and also if the door turns over, to keep the wing from being twisted as the twist is taken on the legs.
3. One of the opened strands of a rope when splicing. Also each one of the parts of a crowfoot.
4. Portion of a vessel's track or plotted course along a single heading. Length of a tack of a sailing vessel on the wind.
Fr: *Bordée;* Ger: *Schlag.*
5. One flange of a steel shape, or angle bar.
Fr: *Aile;* Ger: *Schenkel.*

LEG CLEAT (G. B.). A piece of timber bolted on each side of the hull in small craft, to carry the legs or props which keep the boat upright when dried out in harbor.

LEGISLATION CLAUSE. A time charter clause which stipulates that charterers have the privilege of canceling the contract if at any time legislation discriminating against foreign tonnage is enforced.

LELAYAN. A large trading prao from the west coast of Sumatra with two quarter rudders and a poop with galleries. The hold runs fore and aft and is covered by a roofing. At the bows the planking forms an outboard square platform held together by a heavy crosspiece. It is rigged with three masts. The *lelayan* from Achin has double outriggers.

LENGTH BETWEEN PERPENDICU-LARS. The distance between the forward perpendicular and the after perpendicular. It is the length used in making calculations for displacement, and so on. If the stem- or rudderpost are raked, the length is measured between perpendicular lines struck through the intersection of the upper deck (or second deck in shelter- or awning-deck vessel) with front of stem and back of rudderpost. If the stem is bent to form a cutwater, the front of the straight middle part is extended up to intersect the upper deck. In vessels built with a cruiser stern it is either the length measured as above (or to the forward side of the rudderstock if there is no sternpost), or 96 per cent of the vessel's length from front of stem to the aftermost part of the cruiser stern, whichever is the greater.

Fr: *Longueur entre Perpendiculaires;*
Ger: *Länge zwischen den Loten; Konstruktionslänge.*

See **After Perpendicular, Forward Perpendicular.**

LENGTH OF ENTRANCE. The length from the forward perpendicular to the section at which the entrance ends.

Fr: *Longueur d'Acuité;* Ger: *Zuschärfungslänge.*

LENGTH OF RUN. The length from the after perpendicular to the afterend of the parallel body.

Fr: *Longueur de la Coulée.*
See **Run.**

LENGTH OVERALL. The total length from the foremost to the aftermost points of a vessel's hull.

Fr: *Longueur hors tout;* Ger: *Länge über alles; Grösste Lange.*

LEPA-LEPA. A type of sailing dugout canoe with or without outriggers from South Celebes and Moluccas, of which there are several varieties:

The *lepa-lepa palewai* is a one-man built-up dugout with single outrigger, rigged with a mast and spritsail with short foot and long head. Steered with quarter rudder. Used for fishing.

The *lepa-lepa padari* is a double-outrigger canoe with forked stem and vertical stern. It is rigged with a large square sail of the usual Macassar type with yard and boom. Employed for fishing with a cast net.

In Ambon and Halmahera the *lepa-lepa* is without outriggers.

In Buton it is known as *kole-kole;* in the Gulf of Mandar as *pakur.*

LERRET. The Portland (Great Britain) *lerret* is a double-ended open rowing and sailing boat used on the Chesil Bank for lobstering and crabbing. It is built with great beam, unusually flat floor and clinker planking. It carries two sails: a lug mainsail and a sprit mizzen. When rowed it is propelled by 2, 4, or 6 oars according to size and circumstances. Length 18 ft. Breadth 7.3 ft. Depth 2.7 ft. molded. (Typical.) The boats in general use average from three to four tons burden.

Each oar has a block of wood fixed to the loom by spikes and lashing. This block, called a copse, has a hole through for the iron tholepin fixed to the gunwale. For hauling the boat out on the beach a rope is rove through a hole in the keel just forward of the sternpost.

LESTE. A hot, dry, easterly wind of Madeira and the Canary Islands.

LETE-LETE. A plank-built trading canoe with rocker keel, from Macassar Strait (Celebes). It has a roofing amidships and is rigged with one mast and triangular sail set apex downward.

LET FALL. A command to the crew of a rowboat when the oars have been tossed to drop them in the rowlocks preparatory to getting underway, without letting the blades touch the water.

Fr: *Bordez!;* Ger: *Riemen bei!*

LET FLY. Applies to running gear when let loose quickly and completely.

Fr: *Filer en bande;* Ger: *Fliegen lassen.*

LET GO. To set free, let loose, or cast off as a rope.

Fr: *Larguer;* Ger: *Los Werfen.*

LET RUN. Also to let go by the run. To let a rope or chain go quickly or suddenly.

Fr: *Laisser aller en bande;* Ger: *Plötzlich laufen lassen.*

LETTER OF ASSURANCE. A certificate analogous to the "Navicert." It was issued by the allied powers during the 1914–18 War to various neutral shipping companies after examination and approval of the various cargoes carried in their vessels. It assured both cargo and vessel so certified an undisturbed passage through the British contraband control, to their neutral destination. See **Navicert.**

LETTER OF INDEMNITY. A letter given by the shippers to the shipowners when goods put on board are not in good condition, holding the shipowners harmless in respect of any claim the consignees may make. In exchange for this document clean bills of lading are issued.

In marine insurance this term usually refers to a letter sent by the shipper or consignee agreeing to hold the underwriter indemnified against the consequences of paying a loss without the production of a stamped policy and undertaking to produce the policy should it come to hand. Also called backward letter.

Fr: *Lettre de Garantie;* Ger: *Gutschädigungsbrief; Revers; Garantiebrief.*

LETTERS OF MARQUE. A commission granted to a privateer enabling him under certain conditions to seize the goods and ships of an enemy country and also to make search for contraband of war subject to certain rules and reservations. Also called letters of mart. The practice of sending out privateers furnished with letters of marque is now obsolete and is prohibited by international law.

Fr: *Lettres de Marque;* Ger: *Kaperbriefe.*

LETTERS OF REPRISAL. A special commission, more limited than letters of marque, granted by a government to the owner or master of a merchant ship to obtain reparation for injuries sustained at sea from the subjects of a foreign country, after all attempts by this owner and his government to obtain legal redress have failed.

Fr: *Lettres de Représailles;* Ger: *Kaperbriefe.*

LEUDO RIVANO. A decked or half-decked sailing craft originating from Riva Trigoso (Sestri-Levante) used in the local inshore fisheries or for the transportation of wine casks between the smaller coastal harbors. Some of these boats sail occasionally as far as the Island of Elba to pick up a cargo of wine.

The hull, of Catalan type, is keel-built with sharp stern, considerable deck camber, and carvel planking. The rig is identical to that of the Spanish *balancella* with forward raking mast, lateen mainsail, and jib. The fishing craft are half-decked; those used for transportation are decked fore and aft. The length ranges from 33 to 40 ft.

LEUTO. A decked fishing boat of the Dalmatian coast used for trawling and seining. Also called *liuto.* It is similar in hull form to the *gaeta.* There is one large hatch amidships. Forward on the starboard side there are three small scuttle hatches and on the port side, two. At the stern there is a small cockpit for the helmsman. The rig consists of one mast without rake, lateen mainsail, and one headsail. Length 23 to 26 ft. Breadth 6.5 to 8 ft. Depth 4.9 to 6.5 ft. Deadweight 4 to 5 tons.

Trading boats of this type of 30 to 60 tons and rigged with two masts are now probably extinct.

LEUTO. Sicilian two-masted sailing coaster originating from Trapani, also employed in the sponge fisheries. The full-lined hull is keel-built with straight stem raking aft and square stern. The topsides of the stern are extended outboard at deck level, to form a false overhang as in the pinkie stern. The deck has a pronounced camber. There are two hatchways. The lateen rig consists of a mainmast with forward rake and a small vertical mizzenmast stepped near the sternpost. The bowsprit carries two headsails. Length 49 to 65 ft. Breadth 11 to 21.6 ft. Tonnage 30 to 60.

LEVA LEVA. Australian seagoing dugout canoe of the Ingura and Nungubuyu tribes from Groote Eylandt and the west coast of the Gulf of Carpentaria. The double-ended hull rises at bow and stern. Length 25 ft. Breadth 2 ft. 9 in. (approximate).

LEVANTADES. Gales fro, between North-North-East and East-North-East which occur on the East coast of Spain. They are an intense form of "Levanter" and are most frequent in Spring and Autumn.

LEVANTER. A strong northeasterly wind of the Mediterranean, also called *meltem* or *euroclydon.*

LEVEL. A fish measure used in Great Britain. The equivalent of 12 stone of trawl fish.

LEVER. The first row of half meshes in a net.

Fr: *Levure;* Ger: *Tauben.*

LEVER CONTROLLER. A controller which consists of a heavy iron bed in two parts. On the top there is a groove or pocket in which the chain cable travels. At the afterend is a recess or shoulder into which is fitted a block, free to move up and down, the motion being controlled by a cam and lever. The chain cable passing over is held or allowed to run out, as the movable section is lowered or raised. A guard hoop or bridge piece with heavy fid bar is fitted as extra security for holding down the chain against the shoulder. Also called lever stopper, dead nip stopper.

Fr: *Stoppeur à Pied de Biche;* Ger: *Exzenterhebel-Stopper.*

See **Controller.**

LEVER STOPPER.
See **Anchor Stopper.**

LEWIS BOLT. A bronze bolt, similar to an eyebolt, fitting into a deck socket and secured therein by a wedge, to which lead blocks are made fast.

LIBERTY SHIP. Emergency built single-screw cargo steamer designed by the U. S. Maritime Commission to compensate for the loss of merchant ship tonnage incurred from submarine warfare. The first keel was laid in April 1941. More than 2,300 vessels of this type were built in the U. S. The chief characteristics of the design are minimum cost, rapidity of construction and simplicity of operation. The welded hull is of the full scantling type with transverse framing, two complete decks and five cargo holds. Also called *EC-2 vessel.*

Length over-all..................441 ft. 6 in.
Length between perpendiculars ......416 ft.
Breadth molded ....56 ft. 10¾ in.
Depth molded .....37 ft. 4 in. to upper deck
Draft loaded ....25 ft. 3¼ in.
Deadweight capacity ....10,500 tons
Bale capacity ....468,000 cu. ft.
General cargo capacity ....9,146 tons
Displacement ....14,100 tons
Gross tonnage ....7,185 tons
Net tonnage ....4,380 tons
Indicated horsepower 2,500
Speed ....10–11 knots
Crew 44

Marine Engineering and Shipping Review, New York, vol. 47, April, 1942.

LICENSE. A document issued by the United States Government to all vessels of 20 tons and upward engaged in domestic commerce (coasting trade) and fisheries. The enrollment takes the place of the registration, the latter applying to foreign-going vessels only. Qualifications and requirements for licensed vessels are the same as those required for registration.

LIE AHULL. The condition of a ship lying to when the force of the wind is such that no sail whatsoever can be carried.

Fr: *Être à la Cape Sèche;* Ger: *Zum Treiben liegen.*

LIE ATRY. Said of a ship, lying to in a gale when it is possible to carry some sail. Also called to try.

Fr: *Être à la Cape Courante;* Ger: *Beiliegen.*

LIEN. See **Maritime Lien.**

LIEN CLAUSE. A charter party clause which provides that the owners of the vessel have a lien on all cargoes and all subfreights for hire and general average contribution, and that charterers have a lien on the vessel for all moneys paid in advance and not earned.

Ger: *Lien Klausel.*

LIEN FOR FREIGHT. A lien which the owner or master of a ship has upon the cargo for freight and all lawful charges whether the vessel is chartered or operated as a general ship.

LIEN OF BROKER. The lien which a shipping agent or broker has on the bill of lading and thereby indirectly on the cargo for his charges.

LIE-TO. In general, a ship "lies to" when the conditions or state of wind and sea are such as to prevent her continuing on her course. When referring to sailing craft it means to set merely enough sail, in a gale, to steady the ship; the aim being to keep the sea on the weather bow although the rudder may have but little influence.

Fr: *Capeyer; Être à la Cape;* Ger: *Beiliegen.*

LIFE BELT. See **Life Jacket.**

LIFEBOAT. A boat built of wood or metal and specially designed and equipped for lifesaving purposes, its buoyancy being increased by means of watertight air cases or compartments fitted inside and in some types by outside appliances, such as cork belts. Also called ship's lifeboat. The number of lifeboats carried by merchant vessels is governed by the number of people on board. Lifeboats are of the whaler type, with bow and stern alike. The capacity of air chambers is calculated to give such buoyancy that, with the boat full of water and with its full complement of people, it does not sink. The outside of the boat must be provided with life lines so that persons in the water may catch hold of them.

The standard types of lifeboats as adopted by International Convention for the Safety of Life at Sea (1929) are classified as follows: Class I, which includes open boats with rigid sides, is subdivided into: (a) boats which have internal buoyancy only; (b) those having external as well as internal buoyancy. Class II includes two distinct types: (a) open boats having internal and external buoyancy and upper parts of sides or bulwarks collapsible; (b) decked boats with either fixed or collapsible bulwarks. Class III are open lifeboats with rigid sides constructed of single or double thickness of wood or single thickness of metal but without internal buoyancy air cases.

The number of persons which a lifeboat can accommodate is obtained by dividing the capacity of the boat, in cubic feet, by the standard unit of capacity or standard unit of surface, according to the class of boat as given hereunder:

Class I. A type ....10 cu. ft.
Class II. B type ....9 cu. ft.
Class III. A and B type..3½ cu. ft.

The propulsion of lifeboats with a capacity up to and including 85 persons is by oars (and sails). Boats with a capacity of 86 persons and up to 99 persons are fitted with some form of hand propulsion, mechanical gear, or a small motor (although the boat is not a statutory motor lifeboat). Fifty per cent of normal oar equipment is compulsory. With a capacity of 100 persons and upward the installation of a motor is compulsory, as well as 50 per cent of oar equipment.

Proportions of Class I Lifeboats

$$\frac{Length}{Breadth} = 3; \frac{Length}{Depth} = 7 \text{ to } 8.$$

According to American regulations the minimum capacity requirements for ship's lifeboats are as follows: (1) For those carried by coastwise vessels a capacity of not less than 125 cu. ft.; (2) for those carried by other vessels a capacity of not less than 180 cu. ft.; (3) the boat must be of the double-ended (whaler) type; (4) it must be provided with air tanks.

American Marine Standards Committee, Standard 33, *Lifeboats*, Washington, 1928; Blocksidge, E. W., *Ship's Boats*, London, 1920; *International Convention for the Safety of Life at Sea*, London, 1929.

LIFEBOATMAN. A certificated seaman who has received the necessary training in launching and handling of lifeboats under oars and sail and is able to act as coxswain and take charge of a lifeboat or life raft if necessary. The number of lifeboatmen assigned to each boat varies from 1 for boats which carry 25 persons or less to 5 for boats which carry between 86 and 110 persons.

Fr: *Canotier Brévété;* Ger: *Geprüfte Rettungsbootsleute.*

U. S. Bureau of Marine Inspection and Navigation, *Manual for Lifeboatmen and Able Seamen,* Washington, 1941.

LIFE BUOY. A buoyant object designed to be thrown from a vessel to assist a person who has fallen into the water, to keep himself afloat. Sometimes called safety buoy. It is usually ring-shaped, covered with painted canvas and has beckets on its circumference. According to regulations it must be capable of supporting in fresh water for 24 hours a weight of 32 lb. of iron. Life buoys must be fitted with grab lines of unshrinkable rope about ⅜-in. diameter, secured to the buoy by sewing and in addition, by a double thickness of the covering material at four equidistant points forming loops of 2 ft. 4 in.

Fr: *Bouée de Sauvetage;* Ger: *Rettungsboje; Rettungsring.*

Life buoys are made of solid cork, corrugated copper, kapok, balsa wood. Metallic life buoys are made of 24-gauge corrugated copper and are claimed to be one-third lighter than cork buoys. A certain number of the buoys must have attached to them a life buoy light of the self-igniting type.

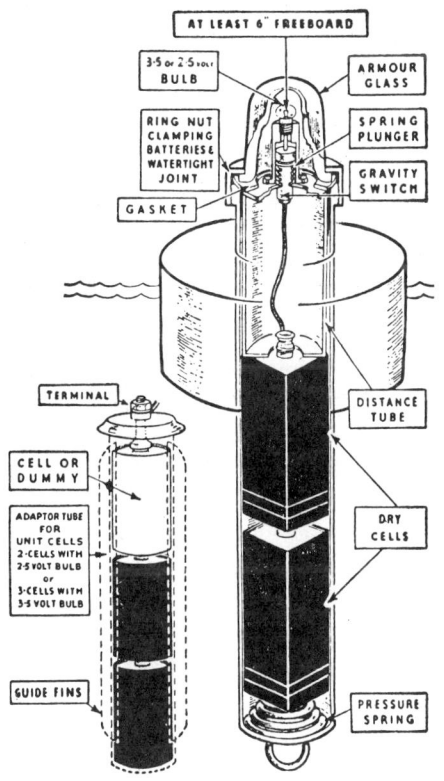

Electric Life Buoy Light. (*Courtesy Shipbuilding and Shipping Record*)

LIFE BUOY LIGHT. A light attached to a life buoy or a life raft. Also called water light. It consists of a sheet-copper canister in which there are chambers containing calcium phosphide and calcium carbide. The latter on contact with water gives off acetylene gas, which is ignited by the phosphine flame emanating from the wet calcium phosphide. The canister is provided with a plug or other device which when removed admits sufficient water to insure prompt and efficient action of the light. The removal of the plug is so arranged and constructed that the weight of the buoy when thrown overboard automatically disengages the plug and insures that the light will ignite itself within one minute after reaching the surface of the water. The electric water light has recently replaced the open flame type in oil tankers and other vessels which carry inflammable cargo. It consists of a plastic outer tube with lead base, small battery and bulb. Electrical connection between bulb and battery is automatic as the weighted tube assumes the vertical position when it floats.

> Fr: *Signal de Bouée de Sauvetage;* Ger: *Schwimmlicht; Wasserlicht; Bojenlicht.*

The light is attached to the buoy by a lanyard 12 ft. or more in length, and has to be capable of burning for a continuous period of not less than 45 minutes, showing a brilliant flame of at least 150 candlepower without emitting obnoxious fumes. Half the statutory number of life buoys on board must be provided with a water light.

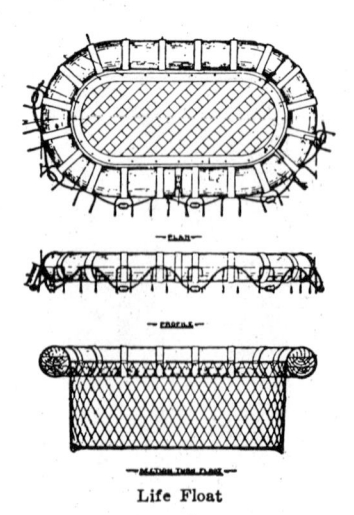

Life Float

LIFE FLOAT. A lifesaving apparatus so constructed as to be entirely reversible, that is, which may be used equally well with either side up. It consists essentially of an elliptical body made of treated balsa wood, or of a sheet-metal tube, which forms the buoyant frame. In the center of the frame there is in some designs a net, in others a box grating made up of several small compartments with lids at top and bottom so that whichever way up the float lands on the water the contents of the boxes can be reached. Lengths of cork cut on a miter board are fitted around the tubular sheet-metal body and fastened with bands of copper wire. A covering of canvas is tightly bound around the cork and painted. A life line is becketed around the outside. Life floats are stowed in such location that they may be launched directly overboard or that they can float freely if there is no time to launch them. Also called Lifesaving float, Carley float.

> Ger: *Flossboot.*

LIFE KITE. A kite flown from a vessel wrecked on a lee shore for sending a line to the beach when, owing to the severity of the wind, a rocket line cannot be shot to the ship.

> Fr: *Cerf Volant de secours;* Ger: *Rettungdrache.*

LIFE LINE. 1. One of several lines stretched fore and aft along the decks to give the crew safety against being washed overboard in heavy weather. Also lines carried along a yard or boom for safety. A rope thrown to any person fallen overboard.

> Fr: *Filière;* Ger: *Manntau; Strecktau.*

2. One of the lines hanging from the span between davit heads for the use of the crew when lowering or hoisting a lifeboat. These lines are knotted at approximately 3-ft. intervals.

> Fr: *Sauvegarde;* Ger: *Greifleine.*

3. A small line made of 2-in. Italian hemp fastened around a lifeboat or other buoyant apparatus and hanging in loops about 3 ft. long so that the users of the apparatus or boat may if necessary hang on to it temporarily. Also called grab line. Each loop is supplied with a cork or wooden float called "seine float."

> Fr: *Filière en Guirlande;* Ger: *Sicherheitsleine; Handleine; Handtau.*

LIFE PRESERVER. A contrivance used

to support the human body in the water. Also called life jacket, life belt. Life belts are made of various materials and in various forms. A well-known type in use for many years on merchantmen is made of sound cork blocks fastened to a cloth lining, with belt and shoulder straps attached so arranged as to place the cork underneath the shoulders and around the body of the person wearing it. It should contain at least 6 lb. of cork and have a buoyancy of 24 lb. According to International Convention, etc., a life jacket whose buoyancy is derived from cork must be capable of supporting 16½ lb. of iron in fresh water for 24 hr. A life jacket whose buoyancy is derived from kapok must be capable of supporting at least 20 lb. of iron after floating in fresh water for 26 hours with 16½ lb. of iron attached. Inflatable life belts which depend on air for their buoyancy are not accepted for merchant ships.

Fr: *Ceinture de Sauvetage;* Ger: *Korkjacke; Schwimmweste; Rettungsgürtel.*

LIFE RAFT. A raft-like construction designed to save life in the event of a shipwreck. Also called pontoon raft. Nowadays nearly all seagoing passenger vessels carry a certain number of life rafts or other buoyant apparatus of approved construction as an equivalent for a proportion of the lifeboat capacity they are required to maintain.

These rafts can be conveniently stowed, are easily transported from one side to the other, may be launched or dropped overboard and have sometimes proved to be better than lifeboats for saving life. A great many types of approved life rafts are used. All depend for their extra buoyancy upon some method of utilizing air receptacles, cork, and so on. One of the types most used is the metallic cylinder raft consisting of two cylinders of metal, cone shaped at the ends and firmly connected to each other with braces. There are slats running longitudinally between the cylinders. It is a statutory requirement that life-rafts be of sufficient strength to hold together when hurled into the sea from their stowage deck. They are equipped with life lines, oars, sea anchor, lifebuoy light. Some life rafts are fitted with collapsible bulwarks made of wood, canvas, or other suitable materials.

Fr: *Radeau de Sauvetage;* Ger: *Rettungsfloss.*

See **Life Float**.

According to the International Convention for Safety of Life at Sea (1929), life rafts have to satisfy the following conditions:
1. be of approved material and construction.
2. be effective and stable when floating either way up.
3. be provided with fixed or collapsible bulwarks made of wood, canvas, or other suitable material, on both sides.
4. have a line securely becketed around the outside.
5. be of such strength that they can be launched or thrown from the vessel's deck without being damaged, and, if to be thrown, to be of such size and weight that they can be easily handled.
6. have not less than 85 cubic decimeters (3 cu. ft.) of air cases or equivalent buoyancy for each person to be carried thereon.
7. have a deck area of not less than 3,720 sq. cm. (4 sq. ft.) for each person to be carried, occupants being effectively supported out of the water.

LIFE RING. One of the small metal rings fitted at intervals of about two feet around the sides of a lifeboat on the under side of the rubber and to which the grab line is attached.

Ger: *Rettungsring.*

LIFE ROCKET. A rocket used for carrying a line over a wreck and establishing communication between ship and shore. The powder charge is contained in a light metallic tube. The distance reached is about 1,300 ft. The line used has a diameter of about 5/16 in. with a length of 240 yards and a minimum breaking strength of 150 lb. These rockets are compound: that is, when the first part of the powder charge has expended its force, the second is ignited and gives an additional impulse to the projectile. The rocket stick, attached to the rocket by a spring, is 9 ft. 6 in. long and has a hole in its lower end through which the rocket line is rove. American regulations provide that all mechanically propelled vessels of 150 tons and over engaged in ocean navigation shall be equipped with at least three line carrying projectiles and the means of propelling them.

Fr: *Fusée Porte Amarre;* Ger: *Rettungsrakete.*

LIFE SAVING SERVICE. A public or private organization entrusted with the saving or attempted saving of vessels, or of life and property on board vessels wrecked or aground or sunk, or in danger of being wrecked or getting aground or sinking within reach of aid from the shore. In the United States all life-saving stations and appliances are made under the care and management of the U. S. Coast Guard Service. In Great Britain a private organization, the "Royal National Lifeboat Institution," founded in 1824 is in charge of the lifeboat service. In France, the "Société Centrale de Sauvetage des Naufragés" and in Germany, the "Deutsche Gesellschaft zur Rettung Schiffbruchiger," are similar organizations.

Fr: *Service de sauvetage;* Ger: *Rettungsdienst.*

LIFE SIGNAL. A device on a life buoy for producing an inextinguishable light which lights automatically when the buoy is being cut loose. Also called life-buoy signal, life-buoy light.

LIFT. 1. One of the components of the force which acts on the rudder in a direction parallel to that of the ship's travel and causes the change of heading.

2. A wire rope or chain used for taking the weight of a yard, boom, derrick, and so on, and enabling it to be topped to the desired angle. Also called topping lift. It leads from the end of the spar through a masthead block.

Fr: *Balancine; Martinet;* Ger: *Toppenant; Hänger.*

See **Heavy Lift, Quarter Lift, Spreader Lift.**

LIFTING. 1. See **Pivoting.**

2. Transferring marks and measurements from a drawing, model, and so on, to a plate or other object, by templates or other means. To lift a template means to make a template to the same size and shape as the structural part of the ship involved, from either the mold loft lines or from the ship itself, from which laying out of material for fabrication may be performed.

Fr: *Gabarier.*

LIFTING MAGNET. An electric magnetic device suspended from a dock crane, used for handling scrap iron and other magnetic material from ship to shore or vice versa. The lifting power is obtained by passing direct current through a coil of wire which contains a soft iron core, the latter becoming a strong magnet capable of picking up and holding the material during transportation. When the desired spot has been reached the current is cut off and the material no longer clings to the iron core.

Fr: *Electro-Aimant de Levage;* Ger: *Lasthebemagnet.*

LIFTING PAD. One of the pads or eyeplates permanently attached on the outside of the shell plating aft for hooking the tackles used in lifting the rudder or propeller. Any such pad attached to a heavy structure to facilitate hoisting, and so on.

Fr: *Pitonnage;* Ger: *Hebe Augplatte.*

LIFTING SAIL. A general term for all sails in which the vertical component due to the pressure of wind acts in an upward direction. The opposite of a driving sail. Jibs, staysails, and lateen sails have a marked lifting component. Square sails on a vertical mast have a slight lifting effect which increases if the mast is raked. The dipping lug is one of the most efficient lifting sails.

LIFT TACKLE. Purchase, usually twofold, with upper block shackled to topping lift and lower block to a deck eyebolt, making it convenient for topping or lowering a boom or derrick as required.

Fr: *Palan d'Apiquage;* Ger: *Toppenantstalje.*

LIGHT. The optical apparatus of a lighthouse, lightship, or light buoy. According to the kind of illuminating apparatus the lights shown by lighthouses are known as: (1) fixed, showing a continuous steady light, (2) occulting or flashing, showing a light varied by the introduction of flashes, eclipses, etc. They are further subdivided into colored lights and lights whose color does not alter throughout the entire system of changes. The rays of light from the luminous source are collected and caused to travel along the desired path by reflection, refraction or a combination of both. The various systems are known as catoptric, dioptric or catadioptric, according to the optical apparatus employed. They are also classified into different ratings or orders according to their focal distances or to the diameter or radius of the lenses of their optical apparatus generally measured horizontally at the level of the focal plane. These orders are as follows:

Order	Focal Distance, in Millimetres
Hyperradial	1330
First order	920
Second order	700
Third order	500
Fourth order	250
Fifth order	187.5
Sixth order	150

The period of a light is the interval between successive commencements of the same phase. In a flashing light it is the interval between the commencement of one flash and the commencement of the succeeding flash. In occulting, alternating, and group-flashing lights it is the time occupied by the exhibition of the entire system of changes included in the same phase.

Illuminants used in lighthouse practice have greatly improved since the days of the oil wick burner, which have now passed. For lights of primary importance either vaporized petroleum or electricity combined with a gas-filled filament lamp are now generally used. On unattended lights, when electricity is not available dissolved acetylene gas burned either as an open flame or in conjunction with a mantle, or compressed oil gas with a mantle is frequently adopted. Cattolica and Luria, *Fari e segnali marittime*, Turin, 1916; Chance, J. F., *Notes on Modern Lighthouse Practice*, Birmingham, 1910; Putnam, G. R., *Lighthouses and Lightships of U. S. A.*, New York, 1933.

LIGHT AIRS. Unsteady, faint puffs of wind. A wind with just sufficient strength to give steerage way to sailing craft. Light airs are classed as force 1 in the Beaufort Scale. Velocity from 1 to 3 nautical miles per hour.

Fr: *Presque calme;* Ger: *Leichter Zug; Leichter Wind.*

LIGHT BOARD.
See Sidelight Screen.

LIGHTBOAT. A small unmanned lightship provided with large gas containers which can supply the illumination medium for a period of several months. These craft are more effective than light-buoys as they carry a more powerful light, with focal plane at a greater height, while avoiding the large expenses of a lightship. They are illuminated by compressed oil-gas or dissolved acetylene. A sun valve is fitted to avoid waste of gas during daylight. Lightboats are considered ships or vessels and come within admiralty jurisdiction. Also called **unattended lightboat, boat beacon, gas boat.**

Fr: *Feu flottant non garde;* Ger: *Unbemannt Feuerschiff.*

LIGHT BOOM. Small spar fitted on each side of a mast and from which cargo clusters are suspended when loading or unloading at night.

LIGHT BREEZE. A wind with a velocity of 4 to 6 nautical miles per hour. Average pressure in lb. per sq. ft. .08. Beaufort's Scale No. 2.

Fr: *Légère Brise;* Ger: *Flaue Brise.*

LIGHT BUOY. A metallic buoy with an illuminating apparatus mounted at the top of a short skeleton tower, showing a fixed or intermittent light. These buoys are mostly used for marking narrow and winding channels. The illuminants used are acetylene, compressed oil-gas, or ordinary lamp oil.

Fr: *Bouée Lumineuse;* Ger: *Leuchtfeuerboje; Leuchttonne.*

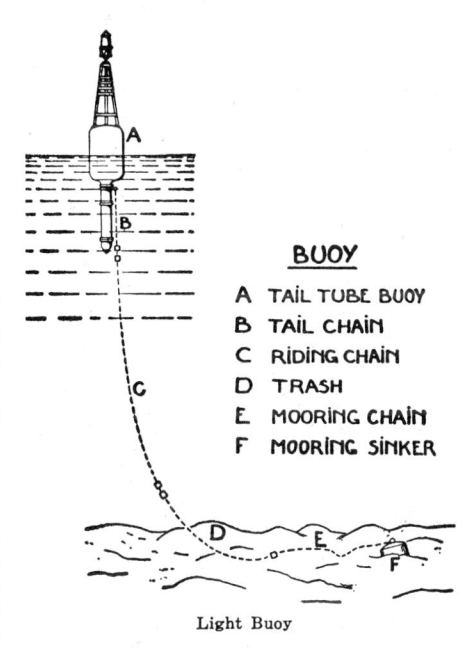

BUOY
A TAIL TUBE BUOY
B TAIL CHAIN
C RIDING CHAIN
D TRASH
E MOORING CHAIN
F MOORING SINKER

Light Buoy

LIGHT CLOSING WELD. A single run of light welding worked continuously along the edge of a plate. A type of weld made by one pass of the electrode or rod. Also called bead weld.

Fr: *Soudure Légère Continue;* Ger: *Leichte Nahtschweissung.*

LIGHT DISPLACEMENT. The weight of a vessel when unloaded. Also called light weight. It includes hull and fittings, engines and boilers, shafting and propellers, water in boilers, condensers, and pipes, feed water, permanent ballast.

Fr: *Déplacement Lège;* Ger: *Leere Verdrängung; Leichtser Deplacement.*

Thery, R., "Le Gain de poids en construc-

LIGHT DRAFT—LIGHT FILLET WELD

tion navale," *Mécanique* (Paris), vol. 21, no. 275 (1937).

LIGHT DRAFT. The vessel's draft at light displacement. The draft when the vessel is floating fully equipped with water in boilers but without crew, fuel, cargo, stores, fresh water, or other loads.

Fr: *Tirant d'eau Lège;* Ger: *Leerer Tiefgang.*

LIGHT DUES. Tolls levied on a ship, usually by scale according to tonnage, toward the maintenance of lights, beacons, buoys, and so on.

Fr: *Droits de Feux;* Ger: *Leuchtfeuerabgaben; Feuergeld; Lichtgebühren; Leuchtfeuergeld.*

See **Dues.**

LIGHTED RANGE. Two lights located some distance apart on a specific true bearing. Lights on ranges may show any of the three standard colors and they may be fixed, flashing or occulting.

Fr: *Feux d'alignement;* Ger: *Richtungsfeuer.*

LIGHTEN. To put cargo, ballast, stores, and so on, in lighters to reduce the ship's draft.

Fr: *Alléger;* Ger: *Erleichtern.*

LIGHTENED PLATE FRAME. A frame having floor plates with large openings cut in them for the purpose of saving weight and to give access to adjoining compartments of the double-bottom.

Fr: *Membrure à Évidements;* Ger: *Erleichterter Spant.*

LIGHTENING HOLE. One of the large apertures punched or cut in floor plates, side girders, tank bracket plates. In double-bottom vessels they provide an access to the different cells for inspection and upkeep, besides taking weight off the structure, which is their principal object. In a general sense any hole cut in a plate which forms part of a vessel's structure to reduce weight without impairing strength.

Fr: *Evidement;* Ger: *Erleichterungsloch.*

LIGHTER. 1. General name for a broad, flat-bottomed boat used in transporting cargo between a vessel and the shore, strongly built, and usually decked. Lighters and barges were formerly classed as one type of craft, but they have within recent years developed into distinct types, some being designed for short sea trips, while others are primarily engaged on harbor, estuary, river, or canal traffic.

The distinction between a lighter and a barge is more in the manner of use than in form and equipment, the term "barge" being more often used when the load is carried to its destination or over a long distance; while the term "lighter" refers to a short haul, generally in connection with loading or unloading operations of vessels in harbor.

Lighters under certain circumstances are held to be ships or vessels and subject to the same maritime laws as other vessels.

Fr: *Allège;* Ger: *Leichter.*

See **Derrick Lighter, Mooring Lighter, Screwing Lighter.**

2. To unload goods from a ship into a lighter. To convey goods by or with a lighter from ship to shore, or vice versa.

Fr: *Mettre sur Allèges;* Ger: *Ableichtern.*

In the East Coast ports of the United States the term lighter is generally used to denote harbor craft in which the cargo is placed on deck only, while a barge carries its freight in the hold under deck.

LIGHTERAGE. 1. A charge for conveyance of goods by lighters or barges in a harbor or between ship and shore. This charge usually includes the loading into and discharging out of lighters.

Fr: *Frais d'Allège; Gabarage;* Ger: *Leichterlohn; Leichtergeld; Leichterkosten.*

2. In general, transportation of goods between ship and shore by means of harbor lighters.

Fr: *Transport par Allèges; Aconage;* Ger: *Leichtertransport; Leichterung.*

See **Free Lighterage.**

LIGHTER CLERK (U. S.). An assistant to the receiving clerk, who keeps a record of the arrival of lighters at the piers and their starting and finishing times.

LIGHTERMAN. One engaged in the navigation and handling of lighters or barges. Also called bargeman. The owner or manager of lighters carrying on business with them in conveying goods is sometimes known as a master lighterman. In law a lighterman is considered a common carrier.

Fr: *Batelier; Aconier; Gabarier;* Ger: *Leichterführer; Leichterschiffer.*

LIGHT FILLET WELD. In fusion welding, a fillet weld in which the sides of the triangle equal at least one-half of the thickness of the plates joined.

Fr: *Soudure d'Angle Normale;* Ger: *Leichtkehlschweissung; Leichtkehlnaht.*

LIGHT GRAIN. The opposite of heavy grain. Barley and oats are included among the light grains. For barley the unit of freight is 2.050 lb. and for oats 1.600 lb.
 Ger: *Leichtgetreide.*

LIGHTHOUSE. A building on some conspicuous point of the coast, a pier or jetty, an island or rock, from which a light is exhibited at night as an aid to navigation. All maritime nations have government departments responsible for the establishment and maintenance of lighthouses.
 Fr: *Phare;* Ger: *Leuchtturm.*
 See **Bow Lighthouse.**

LIGHTHOUSE TENDER. A vessel of small tonnage, usually government owned, specially designed and equipped with the necessary appliances for placing and removing buoys with their moorings, refueling gas buoys, and offshore lighthouses. It is also used for transporting the crews and stores of light vessels, and lighthouse reliefs, as well as for towing light vessels, laying moorings, and locating or dispersing wrecks.
 Fr: *Baliseur;* Ger: *Leuchtturm-Tender; Tonnenleger.*

LIGHT LINE. The line of immersion at which a vessel floats when in ballast draft or light trim. Also called light load line, light waterline.
 Fr: *Ligne de Flottaison Lège;* Ger: *Leichtwasserlinie; Leerlinie.*

LIGHT LINE SPEED. The speed in feet per second of the hook or end of a cargo fall when hoisted or lowered by a winch while no load is attached to it. Also called light hook speed. It is usually four or five times the hoisting speed at full load.

LIGHT LIST. A publication issued in each maritime country by the central authority responsible for the maintenance of aids to navigation. It is issued annually and presents complete information concerning the character and position of lighthouses, lightships, radio beacons, fog signals, lighted and unlighted buoys and beacons. In the United States the list relating to the lights of foreign countries is published by the Hydrographic Office. The U. S. Coast Guard publishes the list referring to those of the U. S. and its possessions.
 Fr: *Livre des Phares;* Ger: *Feuerbuch.*

LIGHT MONEY (U. S.). A duty of fifty cents per net ton levied under a U. S. act of Congress as a duty additional to tonnage duty upon all vessels under foreign flag which enter the ports of the U. S.

LIGHTNING ROD. A pointed insulated metallic rod placed on the truck of a mast. It has a twofold purpose: (1) to prevent as far as possible sudden discharges of electricity from the clouds to the water surface through or in the neighborhood of the vessel; (2) to form a line of least resistance for any such discharge should it take place, and thus prevent damage to the ship.
 Fr: *Paratonnerre;* Ger: *Blitzableiter.*

LIGHT SAILS. General term for all sails made of light canvas, and set only in moderate to fine weather. In square riggers these include royals, skysails, studding sails, and upper staysails. In twentieth century fore and afters these include square sails, ringtails, gaff-topsails, club-topsails, and water sails; and in modern yachts spinnaker, balloon jib, Genoa jib; in schooners, fisherman staysail; in ketches, mizzen staysail.
 Fr: *Voiles Hautes; Voiles Supplémentaires;* Ger: *Beisegel.*

LIGHTSHIP. A sea-going vessel which may or may not be self-propelled and is fitted with a powerful lighting apparatus. It is permanently anchored, either to mark an outstanding danger to navigation where it is impractical to build a lighthouse, or to indicate the approach of a port and mark a point from which passing vessels can take bearings. Lightships serve as beacon by day, as platform for the light at night, and as sound signal or radio station in thick weather. The illuminating apparatus consists generally of a fixed lantern surmounting a steel tubular mast or a lattice girder tower. The sources of illumination used are oil-gas, acetylene and gas-filled electric lamps. Also called light vessel.
 Fr: *Bateau-Phare;* Ger: *Feuerschiff.*
 Cook, G. C., The Evolution of the Lightship, New York, 1913; Putnam, G. R., Lighthouses and Lightships of the United States, New York, 1933; International Lighthouse Conferences (Reports), London, 1929, Paris, 1933, Berlin, 1937.

LIGHTSMAN. A member of the crew on a lightship.

LIGHT WEIGHT.
 See **Displacement.**

LIGNUM VITAE. A hard, close-grained, heavy wood of an oily nature used for block sheaves, mast and flagpole trucks, also stern tube and strut bearings. In the

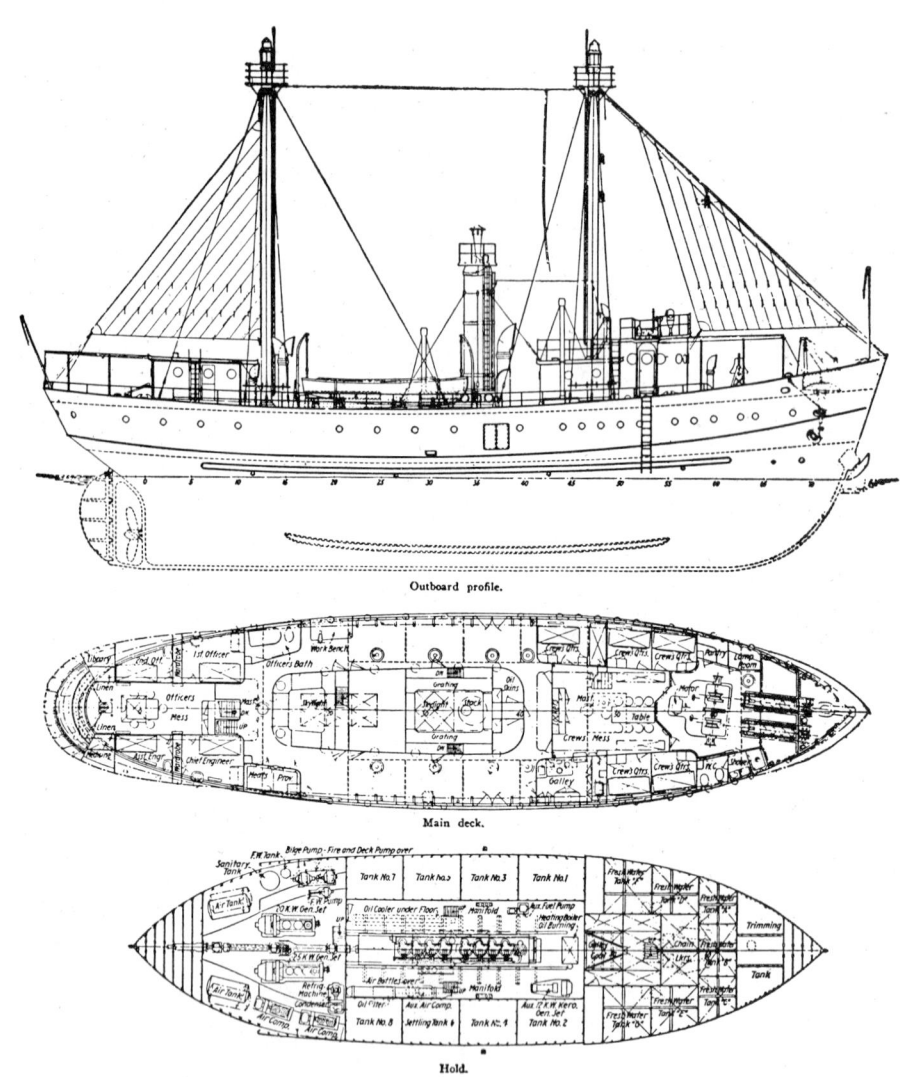

Lightship. (*Courtesy Marine Engineering and Shipping Review*)

latter instance it is fitted in narrow strips so cut that the grain lies radially to insure better wear. It has a crushing strength of about 7,000 lb. per sq. in. and a weight per cubic ft. of 65 to 75 lb.

Fr: *Gaïac;* Ger: *Pockholz.*

LILY IRON, LILLY IRON. A small harpoon with detachable head used in sword fishing. It is rigged with two lines, one fastened to the wooden shank and the other to the head.

LIMB. 1. In astronomy, a horizontal line tangent to the upper or lower edge of the visible disc of the sun, moon, or a planet.

Fr: *Limbe;* Ger: *Rand.*

2. The graduated arc of a sextant from which the reading of the observed angle is made.

Fr: *Limbe;* Ger: *Gradbogen; Kreisbogen; Limbus.*

LIMBER. A passage on each side of the keelson for bilge water, covered by movable

planks called limber boards. A row of limber holes.
 Fr: *Anguiller;* *Canal des Anguillers;* Ger: *Pumpensod; Wasserlauf; Füllungen.*
 See **Limber Hole.**

LIMBER BOARDS. Short pieces of board forming the upper part of the limber passage and made portable in order that any obstruction in the passage may be cleared away. One edge is fitted by a rabbet into the limber strake and the other beveled with a descent against the keelson. In steel vessels with open bottom, the term limber board is used to denote the strake of ceiling planks on either side of the center keelson. It has no features distinguishing it from the rest of the ceiling.
 Fr: *Paraclose;* Ger: *Füllung des Wasserlaufs; Füllungsbretter.*

LIMBER CHAIN. A ⅜ or 7/16-in. galvanized short link chain which is worked back and forth through the limber holes in a wooden vessel, to keep them from choking up.
 Fr: *Chaîne d'Anguiller;* Ger: *Limmerkette; Reinigungskette.*

LIMBER HOLES. Circular holes from 2 to 3½ in. in diameter or elongated holes pierced in the lower part of the floor plates just above the vertical flange of the frame angle bar and in the vicinity of the middle-line keelson or vertical keel for drainage purposes. In general, holes in structure near a deck or flat, worked in to facilitate drainage where desired. Also called watercourse, drainage hole.
 Fr: *Anguiller;* Ger: *Nüstergat; Wasserlaufloch.*

LIMBER STRAKE. The first strake of inside planking from the keelson. Also called buttock strake, futtock plank.
 Fr: *Paraclose;* Ger: *Kielwegerungsgang; Kielwegerungsplanke.*

LIMITED LIABILITY. A term which when used in connection with collision cases refers to the value of the vessel after the accident, plus the earnings for the voyage, collected or collectable.

LINE. General term for ropes or cords of different sizes used for various purposes on board ship.
 Fr: *Ligne;* Ger: *Leine.*

LINE BOAT.
 See **Liner.**

LINE HAULER. A small hand or power driven winch used by fishermen for hauling trawl lines on board. Also called line-winch, power gurdy. It is usually stepped on deck, one hand operating the handle and another taking off the fish as the line is brought on board before it passes over the reels.

LINEN ROPE. Rope made of the fibers of flax. It is lighter and stronger than Manila rope, lasts longer, and is more flexible. Owing to its high cost it is used only on yachts, for running gear such as sheets, halyards, jigs, and tails of wire running rigging, and on naval vessels for signal halyards.
 Fr: *Cordage en Lin;* Ger: *Leinentauwerk.*

LINE OF COLLIMATION. The optical axis of a telescope. Also called **line of sight.** In a sextant the line of collimation passes through the center of the horizon glass, meeting its surface at the same angle as the line drawn from the same point to the center of the index glass.
 Fr: *Ligne de collimation;* Ger: *Kollimationsachse.*

LINE OF NODES. The line in which the plane of the celestial equator and plane of the ecliptic intersect. Due to precession the direction of the lines nodes is continually changing relatively to the stars.
 Fr: *Ligne nodale;* Ger: *Knoten Bahn.*

LINE OF POSITION.
 See **Position Line.**

LINE OF SOUNDINGS. Soundings taken along a predetermined line at stated intervals.
 Fr: *Ligne de sondages;* Ger: *Lotungslinie.*

LINER. 1. Trading vessel used on a particular route with regular sailings. Liners range anywhere from ordinary freighters, which do not differ from the tramp vessels, to large cargo vessels especially built for the freight line service, and to the largest passenger-carrying vessels. Some liners carry freight exclusively, others a varying proportion of freight and passengers, and some passengers exclusively.
 Fr: *Navire Régulier;* Ger: *Linienschiff.*
 See **Cabin Liner, Cargo Liner, Express Liner, Passenger Liner.**
Chamberlain, E. T., *Liner Predominance in Transoceanic Shipping,* U. S. Bureau of Foreign and Domestic Commerce, Trade Information Bull. 448, Washington, 1927; Christie, J. D., *Liner Development During the Past Fifty Years,* North East Coast

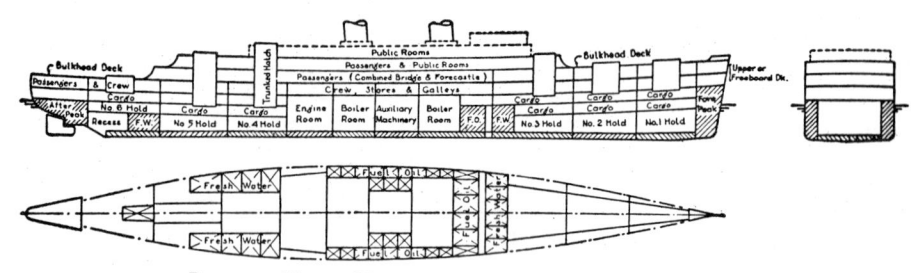

Passenger Liner. (*Courtesy of American Bureau of Shipping*)

Institution of Engineers and Shipbuilders, Newcastle upon Tyne, *Transactions*, vol. 51, 1934-35.

2. A small piece of flat steel used to fill up a narrow space between a plate and a bar or in the seam of two plates so that they can be riveted solidly together in such places where, owing to the arrangements of the parts, the faying surfaces cannot be brought into close contact. Liners may or may not taper in section. They may be used to fill out a lap joint, form a middle layer between two surfaces, or for leveling foundations. Also called Slip-Filling Piece.

Fr: *Cale de Remplissage;* Ger: *Füllstück.*

See **Bulkhead Liner, Dutchman, Frame Liner, Knife-Edge Liner, Taper Liner, Shaft Liner.**

3. A general name for fishing craft with sail or mechanical propulsion, specially built and equipped for hook and line fishing. This term does not denote any particular type of rig or build. Also called dory trawler.

Fr: *Cordier;* Ger: *Angelboot.*

See **Deck Hand Liner, Dory Hand Liner.**

LINER BILL OF LADING. A bill of lading issued for a consignment of goods shipped by a regular liner.

Fr: *Connaissement de Ligne Régulière;*
Ger: *Linie-Konnossement.*

LINER MAN (U. S.). A shipyard worker whose duties are to measure for and to make wooden templates for metal liners, and also to square and put the liners in place after bending or tapering.

LINER NEGLIGENCE CLAUSE. A standard form of hull clause used in marine policies insuring liners and replacing the many varied forms of owner's clauses at one time in use. Also called additional perils clause.

LINER OFF.
See **Layer Out.**

LINER RATES. Freight rates quoted by shipping companies maintaining regular services over advertised routes. Also called conference rates.

LINE ROLLER. A portable wooden roller arranged so that it can be attached to the gunwale of a boat, dory, and the like, and used by fishermen to ease the friction when picking up trawl lines. Also called trawl roller, gurdy.

Ger: *Leinenrolle.*

LINE RUNNER. A man whose business it is to take ashore, make fast and let go ship's mooring lines on a quay, wharf, or pier. Also called boatman, waterman.

Fr: *Haleur; Canotier;* Ger: *Jollenführer.*

LINES. A set of drawings showing the form of the hull projected on three planes perpendicular to each other. Also called body lines, lines drawing. It consists of three plans: (1) an elevation known as sheer plan or profile; (2) a plan showing the form of the hull at several waterlines called half-breadth plan; (3) a plan showing the sectional form of the hull at the square stations or cross sections called body plan.

Fr: *Plan de Formes;* Ger: *Linienriss; Konstruktionsriss.*

In general practice only one side of the ship's form is delineated since all vessels are symmetrical about their longitudinal center plane. In wooden ships the lines represent the skin or outer surface of the planking. The lines of steel hulls represent the outer surface of the frames, or inside of the shell plating. Batey and Batey, "Consideration on the Improved Forms of Modern Cargo Steamers," Institution of Naval Architects (London), *Transactions*, vol. 75 (1933); Vincent, S. A., "Merchant Vessel Lines," *Marine Engineering and Shipping Age* (New York), vol. 35 (March, 1930); Webster, N. B., How to Get Out the Lines of a Ship, Marine

Engineering (New York), vol. 45 (May-June, 1940).

LINES COEFFICIENTS. Also called Form Coefficients. Various coefficients by which the features of the underwater hull form are expressed as a percentage or decimal part of the whole. They are used in naval architecture for design purposes in comparing different hulls regardless of size. The block coefficient, midship section coefficient, load line coefficient and prismatic coefficient are the ones most commonly applied.

Ger: *Formkoeffizienten.*

LINES DRAWING.
See **Lines.**

LINE SHAFT BEARING.
See **Plummer Block.**

LINE SHAFTING.
See **Shafting.**

LINESMAN.
See **Loftsman.**

LINE SQUALL. A squall that results from the sudden undercutting of a warm equatorial air current of high relative humidity by a colder, and hence denser, polar one. It consists of a continuous line of cumulo-nimbus clouds arched across the sky, and usually advances perpendicularly to the line of clouds. It is generally accompanied by heavy rain and often hail. The actual squall of wind lasts but a few minutes but is often extremely violent. During the passage of the squall the barometric pressure will rise with great suddenness and the temperature may drop from 10 to 20° F.
See **Cumulo-Nimbus.**

LINE STORM. A storm occurring in September or March when the sun is near the equinoctial or celestial equator. Also called equinoctial storm.

LINE-THROWING GUN. A lifesaving gun designed to shoot a rocket or a projectile with a line attached to it and carried in a container at the muzzle. The line is shot from the beach (or vice versa) and establishes a connection with the stranded ship by which an endless line and tail block is hauled off, followed by a hawser. With the hawser fast to a mast and the tail block, through which the endless fall is rove, fastened about two feet below it, the apparatus is ready to take the crew off in the breeches buoy sent off by the lifesavers ashore. Also called line-carrying gun.
Line-throwing appliances also include the line-throwing pistol by means of which a rocket carrying a line is fired from a pistol with a small impulse charge, the line being placed on deck alongside the firer.

Fr: *Canon Porte-Amarre;* Ger: *Rettungsgeschütz.*

LINE TRAFFIC. The business of transporting passengers and cargo, with vessels of the "liner" category having fixed schedules as to dates of sailing, route and ports of call, with regular cargo rates.

LINE TRAWLER. General term for fishing boats using long set lines (also called trawl lines) which are stretched over the sea bottom and held in position at each end with a light anchor.

LINE TUB (U. S.). A large shallow tub in which the whale line of a whaleboat was carefully stowed in successive Flemish coils.

LINE OF APSIDES. The line connecting the perihelion and the aphelion.

LINING. 1. A term applied to deep-sea fishing by means of lines with baited hooks. The length of lines and methods used vary according to the nature of the catch and custom. The fishing lines may be thrown from the vessel or may be carried out by dories some distance away from the vessel. The terms short-lining, great-lining, or long-lining refer to the depths of water in which the boats operate. Lining may be divided under two heads: (a) hand-line fishing; (b) long-lining or line trawling.

Fr: *Pêche aux Cordes;* Ger: *Angelfischerei.*

See **Deck Hand-Lining, Dory Hand-Lining, Great Lining, Hand-Lining, Long-Lining.**

2. The process of covering a steel vessel's cargo hold with a wood lining preparatory to loading her with grain or similar bulk cargo.

3. A general term used to denote strengthening pieces affixed to a sail where necessary, to prevent chafing or to reinforce the sail. Also called band, lining cloth. Linings include reef bands, leech lining, top lining, buntline cloths, middle-band, mast lining, footband, reef tackle pieces; and in fore-and-aft sails: clew, head, tack, and corner pieces.

Fr: *Renfort; Doublage;* Ger: *Verdoppellung; Verstärkungsband.*

See **Anchor Lining, Top Lining.**

4. The light wood covering generally of feather and groove boarding applied on the

vessel's side in cabins and storerooms. Also called cleading.

Fr: *Lambrissage;* *Doublage;* Ger: *Bekleidung.*

LINING CLOTH. See **Lining.**

LINT. 1. Name given to each one of the nets which make up a "fleet" of drift nets. It refers more particularly to the center part of each net, the sides or margins being known as "hoddy," or in Scotland as "gales" or "boards."

Fr: *Alèze;* Ger: *Netzwand.*

2. The middle curtain made of small meshed netting in a trammel net.

Fr: *Aunée;* Ger: *Schlange.*

LIP. The thin end on a scarfed piece of timber. The lip should have a thickness of about 25 per cent of the depth of the scarf in order that it can bear calking as required for keel and stem scarfs. Also called scarf lip, nib, jog.

Fr: *Lèvre; Bec;* Ger: *Lippe.*

LIPA. A Philippine canoe originating from the Tawi-Tawi group of the Sulu Archipelago. Also called *lipa-lipa.* The hull is made of a dugout basis with planked sides and has no outriggers. It is used by the Mohammedan Moros for the transportation of passengers.

LIPPEE-LIPPEE. A single-sheet Australian bark canoe of the Gnornbur tribe from Port Essington, Coburg Peninsula (Northern Territory). Its sides are stiffened by gunwale poles and in the bottom short pieces of bark are placed crosswise in order to preserve the shape and give more structural strength. Length 18 ft., breadth 2 ft. Carries 8 people.

LIPPER. A slight ruffling on the surface of the sea. Light spray from small waves under the bow. A small sea coming over the rail. Also called leaper.

LIPPERINGS. See **Slumgullion.**

LIQUID CARGO. Liquid cargoes include mineral oils, whale oil, vegetable oil (palm oil), creosote, molasses, turpentine, and in general any liquid suitable for carriage in bulk. The specific gravity of these cargoes may vary from 0.7 to over 1.0, and their viscosity is often high.

Fr: *Chargement Liquide;* Ger: *Flüssige Ladung.*

LIQUID COMPASS. A magnetic compass in which the card nearly floats in a bowl filled with distilled water to which 35 per cent of alcohol is added to prevent freezing. The bowl is hermetically sealed with pure India rubber and a corrugated expansion chamber is attached to the bottom to allow for expansion and contraction of the liquid. The card is a thin disc either painted or covered with linen upon which the degrees and points are painted, the needles being enclosed in brass. The center of the card is secured to a round brass float which is

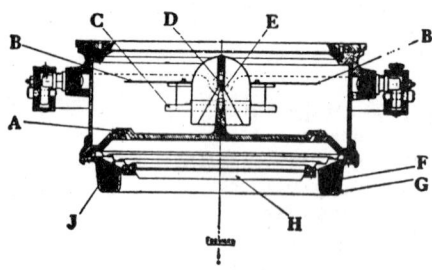

Liquid Compass

A. Bridge
B. Card
C. Magnet
D. Jewel
E. Pivot
F. Lead filling for balance weight
G. Balance weight
H. Bottom glass
J. Expansion diaphragm

so constructed that when resting on the pivot the buoyancy is negative and there is a minimum of friction. On the under side of the float there is a deep conical hollow with a tiny agate cup at its apex, which rests on the pin. The object of having the bowl filled with a liquid mixture is to reduce the weight on the pivot and to dampen the oscillations of the card. Also called spirit compass, fluid compass, wet compass.

Fr: *Compas à Liquide;* Ger: *Fluidkompass; Flüssigkeitskompass; Schwimmkompass.*

LIS-ALIS. See **Alis-Alis.**

LISI. A plank-built canoe with keel and high upturned stem and stern of the Solomon Islands. The framing consists of inserted ribs tied to eyed cleats.

LIST. The leaning or inclination of a vessel. A vessel is said to be listed when she has found equilibrium in any position other than upright, whether owing to an unsymmetric distribution of weights or to any peculiarity of form. Listing is a static condition, as distinguished from heeling, which is dynamic.

Fr: *Gîte;* Ger: *Schlagseite.*

See **Crew's List, Passenger List, Stemming List.**

LISTERBAAT. An open rowing and sailing boat originating from the province of Lister used in the drift-net mackerel fisheries of the southwest coast of Norway. The hull is built with sharp stern, deep keel, and hollow floors. It has usually about six frames and a breasthook at each end, clinker planking, and waterways or runways along the sides from stem to stern. There are five thwarts and the mast is stepped through the second from the bow at about one-third the boat's length. The rig consists of a sprit mainsail and two headsails with a short running bowsprit which passes through an iron ring on the starboard side of the stem. Its heel is held in a wooden bar which crosses the boat's bows. Length, over-all 40 ft.; on keel, 30 ft. 2⅔ in. Beam 15 ft. 1⅓ in. Depth 4 ft. 8 in. (Typical.)

LISTER SKOITE. A small decked fishing vessel employed in the North Sea drift-net fisheries on the southeastern coast of Norway. It takes its specific name from the fishing locality of Lister, where it is said to have originated, although it closely resembles boats from the southwestern provinces of Sweden. It varies in length from 27 to 38 ft. The hull is keel-built with curved stem and sternpost clinker planking. It is sprit-rigged with long bowsprit reaching back to the mast and used as spinnaker boom when running free. The mainsail is a loose-footed spritsail of nearly uniform width. In light winds a club-headed topsail sets on a long pole (30 ft.) which comes nearly as far down as the deck on the forward side of the mast. Length over-all 36 ft. 3 in. Beam 12 ft. 1 in. Depth 6 ft. 8 in. (Typical.)

LITOSILO. A magnesia cement deck sheathing used on steel decks as a substitute for wooden planking. Also called magnasil, magnesite.
See **Decking.**

LITTLE BROTHER. A term used by seamen when referring to a secondary hurricane following a main disturbance.

LITTLE MONSOON. A northwest wind which blows in the Indian Ocean from November to May in the area lying between the 3° and 10° south latitude and near the longitude of Sumatra and Java.

LITTORAL. 1. Of, or pertaining to, a seashore.
Fr: *Littoral;* Ger: *Ufer gehörig.*

2. The interval on a sea coast between high and low water mark.
Fr: *Littoral;* Ger: *Strand.*

LITTORAL DRIFT. Floating or submerged masses of matter, or sunken objects, driven or forced on the seashore by waves or currents.
Fr: *Apports littoraux;* Ger: *Ufer Treibgut.*

LITTORAL RIGHTS. The rights bestowed on the owner of land bounding upon navigable waters subject to statutory rules and governmental regulations. They are termed "littoral" as respects tidal waters and "riparian" as respects non tidal waters.

LITTORAL SEA.
See **Marginal Sea.**

LITTORAL ZONE. The interval on a sea coast between highest and lowest water marks.
Fr: *Zone littorale.*

LIVE HARPOON.
See **Live Iron.**

LIVE IRON. A whaleman's term meaning a harpoon in use or ready for use. Also called live harpoon. (Obsolete.)

LIVE OAK. A compact, fine-grained, very strong and durable wood found in the South Atlantic and Gulf states. Approved by classification societies for all structural parts of wooden ships. It is free from gallic acid but does not take spike fastenings well; bolts and treenails are used in preference. Weight when seasoned about 60 lb. per cu. ft.
Fr: *Chêne vert;* Ger: *Steineichenholz.*

LIVERPOOL HEAD. A sheet-metal ventilation fixture comprising two drums, one inside the other, with staggered openings. It is fitted on the top of ventilators or galley stovepipe to prevent the entrance of sea water, while permitting the passage of air or exhaust gases.

LIVERPOOL HOUSE. A superstructure extending from side to side and situated amidships in large (steel built) sailing vessels. It contained the accommodation for the master and the officers. The steering gear was placed on the top of this house. It extended over one-sixth to two-thirds of the vessel's length, adding largely to structural strength and giving considerable reserve buoyancy, besides preventing decks from being swamped by boarding seas fore and aft.

LIVERPOOL POINT. A rivet point with large face diameter and slightly convex. Used for watertight or oiltight work on thin plating. The countersink extends half-way through the plate.

Fr: *Rivure fraisée bombée.*

LIVERPOOL STEAMSHIP OWNERS ASSOCIATION. An association of shipowners whose tonnage is registered in the port of Liverpool. It was established in 1859 and its membership includes some 63 shipping companies. It has ever since the beginning played an important part in British shipping affairs.

LIVERPOOL VIRUS. A bacillus used for the destruction of rats on board ship, in warehouses, and so on. It is harmless to animals except rats, and mice. The cause of extermination is due to an infectious disease of the intestines which the virus produces and, as rats are cannibalistic in their habits, the disease spreads rapidly.

LIVESTOCK. Live animals. The term includes all domesticated quadrupeds such as sheep, horses, mules, asses and swine. Livestock or provender taken on board for their sustenance does not come under the general heading of cargo except when it constitutes the only article of exportation from the port of departure or, if according to the custom of the port, the word cargo is understood to cover livestock.

Fr: *Bétail;* Ger: *Viehstand.*

LIZARD. A short length of rope having a thimble or bull's-eye spliced into its end and used as a leader for rigging. A traveling lizard is sometimes fitted to the middle of lifeboat's falls for use in taking up the slack when the boat is being hoisted. A lizard is general heading of cargo except when it constitutes the only article of exportation from the port of departure or, if according to the custom of the port, the word cargo is understood to cover livestock.

Fr: *Bétail;* Ger: *Viehstand.*

LIZARD. A short length of rope having a thimble or bull's-eye spliced into its end and used as a leader for rigging. A traveling lizard is sometimes fitted to the middle of lifeboat's falls for use in taking up the slack when the boat is being hoisted. A lizard is also used on a light yard for stopping the yard rope out on the quarter of the yard previous to sending it down from aloft.

Fr: *Guide; Manchette;* Ger: *Brille.*

See **Bunt Lizard, Long Lizard.**

LJUNGSTROM RIG. A rig for small sailing boats, the design of which is based on modern aerodynamics. It consists of a single jib-shaped sail. The luff is attached to a revolving mast which can be spun around with the aid of an endless rope. Friction is reduced by ball bearings where the mast passes through the deck and where it is stepped in the bottom of the boat. About ten revolutions of the mast will roll up the sail entirely. The mast is round and unstayed and provided with a groove in which the luff of the sail is set. The halyards run inside the mast. There is only one stay, an adjusted backstay. The afterpart of the sail is made of heavier canvas; thus it becomes a trysail when canvas is being shortened on account of weather conditions.

In certain cases the rig is provided with a double sail so that each half of the sail can be opened out, one to port and the other to starboard when running before the wind. The strongest point in favor of this rig is its efficiency when going to windward or sailing very close to the wind.

LLOYD'S. A London institution incorporated by act of Parliament in 1871 in which all forms of insurance, except life insurance, can be effected. The corporation does not subscribe policies, the risks being accepted by individual members known as underwriters, each one of them signing for a specified sum for which he alone is responsible. Each member before being elected as a Lloyd's underwriter has to place with the corporation securities to an amount of £15,000 minimum, the amount required being in proportion to the magnitude of the member's commitments. It comprises about 600 underwriting members and about 200 non-underwriting.

See **Custom of Lloyd's, Germanischer Lloyd.**

Grey, H. M., *Lloyd's Yesterday and Today,* London, 1922; Wright and Fayle, *History of Lloyd's,* London, 1928.

LLOYD'S AGENTS. Agents in different ports appointed by the Committee of Lloyd's Underwriters. Their principal duties are to report to headquarters on all losses and casualties, arrivals and departures of ships; further, to assist masters and owners of ships on the Register in case of casualty, etc., and to collect and pass on to Lloyd's Underwriters any special information likely to be of interest to members.

Fr: *Agents du Lloyd;* Ger: *Lloyd's Agent.*

See **Ship's Agent, Forwarding Agent.**

LLOYD'S LENGTH. The length used for classification purposes in accordance with Lloyd's Register of Shipping rules. It is measured from the foreside of the stem to the after side of the sternpost to the Summer load waterline.

LLOYD'S LIST. A daily publication of shipping news issued in London by the corporation of Lloyd's underwriters.

LLOYD'S POLICY. A standard type of marine insurance policy on which most existing forms are based.
Fr: *Police du Lloyd;* Ger: *Lloyd's Police.*

LLOYD'S REGISTER OF SHIPPING. The largest and oldest British classification society, established in 1834, and united with the Underwriters Registry for Iron Ships in 1885. It is entirely independent from the British Underwriters Organization known as "Lloyd's." Lloyd's Register is governed by a committee composed of shipowners, underwriters, and ship and engine builders.

Symbols recorded in the Register book:

✠ 100 A.1. Indicates the highest class for steel vessels and is granted to all vessels built under survey and in accordance with the Society's rules and regulations, and when the scantlings are such as will entitle them to the maximum draft permitted by the dimensions. The notation "With freeboard" is assigned to ships of lighter scantlings having less than the maximum draft permitted by the dimensions.

Other notations, such as "Carrying Petroleum in Bulk," "For Special Service," indicate that the vessel is engaged in a special service and that the scantlings and arrangements have been approved by the society.

The maltese cross indicates that the vessel has been built under survey.

The figure "1" placed after letter "A" indicates that the anchors and cables have been tested by the Society's surveyors and are in accordance with the rules.

The symbol ✠ L.M.C. shown in red type indicates that the engines and boilers have been constructed under survey and that a "Lloyd's Machinery Certificate" has been granted.

The highest class symbol assigned to wooden vessels is the letter "A" in black type, followed by a number ranging from 8 to 18 which is determined by the timber employed in the construction, the type and quality of fastenings, method of construction, and other associated items. Letter "A" in red type denotes that the vessel has lapsed into the second division of the first class. "Æ" is an intermediate class; and letter "E" is the lowest class for wooden vessels.

A red line with a date beneath in place of any of the characters inserted in the Register book indicates that the class has been expunged because the rules have not been complied with. A single black line with a date beneath indicates that the class has been withdrawn through reported defects in hull or machinery. Three dots indicate the withdrawal of class at owner's request.

LLOYD'S SIGNAL STATION. One of the signal stations established by Lloyd's Underwriters on the coasts of Great Britain and abroad. Passing ships may show their designating numbers or letters by the international code of signals to these stations and are then immediately reported by Lloyd's in the (London) *Shipping Gazette* and Lloyd's list.
Fr: *Poste Signalétique du Lloyd;* Ger: *Lloyd's Signalstation.*

LO. Single-outrigger dugout canoe from Eromanga Island, southern New Hebrides, similar to the *niu.*

LOAD DISPLACEMENT. The displacement of a vessel when it floats at its loaded draft or when it has all its weights on board.
Fr: *Déplacement en Charge;* Ger: *Beladene Verdrängung; Beladenes Deplacement.*

LOADED DRAFT. The draft at load displacement.
Fr: *Tirant d'Eau en Charge;* Ger: *Beladener Tiefgang.*

LOADING. The act of putting cargo on board.
Fr: *Charger;* Ger: *Verladen.*

LOADING BERTH. A station in which a ship lies or can lie at a wharf, pier, and so on. The space given to or allotted to a ship to lie in when in a dock or basin. The place alongside a pier or in a roadstead, where a vessel can load or discharge.
Fr: *Poste de Chargement;* Ger: *Ladestelle; Ladeplatz.*

LOADING BROKER. A shipbroker who represents a shipowner at a given port to the extent of finding cargoes and loading vessels on owner's behalf. Such arrangements are generally of a permanent nature, the agent being remunerated by a percentage of all freight and passage money collected by him. One who habitually procures cargoes for vessels on the berth for a certain port or trade.

Fr: *Courtier d'Affrètement;* Ger: *Fracht-Schiffsmakler.*

In the regular liner traffic the loading broker engages shipments in advance and does all preparatory work as between shipper and shipowner up to the time of actual shipment.

LOADING DAYS. The number of lay days allowed for loading cargo as specified in a charter party.

Fr: *Jours de Chargement;* Ger: *Ladefrist; Ladezeit.*

LOADING IN TURN. A charter party term indicating that when several boats are waiting to reach a berth for loading, the loading of each shall commence in order of arrival at the berth, or according to the sequence in which notices of readiness are served. Also called turn loading.

Ger: *Reihenfolge-Beladung.*

LOADING ON THE BERTH. A term meaning that a ship is available for loading parcels of general cargo, as a common carrier.

LOADING SPOT (G. B.). A specified and actual place such as a named wharf or pier: a specific berth at a quay or within a dock where a ship is to load.

LOADING TIME. The period of time within which the ship is to be loaded. It is usually specified in charter parties and sometimes in bills of lading.

Fr: *Période de chargement;* Ger: *Ladezeit.*

LOADING TURN. Rotation or order for ships to berth and load (or discharge) cargo.

Fr: *Tour de Chargement;* Ger: *Reihenfolge der Beladung.*

LOADING WARRANTIES. Expressed warranties sometimes found in marine insurance policies which restrict the classes or cargo or the quantity of some particular classes of cargo to be carried by the vessel.

LOAD LINE. See **Load Waterline.**

LOADLINE CONVENTION (1930). A convention signed in London in 1930 by 40 governments which provides for the establishment of uniform principles and rules with regard to the limits to which ships on international voyages may be loaded. Its provisions were put into force in Great Britain by the Merchant Shipping (Safety and Load Lines Conventions) Act of 1932.

Fr: *Convention sur les lignes de charge. 1930;* Ger: *Freibordvertrag. 1930.*

LOADLINE DISC. A disc 12 in. in diameter marked amidships below the deck line and intersected by a horizontal line 18 in. long and 1 in. wide, the upper edge of which passes through the center of the disc. The letters on each side of the disc indicate the assigning authority: A.B., American Bureau; B.V., Bureau Veritas; L.R., Lloyd's Register, and so on.

Fr: *Disque de Franc-Bord;* Ger: *Ladelinie-Kreis.*

See **Plimsoll Mark.**

LOADLINE SHIP. Any ship which in accordance with the International Loadline Convention of 1930, must carry loadline marks and certificate. International Loadline Ships are those with a gross tonnage of 150 tons or upwards which carry cargo or passengers. Local loadline ships are those of 150 tons gross or more which do not carry cargo or passengers and those of less than that tonnage.

LOADLINE SURVEY. A survey carried out annually by a classification society or Government Agency to see that the conditions under which the loadline of a vessel was originally granted are being efficiently maintained.

Fr: *Visite de franc bord;* Ger: *Freibord Besichtigung; Ladelinie Besichtigung.*

LOAD WATERLINE. The intersection of the surface of the ship with the plane of the surface of the water when the ship is floating with her designed load on board, and is perfectly upright in the water. The line of immersion when a vessel is loaded. The waterline corresponding to the maximum draft to which a vessel is permitted to load either by the freeboard regulations, the conditions of classification, or the conditions of service.

Fr: *Ligne de Charge;* Ger: *Tiefladelinie; Ladewasserlinie.*

The rules which determine the maximum permissible load line in merchant ships with a tonnage of 150 gross or more, engaged on international voyages, have been laid down by the international convention respecting load lines (1930) and have been adopted by most maritime countries. The load lines prescribed by this convention are:

The summer load line, marked "S".
The winter load line, marked "W".
The winter North Atlantic load line, marked "WNA".
The tropical load line, marked "T".
The fresh-water load line, marked "F".

Each of these lines is indicated by a horizontal mark, nine inches long and one inch wide. The marks extend from, and are at right angles to, the vertical line mark twenty-one inches forward of the center of the load line disc.

Fr: *Ligne de Charge;* Ger: *Tiefladelinie; Ladewasserlinie.*

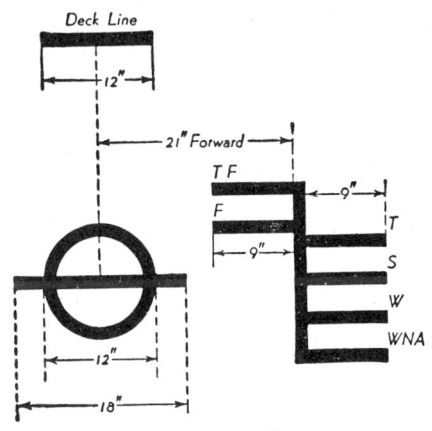

Load Line Marks

Arnott, D., *Load Line Regulations with Special Reference to the International Load Line Convention to 1930,* Society of Naval Architects and Marine Engineers, New York, 1930; Foster-King, J., "Annual Load Line Surveys," Institution of Engineers and Shipbuilders in Scotland, *Transactions,* vol. 81 (1937–38); U. S. Bureau of Marine Inspection and Navigation, *Regulations for the Establishment of Load Lines for Merchant Vessels,* Washington, 1941.

LOBSTER CAR. An oblong rectangular wooden box about 6 ft. long, 4 ft. wide and 2 ft. deep with open seams or numerous small holes to permit free circulation of water. These boxes are moored close to the shore and used by fishermen for holding lobsters alive until they are marketed. Some cars of larger size used by dealers have the inside divided into a series of compartments by horizontal and vertical partitions to prevent lobsters from huddling together and thus killing each other by their own weight.

LOBSTER TRAP. A device to catch lobsters. Lobster traps vary a good deal in shape but basically all are crate-like containers made of wooden laths. The lobster, attracted by a bag of bait and netting hanging inside, crawls through a funnel-shaped net at either end of the trap. Also called lobster pot, creel, lobster basket.

Fr: *Casier;* Ger: *Hummerkorb; Krebsreuse.*

Traps are weighted with flat stones and are slung on a rope, or warp, whose length varies with the depth of the water in which the traps are to be set. On the other end of the rope is a wooden float painted with the lobsterman's identification marks and colors. Lobster traps may be set singly, with a rope and buoy attached to each pot, or they may be set in "trawls" wherein eight or ten pots are fastened together by 20- or 30-ft. connecting ropes.

U. S. Bureau of Fisheries, *Memorandum S. 199,* Washington, 1937.

LOCAL APPARENT NOON. The instant of the transit of the true sun across the meridian.

Fr: *Midi apparent du Lieu;* Ger: *Scheinbarer Ortsmittag.*

LOCAL APPARENT TIME. The hour angle of the apparent sun measured westward from the ship's meridian.

Fr: *Heure Vraie du Lieu;* Ger: *Scheinbare Ortszeit.*

LOCAL ATTRACTION. Any magnetic disturbance, temporary or otherwise, of a compass due to iron, steel, dynamo, electric wiring, and so on, situated in the immediate vicinity of the compass but not included in the stationary metal surrounding it. The effect of cargo containing iron ore, machinery, and so on, may also be classed as local attraction.

Fr: *Attraction Locale;* Ger: *Örtliche Ablenkung.*

LOCAL HOUR ANGLE. The angle at the celestial pole between the meridian of the observer's place and the hour circle of the body. It is measured westward from the meridian of the place 0 to 360 degrees, or from 0 to 24 hours.

Fr: *Angle horaire du lieu;* Ger: *Zeitwinkel.*

LOCAL MEAN NOON. Local transit of the mean sun on the meridian.

Fr: *Midi moyen du lieu;* Ger: *Miltlere ortsmittag.*

LOCAL MEAN TIME. Time reckoned at each particular place from an epoch determined by local convenience. It is based on the hour angle of the mean sun at the inferior meridian. Also called **Ship's mean time.**

Fr: *Temps moyen du lieu;* Ger: *Mittlere Ortszeit.*

LOCAL SIDERAL NOON. Local transit of vernal equinoctial point.

Fr: *Midi Sidéral du lieu;* Ger: *Stern Ortsmittag.*

LOCAL TIME. Solar time reckoned at each particular place from an epoch determined by local convenience such as the transit of the sun's center over the meridian of the place.

If the apparent sun is used as the index, its position measures local apparent time; if the mean sun, local mean time.

Fr: *Heure du Lieu; Temps Local;* Ger: *Ortszeit.*

LOCAL TRANSIT. In astronomy the passage of a celestial body across the observer's meridian.

LOCATION CLAUSE. A marine insurance cargo clause attaching to the interest before shipment in the event of an "open cover." It limits the liability of the underwriters when several shipments have accumulated in one particular place and they are destroyed or damaged by a peril covered in the policy.

LOCATION CLERK (U. S.). An assistant to the delivery clerk, who keeps the record of the location of all cargo discharged from ship to dock.

LOCH FYNE SKIFF. Fishing craft from the west coast of Scotland mostly found around Loch Fyne, the Isle of Bute, and Kilbrennan Sound. Two methods of construction are used. The clinker-built boats are decked forward on a length of 12 to 14 ft. Two thwarts are worked in the afterpart. Present-day carvel-built skiffs are fully decked with fish hatch amidships and cuddy forward. Straight stem and strongly raked sternpost are features common to both types. Recently built craft have an auxiliary engine and canoe or cruiser stern. The sail plan consists of a standing lug mainsail and jib set flying on a short bowsprit. The mast is placed in a long boxlike tabernacle so that it can be lowered. Length over-all 30 to 40 ft. Breadth 9 to 12 ft. Depth 5 ft. Draft forward 2 ft., aft 6 ft. (Average.)

LOCK. An enclosure in a canal or river or at the entrance to a tidal dock, provided with gates at each end, and used in raising or lowering vessels as they pass from one level to another.

Fr: *Écluse à Sas;* Ger: *Schleuse; Kammerschleuse.*

See **Entrance Lock.**

LOCK (to). The action of passing a vessel through a lock.

Fr: *Écluser;* Ger: *Durchschleusen.*

LOCKAGE. Charge against a ship for passing through locks.

Fr: *Droits d'Écluse;* Ger: *Schleusengeld.*

LOCKED HARBOR. A harbor landlocked by shoals or reefs so that vessels cannot readily go in or out.

LOCKED SCARF. General term for various types of scarf joints into which some kind of locking device such as a key, a hook, or a strap is introduced to prevent any sideway or endwise movement of the joint.

LOCKING BAR.

See **Hatch Locking Bar.**

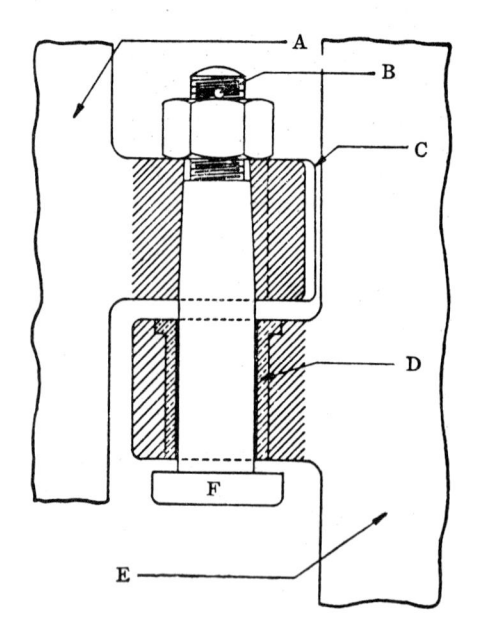

Locking Pintle

A. Rudder C. Rudder Stop E. Rudder Post
B. Split Pin D. Bushing F. Head

LOCKING HEAD. That part of a windlass connected to the driving shaft and driving the wildcats by means of the locking keys. The wildcats are engaged with or disengaged from the locking heads by using handwheels (locking rings) located on either side of the windlass.

LOCKING PINTLE. A pintle with a head on its bottom end to prevent the rudder from unshipping. It is usually the top pintle.

Fr: *Aiguillot à Tête;* Ger: *Schlossfingerling.*
See **Pintle.**

LOCK SIGNAL. A harbor signal relating to the opening or closing of lock gates.
Fr: *Signal d'Écluse;* Ger: *Schleusensignal.*

LOCK STRAKE. In wooden ships: the inner strake of waterway planking when of the two-strake type. The middle strake, if three strakes are worked. So called because it is let in by a score or lock taken out of the beams.
Fr: *Gouttière;* Ger: *Lukenstringer.*

LOCUST. The timber of the acacia tree. An extremely durable straight-grained wood of yellow color. Its use is almost entirely confined to treenails, and dowels for scarfs and cleats. Weight when seasoned about 48 lb. per cu. ft.
Fr: *Acacia;* Ger: *Akazienholz.*

LODGING KNEE.
See **Bosom Knee.**

LODIA. A Russian sailing vessel from the White Sea employed in the coasting trade and also for walrus hunting during the summer months between Cape Kanin and Kara Bay. Length 36 to 60 ft. Breadth 10 to 17½ ft. Depth 7 to 11 ft. Deadweight capacity 25 to 130 tons. (Typical.)
The hull is keel-built with bluff bow, rounded stem, transom stern, and outboard rudder. It is decked and has a poop with cabin. It is rigged with three masts. The fore and main are lug-rigged. The mizzen is a gaff sail with boom. The foremast is stepped just abaft the stem and the foresail is tacked down to a bumkin. There is a bowsprit with whiskers and one headsail.

LODKA. A Siberian rowing boat of the lower Yenisei, flat-bottomed with sharp ends and fair sheer. The larger boats are up to 20 ft. long. It is a clumsy craft constructed of roughly sawed planks, and wood fastened.

LOFTING.
See **Laying Off.**

LOFT PAPER. A very heavy paper especially made to lessen expansion or contraction due to atmospheric conditions and used by shipyards in the manufacture of templates for flat plating in the mold loft.

LOFT RIGGER. One who works in a rigging loft, and prepares standing and running rigging, and cargo gear to be fitted on board ship.

LOFTSMAN. A shipyard worker who lays down the ship's lines taken from plans supplied by the drawing office full size on the mold loft floor and makes full-size paper or wooden templates for various parts of the vessel's structure. A developer is a loftsman particularly skilled in work requiring development of curved plates. Also called linesman (U. S.), developer (U. S.).
Fr: *Traceur;* Ger: *Schnürbodenarbeiter.*

LOG. **1.** An apparatus for measuring the apparent rate of a ship's motion through the water.
Fr: *Loch;* Ger: *Log.*
See **Deck Log, Dutchman's Log, Electric Log, Ground Log, Hand Log, Harpoon Log, Pitometer Log, Screw Log, Submerged Screw Log, Taffrail Log.**
Measurement of Speed at Sea, Engineer (London), vol. 156, August 25, 1933.

2. A piece of wood after the bark has been removed and the sides squared.
Fr: *Bois Équarri;* Ger: *Log; Klotz.*
See **Bilge Log, Bottom Log, Shaft Log, Logbook, Sea Log.**

LOG (to). 1. To enter in the official logbook the name of a seaman with his offense and the penalty attached to it. Also to enter or record in the logbook any special event such as births, deaths and so on.

2. Said of a ship moving at a specified speed according to the indications given by the log.

LOG-BOARD. A slate in a folding frame on which was written at intervals during the day everything connected with the progress of the ship on her voyage, as well as any occurrences worthy of notice. (Obsolete.)
Fr: *Table de Loch;* Ger: *Wachttafel.*

LOGBOOK. A ship's journal or tabulated summary of the performance of the vessel, her engines and other daily events. The logbook is regarded as legal evidence on matters which the master is required by law to enter therein. In a collision suit the logbooks are admissible as evidence when called for and when a testimony is more intelligible by a reference to them. In order to establish a valid claim under a policy of marine insurance the evidence necessary to prove that some accident has overtaken the vessel is furnished by the logbook as well as by the master's protest. Also called **Log.**
See **Engine Room Logbook, Official Logbook, Scrap Logbook, Ship's Logbook.**

LOG CANOE. A double-ended sailing canoe from Chesapeake Bay, used for oyster tonging and fishing. The hull is constructed of a number of pine logs hollowed and shaped with adz and axe and bolted together. There are two varieties: (a) the *poquoson* or Virginia type with high bow and stern in which the hull is composed of a keel log, two garboard logs and a number of wing logs, the latter being naturally-curved logs which form the sides up to the gunwale. The *pocomoke* type in which the sides are built up of sawed lumber attached to the wing logs by ribs or frames like those of an ordinary boat. All have a centerboard 6 to 8 ft. long. A waterway about 15 in. wide extends the whole length on either side of a coaming 6 in. high. The rig consists of one or two masts with leg-of-mutton sails and a jib which tacks down to a short bowsprit. These canoes are good sea boats and fast under sail. Their length ranges from 25 to 35 ft. with a beam of 5½ to 9 ft. and a draft of 1 to 2 ft. Freeboard amidships 12 to 20 in. When used for fishing two wells were fitted abaft the centerboard trunk. Most of these boats have been replaced by planked deadrise boats. Brewington, M. V., *Chesapeake Bay Log Canoes*, Mariner's Museum, Newport News, Publication no. 3 (1937).

LOG CHIP. A thin flat piece of board in the form of a quadrant of a circle, attached to the end of a long line. Also called log ship. It is loaded with lead on the arc to make it float point up.
Fr: *Bateau de Loch;* Ger: *Logbrett; Logscheit.*

LOGGER. Name given in the Netherlands and Germany to a ketch-rigged fishing boat used for lining and drifting in the North Sea. Also called *Zeillogger*. The hull is built with keel, straight, vertical stem, elliptical counter stern. It is decked fore and aft. Length 72 to 95 ft. Breadth 16½ to 20 ft. Tonnage 70 to 200. Crew 10 to 14. The rig includes a running bowsprit with jib and foresail, a miter-cut boomless, gaff mainsail, and a mizzen staysail. Some boats have a fidded main topmast and carry a jackyard topsail, while in others there is a pole mainmast without topmast. The mizzenmast is a pole spar and carries a boomed mizzen and jackyard topsail.

LOGGERHEAD (U. S.). A projecting timber in the stern of a whaleboat around which the whale line was snubbed after the whale had been struck. Also called bollard (G. B.), billethead.

LOGGINGS. The deductions made from a seaman's wages at the end of the voyage for fines or forfeitures which have been duly entered in the official log book. The entries are signed by the master and the mate or one of the crew. They are read over to the seaman and any reply which he makes are also entered.
Ger: *Logbucheintragung.*

LOG GLASS. A sand glass used with a hand or chip log. With a log line divided into lengths of 47.33 feet a 28 seconds glass is used. A 30 seconds glass is used when the line is marked in 50.75 feet lengths.
Fr: *Ampoulette;* Ger: *Logglas.*

LOG GOVERNOR. A steadying device of the wheel or dumbbell type fitted to the line of a taffrail log. It prevents jerky action caused by the length of the line and gives steadiness to the revolutions of the spindle of the indicator.
Fr: *Régulateur de Loch;* Ger: *Log Regulator.*

LOG INDICATOR. The registering mechanism of a taffrail log by which the revolutions of the rotator are recorded and converted into miles and fractions of miles. Also called log register. It consists essentially of a case containing the clockwork and a tube enclosing the spindle and the ball bearings, which take the pull of the line. The forward end of the case is fitted with three dials which record respectively fractions, units, and tens of miles up to one hundred. The whole mechanism is secured to the taffrail by a socket provided with a half gimbal to receive the strain in direct line.

LOG LINE. Line made of hemp for a chip log and of braided cotton twine (¼-in. diameter) for patent screw logs. The length of a chip-log line is 150 fathoms. For patent logs it varies according to the speed of the vessel. On fast craft longer lines are needed. The first 15 or 30 fathoms of the chip-log line, called "stray line" is marked by a piece of red bunting. The line from this point is divided into parts of 47 ft. 3 in. each, called knots. They are marked by pieces of cord tucked through the strands with knots in their next corresponding point. Each knot is subdivided into fifths and marked with a white rag. The line is allowed to run out while a 28-second glass is emptying itself. The result is the rate of speed of the vessel as 47.3 bears the same proportion to 6075.7 (The feet contained in a mean nautical mile) than 28 to 3500: (the seconds contained in an hour.) Patent log lines made of plaited stuff are known by the number of threads used in their manufacture. They are generally sold in 60 fathom coils. Weight 5 ozs. per ft.

Fr: *Ligne de Loch;* Ger: *Logleine.*

LOG RAFT. A cigar-shaped raft of large dimensions used for conveying round timber by sea from place of origin to market. Before assembling the logs, a floating cradle composed of inverted bends spaced about twelve feet apart is constructed and used as a guide or holder in forming the raft. When the cradle has been launched the logs are brought alongside and placed inside the cradle by derrick scows. Heavy chains encircle the body of the raft and hold it together. Log rafts of 400 to 700 ft. length are towed down the Pacific coast for distances of 500 or 600 miles.

Bishop, E. K., Sea-going Rafts on the Pacific, Factory and Industrial Management, vol. 16, no. 1, October (1898); Springer, J. F., Ocean going Log Rafts, Scientific American, vol. 111, no. 20, November 14, 1914.

LOG RAIL. A low rail found on wooden coasters and other small craft. It is made of a strip of wood narrower on top than at the deck and is usually fitted with a capping piece.

LOG REEL. A small wooden reel around which the log line of a ship log is wound.

Fr: *Moulinet de Loch;* Ger: *Logrolle.*

LOG SLATE. A double slate marked and ruled on its inner side like a log book. The daily entries are copied from the slate into the log book.

Fr: *Renard;* Ger: *Logtafel.*

LOI. An East Indian dugout canoe with outriggers from the east coast of Wetar Island (Lesser Sunda Islands) and similar to the *bero.*

LOLL. A ship is said to loll when it is unstable in the upright position due to negative metacentric height, but acquires positive stability at some angle of heel. This can be brought about by excessive free surface, or insufficient ballast in a ship in light condition.

See **Crank, Metacentric Height.**

LOMME. Trading boat originating from Tolkemitt (East Prussia) and specially adapted for navigation in the Kurische and Frische Haffs. The hull is very beamy with full lines. The ratio of length to breadth varies from 3 to 3½ to 1. The framing is of oak with clinker-built planking. Composite construction is occasionally resorted to with steel knees and frames. There is no keel or keelson: the center bottom plank is given 2 to 3 in. extra thickness. The rig varies according to the size of the boats. The smaller units, about 52 ft. in length, are cutter-rigged, and those from 60 to 75 ft. are ketch-rigged with two headsails. A small square topsail is occasionally set on the larger boats. All use pole masts. Large and heavy leeboards are carried.

Although the *Lomme* is chiefly built for trading in the comparatively smooth waters of the West Prussian *Haffs,* the larger units are employed in the small coasting trade along the Pomeranian shores, and others trade as far as the Islands of Bornholm and Gotland, which tends to show that they are comparatively seaworthy. Smaller boats of this type used for fishing and called *Flunder-Lomme, Strand-Lomme* or *Breitlingslomme* are also found in this district. Length 20.6 ft. Breadth 6.5 ft. (Average.)

LONDEH. East Indian outrigger canoe from Sangi and Talaur Islands (North East Celebes). Rigged with one mast and used in the hook-and-line fisheries. Also called liendi.

See **Dondei.**

LONDO.

See **Dondei.**

LONDON CLAUSE. A bill of lading clause in common use which entitles the shipowners to land goods on the quay or to discharge them into craft hired by them immediately on arrival, at the consignee's risk and expense.

LONDON SALVAGE ASSOCIATION. A non-profit, self-supporting British organization established in 1857, with headquarters in London, whose principle function is the protection of commercial interests as regards wrecked and damaged maritime property. The Association owns salvage vessels and equipment, employs special surveyors and has agents all over the world. Its surveyors attend personally at the scene of the casualty and remain on the spot as long as their assistance is required. Their work is not confined to salvage only, but extends to the supervision of damage repairs and dealing with damaged cargo, as well as other matters directly connected with the casualty.

LONG ARM FLOOR TIMBER. In wooden shipbuilding an expression used in connection with a type of framing in which both floor timbers are of the same length, each being molded with a short arm on one side of the center line and a long arm on the other. The short arm of one floor extends on the same side of the center line as the long arm of the other floor, the long arm thus furnishing a lap for the attachment of the first futtock. In this type of frame the first futtock on one side is in the same tier as the second futtock on the other side.

Fr: *Varangue à Branche Longue;* Ger: *Langarmige Bodenwrange.*

LONG BEND CALKING TOOL. A metal calking tool with smooth or carding face, used only in places where it is inconvenient to use the smoothing tool or rough tool. It is called "short bend" or "long bend" calking tool according to the angle formed by the end.

LONG BLAST.
See **Prolonged Blast.**

LONG BOAT. The largest boat formerly carried by merchant sailing vessels. It was equipped with mast, sails and oars and could be used for transporting stores, water, and so on, and in open roadsteads was frequently employed for conveying cargo between ship and shore. Length 20 to 40 ft. Breadth 0.35 to 0.37 of length. Depth 0.38 to 0.40 of breadth. Rise of floors amidships 5 to 8°. Square stern. (Obsolete.)

Fr: *Grand Canot; Chaloupe;* Ger: *Gross-Boot.*

LONG BRIDGE, LONG BRIDGE HOUSE. A bridge house which has a length exceeding 15 per cent of the ship's length. Long bridge houses have the sheer strake and strengthenings raised from the upper deck to the bridge deck, which greatly increases the structural value of these erections.

Fr: *Château Long;* Ger: *Langes Brückenhaus.*

LONG BRIDGE VESSEL. Applies to a vessel in which the length of hull has been increased at the expense of the depth, and which has a full height continuous superstructure covering at least 70% of the length amidships.

Ger: *Lange Brücke Schiff.*

LONG DISTANCE SIGNAL. One of a system of visual signals used when, owing to the distance or state of the atmosphere, the colors of flags could not be distinguished. There were three systems of distant signals in the international code. They involved respectively the use of (1) cones, balls, and drums; (2) balls, square flags, pennants, and whefts; (3) a fixed semaphore. The code signals in all these systems denote things or meanings rather than words. These signals were abolished in 1934.

Fr: *Signal à Grande Distance;* Ger: *Fernsignal.*

LONG-END LINK.
See **Long-Stud Link.**

LONGER. A term used by stevedores to denote a row of barrels or casks stowed fore and aft, and end to end.

LONG FAKE.
See **French Fake.**

LONG FLASHING LIGHT. A coastal light which exhibits a single long flash at equal intervals, and whose duration of light is comparatively long, although shorter than the duration of darkness.

Fr: *Feu à éclats longs;* Ger: *Fener mit langen Blitzen.*

LONG FORECASTLE. Forecastle with a length greater than 20 per cent of the vessel's length.

Fr: *Gaillard Long;* Ger: *Langes Back.*

LONG-HAUL SEINE. A type of shore seine in which the net is comparatively short and is shot a good way out to sea. Two very long ropes are attached to it for hauling. One of these is held ashore and a boat carries out the net, swims it into position, and then brings the end of the other warp to the shore where both warps are then hauled upon so that the fish in a direct line between the net and the shore are caught. The principle of this net is therefore not unlike that of the trawl net.

LONG-HAUL SEINING. A method of fishing in which a seine is dragged between two power boats for a certain distance and then landed by hand in shallow water.

LONG HUNDRED (G. B.). A unit of measurement commonly used by fish tradesmen in Great Britain. It is equal to 132 fresh herrings or 120 mackerel.

LONG ISLAND SCALLOP BOAT. A shallow-draft sailing craft developed in Great South Bay for gathering scallops in the adjoining areas where dredging with power-driven boats is forbidden by law. The length varies from 18 to 45 ft., with a draft of 2 to 3 ft. and a freeboard of about 12 in. amidships. The boats are cat- or sloop-rigged and fitted with a centerboard. The number of scallop dredges employed ranges from 6 for the smaller craft to 35 for the largest. They are tied to deck rings on the weather side. Most of the boats are provided with a cabin aft.

LONGITUDE. The longitude of a place is the distance east or west measured in degrees, minutes and seconds of arc on the equator between the prime meridian and the meridian passing through the place. Celestial longitude is measured on the ecliptic eastward from the vernal equinox.
Fr: *Longitude;* Ger: *Länge.*
See **Difference of Longitude.**

LONGITUDE BY CHRONOMETER. The longitude measured by the difference between mean time at the first meridian as given by the ship's chronometer and ship's mean time.
Fr: *Longitude par différence d'heure;* Ger: *Chronometerlange.*

LONGITUDE BY DEAD RECKONING. The longitude deduced from the course and distance sailed since the last observation. Also called longitude by account.
Fr: *Longitude par l'Estime;* Ger: *Loggelänge.*

LONGITUDE IN ARC. The angle at the pole between the first meridian and the meridian of the observer.
Ger: *Geographische Länge.*

LONGITUDE IN TIME. The difference between the mean time at the first meridian and the mean time at the place of observation.

LONGITUDE LEFT. The longitude from which the ship has departed.
Fr: *Longitude de départ;* Ger: *Verlassene Länge.*

LONGITUDE SCALE. Unit chosen to represent one degree of longitude of a particular part of the globe shown on a chart.
Fr: *Echelle des longitudes;* Ger: *Langenskala.*

LONGITUDINAL. One of the girders fitted on each side between center girder and margin plate in a double bottom. Also called side girder. Longitudinals are usually continuous between solid floors.
Fr: *Support Latéral;* Ger: *Seitenträger.*
See **Deck Longitudinal; Shell Longitudinal.**

LONGITUDINAL CENTER OF BUOYANCY. The location of the center of buoyancy on the middle longitudinal center plane.

LONGITUDINAL CENTER OF GRAVITY. The location of the center of gravity measured on the middle longitudinal center plane.

LONGITUDINAL COEFFICIENT. The ratio of the volume of displacement, up to a given waterline, to the product of its length and immersed area of midship section. Also called cylindrical coefficient, prismatic coefficient. It is equal to the block coefficient divided by the midship section coefficient. Its value is computed as follows:

$$\frac{\text{Volume of displacement (cu. ft.)}}{\text{Waterline length} \times \text{area of midship section (sq. ft.)}}$$

Typical values are:
Passenger vessels .... 0.60 to 0.70
Cargo carriers and tankers..... 0.70 to 0.80
Yachts .... 0.55 to 0.65
Fr: *Coefficient Cylindrique Longitudinal;* Ger: *Völligkeitsgrad der Spantflächenskala; Zylinderkoeffizient.*

LONGITUDINAL FACTOR. The change in longitude from a given point in a Sumner line, brought about by the change of one minute in Latitude.
See **Sumner Line.**

LONGITUDINAL METACENTER. The metacenter corresponding to a longitudinal inclination of a vessel.
Fr: *Métacentre Longitudinal;* Ger: *Längen-Metazentrum.*

LONGITUDINAL METACENTRIC HEIGHT. Height of longitudinal metacenter above center of gravity.
Fr: *Hauteur Métacentrique Longitudinale;* Ger: *Lange metazentrische Höhe.*

LONGITUDINAL MODULUS. Numerical quantity used in ship calculations to express the longitudinal measure of strength of the hull considered as a girder. It is equal to the moment of inertia of the midship section about the neutral axis divided by the distance measured from the neutral axis to the top of the strength deck beam at side calculated in the way of openings.

LONGITUDINAL NUMBER. The numeral under which are tabulated the scantlings of all longitudinal parts such as shell and deck plating, keel keelsons, girders, stringers, and so on. Also called longitudinal numeral.

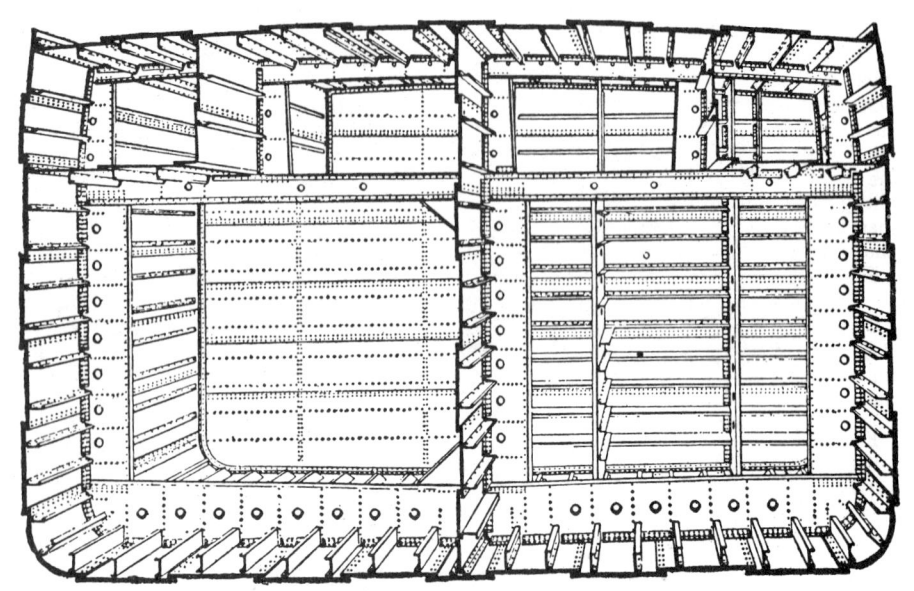

Longitudinal Framing

Fr: *Nombre Longitudinal;* Ger: *Längsnummer.*

LONGITUDINAL STRENGTH. That quality which prevents a ship from breaking in two when in a seaway exposed to hogging and sagging stresses. Longitudinal strength is provided by the hull or ship girder.
See Hull Girder, Hog, Sag.

LONG-JAWED. A seaman's expression to denote a rope in which the twist has come out and the angle of the strand is long.

LONG-LEGGED. Colloquial expression denoting a vessel with deep draft, or, with regard to naval vessels, one with a large cruising radius.

LONG LINES. Fishing gear used in long-lining, which consists of a ground line, back line, or main line into which are spliced smaller short lines called snoods, gangers, or gangings. The snoods are fastened to the main line at intervals which vary according to type of gear. A strong hook is bent to each of them. Each set of lines coiled in a wooden tub is shot from a boat or dory. When set it is anchored and buoyed at each end. Long lines vary with the kind of fish to be captured but are all built on the same plan. They are used for cod, ling, halibut, haddock, and so on. The number of hooks may vary from 20 to 6,000. Also called boulter, trawl lines, set lines, trot lines.

Fr: *Cordes; Lignes de Fond; Harouelles;* Ger: *Grundleinen; Langleinen.*

LONG-LINING. Fishing with long lines or trawl lines. Also called trawl-lining.

LONG LIZARD. A pendant with thimble for carrying the lower (studding sail) boom topping lift out to the fore yardarm. (Obsolete.)

LONG ROLLING SPLICE. A splice chiefly used in lead lines, log lines, and fishing lines where the short splice would be liable to separation through being frequently loosened by water.

Fr: *Épissure de Ligne de Pêche.*

LONG ROVE. The long end of a rope sling which receives the hook.

LONG SEA. A uniform motion of long waves, resulting from a steady continuance of the wind from the same quarter.

Fr: *Mer Longue;* Ger: *Lange Dünung.*

LONGSHOREMAN (U. S.). A man who works at loading or discharging vessels either aboard ship or on the wharf or quay. Longshore laborers may be divided into two sections: those who work on the ship, or stevedores; and those who belong to the shore gang or dock workers. In a generic sense the term "longshoremen" usually refers to the laborers who do the actual physical work, whereas the "stevedore" is the contractor or boss who employs longshoremen.

LONG SPLICE. A splice in which a long piece is unraveled on each rope and the joint made fine so that it does not increase the diameter of the rope appreciably, permitting the splice to run smoothly over a sheave. It is weaker than the short splice and requires more rope.

Fr: *Epissure Longue;* Ger: *Längssplissung.*

LONG STAY. To heave in to a "long stay": said when the anchor is some distance ahead and the cable forms a small angle with the bottom.

Fr: *Ä Long Pic.*
See **Short Stay.**

LONG STROKE. An order to a boat's crew to row with a greater length of stroke, and more outlay of strength.

Fr: *Allongez!;* Ger: *Hol Aus!*

LONG STUD LINK. In an anchor cable: a studded link with parallel sides inserted between a joining shackle and an enlarged link. Relative dimensions of long stud link and common link in a 2 in. cable:

	Diameter	Length	Extreme Width
Common link	2.0 in.	12 to 12.3 in.	7.2 in.
Long stud link	2.4 in.	15.0 in.	8.0 in.

Fr: *Grande Maille;* Ger: *Grosses Glied.*

LONG TACKLE. A tackle composed of two fiddle blocks and fall. Formerly used in hoisting a topsail from the deck to its yard preparatory to bending the sail.

Ger: *Segeltakel.*

LONG TACKLE BLOCK. An elongated shell with two sheaves, the larger one on top, with fall leading the same way. Also called fiddle block.

Fr: *Poulie à Violon;* Ger: *Violinblock.*

LONG TIMBER. One of the frame timbers in the cant bodies, which reaches from the deadwood to the head of the second futtock.

LONG TON. A unit of weight of 2,240 pounds, or 1,016 kilos. Also called English ton, or just ton.

LONG TOPGALLANT MAST. A topgallant mast, royal mast, and skysail mast forming one single spar. Also called pole topgallant mast.

LONG TOW. Tow of the first hackling.

LONTRO. Italian rowboat used in the harpoon sword-fishery in Sicily and Calabria, about 18 ft. long and 4 ft. deep, broader at the stern than at the bow. There is a mast or pole about 17 ft. high surmounted by a curved brace, to support the scunner.

LOOD. Fishing boat of Arab origin found on the coast of Tunisia and used in sponge fisheries around the Kerkenna Islands and in the Sfax district. Also called *loud.* The hull is built with flat bottom amidships and small lengths of keel at each end. It has fine entrance and run. A deck runs from stem to mainmast. The rig consists of a lug mainsail with 6 to 8 rows of reef points and leg-of-mutton or lateen foresail which sets on a very short mast stepped in the bows. The mainmast has a pronounced rake aft. Length 37 ft. Breadth 8.5 ft. Inside depth 2.9 ft. Draft 1.6 ft. Tonnage 3 to 4. (Average.)

LOOF. That part of a vessel where the sides begin to converge towards the stem. The rounded part of a vessel's bow. Also called luff of the bows. (Rare.)

Fr: *Épaule;* Ger: *Backe.*

LOOK-ON NET. A net attached by sailing drifters to the weather quarter. This net is frequently hauled in to see if the fish is striking the fleet. Sometimes called tave (G. B.).

LOOKOUT. A member of the crew stationed on the forecastle or in the crow's nest, whose duty it is to watch for any dangerous object lying near the ship's track, for any other vessel heaving in sight, and so on. Also called lookout man.

Fr: *Homme de Bossoir; Vigie;* Ger: *Ausguckmann.*

By the general maritime law every vessel navigating the thoroughfares of commerce is required to have a lookout. He must be a person of suitable experience, properly stationed and vigilantly employed, especially at night.

LOOKOUT TELEGRAPH. Transmitting apparatus or instruments whereby a lookout man stationed forward can signal to the bridge the position of a light or vessel ahead or on the port or starboard bow.

Fr: *Transmetteur d'Ordres de la Vigie;* Ger: *Ausgucktelegraph.*

LOOK UP. Said of a ship sailing close-hauled when, by the shifting of the wind it is able to steer a course closer to the point of destination.

LOOM. 1. The part of an oar which extends from the blade to the handle.

According to some, the term "loom" applies only to that part which is inside the boat when rowing. The loom is round shaped for the greater part of its length, but slightly elliptical toward the blade.

Fr: *Bras;* Manche; Ger: *Riemenschaft; Ruderschaft.*

2. The glow of a light, usually a powerful one, which is visible over the horizon before the light itself comes into view.

See **Looming.**

LOOMING. A phenomenon due to refraction, by which images of objects which are below the horizon may be observed.

Fr: *Reflet; Lueur;* Ger: *Luftspiegelung.*

LOOP. The bight of a small rope.

Fr: *Boucle;* Ger: *Öse.*

LOOP ANTENNA. Antenna consisting of one or more complete turns of wire on a frame. Used in direction finding apparatus.

Fr: *Cadre;* Ger: *Rahmenantenne.*

LOOSE. To let go: to cast the gaskets or strops from a furled sail. Also called unfurl.

Fr: *Déferler;* Ger: *Losmachen.*

LOOSE-FOOTED. An expression used for denoting a fore-and-aft sail in which the foot is not laced to the boom.

Fr: *A Bordure Libre;* Ger: *Mit losem Fuss.*

LOOSE ICE. See **Open Pack.**

LOOSE SAILS. To unfurl the sails and let them hang loose in readiness for making sail.

Fr: *Déferler les voiles;* Ger: *Segel losmachen.*

LOOSE WATER. Any water within a vessel which has a free surface, such as water in engine-room bilges, partly filled ballast tanks, etc.

See **Free Surface.**

LOP. State of the sea characterized by short choppy waves. It is generally due to a wind blowing in a direction contrary to that of the current or to a sudden change of wind after a regular sea has been set up.

Fr: *Clapotis;* Ger: *Kabbelung.*

LOPI. An East India outrigger canoe from Sumbawa (Sunda Islands).

LOPSIDE. A term used for describing a vessel which when light will not float upright because her sides are unsymmetrical on account of defective construction.

Fr: *Faux-Bord;* Ger: *Schlagseite.*

LORAC. A radio location system operating on long or medium wavelengths and used in long distance offshore surveying operations. It consists essentially of four radio-transmitters.

LORAN. A system of radio navigation developed during World War II by joint effort of the U. S. Navy, Coast Guard, Army Air Forces, and Office of Scientific Research and Development. It takes its name from long range aid to navigation. High frequency radio signals emitted simultaneously by two loran transmitter stations ashore, separated by about 400 miles, are received aboard ship in a loran receiver, which determines accurately the difference in time at which the two signals are received. Curves printed on a navigation chart show loran lines of position for various time differences. These are hyperbolas sweeping about the loran transmitting stations. Inasmuch as ship and aircraft lanes are blanketed by loran signals from several transmitters, the navigator using the loran receiver can determine several lines of position. Their intersection gives him the "fix," or location of the vessel.

There are now installed more than 70 loran transmitter stations, covering approximately three tenths of the earth's surface. In the daytime, loran signals are reliable up to ranges of 700 miles; at night, up to 1,400 miles. Only the most severe electrical storms will produce sufficient static to render loran unusable.

LORCHA. A sailing junk found around Bangkok, used chiefly for carrying rice over the river bars to seagoing vessels loading in the roadsteads. Also called *bai-ao-shiao*. The hull, built of teak and camphor wood, is modeled on western lines with forecastle and poop, straight stem and transom stern. The rig includes three masts with Chinese lugsails. A bowsprit is fitted. The largest have a deadweight capacity of about 200 tons. The *Lorcha's* hull is usually painted red, with bright yellow poop and forecastle.

LOSING RATE. The daily variation of a chronometer which is running too slow.

Fr: *Retard Diurne;* Ger: *Tägliches Verlier.*

LOSS. A vessel lost is one that is totally gone from the owners so that they know nothing concerning her, whether still existing or lost by unknown foundering, sinking by storm, collision, total destruction or shipwreck.

Fr: *Perte;* Ger: *Verlust.*

See **Actual Total Loss, Constructive Total Loss, General Average Loss, Presumed Total Loss, Salvage Loss, Total Loss.**

LOST OR NOT LOST. A term used in marine insurance policies to signify that the contract is retrospective and applicable to any loss within the particular risk insured, provided that the loss is not already known to either of the parties and that neither of them has any knowledge or information not equally known or obvious to the other.

Fr: *Perdu ou Non Perdu.*

LOST OR NOT LOST CLAUSE. 1. A marine insurance policy clause which entitles the insured to claim for loss or damage which occurred before the policy was taken out, provided that neither party was aware of the loss or damage when the policy was drawn up.

2. A bill of lading clause which states that freight is due to the carrier even if the goods are lost on the voyage.

LOTKIO.
See **Gal.**

LOUGH FOYLE YAWL. An Irish sailing and rowing open boat from Northern Ireland used for inshore fishing. It is sharp-sterned and rigged with two spritsails and a jib. Also called skerries yawl. Length (keel) 24 ft. Breadth 6 ft.

LOUGRE. A three-masted lug-rigged boat formerly used in the small coasting trade and fisheries of northern France. Also called *chasse-marée*. The hull had a straight vertical stem. The vertical, transom stern, without counter was customary in fishing boats, while the square or elliptical stern was seen in earlier trading craft. The larger boats, which measured from 50 to 100 tons, were fully decked. The smaller fishing boats were frequently decked at ends only. The rig, similar to that of the *bisquine* from Normandy, consisted of three masts and a short bowsprit. Fishing *lougre* from Fecamp: Length over-all 82 ft. Keel 75.1 ft. Breadth 21 ft. Depth 10.1 ft. Sail area 3,950 sq. ft. Fishing *lougre* from Gravelines: Length over-all 45.2 ft. Breadth 13.6 ft. Depth 9.3 ft.

The foremast was stepped close to the stem and the mizzen right aft next to the sternpost with an outrigger for sheeting the sail. The coasting *chasse-marée* carried topsails on all masts. Fishing boats, especially those from the French Channel ports had very short main- and mizzenmasts and carried a main topsail only. The mainmast was stepped in a tabernacle.

Paris, F. E., *Souvenirs de marine*, vol. 1, Plates 3 and 7, Paris.

LOUVER. A term applied to a series of small openings to permit the passage of air for ventilating purposes. The openings are regulated as to size by means of overlapping shutters. Louvers may be installed in ventilation terminals, ship's machinery, or in joiner bulkheads according to their purpose.

LOW. A meteorological term used to denote a cyclonic depression.

Fr: *Dépression;* Ger: *Depression.*

LOW BUNT. A term describing a sail furled on its yard when the bunt of the sail tapers gradually from the center. Also called rolling bunt.

LOWER. To bring down. To let down gradually. To ease away a rope or tackle to which a weight is attached.

Fr: *Amener;* Ger: *Fieren; Niederlassen.*

LOWER BERTH. The lower of two superposed berths in a cabin or other compartment.

Fr: *Couchette Inférieure;* Ger: *Unterkoje.*

LOWER DECK. The lowest deck in two and three deck vessels, and next to the lowest in vessels having four or more decks.

Fr: *Pont Inférieur;* Ger: *Unterdeck.*

LOWER HIGH WATER. The lowest high water in ports where there are two tides in the same day.

Fr: *Pleine mer inférieure;* Ger: *Niedrigeres Hochwasser.*

LOWER HOLD. The interior of a ship below the lowest deck as distinguished from the 'tween-deck spaces.

Fr: *Cale;* Ger: *Unterraum.*

LOWERING MAST.
See **Collapsible Mast.**

LOWERING SPEED. A term relating to hoisting machinery. The speed in feet per second at which a sling is lowered into the ship's hold or alongside the vessel by a winch.

Fr: *Vitesse d'amenée;* Ger: *Senkgeschwindigkeit.*

LOWER KEEL. A piece of timber occasionally worked between the main and false keels on wooden vessels.

LOWER LIMB. In astronomy, the line tangent to the lower edge of the visible

disc of the sun or moon.
Fr: *Limbe inférieur;* Ger: *Unterrand.*

LOWER LOW WATER. The lower of the two low waters of any tidal day. The mean value of the lower low waters over a considerable period of time is used as the plane of reference (chart datum) for hydrographic work on the Pacific Coast of the United States.
Fr: *Basse Mer Inférieure;* Ger: *Niedrigeres Niedrigwasser.*

LOWER MAST. A term applied to the lowest part of a compound mast composed of two or more poles. Lower masts rest on a step placed as low as possible, usually on the keelson in sailing craft.
Fr: *Bas Mât;* Ger: *Untermast.*

LOWER SHROUDS. The shrouds which extend from the lower masthead down to the deadeyes or rigging screws. Also called lower rigging.
Fr: *Haubans de Bas Mât;* Ger: *Unterwanten.*

LOWER STACK. The lower part of a smokestack, below deck, which connects the funnel proper to the boiler uptakes. Also called lower funnel. It is generally subdivided vertically into as many parts as there are boilers to allow each boiler to be operated individually without diminution of draft.

LOWER THWART. A thwart fitted near the bottom of a lifeboat for the purpose of seating passengers.

LOWER TOPSAIL. The square sail which sets immediately above the courses in a ship with double topsails.
Fr: *Hunier Fixe;* Ger: *Untermarssegel.*

LOWER TRANSIT. Meridian passage of celestial body below the pole.
Fr: *Passage méridien inférieur;* Ger: *Unteren Meridian Durchgang.*

LOWEST LOW WATER. A plane of reference whose depression below mean sea level corresponds with the level of the lowest low water of any tide normally occurring. It is used on French, Greek, and Spanish charts.
Fr: *Niveau des plus grandes basses mers;* Ger: *Niedrigster beobachteter Wasserstand.*

LOWEST LOW WATER SPRINGS. A plane of reference approximating the level of the lowest low water at spring tides. It is used on the nautical charts of Portugal. The plane, in this area, is about one foot below the level of mean low water springs.

Fr: *Niveau des plus basses mers de vive eau;* Ger: *Niedrigstes Springniedrigwasser.*

LOWEST PASSENGER DECK (U. S.). The deck next below the waterline. No passenger can be carried below this deck according to United States Navigation laws.

LOW TIDE. See **Low Water.**

LOW WATER. The periodic low level of water after a periodic high water level due to tidal action. The minimum height reached by a falling tide.
Fr: *Basse Mer;* Ger: *Niedrigwasser.*

LOW WATER DATUM. An approximation to the plane of mean low water that has been adopted as a standard reference plane.
Fr: *Niveau de référence de basse mer;* Ger: *Niedrigwasser Gezeitennull.*

LOW WATER INDIAN SPRING. An arbitrary plane of reference approximating the level of low water of ordinary spring tides, but where there is a large diurnal inequality in the low waters of spring tides it falls considerably below the true mean of such tides. It was first used in a survey of the Indian Ocean, whence the name. Used as reference plane on Indian and Japanese charts.

LOW WATER MARK. The margin of the sea when the tide is out.
Fr: *Niveau de la basse mer;* Ger: *Niedrigwassermarke.*

LOW WATER STAND. The interval of time at low water during which the level of the water does not noticeably vary.
Fr: *Etale de Basse Mer;* Ger: *Stillstand des Niedrigwassers.*

LOXODROME. See **Rhumb Line.**

LOXODROMIC CURVE. See **Curve.**

LOXODROMIC LINE.
See **Rhumb Line.**

LOZZU. Mediterranean double-ended rowboat employed in the coastal fisheries off the Island of Malta. It is built with high projecting stem and sternpost, as other native craft of this particular area.

LUAMPO. Name given by the Galibi Indians of Guiana to the *corial.*

LUBBER LINE. A vertical black line drawn on the forward inner side of the compass bowl. The point of the compass which is directly against the line indicates the direction of the ship's head and the course steered. Four lubber lines are usually marked on the compass bowl: two in the

longitudinal plane of the ship and the other two in the transverse direction.
Fr: *Ligne de Foi;* Ger: *Steuerstrich.*

LUBBER'S HOLE. A hole in the floor of a top next the mast through which one may go farther aloft without going over the rim by the futtock shrouds.
Fr: *Trou de Chat;* Ger: *Soldatengat.*

LUBBER'S KNOT. A knot made by mistake when trying to make a reef knot. It slips, and therefore, should never be used on board ship. Also called **granny's knot.**

LUBEC BOAT. See **Quoddy Boat.**

LUCKY BAG. A compartment or locker in which loose articles of clothing found about the ship are stowed.

LUDERS LINES. Term used in metallurgy to denote two systems of lines at right angles to each other which appear on the surface of a steel plate and which indicate that the plate has been stressed beyond the yield point and that the metal has begun to fail under excessive shearing action.

LUFF. 1. The forward side of a jib-headed fore-and-aft sail. The side next to the stay.
Fr: *Lof; Envergure; Tétière;* Ger: *Stagkant; Vorliek.*

2. Forward side of a quadrilateral fore-and-aft sail. It is often called fore leech or mast leech.
Fr: *Lof; Chute Avant; Chute au Mât;* Ger: *Luvliek; Vorliek.*

3. See **Loof.**

4. See **Luff Tackle, Rigging Luff.**

LUFF (to). To bring a vessel's head nearer to the wind by putting the helm down or increasing the sail area toward the stern.
Fr: *Loffer;* Ger: *Luven.*

LUFF CRINGLE. The loop spliced into the boltrope of a gaff, lug, or spritsail at the junction of the head and luff. Jib-headed sails have but three cringles: head, tack, and clew.
Fr: *Patte de Ralingue de Mât;* Ger: *Klaulagel.*

LUFF EARING. A short line used with fore-and-aft sails to secure the reef cringle on the luff to the foot of the sail or to the boom, in reefing.

LUFFING. The vertical movement of the load or draft by a ship's crane or derrick.

LUFFING MATCH. A struggle for a weather berth between sailing craft during a race.

LUFF ROPE. The hemp or wire rope to which the luff of fore-and-aft sail is sewed. This rope is always sewed on the port side of the sail.
Fr: *Ralingue d'Envergure;* Ger: *Luvliek.*

LUFF TACKLE. A tackle not destined for any particular part of the vessel but used where needed, consisting of a double and a single block each with hook, the standing part being fastened to the single block. The power gained is three or four to one, depending upon whether the upper or the lower block is the moving block. Also called luff purchase.
Fr: *Palan à Croc;* Ger: *Arbeitstalje.*

LUFF UPON LUFF. A purchase consisting of one luff tackle applied to the fall of another. Also called double-rigging luff, stay luff.

LUG FORESAIL. A gaff sail without boom which takes the place of the regular working foresail on a two-masted schooner. It is cut long on the foot and sheets well abaft the mainmast. It is sometimes bent to the foreboom as far as the spar goes.

LUGGER. A small boat used for coasting or fishing, carrying two or three masts with a lugsail on each, and occasionally a topsail. On the bowsprit, which is often of the running type, are set two or three jibs. The rigging is light and simple and the form of the sails enables a lugger to beat close up to the wind. Among English boats the lugrig rarely extends beyond the larger class of fishing boats. On the French coasts they were also employed in the small coasting trade.
Fr: *Lougre;* Ger: *Lugger.*

See **Logger, New Orleans Lugger, Pearl Lugger.**

Luff Tackle

LUGGER TOPSAIL. A fore-and-aft topsail set above a lugsail.

LUG MAINSAIL. The fore-and-aft mainsail of a lug-rigged boat.
  Fr: *Grande Voile de Lougre;* Ger: *Lugger Grossegel.*

LUG PAD. See **Eyeplate.**

LUG PIECE. See **Clip.**

LUGSAIL. A sail of quadrilateral shape with head shorter than foot and luff shorter than leech. It is bent to a yard which hangs more or less obliquely on the mast. It is a good sail for small boats as it gives a large spread of canvas with low center of effort. Also called lug.
  Fr: *Voile au Tiers; Voile à Bourcet; Voile de Lougre;* Ger: *Luggersegel.*

LUGSAIL RIG. A small boat rig, nowadays almost confined to fishing and pleasure craft except in the Mediterranean where this rig is still used by coasters up to 100 ft. long. It consists of quadrilateral sails bent to yards kept in an oblique position, with halyards fastened at a distance which varies from a third to a quarter of the length of yard measured from the forward end according to the type of lug, standing or dipping. Also called lug rig.
  Fr: *Gréement de Lougre;* Ger: *Luggersegel Takelung.*

In the standing lug it does not necessarily follow that the sling is placed at a ¼ length of the yard. This distance varies according to the peak or height of peak required, but the tack of the lug is always brought down close to the foot of the mast so that the greater length of the luff is on the forward side of the mast. The lug rig has seldom found favor for yachting purposes and becomes inefficient in boats exceeding 50 ft. over-all length.

LUHE-JOLLE. A small decked trading boat from the lower Elbe with large beam and rounded bows and stern, cutter-rigged with pole mast and two headsails. Length 29 to 41 ft. Breadth 10.9 to 14 ft. Depth of hold 3.5 to 5 ft. Gross tonnage 7 to 17. (Average.)

LULL. The brief interval of moderate weather between gusts of wind in a gale. An abatement in the violence of the surf.
  Fr: *Accalmie; Embellie;* Ger: *Stille; Ruhepause.*

LUMBER. A term used in the United States for sawed or split timber ready for use, such as beams, joists, boards, planks, staves, hoops, and the like.
  Fr: *Bois de Construction;* Ger: *Gesägtes Nutzholz; Bauholz; Schnittholz.*

LUMBER PORT. An opening just below the hawsepipe used as a cargo port for loading or discharging long pieces of timber.

LUMINOUS BUOY. A life-buoy to which is attached a self-igniting water light. Also called night life buoy.
  Fr: *Bouée de Sauvetage Lumineuse;* Ger: *Nachtrettungsboje; Nachtrettungsring.*
  See **Life-Buoy Light.**

LUMINOUS RANGE. The distance at which a light is visible in a straight line as distinguished from the geographic range where the earth's curvature and height of observers' eye are taken into consideration.
  Fr: *Portée Lumineuse;* Ger: *Sichtweitegrenze.*

LUMPER. 1. A man employed to unload goods from a vessel. This term is applied at the port of London to the men who receive softwood from ship and pile them on the quay. In the United States it is used to denote any laborer employed for the purpose of loading or discharging ship's cargo.
  2. An unskilled laborer about a shipyard.
  Fr: *Débardeur;* Ger: *Schauermann; Hafenarbeiter.*

LUMP FREIGHT. A gross sum stipulated to be paid for the use of the entire ship or a portion thereof.
  Fr: *Fret Forfaitaire;* Ger: *Pauschalfracht.*

LUMP SUM CHARTER. A method of chartering by which a lump sum, as distinct from a rate per ton of cargo, or per month, is paid by charterers to owners. It is principally used when a vessel is chartered to load "on the berth," that is, where a vessel is chartered in anticipation of loading it with a general cargo by advertising the intended voyage. In lump sum charters the charterers usually pay either cost of loading and discharging or limit the cost to owners to an agreed sum per ton, whatever the actual cost may be.
  Fr: *Affrètement à Forfait; Affrètement en Travers;* Ger: *Pauschalcharter.*

LUNAR CYCLE. A period of approximately 19 years after the lapse of which the new and full moon returns to the same day of the year.
  Fr: *Cycle Lunaire;* Ger: *Mondzyklus.*

LUNAR DAY. The interval of the time between the moon's departure from, and return to, the same meridian.
  Fr: *Jour Lunaire;* Ger: *Mondtag.*

LUNAR DISTANCES. A method of determining the longitude at sea based on the rapid proper motion of the moon and its distance from other bodies which lie in its path and which vary very perceptibly in short intervals. The nautical almanacs formerly contained a table giving the calculated distances from the moon of fourteen heavenly bodies used in lunar distances. These are the sun, the four planets, and nine fixed stars. This method has now fallen into complete disuse.
Fr: *Distances Lunaires;* Ger: *Monddistanzen.*
Goodwin, H. B., "The lunar problem in extremis," *Nautical Magazine,* vol. 81, August-September, 1902.
LUNAR INEQUALITY. A variation in the moon's motion of revolution, caused by the perturbative action of the sun and planets upon the moon.
LUNAR MONTH.
See **Lunation.**
LUNAR RAINBOW. A rainbow produced in the same way as a solar rainbow, but generally appearing as whitish or yellowish arch. It can be seen only when the moon is nearly full.
Ger: *Mondregenbogen.*
See **White Rainbow.**
LUNAR TABLES. Navigation tables giving the corrections for refraction, parallax, and semi-diameter in lunar observations.
Fr: *Tables de corrections hunaires;* Ger: *Mondtafeln.*
LUNATION. The period of time taken by the moon to complete the journey around the earth: 29 days, 12 hours, 44 minutes, 2.8 seconds. Also called lunar month.
Fr: *Lunaison;* Ger: *Mondumlauf.*
LUNG-JULUNG. A very small East Indian outrigger canoe employed in line fishing on the north coast of Madura Island.
LUNITIDAL INTERVAL. The interval of time which elapses between the moon's meridian passage and the next following high or low water.
The mean of a number of these intervals is constant for all practical purposes and is given for each port in sailing directions, nautical almanacs, and so on.
Ger: *Mondflutintervall.*
LURCH. A heavy roll, weather or lee, caused by a sea suddenly striking or receding. A sudden roll or sway to one side.
Fr: *Coup de Roulis;* Ger: *Plötzlicher Ruck.*
LURKER (G. B.). An open boat with a length 18 to 20 ft. used in the pilchard fisheries of Cornwall to sight the schools of fish and direct the setting of the seine net. It is rigged with a small spritsail.
LURKIE (G. B.). A small square-sterned open boat rigged with a standing lugsail from the southern Orkney Islands. The same boat is called *sooie* in the northern Orkneys.
LUTCHET (G. B.). A boxlike structure similar to a tabernacle, in which the mast heel does not go below deck.
LUTE STERN. A type of stern found in small fishing boats on the south coast of England. It is a transom stern with an addition formed by extending the sheer strake, covering board and bulwarks, into a sort of openwork counter surrounding the rudderhead and allowing the water to flow freely in and out. This prevents the seas from breaking over the transom when the boat is beached in heavy weather. It also provides more working space aft.
LUTINE BELL. A ship's bell hanging in the main room of Lloyd's Underwriters office in London. It is rung when important announcements are made to members. The bell was salvaged from the British frigate "Lutine" wrecked when carrying a large consignment of gold bars and specie, near Texel island, on the Dutch coast, in the great storm of 1799.
LUTING. A mixture of putty, white lead, and linseed oil having the consistency of heavy cream. It is used by boatbuilders to ensure watertightness of joints and is applied to all faying surfaces of planks in clinker-built boats.
Fr: *Lut.*
LYLE GUN.
See **Line-Throwing Gun.**

M

M. Letter denoted by the international code flag showing an oblique or diagonal white cross over a blue ground. When flown as a single letter signal means: "I have a doctor on board."

MAG. MAGNETIC (Navigation).
M.B. MOLDED BREADTH.
M.D. MOLDED DEPTH.
M. Dk. MAIN DECK.
Merid. MERIDIAN or NOON.
M.H. MAIN HATCH.
M.H.H.W. MEAN HIGHER HIGH WATER.
M.H.W.I. MEAN HIGH WATER LUNITIDAL INTERVAL.
M.H.W.S. MEAN HIGH WATER SPRINGS.
Mid. L. MIDDLE LATITUDE.
Mk. MARK.
M.L.L.W. MEAN LOWER LOW WATER.
M.L.W.I. MEAN LOW WATER LUNITIDAL INTERVAL.
M.M. MERCANTILE MARINE.
M.N.R. MEAN NEAP RISE.
M.O.H. MEDICAL OFFICER OF HEALTH.
M.R. MATES RECEIPT.
M.S. 1. MOTOR SHIP. 2. MAIL STEAMER.
M.S.L. MEAN SEA LEVEL.
M.S.R. MEAN SPRING RISE.
M.T. 1. MEASUREMENT TONS. 2. MEAN TIME.
M.T.I. MOMENT TO ALTER TRIM ONE INCH.
M.T.L. MEAN TIDAL LEVEL.

MACHINE RIVETING. Riveting performed by a single application of steady pressure at the same instant upon the head and point of a rivet. The advantages of machine riveting whether the power is hydraulic or pneumatic are increased output, low cost, and high efficiency.

Fr: *Rivetage Mécanique;* Ger: *Maschinen Nietung.*

See **Hydraulic Riveter.**

MACHINERY CASING. The steel casing which encloses the space above the engineroom in way of the engineroom skylight and hatchway. It forms a trunk providing light and ventilation. Also called engineroom casing. The heat from the engineroom escapes through a skylight with hinged covers fitted at the top of the casing. Doors are fitted in the casing at deck level; giving access to gratings and ladders leading down into the engineroom. Portable strong beams are fitted into the casing trunk for convenience in lifting heavy weights such as cylinder covers, and the like. The engineroom casing in most vessels is of large cubic capacity in order to obtain the maximum machinery space allowance in working out the net tonnage.

Fr: *Encaissement des Machines;* Ger: *Maschinenumbau.*

MACHINERY CHOCK. A heavy timber platform about 2½ in. thick placed under deck auxiliaries such as winches and windlasses and extending over the full area of the bed plate.

MACHINERY SPACE. Term used in connection with the watertight subdivision of passenger vessels according to the regulations of the International Convention of 1929 for the Safety of Life at Sea. It extends vertically from the top of keel to margin line and horizontally between the extreme main transverse watertight bulkheads bounding the spaces occupied by the main and auxiliary propelling machinery, the boilers and permanent bunkers.

Fr: *Tranche des Machines;* Ger: *Treibkraftraum; Maschinenabteilung.*

MacINTYRE TANK. An early form of ballast tank in which the floors are constructed as in a single-bottom ship. Continuous longitudinal girders are run on top of the floors to the required depth of tank and the inner-bottom plating is attached to these girders. This system has been used to convert open-bottom ships into double-bottom ones. It is also convenient when a double bottom is required over a short length only.

Fr: *Double Fond MacIntyre;* Ger: *MacIntyre Doppelboden.*

MACKEREL BREEZE. Expression used by New England fishermen engaged in the mackerel gill-net fisheries to denote a fresh breeze, when the vessel was standing to its nets with mainsail reefed and foresail furled.

MACKEREL POCKET. A large net bag made of coarse twine used by New England mackerel seiners. Also called spiller. It is attached to the side of the vessel where it is kept in position by wooden poles or outriggers at a distance of about 15 ft. from the vessel's rail. When a large school of mackerel is caught the fish are turned into the spiller, from which they are bailed out onto the vessel's deck only as fast as they can be dressed.

MACKEREL SKY. A sky covered with cirro-cumulus or alto-cumulus clouds.
  Fr: *Ciel Pommelé; Ciel Moutonné;* Ger: *Schäfchenwolken Himmel.*

MADE BLOCK. A wooden block made of several parts riveted together.

MADE MAST, BUILT-MAST. A term formerly applied to a wooden mast composed of several longitudinal pieces with their edges meeting in a radial plane: the central piece was called spindle and the others side trees, fore and after fishes, cant pieces, and fillings. These were dovetailed and held to and around the spindle with iron mast bands fitted at a distance of about 3 ft. Nowadays the term "built-mast" refers to a solid built or hollow built wooden mast as used on yachts and other pleasure craft. These are built in comparatively short lengths, with long tapering scarfs, glued together into one homogeneous stick. Modern built-masts are made in a great variety of sections: circular, rectangular, streamlined, and so on.
  Fr: *Mât d'Assemblage;* Ger: *Gebauter Mast.*

Fincham, *Masting of Ships,* London, 1852.

MADREPORE. General name for stony or branching corals of the genus *Acropora* which abound in tropical seas and are often of importance as reef builders.
  Fr: *Madrépore;* Ger: *Steinkoralle.*

MAELSTROM. Famous whirlpool off the coast of Norway in the Lofoten Islands between Mockenaso and Mockeno.

MAE WEST. 1. See **Spinnaker.**
  2. Type of inflated life jacket used by aviators on over-water journeys.

MAGAZINE. A compartment specially designed and fitted out for the stowage of explosives on board. A cool position within easy access of a hatchway or trunk is usually selected for magazine locations. Connections from the fire main with suitable piping are provided for sprinkling the magazine in the event of fire.
  Fr: *Soute aux Poudres;* Ger: *Pulvermagazin; Pulverkammer.*

Great Britain, Ministry of Shipping, *Specification for Building Magazines and Portable Magazines for Powder, Ammunition, etc., Carried as Cargo,* T. 151, London, 1939.

MAGNASIL. See **Litosilo.**

MAGNESITE A deck covering with a minimum thickness of ⅝ to ¾ in., used either as a finished floor or as a sub-floor. In the latter instance it is usually covered with rubber. The composition of commercial magnesites varies within wide limits.

MAGNET. A piece of iron or steel which has the property of attracting iron or steel. The essential character of a magnet is that it is surrounded by a magnetic field. At every point in the field, magnetic force of definite strength and direction is exerted by the magnet. Magnets when used to adjust a compass are applied either fore and aft or athwartships. They are made of hard steel and well magnetized. Their magnetism is considered permanent.
  Fr: *Aimant;* Ger: *Magnet.*
  See **Artificial Magnet, Compensating Magnet, Heeling Magnet, Lifting Magnet, Natural Magnet, Permanent Magnet, Temporary Magnet.**

MAGNET CHAMBER. In a magnetic compass, that part of the binnacle below the compass chamber containing the magnet carriers and compensating magnets.

MAGNETIC AMPLITUDE. The arc of horizon determined by compass between the sun or a star at rising or setting and the East or West point. The difference between the magnetic amplitude and true amplitude gives the deviation of the compass.
  Fr: *Declinaison magnetique Amplitude;* Ger: *Magnetische Amplitude; Magnetische Deklination.*

MAGNETIC AXIS. Straight line passing through the poles of a magnetic needle.

MAGNETIC BEARING. The magnetic bearing of an object is the angle which its direction makes with the magnetic meridian.
  Fr: *Relèvement Magnétique; Cap Magnétique;* Ger: *Magnetische Peilung; Missweisende Peilung.*

MAGNETIC BRAKE. A brake of external disc, solenoid, or torque-motor type fitted to electric deck auxiliaries such as cargo, warping, or boat winches, windlass, capstan, rudder. It is automatically released when current is supplied to the motors, and applied when the current is cut off.
  Fr: *Frein Magnétique;* Ger: *Magnetbremse.*

MAGNETIC CHART. A chart showing lines of equal magnetic variation.
  Fr: *Carte Magnétique;* Ger: *Magnetische Karte.*

Vanssay de Blavous, "Magnetic Charts," *Hydrographic Review* (Monaco), vol. 6, no. 1 (May, 1929).

MAGNETIC COEFFICIENT. One of the several magnetic components affecting the compass needle, the resultant of which constitutes the deviation.

There are five magnetic coefficients known under the letters A, B, C, D, and E.

Coefficient "A" or constant deviation is due to the lubber line not being truly fore and aft together with a small, usually negligible constant deviation, due to horizontal induction in unsymmetrical soft iron.

Coefficient "B" is the fore-and-aft component of the semicircular deviation caused by the sub-permanent magnetism of the ship's hull, together with the effect due to vertical induction in soft iron.

Coefficient "C" is the athwartship component of the semicircular deviation caused by sub-permanent magnetism of the ship's hull.

Coefficient "D" or quadrantal deviation is due to induction in horizontal soft iron.

Coefficient "E" is caused by unsymmetrically placed vertical soft iron.

Fr: *Coefficient Magnétique;* Ger: *Magnetischer Koeffizient.*

A Practical Manual of the Compass, Hydrographic Office, U.S.N., Washington, D. C., 1921.

MAGNETIC COMPASS. An instrument by means of which the directive force of the earth's magnetism upon a freely suspended needle is utilized for a purpose essential to navigation. The needle is so mounted that it moves freely only in the horizontal plane and, therefore, the horizontal component of the earth's force alone directs it. The vertical plane passing through the longitudinal axis of the needle is known as the magnetic meridian. There are two main types of magnetic compasses: the dry-card compass and the liquid compass. The former, known as the Thomson or Kelvin compass, was invented by the late Lord Kelvin and is generally used in the mercantile marine.

Fr: *Compas Magnétique;* Ger: *Magnetkompass.*

MAGNETIC COUPLING. A system of coupling between engine and propeller shafting which consists essentially of one member coupled to the shafting and a second member coupled to the engine with an air gap between the two members. The mechanical torque is transmitted by means of a magnetic flux in the air gap. It is advantageous in that it permits the engines to be started entirely without load, the torque being imposed after they are up to a speed by applying the excitation to the couplings.

If several engines are geared to the same shaft the flexibility of the couplings reduces the wear of the gears. It is mostly used with slower speed engines (400 revolutions per minute and below) where the hydraulic coupling becomes inordinately large.

MAGNETIC COURSE. The course which refers to the magnetic meridian. Also called magnetic heading. The angle between magnetic North and South and fore-and-aft line of the ship.

Fr: *Route Magnétique;* Ger: *Missweisender Kurs.*

MAGNETIC DECLINATION. Difference in direction between true north as determined by the earth's axis of rotation and magnetic north as determined by the earth's magnetism. Also called variation. The variation is designated as east or positive when the magnetic needle is deflected to the east of the north, and as west or negative when the deflection is to the west of true north.

Fr: *Déclinaison Magnétique;* Ger: *Missweisung.*

MAGNETIC DIP. The angle between the direction of a freely suspended magnetic needle resting in the line of total force and the horizontal plane passing through its center; the angle which the magnetic needle freely poised on its center of gravity makes with the plane of the horizon. Also called magnetic declination.

Fr: *Inclinaison;* Ger: *Inklination.*

MAGNETIC EQUATOR. Imaginary line encircling the earth, along which the vertical component of the earth's magnetic force is zero. Also called aclinic line. It nearly coincides with the terrestrial equator.

Fr: *Equateur Magnétique;* Ger: *Magnetisches Äquator.*

MAGNETIC FIELD. The magnetic force of definite strength which surrounds a magnet. The portion of space in the neighborhood of a magnet throughout which the magnet forces produced have sensible values.

Fr: *Champ Magnétique;* Ger: *Magnetisches Feld.*

MAGNETIC FORCE. The force exerted between two magnets. It is repulsive between like, and attractive between unlike poles. Also **Magnetic intensity.**

Fr: *Force magnétique;* Ger: *Magnetische Kraft; Magnetische Intensität.*

MAGNETIC INDUCTION. Name given to the phenomenon by which a magnet imparts magnetism to, or induces magnetism in, a piece of iron placed in its field.

Fr: *Induction Magnétique;* Ger: *Magnetische Induktion.*

MAGNETIC IRON. Iron is magnetically speaking divided into two kinds: hard and soft. Hard iron comprises the metals which offer considerable resistance to being magnetized, but if once magnetized, remain so. Soft iron includes those which instantly acquire magnetism when placed in a magnetic field, but have no power of retaining it when the magnetic field is removed.

Fr: *Fer Magnétique;* Ger: *Magnetisches Eisen.*

MAGNETIC LATITUDE. Latitude North or South of the magnetic equator.

MAGNETIC MERIDIAN. A line passing through the North and South points of the compass needle, when it is not disturbed by local attraction. This defines the direction of the horizontal component of the terrestrial magnetism at any place as indicated by the compass needle, with reference to the geographical North and South as the initial position.

Fr: *Méridien Magnétique;* Ger: *Magnetischer Meridian.*

MAGNETIC MOMENT. The magnetic energy, expressed in Gauss units, developed by the compass needle which gives it the directive force which returns it to the North point when it is deflected. It must be of sufficient magnitude to overcome the moment of inertia caused by the friction of the cap on the pivot and, in the case of a liquid compass, the inertia caused by the friction of the liquid contained in the compass bowl. In dry-card compasses with a card weighing from 15 to 20 grams, the magnetic moment varies from 400 to 500 C.G.S. units. In liquid compasses with cards of normal proportions, the magnetic moment varies from 3,000 to 6,000 C.G.S. units.

Fr: *Moment Magnétique;* Ger: *Magnetischer Moment.*

Bencker, H., "Determination of the Magnetic Moment of Liquid Compasses," *Hydrographic Review,* vol. 5 (1928).

MAGNETIC NEEDLE. A light bar or thin cylinder of magnetized steel which when poised on its center of gravity indicates the line of magnetic force of the earth at the place of observation.

Fr: *Aiguille aimantée;* Ger: *Magnetnadel.*

MAGNETIC POLES. The two points on the globe where the line of total magnetic force is vertical and toward which the magnetic needle points in all adjoining regions.

Fr: *Poles Magnétiques;* Ger: *Magnetische Pole.*

MAGNETIC RANGE. A series of conspicuous objects situated ashore or afloat, for which the correct magnetic bearing has been ascertained, for the purpose of permitting mariners to determine the deviation of the magnetic compass. Magnetic ranges are usually located in or near a harbor, in such position that they can be used by vessels under way when entering or leaving port as well as by stationary vessels when swinging ship.

MAGNETIC SHOAL. Applies to areas of relatively shallow depth of water, observed to produce large errors of the magnetic compass. The best known is that located in the vicinity of Anticosti Island (Gulf of St. Lawrence) and the other off North-West Cape (Western Australia).

MAGNETIC VARIATION.
See **Deviation.**

MAGNETIC STORM. Large-scale disturbance of the magnetic elements occurring simultaneously over the whole of the earth's surface and lasting for a period varying from a few hours to a few days. Magnetic storms usually occur concurrently with major eruptions of sun spots.

Fr: *Tempête Magnétique;* Ger: *Magnetische Störungen.*

MAGNETOMETER. An instrument for direct measurement of the magnetic moment of the compass needle.

MAGNETO-STRICTION ECHO SOUNDER. A supersonic echo sounder in which the transmitter consists of a magnetostriction oscillator made of nickel rods. The working of the oscillator is based on the property of the variation in length of magnetic materials when under the influence of a magnetic field. Nickel appears to be the most suitable magnetostrictive material for the purpose. In magnetostrictive oscillators a frequency of about 16.000 periods per second, which is about two times less than those of the piezo-quartz, has been found to give results, covering every ordinary

requirement. Also called magneto-striction depth finder.
Fr: *Echo-Sondeur à Contraction Magnétique;* Ger: *Magnetostriktion Echolot.*

MAGNITUDE. The brightness of a star expressed according to a numerical system used by astronomers. The lower numbers are assigned to the brighter stars.
Fr: *Grandeur;* Ger: *Sterngrössen.*

MAHOGANY. A native wood of the West Indies and Central America, extensively used in high-class work for deck fittings and cabin panelling. Honduras mahogany, commonly called bay wood, ranks next to teak for durability. It is free from acids which act on metal fastenings; nearly impervious to dry rot; resists changes of temperature without alteration, and holds glue well. Generally used for ship joiner work and planking of small boats. When seasoned its average weight is about 35 lb. per cu. ft. African mahogany is not true mahogany and can only be used for inside joiner work.
Fr: *Acajou;* Ger: *Mahagonyholz.*
See **Philippine Mahogany.**

MAHOWNAH. An open Turkish lighter with a capacity of 30 to 40 tons. The lower mast is fixed, and the topmast, fitted on the starboard side of the lower mast, is collapsible. A sort of sprit weighted at lower end carries a lateen-shaped sail, bent partly on hoops and partly on hanks. When going under bridges in the Golden Horn, topmast and yard come down together. Most craft carry a foresail and some a jib.

MAIDEN TRIP. The first voyage of a vessel after it has been handed over by the builders to the owners.
Fr: *Voyage d'Inauguration;* Ger: *Jungfernfahrt.*

MAIER SHIP'S FORM. A specially designed and patented form given to the underwater body of vessels with a view to reduce towing resistance. Also called Maier form.
Fr: *Carène de Maier;* Ger: *Maierschiffsform.*

The characteristic feature of the Maier form is the peculiar triangular shape of frames from end to end, combined with the wedge-shaped form of the fore-and-aft parts of the vessel. The result is to shorten the path of the streamlines along the hull by about 10 per cent in comparison with ordinary models, thus diminishing the wetted surface and skin friction, as well as residuary resistance, the streamlines being diverted at a small angle. The bow is so shaped that the bow wave is greatly reduced. With the wedge-shaped form aft, the stern wave is very small. As the triangular frame sections cannot be maintained throughout the entire ship, the triangular cut-up bow and stern must merge into the approximately rectangular midship section. This is done by maintaining the slope of all frames at the bilge diagonal parallel to that of the completely triangular bow sections; and to maintain the requisite area of frame, the form at waterline and keel is run in vertically and horizontally respectively. Furthermore, the locus of frame half-area centroids must be as straight as possible and the projection of these loci in the body plan must be coincident for fore-and-after bodies.
Bruhl, W., Versuche und Erfahrungen mit der Maier Schiffsform, Verein Deutscher Ingenieure, Zeitsschrift, vol. 74, no. 3 (1930); "Maier Form Principle of Ship Designing," *Engineering* (London), vol. 138 (October, 1934), p. 433.

MAIL DECLARATION (U. S.). A statement, signed by the master or person having charge or control of the mail before a customs officer, to the effect that every letter, bag, packet, or parcel of letters which was on board has been delivered to the postal authorities. The vessel is not permitted to make entry or break bulk until the mail declaration is handed to the customs.

MAIL FLAG. A distinguishing pennant or flag carried by mail boats and other vessels conveying mail. In Great Britain it is a white pennant with red crown in the center between the words "Royal" and "Mail," also in red. In the United States, vessels which carry mail under contract fly a red pennant with upper and lower blue borders, a spread eagle in the upper corner and the legend "United States Mail."
Fr: *Pavillon Postal;* Ger: *Postflagge.*

Other vessels which are used for the conveyance of mail without contract fly a square blue flag with the letters "U.S.M." in white. Mail pennants have recently been replaced by the letter "Y" of the International Code of Signals. On ships having a signal yard on the foremast it is flown from the starboard yardarm. On other vessels it is flown on the fore halyards with the house flag, from which it is separated by a tack line.

MAIL PENNANT. A pennant flown by ships conveying mails under a post office

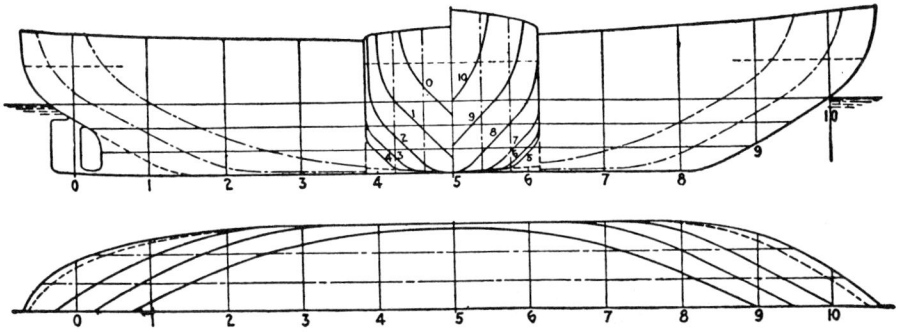

Maier Ship's Form. (*Courtesy Marine Engineering and Shipping Review*)

contract. It is usually flown at the foremast head but if that place is occupied by some other flag it is then usual to employ the starboard fore-yardarm.

Fr: *Flamme Postale;* Ger: *Postwimpel.*

MAIL ROOM. Compartment where mail bags are kept during the voyage.

Fr: *Sou'e aux Dépêches;* Ger: *Postkammer.*

MAIL SIGNAL. A flag signal employed by many shipping lines and flown at the main masthead of ships to indicate that they have mails on board for the port they are entering.

Fr: *Signal Postal;* Ger: *Postsignal.*

MAIL SUBSIDY. Payments made under contract by a government to a shipping line for the transportation of mail under specific requirements as regards speed, equipment, and regularity of schedules. Also called mail subvention. The amounts granted are substantially more than those accorded to non-subsidized vessels by the rules of the international postal service under the Universal Postal Union. The purpose of mail subventions is primarily to encourage the maintenance of fast mail services on regular routes and schedules.

Fr: *Subvention Postale;* Ger: *Postsubvention.*

MAIN. A word employed on board ship to distinguish the principal parts or places from subsidiary or subordinate ones.

Fr: *Grand; Principal;* Ger: *Gross; Haupt.* See **Bilge Main.**

MAIN BREADTH LINE. The greatest width of a ship amidships. If there is tumble home, the main breadth line is well below the waterway. (Obsolete.)

MAIN CHANNEL. Applies to that part of the bed of a river over which the principal volume of waters flow. It is not necessarily the main branch of the river.

MAIN DECK. The principal deck on a vessel which has several decks, or to the deck next below a complete upper deck (awning deck); also the deck situated forward of a raised quarter deck.

Fr: *Pont Principal;* Ger: *Hauptdeck.*

MAIN DRAIN. A piping system installed in engineering spaces, utilizing the fire-and-bilge pumps to remove water from the bilges of the fire rooms and engine rooms. In steam-driven ships, the main circulators are also provided with bilge suctions for the compartments in which they are located.

Fr: *Collecteur Principal;* Ger: *Hauptlenzrohr.*

MAINE WHERRY. A sailing and rowing boat, originating from Ash Point on the coast of Maine, with rounded stem, straight raking sternport, transom stern, hewn Hackmatack frames, carvel or clinker cedar planking. It was used for tub trawling, handlining, and lobstering. The smaller rowing wherry although primarily intended for rowing was often fitted with a centerboard and rigged with a portable mast and spritsail. The sailing wherry, slightly larger, was decked forward as far as the mast and for about 2 ft. aft with waterways and 1 ft. wide between. It carried a boom and gaff mainsail, also a bowsprit and jib. There was no standing rigging. The type is now believed extinct.

Brooks, A. S., *The Boats of Ash Point*, Salem, 1942.

MAIN FLOOD. Principal flood current where several branches of tidal stream occur in the same locality.

MAIN INJECTION VALVE. Large valve fitted to the sea chest which controls the intake of sea water for the main circulating pump.
Fr: *Soupape Principale de Prise d'Eau;* Ger: *Haupt-Injektionsventil.*

MAINSAIL. The square sail set from the main yard. In fore-and-aft-rigged vessels, this term applies to the largest sail set from the mainmast. Mainsail sometimes denotes the whole of the square sails on the mainmast.
Fr: *Grand-Voile;* Ger: *Grossegel.*
See **Boom Mainsail, Lug Mainsail.**

MAIN-TOPSAIL SCHOONER, TWO-TOPSAIL SCHOONER, JACKASS BRIG. A two- or three-masted schooner which carries square topsails on the fore- and mainmasts. Strictly speaking, they should be called "three-mast main-topsail schooner" and "two-mast two-topsail schooner."
Fr: *Goëlette à deux Huniers;* Ger: *Dreimasttoppsegelschoner; Zweitoppsegelschoner.*

MAIN-TRYSAIL KETCH. A ketch rig in which the mainsail is triangular and sets without boom or gaff. The clew is hauled out by a spar called "wishbone."

MAIN-TRYSAIL RIG.
See **Wishbone Rig.**

MAKE. To attain an objective position, as a harbor. To make the land: to sight it in the distance from the sea.
Fr: *Faire; Courir;* Ger: *Ausmachen.*

MAKE FAST. To secure the belaying turns of a rope around a cleat or belaying pin by adding a single hitch.
Fr: *Amarrer;* Ger: *Festmachen.*

MAKER.
See **Iron.**

MAKE SAIL. 1. To get sails on a ship whether starting with bare poles or adding to sails already set. In the latter case each individual sail is *set* (not made).
2. When a ship has been hove to, or stopped, the bracing of the yards so as to give the vessel headway is also described as making sail.
Fr: *Etablir la Voilure;* Ger: *Segel setzen; Segel nahen.*

MAKE-UP FEED. Boiler feed water taken from reserve feed tanks and added to feed water condensed in the main condenser to make up for steam lost in the atmosphere.
Fr: *Eau d'appoint.*

MAKING IRON. A tool somewhat like a chisel with a groove in it used by ship's calkers to finish the seam after the oakum has been driven in. Also called calking iron, creasing iron, common iron.
Fr: *Fer Double; Fer Cannelé;* Ger: *Rabatteisen.*

MAKING LIGHT. Making lights are those which the navigator first sights on approaching land. Also called landfall light. Lights of this description have a long range and the lighting apparatus employed is of the highest order.
Fr: *Feu d'Atterage;* Ger: *Landkennungs-Feuer.*

MALAR PANSHI. A carvel-built Bengalese produce boat. The planks are fastened together by iron clamps. There is no deck. The cargo is covered in with matting amidships. The rig consists of a single mast fitted in a tabernacle. It carries a square sail and topsail. Length 42 ft. Breadth 14 ft. Depth 4.5 ft.

MALLET. A hammer-shaped wooden implement used by sailmakers, wood-calkers, riggers, shipwrights. The head is made of wood and the striking faces are ringed with iron. Also called beetle.
Fr: *Maillet;* Ger: *Klopfkeule.*
See **Calking Mallet, Driving Mallet, Serving Mallet.**

MAMMATO-CUMULUS. A form of cloud showing pendulous sack-like protuberances.

MAMMATUS. Name given to all clouds whose lower surfaces form pockets or festoons. The form is found especially in stratocumulus and cumulo-nimbus clouds.

MAMMY CHAIR (U. S.). Open, box-like sling made to seat two persons and used for transferring passengers from a ship in an open roadstead (Slang).

MAN. 1. To provide a ship or boat with a sufficient number of hands and equipment to navigate it. An order to a boat's crew to embark.
Fr: *Armer;* Ger: *Armieren.*
2. To put the necessary number of men on a rope (halyard brace, etc.) to properly perform the work required.

MANAGEMENT RATE. A charge made on cargo for landing, weighing, taring, storing, bulking, and showing goods for sale in British ports. Also called consolidated rate.

MANAGING OWNER. One of the joint owners whose authority extends to the conduct of all that concerns the employment of a ship or ships.

Fr: *Armateur-Gérant;* Ger: *Korrespondentreeder.*

MANCHE. A general name for various native boats found on the west coast of India and Ceylon. Also called *manji.* The best known are those of Mangalore, Calicut, and Cochin. There are three types of these boats:

(1) The *manji* of Bandor Harbor which is used as a lighter for conveying cargo to and from coasting vessels lying at anchor. Length 25 to 35 ft., beam 6 to 7 ft., depth 4 to 5 ft. These are usually steered with a long paddle. When sailing they rig a settee sail and use a center rudder. (2) The coasting or *panyani manji,* commonly found in the ports of Beypore, Calicut, and Ponani. Typical features are a grab bow, raked stern, and heavy mast raking forward. They carry a large settee sail. The hull is carvel-built and the planking is spiked to the frames and calked with cotton. Average dimensions of the coasting manjiare: length over-all 50 ft., breadth 10 to 12 ft., depth 5 to 7 ft. (3) The *boatila manji.*

See **Kalla Doni, Masula Manche.**

MANDIT. An East Indian fishing craft similar to the Javanese *mayang* employed in the fisheries off Madura Island. Also called *mondet.*

MANEUVERING TRIALS. Trials conducted at sea to ascertain the steering qualities of a vessel and to test working of steering gears and appliances. Maneuvering trials include: ahead steering test, turning circles; emergency astern test; astern run; astern steering gear test; emergency ahead test; auxiliary steering gear test.

Fr: *Essais de giration;* Ger: *Manövrierprüfung Ruderversulk; Steuerfahigkeit Probe.*

MANGANESE BRONZE. A non-ferrous alloy invented by Parsons, British engineer and scientist, in which manganese is introduced as deoxidizing agent, increasing at the same time the strength, ductility and homogeneity of the metal. It is used extensively for components requiring great strength and corrosion resistance, such as propellers, rudders and rudder fittings, stern bearings and stuffing boxes of wooden vessels, propeller blade bolts, sheathing of wooden hulls. The manganese bronze mixture used for manufacturing solid propellers for moderate speed cargo vessels is composed of 58 per cent copper, 39 per cent zinc, 1 per cent iron, 1 per cent manganese, 1 per cent aluminum.

Fr: *Bronze au Manganèse;* Ger: *Manganbronze.*

MANGER (U. S.). 1. The flooring of a chain locker. It is composed of perforated plates which allow seepage water to flow to the drains and at the same time protects the bottom or decking.

2. Also manger board. A low partition extending athwartship immediately abaft the hawseholes. It serves to hinder the passage aft of water which may come in at the hawseholes or from the cable when heaving in. The water, thus prevented from running aft, is returned to the sea by the manger scuppers.

Fr: *Gatte;* Ger: *Schaafhock; Waschbord; Waschschott.*

MANGER PLATE. One of the plates forming part of a breakwater.

Fr: *Tôle de Brise-Lames;* Ger: *Brechwasserplatte.*

MANGU. A dugout canoe of the Birari people of Ossika on the Amur River. It is cut out of *Pinus Sylvestris.* Length 28 ft. Breadth 3 ft. Depth 1 ft.

MANHELPER. A wooden pole, about 10 feet in length, to the end of which a paint brush is fastened at an angle of about 45 degrees. Used for painting inaccessible places, especially a ship's sides when hanging stages are not practical. Also called **Long arm** or **Striker.**

MANHOLE. Round or oval-shaped opening in tank tops, tanks, boilers, and so on, fitted with watertight or steamtight cover.

Fr: *Trou d'Homme;* Ger: *Mannloch.*

See **Sunken Manholes.**

MANHOLE COVER. A watertight, steamtight, or oiltight cover used for closing a manhole. Also called manhole door, manhole plate. The usual type consists of a dished plate or steel casting held in position by dogbolts and fitted with a gasket.

Fr: *Bouchon de Trou d'Homme;* Ger: *Mannlochdeckel.*

MANHOLE DOG. A drop forging in the shape of an arc of a circle, used to hold

a manhole cover in place. Also called crossbar, strongback. There is a boss in the center with stay bolt and nut for tightening up the cover.
>Fr: *Cavalier; Étrier de Trou d'Homme;* Ger: *Mannlochbügel.*

MANHOLE RING. A plate in the form of a ring riveted or welded around a manhole opening as compensation and to provide local stiffness.
>Fr: *Renfort de Trou d'Homme;* Ger: *Mannlochring.*

MANIFEST. A detailed statement of a vessel's cargo, giving the bills of lading numbers, marks, number of packages, names of shipper, names of consignee, weight or total measurement of goods, rate of freight and where payable. Such a statement is sent by the owners or brokers at port of shipment to their agents at destination port.
>Fr: *Manifeste;* Ger: *Ladungsmanifest.*

See **Certified Manifest, Inward Manifest, Outward Manifest, Passenger Manifest.**

MANIFOLD. See **Distribution Box.**

MANILA HEMP. A fibrous material obtained from the leaves of a textile plant named Abaca, *Musa textilis.* Also called Manila. It is native to the Philippine Islands. The raw material is shipped from Manila under supervision of the United States Government inspectors who grade the different qualities. Grades J 1 and J 2 are mostly employed for best ropes and twines. L 1 and L 2 and M 1 and M 2 are used for cheaper ropes. The average length of Manila fibers varies from 5 to 8 ft., but they are often found in lengths of from 10 to 12 ft. Manila hemp is very resistant to wet and not affected by salt water. In the cheaper grades of ropes it is often mixed with other textiles such as sisal, Mauritius, or sunn hemps or jute to improve the color and lessen the cost. It is unequaled for large ropes but too stiff for small cords and twines.
>Fr: *Chanvre de Manille;* Ger: *Manila Hanf.*

MANILA ROPE. A rope made from the fibers obtained from the leaves of the *Musa textilis* or Abaca plant. Manila rope is usually made up of three strands up to 3-in. circumference, and above that size of four strands with a core. It is preferred to Italian or Russian hemp for hawsers and running gear because it is lighter, more flexible, and does not require tarring for preservation. Manila rope is stronger than tarred hemp. It is sometimes called Manila hemp. The smaller sizes of Manila ropes are usually known as 6 thread, 9 thread, 12 thread, and so on, according to the number of yarns they contain. These sizes are used on small craft for bending and/or lacing sails to spars.
>Fr: *Cordage en Manille;* Ger: *Manilatauwerk.*

British Engineering Standards Association, Specifications for Manila Ropes for General Purposes, no. 431, London, 1940; Specifications for Manila Cordage, American Petroleum Institute, Proceedings, 1936; Stang, A. H., *Results of Some Tests of Manila Rope,* U. S. Bureau of Standards, Technologic Paper 198.

MANROPE. 1. One of the side ropes to the accommodation ladder used as handrails.
>Fr: *Tire Veille;* Ger: *Sceptertau.*

2. A general name for ropes used as safety lines on deck, around hatchways, and so on; also the ropes which hang down from a vessel's side to assist in ascending, etc.
>Fr: *Filière;* Ger: *Manntau; Leittau.*

MANROPE KNOT. A knot made by first forming a wall knot and then crowning it. Used for securing the upper ends of gangway manropes.
>Fr: *Noeud de Tireveille;* Ger: *Doppelter Schildknoten; Fallreepsknopf.*

MANUAL WELD. A weld made by hand, without the assistance of a guiding or controlling device.
>Fr: *Soudure Manuelle;* Ger: *Handschweissung.*

MAOTA. A small single-outrigger dugout canoe from the Island of Napuka, Tuamotu Archipelago. The hull is formed of a dugout with pointed ends. The sides are raised by a sewed-on wash strake. These canoes are propelled solely by paddles. Most of them are one-man canoes. Their length ranges from 14 to 16 ft.

MAPLE. A hard, heavy, close-grained wood of light color, durable when permanently immersed, but not so when alternately wet and dry. Used by New England shipbuilders for framing timbers. Hard maple is frequently used for launching-ways and for the planking of slipways. Weight per cu. ft. when seasoned about 43 lb. Also called sugar maple or rock maple.
>Fr: *Erable;* Ger: *Ahorn.*

MARCONI MAIN SCHOONER. A two-masted schooner rig commonly seen on pleasure craft with Marconi (Bermuda) mainsail and gaff foresail.

MARCONI TOPSAIL. A fore-and-aft topsail, the luff of which travels up the afterside of a pole mast by means of slides and a track.

MARCQ ST. HILAIRE METHOD.
See **Intercept**.

MARE CLAUSUM. Legal term used to denote a sea subject to the jurisdiction of a particular nation which, under certain circumstances, may prohibit vessels from sailing on these waters. A closed sea.

MARE LIBERUM. Legal term which applies to the high seas on which vessels of all nations have equal rights.

MARE'S TAILS. Popular name for tufted cirrus clouds.
> Fr: *Cirrus en Queue de Cheval*; Ger: *Windbaum*.
> See **Cirrus**.

MARGIN.
See **Tankside**.

MARGINAL SEA. The marginal sea of a state is that part of the sea within three nautical miles of its shore, measured outward from the mean low water mark or from the seaward limit of a bay or river mouth. Around an island or around land exposed only at some stage of the tide, it is measured outward therefrom in the same manner as from the mainland.
> Fr: *Mer marginale*.

MARGIN CLIP. Angle clip which connects the bilge bracket to the margin plate. Also called margin lug.

MARGIN LINE. An imaginary fore-and-aft line used in floodable length calculations relating to the subdivision of ships. It is situated three inches below the upper surface of the bulkhead deck at the side.
> Fr: *Ligne de Surimmersion*; Ger: *Tauchgrenze*.
> See **Floodable Length**.

MARGIN PLANK. A plank forming the outer boundary of a deck. Also called waterway plank, nibbing plank, joggling plank. Toward the bow and stern it is notched so that the abutting ends of the deck planks may meet it more squarely.
> Fr: *Pièce de Bordure*; Ger: *Randplanke*; *Begrenzungsplanke*.

MARGIN PLATE. A longitudinal plate which bounds the double bottom at turn of bilge. The lower edge is fitted normal to the shell to which it is attached by a continuous angle bar; the top edge is flanged over horizontally and riveted to the tank-top plating.
> Fr: *Tôle de Flanc de Ballast*; *Tôle de Côté*; Ger: *Randplatte*; *Tankrandplatte*.

MARIGAN. Single-outrigger Australian dugout canoe of the Koko-Yimidir tribe from the Cape Bedford, Indian Head coastal range, Queensland. The hull is about 18 ft. long and hollowed out to the extremity at each end. There are no shelf-like projections. A wash strake fastened with sennit is fitted on each side. The outrigger float is connected to the canoe by 5 or 6 pairs of small sticks which run through both wash strakes.

MARIGRAM (U. S.). A graphic representation of the rise and fall of the water in which the hours are given by the abscissas, and the levels of the water by the ordinates, and which commences with a low water and extends to the following low water, passing through a high water. Marigrams which show the variations of the level of the water for a number of tides are obtained by means of a recording instrument or by a tide-predicting machine. In Great Britain called tidal curve, tidal diagram.
> Fr: *Abaque de Marée*; *Courbe de Marée*; Ger: *Gezeiten Diagramm*; *Gezeitenkurve*; *Tidenkurve*.

MARINA (U. S.).
See **Boat Harbor**.

MARINE. 1. Seagoing vessels considered collectively either in the aggregate or as regards nationality, as for instance, "merchant marine."
> Fr: *Marine*; Ger: *Marine*.

2. An adjective meaning relating to navigation or shipping; relating to or connected with the sea; used, or adopted for use at sea. Sometimes called maritime, but maritime is more frequently applied to that which borders on the sea.
> Fr: *Maritime*; Ger: *Schiffahrttreibend*; *Maritim*.

MARINE ADVENTURE. A term applied to the voyage which a ship is to make.
> Fr: *Risque Maritime*; Ger: *Seeunternehmung*.

A marine adventure exists: (1) Where any ship, goods, or other movables are exposed to maritime perils. (2) Where the earning or acquisition of any freight, passage money, commission, profit or other pecuniary benefit, or the security for any advances, loan or disbursements, is endangered by the exposure of insurable property to maritime perils. (3) Where any liability to a third party may be incurred by the owner of, or other person interested in or responsible for insurable property, by reason of maritime perils; a simple example is a shipment of goods sent overseas to be sold at the best price obtainable.

MARINE BAROMETER. A form of mercury barometer for use on board ship, in which the tube is constricted so as to damp the motion of the mercury and so prevent sudden oscillations in a heavy sea when the vessel is laboring. The frame is suspended in gimbals, attached by an arm to vertical structure in the ship.

Fr: *Baromètre à Mercure;* Ger: *Quecksilberbarometer.*
Barometer Manual for the Use of Seamen, London, Meteorological Office, 1926.

MARINE BELT. The belt of sea adjacent to the shore. The belt over which the jurisdiction of the municipal laws of the adjacent land extends is generally understood and agreed upon among nations. It is determined by the law of nations, and the extent of such jurisdiction out over the open seas is three miles from shore. Even within this limit the waters are considered as a part of the common highway of nations, and the jurisdiction of the local authorities exists only for the protection of the coast and its inhabitants, not to subject passing vessels to the local laws of the government of the shore.

That part of the margin of the high seas which is within the jurisdiction of the nation possessing the coast.

Ger: *Seegurtel.*

MARINE BOARD. Name given in Great Britain to the establishments located at different ports for carrying into effect the provisions of the Merchant Shipping Act. One of their chief duties is the granting of certificates of competency to ship's officers and engineers after examination.

MARINE BORER. A general term for various mollusks and crustaceans which attack timber used in marine construction such as ship's hulls, wharf and dock piling. The mollusks which are usually called shipworms include the teredo navalis and the eylotria. The crustaceans commonly known as wood lice include the limnoria, the sphaeroma and the chelura.

Fr: *Taret;* Ger: *Bohrwurm.*

MARINE CHRONOMETER. A very accurate clock slung in gimbals stowed in a special box and used for navigation purposes. It has for its moving power a spring, the force of which is made uniform by a variable lever. It is also furnished with an expansion balance formed by a combination of metals of different expansive qualities in order to compensate for errors due to changes in temperature during voyages. Chronometers carry Greenwich mean time. A ship generally carries three chronometers, which are compared with each other daily. Errors of chronometers are found: (1) by wireless time signals; (2) by visual time signals (time ball); (3) by telegraphic time signals.

See Hack Chronometer, Sideral Chronometer, Standard Chronometer.

Caspari, C. E., *Les Chronomètres de Marine,* Paris, 1894; Gould, R. T., *The Marine Chronometer,* London, 1923; Stechert, C. F., "Das Marine Chronometer," *Archiv der Deutschen Seewarte,* Jahrg: 17 (Hamburg, 1894).

MARINE DOCUMENT (U. S.). One of the official instruments for the registry of vessels and craft. Marine documents consist of certificates of registry, enrollments and licenses. They are of two descriptions (A) Permanent—granted to vessels at their home ports and (B) Temporary—granted to vessels at ports other than their ports of registry.

MARINE ENGINEER. A sea-going engineer, who must be a mechanic as well as an executive officer, ready at all times to make adjustments and repairs during the voyage or in foreign ports, without the assistance of shore labor and equipment. Also called ship's engineer, sea-going engineer.

One of the licensed officers who has charge of maintenance and operation of main engines, auxiliary engines and boilers on board ship. He may be specifically designated by the type of engine for which he has a license, as steam engineer or Diesel engineer.

Fr: *Mécanicien de Marine;* Ger: *Schiffsmaschinist; Seemaschinist.*

MARINE ENGINEERING. The study of marine propulsion machinery and auxiliaries. This study includes the invention, design, building, installation, operation, and repair of marine engines and auxiliaries as fitted on board ship.

MARINE GLUE. A tar-like compound used for paying seams in wooden decks after they have been calked with oakum. The composition varies, but the mixture usually contains pitch, gutta-percha, Stockholm tar, and rosin.

Fr: *Glue Marine;* Ger: *Schiffsleim.*
American Marine Standards Committee Standard no. 34, Marine Glue for Ship's Decks, Washington, 1928.

MARINE INSURANCE. A contract whereby the underwriter undertakes to indemnify the insured in manner and to the extent thereby agreed against marine losses, that is to say, the losses incident to marine adventure. A contract of marine insurance may, by its express terms or by usage of trade, be extended so as to protect the insured against losses on inland waters or on any land risk incidental to any sea voyage.

Fr: *Assurance Maritime;* Ger: *Seeversicherung.*

See **Mutual Insurance, Outfit Insurance.**
Arnould, Sir J., *On the Law of Marine Insurance and Average,* London, 1939; Gale, J. W., *Introduction to Marine Insurance,* London, 1937; Poole, F. W. S., *The Marine Insurance of Goods,* London, 1928; Ritter, C., *Das Recht der Seeversicherung,* Hamburg, 1924 (two volumes); Winter, W. D., *Marine Insurance,* New York, 1929.

MARINE INTEREST. The very high rate of interest which bottomry and respondenta bonds usually carry. Also called bottomry premium. Such interest is allowable, though exceeding legal interest rate, because of the hazard of loss of principal and interest of the loan by the casualty of the voyage.

Fr: *Profit Maritime; Prime à la Grosse; Profit Nautique; Change Maritime; Intérêt Nautique;* Ger: *Bodmereiprämie.*

MARINE POLICY. The instrument, or written contract, whereby insurance is made by an underwriter, in favor of an insured against marine perils, risks or contingencies. Sometimes called policy.

Fr: *Police Maritime;* Ger: *Seeversicherungs Police.*

See **Builders' Policy, Floating Policy, Hull Policy, Interest Policy, Lloyd's Policy, Mixed Policy, Named Policy, Port Risk Policy, Stamped Policy, Time Policy, Unvalued Policy, Valued Policy, Voyage Policy, Wager Policy.**

Eldridge, W. H., *Law of Marine Policies,* London, 1938.

MARINER. A seaman. A sailor. One who directs or assists in the navigation of a ship. A seafaring man of experience. The technical use of the word "mariner" is mostly restricted to legal documents.

Fr: *Marin;* Ger: *Nautiker; Seefahrer.*

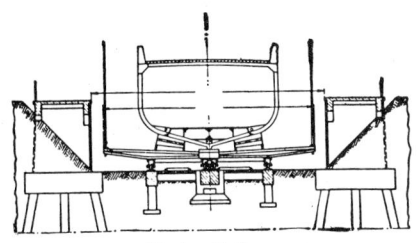

Marine Railway

MARINE RAILWAY. An inclined plane situated on the embankment of a river or in a harbor and equipped with tracks, cradle and winding machinery and on which vessels are hauled up for bottom cleaning and repairs. Also called slipway, or patent slip. Marine railways are built parallel or perpendicular to the embankment, the ships being hauled up sideways or end on as the case may be. The declivity varies from 1/15 to 1/25. Marine railways are generally used for small and medium size vessels the maximum being around 5,000 tons displacement.

Fr: *Slip de Carénage;* Ger: *Schlephelling; Aufschlepphelling.*

Glover, W. G., Marine Slipways, Institution of Engineers and Shipbuilders in Scotland, *Transactions,* vol. 78 (1934–35); Henderson, A., Slipways with side slipping arrangements, Institution of Engineers and Shipbuilders in Scotland, *Transactions,* vol. 75 (1931–32).

MARINE RISK. One of the hazards due to perils of the sea and other incidents of navigation to which a vessel and its cargo is exposed and against which the insured is protected in a marine insurance policy. Also called navigation risk.

Fr: *Risque Maritime;* Ger: *Gefahr der Seeschiffahrt.*

MARINER'S COMPASS. An instrument which indicates the true or magnetic north, enabling the mariner to guide a ship in any required direction and to ascertain the direction of any visible object such as another ship, a heavenly body, or a point of land. Often called just "compass."

Fr: *Compas;* Ger: *Kompass.*

There are two distinct types of compasses in general use at the present time: the magnetic compass, which depends upon the earth's magnetic field to obtain its directive force; and the gyrocompass, which obtains its directive force from the earth's rotation. Deutsche Seewarte, Archiv, Der Kompass an Bord, Hamburg, 1906; Laning, H., *Manual of the Compass,* Annapolis, 1916; Schuck, A., *Der Kompass,* Hamburg, 1918; Suter, E., *The Mariner's Compass,* Glasgow, 1923.

MARINER'S LIEN. The lien on vessel and cargo of a seaman for his wages. It is enforced by a libel in Admiralty and follows the ship and its proceeds into whatever hands they go.

MARINER'S SPLICE. A splice made in a nine-strand hemp or Manila cable. Also called cable splice.

Fr: *Epissure de Cable;* Ger: *Kabeltausplissung.*

MARINE SUPERINTENDENT. One who has the oversight and charge of all vessels belonging to a shipping company and is directly responsible to the managing director for the care, maintenance and upkeep of ships and the manning of the deck department. He is also responsible for the docking and undocking of vessels and supervises the loading and discharging of cargo. In practice, one of the senior captains of the company is usually selected for this post. Sometimes called port superintendent, port captain (U. S.).

Fr: *Capitaine d'Armement;* Ger: *Schiffsinspektor; Beaufsichtiger.*

MARINE SURVEYOR. A duly qualified person who examines ships or any parts thereof to ascertain their condition on behalf of owners, underwriters, and so on. Sometimes called ship surveyor. Classification surveyors are those appointed to supervise and inspect the building and repairing of vessels classed by a register of shipping and to examine them periodically or when damaged. These officers are subdivided into ship surveyors and engineer surveyors.

Fr: *Expert Maritime;* Ger: *Schiffsbesichtiger.*

MARITIME BELT. That portion of the main or open sea adjacent to the shores of a country, over which the jurisdiction of its national and municipal laws extend, and which is under the control of its local authorities. Also called marine belt.

MARITIME COMMISSION. A United States Government Agency created in 1936 to foster the development and to encourage the maintenance of the merchant marine. It is composed of five members appointed by the President with the advice and consent of the Senate. It has taken over the powers and functions of the former Shipping Board.

The principal objectives of this agency are: (1) The creation of a merchant fleet including vessels of all types, the vessels to be so designed as to be readily and quickly convertible into transport and supply vessels in a time of national emergency; (2) the ownership and operation of such a merchant fleet; (3) the training of licensed and unlicensed personnel for American merchant vessels; (4) the planning of vessels designed to afford the best and most complete protection for passengers and crew against fire and marine perils.

MARITIME DECLARATION (G. B.). An extract of the ship's logbook sworn before a notary public by a shipmaster.

MARITIME EXCHANGE. An organization patronized by shippers and carriers interested in the development and fostering of overseas commerce at a port. Its object is to promote in a general way the shipping trade of the port; besides which it usually performs several specific functions such as the collection of shipping statistics, the standardization of charter party and bill of lading clauses, the arbitration of shipping disputes, the establishment or confirmation of local rules and customs governing demurrage, loading and discharging of vessels, receipt and delivery of special kinds of cargoes. In many ports the functions of the maritime exchange are exercised by the local chamber of commerce or by the commercial exchange.

MARITIME LABOR BOARD (U. S.). A government agency established in 1936 by act of Congress for mediation and assistance in all matters related to agreements between shipowners or operators and maritime labor.

MARITIME LAW. That system of jurisprudence which prevails in courts having jurisdiction of maritime causes. Also called marine law. It is a branch both of international and of commercial law. In the United States and in Great Britain maritime law is based upon the custom of merchants, upon generally received authorities on maritime law, statutory enactments, and upon precedents established by judicial decisions. In Continental Europe and in many other nations codes form the basis of maritime law.

Fr: *Droit Maritime;* Ger: *Seerecht.*
Duckworth, L., *Principles of Marine Law,* London, 1930; Saunders, *Maritime Law,* London.

MARITIME LIEN. A lien which, unlike a lien at common law, exists without possession either actual or constructive. It constitutes a right of property in a ship as security for a debt or claim. The appropriation is made by law and vests in the creditor a special property right in the vessel which subsists from the moment the debt arises and follows the vessel into whosoever hands she comes. It is enforceable by seizure and sale under the process of an Admiralty court. In the United States, maritime liens cover claims for seamen's wages, damage by collision, salvage, pilotage, bottomry, damage to cargo, claims for necessaries and by material men. Speaking generally by the weight of authority it may be said that liens irrespective of the time of their creation have the following order of priority: (1) seamen's wages, (2) salvage, (3) tort and collision liens, (4) repairs, supplies, towage, wharfage, pilotage and necessaries, (5) bottomry bonds in inverse order of application, (6) common law liens or nonmaritime claims. Maritime liens are limited to movable things engaged in commerce and navigation. When a ship is libeled she cannot move, load, or discharge until bond is posted for the full amount of the claim.

Fr: *Privilège Maritime;* Ger: *Schiffspfandrecht; Schiffsprivilegien.*
Price, G., *The Law of Maritime Liens,* London, 1940.

MARITIME PERIL. A peril consequent on, or incidental to, the navigation of the sea, that is to say, a peril of the seas, fire, war, pirates, rovers, thieves, capture, seizure, restraint and detainment of princes and people, jettison, barratry, and other perils either of like kinds or which may be designated by the policy.

Fr: *Périls de Mer;* Ger: *Seeunfall; Zufall der See; Seevermögen.*

See **Perils of the Sea.**

MARITIME PORTS CONVENTION. An international convention adopted after the conclusion of the 1914–1918 War by all States members of the League of Nations. Under this convention each of the contracting parties undertakes, subject to the principle of reciprocity, to grant the vessels of every other contracting state equality of treatment with its own vessels, or those of any other state whatsoever, in the maritime ports situated under its sovereignty or authority, as regards freedom of access to the port; the use of the port, and the full enjoyment of the benefits as regards navigation and commercial operations which it affords to vessels, their cargoes, and passengers. The equality of treatment thus established covers facilities of all kinds, such as allocation of berths, loading and unloading facilities, as well as dues and charges of all kinds levied in the name of or for the account of the government, public authorities, concessionaires or undertakings of any kind. The convention does not apply to the coasting trade.

MARITIME SERVICE (U. S.). A voluntary non-military organization established by the U. S. Maritime Commission for the training of licensed and unlicensed personnel for the merchant marine in pursuance of section 216 of the Merchant Marine Act of 1936. The Coast Guard has been assigned to administer this organization. Instruction at shore training stations is supplemented by training at sea in vessels attached to the stations.

MARITIME TERRITORY. In international law, coastal waters which are not territorial waters, although in immediate contact with the open sea. Any strait through which the right of passage of foreign vessels can be forbidden, or bays so landlocked that they cannot be held to form part of any ocean highway are termed maritime territory; for example, the Dardanelles, the Solent, the inland sea of Japan.

Fr: *Territoire Maritime.*

See **Territory.**

MARK. The call given when comparing compasses, taking azimuths or bearings and so on.

MARK BOAT. A boat used as a rendezvous by North Sea fishing vessels when working in fleets. Its presence assists the carriers which take the fish to market and trawlers coming out after refit to locate the fleet. It also forms a convenient point to fish around, making it easier for the Admiral to keep on his ground. The mark boat anchors or shifts position at the order of the Admiral. The fleet operates in touch with its mark boat, the position of which is known to the owners from day to day. It is usually an old trawler.

MARK BUOY. A buoy placed to mark a special position. Also called marker buoy.
Fr: *Bouée de Marque; Bouée-Balise;* Ger: *Markboje.*

MARKER. 1. A small automatic radio-beacon with a range of 4 to 6 miles, located on a buoy, pierhead, or piling structure. It is not intended for long-range accurate bearings but serves as a local mark indicating a channel entrance, turning point, pierhead, etc., in or near a harbor. The use of two or more beacons provides a "fix."
2. A device used in shipyards for marking rivet holes on plates, shapes, and templates. It consists of a short piece of brass pipe, the end of which, being dipped in white lead, leaves a circular imprint on the material. Also called marking pin.

MARKER-OFF (U. S.). A skilled shipyard worker who marks off all material brought to him before it is punched, sheared, planed, and so on. Also called marking-off plater (G. B.), liner-off. Marking-off platers work to drawings supplied from the drawing office and information given from the mold loft, usually in the form of marked battens, and they generally specialize in a certain line, such as framing, floors and intercostals, shell, decks, tank tops, and so on.

MARKET BOAT (U. S.). Fishing craft which make short trips to nearby fishing grounds and sell their catch in a fresh condition. Also a boat carrying produce to market. A ship's boat used to bring off provisions.

MARKET FISH. In the fish trade, those species of fin fishes which do not enter primarily in the canning trade; the salmon, shad and mackerel being exceptions. The opposite of "cannery fish."

MARKING.
See Cable Markings.

MARKING HAMMER. A tool for marking rivet holes on a template.
See Marker.

MARKING PIN.
See Marker.

MARKINGS. Identification and other marks painted on the outside of a ship in accordance with the law. They include ship's name on each side of the bow and on stern, port of registry on stern, scale of feet on either side of the stem and sternpost, official number on main beam, loadline markings on each side, amidships.

MARKS AND DEEPS. The divisions used in marking the hand lead line at the second, third, fifth, seventh, tenth, thirteenth, fifteenth, seventeenth, and twentieth fathoms, each designated by bits of leather and differently colored bunting are called "marks." The intermediate fathoms, estimated by the leadsman, are called "deeps."
Fr: *Graduations de la Ligne de Sonde;* Ger: *Lotleine Markung.*

MARL. 1. To wind a rope with marline, spun yarn, twine, or other small stuff in such a manner that every turn is secured by a marline hitch. A common method for fastening strips of canvas (called parceling) around a rope.
Fr: *Merliner;* Ger: *Marlen; Bekleiden.*
2. To fasten or secure with a series of marline hitches, such as a sail to its boltrope or to a spar, and so on.
Fr: *Merliner;* Ger: *Marlen.*

MARLINE. Two-stranded, lightly tarred or untarred hemp cord laid up left-handed with very little twist. It is commonly used for service, lashings, mousings, and as seizing stuff. It is also employed when securing boltropes to large sails instead of sewing. Common or heavy marline runs about 222 ft. to the pound, medium marline 360, and yacht or light marline 520 ft. Tarred marline is used for serving wire rope of 7/16- to 1-in. diameter. Weight per fathom 0.0327 lb. Untarred marline weighs about 0.028 lb. per fathom and is used for sewing awning backbones.
Fr: *Merlin;* Ger: *Marlleine.*
See Yacht Marline.

MARLINE CLAD ROPE.
See Fiber Clad Rope.

MARLINE NEEDLE. A sailmaker's needle used for making eyelets in sailcloth and marling.
Fr: *Aiguille à Oeillets;* Ger: *Marlnadel; Gatnadel.*

MARLINE SPIKE. A pointed steel tool about 16 in. long, used by riggers and seamen to separate the strands of rope when splicing and also as a lever when putting on seizings, marling, etc. Spikes used with fiber rope have a round head and the body is uniformly tapered to a fine point. Spikes used for wire splicing have an enlarged flattened head with wedge-shaped point. All spikes are provided with an eye near the head for slinging with a lanyard. Also called marlingspike.

Fr: *Epissoir;* Ger: *Marlspiker.*

MARLINE SPIKE HITCH. Hitch used for drawing each turn of a seizing taut. Also called boat knot. It is formed by crossing the bight over the point of a marline spike and sticking the spike through. Used by riggers, or over a stake for tying up a small boat.

Fr: *Noeud de Trésillon;* Ger: *Marlspikerstek; Falscher Stich.*

MARLINE SPIKE SEAMANSHIP. The care, handling, knotting, splicing, and use of the fiber and wire rope.

Fr: *Matelotage.*

MARLING HITCH. A hitch used for marling, lashing hammocks, or making selvage strops. It is similar to the rolling hitch and occasionally called by that name.

Fr: *Demi-Clef à Transfiler;* Ger: *Marlstek; Marlienstek.*

MARRIED FALL. Term used by stevedores to denote one of two cargo falls having the ends fastened to a single cargo hook.

See **Burtoning.**

MARRIED FALL SYSTEM.

See **Burton Tackle.**

MARRIED GEAR. Gear used for handling cargo with two falls brought together and terminating in a single hook.

See **Burtoning.**

MARRY. 1. To join two ropes together for the purpose of reeving by placing them end to end and connecting them by worming or seizing.

Fr: *Marier;* Ger: *Bandseln.*

2. To marry ropes, braces, or falls, i.e., to hold two such ropes together side by side with small seizings placed at a certain distance from each other.

Fr: *Marier.*

3. To open two ropes' ends preparatory to splicing.

MARTINGALE. One of the ropes or chains extending from the jibboom to the end of the dolphin striker to counteract the strain of the head stays. There are usually three martingales: inner jib martingale, middle jib martingale, outer jib martingale. Also called Martingale stay.

Fr: *Martingale;* Ger: *Stampfstag; Kluverdomper.*

See **Flying Martingale, Traveling Martingale.**

MARTINGALE BACK ROPE. Rope or chain stays extending from the lower end of the dolphin striker to each side of the bows. Also called gob line.

Fr: *Moustache; Hauban de Martingale;* Ger: *Stampfstock Achterholer; Stampfstock Geie.*

MARTINGALE BOOM.

See **Dolphin Striker.**

MARTIN'S ANCHOR. Patent double fluked anchor with short stock parallel to the arms (obsolete).

Fr: *Ancre Martin;* Ger: *Martinsanker.*

MARTYGA. A brigantine-rigged sailing coaster with square stern from the Sea of Azov.

MARU-KU-BUNE. A Japanese dugout made of a species of oak tree. Used for salmon fishing in the estuaries.

MASAWA, MASAUWA. A trading canoe from the Trobriand Islands (British New Guinea). It is a single-outrigger dugout with two wash strakes on each side, pointed ends, and transverse carved and painted breakwaters. The outrigger booms, which may be 20 or more in number, are covered by a continuous platform. It is rigged with one short mast and a triangular sail made of pandanus leaf. A similar canoe with three strakes of planking is called *masawa-kikita*; with five, *masavuaka*. The average size canoe has a length of about 25 ft.

MAS-DONI. A small open fishing boat from the Maldive Islands. It has the same features as the mas-odi but is smaller. Length 24 ft. Breadth 8 ft. Crew 4 to 6. (Typical.)

See **Odi.**

MASHUWA, MASHWA. Generic name in the Persian Gulf and in Southern Arabia for an open ship's boat with straight or curved stem and transom stern, usually propelled by oars, but also rigged with one mast on occasion. The smaller ones, about 30 ft. long, are used as ship's boats for Baggalas and Ghanjas. This name also refers to a small open boat with raking stem and rounded stern of Deccan used for fishing and local trading on the Gujarat coast between Bombay and Cam-Bay. The displacement of these boats ranges between 10 and 35 tons. The planking is made watertight by having two sharply edged triangular tongues cut into each landing. To hold the strakes together spikes are driven obliquely from the inner side of the upper plank through the joined tongues and grooves. Trading or fishing *mashwas* are rigged with two masts and settee sails. Holes are made every few feet in the covering board at the tip of ribs and planking to receive wooden uprights. These stanchions support a wash strake which extends right round the vessel, being highest at the stern. The *mashwas* of different ports vary slightly in build. They are considered to be among the fastest sailing craft known, in smooth waters, even when close-hauled. They are very sharp in the bows, and well rounded in the stern, with a 25° forward rake of the masts. Bombay Mashwa: Length overall 60 ft. Length of keel 33 ft. Breadth 15 ft. Depth 9 ft. (Typical.)

MASK. A contrivance for checking a vessel's sternway as it slides down the ways when launching takes place in confined waters. It consists of heavy timbers attached and braced as low as possible at the stern, arranged to present a large flat surface at right angles to the direction of travel. Also called shield.

Fr: *Bouclier;* Ger: *Bremsschild.*

MASSALGEE. Member of an Asiatic crew serving in lascar agreement under the supervision of the deck serang. Cleans, trims and fills ship's lamps.

MAST. A straight piece of timber or a hollow cylinder of wood or metal set up vertically or nearly so and supporting yards, booms, derricks, or gaffs. In fore-and-aft-rigged vessels each mast is commonly made of two parts, called the lower mast and the topmast respectively. On large sailing vessels the masts are composed of several lengths called lower mast, topmast, topgallant mast, and royal mast. Since the adoption of steel spars in recent years, the lower and topmast are usually made of one piece. The royal mast, although made of wood, forms a single spar with the topgallant mast.

The masts of two-masted craft are called foremast and mainmast, except in ketch- and yawl-rigged craft; of three-masted craft, foremast, mainmast, and mizzenmast. In square-rigged vessels with four or five masts the after mast is called spanker mast or jigger mast when it is smaller than the other masts and fore-and-aft rigged. In vessels having four masts these are usually distinguished as foremast, forward mainmast, after mainmast, mizzenmast. When the masts exceed four in number there is no fixed rule. The extra mast is sometimes called middlemast. In fore-and-aft-rigged vessels having five masts they are named as follows: foremast, mainmast, mizzenmast, jigger mast, spanker mast. The name pusher or driver is occasionally given to the aftermost mast of a six-masted schooner. In the seven-masted schooner "Thomas W. Lawson" the following names were given to the masts abaft the mizzen: jigger mast, spanker mast, pusher mast, driver mast.

Steel pole masts of steamers and motor vessels have ceased to exercise their original function of supporting sails, and are now used only for navigational purposes and to provide attachments for cargo booms, the number of which varies from two to ten on each mast. On naval vessels masts serve various military functions, as well.

Masts are supported from forwards by stays, named according to the mast they support. At the sides they are held by shrouds (rigging) and from aft by backstays.

Fr: *Mât;* Ger: *Mast.*

MAST BAND. A metal band fitted with a number of lugs for taking the blocks of various purchases; also a band below the hounds for taking cap and trestle stays.

Fr: *Cercle de Mât;* Ger: *Mastband.*

MAST BED. In wooden boats, the pieces of wood in the decking around a mast hole.

MAST CAP. A collar used to confine two masts or spars together when one is erected at the head of another. It is made of wood, iron-bound, or built up of steel, and has a square hole which fits over the lower masthead and a round one through which the mast above passes and is secured.

Fr: *Chouque;* Ger: *Eselshaupt.*

MAST CARLING. A carling placed on each side of a mast hole between the beams to support the partners.

Fr: *Entremise d'Étambrai;* Ger: *Mastschlingen.*

MAST CLAMP. A stout piece of hardwood, with a round hole in it, secured to two beams to take the strain of the mast in small craft.

See **Mast Hasp.**

MAST CLEAT. A small wedge of wood or metal nailed to a mast or spar so that it may, by the thickness of its head, stop any part of the rigging from slipping in or down. A small cleat on a yardarm to prevent the turns of the reef earing from slipping along the yard. Also called thumb cleat.

MAST CLOTH. The lining in the middle on the afterside of a square sail to prevent the latter from being chafed by the mast. The middle breadth of canvas in a square sail, which receives the chafing of the mast.

Fr: *Triangle de Tablier;* Ger: *Stosslappe.*
See **Mast Cover.**

MAST COAT. A conical covering made of No. 0 to 2 canvas lashed or nailed around the mast just above the wedges and secured to the mast ring at deck level to prevent the oozing of water below. It is usually treated to be fire-resistant and is always painted. Also called petticoat, boot.

Fr: *Braie de Mât;* Ger: *Mastkragen.*

MAST COLLAR. 1. An angle bar formed into a ring and fitted around the mast hole in a steel deck. The horizontal flange is riveted to the deck and the vertical flange is fastened with tap rivets to the mast plating, or welded to it.

2. A wooden circle fitted around a mast and fastened to the deck at the partners. The lower edge of the mast coat is secured to it.

Fr: *Cornière d'Étambrai; Bourrelet d'Étambrai;* Ger: *Mastkragenkranz; Mastlochkragenkranz.*

MAST COVER. Canvas cover laced to a wooden mast located in the wake of a funnel as a protection against smoke. Also called mast cloth.

Fr: *Étui de Mât; Étui de Chauffe;* Ger: *Mastbezug; Rauchbezug.*

MASTER. The commanding officer of a merchant or fishing vessel. Also called master mariner, shipmaster. The term master includes every person except a pilot who has command or charge of a ship. The master of a vessel has general charge of the ship. He must be duly certified for his position. His duties include starting the ship at the proper time and providing a competent crew as well as proper equipment. He must manage the vessel during the voyage and navigate according to the manner which has been agreed upon. Because of his peculiar position and his inability to call in officers of the law to assist him, he is invested with special disciplinary power over all persons on board.

Fr: *Capitaine de Navire;* Ger: *Schiffer; Kapitän; Schiffsführer.*

See **Baggage Master, Berthing Master, Dockmaster, Extra Master, Harbor Master, Prize Master, Sailing Master, Shipping Master, Trinity Master, Wreck Master.**

MASTER AT ARMS. 1. A member of the crew on a passenger vessel who is in charge of police duties in general.

Fr: *Capitaine d'Armes;* Ger: *Schiffsprofoss.*

2. A petty officer aboard a naval vessel who is charged with disciplinary or police duties, called "Jimmy-legs" (U. S.).

MASTER COMPASS. In a gyroscopic compass system; the instrument in which the gyroscope is installed as distinguished from repeater compasses which follow the movements of the master compass.

The master compass itself is not used for navigation. A transmitter is connected to the azimuth gear by means of a pinion so that, as the azimuth gear moves relatively to the binnacle, various contacts in the transmitter are made and broken in a definite series or the transmitter is made to follow it by induction. Through a control panel the transmitter is connected to the repeater compasses placed wherever they may be desired throughout the vessel.

Fr: *Compas Principal;* Ger: *Mutterkompass; Hauptkompass.*

MASTER OF THE HOLD. Term used on British ships to denote a non-navigating petty officer. He travels with the ship and supervises loading, unloading and stowing of cargo and luggage, also ventilation of holds.

MASTER PORTER (G. B.). Agent or firm licensed and controlled by the port authority for sorting out goods landed by a vessel for each receiver. The master porter renders his charges to the receivers of the cargo, but also renders the ship an account of his deliveries (out-turn) after he has completed the operation of sorting.

See **Porter.**

MASTER'S CERTIFICATE. A certificate of competency issued by government authorities showing that the master of a merchant vessel is duly authorized to take charge or command of such a vessel. Also called master's license, master's ticket.

Fr: *Diplôme de Capitaine;* **Ger:** *Patent des Kapitäns.*

U. S. State Department, Treaty Series no. 950, Officers Competency Certificates Convention of 1936, Washington, 1939.

MAST FUNNEL. An iron or copper band at the head of an upper mast around which the rigging fits or is made to rest. Also called jack. It usually consists of a cylinder with two athwartship arms and a shoulder. This contrivance is used in connection with a housing topmast. When housing the topmast the funnel, held by catches, rests on the cap with all the rigging remaining on it until swaying the mast up again.

Fr: *Manchon de Capelage; Gobelet;* Ger: *Trommel.*

MAST HASP. A hinged iron band secured to the thwart of an open boat. Also called mast clamp. In conjunction with the mast step, it holds the mast upright.

Fr: *Collier de Mât;* Ger: *Mastbügel.*

MASTHEAD. 1. The portion of a mast from the eyes of the rigging to the top of the spar.

Fr: *Ton;* Ger: *Masttopp.*

2. To hoist up or send up to the truck or top of a mast. Sometimes called to fullmast, or two-blocks. The opposite is to half-mast. **3.** To masthead a yard means to hoist it as far as it will go.

MASTHEAD KNOT. A multiple noose knot, with four loops, which is used for steadying small masts. Also called jury knot. The center is placed over the masthead, and stays can be bent to the three loops by means of sheet bends: the ends are joined with a bowline knot and one of these is left long enough to take a fourth stay.

MASTHEAD LIGHT. A bright white running light carried by mechanically propelled vessels underway, on or in front of the foremast, or in the fore part of the vessel. It must show an unbroken light over an arc of the horizon of twenty points of the compass, from right ahead to two points abaft the beam on either side, of such a character as to be visible at a distance of at least five miles. Also called steaming light.

Fr: *Feu de Tête de Mât;* Ger: *Topplicht; Topplaterne.*

See **Rules of the Road.**

MASTHEAD MAN. 1. In yachting parlance, one of the members of the crew in large sailing craft who go aloft to lace a topsail, or do other similar work. As there are no ratlines the men have to shin up and are given extra pay.

2. In mackerel seine boats, the man stationed aloft who sights the mackerel school and directs the boat to a position advantageous for capture.

MASTHEAD PENDANT. A pendant attached to each side of a lower masthead with a thimble in the hanging end to which a heavy tackle, called pendant tackle, may be hooked. This tackle was formerly used for setting up the lower rigging or lifting heavy weights.

Fr: *Pantoire de Tête de Mât;* Ger: *Topphänger.*

MASTHEAD RIGGING. The point where stays, shrouds, and backstays encircle a masthead.

Fr: *Capelage.*

MAST HOOP. 1. One of the rings of wood or metal by which the luff of a gaff sail is confined to the mast as the sail is hoisted or lowered. Hoops are seized with marline to cringles in the luff of the sail. Also called mast ring.

Fr: *Cercle de Mât;* Ger: *Legel.*

2. One of the iron bands, $\frac{3}{8}$ to $\frac{5}{8}$ in. thick and $4\frac{1}{4}$ to 5 in. wide, formerly used for binding together the several pieces of a made mast. They were placed 3 to $3\frac{1}{2}$ ft. apart.

Fr: *Frette;* Ger: *Mastband.*

MAST HOUSE. A small deckhouse built around a mast, serving as a support for the derricks or in some cases as a winch platform. Where electric winches are fitted it is used for housing electric control equipment.

MASTING. 1. The masts of a vessel considered collectively.

Fr: *Mâture;* Ger: *Mastwerk.*

2. The determination of the position in which the masts of sailing craft should be placed and the mechanical process by which they are placed. The figures are usually given in percentage of the length between perpendiculars, the distance of the foremast abaft the forward perpendicular being the first figure. In ships which are full-bodied forward, the foremast stands nearer to the bow than in sharp, lean-bowed vessels.

The position of masts varies according to the number with which a vessel is to be furnished, the rig, and in some degree, upon the underwater body. The object to be attained is to place masts so that the center of effort of the whole sail plan will be at a desirable point, the location of which depends on that of the center of lateral resistance of the vessel. As a general rule the center of effort of the sail plan should be placed one-twentieth of the waterline length *forward* of the center of lateral resistance.

Fr: *Mâtage;* Ger: *Bemastung; Mastung.*

See **Center of Effort, Center of Lateral Resistance.**

MAST LADDER. A steel ladder attached to a mast by angle clips and fitted with steel rungs spaced about fifteen inches apart. It usually extends from about two feet above the upper deck or house top to the uppermost navigation light bracket. It has nowadays replaced on many merchant vessels the shroud ratlines for going aloft.

MAST LEECH. The luff of a fore-and-aft sail which sets just abaft a mast.
Fr: *Chûte au Mât;* Ger: *Mastliek.*

MAST PARTNER. Framing or pieces of planking fitted in apertures of the deck for the support of the masts and rabbeted in the mast carlings.
Fr: *Étambrai de Mât;* Ger: *Mastfischung; Mastfisch.*

MAST RING.
See **Mast Hoop.**

MAST ROPE. 1. A rope for hoisting or striking a topmast. Also called top rope, bull rope. It runs from the cap of the lower mast through the sheave hole at the heel of the topmast, then through a block hooked to the cap and from there to the deck.
Fr: *Guinderesse;* Ger: *Stängewindreep.*
2. The luff rope of fore-and-aft sails where the forward edge (luff) is laced or secured to the mast as in gaff sails, Bermuda sails, spritsails, trysails.
Fr: *Ralingue de Mât;* Ger: *Vorderliek.*

MAST SCUTTLE. The narrow slot in the deck immediately abaft the foremast of a sailing drifter into which the mast falls back when lowered on to the gallows or crutch.
See **Tabernacle.**

MAST STEP.
See **Step.**

MAST TACKLE. A purchase secured to a lower masthead for handling heavy weights.
Fr: *Caliorne de bas-mât;* Ger: *Seitentakel.*

MAST THWART. In an open boat, the thwart to which the mast is secured or through which it is stepped.
Fr: *Banc de Mât;* Ger: *Mastducht.*

MAST TRACK.
See **Track.**

MAST TRUCK. A small circular piece of wood, capping the top of a mast. It is usually fitted with sheaves through which signal halyards are rove.

Fr: *Pomme de Mât;* Ger: *Flaggenknopf.*

MAST TRUNK.
See **Tabernacle.**

MAST WEDGE. One of the triangular pieces of wood driven around a mast where it goes through the deck. They confine the mast between the partners.
Fr: *Coin d'Étambrai;* Ger: *Mastkeil.*

MAST WINCH. A small hand winch fastened to the mast and used by sailing craft up to about 15 tons. It is composed of a gipsy, crank-handles, and pawl, and is used for heavy work.
Fr: *Poupée de Pied de Mât;* Ger: *Mastwinde.*

MAST YOKE. The lower cap on a masthead on which the crosstrees are fitted.
Fr: *Chouque Inférieur;* Ger: *Unteres Eselshaupt.*

MASULA, MASULA MANCHE. A plank-built surf boat found all along the eastern coast of the Indian Peninsula and called *padagu* or *salangu* by the Coromandel people. It is a large, clumsy open boat, extremely seaworthy in a heavy surf. It is used for ferrying passengers and goods between ship and shore, also for shooting seines. No iron is used in its construction. The frames are fastened with coir yarns crossing the seams over a wadding of coir which presses on the joint and prevents leakage. The planking is calked with plantain-leaf stalks.
Propulsion is effected with paddles about 12 ft. long consisting of a board about 10 in. wide and 14 in. long at the end of a pole. There is no rig. Length 26 to 35 ft. Breadth 8 to 11 ft. Depth 4 to 7 ft. (Average.)

MAT. Any coarse fabric made of strands of old rope or spun yarn, beaten flat and interwoven.
Fr: *Paillet;* Ger: *Matte.*
See **Cargo Mat, Chafing Mat, Collision Mat, Mooring Mat, Paunch Mat, Sword Mat, Thrum Mat.**

MATCH HOOK.
See **Clip Hook.**

MATE. See **Officer.**

MATE'S BOAT. In the New England menhaden fisheries, one of the two seine boats used in setting the seine and in which the ship's mate is stationed. The other boat in which the captain takes a place is called purse boat.

MATERIALMEN'S LIEN. A maritime

lien on domestic vessels for labor and materials furnished for repairs in a domestic port. This lien does not exist under British law.
Ger: *Unternehmerspfandrecht.*

MATE'S RECEIPT. A receipt given by the chief officer of a vessel when goods are shipped. Also called ship receipt. The master signs the bills of lading in return for the mate's receipt. As a rule the person in possession of the mate's receipt is entitled to the bills of lading, and he gives it in exchange for them.
Fr: *Billet de Bord; Reçu de Bord; Bon de Bord;* Ger: *Steuermanns Quittung; Bordempfangsschein.*

MAT FENDER. A fender made of hemp mats.
Fr: *Paillet de Défense;* Ger: *Mattfender.*

MATINICUS BOAT. A fishing boat originating from Matinicus Island, Maine, and employed in the cod, herring, mackerel and lobster fisheries. It resembles in a general way the Muscongus Bay boat. The hull is sharp forward, round-bilged, square-sterned, lap strake planking with centerboard, washboards, and generally two thwarts. It is rigged with reefing bowsprit and portable mast. These boats can be rowed as well as sailed. Length 22 ft. Breadth 7 ft. (amidships). Breadth at stern 3½ ft. (Typical.)

MA'TO. A small kayak of the Koryak people from Penshina Bay. It differs from that of the western Eskimo in several points. It is shorter, broader, and the round manhole is not covered and occupies the entire width. Near the bow and stern, skin handles are provided for lifting it out of the water either upon shore or upon floating ice. In certain settlements a double-bladed paddle is used; in others (Itkana-Paren) two paddles about 1.3 ft. long, with short handles, are employed. They are tied to the rim of the manhole with a thong so that they can be dropped into the water or placed within the kayak while the occupant casts the harpoon. Length 8.8 ft. Breadth 2.4 ft. Depth 0.9 ft. Weight 32 lb. (Typical.)

MATTES. A name given to shoals of fairly hard soil found in the Mediterranean, formed by accumulated remains of marine plants.
Fr: *Matte.*

MATTHEW WALKER KNOT. A knot similar to the wall knot, used for securing the standing part of a rope or making beckets for buckets. A knot used on the end of a lanyard to prevent unreeving through the deadeyes. It is formed by throwing a half hitch on each strand in the direction of the lay, so that the rope can be continued after the knot is formed. Sometimes called lanyard knot.
Fr: *Noeud de Ride;* Ger: *Taljereepknoten.*

MATTIE (G. B.). Trade name for a brand of herrings in which the roes and milts are not fully developed. Also called virgin herring, matje. Length about 9¼ in. There are from 1,100 to 1,200 in a barrel.

MAUNATA. A heavily built open boat propelled by oars, employed in the Bulgarian net fisheries on the Black Sea. Length 42 to 46 ft.

MAUND (G. B.). A fish measure used in the herring trade. It is the equivalent of 10 long hundreds or 3¾ cwt. of herring.

MAURITIUS HEMP. Hemp obtained from the *agave foetida* plant and only used for ropes when mixed with Manila hemp.

MAYANG, MAYANGAN. An East Indian plank-built fishing boat from Northern Java and Madura Island. The flat-bottomed hull with rocker keel and sheered ends is built of Jati wood. Owing to its great beam the *mayang* is said to have good stability under sail although there are no outriggers except in the smallest boats. Length 40.9 ft. Breadth 9.8 ft. Depth 2.9 ft. (Typical.)

The quarter rudder is of the usual East Indian type and hangs on a projecting crossbeam. A long sweep is also used for steering. The most distinctive features are the rising, blade-shaped, incurving stem and stern, the design of which varies according to local usage. The rig consists of a mast stepped a short distance forward of amidships. The large sail is of trapezoidal shape. The *mayang* is the largest type of fishing craft in Javanese waters. When becalmed it is propelled by short oars.

MAYDAY (G. B.). International radio distress signal used by ships calling for help. Derived from the French *m'aider.*

MAZE. A unit used in the fish trade on the west coast of Scotland and the Irish Sea for the sale of herring by numbers. One maze being the equivalent of 615 or 500 fish according to locality. Also called mease.

MBEMBEO. A large single-outrigger dugout canoe from Tomman Island, New Hebrides, about 24 ft. long, pointed at each end, one end forming a small beak. There is a platform made of close-lying longitudinal bamboos on each side of the hull, which does not extend over the hollowed part.

MEAL FLAG. 1. A white flag displayed by a yacht in harbor at the starboard spreaders or in the rigging, signifying that the owners are at mess.
2. A red pennant flown from the port spreaders, or port yardarm on naval vessels, indicating that the crew are at mess. Also called meal pennant, and, in U. S. naval slang, bean rag.

MEAN DRAFT. The average of the drafts measured at bow and stern.
Fr: *Tirant d'Eau Moyen;* Ger: *Mittlerer Tiefgang; Tiefgang in der Mitte.*

MEAN HIGHER HIGH WATER. The average height, taken over a considerable period of time, of the higher of the two high waters of each day.
Fr: *Pleine mer supérieure moyenne;* Ger: *Mittlere höheres; Hochwasser.*

MEAN HIGH WATER. In tidal terminology refers to the average height of all high waters taken over several years thus eliminating inequalities.
Fr: *Pleine mer moyenne;* Ger: *Mittlere Hochwasser.*

MEAN LATITUDE.
See **Middle Latitude.**

MEAN LOWER LOW WATER. The average height of water of the lower of the two low waters of each day (lumar). A tidal datum plane adopted as reference plane for charts of the Pacific Coast of the United States, Alaska, Hawaii and the Philippine Islands. It is derived through mean low water by correcting the diurnal inequality to a mean level.
Fr: *Basse Mer Inférieure Moyenne;* Ger: *Mittleres Niedrigeres Niedrigwasser.*

MEAN LOW WATER. The average height at any place of all the low waters calculated over a considerable period of time. For navigational purposes this plane of reference is considered the most satisfactory. It has been adopted by the United States Coast and Geodetic Survey for all charts of the Atlantic and Gulf Coasts of the United States and for the Atlantic Coast of the Panama Canal Zone.
Fr: *Niveau moyen des basses mers;* Ger: *Mittleresniedrigwasser.*

MEAN LOW WATER LUNITIDAL INTERVAL. The mean of low water lunitidal intervals at a certain place during a period of one lunar month or more.
Ger: *Mittleres Niedrigivasser Intervall.*

MEAN LOW WATER SPRINGS. A plane of reference whose depression below mean sea level corresponds with half of the mean range of spring tides. It is used on nautical charts of Great Britain, China, Germany, Denmark, Italy, Brazil and Chile.
Fr: *Niveau moyen des basses mers de vive eau;* Ger: *Mittleresspringniedrigwasser.*

MEAN NEAP RISE. The average height of high water above chart datum at neaps.
Fr: *Amplitude moyenne en morte eau;* Ger: *Mittlerer nipptidenhub.*

MEAN NOON. The moment when the mean sun passes the observer's meridian.
Fr: *Midi moyen;* Ger: *Mittlerer Mittag.*

MEAN RANGE. The difference between mean high water and mean low water levels.
Fr: *Amplitude Moyenne;* Ger: *Mittlere Tidenhub.*

MEAN RISE. Height of mean high water above the datum of the chart.
Fr: *Amplitude Moyenne;* Ger: *Mittlerer Steig.*

MEAN SEA LEVEL. The average level of the sea, determined by averaging a long series of observations obtained at equal intervals of time. The level of water at half tide.
Fr: *Niveau Moyen;* Ger: *Mittlerer Wasserstand.*

MEAN SOLAR DAY. The time of the rotation of the earth with respect to the mean sun.
Fr: *Jour Solaire Moyen;* Ger: *Mittlerer Sonnentag.*

MEAN SOLAR YEAR. Average of a long succession of solar years when the irregularity of the sun's motion in the ecliptic and the irregularity of the motion of the first point of Aries are taken into account.
Fr: *Année Solaire Moyenne;* Ger: *Mittlere Sonnenjahr.*

MEAN SPRING RISE. The average height of high water at springs above chart datum.
Fr: *Amplitude moyenne en vive eau;* Ger: *Mittlerer Springtidenhub.*

MEAN SUN. A fictitious sun conceived to move along the equinoctial at a uniform rate, corresponding to the average rate of

the true sun on the ecliptic, the mean sun being alternately in advance and behind the real sun. It is used as reference for reckoning mean time.
Fr: *Soleil Moyen;* Ger: *Mittlere Sonne.*
See **Mean Time.**

MEAN TIDE LEVEL. The average level of high and low waters taken over a considerable period of time.

MEAN TIME. Time as measured by the motion of the mean sun.
Fr: *Temps Moyen;* Ger: *Mittlere Zeit.*
See **Mean Sun.**

MEAN WIDTH RATIO. A factor used in propeller design to denote the average width of a propeller blade outside the hub, divided by the diameter of the propeller.

MEASURED COURSE. A course of one measured mile in length for determining speed and power, standardizing propellers, and determining the relation between speed and propeller revolutions. Also called measured mile course. It is usually indicated by six range buoys for steering purposes, one at each end of the measured mile, one a mile from each end, and one three miles from each end. The ends of the course are fixed by ranges established on shore, each with a front and rear signal or beacon. When these signals are in line the observer is at one end of the course, which is perpendicular to the range lines.
Fr: *Base de Vitesse;* Ger: *Gemessene Seemeile; Meilenfahrt.*

MEASUREMENT. The work of measuring the various dimensions and capacities of a ship in order to get the tonnage for official registration. Also called admeasurement. There are various methods of measuring vessels, according to the national laws of various countries and under the special rules by which vessels are measured when passing through the Suez and Panama canals. Although there are marked differences in these rules, they are all based primarily on the Moorsom system of measurement, which was adopted by Great Britain in 1855 and by the United States in 1864.
Fr: *Jaugeage;* Ger: *Schiffsvermessung.*
See **Builder's Old Measurement, Cubic Measurement, New Measurement, Riddle Measurement, Thames Measurement, Yacht Measurement.**
Lyman, J., Register tonnage and its measurement, American Neptune, Salem (Mass.), vol. 5, 1945; U. S. Bureau of Marine Inspection and Navigation, *Regulations Interpreting Laws Relating to Admeasurement of Vessels,* Washington, 1940.

MEASUREMENT CARGO. 1. Any cargo with a stowage factor above 40 cu. ft. per ton, that is to say, which measures more than 40 cu. ft. to the ton of 2,240 lb. or weighs less than 56 pounds per cubic foot. Also called measurement goods, measurement freight.
Fr: *Marchandises Légères;* Ger: *Massgüter; Massgüterladung.*

2. Light goods which are charged for transport by the bulk of the packages, as distinguished from heavy goods which are charged by weight.
Fr: *Marchandises au Cubage;* Ger: *Massgüter.*

MEASUREMENT RATE. Freight rate charged for all commodities which stow over 40 cu. ft. per ton weight.
Fr: *Fret au Cubage.*

MEASUREMENT TON. A measurement unit of 40 cu. ft. used for goods shipped as measurement cargo.

MEASURE OF INDEMNITY. Expression used in marine policies to indicate the Underwriters liability. When there is a total loss, the liability under a hull policy amounts to the full insured value without deduction on account of previous claims paid, plus any expenses incurred by the assured under the Sue and Labor clause. Where there is a partial loss only, the measure of indemnity under a hull policy amounts to the full reasonable cost of replacing the part lost or damaged, less an allowance in consideration of the old part being replaced by a new one. This deduction is not usually made nowadays because the insurer generally waives this right by a special clause in the policy.

MEAT SHIP. A refrigerator vessel specially designed for the transportation of fresh meat. Also called meat carrier. Meat ships may be classified in two categories:
(1) The frozen-meat ship where the cargo is hard frozen and stowed in suitably-sized "lots" on tank top and 'tween decks with air spaces around each lot at temperatures ranging from 10 to 15° F. Apart from the insulation of the various compartments and the installation of a cooling plant, the frozen-meat carrier differs little in design and structural details from the ordinary cargo carrier.
(2) The chilled-meat ship in which the

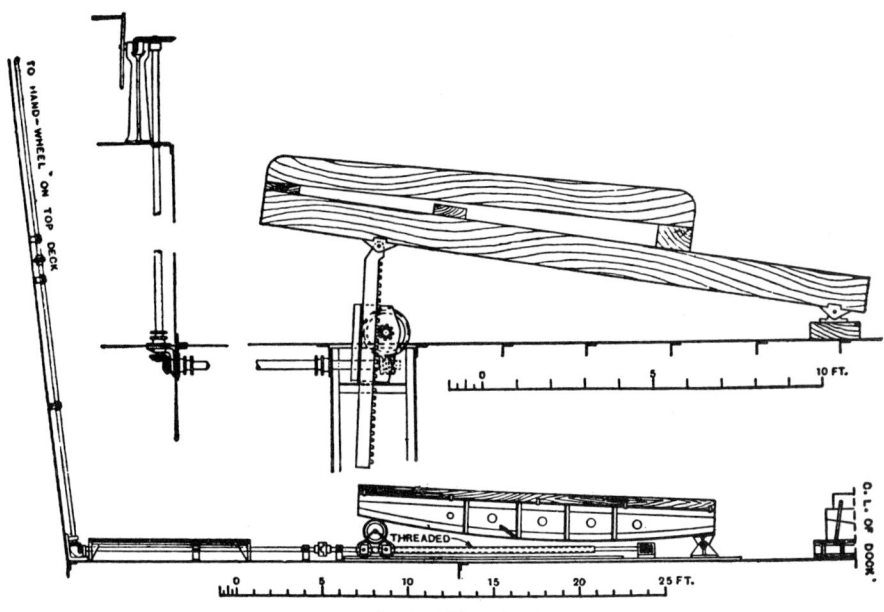

Mechanical Bilge Block

cargo is carried suspended from hooks fastened to rails fitted between the overhead cooling pipes and usually at a temperature ranging from 28 to 35° F. These ships are provided with two or three 'tween decks and shallow lower holds and as the entire weight of the cargo in each compartment is borne by the deck above the scantlings of deck beams, girders and pillars are heavier than in ordinary cargo ships.

Fr: *Transport de Viandes;* Ger: *Fleisch-transportschiff.*

MECHAN FAWKES BOAT. A patent system of construction for open steel boats in which the shell plates are embossed vertically at the butts, obviating the necessity of separate frames. This construction is known as "Mechan Fawkes" patent embossed framing. It can be used for all light craft up to 50 or 60 ft. in length.

MECHANICAL BILGE BLOCK. A bilge block which can be moved into position under water, by means of electric, hydraulic, or hand gear. Also called mechanical side block, movable bilge block, sliding bilge block.

In some designs the blocks hinge around a fulcrum near their inner end and tilt up to grip the bilge. In others, the blocks are set on carriages constructed to slide in grooves cut across the dock bottom and are operated by steel rods and bronze gearing carried up to the coping so that each block can be moved independently in a transverse direction.

Fr: *Tin Mobile; Berceau de Bouchain; Ventrière;* Ger: *Kimmschlitten; Kimpalle.*

The advantage of mechanical bilge blocks is the ease and quickness with which they may be brought into contact immediately after the keel takes the keel blocks. Emergency drydocking of loaded vessels is thus greatly facilitated since it is possible to do away with the necessity of using bilge shores placed by divers, after the vessel is partially dry, when the hull may already have suffered from docking strains. Such blocks also make the use of side shores to keep the ship upright less necessary.

MECHANICAL DAVIT. A general name for davits that move outboard by mechanical gearing, as opposed to ordinary davits which are swung out by hand.

Fr: *Bossoir à Orientation Mécanique;* Ger: *Mechanisch angetriebener Davit.*

MECHANICALLY PROPELLED LIFEBOAT. A lifeboat, other than a motor lifeboat, fitted with propelling gear of approved type having sufficient power to enable the boat to clear readily the ship's side when waterborne and to hold course under adverse weather conditions. If the gear is manually operated it shall be capable of being worked by untrained persons. It shall be capable of being operated when the lifeboat is flooded. Provision must be made for going astern. The volume of internal buoyancy of mechanically propelled boats is increased to compensate for the weight of the propelling gear.

Fr: *Embarcation de Sauvetage à propulsion mécanique;* Ger: *Mechanisch angetriebener Rettungsboot.*

See **Boat Propeller Gear.**

MECHANICAL SIDE SHORE. One of the mechanically operated shores located on each side of a floating dock with a view of mutually adjusting dock and ship, so that the center line of the latter shall coincide with the keel blocks. These shores consist of steel beams working in trunks provided in the side walls and are actuated by rack and pinion.

MECHANICAL VENTILATION. A generic term for various systems of forced or induced ventilation of the compartments of a ship by artificial means. The air is supplied to the compartments, or removed from them by fans or blowers driven by electric motors.

Fr: *Ventilation Artificielle;* Ger: *Kunstlüftung.*

Wright, T., Mechanical Ventilation and Heating as Applied to Ships, Institute of Marine Engineers, London, *Transactions,* vol. 38, 1926.

MECK. A notched staff in a whaleboat, on which the hand harpoon rested. (Obsolete.)

MEDANGARA. A trading prao from Achin, Sumatra, rigged with two masts and steered with two quarter rudders. Its capacity varies from 18 to 36 tons.

MEDCON. Code name for the British Chamber of Shipping East Coast Coal Charter 1922.

MEDICAL SCALES. Government regulations regarding the necessary medical stores and instruments which have to be supplied to seagoing vessels according to the nature and duration of the voyage and trade engaged in.

American Marine Standards Committee, Standard 52, *Medical Equipment for Ocean-Going Vessels;* Standard 53, *Medical Equipment for Coastal Vessels;* Standard 54, *Medical Equipment for Small Vessels;* Washington, 1929. British Board of Trade, *Scales of Medicines, Medical Stores and Instruments for Merchant Vessels,* London, 1936.

MEDICINE CHEST. A chest containing the regulation medical supplies for the use of the crew on a merchant vessel. In the United States, it is compulsory for every vessel of 75 tons or more, with a crew of 6 or more persons to carry a medicine chest. Also called medicine cabinet.

Fr: *Coffre à Médicaments;* Ger: *Arzneikiste.*

MEDITERRANEAN LADDER (G. B.). A plain wooden ladder hinged at its upper end and lying against the ship's side.

MEDITORE. Code name for British Chamber of Shipping Standard Charter Party relating to ore cargoes from Mediterranean ports and Seville River to United Kingdom and continental ports.

MEET HER. An order given to the helmsman to shift the rudder so as to check the swing of the vessel's head in a turn.

Fr: *Rencontrer;* Ger: *Stutzen; Ruderstutzen.*

MEETING RUDDER.
See **Check Helm.**

MEGAPHONE. A trumpet-shaped instrument by which the sound of human voice is increased, so that it may be heard at a greater distance. Recently, an electronic amplifier has been incorporated in hand-held megaphones which increases their audible range several fold. The megaphone is used for giving orders or hailing. Also called speaking trumpet.

Fr: *Gueulard;* Ger: *Sprachrohr; Rufer; Megaphon.*

MEIA-LUA. A roughly built open boat from Portugal very similar to the *saveiro,* from which it differs only by the design of the stem which points higher in the *meia-lua* than in the *saveiro.*

MELON SEED. Small boat originating from Egg Harbor, and used for hunting sea fowls in the shallow marshes and bays bordering the coast of New Jersey, U. S. Its name is derived from the shape of the boat. The hull is wide and shallow with moderately sharp bow and square stern. It is decked with the exception of a cockpit amidships for which there is an adjustable cover. It is fitted with a centerboard and rigged with a single spritsail. Length 13 ft.

4½ in. Breadth 4 ft. 3 in. Also called "Punkin" seed.

MELTEM.
See **Levanter**.

MEMIKENAWA. Japanese fishing sampan from the district of Iwate, northern Japan, employed in long-line fishing. The hull is relatively narrow with a long bow. It is rigged with 2 masts (fore and main). Length over-all 41 ft., waterline 32 ft. Breadth 8.1 ft. Depth 3 ft. Draft 2 ft.

MEMORANDUM CLAUSE. A marine insurance cargo clause which constitutes a limitation of the underwriters' liability in connection with claims for particular average, by exempting him from such claims either absolutely or under certain percentages unless the ship be stranded.

MENAIDE. Double-ended open fishing boat employed for inshore fishing in the Bay of Naples, propelled by a lateen sail and oars. Also called *barca de menaida*. Length 24 to 34 ft. Breadth 6.4 to 8.4 ft. Depth 2.4 ft. Draft 1.1 ft.

MEND. To "mend sail" or to "mend the furl," means to skin the sails up afresh when they have been badly furled.

MENHADEN BOAT. A single-screw vessel used in the menhaden fisheries on the coasts of Florida, North and South Carolina, Virginia and New Jersey. The vessel represents the means of transportation of crew, gear and catch between factory and fishing grounds, and when on the grounds serves as a base from which the purse and striker boats operate.

The hull is of wooden construction and either steam or motor driven. It has a good sheer forward and low stern to facilitate the unloading of fish from the seine to the hold and the lowering and hoisting of the purse boats. The superstructure consists of two deck houses, one forward and one abaft the hold located amidships. There are two masts. The foremast is provided with a lookout nest. Each vessel is equipped with three open boats: the striker boat stowed across the main hatch, and two purse boats swung one on each side from davits near the stern. Length 100 to 175 ft. Draft 9 to 10 ft. Gross tonnage 300 to 600. Net tonnage 60 to 125.

MENTING. A Javanese fishing craft of the *mayang* type but smaller. Also called *kumenting, jumenting, panting*.

MERALTE. Single-sheet bark canoe of the Narrinyeri tribe from Cape Jervis, South Australia.

MERBLANC. Code name for the British Chamber of Shipping White Sea Wood Charter 1899.

MERCAST (U. S.). A radio broadcast system used for the delivery of official Government messages originated by the U. S. Government agencies, addressed to Government-owned, leased or chartered merchant vessels.

MERCATOR SAILING. A navigational method which is characterized by the use of the table of meridional parts. With the assistance of this table, the rules of plane trigonometry suffice for the solution of all problems in dead reckoning.

Fr: *Navigation par latitudes Croissantes;*
Ger: *Segeln nach Vergrosserter Breite.*

MERCATOR'S CHART. A chart built on the principles of Mercator's projection, upon which any rhumb line appears as a straight line. Such a chart is constructed by representing the parallels of latitude at proper intervals, as parallel, horizontal, straight lines, and drawing the meridians perpendicular to the parallels.

On such a chart all the meridians have the same direction and any straight line will cut all meridians at the same angle. But, as on the earth's surface all meridians constantly converge from the equator to the poles, whereas on the chart they are represented as parallel, it is immediately apparent that, except at the equator, all areas have more or less been distorted, and the higher the latitude the greater is the amount of distortion.

Fr: *Carte de Mercator;* Ger: *Merkatorkarte.*

MERCATOR'S PROJECTION. A plan of the earth's surface on which the meridians are represented as being parallel to each other and perpendicular to the parallels of latitude. Each parallel of latitude and each small arc of the meridian is expanded in the vicinity of each parallel in the same ratio. All rhumb lines (loxodromic curves) appear as straight lines on the Mercator projection.

Fr: *Projection de Mercator;* Ger: *Merkatorische Projektion.*

See **Gnomonic Projection, Polyconic Projection, Rhumb Line.**

MERCATOR TRACK. Any straight line on a Mercator chart.
See **Rhumb Line**.

MERCHANTMAN.
See **Merchant Vessel**.

MERCHANT MARINE. The ships and vessels belonging to a maritime nation and employed in commerce and trade. Also called merchant navy (G. B.), mercantile marine.
Fr: *Marine Marchande;* *Marine de Commerce;* Ger: *Handelsmarine.*

MERCHANT MARINE ACT (1920) (U. S.). An act of Congress passed on June 5th, 1920 to repeal certain emergency legislation, and to provide for the disposition, regulation, and use of property acquired thereunder, and for other purposes. The powers conferred on the U. S. Shipping Board Emergency Fleet Corporation were terminated by this act. Also called Jones Shipping Act.

MERCHANT MARINE ACT (1936) (U. S.). An act passed by Congress in 1936 for the fostering, development and maintenance of an American merchant marine sufficient to carry its domestic water-borne commerce and a substantial proportion of the water-borne foreign export and import commerce of the U. S., and to serve as a naval or military auxiliary in time of war or national emergency.

MERCHANT NAVY.
See **Merchant Marine**.

MERCHANT SEAMAN. A name given to a seaman on a private vessel as distinguished from seamen in the Navy or on public vessels.

MERCHANT SHIPPING LAW. That branch of maritime law which gives protection to individuals engaged in maritime commerce both as to their person and their property, whether the wrong be one sounding in tort or in contract. Also called commercial maritime law. It defines the reciprocal rights and obligations of owners, masters, and mariners; gives an adequate remedy to those engaged in supplying the necessities of ships; governs the questions of salvage, general average, marine insurance, charter parties, contracts of affreightment, bills of lading, and so on.
Fr: *Droit Maritime Commercial;* Ger: *Seehandelsrecht; Seeverkehrsrecht.*
Borchard, H. H., *Seeverkehrsrecht,* Berlin, 1928; Maclachlan, D., *Law of Merchant Shipping,* London, 1932.

MERCHANT VESSEL. A privately owned vessel employed and managed by traders for commerce and transportation. Also called trading vessel, merchantman, commercial vessel. As to the legal meaning of the term "merchant vessel" as used in the Hague Convention 1907 and the Declaration of London, the opinions of British and German Prize courts during the 1914-18 war were not in accord. The former apparently restricted the term to vessels employed strictly for purposes of commerce and transportation, their character or use being the test, while the latter extended it to include all vessels not belonging to the state, in which case ownership is the test.
Fr: *Bâtiment de Commerce; Navire Marchand;* Ger: *Handelsschiff; Kauffahrteischiff.*

Merchant vessels or ships may be classified as follows:
1. According to the material employed in their construction and outfit, such as wood, iron, steel, concrete, or a combination of any of these.
2. According to their structural features such as framing system, type of scantlings, arrangement of decks and superstructures.
3. According to their system of propulsion and motive power, that is, paddles, screws, sails, steam, oil engines, or any combination of these.
4. According to the trade and service they are designed for, i.e. passenger vessels, intermediate vessels, tramp vessels, special service vessels (tugs, fishing vessels, dredgers, transports), foreign going vessels, coasting vessels.
Hill, N., "The Functions of the Merchant Ship," Institution of Naval Architects (London), *Transactions,* vol. 62, 1920.

MERCURIAL BAROMETER. A barometer which consists of a long tube containing mercury, with a vacuum at the top of the mercury column and a mercury pot in which the open lower end of the mercury tube is immersed. The height of the mercury column is the measure of atmospheric pressure. Well-made mercurial barometers are fitted with adjustable verniers to permit reading the height of the column to one hundredth of an inch. Aboard ship, the mercurial barometer is mounted in gimbals.
Fr: *Baromètre à Mercure;* Ger: *Quecksilber Barometer.*
See **Aneroid Barometer**.

MERIDIAN. Meridians are imaginary great circles of the earth, passing through the poles.

Fr: *Méridien;* Ger: *Meridian.*
See **Celestial Meridian, Magnetic Meridian, Prime Meridian, Terrestrial Meridian.**

MERIDIAN ALTITUDE. The altitude of a celestial body when on the observer's meridian. It is observed with the sextant and furnishes the simplest and most satisfactory method of determining the latitude of the observer.
Fr: *Hauteur Méridienne;* Ger: *Höhe im Meridian.*

MERIDIAN ANGLE. The meridian angle of a celestial body is the angle at the celestial pole between the meridian of a given place and the hour circle of the body, measured eastward or westward from the meridian from 0 degrees to 180 degrees, or from 0 hours to 12 hours. It is marked East or West according as the body is East or West of the meridian.
Fr: *Angle méridien;* Ger: *Meridian Winkel.*

MERIDIAN DISTANCE. The difference of longitude in time or arc between two places.
Fr: *Distance Méridienne;* Ger: *Meridian Distanz.*

MERIDIAN LATITUDE. The latitude obtained when a celestial body crosses the observer's meridian.
Fr: *Latitude par la méridienne;* Ger: *Meridian Breite.*

MERIDIAN LINE. The line in which the plane of a meridian intersects the plane of the sensible horizon. It meets the celestial horizon in the North and South points.
Fr: *Ligne méridienne;* Ger: *Meridian Linie.*

MERIDIAN PASSAGE. The transit of a heavenly body across the meridian of the place of observation.
Fr: *Passage Méridien;* Ger: *Meridian Durchgang.*

MERIDIAN SAILING. Keeping a vessel on a true North or South course to maintain her on the same longitude.

MERIDIAN ZENITH DISTANCE. The zenith distance of a celestial body when on the meridian of the observer. It is the complement of the meridian altitude.
Fr: *Distance zénitale méridienne;* Ger: *Meridian Zenitdistanz.*

MERIDIONAL DIFFERENCE OF LATITUDE. The quantity which bears the same ratio to the difference of latitude that the difference of longitude bears to the departure.
Fr: *Différence méridienne en latitude;* Ger: *Meridionaldifferenz.*

MERIDIONAL PARTS. In constructing a chart on Mercator's principle, it is necessary to increase the scale of the degrees of latitude as the distance from the equator increases. This is done to preserve the proportion between degrees of latitude and degrees of longitude, the scale of the latter remaining constant. The lengths of small sections of the meridians so increased, measured in minutes of arc of the Equator, are called meridional parts. Also called increased latitudes.
Fr: *Latitudes Croissantes;* Ger: *Meridionalteile.*

MERSEYCON. Code name for the British Chamber of Shipping Coasting Coal Charter 1921 (Mersey Ports).

MESH, MESHING. One of the spaces enclosed by the threads of a net between knot and knot. In measuring a net the distance is taken between two diagonal knots of a square mesh when pulled tightly apart. Thus an 18-in. mesh would have squares of 9-in. sides when floating in the water. There is no universal method of stating the size of a mesh. Thus a mesh (or bar), each side of which is 2 in., may be referred to either as a 2-in. mesh or 4-in. mesh or an 8-in. mesh (sum of four sides); also as an 18-rows-to-the-yard mesh or 6-rows-to-the-foot. By nominal mesh is meant the size of mesh on the spool. Actual or effective mesh means the size after the net has shrunk from use.
Fr: *Maille;* Ger: *Netzmasche; Masche.*
See **Diamond Hang Mesh, Dormant Meshes, False Meshes, Fly Meshing, Square Hanging Mesh, Stale Meshes, Take Up Mesh.**

MESHING NEEDLE. A wooden needle in the form of a shuttle. Used for passing the cord and tying knots in the making of nets.
Fr: *Navette;* Ger: *Filetnadel; Netznadel.*

MESH PIN. See **Spool.**

MESS BOY. Member of a ship's crew who sets tables, serves food, and waits on the tables of the crew's mess room; clears away and washes dishes after meals; cleans mess equipment and mess room. Also called crew messman.
Ger: *Logisjunge; Kajütenjunge.*

MESSENGER. 1. A rope passed around the capstan, and having its two ends lashed together to form an endless line. Formerly used for heaving in the cable. The messenger was bound to the cable by nippers and as the capstan was hove around, the cable was hauled in. As the nippers approached the capstan they were taken off and others put on near the hawse hole. Now replaced by the messenger chain.

Fr: *Tournevire;* Ger: *Kabelar.*
See **Warp.**

2. In an otter trawl net, a wire rope with Manila tail, used for hauling the towing warps inboard and thus bringing both warps together into the towing block after shooting the gear.

Fr: *Vérine.*

3. A general term for lines sent out to lead heavier ropes, such as to lead a mooring line through the shackle of a mooring buoy or to lead a towing line to a disabled vessel.

MESSENGER CHAIN. An endless chain used in transmitting motion from one machine to another, such as driving a windlass or a pump from a winch. Also called gypsy chain.

Fr: *Chaîne de Tournevire;* Ger: *Kabelarkette.*

MESSMAN (U. S.). One who sets table, serves food and waits on table in the officers' mess room; makes beds and cleans wash rooms and living quarters of officers. Also called officers' messman.

MESSROOM. A space or compartment where members of the ship's company have their meals.

Fr: *Carré;* Ger: *Messe.*

MESTIERETO. A Venetian fishing boat of same design and rig as the *bragozzo* but of smaller tonnage, which goes out to the fishing grounds in the morning and returns at night.

METACENTER. The point of intersection of the vertical through the center of buoyancy of a ship in the position of equilibrium, with the vertical through the new center of buoyancy when the ship is slightly inclined, the displacement remaining constant. The height of the transverse metacenter above the center of gravity is a measure of transverse stability.

Fr: *Métacentre;* Ger: *Metazentrum.*

See **Curve of Transverse Metacenter, Longitudinal Metacenter, Pro-** Metacenter, Transverse Metacenter.

METACENTRIC DIAGRAM. A diagram showing the curves of height of metacenter above keel and vertical positions of centers of buoyancy for all drafts to which the vessel may be loaded. They are sometimes set up from a line intersecting the waterlines at 45 degrees.

METACENTRIC HEIGHT. The vertical distance between the center of gravity and the longitudinal or transverse metacenter (in feet or inches). It is termed transverse or longitudinal, as the transverse or longitudinal metacenter is used, and is a measure of stability.

Fr: *Hauteur Métacentrique;* Ger: *Metazentrische Höhe.*

Adams, H. C., "Methods of Finding the Metacentric Height of Vessels for Operating Purposes," Society of Naval Architects and Marine Engineers (New York), *Transactions,* vol. 33 (1925).

METACENTRIC INVOLUTE. The loci of the centers of curvature on the curve of buoyancy of a vessel for varying transverse inclinations.

Ger: *Metazentrische Evolute.*

METACENTRIC SHELF. The curve given by the middle line of the through made by the heeled assymetrical immersed body of the hull. The mean position of this curve is the center of buoyancy but in shape it is almost invariably an irregular curve which cannot be contained by a plane surface.

METAL ELECTRODE. An electrode made of metal, either bare or covered, normally providing the deposit metal of metal-arc welds. Coated metal electrodes have generally supplanted bare electrodes in shipbuilding.

Fr: *Electrode Métallique;* Ger: *Metallelectrode.*

METAL GROMMET. An iron or brass ring sewed into the edge of a hammock, sail or awning. Also called grommet ring. When made of brass it is often in two parts punched together from each side of the canvas and forming an eyelet.

Fr: *Oeuillet Métallique;* Ger: *Gattlagel; Lagel.*

METALLIC LIFEBOAT. A boat made of riveted, welded, or pressed sheets of mild steel or an aluminum alloy. The principal advantage of metallic lifeboats, as compared with wooden boats, is that they are not

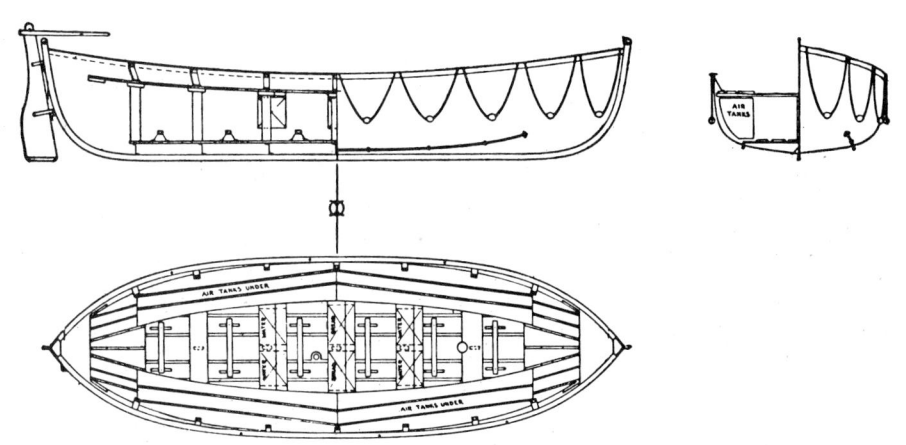

Oar Propelled Metallic Lifeboat. (*Courtesy Welin Davit and Boat Corporation*)

affected by atmospheric temperature and are, therefore, specially suitable for vessels trading in the tropics. Against this there is, however, the disadvantage of corrosion which sets in rapidly in way of chocks, at keel seams, ends of thwarts, and behind buoyancy tanks. The difference in weight between steel and wooden lifeboats is negligible in practice. In order to augment resistance to corrosion boats are frequently built of steel sheets sprayed with molten zinc. The larger types of metallic lifeboats carry up to 145 persons, their loaded weight being about 17¾ tons. They are motor propelled.

A system in which riveting is entirely avoided is occasionally used in the building of metallic steel boats. A plate is bent over on the edge like a hook; a second plate, with its edge of similar hook form, is interlocked with the first and the two short legs of the hooks are closed together by rollers or creases and hammers, making a watertight joint. An inside and outside gunwale are bolted through the plating. The timbers are attached to the shell by means of small lugs. The capacity of buoyancy tanks of all metallic boats is increased by 1.75 cu. ft. for each hundredweight in the boat's hull.

METALLING CLAUSE (G. B.). A marine insurance clause which states that the underwriters are not liable for loss arising from ordinary wear and tear, to which the vessel is subject during the course of the voyage.

METEOROLOGICAL TIDE. A general expression to indicate tides in which time and heights of high and low water are affected by the change in direction and force of wind and the height of the barometer.

METEOROLOGY. The science which treats of the phenomena occurring in the atmosphere surrounding the earth, as well as of their causes and effects. Marine meteorology deals with that portion of the atmosphere which overspreads the oceans and seas.

Fr: *Météorologie;* Ger: *Wetterkunde.*
Allingham, W., *Manual of Marine Meteorology*, London, 1927; Berry, F. A., *Handbook of Meteorology*, New York, 1945; Philip, *Seaman's Handbook on Meteorology*, London, 1918.

METER BOAT. A racing sailboat built to the international rule of measurement and rating 6, 8, 10 or 12 meters as the case may be, according to the formula.

METRIC TON. A unit of weight of 2,204.6 pounds or 1,000 kilograms.

MEWUWO. A West African dugout canoe from Togo, hewed from a cotton tree trunk. Also called *lewu*. It is heavier and larger than the *agowu* and is flat-bottomed. It is employed by the Le people in the coastal fisheries.

MICARTA. Trade name for a patent plastic material consisting of layers of a fibrous product impregnated with synthetic resin, hot-pressed into a dense material with high mechanical strength. It is used for stern tube and propeller strut bearings instead of lignum vitae, and also for rudder pintle bushings.

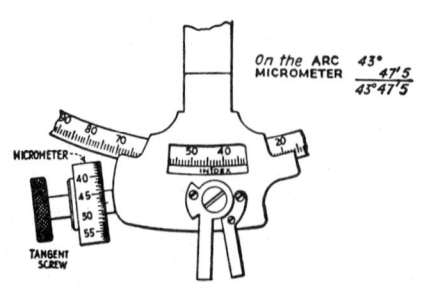

Micrometer

MICROMETER. A screw with graduated head carried by the index bar of a sextant replacing the vernier. Also called sextant micrometer. It is connected to a worm gear which moves the index bar along the toothed limb. One complete revolution of the micrometer head corresponds to one degree along the limb.

MICROSCOPE. In a sextant, a small lens attached to the vernier to facilitate reading the scale.

Fr: *Loupe;* Ger: *Ablese Mikroskop; Lupe.*

MID-CHANNEL. The line of greatest depth in a narrow waterway, as generally followed by vessels entering or leaving a river or harbor.

MID-CHANNEL BUOY. A buoy located in the middle of a fairway or channel.

Fr: *Bouée de mi-chenal;* Ger: *Mittel-Fahwassertonne.*

MIDDLE. To double a rope so that the two parts are of equal length.

MIDDLE BODY. The part of a ship's hull contiguous to the midship section. If the middle body is of uniform cross section throughout its length, and the waterlines are parallel to the center line, it is termed parallel middle body.

MIDDLE GROUND. A shallow area in otherwise deeper water with channels on both sides of it.

Fr: *Banc Milieu; Banc Médian;* Ger: *Mittelgrund.*

MIDDLE-GROUND BUOY. One of the buoys placed at each end of a middle ground, or shoal with navigable channel on either side.

Fr: *Bouée de Banc Milieu;* Ger: *Mittelgrundtonne.*

MIDDLE JIB. A jib, carried by schooners and large trading vessels, which sets next outside the fore-topmast staysail.

Fr: *Faux-Foc;* Ger: *Mittelkluver.*

MIDDLE LATITUDE. A term denoting half the sum of two latitudes. It corresponds to the parallel of latitude situated midway between any two latitudes. Also called mid-latitude.

Fr: *Latitude Moyenne;* Ger: *Mittelbreite.*

MIDDLE LATITUDE SAILING. The approximate solution of a spherical right triangle based on the knowledge that the arc of the parallel of middle latitude between two places intercepted by their meridians is nearly equal to the departure. Also called mid-latitude sailing.

Fr: *Navigation par Latitude Moyenne;* Ger: *Segeln nach Mittelbreite.*

See **Departure.**

MIDDLE-LINE AWNING STANCHION. A stanchion of special design placed amidships to support the ridge spar or awning boom.

Fr: *Support de Faîtage;* Ger: *Mittel-Sonnensegelstutze.*

MIDDLE MAST. A name sometimes given to the third mast of a five-masted vessel. When this term is used the sails and rigging of this mast take on the name "middle."

Fr: *Mât Central;* Ger: *Mittelmast.*

MIDDLE SEAMING. A sailmaker's term which applies to the seam made in the middle of each cloth and parallel to the regular seams, to strengthen the sail and prevent uneven stretching between seams.

MIDDLE STAYSAIL. A triangular or quadrilateral staysail which sets between a topmast staysail and a topgallant staysail.

Fr: *Grand-Voile d'Étai Centrale;* Ger: *Mittelstagsegel.*

MIDDLE WATCH. The watch from midnight till 4 A.M., which follows the first watch. Also midwatch (U. S.).

Fr: *Quart de Minuit;* Ger: *Mittelwache; Zweite Wache; Hundewache.*

MIDDLING SPAR. A round stick or piece of timber suitable for spar making, with a length of 16 to 20 ft. and a girth at the butt of 8 to 12 in. (2 to 3 hands.)

Fr: *Menu Mâtereau.*

MIDNIGHT SUN. A phenomenon which occurs in the arctic or antarctic during the summer when the observer's co-latitude is less than the sun's declination. Under these

conditions the sun does not set.
Fr: *Soleil de Minuit;* Ger: *Mitternachtssonne.*

MIDSHIP FRAME. The frame located at an equal distance from the forward and after perpendiculars; that is, at the midship section.

MIDSHIP LOG. A screw log in which the log line is attached to a boom swung out amidships so that it can be read from the bridge. A connector attached by a shoe to the outboard end of the boom transmits the rotary motion of the log line to a wire and to the log clock secured to the navigating bridge railing.

MIDSHIPMAN. Also cadet. Young man apprenticed as officer to the merchant marine.
Fr: *Elève Officier; Pilotin;* Ger: *Seekadett.*

MIDSHIPMAN'S HITCH. A single loop knot much used about a ship. It consists of a running noose which tightens when the knot passes against an object within the noose.
Fr: *Noeud de Griffe;* Ger: *Hakenschlag; Maulstek.*

MIDSHIP OAR. Also waist oar. **1.** The middle or third and longest oar in a whaling boat, usually eighteen feet in length.
2. The oarsman who pulled the midship oar. He sat on the port side.

MIDSHIPS. A term which describes the position of an object which is midway between the stem and stern, or midway between the sides of the hull.
See **Amidships.**

MIDSHIP SECTION. Also dead flat (U. S.), midship bend, amidships section. **1.** The line formed by the intersection of a transverse vertical plane equidistant from the forward and after perpendiculars with the surface of the hull.
2. A plan of this transverse section on which is indicated the arrangement of the structural parts of the hull with the scantlings of each component part.
Fr: *Coupe au Maître;* Ger: *Hauptspant; Querschnitt.*

MIDSHIP SECTION COEFFICIENT. The ratio of the area of immersed midship section to the product of breadth and draft. In fine-lined vessels where the greatest transverse section is aft of amidships it is the coefficient at the greatest section that applies. Sometimes called maximum section coefficient.
Fr: *Coefficient de Remplissage du Maître Couple;* Ger: *Völligkeitsgrad des Hauptspant; Nullspant Völligkeitsgrad.*

MIDSHIP TACK. An additional tack found on the middle foot of some courses and used in calms and light airs to keep the foot of the sail standing forward thus preventing it from slapping back and chafing against the mast. It is also used in trimming the sail with a quartering wind when the weather clew is raised.
Fr: *Retenue de Basse Voile;* Ger: *Mittschiffshals.*

MIK. See **Boat Crotch.**

MILDEW. Black and green fungus spots on canvas, the growth of which is favored by dampness.
Fr: *Taches d'humidité;* Ger: *Meltau.*

MILITARY BLOCKADE. A blockade designed to shut off an enemy from his sources or bases of supply to make him ineffective and eventually to force him to surrender through lack of food, water, ammunition, or other supplies.
Fr: *Blocus de Guerre;* Ger: *Kriegsblockade.*

MILITARY SALVAGE. Military salvage consists in the rescue of ships and their cargoes from the enemy in time of war. Military salvage cases are dealt with by courts having Admiralty jurisdiction sitting as prize courts.

MILKY SEA. A form of phosphorescence on the surface of the sea which may give light enough to read by.

MILLIBAR. A thousandth part of the unit called a bar and used as a means for reporting barometric pressures. A bar (1,000 millibars) has been established as the measure of atmospheric pressure at sea level and at a temperature of 32° F. 1,000 millibars equals 29.92 in., the ordinary measure of normal atmospheric pressure.

MILL SCALE. An oxide of iron which forms on the surface of steel plates while being rolled. Since mill scale is of a different electrical potential than the main body of the plate corrosive action is frequently set up when the plate is immersed in sea water.
Fr: *Ecailles de Laminage;* Ger: *Walzzunders.*

MINCING HORSE. A bench formerly used on whaling vessels, upon which the horse pieces were laid lengthwise with the

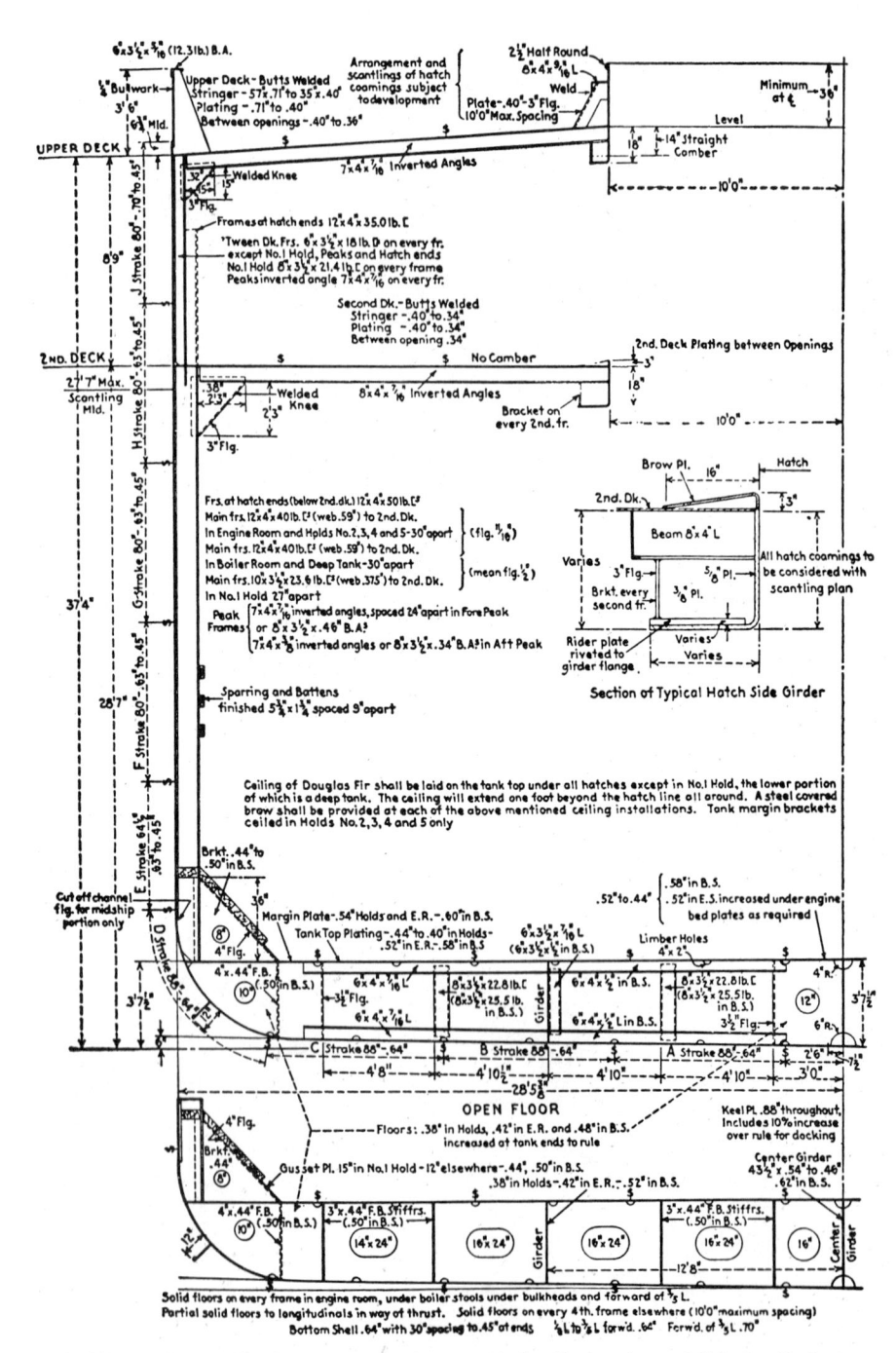

Midship Section, Welded Construction. (*Courtesy Marine Engineering and Shipping Review*)

flesh side downward to be scored or cut into slices varying from ¼ to ¾ in. thick. The knife cut through the skin but was stopped within about an inch of the base, so that the slices were held together like the leaves of a book, and in this condition pitched into the try-pots. They were called minced horse pieces. (Obsolete.)

MINCING KNIFE. A knife about 30 in. long with a handle at each end, formerly used by whalemen to mince the blubber into thin slices.

MINERAL WOOL. An insulating material in blanket form used for heat insulation of hull structure and machinery plant components. Mineral wool generally is made up of rock fibers resulting from melting dolomitic rock and blowing it in a steam spray. These fibers are low in tensile strength and brittle; therefore, to permit installation, they are brought together in blanket form by suitable cements or expanded metal sheathing on both sides, fastened together by fine wires passing through the blanket.

Fr: *Coton Minéral;* Ger: *Mineralwolle.*
See **Insulation.**

MINNOW SEINE (U. S.). A small seine with mesh of about ½ in., used for taking bait, small fish, and so on.

MIRAGE. A delusive appearance caused by abnormal refraction and reflection through air adjacent to the earth's surface, which has air layers of different temperatures or humidity, hence different densities. It appears in many forms, raising the horizon and distant land abnormally, distorting it and often causing images to appear above the horizon or showing them upside down. Suitable atmospheric conditions may occur in any region, but are most frequent over hot deserts. The image when seen across water is generally raised, and is called "looming." Sometimes two or more images of the same object are seen.

Fr: *Mirage;* Ger: *Luftspiegelung.*

MISCIARETTA. See **Cabanella.**

MI-SHUAN. A junk of southern China, known locally as rice carrier, built with keel, sharp bows with stem, and permanent flush deck. The hatches are small, and there is a small superstructure at the stern. The hull has a pronounced sheer aft, and no bulwarks. The rig is 3 masts on the center line. Length over-all 106 ft. Breadth 30 ft. Depth 12.2 ft. (hold). Capacity 500 tons. (Typical.)

MISSING. A vessel is said to be missing when it is so much overdue as to be regarded by its owners as lost. An application is then made to the Committee of Lloyd's to have the vessel "posted," that is, to put up a notice requesting information concerning the vessel. If after a week from this posting no news is received, the vessel is posted as "missing" and on this day the loss is payable by the underwriters. There is no fixed rule in law with regard to the time after which a missing vessel is presumed to be lost but it depends on the circumstances in each case.

Fr: *Sans Nouvelles; Défaut de Nouvelles;* Ger: *Vermisst; Verschollen.*

MISS STAYS. To fail in going about from one tack to the other, when after the ship gets its head to the wind, it comes to a stand, and begins to fall off on the same tack.

Fr: *Manquer à Virer;* Ger: *Wendung versagen.*

MIST. Water vapor suspended in the air in very small drops finer than rain, larger than fog. The term "mist" is applied by seamen to a thin fog which allows navigation to proceed unimpeded. The practical method of differentiating between fog and mist is based upon how far one can see. If the distance which can be seen is under a certain limit the obscurity is termed fog—if over, mist.

Fr: *Brumaille; Brume légère;* Ger: *Mist.*
See **Fog and Visibility Scale.**

MISTIC. A Spanish two- or three-masted, lateen-rigged sailing coaster from Catalonia. The foremast is taller than the mainmast. Both masts rake aft. The mizzenmast, carried only in the larger boats, is vertical and sets a lugsail. The foresail and mainsail are not of the true lateen type. The yard is peaked up higher and the tack projects only very slightly forward of the mast. This particular type of sail is sometimes referred to as "mistic" sail and bears the same relation to the true lateen as the standing lug does to the dipping lug. A standing bowsprit with jibboom carries two to three headsails.

MISTRAL. A northwesterly wind observed in the Gulf of Lyon, the Tyrrhenian Sea, and the middle and lower Adriatic. It is a cold, dry wind, and is the counterpart of the Sirocco. Also called *maestro, maestrale.*
Eredia, F., I venti di mistral, *Rivista Marittima,* no. 2, Rome, 1932.

MISTY. State of the atmosphere characterized by mist.

Fr: *Brumailleux;* Ger: *Diesig.*

MITCH BOARD. An upright piece of timber fitting into a hardwood casing at the deck and forming a crutch for the mast of a sailing drifter to rest upon when lowered. Also called crutch.

Fr: *Miche;* Ger: *Mick.*

MICHELL THRUST BEARING. See **Kingsbury Thrust Bearing.**

MITER. A mode of joining two pieces of timber at an angle. The surfaces to be brought together are so formed that, when connected, the joint makes an angle with the side of each piece that is common to both.

Fr: *Biais; Onglet;* Ger: *Gehrung.*

MITERED JIB. A jib in which the upper cloths above the last run are at right angles to the leech and the others below the last at right angles to the foot. Also called diagonal-cut jib, patent-cut jib.

MITER SEAM. A seam running diagonally from clew to luff across a miter-cut jib-headed sail.

MITTEN MONEY. A local expression used to denote an extra charge added to the regular pilotage fee during winter months.

MIXED POLICY. An insurance policy covering a vessel insured between certain specified places for a given time, it being both a voyage and a time policy.

Fr: *Police à Temps et au Voyage;* Ger: *Zeit und Reise Police.*

MIXED TIDE. A type of tide characterized by two high waters and two low waters in a day, but with morning and afternoon tides differing considerably. This system of tides is intermediate between the diurnal and semidiurnal types, and comprises a great variety of different forms.

Fr: *Marée Mixte;* Ger: *Gemischte Gezeit.*

MIZZEN. Also mizen. 1. The gaff sail on the mizzenmast of a bark or barkentine. Often confused with spanker.

Fr: *Artimon; Brigantine;* Ger: *Besahn; Besan.*

2. The aftermost sail of two-mast fore-and-aft-rigged craft. (Ketch or Yawl.)

Fr: *Artimon;* Ger: *Besahn.*

3. A term which refers to the yards, sails, rigging, and gear belonging to the mizzenmast.

Fr: *Artimon;* Ger: *Besahn.*

See **Storm Mizzen, Yawl Mizzen.**

MIZZENMAST. 1. The aftermost mast of a full-rigged ship, bark, barkentine and three-masted schooner.

Fr: *Mât d'Artimon;* Ger: *Kreuzmast; Besahnmast.*

2. The third mast from forward of a vessel having more than three masts.

3. The after mast in a ketch or yawl.

Fr: *Mât d'Artimon;* Ger: *Besahnmast.*

MIZZEN STAYSAIL. The lower staysail of the mizzenmast. It sets on the mizzen stay.

Fr: *Benjamine; Foc d'Artimon;* Ger: *Kreuz-Stagsegel; Besahn-Stagsegel.*

MLOMU. A Siberian dugout canoe used by the natives near the mouth of the Amur and in the northern part of Sakhalin. It is about 20 ft. long, with pointed bow and square transom.

MOCHIMORO BUNE. Japanese whaling sampan of Yamaguchi district. No rig. Propelled by 6 *yulohs.* Length 36.5 ft. Breadth 8.1 ft. Depth 2.9 ft. Crew 12.

MOCK. A steel pattern representing the exact shape of a portion of the hull where the outside plating has a curvature about more than one axis. Furnaced plates after being heated are hammered to shape on the mock. Also called mock mold, mocked-up mold, bed (G. B.).

Ger: *Plattenmodellbock.*

MOCK FOG. A simulation of true fog, resulting from atmospheric refraction.

MOCKING. A method of building small craft by bending battens to the stem, sternpost and keel without laying off.

MOCKING UP. A name given to the process of duplicating a particular portion of a vessel on the mold loft floor by means of rough frames and sections, so that the necessary molds may be made as though they were being fitted to the ship. Mocking up is used for surfaces which are undevelopable, that is to say which have a double curvature and for which it is not possible to obtain the true shape of area by any geometrical rule.

MOCK MOON. See **Paraselene.**

MOCK SUN. See **Parhelion.**

MOCK-UP. See **Mock.**

MODEL. A ship's model used in a towing tank or model basin for experiments on resistance and powering of vessels when moving through the water.

Fr: *Modèle;* Ger: *Schiffsmodell.*

See **Block Model, Bread and Butter Model, Builder's Model, Half**

Block Model, Half Model, Key Model, Plating Model, Waterline Model.

Some models are made of wood, others are cut from paraffin wax which is cast on to a basketwork frame. The profiling machine employed for this purpose has a pair of rotating cutters which cut down the contour of the model along a waterline. These cutters are controlled by a pantograph, which carries the tracing point along the waterlines of the tracing of the ship. By proper setting of the pantograph the desired size of model can be made from waterlines drawn to any scale. The paraffin between the waterlines is cut away by hand to shape the model. To determine the resistance of a ship from model experiments as developed by Froude, and other scientists, the model is towed at various speeds, the resistances are measured as ordinates to form a curve of resistance.

Davidson, K. M., Importance of Small Models in Naval Architecture, Society of Naval Architects and Marine Engineers, *Transactions*, vol. 49 (New York, 1941).

MODEL TANK. A tank or basin in which ship models are towed at various speeds, and the resistance to propulsion measured. Also called model basin, towing tank. The data are used in predicting the speed and power characteristics of the prototype vessel under investigation. Propellers, self-propelled models, and so on, are likewise tested, and turning characteristics of various hull forms investigated.

Fr: *Bassin d'essai de carènes;* Ger: *Modelltank; Versuchstank; Schlepprinne; Schleppkanal.*

See **Model**.

Davidson, K. M., A Towing Tank for Small Models, Society of Naval Architects and Marine Engineers, *Transactions*, vol. 44, 1936; Saunders, H. E., The Prediction of Speed and Power of Ships, United States Navy Department, Washington, 1933.

MODERATE BREEZE. A wind with a velocity of 11 to 16 nautical miles per hour and a pressure of .67 lb. per square foot. Beaufort's scale No. 4.

Fr: *Jolie Brise;* Ger: *Massige Brise.*

MODERATE GALE. A continuous wind moving with a velocity between 28 and 33 nautical miles per hour. Beaufort's scale No. 7.

Fr: *Grand Frais; Fort Vent;* Ger: *Harter Wind; Steifer Wind.*

MODERATE SEA. A comparatively light running sea. Douglas Scale No. 3.

Fr: *Mer Agitée;* Ger: *Mässig bewegte See.*

MODERATE SPEED. When used in connection with the Rules of the Road at Sea: A speed which permits getting the headway off a ship in a distance less than half the range of the existing visibility.

Fr: *Vitesse modérée;* Ger: *Mässiger Fahrt.*

MODERATE VISIBILITY. Transparency of the atmosphere at sea when objects cease to be visible at a distance of five nautical miles.

Fr: *Visibilité restreinte;* Ger: *Trübe Sichtigkeit.*

MODULUS OF RESISTANCE. A term used in freeboard regulations to denote the moment of inertia of the midship section, divided by the distance from the neutral axis to the strength deck at ship's side.

Fr: *Coëfficient de résistance;* Ger: *Widerstandmodul.*

MOHICAN RIG. A rig of American origin used on sailing canoes.

See **Mohican Sail**.

MOHICAN SAIL. A batten sail used on sailing canoes in the United States. In shape, the sail is an ordinary balance lug cut off at the first reef, thus leaving a short luff and one batten above the boom. The boom is held to the mast by a jaw, above and below which there are leather collars to prevent the spar from rising or falling and render a tack line unnecessary. A parrel or jaw is also used for the batten.

MOHN EFFECT. The erratic transmission of sound emitted by fog signals. It is due to a difference in density of the atmosphere at different points through which the sound travels.

MOKIHI. A raft from New Zealand made of leaves tied in bundles. (Extinct.)

MOLA. Polynesian plank-built canoe from Vella-Lavella Island, northwestern Solomons, similar to the *mon*. It has six strakes of planking. The largest craft have a length of about 45 ft. and a breadth of 3.6 ft.

MOLANGAN. An East Indian double-outrigger canoe used for trolling after tenggire fish off Madura Island. It is rigged with a triangular sail but has no mast. The crew consists of three men. Length 24½ ft. Breadth 1 ft. 6 in. Depth 1 ft. 6 in. (Typical.)

MOLDED BREADTH. The greatest breadth of the hull measured to the outside of frames; that is, inside of the shell plating. In wooden hulls it is measured to outside of planking. It is the breadth used on the lines plan, or sheer draft. Also called Lloyd's breadth or molded beam.
   Fr: *Largeur Hors-Membrures;* Ger: *Berechnungsbreite.*

MOLDED DECK LINE.
See **Beam Line.**

MOLDED DEPTH. The vertical distance measured amidships from the top of the keel (or intersection of the outside of the frame with the center line) to the top of the upper deck beam at gunwale (or of the second deck in a shelter- or awning-deck vessel).
   Fr: *Creux sur Quille;* Ger: *Seitenhöhe.*

MOLDED DISPLACEMENT. A term used in naval architecture. It applies to the displacement computed to the outside of the frames and does not include the submerged volume of planking or shell plating. In wooden hulls this quantity may amount to six or seven percent of the molded displacement. In steel hulls it is only about one percent.
   Fr: *Déplacement hors membres;* Ger: *Form Deplacement.*

MOLDED DRAFT. The keel draft reduced by the amount that the bottom of the keel is below the molded base line; the vertical distance from top of keel to designed waterline; the vertical distance from the waterline to the lowest intersection of the outside planking and the keel. Also called fairbody draft (U. S.), rabbet draft.
   Fr: *Profondeur de Carène;* Ger: *Tauchtiefe; Konstruktionstiefe.*

MOLDED FORM. The form of the ship's structure when the plating or planking is removed. The form over the frames of a ship.
   Fr: *Forme sur gabarits;* Ger: *Form auf Spanten.*

MOLDED LINE. A datum line from which the exact location of the various parts of a ship's hull are determined. It may be horizontal and straight as the molded base line, or curved as a molded deck line or frame line. Molded lines are laid down in the mold loft.
   Fr: *Ligne de tracé;* Ger: *Germallte Linie.*

MOLDING. 1. Half-round iron or strip of wood running fore and aft on the outside of a boat or ship at deck or gunwale level. Also called nosing, ribband, rubber. In ships it is used for finishing or ornamental purposes. In open boats it strengthens the gunwale and acts as a fender.
   Fr: *Liston; Bourrelet;* Ger: *Verzierungsleiste.*

2. The dimensions of a plank or timber reading from outboard to inboard. Opposite of "siding."
   Fr: *Tour;* Ger: *Mallbreite.*
   See **Cable Molding, Hatch Molding, Knuckle Molding, Sheer Molding, Stern Molding.**

MOLDING BOOK. A book prepared by loftsmen, which gives the scantlings of all structural members of the hull with the exception of plates.

MOLD LOFT. A space used for laying down the lines of a vessel to actual size and making templates therefrom for all structural elements entering into a hull. It is necessary that the mold loft be as level as possible and not susceptible to warping; therefore, the floor on which the vessel's lines are drawn consists of two layers of planking laid diagonally and in opposite directions.
   Fr: *Salle à Tracer;* Ger: *Mallboden; Schnürboden.*

MOLD LOFT BATTEN. One of the long flexible battens used in shipyards for laying down the lines of a ship on the mold loft floor and for fairing the sheer in molding. Also called spiling batten, spline. For long easy lines such as sheer lines, battens of rectangular section ranging from ½ by 2 to ¾ by 3 in. are used flatwise; while for greater curves such as the frames, battens of square section varying from ½ by ½ to 1 by 1 in. are used.
   Fr: *Latte de tracé;* Ger: *Streckungsstock.*

MOLDS. Patterns made of thin boards to conform exactly to the shape of frames or other parts of a ship, by the aid of which these structural elements can be bent or fashioned to the required form.
   Fr: *Gabarit;* Ger: *Mallung; Mall.*
   See **Beam Mold, Black-out Mold, Frame Mold, Mock Mold, Sheer Mold.**

MOLE. A substantial masonry structure often serving as a breakwater on its outer side while offering facilities on its inner side for the loading and discharging of ships.

Fr: *Môle;* Ger: *Mole; Hafendamm.*

MOLETA. A Portuguese fishing boat. Rigged with short mast raking forward, carrying a large lateen yard and sail, also two outriggers and a bowsprit on which up to six sails are set. At the stern there is an outrigger spreading two triangular sails. The rudder reaches considerably below the keel level. Length 40 ft. Breadth 13.3 ft. Depth 5.1 ft. (Typical.)

MOLGOGGER. A universal roller used on drifters when shooting the nets and placed on the bulwark abreast of the warp hatch, through which the warp or messenger rope is run out. Also called cage roller, boggey.

MOLOAN. Small East Indian outrigger dugout canoe with portable mast employed in the fisheries off Madura and Sapoodie Islands. Also called *sampan moloan.*

MOMA.
See **Gulba.**

MOMENT OF SAIL. The product of the greatest safe area of sail and the height of the center of effort above the center of lateral resistance.

Fr: *Moment de Voilure;* Ger: *Segelmoment.*

MOMENT OF STABILITY. The moment of the couple tending to return as inclined vessel to the upright.

Fr: *Moment de Stabilité;* Ger: *Stabilitätsmoment.*

MOMENT TO ALTER TRIM, ONE INCH. The longitudinal moment, expressed in foot-tons, required to effect a change of one inch in the trim of the vessel. Also called inch trim moment. It is equal to one-twelfth of the displacement in tons, multiplied by the longitudinal metacentric height in feet, divided by the length at waterline in feet. Abbreviated as M.T.I.

Fr: *Moment pour Faire Varier l'Assiette;* Ger: *Trimmoment.*

MON.. A plank-built boat of the Molucca Islands which is similar in form and construction to the *orembai.*

MONEL. A tough and ductile corrosion-resistant alloy containing 67 to 68 per cent nickel, 28 to 30 per cent copper and 2 to 5 per cent of other metals, principally iron; used for high grade boat fastenings, fittings, propellers and shafting of small craft in salt water service. A similar alloy called K monel contains 2.75 per cent aluminum, 67 per cent nickel and 29 per cent copper. It is non-magnetic and can be used near ship's compasses. There are several other types of monel alloys used in shipbuilding.

Fr: *Metal Monel;* Ger: *Monelmetall.*

Ireland, J., Application of Monel Metal in Engineering and Shipbuilding, Institution of Engineers and Shipbuilders in Scotland, *Transactions,* vol. 72 (Glasgow, 1929); Mueller, R., Die Anwendung von Monel-Metall im Schiffbau. Werft, Reederei, Hafen, vol. 18, no. 11 (Berlin, 1937); Picard, J., Applications du métal monel dans la marine, Aciers spéciaux, métaux et alliages, vol. 3 (Paris, 1928).

MONEY POOL. An agreement entered into by conference lines by which they agree to divide part of the revenue obtained from the transportation of cargo and passengers, usually on the basis of the amount of tonnage employed by each line. The common fund is periodically redistributed. The share of any member violating a price or rate agreement being forfeited, totally or in part in favor of the other members.

MONITOR CANOE. A bark canoe used by the people of the Amur basin in northeast Asia and by those of the Kootenay region in the southeast part of British Columbia and the northeast part of the state of Washington. This craft is peculiar in that both ends are pointed under water; whence its name is derived. With local variations of details the monitor canoe consists of a wooden frame of horizontal slats to which strips of bark are sewed transversely, passing under the boat and ending at the gunwale, the broadest strips being placed amidships. The bark is sewed together with the fibrous roots of fir trees and the seams are well dressed with the gum of the balsam tree. The smallest birch bark canoes are about 12 ft. long, the largest about 36 ft. in length by about 6 ft. in breadth. They are propelled by paddles.

MONKEY BLOCK. A small single block with swivel. The term formerly referred to blocks nailed on topsail yards through which buntlines were led.

Ger: *Grenadierblock.*

MONKEY BRIDGE. Name sometimes given to a fore-and-aft bridge 30 to 36 in. wide on sailing vessels connecting the poop with the forecastle deck, making use of the deckhouses on the way.

MONKEY FACE. A triangular metal plate with a hole drilled at each corner. It is used as a link for shackling the ends of three ropes or chains. It has taken the place of the spectacle clew iron. Also called

MONKEY FIST—MONSOON 518

Shamrock plate; Flounder plate; Eye plate. Mostly used in cargo vessels for joining the topping lift span, the chain preventer and the wire bull rope.

Fr: *Palonnier.*

MONKEY FIST. A heavy knot made of 9- or 12-thread line and worked in the end of a heaving line to weight it. A lead or iron weight is placed inside the knob before the turns are worked taut.

MONKEY FORECASTLE. A short low forecastle open on the after side and used solely for anchor gear (windlass, and so on).

Fr: *Teugue;* Ger: *Halbe Back.*

MONKEY FORESAIL. A square foresail set flying on a sloop or schooner.

Fr: *Fortune; Pafi;* Ger: *Breitfock.*

MONKEY GAFF. A short, standing gaff located above the spanker gaff and projecting from the mizzen topmast head. Used for displaying flags.

Fr: *Corne à Signaux;* Ger: *Flaggengaffel; Obergaffel.*

whale over the ship's side for various purposes connected with cutting in. (Obsolete.)

MONKEY SPAR. A spar of reduced size. A vessel is said to be "monkey rigged" or "monkey sparred" when underrigged or rigged with spars of reduced size. Also called short spar.

MONKEY TAIL.

See **Rudder Horn.**

MONK SEAM. A seam made after sewing the edges of cloths together, one over the other. It is worked with two rows of stitches to give additional strength. Seventy to eighty stitches to the yard is the usual number. Also called prick seam, middle stitching.

Fr: *Couture à Points Piqués;* Ger: *Kappnaht; Durchgenähte Naht.*

MONOMOY SURF BOAT. A double-ended pulling and sailing surf boat with rather full lines, good carrying capacity, and excellent seaworthiness. It has a length of about 26 ft., is carvel-built, and fitted with centerboard. Monomoy boats were carried

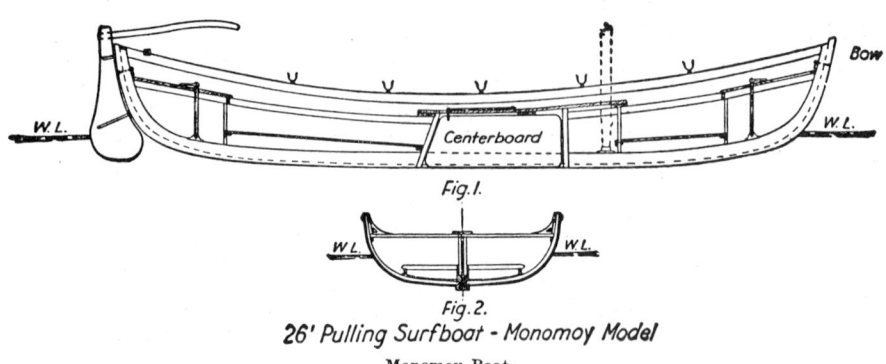

Fig. 1.

Fig. 2.

26' Pulling Surfboat - Monomoy Model

Monomoy Boat

MONKEY ISLAND. Seamen's name for the deck space above the wheelhouse and chartroom where the standard compass is generally placed.

MONKEY POOP. A low house similar to a trunk cabin and projecting up through a raised quarter-deck. It does not extend the full breadth of the ship, nor does it go right aft to the stern.

MONKEY RAIL. A light railing above the quarter boards.

Ger: *Monkireling.*

MONKEY ROPE. Whalemen's term for a rope which was either knotted or belted around a man who was sent down on a

by United States Coast Guard cutters as lifeboats and for general ship's use.

MONOPLANE. A racing boat without break in the longitudinal continuity of the immersed surface, or displacement boat driven at a speed high enough to make it plane.

MONSOON. A name given to seasonal winds found from the Tropic of Cancer to 7° south latitude; and from the coast of Africa through the Indian Ocean and the Bay of Bengal to Japan and the western Pacific. There are two monsoons, the northeast and the southwest. The latter prevails from April to October and the former during the remainder of the year. Monsoons are caused by the unequal heating of land and water and of the several land masses of monsoon regions.

Fr: *Mousson;* Ger: *Monsun.*

See **Little Monsoon, Northeast Monsoon, Southwest Monsoon.**

Barlow, E. W., The Monsoons, *Marine Observer,* vol. 6, no. 63, London, 1929.

MONTAGU RIG. A two-mast fore-and-aft service rig for ship's boats in the British Navy. The sail plan includes a stay foresail, standing lug mainsail, and jib-headed mizzen. A centerboard is fitted to boats with Montagu rig.

MONTEREY SQUID SKIFF. Open boat with short platform at the bow a few inches below the gunwale, a similar platform at the stern and three narrow thwarts. It had a flat bottom, sharp bow, flaring sides and strong sheer. Near the stern the bottom curved up sharply. The width of the stern was intermediate between the dory and sharpy skiff or bateau, being much wider than the former and narrower than the latter. The construction of the stern was purely oriental in style and resembled boats of China. It was formerly used by Chinese squid fishermen on the coast of California and particularly at Monterey. The hull was built of redwood by the Chinese. Length over-all 20 ft. 11 in. Beam 5 ft. 10 in. Depth 2 ft. 4 in. Width of stern 3 ft. 6 in. (Obsolete.)

MONTYCAT. A type of cat-rigged racing boat.

MOON DOG.

See **Paraselene.**

MOONSAIL. A square sail formerly carried in light winds above a skysail. Also called moonraker.

Fr: *Papillon;* Ger: *Mondkieker; Mondreiter.*

MOOR. 1. To secure a ship, boat, or other floating object in a particular place by means of chains or ropes which are made fast to the shore, to anchors, or to anchored mooring buoys.

Fr: *Amarrer;* Ger: *Festmachen.*

2. To ride with both anchors down at a considerable distance apart and with such a scope of chain on each that the bow is held approximately midway between them. Although there is no statutory law against riding to a single anchor, the "custom of seamen" is to moor with two anchors in restricted anchorages where there is insufficient room for each vessel to swing to a single anchor. Failure to do so would constitute negligence and make the offending vessel responsible for damage caused thereby to another ship.

Fr: *Affourcher;* Ger: *Vertauen; Vermuren.*

See **Dropping Moor, Flying Moor.**

MOORAGE. A sum due by law or usage for mooring or fastening ships to posts or piles at the shore or to a wharf.

Fr: *Droit d'Amarrage;* Ger: *Vertauungsgebühren.*

MOOR HEAD AND STERN. A procedure by which a ship is held fast between a bow anchor dropped forward and a stern anchor aft. It is resorted to in narrow anchorages when necessary to avoid swinging to the tide or wind or for any other special reason. A number of large merchant vessels carry a self-stowing stern anchor for this purpose.

Fr: *S'Embosser;* Ger: *Vertauen.*

MOORING. The place in a river, harbor, or dock in which a vessel may be moored; also that to which vessels may be secured.

Fr: *Poste d'Amarrage;* Ger: *Vertauung.*

See **Quarter Mooring.**

MOORING ANCHOR. An anchor used for holding in place a mooring buoy to which ships may secure in lieu of anchoring. They serve also as anchors for buoys marking a channel or shoal. These anchors should not project above the bottom, and therefore, have only one fluke, or are mushroom anchors.

Fr: *Ancre de Corps-Mort;* Ger: *Bojeanker; Bojanker.*

MOORING BITTS. Large hollow cast-iron standards placed in pairs, to which mooring lines are made fast. Also called mooring bollards, timberheads. They are bolted to the deck in such position as to give a good lead to the mooring pipes.

Fr: *Bittes d'Amarrage;* Ger: *Doppelpollern.*

American Marine Standards Committee: Standard no. 2, *Cast-Iron Mooring Bitts,* 1927; Standard no. 23, *Cast-Steel Mooring Bitts,* 1930; British Standards Institution, London, Standard no. 3,005, *Bollards,* 1922.

MOORING BRIDLE. The chains or fasts attached to permanent moorings and taken into the hawse holes.

Fr: *Patte d'Oie de Corps-Mort;* Ger: *Kettenarm.*

MOORING BUOY. A buoy secured to permanent moorings, enabling ships to moor

MOORING CHAIN—MOORING CLUMP 520

Mooring Buoys

A. Cylindrical Mooring Buoy
B. Peg Top Mooring Buoy
C. Pear Shaped Mooring Buoy
D. Wooden Mooring Buoy

Mooring Lines

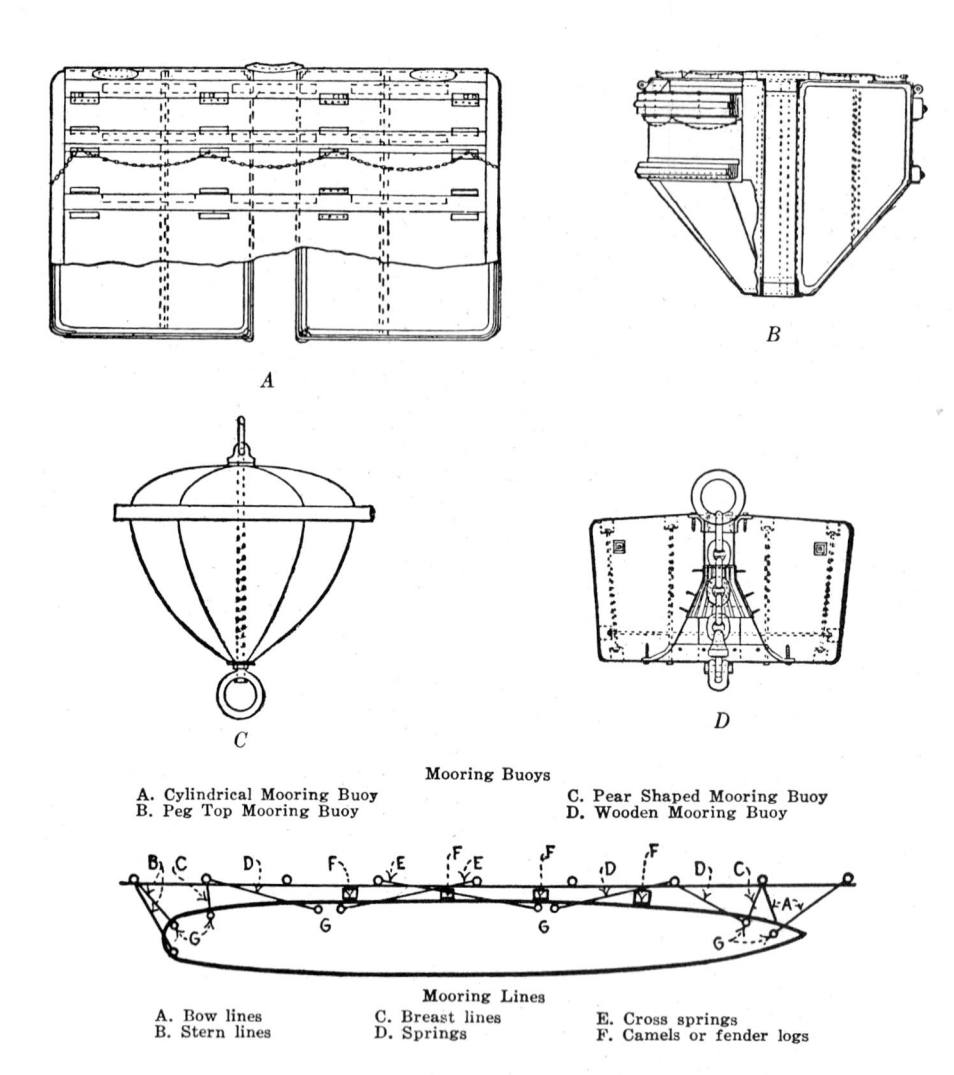

A. Bow lines
B. Stern lines
C. Breast lines
D. Springs
E. Cross springs
F. Camels or fender logs

at specified positions in the harbor instead of having to anchor when they are not tied up alongside a wharf or quay. Also called anchorage buoy. Mooring buoys are usually of cylindrical shape and made of riveted or welded steel plates. The ship's cable is fastened to a heavy ring or shackle fitted on the top.

Fr: *Coffre d'Amarrage; Bouée de Corps-Mort; Bouée d'Amarrage;* Ger: *Muringboje; Festmachetonne; Ankerboje.*

MOORING CHAIN. That part of a buoy mooring chain which lies on the sea bottom and is attached to the sinker.

Fr: *Chaîne dormante;* Ger: *Schlafkette.*

MOORING CHOCK. Cast metal fitting with incurving horns fastened to the deck at sides. It leads hawsers or other lines to the mooring bitts.

Fr: *Chaumard;* Ger: *Lippklampe; Verholklampe.*

See **Chock, Open chock, Roller chock.**

MOORING CLUMP. A mooring weight made of concrete or cast iron and fitted with a heavy iron eye. Mooring clumps are

used as ground tackle, for buoys, etc. Also called mooring block, mooring sinker.
> Fr: *Crapaud;* Ger: *Abbindeblock; Ankerstein; Verankerungsplatte; Muringstein.*

MOORING DOG. A heavy iron bar fastened to the side plating of a vessel near the waterline, to which a mooring line can be secured. Also called mooring staple.

MOORING LIGHTER. A boat or lighter fitted with the necessary appliances for handling and transporting anchors, chains, and cables about a harbor, used for the installation or removal of permanent moorings. Also called chain boat, anchor hoy.

MOORING LINE. Any chain, cable, or hawser by which a vessel is secured to a dock or mooring. Also called mooring hawser. The mooring lines of merchant vessels are usually made of galvanized cast steel flexible wire rope composed of 6 strands with hemp core. Each strand consists of 24 wires around a hemp core. An eye is spliced in the end.
> Fr: *Aussière d'Amarrage; Amarre;* Ger: *Belegtrosse; Muringtau; Festmacheleine; Festmachetrosse; Halteleine.*

MOORING MAT. A thrummed mat bound around a mooring line to prevent chafing at some particular point.

MOORING PENDANT. A small chain which has one end fastened to a mooring buoy and the other to the ground chain.
> Fr: *Itague de Corps-Mort;* Ger: *Vertauschenkel.*

MOORING PIPE. A cast-iron fitting riveted or welded to the bulwarks for leading mooring lines overboard. Also called hawser port.
> Fr: *Ecubier d'Amarrage; Ecubier de Pavois;* Ger: *Verholkluse; Vertaukluse; Seitenkluse.*

American Marine Standards Committee, Standard no. 63, *Mooring Pipes for Ships,* Washington, 1930.

MOORING POST. A strong upright post of wood, stone, or cast-iron fixed firmly in the ground for securing vessels by hawsers or chains.
> Fr: *Borne d'Amarrage;* Ger: *Vertauungspfahl.*

MOORING TELEGRAPH. A telegraph similar in construction to the engine room telegraph and located on the forward end of the forecastle deck. It is connected to a repeater on the navigating bridge and is used by the officer in charge of ground tackle and head lines.
> Ger: *Ankertelegraph.*

MOORINGS. The anchors, chains, bridles, and so on, laid athwart the bottom of a river or harbor, by which a ship is secured. Permanent moorings are laid for many reasons. The most important are as follows: (1) to make the most of a limited space by providing moorings for each class of ship or craft in waters suitable to them; (2) to get ships as near as possible to a common landing place to facilitate the embarkation of passengers, crew, and cargo; (3) to provide the utmost security for ships in crowded waters; (4) to facilitate the administration of a port so that ships may come and go with a minimum of outside help and with certainty of position to be taken up; (5) to preserve a ship's ground tackle from wear and tear.
> Fr: *Corps Mort;* Ger: *Fixe Vertauung.*

See **All-Fours Moorings, Buoy Moorings, Double-Span Moorings, Fore-and-Aft Moorings, Pile Moorings, Screw Moorings, Swinging Moorings, Three-Leg Moorings, Two-Arm Moorings, Two-Leg Moorings.**

Permanent moorings are made up of two or more anchors laid down with large chains which are brought to a central ring for the ship to secure to. The mooring anchors are usually placed at the corner of a square or triangle or up and down stream. In some types of moorings the mooring cable is carried up to the surface of the water and supported by a large-sized mooring buoy, the ship being secured to the buoy by a hawser or by its own chain cable. Another arrangement commonly adopted is to have a small-sized mooring buoy connected to the heavy mooring chain by a small chain or rope which is used only for picking up the riding chain to which the vessel can fasten her cable.

MOORING SCREW. An anchoring device used for securing mooring buoys in soft (clay) bottoms. It is composed of a shaft from 3 to 8 ft. in length with a number of cast-iron flanges having a diameter of 2 to 6 ft. The depth to which the screw is driven into the bottom depends on the nature of the ground.
> Fr: *Ancre à Vis;* Ger: *Vertauschraube; Erdanker; Schraubenanker.*

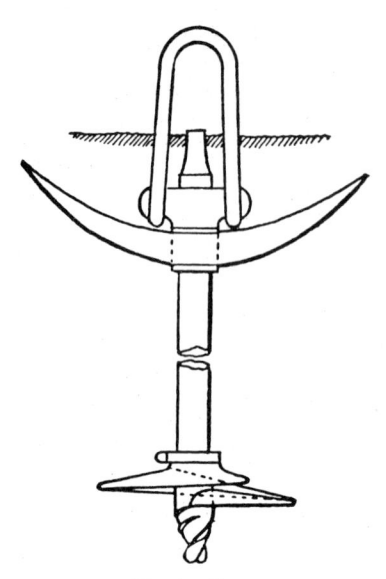

Mooring Screw

MOORING SHACKLE. A swivel used in mooring a ship to shackle two chains together so that they will not become twisted. Also mooring swivel, buoy shackle.

Fr: *Emérillon d'affourche;* Ger: *Vertauschackel.*

MOORING STAPLE.
See **Mooring Dog.**

MOORSOM RULES. A method of calculating the internal capacity of a merchant vessel by expressing it in cubic feet, and dividing it by 100, each 100 cu. ft. to be a ton. This method was worked out by George Moorsom, surveyor general of tonnage in Great Britain in 1854 and has since been adopted by virtually all countries in the world for the measurement of vessels. In their present form the rules differ only in minor respects from those originally formulated by Moorsom. They were adopted by the U. S. in 1864.

Fr: *Jauge Moorsom;* Ger: *Moorsom Vermessungssystem.*

MOORSOM TONNAGE.
See **Measurement.**

MOP. A bunch of thrums or coarse yarn; a piece of cloth fastened to a long handle and used for cleaning floors, drying decks, and clamping down. Also called swab.

Fr: *Guipon; Vadrouille;* Ger: *Mop.*
See **Pitch Mop.**

MORNING WATCH. The watch from 4 A.M. till 8 A.M.

Fr: *Quart de Jour;* Ger: *Morgenwache.*

MOROMI-BUNE. Japanese whaling sampan from Yamaguchi district. Length 39 ft. Breadth 9.5 ft. Depth 3.3 ft. Crew 11. (Typical.) This sampan has no rig and is propelled by 6 yulohs.

MORSE LAMP. A lamp adapted for the transmission of optical signals by the Morse code. Also called blinker, signaling lamp. There are three classes of Morse signaling lamps in general use: (1) fixed electric lamps placed on top of a semaphore standard, on a masthead, or at a yardarm; (2) portable electric lamps deriving their power from a dry battery; and (3) portable oil lamps.

Fr: *Fanal Morse; Fanal à Signaux;* Ger: *Signallampe; Morselampe.*

Morse lamps should be so designed and constructed as to give a candle power equivalent to 10 candles. A cylindrical dioptric lens should be fitted. According to the International Convention for Safety of Life at Sea (1929) all ships over 150 tons gross when engaged on international voyages must have an efficient Morse signaling lamp. This lamp should be distinctly visible at a distance of 3 miles and over an arc of 45 degrees.

MORTISED BLOCK. A block made out of a single piece of wood with the space for the sheave chiseled out.

Ger: *Verzapfter Block.*

MOSES BOAT. An open rowboat formerly used between ship and shore in the West Indian islands for loading hogsheads of sugar. It was broad and flat-bottomed, with lapstrake planking and shaped very much like a walnut shell. There were two classes, termed single or double Moses, according to size. The single Moses boat was about 8 ft. long and just large enough to hold one man and a hogshead of sugar. The double Moses carried two hogsheads. They were worked with pair oars and loaded from cranes or projecting rocks; seldom or never from the beach.

MOTO-MOTO. A double-outrigger dugout canoe from western Papua. Both ends of the hull are raked and produced to a blunt squared point. The sides are heightened by means of a wash strake on which at each side of the bow is a triangular washboard.

These canoes are nowadays schooner-rigged with canvas sails.

MOTORBOAT. A generic term which usually refers to small craft employed as pleasure or work boats propelled by gasoline or internal combustion engines. Motorboats may be classified according to hull form in two categories, i.e. displacement craft and hydroplanes; or, according to engine installation into inboard and outboard engined craft.

Displacement craft are those in which approximately the same amount of water is displaced, no matter at what speed the boat travels. In the hydroplanes, on the other hand, the hull raises itself partly out of the water and the amount of water displaced is less than when at rest.

As defined in the motorboat act of 1940 the term motorboat refers to every vessel propelled by machinery and not more than 65 ft. in length on deck with the exception of tugboats and towboats propelled by steam.

Fr: *Bateau à Moteur; Embarcation à Moteur;* Ger: *Motorboot.*

MOTOR LAUNCH (U. S. N.). Gasoline-engine-driven or Diesel-engine-driven general purpose motorboats, usually of wooden construction, from 24 ft. to 50 ft. in length, undecked, in contradistinction to "motorboats" which are decked boats, and provided with a canopied cabin aft for passengers, and a cockpit amidships.

See **Motorboat.**

MOTOR LIFEBOAT. A lifeboat fitted with an approved type of compression ignition engine suitably enclosed to ensure operation under adverse weather conditions.

According to the provision of the 1948 International Convention for Safety of life at sea, two classes of motor lifeboats are specified; those of class A must carry a sufficient quantity of fuel for 24 hours continuous operation. The speed ahead must be at least six knots in smooth water with full complement and equipment aboard. In motor lifeboats of class B, the speed ahead shall be at least four knots when fully loaded. Provision for going astern is required in both types. All cargo vessels of 1600 tons gross or more and all passenger vessels must carry at least one motor lifeboat or a mechanically propelled lifeboat of approved type. Two motor lifeboats of class A are required to be carried by messenger vessels having 20 or more lifeboats, and each must be fitted with radiotelegraph equipment.

Fr: *Canot à moteur;* Ger: *Motorrettungsboot.*

See **Mechanically Propelled Lifeboat.**

MOTORMAN (U. S.). A marine oiler who lubricates the machinery on a motorship.

MOTOR SAILER (U. S.). Term used to denote in general all craft provided with dual means of propulsion, i.e., sails and motor. It ranges through the entire category from a sailing vessel with little mechanical power to a motor vessel with small sail area.

See **Auxiliary Powered Vessel.**

MOTORSHIP. A mechanically propelled vessel in which the principal motive power is obtained from an internal combustion oil or gas engine. The motor or motors may be directly connected to the main shafting, or fitted with mechanical gearing transmission or driving an electric generator with propeller motor attached to the shafting.

Fr: *Navire à Moteur;* Ger: *Motorschiff.*

See **Diesel Engine, Diesel Electric Drive, Geared Diesel Engines, Semi-Diesel Engine.**

MOTOR TANKER. A tanker propelled by internal combustion engines.

Fr: *Petrolier à moteur;* Ger: *Tankmotorschiff.*

MOTOR WHALEBOAT. A 26 ft. double-ended open motorboat used for lifeboat and picket duty in the United States Navy.

MOTOR WINCH. A winch driven by a separate motor where both are placed on the same bedplate. Gasoline, kerosene, Diesel and semi-Diesel engines have been used for these winches, which are chiefly installed on small motor craft.

Fr: *Treuil à Moteur;* Ger: *Motorbetriebene Winde.*

A governed-speed, constant-running engine drives the hoisting barrel through the necessary gearing and friction clutch. The creeping speeds necessary for breaking out cargo are obtained by slipping the clutch. Light-hook speeds are limited to the full load hoisting speed. Increased flexibility is sometimes obtained by the introduction of a controllable hydraulic coupling between engine and gearing.

MOTSHISO-BUNE. A Japanese open whaling boat from the island of Hirado (Nagasaki district). It has an average length of 41 ft. with a beam of 7 ft. The crew consists of 12 hands and it is propelled by 8 oars. These boats work in fleets of four.

MOURRE DE PORC. A small, flat-floored fishing boat originating in Martigues and Grau du Roi on the coast of Provence. Also called *bateau à éperon*. It is built with large beam; the ratio of breadth to length varies from 0.34 to 0.39. Framing is in three pieces: the floor and two side pieces. The smaller boats of this type are open, the larger ones decked with a hatch amidships and loose hatch covers. Stone ballast is occasionally stowed in wooden boxes. The stem is built clipper fashion and is supposed to resemble a pig's snout ("mourre de porc," in Provencal dialect) from which the boat derives its name. Length 16½ ft. to 30 ft. Breadth 6.3 to 10.5 ft. Depth 2.3 to 3.8 ft. (Average.)

MOUSE. To seize a piece of small stuff across a hook used in the rigging to prevent its unhooking.

Fr: *Moucheter;* Ger: *Einmausen.*

MOUSING. Small stuff, hemp or wire, seized across the opening of a hook to prevent it from clearing itself. It is usually made by taking a number of turns around the shank and crossing the ends and finishing with tight frapping turns to give the necessary tension.

Fr: *Aiguilletage;* Ger: *Mausing.*

MOVABLES. A term used in marine insurance to denote any movable, tangible property which would not, ordinarily, be included under the terms "cargo" or "goods." Money, valuable securities, and other documents come under this heading.

MTEPE. A keel-built open sailing craft from Lamu archipelago (east coast of Africa) with long grab bow and sharp raking stern. The hull is entirely built without nails or iron. The strakes of planking are connected by sewing and doweling. The butts of planks are scarfed. The stemhead terminates with a short stout curved block projecting outboard. The rudder is slung from rope grommets. The rig consists of a vertical mast stepped a little forward of midships and stayed by a forestay and two backstays. It carries a square sail made of palm-leaf matting. Length over-all 60 ft. Length of keel 35 ft. Breadth 18 ft. Inside depth 6 ft. 6 in. (Typical.)

Hornell, J., The Sea-Going Mtepe and Dau of the Lamu Archipelago, Mariner's Mirror, vol. 27, London (1941).

MTUMBWI. A dugout canoe without outriggers used for transportation on the estuaries and between the islands (Tumbatu) of the Kenya coast. It is rigged with a sail which sets on two diagonally crossed poles. Paddles with round blades are also employed for propulsion.

MUD. Fine earthy marine sediment.

Fr: *Vase;* Ger: *Schlamm.*

MUD BERTH. A berth in a tidal harbor where the vessel lies on soft bottom at low water; a berth where a vessel does not remain afloat at all states of the tide.

MUD BOX. A square steel box fitted with a strum plate, located on the suction side of the bilge piping next to the valve chest. It is designed to hinder the entrance of solid matter which might clog the valves.

Fr: *Boîte Égyptienne;* Ger: *Schmutzkasten; Schlammkasten.*

MUD PILOT. A pilot who operates by eyesight, gauging the depth by looking at the bottom and noting the changes in the color of the water. In England the term is also used to denote river pilots who take vessels between London Docks and Gravesend.

Fr: *Pratique.*

MUDYERI. Australian one-piece tied bark canoe of the Wandandian tribe from Shoalhaven River estuary, New South Wales.

MUFFLER. A device through which the exhaust gases from an internal combustion engine are passed in order to deaden the noise from the explosions of the engines. It is generally installed on the upper deck and enclosed in a steel casing (dummy funnel) designed to appear as an ordinary smokestack.

Fr: *Pot d'Échappement;* Ger: *Schalldämpfer; Auspufftopf.*

MULE. 1. Local name given to a ketch-rigged sailing trawler found on the south coast of England (Brixham) of about 30 tons gross.

2. An open fishing boat used off the Yorkshire coast. It is a development of the coble. A sharp stern replaces the coble's flat transom stern. Mules are not as convenient for beaching as cobles, but owing to their sharp stern they are safer for running before a big sea. Length 33.8 ft. Breadth 10 ft. Depth 4.8 ft. Gross tonnage 6. (Typical.)

See **Sea Mule.**

MULETA. A small fishing boat found on the coast of Valencia, Spain, rigged with a lateen sail and jib. This type of boat is characterized by great length in proportion to breadth.

MULEY.
See **Thames Sailing Barge.**

MULLET BOAT. Open boat employed by the Apalachicola fishermen in the mullet fisheries, with seines, off the Gulf of Mexico. It is similar in design to the sponge dinghy but larger. The fore end is decked and waterways run aft to the stern on either side. The sail used is a lateen with long yard and short stubby mast. Length 20 to 22 ft. Breadth 6 to 7 ft. (Average.)

MULTIPLE PLY CANVAS. Canvas in which the warp is made of two threads which lie side by side untwisted. Also called twill canvas. A variety of canvas in which the weft threads do not pass over and under the warp threads in regular succession but pass over one and under two.

Fr: *Toile à Fils Multiples.*

MULTISTEP HYDROPLANE. A form of motorboat in which a series of steps are embodied in the bottom of the hull, offering a series of inclined planes to the surface of the water. This provides a definite lifting effect as soon as the boat attains a certain speed and at the same time reduces the wetted surface, with consequent reduction of skin friction.

Fr: *Hydroplane à Redans Multiples;* Ger: *Gleitboot mit mehreren Stufen.*

MUMBLE BEE. A local name given to a cutter-rigged sailing trawler of the Bristol Channel. The mast is stepped well forward. Over-all length about 35 ft. Tonnage 20 tons gross. It originates from the "Mumbles" in Swansea Bay; hence its name.

MUNTZ METAL.
See **Naval Brass.**

MURMAN CURRENT. A warm current which runs southeastward off the coast of the Kola peninsula. It is formed by the waters of the North Atlantic drift which penetrate the Arctic Ocean. Its influence is shown by keeping these water open to navigation in Winter.

MURO. See **Goa.**

MUSCIARA. Open rowboat employed in the Italian tuna fisheries, in which the fishing master (Rais) takes place with his foreman (Musciarieri) before the fishing operations and during transportation to or from the shore. Length 26.2 ft. Breadth 6.5 ft. Depth 2.3 ft. (Average.) Also called *musciara da rais.*

MUSCIARETTA.
See **Cabanella.**

MUSCONGUS BAY BOAT. Small, square-sterned, sloop-rigged fishing boat, open in the afterpart, and with a cuddy forward. They were built with centerboard and some were clinker-built, while others were set work. The length of these boats varied from 16 to 26 ft., and their width from 6 to 9 ft. They were formerly used in the lobster and shore-cod fisheries of Maine and Massachusetts.

MUSHROOM ANCHOR. A special type of anchor having a bowl-shaped crown, into the center of which the shank is welded. The upper end of the shank is fitted for the reception of a shackle pin as in anchors of ordinary type. It has great holding power in soft bottoms. Used for buoy moorings.

Fr: *Ancre à Champignon;* Ger: *Pilzanker; Schirmanker.*

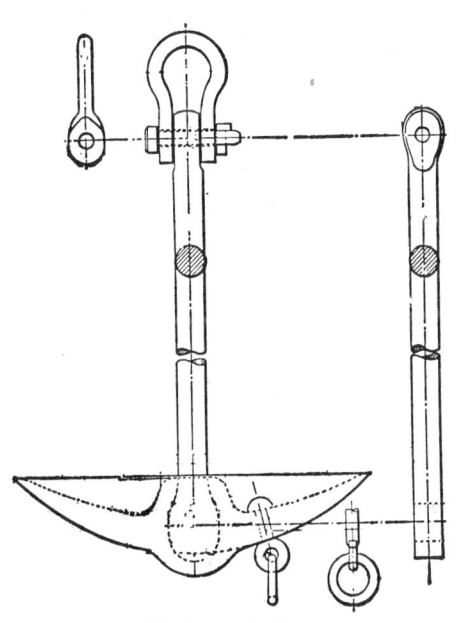

Mushroom Anchor

Owing to its large surface and concavity, the mushroom head is able to arrest moving particles of the sea bottom, and so produce an accumulation of sand or gravel under which it lies deeply buried. This property, technically called "sanding up," is a valuable one, but it is not available in cases of temporary anchorage. Mushrooms are not trustworthy anchors on hard bottoms nor indeed are they to be recommended anywhere unless there is a reasonable certainty of their being sanded up. Another good point for the mushroom consists in its immunity from fouling by the cable. For this reason it is frequently used for mooring lightships.

MUSHROOM VENTILATOR. A small above deck ventilator frequently employed for ventilating cabin spaces, and in which the draft may be regulated by screwing the hood up or down.

Fr: *Chàmpignon d'Aération;* Ger: *Pilzkopflüfter.*

MUSTER. The assembling of a ship's company and passengers for inspection or drill.

Fr: *Appel;* Ger: *Musterung.*

MUSTER LIST.
See **Stations Bill.**

MUSTER ROLL.
See **Bill.**

MUTINY. The unlawful resistance to a superior officer, or the raising of commotions and disturbances on board a ship against the authority of its commander.

Fr: *Mutinerie;* Ger: *Meuterei.*

MUTTE. Small flat-bottomed, round-ended decked boat with overhanging stem and leeboards found in the estuaries and coastal waters of East Frisia, Germany. Also called *Pogge.* Chiefly used for the transportation of peat in the Ems estuary.

See **Spitz-Mutte.**

The rig is composed of a pole mast with gaff mainsail and jib-headed foresail. The larger seagoing boats of this type have a bowsprit, two headsails, and gaff topsail. The so-called *Halb-Mutte* has sharp bow and stern. Tonnage 13 to 30. Length 54 ft. Breadth 7 ft. 4 in. Inside depth 5 ft. (Average.)

MUTTON SPANKER. See **Spanker.**

MUTUAL INSURANCE. A name given to insurance where two or more persons mutually agree to insure each other against marine losses. Mutual insurance associations or clubs (protection and indemnity clubs as they are usually named) are worked on a non profit cooperative basis. They provide for losses not covered under an ordinary marine policy, each owner contributing pro rata to the size and value of the vessels which are entered in the association.

Fr: *Assurance Mutuelle;* Ger: *Wechselseitige Versicherung.*

MU, XIMGU-MU. A keelless plank-built canoe used by the Gilyak people of the lower Amur (eastern Siberia) and Sakhalin Island. It is flat-bottomed with square bilges and vertical sides. The stern is cut off square by a vertical transom board, above which is the steersman's seat.

The pointed bow is formed by two upcurving planks. The bottom is prolonged under the bow planking and terminates in a rough carving representing a bird or other animal. All plank seams are filled with moss from inside and made watertight by seam battens fastened with wooden pegs. In order to protect the hull when the boat is beached or launched, a longitudinal chine piece is fitted outside at each bilge. Length over-all 25 ft. Breadth aft, 3 ft. 4 in.; amidships, 3 ft. 2 in.; forward, 2 ft. 2 in. Depth 1 ft. 6 in.

When traveling in coastal waters a wash strake is fitted to give more freeboard. These craft are seldom sailed. With a fair wind they use a square sail bent to two poles crossing each other diagonally. Each spar is stepped on the side of the boat and held at the head by a line leading aft.

MUZZLE. 1. To muzzle an anchor means to fasten the cable to the throat of the shank, as well as to the ring. It is tied to the former with small stuff or rope strong enough to hold it in place but which will break under a strain if the anchor fouls anything heavy.

2. A term used by Thames bargemen to denote an iron collar encircling the mast and keeping the heel of the sprit in position; the weight is taken by the stanliff.

MUZZLER. A strong head wind. Also called nose ender.

Fr: *Vent contraire;* Ger: *Gegenwind.*

N

N. Letter of the international code of signals denoted by flag having four horizontal rows of alternate blue and white squares. Flown as a single letter signal signifies: "No." Also called **"Negative" flag.**

N.A. NAUTICAL ALMANAC.
n.a.a. NOT ALWAYS AFLOAT.
N.b.E. NORTH BY EAST.
N.b.W. NORTH BY WEST.
N/C NEW CHARTER or NEW CROP (grain trade).
N.Lat. NORTH LATITUDE.
N/m NO MARK (bill of lading).
np or **Np** NEAP (navigation).
N/t. NEW TERMS (grain trade).
N.T. NON-TIGHT.
N.W.T. NON-WATER-TIGHT.

NA-AK. Single-outrigger canoe of Atchin Island (New Hebrides). There are two varieties: the inshore paddling canoe or *na-ak* and the seagoing sailing canoe called *na-ak-wala*. The former is only a dugout with a thin ply running along the whole length of each edge or gunwale. The forepart has a pronounced sheer and terminates with a carved figurehead, usually representing a bird. The seagoing type is double-ended and has two wash strakes on each side. The spars which support the V-shaped sail without need of a mast cross at the foot of the sail and are fastened to the forward outrigger boom inside the canoe.

NABBIE. A lug-rigged open fishing skiff from the west coast of Scotland with a mast raking aft at a great angle, a boomless gaff mainsail, large jib, and reefing bowsprit. Average length on load waterline about 31 ft.

NABOB. See **Vargord.**

NADIR. 1. A shallow-draft fishing boat of the Malacca Strait.
The hull is carvel-built of Kelidang timber, with straight stem and stern. The rig consists of a single lugsail made of screw pine leaf. Length 24 ft. Breadth 6 ft. Depth 3 ft. 3 in. Length of mast 30 ft. **Crew 5.** Carrying capacity 2.4 tons. (Average.)
2. The point of the celestial sphere directly under the observer and opposite to the zenith.
Fr: *Nadir;* Ger: *Fusspunkt; Nadir.*

NAGEGA. A single-outrigger canoe from the Trobriand Islands, British New Guinea, similar to the *masawa* but larger and more seaworthy; consequently, of greater carrying capacity.

NAHANG. A fishing prao without outrigger from Aru Islands, Banda Sea.

NAIL. A small pointed piece of metal, usually with a head, to be driven into a board or other piece of timber. The distinction among tacks, brads, spikes, and nails is chiefly one of size. Spike refers to a cut or wrought nail longer than 10-penny nails, used in boat- and shipbuilding. Long thin nails with a flattish head are known as brads. Ship spikes are from 4 to 10 in. long.
Fr: *Clou; Pointe;* Ger: *Nagel; Spieker.*
See **Boat Nail, Clench Nail, Clout Nail, Deck Nail, Ribband Nail, Roove Clench Nail, Scupper Nail, Sheathing Nail, Spike Nail, Wire Nail.**

There are three leading distinctions referring to the state of the metal from which nails are made: wrought or forged nails, cut nails, and cast nails. Cut nails are made of sheet steel or iron. They are heavier than wire nails. Cast nails are formed by pouring molten metal into a mold. They are brittle and used only where there is little stress. Wrought nails are hand-forged or machine-wrought (pressed). Hand-forged nails are stronger and tougher than the other kinds and will bear clinching. Most wrought-iron nails in common use are machine-wrought. Wire or French nails are made from drawn wire or wire rods. They are more liable to rust than cut or wrought nails and have less holding power.

NAIL PUNCH. A tool used by boatbuilders when driving nails on finished work. Also called nail set. When the head of the nail is about 1/16 inch from the surface, the punch is used to drive the nail home without bruising the wood with the hammer face.
See **Backing-out Punch, Driving Punch, Rove Punch.**

NAKHODA. An Arab shipmaster.

NALAVELGAU. Single-outrigger dugout canoe from Aneityum, southern New Hebrides.

NAME BOARD (U. S.). A painted or carved board where the ship's name is displayed. In sailing ships there was usually one placed on each quarter abaft the mizzen chains. In mechanically propelled vessels there is one on each side of the navigating bridge deckhouse secured to the deck margin plank. On tugs and other harbor craft it is displayed on top of wheelhouse.

Fr: *Tableau;* Ger: *Namenbrett.*
See **Ship's Name.**

NAMED POLICY. The opposite of a floating policy. A marine insurance policy mentioning the name of the vessel, by which the shipment is made and other particulars relating to destination of goods.

Fr: *Police à navire dénommé;* Ger: *Genannte Police; Namenspolice.*

NA-OGA. Single-outrigger seagoing dugout canoe from Siassi Island (Bismarck Archipelago). The ends sheer up and terminate in a long solid beak that rises to a slightly higher level than the body of the hull and is flat on its upper surface. The sides of the dugout are raised by two deep wash strakes sewed on. The rig comprises two masts stepped on ridges projecting from the bottom and are lashed to cross timbers that rest upon the gunwales. Each mast carries a rectangular sail with yard and boom.

NAPIER'S DIAGRAM. A graphic method for extending and utilizing the results of a limited number of observations, for representing the deviation of a ship's compass. The magnetic course corresponding to a given compass course can be deduced from it or inversely, the compass course corresponding to a given magnetic course.

Fr: *Diagramme de Napier;* Ger: *Napiersches Diagramm.*

NAPPEE. Partly dried fish carried in the Far East coasting trade.

NAR. See **Gul.**

NARROW PENNANT. A long narrow piece of bunting generally carried at masthead by naval vessels and other government vessels in commission. Also called long pennant, commission pennant, whip, coach whip.

Fr: *Flamme;* Ger: *Toppwimpel.*

NARROWS. A navigable contracted passage in a river, bay, strait, harbor and so on.

Fr: *Passe; Goulet;* Ger: *Meerenge; Durchfahrt.*

NATIONAL FLAG. See **Ensign.**

NATIONAL MARITIME BOARD (G. B.). A joint organization set up in Great Britain in 1919, to consider standard rates of pay and various rules governing working conditions of seamen. Shipowners, masters, officers, and seamen of all grades are represented in this body which is divided into a number of panels (for example, master's, officer's, sailor's and firemen's, and catering department panels) each of which is composed of an equal number of representatives of the shipowners and the respective category of seafarers.

NATURAL HARBOR. A harbor possessing natural shelter in a large degree. Natural harbors require only the provision of such facilities as quays or piers and sometimes deepening by artificial means to make them serviceable as shipping ports.

Fr: *Port Naturel;* Ger: *Natürlicher Hafen.*

NATURAL MAGNET. A piece of magnetite, naturally occurring, possessing polarity like a magnetic needle. Also called lodestone.

Fr: *Aimant Naturel;* Ger: *Natürlicher Magnet.*

NATURAL SCALE. The ratio that any distance, on a particular chart, bears to the true distance on the earth's surface.

Fr: *Echelle;* Ger: *Natürlicher Masstab.*

NATURAL VENTILATION. Air circulation brought about by the natural tendency of hot air to ascend and give place to heavier cold air, and also by air currents resulting from the ship's motion.

Fr: *Ventilation Naturelle;* Ger: *Natürliche Lüftung.*

Spofford, W., "Natural Ventilation on Board Ship," *Marine Engineering and Shipping Age* (New York), vol. 32 (June, 1927).

NAURI. An Arab deep-sea trading vessel similar to the *dhangi.*

The hull is double-ended and decked fore and aft. It differs from the *dhangi* by its parrot head stem ornament, and by its tiller which fits into the rudderhead instead of being slotted and fitting around it. These vessels run to about 80 tons and trade between the coast of Baluchistan, the Persian Gulf, and Zanzibar. They are rigged with two masts and settee sails.

NAUTICAL. Pertaining to the science or art of navigation, ships, and seamen.

Fr: *Nautique;* Ger: *Nautisch.*

NAUTICAL ALMANAC.
See **Almanac.**

NAUTICAL ASTRONOMY. The branch of the science of navigation in which the position of the observer at sea is determined by observations of celestial bodies, that is, the sun, moon, planets, or stars. Also called Celestial Navigation.

Fr: *Astronomie Nautique;* Ger: *Nautische Astronomie.*

Dutton, B., *Navigation and Nautical Astronomy*, Annapolis, 1939; Legg, P. G., *Introduction to Astronomical Navigation*, London, 1939; Simonds, W. P., *Nautical Astromony*, London, 1925; Williamson, *Navigation and Nautical Astronomy*, London, 1915.

NAUTICAL CHART. A map of water area including the adjoining land, intended primarily for the use of mariners. The main purpose of charts is to assist navigation. Shoals, rocks, and other dangers are shown by special markings and by various symbols; soundings with abbreviations, indicating the nature of the bottom. Depth contours are drawn joining together points of like depths near shore and around shoals. Lighthouses, buoys, and other artificial aids to navigation are represented by descriptive abbreviations and symbols. Currents are indicated by arrows or by explanatory notes. Compass roses printed on the charts give the necessary data concerning magnetic variation and its rate of change. Practically all general sailing charts are on Mercator's projection; gnomonic charts are used for great circle sailing and polygonic charts for plotting surveys.

Fr: *Carte Marine;* Ger: *Seekarte.*
Detz and Adams, *Elements of Map Projection*, Washington, 1931; Flower, G. L., *Rules and Practice Relating to the Construction of Nautical Charts*, U. S. Coast and Geodetic Survey Special Publication 66, Washington, 1920; Putnam, G. R., *Nautical Charts*, New York, 1908; Stewart and Stephen, *Modern Chart Work*, Glasgow, 1923.

NAUTICAL DAY. A day which begins and ends at noon. In the merchant service the nautical day, like the astronomical day, began at noon as the reckoning of the ship's position is made up to noon each day. The hours are carried on to twelve at midnight and thence commencing afresh to twelve next noon. Since 1925 the astronomical day has begun at 00 hours (midnight) and the various national nautical ephemerides now use a day commencing at midnight.

Fr: *Jour Nautique;* Ger: *Nautischer Tag; Etmal.*

NAUTICAL DISTANCE. The arc of a rhumb line intercepted between any two places, expressed in nautical miles.
Ger: *Nautische Entfernung.*

NAUTICAL HYDROGRAPHY. That branch of science which has for its object the measurement and description of seas, lakes, rivers, and other waters with special reference to their use for navigation and commerce. It embraces marine surveying, the determination of winds, currents, and so on, as well as cartography.

Fr: *Hydrographie Maritime;* Ger: *Hydrographie.*
Hawley, J. H., *Hydrographic Manual*, Washington, 1928.

NAUTICAL INSTRUMENTS. General term for the instruments used in the determination of ship's position at sea. It includes: azimuth circle, chronometers, magnetic compasses, gyro compass, radio compass, barometer, lead, sonic depth finder, sounding machine, logs.

Fr: *Instruments Nautiques;* Ger: *Nautisches Instrumente.*

NAUTICAL MILE. The standard unit of measure for marine navigation and for work with the Mercator chart. The nautical mile is 6,080 feet, being for practical purposes the length of one minute of arc of a meridian or of the equator. Also called Admiralty mile (G. B.).

Fr: *Mille Marin;* Ger: *Seemeile.*

NAUTICAL SIGNAL. A signal serving as a means of communication between vessels at sea or between a vessel and the shore. Sometimes called signal. It consists of flags of different colors for use in daytime or lanterns or fireworks for use at night.

Fr: *Signal;* Ger: *Signal.*

Marine signals may be divided into three classes: day signals, night signals, day-and-night signals. Day signals consist of set combinations of flags or shapes. Night signals are made with lights, rockets, torches, and so on, as well as by flashing or waving of a lamp or torch. Rockets and blue lights are used to attract attention and for special purposes. The day-and-night signals are sound signals and wireless telegraph signals. The former are composed of long and short blasts of a whistle or siren or strokes of a bell.

NAUTICAL SURVEYOR. A practitioner of nautical or marine surveying; including triangulation, topography sounding, magnetic and astronomical work, the study of tides, tidal streams and currents, also of oceanography and meteorology so far as they affect navigation. Also called hydrographer.

Fr: *Ingénieur hydrographe;* Ger: *Kartograph; Hydrograph.*

NAUTOPHONE. A sound-producing apparatus of the oscillator type used on shore stations as a fog signal. It consists essentially of an oscillating metal diaphragm attached to a horn which distributes the sound. The diaphragm vibrates under the influence of an electric current acting on an electro-magnet. The vibrating diaphragm is placed against the poles of the electro-magnet and oscillates by the electromagnetic action at its natural frequency. The sound emitted is about 525 to 300 vibrations per second and is somewhat similar in power and tone to that emitted by the reed horn. It emits at full power and the sound is arrested almost instantaneously. Also called electric-diaphragm emitter.

Fr: *Nautophone.*

NAVAL. A term which applies usually to ships of war, a navy, its crews, equipment, and so on, but in some cases also applied to shipping in general.

Fr: *Naval;* Ger: *Marine betreffend.*

NAVAL ARCHITECTURE. The science and practice of designing ships as distinguished from their construction, which belongs to shipbuilding. Naval architecture deals chiefly with such problems as buoyancy, stability, structural strength, speed and resistance, rolling, trim.

Fr: *Architecture Navale;* Ger: *Schiffbaukunst.*

Attwood, E. L., *Theoretical Naval Architecture,* London, 1931; Baker, G. S., *Ship Design, Resistance and Screw Propulsion,* Liverpool, 1933; Hill, G., *Hulls (Yacht). Their Design and Propulsion,* New York, 1940; Lovett, *Applied Naval Architecture,* London, 1920; Peabody, C. H., *Naval Architecture,* New York, 1917; Rossell and Chapman, *Principles of Naval Architecture,* New York, 1939.

NAVAL BRASS. A corrosion-resistant alloy containing 59 to 61 per cent copper, 38 to 40 per cent zinc and 0.5 to 1 per cent tin. Also called Muntz metal, yellow metal. Castings are used for underwater fittings of wooden vessels, flagpole sockets and guides, fittings on wooden handrails, watertight door fittings, belaying pins, and so on. Rolled naval brass is used for skylight fittings, operating rods of watertight doors, turnbuckles, bolts. Its use is generally limited to parts not exposed to the continuous action of sea water.

Fr: *Métal Muntz;* Ger: *Messing; Muntzmetall.*

NAVAL HOODS. Heavy pieces of timber which encircle the hawseholes of a wooden vessel, in order to protect the planking against the chafe of the anchor cables and to support the projecting part of the hawsepipe. Also called hawsepieces, hawse box.

Fr: *Coussin d'Écubier;* Ger: *Klusenback.*

NAVAL LAW. The rules and regulations governing officers and men in the Navy.

NAVAL OFFICER. 1. A commissioned or warrant officer in the naval service of a government.

2. A term sometimes used in the United States to denote an officer of the Treasury Department who, at the larger maritime ports, is associated with the collector of customs. He assists in estimating duties, countersigns permit clearances, certificates, and so on, issued by the collector of customs, and certifies his accounts.

NAVAL STORES. In commerce, manufactured products of gum extracted from pine trees. It includes rosin, turpentine, products of crude turpentine, tar, and rosin oil.

Ger: *Harzprodukte.*

U. S. Agriculture Department Forest Service, Miscellaneous Publications 209, *Naval Stores Handbook,* Washington, 1935.

NAVAL SUBVENTION. Grants made by the Naval Administration to the owners of vessels which fulfill particular requirements as regards construction, speed, equipment, etc., thereby making them readily available or adaptable in wartime as auxiliary vessels, transports, fleet tankers, mine-sweepers, etc. Also called Admiralty subvention.

NAVAL TELESCOPE. A refracting signaling telescope with taper body and having a sliding tube for focusing, in several sizes ranging in power from 12 to 50. Higher-powered telescopes are mounted on stands; lower-powered glasses are usually hand-held.

Fr: *Lunette d'Approche; Longue Vue;* Ger: *Fernrohr.*

NAVEL IRON. See Deck Pipe.

NAVICELLO. A small two-mast Italian sailing coaster from Tuscany, chiefly engaged in the transportation of marble stone from the quarries of Carrara to western Mediterranean ports. Length 60 to 79 ft. Breadth 17.5 to 22.5 ft. Depth 6.2 to 8.5 ft. Tonnage 39 to 84 gross. (Average.)

The hull is keel-built with slightly concave stem and elliptical or sharp stern. There is one hatchway just aft of the mainmast. The fore-and-aft rig consists of the bowsprit which carries one headsail; a short foremast stepped close to the stem and with an angle of rake which varies considerably from one vessel to another. This spar has no shrouds. It is held on each side by a tackle, the lower block of which is fastened to the cathead or the railing. The mainmast is stepped just forward of half length and is fitted with a topmast nearly as long as the lower mast. The usual sail plan is made up of a jib foresail—a quadrangular lower foresail without boom or gaff. The luff of this sail is held to the foremast with wooden hoops, its head is set with two halyards: one from the foremast head, the other from the main crosstrees. It is sheeted on deck. Above the foresail there is a jib-headed sail set flying between the fore and main trucks. The mainsail has a long gaff and no boom. A large gaff topsail is carried above. A bonnet is occasionally laced to the foot of the mainsail. Some boats carry a small mizzenmast with gaff sail. Long sweeps are used in calm weather and when entering or leaving port.

NAVICERT. Abbreviation for "Navigation Certificate." A certificate issued by the diplomatic or consular representatives of a belligerent in a neutral country and testifying that the cargo on a vessel proceeding to a neutral port is not such as to be liable to seizure. Its first use during World War I was due to the difficulties which arose out of the practice of divesting neutral vessels for search in belligerent ports.

Ritchie, H., *The Navicert System During the World War*, London, 1938.

NAVIGABLE. Capable of being navigated; affording passage to ships. In Great Britain a river is deemed navigable as far as the tide ebbs and flows. In the United States the term navigable includes all waters practically available for floating commerce by any method as by rafts or boats.

Fr: *Navigable;* Ger: *Schiffbar; Fahrbar.*

NAVIGABLE SEMICIRCLE. The semicircle in which the direction of the wind as it blows around the center of a cyclone is opposite to the direction of movement of the cyclone along its track. The left-hand side of the track in the Northern Hemisphere.

Fr: *Demi cercle Navigable;* Ger: *Navigierbarer Halbkreis.*

See **Dangerous Semicircle.**

NAVIGABLE WATERS. 1. Rivers, streams, or other stretches of water deep enough and wide enough to afford passage to vessels. Technically, only those waters, whether rivers or not, are called navigable that ebb and flow with the tide. The bed of navigable waters usually belongs to the state and the right of traffic, fishing, and so on, to the public.

See **Right of Navigation.**

2. In the United States those parts of streams or other bodies of water over which Congress has jurisdiction to regulate commerce with foreign nations and among the several states, and which either in their natural or improved condition, notwithstanding interruptions between the navigable parts of such streams or waters by falls, shallows or rapids, compelling land carriage, are used or suitable for use for the transportation of persons or property in interstate or foreign commerce.

Fr: *Eaux Navigables;* Ger: *Schiffbare Gewässer.*

NAVIGABILITY. The state or condition of being navigable.

Fr: *Navigabilité;* Ger: *Schiffbarkeit; Fahrttüchtigkeit.*

NAVIGATING BRIDGE. A raised platform extending from side to side in steam or motor vessels above the railing forward of amidships for the use and convenience of the officers in charge. Also called flying bridge. It affords an uninterrupted view and is supplied with means for communicating by automatic signals with the principal parts of the ship. It provides space for the wheelhouse and chartroom. The bridge superstructure is frequently arranged in two tiers one above the other, and has an outlook station above the upper tier.

Fr: *Passerelle de Navigation;* Ger: *Kommandobrücke.*

NAVIGATION. The nautical art or science of conducting a ship from one place to another. The two fundamental problems in navigation are: first, the determination of the ship's position at any required moment, and secondly, the future course to be steered to reach the desired point. The ship's position is found by one or a combination of the following methods: the observation of heavenly bodies, radiobeacon or radio compass bearings, consecutive soundings, dead reckoning, by observation of objects ashore.

Fr: *Navigation;* Ger: *Schiffahrtkunde.*

See **Celestial Navigation, Celo-Navigation, Geo-Navigation, Improper Navigation, Inshore Navigation, Rules of Navigation.**

Bowditch, *American Practical Navigator*, Washington, 1936; British Admiralty, *Man-*

NAVIGATION LAWS—NAVY 532

ual of Navigation, 1928; Cugle, C. H., *Practical Navigation,* New York, 1943; Dutton, B., *Navigation and Nautical Astronomy,* Annapolis, 1943; Lecky, S. T. S., *Wrinkles in Practical Navigation,* London, 1937; Mixter, G. W., Primer of Navigation, New York, 1943; Weems, P. V. H., *Marine Navigation,* New York, 1940.

NAVIGATION LAWS. Navigation laws are broadly defined as measures of preference and exclusion by which maritime nations endeavor to protect their native or national ships in the foreign shipping trade against foreign competition, and to exclude foreign ships from participation on equal terms with their own marine in their coastal trade, or that of the colonies or possessions they may have. These laws are a branch of, though distinct, from the maritime code which governs the usages of the sea. The various acts and regulations relating to load lines, documentation and inspection of vessels, manning scales and maritime labor relations, entry and clearance of vessels and merchandise, pilotage, sanitation and quarantine, marine casualties and salvage are also included in this term.

Fr: *Code maritime;* Ger: *Navigationsgesetze.*

Arzt, F. K., *Navigation Laws of the United States,* U. S. Bureau of Marine Inspection and Navigation, Washington, 1940; Bacon, E. M., *Manual of Navigation Laws,* Chicago, 1912; Jones, G. M., *Navigation Laws of Leading Maritime Countries,* U. S. Department of Commerce, Special Agents Series 114, Washington, 1916; Shepheard, H. C., History of the United States Navigation and Vessel Inspection Laws, Society of Naval Architects and Marine Engineers, *Historical Transactions* (New York, 1945).

NAVIGATION LIGHTS. The lights any vessel under way must exhibit between sunset and sunrise, so that her classification, position and course may be identified.

Fr: *Feux de position;* Ger: *Fahrtlaterne.*

NAVIGATION LIGHTS BOARD (NAVIGATION LIGHTS INDICATOR). Apparatus fitted in the wheelhouse to indicate any failure of the navigation lights. It consists of a board electrically wired to the masthead lights, side lights, and stern light. Should any one of them go out an alarm bell rings and a colored disc shows which particular light has failed.

Fr: *Tableau des feux de route.*

NAVIGATION SPACES. Enclosed spaces such as charthouse, wheelhouse, radioroom. They are deducted or exempted from the gross tonnage to obtain the net tonnage.

Fr: *Locaux de Navigation;* Ger: *Navigationsraume.*

NAVIGATION SUBSIDY. Payments made by a government to shipping companies owning and operating vessels flying the national flag, under certain conditions as to tonnage, age, size, and speed of each vessel. Special navigation subsidies are those made only to certain companies which maintain special services from ports or regions located outside the usual lanes of trade and travel. Their rate is usually based on number of miles traveled and on tonnage of vessel. Also called navigation bounty.

Fr: *Prime à la Navigation;* Ger: *Fahrtprämien.*

NAVIGATION WATCH. A second setting timekeeper especially designed for the use of navigators and aviators. It is a 1⅞ inch diameter wrist watch and has a large central rotatable dial on which the seconds are shown. It may readily be set to the exact second of time as found by radio or by comparison with a chronometer. Since the second hand cannot be set relative to its dial, the dial is set relative to the hand; means being provided for rotating the dial in either direction.

NAVIGATOR. The officer specially in charge of the navigation of a ship. On most merchant vessels the master is his own navigator. However, in some of the larger trans-Atlantic liners, an officer is specially appointed to direct the ship's course. In warships it is the general custom to have a navigating officer who has no other duties.

Fr: *Navigateur;* Ger: *Nautiker.*

NAVY. The term "navy" was formerly applied to the whole shipping of a country whether used for war, trading, or fishing. In modern parlance "navy" usually means a nation's warships and their auxiliary craft of every kind which operate on, under, or over the sea, and includes the personnel which mans them, as well as the shore establishments connected therewith.

Fr: *Marine de Guerre;* Ger: *Kriegsmarine.*
See **Merchant Navy.**

NDRUA. A Fijian double canoe, now believed extinct, with two unequal hulls connected at a distance of about 5.5 ft. apart by crossbeams. Also called *wangga ndrua*. The fore end of the larger hull was brought to a wedge form with vertical cutwater. Both hulls had a wash strake and inserted ribs. The smaller hull had both ends of truncate form. There was a platform above the crossbeams and about 4 ft. above it a second, smaller platform for the chief. The mast and sail were of same type as those of the *thamakau*.

NEAPED. Said of a vessel when aground at the height of a spring tide.

NEAP LOW WATER. Low water at the times of first and third quarters of the moon.

Fr: *Basse mer de morte eau;* Ger: *Nippniedrigswasser.*

NEAP RANGE. The tidal or difference in height between low water at neap tides.

Fr: *Amplitude en morte eau;* Ger: *Nipptidenhub.*

NEAP TIDE. The tides which, twice in a lunar month, rise least and fall least from the mean level.

Fr: *Marée de Morte Eau;* Ger: *Nippflut; Nipptide.*

See **Tide.**

NEAREST APPROACH. A term used in radar plotting to denote the least calculated distance to which two vessels will close if neither alters course or speed.

NECESSARIES (G. B.). A judicial term which in Admiralty law is used to denote collectively whatever is fit and proper for the service in which a vessel is engaged, or whatever the owner of that vessel as a prudent man would order if present at the time. No distinction can be drawn between necessaries for the ship and necessaries for the voyage, and all things reasonably required for the particular adventure on which the ship is bound are included in this term. Anchors, cables, rigging, fuel, provisions, clothing and slops for the crew, screw propeller, coppering, money for shipwright's bill, dock dues, customhouse fees, and so on, come, among others, under this heading.

NECK. That part of an oar where the loom joins the blade.

NECKING. A molding on the taffrail.

NECORE. Code name of the British Chamber of Shipping Mediterranean Ore charter 1922, for use to east coast ports of England.

NEGATIVE FLAG. A single-letter signal consisting of letter "N" of the International Code of signals. Means "No."

Fr: *Pavillon Négatif;* Ger: *Verneinungsflagge.*

NEGATIVE SLIP. Apparent slip less than zero due to high wave velocity or surface current traveling in the same direction as the ship, or the conjunction of both.

Fr: *Recul Négatif;* Ger: *Negativer Slip.*

See **Slip, Apparent Slip.**

NEGATIVE STABILITY. A ship is said to have negative stability when in unstable equilibrium. It lacks the statical stability which tends to return it to the erect position when inclined.

Fr: *Stabilité négative;* Ger: *Negative Stabilitat.*

See **Unstable Equilibrium.**

NEGLIGENCE CLAUSE. A marine insurance clause covering a shipowner against the loss of freight directly caused by: (1) accidents in loading, discharging, or handling cargo; (2) negligence of master, mariners, engineers, or pilots; (3) explosions, bursting of boilers, breakage of shafts, or any latent defect in the machinery or hull, *provided that* such loss has not resulted from want of due diligence by the owners or managers of the ship.

Fr: *Clause de Négligence;* Ger: *Negligenzklausel.*

NENGAU. A single-outrigger dugout canoe of blunt, almost square-ended form with a projecting shelf at each end, from Tanna Island, New Hebrides. Also called *negau.*

See **Kavineke Nengau.**

NEPHOSCOPE. An instrument designed for determining direction and apparent speed of movement of clouds.

Fr: *Néphoscope;* Ger: *Nephoskop.*

NESS YOLE. A Shetland yole similar to the Fair Island skiff but more heavily built. The frames are not bolted to the keel but connected to it by the garboard strake. It is rigged with a single lugsail. Length over-all 23 ft. Length at keel 15 ft. Breadth 5½ ft. Depth 1½ ft. (Typical.)

NESTED BOATS. A system of boat stowage by which ship's boats are stowed one inside the other after removing the thwarts. By this arrangement it is possible

to carry several boats under a single set of davits, which makes for great economy of space and allows for more boats being carried. Fishing dories stowed this way are said to be stowed "spoon fashion."
Fr: *Embarcations Emboitées.*

NET CAPACITY. The number of tons of cargo which a vessel can carry when loaded in salt water to her summer freeboard marks. Also called cargo carrying capacity, cargo deadweight, useful deadweight.
Fr: *Portée Utile;* Ger: *Ladungsfähigkeit; Ladefähigkeit; Ladungstragfähigkeit.*

NET CHARTER. A charter on net terms is one in which a net rate of freight is paid to the owners who are then relieved of meeting expenses usually borne by the owners when the terms are gross. These expenses include port charges, for loading, discharging, stowing, and trimming the cargo; pilotage dues; towage. Also called net form charter.

NET CHARTER TERMS.
See **Net Charter.**

NET ROPE MAN. On a North Sea herring drifter the member of the crew who hauls and shoots the nets, assisted by the valeman.

NET SLING. See **Cargo Net.**

NET SWING (U. S.). Term used by New England fishermen to denote the heavy rope by which the extremity of a *gang* or *fleet* of drift nets is fastened to the bow of the dragger. It is about 3 in. in circumference and 60 to 70 fathoms long.

NETTING KNOT. Netting knots are of two sorts, the single-sheet bend and the reef knot. Sometimes called mesh knot. The reef knot is chiefly used for small mesh nets such as shrimp trawls.
Fr: *Noeud de Filet;* Ger: *Netzknoten.*

NETTLE. Small white or tarred hemp cord made of two or three reverse spun yarns laid up by hand, used for tying the outer end of batten pockets, also for pointing or grafting of hammock clews, neat seizings, and so on. The term "knittle" is used to refer to small cords formed from the outside yarns of a rope with which the rope's end is pointed or grafted.
Fr: *Lignerolle; Commande pour hanets;* Ger: *Knüttel.*

NET TONNAGE. The carrying capacity of vessels as ascertained according to government regulations and arrived at by measuring the cubic contents of the space intended for revenue earning. Also called net register tonnage. One hundred cubic feet is the standard space taken as the accommodation for one ton of goods. The net register tonnage does not in any way represent the actual carrying capacity of the vessel. It is obtained by deducting from the gross register, superstructures for passengers, crew spaces at the rate of 120 cu. ft. per man, spaces used to accommodate the master, for working the helm, capstan, anchor gear, or storing charts, signals, navigational instruments, boatswain's stores, and spaces adapted only for water ballast.
Fr: *Jauge Nette; Tonnage Net;* Ger: *Netto-Tonnengehalt; Nettoraumgehalt.*

In estimating the tonnage of the machinery and boiler space the following rule is employed for screw vessels: when the tonnage of these spaces is over 13 per cent and under 20 per cent, a deduction of 32 per cent is made off the gross tonnage. In other cases the tonnage of these spaces multiplied by 1.75 is deducted. For paddle vessels the deductions are smaller.

Owing to the lack of uniformity in different countries regarding the spaces which are exempted from tonnage measurement, the League of Nations drew up in 1931 a tentative set of international rules for the measurement of vessels of every maritime state.

NET VALUE CLAUSE. A cargo clause sometimes included in marine policies by which underwriters, in the event of particular average, permit claims to be adjusted by comparing sound and damaged values of goods after deduction of freight, duty, and ordinary charges, payable at destination.

NEUTRAL AXIS. That part of a structure where tensile and compressive stresses are zero.
Fr: *Fibre Neutre;* Ger: *Neutrale Faser; Nullachse.*

When considering the cross section of a ship which is hogging or sagging, and is accordingly stressed by longitudinal bending, the extreme fibers on the one side are in compression while those on the other side are in tension. In some plane between them there exists neither tension nor compression. This axis is termed the neutral axis. Its height, measured from the base line, is usually about 42 per cent of the molded depth.

NEUTRAL EQUILIBRIUM. When the metacenter and center of gravity of a vessel coincide, the metacentric height is zero

and the ship when slightly inclined will not tend to move from the inclined position. The ship is then said to be in a state of neutral equilibrium.
Fr: *Equilibre Indifférent;* Ger: *Indifferentes Gleichgewicht.*
See **Stable Equilibrium, Unstable Equilibrium.**

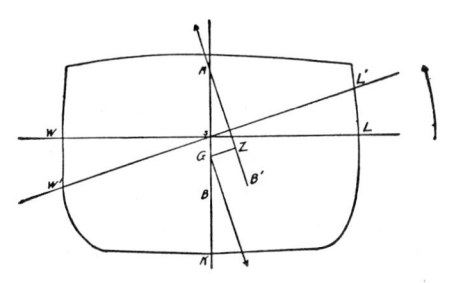

Neutral Equilibrium
B = Center of Buoyancy
G = Center of gravity
M = Metacenter
GM = Metacentric Height

NEVODNIK. A large open, flat-bottomed boat used by the Caspian Sea fishermen to work drag seines in the Volga estuary and along the shallow shores of the coastline. Length over-all 36 ft. Beam 7 ft. 4 in. Depth 3 ft. 6 in. (Typical.)

It has a narrow V-shaped square stern, flaring sides, and a wedge-shaped stem, sharp below the waterline and V-shaped above. It has a cuddy at each end and four thwarts; three of these are well forward and one aft, the central portion of the boat being left unobstructed for stowing the seine.

NEW FOR OLD. The allowance made to the insurer on the hull and equipment of a vessel where old material damaged is replaced by new.
Fr: *Différence du neuf au vieux;* Ger: *Unterschied zwischen alt und neu.*

NEWFOUNDLAND SEALING PUNT. A type of open boat formerly used at Toulinguet, Newfoundland, for hunting seals at sea. It is a clinker-built keel craft with good sheer, sharp bow, strongly raking curved stem, rising floor, flaring topsides, heart-shaped stern with skeg rounded on aftercorner. It is built of cedar on light, bent oak frames and combines lightness with strength and speed, while it turns quickly and easily.

NEW HAVEN STEM. A system of stem construction used in boat building for flat bottom hulls with straight stem. There is no outer stem piece. The side planks are cut with mitered ends and fastened to an inner stem piece with screws or nails. It is covered outside with a sheet of brass bent to form an acute angle and secured to the planking with brads or countersunk screws.

NEW HAVEN YAWL.
See **Baldie.**

NEW MEASUREMENT (G. B.). A formula by which the tonnage of ships was determined in England under the act of 1835, called New Measurement law. The tonnage was obtained by multiplying together the mean length, breadth, and height of measured spaces and dividing the product by 92.4. The new measurement was superseded in 1854 by the Moorsom system.

NEW ORLEANS LUGGER. A half-decked, centerboard boat used in the shore fisheries from New Orleans and in adjacent waters of the Gulf of Mexico. Length overall 40 ft. 6 in. Waterline 39 ft. 9 in. Breadth 12 ft. 6 in. Depth amidships from top of gunwale to keel, 4 ft. 9 in. (Typical.)

The hull is carvel-planked, with half deck forward, wide waterways, and a high coaming around the elliptical shaped cockpit. The latter is provided with hatch covers for about two thirds of its length from forward. The bow is sharp, with straight stem. There is a very shallow keel, moderately rising floor with quick turn of bilge, V-shaped square stern, and outboard rudder with tiller. The rig consists of a pole mast, stepped about 12 ft. abaft the stem, with a large lugsail tacking down to a traveler near the bow. The sheet trims to an iron horse at the stern. These boats are fast under sail and are reputed to be especially well adapted to the shallow and narrow waters along the Louisiana coast.

NEWPORT BOAT. Name formerly given to a Narraganset Bay catboat without centerboard. It was built with a keel having considerable drag. Also called point boat.

NEW YORK SAILING BARGE. A sloop-rigged sailing barge formerly employed in New York harbor and adjacent tidal waters. Length 48.9 to 64.5 ft. Breadth 24.6 to 27.3 ft. Depth 6.6 to 7.1 ft. Tonnage 54 to 72. It became extinct about 1910.

The finely modeled hull was built with shallow keel, round bilges, rounded stem, and transom stern. An outboard rudder with tiller was used for steering. The deck extended fore and aft and, owing to the fact that these craft very frequently carried their cargo above deck; there was only one small hatchway. The pole mast, stepped at a short distance from the stem, was given a strong rake aft and its head plumbed the hatch so that it could be used as a derrick. There was a small standing bowsprit. The sail plan consisted of a boomless mainsail with short standing gaff, the peak halyards allowing this spar to come down alongside the mast when the sail was brailed. Three brails were used. The jib was taken down to the bowsprit end.

NEW ZEALAND SCOW. Seagoing sailing barge used in the New Zealand timber, coal, and cattle coastal trade, and also in the intercolonial trade between New Zealand and Australia. They were named deck scows or hold scows according to their build; the former taking all of their cargo on deck and the latter below hatches.

Up to the early nineties most of these scows were built square across the bow. Since that period they have been built with sharp clipper bow, square stern, and square bilges. The bottom is cross-planked. The hull planking of kauri pine is protected from the attacks of the teredo by a sheathing made of totara wood, which is impervious to wood borers. The craft employed in the log-carrying trade have no bulwarks except at the ends in order to enable the logs to be lifted on board by means of parbuckling chains passed around each one. The outboard rudder is of the barn-door type with steering chains shackled to its after end and led inboard through iron sheaves on each quarter to the wheel barrel. When in deep water the rudder can be lowered a couple of feet below the bottom, and when grounded for loading purposes it is hoisted up by means of a purchase tackle from the top of the sternpost. Two, and sometimes three, centerboards are fitted into the largest of these craft, the third or foremost being a very small affair called a "fin." The average New Zealand scow is rigged as a two or three mast fore-and-aft schooner, although some of them are ketch-rigged and a few as three-masted topsail schooners. The deadweight capacity of these craft ranges from 90 to 300 tons.

P. A. Eaddy, *Neath Swaying Spars*, Wellington, N. Z., 1939.

NIAO-WANG. Chinese fishing boat from Swatow, Kwang-Tung Province. There is a small cuddy aft for the crew. Length 28 ft. Beam 8 ft.

NIB. See **Lip**.

NIBBING PLANK. A margin plank that is notched to take the ends of regular deck planks and insure good calking of the joint.

See **Margin Plank**.

NIB STRAKE. The inner strake of planking of waterways at the ends of the ship.

NICKEL STEEL. Alloy steel which contains up to about five per cent nickel. Used for cast and forged anchor chains and large propeller shafts.

Fr: *Acier au Nickel*; Ger: *Nickelstahl*.

NICKIE. A round-sterned, powerfully built drifter from the Isle of Man rigged with dipping lug foresail, standing lug mizzen, and mizzen staysail. A jack-yard topsail is usually set in fine weather, and the tack of the foresail is set up to an iron bumkin on the stern. Length 40 to 50 ft.

NIGGERHEADS. Bitts used for fastening a towing hawser on tugboats. They are used only for harbor work, a towing hook being used for deep-sea towing. Wooden towing posts are usually of square section from 9x9 to 12x12 in., depending on size of tug.

Fr: *Bittes de remorque*; Ger: *Schleppbeting*.

NIGHT EFFECT. In radio engineering a term applied to difficulty experienced in obtaining accurate radio bearings from about one half hour before sunset until after sunrise.

Ger: *Nachteffekt*.

NIGHT GLASSES. Binoculars with large field and high lightgathering power specially for night use by navigating officers.

Ger: *Nachtglass*.

NIGHT ORDER BOOK. A book kept by the captain, in which before retiring written instructions are entered as to when he is to be called, and any special orders or reminders regarding the ship's navigation which he may consider necessary. The book is placed in the chart room and is signed by each officer when taking watch.

NIGHT PENNANT. A long blue pennant or streamer displayed from the main truck of a yacht or naval vessel at anchor after sunset during such time as no other flags are shown.

NIGHT SIGNAL. A flashing signal made by the exposure and eclipse of a single light for short and long periods of time, representing the dots and dashes of Morse code. The dots and dashes can be made mechanically by an obscuring arrangement but are more usually made by switching on and off specially manufactured electric lamps. In some vessels searchlights are used for this purpose. They are fitted with controllable shutters or iris diaphragms. The ordinary speed of signaling by flashing in merchant vessels is from 7 to 10 words per minute.

Fr: *Signal de Nuit;* Ger: *Nachtsignal.*

NIMBO-STRATUS. A cloud represented by a low, amorphous and rainy layer of a dark color and nearly uniform. Altitude 500 to 2000 feet.

NIMBUS. A thick layer of ragged-edged, shapeless dark clouds, from which steady rain or snow generally falls. Usually an upper layer of cirro-stratus or alto-stratus clouds may be seen through the openings in these clouds. Also called rain clouds.

Fr: *Nimbus;* Ger: *Nimbus; Regenwolke.*

See **Cumulo-Nimbus, Fracto-Nimbus.**

NINEPIN BLOCK. A block shaped somewhat like a ninepin with single sheave pivoted at top and bottom so that it may follow the motion of the rope for which it serves as a guide. Ninepin blocks are placed between bitt crosspieces.

Fr: *Marionette;* Ger: *Leitblock.*

NIP. 1. The place at which a rope bends sharply.

Ger: *Knick.*

2. A short turn or twist in a rope. The part of a rope at the place bound by a seizing or caught by jamming.

Fr: *Coque;* Ger: *Kurze Kinke.*

NIPPED. Said of a ship which is caught between two closing ice fields.

Fr: *Pris; Enclavé;* Ger: *Eingeschlossen.*

NIPPER. A short piece of rope or selvage used for binding the anchor cable to a messenger when heaving up anchor. Iron clamps are used for the same purpose with chain cables. Nippers are not used where the cable is applied directly to the capstan or windlass.

Fr: *Barbarasse; Garcette;* Ger: *Kabelarzeising; Trossenklemme.*

NIPPERING. Fastening two parts of a rope by making turns crosswise between the parts and jamming them.

Ger: *Zeisen.*

NITIH. East Indian keel-built sailing canoe from Madura Island, with pointed rising stem piece and fish-tailed stern. It is rigged with one mast and a triangular sail.

NIU. Single-outrigger dugout canoe of the Tuauru people from southern New Caledonia. It is usually fitted with a wash strake fastened to the dugout by coconut fiber seizings. A massive decking covers the cavity of the hull at each end and between the ends of the wash strakes and the solid ends of the hull. The canoes are from 10 to 26 ft. long and hold 6 to 8 persons. A large paddle serves as a rudder. The rig consists of a mast 19 to 26 ft. high with Oceanic lateen sail made of mats.

NIYON. Plank-built East Indian canoe with double outriggers from Batchian Island (Moluccas). The hull is constructed with high bow and stern which rise gradually narrowing to a sharp point. A shelter with penthouse roof is built amidships and projects on each side beyond the gunwale. Length of canoe 30 to 35 ft.

NO. Generic name for various types of canoes from Rossel Island, Louisiade Archipelago.

They are all dugout canoes with single outrigger. The hulls are long and narrow, raked, and sharply pointed at ends. They are characterized by the decking for some distance at either end and by the addition of wash strakes at center. There are three varieties, the *ma-no* or male canoe; the *pia-no* or female canoe; and the *lia-no* or sailing canoe, which is the largest. The average length of a ma-no is about 21 ft.

NOANK BOAT. Centerboard sloop: Length over-all from 20 to 25 ft. Breadth from 6 to 9 ft. Draught 2 to 4 ft., used in lobstering on the Connecticut shore about Noank and New London. They are shallow, with a flat bottom, sharp bow and wide, heart-shaped transom.

In the middle of the boat there is an elliptical, open space called the cockpit, about 12 ft. long by 7 ft. wide in the clear. Outside of the cockpit the boat is decked over, forming a cuddy forward for the crew and for storage of supplies. The bottom of the cockpit is floored over about one foot above the keelson, and on either side of the centerboard trunk is built a small boxlike well about 3½ ft. long and 1½ ft. high and 1 ft. or more in width, in which the lobsters are kept alive.

NOBBIE, NOBBY. 1. A round-sterned, two-masted, lug-rigged fishing boat found on the south coast of Ireland.

The Manx nobby is a large decked boat resembling the Mount's Bay lugger in type, lug-rigged, with a foremast raking aft considerably and a very small mizzenmast. Both masts carry a standing lug. The headsails consist of a staysail and jib on a reeving bowsprit. Length over-all 40 ft. 9 in. Breadth 11 ft. 11 in. Inside depth 6 ft. 2 in. (Average.)

2. A pointed-stern fishing boat of the Mersey estuary rigged with a jib, a dipping lug foresail, and a standing lug mizzen. The latter is sheeted to a long outrigger or bumkin. It is used for long lining. Length 30 to 35 ft.

See **Lancashire Nobby**.

NO BOTTOM SOUNDING. An expression indicating that the lead used for the sounding did not reach the bottom of the water in which sounding was attempted.

NOCK. 1. The forward side or luff of a staysail with square tack. The term is also applied to the forward upper corner of a gaffsail; more usually called throat.

Fr: *Nerf;* Ger: *Binnennock.*

2. The rounding off of the luff of a gaff mainsail at the tack to allow for the space taken up by the roller reefing gear.

NOCTILUCENT CLOUD. A rare phenomenon produced by the reflection of sunlight from masses of volcanic or meteoric dust high in the stratosphere. Noctilucent clouds are not visible in day time, hence their name. They begin to appear in a clear sky about a quarter of an hour after sunset between latitudes 45° and 50° in the Northern and Southern hemispheres, and mainly between the middle of May and the middle of August. Their color is bluish-white or silvery-white.

NODAL POINT. A point on the shore where the predominant direction of littoral drift changes from upcoast to downcoast or vice versa. Also called **Neutral point**.

Fr: *Point Nodal;* Ger: *Knotenpunkt.*

NODE. The point at which a planet's orbit intersects the plane of the ecliptic. Also called nodal point. The node at which the object ascends from the south to the north side of the ecliptic is the ascending node; that at which the object descends from the north to the south side of the ecliptic is the descending node.

Fr: *Noeud;* Ger: *Knotenpunkt.*

NO HIGHER. An order to keep the vessel from coming closer to the wind.

Fr: *Défie l'aulofée;* Ger: *Nicht höher.*

NO MAN'S LAND BOAT. A name given in the U. S. to a double-ended boat formerly used for lobster and scallop fishing off Martha's Vineyard, Massachusetts.

Its length varied from 16 to 22 ft. It had sharp flaring bows and stern, the lower end of which was rounded off. Cedar wood was used for the planking, which was either clinker- or carvel-built. Some were rigged with two spritsails; others with a loose-footed gaff mainsail and a sprit mizzen. The only standing rigging was a head stay which fastened through a hole in the stemhead: some did not even have this. The boats were half decked and as a rule a centerboard made of weighted oak was fitted on the port side of the keel. (Obsolete.)

Taylor, W. H., "The No man's land Boat," *Yachting,* vol. 52, New York (March, 1932).

NOMINAL HORSEPOWER. A measure of the commercial value of an engine and of the power it might be expected to develop in ordinary work. Various formulas are used by different administrations to calculate nominal horsepower. The British Board of Trade has its own formulas for registration purposes and Lloyd's register for survey fees.

Fr: *Puissance Nominale;* Ger: *Nominelle Pferdestärke.*

NOMINAL PITCH. The distance measured parallel to the axis of rotation between similar positions of a point on the driving face of a propeller blade in successive revolutions.

Fr: *Pas Nominal;* Ger: *Nominelle Steigung.*

NONCONFERENCE CARRIER. A ship placed on the berth as common carrier and furnishing either regular or irregular service without being owned by a member of the conference which operates in that particular trade.

NONCUMULATIVE CLAUSE. A marine insurance hull clause which states that damages sustained by the vessel during each voyage are to be kept distinct and not aggregated.

NONDUMPING CERTIFICATE. Commercial term which refers to a certificate made by the shipper of goods stating that there is no difference between the shipper's export prices and discount and those granted on the same goods in the domestic market. Nondumping certificates are required for goods shipped to Canada, South Africa, Australia, and New Zealand.

NONHARMONIC CONSTANTS. Tidal constants which include the ranges, inequalities, and intervals derived directly from high and low water observations without regard to the harmonic constituents of the tide.

NONMAGNETIC VESSEL. A vessel specially designed and built for detecting the earth's magnetism over different areas on the surface of the ocean. Nonmagnetic vessels are built without practically any steel or iron, the hull being made of wood with copper fastenings. What little iron or steel the vessel carries is placed at such a distance from the standard compass as to have no effect on it. The compass has no soft iron correctors, no Flinders bar, and no magnets. It registers correctly even when the vessel heels.

Fr: *Navire Amagnétique;* Ger: *Unmagnetisches Schiff.*

NONRETURN VALVE. A screw-down valve in which the spindle is not fixed to the valve disc or gate, so that while it may press it down on its seat it is incapable of lifting it. As a result the fluid going through the piping system can lift the valve and pass upward, but it cannot return and flow in the other direction. Valve chests for bilge and ballast systems are equipped with nonreturn valves.

Fr: *Soupape de Non retour;* Ger: *Rückschlagventil.*

NONSPINNING ROPE. A wire rope in which the 6 inner strands are laid in opposite direction to the outer strands.

NONTIDAL CURRENT. A current that is due to causes other than the tide-producing forces. Classed as nontidal are the permanent ocean currents such as the Gulf Stream and the equatorial currents, which are a part of the general ocean circulation; the fresh water discharge of a river, and the temporary currents caused by the wind. These currents lack the periodicity which characterizes the tidal currents.

NONTOPPLING BLOCK. A block so weighted as to remain upright. Running blocks of boatfalls, and cargo whip blocks are usually of this type.

NOON. The time of the sun's transit on the upper branch of the meridian of a place.

Fr: *Midi;* Ger: *Mittag.*

See **Local Apparent Noon, Local Mean Noon, Local Sidereal Noon.**

NOON INTERVAL. In navigation, the number of hours between a celestial observation (usually a morning sight) and local apparent noon, at which time the sun will be on the meridian, and a meridian observation will be taken for latitude.

See **Local Apparent Noon.**

NOON POSITION. The position of a ship as computed by the day's work at each noon, and from which the course for the next twenty-four hours is shaped.

Fr: *Point à midi;* Ger: *Mittagbesteck.*

NOOSE. A loop with a running knot.

Fr: *Noeud Coulant;* Ger: *Laufknoten.*

See **Slip Noose.**

NORDLANDSBAAT. The Nordlandsbaat or nordland fishing boat derives its specific name from the fact that it originates in the northern section of the west coast of Norway, where it is still used, particularly in the cod fisheries of Lofoten Islands. There are various sizes of these boats, classified according to the special branch of the cod fishery in which they engage, but the following particulars are common to all craft. Length over-all 21 ft. to 39 ft. 11 in. Beam 5 ft. 1 in. to 10 ft. 1 in. Depth 19 in. to 3 ft. 2 in. Height of washboards 9½ in. (amidships.)

It is an open boat, keel-built with sharp stern, hollow floors and waterlines; very high stem and sternpost, both of which are nearly vertical above the waterline. It has little freeboard amidships, flaring sides which are generally increased in height by washboards fastened to the gunwales. The planking is clinker-built and fastened with large round-head nails, which project all over the bottom. The number of thwarts depends on the size of the boat. Some of the largest boats have a small cuddy aft underneath a short deck that curves sharply to the center. The original rig is one large square sail with a small square topsail set flying. The mast is stepped nearly in the center of the boat. The arrangement for steering consists of a one-armed yoke extending out from the rudderhead about one foot at right angles to the boat's keel. To this is jointed the tiller several feet long. The fisherman steers simply by moving the tiller fore and aft instead of putting it from port to starboard or vice versa. The smallest boats are used by hand-line fishermen, the next with trawl lines, and the largest with gill nets.

Collins, J. W., *Report on the Fisheries Exhibition,* 1898, at Bergen, Bureau of Fisheries, Report, Washington, 1901.

NORMAN. 1. A steel pin fitted horizontally through the rudder head.

Fr: *Paille de mèche;* Ger: *Normann.*

2. A short bar shipped in one of the

pigeon holes of the capstan head so that a turn may be taken. This term is also used to denote an iron bolt shaped like a staple, and shipped on the windlass to keep the chain clear when running out.

Fr: *Normand;* Ger: *Katzenkopf.*

3. Also *Norman pin.* A device like a belaying pin set horizontally in the head of an anchor bitt or towing bitt, to prevent the cable from flying off when veering rapidly, or in the head of a bollard to prevent hawsers from slipping off.

Fr: *Paille de Bitte;* Ger: *Normann; Betingstange.*

NORSALS. Short lines spaced at regular intervals along the top edge of a drift net to connect it with the balch or top rope. Also called nossles, norsells, ozzles, daffins.

Fr: *Barsouin;* Ger: *Zeisingtau.*

NORSKE VERITAS. Norwegian classification society established in 1864 by the various marine insurance interests, for the survey of steel, wooden, or composite vessels.

Symbols: ✠ 1A1 indicates that the vessel has been built under the supervision of the society and has obtained the highest class. The third figure denotes the efficient state of equipment. A black dot above the maltese cross denotes that the vessel has been built under the supervision of another classification society.

The symbols 1.A.2 or 2A2 are assigned to vessels whose construction conform with the rules for the obtention of the highest class.

Various letters are used as symbols, the meaning of which is as follows: Letter "I" indicates that the vessel is intended for navigation in sheltered waters such as rivers, estuaries and closed-in fjords. "T" refers to steel vessels which have been strengthened for the transportation of ore or similar heavy cargo. "K" indicates that the vessel is intended for navigation along the Norwegian coast to Denmark or to the west coast of Sweden. "Is" indicates that the vessel has been strengthened for ice. "MV" and "KV" signify that the vessel has a Norske Veritas certificate for engines and boilers.

Symbols B.1 to B.5 indicate a special freeboard corresponding with the type of cargo carried on ships having a particular class. A.1 indicates the highest class for wooden or composite vessels. Similar vessels of lower classes have the symbols A2* or A2. and B1 or B2. Under the character of wooden vessels are inserted figures giving the term of years for which the class is assigned.

Any symbol placed within brackets indicates that the class has been withdrawn.

NORTH ATLANTIC DRIFT. The continuation of the Gulf Stream in a Northeasterly direction across the North Atlantic.

Fr: *Courant de derive de l'Atlantique Nord;* Ger: *Nordatlantisch Triftström.*

NORTH ATLANTIC TRACKS. Seasonal routes used since 1891 by the principal transatlantic steamship companies in order to provide for safety from the danger of ice, fog, and collision with fishing vessels on the Grand Banks of Newfoundland:

Route C, northerly from Sept. 1 to Jan. 31. Route B, northerly from Feb. 1 to Aug. 31. Route A, southernmost route. Used only when ice menaces Track B.

The purpose of these tracks is that one lane or strip of the ocean is used by westbound vessels and another for eastbound vessels, thereby reducing the danger of collision in fog and also giving an additional security in cases of wreck or disaster. The greatest width, 20 to 25 miles, is given where most fog is expected. Also called ship lanes.

NORTHEAST MONSOON. A seasonal wind prevailing from October to April in the Mozambique Channel, over the North Indian Ocean, China Sea, and part of the Pacific, and from October to March on the east coast of Brazil.

Fr: *Mousson du Nord Est;* Ger: *Nordostmonsun.*

NORTHEAST PASSAGE. A passage between the Atlantic and Pacific Oceans along the northern coasts of Europe and Asia. It was first completed by the Swedish explorer Nordenskjold in 1878 on the steam whaler "Vega" of 337 tons gross.

Fr: *Passage du Nord-Est;* Ger: *Nordostlich Durchfahrt.*

NORTH EQUATORIAL CURRENT. The North Atlantic Equatorial current is a variable westerly current which covers different areas of the ocean at different times of the year. Its Southern boundary varies from 6 degrees to 12 degrees North latitude. The North Pacific equatorial current is a Westerly drift caused by the Northeast trade winds. It covers the North Pacific from the Revilla Gigedos Islands off the coast of Mexico to the Philippines.

NORTHERN PINE. A general name which also applies to Scotch fir, Norway pine, Baltic fir, Baltic pine, red deal, yellow deal, red and yellow fir. In the U. S. it is found in the North Atlantic and Great Lakes states. Used for deck planking, joiner work, masts, spars, and also for outside planking of small craft of all types. It has less strength and durability than other woods of the same group, such as yellow pine, and therefore requires increased scantlings when used for structural work. Average weight when seasoned 28 to 34 lbs. per cu. ft.

Fr: *Sapin du Nord;* Ger: *Kiefer; Kiefernholz.*

NORTHERS. Applies to sudden and generally violent winds from a Northerly direction which occur between October and April in the Gulf of Mexico, and in a less degree off the East coast of Central America. Their principal characteristics are the suddenness of their approach and the great fall of temperature that invariably accompanies them.

Ger: *Norder.*

NORTHILL ANCHOR. A light folding anchor used in seaplanes and folding boats. It has a stock set through the crown and perpendicular to the plane of the arms, causing one fluke at a time to bite as in the case of the ordinary anchor.

NORTHING. The distance a ship makes good in a true North direction.

Ger: *Nordlicherlauf; Nordlicherfahrt.*

NORTHWEST MONSOON. A generally light wind with frequent rain squalls prevailing from November till March in the Indian Ocean, between the Equator and Latitude 10° Southeastward of the Seychelles Islands.

Fr: *Mousson du Nord Ouest;* Ger: *Nord West Monsun.*

NORTHWEST PASSAGE. A passage in polar waters extending from Davis Strait along the northern Canadian shores to Alaska. It leads through Baffin Bay, Lancaster Sound, Barrow Strait, Melville Sound, McClure Strait into the Beaufort Sea, and was first navigated in 1911 by the Norwegian explorer Roald Amundsen in his 47 ton sloop "Gjoa."

NORWAY BOX (G. B.). A unit of measurement used in the herring trade in Great Britain. It is equal to one-half cran.

NORWAY SPARS (G. B.). Applies to wooden poles imported from Norway, used in shipyards for shores and uprights, and by builders of small craft for masts and spars, as well as for boat hooks, quants and rickers for dan buoys.

NORWAY SPRUCE. A wood of medium value, full of knots and subject to splits and cup-shakes. Also called Norway fir, white fir, white deal.

Fr: *Sapin de Norwège;* Ger: *Fichtenholz.*

NOSE. 1. The stem of a ship or boat.

Fr: *Nez;* Ger: *Schnabel.*

2. Iron or brass fitting protecting the stemhead of a small boat.

See **Soft Nose.**

NOSE ENDER. A wind blowing from dead ahead.

Fr: *Vent Contraire;* Ger: *Gegenwind.*

See **Muzzler.**

NOSING. See **Molding.**

NOTCH. Recess cut in a keel or other timber to receive a floor, frame, futtock, and so on. Indent of prismatic form cut into the edge of a piece of wood so as to make it interlock with another or others.

Fr: *Margouillet;* Ger: *Kerbe.*

See **Stern Notch.**

NOTHING OFF. An order to the helmsman not to allow the vessel to pay off further from the wind.

Fr: *N'arrivons pas!* Ger: *Nichts vergeben!*

NOTICE OF ABANDONMENT. The act by which the insured informs the underwriter of his decision to abandon and claim for a total loss. It may be given in writing or orally but the former is usually preferred. Such a notice is given only in the event of a "constructive total loss."

Fr: *Déclaration d'abandon;* Ger: *Abandon Erklärung.*

NOTICE OF CLAIM CLAUSE. A bill of lading clause which requires notice of loss by the consignee precedent to liability.

NOTICE OF READINESS. Notice served by a shipmaster to the charterers informing them that the vessel is ready to load according to the terms outlined in the charter. Also called stem note.

Fr: *Lettre d'avis;* Ger: *Ladebereitschaftnotiz.*

NOTICE TO MARINERS. Notices of changes in, or additions to, previously published nautical data.

Fr: *Avis aux Navigateurs;* Ger: *Nachrichten für Seefahrer.*

NOT UNDER COMMAND. Said of a vessel when disabled from any cause. Also called not under control.

NOT-UNDER-COMMAND LIGHT. One of the regulation lights which a vessel not under command has to carry in accordance with the Rules of the Road. Also called breakdown light. They consist of two red lights, placed in a vertical line not less than 6 ft. apart, visible all around the horizon at a distance of at least two miles.

    Fr: *Feu d'Impossibilité de Manoeuvre;* Ger: *Manövrierunfähiges Licht; Fahrtstörungslampen.*

NUCLEUS CREW. A depleted or skeleton crew composed of a few trained officers and men which constitutes the manning of a ship which is not actually in service though to all intents and purposes ready for service at short notice.

    Fr: *Noyau d'Equipage;* Ger: *Verminderte Bemannung.*

NUMBER. A flag hoist of alphabet flags to denote a vessel's identity. To make one's number is to present oneself.

    See **Numeral, Cubic Number, Racing Number, Recall Number, Ship's Number.**

NUMERAL. One of the key numbers under which the scantlings and equipment are tabulated in the rules of classification societies. Also called number.

    Fr: *Nombre;* Ger: *Nummer.*

    See **Criterion of Service Numeral, Equipment Numeral, Longitudinal Number, Transverse Numeral.**

Numerals may be regarded as a means of identification to indicate the general size of the vessel and what the scantlings of structural members are in its case appropriate. These numbers are the result of experience and comparison and are arrived at in different ways by the various classification societies.

NUMERAL PENNANT. One of the ten pennants of the International Code used for making numeral signals.

    Fr: *Pavillon Numérique;* Ger: *Nummerflagge.*

NUMERAL SIGNAL. Signal of the international code representing numbers. It is indicated by a code flag over M; a decimal point by a code flag over N; the end of the signal by a code flag over P.

    Fr: *Signal Numérique;* Ger: *Zahlensignale.*

NUMUNISI. A small single-outrigger dugout canoe with rounded sides from Matema Island, Santa Cruz Archipelago.

NUNATAK. A lonely peak, generally glaciated, rising from an ice sheet or from inland ice.

NUN BUOY. A truncated-cone-shaped buoy, broad in the middle and tapering toward each end. In the ordinary nun buoy the underwater part is spherical. In the tall nun both parts are conical.

    Fr: *Bouée à Cône Double;* Ger: *Spitzboje; Spitztonne.*

NUT. Cast iron ball fitted on the end of an anchor stock to assist in bringing the stock flat on the sea bottom.

NUTATION. A periodic variation in the line of intersection of the ecliptic and equinoctial due to the attraction of the sun, moon, and planets on the earth considered as an irregular spheroidal body.

    Fr: *Nutation;* Ger: *Schwanten; Nutation.*

O

O. Flag of the international code of signals diagonally halved in red and yellow. When flown as a single letter signal indicates: "Man overboard."

O.A. OVER ALL.
O.B. OUTBOARD.
Obs. OBSERVATION or OBSERVED (astronomy).
O.D. or O.Dia. OUTSIDE DIAMETER.
O.Dk. OBSERVATION DECK.
O.P. OPEN POLICY.
O.R. OWNER'S RISK.
O.S. ORDINARY SEAMAN.
O.T. OLD TERMS (grain trade).
O.T. OIL TIGHT.

OAI. A single-outrigger fishing canoe of Kaniet Islands, Bismarck Archipelago. The hull is composed of a dugout with sides raised by a wash strake. The ends slope up and form horizontal projections. A gunwale pole runs along the whole length at each side. There is a platform over the outrigger booms. The mast is stepped in the bottom of the canoe and has a decorative wooden fork at the end. The quadrangular mat sail is laced to two spars, the lower one having jaws which rest on the mast.

OAK. The wood of the tree *quercus robur*. Also called Austrian oak or English oak. Its adaptation to the purposes of ship and boatbuilding has long been pre-eminent for strength and durability. It contains gallic acid which corrodes iron fittings and fastenings. It is hard, tough, strong and elastic; the grain is usually straight, uniform and free from knots. English oak is used by boatbuilders for stems, sternposts, aprons, deadwoods, gunwales, keels, keelsons and thwart knees. Weight per cu. ft. 52 lb.

Fr: *Chêne;* Ger: *Eiche.*

See **Live Oak, White Oak.**

OAKUM. A calking material used in waterproofing the seams between strakes of planking. It is a mass of strong, pliable tarred rope fibers obtained from scrap rope, which swell when wet. The fibers are impregnated with pine tar and loosely bundled together. Before oakum is used it is worked or spun into threads which run from 40 to 70 ft. to the pound. The best fibers for marine oakum are Russian and Italian hemp. The fibers may be new, but usually are obtained from cutting old tarred hemp rope into short lengths and pulling the fibers apart.

Fr: *Etoupe;* Ger: *Werg.*

See **White Oakum.**

OANGA TAMO. A single-outrigger dugout canoe found in Blanche Bay, Gazelle Peninsula, and Watom Island in the Bismarck Archipelago. The name "karaveta," a corruption of "corvette," is also given to these canoes.

It has a heavier hull and float than the Oanga Tuna and is built without endpieces. The bow is more or less vertical, somewhat concave, and terminates with a sharp point. The extremity of the stern bears a deeply cut "nose." The larger craft of this type are rigged with a triangular sail between the mast and the bow, and with a trapezoidal sail abaft the mast.

OANGA TUNA. Small, narrow, single-outrigger dugout canoe from Watom Island, Bismarck Archipelago. The endpieces have a forked base which is lashed to the edges of the hull. The fore endpiece rises almost vertically with a slight curve into a long thin erection, which is recurved at the tip. There is a sharp spur at its base.

OAR. A long shaft of wood with a blade or thin enlarged surface at one end and handle at the other, the portion between being called the loom. It is in theory a lever of the second order. The blade immersed in the water forms the fulcrum, and the resultant pressure against the handle, applied to a rowlock or fixed pin in the side of the boat at some point on the loom, drives the boat forward.

Fr: *Aviron;* Ger: *Ruder; Riemen; Seitenruder.*

See **Bow Oar, Cape Ann Oar, Coble Oar, Harpoon Oar, Midship Oar, Rigged Oar, Spoon Oar, Steering Oar, Straight Oar, Stroke Oar, Tub Oar.**

The length of oars varies to suit the particular size of the boat, the position of the thwart, and height of the gunwale above water. For a single-banked boat the length should be about twice the beam at rowlock, plus the freeboard. For a double-banked boat it should be about twice the length of the thwart from which it is used.

OAR BLADE. The flat part of an oar, dipped into the water when rowing. Also

Oar

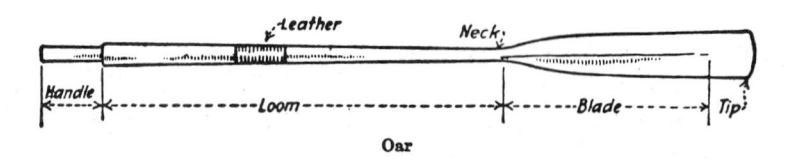

called wash. The blade is either feather- or spoonshaped; the latter shape is only used in smooth water by pleasure or sporting boats. In better oars the blade is copper-tipped.

Fr: *Pelle d'aviron;* Ger: *Ruderblatt; Riemenblatt.*

OARLOCK. A swivel crutch for holding an oar when pulling. Also called **swivel rowlock.** It consists of a forked shank which fits into a socket in the gunwale.

Fr: *Dame de Nage; Tolet à Fourche;* Ger: *Rudergabel; Ruderklampe; Rojegabel.*

See **Rowlock.**

OARLOCK BLOCK. See **Rowlock Chock.**

OARS. Command to a boat's crew to stop pulling and to keep the oars in a horizontal position with blades feathered and ready for the next stroke.

Fr: *Lève Rames;* Ger: *Auf Riemen.*
See **In Oars, Out Oars.**

OARSMAN. One who uses an oar.

Fr: *Canotier;* Ger: *Bootsgast; Ruderer; Rudersmann; Rojer.*

OATH OF ARRIVAL. The oath to truth of the statement of the ship's manifest sworn by the master on arrival in port to the customs officer who boards the vessel.

OATH OF ENTRY. Oath sworn before a collector of customs by the importer of goods or his delegate to the effect that the merchandise listed in the import declaration is a complete account of the shipment, that its description, quantity, and value are correctly stated, and that the consignee named is the actual consignee.

OATH ON DEPARTURE. The oath taken by the master of a ship before a collector of customs when handing to him the copy of the manifest prepared for the customs authorities prior to clearing outward.

OBLIQUITY. The obliquity of the ecliptic is the angle at which the ecliptic is inclined to the equinoctial.

Fr: *Obliquité;* Ger: *Schiefe.*

OBOEN. Australian bark canoe of the Unalla tribe of Raffles Bay, Coburg Peninsula, in the Northern Territory. It is made of a single sheet of bark. The sides are supported by gunwale poles which are spanned together on either side by ropes made of strips of bark. Short pieces of bark are placed crosswise in the bottom in order to preserve the shape and increase the strength of the canoe. Length 18 ft. Breadth 2 ft. Crew 8.

OBSERVATION. Determination of the altitude of a heavenly body usually through the use of a sextant, to find a vessel's position at sea. Also the information so obtained. Sometimes the azimuth, or bearing, of the body is also measured, and forms part or all of the observation. In the latter case, the observation is used to determine the compass error.

Fr: *Observation;* Ger: *Beobachtung.*

OBSERVED ALTITUDE. The elevation of a heavenly body above the visible horizon after the index error, if any, of the instrument by which it has been measured has been applied.

Fr: *Hauteur Observée;* Ger: *Beobachtete Höhe.*

OCCLUDED DEPRESSION. Atmospheric depression in which the cold front closes on the warm front.

Fr: *Dépression occluse;* Ger: *Verschliessende Dépression.*

OCCLUSION. The line of coincidence between a cold front and a warm front in an atmospheric depression. It is due to the warm air being gradually pushed from the earth's surface by the advance of the heavier cold air behind it. Also called **Line of Occlusion.**

Fr: *Occlusion;* Ger: *Okklusion.*

OCCULTATION. The obscuring of a heavenly body from sight by the intervention of some other heavenly body.

Fr: *Occultation;* Ger: *Verdeckung.*

OCCULTING LIGHT. A light in which

the steady luminous rays are interrupted by flashes of darkness as opposed to a flashing light in which the steady darkness is interrupted by flashes of light. The duration of darkness is always less than, or equal to, that of light. For hydrographic purposes a light is characterized as flashing or occulting solely according to the relative durations of light and darkness, without any reference to the illuminating apparatus employed. The revolving apparatus consists of a mechanism termed clock, driven by a falling weight in large lights, or a spring in small ones.

Fr: *Feu à Occultations;* Ger: *Unterbrochenes Feuer.*

OCCULTING QUICK FLASHING LIGHT. A light in which the duration of flashes is interrupted by eclipses shorter than the duration of flashes.

Fr: *Feu scintillant à occultations;* Ger: *Unterbrochenes Funkelfeuer.*

OCEAN BILL OF LADING. A bill of lading in which the name of the cargo receivers is followed by the words "or order," and which, therefore, may be endorsed. Also called port bill of lading (U. S.), order bill of lading (G. B.). The last endorsee is entitled to delivery of the goods on presentation of the bill. The shipowners sign two to four copies, specifying the number signed. When financed by a bank, the latter requires all signed negotiable copies, which is known as a "full set."

Fr: *Connaissement à ordre;* Ger: *Orderkonnossement.*

OCEAN CURRENT. A nontidal current constituting a part of the general oceanic circulation, for example, the Gulf Stream, Kuroshio, equatorial currents.

Fr: *Courant Océanique; Courant Marin;* Ger: *Ozeanische Strömung; Meeresströmung.*

OCEAN-GOING VESSEL (U. S.). Under American laws refers to vessels which under the usual course of their employment proceed outside the line dividing inland waters from the high seas as designated and determined under the provisions of section 2 of the Act of Congress of February 19, 1895.

OCEANOGRAPHY. Dr. G. W. Littlehales has defined oceanography as follows: "oceanography includes investigations which deal with the form and divisions of all the marine area on the surface of the globe: the winds that blow over the surface waters; the contour of the ocean bed from the sea level down to the greatest depths; the temperature, density, salinity, the circulation, the physical and chemical properties of sea water; the currents, tides and waves; the composition and distribution of marine deposits; the nature and distribution of marine organisms at the surface, in the intermediate waters and on the floor of the ocean; modifications brought about in living things by the conditions of their existence; the relations of man to the ocean in the development of trade, fisheries, navigation, hydrography, and marine meteorology."

Fr: *Océanographie;* Ger: *Ozeanographie; Meereskunde.*

Bigelow, *Oceanography,* London, 1931; Fowler, *The Science of the Sea,* London, 1912; Jenkins, J. T., *Text Book on Oceanography,* London, 1921; Sverdrup, H. U., *The Oceans,* New York, 1942.

OCEAN TUG. A type of tug specially designed for long-distance tows at sea where seaworthiness, considerable power, and ample fuel capacity are required.

Fr: *Remorqueur de Haute Mer;* Ger: *Hochsee-Schlepper.*

OCEAN WATERS. Used for defining waters subject to the rules for preventing collisions at sea, the term refers to all waters opening directly or indirectly into the sea and navigable by ships, foreign or domestic, coming in from the ocean, whose draft is as great as that of larger ships which traverse the open sea.

OCTANT. An instrument for measuring the altitude of celestial bodies, of identical principle to that of the sextant, but with a 45° limb instead of a 60° limb.

See **Sextant.**

ODAM. Open sailing coaster from the Laccadive Islands.

A portable decking and roofing made of coconut matting are provided amidships and afford shelter to the crew. A small platform at the stern is for the helmsman. The sides are raised at the stern and ornamented with arabesques in white *chunam.* The framing and planking are pegged or nailed. The rig consists of one mast with lateen sail and jib.

ODDMENTS. Goods left over at the completion of a vessel's discharge and eventually sold by the shipowner to meet claims for short delivery.

Ger: *Ladereste.*

ODI. Generic name for several varieties of

small, open fishing boats of the Maldive and Laccadive Islands.

In some types the bows are very bluff, while others are built on finer lines and have a curved hornlike stem. The carvel planking is sewed with coir twine.

The *mas-odi* or bonito boat from Minicoy (Laccadives) is built with high upturned stemhead, and low, full stern, on which the necessary space is provided for a platform which projects outboard and forms a decking for the afterend. Forward and abaft the mast there are wells in which the live bait is kept. The rig consists of a pole mast stepped slightly forward of amidships in a tabernacle, on which are set two sails: on the foreside a tall and narrow square sail usually made of matting; abaft the mast a boomless gaff sail made of cotton. Length 32 ft. Breadth 9 ft. (Average.)

The *daturu-odi* is an open cargo carrier of the same type but larger than the *mas-odi*; used for trading between the Maldive Islands and Ceylon. It is usually provided with a portable decking or a roofing made of mats. These boats formerly used an outrigger but nowadays they are built with more beam and depth and can therefore dispense with this contrivance. They do not use the fore-and-aft gaff sail of the *mas-odi* but often set a small topsail in fine weather.

ODOGRAPH. An instrument which records to scale on a chart the actual course followed by a ship at sea.

OERTZ RUDDER. A patent rudder built in two parts. The parabolically rounded fore part is constructed as a fixed guide body around the rudder post. The after-part of the rudder, the actual revolving part, joins the fixed fore part in a complete streamline form. The turning axis of the movable back part lies at about one-third of the total fore and aft part. Owing to the distribution of pressure so obtained it is claimed that only 50-70% of the steering power needed for normal plate rudder of the same area is required.

Fr: *Gouvernail Oertz;* Ger: *Oertzruder.*

OFA. Generic name for different types of native craft from Roti Island, Lesser Sunda Islands. The *ofa maeik* is an outrigger canoe. The *ofa baluk* is a trading boat with two masts and lug sails.

OFF. 1. Away from, as from the wind or a course. Clear of, as from the land or a danger. The opposite of "near," as in "off a course," "off the wind," etc.

Fr: *Au large de;* Ger: *Auf.*

2. To seaward of, at a short distance.
Fr: *Au large de;* Ger: *Draussen.*

OFFAL. Trade name given in Great Britain to coarse fish caught with a trawl as distinguished from prime fish. Offal includes plaice, haddock, gurnards, skate, etc.

See **Gurry.**

OFFAL BOAT. A powered boat used on the U. S. Pacific coast for the transportation of offal from the canneries to the refining plants which handle the various by-products of fish.

The offal boat is about 60 to 80 ft. long and designed on the lines of a seine boat with deckhouse forward of a large hold of about 30 to 50 tons capacity, cemented and provided with a sump well.

OFF AND ON. To stand off and on is to approach the land on one tack and recede from it on the other.

Fr: *Au large et à terre;* Ger: *Ab und An.*

OFFICER. One of the certificated members of the ship's staff who under the master's authority assist him in the navigation and operation of the vessel.

According to U. S. navigation laws, vessels of 100 gross tons and under must carry one licensed mate. From 200 to 1000 tons, two officers. Above 1000 tons three officers must be carried if the vessel is engaged in a run of more than 400 miles from the port of departure to the port of final destination. According to British regulations, if the ship is of 100 tons burden or upward she must carry at least one officer besides the master, holding a certificate of only mate, if the ship is engaged in foreign-going trade.

The British Merchant Shipping Act of 1897 provides, independently of the master, two mates for every mechanically-propelled foreign-going vessel of over 200 ft. in length or 700 tons gross tonnage.

On small vessels and sailing ships the officers are usually styled as mates. When the word mate is used without qualification it always denotes the first or chief mate.

Fr: *Officier;* Ger: *Offizier.*

OFFICIAL LOG BOOK. A book carried by all American vessels of 75 tons burden or more, in accordance with U. S. statutes. It may be kept either distinct from, or united with the ship's log. In practice it is usually a separate book.

The official log is purely for statutory purposes and largely for chronicling the history and character of each member of the crew It is not intended to record the ordinary day by day incidents of the navigation of the ship. The information which it is the captain's duty to record is largely personal, and relating to the crew and passengers: (offenses, fines, punishments, illness or injuries, deaths, births, etc.) Statements in case of collisions, groundings, record of boat and fire drills, are also entered. Special provision is made for recording callings, arrivals, departures, freeboard and draught. Spaces are provided for name, duty, etc., of each member of the crew, which should coincide with the list in the ship's articles. Every entry made in the official log book is signed by the master and by the mate.

Fr: *Journal Timbré;* *Journal Réglementaire;* *Livre de Bord;* Ger: *Schiffstagebuch;* *Schiffsjournal.*

See **Logbook.**

OFFING. 1. That part of the open visible sea which is remote from the shore, beyond the midline between the shore and the horizon.

Fr: *Large;* Ger: *Draussen.*

2. To seaward, but in sight of land.

OFFSETS. The coordinates used in naval architecture to determine accurately the outer form of a ship which, geometrically speaking, is a curved undevelopable surface.

Fr: *Devis de Tracé;* Ger: *Aufmasstabelle.*

See **Heights, Half Breadths, Offset Sheets.**

Offsets are measured at right angles to one of the three basic reference planes: (1) vertical longitudinal plane; (2) horizontal plane parallel to the surface of the water; (3) a plane at right angles to each of the first two planes. When set off vertically above the base line they are called heights. When set off horizontally from the center line plane, they are called half breadths or half widths.

OFFSET SHEETS. The sheets on which the offsets are arranged in tabular form. As a rule there are five sheets, as follows: (1) offsets of half breadth on waterlines; (2) offsets of heights on buttocks; (3) offsets of decks and sheer line; (4) offsets of sight edges of shell-plating; (5) offsets of margin plate.

Fr: *Devis de Tracé;* Ger: *Aufmasstabelle.*

OFFSHORE. Generally, clear of the land.

Fr: *Au Large;* Ger: *Vom Land entfernt.*

OFFSHORE DOCK. A single-walled floating dock, fixed in place and depending for its stability on some fixed structure or mechanism, used for lifting vessels out of the water for cleaning and repairs. Also called lifting dock. There are two kinds of lifting docks. One has a pontoon which is sunk to receive the ship and pumped out to raise it. The other has a platform or framework, raised by hydraulic rams, for carrying the ship.

Fr: *Dock flottant type "offshore";* Ger: *"L" Dock.*

OFFSHORE FISH. Species of fish which are usually found at greater depth and farther from the shore than the inshore fish, for examples, cod, haddock, hake, halibut.

OFFSHORE FISHERIES. Fisheries whether trawling, drifting, or lining which are carried on in deep water far from shore with large craft. Also called deep-sea fisheries.

Fr: *Pêche au Large;* *Grande Pêche;* Ger: *Tiefseefischerei.*

OFFSHORE WIND. A wind blowing to seaward, off the land.

OFF SOUNDINGS. Said of a vessel navigating beyond the 100-fathom line of soundings.

OFF THE WIND. 1. Away from the wind; the opposite of "on" or "near the wind."

2. Sailing free.

See **Off.**

OIL BAG. A canvas bag of triangular cross section about 1 ft. long, triced over the side for making a slick in rough seas. When in use it is stuffed with oakum, cotton, kapok, or waste, saturated with oil, and punctured in a number of places by a coarse sail needle. Oil bags are usually made of No. 2 canvas with roping of 15-thread hemp at joints. When secured to a sea anchor, they make a good slick to windward. At bottom a drip pipe filled with oakum may be provided. Vegetable and animal oils are more effective than mineral oils.

Fr: *Fileur d'huile;* Ger: *Ölsack.*

OIL BURNER. Slang term for a steamer burning fuel oil instead of coal. Properly, a mechanical appliance fitted at the mouth of a boiler furnace to atomize the fuel oil.

Fr: *Brûleur;* Ger: *Ölbrenner.*

OILER. 1. See **Greaser.**

2. An oil tanker, in naval parlance. See **Oil Tanker.**

Canvas Oil Bag

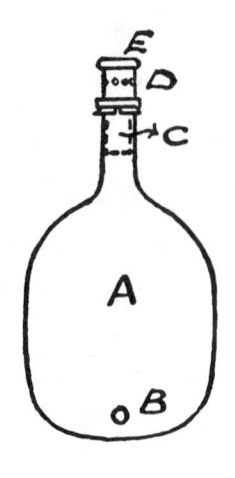

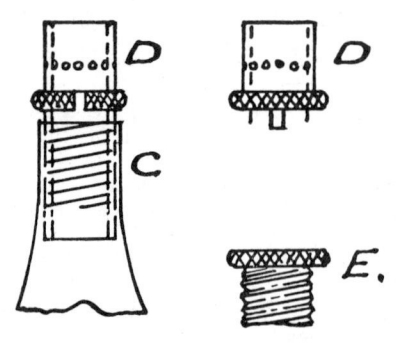

A. Canvas oil bag
B. Eye for lanyard
C. Metal Neck
D. Sleeve
E. Screw cap

OIL FIRING. The method by which low-grade mineral oil (fuel oil) is used as fuel in boiler furnaces to produce steam.

Fr: *Chauffe au Mazout*; Ger: *Ölfeuerung*.

OIL HOSE. A hose used for the transfer of oil cargoes from ship to shore and vice versa. It is constructed of: a helix of flat wire; a cotton duck reinforcement; a rubber layer; another cotton duck reinforcement; a helix of round wire embedded in rubber; an outside rubber cover. It is manufactured in lengths of 30 ft. or less. All fittings and couplings are made of non-ferrous metal. Standard inside diameter 4, 6 or 8 in., capable of sustaining a hydrostatic pressure of 250, 200 and 150 lbs. per sq. in., respectively.

American Marine Standards Committee, Standard O, no. 20, Washington, 1928.

OIL LINE. The system of piping by which oil fuel is transferred from the tanks to the boiler furnaces of a vessel. Also called fuel-oil service and transfer system.

Fr: *Tuyautage de Mazout*; Ger: *Öltankleitung*.

OIL PERMIT (U. S.). A document issued by government authorities allowing a passenger vessel to carry refined petroleum on a particular route where there is no other practical method of transportation.

OIL POLLUTION ACT. An act passed by the U. S. Congress in 1924 which makes it unlawful to discharge oil in coastal navigable waters of the U. S. from any vessel using oil for the generation of propulsion power.

OIL-SEPARATING BARGE. A tank barge fitted with the necessary plant for filtering and reclaiming oil residues accruing from the cleaning of tanks in bulk oil carriers, or found in the ballast tanks of oil-burning vessels when the double bottom is used alternately as oil bunker and as ballast tank. Also called filter barge. The appliances usually consist of oil filters and centrifugal separators. Recently some vessels have been equipped with oil separators, enabling them to dispense with the use of oil-separating barges.

Fr: *Chaland épurateur d'huile; Chaland filtre à Mazout*; Ger: *Ölabscheider Leichter*.

OIL SEPARATOR. An apparatus for separating oil and water coming from ballast tanks, peak tanks, and deep tanks when these have been used as fuel bunkers. It enables the purified water to be discharged overboard when the ship is in harbor or in territorial waters, without infringing on regulations. The oil reclaimed is pumped back into the bunkers.

This apparatus is either installed on board or in an oil-separating barge. One hundred to 200 tons per hour can be dealt with, according to the proportion of oil in the emulsion. A purity of at least 0.05 per cent for the effluent discharged overboard must be attained to satisfy international rules on the pollution of harbor waters.

Fr: *Epurateur d'huile*; Ger: *Bilgewasseröler; Ölabscheider*.

Hele, Shaw, and Beale, "Oil Separators for Bilge and Ballast Water," Institution of Naval Architects (London), *Transactions*, vol. 68, 1926.

OILSKINS. Waterproof coat, trousers, and headgear, of treated cotton, linen, or silk, worn at sea as protection against the elements in heavy weather.

Fr: *Ciré;* Ger: *Ölkleidung; Ölrock; Ölzeug.*

OIL STOP. Lampwick, canvas, felt, etc., soaked in a mixture of shellac and white or red lead, or of pine tar and shellac. Used in steel shipbuilding to prevent leakage of oil where an uncalked member passes through an oiltight surface.

OIL TANKER. A tank vessel specially designed for the bulk transport of petroleum products by sea.

Fr: *Pétrolier;* Ger: *Öltankschiff.*

In tankers with heavy oil cargoes there remains considerable cargo space which cannot be used. Under the 1930 freeboard rules, tankers carrying light oils can be designed to make full use of the available capacity, but vessels carrying heavy oils can be loaded only to about 80 per cent of their internal capacity. The general arrangement of the oil tanker is fairly well standardized. One of the recent changes in design has been the substitution of two longitudinal bulkheads for one centerline bulkhead, combined with summer tanks. The speed of tankers has been gradually increased, and designed speeds of more than 16 knots are now encountered. Another method of tanker construction adopted occasionally is that in which vertical cylindrical tanks are built on the top of the double bottom of an ordinary vessel. These tanks are arranged in pairs and are open to the double bottom, from which strakes of plating are omitted; with this arrangement an ordinary cargo carrier is readily convertible into a tanker and vice versa, the tanks being entirely separated from the hull proper. Cylindrical tanks are used for the transportation of lubricating oils of different grades.

Hudson, J. W., Oil Tankers, Society of Naval Architects and Marine Engineers,
New York, *Transactions,* vol. 44, 1936; Jansen, P., Sea Transport of Petroleum, London, 1938; Lisle, O., Tanker Technique, London, 1936; Morrell, R. W., Oil Tankers, New York, 1931; Pluymert, N. J., Modern Tanker Design, Society of Naval Architects and Marine Engineers, New York, 1939; U. S. Department of Commerce, Bureau of Marine Inspection and Navigation, Rules and Regulations Series 14, Tank Vessels, Washington, 1939.

OILTIGHT. A term applied to any joint having the property of resisting the passage of oil. It requires closer spacing of rivets than a watertight joint.

OILTIGHT HATCH. A steel coaming with an oiltight cover arranged to hinge at one side and closed at the other by toggles or tumble bolts with wing nuts. Oil tightness is obtained by fitting a gasket of greased hemp or rubber which is made to fit in a small channel section around the periphery of the cover, the top edge of the coaming making contact when the cover is closed. The cover is provided with a rest rod to hold it open when desired at an angle of about 45° when the tank has to be aired.

Fr: *Panneau Étanche au Pétrole;* Ger: *Öldichtluke.*

American Marine Standards Committee, Standard 84, *Oil Tight Hatch Covers,* Washington, 1931.

OILTIGHT RIVETING. Riveting adopted where joints are to be oiltight. The spacing of rivets does not in such a case exceed 3 to 3.5 diameters. Rivet holes are punched small and reamed to size.

Fr: *Rivetage Étanche au Pétrole;* Ger: *Öldichtenietung.*

Frear, H. P., *Notes on Rivets and Spacing of Rivets for Oiltight Work,* Society of Naval Architects and Marine Engineers, *Transactions,* vol. 28, New York, 1920.

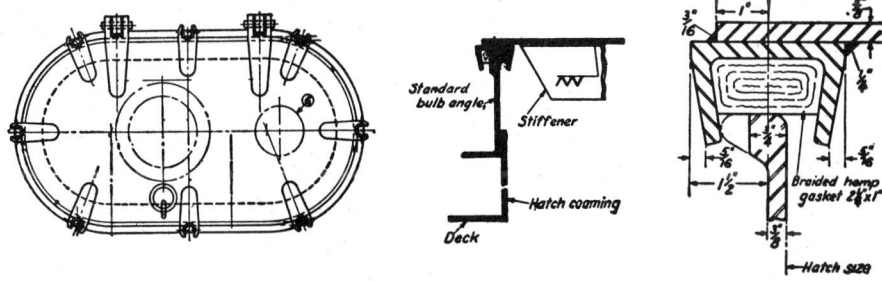

Oiltight Hatch Cover. (*American Marine Standard*)

OIL WASH. A light gas oil used on oil tankers for cleaning tanks after they have been steamed.

OKITAGURI-BUNE. Large Japanese sampan used in the trawlnet and line fisheries of Kanagawa district and the gulf of Tokyo. It is rigged with two masts and has a sail area of about 787 sq. ft. Length overall 50 ft. Breadth 9.6 ft. Depth 3.6 ft. (Typical.)

The absence of sheer and small freeboard forward are due to the fact that this type of boat works in sheltered waters. One of the notable features of the hull is the curvature of the bottom, which raises abaft the stem. The rudder is shorter and broader than usually found in other sampans (height 12½ ft., breadth 3½ ft. at bottom). This type of boat works with trawlnets from January to May and with lines from June to December. The smaller vessels of this type have a length of about 30 ft.

OKO. Generic name of West African dugout canoes from the Bight of Benin, used for fishing by the Meena, Popo, and Nago tribes. Also called *bathray*. The smallest craft, made by the Popo tribes, have an average length of 9.5 ft. and a beam of 1.3 ft. The largest, built by the Nagos, which are used only for inland water transportation, measure up to 82 ft. with a breadth of 10 ft.; their carrying capacity ranges from 15 to 18 tons.

The body, hewed from a hardwood tree trunk, has both ends rounded with shelflike extremities. A breakwater is provided at the bow. There are no thwarts; a number of cross sticks, depending on the size of the canoe, are used to keep the sides in shape. When the length exceeds 16 ft., ribs made of natural crooks are fitted inside. The larger seagoing craft have a wash strake. The body thickness ranges from 13/16 in. to 3 in., according to length.

OLAN MESA. East Indian dugout canoe with double outriggers from the Gulf of Mandar, Celebes.

The small sheer of the ends is augmented by the addition of a short length of wash strake. A railing made of bamboo leaves extends between the end wash strakes. The hull is wall-sided with flat bottom. Rig: one mast with large quadrangular sail. A quarter rudder is used for steering.

OLD-FASHIONED ANCHOR.
See **Stocked Anchor.**

OLD MAN. 1. In shipbuilding, a heavy steel bar bent in the form of a letter Z and used for holding a portable drill. One leg is bolted to the ship's structure and the drill head is placed under the other leg, which holds the drill to its work.

2. In nautical parlance, a colloquialism for the master of a merchantman.

Fr: *Vieux;* Ger: *Ole; Alter.*

OLIMA. A single-outrigger dugout canoe from Squally Islands, Bismarck Archipelago, with sharp ends and no wash strake. The bow end has a pronounced rake and horizontal upper surface. The outrigger is usually carried on the starboard side.

OMNIBUS BILL OF LADING. A bill of lading, usually made out by a forwarding agent, covering numerous small parcels consigned for distribution to an agent at the port of destination; its purpose is to avoid minimum freight charges and bill-of-lading costs for each parcel.

OMPO. East Indian outrigger canoe from Bima, Lesser Sunda Islands.

ON A LAY (U. S.). An arrangement whereby the owner of a vessel lets her to the master to operate on shares, and whereby the master is entrusted with entire possession and control, with the right to employ and navigate the vessel as he sees fit, and with the responsibility of victualing and manning it at his own expense.

ONDOAN. A Philippine dugout of the Visayan Sea used for fishing. It is of the *baroto* type with high, sharp cutwater and light scantlings, and built primarily for speed. It has double outriggers and is propelled by paddles.

ONE-CLASS BOAT. A class of sailing boats or small yachts of one size and design, adopted by a yacht club or group of clubs with the object of requiring all competitors to meet on the same terms in sailing matches.

Fr: *Embarcation Monotype;* Ger: *Einheitsklasse Boot.*

See **Class, One-Design Class.**

ONE-COMPARTMENT SHIP. Term which refers to the ability of a vessel to resist sinking when damaged. A one-compartment ship is a vessel in which the watertight bulkheads are so spaced that one compartment can be flooded without submerging the vessel above her margin line.

Ger: *Einabteilungschiff.*

See **Two-Compartment Ship, Floodable Length, Margin Line.**

ONE-DESIGN CLASS. A class of sailing yachts built from a standard design and identical in construction and rig. Originally designed to keep down the construction cost by elimination of the designer's fee and by adaptability to mass construction. Formerly limited to small boats, it later included yachts up to 70-ft. length.

Fr: *Série Monotype;* Ger: *Einheitsklasse.*
See **One-Class Boat.**

ONKER. A slang word for sailing vessels which bring small timber or firewood from the Baltic Sea to British ports.

ONLY MATE. A term referring to the only officer besides the master on small vessels, such as coasters, fishing boats, and so on. A rank in the British Merchant Service on vessels which carry only one mate.

ON SOUNDINGS. Said of a vessel navigating areas where the depth of water can be measured by using the sounding lead; generally within the 100-fathom curve; "off soundings" when it cannot be so reached.

Fr: *Sondes;* Ger: *Lotbarer Grund.*

ON THE BEAM.
See **Abeam.**

ON THE BERTH. Said of a vessel when it is properly moored to quay or to buoys and ready to load cargo. In chartering, the expression "loading on the berth" or "placed on the berth" means that the ship is available for loading parcels of general cargo.

ON THE BOW. Lying within that part of the horizon included within 45° of dead ahead on either hand.

Fr: *Par le Bossoir;* Ger: *Kranbalksweise.*

ON THE QUARTER. In a position between abeam and astern. Strictly 45 degrees abaft the beam.

Fr: *Par la hanche;* Ger: *In der Vierung; Backstagsweise.*

ONTRO. Double-ended open rowboat employed for swordfishing in the Straits of Messina. Length 19.7 ft. Breadth 3.9 ft. Inside depth 1.8 ft. Crew 4 or 5 oarsmen, 1 harpooner.

The boat has fine lines and light scantlings and is built for speed. It has four thwarts. In the center there is a pole about 11½ ft. high raking aft and provided with rungs. When swordfish are being pursued one of the crew is stationed on a crosspiece rigged at about one-third the height of the spar, to direct the boat. Four oars are used. The aftermost (stroke) has a length of 17 ft. The other two are 17.9 ft. long. The bow oar measures 18.7 ft.

OOARO. A fishing dugout from Gaboon, West Africa, with a length of 10 to 16 ft.

OOTASHETS. A seagoing dugout canoe employed by the Makah Indians of the north Pacific coast for whale hunting near Cape Flattery. It is of the same type as the *wituksut* and is manned by a harpooner, a steersman, and six paddlers. Its length ranges from 35 to 40 ft.

OOZE. Soft deposit covering large areas of the ocean bottom, composed mainly of the shells or other hard parts of minute organisms such as foraminifera, radiolaria, and diatoma.

Fr: *Fange;* Ger: *Schlik.*

OPEN BASIN. Also open dock. A basin or dock in a port with small range of tide, in which dock gates are unnecessary and the shelter is sufficient for vessels to lie alongside. The water in the dock rises or falls according to the state of the tide.

Fr: *Bassin à flot;* Ger: *Aussendock.*

OPEN BERTH. Anchoring berth in an open roadstead.

Fr: *Mouillage forain;* Ger: *Offene Ankerplatz.*

OPEN BOAT. An undecked boat; a boat not protected from the entry of sea water by means of a continuous deck.

Fr: *Embarcation non Pontée;* Ger: *Offenes Boot.*

OPEN BRIDGE HOUSE. A bridge house with forward and after ends open.

OPEN CHARTER. Charter party whereby the vessel may fix for any cargo and for any port or ports.

OPEN CHOCK. A cable chock differing from the closed type in having an aperture in the top to admit ropes.

Fr: *Chaumard Ouvert;* Ger: *Offene Verholklampe.*

See **Chock.**

OPEN CLASS. A classification adopted for the racing of sailing yachts of widely different size and rig. The boats are grouped into divisions according to size and speed. A handicap or time allowance is established to put them on equal footing; the handicap being based on the allotted percentage of the fastest speed made by any yacht in its division.

Ger: *Freie Klasse.*

OPEN COAST. A coast generally clear of dangers to navigation.

Fr: *Côte foraine.*

OPEN COVER. A type of insurance akin to a floating policy but of wider scope. An agreement between the insured and his

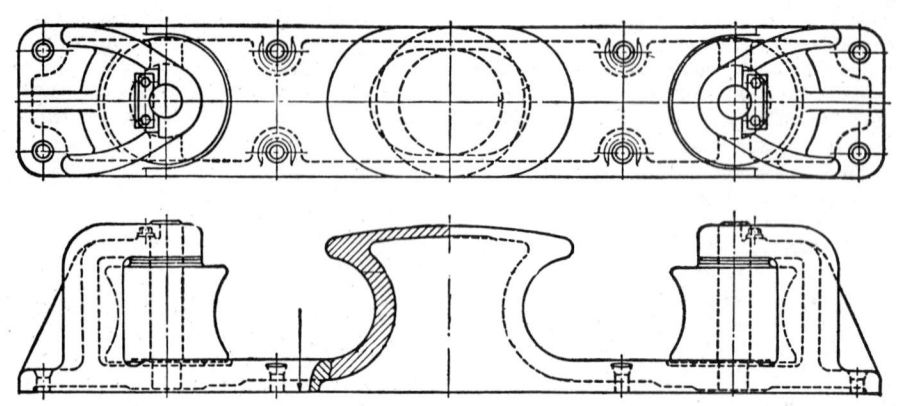

Open Chocks With Center Pillar and Roller Ends. (American Marine Standard)

underwriter whereby the latter accepts all shipments or interests for particular voyages or trades at agreed rates and conditions, subject to a certain limit per vessel.

Fr: *Police Ouverte;* Ger: *Offene Police.*

An open cover generally lasts for one year, and the premium is paid under each policy issued under such contract. The shipper must declare to the insurer all shipments made, but in return for this he avoids the possibility of being uninsured—owing, for instance, to an error. The terms of an open cover are embodied in a "contract note" issued by the brokers.

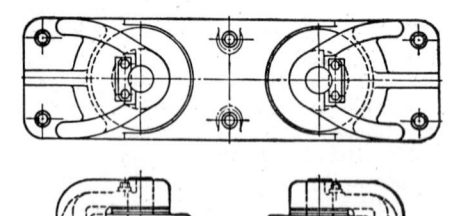

Open Roller Chock. (American Marine Standard)

OPEN DOCK.
See Open Basin.

OPEN GUNWALE. The opposite of "box gunwale." On the open gunwale the capping is omitted.

OPEN HARBOR. A harbor unsheltered, exposed to the sea.

OPEN HAWSE. A ship when moored is said to have an open hawse when the chains lead from the hawse pipes to the anchors without touching each other. When the ship brings a strain on both chains, the head bisects the angle between them. Also called clear hawse.

Fr: *Chaînes claires;* Ger: *Klare Ketten.*

OPENING IRON. A broad-ended, wedge-shaped, wood-calking tool with a rather thin blade, used in opening the seams of planks in large vessels before oakum or cotton is inserted for calking. Also called reeming iron.

Fr: *Fer Taillant;* Ger: *Lasseisen; Scharfeisen.*

OPENING SIDE LIGHT. A side light designed to pivot about its major axis vertically or horizontally. Also called pivoting side light.

Fr: *Hublot ouvrant;* Ger: *Drehfenster; Pivotfenster.*

OPEN PACK. Floes, generally separated, composed of narrow belts and pools, accessible to navigation. Also called loose ice.

OPEN PORT. A port available to commerce without restrictions on account of government regulations or health or physical conditions. A port not closed by ice in the winter. Also called open harbor.

Fr: *Port Ouvert.*

OPEN RAILING. A fence or balustrade consisting of stanchions, handrail, and guard rods which enclose weather decks and superstructures. Also called guard railing. The stanchions are made of round rod or solid drawn-steel tube with ball-shaped swellings through which the guard rods pass.

Fr: *Garde-Corps;* Ger: *Stangengeländer; Stangenreeling.*

OPEN RATES. The condition arising in a specified trade when there exists no rate agreement among shipping lines, each line being free to charge its own freight rates.

OPEN ROADSTEAD. Anchoring place near the open sea, at some distance from a harbor or sea town.

Fr: *Rade Foraine;* Ger: *Offene Reede.*

OPEN SEA. The main sea. That which is not enclosed between headlands or included in narrow straits.

Fr: *Mer libre;* Ger: *Offene Meer; Offene See.*

OPEN SPACE. Term used in tonnage measurement to denote all spaces above the upper deck which may not be fitted with doors or other permanently attached means of enclosing them. All erections and deckhouses included under this classification are exempt from tonnage.

Fr: *Espace Découvert.*

OPEN STERN FRAME. The stern frame of a single-screw vessel in which the sternpost is omitted, the whole rudder area being unsupported between upper and lower bearings.

OPEN TUCK (G. B.). A method of working a tuck seine in slack water. The shape of the set is more or less the same as when a shore seine is worked, except that the two ends of the net are brought on to the larger boat after the smaller has paid the net out, leaving one end with the larger. The fish enclosed by the net are usually frightened down into its bag by creating a disturbance with stones or a tuck pole.

OPERATING DIFFERENTIAL SUBSIDY (U. S.). A subsidy paid by the state to a shipowner or charterer operating a vessel engaged in foreign trade as a compensation over and above the cost of insurance, maintenance, repairs, wages, and subsistence of the crew and other items of expense, upon proof that the owner is at a considerable disadvantage in competition with foreign vessels engaged in the same service, route, or line.

OPPOSED PISTON ENGINE. A marine internal combustion engine in which two pistons are provided for each cylinder, the lower piston being connected to the crankshaft in the usual way. The upper piston is attached by means of a piston rod to a yoke above the upper end of the cylinder. The ends of this yoke are connected by side rods to connecting rods extending downward to two cranks, one on each side of the crank that is driven by the lower piston. The side cranks are set at 180 degrees to the center crank.

Fr: *Moteur à pistons opposés;* Ger: *Gegenkolben Motor.*

OPPOSED RAM STEERING GEAR. Electro-hydraulic gear with cylinders placed athwartships, forward of the rudder head.

Fr: *Appareil à pistons plongeurs opposés;* Ger: *Gegenkolben-Rudermaschine.*

OPPOSITION. Two celestial bodies are said to be in opposition when their longitudes differ by 180°. The opposite of "conjunction."

Fr: *Opposition;* Ger: *Gegenschein; Opposition.*

OPTIONAL CARGO. An expression indicating that the shipper or consignee has the option as to which port the cargo must be delivered. The port is usually made known about 24 hours before the arrival of the vessel.

Ger: *Optionsladung.*

ORA. A plank-built canoe of the Solomon Islands without keel or outrigger. The edge of the topstrakes are continued in an uprising curve to form points of variable height at each end of the canoe. The planks are sewed together. Length 26 to 32 ft. Breadth 3.3 ft. Depth 19 in.

ORCU. A large, double sailing canoe of Mailu Island, southeast New Guinea. The two hulls are dugouts raised by a single wash strake lashed on each side, the wash strakes being connected at each end by a weatherboard or transom.

The two hulls, which are 32 to 35 ft. long, are connected by a platform. They are blunt-ended and nearly always unequal in length. The larger one carries the mast. Steering is by a paddle lashed to the hull and fitted with a tiller. The sail, which is of the kite or crab claw type, is made of plaited rushes or reeds, and its two booms are of a particularly tough and elastic wood. It is hoisted by halyards made fast to one of the booms at the height of the mast, which is about half the length of the boom.

ORDER PORT. A port where a ship, chartered for a range of ports calls to receive orders concerning the next port of discharge or loading it is to proceed to.

Fr: *Port d'Ordres;* Ger: *Orderhafen.*

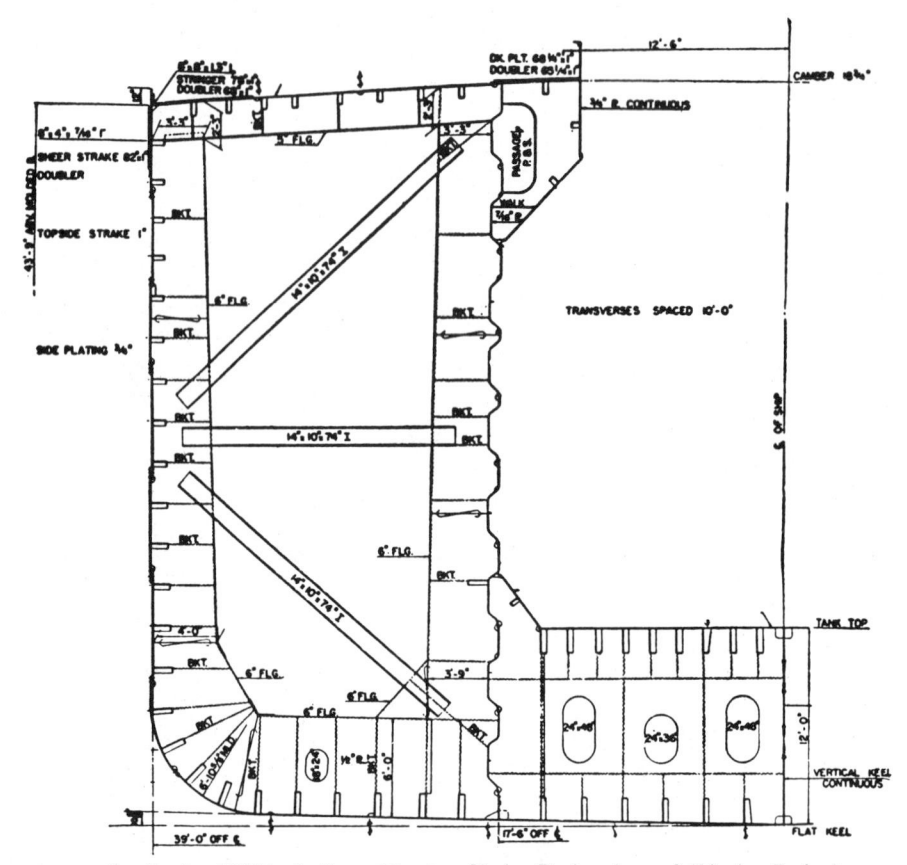

Ore Carrier, Midship Section. (*Courtesy Marine Engineering and Shipping Review*)

ORDINARY SEAMAN. A member of the crew from the deck department who is subordinate to an able seaman but has learned part of the trade. He performs general maintenance and repair tasks on board. After a specified length of time, and on passing an examination he is eligible for signing on as able seaman.

Fr: *Matelot Léger;* Ger: *Leichtmatrose; Jungmann.*

ORDINATES.
See Stations.

ORE CARRIER. A vessel specially constructed for the transport of large ore cargoes in bulk. Also called ore vessel.

Fr: *Transport de Minerai;* Ger: *Erzschiff.*

Ore is a difficult cargo to carry: because of its extreme density a vessel may be loaded down to her marks before the holds are one-quarter full, with the result that all the weight is concentrated in the bottom of the ship. This leads to a snappy roll with consequent liability of straining in a seaway. To eliminate this liability, the ore carrier has a central compartment running fore and aft with buoyancy spaces in the wings and underneath the ore space, thus lifting the center of gravity, reducing the metacentric height, and easing the roll. Ore cargoes are generally loaded by gravity and unloaded by grabs.

Halcrow, W., "Carriage of Heavy Ore Cargoes," Royal Society of Arts (London), *Journal,* vol. 83 (April, 1935).

OREMBAI. A carvel-built sailing boat with tall stem and sternpost found in the Moluccas and adjacent Pacific islands.

There are usually seven strakes of planking on each side of the keel. Each has a row of perforated cleats left in a line down to the center, and those of each strake are spaced so as to coincide transversely with the ones of adjacent strakes above and below. When the planking is completed, the frames are fitted over the vertical rows of cleats and do not lie against the inner surface of the planking. They are tied thereto by cords made of black palm fiber passed over each frame. The *orembai* is rigged with a tripod mast and a square-shaped sail with yard and boom. Length 28 ft.; breadth 5 ft. 6 in.; depth 2 ft. 3 in. (approx.).

ORGAN WHISTLE. A whistle in which steam or air is forced against a thin edge, the principle of the closed organ pipe being the basis of its construction. The organ whistle gives a strong, loud note but its range of audibility is smaller than that of the dome whistle.

Fr: *Sifflet à Anche;* Ger: *Orgelpfeife; Röhrenpfeife.*

ORKNEY SKIFF. Small open sailing boat from the northern group of the Orkney Islands. It differs from the Orkney yole in having less beam, greater draft, and V-pointed sections. The sternpost rakes at an angle of about 45°. There is a straight stem with very little cutaway at the forefoot. It is clinker-built like the yole and rigged with a jib and two large balance lugsails.

See **Orkney Yole.**

ORLOP DECK. A partial deck below the lower deck. This term is also applied to the lowest deck in a ship having four or more decks.

Fr: *Faux-Pont;* Ger: *Orlopdeck.*

ORTHODROME. Arc of great circle used in navigation for plotting the course over great distances.

Fr: *Orthodrome;* Ger: *Orthodrom.*

ORUWA. A single-outrigger dugout canoe from Ceylon. Also called *kulla,* (Tamil). On the gunwale, on each side, a broad vertical wash strake is sewed with coir yarn. The rig consists of a mast stepped at half length which carries a spritsail made of tanned cotton. The canoe is steered with a paddle.

OSCILLATOR. A sound-producing instrument used for submarine echo-sounding and fog signals. It consists of an electric magnet and a large vibrating diaphragm so arranged that when the diaphragm is caused to move to and fro at definite frequency, it produces a high, powerful note which can be interrupted to provide characteristic code notation.

Fr: *Oscillateur;* Ger: *Wechselstromerzeuger; Oszillator.*

OTI. A generic term used by the natives of Ternate and Halmahera (Moluccas) to denote a dugout with double outrigger. The *oti-Mahera* is a kind without wash strake. The *oti banku* is one of a larger type with wash strake.

OTONGO. A dugout canoe used by the Oltscha people of the Lower Amur River, Siberia, propelled by a double paddle in smooth water or by two short single paddles. It is a relatively small craft, hewed from the hammagda tree and pointed at both ends.

OTTEMANSFAR. The *ottemansfar* (eight-man boat) originates from the Faroe Islands and is used in local fisheries. Length over-all 27 ft. Keel 16.5 ft. Breadth 6.3 ft. Depth 2.8 ft. (Typical.)

It is an open sailing and rowing boat of the whaler type with sharp stern and pronounced sheer at the ends. The planking is clinker-built. It is rigged with two masts which set main lugsail and sprit mizzen.

OTTER BOARD. One of a pair of heavy square boards attached on each side of the mouth of a trawlnet to keep it open when the net is being dragged. Also called trawl board, trawl door.

Fr: *Planche de Chalut;* Ger: *Scheerbrett.*

Otter boards are shod with iron and vary in size according to the dimensions of the trawlnet. The boards are attached to the warps by means of chains or iron brackets and arranged in such a way that the pressure of water due to the forward motion causes them to diverge and thus keep the mouth of the net open. The boards are called bracket boards or chain boards according to the system of attachment. In herring trawls a third or extra otter board is occasionally used to lift the headline.

OTTER BOARD BRACKET. The iron fittings of an otter board to which the ends of trawl warps are fastened. Brackets are so arranged as to give the boards the required angle which keeps the mouth of the trawl open when in operation.

Fr: *Ferrement de planche à chalut;* Ger: *Scheerbrettbeschlag.*

OTTER GEAR. See **Paravane.**

OTTER TRAWL. A large, conical net supplied with two otter boards to which the drag ropes are attached. The action of the boards is such that by arrangement of the ropes they incline outward at an angle of about 25° when pulled through the water;

this keeps the mouth of the net open.

Fr: *Chalut à Planches;* *Chalut à Panneaux;* Ger: *Scheernetz;* *Scheerbretternetz.*

This type of trawl is proportionately much lighter than the beam trawl and has greatly increased the catch of round fish such as cod and haddock which swim some distance from the sea bottom. It has a shorter square than the beam trawl but has wings in front. The bag of the net is exactly the same as in the beam trawl. For small craft the advantage of the otter trawl over the beam type is that the former stows into small space on deck so that a vessel may use a much larger otter trawl than beam trawl. A steam trawler will tow an otter trawl with a mouth considerably wider than its own length.

OTTRING. Norwegian open boat used in the herring fisheries and propelled by sail and oar. Also called *stavaring.* Length 33½ ft. Breadth 8 ft. 8 in. Depth 2.8 ft.

The hull is clinker-built with broad strakes of planking, sharp stern, and rising stemhead. The stern is protected by turtle-back-shaped decking. The mast, stepped, amidships, has no rake and sets a large square sail with two rows of reef points near the head and one near the foot.

OUTBOARD. Outside of a vessel's hull. Away from the center or keel line. The opposite of "inboard."

OUTBOARD MOTOR. A portable gasoline motor suitable for attachment to the stern of a small boat. It consists essentially of a horizontal engine driving a vertical shaft at the bottom of which there is a propeller driven through bevel gearing. The majority of outboard motors have two opposed cylinders and are of such weight that they may be conveniently carried by one man. They are fitted to work-boats as well as to pleasure and racing craft.

Fr: *Moteur hors bord;* Ger: *Aussenbordmotor; Anhängemotor.*

OUTBOARD PROFILE. Plan showing a longitudinal exterior view of a vessel, together with deck erections, funnels, masts, rigging details, and so on.

Ger: *Aussenbord Langsschiffsplan.*

OUTBOARD SHAFT.

See Shafting.

OUTBOARD SHOT. Short length of chain cable fitted between the anchor and the first length which permits unshackling a stockless anchor without lowering it out of the hawsepipe. When the outboard shot is provided with a swivel it is also called swivel piece.

Fr: *Extrémité de Chaîne;* Ger: *Vorlauf.*

OUTBOUND FREIGHT. Cargo carried by an outward bound vessel. Also called outward freight or outward cargo.

Fr: *Fret de Sortie;* Ger: *Ausfracht.*

OUTER CASING. In a modern air encased steam boiler, the outer wall of the double casing.

See **Casing.**

OUTER HARBOR. An outer protected area providing comparatively tranquil water even in stormy weather and from which an inner harbor or docks may be entered.

Fr: *Avant-Port;* Ger: *Aussenhafen; Vorhafen.*

OUTER JIB. The jib next to the flying jib.

Fr: *Grand Foc;* Ger: *Zweiter Kluver; Hauptkluver; Aussenkluver; Jager.*

OUTER KEEL. The outer plate of a double-plate keel.

Fr: *Tôle Quille Extérieure;* Ger: *Aussenkiel.*

OUTER RABBET LINE. The lower or outer trace of the groove forming the rabbet.

Fr: *Trait Extérieur de Rablure;* Ger: *Äussere Spundungslinie.*

OUTER STRAKE. A strake of plating between two adjacent sunken strakes which lap over the edges, and which is separated from the frames by liners of same thickness as the sunken strakes.

Fr: *Virure de Recouvrement;* Ger: *Abliegender Gang.*

OUTER WATERWAY. Strake of waterway planking which fits against the frames of top timbers. Also called thick waterway.

Fr: *Fourrure de Gouttière;* Ger: *Leibholz.*

OUTFIT. 1. That portion of the ship's apparel which ordinarily perishes or is consumed in the course of the voyage.

2. All objects necessary to the navigation of the ship, including sails, rigging, spare ropes, provisions for the crew, and so on. In fishing vessels, outfit includes the fishing gear, casks, staves, and so on, needed for the successful prosecution of the voyage.

Fr: *Équipement; Armement;* Ger: *Ausrüstung.*

OUTFIT INSURANCE. When a vessel is specially equipped to engage in some particular trade, such equipment may for the subject matter of a policy separate from the ordinary policy on hull and machinery. The amount insured being usually recoverable only in the event of total loss of the vessel.

Fr: *Assurance sur Équipement;* Ger: *Ausrüstversicherung.*

OUTFITTING. The type of work done during the building of a new ship from shortly after its launching until complete and ready for service.

OUTFOOT. To move faster through the water. Said of a vessel or a boat, when comparing its motion to that of another craft in company.

OUTGAGE. A bevel of about 1/16 in. taken off the top or outside edge of a deck or shell plank and running to zero at center. Its object is to prevent the edges of the plank from splintering when being calked.

OUTHAUL, OUTHAULER. A rope for hauling out the clew of a boom sail or tack of a jib.

Fr: *Hale Dehors;* Ger: *Ausholer.*

See **Foot Outhaul, Head Outhaul.**

OUT OARS. A command to let the oars fall in the rowlocks, with the blades being kept horizontal and ready to start pulling.

Fr: *Armez;* Ger: *Riemen Bei.*

OUT OF TRIM. Not properly trimmed, or ballasted.

OUTPOINT. A vessel under sail is said to outpoint another when it can sail closer to the wind than the latter.

OUTREACH. 1. The extent or length of reach of a cargo derrick or other spar beyond the ship's side.

2. The horizontal distance from the end of a cargo boom to its base.

3. See **Outrigger.** (5).

OUTRIGGER. 1. A counterpoising log of wood or float thrust out to windward of a sailing canoe or boat to prevent its capsizing.

Fr: *Balancier;* Ger: *Ausleger.*

2. Iron brackets for extending oarlocks beyond the sides of a rowboat.

Fr: *Porte-Nage;* Ger: *Ausleger.*

3. A rowboat for racing in smooth waters fitted with these brackets. The outrigger sculling boat with single rower measures from 30 to 35 ft. in length, 12 to 14 in. in breadth and about 9 in. in depth. It is usually built of mahogany and is considered the most perfect specimen of the boatbuilder's art. The eight-oared outrigger, the largest of this type, is from 55 to 65 ft. long by 2 ft. 2 in. to 2 ft. 5 in. in breadth.

Fr, Ger: *Outrigger;* Ger: *Auslegerboot.*

4. A spar of wood or iron rigged out to give spread to standing or running rigging. Also called spreader, bumkin.

Fr: *Boutehors;* Ger: *Luvbaum; Ausrigger.*

5. A structure built athwartships around a mast to support derrick spans and topping-lift blocks. Also called upper mast table, outreach. The blocks are so placed that the pivoting point of topping lift is in a vertical line above the derrick heel to facilitate slewing. The outrigger is sometimes constructed to provide connections for the shrouds and headstays.

Fr: *Hune;* Ger: *Lademast Saling.*

OUTRIGGER CANOE. A canoe with a single float which is extended outboard at the ends of two or more spars named outrigger booms. The geographical distribution of single-outrigger canoes centers in Oceania, South India, and Ceylon, with outlying instances in Madagascar; Geelvink Bay, N.G.; Mokmer; south coast of Wiak Island; north coast of Jobi, Japan; from Cape d'Urville eastwards; New Guinea; Orokolo, Gulf of Papua.

Fr: *Pirogue à Balancier;* Ger: *Ausleger Kanu.*

OUTSAIL. To excel in speed or to outspeed another boat or vessel.

OUTSIDE CABIN. Cabin having a port hole or window in the ship's side.

Fr: *Cabine Extérieure;* Ger: *Aussenkammer.*

OUTSIDE CLINCH. A running knot made by receiving the standing part of the rope through the eye of a simple clinch.

Fr: *Noeud de Bouline Simple;* Ger: *Äussere Klinch; Aussenstich.*

OUTSIDE FASTENINGS. The fastenings or bolts driven from the outside in a wooden hull.

OUTSIDE PLANKING. The planking which forms the outer contour of the hull, including the bottom bilge, side, and topside plankings.

Fr: *Bordé Extérieur;* Ger: *Aussenbeplankung.*

OUTSIDE PORT. A port where cargo discharged from or loaded into seagoing ships is dealt with for the most part by direct transhipment into coasters, lighters, barges, or other small craft without touching the quays.

OUT SQUARE KNEE. A knee in which the angle formed by the arm and the body is obtuse. Also called open bevel knee.

OUT-TURN. The result of the final check of cargo after discharging a vessel with all over-landed, short-landed and damaged cargo reported.

OUTWARD BOUND. Said of a vessel leaving her home port or destined for a foreign port.

Ger: *Nach auswärts bestimmt.*

OUTWARD CLEARANCE CERTIFICATE. A certificate issued by the customs house authorities after the loading of a ship is completed, a full account of the cargo has been given, and all the legal dues paid. The master is not allowed to proceed on the voyage until he has obtained this certificate.

Fr: *Expédition en Douane; Déclaration de Sortie;* Ger: *Ausklarierungs Attest.*

OUTWARD MANIFEST. A manifest of the outward cargo handed over to the custom authorities before the vessel leaves.

Fr: *Manifeste de Sortie;* Ger: *Ausfuhrmanifest.*

OVER. A term used to express the width of a fishing net.

OVERAGE (U. S.). That portion of a shipment above the amount specified in bill of lading, charter party, or manifest, alleged to have been shipped.

OVER-ALL EFFICIENCY. The over-all efficiency of a marine engine installation is the ratio between the power actually developed by the shafts and the power available in the fuel as fired.

Fr: *Rendement Effectif;* Ger: *Mechanischer Wirkungsgrad.*

OVERBOARD. Over the side of a ship, usually into the water; out of or from on board a ship.

Fr: *Par dessus bord;* Ger: *Überbord.*

See **Free Overboard**.

OVERBOARD FALL.

See **Yard Whip**.

OVERCARRIAGE. Goods consigned to one port which are carried to another port because they have been overlooked, owing to improper stowage.

Ger: *Zu weit geführte Ladung.*

OVERCAST. Cloud-covered, as the whole sky covered with one unbroken cloud.

Fr: *Ciel Couvert;* Ger: *Bedeckter Himmel.*

OVERDAYS (G. B.). A trade name for herring remaining on board a drifter for 24 hours after being caught when, because of a poor catch, the boat stays out on the fishing grounds. Overdays are worth about half the price of fresh fish.

OVERDUE. A term employed to denote the nonarrival of a vessel at the appointed time, after making reasonable allowance for sea contingencies.

Fr: *Non Arrivé;* Ger: *Überfällig.*

OVERFALLS. Short, breaking waves caused by a current moving against the wind or moving over a shoal, or by the meeting of contrary currents.

Fr: *Remous; Clapotis;* Ger: *Überbrechende Seen.*

OVER FREIGHT. A freight over and above that stipulated in the charter party. The opposite of "dead freight."

Fr: *Surfret;* Ger: *Oberfracht.*

OVERHAND KNOT. Knot used at the end of ropes to prevent their fraying and as the commencement of other knots. Also called single knot, thumb knot.

Fr: *Noeud Simple;* Ger: *Gewöhnlicher Knoten.*

OVERHANG. The projection of the upper works of a vessel at bow or stern beyond the forward or after perpendicular at waterline level.

Fr: *Elancement;* Ger: *Überhang.*

OVERHAUL. 1. To haul the parts of a tackle, so as to separate the blocks. To open and extend several parts of a tackle so as to separate the blocks in order that they may be again ready for use.

Fr: *Reprendre;* Ger: *Überholen.*

2. To overtake another vessel: to gain in speed on her.

Fr: *Gagner;* Ger: *Überholen; Aufsegeln.*

3. To clear or disentangle a rope: to pull a part of it through a block so as to make it slack.

Fr: *Affaler;* Ger: *Überholen.*

4. To turn over for examination or examine thoroughly with a view to repair.

Fr: *Visiter;* Ger: *Nachsehen.*

OVERHAULING WEIGHT. A weight sometimes fitted to a crane hook or cargo hook so that the light hook runs back when there is no load on the fall.

OVERHEAD WELD. A butt or fillet weld, horizontal or inclined less than 45°

from the horizontal, the weld being made from the lower or underside of the parts joined.

Fr: *Soudure en Plafond; Soudre Surélevée;* Ger: *Überkopfschweissung.*

OVER-LANDED. Refers to discharge of cargo when more goods or a greater number of packages than shown on the manifest and other documents are put ashore. The converse of *short-landed.*

OVERLAP. In welding, overlapping occurs when excessive metal is deposited so that a portion of the bead overlaps the surface of the base metal.

In chartering, a vessel is said to be on overlap time when its charterer keeps it for a period beyond the date of redelivery stipulated in the charter party. The opposite is "underlap."

In yacht racing, overlap denotes the position of two vessels when one overtaking another cannot, without dropping astern, pass on the other side from that on which it is approaching; or when the two vessels cannot turn toward each other without the risk of fouling.

OVERRAKE. Said of heavy seas which come over a vessel's bows when it is at anchor, head to sea.

OVERRIGGED. Said of a vessel having heavier gear than necessary.

OVERSIDE DELIVERY. The process of delivering goods direct from an import vessel to another vessel or lighter moored alongside. A consignee wishing to take his goods overside usually orders a craft to be placed alongside the incoming vessel as soon as the latter begins unloading.

Fr: *Livraison sous Palan;* Ger: *Überbord-Ablieferung.*

OVERSPARRED. Said of a vessel having heavier spars than necessary.

OVERSTOWAGE. Faulty loading, as when cargo for the second port of discharge is stowed above cargo for the first port and therefore the latter cannot be discharged at its destination.

OVERTAKE. To catch up with or gain in speed on another vessel. According to the International Rules of the Road at sea, an overtaking vessel is one which comes up with another from any direction more than two points abaft her beam.

Fr: *Rattraper;* Ger: *Aufkommen.*

OVERTIME. Time worked beyond regular hours. At sea any work connected with the navigation or safety of the vessel, of life on board, or safety of the cargo is not considered as overtime.

Fr: *Heures supplémentaires;* Ger: *Überarbeit.*

OWNERS "PRO HAC VICE." Legal expression indicating that the charterers stand in the place and in lieu of the legal owners and with their responsibilities, though the latter remain none the less the legal owners of the vessel.

OWO. Large East Indian plank-built trading canoe rigged with two masts from Pulo-Nias Island, Western Sumatra. Also called kalambra.

OX BALL (U. S.). Term sometimes applied to a small ornamental ball at the top of a flagstaff or mast. Also called mast ball. In the latter instance it forms the truck.

OXTER PLATE. A shell plate riveted to the stern frame in way of the rudderpost head. Because of the form of the hull at this point it requires furnacing and molding into shape.

Fr: *Tôle de Sommier;* Ger: *Gillungsplatte.*

OYA-SIWO. A cold countercurrent of pale green water which flows southward from the Bering Sea along the southeast coast of Kamchatka, the Kurile Islands, and part of the northeast coast of Japan. It varies both in rate and extent, but is usually much stronger in winter than in summer.

OYSTER CANOE. Canoe with dugout keel and garboards employed for tonging oysters in the Chesapeake Bay and its tributaries. Also called cunner. It is fitted with washboards running along each side from stem to stern, and rigged with two masts with leg-of-mutton sails. Length 27 ft. 6 in. Beam 5 ft. 3 in. Depth 2 ft. 9 in.

OYSTER DREDGE. A fishing apparatus consisting of a short chain bag or net attached to a rectangular steel frame about 4 ft. long. The long sides of the frame are provided with 15 or more long steel teeth which dig into the sea bottom as the instrument is dragged over the oyster bed, tearing the oysters away.

Fr: *Drague à Huitres;* Ger: *Austernkratzer.*

OYSTER SCHOONER. Name given on the east coast of U. S. to a type of small shallow-draft, two-masted schooner with long cutwater, transom stern, raked stem, broad beam, and high bilges with much deadrise; employed in oyster dredging. These boats vary in size from 15 to 45 tons. They are generally from 40 to 50 ft. long with 12- to 16-ft. beam and 5- to 6-ft. draft.

The Mississippi conservation laws which require that all oyster dredging be done under sail are responsible for a fleet of some 50 to 60 of these craft being in commission each year during the oyster season. A few of these craft go into freighting watermelons during the summer months. Most of them hail from Biloxi, Mississippi.

OYSTER SCOW. A type of decked scow employed in the Pacific Coast oyster fisheries in tonging up oysters. It is shallow, with sides slightly tapering from the middle to the square ends. The flush deck slopes a little toward the low rail strip at sides. Length 18 to 20 ft. Breadth 7 to 8 ft.

OYSTER SLOOP.
See **Plunger.**

OYSTER TONGS. A pair of wooden tongs 12 to 20 ft. long, bearing opposing rakelike baskets, used for gathering oysters. Ger: *Zange.*

OZZLES. See **Norsals.**

P

P. Flag of the international code of signals showing a white square on a blue ground. See **Blue Peter**.

P and I. PROTECTION AND INDEMNITY (insurance).

P and R. PARALLAX AND REFRACTION (astronomy).

P and S. PORT AND STARBOARD

Par. PARRALLAX (astronomy).

P.A. POSITION APPROXIMATE.

P.B. PERMANENT BUNKERS.

P.C. PER COMPASS.

P.D. PORT DUES.

P.D. POLAR DISTANCE (astronomy).

P.D. POSITION DOUBTFUL (nautical charts).

P.Dk. POOP DECK.

P.O. PETTY OFFICER.

p.o.c. PORT OF CALL.

P.o.r. PORT OF REFUGE.

p.p. PICKED PORTS.

P.P.I. POLICY PROOF OF INTEREST (marine insurance). See Policy.

p.p.t. 1. PROMPT. 2. PROMPT LOADING.

PACIFIC BLOCKADE. A method of coercion short of war, exercised by a great power for the purpose of bringing pressure to bear on a weaker state.

PACIFIC IRON. Iron fitting at the end of a yard, to which the Flemish horse is spliced. The stunsail boom iron is shipped over the Pacific iron.
See **Gooseneck**.

PACKAGE CARGO. Cargo packed in boxes, barrels, crates, wrapped goods, machinery. Also called package freight.
Fr: *Caissage*; Ger: *Stückgüter*.

PACKER. A shipyard worker who fits lamp wicking, canvas, tarred felt or other material between parts of the structure to insure water or oil tightness joints cannot be made tight by caulking, or when an uncaulked structural member passes through a water or oil-tight surface.

PACKET. A mail boat on a regular run.

PACK ICE. A rough, solid mass of broken ice floes forming a heavy obstruction preventing navigation. A collection of large pieces of floating ice of indefinite extent. A considerable area of floating ice in Polar Seas, more or less flat, broken into large pieces by the action of the wind and waves and driven together in an almost continuous and nearly coherent mass. The principal difference between pack ice and floe ice is that the formation of the pack requires polar ice of many years' standing, while floe ice and ice fields can be formed from one-year ice.
Fr: *Banquise*; *Glace de Pack*; Ger: *Packeis*; *Eisbank*.

PACKING. 1. In the launching cradle, longitudinal timbers which fill the space between the bilge and the upper surface of the sliding ways, under the flatter portions of the ship's bottom. Also called making up, fillings, stopping up.
Fr: *Empilage*; *Billotage*; Ger: *Aufpakkung*; *Aufkeilung*.
See **Cradle**.
2. The gradual gathering and collecting of ice into packs which impede navigation.
Fr: *Embacle*; Ger: *Eisstopfung*.

PACKING LASHING. In launching, chains or heavy wire passed under the keel and over the poppet ribbands from side to side. They prevent the upper ends of the poppets from working outward when the weight of the vessel is transferred to the cradle. Also called poppet lashing, poppet sling, poppet strap.
Fr: *Rousture*; Ger: *Schlittenstützen Laschung*.

PACKING PIECE.
See **Liner**.

PAD. A flat plate welded or riveted to a structural member, to afford attachment for rigging, deck bolts, and the like, or to provide a seat for welding another member.
See **Lifting Pad, Lug Pad**.

PADAGU. Name given to the masula boat by the Coromandel people.
See **Doni**.

PADAO.
See **Padow**.

PADDING. The operation of depositing weld metal by running beads parallel to each other in such a way that the beads are united with one another to form a solid mass.

PADDLE. A short oar with large blade area which does not rest in a rowlock when in use, but is held in the hands and dipped into the water with a nearly vertical motion from forward aft. It may be single- or double-ended, that is, having a blade at one end or both, and is used for propelling canoes, dugouts, and so on. The still hand acts as the fulcrum, and the moving arm provides the power, although the fulcrum hand moves slightly in a direction opposite to the stroke hand to increase the power.

A round-ended blade is considered preferable to a pointed one or one with a straight edge and two angles. The end is usually protected by a strip of brass or copper ¾ in. on each side, turned over the edge for 6 or 8 inches and riveted. A strip of ⅛-in. brass wire run over the edge of the wood and in the angle of the metal tip forms an additional protection.

Fr: *Pagaye; Pagaie;* Ger: *Paddel.*
See Single Paddle, Double Paddle, Paddle Wheel.

PADDLE BOARD. One of the floats placed on the circumference of a propulsive paddle wheel. Also called paddle.

Fr: *Pale; Aube;* Ger: *Radschaufel.*

PADDLE BOX. The structure which encloses the upper part of a paddle wheel. It is supported athwartships by the paddle beams at each end and longitudinally by the sponson beam on which the outer bearing of the paddle wheel shaft rests. Paddle box stays take the downward thrust.

Fr: *Tambour;* Ger: *Radkasten.*

PADDLE BOX STAY. One of the inclined struts running from the side planking or plating to the sponson and spur beams to support the paddle box.

Fr: *Béquille de Tambour;* Ger: *Radkastenstütze.*

PADDLE VESSEL. A vessel or boat propelled by paddle wheels placed amidships on each side.

Fr: *Bateau à Roues; Navire à Aubes;* Ger: *Radschiff.*

This system of propulsion is of low efficiency if compared with the screw propeller, which works entirely underwater. The paddle wheels do not work efficiently in a rough sea, are much exposed to damage by heavy seas and increase the vessel's effective beam inordinately. The small number of revolutions per minute of this type of propeller is responsible for a large weight per IHP of machinery factor. Propulsion by a paddle wheel has, therefore, been confined recently to excursion vessels operating in smooth waters. The salient features of these vessels have remained practically unaltered for many years. A bar keel is often employed and has been found to assist in steering. Scantlings are on the light side in most cases. The propelling machinery consists of a set of diagonal compound engines taking steam at about 120 lb. per square inch with about 28 to 55 revolutions per minute. The latest vessels are equipped with Scotch boilers and coal or oil firing. Average speed from 14 to 16 knots.

Lane, C. D., American Paddle Steamboats (New York); Munro-Smith, R., "The Design of Paddle Wheel Passenger Vessel," *Shipbuilding and Shipping Record* (London), vol. 59 (September 17, 1942); Tripp, G. W., "The Survival of the Paddle Steamer," *Engineer* (London), vol. 153 (May 27, 1932.

PADDLE WALK. See **Paddle Wing.**

PADDLE WHEEL. A form of propeller which rotates about a horizontal axis transverse to the vessel's center line, and located above the waterline. Upon its periphery the wheel bears paddles, or floats, which accelerate the water and undergo a reactive thrust. Paddle wheels are of two types: wheels with fixed floats, and wheels with movable or "feathering," floats. The former have the advantage of simplicity, lightness, low maintenance cost and ruggedness, but the disadvantage that for efficiency wheel diameter must be large, which necessitates low wheel revolutions and precludes the employment of efficient, high-speed engines. The feathering float wheel overcomes these shortcomings but requires greater wheel weight, higher first cost, and higher maintenance. Accordingly, wheels with fixed floats are generally used on the rivers of the western United States, where shipyard facilities are few, whereas in Europe, feathering wheels are extensively used for river towboats and similar vessels.

Fr: *Roue à Aubes;* Ger: *Schaufelrad.*

Paddle wheels are placed either amidship or at the stern of the vessel. Midship wheels, one on each side, are not influenced much by change of trim or pitching of the vessel, but are disadvantageous in that they increase effective beam and cause the vessel to sheer badly when rolling in a seaway. However, this arrangement is preferred for lake and bay steamers using paddle wheels, while towboats and craft operating on narrow rivers and canals are usually stern-wheelers.

Paddle-wheel steamers are gradually disappearing from the modern scene; however, for use in shoal waters and rivers, where disabling damage to screw propellers is probable, they will continue to have their application. They are usually powered by steam reciprocating engines.

PADDLE WING A platform extending

forward and aft of the paddle box. Its function is to support the paddle box laterally and protect the wheel when the vessel goes alongside a quay or landing stage. Also called paddle walk.

Fr: *Jardin de Tambour;* Ger: *Radanbau; Radkastengallerie; Radkastenbalkon.*

PADDY. Name given to rice before the husk is removed.

PAD EYE.

See Eyeplate, Pad.

PADOW. An Indian coasting vessel closely resembling in hull, rig, and general appearance the battels, but smaller. It is frequently confused with the latter. Also called *padao, padau.* No permanent decks are built, forward and aft are two spaces covered with loose planking to form two platforms. The *padow* has a flat, square stern without counter, arched keel and long, overhanging grab bow. Under the after one the crew sleeps. The rig consists of one or two masts raking forward and hoisting the Arab lateen. A jib is also used. Length over-all 60 to 80 ft. Beam 15 to 20 ft. Depth 5½ to 8 ft. Burden from 30 to 60 tons.

PAD PIECE. A piece of wood about 15 in. in length fitted on the outside of ship's lifeboats in way of the stowage chocks to protect the planking. In metal boats a doubling plate takes the place of the wooden pad piece.

Fr: *Matelas; Coussin;* Ger: *Kissen.*

PADUAKAN. A trading boat from Macassar, Celebes. Also called *pediwak.* The hull is built of teak or giam wood, and has hollow sharp bows lower than the main body of the boat. The stem is curved and raking. The transom stern has a tall superstructure supported by cross timbers, and broad open galleries along the sides. There is a deck running fore and aft with one large hatch. *Paduakans* are rigged with tripod masts made

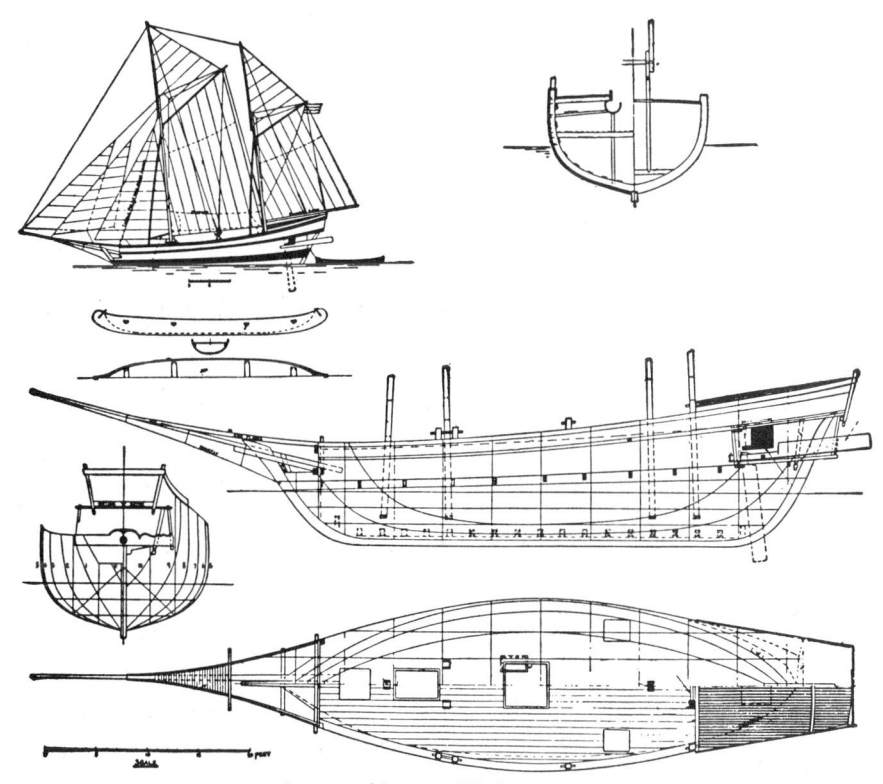

Paduakan. (*Courtesy* "Yachting" *New York*)

of spars joined at the head by a bolt or treenail. The foot of each spar is stepped in a wooden socket and held by a bolt in such a manner that the mast can be lowered backward. The bowsprit is stepped in the forward bulkhead, and is supported laterally by a plank on each side. Length over-all 32 to 90 ft. Beam 9 ft. 4 in. to 18 ft. Depth 4 ft. 4 in. to 12 ft. (Typical.)

The rig consists of one, two, or even three masts. In some cases, both masts are tripods while in others either the foremast or the mainmast is a tripod. The lugsails have nowadays been replaced by gaff sails of the curtain type, that is, brailing to the mast with standing gaffs. The bowsprit carries two to four headsails. Steering is effected by two long, narrow quarter rudders which can be raised to a horizontal position when housed.

In modern craft the standing rigging is made of wire, set up with lanyards. Anchor cables, 2 in. in diameter, are made of palm fiber.

Although these craft take long trips, going as far north as Singapore, they are said to be bad sea boats, pitching heavily and making considerable leeway on account of their high superstructure.

PAE-PAE. A sailing raft from Mangareva, Gambier Islands, made of logs arranged with shorter lengths on outer sides and increasing in length to median longest length. Also called *taketake*.

The mast is a pole stepped at about half length with forward rake, on which is suspended a crab-claw sail with upper and lower sprits. The forward ends of the spars are lashed to the middle line log. These rafts are from 40 to 50 ft. in length and will carry 20 or more persons.

PAGAE. An East Indian dugout canoe from the southern Celebes. It has double outriggers. The *pagae* is employed in the fisheries with a net called *gae*.

PAGALAI KATTU VATHAI. Indian plank-built fishing canoe from Palk Strait, similar to the *vala vathai* but smaller, and with exceptionally long balance board. It is steered with quarter rudders. Length 18 to 37 ft. Breadth 2 to 3 ft. Depth 2½ ft.

PAGARANGAN. A sailing canoe from the Sulu Islands and North Borneo. Also called *pakerangan*. The hull is made of a three-piece dugout base with two or three strakes of planking added to the sides. An extra strake is usually fitted amidships for a short length. Rig: One tripod mast with small boomed square sail or more recently a pole mast and spritsail. Length 30 to 40 ft. Beam 4 to 5 ft.

PAHI. An outrigger sailing canoe of the Society Islands used for fishing. The hull is formed of a round-bottomed dugout. One or two wash strakes are sewed on and finished off with a narrow top strake, forming the gunwale. These craft are fast under sail. They are rigged with one mast and a boomed spritsail and the steering is done with a long paddle.

PAILEBOT. Small, two-masted fore-and-aft trading schooner from Spain.

PAINTED PORTS. Gun ports consisting of alternate black and white squares, painted on the ship's sides. A practice frequently followed on British sailing ships in the late nineteenth century.

Fr: *Fausse Batterie;* *Faux Mantelets;* Ger: *Pfortenband.*

PAINTING.

See **Dazzle Painting.**

PAINT LINE. A line drawn on the outside plating, parallel to the load water line and about twelve inches about it. The sheer is set off at the ends, the amount being about eighteen inches forward and six inches aft. The paint line forms the upper limit of the boot topping.

PAINT LOCKER. A small compartment, usually under the forecastle deck, where ingredients and equipment for painting the vessel are kept. Also called paint room.

Fr: *Magasin à Peinture;* Ger: *Malershellegat.*

PAINT STRAKE. Term formerly used to denote the uppermost strake of outside planking immediately below the gunwale. The sheer strake.

Fr: *Lisse de plat-bord;* Ger: *Gemaltergang.*

PAIR MASTS. A pair of cargo masts stepped abreast each other on either side of the center line, with their heads connected by spans. Also called goal post masts.

PAISAL. East Indian dugout canoe from Amboina, Southern Moluccas. It is about 13 ft. long and has double outriggers. It is handled by one man, and is used for the capture of *jakalan* (bonito) fish.

PAITALIK. Name given by the Kaniagmut people of Kodiak Island to the *bidarka,* or three-hatch kayak.

See **Bidarka, Kayak.**

PAI-TI-SHUAN. The *pai-ti-shuan* or *fukien* trader from Chuan-Chow is a southern keelless junk, with fine lines and very seaworthy. The stern is of the transom type and planked horizontally for about half the distance from the top of the poop to the waterline. Length about 75 ft. Beam 15 ft. at deck.

PAJALA. An East Indian open sailing craft used for fishing and transportation in the Macassar Strait, Bonerate Islands, Buton Island, North Flores and most of the islands east of Madura. The hull is built with keel, carvel planking, rising stem and sternpost which ends in a fine point. The rig consists of a tripod mast with oblong quadrilateral sail. Some of the larger craft have a small second mast aft. The *pajala lompo* used for seining works with a net called *jala lompo*. Length 30 to 42 ft. Capacity 1½ to 4 tons.

PAKATA. A plank-built double-outrigger boat of shallow draft from Batjan Island, Moluccas. Sometimes called *prao paketa*, *pelang pakpak*. It has high pointed ends with ornaments on either of the high projections. The hull is keel-built, with numerous strakes of planking. Each plank is provided with perforated cleats on the inner side for the attachment of frames. There are numerous thwarts or crossbeams with ends projecting beyond the gunwale. A large shelter with a leaf-covered roof is situated amidships. At one end beyond the shelter the outboard ends of the projecting crosspieces are used to provide a narrow outboard platform. The outrigger float, which consists of 3 stout bamboos lashed together, is held by 2 booms. Over-all length about 30 ft.

PAKERANGAN.
See **Pagarangan.**

PAKUR.
See **Lepa-Lepa.**

PALAMPOKO. A decked sailing craft from Macassar, Celebes, with rounded sides and forked stem piece, the latter rising considerably above the gunwales. The rig consists of a tripod mast. These boats carry cargoes of sugar, chalk, salt, and other goods.

PALARI. 1. An East Indian trading boat from southern Celebes and eastern Madura. The hull is similar to that of the *paduakan* from which, however, it differs by the type of stern and its smaller size. It is rigged with one or two masts; the mainmast is a tripod, the foremast a single spar. The *palari* from Madura is generally a one-masted craft.

2. In Macassar the term "palari" refers to a fast-sailing pleasure craft with two masts and an elaborately carved stern.

When becalmed it is propelled by 8 to 12 oars. Length 50 ft. Breadth 10 ft. Depth 3.5 ft. (Average.)

PALASI. A large seagoing dugout canoe from Mindanao, Philippine Islands, similar to a large *vinta* with wash strake and double outriggers. Also called *auang-palasi*.

PALE. One of the interior shores used for steadying the beams of a ship under construction.

PALING SCHUYT. Small Dutch welled sloop with round bows, apple stern, and leeboards. Also called eel boat. It has one or two masts and is mostly employed in the live-eel trade between Frisian ports and London. Average length about 30 ft., burden about 15 tons.

PALINURUS. A gimbaled instrument with time and latitude scales formerly used on board ship to ascertain the true course without tables or calculations. (Obsolete.)

Ger: *Palinurus*.

PALISCHERMO. One of a pair of open boats employed in the Italian tuna fisheries. It is provided with a capstan for lifting the bottom of the end chamber of the *tonnara* net during the last operation or *mattanza*. In Sardinia the craft is called *paliscarmotto*, in the Bay of Naples and adjacent waters *scevo*. Average length 39 ft.

PALLET. A rectangular cargo tray made of wood and designed to be transported by fork lift truck. Its construction is similar to that of a grating. It has no eyes at the corners nor raised edges. Usual size is by about 6 ft. by 4 ft.; it is hoisted into or from the ship's hold with its load. It is used for handling general cargo of a more or less homogeneous nature.

Fr: *Palette*.

PALLETIZATION. A method of stowage of goods on pallets or trays. The system is used with the aid of fork lift trucks and trailer tractors for stacking and transporting on the pier. The saving of labor by this system is considerable.

Fr: *Palettisation*.

PALM. The flattened end of an anchor arm which bites into the ground. Also called wrist, fluke. Spade-shaped palms are best for muddy bottoms because this shape of palm will dig in and hold where no other palm will.

Pointed palms are very efficient in grass and are also preferred for rocky bottom, but are useless in mud. Pointed palms are occasionally fitted with shoes to increase their area and holding power.

In modern stockless anchors such as the Dunn and Baldt, the area of the flukes is so large that the arms are practically all flukes.

Fr: *Patte;* Ger: *Ankerhand; Ankerflue; Ankerflügel; Ankerflunke.*

See **Tripping Palm, Sailmaker's Palm.**

PALOWA. A Philippine coasting craft of the *parao* type but with greater beam, flat bottom, and without outriggers.

PAMPERO. A storm of variable duration, often very violent, which forms in the pampas of Argentina and comes off the land with great suddenness.

Fr: *Pampero;* Ger: *Pampero.*

PAN. A small sheet of flat ice.

Fr: *Poêlon;* Ger: *Pfanne.*

PANAGATAN. A Philippine dugout canoe of double-outrigger type, with scarfed stem and sternpost, and with built-up sides made of bamboo matting fastened to uprights with cotton twine. These are rendered waterproof by applying a sort of sticky white pitch coating on the outer and inner surfaces. The different parts of the structure are fastened together with treenails. There are five thwarts. Used for fishing in the Visayan Sea.

PANAMA CANAL TONNAGE. The registered tonnage as computed by Panama Canal authorities for the assessment of dues for passage of a vessel through the canal. The method of measurement for gross tonnage is similar to that of the Suez Canal, from which it differs only in details. These differences can be summarized as follows: (1) Double-bottom spaces used for oil, fuel, and food and water are included in the gross tonnage, but deducted from the net. Shelter tween-deck space is included in the net tonnage. (2) Deck erections are included as in the Suez Canal tonnage but the deductions are somewhat less. (3) Deductions are allowed for peaks and ballast tanks. There is no percentage limitation. It is generally assumed in practice that the gross tonnage as computed by the Panama Canal measurement rules is approximately 10 per·cent higher than the British official gross tonnage, and the net Panama Canal tonnage about 25 per cent higher than the British net tonnage.

Fr: *Jauge du Canal de Panama;* Ger: *Panama Kanal Vermessung.*

PANAMA CHOCK. A closed rollerchock prescribed by the Panama authorities for all ships going through the Canal. Also: **Panama Bow.** Specially designed to lead towing lines at a sharp angle when in the locks. Also called **Panama lead; Panama towing pipe.** There are two forward near the stem head; and two aft on the poop.

PANCA. A Philippine double-outrigger dugout canoe with planked wash strake. Length 15 to 24 ft. The *panca* is propelled by oars or paddles and is generally used for fishing.

PANCAKE ICE. Small pieces of newly frozen ice, approximately circular, with raised rims of insufficient thickness to prevent navigation. Pancake ice is sometimes separated into round cakes, hence its name.

Fr: *Glace en Forme de Crêpes;* Ger: *Pancakeeis; Pfannkuchen.*

PANCO. A two-masted trading vessel of the Philippine Islands formerly used by the pirates of the Sulu Archipelago. The hull is plank-built with keel. No iron is used in the construction of these craft. The rig consists of two tripod masts with fore-and-aft sails. In the Island of Mindanao it is termed *auang-galay.* Length 80 ft. Breadth 18 to 20 ft.

PANELING. The boarding fitted in cabins and living spaces to the underside of the deck beams and on the ship's sides.

Fr: *Lambrissage;* Ger: *Holzbekleidung; Verkleidung.*

PANGA. A dugout canoe from Panama, double-ended with rising stem and stern. These craft are about 18 ft. long by 4 ft. 6 in. wide and are cut out of one cedar log. Carry produce (bananas) from "up country."

PANGKOH. An East Indian boat from South Borneo named after the trading center of Pangkoh situated at the mouth of the Kahajan River.

PANHEAD RIVET. Rivet with truncated-cone-shaped head, in general use for connecting structural members of a steel ship.

Panhead Rivet

Fr: *Rivet à Tête Tronconique;* Ger: *Flachkopfniet; Einheitskopfniet.*

PANIWALLA. Member of Asiatic crew who carries drinking water to the agwallas (firemen) and koila wallas (coal trimmers) during their hours of duty.

PANSHI. A double-ended open boat with long overhangs covered at the afterend with a bamboo and mat thatch. It is employed for the transportation of goods and passengers on the Estuary of the Ganges River, Bengal. Ironwood is used for the bottom planking, teak for the sides and sal wood for the upper works and beams. Also called panswah.

PANSTONE. Code name for British Chamber of Shipping Charter Party relating to stone cargoes for British ports, channel islands, and continental ports between Brest and the River Elbe.

PANTING. The vibratory motion of the frames and plating of a vessel caused by the force of the waves against bows and stern when the vessel rolls and pitches heavily in a seaway.

Fr: *Effet de Soufflet*; Ger: *Keuchen*.

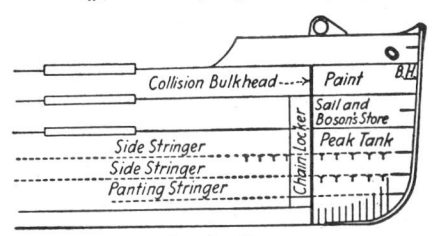

Panting Beam

PANTING BEAM. One of the additional beams fitted at the forward and after ends of screw-propelled vessels in connection with panting stringers. The purpose of this construction is to strengthen the shell plating against panting.

Ger: *Piekverstärkungsbalken*.

PANTING FRAME. One of the forepeak frames constructed of heavier scantlings to withstand the panting action of the shell plating.

PANTING STRINGER. One of the fore-and-aft girders introduced in the bow and stern framing between the side stringers to counteract panting of frames and plating.

PAO-PAO. A small single-outrigger canoe found in the Samoan Islands. Length 10 to 15 ft. Beam at gunwale 8 to 9 in., at bilge 12 to 16 in. Depth 12 to 15 in. It is used for harbor transportation and fishing in sheltered waters. The hull has fine lines, with sharp concave stem and tapered stern. At the extremity of the latter a cube or solid carved knob of wood is left. Also called *pau-pau*.

PAPAGAYOS. Local northeasterly winds of strong or gale force which occur frequently from December to April on the west coast of Costa Rica, Nicaragua and Guatemala. They are accompanied by fine clear weather.

See **Tehuantapeccer**.

PA-PAK-TENG. A long narrow Chinese fishing boat with flat bottom, employed on rivers and estuaries for fishing by moonlight. On one side of the boat there is a bright white board which extends from gunwale to water level. On the other side there is a net stretched vertically on uprights to prevent the fish from jumping overboard. The fish, attracted by the reflection of the moonlight on the white sideboard, leap at it, and some of them jump into the boat. Others are easily netted.

PAPALIMBANG. East Indian trading boat of same type as the *pajala* from Macassar, Celebes. The sides are raised with planking. There is a railing at the stern. It is rigged with a tripod mast.

PAPAU. A single-outrigger dugout canoe from Ontong-Java, northeastern Melanesia, about 14 to 16 ft. long. There is a small upright triangular board at each end acting as breakwater. A single strake of planking is fitted to the sides of the dugout for part of its length and lashed with sennit.

PARACHAL.

See **Basket Boat**.

PARACHUTE FLARE. A distress signal consisting of a cartridge with projectile containing a pyrotechnic candle attached to a parachute by shroud lines. It is fired from a signal pistol and provides a red flare signal which burns for over 30 seconds with a minimum luminous intensity of 20,000 candle power. When discharged vertically upward it attains an altitude of 150 feet or over. Also called **Parachute Distress Signal**.

Fr: *Signal parachute*.

PARACHUTE SPINNAKER. A triangular light weather racing sail conceived by the Swedish yachtsman, Sven Salén, and first used on the yacht "Maybe" in 1927. It is diagonally cut with cloths parallel to the leeches and meeting at the last down the middle of the sail. It is fitted with a headboard, and circular antiwind-cushioning holes are sometimes cut in the last. Its breadth is about double that of an ordinary spinnaker and it sets forward of all head stays. Sometimes called Mae West spinnaker, double spinnaker.

PARADJERA. A two-mast lug-rigged Turkish coaster with long bowsprit and three headsails.

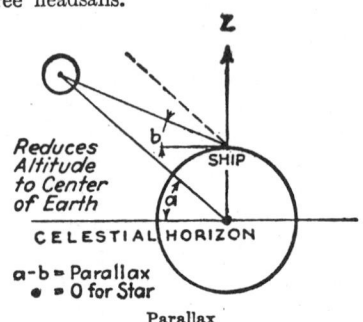

Parallax

PARALLACTIC ANGLE. The angle formed by the hour circle and the vertical circle passing through a celestial body.

Fr: *Angle parallactique;* Ger: *Parallaktisches Winkel.*

PARALLAX. The error in the altitude of a heavenly body, due to the fact that the observer is actually at some position on the earth's surface instead of at the center of the earth. Navigational tables are computed on the assumption that the observer's eye is at the center of the earth. The correction for parallax must be added to the sextant altitude to get the true observed altitude.

Fr: *Parallaxe;* Ger: *Verschub; Parallaxe.* See **Horizontal Parallax.**

PARALLAX AGE. The interval in time between perigean or apogean tides from the moon's corresponding position.

Ger: *Parallaxaltern.*

PARALLAX IN ALTITUDE. The angle at a celestial body between a line drawn from an observer on the earth's surface, and one from the earth's center, when the body is above the horizon.

Fr: *Parallaxe en Hauteur;* Ger: *Höhenverschub; Höhenparallaxe.*

PARALLEL MIDDLE BODY.
See **Middle Body.**

PARALLEL OF ALTITUDE. One of the small circles of the celestial sphere whose planes are parallel to the horizon.

Fr: *Parallèle de Hauteur;* Ger: *Höhen Parallel.*

PARALLEL OF DECLINATION. One of the small circles of the celestial sphere parallel to the celestial equator. All points which have the same declination lie on the same parallel of declination.

Fr: *Cercle de Déclinaison;* Ger: *Deklinationskreis.*

PARALLEL OF LATITUDE. Any one of the small circles on the terrestrial sphere parallel to the equator.

Fr: *Parallèle de Latitude;* Ger: *Breitenparallel.*

PARALLEL RULERS. An instrument used for laying down courses and bearings on a chart. It consists of two rulers connected by crosspieces of equal length, movable about joints, so that while the distance between the two rulers may be increased or diminished, their edges always remain parallel.

Fr: *Règle à Parallèles;* Ger: *Parallellineal.*

See **Roller Rule.**

PARALLEL SAILING. A method of navigation in which courses are followed along meridians and parallels only. Now obsolete.

Fr: *Navigation sur un parallèle;* Ger: *Segeln im Parallel.*

PARANGAN TELATAP. A paddling and sailing dugout canoe employed by the Sea Dyak tribes of Borneo for fishing with a dragnet called *renggae.* The hull is flat-bottomed and the ends are decked. There is a roofed shelter aft and one mast with spritsail.

PARANTHELION. A halo phenomenon similar to a parhelion which occur at a distance of 90 degrees or more in azimuth from the sun.

Fr: *Paranthélie;* Ger: *Nebengegensonne.*

PARANZA. Various types of Italian fishing craft working with a dragnet called *rete de paranza.* Also called *paranzella.*
See **Bilancella.**

PARANZA TRAWL. A Mediterranean trawl, also used in a modified form in the Californian fisheries. Sometimes called pareja trawl. It is similar to the Spanish *pareja* net and the French *filet boeuf* or *grand gangui.* It consists essentially of a bag with two elongated wings. At the end of each wing there is a short stout piece of wood which keeps them open vertically and to which the warps are fastened.

Fr: *Boeuf; Gangui.*

One of the features of this gear is that the strain of the warps is first taken by the cork and ground ropes, then, by wedge-shaped pieces of netting on top and bottom called *scaglietti,* directly to the cod end. This arrangement allows the netting of the wings and throat to bulge out by the force of the water while being towed, causing the meshes to stay open much more than if the strain of the bag was on the netting. The length of the net varies from 160 to 320 ft. with a horizontal spread of 50 to 100 ft. and a vertical opening of 3 to 4 ft. The *paranza* is fished with 2 boats working in pairs. In the Mediterranean these are frequently one-masted lateen-rigged sailing boats or steam vessels. In California, motor-powered boats ranging in size from 56 to 72 ft. in length and in horsepower from 60 to 200 are employed.

PARANZELLA NET. See **Paranza Trawl.**

PARAO. A slow-moving Philippine craft used for transportation of goods and passengers around the coasts of Iloilo, Capiz, Occidental Negros, and Oriental Negros. The hull is composed of a large dugout, which forms the bottom, upon which planked sides flaring outward are built up to increase the capacity. Double outriggers, with floats composed of three poles of bamboo lashed together, provide the necessary stability when under sail. The rig formerly consisted of battened lugsails made of matting, but has lately been changed to the ordinary schooner rig with cotton sail. There is a fairly long bowsprit with jib. Large oars with round blades are used as a secondary means of propulsion. Length 68 ft. Breadth 7.5 ft. (Approximate.)

PARASELENE. A halo phenomena similar to a parhelion but with the moon as a source of light. Also called mock moon, moon dog.

Fr: *Parasélène;* Ger: *Nebenmond.*
See **Parhelion.**

PARAVANE. A special type of water kite, designed to prevent ships from striking a moored mine, and consisting of a streamlined body with plane controlled by a depth-control device, a rudder, and a cutterhead. Two paravanes are towed, one on each side of the ship, by means of specially constructed wire towropes attached to a fitting which bears on, or is supported at, the forefoot of the vessel and can be raised to the weather deck for rigging the towropes. When towed through the water the paravane moves out from the ship's side laterally, at its set depth, and, by means of the towrope, deflects mines moored in the vessel's path. The mine mooring, when thus deflected, slips along the towrope until it reaches the paravane, where it is severed by a cutter secured to the paravane. As soon as the mine mooring is cut, the buoyancy of the mine brings it to the surface, where it can be destroyed by gunfire. The paravanes and their towropes thus form a protective wedge whose apex is the point of tow.

PARBUCKLE. A device for raising or lowering a heavy body along an inclined or vertical plane. A bight of rope is thrown around a post or other secure fastening at the level to which the object is to be raised or lowered. The two ends of the rope are then passed under the object, brought all the way over it, and led back toward the bight. The two ends are then hauled or slackened together to raise or lower the object as may be required, the object itself acting as a movable pulley.

Fr: *Trévire;* Ger: *Schrottau.*

PARCEL. A comparatively small quantity of homogenous cargo shipped with other varieties.

Fr: *Parcelle; Lot;* Ger: *Parcelladung.*
See **Parceling.**

PARCEL (to). To protect a rope from the weather by winding strips of canvas or other material around it, with the lay, preparatory to serving.

Fr: *Limander;* Ger: *Beschmarten.*
See **Serve.**

PARCELING. Long strips of canvas 2 to 3 in. wide, daubed with tar, and wound about a rope, previous to its being served. Parceling is laid over the worming and marled down in place. Also called parcel.

Fr: *Limande;* Ger: *Schmarting.*

PARCEL RECEIPT. A receipt issued by a shipping line to the shipper of a small package or parcel in lieu of a bill of lading. It avoids the conditions and costs imposed on a minimum bill of lading.

PARCEL TICKET. A receipt issued by a shipping company in lieu of a bill of lading for small parcels, for which a nominal sum is charged for freight. Also called ticket.

PAREGGIA.
See **Bovo.**

PAREJA. A generic term for Spanish sailing or screw trawlers working singly or in pairs with the *pareja* net, each boat towing one of the warps. Also called *parella, barca* *de parella, barca de pareja, barca de bou.* The *pareja de vela* or sailing *pareja* is called *barca de bou* when used for single-boat fishing, in which case two spars are rigged, one at each end, on which the warps are fastened. The boat is then made to drift with the wind on the beam. All boats of this type are built of native grown soft wood. The tonnage of sailing craft varies 8 to 40 tons, that of mechanically propelled boats from 30 to 70 tons. None of the boats is fitted with gallows; the gear is towed from the stern. All boats are decked fore and aft. The rig of the sailing boats consists of a lateen sail which sets on a short mast. The larger boats of this type carry a small mizzenmast with no rake, and lateen sail sheeted to an outrigger.

When sailing before the wind the *barca de bou* or *pareja* sets two triangular sails called *polaccas*, which are boomed out on two spars about 40 ft. long called *tangones*. The sail set to starboard is called *polacca del car*; that on the port side *polacca de la pena*. The smaller type of sailing *pareja*, which has displacement of about 5 tons, is built with two grounding keels to facilitate beaching on sandy shores.

PAREJA FISHING. Spanish method of trawling with two vessels. Also called paranzella fishing. The warps connecting the boats to the trawl are smaller than with the ordinary gear and are very long. The net is made of lighter twine but is much larger in extent than the ordinary trawl. The vessels keep a certain distance apart during trawling operations and tow the gear at a much slower speed than single boats.

PARENT METAL. A welding term used to denote the material of the parts to be welded. Also called base metal.

Fr: *Métal de Base;* Ger: *Grundmaterial.*

PARHELION. A form of halo consisting of a more or less distinctly colored image of the sun at the same altitude as the latter above the horizon and usually at about 22 degrees from the sun in azimuth. Also called mock sun, sun dog.

Fr: *Parhélie;* Ger: *Nebensonne.*

PARK AVENUE BOOM. A boom invented by Manfred Curry and used by racing yachts. It is claimed to have the following advantages over a straight boom: (1) It prevents a down draft of wind from passing under the sail. (2) It assures an aerofoil curve extending to the foot of the mainsail.

PARREL. Also parral. Rope, chain, or iron collar by which a running yard or gaff is kept against the mast, but which allows vertical motion.

Fr: *Racage;* Ger: *Rack.*

See **Jaw Parrel, Rib and Truck Parrel, Tub Parrel.**

PARREL LASHING. The lashing by which the eyes of a parrel rope are secured.

Fr: *Aiguillette de Racage;* Ger: *Racksorrung.*

PARREL RIB. One of the pieces of wood with two holes through which the two parts of a parrel rope are rove, with a bull's-eye between. Sometimes called rib. The inner smooth edge of the rib rests against the mast and slides readily up and down, when the spar is hoisted or lowered.

Fr: *Bigot de Racage;* Ger: *Rackschlitten.*

PARREL ROPE. A rope rove through the trucks and ribs of a parrel.

Fr: *Batard;* Ger: *Racktau.*

PARREL TRUCK. Balls of wood strung on the jaw rope of a gaff or on the rope parrel of a yard to lessen friction when the spar is hoisted or lowered.

Fr: *Pomme de Racage;* Ger: *Rackklotje.*

PART. In a tackle, the different sections of the fall.

Fr: *Brin;* Ger: *Part.*

See **Hauling Part, Running Part, Standing Part.**

PARTIAL AWNING DECK VESSEL. A vessel with raised quarter-deck connected to a bridge house, the latter merging into the forecastle, thus completely covering the whole length of the vessel. Also a vessel with long poop connected to bridge house and forecastle, with raised foredeck between bridge and forecastle. The partial awning deck erection is used for light cargo or passenger accommodation. It affords protection to engine and boiler room openings and forms, with the raised quarter-deck or long poop, a full length erection for which due allowance is made in assigning the load line.

Fr: *Navire à Awningdeck Partiel;* Ger: *Teilweises Sturmdeckschiff.*

PARTIAL FLOOR. A floor which does not extend over the full breadth of the bottom.

Ger: *Teil-Bodenwrange.*

PARTIALLY UNDERHUNG RUDDER. A rudder in which part of the blade is located below the bottom pintle.

PARTICULAR AVERAGE. An average

loss which is charged upon cargo or ship. A particular average generally arises from an unavoidable accident such as fire, stranding, collision, or damage to cargo if due to storms. The loss sustained and the particular average is borne by the actual owners or insurers of the property lost or damaged.

Fr: *Avarie Particulière;* Ger: *Besondere Haverei; Partikuläre Havarie.*

PARTICULAR CHARGES. A marine insurance term used to denote expenses incurred by or on behalf of the insured for the safety or preservation of the subject matter insured, other than general average and salvage charges. Also called special charges. None of the particular charges are included in the definition of "particular average."

PARTING STRAP. A strap, which is weaker than the rope or wire used with it, so that the strap will part before the wire.

PARTITION BULKHEAD. A lightly constructed partition used for subdividing a main compartment. Also called nonstructural bulkhead, joiner bulkhead. Such bulkheads are limited to one deck height and are neither oiltight nor watertight.

Fr: *Cloison de Séparation;* Ger: *Trennungsschott.*

PARTNERS. Pieces of timber let in between two beams to form a framing for the support of any part which passes through a deck such as a mast, pump, capstan, shafting, and so on.

Fr: *Étambrai; Entremise d'étambrai;* Ger: *Fischung.*

See Mast Partner.

PARTNER PLATE. A stout deck plate, of width two and one-half times the mast diameter, through which the mast hole is pierced. Also called mast partner plate. It is generally stiffened by a bulb angle coaming which acts as a bearing for mast wedges.

Fr: *Tôle d'étambrai;* Ger: *Fischungsplatte.*

PASS. To reeve and secure. For example, to pass a line is to reeve and secure it; to pass a stopper is to reeve and secure the stopper.

PASSAGE. 1. An outward or a homeward trip; also a journey by water from one port or place to another, as distinguished from the term "voyage" which refers to an outward and homeward journey. Also called crossing.

Fr: *Traversée;* Ger: *Fahrt; Überfahrt; Reise.*

See Meridian Passage, Sanitary Passage.

2. A vessel is said to be "on passage" from the time it leaves its last port of loading until the time it arrives at its port of destination. When referring to commodities bought or sold, "on passage" means in transit.

PASSAGE BROKER. A term applying in Great Britain to a duly licensed broker who sells or lets steerage passages in any ship proceeding from the British Isles.

Fr: *Agent de Passages;* Ger: *Auswanderungsagent.*

PASSAGE MONEY. The charge made for the conveyance of a passenger in a ship.

Fr: *Frais de Passage;* Ger: *Passagegeld; Überfahrgeld.*

PASSAREE. A rope for guying out the clew of a square foresail when running. It was rove through a block on the passaree boom or lower studding sail boom. Also pazaree, placery. (Obsolete.)

PASSENGER. One who travels on a ship by virtue of a contract with the carrier, and who is paying a fare. The term "passenger" includes any person carried in a ship other than the master, the crew, and the owner and his family and servants.

Fr: *Passager;* Ger: *Passagier; Fahrgast.*

See Cabin Passenger, Consular Passenger, Deck Passenger, Steerage Passenger, Tourist Class Passenger.

PASSENGER ACCOMMODATION. Living quarters provided exclusively for the use of passengers on board ship. In each maritime nation statutory regulations determine the capacity, deck area, and other requirements allowed per passenger according to class (cabin or steerage).

The number of steerage passengers allowed according to the United States passenger act of 1882 is limited to one passenger to every 18 clear superficial feet of deck space, in addition to which 5 superficial feet of open or promenade space must be allotted to every passenger on weather deck not included in the tonnage of the vessel. The space allotted to exclusive use of cabin passengers must be in the proportion of at least 36 clear superficial feet to each passenger. In the measurement of deck space—dining rooms, lounging rooms, smoking

rooms, lavatories, toilet rooms and bath rooms are included.
Fr: *Emménagements pour Passagers;* Ger: *Passagiereinrichtungen; Wohnräume für Fahrgäste.*
Graham, G., "Arrangement of Passenger Accommodation," *Shipbuilding and Shipping Record,* Dec. 30, 1938 (Special Number); Hillhouse, P. A., "The Interior Architecture of Ships," North East Coast Institution of Engineers and Shipbuilders (Newcastle upon Tyne), *Transactions,* vol. 46 (1930).

PASSENGER BOAT. Any craft regardless of size, type, equipment or means of propulsion used as a means of transportation for passengers on water. According to international lifesaving appliances rules, any vessel which carries more than twelve passengers is considered a passenger vessel. Cargo vessels of the United States of America are permitted under the Merchant Marine Act of June 5, 1920, to carry a maximum of sixteen passengers without being classed as passenger vessels.
Fr: *Navire à Passagers;* Ger: *Fahrgastschiff.*
British Board of Trade, *Instructions as to the Survey of Passenger Steamships,* London, 1942; Paterson, G. M., "The Design of a Large Passenger Ship," Cambridge University Engineering and Aeronautical Societies *Journal,* vol. 1, 1926; Wall, A. T., "Ship Design and Arrangement from the Passenger's Viewpoint," Institution of Naval Architects (London), *Transactions,* vol. 71, 1929.

PASSENGER CERTIFICATE. A document issued by the Board of Trade to every British vessel carrying any number of passengers in excess of 12. It is granted to the owners of vessels built under Board of Trade supervision and has to be renewed every 12 months. In granting this certificate, ships ranging from foreign-going vessels to excursion craft plying in smooth waters are dealt with; different certificates being issued according to service.

PASSENGER DECK. As defined by the Passenger Act of 1882: Sec. 1, this term refers to every deck or portion of a deck which is above the lowest passenger deck, i.e., the deck next below the waterline.

PASSENGER FERRY. A ferryboat specially arranged for the conveyance of passengers.
Fr: *Transbordeur à Passagers;* Ger: *Personen Fahrboot.*

PASSENGER LINER. A ship or vessel employed in carrying passengers, mails, and goods at stated intervals between regular ports.
Fr: *Paquebot;* Ger: *Packetschiff.*
Biles, J. H., "Atlantic Ships," Institution of Engineers and Shipbuilders in Scotland, *Transactions,* vol. 73 (1929–30); Gaede, G. G., "American Superliners," Society of Naval Architects and Marine Engineers (New York), *Transactions,* vol. 47, 1939; Rigg, E. H., "Modern Atlantic Liners," Society of Naval Architects and Marine Engineers, New York, *Transactions,* vol. 44, 1936.

PASSENGER LIST. An accurate list, signed by the master, of all passengers on board a vessel, specifying the name, sex, calling, nationality, port of embarkation, and proposed destination. Also called passenger manifest (U. S.). It is usually handed over and submitted for inspection to the customs officers when the ship enters a port. On British emigrant ships the passenger list is compulsory for all voyages from the British Isles to any port out of Europe and not within the Mediterranean, also for Colonial voyages. It is countersigned by the emigration officer.
Fr: *Liste des Passagers;* Ger: *Passagier Liste.*

PASSENGER MANIFEST. An official document prepared by the ship's staff from the passenger list for the immigration authorities. It contains a number (39 in U. S. A.) of questions on age, race, status, education, nationality, political opinions, length of stay, and so on, and enables the officials to keep track of persons who enter the country, whether as permanent residents or transient visitors.

PASSENGER SPACES. Spaces for the exclusive accommodation and use of passengers. In flooding or subdivision calculations baggage rooms, store and provision rooms, mailroom, are not included in passenger spaces. Crew spaces below the margin line are regarded as passenger spaces for permeability and criterion numeral calculations.

PASSERA. See **Battellina.**

PASSPORT. A document issued to a neutral vessel in time of war. It is, in fact, the authority under which a vessel is allowed to proceed on her voyage and gives proof of the vessel's nationality. In the document there must be entered the full description of the vessel, the crew, the names of the owners and of the master, the port of registry, the port of lading, and the port of destination. Sometimes called sea brief, sea letter, sea pass.

Fr: *Congé;* Ger: *Seebrief; Seepass.*

PASS THE WORD. To repeat an order or information to the crew.

PATCH. 1. Broken pieces of floe ice of various sizes which have drifted free of the pack.

2. A piece of plating riveted or welded over a break, crack, hole, or wasted place of another plate.

Fr: *Placard;* Ger: *Flick.*

See **Hard Patch, Soft Patch.**

3. Term used by sailmakers to denote one or more reinforcing layers of canvas sewed on a sail or awning at corners or other places where strain is most severe or where chafing is likely to occur. Patches go at the clew, tack, head and at each reef point of the average sail. Also used for repairing rented canvas. A piece of canvas sewed on a sail or awning to cover a rent or strengthen a weak spot.

Fr: *Renfort;* Ger: *Lappen.*

See **Clew Patch, Reef Tackle Patch.**

PATENT ANCHOR. A stockless anchor, housing in the hawsepipe and generally designated by the name of the patentees. Baldt and Dunn anchors are examples.

See **Anchor, Stockless Anchor.**

PATENT BLOCK. A block in which the sheaves work on friction rollers composed of a set of small revolving bronze cylinders which act as bearings for the pin.

Fr: *Poulie à cylindres;* Ger: *Patentscheibeblock.*

PATENT EYE. A metal eye secured to the end of a wire rope in place of a spliced eye.

See **Poured Socket.**

PATENT LINK. A chain link made of two interlocking parts which can be taken apart and inserted in the chain cable when required.

Fr: *Maille démontable;* Ger: *Kentergied.*

See **Kenter Shackle.**

PATENT SLIP. See **Marine Railway.**

PATTIMAR. An Indian coasting vessel with two masts and lateen sails. Also called *patamar. Pattimars* have long overhanging stems, and the stern is either rounded or square, with very little overhang and no counter or rudder truck. They are open boats without properly laid decks. A short portion forward and a larger space aft is roughly planked over, and the remainder of the boat is lightly covered with bamboo splits laced together and resting on the beams and of sufficient strength to support a man's weight. They range in size from 60 to 180 tons. A 100-ton *pattimar* has approximately length over-all 100 ft.; breadth 20 ft.; depth 10 ft.

Between the main and the mizzen masts a tent-shaped structure supported on wooden uprights and covered with bamboos and matting is built up to form a shelter house for the crew. The large *pattimars* are employed in the timber trade between the ports of Malabar and Bombay. The usual sails are two large lateens and a jib, but some of the largest boats rig a small jigger mast right aft.

PAUNCH MAT. A thick strong mat made by interweaving strands of old rope, used to protect the yards and rigging from chafing when sailing close-hauled. Also called panch mat.

Fr: *Paillet de Brasseyage;* Ger: *Stossmatte.*

PAWL. A short piece of steel hinged at one end to the pawl head of a capstan. It drops by gravity into the cogs of the pawl rim as the capstan revolves, acting as a catch or brake to prevent any backward motion when the power is removed. Also called click, drop pawl.

Fr: *Linguet;* Ger: *Pall.*

See **Cross Pawl, Launching Pawl.**

PAWL (to). To prevent any backward motion of a capstan by letting the pawls drop in the pawl rim.

Fr: *Mettre les Linguets;* Ger: *Pallsetzen.*

PAWL BITT. The central bitt in a wooden windlass, fitted with a pawl which acts on the barrel. Used only in small vessels. This bitt supports the rocking lever and ratchet movement.

Fr: *Bitte à linguet;* Ger: *Pallbeting; Pallpfosten.*

PAWL HEAD. The lower part of a capstan barrel where the pawls are located.

Fr: *Cercle à Linguets;* Ger: *Pallrad.*

PAWL RIM. A circular rim made of cast iron provided with notches on which the capstan pawls drop by gravity, so as to prevent the capstan from turning back.

Fr: *Couronne; Saucier;* Ger: *Pallkranz.*

See **Top Rim.**

PAY. To fill the calked seams of a deck with hot pitch or marine glue. To coat or cover with tar or pitch or with a composition of tar, resin, and so on. In small boats and yachts the seams are puttied with white lead instead of being paid.

Fr: *Brayer;* Ger: *Auspechen.*

The pitch is poured into the seams from a paying ladle with a spout, from which the pitch issues in a fine stream. The spout should be held far enough above or away from the seam to allow the air to escape. The application of pitch should be carried out in two steps, the first filling consisting of a small quantity paid into the bottom of the seam and allowed to set before the second one is applied.

PAYANG. An open fishing boat from the Malay Peninsula, with tall blade-shaped stem and stern. Sometimes called *jalak.*

The keel and garboard are cut from one log. The planking is carvel-built. A loose decking made of planks extends over the whole length with the exception of two frame spaces just forward of the main- or aftermast. The endpieces, keel, and bottom planking are made of hardwood, the upper works of a lighter wood called *medang* or *serayak.* Near the stem there is a carved figurehead representing the head of a dragon. The stern is usually decorated with a necklace made from pinang wood. A platform is provided at each end of the boat for the nets (*pukat-petarang*). Length 48 to 50 ft. Breadth 7 to 7½ ft. Depth 2 to 2.8 ft. Sail area about 1,000 sq. ft. Capacity 6 tons. (Typical.)

The rig consists of two masts with boomed lugsails made of black cloth. The foremast is stepped close to the stem, the main- or aftermast at about one third of the boat's length measured from the stem. A long paddle is used as quarter rudder. Thirteen or fourteen oars 8 ft. 9 in. long are used for rowing in calm weather. A small boat called *sampan payang* about 7 ft. long is used as a dinghy and towed astern.

PAYING SHELL. A funnel-shaped container with spout used for pouring marine glue into the seams of a wooden deck.

PAY OFF. 1. To fall off from the wind in consequence of the force exerted by the rudder or the arrangement of the sails or both.

Fr: *Abattre; Tomber;* Ger: *Abfallen.*

2. To discharge a crew at the end of a voyage.

Fr: *Débarquer;* Ger: *Abmustern.*

PAY OUT. To slack out on a line made fast on board.

Fr: *Filer;* Ger: *Nachstecken.*

PAZAREE.
See **Passaree.**

PE, PEI. A general term for "canoe" in Western Papua, New Guinea. Also *peri.*

PEA.
See **Bill.**

PEA JACKET.
See **Reefer.**

PEAK. 1. The angle formed by the head and leech of a gaff sail. The greater the angle the less peak the sail is said to have. The upper after corner of a quadrilateral fore-and-aft sail.

Fr: *Empointure de pic;* Ger: *Piekohr.*

2. The outer or after end of a gaff.

Fr: *Pic;* Ger: *Piek; Gaffelnock.*

3. A name given to the lower spaces forward of the collision bulkhead and abaft the aftermost watertight bulkhead. Peaks are generally used as trimming tanks owing to their large moment arm about the center of buoyancy. Structural strengthening is necessary in these compartments, owing to the special stresses set up: in the forepeak by the pounding of waves, and in the afterpeak by the vibrations due to the working of the propeller.

Fr: *Coqueron;* Ger: *Piek.*

See **Afterpeak, Forepeak.**

PEAK (to). 1. To raise to a perpendicular position, or nearly so, a gaff, a yard, and so on. Also called to top.

Fr: *Apiquer;* Ger: *Toppen; Auspieken.*

2. To raise the blades of oars out of the water and secure or hold them at a common angle with the surface of the water by placing the inner end of each oar under the batten on the opposite side of the boat.

Fr: *Lève rames;* Ger: *Ruderpieken.*

PEAK BULKHEAD. A watertight bulkhead which forms the boundary of a peak tank. In the stern it is the first bulkhead forward of the sternpost. Forward it is the bulkhead nearest the stern, and when extended up to the freeboard deck it is also called collision bulkhead.

Fr: *Cloison de coqueron;* Ger: *Piekschott.*

PEAK CLEAT. In a whaleboat, one of the small cleats fastened to the ceiling opposite the rowlocks for holding the oars peaked at an angle of about 20 degrees. They were used when the boat was made fast to the whale and allowed the oarsmen to rest. (Obsolete.)

PEAK FRAME. One of the frames supporting the shell plating in the Afterpeak or Forepeak.
Fr: *Membrure de coqueron;* Ger: *Piekspant.*

PEAK HALYARDS. The ropes or tackles by which the peak or afterend of a gaff is hoisted.
Fr: *Drisse de Pic;* Ger: *Piekfall.*

PEAK LINE. A line passing through a small block fastened to the afterend of a gaff. It is used as a flag halyard or to assist in hauling down the peak.

PEAK SPAN. A wire rope or chain fastened with both ends to a standing gaff and giving the spar a lift in two places.
Fr: *Patte d'Oie de Pic;* Ger: *Piekspann; Gaffelhänger.*

PEAK TANK. A ballast tank in the extreme bow or stern, used for trimming ship.
See **Forepeak, Afterpeak.**

PEAK TYE. A length of wire or chain leading from the lower masthead to the peak of a standing gaff to support it.
Fr: *Martinet de Corne;* Ger: *Gaffel Drehreep.*

PEA-POD. A double-ended rowing and sailing type of boat originating from Jonesport, Maine. In model these boats are miniature whaleboats, with a straight keel, round bow and stern profile, moderate sheer, rather flat floor, and moderately hard bilges. They are framed with steam-bent oak frames and are carvel-built, with cedar planking. The rig consists of a small mast with spritsail. Length 14 to 18 ft. Beam 3 ft. 10 in. to 4 ft. 11 in.

The boats are used by lobstermen, who row them standing up and facing forward, long oar locks being fitted for this purpose. They are noted for their good rowing qualities in rough weather.

PEARL LUGGER, PEARLING LUGGER. A local name given in northwest Australia to small ketch-rigged boats employed in pearl fisheries. Length over-all 55 ft. Waterline length 47 ft. Beam 13 ft. Draft 5 ft. 6 in.

The planking is of Australian yarrah wood, copper-fastened, and copper-sheeted over keel and garboard strake, under forefoot, and under the round of bilge below the mizzen shrouds. The deck is of Burma teak, the framing of hardwood. The sails include one headsail set to a short bowsprit. These boats are handy and fast sailers. A few of them are fitted with an auxiliary engine.

PEBBLES. Small stones worn and rounded by the action of water, sand, and ice, found on beaches and on the sea bottom.
Fr: *Galets;* Ger: *Kieselgrund; Kieselstein.*

PEDESTAL SOCKET. See **Davit Stand.**

PEDIWAK.
See **Paduakan.**

PEENING. 1. Rounding and cleaning off the sharp edges of steel plates, castings, or forgings to improve the appearance or prevent damage to persons or clothing. It is done with an air hammer carrying a blunt-nosed chisel with a hollow edge.
Fr: *Panner;* Ger: *Pinnen.*

2. A similar operation carried out on a weld bead laid by arc weldings to relieve internal stresses.

PEGGING. A method used in the hook and line fisheries on the east coast of North America. It is a sort of hand lining which requires constant motion. The sinker with hook attached is let down to the bottom of the sea and the instant it strikes it is pulled back a few fathoms in short sharp jerks. When "pegging" a boat seldom anchors. It drifts over shoals which are swept by swift currents. The boat drifts a few hundred yards and then stems back to the starting point which has been previously located.

PEGGY (G. B.). An ordinary seaman or deck boy told off to scrub the forecastle, fetch the food from the galley, and so on.

PEGON. A fishing craft similar to the *mayang* from western Java.

PELAGIC WHALING. The whaling operations by which whales are reduced on board floating factory vessels out in the open sea. Each floating factory is accompanied by 2 to 5 steam whale catchers. The greatest improvement in pelagic whaling is due to the fact that instead of flensing the whale alongside, factory vessels are now equipped so that the whole whale is hauled aboard on a slipway through the stern.

PELANG. A seagoing paddling and sailing canoe employed in the fisheries of northern Celebes Islands. Also called *pelong.* It has a length of about 27 ft. The *pelang-aio* is a double-outrigger canoe from Halmaheira with a length ranging between 8 to 20 ft. and also called *sema-sema.*

PELANG PAKPAK.
See **Pakata.**

PELELE. Small Javanese fishing canoe of the *jukung* type but without wash strakes, used in Batavia. The *pelele laut* is a dugout canoe with wash strake, employed in the sea fisheries of western Borneo, as distinguished from the *pelele darat,* which works in rivers. The rig consists of a single mast with square sail.

PELETEK. A small canoe employed on the northern shores of Java for placing and removing stake nets called *sero*. It is rigged with a small portable mast.

PELICAN HOOK. A quick-release hook used on boat gripes, cargo gear, and wherever rapid release is desired. It consists of a hinged hook held together by a ring or bridgepiece. When the ring is knocked off, the hook swings open.

Fr: *Croc à échappement;* Ger: *Schlipphaken; Schlippschakel.*

See **Hook.**

PELLET. A circular canvas buoy used by British fishermen in the North Sea for marking their nets. Also called pelt, pallet. It consists of a canvas sphere 62 in. in circumference with a circular wooden base in which there is a hole for securing the mooring rope. In this wooden base is fitted an ordinary nonreturn valve such as is used for the inner tubes of bicycles. The sphere is inflated by means of an ordinary bicycle pump. The canvas is tarred both inside and outside to ensure its being airtight and watertight.

PELORUS. A navigational instrument used for taking bearings, usually mounted outboard on a vertical stand, in the wings of the bridge on each side, or in some other convenient location. Also called dumb compass, dummy compass.

Fr: *Taximètre;* Ger: *Peilscheibe.*

The pelorus consists of a circular flat metallic disc graduated at its edge in degrees, and capable of revolving about a central pivot. This disc revolves within an outer rim which is marked with lubber lines, or graduated in degrees, with 0° at the ship's head. Sight vanes are fitted, free to rotate with respect to the central rotating disc, as an aid in taking bearings. The whole is mounted on gimbals. In use the central disc is adjusted to agree with the ship's compass course, and clamped. A bearing taken on an object sighted through the vanes is read as a true bearing on the graduated disc, or as a relative bearing on the graduated rim.

PELOTA.
See **Basket Boat.**

PENMANJA. East Indian plank-built beamy craft with wash strakes which at the ends connect in the form of a turtle back. It is steered with two quarter rudders, and employed in the fisheries of Karimon-Java Island.

PEMAYANG. Another name for a Javanese craft of the *mayang* type. Also called *pemayangan.*

PENALTY CARGO (U. S.). Cargo or goods which by reason of their effectiveness, hazard, or difficult handling require that a higher rate of wages be paid to labor.

PENALTY CLAUSE. A charter party clause stating the penalty for nonperformance of the charter, proved damages. In voyage charters proved damages cannot exceed the estimated amount of freight.

Ger: *Penalty Klausel.*

PENALTY DOCKAGE (U. S.). A charge against a vessel for use of a berth beyond an agreed time allowance.

PENDANT. A short rope hanging from the head of a mast, a yardarm or the clew of a sail, having a block or thimble spliced on the free end. A whip or tackle is fixed at the block end and the other end is made fast to a yard boom or gaff and serves as a brace, guy, or vang. The word "pendant" is generally used with a qualification defining the position or purpose of the rope. Also called rigging pendant, pennant.

Fr: *Pantoire;* Ger: *Schenkel; Hänger.*

See Burton Pendant, Cat Pendant, Centerboard Pendant, Clear Hawse Pendant, Fish Pendant, Fish Tackle Pendant, Masthead Pendant, Mooring Pendant, Reef Pendant, Rudder Pendant, Whip and Pendant, Winding Pendant.

See **Pennant.**

PENDANT TACKLE. A twofold purchase usually hooked to a lower mast pendant, used for moving weights on deck, setting up the lower rigging, or steadying masts when the rigging becomes slack. Also used as deck tackle.

Fr: *Caliorne de Bas Mât;* Ger: *Seitentakel.*

PENGAIL. Small East Indian canoe from western Borneo employed in the hook-and-line fisheries.

PENJAJAP. Malay coaster with fine lined hull, straight raking stem, transom stern, and galleries built over bow and stern. The length varies from 50 to 65 ft. The rig consists of one, two, or three masts each carrying a lugsail with long leech and with the foot laced to a light boom. Length 56 ft. Breadth 11 ft. 2 in. Depth 7 ft.

The foremast, placed near the bow, has a pronounced rake and projects over the stem. The sides are raised by wash strakes made of wood or of *kadjang* leaves. They are extended aft over the stern forming a gallery supported by cross beams. A loose decking of bamboo strips runs fore and aft and above this there is a shelter made of *kadjang* leaves over the waist of the vessel.

PENJALENG. A Malay trader decked fore and aft, and with poop. The hull is built of jati wood and painted white. The cross sections are flat amidships and sharp at ends with transverse planking closing up bow and stern. There is a permanent roofing amidships over the cargo space. The rig consists of one or two tripod masts and sails made of matting, in the shape of a trapezoid or a triangle. It is steered with a quarter rudder. Length 36 to 80 ft. Breadth 12 to 15 ft. Depth 4.8 to 9 ft. Crew 8 to 20. Capacity 36 tons. (Average.)

PENNA.
See **Tchektirme.**

PENNANT. A flag with the fly usually much longer than the hoist and tapering to a point, used for signaling or for dressing ship. Also called pendant.

Fr: *Flamme;* Ger: *Wimpel.*

See **Answering Pennant, Broad Pennant, Irish Pennants, Mail Pennant, Meal Pennant, Narrow Pennant, Night Pennant, Numeral Pennant, Triangular Pennant.**

PENSACOLA OYSTER BOAT. A boat employed in the Pensacola oyster fishery for tonging oysters. It is made on the sharpie pattern, wide and shallow, with sharp bow, square stern, and flat bottom with carvel planking laid athwartships. Length 21 to 26 ft. Breadth 7 to 8 ft.

The bottom is rockered and it is provided with a skeg and sternpost. There is a half deck forward and a deck 3 to 4 ft. long at the stern, while washboards extend along the sides. It is generally built wholly of yellow pine but red cedar frames are sometimes used. A centerboard is provided. Both the cat and sloop rigs are seen; in either case a gaff mainsail with boom is carried.

PENSACOLA PILOT BOAT. Open sailboat employed in the Pensacola red snapper fishery during the summer. It derives its name from the fact that formerly Pensacola pilots used this type of boat almost exclusively, for boarding vessels at sea. It is a carvel-built, centerboard boat with long sharp bow, round bilge, fine rim, and vertical heart-shaped transom stern. The rudder is managed by a yoke, the yoke lines reaching forward of the mizzenmast. Boats of this type varied in size from 16 to 21 ft. in length, with about 3½ beams to length. They had 3 or 4 thwarts according to size. The stern was decked flush with the gunwale for a length of 2 or 3 ft.

This craft enjoyed at one time the distinction of being the only three-masted open boat used in the fisheries of the United States. Each mast carried a spritsail, the mizzen only having a boom. The masts were adjustable and smaller sails and spars could be substituted locally as the pilot rig.

PENTOR. East Indian canoe from Madura Island used for fishing with a hand net.

PERAMA. A small Turkish coaster with big sheer, rounded stem, and sharp stern. It is rigged with two masts, each mast carrying a lugsail. There are two headsails. Its rig is very similar to that of the Italian *bragozzo* from the Adriatic. Length 48.8 ft. Breadth 12.4 ft. Depth 6 ft. (Average.)

PERCH. A staff or vertical rod on top of a buoy supporting a shape and marking a shoal.

Fr: *Perche;* Ger: *Spier.*

PERIAUGER. A flat-bottom sailing barge with a capacity of 20 to 35 tons. The hull is built without keel. The ends are decked. It is propelled by sweeps or by fore-and-aft sails set on two collapsible masts. Leeboards are fitted on each side. Formerly used in navigating sheltered waters along the east coast of the United States and also on the Mississippi and its affluents. Now extinct.

PERIGEE. That point on the moon's orbit which is nearest to the earth. The opposite of "apogee."

Fr: *Périgée;* Ger: *Perigaum; Erdnähe.*

PERIHELION. The point in the orbit of a heavenly body which is nearest to the sun.

Fr: *Périhélie;* Ger: *Sonnennähe; Perihelium.*

PERILS OF THE SEA. Accidents and casualties of the seas covered under an ordinary policy of marine insurance but excluded under a bill of lading. The purpose of the policy is to secure indemnity against accidents which *may* happen; not against events which *must not* happen such as loss through insufficient packing of goods, wear and tear, inherent vice, damage by rats, worms, and so on. The expression, "perils of the sea," as used on bills of lading includes all kinds of marine casualties such as foundering, stranding, and every variety of damage at sea directly attributable to the violent and immediate action of wind or waves. It does not cover any loss or damage directly referable to neglect on the part of the shipowner or his servants.

Fr: *Evénements de Mer;* Ger: *Gefahren der See; Seegefahren.*
See **Maritime Peril.**

PERILS OF THE SEA CLAUSE. A marine insurance clause which states that the underwriters are liable for loss or damage due to perils of the sea. Sometimes called perils clause.

Ger: *Seegefahren Klausel.*

PERIOD. With reference to a coastal light, the interval in time that elapses between successive beginnings of the same phase. In a flashing light it is the interval between the beginning of one flash and the beginning of the next.

Fr: *Periode;* Ger: *Periode.*

PERIODICAL SURVEY. A survey prescribed by classification societies at regular intervals (generally four years) by which vessels are entitled to retain the characters assigned to them in the register book. These surveys become due at four, eight, and twelve years, respectively from the date of building, and are known as No. 1, No. 2, and No. 3 special surveys.

Fr: *Visite Périodique; Visite de Reclassification;* Ger: *Periodische Besichtigung; Klasse-Erneuerung.*

PERIOD OF ROLL. The time, in seconds, that a vessel, rolling freely in undisturbed water, takes to complete an oscillation from port to starboard or vice versa.

Fr: *Période de Roulis;* Ger: *Rollperiode; Schwingungsperiode.*

PERISHABLE CARGO. Generic term for all goods or products which are subject to destruction, decay, deterioration, disintegration, or any other change from the time they are placed on board until they are unloaded, whether carried in refrigerated space or otherwise.

Fr: *Marchandises Périssables;* Ger: *Verderbliche Ladung.*

PERMANENT BALLAST. Ballast in the form of sand, concrete, scrap, or pig iron, usually carried to enhance stability or trim, to overcome an inherent defect due to the faulty design of a vessel or to changed character of service.

Fr: *Lest fixe;* Ger: *Fester Ballast.*

PERMANENT BUNKER. A compartment with permanent bulkheads designed for the storage of bunker coal.

Fr: *Soute fixe;* Ger: *Fester Bunker.*

PERMANENT FENDER. A fender made of wood faced with flat steel which runs fore and aft or vertically on the outside of the vessel above the waterline and is permanently attached to the shell plating with angle bars, as distinguished from portable fenders which are hung over the ship's sides by lines. Also called fender guard.

Fr: *Ceinture;* Ger: *Scheuerleiste.*

PERMANENT MAGNET. Hard iron which having once been magnetized remains so permanently.

Fr: *Aimant permanent;* Ger: *Fester Magnet.*

PERMANENT MAGNETISM. Magnetism that does not depend on a temporary influence but which remains in a body for long periods.

Fr: *Magnétisme Permanent;* Ger: *Fester Magnetismus.*

PERMEABILITY. The volume permeability of any space on shipboard, as defined for subdivision calculations, is the percentage of that space which can be occupied by water. In other words, it is the ratio, expressed in hundredths, of the total space of a compartment to the remaining free space after deducting the capacity or volume of the cargo and other objects into which water has no access. An average permeability of 60 per cent is used for cargo spaces. For machinery spaces the permeability has been fixed at 80 per cent, for spaces occupied by passengers at 95 per cent.

Fr: *Perméabilité;* Ger: *Flutbarkeit.*

Typical Permeability Values

Cargo	Permeability (in per cent)
Flour in bags	29
Butter in boxes	20
Canned goods in cases	30
Cork in bales	24
Furniture in boxes	80
Machinery in cases	85
Tires in bundles	85
Automobiles, uncrated	95

PERMISSIBLE FACTOR.
See **Subdivision**.

PERMISSIBLE LENGTH. A term used in connection with the watertight subdivision of passenger vessels. The permissible length may be defined as the maximum distance allowed between two transverse bulkheads, due consideration being given to the length of the vessel and nature of service for which the ship is intended. It is equal to the product of the floodable length multiplied by a coefficient called "factor of subdivision."

Fr: *Longueur de Cloisonnement;* Ger: *Zulässige Länge.*
See **Floodable Length**.

PERMIT TO UNLADE (U. S.). A permit issued by the customs collector to the master of a vessel giving him permission to unload. The master applies for the permit on a customs form when making entry of his vessel at the customhouse. No merchandise, passenger, or baggage may be unloaded until permit has been granted. A similar permit, called "permit to lade" is issued before loading commences.

PERNE.
See **Garoupeira**.

PERUVIAN CURRENT.
See **Humboldt Current**.

PETROLEUM. Inflammable oily liquid mixture of numerous hydrocarbons occurring naturally in the earth. Petroleum and its derivatives are extensively used to provide heat, light, and power.

Fr: *Hydrocarbures;* Ger: *Erdöl.*

For marine transportation purposes petroleum and its products are usually classed as follows:

Grade A. Petroleum products having a Reid vapor pressure of 14 lb. per square inch or more. This grade includes only casing-head and very volatile gasolines.

Grade B. Petroleum products having a Reid vapor pressure less than 14 and more than 4½ lb. per square inch. This grade includes gasolines and the lighter crude oils.

Grade C. Petroleum having a "Tag" closed flash point below 86° F. and a Reid vapor pressure of 4½ lb. per square inch or less. This grade includes the majority of crude oils.

Grade D. Petroleum having a "Tag" closed flash point of 86° or more and a Pensky Martens flash point of 149° F. or less. This grade includes kerosene and certain distillates.

A simpler classification also used in shipping:

1. Dangerous oils having a flash point of 73½° F. (23° C.).
2. Ordinary oils having a flash point between 73½° F. and 149° F. (23° C. and 65° C.).
3. Nondangerous oils having a flash point above 149° F. (65° C.).

PETROLEUM SHIP. In British harbor regulations, the name applied to any ship having on board a cargo of petroleum spirit, or having discharged petroleum spirit if the holds and tanks have not been rendered free from any inflammable vapor. Such a vessel when in the harbor must display by day a red flag with white circular center. By night a red light at masthead must be displayed, in addition to any other navigation light required by international rules.

PETTICOAT.
See **Mast Coat**.

PETTY AVERAGE. A term applied to certain expenditures or small charges formerly assessed upon cargo and owners of the ship, such as pilotage, anchorage, towage, quarantine. They are now usually provided for in bills of lading.

Ger: *Kleine Haverei.*

PETTY OFFICER. A leading or chief seaman who has direct authority over a section of the crew and supervises the work done by his group. In naval vessels, a noncommissioned officer in charge of nonrated seamen or firemen.

Fr: *Maître;* Ger: *Maat.*

PETURUSAN. A fishing prao from eastern Java similar to the *alis-alis* but smaller. It is used for working a net called *turu*, from which it gets its name.

PHASE. The particular aspect of a celestial body the appearance of which is subject to periodical changes.

Fr: *Phase;* Ger: *Phase.*

PHASE AGE. The interval in time by which spring or neap tides follow the position in each of the periodic monthly cycles of the moon.

Ger: *Phasenalter.*

PHENOLIC RESIN. A waterproof synthetic lumber adhesive employed as bonding agent in boatbuilding for plywood and laminated timber in contact with sea water. It is unaffected by fresh or salt water and is not attacked by worms or fungi.

PHILIPPINE MAHOGANY. Trade name for three species of Philippine hardwoods, i.e., tanguile, almon and red lauan, none of which are mahogany. Tanguile is the best for boatbuilding purposes. Weight when seasoned about 36 lb. per cu. ft. It is generally used for planking of small boats.

PHONOTELEMETRY. Radio-acoustic sound ranging, as used in marine surveying.

PHOSPHOR BRONZE. A bronze alloy to which exceptional purity is given by skillful fluxing with phosphorus. It is harder and stronger than ordinary bronze, and is very close-grained. Phosphor bronze is of special value for articles which are exposed to sea water and require good wearing qualities. It is generally used for driving nuts of hand steering gears, bevel gear wheels on steering rods, propeller shaft liners, rudder pintle liners, bushings for block sheaves, and the like.

Fr: *Bronze Phosphoreux;* Ger: *Phosphorbronze.*

PHOSPHORESCENT WHEEL. One of the great rotating bands of phosphorescent sea occasionally observed in the Indian Ocean and China Seas. It is a well authenticated but comparatively rare phenomenon of which no explanation is known.

PI. A small dugout with single outrigger used for fishing with nets and spears by the Wanimo tribe of northwestern British New Guinea. The hull is built with two wash strakes and a portable carved stempiece. There is a mast which carries a rectangular mat sail almost as long as the canoe.

PICH-LI. A dugout canoe propelled by paddles and used for transportation by the Seminole Indians of Florida. It is hewn out of a cypress log which has previously been buried in mud to gain flexibility and to reduce the chance of splitting and cracking. No fire is used. The only tool used by the natives is a hand adze. It is believed that in former days large craft of this type were built to carry 30 to 40 occupants.

PICKED PORTS (G. B.). A chartering term used to denote a range of selected ports where better conditions for working cargo are obtainable and generally speaking where harbor dues and other charges are lower than in other ports in the same range. Antwerp, Rotterdam, London, Hull, Liverpool, Avonmouth, Glasgow, Newcastle, Cardiff, used to be picked ports, while Hamburg, Bremen, French Atlantic ports, Londonderry, Limerick, King's Lynn, Llanelly, Ipswich, etc., were known as objectionable ports. In the grain trade a minimum rate of discharge of eight hundred tons per day is obtainable in picked ports.

PICKINGS. Marine insurance term denoting the loss ascertained by "picking off," in the case of some goods such as cotton, the damaged portion of the bale, leaving the bale so picked for sale as in sound condition.

PICKINGS CLAUSE. A clause often included in insurance on cotton shipments. The damaged cotton is picked off, and the underwriter pays the loss thereof less an allowance for increase of weight by absorption of water. He also pays cost of picking and mending the bales and is credited with the proceeds of the damaged cotton and canvas.

PICKLED FISH. A process for preserving fish in which the fish are cleaned, split, and packed in salt, after which brine is added. The most common pickled fishes are the mackerel and the herring.

Fr: *Poisson Mariné;* Ger: *Marinierter Fisch.*

PICKLING. A process for removing the mill scale from steel plates prior to their installation in ship's structure. The plates are placed on edge for a few hours in a heated bath of dilute acids. Hydrochloric and sulphuric acids are among those used. After they are taken out, a stream of water is turned on them, their surfaces being brushed at the same time to remove the scale, which is loosened by the action of the acid.

Fr: *Décapage;* Ger: *Beizung.*

PICOTEUX. Small half-decked or open fishing boat found on the coasts of Calvados (Normandy). It is rigged with a lug mainsail, topsail, and two headsails. Length 15 to 22 ft. Breadth 5 ft. 10 in. to 9 ft. 10 in. Depth 2 ft. 5 in. to 3 ft. 8 in. Now nearly extinct.

PIELEGO. An open boat with flat bottom used for lining in the Venetian lagoons and rigged with one or two masts and boomed lugsails. Length 20 to 30 ft.

PIER. A structure sheltering for harbor; also a jetty thrown out from the shore to protect the entrance of a river harbor, etc.

In the United States a pier is a projecting quay or wharf running at an angle with the shoreline and providing a landing place on each side for vessels to receive and discharge cargo or land passengers.

Fr: *Appontement; Jetée;* Ger: *Hafendamm; Leitdamm; Mole.*

Greene, C., Wharves and Piers, New York, 1917.

PIER CREW. A group or gang of longshoremen stationed on a pier or quay when cargo is handled between ship and shore. Two men act as slingers; the others move the goods to or from the place where they are tiered. Also called Wharfmen.

PIERHEAD. The projecting or offshore end of a pier or a jetty.

Fr: *Musoir;* Ger: *Molenkopf.*

PIERMAN (U. S.). A longshoreman who is stationed ashore and deals with the work of trucking and bringing goods to the ship's side within reach of the ship's gear. In Great Britain called quayman.

Ger: *Kaiarbeiter.*

PIG LINE. Name given by salmon fishermen to a trolling line trailing from a short boom stepped amidships at the stern.

PIGSTY BULWARKS. Wooden bulwarks in which every alternate strake of planking is omitted to allow water to run freely from the decks.

PILE FENDER. A loose pile driven in front of a wharf or pier to absorb the shock of boats coming alongside.

Fr: *Défense en Pilotis;* Ger: *Schutzpfahl; Sturmpfahl.*

See **Dolphin.**

PILE MOORINGS. Permanent moorings in which the vessel is tied up fore and aft to clusters of piles, also called dolphins or Duc d'Albe, to prevent it from swinging with changes of wind and tide and to enable it to load or discharge in lighters.

Fr: *Pieu d'Amarrage; Duc d'Albe;* Ger: *Dallen; Dückdalben.*

PILFERAGE. In marine insurance, clandestine theft, such as the abstraction of articles from a case, in contradistinction to "theft," which applies to a whole package. Also called pillage.

Fr: *Larcin; Petit Vol;* Ger: *Kleiner Diebstahl.*

PILGRIM. A Mohammedan passenger going to or coming from the Hedjaz or Kingdom of Iraq on a pilgrim ship. Special regulations are provided in the International Sanitary Convention of 1926 relating to the transportation of pilgrims. For each pilgrim there must be a superficial 'tween deck area of 16 sq. ft. with a height between the decks or not less than 6 ft. On the upper deck (exposed deck) a free area of not less than 6 sq. ft. or for each passenger, irrespective of age, is required. Two or more places for cooking and also wash places screened from view, including a sufficient number for the exclusive use of women, must be provided on deck in addition to a specified number of latrines.

Fr: *Pèlerin;* Ger: *Pilger.*

PILLAR. A column supporting a deck beam or any other part of the structure in a vessel. Pillars are usually cylindrical, hollow or solid, or may be built up of riveted plates and bars. The head and heel are designed so that they can be securely riveted or bolted.

Fr: *Epontille;* Ger: *Stütze.*

See **Bowsprit Pillar, Built Pillar, Deck Pillar, Diagonal Pillar, Hold Pillar, Hollow Pillar, Portable Pillar, Solid Pillar, Widely Spaced Pillars.**

PILLAR BUOY. A buoy with tall cylindrical central structure on a broad base.

Fr: *Bouée à Pilier; Bouée à Fuseau;* Ger: *Spierentonne.*

PILLAR LADDER. A ladder formed by fitting rungs to a pillar or stanchion and generally used as a means of access to cargo holds.

Fr: *Echelle de Cale;* Ger: *Lukenleiter; Raumleiter.*

PILLOW BLOCK.
See **Plummer Block.**

PILOT. 1. A qualified individual possessing local knowledge of shallows, rocks, currents, and so on, and usually licensed by public authority, who is taken on board at a particular place, to conduct a ship through a river, road or channel, or from or into port. Pilots are established by legislative enactments at the principal seaports, and have rights and are bound to perform duties in accordance with the provisions of the laws establishing them.

Fr: *Pilote;* Ger: *Lotse.*

The original meaning of the word pilot was steersman, but the name is applied to men qualified to navigate a ship over certain stretches of coastal waters or estuaries and in and out of harbors. According to the British Merchant Shipping Act, a pilot is defined as a person not belonging to a ship but who has the conduct thereof.

See **Bar Pilot, Branch Pilot, Compulsory**

Pilot, Exempt Pilot, Gyro Pilot, Hobbing Pilot, Mud Pilot, River Pilot, Sea Pilot.

2. A book containing sailing directions for certain waters and giving all particulars for navigating them.

Fr: *Routier;* Ger: *Segelhandbuch; Seehandbuch.*

PILOTAGE. 1. The office of the pilots of a port. Also called pilot station.

2. The art of conducting a vessel in or out of a harbor or in the neighborhood of navigational dangers. Also called piloting. In most maritime nations pilotage is a public service established to provide pilots for vessels entering or leaving harbors, or in narrow waters.

Fr: *Pilotage;* Ger: *Lotsenkunst; Lotsen.*

See **Compulsory Pilotage, Free Pilotage.**

3. The remuneration which is paid to a pilot for his services and creates a maritime lien upon the ship.

Fr: *Droits de Pilotage;* Ger: *Lotsengeld; Lotsengebühren.*

Digby and Cole, *Pilotage Law,* London, 1913; Jones, Grosvenor M., *Pilotage in the United States,* U. S. Bureau of Foreign and Domestic Commerce, Special Agents Series 136, Washington, 1917; Schwerin, B. von, Der Lotse, Berlin, 1921.

PILOTAGE AUTHORITY. The authority from which pilots derive their mandate to act in their proper capacity; it includes all bodies or persons authorized to appoint or license pilots or to fix or alter rates of pilotage.

Fr: *Administration du Pilotage;* Ger: *Lotsenbehörde.*

See **Customs Authorities, Port Authority.**

PILOTAGE CERTIFICATE. A certificate granted in Great Britain to a master or mate who has qualified for such a certificate and is thereby entitled to pilot his own vessel into a certain port. It is chiefly used by coasters and should not be confused with a pilot's license. Since 1906 this certificate has been granted only to British subjects.

PILOTAGE GROUND. The access to a bay, inlet, river, harbor, or port beginning at the exterior point where a pilot may take leave of an outward bound vessel and extending to the places fixed upon by law or usage for the anchorage or mooring of inward-bound vessels.

PILOTAGE RATES. The scales or tariff used for fixing the amount to be paid by a vessel as remuneration for the services of a pilot. Pilotage rates are usually established by municipal or port authorities in the case of a harbor and its approaches, by government or state authorities in the case of rivers, channels and other pilotage waters. The basis of assessment varies and is determined by the local port authority. It may be fixed according to draft, tonnage, type of vessel, distance sailed with the assistance of a pilot, and in some instances time of the year.

Fr: *Tarif de Pilotage;* Ger: *Lotsenrate.*

PILOTAGE WATERS. The areas where the navigational dangers are such as to necessitate the services of a pilot. Also called pilot's water. In a less restricted sense, pilot waters include coastal waters where a ship is navigated from headland to headland without the assistance of a pilot, and also channel navigation, that is, narrow channels, rivers, harbors, and their approaches, where the services of a pilot are indispensable.

Fr: *Zône de pilotage;* Ger: *Lotsenfahwasser; Lotsenstrecke; Lotsenrevier.*

PILOT BOAT.

See **Pilot Vessel.**

PILOT CHART. A track chart on Mercator's projection published by the U. S. Hydrographic Office, which gives in graphic form information relating to meteorology, hydrography, and navigation that will assist the mariner. The light curved lines which cross the chart are curves of magnetic variation.

The blue data consist essentially of a representation of the average conditions of wind and weather for the month *following* the date of issue. The small circles and arrows indicate graphically the probable percentage of calms, and the frequency and force of the prevailing winds. The length of the arrows is in proportion to the relative frequency of prevailing winds. The number of feathers indicates the force of the wind according to Beaufort's scale. The dotted blue lines show the percentage of days on which fogs were observed during that month for several years. The dashed blue lines show the limits of the trade winds.

The red data comprise information collected during the month *preceding* the date of issue of the chart. The latest reported position of derelicts and their drift are indicated by a dotted line. The heavy red lines show the paths of storms for the month which the chart relates.

Pilot charts are issued each month for the North Atlantic, Central American waters, North Pacific, and Indian Ocean. For the South Pacific, they are issued quarterly.

PILOT FLAG. Flag hoisted by a vessel when a pilot is required. The following flags are used for this purpose by international agreement:

a. Flag G of the International Code of Signals.

b. Signal P.T. of the International Code.

c. Ensign with white border flown at foremast truck.

Fr: *Pavillon de Pilote;* Ger: *Lotsenflagge.*

PILOT HOUSE. The enclosed space on the navigating bridge from which a ship is usually controlled when under way.

PILOTING (U. S.). The method of directing a vessel from place to place by soundings or by referring to visible landmarks such as lighthouses, beacons, buoys, prominent rocks, and cliffs.

Fr: *Navigation au bornage.*

PILOT JACK. A small flag consisting usually of the union of the ensign surrounded by a white rectangular border. It is displayed at the fore truck when in need of a pilot.

PILOT LADDER. Rope ladder in which each rung is made of a flat piece of wood pierced by four holes, two at each end, through which the four side ropes are rove. Strong cross seizings are put on just below the rung on each side bending the two side ropes together. Recently, such ladders have been made of chain, with steel rungs. Also called jack ladder.

Fr: *Echelle de Pilote;* Ger: *Lotsentreppe; Lotsenleiter.*

American Marine Standards Committee, Standard 25, *Pilot Ladder*, Washington, 1927.

PILOT RULES (U. S.). The rules supplementing the Inland Rules of the Road. They are established and published by the Board of Supervising Inspectors of Steam Vessels.

PILOT'S CRUISING GROUND. The area bordering a coast where pilots cruise, to be picked up by vessels bound to ports, inlets, harbors, rivers, or bays, into which a pilot is commissioned to take them.

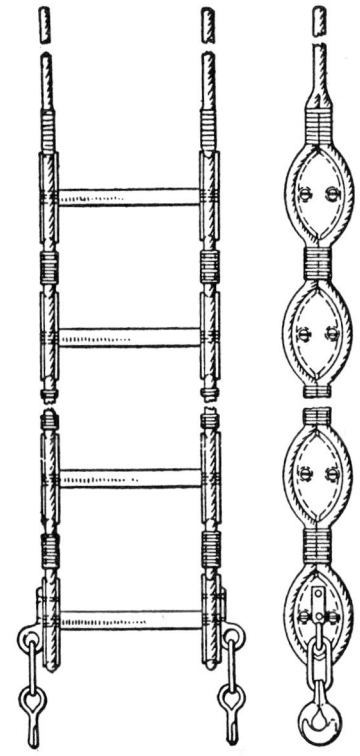

Pilot Ladder

PILOT SIGNALS. These include: (a) visual signals to summon a pilot; and (b) visual signals displayed by pilot vessels or by other vessels having a pilot on board.

(a) Signals to summon a pilot by day are the International Code flags P.T. or the International Code flag G. A white bordered ensign (Pilot Jack) hoisted at the fore truck is occasionally used in some countries. By night a blue pyrotechnic light burned every fifteen minutes or a white light flashed at frequent intervals is used, also the letters P.T. in Morse code.

(b) Signals exhibited by pilot vessels or by vessels having a pilot on board consisting by day of the International Code flag H (white and red divided vertically) or a white bordered ensign (Pilot Jack) at the main truck. In Great Britain a white and red flag divided horizontally is also used for the same purpose. By night a white all-round light is shown over a similar red light 8 ft. below and flare-up signals are displayed.

Fr: *Signal de Pilote;* Ger: *Lotsensignal.*
See **Pilot Flag.**

PILOT SKIFF. A fishing boat used in the mullet fisheries off the coast of the Carolinas, in the United States. The hull is round-bottomed with square or sharp stern and lap strake planking. A long oar is used for steering when going through the surf. Length 25 to 28 ft. Breadth 4 to 6 ft. Depth 20 in. (Average.)

PILOT'S LIEN. A maritime lien for services rendered by a pilot in piloting a vessel into a harbor.

Fr: *Privilège sur Droits de Pilotage;* Ger: *Pfandrecht des Lotsengeldes.*

PILOT'S LUFF.
See **Half Board.**

PILOT VESSEL. A steam, motor, or sailing vessel of small dimensions specially built and equipped for dropping or picking up pilots who serve the large deep-water vessels entering or leaving port. Also called pilot boat.

Fr: *Bateau-Pilote;* Ger: *Lotsenfahrzeug; Lotsenversetzschiff.*

It is only within recent years that mechanically propelled craft have replaced sailing craft as pilot boats. The latter were rigged as cutters or schooners and the lines of the hull were designed for speed as well as seaworthiness, their outward appearance being more like that of a yacht than a merchant vessel. The steam or motor propelled pilot boat as found nowadays, although of small dimensions, is expected to encounter heavy weather, and speed as well as seaworthiness are of importance in its design. Pilot vessels are permanently stationed in certain zones indicated in the sailing directions or pilots used by shipmasters.

PIN. The metal axle upon which the sheave of a block revolves. It is usually made of mild steel and of such size as to withstand a shearing stress at least equal to the breaking load of the rope.

Fr: *Essieu;* Ger: *Scheibennagel.*

See **Belaying Pin, Bitt Pin, Chock Pin, Drift Pin, Jack Pin, Marking Pin, Mesh Pin, Norman Pin, Shackle Pin, Shadow Pin, Slab Pin, Stay Pin, Tack Pin, Tholepin, Togglepin.**

PINASSE. A French name for a long, narrow boat with sharp stern, used for fishing on the southern shores of the Bay of Biscay. The stem rises after the fashion of a Venetian gondola and both ends are decked, the camber on the afterpart of the decks being more pronounced than that on the fore part. The hull is V-shaped with flat bottom. The shape of the hull may be described as being of the multi-chine form in cross section. The *pinasse* of Arcachon was in form and build an exact replica of the *tillole,* which it has replaced in the sardine fisheries on the coast between La Rochelle and Bayonne.

The length of these boats formerly varied from 23 to 40 ft. but the modern *pinasse* has been increased in length up to 50 ft. The floors are slightly rounded and a keel has been added. The deck has two large openings: the forward one is used for stowing four or five nested dories, which are launched when the boat is on the fishing grounds. Abaft the engine there is another opening used as a cockpit for the crew and helmsman.

The *pinasse* of today is supplied with a fairly high-powered motor as speed is essential for crossing the surf in heavy weather. Some of the boats are fitted with a universal joint in the shafting in order that when going over shoals the propeller may be raised.

A smaller variety of this type, known as *pinasse de Parc,* is used solely for working the oyster beds in the lagoons. There is no deck and it has a smaller motor.

PINCH. To sail a boat so close to the wind as to allow the sails to shiver.

PINK. 1. A term sometimes applied nowadays to the Dutch *hoogaars* when used for fishing.

2. In the Mediterranean: a three-mast lateen-rigged coaster.

Other types of pinks are now extinct.

PINK STERN (U. S.). A sharp stern in which the bulwarks were carried abaft the sternpost, finishing with a narrow raking transom. The underside of this false overhang was open so as not to hold water. This stern was typical of all New England pinky boats. It was used as a support for the main sheet horse as well as for a boom crutch and it protected the helmsman and the rudder.

PINKY. A New England type of fishing schooner which originated in Essex, Mass., about 1820. It was a development of the Chebacco Boat. Also called Pinkey or Pink. Length over-all 45 ft. Breadth 13 ft. 7 in. Depth 6 ft. 6 in. (Typical.)

The hull was full-bodied with bluff bows, knee stem and billethead, good rise of floors, sharp raking stern, with fine run and considerable keel drag. There was a pronounced sheer at the ends. The bulwarks aft rose abruptly and extended several feet beyond the sternpost, forming the so-called pinky stern, peculiar to this type. The deck extended from stem to stern. The forward deck from bows to main hatch was raised 4 to 6 in. higher than the deck aft of it and had a low deckhouse. The cuddy was in the bows. Some of the boats had a fish well. The rig was that of a two-masted baldhead fore-and-aft schooner with short bowsprit and one headsail. The foremast was stepped well forward. The tonnage was seldom over 30. The type is now extinct. Chapelle, H. I., *American Sailing Craft*, New York, 1936.

PINNACE. Large double-banked, square-sterned pulling and sailing boat formerly used as a tender to merchant and war vessels. The pinnace was smaller than the launch. Average dimensions: Length 24 ft. Breadth 6½ ft. Depth 2 ft. 8 in. Originally a small vessel propelled by sails and oars and usually schooner-rigged.

Fr: *Grand Canot;* Ger: *Pinasse; Grossboot.*

PINNACLE. A sharp pyramid or cone-shaped rock, under water or showing above it.

Fr: *Aiguille;* Ger: *Spitze.*

PIN RAIL. A rail placed at the side of a vessel for holding belaying pins.

Fr: *Ratelier;* Ger: *Nagelbank.*

PIN RIVETING. A process of riveting which uses, instead of a rivet with an initially formed head, a plain cylindrical piece of material, the two heads being formed simultaneously during the process of riveting. The cylindrical blank is heated once only and the riveting machine is so designed that it applies pressure uniformly at both ends. Its proponents claim that a lower pressure is required; that the rivet hole is filled with greater certainty, and that there is complete contact of both heads with the plate surfaces.

PINTLE. The heavy pins or bolts on the forward edge of the rudder frame, by which the rudder is hinged to the gudgeons of the stern- or rudderpost, around which it pivots. Also called rudder pintle.

Fr: *Aiguillot;* Ger: *Fingerling; Ruderhaken.*

See **Bottom Pintle, Fitted Pintle, Locking Pintle, Solid Pintle.**

PINTLE BEARING. A hemispherical steel disc fitted into the bottom gudgeon of a rudder frame to minimize the friction of the rudder about its axis. Also called rudder riser. It is used in connection with a rounded pintle.

Fr: *Grain de Gouvernail;* Ger: *Tragscheibe; Ruder Tragläger.*

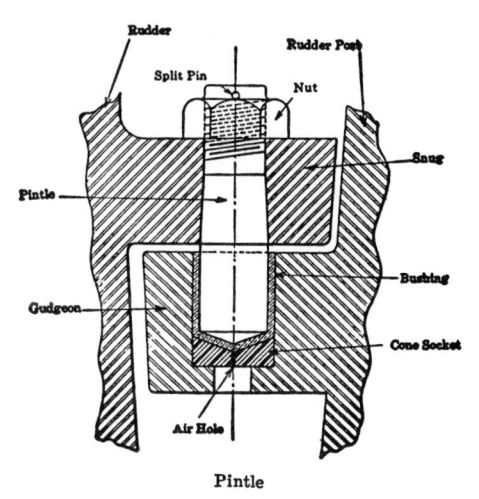

Pintle

PINTLE BOSS. See **Rudder Snug.**

PINTLE SCORE. One of the recesses under each pintle in a rudderstock which allow the rudder to be unshipped readily. Also called rudder score.

Fr: *Lanterne;* Ger: *Ruderhaken Ausschnitt.*

PINWHEELING (U. S.). Turning a multiple screw vessel within the smallest possible space by backing one propeller and going ahead with the other.

PIPE. A cask used in the wine and spirit trade. Its capacity varies according to contents—for Port wine, 115 (American) gallons; for Madeira, 92 gallons; for Marsala, 93 gallons; for Lisbon, 117 gallons; for Vidona, 100 gallons.

Fr: *Pipe;* Ger: *Pipe.*

PIPE BERTH. A berth made of wrought-iron, steel, or aluminum piping, generally of 1¼ in. diameter.

Ger: *Rohrkoje.*

American Marine Standards Committee, *Metal Frame Berths and Accessories for Ships,* Pamphlet 65, Washington, 1930.

PIPE CASING. Protective wooden casing fitted around air and sounding pipes in cargo spaces and coal bunkers. It is usually made of 2 inch white pine planks. Also called **Pipe boxing**.

Fr: *Boite de protection; Encaissement;* Ger: *Bohrschutzkaste.*

PIPE TUNNEL. A centerline tunnel extending forward of engine and boiler rooms between tank top and shell plating, in some vessels, in which bilge, ballast, and all other piping systems are housed.

Ger: *Kieltunnel; Rohrtunnel.*

PIRACY. Robbery, murder, or forcible depredation on the high seas, without lawful authority, in the spirit and intention of universal hostility. Piracy includes acts which, while differing very much in detail, have one thing in common: they are done without authority from any sovereign state and under conditions which make it unfair to hold any state responsible for their commission.

Fr: *Piraterie;* Ger: *Seeraub; Seeräuberei.* See **Pirate**.

"Piracy Laws of Various Countries," Research in International Law, Harvard Law School, Cambridge (Mass.), 1932.

PIRAGUA. A dugout paddling canoe used by the Caribs of British Guiana. The hollowed-out hull has its sides spread apart by seven crosspieces resting upon and lashed to the gunwales. The ends are formed by separate V-shaped sections fitted to the central part and pitched to make the seams tight. The endpieces extend some distance above the gunwales. Length 18 ft. 10 in. Breadth 3 ft. 8 in. Depth 18 in. (Typical.)

PIRATE. A name given to marauders plundering indiscriminately for personal ends. In marine insurance it includes passengers who mutiny and rioters who attack the ship from the shore. The practice of nations gives to everyone the right to pursue and exterminate pirates without previous declaration of war, but those who surrender or are taken prisoners must be brought before the proper tribunal and dealt with according to law.

Fr: *Pirate;* Ger: *Seeräuber.*

See **Piracy**.

PIROGUE. An open, flat-bottom keelless dugout canoe in Louisiana, U. S., made of a single cypress log and used for fishing in the rivers and bayous. It has round and flaring sides, sharp hollow bow, and V-shaped stern without overhang, four thwarts and a seat at each end. Oars are employed for propulsion. Length 17 ft. 8 in. Breadth 30 in. Depth 11½ in. (Typical.)

PIRATE SHIP. A ship devoted by the persons in dominant control to the purpose of committing acts of piracy or to the purpose of committing any similar act within the territory of a state by descent from the high sea, provided that the purposes of the persons in dominant control are not definitely limited to committing such acts against ships or territory subject to the jurisdiction of the state to which the ships belong. A ship may retain its national character although it has become a pirate ship. The retention or loss of national character is determined by the law of the state from which it was derived.

Fr: *Pirate;* Ger: *Piratenschiff; Seeräuberschiff.*

PITCH. 1. A term applied to the distance a propeller will advance during one revolution when revolving in any unyielding medium. The average value of the pitch is from 1.2 to 1.4 of the propeller diameter. It is proportionate to the power of the engines and speed of the vessel. In ordinary propeller design, pitch is uniform. In some special types varying pitches are adopted.

Fr: *Pas;* Ger: *Schraubensteigung; Steigung.*

See **Axially Increasing Pitch, Increasing Pitch, Nominal Pitch, Radially Increasing Pitch, Uniform Pitch, Variable Pitch.**

2. A permanent waterproof homogeneous substance used for filling the seams of wooden decks to aid the calking in keeping them watertight under all conditions of service.

Pitch should be of such consistency that it will not become brittle enough to crack in the seams through contraction at low temperature (0° F.) in cold climates, or soften to the point of becoming sticky under high temperature (125° F.) in tropical climates. When properly paid into clean, dry calked seams it sets in a homogeneous mass with a uniform texture, of jet black color and glossy finish. There are two grades of glue for use on shipboard. Grade A is composed of selected natural or residual bitumens blended with appropriate vegetable pitches, and contains no coal tar. Grade B is basically similar in character to Grade A but includes coal tar in proportion not exceeding 50 per cent.

Fr: *Brai;* Ger: *Pech.*

See **Bastard Pitch, Marine Glue**.

3. The spacing measured from center to center between two rivets in the same row. It should not be confused with the distance of rivets. For watertight work the pitch varies from 3½ to 5 diameters, for oiltight work 3½ to 4, for nonwatertight work 6 to 8 diameters.

Fr: *Ecartement;* Ger: *Abstand; Nietenentfernung.*

PITCH (to). To plunge with alternate fall and rise of bow and stern, as when a ship passes over waves. To oscillate about a transverse horizontal axis through the waist of the ship.

Fr: *Tanguer;* Ger: *Stampfen.*

PITCH (G. B.). The area on a quay or pier on which the slings or drafts of goods are made up when loading, or landed when discharging.

PITCHING. The angular motion which a ship makes about a transverse axis through her center of gravity in a seaway. The laws governing pitching are identical with those for rolling, but there are important numerical differences, the principal of which are due to the fact that the longitudinal stability is very large and the period consequently short, and that the resistance to pitching is relatively great.

Fr: *Tanguage;* Ger: *Stampfbewegung.*

To keep decks dry it is important that the ship should pitch with the wave instead of remaining level and thus shipping water. In a large number of vessels the period of pitching is about one-half of that for rolling, but the maximum angles are considerably less.

PITCH MOP. A kind of brush with which melted pitch or any other substance is laid on the outside of the ship's hull.

Fr: *Guipon;* Ger: *Pechquast.*

PITCHPOLE. Said of a boat which, through the force of a breaking sea, is turned over stern over bow, or vice versa, in a sort of half somersault motion.

PITCHPOT. A large iron pot used for heating pitch before paying the seams of a wooden deck. Also called pitch kettle.

Fr: *Marmite à Brai;* Ger: *Pechtopf; Pechgrapen.*

PITCH RATIO. The ratio of propeller pitch to diameter. It varies in general practice from 1.1 to 1.6. Froude's curves for propeller design indicated that the highest efficiency is obtained from screws having pitch ratios of about 1.5.

Fr: *Pas Relatif;* Ger: *Steigungsverhältnis.*

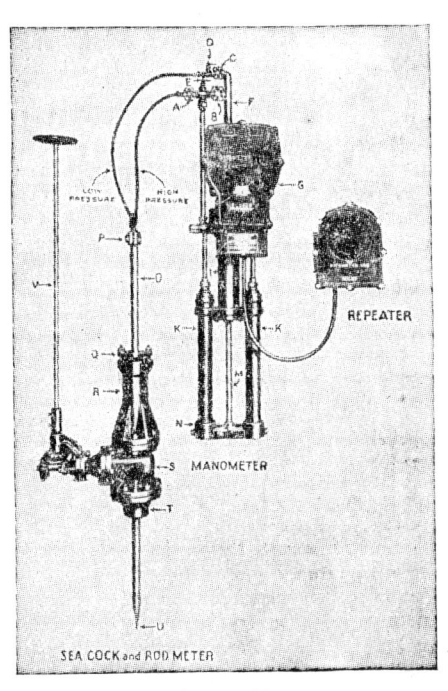

Pitometer Log

PITOMETER LOG. A type of mechanical ship's log indicating the speed of a ship through the water and registering the distance traveled. The indications are a measure of differential water pressures acting on a pitot tube projecting into the water through the bottom of the ship.

Fr: *Loch à Tube Pitot;* Ger: *Pitot Rohr Log.*

Two types are used: the mercury balance type, and the rotary balance type. In the former, the sea valve is riveted or welded to the skin of the ship near the center line, close to the bow. The pilot tube, or rod meter, projects through the valve into water undisturbed by the ship's motion. The flat tip of the rod contains a dynamic orifice in the leading edge, and two static orifices, one on each side of the tip. The dynamic orifice receives the pressure due to the ship's velocity, as well as that due to the static head of water above the tip. The static orifices receive only pressure due to the static head. The two pressures are transmitted up the rod to the two legs of a differential mercury manometer mounted within the ship, below the water line. The difference between the two pressures is indicated on the manometer, and corresponds to the speed of the ship. A float on the surface of the mercury in one leg of the manometer rotates a dial as it moves up or down, indicating speed in knots. Distance run is registered on a counter by means of a mechanical integrator operating in conjunction with a cam attached to the speed dial. Speed and distance indications are both reproduced electrically in different parts of the ship by means of repeaters.

Sanborn, F. B., "The Pitot Tube as a Marine Speedometer and Its Development," *Engineering News* (London), May 4, 1911; "The Pitometer Log," *Marine Engineering and Shipping Age*, vol. 33 (April, 1928); "The Pitometer Log," *Motorship* (New York), vol. 18 (Nov., 1933).

PITTING. A type of electrolytic corrosion characterized by little cavities formed on the surface of iron and steel plates, propeller blades, and so on. It is attributed to the presence of small isolated particles of mill scale or other impurities which, by setting up electrolytic action in the immediate vicinity, gradually causes deeper and deeper wastage of the part so affected. Pitting of shell plating is most frequently found between light and load waterlines, and near the propellers.

Fr: *Piqûre;* Ger: *Lochfrass.*

PITWOODCON. The code name for British Chamber of Shipping Pitwood Charter from France to Bristol Channel Ports applicable since 1924.

PIVOTING. An incident which occurs at the launch of a vessel. It is due to the difference in supporting forces of the fore and after extremities of the ship when leaving the ends of the standing ways. When, owing to its buoyancy, the stern lifts before the center of gravity of the whole structure is beyond the ends of the ways and the hull pivots about the fore poppets, the equilibrium draft is not reached. As the forefoot leaves the standing ways, the fore end of the ship drops down heavily into the water. Also called lifting, dipping.

Fr: *Salut;* Ger: *Dumpen.*

PIVOTING POINT. The point of contact between the turning circle and the middle line of a ship. It is situated forward of midships, the distance being greatest in ships having the least resistance to lateral drift. The position of the pivoting point varies in different ships and also at different points of the turn. It depends upon the underwater form of hull and especially upon the comparative draft forward and aft, and also upon the distribution of weights. In most ships it may be taken as one-sixth to one-third of the ship's length from the stem.

Fr: *Point Giratoire;* Ger: *Drehachse; Drehpunkt.*

PIXPINUS. Code name for the British Chamber of Shipping Pitchpine Wood Charter, 1906.

PLACE. The point on the celestial sphere to which a heavenly body is referred by the observer.

Fr: *Lieu;* Ger: *Ort.*

See **Apparent Place, True Place.**

PLACERY BOOM. A boom used in square-rigged vessels. Also called passaree boom. It is from 30 to 40 ft. long, and projects like an outrigger forward of the fore-rigging, at right angles from the ship's side. It is held by a wire topping lift which runs from the foremast to the end of the boom. It has two guys fore and aft to keep it steady. The placery boom was formerly used to haul out the clew of the foresail when sailing before the wind with lower studding sail set.

PLAGUE.

See **Bubonic Plague.**

PLAIN-LAID ROPE. Rope in which the yarns are spun from right to left, making the rope yarn right-handed. Called also right-handed rope, hawser-laid rope. The strand formed by a combination of such yarns becomes left-handed; and three strands twisted together form a right-handed or plain-laid rope.

Fr: *Cordage Commis à Droite;* Ger: *Rechtsgeschlagenes Tauwerk.*

See **Hawser-laid Rope.**

PLAIN SAIL. The sails normally carried by a vessel in ordinary weather. They are supplemented by light sails in fine weather and replaced in heavy weather by storm sails.

Fr: *Voiles Majeures;* Ger: *Hauptsegeln; Ziehende Segeln.*

See **Working Sails.**

PLAIN SCARF. A scarf made by cutting a taper on each of the pieces to be joined, without leaving a nib or lip at the end.

Fr: *Ecart Simple;* Ger: *Glattenlaschung.*

PLAIN WHIPPING. A whipping tied by laying a loop along the rope and then making a series of turns over it. The working end is stuck through this loop and the standing end hauled back out of sight.

PLANE SAILING. The art of navigating a ship upon principles deduced from the supposition of the earth being an extended plane. On this premise, the meridians are considered as being parallel, the parallels of latitude at right angles to the meridians and the length of a degree on the meridians, and the equator and parallels of latitude everywhere equal.

Fr: *Navigation loxodromique;* Ger: *Plansegeln.*

PLANET. Nonluminous heavenly bodies, seen only by reflected sunlight, which are satellites of the sun and are continually changing position with respect to the fixed stars. Planets may be distinguished from stars by the fact that they do not t̶ ̶ ̶le, and also because they appear in su ̶ntly powerful telescopes as finite discs instead of points of light.

The known major planets are nine in number: their names in order of increasing distance from the sun are: Mercury, Venus, Earth, Mars, Jupiter, Saturn, Uranus, Neptune, Pluto. The planets which are nearer than Earth to the sun are known as "inferior planets," the others as "superior planets." Mercury and Venus are inferior planets, the remainder are superior planets.

The only planets of use to the navigator are Venus, Mars, Jupiter and Saturn and are known as the *navigational planets.*

Those planets which are nearer the sun than is the earth are called *inner planets* or *inferior planets;* and those that are farther from the sun than is the earth are called *outer planets* or *superior planets.*

PLANETARY HOIST. A chain hoist with an epicyclic train of gears in the upper block. Used by the engine room force for lifting heavy machinery parts, also for dry dock repairs and overhauling. Also called differential hoist.

Fr: *Palan Différentiel;* Ger: *Differentialflaschenzug.*

PLANK. A long narrow piece of sawed timber fastened on the outside or inside of frames, beams, and so on. A board when over 1½ in. thick is usually called a plank. A piece of sawed timber from 2 to 6 in. in thickness and 11 in. or more in width. In the United States all timber of square section from 1½ to 8 in. in thickness is called plank.

Fr: *Bordage;* Ger: *Schiffsplanke; Planke.*

PLANKAGE. A charge on vessels in dock for the use of planks for loading or unloading.

Ger: *Bohlwerksgelder.*

PLANKER (U. S.). A shipyard worker engaged in the construction of wooden ships. After the frame of the vessel has been erected and the dubbers have smoothed the timbers, the plankers "stitch" the planks on the framing by boring, driving and wedging treenails, and later fasten the planks with spikes. They also lay the decks, fastening them with bolts, drifts or screws. Also called ceiler.

PLANK FLOOR. A term used in wooden shipbuilding to denote sawed floors made from straight grained timber as distinguished from those made from crooked timber.

PLANKING. A general term for the wooden covering of the frames externally or internally and the covering of the beams.

Fr: *Bordé;* Ger: *Beplankung.*

See Anchor Stock Planking, Bottom Planking, Carvel Planking, Clinker Planking, Cross Planking, Deck Planking, Diagonal Planking, Diagonal and Longitudinal Planking, Double Fore-and-Aft Planking, Garboard Planking, Herringbone Planking, Outside Planking, Ribband Carvel Planking, Sewed Planking, Spline Planking, Strip Planking, Swept Planking, Tapered Planking, Top and Butt Planking, Treble Planking.

PLANK KEEL. A type of keel used in small fishing and pleasure craft where the hull form is such that the garboard planks stand almost vertical at midship section. It is composed of an inside and outside keel plank, the latter being broader than the inner keel to receive the raw edges of the garboard strake.

PLANK SHEER. In wooden shipbuilding, a horizontal fore-and-aft-timber which forms the outer limit of the upper deck at the sides. Also called covering board, washboard. It is fitted in short lengths with butts scarfed and edge-fastened, and is bolted to the deck beams and sheer strake. The bulwark stanchions cut through the plank sheer.

Fr: *Plat-bord;* Ger: *Schandeckel.*

PLANKTON. Collective name for the animal and vegetable life floating or drifting at various depths in large bodies of water.

Fr: *Plankton;* Ger: *Plankton.*

PLANKTON NET. Conical-shaped net with fine mesh used to capture eggs or fish in larval stage as well as other small aquatic or marine organisms.

PLANK STAGE. A stage suspended by rope lanyards at each end and used to support men when working on the ship's side, superstructures of funnels. The ropes are secured to a small cross-piece of wood called a "horn" which projects from the stage and keeps it at a convenient distance from the ship's side.

PLAN POSITION INDICATOR. The display unit of a marine radar set which presents to the observer a picture of the area around the ship, showing all objects on the surface of the sea in their correct position in range and azimuth.

PLAT. Braided foxes formerly used to serve hemp cables in the hawsepipes.

PLAT (to). To braid; used in dealing with smallstuff.

PLATE. See **Goguet.**

PLATEAU. A wide elevation of the ocean bottom rising steeply on all sides from a depression.

Fr: *Plateau;* Ger: *Plateau.*

PLATE CLAMPS. A contrivance used by longshoremen for lifting steel plates. It consists of 2 hook-shaped clamps attached to a length of chain. Each clamp is fitted with an adjustable jaw which closes when the sling takes the strain. Also called **Plate Hooks.**

Ger: *Plattenklemme.*

PLATE COLLAR. Small piece of plating used for closing the notch made in a deck or a watertight bulkhead where a frame or a longitudinal passes through. When the notch is open at both the heel and toe sides of the continuous bar, a two piece collar is fitted. All plate collars are welded.

PLATE DOOR. A steel door consisting of a plate secured by bolts to a bulkhead. Also called **Detachable plate.**

Fr: *Porte montée sur boulons;* Ger: *Plattentür.*

PLATE EDGE PLANER. A machine used in shipyards for planing the edges of steel plates. It is so designed that the cutter moves against the work, the plate being held by clamps.

Fr: *Raboteuse;* Ger: *Blechkantenhobelmaschine.*

PLATE ERECTOR (U. S.). One who erects, sets, fits, and fairs in position the plates and sections which form the hull of the vessel. Also called bolter-up, plater (G. B.). Those engaged upon the plating for the interior of the vessels, such as bunkers, bulkheads, and so on, are called inside platers. Those engaged upon the outside plating are called shell platers or outside platers. Men engaged on light work are known as light platers and receive smaller salary than heavy platers.

Fr: *Charpentier en Fer;* Ger: *Plattierer.* See **Marking-off Plater.**

PLATE HANGER. A shipyard worker who places the plates on the frames in their proper position, bringing the rivet holes in line so that the bolter-up will have less difficulty in placing his bolts and tightening them up.

PLATED MAST. A hollow metal cylinder made of riveted or welded plating, usually strengthened inside by longitudinal angle bars. Also called metal mast. Solid-drawn tubes have also been used as masts. There is a tendency to dispense with angle-bar stiffeners, compensation being attained by increasing the thickness of plates. The diameter of a mast, thickness of plating, butt-straps, riveting, and so on, should conform to the cognizant classification society's requirements.

Welded masts and derrick posts are constructed with two plates in the round, the circumferential butts being shifted clear of each other. The edges of the plates are double-beveled as for large pillars. In place of the full inside and outside doublings usually fitted in riveted construction, flats or narrow thick doublings are fitted inside, these being welded with a light continuous fillet on each edge. The outriggers and other fittings are welded direct to the mast.

Fr: *Mât en tôles;* Ger: *Plattenmast.*

PLATER'S SQUAD. A shipyard squad consisting of three or four platers, one marker boy, and a variable number of helpers. They erect, set, and fit the plates and sections for the riveters.

Fr: *Equipe de Charpentiers en Fer;* Ger: *Plattierergang.*

PLATE SHOP. A shipyard shop where various machine tools for cutting, punching, shearing, planing and otherwise preparing the various parts of the hull that have been marked in the lay-out shed. All work is done cold. Also called **Structural Shop.**

Fr: *Nef d'usinage des tôles;* Ger: *Blechbearbeitungswerkstatt.*

PLATER'S WEDGE. A steel wedge about ¾ inch thick used by shipfitters and platers when erecting the various structural parts of the hull preparatory to riveting or welding.

PLATEWOOD. Code name for American Charter Party used for shipments of resawed lumber from Canada or the United States to River Plate ports.

PLATFORM. A portable flooring made of checkered steel plating, standing at a height of 1 to 3 ft. above the tank top and supported by frame work. It is used in stokeholds and engine rooms. The plates are made of small size so that they may be readily lifted for access to the piping and bilges lying below.

Fr: *Parquet;* Ger: *Plattform.*

See **Compass Platform, Grating Platform, Leadsman Platform, Tunnel Platform, Winch Platform.**

PLATFORM DECK. A partial deck built in the hold of a ship below the lowest complete deck, usually without camber. Sometimes called platform. Where more than one is installed they are termed first, second, and so on, from the top.

Fr: *Plateforme de Cale;* Ger: *Plattformdeck.*

PLATFORM SLING. A wooden platform with rope or wire bridles fastened to the corners or sides, through which the cargo hook is passed. Also called airplane sling, board sling, tray. To prevent crushing of boxes or containers by the bridles wooden spreaders are provided to keep the two parts of each bridle apart. In some slings of this type two pieces of angle iron with rings through which the parts of the bridles can pass are attached to each bridle. When the sling is loaded the angle irons are placed on the upper corners of the containers on the top of the draft. They hold the packages firmly in place and distribute the pressure of the bridles over a large surface. Platform slings are used for handling case goods such as lard, crated or boxed fruit, milk cases, also small heavy units such as copper pencils, billets, and so on.

Fr: *Plateau à Caissage;* Ger: *Trog.*

American Marine Standards Committee, Standard 83, *Platform Slings for Cargo Handling* (specifications), Washington, 1932.

PLATING MODEL. A shipbuilder's half block model prepared from the sheer plan, usually to a scale of ¼ in. to the foot for large vessels or to a larger scale for small ones. The position of frames, the edges and butts of shell plates, the location of decks and generally all features which influence the arrangement of shell plates are laid off on its surface. It is usually made at an early stage of the design so that the necessary dimensional data can be lifted for ordering the plates from the steel mills.

Bisset, G. A., *Models and Their Lining Off, Marine Engineering,* vol. 25, New York, 1920.

PLATTE. A name given on the coast of Normandy to a small fishing boat with round or pointed stern, used for shrimping or inshore trawling. It is generally rigged with two masts and lugsails, a reefing bowsprit, and one headsail. The mainsail is boomed. Length over-all 32 ft. 4 in. Length at keel 25 ft. 5 in. Breadth 10 ft. 4 in. Depth 4.2 ft. (Typical.)

PLEDGET. A roll of oakum used for calking the seams of planks.

Fr: *Quenouillon;* Ger: *Wergzopf.*

PLIMSOLL LINE (G. B.). A term which refers to the freeboard mark painted on the ship's sides. So called from Samuel Plimsoll who was the promoter of three merchant shipping acts passed by British parliament in 1874–75–76, which brought the freeboard question to a definite solution. Also called Plimsoll mark.

See **Load Water Line.**

PLOTTER. See **Protractor.**

PLOTTING. Laying down on a chart the position of the vessel, or of a place or of the ship's course.

PLOW STEEL ROPE. A wire rope made of open-hearth high carbon steel with a tensile strength ranging from 200,000 to 260,000 pounds per square inch sectional area. It combines lightness with great strength. Improved plow steel rope has about 15 per cent more tensile strength than the ordinary plow steel rope. It has the greatest tensile strength of all steel wire used in the production of rope.

See **Wire Rope.**

PLUG. 1. A cylindrical piece of wood set over the head of a deck bolt and cut flush with the surface of the deck. Also called bung. Similar plugs are used in wooden vessels over the fastenings of the outside planking, the depth of the plug being about two-thirds its diameter.

2. A wooden pin fitted into a plughole

in the bottom of a ship's boat, for the purpose of draining water from the boat when it is hoisted out and stowed.

Fr: *Tampon;* Ger: *Holzpfropf.*

See Ball Plug, Docking Plug, Side-Light Plug, Ullage Plug.

PLUG HATCH. A thick airtight hatch with tapered edges lined with insulating material, fitted over a refrigerator hold to prevent the escape of cold air. Does not carry the cargo weight in the 'tween decks or tarpaulins on weather decks, these being carried by ordinary superimposed wooden hatch covers. Also called insulated hatch cover.

Ger: *Isolierlukendeckel.*

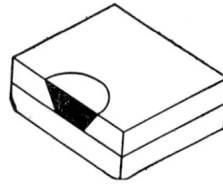

Plug Weld

PLUG WELD. A weld used in joining two members face to face as in a lap joint. A circular hole is punched or drilled in one of the parts and the hole thus formed is filled with weld metal, which fuses into both plates. When the hole extends through both plates it is spoken of as a "rivet weld."

Fr: *Soudure en Bouchon;* Ger: *Lochnaht; Schlitznaht.*

PLUIT. A Dutch flat-bottomed sailing boat with well, employed in the eel fisheries of the Zuiderzee. The hull is clinker-built, and is similar to that of the *schokker.* The boat is rigged with a pole mast and mainsail with curved gaff. Two headsails are carried. Displacement 9 to 12 tons.

PLUMBING. An operation performed during the construction of a vessel by which the frames are hoisted into their respective positions and given the proper rake or angle of inclination to bring them into a plane perpendicular to that of the keel.

Fr: *Balancement;* Ger: *Lotung.*

PLUMMER BLOCK. One of the bearings supporting the tunnel shafting. They are usually provided with a water cooling system. Also called Line shaft bearing, Pillow Block, Spring bearing, Tunnel shaft bearing.

Fr: *Palier d'arbre;* Ger: *Lauflager; Tunnelwellenlager.*

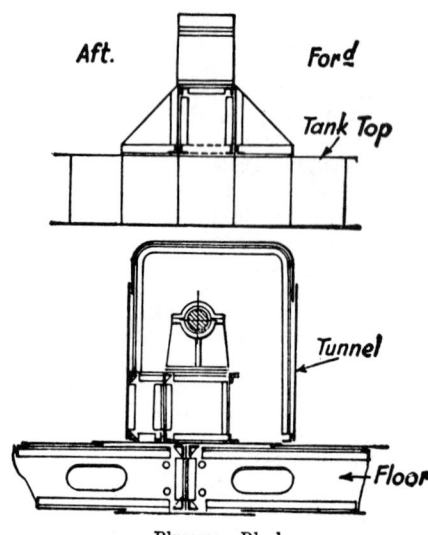

Plummer Block

PLUM PUDDING. Term used by American whalemen to denote a muscular, fibrous substance which permeates the tongue of the humpback and sperm whales.

PLUNGER. Name given to various sailing craft employed in the Pacific coast oyster fisheries for transportation between the oyster stations or to carry oysters to market. Also called oyster sloop. Most of them are built with flush deck and a large central cockpit divided by a centerboard. The larger type is keel-built with low cabin trunk. All are cat-rigged.

PLY. 1. To make regular voyages between certain ports.

Ger: *Regelmässige Fähren.*

2. To work to windward. Also called beat.

Fr: *Louvoyer;* Ger: *Lavieren.*

PLYING HAMMER. A type of hand-riveting hammer.

PLYMOUTH HOOKER. A cutter-rigged hook-and-line fishing boat from the south coast of England. The hull is square-sterned, decked forward with large waterways and a large open well. The pole mast is stepped nearly in the middle and has a slight forward rake. The mainsail has no boom and the afterleech is almost vertical. The larger boats of this type use long lines and are called boulter boats. The smaller ones using hand lines are called whiting boats. Length 30 to 32 ft. Breadth 8 to 9 ft.

PLYWOOD. A material made by gluing together, under pressure, three or four thin sheets of wood so arranged that the grain of alternate layers run in opposite directions. Wood so prepared is light and strong and does not twist to any appreciable extent. It is used in shipbuilding for cabin partitions, door and ceiling panels, and hollow spars. Asbestos plywood and metal-faced plywood are used for fire-resisting bulkheads in passenger accommodations. In the construction of small boats it is an excellent material for decks, cabin roofs, deck houses and, with some limitations, for outside planking.

Fr: *Contreplaqué;* Ger: *Sperrholz.*

PNEUMATIC HOLDER-ON. A tool used in connection with a pneumatic riveting hammer by the rivet holder. It consists of a cylinder carrying a piston behind which air is admitted. The rod extends through the front head and is cupped out to go over the rivethead. It replaces the holding-up hammer used in hand-riveting.

Fr: *Tas Pneumatique;* Ger: *Pressluft Behälter.*

PNEUMATIC RIVETING. A process by which rivets are closed up by a pneumatic hammer which delivers a succession of rapid blows on the point, under a pressure of about 100 lb. per square inch. Pneumatic hammers are capable of dealing with rivets up to 1¼ in. diameter.

Fr: *Rivetage Pneumatique;* Ger: *Pneumatische Nietung; Pressluftnietung.*

PNEUMATIC STEERING GEAR. A steering gear, not now in general use, in which an auxiliary engine and air compressor are installed in a suitable position near the tiller, the action of the gear being controlled from the bridge. The disadvantage of this system is its low efficiency and the difficulty in preventing the expanding air and moisture from depositing ice in the pipes in cold weather.

Fr: *Appareil à gouverner à Air comprimé;* Ger: *Pressluft Rudermaschine.*

PNEUMERCATOR. A type of remote-indicating gauge which shows the amount of liquid in a tank. It consists of a balance chamber, a mercury gauge, a control valve, piping connecting the units, and a supply of compressed air. The column of mercury is balanced against the pressure in the balance chamber, which in turn is dependent upon the height of the liquid in the tank. Of late, some U. S. vessels have adopted electric tank-level indicators in place of pneumercators.

POCKET. 1. One of the spaces at the side of a 'tween deck between frames and stringer bar. These spaces are often filled with cement.

Fr: *Accotar;* Ger: *Aufklotzung.*

2. The space between a boiler casing and the ship's side under deck. Generally used as a bunker.

Ger: *Taschenbunker.*

3. The lacing together of top and bottom sides in a trawlnet between the batings and the belly, which prevent the fish from escaping once it has passed beyond the flapper.

Fr: *Bourse; Poche;* Ger: *Tasche.*

4. Cargo term applied in Far Eastern ports to a small bag about half the size of an ordinary bag, containing such articles as hops, myrabolans, and so on. It is often carried at reduced rate and used as broken stowage.

POCKET BUNKER. A ready service bunker of small dimensions.

Ger: *Taschenbunker.*

POCKET PIECE. One of the two fore-and-aft timbers which form the lower limit of a centerboard trunk when the keel is cut off at each end of the slot. The pocket pieces are scarfed to the sides of the keel forward and abaft the headledges.

POD. A group of whales.

PODYESNAYA. A decked fish carrier used in the seine fisheries of the Caspian Sea, with moderately sharp bow and stern, narrow floor, round bilge, and flaring sides. The narrow V-shaped stern extends nearly down to the waterline, where it joins the sternpost, which, as in all Astrakhan vessels, has a very strong rake. With the exception of the helmsman's cockpit at the stern, the vessel is decked from end to end and has a strong sheer. The upper part of the stem is also V-shaped, but is much narrower than the stern. The size of these vessels ranges from 20 to 65 tons. Length over-all 41 ft. Breadth 14 ft. Depth of hold 4½ ft. (Typical.)

The rig consists of 3 masts with lugsails. The short foremast is stepped in a fore-and-aft timber that runs from the stemhead to a beam a few feet farther aft, and is supported on each side by a shroud set up by a tackle. The mainmast is a little more than one-third the boat's length from the stem, and the mizzenmast is just forward of the cockpit.

POGGE.
See **Mutte.**

POINT. 1. A comparatively low and sharp promontory. A narrow piece of land extending into a body of water.
Fr: *Pointe;* Ger: *Landspitze.*

2. Also *compass point.* One of the thirty-two divisions of the compass card. There are in each point 11° 15'. The point is subdivided into half points, each of 5° 37' 30", and quarter points, each of 2° 48' 45". Midway between each cardinal and intercardinal point is a point with a name formed by combining that of the cardinal and intercardinal point, the former being placed first; as for example north-northeast, east-northeast, and so forth. Midway between the points already indicated are points bearing the name of the nearest cardinal or intercardinal point followed by the word "by" and the name of the cardinal point in the direction in which it lies, as for instance north by east, northeast by north, and so on.
Fr: *Quart; Rhumb;* Ger: *Kompasstrich.*
See **Amphidromic Point, Cardinal Point, Dew Point, Fire Point, Intercardinal Point, Equinoctial Points, First Point of Aries, First Point of Libra, Lubber Point, Pivoting Point, Quarter Point, Reef Point, Rivet Point, Solstitial Points, Stepping Point.**

POINT (to). 1. To taper a rope at the end for neatness or for convenience in reeving through a block.
Ger: *Ausschrapen.*

2. A vessel under sail is said to "point high" when it lays a course very close to the wind.
Ger: *Kneifen; Aufkneifen.*

POINTED ROPE. To point a rope means to unlay the ends of the strands, thin out a portion of them, and by twisting the outside yarns into nettles weave a sort of mat around the conical portion so that it may easily go through a hole.
Fr: *Queue de Rat;* Ger: *Gespitztes Tauende.*

POINTER. A timber fitted diagonally in the fore end or afterend of a ship's framing extending from a deck to the keelson or deadwood. Owing to the difficulty which attends the conversion of timber into pointers and breasthooks, the latter are generally made of iron.
Fr: *Guirlande;* Ger: *Schlagholz; Schräges Piekknie.*
See **Bow Pointer, Stern Pointer, Station Pointer.**

POINTING. Finishing off the end of a rope into a stiff cone-shaped point in order to prevent it from fagging out.
Fr: *Queue de Rat;* Ger: *Hundepunt.*

POINT OF DEPARTURE. When starting on a voyage, a fix secured by taking bearings on established landmarks or aids to navigation. Also called departure.
Fr: *Point de Partance;* Ger: *Abfahrtsort, Abfahrtspunkt.*

POINT OF DESTINATION. The point or position at which the reckoning of a voyage, for navigational purposes, ends.
Fr: *Point d'Arrivée;* Ger: *Bestimmungsort.*

POINT OF MAXIMUM SEPARATION. The point of a great circle track that is farthest from the rhumb track. At this point the courses on both tracks are parallel with each other.

POINTS OF SAILING. Sailing points may be defined as the different courses followed by any craft under sail when compared to the direction of the wind. They are named according to the angle between the direction of the wind, and the fore-and-aft line of the vessel. When this angle is near 180 degrees the ship is said to be sailing with the wind aft. When it is about 135 degrees it is sailing with the wind on the quarter, or quartering; when about 90 degrees it is running free. When the angle is between 60 and 30 degrees, the ship is said to be close-hauled, on the wind or by the wind.
Fr: *Allures;* Ger: *Segelstellung.*

POINTU. The names *pointu* and *rafiau* are given locally in the district of **Toulon** to small boats with sharp stern used by fishermen and boatmen around the harbor and roadstead. Their length varies from 15 to 21 ft. They are open or half-decked. The stem has a slight tumble home and rises about 20 to 24 in. above the gunwale. The sternpost is upright. These boats are rigged with a lateen with two rows of reef points and occasionally a small jib. They are as a rule single-handed.

POLACCA. 1. A two- or three-masted Mediterranean vessel. Sometimes called *polacra*. The Spanish and Venetian vessels are brigantine-rigged. The Italian *polacca* is bark-rigged. In the seventeenth and eighteenth centuries the word "polacca" was used to denote a type of vessel; in the nineteenth century and after, mostly a type of rig.
2. A three-cornered headsail of lateen-rigged fishing boats in the Mediterranean. Also called *polaccone*.

POLACRE RIG. A square rig of the eastern Mediterranean in which the lower mast, topmast, and topgallant mast are made of a single spar. The upper yards are lowered right down to the lower yard for furling.

Fr: *Gréement de Polacre;* Ger: *Polacker Takelung.*

There is only one stay from the lower masthead and another from the pole of the upper mast. When the sails are stowed all the yards are close together. There are no footropes on the upper yards. The men stand on the topsail yard to loose and furl the topgallant sails and on the lower yard to loose, reef, or furl the topsail, all yards being lowered sufficiently for that purpose. There is a short bowsprit.

The *bombarda* and Mediterranean brig are occasionally rigged in this fashion, but the type most commonly met with is the brigantine. The rig is also found in Dalmatia, Greece and Turkey, but under a different name in each country.

POLAR ALTITUDE. The arc of meridian intercepted between the pole and the horizon. It is equal to the latitude of the place.

Fr: *Hauteur Polaire;* Ger: *Polhöhe.*

POLAR CHART. A great-circle chart whose point of tangency is one of the poles of the earth.

POLAR CIRCLE. Arctic or Antarctic circle in latitude 66°30′ North or South.

Fr: *Cercle Polaire;* Ger: *Polarkreis.*

POLAR DISTANCE. The arc of the circle of declination intercepted between a celestial object and the pole.

Fr: *Distance Polaire;* Ger: *Poldistanz.*

POLAR FRONT. The surface of discontinuity separating an air mass of polar origin from one of tropical origin.

Fr: *Front Polaire;* Ger: *Polar Front.*

POLAR ICE. Heavy floes of 10 ft. or more in thickness and of considerable age.

Fr: *Glace Polaire;* Ger: *Polareis.*

POLAR PROJECTION. A map projection in which the earth's pole is taken as the center of projection.

Fr: *Projection Polaire;* Ger: *Polar Projektion.*

POLE. The upper end of a mast or of the highest mast which rises above the rigging and terminates with the truck. The part of a mast above the shoulders on which the eyes of the topmast rigging rest. In spar making the term pole refers generally to pieces having five inches diameter or less.

Fr: *Flèche; Fusée;* Ger: *Flaggenpol; Flaggentopp; Stange; Mastspitze.*

POLE COMPASS. A compass elevated above the deck on the top of a pole, so as to be beyond the influence of the ship's magnetism. Also called elevated compass. Access to it was had by means of a short ladder. (Obsolete.)

Fr: *Compas à Pible;* Ger: *Pfahlkompass.*

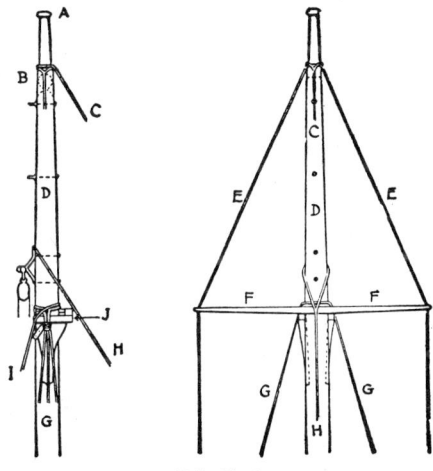

Pole Mast

A. Truck
B. Topmast Sheave
C. Head Stay
D. Topmast
E. Topmast Backstay
F. Crosstrees
G. Shrouds
H. Forestay
I. Runner Pendant
J. Trestletrees

POLE MAST. A mast all in one spar. A mast with a long pole or piece above the hounds. A lower mast and topmast in one piece. When referring to a lower mast only it is also known as a single tree mast.

Fr: *Mât à Pible;* Ger: *Pfahlmast.*

POLICY PROOF OF INTEREST. See **Wager Policy.**

POLICY PROOF OF INTEREST CLAUSE. A marine insurance expression. In a P.P.I. policy the underwriter agrees that no proof of interest other than the policy shall be required in the event of claim. These policies are also known as honor policies. The P.P.I. clause is usually detachable from the policy by perforation or other means. The insured has no power of legal enforcement and relies on the honor of the underwriter to carry out his underwriting.

Fr: *Clause de Police sans Preuve d'Intérêt.*

POLTE. General term for Pomeranian one-mast open or decked fishing boats used for seining on the Stettiner Haff and adjoining waters. There are several varieties called *Tuckerpolte, Taglerpolte, Fischhandelpolte.* The last is used as fish carrier. It is decked and has a length ranging from 39 to 42 ft. The length of the *Taglerpolte* varies from 19 to 32 ft. All are provided with a fish well.

See **Tuckerpolte**.

POLYCONIC CHART. A chart whose construction is based on the polyconic projection.

Fr: *Carte Polyconique;* Ger: *Polykonische Karte.*

See **Projection**.

POLYCONIC PROJECTION. A system of projection used for nautical charts, based upon the development of the earth's surface on a series of cones, a different one for each parallel of latitude, each one having the parallel at its base, and the vertex in the point where a tangent to the earth at that latitude intersects the earth's axis. A degree of latitude in this chart is projected in its true length, and the general distortion of the figure is less than in any other method of projection. It is therefore specially suitable for the plotting of surveys.

Fr: *Projection Polyconique;* Ger: *Polykonische Projektion.*

See **Gnomonic Projection, Mercator's Projection.**

PONTIN. A two-masted fore-and-aft rigged trading coaster used for interinsular traffic in the Philippine Islands. The hull is of Spanish origin and is similar to that of Western craft. It is decked fore and aft. The carrying capacity ranges from 25 to 100 tons. The headrails are very large in order to provide stowage for the wooden anchors carried by these craft. A dugout is used as ship's boat.

PONTOON. A broad, flat-bottomed floating structure without sheer, rectangular in shape, resembling a barge. Also called dummy, flat. It may be moored alongside a vessel to assist in the loading and discharging, or may be used as a float for a crane or derrick, or as a ferry landing.

Fr: *Ponton;* Ger: *Ponton.*

See **Lifting Pontoon.**

The deck, which extends from end to end, provides a clear space, as there are no obstructions of any sort other than the necessary mooring fittings. No cargo is stowed below deck. Pontoons are rectangular or of ship-shape form, the bilge being either square or round. The stern is usually square and the fore end rounded. Some are built of wood; some are composite; and others are steel-built.

In marine insurance policies pontoons are held not included in the category of barges or hulls. In maritime law a pontoon is within admiralty jurisdiction.

PONTOON HATCH. A hatch cover constructed of welded steel forming a series of small box girders, about 12 in. in depth, extending over the entire width of the hatch opening.

At each corner of the cover there is a special casting so designed that a hook can be inserted when lifting the hatches. The rest bars, made of flanged plating, are welded inside the coaming at a distance of about 12 in. from the top.

PONTOON LIFEBOAT. A wide and shallow lifeboat built of steel or wood, in which the bottom is subdivided into a number of transverse, watertight compartments, the depth of which varies from 12 to 30 in. These compartments are bounded by transverse, watertight bulkheads and strengthened by nonwatertight longitudinals.

Ger: *Halbklappboot.*

There are three standard types of pontoon lifeboats. The first type is built with *fixed* watertight bulwarks, and has a well deck, the area of which must be at least 30 per cent of the total decked area. The second type is similar to the first, with the difference that the sides have collapsible bulwarks. The third type is flush-decked with collapsible bulwarks.

POOKHAUN. Small half-decked fishing boat used for rowing and fishing on the west coast of Ireland (Galway). Among the distinguishing features are the strong rake of the sternpost and the pronounced

TOP VIEW

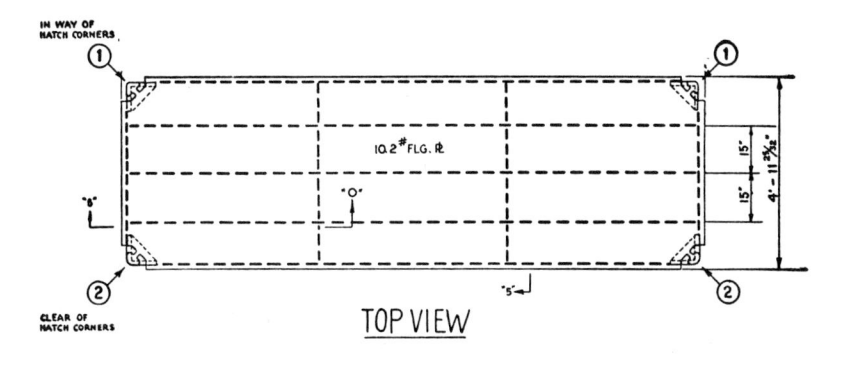

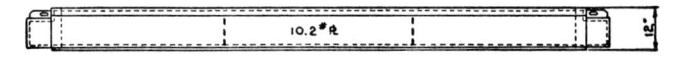

ELEVATION

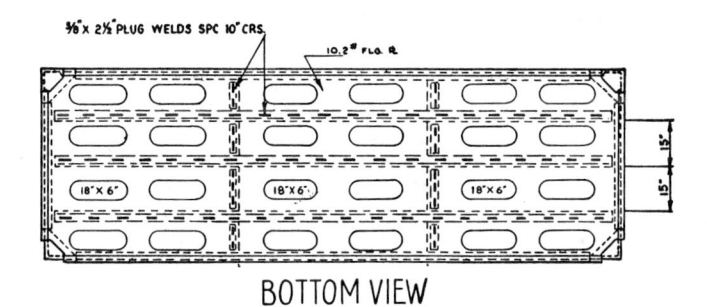

BOTTOM VIEW

Pontoon Hatch Cover

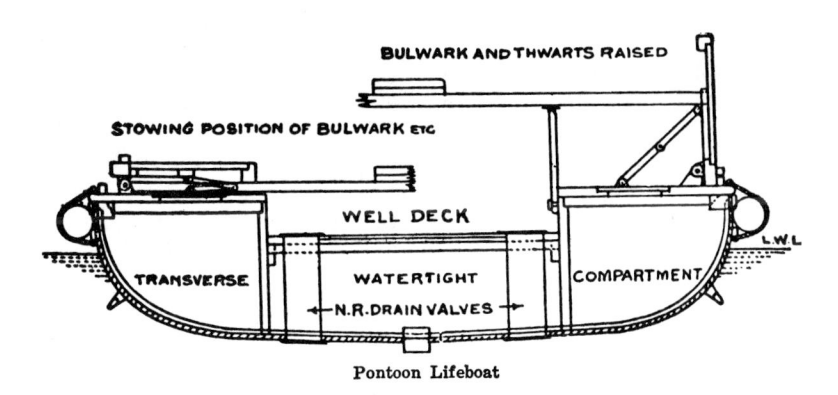

Pontoon Lifeboat

597

tumble home of the topsides. The rig consists of a single mast with dipping lugsail. Length over-all 28 ft. Breadth 8 ft. Draft forward 1 ft. 9 in.; aft 3 ft.

POOP. A short superstructure above the afterpart of the weather deck, extending from side to side, and entirely closed. Its main purpose is to increase the buoyancy of the afterend of the vessel. On sailing ships the poop contains accommodation for the master and officers.
Fr: *Dunette;* Ger: *Hütte.*
See **Sunk Poop.**

POOP DECK. A deck extending from the stern forward over a poop erection. A partial deck over the main deck at the stern.
Fr: *Pont de la Dunette;* Ger: *Hüttendeck.*

POOPING. A contingency which may occur when a large following sea overtakes a vessel. Her stern fails to lift sufficiently above the crest, with the result that the sea then breaks on board, doing considerable damage.
Fr: *Coup d'Acculage;* Ger: *Achterliches See-Übernehmen.*

POOP LINE. In a trawl net a line which runs from the lace hood, at the cod end, to the trawl head, used to facilitate hauling the cod end inboard. Also called poke line.
Fr: *Parpaillot;* Ger: *Pokleine.*

POOP RAIL. The railing around the top of the bulwarks or rail stanchions on the poop deck.
Fr: *Lisse de Dunette;* Ger: *Hütten Reling.*

POOP STAFF. A flag staff at the stern of of a vessel from which the national flag is flown. Also called ensign staff.
Fr: *Mât de Pavillon; Hampe;* Ger: *Flaggenstock.*

POPO. A single-outrigger open canoe of the Ladrone and Caroline Islands, the hull of which is asymmetric, that is, flat on one side and rolled on the other. Also called flying prao. The smaller types vary from 26 to 40 ft. long and 2 to 3 ft. wide, while the largest units, which are now extinct, were 65 ft. long and 7 ft. wide. Only a few of small size still exist.

The flat side helps to keep the craft up to the wind, in the same way as does a leeboard. The canoe-shaped outrigger float is rigged out to windward at the end of the two booms and there is a lee platform which acts as a counterpoise to the outrigger frame. These craft carry a large triangular sail which sets with apex down. They sail very close to the wind, to which they always present the rounded side of the hull. Their speed is said to be very high.

POPPET. A small piece of wood on a boat's gunwale, supporting the wash strake.
Fr: *Macaron;* Ger: *Zapfen.*
See **Launching Poppet.**

POPPET BOARD.
See **Sole Piece.**

POPPET RIBBAND. A steel plate, channel, or heavy plank by which launching poppets are braced longitudinally. Also called poppet stringer, dagger plank.

POPPING THE WHIP (U. S.). Expression used in towing parlance to describe the maneuver wherein the helm of a towing vessel is put hard over so as to change her course sharply in one direction, thereby swinging the towed vessel sharply in the opposite direction, so as to avoid a collision.

PORCUPINE. The fraying of wire rope.

PORPOISING. The tendency of small hulls to jump clear of the water surface when travelling at high speed. This phenomenon is confined almost entirely to flat-bottom racing boats, stepped boats, seaplane floats, skimming boats. Also said of a torpedo that breaks the surface.

PORT. 1. A place for the loading and unloading of vessels recognized and supervised for maritime purposes by the public authorities. The term includes a city or borough for the reception of mariners and merchants and therefore denotes something more than a harbor or havre. A port may possess a harbor but a harbor is not necessarily a port. Any natural creek or inlet on the sea shore with adequate depth of water and sufficient shelter for ships fulfills the essential conditions of a harbor. To make it a port, in the accepted sense of the word, there must be in addition accommodation and facilities for landing passengers and goods and some amount of overseas trade.
Fr: *Port;* Ger: *Hafen.*
Cunningham, Brysson, *Port Administration and Operation,* London, 1925; MacElwee, R. S., *Port Development,* New York, 1925; MacElwee, R. S., *Ports and Terminal Facilities,* New York, 1918; Shankland, E. C., *Modern Harbors,* Glasgow, 1926.

2. The left side of a vessel when looking forward.
Fr: *Babord;* Ger: *Backbord.*

3. One of the rectangular openings in the

sides, bow or stern, of a ship, provided as means of access to the interior in addition to the hatchways. Also called cargo port. They are used for loading or discharging cargo or cattle, or as entrance for passengers.

Fr: *Sabord;* Ger: *Pforte.*

See **Ballast Port, Battle Port, Bow Port, Cargo Port, Coaling Port, Freeing Port, Gangway Port, Half Port, Hawser Port, Helm Port, Lumber Port, Painted Port, Wash Port, Wheel Port.**

PORTABLE DECK. A wood deck built in small sections, called hatches. Each section consists of four 11 inch by 2½ inch planks assembled with steel tie rods. Distance pieces are fitted between the planks to leave about one inch clearance. Portable decks are used in fruit-carrying ships and small freighters which are intended to be used at different times for general cargo.

Fr: *Pont mobile;* Ger: *Tragbar Decksbelag.*

PORTABLE LIGHT. A side light, used on small vessels when under way in bad weather and unable to keep the regulation lights in a fixed position. These lights are kept at hand, lighted, and ready to be exhibited upon the approach of other vessels.

Fr: *Fanal Portatif;* Ger: *Tragbare Laterne.*

PORTABLE STANCHION. A stanchion with hinged heel or head which may be stowed horizontally when desired. Such stanchions are occasionally placed at sides of hatchways to facilitate loading and discharging. Also called portable pillar.

Fr: *Épontille Démontable;* Ger: *Versetzbare Stütze.*

PORT AUTHORITY. Person or persons, corporate or incorporate, who are proprietors of, or entrusted with the duty, or invested with the power of constructing, improving, managing, or maintaining a harbor. Also called harbor authority, harbor board, port trust, port commission.

Fr: *Autorité du Port; Autorité Portuaire;* Ger: *Hafenbehörde.*

The local administration of a port or harbor may be vested in one body or may be divided into several distinct committees, each with jurisdiction over particular functions of the harbor administration; that is, management committee; docks, quays, and warehouse committee; pilotage committee; maintenance committee; marine or navigation committee; finance committee, and so on. Some ports are administered by the state, others by a municipality, others by a statutory trust representing all parties interested, while still others are the property of a private company or corporation.

PORT BAR.

See **Strongback.**

PORTAGE BILL. A statement made out at the end of the voyage by the master, showing total earnings of each member of the crew, including overtime and any gratuities due under special agreement. In this statement the master debits his owners with the gross total earnings of all on board, and he credits them with the sums they may have paid on account of any of the officers or men, such as allotments, advance notes, and so on.

Fr: *Décompte du Capitaine.*

PORT CAPTAIN.

See **Marine Superintendent.**

PORT CHARGES. General term which includes charges and dues of every nature assessed against the vessel, cargo and passengers in a port. Also called port dues. Port charges usually include harbor dues, berth charges, tariff charges, towage, wharfage, customhouse fees, quarantine fees, cost of fumigating, levee dues, watching.

Fr: *Droits de Port;* Ger: *Hafenabgaben.*

See **Handling Charges, Inward Charges, Landing Charges, Harbor Dues.**

Anderson, *Assessment of Harbor Dues,* Institution of Engineers and Shipbuilders in Scotland, *Transactions,* vol. 64 (1921-22); Tutin, J., "Methods of Levying Charges for Services to Shipping," Institution of Naval Architects, *Transactions,* vol. 86 (London, 1944); U. S. Board of Engineers for Rivers and Harbors, *Port and Terminal Charges at United States Ports,* Washington, 1942; *Dues and Port Charges on Shipping Throughout the World,* New York, 1920.

PORT DIFFERENTIAL. A difference in the rates of transportation on certain shipments between inland points and ocean ports over routes competing for the same traffic.

PORT ENGINEER (U. S.). An engineer stationed at the home port of a fleet of vessels who heads the shore staff. Also called engineer superintendent. His principal duties are the engagement, control and discharge of all the engineering staff ashore and afloat, the maintenance, reconditioning, and repair of all ship's machinery, the supervision of reports sent in by the chief engineers of the various ships when at sea, and of the work done ashore. The arrangements for the classification and other surveys of engines and boilers to be carried out are also under his control.

Fr: *Mécanicien Inspecteur; Mécanicien d'Armement;* Ger: *Maschinen Inspektor; Chef-Ingenieur.*

See **Dock Superintendent, Marine Superintendent, Wharf Superintendent.**

PORTER (G. B.). Skilled dock laborers named according to the commodity handled by each group. Those engaged in handling planks and light timber are known as deal porters. Grain porters are those engaged in handling grain. Coal porters are employed in discharging or loading coal into ships.

See **Master Porter.**

PORT FLAP.

See **Port Lid.**

PORT GREVE. In Great Britain, the chief magistrate of a seaport town.

PORT HAND BUOY. A buoy which should be passed to port by vessels entering a harbor, river, or estuary from seaward.

Fr: *Bouée de Babord;* Ger: *Backbord Tonne.*

PORTHOLE. One of the circular openings provided in the sides of a vessel or superstructure to give light and ventilation to living quarters. Also called sidescuttle, air port (U. S.), side light (G. B.). Side lights vary in design but generally consist of a fixed frame, riveted to the outside plating, with a lense frame hinged to it. The lense frame is fitted with a thick, strong lense of glass. When closed it is made watertight by pivoted bolts which press a V-shaped projection on the one frame against a rubber gasket. The diameter of side scuttles generally varies from 6 to 18 inches. The type and position of sidescuttles on passenger vessels is regulated by the rules of the International Convention for the Safety of Life at Sea of 1929.

Fr: *Hublot;* Ger: *Seitenfenster; Ventilationsfenster; Lüftungsfenster.*

American Marine Standards Committee, Standard 78, Circular Hinged and Fixed Lights for Ships, Washington, 1932; British Standards Institute, Standard 3024, "Ship's Side Scuttles and Frames," London, 1926.

PORT HOLIDAY. A day of exemption from work according to local usage or custom of the port.

Fr: *Jour férié du port;* Ger: *Feiertag des Hafens.*

PORT LID. An outside shutter of rectangular shape fitted with two hinges placed on its upper edge and used for closing a wash port. Also called port sash, port flap.

Fr: *Mantelet de Sabord;* Ger: *Pfortendeckel.*

PORT LIGHT. One of the small lighthouses placed at pier heads or at the entrance of a harbor.

Fr: *Feu d'Entrée de Port;* Ger: *Molenfeuer; Hafenfeuer.*

PORT OF ADJUDICATION. A port of a belligerent state or ally to which a seized or captured vessel and its cargo are sent that they may lie there in safety pending prize court proceedings.

Ger: *Zuerkennungshafen.*

PORT OF CALL. A port at which ships usually stop on a given voyage or route to collect or discharge part cargo or passengers, or, to bunker.

Fr: *Port d'Escale;* Ger: *Anlegehafen; Zwischenhafen.*

PORT OF DELIVERY. 1. In maritime law, the port of destination of a ship as distinguished from any port at which the vessel touches in the course of the voyage for other purposes such as for orders or provisions, or in consequence of stress of weather or other necessity.

2. In chartering, the port at which the owners place the vessel at the charterer's disposal.

Fr: *Port de remise;* Ger: *Lieferungshafen.*

PORT OF DESTINATION. Any port to which the vessel may be destined during the voyage. As used in marine insurance (time) policies, the term has been held to mean any port to which the vessel may be destined during the voyage, as well as her home port, and to include any usual stopping place for loading or discharging cargo. A port where the incoming goods are absorbed by the local market or are passed into local factories for manufacturing purposes. Also called entrepot port.

Fr: *Port de Destination;* Ger: *Bestimmungshafen.*

PORT OF DISCHARGE. The port or place at which cargo is discharged. The "last port of discharge" is that one at which the last of the outward cargo is unloaded. It may be the final port of destination, if any part of the cargo is carried there. The term "safe port of discharge," used in charter parties, signifies a port which the vessel can safely enter with its cargo, or which, at least, has a safe anchorage outside, where it can lie and discharge afloat.

Fr: *Port de Déchargement;* Ger: *Losshafen; Abladungshafen.*

PORT OF ENTRY. A port or harbor at which vessels are allowed by customs regulations to load or unload and where the various provisions of the customs and navigation laws are enforced. Also called port of arrival.

Fr: *Port d'Entrée;* Ger: *Einfahrthafen.*

PORT OF LOADING. The place where it is usual for vessels to load.

Fr: *Port de Chargement;* Ger: *Ladehafen.*

PORT OF REFUGE. See **Harbor.**

PORT OF REGISTRY. The port at which a vessel is registered and to which she is considered to belong. Also called home port, port of documentation (U. S.). All documents such as bill of sale, mortgage, assignment of mortgage or hypothecation are not valid until recorded in the office of the collector of customs at the home port of the vessel.

Fr: *Port d'Armement; Port d'Attache;* Ger: *Heimatshafen; Registerhafen.*

PORTOLATA. An open boat with flat bottom, decked at ends, and sharp stern, from the Gulf of Venice used on the Dalmatian coast as fish carrier by the *tartanas, bragozzi* and other fishing craft to take their catch ashore. The old *portolata* was rigged with three masts and dipping lugsails. The modern craft are fitted with an auxiliary motor and one mast.

PORT ORFORD CEDAR. A strong durable wood which grows on the coast of northern California and southern Oregon and is used by boatbuilders of that area as planking and decking material for small boats. It weighs about 31 lb. per cu. ft.

PORT RATES. Government charges imposed on all merchandise arriving at British ports unless dealt with on transshipment terms. They are distinct from charges for services rendered in respect of discharging, loading, or handling goods. Also called tolls.

PORT RISK. In marine insurance, a risk upon a vessel while it is lying in port and before it has taken its departure on another voyage.

PORT RISK POLICY. A marine policy under which the risk ceases as soon as the ship, ready for sea, leaves its moorings to commence the voyage.

Fr: *Police pour risques de Port;* Ger: *Hafenrisiko Police.*

PORT SANITARY STATEMENT. A document issued by the port sanitary authorities to the master of a ship showing the number of cases of, and deaths from, various contagious diseases at the port of departure during the period of two weeks before the vessel sails.

PORT SASH.

See **Port Lid.**

PORT SERVICE SIGNALS. Signals given in a port concerning public holidays, nonworking days, time, weather, mail, medical or customs officer, death on board, water boat, ash lighter, fuel wanted, tug wanted, fire on board, harbor police, mutiny, adjustment of compasses, vessel clearing of sailing, and the like.

Niblack, A. P., "Summary of Data on Port Signals," *Hydrographic Review* (Monaco), vol. 4, no. 1 (May, 1927).

PORTSMOUTH WHERRY. A half-decked clinker-built sailing boat with sharp stern, formerly used in the Solent waters for various purposes, such as fishing, ferrying passengers, and so on. The rig consisted of a sprit mizzen, sprit mainsail, and jib. Length over-all 34 ft. 4 in. Breadth 9 ft. Depth 5 ft. 6 in. (Typical.)

PORT SPEED. A term used to express the rate of loading and discharging operations. It depends on the design and construction of cargo handling appliances, and the arrangement of cargo holds. Sometimes called port efficiency.

Port Speed of Cargo Vessels, Liverpool Journal of Commerce, Shipbuilding and Engineering Edition (November 25th, 1943).

PORT TRUST (G. B.). The public commission or body owning, controlling, and operating port properties as a public trust.

PORT WARDEN. Also port reeve. **1.** An officer of a port whose duties include the safeguarding of a vessel's seaworthiness, as by proper stowage; the holding of surveys on vessels or on cargo ashore; and the measurement of vessels (G. B.).

2. Official having jurisdiction over channels, anchorages, moorings, etc., of a harbor or port (U. S.).

3. An officer maintained in some ports to

oversee the administration of local regulations. A sort of harbor master.
Ger: *Hafen Aufseher.*

PORT WARDEN'S FEES (U. S.). Charges for surveys held on board a vessel or on the wharf to assess damage to cargo. Also for surveys of a vessel whether because of damage or for valuation or measurement.

PORUA. Polynesian single-outrigger dugout canoe from Ndai Island, Gower Island, in the southeastern Solomon Islands. Also called *forua.*

POSITION BUOY. A buoy used for towing astern at night or in foggy weather to enable war ships in formation to keep the proper distance apart. Also called **Towing spar** or **Fog spar.**

POSITION BY OBSERVATION. Position of a ship at sea determined by calculations based on the altitude or position of celestial bodies.
Fr: *Point observé;* Ger: *Observiertes Besteck.*

POSITION FINDER.
See **Radio Compass.**

POSITION LINE. An imaginary line on which a ship at sea must lie to satisfy certain data obtained by the observation of a terrestrial or celestial object. Also called line of positions. If two observations are taken, two position lines are obtained and the point where they intersect is the position of the ship. Position lines are obtained by compass bearings, by radio direction finder, or by astronomical observation.
Fr: *Droite de Hauteurs;* Ger: *Standlinie.*

POSITION LINE SIGHT. One of the sights, taken at any time, from which a line of position is obtained.

POSITION SIGNAL. A signal from the international code in which the degrees and minutes of latitude and longitude are indicated by four numeral pennants preceded by the letter "P." The first two figures denote degrees and the last two the minutes.

POSSESSORY LIEN. A common law lien which arises out of and is dependent upon the possession of the thing by the person asserting the lien. Such a lien may attach to a vessel or freight.

POT. 1. A baited chamber into which fish can enter easily but from which, owing to the special shape of the opening, they are unable to escape. Pots are used mainly for catching crabs, lobsters, whelks, and eels. Also called creel, basket.
Fr: *Casier;* Ger: *Reuse; Fischkorb.*

2. In a pound net, the final enclosure into which the fish are directed by the leader and heart. Also called crib, pound, pocket, bowl. It has a netting bottom and can be raised to secure the fish.
Fr: *Sac;* Ger: *Fangkammer.*
See **Drain Pot, English Pot, Lobster Pot, Try-Pot.**

POTE.
See **Korba.**

POTIK. Local name given in the East Indies to a native fishing craft of the *mayang* type. Also called *kotik.*

POTIN. A Spanish open fishing boat from Leiquito in the province of Vizcaya, similar to the *trainera* but with fuller lines. There are two classes: the larger one comprises the offshore boats called *potines de Altura* which go out to sea a distance of 50 to 70 miles. Length 27.5 ft. Breadth 6.5 ft. Depth 3.1 ft. Tonnage of 3.8. (Average.) The smaller boats are employed for inshore fishing. Length 17.4 ft. Breadth 5 ft. Depth 1.9 ft. All boats are provided with a centerboard, and the usual rig consists of a single mast with lugsail, although some of the largest units may be seen with two masts like the *traineras.*

POTOMAC LONG BOAT. A two-mast, schooner-rigged centerboard sailing barge formerly used for the transportation of cord wood on the Chesapeake Bay and Potomac River. The hull was built with keel, flat floors, round sides, sharp bow, raking stem, and square stern. The deck plan included a foredeck and quarter-deck—with trunk cabin. Gangways about 18 in. wide extended from the foredeck to the quarter-deck on each side of the hatchway. The stem was built with cutwater headsails and short bowsprit. Length over-all 82 ft. Keel 77 ft. Breadth 23 ft. Depth 3 ft. 10 in. (Typical.)
Brewington, M. V., "The Potomac Long Boat," *American Neptune,* vol. I, no. 2, Salem (Mass.), 1941.

POUND AND PINT (G. B.). Slang term used by British seamen to denote the victualing scale as laid down by the Board of Trade regulations.

POUND BOARD.
See **Checker.**

POUNDING. The blow delivered by the sea to a vessel in motion. It is primarily due to the heaving motion of the ship and occurs in irregular and cross seas. The shock produced by pounding can be felt over the whole ship and is followed by a rapid vibration of the elastic portions of the hull.

POUND NET. A set net composed of vertical netting supported and held in place by stakes. It consists of three essential parts. The pot (pound, pocket, bowl), the wings or hearts and the leader or lead. The pound consists of a bag of stout netting with 1-in. meshes the margin of which is supported by upright stakes. The bottom of the pound is spread and secured by ropes which pass through loops near the lower end of the stakes. The wings or heart are vertical fences of netting diverging from the entrance of the net. The mesh is ½ in. and they are supported by stakes. The leader, which may vary in length from about 150 ft. to 1,000 ft. or more, extends from shore or shallow water into deeper water and deflects the fish towards the heart or wings.

Fr: *Paradière; Filet à coeur;* Ger: *Walreuse; Bundgarn.*

U. S. Bureau of Fisheries, Memorandum S-47, *Description of Pound Nets and Trap Nets,* Washington, 1939.

POURED SOCKET. A method of attaching a fitting or connection to a wire rope. The interior of the base of the metal socket is coned. The bare end of the wire rope, after spreading the wires, is bedded in and sealed with molten zinc, which forms a head that holds without distorting the wires. It is the strongest attachment known for use on the end of a wire rope, and will develop the full strength of the rope.

POVERA. An open fishing boat from the north of Portugal with sharp stern and raking stem. It is rigged with a large lugsail and rows 4 to 6 oars on each side. Length of keel 17.3 ft. to 28.8 ft. This type of boat is found all along the coast from the Minho River down to the Douro.

See **Barco Poveiro.**

POWDER FLAG. Flag B of the International Code, hoisted at the fore to denote that the vessel is taking in or discharging powder or highly inflammable fuel.

Fr: *Pavillon d'explosifs;* Ger: *Pulverflagge.*

POWER GURDY.
See **Line Hauler.**

POWER STEERING GEAR. A steering apparatus in which mechanical power is used to work the rudder. Power steering gear is generally of one of the following systems: hydraulic, electric, steam, electric-hydraulic, steam-hydraulic. The power of the engine should be such that the rudder can be put hard over in 30 seconds with the vessel going ahead at full speed.

Fr: *Appareil à Gouverner Asservi;* Ger: *Kraftbetriebene Steuervorrichtung.*

POWER TONNAGE. A term used in United States to classify a ship for the purpose of establishing the rates of pay of engineer officers. It is calculated by adding together the gross tonnage and the indicated horse power of the engines.

POZZOLANA.
See **Barca.**

PRAM. A term of Slavonic origin used in the ports of the Baltic and North seas to denote different types of craft.

In Germany (*Prahm*) and in Holland (*Praam*) this name is given to a flat-bottomed, wall-sided barge built of wood or steel and used as a lighter for discharging or loading cargoes of large vessels anchored in a river or roadstead.

The Norwegian *pram* is an open clinker-built boat with round bottom, long scoop-shaped bow which is square and narrow at the extremity and heart-shaped in cross section. The keel follows the upward curve of the bow and protects the planking when the boat is beached. It has no run and the square stern is somewhat narrower than the midship section. The greatest breadth is aft of amidships. There is usually a small skeg aft. Inside there are four thwarts and a stern seat. When used in the fisheries on the southeastern coast it is rigged with a small mast stepped through the second thwart from the bow, and on this is set a lugsail. Length 17 ft. Breadth 5 ft. 3 in. Depth 19½ in. (Typical.)

Fr: *Prame Norvégienne;* Ger: *Prahm.*

See **Danish Fishing Pram, Pram Dinghy.**

PRAM BOW. A bow in which the planks or plates instead of abutting in the stem are gathered together so as to form a tapering bow, ending in a flat surface, like a small transom, set at a sharp rake forward with the bottom curving up from below to meet it. Also called transom bow, swim bow, scow bow.

Ger: *Prahmbug.*

This form of bow is found in various Dutch and Chinese seagoing craft. Among its advantages are the increase in sailing length when the hull is heeled, also greater deck space forward and low cost of construction. On the other hand, it tends to make the hull pound and makes for a wet craft forward.

PRAM DINGHY. A dinghy having a flat bow of semicircular section sloping about 45 degrees to the water and transom stern. It is the lightest of wood dinghies for its size. Some prams have no keel aft, which makes them unsteady when rowing or towing. They are built with deadrise or round bottom and their length varies from 6½ to 12 ft.

PRAO. Generic name used in Indonesia for undecked native boats or vessels, some of which, however, may have platforms or portable decking, as distinguished from the *kapal*, which denotes permanently decked craft. Also called *prahu, prau, parao, perahu*.

The word belongs equally to the Malay and Javanese languages and from these has spread to others extending as a synonym to the principal Philippine dialects. It is used indiscriminately for dugout or plank-built craft with or without outriggers, whether rowed, paddled, or sailed. The different types are distinguished by specific names according to location of origin, form of hull, size and the duties which they have to perform.

PRAO JULUNG-JULUNG. A native trading craft from the Celebes with double outriggers and bipod mast. The stem rises higher than the stern. Also a decked Malay prao similar to the *penjajap* and rigged with two masts and lugsails, cutaway forefoot and clipper stem. It has galleries, like most of the large decked Malay boats.

PRATIQUE. 1. Permission or license granted by the port medical authorities to a vessel upon arrival from a foreign port after quarantine inspection, to communicate with the shore.

2. A certificate issued in British ports by the medical officer of health upon declaration made by the captain or the ship's doctor on arrival at quarantine station that no member of the crew or passenger is suffering from any contagious disease. Also called certificate of health. Without this document the vessel cannot report at the customhouse.

Fr: *Pratique;* Ger: *Verkehrserlaubnis; Landungsbrief.*

See **Radio Pratique.**

PRAYER BOOK. Name given by seamen to a small holystone about 4 in. by 6 in., used for cleaning a ship's deck in small corners where the ordinary sandstone cannot reach.

Ger: *Gesangsbuch.*

PREAMBLE CLAUSE. An expression used in chartering and giving a brief description of the vessel and principal cargo fittings as taken from a charterer's standpoint.

Fr: *Clause d'énonciation.*

PREASSEMBLING. A procedure adopted in shipyards whereby large structural sections of the hull are built at some distance from the building ways. They are subsequently lifted and transported to their final position on the ways ready for erection as a unit. Forepeak, bulkheads, double bottom sections, afterpeak and deckhouses are among the largest preassemblies. The purpose of preassembling is to speed up production by eliminating the need for crowding a large number of workers into a hull where space is restricted. This system of construction lends itself to the rapid and efficient production of a number of identical ships.

PRECESSION. 1. A variation in the planes of intersection of the ecliptic and equinoctial. It is due to the lunisolar attraction on the protuberant equatorial mass, forming the excess of the terrestrial spheroid above its inscribed sphere and causes the line of intersection of the ecliptic and equinoctial to have a gradual retrograde motion. The first point of Aries moves backward along the ecliptic at a yearly rate of 50 min. 38 sec.

Fr: *Précession;* Ger: *Präzession.*

2. The effect produced by a torque applied to the frame of a gyroscope, tending to alter the plane of spin of the wheel, and make the latter turn about an axis at right angles to that about which the torque is applied, until the plane and direction of spin of the wheel coincide with the plane and the direction of the torque.

Fr: *Précession;* Ger: *Präzession.*

PRECIOUS CARGO. This term includes such articles as gold and silver specie, precious stones, mails, and the like, which are carried by special agreement only, and are placed in a strong room or other locked safe stowage.

Fr: *Marchandises de Valeur;* Ger: **Wertladung.**

PRECIPITATION. A meteorological term which includes any precipitation of water or ice on the earth's surface.

PRECIPITOUS SEA. A mountainous sea with wave heights over 36 ft. Douglas Scale No. 8.

Fr: *Mer Furieuse;* Ger: *Gewaltige See.*

PRE-EMPTION. The belligerent right to requisition neutral cargoes which are contraband of war or conditional contraband, provided a just compensation or purchase price is paid to the owners of the goods. This right may be exercised on the high seas.

Fr: *Droit de Préemption;* Ger: *Vorkaufsrecht.*

PRE-ERECTION. Erecting certain portions of a steel hull, such as bulkheads, bow, stern, deckhouses, and the like, on the ground and transporting them bodily to the ways to be riveted or welded.

See **Prefabrication.**

PREFABRICATE. To assemble portions of a structure at various points, and then assemble the whole at one central location.

PREFABRICATION. The assembling by riveting or welding of comparatively large structural sections of the hull such as bulkheads, fore and after peaks, double-bottom sections, deck houses, etc., in bays or erecting shops previous to their transportation as complete units to the building slip.

PREFERRED MARITIME LIEN. A lien for damages arising out of tort for wages of the crew, general average, and salvage including contract salvage.

PREFORMED ROPE. Wire rope in which the helical form or curve is given to the wires and strands by being pre-shaped (preformed) during fabrication as distinguished from ordinary wire rope in which the various wires are simply forced into shape by twisting. Also called tru-lay rope.

The advantages claimed are: higher resistance to fatigue failure caused by bending and other actions in a loaded rope; no whippings required at ends as the individual wires and strands lie inert or "at ease"; less tendency to kink.

PRELIMINARY ENTRY. Entry under oath made by the master to the customs officer who boards a vessel before the formal entry is made at the customhouse in order to obtain a special license for the landing of passengers, baggage, and express cargo.

PRER. A bamboo raft about 20 to 26 ft. long and 3 ft. wide, used by the natives of Palau Islands (Micronesia) for fishing in shallow waters. It consists of 9 or 10 thick bamboos held in position partly by thin stakes driven transversely through them and partly by lashings. Over the center part an elevated platform is erected, which serves as a station for the fisherman and his gear when line fishing.

PRESS BRAKE. A power press used for flanging plates, in shipbuilding.

PRESS OF SAIL. To carry a press of sail is said of a vessel which carries an extraordinary spread of canvas for some special purpose such as to avoid stranding, to escape an enemy, etc.

Fr: *Forcement de Voiles;* Ger: *Prangen.*

PRESUMED TOTAL LOSS. Term used in marine insurance to denote a vessel that is so overdue as to be posted as missing.

Fr: *Perte Totale Présumée.*

PREVAILING WIND. Average or normal wind over a particular area.

Fr: *Vent Dominant;* Ger: *Vorherrschender Wind.*

PREVENTER. An additional rope or wire fitted with tackle and attached to or placed alongside a heavily laden rope, brace or backstay to relieve effort and prevent accident. In cutter-rigged craft it is sometimes led down from the mast cap aft to the side of the vessel.

Fr: *Patarat;* Ger: *Borgtau.*

PREVENTER BACKSTAY. One of a pair of additional backstays set up temporarily leading from the head of a mast to the ship's side where it is set up with a tackle, and carried in strong winds or when under a press of sail. Also called preventer stay.

Fr: *Faux-Galhauban; Patarat;* Ger: *Borgpardune.*

PREVENTER FID. A bar of iron or wood put through a hole in a mast about two feet above the fid hole.

Fr: *Fausse Clef.*

PREVENTER HAWSER. A hawser used in clearing hawse. It is secured to the chain as a preventer near the slip hook of the clear-hawse pendant.

See **Preventer, Clear-Hawse Pendant.**

PREVENTER PLATE. Steel plate secured to the lower end of a chain plate in wooden sailing ships to assist in taking the stress off the lower rigging.

PREVENTER SHROUD. A shroud rigged as an additional security to assist the

permanent shrouds in supporting a lower mast in heavy weather. They are much used nowadays in yachts and small sailing craft.
Fr: *Faux Hauban;* *Hauban de Fortune;* Ger: *Borgwant; Untere Toppwant.*

PRICKER. 1. A small marlinespike.
Ger: *Marlpfriem.*
2. A small pointed tool with wooden handle used by sailmakers for making eyelet holes in canvas.
Fr: *Poinçon;* Ger: *Pricker; Prigger.*
3. Instrument used by fishermen in the red snapper fisheries of the Gulf of Mexico. It consists of a small metal tube fitted in wooden handles and sharpened at the end, which is thrust through the side of the fish into the bladder as soon as the fish is brought to the surface. This, by removing the air contained in the distended bladder, enables the fishermen to keep the fish alive when placed in the vessel's well until the catch is landed.

PRICKLE BASKET. A unit of measurement used in Great Britain in the oyster trade, equivalent to 10 gal. or half a tub.

PRIDE OF THE MORNING. A morning mist often seen at sea before a fine bright day.

PRIMAGE. 1. A small sum of money formerly paid by the shippers over and above the freight, to the master of a ship for his care of the goods. Sometimes called hat money, average. It is nowadays charged with the freight and retained by the shipowner. The clause "primage and average accustomed" is still occasionally found in bills of lading and has the same meaning as primage. The word average in this connection means a pro rata charge to cover expense of lights, pilotage and wharfage.
Fr: *Chapeau;* Ger: *Frachtaufschlag; Primage.*
2. An addition to freight charges, of 10 per cent usually, in consideration for the use of the ship's cargo handling appliances, or any additional expenditures necessitated by accepting the cargo. It is often returnable as deferred rebate.
Fr: *Primage;* Ger: *Frachtaufschlag; Frachtzuschlag.*

PRIME MERIDIAN. The meridian on the earth's surface from which longitude is measured. The prime meridian used at sea is the one which passes through Greenwich.
Fr: *Premier Méridien;* Ger: *Erster Meridian.*

PRIME RATES (G. B.). A term used to denote collectively the landing, management, and consolidated rates on cargo.

PRIME VERTICAL. The vertical circle intersecting the observer's zenith and passing perpendicularly through the east and west points of his horizon.
Fr: *Premier Vertical;* Ger: *Erster Vertikal.*

PRIMING. 1. A shortening of the interval between the times of successive high waters. It occurs during the moon's first and third quarters and is a phase inequality. Also called acceleration.
Fr: *Gain de la marée; Revif;* Ger: *Gezeitenverfrühung.*
2. The carry over of fine water particles mixed up with steam between boiler and machinery. This leads to formation of scale in superheater tubes, and if it passes direct from the steam drum to machinery, may damage the latter by erosion of moving parts, as well as corrosion.

PRINCIPAL DIMENSIONS. Those dimensions which delineate the over-all size of the ship: length over-all, length between perpendiculars, registered length, molded breadth, registered breadth, molded depth, and registered depth.
See **Dimensions.**

PRISMATIC COEFFICIENT.
See **Longitudinal Coefficient.**

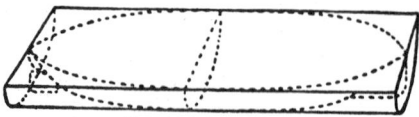

Prismatic Coefficient

PRISMATIC COMPASS. A compass provided with a prism for viewing the compass card and a distant object at the same time. Also called hand bearing compass.

PRISMATIC ERROR. An error found in the mirrors and shade glasses of a sextant, due to lack of parallelism of the two faces of the glass.
Ger: *Prismatische Fehler.*

PRIVATE ARMED VESSEL. A private vessel not built or fitted for naval warfare which carries armament and ammunition for purely defensive purposes and which does not take part in offensive operations.
Ger: *Bewaffnetes Handelsschiff.*

The persons in charge of the navigation of the ship remain the servants of the owners and are paid by the latter. Private armed vessels are subject to all laws, regulations, and liabilities governing merchant vessels. It is generally accepted in international maritime law that a merchant vessel of belligerent nationality may carry armament for the sole purpose of defense, without acquiring the character of a warship. Borchard, E., "Armed Merchantmen," *American Journal of International Law*, vol. 34 (January, 1940); Pearce Higgins, A., "Armed Merchant Ships," *American Journal of International Law*, vol. 8 (1914).

PRIVATEER. An armed vessel privately owned, controlled, officered, and commissioned by a belligerent state to commit hostile acts against enemy ships. The mere arming of a merchant vessel for defensive purposes in time of war does not suffice to convert it into a privateer. The commission issued to a privateer is called "letter of marque." By the Declaration of Paris privateering was abolished but the United States, Spain, Mexico, and Venezuela did not accede to this declaration.

Fr: *Corsaire;* Ger: *Kaperschiff.*

See **Declaration of Paris.**

PRIVATE FLAG. A yacht owner's private signal registered by a yacht club. It is usually rectangular or swallow-tailed in shape. The size of this flag should be one half inch in length for each foot of height of the main truck above water. In a schooner it is displayed from the mainmast, in a ketch or yawl from the mizzen. It is displayed only when under way. It has recently become customary, in racing sloops, to hoist the private flag at the peak and the burgee at the main truck when underway.

Fr: *Pavillon Particulier;* Ger: *Klubflagge.*

PRIVATE PORT. A port primarily owned and operated by an industrial concern, a railway system, and so on. Although termed private, the charges, dues, and services are generally under state or municipal control and regulations.

PRIVATE SIGNAL. A night signal used by ships belonging to the same company when meeting at sea by night. They are seldom employed nowadays since the general adoption of radio communication. They are made by using Coston or blue lights, rockets, or various colored lights.

Fr: *Signal Particulier;* Ger: *Privatsignal.*

See **Private Flag.**

PRIVATE VESSEL. Any vessel not owned or chartered by a State, without any distinction as to the use to which this vessel it put. Also called "Stand on Vessel" or "Right of Way Vessel."

Fr: *Navire Privé;* Ger: *Privatschiff.*

PRIVILEGED VESSEL. The vessel which, according to the rules of the road for two approaching vessels, has the right of way and should under normal conditions keep her course and speed.

Fr: *Navire Privilégié;* Ger: *Wegerechtschiff.*

PRIZE. A vessel captured at sea in wartime and condemned by a prize court. A vessel which on account of its enemy character or unneutral conduct has become the property of a belligerent state.

Fr: *Prise;* Ger: *Prise; Seebeute.*

Colombos, C. J., *Treatise on the Law of Prize*, London, 1940; Garner, J. W., *Prize Law during the World War*, New York, 1927; Tiverton, *Principles and Practice of Prize Law*, London, 1914.

PRIZE COURT. A special tribunal established at the outbreak of war which adjudicates upon cases of maritime capture. The question to be decided by the court is whether according to the law of the nations the ship and cargo in question were liable to capture and if so whether the capture was lawfully made. If the decision be in the affirmative the prize, pronounced good, is then sold and the proceeds placed in the hands of an officer of the government. If the decision be in the negative the vessel is restored to her owners.

Fr: *Conseil des Prises;* Ger: *Prisenhof; Prisengericht.*

A prize court usually sits within the territorial jurisdiction of the belligerent under whose authority the capture is made. As the determination of questions of this character involves the exercise of admiralty jurisdiction, it is customary to confer jurisdiction in cases of maritime capture upon admiralty courts. Hull, H., *Digest of Cases Decided in British Prize Courts*, London, H. M. Stationery Office, 1928.

PRIZE CREW. A detail of officers and men, under the orders of a prize master, placed by a belligerent warship aboard a captured vessel to take her into port for adjudication by a prize court.

Fr: *Equipage de Prise;* Ger: *Prisenkommando.*

PRIZE FLAG. A flag hoisted by the winner of a yacht race as soon as the race has been sailed and the prize winners are aware of the result. It is hoisted beneath the burgee and on the same halyards. The first prize flag is usually a silk miniature of the owner's racing flag. The second and third prize flags are blue and red pendant respectively with conspicuous figures 2 and 3 marked in white upon them.

PRIZE LAW. The system of laws and rules applicable to the capture of prize at sea; its condemnation, the rights of captors, distribution of proceeds, and so on.

Fr: *Droit de Prise;* Ger: *Prisenrecht.*

PRIZE MASTER. A naval officer appointed by the commander of a warship and placed in command of a captured merchant vessel to take her into port for adjudication.

Fr: *Conducteur de Prise.*

PRIZE MONEY (G. B.). A grant out of public funds distributed among the officers and men immediately responsible for the capture of an enemy vessel as a reward for bravery and to encourage success in naval operations.

Fr: *Part de Prise;* Ger: *Prisengeld.*

PRODUCER GAS ENGINE. A reciprocating engine designed to operate on gas generated in a solid fuel producer. A wide range of solid fuels, embracing anthracite, coal briquettes, low-temperature coke, charcoal, peat coke, and wood can be used for producer gas generation. Producer gas engines have been used on small vessels since about 1913. A number of craft fitted with producer gas engines using wood as fuel are employed in Russia on inland waterways. In Germany towboats with this type of engines of 250 to 350 horsepower have been built. The usual arrangement has the gas producer next to the prime mover. There is an appreciable saving of weight in comparison with reciprocating steam engines and cylindrical boilers. On the other hand, the producer gas plant represents additional weight in comparison with internal combustion engines using liquid fuel. The advantage of using a cheaper fuel partly offsets this handicap.

Fr: *Moteur à gaz pauvre;* Ger: *Generatorgasmaschine.*

Development of Producer Gas Motor Boats, Marine Engineering (New York), vol. 18 (November, 1913); Holzapfel, A. C., Gas Power for Ship Propulsion, Institution of Naval Architects, *Transactions,* vol. 54 (London, 1912).

PROFILE.

See Inboard Profile, Outboard Profile, Sheer Plan.

PROGRESSIVE TRIALS. A speed and power trial made on the measured mile for the determination of corresponding values of speed, revolutions, and power over a reasonable range from the maximum down at one displacement and under favorable conditions of wind and weather. Also called standardization trials.

Fr: *Essais Progressifs;* Ger: *Progressive Probefahrten.*

It is generally contended that for practical purposes it is more important to have data for merchantmen on the power, revolutions, propeller slip, and the like, at speeds less than the maximum than at top speed. It is specially important that the vessel be tried at as low a speed as possible consistent with obtaining accurate observations and that between it and full speed there should be one or more trials at intermediate speeds. In practice, three consecutive runs are made on the measured mile for each rate of speed with other factors such as pressure, vacuum, revolutions, kept as steady as possible during the whole run.

PROJECTED AREA. The area of a propeller blade projected on a plane at right angles to the propeller shaft.

Fr: *Surface Projetée;* Ger: *Projektionsfläche.*

PROJECTION WELD. A welded lap joint in which the parts are joined by resistance welding of embossments formed in one or both parts.

Fr: *Soudure par bossages.*

PROLONGATION CLAUSE. A time charter clause which gives the charterers the option of continuing the charter for further periods beyond that originally agreed upon, on giving notice to the owners in writing on an agreed date or time.

PROLONGED BLAST. By the International Rules of the Road, a blast on a whistle or fog horn, from 4 to 6 seconds in duration. Also called long blast.

Fr: *Son Prolongé;* Ger: *Langer Ton.*

PROMENADE DECK. An upper superstructure deck on passenger ships. Also called hurricane deck. It has no bulwarks.

Fr: *Pont Promenade;* Ger: *Promenadedeck.*

PROMETACENTER. The point of intersection between two vertical lines drawn through the two positions of the center of buoyancy of a floating body corresponding to two very slightly differing inclinations. It differs from the metacenter in that neither of the positions is a position of equilibrium.

Ger: *Falsches Metazentrum.*

PROMPT. Chartering term indicating that the vessel is within a week or so of the loading port. A prompt ship is a vessel shortly ready to load. From an importer's point of view, a prompt ship is an import vessel for which the bills of lading do not include any clause granting the consignees a period of time in which to apply for delivery of cargo. The goods therefore become "out of time" immediately the vessel breaks bulk and, if overside delivery is required, craft must be alongside as soon as the stevedores are ready to commence unloading.

PROPCON. Code name for a Baltic and International Maritime Conference charter party applicable to shipments of props and pulpwood from the Baltic to the European continent.

PROPELLER. A propulsive device consisting of a boss or hub carrying radial blades from two to four in number, the rear or driving faces of which form portions of an approximately helical surface, the axis of which is the center line of the propeller shaft. Also called screw propeller. The propeller is generally placed at the afterend of the vessel. In special craft such as ice-breakers and ferryboats a bow propeller is occasionally found.

Each blade is shaped or formed like the others and they are set angularly equidistant from one another with their center line normal or nearly so to the axis of the shaft.

The shape of blades may be oval or elliptical, or broadening somewhat toward the tip with rounded corners. Blade sections are of hydrofoil form.

Cast iron, cast steel, gun metal, monel metal, and various bronzes are used for making screw propellers. Manganese bronze is considered as possessing the best combination of desirable qualities for high-class vessels where the saving in propulsive efficiency is considered worth the increase in first cost.

Fr: *Hélice; Hélice Propulsive;* Ger: *Schraube; Propeller; Schraubenpropeller.*

See **Aerofoil Propeller, Built-up Propeller, Contra Propeller, Feathering Screw Propeller, Hand Operated Propeller, Left-Hand Propeller, Reversible Propeller, Right-Hand Propeller, Shrouded Propeller, Singing Propeller, Solid Propeller, Tunnel Screw Propeller, UniSlip Propeller, Vane Screw Propeller.**

Cast-iron propellers are satisfactory in point of strength and resistance to corrosion, but even when well designed their efficiency is relatively low due to their necessarily thick blades and the frictional resistance offered by their rough surfaces. Bronze propellers can be made with thin smooth blades cast to almost mathematically accurate profile. Cast-steel propellers can be made with thin blades but the latter are rough and liable to warp considerably after casting. In vessels fitted with cast-iron propellers instead of bronze, the engine power has to be increased on an average from 15 to 20 per cent for cargo vessels of 11–12 knots speed.

The design of propellers follows theoretical treatment using Froude's, Rankine's, Greenhill's, Taylor's, or Dyson's mathematical formulas, practical methods of design which include direct comparison with one or more existing propellers of known performance, or methods based on trials of model propellers in model tanks. In addition methods based on actual trials of full-size propellers driving hulls over carefully measured courses are used.

American Marine Standards Committee, *Ship Propeller Details,* Standard 29, 1928, Standard 42, 1928, Standard 55, 1929; Dyson, C. W., *Screw Propellers,* New York, 1924; Peabody, C. H., *Propellers,* New York, 1912; Robinson, S. M., "Propellers for Low Powered Merchant Ships," American Society of Naval Engineers, *Journal,* 1920; Seaton, A. E., *The Screw Propeller,* London, 1909.

PROPELLER APERTURE. The space provided for the propeller, between the propeller post and sternpost. Sometimes called screw aperture, propeller well.

Fr: *Cage d'Hélice;* Ger: *Schraubenbrunnen; Ruderbrunnen.*

PROPELLER ARCH.
See **Bridge Piece.**

PROPELLER AREA RATIO. The ratio between the relative total expanded area of the blades of a propeller and the disc area. It varies as follows on merchant vessels:

Single-screw cargo vessels ..... 0.32 to 0.40
Twin-screw cargo vessels ...... 0.35 to 0.40
Intermediate liners (twin
  screws) .... 0.35 to 0.40
High-speed liners (twin
  screws) .... 0.40 to 0.45
Steam launches .... 0.35 to 0.45
Tugs 0.50

PROPELLER BLADE. Each portion of

PROPELLER BOSS—PROPELLER GUARD

Solid Propeller

Propeller Lock Nut

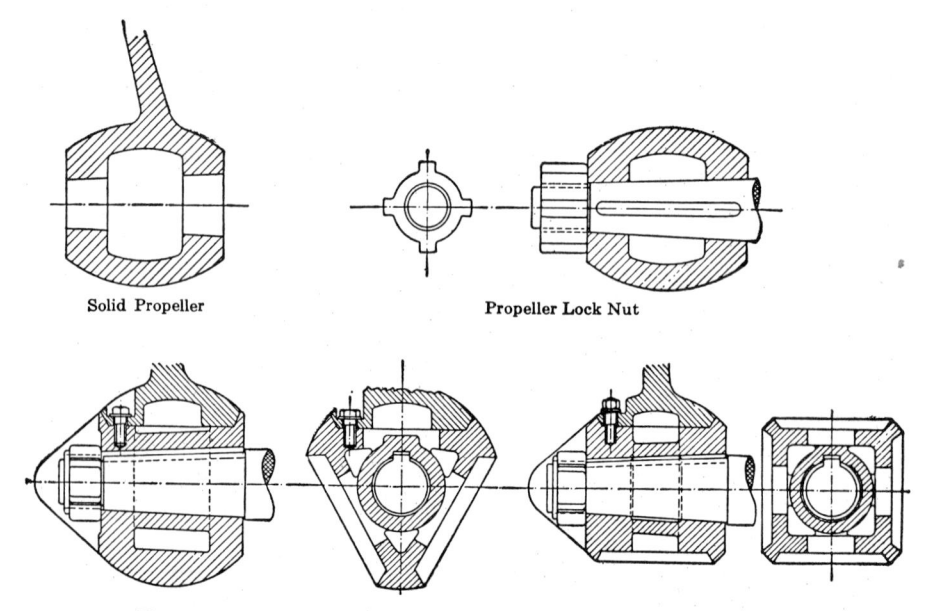

Three Bladed Built-up Propeller

Four Bladed Built-up Propeller

Propeller Boss

a helicoidal sector attached to the hub of a propeller.

Fr: *Aile d'Hélice*; Ger: *Schraubenflügel*.

Propeller blades are made of cast iron, cast steel, or special phosphor or manganese bronze. Icebreakers have nickel steel (3½% nickel) propeller blades which are not so brittle at low temperature. The standard shape of blades takes the form of an ellipse but in practice various modifications of this are adopted with varying results. A polished blade surface increases the efficiency of the propeller and for this reason manganese bronze propellers are fitted in high class vessels. The shape and sections of propeller blades are the subject of much recent tank experiment and research.

PROPELLER BOSS. The central part of a ship's propeller from which the blades stand out. Also called propeller hub. It is taper-bored for the reception of the propeller shaft, and is slotted for the key. It is forced home on the shaft and secured by means of the propeller locknut. A recess is turned out on the forward face to allow for the fitting of a rubber ring to prevent galvanic action.

Fr: *Moyeu d'Hélice*; Ger: *Schraubennabe*.

Standards of Hubs for Built-up Propellers, American Marine Standards Committee, Standard no. 42, Washington, 1928.

PROPELLER CAP.

See **Fairwater**.

PROPELLER EFFICIENCY. The ratio of the thrust horsepower delivered by the propeller, to the shaft horsepower as delivered by the engines to the propeller.

Fr: *Rendement de l'Hélice; Coefficient de rendement propulsif*; Ger: *Maschinennutzleistung Koeffizient; Schraubenwirkungsgrad*.

McEntee, W., "The Limit of Propeller Efficiency," Society of Naval Architects and Marine Engineers (New York), *Transactions*, 1906; Taylor, D. W., *Variation of Efficiency of Propulsion with Variation of Propeller Diameter and Revolutions*, North East Coast Institution of Engineers and Shipbuilders (Newcastle upon Tyne), *Transactions*, vol. 47 (1930).

PROPELLER FRAME. A general term which denotes the whole framing around a propeller and includes the rudderpost, propeller post, bridge piece and sole piece.

Fr: *Cage d'Hélice*; Ger: *Schraubengat*.

PROPELLER GUARD. A framework built of pipe or structural shapes overhanging the propeller blades of a twin-screw vessel with large propellers, to prevent the ship's stern from swinging in close enough to quay walls or other objects which could damage the propellers.

PROPELLER HORSEPOWER. The power received by the propeller. It is equal to shaft horsepower minus the losses at the thrust and line shaft bearings and stern tube bearings.

Fr: *Puissance de Remorque;* Ger: *Nutzpferdestärke.*

PROPELLER HUB.
See **Boss.**

PROPELLER LOCK NUT. Large nut by which a screw propeller is forced home and secured on its shaft.

Fr: *Ecrou de l'Hélice;* Ger: *Propellermutter.*

PROPELLER POST. The forward post of the stern frame on vessels having a centerline propeller. Also called screw post, body post. It provides a support for the stern tube and propeller shaft as well as a joining frame for the converging sides of the ship at the stern.

Fr: *Etambot Avant;* Ger: *Schraubensteven.*

PROPELLER SHAFT. The aftermost section of shafting which carries the propeller. Also called tail shaft, screw shaft. Owing to the severe stresses to which it is subjected this shaft is of larger diameter than the other shafting and, in order to eliminate the corrosive action of salt water, it is partly cased with bronze sleeves. The afterend is tapered and finished off with a screw thread for the propeller nut. The tapered part is fitted with a key to prevent the screw from turning on the shaft.

Fr: *Arbre Porte Hélice;* Ger: *Schraubenwelle; Propellerwelle.*

American Marine Standards Committee, Standard no. 28, *Propeller Shaft Details,* Washington, 1927; British Board of Trade, Standard Conditions and Rules for the Shafts of Marine Steam Engine, London, 1923; "Tailshaft Protection," *Marine Engineer* (London), vol. 60, no. 715 (April, 1937).

PROPELLER WELL.
See **Aperture.**

PROPELLING POWER DEDUCTION. The deduction made from the gross tonnage to determine the net tonnage according to measurement rules.

Fr: *Déduction pour appareil moteur;* Ger: *Maschinenraumabzug.*

Some rules limit propelling power deductions to a fixed maximum percentage of gross tonnage (Suez and Panama Canal rules). Others provide for the deduction of the space actually occupied by the propelling plant and by fixed bunkers. The more general rule is to make propelling power deductions according to the British tonnage rules, which provide for deduction of 32 per cent of the gross tonnage of screw-propelled vessels when the actual volume of propelling plant is above 13 and under 20 per cent of the space included in the gross tonnage. This is called the percentage rule.

PROPELLING POWER SPACES. An expression used in connection with tonnage measurement which includes: engine and boiler rooms, shaft tunnels with their entrances and escapes, light and air casings above the upper deck.

Fr: *Espaces affectés à la puissance motrice;* Ger: *Treibkrafträume.*

PROPULSIVE EFFICIENCY. The ratio of effective horsepower to indicated or shaft horsepower. Also called propulsive coefficient. In propulsive efficiency four terms are included: (a) engine efficiency, (b) hull efficiency, (c) propeller efficiency, (d) hull appendage factor. In ordinary practice a propulsive efficiency of 55 to 60 per cent is accepted as normal.

Fr: *Rendement Propulsif;* Ger: *Propulsionswirkungsgrad.*

Ayre, W., "The Propulsive Efficiency of Cargo Ships," Institution of Engineers and Shipbuilders in Scotland (Glasgow), *Transactions,* vol. 75 (1931); Kent, J. L., "Propulsive Efficiency and Seaworthiness," Institution of Engineers and Shipbuilders in Scotland, *Transactions,* vol. 76 (1932-33); McEntee, W., "The Propulsive Efficiency of Single Screw Cargo Ships," Society of Naval Architects and Marine Engineers (New York), *Transactions,* vol. 27 (1919).

PROTECTION AND INDEMNITY CLUB. A mutual insurance organization formed by a group of shipowners in order to secure cover for various risks that are not covered by the policies such as the first 3 per cent of damages, liability for loss of life and injury, and so on. Also called protection and indemnity association.

These clubs are maintained by a levy based upon the amount of tonnage owned by the members of the club, each making his proportionate contribution to the fund of the club.

PROTEST. 1. A declaration made by the master of a vessel before a notary public in the United States and Great Britain or a tribunal of commerce on the European Continent, or before the consul of the country from which the vessel hails if in a foreign port, on arrival in port, when, through stress of weather, it has not been practicable to adopt ordinary precautions in the matter of ventilation for perishable cargoes; when the condition of the cargo or any part thereof at the time of shipment is such as to lead to the belief that damage or some further damage has occurred during the voyage; when any serious breach of a charter party by the charterer in a foreign port happens; when a vessel experiences bad weather while at sea and when the master has reason to believe that the cargo is damaged or part of the deck load lost overboard. Copies of the protest are frequently demanded by underwriters in the event of a claim. Protests are received as evidence in tribunals on the Continent, but they cannot be made use of as evidence in courts of law in the United Kingdom in favor of the party making the protest except by the consent of both parties concerned.

Fr: *Rapport de Mer;* Ger: *Seeprotest; Verklarung.*

2. A sworn statement made by a survivor of a shipwreck giving full particulars of its cause, and so on, as far as is known.

PROTEST FLAG. International Code flag B flown from the starboard spreader of a sailing yacht during a race. It is a signal to inform the committee that one of the racing rules under which the race is held has been disregarded by another vessel.

Fr: *Pavillon de Réclamation;* Ger: *Protestflagge.*

PROTRACTOR. Navigational instrument, usually in the form of a graduated, semicircle made of transparent material, used for laying down or measuring angles on a chart. Also called plotter.

See **Three-Arm Protractor.**

PROVISION. To provide the necessary foodstuffs for the voyage of a ship.

Fr: *Ravitailler; Avitailler;* Ger: *Verproviantieren.*

PROW. 1. A sailing barge of Bombay harbor. It has long, pointed, slightly sheered bows and a round stern; is very beamy, and is rigged with a single mast, raking forward, on which is set a lateen sail. There are no headsails. Small decks are fitted at the ends and bulkheads enclose these spaces. Length over-all 65 to 80 ft. Beam 20 to 28 ft. Depth 6½ to 8 ft. Tonnage 50 to 100.

2. The part of the bow above water.

PSYCHROMETER. An instrument which measures relative humidity of the atmosphere, by comparing the simultaneous readings of wet-bulb and dry-bulb thermometers.

Fr: *Psychromètre;* Ger: *Psychrometer.*

PUBLIC ARMED VESSEL. An armed vessel converted to a public purpose, commissioned by a government and manned by naval officers and crew.

PUBLIC ENEMIES. In maritime law, enemies of the country. The forces of a country which is at war with that to which the carrier belongs. It does not include pirates or mob violence of any kind and covers only enemies of the country of the carrier, not of the shipper. Where rebellion goes so far as to produce *de facto* a state of war the carrier would be protected by the public enemies clause. Also called King's enemies (G. B.).

PUBLIC HEALTH SERVICE (U. S.). A bureau of the Treasury Department entrusted with the responsiblity of preventing the introduction of contagious diseases from foreign ports. Its inspectors detain ships at quarantine stations until they are satisfied it is safe for them to dock. In addition, the Public Health Service is charged with inspection of all new ships under the American flag with regard to the sanitary conditions of living quarters, drinking water, deratization. It issues the following certificates: (1) certificate of rat-proof construction (new ships). (2) certificate covering the drinking-water and culinary water systems (new ships). (3) deratization certificate (vessels in service). (4) certificate of compliance.

See **Quarantine.**

PUBLIC PORT. A commercial port owned and operated directly by a state or municipality. When some of the port properties are owned privately and others by the state or municipality a varying degree of public degree is exercised and the port may be classified as "semipublic port."

PUBLIC ROOM. In a passenger vessel, one of the rooms for the use of all passengers of the same class, i.e., dining room, smoke room, lounge, and so on.

Fr: *Salle de Réunion;* Ger: *Gesellschaftsraum.*

PUBLIC STORE AND GENERAL ORDER CLERK (U. S.). One who keeps a record of all packages designated by the customs for examination and appraisal at the appraisers stores or public stores.

PUBLIC TRUST PORT. A commercial port owned by and administered through a public trust composed of nonsalaried representatives of the municipality and of the various commercial and labor interests centered at the port.

PUBLIC VESSEL. A vessel owned or chartered by a State or by the ruler of a State for carrying out public duties such as the transportation of troops, ammunition, stores, scientific expeditions. Men-of-war and naval auxiliaries are immediately identified with the personality of the State. Both on the high seas and in foreign ports they are floating portions of the territory of their state. They may not, as neutrals, be visited, searched, or detained by belligerents. Public vessels include dispatch vessels, school ships, naval colliers, revenue vessels, lighthouse tenders, and generally all vessels employed in the service of the state for public purposes only. According to the U. S. Tariff Act of 1922 only such vessels which are not permitted by the law of the nations to which they belong to be employed in the transportation of passengers or merchandise in trade are considered as public vessels.

Fr: *Navire Public;* Ger: *Staatsdienstschiff.*

Great Britain, Foreign Office, Miscellaneous Papers 2 and 3, 1938, *International Convention for the Unification of Certain Rules Concerning the Immunity of State Owned Ships;* Matsunami, N., *Immunity of State Ships,* London, 1924; U. S. Naval War College, "The Classification of Public Vessels," *International Law Topics,* Washington, 1915.

PUCKER. A wrinkled seam in sailmaking.

PUCKER (to). A term used by sailmakers. To pucker two cloths of unequal length which are sewed together means to eliminate the difference in length by eating the slack on the seam of the longer. Also called to eat in.

Fr: *Boire le mou;* Ger: *Falten; Einhalten.*

PUDDING (U. S.). A thick wreath of yarns, strands, matting and oakum for fending and chafing purposes, tapering from the middle toward the ends, grafted all over and placed on a boat's stem. A lay of strand around a metal ring, when a hemp rope is to be fastened to it, to prevent excessive chafing of the rope. In Great Britain called puddening.

Fr: *Emboudinure;* Ger: *Schamfielungsmatte; Schamfielkissen.*

PUDDING CHAIN. Short link chain occasionally used for running rigging. It runs well over sheaves and is easy to belay. It is used for jib halyards and sheets in small trading vessels, but has lately been generally replaced by flexible wire.

Ger: *Takelungskette.*

PUDDING FENDER. A fender with tapering ends made of old rope, unlaid and served with spun yarn to about 6 in. in diameter, covered with canvas or with rope matting. Also called dolphin. Pudding fenders when used on ship's boats are attached to a coir rope.

Fr: *Boudin de Défense;* Ger: *Taufender; Leguan.*

PUFFER. Slang name given in the British Isles to a small type of steam or motor bulk carrier from the Clyde. It differs from the orthodox steam lighter in having a poop and raised forecastle head. It has one hatchway. Typical dimensions, Length 84 feet, Breadth 20 feet, Depth 9'4", Gross tonnage 150, Deadweight 190 tons, Grain Capacity 9500 cubic feet.

PU-HOE. A dugout paddling canoe with single outrigger from the Society Islands. Length 15 to 28 ft. Breadth 16 to 19 in. Depth 12 to 18 in. (Average.)

PULL. The effort exerted on an oar.

PULL (to). To row. To propel a boat by oars. To transport by rowing. In nautical parlance the word "row" is seldom used.

Fr: *Nager;* Ger: *Rudern.*

PULPIT. A platform for the harpooner, on the end of the bowsprit in a sword-fishing boat.

PULVERIZED COAL. General name for any carbonaceous fuel passed through a preliminary crusher and having its moisture content reduced 1 to 5 per cent according to the nature of the fuel, and subsequently ground to an extremely fine powder. Also called pulverized fuel. The state of fineness of this powder should be such that 85 per cent will pass through a mesh of 40,000 holes to the square inch. The coal powder is blown into the furnace by a soft air blast, ignition and complete combustion taking place almost instantaneously with maximum temperature. Any coal can be used for pulverizing, low grade, cheap fuels being as serviceable as high class bunker coal. Powdered coal as delivered to ship's bunkers weighs about 37 lb. per cubic foot, whereas, the ordinary run of mine coal weighs about 47 lb. per cubic foot.

Fr: *Charbon Pulverisé;* Ger: *Pulverkohle.*

Brand, J. C., "Pulverised Fuel for Marine Purposes," Institution of Naval Architects (London), *Transactions,* vol. 69 (1927); Jackson, R., "Modern Developments in Pulverized Coal Firing," Institution of Engineers and Shipbuilders in Scotland (Glasgow), *Transactions,* vol. 70 (1926-28).

PUMP. The number and type of pumps required on board a merchant ship according to classification rules or government regulations vary in relation to the tonnage of the vessel, her type or trade, and her mode of propulsion. Sailing vessels are required to carry two hand pumps with hold suctions, and, if iron or steel built, a supplementary pump must be fitted to the forepeak. On mechanically propelled cargo vessels a minimum of two steam or motor pumps and one hand pump is required, the latter having its suction pipe connected to the bilge piping. The 1929 Conference for Safety of Life at Sea provides that passenger vessels, if more than 300 ft. long, should carry three mechanically driven pumps. Pumps for marine service can be classed into three groups: (1) centrifugal pumps; (2) reciprocating pumps, steam or motor driven; (3) rotary pumps.

Fr: *Pompe;* Ger: *Pumpe.*

See **Admiralty Pump, Ballast Pump, Bilge Pump, Fire and Bilge Pump, Centrifugal Pump, Donkey Pump, Downton Pump, Fire Pump, Hand Pump, Hand Deck Pump, Head Pump, Sanitary Pump, Stripping Pump, Submersible Pump, Variable Delivery Pump, Water Service Pump.**

Bleicken, B., "Neuere Bordpumpen aller Art," *Schiffbau,* Berlin, vol. 35 (Nov., 1934); Frohwein, P. H., *Marine Pumps,* Scranton, Pa., 1933; Schaefer, D., "Bordpumpen," *Verein Deutscher Ingenieure. Zeitschrift,* Berlin, vol. 80, no. 27 (1936).

PUMP BRAKE WINDLASS. A hand windlass worked by means of two long brake beams fastened by connecting rods to a pawl and ratchet gear. With this gear the cable holder is made to revolve on each up-and-down motion of the brake beams.

Fr: *Guindeau à Pompe; Guindeau à Bringuebale;* Ger: *Pumpspill.*

PUMPING. Unsteadiness of the mercury in the barometer caused by the fluctuations of the atmospheric pressure produced by a gusty wind or due to the oscillation of the ship.

Fr: *Pistonnage;* Ger: *Pumpen.*

PUMPING PLAN. A drawing of the entire length of the ship comprising sectional elevation and plan of the inner bottom and showing the subdivision of the double bottom, the holds, deep tanks, oil storage and settling tanks, and bunkers. The sizes and positions of suctions, air pipes, sounding pipes, and so on, are shown, also the approximate arrangement of piping outside the machinery space. Bilge suction wells are also shown and, in oil fuel ships, such cofferdams as may be required between tanks carrying oil and those carrying fresh water, and the gutterways at the base of oil fuel bunkers.

Fr: *Plan de Tuyautage de Coque;* Ger: *Lenz- und Ballasteinrichtungsplan.*

PUMPMAN. Petty officer who tends to and maintains one or more power-driven pumps for handling liquid cargoes such as oil or molasses from or to a ship. He keeps a close watch on the temperature of the cargo and equipment, to keep the cargo below flash and fire points; arranges and connects suction and discharge pipe lines and hose and operates valves as required. He must hold a certificate of competence for pumpman.

PUMP ROOM. A compartment in tank vessels where the pumping plant for handling cargo is installed. It runs right across the vessel from deck to bottom, with the pumps placed as low as possible in order to facilitate draining. In some instances, to suit the vessel's trim, the pump room is placed just forward or abaft the bridge superstructure, and in others it is located aft, forward of the after cofferdam.

Fr: *Chambre des Pompes;* Ger: *Pumpenraum.*

In oil tankers over 400 ft. long two pump rooms are provided as a rule, for loading and unloading purposes and, in addition, a ballast pump room is sometimes arranged for in the forehold or abaft the forepeak tank.

PUMP STRAINER.

See **Rose Box.**

PUMP STRUM.

See **Rose Box.**

PUMP WELL. In small vessels with hand pumps, a compartment or casing extending

PUNCHED HOLE—PUNCHING

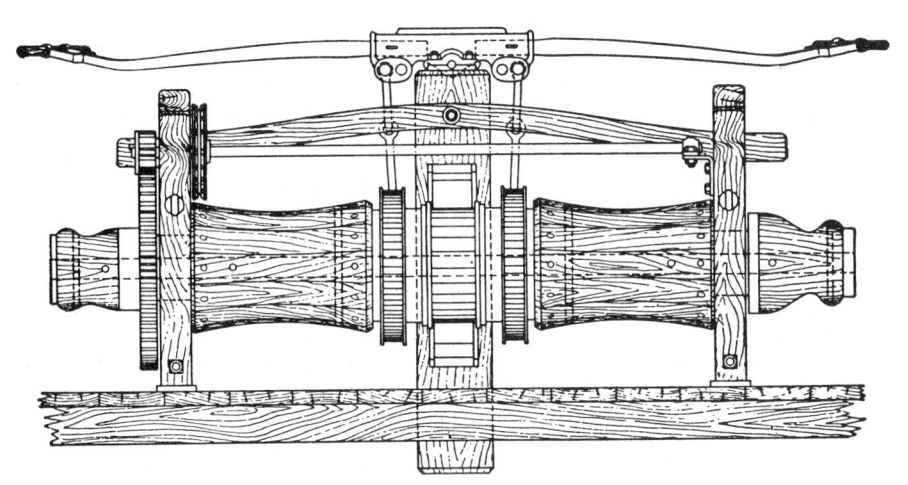

Pump Brake Windlass

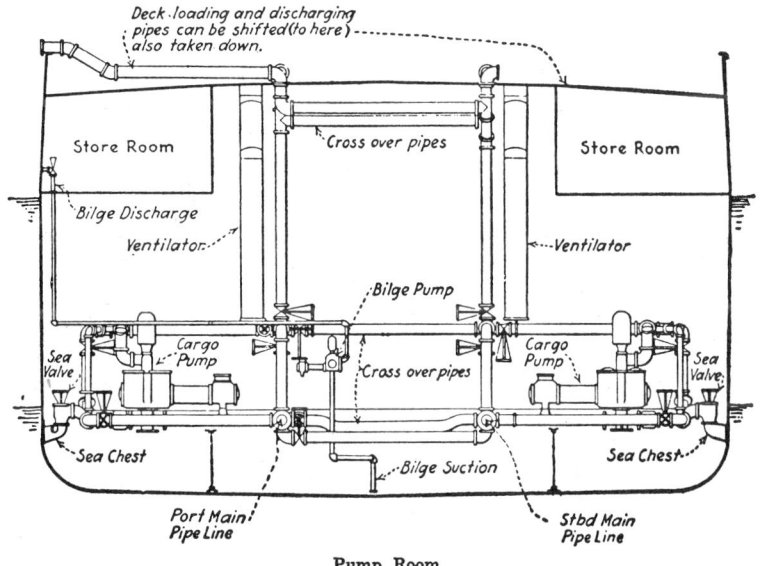

Pump Room

from the ship's bottom to the 'tween deck or the upper deck as the case may be, and containing the pumpstocks, and so on. It is used for removing bilge water which collects in the limbers, or water that enters in the event of a leak.

Fr: *Archipompe;* Ger: *Pumpensod; Pumpensumpf.*

PUNCHED HOLE. A hole produced by pushing the waste material through a hole in a die, the metal yielding by shearing around the edge of the hole. Holes are generally punched from the side which will form the faying surface.

Fr: *Trou Poinçonné;* Ger: *Ausgestanztes Loch.*

PUNCHING. A process for making holes in plates and shapes by means of a punch and die. On account of the ductility of the metal the hole so formed is slightly conical.

The usual practice in shipbuilding is to use coned neck rivets with punched holes so that the neck of the rivet will fit the cone of the hole caused by the punch.

Fr: *Poinçonnage;* Ger: *Ausstanzen.*

PUNGAY. Indian dugout canoe employed in fishing on the coast of North Kanara. It has a capacity from 1 to 3 tons and is worked by a crew of 8. In hull form it is similar to the *odam* canoe from Malabar.

PUNGY. Also pungie. A type of keel schooner once common on the Chesapeake Bay, United States, of the "Baltimore Clipper" model. These vessels had much deadrise, raking stem and sternpost, and considerable drag to the keel. The stem at rabbet was usually curved, the head long and pointed in profile. The stern was broad and square, with thin quarters. The transoms had little overhang, and were usually in the old fashion (upper and lower transom). The hull was wide and the bows full on deck but sharp below. Bulwarks were usually open, or a log rail, like that of a small boat, was fitted; rails were very low. Length on deck 58 ft. Beam 17 ft. 6 in. Draft of water at post 6 ft. 1 in. (Typical.)

These schooners were employed in oyster dredging, in the fruit trade to the West Indies, and as ordinary traders. They had the reputation of being fast sailers but wet; their capacity was small. The masts raked sharply. The rig consisted of gaff sails, main gaff topsail, single jib, and main topmast staysail. Some had a fore-topmast.

PUNI. A single-outrigger dugout canoe of the Manihiki Islands, Polynesia.

PUNT. Flat-bottomed, open boat of simple construction with flaring sides, raking transoms at bow and stern, and rockered fore-and-aft bottom line. Also called flat. The punt is usually built for rowing or poling but is occasionally used as a sailing craft, in which case a centerboard is provided. In some localities punts are fitted with engines and used for fishing.

The term "Punt" was formerly applied in a generic sense to various craft used as ferries, barges and lighters. Nowadays it is usually confined to a lightly built, flat-bottomed pleasure craft very long in proportion to its breadth, with square ends and sides slightly narrowing from the center toward the bow and stem. It is propelled by poles. The word also refers to a roughly built flat-bottomed heavy duty boat with square ends used for painting or other work on the ship's side when in port. It is usually propelled by sculling. Length 10 to 14 feet.

Fr: *Plate;* Ger: *Scheuerprahm; Stechkahn; Pünte.*

See **Fenland Punt, Galley Punt, Hastings Punt, Itchen Punt, Newfoundland Sealing Punt, Quay Punt, Sailing Punt, Southwold Beach Punt.**

PUNTER. A Dutch flat-bottomed craft similar to the *hoogaars* with sharp rising stem, but of smaller tonnage. Larger *punters* are half-decked. Smaller boats are open. Those used for fishing are fitted with a well. The rig generally adopted consists of jibheaded mainsail with boom and foresail. Length over-all 20 to 40 ft.

PURCHASE. A general term for any mechanical arrangement of tackle which increases the force applied by a combination of pulleys. The French word *caliorne* and the German term *gien* usually refer to a threefold or a fourfold purchase.

In all cases where the two blocks of a purchase are alike, the hauling part leads from the block to which the standing part makes fast, while in cases where one of the blocks has an extra sheave, the hauling part leads from this block and the standing part from the other.

Fr: *Caliorne;* Ger: *Takel; Gien.*

See **Bell Purchase, Cant Purchase, Cat Purchase, Double Purchase, Fourfold Purchase, Kent Purchase, Single Purchase, Tack Purchase, Topping Lift Purchase, Treble Purchase, Twofold Purchase, Union Purchase, Union Purchase System, Vang Purchase.**

PURPLE LIGHT. The glow of purple or rosy color which can be observed over the western sky after sunset and the eastern sky before sunrise.

PURSE BOAT. A double-ended open rowboat of rugged construction used in the menhaden fisheries of the Atlantic coast. Also called seine boat. During fishing operations the two seine boats work in pairs, each carrying half of the seine net stowed near the stern immediately forward of the after thwart. The frames, gunwales and thwarts are made of hardwood, the planking and flooring of white cedar or a similar wood. Platforms of 2 to 3 ft. in length are built about one foot below the gunwale at each end. There are 4 thwarts, 1 aft and 3 forward. To maintain the boat on an even keel when the seine is carried, the stern is built with full buttocks which gives greater buoyancy aft and the side planking is raised from 2 to 3 inches. Purse boats vary in length from 28 to 35 ft., with a breadth of 6 to 7 ft. and a depth of 2 to 3 ft. They are pulled with 16 ft. oars. One of the boats is provided with a crane or small davit which fits into the port gunwale about 10 ft. from the bow. When in position it stands about 18 in. above the gunwale. Two snatch blocks, through which passes the purse line when emerging from the water, facilitate pursing the net. Motor-driven purse boats have recently been introduced.

PURSE LINE. A line which runs through metal rings fastened at the bottom of a purse seine by which the net is closed after a school of fish has been surrounded. Also called draw string. Every purse line is divided into two or three parts of equal length connected by a link and swivel at each end.

PURSE NET. A net which consists of one long deep pocket, the mouth of which may be drawn close with cords or closed quickly.

Fr: *Filet Coulissant;* Ger: *Ringnetz.*

PURSER. A clerical officer on board a passenger vessel whose duty it is to take care of the ship's books, crews' lists, passenger lists, and all documents relating to the cargo.

Fr: *Commissaire;* Ger: *Zahlmeister.*

Hill, C. E., *Purser's Manual and Marine Store Keeping,* New York, 1941.

PURSE SEINE. A seine net built like a long shallow curtain without any bag in the middle. Its upper edge is buoyed by a cork line; the lower edge is weighted with sinkers strung on the lead line, the latter being about 10 per cent shorter than the cork line. Along the entire length of the lead line a number of rings are fastened at regular intervals with short ropes called "bridle lines." Through these rings runs the purse line, purse rope, or purse string, by means of which the bottom of the net is closed. At each end of the net are the "up-and-down lines," between the cork and lead lines. Along each of the up-and-down lines is a series of small rings through which runs the brail rope. The brail rope or brail line is used to lift up the lead line to the cork line, one end of it

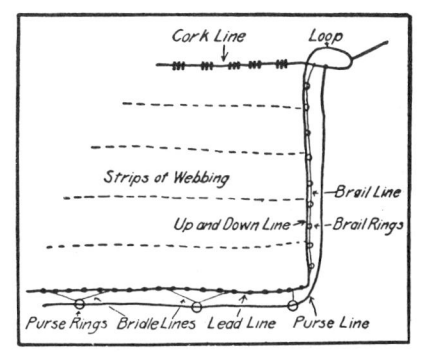

A sketch (not drawn to scale) of the end of a purse seine showing the relative positions of the different lines and rings. The brail and the purse lines and either the haul or the skiff line are tied to the loop.

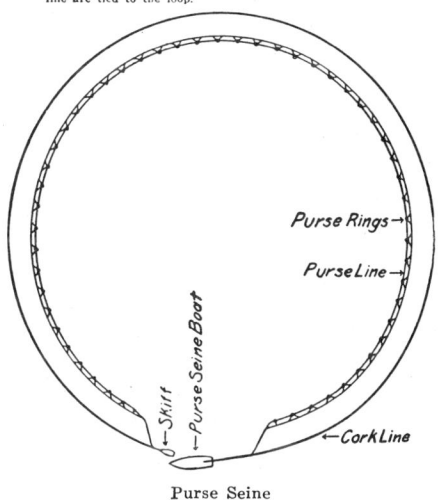

Purse Seine

being fastened to the lead line, the other end to the cork line. One end of the net (called skiff end) is tied to the skiff with a heavy line about 12 fathoms long. The other end (called haul end) is fastened to the seine boat with a line about 100 fathoms long.

Fr: *Senne à Coulisse; Senne Tournante;*
Ger: *Beutelnetz; Beutelgarn; Drehwade.*

Purse seines used for tuna fishing are about 275 to 350 fathoms long and 28 to 34 fathoms deep, with 5- to 7-in. meshing. In the sardine fisheries the nets are 200 to 230 fathoms long and 25 to 30 fathoms deep. Mackerel and menhaden seines in general use on the Atlantic coast of the United States and Gulf of Mexico are from 180 to 250 fathoms long and 8 to 20 fathoms deep. For mackerel the mesh is commonly 1⅞ or 2 in. and for menhaden from 1¾ to

2¾ in. They are made of a light cotton twine graded from a very small size on the ends to a heavier and stronger size in the bunt.

Cod seines used in Nova Scotia, New Brunswick, Labrador, and Newfoundland fisheries are 100 to 130 fathoms long and 10 to 15 fathoms deep. The mesh is 3 in. in the bunt and graduated to 5 in. at the extreme ends. Herring seines used in British North American and Newfoundland fisheries are 50 to 150 fathoms long and 4 to 10 fathoms deep, with a meshing of 1½ to 1¾ in. in the bunt and 2 in. in the arms.

Scofield, W. L., *Purse Seines for California Sardines*, California Fish and Game, vol. 12, no. 1 (1926); Skogsberg, T., *Investigation of the Purse Seine Industry of Southern California*, California Fish and Game, Fish Bulletin no. 9 (1925).

PURSUIT. See **Right of Pursuit.**

PUSH NET. A small net attached to a long handle and pushed by hand through the water in front of the fisherman; used for shrimps. The meshing varies from 1/10th to ½ in.

> Fr: *Pousseux;* Ger: *Stosswade; Scheerenwade; Schiebenetz; Bügelhamen.*

PUT ABOUT. To tack. To go on the other tack.

> Fr: *Changer d'Amures;* Ger: *Über Stag gehen; Stagen.*

PUT BACK. To return to the point of departure.

> Fr: *Rentrer;* Ger: *Zurückfahren.*

PUT IN. To enter a harbor, especially when deviating from the regular course to seek shelter or for some other fortuitous cause.

> Fr: *Relacher;* Ger: *Einlaufen.*

PUT TO SEA. To leave a port or roadstead and go to sea.

> Fr: *Prendre la mer;* Ger: *In See stechen; Auslaufen.*

PUTTY GUN. A device used by calkers to fill with a mixture of red lead and putty spaces between faying surfaces which do not fit properly. A screwed plug forces the putty into the joint under great pressure and fills all the cavities. Also called red lead injector.

> Fr: *Pompe à Mastic;* Ger: *Kittspritze.*

Q

Q. Square yellow flag of the international code of signals. Also called **Quarantine flag** when used as a sanitary signal.

See **Quarantine flag.**

QUADRANT. A reflecting astronomical instrument for measuring angles with a quarter circle graduated arc.

Fr: *Quadrant;* Ger: *Quadrant.*

Q.S.S. QUADRUPLE SCREW STEAMER.

Q.S.M. QUADRUPLE SCREW MOTOR SHIP.

Q-SHIP. A merchant vessel fitted with hidden armament for antisubmarine warfare. Ostensibly unarmed merchantmen, they acted as a lure for surface gunfire attack by U-boats, until the latter came within range—at that time the Q-ship dropped its peaceful role and returned fire. Used successfully in World War I.

QUADRANTAL COMPASS CARD. A compass card occasionally found on merchant ships and in which the four quarters of the card are each graduated into ninety degrees, with zero at North and South and ninety at East and West. By this method the directions of the cardinal points are named simply North, East, South and West, while intermediate directions are named in degrees from North or South towards East or West as the case may be.

Fr: *Rose quadrantale;* Ger: *Quadranten Kompassrose.*

QUADRANTAL CORRECTOR. One of the two hollow spheres made of pure soft iron, free from retained magnetism, secured by screw bolts to slotted supporting arms at each side of the binnacle on the athwartship line through the compass. The centers of the spheres are in the same horizontal plane as the compass needles. The earth's magnetism magnetizes these spheres through induction. The induced magnetism of the spheres then tends to force the compass needle back into the direction of magnetic north, in compensation for the horizontally placed symmetrical soft iron in the ship. Also called compensating globe.

Fr: *Globe Compensateur;* Ger: *Quadrantalkugel.*

QUADRANTAL DEVIATION. A deflection of the compass needle from the magnetic meridian caused by the induced magnetism in a ship's horizontal soft iron. It changes its sign, or becomes easterly or westerly, in alternate quadrants.

Fr: *Déviation Quadrantale;* Ger: *Viertelkreisartige Deviation.*

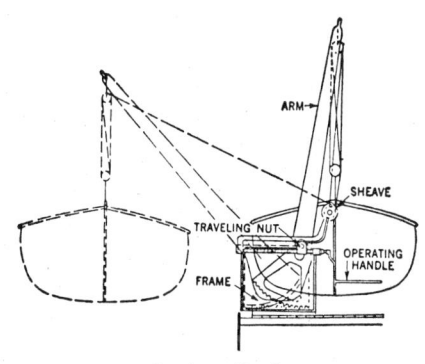

Quadrant Davit

QUADRANT DAVIT, QUADRANTAL DAVIT. A straight steel davit in which the lower end forms a semicircular arc cogged on its circumference. The cogs on the arc or quadrant work in a flat rack fastened to the deck as the boat is swung out.

Fr: *Bossoir à Secteur;* Ger: *Quadrantdavit.*

QUARANTINABLE DISEASES. Those under which a vessel or its occupants may be detained by the medical authorities of the port on arrival. They include: Anthrax; Cholera; Leprosy; Bubonic plague; Psittacosis; Smallpox; Typhus; Yellow Fever.

QUADRANT TILLER. A rudder tiller in the form of an arc of a circle, a half circle, or a complete circle. It consists of a casting or of a forged hub with arms, the circumferencial part being built up of plates and angles. Also called sectional tiller.

Fr: *Mèche à Secteur; Barre à Secteur;* Ger: *Quadrant Ruderpinne.*

QUADRATURE. The relative position of two celestial bodies when the difference of their longitudes is 90°.

Fr: *Quadrature;* Ger: *Quadratur.*

QUADRUPLE-EXPANSION ENGINE. A multiple expansion reciprocating steam engine with four stages.

QUAGGY (G. B.). The condition of timber which is heart-shaken, occurring often in trees growing on loose sandy soil.

QUARANTINE. The period during which a vessel is detained in isolation until free from any contagious disease among the passengers or crew. The word is now applied to the sanitary regulations which are the modern substitute for quarantine.

Fr: *Quarantaine;* Ger: *Quarantäne.*

See **Pratique.**

U. S. Public Health Service, Report 114, *Information Regarding Quarantine and Immigration for Ship Surgeons,* Washington, 1940; U. S. Public Health Service, *Quarantine Laws and Regulations of the U. S.,* Washington, 1920; U. S. State Department, Treaty Series 762, *Convention Revising the International Sanitary Convention,* Washington, 1928.

QUARANTINE ANCHORAGE. The area at the harbor entrance, usually designated by yellow buoys, within which vessels anchor for the exercise of quarantine regulations.

QUARANTINE BOAT. Small craft of various types which meet incoming vessels on their arrival in port. Carries the health officer responsible for the enforcement of quarantine regulations.

Fr: *Bateau de la Santé;* Ger: *Quarantänefahrzeug.*

QUARANTINE BUOY. One of the yellow buoys at the entrance of a harbor indicating the place where vessels must anchor for the exercise of quarantine regulations.

QUARANTINE DECLARATION. A document signed by the captain and the ship's doctor before the port health officer when a ship arrives at the quarantine station. It gives the name of the ship, tonnage, number of crew, first port of voyage and date of sailing, intermediate ports called at, number of passengers for the port at which the vessel is arriving, number of transit passengers, cases of infectious diseases during voyage, deaths, nature of cargo, name of agents. The port health officer then proceeds with the medical inspection of passengers and crew. Also called **entry declaration.**

QUARANTINE DUES. A charge against all vessels entering a harbor to provide for the maintenance of medical control service. Also called quarantine fees.

Fr: *Droits de Quarantaine;* Ger: *Quarantänegeld.*

QUARANTINE FLAG. A yellow flag used as a sanitary signal. It is displayed by all vessels entering a harbor; also when a contagious or infectious disease exists on board, or when the vessel has been placed in quarantine.

Fr: *Pavillon Sanitaire;* Ger: *Quarantäne Flagge.*

QUARANTINE HARBOR. A place where vessels in quarantine are stationed when arriving from contaminated ports.

Fr: *Port de Quarantaine;* Ger: *Quarantänehafen.*

QUARANTINE SIGNAL. Signals flown by vessels required to show their state of health. By day "Q" of the International Code signifies "Ship is healthy—free pratique requested." Flag "Q" over first substitute signifies that the ship has had cases of infectious diseases or that there has been unusual mortality among rats on board. Flag "Q" over flag "L" signifies "Ship is infected." By night a vessel entering harbor exhibits a red light over a white light more than 6 ft. apart, which signifies that the ship is awaiting free pratique.

Fr: *Signal Sanitaire;* Ger: *Quarantänesignal.*

QUARANTINE STATION. A medical control center located in an isolated spot ashore where patients with contagious diseases from vessels in quarantine are taken. It is also used for passengers and crews of vessels arriving from suspected ports while fumigation or any other disinfection is carried out on board ship.

Fr: *Lazaret; Station quarantenaire;* Ger: *Quarantänestation.*

QUARTER. 1. The curved portion of a ship on either side at the stern. The upper part of a vessel's sides near the stern. The term "quarter" literally implies one quarter of the ship, but usually applies to 45° abaft the beam.

Fr: *Hanche;* Ger: *Vierung.*

2. The part of a yard just outside the slings.

Fr: *Brasseyage;* Ger: *Achtkant.*

3. To sail with the wind on the quarter. To quarter the sea means to bring the sea first on one quarter and then on the other. This is frequently resorted to when running before a heavy sea in a small boat.

QUARTER BEAM LENGTH. A factor used in yacht measurement formulas. It is the length of the hull taken parallel with the fore-and-aft vertical plane at a distance from it equal to one-quarter of load waterline breadth and one-tenth of this breadth above the load waterline.

QUARTER BLOCK. 1. A term applied to single lead blocks placed under a yard close in, amidships, for the sheets and clew lines of a sail set above to reeve through. They are frequently shackled to the sling yoke.

Fr: *Poulie de sous vergue; Poulie de bas cul;* Ger: *Marsschotenblock.*

2. One of the lower blocks of the spanker sheet purchase. It is hooked to an eyeplate at the side of the deck.

3. Metal sheave which acts as fairleader for the wheel chains or ropes to the tiller or quadrant.

Fr: *Réa de retour de drosse;* Ger: *Steuerreep Leitrolle.*

QUARTER BOARDS. Light ⁾ ding which extended around the qua ₃ and stern above the quarter rail. (Obsolete.)

QUARTER BOAT. Any boat hung on davits over the ship's quarter.

QUARTER BREAST. A breast line extending from the ship's quarter and holding the stern of the vessel to the dock or quay.

Fr: *Traversier Arrière;* Ger: *Heck Dwarstau.*

QUARTER-DECK. 1. A term applied to the afterpart of the upper deck. In a general way this term was used to indicate the portion of the upper deck extending from the mainmast to the stern. If there is a poop, as far aft as the poop.

Fr: *Gaillard d'Arrière;* Ger: *Halbdeck; Achterdeck; Quarterdeck.*

2. In naval vessels, that portion of the weather deck which is reserved for the use of officers.

QUARTER FAST.
See Quarter Rope.

QUARTER FENDER. A puddening fender used in square-sterned open boats. They extend from near the rudder on each quarter to well forward of the stern. The puddening is made of old rope marled down, parcelled and covered with a hitching of nine-thread manila.

QUARTER GALLERIES. Ornamented projections from the quarters of a square-sterned ship, which were intended to decorate and provide a finish to the quarters. They are still found on some Arab craft.

Fr: *Bouteilles;* Ger: *Windvierungsgalerien.*

QUARTERING SEA. A sea that strikes the ship's quarter or about 45° abaft the beam. A sea running in such direction as to break against the weather quarter of the vessel.

Ger: *Backstagweise See.*

QUARTERING WIND. A wind from the weather quarter or between the fore and aft line and the beam, abaft the latter.

Fr: *Vent sous vergue;* Ger: *Backstagswind.*

QUARTER IRON. Inboard boom iron of a topmast studding-sail boom, located about two-thirds out on the yard, fitted with hinges to clamp and unclamp around the boom. (Obsolete.)

QUARTER KNEE. A lodging knee timber connecting the ship's sides with the transom. A knee fitted horizontally between the gunwale and the crosspiece in a square-sterned rowboat. Also called transom knee.

Fr: *Courbe d'Écusson;* Ger: *Heckknie.*

QUARTER LIFT. One of the boom topping lifts leading from an iron band on the spar up to and through a single block under the eyes of the rigging at the lower masthead, thence down on deck. The band is placed at about quarter length from the end of the spar. Each hauling part is usually provided with a purchase.

Fr: *Balancine de gui;* Ger: *Baumdirk; Baumtoppnant.*

QUARTER LINES. Traces of the vertical planes running fore and aft on either side of the center line half way between that line and the ship's side.

QUARTERMASTER. An able-bodied seaman specially entrusted with the steering of the vessel. There are usually in large vessels two quartermasters in each watch: each one taking a spell of two hours at the wheel. Quartermasters are also detailed for signaling and sounding and have charge of some of the navigating appliances such as log lines, lead lines, sounding machines, and so on.

In naval vessels, quartermasters are petty officers associated with the navigation of the ship, steering, taking soundings, and the like.

Fr: *Timonier;* Ger: *Steurer.*
See Iron Quartermaster.

QUARTER MOORING. See Spring.

QUARTER POINT. The fourth of the distance from one point of the compass to another, equivalent to about two degrees and forty-nine minutes. Also called quarter.

Fr: *Quart de Rhumb;* Ger: *Viertelkompassstrich.*

QUARTER POINT CARD. A compass card which has its circumference divided into 32 points, each point being equivalent to 12½ degrees. It is further subdivided into quarter points and half points. The ¼, ½, and ¾ divisions of each point are read away from a cardinal or intercardinal point. Used on sailing craft, coasters, harbor craft, ship's lifeboats because it is sufficiently accurate and easy to read for the helmsman who has to watch the compass and sail the ship simultaneously.

Ger: *Viertelstrich Kompassrose.*

QUARTER RAIL. On American schooners, a light open railing fitted above the bulwarks and extending around the quarters and stern of the vessel. It serves as guard for the quarter deck. Also called quarterdeck rail, monkey rail.

Ger: *Heckreling; Monkireling.*

QUARTER ROPE. 1. A rope or hawser holding a vessel by the quarter. It acts as a quarter spring. Also called quarter line, quarter fast.

Fr: *Traversier Arrière;* Ger: *Hintere Seitenfeste.*
See **Spring**.

2. In a trawl net one of the lines fastened to the foot of the bosom at each end then rove through a becket on the headrope. Its purpose is to close the net when hauling it on board. Also called leech line.

Fr: *Vire-Vire;* Ger: *Knüppeltau.*

QUARTER RUDDER. A rudder slung in an oblique direction at the side of the stern from a strong crossbeam which projects over each quarter. Most rudders of this type are hung with slings made of rattan or similar material, the friction of which helps to keep them in the desired position. Quarter rudders are still used in native craft of the Pacific islands, Malaya, and so on.

Fr: *Gouvernail Latéral;* Ger: *Seitenruder.*

QUARTERS. 1. See **Accommodation**.
2. Those parts in a trawlnet where the wings join the belly.
3. Individual stations for the crew and passengers for fire drill or boat drill and in all emergencies. In naval vessels, the crew is at quarters when the men are manning their designated stations.

Fr: *Postes;* Ger: *Station.*
See **Firemen's Quarters, Seamen's Quarters**.

QUARTERSAWED PLANK. See Rift Sawed Plank.

QUARTER SAWING. Sawing boards radially from a log so that the annular rings are perpendicular or nearly so, to the face. Quarter-sawed lumber shrinks less, does not sliver and wears more evenly than flatsawed lumber. Also called rift sawing.

QUARTER SLING. One of the supports of a yard on either side of its center.

Fr: *Suspente;* Ger: *Rahestropp.*

QUARTER STANCHION. Name given to stanchions supporting deck beams when two of them are used under each beam and they are placed one on each side of the middle line. Also, a strong stanchion forming the extreme boundary in a squaresterned wooden vessel.

Fr: *Epontille Latérale;* Ger: *Seitenstütze.*

QUARTER TACKLE. A purchase fastened to the quarter of a lower yard to hoist boats or heavy weights. It is composed of a double block and a single block with hook and thimble.

Ger: *Klappaüfer.*

QUARTER TIMBER. In a wooden vessel, one of the timbers secured to the transom frame to help in forming the counter.

Fr: *Branchette;* Ger: *Hinterer Seitenauflanger.*

QUARTER WATCH. One half of the watch on deck.

Fr: *Demi Bordée.*
See **Watch**.

QUARTER WIND. A wind which is blowing four points abaft the beam. The ship is then said to be quartered or veering.

Ger: *Backstagwind.*

QUASI DERELICT. A judicial term sometimes used to characterize a vessel when the conditions are not such as to constitute technically such a vessel derelict; as for instance when a ship is not abandoned but those on board are physically and mentally incapable of doing anything for her safety. Also, when a vessel is found abandoned and there is no indication of the intent of master and crew to return and resume possession; or, according to some, when a vessel is necessarily abandoned because it is afire.

QUASI-PROPULSIVE COEFFICIENT. The ratio of screw efficiency behind a model to that in open water. It is made up of two terms: (1) the efficiency of the screw in open water, which depends upon its revolutions and speed; (2) the product of hull efficiency and relative rotative efficiency. It is frequently used in propeller calculations when selecting and comparing propeller for the most efficient combination of hull and screw. This term is also used to denote the ratio of effective horsepower to propeller (delivered) horsepower; from which, the required horsepower is estimated. Bragg, E. M., "The Quasi Propulsive Coefficient," Institution of Naval Architects, *Transactions,* vol. 86 (London), 1944.

QUAY. A landing place at which vessels receive or discharge cargo. Also called wharf.

A quay is usually a solid masonry wall filled in behind, as distinguished from an open pile structure. In the quay system of harbor planning, the quay wall, warehouse sheds, rail lines, roadway are all parallel to the ship, as distinguished from the pier system, where the platform for handling the goods is at an angle to the other elements.

Fr: *Quai;* Ger: *Kai.*

See **Ex-Quay, Tidal Quay.**

QUAYAGE. 1. The payment made for the use of, or berthing at a quay.

Fr: *Droits de Quai;* Ger: *Kaigeld.*

2. The total length of quays, piers, or wharves of a port where vessels can come alongside for loading and discharging.

QUAY DUES. See **Dockage.**

QUAYMAN. See **Man.**

QUAY PUNT. A small sailing boat found on the estuary of the river Fal (Cornwall), used as a carrier for bringing stores, and the like, to the larger vessels anchored in the roads. These boats are half-decked, with waterways around the cockpit. They are built with straight stem and transom stern. The rig consists of a short pole mast, gaff mainsail with boom, jib-headed mizzen, and foresail which sets on a short iron bumkin. In the summer a larger set of sails is used, and a running bowsprit with jib may be seen, also a standing lug mizzen. Length on water line 25 ft. 9 in. Beam 8 ft. Draft 5 ft. 3 in. Displacement 6.8 tons. (Typical.)

QUAY RATE (G. B.). A reduced charge made on goods landed from a ship when they can be cleared with dispatch from the quay, in place of the ordinary landing rate.

QUAZE. A boat employed on the Danish and German coasts of the Baltic for net fishing and transportation of live fish by sea. Also called *quatze, kvase.* It is built with a large well in which from 1½ to 4 tons of live fish can be carried. The ketch or the cutter rigs are usually adopted and an auxiliary engine fitted. Their gross tonnage varies from 10 to 60. The hull is built with keel and clinker planking, and sharp stern. The sail plan includes main pole mast and small jigger, a boomless gaff or lug mainsail, and two headsails. Pomeranian Quaze: Length 42½ to 53 ft. Breadth 16½ to 18 ft. (Average.)

See **Handelkvase.**

QUEEN. See **Queen Staysail.**

QUEENIE. A four-sided staysail set from the triatic or jumper stay of a schooner yacht.

QUEEN STAYSAIL. A triangular topsail made of working or lighter canvas, set by staysail- or gaff-rigged schooner-yachts forward of the main topmast. Also called queen. Its clew is sheeted to the afterend of a wishbone or sprit. It derives its name from the schooner yacht "Queen" on which it was first used in 1900. It is so cut on the foot as to clear the spring stay.

QUICKEN. Term used in shipbuilding, meaning to give any part or member a sharper curve. To quicken the sheer means to shorten the radius by which the curve is struck. (Rare.)

QUICK-FLASHING LIGHT. A coastal light showing not less than sixty flashes per minute.

Fr: *Feu scintillant;* Ger: *Festfeuer mit Blitzen; Funkelfeuer.*

QUICK FLASHING LIGHT WITH BLINKS. A light in which the duration of flashes is interrupted by eclipses of longer duration than that of the flashes.

Fr: *Feu scintillant à clignotements;* Ger: *Funkelfeuer mit Dunkelpausen.*

QUICK FREEZING. A process in refrigeration of perishable cargoes mainly employed in the transportation of soft fruit, green vegetables and fish. It involves the freezing of the produce very rapidly by exposing it to the influence of very low temperatures in the region of minus 50° F., after which it can be stowed in an insulated hold for any reasonable length of time at a normal refrigerating temperature of a few degrees below freezing point, say plus 25° F.

QUICKSAND. Loose, yielding wet sand which swallows and submerges heavy objects. Sometimes found on sand beaches or banks.
    Fr: *Sable mouvant;* Ger: *Treibsand; Flugsand.*

QUICKWORK. That part of a ship's planking or plating which is under water when it is loaded.
    Fr: *Oeuvres Vives;* Ger: *Lebendiges Werk.*

QUICK WORKS. Term formerly used to denote the vessel's sides above the channels and decks.
    Fr: *Accastillage;* Ger: *Oberwerk.*

QUILTING. Mats nailed to the planking of a vessel when navigating in polar waters as protection against ice.

QUILTING RIVET (U. S.). 1. One of the rivets placed in the middle portion of a doubling plate so as to keep the faying surfaces together at all points. Also called tack rivet (G. B.).
    Fr: *Rivet de Capitonnage.*
2. A rivet used to secure a plate to one below it, well within the bounding row of rivets.

QUILTING WELD. A plug weld used to secure a plate to structure below it, within the bounding welds.

QUINCY. A small, flat-bottomed boat with straight, flared-out sides similar in build to the dory and found on the lower Mississippi.

The flare on the sides has the peculiarity of increasing continually from bow to transom. The latter has a very pronounced rake and forms an open V coming to a point at the waterline. The quincy is seldom used as a sailboat, but when so it is fitted with a centerboard and sets a large leg-of-mutton sail. Its length varies from 18 to 20 ft.

QUINTANT. An instrument similar to the sextant, used for measuring the altitude of heavenly bodies. It has an arc or limb of 72° or one-fifth of a circle.

QUODDY BOAT. A keel-built, double-ended sailing boat found on the coast of Maine in the vicinity of Passamaquoddy Bay. These boats were used in the herring fisheries; also by lobstermen as market boats. Also called lubec carry-away boat. Length over-all 33 ft. 6 in. Length, waterline, 30 ft. Beam 11 ft. 3 in. Depth at hold 4 ft. 6 in. Draft 5 ft. (aft). (Obsolete.)

The hull had strong sheer, raking ends, much drag to the keel, sharp rising floors with rather hard bilges, hollow, well-formed run. The small boats had cuddies and cockpits like the friendship sloops. The larger had a raised foredeck and trunk forward. They had log rails (low plank bulwarks). The rig varied according to size; the smaller boats (20 ft. and over) were cat-rigged. The larger ones (30 to 40 ft.) were sloop-rigged with short bowsprit and mast well forward.

QUOIN. A wooden chock of angular shape used for supporting and wedging up casks or other circular-shaped packages when stowed in a ship's hold so that the quarters will carry the weight. Also called cantick quoin.
    Fr: *Coin d'Arrimage;* Ger: *Staukeil; Kuntze.*
See **Hollow-Quoin.**

R

R. Flag of the international code of signals consisting of a yellow Greek cross on a square red ground. When hoisted singly it means: "The way is off my ship. You may feel your way past me." When used as a towing signal it means "Go slower" when hoisted by the ship towed, or "I will go slower" when shown by the towing ship.

R.A. RIGHT ASCENSION (astronomy).

R.A.M.S. RIGHT ASCENSION MEAN SUN (astronomy).

r.d. RUNNING DAYS (chartering).

R.D.C. RUNNING DOWN CLAUSE (insurance).

Red. REDUCTION (astronomy).

Ref. REFRACTION.

R.F.D. RAISED FOREDECK.

Rm. ROOM.

r.o.b. REMAINING ON BOARD (cargo).

R.P.M. REVOLUTIONS PER MINUTE.

R.T. RYE TERMS (grain trade).

RA. See **Rau**.

RAASCHALUPPE. See **Schaluppe**.

RABBET. A shoulder or recess on the edge of a piece of wood or metal for the reception of the edge of a similar piece. In steel shipbuilding it consists of a groove formed in the stem and equal in depth to the thickness of the plating so as to form an abutment for the bottom and side plating. The principal purpose of the rabbet as used on a wooden hull is to protect the plank ends and permit calking.

Fr: *Rablure*; Ger: *Spundung; Sponung; Falz*.

RABBET DRAFT. See **Molded Draft**.

RABBET LINE. The line formed by the intersection of outside planking of plating at stem, sternpost and side of keel.

Fr: *Trait de rabbure*; Ger: *Sponung Linie*.

See **Inner Rabbet Line; Outer Rabbet Line**.

RABBET PLANK. See **Hog Piece**.

RACE. A strong current of water near the coastline and usually marked by rips. Sometimes caused by the meeting of two tides.

Fr: *Raz de Courant*; Ger: *Stromschnelle*.

RACEABOUT (U. S.). Small sloop-rigged racing yacht, distinguished from a knockabout by having a short bowsprit and a larger sail area.

RACER. See **Racing Yacht**.

RACING. The sudden acceleration in the number of revolutions of a marine propeller, generally due to the pitching of the vessel in a seaway, which causes the screw to emerge partly or totally above the surface of the water.

Fr: *Affolement de l'Hélice*; Ger: *Blindlaufen*.

The racing of screws may be attributed to either of two causes. If the propeller breaks the surface of the water, as the stern rises in a seaway, it will draw down air and the resistance will be immediately much reduced. Racing may also occur if a vessel is among waves, although the propeller may not emerge. This is probably due to the circular motion of the particles of water in the waves. The water which is traveling in one direction at the crest returns in opposite direction in the trough. This circular motion extends to some distance below the surface and if the screws find the resistance augmented or reduced as it is beneath the crest or trough of a wave, it reduces or increases its speed accordingly.

RACING FLAG. A distinguishing flag flown by sailing yachts at the main masthead in place of the club burgee when racing. It is carried as long as the yacht is racing but is hauled down immediately should the boat give up and withdraw.

RACING GIG. A long, narrow rowing boat, very lightly built and adapted for racing. Also called race boat. Modified form of the ship's gig, adapted for pleasure or racing, it is built with straight sheer and upright stem and is heavier than the skiff. It has lapstrake planking of pine or mahogany, and pulls 2 to 6 oars. The largest type has a length of 40 to 42 ft.; the four oared boat is 29 to 40 ft. long, and the smallest 23 to 29 ft. with a common breadth which varies from 40 to 51 in.

Fr: *Yole de Course*; Ger: *Renngig*.

RACING NUMBER. A number allotted by the racing committee to each yacht taking part in the event. It is marked on each side of the mainsail at about two-thirds of the height of the leech above the boom.

The size of the figures varies from 15-18 inches in height.
Ger: *Regattanummer.*

RACING RULES. A code of rules adopted in yacht races. International racing rules, founded on British experience and practice, have been adopted since 1907 by the following countries: Argentine, Austria, Hungary, Denmark, Finland, France, Germany, Great Britain, Holland, Belgium, Italy, Norway, Russia, Spain, and Sweden.

RACING SKIFF. Long, narrow racing boat for one oarsman, outrigged, usually fitted with a sliding seat and covered in fore-and-aft with canvas. It is made from two mahogany boards 2/16th to 3/16th in thickness. Length 30 ft. Breadth 12 to 16 in. Weight from 33 to 44 lb. Also called single shell (U. S.).

Fr: *Skiff;* Ger: *Skiff; Einer; Einskuller.*

RACING YACHT. A type of sailing yacht designed to traverse closed short courses, in comparatively sheltered waters.

Fr: *Racer; Yacht de Course;* Ger: *Rennjacht; Rennboot.*

In a racing yacht speed is the principal object, subject to necessary consideration for seaworthiness and substantial construction. Racing yachts are built with comparatively short and deep keel and shallow forefoot, which makes for quickness in turning. The wetted surface is cut down to a minimum to reduce resistance. The rig is generally more lofty than in cruising yachts.

RACK. See **Belaying-Pin Rack, Ferry Rack, Halyard Rack.**

RACK (to). To seize two ropes together with cross turns.

Fr: *Brider;* Ger: *Recken.*

RACK AND PINION STEERING GEAR. A type of gear in which the rudderhead supports a quadrant having a rack at its periphery. The steering engine drives a vertical shaft with a large pinion that meshes with the rack. Any motion of the engine causes the quadrant and rudder to turn right or left.

Fr: *Appareil à gouverner à secteur denté;* Ger: *Zahnstangengetriebener Steuerapparat.*

RACK BLOCK. A piece of wood with a number of fairlead sheaves set in.

Fr: *Rateau.*

RACKING. 1. Spun yarn or other stuff used to rack two parts of a rope together.

Fr: *Bridure;* Ger: *Kreuzbandsel.*

2. Structural deformation of the transverse section of a ship's hull. A vessel is said to be racked if, when viewed end on, it appears to be leaning or tilting over to one side. Symptoms of racking generally appear at the junction of the frames with the beams and floors.

Fr: *Déliaison;* Ger: *Deformation des Querschnittes; Wrackung.*

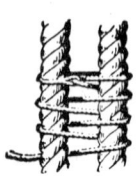

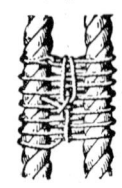

Racking Seizing

RACKING SEIZING. Small stuff passed around two ropes or spars in and over and under, or figure-of-eight fashion. It is used instead of a round seizing when the strain comes upon one rope or part only. Racking seizings are always used with wire rigging.

Fr: *Amarrage en Portugaise;* Ger: *Kreuzsorrung.*

RACKING STOPPER. A rope stopper used on deck for binding the parts of a tackle together and jamming them.

RACKING TURNS. Turns taken figure-of-eight fashion when making a seizing or lashing.

Fr: *Tours Croisés; Portugaise;* Ger: *Kreuztorn.*

RADAR. Radio detection and ranging, a development of World War II. Pulses of ultra-high frequency radio waves emitted by a transmitter aboard ship are reflected by solid objects and are detected upon their return to the sending station. A visual picture of objects projecting above the surface of the sea is presented to the observer on the sending ship. Since conditions of light, darkness, fog, and so on, do not affect its operation, radar is of great aid in navigation. Not only does it afford the navigator a picture of nearby obstacles, such as ships and rocks, showing their range and bearing, but it also depicts a nearby coastline, with accurate location of the ship's position with respect to it.

RADAR AERIAL. That part of a radar set from which electro-magnetic waves are radiated into space and collected. It comprises the reflector and the horn and is usually mounted on the top of a housing which contains the driving motor for rotating it, and also the synchronizing devices for maintaining the picture on the radar screen in correct orientation. The rotation speed varies from 15-30 revolutions per minute.

RADAR BEACON. Electronic signalling device which consists essentially of a receiver which picks up pulses from a radar transmitter, and a transmitter, triggered by the output of this receiver, which puts out signals to be detected by the radar receiver. Radar beacons are specially useful for inshore navigation and pilotage.

Fr: *Balise radar;* Ger: *Funkmessbake.*

RADAR CONSOLE. A console containing the radar transmit-receive unit, and located in a superstructure just below the scanning aerial.

Ger: *Radargerät Konsole.*

RADAR RECEIVER. Electronic device which amplifies radio-frequency signals; demodulates the repetition frequency carrier; further amplifies the desired signal and delivers it to the indicator.

Fr: *Ricepteur radar;* Ger: *Funkmessempfänger.*

RADAR REFLECTOR BUOY. A navigation buoy fitted with a tetrahedron or pentagonal corner reflector as a top mark to facilitate reflection towards the sender.

Fr: *Bouée à reflecteur radar;* Ger: *Messfunkreflektortonne.*

RADDLE. To interlace, as in making boat gripes and flat gasket.

RADIAGRAPH. Portable flame-cutting apparatus used in shipyards. The torch, instead of being operated by hand, as in the ordinary flame cutter runs along a trace, thus insuring better finish when making straight or circular cuts.

RADIAL DAVIT, LUFFING DAVIT. A name given to a boat davit hinged at heel and pivoting in a plane transverse to the ship's keel.

Fr: *Bossoir Oscillant;* Ger: *Barkunen; Radialdavit; Klappdavit.*

RADIALLY INCREASING PITCH. A propeller blade with pitch near the tip greater than that near the hub.

Fr: *Pas Croissant Radial;* Ger: *Radial veränderliche Steigung.*

RADIAL PADDLE WHEEL. A paddle wheel with floats rigidly fixed to the arms as distinguished from the feathering type of wheel.

Fr: *Roue à Aubes Fixes;* Ger: *Rad mit festen Schaufeln.*

See **Paddle Wheel.**

It is seldom found nowadays except where lightness, cheapness, and simplicity are prime factors in determining the choice. The original design of radial paddles has now been modified by making the parts of the arms to which the floats are attached at an angle so that the plane of entry of each float is nearer the perpendicular.

RADIAL PISTON PUMP. A type of pump in which the axes of the pistons are in the same plane, perpendicular to the drive shaft, and are radial to it. The Hele-Shaw variable displacement pump, much used in steering gears, is of this type, and is suited for use in hydraulic transmissions.

RADIATION FOG. Fog formed in stagnant air when the ground is cooled by outgoing radiation until the lowest layer of air is below its dew point. Rarely encountered at sea.

RADIO ALARM SIGNAL. A radio signal used on board ship to announce that a radio distress signal or message is to follow. It consists of twelve dashes sent in one minute, the duration of each dash being four seconds and the duration of the interval between two dashes one second. The purpose of this special signal is to set in operation the automatic apparatus used to give the alarm. Coastal radio stations may use this signal to announce an urgent storm warning.

Fr: *Signal d'Alarme Radiotélégraphique;*
Ger: *Radio-Alarmsignal; Alarmzeichen.*

See **Auto Alarm.**

RADIOBEACON. A land- or lightship-based wireless telegraph station which transmits a regular schedule of signals from which a mobile receiving station, such as that on board ship, may take its bearings to determine its direction in relation to the beacon, or, by using two or more such beacons, to determine its position at sea and distance from the beacons. Radio beacons are used by navigators particularly in foggy weather, at which time the beacon signals are transmitted more frequently. Also called wireless beacon, radiobeacon station.

Fr: *Radiophare;* Ger: *Funkbake; Radiowarte; Funksender.*

The signals from some radiobeacons are intended to enable a mobile receiving station to determine its bearings or direction in relation to the beacon and, in some cases, the distance from the beacon.

Byrnes, I. F., Marine Radio Communication and Equipment, Society of Naval Architects and Marine Engineers (New York), *Transactions*, vol. 48 (1940); Mixter, G. W., A Primer of Navigation (New York, 1943); Putnam, G. R., Radio Beacons and Radio Beacon Navigation (Washington, 1931).

RADIO BEACON STATION.
See **Radio Beacon.**

RADIO BEARING. A bearing obtained with a radio direction finder of wireless transmissions from other ships, aircraft shore stations and radio beacons. The radio bearing is the angle between the meridian of the ship and the great circle track. It therefore has to be corrected before plotting on a Mercator chart. Radio bearings are used for fixing a vessel's position in the same manner as the other lines of position.
Fr: *Relèvement radiogoniométrique;* Ger: *Funkpeilung.*

RADIO BEARING CONVERSION TABLE. A navigational table indicating the correction to be applied to a radio bearing for readily converting it so that it may be plotted on a Mercator chart. The table is used when the distance between the ship and the station is over 50 miles.
U. S. Hydrographic Office, Washington, D. C., 1951. Publication H.O. 205.

RADIO CALL SIGNAL. A call signal from the international series, assigned to each ship and each shore radio station by international agreement. Also called radio call sign. The first letter or the first two letters of the signal show the nationality of the station. In the case of ship stations the call signal consists of four letters, which correspond to those of the ship's number for visual signaling with flags.
Fr: *Indicatif d'Appel Radiotélégraphique;*
Ger: *Radio-Anrufsignal; Rufzeichen.*

RADIO COMMUNICATION. The art of transmitting signals between two points by means of the radiation of electromagnetic waves. Also called **Radio Traffic.**
Fr: *Transmission par radio;* Ger: *Funkverkehr.*

RADIO COMPASS. An instrument used in connection with a compass by which the navigator can ascertain his bearings from fixed points ashore and locate his position by the use of radio signals. Also called direction finder, wireless compass, goniometer.
Fr: *Radio-Goniomètre; Goniomètre;*
Ger: *Funkpeilkompass.*
See **Compass.**

The modern radio direction finder makes use of a closed loop or coil for the reception of wireless signals from a distant transmitting station, or radio beacon. The strength of signals received with the aid of such a loop depends upon its direction relative to that of the transmitting station. When the plane of the loop is directed toward the station the received signal is at its maximum strength, and if the coil is turned through a right angle the signal falls to a minimum intensity. When a bearing has to be taken the desired signals emitted by the radio beacon are tuned in on the loop which is then rotated until the position of the maximum or minimum signal strength is found. This gives the bearing of the transmitting station relative to the ship. By noting the compass reading of the ship's head at the same time, the geographical bearings of the transmitting station is obtained and may be laid off on the chart.
Long, S. H., *Navigational Wireless,* London, 1927.

RADIO COMPASS STATION. A shore station equipped with a radio direction finder and special apparatus for determining the direction of incoming radio waves transmitted by ships.
Fr: *Poste Radio-Goniométrique;* Ger: *Funkpeilstation.*

RADIO DIRECTION FINDER.
See **Direction Finder.**

RADIO DISTRESS SIGNAL. A radio distress signal announcing that the ship sending the signal is threatened by serious

RADIO DISTRESS FREQUENCIES. Frequencies for radiotelegraphy and radiotelephony assigned by international radio regulations. These frequencies are at present 500 kilocycles per second for radiotelegraphy and 2182 kilocycles per second for radiotelephony.
Fr: *Fréquences de détresse;* Ger: *Radio Not Frequenz.*

RADIO EMERGENCY INSTALLATION. Ship's radio installation supplied by a source of energy independent of the propelling power and of the ship's electricity system. Accumulator batteries are generally used. They must be capable of operating the transmitter and receiver for at least six hours continuously besides the auto-alarm and direction finder.
Fr: *Poste radiotélégraphique de secours;*
Ger: *Notfunkstelle.*

and imminent danger and requests immediate assistance. It is emitted on the international distress frequency of 500 kilocycles (600 meters), and consists of a group composed of three dots, three dashes, three dots transmitted three times. In radiotelephony the signal consists of the spoken expression "Mayday." The distress signal must be followed as soon as possible by the distress message giving the position of the vessel in distress, the nature of help requested, and any other useful information.
   Fr: *Signal de Détresse Radiotélégraphique;* Ger: *Radio-Notsignal; Notzeichen.*

RADIO FIX. Determination of the position of a vessel equipped with a radio direction finder by obtaining radio bearings on two or more transmitting stations of known location.
   Fr: *Point par radio;* Ger: *Funkortung.*

RADIO FOG SIGNAL. A signal made by a coastal radio station operating only during periods of fog or low visibility.

RADIOGONIOMETER. An instrument which, when coupled to a suitable fixed aerial system, enables the bearing of arriving radio waves to be determined by rotation of a movable part.
   Fr: *Goniomètre;* Ger: *Funkpeiler; Goniometer-Peilanlage.*

RADIO NAVIGATION. The art of finding a ship's position at sea by using radio signals for directional guidance.
   Fr: *Navigation par radio;* Ger: *Funkortung; Funknavigation.*

RADIO OPERATOR. A member of the ship's staff who controls the operation of all aparatus associated with the ship's radio transmitting and receiving equipment in compliance with official regulations governing its use. He regularly receives and records time signals, weather reports, position reports and other navigation and technical data, and as well handles all radio ship-to-shore and shore-to-ship communications for the vessel and its passengers. He may be assisted by one or more radio operators, depending on the type of ship and voyage. The enlistment of a duly qualified radio operator is compulsory for all classes of vessels required by the 1929 International Convention for the Safety of Life at Sea to be equipped with a radio installation. On U. S. vessels the radio operator must be licensed by the Federal Communications Commission as a first, second, or third class commercial radio operator, and must carry a Certificate of Service as radio operator. He is also called radio officer, wireless telegraph operator, wireless operator, W/T officer.
   Fr: *Radio-Télégraphiste; Opérateur de T. S. F.;* Ger: *Bordfunker; Funkoffizier.*

RADIO PRATIQUE (U. S.). The permission granted by medical authorities to some of the larger passenger vessels whereby they may enter certain specified U. S. ports without stopping at quarantine. A request by radio giving all particulars regarding the sanitary conditions on board must be made from 12 to 24 hours before the expected arrival in port.
   See **Pratique.**

RADIO RANGE. A system of radio-signals designed for the purpose of guiding a ship along a designated track toward, or away from, a specified location. Also called **Radio aids.**

RADIO ROOM. A room from which wireless messages are sent and in which they are received. In large vessels it is usually a soundproof room placed in the upper part of the ship's superstructure in a position of the greatest possible safety, and as high as practical above the load waterline.
   Fr: *Poste Radiotélégraphique de Bord;* Ger: *Funkraum.*

Means of communication either by voice pipe or by telephone or in some other efficient manner are provided between the navigating bridge and the radio room. The installation includes the main transmitting and receiving set and the emergency installation, unless the former comply with all the statutory requirements of an emergency station. The emergency installation must be provided with a source of energy independent of the ship's main generating circuit.

RADIO SAFETY SIGNAL. A radio signal announcing that the station is about to transmit a message concerning the safety of navigation or giving important meteorological warnings. It consists of the group "T.T.T.," transmitted three times. This signal is followed by the letters "DE" and three transmissions of the radio call signal of the station sending it.
   Fr: *Signal Radiotélégraphique de Sécurité;* Ger: *Sicherheitsfunksignal; Sicherheitzeichen.*

RADIO SILENCE. A period of time during which all radio traffic or transmission is foregone by a radio station.
Fr: *Régime silence radio;* Ger: *Funkverbot; Funkstille.*

RADIOSONDE. Miniature weather station carried aloft to heights in the neighborhood of 10 miles by balloons of about 6 ft. diameter. The radiosonde transmits automatically by radio, observations made in the course of upper air explorations or soundings. They are used on ocean weather ships.
Fr: *Radiosonde.*

RADIO TIME SIGNAL. Wireless signal emitted by certain radio stations at stated Greenwich time, by which the navigator is able to ascertain the error in his chronometer. These signals, which were formerly sent by hand are now transmitted automatically. Thereby a precision of half a tenth of a second is attained.
Fr: *Signal Horaire Radio-Télégraphique;* Ger: *Funkentelegraphisches Zeitsignal.*

As a result of the International Time Committee conference in 1925 a new system of rhythmic signals was adopted, which comprises a series of 306 signals transmitted in 300 seconds of mean time. At the commencement of each of the five minutes a dash of half a second's duration is transmitted. This dash is followed by a series of 60 dots; the final signal at the sixth minute being signaled by a dash. Rugby, Bordeaux, Moscow, Saigon, Nauen were the principal stations emitting radio time signals prior to World War II.
Cowie and Eckhardt, *Wireless Longitude*, U. S. Coast and Geodetic Survey, Special Publication 109, Washington, 1924.

RADIO URGENCY SIGNAL. A radio signal transmitted by a ship or land station, indicating that the calling station has a very urgent message to transmit concerning the safety of a ship, aircraft, or some person aboard or within sight. It has priority over all other communications except distress. It consists of three repetitions of the group X.X.X., sent with the letters of each group and the letters of each group and the successive groups clearly separated from each other. In radiotelephony the urgency signal consists of 3 repetitions of the word "PAN." The urgency signal may be transmitted only on the authority of the master.

RADIO WATCH. The service performed by a licensed radio operator on duty in the radio room, listening continuously for signals of other stations transmitting on the international calling and the distress frequency of 500 kilocycles. Also called wireless watch. The operator, regardless of message traffic and signals must listen on 500 kilocycles at least twice per hour during the international silent period, for three minutes beginning at 15 minutes and at 45 minutes past each hour Greenwich mean time.
Fr: *Service d'Ecoute;* Ger: *Funkwache.*

RAFFEE, RAFFIE. A three-cornered sail set over the highest yard. The foot is spread by the yard; the clews haul out to the yardarms, and the head or apex hoists directly in front of the mast to the truck. It is used by fore-and-aft schooners and other small craft rigged to carry a square sail when sailing before the wind or nearly so. Sometimes it is in two pieces, one for each side of the mast.

RAFIAU.
See **Pointu.**

RAFT. A conveyance of primitive design consisting of a quantity of material of sufficient buoyancy fastened together and used for fishing, hunting or transportation by water. Rafts are made of wooden logs, reed bundles, driftwood bark, inflated skins and propelled by sails, paddles or poles. Some sailing rafts are provided with an outrigger. They are also used as a means of conveyance by sea, river or lake, of the materials composing their structure from their place of assembly to a market.
Fr: *Radeau;* Ger: *Floss.*

See **Balsa, Caballito, Jangada, Gay-Beh, Catamaran, Teletap, Log Raft, Life Raft, Shasha, Teppu.**

Suder, H., *Vom Einbaum und Floss zum Schiff*, Institut für Meereskunde, Veröffentlichungen, Neue Folge, Heft 7, Berlin (1930).

RAFTED ICE. A form of pancake ice in which cakes are overriding one another.

RAFTER.
See **Cross Rafter, Side Rafter.**

RAFTING. The piling up of field ice when, due to opposing currents or changing directions of wind, two ice fields impinge on each other. The ice at the edges buckle with the impact and large cakes are thrown up on the adjacent field.

RAG BOLT. An iron pin with barbed shank, used mostly where a common bolt cannot be clinched. Also called barb bolt.
Fr: *Cheville à Barbe;* Ger: *Tackbolzen.*

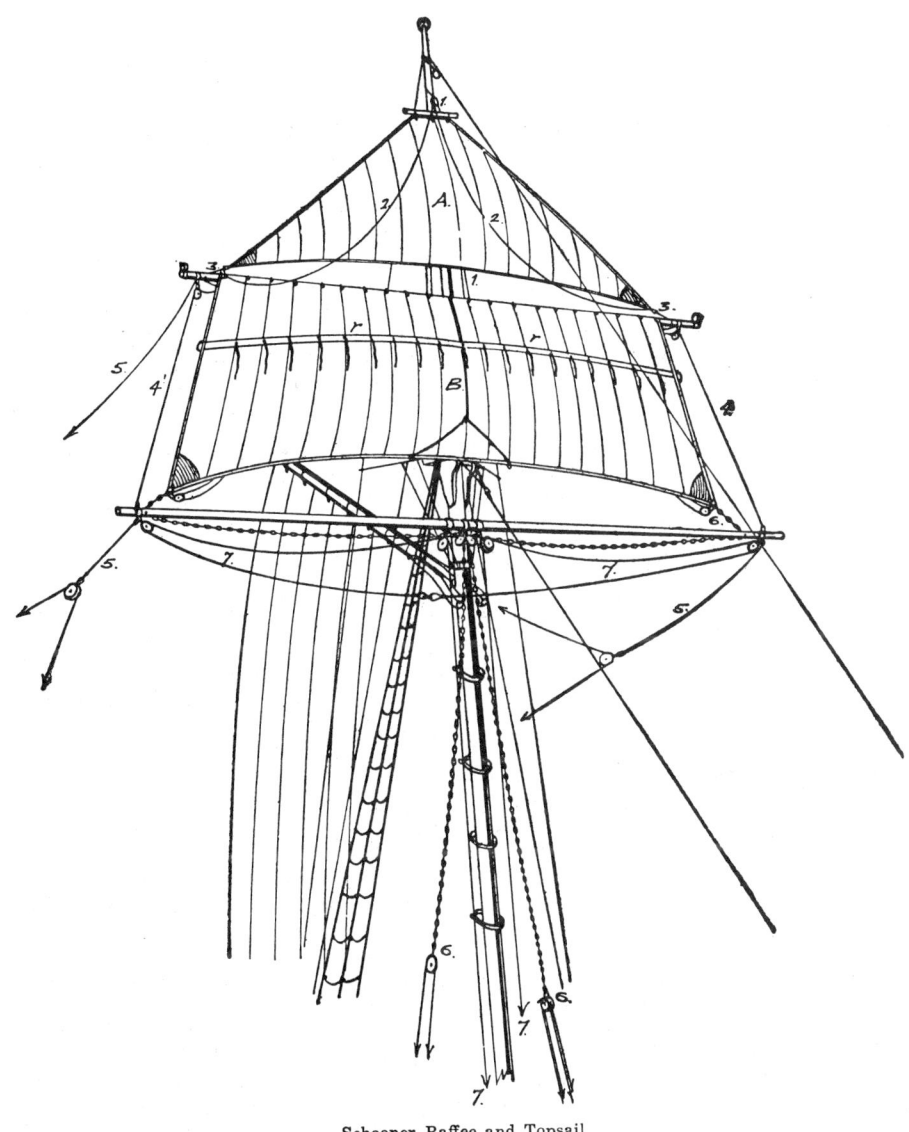

Schooner Raffee and Topsail

A. Raffee
B. Topsail
1. Raffee Halyards
2. Raffee Downhauls
3. Raffee Sheets
4. Topsail Downhauls
5. Topsail Yards, Braces
6. Topsail Sheets
7. Squaresail Outhauls
r. Reef Band and Points

RAGNO A VELA. Sicilian fishing boat from the Gulf of Catania of the bilancella type, with a length of 65 to 75 ft. and carrying capacity of 10 to 15 tons. Crew 5 to 7. These boats fish in pairs, towing a dragnet called "ragno."

RAIL PORT. A port where the largest portion of the traffic is handled from ship direct into rail truck or vice versa.

RAIL SCREEN. A canvas cloth occasionally extended over openwork railing as a protection against wind, rain, and spray. It is usually made of No. 5 or No. 6 canvas, fitted with brass eyelets along the tabling, for lacing at top and bottom. Also called windscreen.

RAIL STANCHION. Stanchions for open railing made of steel pipe or brass, supporting the rods of the railing.

    Fr: *Montant de Garde Corps;* Chandelier; Ger: *Relingstütze; Geländerstütze.*

RAILWAY.
    See **Track.**

RAILWAY DRYDOCK.
    See **Railway.**

RAILWAY FASHION. A system used for rigging a spar. A gaff is said to be rigged "Railway Fashion" when the forward end is held to the mast by a sliding attachment which travels up and down a railway instead of the usual jaws. The same term is applied to a yard provided with a similar device instead of a parrel.

RAILWAY GAFF. A standing gaff fitted on its under side with a track on which the hanks of the head of the sail slide when the sail is hauled out or brailed in.

RAISED DECK BOAT. Term which applies to small pleasure or service craft, where the topsides of the forward superstructure are carried higher than the point where the deck would be in the trunk-cabin type. The flush cabin top is carried across the full width of the boat as far as the stem. A forward cockpit is often featured in this type of construction. From the constructional standpoint, the smooth continuous deck from side to side without break is stronger and easier to fashion than a trunk cabin. It gives a maximum amount of freeboard forward and, as the sides are flared out, it contributes toward dryness in rough weather.

RAISED FOREDECK. The forward portion of an upper deck situated between bridge and forecastle, and raised above main deck level, thus forming a structural discontinuity or break.

    Fr: *Demi-Gaillard;* Ger: *Erhöhtes Vordeck.*

RAISED-HEAD RIVET. Rivet with slightly raised head, the amount of rise being only 5/16 in. for a 1¼-in. rivet as compared with ¾ in. for a button-head rivet of the same diameter.

    Fr: *Rivet à Tête Bombée;* Ger: *Spitzkopfniete.*

RAISED QUARTER-DECK. The after portion of a weather deck or upper deck which is raised a few feet above the forward portion. Strictly speaking, a raised quarter-deck is not an erection, but may be more correctly described as an increase in the depth of the vessel over the after end.

    Fr: *Demi-Dunette;* Ger: *Erhöhtes Quarter-Deck.*

RAISED QUARTER-DECK VESSEL. A flush-decked vessel in which the after part of the upper deck has been raised 3 to 6 feet according to length of vessel, and is commonly known as a raised quarter-deck. This type of construction is often adopted for the smaller sizes of cargo ships engaged in the coasting and shorter oversea trades. This obviates the difficulty sometimes experienced with some cargoes in giving the vessel sufficient trim by the stern, owing to the space occupied by the propeller shaft tunnel. There is a considerable difference between an erection called a raised quarter-deck and such erections as complete or partial awning decks, poops and forecastles. A raised quarter-deck is not a true erection, but a bona fide integral part of the ship's structure, the term erection being used only for purposes of convenience. Raised quarter-deck ships are built with one deck only, and are used principally in the coal and timber trades.

    Fr: *Navire à Demi-Dunette;* Ger: *Erhöhtes Quarterdeckschiff.*

RAISED TANK TOP. A tank top sloping from the centerline towards the bilges. This type of construction is occasionally adopted with a high centerline girder.
    See **Tank Top.**

RAKE. The inclination from the perpendicular of a mast, funnel, stem or sternpost, etc. The overhang of a vessel forward.

    Fr: *Quête;* Ger: *Fall; Neigung.*

RAKE AFT. The inclination towards aft, of a vessel's stern post, mast, etc. The hulls of ordinary trading vessels have no rake aft at the stern, this being confined to small sailing craft such as fishing vessels and yachts. The rake aft of masts on sailing vessels ensures that sails will be lifting rather than depressing when running before the wind or nearly so. However, when sailing close hauled, the angle of heel at which all lifting effect due to rake disappears, is very small. In former days a pronounced rake of spars was a feature of all fast fore-

and-afters. It brought the leeches of sails nearer to the vertical, and thus the unsupported side of the sail was relieved of the pull exercised on it by the actual weight of the sail. The sail set better and was easier to make. The rake of masts also made for efficiency and greater ease in supporting them by shrouds and rigging, and rendered possible the sharper bracing of yards.

Fr: *Quête;* Ger: *Hacke.*
See **Afterrake, Forerake, Overrake.**

RAKING STEM. A straight stem having a forward rake or extending beyond the forward perpendicular. A raking stem tends to minimize under-water damage in case of collision, and promotes better stream-line flow at the bow. In addition, it increases reserve buoyancy and improves seaworthiness.

Fr: *Etrave Élancée;* Ger: *Ausschiessender Vorsteven.*

RALLY. One of a series of drives with battering rams by which the launching wedges are gradually and evenly driven in all along the whole length of the ship, just before launching, in order to transfer the weight of the hull from the keel blocks and shores to the cradle and sliding ways.

Fr: *Volée.*

RAM.
See **Ram Schooner.**

RAMARDOO. Australian one-piece sewed bark canoe of the Leewalloo tribe from Pellew Islands, Gulf of Carpentaria.

RAMARK (U. S.). A type of radar beacon developed by the U. S. Coast Guard for marine use. It produces a narrow ray of light on the P.P.I. scope at the bearing of the beacon even when the ramark is well beyond maximum range for which the P.P.I. is set.

RAM BOW. A curved bow receding above the waterline. It is seen on American cat boats and on some canoes. Also called tumble-home bow.

RAM LINE. A small rope or line formerly used for the purpose of forming the sheer or hang of the decks, for setting the beams fair, etc. (Obsolete.)

RAMMING UP.
See **Wedging Up.**

RAMP. To ramp a sailing boat along: i.e., to sail her rather full when on the wind.

RAM SCHOONER. A three-mast, bald-headed schooner used inside the Chesapeake and on the Delaware Canal. Also called ram.

RANCHINA. A decked fishing boat found in the White Sea, resembling the lodia but with more rise of floors. The hull is clinker-built. The largest boats have the same rig as the lodia; the smaller carry two masts only. Deadweight capacity is 25 to 70 tons.

RANDAN (G. B.). A pleasure rowboat with stern seat and three thwarts.

RANDAN FASHION. A system of rowing with a pair of oars and a pair of sculls. The stroke and bow men each use one oar, and the man between them uses two sculls.

RANGE. 1. A large cleat with two arms bolted in the waist of a sailing ship to which tacks and bow lines are belayed.

Fr: *Taquet d'Amure;* Ger: *Belegknecht.*

2. A geographical section of a coast, or waters, to which the same rate of freight applies. A vessel can load (or unload) at any one or more of the ports included when chartered to load on the range specified. A term which refers to the provisions in a charter party by which the loading or discharging port is not specified. This provision requires the vessel to report at some specified place for orders as to its final destination.

Ger: *Grenze.*

3. A specified length of anchor cable hauled up on deck.

Fr: *Bitture;* Ger: *Bucht.*

RANGE (to). 1. To sail or steer in a parallel direction and near to, as, to range a coast.

Fr: *Ranger;* Ger: *Entlang segeln; Hinfahren.*

2. To place in a line or row, such as an anchor cable.

Fr: *Elonger;* Ger: *Längsseit anlegen; Auslegen.*

3. A vessel at anchor is said to range when she sheers about.

RANGE BEACON. One of two beacons which give a line of position to guide a vessel through a channel.

Fr: *Balise de direction;* Ger: *Leitbake.*

RANGE CLEAT.
See **Range (1).**

RANGEFINDER. An optical instrument by means of which the navigator is able to measure directly his distance from any visible object by one observation performed in a few seconds and without any calculation or reference to tables. Also called telemeter.

Fr: *Télémètre;* Ger: *Entfernungsmesser.*
See **Stadimeter.**

The rangefinder consists of two horizontal telescopes mounted in a common frame with two objectives situated one at each end of the frame and the eyepieces at the center, suitable reflectors being provided beyond the objectives to direct the beams of light along the frame towards the eyepieces. The field of view seen through the right eyepiece is divided by a fine horizontal line called the separating line so that there are two fields of view, the upper and the lower. By moving the deflecting prism the two images can be brought into coincidence. The rangefinder scale moves with the deflecting prism and when coincidence is made, the range is read direct from the scale seen in the left eyepiece. The scale may be graduated in yards, meters, cables, or any other unit.

RANGE LIGHT. 1. The white running light carried by mechanically propelled vessels under way at the after or second masthead in accordance with the Rules of the Road. This light is compulsory for all vessels of 150 ft. or more in length, and optional for others. Also called after range light.

Fr: *Feu de Pointe; Feu Additionel; Feu de Mât Arrière;* Ger: *Richtungsfeuer.*

2. One of two lights placed in line to indicate a course to steer or a danger to avoid, as an aid to navigation. Also called leading light. They are mostly used in narrow waters where an accurately straight course is to be steered. The higher light is placed more remotely, but in the same vertical plane as the lower one. The difference in the height of the two lights should be at least six feet for every mile of the distance at which they must show. A single leading light is occasionally adopted, in which case the light is so arranged as to throw a narrow beam along the channel so that a vessel unable to sight the light is out of the channel. The objection to the use of a single leading light is that there is a possibility of the luminous source being slightly out of position, which would at once alter the angle covered; whereas, when two lights are used even should such an accident occur there is no possibility of the line between the two altering.

Fr: *Feu de Direction;* Ger: *Leitfeuer; Kursfeuer; Richtfeuer.*

RANGE OF STABILITY. The number of degrees of heel from the upright position over which the righting arm is positive. It is shown by the stability curve. It may be defined as the angle at which the righting arm becomes zero.

Fr: *Limite de Stabilité;* Ger: *Stabilitätsgrenze.*
See **Righting Lever.**

RANTERPIKE. Three-masted topsail schooner or brigantine of the River Clyde of about 250 tons. The topmasts were fitted abaft the lower masts. These vessels were generally engaged in the transportation of pig iron from Glasgow to Liverpool. The type is now extinct. Also called *rantipike.*

RAP-FULL. With all sails filled, and not quite close-hauled.

RAPID TRANSIT FALL. An extra fall used in conjunction with the burton fall and midship fall, in the method of discharging cargo called "rapid transit." Its purpose is to give greater speed to the burtoning movement. Also called trolley fall, hurry-up fall (U. S.).

RAPIERS METHOD. A system used in navigation for drawing the great circle track on a Mercator chart by noting the maximum separation in latitude, and then drawing through this point a line parallel between the two places. Having these three points the track may be freely drawn by hand.

Fr: *Méthode de Rapiér.*

RAPSON'S SLIDE. A device for controlling the movements of the tiller. It consists of a carriage which slides transversely across the ship on a guide. The carriage contains a block with a hole in it which can turn about a vertical axis, and can also slide horizontally along the fore end of the tiller. It is a compensating gear because as the rudder angle is increased and the moment of pressure on the rudder blade increases, the turning moment exerted by the tiller increases as well.

Fr: *Chariot de Barre;* Ger: *Gleitklotz.*

RASING KNIFE.
See **Scriber.**

RATCHET WINDLASS. A simple form of hand-worked windlass consisting of a horizontal drum pierced with suitable apertures directed towards its center. Also called handspike windlass. Levers or handspikes are inserted in these to turn the windlass around when the anchor is weighed. It is

provided with a ratchet wheel and pawls.
Fr: *Guindeau à Barres;* Ger: *Bratspill.*

RATER. A small yacht or boat of the type commonly in vogue in the smaller classes of the Yacht Racing Association. (Slang.)
Ger: *Schätzer.*

RAT GUARD. A sheet-metal disc constructed in conical form with a hole in the center and split from the center to the edge. It is installed over mooring lines to prevent rats from boarding the ship from the shore over the line.
Ger: *Rattenschwanz.*

RATING. The grade or position of a seaman on board ship.
See **Yacht Measurement.**

RATING CERTIFICATE. A certificate delivered by a yacht club after a yacht has been officially measured for racing. It gives the exact rating according to the measurement formula in use by the club.
Fr: *Certificat de Jauge;* Ger: *Klassenschein.*

RATING CLASS. A term applied in yacht racing to a group of boats which vary as to length, beam, displacement, sail area and other factors and are rated according to a measurement formula, the result of which must come within a specified rating length. Such groups include the 6 and 12 meter classes; the R.Q.M. and 30 square meter classes; the sloops of the J or 76 rating class. Rating class yachts compete without time allowance.

RATING RULE. The rules according to which the dimensions and other particulars of a racing yacht are taken and computed in, or to issue a rating certificate.
Fr: *Formule de jauge;* Ger: *Messformel; Vermessungsregel.*

RATIONAL HORIZON. The great circle whose plane is parallel to the sensible horizon and which, passing through the center of the earth, extends to the celestial sphere. Also called celestial horizon.
Fr: *Horizon Rationel; Horizon Vrai;* Ger: *Wahrer Horizont; Astronomischer Horizont.*

RATIO OF TIDAL RANGES. The ratio between the heights of high water and low water at a reference port, and that at a subsidiary port.
Fr: *Rapport des Amplitudes;* Ger: *Verhältnis der Tidenhub.*

RATLINE. One of the small lines crossing the shrouds and forming rope runs used by seamen for going aloft. They are fixed about 15 in. apart by a seizing at each end and a clove hitch to each shroud in between. Ratlines are made of ratline stuff.
Fr: *Enfléchure;* Ger: *Webeleine.*
See **Catch Ratline, Ratline Stuff, Sheer Ratline.**

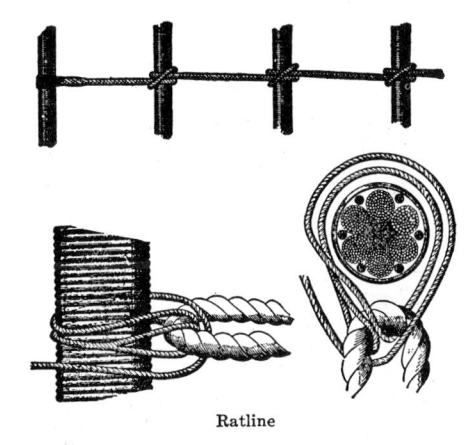

Ratline

RATLINE STUFF. Six, twelve, fifteen, eighteen or twenty-four thread right-hand tarred hemp rope, used for ratlines, heavy serving, heaving lines, anchors, boat lashings, and so on.
Fr: *Quarantenier;* Ger: *Webeleingut.*
Ratline stuff is a little larger than seizing stuff with the same number of threads and it is laid up with less twist, which renders it more pliable. Sizes are designated by the number of threads.

RATPROOFING. The incorporation in a ship's design and construction of features which will prevent infestation by rats. Close attention is given to sealing crevices and narrow passages which might afford harbor for rats.
See **Deratization.**

RATTAN ROPE. Rope made of split and twisted rattan. These ropes were exclusively employed in the Far East for all running gear and cables until the middle of the nineteenth century. They have, to some extent, been replaced recently by hemp or wire rope. Rattan rope is made of the stem of a cane of the genus *Calamus.* Cables up to 42 in. circumference are made of rattan in Eastern seas. They are said to be stronger than hemp and not so easily chafed by rocks.

Fr: *Cordage en Kaire;* Ger: *Rotangtauwerk.*

RATTLE DOWN. To hitch and seize the ratlines to the shrouds. The work of seizing ratlines to the forward and after shroud with small stuff passed through an eye splice at each end of the ratline, and half hitching it around each shroud.

Fr: *Enflécher;* Ger: *Ausweben.*

RAU. East Indian dugout canoe with double outriggers from Kei Islands, Banda Sea. The ends are flat and are used as platform for harpooning fish. In Timor-Laut Islands, called *ra*.

RAVE HOOK. A hooked iron tool used for removing or "reefing out" old oakum from the seams of planks before calking afresh. Also called reef hook, reefing hook.

Fr: *Bec à Corbin;* Ger: *Nahthaken.*

Rave Hook

RAZING. The operation of cutting-in the ship's lines on the mold loft floor or on the scrieve board with a razing knife or scriber, so that they cannot be easily wiped off. Also called rasing, scribing.

Fr: *Rouanner; Racher;* Ger: *Anreissen.*

RAZSHIVA. A sailing barge used for transportation on the Caspian Sea and Volga estuary. The type used on the Volga has a length ranging from 56 to 168 ft. The seagoing *razshiva* has a carrying capacity which ranges from 70 to 140 tons.

REACH. 1. A straight course between the bends of a river. A straight part in a navigable river.

Fr: *Ouvert;* Ger: *Stromstrecke.*

2. Any course sailed with started sheets that is not directly before the wind. A long tack with the wind nearly abeam but always forward of it. Sailing with a beam wind.

REACH (to). To make way to windward by a long tack without going about. A sailing boat under way is said to be reaching when neither beating to windward nor running before the wind. To headreach is to forge ahead when lying to; to forereach is to forge to windward when tacking.

REACH BOAT. Rowing and sailing boat, originating from Moose-a-bec Reach, Jonesport, in eastern Maine, U. S. A., and employed in general fisheries. It is double-ended with clinker planking, has two or three thwarts, and is 10 to 18 ft. long. All but the smallest boats are rigged with one or two spritsails.

REACHING FORESAIL. A triangular sail which sets on the forestay and whose shape is approximately that of an equilateral triangle, owing to the length of its foot which overlaps the mainsail for a considerable distance. Also called Genoa foresail, Genoa jib.

REACTION TURBINE. A turbine which depends for its operation upon the reactive force exerted by steam expanding through rows of blading mounted on a wheel free to rotate.

Fr: *Turbine à Réaction;* Ger: *Gegendruckturbine.*

READY ABOUT. The order to prepare for tacking.

Fr: *Pare à Virer;* Ger: *Klar Zum Wenden.*

REAM. To enlarge or fair rivet holes by means of a reamer.

Fr: *Aléser;* Ger: *Aufreiben.*

REAMER. 1. A fluted tool used for finishing and truing punched or drilled rivet holes. Also called rimer.

Fr: *Alésoir;* Ger: *Raumahle; Riebahle.*

2. One who enlarges rivet holes where they overlap slightly, are not perfectly cylindrical, or where it is desired to enlarge the diameter so that the rivet will completely fill the hole. He operates a pneumatic or electric portable drill. In Great Britain called rimer.

3. Also *reemer*. One who drives a beetle or horsing iron into the seams of hull or deck planking to open them before calking. He usually works on repair jobs.

REAMED HOLE. A hole which has been enlarged by a reamer to the exact diameter required.

Fr: *Trou Alésé;* Ger: *Aufgeriebenes Nietloch.*

REBATE. An allowance or discount on the freight rate made by the carrier to the shipper.

Fr: *Ristourne; Rabais;* Ger: *Ristorno; Rabatt.*

See **Deferred Rebate.**

RECALL NUMBER. A signal consisting of a white number on a black ground, displayed by the sailing committee in yacht racing when one of the competing craft is on or across the starting line at the time of the starting signal or before it is made.

A suitable sound signal is made simultaneously and the yacht must put back and recross the line to the satisfaction of the committee.

Fr: *Pavillon de Rappel;* Ger: *Widerrufsflagge.*

RECAPTURE. To retake by force a captured ship from the control and possession of the captor. The retaking may assume the form of rescue by persons on board the captured ship, or it may be accomplished by persons disconnected with the vessel and attached to another craft.

Fr: *Rescousse;* Ger: *Wiedernahme.*

RECEIVED FOR SHIPMENT BILL OF LADING. A term used in contradistinction to shipped bill of lading, which is the standard document. Some bankers object to such bills of lading on the ground that the security they offer is imperfect. Such bills are, however, a commercial necessity in respect of goods shipped at intermediate ports at which the vessel calls for a few hours only.

Fr: *Connaissement Reçu pour Embarquement;* Ger: *Übernahmekonnossement; Empfangskonnossement.*

RECEIVER OF WRECKS (G. B.). An official stationed at the customhouse, to whom the master of a vessel just arrived must report any derelict, wreck, or iceberg met on the voyage, or any collision that may have taken place.

Ger: *Strandvogt.*

RECEIVING CLERK. One who is in charge of the reception of all cargo on the pier. He keeps the ship foreman posted as to what cargo is available and when more is expected to arrive. He also keeps a daily record of tonnage loaded.

Ger: *Eingangsexpedient.*

RECEIVING NOTE (G. B.). A document issued by a shipper to tne chief officer of a vessel asking him to receive on board the goods specified in the note.

RECESSED BULKHEAD. A bulkhead which is stepped or recessed in the form of a plated, horizontal flat at some point of its height. Also called stepped bulkhead. Such steps or recesses do not, as a rule, extend to the ship's side, inasmuch as such a watertight flat presents a vulnerable part in the event of a collision.

Fr: *Cloison en Baïonnette;* Ger: *Knickschott.*

RECIPROCAL BEARINGS. The bearings of two compasses, each taken from the other. The true bearing of A from B is the reciprocal of the true bearing of B from A.

Fr: *Relèvements Réciproques;* Ger: *Gegenseitige Peilungen.*

See Bearings.

RECIPROCATING ENGINE. An engine in which the rectilinear movement of the piston is transformed into circular motion through a crosshead, connecting rod, crankpin and crankshaft. The vertical, inverted, direct-acting, reversible type of reciprocator has been universally adopted for every sort and almost any size of ship with screw propulsion. When steam is the prime mover, the engines are of the multiple expansion condensing type.

Fr: *Machine Alternative;* Ger: *Kolbenmaschine.*

Steam reciprocating engines are classified by the number of times the steam expands as it passes through the engine, one cylinder being usually provided for each expansion. The principal advantages of the reciprocating engine drive are: excellent control at all loads, ease of reversing, and the fact that efficient speed range of engine and propeller are overlapping. Its disadvantages are: heavy weight and large space requirements, low maximum power output per cylinder, and inefficient use of low pressure steam. As a result of the latter, fuel consumption is rather high. An average figure for triple-expansion reciprocating engines utilizing superheated steam is 1.15 to 1.20 lb. of oil per horsepower hour, as compared with .60 for geared turbine drive.

Hunters, S., "Reciprocating Marine Steam Engine Development during the Past Fifty Years," Northeast Coast Institution of Engineers and Shipbuilders (Newcastle upon Tyne), *Transactions,* vol. 51 (1933–34).

RECIPROCATING PUMP. A pump in which the pistons move axially in cylinders, and remain in the same plane as drive shaft.

RECOVER (to). To swing the oar back from the end of one stroke to the beginning of the next one.

RECOVERY. The point at the end of the stroke where the oar comes out of the water and is brought back to the position of the beginning of the stroke.

REDELIVERY CLAUSE. Similar to the delivery clause but in effect at termination of charter.

Fr: *Clause de Redélivraison;* Ger: *Rücklieferungsklausel.*

See Delivery Clause.

REDELIVERY NOTICE. Written notice given by the charterers to the owners of a vessel, stating at which port and on about what day the vessel will be redelivered at termination of charter. Ten days is generally accepted as the minimum time for the owners to be notified.

Fr: *Avis de Remise;* Ger: *Rücklieferungsanzeige.*

RED-LEAD INJECTOR.
See **Putty Gun.**

REDNINGSKOÏTE. A seagoing sailing boat especially designed and built for the Norwegian government lifesaving service for the particular benefit of the fisheries, to assist open fishing boats that are unable to gain the land unaided or to rescue men from capsized boats. The boats are most frequently called upon to tow to windward fishing boats which are in danger of being blown on the coast or are stranded upon some dangerous lee shore. One of these boats will if necessary pick up and tow into port four or five fishing boats which otherwise would drift helplessly away. Length over-all 44 ft. Beam 14 ft. 4 in. Depth 7 ft. 10½ in. Draft 7 ft. 6 in. Minimum freeboard 3 ft. 5 in. Displacement 925 cu. ft. Sail area 1.061 sq. ft. (Typical.)

These boats are sturdy seagoing craft which must be out in the severest weather and are consequently given a high degree of buoyancy, seaworthiness, and stability. They also render assistance to merchant vessels, piloting them to safety when regular pilots are unobtainable. They are sharpended, flush-decked boats with curved stem, moderately sharp bow with slightly convex lines, hollow floor, deep lead keel, well-formed run, curved sternpost, moderate sheer, and low open bulwarks. The *redningskoïte* is rigged with running bowsprit, pole masts, and two headsails.

REDUCTION GEAR. A term meaning speed-reducing gears and usually applied to the gears used in geared turbine main propulsion plants to reduce the speed of the turbine to a value suitable for driving the propeller, thus avoiding the low efficiency resulting from excessive propeller speeds, and enabling the turbine to operate efficiently at high speed.

See **Geared Turbine.**

Reduction gears are classified as single-reduction and double-reduction. In the former, a high-speed pinion, driven by the turbine, engages directly with a low-speed gear (the main, or bull gear) mounted on the forward end of the propeller shaft, thus accomplishing the entire reduction in one step. In the double-reduction unit, an intermediate gear and pinion are interposed between the high-speed pinion and the low-speed gear, thus effecting the reduction in two steps. Single-reduction gears have speed reduction ratios up to 20 to 1; double-reduction units with ratios as high as 40 to 1. In efficiency, they range from 97.5 per cent to 98.5 per cent for single reductions and from 95 per cent to 97 per cent for double reductions.

REDUCTION OF LATITUDE. The correction applied to the geographical or latitude on the spheroid to obtain the Geocentric or true latitude. It is due to the fact that the Earth is an oblate spheroid.

REDUCTION OF SOUNDINGS. The adjustment of soundings to the selected chart datum.

Fr: *Réduction des sondes;* Ger: *Reduktion der Lotung.*

REED.
See **Reed Horn.**

REED HORN. A fog signal apparatus in which the sound is produced by means of a metal reed or thin blade vibrating under the influence of a stream of compressed air. The note is fairly high, but the power and consequently the audible range are low.

Fr: *Trompette à Anche;* Ger: *Zungenpfeifen Nebelhorn.*

REEDING TOOL. A finishing tool used in calking steel plates, and so on, following the splitter and maker.

REEF. 1. One of the horizontal portions of a sail which may be rolled or folded up in order to reduce the area of canvas exposed to the wind. Reefs are usually situated at the head of square and lateen sails and at the foot of fore-and-aft and lug sails. The courses of large vessels are either reefed with points or with small cords called reef lines or reef points.

Fr: *Ris;* Ger: *Reff; Reef.*

See **Bag Reef, Balance Reef, Barrier Reef, Cunningham Reef, French Reef, Roller Reef, Slab Reef.**

2. A rocky or coral elevation at the bottom of the sea which is dangerous to navigation and which may be uncovered at certain stages of the tide.

Fr: *Récif;* Ger: *Riff.*

REEF (to). 1. To reduce the size of a sail by rolling or folding up part of it and securing it by tying reef points. A square sail reefs at the head, a fore-and-aft sail at the foot. In square sails the reef points are tied around the yard as well as the sail. In fore-and-aft sails they may, or may not, be tied around the boom which extends the foot of the sail.

Fr: *Prendre un Ris;* Ger: *Reffen.*

2. To shorten a spar, such as a running bowsprit or topmast, the latter spar being fitted in such case with a second fid. The depth of such a reef is usually about one-sixth the length of the topmast. The term "housing" applies only when lowering the spar entirely; that is to say, within the cap.

REEF BAND. A strip of canvas sewed horizontally across a sail as a strengthening in which, at regular intervals, are short pieces of rope for reefing.

Fr: *Bande de Ris;* Ger: *Reffband.*

REEF CRINGLE. A rope grommet worked around a thimble in the leech of a sail at the end of a reef band, through which the earing reeves.

Fr: *Patte de Ris;* Ger: *Refflagel.*

REEF EARING. On square-rigged vessels, a piece of Manila rope about ⅝ in. in diameter, with an eye spliced in one end and the other end pointed or carefully whipped. It is used to secure the reef cringle of a topsail to the yardarm. It is usually kept below and given to an experienced seaman when he is starting aloft to reef. On fore-and-afters, reef earings are short, plaited lengths passed through the reef cringle and around the boom several times to secure the leech to the spar after the reef points are tied and the sail is hoisted again.

Fr: *Raban d'Empointure;* Ger: *Reffbindsel; Reffjolle.*

REEFER. 1. A vessel designed and equipped for the transportation of food products under cold storage. A refrigerator vessel.

2. A short, double-breasted coat made of thick cloth. Also called pea jacket.

REEFING BATTEN. A vertical sail batten which runs parallel to the mast of a sharpie or canoe, used for reefing the sail by hauling it close to the mast with brails known as hulling lines.

REEFING BECKET. A sennett strap fitted with an eye and toggle; used in reefing when sails are rigged with French reefs. The toggle part is seized to the iron jackstay on the yard and the tail of the strap is taken around the rope jackstay on the sail, the eye being then placed over the toggle.

Fr: *Garcette de Ris;* Ger: *Reff Knebelsteert.*

REEFING JACKSTAY. The rope rove through the grommets of a reef band for reefing with the use of a toggle on the jackstay. Also called jack line or reef line.

Fr: *Filière de Ris;* Ger: *Reffleine.*

REEFING PLANK. A plank lashed across the ends of the stern davits on a Grand Banks fishing schooner. The crew stood upon it while reefing the mainsail.

REEF KNOT. A knot consisting of two successive overhand knots used for joining together two ropes of the same size. Commonly used for reefing sails because of the ease with which it may be spilled.

Fr: *Noeud Plat;* Ger: *Reffknoten.*

REEF LACING. A small line passed in the reef eyelets along the reef band of a boomed sail when reef points are not used.

Fr: *Hanet de Ris;* Ger: *Reffleine.*

REEF LINE.
See **Reefing Jackstay.**

REEF NET. A fixed net of Indian origin used in the Puget Sound salmon fisheries. It is a set net held in place by four anchors and worked with two double-ended boats 25 to 40 ft. in length. On the bow of each boat is a lookout pole or stand on which a fisherman is stationed to observe the movements of the fish.

Lowman, B. A., "Reef Nets in Puget Sound Salmon Fishery," Pacific Fisherman, vol. 37 (June, 1939).

REEF PENDANT. Short ropes rove through the cringles on the lower leech of a gaff sail and often through a hole on the boom cleat, by which the clew of the sail is secured to the boom preparatory to reefing.

Fr: *Itague de Ris; Bosse de Ris;* Ger: *Schmierreep.*

REEF PENDANT BEND. A bend used when making fast a reef pendant around a boom when the reef is hardened down with the reef tackle. Also called reeving line bend.

REEF POINT. One of a set of short ropes fixed in a line along a reef band to secure the sail when reefed. Their length is nearly double the circumference of the yard.

Fr: *Garcette de Ris;* Ger: *Reffseising; Reffbandsel; Reffknüttel.*

REEF SQUID. A lashing or earing used by fishermen on the south coast of England to lash the outer cringle of a lugsail when reefing.

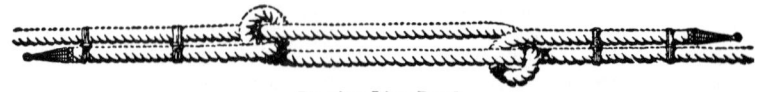

Reeving-Line Bend

REEF TACKLE. A small purchase used in reefing a square sail. It consists of a single block hooked into an eye at the outer end of the yardarm, with another block hooked to the leech of the sail in a special cringle situated below the lower reef band. When reefing, the reef cringle is hauled up and out to the yardarm. A reef tackle is also used with gaff sails to haul the reef earing out along the boom.

Fr: *Palanquin de Ris;* Ger: *Refftalje.*

REEF TACKLE PATCH. A strengthening patch fitted below the lowest reef band of a square sail where the reef tackle is shackled.

Fr: *Renfort de Palanquin;* Ger: *Refftaljenlapp.*

REEL. A revolving frame, varying in size, used for winding up hawsers, hose, lead lines, log lines, and the like.

Fr: *Touret;* Ger: *Rolle; Trommel.*

See **Hawser Reel, Log Reel.**

REEM. To widen or open the seams of planking with a reeming iron so that the oakum may be more readily admitted.

Fr: *Patarasser;* Ger: *Aufweiten; Klameien.*

REEMING BEETLE. A (wood) calker's largest mallet used with the hawsing iron for opening the seams of planks. It is a long-handled maul similar to a calking mallet but larger, and fitted with soft steel rings, instead of tempered steel rings. Also called hawsing beetle or Horsing beetle.

Fr: *Maillet à Patarasser;* Ger: *Klamei Hammer.*

REEVE. To pass or run through any hole in a block, thimble, cleat, ringbolt, and so on, as to reeve the end of a rope.

Fr: *Passer;* Ger: *Scheren; Durchholen.*

REEVING LINE. 1. One of the ropes fixed occasionally to square sails in heavy weather for reefing or furling them more conveniently.

2. Small rope or line fastened to a heavier one to facilitate passing the end of the latter through a block, and so on.

Fr: *Passeresse;* Ger: *Scherleine.*

REFLOAT. To set afloat again. To pull a vessel off after it has been aground.

Fr: *Renflouer; Déséchouer;* Ger: *Flottbringen; Abbringen; Aufschleppen.*

REFRACTION. The change of direction assumed by rays of light passing through atmospheric mediums of varying density. Atmospheric refraction ordinarily elevates a celestial object so that it appears to the

Refraction

observer to be higher in the sky than it really is. It changes according to the density, temperature, and moisture of the atmosphere.

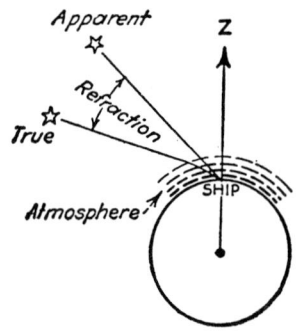

Fr: *Réfraction;* Ger: *Strahlenbrechung; Refraktion.*

Barlow, E. W., "Deceptions of Vision Due to Atmospheric Conditions at Sea," *Marine Observer,* London, vol. 12, January, 1935.

REFRIGERATED CARGO. Any cargo which is stowed at a low temperature in order to preserve the goods during transportation. Refrigerated cargoes are divided into three general classes, frozen, chilled, and air-cooled, according to the temperature at which they are kept.

Fr: *Marchandises Frigorifiées;* Ger: *Kühlraumladung.*

See **Frozen Cargo, Chilled Cargo, Air-Cooled Cargo.**

Gordon, J. S., "The stowage of refrigerated cargo on board vessels," Fourth International Congress of Refrigeration, *Proceedings,* London, 1924.

REFRIGERATED VESSEL. A vessel specially designed and equipped for the transportation of food products such as meat, fruit, fish, butter, eggs, under cold storage, having a large proportion or the whole of its cargo space insulated for this purpose. Also called refrigerator vessel.

The insulation consists essentially of layers of nonconducting materials which cover up all exposed steel work in the cargo spaces, the latter being kept at a certain temperature by the refrigerating plant. According to the nature of the cargo, there is a great difference in the fitting-out of the insulated holds and 'tween decks, not only in the degree of refrigeration required, but also in the stowage of the products, such as chilled or frozen meats, fruit, or any other variety of refrigerated cargo. The cubical loss of capacity occurring as a result of insulating a compartment may be estimated at 18 to 23 per cent, the thickness of insulation depending on the temperature to be maintained in the compartment, and on the range of outside temperatures which are encountered during the voyage. The hatches are reduced to minimum dimensions and are fitted in greater number so that the cargo may be disposed of in the shortest possible time. They are all of the portable plug type. Owing to their comparatively high speed, the great majority of refrigerated vessels can accommodate a certain number of passengers; thus they come under the heading of intermediate passenger liners.

The term *general refrigerated vessel* is used to denote ships equipped for the transportation of mixed refrigerated cargo at the various temperatures required for each product. In some of these vessels arrangements are made for the simultaneous circulation of brine at six distinct temperatures.

See **Meat Ship, Fruit Carrier.**

Fr: *Navire Frigorifique;* Ger: *Ladekühlraumschiff.*

Farmer, J. D., "Recent Developments in Marine Refrigeration," Institute of Marine Engineers (London), *Transactions,* vol. 48 (1936); Willcox and Farmer, "The Design of Refrigerated Vessels," Institution of Engineers and Shipbuilders in Scotland, *Transactions,* vol. 74 (1930–31); Woods, A. R. T., "Transport of Refrigerated Cargoes under Modern Marine Practice," Institution of Naval Architects (London), *Transactions,* vol. 77 (1935).

REFRIGERATING PLANT. An installation of machinery for the purposes of cooling designated spaces aboard ship and for manufacturing ice.

Most modern mechanical refrigerating plants are of the vapor-compression type, using such refrigerant fluids as ammonia, sulfur dioxide, carbon dioxide, ethyl chloride or freon, which boil at temperatures from –110° F. to 50° F. These gases are converted to liquids under high pressure, by cooling to the boiling point at that pressure. The liquid may then be evaporated, the heat necessary for evaporation being drawn from the substance the temperature of which it is desired to lower. The fluids listed above are *primary* refrigerants; the substances from which they extract heat are *secondary* refrigerants. The most common of the latter is brine. The secondary refrigerant serves as a vehicle to convey the heat from the space to be cooled, delivering it to the primary refrigerant. The standard method of designating capacity of a **refrigerating plant** is in terms of tons of refrigeration. The American ton of refrigeration corresponds to the extraction of heat at the rate of 200 B.T.U. per minute.

Fr: *Appareil Frigorifique;* Ger: *Kühlmaschine.*

REFRIGERATION.

See **Refrigerated Vessel.**

REFRIGERATION TON. A commercial unit of refrigeration. It is the heat absorbed by one ton (2000 lb.) of pure ice melting to water at 32° F. in 24 hrs. It is equal to the elimination of 12,000 British thermal units per hour.

REFUSE STAYS. A vessel which fails to tack or balks at going about is said to refuse stays.

Fr: *Refuser à Virer.*

REGISTER. See **Certificate of Registry.**

REGISTERED BREADTH. The width measured to the outside of the shell plating at the widest frame.

Fr: *Largeur réglementaire;* Ger: *Breite für Register.*

REGISTERED DEPTH. The depth measured amidships, from the top of the double bottom or from the top of the floor, if there is no double bottom, or from a point not exceeding three inches above these points where ceiling planking is fitted to the top of the tonnage deck beam at the center line. It is a legal measurement defined in the tonnage rules. Also called depth of hold.

Fr: *Creux de Cale;* Ger: *Raumtiefe; Vermessungstiefe.*

REGISTERED LENGTH. The length measured from the forepart of the stem on the line of the forecastle deck, to the afterside of the head of the sternpost or to the center of the rudderstock where no sternpost exists.

Fr: *Longueur Réglementaire;* Ger: *Registerlänge.*

REGISTER TONNAGE. The official tonnage, gross or net, as determined by the legal mode of measurement, and as shown on the tonnage certificate.

Fr: *Jauge Officielle;* Ger: *Festgestellter Tonnengehalt.*

REGISTRAR GENERAL OF SHIPPING AND SEAMEN (G. B.). A British Government Agency placed under the Ministry of Transport. Its functions cover: the maintenance of a central register of British ships in which are recorded all matters pertaining to these ships, including mortgages and other incumbrances; the allocation of official numbers, signal letters, radio call signs; changes of names of ships; examination and custody of ship's articles, log books, crew lists; records of deaths, births and marriages on board ships; recording of engagements, discharges and certificates of seamen; issuance of certificates of competency for officers; records of Naval Reserve officers and men, also arrangements for training periods of reservists.

REGISTRY. A duty imposed on shipowners in order to secure to their vessels the privileges of ships of the nation to which they belong. Also called registration, documentation. Registration is made by the principal custom officer of the port chosen. It includes: name of the ship, name of owners, tonnage, build, and description of the vessel, particulars of its origin, name of the master, name of the one entitled to the custody of the certificate of registration. The vessel is considered to belong to the port at which it is registered.

In the United States three terms are used to denote the registration of vessels according to their trade and tonnage:

Vessels in foreign trade are "registered."

Vessels in coasting and Great Lakes trade are "enrolled."

Vessels under 20 tons (coasting trade and fisheries) are "licensed."

All are referred to as "documented."

Fr: *Nationalisation;* Ger: *Registrierung.*

U. S. Bureau of Marine Inspection and Navigation, *Documentation, Entrance and Clearance of Vessels,* Washington, 1940.

REGULAR SHACKLE. A shackle which is secured to a block by the pin so that if this is removed, the fitting is freed from the block. The opposite of an "upset shackle."

REGULAR TURN. A chartering term which denotes that the vessel will on arrival be placed in regular rotation on the list of tonnage awaiting berthage. This is the opposite of "free of turn."

Time for lay days will not count until the ship is actually in berth. In different ports the term "regular turn" has been construed as meaning: (1) turn with sailing ships only; (2) turn with steam and sailing ships; (3) turn according to arrival at berth; (4) turn according to date of entry in the dock book.

REGULATION LIGHT. Any of the lights which have to be carried by vessels whether under way, at anchor, or in any other circumstances according to the rules set forth by the International regulations for preventing collisions at sea.

Fr: *Feu Réglementaire;* Ger: *Anordnunglicht.*

REGULATOR (U. S.). A shipyard worker who adjusts correctly the structural steel members placed in position by erectors.

REINFORCED CONCRETE VESSEL. A vessel constructed of concrete reinforced by steel rods, the latter having a small cross-section area in proportion to the area of the concrete. Reinforced concrete as a shipbuilding material for seagoing vessels has been used experimentally as an alternative to steel during wartime owing to the abnormal conditions then prevailing. It is claimed to be particularly suitable for coasting vessels, tugs, harbor and dock vessels, lighters and barges of all types, floating piers, caissons, pontoons, and floating docks.

Fr: *Navire en Ciment Armé;* Ger: *Eisenbetonschiff.*

There is no definite conclusion as to the limit of size for concrete built vessels, but as the length increases, there comes a point at which the amount of steel necessary to take up the stresses is so great that concrete can no longer be usefully employed. The largest concrete vessels built during World War I were oil tankers having a length of 420 ft. with a deadweight capacity of 6380 tons. Among the advantages claimed for concrete vessels are: (1) Quicker construction with very little skilled labor required; (2) longer life owing to the freedom from dry rot or corrosion as in wood or steel; (3) reduced costs of repairs and upkeep.

The disadvantages are: (1) greatly increased weight of hull and consequently greater displacement for the same deadweight, the hull weight, excluding machinery, for instance, for a 300-ton deadweight concrete vessel being about 290 tons as against 120 tons for a steel hull; (2) increase of net tonnage with corresponding port dues; (3) longer time necessary for bottom repairs if damaged.

The world's tonnage in seagoing concrete vessels in 1919 was reckoned at 150,000 tons deadweight, several hundred lighters and other small craft for enclosed waters not being included in the above total. The best concrete for shipbuilding purposes is that which is densest. The steel used for rods is usually of shipyard quality mild steel, 28 to 32 tons tensile strength. The generally recognized method of construction was to cast the concrete in molds made of tongued and grooved boarding.

Boon, A. A., Der Bau von Schiffen aus Eisenbeton, Berlin, 1918; Eisenbetonschiffbau und Stahlersparnis, Zement (Berlin), vol. 26, no. 44, 45 (1937); Ferguson, L. R., "Concrete Ships," American Society of Marine Draftsmen. *Journal*, vol. 4 (1918); Fougner, Sea Going and Other Concrete Vessels, London, 1922; Ruediger, M., "Der Eisenbeton." Schiffbau, vol. 20, Berlin, 1919.

REINING. The strengthening border about 5 or 10 meshes deep at the foot of each lint in a fleet of driftnets.

Fr: *Souillardure*; Ger: *Unterwant*.

REINSURANCE. Insurance effected by an underwriter upon a subject against certain risks with another underwriter on the same subject, against all or a part of the same risks, but not exceeding the same amount.

Fr: *Réassurance*; Ger: *Rückversicherung*.

REISEKAHN. A sailing lighter found in coastal waters of East and West Prussia, originating from the Kurisches Haff and built in the region between Memel and Elbing. The hull is flat-bottomed with carvel planking, broad stem and sternpost, and high sheer at ends. Leeboards are fitted. The smaller units are one-masted, but the ketch rig is most commonly used. The largest boats have a peculiar rig consisting of two masts of equal length and a small jigger mast stepped on the counter. Two headsails are used. Length 72 to 154 ft. Breadth 17 to 31 ft. Draft 4 to 5 ft. Deadweight 80 to 320 metric tons.

RELATIVE BEARING. A bearing stated as a direction relative to the line of the ship's keel and expressed in points or degrees from the ship's head, beam or stern.

RELATIVE HUMIDITY. The degree of saturation of the atmosphere defined as the ratio of the amount of water vapor present in a given volume of air to the amount

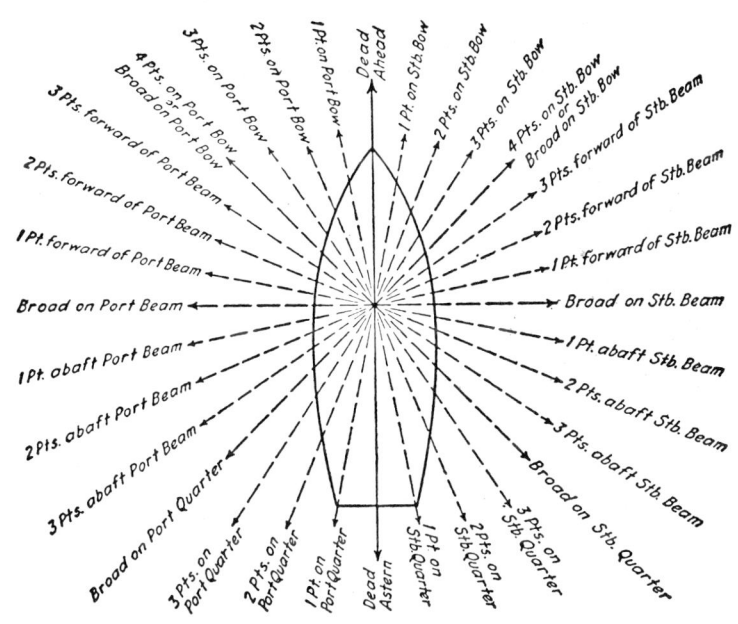

Relative Bearings

necessary to saturate the same volume of air at the same temperature. Also called hygrometric state. In the Beaufort notation a relative humidity of less than 60 per cent is described as dry air.

RELATIVE ROTATIVE EFFICIENCY. The ratio of propeller efficiency behind the vessel to the efficiency of the same propeller obtained in open water.

RELIEVE. To release from a post, duty, or station.

    Fr: *Relever;* *Faire la Relève;* Ger: *Ablösen.*

RELIEVING BOARDS. A term sometimes applied to dunnage planks or boards placed every few feet over cases and other containers stowed in the bottom of a hold to take up or equalize the strain imposed by the cargo above.

RELIEVING TACKLE. Tackle fitted to the tiller of ships not provided with spring buffers or a rudder brake, to prevent the shocks caused by the impact of the sea on the rudder from being transmitted directly to the hand-operated steering wheel, and also to provide a means of securing the tiller in case of emergency. Sometimes called kicking tackle, rudder tackle. The relieving tackle consists of a rope rove through multiple sheave blocks "endless fall" fashion, forming two separate tackles which are connected, one on each side, between the tiller and bulwarks or pedestals so as to provide frictional resistance to the movement of the rudder.

    Fr: *Palan de Garde;* Ger: *Nottalje; Steuertalje.*

REND. Large open split or shake in timber, particularly in planks, where they are occasioned by exposure to the wind or sun.

    Fr: *Eclat;* Ger: *Riss.*

RENDER. The free passage of a rope through a block, a bull's-eye, a deadeye, etc.

    Fr: *Courant;* Ger: *Durchscheren.*

RENNEL'S CURRENT. A current setting in a Northwest direction across the entrance of the English Channel. Caused by a rise in water in the Bay of Biscay following a succession of Westerly gales.

    Fr: *Courant de Rennel;* Ger: *Rennelström.*

REPAIR. General overhaul of a vessel in drydock. (Seldom used.)

    Fr: *Radouber;* Ger: *Ausbesserung.*

See **Damage Repairs, Temporary Repairs.**

REPEATER. One or three pennants of the International code of signals which indicate respectively that the first, second, or third flag in a hoist of signals is duplicated.

    Fr: *Substitut;* Ger: *Wiederholungsflagge.*

REPEATER COMPASS. An apparatus which is electrically connected to a master magnetic or gyrocompass and which follows exactly the movements of the master compass. Also called receiver compass. It consists of a small, step-by-step motor which drives a compass card through a train of gears, the reduction being 180 to 1. Repeater compasses are used with advantage as substitutes for the usual auxiliary compasses. The latter are less satisfactory and have to be constantly checked with the ship's standard compass.

    Fr: *Compas Répétiteur;* Ger: *Tochterkompass.*

REPLACEMENT CLAUSE. A clause inserted in marine insurance policies on machinery, by which the insurer's liability is restricted to the cost of repairing or replacing the particular part lost or injured.

REPRISALS. Act of force short of legal war. Means of obtaining separation before proceeding to war. Reprisals are well-understood and acknowledged means among nations of obtaining justice otherwise denied, and do not constitute an act of war.

    Fr: *Représailles;* Ger: *Repressalien.*

REQUEST NOTE. A special permit to land perishable or other goods before the ship has reported and cleared the customs.

RESERVE BUOYANCY. The watertight volume of a vessel above the designed waterline. It is usually expressed as a percentage of the total volume of the vessel or total buoyancy, and is thus a measure of the additional weight which could be placed on the ship before it would sink through loss of buoyancy. It is an indication of the seaworthiness of the vessel.

    Fr: *Réserve de Flottabilité;* Ger: *Reserve Auftrieb; Reserveschwimmfähigkeit; Reservedeplacement.*

RESIDUAL ERRORS. In a magnetic compass the deviation remaining on the different headings after compensation.

RESIDUARY RESISTANCE. In speed and power calculations, the towrope resistance less frictional resistance. Residuary resistance is considered to be composed of wave-making and eddy-making resistances.

    Fr: *Résistance Résiduaire;* Ger: *Normalwiderstand.*

RESIDUE CARGO (U. S.). A term which refers to cargo shown by the manifest to be destined to a port other than the port at which the vessel first arrived and made entry.

RESISTANCE. The force required to move a floating body at a given speed of translation through water.

See **Air Resistance, Center of Lateral Resistance, Curve of Resistance, Hollows of Resistance, Lateral Resistance, Residuary Resistance, Skin Resistance, Towrope Resistance, Wake Resistance, Wave Resistance.**

Baker, G. S., Laws of Ship Resistance, Engineer, London, vol. 152, November-December, 1931.

RESISTANCE WELDING. A process of pressure fusion welding in which the necessary heat is obtained by passing a heavy electric current across the resistance set up between the contact areas of the parts to be welded. Electrical resistance welding comprises a variety of processes such as butt welding by the upset and flash methods, spot welding, and seam welding.

Fr: *Soudure par Résistance;* Ger: *Widerstandsschweissung.*

RESISTOR HOUSE. A deckhouse containing the electrical equipment controlling deck machinery.

RESPONDENTIA. A loan obtained by the master of a vessel on the security of cargo alone. In other respects the contract is of the same character as bottomry.

Fr: *Prêt à la Grosse;* Ger: *Bodmerei.*

RESTRAINT OF PRINCES. A phrase used in bills of lading to denote a limitation upon the liability of a shipowner when the ship is detained by governmental authority against the will of the owners. It covers belligerent acts of states other than that of the owners of the vessel.

Fr: *Arrêt du Prince;* Ger: *Zwang durch Fürsten.*

RESTRICTED CLASS. A class or group of racing boats which, although differing in hull design, rig sails, spars, and so on, conforms to certain racing rules concerning dimensions and some specified particulars. The object of these rules is to eliminate freak features such as excessive overhangs, insufficient freeboard and poor seagoing ability.

Ger: *Beschränkte Klasse.*

RETARD. In tidal terminology: refers to the interval between transit of the moon at which the tide originates and the appearance of the tide itself.

Fr: *Retard;* Ger: *Verzögerung.*

RETARDATION OF TIDE.
See **Lagging.**

RETENTIVE MAGNETISM. The temporary magnetism communicated to an iron ship when its head is kept in one direction for some time, as, for instance, when it is moored to a pier, or when a continuous course for several days is steered.

Fr: *Magnétisme Rétenteur;* Ger: *Behaltender Magnetismus.*

RETENTIVITY. The property by virtue of which hard iron resists being magnetized, and when magnetized resists being demagnetized. Also called coercive force.

Fr: *Rétention Magnétique;* Ger: *Koerzitivkraft.*

RETROGRADE MOTION. A planet has retrograde motion when its right ascension is increasing.

REVENUE TON (U. S.). A unit of cargo measurement found in all ports of the United States. It cannot be defined in units either of weight or of space occupied by the cargo, as it varies from port to port, from line to line, and from ship to ship, depending on the customs of the port and the nature of the cargo carried by the individual vessel. For any one port, however, and particularly for any one group of ships specializing in the same trade and carrying approximately the same kind of commodities the revenue ton represents a tangible unit of cargo measurement and is frequently used as the only means of expressing the total cargo of the ships.

All United States ships show on their manifests their total revenue tonnage, and very often they also indicate in long tons the total weight of the cargo.

REVERSE BAR. A bar riveted to the upper edge of the floor plate on the side opposite to the frame bar, and back to back to the latter above the head of the floor. It is slightly smaller in section than the frame bar. Also called reverse frame.

Fr: *Cornière Renversée; Cornière Contre-Membrure;* Ger: *Gegenwinkel; Gegenspantwinkel.*

REVERSE TILLER. A tiller which extends abaft the rudderhead.

Fr: *Barre Renversée;* Ger: *Umgekehrte Ruderpinne.*

REVERSIBLE LAY DAYS. Reversible lay days, as mentioned in a charter party, are those under which the charterer has the option of averaging the time allowed for loading and discharging. The total time for the two operations being taken into account.
 Fr: *Jours de Planche Réversibles;* Ger: *Vertauchbare Liegetage; Reversible Lade- und Loschzeit.*

REVERSIBLE PROPELLER. A form of propeller successfully used with small craft. It usually has only two blades, each of which is mounted on a pivot or in a socket so that it may be rotated about an axis along its length sufficiently to change the general direction of its obliquity from right to left hand. In this manner, with the shaft turning constantly in one direction, the propeller may be transformed from go ahead to back, or vice versa. Also called variable pitch propeller, feathering screw.
 Fr: *Hélice Réversible;* Ger: *Umsteuerschraube; Drehflügelschraube.*

It is evident, however, that a propeller of the usual form, right-hand for instance, cannot be transformed into a true left-hand propeller by any such twist of the blades. Furthermore, the blade necessary for satisfactory operation with a reversing propeller must be a mean between the two forms required for right- and left-hand propellers. For this reason it is unable to operate with optimum efficiency in either position, and such propellers are not advisable when considerations of efficiency are of importance. They are, however, of great convenience when used with many modern internal combustion engines, in which the shaft is allowed to rotate continuously in one direction, while reversing is effected by shifting the blades in the manner indicated above. For an intermediate position the plane of the blades will lie nearly transverse and the boat will be driven neither ahead nor back.
Lockwood Taylor, J., "The Variable Pitch Marine Propellers," Institution of Mechanical Engineers (London), *Journal and Proceedings*, vol. 152, 1945.

REVERSIBLE WINCH. A winch with power control of the load when either lowering or raising. This is obtained by reversing the engine when the load is lowered. The lowering is slower than when lowering by gravity, as in nonreversible winches.
 Fr: *Treuil à Changement de Marche;* Ger: *Winde mit Umschaltgetrieb.*

REVERSING CURRENT. A tidal current that flows alternately in approximate opposite directions with a slack water at each reversal of direction. Currents of this type usually occur in rivers and straits where the direction of flow is more or less restricted to certain channels.

REVOLUTION INDICATOR. An electrical apparatus by which the direction and number of revolutions per minute of the main engines are indicated on the navigating bridge. The indications are given by means of two concentric pointers over the face of a graduated circular dial situated in a prominent position of the bridge.
 Fr: *Compteur de Tours;* Ger: *Umdrehungsanzeiger; Umdrehungsfernanzeiger.*

REVOLVING LIGHT. Coastal light which appears and disappears successively and emits rotating beams of light. It is actuated by means of a screen revolving around the source of light. It is distinguished from the occulting and flashing light because there is a gradual waxing and waning of the light while in the other types the eclipses and reappearances are of extreme suddenness. This term was suppressed by international agreement in 1930.
 Fr: *Feu Tournant;* Ger: *Drehfeuer.*

REVOLVING RADIO BEAM. Directional radio sending station which sends a sharply directive signal by which a vessel with only a receiving set may determine direction from the station. Every time the revolving beam passes true North, a distinctive all around signal is emitted which all vessels within hearing can pick up. The listening vessel notes the time at the "North" signal, and then marks the time until the very sharp minimum occurs, when the signal fades out temporarily. The time interval between the "North" signal and the sharp minimum gives the bearing of the vessel from the station.
 Fr: *Radiophare tournant;* Ger: *Drehfunksender; Rotierender; Funksender.*

REVOLVING STORM. Name commonly given to the violent storms which, while advancing bodily in a definite direction, rotate about an axis with great rapidity. Also called cyclonic storm, cyclone. The circulation of the wind is clockwise in the southern hemisphere and counterclockwise in the northern. Revolving storms are so named because the wind in these storms revolves around an area of low pressure at

the center. Hurricanes, cyclones, and typhoons are names given to revolving storms.
Fr: *Cyclone;* Ger: *Wirbelsturm.*

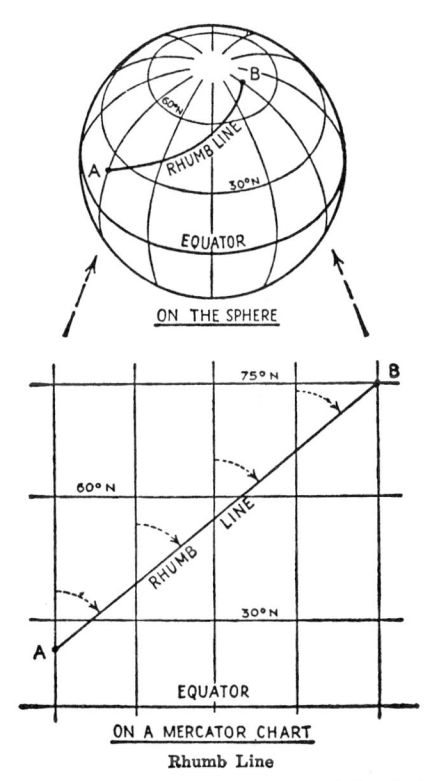

ON THE SPHERE

ON A MERCATOR CHART

Rhumb Line

RHUMB. Thirty-second part of the circle of the horizon 11 degrees 15 minutes in azimuth. A point of the compass.
Fr: *Air de vent; Quart; Rhumb;* Ger: *Windstrick; Rhumb.*

RHUMB DISTANCE. The length of the track a ship makes when sailing from one place to another without changing her course.

RHUMB LINE. The curve on the earth's surface which cuts all the meridians at the same angle. Also called loxodromic curve, loxodrome.
Fr: *Loxodromie;* Ger: *Loxodromische Linie; Loxodrome.*

RHUMB SAILING. The course of a vessel when she keeps on the rhumb line which passes through the place of departure and the place of destination.
Fr: *Route loxodromique;* Ger: *Segeln in der Loxodrome.*

RIB AND TRUCK PARREL. A parrel consisting of a rope on which series of trucks and ribs are strung.
Fr: *Racage à Pommes et Bigots;* Ger: *Taurack.*

RIBBAND CARVEL PLANKING. A system of planking similar to that of the carvel-built boat with the addition of inside battens covering the seams. Each batten is fastened to both planks and ties the whole skin together making a stronger hull than plain carvel.
Ger: *Nahtspanten Beplankung.*

For a given weight of material ribband carvel planking is the strongest type. The ribbands are notched into the ribs or frames, which are made heavier to allow for notching. The planks are slightly thinner than in the ordinary carvel system. This type of planking is most suitable for light, fast boats which have to stand the stress of large sail area. It gives excellent results in strength and tightness.

RIBBAND NAIL. A nail having a large round head with a ring to prevent the head from splitting the timber or being drawn through. Used principally for fastening ribbands.
Fr: *Clou à lattes;* Ger: *Sentennagel.*

RIBBAND SHORE. One of the shores placed at frequent intervals outside the ground ways with the head abutting against the launching ribband and the heel fixed against the sides of the slip or otherwise secured. Their purpose is to hold the standing ways and prevent the ribband from being torn off.

RIBBED PLATE. A plate strengthened by ribs formed in its surface.
Fr: *Tôle à Nervures; Tôle Striée;* Ger: *Riffelblech; Geripptes Blech.*

RIBBON. Narrow strip of contrasting color painted on the outside plating along the weatherdeck line or at the loadwater line above the boot topping, in some ships.

RICKER. A stout pole, used for making a boat's mast, a boat-hook stave, and so on.

RIDDLE MEASUREMENT. A British rule of tonnage measurement officially adopted by Act of Parliament in 1835 and enforced until it was superseded by the Moorsom system in 1854.

RIDE. 1. To lap over, said especially of rope when the part on which the strain is brought lies over and jams the other parts.
Fr: *Mordre;* Ger: *Beklemmen.*

2. To float or move upon the water in a buoyant manner.

Fr: *Etaler;* Ger: *Liegen; Reiten.*

3. To lie at anchor; said of a vessel when kept at some particular spot by her anchor. A vessel at anchor is said to be "riding weather tide" when the wind is against the tide and "riding lee tide" when wind and tide are in the same direction.

Fr: *Etre au Mouillage;* Ger: *Vor Anker reiten; Vor Anker liegen.*

RIDE ATHWART. Said of an anchored vessel lying broadside to the wind with current running in opposite direction to that of the wind, and the latter is not of sufficient force to turn the vessel around.

RIDE DOWN. To force anything down to its proper place by throwing weight upon it.

Fr: *Peser;* Ger: *Herunterreiten.*

RIDE EASY. Said of a ship at anchor when she bears little strain on the cable and does not pitch severely.

Ger: *Bequem vor Anker liegen.*

RIDE HARD. Refers to a ship at anchor when she pitches violently thereby straining her cables.

Fr: *Fatiguer au mouillage;* Ger: *Schwer vor Anker reiten.*

RIDE OUT. Refers to a ship lying at anchor or hove to in heavy weather when sufficiently seaworthy to keep safely afloat.

Fr: *Etaler;* Ger: *Abreiten; Reiten.*

RIDER. In wooden ships one of a series of doubling timbers bolted to the frame timbers. They reach from keelson to lower deck beams and strengthen the framing.

Fr: *Porque;* Ger: *Kattspor; Binnenspant.*

RIDER FRAME. A frame welded or riveted to another frame in order to stiffen it.

RIDER KEELSON. In large wooden hulls, a keelson timber placed on the top of a main keelson to give additional longitudinal strength. Also called false keelson.

Fr: *Fausse Carlingue;* Ger: *Kielschweinsohle.*

RIDER PLATE. 1. A horizontal fore-and-aft plate riveted to the top angles of a centerline keelson running above the floors.

Fr: *Tôle Supérieure;* Ger: *Gurtplatte; Gürtungsplatte.*

2. In a composite built hull, one of the narrow plates extending from keel to sheer strake and inclined at forty-five degrees to the vertical. Rider plates are riveted outside the frames. Their purpose is to improve the longitudinal strength of the structure.

Fr: *Bande Diagonale;* Ger: *Diagonalschiene.*

RIDERS. The upper tier of casks or barrels stowed in a ship's hold.

RIDE TO HAWSE. Said of a vessel which has both bow anchors down.

Ger: *Vermuren.*

RIDGE. 1. A relatively narrow extension of an anticyclone or high pressure area.

2. A long and narrow elevation from the bottom of the ocean with steeper sides than those of a "rise."

Fr: *Dorsale;* Ger: *Rücken.*

RIDGEPOLE.

See **Awning Boom.**

RIDGE ROPE. 1. One of two ropes running out on each side of the bowsprit, which the men can hold to.

Fr: *Filière de Beaupré;* Ger: *Laufstag.*

2. A rope rove through the eyes of metal stanchions fitted in the top rail of small craft.

Fr: *Filière de Garde Corps;* Ger: *Strecktau.*

3. The centerline rope of an awning or backbone into which the crow's foot is tucked, when the awning is short. Also called center ridge rope.

Fr: *Tétière de Tente;* Ger: *Mittelliek.*

4. The rope running along the side of a ship to secure the sides of an awning when spread. It is rove through holes at the top end of the awning stanchions.

Fr: *Filière de Tente;* Ger: *Sonnensegel Strecktau.*

RIDGE SPAR.

See **Awning Boom.**

RIDING ANCHOR. In a ship with two anchors down, that to which the vessel is riding strongest.

Fr: *Ancre travaillante;* Ger: *Tragender Anker.*

See **Guilleux.**

RIDING BITTS. Heavy wooden bitts with an iron casing around which the anchor cables were turned when a vessel was riding to anchor. They were in use before friction cable holders were introduced and served also to check the anchor cables when anchor was let go in deep water.

Fr: *Bittes de mouillage;* Ger: *Betinge.*

RIDING BOOM. A spar working on a hinge or gooseneck riveted to the ship's side and lowered to a horizontal position at right angles to the side of the vessel. To this boom, which is supported by a lift and maintained in position by fore-and-aft guys, the ship's boats tie up when the vessel is anchored. Also called swinging boom, boat boom, guest warp boom.

Fr: *Tangon d'Embarcations;* Ger: *Bootsbaum; Backspiere; Backbaum.*

RIDING CHAIN. In permanent moorings, the length of chain cable which connects the vessel to the ground chain.

Fr: *Pendeur de Corps-Mort.*

RIDING CHOCK. See **Controller.**

RIDING LIGHT. The regulation light or lights which a vessel must carry when at anchor. Also called anchor light. Vessels of 150 ft. or more in length carry two riding lights. The regulations require these lights to show a white light which shall be visible for a distance of at least two sea miles. The diameter of lenses for anchor lights of sea going craft should not be less than 8 in. If oil lights are used, the wicks should not be less than 1¼ in. for colza oil and ¾ in. for paraffin oil.

Fr: *Feu de Mouillage;* Ger: *Ankerlicht; Ankerlaterne.*

RIDING SAIL. A triangular sail set on the mainmast on the Newfoundland Bank fishing schooners. Also called trysail. It is hauled out with tackles and made fast aft to the main boom and stern of the vessel. It helps to keep the vessel head to wind when at anchor on the banks, and lessens the rolling.

Fr: *Voile de Batture; Dériveur;* Ger: *Treiber.*

RIDING STOPPER. A stopper which secures the anchor cable when the vessel is riding at anchor, thus relieving the strain on the windlass.

Fr: *Bosse de Mouillage; Stoppeur;* Ger: *Ankerstopper.*

RIDING TURN. 1. A turn on the parts of a rope on which the strain is brought. It lies over the other turns and jams.

2. A second layer of turns put on over the ground or first turns in a seizing or whipping. Also called rider.

Fr: *Tour Croisé;* Ger: *Obere Schlagtorn.*

RIFT-SAWED PLANK. A plank sawed radially from the log so as to have the annual rings perpendicular or nearly so to the face. Plank sawed in such a way that the broad faces of the strake are at right angles to the annual rings.

RIG. The rig of a vessel is the distinctive manner in which her masts and sails are disposed. There are two main types of rigs: the square and the fore-and-aft rig. These two rigs are frequently combined on the same vessel but whenever a vessel carries square sails it is said to be square-rigged. It must be noted that there is no hard and fast rule to distinguish vessels closely resembling each other. The tendency of all modern rigs is gradually to do away with square sails, which are replaced by fore-and-aft ones.

Fr: *Gréement;* Ger: *Zeug; Takelung.*

Massenet, Vallerey, Letalle, *Gréement et manoeuvre du navire,* Paris, 1921; Middendorf, F. L., *Bemastung und Takelung der Schiffe,* Berlin, 1903; Moore, Sir A., *Last Days of Mast and Sail,* Oxford, England, 1925; Underhill, H., *Sailing Ship, Rigs and Rigging,* Glasgow, 1937; Morris, E. P., *The Fore and Aft Rig in America,* New Haven (Conn.), 1927.

RIGGED OAR. An oar which slips into a tholepin, becket, or rowlock at the stern of a boat, used both for sculling and steering.

Fr: *Godille;* Ger: *Wrieckriem.*

RIGGER. 1. A shipyard worker who, during the vessel's construction, sets in place heavy structural parts such as stem, sternpost, masts, and spars, and assists in hoisting, lowering, and handling all structural components. Also called erector.

See **Crane Rigger, In-Rigger, Loft Rigger.**

2. In Great Britain one of a gang of men engaged to shift a vessel from one part of a harbor to another. Such men are employed between the period when one crew is paid off and another engaged.

3. One who installs all gear and fittings of wire and fiber rope on a ship. He fabricates and installs shrouds, stays, lifts, braces, radio aerials and other rigging fitted to masts and spars; lays out and cuts materials according to drawings and specifications; splices fiber and wire rope where necessary; bolts or ties rigging in place. Also called Ship Rigger.

Fr: *Gréeur;* Ger: *Takler.*

RIGGER'S HORN. A docked horn worn by riggers on their belt and containing tallow for greasing the strands of rope. Also called grease horn. Sailmakers use a similar

horn for sail needles to keep them from rusting.
Ger: *Fetthorn.*

RIGGER'S SCREW. A contrivance used in splicing rope. Also called rigger's vise, splicing vise. It acts as a press for forming the splices; at the same time it acts as a vise for securing and holding the rope while the splice is being made. There are two types, one for Manila or hemp rope, the other for wire rope, the difference between them being in the shape of the jaws.

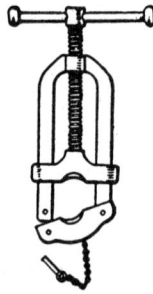

Rigger's Screw

Fr: *Presse de Gréeur;* Ger: *Schraubenklemme; Bandselschraube.*

RIGGING. A general term for all ropes, chains and gear used for supporting and operating masts, yards, booms, gaffs, and sails. Rigging is of two kinds, standing rigging and running rigging. More generally, the whole apparatus of spars including the masts, yards, sails and cordage, by which the force of the wind is utilized to move a sailing vessel against the resistance of the water.

Fr: *Gréement;* Ger: *Takelage; Takelwerk.*

See **Masthead Rigging, Rod Rigging, Running Rigging, Standing Rigging.**

The Rigging of Merchant Ships, Liverpool Journal of Commerce, Shipbuilding and Engineering Edition (January 13, 1944).

RIGGING BATTEN. A batten of wood placed about the rigging in a sailing vessel to save the gear from chafing. Also called scotchman.

Fr: *Pare Manoeuvre;* Ger: *Schalstück; Schamfielungslatte.*

RIGGING CLEAT. A cleat with a heel hollowed out for fixing to a shroud with seizings. Also called shroud cleat, lashing cleat.

Fr: *Taquet de Hauban;* Ger: *Wantklampe.*

RIGGING LOFT. A large shop or room where rigging is fitted and prepared for use on shipboard.

Fr: *Garniture;* Ger: *Taklerei; Taklerwerkstatt.*

RIGGING LUFF. A purchase used for setting up lower rigging and stays. It consists of two double blocks or two single blocks. Also called luff purchase.

Fr: *Palan à Croc;* Ger: *Handtalje.*

RIGGING PLAN. A drawing which gives the distribution and areas of all sails, also their centers of effort, the position of center of lateral resistance and the height of center of effort above the center of lateral resistance. Also called sail draught (G. B.), sail plan.

Fr: *Plan de Voilure;* Ger: *Takelungsplan.*

RIGGING SCREW. See **Turnbuckle.**

RIGHT. To return to a normal position, as, a vessel righting after heeling over.

RIGHT ASCENSION. The angle at the celestial pole intercepted between the meridian passing through the first point of Aries and that passing through the position of a heavenly body. It is always measured eastward along the equinoctial and is expressed in time from 0^h to 24^h, each hour being equivalent to 15° of arc.

Fr: *Ascension Droite;* Ger: *Rechtsaszension; Geradeaufsteigung.*

RIGHT ASCENSION OF MERIDIAN. The angle that the plane of the observer's meridian makes with a plane passing through the axis of the Earth and the first point of Aries.

Fr: *Ascension méridienne;* Ger: *Gerade Aufsteigung der Meridian.*

RIGHT ASTERN. In line with the ship's longitudinal axis and astern.

Fr: *Droit Derrière;* Ger: *Rechts Hintenaus.*

RIGHT HAND BUOY. A buoy to the right of a navigable channel when coming from seaward. These buoys bear odd numbers starting with the first buoy from seaward.

RIGHT-HANDED ROPE. See **Plain-laid Rope.**

RIGHT-HAND LAY. In rope making: the lay wherein the strands are twisted in a counterclockwise direction.

Fr: *Commettage à Droite;* Ger: *Rechtsschlag.*

RIGHT-HAND PROPELLER. A propeller in which the rotation of the blades is from left to right with the ship going ahead and the observer facing forward.

Fr: *Hélice à pas à Droite;* Ger: *Rechtsgängiger Propeller; Rechtsgehender Propeller.*

RIGHTING COUPLE. The mechanical couple formed by the force of gravity acting downward through the center of gravity and the force of buoyancy acting upward through the center of buoyancy, which tends to restore a vessel to the upright after it has been inclined.

Fr: *Couple de Redressement;* Ger: *Aufrichte Kräftepaar.*

RIGHTING LEVER. The perpendicular distance between the vertical lines of force of gravity and buoyancy, one down through the center of gravity and one up through the center of buoyancy, when the ship is inclined from the vertical, when the relative positions of the center of gravity and center of buoyancy are such as to produce a righting couple. The righting lever may also be defined as the product of the transverse metacentric height and the sine of the angle of ship's inclination.

Fr: *Bras de Redressement;* Ger: *Hebelarm.*

RIGHTING MOMENT. The moment of the righting couple which tends to restore a vessel to the upright when it has been inclined. It is expressed in foot-tons and equals the displacement of the vessel multiplied by the righting lever.

Fr: *Moment de Redressement;* Ger: *Stabilitätsmoment; Aufrichtungsvermögen.*

RIGHT OF ANGARY. The right of a State, whether belligerent or neutral, whether in time of peace or war, to requisition ships and goods situated in its territory, subject to adequate compensation. It has been recognized by both constitutional and international law.

Fr: *Droit d'Angarie;* Ger: *Angarierecht.*

Henckels and Crocker, *Memorandum of Authorities on the Law of Angary,* U. S. State Department, Washington, 1919; Puget, H., "Le Droit d'Angarie," *Revue Maritime* (Paris), N. S., vol. 2 (1922); Rolin, A., "Le Droit d'Angarie," *Revue de droit International et Législation Comparée* (Brussels), Series 3, vol. 1 (1920); Woolsey, L. H., "Taking of Foreign Ships in American Ports," *American Journal of International Law,* vol. 35, Washington (1941).

RIGHT OF APPROACH. The right granted by international law to a war vessel to come near enough to a suspected merchant vessel for close inspection to ascertain her nationality. There must be no interference with her voyage and the vessel approached is not required to lie to.

Fr: *Droit de Reconnaissance;* Ger: *Annäherungsrecht.*

RIGHT OF CONVOY. The exemption of visit and search of neutral vessels on the high seas by a belligerent war vessel when the former are sailing in convoy under the protection of a warship of their own nationality whose commander asserts that there is no contraband on board the convoyed vessels. This doctrine has never been admitted by Great Britain. It has, however, been accepted by the United States and several European states, these states having frequently conceded the right by treaty.

Fr: *Droit d'Escorte;* Ger: *Geleitungsrecht.*

RIGHT OF FISHERY. The right by which vessels or craft are allowed to fish. On the high seas it is common to all mankind. The right of fishing within territorial waters is usually vested exclusively in the subjects of the particular state by international law. On the seashore it is prima facie vested in all subjects of the country as a common right. Laws and regulations impose limitations in respect of seasons, kinds of fish, and modes of fishing.

Fr: *Droit de Pêche;* Ger: *Fischereirecht.*

RIGHT OF MOORING. The right by which vessels or craft are permitted to anchor in certain waters. It includes the right to fix moorings in the soil or bed of the foreshore. The right of mooring is incidental to the right of navigation and can only be exercised by vessels which are themselves used in navigation. Coaling lighters or hulks, for example, would not be considered as entitled to the right of mooring unless specially authorized.

Fr: *Droit d'Ancrage;* Ger: *Verankerungsrecht.*

RIGHT OF NAVIGATION. The right by which every ship, whatever her nationality, is entitled to navigate certain waters. The right of navigation in territorial waters, as well as on the high seas, is common to all except in wartime.

It does not include the right to land upon, or embark from the seashore or land adjoining, except at such places as are appropriate to this purpose. In the event of peril or necessity, the landing of goods or persons is permissible on any part of the seashore. The public right to navigate all tidal navigable rivers has the same incidental rights as the right of navigation over territorial waters.

Fr: *Droit de Navigation;* Ger: *Schiffahrtsrecht.*

RIGHT OF PURSUIT. The universally recognized rule by which men-of-war of a littoral state can pursue into the open sea, seize, and bring back into port for trial any foreign merchant vessel that has violated the law while in the territorial waters of that state.

Fr: *Droit de Poursuite;* Ger: *Verfolgungsrecht.*

RIGHT OF SEARCH. In maritime law, the right of a commissioned belligerent vessel to stop neutral merchantmen on the high seas and make such examination and search as may be considered necessary if, after examination of the ship's papers by the visiting officer, there is suspicion of fraud against the vessel.

Fr: *Droit de Recherche;* Ger: *Durchsuchungsrecht.*

See **Search.**

Fell, Das Durchsuchungsrecht im Seekrieg, Würzburg, 1908.

RIGHT OF SEIZURE. The right of State or municipal authorities to take possession of a vessel in territorial waters, for a breach of the revenue laws or laws of trade and navigation of a particular nation.

The utmost length to which the exercise of this right on the high seas has ever been carried, in respect to vessels of another nation, has been to justify seizing them within the territorial jurisdiction of the State against whose laws they offend, and pursuing them in case of flight, seizing them upon the high sea and bringing them in for adjudication before the tribunals of that state.

Fr: *Droit de Saisie;* Ger: *Ergreifungsrecht.*

RIGHT OF VISIT, RIGHT OF VISITATION. The right, according to international maritime law, of a belligerent vessel to stop and visit neutral merchantmen for the purpose of ascertaining whether these vessels are of the nationality they purport to be, and whether they are attempting to break blockade, are carrying contraband goods, or are rendering unneutral service to the enemy.

The right of visit may be exercised in time of war by all commissioned vessels and military aircraft of belligerents. In time of peace men-of-war of all nations have the right of visit only in case of suspicion of piracy. The region where the right may be exercised is the maritime territory of either belligerent and the open sea.

Fr: *Droit de Visite;* Ger: *Visitationsrecht.*

RIGHT OF WAY SIGNAL. A local signal used in channels or harbors, giving certain ships the right of way, and thereby suspending the usual rules of the road.

RIGHT SEMI-CIRCLE. That half of a tropical storm which lies to the right when looking along the track in the direction of movement of the storm. The other half is called left semi-circle.

Fr: *Demi cercle de droite;* Ger: *Rechten Halbkreis.*

RIGOL.

See **Wriggle.**

RIME. To enlarge a grommet or a cringle in sailcloth, forcing it open with a fid. Also called riming up.

RIMER. See **Reamer.**

RIMING STOOL. A hardwood stool with circular top supported by three legs. Holes of various diameters are bored through the top. It is used by sailmakers for enlarging cringles or grommets. These are placed over a suitable hole and a fid is driven through by means of a mallet.

RINDGALL. A local defect in structural timber produced by the growth of fresh layers over an injury sustained by the outside of the tree during growth, as a result of which the subsequent growth does not adhere to the wood previously formed.

RINGBOLT. An eyebolt with a ring worked through the eye. Ringbolts are made with lag screw ends for attachment to wood, with plain ends for riveting, or threaded ends for bolting.

Fr: *Piton à Boucle;* Ger: *Ringbolzen.*

RING NET. A net resembling a purse seine, from which it differs principally by the rounded ends starting at a distance of 4 to 12 fathoms from the extremities and by the landing bag either at the center or at one end. This bag is made of heavier twine and is the portion of the net into which the catch is concentrated preparatory to brailing. Also called purse lampara, semi-purse net.

The sardine ring net of California has a length of 100 to 250 fathoms, depth 20 to 50 fathoms; Meshing: wings 3 to 10 in., other parts ⅝ to 1¼ in. The outstanding feature of the ring net is the speed with which it can be operated. A ring net can make two or three hauls while a purse seine crew is making one.

Fry, D. H., *The Ring Net in the Fisheries of California,* Division of Fish and Game of California, Fish Bulletin no. 27, Sacramento, 1931.

RING PLATE. Eyeplate with a ring worked through the eye.

Fr: *Plaque à Boucle;* Ger: *Ringplatte.*

RING ROPE. A rope by which the anchor ring is hauled up to the cathead after the anchor has been catted.
Ger: *Taustopper.*

RINGSAIL. A studding sail formerly used with a gaff sail. Also called ringtail. It consisted of a narrow strip of canvas set out beyond the leech of the sail. Its head was stretched out on a small yard hoisted to the gaff end and its foot on a similar spar named ringtail-boom. (Obsolete.)
Fr: *Bonnette d'Artimon; Paille-en-Cul;* Ger: *Brotwinner.*

RINGSTAFF.
See **Staff.**

RING STOPPER. The rope or chain securing the upper end of the shank of an old-fashioned anchor on the billboard to a toe of the tumbler arm.
Fr: *Serre Bosse; Bosse de Bout;* Ger: *Porteurleinkette.*
See **Cat Stopper.**

RINGTAIL BOOM. A boom extending beyond the boom or main boom for spreading a ringtail.
Fr: *Bôme de Paille en Cul;* Ger: *Brotwinnerspiere.*

RINGTAIL TOPSAIL. A triangular shaped sail used on fore-and-aft-rigged vessels. It is set abaft a leg-of-mutton spanker and extends from boom to topmast head.
MacDonald, P. A., Mutton Spankers and Ringtail Topsails, The American Neptune, vol. 5, no. 3, July (1945), Salem, Mass.

RIP CURRENT. A strong surface current of short duration flowing outward from the shore. Also called rip tide. It usually appears as a visible band of agitated water and is the return movement of water piled up on the shore by incoming waves and wind.

RIPE HERRING. Trade term for herring which has all its roe and is just on the point of spawning or is actually spawning when captured.
Fr: *Hareng gai;* Ger: *Rogener; Milchener.*

RIP LINE.
See **Belly Line.**

RIPPER.
See **Jig.**

RIPPING IRON. A wood-calker's tool used for clearing a seam of pitch and oakum previous to calking afresh. Also called rasing iron, reefing iron, clearing iron.

Fr: *Pataras Taillant;* Ger: *Schoreisen.*

RIPPLE. The light fretting or ruffling on the surface of the water caused by a breeze.
Fr: *Ride;* Ger: *Kräuselung; Kabbeln; Kabbelung.*

RIPS. Agitation on the surface of the water caused by the meeting of currents or by the impinging of one current upon another moving in a different direction. Rips are more a vertical oscillation than a wave of translation.
Fr: *Clapotis;* Ger: *Stromrippling.*
See **Tide Rips.**

RIP TIDE.
See **Rip Current.**

RISE. A long and broad elevation which rises gently from the ocean bottom.
Fr: *Seuil;* Ger: *Erhöhung.*

RISE AND FALL. The up-and-down movement of the tide resulting from the attraction of the moon and the sun on the aqueous envelope of the earth as it revolves on its axis.
Fr: *Elévation et Abaissement;* Ger: *Steigen und Fallen.*

RISE AND SHINE. A call to turn out of hammocks or bunks. Also called lash and carry.

RISE OF BOTTOM.
See **Deadrise.**

RISE OF FLOOR.
See **Deadrise.**

RISER. 1. A fore-and-aft plank fastened to the inner side of an open boat framing next to the gunwale, serving as support for the thwarts. Also called rising or wearing. There is one riser on each side of the boat, fastened to each frame with a through fastening or a brass screw.
Fr: *Serre de bancs;* Ger: *Duchtenweger.*
2. One of the heavy strakes of the bottom planking adjacent to the garboard strake.
3. A fore-and-aft bearer supporting a deck in a wooden ship.

RISING FLOOR. One of floors at the ends of the hull which rises sharply above the level of the midship floors.
Fr: *Varangue Acculée;* Ger: *Eingezogenes Bauchstück.*

RISING LINE. A curved line drawn on the sheer plan to determine the height of the ends of the floor timbers throughout the ship's length. It also determines whether the shape of the bottom is full or sharp.

RISING TANK—RIVETER 654

Fr: *Lisse des Façons;* Ger: *Flursente; Kimmsente.*

RISING TANK. Double-bottom spaces in which the inner bottom is higher at center line than at sides. This arrangement has the advantage of allowing moisture from the cargo to drain into the bilge pockets on each side.

RISING TIDE. The actual rising of the water from low water to the next high water.

Fr: *Marée montante; Flux; Montant;* Ger: *Flut.*

RISING WOOD. In large wooden vessels, the topmost timber of the keel where, in order to get the required molded size, the keel is made up of two timbers. The rising wood receives the scoring of the floor timbers.

Fr: *Contre-Quille;* Ger: *Gegenkiel.*
See **Deadwood.**

RISK OF CAPTURE CLAUSE. A clause attached to marine policies in general, whether the subject matter insured is hull, freight, cargo, or otherwise, and which states that the underwriters accept all the risks excluded by the "free of capture and seizure" clause.

Fr: *Clause de Capture;* Ger: *Arrestierungsklausel.*

RISK OF CRAFT. A marine insurance term which refers to the risks incurred by goods during transportation by lighter or craft to the side of a vessel moored in a waterway or roadstead. Also called risk of boats.

Fr: *Risque d'Allège;* Ger: *Leichterrisiko.*

RIVE. In herring curing, to string fish on spits, or thin sticks of wood about 4½ feet long, thrust under one gill cover and out of the mouth. The fish are then ready for smoking.

RIVER PILOT. A pilot whose license authorizes him to operate on certain specified rivers.

Fr: *Pilote de Rivière;* Ger: *Flusslotse; Revierlotse.*

RIVER PORT. A seaport which lies on the banks of a river.

Fr: *Port Fluvial;* Ger: *Flusshafen.*

RIVET. A metal pin used for connecting the various structural parts composing a ship's hull. It consists of a cylindrical shank or body, terminated at one end by an enlarged portion or head. The other end is formed into a point when the rivet is driven.

Excluding special materials occasionally used, rivets in general are made of wrought iron or medium or high tensile steel.

Fr: *Rivet;* Ger: *Niet.*

See **Boat Rivet, Bullhead Rivet, Panhead Rivet, Raised-Head Rivet, Snaphead Rivet, Straight-Neck Rivet, Tack Rivet, Tap Rivet, Tapered-Neck Rivet.**

Wrought iron, often called malleable iron, has been used for the manufacture of rivets since the introduction of iron shipbuilding, and its malleability, among other properties it possesses, renders it very suitable for the purpose. Steel, though of a higher tensile strength, does not possess the same malleability and it is for this reason that a higher price is paid for driving such rivets. Practically all rivets used in British shipyards are made of iron, while in the United States, medium steel rivets are most frequently used. It is generally recognized that iron rivets are less liable to corrosion than steel rivets. In the normal type of merchant vessel the cost of rivets and riveting, considered as a percentage of the cost of the total iron and steel, represents about 7½ per cent of the total material and from 35 per cent to 40 per cent of the labor expended on the hull. Rivets are named from the form of the head and point. They are hammered or closed up when in a heated state so as to draw the parts to be connected more firmly together by the contraction of the shank when cooling.

American Society for Testing Materials, *Ship Rivets, Specifications,* A 131:39; Boardman, R., "Rivets and Their Significance in Shipbuilding," North East Coast Institution of Engineers and Shipbuilders (Newcastle upon Tyne), *Transactions,* vol. 48 (1927-28).

RIVET BUSTER (U. S.). A pneumatic tool, in principle similar to the chipping hammer, used for cutting off the heads of rivets during repair work, or for replacement of poorly driven rivets. By substituting the desired tool, it can be used as a chisel or a backing-out punch. A modern rivet buster is driven by compressed air at about 100 lb. per sq. in. pressure, weighs 35 lb., has an 11-in. stroke, and can strike 700 blows per minute.

RIVETER. 1. A man employed in hammering or closing up rivets, by hand or with a machine. Also called rivet driver.

Fr: *Frappeur; Riveur;* Ger: *Nietenkopfschläger; Nieter.*

2. A machine used for closing up or forming the points of rivets by pressure only.

Also called riveting machine.
> Fr: *Presse à River;* Ger: *Nietungspresse.*

See **Hydraulic Riveter.**

RIVET HEAD. The protruding part of a rivet, formed during its manufacture, and providing the necessary holding power on one side of the joint.
> Fr: *Tête de Rivet;* Ger: *Nietkopf; Setzkopf.*

RIVET HOLDER. The laborer on a rivet squad who holds up the head of a rivet with a heavy hammer or dolly bar after it has been inserted in the hole and while the point is being clinched. Also called holder-up, backer-up, holder-on, dollyman.
> Fr: *Appuyeur; Teneur de Tas;* Ger: *Nietenbehälter; Vorhälter.*

RIVET HOLE. Hole drilled or punched through a plate or shape, for rivet connection.
> Fr: *Trou de Rivet;* Ger: *Nietloch.*

RIVETING. The art of fastening two pieces of material together with rivets. The turning over or clinching of the points of rivets, which are hammered sharply while red hot, the hammer beating over the point on all sides.
> Fr: *Rivetage;* Ger: *Nietverbindung; Vernietung; Vernieten.*

> See **Butt Riveting, Chain Riveting, Hand Riveting, Hydraulic Riveting, Lap Riveting, Machine Riveting, Oiltight Riveting, Pin Riveting, Pneumatic Riveting, Watertight Riveting, Zigzag Riveting.**

Rossell, H. E., *Riveting and Arc Welding,* New York, 1934.

RIVETING RAM.
See **Hydraulic Riveter.**

RIVET PASSER. Shipyard worker to whom the rivet heater hands the rivets, and who in turn passes them along to the holder-on. Sometimes called passer.
> Fr: *Passeur de rivets;* Ger: *Nietenträger.*

RIVET POINT. The end of a rivet upset by the riveting hammer when closing up. Also called rivet tail.
> Fr: *Rivure;* Ger: *Schliesskopf.*

Countersunk points are used for shell and deck plating where flush surfaces are required, and where the point may require calking. Snap points (similar in shape to buttonheads) are used in structural work generally where flush surfaces are not required, and especially in sheer strakes of shell plating, in order to avoid loss of material by countersinking. They are also used with hydraulic riveting machines. Oval or Liverpool points are occasionally used with light plating where watertightness under pressure is not required. Hammer points are used where specially required.

RIVET SHANK. The cylindrical body of a rivet between head and point.
> Fr: *Fût de Rivet;* Ger: *Nietschaft.*

RIVET SNAP. A set used in forming rivet points. Its working face is in the form of a hemispherical recess.
> Fr: *Bouterolle;* Ger: *Setzeisen; Döpper.*

RIVET SQUAD. A squad employed in a shipyard for riveting the different parts of a ship under construction. Also called riveter's squad. It usually consists of 3 men and 1 or 2 boys, one of the latter heats the rivets, the other conveys them and inserts them into the hole. Two of the men clinch the point while the third holds up the head. When pneumatic riveting hammers are used only one man is employed for clinching the point.
> Fr: *Equipe de Riveurs.*

See **Frame Squad, Plater's Squad.**

RIVET TOOL. A metal calking tool used for calking heads and points of countersunk rivets.

RIVET WELD.
See **Plug Weld.**

RO, ROH. Malay double-outrigger canoe from Wetar, Lesser Sunda Islands, with wash strake at stern only, tall curved stem and stern pieces having painted ornamentation, which extends under the gunwale. Sometimes called *bero.*

One of the distinctive features of the Wetar Island craft is the fitting of two small platforms enclosed by coamings, projecting outboard on each side. There are several varieties of this type; one is called *roh talor,* another *roh dugen.* They are used for fishing and traveling. The rig consists of a single tripod mast with quadrilateral sail.

ROACH. The concave or convex curve given to any side of a sail. Roach refers correctly to a concave curve only, but it is in general use to describe a convex curve as well. The words round or sweep to denote a convex roach.

In square sails the roach forms an arc of a circle passing through the middle, at the foot and clews, for clearing the stays which reach between the masts. At the foot of courses, however, the roach is not circular. Three-fifths of its length at the middle are made parallel to the head. In gaff sails the foot, luff, and head are roached, the cloths being cut with a curve according to the fullness or draught desired. Jibs are roached along the stay by broad-seaming and gathering the cloths along the luff rope so that they remain comparatively slack, and also along the foot.

Fr: *Echancrure;* Ger: *Gillung; Wölbung; Rundung.*

ROAD, ROADSTEAD. An area of water where ships can ride safely at anchor. More or less open anchorage affording less protection than a harbor. An open anchorage generally protected by shoals.

Fr: *Rade;* Ger: *Reede.*

ROARING FORTIES. Strong westerly winds encountered between 40 and 50 degrees South latitude. Similar winds in the Northern hemisphere are termed Brave West Winds in nautical phraseology.

ROBAND. Short bits of Manila, spun yarn, or plaited line used for fastening the luff of a fore-and-aft sail to the mast loops or stay-hanks, and the head of a square sail to the jackstay. Also used for securing the head of a gaff sail to the gaff when the latter is fitted with a jackstay. Sometimes called robbin, roving.

Fr: *Raban de Têtière; Raban d'Envergure; Hanet d'Envergure;* Ger: *Anschlagbindsel.*

ROBAND HITCH. A binding knot which consists of several turns finished off with a half hitch. Used for fastening the robands of a sail to the jackstay.

Fr: *Amarrage d'Envergure;* Ger: *Rahbandselstek.*

ROCKERED KEEL. A keel with slight fore-and-aft curvature, most frequently used in small hulls 10 to 24 ft. long. These keels are bent or sawed from solid timbers. Also called rocker keel.

Fr: *Quille cambrée;* Ger: *Gekrümmter Kiel.*

ROCKET APPARATUS. A lifesaving apparatus from which a line-carrying rocket is fired. It consists of an adjustable metal tripod with suitable fittings to receive and support the rocket before it is fired.

Fr: *Appareil lance-Fusée; Appareil porte Amarre;* Ger: *Raketenapparat.*

ROCKET LINE. A line used in connection with a lifesaving rocket apparatus. It is made of three-strand Italian hemp (barked or tanned) 1 in. in circumference and about 250 fathoms in length. Also called whip line.

Fr: *Ligne porte Amarre;* Ger: *Raketenleine.*

ROCKET SOCKET. A gunmetal socket with tampion, installed in the handrail on each side of the flying bridge, for firing distress signals.

ROCKING SHACKLE. A large shackle placed on the top of a trunk mooring buoy, to which the ship's cable is fastened.

Fr: *Manille de corps mort;* Ger: *Muring Schakel.*

ROD BOLT. A rod threaded at both ends and driven by screwing a nut on the end to be used as a head. The point is secured with a nut and washer after being driven. The rod bolt is used in wooden hulls where bolts of required lengths cannot be obtained from standard sizes.

RODE. The line or rope to which a small boat rides when anchored.

ROD FENDER. A bundle of canes or rods hanging at the side of a pier or quay to prevent damage by vessels lying alongside. Also called faggot fender, cane fender. Frequently fabricated of Bejuca, a Filipino cane.

Fr: *Défense en Fascines;* Ger: *Rutenfender; Buschfender.*

ROD RIGGING. Standing rigging in which steel rods or bars are substituted for wire rope in shrouds and stays. Also called bar rigging.

Ger: *Stangentakelung.*

This type of rigging has recently been adopted for large and small racing yachts, using in some cases stainless steel bars of streamline section to reduce wind resistance. It is also used on some trading vessels, where round steel rods are employed.

ROGUE'S YARN. A fine jute yarn run through the middle of one strand in a rope for identification. Also called identification thread. It is twisted the contrary way or is different in color or material from the other yarns. Usually it is red or green.

Fr: *Fil de Marque.*

ROKO. Polynesian plank-built fishing canoe with single outrigger from Guadalcanal Island, southeastern Solomon Islands. The stern peak rises from the top strake. At the bow there is a quadrangular splash board in front of the washboards. The boats carry a crew of 2 to 6.

See **Bena.**

ROKO-DA. A large dugout canoe without outrigger from South and Little Andaman

Islands. These craft, which are of very clumsy construction, are mere rounded trunks hollowed out. The largest can carry as many as thirty people.

ROLLER. A long, heavy, swelling wave moving with a steady sweep, breaking or nearly breaking at the top.

Ger: *Roller*.

See **Blind Rollers, Dory Roller, Line Roller, Seine Roller.**

ROLLER CHOCK. 1. Fairlead with horizontal roller fitted at side of stem head in row boat.

Fr: *Davier*; Ger: *Leitrolle*.

2. A warping chock fitted with one or more vertical rollers in order to minimize friction of mooring lines. Also called roller fairlead.

Fr: *Chaumard à Rouleau*; Ger: *Verholklampe mit Rolle*.

ROLLER FENDER. A fender which consists of a number of wooden battens about 3 inches by 3 inches and 2 ft. 8 inches long, rove Jacob's ladder fashion on three ½ inch wire ropes, the battens being some 3 inches to 6 inches apart. The whole is rolled round a 3 foot spar of 6 inches diameter, to the ends of which wire lanyards are shackled.

ROLLER GEAR. In general, various furling and reefing appliances used in connection with fore-and-aft sails of small vessels, such as coasters, pilot boats, and sailing yachts. Also called roller reefing gear.

With gaff sails, roller gear is used only for reefing. The boom is made to revolve by means of worm and wheel, or ratchet apparatus fastened to the mast at the end of the boom. When fitted to headsails it consists in some systems of a wooden roller revolving on a wire stay set on the stemhead or end of a bowsprit. A pull on the line wrapped around the drum at the tack rolls the sail up. Another method consists of rolling the sail which sets flying on a wire luff rope. The sail is then rolled along its own luff rope by merely pulling on a line which is wound around a reel placed just below the tack. By hauling on the sheet the sail is unfurled.

ROLLER REEF. A reefing system in which the surface of the sail is reduced by rolling it around a spar instead of securing it with reef points. Frequently used in small fore-and-aft rigged pleasure boats.

Fr: *Ris à Rouleau*; Ger: *Drehreff*.

See **Roller Gear.**

ROLLER RULE. A brass rule fitted with a roller on each end, so that when moved, it remains always parallel to its initial position. Used in plotting, as a substitute for parallel rules.

See **Parallel Rules.**

ROLLER SHEAVE. Sheave of a block fitted at its center with metal bushing and rollers or ball bearings which revolve around the pin. The friction is absorbed by the rollers and is very much less than in plain sheaves. Roller sheaves are generally used for halyards and purchases where the rope must render quickly and easily. Also called patent sheave.

Fr: *Réa à Rouleaux*; *Réa à Billes*; Ger: *Patentscheibe*; *Blockrollenbüchse*.

ROLLING. The transverse oscillating rotation of a vessel about a longitudinal axis, which results when it meets waves with crests approximately parallel to the length of the ship. When a vessel rolls, it disturbs a much larger cross section of water than when it is steady. This increases its resistance to propulsion, and requires a corresponding increase in the propulsive power necessary for a given speed.

Fr: *Roulis*; Ger: *Schlingern*.

Baker, G. S., "Rolling of Ships under Way," North East Coast Institution of Engineers and Shipbuilders (Newcastle upon Tyne), *Transactions*, vol. 56 (1939).

ROLLING CAISSON. A caisson in which the weight is always kept greater than the displacement and which moves on a track and rollers.

Fr: *Porte Roulante*; Ger: *Rollendes Torschiff*.

See **Caisson.**

ROLLING CHOCK. 1. A support for engines and boilers. Sometimes improperly used to denote bilge keels.

See **Bilge Keels.**

2. A piece of wood fastened to the middle of an upper yard, half encircling it and secured by an iron or rope parrel, to steady the yard. Also called rolling cleat, parrel cleat.

Fr: *Matagot*; Ger: *Rahklampe*.

ROLLING HITCH. A knot which consists of two round turns and one half-hitch used for fastening a line to a spar or when hanging off a rope with a stopper where a knot that will not slip is needed. Also called magnus hitch.

Rolling Hitch

Fr: *Noeud de Fouet;* Ger: *Rollstek; Kneifstek.*

ROLLING SPAR. See **Boat Spar.**

ROLLING SWELL. The motion of a sea where the waves are very far apart, forming long deep troughs between them.

Ger: *Rollende Dünung.*

ROLLING TACKLE. A tackle set up between the yardarm and the mast to steady a yard in heavy weather and relieve the strain on the crane, slings, or parrel.

Fr: *Palan de Roulis;* Ger: *Rolltakel.*

ROLL SET.
See **Roll Template.**

ROLL TEMPLATE. In shipbuilding, a series of small templates with curved surface fitted to a shell plate at the frame lines, and used by the men at the plate-rolls to give the plate the desired curvature. Also called roll set.

ROOM AND SPACE. The distance from the molding edge of a frame timber to the molding edge of the next one. It is usually equal to the breadth of the two timbers plus two to four inches. Also called timber and space.

Fr: *Maille;* Ger: *Inholz und Fach.*

ROOT. The short leg of a wood knee.

ROOVE. A diamond-shaped slightly convex washer or ring, over which the end of a nail is clinched. Also called bur.

Fr: *Rouelle; Jouette;* Ger: *Klinkscheibe.*

ROOVE CLINKER NAIL. A copper nail clenched by hammering the point after placing it over a little diamond or conical-shaped piece of metal called "roove" or "bur." Used for clinker planking of boats. Also called riveted-nail.

Fr: *Clou Rivé Sur Jouette;* Ger: *Gatnagel.*

ROOVING. Riveting the point of a nail over a small copper washer called a roove. This is considered good practice in boat building when using copper nails, to prevent them from drawing, owing to the softness of the metal.

ROPE (to). To sew bolt-rope to the edges of a sail or awning. It is then known as roping.

Fr: *Ralinguer;* Ger: *Anlieken.*

ROPE. A general term for cordage over one inch in circumference. If smaller it is known as cord, twine, line or string, if finer still as thread or double yarn. Ropes have special names according to the number and arrangement of strands and the way these are laid. A rope is usually composed of three strands, although four-stranded ropes are also found on board ship. Technically speaking, a rope is a construction of metallic wires or twisted hemp, Manila, cotton, flax, or jute fibers, so intertwined as to form a thick cord capable of sustaining relatively severe strains. The size of ropes is designated by the circumference or the diameter. The length is given in fathoms. The weight of fiber ropes depends on the quantity of softening oil used, and the degree of twist in every stage of their manufacture; it is therefore difficult to obtain accurate weights for any particular size.

Fr: *Cordage; Filin;* Ger: *Tau; Seil; Reep.*

Carter, H. R., *Modern Flax, Hemp and Jute Spinning and Twisting,* London, 1925; Stopford, P. J., *Cordage and Cable,* Glasgow, 1925; Woodhouse, T., *Cordage and Cordage Hemp Fibers,* New York, 1919.

ROPE CLAMP. A device used for holding together two parts of a bight of wire rope in lieu of an eye splice. It consists of two flat ground pieces of metal secured by bolts passing through the centers of both sections.

Rope Clip

ROPE CLIP. A mechanical means of securing a wire rope round a thimble as an alternative to splicing. It consists essentially of a base piece, or bridge, channeled and grooved to receive the wire, and a "U" bolt passing through the bridge piece and secured by two nuts. Not less than three clips should be used to secure any wire rope. The bridge piece should always be fitted on the working part and the "U" bolt on the tail or dead end of the rope.

ROPE FENDER. A fender made of short pieces of old rope plaited together, the poorer sections being used as filling and the covering made by lacing a strand over the filling.

Fr: *Défense en Cordage;* Ger: *Taufender; Stosstau.*

ROPE LADDER. A generic term for different kinds of flexible ladders in which the rungs are held on each side by one or two ropes. Rope ladders as used on board ship are of three types: the pilot ladder, the round-rung ladder, and the Jacob's ladder. They are used for convenience when boarding from small boats or embarking in them from the deck edge; also in the rigging of large sailing ships.

Fr: *Echelle de Corde;* Ger: *Sturmleiter; Fallreepsleiter.*

ROPEMAKER'S EYE. An eye formed in the end of a cable in laying it up. Two of the strands are two legs of a rope, and when laid up they form an eye; the third strand is then also formed into an eye. A ropemaker's eye is often made in the end of a jib stay when fitted with a slip at the jibboom end. It has a thimble to receive the slip.

Fr: *Oeil d'Étalingure.*

ROPE SHACKLE. Shackle fitted with an oval pin and forelock.

ROPE SLING. A length of rope, usually between 12 and 24 ft. long, with the ends spliced together. Generally used for handling boxes, barrels, bales, bags, and so on.

Fr: *Elingue en Filin;* Ger: *Taustropp.*

Open Socket   Closed Socket
Rope Socket

ROPE SOCKET. A wire rope fitting used for fastening the ends of two ropes instead of splicing them. Also called patent eye. Sockets are of two types, the open and the closed socket. The open socket is fitted with a pin or bolt with cotter. The spread end of each rope is soldered in the socket with pure metallic zinc.

Ger: *Seilhülsen; Seilgehäuse.*

See **Poured Socket.**

Sockets for wire ropes for general engineering purposes, Specification B.S. 463 (revised), British Standards Institution, London (1943).

ROPE YARN. A yarn or thread made up of a number of fibers loosely twisted together. Several rope yarns twisted together form a strand.

Fr: *Fil de Caret;* Ger: *Kabelgarn.*

ROPE YARN KNOT. A knot used for knotting rope yarns. Also called marline knot.

Fr: *Noeud de Fil de Caret;* Ger: *Kabelgarnknoten.*

ROPING. See **Bolt Rope.**

ROPING TWINE. Twine used for sewing sail cloths to bolt ropes. It is generally 9-, 10-, or 11-ply.

Fr: *Fil à Ralinguer;* Ger: *Liekgarn.*

ROREHE. East Indian fishing craft similar to the *orembai* type, found in the Moluccas and North Celebes Islands. It is manned by a crew of 9 to 12. Length 26 ft. Breadth 6.5 ft. (Typical.) Also called *jonaai.*

ROSE.

See **Strum Plate.**

ROSE BOX. A square or round box, 9 in. x 12 in., made of galvanized iron, perforated with holes and fitted at ends of bilge suctions in order to prevent these pipes from becoming obstructed with solid matter. Also called strum box, strainer box.

Fr: *Crépine;* Ger: *Saugekorb.*

ROSE LASHING. A lashing in which the parts are passed alternately over and under, the end being expended around the crossing. Also called rose seizing.

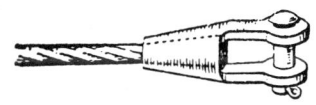

Fr: *Aiguilletage en Portugaise;* Ger: *Rosenzurrung.*

ROSLAGSSKUTA. A small sloop-rigged coaster from the east coast of the province of Upland, Sweden. The foresail tacks down to the stem head.

ROSLYN RIG. A two-mast rig used by small boats. It consists of a jib, sliding-gunter mainsail, and leg-of-mutton mizzen. The mainsail clew is cut short and bent to a small vertical club. Mainsail and mizzen are extended by horizontal sprits.

ROSLYN YAWL. A large sharpie which carries two headsails and a jigger mast. It is supposed to have originated from Roslyn, Long Island.

ROSSEL CURRENT. The continuation of the South Pacific equatorial current after its division near the Fiji Islands. It flows westward among the islands and at length passes through the Torres Strait. The southern branch of the equatorial current sets to the southwestward and flows along the coast of Australia; hence it is known as the Australia current.

ROTARY CURRENT. An offshore tidal current which changes direction continually. No period of slack water occurs, the current running with a fairly constant velocity. Rotary currents may be grouped under three types, i.e., semi-daily, daily and mixed types.

ROTATING DIRECTION FINDER. A radio direction finder in which the loop antenna is rotated for taking bearings.
   Fr: *Radio Goniomètre;* Ger: *Rotierende Funkpeiler.*

ROTATING RADIO BEACON. A wireless station which emits a beam of waves which sweeps around the horizon. Also called revolving radio beacon. The beam thus emitted rotates at a constant velocity and a direction-finding receiver is not needed; the bearing of the station can be calculated by using a stop watch.
   Fr: *Radiophare à cadre Tournant;* Ger: *Rotierende Funkbake.*

ROTATOR. A brass fitting towed at the end of a log line. It consists of a central shank with helical fins running lengthwise around it. When dragged through the water the fins cause it to rotate and the number of revolutions is recorded by the indicator fastened to the taffrail.
   Fr: *Hélice de Loch;* Ger: *Logschraube; Flügelwelle.*

ROTTEN CLAUSE. A marine insurance clause which provides that if the vessel is found unseaworthy on a regular survey by reason of being rotten or unsound the underwriters are released of all obligations.

ROTTEN ICE. Ice floes which have become honeycombed in the course of melting.
   Fr: *Glace pourrie.*

ROTTEN STOPS. Light pieces of basting thread, cheap string, or twine tied around a sail to hold it together in a bundle while it is being sent aloft "in stops."
   Fr: *Fils; Genope.*

ROUGH MAST. A piece of timber suitable for spar- or mast-making.
   Fr: *Bois de Mâture;* Ger: *Unbehauener Mast.*

ROUGH NET (G. B.). A gill net used by sailing drifters in Scotland. Length 21 yd. Depth about 10 yd. Meshing 30 rows to the yard.

ROUGH SEA. A disturbed sea. Height of waves 5 to 9 ft. Wave lengths 7 to 14 ft. Douglas Scale No. 4.
   Fr: *Mer Houleuse;* Ger: *Grobe See.*

ROUGH SIDE (U. S.). That side of a steel bulkhead on which the stiffeners are fitted. In Great Britain called stiffening side.
   Ger: *Versteifungsseite.*
   See **Calking Side.**

ROUGH SPAR. A spar in the rough. Cut timber before being worked into masts, and so on. Also called rough tree.
   Fr: *Espar Brut;* Ger: *Unbehauenes Rundholz.*

ROUGH TIMBER. The timber to its full size, as felled with lop, top, and bark off. Also called rough log.
   Fr: *Bois en Grume;* Ger: *Unbehauenes Holz.*

ROUGH TOOL. A tool used for finishing flush calking, also for calking countersunk rivets where the rivet tool cannot be used. The cutting edge is straight with carding face.

ROUGH-TREE. One of the stanchions supporting a rough-tree rail. (Obsolete.)
   Fr: *Batayoles;* Ger: *Schanzkleidstützen.*

ROUGH-TREE RAIL. The rail at the top of the bulwarks and below the topgallant bulwarks in wooden vessels. The term originated from the former practice in merchant vessels of carrying their rough, or spare spars in crutches along the waist. (Obsolete.)
   Fr: *Lisse de batayole.*

ROUND. 1. Generic term for round bars of steel or nonferrous metal up to 7 in. in diameter.
   Fr: *Rond; fer Rond;* Ger: *Rundeisen.*
   2. The outward curve given to the leech or foot of a sail, as opposed to the roach.
   Fr: *Rond;* Ger: *Gillung; Rundung.*
   3. The first row of half meshes running from right to left when commencing a piece of netting.
   Fr: *Pigeon.*

ROUND BAR DAVIT. The most common type of davit generally used on cargo vessels. It consists of a vertical pillar of round section with the upper portion bent in a fair curve and having sufficient outreach so that the boat should clear the ship's side when the vessel heels at an angle of 15°. This type of davit is usually stepped in a socket attached to the ship's side or on the first deck below the one where the boats are stowed, near the side. Also called rotary davit.
   Fr: *Bossoir Pivotant;* Ger: *Drehdavit.*

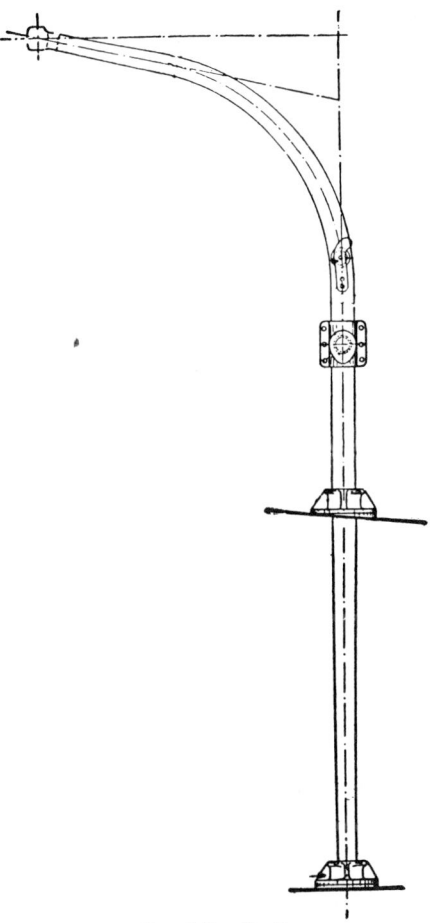

Round Bar Davit

ROUND CHARTER. The chartering of a vessel for a round trip or voyage outward and homeward.

Fr: *Affrètement aller retour;* Ger: *Rundreise Befrachtung; Rundreise Vercharterung.*

ROUNDHOUSE. 1. Name formerly given to a square cabin built on the afterpart of the quarter-deck. The poop deck formed its roof. (Obsolete.)

2. A privy or lavatory on the upper deck near the bow.

3. A deckhouse in the afterpart of a sailing ship for the accommodation of petty officers and apprentices.

ROUNDING. Old rope or strands served around a rope to prevent its chafing. Used by fishermen for the ground rope of dragnets.

Fr: *Garni;* Ger: *Wuhling.*

ROUND LINE, ROUNDLINE. Three right-handed yarns used for heavy service, such as eyes of the lower rigging, heavy seizings, and so on.

Fr: *Quarantenier;* Ger: *Stickleine.*

Roundline is made of tarred hemp and in laying the yarns a top is used to give closeness and regularity to the lay. It is somewhat larger than houseline.

ROUND OF BEAM.

See **Camber, Round Up.**

ROUND-RUNG LADDER. A light rope ladder used in the rigging. The rungs are about one inch in diameter and 15 in. long with a groove cut in each end. Each rung is passed with the aid of a fid, between the strands of the side ropes. A seizing is put on the rope above and below each rung.

ROUND SEAM. A seam formed by sewing the edges of canvas together without lapping. It is used only with the lightest kinds of canvas. About 112 stitches are worked to the yard.

Fr: *Couture à Point debout;* Ger: *Kappnaht; Runde Naht.*

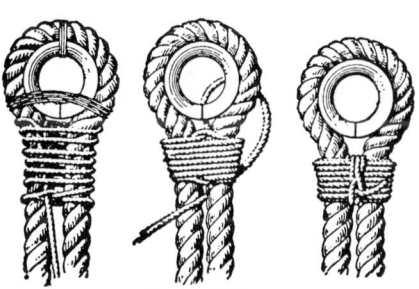

Round Seizing

ROUND SEIZING. A seizing used to hold two ropes together or two parts of the same rope together to form an eye. It is used only when the stress on both parts of the rope are equal, as, for example, in block straps, rigging eyes, and so on. It has riding turns, or riders over the first layer of turns.

Fr: *Amarrage plat avec Bridure;* Ger: *Augbindsel.*

ROUND SENNIT. Sennit formed by plaiting an even number of strands in two's around a small core or heart.

Fr: *Tresse Ronde;* Ger: *Runde Platting.*

ROUND THIMBLE. A round thimble

used for sail earings, tackle block straps, and so on. Heavy, wide scored galvanized sail thimbles are made in diameters ranging from 1 in. to 6 in. Welded iron thimbles for small sails are from ¾ in. to 2¼ in. in diameter. Solid brass and gunmetal thimbles are made in diameters from ½ in. to 2 in.

Fr: *Cosse Ronde;* Ger: *Runde Kauschen.*

ROUND (to). 1. To get past or get round.

Fr: *Doubler;* Ger: *Umsegeln.*

2. To come to the wind. To haul by the wind when sailing large.

Fr: *Venir au Lof;* Ger: *Beidrehen.*

ROUND TURN. To wind a rope once around a bitt, spar, or any other object.

Fr: *Tour Mort; Tour plein;* Ger: *Rundtorn.*

ROUND TURN IN THE HAWSE. A foul hawse after a ship with two anchors out has swung through 720 degrees, or twice around.

Fr: *Double Tour dans les Chaînes;* Ger: *Rundtorn in den Ketten.*

ROUND UP. To haul up, as the slack of a rope through its leading block. To haul through the parts of a purchase so as to bring the two blocks together. Also called round in.

Fr: *Embraquer;* Ger: *Einholen.*

ROUND WIND. A wind that follows the sun, occasionally called a sun wind. A well-known phenomenon in fine summer weather around the British Isles.

ROUSE. To haul heavily or with great force.

Fr: *Souquer;* Ger: *Steifholen.*

ROUSE OUT. To turn out or call up on deck from their berths the crew, the watch, or some of the hands.

ROVE. The long end of a rope sling which passes through the bite and is put on the cargo hook when the draft is lifted.

See **Long Rove.**

ROVE IRON.

See **Rove Punch.**

ROVE PUNCH. A hollow pointed punch used by boatbuilders for hardening home against the planking points of nails over which roves have been previously placed. Also called roving iron, boss punch, rove iron. One man holds the head of the nail with a heavy flat-headed hammer while the rove is driven home and the nail clenched from inside by another hand.

See **Backing-out Punch, Driving Punch, Nail Punch.**

ROVERS. A term used in marine insurance policies, the meaning of which is closely akin to that of piracy.

ROVING.

See **Roband.**

ROW. To impel a boat along the surface of the water by means of oars. To propel a boat with one man at each oar. Also called pull.

Fr: *Nager;* Ger: *Rudern.*

ROWBOAT. An open, double-ended or transom-sterned boat with flat, round or V-bottom and depending principally on oars for propulsion. Also called rowing boat, pulling boat.

Fr: *Canot;* Ger: *Ruderboot.*

ROW DRY. An order given to the oarsmen to row in such a manner as not to splash water.

ROWLOCK. A generic name for various arrangements or contrivances serving as a fulcrum for an oar in rowing. Also called oarlock. It may consist of a notch in the washboard or a pair of pins, or a metal fork or stirrup pivoted in the gunwale or on an outrigger supporting the oar, or of a single pin passing through a hole in the oar or having the oar attached to it by a grommet.

Fr: *Dame de Nage; Tolet;* Ger: *Rundsel; Dolle; Rojepforte.*

See **Becket Rowlock.**

ROWLOCK BOLSTER.

See **Poppet.**

ROWLOCK CHEEK.

See **Rowlock Chock.**

ROWLOCK CHOCK. A strengthening piece made of hard wood, fitted in way of a rowlock. Also called rowlock cheek, swell piece.

Fr: *Joue de Tolet;* Ger: *Rojegabel Backe.*

ROWLOCK COVER.

See **Poppet.**

ROWLOCK PLATE. A small countersunk plate fixed with screws in the rowlock cover, and pierced with a hole for the shank of the crutch.

Fr: *Bague de Tolet;* Ger: *Rudergabel Platte.*

ROWSER CHOCK.

See **Closed Chock.**

ROYAL. A small square sail, usually the uppermost on modern vessels, carried next above a topgallant sail on the royal mast and used only in light winds. It is taken in with clew lines and has no buntlines or leech lines, owing to its small size. Royals are carried only in light breezes because their masts are poorly supported and also because their position is such that they act with a long leverage and have a tendency to bury the ship and retard her progress.

Fr: *Cacatois*; Ger: *Royal*; *Reuel*.

ROYAL FISH. A term applied in Great Britain to whale, sturgeon, and porpoise, which, whether cast upon the shore or caught within the realm, are the property of the Crown and not of the finder.

ROYAL POLE. That part of a royal mast which extends from the eyes of the royal rigging to the shoulder of the truck, provided there is no skysail yard.

Fr: *Flèche de Cacatois*; Ger: *Royalstange*; *Royaltopp*.

RUA-CHALOM. A shallow-draft sailing boat from the Gulf of Siam, with straight raking stem and sternpost, good beam, decked fore and aft. The smaller boats of this type are used in the fisheries, the larger ones for trading on the coast. Two quarter rudders are fitted for steering; the weather rudder is the only one used, the lee rudder being always cocked up at the end above the stern. The rig consists of one mast with a large square-headed lug sail. Four sweeps are used in calm weather. The *rua-chalom* is found as far south as Bandon.

RUA-PET. Deep-hulled sailing boat of the Gulf of Siam. A light non-watertight decking is built across the boat from the stern to the mainmast. The remarkable buoyancy and seaworthiness makes this craft fit for navigating rough waters. The high bows are spoon-shaped with a broad flare, and the stern is sharp pointed. The *rua-pet* has a rockered bottom with greatest draft abaft amidships when under normal trim.

The rig consists of two masts with standing lugsails made of rectangular pieces of yellow palm matting. A boom is laced along the foot of each sail. The mainmast is stepped a little forward of amidships and has a pronounced rake aft. The foremast is very small compared with the other mast and placed right in the eyes of the boat. These boats vary in size from about 20 to 50 ft. in length. The mainsail has 3 to 5 times the area of the foresail. Length 36 ft. Breadth 11 ft. Depth 6 ft. (Typical.)

RUA-PLA. A small four-oared fishing boat of the *rua-chalom* type used in the fisheries on the east coast of the Gulf of Siam.

RUA-TA. A two-masted lug-rigged craft found in the eastern waters of the Gulf of Siam and trading along the coasts of Cambodia and Cochin China. The largest run up to 60 ft. in length and are named after the huge oculi painted on the bows.

RUA-YAYAP. Name given on the east coast of the Gulf of Siam to the Malay *penjajap*.

RUBBER. 1. Half-round or pear-shaped piece of hardwood fitted outside the gunwale on the sides of a wooden open boat, and secured to alternate frames with rooveclenched nails. It forms a protection for the gunwale and acts as a longitudinal stiffener.

Fr: *Liston*; Ger: *Scheuerleiste*; *Wallschiene*.

2. An implement used by sailmakers to flatten or rub the seams of a sail.

Fr: *Frottoir*.

3. See **Molding**.

4. A stout piece of old net cut into strips 2 or 4 ft. long, laced underneath the cod end of a trawl net to avoid abrasion when pressed by the weight of fish against the sea bottom. Also called false belly, rubbing piece.

Fr: *Peau de Bouc Tablier*.

RUBBING STRIP. 1. An external stiffener extending longitudinally on the sides of a vessel a short distance above the water line to protect it against damage from the bending and battering effects of quay-walls, piles, etc., or when going alongside other vessels. Also called rubbing piece, fender, rubbing strake. Fenders usually extend about two-thirds of the vessel's length amidships and are formed either of rectangular pieces of timber firmly secured to the side plating, or of heavy half-round or thick, flat iron bars. They are fitted to small vessels such as coasters, cross-channel vessels, and tugboats, which are frequently in and out of harbor.

Fr: *Ceinture*; Ger: *Reibholz*; *Abweiser*.

2. A strip of heavy plating riveted under a keel plate to afford protection in docking or grounding.

3. A protecting piece of hardwood which runs from stem to stern on each side of a small boat.

Fr: *Liston*; Ger: *Wallschiene*.

RUBBLE. Loose, angular and water-worn stones along a beach.

Fr: *Gravier*; Ger: *Rollstein*.

RUDDER. A device used for steering and maneuvering a vessel. The most common type consists of a flat plane surface of wood or steel hinged at the forward end to the

RUDDER ANGLE INDICATOR—RUDDER BRAKE

stern- or rudderpost and rounded at the after end to make a fair ending to the lines of the vessel.

Fr: *Gouvernail;* Ger: *Ruder.*

See **Balanced Rudder, Bow Rudder, Center-Plate Rudder, Drop Rudder, Full Rudder, Hawser Rudder, Jury Rudder, Meeting Rudder, Rudder Blade, Semibalanced Rudder.**

When made of metal it may either be built of plates, angles, or forgings, or it may be a casting. When the rudder lies in a fore-and-aft position the water flowing past it causes equal pressure on both sides. When turned so that one side is more exposed than the other to the stream, an unbalanced force is produced, which pushes the stern around, thus causing the vessel to swerve from her original course.

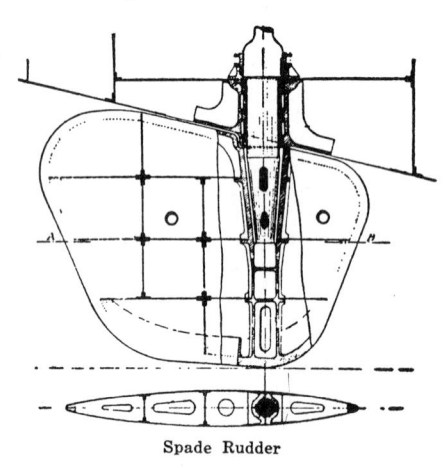

Spade Rudder

RUDDER ANGLE INDICATOR. An electrical or mechanical appliance to indicate at a steering station the angle the rudder makes with the keel line of the ship. Also called rudder telltale.

Fr: *Répétiteur d'Angle de Barre;* Ger: *Ruderzeiger.*

RUDDER AREA. The area of the immersed surface of the rudder blade at designed draft. It is usually expressed as a proportion of the area of lateral plane of the vessel.

Fr: *Aire du Safran;* Ger: *Ruderfläche.*

Average values of rudder areas as fractions of lateral plane area:

Express liners 1/85
Passenger liners ....1/50 to 1/70
Cargo vessels 1/50
Coasters and sailing vessels.1/40 to 1/50
Tugs ....1/30 to 1/40

RUDDER ARM. One of the forgings which project radially from the rudderstock to which the rudder plate is fastened. The arms are shrunk on the stock and fixed against rotation by a key. Also called rudder stay, rudder band.

Fr: *Bras de Gouvernail;* Ger: *Ruderarm.*

RUDDER BAND.

See **Rudder Arm.**

RUDDER BEARING. A fitting made in two parts, bolted to the rudderhead and fastened by means of a wide flange at the top of the rudder trunk. The upper portion is usually fitted with a flat ring, lubricated with oil, on which the rudder carrier turns.

Fr: *Presse Étoupe de Mèche;* Ger: *Ruderschaft Stopfbüchse.*

RUDDER BLADE. The main flat portion of the rudder which provides the necessary surface for the impinging action and side pressure of the water. It is attached to a vertical shaft, the rudderstock, by which it is actuated. Also called rudder body.

Fr: *Safran;* Ger: *Ruderblatt.*

The area of the rudder blade is proportional to the longitudinal immersed plane area of the vessel. This ratio varies according to the type of vessel and the steering qualities required. Narrow deep rudder blades develop more pressure and require a smaller force to handle than do wide shallow ones.

RUDDER BRACES. A term applied to rudder pintles and gudgeons when spoken of collectively. Also called rudder hangings, rudder irons.

Fr: *Ferrures de Gouvernail;* Ger: *Ruderschmiege.*

RUDDER BRACKET. One of the stops fitted on deck for the same purpose as the rudder stops, making contact at the proper angle with the tiller or quadrant. They are arranged so as to check the rudder before the rudderstops, if there are any, come into play. Also called rudder deck-stop, rudder chock.

Fr: *Butoir de Gouvernail;* Ger: *Ruderklick.*

RUDDER BRAKE. A kind of compressor or locking device fitted on the rudderhead to keep the rudder steady in case of damage or when changing from one gear (power) to the other (hand). The American Bureau rules require a rudder brake in all vessels over 350 ft. long. Lloyds rules requesting that all vessels 250 ft. long or over shall have power-operated steering gear also makes the provision of a rudder brake compulsory for ships above 250 ft. in length.

Fr: *Frein de Gouvernail;* Ger: *Ruderbremse.*

RUDDER BUSHING. The brass or metal sleeves fitted around the rudder pintles.

Fr: *Chemise d'Aiguillot;* Ger: *Fingerling Überzug.*

RUDDER CARRIER. A fitting placed inboard either where the rudderstock traverses the shell plating or directly under the tiller. In addition to taking the radial thrust of the rudderstock it carries the whole weight of the rudder, the stock, and the tiller.

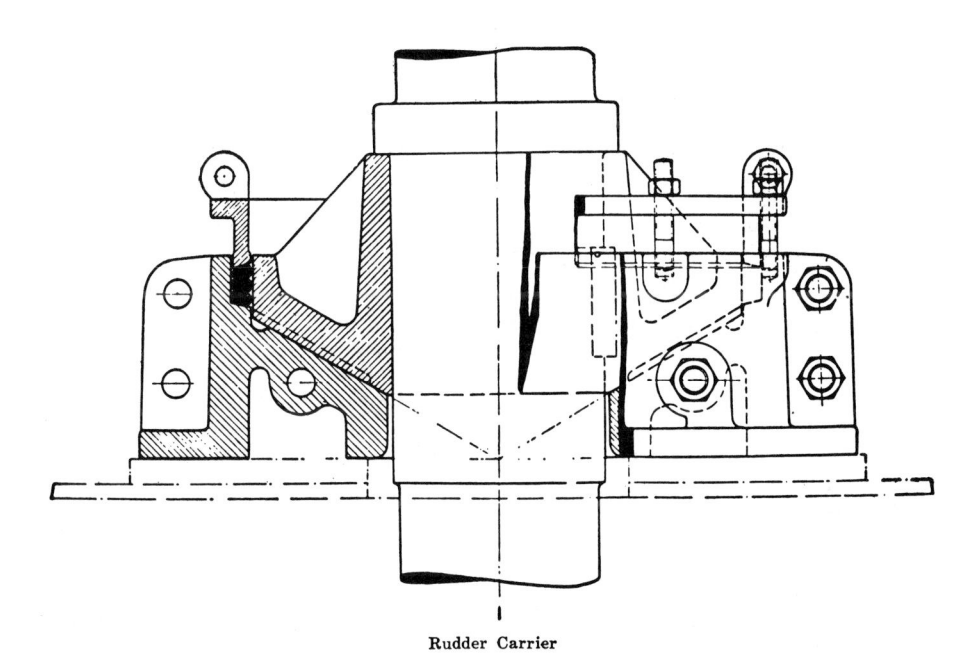

Fr: *Support de Gouvernail;* Ger: *Rudertraglager.*

The rudder carrier consists of a heavy cast pedestal secured to the deck or to the shell plating, provided with a heavy bronze bushing in which the rudderstock rotates, while on the top of the pedestal there is fitted a heavy bronze thrust ring on which the under side of the tiller rests. Both the radial and the thrust bearings are lubricated by oil boxes attached to the tiller. The thrust ring and radial bushing are each made in halves and special arrangements to facilitate examination or renewal of these parts without disturbing any other fittings are provided.

RUDDER CHAIN. One or two chains secured to the rudder horn and leading to each quarter of the vessel. In case of breakdown of the steering gear they were used for keeping the rudder under control. They are nowadays replaced by the rudder brake.

Fr: *Sauvegarde de Gouvernail;* Ger: *Sorgketten.*

RUDDER CHOCK. A wedge used to prevent the working of a wooden rudder when at anchor or when otherwise desired. Pieces of wood to fay or fill up the excavation on the side of the rudderhole so that the rudder may be fixed in midship position if necessary. (Obsolete.)

Fr: *Coin de Gouvernail;* Ger: *Ruderkeil.*

See **Rudder Bracket.**

RUDDER COAT. A tarred canvas covering nailed to the counter of wooden craft and to the rudderhead, with slack enough to permit the latter to turn. Its object was to prevent water from rushing up through the rudder trunk.

Rudder Carrier

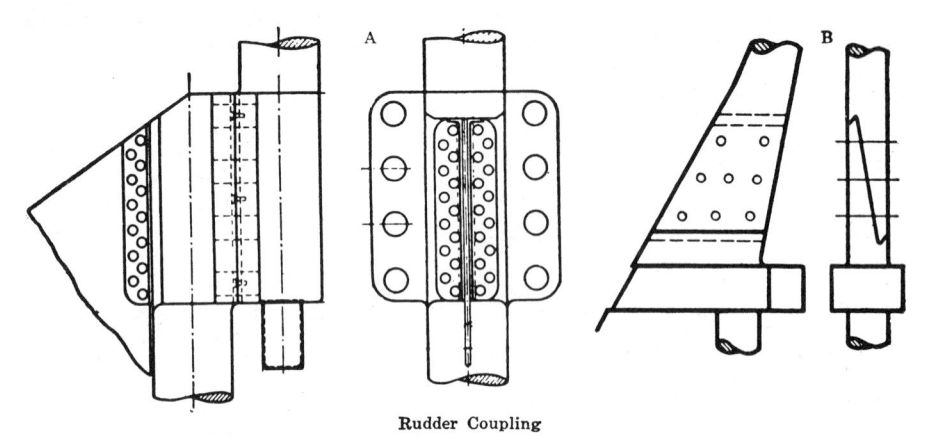

Rudder Coupling
A. Vertical Rudder Coupling   B. Scarfed Rudder Coupling

Fr: *Braie de Gouvernail;* Ger: *Ruderkragen.*

RUDDER COUPLING. A strong coupling with machined flanges, either vertical or horizontal by which the rudderstock is connected to the rudderhead. It is generally so arranged as to permit the rudder to be lifted without disturbing the tiller and steering gear.

Fr: *Accouplement de Mèche;* Ger: *Ruderkupplung.*

RUDDER CROSSHEAD. An athwartship metal piece bolted and keyed to the top of the rudderhead, to which the links of the steering gear are secured.

Fr: *Traverse de Gouvernail;* Ger: *Kreuzkopf.*

RUDDER EYE. Eyebolt fitted at the top of the rudderstock. Used for taking the weight of the stock when shipped or unshipped.

Fr: *Piton de Cervelle;* Ger: *Ruderheissring.*

RUDDER FRAME. The framing of a rudder to which the plating forming the rudder blade is attached.

Fr: *Cadre de Gouvernail;* Ger: *Ruderrahmen.*

RUDDERHEAD. The upper part or continuation of the rudderstock, above the blade, on which the quadrant or tiller is fitted. Also called upper stock.

Fr: *Tête de Mèche;* Ger: *Ruderkopf.*

RUDDER HEAD BEARING. A stuffing box consisting of two thick cast iron blocks with lignum vitae face-pieces fitted segmentally around the rudder head at deck level, to hold same against stresses induced by the tiller. Also called **Steady block; Deck stuffing box.**

Fr: *Presse étoupe de miche;* Ger: *Ruderkeillager.*

RUDDER HOLE. Round aperture in a ship's deck above the rudder trunk, through which the rudder head passes.

RUDDER HORN. A forked iron fitted to the back of a rudder, to which the rudder chains are attached. Also called monkey tail. (Obsolete.)

Fr: *Ferrure de Sauvegarde;* Ger: *Ruderhorn.*

RUDDER LOCK. A metal or wooden cleat fitted in a pintle score to prevent the rudder from being accidentally unshipped.

Fr: *Clef de Gouvernail;* Ger: *Ruder Schloss.*

RUDDER LUG. One of the projections cast with, or forged on the rudder frame for hanging and hinging the rudder. Also called rudder snug, gudgeon.

RUDDER MOMENT. The twisting stress brought to bear upon the rudder stock. It is made up of the pressure upon the rudder blade mulitiplied by the lever expressed in foot-tons.

Fr: *Moment d'évolution;* Ger: *Rudermoment.*

RUDDER PENDANT. One of the two short wire ropes which terminate the rudder chain, and are made fast to the stern.

Fr: *Pantoire de Sauvegarde;* Ger: *Sorgleine.*

RUDDER PIT. A small well in the floor of a drydock near the entrance. It provides the necessary depth to unship the rudder for examination or repairs. Also called rudder well.
Fr: *Fosse à Gouvernail;* Ger: *Rudergrube.*

RUDDER QUADRANT. A casting or forging by means of which the turning power is transmitted to the rudderhead. It has a double groove or channel in its curved edge—one for the port and one for the starboard steering chain. These are fastened to it so that while one winds, the other unwinds, both leaving the quadrant tangentially and exerting a constant leverage or turning effect. Although termed a quadrant it is not in form necessarily the quarter of a circle; it may be half a circle or even a complete circle. On large vessels where the rack and pinion type of gear is installed, a toothed quadrant is geared to the steering engine.
Fr: *Secteur de Barre;* Ger: *Rudersektor; Ruderquadrant.*

RUDDER RATIO ADJUSTMENT. An adjustment in a Gyro-Pilot which provides a means of varying the ration between degrees of deviation from the ship's course, and degrees of rudder movement. As some ships are more sensitive to rudder movements than others, a lever system is so arranged that the effective length of the arms can be varied.

RUDDER SNUG. Cast or forged projections provided on the foreside of the rudderstock to take the pintles when these are of the "fitted" type. Also called pintle boss.

RUDDER STAY.
See **Rudder Arm.**

RUDDERSTOCK. That part of a rudder which acts as a vertical shaft through which the turning force of the steering gear is transmitted to the rudder body. Also called rudder main piece.
Fr: *Mèche Inférieure;* Ger: *Ruderpfoste.*

RUDDER STOPS. Small projections fitted on the rudder stock and on the stern post (one or the other or both) the faces of which make contact when the rudder has reached its maximum permissible angle. Also called rudderpost stoppers.
Fr: *Butoirs de Gouvernail;* Ger: *Ruderauschlagknagge; Ruderknagge.*

RUDDER STUFFING BOX. A stuffing box fitted at the upper end of the rudder trunk to prevent ingress of water.
Fr: *Presse étoupe de mèche;* Ger: *Ruderstopfbuchse.*

RUDDER TELLTALE.
See **Rudder Angle Indicator.**

RUDDER TILLER. A heavy bar or lever with one end bored to fit on the rudderstock, and the other arranged for connection to the steering chains. The function of the tiller is to turn the rudder, the necessary power in most ships being obtained from a steam, electric, or hydraulic steering engine.
Fr: *Barre de Gouvernail;* Ger: *Ruderpinne.*
See **Chain Tiller, Emergency Tiller, Quadrant Tiller, Reverse Tiller, Single Arm Tiller, Spring Tiller, Steam Tiller.**

RUDDER TORQUE. The product of the total pressure on a rudder blade multiplied by the distance of the center of pressure from the centerline of the rudder stock.
Fr: *Moment de torsion;* Ger: *Ruderdrehmoment.*

RUDDER TRUNK. A square or round casing built around the rudderhead to prevent water entering the hull where it traverses the counter. Also called rudder well, rudder tube, rudder case. It extends from the counter to a platform or deck. In wooden ships it is formed by the rudderpost back timber and by building up on the horn timbers. It is staved up inside. A thick oak collar forms the bearing for the rudderhead at deck level.
Fr: *Jaumière;* Ger: *Ruderkoker.*

RUDDER WELL.
See **Rudder Pit.**

RULES OF NAVIGATION.
See **Rules of the Road.**

RULES OF OLERON.
See **Law.**

RULES OF THE ROAD. The rules and regulations accepted by international agreement and enforced by law in maritime countries, which govern the movements of ships when approaching each other under such circumstances that a collision may possibly ensue. Also called rules of navigation.
Fr: *Règles de Route;* Ger: *Seestrassenordnung.*
They establish a well-devised and com-

plete system of vessel's lights and furnish the rules of navigation applicable to all the ordinary cases of vessels approaching each other under such circumstances as to involve the risk of collision, leaving extraordinary cases in respect to which no safe general rule can be devised, to the practical good sense and professional skill of those in charge of such vessels. Any departure from the rules, to be justifiable, must only be made to avoid imminent danger.

The present international rules were drawn up by a conference of representatives of the maritime nations of the world at Washington, D. C., in 1889, and were subsequently adopted by the respective nations concerned. These rules superseded international rules introduced in 1863 by England and France, and similar rules adopted by the United States in 1864, which in turn had been adopted, with amendments before 1886 by the United States, England, France, Germany, Belgium, Norway, and Denmark. In the United States they became effective in 1897. The international rules were again amended at an international conference meeting in London in 1929, and when ratified as amended by the individual nations concerned will become the law of the sea to all vessels on the high seas, that is, outside the limits of excepted inland waters. Signatories of the 1929 convention included, in addition to the nations already named, Australia, Canada, Spain, Finland, Irish Free State, India, Italy, Sweden, Netherlands, Union of Soviet Socialist Republics and Japan. To date (1946) these amendments have not become the law in any country and the International Rules of 1889 are still in effect.

Farwell, R. G., *The Rules of the Nautical Road,* Annapolis, 1941; La Boyteaux, *Rules of the Road at Sea,* New York, 1925; Moore, H. S., *Rules of the Road at Sea,* London, 1922; Sebba, J., *Seewasserstrassenordnung,* Berlin, 1928.

RUMBOWLINE. A name given to coarse soft rope made from yarns and fibers of inferior quality and used for temporary lashings. It is also called "twice-laid" rope.

Fr: *Vieux Filin Blanc;* Ger: *Lodding.*

RUMMAGE. To clear or to move about the cargo of a ship in a search for smuggled goods.

Ger: *Durchsuchen; Durchstöbern.*

RUN. 1. A trough for the water caught by a coaming or breakwater, built across the forecastle and leading overboard.

2. The immersed part of the hull aft of the parallel body or, if the latter is nil, aft of the cross section of the greatest area.

Fr: *Coulée; Façons de l'Arrière.*

See **Angle of Run, Length of Run.**

3. A welding term used to denote the metal deposited by fusion during one passage of the filler metal along the joint. Also called pass.

Fr: *Passe;* Ger: *Lage.*

See **Backing Run.**

RUN (to). 1. To scud or navigate with the wind aft in very heavy weather with sufficient headway to keep the ship ahead of the sea.

Fr: *Fuir;* Ger: *Lenssen.*

2. To sail before the wind as distinguished from reaching or sailing close-hauled.

Fr: *Courir largue;* Ger: *Vor dem Wind segeln.*

3. To move over a definite course.

Fr: *Courir;* Ger: *Fahren.*

RUNABOUT. Small open or decked motor boat with a length ranging usually from 16 to 30 ft. designed particularly for fast day runs of not more than a few hours in sheltered waters. No overnight accommodations are provided. Sometimes called a water taxi.

RUN AGROUND (to). Said of a ship accidentally driven ashore in a stranded manner or condition.

Fr: *Faire côte;* Ger: *Auflaufen.*

RUN AWAY. To seize a line and haul on the run.

RUN BOAT. A sail- or motorboat from 40 to 60 ft. long, with a capacity of 75 to 100 barrels. Employed as carrier in the Chesapeake Bay crab industry, when the crabbing is done in regions where it is inconvenient or impractical for the crabber to deliver his catch to the dealers. When the boat is owned by the dealer and its captain is working on a commission it is referred to as a run boat. When the captain is buying crabs on his own responsibility and selling them where he chooses it is called a buy boat.

RUN DOWN. To run down a port means to sail North or South until the latitude of the port is reached, then head due East or West on that parallel until the port is in sight.

RUN INTO. To collide head on with a ship. To sink a ship by collision. Also called to run down.

Fr: *Aborder;* Ger: *Rammen.*

RUN IN WITH. To sail close to.

RUNNER. 1. A line fastened at one end to a fixed object such as an eye bolt on deck. It reeves through a single block and has an eye at the other end to which a tackle is clapped on. The term is also loosely applied to any line rove through a block.
> Fr: *Cartahu Simple à poulie courante;* Ger: *Klappläufer.*

See **Cargo Runner.**

2. In yachting parlance, a preventer backstay.

3. A man whose business is to take ashore, make fast, and let go the ship's lines on a quay, wharf, or pier. Also called line runner, boatman.

4. One of the men specially engaged to shift a vessel, of which the crew has been paid off, from one port to another. They are shipped "by the run."

RUNNER AND TACKLE. The same purchase as a luff tackle applied to a runner. The runner is a thick rope rove through a single block and usually has a hook attached to one end and one of the tackle blocks to the other. In applying it, the hook of the runner as well as the lower block of the tackle are fixed to the object intended to be moved.
> Fr: *Bastaque; Palan sur Itague;* Ger: *Mantel.*

RUNNER CREW. See **Runners.**

RUNNER TACKLE. A luff tackle added to the end of a whip.

A Runner or Single Whip Reversed.

Runner

Fisherman's Bend
Tail Block "B"
Studding Tack Bend

RUNNING AGREEMENT. A form of articles of agreement used by foreign-going vessels, which may extend to two or more voyages when the average length of the voyage is less than six months.

RUNNING BLOCK. A block fixed, or attached to the object to be raised or moved.
Fr: *Poulie mobile;* Ger: *Laufender Block.*

RUNNING BOWLINE. A bowline made over the standing part of its own rope so that it will form a sliding noose.
Fr: *Laguis;* Ger: *Laufender Pfahlstek.*

RUNNING BOWSPRIT. A bowsprit which can be run in or rigged in when headsails are taken off. Also called running in bowsprit, sliding bowsprit, reefing bowsprit. Running bowsprits are made of wood and only used in small craft. They are occasionally fitted to be rigged in partially when reefing the headsails. The spar travels in and out over a roller let in the stemhead between chocks or at side of stemhead. The heel passes between two heavy wooden uprights named bowsprit bitts. An iron pin through these bitts, with corresponding hole in the spar, keeps it from running in. Strong crossbars over the bitts keep the heel from rising.
> Fr: *Beaupré rentrant;* Ger: *Loses Bugspriet; Einlaufendes Bugspriet; Einziehbares Bugspriet.*

RUNNING DAYS. Days counted in succession without any allowance for holidays. The term is used in settling lay days or days of demurrage. In British shipping circles it is not admitted that Sunday is a running day in the sense of being a working day. A running day is a day of twenty-four hours and is usually reckoned from midnight to midnight.
Fr: *Jours Courants;* Ger: *Laufende Tage.*

RUNNING DOWN CLAUSE. See **Collision Clause.**

RUNNING FIX. A position determined by the intersection of two lines of position established at different times but adjusted to the same time by applying the run of the ship between the observations.
See **Fix.**

RUNNING FREE. See **Going Free.**

RUNNING GAFF. A gaff in which the forward or inner end is fitted with jaws which partly encircle the mast and are confined to it by a parrel which allows the spar to slide up and down the mast. It is hoisted by the throat and peak halyards.
Ger: *Laufende Gaffel.*

RUNNING HITCH. See **Slip Knot.**

RUNNING HOOK. A hook fitted in the bow of an open boat, to which the tack of the foresail is shifted when running.

RUNNING LIGHTS. A general term

applied to the various lights carried from sunset to sunrise by different classes of vessels when under way, in accordance with the International Regulations for Preventing Collisions at Sea. Also called navigation lights. The color, position, and visibility of these lights are defined by these rules.

Fr: *Feux de Position;* Ger: *Positionslaterne; Fahrtlaterne.*

The glass of running lights consists of dioptric lenses so arranged as to throw a beam of light in a plane parallel to the sea level. The outer surface of the lenses consists of a central belt with a number of steps above and below this belt, which are known as dioptric elements. When a dioptric lens is not used the lantern must have a plain glass front, cylindrical in form, and in thickness at least 5/16ths of an inch. Sixty- to one-hundred-watt lamps (single filament) giving a lighting of 50 to 80 candlepower are used. With oil lights a candlepower of at least 12 candles is required of the burners used with side and masthead lights. To minimize the chances of breakdown, electric navigation lights are generally fitted with two lamps for each lantern, or with a double filament lamp each of these lamps being connected by separate wiring to the main source of supply. The running light system is controlled from a panel in the wheel house with indicators showing which lights are on.

RUNNING LINE. A line coiled in a rowboat and run from the ship to a dock, a pier, a buoy, or another ship. Synonym of "guess warp."

RUNNING PART. The movable or hauling part of a fall in a tackle.

Fr: *Courant;* Ger: *Laufender Part.*

RUNNING RIGGING. That part of the rigging which includes the moving or movable ropes hauled upon to brace the yards, make and take in sails, operate gaffs and booms, raise and lower upper masts, hoist weights, and so on. Such gear is chiefly made of Manila rope, but Italian hemp, cotton rope and flexible steel wire or chain are also used. The principal ropes forming the running rigging are: tacks, sheets, braces, halyards, vangs, guys, boom topping lifts, outhauls and downhauls, brails, reef points, reef lines, and reef tackles, buntlines, clew lines, clew garnets, and bowlines.

Fr: *Gréement Courant;* Ger: *Laufendes Gut.*

RUNNING SURVEY. A preliminary marine survey carried out by a vessel under way without using the methods and equipment employed by surveying vessels. The position of the vessel having been established, courses are laid out along the coast and bearings of all prominent marks are taken. As the ship proceeds, keeping accurate run of the course and distance, a bearing is taken of each new object sighted as well as several bearings of all objects passed. The ship's course is plotted as the base line, and the intersections of different bearings of the same landmark fixes the position of that object on the chart.

Ger: *Fliegende Vermessung.*

RUNNING TUCK. A method of working a tuck seine where there is a more or less strong current. The method of shooting is the same as in the open tuck. After this the larger boat is anchored and the arms of the net are brought together by the force of the current.

RUN OUT. To carry out the end of as a warp or hawser for the purpose of mooring or warping it to any object.

Fr: *Elonger;* Ger: *Ausbringen; Auslaufen.*

RUSSCON. Code name of the British Chamber of Shipping Black Sea Berth Contract, 1912, for grain.

RUSSIAN HEMP. Hemp grown in the districts of Orel, Kursk, Mohilev, and Smolensk. The grade M.R.H. is commonly used for the manufacture of ropes. The fibers are about 3 ft. in length.

Fr: *Chanvre de Russie;* Ger: *Russischer Hanf.*

RUSSPRUSS. Code name for the British Chamber of Shipping Wood Charter, Kronstadt, Riga and Memel, 1899. This charter has since 1926 been replaced by the "Baltwood" form.

RUST. The produce of corrosion which consists of an oxide of iron, of reddish brown color, formed on the surface of iron and steel. Rust scale is four to six times bulkier than the parent metal from which it is formed and it is this bulky nature which causes corrosion to exert a bursting effect on riveted joints. As used in bills of lading the word rust is usually held to include rust caused by sea water as well as rust resulting from atmospheric dampness or from sweat.

Fr: *Rouille;* Ger: *Rost.*

RUST JOINT. A jointing material composed of cast-iron borings or filings, sal-ammoniac and flowers of sulfur mixed to a paste with water, formerly employed to secure rigid connection between pipes or to secure watertightness where calking is deficient. Also called rust putty.

Fr: *Mastic de Fer; Potée;* Ger: *Rostkitt.*

RYBNITZA. A fish carrier with a crew of 7 men employed in the seine fisheries on the estuary of the Volga and Caspian Sea. The carrying capacity of this type varies from 8 to 50 tons of live fish transported in a well or tank. It has a flush deck and is rigged with two masts. The foremast stands just abaft the stem and the mainmast is stepped about three-fifths of the boat's length from the stern. Length **51 ft. 8 in.** Beam **17 ft. 2 in.** (Typical.)

RYDE WHERRY. Open sailing and pulling boat of same type and rig as the Portsmouth wherry. It had a cuddy forward, high weatherboards and thwarts for nearly two-thirds of its length from forward, and was steered by yoke lines. It was used chiefly for carrying passengers to and from the Isle of Wight. Now extinct.

RYE TERMS. A chartering term which applies to dealings in various kinds of grain in addition to rye. When goods are sold on "Rye Terms" the sellers guarantee their condition on arrival with certain exceptions which are definitely stipulated in the contract. Samples are taken at port of discharge jointly by agents of shippers and of holders of bills of lading. Any deterioration of claim for such to be fixed by arbitrators.

S

S. Flag of the international code of signals having a white ground with central blue square about one-ninth of the flag's total area. When flown singly means: "Engines going full speed astern." When used as a signal between tug and tow it means: "My engines are going astern" when displayed by the tug and "Go astern" when displayed by the ship towed.

S. Freeboard mark which indicates the load line in summer. It gives the freeboard derived from the tables of the assigning authority.

S.A. SAFE ARRIVAL (marine insurance).
S.B.S. SURVEYED BEFORE SHIPMENT.
S.C. SALVAGE CHARGES.
S.D. SEMIDIAMETER (astronomy).
S/D SEA-DAMAGED (grain trade).
S.D. SHORT DELIVERY.
Shl.Dk. SHELTER DECK.
S. and H. (exct.) SUNDAYS & HOLIDAYS EXCEPTED.
Sid. SIDEREAL (astronomy).
S.L. SALVAGE LOSS.
Sld. SAILED.
S/N SHIPPING NOTE.
S.O.L. SHIPOWNER'S LIABILITY.
S.O.S. DISTRESS SIGNAL.
S.P. STERN POST.
S.P.A. SUBJECT TO PARTICULAR AVERAGE (the opposite of F.P.A., i.e., FREE OF PARTICULAR AVERAGE).
S.P.D. STEAMER (or SHIP) PAYS DUES.
Spg. SPRING (tides).
S.R. and C.C. STRIKE, RIOTS AND CIVIL COMMOTION (marine insurance).
S.S. SCREW STEAMER.
Stg. STRINGER.
Str. STEAMER.
Std. STANDARD (timber trade).
S/L.C. SUE AND LABOR CLAUSE.
S/LOSS SALVAGE LOSS (insurance).
S.S. and C. SALVAGE and SALVAGE CHARGES (insurance).
S.T.A. SHAFT TUNNEL ALLEY.
S.M. SCREW MOTOR SHIP.

SACADA. The *barco de Sacada*, originating from Peniche (Portugal), is similar to the *cahique*, but of lighter construction. The hull, with straight stem and round stern, is decked fore and aft and has four hatches. The rig consists of two masts with lateen sails. The fore- or mainmast, stepped near the bow, has a forward rake of about 15 degrees. The mizzen or aftermast is stepped well in the stern and rakes slightly aft.

SACOLEVA. A light-built, shallow-draft Greek sailer of 30 to 60 tons, with high sheer at both ends, rigged with 1, 2 or 3 masts. In the 3-masted *sacoleva* the foremast carried square sails, whereas the two aftermasts were very small and lateen- or lug-rigged. In the 2-masted trading boats the mainmast is placed at a distance of about one-third of total length from the stem and carries a fidded topmast on which a square topsail and occasionally a topgallant sail are set. The mizzen mast is stepped right aft and carries a jib-headed or lateen mizzen. Fishing boats are rigged with fore- and mainmast settee sails and jibs. One-masted boat: Length over-all 41 ft. Length, keel, 30½ ft. Breadth 12 ft. 3 in. Depth 4 ft. 1 in. Two-masted boat (fishing): Length over-all 49 ft. Breadth 13 ft. Depth 5.9 ft.

The 3-masted *sacoleva* is now extinct, and the 2-masted type does not set square sails above the lugsails. Owing to the very small freeboard amidships, canvas weathercloths supported by a light spar are provided in the waist to protect the cargo from being damaged by spray.

SADDLE. 1. An aid to shipfitting consisting of two uprights and a cross bar welded together, used in welded construction fitting as a quick and easy means of pulling angles and stiffeners up to their proper places. The saddle is welded in place, and a wedge is used in conjunction with it.

2. A semicircular support built of plates and angles on which cylindrical boilers are seated. Also called boiler saddle.

Fr: *Berceau de Chaudière;* Ger: **Kessellager**.

3. See **Tongue**.

SADDLE BACK. The sloping plates under a centerline coal-hatch by which coal is diverted to the side bunkers.

SADDLE HATCH. A small bunker hatchway situated over the boilers or between them and the engines. It consists of a trunk or shaft whose sides open into the upper or lower side bunkers, and whose bottom is shaped like an inverted V or saddle. This

formation diverts the coal into the bunkers and gives clearance below it.
Ger: *Sattelbunkerluke.*

SADDLE PLATE. See **Cradle Plate.**

SADDLE STRAP. See **Cradle Plate.**

SAFETY CERTIFICATE. A government certificate issued to passenger vessels which comply with the requirements of the 1929 International Convention for Safety of Life at Sea concerning watertight subdivision, and lifesaving appliances.
Fr: *Certificat de Sécurité;* Ger: *Sicherheitszeugnis.*

SAFETY HOOK. A cargo hook with a piece hinged to swing down and lock over the point. It prevents the sling from slipping off the hook. Also drop lip hook.

SAFETY RADIOTELEGRAPHY CERTIFICATE. A certificate issued to all ships of 1600 tons gross or more, engaged on international voyages, which comply in an efficient manner with the requirements prescribed in the International Radiotelegraph Convention of 1927.
Fr: *Certificat Radiotélégraphique de Sécurité;* Ger: *Funksicherheitszeugnis.*

SAG. That form of longitudinal deformation under stress in which the middle part of a ship's structure sinks below the extremities. The converse of hogging. In this condition the weight exceeds the buoyancy over approximately the midship halflength, with more buoyancy than weight at both ends, therefore the tendency of the vessel is to arch down or sag at about midlength. Such a condition results in a bending moment which stresses the top members of the vessel in compression and the bottom members in tension. The stresses are termed sagging stresses.
Fr: *Contre-Arc;* Ger: *Durchsacken; Stapelung.*
See **Hog.**

SAG (to). A vessel sags to leeward when it moves rapidly to leeward owing to the force of the wind, sea, or current. Also called to drop to leeward.
Fr: *Dépaler;* Ger: *Abtreiben.*

SAGGING MOMENT. The moment at any given point of the forces which tend to cause a vessel to sag. The opposite of hogging moment.
Fr: *Moment Fléchissant de Contre-Arc;* Ger: *Durchsackungsmoment.*

SAIK. A Turkish sprit-rigged ketch with very tall mainmast and short mizzen. It carries above the main spritsail, a square topsail, and a flying square foresail is set for running before the wind. One headsail is set.

SAIL. A piece of cloth, fabric, texture, or tissue of some kind spread to the wind to cause, or assist in causing, a vessel to move through the water. Sails are usually made of several breadths of canvas sewed together with a double seam at the border and edged all around with a rope called bolt-rope. They generally take their names, partly at least, from the mast, yard, or stay upon which they set. Thus the mainsail, main topsail and main topgallant sails are respectively the sails on the mainmast, maintopmast and main topgallant mast. The tendency of all modern rigging is to do away with square sails in favor of those set fore and aft, which are handier.
Fr: *Voile;* Ger: *Segel.*

Sails are made of flax canvas, cotton or similar material of various thickness and strength according to the size and purpose for which they are intended. The total wind pressure of a sail may be resolved into three components: (a) a fore-and-aft component which drives the vessel forward; (b) a transverse component which tends to incline the

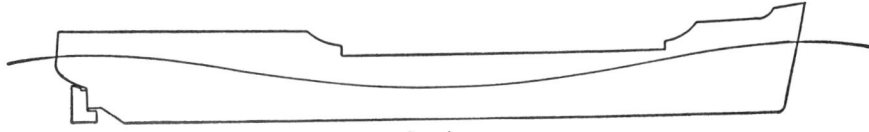

Sagging

vessel; (c) a vertical component which tends to lift or depress the vessel according to the design or shape of the sail and its location.

SAIL (to). 1. To move along over the water by the action of the wind upon sails. Said of a ship.
Fr: *Naviguer à la Voile; Faire Voile;* Ger: *Segeln.*

SAIL AREA—SAIL-CARRYING POWER

2. To move along over the water. To begin a journey on board ship.
Fr: *Appareiller;* Ger: *Abfahren.*

SAIL AREA. The measure of the surface of the sails. The most efficient method of determining the amount of sail for a design is by direct comparison with another boat of approximately the same type. Among the various methods for determining sail area, a coefficient consisting of the ratio of sail area to area of immersed midship section is one of the most useful.
Fr: *Surface de Voilure;* Ger: *Segelareal; Besegelung.*

The numerical value of this ratio for different types of sailing vessels is as follows:

Vessel	Ratio
Square-rigged vessel ...	35 to 50
Topsail schooner	40 to 50
Sailing trawler	24 to 29
Fore-and-aft schooner..	50 to 65
Cruising yachts	45 to 55
Racing yachts	70 to 100

Sail areas for open boats are usually determined by the ratio of sail area to that of a circumscribed rectangle at waterline having the same length and breadth as the boat.

| Cruising gig .... | 2.5 |
| Dinghy .... | 1.5 |

SAIL BATTEN. A short and slender strip of wood placed in the leech of a lateen or racing sail to support and hold the form.
Fr: *Latte de Voile;* Ger: *Segellatte.*

The sail batten is made of a strip of pine or white ash of lathlike form and of width, length, and thickness in proportion to the size or breadth of the sail, but tapering at each end. The battens are slipped into sheaths or pockets formed across the sail. Battens usually extend only partly across the sail. In some racing sails the battens are not sheathed in a pocket. Knittles are fitted for the purpose and the battens are then laced to the sail, one on each side of the canvas.

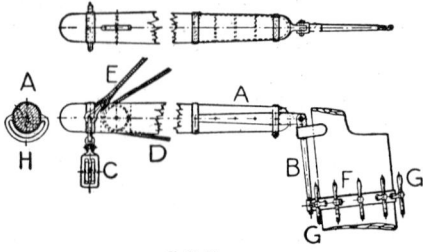

Sail Boom
A. Boom
B. Gooseneck
C. Sheet Block
D. Sail Outhaul
E. Topping Lift
F. Spider Band
G. Belaying Pin
H. Horse

SAIL BOOM. A spar by which the foot of a sail is extended. Sail booms take their names from the sails to which they are attached. They constitute the only means by which some sails can be taken beyond the ship's sides (gaff sails, jibs, and spinnakers) and they help to keep the sails flat. The inner end of the boom is fastened to the mast by jaws or by a gooseneck.

Average boom diameters in fractions of total length:

At mast (fore end)	0.012
At middle	0.015
At end	0.011

SAIL-CARRYING POWER. The amount of sail that can be carried by sailing craft in relation to the service for which they are intended. Also, the angle to which a vessel heels, when carrying her working sails, under the action of a given wind pressure.

In practice sail-carrying power is found by the following formula:

$$\text{Sail carrying power} = \frac{\text{Displacement} \times \text{metacentric height}}{\text{Sail area} \times H}$$

$H =$ Vertical distance in feet between center of lateral resistance and center of effort.

(Displacement in tons. Metacentric height in feet.)

In these calculations the wind pressure is assumed to act at right angles to the lateral plane and with a pressure of one pound per square foot of sail area, which is equivalent to a fresh breeze of force 6, Beaufort scale.
Fr: *Stabilité sous Voiles; Coefficient de Stabilité sous Voiles;* Ger: *Steifheit; Steifigkeit unter Segel.*

Inasmuch as sail-carrying power is dependent on statical stability, if GM is known, the area of sail which the vessel will carry with a given wind pressure can be determined. On large merchant ships, however, the amount of sail is in practice limited by the maximum practicable mast height. The area of sail could be increased if any way could be devised for spreading it. Varying character and stowage of cargo, result in wide variations in the metacentric height, which in turn involves considerable changes in the sail-carrying power.

Average Values of Sail-Carrying Power for Trading Vessels

Square-rigged barks and ships..	21 to 25.5
Topsail schooners	19.5
Fore-and-aft schooners	16.5
Ketches	18
Pilot Cutter	24

SAILCLOTH. A term specifically applied in Great Britain to light canvas manufactured in 12-15 and 18 inches width and used for lifeboat sails. Also called **Yacht canvas**.
Fr: *Toile a Voile*; Ger: *Segeltuch*.

SAIL COVER. A protective canvas **cover** placed over a furled sail. Also called **sail coat**. It is made of cotton canvas, or, for very small boats, of cotton drill, and is painted with a specially prepared paint. The tabling has eyelets to take a long lacing or hooks.
Fr: *Etui*; Ger: *Segelkleid*.

SAIL HOOK. A metal hook from 3 to 5 inches long with a sharp point at one end and a swivel at the other. A lanyard spliced to the swivel is made fast to the sail-maker's bench. The hook is stuck in the canvas for keeping it tightly drawn over the knees while working. Also called **Bench hook**.
Fr: *Croc de voilier*; Ger: *Segelhaken*; *Segelmacherhaken*.

SAILING ICE. In polar navigation refers to loose or broken ice through which a ship can proceed. Also called **Open ice**.
Ger: *Offenes Eis*.

SAILING. The rules or methods of navigation by which a ship's track is determined and represented on a chart and by which the problems relating to navigation are solved. These are: composite sailing, current sailing, Great Circle sailing, Mercator sailing, middle latitude sailing, parallel sailing, plane sailing, traverse sailing, windward Great Circle sailing, windward sailing.

SAILING CRAFT. Small vessel with sail propulsion exclusively.
Fr: *Bateau à Voiles*; Ger: *Segelfahrzeug*.

SAILING DIRECTIONS. Printed books issued by hydrographic offices to supplement charts. They give all pertinent information concerning waters, coasts, harbors, and so on.
Fr: *Instructions Nautiques*; Ger: *Segelanweisungen*.

SAILING DRIFTER. A ketch or dandy-rigged fishing vessel with a tonnage ranging between 30 and 180, according to the distance from the fishing grounds, used in the herring and mackerel fisheries with drift nets. In Great Britain called driver.
The sailing drifter is usually of wood construction, with a lowering mainmast for lying to the nets. The mizzen or jigger mast has a forward rake in order to bring the center of sail area further forward. Sailing drifters usually carry a small auxiliary boiler which supplies the necessary power for the capstan by which the nets are hauled in.

SAILING LENGTH. A term used in yacht measurement rules. It applies to the length on water line with certain additions which include the length of overhangs at bow and stern, and measurement of the fullness of girth of the said overhangs.

SAILING MASTER. A yacht's officer in charge of its navigation.

SAILING ON A BOWLINE. In nautical parlance means sailing on a wind or close hauled when the bowlines would be hauled taut. Sailing on an easy bowline indicates that the vessel is sailing with the sails well full, and is not jammed up into the wind.

SAILING ON HER OWN BOTTOM. Said of a trading or fishing vessel that has paid for herself.

SAILING PUNT (G. B.). Pleasure boat of boxlike construction, with sides formed of single strakes inclining outward, the whole structure being held together by timber knees secured to stout floor pieces spaced about 1 ft. 9 in. apart. A large dipping lug is used for sailing. A punting platform is constructed at the afterend. Length 25 ft. Width 3.8 ft. Depth 1.3 ft. Sail area 200 sq. ft. Two leeboards are provided.

SAILING RULES. Rules adopted by national or international racing associations relating to the management and sailing of races, protests, and so forth.

SAILING THWART. A fore-and-aft plank which runs on the top of the thwarts, through which the mast of a sailboat is stepped. When running from stem to first thwart it is called gangplank. Also called gangboard, mast carling.
Fr: *Banc de Mât*; Ger: *Bootsfisch*; *Segelducht*.

SAILING TRIM. 1. A vessel loaded to her designed draft or in such manner as to make her seaworthy is said to be in sailing trim.
Ger: *Segelfähigkeit*.

2. The arrangement or position of the yards and sails in order that the wind may act upon them at the desired angle.
Fr: *Orientation*; *Allure*; Ger: *Segelstellung*.

SAILING VESSEL. Any ship provided with sufficient sail area for navigation under sails only, whether or not provided with auxiliary power.
Fr: *Voilier*; Ger: *Segelschiff*.

SAILING WHALEBOAT. A whaleboat

formerly issued to vessels of the United States Navy, fitted with a centerboard and with jib-headed ketch rig.

SAIL LARGE. To sail free; to sail other than close-hauled or into the wind.

Fr: *Courir Largue;* Ger: *Raum segeln.*

SAIL LOCKER. A compartment where sails are stowed when not in use.

Fr: *Soute aux Voiles;* Ger: *Segelkoje; Segellast; Segelkammer.*

SAIL LOFT. A loft where sails, awnings, tarpaulins, canvas covers, and so on, are cut out and fabricated.

Fr: *Voilerie;* Ger: *Segelwerkstatt; Segelboden.*

SAILMAKER. One who fabricates and assembles canvas articles used on ships and boats, such as sails, awnings, covers and so on. He attaches ropes and metal fittings to canvas. On sailing vessels he was assisted by a sailmaker's mate and had charge of the upkeep of sails. He did not keep watch and was quartered with carpenter and carpenter's mate.

Fr: *Voilier;* Ger: *Segelmacher.*

SAILMAKER'S BENCH. A wooden seat about 7 ft. long and 15 in. high upon which the sailmaker sits when sewing canvas.

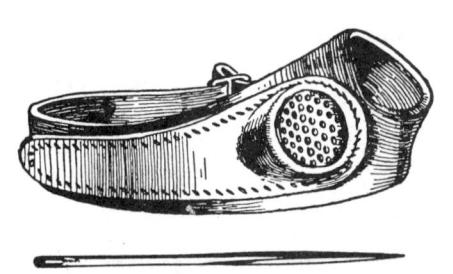

Sailmaker's Palm and Needle

SAILMAKER'S PALM. An instrument used instead of a thimble by sailmakers and seamen in sewing canvas. Also called palm. It consists of a piece of stiff rawhide with an inverted thimble near the base of the thumb, by which the needle is forced through the canvas. A strap over the back of the hand holds it in place and there is a hole through which the thumb protrudes.

Fr: *Paumelle;* Ger: *Segelhandschuh; Segelmacherplatte.*

SAILMAKER'S SPLICE. A splice which differs from the usual mariner's splice in that the strands instead of being tucked over and under the opposite strands, follow round and round with the lay of the rope. This splicing is generally used for joining the ends of bolt ropes. Also called round splice.

Fr: *Epissure de Voilier;* Ger: *Segelmacher Splissung.*

SAILMAKER'S WHIPPING. A whipping used on the ends of reef points and similar gear which are exposed to continual frapping and chafe. It is made by stitching the twine through the rope with a needle. Also called palm and needle whipping.

Fr: *Surliure de Transfilage.*

SAILMAKING. The art of making sails, which includes designing, cutting, sewing, roping, tabling, and putting in linings, grommets, reef points, cringles, holes.

The sailmaker, having been supplied with the spar plan, proceeds first to determine for each sail the proper distribution of the areas of the drawing power; the amount of draft to be put in, and the dimensions. The width, or cross measurement, is expressed in number of cloths, and the depth in yards.

For a square sail, the number of cloths in the head, number in the foot, and the depth in yards are determined.

For a triangular fore-and-aft sail, the number of cloths in the foot and the depth in yards of the luff are determined.

For a four-sided fore-and-aft sail, the number of cloths in the head, number in the foot, and the depths of mast or foreleech and of afterleech are determined.

These particulars having been obtained, a plan called the "casting or cutting plan," which gives the shape and length of each cloth in the sail, is drawn up for the cutter, who then proceeds to cut out the sail, cloth by cloth in consecutive order. The cloths are then sewed together, spread out, and the tablings turned in. Strengthening pieces, or linings, are then seamed on where necessary. The next operation is to rope the edges by sewing the bolt rope. Cringles formed by a strand of bolt rope are then inserted at clews and earings and elsewhere as necessary. Reef holes, head holes, clew and buntline holes, stay holes, and so on, are then pierced; and the sail is then completed.

Davis, C. G., *How Sails Are Made and Handled,* New York, 1931; Gray, A., *Sailmaking Simplified,* New York, 1940; Kipping, R., *Sails and Sailmaking,* London, 1928; Millot, M., Traité de Voilure, Paris, 1926; Terence, North, *Yacht Sails,* London, 1938.

SAIL MOMENT. The area of sails and pressure of wind upon them multiplied by

the distance of the center of effort above the center of lateral resistance, which represents the length of leverage.
>Fr: *Moment d'Inclinaison de la Voilure;* Ger: *Winddruckmoment; Segelmoment.*

SAIL NEEDLE. A steel needle of triangular section for half its length from the point and then round, used for sailmaking. Also called long spur needle. Sail needles are made in different sizes and numbered from 6 to 17½, the higher the number, the smaller the needle. Small ones are used for light cloth and large ones for heavy canvas.
>Fr: *Aiguille de Voilier; Carrelet;* Ger: *Segelnadel.*

See **Bolt Rope Needle, Marline Needle, Tabling Needle.**

SAILOR. A mariner. One whose occupation is to aid in the operation of a vessel.
>Fr: *Matelot;* Ger: *Matrose.*

See **Turnpike Sailor.**

SAILORIZING. To practice the work of a sailor, especially that concerned with rope and canvas, such as the making of knots, splices, braided mats, and so on.

SAILOR-MONGER (U. S.). A judicial term used to denote a person employing or operating with other lawless persons who board vessels upon entering a port and, by the help of intoxicants and the use of other means often savoring of violence, get the crews ashore and "sell" them to outgoing vessels for gain.

SAILOR'S WHIPPING. A whipping made by laying an end down, taking a number of turns about it, hauling taut and laying out. The second end is then laid back around the rope and additional turns are made around the end with the loop that is formed.

SAIL SLIDE. A small metal casting or punching used in connection with a mast, boom, or gaff track and made with lips to slide on it when the sail is set or taken in. When used with fore-and-aft sails, slides have a raised opening at the back where they are seized with marline at each grommet in the sail. They are usually made of cast iron, cast bronze, or pressed brass. Sometimes called slide.
>Fr: *Griffe;* Ger: *Jackstagreiter; Gleitschuh.*

SAIL TACKLE. A tackle used for sending sails aloft; usually a top-Burton.
>Fr: *Cartahu Double;* Ger: *Segeltakel.*

SAIL TRACK. A T-shaped rail fitted to the underside of a gaff, the afterside of a mast, or the end of a boom, in which slides travel up and down or fore and aft as the sail is hauled out or hoisted and lowered. Also called mast track, railway, tramway. In square-rigged vessels the same device is sometimes fitted on the forward side of the mast, thus doing away with the upper topsail and upper topgallant parrels.
>Fr: *Chemin de Fer;* Ger: *Gleitschiene; Gleitbahn.*

ST. ELMO'S FIRE. The luminous brush discharge frequently seen on the extremities of masts and yards at sea and also occasionally on stays and other parts of the ship, when atmospheric electricity of low intensity induces electricity on the ship or other object that happens to be under its influence. Also called corposant. This induced electricity concentrates at the extremities of structures where it becomes visible.
>Fr: *Feu de St. Elme;* Ger: *St. Elmfeuer.*

ST. IVES GIG. A long, open boat primarily designed for pulling, but also fitted for work under sail and used by fishermen of Cornwall. The hull is clinker-built with fine bows and narrow transom stern. When under sail it is rigged with a large, dipping lug on the foremast and standing spritsail on the mizzen, with long outrigger. There are 6 thwarts. Length over-all 26 ft. 6½ in. Breadth 6 ft. 4½ in. Depth, inside from top of keel, 2 ft. 6 in. (Average.)

ST. THOMAS CANOE. A planked sailing canoe with sharp pointed bows and dory stern used by the fishermen of St. Thomas, Virgin Islands. The bottom of the hull is made from a hollowed-out log. Frames are fitted inside this, to which the planks forming the topsides are fastened. A keel is fitted along the bottom. A cat-rigged mainsail is used for sailing. Oars are provided for use in calm weather. Length 15 to 20 ft. Breadth 3 to 4 ft. Depth 2 to 2½ ft. (Typical.)

SAINT HILAIRE METHOD.
See **Intercept.**

SAINT JOHN WOOD BOAT. A type of seagoing sailing barge which originated at St. John, New Brunswick and was formerly used along the Maine coast for bringing cordwood to the lime kilns located near Rockland. The hull, almost wholly built of spruce, had bluff bows, and square transom stern with outboard rudder. Most of the load was carried on deck. The rig was that of a two-masted baldheaded schooner with or without bowsprit. The foremast was stepped as far forward as possible. The type is now extinct.

SALANGER.
See **Chelinga**.

SALANGU.
See **Masula**.

SALAPOORIAH. Small sailing lighter with a capacity of 10 to 15 tons found on the Bosporus, with slightly curved stem and pointed stern. The rig is peculiar as there is no mast. In its stead is a short post carrying on the port side a yard or sprit which is kept upright by a counterpoise on its lower end, and is steadied by a stay and backstays. The sail runs on hoops and is hoisted by a single block and fall at the head. The sheet leads to a short horse under which the tiller works. The sprit hangs in a chain from the head of the post. This enables the lighter to pass under the low bridges that span the Golden Horn.

SALINITY. Number of parts of salt contained in one thousand parts of sea water. The average salinity of sea water is approximately 35, but it varies in different localities from 33 to 37 parts.

Fr: *Salinité*; Ger: *Salzgehalt*.

SALINITY INDICATOR. An electrical instrument in use aboard some high-powered vessels fitted with watertube boilers to warn the engineers immediately of the entry of salts in the fresh water system supplying feed water, and to indicate at all times the saline content of the fresh water. Its operation is based on the principle that proportional variation of the electrical conductivity of water takes place with the variation of its electrolytic impurities.

See **Salinometer**.

SALINOMETER. A hydrometer or floating instrument used to ascertain the percentage of salt in sea water. It indicates the saline contents in thirty seconds, that is, 1 part of salt to 32 parts of water. Electrical chlorine indicators of greater sensitivity are used for checking the salinity of water distilled by the evaporators.

See **Salinity Indicator**.

SALISH CANOE. A dugout canoe used for transportation of people and trading supplies, baggage and provisions by the coastal Indian tribes located between Puget Sound and the 50th parallel of north latitude. Also called chinook canoe. The family or transportation canoes are from 25 to 35 ft. long and 4 to 6 ft. beam. The so-called "voyaging canoes" are from 35 to 65 ft. long and 6 ft. beam.

In the smaller craft of this type the whole hull is hollowed from a single log. In the larger, separate bow and stern piece are added. The bow has a swanlike, barbed shape with sloping cutwater. The stern is vertical and blunt. The bottom is flat with straight flaring sides. The stem and stern pieces are scarfed and joined with dowels to the body of the canoe. Flat gunwale strips run along each side and are carried up to the top of the stem piece, where they are cut off square. This type, which is also called the Southern Indian canoe, is heavier, roomier, stronger and less cranky than the Haida or Northern Indian canoe.

SALISIPAN. A dugout from the southern Philippines similar to the *panca*, with a wash strake made of palm leaves (nipa), which serves also as protection for the paddlers against arrows and darts when fighting. These boats are light and very fast. They were formerly used by the Moros on their piratical expeditions.

SALLYING. The rolling motion given to a small vessel by having the crew run from side to side, in order to loosen ice around the vessel.

Ger: *Abspringen lassen*.

SALMON BOAT. The Columbia River salmon boat is an open, carvel-built double-ended boat fitted with centerboard. It has a long low floor and round bilge, flares slightly at the top, and has a very shallow keel, with little or no rake to the stem and sternpost, both of which are straight. It is decked for 2 or 3 ft. at each end and has waterways extending along both sides. A coaming 2 or 3 in. high runs around the inner edge of the waterways and decked spaces. It has 4 thwarts and is rigged with a single mast stepped in the bow and spritsail. Length over-all 25¾ ft. Beam 6¾ ft. Depth 2 ft. (Typical.)

Ger: *Lachsfänger*.

The Columbia River salmon boat is employed in the river and coast gill-net salmon fisheries of the Pacific from the lower counties of California to Alaska. The Sacramento River salmon boats are smaller, their length ranging from 15 to 20 ft. They are rigged with a leg-of-mutton sail.

The Solway Firth (Great Britain) salmon boats are half-decked with pointed stern and raking sternpost. They are rigged with lowering mast, standing lugsail, and jib. A fish well is provided. Length over-all 20 ft.

Breadth 6 ft. 6 in. Depth 2½ to 3 ft. (Average.)

SALMON COBLE. A flat-bottomed, square-sterned, clinker-built open fishing boat from 16 to 22 ft. in length with pronounced sheer forward used on the west coast of Scotland for the salmon fishery. The salmon coble has well-rounded bows and very sharply rounded bilges with sides nearly parallel. The freeboard is low, particularly aft, where there is an open space for stowing the nets. These boats are generally tarred outside. They row 4 oars, double-banked.

SALMON GILL NET. Drift gill nets with a length of 150 to 200 fathoms and a meshing of 5¾ in. They are handled from small boats and allowed to drift with the current. They are used in Bristol Bay, Columbia River, Skeena River (B. C.), and other points along the American Pacific coast.

SALMON TAIL. An extension plate added to the trailing edge of the rudder to give increased turning power when navigating in narrow waters, such as the Suez Canal and lower Danube. Also called Danube rudder, Suez rudder.

SALOON DECK. In passenger steamers, the deck where passengers' quarters are situated, in the intermediate type of vessels when there is only one such deck.

Fr: *Pont des Emménagements;* Ger: *Salondeck.*

SALOON STORES. Supplies intended for sale on board the vessel. They are subject to duty and must be entered as merchandise.

SALTER. One of a dressing gang in the cod fisheries, who is stationed in the hold of the vessel. He strews salt on the fish and stows it away after it has been cleaned and dressed by the other men working on deck.

Fr: *Saleur;* Ger: *Einsalzer; Salzer.*

SALT HORSE. Salt beef which in former days was the seamen's staple diet. Also called salt junk.

SALTING. The filling of all open spaces in wooden vessels between frame timbers, from light waterline to plank sheer or clamp, with coarse salt. The moisture acting on the salt enclosed between planking and ceiling causes a sort of brine to flow down over the wood and this pickle acts as a preservative against decay. Classification soc'eties add a period of one to two years to a vessel's class when salted.

Fr: *Salaison;* Ger: *Salzung.*

SALT STOPS. Short pieces of thin plank perforated with 1/16 in. holes, wide enough to reach from the inside of planking to inside of ceiling and long enough to fill the open space between frame timbers. Their purpose is to hold salt placed between the frame timbers. Also called salt ledges.

Fr: *Clef de Sel;* Ger: *Salzpropf.*

See **Salting.**

SALT WATER SOAP. A sodium soap, suitable for sea water, made with coconut oil or palm-kernel oil by the cold or semiboil processes, which is suitable for use with sea water. Also called marine soap.

SALVAGE. The property which has been recovered from a wrecked vessel, or the recovery of the ship herself.

Ger: *Geworbenes Gut.*

See **Civil Salvage, Military Salvage.**

SALVAGE AGREEMENT. An agreement containing the conditions by which the owner or master of a vessel in distress accepts the proposed services of a salvor, in return for remuneration. The agreement should be in writing, signed by both parties, and witnessed. The owner or master of the vessel is under obligation to disclose all important facts which might affect the salvage services.

Fr: *Contrat de Sauvetage;* Ger: *Bergungskontrakt; Hilfslohnvertrag.*

A standard form of agreement is published by the Committee of Lloyds. Under this agreement the salvor agrees to use his best endeavors to salve the vessel, and take her to an agreed place of safety, and to provide all proper mechanical and other assistance and labor. The amount of remuneration in the event of success is definitely fixed, with a proviso that in the event of any objection being afterward raised, or any differences arising between the parties, the matter shall be dealt with by arbitration before the Committee of Lloyds or before an arbitrator appointed by them. Salvage agreements are usually made on the "no-cure—no-pay" basis. Salvors are entitled to make reasonable use of the gear and tackle of the distressed ship.

SALVAGE CLAUSE. A marine insurance policy clause which states the proportion of salvage charges for which underwriters are liable.

See **Towing and Salvage Clause.**

SALVAGE LIEN. A maritime lien which exists when a ship or goods comes into the posession of one who preserves them from

peril at sea. All salvage services carry with them a maritime lien on the things saved.
Fr: *Privilège sur Frais de Sauvetage;* Ger: *Pfandrecht der Bergung.*

SALVAGE LOSS. A loss which it is presumed would, but for certain services rendered, have become a total loss. The charges incurred are "salvage charges." The property salved is the "salvage." When referring to goods a salvage loss is one resulting from shipwreck or from a situation where, by the perils of the sea, the vessel is prevented from proceeding on her voyage and the cargo, or the part that is saved is obliged to be sold at a place short of the port of destination. The term is used in marine insurance when, at a point short of destination, it can be shown that it would cost more to forward damaged goods to their destination than the goods would realize on the spot. The underwriters usually pay the difference between the total insured value and the net proceeds of the goods, such a settlement being known as a "salvage loss."
Ger: *Bergungsverlust.*

SALVAGE SERVICE. A service which saves or helps to save maritime property or lives of persons belonging to any vessel, when in danger either at sea or on the shore of the sea or in tidal waters, if and so far as the rendering of such service is voluntary and attributable neither to legal obligations nor to the interest of self-preservation, nor to the stress of official duty.
Fr: *Sauvetage;* Ger: *Bergung; Schiffsbergung.*

SALVAGE TUG. A seagoing tug which although primarily designed for towage work is also provided with appliances and gear for assisting vessels in an emergency. It differs chiefly from the salvage vessel by its smaller tonnage since it is designed to work at a comparatively short distance from its base. Also called wrecking tug (U. S.).
Fr: *Remorqueur de Sauvetage;* **Ger:** *Rettungsschlepper.*

SALVAGE VESSEL. A vessel of undefined type as to size and build fitted with special equipment for salving stranded vessels and for towing. Salvage vessels are usually converted craft, although some remarkable salvage vessels have been specially built for this work.

Fr: *Bâtiment de Sauvetage;* Ger: *Bergungsschiff; Bergungsfahrzeug.*

It was formerly considered that composite-built hulls were better suited for salvage work than steel hulls, but most modern salvage vessels are built of steel. Besides the usual towing appliances and gear found on board, the salvage vessel is equipped with powerful salvage pumps, both fixed and portable; an air compressor supplying the necessary power to the different pneumatic tools for chipping, drilling, and riveting under water; a self-contained welding and cutting plant; portable motor pumps and electric submersible pumps; (the necessary current for the latter being supplied by a special alternating current generator); a small workshop for emergency jobs; and a number of diving suits and appliances.

SALVAGING. The work of raising, refloating, and recovering sunken ships or cargoes. Also called wrecking (U. S.).

The methods used in salvaging depend principally on the location and depth of water in which the wreck lies. In deep water, wrecks are raised by means of pontoons or by the application of compressed air to expel the water to give the hull sufficient buoyancy to float. For refloating ships stranded on rocks or sand, temporary bottom repairs are made by divers, and portable pumps are used to free the damaged compartments of water, thus enabling the vessel to float on her own bottom.
Davis, R. H., *Deep Diving and Submarine Operations,* London, 1936; Gowan and Hadfield, *Deep Sea Salvage,* London, 1933; Grundt, Lavroff, Nechalew, *Schiffsbergung,* Berlin, 1927; Macfarlane, A. P., "Ship Salvage," Institute of Marine Engineers (London), *Transactions,* vol. 55 (1943); Pilkington, A. R., *Salvage Operations at Sea,* Lloyd's Calendar, London, 1936.

SALVED VALUE. The value on which salvage is awarded. It generally means the value of ship and cargo when they have been brought to a place of safety by the salvors.

SALVOR. One who assists a vessel in distress, acting at the time as a volunteer, and not under any contract or duty which binds him to that particular service. Also called wrecker (U.S.). Members of the crew of a vessel are not entitled to a salvage allowance in salving their own ship. There must be skill and enterprise on the part of the salvor, and the service rendered must be of a dangerous nature to constitute salvage.
Fr.: *Sauveteur;* Ger: *Berger.*

SAMBUK. An Arab sailing vessel from

the Red Sea with low curved quarter galleries, stern windows or counter, rigged with two masts and lateen sails. *Sambuks* are also used in the pearl fisheries of the Persian Gulf with dugout canoes as tenders. A large pearling *sambuk* may have as many as 10 canoes. The largest trading *sambuks* carry about 80 tons. In some boats the stern is raked, in others upright. The stem has a great overhang. The capacity of the average boat ranges from 15 to 50 tons. The larger craft are decked but the smaller boats are usually open amidships. Length over-all 77 ft. Waterline 67.2 ft. Keel 49.2 ft. Breadth 17.7 ft. Depth, molded, 9.1 ft. Sail area 2012 sq. ft. (Typical.)

The masts rake forward. The tack of the main sail is brought to the stemhead. The halyards lead to the taffrails, having a pendant and treble purchase block, which becomes the backstay, to support the mast. This, with three pairs of shrouds, complete the rigging, which is entirely of coir rope.

See **Dhow**.

SAMMA-AMI-BUNE. Japanese fishing sampan of Wakayama district in southern Japan chiefly engaged in the mackerel fisheries with drift nets. Also called *sampa-bune*, *samba bune*. The hull has a pronounced sheer at both ends and the rudder is very long and narrow. There are two masts and the total sail area is about 675 sq. ft. Length, waterline, 35 ft. Breadth 7.5 ft. Depth 3.3 ft. Displacement 10.4 tons. Crew 16 to 18.

SAMPAN. Generic term used in the East Indies, Malaya, China, and Japan to denote a small open boat or skiff. The word "sampan" is said to be a corruption of "shan-pan," which in Chinese means three planks.

The Chinese sampan is a general utility boat used in sheltered waters as passenger ferry, or also for the transportation of goods. The seagoing sampan is used for fishing. It is a flat-bottomed boat, wedge-shaped in plan, of considerable width in proportion to length, with low transom bow and rising transom stern with pronounced rake. The afterend runs out into two upward curving timbers which project well beyond the transom. There is no keel. Rowing sampans are propelled with two short oars handled by one man, the latter facing the bow. The rowlocks consist of pieces of twisted rattan. The Chinese sailing sampan is rigged with one mast and battened lugsail. A daggerboard is provided forward and in conjunction with a deep narrow rudder enables these craft to sail fairly close to the wind. Maximum length about 30 ft. Breadth 8 to 10 ft. at the stern.

The Japanese sampan is of a totally different type. It is built with long raking sharp stem, vertical square stern, and broad flat keel of great thickness. The smaller craft are propelled by a single scull rigged out on the port side near the stern. More sculls are used on both sides as the dimensions increase. Sailing sampans are rigged with one, two, or three masts and square sails. A large number are now fitted with motor and screw propulsion.

In the East Indies the word "sampan" is with few exceptions used to denote a plank-built boat in contrast to the dugout canoe. Some of these are provided with outriggers. In most instances they are rigged with one mast and a four-sided or a triangular sail. Some are steered with a centerline rudder, others by a quarter rudder.

SAMSON KNEE.

See **Bitt Standard**.

SAMSON LINE. Light white line made out of 2 or 3 strands of hemp. Usually manufactured in coils of 30 fathoms.

SAMSON POST. 1. In small craft, a single bitt placed amidships just forward of the mast, to which the anchor cable is made fast.

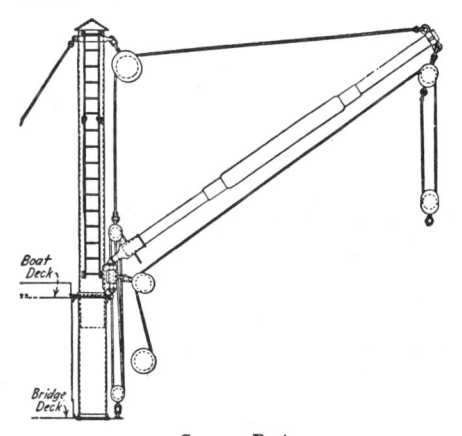

Samson Post

2. A short heavily built tubular mast placed about midway between the centerline and the bulwarks from which a derrick is supported and stayed. It is used for handling light cargo and is nowadays sometimes replaced by electric or hydraulic deck cranes. Also called derrick post, king post.

Fr: *Mât Auxiliaire;* Ger: *Ladebaumpfosten.*

3. A hold stanchion resting on the keelson and supporting a deck beam. (Obsolete.)

SAND. Loose siliceous material consisting of small hard grains resulting from the disintegration of rocks on or near the coastline through the action of the waves.

Fr: *Sable;* Ger: *Sand.*

SANDALE. A coaster of the eastern Mediterranean displacing 15 to 50 tons. Rigged with 2 masts and lateen sails.

SANDBAGGER. A small sloop-rigged centerboard racing boat with enormous sail plan. The type originated about 1850 in western Connecticut ports and New York City. Sand bags were used as movable ballast and were shifted to windward every time the boat came about while tacking. The foot of the jib was laced to a club with fore end swivelled to a gooseneck that slid back and forth on an iron horse fastened to the bowsprit. The hull was built with plumb stem, transom stern and outboard rudder. The type disappeared in 1885 when shifting ballast by deadweight was ruled out. Typical dimensions: Length over-all 18 to 27 ft.; breadth 7 ft. 3 in. to 11 ft.; average depth 2 ft. 2 in.

Chapelle, H. I., History of American Sailing Ships, New York, 1935.

SAND JACK. A rectangular cast-iron box filled with sand, having a side outlet near the bottom, which can be closed with a plug. The box is filled to about 1 in. from the top and placed between the keel and the cribbing and keel blocks, so that when the vessel is ready for launching, it may be lowered onto the cradle by removing the side outlet plug in the jack, allowing the sand to run out.

Fr: *Tin à Sable;* Ger: *Sandtopf.*

SANDOLO. 1. A small boat of Arab origin employed in the sponge fisheries around the Kerkenna Islands on the Tunisian coast. The bottom is flat with negative sheer. At each end is a small keel piece extending about 2 ft. The sharp stern is surmounted by a sort of gallery of typical Arabic design. There is a small deck at each end. The rig is peculiar, consisting of a lug mainsail and Bermuda foresail. The mainmast is stepped at one-third length from the stem. The step is so arranged that the mast can be given three different angles of rake. The only standing rigging consists of the stay, which terminates with a tackle fastened to the stem head. Length over-all 27 ft. Breadth 6.7 ft. Depth 2.5 ft.

2. Small open boat from the Adriatic, with flat bottom, sharp bow, square stern and flaring sides, employed in the Venetian lagoon fisheries and on the Istrian coast. Also called *cio.* Length 22.3 ft. Breadth, at chine, 3 ft.; at gunwale, 4.1 ft. Depth 1.4 ft. It is frequently termed *battana* in Istria.

SAND STRAKE.

See **Garboard Strake.**

SANITARY PASSAGE. A document issued by the harbor sanitary authorities to passengers landing from a vessel suspected of carrying latent germs of a contagious disease, in order that they can be kept under observation by the local health authorities upon reaching their final destination.

SANITARY PUMP. A pump which supplies salt water to the flushing system and to baths, sometimes directly, but more usually into a gravity tank, the overflow of which is carried to the closets and troughs.

Fr: *Pompe Sanitaire;* Ger: *Klosettpumpe; Sanitärpumpe.*

SANITARY TANK. A gravity tank which provides a constant supply of sea water throughout the ship for washrooms, baths, and so on. It is usually placed on top of machinery casing, and is kept full by the sanitary pump.

Fr: *Château d'eau;* Ger: *Spüllwassertank; Hochbehälter; Klosettank.*

SANTA ANA. A hot easterly wind of considerable strength which blows off Santa Barbara Channel and at San Pedro (California).

SAP. The lighter colored portion of timber. As it contains a greater quantity of moisture than heartwood it is more liable to the attacks of disease. In process of time the sapwood becomes heart wood. Sapwood should be removed from all timber to be used in ship or boat construction, as it soon decays.

Fr: *Aubier; Faux-Bois;* Ger: *Splint.*

SAPA. An East Indian type of sailing canoe from Flores and Timor, Lesser Sunda Islands, of which there are several varieties: the *sapa,* the *sapa-bajo,* and the *sapa-sangge,* the last-named being the largest. The hull is of dugout type, to which 3 or 4 strakes of planking are added. The stem is similar to that of the *sope* and is taller than the sternpost.

The stem and stern pieces of the *sapa-sangge* terminate with a scroll. The rig consists of a pole mast stepped in the forepart of the boat, and a boomed spritsail. A quarter rudder is used for steering. Length 14.7 ft. Breadth 2.3 ft. Depth 1.5 ft.

The boats are very seaworthy, and are used for inter-island transportation.

SAPIAOWAN. A dugout with overhanging bow and stern from the Philippine Islands. It is full-bodied above water, flat-bottomed and of U-shape cross section. The *sapiaowan* is propelled by 14 paddlers seated on 7 thwarts, and is chiefly used for fishing with a large seine known as *sapao*, or in coral gathering. The bow and stern are of triangular shape.

SAPIT. A keel-built trading boat of the Samal and Moro people from Tawi-Tawi Islands, Sulu Archipelago. The upper works of the hull are carved and decorated from stem to stern. It is steered with a rudder. The rig is composed of a tripod mast with boomed lugsail and a bowsprit. A *cayang* or canopy made of woven palm leaves serves as shelter for the crew. The *sapit kadiaman* are used by the Bajao people as floating dwellings. Length 19 to 26 ft. Breadth 6½ ft. (approximate).

SAPU. An East Indian dugout canoe. See **Tala.**

SARDARA. Open six-oared seine boat from the east coast of Sicily. Also called *barca i Sardi*. These boats work in pairs and are assisted by a third smaller boat (*lampara*) which carries a light to attract fish when working at night. The *sardara* from the Gulf of Catania is distinguished by the design of the stem, which rises above the gunwale and terminates in a horn-shaped head curving outboard. Length 28½ to 33 ft.

The *sardara* from Syracuse is smaller and does not carry the stemhead ornament found on the boats from the Gulf of Catania. Length 22.9 ft. Breadth 5.9 ft. Depth 2.3 ft. (Average.)

All boats are rigged with a portable mast and lateen sail. A jib is occasionally set.

SARDELLARA. A boat used in the sardine fisheries with driftnets on the Venetian lagoons and adjacent waters. Length 29 to 36 ft. Tonnage 1 to 3. Crew 3 or 4.

SARDINAL. A small half-decked fishing boat found on the Algerian coasts and working with the *lamparo* and sardinal nets. It is rigged with one mast and a lateen sail. Length 26 ft. Breadth 8 ft. 3 in. Depth 2 ft. 4 in. (Typical.)

SARDINIÈRE. General name for different types of open fishing boats used in the sardine fisheries off the coasts of Brittany and the Vendée district south of the Loire Estuary.

They were formerly lug-rigged with 2 or 3 masts. Recently most of the sailing boats have been replaced by decked motor launches and only a few of the original types are still in existence. The sailboats from Brittany differ in hull and rig from the Vendée or southern type. The former have a straight stem with slight rake aft and are rigged with dipping foresail and standing mainsail. The foretack is fastened to the stemhead and there are no headsails. The foresail is frequently a larger sail than the main or after sail. In the boats from Vendée the stem is rounded, with cutaway forefoot. They are rigged with standing foresail and mainsail, reefing bowsprit and jib. Topsails are carried on both masts. A small jiggermast with dipping lug is occasionally seen on this type. Boats from Brittany: Length, over-all, 34 ft. Length, keel, 31 ft. Breadth 10½ ft. Draft aft 5 ft. 2 in. Sail area 800 sq. ft. Boats from Vendée: Length 23 ft. Breadth 8 ft. 3 in. to 9 ft. 2 in. Depth 3 ft. 8 in. to 4 ft. Sail area 750 to 840 sq. ft.

In Brittany the round-stern sardine boats are known as *chaloupes* and those with transom stern as *canots*.

SARDINE LAUNCH. A powered boat used in the sardine fisheries of Monterey Bay (Calif.) and adjacent waters. The wooden hull has a clipper stem, wide flaring gunwales and canoe stern. The deck is slightly cambered. A small hatch forward of the pilot house gives access to the hold but the space below deck is seldom used for stowing fish. The mast is a 4 to 6 ft. pole used only to support an electric light for night work. In traveling to and from the fishing grounds the launch has a lighter in tow. The average length of sardine launches is about 45 ft. with engines ranging from 10 to 50 horsepower.

SARDINE LIGHTER. A seagoing lighter used in the sardine fisheries on the coast of California for transporting the catch from the fishing grounds to the cannery. It has no means of propulsion and is towed by a sardine launch. The capacity of these lighters ranges from 12 to 60 tons. Some are round-bottom, others flat-bottom craft. Most of the deck space is taken by a hatchway leaving only narrow waterways at sides. Nearly all are square-sterned.

SARGASSO. A floating mass of seaweed, especially the gulf weeds, which are so common in the warm portions of the Atlantic Ocean.

Fr: *Sargasse;* Ger: *Sargassokraut.*

SARGASSO SEA. The area of water in the South Atlantic which lies eastward of the Bahama Islands between Latitude 25° and 30° North and Longitude 38° and 60° West and where large quantities of seaweed float on the surface.

Fr: *Mer des Sargasses;* Ger: *Sargasso Meer.*

SARY. Open boat employed on the lagoons and estuaries of the southeast coast of Madagascar. It is built of planks carefully fitted together with rising ends like a whaleboat. It is about 30 ft. long, with 8-ft. beam. No nail or other metal fastening is used in its construction. The planks are tied together with twisted cords of a palm fiber called *anivona.* There is no framework to which the planking is fixed, but the thwarts act as stiffeners of the fabric, passing right through the sides. Strips of bamboo are used to calk the seams, and loops of the same material are used for the rowlocks.

SASH. One of the hinged flaps forming the top of a skylight. Also called skylight sash.

Fr: *Battant de Claire Voie;* Ger: *Oberlicht Flügel.*

See **Port Sash.**

SAUCER. 1. An iron concave-shaped socket let into the step of a capstan, on which the spindle turns.

Fr: *Saucier;* Ger: *Pfanne; Spillspur.*

2. One of the metal steps bolted to the afterside of a wooden rudderpost under a brace, so that the plug of the pintle will rest on it and keep the pintle straps from coming in contact with the braces, thereby reducing rudder-turning friction. (Obsolete.)

Fr: *Grain.*

SAUGE. A small open boat used in the western Mediterranean for fishing. Lateen rig.

SAUTERELLIER. A small open boat used for shrimping with a trawl net in the district of St. Valéry sur Somme, Normandy. Length 19½ ft. Breadth 9¼ ft. Draft 3 ft.

SAVE ALL. A small receptacle made of thin copper or galvanized sheet iron, fitted under a sidelight to collect water. Its width is about 2 in., depth 1 in. The moisture collected is periodically sponged out by hand. In some cases a small pipe is fitted to carry away the drippings. Also called drip pan.

See **Water Sail.**

SAVEIRO. A rocker-bottomed open rowing boat with very high pointed stem and stern, used on the coasts of Portugal in the sardine fisheries for hauling seine nets on the beach. These boats are found from the estuary of the river Douro as far south as Cape Sines. They are of box-shaped cross section and are fitted with iron knees and rubbing pieces at the extremities and bilges. They vary in length from 20 to 30 ft. A simple sail is occasionally set but they are usually propelled by long sweeps. On the coast of the State of Bahia, Brazil, the term *saveiro* is used to denote various small trading or fishing craft with 1 or 2 masts. The *saveiro de carga* has a rig similar to that of a 2-masted *lancha* with square foresail and loose-footed gaff mainsail, both masts having same step piece. The *saveiro de caes* of the State of Bahia is rigged with a single lateen sail and has a capacity of 20 to 25 tons.

SAWED FRAME. Wooden frame sawed in a natural crook shape as nearly as possible to the designed contour. Also called cut frame. Each frame is usually double and is built up of several short lengths. The usual practice is to use sawed frames for boats which have a waterline length over 40 ft. A combination of bent and sawed frames is occasionally used in the building of hulls with a length ranging from 25 to 40 ft., every alternate or every third frame being sawed timber.

Natural crooked timber being obtained with difficulty, straight grained material is usually used. It is inferior to natural crooks for strength.

Fr: *Membrure Chantournée;* Ger: *Geschnittenes Spant.*

As the frame curvature must be considered, the several lengths that compose the frame must be cut and secured in such a manner that short grain, which cannot entirely be avoided at the ends of each piece, will not weaken the frame when assembled. Accordingly, it is customary to make each frame double, two sets of pieces being fastened side by side, with the short-grain portion of one alongside the long grain of an adjacent one, thus making the frame of equal strength from end to end.

SAYEH. Small Arab vessel of *sambuk* type, much used for pearling at Kuwait in the Persian Gulf. Also called *say, shewe.* Its displacement rarely exceeds 15 tons. See **Sambuk.**

SCAFFA. A Scottish herring boat similar in hull form to the *Zulu,* except for the stem, which was built with a rounded forefoot instead of the square, vertical *Zulu* stem. Most of these boats were clinker-built. They came from Moray Firth ports. Now extinct.

SCAFFIE YAWL. A small one-masted boat originating at Portknockie, Scotland, and built on the lines of a *scaffa* with round stem and raking sternpost. The rig consists of a dipping lugsail cut comparatively short in the foot, and a jib set on a long bowsprit. Length over-all 25.5 ft. Breadth 8.5 ft. Depth, inside, 3.6 ft.

SCAITH. An open herring boat originating from Banff, Scotland. It was rigged with 3 masts and lugsails. Spar bowlines were used to keep the luffs of the sails to windward. Length 41 ft. Breadth 13 ft. Depth of hold 4 ft. 9 in. Now extinct.

SCALE DISCHARGE (G. B.). In chartering, the conditions under which the discharging of bulk cargo is to be effected as stipulated in the charter party. The scale may, for instance, range from 600 tons per day at 6½ pence to 3000 tons per day at 1 shilling and 8 pence. Scale discharge is usually at the option of the receiver who must declare in writing before breaking bulk which option he intends to use.

SCALE EFFECT. A term used in model basin work to denote the variation between ship and model performance, due to differences in absolute size, to nonsimilarity of water flow, or to causes arising from lack of proper application of the theory of similitude governing the action of geometrically similar bodies.

SCAN. A term used in radar to denote the automatic and continuous exploration through 360 degrees of azimuth by the continuous variation of the direction of pulses of radio-frequency energy.

SCANDALIZE. To leave a sail partially set. To reduce sail in an unusual manner, as, for instance, to lower the peak of a gaff sail without touching the throat halyards, or, also, to trice up the tack and lower the peak until the gaff is perpendicular to the mast. To tie down the luff and leech of a jib-headed sail without reefing otherwise. To lower a square topsail and haul out the reef tackle without slacking the sheets or tying reef points. To hoist or trice the tack and clew of a fisherman's staysail.

Fr: *Arriser.*

SCANFIN. Code name for the British Chamber of Shipping and Timber Trade Federation Wood Charter (1899) from Scandinavian countries and Finland to the United Kingdom. A new form came into force in 1924.

SCANNING AERIAL. A rotating radar of the flat parabolic type, normally mounted on the roof of the wheelhouse or other superstructure, above and as close as practical over the transmit-receive unit. The signals received by the aerial are transmitted back to the transmit-receive unit through the wave guide run.

SCANT. The handling of a vessel under sail when obliged to head as closely to the wind as possible to make a port or any other desired point.

Fr: *Chicaner;* Ger: *Schrallen.*

SCANTLINGS. 1. The dimensions of all structural parts such as frames, girders, plating used in building a vessel. The various classification societies publish rules giving the scantlings to which the builders must adhere.

Fr: *Énchantillons;* Ger: *Materialstärken; Verbandstärken.*

Foster King, J., "Scantling Developments in Iron and Steel Ships," *Engineering* (London), vol. 120 (September, 1925).

2. In the timber trade, pieces of softwood measuring 2, 2½, 3 in. in thickness, with a width ranging from 3 to 5½ in. In wooden shipbuilding, converted timber under 5 in. sq.

SCANT WIND. A wind which compels a vessel under sail to head as closely to the wind as she can in order to make the desired course. Also called scrimp wind.

Fr: *Vent en Pointe;* Ger: *Knapper Wind; Schraler Wind.*

SCARF. 1. A joint by which the ends of two structural pieces of timber or metal are united so as to form a continuous piece. Also called scarph (G. B.). A lapped joint made by beveling off, notching or otherwise cutting away the sides of two timbers at ends, and bolting, riveting, or strapping them together so as to form one continuous piece without increase in sectional area at the joint.

Fr: *Ecart;* Ger: *Laschung; Lasch.*

See Box Scarf, Coated Scarf, Edge Scarf, Flat Scarf, Half and Half Lap Scarf, Hook Scarf, Key Scarf, Locked Scarf, Plain Scarf, Tabled Scarf, V Scarf.

2. In whaling, the line or score around a whale made by the spades in cutting-in. It is the dividing line between two blankets.

SCARF (to). To join the ends of two timbers or metal parts so as to form a continuous piece in appearance. The joining of wood or metal by sloping off the edges and maintaining the same cross section throughout the joint. In Great Britain, scarph.

Fr: *Ecarver;* Ger: *Laschen; Verlaschen.*

SCARF CLOUD. A name sometimes given to a cirrus cloud surmounting cumulo-nimbus clouds.

SCARF NIB.
See Lip.

SCARF TACK. A small copper nail used in boatbuilding for a variety of purposes. The smallest are used for securing leather on oars, tacking down canvas, small beadings and so on. The larger sizes as used for plank scarfs are through fastened and secured by clenching.

SCEND. The amplitude of the vertical motion of a ship due to the range of the waves.

Fr: *Levée;* Ger: *Aufsteigung.*

SCEND (to). To lift or heave upward in a seaway.

SCEVO. See Palischermo.

SCHALUPPE. 1. A fishing boat from Pomerania and Rügen Island in the Baltic with tonnage ranging from 12 to 85. The hull has less sheer than the *Jacht* and has a flat V-transom stern. It is rigged with a long headed gaff mainsail, above which a gaff topsail is set on a tall fidded topmast. The largest boats also carry a square topsail and topgallant sail set flying. There is a bowsprit with jibboom and 3 headsails. When rigged with yards it is called *Raaschaluppe.*

2. On the North Sea coast of Germany (Heligoland, etc.) an open or half-decked flat-bottomed fishing boat of about 30 to 32 ft. length and 9 ft. beam. It is rigged with one mast sprit mainsail, forestaysail, and jib. On the eastern Frisian coast the *Schaluppe* is decked fore and aft and is ketch-rigged with loose-footed gaff mainsail. Length about 40 ft. Breadth 11½ to 16½ ft.

SCHEERBOOT. A small centerboard-sailing-boat employed in the shallow water fisheries on the Pomeranian coast (Baltic Sea) with round bottom, short flat keel, and good sheer. It has a sharp raking stern, rounded stem, and flush deck. The hull is divided into 4 compartments. The cabin extends from stem to mast. Next is the centerboard trunk with ballast stowed on each side. The fish well forms the third compartment. The stern space is used for gear and nets and is provided with a steersman's cockpit. The rig is that of a cutter with tall pole mast stepped about 5 ft. forward of half-length. The sails include a jib, set flying, a stay foresail, a gaff mainsail with long head and short foot, its luff laced to the mast. There is no boom. The topsail has an unusually long yard. Length over-all 38 ft. Length of keel 28.2 ft. Breadth 12 ft. Depth 4.4 ft. (Typical.)

SCHIFAZZO. A lateen-rigged Sicilian coaster with 1 or 2 masts and displacement ranging between 15 and 35 tons, used for sponge fishing and small coasting trade in the Mediterranean. It has a round stem and stern post, the length varies from 30 to 50 ft., the beam being about one third of the length. It is built with a large sheer and a pronounced camber to the deck. Swifters are used as shrouds for holding the masts. The bowsprit, which is fairly long, has no steeve.

SCHILETTO.
See Bragozzo.

SCHITIKI. A Siberian dugout with sides raised by planks fastened by wattling of willow twigs and calked with moss. It is about 30 ft. long, 12 ft. wide and carries a sail and rigging made of elk leather.

SCHLOOPKA. An open Black Sea fishing boat strongly built with strong sheer, a large flare forward, and a graceful run to a high transom. The frames are so close together that bottom boards are seldom used.

SCHNIGGE. Fishing or trading boat of Frisian origin found on the German North Sea coasts. Also called *Snik.* It is decked, flat-bottomed, and fitted with leeboards. The hull is similar to that of a Galeass but with fuller buttocks and carries fore-and-aft rig with one or two pole masts, a standing bowsprit, and three headsails. Trading boats of this type are nearly extinct. Length 50 to 56 ft. Hold depth 4 to 5 ft. 8 in. Breadth 14 to 16 ft. Gross tonnage 15 to 40 (average).

SCHOKKER. Small, flat-bottomed Dutch boat originating from the island of Schokland. It is fitted with leeboards and a straight stem raked at an angle of about 60° to the waterline. The hull is carvel-planked, with a half deck forward. The stern post is well-raked and the shape of the stern is similar to that of a *hoogaars*. The rig includes a gaff mainsail, a small mizzen, a staysail and a jib. *Schokkers* are mostly used for dip-net fishing or as pleasure craft on the Zuider Zee waters. The stem is a straight beam, cut off square at the upper end. This upper end carries on one side a second narrower beam, and the anchor, which usually consists of a grapnel, is carried between the two. Length 42 ft. Breadth 14 ft.

SCHOLBOOT. Name given by Dutch fishermen to small flush deck North Sea steam trawler of about 150 tons, 200 horsepower and a length from 90 to 100 ft., employed in the offshore plaice fisheries.

SCHONERGALEASSE. A sailing coaster from Germany and the Scandinavian countries with a tonnage ranging from 60 to about 250. It has the hull form of the *Galeass* and is rigged as a fore-and-aft 2-masted schooner.

SCHONERGALIOT. Sailing coaster with a tonnage ranging from 95 to 270, found in the Dutch and German coastal waters. It has the rig of a fore-and-aft schooner and the hull form of a *galiot*. Now extinct.

SCHONERKUFF. Sailing coaster from Germany and the northern Holland area rigged as a 2-masted fore-and-aft schooner with the hull form of the *kuff*. Tonnage 68 to 210. Probably extinct.

SCHOOL FISH. Term used in the trawlline cod fisheries to distinguish the fish moving over the bottom in large schools seeking fresh feeding grounds from the so-called gurry fish, which are the few straggler fish which remain on the banks after the larger schools have migrated.

SCHOONER. A fore-and-aft rigged vessel with 2 to 6 masts, common in the coasting and fishing trades. Also called fore-and-aft schooner. In schooners rigged with 3 or

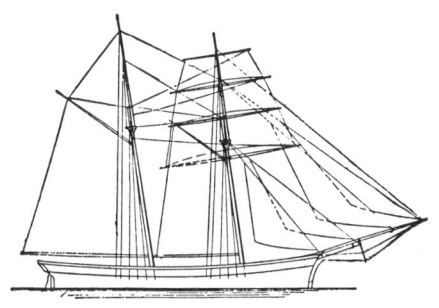

Topsail Schooner

more masts the spars and rigging are of uniform dimensions and scantlings for all masts, with the exception of the main boom on the aftermast, which is heavier and longer than the others. In European waters large trading schooners have not found favor, the bark-rig being preferred for coasting and foreign trades when more than 3 masts are carried. In the United States, 5- and 6-masted schooners have been built for the timber trade on the Pacific coast and the coal trade between Atlantic ports.

Fr: *Goëlette franche; Goëlette Latine;* Ger: *Gaffelschoner; Vor und Achter Schoner; Jacht Schoner.*

See **Bald-Headed Schooner, Bermuda Schooner, Cat Schooner, Five-Masted Topsail Schooner, Hermaphrodite Schooner, Main Topsail Schooner, Oyster Schooner, Ram Schooner, Scow Schooner, Square Topsail Schooner, Staysail Schooner, Steam Schooner, Syrian Schooner, Tern Schooner.**

If compared with the square rig, the fore-and-aft schooner has the advantage of being a better craft when sailing close-hauled and requiring a smaller crew than square-rigged vessels of the same tonnage. The first 4-masted schooner (William L. White), was built in 1880, the first 5-masted schooner (Governor Ames) in 1888, and the first 6-masted schooner (George W. Wells) in 1900. One 7-masted schooner, the "Thomas W. Lawson," built in 1902, was the only boat with more than 6 masts. In Nova Scotia inshore fishermen use schooner-rigged open boats about twenty feet in length which are probably the smallest craft with this rig.

Chapelle, H. I., *The History of American Sailing Ships*, New York, 1935; Church, A. C., "The Evolution of the Fishing Schooner," *Atlantic Fisherman*, New York, vol. 6, October, 1925.

SCHOONER BARGE. A type of seagoing barge found on the Atlantic coast of the United States, usually towed, but fitted with short masts and sails so that it is not entirely helpless if it breaks away from the tug. Schooner barges are towed singly or in fleets of two or three. Some of them have a deadweight capacity of over 3000 tons.

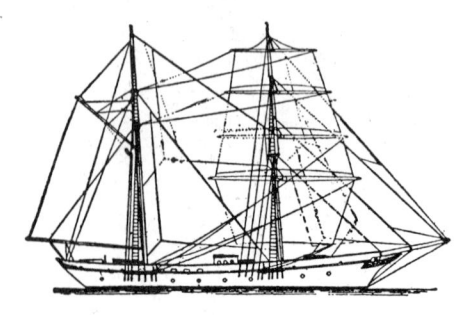

Schooner Brig

SCHOONER BRIG. A two-masted vessel with square-rigged foremast and fore-and-aft rigged mainmast. The term hermaphrodite brig has been used by the leading American writers to describe this rig. Half brig is a common New England term for the same rig. Most American brigs since 1860 have been actually hermaphrodite brigs, although that term was not used in the official records.

Fr: *Brick-Goëlette;* Ger: *Schonerbrigg; Mufferdeibrigg; Briggschoner.*

SCHOONER-BRIGANTINE. A two masted sailing vessel with unorthodox rig. The foremast consists of a lower mast and topmast on which are crossed double topsails and a single topgallant. There is no sail below the fore yard. Between the masts, instead of the usual gaff-foresail, there is a range of staysails.

SCHOONER KETCH. A name sometimes given in America to a 3-masted schooner in which the mizzenmast is shorter than the mainmast.

SCHOONER RIG. A fore-and-aft rig with 2 to 6 masts, used for merchant vessels, fishing craft and yachts. It is safer and handier than the cutter or sloop rigs when the tonnage rises above 60 or 80, as it is lighter and capable of easier handling in a seaway. The 2-masted schooner rig is generally considered more suitable for hulls with an over-all length ranging from 36 to 130 ft., and the 3-masted rig for hull lengths between 70 and 150 ft.

Fr: *Gréement de Goëlette;* Ger: *Schonerzeug.*

SCHOONER STAY (U. S.). The whip rigged between the heads of two derricks when they are topped for working cargo.

SCHOONER YAWL. Two-masted schooner in which the main boom is cut short to avoid its reefing dangers and difficulty of handling. This is compensated by a small jiggermast and sail to restore the area and balance of sail plan.

Fr: *Yawl Goëlette;* Ger: *Schoner Yawl.*

SCHOUW. In Holland, a class of flat-bottomed open or partly-decked craft with hull of prismatic cross section, pram-shaped bows, and flat or round stern. Also called schuyt. It is a handy and comparatively fast type of boat of simple construction, owing to the flat surfaces of contour. The rig consists of a loose-footed gaff mainsail and jib-headed foresail. The seagoing fishing *schouw* has a bowsprit and jib. A fish-well is provided. Large leeboards are carried. Their length ranges from 18 ft. to 37 ft. In recent times these boats have been replaced by the *hoogaars* type.

SCHUTE. In Germany, a small sailing boat from the Frisian Islands. The hull is built with sharp ends, flat bottom and otherwise similar to the *Mutte.* Tonnage 10.

See **Scow, Segelschute.**

SCHUYT. See **Schouw.**

SCINTILLATING LIGHT. A fixed light with very rapid flashes.

Fr: *Feu Scintillant;* Ger: *Flinkerndes Feuer.*

SCINTILLATION. The more or less rapid change of apparent brightness of a star sometimes accompanied by color changes. It is due to minor changes in the refractive power of the atmosphere, and is always greatest towards the horizon and least in the zenith. Also called **Twinkling.**

Fr: *Scintillement;* Ger: *Funkenspruhen.*

SCOFF. A slang term meaning to eat.

SCOOP. 1. See **Baler.**
2. See **Dip Net.**

SCOPE. The length of cable measured from hawsepipe to anchor, by which a ship rides. Also called riding scope.

Fr: *Touée;* Ger: *Ausgesteckte Kettenlänge.*

SCORE. The groove made in the cheeks of a wooden block for receiving the strap. A block may be single or double-scored.
Fr: *Engoujure; Goujure;* Ger: *Kerbe; Blockkeepe.*
See **Pintle Score**.

SCOTCH BOILER. See **Firetube Boiler**.

SCOTCHMAN. Iron or wooden batten fastened to the standing rigging to prevent chafing.
Fr: *Pare-Manoeuvre;* Ger: *Schottmann; Schamfielungslatte.*

SCOTTISH-CUT SAIL. A diagonally cut jib-headed sail in which the cloths at the head run parallel to the leech and those at the foot parallel to the foot, both sections joining at the last. In this cut the sail is fitted with a hemp luff rope. It is a strong cut for storm jibs, trysails, or raffees and is in general use for all headsails of trading vessels.

SCOTTISH RIG. Term applied to the rigs of 4-masted barks. The barks carrying single topgallant sails and a fidded jigger topmast were known as "English-rigged," those with double topgallant sails and pole jiggermast as "Scottish-rigged."

SCOURING. A method used for refloating stranded vessels by which the power of flowing water to scour sand, mud or gravel, is used to scour out such materials from under the bottom of a stranded vessel, so that it can sink to the draft required for floatation.
Fr: *Affouillement;* Ger: *Auschwemmung.*

SCOURING BASIN. A basin in which a quantity of water is impounded during the flood tide and the contents retained until a suitable time, about low water, when the gates are opened again and a volume of water is let out to maintain desired depth of entrance channel by scouring the bottom. Also called sluicing pond.
Fr: *Bassin de Chasse;* Ger: *Spülbecken.*

SCOW. A flat-bottomed boat with sloping ends. The bow and stern are square across instead of coming to a point. Some have the same width fore and aft while others narrow slightly toward the ends. As a general service boat it is easy to build, easy to beach, very stable, and of great carrying capacity. Variations of the type are known as John boat, batteau, punt, beach skiff, pram, square-ender. Large sizes are used for commercial purposes as lighters or as houseboats. A scow is held to be a vessel for the purpose of Admiralty jurisdiction. The fact that pile-driving machinery or a derrick is installed upon these craft does not affect the principle.
Fr: *Gabarre; Chatte;* Ger: *Lichterschiff; Punte; Schute.*

See **Bilge Board Scow, Deck Scow, Garbage Scow, New Zealand Scow, Oyster Scow, Tray**.

The word scow as used in the Atlantic coast ports of the United States refers to harbor craft with decked ends in which the load is carried in an open hold as distinguished from the *lighter* which has the entire load placed above deck.

SCOWING. A procedure used by small boats when anchoring on ground suspected to be foul. The cable is unshackled from the ring and the end made fast round the shank and flukes of the anchor with a clove hitch, and stoppered with spun yarn at the crown. When the cable is hauled upon the stop breaks, and the fluke can then readily be lifted out of its bed.

See **Becuing**.

SCOW SCHOONER. A 2-masted schooner with punt-shaped hull, false cutwater, and centerboard, used as market boat or lighter in San Francisco Bay. Most of the boats have nowadays been provided with motors and their rig has been removed. Length over-all 69 ft. Tonnage length 63.5 ft. Breadth 23 ft. 8 in. Depth of hold 5 ft. 5 in. (Typical.)

SCOW SLOOP. A sloop-rigged sailing barge formerly used in the stone, firewood, and ice trades in New England coastal waters and rivers, as well as on Chesapeake Bay and tributaries from the Susquehanna River to Baltimore. The hull was punt-shaped and wall-sided. Some carried one leeboard on the port side. Others had two leeboards or a centerboard. Length over-all 60 ft. 3 in.; breadth 14½ ft.; depth 4 ft. 4 in.; sail area (jib and mainsail) **1717** sq. ft. (Typical.)

SCRAPE. A fishing implement used in Chesapeake Bay for catching soft crabs. It consists essentially of a triangular iron frame with a base varying in width from 2 to 5 ft. A cotton mesh bag is attached to the upper side and extends about 6 ft. behind the scrape. It is dragged by a rope fastened to the apex. Each scrape boat operates with two scrapes; one on each side.

Clock

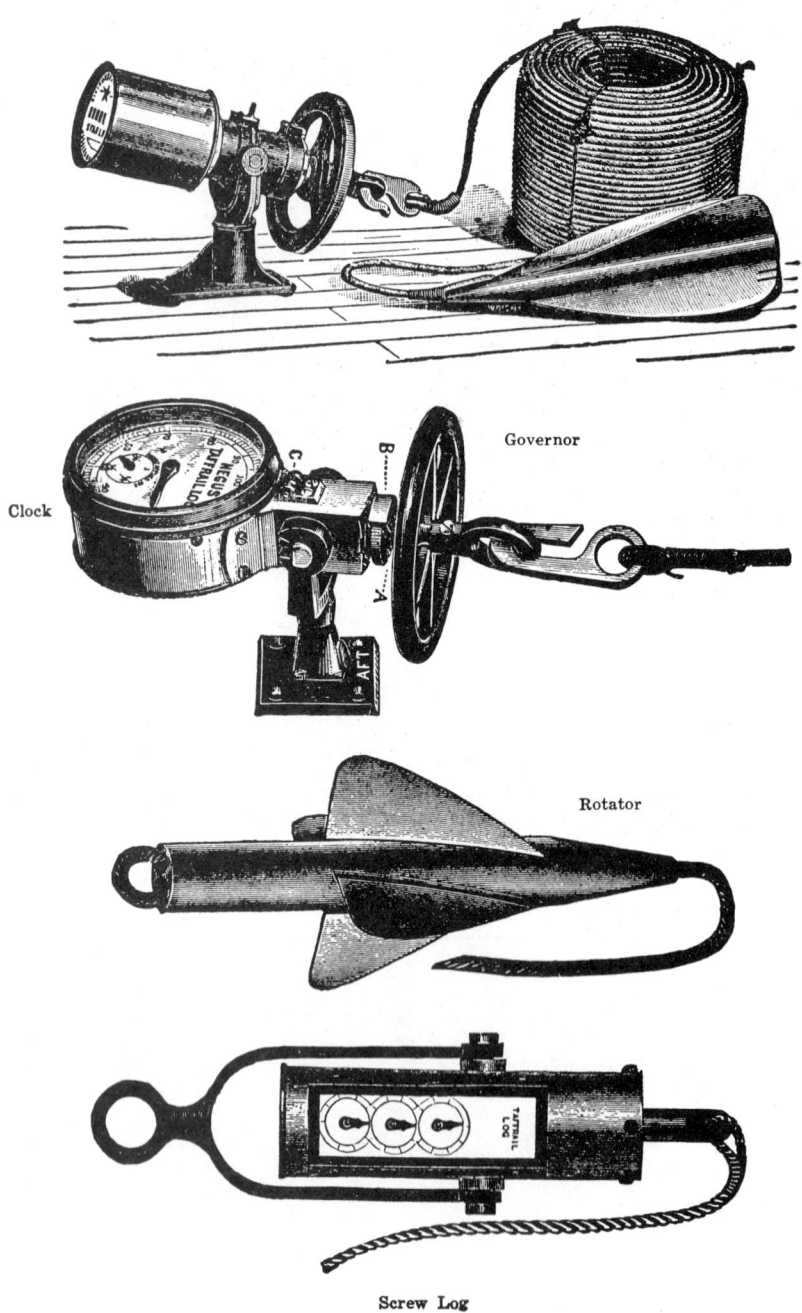

Governor

Rotator

Screw Log

SCRAPE BOAT. Small sailing boat from Chesapeake Bay, employed for catching crabs with an apparatus called "scrape." It is a broad, square-sterned craft with short deck forward. The waterways and coaming on each side extend right aft to the transom. The rig consists of a mast stepped in the bow with leg-of-mutton mainsail and jib foresail which tacks down to a short bowsprit.

SCRAPER. A sharp-edged steel implement used for scraping paint work, decks, cleaning ship's bottom and so on. Some scrapers have both ends flat tapered with one end bent at right angles. Others consist of a triangular metal blade with sharp edges, attached to a wooden handle.

Fr: *Gratte;* Ger: *Schrabber.*

SCREEN BULKHEAD. A light bulkhead made of plain or corrugated sheet iron or wood frequently fitted in cargo vessels as a partition between boiler and engine rooms. It is dust-tight only.

Fr: *Cloison-Écran;* Ger: *Schutzschott.*

SCREEN DOOR. A wooden door frame over which single or double wire mesh is stretched.

SCREW ANCHOR.
See **Mooring Screw.**

SCREW BOLT. A bolt with one end threaded. Also called nut bolt. For most purposes galvanized iron screw bolts are preferred in shipbuilding to clinch bolts. They can be drawn up tighter and are stronger. It is usual to burr the head over after tightening up.

Fr: *Cheville à Écrou;* Ger: *Schraubbolzen.*

SCREW CONTROLLER. A cable controller in which two hinged claws are brought together by a screw spindle with crank handle and are thus made to exert sufficient pressure sideways to prevent the cable from running out. Also called screw stopper.

Fr: *Stoppeur à Vis;* Ger: *Reibungstopper; Friktionstopper.*

SCREW CURRENT. The column of water projected by the motion of a screw propeller. When the propeller turns in its ahead direction this current comes from forward and is discharged aft. When the propeller is backing the current comes from aft and is discharged forward.

The screw current may be subdivided into two components, i.e.: the suction screw current which is that portion of the screw current moving into the propeller disc; and the discharge screw current which is that portion being driven out from the propeller.

Fr: *Sillage;* Ger: *Propellerabstrom.*

SCREW GAMMONING. Chain or plate used as gammoning and tightened up by means of screws and nuts.

Fr: *Liure à Tendeurs;* Ger: *Schraubzurring; Bugsprietbügel.*

SCREWING LIGHTER. A dumb lighter used for driving screw anchors in the bottom of a harbor or roadstead when installing permanent moorings. It is built with a well in the center and is provided with sheer legs and a heavy hand-capstan for handling mooring screws. Length 68 ft. Breadth 31 ft. Depth 6½ ft. (Average.)

SCREW LOG. An instrument automatically registering the distance traveled by a vessel. Also called patent log, mechanical log, speedometer, towing log. It generally consists of a rotator or torpedo-shaped brass body with projecting fins called the screw, which is towed astern at the end of a log line 200 to 600 ft. in length, the forward motion of the ship causing it to rotate with a velocity which varies directly with the speed of the vessel. Through a series of gears, dials are made to register the distance corresponding to the revolutions of the screw. In ships over 400 ft. in length the log may be streamed from a 25- to 35-ft. boom hinged under the forepart of the bridge.

Fr: *Loch Enregistreur;* Ger: *Patentlog.*

SCREW MOORINGS. A type of mooring employed in harbors with soft, muddy bottoms, and in which anchors are replaced by mooring screws.

See **Mooring Screw.**

SCREW SHACKLE. A shackle with threaded pin.

Fr: *Manille à axe vissé;* Ger: *Schraubenschackel.*

SCREW STEERING GEAR. Hand- or power-operated, direct-connected type of steering gear consisting of a shaft provided with left and right hand threads carrying heavy sleeve nuts which travel on the screw shaft. The nuts are connected to the rudder crosshead and travel in opposite directions, the rotation of the shaft causing the rudder to swing. Screw gears are hand, steam, or electrically operated and are found in smaller craft as well as in vessels of moderate tonnage.

    Fr: *Appareil à Gouverner à Vis;* Ger: *Schraubenspindel-Steuervorrichtung.*

timber bolted to the knee of the head under the bowsprit in place of a figurehead. Also called scroll head. It is finished off by a volute turning outward.

    Fr: *Volute;* Ger: *Krulle.*

SCUD. Loose, vapory fragments of clouds

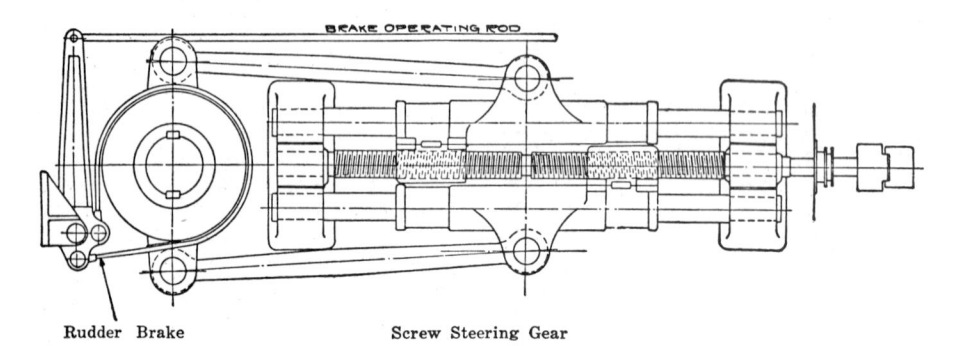

Rudder Brake   Screw Steering Gear

SCRIBE. To mark one timber off against another, so that when the first timber is cut to the marks it will fit the other.

    Fr: *Triquer;* Ger: *Schreiben.*

SCRIBER. A sharp tool used by loftsmen for marking ship's lines on the mold loft floor. Also called scriving knife, razing knife.

    Fr: *Pointe à tracer;* Ger: *Reissahle.*

SCRIBNER·DOYLE. A method used by shippers for measuring mahogany logs on the West African coast.

SCRIMSHAW. Artistic work, consisting chiefly of carving and etching in jaw bones or teeth of whales and sharks, formerly done by whalemen.

SCRIVE BOARD. An auxiliary mold loft floor placed conveniently near the frame bending slabs on which the full-sized body plan of a ship is drawn, the lines being cut into the surface of the wood by means of a sharp tool called scriving knife. For convenience in copying the lines it is usually made so that it can be divided into portable parts and taken to the mold loft to have the lines copied on it, and then transported to its proper position and put together again. It is used as a ready reference for the bending of frames, floors, and so on, or to take dimensions from. It gives complete information as to the shape and dimensions of every part of each transverse frame.

    Fr: *Panneau de Tracé;* Ger: *Spantenplan.*

SCROLL. A curved piece of ornamented

drifting rapidly under rain clouds. Meteorological name "Fracto-Stratus."

    Fr: *Diablotin;* Ger: *Leichtes Dunstgewölk.*

See **Fracto-Nimbus.**

SCUD (to). To run before a gale under enough canvas to keep the vessel ahead of the sea without being pooped.

    Fr: *Fuir;* Ger: *Lenssen; Lenzen.*

SCUDER. On a North Sea herring drifter, one of the crew who assists the mate in scuding the fish and hauling the warp up from below. Also called net rope scuder.

SCULL. 1. A short oar of such length that a pair of them (one on each side) can be managed by a single rower sitting in the middle of the boat.

    Fr: *Aviron de couple;* Ger: *Skull.*

2. An oar used to propel a boat by working it from side to side over the stern, the blade, which is always kept in the water, being turned diagonally at each stroke.

    Fr: *Godille;* Ger: *Wrickriem; Wriggruder.*

3. The act of rowing with short oars named sculls. Both oars are managed by a single rower.

    Fr: *Nage de marinier;* Ger: *Skullen.*

4. To work an oar over the stern of a boat, giving the oar a figure-of-eight motion so as to drive the boat ahead. It is in effect the half stroke of the screw rapidly reversed.

Fr: *Godiller;* Ger: *Wricken.*

SCULLING NOTCH. A half-round notch cut out in the top of the transom of a boat to support a sculling or steering oar. Also called stern notch.

SCUNNER. Lookout man stationed in the foretop of a sealing vessel, whence he directs the course of the vessel so far as its movements through the ice are concerned; avoiding the heavy pans and wheeling aside the lighter ones. A barrel-man is stationed above the scunner.

SCUPPER. One of the drains set in decks to carry off accumulation of rain or sea water. Also called deck drain. The scuppers are placed in the gutters of waterways on open decks and in the corners of enclosed decks, and connect to pipes which eventually lead overboard.

Fr: *Dalot;* Ger: *Speigat.*

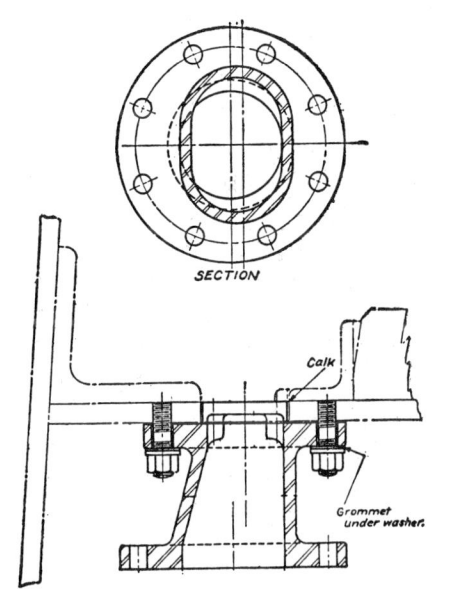

Deck Scupper. (*American Marine Standard*)

American Marine Standards Committee, Standard 48, *Scupper Valves*, Washington, 1928; American Marine Standards Committee, Standard 56, *Ship Scuppers and Drains*, Washington, 1929.

SCUPPER HOLE. A drain hole cut through the gunwale angle bar and adjoining shell plate to allow water to run directly overboard from the gutter or waterway.

Fr: *Dalot;* Ger: *Speigat.*

SCUPPER HOSE. A canvas hose temporarily attached to the outside of a scupper hole and reaching to the water level, to conduct the water clear of the ship's side.

SCUPPER NAIL. A short nail with very broad head used for nailing tarpaulin leather flaps, or scuppers, and so forth, on wooden vessels.

Fr: *Clou à Maugère;* Ger: *Persenning Nagel.*

SCUPPER PIPE. One of the pipes by which the water from a deck scupper is drained by gravity to the bilges or over the ship's side. Those in the weather portions of the decks are led overboard. Those in fully enclosed superstructures on the freeboard deck and on decks below the freeboard or bulkhead deck are led to the bilges. They may also be led overboard if fitted with nonreturn valves as required for the sanitary discharges.

Fr: *Conduit de Dalot; Tuyau d'Orgue;* Ger: *Speigatrohr; Abfallrohr.*

SCUPPER VALVE.
See **Storm Valve.**

SCUTTLE. A small opening of square, circular, or elliptical shape cut through a hatch deck or bulkhead to provide access or for the stowage of fuel, water, small stores, and so on. A similar hole in the side or bottom of a ship. The cover for such an opening.

Fr: *Bouchon; Ecoutillon;* Ger: *Springluke; Schuttloch.*

See **Bunker Scuttle, Cap Scuttle, Gammoning Scuttle.**

American Marine Standards Committee, Standard 90, *Watertight Deck Scuttles*, Washington, 1933.

SCUTTLE (to). To intentionally sink a ship by opening the seacocks or by cutting holes through the ship's bottom or sides.

Fr: *Saborder;* Ger: *Anbohren.*

SCUTTLE BUTT. 1. A drinking fountain or faucet aboardship. Name formerly applied to a large cask or butt carried on deck and containing drinking water for the use of the crew. In modern vessels, a steel tank with a capacity proportionate to the crew, well insulated, and fitted with a drip pan and faucets. In some ships the scuttle butt is provided with cooling coils connected to the refrigerating system.

Fr: *Charnier;* Ger: *Trinkwassertonne; Wasserfass.*

2. A sailor's slang for rumors.

SCUTTLE HATCH, SCUTTLE HATCH COVER. A metal cover used for closing a scuttle.
  Fr: *Ecoutillon;* Ger: *Deckloch; Kistluke.*

SEA. The waves, spoken of collectively and prevailing at the time spoken of. Waves caused by the wind actually blowing at the time of observation. Waves set up by wind prevailing at the place and time of observation.
  Fr: *Mer;* Ger: *See; Meer.*
  See **Beam Sea, Choppy Sea, Confused Sea, Crossed Sea, Following Sea, Head Sea, Heavy Sea, High Sea, Hollow Sea, Long Sea, Moderate Sea, Precipitous Sea, Quartering Sea, Rough Sea, Short Sea, Slight Sea, Smooth Sea, Sugar Loaf Sea, Very High Sea, Very Rough Sea.**

SEA ANCHOR. A drag thrown overboard to keep a vessel to the wind and sea. Also called drogue, drift anchor. Drogues are frequently used when handling a boat in surf, in which case a conical canvas bag is used.
  Fr: *Ancre flottante;* Ger: *Treibanker.*

SEA BAG. A canvas bag about 1 ft. in diameter and 3 ft. in length used by seamen to store their belongings, such as clothing, bedding, dishes, and many other articles which they carry about with them from ship to ship. Also called duffle bag. It is usually made of No. 2 canvas.
  Fr: *Sac d'équipage;* Ger: *Tragesack.*

SEA BOAT.
  See **Accident Boat.**

SEA-BORNE TRADE. The transportation by sea of passengers, merchandise, or other property by merchant vessels.
  Fr: *Transports Maritimes; Commerce Maritime;* Ger: *Seehandel.*

SEA BOTTOM. The bed of a body of water. It is characterized according to its nature as muddy, rocky, sandy, and so on. Sometimes called bottom.
  Fr: *Fond;* Ger: *Meeresgrund.*

SEA BREEZE. A breeze that blows from the sea. It is due to the difference in temperature of the land and the sea. During the day the land becomes heated more than the sea, an area of low pressure is formed over the land, and a breeze sets in from seaward. The opposite of a land breeze.
  Fr: *Brise de Mer;* Ger: *Seebrise.*
  See **Land Breeze.**

SEABRIGHT SKIFF. Beach boat used by fishermen along the coast of New Jersey and especially adapted for landing in a heavy swell with fares of fish. The hull is constructed with slightly rounded stem, square transom stern and flat keel. The ends are decked. Before the advent of motors they were rigged with a single spritsail or with a lugsail and small jib. Today all are fitted with auxiliary engines. The length ranges from 18 to 30 ft.

SEA BUOY. The first buoy encountered coming from sea marking a channel or entrance to a harbor.
  Fr: *Bouée Extérieure;* Ger: *Ansegelungstonne.*

SEA CHEST. The intake between the ship's side and a sea valve.
  See **Suction Box, Seaman's Chest.**

SEA CLUTTER. Radar echoes reflected from the surface of the sea and obscuring some areas of the radar indicator. The amount of sea clutter depends on type of radar used; antennae height state of the sea and atmosphere. Also called **Sea return.**

SEA COCK. A cock fitted to the ship's side plating. Used in flooding ballast tanks, supplying water to sanitary and fire pumps, also as boiler blow down. They are fitted with special gland covers with spanner guards to prevent the spanner being removed while the cock remains open.
  Fr: *Prise d'eau à la mer;* Ger: *Seehahn.*

SEA CONNECTIONS. A general term for valves and cocks attached to the ship's outside plating, some of which are located under water for the supply of sea water to ballast and fire pumps, others above the load water line as discharge of bilge and ballast and circulating pumps, boiler blow downs and so on. All sea connections must be fitted directly to the ship's side without the intervention of pipes. Where brass valves are used zinc rings are fitted around the openings to counteract galvanic action.
  Fr: *Prisees d'eau à la mer;* Ger: *Bodenventil.*

SEA-DAMAGED TERMS. An expression used in connection with grain contracts, which provides either that damage by sea water shall be for seller's account or that grain damaged by sea water or condensation shall be rejected by buyers.

SEA FISHERIES. All fisheries pursued

in salt water as distinguished from the lake, stream, or fresh water fisheries.

Fr: *Pêche Maritime;* Ger: *Seefischerei.*

SEA FOG. Fog formed when warm, damp air passes over a cold sea surface the temperature of which is lower than the dew point of the air. The air then becomes cooled below its dew point and condensation results. Sea fog is comparatively shallow, and it frequently happens that the topmasts of ships may be seen protruding through it. At times its base does not rest on the sea and there are a few feet of clear air immediately above the water line; hence the necessity of placing look-out men as high up and as low down as possible when steaming in a fog.

Fr: *Brouillard marin;* Ger: *Küstennebel.*

SEA GASKET. A long line passed around a yard or other spar and the sail which is to be secured to it. Also called furling line, long gasket. It is used at sea when neatness is not required.

Fr: *Raban de Ferlage; Chambrière;* Ger: *Beschlagleine.*

SEA GATE. One of a pair of supplementary gates opening outward at the entrance of tidal basin in exposed situation as a safeguard against a heavy sea.

Ger: *Seethor.*

SEAGOING TUG. A tug built for channel and small coasting work, in which the hull form is similar to that of other seagoing vessels. The crew's accommodation and bunker capacity are on a larger scale than in a harbor tug.

Fr: *Remorqueur de Mer;* Ger: *Seeschlepper.*

SEAGOING VESSEL. A vessel fit to withstand the ordinary strains of a sea voyage and which in the ordinary course of its business does actually go to sea. For certain statutory purposes the following classes of vessels are not deemed to be seagoing even though they may be seagoing for the purposes of other statutes: pleasure yachts, tugs, lighters, barges. A vessel engaged actually and intentionally in navigation outside the headlands of a harbor or outside the boundaries of inland waters is seagoing throughout the voyage although only part of it may be at sea. In Great Britain it is held that a vessel fit to go to sea but actually used entirely upon navigation of inland rivers is not seagoing for statutory purposes. The term "seagoing vessel" as used in maritime law applies to those craft which in the ordinary course of events are employed in deep-sea navigation although they may occasionally be navigating rivers or inland waters.

Fr: *Navire de Mer;* Ger: *Seeschiff; Seefahrzeug; Überseeschiff.*

SEAHIGH. An elevation of the deep sea floor of approximately 3,000 feet or more, the morphology of which is insufficiently well known to be covered by a more precise definition.

SEA HORSE. A large white-crested wave.

SEA ICE. Ice formed by direct freezing of the ocean waters. As trapped brine works its way out of sea ice in time, the ice generally yields fresh water when melted six months after formation. Also called **Salt water ice.**

Fr: *Glace de mer;* Ger: *Meereis.*

SEA KINDLINESS. A term relating to the ease of motion or behavior of a vessel in heavy weather particularly in regard to rolling, pitching, and shipping water on deck. It should not be confused with seaworthiness, which implies that the vessel is able to sustain without structural damage heavy rolling or pitching. Sea kindliness is a desirable but not essential adjunct to seaworthiness.

Fr: *Aptitude à la mer; Tenue à la mer;* Ger: *Seetüchtigkeit.*

Macdonald and Telfer, "Sea Kindliness and Ship Design," North East Coast Institution of Engineers and Shipbuilders (Newcastle upon Tyne), *Transactions,* vol. 54 (1938).

SEA LADDER. A ladder on a ship's side, formed of rungs riveted, welded, or otherwise fastened to the sides from load-line level to weather deck.

SEA LAWYER. A seaman who is prone to argue, especially against recognized authority.

SEALER. Seal-hunting boat. Any craft used for seal hunting. In the Baltic the sealer is a light, clinker-built boat with a swim bow which enables it to override and break through the ice. The keel is deep and is shod with iron. A large square sail is carried. Length 26.3 ft. Beam 9.7 ft. (Typical.)

Fr: *Phoquier;* Ger: *Seehundfänger; Robbenboot.*

SEA LETTER.
See **Passport, License.**

SEA LEVEL. The level of the surface of the sea midway between high and low water.
Fr: *Niveau de la mer*; Ger: *Wasserstand*.
See **Mean Sea Level, Mean Tide Level**.

SEA LINE. 1. The line where sea and sky seem to meet. The apparent horizon. 2. The coast line or seaboard. 3. A long line used for sea-fishing in deep water. Also called **Boulter**. (G. B.)

SEALING BEAD.
See **Calking Weld**.

SEAM. 1. An edge joint of two plates, whether flush or lapped or the joint between adjacent planks. Also, the slight crevice between the ends or edges of butt laps.
Fr: *Couture*; Ger: *Naht*.
See **Calk Seam**.
2. The junction of two pieces of canvas when they are sewed together.
Fr: *Couture*; Ger: *Segelnaht*.
See **Cord Seam, Flat Seam, Miter Seam, Monk Seam, Round Seam, Slack Seams**.

SEA LOG. The log book kept at sea, as distinguished from the harbor log, kept in port.

SEAMAN. In its broad sense the term seaman refers to any person employed or engaged to serve in any capacity on board a vessel. Also called sailor, mariner. With respect to the laws affecting seamen the term is generally used in the sense which it is given in the construction of the British statutes relating to merchant shipping as "any person (except masters, pilots and apprentices) employed or engaged in any capacity on board any ship." In most countries seamen are required to pass an examination as to eyesight, hearing, and physical condition, and to give evidence as to service and capabilities. In law the term "seaman" usually refers to any man serving on board a seagoing vessel below the rank of officer.
Fr: *Homme d'équipage*; *Gens de Mer*; Ger: *Schiffsmann*; *Seemann*.
See **Able-Bodied Seaman, Merchant Seaman, Ordinary-Seaman**.

Healey, J. C., *Foc'sle and Glory Hole, Study of the Merchant Seaman*, New York, 1936; International Juridical Association, *Report on Status and Working Conditions of Seamen in the American Merchant Marine*, New York, 1936; Neuhauser, W., *Der Arbeitsvertrag des Schiffsmannes in der deutschen Seeschiffahrt*, Rostock, 1934.

SEAMAN APPRENTICE. A youngster who works under close supervision and receives theoretical instruction, ashore and aboard ship, in preparation for qualified employment on the deck department or ships of the American merchant marine.

SEAMAN'S CHEST. A wooden box usually forming all the luggage of a sailor in the merchant service. It is fitted with one or more tills and is usually long and very narrow, the back sloping slightly so that the cover is narrower than the bottom.
Fr: *Coffre de Marin*; Ger: *Seemannskiste*; *Matrosenkiste*.

SEAMAN'S HEAD. Formerly, the space next to the knee of the head where the sanitary arrangements for the crew were found. It consisted of a pair of long latrine troughs with holed lids, lying fore and aft on each side above the knee timbers and abreast of the inner part of the bowsprit. These troughs were concealed from outboard by painted canvas cloths called "head screens" fastened to an iron rod known as the "iron horse." Nowadays, a compartment with toilet facilities for the crew.
Fr: *Poulaine*; Ger: *Mannschaftsabort*.

SEAMANSHIP. A general term for the art by which vessels of all classes and sizes are handled in all conditions of weather. The principles of seamanship may be stated in a literary form but a mastery of it can be acquired only by actual practice at sea. Though the art of seamanship is distinct both from the art of shipbuiding and the science of navigation it has naturally developed with them.
Fr: *Manoeuvre*; *Matelotage*; Ger: *Seemannschaft*; *Seemannskunst*.
See **Deck Seamanship, Marlinspike Seamanship**.

Cooke, F. B., *Seamanship for Yachtsmen*, London, 1923; Cornell, F. M., *American Merchant Seamen's Manual*, New York, 1938; Nicholls, A. E., *Seamanship and Nautical Knowledge*, Glasgow, 1937; Prince, W., *Seamanship as Applied to Towing*, London, 1934; Riesenberg, F., *Standard Seamanship*, New York, 1936; Tait, J., *New Seamanship and Nautical Knowledge*, Glasgow, 1933; Turpin, E. A., *Merchant Marine Officer's Handbook*, New York, 1942.

SEA MARK. An elevated object on land which serves as a guide to navigators in approaching a coast or harbor. Buoys, lighthouses, beacons, lightships, are included collectively under this term.
Fr: *Amer*; Ger: *Seemarke*; *Seezeichen*.

SEAMEN'S LIEN. A maritime lien on seamen's wages. It attaches to ship and freight and the proceeds of both and follows them into whatever hands they come.

Fr: *Privilège sur salaires de l'équipage.*

SEAMAN'S PASSPORT. In the U. S. a passport issued to merchant seamen; valid only for travel occasioned by the seaman's shipping assignment.

See **Certificate of Identification.**

SEAMEN'S QUARTERS. Place of lodging for deck hands.

Fr: *Poste des Matelots;* Ger: *Matrosenlogis.*

SEAMEN'S REGISTER (G. B.): A record kept by the Registrar General in London containing the official number and date of registration of each foreign-going ship under the British flag and her registered tonnage, the length and nature of her voyage or employment, the names, ages, wages, nationality, and so on, of the master and crew.

SEAMING TWINE. Linen, cotton, or flax twine used for sewing sails and canvas in general. Also called sail twine. It is known by the ply, that is, the number of threads, which varies from 2 to 8. Two kinds most commonly used are the 4-ply and 5-ply. Flax twine is occasionally dipped in tar softened by a proper proportion of oil.

Fr: *Fil à Voile;* Ger: *Segelgarn; Nähgarn.*

SEAM LAP. A joint between two plates in the direction of their length, in which their edges are overlapped a sufficient width to receive one or more line of rivets. Also known as edge lap, landing.

Fr: *Recouvrement des Cans;* Ger: *Nahtüberlappung; Längsnaht.*

SEAMLESS BOAT. A metal boat without frames or seams, composed of two sides riveted to a steel keel bar of T-bulb section. Each side consists of one sheet of mild steel sheered in the flat from an expansion mold to the shape which when pressed gives the desired model. The plate is furnaced, and upon reaching the required degree of heat, is pulled onto the press which lies in close proximity to the furnace. It is then automatically guided and secured in the proper position. The lower part of the hydraulic press rises till the plate comes in contact with the upper half of the shaping die. A stroke of from 3 to 5 ft. is sufficient to bring the concave and convex dies together and this one operation molds the half-hull. The lower part of the press is then brought back to its starting position. After the plate has been extracted from the mold it is immediately galvanized, by the electrolytic process. The keel bar is also bent in a hydraulic press and fixed on a stand where the two shelves are secured one on either side. These three thicknesses having been correctly punched, are riveted by hydraulic machines, after which the hull is ready for trimming, painting, and the fitting of interior work. Wooden thwarts, bottom boards, stern sheets and gunwales are then fitted as usual.

Fr: *Embarcation Seamless;* Ger: *Nahtloses Stahlboot.*

This type of construction is satisfactory for standard boats built in quantities, but owing to the expense of making dies for the presses, the cost is prohibitive for a single boat of a new type. Other objections to this system are: the straining of the plate which takes place at or about the bilge; the necessity of welding together two or more plates to obtain the necessary amount of material for the half girth amidships, if large boats are to be built; and the heavy and expensive plant necessary to work the plates.

SEAMOUNT. A term used in submarine topography and applied to an isolated submarine mountain rising more than 500 fathoms (3000 ft.) above the sea floor.

SEAM STRAP. Long, narrow strip of plating used to connect the side joints or edges of two plates. Narrow strip of plating serving as a connecting strap between the edges of plates when these are not lapped. Also called edge strip, seam strip, butt strap.

Fr: *Couvre joint longitudinal;* Ger: *Nahtstreif.*

SEAM STRIP.

See **Seam Strap.**

SEA MULE. A square, box-shaped floating structure equipped with a substantial power plant; employed in harbors and sheltered waters for handling barges, scows, lighters and other dumb craft. It is so arranged that it can be attached to the stern of any barge-like structure which it is to propel. The engine drives a large-diameter, coarse-pitch screw through a joint capable of being operated in a vertical direction by means of a ratchet, so that when the sea mule approaches shoals or shallow water, by working the ratchet the propeller can be lifted up from the bottom of the aperture to avoid damage.

SEA PAINTER. A long rope, not less

than 2¾ in. in size, for use in maneuvering a ship's boat away from side of ship when lowered underway. It is led from forward, and secured to the center of the forward thwart with a strop eye and toggle so as to permit quick releasing. It tends to throw the bow of the boat out when the boat is waterborne.

SEAPEAK. A seamount roughly circular or elliptical in plan, with a pointed top.

SEA PIE. A seaman's dish composed of fish or meat and vegetables in layers between crusts, the number of which determines whether it is a "double-decker" or a "three-decker."

SEA PILOT. A pilot who navigates large vessels to and from open waters.

Fr: *Pilote de Mer;* Ger: *Seelotse.*

SEAPORT. A port located either on the seacoast or within a sheltered estuary near the sea. Also refers to any port of major importance where unimpeded connection with the sea exists although the port be located some distance from the open water.

Fr: *Port de Mer; Port Maritime;* Ger: *Seehafen.*

SEARCH. The act by a belligerent war vessel of searching a neutral vessel and her cargo in exercise of the right of search when the visit has given no satisfaction or if there is grave suspicion of fraud against the vessel. It is effected by one or two officers of the war vessel accompanied by some of the crew. If the search proves satisfactory to the visiting officers a memorandum is made in the vessel's official log book by the senior visiting officer and the ship is allowed to proceed on her course.

Fr: *Recherche;* Ger: *Durchsuchung.*

When conditions make it impossible to carry out the search at sea, owing to the size of the vessel, the great amount of cargo, the danger of attack from enemy submarines, or the elaborate arrangements made by the enemy for concealing the identity of the various consignments of goods at the time of the search, it has nowadays become the practice to take the vessel into a belligerent port for search.

SEARCH (to). To search a ship for contraband goods, stowaways, and so on. Also called to overhaul.

Fr: *Visiter;* Ger: *Visitieren.*

SEARCHER. Name given by North Sea fishermen when working in fleet to a trawler whose duty it is to leave the fleet to explore and test localities suggested by the Admiral, to see where fish are to be found.

SEARCHLIGHT. A powerful electric light with large reflector, visible over a long distance. When fitted with a shutter, it may be used for signaling. Searchlights are compulsory for vessels going through the Suez Canal.

Fr: *Projecteur;* Ger: *Scheinwerfer.*

SEA RETURN. Indication on a radar indicator caused by radio waves being reflected by the surface of the sea. Also called **Cutter.**

SEA ROOM. A position offshore which offers no dangers to navigation.

Fr: *Mer Libre;* Ger: *Seeraum.*

SEA SCALE.

See **Douglas Scale.**

SEA SLED. A type of construction adopted for small craft of high speed in which the ordinary V bottom is inverted, in order to collect a layer of air under the bows of the boat. This helps to cushion the boat and reduces skin friction. A variation of this type provides a tunnel in the center of the boat's bottom in order to obtain greater air collecting powers for cushioning and to improve the directional handling qualities. Also called inverted V-bottom boat.

Perring, G. W. A., Design of High Speed Motor Boats, Institution of Engineers and Shipbuilders in Scotland, *Transactions,* vol. 69, 1925-26.

SEA SMOKE. A type of fog which occurs when cold air blows over a relatively warm sea. Also called **Warm water fog.**

Ger: *Seerauch.*

SEASONED TIMBER. Timber which has become hard and dry by the escape of natural moisture.

Fr: *Bois Sec;* Ger: *Lufttrockenes Holz.*

See **Seasoning.**

SEASONING. The process by which moisture is extracted from timber to be used for ship- or boatbuilding. As a rule timber is either air-dried (natural seasoning) or kiln-dried (artificial seasoning).

See **Water Seasoning.**

In the natural seasoning or air-drying process the material is piled up in open sheds and small slips of wood are placed between the various pieces allowing fresh air to circulate freely around each piece.

Air-drying of timber takes months and sometimes years, but the wood shrinks into a more homogeneous and hard material than with any other process.

In artificial seasoning, or kiln-drying process, the material is placed in an oven where

the moisture evaporates faster so that wood does not have time to shrink back into the microscopic spaces left by the evaporated moisture. Thus kiln-dried timber is more apt to pick up moisture from the atmosphere than naturally seasoned wood.
Most naval architects' specifications call for boat lumber to be dried to a point where it will not contain more than 15 per cent moisture.
Bateson, R. G., *Timber Drying*, London, 1938; Henderson, H. L., *The Air-Seasoning and Kiln-Drying of Wood*, Albany (New York), 1936; Wagner, J. B., *Seasoning of Wood*, New York, 1917.

SEA STORES. A general term for provisions, materials, and supplies taken on board for the maintenance of passengers and crew, and the navigation, propulsion, and upkeep of ship and machinery during the voyage. The victuals and provisions collected together for the subsistence of a ship's company. Provisions and supplies for use at sea.

Fr: *Approvisionnements de Bord;* Ger: *Schiffsvorräte.*

SEATING. That part of a floor timber which fays on the deadwood, or the part of a transom which fays against the stern post. See **Engine Seating.**

SEATRAIN, SEA-TRAIN. A seagoing train-ferry for the transportation of railway cars on one or several decks, over comparatively long distances in open waters. The cars are taken on board through a stern opening or are lowered bodily through a hatchway. This term is also used to denote collectively a number of vessels of merchant ship type as well as naval auxiliaries which follow a battle fleet engaged in long range operations and carry supplies, stores, and ammunition for the maintenance of the fleet, although the term "train" is more frequently applied to such activities.

Ger: *Trajektschiff.*

Burrill, L. C., The design and construction of the rail-car carrying steamship *Seatrain*, North East Coast Institution of Engineers and Shipbuilders (Newcastle upon Tyne), *Transactions*, vol. 46 (1930).

SEA TRIALS. A series of trials conducted by the builders, during which the owner's representatives on board act in a consulting and checking capacity.

Fr: *Essais à la mer;* Ger: *Probefahrt.*

SEATTLE HEAD. A T-shaped fixture fitted on the top of a galley smoke pipe to prevent down-drafts.

SEA VALVE. A valve or cock placed at or near the outside plating of a vessel below the waterline to admit water for purposes such as supplying sea water to the fire pumps, filling or discharging ballast tanks, blowing down the boilers, and so on. Also called outboard valve, seacock.

Fr: *Prise d'eau à la mer;* Ger: *Bodenventil; Seehahn; Seeventil.*

SEAWARD. Toward the sea or offing.
Fr: *Au Large;* Ger: *Seewärts.*

SEAWAY. 1. The progress a vessel is making through the water.
Fr: *Sillage;* Ger: *Fahrt.*

2. A navigable portion of the sea. The position of a vessel where a moderately heavy sea is running.

3. The undulatory movement of the sea when clear of shoal water.
Fr: *Levée;* Ger: *Seegang.*

SEAWEED. General name for marine plants of the Algae class which grow in long narrow ribbons. Also called sea grass. Seaweed forms excellent manure; when thrown by the tide and thus used it is called "sea wrack." It is also one of the principal sources of iodine.

Fr: *Varech;* Ger: *Seetang; Seegrass; Seekraut.*

Newton, *Hand-book of British Seaweeds*, London, 1931.

SEAWORTHINESS. The sufficiency of a vessel in materials, construction, equipment, crew, and outfit for the trade or service in which it is employed. Also called navigability. Any sort of disrepair in the ship by which it or the cargo may suffer, bad stowage of the cargo if such as to make it difficult and dangerous to navigate the ship, overloading, all are breaches of the warranty of seaworthiness. Where nothing is said on the subject, seaworthiness is an implied condition of hiring of shipping.

Fr: *Etat de Navigabilité;* Ger: *Seetüchtigkeit; Seefähigkeit.*

Burrill, L. C., "Seaworthiness of Collier Types," Institution of Naval Architects (London), *Transactions*, 1931; Erbach, R., "Freibord und Seefähigkeit," Schiffbautechnische Gesellschaft (Berlin), *Jahrbuch*, 1929; Ives, B. J., *Elements of Seaworthiness*, North East Coast Institution of Engineers and Shipbuilders (Newcastle upon Tyne), *Transactions*, vol. 41, 1925.

SEAWORTHINESS CERTIFICATE. A certificate issued by a classification surveyor or other qualified person to allow a vessel to proceed after she has met with an accident. It is frequently issued to enable a vessel to proceed, after temporary repairs have been effected, to another port where permanent repairs are then carried out.

Fr: *Certificat de Navigabilité*; Ger: *Seetüchtigkeitsattest*.

SEBIR. An East Indian canoe employed in the pearl fisheries of the Aru Islands. It is similar to the *belang* although the stem and stern differ somewhat from the latter craft. The stem ends in two projecting horizontal baulks placed above each other, sometimes with a vertical plank on the outboard end, used by the divers for hauling themselves on board. The stern is composed of a long and narrow uprising piece decorated with carvings.

SECONDARY CYCLONE. A small circular depression subsidiary to a cyclone. It is usually formed by the bends of the isobars on the equatorial side of cyclones. It also forms on the edge of anticyclones.

SECONDARY DEPRESSION. Small atmospheric depression on the periphery of a larger primary depression, the isobars forming a loop around which the wind may blow with considerable force.

Fr: *Depression Secondaire*; Ger: *Teiltief*.

SECONDARY PORT. A port for which tidal differences from a standard port have been calculated and published in tide tables.

Fr: *Port Secondaire*; Ger: *Anschlussort*.

SECOND ASSISTANT ENGINEER (U. S.). An engineer in charge of a watch. In Great Britain called third engineer. This engineer has charge of the boiler room and the auxiliary machinery within the fireroom. His position is particularly important in steamers because the efficiency of the propelling machinery is largely dependent upon the condition of the boilers and the manner of fuel consumption.

Fr: *Troisième Mécanicien*; Ger: *Zweiter Maschinenassistent*.

SECOND DOG WATCH. The dog watch from 6 to 8 P. M. Also called last dog watch.

SECOND HAND (G. B.). A certificated seaman acting as an assistant to the skipper of fishing vessels of more than 25 tons, for navigating purposes.

SECTION. See **Bar**.

SECRET BLOCK. A block designed to prevent fouling by building the shell completely over the sheave, with access only large enough on each side for the rope.

SECTIONAL BOX DOCK. A self-docking, floating dry dock in which the joints of the various sections are vertical and are continued all around the profile of the dock. It is thus possible to make connections between the different portions as strong as the net sections of the plating. This type of dock is as strong as the box dock with the advantage of being self-docking. It can be employed for docks of the largest size.

Fr: *Box dock en sections*.

SECTIONAL PONTOON DOCK. A self-docking, floating dry dock in which the two walls are continuous structures, but where the pontoon is made in separate sections, attached to the walls by flat, horizontal bolted joints. Also called sectional dock. Any pontoon section can be unbolted from the rest of the dock, and lifted by it for painting and repairs. This system has been frequently adopted for small and medium size docks.

Fr: *Dock à pontons sectionnés; Dock Auto-carénable; Dock auto-carénant*; Ger: *Teildock; Sektiondock*.

SECTION MODULUS. In calculating the longitudinal strength of the hull of a vessel, the section modulus of the ship girder is defined in the Load Line Regulations of the United States as follows, "The longitudinal modulus I/c is the moment of inertia I of the midship section about the neutral axis divided by the distance c measured from the neutral axis to the top of the strength deck beam at side, calculated in way of openings but without deductions for rivet holes. Areas are measured in square inches and distances in feet. Below the strength deck, all continuous longitudinal members other than such parts of under deck girders as are required entirely for supporting purposes are included. Above the strength deck, the gunwale angle bar and the extension of the sheer strake are the only members included."

See **Hog, Sag, Hull Girder**.

SECTIONS. Rolled bars of iron or steel of various cross sections used in shipbuilding. Also called shapes.

Fr: *Profilés*; Ger: *Profile*.

SECTOR. A portion of a circle defined by bearings within which a light shows a special character or color or is obscured.

Fr: *Secteur*; Ger: *Sektor*.

SECTORED LIGHT. A light made to show different colors in different sectors

within its range, or the same color over definite sectors.
Fr: *Feu à Secteur;* Ger: *Sektorfeuer.*

SECUNNY. Indian seaman acting as steersman or quartermaster.

SEEPRAHM. A non-propelled steel-built seagoing lighter from the lower Weser (Germany), with round bilges, sharp stem, round stern, four hatchways, usually equipped with two 3-ton deck cranes. Dimensions, etc. (typical): Length 170 ft. Breadth 27.3 ft. Load draft 8.5 ft. Deadweight capacity 600 tons.

SEGELSCHUTE. A sailing barge from the lower Elbe similar to the *Ever*, used for transportation on rivers and in coastal waters as far as Denmark.

The hull is flat-bottomed. It is decked and has one or two hatchways. Most of these craft were built with sharp stern. They were ketch-rigged with collapsible masts, enabling them to go under bridges. Length 59 to 72 ft. Breadth 15½ to 17 ft. Hold depth 4.1 to 5.9 ft. Tonnage 25 to 45 gross. (Average.)

SEICHE. A sudden and temporary oscillation or fluctuation of the water level in a land-locked part of the sea.
Fr: *Seiche;* Ger: *Seiche; Seeschwankung.*

SEINE. A type of net of which there are many varieties used for the capture of fish found near the surface of the water either along the coast-line or out at sea. It consists essentially of a long and narrow netting with or without a bag which hangs vertically in the water, one edge being provided with floats and the other with sinkers. After the school of fish has been encircled the ends are brought together or hauled ashore.
Fr: *Senne;* Ger: *Wade.*
See **Bait Seine, Beach Seine, Capelin Seine, Deep Sea Seine, Drag Seine, Drift Seine, Long Haul Seine, Minnow Seine, Purse Seine, Shore Seine, Stop Seine, Tuck Seine.**

SEINE BOAT.
See **Seiner.**

SEINE FLOAT. A small cork or wooden float in each loop of the life line extending around a lifeboat or buoyant apparatus, to prevent the line from twisting and to give a better security for the person holding on. A similar float is used with seine nets, hence its name.
Fr: *Flotte;* Ger: *Schwimmer; Flott.*

SEINER. Generic term for various craft employed in the seine net fisheries. Also called seine boat. The typical seiner as used for salmon and sardine purse seining on the Pacific coast of the U. S. is a powered boat with vertical stem, square stern, decked fore and aft with pilot and deck houses forward. At the afterend there is a turntable on which the seine net is stowed. For working the net there is a power winch with two gypsy heads located amidships, near the hatchway. Most of these boats are built of wood and propelled by Diesel engines. Length 55½ to 85 ft. overall. Beam 15 to 22 ft. Draft 5½ to 11 ft.
Fr: *Senneur;* Ger: *Wadenfischer.*

SEINE ROLLER. A large wooden roller about 9 to 10 ft. long and 6 in. in diameter, fitted at the stern of a purse seine boat to lessen the friction between the railing and the seine when the latter is being hauled on board or paid out.

SEINING. The act or method of using a seine net. On the Pacific coast of the U. S. the purse seine is worked in the following manner: when a school of fish is sighted a skiff or small pulling boat about 20 ft. long is dropped overboard from the stern of the seine boat, which continues to steam ahead while the men in the skiff row in the opposite direction, with the result that the net is drawn off the turntable into the water as the vessel encircles the school. The seine boat returns to the skiff when the net has been entirely paid out. The two ends of the purse line are recovered and taken to the purse winch and hauled in. While the bottom of the net is being closed by this means, fishermen drive the fish away from the opening where the two ends of the net meet. When finally the bottom of the net has been entirely closed and the fish are crowded together the catch is taken on board with a dip net, called a brailer.
Fr: *Pêche à la Senne;* Ger: *Wadenfischerei.*
See **Long-Haul Seining.**

SEISMIC WAVE. A heavy disturbance of the sea, taking the form of rollers caused by a submarine earthquake. Also called earthquake wave. Sometimes erroneously called tidal wave.
Fr: *Vague Sismique;* Ger: *Seismische Welle.*

SEIZE. To bind, lash, or make fast a rope to another, a rope to a spar, and so on, with

SEIZING—SEIZING STUFF

several turns of small stuff such as spun yarn, marline, or specially made seizing stuff.

Fr: *Genoper; Amarrer;* Ger: *Zurren; Bindseln.*

SEIZING. 1. Small 4-stranded rope 0.5 to 0.7 in. in diameter and 24 ft. in length by which each deeping of a drift net is fastened to the warp. When hauling the nets in, the seizings help to keep the strain even on each deeping.

Fr: *Barsouin;* Ger: *Zeising.*

Fr: *Amarrage;* Ger: *Bindsel; Bandsel; Sorring.*

See **Cross Seizing, Flat Seizing, Half-Crown Seizing, Racking Seizing, Rose Seizing, Round Seizing, Throat Seizing.**

SEIZING LINE. Small stuff made of tarred hemp yarns and used for permanent seizings.

Fr: *Ligne d'Amarrage;* Ger: *Bindselleine; Bandselleine.*

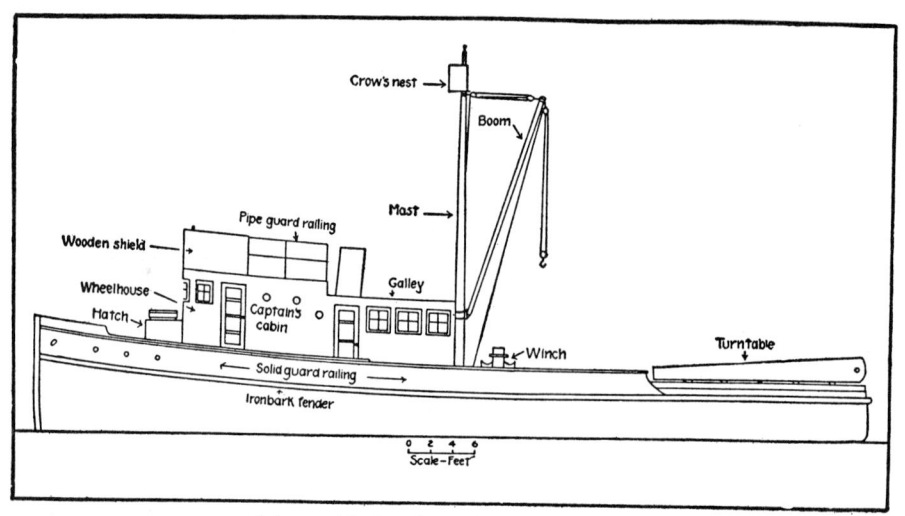

Seiner. (*Outboard profile of purse seiner*)

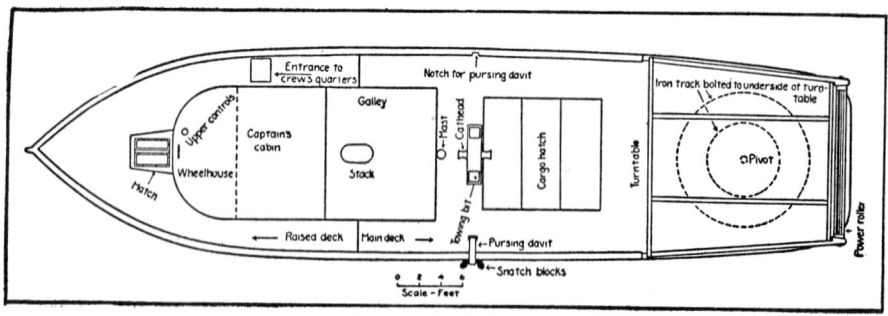

Seiner. (*Deck Plan*)

2. A binding made with small stuff of one rope to another, a rope to a spar, or different parts of the same rope. Seizings take their names from their appearance or the use they are put to. Throat seizings, middle seizings, and end seizings are named from the part of the rope where the seizing is applied.

SEIZING STRAND. See **Seizing Wire.**
SEIZING STUFF. Line or cord used for making seizings and worming. Fiber seizing stuff is heavier and stronger than houseline or roundline. For very small seizings, small waxed or tarred seizing twine or whipping twine is used. For heavier seizings tarred

marline and for still heavier ones, spun yarn. The different sizes of fiber seizing stuff are distinguished by the number of yarns or threads of which they are composed. Seizing stuff most commonly used is three strand right hand stuff made of 4-, 6-, or 9-yarns of tarred hemp.

Fr: *Ligne d'Amarrage;* Ger: *Bindselgut; Nähtaue.*

See **Seizing Wire.**

SEIZING TWINE. Twine used for small seizings.

Fr: *Fil d'Amarrage;* Ger: *Bindselgarn.*

SEIZING WIRE. Small stuff made of galvanized annealed steel wire and used for serving and making seizings on wire rope, also for lashings. Sometimes called seizing strand. The smaller sizes, from 1/16 to ⅛ in. in diameter, are composed of 7 wires twisted into a single strand. For 3/16 and ¼ in. diameters, the construction is 1 by 19.

SEIZURE. The taking possession of a ship and its cargo in time of peace or war for a violation of public law, as for instance, illicit trade. Seizure is not equivalent to, but is less exigent than, capture, as the latter word involves keeping what has been seized.

It includes seizure by revenue officers of another State and seems to cover every act of a ship either by a lawful authority or by overpowering force whether such seizure be justified by law or not or whether it is belligerent or not..

Fr: *Saisie;* Ger: *Besitzergreifung; Beschlagnahme.*

SEKAH. An East Indian keel-built fishing boat from Billiton Island with raking stem and vertical stern. It has a portable decking and a centerline rudder of European type. There is one mast.

SEKO BUNE. Japanese whaling sampan. There are two types of *seko bune,* one from Koochi district, the other from Yamaguchi district. The first type is distinguished by the elongated shape of the fore part and stem, which is more pronounced than in any other fishing sampan. Length 33.6 ft. Breadth 6.1 ft. Depth 2.6 ft. It is rigged with one mast and has a crew of 12.

The second type has as distinctive feature long washboards which extend for about four fifths of the boat's length from the stem. It is not rigged, and is propelled by 6 *yulohs.* Length 36 ft. Breadth 6.2 ft. Depth 2.8 ft. Crew 11.

SEKONG. An East Indian sailing canoe of the *jukung* type with double outriggers, bladelike stem and stern, and deep wash strake, found in eastern Java, Bali, Madura, and Lombok and used for fishing and transportation. Also called *prao sekong.* The sides have a certain amount of tumble home at the wash strake. It is steered with a quarter rudder. Two different rigs are employed. The first one consists of a short mast and quadrilateral sail. The second, which is most frequently seen, has no mast. The triangular-shaped sail has the foot of its yard stepped in the bottom of the boat; a bamboo pole or strut leading aft keeps the yard at the desired angle. Length 21.7 to 34.4 ft. Breadth 2.7 ft. Depth 1.3 to 1.6 ft. In Kubran and Surabaya the *sekong* is called *jukung.*

See **Jukung.**

SEKSKEIPING. A Norwegian open boat used for fishing and other purposes in the Nordfjord and surrounding waters. Also called *kirkebaat.* It is a twelve-oared boat, and is the largest craft built in that district. Length 32 ft. Breadth 7.2 ft. Depth 2.2 ft. (Typical.)

SEKSRING. A Norwegian open boat from the Nordland coastal district propelled by 3 pairs of oars. Also called faering.

See **Nordlandsbaat.**

SELATAN. A strong southerly wind which blows during the Southeast monsoon in the North Celebes.

SELF-BALING BOAT. A type of lifeboat in which a watertight deck runs throughout the length of the boat slightly above the load waterline. The space below this is thus converted into a watertight compartment. Extending from the deck down through the

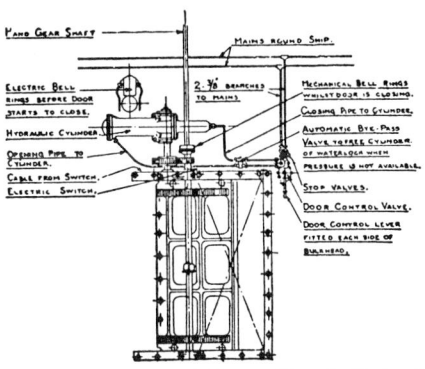

Self-Closing Bulkhead Door. (*Stone's System*)

bottom of the boat there are several watertight trunks, open at top and bottom, through which any water which accumulates on the deck is carried off. The trunks are in effect scuppers.

Fr: *Embarcation à Vidange automatique;* Ger: *Selbstentleerendes Boot.*

SELF-CLOSING DOOR. An installation used on passenger vessels in which watertight doors are remotely operated by a hydraulic pressure system, allowing them to be closed simultaneously from the bridge by the officer in charge or to be closed separately at the door from either side of the bulkhead. Also called automatic closing door.

Fr: *Porte à Fermeture automatique;* Ger: *Krafttür.*

Before the door closes a bell at each door gives warning. The power is derived from a pump situated in the engine or boiler room. It is also possible to open a door locally by means of a handle on the local control valve, but when the handle is released the door again closes automatically.

SELF-DOCKING DOCK. A floating dock divided into sections, any one of which can be lifted on the remainder of the dock for cleaning, painting and repairs. The various types of self-docking docks are: (1) the bolted sectional dock; (2) the sectional pontoon dock; (3) the offshore dock; (4) the sectional box dock; (5) the multi-sectional dock; (6) the depositing dock.

Fr: *Dock auto-carénant.*

SELF-DRAINING COCKPIT. A cockpit separated from the cabin by a watertight bulkhead. The sides and floor are also made watertight, the latter sloping slightly aft. Drain pipes with nonreturn valves are provided to discharge the water through the outside skin. Also called self-emptying cockpit, or self-bailing cockpit.

Fr: *Cockpit à Auto-Vidange;* Ger: *Selbstentlerender Cockpit.*

SELF-REEFING TOPSAIL. A square topsail fitted with gear by which it can be furled without sending men aloft. Also called self-reefing topsail. The gear consists of two yards, the lower one on which the sail is bent being suspended from the upper one by 2 or 4 claw rings fitted with wooden rollers. At each end of the lower yard is a drum from which a light chain runs, through a sheave on the upper yard, to a block on the mast. Passing through this it joins the chain from the other yard arm, and on the bight so formed is a block with a single hauling part to the deck. Pulling on this rolls up the sail.

Fr: *Hunier à Rouleau.* Ger: *Selbsttätiger reffender Marssegel.*

This gear is still used by French Newfoundland fishing boats. Roller gear topsails are not suitable for large sailing vessels, since when they are fitted to large yards the sails are too cumbersome to be easily handled and in reefing the sail often splits. The best-known systems of roller gear topsails are Cunningham, Collins, and Pinkney's. In Cunningham's patent the topsail yard itself rolls and winds the sail, while in Collins' and Pinkney's rig the sail rolls around a rolling spar fitted on the foreside of the yard. The Cunningham system has a light spar on the afterside termed the chafing spar, which carries the foot ropes. It rolls only to a close reef and is very heavy to hoist. In Collins' and Pinkney's system the sail can be rolled up entirely by slacking away the sheets, thus doing away altogether with furling aloft.

Middendorf, F. L., *Bemastung und Takelung der Schiffe,* Berlin, 1903.

SELF-LUBRICATING BLOCK. A block fitted with a bronze bushing in which a cavity containing a special lubricant is provided. The cavity is pierced with radial holes leading toward the pin. A porous substance, such as leather, is placed in the oiling grooves in order to allow the lubricant to pass through gradually. Also called self-oiling block.

Fr: *Poulie à graissage automatique;* Ger: *Selbstschmierender Block.*

SELF-LUBRICATING SHEAVE. A sheave made with a perforated bronze bushing in which the perforations are filled with a special lubricant (graphite). As the bearing wears, the lubricant is distributed over the pin.

SELF-RIGHTING BOAT. A coastal lifeboat which has high bow and stern air tanks, and which is fitted with a heavy keel of iron or lead. The buoyancy is carried sufficiently high, so that the boat tends to right itself when capsized, and this tendency is increased by the keel being made as heavy as practicable. In practice the weight of the keel is from one fifth to one third of the boat's total weight.

Fr: *Embarcation inchavirable;* Ger: *Selbstaussrichtendes Boot.*

The features which make a boat self-righting are obtained only by the sacrifice of other desirable qualities, and accordingly this type is not always adopted for coastal lifesaving craft. The self-righting type, owing to its deep and heavy keel, cannot be adopted where a shallow-draft lifeboat is required or where launching is laborious and difficult.

SELF-SYNCHRONOUS TRANSMISSION. Electrical operating gear consisting of a Selsyn transmitter, electric leads and a Selsyn receiver. Also called Selsyn system. Selsyn transmitters and receivers are alternating-current motors so designed that the rotor of the receiver follows accurately in speed and magnitude of angular displacement the motion of the transmitter rotor. As applied to steering control, for example, the motion of the steering wheel, which is carried on an extension of the shaft of a Selsyn transmitter rotor, is transmitted via the Selsyn receiver at the steering engine to the steering engine control mechanism, which in turn governs the motion of the steering engine and causes the engine to move the rudder to the desired angle.

See **Telemotor, Follow up System.**

This system of control offers certain advantages not present in other methods, such as the telemotor, in that it is applicable to any vessel, is simple and reliable, has no friction losses, is not subject to air-lock, does not get out of step, and connections can be made to pierce ship structure at the most advantageous locations.

SELF-TRIMMER.
See **Self-Trimming Vessel.**

SELF-TRIMMING VESSEL. A vessel so arranged structurally that loose bulk cargo will flow freely into holds, so that little, if any, trimming by hand is required to ensure the cargo completely filling the holds. Also called self-trimmer. Cargoes such as grain or coal are those most commonly handled in this way and vessels of the turret, trunk, cantilever, and arch-framed type are illustrative. Ore-carrying vessels are frequently fitted with longitudinal wing bulkheads extending throughout the lower part of the hold making a sufficient angle with the tank top to trim the ore toward the centerline, so that unloading grabs can clean out the hold. One of the main features of self-trimmers is the great width of hatches, which may be as much as from 40 to 65 per cent of the molded breadth, in order to reduce the under-deck space at sides, and the distance from hatch ends to watertight bulkhead, which is not more than 12 ft. Topside ballast tank vessels are very efficient in this way as there is practically no lost space.

Fr: *Navire Self Trimmer;* Ger: *Selbsttrimmerschiff.*

In British ports and also in some Continental ports (Antwerp, Rotterdam) vessels are classified for the purpose of trimming expenses into (a) self-trimmers, (b) easy trimmers, (c) ordinary trimmers. The holds of a self-trimmer are entirely clear, single deck holds having hatches large enough to fill the holds without any trimming being

Self-Trimming Vessel

required, leveling of the hatch openings excepted. The so-called "distance" of such holds does not exceed 32 ft. The holds of an easy trimmer are single holds which, without being self-trimmer holds, have a "distance" of 39 ft. maximum. Ordinary holds are single-deck holds where (1) the "distance" exceeds 39 ft. and (2) an "end" exceeds 11.4 ft. The "distance" is calculated by adding the two ends and the two wings of each hatch and dividing by the number of hatches. Measurements are taken at deck level, from hatch coaming to ship's side or bulkhead respectively.

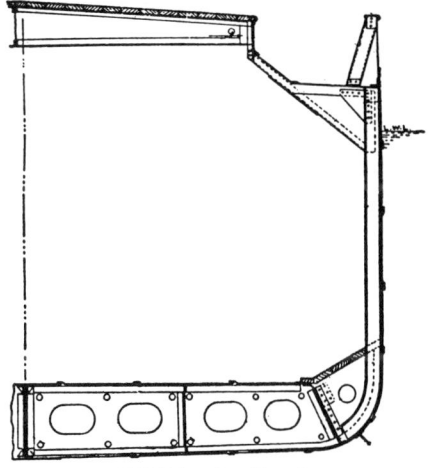

Mitchell, E. H., *Special Features in the Design and Loading of Self Trimming Colliers;* Institute of Naval Architects, *Transactions,* vol. 73 (London, 1939).

SELF-UNLOADING VESSEL. Vessel designed for the carriage of bulk cargoes such as coal, ore, gypsum, cement, and fitted with cargo handling machinery which renders it totally independent of unloading plant ashore as well as shore labor. This type of vessel is adapted only to cargo which will flow by gravity and is of sufficiently hard and irregular nature to avoid interlocking and bridging.

Fr: *Navire Auto Déchargeur;* Ger: *Selbstumladungsschiff.*

The unloading system generally consists of two horizontal conveyors placed at the bottom of the hold, symmetrically arranged at the forward end of the ship (through a combining hopper). These deliver cargo to the heel of an inclined elevator, which in turn delivers to the heel of a boom conveyor which can be swung over either side through a total arc of about 200 degrees. To obtain a flow of cargo to the conveyors, the cargo hold is built with a bottom approximating in cross section the shape of a flattened W.

SELSYN MOTORS. Abbreviation for Self Synchronizing Motors. Applies to two specially designed synchronous electric motors connected to a single alternating current source in such a manner that any position or any speed and direction of rotation of the rotor in one machine is accomplished by a similar position, or similar speed and direction of rotation of the rotor in the other machine. Used for distant control of steering gear, electric telegraph, electric telemotor.

SELVAGE. The side edges of a piece of net as distinguished from the head and foot (heading and reining). Also called guarding.

Ger: *Randmaschen.*

SELVAGEE STRAP. A strap made by warping a piece of small stuff around two or more nails or spikes placed at some distance apart. The ends of the small stuff are spliced or tied together with a reef knot and the whole is firmly marled. It is stronger than a spliced strap.

Fr: *Erse en Bitord;* Ger: *Garnstropp; Wantstropp.*

SELVEDGE. The edge of a sail cloth finished in such a manner as to prevent the raveling out of the weft. Also called selvage.

Fr: *Lis;* Ger: *Einstrich.*

SEMAN. A plank-built boat with double outriggers from East Halmahera, Moluccas, found chiefly in Tobelo, Kao, and Buli. Also called prao seman. The planked hull is built upon a very narrow dugout base which serves the purpose of a keel. In some boats the keel is nearly straight, but many of the medium-sized craft have the dugout portion strongly curved, with stem and stern pieces continued upward with strong sheer. Length over-all 20 ft. Breadth 4½ ft. Depth 3¼ ft. (Typical.)

SEMAPHORE. 1. A signaling apparatus employing moving arms or plates affixed to a high post or pole.

Fr: *Sémaphore;* Ger: *Semaphor.*

2. A method of hand-signaling with two flags, used by naval vessels. Frequently called wigwag.

SEMAPHORE FLAG. Letter "J" of the international code of signals which when hoisted singly or under a group of signal letters signifies: "I am going to send a message by semaphore." It is kept while message is being made.

Fr: *Pavillon sémaphorique;* Ger: *Semaphor Flagge.*

SEMAPHORE SIGNAL. Long distance signal made with the arms of a semaphore stationed on board ship or ashore.

Fr: *Signal Sémaphorique;* Ger: *Semaphorsignal; Küstentelegraphsignal.*

SEMA-SEMA. An East Indian craft. See **Pelang.**

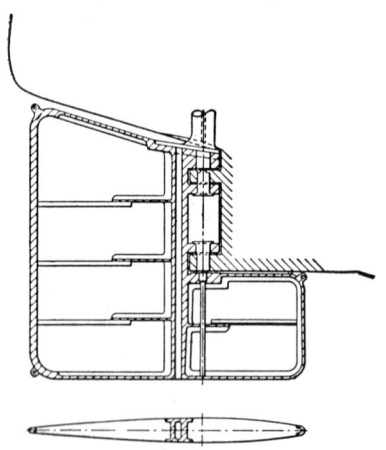

Semi-balanced Rudder

SEMI-BALANCED RUDDER. A balanced rudder in which the blade forward of the stock does not extend vertically to the full height of the blade situated abaft the stock. The forward blade area is about 10 per cent less in surface than with the fully balanced rudder.

Fr: *Gouvernail Partiellement Compensé;* Ger: *Halbschweberuder.*

See **Balanced Rudder.**

SEMICIRCULAR CORRECTOR. In a compensating binnacle, one of the bar magnets symmetrically placed in long horizontal holes athwartship and fore and aft within the binnacle. The magnets are round bars of hard steel 8 in. long and 0.4 of an inch or 0.2 of an inch in diameter (for a 10-inch card). Each magnet is painted blue on one half of its length and red on the other half, to mark the end of possessing the same kind of magnetism as the earth's north and south polar regions respectively. The fore-and-aft corrector holes are in two vertical rows at equal distances of about 5 in. from the middle of the binnacle. The athwartship corrector holes are in one vertical row about the same distance forward or aft from the center of the binnacle. The holes in each vertical scale are spaced to give equal augmentation or diminution of corrective force, when one of the corrector magnets is shifted up or down from hole to hole in order. These are marked with numbers proportional to the corresponding corrective force.

Fr: *Aimant Correcteur Semi Circulaire;* Ger: *Halbkreisförmiger Kompensationsmagnet.*

SEMICIRCULAR DEVIATION. The deviation which, as the ship turns around, changes its sign in each semicircle, that is, easterly in one semicircle and westerly in the other. It is due to the subpermanent magnetism of the ship and is also affected by the vertical induction in soft iron.

Fr: *Déviation Semi Circulaire;* Ger: *Halbkreisartige Deviation.*

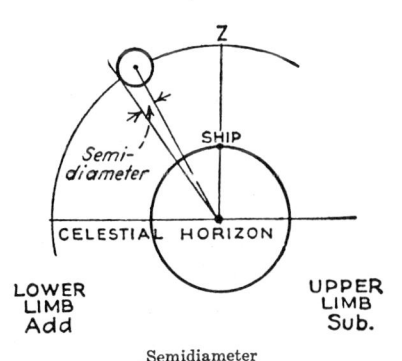

Semidiameter

SEMIDIAMETER. A correction of sextant altitude when observing heavenly bodies such as the sun and moon which have a sensible diameter and where the point brought tangent to the horizon may be the top of the disc or "upper limb," or the bottom of the disc or "lower limb."

The quantities given in navigational tables are calculated for the center of heavenly bodies, so that if the upper limb is observed, the semidiameter must be subtracted, and if the lower limb is observed, the semidiameter must be added to make the final result apply to the center of the body.

Fr: *Demi-Diamètre;* Ger: *Halbmesser.*

SEMI-DIESEL ENGINE. Semi-Diesel engines are two-cycle internal combustion engines where the vaporization of the fuel and the ignition of the charge occur in contact with a hot surface, the heat of this surface being maintained by explosions. Also called hot-bulb engine.

Fr: *Moteur Semi Diesel;* Ger: *Glühkopfmotor.*

Before the engine can be started the necessary heat for vaporizing and igniting is usually obtained by means of a torch or other heating device, which is cut out when the engine has been warmed up. The maximum power developed by semi-Diesel engines is from 300 to 400 h.p., but in general practice the power of each unit is seldom above 200 h.p. The fuel consumption for the larger sizes is about 0.55 pounds per bhp. The weight per bhp varies considerably but the average is about 160 pounds for the larger sizes. This type of engine is obsolete. Pollock, W., Hot Bulb Engines and Suitable Vessels, New York, 1920.

SEMIDIURNAL TIDE. The tides which occur twice a day. They are the best known and are usually marked by a fairly regular interval between times of high water, with maximum height about the time of conjunction of moon and sun, and minimum height about quadrature. The highest of these tides are called *spring* tides; the lowest, *neap* tides.

Fr: *Marée Semi-diurne;* Ger: *Halbtägige Gezeit.*

SEMIPURSE NET.
See **Ring Net.**

SENHOUSE SLIP. A short length of chain of the same strength as the anchor cable, with a slip hook at one end and a shackle at the other. It is shackled to the cable clench, its purpose being to allow the bitter end of the cable to be easily slipped in case of emergency.

SENNIT, SENNET. Braided cordage made from untarred marline rope yarns or spun-yarn plaited by hand. Also called sinnet. There are a number of varieties such as round sennit, square sennit, flat sennit, French sennit, etc. Sennits are used for

making mats, stoppers, manropes, tiller-lashings, and so on.
Fr: *Tresse;* Ger: *Platting.*
See **French Sennit, Flat Sennit, Round Sennit, Square Sennit.**

SENNIT LINE. Braided line such as is used for signal halyards.

SENSIBLE HORIZON. The circle which bounds the horizontal plane extending from the spot where the observer stands.
Fr: *Horizon Sensible;* Ger: *Scheinbarer Horizont.*

SENTINEL. A device used by small craft to increase the holding power of an anchor. It consists of a weight fitted with a large shackle. When the anchor is let go and the required amount of cable veered out, the sentinel is attached over the anchor cable so that it will run freely up and down the cable. A light preventer line is attached to the sentinel and the end is kept on deck. The sentinel is run down the cable until it reaches the bottom and is approximately half way between the anchor and the boat. The sentinel acts as an auxiliary weight at the middle of the cable and as the boat heaves back on the cable the weight must be lifted clear of the bottom before any strain comes on the anchor.

SENTI-SENTEK. Local name given in Tuban, Java, and Madura Island to a double-outrigger canoe used for transportation, similar to the *sekong.*

SEPARATION CLOTH. Large sheet of gunny, burlap, jute cloth, or other fabric used in stowage for separating different grades of bulk grain or similar cargo, also to protect special cargoes such as sugar from moisture. Also called save all.
Fr: *Toile de Fardage;* Ger: *Garniermatte.*

SEQUENCE WELDING. A method of making a continuous fusion weld in sections by carrying it along the joint for a short distance, then stopping and moving to another position and laying another section.

SERANG. Name given on British vessels to an Asiatic boatswain or native boss, acting as liaison between a Lascar crew and the officers.

SERUA. A paddling and sailing East Indian canoe from the Moluccas, smaller than the *orembai,* used in the Island of Geram. It has a shelter with flat roof.

SERVE. To bind or wind a rope tightly with small cord, spun yarn or marline, keeping the turns very close together. The stuff thus used is called service.
Fr: *Fourrer;* Ger: *Bekleiden.*

SERVICE. Tarred spun yarn or marline tightly bound over the worming and parceling around a rope to protect it from wear and weather.
Fr: *Fourrure;* Ger: *Bekleidung.*

SERVICE HORSEPOWER. In cargo ships and in a number of passenger vessels with steam engines this term refers to about 80 per cent of the power developed on trial and is the usual power at which engines are run for the sake of economy and regularity.
Fr: *Puissance Normale;* Ger: *Normale Leistung in Pferdestärke; Dienstpferdestärke.*

SERVICE SPEED. The speed of a vessel with clean bottom loaded to her designed draft with engines exerting average power on a voyage of standard weather frequency. The mean sea speed for a series of voyages. Sometimes called commercial speed.
Fr: *Vitesse Normale; Vitesse Commerciale;* Ger: *Seegeschwindigkeit; Dienstgeschwindigkeit; Normale Geschwindigkeit; Fahrgeschwindigkeit.*
Kent, J. L., "Average Sea Speeds of Ships Under Winter Weather Conditions," Institution of Naval Architects (London), *Transactions,* 1927; Taylor, D. W., *The Speed and Power of Ships,* Washington, 1933.

SERVICE TANKS. In steamships equipped with oil-fired boilers, fuel oil tanks located under the engine rooms or in other spaces near the fire rooms, to maintain a reasonably large supply of oil ready for immediate use. Commonly found in naval vessels.

SERVING BOARD. See **Serving Mallet.**

SERVING MALLET. A cylindrical piece of ash or lignum vitae wood fitted with a handle and having a groove on one side to fit the convexity of a rope. It is used as an aid in serving ropes or wrapping them round with spun yarn, and so on, to prevent chafing. Also called serving board, service board. Diameter of head 3 in., length of head 7½ in., radius of groove ⅝ in., length of handle 12 in.
Fr: *Mailloche;* Ger: *Kleidkeule.*

SERVING STUFF. Spun yarn, hambroline, houseline, or roundline used for serving a rope.
Fr: *Ligne à fourrer;* Ger: *Kleidungsgut.*

SET. 1. Collectively speaking: a number of sails which complement each other and

fit the spars of a vessel or boat. Also called suit.
Fr: *Jeu de Voiles;* Ger: *Segelstell.*
2. The set of a current is that point of the compass toward which the water runs.
Fr: *Direction;* Ger: *Stromrichtung.*
See **Roll Set.**
SET (to). To loosen and extend. To spread to the wind, as a sail.
Fr: *Etablir;* Ger: *Setzen.*
SET-BACK.
See **Skew Back.**
SET BOLT. A bolt used as a punch or drift to force another bolt further in than can be done by driving.
Ger: *Zugbolzen.*
SET IRON. In shipbuilding, a flat bar of soft iron used for transferring the curvature of a frame, etc., from the scrieve board to the bending slab.
SET NET. An entangling net, either gill or trammel net, attached to some fixed object such as the shore, the bottom of the sea, or an anchored boat. It may be set on the surface or it may be submerged. It can only be set on or near the bottom when there is little current.
Fr: *Filet Dormant; Filet Fixe;* Ger: *Stellnetz.*
SET SAIL. To begin a voyage. The term is used for mechanically propelled vessels as well as for sailing vessels.
Fr: *Mettre à la voile;* Ger: *Abfahren.*
SETT.
See **Wrain Staff.**
SETTAGE. A tax laid on incoming vessels for the use of a jetty or pier. (Obsolete.)
SETTEE. Long, sharp, decked, and lateen-rigged craft of the Mediterranean.
Fr: *Sétie;* Ger: *Settie.*
See **Settee Sail.**
SETTEE RIG. A rig adopted for small sailing craft. It requires only low masts and answers well for boats of narrow hull form, the broadest part of the sail being kept low down.
Fr: *Gréement de Sétie;* Ger: *Settie Takelung.*
SETTEE SAIL. A quadrilateral lateen sail with short luff used by Spanish, Portuguese, and Arabian craft. The leech is about five sixths of the length of the head and the luff one fifth to one sixth of the depth of the leech. The foot is gored to provide a circular sweep. One row of reef points runs at one fifth of the depth of the leech from the foot. It is said to be of Arab origin.
Fr: *Voile à demie Antenne; Voile de Sétie; Voile de Chébec;* Ger: *Schebeckensegel.*
SETTING FID.
See **Cringle Fid.**
SETTING MAUL. A wood calking tool used for striking setting, or making irons. Also called making maul. It has a short, thick, barrel-shaped head of hardwood bound on the ends with iron rings, as the calking mallet, and is fitted with a straight round handle.
Fr: *Maillet à Patarasser;* Ger: *Schleihammer.*
SETTINGS. The small lines by which the balch line is fastened to the ground rope in a trawl net.
Ger: *Bandsel; Strippen.*
SETTING UP.
See **Wedging Up.**
SETTLE. To ease slightly, as a fall or tackle.
SETTLING TANK. 1. In ships equipped with oil-burning boilers, a small tank, located in the fire room, not integral with the ship's structure, and fitted with steam-heating coils. It is used as a receiving space for oil which is contaminated with water. The contaminated oil is heated and the water settles by gravity to the bottom of the tank, whence it is drawn off and discharged overboard or to a bilge sump tank. The oil may then be passed through a purifier, to remove every trace of water, and the purified oil is returned to a service tank.
2. In Diesel-engined ships, a similar tank in which impurities are separated by settling out before the oil is drawn off for use.
Fr: *Caisse de Décantation;* Ger: *Absetztank; Klarbehälter; Setzöltank.*
SETT PILING. Piles driven into the ground as a foundation for the building ways. Sometimes a concrete slab is laid on top of the sett piling over the entire bottom of the ways. The piling must often be driven very deep to find solid footing and to guarantee against any settling under the weight of the ship.
SET UP. To haul taut or take in the slack, as in standing rigging, to bring the shrouds or other rigging to a uniform and proper tension by adjusting the turnbuckles or lanyards.

Fr: *Rider; Raidir;* Ger: *Ansetzen.*

SEVERAL FISHERY (G. B.). The right to fish in certain areas granted to private persons and in which places the public has no right to fish. At present a several fishery in Great Britain must have been acquired either by a grant previous to the Magna Charta or by prescription or by Act of Parliament.

SEVERALTY. A law term indicating the reference of disagreements among part owners of a ship or her cargo, to the courts.

SEW. Refers to the depth of water lacking to keep a grounded ship afloat at low tide. If the water has left her 2 ft. she has "Sewed" 2 ft. Also called Sue.

SEWAGE TANK. One of several tanks for the disposal of sewage in a passenger vessel. The contents of the tank are expelled by sewage ejectors using compressed air, with discharge openings located in the ship's bottom.

Fr: *Caisse à eau Sale;* Ger: *Abwasserbehälter.*

Marine Sewage Disposal, Marine Engineer, London, vol. 56, September, 1933, pp. 265/7.

SEWED. Said of a ship resting upon the ground when there is not sufficient depth of water to float her. Also called sewed up. A vessel thus situated is said to be sewed up by as much as is the difference between the level of the water and her floating line.

Fr: *Déjaugé;* Ger: *Trocken gefallen.*

SEWN PLANKING (G. B.). A method of planking dispensing with seam battens and calking and used for the construction of high-speed boats, canoes, and so on. It consists of layers of thin mahogany sewed together with copper wire passing through holes bored in the ribs. It is said to give great strength combined with flexibility. Its inventors are Messrs. S. E. Saunders, Cowes. Another method of accomplishing this is to string the planks edgewise with copper wire and draw them up in place. Narrow planks of about the same width as their thickness are generally used for this system. The planking thus fastened is very flexible, but the costs of construction are high.

Fr: *Bordé Cousu;* Ger: *Angeliekte Beplankung.*

SEXTANT. A portable reflecting astronomical instrument for measuring angles. It is principally employed for measuring the altitude of heavenly bodies at sea, but it can also be useful in determining the horizontal angles between landmarks to fix a position. The instrument consists of a triangular frame one side of which is the graduated arc of a circle about 75° in scope. At the opposite angle an arm is pivoted which swings across the surface of the frame and the graduated arc, and by a system of reflecting mirrors the images whose angle is desired are brought together and the angle read from the arc. Principal parts of a sextant are the frame, the arc and the arm, the index glass, horizon glass, telescope and vernier. A sextant usually measures angles of 120 to 150°. The principle of the sextant is that the angle between the first and last directions of a ray which has suffered two reflections in one plane is equal to twice the inclination of the reflecting surfaces to each other.

Fr: *Sextant;* Ger: *Sextant.*

See **Angle Sextant, Sounding Sextant.**
U. S. Bureau of Standards, "Specifications for Marine Sextants," Circular no. 110, Washington, 1921.

SEXTANT ADJUSTMENTS. The art of correcting the various errors to which a sextant is liable and which can be eliminated.

Fr: *Rectifications du Sextant;* Ger: *Sextantberichtigungen.*

See **Error.**

After adjusting, the instrument should have: (1) the index glass perpendicular to the plane of the instrument; (2) the horizon glass perpendicular to the plane of the instrument; (3) the line of collimation parallel to the plane of the instrument; (4) the horizon glass parallel to the index glass when the index is set at zero.

The sextant has also three so-called unadjustable errors which are: the centering error, the prismatic error, and the shade error.

SEXTANT TELESCOPE. A small telescope used with a sextant. It has a good field of view and brightness of image. It fits into a screw collar and is parallel to the plane of the instrument and in line with the horizon glass. Each sextant is generally provided with two telescopes, as well as an inverting telescope. The long telescope has a magnifying power of 6 to 10 diameters and has two eyepieces with a fine wire through the center of the field and two coarse wires at right angles to it. The short telescope is of Galilean type with a magni-

Sextant

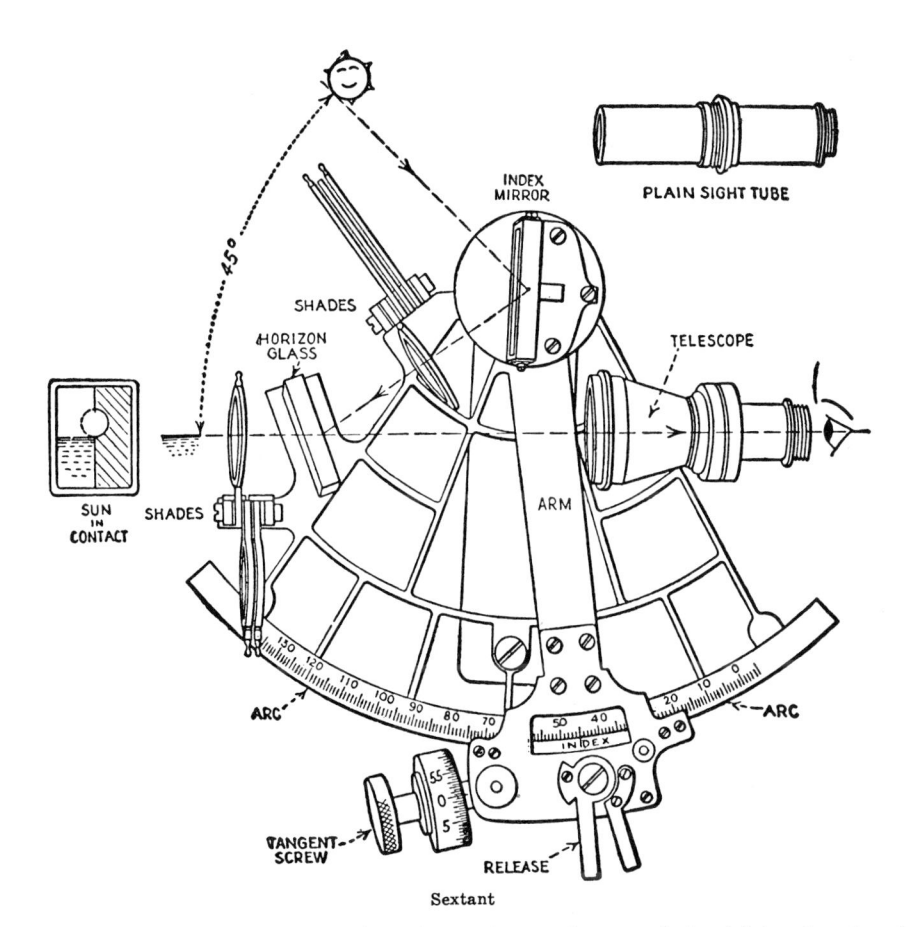

fying power of about three. It consists of a double object glass with double concave eyepiece placed beyond the focus of the object glass at a distance of virtual focus of the eye lens.

Fr: *Lunette Terrestre;* Ger: *Sextantenfernrohr.*

SHACK FISHING. Among American and Canadian fishermen from Nova Scotia, a method of capture in which the men fish from the deck of the boat each with several long lines. Each hand dresses his own fish and gets credit for his catch when sharing.

SHACKLE. 1. A bow-shaped, D-shaped, saddle-shaped, or U-shaped wrought-iron or steel fitting with a pin across the throat, used as a connection between lengths of chain, or to attach other fittings. Shackles used in the rigging have a threaded pin, whereas those used for joining lengths of anchor chains have a smooth, heavy pin, held in place by a small cotter.

Fr: *Manille;* Ger: *Schakel.*

American Marine Standards Committee, Standard 82, "Rigging Shackles," 1931; British Standards Institution, Standard 825, Shackles (Mild Steel) for Lifting Purposes, 1939.

2. *Shackle.* A "shackle" or "length of cable" is the standard length of a piece of chain cable as manufactured, each length being connected to the next one by a joining shackle. Also called shot. In the British navy a length of cable is 12½ fathoms. In the U. S. Navy and in the merchant service, it is 15 fathoms.

Fr: *Maillon;* Ger: *Kabellänge; Kettenende.*

3. To join or make fast with a shackle two ends of a chain or rope.
Fr: *Maniller;* Ger: *Einschakeln.*

SHACKLE BLOCK. An iron-strapped block fitted with a shackle and bolt attachment. If the shackle bolt passes through the eye of the strap the block is called a regular or standard shackle block. If the U passes through the eye it is known as an upset shackle block. When the shackle is made fast in the direction of the circumference of the sheave it is called a front shackle block. When made fast in the direction of the pin it is a side shackle block. The same terminology is used for hook blocks, which are termed front hook or side hook blocks according to the direction of attachment of the hook.

SHACKLE BOLT. A bolt which passes through the eyes of a shackle and is secured by a shackle pin.
Fr: *Boulon de Manille;* Ger: *Schakelbolzen.*

SHACKLE PIN. The small pin of wood or iron that secures a shackle bolt in place. The bolt may be secured by a pin through each end, or by one end headed and a pin through the other, also by a pin through one end and through the eye.

SHACK LOCKER (U. S.). A room or compartment on fishing craft where food is available at all hours.

SHADE DECK. A very light deck not enclosed at sides and supported by stanchions. Such a deck does not usually extend from bow to stern. Its purpose is to provide protection for passengers against the weather.
Fr: *Shade Deck;* Ger: *Schattendeck.*

SHADE-DECK VESSEL. A vessel provided with a full length superstructure of very light construction which is open on the sides. Intended primarily to provide a moderate degree of protection for passengers; since its construction is light and the sides are not enclosed it gives the hull no greater structural strength or buoyancy.
Fr: *Navire à Shade Deck;* Ger: *Schattendeckschiff.*

SHADE ERROR. In a sextant, the angle through which the index must be moved to restore contact between the reflected and direct images of the observed heavenly body if these images do not remain in contact when a shade is interposed in the optical system. This error is usually recorded for each shade or combination of shades.
Fr: *Rectification du Petit Miroir;* Ger: *Spiegelfehler.*

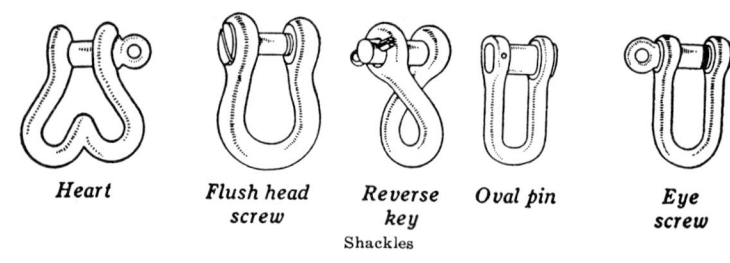

*Heart   Flush head   Reverse   Oval pin   Eye
              screw   key   screw*
                               Shackles

SHADOW. A quadrilateral spinnaker with very short head which hauls out on a temporary gaff rigged out at the masthead. The foot hauls out to the spinnaker boom in the customary manner.

SHADOW PIN. A vertical pin 3 or 4 in. high fitted on the glass cover of a compass and used for taking the sun's azimuth.

SHAFFLE. The fitting on a mast which receives the gooseneck pin of the boom.

SHAFT ALLEY. A watertight passage extending from engine room to stern tube and providing access to the line of shafting. Also called shaft tunnel.
Fr: *Tunnel;* Ger: *Wellentunnel.*

SHAFT BRACKET.
See Propeller Strut.

SHAFT HORSEPOWER. The horsepower obtained from a torsion meter applied to a calibrated section of the line shafting. In steam reciprocating engines the shaft horsepower is approximately 85 to 95 per cent of the indicated horsepower, in diesel engines with direct drive 67 to 76 per cent. The expression "maximum designed shaft horsepower" is used to denote the shaft horsepower at 10 per cent in excess of the normal shaft horsepower, the latter being the shaft horsepower established by the specifications. The maximum designed shaft horsepower is used in determining the various safety factors for the component parts of the machinery. In a turbine installation it is the power developed with all the turbine nozzles open. In a diesel installation it is the maximum overload condition as fixed by the specifications. Also called brake horsepower.

Fr: *Puissance au frein; Puissance sur l'Arbre;* Ger: *Bremspferdestärke; Wellenpferdestärke.*

SHAFTING. The medium by which the motion of the engines is transmitted to the propeller screws. From the crankshaft of the reciprocating engine, the main shaft of a direct-drive turbine, or the bull gear of a geared turbine, the rotational motion is communicated to the propeller by means of sections of shafting carried by bearings and secured to each other by couplings, usually flanged. The after section carrying the propeller is known as the propeller or tail shaft, the section fitted to work in the thrust bearing to transmit the thrust of the propeller to the ship is called the thrust shaft, the section in the stern tube, the stern tube shaft, and the intermediate sections are known as line shafting. The shafting is usually a high-grade steel forging.

Fr: *Ligne d'Arbres.*

SHAFT LINER. A brass liner which encases the propeller shaft as protection against the corrosive action of sea water. It may be fitted by forcing on cold with hydraulic pressure or shrunk on hot. In some cases, particularly with reference to small vessels, the shaft is built with two short liners, one fixed at the forward end in way of the stern gland, the other aft in way of the stern bush. The space between the liners is served with canvas and tarry twine, the whole being coated over with special composition paint.

Fr: *Chemise d'Arbre;* Ger: *Propellerwelle Uberzug.*

SHAFT LOG. A timber connected to the keel and the after deadwood through which the propeller shaft passes. Some shaft logs are made of one piece of wood with shaft hole bored through. Others are built up of two pieces bolted together. The hole is frequently provided with a lead or copper sleeve flanged and fastened to the log at both ends.

Ger: *Wellenklotz.*

SHAFT STRUT. A bracket supporting the afterend of the propeller shaft and the propeller in twin or multiple-screw vessels having propeller shafts off the center line.

Fr: *Support d'Arbre;* Ger: *Wellenbock.*

See **Bossing, Spectacle Frame.**

SHAKE. Cracks, flaws, or clefts which occur in timber. They may have occurred during growth or may be due to unequal shrinkage.

Fr: *Cadranure;* Ger: *Kernriss.*

See **Cup Shake, Heart Shake, Star Shake.**

SHAKE (to). To shake a vessel in the wind. To bring a vessel's head so close to the wind that the sails shiver.

Fr: *Faire ralinguer;* Ger: *Segel Tillen.*

SHAKEDOWN CRUISE. A journey of varying length made by a new vessel for the purpose of running in and adjusting machinery and instruments, as well as familiarizing the crew with the working and handling of the ship. Shakedown cruises of merchant vessels are relatively short, but naval vessels usually voyage several thousand miles.

SHAKE OUT. To shake out a reef; that is, to untie the reef points and spread more canvas.

Fr: *Larguer;* Ger: *Auslassen.*

SHAKES. Parts of casks or barrels knocked down for shipment.

SHALLOP. A lug-rigged, two-masted fishing boat. This term was also applied to an open boat propelled by oars or sails, for use in shallow waters. (Obsolete.)

SHALLOW. An area of water where the depth is relatively slight.

Fr: *Petit fond; Haut fond;* Ger: *Untiefe.*

SHALLOW FLOOR. A floor of comparatively small depth, as found in single-bottom vessels.

Fr: *Varangue Basse;* Ger: *Niedrige Bodenwrange.*

SHAMAL. A northwesterly wind of the Persian Gulf.

SHANGHAI-ING. Unlawful practice of procuring or inducing a person by force, threat or misrepresentation, or while the person is intoxicated, to go on board ship or to enter into a vessel to perform service or labor thereon.

SHANK PAINTER. The rope or chain securing the fluke of an anchor on the billboard to a toe of the tumbler arm.

Fr: *Serre Bosse;* Ger: *Rüstleine.*

SHANTY. A sailor's song, especially one which was sung in former days during heavy work such as mastheading a topsail yard, weighing anchor and in general during all work where unison and strength were required. Shanties were of two kinds: those sung at the capstan and those sung when hauling on a rope. Also called chantey.

SHAOSING OR HANGCHOW BAY JUNK. A three-masted trading junk originating from the port of Shaosing on the Yung Ho River, Province of Chekiang. These junks are chiefly engaged in carrying firewood, charcoal, and cotton from Chekiang ports to Shanghai. The largest are about 100 ft. long and carry up to 3000 piculs (180 tons). The hull is flat-bottomed with swim-headed bows and square transom stern. Portable decking. They have a very light draft and carry leeboards.

Waters, D. W., Hangchow Bay trader and fisher, *Mariners Mirror*, London, vol. 33, January, 1947.

SHAPE. A structural section or girder. See **Bar**.

SHARKI. Local southeasterly wind which blows during the winter months in the Persian Gulf and reaches force 7 (Beaufort Scale). Also called "Kaus."

SHARKS' MOUTH. An opening in an awning where masts and stays pierce it.

SHARP BILGE. A sharply curved bilge, as found in flat-floored hulls. Also called hard bilge.

Fr: *Bouchain Vif*; Ger: *Scharfe Kimmrundung*.

SHARP-BOTTOMED. A hull with considerable rise of floors.

Fr: *A Varangues acculées*; Ger: *Scharf gebaut*.

SHARPIE. Long, flat-bottomed, centerboard boat used for pleasure or fishing in the U. S. The original rig consisted of two short masts which carried a triangular leg-of-mutton sail extended by a horizontal sprit. Racing sharpies have a large single sail laced to a boom. The floor or bottom of a sharpie is usually rockered or rounded up at both ends. Length/Beam ratio is from four to five. As a rule the boat is decked at both ends. The Florida sharpie employed in the Gulf Coast fisheries is the largest of this type of boats. Length over-all 56 ft. Beam 12 ft. Depth from bottom of garboard to top of gunwale 4 ft. (Average.)

It is rigged with two leg-o-mutton sails. The New England Sharpie has an over-all length of about 35 feet, beam 19 feet 9 inches. It is decked at ends with a large cockpit in center. The North Carolina Sharpie used in operating pound nets is smaller than the above: its length over-all is only about 28 feet. The sails are of the jib headed pattern with sprits. The mainsail is loose footed.

Chapelle, H. I., *American Sailing Craft*, New York, 1936.

SHARPSHOOTER. 1. A double-ended, decked sailing boat from the Bahama Islands, with short hollow entrance, long run, and greatest beam forward of amidships. Raking stem and sternpost. The rig consists of a mast stepped in the bow with leg-of-mutton sail. Length over-all 24 ft. Keel 20 ft. Breadth 9 ft. (Typical.)

Chapelle, H. I., Bahama Sharpshooters, Yachting, New York, vol. 53, August, 1932.

2. Local name given in the eighteen sixties to a type of New England fishing schooner because of its reputed sharpness in deadrise and waterlines. Also called file bottom. Now extinct.

SHARP STERN. A pointer stern of triangular section, stem and sternpost being alike, and with outboard rudder. It is frequently found in lifeboat construction. Also called lifeboat stern or whaleboat stern. In the construction of small craft the sharp stern possesses certain advantages: it is cheap to build and perfect longitudinal balance of hull under seagoing conditions is more easily obtained by its use, giving greater comfort in rough weather. The objections are mainly a loss of initial stability due to the lack of buoyancy aft and the curtailing of deck space and of room below deck.

Fr: *Arrière Pointu*; Ger: *Scharfer Heck*.

SHARP UP. The position of the yards in a square rigged vessel when braced as nearly fore and aft as the rigging will allow.

SHASHA. An Arab raft or float made of date sticks, used on the Batira coast of the Gulf of Oman for fishing and for communicating with native craft anchored off shore. It is made of two bunches tied together at the small end to form the stem. The thick ends are joined to form the skeleton of the float which is filled up with palm bark coconut fiber. Their length is about 12 ft. and they hold one or two men.

SHA-TENG. Sampan of Canton River used to ferry passengers. The central part of the boat has a cabin. Length 24 to 28 ft. Breadth 6 to 8 ft.

SHAY. A local name given in Ipswich Bay, Mass., to the Isle of Shoals boat.

See **Isle of Shoals Boat**.

SHEAR LEGS. See **Sheerlegs**.

SHEATHING—SHEAVE

SHEATHING. 1. A covering fastened to the underwater body of wooden, composite, or steel hulls as a protection against ship worms and marine growths of all kinds. Zinc, galvanized iron, or copper are used. In iron-fastened hulls, copper is not used, in order to avoid electrolytic action between dissimilar metals. Over brass or treenail fastenings, copper sheathing is very satisfactory and is frequently used. Heavy brown paper, well tarred and oiled, or sheets of felt are laid between the sheathing and the planking.

Fr: *Doublage;* Ger: *Kupferhaut; Bodenbeschlag.*

See **Deck Sheathing.**

Hot-rolled or cold-rolled copper sheets weighing from 14 to 16 ounces per square foot are generally used for sheathing. The former is more pliable and easier to fit over curves but the cold rolled metal gives a better surface. The sheathing is generally carried up to a height of about 3 in. above designed waterline and kept parallel to it. Wood treated with creosote is often used to sheathe barges and lighters.

2. Light sheet metal covering over insulation applied to bulkhead or overhead plating.

SHEATHING NAIL. A cast nail made of an alloy of copper and tin, used in fastening the metallic sheathing to the hull of a wooden vessel. They are from ¾ in. to 2¼ in. long with large polished countersunk flat heads which do not encourage the adhesion of weeds.

Fr: *Clou à Doublage;* Ger: *Kupferhautnagel.*

SHEATHING PAPER. A coarse paper laid in several thicknesses under the copper sheathing of a wooden vessel.

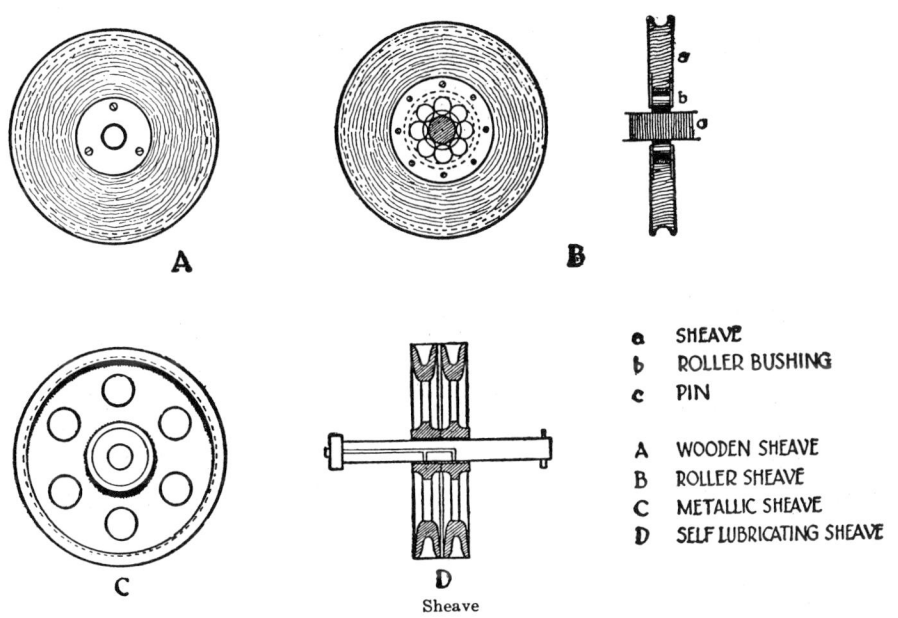

```
a   SHEAVE
b   ROLLER BUSHING
c   PIN

A   WOODEN SHEAVE
B   ROLLER SHEAVE
C   METALLIC SHEAVE
D   SELF LUBRICATING SHEAVE
```

Sheave

Fr: *Papier à doublage;* Ger: *Futterpappe.*

SHEATH KNIFE. A knife without clasp worn by seamen. It fits into a leather sheath attached to a belt.

Ger: *Scheidemesser.*

SHEAVE. A grooved wheel in a block, mast, yard, and so on, over which a rope passes. The sheave, which is bushed, rotates upon the pin. Sheaves are made of wood, bronze, or galvanized cast-iron or steel. For running rigging where severe or heavy intermittent strains are expected, as in the case of runners and topping lifts, brass sheaves are used.

Fr: *Réa;* Ger: *Scheibe.*

See **Dead Sheave, Disc Sheave, Dumb Sheave, Half Sheave, Roller Sheave, Self-Lubricating Sheave, Spoke Sheave.**

Wooden sheaves are made of lignum vitae wood bushed with bronze. Iron or steel sheaves are used with flexible wire rope to prevent galvanic action, which would soon damage the rope. They are of much greater diameter than those for fiber rope (15 to 20 times the rope's diameter). The groove should fit the rope accurately so as to support it for one third of its circumference. In practice the diameter of the groove at the bottom should be 1/16 in. greater than the diameter of the rope, with an angle of flare from 50 to 60 degrees.

Ratio of diameter to thickness (wooden sheaves):
    Heavy purchase falls 4
    Running gear 5
    Boat falls 6

SHEAVE-HO. A cry raised when the blocks of a tackle have come together by hauling or the tackle is two-blocked, and it is necessary to overhaul it.

SHEBAR. Name given by the Swahili people on the east coast of Africa to a small Arab dhow with sharp stern.

SHEEPSHANK. A hitch made in a rope to shorten it. It is formed by making a long bight in the rope, and taking a half hitch near each end. It remains secure only as long as there is a strain on the rope.

Fr: *Jambe de chien;* Ger: *Trompetenstich; Verkürzungstrompete.*

See **Knotted Sheepshank, Toggled Sheepshank.**

SHEEPSHANK WITH REEF. A variety of sheepshank which is more secure than the ordinary or plain sheepshank.

SHEER. 1. The longitudinal curvature of the deck at side between stem and sternpost. In amplitude, it is equal to from 2 to 4 per cent of length in merchant vessels. The lowest point of sheer is located amidships in cargo vessels. Passenger vessels and yachts are generally designed with low point of sheer at 0.6 to 0.7 of the length from the stem. The forward sheer is about two thirds and the after sheer about one third of the total sheer.

Fr: *Tonture;* Ger: *Sprung.*

2. The position in which a ship is sometimes kept when riding at a single anchor in order to keep her clear of it.

See **Plank Sheer, Standard Sheer.**

SHEER (to). To deviate from the line of the course so as to form a crooked and irregular path through the water. This may be due to the ship being difficult to steer, or to careless handling of the helm.

Fr: *Embarder;* Ger: *Scheren.*

SHEER CLEAT.
See **Whaleboat Chock.**

SHEER CURVE.
See **Sheer Line.**

SHEER DRAFT. A drawing which serves principally for the reproduction of a vessel's lines in natural size on the mold loft floor. It consists of three plans, the sheer plan, the half-breadth plan, the body plan. Also called sheer drawing.

Fr: *Plan Longitudinal;* Ger: *Längenriss; Aufriss.*

See **Lines.**

SHEER HEAD LASHING. A lashing secured to the legs of sheers with cross turns and a reef knot. When the legs are separated the lashing is tautened.

Fr: *Amarrage en Portugaise;* Ger: *Kopflaschung.*

SHEER HULK. A vessel or any floating structure fitted with sheer legs and used in a harbor for lifting heavy weights and placing or removing masts.

Fr: *Ponton-Mâture;* Ger: *Hulk mit Mastenkran.*

SHEERING BATTEN, SHEER BATTEN. A wooden batten fixed to the frames after erection, for fairing the landings of shell plates, in relation to the sheer line.

Fr: *Lisse de Construction;* Ger: *Sprietlatte; Spreizlatte; Sente.*

SHEERLEGS. Also shear legs. A triangular weight handling framework consisting of two spars or girders fastened together near the top, with their lower ends spread out to form a base. The legs are steadied by guys, and the hoisting tackle is suspended from the apex. Used in harbors and dockyards for handling heavy weights from ship to shore and vice versa.

Fr: *Bigues;* Ger: *Bock; Mastenkran.*

SHEER LINE. The longitudinal curve of the rail or decks which shows the variation in height above water or freeboard throughout the vessel's entire length. Also called sheer curve.

Fr: *Ligne de Tonture;* Ger: *Decksprunglinie.*

SHEER MAST. A mast made of two poles fitted triangle fashion on the principle of sheers and stepped on each side of the boat. Common to *prahus* and other craft of the Eastern seas.

Fr: *Mât Bipode;* Ger: *Zweibeinmast.*

SHEER MOLD. A long thin plank for adjusting the rail line on the ship's side in

order to form the sheer of the ship. One of its edges is curved to the extent of the sheer intended to be given.
Ger: *Strakmallung*.

SHEER MOLDING. A molding which follows the upper deckline on the outside of the planking or plating. Also called sheer rail.
Fr: *Lisse de Plat-Bord;* Ger: *Schandeckelleiste*.

SHEER OFF. To move away from. The opposite of to bear toward.

SHEER PLAN. A plan showing the longitudinal, vertical section passing through the median line of a vessel. Also called sheer draft, inboard profile.
Fr: *Plan Longitudinal;* Ger: *Längsriss; Aufriss*.

SHEER POLE. An iron bar or wooden batten seized across the shrouds above the upper deadeyes or the turnbuckle serving as a first ratline. Also called sheer batten. It is generally provided with belaying pins.
Fr: *Quenouillette;* Ger: *Bockstange; Spreelatte*.

SHEER RATLINE. A name given to every fifth ratline which extends to the swifter and after shroud.
Fr: *Enfléchure Bâtarde;* Ger: *Springwebeleine*.

SHEER STRAKE. Strake of shell plating running next to the main, or strength-deck, its upper edge having the curvature or sheer of the vessel. The sheer strake forms with its adjacent stringer plate the top flange of the ship girder, and for this reason is always of increased thickness.
Fr: *Virure de Carreau;* Ger: *Farbegang; Scheergang*.

SHEET. 1. A rope or chain fastened to one or both of the lower corners of a sail, and used to extend it or to change its direction. The ropes, in the square sails above the course, by which the clews are extended. In the courses, each clew has a tack and sheet, the tack being used to extend the weather clew, and the sheet the lee clew. In fore-and-aft sails, except gaff topsails, the sheet secures the after lower corner and the tack the forward lower corner. In studding sails the tack secures the outer clew and the sheet the inner one.
Fr: *Ecoute;* Ger: *Schot*.

2. A term which distinguishes the thinner from the thicker plates used in shipbuilding. A plate ⅛ in. in thickness is called a "sheet"; above that thickness it is called a "plate."
Fr: *Feuillard;* Ger: *Feinblech; Eisenblech*.

SHEET ANCHOR. A spare anchor formerly carried in the waist of the ship, as far forward as convenient. Sometimes called waist anchor. It was the largest anchor aboard and was kept ready for use in an emergency, with cable bent. Sheet anchors are nowadays generally called spare bower or best bower.
Fr: *Ancre de Veille;* Ger: *Pflichtanker; Rüstanker*.

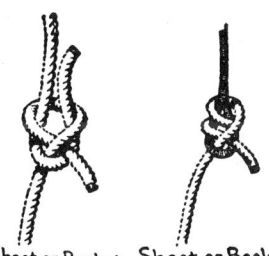

Sheet or Becket Bend Single. Sheet or Becket Bend Double.

Sheet Bend

SHEET BEND. A type of double hitch made by passing the end of one rope through the bight of another, around both parts of the other, and under its own part. Also called single bend, becket bend, swab hitch, signal halliard bend. It is used for joining two ropes, especially when of different sizes, also in bending small sheets to the clews of sails, and in bending flags where snap hooks are not fitted.
Fr: *Noeud d'écoute simple;* Ger: *Einfacher Schotenstek*.

SHEET HOME. To strain or haul on a sheet until the foot of a sail is as straight and as taut as possible.
Fr: *Border Plat; Border à Joindre;* Ger: *Vorscholen*.

SHEET ICE. A thin layer of new ice, smooth and level.
Fr: *Couche de Glace;* Ger: *Flächeneis; Eisschild*.

SHEET IRON.
See **Sheet**.

SHEET IRON BOARD. A platform sling especially designed for handling structural steel of short lengths and other similarly heavy and hard commodities. It is 9½ ft. long, 4 ft. wide. A narrower type

12 ft. long, 2 ft. wide, is used for small strips of sheet iron, reinforcing steel, pipes, tubes and other similar metal shipments.

SHEET LIGHTNING. The reflection of fork lightning. Also called summer lightning.

Fr: *Exhalaison;* Ger: *Wetterleuchten; Flächenblitz.*

SHEETS. The spaces in the forward and afterends of a row boat, not occupied by oarsmen.

See **Flowing Sheets, Foresheets, Off-set Sheets, Stern Sheets.**

SHEET WINCH. Small hand winch with vertical barrel, used on sailing yachts for handling jib sheets, with an average load from three-quarters to one and one-half tons. A similar winch with horizontal barrel attached to the bulwark railing was used on merchant sailing vessels for trimming the fore and main sheets.

Ger: *Schotenwinde; Relingswinde.*

SHELF. 1. An inner timber or line of timbers which follows the sheer of the vessel and is bolted to the underside of the beams to strengthen the frame and sustain the deck. The term "lock shelf" is used when the beam is locked to the shelf by means of a key piece, a coak or any other projection which fits into a corresponding score in the underside of the beam.

Fr: *Bauquière;* Ger: *Balkweger.*

2. In launching, a series of brackets riveted to the shell plating forming a bearing surface for the heads of the forepoppets. Also called poppet shelf. It is used when launching large heavy vessels to prevent the poppets from slipping upward.

3. The zone of the ocean bottom extending from the line of permanent immersion to the depth where there is a marked steep descent toward the great depths.

Fr: *Plateau;* Ger: *Schelff.*

See **Continental Shelf, Metacentric Shelf.**

SHELF ICE. A form of land ice in the Antarctic produced by an accumulation of horizontal layers of snow which has reached the intermediate opaque "Neve" stage, before passing into true glacier ice. Portions of the shelf ice break off to form tabular bergs.

Ger: *Eiszunge.*

SHELL. 1. The wooden or metal casing of a block in which the sheaves revolve. It may be all wood, with a rope strap, wood with internal iron strap, or all metal. Ash or elm are used for wooden shells; steel or composition for metal shells.

Fr: *Caisse;* Ger: *Gehäuse.*

2. The outer hull of a ship.

See **Paying Shell.**

SHELL BOSSING. A local swelling of the shell plating and frames found in twin- and quadruple-screw vessels where the propeller shafts pierce the hull. Also called shaft bossing. It terminates nearly at right angles to the shell, where the shaft enters in a casting called a spectacle frame. Shaft bossings not only reduce resistance but also have the advantage of strengthening the afterend of the ship and obviate the

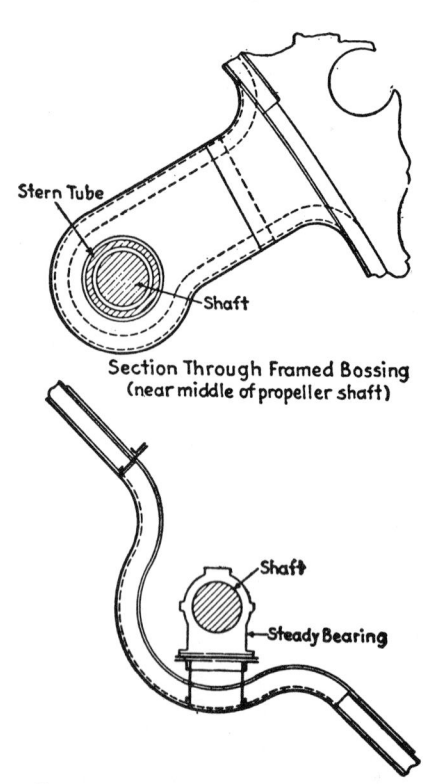

Shell Bossing. (Courtesy Society of Naval Architects and Marine Engineers, N. Y.)

possibility of damage to exposed shafts, as is the case when struts are fitted. Propulsion resistance is increased 10 to 12 per cent in twin-screw ships if bossings are installed.

Fr: *Aileron;* Ger: *Wellenhose.*

SHELL CHOCK. One of the closely fitting chocks placed in the waterway spaces of a 'tween deck between the stringer bar and shell plating. Various materials such as wood covered with cement, a mixture of coke and cement, or concrete are used. Experience having shown that cement or concrete, being inelastic, have a tendency to crack and break away from the shell and frames, the latest practice is to use a mixture of large gravel and an asphalt by-product with a high melting point. The gravel is laid first within the space and then the asphalt is poured in hot.

Fr: *Accotar;* Ger: *Aufklotzung.*

SHELL EXPANSION PLAN. A plan which provides information for the ordering, manufacturing, and fitting of outside shell plating.

Fr: *Plan de développement de bordé;* Ger: *Plattenabwicklungszeichnung.*

The principal data usually indicated on this plan are: ordered dimensions and marks of each plate; position, form and thickness of all doubling plates; sizes and location of cargo ports, sidelights, and all other openings; location of watertight bulkheads, tank margins and divisions, decks, stringers, bilge keels and fenders; breadths of landings, lapped joints, and butt straps; size and spacing of rivets.

Since the outside hull form of a ship cannot be geometrically developed, this plan is not a correct expansion of the shell plating. It is necessary therefore to make a wooden model called the plating model, and lay off the plates on it.

SHELL LANDINGS. The points of intersection of the frames with the edges of the various shell plates as shown on the shell expansion plan.

SHELL LONGITUDINAL. In a longitudinally framed hull one of the closely spaced stiffeners riveted or welded to the shell plating.

Fr: *Membrure Longitudinale de Bordé;* Ger: *Aussenhautlängsspant.*

SHELL PLATING. A collective term for the outer plating of a vessel, comprising bottom plating, bilge plating, and side plating.

Fr: *Bordé Extérieur;* Ger: *Aussenhaut.*

Shell plating is laid in longitudinal strakes, the first one being nearest to the keel. Plates vary in thickness according to their position, being thickest amidships and tapering in thickness toward each end of the hull. For convenience in working, shell plates are numbered and lettered, each strake corresponding to a letter, the strake nearest to the keel being known as "A" strake. The numbers of plates may run from forward aft or conversely.

SHELTER. A light superstructure built at each end of the navigating bridge to afford a shelter for navigating officers. Also called wing shelter, bridge shelter.

Fr: *Cagnard;* Ger: *Schutz; Windschutz.*

SHELTER DECK. A deck similar to an awning deck, differing from it in that the 'tween deck space below is not included in the vessel's net register tonnage. This omission is allowed under existing tonnage laws on condition that somewhere in the deck an opening referred to as "tonnage opening" is arranged for without *permanent* means of closing it, and that no part of the 'tween deck space under the shelter deck is partitioned off or enclosed in a *permanent* manner.

Fr: *Shelter Deck;* Ger: *Schutzdeck.*

SHELTER-DECK VESSEL. A type of ship with a full length superstructure above the principal deck, the superstructure being of lighter construction than would be required for a ship of full scantlings to the uppermost continuous deck. Also called complete superstructure vessel. Shelter-deck vessels may be of the three-island type, or with erections of various kinds built over the shelter deck. The shelter 'tween deck spaces can be excluded from the net tonnage (except in calculating the Suez Canal charges) and dues need be paid only on such spaces as are actually occupied by cargo. The ship is made subject to certain restrictions on freeboard and draft, corresponding to permitted methods for temporary closing of openings and scuppers in the shelter deck space.

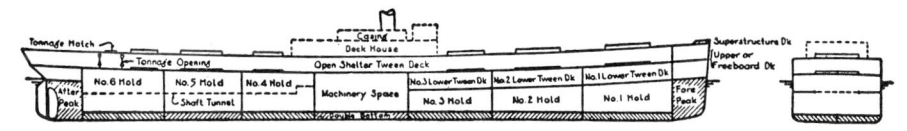

Shelter Deck Vessel. (*Courtesy American Bureau of Shipping*)

SHELVING SHORE—SHERINGHAM CRABBER 720

Shelter Deck Vessel

A. Main Deck	J. Gunwale Bar	T. Tank Top Plating	7. Hold Pillar
B. Shelter Deck	K. Shell Bar	U. Side Girder	8. Deck Girder
C. Hatch Coaming	L. Stringer Bar	V. Centre Girder	9. Bulkhead
D. Hatch Beams	M. Beam Knee	1. Keel Plate	10. Hold Ceiling
E. Hatch Carrier	N. Frame	2. Garboard Strake	11. Bilge Ceiling
F. Hatch Cover	O. Tankside Bracket	3. Bottom Strake	12. Spar Ceiling
G. Bulwarks	P. Gusset Plate	4. Bilge Strake	
H. Half Beam	R. Margin Plate	5. Side Plating	
I. Stringer Plate	S. Floor Plate	6. Sheer Strake	

Fr: *Navire Shelter Deck;* Ger: *Schutzdeckschiff.*

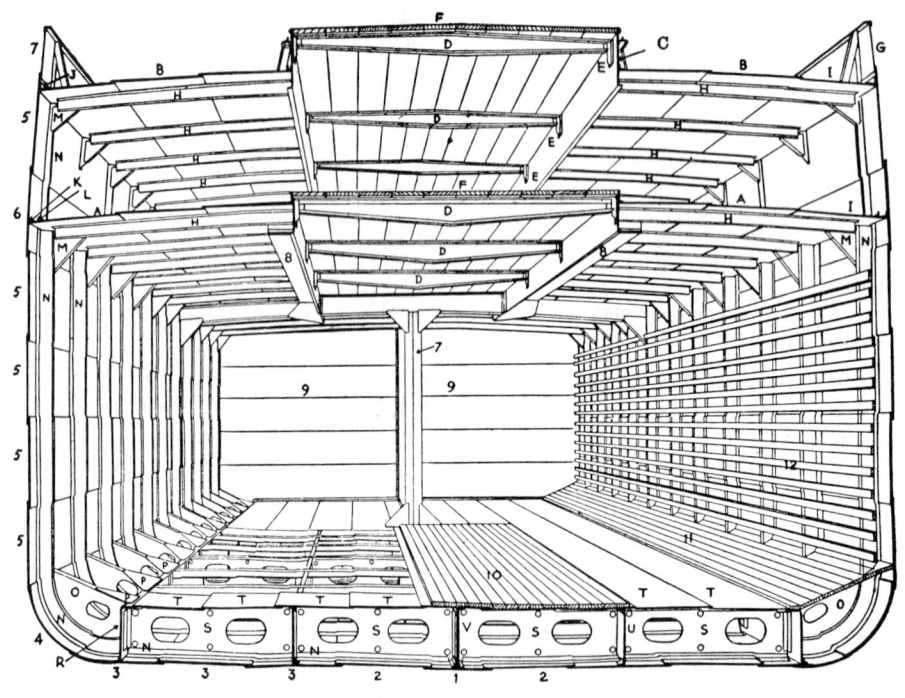

Shelter-deck vessels when considered as cargo carriers have approximately 10 per cent more cubic capacity per ton deadweight than the single-deck or two-deck vessels. Their gross tonnage is about 13 per cent less and their net tonnage 12 per cent. The cost of the shelter-deck vessel is practically the same as that of the single-deck vessel, but is slightly higher per ton deadweight than that of the two-decker.

In the U. S. "shelter-deck vessel" usually refers to any vessel having a continuous weather deck as opposed to the type having raised forecastle, bridge, and poop; and in referring to tankers applies to a vessel having three continuous steel decks, the uppermost of which is the strength deck.

Sjöstrom, C. H., "Shelter Deck Cargo Ship," *Marine Engineering and Shipping Age,* vol. 40 (October, 1935).

SHELVING SHORE. A shore gradually sloping towards the sea.

SHERINGHAM CRABBER. An open beach boat from the east coast of England originating from Sheringham and used for inshore fishing with lines or crab pots. The hull is clinker-built, with sharp stern, rounded stem, and drop rudder. The frames are bent and joggled, closely spaced amidships, but wide apart toward the ends. The heavy top strake is pierced by rowlock holes. There are three thwarts, the forward one or mast thwart has double knees and hanging knee. The rig consists of a dipping lug. The tack hooks just forward of the stemhead. When fishing the sail is rolled round the yard and it and the mast are stowed forward out of the way. When the boat is beached it is carried up by the oars, which are passed right through the rowlock holes. Four men can usually walk up the boat in this manner. Length over-all 16 to 19 ft. Breadth 6 ft. 3 in. to 7 ft.

SHETLAND HERRING BOAT. Sailing craft similar in construction to the *fife* but different in rig, the lugsails being replaced by a gaff mainsail and small lug mizzen sheeted on a long outrigger. There are two headsails. Length of keel 45 to 65 ft.

SHETLAND YAWL. A name sometimes given to the *haaf boat* or *sixern*.

SHEWE. A small Arab dhow used in the pearl fisheries of the Persian Gulf. It is similar to the *sambuk* but smaller, its tonnage rarely exceeding 15 tons. There is a slight difference in the manner in which the timbers of the stempost are carried up into a pillar above the bow.

SHIBARI-AMI-BUNE. Japanese fishing sampan from Hiroshima district working with an offshore seine net. The rig consists of one mast. Length, waterline, 32.5 ft. Breadth 11.2 ft. Depth 3.7 ft. Displacement 10.5 tons.

SHIELD. See **Mask**.

SHIELDED ARC WELDING. The customary type of electric arc welding, in which the arc is shielded from injurious contact with the surrounding atmosphere during the fusion process by a protective layer of inert gases. These gases are produced by coating the weld rod with the proper flux. This also results in the formation of an easily removable slag after the arc has moved along, which covers and protects the weld from further oxidation during cooling.

SHIFT. 1. To move from one berth to another a vessel in harbor or dock.

Fr: *Déhaler;* Ger: *Verholen.*

2. To change direction, as the wind.

Fr: *Sauter;* Ger: *Umspringen; Umlaufen.*

SHIFTING. 1. The transverse alteration in the position of a ship's cargo with special reference to bulk cargoes. It is generally caused by the inclination of the vessel, either by the amplitude of rolling or by a heavy list during a certain length of time.

Fr: *Ripage;* Ger: *Ubergehung; Verschiebung.*

2. A tugboat charge for moving a vessel from one berth to another in a harbor.

Fr: *Frais de Déhalage;* Ger: *Verholungskosten.*

3. Any object or gear which is only temporarily fixed or attached on board.

Fr: *Volant; Mobile;* Ger: *Schlinger.*

SHIFTING BACKSTAY. Backstay used with fore-and-aft rig, but only as necessity requires. Also called running backstay, preventer, runner. Such stays are shifted when the vessel goes about so that the weather ones will be taut and the lee ones slack. Shifting backstays are set up with their own permanent tackle and act as preventer stays for the topmast when the vessel is under a press of sail. Running backstays are on the border line between running and standing rigging. They perform the function of standing rigging in that they help stay the mast but they are handled like running rigging in that the lower end terminates with an eye to which a tackle is attached.

Fr: *Galhauban Volant;* Ger: *Schlingerpardune; Borgtau.*

SHIFTING BALLAST. Pigs of iron, bags of sand, and so on, used as ballast in open sailing boats and capable of being moved about to trim the vessel. Also called portable ballast.

Fr: *Lest Volant;* Ger: *Luvballast; Fliegender Ballast; Lebender Ballast.*

SHIFTING BEAM. A portable beam fitted in a hatchway for the purpose of supporting the hatch covers. The ends of the beams are fitted in slotted carriers attached to the inside of the hatchway coamings. Also called hatch beam, bridle beam, hatch web.

Fr: *Barrot mobile;* Ger: *Schiebebalken.*

SHIFTING BOARDS. Fore-and-aft bulkhead made of loose planking, temporarily fixed to the middle-line pillars in a ship's hold to prevent bulk cargo, especially grain, from shifting due to the motion of the ship. Sometimes called portable grain bulkhead. Vessels which generally carry grain in bulk are required by statutory regulations to have shifting boards in all holds and 'tween decks in which it is so carried. In many vessels shifting boards are replaced by a permanent steel grain bulkhead. Shifting boards are also used as closing appliances for tonnage openings in end bulkheads.

Fr: *Bardis;* Ger: *Losnehmbares Getreideschott; Schlingerschott.*

SHIFTING CHOCK. A boat chock fitted with hinges and provided with a catch so that the boat may be launched outboard

SHIFTING IRON—SHIP (to) 722

without any preliminary lifting by boat tackles.

Fr: *Chantier à Rabattement;* Ger: *Klappbare Bootsklampe.*

SHIFTING IRON. One of the fittings in the form of iron clasps or hook bolts secured to the hold pillars of a vessel carrying grain in bulk, to support the shifting boards.

SHIFTING SAND. Sand of small particle size which drifts with the action of the water or wind.

Fr: *Sable Mouvant;* Ger: *Treibsand.*

SHIFTING-STOCK ANCHOR. An anchor fitted with a movable stock which has one extremity bent at a right angle which permits it to be brought along the shank by taking out a forelock.

Fr: *Ancre à Déjaler;* Ger: *Anker mit beiklappbarem Stock.*

applied to thin layers of metal or other material used to true up a bed plate or a machine, or inserted in bearings to regulate clearance.

SHIN. To climb a mast, rope or spar by using hands and legs only when there are no rungs, steps or the like.

SHINGLE. Coarse gravel or small, rounded stones. Formerly used as ballast for sailing vessels. It measures about 23 cu. ft. to the ton.

Fr: *Galet;* Ger: *Grant; Meerkies; Gerölle.*

SHIP. A ship may be defined as a vessel of considerable size adapted to navigation. The word is used as a general term for seagoing vessels of every kind. A ship may also be defined as a masted vessel larger than a boat and suitable for navigation on the high seas. In maritime law and prize law

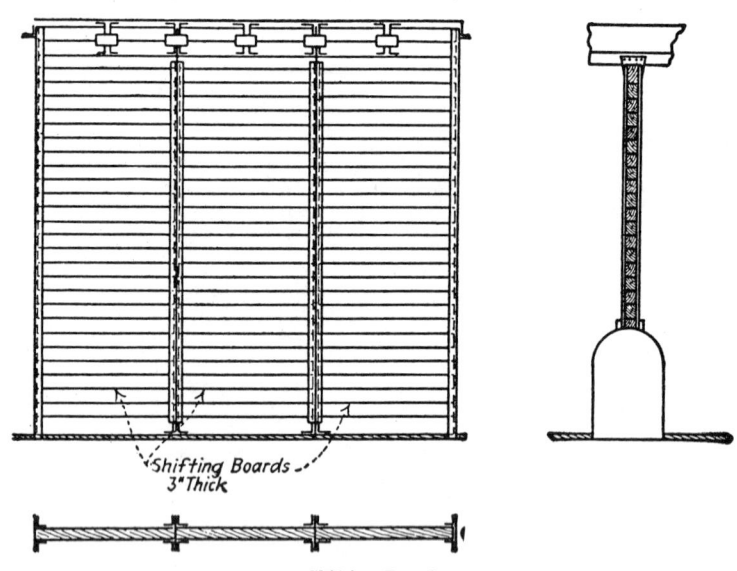

Shifting Boards 3" Thick

Shifting Boards

SHIFT OF BUTTS. A carefully planned disposition of the butt joints throughout the whole surface of plating or planking in order to prevent the occurrence of any line of weakness due to the alignment of joints, which would form a line of probable rupture compared with a solid surface.

Fr: *Décroisement des Abouts;* Ger: *Stossverteilung.*

SHIM. A piece of wood or iron, inserted in a slack place in a frame, plank, or plate to fill out a fair surface or line. Also

the word ship is equivalent to vessel and it is not the form, the construction, the rig, the equipment or the means of propulsion that makes a ship, but the purpose and business of the craft as an instrument of marine transportation. A ship is born when she is launched and becomes a subject of admiralty jurisdiction from the moment her keel touches the water.

Fr: *Navire;* Ger: *Schiff; Fahrzeug.*

SHIP (to). 1. To ship the oars means to

put them in the rowlocks ready for use. To place an object in its working position.
Fr: *Border; Armer;* Ger: *Klarmachen.*
2. To bring within the ship; to load.
Fr: *Embarquer;* Ger: *Einschiffen; Verladen.*
3. See **Sign on (to).**

SHIP BISCUIT. Hard biscuit consisting of flour, water or milk and salt, which does not deteriorate when stored for long periods and therefore is suitable for use on board ship. Also called hard bread, hardtack, pilot bread, sea biscuit, ship's bread.
Fr: *Biscuit de Mer;* Ger: *Schiffsbrot; Hartbrot.*

SHIPBREAKING. The demolition or cutting up of vessels which are unfit for sea or obsolete, and are therefore commercially unproductive. Such vessels, after having been stripped, are cut up into scrap for use in steel works.
Fr: *Démolition de Navires;* Ger: *Abwrackung.*
Rossell, H. E., Scrapping Warships, Society of Naval Architects and Marine Engineers, *Transactions,* vol. 32 (New York, 1924).

SHIP BROKER. Any person or firm securing passenger and freight for line vessels, obtaining cargoes for vessels, seeking charter traffic, providing shippers with their tonnage requirements at the time and place where required, and so on. Those who negotiate the purchase and sale of ships are also styled "ship brokers"; as well as the agents who, on a commission basis represent the owners of a vessel in ports where they have no branch offices.
Fr: *Consignataire de Navires; Courtier Maritime;* Ger: *Schiffsmakler.*
The services of a ship broker extend to berthing and victualing the ship, engaging and paying the crew, arranging charters, canvassing for cargo, collecting freight payments, arranging to load and discharge cargo, settling claims arising from loss or damage to cargo, and in fact, acting in every way on behalf of the owners.

SHIPBUILDER. A builder of vessels as distinguished from a naval architect, who is a designer of vessels. Shipbuilders are usually, but not necessarily, naval architects as well. In the smaller shipbuilding yards there are no naval architects.
Fr: *Constructeur de Navires;* Ger: *Schiffsbauer.*

SHIPBUILDING LIEN (U. S.). A lien for labor and materials furnished toward the original construction of a vessel. It is not a maritime lien and cannot be enforced in an Admiralty court.

SHIP CANAL. An artificial waterway of more or less uniform dimensions, suitable for seagoing vessels.
Fr: *Canal Maritime;* Ger: *Seekanal.*

SHIP CHANDLER. A dealer in cordage, canvas, and all other articles connected with the furnishing of a ship. A merchant who supplies vessels with all kinds of stores.
Fr: *Fournisseur de Navires;* Ger: *Schiffslieferant; Schiffshändler.*

SHIP CHANNEL.
See **Fairway.**

SHIP DUNNAGE. Material such as boards, planks, braces, cordwood, scantling, shiplap, separation cloths, dunnage paper, used for dunnaging in ships' holds.

SHIPENTINE (U. S.). A vessel in which the three forward masts are square-rigged and the aftermast fore-and-aft rigged. In Great Britain called four-masted bark. The names of masts are: foremast, mainmast, mizzenmast and jigger mast. The fore-, main-, and mizzenmasts are usually of same height. This rig has been adopted for vessels with gross tonnage ranging from 1400 (*Tweedsdale,* 1877) to 3500 (*Somali,* 1892).
Fr: *Quatre Mâts Barque;* Ger: *Viermastbarke.*

In the United States the term "four-masted bark" is occasionally used to denote a vessel square-rigged on two masts and schooner-rigged on the other two.

SHIP ERROR (radio). Expression used in electronics when referring to the error of a radio direction finder due to reradiation of radio waves by the metal structure of the ship.

SHIPFITTER. One who lays out the shape, location of rivet holes, and bevelings upon the plates and shapes of which the ship is constructed. In addition to laying out from templates supplied by the loftsman, he also makes or lifts templates himself directly from the ship for parts of special shape and sees that they are properly shaped and fitted into place. The contracting shipfitter is one who takes a contract to lay out the material for some structural part of the vessel such as a keel, a deck, or the shell plating, and to set it up on the ship ready for riveting.
See **Plater.**

SHIP FOREMAN. A stevedore who

superintends the work of loading or discharging an entire vessel with the assistance of several hatch foremen.

SHIP GIRDER. The main body of a vessel, when exposed to longitudinal bending, either hogging or sagging, may be likened to a hollow box girder, which has its principal strength in the top and bottom flanges. The top flange of the ship girder consists of the main deck (uppermost continuous deck) plating, deck stringers, and sheer strakes. The bottom flange consists of the bottom plating, keel, garboard strakes, B & C strakes, and any continuous longitudinal girders in way of the bottom. A continuous inner bottom also contributes to the lower flange.

See **Hog, Sag, Section Modulus.**

The side webs of the ship girder are composed of the side plating, which takes up the shearing stresses. The maximum stress in the deck or bottom when the ship is in longitudinal bending is equal to the bending moment divided by the sections modulus.

SHIP HOUR (U. S.). A unit of labor time which represents the time a ship remains alongside a pier for the purpose of loading or discharging cargo.

SHIPKEEPER. 1. The member of the crew in charge of a whaling vessel when the master is himself taking an active part in the capture or lowers the boats. (Obsolete.)

2. A watchman in charge of a vessel in port when there is no crew on board.

SHIP LETTER. A letter conveyed by a merchant vessel which is not classified or subsidized as mail vessel.

SHIPLOAD. As much cargo as will load a vessel to her proper load line or fill her to capacity.

Fr: *Cargaison;* Ger: *Schiffslast.*

SHIPMASTER'S LIEN. A lien which the master of a ship has by the maritime law and the custom of merchants on the freight, as against the owners, for the payment of seamen's wages and other disbursements.

SHIPMEN (G. B.). In British ports, longshoremen working on board ship, as distinguished from quaymen, who are employed only on land.

SHIPMENT. 1. The act of placing goods on board a vessel. By prompt shipment is meant usually that goods must be shipped within 14 days from the date of the contract.

Fr: *Embarquement;* Ger: *Verschiffung.*

2. The goods themselves when in transit to one consignee.

SHIP MORTGAGE ACT (U. S.). An act passed by Congress in 1920 also known as section 30 of the Merchant Marine Act 1920, which relates to the recording of sales, conveyances and mortgages of vessels of the United States.

SHIPOWNER. One of the persons in whom is vested the title of property of a ship or ships.

Fr: *Propriétaire de Navires;* Ger: *Schiffseigentümer; Schiffseigner.*

See **Berth Owner, Joint Owner, Managing Owner.**

SHIPPED BILL OF LADING. A bill of lading issued only after the goods have actually been shipped on board the vessel, as distinguished from the received for shipment bill of lading.

Fr: *Connaissement Embarqué;* Ger: *Abladekonnossement.*

SHIPPER. The person for whom the owners of a ship agree to carry goods, called "freight," to a specified destination and at a specified price. Also called consigner. The conditions under which the transportation is effected are stipulated in the bill of lading.

Fr: *Chargeur;* Ger: *Ablader; Belader.*

SHIPPER'S EXPORT DECLARATION. A custom house form filled by the shipper of goods to foreign countries. Also called Shipper's Manifest. It mentions the marks, numbers, quantity, description and value of the goods at time and place of export. This document furnishes one of the bases for foreign trade statistics.

Fr: *Déclaration d'Exportation;* Ger: *Ausfuhrdeklaration; Schiffszettel.*

SHIPPER'S GUARANTEE. An indemnity given to a shipowner in exchange for clean bills of lading, for goods to which a clean mate's receipt has not been issued. This practice prevents bills of lading being claused "weak cases," "recoopered," and so on, and may save annoying claims from consignees which will be difficult to rebut.

SHIPPER'S MANIFEST.

See **Shipper's Export Declaration.**

SHIPPER'S PAPERS. The papers or documents employed by the carrier and the shipper in their dealings with each other and also the papers which the shipper requires in his relations with government authorities, underwriters and consignees. They include: bill of lading, insurance policy or insurance receipt, shipping permit, dock receipt, shipper's manifest, consular invoice, exporter's invoice, certificate or origin. Also called shipping papers, shipping documents.

Fr: *Documents d'Embarquement;* Ger: *Verschiffungsdokumente; Verladungspapiere.*

Hodgson, A. J., Shipping Documents (London, 1929).

SHIPPER'S PROTEST. A protest entered before a notary public against the master and owners of a vessel in consequence of the master's refusal after notice to sign bills of lading in the customary form, i.e., without qualifications or exceptions concerning the goods shipped.

SHIPPING. Ships when spoken of collectively. The body of ships that belongs to a country's fleet, that frequent a particular port or harbor, or that are used for a certain purpose. The term is often broadly used in law treatises as including the instrumentalities of transportation by water, their regulations, ownership, and employment and the rights and liabilities connected with or growing out of them.

Bryan, L. A., *Principles of Water Transportation,* New York, 1939; Berglund, A., *Ocean Transportation,* New York, 1931; Calvin and Stuart, *The Merchant Shipping Industry,* New York, 1925; Kirkaldy, A. W., *British Shipping,* London, 1914; MacMurray, C. D., *Shipping and Shipbroking,* London, 1934; Zimmermann, E. W., *Ocean Shipping,* New York, 1921.

SHIPPING BILL (G. B.). A form filled by an exporter of goods and delivered to the customs authorities before shipping goods for export. When the bill has been stamped and signed by the customs, the exporter is at liberty to move the goods. When presented to the customs officer at the dock, the shipping bill is the authority for him to allow the goods to be loaded on board the vessel named on the bill.

Fr: *Certificat d'Embarquement;* Ger: *Zollfreischein.*

SHIPPING BOARD (U. S.). A commission of seven members created by Act of Congress in 1916 to encourage and develop the merchant marine of the United States. It was dissolved in 1933 and was replaced by the Maritime Commission in 1936.

SHIPPING COMMISSIONER (U. S.). A government official of the United States who supervises all matters relating to merchant seamen as required by law. He affords facilities for engaging seamen by keeping a register of their names and characters. He superintends their engagement and discharge. He provides means for securing the presence on board at the proper times of men who are so engaged. Also called shipping master in British ports.

Fr: *Commissaire Maritime;* Ger: *Seemannsamt Beisitzer.*

SHIPPING DOCUMENTS.
See **Shipper's Papers.**

SHIPPING MASTER.
See **Shipping Commissioner.**

SHIPPING NOTE (G. B.). A document which accompanies goods for export when consigned to the dock for shipment. Many exporters use their own form of shipping note. It is generally made in two parts; the first being a receiving note and the second a receipt prepared for the signature of the wharfinger or the ship's mate. The latter, when signed, becomes the Mate's receipt. The shipping note is not in use at all ports. Also **Shipping permit.**

Fr: *Déclaration d'expédition;* Ger: *Vereichnis der verschiften Waren.*

SHIPPING OFFICE (G. B.). An office maintained by the Board of Trade in Great Britain where seamen are engaged under the supervision of a government official known as marine superintendent. Also called marine office.

SHIPPING PERMIT (U. S.). A delivery or receipt note issued by a shipping firm to a shipper of goods when an agreement has been reached in regard to freight rates and date of shipment on the goods to be transported. In Great Britain called shipping note.

Fr: *Permis d'embarquement; Billet d'embarquement; Billet de bord;* Ger: *Ladeorder; Varladungsschein; Schiffszettel.*

The document instructs the receiving clerk at the dock or pier to accept delivery of certain goods for shipment by a named vessel to a given port. It is sometimes made out in two sections, one of which, called receiving note, is returned to the shipper; the other, called mate's receipt, retained by the shipping firm for making up the bill of lading from the particulars contained in the document.

SHIPPING POOL. An agreement between shipping firms by which the payment of a percentage of the freight or passage money collected by any of the conference lines is

divided in certain agreed proportion among the firms belonging to the pool.
Fr: *Pool; Consortium;* Ger: *Schiffahrtspool.*
See **Money Pool, Traffic Pool, Working Pool.**

The form and administration of pools differ according to trade requirements. The simplest form is where a single article or a certain class of articles is pooled without regard to the carriage of other cargo aboard the ship. This form of pool carries with it an allowance for actual stevedoring, and sometimes other expenses that are the same with each line. This is known as the carrying charge. All monies received over and above the carrying charge are pooled and subsequently divided in accordance with the agreed percentage for each line. In the long voyage services it is more customary to pool the entire cargo of each vessel, with the usual allowance for the carrying charge. This equalization of earnings is often extended to a form that takes into consideration the operating costs of each vessel and these varying costs are brought to a common level, which is debited against the total earnings. The net profits are then apportioned in the agreed percentages among the lines party to the agreement.

Sickel, W. G., "Pooling Agreements," American Academy of Political and Social Science, Philadelphia, *Annals,* vol. 55 (Sept., 1914).

SHIPPING RING.
See **Conference.**

SHIPPING TON. A unit of measure used in marine transportation. The U. S. shipping ton has a capacity of 40 cubic feet or 32.14 U. S. bushels, or 31.16 Imperial bushels. The British shipping ton has a capacity of 42 cu. ft. or 32.72 Imperial bushels, or 33.75 U. S. bushels.

SHIPPING VALUE. As used in marine insurance (cargo) policies, the prime cost of the goods to the insured, plus the expenses of and incidental to shipping, and the charges of insurance.

SHIP'S AGENT. A person or firm who transacts all business in a port on behalf of shipowners or charterers. A permanent representative for a shipping line. Also called shipping agent.
Fr: *Consignataire de Navires;* Ger: *Schiffsagent.*

SHIP'S BILL OF LADING. A plain (unstamped) bill of lading retained by the master for record purposes. In case of variance between this and the bill delivered to the shipper, the latter must control. Of the other two copies, one is retained by the shipper and the other is forwarded to the consignee. Also called captain's bill of lading.

SHIP'S CARPENTER. A petty officer, responsible directly to the chief officer, whose duties include the opening and battening down of hatches and cargo ports; the sounding at regular intervals of the double-bottom and other tanks; the handling and upkeep of anchors and cables, wooden masts, and cargo booms; and the maintenance of wooden decks. In vessels fitted with rod-and-chain steering gear he must oil and inspect this gear daily. He has charge of the storm oil tanks and generally speaking must be able to effect all kinds of repairs not made by the engineers' department. As far as possible, the work of the ship's carpenter at sea is confined to dayworker's hours.
Fr: *Charpentier de Bord;* Ger: *Schiffszimmermann.*

SHIP'S CLERK.
See **Cargo Sheet Clerk.**

SHIP'S DOCTOR. A duly qualified medical practitioner whom the statutes of most maritime countries require every seagoing vessel engaged in foreign trade to carry when the number of persons on board is in excess of a specified figure. Also called medical officer, ship's surgeon.
Fr: *Médecin de Bord;* Ger: *Schiffsarzt.*

He attends the passengers and crew in need of medical attention. The treatment of such passengers, however, is under their own control and they may accept or refuse the services of the ship's doctor, who is in no sense the owner's servant. He keeps a journal of his practice and a record of all accidents, sickness, deaths, and births. He inspects the sanitary condition of the vessel with the master and other officers and is in charge of all medical and surgical supplies on board for both passengers and crew.

SHIPSHAPE. Neat and well ordered.

SHIP'S HOLIDAY. A day of exemption from work in accordance with the laws and customs of the nation whose flag the ship carries.
Fr: *Jour férié du bord;* Ger: *Feiertag der Schiffsmannschaft.*

SHIP'S HUSBAND. A duly registered person to whom the management of a ship or ships is entrusted by or on behalf of the owners. He is subject to the same liabilities as if he were the managing owner, although, according to some authorities, lacking power to bind the owners when the ship is in her home port. He has authority to contract for all necessary supplies, repairs, equipment, towage and salvage services to be rendered to the ship, enter into contract for her freight or chartering, hiring of officers and crew, and to do all acts necessary and proper for conducting the ship's affairs in the usual way.

Fr: *Armateur Gérant;* Ger: *Schiffsdisponent; Korrespondentreeder.*

SHIP'S LOG BOOK. A nautical record compiled from entries taken from the rough log book. Also called ship's log, smooth log book, mate's Log. It is kept by the chief officer and signed by the master. In addition to the routine particulars of the navigation of the ship, entries are made of the following matters: any loss or damage to the ship or anything connected therewith, whether occasioned by the violence of the wind or sea or by any extraordinary cause or event, any stranding or collision or breakdown of machinery with full particulars of such damage; time when vessel is berthed and notice of readiness to load or discharge given; any cause operating to hinder or prevent the continuous working of cargo; the quantity of cargo dealt with on each day and an exact record of all times occupied.

Fr: *Journal de Bord; Journal de Route;* Ger: *Logbuch; Schiffstagebuch.*

See **Scrap Log Book, Official Log Book.**

SHIP'S LANTERN. A heavy lantern well protected against injury by contact with ropes, and so on, and placed in the rigging or any other conspicuous place designated in the Rules of the Road, for the purpose of defining a vessel's position at night, and indicating the type of vessel.

Fr: *Fanal de Bord;* Ger: *Schiffslaterne.*

See **Combined Lantern, Globe Lantern, Hurricane Lantern, Rules of the Road, Tricolored Lantern.**

SHIP'S MAGNETISM. The ship's magnetism is chiefly due to induction in the earth's magnetic field. Most of the ship's metal is structural steel, which is intermediate in character between hard steel and soft iron. Deviation of the compass due to the ship's magnetic field.

Ger: *Schiffsmagnetismus.*

SHIP'S MEAN TIME. The hour angle of the mean sun, measured westward, from the ship's meridian. Also called **Mean time at ship,** or **Local mean time.**

Fr: *Temps moyen du bord;* Ger: *Mittlere Ortszeit.*

SHIP'S NAME. The name of every registered (merchant) vessel is marked upon each bow and upon the stern, and the home port is marked on the stern. Names are painted, gilded, or consist of cut, carved or cast Roman letters of light color on a dark background or vice versa, secured in place and distinctly visible. According to United States and British rules for merchant vessels the height of letters should not be less than 4 in. They are usually made of cast naval brass.

Ger: *Schiffsname.*

A pleasure vessel or yacht is required to have its name and port of registry placed on some conspicuous portion of the hull. No change can be made in the name of a ship without written permission of the marine department in charge of the registration of vessels.

SHIP'S NUMBER. Four letters of the International Code of Signals assigned to every registered vessel by the national government to which it belongs. Also called signal letters, call letters. When it desires to make its identity known, the vessel hoists the flags corresponding to these letters. Lists are published by each country containing tables both of signal letters and of ships names arranged alphabetically. The top or first flag (square) indicates the nationality of the ship and, by international agreement one or two particular letters are allotted to each nationality. The number of all ships registered in Great Britain begin with letter "G" or "M." Signal letters are also used for wireless call signals.

Fr: *Numéro Officiel; Lettres Signalétiques;* Ger: *Ordnungsnummer; Signalbuchstaben.*

SHIP'S PAPERS. The papers or documents required for the manifestation of the ownership and national character of a vessel and cargo and to show its compliance with the various laws of the country to which it belongs. They include: certificate of registry, register, clearance certificate, manifest, license, sea letter, passport, muster roll, charter party (if any), bill of health, log book (official), ship's articles, articles of agreement, bills of lading, builder's certificate (optional), bill of sale, freeboard certificate, classification certificates, load-line certificate, radio certificate.

Fr: *Papiers de Bord;* Ger: *Schiffsdokumente; Schiffspapiere.*

SHIP'S REGISTER. The official record of particulars and description of a vessel. Also called register.

Fr: *Immatriculation;* Ger: *Schiffsregister.*

SHIP'S STAFF. The officers belonging to the different departments of a merchant vessel. It includes the deck and engine room officers, the ship's doctor, purser and wireless operator.

Fr: *Etat-Major;* Ger: *Schiffsstab.*

SHIP STEEL. Mild steel manufactured by the open hearth process (acid or basic) and having a tensile strength of 26 to 32 tons per square inch with an elongation not less than 20 per cent on 8 in. for material of 0.375 in. thickness or above, and not less than 15 per cent for thinner material. American Marine Standards Committee, Standard 81, *Structural Medium Steel for Ships (Specifications)*, Washington, 1932; British Standards Institution, Standard 13, *Structural Steel for Shipbuilding*, 1942; Donaldson, J. W., "Steel and Iron in Shipbuilding and Marine Engineering," *Iron and Steel Industry* (London), vol. 11, no. 1 and 3 (1937); Hatfield, W. H., "Steel Metallurgy in Relation to Marine Engineering and Shipbuilding," Junior Institution of Engineers (London), *Journal*, vol. 46 (1936).

SHIP STORES. Provisions and supplies for use on board ship at sea or in port. Ship stores are sealed as nondutiable by the customs.

Fr: *Approvisionnements de Bord;* Ger: *Schiffsbedarf.*

SHIP'S TIME. Local apparent time. Also called nautical time. On board ship the clocks are set every day at 12 o'clock when the sun crosses the meridian. When the difference of longitude is considerable the clocks are sometimes set three times daily, at 11 P.M., 3 A.M., and 5 A.M. The civil mean time of the zone in which a ship happens to be, as contrasted with Greenwich time.

Fr: *Heure du Bord;* Ger: *Schiffszeit; Borduhr.*

SHIP'S WARRANT. A document introduced by Great Britain in 1940 to supplement the "Navicert" system. It is issued to neutral ships whose owners or time-charterers have given satisfactory assurances to the Ministry of Shipping in London that all ships under their control will refrain from carrying on a contraband trade or a trade capable of proving of any benefit to the enemy.

SHIP TIMBER. The term "timber" is applied to wood of sufficient size to be adapted for building or structural purposes, whether standing in the forest or after it has been felled. It is used to denote all pieces of wood of any importance employed in the construction of a ship but in particular for those forming the frame. The word is also applied to the trunk or body of a tree after it has reached a diameter of eight inches.

Fr: *Bois de Construction; Bois de Marine;* Ger: *Schiffbauholz; Schiffsholz.*

Boulton, E. H. B., Timber in Shipbuilding, Institution of Engineers and Shipbuilders in Scotland, *Transactions*, vol. 87, 1944; Robertson, E., Timber in Shipbuilding, Institution of Engineers and Shipbuilders in Scotland, *Transactions*, vol. 79. 1936; Robertson, W. A., Timber and Shipbuilding, Institution of Engineers and Shipbuilders in Scotland, *Transactions*, vol. 80, 1937.

SHIPWORKER. Name given to a foreman stevedore. He is responsible for the correct loading of the whole vessel, which means deciding the sequence in which different holds shall be filled, and noting that each package is stowed so that its own safety and that of neighbouring goods is assured. Also called ship foreman.

Fr: *Chef Arrimeur.*

SHIPWORM. A marine mollusc which bores into submerged wood by means of an almost microscopic hole for a short distance, then turning at right angles continues to bore with the grain of the wood, seldom if ever breaking through the surface. Commencing its boring operations as a tiny mollusc, it fattens and grows until it reaches a length of about 8 to 9 inches and bores a hole of a diameter equal to that of an ordinary lead pencil. The best known and most destructive of these molluscs is the *Teredo navalis*. Damage to ships through worms is more common and rapid in tropical waters than in colder latitudes. Attack by teredos is discouraged by the use of sheathing of copper, or of wood treated with creosote, acid cupric chromate, or copper naphthenate.

Fr: *Taret;* Ger: *Bohrwurm.*

Sigerfoos, C. P., *Natural History, Organization and Late Development of the Terenidae or Shipworms*, U. S. Bureau of Fisheries (Washington), Bull. 27 (1907).

SHIPWRIGHT. A skilled, all-around ship carpenter, experienced in building wooden ships, barges and other classes of craft, including such work as laying out, drawing, fastening, planking, calking, deck laying, hewing. Also called foreman ship carpenter, yard carpenter.

Fr: *Charpentier de Marine;* Ger: *Schiffsbaumeister.*

The shipwright must be experienced in building launching ways and launching cradles, and in the actual launching of ships. In steel shipyards he supervises all wood construction, prepares the ground for the keel blocks, lays the blocks at proper height and inclination, and secures them against tripping. He also sets the uprights and erects the staging around the building berths. He lays wooden decks and hold ceilings. His work on board ship includes: laying of wooden decks, ceilings, sparring, fitting of hatch covers, hatch wedges and wooden framework of awnings (ridge poles and stretchers), boat chocks, machinery chocks under winches and windlass, shore gangways, tunnel platforms, shifting boards and grain feeders, wooden fenders, bulwark rails, lines for regulating erected structure.

SHIPYARD. A yard, place, or enclosure containing building slips for the construction and fitting out of vessels. Shipyards are located on the edge of a body of water of sufficient depth and area to allow of safe launching either endwise or sidewise, and where a channel leading to the sea exists. The area of ground depends upon the number, size and character of the ships to be built, and also upon how much of the fitting out and equipping of the hulls is done at the shipyard. Also called shipbuilding yard.

Fr: *Chantier de Constructions Navales;* Ger: *Schiffswerft.*

Barrie, G., Shipyard Methods and Layout, Institution of Engineers and Shipbuilders in Scotland, *Transactions*, vol. 77, 1934; Ferguson, W. B., Economic Phases of Foreign Shipyard Practice, *Marine Engineering*, New York, vol. 35, February, 1930; Van Donkelaar, A., Modern Dutch Shipyard Arrangement and Practice, North East Coast Institution of Engineers and Shipbuilders (Newcastle upon Tyne), *Transactions*, vol. 48, 1931/32.

SHIVERING. The shaking of the sails when a ship is brought close to the wind. The flutter or shake of a sail caused by trimming the spars or luffing so that the wind strikes on the edge of the sail.

Fr: *Faseyer;* Ger: *Killen.*

SHNIAKA. A boat used on the Murman coast and on the Russian side of the Varanger Fjord. According to some writers the design of this boat is unique and not only differs from the Russian boats but is unlike those of any other country. Also called *shnekke.*

The largest boats range from 25 to 40 ft. in length, with an average of about 25 ft. They are mostly open boats although some of them have a cuddy aft. These boats are built with keel, sharp stern, vertical sternpost, rounded stem with tumble home above the waterline. The ends are covered with tarred canvas flush with the gunwales for a distance of about 5 ft. The rudderhead is fitted with a yoke and long tiller like those used on the Norwegian boats. At a distance of about one-quarter the boat's length from the stem there is a heavy transverse bulkhead. The planking is clinker-built and fastened with a soft line about the size of manila spun yarn, made of tree bark. The keel, stem, sternpost and timbers are made of birch, while the planking is pine or spruce. The rigging consists of one mast stepped between a crossbeam which extends from gunwale to gunwale and a bulkhead. It carries a square sail, trimmed by braces and sheets. When close-hauled the lower part of the luff is hauled forward by a bowline and the upper part is pushed forward with a sprit. Length over-all 32 ft. 11 in. Beam 6 ft. 8 in. Depth 2 ft. 5 in. Height of mast above gunwale 18 ft. Yard 15 ft. Sprit 16 ft. 3 in. Mast abaft stem 12½ ft. Oars 13½ ft.

SHOAL. An elevation of the sea bottom which comes within 6 fathoms of the surface. A detached area of any material except rock or coral which constitutes a danger to navigation and over which seas usually break in heavy weather. A sand bank which shows at low water.

Fr: *Haut-fond;* Ger: *Flache Stelle; Untiefe Watt; Droogte Plate.*

SHOALWATER OYSTER BATEAU. Open, flat-bottomed, flatiron-shaped boat used in the oyster fishery at Bay Center, Shoalwater Bay (Washington). Some of these boats have a centerboard and carry a single lug sail. Ordinarily they sail to and from the oyster grounds, but in light winds they are often towed. Length 24 to 30 ft. Beam 11 to 12 ft.

SHOE. 1. The horizontal connection between the heel of the rudderpost and that of the sternpost in a single-screw vessel.

Fr: *Semelle;* Ger: *Stevensohle.*

2. The outer piece of the cutwater.

See **False Keel, Anchor Shoe, Beam Shoe.**

SHOE BLOCK. A block containing two sheaves which instead of setting parallel to each other are at right angles.
Fr: *Poulie à olive;* Ger: *Schubblock.*

SHOE DONI. A peculiarly shaped fishing craft from the Delta of Godavari River (east coast of India). The hull is wide and flat forward with sharp stem narrowing gradually toward the stern, which is of the square-transom type. The forepart is decked, forming a sort of turtleback. The afterpart is decked for about three feet from the stern. The well is narrow and is protected at its fore end by a transverse coaming. It is steered by means of an oar working in a wooden crutch rowlock fastened to the center of the stern. This oar is used for sculling when there is no wind. There is a deep forefoot and a keel of 6 to 8 in. deep, which extends aft as far as the mast step. The carvel planking is made of narrow teak strakes nailed on the frames. Length over-all 26 ft.; forepart 8 ft. 6 in. Breadth at coaming 3 ft. 7 in. Depth 2 ft. (Typical.)

SHOE PLATE. A furnaced plate which connects the keel and sternpost. Its after end extends right under and around the stern frame, encasing it.

SHOLE. A small piece of timber or plank placed under the heel of a shore.

SHON-TU-CHUAN. Small open Chinese fishing boat from Swatow employed as tender to the *ta-tseng* boats. Length 28 ft. Beam 9 ft.

SHOOKS. Barrel staves bundled for export.
Ger: *Stabholz.*

SHOOT. The act of suddenly luffing a sailboat in the wind while it continues to make headway by force of momentum.
Fr: *Lancer dans le Vent;* Ger: *Aufschiessen.*

SHOOT KNOT. A netting knot of the reef knot description used mostly by inshore fishermen. Also called braiding knot.
Ger: *Schotenstek.*

SHORAN. Name given to a special type of radar system consisting of one ship equipment, and two shore equipments set up at known points. It is based on the fact that radio waves travel through the atmosphere at a very near constant velocity of 186.218 statute miles per second. It gives extremely accurate determination of positions which make it an essential control method for hydrographic surveys. Shoran has become the standard control system for surveys extending from 50 to 100 miles offshore.

SHORE. 1. The land adjacent to the sea or to a large river; land which extends between ordinary high-water mark and low-water mark.
Fr: *Rivage;* Ger: *Ufer.*
See **Lee Shore, Bold Shore, Shelving Shore, Flat Shore, Weather Shore.**
2. A prop fixed under a ship's bottom or at the side to support her when in drydock, aground or on the stocks. Also a timber or metal strut or prop used as an emergency support for a weakened or damaged portion of the ship's structure such as a deck, a bulkhead, and so on.
Fr: *Accore;* Ger: *Stütze.*
See **Back Shore, Bilge Shore, Cap Shore, Dog Shore, Driving Shore, Riband Shore, Side Shore, Skeg Shore, Spur Shore, Trip Shore, Wale Shore.**

SHORE BOAT. A small boat operated from or owned ashore as distinguished from a ship's boat which forms part of the equipment of a vessel. Also a boat plying between a vessel at anchor and generally used for ferrying passengers or crew.

SHORE FAST. Any mooring or docking line by which a vessel is secured to the shore as distinguished from those which run out from the ship towards a buoy, a dolphin, and so on.
Fr: *Amarre de Terre;* Ger: *Landfest.*

SHORE FISHERIES. Under this head are included all those fisheries prosecuted from small boats or from the shore without the aid or use of vessels, although, as in the case of the lobster fishery, vessels may be employed to take the catch of the shore fishermen to market.
Fr: *Petite Pêche;* Ger: *Uferfischerei.*

SHORE RAM. A battering ram for knocking out shores. Length ranges from 22 to 32 ft., depending on the size of the ship to be launched, with ropes to accommodate 20 to 30 men. A steel head is provided to prevent splitting.

SHORE SEINE. A general name for various types of seine-nets worked from the shore, as distinguished from purse seines which are fished in deep water away from the coastline.
Ger: *Landwade.*

SHORESMAN. Term applied to a sole or part owner of a fishing vessel, who superintends onshore all operations relative to the voyage, performing duties such as supplying salt and bait, fishing gear and other necessary equipment.

SHORE UP. To support by means of shores placed on each side.

Fr: *Accorer;* Ger: *Abstützen; Unterstützen.*

SHORE WEIR. A weir located near the shore line, with perhaps one wing extending diagonally into the sea, while the shore answers the purpose of a wing on the other side.

SHORE WHALING. The name given to the whaling operations and treatment carried out from a land station to which whales are towed after capture, as distinguished from ship whaling, in which operations are carried out on board a factory vessel.

Starks, E. C., History of California Shore Whaling, California Fish and Game Commission Bulletin no. 6, Sacramento, 1922.

SHORING. A system of shores as installed to strengthen or support a weakened bulkhead, deck, or area of the ship's hull.

See **Shore.**

SHORT ARM FLOOR TIMBER. One of the floor timbers in the long and short arm type of framing.

Fr: *Varangue à Branche Courte;* Ger: *Kurzarmige Bodenwrange.*

SHORT BLAST. A blast of the whistle or fog horn of less than 4 seconds duration.

Fr: *Son Bref;* Ger: *Kurzer Ton.*

SHORT BRIDGE. A bridge house less than 15 per cent of the vessel's length.

Fr: *Château Court;* Ger: *Kurzes Brückenhaus.*

SHORTEN SAIL. To reduce the amount of sail by reefing or furling.

Fr: *Diminuer la Voilure;* Ger: *Segel mindern; Segel kürzen.*

SHORT FORECASTLE. A forecastle with a length of less than 20 per cent than the ship's length.

Fr: *Gaillard Court;* Ger: *Kurzes Back.*

SHORT-HANDED. Said of a vessel inadequately manned or without the regular number of men.

SHORT-LANDED. The unloading of cargo when less goods or a lesser number of packages than that shown on the manifest or other documents are put ashore at port of destination. Also called short delivery.

Fr: *Manquant;* Ger: *Minderlieferung.*

SHORT SEA. A sea in which the waves are irregular, broken and interrupted so as to break frequently over a vessel's bow, beam, or quarter. A sea whose distance between two crests is shorter than is normal with their height.

Fr: *Mer Courte;* Ger: *Kurze See; Knappe See.*

SHORT SEAS. A chartering term which in Europe refers to the Baltic and White Sea trades.

SHORT-SHIPPED. Goods are said to be "short-shipped" when shut out of a vessel through lack of space, late arrival, or error. They are also called "shut-outs."

Fr: *Non Embarqué;* Ger: *Unverschifft.*

SHORT SPLICE. A splice in which two ends of rope are joined by untwisting only a short part of each, which makes the union thick. Used only where the rope is not required to reeve through a block and where an increased diameter is not objectionable, as in straps, slings, pendants, and so on. It is the strongest way to unite two ropes.

Fr: *Epissure Carrée;* Ger: *Kurzsplissung.*

SHORT STAY. An anchor is hove in to a short stay when the amount of cable out is little more than the depth of water.

Fr: *A pic;* Ger: *Auf und nieder; Kurzer Stag.*

SHORT STOWAGE. A term used in the lumber trade to denote short and small pieces which form part of a shipment in order to obtain maximum stowage. Also called ends. Charters usually specify the percentage of short lengths which must be supplied by the shippers for stowage purposes.

SHORT TACK. To run short boards when working to windward where there is no room, or from some other cause.

SHORT TON. A unit of weight of 2000 pounds. Also called American ton.

SHOT. A length of chain cable, usually 15 fathoms, between two joining shackles.

Fr: *Maillon;* Ger: *Kettenlänge.*

See **Outboard Shot.**

SHOT LINE (U. S.). A 3-stranded, left-laid, flax line, used with line throwing guns. It varies in circumference from 25/64 to 31/32 of an inch.

SHOTTEN HERRING. A herring which has just deposited its eggs. It is dry and thin, and is often used as bait for lining. The trade term "spent" refers to such fish with a minimum length of 10¼ in. About 850 to 1000 per barrel.

Fr: *Hareng Vide;* Ger: *Ihlen; Hohlhering; Abgelaichter Hering.*

SHORT FLOOR TIMBER. 1. The shortest floor timber in the long and short floor type of framing. In this system the long floor extends past the ends of the short floor for an equal distance on each side, these extensions furnishing the lap for attachment of the first futtocks. In this style of frame futtocks of like numbers fall in the same tier, all first futtocks abutting the ends of short floors and second futtocks the ends of long floors.

Fr: *Varangue Courte;* Ger: *Kurze Bodenwrange.*

2. Timber placed across the keel where half floors are used in order to secure the heels of the latter. Also called **cross timber**. Ger: *Lieger.*

SHOULDER. A projection on a block or mast.

Fr: *Noix;* Ger: *Schulter.*

See **Hounds**.

SHOULDER BLOCK. A block with a projection near the upper end so that it can rest against a spar without jamming the rope.

Fr: *Poulie à Talon;* Ger: *Hackenblock; Schulterblock.*

SHOULDER GUN. A line-carrying, breechloading rifle propelling a projectile attached to a line 400 feet or more in length. It is used only on small craft of 300 tons and less for life-saving purposes.

Fr: *Fusil Porte-Amarre;* Ger: *Leinen-Wurfgewehre.*

SHOULDER-OF-MUTTON SAIL. A triangular sail having its foot extended on a boom and its apex attached to the head of a pole mast. Also called **leg-of-mutton sail**. The luff of the sail is attached to the mast by hoops or by a lacing so that any other gear such as stays or jib halyards must be fastened above the peak of the sail.

Ger: *Dreieckiges Bootsegel.*

SHOULDER PIPE. A mooring pipe located in the forepart of the vessel usually at or near the break of the forecastle head, and through which the backspring is led on to the quay or pier.

SHOWER. A fall of rain, snow, sleet or hail, usually of short duration, but often of considerable intensity. Showers fall from isolated clouds separated from one another by clear spaces.

Fr: *Ondée; Giboulée;* Ger: *Schauer.*

SHRIMPER. Generally a small vessel or boat used for the capture of shrimps with a drag net. Also called **shrimp boat**, **shrimp dragger** or **shrimp trawler**.

The craft found in the south Atlantic states where the fishery is prosecuted in open coastal waters are larger and more seaworthy than those of the Gulf of Mexico. The latter work in more restricted areas and to a large extent in sheltered waters. All hulls are made of wood with straight stem, elliptical stern with counter and decked fore and aft. The pilot house is located forward of the fish hold in the Atlantic coast boats and abaft the hold in the Gulf craft. For working the gear there is a short stout mast with derrick or an "A" frame which serves to elevate the drag lines so that the otter boards can be hauled on deck and also to assist in bringing aboard heavily laden trawls. There is a power winch driven either by a separate engine or geared to the main engine. In the Gulf of Mexico the shrimpers have no power winch or mast and the bringing in of the trawl is entirely manual. Length 40 to 65 ft. Breadth 11½ to 18 ft. Draft 3 to 6 ft. Propulsion by heavy oil single screw engines 50 to 170 horsepower.

Fr: *Crevettier;* Ger: *Garneelenboot.*

SHRIMP JUNK. A Chinese junk employed in the shrimp fisheries of San Francisco Bay. The craft vary in size, but the majority are about 50 ft. long and 12 ft. broad with round bottom, no keel, square stern and blunt bows. The rig consists of one mast stepped slightly forward of half length with a battened lugsail. The stern is decked for a length of about 14 ft. and used as living quarters for the crew. Just forward is the open shrimp hold about 12 ft. long. Next forward is a net room of similar size. The remaining space forward is used for lines and gear. On the after deck there is a crude wooden windlass worked by four wooden spokes and used for lifting the nets. Each junk operates 30 to 60 nets of Chinese pattern.

SHRIMP TRAWL. A beam trawl towed by a small boat or in very shallow water by a horse. The length of the beam varies from 10 to 30 ft. according to the tonnage of the boat. The mesh is ¼ in. to 1 in. In some countries small otter boards 32 in. long and 26 in. deep are fitted instead of a beam.

Fr: *Chalut à Crevettes;* Ger: *Garneelenkurre.*

SHRINKAGE. In welding, the contraction which occurs in the base and weld metal upon cooling. When in the direction along the line of the weld it is known as longitudinal shrinkage; when normal to this direction, transverse shrinkage.

Fr: *Retrait;* Ger: *Schrumpfung.*

SHROUD. One of a set of strong wires or hemp ropes extending on each side of a masthead to the sides of the ship to support a mast laterally.

Fr: *Hauban;* Ger: *Want; Wanttau.*

See **Bowsprit Shroud, Bumkin Shroud, Diamond Shroud, Futtock Shroud, Funnel Shroud, Lower Shroud, Preventer Shroud, Topgallant Shroud, Topmast Shroud, Upper Shroud.**

In small vessels, especially if fore-and-aft rigged, the shrouds are fitted in pairs, one piece of rope being doubled to form two legs, a little below the bend these parts being seized together forming a loop. This loop or collar is passed over the head of the mast, both legs coming down on the same side. In large, square-rigged vessels, and in steam or motor-propelled vessels, the lower shrouds are usually made of steel, and are fastened to small separate eyeplates riveted to the mast. The lower ends of the shrouds are fastened to deadeyes or rigging screws at the channel plate. Shrouds take their names from the spars they support.

SHROUD CAP. A thimble-shaped covering made of brass, sheet lead, tarred canvas, or leather and fitted to the upturned ends of shrouds to keep out moisture.

Fr: *Coiffe;* Ger: *Taukappe.*

SHROUDED PROPELLER. A propeller in which there is some form of cylinder surrounding the propeller tips for the purpose of concentrating the flow of water into the propeller disc and avoiding tip losses and losses due to turbulence and tangential flow from the propeller tips. The shrouds are attached to the hull and surround the propeller with a small clearance. This system has been successfully applied to small units of shallow draft, such as tugs and self-propelled barges. The best known example of a shrouded propeller is the so-called "Kort" nozzle.

Fr: *Hélice à Tuyère;* Ger: *Dusenschraube.*

SHROUD HOOP. A steel band with eyes to which the upper ends of the shrouds are fastened.

SHROUDING. A ring of trapezoidal cross section secured over the blade tips of a turbine wheel to prevent steam from spilling out at the ends of the blades and to reduce blade vibration.

SHROUD KNOT. A knot used to unite two ropes. Formerly used for repairing hemp shrouds. It is strong and neat and requires very little rope.

Fr: *Noeud de Hauban Double;* Ger: *Wantknoten.*

SHROUD-LAID ROPE. Right-hand laid cordage with or without a hemp core surrounded by four-strand. It is often found on yachts as it looks neater and does not get so hard when wet as hawser-laid cordage. The latter is, however, about one-fifth stronger for a given size. Shroud-laid rope is supplied to the trade in white Manila 3 to 8 in. in circumference, in white hemp 1½ to 5½ in., and in tarred hemp 1½ to 12 in.

Fr: *Aussière en Quatre;* Ger: *Wantschlag-Tauwerk.*

SHROUD TRUCK. A short wooden cylinder perforated and used as fairleader for running rigging. It is seized to the standing rigging. Also called seizing truck, leading truck.

Fr: *Pomme Gougée;* Ger: *Wantklotje.*

SHUT-OUT CARGO. A shipment of goods which has been booked for a specified vessel, but which on account of lack of space, intervention of authorities or other circumstances has failed either wholly or in part to be loaded in that vessel.

SHUTTER. A piece of wood which fits into the rowlocks of an open boat. Shutters are shipped whenever the oars are not being used. They are fitted with lanyards. Though the word "shutter" is the correct name for these fittings they are often referred to as "poppets."

Fr: *Tape de Dame;* Ger: *Pfortendeckel; Rojepfortendeckel.*

See **Shutter Strake.**

SHUTTER STRAKE. The last outside plank strake of the bottom to be worked in when building a wooden hull. The last plank to complete a strake. Also called shutter.

SIBIDSIBIRAN. A double-outrigger, fishing canoe of the Baroto type from the Philippine Islands, used in the hook-and-line fisheries on the Visayan Sea. The hull is a dugout with built-up sides made of bamboo matting fastened to uprights with coir lashings. It is rigged with a sprit mainsail with boom and a triangular foresail. A quarter rudder is used for steering. Also called *pinayo*.

SICK BAY. A general term which covers all rooms or compartments on board ship assigned for the treatment of the sick, such as the dispensary, operating room, contagious ward, and so on. More frequently used in connection with troop ships or men-of-war.

See **Hospital**.

SICKE. Open seine boat employed in the coastal fisheries of the Gulf of Danzig and the Frische Haff. The hull is double-ended with keel, round bilge, clinker planking, and fish well. It is rigged with two short masts and spritsails. The foremast is stepped near the stem and has a considerable forward rake. Other craft of the same type are the *Angelsicke* and the *Garnsicke*. The latter works with a drag net. *Sicke:* Length 16 to 23 ft. Breadth 4.6 to 6.5 ft. *Garnsicke:* Length 32 ft. Breadth 9.8 ft. (Average.)

SICK SEAM. A term used by sailmakers to denote that the stitches of a seam are worn and giving way.

SIDE (to). 1. To work the timbers of a ship to the required scantlings by trimming the sides.

2. To make two or more sides of a log parallel.

Fr: *Triquage; Dégraissage.*

SIDE BAR. One of the two strengthening flat bars fitted on each side of a built bar keel.

Fr: *Plat de Quille;* Ger: *Kielschiene.*

SIDE BAR KEEL. A keel consisting of a central vertical through plate which extends down from the top of the floors below the garboard plates. The thickness of the projecting part is made up by riveting two side bars or slabs, one on each side. Flanged down against the latter are the garboard plates as in the bar keel. This form of keel, costly to fit and repair, has practically disappeared from present-day hulls.

Fr: *Quille d'Assemblage;* Ger: *Gebauter Kiel.*

SIDE BULKHEAD. A longitudinal bulkhead in the sides or wings.

Fr: *Cloison latérale;* Ger: *Seitenschott.*

SIDE BUNKER. A bunker situated at sides of boilers in boiler-room compartment from tank top to lowest deck, also in lower and upper 'tween-decks at casing sides.

Fr: *Soute Latérale;* Ger: *Seitenbunker.*

SIDE BY SIDE. The position of two ships placed close alongside each other.

Fr: *Bord à Bord;* Ger: *Seite an Seite.*

SIDE COAMING. One of the fore-and-aft coamings at the sides of a hatchway.

Fr: *Hiloire Longitudinale;* Ger: *Langsulle.*

SIDE COUNTER TIMBERS. The two timbers on each side which form the outer limit of the counter in square sterned craft. They are often formed of two pieces scarfed together because of their shape. Also called term pieces.

Fr: *Cornier; Terme;* Ger: *Heckstütze.*

SIDE CURTAIN. Canvas secured fore and aft in canopy-cover openings as a protection against spray; also canvas spread between the rail and the awning ridgeropes as a protection against the wind.

Fr: *Rideau de tente;* Ger: *Seitenkleid.*

SIDED TIMBER. Log in which the sides have been trimmed.

Fr: *Bois Équarri;* Ger: *Vierkantig behauenes Holz.*

SIDE DUNNAGE. The dunnage boards or spar ceiling fitted on the ship's sides to prevent packages from protruding into the frame spaces and interfering with ventilation, or coming into contact with frames or shell, with consequent damage from the condensed moisture there. With some cargoes the boards forming the side dunnage are overlaid with bamboo or split bamboo dunnage mats woven grate-fashion.

SIDE GIRDER.

See **Longitudinal**.

SIDE KEELSON. A beam or girder placed on each side of the bottom about two thirds the distance from the center line to the bilge. This is used as a longitudinal stiffener for the bottom of the hull.

Fr: *Carlingue latérale;* Ger: *Seiten-Kielschwein.*

SIDE LAUNCHING. A method of launching used in restricted waters. The building berth is parallel to the waterfront and the vessel slides down multiple ways in a direction perpendicular to the keel. It has the advantage that the vessel can be built on an even keel. The inclination of the ways is steeper than with the end launching.

Fr: *Lancement en Travers;* Ger: *Querablauf.*

Kirby and Hopkins, "Side Launching of

Ships on the Great Lakes," Society of Naval Architects and Marine Engineers, *Transactions*, vol. 26 (New York) 1918; Schade, H. A., "Side Launching," *Marine Engineering and Shipping Age* (New York), April, 1932.

SIDE LIGHT. See **Porthole.**

SIDE-LIGHT PLUG. A portable metal shutter in the form of a disc fitted on the outside of a side light to protect the glass against the impact of the waves. Also called port lid, side-light shutter, storm shutter. It is held in place by a small projecting lip on the fixed frame.

Fr: *Tape de Hublot;* Ger: *Pfortendeckel; Einlegedeckel.*

SIDE LIGHTS. The red (port) and green (starboard) lights carried by vessels when under way. They are so screened as to show from ahead to two points abaft the beam, which is equivalent to an arc of 112° 30', and must be visible at a distance of at least two miles.

Fr: *Feu de Côté;* Ger: *Seitenlaternen; Seitenlicht; Seitenlampen.*

Side lights must not be carried in the rigging of steam or motor vessels, but whenever possible are to be fitted at bridge ends. They are fixed by a metal tongue on the screen board, the dimensions of this tongue being usually: height 5 in., width 2½ in., thickness ½ in. In side lights that burn oil the height of the back of the lantern case should be at least 12 in. and its breadth at least 10 in. The lantern fixing should always be on the side. Owing to the absorption by coloring, the power of a red light is only 40 per cent of the intensity of the corresponding white light. The corresponding intensity of the green light is 25 per cent.

SIDE-LIGHT SCREEN. A wood or steel framing with a minimum length of 3 ft. in which each one of the vessel's red and green navigation lights is carried and which is so constructed as to prevent these lights from being seen across the bow. Also called lamp screen, light box, lamp board, light board.

Fr: *Ecran de fanal;* Ger: *Laternenkasten; Laternenbrett; Laternenschirm.*

A batten is placed vertically along the forward edge of the fore-and-aft screen and projecting outboard so that its outer edge is tangent to a line drawn through the inner edge of the wick or filament parallel to the keel line. The afterside of the frame is arranged to screen off the light so as to show two points abaft the beam.

SIDE-PLATE RUDDER. A rudder formed of a solid frame forged or cast which includes the bow, the stock, and the transverse uniting stays or arms. Also called double plate rudder. On either side of this frame a comparatively thin plate is riveted. The space between the two plates is filled with wood.

Fr: *Gouvernail à Double Tôle;* Ger: *Zweiplatterruder.*

SIDE PLATING. The shell plating extending from the curve of the bilge up the ship's side.

Fr: *Bordé de Muraille;* Ger: *Seitenbeplattung.*

SIDERAL HOUR ANGLE. The angular distance that the declinational circle of a celestial body is to the Westward of the declinational circle passing through the first point of Aries. Also called **Ascension verse.**

Fr: *Angle horaire sidéral;* Ger: *Sternzeitwinkel.*

SIDERAL MONTH. Mean period required by the moon to make a circuit among the stars. It has a duration of 27 days, 7 hours, 43 minutes, 11.5 seconds.

Fr: *Mois lunaire;* Ger: *Siderischer Monat.*

SIDEREAL. Of or pertaining to the stars.

Fr: *Sidéral;* Ger: *Sideral.*

SIDEREAL CHRONOMETER. One so regulated that it shows the exact time with reference to the apparent movement of a fixed star.

Fr: *Chronomètre Sidéral;* Ger: *Chronometer nach Sternzeit.*

SIDEREAL DAY. The interval between two successive upper transits of the vernal equinox.

Fr: *Jour Sidéral;* Ger: *Sterntag.*

SIDEREAL NOON. See **Noon.**

SIDEREAL TIME. The time defined by the motion of a star as it appears to revolve from East to West. The westerly hour angle of the First Point of Aries.

Fr: *Heure Sidérale;* Ger: *Sternzeit.*

SIDEREAL YEAR. The time required for a complete revolution of the earth around the sun with reference to a specified star.

Fr: *Année Sidérale;* Ger: *Sternjahr.*

SIDE-SET TRAWLER. An otter trawler in which the nets are set and hauled in from the sides of the vessel as distinguished from those which are rigged for setting and hauling over the stern.

SIDE SHACKLE. A shackle which stands so that its narrow edge or side is at right angles to the sheave of the block to which it is fitted.

SIDE SHORE. See **Breast Shore.**

SIDE STRINGER. A fore-and-aft girder running along the side of a ship above the bilge. The stringer may be intercostal and attached directly to the shell plating, or continuous and attached to the inner flanges of the frames.

Fr: *Serre de Côté;* Ger: *Seitenstringer.*

SIDE TANK. A structural ballast tank which forms a continuation of a double bottom up the sides, giving the advantage of a double skin. Also called Macglashan tank.

Fr: *Ballast Latéral;* Ger: *Seitentank; Hoher Wasserballastkasten.*

SIDING. The dimensions of a timber reading opposite to the molding.

Fr: *Droit;* Ger: *Seitenrechte Dicke.*

SIGHT. An instrumental observation of the sun or other heavenly body for determining the position of a vessel at sea. A navigator's expression for taking the altitude of a heavenly body.

Fr: *Hauteur;* Ger: *Höhe.*

See **Back Sight, Position Line Sight.**

SIGHT EDGE. The edges of the plates, in clinker-built plating, which are visible on the outside of the shell, on the top of decks and tank top, and on the opposite side from the stiffeners on bulkheads.

SIGHT ENTRY. See **Bill of Sight.**

SIGHTING (G. B.). The presentation by a consignee or holder of a bill of lading to the master of a ship in order to obtain delivery of the goods. This is called "sighting a bill of lading."

SIGHT THE ANCHOR. To heave an anchor up to the water's edge to make sure it is clear; it is then again let go.

SIGHT VANE. An instrument fitted on the top of a compass or pelorus and used for taking bearings. Also called azimuth sight. The *object vane* is an oblong frame having a fine thread or wire stretched along its middle by which the point to be observed is intersected. The *eye vane* consists of an oblong plate having a very narrow slit which forms the sight through which vision is directed in taking a bearing.

Fr: *Viseur Azimutal;* Ger: *Diopter; Visier.*

See **Pelorus.**

SIGNAL FLAG. A flag used in or adapted for signaling between two ships or between ship and shore. One of a set of flags of different colors, shapes and markings which used singly or in combination have different meanings. Also called signaling flag. Signaling flags for merchant vessels have been agreed upon internationally and as a consequence an international code of signals was brought into force. The flags of the code in use since 1932 include 30 letters of the alphabet, a code flag, 10 numeral pennants and 3 substitutes. By means of hoists not exceeding 4 flags it is possible to make any signal from the code or spell out words not contained therein.

Fr: *Pavillon Signalétique;* Ger: *Signalflagge.*

Only a few colors can be readily distinguished at sea. These are: red, blue, yellow, black, and white; and these cannot be mixed indiscriminately. For clarity at a distance flags should be either red and white, yellow and blue, blue and white, or black and white; besides plain red, white, and blue flags.

SIGNAL HALYARDS. Light lines running through sheaves at the gaff end, masthead, jumper stay, and so on, for hoisting flags. They are made of white hemp, soft-laid, with one of the yarns reverse spun so as to get flexibility. They are usually supplied in three sizes, ¾, 1⅛, 1¼ in. Signal halyards are also made of hard-laid or braided cotton, or of eight strand, three-ply, braided flax twine.

Fr: *Drisse de Pavillon;* Ger: *Flaggenfall.*

SIGNAL LETTERS. A 4-flag signal officially recorded and allocated by various governments to each ship for the purpose of making the vessel's name known at sea. The first letter, or in some cases the first two letters indicate the nationality of the vessel. By international agreement each nation has been allocated one or two letters which form the top or uppermost flags of the signal. Since 1943 the wireless call sign or call letters have been composed of the same letters in the same order.

Fr: *Lettres Signalétiques;* Ger: *Unterscheidungssignal; Signalbuchstaben.*

See **Ship's Number.**

United States Bureau of Marine Inspection and Navigation, Signal Letters of the United States Merchant Marine, Report Series no. 10, Washington, 1941.

SIGNALING MIRROR. A stainless steel or other suitably polished metal mirror with a reflecting surface of 20 sq. in. or more, used for making distress signals from a lifeboat.

SIGNAL MAN. See **Hatchman.**

SIGNAL PISTOL. A pistol used for making distress signals from a small boat. It fires parachute signal cartridges giving a brilliant red flame of 20,000 candlepower or more with a burning duration of 30 seconds, projected vertically to a height of 150 ft.

SIGNAL ROCKET. A pasteboard cylinder with conical head containing pyrotechnic stars of various ingredients and colors and a quantity of powder. When the rocket has attained its greatest height the cylinder bursts and the ignited stars spread through the air, casting a brilliant light.

> Fr: *Fusée de Signalisation;* Ger: *Signalrakete; Leuchtrakete.*

SIGNAL STATION. A position on the coast from which signals are made to ships at sea.

> Fr: *Station de Signaux;* Ger: *Signalstation.*

SIGNAL YARD. A short yard made of wood or steel tubing fixed to the forward side of the foremast and used for signaling purposes. Each yard arm is provided with one or two signal halyard blocks. The yard is held in place by inner lifts, outer lifts, and a pair of short braces which are taken to the backstays. Some passenger vessels have a second signal yard on the mainmast.

> Fr: *Vergue à signaux;* Ger: *Signalraa.*

SIGNING OFF. The discharge of seamen at the completion of the voyage, and payment of wages. It takes place before the same authorities as signing on.

> Fr: *Licenciement;* Ger: *Abmeldung; Abmusterung.*

SIGNING ON. The signing by each member of the crew of the articles of agreement before the beginning of the voyage. This procedure must, in most maritime countries, take place before the proper authority; in Great Britain a superintendent; in the U. S. a shipping commissioner or a collector of customs; in foreign ports, a consular officer.

> Fr: *Enrôlement;* Ger: *Anmeldung; Anmusterung.*

SILK ROOM. Steel walled space provided in vessels designed for the Far East trade and specially adapted for the transport of silk bales. Silk rooms are usually built in 'tween decks. The walls are lined with soft wood paneling and wooden gratings are fitted on the floor. The spaces between beams are packed with cork dust and all precautions are taken to eliminate any risk of sweat owing to the delicate nature and high value of the goods. In some modern vessels the capacity for silk is over 35,000 cu. ft.

> Fr: *Soute à Soieries;* Ger: *Seidenraum.*

SILL. A small angle lug or casting, fixed under a scupper hole outside of the shell plating in order to prevent the water issuing from a scupper hole from trickling down the ship's side. Also called port sill, lip.

> Ger: *Pfortendrempel.*

See **Dock Sill.**

SILT. A fine earthy sediment. A deposit of mud or fine soil from running or standing water. Fine sand, clay, and earth transported by running water and often accumulated in banks at the mouths of rivers.

> Fr: *Vase;* Ger: *Schlick; Schlamm.*

SLIVER PIECE. A boatbuilding term used to denote small pieces of wood of triangular section fastened on each side of the stem or keel of a boat at the back of the bearing or rabbet line to make up for the deficiency of material.

> Ger: *Abgeschnittenes Stück.*

SIM. A single-outrigger dugout canoe with wash strake from Lihir Island, New Ireland, Bismarck Archipelago, of same type as the *bil* from Lamusmus. Length 30 ft. Breadth 1.2 ft. Depth 1.7 ft. (Typical.)

SIMOON. A very short and violent wind met with on the coasts of the Arabian peninsula. It lasts only about 10 minutes and is laden with sand.

SIMPLEX PUMP. A reciprocating pump which has a single water cylinder, as distinguished from a duplex pump with two steam cylinders cast side by side in a single block and two water cylinders constructed in a similar manner.

SIMPSON'S RULES. Mathematical rules for obtaining the area included between a graphic curve and its base line. In these rules arcs of parabolas passing through the extremities of equally spaced ordinates are considered to approximate actual curve.

> Fr: *Règles de Simpson;* Ger: *Simpsonsche Regel.*

SIMULTANEOUS ALTITUDES. Altitudes of two or more heavenly bodies observed at the same time in order to ascertain the ship's position.

Fr: *Hauteurs Simultanées;* Ger: *Gleichzeitige Höhen.*

SINAGOT. A French sailing trawler from the village of Séné in the Gulf of Morbihan. It resembles the sardine boats of southern Brittany in rig but is different in hull form and usage. The scantlings are heavier. It has a greater length of keel and area of midship section with corresponding increase of displacement. The hull is built with straight stem, raking sternpost, high freeboard forward, sharp stern, and short deck forward. The rig consists of two masts with lug sails, each sail having 5 or 6 rows of reef points. There is one headsail which tacks down to a short bowsprit. There is no standing rigging. The average length is 34 ft. with a tonnage of 5 to 6. Crew 2.
Journal de la Marine Le Yacht, Paris, no. 2223 (October 31, 1925), p. 526–27.

SINGHALESE CATAMARAN. A raft made of 3 to 5 logs of hewn mahogany fastened together by lashings, and so disposed that the outer logs are canted to raise their upper edge above the others and thus form a sort of longitudinal trough in the center. The central logs project at the stern some distance abaft the side logs, and afford a position on their lee side for the steering oar. The bow is formed by three short pieces of timber secured to the forward end of the raft and projecting upward at a considerable angle.

A single triangular sail with boom is set on a mast stepped amidships. The largest *catamarans* are from 25 to 30 ft. long. Smaller ones are used for fishing. The larger type is employed for boarding vessels in open roadstead through the surf.

SINGING PROPELLER. A screw propeller in which the blades are so proportioned that under normal working conditions they vibrate at a rate which produces a distinct noise. These sounds may be musical or discordant; some singing propellers emit only one type of sound but in most cases both types are represented. So far as the mechanism of singing is concerned it is now generally agreed that the noise is caused by the vibrations of the blades and that the sonic vibrations are transmitted through the water and picked up by the shell plating in way of the afterend of the ship, which acts as a sounding board. Usually the blades are found to be too thin.
Fr: *Hélice Chantante;* Ger: *Singende Schraube.*

Davis, A. W., "Characteristics of Silent Propellers," Institution of Engineers and Shipbuilders in Scotland, *Transactions,* vol. 83 (1939).

SINGLE. To unreeve the running part of a purchase. To reduce the number of parts of a doubled or trebled rope to one.

SINGLE-ARM TILLER. A tiller which consists of a single bar or lever, as distinguished from a quadrant tiller or a yoke.
Fr: *Barre Simple.*

SINGLE-BANKED. A rowboat in which one oarsman sits on each thwart. Gigs, whaleboats and dinghies are single-banked.
Fr: *Armé en Pointe;* Ger: *Einzigruderig.*

SINGLE BLOCK. A block with one sheave.
Fr: *Poulie Simple;* Ger: *Einscheibiger Block.*

SINGLE BOATER. A North Sea trawler which takes aboard fuel, stores, and ice for about a week, then proceeds to the fishing grounds and stays there until a sufficient quantity of fish has been caught. It then returns home with the catch to unload and start off again. Single boaters do not fish in fleets, as do the box trawlers.

SINGLE BOTTOM. Refers to a vessel which has no inner bottom or tank top.
Ger: *Einfacher Boden.*

SINGLE BURTON. A tackle rove with two single blocks, frequently used on small craft for loading and discharging cargo by hand.
Fr: *Bredindin Simple;* Ger: *Einfacher Klappläufer.*

SINGLE-COLLAR THRUST BEARING. See Kingsbury Thrust Bearing.

SINGLE-DECK VESSEL. A type of vessel particularly suitable for the transport of bulk cargoes which have to be trimmed after loading and which are often discharged with grabs. Large single-deck vessels with a total deadweight up to 10,500 tons have been built for the carriage of coal, grain, and ore. This type of vessel is not suitable for bagged or packaged cargoes owing to possible damage to lower tiers by crushing on account of the great depth of the hold.
Fr: *Navire à un Pont;* Ger: *Eindeckschiff.*

SINGLE-DORY FISHERMAN. In New England, trawl-line vessels which use small dories about 12 ft. in length requiring only one man per dory as distinguished from the double-dory fishermen which use a larger type of dory, about 14 ft. long with 2 men in each dory.

SINGLE-EXPANSION ENGINE. An early type of reciprocating steam engine, in which steam was admitted to one or more cylinders, and expansion took place in the single cylinder or in one stroke, after which the steam was discharged to the condenser.

SINGLE FALL AND SKID METHOD. A system used for loading cargo. The cargo hook is thrown on the wharf or quay and attached to the draft. The latter is then dragged up a cargo skid to the deck. When it swings across the hatch opening, it is checked by the hatch foreman with a rope and then lowered into the hold. Also called Whip and skid system.

SINGLE FASTENING. By single fastening is meant that each strake of planking has one fastening of each kind, wood and metal, into each frame timber.

Fr: *Chevillage Simple;* Ger: *Einfache Verbolzung.*

SINGLE-LEG PROPELLER STRUT. A propeller strut in which the hub or strut bearing is attached to the hull by a single member.

SINGLE PADDLE. A type of canoe paddle with single blade, derived from the North American Indians. It is used continuously on the same side of the boat and its motion, in skilled hands, is noiseless. Single paddles are of two types, the bow paddle and the stern paddle. The latter is heavier and made of hardwood (maple). The bow paddle is usually made of spruce. Bow paddle: Length 4 to 5 ft. Blade 26 to 28 in. Breadth 5 to 5½ in. Stern paddle: Length 4 ft. 9 in. to 5 ft. Blade 24 to 28 in. Breadth 6 to 6½ in.

Fr: *Pagaye Simple;* Ger: *Einziger Paddel.*

SINGLE-PLY CANVAS. Canvas in which each weft or filling thread passes alternately over and under the warp thread.

Fr: *Toile à Fils Simples.*

SINGLE PURCHASE. See Whip.

SINGLE SHELL. See Racing Skiff.

SINGLE STEP HYDROPLANE. A hydroplane with one step in the bottom.

Fr: *Hydroplane à Redan Unique;* Ger: *Einstuf-Gleitboot.*

See Hydroplane.

SINGLE TOPSAIL. A large square topsail with 2 to 4 reef bands. This sail in modern vessels has been replaced by double topsails. Also called whole topsail.

Fr: *Hunier Plein;* Ger: *Einfacher Marssegel.*

SINGLE-TREE MAST. The converse of a built mast, a lower mast made of one piece of timber.

Fr: *Mât d'un Seul Brin;* Ger: *Pfahlmast.*

SINGLE UP. To take in all bights of mooring lines preparatory to getting underway from alongside a quay wall or pier.

Fr: *Dédoubler les amarres.*

SINGLE-VEED WELD. A butt weld where both fusion faces are straight beveled before welding.

Fr: *Soudure en V;* Ger: *V-Schweissung.*

SINGLE-WAY LAUNCHING. A method of end launching in which only one large set of ways is used in conjunction with smaller auxiliary bilge ways. The entire weight of the ship is sustained at the keel which rests on a sliding way. In order to prevent the vessel from swaying sideways, two additional ways are provided, one under each bilge. They are also relied upon as an emergency arrangement in case the ship should stall on the ways.

Fr: *Lancement sur Quille; Lancement sur Savate;* Ger: *Stapellauf mit Mittelschlitte; Kielablauf.*

The single-way launching, although somewhat more hazardous than the two-way system, has some points in its favor. It is simpler and its first cost is considerably less than the double way system. Its use is by no means confined to small craft. Vessels with a launching weight well over 8000 tons have been successfully put in the water by this method, the width of the sliding way being in this case 4 ft. and its thickness varying from 10 to 22 inches.

SINI. Polynesian single-outrigger dugout canoe with deep wash strake from Nissan Islands, Solomon Islands, which carries from 1 to 6 persons, according to length. The hull is sharply pointed and raked at the ends. There are flattened transverse endboards which curve fore and aft respectively. The larger craft have a platform, made of sticks laid longitudinally, over the booms. Also called *tsine tini.*

SIREN. A noise-making apparatus in which a metallic disc with holes equidistantly arranged in a circle is driven on the turbine principle by a jet of air or steam between two fixed plates with inclined holes. Also called syren. Since the escaping air or steam is cut off by the holes, a sound wave of frequency determined by the speed of rotation and the number of holes in the circle is generated The note emitted is generally of medium power, increasing to a maximum and then diminishing. The sound is conveyed by a trumpet-shaped tube.

Fr: *Sirène;* Ger: *Sirene.*

Large passenger vessels are usually equipped with sirens emitting a low note, as an increased range is thereby obtained and the sound is less unpleasant than it is higher up the scale. The siren is frequently placed on the foremast above the crosstrees, where it is out of the way of the cargo gear. When so located the greater part of the ship is, acoustically speaking, in shadow, so that passengers are not disturbed. At the same time it is easier for the navigating personnel to distinguish between their own siren and those of other ships. Lately electric sirens in which the kinetic energy of the motor armature is converted to sound have been fitted to some passenger vessels.

SIRMARKS. Points or stations marked on the molds of frame timbers where bevelings are applied in order to cut the timber to the required bevel at these points. (Obsolete.)

Fr: *Points de Rabattement;* Ger: *Rennzeichen.*

SIROCCO. A hot and dry south or southeasterly wind experienced in the western half of the Mediterranean at all times of the year but more frequently during the months of July and August. It originates from the high land in the Sahara Desert.

SISAL ROPE. A rope made of sisal fiber as a substitute for Manila. Its tensile strength is about 75 per cent that of Manila. Unlike Manila, sisal rope is stiff and harsh, and deteriorates rapidly when exposed to salt water. The henequen or Agave plant from which sisal hemp is made, grows chiefly in East Africa, New Zealand, Mexico and Java.

Fr: *Cordage en Sisal;* Ger: *Sisaltauwerk.*

SISTER BLOCK. A shell with two sheaves of same size one above the other. Also called long-tail block. The falls lead in opposite directions.

Fr: *Poulie Vierge;* Ger: *Stängenwantblock; Puppblock.*

SISTER HOOK.
See **Clip Hook.**

SISTER KEELSON. Longitudinal timbers placed on each side of the main keelson and extending as far forward and aft as possible in order to give additional strength at the middle line of the vessel. They are fastened horizontally to the center keelson and vertically to the floors.

Fr: *Carlingue Latérale; Contre Carlingue;* Ger: *Nebenkielschwein; Seitenkielschwein.*

SISTER SHIP CLAUSE. Insurance clause by which the underwriters agree that in the event of collision between ships of the same ownership they will deal with the matter as if the ships belonged to different owners.

SISTER SHIPS. Ships built on the same design.

SIXAERN. Small sailing and rowing clinker-built boat with great spring at ends, used for long-line fishing around the Shetland Islands. Also called sixarren, sixern, haaf boat. The rig is made up of a single square sail of primitive design, hoisted by halyards bent to the yard and running through a sheave in the mast. The loose end is also made fast to the yard and used as a downhaul. The boat is divided into 6 compartments known locally as: fore head, foreroom, mid-room or ballast room, Owse room, shot or wade room, Kannie or Hurrik. Length over-all 25 to 30 ft. Length at keel 17 to 21 ft. Breadth (extreme) 8 to 9 ft. Inside depth at mast thwart 2½ to 3 ft. 2 in. (Typical.)

SJAEKTER. A small open boat 18 to 20 ft. in length used for fishing in the Kattegat, North Sea.

SKAFFIE. A type of Scotch lugger with curved stem and raked sternpost, apparently of Norse origin. Also called *scaffa.* The rig consists of a dipping lug on the foremast and a smaller standing lug on the mizzen. It is broader, flatter in the bottom and generally deeper in the keel than the *Fifie.* Length over-all 60 ft. Length at keel 36 ft. Breadth 17 ft. 3 in. Depth of hold 7 ft. (Average.)

SKAG (U. S.). A length of heavy chain carried by a barge when in tow, intended to be dropped overboard, if necessary, to steady the barge in its course when navigating narrow channels.

SKAPHE. A single-masted, lug-rigged, fully decked boat originating from the Grecian Archipelago, used for small coasting and sponge fishing. The hull is beamy with good flare, pointed stern, and pronounced rake of stem, with one large hatchway amidships. The mast, very short, is stepped forward and sets a spritsail and one headsail with tack fastened to stemhead.

SKATE. In the trawl-line fisheries, the receptacle in which the lines are coiled before setting. The skate is a piece of canvas about 15 to 18 in. square after it has been hemmed, with two small ropes, each 9 or 10 ft. long, crossed at right angles on the canvas and fastened at each corner and in the center. The trawl is coiled on it and tied up with the ropes.

SKEEMAN. An officer on a British Greenland whaling vessel who directed the stowing of the blubber. (Obsolete.)

SKEET.
See **Baler**.

SKEG. 1. A knee timber which connects and braces the stern post and keel.
Fr: *Courbe d'Étambot;* Ger: *Kielhacke.*
2. Additional timbers fastened under the stern of small craft, acting as a deep keel to keep the boat on a straight course.
Ger: *Totholz; Stevenschwert.*
3. A wood or metal arm extending abaft the keel with a bearing at its afterend. It acts as support for the rudder and protects the propeller.
Fr: *Talonnière; Crosse;* Ger: *Kielhacke; Hacke.*
4. The extension of the after part of the keel in a single screw vessel that supports the rudder post and stern post.
Fr: *Semelle d'Etambot;* Ger: *Stevensohle.*

SKEG BAND. An iron band fitted outside of the sternpost and keel of a rowboat to protect and strengthen the keel and sternpost scarf. It extends from the lower rudder brace to about 2 ft. forward of the scarf.
Fr: *Bande d'Étambot;* Ger: *Hinterstevenschiene.*

SKEG SHORE. A diagonal prop, the upper end of which abuts against the back of the sternpost, formerly used to prevent the launching cradle from sliding down after the keel blocks have been removed.
Fr: *Poulin;* Ger: *Hintere Kielstütze.*

SKEIN. A quantity of yarn, twine, houseline, and so on, put up in a sort of knot.
Fr: *Manoque;* Ger: *Bund.*

SKEKTA. Open rowing and sailing boat from the west coast of Iceland (Breidafjord) lightly built with short keel, long raking stem, rounded forefoot, and sharp curved stern and clinker planked. The rig consists of one mast stepped a little forward of half length, which sets a large square sail, and sometimes a small topsail. Length 20 to 23 ft. Breadth 7.2 to 8 ft.

SKELETON FLOOR. A floor composed of plate brackets on each side of the center girder and at the margin plate. The reverse and frame bars are connected in between by struts with or without bracket plates according to the size of the vessel. Also called bracket floor, open floor.
Fr: *Cadre Varangue; Varangue Squelette;*
Ger: *Offene Bodenwrange.*

SKERRY YAWL.
See **Trondjem**.

SKEW. A type of arrangement of propeller blades, set with an inclination aft instead of being placed at right angles to the hub. Also called skew-back, set-back, rake. It is claimed that in single-screw vessels the raking of the propeller blades is a distinct advantage when there is an eddy formation at the upper levels. In addition, it appears to give better results in rough water when the propeller blades occasionally emerge.
Fr: *Inclinaison;* Ger: *Winkelstellung; Aufflage.*

SKID. 1. A framework of planks or timber fitted to the outside of a ship abreast of the hatches to prevent injury to the ship's side when cargo is loaded or unloaded.
Fr: *Martyr;* Ger: *Ladeschlitten.*
2. Beams sometimes fitted over the decks for the stowage of boats.
See **Boat Skid**.

SKIFF. A flat-bottomed, shallow-draft, open boat of simple construction, with sharp bow and square stern. Skiffs are propelled by motor, sail, or oars. They are used by fishermen and watermen, or as pleasure boats in sheltered waters.
Fr: *Skiff;* Ger: *Skiff.*
See **Beach Skiff, Dory Skiff, Delaware Sturgeon Skiff, Fair Isle Skiff, Loch Fyne Skiff, Monterey Squid Skiff, Orkney Skiff, Pilot Skiff, Thames Skiff.**

SKIMMINGS. In marine insurance policies, the removal from a bag of coffee or other similar commodity of the damaged beans, leaving the bag so "skimmed" for sale in sound condition.

SKIN. 1. The plating of a ship. The inside skin is sometimes called the ceiling, the outside skin, the case. In modern riveted or welded vessels the skin consists of steel plates, laid in adjacent contiguous strakes.

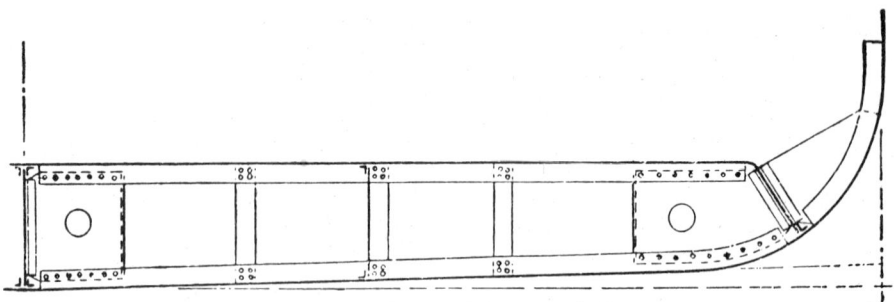

Skeleton Floor

2. That part of a furled sail which remains outside and covers the whole.
Fr: *Chemise;* Ger: *Brok.*

SKIN BOAT. Generally, a primitive open or decked craft used for hunting, fishing or transportation and propelled with paddles or sail, in which the outer shell is made of seal or other animal skins tightly stretched over a light framing usually of wood. With a few exceptions the skin boats are mostly found in the Arctic regions where there are no trees and where large marine animals are common.
Ger: *Fellboot.*
See **Kayak, Umiak, Baidarka.**
Shinji Nishimura, Skin Boats, Tokio (1931); Süder, H., Vom Einbaum und Floss zum Schiff, Institut für Meereskunde, Berlin (1930); Trebitsch, R., Fellboote und Schwimmsacke und ihre Geographische Verbreitung, Archiv für Anthropologie, Band 11, N.F., Braunschweig (1912).

SKIN GIRTH. The girth of the hull taken by following the skin surface from gunwale to gunwale.
Fr: *Périmètre;* Ger: *Schmiegenumfang.*

SKINNER. In the cod and halibut fisheries, one of the men of the dressing gang who, with a glove or a piece of bagging, rubs off the nape skins, also any blood spots, and drops the fish in a tub of salt water.
Fr: *Gratteur.*

SKIN RESISTANCE. Resistance caused by the friction of the water on the immersed surface of the hull. It depends upon the area of wetted surface, the nature and condition of the wetted surface and the speed of the ship. It is the most important factor in the total resistance, the other factors being the eddy-making resistance and the wave-making resistance. For large vessels of very low speed the skin resistance may approach 90 per cent of the total. For ordinary vessels of moderate speed it is usually between 70 and 80 per cent.
Fr: *Résistance de Frottement;* Ger: *Reibungswiderstand.*
Baker, G. S., "Skin Friction Resistance of Ships," Institution of Naval Architects (London), *Transactions,* vol. 58 (1916).

SKIP.
See **Tray.**

SKIP. A shallow, flat-bottomed, straight-sided wooden box strengthened with iron fittings, with top and one end open, supported by three or four chains or wire ropes leading to a common ring for hanging on a hook. The chain supporting the open end is provided with a trip hook for dumping. Also called skip box. Skip boxes are frequently used for handling miscelleaneous small cargo when the use of slings or slings and netting is disadvantageous.

SKIPJACK. A centerboard, V-bottomed sailing boat common on the Chesapeake Bay and Atlantic coast of the United States. The hull is built of hard pine with clipper stem fitted with billet, headsails and trail boards, and a broad transom stern with outboard rudder. The bottom is planked crosswise. The deck runs from stem to stern. The rig consists of one mast with pronounced rake aft, on which are set a leg-of-mutton mainsail and a stay foresail or jib, which tacks down on a short and much hogged-down bowsprit, as in the bugeye. This type of craft, which derives from the sharpie, is a compromise between the flat-bottomed and the round-bottomed boat. It is used for oyster dredging and as a market boat. It is also a popular form of hull for small yachts. At Provincetown,

Mass., it is called corner boat on account of the sharp angle formed by the topsides and bottom. The largest boats used in the oyster trade have the following average dimensions: Length 42 ft. Beam 14 ft. Depth 3 ft. 9 in. Draft 3 ft. The smaller units vary in size as follows: Length 36 ft. 6 in. to 39 ft. 8 in. Breadth 11 ft. 6 in. to 13 ft. 2 in. Depth 2 ft. 8 in. to 3 ft. 6 in. Draft 2 ft. 6 in. to 3 ft.

Chapelle, H. I., Notes on Chesapeake Bay Skipjacks, American Neptune, Salem, vol. 4, October, 1944.

SKIPPER. 1. A term applied officially in Great Britain to a duly certificated person in charge of a fishing vessel. The presence of a skipper is compulsory for all fishing vessels of 25 tons or more.

2. Name given to the master of a small trading or pleasure vessel.

Fr: *Patron;* Ger: *Schiffer; Führer.*

SKIP WELDING. Method of fusion welding adopted for fillet and butt welds to relieve residual stresses and to prevent distortion. In the "skip" method a short run is made and then another short run is made by skipping some distance, and so on throughout the joint. The operator then returns to the first run and makes a similar short run adjacent to it, proceeding systematically throughout the work. The time between adjacent runs should be such that the first run deposited has had sufficient time to cool and contract. In the "step-back" method a similar procedure is adopted but with a different sequence of runs.

Skip Welding sequence

| 1 | 4 | 7 | 10 | 2 | 5 | 8 | 11 | 3 | 6 | 9 | 12 |

Step-Back Welding sequence

| 9 | 7 | 5 | 3 | 1 | 2 | 4 | 6 | 8 | 10 |

The greater and shorter the number of runs, the more effective the stress relieving becomes.

Fr: *Soudure à pas de Pèlerin.*

SKJEGTE. A sail, and rowboat used in Norway in the south coast fisheries. It is built with deep keel, clinker planking and a runway (*skvetganger*) on each side with coaming extending fore and aft, and is undecked. It is rigged with a spritsail. Its length ranges from 19 to 23 ft.

SKOiTE. A general term which, when used alone, applies to a type of small, Norwegian decked sailing coaster or fishing boat, clinker-built, with transom stern. Its tonnage seldom exceeds 35. It is always single-masted with sloop or cutter rig, the latter being most common. The construction of the stern has special features. The hull proper is sharp or pointed and the transom is formed by extending the deck and bulwarks abaft the rudder and fastening planks across. The so-called counter is entirely flat, and, to prevent the seas from lifting and breaking this structure, it is supported by iron braces which extend downward from the underside of the deck. Length over-all 32 ft. 3 in. Breadth 11 ft. 3 in. Depth 4 ft. 3 in. (Typical.)

See **Bankskoite, Kokarsköt, Listerskoite, Redningskoite.**

SKY-GAZER. A light, triangular sail set flying above the royal. It was used only during the clipper ship era. A triangular skysail.

SKYLIGHT. A wood or metal structure built over a weather-deck opening to afford light and ventilation to the spaces below. The top covers are flat or pitched and are provided with hinges. They can be raised or lowered by screw gear from below. Brass rods are frequently fitted over the glass for protection.

Fr: *Claire Voie;* Ger: *Oberlicht; Deckfenster.*

See **Circular Headed Skylight, Dwarf Skylight, Hipped Skylight**

SKYLIGHT COVER. 1. The top of a skylight having glass panes fitted in it, and usually hinged and operated from below.

2. A canvas hood cut to the required shape and placed over a skylight as a precaution in heavy or wet weather to prevent water trickling down.

Fr: *Capot de Claire Voie; Etui de Claire Voie;* Ger: *Oberlichtkappe; Oberlichtbezug.*

SKYLIGHT GEAR. A lifting gear composed of a quadrant, rods, pinions, lever, and hand wheel for opening and shutting a skylight from below.

SKYLIGHT GRATING. Guards of brass or other metal protecting the glass panes of a skylight.

Fr: *Caillebotis de Claire Voie;* Ger: *Oberlicht Schutzstangen.*

SKYLIGHT QUADRANT. A brass bar in the form of a quadrant hinged to a plate at one end and having a slot in the middle. The plate is screwed to the side of the sky-

light and the sash carries a set screw which slides in the slot. It is used for holding the sash open at any desired angle.
  Fr: *Secteur de Claire Voie;* Ger: *Oberlicht Sektor.*

SKYSAIL. 1. A triangular racing sail used in the staysail schooner rig. Its head sets on snap hooks which run on a taut wire from main truck to fore truck. There is no true sheet, as adjusting the downhaul on the luff gives the desired draft at different points of sailing.
  2. A small square sail set above a royal.
  Fr: *Contre-Cacatois; Papillon;* Ger: *Skysegel; Scheisegel.*
  See **Flying Skysail.**

SKYSAIL POLE. The mast pole extending from the royal rigging to the truck in vessels which carried flying skysails over standing royals.
  Fr: *Flèche de Contre-Cacatois;* Ger: *Scheisegeltopp; Scheisegelstange.*

SKYSCRAPER. A triangular sail which sets from the truck and the skysail yardarms; also called moonraker. It was used during the clipper ship era. Obsolete.
  Fr: *Aile de Pigeon;* Ger: *Dreieckiger Wolkenraper.*

SLAB. The slack part of a sail which hangs down after the leech lines are hauled up.
  Ger: *Gei.*
  See **Bending Floor.**

SLAB CORK. Granulated cork compressed into boardform, baked and held together by the natural cork gum as a binder. Used for insulation of cargo spaces and applied in two or more layers arranged to break joints. Weight 8 to 12 pounds per cubic foot. Also called corkboard.
  Fr: *Liège aggloméré;* Ger: *Korkstein.*

SLAB HATCHES. Hatches made of a number of wooden hatch covers bolted together and securely bound with an iron band. Usually only four are required to cover the hatchway. As they are too heavy to be lifted without a purchase, they effectively prevent cargo pilfering.
  Ger: *Schillenluke.*

SLAB KEEL. An additional plate of heavy steel riveted outside of a plate keel. It gives great local rigidity, and serves as a substantial fender. It is also called false keel, rubbing bar, rubbing strip.
  Fr: *Fausse Quille;* Ger: *Schutzkiel.*

SLAB KNEE.
  See **Welded Knee.**

SLAB LINE. Lines used for confining the slack canvas of a course after it has been taken in. It is rigged in the same manner as a buntline, but is run up on the afterside of the sail to slab-line blocks lashed to the jackstay.
  Fr: *Cargue à Vue; Dégorgeoir;* Ger: *Dampfleine; Schlappleine.*

SLAB PIN. A slightly conical steel pin used as a positive stop on a bending slab or floor.

SLAB REEF. The first or upper reef in a whole topsail.

SLACK. 1. The extra length allowed in cutting out a fore-and-aft sail to obtain a round or curved afterleech.
  Fr: *Mou;* Ger: *Schlacktuch.*
  2. The part of a rope which has no stress upon it.
  Fr: *Mou;* Ger: *Lose.*
  See **Slack Water.**

SLACK AWAY. To pay out without losing control over the rope thus handled. Also called to slack off.
  Fr: *Filer;* Ger: *Wegfieren; Losfieren.*

SLACK CLOTH. A certain quantity of canvas allowed to be gradually gathered up in sewing on the boltrope of a sail, in order to prevent the rope from tearing the sail as a result of stretching in consequence of wear.
  Fr: *Mou;* Ger: *Schlacktuch.*

SLACKEN. To decrease in tension or velocity. To ease up tension on a rope.
  Fr: *Mollir; Donner du Mou;* Ger: *Fieren; Lose geben.*

SLACK IN STAYS. Slow in going about. A vessel in bad trim or handled in a lubberly manner is generally slack in stays.
  Fr: *Lent à Virer;* Ger: *Beim Wenden langsam sein.*

SLACKNESS. The tendency of a vessel under sail to fall off or away from the direction of the wind when the helm is amidships, as opposed to "ardency." Slackness can be corrected by moving the center of effort of the sail plan sufficiently abaft the center of lateral resistance to balance the tendency.
  Fr: *Mou;* Ger: *Leegierigkeit.*

SLACK SEAMS. A certain quantity of canvas allowed for gathering in the seaming up of the afterleech of fore-and-aft mainsails. The puckering of the seams in a gradual manner. The seams sewed after slack is allowed in the cutting out form the curve on the afterleech.

Fr: *Embu;* Ger: *Breiterhaltung.*

SLACK WATER. The period between the flood and ebb or between the cessation of the tidal stream in one direction and its commencement in the opposite direction. The relation of the time of slack water to the tidal phases varies in different localities. In some cases slack water occurs near the times of high and low water, while in other localities the slack water may occur midway between high and low water.

Fr: *Etale;* Ger: *Stauwasser.*

SLAMMING. A feature of the motion of a ship through a seaway. Slamming almost always takes places forward and the greatest effect upon the hull structure is usually shown by damage to the floors and plating at a distance of from one-eighth to one-sixth of the length of the ship from the fore perpendicular. Slamming damage is usually ascribed to dynamic pressures arising from impact of the ship's hull upon the surface of the water, and from the actual impulsive displacement of water caused by the downward movement of the ship when pitching. It is particularly noticeable in cargo vessels with engines aft when making passages in ballast. Also called pounding.

Spanner, E. F., Slamming Damage at Sea Engineering, London, vol. 139, no. 3601 January, 1935.

SLANT. A slant wind; i.e., a transitory breeze or period of its duration.

SLAT DOOR. A wooden door composed of a frame with slats or blinds. Slat doors are fitted in conjunction with joiner doors to state rooms, or independently to some compartments. Also called blind door, jalousie door.

Fr: *Porte à Persienne;* **Ger:** *Jalousie Tür.*

SLAVE JIB. A term used by yachtsmen to denote a working jib, almost permanently set and slightly larger than the spitfire.

SLEEPER. 1. One of the heavy timbers placed upon the ground or on top of piling of a building berth to support the cribbing, keel blocks, and bilge blocks.

Fr: *Traversin de Cale.*

2. One of the knees bolted to the transoms and counter timbers to strengthen the stern framing.

Fr: *Tablette;* Ger: *Heckbalkenknie.*

SLEET. Falling pellets of ice, sometimes mixed with a cold rain.

Fr: *Grésil;* Ger: *Graupeln.*

SLEW. Also Slue. **1.** To turn about a fixed point, as a spar, derrick, and so on.

2. To yaw from side to side while at anchor or being towed.

SLEWING DERRICK. A cargo derrick mounted on the center line of the ship, which works cargo in or out of the ship by slewing inboard or outboard. The slewing motion is controlled by man-power or by small slewing winches acting on the derrick guys.

SLEW LINE.
See **Slew Rope.**

SLEW ROPE. A rope used in slewing a spar or derrick. Also called slue rope, slew line.

SLICE.
See **Launching Wedge, Adjusting Wedge.**

SLICK. A smooth area on the surface of the sea, as one caused by a film of oil or by the sweep of a ship's stern in making a turn. Also called greyslick.

SLIDING BULKHEAD DOOR. A watertight steel door so constructed and operated that it can be moved horizontally (or vertically) into position. These doors are made watertight and are fitted with shafting and bevel gears or other mechanism to permit them to be operated from an upper deck. Also called sliding door.

Fr: *Porte à Glissières;* Ger: *Schiebetür.*

SLIDING GUNTER.
See **Rig.**

SLIDING GUNTER MAST. A mast made in two pieces, the upper part sliding on the aft side of the lower by means of two iron rings. These irons are fitted to the hoisting part of the mast, which is usually termed topmast or gunter yard, and fit the lower mast very loosely. They are made of brass or galvanized iron covered with leather, and are kept well greased. The sail is bent to the topmast and laced to the lower mast. Sliding gunter masts were formerly used on some clipper ships for setting skysails.

Fr: *Mât de Houari;* Ger: *Schiebestänge; Houari.*

SLIDING GUNTER SAIL. A triangular sail with the luff bent partly to a sliding gunter yard and partly to the mast. It is a handy form of open boat sail.

Fr: *Houari;* Ger: *Portugiesisches Segel; Houarisegel.*

SLIDING KEEL.
See **Drop Keel.**

SLIDING WAYS. Heavy timbers forming the lower part of the cradle which slides down the standing ways when the vessel is launched. Also called bilge ways, bilge logs. They are usually made of timbers 12 in. by 12 in. about 35 ft. long. The adjacent sections are held together by link plates and pins so as to provide some degree of flexibility.

Fr: *Coulisse Vive;* Ger: *Schlittenbalken; Läufer; Ablaufschlitten.*

SLIGHT SEA. A fine weather sea with wave heights ranging between ½ and 2 ft. No. 2 Douglas scale.

Fr: *Mer peu agitée;* Ger: *Leicht bewegte See.*

SLING. 1. Rope or chain strap used for encircling any object so as to suspend it, while being raised or lowered. In a more general sense the word "sling" denotes anything that is used to handle loads or join together several packages that make up a draft.

Fr: *Elingue; Estrope;* Ger: *Hängestropp; Stropp; Schlinge.*

See **Bale Sling, Barrel Sling, Boot Sling, Buoy Sling, Canvas Sling, Chain Sling, Platform Sling, Gaff Sling, Let Sling, Quarter Sling, Rope Sling, Web Sling, Wire Sling, Yard Sling, Wide-Board Sling, Soda-Ash Sling.**

2. A single lift of cases, bags, barrels, package or other merchandise bound together in a sling and hooked on to the end of a cargo fall operated by a winch or crane. The normal weight of a sling ranges from 1000 to 2000 pounds with a maximum of 3000 pounds. Also called draft, sling load.

Fr: *Palanquée; Elinguée;* Ger: *Aushebung.*

SLING (to). To place goods or merchandise in a sling for transfer from ship to shore or inversely. This operation is performed as follows: The sling is laid out flat on the dock floor or ship's bottom and the cargo piled on it in such a manner as to have one end of the sling longer than the other. The long end, or rove, is put through the shorter end called "bite," and on the cargo hook. As the draft is lifted, and the sling gets taut, the bite is driven tight on the rove with a piece of wood or an iron bar.

Fr: *Elinguer;* Ger: *Schlingen; Anschlagen.*

SLING BAND. A band around the center of a lower yard to which the slings fasten. Also called sling hoop.

Fr: *Collier de Suspente;* Ger: *Hängerband.*

SLING CLEAT.
See **Becket.**

SLING-DING (U. S.). In New England hand-line fisheries, a galvanized iron rod about ⅜ in. in diameter and 15 to 20 in. long with an eye at each end, from which snoods are hung. The object of the sling-ding gear is to prevent the snoods from fouling.

Fr: *Arbalète.*

SLINGER. A longshoreman who fastens the sling around the draft and hooks on the winch fall. Also called hooker-on.

Fr: *Elingueur;* Ger: *Anschlager.*

SLINGING. A charge made for putting chains or ropes around goods as they lie in a craft or on a quay so that they may be lifted on board. The expression generally used is "slinging and lifting."

Fr: *Frais d'élingage;* Ger: *Anschlagskosten.*

SLINGS. 1. That part of a yard to which the slings are fastened. The center part of a yard.

2. A fitting for hoisting a boat by a boat crane or boom, consisting of a metal ring with four pendants. Two of these pendants are for athwartships steadying lines, and the others shackle to chain bridles permanently bolted to the keel. Customarily used in U. S. Navy ships' boats.

SLING SHOT (U. S.). A line inserted between a ground or trawl line and the anchor, serving as a point of attachment for the buoy line. Also called slip shot (U. S.).

SLIP (G. B.). 1. A note issued by the insurer on acceptance of a risk. It contains brief details of the voyage, goods, conditions, and so on, and is initialed by the insurer. From the duplicate of this slip the policy is issued. Also called binder (U. S.), application (U. S.).

Ger: *Versicherungsschein.*

2. The difference between the pitch of a propeller or the mean circumference of a paddle wheel and its actual advance through the water corresponding to one revolution.

Fr: *Recul;* Ger: *Slip.*

3. The area of water between two piers or wharves.

Fr: *Darse;* Ger: *Becken.*

See **Apparent Slip, Clear-Hawse Slip, Liner, Negative Slip, Patent Slip, Senhouse Slip, True Slip.**

SLIP (to). To let go suddenly. To slip the anchor cable. To detach a ship from her anchor in an emergency by letting go the chain at a shackle when there is no time to heave up the anchor. To let go entirely.

Fr: *Filer par le Bout;* Ger: *Abschlieren; Schlippen.*

SLIP ANGLE. The angle between the tangent to the face of a propeller blade and the line of advance of the blade.

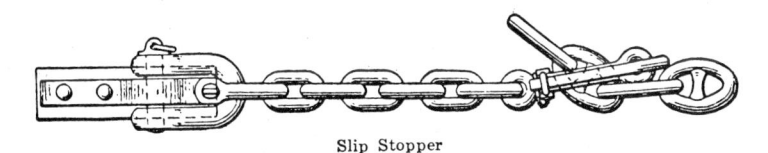

SLIP DOCK. A type of marine railway in which a vessel is partially withdrawn from the water by means of a cradle on rails and the tide is excluded from the lower part of the slipway by a pair of gates and side walls. It is used only where there is a considerable range of tide. It permits the shortening of the underwater portion of the marine railway.

Fr: *Slip de Carénage; Cale de Halage;* Ger: *Schleppdock.*

See **Marine Railway.**

SLIP HOOK. A long-shank, hinged hook with a link over the beak. When the link is knocked off, the hook collapses. It is used for chain plates, cable stoppers, boat gripes, clear-hawse pendants, and so on. Also called pelican hook.

Fr: *Echappement;* Ger: *Schlipphaken; Schlippschakel.*

SLIP KNOT. A simple knot which can be drawn taut easily and which slips with facility. A knot used where a loop is required to jam on to anything when pulled taut. It is similar in action to a running bowline. Sometimes called running knot, running hitch.

Fr: *Noeud Coulant;* Ger: *Weiberknoten; Laufknoten.*

SLIPPERY HITCH. A variation of the clove hitch which provides a convenient way to secure a line to a ring. It can be instantly released by pulling on the free end of the line and is therefore frequently used for sheets and halyards in small sailboats.

Fr: *Noeud de Ride; Noeud de Soldat;* Ger: *Schlippstek.*

SLIPPERY REEF KNOT. A knot similar to the ordinary reef knot but easier to untie. Also called half bowknot.

SLIP ROPE. A rope so arranged that it may be readily let go, as for instance a rope passed through the ring of a mooring buoy with both ends on board ship. By letting go one end and hauling on the other the ship is freed.

Fr: *Amarre en Double;* Ger: *Schlipptau.*

SLIP STOPPER. A chain stopper used

Slip Stopper

for holding the anchor cable when the anchor is down, to relieve the strain on the windlass. It is shackled to a heavy ringbolt in the deck and ends with a pelican hook. A horizontal link of the cable is held fast between tongue and link of the pelican hook. For small ships the slip stopper is sometimes made up of hemp with a stopper knot or an iron toggle in the outer end and a lanyard for lashing to the cable.

Fr: *Bosse à Echappement;* Ger: *Schlipp Stopper.*

SLIPWAY. 1. The space in a shipbuilding yard where foundations for launching ways and keelblocks exist and which is occupied by a ship while it is under construction. It slopes gently down toward the water, with sufficient slope or declivity to cause the vessel to move under the impulse of gravity when disengaged from the holding-up appliances. Also called slip, building berth, building slip, stocks.

Fr: *Cale de Construction;* Ger: *Stapel; Aufschleppe; Bauhelling.*

2. General term for the blocks and shores on which a vessel is built.

See **Marine Railway, Slip Dock.**

SLIVER.

See **Launching Wedge.**

SLOB ICE. A name given to loose broken ice in bays and along the exposed edges of floes. It is usually more or less discolored and contains some miscellaneous flotsam.

Fr: *Glace morcelée;* Ger: *Sickeis.*

SLOEP. A Dutch fishing boat employed in the hook-and-line fisheries of the North Sea. Also called vischsloep, beugsloep, sloepschip. The steel hull is similar to that of the *logger* with vertical stem, elliptical stern and fish well amidships. Its relative dimensions, however, differ. It has more depth and less beam than has the *logger*. Up to about 1890 all *sloepen* were built of wood with transom stern, and were rigged as two-mast fore-and-aft schooners. Since then the ketch rig has replaced the schooner rig as in the *logger*. In 1926 there were still ten of these boats afloat. Length 82.3 ft. Breadth 19.7 ft. Depth 12.4 ft. (molded). (Typical.)

SLOOP. A rig very similar to that of the cutter from which it is distinguished by having a short *standing* bowsprit, and a jib set on a stay instead of the long *running* bowsprit and jib set flying as in the cutter rig. Sloops usually have only one headsail, the foresail and jib forming one sail.

Fr: *Gréement de Sloop;* Ger: *Schlup.*

See **Bermuda Sloop, Friendship Sloop, Sandbag Sloop, Oyster Sloop, Scow Sloop.**

The mast of a sloop is stepped further forward than that of the cutter. The name "knock-about" is frequently used to denote a sloop without bowsprit and with a jibstay leading to the stem head. Originally the distinction between a cutter and a sloop lay primarily in the hull, the sloop having more beam and less draft for same length than the cutter. The practical limits of over-all length of hull for a sloop rig usually range between 14 and 50 ft. The term is also commonly applied to a yacht without bowsprit and with only one headsail which sets on the forestay. In the U. S. the term sloop is often applied to cutter-rigged craft. The sail area is divided roughly into 80 per cent of the total area in the mainsail and 20 per cent in the headsail.

SLOOP BOAT (U. S.). Term formerly used by New England fishermen to denote a keel-built, sloop-rigged fishing boat with clipper bow and long counter stern employed in the local fisheries. Length over-all 49 ft. 3 in. Breadth 14 ft. 2 in. Depth 5 ft. 9 in. (Typical.)

Chapelle, H. I., "The Gloucester 'Sloop Boats'," *Yachting* (New York), vol. 53 (January, 1933).

SLOOP RIG.
See **Sloop.**

SLOPE. The declinity of the ocean bottom extending from the outer edge of the shelf into deeper water.

Fr: *Talus;* Ger: *Abfall.*

SLOP CHEST. A chest containing a complement of clothing, boots, oilskins, tobacco, blankets, and so on, for the use of seamen. Any of the contents may be sold during the voyage to members of the crew. The carriage of a slop chest is compulsory for all vessels registered in the United States, with the exception of whaling and fishing vessels.

Ger: *Kleiderkiste.*

SLUDGE.
See **Slush Ice.**

SLUDGE VESSEL. A tank vessel or lighter with false bottom so arranged that when the discharging grounds, out at sea, are reached, the valves are opened and the sludge flows overboard automatically. The function of sludge vessels is to receive the discharge from sewage disposal plants and carry it out to sea.

Fr: *Marie-Salope;* Ger: *Mudderprahm.*

SLUICE. An opening in the lower part of a bulkhead, fitted with a sliding watertight gate, which has an operating rod extending to an upper deck. It is used to permit the flow of liquids from one compartment to another.

See **Sluice Valve.**

SLUICE KEEL. A bar keel which terminates at the afterend in a casting forming deadwood, and in which one or more apertures are provided. This type of keel is adopted in small tugs to facilitate turning by lessening the area of lateral plane.

Ger: *Schleusenkiel.*

SLUICE VALVE. Valve attached to the foot of a bulkhead. There is no connecting pipe and it is used only for allowing liquid to flow from one compartment into the adjoining one. Also called sluice cock. Sluice valves should be fitted only in positions where they are accessible at all times, as they are very liable to be blocked with dirt. They are operated from a deck above by means of a rod.

Fr: *Diaphragme; Vanne à Glissière;* Ger: *Schleusenventil.*

See **Sluice.**

SLUMGULLION. Term used by American whalemen to denote a mixture of the blood, which issues from the fat-lean, and the salt water and oil which flows from the blubber while the men are handling it as they hoist it aboard ship, stow it away, and prepare it for the try-pots. Also called lipperings, dreenings.

SLUSH. 1. A mixture of tallow black soap and linseed oil applied to wooden masts. Its purpose is to ease the up-and-down movements of parrels.

Fr: *Graisse à Mâture;* Ger: *Stängeschmiere.*

2. A mixture of white lead and tallow, with which the bright parts of machinery are covered to prevent rusting.

Fr: *Galipot.*

SLUSH ICE. The initial stages in the freezing of sea water when it is of gluey or soupy consistency, or, inversely, when field or drift ice breaks up and becomes slushy through a rise in the temperature of sea water. Also called sludge ice, frazil ice. Navigation is not checked by slush ice.

Fr: *Bouillie Glacée;* Ger: *Schlammeis.*

SMACK. A small, decked vessel sailing under various rigs and formerly used for fishing or trading. This name is applied indiscriminately to various types of fishing vessels. British fishermen distinguish between a *smack* and a *boat,* the smack being considerably the larger of the two and engaged exclusively in trawling. It is wholly decked and is often supplied with a steam engine for getting in the gear, whereas the boat is mostly half-decked. Smacks are rigged as cutters, sloops, dandys, or ketches, according to size, and have usually a running bowsprit. The length varies from 60 to 90 ft. In the Atlantic coast fisheries of the United States the use of the term "smack" is generally limited to boats above 5 tons which, according to law, must register at the custom house. They are built with or without well. The larger are usually "dry smacks," having no well.

Fr: *Smack;* Ger: *Schmack.*

See **Boston Smack, Well Smack.**

SMACKEE. A name given to a welled fishing boat of Key West, Florida. The hull is carvel-built with good sheer, sharp bows, rising floor, long run and skeg, and a transom stern with outboard rudder. There is a cockpit aft, well amidships, and cuddy hatch forward. The rig consists of a pole mast stepped well forward, which carries a triangular mainsail and a jib with short bowsprit. Length over-all 24 ft. Beam 8 ft. 3 in. Molded depth 3 ft. Height of mast above deck 32 ft. Length of boom 23 ft. Outboard length of bowsprit 6 ft.

SMALL BITTS. Cast-iron or metal heads extending above a deck or railing, upon which sheets or other running gear is belayed. Also called sheet bitts.

Fr: *Bittons;* Ger: *Schotenpoller.*

SMALL CIRCLE. Any circle on the terrestrial or celestial sphere whose plane does not pass through the center, as opposed to a great circle.

Fr: *Petit Cercle;* Ger: *Nebenkreis.*

SMALL COASTING TRADE. Traffic between ports on the same coast and within specified geographical limits. Also called coastwise trade, limited coasting trade.

Fr: *Petit Cabotage;* Ger: *Kleine Küstenfahrt.*

SMALL LINES. A type of long line similar to the "great line" but of smaller pattern. The snoods are shorter, about 3 ft. long, placed close to each other and the hooks are smaller. Length 50 to 2000 fathoms. Also called spillers.

Fr: *Petites Cordes;* Ger: *Kleine Langleinen.*

SMALLPOX. A contagious disease characterized by a peculiar postular cutaneous eruption. The International Sanitary Convention of 1926 provides that ships which have had, or have, a case of smallpox on board either during the voyage or at time of arrival, are subject to: (a) medical inspection; (b) disembarkation and isolation of the sick; (c) disinfection of all bedding, soiled linen, wearing apparel, etc., which may have been infected; (d) disinfection of parts of the ship which have been occupied by persons with smallpox. Provided these regulations are observed, the ship can be given immediate free pratique.

Fr: *Petite Vérole;* Ger: *Pocken.*

SMALL SAILS. In square-rigged vessels, the topgallants, royals, flying jib, and staysails.

Fr: *Voiles Hautes;* Ger: *Obersegel.*

SMALL STORES. A term sometimes applied to personal necessities such as soap, needles, thread, tobacco, etc.

SMALL STOWAGE. Cargo suited by size and shape to fill space which would otherwise be wasted owing to irregularity in size and shape of the cargo, interruption by stanchions, spaces between beams, and so on. Also called beam filling.

Fr: *Barrotage.*

SMALL STUFF. General name given to all the small lines or ropes under one inch in circumference used on board ship. It includes spun yarn, marline, houseline, roundline, the smaller sizes of seizing and ratline stuffs, and the corresponding sizes of untarred line, made either of flax or Manila. Hemp cordage, generally tarred, of 2, 3, 4, 6, or 9 threads. Also called tarred fittings.

Fr: *Menu filin;* Ger: *Reusel; Dünnes Tauwerk.*

SMELLING THE BOTTOM. Nautical expression which refers to the behavior of a vessel when navigating in shallow water, the effect of which is to reduce her speed and often cause her to sheer off her course or make her slow in answering her helm. Also called feeling the bottom, smelling the ground. The increase of resistance with consequent reduction of speed is largely due to the fact that the restriction on the flow of water around the ship results in the generation of higher pressures in the water and the formation of higher waves. The increase in the velocity of the water flowing past the ship also results in an increase in the bodily settlement of the ship, due to which the vessel may strike the bottom even though her still draft is less than the depth of water.

SMITER (G. B.). A storm jib used on fishing luggers of East Cornwall.

SMITHWORK. All workmanship in connection with the installation and fitting of mast and derrick mountings, cargo gear, boat davits, rails and stanchions, chain plates, cleats, eye- and ringbolts, and so on.

SMITING LINE. A line used for breaking out a light sail sent up in stops.

Ger: *Rucker.*

SMOKE COVER. Canvas cover used to protect sails situated abaft the smokestack in auxiliary vessels.

Fr: *Etui de Chauffe;* Ger: *Rauchbezug.*

SMOKE DETECTOR or SMOKE INDICATOR. Automatic fire detecting system located in the wheelhouse or central fire station of passenger vessels and indicating the slightest trace of smoke in any particular compartment by luminous and audible means.

Fr: *Détecteur de fumée;* Ger: *Rauchmelder.*

SMOKE SAIL. 1. A small sail hoisted in sailing vessels forward of the galley funnel when the ship was riding head to wind to prevent the smoke from being blown aft and to permit it to rise.

Ger: *Rauchsegel.*

2. A piece of sail cloth stretched near a forge when used on deck as a protection.

SMOKE SIGNAL. A daytime distress signal for lifeboats, which while floating on the water produces smoke in sufficient intensity, volume and color as to be visible from aircraft. Recently small, hand-held smoke-producing distress signals have also been devised. When ignited they emit large quantities of colored smoke. These signals are dual, in that they can at will be made to produce a pyrotechnic display for night signaling, in lieu of smoke.

SMOKESTACK. See **Stack.**

SMOKESTACK GUY (U. S.). One of the wires or chains which give lateral support and prevents swaying of the stack. Also called funnel stay, funnel shroud, shroud stay.

Fr: *Hauban de Cheminée;* Ger: *Schornsteinstag.*

SCOTCH HADDIE (U. S.). Trade name for a specially processed haddock, precooked and smoked at the same time. The smokie differs from the finnan haddie in that the fish is not split open, but the whole fish is hung up smoked and cooked, so that it is ready for consumption. In Great Britain called smokie.

SMOKING.

See **Curing.**

SMOOTH. An area of comparatively smooth water, following usually after two or three heavy seas.

Fr: *Embellie;* Ger: *Glätten; Glätte.*

SMOOTHING.

See **Dubbing.**

SMOOTHING TOOL. A metal calker's tool used in touching up leaky rivets, or instead of a splitter for calking heavy plates. the narrow edge being used in splitting. It is also used for removing gates, sprues and other projections from castings.

SMOOTH PLANKING.

See **Carvel Planking.**

SMOOTH SEA. A slightly disturbed sea with waves up to ½ ft. high. No. 1 Beaufort Scale.

Fr: *Mer Belle; Mer Ridée;* Ger: *Ruhige See.*

SMOTHERING. A method of extinguishing fires on board ship, based on the principle of cutting off the supply of air so that combustion cannot be supported, and at the same time blanketing the flames. Three methods of smothering are in general use: (a) by steam; (b) by foam; (c) by carbon-dioxide.

SMOTHERING LINE. A line of piping for conveying steam, carbon dioxide gas or any other extinguishing gas or vapor to the various compartments of the ship, in order to smother a conflagration.

Fr: *Tuyautage de Vaporisation;* Ger: *Feuerlöschleitung.*

SNAKE. To wind small ropes spirally between two larger ones.

Fr: *Transfiler;* Ger: *Schwichten.*

SNAKE PIECE. See **Stern Pointer.**

SNAKING. 1. A method of making a whipping more secure by passing turns across, winding from one to the other.

2. The turns of a rope passed in a zigzag direction, or spirally between two other ropes.

Fr: *Transfilage:* Ger: *Schwichtung*

SNAPHEAD RIVET. Rivet with hemispherical head used where a finished appearance is required in outside work. Also employed with hydraulic riveting machines. Also called buttonhead rivet, cuphead rivet, roundhead rivet.

Snaphead Rivet

Fr: *Rivet à Tête Bouterollée;* Ger: *Schellkopfniet.*

SNAP HOOK. A metal hook closed by a spring snap, generally used for bending headsails to their stays, instead of hanks.

Fr: *Mousqueton;* Ger: *Karabiner.*

SNATCH BLOCK. A single block so fitted that the bight of a rope may be passed through it, without the delay of reeving or unreeving. The iron strap is hinged on one side and the shell is divided to allow the rope to be shipped into the sheave. A snatch block is often used as a lead block for wires and moorings, in which case it is hooked into a ringbolt in the hatch coaming or on deck near a winch.

Fr: *Poulie Coupée;* Ger: *Fussblock; Kinnbacksblock.*

SNEAK BOAT.
See **Sneak Box.**

SNEAK BOX. Name given in New Jersey (U. S.) to a very shallow-draft, decked boat, originally used for shooting and fishing, and which, because of its slight projection above water and easy lines, could be quietly pushed up to the game. Also called sneak boat, devil's coffin. It can be rowed or sailed. Length from 12 to 15 ft. Beam 4½ to 5 ft. The racing sneak box, as built today, is about 20 ft. long with a draft of only 6 in. It is built on the lines of a scow with Marconi rig, and a centerboard.

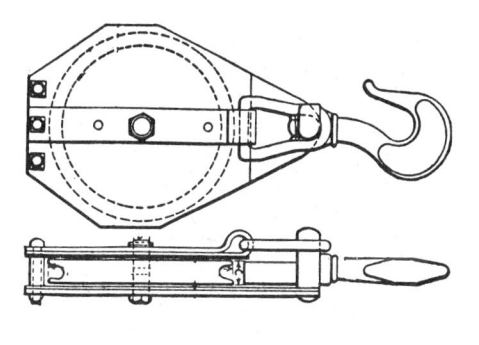

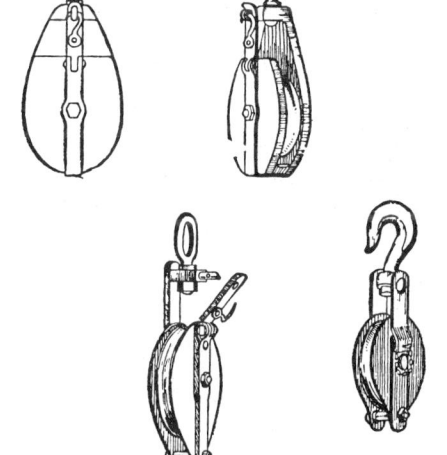

Snatch Blocks

SNIB. One of the handles that can be operated from either side of a watertight door. Also called "dog."

Fr: *Tourniquet.*

SNIK. A small Dutch sailboat built with a fish well, used for trawling in the estuaries of the Schelde and Waal Rivers. It is ketch-rigged with triangular mizzen and two headsails.

SNIPA. A double-ended sail- and rowboat used for inshore fishing and transportation in Sweden. There are several varieties of this type. They are mostly rigged with two masts and narrow spritsails. In Norway a similar boat is called *snekke* and has a length which ranges from 16 to 24 ft. Snipa from Landskrona: Length 14.7 ft. Breadth 5.2 ft. Depth 1.6 ft. Freeboard amidships 12 in. Maximum draft 1.9 ft.

SNIPE. To cut a sharp bevel on the end of a stiffener or beam, frequently done to provide proper continuity of strength in the structure.

SNODDER. A line about 10 ft. long used for heaving in the slack of a trawl net in heavy weather.

SNOOD. A thin strong line by which a hook is attached to the main or back line of a trawl. Also called ganging, gangion, snell. Horse-hair, gut, Japanese gut, and airplane wire are used for the snooding of hooks. In many of the larger lines the snoods are corked so as to lift them off the bottom, in order to prevent the bait being robbed by small creatures.

Fr: *Avançon*; Ger: *Schnur; Vorfach.*

SNORTER. A small rope bent to the end of a light yard over which the eye of the lift and brace fits. Also called snotter. The tripping line leads from the other end to the deck and when hauled upon, pulls off the lift and brace.

Ger: *Ruckleine.*

SNOTTER. 1. A length of rope of 2 to 4 fathoms, with an eye spliced in each end, used for the same purpose as a sling and convenient for reeving through the handles of bags, and so on.

2. A strap by which the heel of a sprit is supported on the mast. It consists of a short piece of rope with an eye spliced in each end. It is put around the mast and one end rove through an eye, the heel of the sprit ships in the other eye.

Fr: *Collier de Livarde*; Ger: *Sprietstropp.*

3. Generally speaking, any rope loop to prevent slipping, as for instance, one by which a block is kept in its place at the end of a boom.

4. A small strap on the yard of a lugsail into which the halyards hook. On the yard of a dipping lug it is placed at about one third the distance of the yard from the forward end, in the yard of a standing lug at about one fourth.

SNOUTER. A trolling line carried on a short pole placed as a jibboom and used by Pacific salmon trollers.

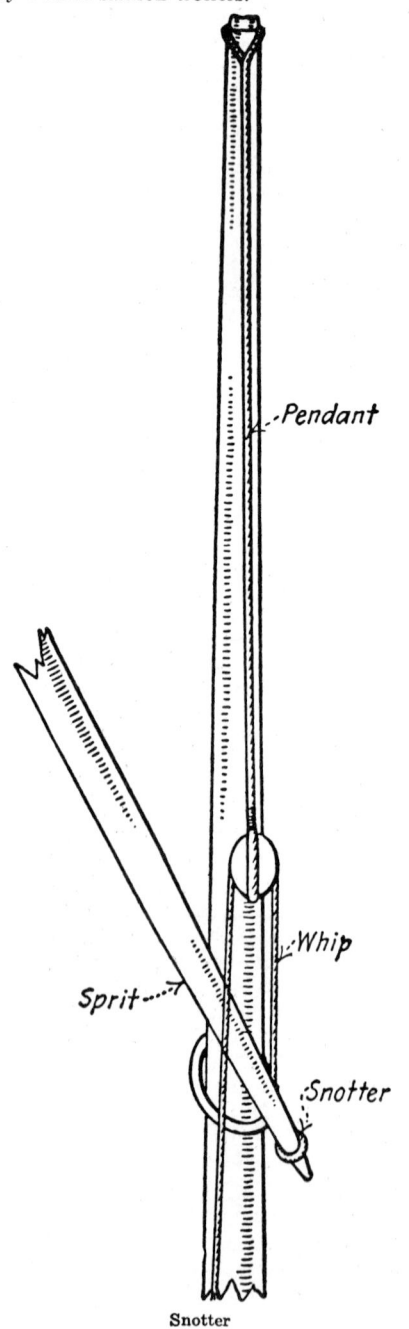

Snotter

SNOW. 1. A snow-rigged vessel.
Fr: *Senau;* Ger: *Schnauschiff.*
2. A rig which differed from the brig by having a trysail mast abaft the main lower mast, to which the boom mainsail was hooped.

SNUB. 1. To let go the anchor and bring a ship up quickly with a short range of cable.
Fr: *Casser l'erre;* Ger: *Kurz anhalten.*
2. The action of checking a line or rope from running out by taking a turn about a cleat, bitts, or similar fitting.
Fr: *Choquer à la demande;* Ger: *Plötzlich anhalten.*

SNUBBING. To draw in sharply at their ends the waterlines or diagonals in the lines plan.

SNUG. To reduce sail when expecting bad weather. To be prepared to meet bad weather. Also called snug down.
Fr: *Faraud;* Ger: *Knagge.*

SNUG HARBOR. A harbor affording good shelter, where vessels can lie securely.

SNY. In wood shipbuilding, the upward curve given to the planking at bow or stern. Also called spile. It is commonly measured by a batten, called a spiling batten, temporarily fastened for this purpose to the frame timbers
Fr: *Epaule;* Ger: *Krümmung.*

SNYING. In steel shipbuilding, the process of giving shell plates a curvature or shape which cannot be obtained with the use of the ordinary press or bending machines, usually a double curvature. The plate is heated in a furnace to bright orange and is then secured to a steel template; after which process it is hammered until the desired curvature is attained. Snying is resorted to only for a few plates of the bow and stern.

SOATAU. A large paddling dugout canoe with single outrigger from Samoa.

SOCKET.
See **Rope Socket.**

SOCKET SIGNAL. A rocket or similar device discharged from a brass socket fitted to the railing. It is fired by a friction tube attached to a lanyard.

SOCKEYE TREATY (U. S.). An international treaty ratified in 1937 by U.S.A. and Canada for the protection and regulation of the Pacific Salmon fisheries in the waters of Juan de Fuca Strait, Puget Sound and Gulf of Georgia. It applies chiefly to Sockeye salmon of the Fraser River, hence its name.

SODA-ASH SLING. A platform sling about 5 ft. 4 in. long, and 2 ft. 5 in. wide used for handling soda ash.

SOFT LAY. In ropemaking: A construction in which the amount of twist given to the yarns and to the strands is less than in the regular or standard lay. Used only where great flexibility is required. Also called long lay.
Ger: *Loser Schlag.*

SOFT NOSE.
See **Fashion Plate Stem.**

SOFT NOSE PLATE. One of the rounded stem plates above the waterline in ships built with a fashion plate stem.

SOFT PATCH. 1. A metal patch, fastened or held in place by means of tap bolts or tap rivets and made watertight by means of a stopwater of red lead and putty or fibrous packing.
2. A temporary patch on piping aboard ship, frequently made by placing a layer of gasketing material and sheet lead, then wrapping with wire.
Fr: *Placard à Joint Plastique.*

SOFT TACK. Seamen's term for leavened bread as distinguished from hardtack or biscuit.

SOFTWOOD. All timber converted from coniferous trees (which have needles instead of leaves). As defined by the British Merchant Shipping Act, this term includes deals, battens, or other lightwood goods of any descriptions other than those classed as "heavy." In the market sense the term softwood as opposed to hardwood, includes pine, fir, spruce, and similar lightwoods generally grown in North America and in Northern Europe. Pitch and Oregon pine are regarded by the trade as on the borderline.
Fr: *Bois Tendre;* Ger: *Nadelholz; Weichholz.*

SOGER. Name given by New England fishermen working with hand lines to hardwood pins ¾ to 1 in. diameter fitted at intervals of about 4 ft. in the vessel's rail to prevent the lines from slipping in a fore-and-aft direction when the tide is running strong.
See **Soldier.**

SOGNEBAAD. Generic name for various open boats of the same design built in the Sognefjord district (Norway) used for inshore fishing. They range in size from 17 to 30 ft. but those not exceeding 22 ft. length are most in use. They are clinker-built, with 4 strakes of planking on a side, curved raking stem, and a sharp stern with raking sternpost. There are 3 frames occupying from one quarter to three eighths of the boat's length, of which the 2 foremost have crossbeams. There is a breasthook at bow and stern placed diagonally. The boats have no gunwales but there is on each side a ribband or clamp running along the inner upper edge of the strake next to the top one. The rig usually consists of a narrow-headed, small square sail set on a mast stepped nearly amidships. Length over-all 22 ft. 7 in. Beam 5 ft. 3 in. Depth 22 in. Stem and sternpost rise about 10 in. above planking. (Typical.)

SOIMA. Open fishing boat found in Russia on Lake Ladoga and the Estuary of the Neva, rigged with two short masts, which carry spritsails. There are no shrouds and the luff of the sail is laced to the mast. These boats vary in size from 20 to 50 ft. in length. The greatest breadth is always abaft amidships. A small well is built for carrying fish alive.

SOKAI-BUNE. A Japanese open boat used for capturing whales in the coastal areas. It is rigged with a mast and square sail and is handled by a crew of 10 with 8 oars.

SOLAR DAY. The period of the rotation of the earth with respect to the sun.
Fr: *Jour Solaire;* Ger: *Sonnentag.*

SOLAR SYSTEM. The astronomical system consisting of the sun and all the celestial bodies which revolve about it.
Fr: *Système Solaire;* Ger: *Sonnensystem.*

SOLAR TIME. Time measured by the hour angle of the sun.
Fr: *Heure Solaire;* Ger: *Sonnenzeit.*

SOLAR WIND. A shifting wind blowing from sea and land alternately at certain hours and sensibly only near the coasts. Solar winds result from the action of the sun raising the temperature of the land so as to draw an atmospheric current from seaward by day. This action is reversed as the earth cools down at night. Also called sun-wind.

SOLAR YEAR. The elapsed time between successive passages of the sun through the vernal equinox. Also called tropical year.
Fr: *Année Solaire;* Ger: *Solarjahr.*

SOLDIER. Slang word for a seaman who shirks his work. Also called soger, blood sucker, gold brick.
Ger: *Bokligger.*

SOLEING. Also soling. The joint where two planks overlap in clinker planking of small boats.

SOLENT BARGE. See Cowes Ketch.

SOLE PIECE. 1. In launching arrangements, a heavy plank on which the lower ends or heels of the poppets rest. Also called poppet board. The sole piece has a groove taken out of its center to receive the tenons

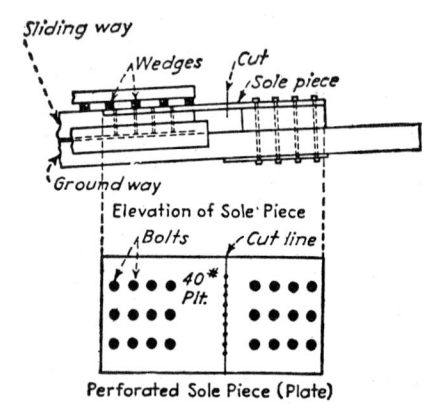

Sole Piece. (Baker, E., *Steel Shipbuilding*, McGraw-Hill Book Company)

raised in the heels of the poppets. Solepiece planks are fitted so that when their inner edge rests firmly upon the sliding ways the outer edge is about ¾ in. open. The purpose of this opening is to give good bearing surface to the wedges.
Fr: *Semelle de Colombiers;* Ger: *Sohle des Schlagbettes.*

2. A timber or steel plate used for releasing the cradle when launching a ship. Also called tie plank, sole plate. The forward portion of these timbers is bolted to the ground way and the after portion to the sliding ways at the forward end of the cradle. Sawing through or burning with a torch it pulls apart under the load and the ship is free to slide down the ways.
Fr: *Savate; Sablière;* Ger: *Schuh.*

3. In boat building, a filling piece on the keel and under the forward deadwood.

4. The fore-and-aft piece forming the lower part of the stern frame in single-screw vessels extending from the propeller post to the rudderpost. Also called heel piece.
Fr: *Semelle d'Étambot;* Ger: *Stevensohle.*

SOLE PLATE.
See **Bed Plate.**

SOLID FLOOR. A floor consisting of a continuous plate or of a range of intercostal plates extending from center line to bilges, and with lightening holes cut through the plating.
Fr: *Varangue Pleine;* Ger: *Volle Bodenwrange.*

SOLID FRAME. A frame consisting of a single bar such as an angle bar, bulb angle or channel, as distinguished from a built-up frame.
Fr: *Membrure Simple;* Ger: *Fullspant.*

SOLID SPAR. A wooden spar made either from a grown stick or fashioned from a larger log; the heart of the tree being as nearly as possible the center of the spar. Also called pole spar.
Fr: *Espar Plein;* Ger: *Volles Rundholz.*

SOLID THIMBLE. A cast-iron or steel thimble for use with wire rope. It has a hole or holes drilled in the heart for attachment. It varies in size from 1½ to 3¾ in.
Fr: *Cosse Massive;* Ger: *Massive Kauschen.*

SOLSTICE. The times of the year when the sun reaches the solstitial points.

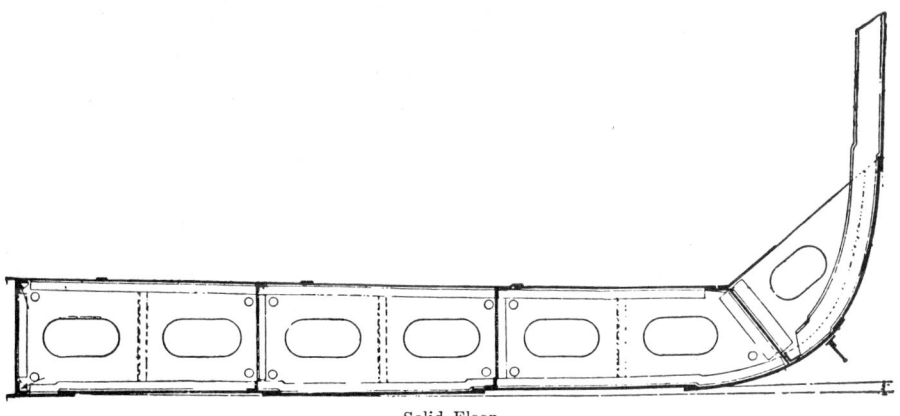

Solid Floor

SOLID LOG BULKHEAD. Structural wooden bulkhead made of heavy horizontal or vertical strakes of planking calked all over to insure watertightness.

SOLID PILLAR. A massive pillar or round section made of a rolled or forged steel bar. Also called round pillar.
Fr: *Epontille Massive;* Ger: *Massive Stütze.*

SOLID PINTLE. A rudder pintle cast or forged solid in one piece with the rudder-arm. Solid pintles are seldom found except in very small rudders.
Fr: *Aiguillot Massif;* Ger: *Massiver Fingerling.*

SOLID PROPELLER. A propeller in which the boss and blades are made of one casting.
Fr: *Hélice Massive;* Ger: *Massive Schraube.*

SOLID RUDDER FRAME. The framing of a rudder in which the arms are cast or forged with the main piece.
Fr: *Cadre Massif;* Ger: *Massiver Ruderrahmen.*

Fr: *Solstice;* Ger: *Sonnenwende.*

SOLSTITIAL COLURE. The great circle of the celestial sphere which passes through the solstitial points of the ecliptic.
Fr: *Colure Solsticial;* Ger: *Solsticial Kolure.*

SOLSTITIAL POINTS. The two points of the ecliptic at the greatest distance from the equinoctial and where the sun reaches its maximum and minimum declination. They are distinguished as the summer solstitial point and the winter solstitial point.
Fr: *Points Solsticiaux;* Ger: *Solstitialpunkte; Sonnenwendepunkte.*

SOMA. Japanese trading junk. It is rigged with one mast stepped very far aft and one square-headed sail bent to a yard which hoists right to the masthead, with sheets and tacks at the clews. Although the yard permits a certain amount of bracing up, these craft do not sail with the wind before the beam.

SONAR. Abbreviation for sound, navigation and ranging. The term includes various types of underwater sound devices used for listening, depth indication, echo ranging and obstacle location.

SONDER. A class of small yacht originated in Germany, in which the sum of the waterline length, extreme beam, and extreme draft must not be greater than 32 ft.

SONDMORSBAAT. The *sondmorsbaat*, or Sondmore boat, is an open sail- and rowboat commonly used in the cod and herring fisheries in the district of Sondmore, Norway. It has sharp flaring ends and a deep keel, and is V-shaped throughout its entire length. The clinker planking consists of 4 strakes on each side with an additional top strake at the bow which extends aft a little more than one third of the boat's length and another at the stern which is about half as long. The distinguishing characteristic of this craft is that it has no gunwale, and the lower bow planks instead of being placed in the usual way extend diagonally upward at an angle of 10 to 15 degrees and meet the other planks coming from the stern about one third of the boat's length from the stem. The ends of the planks are chamfered, so that they lap over the after planks instead of butting against them. The rudder is small, curved on the foreside to fit the sternpost, and is operated with a long tiller similar to that used on the *Nordlandsbaat*. Sondmore boats vary considerably in size, their length ranging from 24 to 39 ft. Length over-all 27 ft. Breadth 6 ft. Depth 2 ft. (Typical.)

The rig consists of a single raking mast, stepped amidships and supported on each side by 4 shrouds, to the lower ends of which are attached pointed wooden toggles. These are inserted into rope beckets held by metal staples to the hull. This arrangement is adopted so that the standing rigging can almost instantly be removed or put in place whenever it is desirable to lower or erect the mast. The mast is in some boats additionally supported by a stay running to the stemhead. A narrow-headed, lugsail is carried, which, when the boat is sailing close-hauled, tacks down to the stem, while the sheet trims to the lee quarter. When the sail is trimmed in this manner, the larger part is forward of the mast, and the center of effort of the sail is considerably forward of the midship section. When there is a forestay it is customary to lace the lower part of the luff to it when the boat is by the wind; but when there is no stay a rope is rove through the cringles in the luff of the sail and taken around the stemhead.

SONIC DEPTH FINDER. An echo-sounding device which uses low frequency sound waves of about 2000 cycles per second. These can de detected by ear. Also called sonic echo sounder. The transmitter consists of a steel diaphragm which is struck a powerful blow by a pneumatic or a spring driven electro-magnetic hammer, thereby emitting a heavily damped sound wave. The receiver is a hydrophone. Both transmitter and receiver are mounted in water-filled tanks fitted inside the ship's plating. In some systems the generation of sound impulse is produced by an oscillator. The time required for the emitted sound to reach the bottom and return to the ship is measured, and serves as an index of the depth.

Fr: *Echo Sondeur à ondes sonores;* Ger: *Schallwellen Echolot.*

See **Echo Sounder, Fathometer, Flying Sounder, Magnetic Striction Echo Sounder, Super-Sonic Echo Sounder, Echo Sounding.**

SOOIE.
See **Lurkie.**

SOPE. Refers to several types of East Indian native-built boats. Some are plank-built with keel and straight stem and are used for the transportation of goods in Karimon Java. In the Celebes this name refers to a keel-built trading and fishing prao rigged with one mast, which carries a kind of boomed low lugsail extending from stem to stern. The capacity of these boats is from 10 to 15 tons. They engage chiefly in the Trepang fisheries.

SOPET. An East Indian dugout canoe from Makassar, the Celebes, similar to the *palary* but smaller.

SORTER (U. S.). One employed in sorting cargo as it is being unloaded from a ship, designates the section where the dock gangs are to place the cargo; sees that the marks of all packages are turned out so that they can be readily identified for delivery to the consignee.

SOUND. An arm of the sea over the extent of which soundings may be obtained. A narrow channel or strait. A narrow passage of water having communication with the open sea at each end lying between a long extent of land on both sides. Sounds are also called belts in the Baltic, firths in the Scottish Isles, and *pertuis* on the French coast.

Fr: *Bras de mer; Pertuis; Goulet;* Ger: *Sund; Meerenge.*

SOUND (to). **1.** To produce vibrations affecting the ear as with a whistle, bell or other instrument used for signaling.

Fr: *Emettre un son;* Ger: *Pfeifen; Tönen.*

2. To measure the depth of water by means of a lead line, a sounding machine or by echo sounding.

Fr: *Sonder;* Ger: *Loten.*

soundings in depths up to about 200 fathoms while the vessel is going at normal speed. Also called mechanical sounding apparatus. It consists essentially of a hand or electrically operated reel on which a sounding wire is reeled, and the sinker, upon which the recording device is fixed, enclosed in a brass case open at one end. The recording device consists of either a glass tube or a mechanical depth recorder with piston and spring. The smooth surface and minute sec-

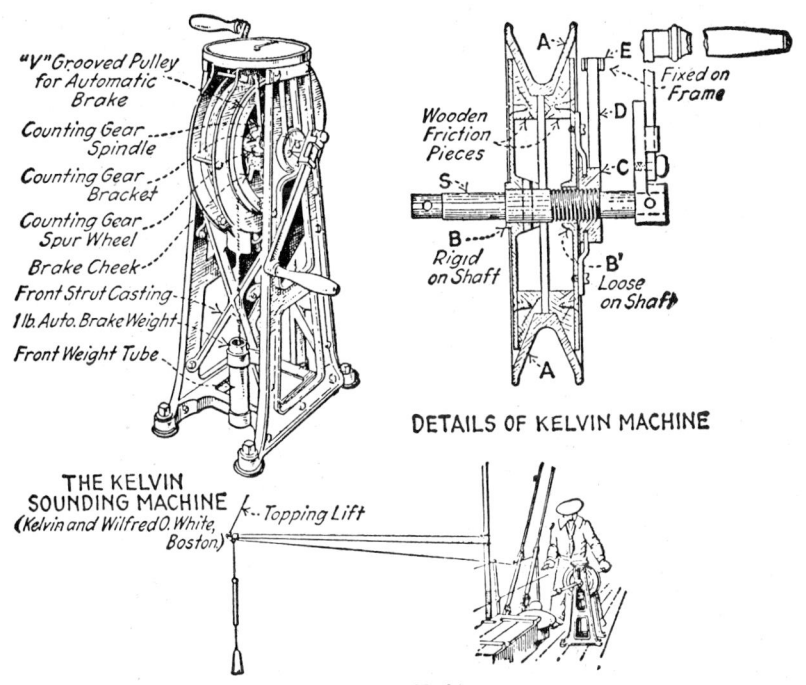

THE KELVIN SOUNDING MACHINE
(Kelvin and Wilfred O. White, Boston)

DETAILS OF KELVIN MACHINE

Sounding Machine

SOUNDING. The depth measured or the number indicating the depth on the chart usually in fathoms. To strike soundings; to come inshore sufficiently to reach the bottom with the hand lead.

Fr: *Sonde;* Ger: *Lotung.*

See **Echo Sounding, No Bottom Sounding.**

SOUNDING BOOM. A small boom which fits into a gooseneck on the shell plating. It is used in connection with a sounding machine for taking casts of the lead from amidships or near the navigation bridge.

SOUNDING MACHINE. A navigational instrument used on board ship for taking

tion of the sounding wire reduces friction to a minimum and permits a rapidity of descent of about 100 fathoms per minute. After casting the lead, reeling in may be accomplished nearly at the same rate.

The weight of the sinker varies according to the speed of the vessel: 26 to 33 pounds for vessels with a speed of 10 to 15 knots, 35 to 44 pounds for faster ships. The fitting of a sounding machine is mandatory for all mechanically propelled American vessels of more than 500 tons gross.

Fr: *Sondeur Hydrostatique;* Ger: *Lotmaschine; Patentlot.*

See **Depth Recorder, Sounding Tube.**

SOUNDING PIPE. A pipe running vertically from an upper deck to the ship's bottom so that the height of water or liquid in any compartment or tank can be measured at all times by means of a sounding rod attached to a line and lowered in the pipe. Also called sounding tube. Sounding pipes are provided at the afterend of each ballast tank or other water spaces, in oil-fuel tanks, and in every hold space. They terminate with a screw plug.

Fr: *Tuyau de Sonde;* Ger: *Peilrohr.*

SOUNDING POLE. A thin graduated pole used for obtaining the water depth in shallow rivers, fairways, and so on, or to ascertain the exact depth above a pinnacle. It has a length of about 10 ft. and its lower end is fitted with an iron cap.

Fr: *Lance de Sonde;* Ger: *Peilstock.*

SOUNDING ROD. A graduated rod or piece of iron or brass used to ascertain the depth of water in the pump well, bilges, ballast tanks, fuel tanks, and so on.

Fr: *Sonde;* Ger: *Peilstock.*

SOUNDING SEXTANT. A sextant used for nautical surveys. It differs from the ordinary sextant in being lighter and handier.

SOUNDING TABLE. A table indicating the capacity in tons of each double-bottom tank, peak tank and deep tank, corresponding to every inch of sounding.

SOUNDING TUBE. A slender glass tube about 2 feet long placed in a protective brass casing and used with a sounding machine. The tube is lowered with a sinker to the sea bottom; the lower end is open and the upper end closed. The tube is coated inside with a chemical substance (chromate of silver). The air within is compressed in proportion to the depth of water. The chemical coating is discolored as far as the pressure has forced the water up the tube. After taking a sounding the tube is removed from the brass case and laid against a special scale which indicates the depth of water.

Fr: *Tube de Sondage;* Ger: *Peilrohr; Lotrohr.*

SOUNDING WIRE. A galvanized wire line made of annealed mild steel and composed of 7 strands tightly twisted, with an outside diameter ranging from 0.027 to 0.054 of an in. according to the weight of the sinker. It is used for taking soundings with the Kelvin or other patented sounding machines.

Ger: *Lotdraht.*

SOUND-POWER TELEPHONE. A type of telephone in which the driving electrical energy is generated at the transmitter by the motion of an iron core attached to diaphragm, within a magnetic field set-up by an ALNICO permanent magnet. The receiving unit is virtually a duplicate of the transmitter, and operates on the same principle, in reverse. This type of telephone was used very successfully in the United States Navy during World War II as a battle telephone. By virtue of its simplicity, it is rugged, reliable, and easy to repair. No external source of electric power is required for its operation.

SOUND SIGNAL. General term for aerial and submarine audible signals as used on board ship and ashore, which includes steam or pneumatic whistles, foghorns, sirens, diaphones, bells, and guns. With the exception of the latter, the dot and dash system is employed in a similar manner to flashing a light. A note frequency of 128 periods per second has been found the most satisfactory for aerial fog signals. All aerial sound signals are strongly affected by atmospheric conditions, and are therefore mostly used in conjunction with radio beacons and direction finders or submarine signals.

Fr: *Signal Phonique;* Ger: *Hörbares Signal; Schallsignal.*

Gill and Harding, "Sound and Radio Aids to Navigation," Society of Naval Architects and Marine Engineers (New York), *Transactions,* vol. 48 (1940).

See **Submarine Signal.**

SOUND VESSEL. A term which formerly referred to a wooden vessel on its first voyage, after which voyage all wooden hulls were considered as having some of their timbers more or less decayed, although still in good order.

SOUTH EQUATORIAL CURRENT. The South Atlantic equatorial current is a strong permanent westerly stream met with from the Eastward of 30 degrees West longitude, to 15 degrees South latitude. The South Pacific equatorial current stretches from 85 degrees West longitude to 135 degrees East longitude.

Fr: *Courant Equatorial du Sud;* Ger: *Südäquatorialstrom.*

SOUTHERLY BURSTER. Name given in south and southeast Australia to a sudden shift of wind, usually from a northwesterly direction. These storms are accompanied by a sudden fall in temperature and are most prevalent from October to March.

SOUTH ISLES YOLE. A boat of construction and design similar to the Westray or North Isles yole, and rigged with two spritsails instead of lugsails.

SOUTHWESTER. A hat of waterproof material, usually oiled linen. The brim is made very broad at the back so as to protect the neck from rain and spray. Also called sou'wester.

Fr: *Suroit;* Ger: *Lackhut; Südwester.*

SOUTHWEST MONSOON. A seasonal wind found from April until October in the Mozambique Channel, in the north Indian Ocean, and part of the Pacific, also in the southern part of the China Sea. From July until October it is found between 5° and 10° north latitude on the west coast of Africa.

Fr: *Mousson du Sud Ouest;* Ger: *Südwestmonsun.*

SOUTHWOLD BEACH PUNT. Small open fishing boat with vertical transom stern, and clinker planking. The rig consists of two masts with lugsails, a dipping foresail, and standing mizzen. The foresail is tacked to an iron bumkin. Also called Alderburgh sprat boat. Length 15.2 ft. Breadth 6.2 ft. Depth 2.3 ft. (Typical.)

SPACE SYSTEM. A method of ventilating a ship's hold loaded with bags of rice. A tunnel is formed of the bags, placed fore and aft, leaving an empty space about a foot wide which forms the ventilating duct.

See **Closed-in Spaces, Deducted Space, Exempted Space, Open Space, Propelling-Power Spaces.**

SPADE RUDDER. See **Underhung Rudder.**

SPALL.

See **Thwart, Cross-spall.**

SPAN. A rope having both ends made fast some distance apart, so that a block or a purchase may be hooked to its bight.

Fr: *Brague; Patte d'Oie;* Ger: *Spanne; Hänger.*

See **Buntline Span, Davit Span, Guy Span, Peak Span, Yard Span.**

SPAN BLOCK. 1. A block seized into the bight of a span.

2. A block at the head of topmast or topgallant mast for studding sail halyards to reeve through.

SPAN IRONS. Whaling term denoting harpoons secured to the sides of a whaleboat above the thwarts, as distinguished from the live irons, which were ready for instant use. (Obsolete.)

SPANISH BOWLINE. A method of forming two loops in a rope neither of which will slip.

SPANISH BURTON. A tackle composed of two single blocks, with both standing parts fastened to the load to be moved. The strap of one block is tailed and rove through the sheave of the other.

Fr: *Bredindin;* Ger: *Staggarnat.*

SPANISH CEDAR. A name popularly given to a tropical tree of the family Meliaceae, in no way related to the cedar specie. It is also called Honduras cedar and is extensively used for planking on racing hulls and cabin trunks. It is soft and has comparatively little strength but holds its shape well and is easy to work. Weight when seasoned 35 lb. per cu. ft.

SPANISH CLEWS. Hammock nettles or clews, not plaited below the ring or eye.

SPANISH FOX. A single yarn twisted up left-handed, or contrary to its lay. Used for small seizings.

Fr: *Lignerolle.*

SPANISH TRAWL. A trawl net without boards, worked by two boats. Also called paranza or pareja.

SPANISH WINDLASS. A device for extracting power when heaving the two parts of a rope together for any purpose. It consists of a well-greased line, a steel or wooden bar, and two marlinespikes.

Fr: *Trésillon;* Ger: *Spanische Winde.*

SPANKER. The triangular or quadrilateral gaff sail set on the afterside of the mizzenmast of a square-rigged ship, brig, or bark. The gaff sail of a bark is usually known as "mizzen." The term "driver" is applied in a more general sense to the fore-and-aft sail with or without gaff set on the aftermast of a ship or bark. When triangular it is called "mutton spanker."

Fr: *Brigantine;* Ger: *Besan; Briggsegel.*

SPANKER GAFF. A standing or running gaff on which the head of a spanker is bent.

Fr: *Corne de Brigantine; Corne d'Artimon;* Ger: *Besan Gaffel.*

SPANKER MAST. The aftermast of a barkentine or schooner-rigged vessel with 4 masts.

SPANKING BREEZE. A fresh, strong breeze. A quartering wind which keeps the spanker full.

Fr: *Bonne brise;* Ger: *Lebhafte brise.*

SPAN LASHING. A lashing used to secure two ropes or spars a short distance apart.

SPANNER STAY—SPAR VARNISH

Ger: *Spannlaschung.*

SPANNER STAY. A horizontal wire extending athwartships between the heads of two kingposts.

SPANNING. A whaling term used to denote a whale swimming in a definite direction and appearing at the surface at more or less regular intervals.

SPAN SHACKLE. An eyebolt with a triangular shackle. Span shackles are fastened to the deck and are used for lashing boats and spars in place. Also called lashing triangle.

Fr: *Echaudis.*

SPAR. A general term for a piece of timber of round section and of great length in proportion to its diameter, used for masts, yards, booms, gaffs, bowsprits, and so on. Spars are cut from strong, sound, straight grain, slow growth, live and straight trees. Metal spars are constructed of riveted or welded plating and also of steel pipe with swaged joints.

Fr: *Espar;* Ger: *Spiere; Rundholz.*

See **Bamboo Spar, Barling Spar, Boom Spar, Boat Spar, Built Spar, Cant Spar, Cut Spar, Foot Spar, Fender Spar, Grown Spar, Hollow Spar, Middling Spar, Monkey Spar, Ridge Spar, Rolling Spar, Rough Spar, Solid Spar, Steel Spar, Towing Spar.**

SPAR AND BOOM GEAR. The arrangement of cargo booms used when handling goods by the Burton system. One boom is guyed over the hatchway, another over the ship's side.

See **Burton System.**

SPAR BUOY. A buoy consisting of a wooden or steel spar anchored by one end. Spar buoys are used in northern latitudes, where icing occurs during the winter, in place of hollow metal buoys, as there is less danger of the spar buoys being swept away or damaged. They are also useful for indicating the direction and force of the current.

Fr: *Bouée Mâtée; Bouée-Espar;* Ger: *Spierentonne.*

SPAR BOWLINE. A bowline provided with a light spar or pole for holding the luff of a lugsail to windward.

Fr: *Foule;* Ger: *Bulienspriet.*

SPAR CEILING. Battens laid in holds and 'tween decks of ships other than colliers, tankers, and timber and ore carriers. They are fitted on the sides from the turn of the bilge upward, and are spaced about 9 in. apart. Their thickness is about 2 in., and width 6 to 7 in. They prevent the cargo from coming into contact with the frames or shell plating, with resulting damage by moisture or sweat. The boards are arranged vertically or horizontally according to the system of framing adopted. Also called sparring, hold sparring, open ceiling, open sparring.

Fr: *Vaigrage à Claire-Voie;* Ger: *Wegerungslatten; Garnierlatten.*

SPAR DECK. An upper deck of comparatively light construction above the main or strength deck.

Fr: *Spardeck;* Ger: *Spardeck.*

SPAR-DECK VESSEL. Vessel having over its main or strength deck another deck of light construction.

Fr: *Navire à Spardeck;* Ger: *Spardeckschiff.*

The upper 'tween deck in this type of vessel, as originally built, was fitted only for the use of passengers or very light cargo. The side plating is of reduced thickness, and is supported only by alternate frames. In later types the thickness of side plating was increased, and it was supported at every frame. The spar-deck type has ill-defined limits, but generally it is a ship having two or more complete decks of lighter construction at sides, than a full-scantling ship, and heavier in scantlings than one of the awning-deck type.

SPARE BUNKER. A coal bunker in cargo vessels which may be used for either coal or cargo. Also called reserve bunker.

Fr: *Soute de Réserve;* Ger: *Reservebunker.*

SPAR FENDER. A short, round piece of wood fastened to a line and hanging over the side to protect the ship's sides. Sometimes called wood fender. Length 4 to 6 ft. Diameter 6 to 10 in.

Ger: *Wreifholz; Holzfender; Reibholz.*

SPARMAKER. A ship carpenter who specializes in sparmaking. He finishes and installs square, octagonal, and round spars, masts, cargo booms, and so on, and applies the fittings.

SPARRING. 1. See **Spar Ceiling.**

2. Equipping a ship with spars.

SPARRING DOWN. Lashing battens or oars across the shrouds for the men to stand on when rattling down.

SPAR VARNISH. 1. A rapid-drying, water-resistant, elastic varnish used on board ships and boats. It is designed to meet all the needs for a general utility varnish suitable for both outside and inside exposure where durability is the chief requisite, and where high gloss or initial hardness of the film are not required

Fr: *Vernis Marin;* Ger: *Bootslack.*

Spar varnish consists of various gums fused and dissolved in hot linseed oil, thinned with turpentine, and incorporating a crystalline mineral such as fluor spar or feldspar for increasing moisture resistance. The dried film should withstand cold water for 12 hr. and boiling water for 60 min. without whitening or dulling.

2. A varnish made of rosin, sulfur, and linseed oil used for wooden spars and outside brightwork where no paint is applied.

Ger: *Harpeus; Harpuis.*

SPAWN. The eggs of fishes, molluscs, crustaceans, and so on, when small and numerous. The mass of eggs that a lobster carries under its tail is known as a "coral" or "berry."

Fr: *Frai;* Ger: *Laich.*

SPEAKING TUBE. A tube, usually of brass, serving to convey the human voice from one part of the ship to another. Also called voice pipe, voice tube. In small vessels it is used for communicating between the bridge and the engine room. It is usually fitted with a whistle at each end for calling attention. On vessels of U. S. registry speaking tubes are permitted only if the distance between the wheel house and forward part of engine room is less than 150 ft.

Fr: *Porte Voix;* Ger: *Sprachrohr.*

SPECIAL CARGO. A term usually applied to goods for which special stowage, supervision and checking are considered desirable because of the value of their contents, the ease with which abstracted articles can be secreted, etc. Jewelry, fancy goods, toilet articles, wearing apparel, furs, laces, bottled spirits and articles of value and portability are included under this heading. Special cargo should not be confused with precious or valuable goods which are carried in a specie room.

SPECIALS. A general name given to valuable fragile, hazardous, or objectionable goods which are usually accepted by ship-operators at an increased rate of freight and for which "special stowage" instructions are issued.

SPECIAL SURVEY. A vessel is said to be built "under special survey" when during the progress of construction from the laying of the keel to completion, the material and workmanship has been examined by the surveyors of the cognizant Classification Society in order to insure that the requirements of the rules and the approved plans are satisfactorily followed.

Fr: *Construction sous Surveillance Spéciale;* Ger: *Erbauung unter Aufsicht.*

SPECIFICATION. A statement of all the particulars of a vessel both general and in detail, including what is shown on the plans as well as what cannot be shown on them. The quality of the materials to be used is described and the scantlings are carefully recorded. It also states how parts not supplied by the shipbuilders are to be obtained. The specification is a legal, technical, and commercial document. Legally it forms part of the contract between owner and builder and states the conditions and requirements to be fulfilled in a manner which leaves no doubt as to the meaning it is intended to convey. Technically, a specification states, beginning with the dimensions, all the essential properties of the proposed vessel and gives a general description indicating the general type of vessel required

Fr: *Spécification;* Ger: *Bauvorschrift.*

The technical qualities include draft, trim, deadweight, quality of material and workmanship, survey and certificates. The specification should be considered in conjunction with plans, and as regards the main structure of the hull it is customary to state that the scantlings shall be as per approved midship section. With regard to ordinary vessels built to classification rules or their equivalent, extra requirements for special trade conditions should be clearly and definitely expressed in the specification.

SPECK FALL. One of the falls formerly used by whaling vessels for hoisting blubber and bone when flensing a whale lying alongside. It was rove through a single block attached to the blubber guy. (Obsolete.)

SPECTACLE CLEW. A steel contrivance used at the clews of square sails. It consists essentially of three rings cast together at different angles but in the same plane, so that three ropes or blocks can be hooked into it and lead in different directions. Also called spectacle iron, clew iron.

Fr: *Trèfle;* Ger: *Brille; Brillenlegel.*

SPECTACLE EYE. A steel fitting with

two eyes attached to the head of a round bar davit to receive the span and guy.

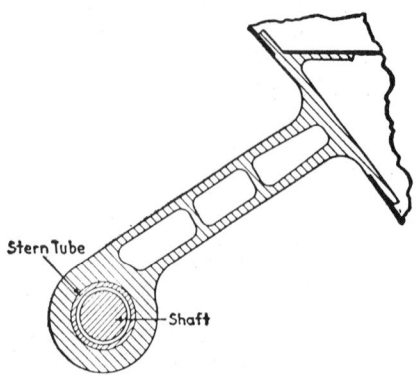

Spectacle Frame. *(Courtesy Society of Naval Architects and Marine Engineers, N. Y.)*

SPECTACLE FRAME. A single casting which contains the bearings for and supports the ends of the propeller shafts in twin- or multiple-screw vessels. It consists of arms of pear-shaped cross section which extend outboard on each side of the ship's centerline to bosses which take the propeller shaft bearings. In large merchant vessels the spectacle frame replaces shaft struts or bracket.

Fr: *Aileron;* Ger: *Wellenbock.*
SPECTACLE IRON.
See **Spectacle Clew.**

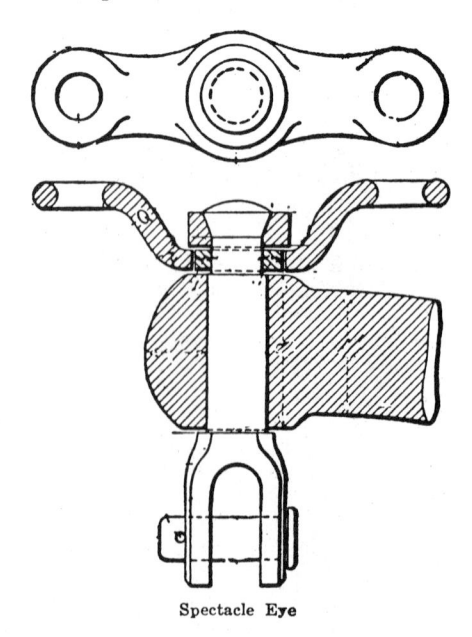

Spectacle Eye

SPECTACLE PLATE.
See **Davit Spreader.**
SPECTIONEER. Also **Specksioneer.** A whaling term formerly used in the Greenland fishery for denoting the officer under whose direction the whale was cut up.
SPEED-LENGTH RATIO. The ratio of the speed in knots to the square root of the waterline length (ft.). It is the speed constant for ships of geometrically similar form.
Fr: *Coefficient de Vitesse Relative;* Ger: *Relatives Geschwindigkeitsverhältnis.*
SPEED MADE GOOD. The actual velocity of the ship in knots along the course, measured in relation to the ocean bottom or to fixed objects ashore.
SPEED OF ADVANCE. The speed of translation of a screw propeller in the direction of its axis with reference to the body of water in which it works. A propeller having a pitch P and making N revolutions per minute would advance a distance PN if there were no slip. It is less than the ship's speed by the amount of the wake.
Fr: *Avance par Tour;* Ger: *Fortschrittsgeschwindigkeit.*
SPEED TABLE. A navigational table which gives the speed in nautical miles per hour made by a vessel on a measured mile in any given number of minutes and seconds. It is entered with the number of minutes taken to run the measured mile at the top of the page, and additional seconds in the left column, opposite which the body of the table gives the speed in knots.
SPENCER. A trapezoidal gaff sail, generally without boom, formerly set on the fore and main square-rigged lower masts of barks and ships. On some vessels the luff of the sail was attached to mast hoops which hoisted up and down on a spencer mast stepped just abaft the principal mast. On other vessels the head of the sail was bent to a standing gaff and was brailed in on the mast. Spencers were replaced by staysails in the early seventies.
Fr: *Voile de Senau; Voile Goëlette;* Ger: *Treisegel; Schnausegel.*
See **Spencer Mast.**
SPENCER MAST. A small mast stepped abaft a fore or main lower mast, to which a spencer was bent by means of hoops. (Obsolete.)
SPENT. Term used to denote the condition of a ship as regards draft stability, and

so on, with fuel, stores and fresh water consumed, cargo spaces empty and ballast tanks full, as at the end of a voyage. The converse of ready for sea. Also called burned-out condition.

SPENT FISH. Fish exhausted of spawn. Ger: *Hohlfisch*.

SPERMACETI. The white flakes of fatty substance or wax that separate from sperm oil when it cools after boiling. It is used in the preparation of candles and cosmetics. It the East it is also used in cookery. Refined spermaceti is white, translucent, and crystalline. It is tasteless, odorless, and very brittle.
Fr: *Cétine; Blanc de Baleine*; Ger: *Walrat*.

SPERM OIL. Waxy oil extracted from the head cavity of the sperm whale and the bottlenose whale. It differs from whale oil and fish liver oil in that it is composed chiefly of waxes and not fats. The most valuable constituent of sperm oil is spermaceti. Commercial sperm oil is usually composed of one third head oil and two thirds body oil.
Fr: *Huile de Spermaceti*; Ger: *Walratöl; Pottwalöl; Spermöl*.

SPHERICAL BUOY. A buoy showing a domed top above water, generally used for marking the ends of a middle ground.
Fr: *Bouée Sphérique*; Ger: *Kugelboje; Kugeltonne*.
See **Middle Ground**.

SPHERICAL NAVIGATION.
See **Spherical Sailing**.

SPHERICAL SAILING. The method of solving problems in navigation based upon principles reduced from the spherical figure of the earth, whereas in plane sailing the earth's surface is assumed to be a plane surface.

SPIDER. A triangular metal outrigger, used to keep a block clear of the mast or the ship's side. Also called strut.
Fr: *Pistolet*.

SPIDER BAND. An iron band around a lower mast, near the deck, with sockets attached into which belaying pins are thrust. Also called spider iron.
Fr: *Cercle de Tournage*; Ger: *Belegnagelband; Nagelband; Kavielnagelring*.
See **Futtock Hoop**.

SPIDER IRON.
See **Spider Band**.

SPIEGEL. Small Dutch sloop similar in hull form to the *boeier*. The spiegel rig differs from the boeier in two respects: (a) the mainsail of the spiegel is a little wider at the head than that of the boeier; (b) there are three headsails instead of two, a bowsprit and small jib forming part of the spiegel rig. The mast is very lofty in proportion to the length of the boat.

SPIKE. A name given to a large, cut or wrought nail of square section, made of galvanized iron, steel, or composition. Also called boat spike, spike nail, deck nail. Spikes are used by boatbuilders for fastening thick planking. They are shaped like nails. The word "spike" is loosely applied to large nails, generally roseheaded. The length at which nails come under the heading of spike is approximately 3 in. Boat spikes are from 3 to 14 in. long, with diamond-, button-, or nailhead, square shank, and chisel point, 7 to 17 to the pound.
Fr: *Clou*; Ger: *Spiker*.

SPIKE FASTENING. A temporary fastening used to hold the planks in place until they can be finally fastened. Also called working fastening.
Fr: *Cloutage*; Ger: *Spikerbefestigung*.

SPIKE IRON. A wood calking tool with narrow, blunt edge, used for calking around corners, boltheads, spikes, and other close places.
Fr: *Fer à clous*.

SPIKE TACKLE. A tackle formerly used by whalers to hold the whale alongside while flensing it. (Obsolete.)

SPIKE TUB. A wooden tub formerly used for receiving the fat, blubber, and so on, of whales until it was rendered. (Obsolete.)

SPILE. A small wooden peg used by shipwrights to stop the hole left by a spike when it is withdrawn.
Fr: *Coupe-eau*; Ger: *Speiler*.

SPILING. A method used in ship construction by which the desired shape or curvature of a structural part is inscribed on a template or batten and transferred to the material to be used before cutting.

SPILINGS. Dimensions taken from a straight edge or rule or template to different points on a curve.

SPILING STAFF. A strip of wood with straight edges, about ½ in. thick and 2 to 3 in. wide used by boatbuilders to take the spiling of a plank. Also called spiling batten.

SPILL. To throw the wind out of a sail. To relieve a sail or part of it from the pressure of the wind, in order to furl or reef it. This is done by collecting the sail together or by bracing it so that the wind strikes the leech.
Fr: *Etouffer;* Ger: *Verschütten.*

SPILLAGE. Goods which have escaped from their containers. They are collected and either appropriated to the merchants concerned in proportion to their respective consignments or are sold to meet possible claims. Also called sweepings.
Fr: *Balayures;* Ger: *Kehrling; Fegsel; Fegel.*

SPILLER. 1. A square compartment made of netting, which adjoins the pot of a pound net and is used as a container for fish. A small tunnel leads the fish from the pot into the spiller, from which fishermen lift them out.
Ger: *Fangkammer.*
2. In the mackerel fisheries of Nova Scotia, a seine inserted into a larger seine for taking out the fish.

SPILLERS. A term used in Cornwall and Devon for "small lines" employed for the capture of whiting, with about 2000 hooks.

SPILLING LINE. 1. A buntline fitted to square sails to spill the wind and assist in getting the sail secured. It is fastened to the yard rope through a bull's-eye on the footrope and comes up on the after side of the sail. It "spills" the wind out of the sail by crumpling the canvas up the yard.
Fr: *Fausse Cargue; Dégorgeoir; Etrangloir;* Ger: *Dampgording.*
2. A small rope rigged on the fore side of a square sail for picking up the reef line in reefing topsails.
3. Any line used for spilling the wind out of a sail by brailing in an edge and keeping it from bellying out.

SPILL PIPE.
See **Deck Pipe.**

SPINDLE. The center of a made mast. The main piece of a made mast. Also called heart.
Fr: *Mèche;* Ger: *Herzstück.*
See **Made Mast, Vane Spindle.**

SPINDRIFT. See **Drift.**

SPINNAKER. A large and baggy loose footed triangular sail, first introduced aboard the British cutter "Sphinx" in 1866, and used by cruising and racing yachts when running before the wind. It is set flying on the side opposite to the mainsail. The head is hoisted by halyards which pass through a block at the masthead. The tack is secured to the outer end of a boom, and the clew is sheeted to the deck forward of the mast. Pacific coast lumber schooners carried spinnakers varying in form and size according to the master's ideas. They had a boom and hoisted to the trestletrees.
Fr: *Spinnaker;* Ger: *Spinnaker.*
See **Parachute Spinnaker.**

SPINNAKER BOOM. A long light spar for extending the foot of a spinnaker. It swings out on the side opposite to the main or foreboom.
Fr: *Tangon de Spinnaker;* Ger: *Spinnakerbaum.*

SPIRIT FLAG (G. B.). A red flag with white disc in the center. It is flown by tankers in port when carrying gasoline and spirits.

SPIRKETING. A thick strake or strakes of ceiling worked inside the hull upon the beam ends or next above the waterways of a 'tween deck. Where there are no waterways, the spirketing is the thick strake worked on the topside of the beams. (Obsolete.)
Fr: *Virure Bretonne;* Ger: *Setzweger.*

SPIRKETING PLATE. 1. Vertical side stringer plate attached inside the frames at a lower deck or tier of hold beams.
Ger: *Setzwegerplatte.*
2. A small bulwark plate attached to the stemhead and tapered downward as it goes aft.

SPIRUNARA. Sicilian fishing boat employed for catching anchovy with a net called *spigone.* Occasionally used in the small coasting trade. Sometimes called *spigonara.*

SPIT. A relatively small extension of a coastline into the sea.
Fr: *Epi;* Ger: *Spitze; Landzunge.*

SPITZ-MUTTE. A small boat resembling the *Mutte,* but having sharp ends. The larger boats of this type are rigged with a gaff topsail and jib. Some carry a jiggermast.

SPLICE. A method of joining rope by interweaving the strands. A splice is a more intimate junction of parts than a knot, the lay of the rope being opened and the ends tucked in so that the size and character of the rope at the place where the splice is made are not greatly changed. It is generally admitted that splicing of wire rope diminishes its strength, this loss being in proportion to the size of the rope. In small sizes, from ⅜ to ¾ in. diameter, it is only about 5 per cent, but it may, in larger ropes, reach 30 per cent.

Fr: *Epissure;* Ger: *Splissung.*

See **Chain Splice, Drawing Splice, Eye Splice, Flemish Eye Splice, Horseshoe Splice, Irish Splice, Long Splice, Long Rolling Splice, Mariner's Splice, Sailmaker's Splice, Short Splice, Tail Splice.**

Graumont and Hensel, Splicing Wire and Fiber Rope (New York, 1945); Lawrence Day, *Sailors Knots,* London, 1936; Scot Skirving, *Wire Splicing,* Glasgow, 1932.

SPLICE (to). To unite or join together two ropes or the parts of a rope by interweaving the strands of the ends.

Fr: *Episser;* Ger: *Splissen.*

SPLICING FID. A tapered wooden pin, 12 to 24 in. long, rounded at the end, and made of hickory or lignum vitae wood. It is used by riggers and sailmakers for opening the strands of a rope, and so on. Diameter at butt 1 to 3 in. Also called driving fid, hand fid.

Fr: *Burin;* Ger: *Splisshorn; Fid.*

SPLICING SHACKLE. A shackle at the end of a length of chain, around which the end of a rope is taken and spliced when chain and rope are secured together.

Ger: *Splissschakel.*

SPLICING VISE.

See **Rigger's Screw.**

SPLINED DECK. A wooden deck in which the seams, after being calked, have wedge-shaped strips of a darker wood such as mahogany or teak, fitted in them, instead of the usual paying. These strips are glued in the seams and a few copper brads are added to back up the glue.

SPLINE PLANKING. A system used for topside planking of racing yachts, teak splines being let into the seams after the calking. There is no paying or puttying.

SPLINING. A method of ensuring watertightness of outside planking in which the seam is first calked in the usual manner, the filling material being kept well back from the outer surface of the planking. Thereafter long and accurately fitting strips of teakwood known as "splines" are glued into the seam over the calking. It is mostly used for topsides, but is occasionally used for decks in high-class yacht-building.

SPLIT FALL. Term used by stevedores to denote one of the cargo falls when each fall is provided with a cargo hook, as distinguished from the married fall, in which the ends of both falls are attached to a single hook.

See **Double Whip.**

SPLIT HERRING. A herring which has its viscera taken out, and is then prepared for kippering.

Fr: *Hareng Braillé;* Ger: *Spaltenhering.*

SPLIT JIGGER. A sail used on large four-masted barks where the gaff sail of the jigger mast was, owing to its unhandy size, rigged with lower and upper gaffs. Also called divided jigger.

See **Double Gaff Rig.**

SPLIT LINK. Chain link made of two symmetrical halves riveted together.

Fr: *Maille Brisée;* Ger: *Splitterglied.*

SPLIT LUG. A lugsail split in two in the wake of the mast. The yard is slung at two fifths its length from the forward end as in the dipping lug. The luff of the afterpart is partly fitted with mast hoops and is partly laced to the mast. The afterpart of the sail is used as a standing lug, while the fore part, fitted with two sheets, acts as a jib. In going about neither tack is cast off. It was formerly used for ships' boats of the

Split Lug
A. Head of Sail   C,C¹. Luff
B,B¹. Leech   D,D¹. Foot
1. Halyards 2. Reef Points 3. Sheets 4. Tacks

British Navy, and until recently by Scottish fishing boats.

SPLIT SPRIT.

See **Wishbone.**

SPLIT TACKS. Said of one of two vessels

that have been sailing on the same tack when one goes about and the other keeps on the same tack.
See **Tack**.

SPLITTER. 1. The member of a dressing gang on a cod or halibut fishing vessel who, continuing the opening made by the throater, splits the fish close by the side of the backbone from the body. He is equipped with a peculiarly shaped knife, the blade of which is somewhat curved flatwise.
Fr: *Trancheur;* Ger: *Fischspalter*.
2. A tool used in conjunction with a pneumatic piston for calking plate laps and the ends of angles, also for the first operation in calking butts. The cutting edge may be straight or slightly curved. This tool is also used for chipping square edges to a bevel to facilitate calking.
Fr: *Matoir à Gorge;* Ger: *Spalteisen*.

SPLITTING KNIFE. A knife with a flatwise curved blade, used by the splitter on a cod or halibut fishing vessel, when dressing fish.

SPLITTING OUT. The removal of keel blocks and shores from under a vessel about to be launched, by inserting cold chisels in the cap pieces and splitting them away. It follows the wedging up as rapidly as possible, and thus completes the transfer of the weight of the vessel to the launching ways.

SPLITTING STRAP. A loop passed through straps located at suitable points around a large trawl net so as to divide the catch into convenient portions while unloading the cod end. The splitting strap and cod end are hove to the surface by the haul-up line and lifted aboard by the fishing tackle.

SPOIL GROUND. A sea area within which material dredged from other areas is deposited. Also called dumping ground.
Fr: *Emplacement de Déblais;* Ger: *Abladeplatz*.

SPOKE SHEAVE. A metal sheave with spokes, as distinguished from a disc sheave.
Fr: *Réa à rais;* Ger: *Spakenscheibe*.

SPONGE BOAT. A motor sailer of Greek type employed in the sponge fishing industry of the Gulf of Mexico. The wooden hull of heavy construction has a pronounced bow sheer, rounded stem, square tuck stern with outboard rudder and is fully decked. An unusual feature is that the planking is so worked that no calking is necessary. The greater number of spongers are yawl-rigged although there are a few ketches and a few sloops. All are fitted with a motor, the sails being used as auxiliary and for steadying purposes when riding at anchor at night and diving operations are suspended. The over-all length ranges from 28 to 50 ft. with a beam ratio of 3½ to 1 in the smaller boats, and 3 to 1 in the larger. A typical 30-ft. boat has the following measurements: Length over-all 30 ft. Waterline length 26 ft. Beam 11 ft. Draft 3½ ft. Sail area 375 sq. ft. Motor 25 h.p.

SPONGE DINGHY. Small open boat used around Key West for gathering sponges on shallow reefs with sponge hooks. It is a carvel-built keelboat with straight stem and heart-shaped, vertical transom stern with skeg. It has considerable sheer and comparatively low freeboard. Each boat is provided with a stern and bow seat and three thwarts, the middle one on which the sponge fisher sits being adjustable. Length over-all 13 ft. 6 in. Length, keel, 13 ft. Breadth 4 ft. 6 in. Depth 17 in. (Typical.)

Two men go in a boat, one watching for and hooking the sponges from the bottom, the other slowly sculling the dinghy over the ground. These boats are generally carried by a sponging vessel which takes one boat for every two men of the crew.

SPONGE HOOK. An iron or steel hook with 3 curved prongs measuring in total width about 5 or 6 in. The entire length is about 8 in., the upper end being made into a socket for the insertion of a long pole. These hooks are used in shallow waters where it is not necessary to send down divers for the sponges.

SPONSON. In a paddle-wheel steamer, a small outboard platform strongly bracketed to the side plating, and supporting the paddle-wheel bearing.
Fr: *Chaise de Palier;* Ger: *Konsole*.

SPONSON BEAM. In a paddle-wheel steamer, the outer fore-and-aft girder supporting the paddle-wheel box and the outer bearing of the paddle-wheel shaft.
Fr: *Elongis de Tambour;* Ger: *Radgehäuse-Längsträger; Längsträger des Radkastenbalkons*.

SPONSON DECK. A platform extending forward or abaft a paddle box.
Fr: *Jardin de Tambour;* Ger: *Radkastenbalcon*.

SPONTANEOUS COMBUSTION. Ignition produced in coal cargoes and bunkers by the evolution of heat through the chemical action of its own constituents. It is due mainly to the oxidation of fine coal.

Fr: *Combustion Spontanée;* Ger: *Selbstentzündung.*

Anderson, J. A., The Spontaneous Ignition of Coal in Ship's Bunkers, Institute of Marine Engineers (London), *Transactions,* vol. 35, 1924; Stoek, H. H., Fires in Steamship Bunkers and Cargo Coal, U. S. Bureau of Mines, Technical Paper no. 326 (Washington, 1923).

SPOOL. A gauge formed of a round piece of wood, used in making nets by hand. The size of the meshes is regulated by the perimeter of the spool. Length 6 to 8 in. Also called mesh pin, pin, shale, moot, bowl, keevil, kibble.

Fr: *Moule;* Ger: *Strickholz.*

SPOON. A trolling bait fashioned like the bowl of a spoon with a hook or hooks at one end and the line attached to the other. A revolving metallic lure for the capture of fish, used in trolling. Also called spoon bait, trolling spoon.

Fr: *Cuiller;* Ger: *Löffeltoder.*

SPOON BOW. A bow, with full round sections, the shape of which bears a general resemblance to the bowl of a spoon. It is mostly found on yachts, and on stern-wheel steamers designed for shallow river travel. Also called shovel bow.

Fr: *Avant à cuiller;* Ger: *Löffelbug; Löffelartiger Bug.*

SPOON DRIFT. A showery sprinkle of sea water or fine spray swept from the top of the waves by the force of the wind and driven along before it, covering the surface of the sea.

Fr: *Embrun;* Ger: *Wasserflocken.*

SPOON FASHION. See **Nested Boats.**

SPOON OAR. An oar with curved blade, mainly used in smooth waters for light boats.

Fr: *Aviron à Cuiller;* Ger: *Löffelruder.*

SPOON STERN. A special form of cruiser stern in which each waterline is longer than the one below, and ends in a blunt angle at the center line. Also called canoe stern.

SPOT SHIP. A chartering term to denote a vessel which has arrived at the port of loading and is ready to receive cargo. Occasionally the expression "spot ship" means a laid-up vessel with skeleton crew on board and ready to sail on comparatively short notice.

SPOT WELD. A resistance welding process in which overlapping parts are welded at one or more spots by the application of an electrical current of low voltage and high amperage on opposite sides of the joint by two opposing contact points.

Fr: *Soudure par Points;* Ger: *Punktschweissung.*

SPRAT. Small herring found in the North Sea and the Baltic. Also called garvie herring.

Fr: *Esprot;* Ger: *Sprotte.*

SPRAWL WIRE See **Spreader.**

SPRAY. Water dispersed in particles over any exposed part of a vessel, either by the wind or by the impact of waves against the ship's sides.

Fr: *Embrun;* Ger: *Spritzwasser; Sprühregen.*

SPRAY HOOD. A canvas hood extended by iron spreaders, used in open boats to protect the occupants from rain and spray. Also called canopy.

Fr: *Capot d'embarcation;* Ger: *Bootsbezug.*

SPREADER. 1. A horizontal steel bar rigged out in small sailing craft with sharp bows to give more spread to the head sheets, on the same principle as the whiskers which spread the jibboom guys. Also called whisker, whisker boom.

Fr: *Barres de Civadière;* Ger: *Blinde Rahe; Kluver Backstag Ausleger.*

2. One of the extensions bolted on each side of the cross trees to spread the topmast backstays in a schooner, or the topgallant and royal backstays in square-rigged vessels.

Fr: *Barres de Télégraphe;* Ger: *Backstag Ausleger.*

3. A short boom or beam of timber projecting from each bow in a square-rigged vessel. It is made to extend the weather clew of the foresail.

Fr: *Porte-lof;* Ger: *Butluv; Luvbaum.* See **Cross Tree.**

4. A device used in the hand-line fishery to separate the snoods and prevent them from fouling. It consists of a small iron rod slightly curved and with an eye at each end from which a snood hangs. Also called sprawl wire.

Fr: *Arbalète;* Ger: *Spreit.*

See **Davit Spreader, Jumper Stay Spreader.**

SPREADER LIFT. One of a pair of lifts running between the spreader crosstrees, and the mast to keep them from sagging.

SPREAD FIRES. To open or spread banked fires in a coal-fired boiler over the whole surface of the grates, and at the same time to supply them with the requisite quantity of coal for raising steam.

SPREAD YARD. A small boom lashed across the forecastle deck in small sailing vessels, serving as outrigger to the jibboom guys. It replaced the whiskers. (Obsolete.)

SPRING. 1. A shore mooring line diagonal to the keel and exerting a force, when power is applied to it, both in the direction of the keel and at right angles to it. It is therefore used for moving a vessel lying alongside a quay or pier ahead or astern, breasting her in at the same time. Also called spring line, spring rope.

Fr: *Amarre de Poste; Garde Montante;* Ger: *Springtau.*

2. Offshore line or hawser made fast at one end to an anchor cable, the other end to the ship's quarter, by which the vessel is handled broadside to the anchor. Also called spring line, quarter mooring.

Fr: *Croupiat; Croupière;* Ger: *Ankerspring.*

3. A crack running obliquely through any part of a wooden mast or yard, which renders it unsafe to carry the usual sail thereon. The spar is then said to be sprung.

Fr: *Fente; Crevasse;* Ger: *Sprung.*

See **After Spring, Grass Spring, Forward Spring.**

SPRING (to). To split or crack, such as a mast or spar. To injure by straining.

Fr: *Fendre; Craquer;* Ger: *Zwängen.*

SPRING BEARING. A bearing installed to support line shafting. It consists of a pedestal fitted with a bottom brass lined with white metal. Also called steady bearing, plummer block, line shaft bearing, pillow block.

Fr: *Palier d'Arbre;* Ger: *Lauflager; Tunnel Wellenlager.*

SPRING LAY ROPE. A six strand composite rope made of alternate fiber and wire strands around a fiber core. Each strand consists of three 19 plow steel wire strands and three Manila fiber strands laid around a heavy fiber core. It is used for mooring lines.

SPRING LINE. Trolling line carried from the tip (outboard end) of a fish pole. See **Spring.**

Spring Lay Rope

SPRING RANGE. The average difference in height between high and low water at time of new or full moon.

Fr: *Amplitude en Vive eau;* Ger: *Springtidenhub.*

SPRING STAY. 1. A horizontal stay which extends between lower mastheads.

2. An arrangement of gear by which cargo is hoisted or lowered, consisting of a pendant from each masthead. These are shackled at their ends over the hatch where the stay tackle or hatch tackle is hooked.

Fr: *Maroquin;* Ger: *Ladestag.*

3. A term used to denote, in racing and cruising ketches, stays which run between the main and mizzenmasts. One of them runs from the truck of the mainmast through a sheave at the truck of the mizzenmast and down the fore side to a turnbuckle on deck. The other runs from the truck of the mainmast to a point on the mizzenmast sufficiently high to clear the leech of the mainsail.

Ger: *Springstag.*

SPRING TIDE. The tides of maximum range. They are the result of the additive action of the moon and sun. They take place twice in a lunar month, when the moon is in conjunction or opposition, that is, at new and full moon.

Fr: *Marée de Vive Eau;* Ger: *Springflut; Springtide.*

SPRING TILLER (G. B.). A tiller connected by buffer springs to a quadrant, or sectional tiller, which works loosely on the rudderhead. The steering engine is geared to the periphery of the quadrant by a pinion wheel, thus reducing the concussion transmitted to the engine when the rudder is struck by the force of the seas. It is also known as elastic quadrant.

SPRIT. 1. A pole set diagonally across a fore-and-aft sail to extend that sail by the peak. The lower end of the sprit rests on a sort of becket called "snotter," which encircles the mast.

Fr: *Livarde; Baleston;* Ger: *Spriet.*

2. A light spar to which the luff of a jib-headed gaff topsail is laced and extended above the truck. It differs from a jackyard in that it sets parallel to the topmast, whereas the latter is carried at an angle. Also called hoisting pole.

Fr: *Vergue de Flèche;* Ger: *Toppsegelraa.*

See **Split Sprit.**

SPRIT JIB. A jib fitted with a sprit which extends from clew to luff, bisecting the angle of the clew and perpendicular to the stay.

Fr: *Foc à Livarde;* Ger: *Sprietkluver.*

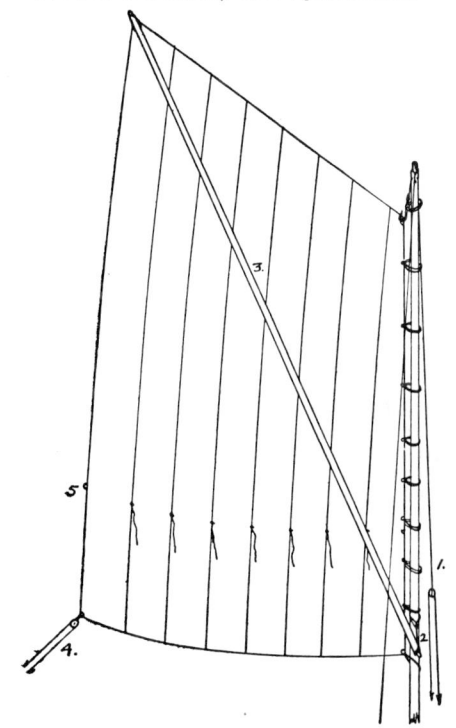

Spritsail
1. Throat halyards
2. Heel of sprit and snotter
3. Sprit boom
4. Sheet
5. Reef Cringle

SPRITSAIL. A quadrilateral sail extended by a spar reaching diagonally from the mast to the upper aftercorner of the sail.

Fr: *Voile à Livarde;* Ger: *Sprietsegel.*

In small boats the luff of the sail is usually laced to the mast to which it is permanently bent. It is a favorite rig for some types of craft on account of the simplicity of running gear However, a sprit is an awkward spar to handle, and needs to be longer and heavier than a gaff to set a similar sail. The upper corner of the sail is sustained by a loop or becket in the boltrope fastened to the upper end of the sprit. The lower end of the spar is set up tight with a becket at the heel of the mast, (called "snotter") or just above the rail level.

In the Levantine spritsail the sprit itself is rigged as usual but the sail runs on rings along an almost horizontal stay from masthead to sprit end. This arrangement is very satisfactory in waters where squalls and sudden shifts of wind are common.

SPRITSAIL RIG. A rig used for small boats, seagoing barges, fishing craft, and so on, which carry spritsails. The economy and simplicity of the gear and general handiness of this rig, dispensing with gaff and boom, have made it a great favorite for fishing vessels where winds are strong. Also called sprit rig.

Fr: *Gréement à Livarde;* Ger: *Spriet Takelung.*

SPRITSAIL SHEET KNOT. A stopper knot which consists of a double wall and double crown made by the two ends, used formerly in the clews of sails, and nowadays as a stopper knot.

SPRITSAIL TOPSAIL. A jib-headed gaff topsail with its luff extended well above the mast truck by a light spar called "sprit" or "hoisting pole." It is set flying from the deck and the clew is sheeted to the gaff end.

Fr: *Flèche Pointu à Vergue;* Ger: *Dreikant Raatoppsegel.*

SPRIT TOPSAIL. A quadrilateral topsail set flying from the deck. Its head is laced to a spar called a sprit, which sets at an angle across the topmast after the fashion of a lugsail. This sail does not project beyond the gaff end, as does a club topsail, and should not be confused with the spritsail topsail. Also called lug topsail.

Fr: *Flèche à Vergue;* Ger: *Schiebblindes Toppsegel.*

SPRUCE. A light, soft and moderately strong wood of which there are many varieties. The only two kinds used for shipbuilding in the U. S. are the black and the white spruce. Floors, keelsons and longitudinal members of the vessel's framework are made of spruce. In boatbuilding it is used for the planking of light skiffs likely to be exposed to weather and general knocking about. The framework of small speedboats is frequently made of spruce. For masts and spars the variety known as sitka or silver spruce is highly desirable. On steel vessels it is used for hold ceiling, hatch covers, and lining of refrigerated spaces. Seasoned weight per cu. ft. 26 to 32 lbs.

Fr: *Spruce;* Ger: *Spruceholz.*

SPUN YARN. Small stuff made of 2, 3, or 4 yarns of hemp tarred and laid up without being twisted together themselves.

Fr: *Bitord;* Ger: *Schiemannsgarn.*

SPUR. 1. A shore or piece of timber extending from the bilge ways and fayed to the bottom of the ship on the stocks. Shores slightly inclined, which are often fitted in pairs, alternate with the keel blocks.

Fr: *Accore;* Ger: *Schlittenständer.*

2. A prong on the arm of a stockless anchor to assist it in catching hold of the bottom.

Fr: *Ergot;* Ger: *Sporn.*

SPUR BEAM. A diagonal beam forming the margin of the sponson and connecting the end of the sponson beam to the ship's side in a paddle vessel.

Fr: *Élongis de Jardin;* Ger: *Radkasten-Galleriebalken.*

SPUR-GEARED WINCH. A winch in which the engine or motor is connected to the main shaft through spur gearing. Steam winches are usually spur-geared, whereas electric winches are frequently worm-geared, or drive through a hydraulic transmission. Spur gears are of the straight or herringbone type. The hoisting speed of spur-geared winches is limited by the peripheral speed of gears which, in practice, have their limit within a comparatively narrow margin when compared to worm gearing. If driven at high speed with no load, spur gearing is very noisy.

Fr: *Treuil à Engrenages Droits;* Ger: *Stirnradgetriebene Winde.*

SPURLING LINE. 1. A rope stretched across the two forward shrouds. It has thimbles spliced into it and serves as fairleader for running rigging.

Ger: *Wegweiserleine.*

2. A line or chain connected with the drum of a steering wheel, by means of which a telltale is made to show the position of the helm. (Obsolete.)

SPUR SHORE. One of several heavy spars resting against the side of a vessel to hold it clear of a quay or wharf when it is necessary to leave room for lighters between ship and shore. The ship end is held by one or more lanyards made fast to the deck or rail. The shore end is fitted with a truck or rollers to accommodate it to the different stages of the tide. Two breast tackles or heel chains leading from the heel of the spur shore to the string piece of the wharf are used for keeping the shore hard up against the vessel's side.

Ger: *Abhalter.*

SPUR TEETH GROMMET. A sailmaker's metal eyelet with an external diameter ranging from thirteen-thirty-seconds to one-thirteen-sixteenths inch inserted in canvas with a punch and die. The ring is provided with a number of spurs giving it a stronger grip than the plain eyelet.

Fr: *Oeillet à dents;* Ger: *Sporn Gattchen.*

SQUALL. A sudden and violent gust of wind or a succession of gusts, usually accompanied by rain, snow, or sleet. It is frequently associated with a temporary shift of wind. It arises suddenly, lasts for some minutes, and usually dies away as suddenly.

Fr: *Grain;* Ger: *Bö.*

See **Arched Squall, Bull's-Eye Squall, Line Squall, White Squall.**

Barlow, E. W., Squalls at Sea, Marine Observer, vol. 7, Jan.-February, 1930.

SQUALLY. The state of the atmosphere when frequently disturbed by sudden and violent gusts of wind. Also called squally weather.

Fr: *Temps à Grains;* Ger: *Böig.*

SQUARE. 1. A unit of measure used in the timber trade, equivalent to 100 superficial feet.

2. The upper part of the shank where the anchor stock goes through.

Fr: *Carré;* Ger: *Vierkant.*

3. In a trawl net, that part of the net laced to the fore end of the batings. The central upper portion of the net which overhangs the sea bottom in front of and above the ground rope. It measures about half the length of the whole net.

Fr: *Grand Dos;* Ger: *Vierkant; Dach; Square; Querstück.*

SQUARE (to). 1. To lay the yards at

right angles to the keel by means of the braces, at the same time bringing them to a horizontal position by the means of lifts.

Fr: *Brasser Carré*; Ger: *Vierkant Brassen*.

2. To square the ratlines, means to get them horizontal and parallel to each other.

Fr: *Aligner*; Ger: *Wanten nachweben*.

SQUARE BODY. That part of a ship's hull situated between the forebody and the afterbody, which is parallel-sided and has a constant cross section. The portion of the vessel more or less amidships, in which there is no variation in hull form below the waterline. Also called parallel middle body.

Fr: *Section Cylindrique*; Ger: *Paralleles Mittelschiff*.

See **Middle Body.**

SQUARE CLOTHS. In sailmaking, the cloths cut square to the depth or cut by a thread of the canvas as distinguished from goring cloths.

SQUARE FRAME. The frames in the central portion of a ship or parallel middle body which have their plane perpendicular to the longitudinal axis of the vessel. Also called balanced frame (U. S.).

Fr: *Couple Droit*; Ger: *Richtspant; Querspant*.

SQUARER (U. S.). A worker in a shipyard building wooden ships. He follows the plankers and fairs up the surfaces after the planking is fastened to the frames or beams. He uses the adze and broadax.

SQUARE-HANGING MESH. Meshes hanging with two sides parallel to the head and foot of a net.

SQUARE MARKS. Bits of twine on braces and other running gear to serve as a guide. Some indicate that the yards are square; others that they can be braced up no farther. Also called sharp-up marks.

Fr: *Repères*; Ger: *Zeichen*.

SQUARE RIG. A general term for all rigs where sails are extended by yards slung athwartship and trimmed with braces. In some fore-and-aft rigs, such as the lateen, lug, and sliding gunter rigs, spars called yards are also used, but as they are set in a fore-and-aft direction and are not controlled by braces, they are not included under this term. In square-rigged vessels, the theoretical center of effort of the sail plan is situated forward of the center of lateral resistance. This is the reverse of the conditions existing in fore-and-aft-rigged craft, and is done to facilitate paying off in any sudden change of wind and thus to prevent the sails from being taken aback. A square-rigged vessel can spread a large amount of canvas with the wind abeam or abaft the beam, often outsailing a fore-and-after of the same size and type. The square rig is also efficient in heavy weather, providing the standing rigging is well set up.

Fr: *Gréement à Traits Carrés*; Ger: *Rahtakelage*.

SQUARE-RIGGED VESSEL. A sailing ship with square rig on two or more masts.

Fr: *Navire à Traits Carrés*; Ger: *Quersegelschiff*.

SQUARE SAIL. Rectangular sails set from yards which pivot about their middle. In all quadrilateral sails the upper edge is called the "head"; the sides or skirts are called "leeches," and the bottom or lower edge is called the "foot." If the head is parallel to the foot the lower corners are termed "clews" and the uppermost corners "earings."

Fr: *Voile Carrée*; Ger: *Raasegel; Rahsegel*.

SQUARE SENNIT. Sennit made with any multiple of four strands, and with no heart.

Fr: *Tresse Carrée*; Ger: *Viereckige Platting*.

SQUARE STATIONS. A series of vertical lines equally spaced from stem to stern on the sheer plan. Also called sections, vertical stations.

Fr: *Sections transversales*; Ger: *Spantebene*.

SQUARE STERN. See **Flat Stern.**

SQUARE-TOED FRIGATE (U. S.). Local name given in Quincy, Mass., to the scow sloops engaged in the granite trade. (Obsolete.)

SQUARE TOPSAIL. A square sail set above the lowest sail or course and carried on a topsail yard in square-rigged ships.

Fr: *Hunier*; Ger: *Marssegel*.

Topsails take their name from the mast upon which they stand. In modern trading vessels the huge single topsail has been divided into two parts, called respectively the upper topsail and the lower or middle topsail. Single topsails are still carried in most Indian square-rigged craft, and it is only in a few of the largest barques that double topsails are set. Many important evolutions of a sailing vessel are made, under topsails, especially in time of emergency, and they are justly accounted as being among the principal sails in a ship.

SQUARE TOPSAIL SCHOONER. A vessel which carries square topsails on the foremast, the main and mizzen masts being rigged with a gaff sail and topsail. Also called topsail schooner.

Fr: *Goëlette Carrée; Goëlette à Humiers;* Ger: *Schonerbark; Rahschoner.*

The topsail schooner is the simplest of the square-rigged craft, and spreads an upper and lower topsail on the foremast. When a similar rig is carried on the mainmast, the rig is known as a "two-topsail schooner." A topsail schooner is generally a three-masted vessel with yards on the foremast, and fore-and-aft sails on the other masts. The square foresail is not bent to the yard, but is set flying when running. The topsail schooner has a gaff foresail.

SQUARE TUCK. A thwartship termination of the stern, used only in small craft, being a substitute for the ordinary arrangement of transoms, and so on.

SQUARE-TUCK STERN. A flat stern without counter. The plank ends abut in the fashion timber or tuck timber. This type of stern is still found in small coasting craft (*Jagt*, and so on) and in pleasure craft with outboard rudder.

Fr: *Arrière à écusson;* Ger: *Plattgatt.*

SQUARE YARD. A yard to which the head of a square sail is bent. Square yards are trimmed by braces, supported in their center by slings, ties, or halyards, and at their extremities by lifts. Lower yards, lower topsail yards, and lower topgallant yards, are standing, being confined to their respective masts by trusses which permit angular movement only. All other yards are connected to the mast by a parrel or a slide track which permits a vertical as well as an angular movement.

SQUARE YARDS. A ship is said to have "square yards" when there is only a comparatively small difference between the length of the upper and lower yards.

Fr: *Grande Croisure.*

SQUARING. The checking up of a vessel's frames to assure their proper position in the transverse and longitudinal planes when they are erected and during the construction of the hull. Also called fairing, regulating (U. S.).

Fr: *Balancement;* Ger: *Einloten.*

SQUARING OFF. Trimming off the projecting edges of the strakes after a wooden vessel is planked. Also called dubbing.

Fr: *Dresser;* Ger: *Abdechseln.*

SQUAT (U. S.). The change of trim by the stern due to the motion of a vessel through the water.

Fr: *Déjauge.*

SQUATTING. The tendency of a fast boat to go down by the stern as it gets underway. Squatting speeds occur when the speed length ratio attains 1.1 to 1.2.

SQUAW NET. Used in the salmon fisheries of the Columbia River, Pacific coast. It consists of an oblong sheet of gill netting about 12 ft. long and 8 ft. deep, its lower edge weighted to keep it down, and its upper edge attached to a pole that floats on the surface and which is held by a line or lines to another projecting pole that is securely fastened to the shore so that it will not swing around with the strain of the current upon the net. It derives its name from the fact that it is the same net used by Indian squaws.

SQUEEGEE. A strap with toggles in the end, used to confine a studding sail while it is being set.

See **Squillagee.**

SQUID JIG. Name given by Newfoundland Bankers to a small piece of lead about 3 in. long and of oval shape which has a number of radially arranged fishhooks curving upwards. Also called ripper, pirn. It is kept constantly moving from a boat, and is used for catching squid for baiting the cod lines.

Fr: *Faux;* Ger: *Aufschlitzer.*

SQUILLAGEE. An implement somewhat resembling a wooden hoe, with an edge of India rubber or thick leather, used for scraping water from wet decks. Also called squilgee, squeegee.

Fr: *Séchoir; Rateau;* Ger: *Backschwabber; Absetzer; Deckraufe.*

STABBER. A sailmaker's tool, similar to an awl. It has three edges and is used for marking eyelet holes.

Fr: *Alène de Voilier.*

STABILITY. The tendency of a body to return to its original position after it is displaced therefrom. In a ship, stability is indicated by several characteristics. Initial stability is measured by the metacentric height. The range of stability, maximum righting arm, and angle of heel at which the maximum righting arm occurs are all important in considering the ship's stability. Also, the area under the curve of righting moment, which is a measure of the work required to capsize the ship, is a function of stability.

Fr: *Stabilité;* Ger: *Stabilität.*

See **Metacentric Height, Initial Stability, Righting Lever, Range of Stability, Static Stability, Dynamic Stability, Curve of Stability.**

Hillhouse, P., *Ship Stability and Trim*, London, 1919; La Dage and Van Gemert, Stability and Trim, New York, 1946; Macdonald, K., *Practical Ship Stability*, Glasgow, 1933; *Report of the Special Committee on Stability and Loading of the American Standards Committee*, U. S. Department of Commerce, Washington, 1929; Vickery, C. A., *Stability of Ships*, London, 1926.

STABILITY OF MOTION. The inherent tendency of a vessel to regain a straight course when the helm is brought amidships after turning.

Fr: *Stabilité de route;* Ger: *Kurzbeständigkeit; Fahrstabilität.*

STABILITY TEST.

See **Inclining Experiment.**

STABILIZING BULGE. A combination of built-in antirolling tanks consisting of outside bulges incorporated over a considerable length on each side of the hull. The bulges form the arms of a U tube, each one of the tanks being connected by an air duct of one frame space width, from the upper margin plate to the corresponding tank on the other side of the ship.

Ger: *Anschwellung; Stabilität Anschwellung.*

In each tank, air duct valves controlled from above are fitted to throttle or to shut off the air passing between the tanks. By means of these valves the phase of the oscillating water in the tanks, set in motion by the rolling of the ship, can be controlled in such a manner as to work against the roll.

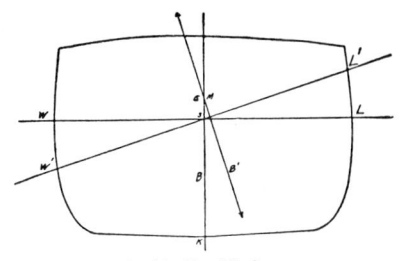

Stable Equilibrium
B = Center of buoyancy
G = Center of gravity
M = Metacenter
GM = Metacentric Height
WL = Water Line

STABLE EQUILIBRIUM. A ship is in stable equilibrium if, when it is slightly inclined from the upright position, the vertical forces of weight and buoyancy will tend to return it to the upright. The metacenter is then above the center of gravity, and the metacentric height is positive.

Fr: *Equilibre Stable;* Ger: *Stabiles Gleichgewicht.*

See **Neutral Equilibrium, Unstable Equilibrium, Metacenter.**

STACK. A metal trunk through which the combustion gases are led from the uptakes to the open air. Also called funnel, smoke pipe, smokestack. It is built of light plating, generally double, with an air space between outer and inner stack to prevent heat losses by radiation, thus keeping the temperature of the gases as high as possible while they are passing through the stack, a condition which is advantageous for good draft. The two stacks are tied at intervals by plate brackets or tie plates. The cross-sectional area of the stack is derived from the grate surface of boilers, the average proportion being 1 sq. ft. in the stack to every 6 or 8 sq. ft. of grate area. The inner stack is circular, the outer elliptical.

Fr: *Cheminée;* Ger: *Schornstein.*

See **Air Funnel, Dummy Funnel, Lower Funnel, Mast Funnel.**

STACK COVER. A metal plate for covering the top of a smoke stack, to prevent rain and snow from penetrating inside when the vessel is laid up.

STADIA. A graduated rod used in conjunction with a telemeter for measuring short distances in surveying operations.

STADIMETER. An instrument used to measure the distance from the observer to a more-or-less distant object, such as another vessel, when the height of a specified portion of the latter (such as the masthead), is known. It is in effect a hand-held rangefinder.

STAFF. A pole on which a flag is hoisted and displayed. Also called flagstaff, flagpole.

Fr: *Hampe de Pavillon; Baton de Pavillon; Mât de Pavillon;* Ger: *Flaggenstock; Flaggenpol; Flaggenstange.*

See **Buttock Staff, Futtock Staff, Jack-Staff, Poop Staff, Ship's Staff, Spiling Staff, Tide Staff, Wring-Staff.**

STAFF GAUGE.
See **Pole.**

STAGE BEARER.
See **Thwart.**

STAGE BENT.
See **Upright.**

STAGE LASHING. Tarred cordage made of soft-laid hemp and used for securing material which has already been placed in position. It is never used for hoisting, slinging, or lifting purposes. It varies in size from 1½ to 4½ in.

STAGE PLANK. A plank between staging uprights on which men stand when working on the outside of the hull in a shipyard.

STAGE POLE. Vertical scaffolding placed in shipyards around the building ways to support the necessary staging during the construction of vessels.

Fr: *Forant;* Ger: *Stellage Stütze.*

STAGGERED INTERMITTENT WELDING. A process of fusion welding in which increments on one side of the standing member are placed midway between adjacent increments on the other side.

Fr: *Soudure Discontinue Alternée;* Ger: *Zickzachschweissung; Zickzack Unterbrochene Schweissung.*

STAGING. 1. Upright supports fastened together with horizontal and diagonal braces forming supports for planks which constitute a working platform around a ship under construction.

Ger: *Stelling; Hellinggerüst.*

2. Planks suspended over the ship's side, from which men work to clean, paint, or repair the hull. Also called hanging stage.

Ger: *Stellage.*

See **Cutting Stage, Hanging Stage, Landing Stage.**

STAINLESS STEEL. A corrosion-resisting alloy steel with 18 per cent chromium and 8 per cent nickel, available commercially in sheets, strip, seamless tubes and bars. Corrosion-resistance is primarily due to its chromium content but is enhanced by other constituents. Used in naval vessels for stacks, uptakes, and in other locations where resistance to corrosion is paramount. It has also come into wide use for sanitary spaces, cold storage compartments, and in food preparation units.

Fr: *Acier Inoxydable;* Ger: *Unverrostbarer Stahl.*

See **High-Elastic Limit Steel, High-Tensile Steel, Ship Steel.**

Saunders, H. E., *Corrosion-resisting steel and its application to ships,* Society of Naval Architects and Marine Engineers (New York, 1929).

STAINLESS STEEL ROPE. A rope in which the wires are made of a stainless steel. It is the strongest wire rope available, affords permanent resistance to corrosion, takes a minimum of stretch, is highly flexible, and is practically nonmagnetic.

Fr: *Filin d'Acier Inoxydable;* Ger: *Rostfreies Tauwerk.*

Owing to its slippery nature it is difficult to splice and for this reason sockets or other fittings are generally adopted. On account of its high cost it is seldom used except for yacht rigging, where it is generally conceded to be the most suitable, particularly in the smaller sizes (3/32 in. and under), since in these sizes galvanized wire breaks down rapidly.

STAITHS (G. B.). Landing stages with lines of rails projecting over a river, canal, or quay wall, from which vessels can be loaded with coal, ore, or other bulk cargo by dumping the contents of railway trucks right into the vessel's holds.

Fr: *Verse;* Ger: *Kippbrücke.*

STAKEBOAT (U. S.). On the lower Hudson river, a floating structure permanently anchored, and without motive power of its own, used to facilitate making up tows for upriver traffic. The scows are brought to the stakeboat by harbor tugs, and thereafter are picked up by other tugs for the trip upriver.

STAKE NET. Any one of various fixed gill nets consisting of netting hung on stakes driven into the ground, with or without additional contrivances for entrapping the fish.

Fr: *Parc sur filets;* Ger: *Staaknetz; Hamen; Ketscher.*

STAMPED POLICY (G. B.). A policy stamped in accordance with the stamp act of 1891. Under English law all policies of sea insurance are subject to payment of duty, the requisite amount of the duty being stamped on the policy before the policy is signed by the underwriters.

Fr: *Police Timbrée;* Ger: *Taxierte Police.*

STANCHION. 1. In steel ships, a vertical structural member between decks, usually of round hollow section.

2. In wooden vessels, a rough log used as a pillar in the ship's hold.

Fr: *Montant; Epontille;* Ger: *Stütze.*

See **Awning Stanchions, Bulwark Stanchion, Hatch Stanchion, Middle Line Awning Stanchion, Pillar, Quarter Stanchion, Rail Stanchion, Step Stanchion.**

STANCH. Also Staunch. Said of a vessel when the hull is sound, watertight, free of water, and fit in every way to receive and carry her lading.

Fr: *Fort;* Ger: *In gutem Zustande; Fest.*

STAND. The interval between the last of the ebb tide and first of the flood tide, or vice versa, during which there is no sensible change in the height of the tide.

Fr: *Etale;* Ger: *Wasserstand.*

See **Boat Stand, Davit Stand, High Water Stand, Low Water Stand, Steering Stand.**

STAND (to). 1. A term, meaning to hold a course at sea.

Fr: *Tenir;* Ger: *Anliegen.*

2. A sail is said to stand well when it does not lift or shake.

STANDARD. A capacity measurement used in the timber trade and which has a different meaning in various localities:

1 Gothenburg standard contains 120 cu. ft.
1 Petrograd standard contains 120 pieces of 1½ in. × 11 in. × 12 ft. = 165 cu. ft.
1 London standard contains 120 pieces of 3 in. × 9 in. × 12 ft. = 270 cu. ft.
1 Drammen standard contains 120 pieces of 2½ in. × 6½ in. × 9 ft. = 127⅞ cu. ft.
1 Quebec standard-hundred contains 100 pieces of 2½ in. × 11 in. × 12 ft. = 229⅙ cu. ft.
1 Christiana standard-hundred contains 100 pieces of 1¼ in. × 9 in. × 11 ft. = 103⅛ cu. ft.
1 Batten standard contains 120 pieces of 2½ in. × 6½ in. × 12 ft. = 162½ cu. ft.

STANDARD CHRONOMETER. The chronometer with which the others aboard a vessel are compared, and to which all observations involving time are referred.

Fr: *Chronomètre Étalon;* Ger: *Normal Chronometer.*

STANDARD COMPASS. A term applied to a magnetic compass used generally as azimuth compass, to which all other compasses are referred and by which the ship is navigated. It is placed in a position as remote as possible from magnetic influence and is adjusted with great care. All courses are referred to its reading.

Fr: *Compas Étalon;* Ger: *Normal Kompass; Regel Kompass.*

STANDARDIZATION TRIALS. See Progressive Trials.

STANDARD KNEE. In a wooden vessel, an inverted knee timber, fayed to the deck and against the ship's side.

STANDARD PORT. A port for which full tidal predictions are given in the tide tables and to which tidal differences for secondary ports are applied.

Fr: *Port de Référence; Port Principal;* Ger: *Basishafen; Bezugsort.*

STANDARD SHEER. The sheer as established in conformity with the 1930 rules of the International Convention on Load Lines. It can be described as forming two branches of a parabola, tangent to a line drawn parallel to the keel through the sheer line amidships. The ordinate at the stem is double that at the stern.

Fr: *Tonture réglementaire;* Ger: *Normaler Sprung.*

STANDARD TIME. Time based upon the transit of the sun over a certain specified meridian, called the time meridian, and adopted for use over a considerable area, usually a belt of 15° longitude. With a few exceptions standard time is based upon some meridian which differs by a multiple of 15 degrees from the meridian of Greenwich. Also called zone time.

Fr: *Heure du Fuseau; Heure Légale;* Ger: *Gesetzliche Zeit; Zonenzeit.*

STAND BY. To be in readiness. To be prepared to execute an order.

Fr: *Etre Paré;* Ger: *Klar stehen; Bleiben bei.*

STAND CLEAR. To keep out of the way. To keep away from.

Fr: *Dégager;* Ger: *Klar bleiben.*

STAND IN. To be coming in toward the shore. To head for harbor or anchorage.

Fr: *Courir Sur;* Ger: *Gegen Land steuern; Anlaufen.*

STANDING BEVEL. The bevel between the surfaces of a frame when the angle so formed is obtuse. Also called open bevel.

Fr: *Équerrage en Gras;* Ger: *Schmiegung ausser dem Winkel.*

STANDING BLOCK. A block fastened to some permanent support, as distinguished from a running block, which is attached to the object to be raised or moved.

Fr: *Poulie fixe;* Ger: *Fester Block.*

STANDING BOWSPRIT. A bowsprit permanently fixed, as distinguished from a running bowsprit.

Fr: *Beaupré fixe;* Ger: *Fester Bugspriet.*

STANDING BY. Delay caused to a vessel's discharge or loading by bad weather, absence of lighters, and so on, the cost of such delay being a matter for arrangement between the parties concerned.

STANDING GAFF. A gaff kept hoisted and peaked on which a fore-and-aft sail is set by means of an outhaul and furled with brails. It is kept in position by a peak span leading to the lower masthead, is steadied by vangs on either side, and confined to the mast by a gooseneck.

Fr: *Corne Fixe;* Ger: *Feste Gaffel.*

STANDING JIB. A large jib formerly carried by ships and barks, but later replaced by the inner and outer jibs.

Fr: *Grand Foc;* Ger: *Stehender Kluvfock.*

STANDING LUG. A lugsail in which the tack secures at the foot or abaft the mast. The fore end of the yard projects forward of the mast for a distance varying from a third to a quarter of the total length of yard. The yard is not dipped in tacking or jibing, and the sail lies *on* the mast and one tack and *off* the mast on the other.

Fr: *Voile à Bourcet à amure Fixe; Voile de Lougre Fixe;* Ger: *Festes Luggersegel; Stehendes Luggersegel.*

STANDING PART. In knotting, the main part of a rope, as distinguished from the bight and the end. That part of a tackle fall made fast to the standing block.

Fr: *Dormant;* Ger: *Stehender Part; Fester Part.*

STANDING RIGGING. Semipermanent rigging which acts chiefly to support the masts; that is, shrouds, stays, backstays, and so on. When once in position these are not moved except when they require adjustment or renewal. Yards, gaffs, and booms have some standing rigging for their support, or for other purposes. Standing rigging is usually made of wire rope, except in some very small craft. It consists generally of mild steel wire of 6×7 construction, with a tensile breaking strength of 45 to 55 tons per sq. in., or of galvanized plough steel wire with a tensile breaking strength of 95 to 105 tons per sq. in.

Fr: *Gréement Dormant;* Ger: *Stehendes Gut.*

Recently stainless steel wire has come into favor for the standing rigging of sailing yachts and for other special craft. It is then used in the form of a strand or wire line composed of 19 wires and known as the 1×19 construction. The ropes usually included in the standing rigging of sailing vessels are: lower rigging, topmast rigging, topgallant rigging, stays, backstays, bobstay, bowsprit shrouds, martingale stay, jibboom guys, and lifts. Standing rigging should give the greatest possible rigidity to the masts in a fore-and-aft direction. However, some lateral flexibility should be allowed since, unless a mast can bend from side to side under the pressure of canvas, a dangerous compression strain is set up which may buckle the mast.

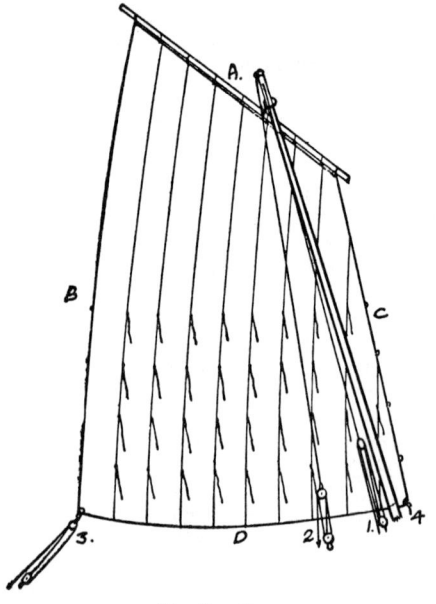

Standing Lug

A. Head of Sail
B. Leech
C. Weather
D. Foot

1. Halyards
2. Shroud or Stay
3. Sheet
4. Tack Hook

STANDING TIMBER. Timber during the period that it forms part of the growing tree.

Fr: *Bois Sur Pied;* Ger: *Stehendes Holz.*

STANDING TOPSAIL.

See **Gaff Topsail.**

STANDING WAYS. Heavy structure fastened to the building berth, consisting of solid balks of timber 15 in. to 72 in. in breadth, laid down on closely spaced supporting blocks. Also called fixed ways, ground ways. In lengthwise direction the standing ways may be either straight or

very slightly cambered. They extend from the vessel's stem right aft and into the water a sufficient length to insure the required depth of water at the afterend of the ways. Their slope varies from 1/12 to 1/24.
Fr: *Coulisse Morte;* Ger: *Schlagbalken; Ablaufbahn.*
See **Sliding Ways, Launching.**

STAND OFF AND ON. To remain near, as a coast, by sailing toward it, and then away from it.
Ger: *Ab und zu liegen.*

STAND ON. To continue on the same course or tack. To hold the course and speed.
Fr: *Garder Maintenir;* Ger: *Durchliegen.*

STAND ON VESSEL.
See **Privileged Vessel.**

STAND OUT. To sail out from a harbor and direct a course to seaward.
Fr: *Cap au Large;* Ger: *Herausliegen.*

STAND UP. A vessel under sail stands up when she carries her canvas without heeling heavily.
Fr: *Porter la toile.*

STAPLE. A loop of metal, or a bar bent and formed with two points to be driven in at both ends or welded to a pad for holding a hook, pin, or bolt. Also called dog.
Fr: *Crampe;* Ger: *Krampe.*
See **Staple Angle.**
See **Mooring Staple.**

STAPLE ANGLE. A short length of forged, stamped or cast angle bar forming a close fit around a continuous structural member at the point where it passes through a deck or bulkhead. It is calked for water-tightness. Also called angle collar, stapling, staple.
Fr: *Cornière d'Étanchéité;* Ger: *Winkelkragen.*

STAPLE KNEE. Long iron knee made in the form of a staple, with one arm secured to the deck beam above, and the other bolted to the deck beam below. The body was fastened to the ship's frame. (Obsolete.)
Ger: *Doppelknie.*

STAPLING.
See **Staple Angle.**

STAR. A type of racing sailboat belonging to an international one-design class. The hull is chine-built with fin keel. The over-all length is 22 ft. 7½ in. It is rigged with a marconi mainsail and jib. Also called star boat.

STARBOARD HAND BUOY. A buoy which should be kept on the right-hand side of a vessel entering a harbor, river, or estuary from seaward, or with the main stream of flood tide.

STAR BOAT. See **Star.**

STARRING. The process of sounding around a point, island, or rock, on lines of sounding which radiate from its center.
Fr: *Sondage en Etoile.*

STAR SHAKE. One of a number of clefts radiating from the pith toward the circumference in a piece of timber. They widen toward the bark.

START. To start a sheet, when sailing to windward, means to slacken it because the boat does not respond quickly enough to the helm under the pressure of the wind.
Fr: *Choquer;* Ger: *Auffieren.*

STAR TELESCOPE. A bell-shaped telescope with large object glass for use with a sextant. It is an erecting telescope of magnification about 3 and minimum apparent field of 15 degrees. It has less magnifying power than the ordinary inverting telescope but is the only practical one for taking sights from the deck of a small craft.
Fr: *Lunette de nuit;* Ger: *Sternfernrohr.*

STARTING RAM. A device provided for starting a vessel on the launching ways in the event that it refuses to move by gravity after the releasing arrangements have been put into effect. Also called starting jack. It consists of a hydraulic ram placed under the forefoot or at the upper end of each sliding way which is capable of applying pressure parallel to the ways, and toward the water.
Fr: *Vérin de Poussée; Vérin de Chasse;* Ger: *Anlasshebel.*

STARTING SIGNAL. One of the various signals used by a race committee at the commencement of a yacht race. Starting signals include, first, a warning signal, second, a preparatory signal shown a few minutes after the warning signal, and third, a starting signal hoisted a few minutes after the preparatory signal. Attention is called to each visual signal by a sound signal, gun, or whistle. If several classes of yachts are to be started, those following the first class usually start on the next signal, the warning and preparatory signals being omitted.

Fr: *Signal de départ;* Ger: *Abfahrtsignal.*

STATICAL STABILITY. The stability characteristics of a ship when at rest at a given angle of keel, as distinguished from dynamic stability, which is a measure of the work done up on a ship in motion to incline her to a given angle.

Fr: *Stabilité Statique;* Ger: *Statische Stabilität.*

See **Dynamical Stability, Stability.**

STATION. The allotted place or the duties of each person on board ship in emergencies.

Fr: *Poste;* Ger: *Station.*

See **Anchor Stations, Boarding Station, Boat Station, Fire Station, Lloyds Signal Station, Quarantine Station, Radio-Compass Station, Signal Station, Square Station.**

STATION POINTER. An instrument used for plotting an observer's position by means of two observed horizontal sextant angles between three objects. Also called three-arm protractor. It consists of a graduated brass or plastic circle from the center of which three arms radiate; the middle one is fixed, but the other two are free to rotate around the circle. To each of these movable arms a vernier, with clamp and tangent screws is attached. When two angles have been observed these angles are set on the two movable arms of the station pointer, which is then placed on the chart and moved about until the edge of the middle arm is on the middle object observed and the edges of the other arms on the other two objects. Then the center of the graduated circle gives the ship's position at the time of the observation.

Fr: *Stigmographe;* Ger: *Kompasskreis.*

STATIONS. Projected lines in the body plan through which the sections parallel to the vertical longitudinal plane cut the molded surface of the hull. In merchant ship design they are spaced so as to divide the length between perpendiculars into either ten or twelve equal spaces. Beyond the limits of the parallel middle body the intervals are halved and near the ends, where the curvature becomes more pronounced, quarter intervals are generally used. Also called **square stations, ordinates, transverse sections.**

STATIONS BILL. A list which shows the names of all members of the crew and details of their various duties in connection with fire and boat drills, giving the particular lifeboat to which they belong. Also called muster list or muster roll. It assigns duties to the different members of the crew in connection with: (1) the closing of W. T. doors, valves, etc.; (2) the equipment of boats and rafts generally; (3) the launching of boats attached to davits; (4) the general preparation of the other boats and rafts; (5) the muster of passengers; (6) the extinction of fire. The same list also assigns certain duties to the members of the steward's department in passenger vessels, such as: warning the passengers, seeing that passengers are clothed and have their lifebelts on, assembling of passengers, keeping order in the passages and stairways and generally controlling the movements of all passengers.

Fr: *Rôle d'Appel;* Ger: *Musterrolle.*

STATUTORY DECK LINE. A horizontal line 12 in. in length and 1 in. in breadth marked amidships on each side of the ship and from which freeboard is measured. Its upper edge passes through the point where the continuation outward of the upper surface of the freeboard deck intersects the outer surface of the shell plating.

Fr: *Ligne de Pont Réglementaire;* Ger: *Gezetzliche Decklinie.*

STAVARING.

See **Ottring.**

STAVE. 1. To crush in. To knock a hole in. When violent damage is done to the upper part of a ship's hull, it is said to be stove.

Fr: *Crever;* Ger: *Rochstasten; Einschlagen.*

2. In the timber trade, narrow pieces of softwood about 42 in. long, and of various widths and thicknesses.

Fr: *Merrain;* Ger: *Daubenholz.*

STAVERSCHE JOL. A Dutch open fishing boat with well from Stavoren, Friesland, used for catching herring and sardines on the Zuider Zee. It is distinguished from other small craft of this region by its deep keel and the absence of leeboards, and is probably of Scandinavian origin. The hull is built with ample freeboard, transom stern, rounded stem, and pronounced sheer forward. Owing to its good seagoing qualities this type of boat is frequently chosen by yacht owners. The rig consists of a boomless gaff mainsail and foresail. Length, waterline, 17.3 ft. Beam 7.2 ft. Tonnage 4 to 6. Crew 2 or 3.

STAY. A strong rope, generally of wire, forming part of the standing rigging, used as a support for spars and more especially masts. Stays lead from the head of a mast down to another mast or down to the deck. The stays leading forward or aft are called fore-and-aft stays, while those leading across the ship are named backstays.

Fr: *Étai;* *Draille;* Ger: *Stag;* *Leiter.*

STAY (to). To incline forward, aft, or to one side by means of stays and shrouds.

Fr: *Etayer;* Ger: *Wenden.*

See **To Tack.**

STAY FORESAIL. See **Fore Staysail.**

STAY HOLE. Hole in the luff of a staysail or jib for the lacing, rings, or hanks, by which it is confined to the stay.

Fr: *Oeillet d'envergure;* Ger: *Stagliek Gattchen.*

STAY PIN.

See **Stud.**

STAYSAIL. A triangular or trapezoidal fore-and-aft sail hoisted on a stay. It is held down by its tack, and is confined to the stay by iron thimbles, rings, hanks, bridles, or lacings, toggled into the stay holes or into eyelets.

Fr: *Voile d'Étai;* Ger: *Stagsegel.*

See **Advance Staysail, Fisherman's Staysail, Forestaysail, Fore-Topmast Staysail, Middle Staysail, Mizzen Staysail, Queen Staysail, Storm Staysail, Vanderbilt Staysail.**

STAYSAIL RIG. A fore-and-aft rig adopted for racing and cruising ketches and schooners, in which the gaff or triangular foresail is discarded, and is replaced by two staysails between each mast. It gives a greater sail area and increased efficiency when sailing on the wind.

Fr: *Gréement à Voiles d'Étai;* Ger: *Stagsegeltakelung.*

The main advantages of this rig are the ease with which sail can be taken in or set and the more effective staying. One disadvantage is its inability to hold a high wind. Also, when sailing before the wind, one third of the sail area is lost, the sails between the two masts being useless. This rig is simple to handle. The sail plan is cut up and can easily be lowered and hoisted, but the upper staysails do not stand when sailing off the wind. Close-hauled it is fairly efficient, but with the wind free it is very ineffective. It was never adopted on commercial sailing craft, because of the need of many additional sails when running before the wind.

STAYSAIL SCHOONER. A rig in which the conventional gaff or Bermuda foresail is replaced by a number of smaller triangular sails which fill the rectangular area between the deck, the two masts, and the main topmast stay. According to aerodynamic theory this outfit of canvas has greater efficiency than the single sail, whether of the gaff-headed or marconi type.

Fr: *Goëlette à Voiles d'Étai;* Ger: *Stagsegelschoner.*

STAYSAIL STAY. A stay which is not used to support a mast, its duty being to carry a triangular sail, staysail, or jib when no stay is available for this purpose.

Fr: *Draille;* Ger: *Leiter.*

STAY TACKLE. A tackle made fast to a stay and used for hoisting weights to a midships position and lowering them into the hold, or the reverse. Stay tackles are hooked to the collar of the lower stay or some point aloft where they plumb the deck nearly amidships, for hauling in and landing on deck articles hoisted by the yard tackle.

Fr: *Palan d'Étai;* Ger: *Stagtakel.*

STEADY. An order to the helmsman to keep the ship's head in the direction the vessel is on at the moment the order is given. Also "steady as you go."

Fr: *Comme ça;* Ger: *Recht so.*

STEADY BEARING. A bearing for line shafting, which incorporates both upper and lower brasses lined with white metal, to take care of bending stresses in the shaft.

See **Spring Bearing, Shafting.**

STEADY COURSE. An expression used in connection with the Rules of the Road. A vessel is said to be on a steady course not only when her heading does not change, but whenever her future positions are clearly ascertainable from her present positions and movements.

STEADYING SAILS. A general name given to sails carried by small, mechanically propelled boats in order to reduce rolling or to help to keep the desired course in rough weather.

Fr: *Voiles d'appui;* Ger: *Stützsegel.*

STEADY WIND. A wind constant in force and direction.

Fr: *Vent Fait;* Ger: *Beständige Brise; Stehender Wind; Stetige Brise.*

STEALER. A trapezoidal shell plate of about double width at one end, located near the stem or stern. It takes the combined

butts of a through strake and of a drop strake. Also called stealer plate.
See **Drop Strake.**

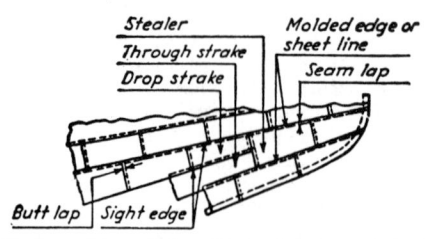

Stealer. (*From Baker, E., Steel Shipbuilding, by permission of McGraw-Hill Book Co. N. Y.*)

STEAM CAPSTAN. A capstan operated by a steam engine. The engine is usually nonreversing and transmits its power to the capstan spindle through a worm and worm wheel.
Fr: *Cabestan à Vapeur;* Ger: *Dampfspill.*

STEAM GUY. A single-wire derrick guy replacing the ordinary guy with wire pennant and rope tackle. When trimming the derrick it is taken to a winch.

STEAMING LIGHT. The white light carried by steam and motor vessels under way, on the foremast or in the fore part of the vessel, and visible from ahead through an arc of 112½° on either hand at a distance of at least 5 miles, in accordance with the Rules of the Road. Also called masthead light.
Fr: *Feu de Tête de Mât;* Ger: *Topplicht; Topplaterne; Topplampe.*

STEAMING-OUT LINE. A pipe system with a branch in each cargo hold, by which live steam can be turned on for fire-fighting purposes, or for freeing oil tank spaces of gas. Also called steam smothering line.
Fr: *Tuyautage de Vaporisation;* Ger: *Dampffeuer-Löschleitung.*

STEAMING RANGE.
See **Cruising Radius.**

STEAMING TIME. The distance in nautical miles between two ports, divided by the average daily run of the vessel.

STEAM SCHOONER. A special type of bulk cargo vessel mainly used in the lumber trade of the Pacific coast of the United States. Although these vessels were originally the outgrowth of lumber sailing schooners, the modern steam schooners depend wholly upon their engines. Their general structure resembles that of sailing schooners. They have a greater proportionate beam than the ordinary steamer, high freeboard, great sheer forward, and a long unobstructed deck space between the forecastle and the bridge, which is placed far aft. Large quantities of lumber are frequently carried on this open deck space as "deck load." Their length ranges from 100 to 200 ft. with a maximum capacity of 500 tons. They are locally known as "single-enders" when the engines are placed abaft the cargo spaces; and "double-enders" when there is an extra hold aft of the engine room. The latter have three masts.
Dickie, D. W., The Pacific Coast Steam Schooner, Society of Naval Architects and Marine Engineers, *Historical Transactions* (New York, 1945); "Pacific Coast Steam Schooners," *Marine Engineering* (New York), vol. 23 (1918).

STEAM SCHOONER GUY.
See **Guy Span.**

STEAMSHIP. A mechanically propelled vessel in which the principal motive power is steam, as opposed to a sailing vessel or motorship. Also called steamer.
Fr: *Vapeur;* Ger: *Dampfschiff.*

STEAM SMOTHERING LINE.
See **Steaming Out Line.**

STEAM STEERING GEAR. A steering apparatus in which a vertical or horizontal steam engine supplies the necessary power for moving the rudder. These engines are simple and reliable, but are noisy and very inefficient. Their efficiency is about 5 per cent. Their initial cost is low compared with that of other systems.
Fr: *Appareil à Gouverner à Vapeur;* Ger: *Dampfrudermaschine; Dampfsteuerapparat.*

STEAM TILLER. A steering gear in which the steering engine is fastened to and moves with the tiller. The motion is conveyed through a pinion geared to a fixed quadrant. Steam connection between moving and stationary parts is obtained by means of ball and socket joints.
Fr: *Servomoteur Sur Barre;* Ger: *Ruder mit Antriebskraft auf der Pinne.*

STEAM TRAP. A device for removing entrained or condensed water from steam in a marine steam power plant. They are mechanical, of the bucket or float type, or thermostatic. Also called drainer.
Fr: *Séparateur;* Ger: *Kondenstopf.*

STECHSCHWERTBOOT. Single-masted, half-decked sailing trawler from Stralsund, Pomerania, with fore-and-aft rig. Length 22.9 to 26.2 ft. Breadth 9.8 ft. Depth 3.9 ft.

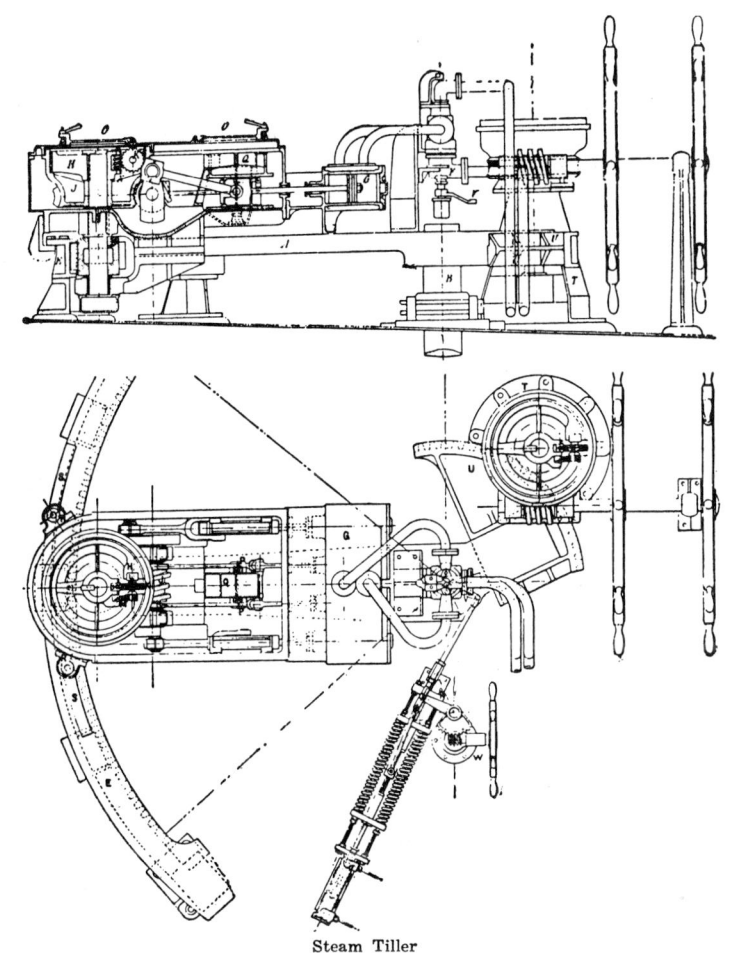

Steam Tiller
A. Tiller   B. Rudder Head   E. Rack   G. Engine Cylinders
W. Trick wheel connected to telemotor   U. Emergency quadrant

STEEL GRATING. A structure of metal bars so arranged as to give a support or footing over an opening while providing spaces between the bars for the passage of light and air. Also called grill flooring. The most common applications of gratings on board ship are for covering boiler hatches or fidley hatches, floors of oil-fired boiler rooms, walkways and galleries in engine and boiler rooms, ladder steps, and so on. The width usually ranges between 16 in. and 2 ft. They are constructed of flat bars on edge, or of rods ⅝ or ¾ in. in diameter carried by side bars 2¼ to 2½ in. deep.

STEEL SPAR. A built-up spar made of plates riveted or welded together, or of steel tubing with swaged joints.

Fr: *Espar Métallique;* Ger: *Stählernes Rundholz.*

STEER. To guide a vessel by the movements of a rudder or helm.

Fr: *Gouverner;* Ger: *Steuern.*

STEERAGE. 1. The part or space of a passenger vessel, in the 'tween decks, allotted to the passengers who travel at the cheapest rate.

Fr: *Entrepont;* Ger: *Zwischendeck; Steerage.*

2. The effect of the helm on a ship in motion. The manner in which a ship is affected by the helm.

Fr: *Gouverne;* Ger: *Steuerung; Wirkung des Steuers.*

STEERAGE PASSENGER (G. B.). According to British law the expression "steerage passenger" means all passengers except cabin passengers.

Fr: *Passager d'Entrepont;* Ger: *Zwischendeckpassagier.*

STEERAGEWAY. That degree of forward movement or headway of a ship which renders her subject to the helm. The expression "bare steerage way" has been held to mean the lowest speed consistent with the maintenance of headway.

Fr: *Erre pour Gouverner;* Ger: *Steuerfahrt.*

STEER CLEAR OF. To keep away from.

Fr: *Gouverner au Large de;* Ger: *Klar steuern.*

STEERER.

See **Steering Gear, Automatic Steerer, Boat Steerer.**

STEERING. The act of directing a ship on her course. Also the effect of the helm on a ship.

Fr: *Gouverne;* Ger: *Steuern.*

See **Automatic Steering.**

STEERING CHAIN. Unstudded short link chain transmitting motion from a steering engine drum or steering wheel, to the quadrant or rudder tiller.

Fr: *Chaîne de drosse;* Ger: *Steuerkette.*

STEERING COLUMN. A pedestal of nonmagnetic metal which supports the steering wheel. An indicator is usually fitted on the top or at the side of the column to show the rudder angle, and there is frequently a similar indicator to show the angle transmitted by the steering wheel. Also called steering stand.

Ger: *Steuerstand.*

STEERING COMPASS. The compass placed next to the steering wheel, by which the course is steered. These compasses are usually supplied with a magnifying prism placed over the lubber's line, thus enabling the helmsmen to detect any movement of the ship's head more readily than would be possible by reading the card direct.

Fr: *Compas de Route;* Ger: *Steuerkompass.*

STEERING CRUTCH. A crutch fitted on the quarter of a lifeboat as a support for the steering oar.

STEERING ENGINE. A steam, electric, or hydraulic power machine used for working the rudder and having its valves or operating gear actuated by leads from the navigating bridge.

Fr: *Servo moteur de barre;* Ger: *Rudermaschine; Steuermaschine.*

STEERING GEAR. The steering wheel, leads, steering engine, and fittings by which the rudder is turned. Also called steering apparatus, steerer.

Fr: *Appareil à Gouverner;* Ger: *Steuervorrichtung; Steuerapparat.*

For vessels over 500 tons and even smaller it is considered advisable to fit mechanical steering gears. According to American Bureau rules all vessels exceeding 250 ft. in length must be provided with a steering engine. The Bureau Veritas rules specify mechanical steering gear for vessels over 800 tons and 500 horsepower. A steering apparatus includes three distinct items:

1. The tiller or quadrant fixed on the rudderhead.
2. The engine or hand wheel giving the necessary power for moving the tiller which may be placed close to the steering apparatus or at a distance.
3. The controlling or transmission gear for the engine.

STEERING GROMMET. A wire grommet served with marline or spun yarn and fastened to the sternpost of an open boat for holding a steering oar.

Fr: *Erseau d'Aviron de Queue;* Ger: *Ruderstropp.*

STEERING LIGHT. The small white light sometimes carried abaft the smokestack or aftermast by a vessel when towing, as an aid for the vessel towed to steer by.

Fr: *Feu de Gouverne;* Ger: *Steuerlicht.*

STEERING OAR. A long oar used as a rudder, especially in lifeboats where a hinged rudder becomes ineffective in a seaway, and where the seas are liable to keep the rudder blade out of the water at times. It is also used where a boat must be turned quickly. A steering oar fits into the steering crutch next to the sternpost, or in a rope grommet. In lifeboats it is often painted white to distinguish it from the other oars.

Fr: *Aviron de Queue;* Ger: *Steuerruder; Steuerremen.*

STEERING OAR BRACE. The fulcrum of a whaling boat's steering oar located on a sort of bumkin, projecting over the port side just forward of the sternpost. Also called steering brace.

STEERING QUALITIES. The tendency of a vessel underway to answer readily to any movement of the rudder. Steering qualities are principally affected by the area of the rudder blade, the shape of the deadwood fore and aft, and the time taken to put the helm over. They are proportional to the immersed area of the rudder and inversely proportional to the ship's immersed lateral plane.

Fr: *Qualités Évolutives;* Ger: *Steuerfähigkeit; Kursbeständigkeit; Steuermacht.*

See **Steering, Weatherly Qualities.**
Davidson and Schiff, "Turning and Coursekeeping Qualities," Society of Naval Architects and Marine Engineers, *Transactions,* vol. 54, New York, 1946; Johns, A. W., "Ship Form and Steering." *The Engineer* (London), vol. 136 (1923).

STEERING ROD. A length of straight rod running along the waterways and connected to the wheel chains. Also called wheel rod.

Fr: *Tringle de Drosse;* Ger: *Ruderstange.*

STEERING STAND. A small raised platform or grating placed next to a hand steering wheel, for the helmsman to stand on.

Ger: *Steuerplicht.*

STEERING TELEGRAPH. An apparatus similar to the engine telegraph, arranged for the transmission of orders from the navigation bridge to the steering-engine room or any other steering station.

Fr: *Transmetteur d'Ordres de Barre;* Ger: *Steuertelegraph; Rudertelegraph.*

See **Selsyn.**

STEERING WHEEL. A wheel which controls the movements of a ship's rudder, and so constructed that the spokes are continued through the felloes or rim for a distance sufficient to provide a good grasp for the hands of the helmsman.

Fr: *Roue de Gouvernail;* Ger: *Steuerrad.*

The size, in merchant vessels, may vary from 1 ft. 6 in. to 6 ft. in diameter, the larger wheels being fitted in small vessels without mechanical steering apparatus. The smaller ones are mostly made of solid metal. Wooden wheels are made of teak with solid nave cast in brass and shaped to receive the inner ends of the spokes. The latter are turned to make ornamental shape with felloes made up of three thicknesses. A heavy brass ring is sunk into grooves in the felloes. There is usually one steering wheel on the navigating bridge or in the wheel house, also one or sometimes two aft on or below the poop for the emergency steering gear. In modern vessels with self-synchronous electric steering control, the steering wheel is frequently a metal disc from 2 to 3 ft. in diameter with heavy rim, suited to the hand grasp.

STEERING WHEEL BECKET. A short line with one end fastened to the deck, used in small craft for holding the tiller or steering wheel in any desired position. Also called tiller becket.

Fr: *Raban de Barre;* Ger: *Ruderpinne Haltetau.*

STEER SMALL. To steer with little movement of the helm. The opposite is "steer large."

Fr: *Gouverner avec Peu de Barre.*

STEERSMAN. See **Helmsman.**

STEEVE. 1. The inclination above horizontal given to the bowsprit. This angle varies according to size and type of vessel. It is advantageous in small vessels, as it gives more height above water for working the headsails in a seaway.

Fr: *Inclinaison;* Ger: *Steigung; Neigungswinkel des Bugspriet.*

Average Values of Steeve

Vessel	Angle in degrees
Three-masted bark	17 to 19
Fore-and-aft trading schooners	12½ to 17
Fore-and-aft schooner yacht	10 to 12
Trading ketch	8
Cutter	2

2. Short spar with a block at one end, used for stowing bale goods in a ship's hold.

STEEVE (to). To elevate a spar at an angle.

Fr: *Apiquer.*

STEEVING. The stowing of cotton, wool or other bale cargo, with jackscrews.

Ger: *Trawen.*

STEM. 1. The upright post or bar of the bow. It may be a casting, forging, or weldment, or made of wood.

Fr: *Etrave;* Ger: *Vorsteven; Vordersteven.*

See **Bar Stem, False Stem, Fashion Plate Stem, Free Stem, Newhaven Stem, Raking Stem.**

2. An agreement respecting the quantity of cargo, date of loading and time to be occupied in loading. It generally refers to bulk cargoes.

STEM (to). 1. To make headway, especially to make progress in opposition to some obstruction such as a current, head wind, tide, and so on.

Fr: *Etaler;* Ger: *Vorwärtsdringen; Totsegeln.*

2. To stem a vessel means to load it, or arrange to load it, within a certain period of time (G. B.). In the coal trade vessels are stemmed to begin to load on a particular date agreed between charterer and shipowner. Such a date is known as the stem date.

STEM ANCHOR. An anchor similar to a bower anchor in size but stowed in a stem hawsepipe. Also called center anchor. The stem anchor replaces the spare bower.

Fr: *Ancre d'Étrave.*

STEM BAND. A piece of flat or half-round iron fastened outside on the stem of a wooden boat as protection. It extends over the stemhead to about 2 ft. abaft stem and keel scarf. Also called stem iron nose.

Fr: *Bande d'Étrave;* Ger: *Vorstevenschiene.*

STEM DINGHY. A dinghy with pointed bows, as distinguished from a pram dinghy.

STEM FOOT. The forward end of the keel, into which the stem is fitted.

STEM IRON. See **Stem Band.**

STEMMING. The application made by a ship's agent to the port authorities for a discharging berth just before the vessel's arrival at the port of destination.

Ger: *Einschreiben.*

STEMMING DATE. The date and time specified in a charter party at which the loading is to commence and upon which lay time commences. Also called stem date.

STEMMING LIST (G. B.). A list computed by the harbor authorities indicating the rotation of vessels awaiting berthage at a loading port.

STEM NET. In a fleet of drift nets, the one nearest the stem of the vessel.

STEM NOTE.

See **Notice of Readiness.**

STEM PIECE. 1. The lower timber of the knee of the head, scarfed to the gripe or to the keel. Also called independent piece.

Fr: *Dossier;* Ger: *Rückenstück.*

2. One of the pieces of wood worked against the stem on each side for the purpose of increasing the distance between the knightheads and to avoid cutting away the latter to form the hole for the bowsprit. Also called snaped timber.

STEM PLATE. Plate fitted flat against the inside lower portion of the stem in composite vessels, for additional strength.

Fr: *Tôle d'Étrave;* Ger: *Vorstevenplatte.*

STEMSON. A piece of compass timber worked abaft the apron. Its lower end scarfs to the keelson. Its upper end is continued as high as the middle or upper deck, and its purpose is to support the scarfs of the apron. Also called stem knee.

Fr: *Marsouin Avant;* Ger: *Stevenknie; Reitknie; Schlempknie.*

STEP. Also mast step. **1.** The recessed block or framing in which the heel of a mast is placed. It is fitted on the keelson or on a lower deck.

2. The hole or mortise into which a mast tenon steps.

Fr: *Emplanture;* Ger: *Mastspur.*

STEP-BACK WELDING.

See **Skip Welding.**

STEPPED BOTTOM. A form of bottom construction peculiar to hydroplanes and racing craft designed for high speed. It introduces one or two steplike breaks in the continuity of the bottom past which the water flows. The effect of this is to create an air space behind the step and reduce the amount of wetted surface, with a corresponding gain in speed.

Fr: *Fond à Redan.*

STEPPING POINT. See **Bearding Line.**

STEP STANCHION. Stanchion placed near a hatchway and used as a hold ladder. Also called notch stanchion, cleat stanchion.

Fr: *Epontille à échelons;* Ger: *Treppenstütze.*

STERN. The afterpart of a ship or boat.

Fr: *Arrière;* Ger: *Heck; Gatt.*

See **Apple Stern, By the Stern, Canoe Stern, Counter Stern, Cruiser Stern, Elliptical Stern, Fantail Stern, Flat Stern, Irish Sea Stern, Lute Stern, Pink Stern, Sharp Stern, Spoon Stern, Square Stern, Square Tuck Stern, Transom Stern, V Stern, Yacht Stern.**

STERN ALL. A command to a boat's crew to back water on both sides, to acquire sternway.

Fr: *Sciez Partout;* Ger: *Überall streichen.*

STERN ANCHOR. A stockless anchor about one-fourth the weight of a bower and used for lying at anchor where the space for swinging is restricted, or for maneuvering in narrow waters.

Fr: *Ancre de croupiat;* Ger: *Heckanker.*

STERN BOSS. The enlarged part of the propeller post in a single-screw vessel, through which the propeller shaft passes. Also called stern bossing.

Stem

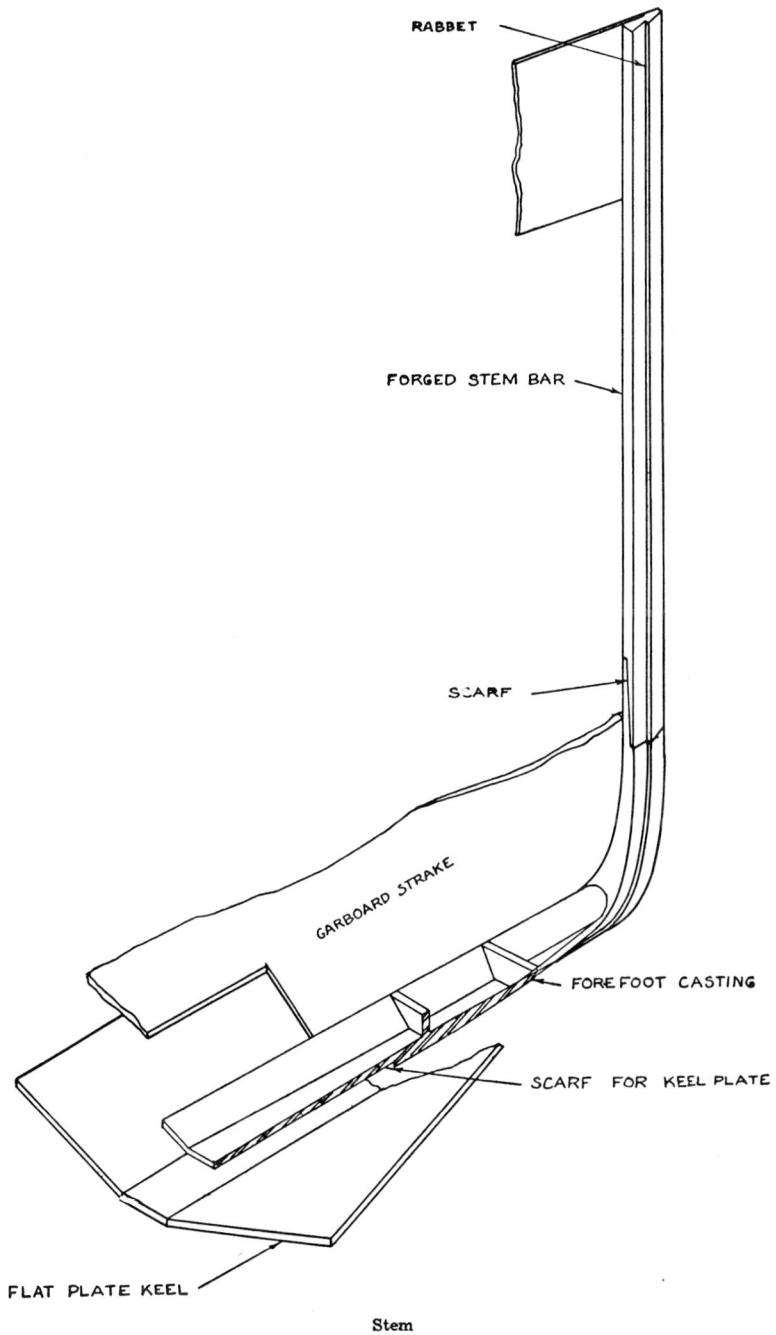

Fr: *Lunette;* Ger: *Schraubenöffnung.*

STERN BUSH. A grooved brass or composition bushing fitted at the after end of the stern tube on which the propeller shaft bears. The material of the bearing surface may consist of one of the following alternatives. 1. Lignum vitae blocks with grain on edge driven into grooves; 2. rubber bearing surfaces vulcanized to brass backing strips for attachment to the grooves; 3. phenolic composition blocks driven into the grooves (See **Micarta**); 4. Babbitted bearings with forced lubrication from a special feed system. In the first three cases grooves are left between the strips so as to allow for water passing through for lubrication. Also called stern tube bearing, stern tube bushing.

Fr: *Boîte à Gaïac; Coussinet d'Étambot;* Ger: *Stevenrohrbüchse; Stevenrohrlager.*

STERN CHOCK. A round or oval casting or frame inserted in the bulwark plating at the stern of the vessel for leading mooring lines. Also called stern pipe.

STERN DAVIT. One of a pair of davits projecting beyond the counter of a square-sterned vessel, from which the stern boat is handled.

Fr: *Bossoir de Portemanteau;* Ger: *Heckdavit.*

STERN FAST.
See **Stern Rope.**

STERN FRAME. A heavy casting, forging, or weldment forming the afterend of the ship's structure, and supporting the rudder. It also serves as a frame for connecting the ends of the shell plating. Sometimes called sternpost.

Fr: *Étambot;* Ger: *Hintersteven.*
See **Post.**

In single- and triple-screw vessels it includes the propeller and rudderposts. In wooden vessels, it includes the framing of timber composed of the sternpost transoms, and fashion pieces which receives the ends of the planking and supports the rudder.

STERN GLAND. A short, hollow cylindrical casting having a flange at one end, used for compressing the packing in the stern tube stuffing box. It is placed at the forward end of the stern tube on the afterpeak bulkhead. Also called stern tube gland.

Fr: *Presse-Étoupe Arrière;* Ger: *Sternbüchse; Stevenrohrbüchse.*

STERN KNEE. A heavy knee which forms the lower piece of the deadwood aft and connects the sternpost to the keel in a wooden vessel. Also called sternpost knee, heel knee.

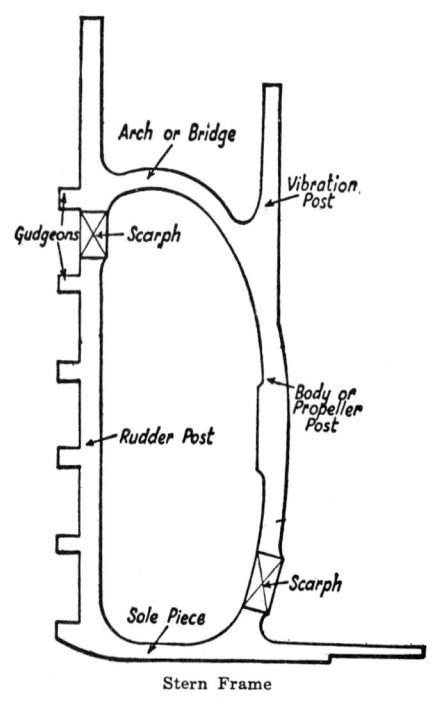

Fr: *Courbe d'Étambot;* Ger: *Reitknie; Hinterstevenknie.*

STERN LIGHT. A white light carried at the stern and throwing an unbroken light over an arc of the horizon of 12 points (135 degrees) of the compass or of 6 points from right aft on each side of the vessel, in accordance with the Rules of the Road. It is placed as nearly as practicable on the same level as the side lights and must be visible for a distance of at least one mile.

Fr: *Feu de Poupe;* Ger: *Hecklicht.*

STERN LINE.
See **Stern Rope.**

STERN MOLDING. Half-round battens, or ornamental work fitted around the stern of a vessel.

Fr: *Couronnement;* Ger: *Heckverzierung.*

STERN PIPE. A hawsepipe similar to the stem pipe, and placed on the center line at the stern. It is used for housing a stockless stream anchor.

Fr: *Ecubier de remorque; Ecubier d'embossage;* Ger: *Taukluse; Hinteres Klusenloch.*

STERN POINTER. In a wooden vessel, one of the timbers fayed and bolted diagonally upon the ceiling at the stern for the security of the heels of half timbers. Also called crutch, snakepiece.
   Fr: *Echarpe;* Ger: *Hinterpiekband; Piekstück.*

STERNPOST. See **Stern Frame**.

STERN ROPE. A mooring or docking line leading aft and making an angle of less than 45° with the fore-and-aft line of the ship. Also called stern fast.
   Fr: *Amarre de Bout;* Ger: *Achtertau; Hecktau.*

propeller shaft passes, extending from the sternpost to the stuffing box bulkhead. Also called shaft tube. It consists of a hollow cast-iron or cast-steel cylinder fitted with brass bushings. These are lined with lignum vitae, white metal, plastic, or vulcanized rubber bearing surfaces upon which the propeller shaft rotates. The forward end of the stern tube is connected by a flange to the afterpeak bulkhead, which in conjunction with the stuffing box fitted around the shaft makes a watertight joint at this point.
   Fr: *Tube d'Étambot; Tube de Sortie d'Arbre;* Ger: *Stevenrohr.*

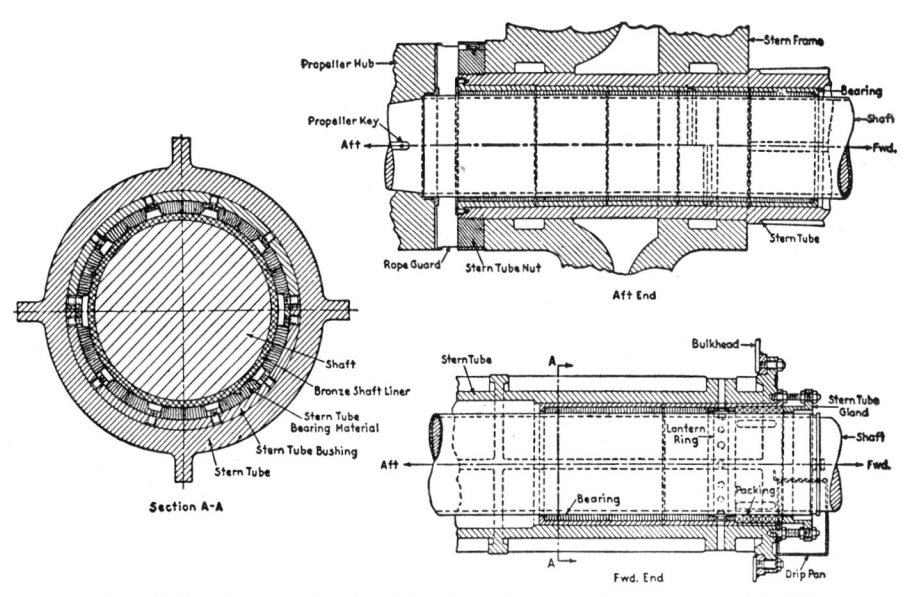

Stern Tube. (*Courtesy Society of Naval Architects and Marine Engineers, N. Y.*)

STERN SHEETS. The space in an open boat abaft the afterthwart, and provided with seats for passengers.
   Fr: *Chambre;* Ger: *Hinterteil.*

STERNSON. The curved timber uniting the upper deadwood to the sternpost in wooden ships.
   Fr: *Marsouin Arrière;* Ger: *Hintersteven Reitknie.*

STERN TIMBER. One of the fore-and-aft timbers which make up the framing of the upper counter or transom and support the taffrail. Also called transom timber.
   Fr: *Jambette de Tableau;* Ger: *Heckspanten; Spiegelhölzer; Heckstütze.*

STERN TUBE. A tube through which the

Water can enter the stern tube from the afterend through suitable grooves cut in the bearing surfaces, and forms a satisfactory lubricant when not mixed with sand or mud. In twin-screw vessels, stern tubes are supported aft by the spectacle frame, and a stuffing-box bulkhead is worked at the forward end.

West, A. C., "Stern Tubes and Tail-End Bearings," Institute of Marine Engineers (London), *Transactions,* vol. 46 (July, 1934).

STERN TUBE BEARING.
   See **Stern Bush**.

STERN TUBE BEARING STRIPS. Strips of lignum vitae wood or hardened rubber fitted on the periphery of the stern bush, which form the bearing surface for the propeller shaft.

Fr: *Lamelles de Gaiac;* Douvelles; Ger: *Pockholzstuben; Pockholzstreifen.*

STERN TUBE CHECK RING.
See **Stern Tube End Plate.**

STERN TUBE END PLATE. A flat ring with an inside diameter about one inch less than the inside diameter of the stern tube bushing, to which it is tap bolted. Its purpose is to prevent the stern tube bearing strips from slipping out. Also called stern tube check ring.

Fr: *Couronne d' Arrêt;* Ger: *Stoppring; Stevenrohrschlussring.*

STERN TUBE NUT. A large malleable iron nut which fits on the afterend of the stern tube. It is tightened hard up against the stern frame and is locked by means of a keeper plate. Also called stern tube ring nut.

Fr: *Écrou de Serrage du Tube d'Étambot;* Ger: *Stevenrohrmutter.*

STERN TUBE RETAINING STRIP. One of the several bronze strips of trapezoidal cross section fastened to the periphery of the stern tube bushing and holding the bearing material in place.

Fr: *Clef de tenne des Douvelles;* Ger: *Stevenrohr Längsschiene.*

STERN TUBE STUFFING BOX. The receptacle for the packing around the propeller shaft at the forward end of the stern tube.

Fr: *Presse-étoupe arrière;* Ger: *Stevenrohr Stopfbüchse.*

STERN WAVES. The wave series having its origin at the stern of a vessel moving through the water. The series of waves produced at the stern does not increase propulsive resistance as much as that formed by the bow. Also called waves of replacement.

Fr: *Vagues de l'Arrière;* Ger: *Heckwelle.*

STERNWAY. The backward motion of a boat. The movement of a vessel carried or impelled backward.

Fr: *Erre en Arrière;* Ger: *Rückwärtsfahrt.*

STERN-WHEELER. A paddle-wheel vessel in which the wheel is at the stern, as distinguished from the side-wheel steamer. Stern-wheelers are common on the rivers of the United States, where they are used as freight boats, and to tow barges.

Ger: *Hinterradschiff.*

STERN WINDOW. One of the square openings for light and ventilation formerly seen in square-sterned ships. They are still found in some Arab and Indian native-built vessels, also on some of the small sailing coasters in Northern European waters.

Fr: *Fenêtre;* Ger: *Kajütspforte; Spiegelfenster.*

STEVEDORE. A person or firm employed in loading and unloading vessels. One whose occupation is the stowage of cargo in a ship's hold. Also called longshoreman. The private stevedore in return for a fixed rate of remuneration, generally so much per ton, provides the men, gear, and all other adjuncts for working the cargo in or out of a vessel. Some shipowning firms do their own stevedoring and maintain a special staff and organization for this purpose. Owing to the varied nature of the goods handled, the work is classified as technical.

Fr: *Arrimeur;* Ger: *Stauer.*

See **Contract Stevedore, Foreman Stevedore, Stevedore Gang.**

A stevedore is not an independent contractor doing work which when completed is to be turned over to the master for his approval or disapproval. Instead he must load the vessel at all times under the direction of, and subject to, the control of the master.

STEVEDORE GANG. Also longshoremen's gang. A group of longshoremen or stevedores working as a unit in handling cargo through one hatchway. Each gang includes three squads: one working in the holds or 'tween-decks, the second on deck, and the third on the pier or quay. Each gang is in charge of a hatch boss (U. S.) or foreman stevedore (G. B.).

The size of gang and distribution of crew depend on the kind of cargo handled, whether the cargo is loaded or discharged and on the custom of the port. For loading general cargo in the ports of London and New York the average number of men forming a gang may vary from 18 to 24 men, stationed as follows: 9 to 12 in the hold (holdsmen); 3 to 5 on deck (hatch tenders, winchmen); 6 to 7 ashore (piermen, quay men).

STEVEDORE'S KNOT. A type of double figure-eight knot, occasionally used to prevent a rope from unreeving.

STEVEDORING. The operations of loading and discharging ships. Specifically defined, stevedoring applies to the transfer of commodities from the ship to the first place of rest on the pier and to the direct transfer of commodities from the ship to a railroad car or lighter and vice versa. In discharging cargo, stevedoring therefore includes the sorting of the commodities as the piling on the pier; in loading cargo, it includes the stowing of the cargo in the various compartments of the ship.

STEVNSBAD. Open or half-decked keel-built Danish fishing boat originating from the village of Stevns (hence its name) and employed in the herring fisheries of the Sund. It is rigged with a sprit mainsail, topsail, and two headsails. Length 25 ft. Breadth 9 ft. Depth 3 ft. 6 in. (Typical.)

STEWARD. One of the ship's company, who attends to domestic matters. In a cargo vessel, the duties of the steward are mainly confined to provisioning, and catering for the officers and crew. In passenger vessels, the functionary called "chief steward" has charge of the table and culinary departments for the passengers and crew, the servants, and the whole of the passengers quarters, the term steward being also applied to his male helpers.

Fr: *Steward;* Ger: *Steward.*

See **Bedroom Steward, Chief Steward, Deck Steward, Glory Hole Steward.**

STEWARDESS. A woman who waits upon female passengers on board ship.

Fr: *Femme de Chambre de Bord;* Ger: *Stewardess; Aufwärterin.*

STICK. A piece of timber suitable for making a mast or spar. Sticks are classified as "square sticks" or "round sticks," according to their cross section.

See **Girth Stick, Gob Stick, Hand Mast, Head Stick, Inch Mast.**

STICK LENGTH. The total length of a spar. It includes the bury or housing, the hounding or hounded length, and the pole or head.

STICK UP. A small leg-of-mutton sail used on the Chesapeake Bay crabbing boats. Also called jigger. It sets on a short mast with pronounced forward rake, stepped just abaft the stem.

STIFF. 1. The power or ability of a vessel to offer resistance to inclination from the upright caused by external forces. Large metacentric height induces stiffness, a condition which causes quick, "snappy" rolling in disturbed waters. The opposite of "crank."

Fr: *Stable;* Ger: *Stabil; Steifheit.*

2. A ship having a large or excessive amount of initial stability.

STIFFENER. Sections or shapes used for increasing the rigidity of plating, as bulkhead stiffeners. Also called stiffening bar.

Fr: *Cornière de Renfort; Cornière de Raidissage;* Ger: *Versteifungsprofil; Verstärkungswinkel.*

See **Bulkhead Stiffener.**

STIFFENING. Weights, ballast or cargo, kept in a ship when the vessel is unloaded or nearly so in order to increase her stability and to prevent her from becoming crank. In former days stiffening booms or spars were used for this purpose, lashed to the hull on each side. The term also means sufficient ballast for the safe movements of a vessel within docks or in a river, but not necessarily sufficient for a seagoing trip.

Ger: *Steifheitsballast.*

STIFFENING BAR.

See **Stiffener.**

STIFFENING ORDER (G. B.). Order issued by the customs in British ports by which permission is granted to a ship to take in ballast or heavy cargo prior to her being totally unloaded, thereby improving the conditions of stability.

Fr: *Permis de Lestage;* Ger: *Ballastorder.*

STIFFENING SIDE (G. B.). That side of steel plating on which the stiffeners or frames are fitted. In the U. S., rough side.

Ger: *Versteifungsseite.*

STIRRUP. One of a number of short pieces of served rope suspended from a yard. They are fastened to the footropes, which they support at the required distance from the yard.

Fr: *Etrier;* Ger: *Springperd.*

STOCK. A crosspiece fitted at the end of the shank opposite to the arms and lying transversely to the plane of the arms in a stocked anchor. Also called anchor stock. The stock is held in position in the shank by a raised lug or shoulder on one side and a key on the other. It has a ball cast on one end. The other end is bent at right angles a few inches from its extremity and also terminates in a ball which is removable. The bend at the end allows it to be partly drawn and folded along the shank. When a strain comes upon the cable, the stock cants the anchor, causing the arm to lie at a downward angle to the ground so that the pea enters and buries itself. The balls at the ends of the stock keep it from sinking too deeply in the ground before it is in proper position.

Fr: *Jas;* Ger: *Ankerstock.*

See **Rudder Stock.**

STOCK AND BILL TACKLE. A purchase used in getting a stock anchor on and off the foredeck. It is hooked to straps on the stock or the bill of the anchor and leads across the deck.

Fr: *Palan de Mouillage.*

STOCKED ANCHOR. An anchor made of a steel shank to one end of which two curved arms are forged. The other end of the shank is bored to receive the stock, which is attached at right angles to the arms and shank. The horizontal distance measured between the extremity of the arms is 0.7 of total length of shank. Also called common anchor, old-fashioned anchor, solid anchor, admiralty anchor.

Fr: *Ancre à Jas;* Ger: *Stockanker; Normalanker.*

See **Housing Anchor.**

A disadvantage of the old-fashioned anchor that should be noted is that when the stock strikes the bottom it may get buried in the ground and the pull on the cable may bend or fracture it. The difficulty of stowing and the length of time taken for fishing and catting the stock anchor are the most objectionable features of this type. When the fluke is properly buried it has good holding qualities. A stock anchor when carried out by a boat for streaming has better holding power than the stockless type.

STOCKHOLM TAR. Tar obtained by the crude distillation of pine stumps and roots. It is used in wooden shipbuilding and in the manufacture of cordage.

STOCKLESS ANCHOR. A type of anchor which has no stock and in which the arms are not fixed to the shank but are free to turn about a pin, a trunnion, or a ball socket in the crown.

Fr: *Ancre sans Jas;* Ger: *Stocklosanker.*

The advantages of stockless anchors when compared with stocked anchors with fixed flukes are as follows: Greater holding power is obtained by the fact that both flukes embed themselves in the sea bottom. The elimination of the stock makes for ease of housing; that is, it becomes possible for the shank of the anchor to be pulled into the hawsepipe, and as the flukes rotate freely, they draw up hard against the ship's side. The anchor is thus stowed quickly and conveniently and is ready for instant use.

Stockless anchors are usually made in two parts; the head, or crown, and the flukes form one part, always made of cast steel. The shank (which may be, according to the type, of forged or cast steel) forms the second part. The connection between the shank and the flukes is made on the ball-and-socket principle or by means of trunnions on the head of the shank so arranged that the flukes are always at an angle of about 45° to the side of the shank lying next to the bottom of the sea. The two parts forming the anchor are usually assembled by drawing the shank through an opening provided in the head, wedge-shaped pieces or a riveted fluke pin being afterward inserted to prevent it from coming out. Some of the patent anchors have the flukes and crown secured to a forged shank by a through bolt of steel, the axis of which is parallel to the points of the flukes. Also called swinging fluke anchor, housing anchor, double fluke anchor.

STOCKS. The timbers on which a ship rests while being built. Generally, the keel-blocks, bilge blocks, and shores upon which a vessel is built.

Fr: *Attinage;* Ger: *Unterstützung.*

STOKEHOLD. That space in a ship's boiler room from which the fires are fed and cleaned. Also called fire room.

Fr: *Chaufferie; Rue de Chauffe;* Ger: *Heizraum.*

STOKER. A hand belonging to the engine room force of a steam vessel and whose duties consist in feeding the furnaces and attending to the boilers in a general way. In coal-burning ship: shovels coal from locations where it was dumped by coal passers into furnace, spreading the coal so as to form an efficiently-burning fire; rakes and slices fires periodically or as directed by water tender to clean them of clinkers and ash and make them burn more brightly; helps coal passer to dispose of ashes overboard. In an oil burning ship: cleans oil burning equipment in boiler room as routine or under direction of water tender; shuts down oil burners that are clogged with carbon or otherwise operating inefficiently and replaces them with clean ones; cleans oil strainers; cleans spilled or accumulated oil from working spaces in the fire room. Also called fireman.

Fr: *Chauffeur;* Ger: *Heizer.*

STOLE MESHES. A process in net-making in which a mesh is taken away by netting two meshes of the preceding row in one.

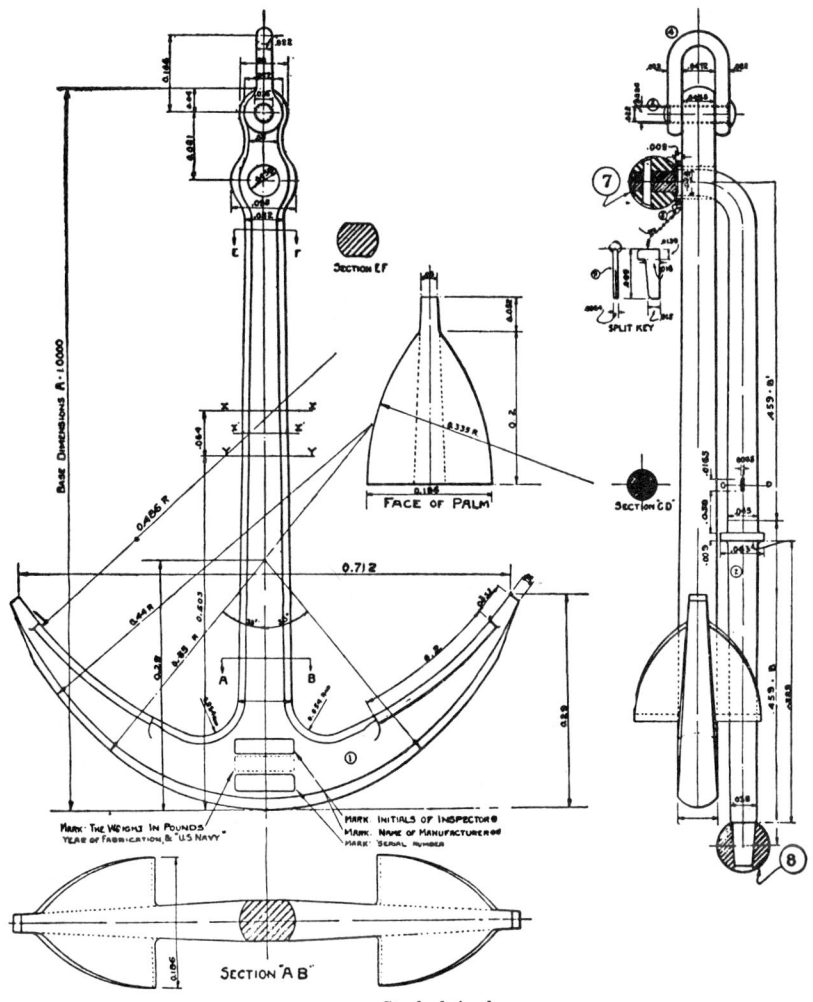

Stocked Anchor

STOMACH PIECE.
See **Apron.**

STOOL. A support for shaft gearing, piping, light auxiliary machinery, and so on, usually built up of plates and angles.

Fr: *Support; Chaise;* Ger: *Stuhl.*

See **Backstay Stool, Boiler Stool, Derrick Stool, Riming Stool.**

STOP. 1. A small projection at the head of a lower mast supporting the trestletrees. Any projection on a mast or spar to support something or keep it from slipping down.

Fr: *Noix;* Ger: *Knagge; Schulter; Stumpfer Abfass.*

2. Small stuff used to tie up anything. A fastening of small stuff used for securing a sail to a boom or gaff after it is furled. Piece of small stuff or narrow band of canvas used for securing a sail or awning temporarily.

Fr: *Amarrage;* Ger: *Nitzel; Knüttel.*

See **Awning Stops, Awning Side Stops, Clothes Stops, Deck Stops, Hammock Stops, Keel Stop, Rotten Stops, Rudder Stops.**

STOP (to). To tie up with small stuff, as a sail when sent aloft, or an awning when furled to prevent the wind from blowing it away.

Fr: *Mettre Sur Fils;* *Serrer en Bonnette;*
Ger: *Befestigen;* *Stoppen.*

STOP FOR FREIGHT. A written request made by a shipowner, as carrier, to the custodian of goods asking for the detention of the latter until the amount of freight specified in the request has been paid. The stop must be delivered at the time of the landing of the goods. It is canceled by the issue of a "removal of stop."

STOPPER. A short length of rope or chain, or a steel fitting used on board ship for checking the running of a rope or chain cable, or for holding it firmly while it is being belayed. A rope stopper is made up of a short length of Manila secured at one end to the structure of the ship, the other end being passed around the rope to be stoppered with a jamming hitch.

Fr: *Bosse;* Ger: *Stopper.*

See **Bow Stopper, Cable Stopper, Cathead Stopper, Chain Check Stopper, Chain Stopper, Check Stopper, Dog Stopper, Hatch Stopper, Housing Stopper, Lanyard Stopper, Lever Stopper, Riding Stopper, Ring Stopper, Rocking Stopper, Slip Stopper, Trip Stopper, Wire Rope Stopper, Wire Stopper.**

A stopper for a chain cable may consist of wire rope or chain from 4 to 6 ft. long. At one end it is spliced into the eye of a hook and at the other it has an eye formed around an iron toggle. The hook is placed in a ringbolt in the deck, and the body of the stopper lashed to the chain by two tails of soft Manila rope. When a ship is at anchor cables can be held by such stoppers to relieve the strain of the windlass.

STOPPER (to). To check or hold fast any rope or cable by means of a stopper.

STOPPER HITCH. A hitch similar to the rolling hitch except that the second turn is crossed over the first turn. It is more secure than the rolling hitch.

Fr: *Noeud de Bosse;* Ger: *Stopperstek.*

STOPPER KNOT. A general name for the different knots used for preventing the end of a rope from flying loose or slipping through some block or fairlead. The overhand knot, figure-of-eight knot and Matthew Walker knot are the most commonly used.

Fr: *Noeud de Bosse;* Ger: *Stopperknoten.*

STOPPING UP. Rolling up or gathering tightly a sail or awning and holding it in this condition with more or less evenly spaced turns of light twine called stops or rotten stops.

Fr: *Serrer en Bonnette;* Ger: *Stoppen.*

STOPPING-UP PIECES. Timbers used in a launching cradle for filling up the space between the upper side of the bilgeways and the ship's bottom. Also called stoppings up, packing.

Fr: *Billotage; Empilage;* Ger: *Aufklotzung; Aufkeilung.*

STOPS. Short pieces of rope or canvas bands for furling fore-and-aft sails.

STOP SEINE. A short seine shot across the arms of a larger one (called "main seine") to complete the circle, thus enclosing the fish in a kind of pound

STOP VALVE. A valve which acts to permit or prohibit the flow of a fluid through a pipe.

Fr: *Soupape d'Arrêt; Robinet d'Arrêt;* Ger: *Absperrventil; Absperrhahn.*

See **Globe Valve, Gate Valve.**

STOPWATER. 1. A dowel of white pine or other softwood driven in a seam between the keel and one of the adjoining parts where the wood is too thick to allow calking. The hole for a stopwater should be bored directly across the seam and so situated that the center of the hole comes on the seam.

Fr: *Coupe Eau; Clef de Calfat;* Ger: *Scheidenagel.*

2. In steel shipbuilding, any device whereby faying surfaces are made watertight by any method other than calking in such parts of the structure as are inaccessible to the calker. Also called stopper, oil stop. The materials generally used for this purpose are: tar, felt, flatwoven lampwick, strand lampwick, tarred paper, red-lead putty.

STORAGE. A port charge for goods held in transit sheds or warehouses under fixed or special arrangement for periods of time beyond that considered in the term "wharfage."

Fr: *Frais de Magasinage; Frais d'entreposage;* Ger: *Lagergeld; Lagermiete.*

STORBAAD. A Norwegian open sailing boat used for setting and hauling trawl lines for the larger decked craft such as the *bankskoite, storskoite,* and *smaskoite* in the same way as dories are employed in the Newfoundland cod fisheries. It is clinker-built with sharp stern and curved sternpost, and is sprit-rigged with 2 masts. The foremast is stepped just abaft the stem and the mainmast forward of amidships. There are 5 thwarts. This type of boat has now been replaced by the dory. Length over-all 22 ft. 1 in. Beam 8 ft. 9 in. Depth 3 ft. 9 in. (Typical.)

STOREKEEPER. Unlicensed member of the crew carried on some merchant vessels. He is charged with the custody of all stores and issues them as needed. Some ships carry both deck and engine storekeepers.

Fr: *Magasinier;* Ger: *Lageraufseher.*

STOREROOM. Any space or compartment in which are stowed the various stores and supplies used on board ship.

Fr: *Magasin;* Ger: *Vorratskammer; Vorratsraum.*

STORM. A wind of force 11 on Beaufort's Scale, sometimes accompanied by rain, snow, hail, or lightning, which reaches a velocity of 56 to 65 nautical miles per hour. The terms "cyclone" and "cyclonic storms" are often used interchangeably.

Fr: *Tempête;* Ger: *Sturm.*

See **Law of Storms, Magnetic Storm, Revolving Storm.**

Bigelow, F. H., *Storms, Storm Tracks, etc.;* U. S. Weather Bureau Bulletin no. 20, Washington, 1907.

STORM CANVAS. An expression used to denote the storm staysails, trysails, storm mizzen, double-reefed foresail, fore and main lower topsails, and fore-topmast staysail in a square-rigged ship.

Fr: *Voile de Cape;* Ger: *Sturmsegel.*

STORM COVER. A hinged cover made of sheet iron fitted over stokehold fiddley openings to cover the gratings in heavy weather.

STORM JIB. A small jib of heavy flax canvas used as a storm sail. Also called spitfire jib. It is generally of Scottish or diagonal cut.

Fr: *Tourmentin;* Ger: *Sturmkluver.*

STORM MIZZEN. A triangular sail used in stormy weather instead of the usual gaff mizzen.

Fr: *Artimon de Cape;* Ger: *Sturmbesahn.*

STORMOGRAPH.

See **Barograph.**

STORM OIL. Oil used in case of emergency to prevent the breaking of waves and to some extent to prevent them from forming. Also called wave-quelling oil, sea-quelling oil. It is used in heavy weather when boarding a wreck, hoisting and lowering boats, for taking a disabled vessel in tow, when crossing rollers or surf on a bar. Thick and heavy animal and vegetable oils such as sperm, linseed, cottonseed, and olive oils are the best. Mineral oils are less effective.

Fr: *Huile de Filage;* Ger: *Wellenöl.*

See **Oil Bag.**

The oil should be released in a slow and steady flow. In ordinary merchant vessels it is usually distributed from a waste pipe on each bow, either by filling the closet bowls with oakum and oil, or by placing in the bowls a can with a tap slightly open so as to ensure a slow drip. Another way is to use a canvas bag hung over the side at any point where it is found to give the best results. The quantity used need not exceed a few gallons even for a large ship. The efficacy of oil is chiefly due to the fact that when it spreads over the surface of water, it maintains itself as a distinct layer whose particles do not take up the orbital motion of particles of water in the sea waves. The carriage of storm oil is compulsory on all mechanically propelled, seagoing vessels of the United States with a gross tonnage of 200 or more; the quantity ranging from 30 gallons for vessels of 200 tons to 100 gallons for those of 5000 tons or more.

STORM OIL TANK. A metal container placed under the forecastle deck near the stem in some ships for storing storm oil. Each tank (port and starboard) is fitted with a drainpipe leading overboard through the shell plating.

STORM RAIL. A rail of galvanized pipe fitted around the outside of deckhouses accessible to passengers. A similar rail made of mahogany and fitted in passageways of accommodation.

STORM SAIL. A stout sail, generally of No. 1 canvas, and of reduced dimensions for use in heavy weather. A sail made of very stout canvas, of smaller size than the corresponding working sail. Storm sails are usually roped with hemp.

Fr: *Voile de Cape;* Ger: *Sturmsegel.*

STORM SIGNALS. Visual signals hoisted at coastal stations to indicate the approach of gales, and so on.

Fr: *Signaux de Mauvais temps;* Ger: *Sturmsignale; Sturmwarnungssignale.*

Niblack, A. P., "Summary of Data on Uniformity in Storm Warning Signals," *Hydrographic Review* (Monaco), vol. 3, no. 2 (July, 1926).

STORM STAYSAIL. A staysail of reduced dimensions for use in heavy weather.

Day Signals

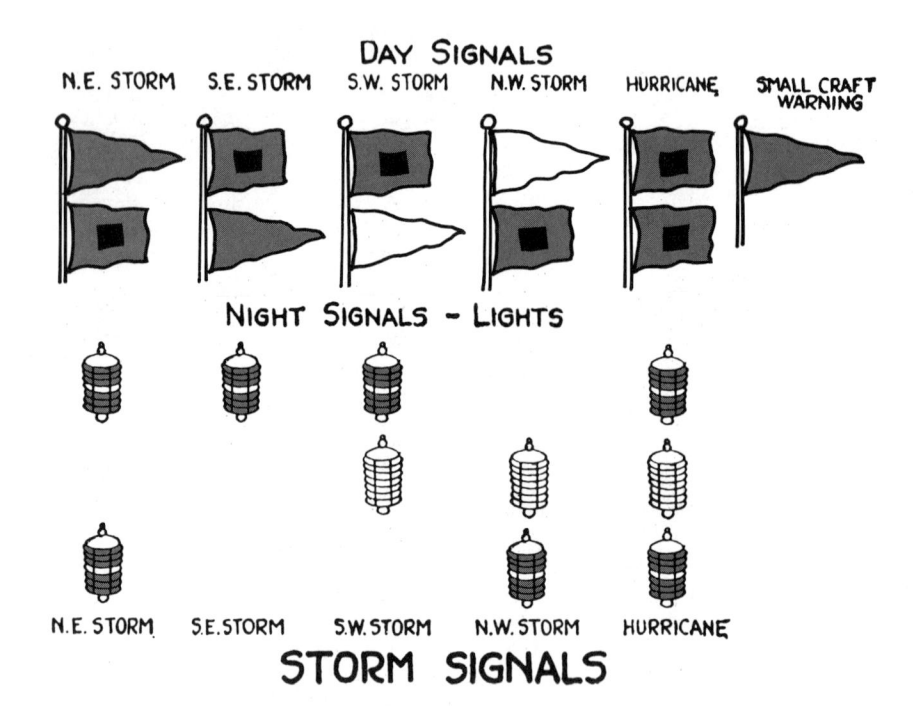

N.E. STORM S.E. STORM S.W. STORM N.W. STORM HURRICANE SMALL CRAFT WARNING

Night Signals – Lights

N.E. STORM S.E. STORM S.W. STORM N.W. STORM HURRICANE

STORM SIGNALS

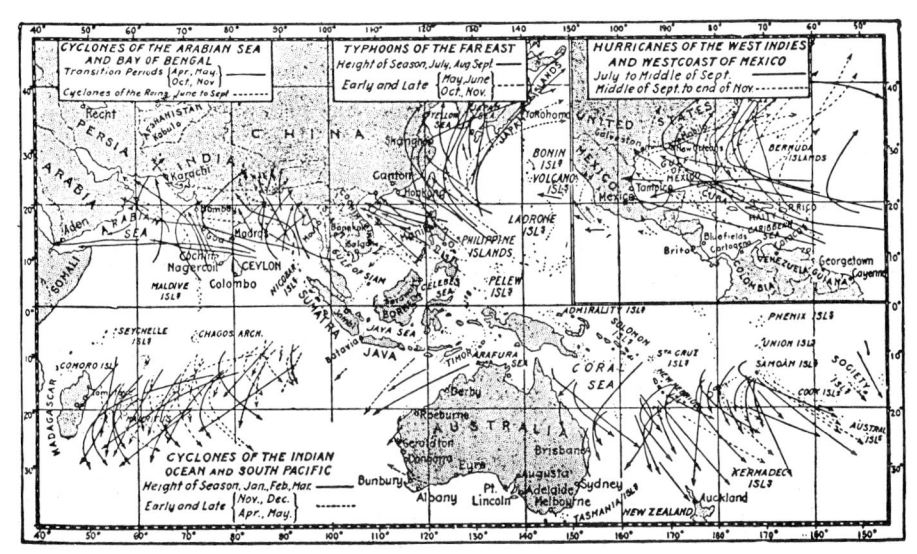

Storm Tracks

Fr: *Voile d'étai de Cape;* Ger: *Sturm Stagsegel.*

STORM TIDE. A rise of sea level which precedes or accompanies a tropical revolving storm.

STORM TRACK. The line of progressive motion followed by the path or vortex of a cyclonic storm. In the Northern Hemisphere the path follows a right-hand curve; in the Southern Hemisphere, a left-hand one.

Fr: *Trajectoire;* Ger: *Sturmbahn.*

STORM TRYSAIL. A triangular or quadrilateral loose-footed sail carried abaft the mast, made of strong flax canvas, and used in heavy weather in lieu of the ordinary working sails when there is too much wind for the latter, even if fully reefed. Cringles are worked in the luff tabling and the sail is fastened to the mast by parrel lines suitably spaced.

Fr: *Artimon de Cape; Dériveur;* Ger: *Sturm Treisegel.*

STORM VALVE. A simple form of check valve placed at the end of soil or scupper pipes discharging through the ship's side near the waterline. It allows the water to discharge overboard but prevents sea water from backing up in the pipe. Also called flap valve, clack box.

Fr: *Boîte à Clapet;* Ger: *Sturmventil; Selbstschlussventil.*

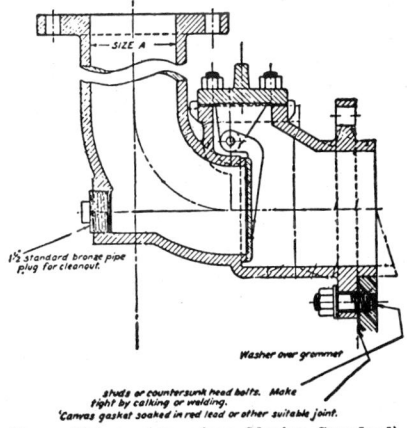

Storm Valve. (*American Marine Standard*)

STOSH. See **Ground Bait.**

STOVE IN. Said of the outside of a ship or boat when pushed in or broken in by accident.

Fr: *Défoncé;* Ger: *Eingestossen.*

STOW. 1. To furl or roll up as a sail, an awning, and so forth.

Fr: *Serrer;* Ger: *Festmachen.*

2. To arrange compactly the goods or cargo in a ship's hold, and 'tween decks.

Fr: *Arrimer;* Ger: *Stauen.*

3. To put anything away for sea. To put gear in its proper place.

Fr: *Saisir;* Ger: *Wegstauen.*

STOWAGE. 1. Stowage is that important branch of the art of seamanship which applies to the loading of a vessel and has for its aims the handling, placing, and packing of goods, in such a manner as to ensure the preservation of crew and ship from danger or injury arising from the manner in which the cargo is stowed, the protection of the cargo space from damage, loss or deterioration; the economy of cargo space on which depends the vessel's earning capacity; and the highest possible rate of port speed, that is, the rate at which the vessel is capable of loading and discharging her cargo.

Fr: *Arrimage;* Ger: *Stauung; Stauen.*

2. The amount of cubic space occupied by a ton weight of cargo when actually laden in the ship's hold. Stowage consists of measurement plus breakage.

Fr: *Encombrement;* Ger: *Stauraum.*

3. A support or fastening for any gear such as anchors or ship's boats (U. S.).

See **Broken Stowage, Deep Stowage, Overstowage, Short Stowage, Small Stowage.**

Bridger and Watts, *The Stowage of Cargo,* London, 1927; Hillcoat, C. H., *Notes on the Stowage of Ships,* London, 1918; Leeming, J., *Modern Ship Stowage,* Washington, 1942; Stevens, R. W., *Stowage of Ships and Their Cargoes,* London, 1894; Thomas, R. E., *Stowage,* London, 1928.

STOWAGE CERTIFICATE. A certificate handed to the master by a sworn surveyor in which it is stated that the cargo has been stowed properly and efficiently.

Fr: *Certificat d'Arrimage; Procès Verbal de bon Arrimage;* Ger: *Stauungsattest; Stauungsschein.*

STOWAGE FACTOR. The figure which expresses the number of cubic feet occupied by one ton of 2240 pounds of a commodity when stowed and dunnaged in the usual manner. This factor is computed by dividing 2240 pounds by the weight, in pounds, of a cubic foot of this particular commodity.

Fr: *Coefficient d'Arrimage;* Ger: *Raumbedarf.*

STOWAWAY. A person hiding on a departing vessel, for the purpose of obtaining free passage or passage without authorization.

Fr: *Passager Clandestin;* Ger: *Blinder Passagier; Überschmuggler; Einschleicher.*

STOW NET. A conical bag net set in a moving body of water and used for the capture of shrimp, sprat, and herring.

Fr: *Chalut à l'étalage;* Ger: *Ankerhamen.*

The stow net is fastened to the anchor chain of a vessel moored in a tideway and may be as much as 200 ft. long. Its mouth is held open by 2 spars 20 to 30 ft. long called balks. The gape or vertical distance between the balks is from 5 to 6 fathoms. The net itself is made in 3 or 4 long sections joined along their selvages.

STRAIGHT BILL OF LADING. A nonnegotiable shipping document which provides that a shipment is to be delivered direct to the party whose name is shown as consignee.

Fr: *Connaissement Nominatif; Connaissement à Personne Dénommée;* Ger: *Nicht indossables Konnossement; Namenskonnossement.*

STRAIGHT BOW. A rectilinear wedge-shaped bow, raked, or perpendicular to the water plane, in distinction to a clipper bow or spoon bow. Also called straight stem.

Fr: *Etrave Droite;* Ger: *Senkrechter Bug; Gerader Steven.*

See **Clipper Bow, Spoon Bow.**

STRAIGHT DECK. A wooden deck in which all planks run parallel to the fore-and-aft line of the boat.

Fr: *Pont à Bordages Rectilignes.*

See **Laid Deck.**

STRAIGHT FRAMED SHIP. A simplified form of hull whose transverse sections are completely delineated by straight lines, and in which such features of the shell surface as round of bilge flare, stern hollow, and clubbing of forefoot, are practically eliminated in order to simplify construction. It has no sheer and the length of parallel middle body is about 45 per cent of total length.

The constructional advantages claimed for this type of hull form include the possibility of fabrication of all steel work in bridge-building yards; greater speed of construction as compared with curved frame hulls; elimination of most of the fairing process in the mold loft; simplification of repair after damage; better riveting, owing to more satisfactory marking off; superior steering qualities. During the 1917–1921 period this system was put into practical use in various types of cargo vessels ranging from small 1200 ton coasters to cargo liners of over 12,000 tons deadweight. In World

War II, it was not found necessary to resort to this type of construction in order to build the great number of cargo ships finally constructed.

Robb, A. M., "Straight-Frame Ships," Institution of Engineers and Shipbuilders in Scotland, *Transactions*, vol. 68 (1925).

STRAIGHT-NECK RIVET. Rivet with shank of uniform diameter used with drilled holes only. Also called straight-shank rivet.

Fr: *Rivet à Fût Droit;* Ger: *Geradeschaft-Niet.*

STRAIGHT OAR. An oar with straight blade as distinguished from a spoon oar.

Fr: *Aviron Droit;* Ger: *Gerades Ruder.*

STRAIGHT TIMBER. Timber which has no curvature, such as used for keels, keelsons, shelfs, sternposts.

Fr: *Bois Droit;* Ger: *Gerades Holz.*

STRAIN. To undergo structural distortion under force, as the hull of a ship in a high sea.

Fr: *Travailler;* Ger: *Sich Begeben; Arbeiten.*

STRAIT. A relatively narrow waterway between two large bodies of water. In the absence of special agreement to the contrary the waters of a strait are territorial waters in those parts where the width of the strait does not exceed 6 nautical miles.

Fr: *Détroit;* Ger: *Strasse; Meerenge.*

See **Territorial Straits.**

STRAKE. A range of planks or plates abutting against each other and extending the whole length of the ship.

Fr: *Virure;* Ger: *Gang; Plankengang; Plattengang.*

See **Air Strake, Binding Strake, Bilge Strake, Block Strake, Bottom Strake, Broad Strake, Clamp Strake, Closing Strake, Diminishing Strakes, Drop Strake, Garboard Strake, Inner Strake, Knuckle Strake, Landing Strake, Limber Strake, Lock Strake, Nib Strake, Outer Strake, Rubbing Strake, Sand Strake, Sheer Strake, Shutter Strake, Thick Strake, Wash Strake.**

STRAKE BOOK. A book used in shipyards in which the ordered dimensions and marks of each ship plate are indicated.

STRAND. 1. The shore or beach of the sea or ocean. Land bordering a sea or river.

Fr: *Estran;* Ger: *Strand; Ufer.*

2. One of the component parts which when twisted or laid up together form a rope. Strands are made of yarns or wires and are twisted together in a direction opposite to that in which the yarns are twisted.

Fr: *Toron;* Ger: *Ducht; Kardeel; Litze; Faser.*

See **Seizing Strand.**

STRAND (to). 1. To drift or be driven ashore. To run aground. Stranding occurs when a ship takes the ground not in the ordinary course of navigation but by accident or the force of wind or sea, and remains stationary for some time. The stranding of a ship within the meaning of a marine policy does not include the taking of the ground in a tidal harbor in the place where it is intended it should, even if in so doing the bottom of the vessel strikes against some hard substance by which it is damaged.

Fr: *Etre Jeté à la Côte; Echouer;* Ger: *Stranden.*

2. To break one or more strands in a rope by chafing or by excessive straining.

STRANDED WRECK. A wreck which has some part of it projecting above water.

STRAND FISHERIES. Fishery pursued from the shore with the use of open boats only.

Fr: *Pêche à l'Estran;* Ger: *Strandfischerei.*

STRANDING. The destruction or loss of of a vessel by its being sunk or broken up by the violence of the sea or by its striking or stranding upon a rock, shoal, or the like. The term stranding refers most particularly to the driving or running aground of a vessel. It may be either accidental or voluntary. Voluntary stranding takes place where the ship is run aground either to preserve her from a worse fate, or for some fraudulent purpose. In marine insurance a "touch and go" is not considered a stranding. In order to constitute a stranding the ship must be stationary for a certain length of time.

Fr: *Naufrage;* Ger: *Schiffbruch.*

STRAP (U. S.), STROP (G. B.). 1. A ring or rope or band of iron put round a block or deadeye suspending it or holding it in place.

2. A piece of rope with the ends spliced together used for attaching a tackle to anything or for slinging any weight to be lifted.

Fr: *Estrope; Erse;* Ger: *Stropp.*

See **Bow Strap, Parting Strap, Selvagee Strap, Splitting Strap, Bosom Piece, Belly Strap, Head Strap, Jaw Strap, Kicking Strap, Saddle Strap.**

STRAP (to) (U. S.). To fasten a strap of rope or iron around a block, a deadeye, a bull's-eye, and so on. In Great Britain called to strop.

Fr: *Estroper;* Ger: *Stroppen.*

STRAP-BORED BLOCK. A block with its sheave entirely enclosed except for the holes left on each side for reeving the rope. These blocks were used for clew lines and clew garnets on topsails and courses to prevent fouling by reef points. Also called secret block, clew-line block.

Fr: *Poulie de Cargue Point.*

STRAPPER (U. S.). In the construction of wooden ships, one who ties frames or deck beams by the application of steel or iron straps placed diagonally across these members. The straps are set in so that the face of the strap comes flush with the face of the frame or beam.

STRATO-CUMULUS. Large globular masses or rolls of dark clouds often covering the whole sky, especially in winter. It generally appears as a gray layer irregularly broken into masses, of which the edge is often formed of smaller masses, often of wavy appearance like alto-cumulus. Sometimes it characteristically appears as great rolls arranged in parallel lines, pressed close together. Blue skies may be seen through the lighter intervening spaces. In Great Britain called roll-cumulus.

Fr: *Stratocumulus;* Ger: *Wulst-Cumulus.*

See **Alto-Cumulus, Cumulus.**

STRATUS. A uniform layer of cloud resembling a fog, but not resting on the ground. When this sheet is broken into irregular shreds and patches by wind, or by mountain peaks, it is called fracto-stratus.

See **Alto-Stratus, Cirro-Stratus, Strato-Cumulus.**

STRAY MARK. A conspicuous rag of bunting placed on the log line at 10 to 12 fathoms from the log chip to mark off the stray line. Also called **Fore runner.**

Fr: *Marque de houache;* Ger: *Vorlauf Merkzeichen.*

STRAY LINE. 1. The unmarked part of a log line which is allowed to run out to let the log chip go clear of the vessel before beginning to count.

2. Any similarly unmeasured initial portion of a metered line or wire, such as an oceanographic sampling wire.

Fr: *Houache;* Ger: *Vorlauf.*

STREAM. 1. A course of water flowing along a bed in the earth.

2. A current in the sea formed by the action of the wind.

Fr: *Courant;* Ger: *Strom; Strömung.*

See **Gulf Stream, Japan Stream, Tidal Stream.**

STREAM (to). To shoot overboard as a patent log, an anchor buoy, and so forth.

Fr: *Filer;* Ger: *Werfen.*

STREAM ANCHOR. An anchor stowed at the stern and employed with a bower anchor in narrow waterways where there is no room for the vessel to swing with the tide. Also called stern anchor. It is usually a light anchor, its weight being from 25 to 50 per cent that of a bower. It is occasionally used as a kedge anchor and is about twice as heavy as the latter. Stream anchors in modern vessels are frequently of the stockless type.

Fr: *Ancre de Détroit; Ancre de Touée;* Ger: *Stromanker; Heckanker.*

STREAM CHAIN. A close-link chain used with a stream anchor. Stream chain is occasionally used as anchor or mooring chain on small vessels.

Fr: *Chaîne de Touée;* Ger: *Stromankerkette.*

STREAM CURRENT. The accumulation of a drift current into a collective mass by the effect of some obstacles such as islands or confined outlets, the mass running off by its own gravity in a direction imposed upon it by the obstacle. Stream currents are frequently very heavy.

Ger: *Seestrom.*

STREAMING. A tugboat charge for assisting a vessel out of its berth and into the channel. The opposite of "docking."

STREAMLINED RUDDER. Also called hydrofoil rudder. A plated rudder which, owing to its hydrofoil shape, produces the minimum resistance in passing through the water. Whereas with a flat-plate rudder a considerable loss in efficiency is caused by the propeller, especially in single-screw vessels, with a streamlined rudder, there is little interference with the slip stream. The best results, according to tests carried out in model tanks, are obtained with

streamline sections having a thickness between 0.2 and 0.25 of the breadth in the direction of the stream. Streamlined, plated rudders are also designed to lessen the load on the rudderpost, on account of their buoyancy.
Fr: *Gouvernail Profilé;* Ger: *Strombetätigtes Ruder; Stromlinienruder.*
STREAMLINE WAKE. Wake due to the streamline motion of the water closing in behind the stern.
STREAMLINING. As applied to the superstructures of modern fast passenger vessels, the design and installation of deck houses and erections of streamline form. This involves the elimination and rounding off, or fairing, or sharp corners and excrescences, with a view to decreased wind resistance, improved efficiency, and eye appeal.
Fr: *Profilage; Carénage.*
STREAM NET. A fixed wall of netting held by stakes along the shore, into which the fish thrust their heads. Owing to the opening of their gills they are unable to withdraw and so become entangled.
Fr: *Filet de Barrage;* Ger: *Sperrnetz.*
STRENGTH DECK. The uppermost complete deck which offers resistance to longitudinal bending. The uppermost deck incorporated into, and forming an integral part of the longitudinal girder within the half-length amidships. By extension, any continuous deck which is accounted for as part of the ship girder.
Fr: *Pont de Résistance;* Ger: *Gürtungsdeck; Festigkeitsdeck.*
STRESS OF WEATHER. Also press of weather. **1.** Continued and sustained violence of the elements.
2. Constraint imposed by continued bad weather.
Fr: *Gros Temps; Temps Forcé;* Ger: *Unwetter; Schweres Wetter; Ungestümes Wetter.*
STRETCH. The reach or extent of progression on one tack of a ship under sail.
Fr: *Bord;* Ger: *Strecke.*
STRETCH (to). To sail by the wind under all sail.
Fr: *Torcher la Toile;* Ger: *Prangen.*
STRETCHER. Thwartship pieces of wood against which oarsmen brace their feet. Also called boat stretcher, footboard.
Fr: *Marchepied de nage;* Ger: *Fusslatte; Fussleiste; Fusstock; Fussbrett.*
See **Awning Stretcher.**
STRETCHER CLEAT. A cleat fitted at bottom of a rowboat and supplied with notches for holding the foot board in place.
STREUERBOOT. A one-mast open boat engaged in the flounder fisheries with a dragnet called *Streuer,* on the Pomeranian coast. The hull is flat bottomed with clinker planking. Leeboards are provided. Length 24 ft. Breadth 8½ ft. Depth 3 ft. (Average.)
STRICKWADENBOOT. Half-decked seine boat from the coast of Pomerania. The hull is built with keel, clinker planking, and centerboard. The rig consists of one mast. Length over-all 23 ft. Breadth 9½ ft. Depth 3 ft. 4 in. (Average.)
STRIKE. 1. A topmast is said to be struck when after swaying and taking out the fid it is sent down on deck and the rigging taken off.
Fr: *Dépasser;* Ger: *Streichen.*
2. To lower, dip, or haul down, especially when referring to a flag mast or yard, or the ensign in token of submission.
Fr: *Amener;* Ger: *Streichen.*
3. A ship strikes when it in any way touches the bottom. To run ashore or aground. To run upon a bank, a shoal, and so on.
Fr: *Talonner;* Ger: *Aufstossen; Stossen.*
STRIKE BELOW. To lower into the hold as cargo or any other object. To lower below the upper deck and stow any article as, in naval vessels, to strike ammunition below.
STRIKE CLAUSE. A clause inserted in bill of lading and charter parties when labor difficulties are foreseen or probable, by which the ship is not responsible for loss, damage, or delay caused by or arising out of strikes or labor disturbances.
Fr: *Clause de Grève;* Ger: *Streikklausel.*
STRIKE MAST.
See **Collapsible Mast.**
STRIKE OUT. To hoist up from below deck and out on a pier or quay, as cargo.
STRIKER. 1. In the Menhaden fisheries, the man who in a small boat rows in the direction of the school which has been sighted by the lookout men aloft. Also called striker man. Upon resighting the fish he signals with an oar their location and direction of travel to the captain. He then rows until he is in such a position that the fish are between his boat and the boats which carry the seine. When in that position he endeavors to halt the progress of the school by splashing the water with his oars,

thus preventing their escape while the seine is being set.

2. The man assigned to the pulpit of a sword-fishing vessel, who strikes the fish with the harpoon.

See **Dolphin Striker**.

STRIKER BOAT. Name given on the Atlantic coast of the United States to a small, round-bottom rowboat very light in weight and exceptionally seaworthy, with sharp bow and square stern used in the Menhaden fisheries, for keeping track of the schools of fish and for indicating to the seine boats the direction in which they are moving. Also called drive boat. Length 12 ft. Breadth 4½ ft. Depth 1 ft. 9 in. amidships. (Approximate.)

The hull of these boats is built of white cedar and they are rowed with a pair of 7-ft. oars by the striker man, who stands on a small platform while rowing.

On the Pacific coast the striker boat, also called bait boat or chum boat, is a decked motorboat with a length of 35 to 40 ft., used for the capture of mackerel by means of hook and line. The fishing gear consists of a short bamboo pole, a short line with wire leader, and a feather lure (the striker) with a barbless hook.

STRIKE THE BELL. Expression used at sea to denote the divisions of the daily time from their being marked by bells which are struck every half hour, the term "bell" being employed aboard ship as "o'clock" is ashore.

Fr: *Piquer;* Ger: *Schlagen.*

STRING. A term used in the trawl-line fisheries. On the East Coast each string is composed of a 60-fathom ground line to which are attached the *gangings* spaced 4 fathoms apart, each one having a length of 2 fathoms. Eight strings (128 hooks) form a basket or skate of line. In the Pacific coast halibut fisheries, the term is used to denote several skates or trawl-line fastened together.

See **Drawing String, "G" String**.

STRINGER. Fore-and-aft strength member girder. There are two sets of these girders in the framing of the usual cargo ship, the keelsons or longitudinals at the bottom, and the side stringers on the sides above the bilges.

Fr: *Serre;* Ger: *Stringer.*

See **Hold Stringer, Panting Stringer, Poppet Stringer, Side Stringer**.

STRINGER BAR. An angle bar connecting the stringer plate of a deck to the shell or frames.

Fr: *Cornière Gouttière;* Ger: *Stringerwinkel.*

STRINGER LUG. Short lengths of angle bar forming the connection between 'tween-deck stringer plate and shell plating. Also called shell lug, chock.

Fr: *Taquet de Gouttière;* Ger: *Aufklotzungwinkel; Kurzer Stringerwinkel.*

STRINGER PLATE. The outer strake of plating on a deck or the plates attached to the top flanges of any tier of beams at the sides of a vessel. Also called deck stringer. These plates assist in connecting the deck beams to the sides of the ship. They stiffen the shell plating in the vicinity of the stringers and contribute to the longitudinal strength of the hull.

Fr: *Tôle Gouttière;* Ger: *Stringerplatte.*

STRINGPIECE MAN. In a stevedore gang, one of the longshoremen stationed on the edge of the pier at the stringpiece to assist in handling the sling loads to or from the vessel at the end of the hook movement. There are generally two stringpiece men to each gang.

STRIP. To remove all rigging from a ship, a mast, or a spar. Also called cast off.

Fr: *Dégarnir;* Ger: *Abtakeln.*

STRIPPER.

See **Stripping Line**.

STRIPPING LINE. An auxiliary suction system in an oil tanker used for draining residual oil when the main suction line ceases to be effective. Also called stripper. It runs fore and aft, with a suction in each tank, and is connected to a stripping pump.

Fr: *Collecteur d'Assèchement;* Ger: *Nachlenzleitung.*

STRIPPING PUMP. A pump of about one fourth the capacity of one main cargo pump fitted in oil tankers to remove the residual oil in the tanks after the main cargo pumps cease to be effective. It is connected to a separate suction line. It is brought into action when the flow of oil to the pump suctions becomes intermittent causing heavy wear and tear on the main pump suctions and discharge valves.

Fr: *Pompe d'Assèchement;* Ger: *Nachlenzpumpe; Jaegerpumpe.*

STRIP PLANKING. A form of carvel planking in which the planks or strips are very narrow (1 in. to 1½ in. wide) and slightly tapered, wedged down close, with the edges fastened to each other. It can be used on any hull form designed for carvel planking. The strips are put on from the keel upward and are narrow enough to be edge-fastened by galvanized wire nails driven parallel to the face of the strip.

With a little paint or marine glue smeared on the edges, the seams become permanently watertight and need no calking. Each strip must be tapered from end to end as the girth of the boat varies from stem to stern. In the event of damage to any of the lower planks it is almost impossible to set in a new plank without taking off (and trimming) all the planks above the damaged area.

STROKE. 1. The type of rowing, or the manner of handling oars, especially with regard to the length, speed, or frequency of motion. The number of dips of the oars in the water within a given time. A single pull of the oar.

The average number of strokes per minute for ship's boats formerly in use were:

Launch	25 to 29
Pinnace	26 to 30
Cutter	31 to 36
Whaler	31 to 36
Gig	24 to 26

Fr: *Nage;* Ger: *Gang; Schlag.*

See **Breast Stroke, Cutter Stroke, Dago Stroke, Feathering Stroke, Galley Stroke, Gig Stroke, Long Stroke.**

2. A rower who pulls an oar nearest the stern in single-banked boats, usually on the port side, and sets the stroke for all the rowers. Also called strokesman or stroke oar.

Fr: *Chef de Nage;* Ger: *Schlagmann; Schlagriem.*

STRONGBACK. 1. Portable wooden fore-and-aft beam extending from stem to stern on a lifeboat, over which the boat cover is stretched.

2. Bar placed across a cargo door or port to secure it in a closed position. In general, a bar placed across any access cover to assist in holding it in the secured position.

Fr: *Traverse;* Ger: *Betingbalken.*

See **Deck Strongback, Hatch Beam.**

STRONG BREEZE. A strong wind with an average velocity of 24 nautical miles per hour and a pressure of 2.3 lb. per square foot. Beaufort's scale no. 6.

Fr: *Vent Frais;* Ger: *Steife Brise.*

STRONG GALE. A continuous wind moving with a velocity between 41 and 47 nautical miles per hour. Beaufort's scale no. 9.

Fr: *Coup de Vent;* Ger: *Sturm.*

STRONG ROOM. A specially constructed compartment in passenger liners for storing valuable cargo, such as bullion, silk, species, and the like. It is usually situated low in the ship, where it is not readily accessible. Adjacent compartments are usually so arranged that they seldom require to be opened.

Fr: *Soute aux Valeurs;* Ger: *Geldraum.*

STRUCTURAL BULKHEAD. A bulkhead, generally water- or oiltight, which forms one of the boundaries of the main compartments and contributes to the strength of the hull. Its depth usually extends through several decks.

STRUM PLATE. A plate fitted in pump suctions, deck scuppers, sea cocks, having a number of small holes in it to allow water to pass, but designed to stop foreign matter that would clog the piping. Also called rose, strainer plate.

Fr: *Tôle Crépinée;* Ger: *Siebplatte.*

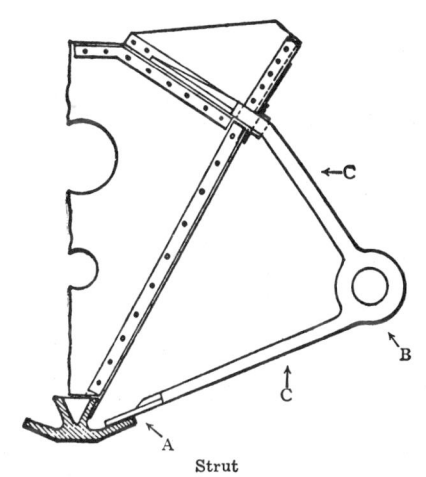

Strut
A. Palm   B. Barrel   C. Arm or Leg

STRUT. Bracket supporting the outboard end of a propeller shaft in twin- or multiple-screw vessels having propeller shafts fitted off the center line. Also called propeller strut, propeller bracket, shaft strut. It usually consists of a barrel fitted with a bushing to form a bearing for the shaft, connected to the shell by one or two streamlined arms. The inboard end of each arm is fitted with a palm for attachment to the shell.

Fr: *Support d'arbre;* Ger: *Wellenträger; Wellenbock.*

See **Single Leg Propeller Strut, Two Leg Propeller Strut.**

STRUT STAY. See **Jackstay.**

STUD. A wedge of cast steel inserted when cold into the heated link of anchor cable and shrunk into place. Its effect upon the distribution of stress is to reduce the maximum tensile stress by about 20 per cent and the compressive stress by about 50 per cent. Also called cable stud or stay pin.

Fr: *Etai;* Ger: *Stütze.*

STUD BOLT. A bolt threaded at both ends. One end is screwed into a tapped hole in the base structure to which attachment is to be made. Stud bolts threaded at one end only and attached to the base structure by welding, have come into general use.

Fr: *Goujon;* Ger: *Schraubenbolzen.*

STUDDING. The vertical timbers or framing of a wooden deck house, fitted between the sill and the plate.

STUDDING SAIL. One of the light sails set from studding sail booms, which are portable extensions of yardarms. Also called stunsail. They are extended upon different yards of the fore- and mainmast and are named according to their stations as lower, topmast, and topgallant studding sails. Royal studding sails were sometimes carried. They are controlled by halyards leading through jewel blocks at the yardarms, outhauls, and sheets. They are very seldom seen nowadays. Studding sails are all quadrilateral in shape except the lower ones, which are occasionally triangular.

Fr: *Bonnette;* Ger: *Leesegel.*

See **Flying Studding Sail.**

STUDDING SAIL BOOM. A spar that rigs in and out upon a lower topsail or topgallant yard for stretching the foot of a studding sail.

Fr: *Bout-dehors de Bonnette;* Ger: *Leesegelspieren.*

STUDDING SAIL HALYARD BEND. A bend made by taking a round turn with the end coming around the standing part, then under both turns and tucking over and under the turns.

Fr: *Noeud de Drisse de Bonnette;* Ger: *Leesegelfallstich.*

STUDDING SAIL TACK BEND. A bend for securing a rope round a spar. It will remain secure only so long as a strain is kept on the line. Also called buntline hitch.

STUDDING SAIL YARD. The spar to which the head of a studding sail is bent.

Fr: *Vergue de Bonnette;* Ger: *Leesegelraa.*

STUD LINK. Link in chain cable fitted with a stud or stay pin across it. Stud links are stronger than studless ones and are less susceptible to kinking. Also called studded link. When made of cast steel the stud is cast integral with the link.

Fr: *Maille à Étai;* Ger: *Stegglied; Stegschake.*

Stud Link Chain Cable
A. Common link
B. Enlarged link
C. Long stud link
E. End link
D. Joining shackle

STUD LINK CHAIN. Chain in which each link has a short distance piece known as a stud or stay pin worked at its mid-length at right angles with its major axis, in order to maintain the shape of the link. It has been proved by experiments that the resistance of stud link chain is about 20 per cent higher than that of open link chain. It has the further advantages that it does not foul so readily and offers greater resistance to cross stresses and blows tending to deform or rupture the chain by forces other than those of pure tension.

Fr: *Chaîne Étançonnée;* Ger: *Stegkette.*

STUDSAIL. See **Bonnet.**

STUFF. A mixture of tallow, turpentine, etc., applied to the spars or planking of wooden vessels. Turpentine and resin is used for lower masts, tallow on the topmasts. For the sides: turpentine, oil and varnish; for the bottom: tallow, sulfur and resin. Black lead and water are used in fishing vessels to give smooth sides.

Fr: *Coroi;* Ger: *Schmiere.*

See **Diminishing Stuff, Lanyard Stuff, Nettle Stuff, Ratline Stuff, Small Stuff, Seizing Stuff, Serving Stuff, Thick Stuff.**

STUFFING BOX. A device designed to prevent leakage around a moving part that passes through a hole in a vessel or in a compartment containing water, steam, or oil. It consists of a tubular box, and a packing gland or follower to compress the contained packing between the moving part and the stuffing box proper.

Fr: *Presse-étoupe;* Ger: *Stopfbüchse.*

STUFFING BOX RECESS. A recess provided at the afterend of the shaft tunnel to give the necessary space for withdrawing and manipulating the propeller shaft. Its length is usually from 4 to 5 frame spaces, being based on the space required for such an operation. Also called tunnel recess.

Er: *Niche de Presse Etoupe;* Ger: *Wellentunnel Nische.*

See **Thrust Recess.**

STUMP MAST. Short upper mast without pole.

Ger: *Stumpfermast.*

STUMP POLE. A mast pole shortened to minimum length above the uppermost eyes of the rigging.

Ger: *Stumpfertopp.*

STUMP TOPGALLANT MAST. A topgallant mast which ends close to the shoulder of the spar. There is no pole, or merely a very short one.

Ger: *Stumpferbramstänge.*

STUMPY.

See **Thames Sailing Barge.**

SUBASSEMBLY. In shipbuilding a portion of the structure of the hull assembled into a unit, usually to a high state of completion.

SUBCHARTER. An agreement made by the charterer of a vessel to sublet in part or totally the said vessel to other persons. It is an independent contract between charterer and subcharterer in no wise connected with the original charter except as regards the determination of the charterer's right to subcharter. It does not create any contractual relationship between subcharterer and owner of vessel.

Fr: *Sous-Affrètement;* Ger: *Unterverfrachtung; Untervercharterung.*

SUBDIVISION. The partitioning of the hull's internal volume transversely, and longitudinally into a number of compartments in order to reduce the quantity of water which may gain access to it through stranding, collision, or any other accidental cause. Also called compartmentation.

Fr: *Compartimentage; Cloisonnement;* Ger: *Schotteneinteilung; Schottenstellung; Wasserdichte Unterteilung.*

The question of subdivision is of primary importance in passenger vessels, where a proper system of watertight bulkheads can be instrumental in keeping a ship afloat after serious damage. Following the loss of the "Titanic" in 1912 new regulations for the subdivision of passenger vessels were drawn up by an International Conference in 1914. The 1914–1918 War having prevented the ratification of the 1914 Conference regulations by several Governments, another Conference for the Safety of Life at Sea took place in London in 1929 and its provisions now apply to all ships belonging to countries of the signatory Governments. The contracting Governments to the 1929 Convention for the Safety of Life at Sea, are: Commonwealth of Australia, Belgium, Canada, Denmark, Spain, Irish Free State, United States of America, Finland, France, Germany, United Kingdom of Great Britain, India, Italy, Japan, Norway, Netherlands, Sweden, Union of Socialist Soviet Republics.

Anderson, A. C. F., "The Subdivision of Large Passenger Steamers," Institution of Naval Architects (London), *Transactions,* vol. 65 (1923); Bates and Wanless, "Subdivision of United States Maritime Vessels," Society of Naval Architects and Marine Engineers (New York), *Transactions,* vol. 50 (1942); Biedermann, P., "Schotteinteilung bei Frachtschiffen der Schutzdeckbauart," Verein Deutsche Ingenieure, *Zeitschrift,* vol. 80, no. 5 (1936); Tawresey, J. G., "Safety at Sea," Society of Naval Architects and Marine Engineers (New York), *Transactions,* vol. 44 (1936).

SUBDIVISION DRAFT. The draft of a passenger vessel when immersed to her subdivision load line assigned in accordance with the rules of the International Convention of 1929 for the Safety of Life at Sea.

Fr: *Tirant d'eau de Compartimentage;* Ger: *Schottentiefgang.*

SUBDIVISION LENGTH. The length between perpendiculars measured at the extremities of the subdivision load line.

Fr: *Longueur de Cloisonnement;* Ger: *Abteilungslänge.*

SUBDIVISION LOAD LINE. The waterline corresponding to the maximum draft, beyond which a ship cannot be loaded and still maintain the degree of subdivision required by the service for which it is designed.

Fr: *Ligne de Charge de Cloisonnement;* Ger: *Abteilungsladelinie; Schotten Ladelinie.*

SUBJUNIOR OFFICER (U. S.). A student officer who has completed his theoretical work in a nautical school and is placed by the Maritime Commission aboard a merchant vessel for a period of two months in order that he may complete his sea experience before qualifying for examination as third mate.

SUBMARINE BELL. A fog-signal device used principally in connection with lightships, buoys, and beacons. It consists of a bell suspended below the surface of the water. The clapper is actuated either electrically, by compressed air or, if fitted to a buoy, by the motion of the buoy. The range of audibility varies from 10 to 30 miles. Also called submarine fog signal.

Fr: *Cloche sous marine;* Ger: *Untersee Glocke.*

Carter, W. R., Submarine Signaling, *American Society of Naval Engineers Journal,* August (1914).

SUBMARINE SIGNAL. Underwater sound signal in which the sound is produced by a submarine bell or by an electric oscillator installed on a coastal station or on a lightvessel. The latter has proved superior to the submarine bell since it gives a sustained sound instead of a single note. The range of submarine signals far exceeds that of aerial signals. There are several systems of receiving apparatus in use. The one most generally adopted consists of two microphones fitted well below the water line on the outer plating of the ship, one on each bow. These microphones are connected to telephone receivers on the navigating bridge, a two-way switch enabling the operator to listen on either side of the ship at will.

Fr: *Signal sous marin;* Ger: *Unterwasser Schallsignal.*

SUBMARINE SENTRY. A sounding machine consisting of a kite towed by the vessel. Because of its construction, it submerges and remains at a constant depth below the surface. Should the vessel pass into shallow water, the trigger, on touching the bottom, is dislodged and the kite rises to the surface, sounding a bell or gong on board.

Ger: *Lotscheit; Tiefenmelder.*

SUBMERGED SCREW LOG. An electric log consisting of a seacock or valve fitted on the ship's bottom. Also called submerged speed indicator. Through the seacock protrudes a composition fitting having one opening facing forward for the admission of water, another opening facing aft for the escape of water. Between these two openings a small rotator or propeller of extreme sensitiveness is placed. This is set in motion by the slightest flow of passing water, thus responding to any movement of the vessel or any change of speed. The submerged mechanism is so arranged that a contact occurs at a given number of revolutions of the rotator. Each time a contact is made an electric impulse is transmitted to an instrument box placed on the navigating bridge where, by means of a make and break arrangement, it is repeated in synchronism with the submerged mechanism and is indicated on a dial or distance recorder. The whole of the apparatus which protrudes through the ship's bottom can at any time be drawn up into the interior of the ship, and, after closing the seacock, can be removed for examination. The best known logs of this type are the Chernikeeff, Forbes, and Nicholson's logs.

See **Pitometer Log.**

SUBMERSIBLE PUMP. A portable centrifugal pump actuated by an integral electric motor, the whole assembly being capable of functioning when entirely submerged. This type of pump is included in the statutory equipment of oceangoing passenger vessels. The source of power must be situated above the bulkhead deck.

Fr: *Moto-pompe électrique submersible;* Ger: *Tauchpumpe; Notlenzpumpe.*

SUBPERMANENT MAGNETISM. The magnetism in the steel and hard iron of a ship, which acts like a permanent magnet. The metal becomes magnetized during the shipbuilding process, since it lies in the earth's magnetic field, and is subjected to stresses while being formed, bent, and riveted or welded. It causes semicircular deviation.

Fr: *Magnétisme Sub-Permanent;* Ger: *Halbfester Magnetismus.*

See **Deviation, Semicircular Deviation.**

SUBPUNCHING (U. S.). The process of punching rivet holes a size or two smaller than their final diameter and reaming them out to full size after assembling and bolting up to adjacent structural parts. Also called small punching.

SUBROGATION. In marine insurance, the act by which an underwriter, having settled a loss, is entitled to place himself in the position of the insured, to the extent of acquiring all the rights and remedies in respect of the loss which the insured may have possessed, either in the nature of proceedings for compensation or recovery in the name of the insured against third parties, or in obtaining general average contribution thereto.

Fr: *Subrogation;* Ger: *Unterschiebung.*

SUBROGATION CLAUSE. A marine insurance cargo clause which prevents the underwriters from suing the carrier in the name of the insured in order to seek reimbursement on a loss due to the carrier's negligence.

SUBSIDY. General term for financial aid granted by a government to the various branches of its shipping industry either with or without any requirement of special service as compensation. Also called bounty, subvention.

Fr: *Subvention; Prime;* Ger: *Schiffahrtsprämien; Schiffahrtssubvention.*

See **Construction Differential Subsidy, Construction Subsidy, Equipment Subsidy, Mail Subsidy, Navigation Subsidy, Operating Differential Subsidy.**

Saugstad, J. E., "Shipping and Shipbuilding Subsidies, U. S. Bureau of Foreign and Domestic Commerce," Trade Promotion Series, 129, Washington, 1932; Schiedewitz, E. W., Subventionierung der Weltschiffahrt, Hamburg, 1931.

SUBSTITUTE FLAG. A flag used in a code to repeat a signal flag of the same class as that immediately preceding it. Also called repeater. The use of substitutes is to enable the same signal flag to be repeated one or more times in the same group while carrying only one set of flags. In the International Code of Signals there are three substitutes called first, second, and third substitutes. The first substitute always repeats the uppermost signal flag of that class of flags which immediately precedes the substitute. The second substitute repeats the second signal flag counting from the top. The third substitute repeats the third signal flag counting from the top.

Fr: *Substitut;* Ger: *Wiederholungsflagge.*

SUBSTITUTION CLAUSE. A bill of lading clause by which the shipping company is at liberty to carry the goods by the vessel named in the bill of lading or any other vessel either belonging to the company or other persons.

Fr: *Clause de Substitution de Navire;* Ger: *Substitutionsklausel.*

SUCTION. A term commonly applied by seamen and pilots to several distinct hydraulic phenomena associated with moving vessels. These independent actions are:

(1) the direct impulse embodied in the streams of water projected astern by screw or paddle independently of any motion of the ship itself; (2) the direct effect of the mass of water which follows a ship bodily when it is moved slowly through restricted waters; (3) the indirect, or lateral pressure, effect of the fore-and-aft acceleration of the water displaced from bow to stern during normal motion through the water at full speed. In the first two, the force exerted is aligned with the water's motion. In the last, the force developed hydraulically acts at right angles to the line of the water's motion.

Fr: *Suction;* Ger: *Sog.*

See **Bilge Suction.**

Bodilly, R. B., Interaction Between Vessels, New York, 1924; Reeve, S. A., Hydraulic Interaction Between Passing Vessels, *U. S. Naval Institute Proceedings,* vol. 37, 1921.

SUCTION BOX. A cast or built-up box fitted inside the ship's skin below water, for the purpose of supplying sea water to the circulating pump. Also called sea chest, inlet box. A strainer plate is fitted on the opening and the main injection valve is bolted on the inlet side of the chest.

Fr: *Caisse de Prise d'Éau;* Ger: *Saugekasten; Seewasserkasten.*

SUCTION DREDGE. A type of dredge extensively used where the material to be excavated is mud, sand, or other soft matter which can be mixed with water and pumped through pipes. Also called hydraulic dredge, pump dredge.

Fr: *Drague Suceuse;* Ger: *Saugebagger.*

The excavating machinery consists of a suction pipe which can be lowered through a well or over the side or end of the hull; a centrifugal pump for sucking or drawing a stream of water through the suction pipe, and a discharge pipe through which the pump discharges the water thus sucked in. The end of the suction pipe is lowered to the soft bottom and partly buries its end in the material. In most dredges of this type the end of the suction pipe is provided with revolving cutters or with water jets to loosen the material so that it will be more easily drawn into the suction pipe. The discharge pipe may lead to hoppers in the dredge or it may be extended to the shore and discharged at some chosen point.

SUE AND LABOR CLAUSE. A clause printed in policies of marine insurance. The object of this clause is to encourage exertion on the part of the insured and induce him to take every step practicable for the protection or recovery of the thing insured. Permission is granted to the insured or his servants to take steps in mitigation of any loss for which the insurer would be liable. The insurer agrees to pay his proportion of any expenses so incurred. Also called sue, labor, and travel clause.

Fr: *Clause d'Agir et de Travailler;* Ger: *Gerichtskosten- und Arbeitslohnklausel.*

SUEGEE. A mixture of caustic soda, soft soap and water used on board ship for scrubbing paint work. Also called suji-muji.

Ger: *Sodalösung.*

SUEZ CANAL TONNAGE. The tonnage on which transit dues are calculated for vessels going through the Suez Canal. The Moorsom system of measurement is used with the following differences as compared with the British tonnage regulations:

1. All enclosed spaces are included in the gross tonnage.
2. Unenclosed spaces are excluded, also the fore end of the forecastle from the stem over a length equal to ⅛ the length of the ship and the poop from right aft over 1/10 the length of the ship, the length of the bridge as is equal to the length of the machinery space deck openings.
3. Shelter deck space is included except immediately opposite any openings in the side.
4. No deduction is made for peak ballast tanks, but a deduction of 5 per cent in gross tonnage is made.
5. The maximum deduction allowed off the gross tonnage is 50 per cent.

It is generally assumed in practice that the gross register tonnage as computed by the Suez Canal rule is approximately 5 per cent higher than that computed by the British official rule and the net Suez Canal tonnage about 30 per cent higher than the British net tonnage.

Fr: *Jauge du Canal de Suez;* Ger: *Suez Kanal Vermessung.*

SUEZ RUDDER.
See **Salmon Tail.**

SUFFERANCE WHARF. A wharf or pier appointed by the customs on which dutiable and other goods may be landed and loaded under certain conditions without paying duty.
See **Bill of Sufferance.**

SUGAR-LOAF SEA. A sea in which the waves rise into sugar-loaf shapes, with little wind.

SUGG. To rock with the action of the sea when stranded.

SUJI-MUJI.
See **Suegee.**

SUMATRA. Strong southwesterly gust of wind experienced during the southwest monsoon season in the Strait of Malacca.

SUMMER LOAD LINE. The deepest waterline to which a merchant vessel is legally allowed to load for voyages within specified geographical zones in summer months. It is indicated by the letter S on the ship's side.

Fr: *Ligne de charge d'été;* Ger: *Sommer Tiefladelinie.*

SUMMER TANK. One of the tanks in a tank vessel in which additional oil is carried during the summer months when freeboard regulations allow the draft of tankers to be increased or when light oils are carried. These tanks extend on both sides of the expansion trunk immediately above the main tanks. Some of them are frequently arranged for the carriage of fuel or Diesel oil for the ship's use.

Fr: *Citerne d'Été;* Ger: *Sommertank.*

SUMNER LINE. A position line used in navigation, based on the important discovery made by Captain T. H. Sumner in 1837 that a line of position on some part of which the ship is situated can be obtained from a single altitude observation, the line always being at right angles to the bearing of the body.

Fr: *Droite de Sumner;* Ger: *Sumner's Linie; Sumner Standlinie.*

U. S. Hydrographic Office, *The Sumner Line of Position,* Publication 204, Washington, 1933.

SUMNER'S METHOD. The method of finding a ship's position at sea by the projection of one or more lines of equal altitude on a Mercator chart.

Fr: *Méthode de Sumner;* Ger: *Sumner Standlinie.*

SUMP. A small well fitted in the main compartments, usually at the afterend, to facilitate drainage of bilge water. Also called drainage sump, drainage well.

Fr: *Puisard;* Ger: *Sumpf; Drainagebrunnen.*

SUMPA. Decked fishing boat with large well, used as a tender on the Latvian coast for the transportation of live fish. These boats vary in length from 25 to 45 ft. with a beam of 15 to 25 ft. The well has a capacity of 1½ to 2½ tons of fish.

SUNASUNA. Polynesian single-outrigger dugout canoe from Vella Lavella Islands, Northwestern Solomon Islands, similar to the *bul* of Lavongai Island. It has carvings at both ends with a bird's head on the bow.

SUN DECK. 1. The uppermost deck on large passenger liners. Also called sports deck. It is frequently used as a boat deck, providing at the same time room for various sports such as tennis court, squash racket court, etc. The officers' accommodation and radio room, with the necessary accommodation for wireless operators is usually arranged for on this deck.
2. On cargo vessels and other small vessels this term also refers to an uppermost deck constructed of light boarding and usually covered with canvas and painted. It is intended merely as a sun protection for the navigating bridge and not as a promenade space.
Fr: *Sun Deck;* Ger: *Sonnendeck.*

SUN DOG. A mock sun shining near the sun, caused by peculiar atmospheric conditions.
Fr: *Parhélie;* Ger: *Nebensonne.*

SUNDSBAT. A Danish open boat employed in the Sound and Kattegat inshore net fisheries. The hull is clinker-built with rounded stem and sternpost, and has 5 thwarts. The rig consists of 4 sails: a sprit mainsail with topsail bent to a spar nearly as long as the mainmast, a large jib-headed foresail, and a very small jib which tacks down to a short bowsprit. Length over-all 16 to 24 ft. Length of keel 10 to 16 ft. Breadth 4¼ to 8 ft.

SUNKEN MANHOLE. A manhole in which the cover is below deck or tank-top level.
Ger: *Versenktes Mannloch.*

SUNKEN POOP. A poop which has its deck raised only a partial deck height above the level of the upper or weather deck. Also called monkey poop.
Ger: *Versenkte Hütte.*

SUNK FORECASTLE. A forecastle which extends partly above and partly below the upper or weather deck.
Fr: *Demi Gaillard;* Ger: *Versenktes Back.*

SUNK NET. A drift net fished with the warp above the net as distinguished from a swum net where the warp is under the net.
Ger: *Sinkfleet.*

SUNN HEMP. Hemp made from the fibers of an Indian plant, *Crotalaria juncea*. It is also found in the East Indies. It is largely used by ropemakers. Also called Bombay hemp, Madras hemp.
Fr: *Chanvre du Bengale;* Ger: *Sunnhanf.*

SUNNMORSBAAD. A generic name by which various Norwegian open boats employed in the fisheries of the Sunnmore district are known. They are distinguished from each other by the number of oars they use. The boats of Sunnmore include: (1) the *ottring* or 8-oared boat; (2) the *fjoringfar* also an 8-oared boat, but of smaller size than the *ottring;* (3) the *seksring* or 6-oared boat; (4) the *faering* or 4-oared boat. The *seksring* is occasionally called *treroring.*

SUN PILLAR. A vertical column of light occasionally seen above the sun at sunrise or sunset, attributed to the reflection of sunlight from horizontal ice crystals.
Fr: *Colonne Solaire;* Ger: *Sonnensäule.*

SUN VALVE. See **Unattended Light.**

SUPERCARGO. 1. A person appointed by the owners of the cargo on a merchant ship whose business it is to manage the sales or purchase of goods and to superintend all the commercial aspects of the voyage. The supercargo sails from port to port with the vessel to which he is attached and has complete control over the cargo and everything which immediately concerns it. Under certain circumstances he is responsible for the cargo, but he has no power to interfere with the management of the ship.
2. In the American merchant marine refers to an unlicensed member of the crew who performs general clerical duties aboard ship such as filing various papers, typing correspondence, ship's accounts, store lists, personnel roster, and so on. He receives freight aboard ship, checking all items against manifest; under the joint supervision of chief officer aboard and chief stevedore ashore he supervises the stowage of freight and sees that freight is discharged at proper port. He may inspect the condition of perishable freight prior to stowage, notifying chief officer of any unsatisfactory condition discovered. Also called freight clerk.
Fr: *Subrécargue;* Ger: *Kargadeur; Superkargo.*

SUPERHEAT. When steam is heated above the temperature necessary for its formation at a given pressure, it is said to be superheated. Modern steam-driven marine engineering plants utilize superheated steam to increase their efficiency.

SUPERINTENDENT ENGINEER. See **Port Engineer.**

SUPERIOR MIRAGE. Optical phenomenon most often experienced in high latitudes and whenever the sea surface temperature is abnormally low and in which an inverted image is seen over the real object.

See **Mirage.**

SUPERIOR TRANSIT. The crossing of the meridian at the higher altitude by a celestial body whose declination is of the same name as, and of less latitude than that of the observer.

Fr: *Passage Supérieur;* Ger: *Obere Kulmination.*

SUPERLINER. A term reserved to passenger ships which represent radical departure either in size or speed over previous practice.

Gaede, G. C., American Superliners, Society of Naval Architects and Marine Engineers, New York, *Transactions,* vol. 47, 1939.

SUPERSONIC ECHO SOUNDER. Echo-sounding equipment in which inaudible high-frequency sonic waves with frequency ranging from 30 to 40 thousand per second are made use of. Also called ultra sonic depth finder. These vibrations travel in water at the same speed as audible sounds but, through their inaudibility, avoid interfering noises of audible frequencies such as propeller noises and water noises produced by the sea on the hull, which affect the receiver. Supersonic waves also obtain a comparatively sharp beam of transmitted energy to the sea bottom with reasonable dimensions of transmitter thus avoiding a distribution of energy over a wide area of sea bottom. They are based on the piezo-electrical property of quartz for transmitting vibrations; the transmitter consisting of two steel plates of adequate thickness with a mosaic of small sheets of quartz sandwiched between them.

Fr: *Echo-Sondeur à Ultra Sons; Echo-Sondeur Ultra Sonore;* Ger: *Ultraschallwelle Echolot.*

See **Echo-Sounding.**

SUPERSTRUCTURE. Any structure extending above the upper or main deck, as a continuation of the main framing such as a bridge house, poop, forecastle, or a decked structure on the freeboard deck extending from side to side of the ship. Also called deck erection. A raised quarter deck is considered a superstructure.

Fr: *Superstructure;* Ger: *Aufbau; Überbau.*

SUPERSTRUCTURE DECK. 1. A continuous deck of light scantlings upon which the superstructures (poop, bridge, forecastle) are built. It is usually the first deck above the strength deck and is often known as the awning or shelter deck.

2. The deck forming the top of a superstructure.

Fr: *Pont des Superstructures;* Ger: *Aufbaudeck.*

SUPPLEMENTARY ARC. In a sextant, an extra arc attached to the limb inside the curve of the regular arc. It is made of aluminum and is used solely for the purpose of taking 2 or 3 land bearings quickly. It is graduated to 10 seconds only to facilitate rapid reading by eye.

SUPPLY-EXHAUST VENTILATION. A combined supply and exhaust system of mechanical ventilation which finds most general application in the ventilation of passenger quarters. Also called plenum-exhaust ventilation. Air is supplied direct to staterooms and extracted through louvres fitted in the doors or bulkheads, the movement of the air being induced toward adjacent lavatories and toilets where an exhaust system is in operation.

Fr: *Ventilation Mixte;* Ger: *Gemischte Lüftung.*

SUPPLY VENTILATION. A system of mechanical ventilation by which fresh air is forced into the various compartments. Also called plenum ventilation, pressure ventilation. The plenum system is a supply system only, the vitiated air exhausting through natural ventilators including stairways, doors, and so on. It is largely adopted in accommodation for third-class passengers and crew. The supply system offers an additional advantage in that it is readily adaptable for temperature control. A heating element is then incorporated with the fans so that the air may be delivered at any desired temperature.

Fr: *Ventilation par Refoulement;* Ger: *Drucklüftung.*

SURCHARGE. A marine insurance term used to denote additional rates superim-

Fig. 3

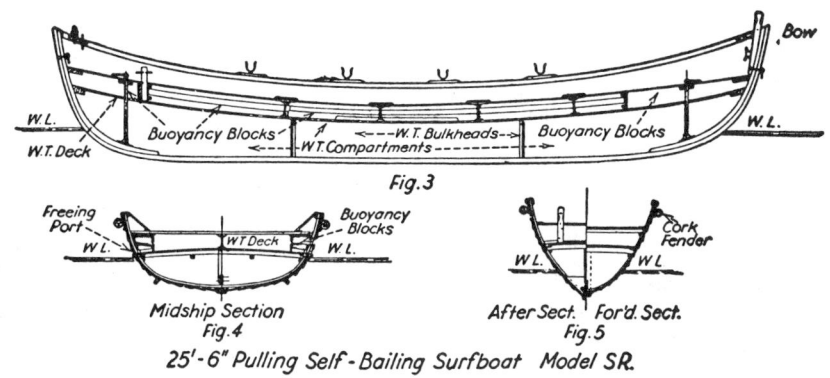

Fig. 4 Midship Section

Fig. 5 After Sect. | For'd. Sect.

25'-6" Pulling Self-Bailing Surfboat Model S.R.

Surf Boat

posed on the basic rate for the insurance of cargo bound through war or similar perilous areas. Also called cargo surcharge.
Fr: *Surprime;* Ger: *Zuschlaggebühr.*

SURF. The waves of the sea which break upon a shore or a shoal. Also called breakers.
Fr: *Brisants;* Ger: *Brandung.*

SURF BOAT. Open rowboat specially designed for beaching and launching through the surf. Its design varies according to local conditions and duties. In most cases the hull is double-ended with flat floors and heavy scantlings. Some are used as coastal life boats, others as work boats for the transportation of goods from ship to shore.
Ger: *Brandungsboot; Surfboot.*

SURF DAYS. Days on which the working of cargo when carried out by means of boats or lighters in open roadsteads or bar ports is not practicable or is not reasonably safe on account of the state of the sea.
Ger: *Brandungstag.*

SURGE. 1. The tapered parts of the whelps in a capstan.
Ger: *Rippen der Spillklampen.*
See **Whelp.**

2. Horizontal oscillation of water with comparatively short period and high velocity. A compound or reacting wave action, usually a continuation of the vessel's wash acting and reacting in opposite directions.
Fr: *Lame de Houle;* Ger: *Sturzsee; Woge.*

3. A general change of atmospheric pressure superimposed upon the changes which are due to the movements of depressions and anticyclones.
Fr: *Variation Générale;* Ger: *Aufwallung.*

SURGE (to). 1. To slip back. To let go a piece of rope suddenly. To slack a rope suddenly when it renders around a belaying pin, a winch, windlass or capstan.
Fr: *Choquer;* Ger: *Schricken; Aufschricken.*

2. To rise and fall, as a ship does when riding at anchor.
Ger: *Wogen.*

SURGING. One of the various motions of a ship in a seaway; may be defined as the variation in speed of translation (forward) through the water. It is a bodily movement of the ship as a whole.
Lockwood Taylor, J., Surging of Ships, Engineer, London, vol. 151, March 6, 1931.

SURVEY. 1. The measurement of an area in all its details for the purpose of compiling a chart.
Fr: *Levé;* Ger: *Aufnehmung; Aufnahme.*

2. Examination or inspection of a ship or part of its cargo or equipment to determine its condition, responsibility for damage, and disposition to be made.
Fr: *Visite; Expertise;* Ger: *Besichtigung.*

See **Coast and Geodetic Survey, Damage Survey, Hydrographic Survey, Periodical Survey, Running Survey, Special Survey.**

SURVEYING BOAT. Any of various types of small boats, such as launches, pinnaces, whaleboats, dorys, gigs, dinghys, etc., used as tenders by a surveying vessel where, owing to shallowness of water or for other reasons, it is necessary to carry out nautical surveys from small craft.

Fr: *Embarcation Hydrographique;* Ger: *Peilboot.*

Coastlining, searching for pinnacle rocks in shallow waters, sounding and sweeping are carried out by surveying boats. As they may have to work at a considerable distance away from the land or from the parent ship and may be exposed to heavy seas, only thoroughly seaworthy boats are employed. Their weight and size are restricted by the fact that they must be capable of being hoisted on board their parent ship in open waters. They are usually fitted with engines.

Nares, J. D., "Surveying Boats," *Hydrographic Review* (Monaco), vol. 10 (1933).

SURVEYING VESSEL. Mechanically propelled seagoing vessel, specially built and equipped to carry out hydrographic and other nautical surveys in coastal waters and on the high seas. Surveying vessels are in most instances government-owned.

Fr: *Navire Hydrographe;* Ger: *Vermessungsfahrzeug.*

SUSPECTED BILL OF HEALTH. A suspected bill of health indicates that there were rumors of contagious diseases at the *last* port *at which the vessel called* but that they had not appeared before the vessel's departure. Also called touched bill of health.

Fr: *Patente de Santé Suspecte;* Ger: *Zweifelhafter Gesundheitspass.*

SWAB. A mop from 1½ to 3 ft. long, made of a middled and seized piece of rope with the strands raveled out or with rope yarns wound into a skein, put through a grommet and there seized and snaked. It is fastened to a rope lanyard and then to a swab handle, and is used for swabbing and drying decks. Also called deck swab.

Fr: *Faubert;* Ger: *Schwabber.*

SWAB HITCH. A form of hitch similar to the sheet bend, in which the end is bent to an eye instead of a loop. Used for attaching a line to a swab.

SWALLOW. 1. The aperture between the sides in the shell of a block, through which the rope reeves. The space or opening in a block which takes the rope above the sheave.

Fr: *Gorge;* Ger: *Schlund.*

2. The oval or round opening in a mooring chock.

SWAMP. To overset, sink, or cause to become filled with water, as a boat.

Fr: *Remplir;* Ger: *Vollaufen.*

SWAN NECK VENTILATOR. An uptake ventilator which has its upper extremity bent through an angle of 180°. Also called gooseneck ventilator.

Fr: *Col de Cygne;* Ger: *Schwanenhals Lüfter; Schwanenhals.*

SWASH BULKHEAD (U. S.). A middleline bulkhead with numerous openings built in peak-tank or deep-tank to provide against violent movement of free water when these tanks are partly filled. In Great Britain called wash bulkhead.

Fr: *Cloison Chicane;* Ger: *Schlingerschott; Schlagschott.*

SWASH PLATE. Plates fixed in tanks to prevent or inhibit excessive movement of contained liquid, and thus decrease the deleterious effect on stability of the consequent free-surface effect. Swash plates are lighter than strength structure, and are pierced with lightening holes.

SWAY. 1. To hoist or raise, particularly when referring to masts and spars. To "sway up" a topmast means to raise it so that the fid may be taken out before striking. To "sway on end" means to hoist to a perpendicular position from the deck.

Fr: *Guinder;* Ger: *Aufheissen.*

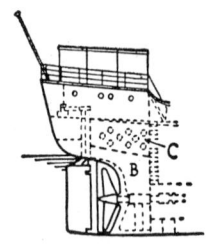

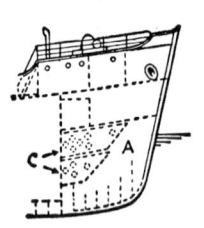

Swash Plate
A. Fore Peak   B. After Peak   C. Swash Plates

2. Also, the effort made by throwing the weight of the body on a rope when hoisting.

SWAY ACROSS. To move a yard to a horizontal position.

Fr: *Croiser;* Ger: *Kaien.*

SWEAT. The condensation of moisture on cargo and on metal surfaces in a ship's hold due to changes of temperature which develop chiefly when the vessel passes from warm to cooler waters especially if ventilation is insufficient. The condensation on the uninsulated inner surface of the shell, or on uninsulated cold-water piping.

Fr: *Buée de Cale;* Ger: *Schiffsdunst; Schwitzwasser.*

Colvin, Hahne, Colby, "Care of Cargo at Sea," Society of Naval Architects and Marine Engineers (New York), *Transactions*, vol. 46 (1938); Duly, S. J., "Condensation on Board Ship," Royal Society of Arts (London), *Jour.*, vol. 86 (1938); Duly, S. J., "Damage to Cargo Due to Ship's Sweat," Royal Society of Arts (London), *Jour.*, vol. 76 (December, 1927); *Marine Moisture Damage*, Association of Marine Underwriters of British Columbia, Bulletin 10, 1940.

SWEAT BOARD. A wood lining fitted over sleeping berths in seamen's quarters as a protection against sweat from the steel deck above.

SWEEP. 1. A term formerly used in naval architecture to denote various arcs of circles describing the form of frames in the body plan. There were 5 sweeps: the floor sweep, the lower breadth sweep, the reconciling sweep, the upper breadth sweep, the top-timber or back sweep. (Obsolete.)

2. A semicircular frame on which the end of a tiller or rudder yoke travels.

Fr: *Tamisaille;* Ger: *Leuwagen; Gleitbahn.*

3. An apparatus used in hydrographic surveys for the detection of rocky pinnacles, ledges, boulders, coral reefs. Also called wire drag. It consists of a horizontal bottom wire supported at intervals by adjustable upright cables suspended from buoys on the surface. These uprights can be lengthened or shortened for various required depths. They are kept in a nearly vertical position by means of weights attached to their lower ends. The end weights and buoys are larger than the intermediate and the towing gear is attached to them. The wire sweep is a modification of the drag for use in areas where the general depths are considerably greater than the depths to be verified and where few, if any, obstructions are believed to exist.

Fr: *Drague;* Ger: *Dregtau.*

4. A long and heavy oar used in small boats, barges, and so on, for steering or occasionally to assist the motion of the boat in a calm. A long oar used for sculling.

Fr: *Aviron de Galère;* Ger: *Lange Riemen; Lange Ruder.*

5. The curve in the leech of a sail.

Fr: *Echancrure;* Ger: *Gillung.*

See **Roach.**

SWEEPING. Various methods employed in hydrographic surveys to discover the irregularities of the sea bottom in navigable channels.

Fr: *Draguer;* Ger: *Dreggen.*

Edgell, J. A., "Notes on Wire Drag Surveys," *Hydrographic Review* (Monaco), vol. 13 (1936); "Methods of Sweeping Used in Various Countries," *Hydrographic Review* (Monaco), vol. 11 (1934), pp. 67–80.

SWEEPINGS. See **Spillage.**

SWELL (G. B.). 1. A fish measure of common use in Great Britain. The equivalent of 1 cran (3¾ cwt.) of fish stowed in 3 boxes.

2. Undulating movement of the sea surface persisting after the originating cause of the motion has ceased. It is caused either by wind at a distance from the place of observation or by winds which persisted in the locality previous to the time observation.

Fr: *Houle;* Ger: *Dunung; Deining.*

See **Cross Swell, Ground Swell, Rolling Swell.**

Bouasse, H., *Houle, Seiches, Rides et Marées*, Paris, 1924.

SWELL DAMAGE. The damage to anchored or moored craft, shore installations and so on, caused by a swell or system of waves which are generated by a moving ship in constricted waters. These waves travel at a velocity of about one-half the speed of the vessel and proceed on a course diverging 45 degrees from the course of the ship. Considerable swell damage may result from the passage of sizable vessels through constricted passages at high speed.

SWEPT PLANKING. A method of planking used for wooden decks in which the planks are made to follow the sweep of the sides and are notched or nibbed into a center plank called a king plank. It is used only for small boats and yachts. Also called sprung planking.

SWIFTER. 1. The forward or after shroud of lower rigging when there is an odd number of shrouds.

Fr: *Hauban Bâtard;* Ger: *Hoofdtau.*

2. A small line joining the outer ends of capstan bars to confine them to their sockets while the capstan is being turned.

Fr: *Raban;* Ger: *Strecktau.*

3. A rope fender encircling a boat longitudinally and protecting its sides.

Fr: *Ceinture;* Ger: *Stosskissen.*

SWIFTERING LINE. A line for swiftering the shrouds before ratlines are put on.

Also used between stays and preventer stays. (Obsolete.)

Fr: *Pantoquière*; Ger: *Schwichtleine*.

SWIG. To tighten a line which is fastened at one end to a fixed object and at the other to a moving one, by hauling thereon at right angles to its lead and. for each haul, taking up the slack at the fixed point of attachment. It gives greater power than by hauling at the free end of the rope.

Fr: *Etarquer*; *Faire Abattage*.

SWILL. Name given on the east coast of England to a basket of double pannier shape, made of unpeeled willow and holding about 660 herring or 5 long hundred. It was formerly used to transfer fish from boat to shore, and is still used as a fish measure.

SWIM-END BARGE. A type of open lighter commonly used in the port of London, with overhanging blunt ends. It has a length of 80 to 90 ft., 18 to 20 ft. beams, and a deadweight capacity of 100 to 120 tons.

SWING. 1. To move or float around with the wind or tide, as a ship riding at a single anchor.

Fr: *Eviter*; Ger: *Schwoien*; *Schwaien*; *Aufdrehen*.

2. The procedure followed for bringing a ship's head to every point of the compass in succession in order to ascertain the amount of local deviation or compass error on each heading by comparison of the compass and true bearings of some distant object ashore, or of the sun. Also called to swing ship.

Fr: *Faire Éviter*; *Éviter*; Ger: *Rund Schwoien*.

The vessel is placed on a given compass heading, such as north, the deviation is obtained, and the ship is then swung to the right, steadying on successive headings varying by 15, 30, or 45 degrees according to conditions, deviations being observed on each heading. As soon as a complete set is made with the right rudder, another similar set is obtained with the left rudder. Intervals of 15 degrees are considered preferable if accurate results are to be obtained for the intermediate points. The vessel should remain on each course several minutes before the observation is made.

SWING CLEAR. To ride at anchor, particularly in tidal waters, without colliding with any object.

SWINGING. The turning of a vessel at anchor from one direction to another under the influence of tide or wind.

Fr: *Evitage*; Ger: *Schwoien*.

SWINGING BOOM. A spar formerly used as outrigger for a lower studding sail. Also called lower studding sail boom. (Obsolete.)

Fr: *Tangon de Bonnette Basse*; Ger: *Schwingbaum*; *Backspiere*.

SWINGING BUOY. One of the buoys placed in a harbor, river or a roadstead to assist turning a ship in a circle for compass adjustment. The buoys are arranged so as to be in line with magnetic range beacons ashore. The ship's head is made fast with a line to a large nun buoy which serves as the center of the circle. Four smaller buoys are anchored, one on each cardinal point of the compass, for swinging the ship's stern by means of a small stern line, thus enabling the vessel to make a complete circle.

Fr: *Bouée d'évitage*; Ger: *Deviationsboje*.

SWINGING DERRICK SYSTEM. A rig for transferring cargo from ship to shore, or vice versa, in which one cargo boom is used. The boom is held by two guys, the inboard guy and the outboard guy. As each sling is taken out of the hold the outboard guy is hauled over by manual or mechanical power so as to bring the sling over the ship's side. After lowering the draft on the pier, the boom is hauled back by the inboard guy. A weight attached to this guy is frequently provided for this. This rig is often used for bags, barrels, drums and light cargo. Also called **Single boom system**.

SWINGING-FLUKE ANCHOR.
See **Stockless Anchor**.

SWINGING MOORINGS. All types of permanent moorings where there is only one riding chain, the vessel being allowed to swing freely to wind and tide.

SWINGING THE LEAD. Slang expression denoting wilful evasion of duty or work on the part of a member of the crew.

SWING OUT. To move about in a horizontal plane a ship's boat, an anchor, or any other object suspended from a davit, to get it over the ship's side before lowering.

Fr: *Déborder*; Ger: *Ausschwingen*.

SWIVEL. 1. A hoop or link in which provision is made, by means of a shank and collar, for circular movement. Used for chain cables, blocks, and so on.

Fr: *Emérillon*; Ger: *Wirbel*.

2. A mooring appliance consisting of a large swivel and link secured to two tri-

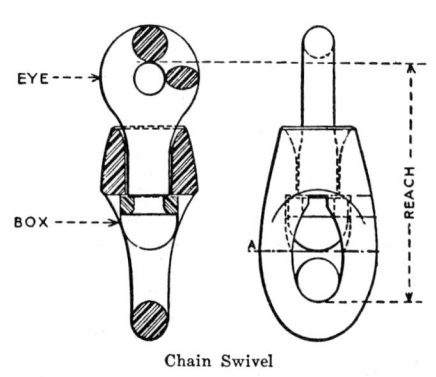

Chain Swivel

angular or three-eyed forgings called spectacles or large eyes. To these eyes studless links are attached; two links to one eye and one to the other on each forging. Swivels are used for keeping turns out of the cables when the ship is moored. Also called mooring swivel.

Fr: *Emérillon d'affourche;* Ger: *Muringswirbel; Vertauwirbel.*

The mooring swivel is shackled upon cables just forward of the stem in such a way that the parts leading from the hawsepipes are connected to the inner shackles and the parts leading to the anchors to the outer shackles. As the ship swings, the swivel turns and keeps the cables clear.

SWIVEL HOOK. A hook secured to anything by means of a swivel. In a swivel hook block the suspending hook is swiveled to the block so that the latter is free to turn, to present the sheave in any direction.

Fr: *Croc à Emérillon;* Ger: *Wirbelhaken.*

SWIVEL PIECE. The combination of shackles, swivel, and special links which form the outboard end of an anchor cable. Swivel pieces are made up in various combinations. The following sequence is commonly adopted: (1) the bending shackle which goes next to the anchor; (2) heavy open link or long end stud link; (3) stud or open link; (4) swivel; (5) stud or open link; (6) connecting shackle joining the swivel piece to the first length of cable.

Fr: *Etalingure à Emérillon;* Ger: *Vorläufer; Wirbelstück; Ketten Wirbel.*

SWORD MAT. A mat made of rope yarns woven close together, used as chafing gear.

Fr: *Sangle au Métier;* Ger: *Schwertmatte; Brook.*

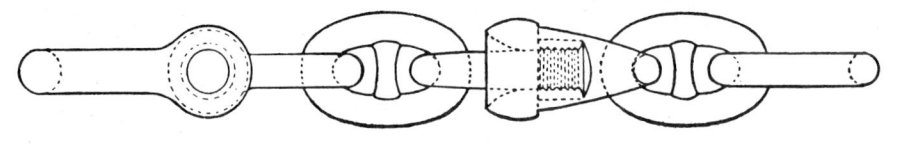

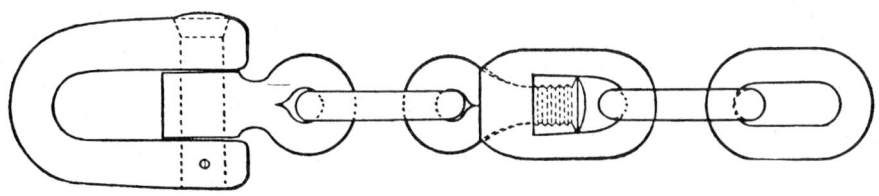

Swivel Piece

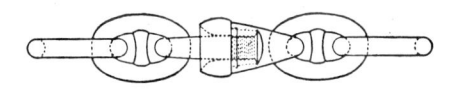

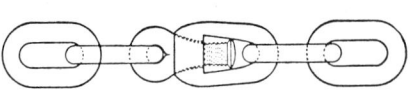

Swivel Piece

SWORN BROKER. A broker bound, affirmed, or attested by an oath.

Fr: *Courtier Juré;* Ger: *Schwurmakler.*

SWUM NET. A drift net with the warp sunk beneath the net.

Ger: *Treibfleet.*

See **Sunk Net.**

SYNCHRONISM. The condition obtained when the rolling or pitching period of a vessel at sea coincides with the wave periods, thereby causing violent rolling or pitching.

Fr: *Synchronisme;* Ger: *Gleichzeitigkeit.*
SYNCHRONOUS WAVE. Waves are synchronous when the half-period of the wave is equal to the ship's own period in still water, or in other words when the ratio of the period of the vessel and that of the period of the wave is 1 to 2.

Fr: *Houle Synchrone;* Ger: *Gleichzeitige Welle.*

SYNODIC MONTH. The period of time which elapses between one conjunction of the moon and sun and the next one. The synodic month is used in the study of the phases of the moon and the tides.

Fr: *Mois Synodique;* Ger: *Synodischer Monat.*

SYNOPTIC CHART. A special chart used in weather forecasting on which a large number of simultaneous observations are plotted showing the actual barometric pressure, temperature, humidity, direction and force of wind, state of sea, weather experienced, clouds, and so on, at the time for which the chart is compiled. Also called synchronous chart.

SYRIAN SCHOONER. A two-masted fore-and-aft schooner of about 80 tons, found in eastern Mediterranean waters and plying between the Syrian coast, Cyprus, and the Egyptian ports. It carries two tall raking masts, a bowsprit and jibboom, and a long main boom. The sail plan includes 3 headsails, a jib-headed foresail, main staysail, main topmast staysail, and jib-headed mainsail. The mainsail is loose-footed and the clew is set flying to the boom end. The boom projects a considerable distance over the transom. The foresail is boomless and the main staysails are fitted with booms. These vessels are said to be smart and handy under sail. Local name *Shaktura.*

SYZYGY. The point of an orbit, as of that of the moon, when it is in conjunction or opposition. Generally used in regard to the sun and moon.

Fr: *Syzygie;* Ger: *Syzygium.*

See **Conjunction, Opposition.**

SYZYGY TIDE. The tide which takes place on the afternoon of the day the sun and moon are in syzygy.

Fr: *Marée de Syzygie;* Ger: *Syzygiumgezeit.*

T

T. Flag of the international code of signals showing red, white and blue equal vertical divisions. When hoisted singly it means: "Do not pass ahead of me." When used as a towing signal it means: "I am increasing speed," when flown by the ship towing, and "Increase speed" when shown by the ship towed.

T. Freeboard mark which indicates the load line in tropical zones. It is arrived at by deducting from the summer freeboard one-quarter of an inch per foot of summer draft measured from the top of the keel to the center of the disc.

T. ANTENNA. Aerial consisting of one or more horizontal wires with leading connection made approximately at center.

Fr: *Antenne en T;* Ger: *T. Antenne.*

T. F. Freeboard mark which indicates the loadline when the vessel is loaded in fresh water in tropical zones during summer.

T. TRUE (with reference to direction).
T. TEE IRON.
T TROPICAL WATERS (with reference to freeboard).
T TIME.
t.l.o. TOTAL LOSS ONLY (see **Loss**).
T. and P. THEFT AND PILFERAGE.
T. and S. TOUCH AND STAY.
T.Dks. 'TWEEN-DECKS.
T.F. TROPICAL FRESH WATERS.

T.I.B. TRIMMED IN BUNKERS.
t.s.m.s. TWIN-SCREW MOTOR SHIP.
T.S.S. TWIN-SCREW STEAMER.
Tr.S.S. TRIPLE-SCREW STEAMER.
Tr.S.M.S. TRIPLE-SCREW MOTOR SHIP.

TABABERI. A double-outrigger dugout canoe from Geelvink Bay, Dutch New Guinea, with flat square stern and long rising stem. These canoes are usually rigged with a tripod mast and oblong sail made of matting.

TABERNACLE. A vertical trunk to take the heel of a lower mast that does not pass through a deck. Also called mast trunk. It is sometimes built so that the mast can be lowered, in which case a heavy bolt is fitted through the sides of the tabernacle and serves as a pivot for the mast. In small fishing vessels the tabernacle is constructed of three upright timbers extending for some distance above the deck.

Fr: *Caisse de Pied de Mât;* Ger: *Mastbock; Mastkoker.*

TABLE. 1. Outer part of a keel, stem, or sternpost projecting beyond the rabbet line. Also called depth.

Fr: *Tableau.*

TABLE (to). To strengthen a sail by making broad hems on the head, leeches, and foot for the attachment of the bolt rope.

Fr: *Gainer;* Ger: *Stosslappen setzen.*

See Azimuth Tables, Bending Table, Derrick Table, Deviation Table, Tide

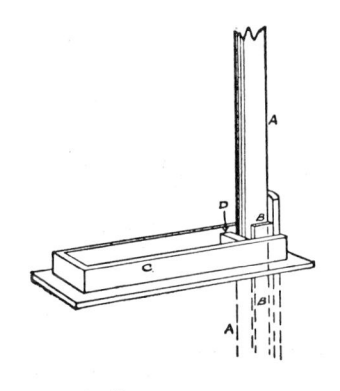

Tabernacles

A. Mast
B. Partners
C. Trunk or Mast Box
D. Chock or Choke

A. Mast
B. Partners
C. Band
D. Heel

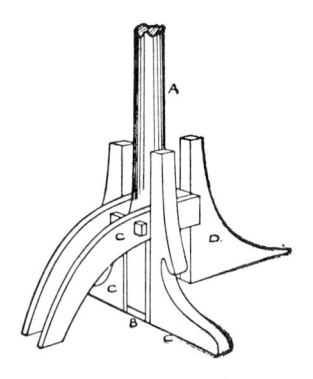

A. Mast
B. Heel of Mast
C. Tabernacle
D. Fore Knee

Tables, Traverse Table, **Upper Mast Table, Winch Table**.

TABLE CLOTH. A type of cloud hanging over Table Mountain, near Capetown, before a southeasterly gale.

TABLED SCARF. A scarf in which one part is tenoned to occupy a mortise or recess in its counterpart.

Fr: *Ecart à Entablement;* Ger: *Schakwerklaschung.*

TABLEMOUNT. A seamount, roughly circular or elliptical in plan, and generally deeper than 100 fathoms, the top of which is a comparatively smooth platform.

TABLE OF COMPUTED ALTITUDE AND AZIMUTH. Navigational tables designed to permit rapid computation of calculated altitude and azimuth of a heavenly body, with minimum effort on the part of the navigator. Also called H. O. 214. They consist essentially of tabulated solutions of the astronomical triangle, so arranged as to yield the navigator his calculated altitude and azimuth by inspection.

The tables are applicable equally to sights of the sun, moon, planets and navigational stars. They are designed for use in connection with celestial bodies both of the same name as and contrary name to the latitude and apply to both Northern and Southern Hemispheres. For greater convenience they are divided into 9 volumes, the values for 10 degrees of latitude being included in a single volume.

U. S. Hydrographic Office, Publication 214, Washington.

TABLING. 1. A reinforcing border of canvas around a sail to which the boltrope is sewn. It is made by turning over the edge of the cloth and sewing it down with an average of 68 to 72 stitches to a yard. At the head, the tabling is on the afterside of a square sail, but around the rest of the sail on the foreside.

Fr: *Gaine;* Ger: *Umschlag Stosslappen.*

Tabling breadths for trading vessels average:

Courses	4 to 6 in.
Topsails	3 to 5 in.
Topgallants and royals...	3 in.
Jibs, on the leech and stay	3 in.
on the foot	2½ in.
Gaffsails, Leech, at middle;	3½ in.
broader at clew and peak; foot	2½ in.

2. The letting of one piece of timber into another by alternate scores of projections from the middle so that they cannot be drawn asunder lengthways or sideways.

Fr: *Assemblage à Patte de Loup;* Ger: *Hakenlaschung.*

TABLING NEEDLE. A needle used for sewing service leather to those parts of a boltrope likely to chafe against the rigging. The length ranges from 5 to 5½ in.

Fr: *Aiguille à Basaner;* Ger: *Stosslappnadel.*

TABULAR BERG. A flat-topped iceberg carved from the greater ice barrier. Also called snowberg.

TACHOMETER. A mechanical device for indicating shaft revolutions per minute. Some types also average the revolutions per minute of two or more shafts.

Fr: *Tachymètre.*

TACK. 1. The rope holding down the weather clew of a course.

Fr: *Amure;* Ger: *Hals.*

2. The direction of a vessel's head with regard to the trim of its sails; as, on the starboard tack, it has the wind on the starboard side. The run of a vessel on one tack.

Fr: *Bordée;* Ger: *Gang; Schlag.*

3. The lower forward corner of a fore-and-aft sail. That part of a sail to which the tack is fastened, the weather clew of a course.

Fr: *Point d'Amure;* Ger: *Hals.*

See **Lazy Tack, Lee Tack, Midship Tack**.

TACK (to). To change the course of a ship when sailing by the wind by turning her head toward the wind so that it will sail at the same angle with the wind on the other side. To change from the port tack to the starboard tack, or vice versa. Also called go about, stay.

Fr: *Virer de Bord Vent Devant; Louvoyer;* Ger: *Lavieren; Uber Stag Gehen.*

See **Cross Tack, False Tack, Short Tack, Split Tack**.

TACK AND HALF TACK. A long tack followed by a short one.

TACK CRINGLE. The iron ring spliced into a fore-and-aft sail at the junction of the luff and the foot. The iron shapes spliced into the lower corners of square sails.

Fr: *Patte de Point d'Amure;* Ger: *Halslegel.*

TACKER (U. S.). A welder's helper who does most of the temporary welding, such as the welding of clips and saddles for assembling or erecting structural members prior to final welding. So called because the majority

of his work consists of tack welding.
See **Tack Welding**.

TACK HOOK. A hook fitted on the stem of an open boat for fastening the tack of the foresail.

TACKING TO LEEWARD. A practice sometimes resorted to when running before the wind, to keep all sails drawing, especially with fore-and-aft rigged vessels. The ship is run for some time with the wind on one quarter, then gybed and run an equal distance with the wind on the other quarter.
See **Gybe**.

long used for separating each group of flags when more groups than one are shown on the same halyard.

Fr: *Queue*; Ger: *Flaggensteert; Flaggenleine*.

TACKLE UPON TACKLE. A purchase consisting of one luff tackle applied to the fall of another. Also called luff upon luff.

Fr: *Palan sur Garant*; Ger: *Takel auf Takel*.

See **Luff Tackle**.

TACK PIN. A long belaying pin on a fife rail.

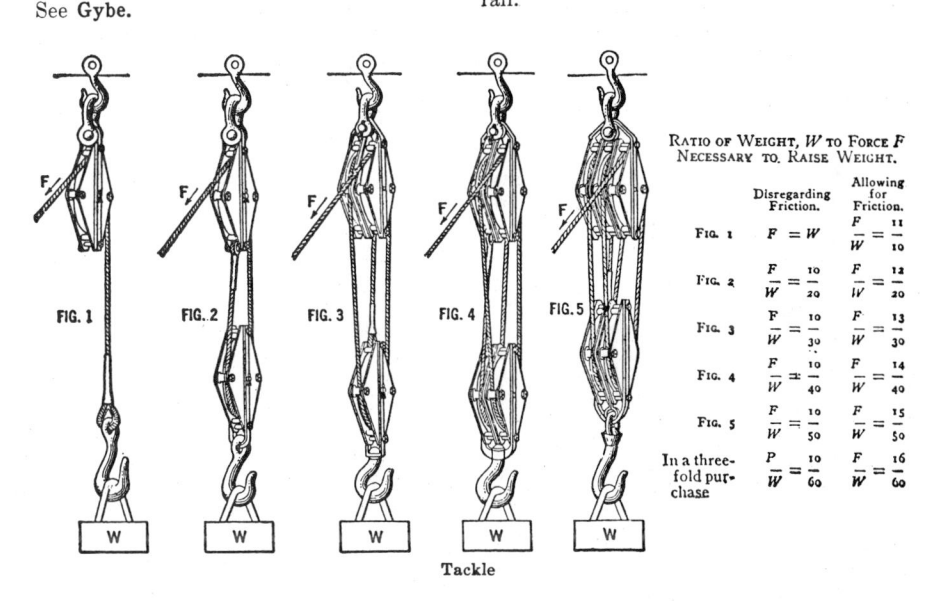

Tackle

	Disregarding Friction.	Allowing for Friction.
Fig. 1	$F = W$	$\dfrac{F}{W} = \dfrac{11}{10}$
Fig. 2	$\dfrac{F}{W} = \dfrac{10}{20}$	$\dfrac{F}{W} = \dfrac{12}{20}$
Fig. 3	$\dfrac{F}{W} = \dfrac{10}{30}$	$\dfrac{F}{W} = \dfrac{13}{30}$
Fig. 4	$\dfrac{F}{W} = \dfrac{10}{40}$	$\dfrac{F}{W} = \dfrac{14}{40}$
Fig. 5	$\dfrac{F}{W} = \dfrac{10}{50}$	$\dfrac{F}{W} = \dfrac{15}{50}$
In a three-fold purchase	$\dfrac{P}{W} = \dfrac{10}{60}$	$\dfrac{F}{W} = \dfrac{16}{60}$

Ratio of Weight, W to Force F Necessary to Raise Weight.

TACKLE. A combination of ropes and blocks working together, or any similar contrivance affording a mechanical advantage to assist in lifting or controlling a weight or applying tension on board ship. Tackles vary in design according to their different uses, every form or adaptation having its own specific name. The theoretical power of a tackle is equal to the number of parts of rope entering the moving block or blocks. A deduction ranging between 10 and 50 per cent must be applied for friction, according to the type of tackle and the working of the sheaves.

Fr: *Palan*; Ger: *Takel; Talje*.

TACK LINE. 1. A line spliced into the eye at the bottom of the tabling for securing a flag to the halyards and separating the different flags of a signal.

2. A length of signal halyard about 6 ft.

Ger: *Koveinnagel*.

TACK PURCHASE.
See **Tack Tackle**.

TACK RIVET.
See **Quilting Rivet**.

TACK TACKLE. Tackle used to bowse down the tack of a sail to its proper place, particularly applied to the sails of fore-and-aft-rigged craft. Also called tack purchase.

any fore-and-aft-rigged craft.

Fr: *Palan d'Amure*; Ger: *Halstalje*.

TACK TRICING LINE. In a fore-and-aft-rigged vessel, the line which draws the tack of a gaff sail upward in order to spill the wind without lowering the gaff. Also called tack trice.

Fr: *Capucin*; Ger: *Hals Aufholer*.

TACK WELD. A short weld used principally for assembly preparation purposes, for temporarily holding material in place that is to be solidly welded, until the proper alignment and position are obtained. Also occasionally used in permanent assembly of secondary structures in welded vessels.

Fr: *Soudure d'Agrafage.*

TACK WELDING. A welding term used to denote short, light, separate welds made at points on the welding line, for the purpose of holding temporarily the pieces to be welded during the making of the final weld, or for attachments not subject to high stress. Also called tacking.

TACTICAL DIAMETER. The perpendicular distance from the original course to the position where a ship has turned through 180°, after the helm is put over.

Fr: *Diamètre d'Évolution;* Ger: *Durchmesser des Evolutionskreises.*

TAFA-ANGA. A plank-built single-outrigger seagoing canoe from the Tongan Archipelago. The construction of the hull is the same as that of the Samoan Va' a-Alo or Bonito boat. Length 20 to 30 ft. Breadth of 20 to 22 in. in the middle. The ends are decked over.

TAFFAREL. Small open boat found in Malta and adjacent waters. Length 20 to 23 ft. Breadth 4 to 4½ ft. Depth 30 in. Deep curved rudder. The rig consists of a jib, rigged on a small bowsprit, and a spritsail. The foot of the sprit is not tied to the mast, but rests on one of the notches cut in the thwart, a little abaft the mast.

TAFFRAIL. In a wooden vessel, the upper part of the ship's stern, usually ornamented with carved work or molding, the ends of which unite to quarter pieces. The railing about a ship's stern.

Fr: *Couronnement;* **Ger:** *Heckreling; Heckbord.*

TAFFRAIL LOG. A screw log in which the register or recording dial is secured to the taffrail. In twin-screw ships the taffrail register is frequently fitted on a short spar 4 to 5 ft. in length in order that the rotator may be streamed well clear of the ship's wake.

Ger: *Heckrelingslog; Decklog.*

See Log, Patent Log.

TAGLER. Open fishing boat somewhat smaller in size than the *Tucker,* used for drifting in the Stettiner Haff, at the mouth of the Oder River. Also called *Tagler Kahn.* The over-all length varies from 37 to 50 ft. with a beam of 16½ to 19 ft. The largest boats have a centerboard. They are rigged with one mast which carries a gaff mainsail, topsail, and forestaysail. A jib is also seen on the larger type.

TAGURI-AMI-BUNE. Japanese trawling fishing sampan from Fukui district, rigged with one mast and a square sail about 317 sq. ft. in area, made of sedge mat. Length over-all 35 ft. Breadth 7.1 ft. Depth 2.6 ft.

TAHPOOY. A small sailing coaster found on the coasts of Guiana and Venezuela with a capacity of 20 to 100 tons. The smaller units are cutter-rigged, while the larger ones are fore-and-aft schooners. The bows are of swimhead type, being trapezoidal in shape with the broadest part on the top. The smaller or lower base is connected to the keel by a kind of forefoot. In order to lessen resistance, the bows are given an inclination of 30° to 40°. The stern is round with outboard rudder. The lines of the run are fine. Length 32 to 82 ft. Breadth 10 to 21½ ft. Draft forward 2 ft. Draft aft 4½ ft.

TAHRAY. West African planked boat employed by the Wolof people in the fisheries at the estuary of the Senegal River. The hull is flat-bottomed, wall-sided, and slightly rockered fore-and-aft, with square bilges. The bow and stern terminate in a solid end piece of rectangular section, about 4.9 ft. long, which projects beyond the transoms. The framing consists of floors and knee timbers. There are 3 thwarts. The mast thwart is connected to the sides by 4 lodging knees. There are 3 strakes of side planking. The top or gunwale strake is strengthened by a half-round batten. The boat is rigged with a vertical mast and a boomed sprit sail. Length over-all 24.6 to 31.1 ft. Breadth 7.4 ft.

TA-HUNG. A 4-masted Northern junk, trading between Antung and Shanghai and varying in size from 50 to 250 tons. Also called *tuyang shuan* or *antung junk.* The hull is built with considerable sheer, flat bottom and flush deck. Three or four heavy wales made from split trunk trees give the necessary longitudinal strength. The bow and stern terminate in heavy stem and transom beams. The bottom planking is laid fore and aft, except at the ends where it is laid transversely. Transverse bulkheads are spaced 2 to 6 ft. apart. The side and bottom planking form a sharp angle at bilge. The bow framing consists of a heavy cross timber laid in the angle formed by the bottom planking and the foremost bulkhead. Where it abuts against the sides stout ribs grown to shape are laid against the turn of the bow and sides. A similar arrangement is provided aft to strengthen the turn of the stern. The hatch coaming which extends from the foremost bulkhead for about two thirds of the length is some 3 ft. in height and horizontal, not following the sheer of the hull. The breadth of hatchways is about one third of the vessel's beam. A deck house is built over the afterdeck. Abaft the deck house, which ends at the transom, a short overhanging gallery is built out from deck level and terminates in a false transom some 5 ft. in height. The rudder-raising windlass is located in this gallery, and the mizzenmast or masts are stepped at sides. It is supported by numerous knees fastened to the inner sides of the wales and the undersides of the deck planking. The most general method used for fastening planking and timbers is with wrought-iron clamps. Nails are seldom used. Length over-all 70 to 110 ft. Breadth 15 to 32 ft. Depth of hold 6½ ft.

The rig consists of 3 or 4 pole masts. The fore- and mainmasts are stepped in tabernacles on the center line, the former having a slight forward rake and the mainmast a slight rake aft. There are one or two quarter mizzenmasts stepped on the gallery. Just off the center line on the starboard bow there is a cathead projecting for about 5 ft., its outer end cleft and fitted with a sheave. Abaft the sheave there is an iron hoop which serves as a support for a jibboom when it is shipped. On each quarter (where 2 mizzenmasts are carried) there is a light fore-and-aft quarter boom and a transverse check boom for handling the mizzens. These sails are made of dark brown cotton and stiffened with bamboo battens spaced 20 in. apart. They consist of narrow vertical cloths sewed together. The mizzens have 1 bonnet, the foresail 2, and the mainsail 3. They are laced together and fitted with boltropes. The ground tackle includes 3 to 6 anchors or grapnels with cables made of bamboo fiber served to prevent chafe. Yulohs are provided for use in cabin weather or when in or near harbor. The bearing pins for these are in chocks of wood which can be shipped on either side forward and project outboard.
Waters, D. W., The Antung Trader, *Mariner's Mirror*, vol. 24, January, 1938.

TAIL. 1. A rope spliced around a block, with an end of sufficient length by which the block may be secured to another rope instead of using a hook.

Fr: *Fouet;* Ger: *Steert.*

See **Cat Tail, Cow's Tail, Monkey Tail, Salmon Tail.**

2. The tapered end of a clew, head, or tack rope which extends only a short length beyond the cringle.

3. The direction in which the stern of a ship at anchor swings. It is said to tail inshore or downstream.

Fr: *Eviter;* Ger: *Steigen und fallen.*

TAIL (to). To taper a rope's end by unlaying it for a certain distance, putting a stop on it, unraveling the yarns in each strand and tapering them with a knife. After treating the yarns with wax the rope is relaid. Also to point.

TAIL BLOCK. A single block having a short piece of rope or tail by which it can be clapped on to any gear.

Fr: *Poulie à Fouet;* Ger: *Steertblock.*

TAIL ON. To take hold of a rope and haul away. Also called tally on.

Fr: *Se mettre sur;* Ger: *Anholen.*

TAIL SHAFT.
See **Shafting.**

TAIL SPLICE. A splice used for joining a Manila, hemp, cotton or linen rope to a wire rope by interweaving the strands of the ends. Frequently used on sailing yachts.

TAIL TACKLE. A watch or luff tackle in which a tail is substituted for the hook in the double block, so that it can be fastened to ropes or parts of rigging.

Fr: *Palan à Fouet;* Ger: *Steerttalje.*

TAINT. Damage to goods due to other cargo having been wetted by sea water in heavy weather. Also called taint damage. It is a result of a peril of the sea. When taint damage is due only to contact with other cargo or is caused by odors from other cargo stowed in the same hold it is not a peril of the sea.

TAKA. Small Turkish coaster 26 to 32 ft. in length, with a capacity of 4/5 tons, found along the Asiatic shores of the Black Sea. Also called *filuka.* The hull is clinker-built with high stem and transom stern, outboard rudder, decked fore and aft. The rig consists of a collapsible mast with standing lug mainsail. Headsails are occasionally set. The mainsail has 3 rows of reef points at the foot and 2 at the head. When becalmed these boats are propelled by 4 sweeps.

TAKE A TURN. To pass a rope once or several times round a belaying pin, bitts or any other object to keep it fast. Also, **to catch a turn.**
Fr: *Tourner;* Ger: *Tornnehmen.*

TAKEN ABACK. Said of a vessel's sails when caught suddenly or unexpectedly by the wind in such a way as to press them aft, or so as to impart a tendency to force the ship astern.
Fr: *Pris Vent Dessus;* Ger: *Back bekommen.*

TAKE IN THE SLACK. To draw in the loose or released part of a rope until it becomes taut.
Fr: *Embraquer le Mou;* Ger: *Lose einholen.*

TAKE-UP MESH. A method of mending fishing nets by which the adjacent row of meshes is decreased by one mesh. Also called stealing mesh.

TAKIA. A small, single-outrigger dugout canoe from the Fiji Islands.

TAKINGS AT SEA. An expression used in marine insurance policies. It relates to the stopping, in wartime, and the taking into port for examination of neutral merchantmen suspected of carrying contraband of war to the enemy.

TAKING OFF. The operation of taking the necessary outside measurements upon an actual ship, so as to enable her lines or form to be drawn from these measurements.

TAKING ULLAGE. Measuring the height of empty space above the level of the oil in a tank.
Fr: *Prendre le Vide.*
See **Ullage.**

TA-KU. Chinese fishing junk from Hangchow-Bay, about 44 ft. long, which works with a bag net. Also called *ku-shuan.* The hull is built with flat bottom, no keel, and 2 strakes of half-sawed logs. The rig consists of 2 masts, main and very short mizzen, stepped abaft the rudder.

TAKUP. Single-outrigger dugout canoe with wash strake, from Lihir Islands, Bismarck Archipelago. Also called *tagup, dagub.* The stem and stern are prolonged upward by means of end pieces, the narrow head of each terminating in a flat, vertical, triangular expansion which is said to represent a hawk's head. There are from 4 to 6 outrigger booms. Length 30 ft. Breadth 1.2 ft. Depth 1.7 ft. (Typical.)

TALA. A small East Indian dugout canoe with double outriggers employed for the inshore fisheries at Amboina, Southern Moluccas. Also called *sapu.* The hull is long and narrow with slab sides. No wash strake is provided. The outrigger floats are usually made of the large leaf stalks of the sago palm.

TALK BACK HAILER. Trade name for a telecommunication device used on board ship. By means of a control panel on the navigating bridge, and various substations throughout the ship covering operational and emergency areas, anyone standing anywhere in any of those areas can hear a command from the bridge, and can reply to the bridge from wherever he may be, and without interrupting whatever he may be doing. Also called **Master communicator.**

TALLY. A record taken of the number of packages, bales, bags, and so on, delivered to or from a vessel.
Fr: *Pointage;* Ger: *Anschreibung.*

TALLY BOARD. 1. A small piece of board attached to the line or tail block sent out by rocket apparatus to a stranded vessel. Instructions in several languages of how to use and where to make the line fast are carried on the board.
2. A board used as a tally sheet.

TALLY CLERK.
See **Tallyman.**

TALLYMAN. The person who records cargo discharged or loaded by a vessel. Also called checker, tally clerk. One of the tallymen is usually appointed by the ship or ship's agent and another by the merchant, shipper, dock company or custom authority. Comparison between the several tally books kept by the several parties are then made at the end of each day.
Fr: *Pointeur;* Ger: *Tallymann; Zahlleute; Ladungsanschreiber.*

TAMARACK. A coarse, hard, durable wood, with good holding power for fastenings. Natural crooks make excellent knees. Weight when seasoned about 37 lbs. per cu. ft. Also called hackmatack, juniper, or eastern larch.
Fr: *Génévrier;* Ger: *Wachholderholz.*

TAMBANGAN. A generic term used in the western half of the East Indies for a type of small dugout canoe with flat bottom used for ferrying passengers from ship to shore, across estuaries, and so on, also, as a tender for larger boats. When used in open waters they are rigged with a small forward raking mast and triangular sail set with the apex downward. They are paddled in Bandjermasin district, South Borneo, and Palembang district, Sumatra, while in other localities oars are used. For steering, a paddle or a centerline rudder of European pattern is employed. Larger canoes of this type rigged with 2 masts are also used for crossing from Surabaya to Madura Island.

The *sasak tambangan*, used only in smooth waters, consists of 2 canoes lashed together and with a platform between them.

The *jukung tambangan* from Bandjermasin is used to ferry passengers across rivers or for short trips along the coast.

TAMBILAI. Polynesian single-outrigger dugout canoe from Suva and Levuka Islands, Fiji Islands. The hull is left solid for several feet at each end, and it has a deep vertical cutwater.

TAMBUL. A single-outrigger dugout canoe from northwest Lavongai Island, New Hanover, Bismarck Archipelago, with no sheer and slender ends. The stem and stern carry fretwork carvings.

TANCOOK WHALER. Half-decked, double-ended, schooner-rigged centerboard boat originating from Tancook Island, Mahone Bay, and used for fishing with hand lines on the coast of Nova Scotia. There is a long working cockpit extending from amidships aft, and a cuddy forward for the crew. Boats built recently have a stern with counter and small transom. They have no centerboard, and are fitted with an auxiliary motor. The rig consists of 2 vertical masts and short bowsprit, forestaysail with short boom, gaff foresail and mainsail, fisherman's staysail with yard. Length overall 43 ft. 6 in.; waterline 33 ft. Breadth 10 ft. Draft aft 6 ft. 2 in. Sail area 822.4 sq. ft. Motor 25 hp. (Typical.)

Bell, E. A., "The Passing of the Tancook Whaler," *Yachting* (New York), vol. 53 (February, 1933).

TANDI. A single-outrigger, Australian dugout canoe of the Koka Ompindamo people from Princess Charlotte Bay, North Queensland. At each end of the hull there is a flattened projection from 15 to 20 in. long. A wash strake is usually provided on each side with a coil of bark running like a thick rope between the wash strake and the hull. The outrigger booms are double and pass through both gunwales or wash strakes. Their number varies from 4 to 8 according to the size of the canoe.

TA-NEI-WAN. Chinese seine boat from Swatow, Kwang-Tung Province. These boats work in pairs. Length 43 ft. Breadth 13½ ft. (Typical.)

TANG. A metal fitting used on sailing yachts for the attachment of standing rigging to the mast, replacing the loops or eyes and eliminating all splicing. It is usually made in the form of a pad hook or a mast band with broad-based hooks which take the downward thrust of shrouds and stays.

TANGENT METHOD. An artifice of navigation used in the Sumner's method for describing the circles of position on the Mercator chart. The tangent method is based upon the assumption that for a short distance, the tangent drawn through a point taken upon the circumference of a circle will coincide very nearly with the arc of the circle.

Fr: *Méthode de la tangente;* Ger: *Tangentenmethode.*

TANGENT SCREW. The screw attached to the vernier of a sextant for making the final adjustment when making an observation. It works tangentially to the arc.

Fr: *Vis de Rappel; Vis Tangente;* Ger: *Feinschraube.*

TANGLE NET. A general name for those nets in which fish are captured by entangling themselves in its complicated folds. Also called flounder net.

Fr: *Filet Maillant;* Ger: *Stassnetz.*

TANG-O. A double-outrigger dugout canoe from the east coast of Cape York Peninsula, Queensland, 24 to 30 ft. long and manned by 3 or 4 men.

TANG-VAY. Small fishing junk, decked fore and aft, and rigged with one mast, found in southern China and Indo-China.

TANJU. Double-outrigger Australian dugout canoe of the Barunguan tribe from Port Stewart, North Queensland. The outrigger floats are supported by a pair of long flexible booms lashed to the top of the gunwales, one being nearly amidships and the other near the stern. The body of the canoe has a rounded bow with projecting flat extension. The truncated stern is cut off vertically.

TANK BARGE. A special type of steel

barge used in the transportation of liquid cargoes. These barges are fitted with tanks in the same way as tank vessels but have no means of self-propulsion. Some tank barges are large seagoing craft, measuring up to 370 ft. in length. They are usually provided with pumping engines for handling the cargo.

Fr: *Chaland Citerne;* Ger: *Tankleichter; Tankkahn.*

TANKER. A vessel specially designed and constructed for the carriage of fluid cargoes in bulk. Also called tank vessel. The vessel's holds are subdivided by longitudinal and transverse bulkheads so that each compartment forms a separate tank. Petroleum and similar oils, spirit, propane, sulfuric acid, molasses, wine, and whale oil are among the cargoes carried in tank vessels. The fluid is pumped into and out of the tanks by a system of piping and the ship's pumping plant. The propelling machinery is placed aft and, in case of inflammable cargoes, is separated from the tanks by a cofferdam formed by two complete transverse bulkheads spaced 2 to 5 ft. apart.

Fr: *Bateau Citerne;* Ger: *Tankschiff; Tankfahrzeug.*

See **Fuel Ship, Oil Tanker, Twin-Bulkhead Tanker.**

In order to avoid large areas of free liquid surfaces which are detrimental to the ship's structure the usual practice is to divide the cargo space into 3 fore-and-aft sections using 2 longitudinal bulkheads or by constructing small tanks in each wing, named summer tanks, in addition to a centerline bulkhead. Molasses tankers are built with alternate long and short tanks for the better distribution of cargo and also to suit cargoes of different specific gravities. A double bottom is fitted for water ballast so that the main cargo tanks can be used solely for the purpose intended.

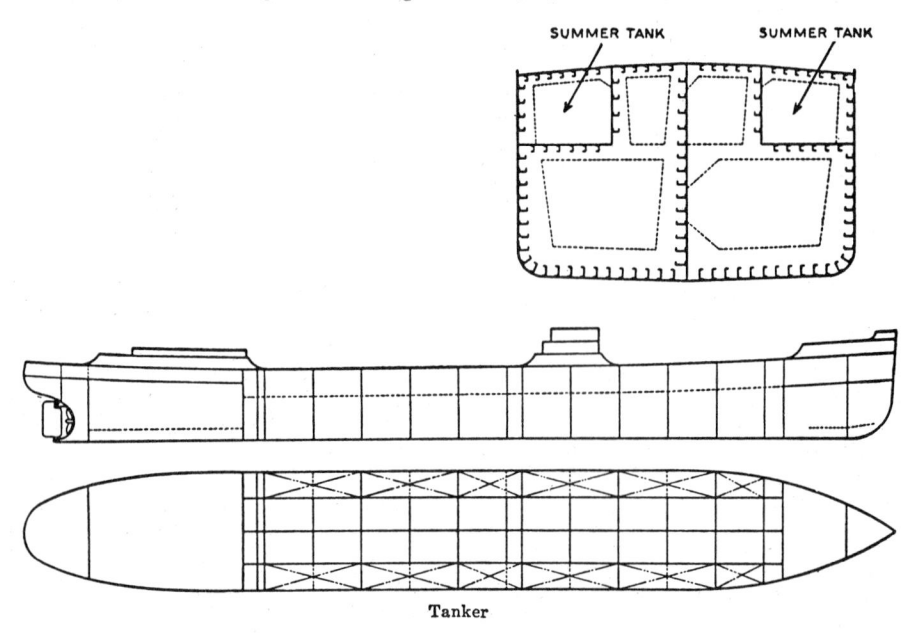

Tanker

Hudson, J. W., "Oil Tankers," Society of Naval Architects and Marine Engineers (New York), *Transactions,* vol. 44 (1936); Jansen, P., *Sea Transport of Petroleum,* London, 1938; Lisle, O., *Tanker Technique,* London, 1936; Morrell, R. W., *Oil Tankers,* New York, 1931; Pluymert, N. J., *Modern Tanker Design,* Society of Naval Architects and Marine Engineers, *Transactions,* vol. 47, New York, 1939.

TANKERMAN (U. S.). A seaman to whom competent authorities have granted a certificate or license showing that he is trained in and capable of performing all duties on tank vessels which relate to the handling of liquid cargoes. The kinds or grades of liquid cargo the holder is qualified to handle are stated on the certificate.

Wooler, R. G., Tankerman's Handbook, New York, 1946.

TANK HEATING LINE. A system of low pressure steam piping installed in the bunker tanks of oil burning steamers and in the cargo spaces of tankers to preheat the oil before pumping out. Also called heater coils.
Fr: *Serpentins de Réchauffage;* Ger: *Dampfheizungsstränge.*

TANK-SIDE KNEE.
See **Bilge Bracket.**

TANK TESTER. A shipyard worker who inspects tanks for water- and oiltightness. He cuts, chips, splits, files, and calks angles, seams, and rivets. He tests by sounding with a light hammer to detect looseness of rivets and uses a thin-bladed knife called a "feeler knife" to test closeness of joints, and repairs the defect found.

TANK TOGGLE. A short, heavy piece of wood placed inside a portable tank, across the manhole, to which a strap is fixed for hooking a block to lift the tank.

TANK TOP. Plating forming the top part of a double bottom. In cargo holds it is the flooring on which the cargo rests. Also called inner bottom.
Fr: *Plafond de Ballast;* Ger: *Tankdecke; Tanktop; Doppelbodendecke.*

TANK VESSEL.
See **Tanker.**

TANNED SAIL. A sail soaked in an oak bark or cutch solution to keep it from mildewing.

TANNING. General name for various dressings employed to counteract deterioration through rot or mildew of sails and nets. Cutch (an East Indian gum), oak bark, tar, creosote, ocher, and linseed oil are among the best-known preservatives, besides a number of patented compositions. The usual dressing put on sails consists of a mixture of boiled linseed oil, ocher, and paraffin. In Great Britain bargemen use fish oil instead of linseed oil.
Fr: *Tannage;* Ger: *Gerbung.*

TANO. Australian double-outrigger dugout canoe employed by the Koka-Yao tribesmen on the east coast of Cape York Peninsula for dugong hunting. It has a length ranging from 24 to 30 ft. The bow is rounded off and terminates at gunwale level in a shelflike projection used as a platform by the harpooner. A similar but smaller projection forms the stern. The 2 outrigger booms cross over the gunwales, one nearly amidships, the other near the stern.

TAPAKE.
See **Lapis.**

TAPERED NECK RIVET. A panhead or snaphead rivet used with punched holes. Also called cone-neck rivet, swell-neck rivet. Part of the shank, immediately below the head, is slightly tapered or swollen so as to fill the natural countersink of the hole. Used for shell plating, tanks, and so on, above 16 mm. diameter.
Fr: *Rivet à Fût Renflé;* Ger: *Schaftanschwellungsniet.*

TAPERED PLANKING.
See **Diminishing Stuff.**

TAPER LINER. A liner having a wedge shape, used to fill up the triangular spaces between the faying surfaces of shell plating when the butts of plating are arranged clinker fashion. Also called tapered liner, tapered slip.
Fr: *Cale Etirée;* Ger: *Spitzfüllstück.*

TAP RIVET. A threaded bolt with a head shaped like a rivethead. Used for connecting shell plates to castings (stem, stern, frame, shaft brackets). Also called stud rivet.
Fr: *Prisonnier;* Ger: *Nietschraube.*

TARPAULIN. A double-warp, single-weft, plain-woven jute or hemp fabric, waterproofed with boiling tar or chemically treated, used as covering over wooden hatch covers.
Fr: *Prélart; Toile à Prélart;* Ger: *Persenning; Persenningtuch.*

Seagoing vessels carry 3 tarpaulins over weather-deck hatches. They are secured to the sides of the hatch coamings by battens driven tight with wedges. The linear dimensions exceed those of the hatch by about 3 ft., making an overlap of about 18 in. at each hatch end. In 'tween decks the usual practice is to provide one tarpaulin over the upper 'tween-deck hatches and none on the lower 'tween-decks. Tarpaulin canvas is made up in 36 or 45 in. widths. Number 1 to 4 canvas is generally used. The British Board of Trade recommendations specify that the material used be entirely free from jute and that the minimum weight per square yard before treatment should be as follows: 19 ounces if tarred, 18 ounces if chemically dressed, 16 for black dressed material.

Hardy, E., Ship's Canvas, The Shipbuilder, Newcastle upon Tyne, vol. 51 (January, 1944)

TARRED FITTINGS. Collective term for small tarred hemp lines such as ratline, marline, houseline, hambroline, seizing, rounding, spun yarn, which are made on special machinery or by hand and are usually designated by the number of threads or yarns they contain. They are used with wire or Manila rope for worming, serving, and whipping. Also called marine fittings.

TARRED ROPE. Fiber rope is tarred when it is to be exposed to the weather. Tarred rope is only about 75 per cent as strong as untarred or white rope, and becomes less strong with time. Also called black rope.

Fr: *Filin Gourdronné*; Ger: *Geteertes Tauwerk*.

Tarred rope is made by passing the strands through copper tar tanks heated to 220° F. The excess of tar is removed by rollers or by passing the strands through holes surrounded with oakum and then dried. Stockholm tar is usually employed but coal tar is sometimes used. Ropes take up about one quarter of their weight in tar. Tarred ropes are weaker than white cordage on account of the effect of heat on the fibers which injures their elasticity. Most tarred rope is tarred "in the yarn"; that is, the individual yarns are tarred before they are processed into rope. Small diameter lines of about ¼ to ⅜ in. are tarred "in the rope"; that is, the finished rope is tarred.

TARTANA. Single-masted vessel found in the western Mediterranean and adjacent seas, used for trading and fishing. Tartanas are built in different sizes, the largest having an approximate length of 65 ft. with a beam of 15 ft., while the smallest are only 27 ft. long with a beam of 9 ft. 4 in. A great number have been fitted with auxiliary motors. Tartanas have a high freeboard and are generally decked. They are built with pointed stern, high stem, and sternpost. The mast is upright, and is held in place by shrouds with ratlines, and the rig consists of a lateen sail and one or two jibs set from a bowsprit.

Tartana

Fr: *Tartane;* Ger: *Tartane.*

TARTANELLA. A small fishing Tartana on the Dalmatian coast, decked fore and aft, with pronounced sheer forward, rigged with a long bowsprit and large headsail. Capacity 2 to 4 tons.

TARTANON. A double-ended, open fishing boat from the coast of Algeria. Length 13 to 16 ft. Breadth 4.9 to 6.9 ft. (Average.)

TASTING. The act of chipping a plank or timber with an adze, or boring it with a small auger for the purpose of ascertaining its condition.

TATAI. A single-outrigger, Polynesian dugout canoe from the Island of Pukapuka, Tuamotu Archipelago, with wash strake sewed to the underbody and both ends decked in. The smaller craft are one-piece dugouts; the larger have bow and stern pieces.

The *tatia-tokatai*, or one-man canoe, has a length of 10½ ft., a beam at gunwales of 10 in., and a depth of 17 in.

The *tatai-tokalua*, or two-man canoe, has a length of 19 ft., beam of 11 in., a depth of 16 in.

PATAKU. A small, single-outrigger dugout canoe from the western division of Papua, British New Guinea. This name is also given at times to simple dugouts without wash strakes or outrigger, employed on the creeks and small rivers in the same district. Also called tatagu.

TATARA. Open, double-ended rowboat from Botel Tobago (a small island off the southern end of Formosa) with stem and stern rising vertically and terminating in a point, greatest beam amidships, gradually decreasing toward each end. The base of the hull consists of a narrow salient keel scarfed by means of a lock joint at each end to a narrow and curved post. On each side of the keel are 3 wide strakes of planking. The ends of the upper or wash strake form the curved-up end pieces. The ends rise to a height of 4 ft., measured from the base, whereas the depth amidships is only 2.4 ft. The beam is 1.2 ft. It is propelled by 1 or 2 men with short sculls, and is said to be unseaworthy in even a mild swell, and to become completely unmanageable in any sort of wind.

TATAYA. A native surf boat of the Batanes Islands, Philippines, built like a dory.

TA-TSENG. A type of southern junk hailing from Swatow and other localities at the mouth of the river Han, used for trawling off Lamock Islands. Also called Swatow fishing junk. These junks have fine lines at ends but are comparatively beamy amidships. The bow tapers up from the waterline to a T-shaped stemhead. The stern is of the Chinese transom type. They usually have 2 or 3 masts, although some of the smaller ones are single-masted. The mainmast is much taller than the other masts. The sails are round-leeched and are stiffened by a large number of battens. These junks work in pairs, towing a long trawlnet. They generally fish in fleets. The rig consists of 1 to 3 masts. Length over-all 23 ft. to 51 ft. Breadth 8.8 ft. to 14 ft. Depth of hold 2.1 ft. to 4.5 ft. (Typical.)

TA-TUI-SHUAN. A Chinese fishing junk from Hangchow Bay, about 47 ft. in length; capacity about 300 picul. These boats work in pairs with a drag net. The hull is built with flat bottom, low stern, two grounding keels and rounded sides, with topsides built of 3 strakes of half-sawed logs.

TAURUA. A double canoe of the Tubuai Islands, used for fishing.

TAVAKA. A single-outrigger dugout canoe with decked ends, from Futuna Islands, New Hebrides. The sides are raised by a wash strake. An ornament supposed to resemble the tail of a fowl is affixed at the stern. The larger canoes of this type are formed of two logs firmly and skillfully wound together end to end by sennit. They are used for catching flying fish.

TAVE (G. B.).
See **Look-on Net.**

TCHEKTIRME. Turkish coaster, decked fore and aft, about 50 ft. in length, with bluff bows, high inboard curving stem and stern, and high bulwarks amidships. Also called *Tchektima*. The rig consists of a lower mast with topmast, carrying a square foresail, topsail and sprit mainsail. The head of the spritsail runs on hanks along a wire leading from mast cap to sprithead.

The topsail braces are rove through blocks at the end of the sprit. Headsails include two jibs and a forestaysail which sets on a bowsprit with jibboom. The elaborate carvings of the stern have nowadays entirely disappeared. These boats are chiefly engaged in the timber trade between the Dardanelles and the Bosporus, and seldom venture out in the open sea.

TEAK. East Indian hardwood. Found in India, Burma, Siam, and Java. Formerly used for the framing and planking of wooden vessels chiefly because it contains a resinous oil which prevents the rusting of iron fastenings and is very resistant to the attacks of ship worms. Mostly used today for decks, deckhouses, handrails, planksheers of decks and erections, foundations for deck machinery, binnacles, etc. Also called teakwood. Weight per cubic foot 45 to 52 pounds.

Fr: *Teck;* Ger: *Tiekholz.*

TEE BAR. A steel bar with a cross section like the letter "T." Also called "T" beam.

Fr: *Fer à T;* Ger: *T-Profil.*

TEE BULB BAR. A tee bar with bulb on toe of its web. Also called bulb tee.

Fr: *Fer T à Boudin;* Ger: *T-Wulstprofil.*

TEHUANTEPECER. A violent wind blowing from the north in the Gulf of Tehuantepec, Central America.

TEIKOKU KAIJI KYOKAI. Imperial Japanese Marine Corporation, the Japanese classification society established in 1899 in Tokyo. Its rules and regulations for the building and survey of steel vessels are similar to those of the British Corporation. In 1919 the Japanese Marine Corporation made an agreement with the American Bureau, the British Corporation and the Registro Italiano for the mutual recognition of the classification and survey of vessels.

Symbols: N.S.* (Nippon Standard). Indicates the highest class and that the vessel has been under the society's supervision during construction.

N.S. The same letters without the star indicate the highest class without survey during construction.

N.S.*f. Indicates that the vessel has been surveyed during construction and built to modified scantlings approved by the society for the freeboard assigned. The same symbol without the star indicates that the vessel has been surveyed after construction and has had a freeboard assigned by the society.

The letter "M" preceding any of the above symbols indicates that the machinery and boilers have been surveyed by the society.

A single horizontal black line inserted through the symbol shows that the class has been withdrawn or suspended for noncompliance with the rules. When the symbol is inserted between brackets it shows that the class has been withdrawn at the owners' request.

TEINAERINGUR. Open rowing and sailing boat formerly employed in the fisheries on the south coast of Iceland. The hull was very strongly built with rounded stem, sharp raked stern, and good sheer. It was rigged with two masts, main and mizzen, and a short bowsprit. It had two headsails, a gaff mainsail without boom and a sprit mizzen. This rig was altered later, the gaff mainsail being replaced by a spritsail.

Length 16 to 28.4 ft. Breadth 3.9 to 7.2 ft. This type is now believed extinct.

TEKLETEK. An East Indian sailing canoe employed for trading and fishing off Sapudi Islands, east of Madura.

TEK-PAI. A Catamaran from the Isle of Formosa made of bamboo logs fastened together by lashings of rattan which firmly bind 6 or 7 crosspoles on the top. The forepart is strengthened by lacings of rattan woven in and out between the logs. The smaller ends of the bamboo logs are set at the bow and have a strong upward curve which enables the raft to ride better in a sea. Along each side above the crosspiece, and securely tied to them, is a small bamboo forming a sort of gunwale upon which are fastened two rowlocks, each with a long tholepin. A heavy mast step is lashed to two crosspieces. The mast is placed a little forward of amidships and carries a single lug sail of matting. Length 23 to 35 ft. Width 4 to 10 ft.

See **Balsa, Jangada.**

The number of bamboo logs varies from 6 to 14. The largest rafts of this type are used as surf boats and have 3 leeboards, 1 in the center, and 2 at the side. A long oar is used for steering.

TELEGRAPH BLOCK. A pyramid-shaped block with a number of small sheaves used for making signals and permitting several flags to be hoisted simultaneously.

TELEGRAPH BUOY. A spherical or can-shaped buoy painted green and surmounted by a globe, and occasionally by a flag, which marks the end of a submarine telegraph cable. Below the top mark two lanterns showing fixed white lights are placed horizontally for use by night.

> Fr: *Bouée de cable sous-marin;* *Bouée de Télégraphe;* Ger: *Kabeltonne; Telegraphenboje.*

TELAJANGAN. A Javanese fishing canoe from the districts of Besuki and Pasuruan, with outriggers and forked stern shaped like a fishtail, and wash strake of planking or palm leaf. Two types of rig are used as in the *sekong*, one with short mast and triangular sail with yard and boom, the other without mast, the yard being held in place by a pole stepped near the stern.

TELEMOTOR. A hydraulic follow-up system by which the motion of the steering wheel is transmitted to a steering engine. Also called telemotor system. It consists of a transmitting cylinder located near the wheel connected by pipes to a similar receiving cylinder near the engine, each cylinder being fitted with a piston. The entire system is filled with a nonfreezing mixture of glycerine and water, or a special oil. Movement of the steering wheel displaces a quantity of fluid which produces a corresponding movement of the receiving piston, thus operating the steering engine control mechanism. This system is simple, but is subject to malfunctioning if air leaks into it at any point.

Fr: *Télémoteur;* Ger: *Telemotor.*

See **Follow-up Gear.**

TELESCOPE. An optical instrument designed to magnify in a high degree and to reveal in sharp focus a very small part of the wide area seen with the unaided eye. Also called spyglass. It collects as much light as its large object glass will take from a relatively small area of the field or object in order that this light may form a brilliant image, at high magnification. It consists of a brass tube having a concentric extension tube within, bearing an object glass and an eyepiece. The object glass is formed of two lenses with different refractive and dispensive properties, one a double convex lens of crown glass, the other a plane concave lens of flint glass. The eyepiece is a combination of lenses. The two lenses are kept apart at a definite distance in the brass tube which forms the eyepiece. The magnifying power depends on the ratio of focus between the object glass and the eyepiece and their distance. At various points in the interior of the telescope are placed thin discs of metal with a central aperture. These rings are termed "stops." Their purpose is to intercept the extreme rays near the edge of the lens and also cut off any extraneous light.

Fr: *Longue Vue;* Ger: *Teleskop; Fernrohr.*

See **Day and Night Telescope, Dioptric Telescope, Inverting Telescope, Naval Telescope, Sextant Telescope, Star Telescope, Water Telescope, Zenith Telescope.**

TELESCOPE SHADE. A dark glass that can be screwed on to the eye end of a sextant telescope.

Ger: *Okularblende.*

TELESCOPIC TOPMAST. A topmast arranged to telescope into the lower mast by suitable sheaves and a wire line, used principally in vessels which have to navigate canals and rivers with bridges.

Fr: *Mât de Flèche Télescopique;* Ger: *Teleskopartige Stänge.*

TELLTALE COMPASS. A compass, generally of the inverted type and suspended from the deck, placed in the master's quarters for his convenience.

TEMBON. In Cheribon, a Javanese fishing dugout with wash strakes, or *jukung* type. Also called *jukung tembon.*

TEMPLATE. Mold or pattern made to the exact size of a piece of work that is to be laid out or formed, and on which such information as position of rivet holes, size of lap, and so on, is indicated. Templates in ship work are usually made of thin board or paper.

Fr: *Gabarit;* Ger: *Schablone.*

TEMPORALES. A strong Southwest to West wind accompanied by heavy rain which prevails during July and August on the West coast of Costa Rica and Nicaragua.

TEMPORARY BUNKER. A portion of the forehold generally in front of a permanent cross bunker, partitioned off with wood and found on coal-burning steamers which make long voyages without recoaling.

Fr: *Soute Provisoire;* Ger: *Fliegender Bunker.*

TEMPORARY MAGNET. Soft iron which loses its magnetism when the magnetizing source is removed or discontinued.

Fr: *Aimant Induit;* Ger: *Induktionsmagnet.*

TEMPORARY MAGNETISM. The magnetism which changes in amount with every change of heading of the ship. It is induced in soft iron by the earth's magnetic field. Also called transient magnetism.

Fr: *Magnétisme Temporaire;* Ger: *Flüchtiger Magnetismus.*

TEMPORARY REPAIRS. Repairs necessitated by the action of a peril insured against and for which underwriters may be held liable.

They are classified as follows: (1) those effected as a port of refuge because the cost of permanent repairs at this port would be excessive; (2) those effected at a port of refuge because of lack of necessary facilities for permanent repair work; (3) those made at port of destination because of lack of facilities for permanent work in order that the vessel may proceed to another port where the damage can be repaired at less cost; (4) those incurred at a port of refuge for the common safety of all interests.

Fr: *Réparations Provisoires;* Ger: *Vorläüfige Reparaturen; Zeitweilige Reparaturen; Notausbesserungen.*

TEND. 1. To lead in a certain direction, as, for instance, the anchor cable. Also called grow.

Fr: *Appeler.*

2. The equivalent of "attend" in nautical language. Used when referring to mooring lines or other ropes.

TENDER. 1. A vessel is said to be tender when its center of gravity is too high, giving it too small a metacentric height, with resulting insufficient statical stability. This condition makes a vessel top-heavy and is conducive to capsizing. Small off-center weights will cause the vessel to list considerably under these conditions.

Fr: *Volage;* Ger: *Rank.*

2. A small vessel or craft employed to attend a larger one, taking ashore or bringing aboard passengers, goods, stores, and so on.

Fr: *Annexe;* Ger: *Beiboot; Tender.*

See **Hatch Tender, Lighthouse Tender, Water Tender.**

TENDER CLAUSE. A hull clause in a marine insurance policy whereby the underwriters are entitled to decide the port to which a damaged vessel shall proceed for repairs or docking. The underwriters also have the right of veto in connection with the place of repair and repairing firm proposed by the owners. Whenever the extent of the damage is ascertainable the underwriters may require tenders to be taken for the repair of such damage.

Ger: *Tenderklausel.*

TEND SHIP. 1. To watch the swinging of a ship at anchor at each turn of the tide, taking advantage of any conditions which may make the ship swing to that side which will keep the hawse clear.

2. To use the helm to preserve the sheer of a vessel at anchor and to prevent her dragging the chain in a bight over the anchor and fouling it.

Fr: *Faire Éviter; Garder l'Évitage;* Ger: *Handhaben beim Schwoien.*

TENON. The end of a piece of wood shaped in the form of a rectangular prism, which is received into a recess in another piece, having the same shape and size. This recess is called a mortise.

Fr: *Tenon;* Ger: *Zapfen.*

See **Head Tenon, Heel Tenon.**

TENTING. Tenting an awning consists of casting off the stops from the jackstay and making them fast to ringbolts in the deck. This is done either to catch fresh water or to keep the wind out of the awning during a squall.

TENTOO. Japanese fishing sampan from the Aomori district in northern Hondo. It is employed in the cod fisheries from December to March, in the herring fisheries in April and May, and in the capture of sharks in October and November. These boats work as far as 40 to 50 miles from shore when looking for cod. They are rigged with one mast and square sail. Length overall 36 ft. Breadth 7½ ft. Depth 2.6 ft. Draft 1.8 ft. Displacement 5.2 tons.

TEPPU. An Indian raft or catamaran from Vizagapatam, made up of two halves lashed together fore and aft. Each half consists of a long log bearing a washboard sewed upon the outer edge and a pointed beak piece pegged on the fore end. On coming ashore the rope lashings are cast off; whereupon the two halves fall apart and are carried separately up the beach.

TEPUKEI. An outrigger of the Santa Cruz and Reef Islands, Melanesia. It carries a wide stage which is loaded with cargo on one side and has a sun shelter on the other. It is rigged with one mast and crab-claw sail. Although very unseaworthy, these canoes have been known to go as far as the Solomon Islands.

TEREDO.
See **Shipworm.**

TERMITANE. A type of Sicilian fishing boat similar to the *capaciota* built at Termini Imerese. Their length ranges from 26 to 31 ft.

TERM PIECE.
See **Side Counter Timber.**

TERN SCHOONER. A three-mast fore-and-aft-rigged schooner.
Fr: *Goëlette à trois mâts;* Ger: *Dreimast Gaffelschoner.*
Chapelle, H. I., "The Nova Scotia Tern Schooners," *Yachting* (New York), vol. 56 (August, 1934).

TERRE ALTOS. A Northwest squall lasting 5-6 hours, which occurs in the coastal region of Rio de Janeiro.

TERRESTRIAL EQUATOR. The great circle on the earth's surface, every point of which is equidistant from either pole. Its plane is perpendicular to the earth's axis.

Fr: *Equateur;* Ger: *Äquator.*

TERRESTRIAL MAGNETISM. The magnetic properties of the earth which give the compass needle its directive power and cause it to dip.
Fr: *Magnétisme terrestre;* Ger: *Erdmagnetismus.*

TERRESTRIAL MERIDIAN. The great circle on the earth's surface passing through the poles and the station of the observer.
Fr: *Méridien Géographique;* Ger: *Erdmeridian.*

TERRESTRIAL POLE. One of the points at which the earth's axis of rotation intersects the earth's surface.
Fr: *Pôle Terrestre;* Ger: *Erdpol.*

TERRITORIAL STRAITS. Straits which are less than 6 nautical miles wide are known as territorial straits. When a strait of this kind divides the land of one and the same state, it belongs to the territory of such state. If a strait divides the land of two different states, it belongs to the territory of both, and the boundary line runs through mid-channel.
Fr: *Détroit territorial;* Ger: *Territoriale Meerenge.*

TERRITORIAL WATERS. The waters under territorial jurisdiction of a state. It is generally admitted that the three-mile limit marks the outer boundary of that part of the marginal sea which is under the territorial jurisdiction of the littoral state. Such a rule is not inconsistent with the exercise of other rights (neutrality, customs, fisheries) over the high seas beyond the three-mile limit. With regard to bays and gulfs, territorial waters follow the sinuosities of the coast unless an established usage has sanctioned a wider limit. Also called territorial sea.
Fr: *Eaux Territoriales;* Ger: *Territorialgewässer; Küstenmeer; Hochheitsgewässer.*

Although the 3-mile limit, in case of war, has become inadequate in consequence of the increased range of modern gunnery, no other rule has been generally recognized. Some nations have adopted a wider limit but so far they have never, in practice, successfully asserted it against a recalcitrant state.
Bustamante, A. S., *The Territorial Sea*, New York, 1930; Coulson and Forbes, *Law Relating to Waters*, London, 1910; Jessup, P. C., *The Law of Territorial Waters*, New York, 1927.

TEST HEAD. The head or height of a column of water which will give a prescribed pressure on the vertical or horizontal sides of a compartment or tank when subjecting it to hydrostatic test for tightness, strength, or both.

THALWEG. The line of deepest soundings along the course of a river. In international law the term is judicially construed to denote the main navigable channel of a waterway which constitutes a boundary line between two nations or states.

Fr: *Thalweg;* Ger: *Talweg; Stromstrich.*

THAMAKAU. A single-outrigger, sailing canoe of the Fiji Islands. The tack of the triangular canoe sail is set right forward with the point of the yard resting in a slot worked in the deck to receive it, the lower spar acting as a sort of cocked-up boom. The tack is always shifted from end to end of the canoe when going about, as the outrigger is always carried to windward. This type is almost extinct.

THAMES MEASUREMENT. A measurement rule adopted in 1855 by the Royal Thames Yacht Club and still retained in Lloyds Register of British Yachts. Also called Thames tonnage. It is frequently used for estimating the cost of building an average cruising yacht at "so much per ton Thames Measurement," and is given by the following formula (all dimensions in ft.):

$$\text{Thames Measurement} = \frac{(\text{Length} - \text{Breadth}) \times \text{Breadth} \times \tfrac{1}{2} \text{Breadth}}{94}$$

Fr: *Jauge de la Tamise;* Ger: *Themsemass.*

THAMES SAILING BARGE. A type of barge intended for navigation on tidal rivers and short sea trips. Also called topsail barge, spritsail barge (G. B.). The hull is long, wall-sided, flat-bottomed, and very deep in the water. These vessels, in common with other flat-bottomed craft, have leeboards. They are mostly sprit-rigged, having a sprit mainsail and a very small sprit-rigged mizzen called a jigger. They carry a topsail, foresail, and jib. The mast is usually fixed on deck in a tabernacle and is collapsible. They sail rapidly in a fresh breeze, very close to the wind, and can face almost any weather. The muley is a similar barge with a ketch mizzen. The stumpy has no topmast or bowsprit and the boomy is rigged with a gaff and boom mainsail.

Carr, F. G., *Sailing Barges*, London, 1931.

THAMES SKIFF (G. B.). Small rowing boats used on the Thames River. There are two types, known as the waterman's skiff and the pleasure skiff.

THAMES WHERRY (G. B.). Open sailing boat formerly rigged with sprit mainsail, foresail, and sprit mizzen, but later with lugsails.

THAUAV. A single-outrigger canoe of the Western Caroline Islands, employed for coastal and lagoon transport. The fore end sheers sharply and terminates in a broad truncate extremity. The afterend is wider than the fore end and nearly horizontal. A platform of rectangular form is built over the central section of the hull and projects a short distance outboard on each side.

THEFT. The word "theft" in marine insurance is understood to mean theft of a whole package in contradistinction to "pilferage"; that is, clandestine theft. The risk of theft is not covered under an ordinary form of marine policy, unless specially added thereto. A theft committed by anyone of a ship's company, whether crew or passenger, is not covered in the ordinary form of marine policy under the word "thieves," the latter word referring especially to what is termed "assailing thieves"; that is, robbery with violence.

Fr: *Vol;* Ger: *Diebstahl.*

THERMAL CONVECTION. A term used in meteorology to denote the ascent of a limited mass of air through its environment.

Fr: *Convection thermique;* Ger: *Thermisches Übertragung.*

THERMIT WELDING. A method of welding which depends upon the production, by a reaction between finely divided aluminum and iron oxide, of a supply of clean superheated liquid steel at a temperature of approximately 5000 degrees F.

Fr: *Soudure Alumino-Thermique;* Ger: *Thermitschweissung.*

In practice a mold is built around the fracture or parts to be welded, so shaped as to provide a surplus of metal, and also with sufficient provision for the formation of headers. Above this mold a crucible is suspended, filled with a mixture of iron oxide and finely divided aluminum. When the mixture is ignited reaction takes place with extreme rapidity, forming liquid steel. This supply of liquid steel then flows into the mold, its very high temperature serving to fuse the exposed survases to be welded, thus insuring a knitting together of the new steel with existing fractured portions. Thermit welding has been successfully used in marine work for repairs to large castings such as stern frames, rudders, and heavy forgings such as propeller posts, rudder-stocks, tiller arms, piston rods, and crank shafts.

THERMOGRAM. The continuous record of temperature made by a self-registering thermometer or thermograph.
See **Thermograph.**

THERMOGRAPH. A registering thermometer. In the ordinary thermograph a bimetallic strip is used to measure the temperature. The unequal expansion or contraction of the two dissimilar metals causes the strip, wound on a coil, to bend or unbend. This operates a pen arm, the movement of which is proportional to the temperature change causing it. This movement is recorded on a chart graduated with a temperature scale.
Fr: *Thermomètre Enregistreur;* Ger: *Registrierendes Thermometer.*

THERMOMETER SCREEN. A wooden box with louvered sides in which dry and wet-bulb thermometers are housed, with protection from the direct rays of the sun and other atmospheric exposure. Also called instrument shelter.

THERMOPILE. A device for measuring temperature (difference), consisting of a closed electric circuit made of two different metals and an electric meter. It consists of a number of thermocouples in series, all junctions of type A-B being thermally connected, as are all of type B-A.

THICK AND THIN BLOCK. A block which has two sheaves, one thicker than the other, so as to accommodate two ropes of different sizes.
Fr: *Poulie à Violon;* Ger: *Violinblock.*

THICK STRAKE. Heavy ceiling planks worked over the head of the floor timbers and first futtocks to prevent the heads and heels of these timbers from being forced in.
Fr: *Serre d'Empâture;* Ger: *Kimmwegerungsgang.*

THICK STUFF. Sided timber exceeding 4 in. but not more than 12 in. in thickness, cut the whole depth of the tree.
Fr: *Gros Bordages;* Ger: *Bauchdielen.*

THICK WEATHER. Condition of the atmosphere when visibility is impaired or greatly reduced by fog, mist, rain, snow, and so forth.
Fr: *Temps Bouché;* Ger: *Dickes Wetter.*

THIEF KNOT. A knot identical with the reef knot except that the standing part of the two ropes are on opposite sides of the knot. Because of this it is liable to slip under strain.

THIEF NET. A net used for catching herring which fall out of the main net when the latter is hauled on board the drifter. Also called scum net.

THIEF-SAMPLER (U. S.). A device used on tank vessels for estimating the quantity of water lying at the bottom of a tank containing oil. Also called water finder.
Fr: *Déceleur d'Eau.*
It consists of a small brass instrument about 2 ft. long, marked in inches, to which a strip of "caramel" or other indicating paper is fastened by a sliding ring, thus securing the paper alongside the gauge. The instrument is lowered to the bottom of the tank and kept there for 3 or 4 minutes. The water, if any, will dissolve the burnt sugar (caramel) on the paper, or will affect the indicator, which will be discolored, and the gauge will show how many inches of water there are at the bottom of the tank. The water finder is only used with black oil. For light oils a chalked sounding rod can be used.

THIGH THWART. A thwart in the foresheets of a whaleboat used by the boat steerer to steady himself during the capture. The edge is notched to fit the boat steerer's left thigh and so steady him at his job of darting and lancing. Also called clumsy cleat. (Obsolete.)

THIMBLE. A round or heart-shaped fitting made from gun metal, galvanized iron, solid or light brass, with a deep score in its outer surface, around which an eye may be spliced in hemp or wire rope. Its purpose is to protect the eye from the destructive effect of a link or shackle pin passing through it.
Fr: *Cosse;* Ger: *Kausche.*
See **Dog-Bitch Thimble, Hawser Thimble, Heart-Shaped Thimble, Lanyard Thimble, Round Thimble, Solid Thimble, Union Thimble.**
British Standards Institution, Standard 464, *Wire Rope Thimbles,* London, 1932.

THIMBLE-HEADED TRYSAIL. Triangular boomless storm sail, the area of which is approximately that of the close-reefed sail it replaces. It is usually provided with one deep reef.

THIN WATERWAY.
See **Inner Waterway.**

THIRD ENGINEER.
See **Second Assistant Engineer.**

THIRTY DAYS CLAUSE. A marine insurance hull clause specifying that insurance is to continue for a period of thirty days after the vessel's arrival at its final port of destination.

THIRTY-TWO POINT LIGHT (U. S.). A regulation light so constructed as to show a clear, uniform and unbroken light visible all around the horizon.

THOLE PIN. A wooden or steel pin which fits in the hole bored in the gunwale of a boat to keep the oar in place when rowing. Also called thole. The oar may be placed between the two pins or secured to a single pin by means of a grommet.

Fr: *Tolet;* Ger: *Ruderdolle; Bootsdolle; Dolle; Rojedolle.*

scribed in terms of three figures. It is always fitted to gyroscopic compasses. Also called **Circular notation card, Full circle division.**

Fr: *Rose à divisions en degrés;* Ger: *Volkreisteilung Kompassrose.*

THREE-ISLAND VESSEL. A vessel with erections consisting of poop, bridge, and forecastle, these erections covering approximately 50 per cent of the vessel's length. This class of ships embraces a variety of types differing in the percentage length of erections as well as their interrelation. They are mostly used as general cargo carriers, and are built with **1, 2, or 3 continuous decks.**

Fr: *Navire à deux Coffres; Navire à trois Superstructures;* Ger: *Dreiinselschiff.*

THREE-LEG MOORING. A type of mooring which consists of three anchors

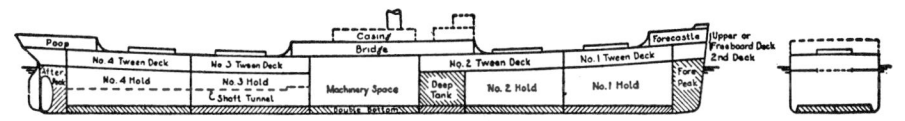

Three-Island Vessel. (*Courtesy American Bureau of Shipping*)

THONNIER. A French sailing troller from Brittany used in the tuna fisheries of the Bay of Biscay. The wooden hull has fine lines, rounded stem, a square stern with long overhang and raked sternpost. Ketch rig. Length 71.6 ft. Breadth 19.1 ft. Draft 9 ft. Displacement 58 tons. Sail area 2863 sq. ft. (Typical.)

Journal de la Marine le Yacht, Paris, vol. 44, Nov. 6, 1926.

THOROUGHFOOT. To coil down a rope against the lay, bringing the lower end up through the center of the coil, and coiling down with the lay. This is done to straighten the kinks from new rope.

THREAD. The smallest component part of a rope fiber; spun into yarn. Also called fiber.

Fr: *Fibre;* Ger: *Faser.*

THREE-ARM PROTRACTOR.
See **Station Pointer.**

THREE FIGURE COMPASS CARD. A compass card graduated in degrees, clockwise from 000 (North) to 359. When using this card the ship's direction is always de-

with ground chain forming an angle of 120 degrees between each other. The ground chains join into a central piece or swivel from which the riding chain is led to the buoy. Also called three-arms mooring.

Fr: *Corps Mort à Trois Branches.*

THREE LETTER POINT. One of eight points of the compass card between the cardinal and intercardinal points such as, for instance, North-North-East and West-South-West, which in current usage are indicated by three letters—N.N.E. and W.S.W.

THREE LETTER SIGNAL. A three flag signal from the international code used for messages relating to points of the compass, relative bearings, standard time and general vocabulary section.

Fr: *Signal à trois pavillons;* Ger: *Drer Flaggen Signal.*

THREE-MASTED BARK. A three-masted vessel, square-rigged on the fore and main, and fore-and-aft-rigged on the mizzen mast. This rig is best suited for vessels with a gross tonnage of 300 to 2000.

Fr: *Trois mâts barque;* Ger: *Dreimastbark; Barkschiff.*

The distribution of sail area between the different masts, according to Middendorf, is approximately as follows: bowsprit, 0.0864 to 0.0991; fore, 0.3864 to 0.3791; main, 0.4090 to 0.3826; mizzen, 0.1182 to 0.1392.

THREE-QUARTER LUG. A lugsail with the yard slung at one fourth of its length from the forward end. The tack hooks at a short distance forward of the mast to an eye in a fore and aft batten.

3. Swelling of the anchor shank where it joins the arms.

Fr: *Collet; Aisselle;* Ger: *Ankerhals.*

4. That part of the shell of a block nearest the hook or eye.

Fr: *Collet;* Ger: *Tauraumende.*

5. The midship part of a floor timber over the keel where its depth is greatest.

Fr: *Collet;* Ger: *Dunnung.*

6. The minimum thickness of a fusion weld along a straight line passing through

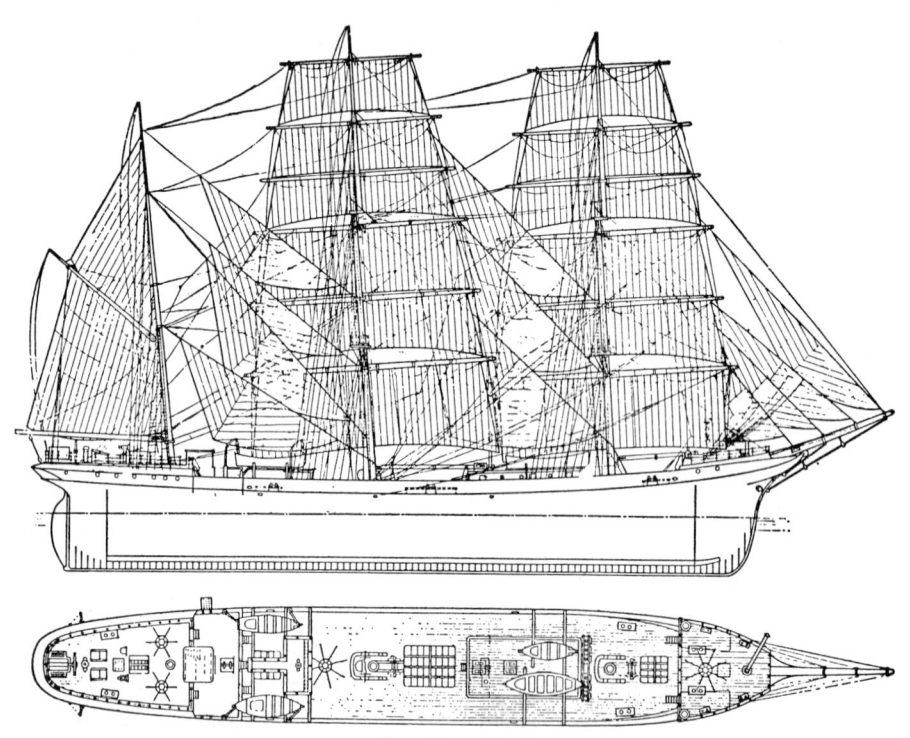

Three-Masted Bark

THREE TWELVES. Slang expression used when referring to a prototype of early Diesel-driven oil tanker of about 12,000 tons deadweight, 12 knots speed and 12 tons per day fuel consumption.

THROAT. 1. The forward or inner end of a gaff where the cheeks are fitted so as to enclose the mast. Also called jaw.

Fr: *Mâchoire;* Ger: *Klaue.*

2. The upper forward corner of a quadrilateral fore-and-aft sail where head and luff join. Also called nock.

Fr: *Point de Mât; Empointure de Mât;* Ger: *Klauohr; Nockohr.*

the bottom of the cross-sectional space provided to contain it.

7. The center part of a knee or breasthook. The inside of knee timbers at the middle or turn of the arms.

Fr: *Gorge; Collet;* Ger: *Hals; Kehle; Knick.*

THROAT BOLT. 1. Eyebolt passing through the fore end of a wooden gaff and into which the throat halyards are hooked.

Fr: *Piton de Drisse de Mât;* Ger: *Klaufallbolzen.*

2. A bolt driven through the throat of a knee or a hook.

Ger: *Halsbolzen.*

THROAT BRAIL. A brail reeving through a block at the jaws of a gaff and made fast to the clew of the sail.

Fr: *Étrangloir;* Ger: *Brookgeitau; Halsgording.*

THROATER. The member of a dressing gang on a cod or halibut fishing vessel who cuts down the belly and lays open the abdominal cavity of the fish immediately after its capture.

Fr: *Piqueur.*

THROAT HALYARDS. The rope or purchase hooked to the jaws of a gaff and by which it is hoisted.

Fr: *Drisse de Mât;* Ger: *Klaufall.*

THROAT SEIZING. A round seizing made without cross turns at the point where two ropes cross. Used for the same purpose as a horseshoe splice.

Throat Seizing

Fr: *Amarrage Plat Double;* Ger: *Hartbinsel.*

THROUGH BILL OF LADING. A bill of lading drawn up to cover goods to their final destination when transhipment and even railway carriage are necessary to complete the journey. Such bills place the entire liability on the carrier making the contract, and his liability does not cease even when he has to pass the goods on to other carriers, unless the bill of lading bears a special clause so specifying.

Fr: *Connaissement Direct;* Ger: *Durchgangkonnossement; Durchstehendes Konnossement.*

Cricher, A. Lane, *Uniform Through Bill of Lading,* U. S. Department of Commerce, Trade Information Bulletin 598, Washington, 1928.

THROUGH FASTENING. A fastening that passes completely through two pieces of timber to be joined and is secured either by a nut or by clinching on a clinch ring. The outboard end of through fastenings is countersunk and plugged.

Fr: *Chevillage à Travers Bois;* Ger: *Durchverbolzung.*

THROUGH PLATE. The converse of intercostal plate. A plate which is continuous through adjacent structure.

Fr: *Tôle Continue;* Ger: *Durchlaufende Platte.*

See **Intercostal Plate.**

THROUGH-PLATE CENTER KEELSON. A longitudinal girder consisting of a continuous vertical center through plate extending from the keel to the top of the floors.

Fr: *Carlingue Centrale Continue;* Ger: *Durchlaufendes Mittelkielschwein.*

THRUM. Short bits of rope yarns used in thrumming canvas for making mats. Also called foxes.

Fr: *Lardage;* Ger: *Fuchjes.*

THRUM (to). To make a rough surface on a mat, and so on, by inserting short strands of yarn.

Fr: *Larder;* Ger: *Bespicken; Spicken.*

THRUM MAT. A mat or piece of canvas with short strands of yarn stuck through it to form a pile. It is used in the rigging to prevent chafing and also as collision mat. Also called thrummed mat, thrumbed mat.

Fr: *Paillet Lardé;* Ger: *Gespickte Matte.*

THRUST BEARING. The bearing to which the propeller thrust is transmitted to the hull through the shafting. It is usually located at the forward end of the shaft line. On ships driven by reciprocating engines or electric motors it is usually mounted on a separate casting. In most geared turbine installations it is incorporated in the reduction gear casing. Also called thrust block.

Fr: *Palier de Butée; Buttée;* Ger: *Drucklager.*

Gibson, J. H., *Thrust and Journal Bearings,* Institute of Marine Engineers, London, *Transactions,* vol. 45, April (1933).

THRUST BLOCK. See **Thrust Bearing.**

THRUST COLLAR. One of the collars on a thrust shaft by which the thrust of the propeller is transmitted to the thrust bearing.

Fr: *Collet de Butée;* Ger: *Kammzapfen.*

THRUST DEDUCTION. The thrust used in overcoming the suction exerted on the afterbody of a ship by the propeller. Hence, the thrust lost through interaction between propeller, thrustblock and ship. Also called augment of resistance. Thrust deduction is affected by the type of hull, the number and location of the propellers, the number of blades of each and to a lesser extent is dependent on the propeller diameter.

Fr: *Coefficient de Suction;* Ger: *Strahlverlust; Schubverlust.*

Telfer, E. V., The Wake and Thrust-Deduction of Single-Screw Ships, North East Coast Institution of Engineers and Shipbuilders (Newcastle upon Tyne), *Transactions* (1936).

THRUST DEDUCTION COEFFICIENT.
The ratio of the thrust deduction to the total thrust of the propeller. If 1 represents the total propeller thrust and t the thrust deduction, $1-t$ is the proportion of total thrust which is useful or effective in driving the hull.
Fr: *Coefficient de Poussée Corrigée;* Ger: *Schubbeiwert.*

THRUST RECESS. The enlarged end of a shaft tunnel located off the engine room and containing the thrust shaft and thrust block.
Fr: *Niche de la Butée;* Ger: *Drucklager Nische.*
See **Stuffing Box Recess.**

THRUST SHAFT. The length of shafting provided with one or more collars which transmits the thrust of the propeller to the thrust bearing.
Fr: *Arbre de Butée;* Ger: *Drucklagerwelle.*

THUMB CLEAT. A one-horned cleat resembling a thumb, used about the rigging to prevent ropes from slipping or to give them the desired lead.
Fr: *Oreille;* Ger: *Nockklampe.*

THWART. 1. One of the athwart benches in an open boat. Their number is governed by the length of the boat and varies from 4 to 7 in ship's lifeboats. When the unsupported length exceeds 5 ft. a stanchion is usually fitted.
Fr: *Banc de Nage;* Ger: *Rojebank; Ruderbank; Ducht.*
2. One of the horizontal ledger boards between two staging uprights on which stage planks rest. Also called stage bearer, spall.
See **Lower Thwart, Mast Thwart, Sailing Thwart, Thigh Thwart.**

THWART KNEE. Iron or wooden knee connecting each thwart to the gunwale in an open boat.
Fr: *Courbe de Banc;* Ger: *Duchtknie.*

TIAO-PAI. Chinese craft from Swatow, Kwang-Tung Province, used for fishing by moonlight in shallow waters. Boards painted white about 2½ ft. wide are hung outside the projecting outboard, sloping a little toward the water. Fishermen go out in these boats on bright clear nights. Two boats are fastened together and as the moonlight falls on the boards the fish leap over them into the boats and are captured. Length 25½ ft. Breadth 2¾ ft. (Typical.)

TIAO-TSAO. Chinese fishing boat from Swatow. The center of the boat is open. There is a fish well forward and the afterpart is decked over for the crew. Length 36 ft. Breadth 11½ ft. (Typical.)

TICK NOTE (G. B.). A slip of paper issued to a lighterman or stevedore on which are recorded the marks and number of packages to be delivered to a particular lighter or to be landed on the quay.

TIDAL AMPLITUDE. The height of a tidal rise above a given level, generally the chart datum or mean sea level.
Fr: *Amplitude de Marée;* Ger: *Tidenhub.*

TIDAL BASIN. A dock in a tidal harbor or river in which the water is kept at a desired level by means of floodgates. Also called tidal dock.
Fr: *Bassin de Marée;* Ger: *Tidebecken.*

TIDAL CONSTANTS. Tidal relations that remain practically constant for any particular locality. Quantities such as the average lunitidal interval and mean rises and ranges of springs and neap tides are used in defining the tides at any place. Tidal constants are classified as harmonic and nonharmonic.
Fr: *Constantes de Marée;* Ger: *Tidekonstante.*

TIDAL CONSTITUENT. A component factor of the tidal undulation due to a particular cause, such as the moon's declination or the sun's distance from the earth.
Fr: *Composante de Marée;* Ger: *Tidekomponent.*

TIDAL CURRENT (U. S.). A current caused by the tide-producing forces of the moon and sun. Tidal currents are a part of the same general movement of the sea that is manifested in the vertical rise and fall of the tides. Also called tidal stream (G. B.).
Fr: *Courant de Marée;* Ger: *Gezeitenstrom.*
Schumacher, A., "Die Gezeitenströmungen," *Archiv der Deutschen Seewarte* (Hamburg), vol. 41 (1923).

TIDAL CURVE. See **Marigram.**

TIDAL DATUM. A datum selected by hydrographers from the level of which tide measurements can be made. It is sometimes of vital importance to the mariner that a chart should indicate the least depth of water possible; hence the datum selected is usually that of the lowest level to which the tide falls under normal conditions. Also called tidal plane of reference.
Fr: *Zéro des Marées;* Ger: *Normalnull.*

TIDAL DIAGRAM. See **Marigram.**

TIDAL DIFFERENCES. Quantities of either time or height which, when applied to the predicted time or height of high water or low water at a standard port, give the corresponding time or height at a secondary port for which the tidal differences are given in the tide tables.
> Fr: *Différences de Marée;* Ger: *Gezeitenunterschiede.*

TIDAL FALL. The amount the depth of water decreases during a falling tide, or the difference between the height of high water and the following height of low water.
> Fr: *Marnage;* Ger: *Tidenfall.*

TIDAL HARBOR. A harbor in which the tide ebbs and flows, in distinction from a harbor which is kept at high water level by means of docks with gates.
> Fr: *Port à Marée;* Ger: *Fluthafen; Tidehafen.*

TIDAL LIGHTS. The lights shown at the entrance of some harbors in order to indicate the depth of water and the direction in which the tidal stream is running.
> Fr: *Feux de Marée;* Ger: *Gezeitfeuer.*

TIDAL OSCILLATION. One vertical oscillation of a tide wave about the mean sea level. It includes one high water and the succeeding low water.
> Ger: *Flutwelle Oscillation.*

TIDAL PLANE OF REFERENCE.
See **Tidal Datum.**

TIDAL PREDICTION. Daily prediction of the times and heights of tides for each day at various ports called standard ports. These predictions are based on data obtained by a method of harmonic analysis. They are published in the tidal tables issued by maritime nations.
> Fr: *Prédiction des marées;* Ger: *Gezeiten Vorausberechnung; Hochwasservoraussage.*

TIDAL QUAY. A quay in an open harbor or basin in which the shelter allows vessels to lie alongside and the depth of water enables them to remain afloat in any tide.
> Fr: *Quai à Marée;* Ger: *Flutkai.*

TIDAL RANGE. The arithmetical mean between the heights of successive high and low waters, or successive low and high waters.
> Fr: *Amplitude de la Marée;* Ger: *Tidenhub.*

See **Ratio of Tidal Ranges.**

TIDAL RISE. The amount that the water rises during the rising tide or the difference between the height of high water and the preceding height of low water.
> Fr: *Hauteur de la pleine mer;* Ger: *Tidenstieg.*

TIDAL STREAM.
See **Tidal Current.**

TIDAL UNDULATION. The sea level that causes tides and tidal streams in the vicinity of land. Also tidal wave.
> Fr: *Onde de marée;* Ger: *Gezeitenwelle.*

TIDAL WATERS. All waters which flow and reflow under the influence of the tides. Arms of the sea, bays, creeks, coves, or rivers in which the tide ebbs and flows are properly denominated tidal waters. The term tidal water is not limited to water which is salt, but embraces also so much of the water of fresh rivers as is propelled backward by the ingress and pressure of the tide. Also called tide waters.
> Fr: *Eaux Maritimes;* Ger: *Flutgebiet.*

Such waters are included in the term "high seas" for the purpose of jurisdiction whether the cause of action in Admiralty law be one of contract or one of tort.

TIDAL WAVE. A term erroneously applied to almost any unexpected wave that inundates the seacoast or the shore of a lake. These waves are rarely if ever due to the tides. They may usually be traced to some more-or-less distant earthquake or violent storm.
> Fr: *Raz de Marée;* Ger: *Flutwelle.*

Patton and Marmer, "The Waves of the Sea," U. S. National Research Council, Bulletin no. 85, Washington, 1932; Rothe, E., "Les raz de marée," *Revue générale des sciences* (Paris), May, 1924.

TIDE. Oscillations of the ocean occasioned by the combined action of the sun and moon. The relative effect of these two bodies is directly proportional to their mass and inversely proportional to the square of their distance.
> Fr: *Marée;* Ger: *Flut; Gezeit; Tide.*

See **Age of Tide, Change of Tide, Diurnal Tide, Double Tide, Equatorial Tide, Equinoctial Tide, Falling Tide, Half Tide, High Tide, Lee Tide, Low Tide, Meteorological Tide, Mixed Tide, Neap Tide, Rip Tide, Rising Tide, Semidiurnal Tide, Spring Tide, Syzygy Tide, Weather Tide.**

Darwin, G. H., *The Tides,* London, 1911;

Marmer, H. A., *The Tide*, New York, 1926; Warburg, H. D., *Tides and Tidal Stream*, Cambridge, 1926; Wheeler, W. H., *Practical Manual of Tides and Waves*, London, 1906.

TIDE AND HALF TIDE. A phenomenon which occurs in channels where a tide current is formed and the stream continues to flow up for 3 hours after it is high water. When continuing to flow during 1½ hours after high water it is then known as "a tide and quarter tide."

TIDE-BOUND. Said of a vessel prevented from proceeding because of insufficient depth of water at low tide.

TIDE CRACK. A term used in ice terminology to denote the line of junction between an immovable ice-foot and fast ice, the latter being subject to the rise and fall of the tide.

TIDE GATE. A place where the tide runs with great velocity.

TIDE GAUGE. 1. A graduated staff, erected at the end of a quay or wharf in communication with the open sea, from which the rise and fall of the tide can be ascertained at any moment.

2. An apparatus for recording the movements of the sea level in tidal waters.

Fr: *Echelle de Marée; Marégraphe;* Ger: *Flutmesser; Gezeitpegel.*

Schureman, P., *Standard Automatic Tide Gauge*, U. S. Coast and Geodetic Survey, Special Publication 196, Washington, 1935.

TIDEMARK. The point or line on the sea shore reached by high water or low water. Also called water mark.

Fr: *Laisse;* Ger: *Küstensaum.*

TIDE POLE. A staff made of a board 5 to 6 inches wide and 1 inch thick, graduated to feet and tenths and used for measuring the rise and fall of the tide.

Fr: *Echelle de Marée;* Ger: *Lattenpegel.*

See **Tide gauge**.

TIDE POLE REFERENCE POINT. The zero point or reference mark on a tide pole to which tidal heights are referring.

Fr: *Zero de l'échelle;* Ger: *Pegelnull.*

TIDE-PREDICTING MACHINE. An instrument which predicts the tides by mechanically summing up the harmonic constituents of which it is composed. Also called tide predictor.

Fr: *Machine à calculer les Marées;* Ger: *Gezeitenrechenmaschine.*

TIDE RACE. A tidal current occurring when the tide wave, advancing inshore, is arrested by a promontory. The water attains a height which causes it to flow off obliquely with considerable velocity.

Fr: *Mascaret;* Ger: *Stromschnelle.*

See **Propeller Race**.

TIDE RIPS. A vertical oscillation of the sea caused by tidal streams. Short ripplings which result from eddies or from the passage of the tide over uneven bottom.

Fr: *Ridins de Marée;* Ger: *Stromkabbelung.*

TIDE RODE. Swinging by the force of the tide when at anchor. Riding at anchor with head to tide and not to wind.

Fr: *Evité à la Marée;* Ger: *Stromgerecht.*

TIDE SAIL. A ship is said to be on a tide sail when ready to leave dock by the next tide.

TIDE SIGNALS. Signals hoisted on a signal mast at the entrance of a harbor to indicate the depth of water above mean sea level. Also called tidal signals.

Fr: *Signaux de Marée;* Ger: *Flutsignale.*

TIDE STAFF. See **Tide Gauge**.

TIDE TABLES. Daily predictions of the times and heights of the tide for one year arranged in tabular form. In the United States they are issued in two volumes, one for the Atlantic Ocean and tributary waters and the other for the Pacific and Indian Oceans and tributary waters.

Fr: *Annuaire des Marées;* Ger: *Gezeitentafeln.*

Bencker, H., "Study of Tide Tables Published by Different Nations," *Hydrographic Review* (Monaco), vol. 6, no. 1 (1929); *Manual of Tide Observations*, U. S. Coast and Geodetic Survey, Special Publication 196, Washington.

TIDE WAVE. The alteration in the level of the sea propagated from East to West and caused by the combined attraction of the sun and moon. Also called tidal wave.

Fr: *Onde de marée;* Ger: *Gezeitenwelle.*

TIE. 1. Part of the purchase used for hoisting a yard. Also called tye. It consists of a rope or chain attached at one end to the middle of an upper topsail or topgallant yard, rove through a sheave hole or through a hanging block at the top of the mast, and having a fly block made fast to its outer end for the halyards to reeve through. Another arrangement consists of a chain with the standing part fastened to the mast;

it is rove through an iron block called the tie-block, attached to the middle of the yard, and through a sheave hole or hanging block at the head of the mast; the other end being hooked to the fly block through which the halyard purchase is rove.
Fr: *Itague*; Ger: *Drehreep*.
2. One of the small bands of canvas used for securing a sail when stowing it upon its spar.

TIE BAR. Angle bar of short length fitted to the margin plate and tank side bracket instead of a gusset plate.
Ger: *Fächerwinkel*.

TIE BEAM. A wood or steel batten fitted over each range of hatch covers, for extra security, after the tarpaulins have been battened down. It is held by a strong screw bolt at each end.

TIE BLOCK. Also tye block. **1.** A steel single block on a topsail or topgallant yard through which the tie of the halyards is rove.
2. The gin block through which the halyard runner reeves.
Fr: *Poulie d'itague*; Ger: *Drehreepblock*.

TIE PLANK. In launching, a heavy plank or log which holds the ship from sliding down the ways after the keel blocks have been removed.
Fr: *Savate*; Ger: *Shuh*.

TIE PLATE. A fore-and-aft strake of plating fitted under a wooden deck and extending under the coamings of deck houses, alongside hatch openings, and at each line of stanchions.
Fr: *Virure d'Hiloire*; Ger: *Lukenstringer*.

TIERER. A man formerly stationed in the chain locker for stowing the anchor cable when weighing anchor. Owing to the weight of cables in modern vessels tierers are now dispensed with. The cables are stowed in deep and narrow chain lockers where there is little chance of kinking.
Ger: *Ankertau Aufschiesser*.

TIERING. The act of stowing regularly and symmetrically, in long fore-and-aft flakes, chain cables in their chain lockers with the aid of chain hooks and hook ropes.
Ger: *Aufschiessen*.

TIE-TIE. Stops of small cord occasionally used for securing a hammock, taking the place of hammock lashing.
Fr: *Hanet de Hamac*; Ger: *Hängemattensnitzel*.

TILLER.
See **Rudder Tiller**.

TILLER HEAD. The free end of the tiller to which the tiller ropes or chains are attached.
Ger: *Kopf der Ruderpinne*.

TILLER LINE. Line used on small sailing craft steered with a hand tiller, to ease the pull on the helmsman's arms. The ends of the line are fastened to the boat's sides and it is passed amidships once or twice around the tiller head. The friction of the line on the tiller relieves the strain on the helmsman.

TILLER ROPE.
See **Wheel Rope**.

TILLOLE. A small open boat with flat floors and raking ends used for seining and oystering in the basin of Arcachon. It is rigged with a small mast and lugsail. Different names are given to these boats according to size. The smallest is known as *tillole de saou*. Length 26 ft. Breadth 5 ft.. Depth 2 ft. Next comes the *tillole bâtarde*. Length 29 ft. Breadth 7 ft. Depth 2 ft. 3 in. The largest is the *tillole de côte*. Length 31 ft. 6 in. Breadth 8 ft. 3 in. Depth 4 ft.

These boats are built entirely of the local pine tree known as *pin des landes* and are assembled in a most primitive way. The builder has no tools other than a saw, an adze, and a knife. The planking is made of boards about 27 ft. long, 13 in. broad, ⅔ in. thick, and is clinker-laid. There are 4 transverse frames. The knees are hewed out of a log. The stringers are made of the trunk of a small tree sawed in halves and used in the rough, the outer side only being fitted. The fastenings are treenails made of heather stumps. It is stated that an experienced builder assisted by a helper can build such a boat in two days. The lugsail carried by the *tillole* has its tack fastened to the weather gunwale and is hoisted by a single halyard, the standing part of which is fastened aft near the helmsman. When going about, the halyard is cast off and the sail comes down, ready to be tacked on the other gunwale. The maststep has several holes enabling the mast to be raked both fore and aft, and transversely. The rudder is daggershaped, and extends well below the keel. It is so fastened that besides its normal position in the same plane as the sternpost, it can also, if required, be moved laterally on the lee side. This is resorted to when the boat heels over considerably, as it prevents the blade from emerging above water.

TILT. Canvas awning rigged up from stem to stern on a rowboat.
Fr: *Tendelet*; Ger: *Bootssonnensegel*.

TIMBER CARRIER. A vessel specially

designed for the transportation of timber. The single-deck type of ship with short bridge is considered the best timber carrier. To obtain the most efficient stowage, cargo holds are made as free as possible from projecting structures such as stringers and web plates, large knees, deep deck and hatch beams, deck girders, pillars, and so on. To avoid this the hatch-side coaming is made continuous fore and aft above deck. At the height of the continuous hatch-side girder a winch platform is built between hatchways. To increase the safety and carrying capacity of the vessel the double bottom is specially subdivided into permanent ballast tanks and regulating tanks. The purpose of the latter is to nullify any reduction in stability resulting from using up bunkers and feed water during the voyage; also to counteract the reduction in stability due to the saturation of the deck cargo by rain, salt water, and so on.

Fr: *Transport de Bois;* Ger: *Holztransportschiff.*

Schröder, Konstruktion: Doppelbodenteilung und Stabilität holzladender Schiffe, *Werft, Reederei, Hafen,* vol. 7 (January, 1927).

TIMBER HEAD. Projecting timbers rising above deck and used as bitts. Also called kevel head.

Fr: *Tête d'Allonge; Jambette;* Ger: *Poller; Pollerkopf.*

TIMBER HITCH. A turn around a spar, around the standing part, and then several around its own part. It is a quick way of securing a rope temporarily around a spar or piece of timber. Much used in handling cargo.

Timber Hitch

Fr: *Noeud de Bois;* Ger: *Balkenstek.*

TIMBER KNEE. Natural grown crook, or heavy iron bar used for strengthening, connecting or supporting different structural parts of a wooden hull. Also called knee timber, knee piece. Root knees are the best. Suitable wood for knees must be tough and have good holding power for fastenings. Oak, hackmatack, Douglas fir, and apple tree are usually preferred.

Fr: *Courbe;* Ger: *Knieholz.*

TIMBER LOAD LINE. A special load line prescribed by the 1930 International Load Line Convention respecting load lines for vessels which carry timber deck cargoes. There are five timber load lines, which vary according to seasons and zones as follows:

Summer load line marked "LS."
Winter timber load line marked "LW."
Winter North Atlantic timber load line marked "LWNA."
Tropical timber load line marked "LT."
Fresh water timber load line marked "LF."

Fr: *Ligne de Charge pour Bois en Pontée;* Ger: *Holzlastladelinie.*

TIMBER OF THE HEAD. One of the timbers which connected the main, middle, and lower headrails in large vessels. There were usually three on each side of the stem. (Obsolete.)

TIME AMPLITUDE. The difference between the hour angle of a celestial body at rising and 18 hours or between the hour angle at setting and 6 hours.

TIME AZIMUTH. An azimuth determined by calculation from latitude, declination and hour angle.

Ger: *Zeitazimut.*

TIME BALL. A ball dropped from a staff at an observatory to notify certain pre-arranged time—generally noon.

Fr: *Ballon horaire;* Ger: *Zeitball.*

TIME CHARTER. A form of charter party issued when the vessel is chartered for an agreed period of time. It places the vessel in the possession of the charterer. It may, however, provide that the owner shall man and provision the vessel. In ocean traffic the usual practice is for the charterer to pay to the owner for the hire of the ship an agreed rate per deadweight ton per month and also to furnish the fuel and pay all expenses at the ports except crew and provision expenses. A time charter may, however, base the rate of pay upon the vessel's net register tonnage.

Fr: *Time Charter;* Ger: *Zeitcharter.*

Janssen, H., *Die Zeitcharter,* Leipziger Rechtwissenschaftliche Studien, Leipzig, 1923.

TIME FREIGHT. Periodical payment for a ship's hire as distinct from lump freight. Also called charter hire.

Ger: *Zeitfracht.*

TIMENOGUY. A rope or line stretched from one point to another for the purpose of preventing gear from fouling. A piece of light rope with a bull's-eye spliced in the end. It serves to support long and heavy lines like the main brace which passes through the bull's-eye.

Fr: *Manchette;* Ger: *Brille.*

TIME OF HIGH WATER. The instant at which high water occurs.

Fr: *Heure de la Pleine mer;* Ger: *Hochwasserzeit.*

TIME OF LOW WATER. The instant at which low water occurs.

Fr: *Heure de la basse mer;* Ger: *Niedrige Wasserzeit.*

be extended for a further period not exceeding thirty days.

Fr: *Police à Temps;* Ger: *Zeitversicherungspolice.*

TIME SHEET. A document in which are recorded daily all particulars relating to the loading or discharging of cargo. It indicates the duration of and reason for any stoppage of work and is used as a basis for the calculation of demurrage.

TIME SIGHT. A navigational method in which after taking the altitude of a celestial body, the longitude is determined

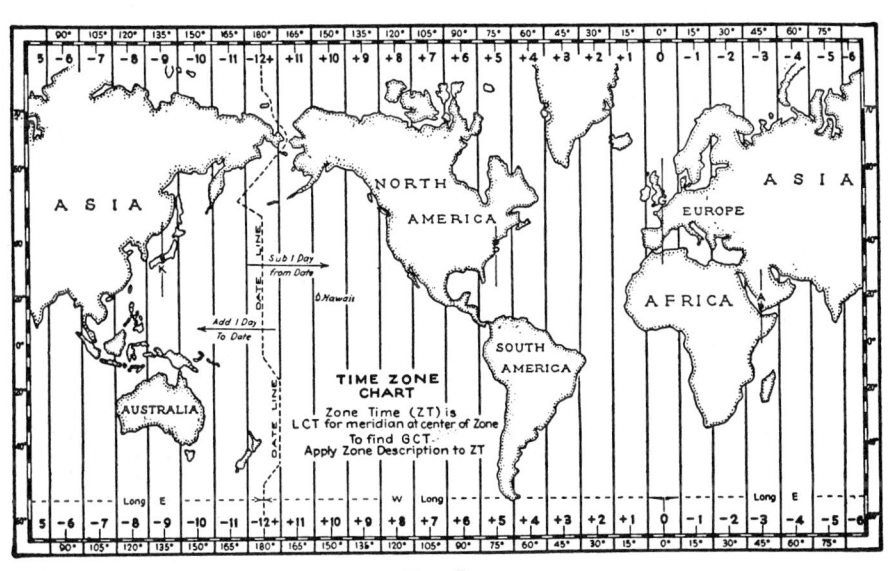

Time Zone

TIME PENALTY CLAUSE. A clause usually incorporated in marine policies on chartered freight (amount paid for the hire of a vessel) by which the insurer is not liable for claims consequent on loss of time, whether arising from a peril of the sea or otherwise.

Fr: *Clause de Retard;* Ger: *Zeitverlust Klausel.*

TIME POLICY. A policy made for fixed periods, in Great Britain not exceeding one year and thirty days. The risk assumed is for any loss which may occur during the life of the policy, irrespective of the voyage or voyages undertaken. Time policies may be issued with a continuation clause, under which, in certain circumstances, risk may

by comparison of local time with Greenwich time.

Ger: *Zeitbeobachtung.*

TIME SIGNAL. One of the daily signals used to mark Greenwich Mean Time and to determine the error and rate of chronometers. Radio time signals are now in general use as time signals by most ships. Visual time signals still exist in many ports for the benefit of shipping, the usual type being the time ball dropped by electric signal.

Fr: *Signal Horaire;* Ger: *Zeitsignal.*

See **Time Ball.**

TIME ZONE. One of the 24 divisions of the earth included between two meridians spaced 15° one hour apart, used for keeping standard time in all places situated between any two of these adjacent meridians. The adoption of this system insures that all vessels, when within certain defined limits of longitude, normally keep the same time.

Fr: *Fuseau Horaire;* Ger: *Zeitzone.*

TIMON. Code name for a standard time charter form issued by the Baltic and International Maritime Conference. It differs from the Baltime form of charter in that it allows redelivery of vessel to owners at any port mutually agreed upon.

TINABLA. A small coasting vessel with double outriggers found in the Philippine Islands, very similar to the *parao.*

TINDAL. A member of Asiatic crew serving under lascar agreement. Acts as deputy to the deck serang and for boatswain's mate but supervises Asiatic crew only. Also called deck tindal.

TINGLE. A sheet of copper, lead, or other soft metal used for making temporary repairs on a small wooden boat when it has been holed.

TINI.
See **Sini.**

TIP. A mechanism for tilting an open-top railway truck to spill out the bulk material from the car into the ship's hold. Also called dumper, car dumper.

Fr: *Verse;* Ger: *Kipp; Wagenkipp.*

TIP CLEARANCE. The smallest distance between the hull and the circumference of the circle described by the propeller.

TIPPING. One of the dangers incident to launching which occurs when the ship's center of gravity passes over the ends of the standing ways and there is too little buoyancy of the immersed portion of the ship to provide a counteracting moment. Also called backward dip. The fore end of the vessel lifts clear of the sliding ways and the whole weight of the hull, less the buoyancy of the waterborne portion, bears upon the extreme end of the standing ways. Under these conditions the vessel may slew across the launching ways by the force of wind or tide, or the intense local pressure upon the bottom may be sufficient to crush in the plating and framing in way of the way ends.

Fr: *Cabanement;* Ger: *Abkippen.*

TIRA. A double canoe of the Society Islands, Polynesia, used in bonito fishing.

TISSOT. A rope or chain used by a drifter when the nets are shot, to prevent the warp chafing on the vessel's rail. It is usually a 6-in. coir rope of 12 fathoms. Also called lash, tizzard, guy rope.

TJALK. A Dutch flat-bottomed craft of large carrying capacity, employed in the coastal trade and on inland waterways. The full-ended broad and shallow hull is built with rounded bilges and a heavy flat keel plank. Sometimes a shallow vertical keel is used. The stem terminates in a short beak head.

The sternpost is spoon-shaped with outboard deadwood and vertical sternpost. The topsides have a pronounced tumble home at bow and stern. There is a flush deck running fore and aft. Some boats have a raised afterdeck. The amount of sheer varies according to the trade for which the boats are designed. Craft sailing in open waters have more sheer than others and a higher sheer aft than forward. The pole mast is stepped well forward in a tabernacle. The bowsprit lies at the side of the stem and is of the reefing type. The mainsail has a short gaff and long boom. There is a gaff topsail, staysail, and one or two jibs. The size of these boats varies widely, the largest being up to 160 tons gross, although the majority of them range from 12 to 50 tons, with a length of 37.6 to 62 ft., a breadth of 10.6 to 17.2 ft. and a hold depth of 3.2 to 6.5 ft.

TJEMPLON. 1. A large Javanese plank-built boat with full lines and flat floors, formerly used for transportation of freight between Semarang and Japan. It was a poor sailer. This type is believed to be extinct.

2. A fishing dugout canoe of *jukung* type from Semarang, employed in the fisheries with the *payang* or native trawl net. Length 15 ft. Breadth 3 ft. (Approximate.)

TJENRANA. A trading prao from the western Celebes of hull form like that of the *padewakan.* The stem piece is curved and of great height, with raised curved sternpost. The deck extends from abaft the tripod mast to the shelter built over the stern. It has a pronounced camber.

TJOTTER. Small, half-decked Dutch sloop used as pleasure craft or for fishing on the Zuider Zee. The rig consists of a long pole mast without shrouds. The mainsail has a very short head and the small gaff is of the typical Dutch curved shape. The foresail tack is fastened to a small steel bowsprit, in which it differs from the *boeier.* The average length of these boats ranges from 14 to 26 ft. The hull lines are similar to those of the *boeier,* with apple bows and stern, rounded bilges and broad, fan-shaped leeboards. It is usually built of oak. Displacement is about 6 tons.

TOAD'S BACK. An octagonal piece of cast iron bolted to the deck and formerly used in some ships as step for a trysail mast. (Obs.)

TOE. The edge of the flange of a structural shape or angle.

TOE CLEAT. A piece of wood fitted immediately below the gunwale of a rowboat to support the end of the crutch shank.
>Fr: *Taquet de Pied de Tolet;* Ger: *Rojeklampe.*

TOE LINK. The lower link of the chains. It was secured to the ship's side by the chain bolt. (Obsolete.)

TOGGLE. A pin of wood or metal employed to connect two ropes, which may have to be cast loose suddenly in an emergency. The pin slips through between the ropes, under a loop in one rope and across an eye called a becket, formed in another rope. Bowlines are fastened to their bridles in this manner and the method is also used to secure ring lifebuoys, code flags, and so on, so that they may be let go quickly. Toggles are generally made of lignum vitae or hickory wood.
>Fr: *Cabillot;* Ger: *Knebel.*
>See **Buntline Toggle, Tank Toggle.**

TOGGLE BOLT. A bolt used to confine an iron band or strap in its place, such as the band by which a boat's mast is secured to a thwart, or a flagstaff to the railing.
>Ger: *Knebelbolzen.*

TOGGLE IRON (U. S.). In whaling, a harpoon with a hinged head which turns at a right angle to the shank when pulled. Also called hand harpoon (G. B.).

TOGGLE PIN. A metal pin with an eye at the head and a point so arranged that a portion of it may pivot, thus forming a T-shaped locking device.
>Ger: *Klappbolzen.*

TOGGLED SHEEPSHANK. A sheepshank which can be made when both ends of the rope are fastened. It will not loosen if the rope is slackened.

TOI. See **Wetka.**

TOLL. A tax levied by a dock or canal company upon the traffic conveyed. Tolls are payable by the owner of the goods and not by the vessel or craft carrying them. Also called toll money.
>Fr: *Péage;* Ger: *Wegegeld.*
>See **Wharfage.**

TOLLESBURY FASHION. A method of stowing anchor with the anchor stock close up to the hawsepipe at right angles to the stem, and crown aft, level with rail and secured by lashings.

TOMAHAWK (G. B.). A smooth-faced hammer used as a calking tool by hand riveters for dressing around a rivet point, and frequently used in watertight work. It gives a nice finished appearance to the rivet but has a tendency to cut deeply into the material and is not, therefore, used in light and medium work.

TOMAHAWKING (G. B.). A kind of calking process practiced in shipyards by one riveter holding a tomahawk, at the circumference of the edge of the rivet point, while another riveter strikes the tomahawk with his own. When efficiently done all round the point, tomahawking makes a rivet thoroughly watertight. An analogous process used in U. S. shipyards is called gardening-up. Pneumatic hammers are used in this case.
>Fr: *Couronnage.*

TOMFOOL'S KNOT. A knot in which two loops are formed.

TOMMING DOWN. The opposite of "shoring up." A piece of timber is braced under a deck beam and on a plank in order to hold down the cases or bales.
>Fr: *Epontiller;* Ger: *Abstützen.*

TON BURDEN. The unit of deadweight load. Tons burden or the burden of a ship means the number of tons weight required to weigh the vessel down in the water from her light to her load line. This may be expressed either in tons of 2240 pounds or in displacement tons of 35 cu. ft.
>Fr: *Tonne de Portée;* Ger: *Lasttonne.*

TONG BOAT (U. S.). Small open sailing skiff 15 to 25 ft. in length, rigged with one mast and spritsail, employed in North Carolina for gathering oysters.

TONGKANG. A seagoing, sailing barge used in the coastal timber trade between the Malay Peninsula and the nearby islands of Mersing, Singapore, and Kotak Tinggeh. Also called *tongkung, tongkang malayu.*

The hull is built with keel and keelson. Each frame is made up of 3 pieces grown to shape. Several wales, external and internal, provide longitudinal strength. Amidships there is a capacious open hold which extends from forecastle to poop; these being the only decked spaces. Over the counter a rectangular platform (gallery) projects for about 16 ft. abaft the hull proper. The rig is composed of main and mizzen masts, without rake, stepped and housed under forecastle and poop so as to have a clear hold. A long, sharply steeved bowsprit rigged with shrouds carries 3 headsails. The mainsail and mizzen are of the usual western design with gaff and boom. The standing rigging is made of wire rope. Length 97 ft.; forecastle, 33 ft.; poop, 21 ft.; gallery, 16 ft. Breadth 30 ft. Depth 15 ft. (Typical.) Waters, D. W., "The Tongkang," *Mariners Mirror*, vol. 26 (London, 1940).

TONGUE. 1. A block of wood placed vertically between the jaws of a gaff to facilitate the sliding of the spar up and down the mast when the throat halyards are handed. It works on a pin driven through the jaws from side to side, so that it can play in a fore-and-aft direction to suit the angle assumed by the gaff when raised. Also called tumbler, saddle, clapper.

Fr: *Sabot;* Ger: *Gaffelschuh.*

2. A mass of ice projecting under water from a floe or an iceberg, and generally distinguishable at a considerable depth in smooth water. It differs from a calf in being fixed to and forming part of the larger body.

TONI. A canoe-shaped fishing boat used in Bombay. The lower part of the hull is hollowed out of a single tree. A portion of side planking is fastened to it by nails and coir lashings, the seams being calked and made watertight. The length of these boats varies from 25 to 30 ft. They are also used for the transportation of passengers and are propelled either by oar or sail, the rig consisting of a settee sail set on a small mast raking forward. The clew of the sail trims forward of amidships. The bottom of the Toni is without keel except at ends where a short rockered skeg is worked on. Length over-all 30 ft. Beam 4½ ft. Depth 2½ ft. (Typical.)

TONNAGE. 1. The size of a vessel.

2. The amount of a ship's cargo.

3. In considering merchant vessels, usually the capacity of the vessel in tons as determined by the legal mode of measurement.

See Deadweight Tonnage, Displacement Tonnage, Freight Tonnage, Gross Tonnage, Moorsom Tonnage, Net Tonnage, Power Tonnage, Register Tonnage, Riddle Tonnage, Panama Canal Tonnage, Suez Canal Tonnage, 'Tween-Deck Tonnage, Underdeck Tonnage.

Blocksidge, E. W., *Register Tonnage of Merchant Ships,* Liverpool, 1933; Johnson, E. R., *Measurement of Vessels for the Panama Canal,* Washington, 1913; League of Nations, *Communications and Transit,* Technical Committee on Maritime Tonnage Measurement, Draft Regulations, Geneva, 1931; Prior, L. N., *Vessel Tonnages,* U. S. Bureau of Marine Inspection and Navigation Bulletin, January, 1937; Van Driel, *Tonnage Measurement,* The Hague, 1925.

TONNAGE BOARDS. Heavy planks used as temporary closure for tonnage openings.

TONNAGE BREADTH. The breadth taken horizontally from face to face to the inside of the frames or to the inside of the ceiling on the frames, provided the ceiling is not more than 3 in. thick.

Fr: *Largeur de Jauge;* Ger: *Vermessungs Breite.*

TONNAGE CERTIFICATE. A document issued by the competent authorities and delivered to the ship stating the vessel's name and nationality, port of registry, principal dimensions; and all particulars of the under-deck tonnage, the items included in the gross tonnage and those items which have been deducted in order to obtain the net register tonnage; also, particulars of all spaces which have been exempted from measurement. Also called certificate of measurement. In the United States this certificate is issued by the Department of Commerce, Bureau of Navigation; in Great Britain by the Registrar of Shipping; in France by the Ministry of Finance.

Fr: *Certificat de Jauge;* Ger: *Messbrief.*

The validity of this document is unlimited providing that no alterations are made in the ship's structure which may alter the internal spaces measured for tonnage. International conventions or agreements exist between different maritime powers for the mutual acceptance of tonnage certificates under certain conditions.

TONNAGE COEFFICIENT. The decimal by which the product of length, breadth, and depth of a vessel must be multiplied to obtain the gross tonnage.

Fr: *Coefficient de Tonnage;* Ger: *Vermessungs Koeffizient.*

TONNAGE DECK. The deck from which a ship's tonnage is measured. The tonnage deck in vessels having more than one deck is the second one from the keel, and in other vessels the upper deck.

Fr: *Pont de Tonnage;* Ger: *Tonnagedeck; Vermessungsdeck.*

TONNAGE DEPTH. The depth of hold for tonnage calculations. In transversely framed vessels, it is taken from the top of the tank top or hold ceiling at cen-

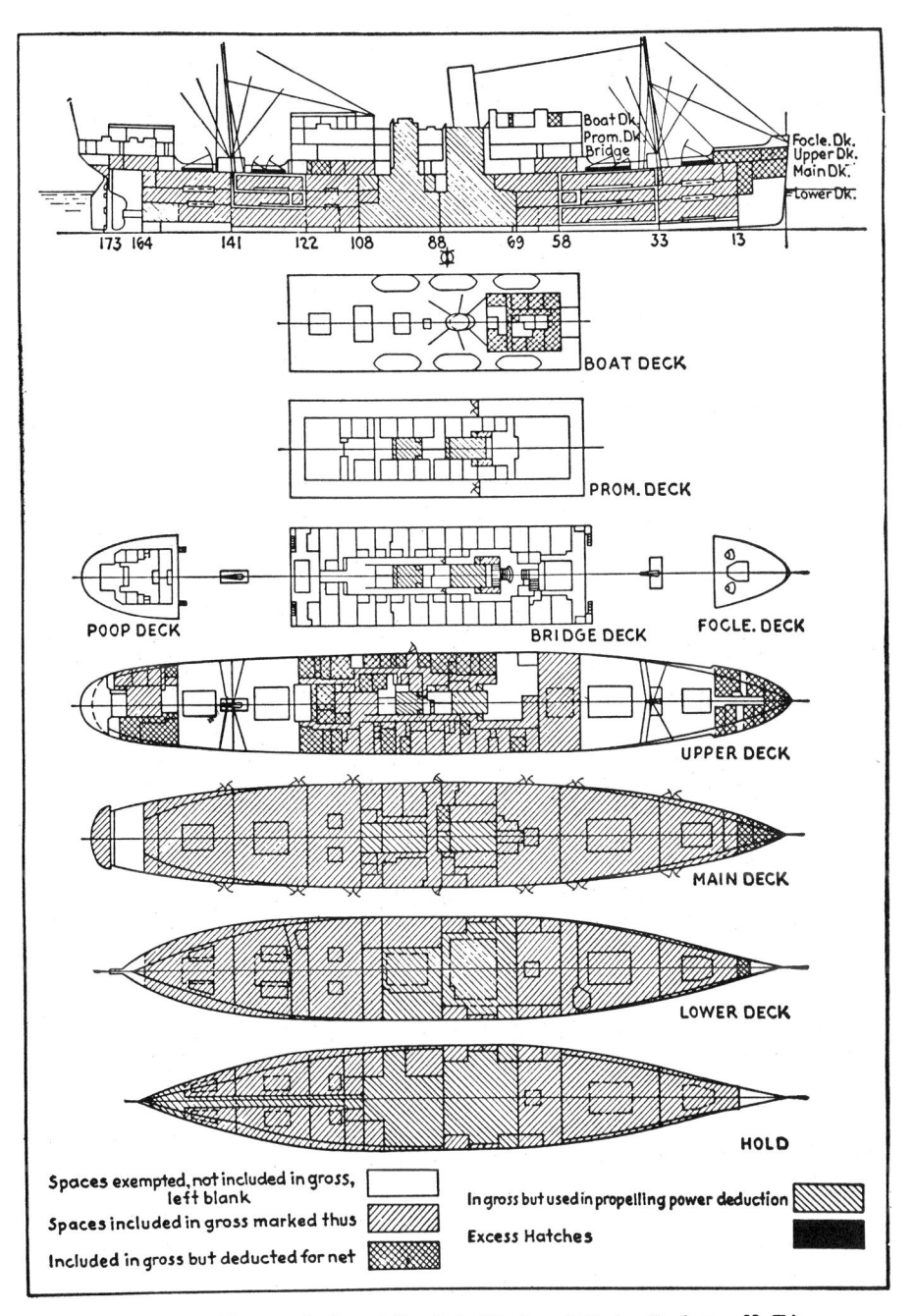

Tonnage. (*Courtesy Society of Naval Architects and Marine Engineers, N. Y.*)

ter line to the under side of the tonnage deck. In longitudinally framed vessels, the depth is taken from the top of bottom longitudinals or ceiling to the top of beams at center.
Fr: *Creux de jauge;* Ger: *Vermessungstiefe.*

TONNAGE DUES. Fee levied by port authorities on the net register tonnage of vessels entering a harbor. Also called tonnage tax, harbor tonnage dues. They are payable by the shipowner and go to assist in the maintenance of buoys, moorings and river channels, or the upkeep of the docks.
Fr: *Taxes de Tonnage; Droits de Jauge;* Ger: *Tonnagegeld.*

TONNAGE HATCH. A small hatchway fitted aft on the shelter deck in accordance with tonnage rules so that the space below deck may be exempt from tonnage measurement. Its after coaming must be not less than one twentieth of the vessel's length forward of the sternpost; and its forward coaming not less than one fifth of the vessel's length from the fore edge of the stern. Its width is to equal that of the after cargo hatch. Its length is usually about 4 ft. It is fitted with a coaming extending 12 in. above deck and is closed by wooden covers which may be lashed from underneath with hemp. Tarpaulins may not be used.

TONNAGE LENGTH. The length measured along the center line of the upper surface of the tonnage deck, the extremities being the points where the inside lines of the framing ceiling or cargo battens meet.
Fr: *Longueur de Jauge;* Ger: *Vermessungslänge.*

TONNAGE OPENING. 1. A well in the uppermost deck of a shelter-deck vessel which has only temporary means of closing; that is, portable planks supported by portable beams. This arrangement is designed to secure exemption from tonnage measurement of the space included between the shelter and upper decks.
Fr: *Ouverture de Tonnage;* Ger: *Vermessungsöffnung.*
2. Opening in a cargo space bulkhead for passage and transfer of cargo.

TONNAGE PLAN. A body plan of the tonnage sections, drawn up to the top of the inner bottom or floor ceiling and inside of frames and cargo battens, with sufficient dimensions and areas to permit the gross tonnage to be calculated from this drawing.

TONNAGE SCALE. A tariff of freight rates which does not determine the actual freight to be charged on a given commodity, but serves merely to establish the difference which is to exist between rates chargeable to different commodities. Also called tonnage schedule. Tonnage scales are built upon one basic commodity which differs according to the geographic peculiarities of the particular trade to which the scale is to apply. The actual freight charge is arrived at through individual negotiation. These scales are still used in East Indian trade and are based exclusively on weight and measurement, without regard to the value of the commodity.

TONNAGE TAX (U. S.). A federal tax levied on all commercial vessels used as instruments of commerce, for the privilege of entering, trading, leaving or lying in a port or harbor of the U. S. or navigating the public waters of the country. The amount, calculated on the tonnage of the vessel, varies according to the ownership, port of registration, trade in which engaged, and number of calls made per year at U. S. ports. Harbor fees, wharfage fees, pilotage charges, quarantine charges, and canal lock tolls are not included in the tonnage tax.

TOOL HOUSE FOREMAN (U. S.). One who maintains and keeps in repair all equipment used on docks and in the loading and unloading of vessels. He is assisted by tool house men. Also called gearman.

TOP. 1. A platform of semicircular or semielliptical shape, which rests upon the trestletrees at the head of a lower mast. It serves to spread the topmast shrouds. Tops are named after the mast to which they belong as maintop, foretop, mizzentop. The topmast shrouds are set up to the rim with deadeyes or turnbuckles. In merchant vessels the tops are made as small and as light as possible in order to reduce the chafing of sails and gear against the rim.
Fr: *Hune;* Ger: *Mars.*
See **Cabin Top, Raised Tank Top, Tank Top.**
2. The largest type of Malay trading vessel, formerly seen in Achin, Borneo, the Celebes, but now believed to be extinct. The hull was decked with planks from stem to stern with a hatchway abaft each mast. The transom stern was elaborately decorated with carvings. There was a sunken poop only slightly rising above deck. The rig con-

sisted of two masts with quadrilateral mainsail and triangular mizzen. The largest boats of this type had a capacity of about 200 tons and carried 3 masts. Length 40 to 90 ft. Breadth 8.8 to 18.8 ft. Depth 10 to 13 ft.

TOP (to). To raise one end, as of a yard or boom, higher than the other by means of the lifts.

Fr: *Apiquer;* Ger: *Auftoppen; Aufpieken.*

TOP-AND-BUTT PLANKING. A peculiar way of planking the outside of a ship with planks that are widest at one-third the length and taper toward the ends, by bringing the butt of one plank to the top of the other so as to make a constant height of strake in two layers.

Fr: *Bordé à Joints en Ligne Brisée.*

TOPAS. Member of Asiatic crew serving under lascar agreement in the steward's department and employed in cleaning and sanitary work generally. The "Stock Topas" is one who attends to livestock (sheep, goats, poultry) carried on board for feeding the Asiatic crew.

TOP BLOCK. A large single iron-bound block hung to an eye bolt in the cap used for swaying or striking a topmast.

Fr: *Poulie de Guinderesse;* Ger: *Windreepblock.*

TOP BURTON. A long tackle formed of a fiddle or double block and a single block. The double block is fitted with a hook, the single block with a long strap, hook, and thimble. The upper block hooks to a pendant at topmast head. The fall is made long enough to allow the lower block and hauling part to come down on deck. It was formerly used for raising or lowering yards, sails, setting up rigging, and so on.

Fr: *Candelette;* Ger: *Stängetalje.*

TOPETO. A Venetian boat originating from Chioggia, used as a fish carrier by the *bragozzi.* It is built with flat bottom, is wall-sided amidships, and has a long, raked bow. Length 23 ft. Breadth 7 ft. 10 in. Inside depth 2 ft. 9 in. Draft 4 in. (Typical.)

TOPGALLANT.

See **Topgallant Sail.**

TOPGALLANT BREEZE. A moderate to fresh breeze in which topgallant sails may be used.

Ger: *Bramsegelkühlte; Bramsegelsbrise.*

TOPGALLANT BULWARKS. In a sailing vessel that part of the bulwarks which extends above the main rail and up to the topgallant rail.

Fr: *Bastingages;* Ger: *Oberschanzkleid.*

TOPGALLANT FORECASTLE. A superstructure just abaft the stem. Its height is the same as that of the other superstructures, and its length is generally between one tenth and one eighth of the ship's total length.

Ger: *Feste Back.*

TOPGALLANT MAST. The mast next above a topmast, and may consist of a separate spar or a single stick with the topmast. Its use is confined to square-riggers.

Fr: *Mât de Perroquet;* Ger: *Bramstänge.*

TOPGALLANT RAIL. The railing above the topgallant bulwarks in sailing vessels.

Fr: *Lisse de Bastingages;* Ger: *Oberschanzkleidreling.*

TOPGALLANT SAIL. A quadrilateral sail, square on the head and roached on the foot, extended above the topsails in the same manner as topsails are extended above the lower yards. In modern vessels topgallants are usually divided into upper topgallant sail and lower topgallant sail. They are seldom made to be reefed, but they have buntlines and leechlines. Also called topgallant.

Fr: *Perroquet;* Ger: *Bramsegel.*

See **Gaff Topgallant Sail.**

TOPGALLANT SHROUD. The shrouds which extend from the topgallant mastheads to the outer ends of the topmast crosstrees and, in some ships, to the tops. Also called topgallant rigging.

Fr: *Hauban de Perroquet;* Ger: *Bramwanten.*

TOP HAMPER. In sailing vessels refers to the upper rigging and spars and to unnecessary gear kept aloft—in general, to articles of outfit such as boats, masts, spars or other gear as well as superstructures, funnels, ventilators, etc.

Fr: *Fardage;* Ger: *Obere Takelage.*

TOP KEEL. The topmost timber of the keel in a vessel where, in order to obtain the required molded size, the keel is made up of two timbers. In such keels the scarfs of the two keels are shifted so that there is the greatest possible distance between the location of the scarfs on the timber immediately below. The grain of the two pieces should run at right angles.

Fr: *Contre-Quille;* Ger: *Gegenkiel.*

TOP LINING. An extra piece of canvas sewed on the after surface of a square sail to take the chafe of the top.
Fr: *Tablier;* Ger: *Stosslappen.*

TOPMARK. A characteristic shape affixed to the top of a buoy or beacon to identify it.
Fr: *Voyant;* Ger: *Toppzeichen.*

TOPMARK BUOY. A buoy with a topmark upon it, such as a sphere, a cone (pointing either up or down), a cage, a diamond, two cones base to base, two cones point to point, and so forth.
Fr: *Bouée à Voyant;* Ger: *Bakentonne.*

TOPMAST. The spar next above a lower mast and below the topgallant mast in a square-rigger. In fore-and-aft-rigged vessels, the upper and smaller spar. The topmast as a separate spar with cap and yoke is now obsolete in cruising and racing yachts. Smaller trading or fishing vessels only are seen with anything but pole masts.
Fr: *Mât de Hune; Mât de Flèche;* Ger: *Marsstänge; Stänge.*
See **Fidded Topmast, Telescopic Topmast.**

TOPMAST SHROUDS. The shrouds running from topmast heads to top rims in square-rigged vessels. In fore-and-aft-rigged vessels they are extended by crosstrees and secured on deck with lanyards or rigging screws. Also called topmast rigging.
Fr: *Haubans de Hune;* Ger: *Stängewanten.*

TOPO. Also toppo. Flat-bottom, half-decked sailing and rowing boat, 23 to 34 ft. long, used in the lagoon fisheries of Venice, Mugia, and Zaole (near Trieste). The construction of the hull is very similar to that of the *battello,* with long overhanging stem, round stern, no keel, deep rudder, and 2 thwarts. The rig consists of a portable mast stepped at a distance of about one-third the total length from the stern and fastened with a hasp to the after thwart. There are 2 sails, a lug mainsail with boom and a jib-headed foresail which tacks down to stemhead and sheets amidships. These boats fish with a trawl net called *grippo.* Length 34 ft. Breadth 7.8 ft. Depth inside 2.8 ft. Crew 1 to 5. (Typical.)

TOPPING LIFT. See **Lift.**

TOPPING LIFT BULL ROPE. A wire rope used for topping a cargo boom, the end of which is fastened to a triangular bail or yoke. The hauling part is taken to the niggerhead of a winch. When the boom is topped, it is permanently secured by the topping lift chain.
Fr: *Martinet;* Ger: *Baumaufholer.*

TOPPING LIFT CHAIN. A short length of close-link chain for securing a cargo derrick at the desired height after it has been raised. The upper end is fastened to a triangular bail or yoke. One of the links at the lower end is shackled to a hook bolt.
Fr: *Chaîne de Martinet;* Ger: *Hängekette.*

TOPPING LIFT BAIL. A bail with apex shackled to the end of a derrick span (topping lift). A length of rope, called winch end whip or bull rope, is secured to one angle of the bail and a length of chain to the other. When the bail reaches the desired height above deck, as the boom rises, it is shackled to an eye plate and the winch end whip can be freed. Also **Union plate.**
Fr: *Palonnier;* Ger: *Herzstuck; Hangerbügel.*

TOPPING LIFT BLOCK. A masthead cargo block through which a derrick topping lift reeves. For handling heavy loads a topping lift tackle is rigged and there are two topping lift blocks, masthead topping lift block and derrick head topping lift block. Also called **Span block.**
Fr: *Poulie de martinet;* Ger: *Hangerblock.*

TOPPING LIFT CROSSHEAD. A cruciform deck fitting for belaying topping lifts. It is provided at the top with a worked eye for the standing part of the lift and a cleat for belaying the running part. It is met with in sailing yachts.
Ger: *Hangerbügel.*

TOPPING LIFT FALL. The fall used with a topping lift for raising or lowering a boom or derrick.
Fr: *Martinet;* Ger: *Hängeseil.*

TOPPING LIFT PURCHASE. A double- or treble-block purchase fastened to a topping lift pendant for raising a derrick.
Fr: *Palan de Martinet;* Ger: *Hängetalje.*

TOPPING LIFT SPAN. A single part derrick topping lift generally used with loads not exceeding three tons. It consists of a heavy wire reaching from the derrick head through a single lead block attached to the upper mast table. Below the block there is a tackle with hauling part leading to the winch.

TOPPING LINE. The line that lifts a cargo boom. Also **Topping lift.**
Fr: *Martinet;* Ger: *Hängeseil.*

TOPPING OFF. 1. The act of stowing cargo in the top of a hold or 'tween deck to fill in the uppermost portion of the compartment. Bagged cargo is frequently used for this purpose.
2. Filling up fuel tanks or water tanks which are partially full.

TOP QUARTERS. In an otter trawl, those parts of the net where the upper wings join the square.

TOP RIM. The circular sweep which forms the edge of a mast top. It covers the ends of the crosstrees and trestletrees, and prevents the chafing of the topsail against them.
Fr: *Guérite;* Ger: *Marsrand.*

TOP ROPE. See **Mast Rope.**

TOPSAIL HALYARD BEND. A knot similar to the topsail sheet bend, with the addition of an extra turn taken around the spar.

TOPSAIL SCHOONER. A vessel with three or more masts fore- and aft-rigged throughout, but with the additional square sails on the foremast. No sail is bent to the lower yard although a square running sail is set flying below it. Above this yard there are either single or double topsails and topgallants, single or double. In recent times two square sails, upper and lower topsails, became the accepted rig, while in some instances only a small single topsail was carried. There are three or four headsails.
Fr: *Goelette à huniers;* Ger: *Toppsegelschoner.*

TOPSAIL SHEET BEND. A bend which is used for bending the sheet to the clew of a sail. It is not shaken loose by the flapping of the sail. Also called studding sail tack bend.

TOPSIDES. The upper part of a ship's sides above the designed waterline up to the rail.
Fr: *Accastillage;* Ger: *Obere Seitenteile.*

TOPSIDE SCANTLINGS.
See **Types.**

TOPSIDE TANK. Ballast tanks placed at the ship's side just under the weather deck with the twofold object of immersing the vessel when traveling light, in order to minimize propeller racing, and also of reducing what has been recognized in some vessels as an excessive amount of initial stability, or metacentric height when light.

These tanks are formed by a section of the deck which acts as topside plating and a fore-and-aft bulkhead set diagonally from side to deck. Also called gunwale tank, corner tank, wing tank, cantilever tank.
Fr: *Ballasts Latéraux;* Ger: *Seitlicher Deckballasttank; Topseitentank; Flügeltank.*

TOP TACKLE. A double purchase used in sending a fidded topmast up or down.
Fr: *Palan de Guinderesse;* Ger: *Stängewindreeptakel.*

TOP TIMBER. In a wooden vessel, the timber next above the futtocks in a built-up frame. The uppermost timber in a frame.
Fr: *Allonge de Pavois;* Ger: *Oberer Auflanger.*

TOP WINGS. The outlying portions of an otter trawl net which extend forward from the square on each side of the trawl boards. Also upper wings.
Fr: *Petite Aile;* Ger: *Obernetz Flügel.*

TORCH CUTTING.
See **Flame Cutting.**

TORNADO. A whirlwind of extreme intensity, lasting for about half an hour, and advancing with a speed of 20 to 40 miles per hour. It has a diameter of 100 to 500 yards and carves a belt of complete destruction along its line of progress.
Fr: *Tornade;* Ger: *Wirbelsturm.*

TORT. The word "tort" in its maritime signification embraces all unlawful or injurious acts done or committed on the sea or on navigable waters connected with the sea. Also called maritime tort. Their character as marine torts and the jurisdiction of Admiralty Courts over them depends exclusively on the place where they are committed.
Fr: *Délit;* Ger: *Unrecht; Beleidigung.*
The term when used in reference to Admiralty jurisdiction is not confined to wrongs or injuries committed by direct force but also includes wrongs suffered in consequence of the negligence or malfeasance of others where the remedy in common law is by an action on the case.

TORTOLA CUTTER. A Caribbean, native-built, decked boat from Tortola, Virgin Islands, used for the transportation of passengers and goods between the islands.
The hull is of exceptionally strong construction, with sawed frames of native hardwood, short overhangs, transom stern, straight stem, slightly raked, and deep forefoot. There is a small scuttle forward, a cargo hatch amidships and steering well aft.

The rig consists of a short leg-of-mutton mainsail, with long foot and an overlapping jib. Sail area of approximately 300 sq. ft. on a 20-ft. waterline length. Length, over-all 21 ft. 6 in.; waterline 18 ft. 2 in. Breadth 7 ft. 10 in. Draft 3 ft. 8 in. (Typical.)

TOSHER. Small fishing boat, 18 to 22 ft. long, from the west coast of Great Britain, yawl-rigged, and used for catching mackerel, with trolling lines fastened to long poles. The term "tosher" is also used in a general sense to indicate a type of fishing boat smaller than another of the same type. For instance, the Ramsgate tosher is smaller than the Ramsgate smack. The Mevagissey tosher is smaller than the Mevagissey standard lugger, and so on.

TOSS. To toss oars means to lift them up at the end of a stroke to a perpendicular position, with blades fore and aft and handles resting in the bottom of the boat. It is done either as a salute or preparatory to shipping or unshipping in warships' boats.

Fr: *Mâter les Avirons;* Ger: *Riemen pieken; Riemen Hoch.*

TOT (G. B.). A drinking cup of smaller capacity than a half pint, in which the spirit ration was served on board ship. (Obsolete.)

Fr: *Boujaron.*

TOTAL LOSS. Total loss may be either actual, constructive, or presumed. Where the subject matter insured is destroyed, or so damaged as to cease to be a thing of the kind insured, or where the insured is irretrievably deprived thereof, there is actual total loss. There is also actual total loss when a ship is consumed by fire or destroyed by the perils of the sea.

Fr: *Perte Totale;* Ger: *Totalverlust.*

See **Constructive Total Loss, Presumed Total Loss.**

TOTAL LOSS ONLY. A phrase used in marine insurance policies which exempts the underwriters from liability for all partial losses.

Ger: *Nur für Totalverlust.*

TOUCH. The broadest part of a plank worked top and butt fashion, or the middle of a plank worked "anchor-stock" fashion. (Obsolete.)

TOUCH (to). 1. To graze the bottom with the keel for a moment without lessening of speed.

Fr: *Toucher;* Ger: *Berühren.*

2. To have the weather leeches of the sails shake by steering very close. to the wind.

Fr: *Arriser;* Ger: *Flattern; Tillen.*

3. To call at a port for a very short time, such as for landing or taking passengers; for orders, etc.

Fr: *Toucher;* Ger: *Anlaufen.*

TOURIST CLASS PASSENGER. A special class of passenger for whom improvements in food, accommodation, and facilities for recreation are provided at passage rates slightly above those charged for the regular third-class passage. The adoption of this new class on the North Atlantic routes was due to restrictions placed on the immigrant traffic in 1929 which reduced considerably the number of aliens admissible under United States Immigration Laws.

TOW. 1. A vessel or a number of vessels which are being towed. The word is also used to denote a tug towing one or more floating structures, but it refers more particularly to the craft which are towed. For the purpose of collision liability tug and tow in English law are treated as one vessel.

Fr: *Remorque;* Ger: *Schleppzug; Schleppschiff; Hinterhangfahrzeug.*

2. Short and coarse fibers of little value separated from the longer and more valuable fibers through "hackling" in the manufacture of rope. Tow is occasionally used in the manufacture of inferior qualities of rope.

Fr: *Filasse;* Ger: *Schmickel.*

TOW (to). To draw a vessel through the water or pull it along by means of a rope or chain.

Fr: *Remorquer;* Ger: *Schleppen.*

See **Towrope.**

TOWAGE. 1. A port charge against a vessel for employment of tugs to assist into or out of a harbor, or docking, undocking, or shifting from one berth to another within the harbor. Towage rates vary with the tonnage of vessel, distance of haul, class of vessel. Also called tugboat charge, towage dues.

Fr: *Frais de remorquage;* Ger: *Schlepplohn; Schlepperbeihilfe.*

2. The act of towing. The employment of one vessel to expedite the voyage of another vessel when nothing more is required than the acceleration of her progress.

Fr: *Remorquage; Touage;* Ger: *Schleppen.*

TOWAGE DUES.
See **Towage.**

TOWAGE LIEN (U. S.). A maritime lien for services rendered in towing a ship. In Great Britain this lien is not recognized.

TOWAGE SERVICE. The employment of one vessel to aid in the propulsion of or to expedite the voyage of another when there is no circumstance of peril and nothing more is required than the acceleration of progress. Unlike salvage, it rests exclusively upon a contract duly made between competent parties.

Fr: *Assistance*; Ger: *Schlepperbeihilfe*.

TOWBOAT. See **Tug**.

TOWER'S LIABILITY CLAUSE (G. B.). A special form of "Running Down Clause" used in British marine insurance policies covering tugs and such vessels which habitually tow other craft. It covers in full the legal liability of the owner of the tug for damage done by or to craft in tow of his vessel, as well as such liability as he may incur through collision of the tug with other vessels or fixed or floating structures.

TOW FORESAIL. A large forestaysail considerably overlapping the mainsail; used by sailing trawlers when towing their gear.

TOW HOOK. A large, cast steel hook used by tug boats to which the end of the towing hawser is made fast. It is usually fitted with a compressive spring to absorb the shocks on the hawser. Also called towing hook. The hook is usually hinged at its shank, and is kept in position by a link and tripper over the end. The moment the tripper is hit upwards, the link disengages from the end of the hook and the strain of the rope pulls it over on its hinge until the mouth is wide open, thus releasing the rope instantly.

Fr: *Crochet de Remorque*; Ger: *Schlepphaken*.

TOWING AND SALVING CLAUSE. A charter party clause giving the vessel liberty to tow or be towed, assist vessels in distress and deviate for the purpose of saving life and property. Also called towage clause.

TO WINDWARD. Toward the direction from which the wind is blowing. Also called to the wind.

Fr: *Au Vent*; Ger: *Windwärts*.

TOWING BEAM. See **Tow Rail**.

TOWING BITTS. Bitts on the afterdeck of a tugboat, between which the towline is led, from the towing engine through the towing chock. Also called towing posts, towing bollards, timberheads. The towline strain can be taken off the towing engine by the use of tackle led from the towing bitts, or the towline can be made up directly to the towing bitts.

Fr: *Bittes de remorque*; Ger: *Schleppbetinge*.

See **Towing Winch**.

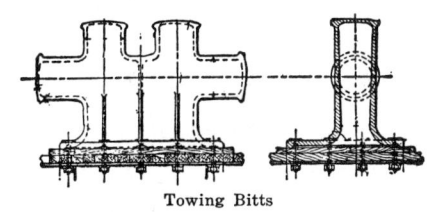

Towing Bitts

TOWING BLOCK. A small iron frame used in trawlers and fastened to the top of the rail abaft the after gallows on the towing side for the purpose of holding the drag ropes together and within reach. It enables the crew to feel the pull, so that if it becomes excessive, the speed may be reduced in order to prevent damage to gear.

Fr: *Chien*; Ger: *Sliphaken*; *Hakentauroller*.

TOWING BOLLARDS. Bollards of larger size than the mooring bollards and used for fastening a towing hawser. On merchant ships the usual practice is to install four pairs of towing bollards, two forward and two aft.

Fr: *Bittes de remorque*; Ger: *Schleppbetinge*; *Schleppollern*.

TOWING BRIDLE. A heavy chain or hawser to the bight of which a towline is attached when a vessel is being towed.

Fr: *Branche de Remorque*; Ger: *Lenktau*.

TOWING EFFICIENCY. The ratio of combined resistance of the tow and tug to power developed by the tug while towing. It seldom exceeds 0.65, and is less in many cases.

TOWING HAWSER. See **Tow Rope**.

TOWING LAUNCH. A boat from 25 to 40 ft. in length fitted with comparatively powerful engines, used in harbors for the towage of lighters and other small craft. Also called launch tug.

Fr: *Vedette de Remorquage*; Ger: *Schleppbarkasse*.

TOWING LIGHT. One of the 2 or 3 white lights placed 6 ft. apart in a vertical line, carried by a mechanically propelled vessel, in accordance with the Rules of the Road, when towing another vessel, and showing

an unbroken light over an arc of the horizon of twenty points of the compass. It must be of such a character as to be visible at a distance of at least 5 miles.
Fr: *Feu de Remorque;* Ger: *Schlepperlaterne.*

TOWING PAINTER. A length of tarred hemp or light chain for towing a dinghy or other small boat. It is usually fastened to an eyebolt clinched fore and aft through the stem near the waterline.
Fr: *Bosse de Remorque;* Ger: *Schleppleine.*

TOWING POSTS. See **Towing Bitts.**

TOWING SHACKLE. Heavy shackle used for joining two towing hawsers.
Fr: *Manille de Remorque;* Ger: *Schlepptau Schackel.*

to broach frequently while being towed, and is usually painted bright yellow or white to improve its visibility.

TOWING SPEED. The speed at which a tug usually tows, ordinarily from 0.4 to 0.7 of its maximum speed.
Fr: *Vitesse de Remorquage;* Ger: *Schleppgeschwindigkeit.*

TOWING WINCH. In a tugboat a winch with large single barrel on which the towing line is reeled, providing an elastic spring or cushion which relieves the hawser from sudden jerks and strains and permits the use of wire hawsers. Also called **towing machine, towing engine.**
Fr: *Treuil de Remorquage;* Ger: *Schleppwinde; Trossenwinde.*

In the steam towing machine the pull and

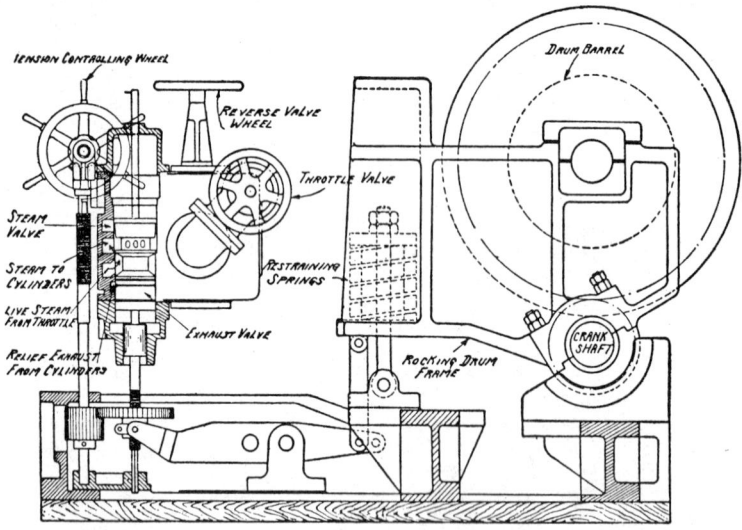

Towing Winch

TOWING SIGNAL. Signals used between tug and tow to indicate a change of course or any other movement as circumstances may require. These signals are made by hand with code flags, using one flag for each signal, or by hoisting a flag at the stay or fore shrouds or at the gaff. By night, flashing is used.
Fr: *Signal de Remorque;* Ger: *Schleppsignal.*

TOWING SPAR. A spar towed astern from vessels navigating in convoy, used as a mark by following vessels in thick weather. Also called fog buoy. It is constructed so as

strain of the tow is held entirely by the steam pressure on the pistons. An automatic control gear, provided with special admission and reverse valves, allows under normal conditions only sufficient steam to hold the tow, the valve being only open a small amount.

When an extra strain comes and causes the line to run out, the valve quickly opens, checking the run and recovering the line through the action of the reverse valve.

Kemble, T. S., Towing Problems, Society of Naval Architects and Marine Engineers, New York, *Transactions,* vol. 17, 1909.

TOWLINE.
See **Towrope.**

TOW-MENG. A type of Cantonese junk employed mostly during the prevalence of eastern monsoon winds. Also called monsoon junk. It is subdivided into numerous watertight compartments. The hull is built with raking V-shaped square bow, with keel extending over nearly the forward half-length, a round bottom curving up sharply at stern, and V-shaped square stern. The tow-meng is decked fore and aft, and is rigged with 3 masts. Length over-all 63 ft. Breadth 14½ ft. Hold depth 6½ ft.

TOW RAIL. Arched iron or wood beam carried across the afterdeck of a tug which prevents the towrope from sweeping and damaging any projections such as skylights, cabin tops, and so on. Also called towing rail, towing beam. The towing hawser rests on these beams when slack. If made of iron, towing rails are capped with hardwood to protect the towrope.

Fr: *Arceau de Remorque;* Ger: *Schleppbogen; Schleppgalgen.*

TOWROPE. A heavy hawser of fiber or wire, by which a vessel tows another ship or is towed. Also called towline, towing hawser.

Fr: *Remorque;* Ger: *Schlepptau; Schlepptrosse.*

When it is made of fiber the best boltrope is used, the circumference ranging from 5 in. up. It is manufactured in coils of 200 fathoms length. Towlines employed by tugs are generally very large hemp ropes, seldom less than 7 in. in circumference. As a rule, half of the length is composed of wire as being easier to shorten or pay out when necessary, and quicker to slip, and half of either hemp or coir rope which gives the required elasticity. For long, deep-sea tows, 90 fathoms of 12-in. water-laid Manila coupled to 45 to 60 fathoms of 4½ steel wire, are also used. A few fathoms of chain are sometimes shackled between the Manila and wire ropes to form a catenary which takes up any sudden jerks or strains.

Up to about 1874, towropes were always made of hemp, Manila, or coir. Although the two latter possess great elasticity, the internal friction which is caused when they are stretched quickly wears them out. Hemp hawsers are in this respect much superior to Manila or coir. As usually made, hemp hawsers have a maximum stretch of about 14 per cent before breaking and it is this large stretch which renders hemp so useful for towing purposes. Steel wire rope combines the maximum strength with the minimum of weight. Wire ropes employed for deep-sea towage are made of 6 strands—37 wires to the strand—with hemp center core, circumference 3¼ to 8¾ in. They should not be galvanized. The most suitable length of towrope is that which permits synchronism between tug and tow.

Synchronism is determined by reference to the half-lengths of tug and tow. The distance between the center of the tug and the tow should be either a wave length or some multiple of it. For long distance towage the towrope is usually homogeneous throughout its length, either all hemp, all Manila, or all wire. Rope springs are not necessary with a wire rope, providing a suitable length of the latter is used.

TOWROPE RESISTANCE. The force equal and opposite to the total resistance overcome in towing a ship. It equals the combined frictional resistances of the eddy-, air- and wavemaking resistances. The reaction which a vessel opposes to an extraneous force by which it is dragged or driven through the water and particularly to forward motion in the direction of the length of the vessel. Modern investigation and experiments in model basins have led to the division of the towrope resistance into two parts, that is, the residuary resistance and the frictional resistance.

Fr: *Résistance de Carène;* Ger: *Schleppwiderstand; Formwiderstand.*

TO-XINH. An open boat of sampan type similar to the *tuyen-luoi* from Port Wallut Bay, Indo-China. It is usually propelled by a rower who stands forward, and a sculler aft.

TRABACCOLO. Coasting vessel of the Adriatic Sea, originating from Chioggia, near Venice. Their capacity varies from 25 to 100 tons and their cargoes are usually firewood, boards, and building stone. The rig consists of 2 masts without rake. The foresail is a dipping lug, the mainsail a standing lug. Both sails are boomed. A single headsail is carried on a reefing bowsprit. The position of the masts is determined as follows: the length of hull between perpendiculars is divided into nineteen parts and the mainmast is stepped at the fifth division counting from the stern and the foremast at the fifteenth division. The length of foremast from heel to hounds is three times the beam and the mainmast is 1 ft. 8 in. shorter. The bluff-ended hull is built of oak with the exception of the clamps, and beams not adjacent to hatchways, which are all of larch. The deck planking is of pine. The fastenings are of galvanized iron. The frames are composed of 5 pieces; floor, futtocks, and bilge pieces, which overlap and bind the futtocks on the floors. In the smaller boats bilge pieces are dispensed with. There is one large hatch amidships and two small ones at the ends.

Trading trabaccolo: Length between perpendiculars 95 ft. Breadth 19.7 ft. Molded depth 7.2 ft. Loaded draft 6.5 ft. Displacement 150 tons. Sail area 3525 sq. ft.

Fishing trabaccolo: Length 38 to 71 ft. Breadth 9.8 to 16.8 ft. Depth 3.3 to 7 ft. Tonnage 8.5 to 39 gross.

TRACE. Term applied in radar to the deflection which commences at the moment an electronic pulse is transmitted, and which shows as a radial line on the plan position indicator. Also termed **"Sweep."**

TRACK. A T-shaped device fitted to the underside of a gaff, the after side of a mast, or to the end of a boom in which slides travel up and down or fore and aft as the sail is hauled out or hoisted and lowered. In square-rigged vessels the same device is sometimes fitted on the forward side of the mast, thus doing away with the upper topsail and upper topgallant parrels. Also called sail track, mast track, railway, tramway.

Fr: *Chemin de Fer;* Ger: *Gleitschiene; Gleitbahn.*

TRACK (to). To tow a vessel by a towline led ashore.

Fr: *Remorquage à la Cordelle;* Ger: *Treideln.*

TRACK CHART. Blank sheets constructed on the Mercator projection for different latitudes, upon which the ship's track is plotted during a passage. Also called skeleton chart.

Fr: *Routier;* Ger: *Segelkarte; Übersegler; Kurskarte.*

TRADE. The waterborne commerce between given ports.

See **Board of Trade, Coasting Trade, Colonial Trade, Contraband Trade, Fishing Trade, Home Trade, Sea-Borne Trade, Small Coasting Trade.**

TRADE WINDS. One of the great aerial currents which form part of the general circulation of the atmosphere, and are governed by the distribution of pressure. The word "trade" in this term means "track" as the trade winds are those which keep to a fixed track.

Fr: *Vents Alizés;* Ger: *Passatwinde.*
Hepworth, Dunes and Gold—The Trade Winds of the Atlantic, Meteorological Office, London, 1910.

TRADING VOYAGE. A marine insurance term which refers to a voyage during which the vessel is at liberty to touch, stay, trade, or go forward and backward at sea. During a trading voyage the goods may be put ashore temporarily for the purposes of barter and returned to the ship after an unsuccessful attempt to barter.

TRADING WARRANTIES. Charter party warranty clause which implies that the vessel shall remain within the geographical boundaries set forth by the underwriters.

Ger: *Fahrtbegrenzungsklausel.*

TRAFFIC POOL. A method of apportioning traffic in accordance with agreed percentages between conference lines. It differs from the traffic agreement which limits the volume of freight that certain lines may carry. Its object is to control competition between conference lines.

Ger: *Verkehrskonzern.*

TRAFFIC SIGNALS. Port signals which include those concerning interruptions of traffic; explosive, anchorage or prohibited anchorage distinguishing marks; lock, docking, berthing, and bridge signals.

Fr: *Signaux de mouvements de port;* Ger: *Verkehrssignal.*

TRAHANDILLA. A Maltese sailing and pulling open boat, rigged with a spritsail.

TRAIL. To let go the oars of a rowing boat, allowing them to swing in the rowlocks or to be held by small lines until the blades, drawn by the onward motion of the boat, hang alongside.

TRAIL BOARD. Also headboard. **1.** One of the ornamental boards extending on each side from abaft the hawse to the figurehead between the trail knees.

2. The close boarding between the head-rails.

Fr: *Frise;* Ger: *Gallionsbrett.*

TRAILING LINE. A small line attached to an oar to prevent its loss if let go. It is secured to the loom of the oar by an eye splice forming a slip noose and to the rising in the boat.

Fr: *Sauvegarde d'Aviron;* Ger: *Riemen Bandsel.*

TRAIL KNEE. One of the timbers furnishing lateral support for the knee of the

head. There are usually two trail knees on each side, reaching from the figurehead to abaft the hawse. (Obsolete.)
Fr: *Jottereau;* Ger: *Schloiknie.*
TRAIL NET. In a fleet of drift nets, the one farthest from the vessel.
TRAIN.
See **Fleet, Fleet Train.**
TRAINIÈRE. 1. An open sailing and rowing boat found in the southern waters of the Bay of Biscay, as far as Bilbao. Also called *trainera* or *lancha trainera*. A few specimens of this type are still believed to exist, although they are becoming rare owing to the large crew required for working them. The hull is flat-floored with very fine run and round stern. The masts have no standing rigging and are held by the step, thwart, and halyards. The foremast, placed close to the stem, is nearly upright; the mainmast is stepped at equal distance from stem and stern. It has a pronounced rake aft and a mast step so arranged that it can be inclined transversely. Length 33 ft. Breadth 6 ft. Depth 2 ft. 8 in. (Average.)

It is claimed that by righting the mast to windward, the boat is able to carry more canvas without reefing than would be the case with an ordinary mast step. The mainsail, called *papayua* by the local fishermen, is tacked down to a short iron bumkin fastened just outside the gunwale. When sailing close to wind, a rough and ready leeboard made of a plank is used.

2. Steam launch of about 15 to 20 horsepower, used on the southern shores of the Bay of Biscay, for handling seine nets in the sardine fisheries.

TRAIN FERRY. A ferryboat fitted with rail lines for transporting railway cars and trucks. Some are double-ended, others are open at the stern only, with the bows completely closed in and of ordinary ship shape.
Fr: *Bac Porte-Trains;* Ger: *Eisenbahnfähre; Eisenbahnfahrschiff.*

"Train Ferries," *Marine Engineering and Shipping Age*, vol. 35 (1930); "Transport by Train Ferries," *Engineering* (London), vol. 128 (October 4, 1929).

TRAMMEL. A set net suspended from a cork rope and anchored with stones at each end. It consists of three curtains of netting suspended from a common cork rope. The middle small-meshed net, called a "lint," is sandwiched between two other large-meshed nets called "wallings" or "armorings." A fish striking either side swims through the first wall it encounters, hits the second layer, and pushes through one of the openings in the third layer to form a sack in which it is trapped. The weight and struggle of the fish causes the open end of the bag to rest on the strands of the guard netting which closes it effectively. It is used for the capture of ray, plaice, pollack, sharks, and so on.
Fr: *Tramail;* Ger: *Ledderungsnetz; Trammelnetz.*

TRAMONTANA. A cold northerly day wind observed in the Adriatic. Also called *borea, aquilone, rovaio, ventavolo.*

TRAMP. A freight vessel that does not run in any regular line but takes cargo wherever the shippers desire. Also called ocean tramp. Tramp vessels are hired to carry cargo of any kind not requiring vessels of special design. They are operated singly over any ocean route and to any destination not prohibited by physical conditions, such as insufficient harbor depth, or legal requirements.
Fr: *Tramp;* Ger: *Unregelmässiger Fahrer; Trampschiff.*

Tramp vessels are chartered either for a particular trip or for a stipulated period. They usually carry full cargoes of bulky commodities, such as coal, ore, grain, sugar, also manufactured products such as iron or steel which are moved in vessel load lots. They are occasionally placed "on the berth" by the owners or shipbrokers for smaller shipments of general cargo.

They are built for maximum economy and freight capacity without sacrifice for ability to enter harbors and channels of every water depth.

Campbell and Ramsay, "Shipowner's Choice of a New Cargo Ship," Institution of Engineers and Shipbuilders in Scotland, *Transactions*, vol. 77 (1933-34); Runciman, W. L., "Tramp Ship Design," North East Coast Institution of Engineers and Shipbuilders (Newcastle upon Tyne), *Transactions*, vol. 49 (1932-33).

TRAMPING. Sea trade which is not confined to any particular route or harbors but which operates to all or any ports of the world.
Fr: *Tramping;* Ger: *Trampschiffahrt.*
See **Tramp.**

Hurd, A. S., *The Triumph of the Tramp Ship*, London, 1922; Nubel, O., *Probleme der Trampschiffahrt*, Hamburg, 1936.

TRAMWAY. See **Track.**

TRANKI. Open double-ended sailing craft, used by divers in the Persian Gulf pearl fisheries.

TRANSFER. 1. The distance gained by a vessel to the right or left of the original track from the time the helm is put hard over until the ship has turned to its new heading.
2. The movement of cargo between ship and wharf.

TRANSIRE. A customhouse document furnished to a coasting vessel in place of the normal clearance. It embodies a detailed statement of the vessel's cargo, consignor and consignee's name, and so on, and must be signed by the master and countersigned by a customs officer.
Fr: *Passavant;* Ger: *Ausklarierungsschein.*

TRANSIT. 1. The passage of a celestial body over a specified meridian of the earth. The passage is designated as "upper" transit or "lower" transit, according to whether it is over that part of the meridian lying above or below the polar axis.
Fr: *Passage méridien;* Ger: *Kulmination.*
2. Two objects (lights, beacons, and so on) seen in line with one another are said to be "in transit."
Fr: *Alignement;* Ger: *Transit; Durchfuhr.*

TRANSIT BEARING. A bearing taken of two objects when in line.

TRANSIT CARGO. Goods on board which upon their arrival at a certain port are not to be discharged at that port.
Fr: *Marchandises de Transit;* Ger: *Transitladung.*

TRANSIT PORT. A port where goods received are merely en route and from which they have to be transferred and dispatched to their ultimate destination by coasters, river craft, barges, and so on. Also called transshipment port.
Fr: *Port de Transit;* Ger: *Transithafen.*

TRANSIT SHED. A covered structure on a wharf or quay for the temporary storage of goods in transit between ship and railhead or warehouse. Legally the transit shed is part of the ship, that is, goods may be removed from the ship and placed in the shed on the account of the shipowner and still be under his control before payment of freight and without depriving him of his lien on the goods for his freight, as is the case when the goods have passed beyond the transit shed into a warehouse or into consumption.
Fr: *Hangar de Quai;* Ger: *Kaischuppen.*

TRANSMITTING MAGNETIC COMPASS. A master magnetic compass which, by means of an electrical "pickup" system, a valve amplifier and "follow-up" system, is enabled to operate one or more repeater compasses. In the larger types of transmitting magnetic compasses, the transmission capacity is equal to that of the gyrocompass.

TRANSOM. 1. In steel ships, the framework of the stern at the sternpost. The floor, frame, and beam which form the aftermost transverse member are named, respectively, transom floor, transom frame, and transom beam. They are usually of heavier scantlings owing to the overhang of the counter which they support. The transom may be vertical or raking.
Fr: *Arcasse;* Ger: *Heck; Heckwerk.*
2. The upper part of the stern above the counter in a square sterned vessel. The transverse planking which forms the afterend of a small square-ended boat.
Fr: *Tableau;* Ger: *Spiegel.*
3. A seat or couch built at the side of a stateroom or cabin. It usually has lockers or drawers underneath. Also called transom berth.
Fr: *Caisson.*
See **Deck Transom, Filling Transom, Helm Port Transom.**

TRANSOM BEAM. A deck beam at the afterend of the vessel, situated over the sternpost and bracketed at each end to the transom frame. The cant beams extend radially abaft the transom beam.
Fr: *Barrot d'Arcasse;* Ger: *Heckbalken; Warpbalken.*

TRANSOM BOARD. Heart-shaped board in cutter-built rowing boats, secured to the backboard by horizontal knees.
Fr: *Ecusson;* Ger: *Heckbalkenplanke.*

TRANSOM COUNTER. A type of stern in which the upper counter is terminated by a flat, or slightly arched surface called transom board, on which the ship's name and port of registry is generally indicated. It was the most common form of stern found in wooden vessels.
Fr: *Arrière à tableau;* Ger: *Spiegelheck.*

TRANSOM FLOOR. A floor connected amidships to the top of the sternpost on which the heels of the cant frames abut.
Fr: *Varangue d'Arcasse;* Ger: *Heckbalkenplatte.*

TRANSOM FRAME. In wooden hulls, one of the horizontal timbers of the stern which connects the fashion timbers to the sternpost. In steel ships the aftermost frame of the square body. It is riveted to the head of the sternpost and from it the cant frames radiate. It has a deep floor plate so that the

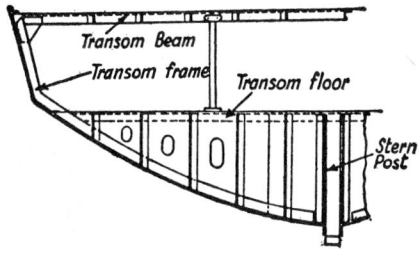

Transom Frame

stern framing may be efficiently connected by deep brackets.

Fr: *Membrure d'Arcasse;* Ger: *Heckspant; Gillungspant.*

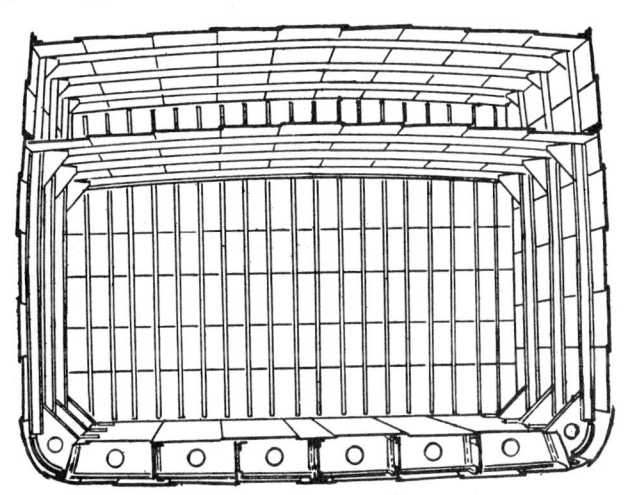

Transverse Framing System

TRANSOM STERN. A form of stern in which the upper part of the hull aft terminates in a large flat surface, vertical, or nearly so, and square to the central longitudinal plane. Also called round-tuck stern. Transom-sterned craft have the advantage of somewhat longer buttock lines than sharp-sterned boats. There is, however, a considerable amount of eddy making at the tuck if it is much immersed. Transom sterns are frequently designed with a slight rake aft and if viewed from above may be slightly rounded or shaped like a widely opened V.

Fr: *Arrière à Tableau;* Ger: *Spiegelheck; Querholzheck; Overholzheck.*

TRANSPORT. A ship owned or hired by a state to convey troops, or military or naval supplies to their port of destination.

Fr: *Transport;* Ger: *Transportschiff.*

TRANSSHIPMENT. The transfer of goods from the vessel stipulated in the contract of affreightment to another vessel before the place of destination has been reached. Transshipment without legal excuse is a violation of the contract and subjects the carrier to liability if the goods be lost. In marine insurance, the unnecessary transshipment of cargo from one ship to another is considered such a variation of the risk as to discharge the underwriters of the risk unless liberty to transship is given by the policy.

Fr: *Transbordement;* Ger: *Umladung; Verschiffung.*

TRANSVERSE. Term applied in the longitudinal (Isherwood) system of construction, to each one of the widely spaced deep frames. They are continuous and have notches cut out to permit the longitudinals to pass through.

TRANSVERSE FRAMING. In ship construction, a system of framing in which closely spaced frames of similar scantlings are used to provide the main strength framing of the ship, upon which the shell, keel, and decks are attached, in contradistinction to longitudinal framing, in which many closely spaced longitudinals are used, with greater frame spacing, lighter frames, and occasional web frames.

Fr: *Construction Transversale;* Ger: *Querspannung.*

See **Frame, Longitudinal Framing.**

TRANSVERSE METACENTER. The point of intersection of the vertical through the center of buoyancy of a ship in the upright position with the vertical through a new center of buoyancy when the ship has a slight heel.

Fr: *Métacentre Latitudinal;* Ger: *Breites Metazentrum.*

TRANSVERSE METACENTRIC HEIGHT. Height of transverse metacenter above center of gravity, abbreviated as G. M.

Approximate Transverse G. M.:
Passenger liner ....1 to 2 ft.
Cargo vessel ....2 ft.
Collier ....1 ft. 6 in.
   loaded to 10 ft. in ballast
Tug ....1½ to 2 ft.
Sailing vessel ....3 to 4 ft.
Trawler ....2 to 3 ft. 4 in.

Fr: *Hauteur Métacentrique Transversale;* Ger: *Metazentrische Breitenhöhe.*

See **Transverse Metacenter.**

TRANSVERSE NUMERAL. The numeral which gives the scantlings and spacing of the transversely disposed part of a ship's structure, in accordance with classification rules. Also called framing-numeral.

Fr: *Nombre Transversal;* Ger: *Quernummer.*

TRANSVERSE WAVES. A series of waves, produced by the motion of the vessel, which carry their crests transversely to the line of travel. The length of these waves bears a definite relation to the speed of the ship. One set is produced at the bow, another at the stern.

Fr: *Vagues Transversales;* Ger: *Querlaufende Wellen.*

TRAP.

See **Fish Trap, Flapper.**

TRAPEZOIDAL RULE. A mathematical rule used in ship calculations for computing the area of curvilinear figures. The base line is divided into any number of convenient equal parts and perpendiculars are erected meeting the curve. To half the sum of the first and last perpendiculars the sum of all the intermediate ones is added; the sum multiplied by the common interval gives the area.

Fr: *Règle des Trapèzes;* Ger: *Trapezregel.*

TRAP NET. An inshore fishing apparatus consisting of a series of funnels, with their mouths kept open by hoops, opening into each other and finally closing into a sack forming a trap. The whole is covered by netting and the fish coming from either direction are led to the trap by a leader extended on stakes running from the shore. This type of net, of which there are many variations is fastened to the bottom. Also called fyke net.

Fr: *Verveux;* Ger: *Reuse.*

TRAVELER. The ring of a sheet block which travels on a deck or boom horse. An iron ring, thimble, or strap which travels on a spar, a bar, or a rope.

Fr: *Rocambeau;* Ger: *Leiterring.*

See **Boom Traveler, Clew Traveler, Jib Traveler.**

TRAVELING BACKSTAY. A backstay fitted to a traveler on the topmast by which the mast is supported at the place to which the topsail yard is hoisted. It was used with single topsails.

Fr: *Faux Galhauban;* Ger: *Borgpardune.*

TRAVELING MARTINGALE. A martingale fitted to the bowsprit of a small vessel, used only when the jib is set.

TRAVERSE. To lay athwart, as a yard or spar.

Fr: *Croiser;* Ger: *Kreuzen.*

TRAVERSE BOARD. A board formerly used for recording the ship's course during a watch. It consisted of a disk or board marked with all the points of the compass, and having eight holes bored upon each point. The course for each half hour was noted by placing a peg in one of the holes corresponding to the ship's course.

Fr: *Renard;* Ger: *Pinnkompass; Besteckkompass.*

TRAVERSE SAILING. A variety of plane sailing in which the ship makes two or more courses in succession, the difference of latitude and departure being added algebraically and a single resultant course and distance found.

Fr: *Route Moyenne;* Ger: *Koppelkurs segeln.*

TRAVERSE TABLE. A table giving the difference of latitude and departure corresponding to any given course and distance.

It contains the lengths of the two sides of a right-angle triangle, for every degree of course, and for every mile of the hypotenuse up to a maximum distance which varies in different publications.

Fr: *Table de Point;* Ger: *Koppeltafel; Grad- und Strichtafel.*

TRAWL. A large conical net made of Manila, cotton, or hemp twine. It has its lower part cut well back in the form of a U so that the fish when distributed are already enclosed at the sides and top. The lower edge is fitted with a heavy ground rope, with the object of preventing the escape of fish underneath the net. Toward the narrow end of the net there is the cod end or trap in which the fish are finally caught.

Fr: *Chalut;* Ger: *Grundschleppnetz; Kurre; Schleppnetz.*

See **Beam Trawl, Herring Trawl, Otter Trawl, Paranza Trawl, Shrimp Trawl, Spanish Trawl.**

The size of a trawl depends upon the dimensions and power of the towing vessel, the largest being about 250 ft. long by 125 ft. wide at the opening. The size of meshes varies from ½ in. from knot to knot in the pocket, to 3 in. in other parts. Manila is employed where rough work has to be done as in the otter trawl and larger beam trawls, cotton and hemp in the smaller beam trawls and shrimp trawls.

See **Long Line.**

TRAWL BEAM. See **Beam Trawl.**

TRAWL-BOARD SHACKLE. A shackle fitted with a flat and square-headed screw pin, with which the trawl warp is attached to the otter board. Also called warp shackle.

TRAWL BRIDLE. One of the ropes connecting the beam of a trawl to its warp or main rope. They are shackled to swivel eyebolts on the trawl heads.

Fr: *Bras de Chalut;* Ger: *Breidel.*

TRAWL DOOR.
See **Otter Board.**

TRAWLER. A sail- or mechanically-propelled vessel engaged in sea fisheries with a drag net, the most modern development of which is the otter trawl. Also called dragger. Modern deep-sea trawlers are single-screw steam or motor vessels designed with high sheer forward, in order to provide a dry fore deck upon which the dressing and sorting of the catch is carried out at sea, and low freeboard aft to reduce the vertical movement in the warps to a minimum. The after deck is raised from the trawl winch aft. Deck ponds for holding the fish after the pocket of the trawl net has been emptied on deck are provided in the well. The crew is housed in the forecastle. The size of draggers has been greatly increased due to the greater distance covered to reach fishing grounds, and to the larger cargoes of fish brought to port as compared to former times. Their length ranges from 75 to 250 ft. with a horsepower of 100 to 1200 and a free speed of 8 to 12 knots. Owing to the additional strain imposed on the hull when towing the fishing gear in rough weather, the scantlings are usually in excess of the requirements for trading vessels of the same tonnage. The speed of the vessel when towing is usually between 2½ and 5 knots depending on weather conditions and nature of sea bottom.

Fr: *Chalutier;* Ger: *Schleppfischer.*

See **Line Trawler, Side-Set Trawler.**
Nicholas, W. H. C., Evolution of the Modern Steam Trawler, Institution of Naval Architects, *Transactions,* vol. 77 (1935); Schleufe, F., "Neuzeitliche Fischdampfer," *Werft. Reederei, Hafen,* vol. 19 (February, 1938); Taylor, A. R., "Fishing Vessel Design," Institution of Naval Architects (London), *Transactions,* vol. 85 (1943).

TRAWLER BOAT. A small boat used in the winter trawl fisheries on the coast of Virginia and North Carolina. These boats, originally built for oyster and crab dredging in lower Chesapeake Bay, are generally from 40 to 50 ft. long, 12 to 16 ft. broad, and have a draft of 5 to 6 ft. Their deadweight capacity is about 20,000 pounds. They work with an otter trawl. Their catch consists chiefly of scup, croaker, flounder, and sea bass.

TRAWLER DRIFTER. A North Sea type of fishing vessel fitted out for trawling or drifting. Fittings include not only the usual trawl gallows and winch but also a lowering mast, a special compartment for stowing the fleet of nets, and the necessary fittings at the bow for paying out the warp. Trawler drifters are thus equipped to enable them to use drift nets during the herring season, which is of brief duration, and subsequently to be used as trawlers.

TRAWLER'S KNOT. A netting knot of the single sheet bend type used by North Sea fishermen. Also known as herring knot, round knot, beating knot.

TRAWL GALLOWS. Four strong fittings

placed on both sides of a trawler, generally formed by an H bar with bracket attachments to the deck. The purpose of the gallows is to raise the otter boards when work-

TRAWLHEAD. A strong heart-shaped iron frame fitted at each end of a trawl beam. The lower part is called the shoe. The after side is straight and slopes upward

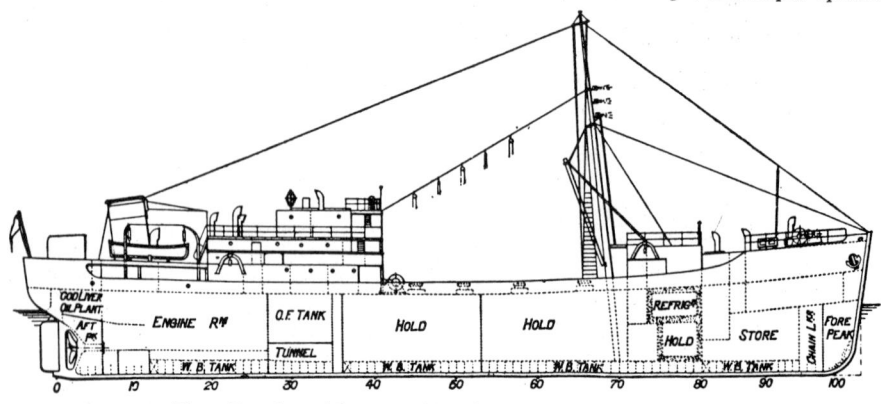

Motor Trawler. (*Courtesy Shipbuilding and Shipping Record*)

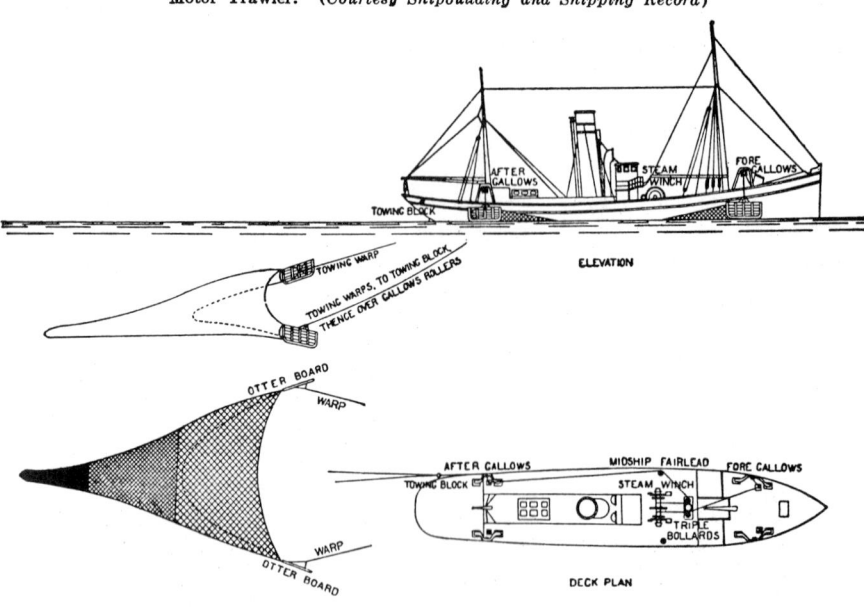

DIAGRAM OF STEAM TRAWLER
SHOWING FISHING GEAR
Trawling. (*Courtesy Bureau of Fish and Wild Life*)

ing the trawl. Each gallow is provided with a heavy steel pulley at the top, through which the trawl warp is rove.

Fr: *Potence de Chalut;* Ger: *Fischnetzgalgen; Fischgalgen.*
See **Otter Board.**

from the hindmost point or heel and then curves down in a single unbroken arc, which forms the front of the frame, to join the shoe. A square socket is bolted to the top of the frame to receive the end of the beam, and eyebolts are fitted at the extreme front of each head to take the ropes or wires by which the trawl is towed. The sides of the net are seized or lashed at a point close to the ground. The shoe of the trawlhead is generally made of double thicknesses. Also called head iron, trawl iron, runner.

Fr: *Patin de Chalut;* Ger: *Klaue; Bügel.*

TRAWLING. A method of fishing, also called dragging, which consists in dragging or towing at a reduced speed over the sea bottom a large conical net called trawl. The mouth or opening of the trawl is kept open by trawl boards or by a wooden spar or beam. The speed of the net over the sea bottom must be sufficient to prevent the caught fish from escaping through the opening or mouth of the net. On the other hand, if the speed is excessive the net will not keep to the bottom and thus becomes inefficient. The speed of a trawler when fishing should be between 2 and 5 knots per hour, this being the effective speed over the bottom, due allowance being made for tidal currents. A thorough knowledge of the nature of the sea bottom and of the currents prevailing on the fishing grounds is essential for trawling operations to be carried out successfully.

To begin trawling the vessel is maneuvered until she gets the wind on the beam. The net is then put over on the lee side. The forward otter board is lowered first, about 10 fathoms of the drag rope attached to this board being run out before the winch barrel controlling the other drag rope is put into operation. Both ropes are then run out simultaneously until the net is at a suitable distance from the vessel, depending on the local depth of water. The main barrels of the winch are then put out of action by means of a clutch gear and the drag ropes are pulled sideways inboard by a messenger chain worked from the winch drums so that they may be attached to the after towing bollard on that side of the ship over which the net was lowered.

When the net is being hauled on board these operations are repeated in the reverse order. When the net has been pulled alongside it is finally hoisted above deck by heaving apparatus provided at the masthead. When in this position the end of the pocket is unlaced and the fish allowed to fall in the deck ponds. Sailing trawlers rarely work in depths over 20 fathoms. Steam and motor vessels frequently work in depths of 200 fathoms, and commercial trawling in 500 fathoms is not unknown.

Fr: *Chalutage;* Ger: *Schleppnetzfischerei; Kurrenfischerei.*

Alexander-Moore-Kendall, Otter Trawl Fishery, United States Bureau of Fisheries, Document no. 816, Washington, 1915.

TRAWL IRON.
See **Trawlhead.**

TRAWL NET.
See **Trawl.**

TRAWL WARP. The rope or ropes by means of which a trawlnet is towed through the water. Beam trawls are towed by a single warp attached to the trawl bridle. The ends of the bridle are shackled to the trawlheads. It is usually a four-strand cable-laid white Manila rope. Otter trawls are worked with two wire warps of 2¼ or 2¾ in. in circumference although in some small boats a bridle is used, which makes for easy maneuvering when working in fleets. Also called drag rope.

Fr: *Fune;* Ger: *Schlepptau; Schleppleine.*

TRAWL WINCH. A steam or electric winch especially designed to meet the requirements of trawling operations. It is provided with two large barrels, one for each warp, which can be worked together or separately by the action of clutches. A small gypsyhead on each side is provided for the final hoisting of the net on board and also for pulling the drag ropes sideways.

Fr: *Treuil de Pêche;* Ger: *Netzwinde.*

Trawl winches vary in size according to the depths which are likely to be encountered on the fishing grounds and the size of the vessel. They are provided with coiling gear for the warps placed on the forward side of the winch which consist of vertical rollers running on a horizontal track. These rollers are connected through rack and pinion to a hand wheel abaft the winch from which they receive their motion. Motor trawlers of small size with engines developing up to about 200 bhp. have usually the winch directly connected to the main engines in order to avoid the installation of a separate motor. The operation of the winch in this case is effected by a pulley and belt drive operated from the forward end of the main shaft which, through a second fore-and-aft shaft placed at deck level, drives the winch through gearing. "Electric Winch for Trawls," *Engineer* (London), vol. 163, no. 4231 (1937).

TRAWL WIRE.
See **Spreader.**

TRAY. A small rectangular wooden platform made of heavy boards and with a coaming of 8 to 12 in. high all around. A line fastened at each corner connects to a ring at the point of attachment of the cargo hook. It is used for loading and unloading small case goods such as lard, fruit, canned milk, etc. Also called skip, platform sling, scow.
Fr: *Plateau;* Ger: *Trog.*
TREAD. The length of a vessel's keel.
TREATY PORT. On the China coast, a harbor or town where foreigners were allowed to trade. Many so-called treaty ports are interior cities. (Obsolete.)
Fr: *Port à Traité;* Ger: *Vertragshafen.*
En-Sai Tai, *Treaty Ports in China,* New York, 1918.
TREBLE BLOCK. A block with three sheaves.
Fr: *Poulie Triple;* Ger: *Dreischeibiger Block.*
TREBLE PLANKING. A method of planking which calls for the laying of two inner layers of planking laid diagonally in opposite directions from sheer to keel, and one thicker outer layer of fore-and-aft planking. The combined diagonal and fore-and-aft planking increases the longitudinal strength while at the same time reducing the total weight of the hull as compared with ordinary planking. Reductions in frames, scantlings, and broader spacing are permissible with this system. A saving in hull weight of 10 to 11 per cent has been attained.
Fr: *Bordé Triple;* Ger: *Dreifache Beplankung.*
TREBLE PURCHASE. A tackle consisting of two treble blocks. It is so reeved that its standing and hauling parts both come out of the center sheave in each block, and the standing part is made fast to a becket or lug in the tail of the block through which the hauling part is led. Also called threefold purchase.
Fr: *Caliorne à Trois Réas;* Ger: *Dreischeibiger Gien.*
TREBLING. Strengthening planks put on a wooden vessel's bows to enable her to withstand more efficiently the pressure of ice.
Ger: *Eisverstärkung.*
TREENAIL. A cylindrical pin of hard wood used for fastening planks or timbers. Treenails are often made of oak and teak-wood, but the best material is locust, on account of its great durability, toughness and freedom from shrinkage. Treenails are used for outside planking below waterline. They are driven from the outside through the ceiling, and are wedged at both ends.
Fr: *Gournable;* Ger: *Holznagel; Dubel.*
There are three types of treenails. The first is straight and is driven in a hole about 1/16 in. smaller than the treenail. The second has one half sized about ⅛ in. smaller than the other half. The third type is tapered. On account of the large diameter of holes they require, treenail fastenings are not adopted as a rule for vessels of less than about 50 tons.
TREENAIL WEDGE. A small oak wedge inserted at each end of a treenail to increase its holding power.
Fr: *Epite;* Ger: *Deutel.*
TREMANNINGAR. An open boat from the Island of Gotland (Sweden) engaged in the drift-net herring fishery. The *tremannigar* or "three men boat" is so called because it is handled by a crew of 3. The boat has a fine sheer, deep keel, curved stem and sternpost with pronounced rake. It is clinker-built with 7 strakes to a side, 15 frames, and 5 thwarts. The rig consists of 2 masts with spritsails and jib tacking to stemhead. Length over-all 25 ft. 2½ in. Beam 6 ft. 7 in. Depth 2 ft. 6½ in. (Typical.)
TRENCH. A narrow and elongated depression of the sea bottom lying along the edge of a continent.
Fr: *Fossé;* Ger: *Graben.*
TREND. 1. The angle made by the anchor cable with the line of the keel.
Fr: *Gisement;* Ger: *Richtung.*
2. The lower part of the shank of an anchor measured at a distance from the throat equal to the length of one of the arms.
TRERORING.
See **Sunmorsbat.**
TRESTLETREES. Fore-and-aft framing resting on the hounds of a lower mast or topmast, and supporting the weight of the crosstrees and top. The fid of the mast above rests on the trestletrees. Also called trestles.
Fr: *Elongis;* Ger: *Längssalings.*
TRET. Allowance for ordinary wear and tear or depreciation during a voyage.
TRIAL RANGE.
See **Measured Course.**
TRIAL TANK. A tank in which experiments on the resistance of ships are carried

out by towing ship models, in accordance with the theory of mechanical similitude. Also called towing tank, model tank. Trial tanks are usually of sufficient length to give the model a free run on a distance from 300 ft. to 1000 ft. To this length are added a basin, and a pit at one end, for convenience in adjusting the model and overhauling the towing carriage. The tanks are 20 to 40 ft. wide and 10 to 20 ft. deep. The models are commonly 12 to 20 ft. long and are made to scale. The towing carriage is a large steel bridge 5 to 45 tons in weight which spans the tank just above water level and can be driven at high speeds along it upon leveled rails fixed to the tank walls. The carriage carries the experimenter with

It also gives the speed, maximum horsepower developed by the engines, and the consumption of fuel necessary to obtain the speed and power.

Fr: *Voyage d'Essai;* Ger: *Probefahrt.*
See **Progressive Trials.**

Baker, G. S., "Measured Mile Trials," North East Coast Institution of Engineers and Shipbuilders (Newcastle upon Tyne), *Transactions,* 1923; Stevens, E. A., "Practical Methods of Conducting Trials of Vessels," Society of Naval Architects and Marine Engineers (New York), *Transactions,* 1909; Telfer, E. V., "The Practical Analysis of Merchant Ship Trials and Service Performance," North East Coast Institution of Engineers and Shipbuilders (Newcastle upon Tyne), *Transactions,* 1926; Weingart, W.,

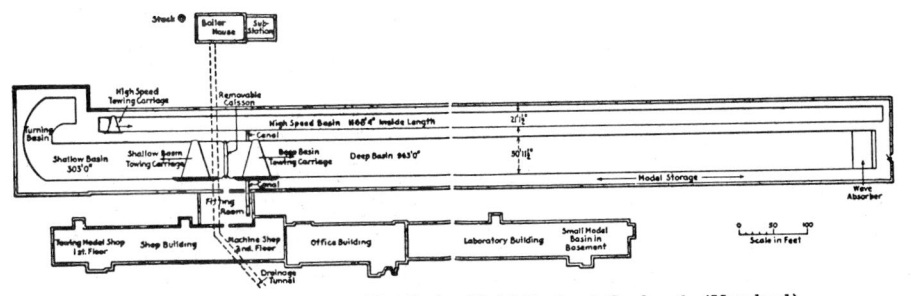

Trial Tank (Model Basin). The Taylor Model Basin at Carderock (Maryland)
(*Courtesy Society of Naval Architects and Marine Engineers*)

the measuring apparatus. The model is towed through the water at various speeds, its resistance is measured and the wave patterns it creates in the water are filmed and studied. This enables the naval architect to see whether the ship will attain the desired speed economically. If not, changes in hull form are made on the model and the model is again tested.

Fr: *Bassin d'essai de carènes;* Ger: *Modelltank; Versuchstank; Schlepprinne.*

See **Model Basin.**

Davidson, K. M., "A Towing Tank for Small Models," Society of Naval Architects and Marine Engineers, *Transactions,* vol. 44 (1936); Saunders, H. E., "The Prediction of Speed and Power of Ships," United States Navy Department, Washington (1933).

TRIAL TRIP. A trip during which successive runs in opposite directions on a measured mile are made in order to ascertain the capabilities and efficiency of the propelling machinery when under full power.

Die Pratiksche Auswertung von Probefahrten und Reiseergebnissen," *Werft, Reederei, Hafen,* vol. 7 (1927), p. 122.

TRIANGLE OF POSITION.
See **Astronomical Triangle.**

TRIATIC STAY. 1. In mechanically propelled vessels, a wire extending from the fore-topmast to the main topmast or from the fore-topmast to the top of the stack, used for signaling. Also called signal stay.

2. A wire secured to the topmast head of a fore-and-aft rigged vessel and leading to the lower masthead of the mast next abaft it, acting as a support to the topmast.

Fr: *Etai de Chouque;* Ger: *Toppreep.*
TRICE.
See **Bobstay Trice, Tricing Line.**
TRICE (to). To haul up or lift by means of a lashing or line.

Fr: *Retrousser; Relever;* Ger: *Aufholen.*
TRICING LINE. 1. In a fore-and-aft-rigged vessel, a line which draws up a sail.
2. A small rope used for hauling up or

tricing up any object either to stow it or get it out of the way.
Fr: *Lève-Nez;* Ger: *Aufholer; Schlappgording.*

TRICING STAY. A guiding rope running parallel to a mast, to which the edge of a sail is attached by a number of hanks so that it can travel up and down when required. Also called bight stay, leader.
Fr: *Mât de Corde;* Ger: *Segelleiter.*

TRICK. A period of two hours of the helmsman at the wheel. A turn or spell of duty.
Fr: *Tour; Tour de Barre;* Ger: *Dienstzeit; Torn; Rudertorn.*

TRICOLORED LANTERN. A lantern carried by mechanically propelled vessels engaged in trawling, as required by the Rules of the Road. It shows a white light from right ahead to two points on each bow, and a green and red light over an arc of the horizon from two points on each bow to two points abaft the beam on the starboard and port sides respectively.
Fr: *Fanal Tricolore;* Ger: *Dreifarbenlaterne.*

TRIGGER BAR. See **Tumbler.**

TRIM. The longitudinal deviation of a vessel from her designed waterline at a given draft. The condition of a ship with reference to her longitudinal position in the water. The difference between the draft forward and aft.
Fr: *Assiette;* Ger: *Trimm.*
See **Cork Light Trim, Moment to Alter Trim, Sailing Trim, Veering Trim.**

TRIM (to). 1. To haul or dispose the yards and sails in such a manner that the wind strikes them at the desired angle.
Fr: *Orienter;* Ger: *Stellen; Trimmen; Kanten.*

2. To work a piece of timber into proper shape by means of an ax or adze.
Ger: *Ausrüsten.*

3. To arrange the weights in a vessel in such a manner as to obtain desired immersion at the bow and stern.
Fr: *Arrimer;* Ger: *Verstauen; Trimmen.*
See **Trimming.**

TRIM BY THE HEAD. A vessel is said to trim by the head when its draft forward is greater than aft.
Fr: *Piquer; en Contre Différence;* Ger: *Kopflastig.*

TRIM BY THE STERN. A vessel is said to trim by the stern when it draws more water aft than forward.

Fr: *Sur Cul; en Différence;* Ger: *Steuerlastig.*

TRIMMER (G. B.). A man employed in the boiler-room force to trim and transfer coal from the bunkers to the firing platform. Also called coal passer. He assists the firemen in cleaning fires, in the removal of ashes from the fireroom and in other fireroom work, thereby acquiring the primary experience necessary to qualify as fireman. The trimmers usually number two thirds of the firemen.
Fr: *Soutier;* Ger: *Kohlentrimmer; Kohlenzieher.*
See **Self-Trimmer.**

TRIMMING. The shoveling of bulk cargo such as coal, grain, or ore into the different holds, or parts thereof, which cannot be reached by gravity flow. Bulk grain is trimmed or shoveled together to facilitate filling into bags or discharging by bucket or pneumatic elevator.
Fr: *Arrimage à la Pelle;* Ger: *Trimmen.*

TRIMMING HATCH. Small hatch pierced in the 'tween decks of a vessel loading grain in bulk, through which grain is poured so as to bring it close up to the deck at the sides. Also called trimming hole.
Ger: *Trimmluke.*

TRIMMING TANK. The tanks situated at the bow and stern of a vessel, used frequently for adjusting the trim, on account of their large leverage about the center of flotation.
Fr: *Caisse d'Assiette;* Ger: *Trimmtank.*
See **Peak Tank.**

TRIM NET (G. B.). A bag net similar to the stow net, but much smaller and with a triangular-shaped opening.

TRINITY HOUSE. The Corporation of Trinity House is an association of British mariners dating back to 1514, specially concerned with the lighting, buoying, and pilotage on the coasts of England. Its practical duties are the erection and maintenance of lighthouses, light vessels, buoys, and beacons. In Scotland the same duties are performed by the Northern Lighthouse Board and in Ireland by the Irish Lighthouse Board. Trinity House also has the care and supervision of pilots in England. It is managed by a board whose members are known as the "Elder Brethren," two of whom are elected from the Navy and eleven from the Merchant Service. The Elder Brethren or

Trinity Masters act as nautical assessors in Admiralty courts.

Barrett, C. R. B., *Trinity House of Deptford*, London, 1893; Mayo, W. H., *Trinity House*, London, 1905.

TRINITY HOUSE FLAG (G. B.). The flag of the Master of Trinity House. It has the red cross of St. George on a white ground, with an ancient ship on the waves in each quarter. In the center is a shield with the same device, surmounted by a lion.

TRINITY MASTERS (G. B.). Name given to the Elder Brethren of Trinity House Corporation, summoned in actions of collision, damage, salvage and other actions involving nautical questions, at the request of the parties or by order of the Admiralty court. Their duties are purely advisory. Trinity masters act as nautical assessors in the House of Lords, the Admiralty Division of the High Court of Justice, and the Court of Session in Scotland.

TRINKET. The uppermost sail, topgallant or royal, in a square-rigged ship.

TRINQUART. Small fishing boat used on the coasts of Normandy during the herring season.

TRIP. A single or one-way journey. Also called crossing.

Fr: *Traversée;* Ger: *Einmalige Fahrt.*

See **Maiden Trip, Trial Trip.**

TRIP (to). 1. To swing a yard or spar to a vertical position for lowering.

Ger: *Trippen.*

2. To raise an anchor from its bed at the bottom by hauling on a line previously made fast to the crown.

3. To swing a yard into a perpendicular position by using a tripping line.

Fr: *Apiquer;* Ger: *Kaien.*

4. To trip a topmast: to hoist it sufficiently to allow the fid to be knocked out preparatory to housing or lowering.

Fr: *Soulager;* Ger: *Lüften.*

5. To let go, such as an anchor from the anchor bed.

TRIP CHARTER. A charter party used when a vessel is chartered for a single voyage. The owner retains and operates his vessel; his payment is based upon the amount of cargo transported, in terms of tons or any other cargo unit. Also called voyage charter.

Fr: *Affrètement au Voyage;* Ger: *Reisebefrachtung.*

TRIP HALYARDS. A rope or tripping line used for bringing the yard of a fore-and-aft topsail to the desired angle.

TRIPLE-EXPANSION ENGINE. A multiple-expansion steam reciprocating engine in which the expansion is conducted in two stages, there being one high-pressure cylinder, one intermediate-pressure cylinder, and one or two low-pressure cylinders.

TRIPOD MAST. A mast made of three legs. Tripod masts permit the lower rigging to be omitted. The two after legs, which take the place of the rigging, are connected to the masthead below the trestletrees.

Fr: *Mât Tripode;* Ger: *Dreibeinmast.*

TRIPPING BRACKET. One of the flat bars or plates placed at various points on deck girders, stiffeners, or beams as a reinforcement to prevent their free flanges from turning.

TRIPPING GEAR.

See **Tumbler.**

TRIPPING LINE. 1. A line fastened to the point or apex of a drogue or sea anchor for hauling it on board of the boat.

2. A line fastened to the fluke of the anchor. Used on rocky bottom where the flukes may be caught and cannot be dislodged by the pull on the cable. The free end is fastened to a buoy.

Fr: *Orin;* Ger: *Ankerbojereep.*

3. A small line fastened to the snotter of a light yard when sent down for guiding it. Also called squilgee, fancy line.

Fr: *Halebreu; Retenue;* Ger: *Aufholleine; Trippleine.*

TRIPPING LINK. A link consisting of a hook closed by a ring, and opened by a pull on a tripping line. Also called sliphook.

Fr: *Echappement;* Ger: *Sliphaken.*

TRIPPING PALM. Projecting pieces fitted on the head of a stockless anchor causing the flukes to turn about their axis when the anchor is down and a pull comes on the cable. Also called canting piece.

Fr: *Ressaut;* Ger: *Schlagstück.*

TRIP SHORE. One of several shores installed under the after end of the keel of a ship about to be launched when the keel blocks and cribbings have been removed. They assist in supporting the weight in the area below high-water level up to the time of launching. They have rounded ends and fall down as the ship begins to move. Also called tumble shore.

Fr: *Béquille; Bonhomme; Chandelle;* Ger: *Fallstütze.*

TRIP STOPPER. A short chain secured with eyebolts to the ship's side and used for canting a stocked anchor in letting go.

Fr: *Mouilleur.*

See **Stock and Fluke Fashion.**

TROCHOIDAL WAVE. A wave, the contour of which is the curve traced out by a point on a radius of a circle, when the latter is rolled on the underside of a given line. This is the wave contour which is usually adopted for use in connection with longitudinal strength calculations of bending moments acting upon a vessel among waves.

Fr: *Houle Trochoïde;* Ger: *Trochoide Welle.*

TROINIK. A double-ended, open boat employed by the Samoyeds in the fisheries of the White Sea. It consists of a dugout basis with two strakes of sewed planking on each side. There are 4 to 6 transverse ribs by which the wash strakes are fastened to the dugout basis. The thickness is about three quarters of an inch at bottom and three eighths at the sides of the dugout. Two bilge logs are fitted for dragging the boat over the ice. Propulsion is assured by oars. A long sweep is used for steering. A portable mast with spritsail is used in fair winds. Length 13 to 19 ft. Breadth 1.9 to 2.8 ft. (Average.)

TROLL.

See **Trolling Line.**

TROLLER. Generic name for a power boat, sailboat or rowboat used for trolling. Also called trolling boat. The seagoing troller is decked and fitted with a motor of sufficient power to drive it at a normal working speed of 7 to 8 knots. On the Pacific coast of North America trollers are the most numerous class of craft to be found. They troll for salmon, tuna, and albacore. There is a wide range of design. In northern California the boats have the Italian-style clipper bow. The Columbia River type is a "double-ender" about 25 ft. long with low cabin forward and usually fished by one man. Farther north, the elliptical stern is usually found with raised fore deck merged into the pilot house. This is a larger type with a length of 35 to 40 ft. and accommodations for 2 or 3 men. The largest boats with a length of 45 ft. or more are listed as albacore boats and carry a

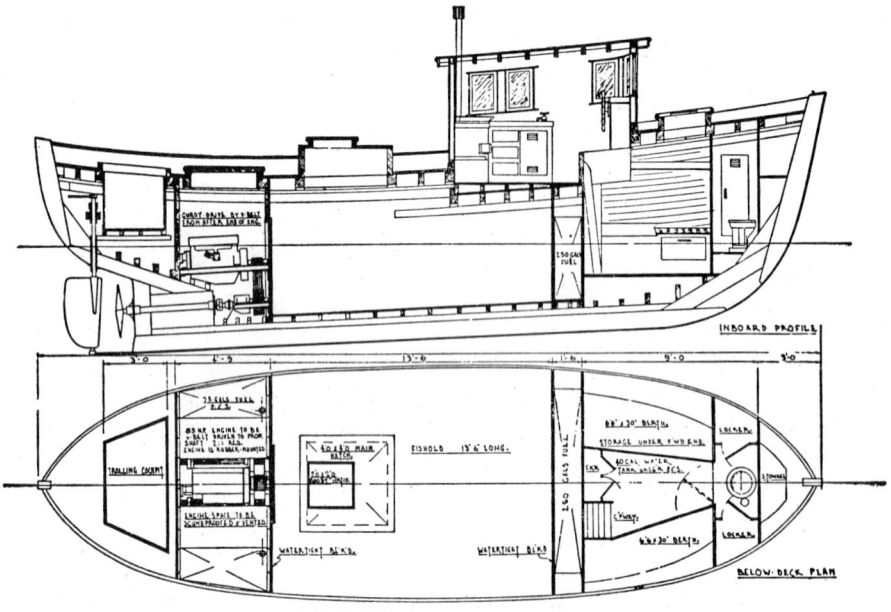

Troller

larger crew than is necessary for salmon trolling. Some of these accommodate 8 to 10 men and are propelled by engines of 100 hp. or more.

The wooden hull is strongly built with slightly rounded stem, straight keel and canoe, elliptical, or transom stern. The pilot house is located amidships with raised fore deck or cabin trunk forward and fish hold aft. At the extreme stern is a trolling cockpit 2 to 3 ft. deep which in some craft is provided with a steering wheel and motor controls. The rig consists of a small mast with derrick stepped just aft of pilot house. Some boats carry a jib-headed steadying sail.

TROLLING. A method of fishing which consists essentially in dragging through the water a bait or bright object to which a hook is attached. Also called whiffing, railing. It is employed for the capture of predaceous surface-feeding fishes such as albacore, blue fish, tarpon, tuna, bonito, and various species of mackerel. This method of fishing is carried out by rowboats, sailing boats, and power boats. The rowboat trollers use but one line attached to a thwart and trailing out from the stern of the boat. The arrangement of trolling gear in sailing and power boats varies widely but the lines are generally attached to wooden poles rigged out on each side. French tunny boats from Brittany carry one set of poles. Northern Pacific salmon motor-trollers carry two sets of poles: two bow poles about 20 ft. long and a second pair winged out amidships, each 30 ft. long. An extra pole is carried at the stern. The hooks are baited in some instances, but artificial lures such as metal spoons, Japanese feathers, and horsehair, are mostly used. While a first-class trolling vessel can ride out a heavy gale, fishing is impossible in heavy weather and is brought virtually to a standstill when the sea is rough. The best speed for working the gear is from 4 to 5 knots.

Fr: *Pêche aux Lignes Traînantes*; Ger: *Schleppangelfischerei*.

TROLLING LINE. One of the lines used in troll fishing or trolling, and carried by the fish poles winged out on each side of a trolling boat. Also called troll. Trolling lines are usually made of hard-laid cotton with smaller linen leader lines followed by a piano wire leader to the spoon or bait.

Fr: *Ligne Traînante*; Ger: *Laufangelleine; Schleppangelleine; Schiessleine*.

In order to control the depth of fishing, sinkers of spherical or oval shape are attached to the lines. A boat usually carries an assortment of sinkers from 4 to 14 lb. The lines are dragged through the water as the boat moves along. Various length of lines are used; in the Pacific salmon fisheries the outer lines are on the average about 60 ft. and the inside lines about 40 ft.

In powered boats it is customary to use from 5 to 7 lines. The two outer lines lead from the ends of the poles. The next pair are attached to intermediate tips fastened halfway out on the main poles; while two inboard lines are attached to small upright rods on either quarter. The outer trolls are brought within reach by means of a short piece attached to each fishing line 15 or 20 ft. from the point where it is fastened to the pole, and leading inboard.

TROPIC. One of the two small terrestrial circles parallel to the equator and in latitude 23° 27′ north and south of it.

Fr: *Tropique*; Ger: *Wendekreis*.

TROPICAL DISTURBANCE. In meteorology, a cyclonic wind system of the tropics not having sufficient force to justify the use of the word storm.

TROPICAL YEAR. The interval in time between one vernal equinox and the following one. It works out at 365 days, 5 hours, 48 minutes, 46 seconds.

Fr: *Année tropique*; Ger: *Tropisches Jakr*.

TROPIC LOW WATERS. Low waters occurring at the time of the moon's semimonthly North and South declinations, when the diurnal inequality is at a maximum.

Fr: *Basses Mers de Marée Tropique*; Ger: *Tropisches Niedrigwasser*.

TROPIC TIDES. Tides in which the diurnal inequality is so increased as to cause only one low water each day. Their predominating factor is the declinational changes in the moon and sun. These tides are prevalent in the tropics and are therefore called tropic tides. The maximum heights occur with maximum declination of the moon.

Fr: *Marée Tropique*; Ger: *Tropische Tide*.

TROPOPAUSE. The upper limit of the troposphere. The layer of the atmosph

which separates the troposphere from the stratosphere.
Fr: *Tropopause.*

TROPOSPHERE. The lowest layer of the atmosphere surrounding the earth. It varies in height between 6 miles at the temperate zone and 10 miles at the tropics.
Fr: *Troposphère;* Ger: *Troposphäre.*

TROT LINE. A trawl line used for catching crabs in Chesapeake Bay. It is from 3/16 to 3/8 of an inch in diameter, and from 800 to 2000 ft. long. It is rigged with snoods 6 or 8 in. long.
See **Long Line.**

TROT-LINE BOAT. Open rowboat with sharp stem, square stern, flat bottom, and clinker planking, employed in the crab fishery of Chesapeake Bay. A portable mast which carries a small sail is stepped through the forward thwart. Sailing is resorted to only in going to and from the crabbing grounds.

TROUGH. A line separating the falling from the rising barometer in a wind system.
Fr: *Dépression barométrique;* Ger: *Tief.*

TROW. Bargelike vessel with flat bottom, bluff bows, wide transom stern and wall-like parallel sides used on rivers and for small coasting work around the British Isles. The hold is completely open, with 2 or 3 beams across the top. There are no bulwarks amidships; canvas washcloths supported by pole battens are fitted on each side of the hold instead. The ends are decked and sheered. The tonnage of seagoing trows varies from 100 to 200 tons. They were formerly ketch-rigged.
Greenhill, B., "The Story of the Severn Trow," *Mariners Mirror,* vol. 26, 1940.

TRUCK CLERK (U. S.). An assistant to the receiving clerk who receives all freight delivered by trucks on the pier.

TRUE ALTITUDE. The altitude of a heavenly body above the rational or celestial horizon, or the apparent altitude corrected for refraction, semidiameter, and parallax (if any).
Fr: *Hauteur Vraie;* Ger: *Wahre Höhe; Berechnete Höhe.*

TRUE BEARING. The true bearing of a celestial or terrestrial object is the angle from the direction of the true north to the direction of the object and is measured clockwise from 0° to 360°.
Fr: *Relèvement Vrai; Cap Vrai;* Ger: *Rechtweisende Peilung.*

TRUE COURSE. The course which refers to the true meridian. The angle between true North and South and the fore-and-aft line of the ship. Also called true heading.
Fr: *Route Vraie;* Ger: *Rechtweisender Kurs.*

TRUE PLACE. The true place of a heavenly body is the point on the celestial sphere to which it would be referred by an observer placed at the center of the earth viewing it through a uniform medium.
Fr: *Lieu Vrai;* Ger: *Wahrer Ort.*

TRUE POSITION. The position of a vessel as found by bearings of objects whose positions are known.
Fr: *Point Vrai;* Ger: *Wahres Besteck.*

TRUE SLIP. The difference between the speed at which the water is fed to the screw and that with which it is projected at the stern, both speeds being measured in relation to the vessel's motion.
Fr: *Recul Effectif;* Ger: *Effektiver Slip; Tatsächlicher Slip.*

TRUE TIME. The time given by two consecutive crossings of the sun on the same meridian.
Fr: *Heure Vraie;* Ger: *Wahre Zeit.*

TRUE WIND. The direction of the wind as observed from a stationary object.
Fr: *Vent Vrai;* Ger: *Wahrer Wind.*

TRUNDLE HEAD. The circular portion of a capstan head designed to take the ends of capstan bars.
Fr: *Chapeau;* Ger: *Spillkopf.*

TRUNK. 1. Long leg of a knee timber.
2. A strongly framed erection in a trunk vessel which extends from forecastle to bridge and from bridge to poop. Its breadth is about 50 to 75 per cent that of the vessel, and its height is the same as that of the other superstructures; the poop, bridge, forecastle, and trunk thus forming a continuous platform. The hatchways, ventilators, and deck openings are on the trunk deck, the area of which is increased by extending the deck plating beyond the trunk sides.
Fr: *Coffre;* Ger: *Koffer.*
See **Trunk-Deck Vessel.**
3. A unit of weight used in the fresh fish trade on the south coast of England, Brixham. It is the equivalent of 85 pounds of round fish or 100 pounds of flat fish. In the herring trade 7/16 cran or 1/6 cran of iced herring.

larger crew than is necessary for salmon trolling. Some of these accommodate 8 to 10 men and are propelled by engines of 100 hp. or more.

The wooden hull is strongly built with slightly rounded stem, straight keel and canoe, elliptical, or transom stern. The pilot house is located amidships with raised fore deck or cabin trunk forward and fish hold aft. At the extreme stern is a trolling cockpit 2 to 3 ft. deep which in some craft is provided with a steering wheel and motor controls. The rig consists of a small mast with derrick stepped just aft of pilot house. Some boats carry a jib-headed steadying sail.

TROLLING. A method of fishing which consists essentially in dragging through the water a bait or bright object to which a hook is attached. Also called whiffing, railing. It is employed for the capture of predaceous surface-feeding fishes such as albacore, blue fish, tarpon, tuna, bonito, and various species of mackerel. This method of fishing is carried out by rowboats, sailing boats, and power boats. The rowboat trollers use but one line attached to a thwart and trailing out from the stern of the boat. The arrangement of trolling gear in sailing and power boats varies widely but the lines are generally attached to wooden poles rigged out on each side. French tunny boats from Brittany carry one set of poles. Northern Pacific salmon motor-trollers carry two sets of poles: two bow poles about 20 ft. long and a second pair winged out amidships, each 30 ft. long. An extra pole is carried at the stern. The hooks are baited in some instances, but artificial lures such as metal spoons, Japanese feathers, and horsehair, are mostly used. While a first-class trolling vessel can ride out a heavy gale, fishing is impossible in heavy weather and is brought virtually to a standstill when the sea is rough. The best speed for working the gear is from 4 to 5 knots.

Fr: *Pêche aux Lignes Traînantes;* Ger: *Schleppangelfischerei.*

TROLLING LINE. One of the lines used in troll fishing or trolling, and carried by the fish poles winged out on each side of a trolling boat. Also called troll. Trolling lines are usually made of hard-laid cotton with smaller linen leader lines followed by a piano wire leader to the spoon or bait.

Fr: *Ligne Traînante;* Ger: *Laufangelleine; Schleppangelleine; Schiessleine.*

In order to control the depth of fishing, sinkers of spherical or oval shape are attached to the lines. A boat usually carries an assortment of sinkers from 4 to 14 lb. The lines are dragged through the water as the boat moves along. Various length of lines are used; in the Pacific salmon fisheries the outer lines are on the average about 60 ft. and the inside lines about 40 ft.

In powered boats it is customary to use from 5 to 7 lines. The two outer lines lead from the ends of the poles. The next pair are attached to intermediate tips fastened halfway out on the main poles; while two inboard lines are attached to small upright rods on either quarter. The outer trolls are brought within reach by means of a short piece attached to each fishing line 15 or 20 ft. from the point where it is fastened to the pole, and leading inboard.

TROPIC. One of the two small terrestrial circles parallel to the equator and in latitude 23° 27' north and south of it.

Fr: *Tropique;* Ger: *Wendekreis.*

TROPICAL DISTURBANCE. In meteorology, a cyclonic wind system of the tropics not having sufficient force to justify the use of the word storm.

TROPICAL YEAR. The interval in time between one vernal equinox and the following one. It works out at 365 days, 5 hours, 48 minutes, 46 seconds.

Fr: *Année tropique;* Ger: *Tropisches Jakr.*

TROPIC LOW WATERS. Low waters occurring at the time of the moon's semimonthly North and South declinations, when the diurnal inequality is at a maximum.

Fr: *Basses Mers de Marée Tropique;* Ger: *Tropisches Niedrigwasser.*

TROPIC TIDES. Tides in which the diurnal inequality is so increased as to cause only one low water each day. Their predominating factor is the declinational changes in the moon and sun. These tides are prevalent in the tropics and are therefore called tropic tides. The maximum heights occur with maximum declination of the moon.

Fr: *Marée Tropique;* Ger: *Tropische Tide.*

TROPOPAUSE. The upper limit of the troposphere. The layer of the atmosphere

motion for bracing or topping a yard. It is fastened to the mast by an iron band and to the yard by two truss bands.
Fr: *Drosse;* Ger: *Rack; Joch.*

TRUSS BAND. See **Truss Hoop.**

TRUSS BOW. See **Truss Yoke.**

TRUSS HOOP. One of the two steel bands fitted around the middle part of a standing yard and forming the attachment of the truss yoke to the yard. Also called truss band. The same term is often applied to the band on the mast which connects the truss yoke to the mast.
Fr: *Cercle de Drosse;* Ger: *Rackband; Mastring.*

TRUSS YOKE. A forging by which a yard is held out from the mast so that when braced round it may clear the rigging. Also called truss bow.
Fr: *Arc-Boutant de Drosse;* Ger: *Tragbügel.*

TRY. To try or to lie-to in a gale is, to keep a ship's bow to the sea by judicious balance of canvas and, with as much as it can safely show, prevent its rolling to windward in the trough of the sea.
Fr: *Etre à la cape courante; Capeyer;* Ger: *Beiliegen.*

TRYING. See **A-try.**

TRY-POT. Large metallic pot with capacity ranging from 120 to 200 gallons, formerly used on whaleships for converting whale blubber into oil. The try-pots were placed within the tryworks with their bottoms resting upon the arches or furnaces. (Obsolete.)

TRYSAIL. Quadrilateral fore-and-aft sail with boom and gaff, carried abaft the mainmast of a brig and hoisting on a small mast called trysail mast, or on the lower mast. When carried at the foremast of a brig it is called spencer. Spencers are usually boomless, the clew being held by two sheets. They hoist on spencer masts. (Obsolete.)
Fr: *Voile de Senau;* Ger: *Schnausegel.*
See **Gaff Trysail, Main Trysail Rig, Storm Trysail, Thimble-Headed Trysail, Wishbone Trysail.**

TRYSAIL MAST. A small mast or spar stepped abaft the lower mainmast of a brig-rigged vessel, which was then called snow. It was from one-third to one-half the diameter of the mainmast. Its foot was octagonal and stepped in a block of wood fastened to the deck or on a clasp hoop with eye. The head was secured by an iron plate to the after part of the cap. (Obsolete.)
Fr: *Mât de Senau;* Ger: *Schnaumast.*

TRY WORKS. A brick structure about 8 to 10 ft. long, 7 or 8 ft. wide and 4½ ft. high, built athwartship between the foremast and the mainmast of a whaling vessel and formerly used for converting whale blubber into oil. The first course of bricks, or base, was laid in openwork, forming channels through which the water could freely circulate. The fireplaces, called "arches," were strengthened by pieces of iron and fitted with sliding doors. The trypots were placed within the try works. (Obsolete.)

TSAO-SHUAN. A junk from Chao-Chow, Kwangtung, coast resembling in construction the Swatow fishing junk, but of much larger size, some having a capacity of 250 to 300 tons. Also called *chao-chow trading junk*. Length 132 ft. Breadth 33 ft. Hold depth 16 ft.

TSHAPPA. A scow propelled by sweeps found on the Black Sea coast of Asia Minor.

TSINE. A single-outrigger dugout canoe from the Nissan group (Solomon Islands). Also called *sini*. These canoes varied in size from a few ft. long, to hold one person, to those sufficient in size to carry 5 or 6 occupants.

TSUKUPIN. A large single-outrigger canoe from Yap, Caroline Islands, in which the two ends, which are of swan-neck form, rise to a considerable height. It is rigged with one mast and triangular sail with apex downward. Used locally in the flying-fish fisheries.

TSUNAMIS. Term applied in oceanography to ocean waves of enormous dimensions generally caused by submarine earthquakes.

TUB. 1. A barrel used on board ship to soak salt beef and salt pork before cooking. Also called steep tub.
Fr: *Charnier;* Ger: *Fleischständer; Frischbalje.*

2. A section of a trawl line; also the receptacle in which such line is coiled when ready for setting. It is usually made of a section of a flour barrel sawed off an inch or two above the lower quarter hoops and

See **Cabin Trunk, Centerboard Trunk, Coaling Trunk, Escape Trunk, Expansion Trunk, Mast Trunk, Rudder Trunk, Ventilator Trunk.**

TRUNK BUOY. A cylindrical mooring buoy made of steel plating with a central watertight trunkway. Also called trunk mooring buoy. The end of the mooring pendant is brought up through the trunk. The pin of a large shackle (buoy shackle) is passed through the end link of the pendant and the ships shackle their cable direct to this shackle.

Fr: *Bouée à Puits;* Ger: *Vertauboje.*

TRUNK CABIN. A cabin which extends only a partial deck height above the deck; a cabin half below and half above the level of a deck. It is commonly found on small pleasure and service boats and consists of a trunk which does not extend over the full width of the hull and leaves deck space forward and at the sides. The side decking is made wide enough to provide passage and there is a handrail on the cabin top for use in rough weather. The sides of the trunk are usually provided with ports or rectangular windows insuring natural light and ventilation below.

Ger: *Kofferkajüte.*

TRUNK DECK. The upper surface of the fore-and-aft trunk of a trunk-deck vessel.

Fr: *Trunk Deck;* Ger: *Kofferdeck.*

See **Trunk-Deck Vessel.**

TRUNK-DECK VESSEL. A vessel of the full-deck type having, on the upper deck, in addition to ordinary erections such as poop, bridge, and forecastle, a continuous trunk extending over at least 70 per cent of the vessel's length. The top of the trunk forms the working deck and is fitted with hatchways, winches, and so on. This type of vessel is especially suitable for bulk cargoes like grain, the trunk forming a very efficient self-trimmer.

Fr: *Navire Trunk-Deck;* Ger: *Kofferdeckschiff; Trunkdeckschiff.*

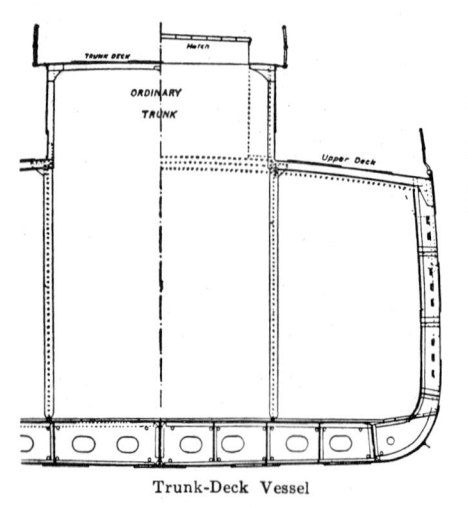

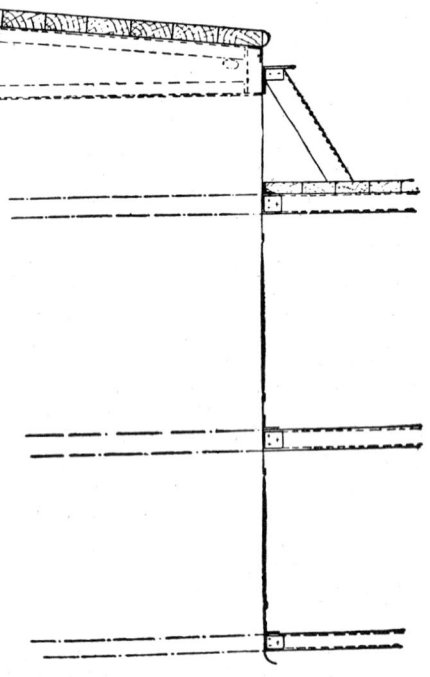

Trunked Hatchways

TRUNKED HATCHWAYS. A line of hatchways united vertically by a casing between the decks forming a trunk and separating these hatchways from the deck space around them.

Fr: *Panneau à Tambour;* Ger: *Schachtluke.*

TRUNK PLANK. A plank or hardwood 6 or 8 ft. long, 9 in. broad, 2½ or 3 in. thick, used when stowing bales of cotton in a ship's hold with cargo jacks.

TRUNO. Australian one-piece sewed bark canoe of the Niggerikudi tribe from Lower Batavia River, Cape York Peninsula.

TRUSS. A heavy swivel with a horizontal and a vertical pivot forming the center of

Trunk-Deck Vessel

has holes in the bottom to let the water out. A tub of haddock trawl has 500 hooks strung on about 292 fathoms of ground lines. A tub of cod trawl, 300 hooks on approximately 287 fathoms of line.

3. A unit of measurement used in Great Britain in the oyster trade and equal to 21 gallons, 1 quart and ½ pint or nearly three imperial bushels. Also 3 pecks (33 to 42 lb.) of shrimps.

See **Fall Tub, Line Tub, Spike Tub.**

TUB OAR. In a whaling boat, the fourth oar, the one next to the after oar; also the oarsman sitting on the starboard side. It was supported by a double-decked rowlock, that is, it had a higher branch supporting a higher notch. This lifted the oar sufficiently to clear the line tub. (Obsolete.)

TUB PARREL. A yard parrel made up of vertical wooden staves held together by an iron hoop or of a plate iron cylinder flared at top and bottom.

Fr: *Barillet; Racage à Barillet;* Ger: *Tonnenrack.*

TUB TRAWLING.
See **Long Lining.**

TUBULAR DERRICK. A steel derrick consisting of large sections of tubing joined together, or made of one single, solid-drawn tube. In the first instance the sections are joined by welding, or by swaging and shrinking.

Fr: *Mât de Charge Tubulaire;* Ger: *Röhrenform Ladebaum.*

In swaging and shrinking, the joints are made by inserting the end of the smaller cold pipe into the end of the larger heated pipe to a full red heat, and while in this position swaging the larger pipe into close contact with the inserted cold pipe. The joint so swaged is then allowed to cool and shrink. The tubing for derricks is generally made of open-hearth steel with a tensile strength of not less than 50,000 lb. per sq. in. with an elongation not under 20 per cent in 8 in.

American Marine Standards Committee, Standard 26, *Tubular Steel Cargo Booms,* Washington, 1927.

TUCK. That part of the vessel where the afterends of the outside planking end either on the wing transom or against the tuck timber. The word "tuck" strictly means a point and not a surface. It is the technical term for the point in which the rising line meets the sternpost. It is, however, frequently used to mean the surface of the stern between the tuck proper and the counter, especially when that surface is flat.

Fr: *Coude; Genou;* Ger: *Gillung.*

See **Square Tuck.**

TUCK BOAT. In the seine fisheries, a boat which carries the tuck net or tuck seine.

TUCKED SHEET BEND. A bend used for reeving knotted rope or twine through a small hole.

TUCKER. Open, clinker-built fishing boat with sharp stern found in the Stettiner Haff (Baltic Sea) and very similar to the *Tagler,* although larger. The length of keel varies from 60 to 63 ft., with a beam of about 21 ft. The rig includes a main lugsail, forestaysail, jib and topsail. In light winds a jigger is set. Also called tuckerkahn.

TUCKERPOLTE. A Baltic sailing trawler, found on the coast of Prussia (Swinemünde) and employed in the eel and flounder fisheries. These boats work in pairs each towing one warp and drifting before the wind. They are decked, and are fitted with a fish well amidships. They are rigged with one mast. Length 42.6 ft. Breadth 17 ft. Depth 6 ft. Tonnage 14.1. (Typical.)

TUCKING (G. B.). 1. A method of fishing a seine in deep water away from the shore. Two boats are generally used, a large and a small one, both ends of the net being eventually taken to the large boat. There are two ways of tucking, named "open tuck" and "running tuck."

2. Clearing a seine with the aid of a tuck net.

See **Open Tuck, Running Tuck.**

TUCK NET.
See **Purse Seine.**

TUCK NET BOAT.
See **Volyer.**

TUCK PLATE. A vertical shell plate fitted at the side of the bridge between the head of the sternpost and stern plating.

Fr: *Tôle de Sommier;* Ger: *Gillungsplatte.*

TUCK POLE. A pole used in connection with a tuck seine to frighten the fish into the bag of the seine.

TUCK RAIL. A railing fitted above the wing transom forming an abutment and finish to the ends of the planks in square-sterned vessels.

TUCK SEINE (G. B.). A small seine about 100 fathoms in length and 18 in depth, used in pilchard fishing. It is shot by a Vollyer boat inside the main seine, after the wings have been brought together, to bring the fish to the surface and take the catch.

TUCK TIMBER. The aftermost frame timber in vessels built with a square tuck stern and in which the after ends of the planking are rabetted.

TUFA. Decayed rocky matter found on the sea bottom and similar to gray clay.
 Fr: *Tuf*.

TUGBOAT. A mechanically propelled vessel of small tonnage with little or no cargo capacity, used for towing or assisting vessels at sea, in or out of harbors, rivers, and docks, also for coastal or harbor towage of barges, lighters, and other small craft. Also called towboat, tug.
 Fr: *Remorqueur*; Ger: *Schlepper*.

The engine power of tugboats is high in relation to the general dimensions of the vessel, the ratio of displacement to weight of machinery running from 2.3 to 3 for the larger boats. As the pull of the towrope tends to lift the stern out of the water the common practice is to build tugs on a sloping keel, that is to say, with a bigger draft of water aft than forward. In the design of seagoing tugs, care is taken to obtain ample stability combined with good weathering and steering qualities.

Munro Smith, R., "The Design of Screw Tugs," *Shipbuilding and Shipping Record* (London), vol. 60 (November, 1942); Shoosmith, G. T., "Steam Tugs," Institute of Marine Engineers (London), *Transactions*, vol. 54 (1942); *Les Remorqueurs*, Bureau Veritas, Bulletin Technique (Paris), vol. 18, no. 9 (1936).

TUGBOAT STERN. Elliptical stern in which a pronounced tumble home is given to the bulwarks.

TUKANG. Small, planked boat with straight keel, raked stem, and sternpost employed in the fisheries of the Malacca Strait. It is rigged with one mast and a boomed lugsail. Length 26 to 33 ft.

TUMBLE HOME. The inward inclination of a ship's sides near the upper deck. The opposite of "flare."
 Fr: *Rentrée*; Ger: *Einfall; Spanteneinfall*.

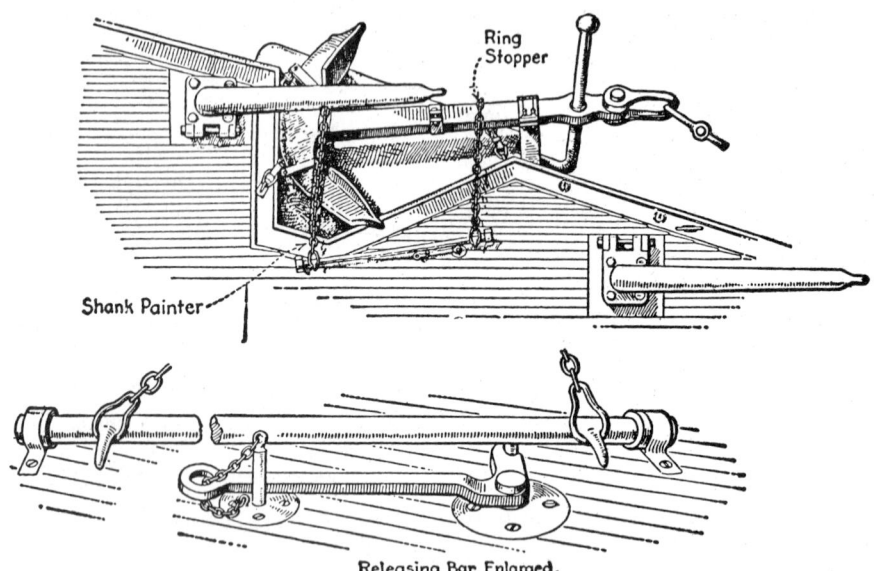

TUMBLER. A device for tripping or casting loose stocked anchor. Also called anchor tripper, trigger bar, releasing bar, tripping gear. It consists of a revolving iron bar set horizontally on the deck and fitted with a lever and two horns or pins. The latter are curved and hold the ends of the cat-stopper and shank-painter. By raising the lever the bar revolves and releases the securing chains from the pins allowing the anchor to drop overboard.
 Fr: *Mouilleur*; Ger: *Ankerschlipper; Schlippvorrichtung*.

See **Tongue**.

TUMBILUNG. East Indian dugout canoe with double outriggers from Sangi and Talaud Islands, northeastern Celebes. Although small, these craft, which are rigged with two masts, venture far out to sea to fish with hook and line.

TUNA BOAT (U. S.). General term for various types of power or sailing craft engaging in the capture of tuna fish with trolling lines or with hook and rod. Also called tunny boat (G. B.).
  Fr: *Thonnier; Bateau Thonnier;* Ger: *Thunfischer.*
See **Tuna Clipper, Thonnier**.

made of silky feathers and a piece of fish's skin which conceals the hook. The tunas are swept on board by a carefully timed heave and swing. If the fish are large, two poles are yoked together and the fishermen work in teams.
Godsill, *Fishing Methods of the Bluefin Tuna*, Natural Resources Department, Fish and Game Division (California), Fish Bulletin 33 (1931).

TUNDRAKA GAI. East Indian fishing canoe with raised wash strakes from Pulo Nias Island (eastern Sumatra) employed for lining. *Tundraka* is the generic term for boat on this island. The smaller boats are dugouts handled by a crew of 2 or 3, and

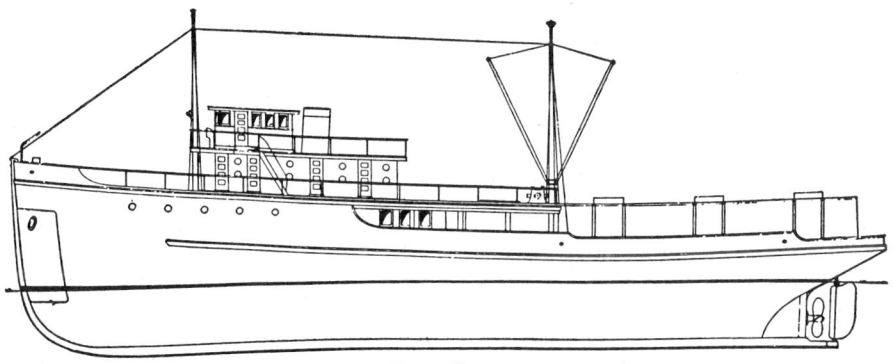

Tuna Clipper

TUNA CLIPPER. A Diesel-powered fishing boat from California employed in tuna fisheries all along the western coast of North America and as far south as the Galapagos Islands and the coast of Ecuador. Also called tuna bait boat (U. S.). Length 65 to 148 ft. Breadth 17.8 to 29½ ft. Maximum depth 19 ft. Engine power 115–800 h.p. Crew 17. (Typical.)

These boats range from 65 to 148 ft. in length, have a raised forward deck with deckhouse and engine room well forward. Most of them are built of wood. The fish hold is insulated with cork slabs, and refrigerating machinery is installed for keeping the catch fresh under subtropical conditions and during the return trip. On the afterdeck are large bait tanks in which living sardines or anchovies are kept. Sea water is constantly circulated through the tanks to keep the bait alive until the fishing grounds are reached. Fishing is carried on from iron racks which hang outboard around the vessel's stern. Each man wields a heavy bamboo pole with a short line attached to its tip. This line carries a lure

are used for transportation over short distances.

TUNNEL (U. S.). Part of a pound net which leads from the narrow end of the heart into the pot. The bottom of the tunnel is closed by the apron.
See **Pipe Tunnel, Shaft Alley**.

TUNNEL ESCAPE. An opening or trunkway provided at the afterend of the shaft tunnel as an emergency exit.
  Fr: *Échappée de Tunnel;* Ger: *Tunnel Notausgang.*

TUNNEL FRAME. One of the frames supporting the plating of a shaft or access tunnel.
  Fr: *Membrure du Tunnel;* Ger: *Tunnel Spant.*

TUNNEL PLATFORM. A wooden platform fitted at the side of the tunnel shafting to provide a working passage.
  Fr: *Plancher de Tunnel.*

TUNNEL RECESS. See **Recess**.

TUNNEL SCREW PROPELLER. A method of propulsion adopted for shallow-draft vessels in which the hull is formed into a tunnel over the propeller, the tips of the blades emerging when the vessel is at rest. When the engines are set in motion the water rises and completely fills the tunnel. The screw is well able to produce a thrust commensurate with its full diameter, which produces improved propulsive efficiency.

Fr: *Hélice sous voûte;* Ger: *Tunnelschraube.*

TUNNEL SHAFT BEARING.
See **Plummer Block.**

TUNNEL WELL. A drainage well at the afterend of the shaft tunnel to collect water used for cooling the shaft bearings, and leakage from the stern tube.

Fr: *Puisard du Tunnel;* Ger: *Tunnel Brunnen.*

TUPPAL. A single-outrigger Australian dugout canoe of the Kokolamalama natives of Princess Charlotte Bay, North Queensland. The outrigger float, placed on the starboard side of the canoe, is supported by six pairs of horizontal sticks (booms) lashed to crossed sticks driven obliquely into the float. The outrigger booms are passed through rectangular holes cut in the wash strakes. The latter are lashed to the gunwales of the canoe after the spaces between them and the hull have been packed with paper-bark pads.

TURBINE. A type of engine in which the kinetic energy of steam is transformed into direct rotary motion through the impulse or reaction of steam jets impinging at high velocity on rotary vanes. Its weight is less than that of a reciprocator of equal power, and the maximum power which can be developed is practically unlimited. It is therefore suited for fast passenger vessels requiring large power. The rotating principle upon which the turbine operates reduces vibration considerably compared with steam or internal combustion reciprocators, an important advantage for passenger vessels. On the other hand the steam turbine is not reversible. The reversing of propellers with direct or gear drive is accomplished by means of a separate turbine, the power of which varies from 25 to 50 per cent of the ahead full power.

The driving of the propellers in turbine ships is either of the direct drive or of the so-called geared-turbine type. Earlier turbine vessels were provided with direct drive which has now been almost superseded by geared driving. Direct drive involves the installation of large and heavy slow-speed turbines and the adoption of higher propeller speeds than are conducive to high propulsion efficiency.

Fr: *Turbine;* Ger: *Turbine.*

See **Exhaust Turbine, Geared Turbine.**

TURBO-ELECTRIC DRIVE. A form of main propulsion which consists essentially of a high-speed steam turbine directly coupled to an electric generator; and a propelling motor coupled to the main shafting and connected by cable to the generator. As the reversing is carried out electrically this system has the advantage of eliminating astern turbines and at the same time making full power astern immediately available. The line of shafting is very short.

Fr: *Propulsion Turbo-Electrique;* Ger: *Turboelektrischer Antrieb.*

A high propeller efficiency is obtained as the system lends itself practically to any desired speed reduction between the turbine and the propeller; each may therefore be designed to operate at a speed corresponding to its highest efficiency. On the other hand, first cost and weight per horsepower are higher as compared with geared turbine plants, but maintenance and operating costs are lower. The turbo-electric drive lends itself particularly well to the propulsion of large passenger and intermediate vessels. Berg, E., Electric Propulsion of Ships, North East Coast Institution of Engineers and Shipbuilders (Newcastle upon Tyne), *Transactions,* vol. 43, 1926; Robinson, S. M., *Electric Ship Propulsion,* New York, 1922.

TURBO-RECIPROCATING ENGINES. A system of propulsion in which the utilization of the expansive properties of steam is carried to the limit by the addition of an exhaust turbine which eliminates the losses, occurring in a reciprocating engine, due to the impossibility of further expansion. Also called combination engines.

Fr: *Machines Turbo-Alternatives;* **Ger:** *Gemischtes Maschinensystem; Kolbenmaschine mit Abdampfturbine.*

See **Exhaust Turbine.**

In triple-screw vessels the arrangement consists of two-wing triple or quadruple expansion engines exhausting into a central low pressure, a head turbine driving the center shaft and propeller. An alternative design for quadruple-screw vessels is that of two reciprocating engines driving the inner shafts and two low-pressure turbines for the wing shafts. In each case all reversing is done by the reciprocators only; which, when running astern, exhaust directly to the condensers by means of a suitable arrangement of valves. The saving in fuel by this combination is generally about 15 per cent over that of the triple or quadruple expansion engines.

Parsons and Walker, "The Combination System of Reciprocating Engines and Steam Turbines," Institution of Naval Architects (London), *Transactions*, vol. 50 (1908).

TURBULENCE. Irregular motion of the atmosphere. It occurs when air currents are flowing over a comparatively uneven surface, such as the surface of the earth, or when two atmospheric currents flow past or over each other in different directions or at different speeds.

dependent upon priority of stem, readiness of vessel to load, suitability of berth, and sufficiency of cargo to maintain continuous loading.

Fr: *Tour de Rôle; Tour de Place; Tour de Mise à quai;* Ger: *Reihenfolge.*

2. The change from flood tide to ebb tide and vice versa.

Fr: *Renversement;* Ger: *Stromwechsel.*

See Colliery Turn, Free of Turn, Loading Turn, Regular Turn.

TURNBUCKLE. A device for adjustment of length fitted at the lower end of shrouds, stays, smokestack guys and so on, in lieu of deadeyes and lanyards. Also called rigging screw. It consists of an internally threaded collar turning on two screws

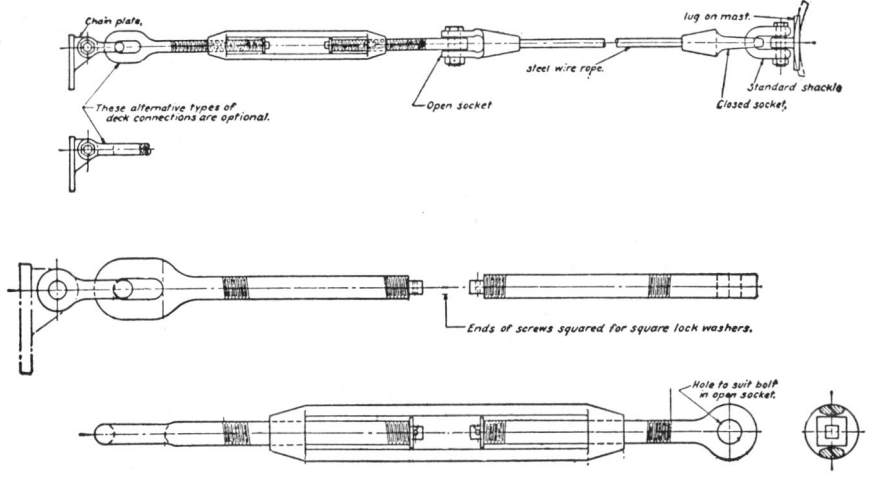

Turnbuckle. (*American Marine Standard*)

TURK'S HEAD. A knot of turbanlike form made around a cylindrical object such as a rope, a stanchion, or a rail. There are several varieties. The standing Turk's head is one tied with any number of strands. The common or running Turk's head is tied with a single strand. The knot is used for various practical purposes on board ship, as on footropes, jacobs ladders, and hand ropes where any slipping is to be avoided.

Fr: *Bonnet Turc; Tête de Maure;* Ger: *Türkenbund; Türkischer Knopf.*

TURN. 1. The rotation, in accordance with local regulation of custom of the port, in which berths for loading or discharging are given to vessels awaiting in a harbor or anchored in a roadstead. Also called stem. The allocation of loading berths is usually

threaded in opposite directions. In some types one end may have a swivel and the other a screw. The link or collar is operated by means of a wrench or lever. When the link is turned the two screws move apart or together simultaneously, lengthening or shortening the whole.

Fr: *Ridoir;* Ger: *Wantschraube; Spannschraube.*

American Marine Standards Committee, Standard 4, Washington (1928); British Standards Institution, Standard 716, Wire Rope Rigging Screws, London (1936).

TURNED KNEE. A knee plate formed by turning down the end of a bulb bar and welding a triangular plate to it, which forms a square upper corner. When the beam is made of a bulb tee or channel the bar is split and the lower part turned down.

TURN IN. To turn in a deadeye means to secure by seizing the end of the shroud or stay around a deadeye. To turn in a block means to strap it.

Fr: *Rabattre;* Ger: *Einbinden.*

TURNING BASIN. An area of water or enlargement of a channel used for turning vessels. Also called maneuvering basin.

Fr: *Bassin d'évitage;* Ger: *Wendebecken.*

TURNING CIRCLE. The path approaching the form of a circle described by a vessel with helm at full angle while turning through 32 points of the compass with engines running at full speed. The approximate diameter of the turning circle is about 6 times the length of ship for single-screw

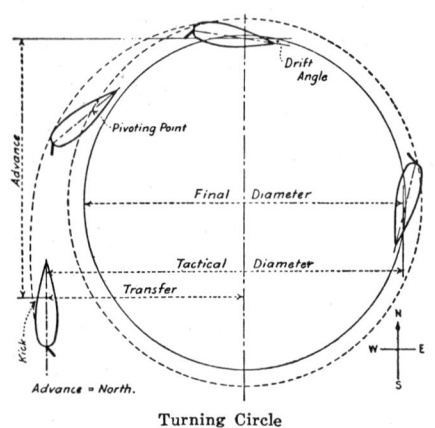

Turning Circle

cargo vessels and about 3 to 4½ times for twin-screw vessels.

Fr: *Cercle de Giration;* Ger: *Drehungskreis.*

Hovgaard, W., "Turning Circles," Institution of Naval Architects (London), *Transactions,* vol. 66, 1924.

TURNING GEAR. See Jacking Gear.

TURN OF BILGE. The lower outer part of the bilge where the curvature is greatest. The turn from the flat of the bottom to the upward rise of the sides. The place of maximum curvature of the outside form of the hull along the middle body, where the bottom turns into the side.

Fr: *Arrondi de Bouchain;* Ger: *Kimmrundung; Kimmwölbung.*

TURN OUT. To turn out a reef means to unknot the reef points to enlarge the area of the sail.

Fr: *Larguer;* Ger: *Ausstecken.*

TURNPIKE SAILOR. A colloquial name given to a sham seaman who begs under the pretense of having been shipwrecked.

TURN ROUND. The whole series of operations connected with the arrival and departure of a vessel, including the discharge of its cargo and the process of reloading.

Fr: *Rotation;* Ger: *Umschlag.*

TURNTABLE. A movable platform on a pivot placed at the stern of purse seine vessels. The net is stowed on this platform. The afterend of the turntable is fitted with a roller about one foot in diameter with strips of hardwood fastened along its periphery to increase the friction when the net is hauled on board. Power for the roller is supplied by a shaft which runs along the bulwarks and is connected to the purse winch by a sprocket and chain.

Fr: *Plaque Tournante;* Ger: *Drehscheibe.*

TURN TURTLE (to). To capsize.

TURRET DECK. The top of the trunk of a turret vessel. The turret deck has no sheer nor camber. Its breadth is about half the ship's breadth and its minimum height above the harbor deck is usually one quarter of the hold depth measured from the harbor deck.

Fr: *Pont Turret;* Ger: *Turmdeck.*

TURRET-DECK VESSEL. Also turret vessel. A vessel in which the sides are built with an abrupt round over or tumble home. From about the level of the main deck they are carried up in a reverse curve to a narrow deck termed turret deck. The height of the turret is about one quarter of the hold depth. This type of vessel, the first of which was built at Sunderland in 1892, was especially adapted for the carriage of bulk cargoes, but in late years it has been superseded by the trunk deck vessel.

Fr: *Navire à Turret Deck;* Ger: *Turmdeckschiff; Turmdecker.*

Turret vessels were built without sheer and generally had erections on the top of the turret deck, such as poop, bridge, and forecastle. They were originally designed to save tonnage under the Suez Canal system of measurement. Cutting away the outboard parts of the upper 'tween decks served the double purpose of reducing the tonnage measurement and port charges, and providing a center trunk which acted as an expansion chamber. This made the vessel self-trimming when loaded with grain or similar cargo. The size of turret vessels ranged from 280 to 455 ft. length and 1970 to 7700 tons gross. The last ship of this type was built in 1911.

Kendall, S. O., Turret Deck Cargo Steamers, North East Coast Institution of Engineers and Shipbuilders (Newcastle upon Tyne), *Transactions,* vol. 11 (1892).

TURTLE BACK. See **Whaleback.**

TURTLE DECK. A term applied to a weather deck forecastle or poop, which is rounded over at sides in order to shed the water rapidly in heavy weather. Also called turtle back, turtle-back deck.

Fr: *Pont en Dos de Tortue;* Ger: *Schildkrötendeck; Walrückendeck.*

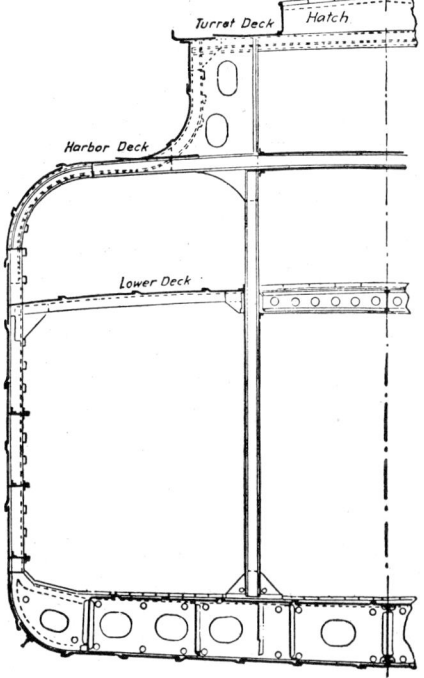

Turret-deck Vessel

TURTLE SPEAR. An appliance used in the turtle fisheries of Florida. It consists of a steel spear attached to a pole 12 to 16 ft. long which is thrown from a boat into the back of the turtle. The turtle is drawn in and secured by means of a line attached to the spear.

TUYEN-LUOI. A flat-bottomed fishing sampan from Port-Wallut Bay, Indo-China. Also called *tuyen-dang.* The hull has a length from 19 to 26 ft. and is made of hardwood. It is covered for most of its length by a round-shaped roof made of bamboo matting and is used as dwelling by the fishermen and their families. It is propelled by two rowers using yulohs.

TWAKOW. A Chinese sailing boat used as cargo lighter in Singapore. It is decked at both ends. The rig consists of 2 masts and 2 Chinese lugsails. The foremast is stepped well forward. Length 57 ft. 6 in. Breadth 22 ft. Depth 7 ft. 6 in. (Average.)

'TWEEN DECK. Any deck below the upper deck and above the lowest deck.

Fr: *Entrepont;* Ger: *Zwischendeck.*

'TWEEN-DECK BUNKER. A bunker located between two decks.

Fr: *Soute d'Entrepont;* Ger: *Zwischendeckbunker.*

'TWEEN-DECK TANK. A deep tank extending athwartship from side to side of the vessel between the upper deck and the 'tween deck next below. These tanks are usually located amidships, forward and abaft the engine-room trunk.

'TWEEN-DECK TONNAGE. The cubical capacity of each space between decks situated above the tonnage deck.

Fr: *Jauge d'Entrepont;* Ger: *Zwischendeckvermessung.*

TWICE-LAID ROPE. Rope made from old yarns laid up a second time.

Fr: *Cordage Refait;* Ger: *Umgeschlagenes Tauwerk.*

TWICE-LAID STUFF. Small stuff made by hand from junk.

TWIDDLING LINE. 1. Line fastened to a steering wheel to keep it steady or to secure it. (Obsolete.)

Fr: *Raban de Gouverne; Bosse de la Roue de Gouvernail;* Ger: *Fangtau; Haltetau.*

2. Line fastened to the rudder yoke of an open boat.

TWIG. In sailing ship parlance, to twig the fore means to see that all sails on the foremast are properly furled and the yards squared.

TWIGGING LINE. A line attached to the bowl or to the gimbals of a compass to remedy its sluggishness by jerking. (Obsolete.) Also twiddling line.

TWILIGHT ARCH. The boundary between the illuminated segment and the dark sky above as seen in the later stages of twilight.

Fr: *Cercle crépusculaire.*

TWIN-BULKHEAD TANKER. A tank vessel in the construction of which the conventional centerline bulkhead with summer tanks is replaced by two longitudinal bulkheads, placed about one fourth of the vessel's beam from each side, the summer tanks being dispensed with.
Ger: *Dreitankschiff*.

This type, which was first introduced about 1923, has gradually taken the place of the older type. It is claimed that the twin bulkhead system of construction provides for increased longitudinal strength, less steel weight, and less area of oiltight surface for the same quantity of cargo carried. Among other features of this type the staggering of transverse bulkheads in center and wing tanks is noticeable; also the absence of deadrise in the bottom under the center tank. The deadrise begins outside the longitudinal bulkheads.

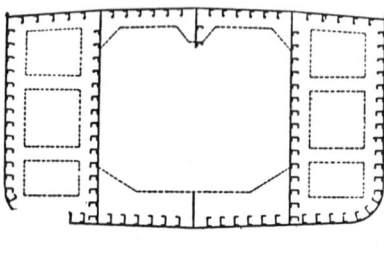

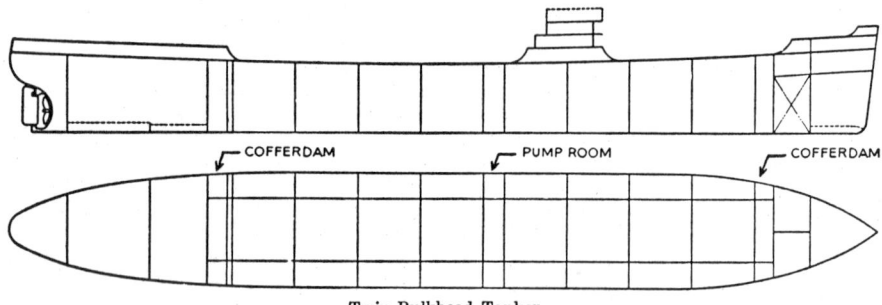

TWINE. A thread made up of a number of fibers twisted together.
Fr: *Fil; Fil de Caret*; Ger: *Garn; Bindfaden*.
See **Cotton Twine, Roping Twine, Seaming Twine, Seizing Twine, Whipping Twine.**

TWINGUTU. A single-outrigger, dugout canoe from the Tongan Archipelago, adapted for sailing as well as paddling. Also called *tuingutu*. The smaller canoes of this type are from 16 to 18 ft. long, and the larger about 20 to 30 ft. A narrow wash strake about 5 to 6 in. in height is sewed with sennit on the topsides. Each end of the dugout is solid for a length of about 12 in. The intervening space between this solid part and the nearby outrigger boom is usually decked over with transverse planking, the innermost board of which has a mast hole in the center. The rig used is derived from a European type.

TWISTED PLATE. A plate not having its four corners in the same plane. Also called snyed plate.
Fr: *Tôle Gauche*; Ger: *Gezogene Platte*.

TWISTED-THREAD CANVAS. A quality of canvas in which the warp or both the warp and weft are made of two threads twisted together. Fr: *Toile à Fils Retors*.

TWO-ARM MOORING.
See **Two Leg Moorings.**

TWO-BLOCKS. 1. A tackle is two-blocks when it has been hauled upon until the blocks meet. Further effort is wasted until the tackle has been overhauled. Also called chockablock, block and block.
Fr: *A bloc*.
2. Hoisted for full due, as, a signal flag or pennant.

TWO-COMPARTMENT SHIP. A vessel so subdivided that flooding of any two main compartments will not bring the margin line below the water, or cause the ship to capsize.
See **Floodable Length, Margin Line, One-Compartment Ship.**

TWOFOLD PURCHASE. A tackle made up of 2 double blocks. The standing and hauling parts are both at the same block. The power gained is about 4 to 1.

Twin-Bulkhead Tanker

Fr: *Palan Double;* Ger: *Vierläufer.*

TWO-LEG MOORINGS. Permanent moorings which consist of two anchors connected to each other by a suitable length of ground chain. The middle of the span is provided with a swivel to which the riding chain is fastened. Also called span moorings.
Fr: *Corps Mort à deux branches.*

TWO-LEG PROPELLER STRUT. A strut with two arms set at an angle for supporting the outboard portion of the propeller shaft.
See **Strut.**

TWO-TOPSAIL SCHOONER.
See **Square-Topsail Schooner.**

TYE.
See **Tie.**

TYE BLOCK.
See **Tie Block.**

TYFON SIGNAL APPARATUS. A patented sound signaling apparatus used in lieu of a steam whistle. In it the sound-producing medium, compressed air or steam, impinges against a bronze diaphragm comprising from 1 to 6 leaves secured by a screw ring and controlled by a nonreturn, spring-loaded valve. When the control valve is opened the compressed air or steam enters the pipe causing the diaphragm to vibrate at its natural frequency. As the diaphragm vibrates it covers and uncovers the end of the inlet pipe, so that at each vibration of the diaphragm the inlet pipe is opened and closed completely and consequently the whole of the driving power of the compressed air or steam is utilized in producing sound. The pitch of the note is determined by the length of the horn.
Fr: *Typhon;* Ger: *Tyfon.*

TYPHOON. A cyclonic storm of the China Seas and the coasts of Japan which occur at the seasons of the changes of the monsoons. Their velocity exceeds 65 nautical miles per hour and force 12 of Beaufort's scale. They correspond to the hurricanes of the West Indies.
Fr: *Typhon;* Ger: *Taifun.*
Hennessy, J., "Typhoons of the North Pacific and China Seas," *Marine Observer,* vol. 2, August, 1925.

TYPHUS. A contagious, louse-borne continued fever lasting from 2 to 3 weeks. According to regulations provided for in the International Sanitary Convention of 1926, ships which during the voyage have had or have at the time of their arrival, a case of typhus on board, are subject to the following precautions: (1) medical inspection; (2) disembarkation, isolation, and delousing of the sick; (3) disinfection of any wearing apparel, and so on, which has been used; (4) disinfection of all parts of the ship which have been occupied by the sick.
Fr: *Typhus;* Ger: *Typhus.*

U

U. Flag of the international code of signals showing two white and two red squares of equal size alternately set. When hoisted singly means "You are standing into danger."

u.c.b. UNLESS CAUSED BY (marine insurance).

U.Dk. UPPER DECK.

U.K. fo. UNITED KINGDOM FOR ORDERS.

U.K.H.H. Range of ports which include all ports in the United Kingdom and those between Havre and Hamburg inclusive.

U.W. UNDERWATER.

UARO. West African dugout canoe from the coast of Gabon. The cutwater rises with a pronounced curve into a long pointed beak projecting outboard horizontally. The stern is produced into a narrowing flat shelf cut square at the end. There is a sort of bow keel forward. Three thwarts are provided, the forward one serving as mast thwart. The average length of these craft ranges from 10 to 13 ft., the largest being 16 ft. long. The timber used is *Okume*. Propulsion is by paddles and sail.

UCHE. A single-outrigger canoe from the Hermit Islands (Bismarck Archipelago). The smaller canoes of this type are dugouts with rounded sides, in cross section forming three quarters of a circle. In the larger ones the dugout is not much more than a high keel on which several strakes of planks are sewed. It has a cross section of trapezoidal form.

The dugout rakes up at each end and the curve is continued by an end piece. A narrow platform made of cane lies close to the hull over the outrigger booms. The mast stands in a sling outboard in an angle between the side of the hull and a boom. The sail is oblong and has a yard and boom. The latter is provided with jaws that embrace the mast.

UCHISE-AMI-BUNE. Japanese trawler-sampan of which there are 4 local types. The largest is from the Hiroshima district, southern Japan. When trawling the boat lays broadside to the wind and spreads the mouth of her trawl by leading the warps from the outboard ends of 2 long spars 18 and 35 ft. long which project over the bow and stern. This type is rigged with 4 masts and has a sail area of about 1782 sq. ft. The foremast has a very pronounced forward rake. The second and third (main) masts have no rake. The fourth has a slight rake aft. The rudder is broad and shallow, which is exceptional in Japanese sampans. Length over-all 47.5 ft. Breadth 12.5 ft. Depth 3.4 ft. Crew 3. (Typical.)

The second type, from Osaka district is a three-masted boat with portable washboards forward. These are removed when shooting the gear. The boats are also used for trading from May to November. Length over-all 44 ft. Breadth 10.2 ft. Depth 2.8 ft. Draft 1.5 ft. Displacement 7.3 tons. Crew 5. (Typical).

In the Aichi district there are two types of trawlers, both of which are used in sheltered waters. One of these is notable for the shape of the stem, which is quite unusual for a sampan, and is somewhat like that of a clipper ship. The deck is permanently fastened to the beams and built with hatch openings. Length over-all 38 ft. Breadth 7.4 ft. Depth 2.8 ft. Displacement 2.7 tons. Crew 2. (Typical.)

The other boat of the Aichi district is of the usual Japanese design with narrow stern. Length 35.8 ft. Breadth 6.8 ft. Depth 2.7 ft. Displacement 2.03 tons. Crew 2. (Typical.)

Both types from Aichi are rigged with two masts.

ULLAGE. The amount that a partially filled tank or cask lacks being full. The wantage or estimated measure of the empty part of a tank, cask, and the like.

Fr: *Vide*.

ULLAGE BOARD. A device used by tankermen for taking ullage in a tank. It consists of a wooden batten about 9 ft. long, marked in feet and inches. There is a crosspiece at one end to allow it to rest on the edge of the ullage hole in the hatch cover. Also called ullage stick.

ULLAGE FOOT. A gauge attached to a tape line and used on tank vessels for measuring deep or long ullages. It consists of an elongated weight with graduations on a scale, which forms one side of the weight.

ULLAGE HOLE. One of the circular apertures fitted with a brass plug in the hatch covers of a tanker. Used for taking ullage. Also called sounding hole.

Fr: *Trou de Jauge;* Ger: *Schauloch.*

ULLAGE PLUG. A fitting provided in oil-tight hatch covers to permit examining or measuring of the oil level in the tank below without opening the hatch. It consists of a steel ring riveted or welded to the cover with an opening 10 to 12 in. in diameter. The ring has a circular lip on which a steel cover with a gasket is arranged to clamp down by means of a strongback. On small tankers a 6-in. pipe flange with screwed plug is used.

Fr: *Bouchon de Jauge;* Ger: *Schaulochpflock; Schaulochstöpsel.*

UMBRELLA. A metal shield in the form of a frustrum of a cone riveted to the outer casing of the stack over the air casing to keep out the weather. The same device is occasionally fitted at the top of the inner casing to protect the space between the two casings. Also called apron, bonnet, cape, funnel hood.

Fr: *Parapluie de Cheminée;* Ger: *Schornsteinkragen.*

UNAFFECTED ZONE. In fusion welding, that portion of the base metal outside the heat-affected zone, wherein no change in the physical properties and/or structure has taken place.

UNATTENDED LIGHT. A light (aid to navigation) which does not require the presence of a keeper or attendant, and is only in action when natural light (daylight) fails. Also called unwatched light. The source of light, which is usually dissolved acetylene in steel cylinders, is controlled by a mechanism called a sunvalve. The action of this valve is based on the fact that a dull black or nonreflecting surface which absorbs all light falling upon it will develop a higher temperature than an all-reflecting body similarly exposed. It is constructed with light-reflecting metal disposed vertically and symmetrically around a central dead-black metal cylinder, the whole being protected by a glass sleeve. On exposure to light, the light-absorbent cylinder expands slightly, whereas the reflecting rods remain unaltered. This slight difference is mechanically magnified sufficiently to close the gas admission valve which provides the illuminant, leaving a small invisible pilot flame alight. At sunset, when natural light fails, the contraction of the absorbent element allows the gas valve to open and the gas passes again. This system is occasionally adopted for lighthouses and lightships accessible only with difficulty, and is also used very extensively for buoys to mark channels and fairways.

Fr: *Feu Non Gardé;* Ger: *Unbewachtes Feuer.*

UNBALANCED RUDDER. A rudder whose area does not extend forward of the axis of rotation. See **Balanced Rudder.**

UNBALLAST. To discharge the ballast from a ship.

Fr: *Délester;* Ger: *Ballast ausschiessen.*

UNBEND. 1. To untie one rope from another.

Fr: *Démarrer;* Ger: *Lösen; Abstecken.*

2. To remove the sails from their yards, gaffs, or stays.

Fr: *Désenverguer; Déverguer;* Ger: *Abschlagen; Segel abschlagen.*

3. To cast loose a cable from its anchor.

Fr: *Détalinguer;* Ger: *Losmachen; Losschakeln.*

4. To remove the gear of a boom mast, yard, and so on.

Fr: *Dégarnir;* Ger: *Losbinden.*

UNBITT. To remove the turns of a cable from the bitts.

Fr: *Débitter;* Ger: *Betingschlag loswerfen.*

UNCOIL. The converse of coiling.

Fr: *Délover;* Ger: *Aufrollen.*

UNDECKED. Not having a full deck, as, for example, a rowboat. Also called open.

Fr: *Non Ponté;* Ger: *Ungedeckt.*

UNDER BOWING. Making use of a foul tide by a ship under sail with the wind blowing across a tidal stream by pointing the ship full and by, and having the tide coming up against the lee bow. This will set the ship to windward. Also called lee bowing.

UNDERCANVASSED. Said of sailing craft when the spread of canvas is too small in relation to the size of hull.

Fr: *Insuffisamment Voilé;* Ger: *Zu leicht getakelt; Unterbesegelt.*

UNDERCUT. In fusion welding, a wastage of the parent metal alongside a weld in the form of a grooving. It is generally due to careless laying of the bead and causes weakness in the parent metal at the joint.

UNDERDECK TONNAGE. The cubic capacity of the vessel below the tonnage deck, without the deductions necessary to arrive at the net register tonnage. The underdeck tonnage is seldom needed for commercial purposes.

Fr: *Jauge sous le Pont;* Ger: *Unterdeck Tonnengehalt.*

UNDERFOOT. The condition when an anchor is under the ship's forefoot. Said of an anchor dropped while the ship has headway.

UNDERHAUL. A term used when a vessel at anchor rides at an angle to its normal heading, as a result of a subsurface current.

UNDERHUNG RUDDER. A rudder entirely supported from within the hull, deriving no support from the sternpost. Also called spade rudder. See page 607. The rudder blade in this type is made wide and shallow in order to elevate the center of pressure and thus reduce the bending stresses on the stock.

Fr: *Gouvernail Suspendu;* Ger: *Hängeruder; Steckruder.*

Denny, M. E., "Design of Balanced Rudders of the Spade Type," Institution of Naval Architects (London), *Transactions,* vol. 66, 1924.

UNDERMANNED. Said of a vessel whose crew is composed of an insufficient number of men.

Fr: *Mal armé;* Ger: *Schwach bemannt.*

UNDERMASTED. Inadequately or insufficiently masted. Also called undersparred. Any sailing craft in which the masts or spars are either too light or too short, so that it cannot spread the sails necessary to obtain the speed of which it is capable.

Ger: *Zu leicht bemastet.*

UNDERRUN. 1. To underrun a tackle is to separate its parts and clear the fall.

Fr: *Dépasser;* Ger: *Nachsehen und klaren; Klar scheren.*

2. To haul a boat along under a hawser, lifting the latter out of the water. To follow up a rope, chain, hawser, or cable by hauling in from a boat which moves in the direction in which the cable is laid out.

Fr: *Paumoyer.*

UNDERRUNNING. A labor-saving method employed in the trawl-line fisheries by which the removal of the fish and rebaiting of the hooks is performed in a single operation by the dory men without taking the gear back to the vessel.

UNDER SAIL. With sails set. Underway.

Fr: *Sous Voiles;* Ger: *Unter Segel.*

UNDERSAIL. To sail under the shelter of the land.

Ger: *Längs der Küste segeln.*

UNDERSET. A current of water below the surface in a direction contrary to that of the wind or of the water on the surface. The opposite of surface current. Undersets occur most frequently in straits where there are strong surface currents due mainly to wind.

Fr: *Contre-Courant;* Ger: *Unterströmung.*

UNDER THE WIND. On the side away from the wind. Also called to leeward.

Fr: *Sous le Vent;* Ger: *Leewärts.*

UNDERTOW. A current below the surface of the water, flowing in the opposite direction to the water at the surface. The current of water below the surface receding from waves breaking on a shelving beach.

Fr: *Ressac;* Ger: *Widersee.*

UNDERWAY. Refers under normal circumstances to a vessel that has weighed anchor or has left its moorings and is making progress through the water. However, a vessel with its anchor down but neither held by it nor under its control is underway. A vessel driven from her anchorage or moorings by a gale of wind, even if wholly unmanageable, is a vessel underway. Every ship not actually brought up is underway. A vessel is underway, even though not making any progress through the water, if its anchor is not down and holding, or if it is not moored to some fixed object.

Fr: *En route;* Ger: *Im fahren; Unterwegs sein.*

UNDERWRITER. In marine insurance, one who subscribes his name to the policy indicating his acceptance of the liability mentioned therein, in consideration for which he receives a premium. Any person capable of entering into an agreement can underwrite a marine risk, that is, sign his name at the foot of a policy as an insurer of a specific amount set against his name. The signature constitutes a separate agreement on the part of each of the underwriters. Every Lloyd's underwriter is called upon by the Committee of Lloyd's to deposit securities to the value of at least £5,000 in the hands of trustees approved by the committee.

Fr: *Assureur Maritime;* Ger: *Assekuradeur; Versicherer.*

See **Cargo Underwriter, Hull Underwriter.**

UNDOCK. To take a ship out of a dock.

Fr: *Sortir du bassin;* Ger: *Aus dem Dock holen; Ausdocken.*

UNEQUAL-ANGLE BAR. Angle bar in which one flange is wider than the other.

Sometimes called unequal flange bar, unequal leg bar.
Fr: *Cornière à ailes inégales;* Ger: *Ungleichschenkeliger Winkel.*

UNFURL. To spread or shake out of a furled state a sail or a flag.
Fr: *Déferler; Larguer;* Ger: *Wehen lassen; Losmachen.*

UNIDENTIFIABLE CARGO. Goods reaching their destination so damaged as to have lost all their marks of identification. The practice of American Underwriters is to settle as for a total loss and take over the proceeds. In Great Britain such losses are treated as particular average claims, the underwriters making payments on account to the assured, and paying the balance of the claims after the unidentifiable goods have been sold, and the proceeds apportioned among the various consignees.
Fr: *Marchandises non-identifiables;* Ger: *Unbezeichnete Güter.*

UNIFORM PITCH. The pitch of a propeller blade which has its driving face lying entirely in a true helical surface. The blade has no variation in pitch either radially or axially. Also called true screw.
Fr: *Pas Constant;* Ger: *Konstant Steigung.*

UNIMAGDA.
See **Awarpe.**

UNION GEAR. Gear used for handling cargo with two falls fastened to a single hook.
See **Burton System.**

UNIONMELT. A patented, machine electric welding process widely used in the mass production of cargo vessels in the United States during World War II. The machine makes a down-hand weld on the flat, either on a butt or lap joint, traveling on a small two-rail track set up in 6-ft. interlocking lengths. The welding rod is fed by the machine from a continuous coil as the machine travels along the track. At the same time the hot weld bead is automatically covered with a special flux from a hopper, thus reducing oxidation and keeping the fusing metal from chilling too fast. The welding crew consists of an operator and two helpers, who with one machine, can make from 200 to 300 linear feet of weld in 8 hours.

UNION PURCHASE SYSTEM.
See **Burton Tackle.**

UNION SYSTEM.
See **Burton Tackle.**

UNION THIMBLE. Two thimbles inserted in each other. Also called lock thimble.
Fr: *Cosse Baguée;* Ger: *Verkettete Kausche.*

UNISLIP PROPELLER. A propeller so designed that the pitch increases from root to some point on the blade and thereafter decreases toward the tip.

UNIVERSAL RULE. An American yacht measurement rule first proposed by N. G. Herreshoff in 1903 and in general use in the United States and Canada. It is claimed to be less complicated than the European International Rule, particularly as regards the measurement of sail area. Since 1933 the Universal rule has been in effect in Europe for 56-ft., 65-ft., and 76-ft. racing classes. It is expressed as follows:

$$\text{Rating} = 0.18 \frac{L \times \sqrt{S.A.}}{3\sqrt{D}}$$

L = Length in ft.;
S.A. = Sail Area in sq. ft.;
D = Displacement in cu. ft.

UNIVERSAL TIME. Greenwich mean civil time.

UNKINKABLE LAY. A rope lay similar in general appearance to the plain or hawser lay. The individual yarns are spun with the same direction of twist as the strand instead of being in the reverse direction, as is true of all ordinary ropes.

This results in the elimination of the natural tendency of an ordinary rope to kink when allowed to go slack or to twist when working in multiple blocks. It is therefore frequently used for lifeboat falls and similar gear.
Fr: *Cablage antigiratoire.*

UNLASH. To loose, unfasten, or separate, as something lashed or tied down.
Fr: *Dessaisir;* Ger: *Losmachen.*

UNLAY. To untwist the strands of a rope.
Fr: *Décommettre;* Ger: *Aufschlagen.*

UNMOOR. 1. To loose or free a vessel from her moorings.
Fr: *Démarrer;* Ger: *Losmachen.*
2. To cause a vessel to ride with one anchor after having been moored.
Fr: *Désaffourcher;* Ger: *Abankern.*

UNNEUTRAL SERVICE. In international law, the actions of neutral merchant vessels which violate neutrality by carrying contraband of war, by carrying supplies to belligerent vessels on the high seas, or by breaking blockade and generally by affording aid to the enemy.

UNREEVE. To haul a line or rope out of a block, fairlead, and so on.
Fr: *Dépasser;* Ger: *Ausscheren.*

UNRIG. To take down the rigging. To lower a cargo boom and remove its gear. To strip a ship of both standing and running rigging.
Fr: *Dégréer;* Ger: *Abtakeln.*

UNSEAWORTHINESS. The state or condition of a vessel when it is not in a proper state of maintenance, loading, equipment, crew, repair, or in any other respect ready to encounter the ordinary perils of the sea. In marine insurance the condition of unseaworthiness is difficult to establish except in flagrant cases. The burden of proof lies on the insurer, the presumption being that a vessel is seaworthy until the contrary is proved.
Fr: *Innavigabilité;* Ger: *Seeuntüchtigkeit; Fahruntüchtigkeit; Seeunfähigkeit.*

UNSHACKLE. To disconnect two lengths of rope or chain which are joined by a shackle.
Fr: *Démaniller; Démailler;* Ger: *Ausschakeln.*

UNSHIP. To detach or remove anything on board ship from the place where it is fixed or fitted.
Fr: *Rentrer; Démonter;* Ger: *Einlegen.*

UNSLING. To take the slings off, as a yard. To release from slings cargo being loaded or discharged.
Fr: *Désélinguer;* Ger: *Aushängen; Ausschlingen.*

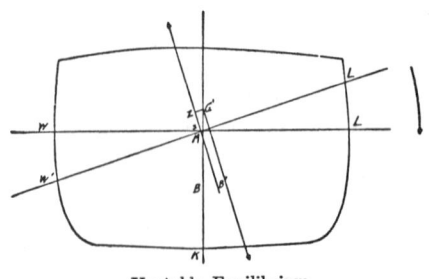

Unstable Equilibrium
B = Center of buoyancy
G = Center of gravity
M = Metacenter
GM = Metacentric Height

UNSTABLE EQUILIBRIUM. A condition of equilibrium in which a floating body, if displaced from its original position by an outside force, will continue to move away from its original position after the disturbing force is removed.

If a vessel having its metacenter below the center of gravity is slightly inclined by an outside cause, the action of the forces of weight and buoyancy will tend to make it move still further away from the upright. The vessel is in a state of unstable equilibrium.
Fr: *Equilibre Instable;* Ger: *Labiles Gleichgewicht.*
See **Stable Equilibrium.**

UNSTOW. See **Break Out.**

UNSTOWED. Goods or equipment lying loose on deck or below decks.

UNVALUED POLICY. A marine insurance policy which does not specify the value of the subject matter insured, but leaves the insurable value to be subsequently ascertained subject of the limit of the sum insured. Also called open policy.
Fr: *Police non évaluée;* Ger: *Offene Police.*

UOMI-BUNE. A Japanese open boat used for operating the scare cord net (*nekosaiami*) in conjunction with the *ama-bune* and the *onaka-bume* boats. It is the master's or leading boat. The hull is built with straight raking stem and narrow flat bottom, straight for about two thirds of its length from the stern, and then rising sharply toward the bow. The open stern and lap strake planking are of the usual Japanese pattern. There is a frame or gallows above the stern for resting the mast when unshipped. Length over-all 21 ft. 8 in. Breadth 5 ft. 7½ in. Inside depth 20 in.

UP. The helm of a vessel under sail is said to be up when it is put so as to bring the rudder to leeward of the sternpost.
Fr: *Barre au Vent;* Ger: *Ruder in Lee.*

UP AND DOWN. The anchor cable is up and down when the anchor is under or nearly under the forefoot.
Fr: *à Pic;* Ger: *Auf und nieder.*

UP-AND-DOWN FALL. The derrick fall which, in burtoning, raises and lowers the draft, while the burton fall carries the draft athwartship. Also called hatch whip, midship fall.
See **Burton System.**

UP-AND-DOWN LINE.
See **Breast Line.**

UP-AND-DOWN TACKLE. A tackle composed of a single and a double block. The double block is fitted with a lashing, the single block with a hook.

Fr: *Palan Renversé.*

UP BEHIND. An order to cease pulling on a rope and slack up roundly so that the gear may be belayed.

UPPER BERTH. The higher of two superimposed berths in a cabin or other accommodation.
Fr: *Couchette Supérieure;* Ger: *Oberkoje.*

UPPER DECK. In merchant ships, a continuous deck extending below a shelter or shade deck. On passenger vessels the upper deck is situated below the promenade deck and above the main deck. In the tonnage rules the upper deck is defined as the topmost watertight deck extending continuously throughout the whole of the vessel's length.
Fr: *Pont Supérieur;* Ger: *Oberdeck.*

UPPER MAST. Any mast above a lower mast.
Fr: *Mât Supérieur;* Ger: *Obermast.*

UPPER MAST TABLE.
See **Outrigger.**

UPPER SHROUDS. In Bermuda-rigged craft, the shrouds running to the masthead, as distinguished from those which go only part way up, which are known as lower shrouds.
Fr: *Haubans de Tête de Mât.*

UPPER TOPSAIL. The topsail which hoists above a lower topsail. In modern ships with double topsails, the upper topsail on each mast has no clew lines, the clews of the sail being shackled to the lower topsail yard which is connected with the upper (topsail) yard by a tackle called the upper topsail downhaul.
Fr: *Hunier Volant;* Ger: *Obermarssegel.*

UPPER WORKS. The part of a ship's hull above the water line when it is floating at its normal loaded draft. The sides of a vessel from waterline to covering board. Also called dead works.
Fr: *Accastillage; Oeuvres Mortes;* Ger: *Oberwerk; Totes Werk.*

UPRIGHTS. Poles placed vertically at a small distance from a ship's hull during construction, to support the staging planks on which the riveters and other workmen stand. Also called staging uprights, stage bent (U. S.). They are longer and thicker than the shores. Their average length is from 50 to 70 ft., occasionally 80 or 100 ft. The customary method of using uprights is to saw them down the center and bolt the two halves together with a space between, so that the stage planks are supported by the bolts. There is an increasing tendency to use steel uprights built of angle bars and plates or tubular uprights in place of wooden poles. They have longer life, are more conveniently handled and enable staging to be erected more quickly.
Fr: *Étamperche;* Ger: *Hellingmast.*

UPSET. A defect in structural timber produced by the separation of the grain when the fibers have been crippled by compression.

UPSET SHACKLE. One in which the shackle is passed through the block while it is being assembled, so that the bolt or pin can be removed without the shackle coming free of the block. A shackle standing in the block upside down or pin up. The converse of a "regular shackle."

UPSETTING. The process of heating a metal shape and then compressing it by hammering or squeezing so that the heated part is thickened.
Fr: *Refouler;* Ger: *Stauchen.*

UPSETTING ANGLE. The angle of heel of a vessel afloat which corresponds to the statical upsetting moment, that is to say, when the value of the couple tending to return the vessel to the vertical is nil.
Fr: *Angle de Chavirement;* Ger: *Kenterwinkel.*

UPSETTING ARM. The perpendicular distance between two vertical lines passing through the center of gravity and the center of buoyancy when the relative positions of the two centers produces a couple which tends to overturn or capsize the vessel. Also called upsetting lever. The opposite of righting lever.
Fr: *Bras de Chavirement;* Ger: *Umschlagarm.*

UPSETTING MOMENT. The product of displacement and upsetting arm, expressed in foot-tons.
Fr: *Moment de Chavirement;* Ger: *Kippmoment; Kentermoment.*

UPSETTING POINT. The point on a transverse stability curve where the relative position of the center of gravity and center of buoyancy is such as to produce a couple which tends to capsize the vessel.
Fr: *Point de Chavirement;* Ger: *Kenterpunkt.*

UPTAKE. Conduit made of light plating connecting the smokebox with the base of smokestack or lower funnel. It conveys the smoke and hot gases of combustion from the boilers to the stack and is often made of double thickness with an insulating air space of 2 to 3 in. between to prevent excessive radiation. Also called breaching.

> Fr: *Culotte; Conduit de Fumée;* Ger: *Kesselschacht; Schornsteinschacht; Rauchfang.*

See **Divided Uptakes.**

UPTAKE VENTILATOR. Any ventilator by which hot, moist, or vitiated air is removed from the different compartments of a ship. Also called upcast ventilator.

Fr: *Manche d'Evacuation;* Ger: *Ausziehlüfter.*

USEFUL DEADWEIGHT.
See **Net Capacity.**

USEFUL LOAD. The fraction of a vessel's total displacement, when it is floating at designed draft, which is devoted to the purpose for which the vessel is intended. In merchant vessels it includes cargo, fuel, stores and water (drinking and reserve-feed). Useful load refers exclusively to weight, not volume. Also called net capacity, dead load.

> Fr: *Portée Utile;* Ger: *Nutzladefähigkeit.*

V

V. Flag of the international code of signals showing an oblique or diagonal red cross on a white ground. When hoisted singly means: "I require assistance."

Var. VARIATION (navigation).
Vert. VERTEX or VERTICAL.
V.K. VERTICAL KEEL.

VA'A. A general term used throughout Polynesia and Melanesia for a dugout or planked outrigger canoe. The spelling varies according to the various dialects spoken in the particular island or group of islands. Also *vaka, waka, wangga, vaga, va.*

VA'A-ALO. A plank-built canoe of Samoa, with a length ranging between 15 and 25 ft., built on the same lines as the *pao-pao*. The keel piece or underbody extends the full length of the hull and is hollowed-out on the top. From this, the sides are built up of pieces several feet in length, adzed out of solid wood. Each piece is carefully fitted to its neighbor and a "lip" ¾ in. high of the solid wood is left all around the edge on the inside. Small holes are bored through this lip with corresponding holes in the adjacent one, through which lashings of sennit are passed and tightly knotted. A single outrigger of balsalike wood is lashed on. A deck is put over the bows. These boats are manned by two paddlers and a fisherman. They troll in deep water outside the breakers.

VA'A-KATEA. A Cook's Island double canoe.

VA'A-POTI. A double-ended, planked, outrigger canoe from the Marquesas Islands.

VA-FATEN. A single-outrigger, dugout canoe from the western area of the Caroline Islands. It has an elegantly shaped hull with prominent finlike projection at each end. A central platform covers part of the central portion of the dugout and extends outboard upon the outrigger booms for a short distance.

VAGA-UE. A large built-up sailing canoe from Samarai Island and Milne Bay (British New Guinea). It is rigged with a very large flat oval-shaped mat sail. The over-all length of these craft is about 50 ft., and the sides are built up with 3 or 4 strakes of planking, giving a molded depth of 4 or 5 ft.

VAKA HEKE FA. A single-outrigger dugout canoe with whaleback-covered ends, employed in the fisheries of Niul Island, Tongan Archipelago. Length 17 to 25 ft. Breadth 12 to 16 in. Depth 18 to 24 in. (Average.)

VAKA TUI TUTA, VAKA TUI AUTALI. A Polynesian single-outrigger dugout canoe from Pukapuka Island, Tuamotu Archipelago. The hull is composed of 3 to 5 transverse sections carefully fitted together and fastened to each other by sennit lashings made of coconut husk fiber. both ends are decked over and fitted with a breakwater. The bow is pointed, the stern, fishtail shaped. A heavy wash strake and gunwale pole run fore and aft on each side. Transverse lifting poles are provided at each end to carry the canoe when beached. The *vaka tui autali* is distinguished from the *vaka tui tuta* by the difference in the method of attachment of the hull sections and other structural parts. In the *tui autali*, raised inside flanges about 2 in. high are left to all structural parts at the joints. The connection is made by passing the lashing through holes drilled through each flange. In the *tui tuta* there are no flanges and the connection is made by sewing the lashing passing through and through inside and outside. The rig consists of a mast which can be stepped at either end of the canoe, the outrigger being always kept to windward. A spritsail is set when sailing. A paddle is used for steering. The length of these craft ranges from 22 ft. for a 4-seater canoe, to 60 ft. for a 13-seater, which can accommodate about 30 people.

VALA-VATHAI. A type of Indian boat from Palk Strait. There are two varieties. One is a dugout or plank-built craft-rigged with one mast stepped forward, and a square-headed lugsail. The balance board consists of a long plank stayed by a shroud which leads to the masthead on either side. Men are stationed on the weather end of the plank. The other or northern variety of *vala-vathai* is a narrow, carvel-built, round-bottomed craft of canoe form rigged with 3 masts and square-headed lugs. It is steered with a large centerline rudder hung on pintles, and is provided with leeboards. Length 43 ft. Breadth 4½ ft. Depth 2½ ft.

VALEMAN. One of the crew in a North Sea herring drifter who sees that the nets are kept in proper order for fishing.

VALLAM.
See **Ballam.**

VALLEY. In oceanography, the prolongation of a land valley at the bottom of the sea into or across the continental or insular shelf.
Fr: *Vallée;* Ger: *Tal.*

VALUATION CLAUSE. A marine clause usually inserted in insurance policies on hulls of vessels, whereby it is agreed that the insured value shall be taken as the repaired value in ascertaining whether a constructive total loss has arisen.
Fr: *Clause d'Évaluation;* Ger: *Wertklausel.*

VALUED POLICY. A valued policy in marine insurance is one which specifies the agreed value of the subject matter insured. This statement of value is conclusive between the parties in case of total or partial loss even though it is in excess of the actual value of the subject matter. Ships and freights are generally insured under valued policies.
Fr: *Police Évaluée;* Ger: *Pauschalpolice.*

VALVE CHEST.
See **Distribution Box.**

VANAGI. A single-outrigger, dugout canoe found in the coastal area extending from Cape Possession to Cape Rodney of Papua, British New Guinea. Also called *vai.* The bow is usually prolonged horizontally into an elongated quadrangular projection with a square end. The sides of this projection are often furnished with shelflike wings which are perforated for tassels. There is a long platform supported by the outrigger booms which extends outboard on both sides. These canoes were formerly rigged with a rectangular matwork sail, fastened on each side to a vertical pole by a series of loops of light rope.

VANDERBILT STAYSAIL. A quadrilateral fore-and-aft reaching sail used on cruising and racing staysail-ketches and schooners. The head is set flying, and the luff is hanked to a track. It is loose-footed.

VANE. A small piece of bunting or a thin piece of sheet metal carried at the truck, free to rotate on a spindle. Also called fly. It indicates the direction of the wind.
Fr: *Girouette;* Ger: *Windfahne; Flügel.*
See **Dog Vane, Sight Vane.**

VANE-SCREW PROPELLER. A partly-immersed propeller of large diameter adopted for shallow-draft river vessels. Also called vane wheel. The center of the shaft is well above water so that the screw is immersed to approximately 40 per cent of its diameter when the vessel is fully loaded. The blades, which have broad tips, stop short of the boss and are connected thereto by two stout arms. A propulsive efficiency of 70 per cent has been obtained with this type. Its disadvantages are that it is relatively noisy in operation, and is sensitive to changes in trim and draft.
Twin Vane-Wheel Propulsion of Ships, Marine Engineering and Shipping Age, vol. 27 (1922), p. 565.

VANE SPINDLE. The spindle at the truck on which a vane works.
Fr: *Axe de Girouette;* Ger: *Flügelpinne.*

VANG. A purchase with pendant leading from the peak of a gaff or derrick to the deck at the vessel's sides, in order to steady the spar in the desired position, and to restrain it from slewing. Also called guy.
Fr: *Garde; Retenue;* Ger: *Geer; Geie.*

VANG PURCHASE. A purchase used for steadying a gaff or derrick. Also called guy tackle. It has one block fastened to the vang pendant and the other shackled to an eyeplate.
Fr: *Palan de Garde;* Ger: *Geieläufer.*

VANISHING POINT. The angle at which a ship, on being gradually inclined, becomes unstable. The point at which the statical stability of a ship in an inclined position disappears.
Ger: *Verschwindeflucht Punkt.*

VANISHING TIDE. A tide in which only one high and one low water occur during the day. It is due to the fact that the other high and low water melt together into a period of several hours with nearly constant water level.

VAPOR COCK. A cock with wire gauze protected gooseneck fitted to the hatch covers of oil tankers as an escape for the gas given off by the cargo.

VAPOR PIPE.
See **Vent.**

VAQUELOTTE. Small fishing boat of Normandy with half deck and carvel or clinker planking. The *vaquelotte* is cutter-rigged with 2 headsails. The mast is usually placed at about one-third length from the stem. In some boats the mast is stepped at a distance of 1½ to 2 ft. from the stem. They carry a lug mainsail with tack fastened to the stemhead, and a small jigger mast aft. Length 20 to 25 ft. Breadth 7½ to 9 ft. Depth 4½ to 5 ft. (Average.)

VAR. A single-outrigger canoe of Ponape, the Caroline Islands. Also called *wuar,* Length 26.5 ft. Breadth 13.5 in. Depth 17.5 in. (Typical.)

VARGORD. Term used by the fishermen of Cornwall to denote a light spar or pole used instead of a bowline for keeping to windward the luff of a lugsail. It had a small fork at the upper end which was stuck into one of 3 or 4 cringles called "war eyes" worked on the boltropes for this purpose. The lower end of the *vargord* rested in one of 3 or 4 notches in a piece of timber called "timmy noggy" or "nabob."

VARIABLE DELIVERY PUMP. A rotary piston pump driven at a constant speed, in one direction and so designed that the stroke of the pistons may be varied, with the result that the rate at which the fluid is delivered can be adjusted as desired from zero to the full capacity of the pump. Also called variable stroke pump. Variable delivery pumps are used on board ship to provide the necessary pressure to the cylinders of hydraulic steering gear, and hydroelectric winches.

Fr: *Pompe à débit Variable;* Ger: *Veränderliche Leistungspumpe.*

VARIABLE PITCH. A variable pitch screw is one in which the blade surfaces are made up of portions of various helices, so that pitch varies continuously from one part to the next.

Fr: *Pas Variable;* Ger: *Veränderliche Steigung.*

VARIABLES OF CANCER AND CAPRICORN. The regions of the ocean included between latitudes 23½ degrees North and South of the equator where the winds are light and very variable. Also called **Horse latitudes,** by seamen.

VARIABLE WINDS. Refers to the variable winds of Cancer and variable winds of Capricorn which occur between the trade winds and the westerlies.

Fr: *Vents Variables;* Ger: *Veranderliche Winde.*

VARIATION. See **Magnetic Declination.**

VARIATION CHART. A chart which shows by means of isogonic lines or curves all places where variation of the magnetic from the geographical meridian has the same value.

VARIATION NEEDLE. A magnetic needle placed on a pivot and so balanced that it moves only in a horizontal plane or azimuth. Also compass needle. It indicates the angle which the magnetic meridian makes with the geographical meridian at the place of observation.

Fr: *Aiguille du Compas;* Ger: *Kompassnadel.*

VARRINHO. A flat-bottomed, open fishing boat found on the coasts of Portugal. Portable washboards are fitted above the gunwale in rough weather. The framing is composed of a heavy floor at each end (bilge) of which two knee pieces are fastened with a straight frame or futtock, to which the side planking is secured.

VASCELLO. Nonself-propelled, open, bargelike craft employed in the tunny fisheries of Italy. The ends are generally decked over. It is divided internally into several compartments. During the fishing operations it is located at one end of the *tonnara* net. The *caporais* is stationed at the opposite end. Length 52 to 78 ft. Breadth 14 to 16 ft. Depth 3.3 to 4 ft.

VAST. See **Avast.**

V-BOTTOM BOAT. A boat in which the transverse half section is composed of two planes forming a sharp angle at the bilge. Also called straight-framed boat, deadrise boat, hard chine boat, double wedge boat. Straight-framed boats, such as sharpies, dory boats, and the like, are superior in certain respects when compared with round-section hulls. Sharpie-built motorboats running at planing speeds have proved superior to motor craft with rounded sections. Fast V-bottom craft are likely to be drier than those with round bilges, as the sharp angle at the chine has a tendency to throw the bow wave outward instead of allowing it to rise well above the waterline. The roughwater qualities of this type of boat are chiefly dependent upon the steepness of the sectional angles.

Fr: *Embarcation à Bouchains à arêtes Vives;* Ger: *V-Bodenboot; Knickspantboot.*

V-bottom boats are unquestionably faster than the round-bilge type but they have several disadvantages. One of these is the hard angle of the chines in the bows, which causes light broken spray to be blown aboard when the wind is on the beam or nearly so. Another drawback is that the rolling motion of a V-bottom boat is of quicker period than the round-bilge boat, due to its greater initial stability. As for construction, a really sound V-bottom hull is nearly as expensive to build, especially if it has a flaring forward bottom and plenty of shape in the topsides. There are two extra seams on each side in the chine rabbets which have to be carefully worked to insure watertightness.

Goeller, F. W., *How to Build "V" Bottom Boats,* New York, 1917.

VEER. Also veer out. **1.** To pay out or let out a greater length of chain or rope.
2. To slack off and allow to run out.
Fr: *Filer;* Ger: *Fieren; Abfieren.*

VEER (to). The act of veering. Said of a change in the direction of the wind in a clockwise direction, as for instance from west to north. The opposite of backing.
Fr: *Haler;* Ger: *Umspringen.*

The discussions which have taken place from time to time at the meetings of the International Meteorological Committee as to the use of the words veering and hauling in reference to the wind, have proved fruitless because of the reversal of the directions of the wind in circular storms in the northern and southern hemispheres. It is thought therefore that the use of the words right or clockwise, and left or anti-clockwise clear up this difficulty besides giving greater definiteness in any translation of these terms into foreign languages.

VEER AFT. If the wind is abeam and changes its direction toward aft it is said to "veer aft." The opposite is "to haul forward."
Fr: *Adonner;* Ger: *Raumen.*

VEER AND HAUL. To pull and slacken alternately.
Fr: *Haler à Coups;* Ger: *Fieren und holen.*

VEER AWAY. To let out or slacken gradually a rope, cable, hawser, and so on.
Fr: *Filer;* Ger: *Ausstechen.*

VEERING TRIM. A term formerly used by whalemen. A whaling vessel was said to be in veering trim when the sails were set for quick handling and dodging among the ice. Generally under reefed topsails.

VELACCIERE. Three-masted Sicilian sailing coaster, square-rigged on the foremast, and lateen-rigged on the main and mizzen. The foremast is a pole spar with polacre rig. The jibboom carries one headsail.

Velacciere

VELACHERO. A Spanish, two-masted sailing coaster with square-rigged foremast and lateen-rigged mainmast.

VELO-VELO. See **Takia.**

VELOX BOILER. A type of forced-circulation boiler.
See **Forced-Circulation Boiler.**

VENDAVAL. Strong southwest wind over Spain and in the Straits of Gibraltar. A west wind on the coasts of Central America.

VENT (U. S.). In oil tank vessels, a vertical pipe fitted in the hatch cover of each main and summer tank to provide means of ventilating the tanks. In Great Britain called vapour pipe. In some cases the open end of the pipe terminates with a gooseneck return bend. When light or gassy oils are carried, an automatic relief valve with double discs, seats, and springs is fitted, which provides for vacuum as well as pressure in the tank.
Fr: *Tuyau de Dégazage;* Ger: *Abgasrohr.*

VENT HEADER. The end of a vent pipe system which rises above the weather deck in an oil tanker. When light or gassy oils are carried a pressure-vacuum relief valve is fitted. In other cases there is a gooseneck with a wire gauze safety screen.

VENTILATING BLOWER.
See **Blower.**

VENTILATION. The process of replacing foul or vitiated air in any of the ship's compartments with pure air.
Fr: *Ventilation;* Ger: *Lüftung.*
See **Exhaust Ventilation, Mechanical Ventilation, Natural Ventilation, Plenum-Exhaust Ventilation, Plenum Ventilation.**

Bullen, F. L., *Ventilation of Ships,* London, 1935; Glass, W. H., "Air Conditioning in Ship's Passenger and Cargo Spaces," North East Coast Institution of Engineers and Shipbuilders (Newcastle upon Tyne), *Transactions,* vol. 56 (1940); Nichols, J. F., "Ventilation of Ships," Society of Naval

Architects and Marine Engineers (New York), *Transactions*, vol. 42 (1934).

VENTILATOR COAMING. That part of a ventilator trunk which extends above a weather deck and to which the ventilator cowl is fitted.

Fr: *Fût de Manche à Air;* Ger: *Lüftersull; Ventilatorsockel.*

VENTILATOR COVER. A canvas hood placed over a ventilator coaming when closed with a plug in heavy weather.

Fr: *Capuchon;* Ger: *Ventilatorkappe.*

VENT LINE (U. S.). A cargo tank ventilating system installed on oil tankers which carry highly inflammable liquids. In Great Britain called gas line. It consists of a main with branch fitted to each tank hatch cover. The branches lead upward from each tank to the main which runs under the fore-and-aft bridge and is carried up the mast, to a height of 30 ft. in some cases. The upper end, or vent header is fitted with a pressure-vacuum relief valve at the outlet to the atmosphere.

Fr: *Collecteur de Dégazage;* Ger: *Gasleitung; Entgasungsleitung.*

VENT PIPE.
See **Air Pipe.**

VERIFICATION OF FLAG. A procedure recognized in international law, by which a ship of war is entitled to chase and stop another vessel when it has reason to suspect that the latter is flying false colors, in order to verify the facts. The warship has to display previously her own national colors, and if necessary to affirm her colors by firing a blank shot known as "informing gun."

Fr: *Enquête du Pavillon;* Ger: *Flaggenprüfung.*

VERNAL EQUINOX. The equinox which falls in the spring on or about March 21. The point where the celestial equator intersects the ecliptic.

Fr: *Equinoxe du Printemps;* Ger: *Frühlingspunkt; Widderpunkt.*

See **Equinoctial Points.**

VERNIER. Short graduated scale attached to the index bar of a sextant and made to slide along the divisions of the arc or limb to enable the user to read angles accurately to a small fraction of a division of the arc. It is fitted with a tangent screw for making the final adjustments.

Fr: *Vernier;* Ger: *Vernier; Nonius.*

VERTEX. 1. The point of a great circle which is nearest to the pole.

2. The point on a great circle track which reaches the highest latitude.

Ger: *Scheitelpunkt.*

VERTICAL CIRCLE. A general term embracing all great circles which are perpendicular to the observer's horizon, hence passing through his zenith and nadir. Also called circle of altitude.

Fr: *Vertical;* Ger: *Vertikalkreis; Höhenkreis.*

VERTICAL-CUT SAIL. A sail in which the cloths run parallel to the leech. Also called up-and-down cut sail. This type of cut is always used for the square and gaff sails of trading vessels. It is the best cut for a loose-footed gaffsail, as the biggest strain on it is from luff to leech. No battens are required to make the round of leech stand as in a cross-cut sail. It has the advantage of having the reef points sewed into the seams where the cloth is double.

VERTICAL INTENSITY. The magnetic force in a vertical plane of the compass needle.

VERTICAL IRON. The various structural parts of a steel vessel which act in a vertical plane and which are of account in the compensation of magnetic compasses.

Ger: *Vertikale Eisenmassen.*

VERTICAL KEEL (U. S.).
See **Center Girder.**

VERTICAL WELD. A weld made on a surface lying vertically or at an angle less than 45 degrees to the vertical, the weld lying along the vertical axis of the parts jointed, or being inclined at an angle less than 45 degrees to that axis.

Fr: *Soudure Montante; Soudure Verticale;* Ger: *Vertikale Schweissung.*

VERTICAL WINDLASS. A power windlass in which each wildcat is mounted close to the deck on a vertical shaft, the driving engine or motor being located on the deck below. In some installations a capstan capable of independent operation is provided above the wildcat. This type is usually seen on large passenger vessels. Also called capstan windlass.

VERY HIGH SEA. A state of sea disturbance between high sea and precipitous sea with wave heights ranging from 23 to 36 ft. Number 7 of International Scale of Sea Disturbance.

Fr: *Mer Très Grosse;* Ger: *Sehr hohe See.*

VERY ROUGH SEA. A very disturbed sea with wave heights ranging from 9 to 15 ft. Number 5, International scale of sea disturbance.

Fr: *Mer Très Houleuse;* Ger: *Sehr grobe See.*

VERY SIGNAL. A night signal consisting of red, white, and green stars fired with a special pistol and used in a special code. The cartridges are so corrugated that the different colors may be identified by touch at night.

Fr: *Signal pyrotechnique Very;* Ger: *Very Kunstfeuersignal.*

VESSEL. A general term for all craft capable of floating on water and larger than a rowboat. The term vessel includes every description of water craft or other artificial contrivance used or capable of being used as a means of transportation on water. Barges, dredges, scows, and similar nondescript craft having no means of propulsion and depending entirely on external appliances for motive power are vessels within Admiralty jurisdiction. Lighters used in loading and unloading vessels are, while on navigable waters, subject to Admiralty process.

Fr: *Bateau;* Ger: *Fahrzeug.*

Dredges, floating bath houses, floating elevators, wharf boats, rafts, canal boats, have all been held to be within the jurisdiction of Admiralty courts, so far as actions for tort are concerned. Floating dry docks have been held to be within the jurisdiction of Admiralty in actions of the nature of tort, but not within the jurisdiction in possessory actions when the ownership of the property is sought to be established.

VESSEL BOND (U. S.). 1. A bond given by master agent or consignee of a foreign vessel in accordance with the requirements of the United States customs regulations when a preliminary entry of the vessel is made immediately after report of arrival. The purpose of the bond is to indemnify the U. S. for any loss or liability which might occur when a special license is granted for the landing of merchandise, baggage or passengers before formal entry of vessel at the customhouse.

2. Execution of a bond by which the master of a ship lying in a foreign port may bind the owners to procure the release of his vessel. See **Bottomry Bond.**

VETKA. Small, plank-built boat used by the Chukchi people of Eastern Siberia for hunting and fishing on the estuary of the Anadyr River. The flat-bottomed hull is made of 3 planks hewed out with an ax. The bottom board is about three quarters of an inch thick, pointed at both ends. Each side consists of a single board 8 to 10 in. wide and about one quarter of an inch thick, sewed on the bottom board with sinew of deer. The seams are sealed with pitch. It is propelled by a light, double-bladed paddle. Length 15 ft. Breadth 1½ ft. (Average.)

VIBRATORY HORN. A sound-signaling device fitted on motor boats and other small craft with a length of 16 ft. or more. It consists essentially of a diaphragm and a high-speed rotor with notches cut on the periphery. A push rod transmits its motion to the rotor through a train of gears or through a spiral spindle. In electric-driven horns the rotor is actuated by a push button connected to a series-wound 6-volt motor conveniently located in a separate watertight case. The sound produced is clear, distinct and uniform at a distance of two thousand feet.

VIBRATING NEEDLE. A magnetic needle used by compass adjusters to find the relative intensity of the horizontal component of a ship's magnetism. It consists usually of a needle about 3 in. long, designed so to vibrate 30 times a minute when on shore and removed from the influence of all local disturbance.

VIBRATIONAL PERIOD. The vibrational period of a magnetic compass card is the time taken to perform a complete oscillation when it is deflected horizontally through any angle not exceeding 40 degrees and left to itself to vibrate freely. The time of oscillation depends upon the moment of inertia of the card, the magnetic moment of the needles, and the horizontal intensity of the magnetic field.

Fr: *Période Vibratoire;* Ger: *Schwingungsperiode.*

VICTORY SHIP (U. S.). A standard type of single-screw cargo vessel designed by the United States Maritime Commission in 1942 as a war emergency project, as a faster and more efficient cargo carrier than the earlier Liberty Ship. There are two types of Victory Ships, the VC2-AP2 and the VC2-AP3. The hulls are identical, but the VC2-AP3 is one knot faster. Length between perpendiculars 436 ft. 6 in. Beam molded 62 ft. Depth molded 38 ft. Loaded draft 28 ft. 6 in. Displacement 15,200 tons. Deadweight capacity 10,700 tons. Tonnage, gross

7,612; net 4,553. Sea speed VC2-AP3 15½ knots; VC2-AP3 16½ knots.
See **Liberty Ship, Maritime Commission.**
VICTUALING BILL. A customhouse form which has to be filled by the master before a vessel can sail. It contains a list of all bonded or drawback goods taken on board for use as ship's stores during the voyage, and when signed by the customs authorities constitutes one of the captain's clearance papers.
Ger: *Proviantschein.*
VICTUALING SCALE. The scale of provisions to be allowed and served out daily to the crew during the voyage. It is inserted in the articles of agreement. All maritime countries have an official minimum scale approved by law.
Fr: *Equivalence des Rations;* Ger: *Speiserolle.*
VIGIA. Navigational warning on a chart to denote a possible pinnacle, rock, or shoal, the position of which is uncertain.
Fr: *Vigie;* Ger: *Warnungszeichen.*
VINDA. Australian sewed bark canoe from Whitsunday and adjacent islands, Queensland, made of 3 sheets cut into more or less diamond shape. One sheet forms the bottom; the other two the sides. The peel of fibrous roots is used as thread. On each side there is a gunwale pole running from just behind the bow to the extremity of the stern. One or more ribs are fitted to hold in place extra pieces of bark placed on the bottom and strengthening the sides of the craft. The smallest one-man canoes have a length of 6 to 7 ft. Also called *winta.*

VINTA. A paddling and sailing canoe with double-outriggers, of the southern Philippine Islands (Moro Gulf and Sulu Archipelago), used for fishing and transportation. The hull is a dugout, with the sides raised by a wash strake made of *nipa* leaves or planking sewed on with coir yarn. The stem and stern are forked. The lower point of the stem fork is nearly horizontal. On the upper point a triangular or swallow-tail splash board is fastened. The two points forming the stern fork are ornamented with open-work carvings. Inside, the boat is divided into five sections. The three central ones are covered with portable decking of split bamboo. The forward and after sections are left open for the paddlers. The outrigger booms are lashed on a series of double cross spars, the lower being about 4 ft. long. The upper ones extending only about 2½ ft. outboard serve to strengthen the lower spars at its weakest point, that is, just beyond half length.

The rig varies according to locality. Some boats have a bipod or tripod bamboo mast which carries a kind of large lugsail, with foot laced to a boom on which the sail is rolled when furled. Others have a single mast with spritsail. They cannot tack or sail close to the wind.

The *vintas* are said to be very fast under sail and wonderfully seaworthy for their size, taking trips which may last 4 or 5 days in open waters. They are much used on account of their speed for smuggling between the Sulu Islands and Borneo. According to some their capacity ranges from 4 to 40 tons burden.

VIOL BLOCK. A block similar to a snatch block but without hinge, so that the bight of a rope may be dropped into the sheave.
Fr: *Galoche.*
VISIBLE HORIZON.
See **Apparent Horizon, Horizon.**
VISIBILITY. The transparency of the atmosphere as perceptible to the eye. The range of vision for an object such as a ship under the conditions of light and atmosphere existing at a particular time.

Navigational visibility is that affecting the speed of a vessel with reference to the distance within which the vessel could be brought to a standstill before the course of any other vessel emerging from the fog would cross her course.
Fr: *Visibilité;* Ger: *Sichtbarkeit.*
See **Arc of Visibility.**
VISIBILITY SCALE.

0—Dense fog	Objects not visible at 50 yd.
1—Thick fog	Objects not visible at 200 yd.
2—Fog	Objects not visible at 400 yd.
3—Moderate fog	Objects not visible at ½ mi.
4—Thin fog or mist	Objects not visible at 1 mi.
5—Visibility poor	Objects not visible at 2 mi.
6—Visibility moderate	Objects not visible at 5 mi.
7—Visibility good	Objects not visible at 10 mi.
8—Visibility very good	Objects not visible at 30 mi.
9—Visibility exceptional	Objects visible for more than........30 mi.

Fr: *Echelle de Visibilité;* Ger: *Sichtbarkeit Skala.*

VISIT. The act of boarding and examining a neutral merchant vessel's papers in exercise of the right of visit. Also called visitation. The usual modern practice is for the visiting ship to send a boat with an officer in charge alongside the merchant vessel. No one but the officer and an assistant wearing side arms go on board for the purpose of examining the ship's papers.

The commander of the belligerent cruiser may also summon the master or chief officer of the suspected vessel to come on board the cruiser and bring his papers with him for examination. After completion of the examination the visiting officer enters on the official log book of the merchantman a memorandum of the visit. A similar memorandum of the visit is made on that document among her nationality.
Fr: *Visite;* Ger: *Visite.*
See **Right of Visit.**
Frascona, J. L., *Visit Search and Seizure on the High Seas,* Rahway, New Jersey, 1938.

VISOR (U. S.). A small inclined awning supported by a pipe frame running around the pilot house, over the windows, to exclude the glare of the sun and to prevent the rain from coming in over the top of the window sashes.

VIZAGAPATAM CATAMARAN. A type of catamaran found on the Madras coast, adapted for use at sea. The logs, besides being fastened together with wooden pegs, are provided with a vertical wooden board on each side to break the force of the waves. The stern is left open. A small primitive rudder is fitted at the afterend of the central log. A leeboard is also used. This craft is rigged with one mast and boomed lugsail.

VLET. Clinker-built, half-decked fishing boat with pram bow and transom stern found in the northern waters of the Zuiderzee. It is generally used as a tender by larger craft, although some of them from the Helder work as single boats in the North Sea. The rig consists of a sprit mainsail and stay foresail. Maximum length 28 ft.

VOIROLLE. Open fishing boat from the coast of Normandy of about 3 tons burden. The rig is 2 masts with lugsails.

VOITH-SCHNEIDER PROPELLER. A patent propeller which consists of a circular disk set flush into the bottom of the hull, with its axis of rotation vertical, and bearing near to the periphery a number of spadelike blades which project out into the water and are rotatable about their longitudinal axes somewhat like the feathering floats on a paddle wheel.

By adjusting the disposition of the blades, this type of propeller can be used to steer the ship as well as to propel it. This propeller has been installed in a number of shallow-draft vessels and has proved to be entirely practical. It is no more efficient than a comparable paddle wheel or screw propeller, but its peculiar advantage of utilizing the propeller thrust for steering purposes makes it eminently suitable for the propulsion of vessels which normally operate in crowded and restricted waters and require large steering power at low speed. The Voith-Schneider gear is a development of the Fowler wheel, installed in the U. S. ship "Alarm" in 1874, which was simply a feathering paddle wheel placed with its axis vertical.

Goldsworthy, E. C., Voith-Schneider System of Propulsion, American Society of Naval Engineers, *Journal,* vol. 52, February (1940); Kreitner, H., "Die hydraulischen Grundlagen des Voith-Schneider Antriebes," *Werft, Reederei, Hafen* (1931), vol. 11, p. 185.

VOLUME COEFFICIENT. The percentage difference in volume of an oil caused by a change of temperature of one degree. It is usually expressed as a fraction of the total volume. It must be known in order to allow for ullages to be left in the cargo tanks of oil tankers when loading, to obviate overflowing due to oil expansion.
See **Ullage.**

VOLUME OF DISPLACEMENT. The volume of water displaced by a vessel. The volume of displacement is given in cubic feet and equals thirty five times the displacement (in tons) in salt water or thirty six times the displacement (in tons) in fresh water. When metric units are used the volume of displacement is expressed in cubic meters and is equal to the vessel's weight in metric tons multiplied by 0.9756.
Fr: *Volume de Carène;* Ger: *Rauminhalt der Verdrängung.*

VOLUNTARY STRANDING. Stranding which occurs when, in an emergency, a vessel is voluntarily headed for the shore to avoid impending damage of shipwreck; or to save the lives of the crew; or so that the cargo may be better salved by choosing the place of running aground; or to escape capture. According to the maritime laws of some countries (Netherlands, Germany, Chile, Argentine) the damage caused by voluntary stranding is admitted as general average.
Fr: *Echouement Volontaire;* Ger: *Freiwillige Aufstrandsetzung.*
See **General Average.**

VOLYER. A carvel-built open boat with sharp bow, and transom stern, fitted with 4 thwarts, used in British fisheries for working large pilchard seines. Also called follyer, tuck net boat. Its greatest breadth is near the after thwart. When the wings of the seine have been brought together after encircling a shoal of fish the volyer proceeds over the cork line and shoots a tuck seine inside the large seine. By means of this small seine the fish are brought to the surface and captured. The volyer is lug-rigged with large main- and small foresail. Length 20 ft. Breadth 6.6 ft. Depth 3 ft. Capacity about 15 tons. (Typical.)

VORTEX. The center of a tropical revolving storm where the barometer is lowest and there is comparative calm with a very high sea running in all directions. In the Northern hemisphere it is, the most Westerly point reached by the center of a tropical revolving storm when recurvature takes place. Also called **Boiling pot**.
  Fr: *Centre-Oeil;* Ger: *Orkanzentrum-Orkanauge.*

VOYAGE. A journey by sea which includes the outward and homeward trips which are called passages. In marine insurance a voyage is deemed to commence at any time at which the vessel begins to load cargo or sails in ballast to a loading port. Such voyage continues during the entire ensuing period until either the ship has made one outward and one homeward passage (including an intermediate passage if made), or has carried and discharged two cargoes, whichever may happen first, and in either case until she begins to load a subsequent cargo or sails in ballast for a loading port.
  Fr: *Voyage;* Ger: *Rundreise.*

VOYAGE POLICY. A marine insurance policy which covers the subject matter for the fixed insurance only during the voyage named in the policy.
  Fr: *Police au Voyage;* Ger: *Reisepolice.*

V-QUARTERED BOAT. A flat-bottomed boat in which the quarters are shaped into a sweeping V. This build of the quarters gives better sailing qualities than the deep-sterned flatboat. The V-cut or slit is covered inside with a piece of timber called a half keelson. This type of hull is used for sailing dinghies and is generally associated with deep rudder and daggerboard.

VRAKEKA. An open Swedish herring boat from Blekinge with raking stem, narrow square stern, and good sheer. Some boats are rigged with a single mast and others as ketches with sprit mainsail and mizzen, and two headsails. The single-masted boats, which have now become obsolete, carried a large dipping lug with 8 reef bands. Length over-all 19 ft. Length on keel 13 ft. Beam 6 ft. 3 in. Depth 2 ft. 3 in. (Approximate.)

V SCARF. A scarf used for connecting small masts, booms, and so on. It is made by cutting a V in one piece and a tongue in the other to fit into the V. It is bolted and secured with two iron bands or served with wire seizing. The length of the scarf as compared to the diameter of the spars should be about 12 to 1.

V STERN. A form of transom stern which approaches the counter stern when viewed in profile. The transom is set at a considerable angle to the vertical.
  Fr: *Arrière en V.*

VULGAR ESTABLISHMENT. The vulgar establishment of a port is the interval of time between the instant of the moon's transit across the meridian on the day of the new or full moon and the following high water. Also called common establishment. It is denoted on nautical charts by the abbreviation H.W.F.C. (high water full and change). For practical purposes this establishment is constant.
  Fr: *Etablissement du Port;* Ger: *Hafenzeit.*

VUZZITEDDI. Small, open sailing boat with 2 or 3 thwarts used in the coastal fisheries of Sicily. It is rigged with one mast and lateen sail.

VUZZO. Open, double-ended sail- and rowboat employed in the local fisheries of the Bay of Naples and adjacent waters. Its length varies from 13 to 19 ft. The rig consists of a portable mast, stepped near the stem and raking forward, which carries a lateen sail. Also called *vuzzariello, gozzo*. The *vuzzo* or *gozzo* from the coast of Calabria has a length of 26 to 29 ft.

W

W. Flag of the international code of signals having a central red square set in a larger white square with an all-round blue border. When hoisted singly it denotes: "I require medical assistance." When used as a towing signal it means: "I am paying out the tow line."

W. Freeboard mark which indicates the maximum load line in winter. It is arrived at by adding to the summer freeboard one-quarter of an inch per foot of summer draft.

W.A. WITH AVERAGE (marine insurance).

W.B.S. WITHOUT BENEFIT OF SALVAGE (insurance).

W.L. WATERLINE.

W.M. WEIGHT OR MEASUREMENT (cargo).

W.N.A. Freeboard mark indicating the minimum freeboard for seagoing vessels with a length of 330 ft. or less which make voyages across the North Atlantic Ocean, north of latitude 36° during the winter months.

W.P.A. WITH PARTICULAR AVERAGE.

W.R.O. WAR RISKS ONLY (insurance).

W.T. WATERTIGHT.

W.T. WARTIME (navigation).

W.W. WEATHER WORKING DAYS.

WAAG. A single-outrigger, dugout canoe used in the harbor streams and lagoons of Kusaie Island, the Carolines. Also called *oak*. The hull is round-bottomed with sharp ends, both of which are either low, or one upturned and pointed, and the other low. Most of these canoes are propelled by paddles, although some of the larger are fitted for sailing. Maximum length 28 ft.

WA-A-KAUKAHI. A single-outrigger dugout canoe used for fishing in the Hawaiian Islands. The sides are raised by a wash strake fastened to the underbody with nails driven through the overlap from the outside and clinched on the inner side. The wash strakes of the present-day canoe merge at both ends into the solid bow and stern end pieces, each of which is hewed out of a single block. The outrigger is always fitted on the port side. The rig consists of a spritsail with luff laced to the mast and foot laced to a boom.

WA-A-KAULUA. A double-dugout canoe with wash strake from the Hawaiian Islands. Both hulls had the same length. The wash strake was a thin plank from 6 to 8 in. high, sewed upon the edge of the dugout except for a length of several feet at each extremity, where it was replaced by a shaped board carved out of the solid. When one hull was longer than the other the canoe was called *wa-a-ku-e-e*. Now extinct.

WABATA. A small canoe from Geelvink Bay, New Guinea.

WACHE. A single-outrigger, dugout canoe from 16 to 30 ft. long of Humbolt Bay, Dutch New Guinea. Also called *waka*. Each side of the dugout is raised by a wash strake. The ends are curved and decorated by painted carvings, often showing a mixed group of fishes surmounted by a seated parrot. The masthead is forked to receive the halyard and is usually ornamented with cassowary feathers. The rectangular sail made of pandana leaves is tall and narrow and fastened to a yard and boom.

WAFT.
See **Weft.**

WAGA. A single-outrigger, sailing dugout from Orangerie Bay and Louisiade Archipelago, British New Guinea, with long pointed ends, on the top of which a triangular flat board is fitted to form a shelf. There is a platform over the outrigger booms. The short longitudinal poles lashed between two booms. It is steadied by a curved mast shore. The pandana leaf sail has long, straight mast is stepped forward of half length on sides and rounded ends. Also called *vaga*.
See **Keama.**

WAGER POLICY. A marine insurance policy where the interest of the insured, although actually existing, would be difficult to define. Also called honor policy, policy proof of interest. These policies contain such clauses as "Full interest admitted" (F.I.A.) or "Policy Proof of Interest" (P.P.I.), thus exempting the insured from the necessity of proving his interest in the event of loss. They are not enforceable in British courts of law, but, as the name implies, are a matter of honor between underwriters and insured. In the United

States, France, Germany, Italy, and Holland, wager policies are enforceable in law courts.
Fr: *Police d'Honneur; Police de Pari;* Ger: *Wettpolice.*

WAI. A small dugout canoe from western and northern New Guinea.

WAIDON. A large dugout canoe from western and northern New Guinea, with horn-shaped ends, terminating in a knob.

WAIST. The central part of a ship. The portion of the upper deck between poop and forecastle.
Fr: *Coffre; Vibord;* Ger: *Kuhl.*

WAIST BOAT. In whaling vessels, the second mate's boat, carried in the ship's waist on the port side. (Obsolete.)

WAIST BREAST. A breast line from amidships, keeping a vessel to the dock; sometimes used in mooring or docking.

WAIST PLATE. The shell plate or bulwark plate which sweeps down at the break of the poop, bridge house, or forecastle deck to the next deck below.

WAIVER CLAUSE. A clause found in all marine policies whereby it is agreed that either party to the contract may take such steps or incur such expense as to minimize the loss without prejudice to the rights of the insured or insurer under the contract.
Fr: *Clause de Non Préjudice d'Abandon.*

WAKA-AMI-BUNE. An open Japanese fishing boat used on the coast of Hokkaido in the herring pound-net fisheries. The hull is carvel-built, without keel, and sharp flaring overhanging bows, strongly raking stem, narrow flat bottom, sides nearly vertical, raised after section, square stern with projecting sides, deep rudder extending well below the bottom, and stout crossbeams fitted to receive mast. Length over-all 35 ft. 10 in. Beam 9 ft. 4½ in. Depth 2 ft. 5 in. (Typical.)

WAKA-KORARI. A Moriori seagoing canoe of the Chatham Islands. The scow-shaped hull is made of a framework of tarata wood, which encloses bundles of flower stalks of the flax plant (*Phormium tenax*), the latter supplying the required buoyancy. The framework consists of a double keel or pair of runners about 10 in. apart and 2½ in. wide and ¾ in. thick. The bottom framing is made up of lengths of supplejack and *matipo* wood laid 2 in. apart. The flooring consists of closely packed flower stems of the flax plant about 6 in. in thickness tightly lashed to the bottom framework. The side framing is set vertically at right angles to the bottom framing, and is made up of the same material. The frames, which run from the stern to the point where the square bow curves upward, are 12 in. in length and spaced 2 in. apart. Lashed upon the outside of this frame is the side padding, constituted of flax sticks and fern stalks. The whole is surmounted by a gunwale formed of a pile of *matipo* shrub. Immediately below the gunwale and between it and the thwarts, on the inside of the structure, a roll of fern stalks tightly bound together by lashings 2 in. apart is laid from end to end of the canoe. These give extra buoyancy when the craft is deeply laden. As a further longitudinal strengthening of the structure a pole is fixed on each side under the thwarts, of which there are 5. According to some writers, the Moriori craft, in which the elements derived from a raft and a canoe are combined, was a development necessitated by the absence at Chatham Islands of any timber from which a dugout canoe could be made. Length 30 to 35 ft. Width 4 to 5 ft. These craft are extinct.
Skinner, H. D., Moriori Sea-going Craft, "Man," vol. 19, London, May (1919), no. 34.

WAKA-RIMU. A Moriori canoe of composite structure similar to the *waka-koraki.* It differs from the latter in that bull kelp is used instead of flower stalks of the flax plant in its construction.

WAKA TETE. A five-piece fishing canoe of New Zealand, without outrigger.

WAKE. The disturbed column of water around and behind a moving ship which is set into motion by the passage of the vessel. Also called wake current. This forward-moving water has a marked influence upon the efficiency of the propeller. It is greatest near the surface and close to the ship. For propeller purposes wake may be defined as the average speed in way of the propeller disk of the following current in which the propeller works, with reference to undisturbed water.
Fr: *Sillage;* Ger: *Totwasser; Kielwasser; Sog; Nachstrom; Mitstrom.*

Baker, G. S., Wake, North East Coast Institution of Engineers and Shipbuilders (Newcastle upon Tyne), *Transactions,* vol. 51, 1935; Calvert, G. A., "On the Measurement of Wake Currents," Institution of Naval

Architects (London), *Transactions*, vol. 35, 1893; Kempf, G., Mitstrom und Mitstromschrauben, *Jahrbuch*, Schiffbautechnische Gesellschaft, vol. 32 (Berlin, 1931).

WAKE COEFFICIENT. The ratio of the speed of the wake to the speed of the ship with reference to undisturbed water.

Fr: *Coefficient de Sillage*; Ger: *Mitstrom Koeffizient*.

Taylor, D. W., "Wake Propeller Coefficients," Institution of Naval Architects (London), *Transactions*, 1925, vol. 67.

WAKE FRACTION. The speed of the wake divided by the speed of the ship with reference to undisturbed water. Also called wake factor, wake value. Wake fraction is affected by the lines of the vessel, the number of propellers and their location. It varies for an individual propeller over the length of blade and is not a constant for any given point of the blade during a single revolution.

Fr: *Coefficient de Sillage*; Ger: *Sogziffer*.

WAKE GAIN. The increase in the effective thrust of a propeller, for a given power delivered to it, resulting from the forward motion of the water forming the wake behind the vessel's hull.

WAKE RESISTANCE. The resistance caused by a forward moving body of water called the frictional wake, at the stern of a vessel in motion. Also called eddy-making resistance. Its importance lies in the fact that the propeller works in water which has this forward velocity, causing an increased thrust.

Fr: *Résistance de Remous*; Ger: *Wirbelwiderstand*.

See **Wake**.

WAKE SPEED. The velocity of the stream or column of water which follows at the stern of a vessel underway.

Fr: *Vitesse de Sillage*; Ger: *Geschwindigkeit des Kielwassers*.

WALA. A single-outrigger, dugout canoe from East Malekula, New Hebrides, with long, pointed ends and 3 wash strakes, which form a boxlike superstructure with square ends.

WA-LAB. A single-outrigger, sailing canoe from the Marshall Islands. Also called *wa-lap*. The hull is built upon a dugout keel portion, with the sides raised by the addition of several irregularly shaped strakes of planking. These strakes abut at each end against upcurved stem and stern pieces. No frames are employed. The hull is stiffened internally by the two platform bulkheads and several thwarts. The mast is stepped in a socket outside the weather gunwale. It exceeds by several feet the length of the canoe and is made of 2 parts scarfed and seized. The sail is triangular with boom and yard, and is made of matting. It is set apex down, the tack resting against a pin step in the bows. Length 21 ft. Beam 30 in. Depth 32 in. Length of mast 23 ft. Yard and boom 24 ft. (Typical.)

WALE. 1. In an open boat the strake of planking running beneath the outer edge of the gunwale. Also called outer wale.

Fr: *Préceinte*; Ger: *Bordleiste*.

2. In a wooden vessel, a strake of outside planking broader and thicker than the others, and extending along the sides at different heights from stem to stern. Wales were reckoned from the waterline as first, second, and third bends. The beam knees and futtocks were bolted to them, and they were the main strength members in the ship's sides. The term has now become obsolete, as the planks between sheer and garboard strakes are usually all alike in thickness and method of fastening.

Fr: *Préceinte*; Ger: *Bergholz*.

WALE SHORE. See **Breast Shore.**

WALK BACK. 1. To reverse the action of a capstan so as to come up or ease the rope around it.

Fr: *Dévirer*; Ger: *Zurückdrehen*.

2. An order given to men hauling on a rope to keep the gear in hand, but walk back with it toward the belaying point.

WALLING See **Armoring.**

WALL KNOT. A knot made at the end of a rope by back-splicing the ends, thus forming a knob. Used for finishing off seizings, and on the end of a rope to prevent the rope from unreeving. Also called single wall knot.

Fr: *Cul de Porc Simple*; Ger: *Schauermannsknoten*; *Einfacher Taljereepsknoten*.

WALTELLE. A shallow-draft, open sailboat employed in the drag-net fisheries of the Kurische Haff, East Prussia. It is similar in type and rig to the *Keitelkahn and Kurrenkahn*, but of smaller size. Length 19 ft. Breadth 3.9 ft. Depth 1.6 ft. (Typical.)

WANG. 1. Single-outrigger, dugout canoe of the Webias people from northwestern New Caledonia.

2. A single-outrigger, dugout canoe from the Fiji Islands with covered ends, suited for sea work.

WANGGA. The equivalent of *vaka:* a generic term for an outrigger canoe in Austronesia.

WANGGA HUAHUA. A single-outrigger, paddling dugout canoe from Pentecost Island, New Hebrides. Each end of the canoe is made into a long flat shelf.

WANING MOON. A crescent moon with the open side toward the West.

Fr: *Déclin de la lune;* Ger: *Mondneigung; Abnehmender Mond.*

WAONA. A paddling and poling dugout canoe with single-outrigger. Some of the larger boats of this type are rigged with a mast and small sail. They are employed by the Mailu people of British New Guinea.

WAO-TETEAR. A plank-built canoe from Kei Islands, of type similar to the *belang*, but much smaller.

WAPAI. A large double-outrigger dugout canoe from Manokwari, New Guinea, about 30 ft. in length, with 25 in. beam. The outrigger framing consists of 7 crossbeams and 2 floats on each side. A shelter about 10 ft. long is built amidships. It extends outboard and is supported by 4 transverse booms. A stiffening bamboo bracing pole is lashed upon the booms.

The stem is provided with an additional piece with elaborate scroll design, open-work ornamentation. It is carved from a plank broad at the base and rising nearly vertically, terminating with a point. The rig consists of a tripod mast and oblong lugsail.

WAPP. Also wap, whap. A shroud stopper.

Fr: *Bosse de Hauban;* Ger: *Wantstopper.*

WAR CONTRABAND. Goods which neutrals may not, according to international law, carry in time of war to either of the belligerent nations without subjecting themselves to the loss of the goods, also to the loss of the ship and other cargo, if intercepted. Also called contraband of war.

Fr: *Contrebande de Guerre;* Ger: *Kriegskonterbande.*

The meaning of the term is generally defined by treaty provisions enumerating the articles which shall be deemed contraband of war. Contraband articles contaminate noncontraband if belonging to the same owner.

Favraud, *Contrebande de guerre, blocus, droit de visite*, Paris, 1916; Pyke, H. R., *Law of Contraband of War*, Oxford, 1915.

WARD ROOM. Messroom assigned to officers in a warship.

WAREHOUSE RECEIPT. See **Warrant**.

WAREHOUSE TO WAREHOUSE CLAUSE. Marine insurance clause whereby the period of the policy insures the goods from time of leaving the store or warehouse at the place named in the policy, and continues during the ordinary course of transit until the goods are discharged at the final port. Thereafter the insurance continues while the goods are in transit, or awaiting transit, until delivered to final warehouse at the place named in the policy.

Fr: *Clause Magasin à Magasin.*

WA-RIRIK. A double-ended, plank-built boat with single-outrigger, used for fishing in the Gilbert Islands, Micronesia. Also called oa. It is rigged with a large triangular sail set with apex downward. Length 15 to 24 ft. Breadth 15 to 24 in. Depth 24 to 36 in.

WARNING LIGHT. A lighthouse marking some dangerous rock, headland, or other obstruction to navigation. The classification of warning lights usually includes light vessels, lighted buoys, and beacons.

Fr: *Feu d'Avertissement;* Ger: *Warnungsfeuer.*

WARP. 1. A fiber or wire rope, by which a vessel is moved about when in harbor. Warps are made fast to buoys or other fixed objects and when heaved upon bring the vessel gradually alongside or away from a pier, quay, jetty, and so on.

Fr: *Aussière de Halage; Touline;* Ger: *Pferdeleine; Verholleine; Warptrosse; Verholtrosse.*

2. A unit used by herring fishermen on the east coast of Great Britain (Yarmouth). It is equal to 4 fish. Thirty-three warps make a long hundred (132 fish).

3. A lengthwise measurement of canvas. The threads along the length of sail cloth. Also called chain.

Fr: *Chaîne;* Ger: *Kette.*

See **Box Warp, Fire Warp, Ground Warp, Guess Warp, Herring Warp, Trawl Warp.**

WARP (to). To move a vessel from one place to another in a port, river, harbor by means of warps fastened to buoys, anchors or some fixed object ashore.

Fr: *Déhaler; Touliner;* Ger: *Verholen; Warpen.*

WARPING. In welding, the slight bulge-out or upset which occurs in the base metal in way of the line of welding when the temperature has fallen to that of the surrounding atmosphere.

Fr: *Déformation;* Ger: *Krümmung.*

WARPING BRIDGE. A bridge or platform situated at the afterend of the vessel and used only while docking. Also called after bridge, docking bridge.

Fr: *Passerelle Arrière;* Ger: *Achterbrücke.*

WARPING BUOY. A buoy so placed that it can be used with lines for moving or directing the movements of ships by warping.

Fr: *Bouée de Halage;* Ger: *Verholboje.*

WARPING CAPSTAN. A power capstan used for handling mooring or towlines. No provision is made for hand operation and it has no cable holder. Also called gypsy capstan, gypsy.

Fr: *Cabestan de touage;* Ger: *Verholspill.*

WARPING WINCH. A steam- or electric-powered winch used for warping a vessel alongside a pier or quay and also for moving the ship from one place to another about a dock or harbor by means of hawsers, without the assistance of tugs or of the main propelling engines. Also called mooring winch. It is usually located aft and is of the single or compound geared type. It is designed to develop a pull on the lines equal to at least half the breaking strength of the mooring lines and warps required to be carried by the vessel. It should be capable of withstanding the full breaking strength of these lines without damage. The construction is the same as that of a cargo winch without drum and with the addition of long extensions of the main shaft which carry at each end a warping head. The warping winch is occasionally used for handling cargo booms and is so placed that it can also be used for emergency steering with relieving tackles.

Fr: *Treuil de déhalage;* Ger: *Verholwinde.*

WARP-LAID ROPE. The same as cable-laid rope excepting that the primary strand and the finished cable have a shorter lay.

See **Cable-Laid Rope.**

WARP YARN. The thread which is extended lengthwise in a loom and across which the weft yarn is thrown in the process of weaving. Also warp thread.

Fr: *Fil de Chaîne;* Ger: *Kettengarn.*

WARRANTY. A warranty in a contract of marine insurance is a condition which must be exactly complied with, whether it be material to the risk or not. If not so complied with, the insurer is discharged from liability as from the date of the breach of the warranty. There are two forms of warranty, implied and express warranty.

Fr: *Garantie;* Ger: *Garantie.*

See **Express Warranty, Implied Warranty, Institute Warranties, Loading Warranties, Trading Warranties.**

WARRANTY OF LEGALITY. An implied warranty in a charter party, that the adventure is a lawful one and that it shall be carried out in a lawful manner.

WARRANTY OF NEUTRALITY. An implied warranty, in marine insurance policies, that the ship and/or cargo shall have a neutral character at the commencement of the risk and that so far as the insured can control the matter, its neutral character shall be preserved during the risk.

WAR RISK. In marine insurance, one of the risks arising from consequences of hostilities or warlike operations. The word "hostilities" is here intended to describe an actual operation, offensive or defensive, in the conduct of war. The perils insured under war risks must be due directly to some hostile action to be a war risk. Should the peril be a marine risk and be but aggravated or increased by the operation relied on as a warlike operation, then the risk is not a war risk.

Fr: *Risque de Guerre;* Ger: *Kriegsgefahr; Kriegsrisiko.*

Hasket Derby, S., "What Are Warlike Operations Under F. C. and S. Clause in Marine Policies?" *California Law Review*, vol. 33, March, 1945; Heynen, H., *Die Kriegsseeversicherung*, Altona, 1928; Schonfeld, J., *Risque de Guerre en Matière d'Assurances Maritimes*, Paris, 1916.

WARSAW-OXFORD RULES. A set of rules adopted and endorsed by the International Law Association in 1931 for international cost-insurance and freight contracts. These rules cover such points as time of shipment, evidence of date, rights and obligations of seller and buyer as to insurance, bills of lading, loss and damage after shipment.

WARY. Flat-bottomed, open boat used for inshore fishing in Newfoundland and

Nova Scotia, equipped with a small motor.

WASH. 1. The loose or broken water left behind a vessel as it moves along. The water thrown aft by screw or paddle wheels.
Fr: *Remous;* Ger: *Wellenschlag.*
2. The blade of an oar (G. B.).
See **Blade.**

WASH BOARD. 1. A strake of thin planking fitted above the gunwale in open boats or around the edge of a cockpit. It increases the freeboard and keeps out the spray. Also called Weatherboard, Waste board, Wash strake.
Fr: *Fargue;* Ger: *Setzbord; Waschbord; Dollbord.*
2. Angular pieces of wood placed under the lower cheeks.

WASH BULKHEAD.
See **Swash Bulkhead.**

WASH PLATE. Vertical fore-and-aft plate fitted in deep tanks and peaks for lessening the movements of loose water in these compartments, and decreasing the free-surface effect. Also called swash plate (U. S.).
Fr: *Tôle de Roulis.*

WASH PORT.
See **Freeing Port.**

WASTE-HEAT BOILER. An auxiliary boiler installed on motor ships to provide steam for operating auxiliaries, and at the same time to improve the over-all efficiency of the installation. These boilers are usually provided with fuel oil burners in conjunction with a small fuel oil burning plant, so that they are available for use in port when the main engines are not in operation, the steam being used to drive cargo winches, pumps, and so forth.
Fr: *Chaudière de récupération;* Ger: *Auspuffkessel; Abgaskessel.*

WATCH. 1. The part of a ship's company which is employed in working it at one time. Deck hands are usually divided into port and starboard watches, and the engine-room and fireroom forces into three watches. In cases of emergency or when the ship is getting under way, coming to anchor, or performing some evolution requiring all available men, both watches (all hands) are called.
Fr: *Bordée;* Ger: *Wache; Schiffswache.*
2. The sixth part of a day on board ship during which a watch of men are on duty. In ships sailing under Danish, Swedish, and Dutch flag, it is customary to divide the day into five watches: from midnight to 4 A.M. then from 4 A.M. to 8 A.M., the first two watches being short, four-hour watches. Then comes a 5-hour watch from 8 A.M. to 1 P.M. followed by a 6-hour watch from 1 P.M. to 7 or 7:30 P.M. and finally the last watch of 5 hours, from 7 P.M. to midnight. In this system there are no dog watches.
Fr: *Quart;* Ger: *Wache; Schiffswache.*
See **Afternoon Watch, Anchor Watch, Calashee Watch, Deck Watch, Dog Watch, First Dog Watch, First Watch, Forenoon Watch, Middle Watch, Morning Watch, Quarter Watch, Radio Watch, Second Dog Watch.**

WASHSTRAKE. In decked craft a board or plank forming the lower part of the bulwarks and resting on the covering board. Also called **Washboard.**
Fr: *Fargue;* Ger: *Sétzbord.*

WATCH (to). To appear above the surface of the water, for example, the anchor buoy is said to watch when it is visible above the water surface.

WATCH AND WATCH. The arrangement whereby one half of the crew of a vessel is on duty for 4 hours and the other half for the next 4 hours.
Fr: *Quarts à Courir;* Ger: *Wache um Wache.*

WATCH ASHORE. A system of watches in use on colliers of the northeast coast of Great Britain. Also called watch aboard. The seamen work in separate loading watches, each watch loading the ship alternately. The firemen on the arrival of the ship in loading port wipe the engines down and finish, and except for slight repairs these men do not rejoin the ship until sailing time, or when required for raising steam to be ready for sea.

WATCH BELOW. That part of a ship's company which is off duty when watches are kept.
Fr: *Quart en Bas;* Ger: *Freiwache.*

WATCH BUOY. Small buoy placed near a light vessel to indicate whether it is dragging at its moorings. Also called marker buoy.
Fr: *Bouée de Veille;* Ger: *Markierungsboje.*

WATCH CAP. 1. Canvas or sheet-iron cover placed over the stack of a vessel when it is laid up, or when the boilers are secured. Also called stack cover.

Fr: *Capuchon de Cheminée;* Ger: *Schornsteinkappe.*

2. A streamlined shield placed over the forward part of the stack opening, designed to keep stack gases from eddying and being carried forward to the navigating bridge.

WATCH ENGINEER.
See **Assistant Engineer.**

WATCH OFFICER. The officer in charge of a watch. Upon him the responsibility of the safe and proper navigation of the vessel rests during the whole of his watch on deck.

Fr: *Officier de Quart;* Ger: *Wachhabender Offizier; Wachoffizier.*

WATCH ON DECK. The opposite of "watch below."

Fr: *Quart en haut;* Ger: *Wache in See.*

WATCH TACKLE. A small, handy purchase used for various purposes about the decks. It may be either a luff or gun tackle rove with a fall of 2 in. or less. One block is usually provided with sister hooks, and the other with a tail.

Fr: *Mousse; Palan de Dimanche;* Ger: *Handtalje.*

WATER BAILIFF. An officer in various port towns of Great Britain charged with the enforcement of shipping regulations, the searching of vessels, and the collection of customs. Also an official responsible for the by-laws relating to sea fisheries.

WATER BALLAST. Sea water carried in double-bottom tanks, peak tanks, deep tanks, or other compartments in order to obtain satisfactory conditions of draft, trim, or stability.

Fr: *Lest d'eau;* Ger: *Wasserballast.*
Bocler, E., "The Ballasting of Merchant Ships," North East Coast Institution of Engineers and Shipbuilders (Newcastle upon Tyne), *Transactions,* vol. 58 (1942); Chaston, E. C., "The Ballasting of Tramp Steamers," North East Coast Institution of Engineers and Shipbuilders (Newcastle upon Tyne), *Transactions,* vol. 18 (1902); Frear, H. P., "Use of Water Ballast for Colliers in the Pacific Coast Trade," Society of Naval Architects and Marine Engineers, New York, *Transactions,* vol. 5 (1897); Thearle, S. J. P., *The Ballasting of Steamers for North Atlantic Voyages,* Institution of Naval Architects (London), *Transactions,* vol. 45 (1903).

WATER BOAT. A small, self-propelled tank boat used in harbors for supplying fresh water to seagoing vessels. Water boats are supplied with pumps of large capacity and hose connections necessary for rapid discharge of water into the ship's tanks.

Fr: *Bateau-Citerne;* Ger: *Wasserfahrzeug; Wasserprahme; Wasserboot.*

WATERBORNE. 1. Said of a boat or vessel when supported by the water and clear of the ground upon which it has rested.

Fr: *A flot;* Ger: *Schwimmend; Flott.*

2. Carried or transported by water; conveyed by ship or boat. Specifically when referring to trade, commerce or traffic.

3. Said of goods placed aboard a ship or boat.

WATER BOTTOM (U. S.). The space between the outer bottom and tank top plating used for carrying water ballast, fresh water or fuel oil. Also **Double bottom.**

Fr: *Double fond;* Ger: *Doppelboden.*

WATER BREAKER. A small cask carried in ship's boats, containing drinking water.

Fr: *Baril de Galère;* Ger: *Bootsfass.*

WATERCOURSE. See **Limber Hole.**

WATER CLERK. A shipbroker's employee in the days when ships arrived unchartered at a port and the shipmaster himself was the owner. The brokers secured the ship through the water clerk. To effect this he had to go on board to obtain the clearance from the master. Nowadays the owner himself effects the chartering through his broker.

Ger: *Hafenkommis.*

WATER CRAFT. Generic term for every sort of boat or vessel capable of being used as a means of transportation by water.

WATER FINDER. A graduated rod about twelve inches long to which is attached water-finding litmus paper or paste. It is used by tankermen when taking ullages to determine the amount of water present in a tank. Also **Thief sampler.**

WATERGUARD.
See **Customs Guard.**

WATER HOLE. A hole cut in the lower part of a watersail to prevent its being damaged by a sea.

WATER-LAID ROPE. Three- or four-stranded rope laid up left-handed, made by wetting the fibers with water before spinning, instead of using oil or tallow. Water-laid rope has less tensile strength than plain-laid cordage of the same diameter. It has more elasticity and is, therefore, frequently used for salvage and towing purposes. It is also used for log and lead lines.

Fr: *Cordage Câblé au Mouillé.*

WATER LIGHT. See Lifebuoy Light.

WATERLINE LENGTH. Length measured from front of stem to back of rudder post at designed waterline level.

Fr: *Longueur à la Flottaison;* Ger: *Wasserlinielänge.*

WATERLINE MODEL. A model which indicates the external shape of the vessel at the various levels that are used in drawing up the ship's lines.

WATERLINES. 1. The intersection of horizontal planes with the hull of a ship.
2. Horizontal lines parallel to the base line in the body plan.
3. Horizontal lines parallel to the base line in the sheer plan, or curved lines in the half-breadth plan.

Fr: *Lignes d'Eau;* Ger: *Konstruktionswasserlinien.*

See **Body Plan, Half-Breadth Plan, Sheer Plan.**

WATERLOGGED. Saturated or filled with water. The condition of a ship when by leaking and receiving a great quantity of water into its hold it has become unmanageable or nearly so, and is kept afloat only by the buoyancy of her cargo.

WATERMAN. A boatman. A ferryman. A man who manages water craft. One who plies for hire in docks, harbors, or on rivers. A boatman who attends to the berthing of vessels. Also called line runner.

Fr: *Canotier; Passeur;* Ger: *Fährmann.*

WATERMAN'S KNOT. A crossed seizing between two eyes in ropes.

See **Clove Hitch.**

Fr: *Demi Clefs Renversées;* Ger: *Webeleinstek.*

WATER MARKS. Scale of feet or meters cut on each side of stem- and sternpost, or affixed to them, to denote the ship's draft. Also called draft marks. The letters on trading vessels are 6 in. high and are painted white on dark ground or vice versa. The lower line of each figure denotes the draft.

Fr: *Échelle de Tirants d'Eau;* Ger: *Tiefgansmarken.*

WATERPLANE COEFFICIENT. The ratio of the area of the load waterplane to the circumscribing rectangle.

Ships with fine ends 0.70
Ships of ordinary form........ 0.75
Ships with bluff ends 0.85

Also called load waterline coefficient.

Fr: *Coefficient de Remplissage à la Flottaison;* Ger: *Völligkeitsgrad der Konstruktionswasserlinie; Wasserlinienvölligkeitsgrad.*

WATERPROOF GLUE. Ordinary glue to which a very small quantity of formaldehyde (1 to 3 per cent) is added when the glue solution is in the hot state just before using.

WATER SAIL. 1. A sail formerly set under a lower studding sail boom or Passaree boom. The name today refers to a long rectangular sail of little depth extended under a boomed mainsail when running before the wind. It is either laced to the boom or to a row of eyelets which run along the foot of the boom. Also called save all.

Fr: *Bonnette de Sous-Gui;* Ger: *Wassersegel.*

2. A triangular sail which sets under the bowsprit and is used by the British fishing luggers from East Cornwall when on a passage to or from the fishing grounds.

WATER SEASONING. A method of seasoning which consists in storing timber, usually in the form of logs, under water. The water acts not only by excluding the air but also by dissolving the impurities in the timber, rendering it more durable and less liable to warp.

WATER SERVICE PUMP. 1. A pump for circulating cooling water through shaft bearings, and the crosshead guides of a reciprocator.
2. The combined fire and bilge pump. Also called general service pump.

Fr: *Pompe de Service;* Ger: *Verkehrspumpe.*

WATERSHED. A fitting over a door or window on an exposed deck to prevent water from entering from above.

WATER SKY. Dark streaks showing on the sky in high latitudes. They are due to the reflection of water spaces or of the open sea in the neighborhood of large areas of sea ice.

Fr: *Ciel d'Eau;* Ger: *Wasserhimmel.*

WATERSPOUT. A phenomenon at sea of the same character as a whirlwind or tornado on land, causing a rain cloud to be drawn down as a tapering funnel to the surface of the water.

Fr: *Trombe;* Ger: *Wasserhose.*

Visher, S. S., "Waterspouts," *Geographical Society of Philadelphia, Bulletin,* vol. 28, July, 1930.

WATERSTOP RING. A rubber ring fitted around the propeller shaft at the forward face of the propeller boss to prevent water seepage to the after-end of the shaftliner. Compression of the ring is effected either by the propeller nut or by a glandring adjusted independently.

WATER TELESCOPE. A metal tube 4 to 8 ft. long and 5 to 6 in. in diameter fitted with a plate glass inserted at the end. It is used by fishermen and others to see underwater.

Fr: *Lunette d'Eau;* Ger: *Wasserkieker.*

WATER TENDER (U. S.). An unlicensed petty officer who directs the maintenance of specified steam pressure in a ship powered by cylindrical or water tube boilers. He checks boiler gages to determine the need for water in the boilers and regulates valves and equipment such as heaters, pumps or injectors of the water feeding system; notes reading of steam pressure gages to determine need for increasing or diminishing boiler fires and regulates fuel oil valves or directs the trimming of coal fires as necessary to keep desired steam pressure constant. Must hold certificate of competence for water tender.

Fr: *Alimenteur;* Ger: *Donkeymann.*

WATERTIGHT. Impervious to the passage of water, as applied to ship's structure, closures, and joints.

Fr: *Étanche à l'Eau; Étanche;* Ger: *Wasserdicht.*

WATERTIGHT BULKHEAD. One of the main vertical partitions in a ship. It is strongly built, with joints which are tight enough to withstand the pressure of the hydrostatic head and prevent water escaping into adjoining spaces if the compartment fills with water.

Fr: *Cloison Étanche;* Ger: *Wasserdichtes Schott.*

The minimum number of main transverse watertight bulkheads is 4 for vessels with the machinery amidships and 3 when the machinery is aft. Watertight bulkheads also contribute to the structural strength of the ship, and act as safeguards against the spread of fire.

WATERTIGHT DECK. A deck so constructed as to prevent water from passing through in an upward or downward direction, if flooding occurs.

Fr: *Pont Étanche;* Ger: *Wasserdichtes Deck.*

WATERTIGHT DOOR. A metal door in a watertight bulkhead so constructed that when closed it will prevent water under pressure from passing through. The two designs of doors most commonly found on board ship are the hinged door and the sliding door. The latter may be of the horizontal or vertical type. The framing of the doorway and the door itself are sufficiently strong to withstand the pressure to which they are exposed in the event of flooding.

Fr: *Porte Étanche;* Ger: *Wasserdichte Tür.*

WATERTIGHT FLAT. A partial deck made watertight.

Fr: *Plateforme Étanche;* Ger: *Wasserdichte Plattform.*

WATERTIGHT FLOOR. A solid floor placed at the end of a ballast tank, or well, also under transverse bulkheads, forming one of the subdivisions of the double bottom.

Fr: *Varangue Étanche;* Ger: *Wasserdichte Bodenwrange.*

WATERTIGHT FRAMES. Frames having solid floor plates between the frame bar, reverse bar and longitudinal girders, in ships built with double bottom, thus dividing the double bottom space into a number of watertight compartments.

Fr: *Couple Étanche;* Ger: *Wasserdichter Spant.*

WATERTIGHT HATCH. A steel hatch cover, the bearing edges of which are pressed down onto the coaming by dogs. A gasket is installed to insure watertightness.

Fr: *Panneau Étanche;* Ger: *Wasserdichte Luke.*

WATERTIGHT RIVETING. Riveting for joints which are to be watertight. To ensure efficient calking, the spacing of rivets should not exceed 4 to 4½ diameters.

Fr: *Rivetage Étanche à l'Eau;* Ger: *Wasserdichte Nietung.*

WATER-TUBE BOILER. A steam generator in which the water is carried in tubes and is heated from hot gases surrounding the tubes. The main advantages of water-tube boilers as compared with the fire-tube type are rapid generation of steam, compactness and lighter weight. The saving in space amounts to 10 to 15 per cent and the average gain in weight is 35 to 45 per cent. Although rapid development is taking place in the use of water-tube boilers for merchant steamers a number of steam propelled cargo vessels is still equipped with

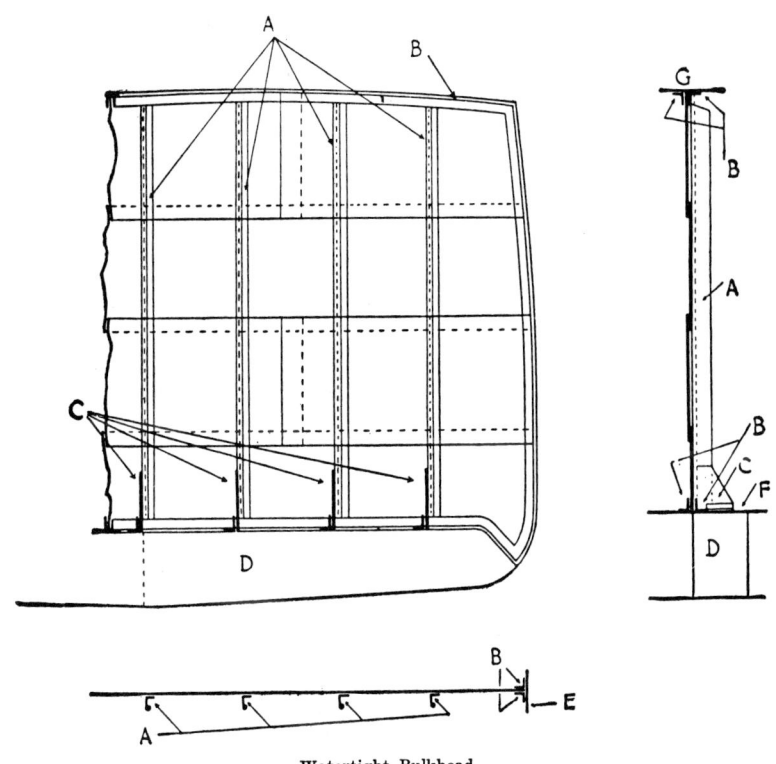

A. Stiffener   **B. Boundary bar**   **C. Bracket**   Watertight Bulkhead   **D. Double bottom**   **E. Shell plating**
F. Tank top   **G. Deck plating**

fire-tube steam generators. On the other hand, oil-fired water-tube boilers are now exclusively adopted for all the largest ocean liners with a service speed of over 20 knots as in this class of vessels space occupied, weight, and steaming capacity are the main considerations. During World War II, the majority of cargo ships constructed used this type of boiler, as do almost all warships.
    Fr: *Chaudière Aquatubulaire;* Ger: *Wasserrohrkessel.*

King and Cox, Development of Marine Watertube Boilers, Society of Naval Architects and Marine Engineers, *Historical Transactions* (New York, 1945); Whayman, W. M., Watertube Boilers for Merchant Ships, Institute of Marine Engineers (London), *Transactions,* vol. 42 (1930–1931).

WATERWAY. 1. In a wooden vessel, one of the thick strakes of planking at the sides of a deck, worked over the ends of beams and inside of top timbers, to which, as well as to the ends of beams, they are bolted. They serve to connect the sides of a ship to the decks and form a gutter to carry off any water by means of scuppers.
    Fr: *Gouttière;* Ger: *Wassergang; Leibholz.*

2. In a steel ship, the gutter formed along the sides of a steel weather deck by the waterway angle bar and the gunwale bar so that deck drainage may lodge therein until it escapes through the scuppers. Also called gutter waterway.
    Fr: *Rigole; Cunette;* Ger: *Rinne; Wasserlauf.*

See **Innerwater Way, International Waterway, Outer Waterway.**

WATERWAY BAR. An angle bar on top of the upper deck stringer plate running parallel to the gunwale bar and forming therewith a gutterway which leads the water to the scuppers. It serves as an abutment for the wooden deck planking. Also called gutter bar.

Fr: *Cornière Rigole;* Ger: *Rinnsteinwinkel; Wasserlaufswinkel.*

WAVE. Oscillatory movement of the sea which results in an alternate rise and fall at the surface. Waves are produced by the wind blowing at the time and place of observation as distinguished from swells, which usually result from a storm at a place more or less distant.

Fr: *Lame; Vague;* Ger: *Welle.*

See **Bow Wave, Diverging Waves, Seismic Waves, Stern Wave, Synchronous Wave, Tidal Wave, Transverse Waves, Trochoidal Wave.**

Cornish, Vaughan, *Ocean Waves,* Cambridge, 1934; Patton and Marmer, "The Waves of the Sea," U. S. National Research Council, Bulletin 85, Chapter 6, Washington, 1932; Thorade, H., *Probleme der Wasserwellen,* Hamburg, 1931; Wheeler, *Practical Manual of Tides and Waves,* New York, 1906.

WAVE AMPLITUDE. One half the vertical distance from trough to crest of an ocean wave.

Ger: *Wellenschwingungsweite.*

WAVE CREST. The highest part of a wave. The line along the top of a wave.

Fr: *Crête;* Ger: *Kamm.*

WAVE HOLLOW. The depression between two wave crests. Also called trough.

Fr: *Creux;* Ger: *Wellental.*

WAVE LENGTH. The length of wave is the distance in feet between consecutive crests or troughs measured in a direction perpendicular to the crest lines. The horizontal distance from crest to crest or from hollow to hollow.

Fr: *Distance de Crête en Crête;* Ger: *Wellenlänge.*

WAVE PERIOD. Time in seconds taken by a wave to move through a distance equal to its own length. Time between the passage of two succeeding wave crests past a fixed point.

Fr: *Période de Houle;* Ger: *Wellenumlauf; Wellenperiode.*

WAVE PROFILE. The wave outline against the ship's side with reference to the bow wave, which for a given speed and ship assumes a fairly constant size, shape, and position relative to the ship's length. When dealing with strength calculations, a trochoidal deep sea wave is assumed and its profile is considered as conforming closely to a mathematical law, with length equal to that of the ship on the designer's waterline, and height from trough to crest equal to one twentieth the length.

Fr: *Profil de la Houle;* Ger: *Wellenlinie.*

See **Trochoidal Wave.**

WAVE RESISTANCE. The energy expended by a ship in the formation of the systems of waves at bow and stern. It is second in importance only to frictional resistance. Its value lies between 10 and 30 per cent of the total resistance for most ships. Also called wave-making resistance.

Fr: *Résistance due aux Vagues;* Ger: *Wellenwiderstand.*

Wigley, W. C. S., "Ship Wave Resistance," Institution of Naval Architects (London), *Transactions,* vol. 77 (1935).

WAVE SLOPE. The angle of inclination of the surface of a wave at any point, to the horizontal.

Fr: *Déclivité de la Houle;* Ger: *Wellengefälle.*

WAVE VELOCITY. The rate at which the wave crest travels forward. It is obtained by dividing the wavelength by the period, the result being the velocity in feet or meters per second.

Fr: *Vitesse de Houle;* Ger: *Wellengeschwindigkeit.*

WAVE WAKE. Wake due to the orbital movement of the water set up by the ship's wave pattern.

WAXING MOON. A crescent moon with the open side to the East.

Fr: *Crossement de la lune;* Ger: *Zunehmender Mond.*

WAY. The progress or motion through the water of a vessel. A vessel gathers way when its rate of sailing increases. It loses way when the rate diminishes.

Fr: *Erre;* Ger: *Fahrt.*

See **Give Way, Sternway, Underway.**

WAY ENOUGH. An order to a boat's crew when the craft has enough way on to reach her destination. The crew takes one more stroke, then tosses and boats the oars and unships the rowlocks.

Fr: *Laisse Aller; Laisse Courir;* Ger: *Lass Laufen.*

WAYS. The timber sills upon which a ship is built.

See **Launching Ways.**

WAYS-END. The end of the building slip and launching ways, which extends to the water.

Fr: *Avant-Cale;* Ger: *Vorhelling.*

WEAR (to). To bring a vessel sailing close-hauled to another tack by putting the helm

up and turning her head away from the wind. The opposite of to tack. Also called ware.
Fr: *Virer Lof Pour Lof;* Ger: *Vor dem Wind halsen.*
See **Gybe.**

WEAR AND TEAR. The decay and deterioration of the hull, engines, boilers, equipment, and outfit of a vessel in the course of a voyage.
Fr: *Usure;* Ger: *Verschleiss; Abnutzung; Altersschaden.*

WEARING.
See **Rising.**

WEATHER. The state of the atmosphere with respect to its cloudiness, humidity, motions, pressure, temperature, or any other meteorological phenomena.
Fr: *Temps;* Ger: *Wetter.*
See **Bad Weather, Stress of Weather, Thick Weather.**

WEATHER (to). 1. To bear up against and come safely through, as a ship in a storm, and so on.
Fr: *Etaler;* Ger: *Aushalten.*
2. When two ships are sailing close-hauled on parallel courses and one gains directly to windward of the other, the former is said to weather the latter.
3. To pass to windward of an object.
Fr: *S'Élever; Doubler;* Ger: *Umsegeln; Leewärts vorübersegeln.*

WEATHERBITT (to). 1. To take an extra turn of cable about the anchor bitts or windlass end as a precaution in bad weather. (Obsolete.)
2. The bitt to which the weather cable is secured when a ship is moored. (Obsolete.)

WEATHERBOARD. Also storm board.
1. A board which fits in the doorway of a cabin or other enclosed space on a weather deck to prevent the inrush of water in bad weather.
2. Pieces of board fitted over open ports to turn the water or rain off.
Fr: *Auvent;* Ger: *Wasserboard; Waschbrett.*

WEATHER CLEW. 1. The tack, or forward corner, of a fore-and-aft sail.
2. The largest middle cloth of a lugsail. So called by fishermen and sailmakers.
Fr: *Point d'Amure;* Ger: *Luv Schothorn.*

WEATHER CLOTH. A shelter cloth made of canvas and made fast to the weather mizzen rigging of a sailing vessel or on the sides and front of the bridge in a steamer, also around the crow's nest to keep spray and rain off the watch-standers. Also called dodger. Bridge dodgers are made of no. 1 to no. 3 canvas, roped, and fitted with grommet eyes for lacing or lashing to jackstay.
Fr: *Cagnard;* Ger: *Schutzkleid; Schauerkleid.*

WEATHER DECK. An uncovered deck exposed to the weather. The upper, awning, shade or shelter decks or the uppermost continuous deck, exclusive of forecastle, bridge and poop, which are also exposed to the weather.
Fr: *Pont Découvert; Pont Exposé;* Ger: *Freideck; Wetterdeck.*

WEATHER FLAG. A pennant or a square flag displayed as a weather signal.
Ger: *Wettersignal Flagge.*
See **Weather Signal.**

WEATHER GAUGE. The advantage of the wind. It refers to the position of a ship under sail when she is windward of another ship.
Fr: *Avantage du vent; Dessus du vent;* Ger: *Luv Wind Seite.*

WEATHER HELM. A ship is said to carry weather helm when it has a tendency to come up to the wind and requires the helm up constantly to keep a straight course. The opposite of "lee helm."
Fr: *Barre au Vent;* Ger: *Luvruder.*

WEATHERLINESS. The ability of a sailing boat to carry sufficient canvas in a hard breeze to enable her to get to windward. In order to ensure weatherliness, the sail plan is usually designed to keep the center of effort abaft the center of lateral resistance.
Ger: *Luvgierigkeit.*

WEATHERLY. Said of a sailing craft making little leeway when close-hauled, in a stiff breeze and heavy sea.
Fr: *Boulinier;* Ger: *Luvgierig.*

WEATHERLY QUALITIES. Easy behavior of the ship at sea and a sufficient amount of freeboard, so as not to be readily swept by the waves.
Fr: *Qualités Nautiques;* Ger: *Seefähigkeit.*
See **Steering Qualities.**

WEATHER PERMITTING CLAUSE. A charter party clause which specifies that lay days do not count when weather conditions are such as to prevent the normal working of cargo.

WEATHER QUARTER. The quarter of a ship which is on the windward side.
Fr: *Hanche du vent;* Ger: *Windvierung.*

WEATHER SHORE. The land lying in the direction from which the wind is coming.
Ger: *Luvwall; Upperwall.*

WEATHER SIDE. The opposite of "lee side." The side of the vessel from which the wind is blowing.
Fr: *Bord du Vent;* Ger: *Luvseite.*

WEATHER SIGNAL. A local signal which usually consists of flag hoists indicating the weather forecast. It should be distinguished from storm-warning signals.
Fr: *Signal d'indication du temps; Signal atmosphérique;* Ger: *Wetter Anzeigesignal.*

WEATHER SYMBOLS. A code of letters indicating the state of weather. It was originally introduced by Admiral Beaufort and has been in use since 1838.

b. —Blue Sky
b.c.—Partly Cloudy
c. —Cloudy
d. —Drizzle
e. —Wet air without rain falling
f. —Fog
g. —Gloomy
h. —Hail
l. —Lightning
m. —Mist
o. —Overcast
p. —Passing showers
q. —Squalls
kq.—Line squall
r. —Rain
r.s.—Sleet
s. —Snow
t. —Thunder
t.l. —Thunderstorm
u. —Ugly, threatening sky
v. —Unusual visibility
w. —Dew
x. —Hoar frost
y. —Dry air (less than 60 per cent humidity)
z. —Haze

Under the International Meteorological Convention of 1921 a capital letter is used to denote intensity of the phenomenon to be noted. Slight intensity is indicated by a small suffix.
Ger: *Wetterskala.*

WEATHER TIDE. A tide which will carry a ship under sail to windward.
Fr: *Marée Portant au Vent;* Ger: *Luvwärts setzende Gezeit.*

WEATHERTIGHT DECK. A term applied to an exposed deck through which in normal sea conditions water will not penetrate in a "downward" direction.
Ger: *Wetterdichtes Deck.*

WEATHERTIGHT DOOR. A term applied to outside doors on an upper deck, which are designed to keep out rain and spray only.
Ger: *Wetterdichte Tür.*

WEATHER WORKING DAYS. Days on which the weather permits working during customary hours for such work at a port. It refers particularly to freight which might suffer damage from being unloaded during rain. Days during which exposure would not seriously damage the particular cargo or goods to be handled.

WEAVING. 1. See **Brading.**
2. In electric arc welding, a semicircular motion of the arc terminal to the right and left of the direction of deposition which serves to increase the width of the deposit, decrease overlap, and assist in slag flotation. Also called weaving the bead.

WEB. The central portion of a structure as distinguished from its flanges and bosses. A girder web is the main vertical plate which becomes the connection between the top and the bottom flanges and which absorbs most of the shearing forces.
Fr: *Ame;* Ger: *Steg.*
See **Hatch Web.**

WEB FRAME. A frame composed of a web plate with bars riveted or welded to each edge. Web frames are fitted at every fourth, fifth or sixth ordinary frame when there are no hold beams or in spaces such as engine or boiler rooms where there is a great depth of side unsupported between the bottom and the lowest deck.
Fr: *Porque;* Ger: *Rahmenspant.*

WEB FRAMING. The web system of framing consists principally in making a large reduction in the scantlings of the ordinary frames and regaining the strength thus lost by converting every fifth or sixth frame into a deep girder or web frame. This type of framing has now been abandoned for cargo ships owing to the loss of stowage capacity, particularly with case goods, but is in general use for warships.
Fr: *Construction à Porques;* Ger: *Rahmenspannung.*

WEB PLATE. A wide girder plate, as in a web frame or hatch beam, usually reinforced by angle bars on both sides.

WEB SLING. A rope sling in which the sides are connected by rope webbing or strong canvas. It is used for bagged cargo that might be cut or burst open by the pressure of an ordinary rope sling. Animals are also taken aboard with web slings. Also called animal slings.
Fr: *Elingue Entoilée;* Ger: **Brooke.**

WEDGE OF EMERSION. The portion

of a ship which emerges from beneath the water plane when the vessel is inclined or given a list without changing its displacement.
Fr: *Onglet d'Émersion;* Ger: *Auftauchendes Keilstück.*

WEDGE OF IMMERSION. The portion of a ship's body which becomes immersed when the vessel is given a transverse inclination without alteration in its displacement.
Fr: *Onglet d'Immersion;* Ger: *Eintauchendes Keilstück.*

of the sliding ways and the cradle. As these wedges are driven in on each side they tend to lift the ship, thereby removing the weight from the shores and transferring it to the sliding ways. Sometimes called setting up.
Fr: *Billarder;* Ger: *Aufkeilen; Abkeilen.*

WEEPING. A slight leak.
Fr: *Suintement;* Ger: *Triefung.*

WEFT. Also wheft, waft, waif. **1.** A flag tied or stopped in the middle or with the fly tied to the staff. Also, a flag rolled up lengthwise with one or more stops. It was

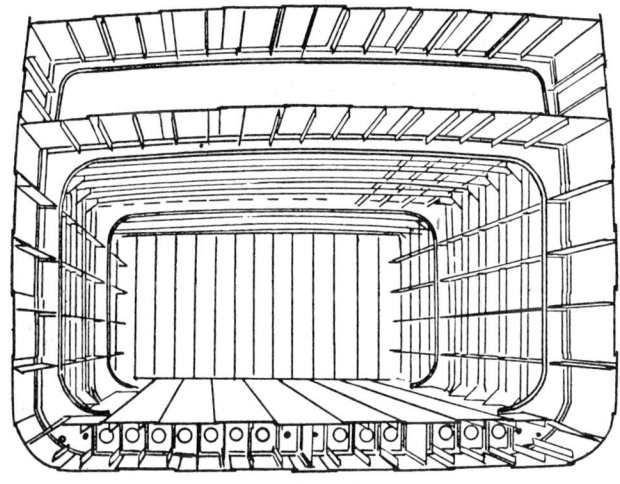

Web Framing

WEDGE RAM. A heavy baulk of timber 6 to 8 ft. long fitted with an iron capping at each end and used for driving the launching cradle hard up against the ship's bottom, thereby facilitating the knocking out of the shores and keel blocks shortly before launching of the vessel. It is provided with a rope through the ram near each end to accommodate a four-man gang.

WEDGES. Pieces of wood fastened on each side of the stem in a rowboat, to take the chafe of the painter or post. Also called whiskers.
See **Adjusting Wedge, Hatch Wedge, Mast Wedge, Plater's Wedge, Treenail Wedge.**

WEDGING UP. An operation performed immediately before launching a vessel. It transfers the weight of the hull to the sliding ways from the shores and blocks which support it during the process of construction. This is accomplished by means of long wedges which are inserted between the top

used as one of the distant signals of the International Code but has now been abolished.
Fr: *Pavillon Couplé;* Ger: *Flagge im Schau.*

2. A small flag with sharpened staff with which a whale is marked by its captor.

3. In sailmaking, the width measurement of sail cloth, the length measure being the warp. The threads taken together which run across the warp from side to side. Also called woof, filling.
Fr: *Trame;* Ger: *Einschlag; Einschutz.*

WEFT YARN. Each thread woven into and crossing the warp at right angles. Also called filling thread.
Fr: *Fil de Trame;* Ger: *Schutzgarn.*

WEIGH. To raise or lift an anchor. To get underway or in readiness to sail.
Fr: *Lever l'Ancre; Déraper;* Ger: *Lichten; Anker aufgehen.*

WEIGHING. The costs charged for weighing goods.

Fr: *Frais de Pesage;* Ger: *Wiegegebühren; Wiegegeld; Wiegekosten.*

WEIGHING LINE. A rope with one end made fast to the crown of an anchor, and the other end to the anchor-buoy rope. Used for recovering the anchor if the cable parts or is slipped.

Fr: *Orin d'Ancre;* Ger: *Ankerbojereep.*

WEIGHT OR MEASUREMENT. Tons weight or measurement at ship's option when calculating freight charges. Freight shipped can be taken either by weight of 20 cwt. or by measurement of 40 cubic at ship's option.

Fr: *Poids ou Cubage;* Ger: *Mass oder Gewicht.*

See **Deadweight, Light Weight, Overhauling Weight.**

WEIR. A sort of fence set in a stream or along a shore line to catch fish. It differs from a pound because it is mainly constructed of brush hedging or narrow boards with or without nettings. The terms *weir* and *pound* are to a great extent used interchangeably in the United States. Also called brush weir, fish weir.

Fr: *Parc;* Ger: *Reuse; Fischreuse.*

See **Bar Weir, Dry Weir, Shore Weir.**

Fish weirs are fixed solid structures made of stones or stakes and wattlings, or a combination of both. The simplest form is a V with the end toward high-water mark and the apex toward low water. In the apex there is very often a special cage or trap for the concentration or retention of the catch. Coastal weirs are generally built where there is a large expanse of ground left uncovered at low water. Weirs are usually kept in position all year round.

WELCON. Code name for the British Chamber of Shipping Coasting Coal Charter, 1913.

WELDED HULL. A vessel in which the greater part of the joining or uniting of the different structural parts is effected by welding instead of riveting. It has been demonstrated in practice that by the use of welding in conjunction with a structural design specially planned for that system of connection, it was possible to build a satisfactory hull one-third lighter than a riveted hull for the same service and cheaper by about 11 per cent. In the mass production of cargo vessels during World War II, new structural designs utilized welding for most fabrication and erection of structure, with consequent economy and rapidity of construction.

The science of welding in its application to shipbuilding has progressed very rapidly in the past decade, and a considerable amount of investigation and research has recently been undertaken with good results. The constitution of the electrode in relation to that of the steel with which the ship is being built, the nature of the flux, the rate of welding, the length of arc, and so on, all have been carefully investigated. Since results in welding depend largely upon the skill of the operator, great care must be observed in the selection of skilled workmen for carrying out this class of work and for inspection of the work.

WELDED KNEE. A beam knee formed by welding a small plate to the beam end. Also called slab knee.

Fr: *Gousset Soudé;* Ger: *Geschweisstes Knie.*

WELDLESS DERRICK. A tubular derrick made of a drawn-steel tube with varying diameters from the center toward the ends. Also called telescopic derrick.

Fr: *Mât de Charge Étiré;* Ger: *Nahtloser Ladebaum.*

WELDWOOD. Trade name for a plywood used for boat-building in which the bonding material which joins the layers together is a synthetic thermoplastic resin unaffected by moisture, decay or time. The manufacture is conducted in hot plate presses which bind the components together by the combined action of heat and pressure.

WELL. The portion of a weather deck with bulwarks between bridge and forecastle front bulkheads.

Fr: *Puits; Baignoire;* Ger: *Brunnen; Well.*

See **Bilge Well, Centerboard Well, Fish Well, Propeller Well, Pump Well, Rudder Well, Tunnel Well.**

WELL BOAT. A fishing boat provided with a well in which sea water circulates to keep fish alive from the time they are caught on the fishing grounds until the vessel reaches her port of destination. Also called wet smack, well smack.

Fr: *Bateau à Vivier;* Ger: *Bunnschiff.*

The well is not a tank fitted into a suitable hull, but is part of the main structure. Two watertight bulkheads are built across the vessel from keelson to deck, enclosing a large space just in the center of the smack. A constant supply and circulation of sea water is kept up within it through large holes in the bottom of the vessel in that part of it between the bulkheads. The vessel is in fact built in 3 compartments. The entrance to the well is through a narrow hatchway on deck, called curb or funnel, the 4 sides of which are carried down for about 3 ft. to what is called the well deck, situated above the level of the waterline and extending all around the hatchway to the bulkheads and sides of the vessel.

WELL DECK. The open deck running between forecastle and bridge-house in a well-deck vessel.

used for river and small coasting trade around estuaries of the Weser and Elbe Rivers. The rig consists of one mast with boom mainsail, gaff topsail, stay foresail and jib. Leeboards are fitted on each side. The hull is similar to that of the *ewer*.

WEST COUNTRY WHIPPING. A whipping made with a series of overhand knots on alternate sides until the whipping is of sufficient length. The ends are joined by a reef knot. Also called French whipping.

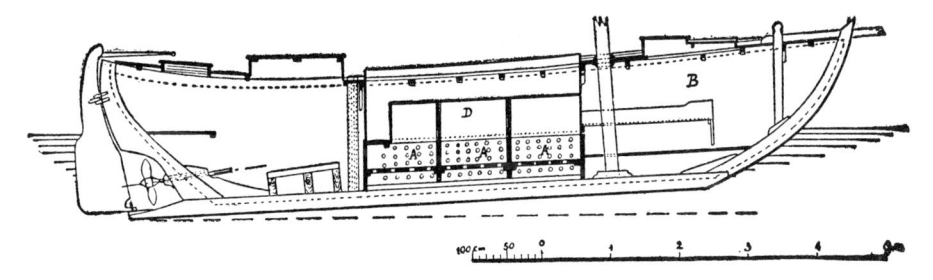

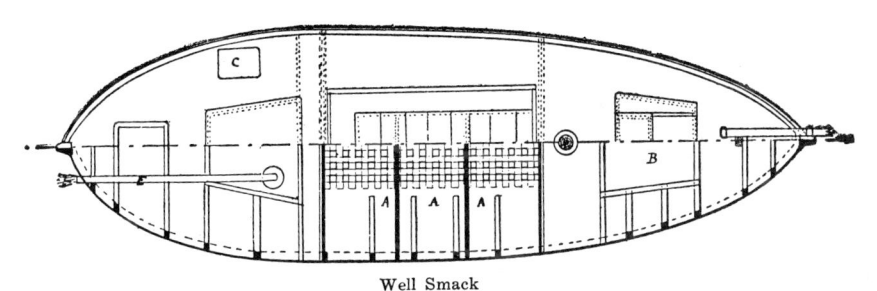

Well Smack
A. Well   B. Crew   C. Fuel tank   D. Well trunk   E. Exhaust pipe

Fr: *Pont du Coffre;* Ger: *Brunnendeck; Welldeck.*
See **Well-Deck Vessel.**

WELL-DECK VESSEL. Vessel having a forecastle with a long poop and bridge combined. A vessel with raised quarter-deck and bridge house combined and forecastle. One of the advantages of the well is that when seas are shipped over the bows the well forms a trap for the water and prevents it from sweeping the weather deck fore and aft.

Fr: *Navire à Coffre; Navire Well-Deck;* Ger: *Welldeckschiff.*

WELL SMACK. See **Well Boat.**

WESERKAHN. A German sailing barge

Fr: *Surliure à Demi-Clefs;* Ger: *Takelung mit einfachen Knoten.*

WESTERLIES. The prevailing winds of the temperate zone, especially steady in the Southern Hemisphere.

WESTRAY YOLE. A double-ended clinker-built open boat of Scandinavian origin found in the Orkney Islands with pointed stern, flat floors, and rather flaring sections. Also called North Isles yole, Orkney yole (G. B.). It is similar in design to the Shetland boat known as "ness yole," but has a proportionally greater beam and fuller stern. The rig for boats with an over-all length of 20 ft. or over usually consists of 2 masts with standing lugsails or spritsails and a jib set flying. The mainsail is extended by a traveler which works on a long boom.

WET BASIN. See Wet Dock.

WET DOCK. An enclosed dock into which vessels are admitted at high water and kept afloat if necessary by pumping to maintain the desired level of water. Particularly, basins at places with a large range of tide in which the water is maintained at a fairly uniform level by gates which are closed when the tide begins to fall. Also called wet basin, closed dock.

Fr: *Bassin à Flot;* Ger: *Flutbecken; Schleusendock.*

WET FISH (G. B.). Fresh, uncured, sea fish as distinguished from shellfish.

WETKA. A dugout canoe from Northern Siberia used for fishing and transportation by the Yakut people on the lower Lena River and Archipelago. These craft are hewed from trees found to the south of the Arctic circle and transported overland to the coast. The largest have a length of 30 ft. with a capacity of about 1,800 pounds. Length 16 ft. Breadth 2 ft. Depth 11 in. (Average.) They are termed *wetka* in Russian, and *toi* in Yakut.

WET SMACK. See Well Boat.

WETTED SURFACE. The surface area of the underwater body of a vessel including are area of the appendages which have appreciable length, such as bilge keels, propeller bossings, and rudder. It enters into the calculations relating to frictional resistance, horsepower, and weight of shell plating.

Fr: *Surface Mouillée;* Ger: *Benetzte Oberfläche.*

Taylor, D. W., Wetted Surface of Ships, Society of Naval Architects and Marine Engineers, New York, *Transactions,* vol. 1, 1893; Vincent, S. A., Estimating the Wetted Surface, *Marine Engineering and Shipping Age,* New York, vol. 34, February, 1929.

WHALEBACK. Small steel-built erection of arched form at the stern to protect against injury or damage from the breaking on board of heavy seas. Also called turtleback.

WHALEBACK VESSEL. A tubular, bargelike type of vessel which originated on the Great Lakes of North America in 1889 and was primarily designed for the transportation of bulk cargoes. A few of these vessels were subsequently also used for ocean navigation. The distinguishing features of the design were the spoon-shaped bow and the rounded topsides which formed an easy curve with the deck, the latter being of convex shape and without bulwarks in order to let the seas run freely over the hull. The hatchways were sealed with bolted plates. The only erection forward consisted of a circular deckhouse in the bows, which supported a small platform under which the windlass was housed. A larger erection aft supported by three turrets consisted of a double deck, the upper of which accommodated lifeboats. On the lower were the captain's and officers' quarters, the galley, charthouse and wheelhouse. Internally there was a collision bulkhead forward and second watertight bulkhead abaft the cargo space, just forward of the boiler and engine room. A cellular, double bottom was provided.

The advantages claimed for this type of hull were: saving in steel weight, due to lighter scantlings, self-trimming cargo hold, economy in construction, saving of over 50 per cent in horsepower at 7 or 8 knots speed, and greater freedom from rolling and pitching in a seaway. After several years experience, whaleback vessels were no longer built. They were considered unsuited for deep-sea voyages. The spoon-shaped bow was not conducive to economical propulsion, and when pounding against head seas, was especially liable to damage. The poor accommodations for the crew on long voyages and the absence of any safe means of communication between the forward turret and the afterend of the ship also prevented the general adoption of the type for ocean traffic.

WHALEBOAT. 1. An open rowboat with sharp stern employed for the capture of whales before the advent of whale catchers. Length 27 ft. Beam 6 ft. Depth 2 ft. 6 in. (Average.) The bows were covered in for the distance of a few feet forming a sort of platform through which rose 2 wooden posts, the forward one being called the gun-bollard head on which the harpoon gun was mounted, whereas the whale line was run around the other, further aft. At the stem, between the head bollards a pulley was sunk over which the whale line rode. On the port bow beside the gun bollard a small tub was fitted, into which part of the whale line known as the foregoer was coiled. The after part of the boat as well as a part amidships was fitted up for the reception of the whale line. The whaleboat was manned by 5 oarsmen and a boat steerer.

The true whaleboat, as formerly used by whaling vessels, was quite different from the ship's boat commonly known nowadays under the name of "whaler." It had a moderate beam, a long rather flat floor, an easy turn of bilge, a very bold sheer, and *no deadwood* either forward or aft. This absence of deadwood resulted in a sharp rake to the stem- and sternposts, which rounded boldly in to meet the shallow keel. The lines were considerably fuller at the bow than at the stern, and this leanness of the afterbody was one of the characteristic features of the type. The planking of these boats was never more than ½ in. in thickness and the seams instead of being calked were covered by a light batten run along them on the inside. The true whaleboat was single-banked and was designed to be steered with an oar, though a rudder was sometimes fitted to the curved stern. The crutch for the steering oar was carried on a bumkin projecting from the quarter of the boat.

2. A long, narrow, flat-floored open boat, sharp at both ends, used on warships and merchant vessels. Also called whaler. Its length ranges between 20 and 40 ft., with a beam equal to about one fifth of its length. It is carvel- or clinker-planked and is fitted with buoyancy tanks. The stem and stern are rounded off as in the boats formerly used in whaling. It is rowed single or double banked. In United States warships, whaleboats fitted with a Diesel engine are used as lifeboats.

Fr: *Baleinière;* Ger: *Walboot.*

WHALEBOAT CHOCK. A groove or notch in the stem of a whaleboat through which the whale line leads, to prevent it from running over the boat's side, and thereby running the risk of a capsize. It is either bushed with lead or fitted with a bronze roller. Also called sheer cleat.

WHALEBONE. The horny laminated substance found in the mouth of baleen whales in extensive rows each consisting of upward of 300 blades which average 10 ft. in length. Also called baleen, whale fin. Whalebone was at one time valuable as a product of commerce but is now used only in small quantities for the bristles of chimney sweeps, brooms, and as a stiffener in silk fabrics.

Fr: *Baleine;* Ger: *Walfischbein.*

Stevenson, C. H., *Whalebone, Its Production and Utilization,* U. S. Bureau of Fisheries, Document 626, Washington, 1907.

WHALE CATCHER. Small, oil-burning, steam-propelled vessel, staunchly built. Also called whaling vessel. Modern vessels of this type have a length of 130 to 145 ft., are propelled by a single screw with 1,000- to 1,600-hp. engines and a speed of about 11 to 15 knots. Speed, rapid turning, and ability to "get off the mark" are essential qualifications of the successful whale catcher.

Fr: *Chasseur de Baleines;* Ger: *Walfangboot; Walfischfänger.*

These vessels are equipped with a considerable machinery installation and this, as well as the hull, is of special design. The hull is built with scantlings greatly in excess of classification societies' requirements, the forward frames being closely spaced, with special gun and ice stiffening provided. Steam heating pipes are run in the whaleline bins to prevent them from freezing into a solid mass. Similarly, steam lines are fitted in the oil bunkers to keep the fuel liquid. These vessels are equipped with radio and direction finding instruments for working in close cooperation with factory ships.

WHALER.

See **Whale Boat, 2.**

WHALE LINE. A three-strand Manila rope used as harpoon line in whale fishery, about 6½ in. in circumference to which the foregoer is attached. It is 500 to 600 fathoms in length, and is made with great care from selected material. Also called whale rope.

Fr: *Ligne de Harpon;* Ger: *Harpuneleine; Walfischleine.*

On whale catchers the line is coiled in a bin below deck. From the bin the line passes through a wood-lined tube to the deck. There it is wound several times around the double drum of the winch. It is then rove through a large block at the masthead. This block or gin is not rigidly fixed, but, by an ingenious arrangement of ropes and springs, it takes the violent strain on the line resulting from the struggle of the whale and the jump of the sea. It then continues under a pulley on deck behind the gun platform, and finally over another pulley.

WHALE OIL. Oil extracted from the blubber and body tissues of various species of whales.

The blubber is heated in open vats by direct contact with steam. The oil after it has been cooked out is skimmed off, and the residue is pressed in a hydraulic press. In rendering the carcass the chunks of meat and bone are placed in digestors, where the

WHALE-OIL FACTORY VESSEL

Whale Catcher

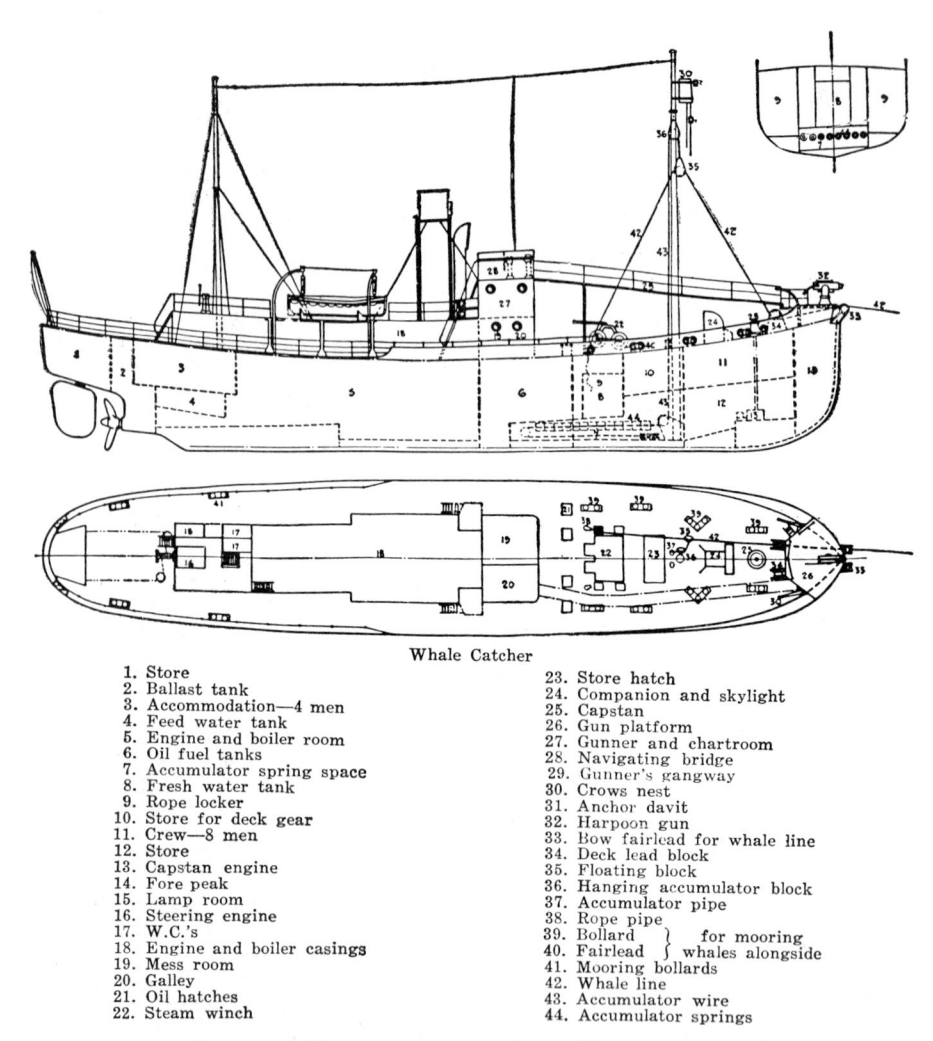

1. Store
2. Ballast tank
3. Accommodation—4 men
4. Feed water tank
5. Engine and boiler room
6. Oil fuel tanks
7. Accumulator spring space
8. Fresh water tank
9. Rope locker
10. Store for deck gear
11. Crew—8 men
12. Store
13. Capstan engine
14. Fore peak
15. Lamp room
16. Steering engine
17. W.C.'s
18. Engine and boiler casings
19. Mess room
20. Galley
21. Oil hatches
22. Steam winch
23. Store hatch
24. Companion and skylight
25. Capstan
26. Gun platform
27. Gunner and chartroom
28. Navigating bridge
29. Gunner's gangway
30. Crows nest
31. Anchor davit
32. Harpoon gun
33. Bow fairlead for whale line
34. Deck lead block
35. Floating block
36. Hanging accumulator block
37. Accumulator pipe
38. Rope pipe
39. Bollard } for mooring
40. Fairlead } whales alongside
41. Mooring bollards
42. Whale line
43. Accumulator wire
44. Accumulator springs

material is cooked with steam under pressure for a number of hours. The water and oil are then drawn off and the residue is pressed. The oil obtained from the carcass is not of as high quality as blubber oil.

WHALE-OIL FACTORY VESSEL. A vessel used as a tanker for the transportation of whale oil and supplied with the necessary plant for extracting from the captured whales oil and other by-products. Also called whaling factory ship. The actual factory is in the 'tween decks and the weather deck is used as working deck for cutting up whales. The vessel also acts as mother ship to a fleet of 5 to 7 small vessels known as whale catchers, which draw their supplies of fuel from the mother ship.

Ger: *Walölschiff; Walverarbeitungsschiff*.

When killed, a whale is inflated with compressed air and is then towed to the factory, where it is moored alongside. The size of whales varies from 40 to 200 ft. in length, the weight being sometimes as much as 100 tons. The whale is hauled on board up a specially designed slipway at the stern by powerful winches. The blubber, or fatty outer portion of the carcass, is cut off and reduced in steam-heated boilers to extract the oil, which is refined and stored in the main tanks. The thick residue known as grax is collected in troughs and pumped through a receiver to the grax press to extract further oil. The remainder of the carcass is then taken to the forward end of the ship to the meat factory. Here the flesh and bones are passed through hatchways direct into steam boilers in order to extract the oil and other residues.

Christensen, "The Whaling Factory Ship 'Vikingen'," North East Coast Institution of Engineers and Shipbuilders (Newcastle upon Tyne), *Transactions*, vol. 47 (1930).

WHALE ROPE.
See **Whale Line**.

stern, in which case the vessel must be swung around completely and the chase resumed at top speed.

Fr: *Chasse au Cétacés;* Ger: *Walfischfang.*

See **Pelagic Whaling, Shore Whaling.**

After the harpoon is fired the whale soon dies, provided the hit was accurate and the explosive charge detonated. The whale is then heaved upon and maneuvered alongside. A spear with compressed air connection is rammed in and the whale pumped up. It is then flagged and let go, in order to continue the hunting for other mammals.

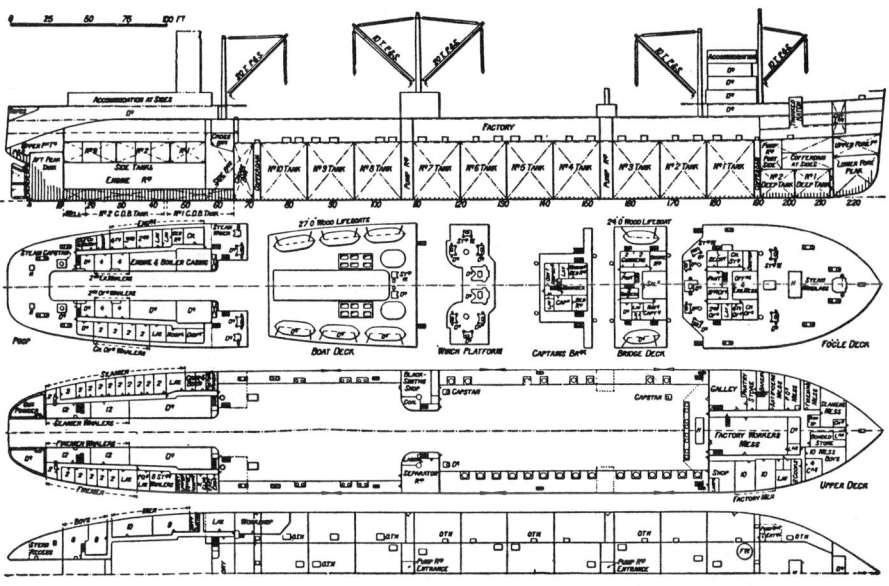

Whale-Oil Factory Vessel. (*Courtesy Shipbuilding and Shipping Record*)

WHALING. The capture of whales, which is nowadays carried out solely by means of mechanically propelled steel-built whale catchers, with a harpoon gun placed in the bows. When the whale is first sighted the vessel makes toward it as speedily as possible and on the submerging of the whale the catcher is taken slowly over the spot where it was last seen. After successfully maneuvering the boat to a point near the spot where the whale comes to the surface to breathe, the gunner stands by, ready to shoot. If whale comes to the surface close to he ship, the latter must, without loss of time, be maneuvered into position to enable the gunner to get a harpoon home at effective range. On the other hand, it may come up half a mile away, perhaps dead

When satisfied with the result of the day, the catcher tows the whales to the factory vessel, receives fresh equipment, and goes out again. Modern whaling is at present almost entirely concerned with the capture of Blue Whales and Fin Whales and the capture of the remaining species are negligible in comparison. Of the eight commercially important whales, two are toothed whales: the Sperm and the Bottle Nose. Two are true whales: the Nordcaper and the Greenland Whale. Four are finner whales: the Blue Whale, the Common Fin whale, the Sei, and the Humpback. Whale meat is coarser in texture and darker than beef.

Among whalemen it is regularly eaten fried as steaks. Norwegians salt down quantities of it for their own use at home. In Japan it is eaten fresh or canned. Fresh whale meat contains: water, 71.2 per cent; protein,

23.1 per cent; ash, 1.2 per cent; fat, 4.2 per cent.

Bennet, A. G., *Whaling in the Antarctic*, Edinburgh, 1931; Hjort, J., *Pelagic Whaling in the Antarctic*, Oslo, 1934; Jenkins, J. T., *Whales and Modern Whaling*, London, 1932; Turner, *Whaling in the South Atlantic*, Cairo, 1924; U. S. State Department, **Treaty Series 933 and 944**, *Regulation of Whaling (International)*, Washington, 1938–39.

WHALING GUN. A small breech- or muzzle-loading gun with a bore of about 3½ in., from which a harpoon is shot.

Fr: *Canon Porte-Harpon;* Ger: *Harpune Geschütz.*

WHALING VESSEL.
See **Whale Catcher.**

WHAMMEL BOAT. The whammel or salmon drift net boat as found on the Solway Firth, west coast of Scotland, is a carvel-built, half-decked craft fitted with wooden buoyancy tanks under deck on each side of the boat amidships. The hull is double-ended, with moderately raked sternpost, straight stem and curved forefoot. There is a deep keel to which is fastened an extra iron keel bolted at intervals right through the wooden keel to the floors. The rig consists of a standing lug and jib, the mast being placed approximately one-third of the over-all length from the stem. The lug sail has a boom fitted with jaws. Length over-all 19 ft. 3 in. Length of keel 17 ft. 1½ in. Beam 6 ft. 3½ in. Depth inside 2 ft. 9 in. Sail area 124.74 sq ft. (Typical.)

WHARF. A structure of timber or iron built on the shore of a harbor extending into deep water so that vessels may lie alongside close together. Also called pier.

Fr: *Appontement; Embarcadère;* Ger: *Pier; Landungsplatz.*

See **Quay, Sufferance Wharf.**

WHARFAGE. The exact meaning of this term varies in different ports. It can be defined in a general way as a charge assessed against all cargo conveyed on, over, or through a wharf, quay, or pier. Sometimes called transfer charge tolls, port toll.

Fr: *Péage;* Ger: *Kaigebühren; Kaikosten; Umschlagsgebühren.*

See **Double Wharfage.**

In some British ports the term "wharfage" is used to denote a charge made in respect of the landing and handling of freight across a quay where no labor is supplied by port authorities for the purpose. If the port authorities supply the labor it is termed a "landing rate." In the port of London the expression "wharfage and porterage" refers to a charge for dealing with export cargo, which covers receiving from truck, conveying to export shed, and delivering to ship's side for lifting on board.

WHARFBOAT (U. S.). A floating structure used as warehouse and office and not capable of navigation. It is not a vessel within Admiralty jurisdiction.

WHARF DEMURRAGE (U. S.). A charge against the cargo paid per day and per ton after the expiration of 24 hours from the time of discharging for goods left on a wharf or quay.

WHARFINGER. The proprietor or manager of riverside premises specially adapted to the berthing and discharge of ships and barges and the storage of goods. Also called warehouseman. The owner, operator, or manager of a wharf (U. S.). In Great Britain this term refers to a shipowner's representative at the docks. Goods arriving for shipment are received by him and checked. While the vessel is being loaded the wharfinger arranges for a tally to be made. When the vessel has been loaded he supplies the office with full particulars.

Ger: *Kaimeister; Kaibesitzer.*

WHARFMAN. One who performs various duties about a dock or wharf, such as fastening ship to dock by catching heaving line from ship, pulling mooring line to dock and slipping eye of hawser over mooring post, casting off mooring hawsers when ship is ready to clear dock, moving gangplank or gangway, and so on. Also called dockman or pierman.

WHARF SUPERINTENDENT (U. S.). The official of a shipping line in direct charge of the company's wharf.

WHEEL CHAIN. One of the chains used for connecting the steering wheel or steering engine with the tiller. Also called tiller chain.

Fr: *Chaîne de Drosse;* Ger: *Ruderkette; Steuerkette.*

WHEEL GRATING. Small wooden grating under the steering wheel, and on which the helmsman stands.

Fr: *Caillebotis de timonier;* Ger: *Rudergrating.*

WHEELHOUSE. A house built of wood or steel over the steering wheel as a protection for the helmsman. Also called pilothouse. In large vessels it is also used for navigational purposes and is located amid-

ships on the navigating bridge. It contains the various ship control instruments and apparatus by which the vessel's speed and direction are controlled.
Fr: *Abri de Navigation;* *Timonerie;* Ger: *Ruderhaus.*

WHEELMAN.
See **Helmsman.**

WHEEL PORT.
See **Aperture.**

WHEEL ROPE. One of the two wires which run from tiller head to the barrel of a steering wheel or engine. Sometimes called tiller rope. Also, a type of very flexible wire rope used in small pleasure craft, connecting the steering wheel with the tiller. It is usually made of bronze with 6 strands and 42 wires in each strand.
Fr: *Drosse;* Ger: *Steuerreep.*

WHELK. A marine mollusc used as bait by trawl-line fishermen.
Fr: *Buccin;* Ger: *Kinthorn; Hornschnecke; Trompetenschnecke.*

WHELP. 1. One of the projecting ribs fitted on the periphery of a capstan barrel, mooring winch barrel, windlass gypsy heads, and so on, to give better grip to the lines.
Fr: *Nervure;* Ger: *Spillklampe.*
2. One of the sprockets on the wildcats of a windlass which engage the links of the chain cable.
Ger: *Kettennuss.*

WHERRY. 1. A narrow, open, racing or exercise boat rowed by one person with sculls.
2. A sailing craft found on the east coast of Great Britain, somewhat similar to the Thames barge. It has great beam and is chiefly intended for inland or estuary navigation. The hull is built with a pronounced flare of the upper works, low freeboard, fine lines forward and aft, a pointed stern, and good sheer. The rudder is large and broad. The tonnage of these craft varies from 20 to 30. Length 50 to 60 ft. Beam 12 to 16½ ft. Depth 3 ft. 3 in. Loaded draft 2½ to 4 ft. The rig consists of a collapsible mast with weighted heel which carries a loose-footed gaff mainsail, the after leech of which is nearly parallel to the mast. The mast is placed well forward on a short deck and is pivoted to a heavy tabernacle which extends to the keelson. A long open hatch extends from abaft the mast to the forward end of the raised cabin in the stern with narrow waterway on either side. Wherries are chiefly used for the conveyance of heavy merchandise such as bricks, lime, corn, flour, meal, and so forth, on the Norfolk Broads and adjacent waters.
3. A light ship's boat with transom stern pulled by 2 or 3 men, each using two oars. There are no sails.
Fr: *Wherry;* Ger: *Jolle.*
See **Norfolk Wherry, Cape Roseway Wherry, Maine Wherry, Portsmouth Wherry, Ryde Wherry, Thames Wherry.**

WHIFF (to). To angle from a moving boat with hand lines towing the bait near the surface. See **Trolling.**

WHIFFING LINE. A fishing line used for the capture of pelagic fish such as mackerel and pollack. These lines are towed from a boat underway, the depth of the hook below the surface being regulated by the weight of the sinker. Several lines are used simultaneously from the same boat, the lines being kept clear from one another by fishing them from outriggers and using different weights.
Fr: *Ligne Courante; Ligne Trainante;* Ger: *Schleppangelleine; Laufangelleine.*

WHIP. A rope rove through a fixed single block. A simple kind of tackle consisting of a single block with a rope rove through it. It offers no mechanical advantage but it serves to change the direction of hauling. Also called gantline, single whip, single purchase.
Fr: *Cartahu Simple; Cartahu;* Ger: *Jollentau; Jolltau; Wippe; Jolle.*
See **Ash Whip, Bunt Whip, Cargo Whip, Coaling Whip, Double Whip, Double Whip System, Hatch-Whip, Popping the Whip, Yard Whip.**

WHIP (to). 1. To wind the end of a rope

with twine to prevent it from fagging or fraying.

Fr: *Surlier;* Ger: *Takeln; Betakeln.*

2. To hoist by a whip.

WHIP AND RUNNER. A whip which has its block made fast to a pendant, the latter being rove through a single block. A single whip hooking to the hauling part of a runner. Also called whip and pendant.

Fr: *Bastaque Simple;* Ger: *Steerttalje.*

WHIP AND SKID SYSTEM. A method employed for loading cargo in which a single boom with its attendant fall is used, together with an inclined skid leading from the pier to the deck of the ship. The boom is held by its guys in a fixed position, plumbing the hatchway. The draft is dragged up the inclined skid and over the bulwarks. It then swings over to the hatch by its own weight. The winch is then reversed and lowers it into the hold. Also called single fall and skid system.

WHIPPING. Working light cargo with a single whip held by hand and taken around the gipsy head of a winch which is kept running continuously.

Ger: *Wippen.*

WHIPPING TWINE. The smallest cordage used on board ship. It is made up of 2 threads of flax, well coated with wax, and is used for whippings, worming, and so on.

Fr: *Fil à Surlier; Fil Ciré; Fil à Congréer;* Ger: *Takelgarn.*

WHIRLPOOL. An eddy or vortex where the waters are continually in rapid rotary motion.

Fr: *Tourbillon;* Ger: *Wasserwirbel.*

WHIRLWIND. A wind moving rapidly in a circular, vertical spiral path. A mass of air rotating rapidly round a vertical or slightly inclined axis, this axis having at the same time a progressive motion over the surface of the sea.

Fr: *Tourbillon;* Ger: *Wirbelwind.*

WHISKER JUMPER. A steadying line which goes over the end of a whisker boom with an eye and sets up to the cutwater. In some cases it may lead through a clump block on the cutwater to the ship's head where it is set up.

Fr: *Calebas d'Arc-Boutant de Beaupré;* Ger: *Blinder Raa Domper.*

WHISKER POLE. A light boom with jaws at one end and a short spike on the other. The jaws rest against the mast and the spike is pushed through the clew of a jib, holding the sail out at right angles to the fore-and-aft line of the boat. It is used by small boats when sailing wing and wing.

Fr: *Tangon de Vent Arrière.*

WHISKERS. Outriggers extending horizontally from the bowsprit cap for spreading the jibboom and flying jibboom guys. Also called whisker booms, spreaders. They have now been replaced by iron outriggers extending from the catheads with cleats in them for the guys to reeve through and set up to the fore chains. This gear has frequently been used in small trading vessels.

Fr: *Arc-Boutants de Beaupré; Arc-Boutants de Bossoirs;* Ger: *Blinde Raa.*

WHISTLE. A sound-emitting apparatus used for marine signaling in which steam or compressed air is forced into a cavity or against a thin edge.

Fr: *Sifflet;* Ger: *Pfeife.*

See **Bell Whistle, Boatswain's Whistle, Chime Whistle, Organ Whistle, Siren, Tyfon Whistle.**

A ship's whistle is not considered efficient unless in still weather it can be plainly heard at a distance of at least 2 miles. A clear sharp blast is essential in whistle design, the significance of signals depending on the kind and succession of blasts whether long or short. For this reason drainage of steam whistle pipes is as thorough as possible. The note obtained from a whistle depends on the length of the vibrating column (or length of whistle) and the pressure.

WHISTLE BUOY. A buoy fitted with an apparatus by which air drawn in and compressed by the movements of the waves is made to escape through a whistle and so give warning of danger. The sound is irregular. Also called whistling buoy.

Fr: *Bouée à Sifflet;* Ger: *Heultonne.*

WHISTLE CONTROLLER. An electrical device for operating a ship's whistle. Also called electric whistle control. It consists essentially of one or more control switches located on the navigating bridge and electrically connected to a relay placed in the engine room. The closing of the control switch in the bridge causes the relay to close, which completes a circuit through a solenoid situated just below the whistle valve. The apparatus can be set to give blasts of a definite duration at regular intervals as required by the Rules of the Road in foggy weather. It is usually fitted in such a manner as to be independent of other electric circuits.

Ger: *Pfeifen Kontrollsystem.*
WHISTLE LANYARD. A small line running from the whistle to the wheelhouse or navigating bridge, used for blowing the whistle. It is usually made of galvanized steel or phosphor bronze wire with a braided cotton log-line fore end. Also called whistle pull.
WHITECAP. The crested foam on the tops of waves in a breeze. A wave with a broken crest showing as a white patch. Also called white horse.
Fr: *Mouton;* Ger: *Schaumwelle; Lamm.*
WHITE CEDAR. An excellent wood for pleasure boats and canoes. It is exceedingly light, very soft, pliant, and of good durability. It is unsurpassed for canoes, and is one of the best woods for planking yachts up to about fifty ft. length, also for decks and cabin tops, when canvassed. It weighs 20 to 27 lb. per cu. ft. when seasoned. Also called American cedar, Oregon cedar, black cedar.
WHITE HORSE. Whaleman's term for the headskin of a whale, which was impenetrable to hand-thrown harpoons, and upon which the iron bent without piercing it.
See **Whitecap.**
WHITE LINE. A general term for cod line, houseline, nettle line, and lacing line. It is made up of 2 or 3 yarns of light Italian hemp in 20 fathom length and sold by weight. Thus a 2½-pound line means that 20 fathoms weighs this amount. It is usually manufactured in weights ranging from ½ to 5½ pounds, and is used for making reef points, stops, lashings, lacings, lanyards, also by fishermen for trawl lines and hand lines.
WHITE OAK. An American wood extensively used in yacht and other small-craft construction. When of good quality, it is an excellent wood for steamed frames, deck beams, carlines and keels for boats from 20 to 80 ft. in length. Also used for fenders, wearing strips, bitts and chock rails. It requires long seasoning and should not be used for outside planking. It contains gallic

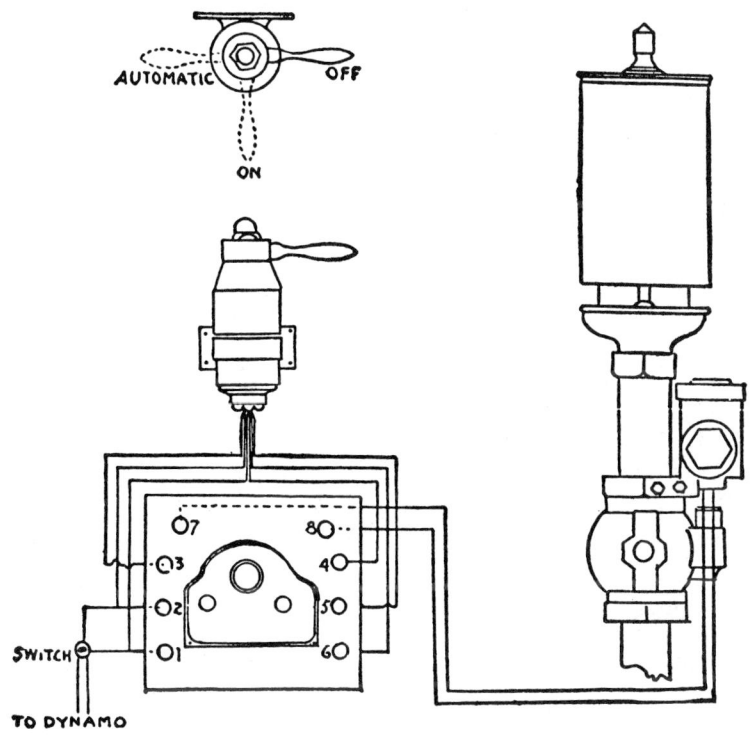

Whistle Controller

acid and requires heavily galvanized fastenings. Weight when seasoned 45 to 48 lb. per cu. ft.
Fr: *Chêne Blanc;* Ger: *Weisseichenholz.*

WHITE OAKUM. Oakum made from untarred hemp.
Fr: *Etoupe Blanche;* Ger: *Ungeteertes Werg.*
See **Oakum.**

WHITE PINE. A soft light-weight wood of little value for structural shipbuilding purposes. It is used for canvas-covered decks and joiner work that will be painted, also for outside planking of light skiffs, canoes and other small craft. It swells considerably when wet and is therefore extensively used for stopwaters in scarfs, for plugs over deck bolts, and for wedges for calking the ceiling of wooden ships. Weight when seasoned 27 to 29 lb. per cu. ft.
Fr: *Pin de Floride; Pin blanc;* Ger: *Weymouthskiefer.*

WHITE RAINBOW. A rainbow sometimes seen in a thick fog. Also called fog bow.

WHITE ROPE. Any rope made of untarred hemp, used for log and lead lines.
Fr: *Filin Blanc;* Ger: *Ungeteertes Tauwerk; Weisses Tauwerk.*

WHITE SQUALL. A whirlwind of small radius arising suddenly in fair weather without the usual formation of clouds. White squalls rarely occur outside the tropics.
Fr: *Grain Blanc;* Ger: *Sturmbö; Weisse Bö.*

WHITE WATER. Water over shallow sand banks.

WHITING BOAT.
See **Plymouth Hooker.**

WHITING LINE. A 3-strand, 6-thread fishing line made of 2-pound white line, used for catching whiting.
Fr: *Ligne à Merlan;* Ger: *Wittling Schnur.*

WHOLE GALE. A continuous wind moving with a velocity between 48 and 55 nautical miles per hour. Force 10, Beaufort's scale.
Fr: *Fort Coup de Vent;* Ger: *Starker Sturm.*

WHOLESOME. The behavior of a vessel in a heavy gale. A wholesome ship is one that will try, hull, and ride well without heavy laboring in the sea.
Fr: *Marin;* Ger: *Seetüchtig.*

WIDE-BOARD SLING. A type of platform sling consisting of 3 wooden strips each 7 ft. long, 4 in. wide and 2 in. thick, with similar strips 3 ft. long bolted across at each end and in the middle. Nine-ft. wire bridles with wooden spreaders 3 ft. long are used. These slings are used most frequently for bagged cargo, canned goods, and other case goods.

WIDELY SPACED STANCHIONS. Hollow or built stanchions of great strength, connected to deck girders and widely spaced to offer minimum interference to the stowage of cargo.
Fr: *Epontilles à Grand Écartement;* Ger: *Weitstehende Stütze.*

WILD. A term applied to a vessel that steers badly, also to some gear out of order.
Fr: *Volage;* Ger: *Wild.*

WILDCAT. A steel casting in the form of a deeply grooved drum with whelps which engage the links of the anchor cable. Also called cable holder, cable lifter, chain grab. It is connected by locking keys to the driving shaft of the windlass or capstan in order that the cable may be operated independently of the engine when paying out. It is also controlled by a frictional band brake so that when the wildcat is uncoupled, the cable may be held fast or paid out slowly or quickly as required. On many high-class passenger vessels where obstructions on the weather deck are kept to a minimum, wildcats are mounted on vertical shafts snug to the deck, with the driving engine located on the deck below.
Fr: *Barbotin;* Ger: *Kettenscheibe; Kettentrommel; Kettenmitnehmer.*

WILLIWAW. A violent and unpredictable wind arising suddenly in Aleutian waters, especially in close proximity to the mountainous coasts of the islands in that region. A similar wind off the Patagonian channels and Magellan Strait.

WILLY-WILLY. A violent wind storm accompanied by rain, found off the northwest coast of Australia.

WINCH. A hand- or power-driven machine having one or more drums or barrels on which to wind a chain or rope, and used on board ship for hoisting or hauling. Ship's winches may be classified (1) according to uses: boat winches, brace winches, cargo winches, mast winches, warping winches, trawl winches; (2) according to the number and kind of drums; (3) according to the type of gearing: single or double gearing, friction gearing, spur gearing, worm gearing, herringbone gearing; (4) according to system of powering: hand, steam, electric, hydraulic or motor drive.

Fr: *Treuil;* Ger: *Winde.*

WINCH HEAD.
See **Gipsy.**

WINCHMAN. A longshoreman from the deck gang who hoists and lowers cargo in and out of a ship's hold using a power winch. Also called winch runner. He manipulates levers or switches to control raising, lowering or swinging of load attached to cargo hook and follows hand signals of hatch tender when the load is out of his sight.

Fr: *Treuilliste;* Ger: *Windenmann.*

WINCH PLATFORM. A strongly built mast table which serves as foundation for cargo winches around a mast. Also called winch table.

WINCH TABLE.
See **Winch Platform.**

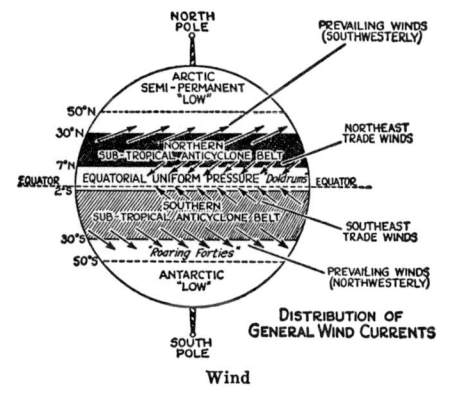

Wind

WIND. 1. Currents in the atmosphere conveying air with more or less velocity from one part of the earth's surface to another. Winds may be divided into three classes: (1) permanent winds such as the trade winds of the torrid zone; (2) periodical winds such as the monsoons of the Indian Ocean, and (3) variable winds such as the winds of the temperate and frigid zones.

2. Air in motion at any rate of speed.

Fr: *Vent;* Ger: *Wind.*

Perrel, *Treatise on Winds,* New York, 1925.

WIND (to). To bring a ship around end for end. To wind a tow means to give it a sheer, cast off the tow rope and use the tug's bow to assist the tow around.

Fr: *Virer cap pour cap.*

WIND-BOUND. Said of a sailing vessel which is prevented from leaving because the wind is unfavorable.

Ger: *Von widrigen Winden aufgehalten.*

WIND CATCHER. Portable sheet metal fitting, inserted in a sidelight to deflect wind, thereby increasing ventilation in passengers' accommodation or living quarters. Also called wind scoop, air scoop.

Fr: *Bonnette de Hublot;* Ger: *Luftfänger; Windfänger.*

WIND DRIFT. The general movement of the wind disregarding minor deflections. The general movement of clouds, or flotsam carried along by the wind.

WINDER. A tool used on the bending blocks for handling bars or shapes when heated.

WINDING PENDANT. A pendant hooked at the fore- or mainmasthead with its bight secured as far out as necessary on the foreyard or mainyard, and having a heavy tackle, called a "winding tackle," depending from its lower end. It was used for lifting heavy weights.

WINDING WEAZE (or WEEZE). A crescent-shaped tool used for manual bending of frame bars on the bending slabs.

Fr: *Levier à Secteur.*

WINDJAMMER. A sailing vessel, generally square-rigged. Colloquially, a merchant sailing vessel.

Ger: *Windjammer.*

WINDLASS. A special form of winch used to hoist the anchors, house them safely, and warp the ship when in harbor. It has two drums designed to grab the links of the anchor cables and is fitted with ratchet or braking device suitable for paying out cable.

Fr: *Guindeau;* Ger: *Ankerspill; Ankerwinde; Ankerlichtmaschine.*

See **Pump-Brake Windlass, Ratchet Windlass, Spanish Windlass.**

There is a great variety in the design of windlasses of modern vessels. Certain general features, however, are common to them all. The engine turns a shaft, either horizontal or vertical, on which is mounted a wildcat, over which the chain passes and by which its links are engaged. Each wildcat turns loosely on the shaft, but may be rigidly secured to it by some form of connection, and much of the individuality of different types of windlasses lies in the nature of this connection. The cable lifter is secured to the shaft for heaving the chain

Windlass. (*Courtesy Hyde Windlass Company*)

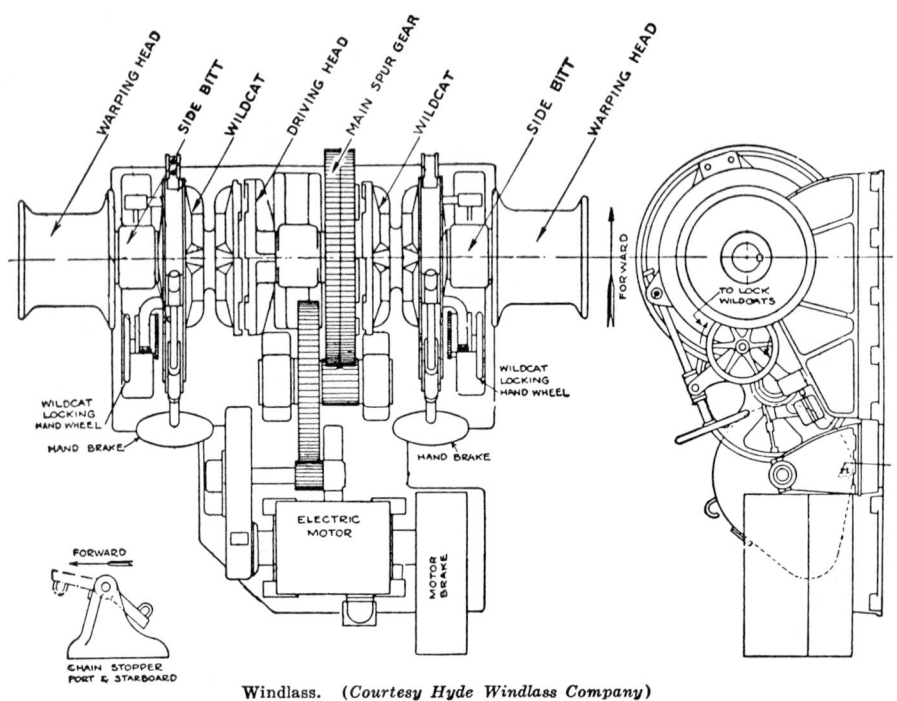

in or paying out, but is disconnected in veering chain and in riding by the windlass, being controlled when so disconnected by a friction brake. Steam engines of the reversible type, electrohydraulic drive, or electric motors are used for driving the windlass. Windlasses operated by compressed air are found on lightships. The windlass must be capable of exerting a heavy pull at a slow speed to break out the anchor and must be capable of housing the anchors gently into the hawsepipe. The cable speed varies from 5 to 60 ft. per minute.

WINDLASS BITTS. See **Carrick Bitts.**

WINDLIPPER. The first effects of a breeze or wind on smooth water, before the waves are raised.

Fr: *Risette.*

WINDLOP. Short wind waves generally found in narrow waters, as distinguished from ocean waves.

Fr: *Clapotis.*

WIND RODE. Said of a ship at anchor when riding head to wind and little or not affected by the direction of tide or current.

Fr: *Evité au Vent;* Ger: *Windgerecht.*

WIND ROSE. A diagram used on a pilot chart or weather chart to indicate clearly and concisely the average direction and force of the wind. The arrows which accompany each rose fly the wind and indicate by their length and thickness the frequency and force, also the direction of the wind. On American charts the arrows are feathered, the number of the latter showing the wind force according to Beaufort's Scale.

Fr: *Rose des Vents;* Ger: *Windrose.*

WINDSAIL. A sort of tube or funnel made of canvas spread by wooden hoops or wire rings, serving to convey a current of fresh air below deck. On either side of the top are canvas wings designed and set to catch the wind. It is suspended from a stay by halyards and the wings are held by guys. Wind sails are made of no. 5, no. 6 or no. 7 canvas, roped with 21-thread Manila or hemp.

Fr: *Manche à Vent;* Ger: *Windsack.*

WIND SCOOP.
See **Wind Catcher.**

WINDWARD. The general direction from which the wind blows. It is a point of reference in designating a movement or a location.

Fr: *Au Vent;* Ger: *Luvwärts.*

WINDWARD FLOOD. A flood tide setting against the direction of the wind.

WINDWARD GREAT CIRCLE SAILING. A term which refers to sailing ship navigation when in consequence of head winds a vessel cannot be kept on direct Great Circle track and is put on the tack by which it will deviate the least amount from the true Great Circle track.

WINDWARD SAILING. Method of navigating of a vessel under sail in which the ship endeavors to gain a point situated in the direction from which the wind is blowing. The ship is therefore made to sail as near as possible to the wind by frequent tacking.

Fr: *Gagner au Vent;* Ger: *Überluven.*

WINDWARD TIDE. A tide which sets to windward.

WING. 1. That part of a ship's hold or space between decks which is next to the vessel's side. Also any structural part or objects which are placed at some distance off the center line, such as wing tanks.

Fr: *Abord;* Ger: *Schlag.*

2. The narrow, straight sides of a trawlnet between the back and the ground rope which form the opening or mouth, and extend from the otter boards or trawl heads.

Fr: *Aile;* Ger: *Flügel.*

WING AND WING. The condition of the sails on a fore-and-aft-rigged vessel when running before the wind with her booms on opposite sides, the foresail on one side, the mainsail on the other.

Fr: *En Ciseaux;* Ger: *Mit beiden Bäumen abgefiert.*

See **Bottom Wings, Goose Winged, Paddle Wing, Top Wings.**

WING BOARDS. Shifting boards fitted at sides in the hold of a collier so as to shut off the empty spaces left under the gunwales when hand trimming is dispensed with.

WING BRACKET. Triangular plate riveted or welded to the margin plate, connecting the foot of a frame bar to the inner bottom. Also called margin plate bracket.

Fr: *Gousset de Pied de Membrure;* Ger: *Kimmstutzplatte.*

WINGER. An outside tier or casks stowed in the wings of the hold.

WING HOUSE. A small deckhouse at the side of the upper deck which serves various purposes, such as paint locker, lamp room, latrine, and so on.

WINGING. The placing of weights or cargo on board toward the sides. It increases the transverse moment of inertia and tends to lengthen the period of roll of the ship without decreasing the stability.

Fr: *Arrimage en Abord;* Ger: *Hochstauung.*

WING SAIL. A quadrilateral sail bent to hoops on the mainmast and to the gaff of a ketch.

WING SHELTER. One of the small shelters closed on three sides and located at each end of the navigating bridge for the protection of watch officers against the weather.

Fr: *Abri de passerelle;* Ger: *Nockhaus.*

WING TANK. Ballast tanks located outboard and usually just under the weather deck. Sometimes formed by fitting a longitudinal bulkhead between the two uppermost decks and sometimes by working diagonal plating between the ship's side and the weather deck.

Fr: *Ballasts latéraux;* Ger: *Seitentank.*

WING TRANSOM. In wooden ships, a transverse timber which extends between the fashion pieces, crossing in front of the sternpost near the head. In square-sterned ships it forms the base of the stern. The heels of the counter timbers rest on the wing transom. Also called helm transom.

Fr: *Lisse d'Hourdi;* Ger: *Heckbalken.*

WIPER. One who cleans machinery on board ship, using cloths, cotton waste and solvents as necessary; otherwise assists in keeping the engine room clean; helps dismantle and repair machinery under direction of engineer in charge and assists in general maintenance work, such as chipping or scaling boilers, cleaning fire boxes and tubes.

WIRE BRUSH. A brush or broom with bristles made of steel wire, Used for cleaning ship's bottom and sides when in dry dock.

Fr: *Brosse métallique;* Ger: *Stahlbürste.*

WIRE DRAG.
See **Drag.**

WIRELESS HOUSE. A small deckhouse usually situated on the uppermost deck in which radio equipment and operators are housed. Also called radio room.

Fr: *Poste de Radio;* Ger: *Funkapparateraum.*

WIRELESS LOG. A statutory log book carried on all vessels equipped with radio apparatus. It is kept in the radio room and contains for each watch the names of operators and watchers as well as all incidents and occurrences connected with the wireless service; particularly all distress messages and distress traffic in full. The date and time of testing the automatic alarm receiver is noted in the book.

Fr: *Journal Radio-électrique;* Ger: *Funktagebuch.*

WIRELESS OPERATOR. A member of the ship's staff responsible for the operation and care of wireless apparatus. Also called radio operator. The enlistment of a duly qualified wireless operator is compulsory for all classes of vessels, which are required by the 1929 International Convention for the Safety of Life at Sea to be fitted with a radio-telegraph installation.

Fr: *Radio Télégraphiste; Operateur de Télégraphie sans Fil;* Ger: *Funker; Funkoffizier; Bordfunker.*

WIRE LINE. Small stuff made of twisted wire strands, used for seizings, lacings, earings, in sizes ranging from 1¼ in. circumference to ⅜ in.

Fr: *Ligne d'Amarrage Métallique;* Ger: *Drahtleine.*

WIRE NAIL. A round shank nail occasionally used in boatbuilding when the planking is made of softwood or is under ⅝ in. in thickness.

WIRE NETTING. Network made of wire rope or line, used for cargo nets, bulwark netting, and so on.

Fr: *Filet Métallique;* Ger: *Drahtnetz.*

WIRE ROPE. Rope made of metal wires twisted into strands and strands twisted into rope. The strands are in most types twisted around a heart or core made of hemp or wire. The larger the number of wires per strand or the larger the number of strands, the greater the flexibility. In some ropes each strand has a hemp core. The purpose of this core is to increase the flexibility, to retain a lubricant which adds to the life of the rope and also to minimize internal friction from contact of the wires with each other.

Fr: *Filin d'Acier; Filin Métallique;* Ger: *Drahttauwerk; Drahtseil; Stahldrahttauwerk.*

The materials used for wire rope are: plow steel, cast steel, stainless steel, bronze, iron. The first mentioned is the strongest and the last one, seldom required for ship's work, the weakest. Wire rope is usually designated by its diameter. Its construction or formation is described by two numbers, the first gives the number of strands, the second the number of wires in each strand. American Marine Standards Committee,

Standard 66, *Standard Wire Ropes for Marine Uses (specifications)*, Washington, 1930; British Standards Institution, Standard 365, *Wire Rope for Shipping Purposes*, 1929; Grant, D. E., *Wire Ropes and Cordage*, Gateshead (England), 1941.

WIRE SLING. A sling made of flexible steel wire rope. One well suited for cargo handling is made of 6-stranded 1-in. rope with 37 wires in each strand. A thimble is provided at each end. Used for handling heavy cases, machinery, etc.

Fr: *Elingue en Fil d'Acier;* Ger: *Drahtseilstropp.*

WIRE STOPPER. A contrivance used for holding a wire hawser. Also called wire nippers. It secures the rope between two jaws and dispenses with belaying or fastening to bitts, which is usually detrimental to wire roping. It is used in some vessels when a stern anchor is worked by steel wire rope. It consists essentially of a steel block in two parts hinged together by a screw pin.

Fr: *Griffe;* Ger: *Trossenklemme; Drahtkneifer; Drahtstopper.*

The interior of the block is wedged on one side and straight on the other and a wedge piece, grooved to fit the lay of the hawser, is attached to the block. When any strain is brought upon the hawser, the wedge is drawn into the block, thereby jamming the block. By changing the wedge piece, the stopper can be used for different sizes of rope.

WISHBONE. A sort of gaff or sprit consisting of two bowed spars of laminated built-to-shape wood. Also called split sprit, double sprit, wishbone gaff.

Fr: *Double Corne; Double Pic;* Ger: *Spreizgaffel.*

Both sprits are connected to the mast at their forward ends by a gooseneck. Their afterends are transversely joined by a crosspiece, to which the clew of the sail is hauled out between the two. The whole contrivance pivots at its connections to its own mast and is sheeted to the mast immediately abaft. Double sprits which hoist and lower with the sail are occasionally used to avoid the necessity of hauling the canvas through the sprits. Double sprits have also been used to replace booms or clubs on staysails.

WISHBONE RIG. A fore-and-aft yacht rig in which the clews of sails are hauled out by a spar called wishbone or open sprit. The object of this rig is to wing out the sails when sailing before the wind and also to take the strain from the mast next abaft when extending the clew, the angle of the wishbone being such that the pull of the clew lies along the axis of the spar. Also called main trysail rig, kitesail rig.

Fr: *Gréement à Double Pic;* Ger: *Spreizgaffel Takelung.*

Fenger, F. A., "The Most Criticized Rig," *Yachting*, New York, vol. 68, August, 1940.

WISHBONE TRYSAIL. A triangular or jib-shaped sail used by racing or cruising ketches and schooner yachts in which the luff of the sail runs along the mainmast track, and the clew is extended by a wishbone or double sprit. Also called main trysail. It is claimed that the efficiency of such a sail is directly improved by the fact that the clew is raised to the top half of the whole area and has the long, efficient, entering edge. It was first designed and tried on models by N. G. Herreschoff and later adapted by two other designers, Fenger and Jasper Morgan.

Ger: *Spreizgaffel Segel.*

WITH AVERAGE. A form of insurance which includes both particular and general average claims. The opposite is "free of average."

WITHE. Also wythe. An iron ring at the end of a mast, boom, or yard through which another spar can be run out. A boom iron.

Fr: *Blin;* Ger: *Spierenbügel.*

See **Boom Iron.**

WITH FREEBOARD (G. B.). Applies to the freeboard of "complete superstructure" type of vessels where the freeboard is calculated and marked from the superstructure deck, unless a tonnage opening is provided in the superstructure deck, in which case the freeboard is calculated from the second deck. Since 1949, Lloyd's Register has introduced new rules and tables of scantlings and the restriction "with freeboard" formerly assigned to shelter deck vessels has been abolished.

Fr: *Avec Franc-bord.*

WITUKSUT. A seagoing, dugout canoe used for traveling by the North American Indians of Cape Flattery and southern Vancouver (Makah Clyoguot and Nittinat people). Also called *tleiks*. It has the gracefully curving bow, sloping cutwater, plumb stern and flat bottom by which all large canoes of the chinook type are conspicuous. The upper part of the bow and stern are carefully designed with a view to artistic effect and are made separately and connected to the body of the canoe with scarfs and pegs. The length ranges from 25 to 35 ft. with a breadth of 4 to 6 ft.

WOM. A West African dugout canoe from Sherbro Island and adjacent estuaries on the coast of Sierra Leone. It is also termed bonga canoe by the Europeans. The smallest size used by a single man is employed almost exclusively in hand-lining in the river estuaries. The largest, which may attain a length of 30 ft. or more, is manned by 3 paddlers, and is used in fishing for shad by means of the cast net.

WONG. Single-outrigger, dugout canoe of the Yengen and Wagap people from eastern New Caledonia.

WONGA. Single-outrigger, dugout canoe of the Ponerihuen people from eastern New Caledonia.

WOOD CALKER. A shipyard laborer who fills the seams in the planking with cotton, oakum, white lead, putty or pitch, to make them watertight.

Fr: *Calfat;* Ger: *Kalfater.*

WOODLOCK. A close-fitting piece of wood placed below a rudder pintle nearest the waterline to prevent the rudder from unshipping. One end abuts under the lower side of the gudgeon and the other against the score. It is secured when in place by driving a bolt through it into the rudder stock.

Fr: *Clef de Gouvernail;* Ger: *Ruderschlossholz.*

WOOF.
See **Weft.**

WOOLD (to). To wind a rope or chain around a spar at the place where it is fished or scarfed for confining and strengthening it.

Fr: *Rousturer;* Ger: *Bewuhlen.*

WOOLDER. A hardwood stick about 3 ft. long, 1¾ in. in diameter at its center, and 1¼ in. at either end, used for tightening a rope at a knot, strapping blocks, winding close turns of rope around a broken spar, and so on. Also called woolder stick.

Fr: *Trésillon;* Ger: *Knebel; Drehknüppel.*

WOOLDING. A strong lashing tautened by the insertion of wedges.

Fr: *Rousture;* Ger: *Wuhling.*

WORK (to). A vessel is said *to work* when its different members begin to have play in locations where there is rigidity under normal conditions. A cargo "works" when the stowage ceases to be compact.

Fr: *Fatiguer; Jouer;* Ger: *Losarbeiten.*

WORKAWAY. Slang term to denote a person who works his passage on a ship, as distinguished from a stowaway. The workaway is a seaman and a member of the crew. He signs the articles.

WORKED EYE. Hole in a bolt, or thimble where the edges are smooth or rounded as distinguished from a shackle eye which is a straight drilled hole.

WORKING ANCHOR. A term applied in the Northern hemisphere to the Port bower because the wind usually hauls to the right; shifts of wind from S.W. to N.W. being common occurrence.

WORKING CANVAS. The sails used by a vessel when working to windward in moderate or ordinary weather.

WORKING DAY. A working day as used in charter parties is one upon which work would ordinarily be done in the port. This excludes holidays usually observed, but not days on which the usual working is merely prevented owing to the state of the elements, as for example by bad weather, or where a vessel has to discharge into lighters in open waters. The working day as mentioned in charters is usually held to be the 8-hour working day reckoned from 8 A.M. to noon and 1 P.M. to 5 P.M. It can be defined as a day on which work is not prohibited by law, custom, usage, or regulations of the port in which the charter has to be carried out. "Days" and "working days" are generally held to be synonymous terms.

Fr: *Jour Ouvrable;* Ger: *Arbeitstag.*

WORKING JIB. A medium-sized jib used in ordinary weather, as distinguished from a storm jib or a balloon jib.

Ger: *Hauptkluver.*

WORKING LIGHTS. The lights displayed at sea by fishing vessels while sorting the fish or clearing their fishing gear. Also called fishing lights.

Fr: *Feux de Pêche;* Ger: *Arbeitslicht.*

WORKING LINES. Mooring lines, warps, tow lines, and other lines used for tying a vessel to a pier or mooring.

Fr: *Amarre;* Ger: *Festmachetau.*

WORKING POOL. An area of clear water in pack ice or ice fields which gives sufficient sea room for a vessel to maneuver.

WORKING SAILS. 1. Sails made of fairly heavy canvas permanently bent in moderate weather. They are supplemented by the so-called light sails in fine weather and replaced by storm canvas in very strong winds. On a cutter the jib and mainsail are usually referred to as the working sails; on a ketch, the jib, forestaysail, mainsail, and mizzen; and on a fore-and-aft schooner, the jib, forestaysails, foresail, and mainsail.

2. On sailing yachts, a medium-sized sail, as distinguished from a storm or a racing sail.

3. In fishing boats, working sails are those set when working their gear.

Fr: *Voiles Majeures;* Ger: *Hauptsegel.*
See **Working Canvas.**

WORKING TOPSAIL. A topsail which can be carried on a wind in a fresh breeze, used only in connection with fore-and-aft-rigged vessels which carry gaff topsails.

WORM (to). To follow the lay or outline of a rope between the strands with tarred small stuff or filling, to prevent the penetration of moisture to the interior of the rope. It fills out the rope and gives a smooth surface for the serving.

Fr: *Congréer;* Ger: *Schladden; Trensen.*

WORM-GEARED WINCH. A deck winch with the transmission between motor and main shaft through worm gearing. This type of winch is particularly suited for high-class vessels carrying passengers on account of its relatively noiseless operation and also for the fast hoisting speeds which can be obtained.

Fr: *Treuil à Engrenages Hélicoïdaux;* Ger: *Schneckengetriebene Winde.*

WORMING. Small stuff used for worming a rope. Tarred marline or seizing is used for wire ropes. Marline, seizing, houseline, roundline, or hambroline are used for fiber ropes.

Fr: *Ligne à Congréer;* Ger: *Trensing; Trensgarn.*

WRACK. Seaweed cast ashore, particularly, the species of fucus which form the bulk of the wrack collected for manure or for making kelp.

Fr: *Varech;* Ger: *Seetang.*

WRACKING.
See **Racking.**

WRECK. In its widest sense, anything without an apparent owner, afloat upon, sunk in, or cast ashore by the sea. In legal phraseology it has a narrower meaning, being defined as parts of vessels or their cargoes cast upon land by the sea. According to the British Merchant Shipping Act of 1894 the term "wreck" includes jetsam, flotsam, lagan, and derelict, found on or in, the shores of the sea or any tidal water consisting of the hull, cargo, or appurtenances of a vessel. In the law of marine insurance a vessel becomes a wreck, and may be abandoned to the insurers when it becomes so disabled as to be unnavigable. The word "wreck" is also used in the meaning of a ship cast ashore after being abandoned. As regards seamen's wages, the term "wreck" refers to the case where damage is such that the ship cannot continue the adventure in respect to which the seamen's contract was entered into.

Fr: *Épave;* Ger: *Strandgut; Schiffbruch.*
See **Dangerous Wreck, Stranded Wreck.**

WRECKAGE. Goods cast ashore after a wreck. Commonly, jetsam, flotsam, lagan, and derelict.

Fr: *Débris;* Ger: *Wracktrümmer; Schiffstrümmer.*

WRECK BUOY. A buoy painted green, or with red and black horizontal stripes, moored over or near a wreck. The word "wreck," or its equivalent in the language of the country, is painted in white on the upper part of the buoy. Also called wreck-marking buoy.

Fr: *Bouée d'Épave;* Ger: *Wracktonne.*

WRECK COMMISSIONER (G. B.). The member of a court consisting of not more than three appointed by the Lord Chancellor for the purpose of investigating shipping casualties.

Ger: *Strandvogt.*

WRECKER. 1. A salvager of wrecks and wreckage, either legitimate or illegitimate salvage. Also called salvor.

Fr: *Sauveteur;* Ger: *Berger.*

2. Any person engaged in illegitimate salvage of wrecks and wreckage.

Fr: *Pilleur d'Épaves;* Ger: *Wracker; Strandräuber.*

WRECKING.
See **Salvaging.**

WRECKING BLOCK. A large, extra heavy iron strapped block with lashing shackle used for rigging up special derricks for temporary use with heavy loads.

WRECK MASTER (U. S.). 1. A person in charge of salvage operation.

2. A person given charge of a wreck or stranded goods by owners or salvors.

WRIGGLE. Bent steel strip fitted on the outside shell plating above a sidelight to deflect any water which may be trickling down, and prevent it from entering when the sidelight is open. Also called rigol, brow, watershed.

Fr: *Cil; Arceau.*

WRING BOLT. A large ringbolt used in conjunction with a ring staff to force outside planks into position during the construction of a wooden hull. It consists of a ringbolt with two or more forelock holes in the end for taking in the set as the plank is worked near the timbers. Also called wrain bolt.
Ger: *Zwingbolzen.*

WRING STAFF. A stong bar of wood with two wringbolts used by shipwrights for bending planks over the frames so that they can be bolted efficiently. Also called wrain staff, sett.
Fr: *Bridole;* Ger: *Zwinger.*

WU-TSEI-SHUAN. A Chinese seagoing fishing junk from Hangchow Bay (Che-Kiang province) or cuttlefish boat which works with nets. It is rigged with one or two masts stepped forward. Length 30 to 55 ft. Breadth 7 to 8 ft. (Average.)

WYE.
See **Spider Iron.**

WYTHE.
See **Withe.**

X

X. Flag of the international code of signals having a white ground with a blue Greek cross extending full length and breadth of the flag. Hoisted singly it means: "Stop carrying out your intentions and watch for my signals." When used between tug and tow it means: "Get spare towing hawser ready," when made by ship towing. When made by ship towed it means: "I cannot carry out your order."

XEBEC. Three-masted Mediterranean coaster of displacement ranging from 30 to 60 tons. Also called *chébec, sciabecco, jabeque.*

In the 18th and early 19th centuries, large xebecs had square rig on the foremast and lateen sails on the others, with bowsprit and two headsails, and displaced 300 to 400 tons. Nowadays the Italian *sciabecco* is rigged with lateen sails on the fore- and mainmasts and gaff sail on the mizzen. It has neither headsails nor bowsprit. The hull is built with sharp stern and high poop. When becalmed long sweeps are used.

The Spanish *jabeque* is still found in the Balearic Islands. It is lateen-rigged on all 3 masts, and carries a bowsprit with large jib. The foremast rakes forward, the main and mizzen are upright. The lateen yard of the mizzen is nearly perpendicular and the sail sheets on a long outrigger. It is the largest lateen-rigged vessel of the Mediterranean.

On the African coast the *xebec* has lateen sails on all 3 masts. The mainmast, stepped amidships, is vertical; the foremast has a slight forward rake and the mizzen rakes aft. One headsail sets on a light spar, which is lashed to the beakhead of the stem. The **stem** is built with long overhand counter.

Fr: *Chébec;* Ger: *Schebecke.*

Most of these craft are fully decked, although some of the smaller ones are undecked amidships. Sails are made of cotton. The hull is flat floored to enable the boats to be beached without damage. The small *xebecs* have a length of about 50 ft. with a length to breadth ratio which ranges from 3½ to 4 and a maximum draft of 6 ft. The tonnage varies between 25 and 30. According to some writers, the *xebec* from the Tunisian coast is also known under the name of *mistico.*

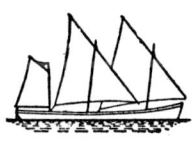

Italian Xebec

927

Y

Y. Flag of the international code of signals showing a series of diagonal alternating yellow and red stripes of equal width and making a 45° angle with the hoist. When hoisted singly at starboard yard arm, at triatic stay or on mast below house flag, it denotes: "I am carrying mails." Used as a signal between tug and tow it means: "I cannot carry out your order."

Y. A. R. YORK ANTWERP RULES (insurance).
Y.M. YACHT MEASUREMENT (tonnage).
Y. R. A. YACHT RACING ASSOCIATION.

YACHT. A vessel used exclusively for pleasure, as distinguished from one used for commerce, war, or scientific purposes. A yacht is also used as a vessel of state to convey persons of distinction by water. From the legal viewpoint, a yacht is a ship, and is subject to most of the rights and liabilities of ships, though it may be bound by the local rules of any yacht club to the exclusion of its legal rights, but not for its liabilities.

Fr: *Yacht;* Ger: *Yacht; Lustyacht.*

See **Barge Yacht, Canoe Yacht, Cruising Yacht, Racing Yacht.**

YACHT DUCK. Sailcloth made of American or Egyptian cotton and used in the fabrication of sails for racing and cruising craft. Yacht duck is graded by weight. The unit of weight, as established by the U. S. Bureau of Standards, is the weight in ounces of a piece of duck with an area of 1026 square inches which is the equivalent of a piece one yard long and 28½ inches wide. Most yacht duck is made in bolts of 18, 22, and 28½ inches width. Cloth for light spinnakers ranges from 36 to 40 inches in width.

YACHT ENSIGN. A flag adopted in United States by Act of Congress and restricted in its use to yachts. In the blue square, in which the 48 stars ordinarily appear, is a circle of 13 stars, in the center of which is a fouled anchor.

YACHT MARLINE. Tarred marline with a weight of 0.0195 lb. per fathom, used for small work in rigging lofts.

YACHT MEASUREMENT. The measuring of a yacht according to a certain rule or formula in order that the vessel can be given classification and time allowance when entered in a competitive event. Also called **yacht rating.** International rating or measurement rule is of Danish origin.

Fr: *Jauge de Course;* Ger: *Rennwert.*
Froude, R. E., "Yacht Racing Measurement Rules and the International Conference," Institution of Naval Architects (London), *Transactions,* vol. 48 (1906); Stephens, W. P., "Yacht Measurement," Society of Naval Architects and Marine Engineers (New York), *Transactions,* vol. 43 (1935).

YACHT ROPE. Rope made from high grade Manila fiber and used for the running rigging on yachts.

YACHT STERN. A variation of the fantail stern in which a small, sharply raked transom takes up the extreme afterend of the counter instead of allowing the planking to sweep up to a sharp point. Also called small transom stern. It is not suitable for small motor cruisers, or for open boats of any size.

See **Fantail.**

YAHTRA ORUWA. A small, single-outrigger, open coaster from the southwest coast of Ceylon, with a capacity of about 50 tons. The hull is built with sewed planking. The rig consists of two pole masts with lugsails. Also called *yahtra doni.*

YANCA'ATWAT. A dugout canoe of the Koryak and Kamchadal of northern Kamchatka. Also called *yanina'atwat, struzhok.* It is hollowed out of poplar or aspen trunks and is so well made that it is no heavier than a skin canoe. It is mostly used on rivers, but the maritime Koryak of northern Kamchatka go out in them on the bays to hunt seals like the Kamchadal people.

YANKEE JIB TOPSAIL. A racing jib topsail in which the luff extends from bowsprit (or stemhead) to masthead. It is cut diagonally, has a wire luff, and is roped at the clew. It sets on the topmast stay with hanks.

YANNO. Deep-sea Japanese fishing sampan employed in the tuna fisheries with lines. There are two types, one from the Shizuoka district, the other from the Shiba district. The first is a three-masted boat. Length over-all 46 ft. Breadth 9.6 ft. Depth 3.7 ft. Draft 2.4 ft. The rig consists of 3 masts with the usual square sails of Japanese pattern. The foremast is stepped just above the forefoot and is about 20 ft. in length.

The second, or middle mast, stepped a short distance abaft the foremast, is about 22½ ft. long. The aftermast or mainmast is stepped well aft as in all Japanese craft, and is about 35 ft. long. Total sail area 940 sq. ft. These boats are built with high washboards extending from the stern to the middle mast and also for a short length on each side of the foremast. They are manned by a crew of 9.

The second type, from Shiba district, is a smaller boat. Length over-all 35.5 ft., breadth 9.0 ft., depth 3.4 ft. It is rigged with one mast, and has a total sail area of 707 sq. ft. It is manned by a crew of 10.

Fr: *Potence;* Ger: *Bock.*

YARD MASTER. One who oversees the operation and moving of locomotives and trains in a shipyard. He oversees the carrying and handling of material about the yard. He directs the operation of cranes.

YARD ROPE. A rope for sending yards up or down. It is kept rove off at masthead.

Fr: *Cartahu de vergue;* Ger: *Raajolle.*

YARD SLING. A chain used for supporting a yard which does not travel up and down the mast, such as lower yards, lower topsail, and lower topgallant yards. It is fastened to the middle of the yard.

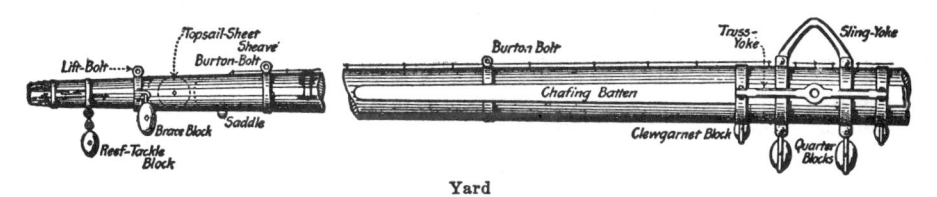

Yard

YARD. A long, nearly cylindrical spar, tapering toward the ends, used for supporting and extending a square, lateen, or lugsail.
Fr: *Vergue;* Ger: *Rahe; Raa.*
See **After Yards, Cross-Jack Yard, Gunter Yard, Jack Yard, Jenny Yard, Jinny Yard, Lateen Yard, Signal Yard, Spread Yard, Square Yard, Square Yards, Studding Sail Yard, Gaff Topsail Yard.**

YARDAGE. The length per unit of weight of ropes and small stuff.

YARD AND STAY SYSTEM.
See **Burton Tackle.**

YARD BECKET. A rope grommet fastened to a yard and used for holding on by men working aloft. Also called hand becket.
Fr: *Poignée;* Ger: *Handperd.*

YARD BOOM. A derrick or cargo boom swung over the ship's side and guyed there. It takes the load off the hatch boom and lowers it clear of the ship's side. Also called yard derrick.

YARD CRAFT. Collectively, tugs, barges, lighters and other small harbor craft used in a dockyard.

YARD CRANE. A projecting iron arm attached to the fore part of the mast cap or to the mast itself and hinged so as to move horizontally. It is used for supporting lower topsail or lower topgallant yards.

Fr: *Suspente;* Ger: *Hängerkette.*

YARD SPAN. An arch-shaped forging with ends attached to the sling hoops of a yard and connected at its center to the truss.

Fr: *Etrier de Brasseyage;* Ger: *Hänger.*

YARD TACKLE. Tackle used in conjunction with a stay tackle and attached to a lower yard, where the latter is used as a derrick. The term is applied specifically to a rather heavy, two-fold purchase kept for handling weights too heavy for a yard whip. Also called quarter tackle.

Fr: *Palan de Bout de Vergue;* Ger: *Nocktakel.*
See **Yard Whip.**

YARD TOPSAIL. See **Donkey Topsail.**

YARD WHIP. A cargo whip fastened to the extreme end of a yard or derrick boom and used for swinging outboard or inboard the sling of cargo lifted or lowered by the hatch whip. It was formerly used in square-rigged ships when watering at sea with casks. Also called burton fall, water whip.

Fr: *Cartahu d'en Dehors;* Ger: *Nocktakel.*

YARN. Any of the fiber threads which, when twisted together, form a strand.
Fr: *Fil;* Ger: *Garn.*
See **Rogue's Yarn, Rope Yarn, Spun Yarn, Warp Yarn, Weft Yarn.**

YAW. A temporary deviation of a ship from her course caused by bad steering, the action of the waves, or by an injudicious arrangement of the sails.

Fr: *Embardée;* Ger: *Gieren.*

YAW (to). To steer wildly or out of the line of the course, as when running with a heavy quartering sea.

YAWING. The rotary oscillation of a ship about a vertical axis approximately through its center of gravity.

YAWL. 1. A rig for small craft consisting of two masts, the after one being much the smaller and stepped abaft the sternpost. The aftermast is called a jigger, mizzen, or dandy mast. It is a cutter-rigged vessel with a jigger mast stepped in the counter, and a short main boom. The after sail is not necessarily a gaff sail. In the smaller class of yawls a lug or jib-headed sail takes the place of the gaff sail. The clew of the yawl's jigger is hauled out abaft the stern on an outrigger. The jigger mast is customarily less than one-half the height of the mainmast and usually stepped as far aft as the design and construction of the boat will allow, with an outrigger or boomkin of sufficient length to give proper control over the sheet. The area of the jigger is usually 10 to 16 per cent of the total sail area.

Fr: *Cotre à Tapecul; Yawl;* Ger: *Yawl; Jolle; Hecksegelkutter.*

2. A rowboat with stem and stern alike, both ends being sharp as on lifeboats. Norway Yawls are square-sterned and shovel-nosed, the so-called pram dinghy being in effect such a yawl abbreviated.

3. A man-of-war's boat resembling a pinnace but somewhat smaller, carvel-built and generally rowed with 4 or 6 oars (G. B.).

4. In Kilkeel, North Ireland, a small, open fishing boat with sharp stern and rigged with a foresail and single lug. It is also called skiff.

See Cat Yawl, Canoe Yawl, Donegal Yawl, Greencastle Yawl, Groomport Yawl, Lough Foyle Yawl, New Haven Yawl, Roslyn Yawl, Scaffie Yawl, Schooner Yawl, Shetland Yawl, Skerry Yawl.

YAWL MIZZEN.
See Jigger.

YECABUQUTS. A dugout canoe from the north-west Pacific coast employed by the Makah Indians from Cape Flattery for seal hunting. It is handled by two men, one in the bow with harpoon, the other paddling. Length 20 to 22 ft. Breadth 2½ ft. (Average.)

YEL. An East Indian dugout canoe with double-outriggers, from Weda Bay, eastern Moluccas. Some of these boats have the depth increased by the addition of a wash strake. They carry a shelter with sides built outboard upon the supports of the booms. The bow and stern pieces are short and inconspicuous. Length over-all 25 ft. Breadth 2½ ft. Depth 2½ ft. (Typical.)

YELLOW FEVER. An infectious, mosquito-borne disease of warm climates which spreads from place to place. The International Sanitary Convention of 1926 provides that a ship shall be regarded as infected by yellow fever if there is a case on board or if there was one at the time of departure or during the voyage. The ship is regarded as suspect if, having had no case of yellow fever, it arrives after a voyage of less than 6 days from an infected port or from a port in close relation with an endemic center of yellow fever, or if it arrives after a voyage of more than 6 days and there is reason to believe that it may transport germs emanating from the said port. A ship is regarded as healthy notwithstanding its having come from an infected port, if on arriving after a voyage of more than 6 days, it has had no case of yellow fever on board, and, therefore, there is no reason to believe that it transports adult *Stegomya* mosquitoes, or it is proved to the satisfaction of the Authority on the time of arrival, that: (1) The ship during its stay in the port of departure was moored at a distance of at least 600 feet from the infected shore, or (2) That the ship, at the time of departure was effectively fumigated in order to destroy mosquitoes.

Fr: *Fièvre Jaune;* Ger: *Gelbes Fieber.*

YELLOW JACK. 1. Seaman's name for the quarantine flag "Q."
2. Yellow fever.
See Yellow Fever.

YELLOW METAL.
See Naval Brass.

YELLOW PINE. A strong, close-grained durable wood free of knots, extensively used in ship and boatbuilding for outside and deck planking, keels, keelsons, deadwood, gunwales, and spars. Weight when seasoned

about 45 lb. per cu. ft. Also called Georgia pine, long leaf pine, pitch pine.
Fr: *Pichpin;* Ger: *Pechtannenholz; Pitchpineholz.*

YEN-TAI-SHUAN. A Chefoo trading junk similar in build to the Antung junk and found in the various ports of the Gulf of Petchili. It is rigged with 4 masts. Length 70 to 90 ft. Breadth 20 ft. Capacity 50 to 60 tons.

YOKE. A steel frame or bar having its center bored and keyed for attachment to the rudderhead. Connecting rods or leads from the steering gear are connected to each end of the yoke.
Fr: *Croissant; Tête de Cheval; Traverse;* Ger: *Ruderjoch; Kreuzkopf.*
See **Mast Yoke, Truss Yoke.**

YOKE LANYARD.
See **Yoke Line.**

YOKE LINE. One of the lines attached to each end of the yoke in a rowboat, by which the rudder is moved. Also called yoke lanyard.
Fr: *Tire Veille;* Ger: *Sceptertau; Jochleine.*

YOLE. Clinker-built open boats with raking stem and pointed stern, used for fishing and transportation in the Orkney and Shetland Isles. Yoles have recently been mostly replaced by the larger fifies. They are rigged with one or two masts and a bowsprit. The masts carry spritsails or standing lugs. Most of them are open craft. Some have a small deck at bow and stern, connected by waterways. Most of these boats are nowadays fitted with auxiliary engines. Length over-all 19 ft. Length of keel 14 ft. Breadth 7 ft. 9 in. Depth 2 ft. 8 in. (Typical.)
See **Ness Yole, South Isles Yole, Westray Yole.**

YORK-ANTWERP RULES. A code of rules relating to General Average, agreed upon by British and foreign merchants, bankers, underwriters, and others interested in the shipping business as a result of meetings first held in York and subsequently in Antwerp, their object being to establish a uniform system for adjusting all questions relating to General Average. They were first adopted by the shipping community at York in 1864 and in Antwerp in 1877. They underwent further revisions in 1890 at Liverpool, in 1892 at Genoa, in 1903 at Antwerp, and in 1924 at Stockholm.
See **General Average.**
Cole, S. D., *The Stockholm Conference on General Average,* London; Rudolph, G. R., *The York Antwerp Rules,* London, 1926.

YOUNG ICE. All unhummocked ice of any age or thickness.
Fr: *Glace Nouvelle.*

YOURKEVITCH BOW. A bow form characterised by a fore-body built in such a way that the fore and aft distribution of displacement, combined with a reduction in the angles of entrance, particularly in the vicinity of the load waterline, are very much reduced.

YULOH. A Chinese sculling sweep which consists of two parts, a loom and a blade, both lashed and pegged together so that they are not in a straight line. When in use the *yuloh* is supported on a pin which fits easily into a shallow hole in the loom, with the result that the center of gravity of the whole is below the point of support. The blade in this position, being horizontal, makes the *yuloh* self-feathering, and it must be turned to make a stroke. This is opposite to the European sculling sweep, which must be turned to feather. In northern China, *yulohs* are occasionally made of one piece, which is bent to maintain the self-feathering effect.

Z

Z. International code of signals flag consisting of 4 colored triangles having their apexes meeting at the center of the flag. The black triangle is at the hoist, the blue at the fly, the yellow at the top and the red at the bottom. When hoisted singly the flag means: "I am addressing or wish to communicate with a shore station." When used by a ship towing another it denotes: "I am commencing to tow." If flown by the ship towed it means: "Commence towing."

Z. AZIMUTH (astronomy).
Z.D. ZENITH DISTANCE (astronomy).
Z.T. ZONE TIME.

ZAIMA. A boat from Hodeida, on the Red Sea, with long prow and backward-sloping stern. It is rigged with one mast.

ZARUK, ZARUKA. Arab dhow from the Red Sea with raking stem, pointed stern, and vertical sternpost rising above the deck. The rig consists of 1 or 2 masts with settee sails. Steering is effected by means of a spur projecting abaft the rudder blade, to which are attached the rudder lines. These are made fast each to the outboard end of two spars, which are pivoted at the end of a heavy beam laid athwartship and projecting outboard, so that lines from their inboard ends come handy to the steersman. Small *zaruks* with a length ranging from 26 to 32 ft., owned and manned by Arabs from the Yemen, are used in the fisheries of the coast of Eritrea (Hawakil and Anfile Bays). Each *zaruk* is accompanied by several *uri* (dugout canoes) from which the lines are handled. Length 70 ft. Breadth 18 ft. Depth 10.5 ft. Tonnage 100. (Typical.)
See Bagara.

ZEE BAR, Z BAR. A rolled section or shape with two legs standing perpendicularly to a web, which gets its name from the similarity of its cross section to the letter "Z." Used as a stiffener for bulkheads and shell plating. In small ships it is occasionally used as frame bar. The toe is located on the outstanding point of the flange. The heel is the outside corner where web and flange join.
Fr: *Fer en Z;* Ger: *Z-profil.*

ZEESENBOOT. A half-decked, sailing trawler found in the Baltic on the coast of Schleswig-Holstein and Pomerania, with a keel length of 25 to 31 ft., a breadth of 9 to 12 ft., and a depth of 3.3 to 4 ft. The *Zeesenboot* is ketch-rigged in the Oder Estuary, lug-rigged in the Stettiner-Haff with a loose-footed mainsail and boomed mizzen. Center- or leeboards are fitted. The mouth of the net, when not fitted with otter boards, is kept open by fastening the warps to two spars (*Zeesenbaume*) rigged out at bow and stern. The boat is then kept drifting before the wind with all sails set.

ZEESENERKAHN.
See Zeesenboot.

ZENITH. The point in the celestial sphere vertically overhead.
Fr: *Zenith;* Ger: *Zenit.*

ZENITH DISTANCE. The angular distance of an object from the observer's zenith, found by subtracting the true altitude from 90°.
Fr: *Distance Zénithale;* Ger: *Zenitdistanz.*

ZENITH TELESCOPE. A telescope used in observatories for detecting and measuring small variations of terrestrial latitude. It is directed toward the zenith, and is usually mounted on floating mercury.
Fr: *Lunette astronomique;* Ger: *Astronomisches Fernrohr.*

ZERNOCON. Code name for charter parties relating to grain cargoes from Russian, Black Sea, and Azoff ports to United Kingdom and continental ports.

ZIGZAG RIVETING. Rows of rivets placed parallel longitudinally, but alternately, or in zigzag form in the transverse direction. Also called staggered riveting, reeled riveting.
Fr: *Rivetage en Quinconce;* Ger: *Zickzacknietung.*

ZINC PROTECTOR. Slabs or rings of rolled zinc fastened to the shell plating at points near propellers, stern-tube bushing, gudgeons, sea valves, and other underwater fittings made of bronze or brass, to prevent their corrosion due to galvanic action. Sometimes called zincs. The zinc wastes away, and must be replaced periodically.
Ger: *Schutzplatte.*

ZODIAC. A zone extending 8° on each

side of the ecliptic and divided into twelve equal parts called the signs of the zodiac.

Fr: *Zodiaque;* Ger: *Tierkreis; Zodiakus.*

ZODIACAL BAND. A faint luminous band joining the apexes of the cones of the morning and evening zodiacal lights, lying nearly along the ecliptic and only a few degrees wide.

ZODIACAL LIGHT. A soft faint light, usually white, which may be seen in the tropics on any clear night rising cone-shaped above the western horizon after sunset and above the eastern horizon before sunrise.

Fr: *Lumière Zodiacale;* Ger: *Tierkreislicht.*

ZONE DESCRIPTION. The correction which must be applied to ship's time to obtain the corresponding Greenwich Meridian Civil time. It is the number of the zone prefixed by the plus sign (+) if in West longitude, or the minus sign (−) if in East longitude.

ZONE TIME. Standard time applied at sea according to the time zone in which the vessel is located; each zone being designated by the number of hours which must be applied to the local time to obtain Greenwich time. Ship's clocks are set to zone time.

Fr: *Heure du Fuseau;* Ger: *Zonenzeit.*

ZOPPOLO. An open fishing boat of the Croatian coast. It is hewed out of a single trunk, and the sides are raised by planking. In order to increase stability a broad plank about 10 ft. long is nailed across the boat extending about 1 meter on each side. It serves as an outrigger for the rowlocks. The length is about 4 m., breadth 1 m.

ZULU. Scotch, lug-rigged fishing boat of 15 to 25 tons burden. It has a broad and powerful form with fine sharp bow and stern, an over-all length of 26 to 80 ft. and is completely decked. The rig consists of 2 masts and 3 sails: mainsail, foresail, and mizzen. The mainmast, very lofty, stands well forward and is not supported by shrouds, stays, or any kind of standing rigging. The foresail is run out on a bowsprit standing about 8 ft. beyond the stem. The clew of the mizzen is hauled out on an outrigger. There are usually 7 rows of reef points in the mainsail and 4 rows in the mizzen. The Zulu has an enormous rake to her sternpost and a considerable amount in her keel so that for the same waterline length and mid-sections it has less wetted surface and turns better than the fifie. This type of boat combines the straight stem of the fifie with the raked stern of the skaffie. Large Zulu: Length over-all 79 ft. Breadth 20.4 ft. Depth 12 ft.

ZUMACA. A small sailing coaster from the River Plate estuary and adjacent waters in Brazil. The hull is roughly built. The rig consists of 2 masts with lug foresail and gaff mizzen.

FRENCH INDEX

Abandon, 1
Abaque de Marée, 489
Abattage, 375
Abattre, 130, 274, 574
Abattre en Carène, 124
A bloc, 876
A Bord, 2, 921
Abordage, 164
Aborder, 668
A Bordure Libre, 474
About, 110
Aboutement, 111
Abri de Navigation, 915
Abri de passerelle, 922
Acacia, 467
Acajou, 484
Accalmie 478
Accastillage, 203, 624, 847, 883
Accélération, 2
Accélération Diurne, 226
Accore, 730, 770
Accore de Bouchain, 63
Accore latérale, 63
Accorer, 730
Accotar, 593, 719
Accouplement de Mèche, 666
Achromatique, 3
Acier au Nickel, 536
Acier à Haute Résistance, 372
Acier Inoxydable, 774
Aconage, 454
Aconier, 454
Acquit à Caution, 82, 193
Acquit de Douane, 150
Acte de Guerre, 3
Acte de Nationalisation, 137
Acte de Propriété, 137
Acte de Vente, 64
Administration du Pilotage, 582
Adonner, 888
Aération de Chaufferie, 279
Aérolite, 6
Affaler, 558
Affolement de l'Hélice, 224
Affouillmenet, 689
Affourcher, 519
Affrètement, 6
Affrètement à Forfait, 478
Affrètement aller retour, 661
Affrètement au Voyage, 863
Affrètement Coque-Nue, 212

Affrètement en Travers, 478
Affrèteur, 141, 310
A Fleur d'eau, 28
À flot, 6, 900
Age, 7
Agent en Douane, 193
Agent de Passages, 571
Agents du Lloyd, 462
Aide de Navigation, 8
Aiguille, 585
Aiguille à Basaner, 816
Aiguille aimantée, 483
Aiguille à Oeillets, 494
Aiguille à Ralinguer, 81
Aiguille de Voilier, 677
Aiguille d'Inclinaison, 222
Aiguille du Compas, 887
Aiguilletage, 524
Aiguilletage en Portugaise, 659
Aiguilleter, 434
Aiguillette, 434
Aiguillette de Bout-Dehors, 368
Aiguillette de Racage, 570
Aiguillot, 585
Aiguillot à Tête, 467
Aiguillot Inférieur, 86
Aiguillot Massif, 755
Aiguillot Rapporté, 287
Aile, 289, 445, 921
Aile à Pas réglable, 3
Aile de Pigeon, 744
Aile d'Hélice, 610
Aileron, 718, 762
Aimant, 481
Aimant Compensateur, 171
Aimant Correcteur Semi Circulaire, 707
Aimant Correcteur de Bande, 368
Aimant Induit, 827
Aimant Naturel, 528
Aimant permanent, 578
Aire de vent, 647
Aire du disque, 223
Aire du Safran, 664
Aires des Couples, 305
Aisselle, 832
Ajut, 56
A la cape, 26
À la Cape Sèche, 8
A la Demande, 354

A l'arrière, 6
A l'avant, 303
Alène de voilier, 772
Aléser, 636
Alésoir, 636
Alèze, 211, 460
Algue, 9
Algues, 420
Alidade, 391
Alignement, 9, 151, 854
Aligner, 771
Alimenteur, 232, 902
Allège, 454
Allégeance, 10
Alléger, 454
Allonge, 317
Allonge Coudée, 424
Allonge d'écubier, 361
Allonge de Pavois, 847
Allonge de Revers, 105
Allonge de Voûte Fourchette, 379
Allonge Double, 235
Allongez, 473
Allure, 675
Allures, 524
A Long Pic, 473
Aluminium, 11
Amarrage, 373, 434, 702, 791
Amarrage Croisé, 187
Amarrage d'Envergure, 656
Amarrage en Étrive, 348
Amarrage en Portugaise, 626, 716
Amarrage Plat, 291
Amarrage plat avec Bridure, 661
Amarrage Plat Double, 833
Amarrages de Tente, 29
Amarre, 521, 924
Amarre de Bout, 90, 787
Amarre de Poste, 276, 768
Amarre de Poste Arrière, 7
Amarre de Poste Avant, 304
Amarre de Terre, 730
Amarre en Double, 747
Amarrer, 54, 434, 486, 519, 702
Amarre Traversière, 97
Ambregris, 12
Âme, 178, 365, 906
Amener, 360, 475, 799
Amer, 49, 433, 696

935

Amer à Voyant biconique, 218
Amers de Direction, 442
Amers de Sécurité, 151
à Mi-Drisse, 221
a mi-drisse en berne, 349
Amphidrôme, 234
Amplitude, 13
Amplitude de la Marée, 835
Amplitude de Marée, 834
Amplitude Diurne, 227
Amplitude du roulis, 13
Amplitude du tangage, 13
Amplitude en morte eau, 533
Amplitude en vive eau, 768
Amplitude Moyenne, 501
Amplitude moyenne en morte eau, 501
Amplitude moyenne en vive eau, 501
Ampoulette, 468
Amure, 816
Amure de Revers, 445
Ancre, 13
Ancre à Champignon, 525
Ancre à Déjaler, 722
Ancre à Jas, 790
Ancre à Jet, 418
Ancre articulée, 235, 299
Ancre à Vis, 521
Ancre de Bossoir, 88
Ancre de Corps-Mort, 519
Ancre de croupiat, 784
Ancre de Détroit, 798
Ancre d'Empennelle, 30
Ancre de réserve, 59
Ancre de Touée, 798
Ancre d'Étrave, 784
Ancre de Veille, 717
Ancre engagée, 304
Ancre flottante, 238, 423, 694
Ancre Martin, 495
Ancre sans Jas, 790
Ancre sons de vent, 444
Ancre travaillante, 648
Anémomètre, 17
Angle d'Acuité, 18
Angle de Chavirement, 883
Angle de Dérive, 243
Angle de Gîte, 18
Angle d'inclinaison Magnétique, 18
Angle Horaire, 381
Angle Horaire de Greenwich, 338
Angle horaire du lieu, 465
Angle horaire sidéral, 735
Angle méridien, 507

Angle parallactique, 568
Anguiller, 240, 457
Anneau de Bishop, 66
Année Sidérale, 735
Année Solaire, 754
Année Solaire Moyenne, 501
Année tropique, 865
Annexe, 827
Annuaire des Marées, 836
Anon, 161
Anse, 61, 182
Anspec, 14, 354
Antenne, 19, 435
Antenne en T, 815
Antenne-Prisme, 116
Anticyclone, 19
Aphélie, 20
A Pic, 20, 25, 731, 882
A piqué, 20
A piquer, 160, 574, 783, 845, 863
Apogée, 20
À poste, 376
Apôtre, 423
Apparaux de manutention, 126
Apparaux de mouillage, 16, 340
Apparaux et Agrès, 20
Appareil, 305, 327
Appareil à Gouverner, 782
Appareil à gouverner à Air comprimé, 593
Appareil à gouverner à Bras, 354
Appareil à Gouverner à Commande Directe, 223
Appareil à Gouverner à Commande Indirecte, 392
Appareil à gouverner à Drosses, 138
Appareil à gouverner à secteur denté, 626
Appareil à Gouverner Asservi, 603
Appareil à Gouverner à Vapeur, 780
Appareil à Gouverner à Vis, 692
Appareil à Gouverner Électrique, 255
Appareil à Gouverner Hydraulique, 385
Appareil à gouverner Hydro-Électrique, 257
Appareil à pistons plongeurs opposés, 553
Appareil Auto Alarme, 26

Appareil de commande à Distance, 299
Appareil de Décrochage, 225
Appareil Frigorifique, 641
Appareil lance-Fusée, 656
Appareiller, 674
Appareil porte Amarre, 656
Appareils auxiliaires, 28
Appel, 341, 526
Appeler, 827
Appendice, 21
Appontement, 433, 581, 914
Apports littoraux, 461
Approvisionnements de Bord, 699, 728
Approvisionnements de Pont, 209
Approvisionnements Machines, 261
Approvisionnements non Dédouanés, 81
Appuyer, 360
Appuyeur, 655
Aptitude à la mer, 694
Araignée, 187
Araignée de Hamac, 350
Arbalète, 746, 767
Arbalétrier, 29, 187
Arbre à manivelles, 184
Arbre Coudé, 184
Arbre de Butée, 834
Arbre Intermédiaire, 396
Arbre Porte Hélice, 611
Arc, 373
Arcasse, 7, 854
Arc Boutant de Billot, 31
Arc-boutant de brasseyage, 92
Arc Boutant de Chantier, 31
Arc-Boutant de Chasse, 245
Arc-Boutant de Drosse, 868
Arc-Boutant de Martingale, 231
Arc-Boutant de Traversière, 284
Arc-Boutants de Beaupré, 916
Arc-Boutants de Bossoirs, 916
Arceau, 925
Arceau de Remorque, 851
Archipompe, 615
Architecture Navale, 530
Ardent, 23
Arête d'Entrée, 442
Arête de Sortie, 299
Armateur-Gérant, 487, 727
Armé en Couple, 233
Armé en Pointe, 738
Armement, 75, 556
Armer, 486, 723

Armez, 557
Armez les Avirons, 441
Arqué, 99
Arraisonnement, 72
Arraisonner, 347
Arrêt de Prince, 24, 645
Arrêt de Puissance, 24
Arrêté par la brume, 298
Arrêter, 287
Arrière, 784
Arrière à écusson, 772
Arrière à Tableau, 854, 855
Arrière à Voûte, 180
Arrière Carré, 291
Arrière de Canoe, 121
Arrière de Croiseur, 188
Arrière en V., 893
Arrière Pointu, 714
Arrière Port, 393
Arrière Rond, 258
Arrimage, 796
Arrimage à la Pelle, 862
Arrimage en Abord, 922
Arrimé en Travers, 2
Arrimer, 795, 862
Arriser, 685, 788, 848
Arrondi de Bouchain, 874
Artimon, 320, 410, 514
Artimon de Cape, 294, 793
Ascension Droite, 650
Ascension méridienne, 650
Aspiration aux Bouchains, 63
Aspiration Principale aux Bouchains, 62
Assemblage à Dé, 156, 161, 236
Assemblage à Patte de Loup, 816
Assiette, 862
Assistance, 849
Assurance, 113
Assurance débours, 223
Assurance fret, 310
Assurance Maritime, 491
Assurance Mutuelle, 526
Assurance sur Équipement, 557
Assureur Maritime, 880
Assureur sur Corps, 383
Assureur sur Facultés, 128
Astronomie Nautique, 528
A terre, 24
Atteindre, 278
Atterrage, 432
Attinage, 69, 790
Attraction Locale, 465
Aube, 562
Aubier, 681

Au Large, 546, 698
Au large de, 545
Au large et à terre, 545
Aumée, 23
Au Milieu du Navire, 13
Au mouillage, 16, 25
Aunée, 460
Au Plus Près, 112, 154
Aussière, 362, 371
Aussière d'Amarrage, 521
Aussière de Halage, 897
Aussière en Quatre, 733
Aussière en Trois, 362
Auto Gouvernail, 346
Autorité du Port, 599
Autorité Portuaire, 599
Autorités Douanières, 192
Autorités Portuaires, 354
Au Vent, 28, 849, 905, 921
Auxiliaires de bord, 28
Auxiliaires de coque, 383
Auxiliaires de Machine, 261
Auxiliaires de Pont, 204
Avance, 5
Avance de Fret, 5
Avance Diurne, 321
Avance par Tour, 762
Avançon, 752
Avant, 88, 270, 300, 363
Avant à Bulbe, 103
Avant à cuiller, 767
Avant à dévers, 290
Avantage du vent, 905
Avant à Guibre, 153
Avant-Cale, 904
Avant fin, 444
Avant Plein, 79
Avant-Port, 556
A Varangues acculées, 714
Avarie, 28
Avarie Commune, 328
Avarie Particulière, 571
Avec Franc-bord, 923
Avertisseur automatique d'Incendie, 282
Aviron, 543
Aviron à Cuiller, 767
Aviron de couple, 692
Aviron de Galère, 811
Aviron de Queue, 782
Aviron Droit, 797
Avirons dans l'eau, 375
Avis aux Navigateurs, 541
Avis de Remise, 638
Avitailler, 612
Avoir Son Port d'Attache, 347
Awning Deck, 29
Axe de Girouette, 886

Axe Longitudinal, 136
Azimut, 29

Babord, 598
Bac, 278
Bac Porte-Trains, 853
Badingue, 199
Badinque, 108
Bagage, 33
Bague d'Envergure, 354
Bague de Tolet, 662
Baie, 49
Baignoire, 908
Baille à Drisse, 350
Baille à Salaisons, 356
Balance, 377
Balancement, 591, 772
Balancement des Formes, 273
Balancier, 34, 557
Balancine, 452
Balancine de gui, 621
Balant, 61
Balayures, 764
Baleine, 337, 911
Baleinière, 911
Baleston, 769
Balestron, 155
Balisage, 50, 107
Balise, 49
Balise de direction, 633
Balise Fixe, 288
Balise Flottante, 293
Balise radar, 627
Baliseur, 455
Ballast Latéral, 736
Ballast Sec, 247
Ballasts latéraux, 847, 922
Balle, 35
Ballon, 36, 37, 55
Ballon de Défense, 178
Ballon en Toile à Voile, 122
Ballon horaire, 838
Banc, 39
Banc de Carénage, 338
Banc de Mât, 499, 675
Banc de Nage, 834
Banc Médian, 510
Banc Milieu, 510
Bande, 367, 412
Bandeau, 191, 272, 381
Bande de Cargue Fond, 107
Bande de Ris, 639
Bande de ris Diagonal, 35
Bande d'Étambot, 741
Bande d'Étrave, 784
Bande Diagonale, 217, 648
Bandes Diagonales, 218

Banquise, 561
Banquise Flottante, 294
Baraterie, 44
Barbarasse, 231, 537
Barbe, 377
Barbes de l'Arrière, 6
Barbes de l'Avant, 301
Barbotin, 918
Barbouquet, 189
Bardis, 335, 721
Baril de Galère, 74, 96, 900
Barillet, 869
Barogramme, 43
Barographe, 43
Baromètre, 43
Baromètre à Mercure, 490, 506
Baromètre Anéroide, 17
Baromètre enregistreur, 43
Barque, 42
Barsouin, 540, 702
Barre, 40, 369
Barre à Drosses, 139
Barre à Secteur, 619
Barre au Vent, 369, 882, 905
Barreaux aimantes longitudinaux, 300
Barre de Cabestan, 123
Barre d'Écoutille, 357
Barre de Flinders, 293
Barre de Fortune, 260
Barre de Gouvernail, 667
Barre de Pont, 209
Barre de Rechange, 260
Barre de Secours, 260
Barre en Dessous, 369
Barre Franche, 354
Barre Renversée, 645
Barres de Civadière, 767
Barres de Flèche, 187
Barres de Perroquet, 403, 404
Barres de Télégraphe, 767
Barres de Théorie, 76
Barre Sèche, 375
Barre Simple, 738
Barrette d'Essai, 180
Barreur, 369
Barrière de Glace, 45
Barrière de Récifs, 45
Barrot, 50
Barrotage, 749
Barrot d'Arcasse, 854
Barrot d'Assemblage, 102
Barrot de Fronteau, 96
Barrot de Pont, 204
Barrot Dévoyé, 121
Barrot d'extrémité de Panneau, 358

Barrot en Caisson, 91
Barrotin, 348
Barrot mobile, 357, 721
Bas de Dos, 47
Base de Vitesse, 502
Bas Mât, 476
Basse, 291
Basse Mer, 476
Basse mer de morte eau, 533
Basse Mer Inférieure, 476
Basse Mer Inférieure Moyenne, 501
Basses Mers de Marée Tropique, 865
Basse Voile, 181
Bassin, 45, 228
Bassin à flot, 551, 910
Bassin d'armement, 287
Bassin de Chasse, 689
Bassin de Construction, 102
Bassin de Marée, 834
Bassin de Mi-Marée, 349
Bassin d'essai de carènes, 515, 861
Bassin d'évitage, 874
Bastaque, 669
Bastaque Simple, 916
Bastet de Hamac, 350
Bastin, 163
Bastingages, 845
Batard, 570
Batayoles, 660
Bateau, 72, 183, 890
Bateau à Moteur, 523
Bateau à Roues, 562
Bateau à Vivier, 908
Bateau à Voiles, 675
Bateau Citerne, 822, 900
Bateau de la Santé, 620
Bateau de Loch, 468
Bateau de Pêche, 285
Bateau mi-ponté, 348
Bateau-Phare, 455
Bateau-Pilote, 584
Bateau-Pompe, 282
Bateau-Porte, 117
Bateau Thonnier, 871
Batelier, 42, 454
Bâti, 53
Bâtiment de Commerce, 506
Bâtiment de Sauvetage, 680
Bâtiment-Usine, 272
Bâton de Clin-Foc, 297
Bâton de Foc, 364, 408
Bâton de Pavillon, 289, 773
Bâton de Pavillon de Beaupré, 404
Battant, 296

Battant de Claire Voie, 684
Batterie de Secours, 259
Batture, 291
Bau, 50
Bayonette de Clin-Foc, 297
Beaupré, 90
Beaupré fixe, 776
Beaupré rentrant, 669
Bec, 64
Bec à Corbin, 636
Beffroi, 54
Bélier, 48
Benjamine, 514
Benne Preneuse, 334
Béquille, 445, 864
Béquille de Tambour, 562
Ber, 183, 437
Berceau de Bouchain, 503
Berceau de Chaudière, 79, 672
Berceau de Lancement, 437
Berge, 39
Berthon, 163
Bétail, 462
Biais, 514
Bien pris, 356
Bigot de Racage, 570
Bigues, 716
Billard, 48
Billarder, 907
Billet de bord, 500, 725
Billet d'embarquement, 725
Billot, 186
Billotage, 69, 561, 792
Biscuit de Mer, 723
Bitord, 770
Bitte, 66
Bitte à linguet, 573
Bittes d'Amarrage, 519
Bittes de Beaupré, 91
Bittes de mouillage, 648
Bittes de remorque, 536, 849
Bittes doubles, 234
Bittons, 749
Bitture, 633
Blanc de Baleine, 763
Blin, 343, 357, 923
Blin de Bonnette, 84
Blocs mamelonnés, 57
Blocus, 68
Blocus Commercial, 167
Blocus de Guerre, 511
Bloqué, 59
Bloqué par les Glaces, 387
Bluff, 71
Boëtte, 33
Boeuf, 568
Boire le mou, 613
Bois Courbant, 171

Bois d'Arrimage, 99, 250
Bois Débité, 176
Bois de Construction, 478, 728
Bois de Fardage, 250
Bois de Fer, 400
Bois de Marine, 728
Bois de Mâture, 660
Bois Droit, 797
Bois dur, 356
Bois en Grume, 660
Bois Equarri, 371, 467, 734
Bois Sec, 698
Bois Sur Pied, 776
Bois Tendre, 753
Boîte à Clapet, 795
Boîte à Gaïac, 786
Boîte de Distribution, 226
Boîte de protection, 586
Boîte Egyptienne, 524
Bollard, 66, 79, 142
Bôme, 83, 155
Bôme de Misaine-Goëlette, 301
Bôme de Paille en Cul, 653
Bon de Bord, 500
Bon de Livraison, 30, 212, 311
Bonhomme, 864
Bonne Brise, 311, 759
Bonnette, 802
Bonnette d'Artimon, 653
Bonnette de Grand Miroir, 391
Bonnette de Hublot, 919
Bonnette de Petit Miroir, 378
Bonnette de Sous Gui, 238, 901
Bonnette Maillée, 83
Bonnet Turc, 873
Bon plein, 150, 333
Bon Vent, 273
Boque, 197
Bord, 799
Bord à Bord, 268, 734
Bordage, 589
Bordages de Bouchain, 63
Bord d'Entrée, 442
Bord de Sortie, 299
Bord du Vent, 906
Bordé, 589
Bordé à clins, 152
Bordé à Clins Épaulés, 411
Bordé à Double Clins, 390
Bordé à franc-bord, 130, 296
Bordé à Joints en Ligne Brisée, 845
Bordé à Simples Clins, 153
Bordé Cousu, 710
Bordé de Bouchains, 63
Bordé de Diminution, 221
Bordé de l'Avant, 89
Bordé de Muraille, 735

Bordé de Point, 86
Bordé de Pont, 208
Bordé des Fonds, 86
Bordée, 445, 816, 899
Bordé Extérieur, 557, 719
Border, 723
Border à Joindre, 717
Border au Vent, 33
Border Plat, 291, 717
Bordées de Galbord, 324
Bordé Triple, 860
Bordez, 446
Bord sous le Vent, 445
Bord Tombé, 289
Bordure, 299
Bornage, 394
Borne d'Amarrage, 521
Bosse, 792
Bosse à Bouton, 209, 433
Bosse à Echappement, 747
Bosse à Ridoir, 382
Bosse Avant, 89
Bosse Cassante, 142
Bosse de Bout, 132, 653
Bosse de Hauban, 897
Bosse de la Roue de Gouvernail, 875
Bosse de lof, 89
Bosse d'Embarcation, 75
Bosse de mouillage, 209, 649
Bosse de Remorque, 850
Bosse de Ris, 639
Bosses Cassantes, 438
Bossoir à Orientation Mécanique, 503
Bossoir à Secteur, 619
Bossoir Automatique, 336
Bossoir d'Ancre, 15
Bossoir de Capon, 132
Bossoir d'Écoutille, 358
Bossoir d'Embarcation, 74
Bossoir de Portemanteau, 786
Bossoir de Traversière, 284
Bossoir Oscillant, 627
Bossoir Pivotant, 660
Bossoir Rabattable, 163
Bouchain, 61
Bouchain à grand rayon, 251
Bouchain Vif, 714
Boucher, 144
Bouchon, 693
Bouchon de brume, 298
Bouchon de Jauge, 879
Bouchon de Nable, 75, 228
Bouchon de Soute, 106
Bouchon de Trou d'Homme, 487
Boucle, 474

Boucle de Panneau, 359
Bouclier, 496
Boudin de Défense, 613
Bouée, 107
Bouée à Boyant, 846
Bouée à Cloche, 55
Bouée à Cône Double, 542
Bouée à Culotte, 97
Bouée à Fuseau, 581
Bouée à Gaz, 325
Bouée à Pilier, 581
Bouée à Puits, 867
Bouée à reflecteur radar, 627
Bouée à Sifflet, 916
Bouée à Voyant Sphérique, 331
Bouée-Balise, 494
Bouée d'Amarrage, 520
Bouée d'Avertissement, 198
Bouée de Babord, 600
Bouée de Banc Milieu, 510
Bouée de Barre, 40
Bouée de Bifurcation, 61
Bouée de cable sous-marin, 826
Bouée de Chenal, 140
Bouée de Corps Mort, 115, 520
Bouée de déhalage, 360
Bouée de Direction, 273
Bouée de Halage, 898
Bouée de Jonction, 413
Bouée de Marque, 494
Bouée de Mi-Chenal, 273, 510
Bouée d'Épave, 925
Bouée de Sauvetage, 449
Bouée de Sauvetage Lumineuse, 478
Bouée de Télégraphe, 826
Bouée de Veille, 899
Bouée d'évitage, 812
Bouée d'Orin, 115
Bouée en cône renversé, 119
Bouée en Fer à Cheval, 379
Bouée-Espar, 760
Bouée Extérieure, 694
Bouée Lumineuse, 453
Bouée Mâtée, 760
Bouée peinte par bandes, 143
Bouée Plate, 195
Bouée Sonore Automatique, 27
Bouée Sphérique, 763
Bouée Sphéro-conique, 173
Bouée-Tonne, 130
Bouge, 119
Bougie, 119
Bouilleur Évaporateur, 266
Bouillie Glacée, 749
Boujaron, 848
Bouleau, 66

Bouline, 89
Boulinier, 905
Boulon de Fixation, 375
Boulon de Manille, 712
Bourguignon, 95
Bourrelet, 231, 340, 516
Bourse, 593
Boussole compensée, 171
Bout-dehors de Bonnette, 802
Bout-Dehors de Tapecul, 410
Boutehors, 557
Bouteille Flottante, 243
Bouteilles, 621
Boute-Lof, 105
Bouterolle, 655
Boutre, 217
Box Dock, 91
Box dock en sections, 700
Brague, 759
Brai, 586
Braie, 160
Braie de Gouvernail, 666
Braie de Mât, 497
Branche de Bouline, 89
Branche de Remorque, 849
Branchette, 622
Bras, 23, 92, 340, 474
Bras de Bossoir, 200
Bras de Chalut, 857
Bras de Chavirement, 883
Bras de Gouvernail, 664
Bras de mer, 23, 757
Bras de Redressement, 651
Brasse, 276
Brasser, 92
Brasser à culer, 92
Brasser Carré, 771
Brasser en Pointe, 92
Brasser sous le Vent, 92
Brasseyage, 620
Brayer, 574
Bredindin, 759
Bredindin Double, 236
Bredindin Simple, 738
Brick, 98
Brick-Goëlette, 688
Bride, 289, 435
Brider, 307, 626
Bridole, 926
Bridure, 307, 626
Brigadier, 89
Brigantin, 98
Brigantine, 513, 759
Brin, 570
Bringuebale, 94
Bringueballe, 365
Brin Simple, 203
Brion, 301, 338

Brion Droit, 210
Brion Rogné, 193
Bris, 95
Brisants, 96, 809
Brise, 97
Brise de Mer, 694
Brise de Terre, 432
Brise-Glace, 387
Brise-Lames, 96
Brises Folles, 32
Broche, 243
Bronze, 100
Bronze au Manganèse, 487
Bronze d'aluminum, 11
Bronze Phosphoreux, 580
Brosse métallique, 922
Brouillard, 298
Brouillard intense, 213
Brouillard marin, 695
Bruine, 245
Brûleur, 109, 547
Brumaille, 513
Brumailleux, 514
Brumasse, 362
Brume légère, 513
Brumeux, 298, 362
Buccin, 915
Buée de Cale, 810
Bulb, 103, 281
Bulletin d'information des glaces, 388
Burin, 765
Buttée, 833
Butée à Collets Mobiles, 379
Butoir de Gouvernail, 664
Butoirs de Barre, 209
Butoirs de Gouvernail, 667

Cabanement, 840
Cabestan, 123
Cabestan à barbotin, 15
Cabestan à double Effet, 327
Cabestan à Manivelles, 184
Cabestan à Vapeur, 780
Cabestan de Mouillage, 15
Cabestan de touage, 330, 897
Cabillot, 289, 841
Cabillot de Bossoir, 200
Cabillot de Cargue Fond, 107
Cabillot de Ratelier, 404
Cabillot de Tournage, 54
Cabine, 114
Cabine de Luxe, 114
Cabine Extérieure, 557
Cabine Intérieure, 394
Cablage, 440
Cablage antigiratoire, 881

Cablage Lang, 433
Câble, 114
Câble-Chaîne, 15
Câble Guide, 442
Cabler, 440
Cablot, 116
Cabotage, 159
Cacatois, 663
Cachou, 193
Cadène, 139
Cadranure, 713
Cadre, 179, 474
Cadre d'Assemblage, 102
Cadre de Gouvernail, 666
Cadre Massif, 755
Cadre Varangue, 741
Cage d'Hélice, 609, 610
Cagnard, 230, 719, 905
Caillebotis, 336
Caillebotis avant, 302
Caillebotis de Claire Voie, 743
Caillebotis de panneau, 359
Caillebotis de timonier, 914
Caissage, 561
Caisse, 368, 718
Caisse à eau Sale, 710
Caisse d'Assiette, 862
Caisse de Décantation, 709
Caisse de Déglaçage, 387
Caisse de Pied de Mât, 815
Caisse de Prise d'Eau, 805
Caisse d'Inclinaison, 368
Caisses Anti Roulis, 19
Caisson, 854
Caisson à Air, 107
Caisson d'Extrémité, 261
Cale, 146, 374, 475
Cale à Eau, 211
Cale à Poisson, 285
Calebas d'Arc-Boutant de Beaupré, 916
Cale de Compensation, 103
Cale de Construction, 747
Cale de Halage, 747
Cale d'Empatture, 111, 295
Cale de Remplissage, 458
Cale Etirée, 823
Cale frigorifique, 394
Caler, 241, 381
Cale Sèche, 246
Cale Sous Membrure, 306
Calfat, 924
Calfatage, 118
Calier, 375
Caliorne, 209, 616
Caliorne à Quatre Réas, 305
Caliorne à Trois Réas, 860
Caliorne d'Abattage, 124

Caliorne de Bas-Mât, 499, 575
Caliorne de Braguet, 330
Caliorne de Drisse, 350
Calme, 119
Calmes Equatoriaux, 231
Cambuse, 441
Can, 252
Canadienne, 120
Canal des Anguillers, 457
Canal Maritime, 722
Candelette, 17, 844
Canoe, 120
Canon de Brume, 298
Canon de Détresse, 226
Canon Porte-Amarre, 459
Canon Porte-Harpon, 913
Canot, 72, 661
Canotage, 74
Canot à moteur, 522
Canot d'apparat, 42
Canot de Sauvetage de Côte, 158
Canot de Sauvetage Ponté, 205
Canot de Service, 194
Canotier, 75, 458, 543, 900
Canotier Brévété, 449
Canots de Bossoir, 200
Cap, 122, 363
Capacité Utile, 311
Capacité Volumétrique, 189
Capacité Volumétrique en Balles, 35
Capacité Volumétrique en Céréales, 335
Cap au compas, 168
Cap au Large, 776
Cap de Mouton, 202
Capelage, 498
Capeyer, 448, 867
Capitaine d'Armement, 492
Capitaine d'Armes, 497
Capitaine de Navire, 497
Capitaine de Port, 355
Cap Magnétique, 481
Caponner, 131
Capot, 82, 377
Capot de Claire Voie, 742
Capot de Descente, 168
Capot d'embarcation, 766
Capot d'Habitacle, 65
Capture, 124
Capuchon, 182, 888
Capuchon de Cheminée, 899
Capucin, 816
Cap Vrai, 865
Caractéristique, 140
Cardan, 330
Carénage, 798
Carène de Maier, 484

Carène Liquide, 203
Caréner, 124
Carène Sale, 304
Cargaison, 124, 723
Cargaison Réfrigérée, 144
Cargaison Refroidie, 144
Cargo, 310
Cargue, 94
Cargue à Vue, 743
Cargue Bouline, 445
Cargue de Foc, 410
Cargue-Fond, 107
Cargue Point, 152
Carguer, 94, 151
Carie Sèche, 247
Carlingage de Machines, 261
Carlingue, 419
Carlingue Centrale, 136
Carlingue Centrale Continue, 832
Carlingue de Bouchain, 62
Carlingue en Caisson, 92
Carlingue Intercostale, 396
Carlingue latérale, 733, 739
Carnet de Passerelle, 208
Carré, 507, 769
Carrelet, 676
Cartahu, 324, 914
Cartahu de Bout Dehors, 84
Cartahu de Mât de Charge, 128
Cartahu d'en dedans, 359
Cartahu d'en Dehors, 928
Cartahu de Pavois, 242
Cartahu de vergue, 928
Cartahu Double, 237, 676
Cartahu Simple, 914
Cartahu Simple à poulie courante, 668
Carte Bathymétrique, 47
Carte Cotidale, 179
Carte de Débarquement, 432
Carte de Mercator, 505
Carte d'inclinaison magnétique, 221
Carte d'intensité d'aimantation, 378
Carte Gnomonique, 331
Carte Isobarique, 402
Carte Magnétique, 481
Carte Marine, 528
Carte Polyconique, 595
Casernet, 207
Casier, 465, 601
Casse, 95
Casser l'erre, 752
Cat Yawl, 134
Cavalier, 488
Cavitation, 134

Cay, 134
Cèdre de Virginie, 417
Ceinture, 341, 577, 622, 810
Ceinture de Hamac, 350
Ceinture de Sauvetage, 451
Ceinture Rocheuse, 444
Centre de Carène, 136
Centre de Dérive, 136
Centre de Gravité, 136
Centre-Oeil, 892
Cercle à Linquets, 572
Cercle Azimutal, 29
Cercle crépusculaire, 874
Cercle de Déclinaison, 135, 147, 567
Cercle de Distance, 198
Cercle de Drosse, 867
Cercle de Giration, 873
Cercle de Latitude, 147
Cercle de Mât, 496, 498
Cercle de Mât de Charge, 215
Cercle de Relèvement, 29
Cercle de Tournage, 762
Cercle de Trélingage, 317
Cercle de Vit de Mulet, 334
Cercle Diurne, 226
Cercle Horaire, 381
Cercle Méridien, 147
Cercle Polaire, 594
Cercle Polaire Arctique, 23
Céréales, 335
Cerf Volant de secours, 450
Certificat d'Arrimage, 795
Certificat d'Assurance, 395
Certificat d'Avaries, 196
Certificat de Classification, 149
Certificat de Construction, 101
Certificat de Débarquement, 137, 224
Certificat de Dégazage, 325
Certificat de Dératisation, 214
Certificat de Jauge, 634, 841
Certificat d'Embarquement, 724
Certificat de Navigabilité, 699
Certificat de Sécurité, 672
Certificat de Visite, 137
Certificat d'Origine, 137
Certificat International de Franc-Bord, 399
Certificat Radiotélégraphique de Sécurité, 672
Cesser Clause, 137
Cétine, 762
Chaîne, 139, 896
Chaîne à Mailles Serrées, 154
Chaîne d'acier moulé, 131
Chaîne d'Anguiller, 457

Chaîne d'apiquage, 756
Chaîne de capon, 132
Chaîne de drosse, 782, 914
Chaîne de Fond, 339
Chaîne de martinet, 756, 846
Chaîne de Touée, 798
Chaîne de Tournevire, 508
Chaîne dormante, 520
Chaîne Étanconnée, 802
Chaînes claires, 552
Chaînes de Retenue, 239
Chaise, 791
Chaise de Gabier, 76
Chaise de Mâture, 76
Chaise de Palier, 766
Chaland, 42
Chaland à Clapets, 378
Chaland Basculeur, 249
Chaland Citerne, 822
Chaland de mer, 159
Chaland épurateur d'huile, 547
Chaland filtre à Mazout, 547
Chaland non propulsé, 249
Chaloupe, 470
Chalumeau de découpage, 194
Chalut, 857
Chalut à Crevettes, 733
Chalutage, 859
Chalut à l'étalage, 796
Chalut à Panneaux, 556
Chalut à Perche, 51
Chalut à Planches, 556
Chalutier, 857
Chambre, 365, 787
Chambre de décongélation, 144
Chambre des Cartes, 142
Chambre des Machines, 261
Chambre des Pompes, 614
Chambrière, 53, 317, 695
Chameau, 119
Champ de Glace, 389
Champignon d'Aération, 526
Champ Magnétique, 482
Champs de Glace, 279
Chandelier, 189, 632
Chandelier d'Écoutille, 359
Chandelle, 864
Chandelle de Chouque, 123
Chanfreiner, 140
Change Maritime, 491
Changer, 92, 360
Changer d'Amures, 618
Chanter la Sonde, 119
Chantier à Rabattement, 722
Chantier de Constructions Navales, 729
Chantier d'Embarcation, 73
Chanvre, 369

Chanvre de Manille, 488
Chanvre de Russie, 670
Chanvre du Bengale, 807
Chape, 85, 122, 330
Chapeau, 106, 246, 273, 374, 606, 866
Charbon Pulvérisé, 614
Chargement, 124
Chargement Complet, 314
Chargement en Balles, 36
Chargement en Barils, 45
Chargement en Sacs, 32
Chargement en Vrac, 103
Chargement Liquide, 460
Charger, 463
Chargeur, 173, 310, 724
Chariot de Barre, 634
Charnier, 693, 868
Charpentier de Bord, 726
Charpentier de Marine, 729
Charpentier en Fer, 81, 590
Charte Partie, 141
Charte Partie Nette, 150
Chasse au Cétacés, 913
Chasser, 239
Chasseur, 284
Chasseur de Baleines, 911
Châtaigner, 143
Château, 97
Château Court, 731
Château d'eau, 682
Château Long, 470
Chatte, 208, 689
Chaudière à Circulation Accélérée, 171
Chaudière à Circulation forcée, 300
Chaudière à double façade, 235
Chaudière Aquatubulaire, 903
Chaudière à Tubes de Fumée, 283
Chaudière Auxiliaire, 232
Chaudière de récupération, 899
Chaudière Ignitubulaire, 283
Chaudronnier, 79
Chauffe, 283
Chauffe au Charbon, 157
Chauffe au Mazout, 548
Chaufferie, 790
Chauffeur, 790
Chauffeur de Rivets, 365
Chaumard, 520
Chaumard à Rouleau, 657
Chaumard Avant, 88
Chaumard de Déhalage, 115
Chaumard Fermé, 154
Chaumard Ouvert, 551
Chavirer, 123

Chébec, 927
Chef Arrimeur, 302, 728
Chef de Chauffe, 442
Chef de Nage, 801
Chef Mécanicien, 143
Chemin de Fer, 176, 677, 852
Chemin de Glissement, 438
Cheminée, 773
Chemin Est-Ouest, 213
Chemin Parcouru, 201
Chemise, 742
Chemise d'Aiguillot, 665
Chemise d'Arbre, 713
Chenal, 140, 342
Chêne, 543
Chêne Blanc, 918
Chêne vert, 461
Chevillage, 81, 276
Chevillage à Bout Perdu, 249
Chevillage Double, 235
Chevillage Simple, 739
Cheville, 80
Cheville à Barbe, 630
Cheville à Bout Perdu, 71
Cheville à Croc, 377
Cheville à Écrou, 691
Cheville à Goupille, 302
Cheville à travers bois, 390, 833
Cheville à Virole, 152
Cheville de Cadène, 139
Chevillé en Cuivre, 177
Chicaner, 685
Chien, 849
Choléra, 146
Chouque, 496
Chouque Inférieur, 499
Choquer, 142, 777, 809
Choquer à la demande, 753
Chouque de Beaupré, 91
Chronomètre Étalon, 775
Chronomètre Sidéral, 735
Chute, 246, 374, 455
Chute au Mât, 477, 499
Chute au Point, 6
Chute Avant, 477
Ciel Couvert, 558
Ciel d'Eau, 901
Ciel Moutonné, 481
Ciel Pommelé, 481
Ciel pur, 151
Cigale, 16, 56
Cil, 100, 925
Cinq-mâts barque, 286
Circle de Visibilité, 148
Circumpolaire, 148
Ciré, 549
Cirrus en Queue de Cheval, 489
Ciseau à Boucher, 144

Ciseau de Calfat, 118
Citerne d'Éte, 806
Clair, 150
Claire Voie, 743
Clapotis, 99, 474, 558, 653, 920
Clarté des Glaces, 387
Classification, 149
Clause d'Abandon, 1
Clause d'Abordage, 165
Clause d'Agir et de Travailler, 806
Clause d'Annullation, 119
Clause d'Arbitrage, 22
Clause d'Avaries, 28
Clause de Capture, 654
Clause d'Échec de l'Aventure, 314
Clause de Classification, 149
Clause de Courtage, 99
Clause de Déroutement, 216
Clause de Franchise, 307
Clause de Glaces, 388
Clause de Grève, 799
Clause de Livraison, 212
Clause d'Emploi, 260
Clause de Négligence, 533
Clause d'enonciation, 604
Clause de Non Préjudice d'Abandon, 895
Clause de Police sans Preuve d'Intérêt, 596
Clause de Prolongation de Risque, 175
Clause de Redélivraison, 638
Clause de Retard, 839
Clause de Risques Assurables, 396
Clause de risques d'Allèges, 183
Clause de Substitution de Navire, 805
Clause d'Évaluation, 886
Clause d'Exonération, 266
Clause Franc de Capture et Saisie, 271
Clause Magasin à Magasin, 897
Clauses sur Facultés de l'Institut, 394
Clause "toujours à Flot," 294
Clause Valeur Agréé, 7
Clavette, 302
Clef, 186, 238, 278, 373, 420
Clef d'accorage, 97
Clef de Berceau, 230
Clef de Calfat, 792
Clef de Gouvernail, 666, 924

Clef de Lancement, 230, 438
Clef de Sel, 679
Clef de tenne des Douvelles, 788
Clin Foc, 297, 410
Clin Foc Ballon, 37
Clinomètre, 153
Clipper, 153
Cloche de Bord, 54
Cloche de Brume, 298
Cloche sous marine, 804
Cloison, 103
Cloison Axiale, 136
Cloison Chicane, 810
Cloison Coupefeu, 282
Cloison d'Abordage, 165
Cloison de coqueron, 574
Cloison de Presse étoupe, 6
Cloison de Séparation, 571
Cloison d'Emménagements, 412
Cloison d'Extrémité, 260
Cloison d'Incendie, 282
Cloison-Écran, 691
Cloison en Baïonnette, 637
Cloison en bordages Croisés, 217
Cloison Étanche, 902
Cloison latérale, 734
Cloisonnement, 803
Cloison Ondulée, 179
Clou, 527, 763
Clou à Bordage, 208
Clou à Doublage, 715
Clou à lattes, 647
Clou à Maugère, 693
Clou à river, 152
Clou à Tête Étampée, 155
Clou d'Embarcation, 75
Clou Rivé Sur Jouette, 658
Cloutage, 763
Co-Armateur, 412
Cockpit, 160
Cockpit à Auto-Vidange, 704
Code de signaux, 161
Code International de Signaux, 397
Code maritime, 532
Code Météorologique International, 399
Coefficient Cylindrique Longitudinal, 471
Coefficient d'Aire, 223
Coefficient d'Arrimage, 796
Coefficient de Consommation, 314
Coefficient de Frottement, 312
Coefficient de l'Amirauté, 4

Coefficient de Poussée Corrigée, 834
Coefficient de Ramplissage, 69
Coefficient de Remplissage à la Flottaison, 901
Coefficient de Remplissage du Maître Couple, 511
Coefficient de rendement propulsif, 610
Coefficient de résistance, 515
Coefficient de Sillage, 896
Coefficient de Stabilité sous Voiles, 674
Coefficient de Suction, 833
Coefficient de Tonnage, 842
Coefficient de Vitesse Relative, 762
Coefficient Magnétique, 482
Cofferdam, 161
Coffre, 866, 895
Coffre à Médicaments, 504
Coffre à Pavillons, 288
Coffre d'Amarrage, 520
Coffre de Marin, 696
Coffre d'Expansion, 268
Coiffé, 1, 733
Coiffer, 345
Coin d'Arrimage, 624
Coin d'Écoutille, 359
Coin de Gouvernail, 665
Coin d'Étambrai, 499
Co-Latitude, 163
Col de Cygne, 810
Collecteur d'Assèchement, 800
Collecteur de Dégazage, 889
Collecteur Principal, 485
Collecteur principal de Cale, 63
Collerette de pont, 205
Collet, 188, 832
Collet de Butée, 833
Collier, 164
Collier à Pitons, 184
Collier de Bossoir, 200
Collier de Livarde, 752
Collier de Mât, 498
Collier de Suspente, 746
Colombier, 438
Colonne Solaire, 807
Colure equinoctial, 264
Colures, 165
Colure Solsticial, 755
Combustible Colloïdal, 165
Combustion Spontanée, 767
Commande, 305
Commandements à la Barre, 369
Commande pour hanets, 534

Comme ça—Cornière à Boudin 944

Comme ça, 779
Commerce de Contrebande, 175
Commerce Maritime, 694
Commettage, 440
Commettage à Droite, 650
Commettre, 440
Commis, 151
Commissaire, 617
Commissaire Maritime, 725
Commission d'Adresse, 3
Commission d'Affrètement, 141
Commissionaire Expéditeur, 303
Commodore, 167
Compartimentage, 803
Compartiment Chaudières, 79
Compas, 491
Compas à Liquide, 460
Compas Amorti, 202
Compas à Pible, 595
Compas à Rose Sèche, 246
Compas Azimutal, 29
Compas de Déclinaison, 210
Compas d'Embarcation, 73
Compas de Relèvement, 29
Compas de Route, 782
Compas d'Inclinaison, 222
Compas Étalon, 775
Compas Gyroscopique, 345
Compas Magnétique, 482
Compas Principal, 497
Compas Renversé, 354
Compas Répétiteur, 644
Compensation d'Armement, 264
Composante de Marée, 834
Composante Harmonique, 356
Compris d'Avaries, 28
Compteur de Tours, 646
Computeur, 347
Condamner, 48
Conducteur de Prise, 608
Conduit, 273
Conduit de Dalot, 693
Conduit de Fumée, 884
Conduits de Fumée Lateraux, 227
Conférence, 173
Confiscation, 172
Congé, 150, 572
Congréer, 925
Conjonction, 173
Connaissement, 64
Connaissement à ordre, 545
Connaissement à Personne Dénommée, 796
Connaissement au Porteur, 67

Connaissement de Ligne Régulière, 458
Connaissement Direct, 833
Connaissement Embarqué, 724
Connaissement en droiture, 222
Connaissement Net, 150
Connaissement Nominatif, 796
Connaissement Reçu pour Embarquement, 637
Conseil des Prises, 607
Conseiller Nautique, 25
Conserves en Boîtes, 120
Consignataire de Marchandises, 173
Consignataire de Navires, 723, 726
Consortium, 726
Constante de Latitude, 436
Constantes de Marée, 834
Constantes Harmoniques, 356
Constructeur d'Embarcations, 72
Constructeur de Navires, 723
Construction à Barres Sèches, 375
Construction à Bordages Croisés, 218
Construction à Cantilever, 121
Construction à Clins, 152
Construction à doubles bordages croisés, 235
Construction à Membrures Renforcées, 211
Construction à Porques, 906
Construction Composite, 171
Construction en Arc, 22
Construction Isherwood, 401
Construction Isherwood Sans Goussets, 93
Construction Mixte, 167, 172
Construction sous Surveillance Spéciale, 761
Construction Transversale, 856
Consul, 174
Contrat de Grosse, 87
Contrat de Grosse Aventure, 87
Contrat de Sauvetage, 679
Contre-Alisés, 20
Contre-Arc, 673
Contrebande, 175
Contrebande Absolue, 2
Contrebande Conditionnelle, 173
Contrebande de Guerre, 897
Contre brassé devant, 2
Contre-brasser, 92, 180

Contre-Brasser Devant, 92
Contre-Cacatois, 744
Contre Carlingue, 740
Contre-Courant, 880
Contre-courant équatorial, 263
Contre-Étai, 404
Contre-Etambot, 393
Contre-Étrave, 21
Contre-fil, 186
Contre Hélice, 175
Contre Hublot, 202
Contreplaqué, 593
Contre-Quille, 654, 845
Contribution d'Avarie, 328
Convention sur les lignes de charge, 1930, 464
Convection thermique, 829
Convoi, 177
Convoyage, 177
Convoyeur de Bétail, 133
Coque, 382, 422, 537
Coqueron, 574
Coqueron Arrière, 6
Coqueron Avant, 302
Cordage, 658
Cordage Câblé au Mouillé, 901
Cordage Commis à Droite, 588
Cordage commis à Gauche, 445
Cordage commis en Aussière, 362
Cordage Commis en Grelin, 115
Cordage en Chanvre, 370
Cordage en Coton, 180
Cordage en Fibre, 278
Cordage en Kaire, 636
Cordage en Lin, 292, 457
Cordage en Manille, 488
Cordage en Pitte, 163
Cordage en Sisal, 740
Cordage Mixte, 278
Cordage Refait, 875
Corde, 286
Corde de Dos, 364
Cordes, 472
Cordier, 377, 458
Cordon, 50
Corne, 319
Corne à Signaux, 518
Corne d'Artimon, 759
Corne de Brigantine, 759
Corne Fixe, 776
Cornet de Brume, 298
Cornier, 734
Cornière, 18
Cornière à ailes égales, 263
Cornière à ailes inégales, 881
Cornière à Boudin, 103

Cornière Cadre, 87
Cornière Contre-Membrure, 644
Cornière Couvre-Joint, 85
Cornière d'Appui de Panneau, 359
Cornière de Raidissage, 788
Cornière de Renfort, 788
Cornière d'Étambrai, 497
Cornière d'étanchéité, 18, 776
Cornière d'Hiloire, 157
Cornière Gouttière, 344, 799
Cornière Membrure, 305
Cornière Renversée, 644
Cornière Rigole, 903
Coroi, 801
Corps, 382
Corps Mort, 520
Corps Mort à Coffre, 108
Corps Mort à deux branches, 876
Corps mort à quatre branches, 305
Corps Mort à Quatre Itagues, 10
Corps Mort à Trois Branches, 830
Correction de tonture, 178
Corrections d'Aboutissement, 178
Corrections du compas, 169
Corrosion, 179
Corsaire, 606
Cosse, 829
Cosse à Ride, 434
Cosse Baguée, 880
Cosse d'Aussière, 362
Cosse en Poire, 365
Cosse Massive, 754
Cosse Ronde, 661
Cote, 149, 158
Côte Accore, 79
Côte basse, 291
Côte foraine, 550
Côté Matage, 118
Coton à Calfater, 118
Coton Minéral, 512
Côtre, 193
Côtre à Tapecul, 197, 929
Cotre Bermudien, 57
Coube d'Entremise, 128
Couche de Glace, 716
Couchette, 58, 106
Couchette Inférieure, 475
Couchette Supérieure, 882
Coude, 424, 868
Couenne, 71
Couillard, 106

Coulage, 444
Coulée, 667
Couler, 304
Couleurs, 165
Coulisse de Lancement, 340
Coulisse Morte, 776
Coulisse Vive, 745
Coup d'Acculage, 597
Coup de Roulis, 479
Coup de Semonce, 392
Coup de Vent, 800
Coupe, 334
Coupe au Maître, 510
Coupée, 194, 323
Coupe-eau, 762, 791
Coupe Longitudinale, 391
Couple, 305, 306
Couple de Redressement, 650
Couple de Remplissage, 281
Couple Dévoyé, 121
Couple Droit, 770
Couple Étanche, 901
Couples de Tracé, 306
Courant, 191, 360, 643, 669, 797
Courant côtier, 158
Courant d'Australie, 17
Courant de Dérive, 243
Courant de derive de l'Atlantique Nord, 539
Courant de Flot, 295
Courant de Jusant, 251
Courant de Marée, 833
Courant de Rennel, 643
Courant équatorial, 263
Courant Equatorial du Sud, 757
Courant Marin, 544
Courant Océanique, 544
Courbe, 185, 423, 837
Courbe de Banc, 833
Courbe de Capucine, 77, 428
Courbe d'Écusson, 620
Courbe de dégraissement, 52
Courbe de Déplacements, 225
Courbe de Marée, 489
Courbe d'Éperon, 323
Courbe de Résistance, 191
Courbes des Aires de Couples, 191
Courbes des aires de flottaison, 192
Courbe des Centres de Carène, 191
Courbe des Centres de Carène en Hauteur, 192
Courbe des Centres de Carène en Longueur, 191

Courbe des centres de Gravité de flottaison, 191
Courbe des Charges, 191
Courbe des Longueurs Envahissables, 295
Courbe des Métacentres, 192
Courbe des Poids, 192
Courbe d'Étambot, 740, 785
Courbe Diagonale, 196
Courbe Horizontale, 85
Courbe Oblique, 196
Courbes de Lancement, 438
Courbes des Couples de Redressement, 192
Courbe Verticale, 354
Cour d'Amirauté, 4
Courir, 486, 667
Courir grand largue, 309
Courir Largue, 333, 667, 675
Courir Sur, 774
Couronnage, 840
Couronne, 178, 572
Couronne d'Arrêt, 787
Couronnement, 22, 785, 817
Cours du Fret, 311
Coursive, 10
Courtage, 99
Courtier d'Affrètement, 141, 310, 464
Courtier d'Assurance, 395
Courtier Juré, 812
Courtier Maritime, 722
Coussin, 80, 146, 562
Coussin de Beaupré, 91
Coussin de bout-dehors, 408
Coussin d'écubier, 361, 529
Coussin d'Hiloire, 157
Coussinet d'Étambot, 785
Coût, 113
Coût Assurance et Fret, 179
Coût et Frêt, 179
Couture, 695
Couture à point broché, 291
Couture à Point debout, 660
Couture à Points Piqués, 517
Couture Forcée, 99
Couture piquée et rabattue, 178
Couvre-Joint, 111
Couvre joint longitudinal, 696
Couvrir, 39
Crachin, 245
Crampe, 230, 776
Crapaud, 421, 520
Crapaudine de Bossoir, 200
Craquer, 767
Cravate, 338

Crépine, 659
Crête, 184, 904
Creux, 213, 904
Creux de Cale, 214, 641
Creux de Franc Bord, 307
Creux de jauge, 844
Creux de la Courbe de Résistance, 376
Creux sur Quille, 516
Crevasse, 768
Crever, 778
Crevettier, 732
Crinoline, 185
Crique, 184
Critérium de Service, 185
Croc à Ciseaux, 153
Croc à échappement, 576
Croc à Emérillon, 813
Croc de voilier, 675
Crocher, 338
Crochet de Capon, 132
Crochet de Mât de Charge, 126
Crochet de Remorque, 849
Crochet d'établi, 55
Crochet de Traversière, 285
Croisée, 188
Croiser, 185, 810, 856
Croisette, 404
Croisillon, 188
Croissant, 931
Croix dans les Chaînes, 186
Crosse, 741
Crossement de la lune, 904
Croupiat, 768
Croupière, 768
Crue, 312
Cubage, 189
Cuiller, 410, 767
Cuisine, 322
Cul, 24, 97, 161
Culasse, 85
Cul de porc, 31
Cul de Porc Double, 236
Cul de Porc double et tête d'Alouette, 236
Cul de Porc Simple, 896
Culer, 333
Culmination, 189
Culotte, 884
Cumulus, 190
Cunette, 903
Cuvette, 168
Cycle Lunaire, 478
Cyclone, 195, 647
Cylindre, 246
Cyprès, 195

Dalle, 208
Dalot, 205, 693
Dame de Nage, 543, 662
Dans le Vent, 399
Darse, 45, 747
Date de Cloture, 155
Date de Déclaration, 201
Date de Résiliation, 119
Dauphin, 363
Davier, 657
Dé, 110, 156, 238
Debâcle, 204
Débardeur, 228, 478
Débarquement, 224
Débarquer, 224, 574
Débitter, 879
Déborder, 52, 812
Débouquer, 226
Débris, 925
Décapage, 580
Déceleur d'Eau, 830
Décharge d'Exportation, 241
Décharger, 224
Déchet, 429
Deck steward, 209
Déclaration à la Sortie, 263
Déclaration à l'Entrée, 263, 400
Déclaration d'abandon, 541
Déclaration de Paris, 210
Déclaration de Sortie, 263, 558
Déclaration d'expédition, 725
Déclaration d'Exportation, 724
Déclaration du Capitaine, 124
Déclaration en Douane, 64, 263
Déclarer à la sortie, 262
Déclarer a l'entrée, 262
Déclarer en douane, 262
Déclinaison, 210
Déclinaison Magnétique, 482
Déclinaison magnétique Amplitude, 481
Déclin de la lune, 897
Déclivité de la Houle, 904
Décommettre, 881
Décompte de Fret, 310
Décompte du Capitaine, 599
Décrochement, 95
Décroisment des Abouts, 722
Dédoubler les amarres, 739
Déduction pour appareil moteur, 611
Déductions d'usage, 192
Défaut de Nouvelles, 513
Défense, 278
Défense en Cordage, 658
Défense en Fascines, 656

Défense en Pilotis, 581
Déferler, 95, 474, 881
Déferler les voiles, 474
Défie l'aulofée, 538
Déflecteur de Boussole, 212
Défoncé, 795
Déformation, 898
De Fortune, 414
Dégager, 150, 775
Dégager les Chaînes, 151
Dégarnir, 800, 879
Dégaussage, 212
Dégazage, 325
Dégorgeoir, 744, 764
Dégraissage, 734
Dégréer, 882
Déhaler, 360, 721, 897
Déjaugé, 710, 772
Délaissement, 1
Délester, 879
Déliaison, 626
Délit, 847
Délover, 879
Delta, 212
Démailler, 882
Démaniller, 882
Démarrer, 879, 881
Démâté, 224
Demi, 88
Demi-bau, 348
Demi Bordée, 622
Demi cercle Dangereux, 198
Demi cercle de droite, 652
Demi cercle Navigable, 531
Demi Clef, 349
Demi-Clef à Capeler, 155
Demi-clef à Transfiler, 495
Demi Clefs Renversées, 901
Demi-Diamètre, 707
Demi-Dunette, 632
Demie Varangue, 283, 349
Demi-Gaillard, 632, 807
Demi-Membrure, 350
Demi-quart, 349
Demi-Tape d'Écubier, 348
Démolition de Navires, 723
Démonter, 882
Dépaler, 673
Departement du fret, 310
Dépasser, 150, 799, 880, 882
Dépasser les tours de Chaîne, 151
Dépecer, 292
Déplacement, 226
Déplacement en Charge, 463
Déplacement hors membres, 516
Déplacement Lège, 453

Dépression, 221, 475
Dépression barométrique, 866
Dépression occluse, 544
Dépression Secondaire, 700
Dérapé, 26
Déraper, 96, 907
Dératisation, 214
Dérive, 135, 445
Dérive du Courant, 242
Dérive Latérale, 444
Dériver sur son Ancre, 156
Dériver Vent dessus Vent dedans, 30
Dériveur, 370, 649, 795
Déroutement, 216
Derrière, 6
Désaffourcher, 881
Désarmer, 441
Désarrimage, 96
Descente, 168
Déséchouer, 640
Désélinguer, 882
Désenverguer, 879
Désertion, 216
Dessaisir, 881
Dessus de vent, 905
Détalinguer, 879
Détecteur de fumée, 750
Détecteur d'Incendie, 282
Détection sous-marine, 251
Détention, 23
Détresse, 226
Détroit, 797
Détroit territorial, 828
Devant, 303
Déventé, 52
Déverguer, 879
Dévers, 290
Déviation, 216
Déviation balistique, 37
Déviation due à la Bande, 368
Déviation Quadrantale, 619
Déviation Semi-Circulaire, 707
Dévirer, 896
Devis de Tracé, 547
Diablotin, 692
Diabolo, 77
Diagramme de Napier, 528
Diagramme d'Indicateur, 392
Diamètre de Giration, 281
Diamètre d'Évolution, 818
Diaphragme, 748
Diele, 203
Différence d'Ascension Droite, 24
Différence de Longitude, 220

Différence du neau au vieux, 535
Différence en Latitude, 220
Différence méridienne en latitude, 507
Différences de Marée, 835
Diminuer la Voilure, 731
Diplôme de Capitaine, 497
Direction, 709
Dispache, 28
Dispacheur, 4
Disque, 85
Disque de Franc-Bord, 464
Distance de Crête en Crête, 904
Distance Franchissable, 188
Distance Méridienne, 507
Distance Polaire, 595
Distances Lunaires, 479
Distance Zénithale, 932
Distance zénithale méridienne, 507
Distorsion angulaire, 18
Dock à pontons sectionnés, 700
Dock auto-carénant, 700, 704
Docker, 228
Dock Flottant, 294
Dock flottant type "offshore," 547
Documents d'Embarquement, 725
Doloir, 99
Dôme, 231, 424
Donner du Mou, 744
Doris, 232
Dormant, 776
Dorsale, 648
Dossier, 30, 784
Douane, 193
Douanier, 193
Doublage, 237, 459, 460, 715
Double, 61
Double Corne, 923
Doublé en cuivre, 177
Double fond, 234, 900
Double Fond Cellulaire, 135
Double Fond MacIntyre, 480
Double Hauteur, 233
Double Huniers, 236
Double Noeud de Hauban (Anglais), 235
Double Noeud de Tireveille, 235
Double Pic, 923
Doubler, 233, 662, 905
Doubler le tour de bitte, 234
Double Tour dans les Chaînes, 662
Douvelles, 788

Drague, 241, 811
Drague à Benne Preneuse, 334
Drague à Godets, 100
Drague à Huitres, 559
Drague à Pelle, 222
Drague mixte, 172
Drague Porteuse, 378
Draguer, 167, 811
Drague Suceuse, 805
Draille, 779
Drain Traversier, 187
Dressage, 248
Dresser, 772
Drisse, 350
Drisse d'Araignée, 187
Drisse de Flèche, 320
Drisse de Mât, 833
Drisse de Pavillon, 736
Drisse de Pic, 575
Droit, 736
Droit ad Valorem, 5
Droit d'Amarrage, 519
Droit d'Ancrage, 651
Droit d'Angarie, 651
Droit de Navigation, 651
Droit d'Entrée, 390
Droit de Pêche, 285, 651
Droit de Poursuite, 652
Droit de Préemption, 605
Droit de Prise, 608
Droit de quille, 419
Droit de Recherche, 652
Droit de Reconnaissance, 651
Droit Derrière, 650
Droit de Saisie, 652
Droit de Sortie, 268
Droit de Stationnement, 58
Droit d'Escorte, 651
Droit Devant, 363
Droit de Visite, 652
Droite de Hauteurs, 602
Droite de Sumner, 806
Droit Maritime, 493
Droit Maritime Commercial, 506
Droits d'Amarrage, 107
Droits d'Ancrage, 16
Droits de Balisage, 108
Droits de Balise, 50
Droits de Bassin, 228
Droits d'Écluse, 466
Droits de Douane, 193
Droits de Feux, 454
Droits de Jauge, 844
Droits de Navigation, 355
Droits de Pilotage, 582
Droits de Port, 599
Droits de quai, 58, 228, 623

Droits de Quarantaine, 620
Droits stationnement, 58
Drôme, 84, 200
Drosse, 867, 915
Duc d'Albe, 231, 581
Dunes, 238
Dunette, 598

Eau d'appoint, 486
Eau Morte, 203
Eaux Intérieures, 393
Eaux Maritimes, 835
Eaux Navigables, 531
Eaux Territoriales, 828
Ecailles de Laminage, 511
Ecart, 686
Écart à Clef, 420
Écart à Dés, 156
Écart à Entablement, 816
Écart à mi-bois, 92
Écart à Sifflet, 252
Écart à Trait de Jupiter, 377
Écart Double, 377
Écart du brion, 92
Écartement, 587
Écartement des Membrures, 306
Écart long, 252
Écart Plat, 291
Écart Simple, 588
Écarver, 686
Echancrure, 656, 811
Échappée, 264
Échappée de Tunnel, 871
Echappement, 747, 863
Echarpe, 787
Echaudis, 760
Échelle, 528
Échelle de Beaufort, 52
Échelle de Cale, 375, 581
Échelle de Corde, 659
Échelle de Coupée, 2
Échelle de Déplacement, 203
Échelle de déplacements, 225
Échelle de descente, 168
Échelle de Marée, 836
Échelle de nébulosité, 155
Échelle de Pilote, 583
Échelle de Pont, 207
Échelle de Revers, 405
Échelle des latitudes, 436
Échelle des longitudes, 471
Échelle des milles, 285
Échelle de Tirants d'Eau, 239, 390, 901
Échelle de Visibilité, 891

Echo-Sondeur à Contraction Magnétique, 484
Echo-Sondeur à ondes sonores, 756
Echo-Sondeur à Ultra Sons, 808
Echo-Sondeur Ultra Sonore, 808
Echoué, 7
Échoué à Sec, 371
Echouement Volontaire, 892
Échouer, 49, 339, 797
Éclair en boule, 37
Eclat, 644
Écliptique, 252
Écluse, 286
Écluse à Sas, 466
Écluser, 466
Écope, 36
Écoper, 35
Ecoute, 717
Ecoutes Filées, 296
Écoutille, 357
Ecoutillon, 693, 694
Ecran de fanal, 735
Ecrou de l'Hélice, 611
Ecrou de Serrage du Tube d'Étambot, 788
Écubier, 361
Écubier d'Amarrage, 521
Écubier d'embossage, 132, 786
Écubier de Mouillage, 362
Écubier de Pavois, 521
Écubier de Pont, 139, 208
Écubier de remorque, 786
Ecusson, 854
Effet de Soufflet, 567
Effet Galvanique, 322
Éhochteur, 344
Ejecteur de Dégazage, 325
Elancement, 302, 558
Électro-Aimant de Levage, 452
Électrode, 257
Électrode en Charbon, 124
Électrode Enrobée, 182
Électrode Métallique, 508
Électrode Nue, 42
Électrolyse, 257
Elévateur à grain, 258
Elévateur flottant, 294
Elévation et Abaissement, 653
Elève Officier, 116, 511
Élingue, 746
Élingue Double, 36
Élinguée, 374, 746
Élingue en Chaîne, 139
Élingue en chaîne, double, 234

Élingue en Fil d'Acier, 923
Élingue en Filin, 659
Élingue Entroilée, 906
Élingue limandée, 122
Élingueur, 746
Élonger, 441, 633, 670
Élongis, 128, 860
Élongis de Jardin, 770
Élongis de Tambour, 766
Embâcle, 258, 561
Embarcadère, 914
Embarcation, 72
Embarcation à Bouchains à arêtes Vives, 887
Embarcation à Moteur, 523
Embarcation à Vidange automatique, 704
Embarcation de Pêche, 285
Embarcation Hydrographique, 810
Embarcation inchavirable, 704
Embarcation Monotype, 550
Embarcation non Pontée, 551
Embarcation Seamless, 697
Embardée, 930
Embarder, 716
Embargo, 260
Embarquement, 259, 724
Embarquer, 72, 723
Embellie, 478, 750
Embossage, 300
Embossé, 331
Emboudinure, 613
Embrader sur l'Ancre, 96
Embraquer, 360, 662
Embraquer le Mou, 820
Embrun, 767
Embu, 251, 745
Emerillon, 812
Emerillon d'affourche, 522, 813
Emettre un son, 757
Emménagements, 2
Emménagements pour Passagers, 572
Empanner, 100
Empenneler, 30
Empilage, 69, 561, 792
Emplacement de Déblais, 766
Emplanture, 784
Empointure, 251
Empointure de Mât, 832
Empointure de pic, 574
En Avant, 7
En Avarie, 223
Encâblure, 114
Encaissement, 130, 279, 586

Encaissement des Chaudières, 78
Encaissement des Machines, 480
Encalminé, 52
Enchantillons, 685
En Ciseaux, 921
Enclavé, 537
Encombrement, 796
En Contre Différence, 862
Encornail, 249, 349
En Dérive, 5
En Différence, 862
Enduit au Bitumastic, 66
Enflécher, 636
Enfléchure, 635
Enfléchure Bâtarde, 717
Engagé, 50, 304
Engoujure, 689
En Haut, 10
En Long, 300
En Membrures, 305
Enquête du Pavillon, 889
En Ralingue, 399
Enrôlement, 737
En route, 880
Entablature, 262
En travers, 25
En travers de la touée, 25
Entrée au Bassin, 228
Entrée en Douane, 263, 400
Entremise, 128
Entremise de Bossoir, 200
Entremise d'Étambrai, 496, 571
Entremise sous Barrots, 206
Entrepont, 781, 875
Entrepôt de Douane, 82
Entrer, 262
Entrer au Bassin, 228
Entrer en déchargement, 95
Entrer en douane, 262
Entretoise de Soute, 106
Enverguer, 56
Envergure, 362, 477
Épaule, 473, 753
Épaulement, 411
Épave, 214, 925
Épave rejetées, 407
Épaves Flottantes, 296
Éperon, 50, 423
Epervier, 131
Ephémérides Nautiques, 10
Epi, 338, 764
Épinglette, 365
Episser, 765
Epissoir, 495
Epissure, 765

Épissure à Oeil, 270
Epissure Carrée, 731
Epissure de Cable, 492
Epissure de Ligne de Pêche, 472
Epissure de Voilier, 676
Epissure en Greffe, 379
Epissure Longue, 473
Epite, 860
Epontille, 580, 774
Epontille à échelons, 784
Épontille Creuse, 376
Épontille d'Assemblage, 102
Épontille de Cale, 375
Epontille Démontable, 599
Epontille d'entrepont, 208
Epontille Diagonale, 218
Epontille Latérale, 622
Epontille Massive, 755
Epontiller, 841
Epontilles à Grand Écartement, 918
Epuisette, 222
Epurateur d'huile, 548
Equateur, 828
Equateur Magnétique, 482
Equation du Temps, 263
Équerrage, 60
Équerrage des Couples, 305
Équerrage en Gras, 775
Équerrage en maigre, 154
Équilibre de Résistance, 383
Équilibre Indifférent, 535
Équilibre Instable, 882
Équilibre Stable, 773
Equinoctial, 264
Équinoxe d'Automne, 28
Équinoxe du Printemps, 889
Equipage, 184
Equipage de Prise, 607
Equipe de Charpentiers en Fer, 590
Equipe de Riveurs, 655
Equipe de Secours, 259
Équipement, 556
Equivalence des Rations, 891
Erable, 488
Ergot, 770
Erre, 903
Erre en Arrière, 788
Erre en Avant, 364
Erre pour Gouverner, 782
Erreur de Collimation, 164
Erreur de Gaussin, 326, 386
Erreur de Latitude, 436
Erreur d'Index, 391
Erreur du Compas, 169
Erreur Instrumentale, 391

Erse, 797
Erseau, 338
Erseau d'Aviron de Queue, 782
Erseau de Défense, 338
Erse en Bitord, 706
Escarbilleur, 24
Escarbilleur Hydraulique, 24
Escorte, 177
Espace Découvert, 553
Espace Déduit, 210
Espace Exempté, 267
Espaces affectés à la puissance motrice, 611
Espaces Clos, 154
Espaces deductibles, 210
Espar, 760
Espar Brut, 660
Espar Creux, 376
Espar d'Assemblage, 102
Espar Débité, 193
Espar en bois de Brin, 341
Espar Métallique, 781
Espar Plein, 755
Esprot, 767
Essai à la Lance, 380
Essai d'appareil à gouverner de secours, 259
Essai de Stabilité, 391
Essai hydrostatique, 386
Essais à la mer, 699
Essais au point fixe, 229
Essais de giration, 487
Essais Progressifs, 608
Essieu, 584
Estain, 276
Estran, 49, 303, 797
Estrope, 746, 797
Estroper, 798
Estuaire, 265
Etablir, 709
Etablir la Voilure, 486
Etablissement du Port, 893
Etablissement moyen, 502
Étai, 779, 802
Etai de Chouque, 124, 861
Etai de Flèche, 364
Etale, 775
Etale de Basse Mer, 476
Etale de Pleine Mer, 372
Etaler, 648, 784, 905
Étaler sur les avirons, 375
Étalingure, 56, 152
Étalingure à Émérillon, 813
Étalingure d'Ancre, 115
Étalingure de Puits, 66
Étambot, 786
Etambot Arrière, 31
Etambot Avant, 611

Etambot en tôles façonnés—Ferrure de Sauvegarde 950

Etambot en tôles façonnés, 271
Étambrai, 571
Étambrai de Mât, 499
Etamine, 106
Étamperche, 883
Étanche, 902
Étanche à l'Eau, 902
Étancher, 307
Etarquer, 812
Etarquoir, 410
Etat de Navigabilité, 699
Etat-Major, 728
Etayer, 779
Etêteur, 363
Etouffer, 764
Etoupe, 543
Etoupe Blanche, 918
Étrangloir, 172, 764, 833
Etrave, 45, 783
Etrave Droite, 796
Etrave Élancée, 633
Etrave en Tôles, façonnées, 276
Être à la Cape, 448
Être à la cape courante, 448, 868
Être à la Cape Sèche, 448
Être Ardent, 338
Être au Mouillage, 648
Être Dépalé, 245
Être Drossé, 245
Être Jeté à la Côte, 797
Être Paré, 775
Etrier, 238, 379, 789
Etrier de Brasseyage, 929
Étrier de Trou d'Homme, 488
Etui, 675
Étui de Chauffe, 497, 749
Etui de Claire Voie, 743
Étui de Mât, 497
Etui d'Embarcation, 73
Etui d'habitacle, 169
Evénements de Mer, 578
Evidement, 454
Evitage, 812
Evité à la Marée, 836
Evité au Vent, 921
Eviter, 812, 819
Excedent d'Ecoutilles, 267
Exercice, 244
Exercice d'Embarcations, 74
Exercice d'Incendie, 282
Exfoliation, 267
Exhalaison, 718
Expedier, 150
Expéditeur, 173, 210
Expédition à l'Entrée, 150
Expédition d'Entrée, 400
Expédition de Sortie, 151

Expédition en Douane, 150, 557
Expertise, 809
Expertise d'Avarie, 197
Expert Maritime, 492
Expert Mécanicien, 261
Extrémité de Chaîne, 556
Extrémité de Varangue, 295

Face Antérieure, 30, 240
Face poussant, 272
Faces de Placage, 277
Façons de l'Arrière, 668
Façons de l'avant, 263
Facteur de Cloisonnement, 272
Facture Consulaire, 174
Facture d'Expédition, 268
Faire, 486
Faire Abattage, 812
Faire abattre, 130
Faire Ajut, 56
Faire Cap Sur, 363
Faire Chapelle, 140
Faire côte, 668
Faire croupiat, 156
Faire Escale, 118
Faire Éviter, 812, 827
Faire la Relève, 644
Faire le Sac, 32
Faire Marche Arrière, 278
Faire Marquer, 221
Faire Mordre, 146
Faire Peneau, 160
Faire ralinguer, 713
Faire route pour, 87
Faire Servir, 280
Faire Tête, 98
Faire un Lan, 99
Faire Voile, 673
Faitage de Tente, 28
Fait de Guerre, 3
Falaise, 152
Falaise de glace, 388
Fanal à Signaux, 522
Fanal Combiné, 167
Fanal de Bord, 727
Fanal d'embarcation, 75
Fanal Morse, 522
Fanal Portatif, 599
Fanal Tricolore, 862
Fange, 551
Faraud, 753
Fardage, 845
Fargue, 88, 899
Faseyer, 729
Fatiguer, 428, 924
Fatiguer au mouillage, 648

Faubert, 354, 810
Fausse Batterie, 564
Fausse Cargue, 764
Fausse Carlingue, 648
Fausse Cheminée, 249
Fausse Clef, 605
Fausse Mèche, 28
Fausse Penture, 249
Fausse Quille, 275, 744
Fausse Varangue, 349
Faute Nautique, 264
Faux, 286, 772
Faux-Bois, 682
Faux-Bord, 474
Faux bras, 75
Faux-bras à dépasser les tours de chaîne, 151
Faux-bras de Tangon, 342
Faux-Bras Élongé en Créance, 341
Faux-Cartahu, 249
Faux Cirrus, 20
Faux Élongis, 60
Faux Étai, 413
Faux-Etambot, 275
Faux-Foc, 510
Faux Fret, 202
Faux-Galhauban, 605, 856
Faux Hauban, 606
Faux Mantelets, 564
Faux-Marchepied, 292
Faux Plet, 132
Faux-Pont, 555
Faux Tillac, 348
Faux-Tin, 122
Feau d'Atterage, 486
Feeder, 277
Fémelot, 341
Femme de Chambre de Bord, 789
Fendre, 768
Fenêtre, 788
Fente, 768
Fer à Boudin, 103
Fer à clous, 763
Fer à T, 825
Fer Cannelé, 486
Fer de Calfat, 118
Fer Demi-Rond, 349
Fer Double, 486
Fer en Z, 932
Fer Magnétique, 483
Fermer, 92
Fer Plat, 290
Ferrement de planche à chalut, 555
Fer Rond, 660
Ferrure de Sauvegarde, 666

Ferrure de tête, 215
Ferrures de Gouvernail, 664
Ferryboat, 278
Fer T à Boudin, 825
Fer Taillant, 194, 552
Fer U, 140
Fesses, 111
Feu à changement de coloration par groupes, 340
Feu Additionel, 634
Feu à Éclats, 290
Feu à Éclats Groupés, 340
Feu à éclats longs, 470
Feu Alternatif, 11
Feu alternatif à éclats groupés, 10
Feu alternatif à occultations, 11
Feu alternatif à occultations groupées, 11
Feu alternatif clignotant, 10
Feu alternatif fixe à élcat, 10
Feu alternatif fixe à éclats groupés, 10
Feu antérieur, 312
Feu à Occultations, 545
Feu à Secteur, 701
Feu Coston, 179
Feu à Occultations Groupées, 340
Feu d'Avertissement, 897
Feu de Côté, 735
Feu de Direction, 634
Feu de Gouverne, 782
Feu de Mât Arrière, 634
Feu de Mouillage, 649
Feu d'Entrée de Port, 600
Feu de Pointe, 634
Feu de Poupe, 786
Feu de Remorque, 850
Feu de St. Elme, 677
Feu de Tête de Mât, 363, 498, 780
Feu d'Impossibilité de Manœuvre, 542
Feu Dioptrique, 221
Feu Fixe, 288
Feu Fixe à Éclats, 287
Feu Fixe à Éclats Groupés, 288
Feu flottant non gardé, 453
Feuillard, 717
Feu intermittent, 397
Feu isophase, 397
Feu Non Gardé, 879
Feu Pyrotechnique, 226
Feu Pyrotechnique Holmes, 376

Feu Réglementaire, 641
Feu scintillant, 293, 623, 688
Feu scintillant à clignotements, 623
Feu scintillant à occultations, 545
Feu scintillant intermittent, 397
Feu Tournant, 646
Feux Couverts, 39
Feux d'alignement, 454
Feux de Côte, 159
Feux de Marée, 835
Feux de Pêche, 924
Feux de position, 531, 670
Fibre, 831
Fibre Neutre, 534
Fièvre Jaune, 930
Figure d'Étrave, 280
Fil, 335, 876, 929
Fil à Congréer, 916
Fil à Ralinguer, 659
Filasse, 848
Fil à Surlier, 916
Fil à Voile, 697
Fil Ciré, 916
Fil d'Amarrage, 703
Fil de Caret, 659, 876
Fil de Chaîne, 898
Fil de Marque, 656
Fil de Pêche, 180
Fil de Trame, 907
Filé, 296
Filer, 574, 744, 798, 888
Filer en bande, 112, 446
Filer en grand, 112
Filer le loch, 366
Filer par le Bout, 747
Filet, 286
Filet à coeur, 603
Filet à Poche, 33
Filet Coulissant, 617
Filet de Barrage, 799
Filet de Beaupré, 409
Filet d'Elingue, 127
Filet Dérivant, 244
Filet Dormant, 709
Filet Fixe, 288, 709
Filet Maillant, 330, 821
Filet Métallique, 922
Filets de Pavois, 105
Fileur d'huile, 547
Fileux, 134, 420
Filière, 450, 488
Filière de Beaupré, 91, 646
Filière de Garde Corps, 648
Filière d'Envergure, 56, 404
Filière de Ris, 404, 639

Filière de Tente, 29, 648
Filière en Guirlande, 450
Filin, 658
Filin à Croc, 377
Filin à Rides, 433
Filin Blanc, 918
Filin d'Acier, 922
Filin d'Acier Inoxydable, 774
Filin de Hissage, 128
Filin en Acier Fondu, 131
Filin Gourdronné, 824
Filin Métallique, 922
Fils, 660
Fincelle, 363
Fin Keel, 281
Firth, 284
Fixer, 287
Flamber, 96
Flamme, 528, 577
Flamme de Commandement, 99
Flamme du Code, 19, 161
Flamme Postale, 485
Flare Up, 290
Flèche, 595
Flèche à Vergue, 404, 768
Flèche Ballon, 37
Flèche Bômé, 156
Flèche Carré, 232, 404
Flèche de Cacatois, 663
Flèche de Contre-Cacatois, 744
Flèche Pointu, 409
Flèche Pointu à Vergue, 769
Flèsche, 320
Fleuriau, 306
Flot, 295
Flottabilité, 107
Flotte, 222, 293, 701
Flotteur, 107
Flux, 295, 654
Foc, 408
Foc à Double Écoutes, 234
Foc à Livarde, 769
Foc Ballon, 37
Foc d'Artimon, 514
Foc de Gênes, 328
Foc de Près, 328
Foc en l'Air, 410
Foëne, 286
Fond, 106, 299, 694
Fond à Redan, 784
Fond de Bonne Tenue, 375
Fond de mauvaise tenue, 304
Fond de Rablure, 31
Fond plat, 290
Fonds, 61
Fonds de Pêche, 285
Fontaine de Bossoir, 200, 201

Forant—Glace Épaisse 952

Forant, 774
Force d'un Courant, 242
Force magnétique, 483
Force Majeure, 3
Forcement de Voiles, 605
Forcer, 187
Forme de Radoub, 246
Forme sur gabarits, 516
Formule de jauge, 635
Formule de Kirk, 422
Fort, 775
Fort Coup de Vent, 918
Forte Mer, 367
Fort Vent, 515
Fortune, 297, 518
Fortune de mer, 199
Fosse, 210, 241, 860
Fosse à Gouvernail, 667
Fouet, 819
Foule, 760
Four à réchauffer, 56
Fournisseur de Navires, 723
Fourrer, 335, 708
Fourrure, 418, 708
Fourrure de Gouttière, 556
Fourrure de Préceinte, 67
Fragments plats de Banquise flottante, 294
Frai, 761
Fraisage, 180
Frais à l'Entrée, 400
Frais Consulaires, 174
Frais d'Agence, 7
Frais d'Allège, 454
Frais d'Armement, 223
Frais de cale sèche, 247
Frais de Déhalage, 721
Frais de Grue, 183
Frais d'élingage, 746
Frais de Magasinage, 792
Frais de Manutention, 352
Frais de mise à Terre, 433
Frais de Navigation, 355
Frais d'entreposage, 792
Frais de Passage, 571
Frais de Pesage, 908
Frais de remorquage, 848
Franc Bord, 307
Franc d'Avaries, 308
Franchise, 306
Franco Bord, 308
Franco Chargement et Déchargement, 308
Franco Déchargement, 432
Franco Quai, 268
Frapper, 56
Frappeur, 654
Frein, 419

Frein de Gouvernail, 665
Frein Magnétique, 481
Frêne, 24
Fréquences de détresse, 628
Fret, 113, 309
Fret ad Valorem, 5
Fret au Cubage, 502
Fret Brut, 339
Fret de Distance, 225
Fret de Retour, 391
Fret de Sortie, 556
Fret Forfaitaire, 478
Fret proportionnel, 225
Frette, 498
Frise, 852
Front, 312
Fronteau, 95
Front froid, 163
Front Polaire, 23, 595
Frottoir, 663
Frustration, 314
Fuir, 668, 692
Fumigation, 315
Fune, 30, 859
Fuseau Horaire, 840
Fusée, 595
Fusée de Signalisation, 737
Fusée Porte Amarre, 451
Fusil Porte-Amarre, 732
Fût de Manche à Air, 889
Fût de Rivet, 655

Gabarage, 454
Gabarier, 42, 452, 454
Gabarit, 516, 827
Gabarit de barrot, 51
Gabarit de Membrure, 306
Gabarre, 689
Gaffe, 74, 232
Gaffeau, 232
Gaffion, 232
Gagner, 278, 302, 558
Gagner au Vent, 921
Gaiac, 456
Gaillard Court, 731
Gaillard d'Arrière, 621
Gaillard Long, 470
Gain de la marée, 606
Gaine, 816
Gainer, 815
Galbord, 324
Galet, 722
Galets, 575
Galhauban, 31
Galhauban Volant, 721
Galiote, 300, 322

Galipot, 67, 749
Galoche, 149, 891
Galon, 39
Galvanisation, 322
Gambes de Revers, 318
Gambeyer, 221
Gamelle, 421
Gangui, 568
Garant, 274
Garant de Bossoir, 74
Garant de Capon, 132
Garant de Mât de Charge, 126, 128
Garantie, 898
Garantie Expresse, 268
Garantie Implicite, 390
Garanties de l'Institut de Londres, 394
Garcette, 325, 537
Garcette de Ris, 639
Garçon de Cabine, 53
Garçon de Pont, 209
Garde, 886
Garde-Corps, 553
Garde Côte, 159
Garde montante, 364, 768
Garde Montante de l'Arrière, 7
Garde Montante de l'avant, 303, 304
Garder l'Évitage, 827
Garder Maintenir, 777
Gare, 440
Garni, 661
Garnir, 98, 335
Garniture, 95, 327, 650
Garniture de Plomb de Sonde, 23
Gatte, 487
Génévrier, 820
Genope, 660
Genoper, 307, 702
Genou, 283, 869
Genou de Fond, 349
Gens de Mer, 696
Géocentrique, 328
Gibbeux, 329
Giboulée, 732
Girouette, 3, 886
Gisement, 860
Gité, 10, 367, 460
Glace d'ancre, 16
Glace de Baie, 49
Glace de banquise, 45
Glace de mer, 695
Glace de Pack, 561
Glace Dérivante, 243
Glace en Forme de Crêpes, 566
Glace Épaisse, 367

Glace morcelée, 748
Glace Moutonnée, 383
Glace Nouvelle, 931
Glace Polaire, 595
Glace pourrie, 660
Glacière, 387
Glène, 161, 274
Glène Filante, 311
Glène Plate, 292
Glissière, 125
Globe Compensateur, 619
Glue Marine, 491
Gobelet, 498
Godille, 649, 692
Godiller, 693
Goëlette à deux Huniers, 486
Goëlette à Humiers, 772
Goëlette à huniers, 847
Goëlette à phares abaissés, 35
Goëlette à trois mâts, 828
Goëlette à Voiles d'Étai, 779
Goëlette Bermudienne, 58
Goëlette Carrée, 772
Goëlette de Cape, 320
Goëlette franche, 687
Goëlette Latine, 687
Golfe, 259
Gong de brume, 298
Goniomètre, 628, 629
Gord, 286
Goret, 373
Gorge, 810, 832
Gorgère, 194
Gouffre, 117
Goujon, 802
Goujure, 689
Goulet, 344, 393, 528, 757
Goupille, 302
Gournable, 860
Gousset, 93, 344, 423
Gousset à Bord Tombé, 289
Gousset de barrot, 51
Gousset de Pied de Membrure, 921
Gousset Soudé, 908
Gouttière, 467, 903
Gouvernail, 664
Gouvernail à Tôle simple, 136
Gouvernail Avant, 90
Gouvernail à Double Tôle, 735
Gouvernail Compensé, 34
Gouvernail de Fortune, 414
Gouvernail Latéral, 622
Gouvernail Oertz, 546
Gouvernail Partiellement Compensé, 706
Gouvernail Profilé, 799
Gouvernail Suspendu, 880

Gouverne, 782
Gouverne Automatique, 27
Gouverner, 781
Gouverner au Large de, 782
Gouverner avec Peu de Barre, 783
Gouverner sur, 52
Gradin, 10
Graduations de la Ligne de Sonde, 494
Grain, 684, 770
Grain Arqué, 22
Grain Blanc, 918
Grain de Gouvernail, 585
Graisse a Mâture, 749
Graisseur, 337
Grand, 485
Grand Cabotage, 377
Grand Canot, 437, 470, 585
Grand Cercle, 337
Grand Dos, 770
Grande Aile, 87
Grande Croisure, 772
Grande Maille, 262, 396, 473
Grande Marée, 264
Grande Pêche, 547
Grande Sonde, 211
Grandes Cordes, 337
Grandeur, 484
Grande Voile de Lougre, 478
Grand Foc, 556, 776
Grand Frais, 515
Grand Miroir, 391
Grand Pavois, 242
Grand Pavois Longitudinal, 242
Grand Pavois Transversal, 242
Grand vent, 373
Grand-Voile, 486
Grand-voile Bômée, 84
Grand-Voile d'Étai Centrale, 510
Grappin, 335
Gratte, 691
Gratteur, 742
Gravier, 663
Gréement, 649, 650
Gréement à Antenne, 435
Gréement à Double Pic, 923
Gréement à Livarde, 769
Gréement à Traits Carrés, 771
Gréement Aurique, 300
Gréement à Voiles d'Étai, 779
Gréement à Voiles en Pointe, 300
Gréement Bermudien, 57
Gréement Courant, 670
Gréement de Cat boat, 132

Gréement de Barque, 43
Gréement de Fortune, 414
Gréement de Goëlette, 688
Gréement de Lougre, 478
Gréement de misaine, 302
Gréement de Polacre, 595
Gréement de Sétie, 709
Gréement de Sloop, 748
Gréement Dormant, 776
Gréement Houari, 343
Gréement Marconi, 57
Greenheart, 337
Gréeur, 649
Grelin, 115
Grenier, 95
Grésil, 745
Greule de Raie, 356
Griffe, 677, 923
Griffe de corne, 320
Gril de Carénage, 338
Grisette, 246
Grondeur, 341
Gros Bordages, 830
Grosse Erse, 324
Gros Temps, 799
Grue de Bord, 205
Grue de Capon, 15
Grue de Quai, 229
Guérite, 182, 847
Gueulard, 504
Gueule de loup Double, 234
Gueule de Raie, 133
Gui, 83
Guibre, 423
Guibre à Volute, 279
Guide, 462
Guideau, 442
Guide de Cargue Fond, 107
Guidon, 109
Guidon de Club, 156
Guignette, 207
Guindant, 374, 381
Guindeau, 919
Guindeau à Barres, 635
Guindeau à Bringuebale, 614
Guindeau à Pompe, 614
Guinder, 810
Guinderesse, 368, 499
Guindineau, 199
Guipon, 522, 587
Guirlande, 96, 594
Guirlande Arrière, 189
Guirlande d'Ecubiers, 238
Guirlande d'Étrave, 89

Habitacle, 65
Habitacle à Compensateurs, 171

Hachot, 358
Hacke, 31
Hale, 242
Hale à Bord, 393
Halebas, 238
Halebas de Corne, 275
Halebreau, 863
Hale Dehors, 557
Hale dehors de pic, 363
Haler, 360, 888
Haler à Coups, 888
Haleur, 458
Halo, 350
Hamac, 350
Hameçon, 285
Hampe, 598
Hampe de Pavillon, 289, 773
Hanche, 620
Hanche du vent, 906
Handicap, 351
Hanet, 423
Hanet d'Araignée de Hamac, 350
Hanet de Hamac, 837
Hanet d'Envergure, 656
Hanet de Ris, 639
Hanet de Tente, 29
Hangar de Quai, 854
Hareng Braillé, 765
Hareng d'Été, 331
Hareng gai, 315, 653
Harenguier, 370
Hareng Vide, 732
Harmattan, 356
Harouelles, 472
Harpoire, 301
Harpon, 356
Hauban, 733
Hauban Bâtard, 811
Hauban de Beaupré, 91
Hauban de Cheminée, 750
Hauban de Foc, 409
Hauban de Fortune, 606
Hauban de Martingale, 495
Hauban de Perroquet, 845
Haubans de Bas Mât, 476
Haubans de Clin-Foc, 297
Haubans de Hune, 846
Haubans de Tête de Mât, 883
Haute Mer, 372
Hauteur, 11, 368, 736
Hauteur Apparente, 20
Hauteur Circumméridienne, 268
Hauteur de la basse mer, 369
Hauteur de la pleine mer, 369, 835
Hauteur d'entrepont, 207

Hauteur Observée, 544
Hauteur Méridienne, 507
Hauteur Métacentrique, 508
Hauteur Métacentrique Longitudinale, 471
Hauteur Métacentrique Transversale, 856
Hauteur Polaire, 595
Hauteurs Égales, 263
Hauteurs Simultanées, 738
Hauteur Vraie, 866
Haute Varangue, 210
Haut fond, 713, 729
Héler, 347
Héliaque, 369
Hélice, 609
Hélice à Ailes rapportées, 103
Hélice à pas à Droite, 650
Hélice à Pas à Gauche, 445
Hélice à pas réglable, 3
Hélice à Tuyère, 733
Hélice Chantante, 738
Hélice de Loch, 660
Hélice Massive, 755
Hélice Propulsive, 609
Hélice Réversible, 646
Hélice sous voûte, 872
Héliocentrique, 369
Herminette, 5
Hernier, 266
Heu, 382
Heure Astronomique, 25
Heure Civile, 148
Heure de Fuseau, 933
Heure de la basse mer, 839
Heure de la Pleine mer, 839
Heure du Bord, 728
Heure du Fuseau, 775
Heure du Lieu, 466
Heure Légale, 775
Heure Sidérale, 735
Heure Solaire, 754
Heure Solaire Vraie, 21
Heures supplémentaires, 559
Heure Vraie, 866
Heure Vraie du Lieu, 465
Hiloire, 157, 358
Hiloire de Fronteau, 103
Hiloire Longitudinale, 734
Hiloire Renversée, 357, 359
Hiloire Transversale, 260, 363, 444
Hisser, 366, 374
Ho, 8
Homme de Barre, 369
Homme de Bossoir, 473
Homme d'équipage, 696
Hopital, 380

Horizon Apparent, 20
Horizon Rationel, 635
Horizon Sensible, 708
Horizon Vrai, 635
Houache, 302, 798
Houari, 343, 745
Houle, 811
Houle Battée, 187
Houle de fond, 340
Houle de l'avant, 364
Houle Synchrone, 814
Houle Trochoïde, 864
House Boat, 381
Hublot, 600
Hublot Fixe, 288
Hublot ouvrant, 552
Huile de Filage, 793
Huile de foie de Morue, 161
Huile de Moteur, 220
Huile de Poisson, 286
Huile de Spermaceti, 763
Hummock, 383
Hune, 557, 844
Hunier, 771
Hunier à Rouleau, 704
Hunier Fixe, 476
Hunier Plein, 739
Hunier Volant, 883
Hydrocarbures, 579
Hydroglisseur, 385, 386
Hydrographie, 386
Hydrographie Maritime, 529
Hydromètre, 386
Hydrophone, 386
Hydroplane, 386
Hydroplane à Redans Multiples, 525
Hydroplane à Redan Unique, 739
Hygromètre, 386
Hygromètre Enregistreur, 386

Iceberg, 387
Immatriculation, 728
Inclinaison, 221, 482, 741, 783
Indemnité pour temps gagne, 226
Indicateur de Tirant d'Eau, 239
Indicatif d'appel, 119
Indicatif d'Appel Radiotélégraphique, 628
Induction horizontale, 378
Induction Magnétique, 483
Inégalité Diurne, 226
Ingénieur Hydrographe, 385, 386, 529

Innavigabilité, 882
Inspecteur de l'immigration, 390
Instable, 184
Instructions Nautiques, 675
Instruments Nautiques, 529
Insuffisamment Voilé, 879
Intercostal, 396
Intérêt Nautique, 491
Inventaire de Pont, 208
Isobare, 402
Isobathe, 276
Isolation, 394
Isolement, 394
Isotherme, 402
Isthme, 402
Itague, 837
Itague d'Affourchage, 151, 222
Itague de Corps-Mort, 521
Itague de Ris, 639

Jambe de chien, 716
Jambette, 838
Jambette de Pavois, 105
Jambette de Tableau, 787
Jambette de Voûte, 180
Jambette d'Hiloire, 157
Jardin de Tambour, 563, 766
Jas, 790
Jaugeage, 502
Jauge Ancienne, 101
Jauge Brute, 339
Jauge de la Tamise, 829
Jauge du Canal de Suez, 806
Jauge Moorsom, 522
Jauge Officielle, 642
Jauge Nette, 534
Jauge sous le Pont, 880
Jaumière, 369, 667
Jet à la Mer, 407
Jetée, 96, 407, 581
Jeu de Voiles, 709
Joint, 325
Joint à Clin, 434
Joint à Franc-Bord, 111
Joint à Recouvrement, 434
Joint Glissant, 268
Jolie Brise, 515
Jonque, 413
Jottereau, 143, 853
Jottereaux, 381
Joue, 143, 378
Joue de Guidage, 438
Joue de Safran, 143
Joue de Tolet, 662
Joue de vache, 143, 149
Jouer, 924

Jouette, 658
Jour Astronomique, 25
Jour Civil, 148
Jour Férié, 375
Jour férié de bord, 726
Jour férié du port, 600
Jour Lunaire, 478
Journal de Bord, 727
Journal de la Machine, 261
Journal de Mer, 208
Journal de Route, 727
Journal des Montres, 147
Journal Radio-électrique, 922
Journal Réglementaire, 547
Journal Timbré, 547
Jour Nautique, 529
Jour Ouvrable, 924
Jours Courants, 669
Jours de Chargement, 464
Jours de Grâce, 201
Jours de Planche, 440
Jours de Planche Réversibles, 646
Jours de Surestaries, 213
Jours Francs, 151
Jour Sidéral, 735
Jour Solaire, 754
Jour Solaire Moyen, 501
Juage d'Entrepont, 875
Juage du Canal de Panama, 566
Juglinage, 411
Jumeler, 284
Jumelle, 284
Jumelle de Frottement, 285
Jumelles, 65
Juridiction Maritime, 4
Jusant, 251

Ketch, 420
Kiosque de Veille, 142

La Gueule de Loup, 67
Laguis, 669
Lagune, 429
Laisse, 836
Laisse Aller, 904
Laisse Courir, 904
Laisse de Haute Mer, 372
Laisser aller en bande, 446
Laisser Arriver, 52
Laisser Porter, 52
Laisser Suivre, 311
Lait de Ciment, 135
Laiton, 95
Laiton Rouge, 343

Laize, 155
Laize de Pointe, 334
Lamanage, 72
Lamaneur, 75, 373
Lambourdes, 340
Lambrissage, 460, 566
Lame, 904
Lame de Houle, 809
Lamelles de Gaiac, 788
Lampe de Sureté, 289
Lampe d'habitacle, 65
Lampiste, 431
Lampisterie, 431
Lance Amarre, 360
Lance de Sonde, 758
Lancement, 437
Lancement en Long, 260
Lancement en Travers, 734
Lancement sur Double Coulisse, 237
Lancement sur Flancs, 237
Lancement sur Quille, 739
Lancement sur Savate, 739
Lancer dans le Vent, 99, 730
Languette, 4
Lanterne, 585
La Ralinque, 81
Larcin Petit Vol, 581
Lardage, 833
Larder, 833
Lardon, 250
Large, 547
Largeur, 50
Largeur au fort, 269
Largeur de Jauge, 842
Largeur Hors-Membrures, 516
Largeur réglementaire, 641
Largue, 307, 434
Larguer, 131, 446, 713, 874, 881
Larguer les Amarres, 131
La Rose du Compas, 170
Last, 435
Latitude, 436
Latitude Circumméridienne, 268
Latitude de départ, 436
Latitude Ex-Méridienne, 268
Latitude Géocentrique, 328
Latitude géographique, 328
Latitude Moyenne, 510
Latitude observée, 436
Latitude par la méridienne, 507
Latitude par l'Estime, 436
Latitudes Croissantes, 507
Latitude Terrestre, 328
Latte de Hune, 317

Latte de Pied, 151
Latte de ragage, 138
Latte de tracé, 516
Latte de Vaigrage, 125
Latte de Voile, 674
Lazaret, 441, 620
Le Gaillard, 301
Légère Brise, 453
Lent à Virer, 744
Le Ratelier de Mât, 279
Lest, 36
Lest d'eau, 900
Lest fixe, 578
L'estime, 202
Lest Volant, 721
Le Taquet, 151
Le Tirant d'Eau, 239
Lettre d'avis, 541
Lettre de Garantie, 447
Lettres de Marque, 447
Lettres de Représailles, 447
Lettres Signalétiques, 727, 736
Levé, 809
Levée, 365, 366, 686, 699
Levé Hydrographique, 386
Lève-Nez, 862
Lève rames, 544, 574
Lever l'Ancre, 366, 907
Levier à Griffe, 60
Levier à Secteur, 919
Lèvre, 460
Levure, 447
Liberté des Mers, 308
Libre de glace, 389
Licenciement, 737
Liège aggloméré, 744
Lieu, 588
Lieu Apparent, 20
Lieue Marine, 444
Lieu Vrai, 866
Ligne, 457
Ligne à Cabillaud, 347
Ligne à Congréer, 925
Ligne à Dorys, 161
Ligne a Flétan, 350
Ligne à fourrer, 708
Ligne à Main, 352
Ligne à Merlan, 918
Ligne à Morue, 161
Ligne antiméridienne, 199
Ligne Courante, 915
Ligne d'Amarrage, 703
Ligne d'Amarrage Métallique, 922
Ligne d'Arbres, 713
Ligne d'Arêtes, 217
Ligne d'Attrape, 360
Ligne d'Eau Zéro, 45

Ligne de Charge, 464, 465
Ligne de Charge de Cloisonnement, 803
Ligne de charge d'été, 806
Ligne de Charge pour Bois en Pontée, 838
Ligne de collimation, 457
Ligne de Flottaison Lège, 455
Ligne de Foi, 477
Ligne de Fond, 86
Ligne de Grande Sonde, 211
Ligne de Harpon, 911
Ligne de Loch, 469
Ligne de Pêche, 286
Ligne de Petite Sonde, 352
Ligne de Pont, 207
Ligne de Pont Réglementaire, 778
Ligne de Quille, 419
Ligne de Relèvement, 442
Ligne de Revers, 381
Ligne de sondages, 457
Ligne de Sonde, 444
Ligne des Sondes, 276
Ligne de Surimmersion, 489
Ligne de Tonture, 716
Ligne de tracé, 516
Ligne Isocline, 402
Ligne Isodynamique, 402
Ligne Isogone, 402
Ligne méridienne, 507
Ligne nodale, 457
Ligne porte Amarre, 656
Lignerolle, 534, 759
Lignes cotidales, 179
Lignes d'Eau, 901
Lignes de Fond, 472
Ligne Traînante, 865, 915
Limande, 569
Limander, 569
Limbe, 456
Limbe inférieur, 476
Limite de Stabilité, 634
Limnorie, 338
Linquet, 573
Lis, 706
Lisière des glaces, 389
Lisse d'angle, 144
Lisse de Bastingages, 845
Lisse de batayole, 660
Lisse de Construction, 306, 716
Lisse de Dessus de Quille, 194
Lisse de Dunette, 598
Lisse de Pavois, 105
Lisse d'Éperon, 363
Lisse de Plat-Bord, 344, 564, 717
Lisse de Rabattue, 244

Lisse des Bouchains, 62
Lisse des Façons, 654
Lisse d'Hourdi, 922
Lisse d'Ouverture, 187
Lisse Oblique, 217
Lisses d'exécution, 356
Lisses Planes, 218
Lisse Verticale, 400
Liste des Passagers, 572
Liston, 50, 516, 663
Liston de la Voûte, 424
Lit, 269
Littoral, 461
Liure à Tendeurs, 691
Liure de Bâton de Foc, 368
Liure de Beaupré, 323
Livarde, 769
Livet en Abord, 207
Livet Milieu, 207
Livraison sous Palan, 559
Livre de Bord, 547
Livre des Phares, 455
Livret de marin, 175
Locaux à marchandises, 128
Locaux de Navigation, 532
Loch, 467
Loch à Touret, 352
Loch à Tube Pitot, 587
Loch de Fond, 340
Loch Électrique, 255
Loch Enregistreur, 691
Lof, 477
Loffer, 360, 477
Logement, 381
Logement d'Ancre, 16
Log Forbes, 299
Loi d'Archimède, 439
Loi de Froude, 313
Loi du Pavillon, 439
Lois de Similitude, 440
Longitude, 471
Longitude de départ, 471
Longitude par différence d'heure, 471
Longitude par l'Estime, 471
Longitudinal, 300
Longueur à la Flottaison, 901
Longueur d'Acuité, 446
Longueur de Cloisonnement, 579, 803
Longueur de Jauge, 844
Longueur de la Coulée, 446
Longueur entre Perpendiculaires, 446
Longueur Envahissable, 295
Longueur Hors-Tout, 269, 446
Longueur Réglementaire, 642
Longue Vue, 530, 826

Lot, 569
Lougre, 477
Loupe, 510
Louve, 369
Louvoyer, 52, 592, 816
Lover, 161
Loxodromie, 647
Lubréfiant de Lancement, 438
Lueur, 474
Lumière Zodiacale, 933
Lunaison, 479
Lunette, 786
Lunette Astronomique, 400, 932
Lunette d'Approche, 530
Lunette d'Eau, 902
Lunette de nuit, 777
Lunette d'Étambot, 85
Lunette Terrestre, 711
Lusin, 381
Lut, 479

Macaron, 598
Machine à Balancier, 50
Machine à calculer les Marées, 836
Machine Alternative, 638
Machine à Sonder, 297
Machines Turbo-Alternatives, 872
Mâchoire, 406, 832
Madrépore, 481
Magasin, 793
Magasin à Peinture, 564
Magasin du Maître d'Équipage, 76
Magasinier, 793
Magnétisme Induit, 392
Magnétisme Permanent, 578
Magnétisme Rétenteur, 645
Magnétisme Sub-Permanent, 804
Magnétisme Temporaire, 827
Magnétisme Terrestre, 828
Maillage, 94
Maille, 306, 507, 658
Maille à Étai, 802
Maille amovible, 216
Maille Brisée, 765
Maille Courante, 168
Maille de bout, 260
Maille de Capon, 133
Maille demontable, 216, 420, 573
Maille de Renfort, 396
Maille d'Extrémité, 260
Maille Ordinaire, 168

Mailler, 428
Maillet, 486
Maillet à Épisser, 167
Maillet à Patarasser, 640, 709
Maillet de Calfat, 118
Mailloche, 708
Maillon, 711, 731
Main Courante, 353
Main d'Ancre, 16, 357
Main de Fer, 334
Main Sur Main, 353
Maître, 579
Maître Baggagiste, 33
Maître de pêche, 284
Maître d'Équipage, 76
Mal armé, 880
Mamelon, 424
Manche, 379, 474
Manche à Air à Pavillon, 55
Manche à Charbon, 157
Manche à Escarbilles, 24
Manche à Incendie, 282
Manche à Ordures, 324
Manche à Saletés, 324
Manche à Vent, 921
Manche d'Aspiration, 238
Manche d'Évacuation, 267, 884
Manchette, 53, 462, 839
Manchon de Capelage, 498
Manchon d'écubier, 362
Manger au Vent, 251
Manifeste, 488
Manifeste d'Entrée, 400
Manifeste de Sortie, 558
Manille, 711
Manille à axe vissé, 691
Manille à Violon, 357
Manille d'Ajust, 412
Manille d'Affourchage, 411
Manille de Capon, 133
Manille de corps mort, 656
Manille de Jonction, 412
Manille de Remorque, 850
Manille d'Étalingure, 16
Manille en D., 196
Maniller, 712
Manoeuvrabilité, 351
Manoeuvre, 244, 696
Manoeuvre des Embarcations, 74
Manoeuvre des Portes Étanches, 165
Manoeuvre d'Incendie, 282
Manoque, 354, 741
Manquant, 731
Manquer à Virer, 513

Mantelet Brisé, 349
Mantelet d'écubier, 361
Mantelet de Sabord, 600
Mantelet Plein, 68
Marchandises, 333
Marchandises au Cubage, 502
Marchandises Congelées, 313
Marchandises Dangereuses, 198
Marchandises de Transit, 854
Marchandises de Valeur, 604
Marchandises Diverses, 328
Marchandises Frigorifées, 640
Marchandises Inflammables, 392
Marchandises Légères, 502
Marchandises Lourdes, 203, 367
Marchandises non-identifiables, 881
Marchandises Périssables, 578
Marche Chronométrique, 147
Marche Diurne, 196
Marchepied, 299
Marchepied de Bout de Vergue, 292
Marchepied de Nage, 299, 799
Marée, 835
Marée de Morte Eau, 533
Marée descendante, 274
Marée de Syzygie, 814
Marée de Vive Eau, 768
Marée diurne, 227
Marée Mixte, 514
Marée montante, 654
Marée Portant au Vent, 906
Marée Portant sous le Vent, 445
Marée Semi-diurne, 707
Marée Tropique, 865
Marégraphe, 27, 836
Margouillet, 541
Marier, 495
Marie-Salope, 748
Marin, 491, 918
Marinage, 190
Marine, 489
Marine de Commerce, 506
Marine de Guerre, 532
Marine Marchande, 506
Marionette, 537
Maritime, 489
Marmite à Brai, 587
Marnage, 835
Maroquin, 768

Marque de franc-bord, 307
Marque de franc-bord en eau douce, 312
Marque de houache, 798
Marque de jour, 201
Marsouin, 301
Marsouin Arrière, 787
Marsouin Avant, 784
Marteau à Air Comprimé, 8
Marteau à Piquer, 145
Martinet, 452, 846, 847
Martinet de Corne, 575
Martingale, 495
Martingale de Clin-foc, 297
Martyr, 143, 741
Mascaret, 85, 836
Masqué, 1
Masquer, 30
Masquer sous le vent, 98
Massif, 203
Mastic de Fer, 671
Mât, 496
Mât à Clef, 279
Matage, 118, 498
Matage d'About, 111
Matagot, 657
Mât à Pible, 595
Mât à Portique, 333
Mât Arrière, 6
Mât Auxiliaire, 682
Mât basculant, 163
Mât bipode, 66, 716
Mât Central, 510
Mât Creux, 376
Mât d'Artimon, 410, 514
Mât d'Assemblage, 481
Mât de Calcet, 70
Mât de Charge, 214
Mât de charge d'en dedans, 358
Mât de Charge en Treillis, 436
Mât de Charge Étiré, 908
Mât de charge hydraulique, 384
Mât de charge pour poids lourds, 367
Mât de Charge Tubulaire, 869
Mât de Corde, 379, 862
Mât de Flèche, 846
Mât de Flèche Télescopique, 827
Mât de Fortune, 414
Mât de Houari, 745
Mât de Hune, 846
Mât de misaine, 302
Mât de Pavillon, 289, 598, 773
Mât de Perroquet, 845
Mât de Senau, 868

Mât de Tapecul, 410
Mât d'un Seul Brin, 739
Matelas, 563
Matelot, 2, 677
Matelotage, 495, 696
Matelot Léger, 554
Mât en tôles, 590
Mât en Treillis, 436
Mâtereau, 84
Mâter les Avirons, 848
Mateur, 118
Matoir, 118
Matoir à Gorge, 766
Mât Supérieur, 883
Matte, 127, 500
Mât Tripode, 863
Mâture, 498
Mauvais Évitage, 304
Mauvais Fond, 304
Mazout, 314
Mécanicien chef de quart, 25
Mécanicien d'Armement, 600
Mécanicien de Garantie, 341
Mécanicien de Marine, 490
Mécanicien Inspecteur, 600
Mèche, 764
Mèche à Secteur, 619
Mèche Inférieure, 667
Médecin de Bord, 726
Mélèze, 434
Mélèze d'Amérique, 347
Membrure, 305, 306
Membrure à Évidements, 454
Membrure Chantournée, 684
Membrure Composite, 102
Membrure d'Arcasse, 855
Membrure d'Assemblage, 102
Membrure de Brin, 341
Membrure de coqueron, 575
Membrure de Tunnel, 871
Membrure Épaulée, 411
Membrure Etuvée, 56
Membrure Intermédiaire, 396
Membrure Longitudinale de Bordé, 719
Membrure Longitudinale de Pont, 208
Membrure Ployée, 56
Membrure Renforcée, 210
Membrures diagonales, 217
Membrure Simple, 755
Menille, 186
Menu filin, 750
Menuisier de marine, 412
Menu Mâtereau, 510
Mer, 694
Mer Agitée, 515
Mer Belle, 750

Mer Confuse, 173
Mer Contraire, 187
Mer Courte, 146, 731
Mer Creuse, 376
Mer Debout, 364
Mer de l'Arrière, 299
Mer des Sargasses, 684
Mer de travers, 51
Mer Furieuse, 605
Mer Grosse, 371
Mer Houleuse, 660
Méridien, 507
Méridien Géographique, 828
Méridien Inférieur, 392
Méridien Magnétique, 483
Mer libre, 553, 698
Merlin, 494
Merliner, 494
Mer Longue, 472
Mer marginale, 489
Mer peu agitée, 746
Merrain, 778
Mer Ridée, 750
Mer Très Houleuse, 890
Mer Très Grosse, 889
Métacentre, 508
Métacentre Longitudinal, 471, 856
Métal d'Apport, 280
Métal de Base, 570
Métal Monel, 517
Métal Muntz, 530
Météorologie, 509
Méthode de la tangente, 821
Méthode de Rapiér, 634
Méthode de Sumner, 806
Mettre à la voile, 709
Mettre en Panne, 98, 365
Mettre en Pantenne, 160
Mettre le cap sur, 52
Mettre les Linquets, 573
Mettre sur Allèges, 454
Mettre Sur Fils, 792
Miche, 514
Midi, 539
Midi apparent du Lieu, 465
Midi moyen, 501
Midi moyen du lieu, 465
Midi Sidéral du lieu, 466
Midi vrai, 20
Mille géographique, 328
Mille Marin, 529
Mi-Marée, 349
Minot, 105
Mirage, 513
Miroir Azimutal, 29
Misaine, 302
Misaine-Goëlette, 319

Mise à la Chaîne, 23
Mises dehors, 223
Mobile, 721
Modèle, 514
Modèle demi-bloc, 348
Mois lunaire, 735
Mois Synodique, 814
Môle, 517
Mollir, 251, 744
Moment de Chavirement, 883
Moment de Redressement, 651
Moment de Stabilité, 517
Moment de torsion, 667
Moment de Voilure, 517
Moment d'évolution, 666
Moment d'Inclinaison de la Voilure, 677
Moment Fléchissant, 56
Moment fléchissant d'Arc, 374
Moment Fléchissant de Contre-Arc, 673
Moment Magnétique, 483
Moment pour Faire Varier l'Assiette, 517
Montage, 81, 264
Montant, 295, 654, 774
Montant de Bittes, 66
Montant de Cloison, 104
Montant de Garde Corps, 632
Montant de Tente, 29
Montez, 440
Montre d'Habitacle, 209
Montre d'habitade, 347
Moque, 365
Moque à réa, 156
Moque à rouet, 156
Moraillon, 357
Mordre, 647
Moteur à Combustion Interne, 397
Moteur à faz pauvre, 608
Moteur à pistons opposés, 553
Moteur à transmission par engrenages, 327
Moteur Diesel, 220
Moteur hors bord, 556
Moteur Semi Diesel, 707
Moto-pompe électrique submersible, 804
Mou, 744
Moucheter, 524
Mouchoir, 93
Mouchoir en Losange, 218
Mouillage, 14
Mouillage forain, 551
Mouillé, 25
Mouiller, 16
Mouiller de l'arrière, 15

Mouilleur, 17, 864, 870
Moule, 767
Moulinet de Loch, 469
Mousqueton, 288, 751
Mousse, 298, 900
Mousson, 519
Mousson de Nord Est, 540
Mousson du Nord Ouest, 541
Mousson du Sud Ouest, 759
Moustache, 333, 495
Mouton, 917
Mouvement diurne, 227
Moyeu d'Hélice, 610
Musoir, 581
Mutinerie, 526

Nable, 74, 228, 240
Nable de Pont, 208
Nadir, 527
Nage, 801
Nage Courte, 194
Nage de Baleinière, 329
Nage de marinier, 692
Nage de Parade, 329
Nager, 613, 662
Nager à culer, 32
N'arrivons pas, 541
Nationalisation, 642
Naufragé, 130, 797
Nautique, 528
Nautophone, 530
Naval, 530
Navette, 507
Navigabilité, 531
Navigable, 531
Navigateur, 532
Navigation, 531
Navigation à la Pêche, 286
Navigation Astronomique, 135
Navigation au bornage, 583
Navigation au Long Cours, 302
Navigation côtière, 159
Navigation Fautive, 390
Navigation Loxodromique, 504, 589
Navigation Orthodromique, 337
Navigation par Arc de Grand Cercle, 337
Navigation par latitudes Croissantes, 505
Navigation par Latitude Moyenne, 510
Navigation par radio, 629
Navigation sur un parallèle, 568

Naviguer à la Voile, 673
Navire, 722
Navire à Aubes, 562
Navire à Awning Deck, 29
Navire à Awningdeck Partiel, 570
Navire à Coffre, 909
Navire à Demi-Dunette, 632
Navire à deux Coffres, 831
Navire à Échantillons Pleins, 315
Navire à Émigrants, 260
Navire à Flancs Ondulés, 179
Navire Amagnétique, 539
Navire à Moteur, 523
Navire à Moteur Auxiliaire, 28
Navire à Passagers, 572
Navire à Pont Ras, 296
Navire à trois Superstructures, 831
Navire à Shade Deck, 712
Navire à Spardeck, 760
Navire à Superstructure continue, 171
Navire à Traits Carrés, 771
Navire à Turret Deck, 874
Navire à un Pont, 738
Navire au plus près, 154
Navire Auto Déchargeur, 706
Navire Auxiliaire, 17
Navire Câblier, 115
Navire Charbonnier, 164
Navire de charge, 310
Navire de Charge Régulier, 127
Navire de Mer, 695
Navire en Ciment Armé, 642
Navire Frigorifique, 641
Navire Hopital, 380
Navire Hydrographe, 810
Navire Long Courrier, 302
Navire Marchand, 506
Navire Parlementaire, 129
Navire patrouilleur des glaces, 389
Navire Privé, 607
Navire Privilégié, 607
Navire Public, 613
Navire Régulier, 457
Navire Self Trimmer, 705
Navire Shelter Deck, 720
Navire Trunk-Deck, 867
Navire Well-Deck, 909
Nebulosité, 155
Nef d'usinage des tôles, 591
Néphoscope, 533
Nerf, 538
Nervure, 915

Net, 150
Nez, 541
Niche de la Butée, 834
Niche de Presse Etoupe, 803
Nid de Pie, 188
Nimbus, 537
Niveau de la basse mer, 476
Niveau de la mer, 696
Niveau de référence de basse mer, 476
Niveau des plus basses mers de vive eau, 476
Niveau des plus grandes basses mers, 476
Niveau Moyen, 501
Niveau moyen des basses mers, 501
Niveau moyen des basses mers de vive eau, 501
Noeud, 56, 357, 373, 424
Noeud Coulant, 539, 747
Noeud d'Arrêt, 280
Noeud de bec d'oiseau, 67
Noeud de Bois, 838
Noeud de Bois et Barbouquet, 349
Noeud de Bois et Demi-Clef, 349
Noeud de Bosse, 792
Noeud de Bouline, 89
Noeud de Bouline Double, 394
Noeud de Bouline Simple, 557
Noeud de Chaise Double, 311
Noeud de Chaise simple, 89
Noeud d'écoute double, 236
Noeud d'écoute simple, 717
Noeud de Drisse, 350
Noeud de Drisse de Bonnette, 802
Noeud de Fil de Caret, 659
Noeud de Filet, 534
Noeud de Fouet, 658
Noeud de Griffe, 511
Noeud de Hauban (Anglais), 218
Noeud de Hauban Double, 733
Noeud de Hauban Simple, 311
Noeud de Ride, 182, 500, 747
Noeud de Soldat, 182, 747
Noeud d'Étalingure, 115, 362
Noeud de Tireveille, 488
Noeud de Tireveille Simple, 218
Noeud de Trésillon, 495
Noeud de Vache, 129
Noeud d'orin, 285

Noeud Plat, 639
Noeud Simple, 558
Noeud sur le Pouce, 285
Noix, 381, 732, 791
Nombre, 542
Nombre d'Équipement, 264
Nombre Longitudinal, 472
Nombre Transversal, 856
Non Arrivé, 558
Non Embarqué, 731
Non Ponté, 879
Normand, 540
Note de Délégation, 10
Noyau d'Equipage, 542
Noyer, 295
Nuage, 155
Numéro Officiel, 727
Nutation, 542

Obéir à, 18
Obliquité, 544
Observation, 544
Occlusion, 544
Occultation, 544
Océanographie, 545
Oeil, 269
Oeil à la Flamande, 292
Oeil de Fourche d'Étai, 435
Oeil de Pie, 270
Oeil d'Étalingure, 659
Oeillet à dents, 770
Oeillet d'envergure, 779
Oeillet de Tétière, 363
Oeillet de Transfilage, 270
Oeilleton, 429
Oeuillet, 338
Oeuillet Métallique, 508
Oeuvres Mortes, 203, 883
Oeuvres Vives, 624
Officier, 546
Officier de Pont, 208
Officier de Port, 229
Officier de Quart, 900
Officier de Santé, 365
Officier Général, 288
Ohé, 8
Onde de marée, 836
Onde de sauvegarde, 226
Ondée, 732
Onglet, 514
Onglet d'Émersion, 907
Onglet d'Immersion, 907
Opérateur de Télégraphie sans Fil, 922
Opérateur de T.S.F., 629
Opposition, 553

Ordre de Livraison, 212
Oreille, 378, 834
Organeau, 16, 56
Orientation, 675
Orienter, 862
Orin, 863
Orin d'Ancre, 908
Orme, 258
Orthodrome, 555
Oscillateur, 555
Ouragan, 384
Outrigger, 557
Ouvert, 636
Ouverture de Tonnage, 844

Pack, 389
Pafi, 518
Pagaie, 562
Pagaye, 562
Pagaye-Double, 236
Pagaye Simple, 739
Paille de Bitte, 48, 66, 540
Paille de mèche, 539
Paille-en-Cul, 653
Paillet, 499
Paillet d'Abordage, 165
Paillet de Brasseyage, 573
Paillet de Défense, 500
Paillet de Portage, 138
Paillet d'Étai, 33
Paillet Lardé, 833
Palan, 817
Palan à chaînes, 139
Palan à Croc, 477, 650
Palan à Deux Poulies simples 236, 343
Palan à Fouet, 819
Palan d'Amure, 817
Palan d'Apiquage, 452
Palan de Bout de Bergue, 929
Palan de Capon, 133
Palan de Dimanche, 109, 900
Palan de Garde, 644, 886
Palan de Guinderesse, 847
Palan de Hune, 109
Palan de Martinet, 846
Palan d'Embarcation, 77
Palan de Mouillage, 790
Palan de Retenue de Gui, 84
Palan de Roulis, 658
Palan d'Étai, 779
Palan d'Etarque, 410
Palan de Traversière, 287
Palan d'Hune, 106
Palan Différentiel, 589
Palan Double, 877
Palangre, 86

Palanquée, 746
Palanquer, 90
Palanquin de Ris, 640
Palan Renversé, 883
Palan sur Garant, 817
Palan sur Itague, 669
Pale, 562
Palette, 655
Palettisation, 565
Palier d'arbre, 592, 768
Palier de Butée, 833
Palonnier, 518, 846
Panier, 45
Panneau, 351, 357
Panneau à Tambour, 867
Panneau d'Aération, 279
Panneau d'échappée, 265
Panneau d'Écoutille, 358
Panneau de Déchargment, 126
Panneau de Descente, 83, 168, 429
Panneau des Chaufferies, 79
Panneau des Machines, 261
Panneau de Tracé, 692
Panneau de Vaigrage, 134
Panneau Étanche, 902
Panneau Étanche au Pétrole, 549
Panneau Grillagé, 335
Panner, 575
Pantoire, 576
Pantoire de Bras, 92
Pantoire de Candelette, 109
Pantoire de Capon, 132
Pantoire de Sauvegarde, 666
Pantoire de Tête de Mât, 498
Pantoire de Traversière, 287
Pantoquière, 187, 812
Papier à doublage, 715
Papiers de Bord, 727
Papillon, 197, 519, 744
Paquebot, 572
Paquebot de Manche, 186
Paquebot Mixte, 397
Paraclose, 457
Paradière, 603
Parallaxe, 568
Parallaxe en Hauteur, 568
Parallaxe Horizontale, 378
Parallèle de Hauteur, 568
Parallèle de Latitude, 147, 568
Paranthélie, 568
Parapluie de Cheminée, 879
Parasélène, 569
Paratonnerre, 455
Parc, 286, 908
Parcelle, 569
Parc sur filets, 774

Par dessus bord, 558
Pare à Virer, 636
Pare Manoeuvre, 650, 689
Parer, 150
Parhélie, 570, 807
Par la hanche, 551
Par l'Avant, 112
Par le Bossoir, 551
Par le travers, 1, 2
Parpaillot, 161, 598
Parquet, 591
Part de Prise, 608
Pas, 586
Pas Constant, 881
Pas Croissant, 391
Pas Croissant Axial, 29
Pas Croissant Radial, 627
Pas Nominal, 538
Pas Relatif, 587
Passage de Nord-Est, 540
Passage inférieur, 392
Passage Méridien, 506, 507, 854
Passage méridien inférieur, 476
Passager, 571
Passager Clandestin, 796
Passager de Cabine, 114
Passager d'Entrepont, 782
Passager de Pont, 208
Passager sans installation de couchette, 208
Passage Supérieur, 808
Passavant, 300, 854
Passe, 273, 528, 668
Passeport, 150
Passer, 640
Passerelle Arrière, 898
Passerelle de Débarquement, 323
Passerelle de manoeuvre, 228
Passerelle de Navigation, 531
Passerelle haute, 297
Passeresse, 640
Passeresse de Paillet, 373
Passeur, 901
Passeur de rivets, 655
Pas Variable, 887
Patarasser, 379, 640
Pataras Taillant, 653
Pataras Travaillant, 362
Patarat, 605
Patente de Santé, 64
Patente de Santé Brute, 304
Patente de Santé Nette, 150
Patente de Santé Suspecte, 810
Patin de Chalut, 859
Patron, 743

Patron d'Embarcation, 182
Patte, 185, 566
Patte à futaille, 45, 120
Patte d'ancre, 15
Patte de Bouée, 108
Patte de Bouline, 89
Patte de Cargue Fond, 107
Patte de Chat, 133
Patte d'Embarcation, 76
Patte d'Empointure, 363
Patte de Point d'Amure, 816
Patte de Point d'Écoute, 151
Patte de Ralingue de Mât, 477
Patte de Ris, 639
Patte d'Oie, 98, 759
Patte d'Oie de Corps-Mort,˅ 519
Patte d'Oie de Pic, 575
Paumelle, 676
Paumoyer, 880
Pavillon, 288, 378
Pavillon Affirmatif, 6
Pavillon Couplé, 907
Pavillon de Beaupré, 403
Pavillon de Compagnie, 381
Pavillon de Départ, 71
Pavillon de Pilote, 583
Pavillon de Rappel, 637
Pavillon de Reclamation, 612
Pavillon de Secours, 226
Pavillon d'explosifs, 603
Pavillon d'Invités, 341
Pavillon du Code, 161
Pavillon National, 262
Pavillon Négatif, 533
Pavillonnerie, 288
Pavillon Numérique, 542
Pavillon Particulier, 607
Pavillon Postal, 484
Pavillon Sanitaire, 620
Pavillon sémaphorique, 706
Pavillon Signalétique, 736
Pavois, 105
Pavoiser, 242
Payol, 86
Péage, 840, 914
Péages, 355
Peau de Bouc Tablier, 663
Pêche à la Senne, 701
Pêche a l'Estran, 797
Pêche au Large, 547
Pêche aux Cordes, 459
Pêche aux Filets Dérivan˒, 244
Pêche aux Grandes Cordes, 337
Pêche aux Lignes à Main, 352
Pêche aux Lignes Courantes, 243

Pêche aux Lignes Traînantes—Plein Fret 962

Pêche aux Lignes Traînantes, 865
Pêche aux Petites Cordes, 352
Pêche Cotière, 394
Pêche Maritime, 695
Pêcherie, 285
Peinture Aluminium, 12
Peinture Anticorrosive, 19
Peinture Antifouling, 19
Peinture au liège, 178
Peinture de Carène, 86
Peinture de Flottaison, 85
Peinture de Pont, 208
Peinture Ignifuge, 282
Peinture Pour Cheminée, 316
Peinture Sous-Marine, 86
Pèlerin, 581
Pelle d'aviron, 544
Pendeur de Corps-Mort, 649
Pendeur de Dérive, 135
Penon, 231
Perceur, 245
Perche, 577
Perdant, 274, 429
Perdre, 129, 274
Perdu ou Non Perdu, 475
Périgée, 577
Périhélie, 577
Périls de Mer, 493
Périmètre, 331, 742
Période, 578
Période de Houle, 904
Période de chargement, 464
Période de Roulis, 578
Période Vibratoire, 890
Perméabilité, 578
Permis de Lestage, 789
Permis d'embarquement, 725
Permis d'Enlèvement, 229
Perpendiculaire Arrière, 6
Perpendiculaire Avant, 303
Perroquet, 845
Perte, 474
Perte Totale, 848
Perte Totale Présumée, 605
Perte Totale Réelle, 3
Pertuis, 757
Peser, 648
Peste, 100
Petit Cabotage, 749
Petit Cercle, 749
Petit Cheval, 232
Petit Coup de Vent, 312
Petite Aile, 847
Petite Brise, 328
Petite Pêche, 730
Petites Bittes de Guindeau, 129
Petites Cordes, 347, 749

Petite Sonde, 351
Petite Vérole, 749
Petit Foc, 303, 393
Petit fond, 86, 291, 713
Petit Miroir, 378
Petit Pavois, 242
Petit Quart, 231
Petit Treuil, 183
Pétrolier, 549
Pétrolier à moteur, 523
Phare, 455
Phare de Misaine, 365
Phares de l'Arrière, 7
Phase, 579
Phoquier, 695
Pic, 574
Pichpin, 931
Pièce, 81
Pièce de Bordure, 87, 489
Pièces de Forge, 303
Pièces de Moulage, 131
Pied Emplanture, 368
Pierre à briquer, 376
Piétage, 239
Pieu d'Amarrage, 581
Pigeon, 660
Pilleur d'Épaves, 925
Pilotage, 582
Pilotage Libre, 308
Pilotage Obligatoire, 172
Pilote, 581
Pilote côtier, 160
Pilote de Barre, 44
Pilote de Mer, 698
Pilote de Rivière, 654
Pilote Obligatoire, 172
Pilotin, 21, 511
Pin blanc, 918
Pin de Floride, 918
Pin d'Oregon, 237
Pin Noir, 67
Pipe, 585
Piquer, 800, 862
Piqueur, 833
Piqûre, 588
Pirate, 586
Piraterie, 586
Pirogue, 120, 249
Pirogue à Balancier, 34, 557
Pirogue à Deux Balanciers, 236
Pirogue à Deux Corps, 234
Pirogue en écorce, 43
Pistolet, 763
Pistolet d'Amure, 105
Pistolet de Bras, 92
Pistonnage, 614
Piton à Boucle, 652

Piton à oeil, 269
Piton à Plaque, 270
Piton de Bossoir, 200
Piton de Cervelle, 666
Piton de Drisse de Mât, 832
Piton de Sous Barbe, 77
Pitonnage, 452
Pivot de Boussole, 170
Placage, 272
Placard, 138, 237, 573
Placard à Joint Plastique, 753
Placard maté, 356
Plafond, 134
Plafond de Ballast, 823
Plage, 49
Planche à Roulis, 106
Planche à Terre, 100
Planche de Chalut, 555
Planche de Débarquement, 100
Planche d'Ouverture, 187
Plancher de Tunnel, 871
Planchette d'équerrage, 60
Plan d'Arrimage, 127
Plan de Dérive, 435
Plan de développement de bordé, 719
Plan de Formes, 458
Plan de Tuyautage de Coque, 613
Plan de Voilure, 650
Plan Horizontal, 348
Plankton, 590
Plan Longitudinal, 716, 717
Plaque à Boucle, 653
Plaque à cintrer, 56
Plaque de Fondation, 53
Plaque Indicatrice, 428
Plaque Tournante, 874
Plat, 290
Plat-bord, 589
Plat de Quille, 734
Plate, 616
Plateau, 590, 718, 860
Plateau à Caissage, 591
Plateau Continental, 174
Plateforme, 290
Plateforme de Cale, 591
Plateforme de Sonde, 444
Plateforme Étanche, 902
Plein, 314
Plein Chargement, 314
Pleine Mer, 372
Pleine Mer de Syzygie, 372
Pleine mer inférieure, 475
Pleine mer moyenne, 501
Pleine Mer Supérieure, 371
Plein Fret, 315

Pleine mer supérieure moyenne, 501
Plet, 274
Plomb, 442
Plombe de Sonde, 442
Plumer, 277
Poche, 593
Poêlon, 566
Poids Lourd, 367
Poids ou Cubage, 908
Poignée, 338, 351, 929
Poinçon, 606
Poinçonnage, 616
Point, 151, 287
Pointage, 820
Point à midi, 539
Point Amphidromique, 13
Point Cardinal, 124
Point Corrigé, 265
Point d'Amure, 815, 905
Point d'Arrivée, 201, 594
Point de Chavirement, 883
Point d'Eclair, 290
Point de Drisse, 363
Point de Mât, 832
Point de Partance, 213, 594
Point d'Inflammabilité, 282
Pointe, 94, 527, 594
Pointe à tracer, 692
Pointe de Laize, 334
Point Estimé, 203
Pointeur, 820
Point Giratoire, 588
Point Intercardinal, 396
Point Nodal, 538
Point observé, 602
Point par radio, 629
Points de Rabattement, 740
Points Equinoxiaux, 264
Point solsticial d'été, 284
Point solsticial d'hiver, 284
Points Solsticiaux, 755
Point Vélique, 136
Point Vrai, 866
Poisson Mariné, 580
Poisson Plat, 290
Poisson Séché, 242
Pôle bleu, 71
Pôle Céleste, 135
Poles Magnétiques, 483
Pôle Terrestre, 828
Police à navire dénommé, 528
Police à Temps, 839
Police à Temps et au Voyage, 514
Police au Voyage, 893
Police avec Intérêt, 396
Police de Pari, 895

Police d'Honneur, 895
Police du Lloyd, 463
Police Évaluée, 886
Police Flottante, 294
Police Maritime, 491
Police non évaluée, 882
Police Ouverte, 552
Police pour risques de Port, 601
Police sur Corps, 383
Police Timbrée, 774
Pomme de Mât, 499
Pomme de Racage, 570
Pomme d'Etrier, 218
Pomme Gougée, 165, 733
Pompe, 614
Pompe à Balancier, 351
Pompe à Bras, 353
Pompe à débit Variable, 887
Pompe à Eau Douce, 312
Pompe à Incendie, 283
Pompe à Mastic, 618
Pompe attelée, 392
Pompe Centrifuge, 136
Pompe d'Assèchement, 800
Pompe des Ballasts, 36
Pompe de Service, 901
Pompe Downton, 238
Pompe Sanitaire, 682
Pont, 204
Pont à Bordages Courbes, 429
Pont à Bordages Rectilignes, 796
Pont de Cloisonnement, 103
Pont Découvert, 905
Pont de Franc Bord, 307
Pont de la Dunette, 598
Pont d'Embarquement, 259
Pont de Refuge, 355
Pont de Résistance, 799
Pont des Embarcations, 74
Pont des Emménagements, 679
Pont des Superstructures, 808
Pont de Tonnage, 842
Pont du Château, 97
Pont du Coffre, 909
Pont du Gaillard, 301
Pontée, 205
Ponte en Dos de Tortue, 875
Pont Étanche, 902
Pont Exposé, 905
Pont Inférieur, 475
Pont mobile, 599
Ponton, 382, 596
Ponton à Charbon, 157
Ponton de Relevage, 119
Ponton-Grue, 294
Ponton grue à portique, 294

Ponton-Mâture, 716
Pont Plat, 296
Pont Principal, 485
Pont Promenade, 608
Pont Ras, 296
Pont Supérieur, 883
Pont Turret, 875
Pool, 726
Porque, 648, 906
Port, 354, 598
Port à Barre, 44
Port à Marée, 835
Portant, 381
Port à Traité, 860
Port Artificiel, 24
Port Autonome, 28
Port d'Armement, 601
Port d'Attache, 601
Port de Chargement, 601
Port d'Échouage, 247
Port de Déchargement, 601
Port de Destination, 600
Port de Mer, 698
Port d'Entrée, 601
Port de Pêche, 285
Port de Quarantaine, 620
Port de Référence, 775
Port de Refuge, 355
Port de remise, 600
Port d'Escale, 600
Port de Transit, 854
Port d'Ordres, 553
Porte, 326
Porte à Charnières, 373
Porte à coufissement horizontal, 378
Porte à Fermeture à Distance, 327
Porte à Fermeture automatique, 704
Porte à Glissières, 745
Porte à Persienne, 745
Porte d'Èbe, 251
Porte de Charbonnage, 157
Porte de Chargement, 126
Porte de coupée, 324, 343, 350
Porte de Flot, 295
Portée Lumineuse, 478
Porte Étanche, 902
Porte étanche à charnières, 373
Portée Utile, 108, 534, 884
Porte-Haubans, 140
Porte Lof, 105, 143, 767
Porte montée sur boulons, 590
Porte-Nage, 557
Port en Lourd, 203
Port en Rivière, 265

Porter, 241
Porter au Large, 52
Porter la toile, 777
Porte Roulante, 657
Porteur de Déblais, 378
Porte Voix, 761
Port Fluvial, 654
Port Franc, 309
Port Intermédiaire, 396
Port Maritime, 698
Port Naturel, 528
Port Principal, 775
Port Ouvert, 552
Port Secondaire, 700
Ports exdus, 267
Portugaise, 626
Poste, 58, 778
Poste d'Amarrage, 519
Poste de Chargement, 463
Poste de Déchargement, 224
Poste de Mouillage, 16
Poste d'Équipage, 184
Poste de Radio, 922
Poste des Chauffeurs, 282
Poste des Matelots, 697
Poste d'Évitage, 151
Poste Électrogène de Secours, 259
Poste Radio-Goniométrique, 628
Poste Radiotélégraphique de Bord, 629
Poste Radiotélégraphique de Secours, 628
Poste Radiotélégraphique de Terre, 159
Poste Reservé, 21
Postes, 622
Postes d'Embarcations, 76
Postes de Mouillage, 16
Postes de Sécurité, 176
Postes d'Incendie, 283
Poste Signalétique du Lloyd, 463
Pot au Noir, 231
Pot d'Échappement, 524
Potée, 671
Potence, 929
Potence de Chalut, 858
Poulaine, 696
Poulie, 68
Poulie à Croc, 377
Poulie à cylindres, 573
Poulie à Fouet, 819
Poulie à graissabe automatique, 704
Poulie à olive, 730
Poulie à Ringot, 53

Poulie à Talon, 732
Poulie à Violon, 473, 830
Poulie Basse, 360
Poulie Coupée, 751
Poulie d'Assemblage, 102
Poulie de bas cul, 621
Poulie de bout de Vergue, 408
Poulie de Capon, 132
Poulie de Cargue Point, 798
Poulie de charge, 215
Poulie de Guinderesse, 845
Poulie de Ligne de Sonde, 442
Poulie de martinet, 846
Poulie de Mât de Charge, 125
Poulie de pied de corne, 215
Poulie de Retour, 442
Poulie de sous vergue, 621
Poulie de Traversière, 284
Poulie différentielle, 220
Poulie d'itague, 837
Poulie double, 234
Poulie Ferrée, 401
Poulie fixe, 775
Poulie Havraise, 397
Poulie mobile, 669
Poulie quadruple, 305
Poulie Simple, 738
Poulie Triple, 860
Poulie Vierge, 740
Poulie volante, 297
Poulin, 741
Poupée, 330
Poupée de Pied de Mât, 499
Pousseux, 618
Prame Norvégienne, 603
Pratique, 373, 524, 604
Préceinte, 896
Précession, 604
Prédiction des marées, 835
Prélart, 823
Première Allonge, 283
Premier maître d'Hôtel, 144
Premier Méridien, 606
Premier Quart, 284
Premier Vertical, 606
Prendre de l'Erre, 278
Prendre la mer, 618
Prendre le Vide, 820
Prendre un Ris, 639
Prendre un tour de bitte, 66
Près et Plein, 314
Presque calme, 453
Presse à Cintrer, 104
Presse à Jugliner, 411
Presse à River, 655
Presse de Gréeur, 650
Presse-Étoupe, 803

Presse-Étoupe Arrière, 786, 788
Presse Étoupe de Mèche, 664, 667
Presse Étoupe de Mèche, 666
Prêt à la Grosse, 87, 645
Prêt à Retour de Voyage, 87
Prévision du type de temps, 328
Primage, 606
Prime, 805
Prime à la Construction, 174
Prime à la Grosse, 491
Prime à la Navigation, 532
Prime de Célérité, 225
Principal, 485
Pris, 537
Prise, 124, 607
Prise d'eau à la mer, 694, 699
Prisonnier, 823
Pris Vent Dessus, 820
Privilège, 224
Privilège de Droit Commun, 168
Privilège de Pavillon, 288
Privilège du Prêteur à la Grosse, 87
Privilège Maritime, 493
Privilège sur Droits de Pilotage, 584
Privilège sur Frais de Sauvetage, 680
Privilège sur le chargement, 126
Privilège sur salaires de l'équipage, 697
Procès Verbal de bon Arrimage, 796
Profilage, 799
Profil de la Houle, 904
Profilé, 40
Profilés, 700
Profit Maritime, 491
Profit Nautique, 491
Profondeur de Carène, 516
Profondeur sur radier, 214
Profondeur Vérifiée, 176
Projecteur, 698
Projection de Mercator, 505
Projection Gnomonique, 332
Projection Polaire, 595
Projection Polyconique, 596
Promontoire, 363
Prompe de Cale, 63
Propriétaire de Navires, 724
Propulsion cycloidale, 195

Propulsion Diesel-Electrique, 219
Propulsion Electrique, 254
Propulsion hydraulique, 407
Propulsion Turbo-Electrique, 872
Puisard, 63, 240, 806
Puisard du Tunnel, 872
Puissance au frein, 713
Puissance de Remorquage, 252
Puissance de Remorque, 611
Puissance Effective, 252
Puissance Indiquée, 392
Puissance Nominale, 538
Puissance Normale, 708
Puissance sur l'Arbre, 713
Puits, 908
Puits à Cables, 116
Puits aux Chaînes, 139
Puits de Dérive, 135
Psychromètre, 612

Quadrant, 619
Quadrature, 619
Quai, 623
Quai à Marée, 835
Qualités Évolutives, 783
Qualités Nautiques, 905
Quarantaine, 620
Quarantenier, 350, 635, 661
Quart, 594, 647, 899
Quart à Poche, 88
Quart de Jour, 522
Quart de Matin, 302
Quart de Minuit, 510
Quart de Rade, 17
Quart de Rhumb, 622
Quart en Bas, 899
Quart en Haut, 900
Quarts à Courir, 899
Quatre Mâts Barque, 723
Quenouillette, 180, 318, 717
Quenouillon, 591
Quête, 632, 633
Queue, 30, 31, 817
Queue de Capon, 131
Queue de Rat, 156, 594
Queue de Traversière, 284
Quille, 418
Quille à bulbe, 103
Quille cambrée, 656
Quille d'Assemblage, 734
Quille de Roulis, 62
Quille d'Échouage, 339
Quille en Caisson, 248
Quille massive, 43
Quille Plate, 291

Rabais, 636
Rabais de Fidélité, 211
Rabais Différé, 211
Raban, 325, 811
Raban de Barre, 783
Raban de Dos, 364
Raban de Ferlage, 695
Raban de Gouverne, 875
Raban d'Empointure, 363, 639
Raban d'Envergure, 656
Raban de Sac, 241
Raban de Tente, 104
Raban de Têtière, 656
Rabanter, 316
Rabattre, 379, 874
Rabattue, 243
Rablure, 625
Raboteuse, 590
Racage, 407, 570
Racage à Barillet, 868
Racage à Pommes et Bigots, 647
Racer, 626
Rachat de Planche, 225
Racher, 636
Radan de cul, 161
Rade, 656
Radeau, 630
Radeau de Sauvetage, 451
Rade Foraine, 553
Radier, 21, 228
Radio-Goniomètre, 628, 660
Radiophare, 627
Radiophare à cadre Tournant, 660
Radiophare à faisceau tournant, 223
Radiophare à Rayonnement Circulaire, 148
Radiophare Directionnel, 223
Radiophare Tournant, 646
Radiosonde, 633
Radio-Télégraphiste, 629, 922
Radoubage, 336
Radouber, 644
Rafale Fougue, 344
Rafraîchir, 312
Ragage, 138
Ragréeur, 145
Raidir, 366, 710
Ralingue de Chûte, 445
Ralingue de Fond, 299
Ralingue de Mât, 499
Ralingue d'Envergure, 364, 477
Ralingue de Ventre, 35
Ralinguer, 658
Rallier, 360

Rambarde, 341, 353
Rambarde de Gaillard, 301
Ranger, 633
Rapetissure, 47
Rapport d'Avarie, 197
Rapport de Compensation, 35
Rapport de Mer, 612
Rapport des Amplitudes, 635
Ras, 294
Rateau, 273, 772
Ratelier, 585
Ratelier de Manoeuvre, 54
Rations d'embarcations, 75
Rattraper, 559
Ravitailler, 612
Rayon d'Action, 188
Rayon vert, 337
Raz de Courant, 625
Raz de Marée, 835
Réa, 715
Réa à Billes, 657
Réa à rais, 766
Réa à Rouleaux, 657
Réa de retour de drosse, 621
Réa Plein, 224
Réassurance, 643
Rebattage, 356
Rebord des glaces, 389
Récépissé-Warrant, 230
Récepture de sécurité, 259
Recherche, 698
Récif, 638
Recouvrement, 434
Recouvrement d'Abouts, 260
Recouvrement des Cans, 432, 697
Rectification du Petit Miroir, 712
Rectifications du Sextant, 710
Reçu de Bord, 500
Recul, 31, 746
Recul Apparent, 21
Recul Effectif, 866
Recul Négatif, 533
Reçu Provisoire, 229
Redresser, 251, 272
Redresser sur Place, 273
Réduction des sondes, 638
Reflet, 474
Reflux, 274
Refouler, 883
Réfraction, 640
Refuser, 360
Refuser à Virer, 641
Régime silence international, 399
Régime silence radio, 630, 633
Règle à Parallèles, 568

Règle de jauge Internationale,
  399
Règle des Trapèzes, 856
Règlement d'Avaries, 28
Règles de la Haye, 347
Règles de Route, 667
Règles de Simpson, 737
Régulateur de Loch, 468
Régulation du compas, 168
Relacher, 618
Relevé de Varangues, 203
Relèvement, 52
Relèvement au compas, 168
Relèvement des quatre quarts,
  305
Relèvement Magnétique, 481
*Relèvement radiogonio-
  métrique*, 628
Relèvements Croisés, 185
Relèvements Réciproques, 638
Relèvement Vrai, 866
Relever, 644, 861
Remorquage, 848
Remorquage à la Cordelle, 852
Remorque, 848, 851
Remorquer, 848
Remorqueur, 870
Remorqueur de Bassin, 229
Remorqueur de Haute Mer,
  545
Remorqueur de Mer, 695
Remorqueur de Port, 355
Remorqueur de Sauvetage, 680
Remous, 32, 558, 899
Remplir, 810
Remplissage, 280, 281
Remplissage d'Arcasse, 281
Remplissage de la Guibre, 272
Remplissage sous barrots, 50
Renard, 230, 469, 856
Recontrer, 504
Rendement de Carène, 383
Rendement de l'Hélice, 610
*Rendement des Appareils
  Évaporatoires*, 78
*Rendement des Appareils
  Moteurs*, 261
Rendement Effectif, 558
Rendement Propulsif, 611
Renflouer, 640
Renfor d'hiloire, 157
Renfort, 237, 459, 573
Renfort de Chapeau, 106
Renfort de Palanquin, 640
Renfort de Point, 152
Renfort de Remplissage, 55
Renfort de Trou d'Homme. 488
Rentrée, 870

Rentrer, 617, 669, 882
Rentrer les Avirons, 441
Rentrez, 393
Renverse de la Marée, 140
Renversement, 873
Renverser, 30
Réparations d'Avaries, 28, 197
Réparations Provisoires, 827
Repère de marée, 57
Repères, 771
Répétiteur d'Angle de Barre,
  369, 664
Répondre, 18
Repoussoir, 243
Reprendre, 292, 558
Représailles, 644
Reprise à l'Envers, 31
Rescousse, 637
Réserve de Flottabilité, 644
Résistance à La Dérive, 436
Résistance à l'air, 8
Résistance de Carène, 851
Résistance de Frottement, 742
Résistance de Remous, 896
Résistance due aux Vagues,
  904
Résistance Résiduaire, 644
Ressac, 880
Ressaut, 863
Retard, 645
Retard Diurne, 474
Rétention Magnétique, 645
Retenue, 33, 142, 344, 863,
  886
Retenue de Basse Voile, 511
Retenue de Bossoir, 200
Retenue de Gui, 84
Retenue de Mât de Charge,
  215
Retour, 443
Retrait, 733
Retrousser, 861
Revêtement de Pont, 207
Revif, 606
Revolin, 252
Rhumb, 594, 647
Ribord, 99
Ricepteur radar, 627
Ride, 433, 653
Rideau de tente, 28, 734
Rider, 710
Ridins de Marée, 836
Ridoir, 873
Ridoir à Fourreau, 86
Ridoir à Lanterne, 86
Rigole, 903
Ringot, 53
Ripage, 721

Ris, 638
Ris à Filière, 311
Ris à Rouleau, 657
Ris Cunningham, 190
Ris Diagonal, 35
Risée, 133
Risette, 921
Risque d'Allège, 654
Risque de Guerre, 898
Risque Maritime, 489, 491
Ristourne, 636
Rivage, 730
River sur Virole, 152
Rivet, 654
Rivet à Fût Droit, 797
Rivet à Fût Renflé, 823
Rivetage, 655
Rivetage à Clins, 434
Rivetage a Franc Bord, 111
Rivetage à la Main, 353
Rivetage en Chaîne, 139
Rivetage en Quinconce, 932
Rivetage Étanche à l'Eau, 902
Rivetage Étanche au Pétrole,
  549
Rivetage Mécanique, 480
Rivetage Pneumatique, 593
Rivet à Tête Bombée, 632
Rivet à Tête Bouterollée, 751
Rivet à Tête fraisée, 104
Rivet à Tête Tronconique, 566
Rivet de Capitonnage, 624
Riveteuse Hydraulique, 385
Riveur, 654
Rivure, 655
Rivure fraisée bombée, 462
Robinet d'Arrêt, 792
Rocambeau, 856
Rocambeau d'Écoute, 152
Rocambeau de Foc, 410
Rôle d'Appel, 778
*Role d'Appel aux Postes
  d'Embarcations*, 76
*Rôle d'appel aux Postes d'In-
  cendie*, 282
Rôle d'Équipage, 24, 184
Romaillet, 336
Rompre, 129
Rond, 239, 660
Rose, 169
Rose à divisions en degrés, 831
Rose des Vents, 921
Rose quadrantale, 619
Rotation, 874
Rouanner, 636
Roue à Aubes, 562
Roue à Aubes Articulées, 277
Roue à Aubes Fixes, 627

Roue de Gouvernail, 783
Rouelle, 658
Rouf, 207
Rouille, 670
Roulis, 657
Rousture, 561
Rousturer, 924
Route, 181
Route au Compas, 169
Route Corrigée, 181
Route de Navigation, 433
Route Loxodromique, 647
Route Magnétique, 482
Route Moyenne, 856
Route par arc de grand cercle, 337
Route parcourue, 226
Route Vraie, 866
Routier, 582
Rue de Chauffe, 790

Sable, 682
Sable mouvant, 624, 722
Sablière, 754
Sabord, 599
Sabord de Chargement, 127
Sabord de Coupée, 324
Sabord de Décharge, 308
Sabord de Lestage, 36
Saborder, 693
Sabord de Soute, 157
Sabord d'Étrave, 89
Sabot, 842
Sac, 55, 602
Sac d'Écubier, 403
Sac d'Équipage, 694
Safran, 664
Saisie, 703
Saisine, 434
Saisine à Ridoir, 382
Saisine d'Embarcation, 75
Saisir, 434, 796
Salaison, 679
Saler en Vert, 420
Saleur, 679
Salinité, 678
Salissure, 304
Salle à Tracer, 516
Salle de Réunion, 612
Salut, 221, 588
Salut du Pavillon, 288
Sangle, 338
Sangle au Métier, 813
Sangle d'Embarcation, 55, 74
Sangle de Sondeur, 96
Sans Bonification pour Temps Gagné, 308

Sans Différence, 266
Sans Nouvelles, 513
Sans nuages, 155
Sapin, 281
Sapin de Norvège, 541
Sapin de Nord, 541
Sargasse, 684
Sas, 263
Saucier, 573, 684
Saudure a Franc-Bord, 111
Saumâtre, 94
Sauter, 360, 721
Sauvegarde, 78, 450
Sauvegarde d'Aviron, 852
Sauvegarde de Gouvernail, 665
Sauvetage, 148, 680
Sauveteur, 680, 925
Savate, 16, 754, 837
Scaphandrier, 227
Scier, 32
Sciez Partout, 784
Scintillement, 688
Seau à Escarbilles, 24
Seau en toile, 122
S'écarter, 331
Sèche, 290
Séchoir, 772
Second, 143
Second Charpentier, 129
Second Maître d'Équipage, 77
Second Mécanicien, 283
Secteur, 700
Secteur Dangereux, 198
Secteur de Barre, 667
Secteur de Claire Voie, 744
Secteur de Visibilité, 22
Section Cylindrique, 771
Sections longitudinales, 111
Sections Obliques, 218
Sections transversales, 771
Segment Capable, 198
Seiche, 701
S'elever, 150, 360, 905
Selle de Calfat, 118
Sémaphore, 706
S'embosser, 17, 519
Semelle, 729
Semelle de Colombiers, 754
Semelle d'Etambot, 741, 754
Se mettre au plein, 339
Se mettre sur, 819
Senau, 753
Senne, 701
Senne à Coulisse, 617
Senne droite, 49
Senne Tournante, 617
Senneur, 701
Séparateur, 780

Série Handicap, 351
Série Monotype, 551
Serpentin de réchauffage, 365, 823
Serre, 800
Serre-Bauquière, 148
Serre Bosse, 653, 713
Serre de Bancs, 653
Serre de Cale, 375
Serre de Côte, 736
Serre d'Empatture, 62
Serre d'Empâture, 830
Serre-Gouttière, 144, 393
Serrer, 316, 351, 382, 795
Serrer en Bonnette, 792
Serrer la Côte, 382
Service Contractuel, 175
Service d'Ecoute, 630
Service de Sauvetage, 452
Service de Surveillance des Glaces, 389
Service Hydrographique, 386
Servomoteur de barre, 782
Servomoteur sur barre, 780
Sétie, 709
Seuil, 229, 653
Sextant, 710
Shade Deck, 712
Shelter Deck, 719
Sidéral, 735
Sifflet, 916
Sifflet à Anche, 555
Sifflet à Cloche, 55
Sifflet de Manoeuvre, 77
Sifflet Harmonique, 144
Signal, 529
Signal à Grande Distance, 470
Signal atmosphérique, 906
Signal à trois pavillons, 831
Signal Auto-Alarme, 26
Signal Côtier, 159
Signal d'Alarme Radiotélégraphique, 627
Signal d'approche, 21
Signal d'Avertissement, 134
Signal de Barre, 45
Signal de Bouée de Sauvetage, 450
Signal de Brume, 298
Signal d'Écluse, 467
Signal de départ, 778
Signal de Détresse, 226
Signal de Détresse Radiotélégraphique, 629
Signal de Nuit, 537
Signal de Pilote, 584
Signal de Port, 229

Signal de Poste, 59
Signal de Remorque, 850
Signal d'Indication du Temps, 906
Signal géographique, 328
Signal Horaire, 839
Signal Horaire Radio-Télégraphique, 630
Signal Numérique, 542
Signal Parachute, 567
Signal Particulier, 607
Signal Phonique, 758
Signal Postal, 485
Signal pyrotechnique Very, 890
Signal Radiotélégraphique de Sécurité, 629
Signal Sanitaire, 620
Signal Sémaphorique, 706
Signal sous marin, 804
Signaux de Marée, 836
Signaux de Mauvais temps, 793
Signaux de mouvements de port, 852
Signaux d'Entrée et de Sortie de Port, 262
Signaux de Port, 355
Sillage, 691, 699, 895
Sillon, 317
Sirène, 740
Skiff, 626, 741
Slip de Carénage, 491, 747
Smack, 749
Socle insulaire, 394
Sole, 304
Soleil Apparent, 21
Soleil de Minuit, 511
Soleil Moyen, 502
Solstice, 755
Sombrer, 304
Sommier, 22, 97
Son, 67
Son Bref, 731
Sondage Acoustique, 3
Sondage en Etoile, 777
Sonde, 442, 757, 758
Sonder, 130, 366, 757
Sondes, 551
Sondeur, 297, 444
Sondeur Hydrostatique, 757
Son Prolongé, 508
Sortir du bassin, 880
Soudre à Clin, 280
Soudre Surélevée, 559
Soudure Acoustique, 252
Soudure à l'Arc, 254

Soudure Alumino-Thermique, 829
Soudure à pas de Pèlerin, 743
Soudure à Plat, 291
Soudure au Chalumeau, 325
Soudure Autogéné, 317
Soudure Automatique, 27
Soudure bout à bout, 111
Soudure Continue, 175
Soudure d'Agrafage, 818
Soudure d'Angle, 280
Soudure d'Angle Normale, 454
Soudure d'Angle Renforcée, 315
Soudure Discontinue Alternée, 774
Soudure en Bouchon, 592
Soudure en Chaîne, 139
Soudure en Plafond, 559
Soudure en V, 739
Soudure en "X", 236
Soudure Légère Continue, 453
Soudure Manuelle, 488
Soudure Montante, 889
Soudure par Fusion, 317
Soudure par Points, 767
Soudure par Résistance, 645
Soudure par bossages, 608
Soudures Alternées, 397
Soudure Verticale, 889
Soufflage, 68, 237, 317
Souillardure, 31, 643
Souille, 241
Soulager, 863
Soupape auxiliaire de prise d'eau, 371
Soupape d'Arrêt, 792
Soupape de Non retour, 539
Soupape Principale de Prise d'Eau, 486
Souquer, 662
Souquer sur les Avirons, 441
Sous-Affrètement, 803
Sous Barbe, 77
Sous le Vent, 9, 444, 445, 880
Sous Palan, 307, 308
Sous Voiles, 880
Soute, 106
Soute à Bagages, 33
Soute à Combustible Liquide, 314
Soute à Soieries, 737
Soute aux Dépêches, 485
Soute aux Poudres, 481
Soute aux Valeurs, 801
Soute aux Voiles, 676
Soute de Cale, 375
Soute d'Entrepont, 875

Soute de Réserve, 760
Soute fixe, 578
Soute Latérale, 734
Soute Provisoire, 827
Souter, 106
Soute Transversale, 186
Soutier, 862
Spardeck, 760
Spécification, 761
Sphère Céleste, 135
Spinnaker, 764
Spruce, 770
Stabilisateur Gyroscopique, 346
Stabilité, 773
Stabilité de route, 773
Stabilité des formes, 303
Stabilité Dynamique, 250
Stabilité Initiale, 393
Stabilité négative, 533
Stabilité sous Voiles, 674
Stabilité Statique, 778
Stable, 789
Staries, 440
Station de Signaux, 737
Station quarantenaire, 620
Stelle, 360
Steward, 789
Stigmographe, 778
Stoppeur, 116, 176, 649
Stoppeur à Pied de Biche, 448
Stoppeur à Vis, 691
Stratocumulus, 798
Subrécarque, 807
Subrogation, 805
Substitut, 644, 805
Subvention, 805
Subvention Postale, 485
Suçon, 117
Suction, 805
Suintement, 907
Sun Deck, 807
Superstructure, 206, 808
Support, 189, 322, 791
Support d'arbre, 713, 801
Support de Barrot Mobile, 51, 358
Support de Bôme, 322
Support de Faîtage, 510
Support de Guiole, 358
Support de Gouvernail, 665
Support de Gui, 84
Support de Mât de Charge, 215
Support d'Embarcation, 76
Support Central, 135
Support en Caisson, 91
Support Latéral, 471
Surbau, 157, 358

Sur Cul, 112, 862
Surestarie, 212
Surface des Ailes, 67
Surface développée, 216
Surface de Voilure, 674
Surface Mouillée, 910
Surface Projetée, 608
Surfret, 558
Surjalé, 304
Sur l'arrière, 25
Sur l'arrière de, 1
Sur l'arrière du travers, 1
Sur l'avant du travers, 54
Sur Lest, 36
Surlier, 916
Surliure à Demi-Clefs, 909
Surliure de Transfilage, 676
Suroit, 759
Surpatté, 304
Surprime, 809
Surtaxe de Pavillon, 289
Sur Tête, 112
Suspente, 622, 929
Synchronisme, 814
Système Solaire, 754
Syzygie, 814

Tableau, 528, 815, 854
Tableau des feux de route, 532
Table de Déviation, 216
Table de Loch, 467
Table de Point, 857
Tables de corrections hunaires, 479
Tablette, 207, 745
Tablette de Mât de Charge, 215
Tablier, 846
Taches d'humidité, 511
Tachymètre, 816
Taillemer, 194, 275
Talonner, 799
Talonnière, 741
Talus, 748
Tambour, 44, 290, 562
Tambour de Soute, 157
Tamisaille, 811
Tampon, 592
Tampon d'écubier, 361
Tangon, 83
Tangon de Bonnette Basse, 812
Tangon d'Embarcations, 649
Tangon de Spinnaker, 764
Tangon de Vent Arrière, 916
Tanguage, 587
Tanguer, 587
Tannage, 43, 823

Tanvez, 88
Tape Ajourée, 336
Tapecul, 197, 410
Tape de Conduit à Charbon, 157
Tape d'Écubier, 68
Tape de Dame, 733
Tape de Hublot, 735
Tapon, 75
Taquet, 153
Taquet à une Oreille, 23
Taquet d'Amarrage, 205
Taquet d'Amure, 633
Taquet de Barrot, 50
Taquet de Bitte, 66
Taquet de Bout de Vergue, 160
Taquet de Choc, 78
Taquet de Gouttière, 800
Taquet de Hauban, 650
Taquet de Lancement, 406
Taquet de Liure, 323
Taquet de Pied de Tolet, 841
Taquet de Pont, 205
Taquet de Suspension, 53
Taquet de Tournage, 54
Taquet de Vaigre, 374
Taquet d'Hiloire, 358
Taret, 490, 728
Tarif de Pilotage, 582
Tartane, 824
Tas, 231
Tas Pneumatique, 406, 593
Tasseau, 151
Taud, 359
Taux d'Affrètement, 142
Taux de Fret, 311
Taxes de Tonnage, 844
Taximètre, 576
Teck, 825
Télémètre, 634
Télémoteur, 826
Tempête, 793
Tempête Magnétique, 483
Temps, 905
Temps à Grains, 770
Temps Bouché, 830
Temps Corrigé, 178
Temps écoulé, 254
Temps Forcé, 799
Temps Local, 466
Temps Moyen, 502
Temps Moyen de Greenwich, 337
Temps Moyen du bord, 727
Temps Moyen du lieu, 465
Temps Sidéral de Greenwich, 338
Tendelet, 72, 121, 837

Teneur de Tas, 655
Tenir, 775
Tenir bon, 375
Tenon, 827
Tenon de Chouque, 364
Tenon d'Emplanture, 368
Tente, 28
Tenue à la mer, 695
Terme, 734
Terme de Benzon, 57
Terre sous le Vent, 445
Territoire Maritime, 493
Tessure, 292
Tête, 363
Tête d'Allonge, 838
Tête d'Alouette, 188, 434
Tête d'Alouette Double, 234
Tête de Bossoir, 200
Tête de Cheval, 931
Tête de Corne, 215
Tête de mât de charge, 215
Tête Maure, 873
Tête de Mèche, 666
Tête de Rivet, 655
Tête de Varangue, 295
Tétière, 362, 477
Tétière de Tente, 648
Teugue, 16, 517
Thalweg, 829
Thermomètre Enregistreur, 830
Thonnier, 871
Tiens bon, 28
Tille, 189
Time Charter, 838
Timonerie, 915
Timonier, 621
Tin à Sable, 682
Tin de Construction, 418
Tin Latéral, 62
Tin Mobile, 503
Tirage en Vase clos, 154
Tirage Forcé, 300
Tirage induit, 392
Tirant d'Eau de Compartimentage, 803
Tirant d'Eau en Charge, 463
Tirant d'Eau Lège, 454
Tirant d'Eau Maximum, 269
Tirant d'Eau Moyen, 501
Tireveille, 239, 488, 931
Toile à Fils Multiples, 525
Toile à Fils Retors, 876
Toile à Fils Simples, 739
Toile à Hamac, 350
Toile à Prélart, 823
Toile à Voile, 121, 675

Toile de Coton, 179	Touer, 418	Transmission Directe, 223
Toile de Fardage, 127, 708	Toujours à flot, 12	Transmission électro-magnétique, 258
Toile de Jute, 109	Touline, 897	
Toile de Lin, 292	Touliner, 897	Transmission Hydro-Mécanique, 384, 385
Tôle à Bord Tombé, 289	Tour, 516, 862	
Tôle à double courbure, 235	Tourbillon, 916	Transmission par engrenages réducteurs, 327
Tôle à Empreintes, 142	Tour Croisé, 649	
Tôle à Nervures, 647	Tour de Barre, 862	Transmission par radio, 628
Tôle Chaudronnée, 317	Tour de Chargement, 464	Transport, 855
Tôle Continue, 833	Tour de Mise à quai, 873	Transport à Bestiaux, 134
Tôle Crépinée, 801	Tour de Place, 873	Transport de Bois, 838
Tôle d'About, 111	Tour de Rôle, 873	Transport de Fruits, 313
Tôle de Bossage, 85	Tourelle de Fanaux, 88	Transport de Minerai, 554
Tôle de Brise-Lames, 487	Touret, 640	Transport de Viandes, 503
Tôle de Côte, 489	Touret à Aussière, 362	Transporteur, 129
Tôle de Flanc de Ballast, 489	Tourmentin, 303, 793	Transporteur en Commun, 167
Tôle de Liure, 323	Tour Mort, 662	Transport par Allèges, 454
Tôle de parquet, 295	Tourner, 54, 820	Transports Maritimes, 694
Tôle de ragage, 138	Tournevire, 508	Travailler, 797
Tôle de Roulis, 899	Tourniquet, 230, 751	Traverse, 187, 801, 931
Tôle de Sommier, 559, 869	Tour plein, 662	Traverse de Fausse Mèche, 249
Tôle d'étambrai, 571	Tours Croisés, 626	Traverse de Gouvernail, 666
Tôle d'Étrave, 784	Tours dans les Chaînes, 254, 304	Traversée, 571, 863
Tôle Diaphragme, 219		Traverser, 284
Tôle Doublante, 237	Tourteau de Poisson, 286	Traversier, 97
Tôle Emboutie, 225	Tous Risques, 10	Traversier Arrière, 6, 621, 622
Tôle Façonnée, 276	Toute, 355	Traversier Avant, 88, 303
Tôle façonnée à chaud, 317	Tracé à la Salle, 441	Traversière, 287
Tôle Gauche, 876	Traceur, 467	Traversin, 187
Tôle Gouttière, 209, 800	Traceur de Route, 181	Traversin de Bitte, 186
Tôle Intercostale, 396	Trait de rabbure, 625, 627	Traversin de Cale, 186, 745
Tôle Ondulée, 179	Trait Extérieur de Rablure, 556	Trèfle, 761
Tôle Quille Extérieure, 556		Trélucher, 408
Tôle Quille Intérieure, 393	Trait Intérieur de Rablure, 393	Trésillon, 365, 759, 924
Tôle Striée, 647		Tresse, 305, 708
Tôle Supérieure, 648	Trajectoire, 795	Tresse Carrée, 771
Tolet, 662, 831	Tramail, 853	Tresse Plate, 291, 355
Tolet à Fourche, 74, 544	Trame, 907	Tresse Ronde, 661
Tôle varangue, 295	Tramp, 853	Treuil, 919
Tomber, 246, 574	Tramping, 853	Treuil à Air Comprimé, 9
Ton, 237, 498	Tranche des Machines, 480	Treuil à bras, 183
Tonnage Brut, 339	Trancheur, 766	Treuil à Changement de Marche, 646
Tonnage Net, 534	Transbordement, 855	
Tonneau d'Affrètement, 311	Transbordeur, 278	Treuil à Embrayage à Friction, 312
Tonneau de Mer, 311	Transbordeur à Passagers, 572	
Tonne de Déplacement, 225	Transfilage, 404, 429	Treuil à Engrenages Droits, 770
Tonne de Jauge, 339	Transfiler, 751	
Tonne de Portée, 841	Transformateur Föttinger, 385	Treuil à Engrenages Hélicoïdaux, 925
Tonture, 716	Transmetteur d'Ordres Arrière, 228	
Tonture réglementaire, 775		Treuil à Escarbilles, 24
Torche, 290	Transmetteur d'Ordres aux Machines, 262	Treuil à Marchandises, 128
Torcher la Toile, 799		Treuil à Moteur, 523
Tornade, 847	Transmetteur d'Ordres Électrique, 255	Treuil de Bossoir, 77
Toron, 797		Treuil de Brasseyage, 93
Toronnage, 303, 440	Transmetteur d'Ordres de Barre, 783	Treuil de charbonnage, 157
Touage, 848		Treuil de déhalage, 898
Toucher, 848	Transmetteur d'Ordres de la Vigie, 473	Treuil de Pêche, 859
Touée, 361, 688		Treuil de Remorquage, 850

Treuil électrique, 257
Treuil Hydro-Électrique, 257
Treuilliste, 919
Trévire, 569
Triangle de Position, 25
Triangle de Tablier, 497
Tringle de Drosse, 783
Tringle de quille, 419
Trinquette, 302, 303
Trinquette Ballon, 37
Triquage, 734
Triquer, 692
Troisième Mécanicien, 700
Trois mâts barque, 832
Trois-mâts carré, 315
Trois-mâts Goëlette, 43
Trombe, 901
Trompette, 378
Trompette à Anche, 638
Troncon de l'avant, 88
Tropique, 865
Tropopause, 866
Troposphère, 866
Trou à Charbon, 106, 157
Trou Alésé, 636
Trou Borgne, 68
Trou d'Air, 8
Trou de Chat, 477
Trou de clef de mât, 279
Trou de Jauge, 879
Trou de liure, 323
Trou de Rivet, 655
Trou d'Homme, 487
Trou Poinçonné, 615
Trous rectifiés, 273
Trouvillaise, 199
Trunk Deck, 867
Tube de Sondage, 758
Tube de Sortie d'Arbre, 787
Tube d'Étambot, 787
Tuf, 870
Tunnel, 712
Turbine, 872
Turbine à Action, 390
Turbine à Engrenages, 326
Turbine à Réaction, 636
Turbine d'Échappement, 267
Turbine d'Évacuation, 267
Tuyau d'Air, 8
Tuyau de Ballast, 37
Tuyau de Cale, 63
Tuyau de Dégazage, 888
Tuyau de Sonde, 758
Tuyau d'Orgue, 693
Tuyautage de Ballast, 36
Tuyautage de Cale, 63
Tuyautage de Mazout, 548

Tuyautage de Vaporisation, 751, 780
Tuyère Kort, 425
Typhon, 877
Typhus, 877

Usages du Port, 192
Usure, 905

Vactait, 341
Vadrouille, 522
Va et Vient, 360
Vague, 904
Vague d'Étrave, 91
Vagues de Fond, 68
Vagues de l'Arrière, 788
Vagues Divergentes, 227
Vague Sismique, 701
Vagues Transversales, 856
Vaigrage, 134
Vaigrage à Claire-Voie, 760
Vaigrage Diagonal, 217
Vaigrage Plein, 154
Vaigre, 134
Vaigres de bouchain, 62
Vaigres de Fond, 295
Valet, 230
Valeur Contributive, 176
Valeur en Douane, 82
Valeur non Dédouanée, 82
Vallée, 886
Vanne à Glissière, 748
Vapeur, 780
Varangue, 295, 296
Varangue à Branche Courte, 731
Varangue à Branche Longue, 470
Varangue Acculée, 653
Varangue Basse, 713
Varangue Continue, 175
Varangue Courte, 732
Varangue d'Arcasse, 854
Varangue Étanche, 902
Varangue Intercostale, 396
Varangue Pleine, 755
Varangue Squelette, 741
Varech, 420, 699, 925
Variation Générale, 809
Vase, 524, 737
Vedette, 355
Vedette de Remorquage, 849
Vélage, 119
Venir au Lof, 167, 662
Vent, 919
Vent Apparent, 21

Vent Arrière, 54
Vent Catabatique, 416
Vent Contraire, 526, 541
Vent Debout, 365
Vent de Travers, 52
Vent Devant, 394
Vent Dominant, 605
Vent en Pointe, 685
Vent Étésien, 265
Vent Fait, 779
Vent Fraichissant, 312
Vent Frais, 801
Ventilateur, 71
Ventilation, 888
Ventilation Artificielle, 504
Ventilation Mixte, 808
Ventilation Naturelle, 528
Ventilation par Refoulement, 808
Ventilation par Suction, 267
Vent Largue, 309
Vent Permanent, 586
Vent Portant, 443
Ventre, 55
Ventrière, 503
Vents Alizés, 852
Vent sous vergue, 620
Vents Variables, 887
Vent Vrai, 866
Verge, 16
Vergue, 929
Vergue à signaux, 737
Vergue Barrée, 186
Vergue de Bonnette, 802
Vergue de Flèche, 320, 374, 404, 769
Vergue de Houari, 343
Vergue Sèche, 186
Vérin, 403
Vérin de Chasse, 777
Vérin de Poussée, 777
Vérin de Retenue, 438
Vérine, 508
Vernier, 889
Vernis Marin, 761
Verre de Pont, 207
Verre Mort, 105, 202
Verrine, 331
Verrou Hydraulique, 438
Verse, 774, 840
Vertical, 78, 147, 889
Verveux, 377, 856
Vibord, 895
Vice Propre, 393
Vidange de Cale, 63
Vide, 95, 878
Vide d'Arrimage, 95
Videlle, 370

Vider—Zone littorale 972

Vider, 35
Vieux, 550
Vieux Filin, 413
Vieux Filin Blanc, 668
Vigie, 473, 891
Violon de Ris, 84
Violons, 53, 279
Vire-Lof, 207
Vire-Lof de Trinquette, 302
Virement du Vent, 360
Virer, 365
Virer à Pic, 366
Virer au Linguet, 365
Virer cap pour cap, 919
Virer de Bord, 332
Virer de Bord Vent Devant, 816
Virer Lof Pour Lof, 905
Virer lof pour lof en culant, 91
Vireur, 404
Vire-Vire, 622
Virole, 152
Virure, 797
Virure Bretonne, 764
Virure d'Aération, 8, 9
Virure de Bouchain, 63
Virure de Carreau, 717
Virure de Fond, 87
Virure de Galbord, 324
Virure de Liaison, 65
Virure de Placage, 393
Virure de Pont, 209
Virure de Recouvrement, 556
Virure d'Hiloire, 837
Virure en Pointe, 246
Vis à Bois, 75
Vis de Pression, 149
Vis de Rappel, 821
Viseur Azimutal, 736
Visibilité, 891
Visibilité restreinte, 515
Visite, 809, 892
Visite de Douane, 407
Visite de franc bord, 464
Visite de Reclassification, 578
Visite Périodique, 578
Visiter, 558, 698
Vis Tangente, 821
Vit de Mulet, 334

Vitesse Commerciale, 708
Vitesse Critique, 185
Vitesse d'amenée, 475
Vitesse de Hissage, 374
Vitesse de Houle, 904
Vitesse de Remorquage, 850
Vitesse de Sillage, 896
Vitesse Économique, 252
Vitesse modérée, 515
Vitesse Normale, 708
Vitesses Correspondantes, 178
Vivier, 124, 287
Voie de Lancement, 438
Voie de Lancement à Profil Courbe, 119
Voile, 673
Voile à Antenne, 435
Voile à Bourcet, 478
Voile à Bourcet à amure Fixe, 776
Voile à Bourcet Gambeyant, 222
Voile à Corne, 320
Voile à demie Antenne, 709
Voile à Livarde, 769
Voile Aurique, 301
Voile au Tiers, 478
Voile Barrée, 186, 410
Voile Carrée, 771
Voile de Batture, 649
Voile de Cape, 793
Voile de Chébec, 709
Voile de Fortune, 414
Voile de Jonque, 144
Voile de Lougre, 478
Voile de Lougre Bômée, 35
Voile de Lougre Fixe, 776
Voile de Lougre Volante, 222
Voile de Senau, 762, 868
Voile de Sétie, 709
Voile d'Étai, 779
Voile d'Étai de Cape, 795
Voile Goélette, 762
Voile Latine, 435
Voile Lattée, 48
Voilerie, 676
Voiles d'appui, 779
Voiles de l'Avant, 364

Voiles Hautes, 455, 749
Voiles Majeures, 588, 925
Voiles Supplémentaires, 455
Voile Triangulaire, 409
Voilier, 675, 676
Vol, 829
Volage, 827, 918
Volant, 721
Volée, 633
Volige, 48
Volume de Carène, 892
Volute, 692
Voûte, 180
Voyage, 893
Voyage d'Essai, 861
Voyage d'Inauguration, 484
Voyant, 846

Waretaille, 341
Warrant, 193, 230
Wherry, 915

Yacht, 928
Yacht de Course, 626
Yacht de Croisière, 189
Yawl, 930
Yawl Canoe, 121
Yawl Goëlette, 688
Yole, 329, 412
Yole de Course, 625
Youyou, 221

Zenith, 932
Zéro de l'Échelle, 836
Zéro des Cartes, 141
Zéro des Marées, 834
Zingage, 322
Zodiaque, 933
Zone Contigue, 3
Zone de Franc Bord, 307
Zone de pilotage, 582
Zone des Calmes tropicaux, 379
Zone douanière maritime, 193
Zone Franche, 309
Zone littorale, 461

GERMAN INDEX

Abandon, 1
Abandon Erklärung, 541
Abandonierung, 1
Abandonklausel, 1
Abankern, 881
Abbaumen, 84
Abbindeblock, 521
Abblätterung, 267
Abbrechen, 129
Abbringen, 98, 640
Abdampfturbine, 267
Abdechseln, 772
Abdrift, 242
Abfahren, 52, 674, 709
Abfahrt Pfeifesignal, 276
Abfahrtsignal, 262, 778
Abfahrtsort, 213, 594
Abfahrtspunkt, 213, 594
Abfall, 748
Abfallen, 274, 574
Abfallrohr, 693
Abfallschutte, 324
Abfieren, 888
Abflammen, 96
Abgaskessel, 899
Abgasrohr, 888
Abgelaichter Hering, 732
Abgeschnittenes Stück, 737
Abgestempelter Verladungsschein, 30
Abgewickelte Fläche, 216
Abhalten, 52
Abhalter, 770
Abkeilen, 907
Abkippen, 840
Abkreuzen, 150
Abladekonnossement, 724
Abladeplatz, 766
Ablader, 310
Abladungshafen, 601
Ablagen, 292
Ablauf, 437
Ablaufbahn, 340, 438, 777
Ablaufgerüst, 437
Ablaufschlitten, 746
Ablaufschmiere, 438
Ableichtern, 454
Ablese Mikroskop, 510
Ablieferungschein, 229
Ablieferungsklausel, 212
Ablieferungsschein, 212
Abliegender Gang, 556
Ablösen, 644

Abmeldung, 736
Abmustern, 224, 574
Abnehmbares Glied, 216
Abnehmen, 47
Abnehmender Mond, 897
Abnutzung, 905
Abreiten, 646
Abrinden, 43
Abrüsten, 441
Abschätzungsklausel, 7
Abschlagen, 879
Abschlichten, 248
Abschlieren, 747
Ab Schiff, 268
Abschnüren, 441
Absender, 173
Absetzdock, 213
Absetzer, 772
Absetztank, 709
Absolute Konterbande, 2
Absoluter Total Verlust, 3
Absperrhahn, 792
Absperrventil, 792
Abspringen lassen, 678
Abstand, 587
Abstauen, 146
Abstecken, 879
Abstoppen, 142
Abstossen, 52
Abstützen, 731, 841
Abtakeln, 800, 882
Abteilungsfaktor, 272
Abteilungsladelinie, 803
Abteilungslänge, 803
Abtreiben, 245, 673
Abtrift, 445
Ab und An, 546
Ab und zu liegen, 777
Abwasserbehälter, 710
Abweichung, 210
Abweichungsklausel, 216
Abweichungsparallel, 226
Abweichung vom Kurse, 216
Abweiser, 663
Abweitung, 213
Abwrackung, 723
Abzüge vom Bruttoraumgehalt, 210
Achteraus, 25
Achteraussacken, 274
Achterbrücke, 228, 898
Achterdeck, 621
Achter-Geie, 333

Achterlastig, 112
Achterlicher Wind, 309
Achterliches See-Übernehmen, 598
Achterlich von dwars, 1
Achterliek, 6
Achtermast, 6
Achtersegel, 7
Achterstick, 280
Achtertau, 787
Achtkant, 620
Admiralitätskoeffizient, 4
Adresskommission, 3
Aerolith, 6
Agonische Linie, 7
Ahming, 239
Ähnlichkeitsgesetze, 440
Ahoi, 8
Ahorn, 488
Akazienholz, 467
Akromatisch, 3
Aktionsturbine, 390
Akustisches Lot, 252
Alarmzeichen, 627
Algen, 9
Alhidade, 391
Allgemeine Wetterlage, 328
Alter, 7, 550
Altersschaden, 905
Alte Vermessungs Methode, 101
Aluminium, 11
Aluminium Farbe, 12
Aluminium Folien, 11
Aluminum Metall, 11
Ambos Cirruswolke, 20
Ameris Hering, 331
Am Grund, 7
Amphidromien, 13
Amplitude, 13
Am Wind, 154
Anbau, 21
Anbohren, 693
An Bord, 2
Anbrassen, 92
Anbrechen, 99
Anderthalbmaster, 197, 420
Aneroidbarometer, 17
Anfahren, 304
Anfangskurs, 393
Anfangsstabilität, 393
Angarierecht, 651

Angebrachter Fingerling—Aufbringung 974

Angebrachter Fingerling, 287
Angel, 285
Angelboot, 458
Angelfahrzeug, 377
Angelfischerei, 459
Angeliekte Beplankung, 710
Angelköder, 410
Angelleinfahrzeug, 377
Angelschnur, 286
Angeschwemmtes Strandgut, 407
An Grund geraten, 339
Anhaltung, 23
Anhängemotor, 556
Anhöhe, 39, 424
Anholen, 819
Anholpart, 360
Anker, 13
Ankerarm, 23
Anker aufgehen, 907
Ankeraufwindebaum, 284
Ankerauge, 269
Ankerboje, 115, 520
Ankerbojereep, 863, 908
Ankerdavit, 15
Ankerdeck, 16
Ankereis Grundeis, 16
Ankerfässchen, 74
Ankerflue, 566
Ankerflügel, 566
Ankerflunke, 566
Ankerfütterung, 16
Ankergeld, 16
Ankergerschirr, 16
Ankergeschirr, 340
Ankergrund, 375
Ankerhals, 832
Ankerhamen, 796
Ankerhand, 566
Anker hieven, 366
Anker Katten, 131
Ankerkette, 15
Ankerkette Marken, 115
Ankerketten klarieren, 151
Ankerkluse, 362
Ankerkran, 15
Ankerkreuz, 188
Ankerlaterne, 649
Ankerlicht, 649
Anker lichten, 366
Ankerlichtmaschine, 919
Anker mit beiklappbarem Stock, 722
Anker mitbeweglichen armen 235
Ankern, 17
Ankern mit einem Spring, 17
Ankerplatz, 14, 16, 151

Ankerring, 16
Ankerschaft, 16
Ankerschakel, 16, 357
Ankerschaufel, 15
Ankerschlipper, 17, 870
Ankerschuh, 16
Ankerspill, 15, 919
Ankerspitze, 64
Ankerspring, 768
Anker Station, 16
Ankerstein, 521
Ankerstich, 115
Ankerstock, 790
Ankerstock Form Replankung, 17
Ankerstopper, 649
Anker Talje, 17
Ankertasche, 16
Ankertau, 15
Ankertau Aufschiesser, 837
Ankertelegraph, 521
Anker Wache, 17
Ankerwinde, 919
Ankerzertifikat, 14
Anlandebrücke, 433
Anlasshebel, 777
Anlaufen, 118, 775, 848
Anlegehafen, 600
Anliegen, 775
Anliegender Gang, 393
Anliegende Zone, 3
Anlieken, 658
Anluven, 167, 360
Anmeldung, 737
Anmusterung, 737
Annäherungsrecht, 651
Anordnungslicht, 642
Anpreien, 347, 348
Anreissen, 636
Anruf Zeichen, 119
Ansatzstück, 211
Anschlagbindsel, 656
Anschlagen, 56, 746
Anschlager, 746
Anschlagliek, 364
Anschlagskosten, 746
Anschlussort, 700
Anschreibung, 820
Anschwellung, 68, 773
Ansegelungssignal, 21
Ansegelungstonne, 694
Ansetzen, 710
Anshalten, 905
Anstecken, 56
Ansteuerungstonne, 273
Anteil-Police, 396
Antenne, 19
Antifäulnisfarbe, 19

Antifoulingkomposition, 19
Antikorrosivekomposition, 19
Antizyklone, 19
Antwortwimpel, 19
An und abliegende Plattung, 390
Anweisung, 10
Anwuchs, 304
Anwuchsverhindernde Farbe, 19
Aphelium, 20
Apogaum, 20
Äquator, 828
Äquatoriale Gegenströmung, 263
Äquatorialkalmen, 231
Äquatorialstrom, 263
Äquinoktial, 264
Äquinoktiale Kolure, 264
Äquinoktialpunkte, 264
Äquinoktialtide, 264
Äquinvalenter Träger, 264
Aräometer, 386
Arbeiten, 428, 797
Arbeitslicht, 924
Arbeitstag, 924
Arbeitstalje, 477
Archimedisches Prinzip 439
Arm, 378
Armieren, 486
Armunklar, 304
Arrest, 23
Arrestierungskausel, 654
Arzneikiste, 504
Ascheauswerfer, 24
Ascheejektor, 24
Ascheheisswinde, 24
Ascheimer, 24
Aschekübel, 24
Aschenauslauf, 24
Ascheschutte, 24
Assekuradeur, 880
Assekuranzklausel, 396
Astronomische Navigation, 135
Astronomischer Horizont, 635
Astronomischer Tag, 25
Astronomisches Fernrohr, 932
Astronomisches Grunddreieck, 25
Astronomische Zeit, 25
Atoll, 26
Auf, 545
Aufbanken, 39
Aufbau, 206, 808
Aufbaudeck, 808
Aufbringen, 98
Aufbringung, 124

Aufbucht, 373
Aufbuchtungsmoment, 374
Auf den Strand setzen, 49
Auf der Rückreise begriffen, 377
Aufdrehen, 812
Aufentern, 440
Auffieren, 167, 312, 777
Aufflage, 741
Auffrischender Wind, 312
Aufgebanktes Feuer, 39
Aufgehisst, 26
Aufgeien, 151, 360
Aufgeriebenes Nietloch, 636
Aufheissen, 810
Aufhieven, 366
Aufholen, 861
Aufholer, 105, 862
Aufholleine, 863
Aufkeilen, 907
Aufkeilung, 561, 792
Aufkimmung, 203
Aufklotzung, 69, 203, 593, 792, 818
Aufklotzung Stütze, 31
Aufklotzungwinkel, 800
Aufkneifen, 594
Aufkommen, 251, 559
Aufkreuzen, 150
Aufkrimpen, 30
Aufkrimpender Wind, 31
Auflage der Lukendeckel, 359
Auflanger, 317
Auflaufen, 339, 668
Auflegen, 441
Aufmasstabelle, 547
Aufnahme, 809
Aufnehmung, 809
Aufpakkung, 561
Aufpieken, 845
Aufreiben, 636
Aufrichte Kräftepaar, 651
Aufrichtungsvermögen, 651
Auf Riemen, 544
Aufriss, 716, 717
Aufrollen, 879
Aufschiessen, 161, 730, 837
Aufschlagen, 881
Aufschleppe, 747
Aufschleppen, 640
Aufschlepphelling, 491
Aufschlitzer, 772
Aufschricken, 809
Aufschütten, 39
Aufsegeln, 558
Aufsteigende Bewegung, 366
Aufsteigung, 686
Aufsteigungs Unterschied, 24
Aufstossen, 799

Auftaljen, 90
Auftauchendes Keilstück, 907
Auftoppen, 160, 845
Auftriebskraft, 107
Auf und Nieder, 20, 731, 882
Aufwallung, 809
Aufwärterin, 789
Aufweiten, 640
Aufzug, 374
Augbindsel, 661
Auge, 164, 269
Augenbolzen, 269
Augplatte, 270
Augsplissung, 270
Ausbalancierungsbrett, 34
Ausbauchung, 290
Ausbesserung, 644
Ausbrechen, 96
Ausbringen, 441, 670
Auschakeln, 882
Auschlag Jackstag, 56
Auschwemmung, 689
Ausdehnungstaum, 268
Aus dem Dock holen, 880
Ausdocken, 880
Ausdrückliche Garantie, 268
Ausdünung, 432
Auseisung, 96
Ausfahren, 441
Ausfall, 302
Ausflaggen, 242
Ausflaggen über Masttoppen und Raanocken, 242
Ausfracht, 556
Ausfuhrdeklaration, 263, 724
Ausfuhrmanifest, 558
Ausfuhr Warenrechnung, 268
Ausfuhrzoll, 268
Ausgabe Versicherung, 223
Ausgangschacht, 265
Ausgebung, 1
Ausgeschlossener Raum, 210
Ausgestanztes Loch, 615
Ausgesteckte Kettenlänge, 688
Ausgleichklasse, 351
Ausgleichrennen, 351
Ausguck, 188
Ausguckmann, 473
Ausgucktelegraph, 473
Ausguss, 324
Aushängen, 882
Aushebung, 746
Ausholen, 331
Ausholer, 557
Ausholring, 152
Ausklarieren, 262
Ausklarierung, 150
Ausklarierungsattest, 151, 558

Ausklarierungsschein, 854
Auslage, 281
Auslagen, 223
Aus Land, 24
Auslassen, 713
Auslaufen, 618, 670
Auslaufendergang, 246
Auslegen, 441, 633
Ausleger, 83, 557
Auslegerboot, 557
Ausleger Kanu, 557
Auslieferungsschein, 311
Ausmachen, 486
Ausösen, 35
Auspechen, 574
Auspieken, 574
Auspuffkessel, 899
Auspufftopf, 524
Ausrigger, 557
Ausrüsten, 862
Ausrüstung, 264, 556
Ausrüstung-Bassin, 287
Ausrüstung Dock, 287
Ausrüstungsnummer, 264
Ausrüstversicherung, 557
Aussacken, 246
Ausscheren, 882
Ausschiessender Vorsteven, 633
Ausschiessender Wind, 360
Ausschiffung, 224
Ausschiffungskarte, 432
Ausschlingen, 882
Ausschnitt, 334
Ausschöpfen, 35
Ausschrapen, 594
Ausschwingen, 812
Aussenbeplankung, 557
Aussenbord Langsschiffsplan, 556
Aussenbordmotor, 556
Aussendock, 551
Aussenhafen, 556
Aussenhaut, 719
Aussenhautlängsspant, 719
Aussenhautpflock, 228
Aussenkammer, 557
Aussenkiel, 556
Aussenkluver, 297, 556
Aussenkluverbackstage, 297
Aussenkluverbaum, 297
Aussenkluverdomper, 297
Aussenkluver Stampfstag, 297
Aussenmeridianbreite, 268
Aussensteven, 275
Aussenstich, 557
Äussere Klinch, 557
Äussere Spundungslinie, 556

Ausstanzen, 616
Ausstechen, 888
Ausstecken, 874
Ausstraken, 273
Ausstromlüftung, 267
Austernbrut, 189
Austernkratzer, 559
Australstrom, 26
Austretende Flügelkante, 299
Auswanderungsagent, 571
Auswanderungsschiff, 260
Ausweben, 636
Ausziehlüfter, 884
Autoalarmapparat, 26
Automatische Heulboje, 27
Automatische Heultonne, 27
Automatischer Feuermelder, 282
Automatischer Notruf, 26
Automatische Schweissung, 27
Average Klausel, 29
Axial Variable Steigung, 29
Azimut, 29
Azimut Kompass, 29
Azimutkreis, 29

Back, 301
Backbaum, 649
Back bekommen, 820
Backbord, 598
Backbord Tonne, 600
Backbrassen, 92
Backdeck, 301
Backe, 143, 378, 473
Backen und Füllen, 30
Backhalsen, 91
Backholen, 30
Backlegen, 1, 33
Backreling, 301
Backschwabber, 772
Backspiere, 649, 812
Backstag Ausleger, 767
Backstagsweise, 551
Backstagweise See, 621
Backstagwind, 621, 622
Bagger, 241
Baggerprahm, 378
Baggerschute, 378
Bagien Raa, 186
Bagiensegel, 186
Bai, 49
Bake, 49
Bakengeld, 108
Bakengelder, 50
Bakentonne, 846

Balance Luggersegel, 35
Balancereff, 35
Balancereffband, 35
Balance Ruder, 34
Balanziermaschine, 50
Balanzierspant, 121
Balken, 50
Balkenbucht, 119
Balkenkiel, 43
Balkenknie, 51
Balkenkopf, 50
Balkenmallung, 51
Balkenrost, 338
Balkenstek, 838
Balkhaken, 230
Ballast, 36
Ballast ausschiessen, 879
Ballasteinrichtung, 36
Ballastleitung, 36
Ballastorder, 789
Ballastpforte, 36
Ballastpumpe, 36
Ballastrohr, 37
Ballastwassertank, 37
Ballen, 35
Ballenladung, 36
Ballenladung Inhalt, 35
Ballistischesfehler, 37
Ballon Flieger, 37
Ballonkluver, 37
Ballonkluver Topsegel, 37
Ballonsegel, 37
Ballonstagsegel, 37
Ballon Topsegel, 37
Ball-Signallball, 36
Bandsel, 702, 709
Bandselauge, 435
Bandselleine, 702
Bandseln, 495
Bandselschraube, 650
Bank, 39
Baratterie, 44
Bark, 42
Barkschiff, 832
Barktakelung, 43
Barkunen, 627
Barogramm, 43
Barograph, 43
Barometer, 43
Barre, 40
Barrehafen, 44
Barrelotse, 44
Barresignal, 45
Barretonne, 40
Barriereis, 45
Barrierenriff, 45
Barringsbalken, 76
Basishafen, 775

Bassin, 45
Basttau, 163
Bauch, 55, 106
Bauchaufholer, 106
Bauchband, 55
Bauchbeschlag, 106
Bauchdielen, 830
Bauchen, 32
Bauchgording, 107
Bauchgordingbrille, 107
Bauchgordingknebel, 107
Bauchgordinglapp, 107
Bauchseising, 106
Bauchstropp, 106, 331
Bauchstück, 55, 296
Baudock, 102
Bauhelling, 747
Bauholz, 478
Baum, 83
Baumaufholer, 846
Baumbügel, 84
Baumdirk, 621
Baumfock Baum, 57
Baumgalgen, 322
Baumkrücke, 84
Baumkurre, 51
Baumnock, 215
Baumschleppnetz, 51
Baumtalje, 84
Baumtoppnant, 621
Baumwollstoff, 179
Baumwolltau, 180
Baurisiko Police, 101
Bauvorschrift, 761
Beantworten, 18
Beaufort Skala, 52
Beaufsichtiger, 492
Bebakung, 50
Becken, 747
Bedeckter Himmel, 558
Bafahrungsabgaben, 355
Befestigen, 792
Befestigungskette, 520
Befestigungstau, 30
Beförderungsgeld, 224
Beförderungstage, 224
Befrachter, 141, 310
Befrachtung, 6
Befrachtungsgebühr, 99
Befrachtungskommission, 141
Befrachtungsmakler, 141
Befreiungsklausel, 266
Begrenzungsplanke, 489
Begrenzungswinkel, 87
Behaltender Magnetismus, 645
Behauen, 52
Behauenes Holz, 371
Behauenes Rundholz, 193

Behauer, 145
Beibleiben, 375
Beiboot, 221, 827
Beibrassen, 92
Beidemwinder, 154
Beidrehen, 662
Beiholer, 104
Beilbrief, 101
Beilegen, 98, 366
Beiliegen, 26, 448, 868
Beilieger, 410
Beim Wenden langsam sein, 744
Beim Winde, 112
Beisegel, 455
Beitknie, 301
Beitragspflichtiger Wert, 176
Beizung, 580
Bejahungsflagge, 6
Bekalmen, 52
Bekeidetes Stahltauwerk, 278
Bekleiden, 494, 708
Bekleidete Elektrode, 182
Bekleidung, 150, 460, 708
Beklemmen, 647
Bekneigen, 406
Beladene, 463
Beladener Tiefgang, 463
Beladenes Deplacement, 463
Belader, 724
Belastungskurve, 191
Belegen, 54
Belegklampe, 54
Belegknecht, 633
Belegnagel, 54, 404
Belegnagelband, 763
Belegtrosse, 521
Beleidigung, 847
Bemastung, 498
Benept, 56
Benetzte Oberfläche, 910
Benzon Grenze, 57
Beobachtete Breite, 436
Beobachtete Höhe, 544
Beobachtung, 544
Beobachtungs Uhr, 347
Beplankung, 589
Bequem vor Anker liegen, 648
Berechnete Höhe, 866
Berechnungsbreite, 516
Bergeleistung, 148
Bergen, 316, 381
Berger, 680, 925
Bergholz, 896
Bergung, 148, 680
Bergungsfahrzeug, 680
Bergungskontrakt, 679
Bergungsschiff, 680

Bergungsverlust, 680
Bernstein, 12
Berth Klausel, 59, 294
Berthon Boot, 163
Berühren, 848
Besahn, 410, 514
Besahnmast, 410, 514
Besahn-Stagsegel, 514
Besan, 245, 410, 514, 759
Besan Gaffel, 759
Besankutter, 420
Besanmast, 245
Besansegel, 410
Besatzung, 184
Besatzungsraum, 184
Beschädigungsreparaturen, 197
Beschlagen, 316, 351
Beschlagleine, 317, 695
Beschlagnahme, 703
Beschlagseising, 325
Beschleunigung, 2
Beschleunigungsgebühr, 224
Beschmarten, 569
Beschränkte Klasse, 645
Besegelte Fracht, 225
Besegelung, 674
Besichtigung, 809
Besichtigungsprotokoll, 137
Besichtigungsschein, 137
Besitzergreifung, 703
Besondere Haverei, 571
Bespicken, 833
Beständige Brise, 779
Besteck, 287
Besteckkompass, 856
Bestimmen, 287
Bestimmt, 87
Bestimmungshafen, 600
Bestimmungsort, 594
Betakeln, 916
Beting, 66
Betingbalken, 187, 801
Betinge, 648
Betingsbalken, 186
Betingschlag loswerfen, 879
Betingschlag nehmen, 66
Betingschlag verdoppeln, 234
Betingshörner, 48
Betingsknie, 66
Betingstange, 66, 540
Betingstützplatte, 66
Betonnung, 50, 107
Betonnungssystem, 107
Betriebszuschuss, 264
Betrügerei, 44
Bettung, 148
Beutel, 81

Beutelgarn, 617
Beutelnetz, 617
Bewaffnetes Handelschiff, 606
Bewegliches Schaufelrad, 277
Bewölkung, 155
Bewuhlen, 924
Bezugsort, 774
Biegemoment, 56
Biegsames Drahtseil, 293
Biegungsmoment, 56
Bilge, 61
Bilgeleitung, 63
Bilgenwasser, 63
Bilgepumpe, 63
Bilgerohr, 63
Bilgewasseröler, 548
Bilien, 111
Bindfaden, 876
Bindsel, 702
Bindselgarn, 703
Bindselgut, 703
Bindselleine, 350, 702
Bindseln, 702
Binnenbefestigung, 394
Binnengewässer, 393
Binnenhafen, 393
Binnen Hintersteven, 393
Binnenkiel, 419
Binnenkimm, 62
Binnenkluver, 393
Binnennock, 538
Binnenschwert, 135
Binnenspant, 648
Binnenstich, 394
Binnenvorsteven, 21
Birkenholz, 66
Bitumastik Emailleanstrich, 66
Blanke Elektrode, 42
Blanko Konnossement, 67
Blase, 68
Blauer Peter, 71
Blauer Pol, 71
Blaufeuer, 71
Blaulicht, 71
Blechbearbeitungswerkstatt, 591
Blechkantenhobelmaschine, 590
Blei, 442
Bleiben bei, 775
Bleikiel, 36
Blende, 202
Blendglas, 378, 391
Blinde Hecktasche, 32
Blinde Raa, 916
Blinder Raa Domper, 916
Blinde Rahe, 767

Blinder Kreuzkopf, 249
Blinder Passagier, 796
Blinder Schornstein, 249
Blinde Ruderschaft, 28
Blindes Loch, 68
Blindhölzer, 340
Blindlaufen, 625
Blinkfeuer, 290
Blitzableiter, 455
Block, 68
Blockade, 68
Blockauge, 53
Blockbacke, 143
Blockherd, 24
Blockkeepe, 689
Block mit Beschlag im Gehäuse, 397
Block mit Eisenbeschlag, 401
Block mit innenliegendem Beschlag, 397
Blockmodell, 70
Blockrollenbüchse, 657
Bluff, 71
Blusfeuer, 290
Bö, 770
Bock, 716, 929
Bockstange, 717
Boden, 86
Bodenbeplankung, 86
Bodenbeplattung, 86
Bodenbeschlag, 715
Bodengang, 87
Bodenlinie, 45
Bodenstück, 295
Bodenventil, 240, 694, 699
Bodenventilstöpsel, 228
Bodenwegerung, 134, 295
Bodenwrange, 295, 296
Bodenwrangenblech, 295
Bodmerei, 87, 645
Bodmereibrief, 87
Bodmereipfandrecht, 87
Bodmereiprämie, 491
Bogenstrück, 22, 97
Bohle, 142
Bohlwerksgelder, 589
Bohrassel, 338
Bohrer, 245
Bohrschutzkaste, 586
Bohrwurm, 490, 728
Böig, 770
Bojanker, 519
Boje, 107
Bojeanker, 519
Bojenlicht, 450
Bojereep, 108
Bojestropp, 108
Bokligger, 754

Bolzen, 80
Bonnet, 83
Boot, 72
Bootbeihilfer, 75
Bootdeck, 74
Bootfahren, 74
Bootführer, 182
Bootkleid, 73
Bootsbauer, 72
Bootsbaum, 649
Bootsbeihilfe, 72
Bootsbezug, 767
Bootsbrok, 55, 74, 339
Bootsdavit, 74
Bootsdolle, 831
Bootsfass, 96, 900
Bootsfisch, 675
Bootsgalgen, 76
Bootsgast, 544
Bootshaken, 74
Bootsklampe, 73
Bootskompass, 73
Bootskrabber, 75, 339
Bootslack, 761
Bootslanterne, 75
Boot Slipvorrichtung, 224
Bootsmann, 76
Bootsmannschaft, 75
Bootsmannshellegat, 76
Bootsmannsmaat, 77
Bootsmannspfeife, 77
Bootsmannstuhl, 76
Bootsmannsvorratskammer, 76
Bootsmanöver, 74
Bootsnagel, 75
Bootspflock, 75
Bootspfropfen, 75
Bootsrolle, 76
Bootsschraube, 75
Bootssonnensegel, 837
Bootsständer, 76
Bootsstation, 76
Bootstalje, 77
Bootstaljenläufer, 74
Bootstank, 107
Bootstau, 342
Bootsteurer, 182
Bootstropp, 76
Bootsübung, 74
Bootswinde, 77
Bootszelt, 72, 121
Boottopfarbe, 85
Bordempfangsschein, 500
Bordfunker, 628, 921
Bordkran, 205
Bordleiste, 896
Borduhr, 728
Bore, 85

Borgpardune, 604, 856
Borgtau, 605, 721
Borgwant, 606
Böschungswinkel, 18
Bourguignon, 95
Brack, 94
Brackwasser, 94
Brail, 88
Bramsegel, 845
Bramsegelkühlte, 845
Bramsegelsbrise, 845
Bramstänge, 845
Bramwanten, 845
Brandrolle, 282
Brandung, 809
Brandungsboot, 809
Brandungstag, 809
Brandungswellen, 96
Brassarm, 92
Brassbaum, 92
Brasschenkel, 92
Brasse, 92
Brassen, 92
Brassenwinde, 93
Bratspill, 634
Bratspillbeting, 129
Braver Westwing, 95
Breakdown Klausel, 95
Brechsee, 96
Brechwasser, 96
Brechwasserplatte, 487
Breidel, 856
Breil, 197
Breiltau, 199
Breitbeil, 99
Breite, 50, 436
Breite für Register, 641
Breitegang, 67
Breitenfehler, 436
Breitenkomplement, 163
Breitenkonstante, 436
Breitenparallel, 147, 568
Breitenskala, 436
Breitenunterschied, 220
Breiter Bug, 79
Breiterhaltung, 745
Breites Metazentrum, 856
Breite über Alles, 269
Breitfock, 297, 518
Breitwimpel, 99
Bremsketten, 239
Bremspferdestärke, 713
Bremsschild, 496
Brennen, 96
Brennkraftmaschine, 220
Brennöl, 314
Brennpunkt, 282
Brigg, 98

Briggschoner, 688
Briggsegel, 759
Brille, 462, 761, 839
Brillenlegel, 761
Brise, 97
Brok, 742
Brokmatte, 55
Bronze, 100
Brook, 813
Brooke, 906
Brookgeitau, 833
Brotwinner, 653
Brotwinnerspiere, 653
Bruch, 95
Brückenbau, 97
Brückenbuch, 208
Brückendeck, 97
Brückenhaus, 97
Brunnen, 63, 908
Brunnendeck, 909
Brustholz, 194
Brustleine, 96
Brutto Charter, 339
Bruttofracht, 339
Bruttoraumgehalt, 339
Brutto-Tonnengehalt, 339
Büchsenlaschung, 92
Bucht, 49, 61, 182, 259, 274, 633
Buchtsplissung, 379
Buckelig, 329
Bückling, 356, 422
Bug, 88, 363
Bug Achterleine, 364
Buganker, 88
Bugaufklotzung, 88
Bugaufklotzungplatte, 88
Bugband, 89
Bugbefestigung, 89
Bugbeplattung, 89
Bug Dwarstau, 88
Bügel, 859
Bügelhamen, 618
Bugfender, 88
Bugfigur, 280
Bugflagge, 403
Buggording, 107
Buggording Spann, 107
Bugklampe, 88
Bugleine, 89
Buglippe, 88
Bugmann, 89
Bugpforte, 89
Bugpumpe, 363
Bugriem, 89
Bugruder, 90
Bugsente, 356
Bugspriet, 90, 323

Bugspriet Beting, 90
Bugsprietbett, 91
Bugsprietbettung, 91
Bugsprietbügel, 691
Bugspriet Eselshaupt, 91
Bugsprietsurring, 323
Bugsprietwuhling, 323
Bugspring, 304
Bugstag, 91
Bug und Heck Vertauung, 300
Bug Vorleine, 303
Bugwelle, 91
Buhne, 339
Buk, 106
Bukbandsel, 106
Bukslapp, 107
Buleine, 89
Bulien, 89
Buliespriet, 89, 760
Bulin, 89
Bulinenlagel, 89
Bulkladung, 103
Bullauge, 105, 202
Bullentau, 84
Bulschleine, 35
Bumboot, 105
Bün, 287
Bund, 741
Bundgarn, 603
Bunker, 106
Bunkeranker, 106
Bunker Deckel, 106
Bunkergat, 157
Bunkerklausel, 106
Bunkern, 106
Bunkerschacht, 157
Bunkerschutte, 157
Bunkerschuttloch, 106
Bunkerstütze, 106
Bunkertür, 157
Bunnschiff, 908
Bürgerlicher Tag, 148
Bürgerliche Zeit, 148
Busch, 110
Buschfender, 656
Butluv, 105, 767
Buttleine, 350

Cantilever-Bauart System, 121
Cat Takelung, 132
Cat Yawl, 134
Cancelling Klausel, 119
Centrifugal Pumpe, 136
Cesser Klausel, 137
Charakteristik, 140

Charter, 141
Charterer, 141
Chartergeld, 141
Chartermässige Liegezeit, **224**
Charterpartei, 141
Chartersatz, 142
Chef-Ingenieur, 600
Chinesisches Luggersegel, 144
Cholera, 146
Chronometergang, 147
Chronometerjournal, 147
Chronometerlange, 471
Chronometer nach Sternzeit, 735
Clubflagge, 156
Cockpit, 160
Codleine, 161
Commodoreständer, 99
Contraruder, 176
Costonsches Kunstfeuer, 179
Cotleine, 161, 241
Courtage Klausel, 99
Cumulus, 190
Cunningham Patent Reff, 190
Cyclonartig Depression, 195
Cykloide Antrieb, 195
Cypresse, 195

Dach, 770
Dachsparrenholz, 187
Dallen, 581
Dammriff, 45
Dampferwege, 433
Dampffeuer-Löschleitung, 780
Dampfheizungsstränge, 823
Dampfklappe, 197
Dampfleine, 744
Dampfrudermaschine, 780
Dampfschiff, 780
Dampfspill, 780
Dampfsteuerapparat, 780
Dampgording, 764
Das Aussenliek, 6
Datumgrenze, 199
Dau, 217
Daubenholz, 778
Davitaugplatte, 200
Davitbrasse, 200
Davitgeie, 200
Davit Halslager, 200
Davit Klampe, 200
Davitkopf, 200
Davitlagerbock, 200
Davitspur, 200
Davitständer, 200, 201
Deck, 204
Deckanstrich, 208

Deckbalken, 204
Deckband, 96, 207
Deckbeplankung, 208
Deckbeplattung, 208
Deckbolzen, 204
Deckfenster, 743
Deckflansch, 205
Deckgang, 209
Deckglass, 207
Deckgüter, 205
Deckhandpumpe, 351
Deckhaus, 207
Deckhaus Sullplatte, 381
Deckhilfsmaschinen, 204
Deckholzschraube, 204
Deckklampe, 205
Deckkluse, 139, 208
Deckkran, 205
Deckladung, 205
Decklast, 205
Decklinie, 207
Deckloch, 694
Decklog, 818
Decknotizen, 208
Deckoffizier, 208
Decksbelag, 207
Deckschraube, 204
Decksenventar, 208
Decksfahrgast, 208
Deckshöhe, 207
Decksinventar, 208
Deckslangsspant, 208
Decksmann, 206
Decksnagel, 208
Deckspassagier, 208
Deckspringlinie, 716
Decksstringer, 209
Decksteward, 209
Deckstopper, 176
Deckstütze, 208
Decks Verschraubung, 208
Decktalje, 209
Decktaufe, 772
Deckträger, 206
Decktreppe, 207
Deckvorräte, 209
Deckworp, 209
Deckwrange, 207
Deficiency Klausel, 211
Deformation des Querschnittes 626
Deich, 39
Deichsel, 5
Deining, 811
Deklaieren, 262
Deklination, 210
Deklination Busole, 210
Deklinationskreis, 568

Deklinationsungleichheit, 210
Delivery Klausel, 212
Delta, 212
Deplacementschwerpunkt, 136
Deplacementskoeffizient, 69
Deplacementskurve, 225
Deplacementsskala, 225
Deplacementstonne, 225
Deplacements Völligkeitsgrad, 69
Depression, 221, 475, 866
Derivationswinkel, 243
Desertion, 216
Destillierapparat, 266
Detachierapparat, 224
Deutel, 860
Deviation, 216
Deviationsboje, 812
Deviationsklausel, 216
Deviationstabelle, 216
Diagonalband, 217
Diagonalbauart, 218
Diagonale Bespannung, 217
Diagonalgebauter Schott, 217
Diagonalknie, 196
Diagonalschiene, 217, 218, 648
Diagonalschienen, 218
Diagonalwegerung, 217
Diamantbake, 218
Diamantknoten, 218
Diamantplatte, 218
Dicht am Lande halten, 382
Dicht am Winde halten, 382
Dichtung, 325
Dichtungsfläche, 277
Dickes Wetter, 830
Diebstahl, 829
Die Kompassrose, 170
Die Nagelbank, 279
Dienstgeschwindigkeit, 708
Dienstpferdestärke, 708
Dienstunfähig, 223
Dienstzeit, 862
Dieselöl, 220
Diesig, 513
Differentialflaschenzug, 220, 589
Dingi, 221
Diopter, 736
Dioptrisches Feur, 221
Dippen, 221
Dippende Luggersegel, 222
Direkter Antrieb, 223
Dirkläufer, 126
Dispacheur, 4
Dispachierung, 28
Dispatchgeld, 224

Distanzfracht, 225
Divergierende Wellen, 227
Dochtwieke, 180
Dock, 45
Dockarbeiter, 228
Docken, 228
Dockgebühr, 58
Dockgeld, 228, 229
Dockhaupt, 229
Dockmeister, 229
Dockschlepper, 229
Docksignal, 229
Docksohle, 21
Docktelegraph, 228
Doldrums, 231
Dollbaum, 344
Dollbord, 400, 899
Dolle, 662, 831
Domperkette, 368
Donkey, 232
Donkeykessel, 232
Donkeymann, 232, 902
Donkeypumpe, 232
Doodshoft, 365
Doppel-Ausleger Kanu, 236
Doppelboden, 234, 900
Doppelbodendecke, 823
Doppelboot, 234
Doppeldiagonal Beplankung, 235
Doppelender, 234
Doppelenderkessel, 235
Doppelfarbige Laterne, 167
Doppelglas, 65
Doppelhaken, 153
Doppel Hankenkette, 234
Doppelhaut, 237
Doppelkanu, 234
Doppelknie, 777
Doppelmasten, 333
Doppelpaddel, 236
Doppelpart, 61
Doppelpeilung, 305
Doppelpoller, 234
Doppelpollern, 518
Doppelring, 330
Doppelruderig, 233
Doppelständer, 109
Doppelte Auflanger, 235
Doppelte Befestigung, 235
Doppelte eincheibige Talje, 343
Doppelte Marssegel, 236
Doppelter Fallreepsknoten, 236
Doppelter Hakenschlag, 234
Doppelter Hollander, 234
Doppelter Pfahlstich, 311

*Doppelter Schauermanns-
 knoten*, 236
Doppelter Schildknoten, 489
Doppelter Schotenstek, 236
Doppelte Schlinge, 36
Doppeltes Jollentau, 237
Doppelte Steertalje, 237
Doppelte Talje, 236
Doppelte Verbolzung, 235
Doppeltgekrummte Platte, 235
Doppelung, 237
Doppelungsplatte, 237
Doppelwertbestimmung, 248
Döpper, 655
Dorn, 243
Dorsch Schnur, 161
Dory, 232
Downton Pumpe, 238
Dragg Anker, 423
Dragger, 335
Drahtkneifer, 923
Drahtleine, 922
Drahtnetz, 922
Drahtseil, 922
Drahtseilstropp, 923
Drahtstopper, 923
Drahttauwerk, 922
Drainagebrunnen, 806
Draussen, 546, 547
Dreganker, 240, 335
Dreggen, 811
Dregtau, 811
Drehachse, 588
Drehdavit, 660
Drehen, 360
Drehfenster, 552
Drehfeuer, 646
Drehflügelschraube, 646
Drehfunksender, 646
Drehknüppel, 365, 924
Drehkreisdurchmesser, 281
Drehpunkt, 588
Drehreep, 837
Drehreepblock, 837
Drehreff, 657
Drehscheibe, 874
Drehungskreis, 874
Drehvorrichtung, 404
Drehwade, 617
Dreibeinmast, 863
Dreieckiger Wolkenraper, 744
Dreieckiges Bootsegel, 732
Dreieckiges Segel, 409
Dreifache Beplankung, 860
Dreifarbenlaterne, 862
Dreiinselschiff, 831
Dreikant Raatoppsegel, 769
Dreikanttoppsegel, 320, 409

Dreimastbark, 832
Dreimast Gaffelschoner, 828
Dreimastschoner, 43
Dreimasttoppsegelschoner, 486
Dreischeibiger Block, 860
Dreischeibiger Gien, 860
Dreitankschiff, 876
Drempel, 229
Drempel Tiefe, 214
Drer Flaggen Signal, 831
Drift, 242
Driftfahrt, 242
Driftströmung, 242, 243
Droogte Plate, 729
Druckfläche, 272
Drucklager, 833
Drucklager Nische, 834
Drucklagerwelle, 834
Drucklüfter, 267
Druckluftgetriebene Winde, 9
Drucklüftung, 808
Dshunke, 413
Dubel, 238, 860
Dublieren, 233
Ducht, 797, 834
Duchtenweger, 653
Duchtknie, 834
Dückdalben, 581
Dukdalben, 231
Dumpen, 588
Dünnes Tauwerk, 750
Dunnung, 832
Dunst, 362
Dunstig, 362
Dunung, 811
Durchbolzen, 390
Durcheinanderlaufende See, 173
Durchfahrt, 529
Durchfuhr, 854
Durchgangkonnossement, 833
Durchgehen, 167
Durchgenähte Naht, 518
Durchgesegelte Strecke, 201
Durchholen, 640
Durchkaien, 345
Durchlaufende Bodenwrange, 175
Durchlaufende Platte, 833
Durchlaufendes Aufbauschiff, 171
Durchlaufende Schweissung, 175
*Durchlaufendes Mittelkiel-
 schwein*, 833
Durchliegen, 777
*Durchmesser des Evolutions-
 kreises*, 818

Durchsacken, 673
Durchsackungsmoment, 673
Durchscheren, 644
Durchschlag, 243
Durchschleusen, 466
Durchschnittene Bodenwrange, 396
*Durchstehendes Konnosse-
 ment*, 833
Durchstöbern, 668
Durchsuchen, 668
Durchsuchung, 698
Durchsuchungsrecht, 652
Durchverbolzung, 833
Dusenschraube, 733
Düster, 334
Dwars Ab, 1, 2
Dwarsfeste, 97
Dwarsholz, 187
Dwarssalin, 187
Dwarsseegang, 51
Dwarsstütze, 97
Dwars Wegtreiben, 182
Dweil, 354
Dynamische Stabilität, 250

Ebbe, 274
Ebbelinie, 476
Ebbemarke, 476
Ebbetor, 251
Ebbstrom, 251
Ebbströmung, 251
Echolot, 252
Eckig Verformung, 18
Effective Pferdestärke, 252
Effektiver Slip, 866
Ehochteur, 344
Eiche, 543
Eichel, 3
Eierkauschen, 365
Eigentumszertifikat, 137
Eilgeld, 224
Eimerbagger, 100
Einabteilungschiff, 550
Einbaum, 248
Einbinden, 874
Einbootungsdeck, 259
Eindeckschiff, 738
Einer, 626
Einfacher Boden, 738
Einfacher Hakenschlag, 67
Einfacher Klappläufer, 738
Einfacher Marssegel, 739
Einfacher Schotenstek, 717
Einfacher Taljereepsknoten, 896
Einfache Sektionsdock, 91

Einfache Verbolzung, 739
Einfahrt, 393
Einfahrthafen, 601
Einfahrtsignal, 262
Einfall, 870
Einfuhrdeklaration, 263
Einführen, 262
Einfuhrkosten, 400
Einfuhrmanifest, 400
Einfuhrzoll, 390
Eingangsdeklaration, 263
Eingangsexpedient, 637
Eingangspforte, 324
Eingebogener Spant, 56
Eingeeist, 387
Eingeengt, 59
Eingefügter Fingerling, 287
Eingeschlossen, 537
Eingeschlossene Räume, 154
Eingestossen, 795
Eingezogenes Bauchstück, 653
Einhalten, 613
Einhängemasche, 275
Einheitsklasse, 551
Einheitsklasse Boot, 550
Einheitskopfniet, 566
Einholen, 360, 662
Einholer, 393
Einklarieren, 262
Einklarierung, 150
Einklarierungsattest, 150, 400
Einklarierungtag, 201
Einkommen, 262
Einlaufen, 617, 667
Einlaufendes Bugspriet, 669
Einlegedeckel, 735
Einlegen, 882
Einloten, 772
Einmalige Fahrt, 863
Einmausen, 524
Einnehmen, 72
Einplattiges Ruder, 136
Einpökeln, 190
Einriemen, 393
Einsalzer, 679
Einschakeln, 712
Einscheibiger Block, 738
Einschiffen, 723
Einschiffung, 259
Einschlag, 907
Einschlagen, 778
Einschleicher, 796
Einschreiben, 784
Einschutz, 907
Einskuller, 626
Einstrich, 706
Einstuf-Gleitboot, 739
Eintatige Gezeit, 227

Eintauchendes Keilstück, 907
Eintretende Flügelkante, 442
Einwanderungskommissär, 390
Einwärts gebogene Krulle, 64
Einwarts gebogenes Krullgallion, 279
Einziehbares Bugspriet, 669
Einziehender Lüfter, 238
Einziger Paddel, 739
Einzigruderig, 738
Eisbank, 561
Eisberg, 387
Eisblink, 68, 387
Eisbrecher, 387
Eisbruch, 204
Eisbunker, 389
Eisdoppelung, 389
Eisdraggen, 388
Eisemeldedienst, 389
Eisenbahnfähre, 853
Eisenbahnfahrschiff, 853
Eisenbetonschiff, 642
Eisenblech, 717
Eisenbügel, 230
Eisenholz, 400
Eisfeld, 389
Eisfrei, 389
Eisfuss, 389
Eisgang, 258
Eisgürtel, 389
Eishocker, 383
Eishügel, 383
Eiskante, 389
Eisklausel, 388
Eisklippe, 388
Eispatrouille, 389
Eisraum, 389
Eisschild, 717
Eisschollenberg, 294
Eisstopfung, 561
Eisstücke, 57
Eisverstärkung, 389, 860
Eiswachschiff, 389
Eiszunge, 718
Ekliptik, 252
Elektrische Ladewinde, 257
Elektrischer Antrieb, 254
Elektrischer Log, 255
Elektrischer Steuerapparat, 255
Elektrischer Telegraph, 255
Elektrisch-Hydraulische Ladewinde, 257
Elektrisch-Hydraulisch Steuervorrichtung, 257
Elektrode, 257
Elektrolyse, 257

Elektromagnetische Kupplung, 258
Elementarereignisse, 3
Elger, 286
Elliptisches Heck, 258
Empfänger, 173
Empfangskonnossement, 637
Employmentklausel, 260
Endglied, 260
Endkurs, 281
Endluftkasten, 261
Endschott, 260
Englischcher Fallreepsknoten, 235
Entgasung, 325
Entgasungsattest, 325
Entern, 72
Entfernen, 360
Entfernungsflagge, 2
Entfernungsmesser, 634
Entflammungspunkt, 290
Entgasungsleitung, 889
Entlang segeln, 633
Entlassungsschein, 137, 224
Entmagnetisierung, 212
Entmastet, 224
Entrattung, 214
Entrattungsschein, 214
Erbauung unter Aufsicht, 761
Erdanker, 521
Erdmagnetismus, 828
Erdmeridian, 828
Erdnähe, 577
Erdol, 579
Erdpol, 828
Ergreifungsrecht, 652
Erhöhte Pole, 258
Erhöhtes Quarter-Deck, 632
Erhöhtes Quarterdeckschiff, 632
Erhöhtes Vordeck, 632
Erhöhung, 653
Erleichtern, 454
Erleichterter Spant, 454
Erleichterungsloch, 454
Erreichen, 278
Erster Maschinen Assistent, 283
Erster Meridian, 606
Erster Vertikal, 606
Erste Wache, 284
Erwachsenes Rundholz, 341
Erzschiff, 554
Esche, 24
Eselshaupt, 496
Eselstütze, 123
Eskorte, 177
Etesischer Wing, 265

Etmal, 201, 529
Expansionsfalt, 268
Expansionsluke, 268
Expansionsschacht, 268
Expedient, 128
Export Bonifikation, 241
Exzenterhebel-Stopper, 448
Exzentrizitätsfehler, 251

Fabrikschiff, 272
Fabriksmässig gebautes Schiff, 272
Fächerplatte, 181, 272, 344
Fächerwinkel, 837
Faden, 276
Fahne, 165
Fahrbar, 531
Fahrboot, 278
Fähre, 278
Fahren, 668
Fahrgast, 571
Fahrgastschiff, 572
Fahrgeschwindigkeit, 708
Fährmann, 901
Fahrrinne, 140, 344
Fahrstabilität, 773
Fahrstreckenaktionsradius, 188
Fahrt, 364, 571, 699, 904
Fahrtbegrenzungsklausel, 852
Fahrtbekommen, 278
Fahrtfehler, 436
Fahrtflagge, 71
Fahrtlaterne, 532, 670
Fahrtprämien, 532
Fahrtrouten, 433
Fahrtstörungslampen, 542
Fahrttüchtigkeit, 531
Fahruntüchtigkeit, 882
Fahrwasser, 273
Fahrwasserkanal, 140
Fahrwassertonne, 140
Fahrzeug, 72, 183, 722, 890
Fall, 350, 632
Fallbalje, 350
Fallgien, 350
Fallreep, 323
Fallreepsknopf, 488
Fallreepsknoten, 218
Fallreepsleiter, 659
Fallreepspforte, 324
Fallreepstreppe, 2
Fallstek, 350
Fallstütze, 864
Fallwind, 252
Falscher Stich, 495
Falsches Metazentrum, 609

Falten, 613
Falz, 625
Fang der Bucht, 132
Fangkammer, 365, 602, 764
Fangleine, 75, 441
Fangtau, 875
Farbegang, 717
Farke, 373
Faser, 797, 831
Fasertauwerk, 278
Fassladung, 45
Fass Lange, 45
Fasstonne, 130, 419
Faul, 304
Fauler Boden, 304
Fauler Grund, 304
Fäulnissichere Farbe, 19
Fautfracht, 202
Feeder, 277
Fegel, 764
Fegsel, 764
Fehlerhafte Navigation, 390
Fehlfracht, 202
Fehlweisung, 169
Feiertag der Schiffsmannschaft, 726
Feiertag des Hafens, 600
Feinblech, 717
Feinschraube, 821
Feldeis, 279
Fellboot, 742
Felsenreihe, 444
Felsige Küste, 400
Fender, 278
Fener mit langen Blitzen, 470
Fernrohr, 530, 826
Fernsignal, 470
Fernsteuerapparat, 299
Fest, 775
Feste Back, 845
Feste Gaffel, 776
Fester Ballast, 578
Fester Block, 775
Fester Bugspriet, 776
Fester Bunker, 578
Fester Liegeplatz, 21
Fester Magnet, 578
Fester Magnetismus, 578
Fester Part, 776
Festes Feuer mit Blinker, 287
Festes Luggersegel, 776
Festes Seitenfenster, 288
Festes- und Blinkfeuer, 287
Feste Wegerung, 154
Festfeuer, 288
Festfeuer mit Blink-Gruppen, 288
Festfeuer mit Blitzen, 623

Festgestellter Tonnengehalt, 642
Festhalten, 375
Festhieven, 28
Festigkeitsdeck, 799
Festmachekette, 520
Festmacheleine, 521
Festmacheleinen, losmachen, 131
Festmachen, 316, 486, 519, 795
Festmachertonne, 108
Festmachetau, 276, 924
Festmachetonne, 520
Festmachetrosse, 521
Festsitzen, 7
Festtag, 375
Fest und Blitz Wechselfeuer, 10
Fest und Grupperblitz Wechselfeuer, 10
Fetthorn, 650
Feuerbuch, 455
Feuerfeste Farbe, 282
Feuergefährliche Ladung, 392
Feuergeld, 454
Feuerlöschboot, 282
Feuerlöschleitung, 750
Feuerlöschmanöver, 282
Feuerlöschpumpe, 283
Feuerlösch Station, 283
Feuerplatte, 317
Feuerrolle, 282
Feuerschiff, 455
Feuerschlauch, 282
Feuerschott, 282
Feuerübung, 282
Feuerung, 283
Fichtenholz, 540
Fid, 765
Fieren, 142, 475, 744, 888
Fieren und holen, 888
Filetnadel, 507
Fingerdock, 213
Fingerling, 585
Fingerling Überzug, 665
Fischangel, 285
Fischblock, 284
Fischblocksteert, 284
Fischdavit, 284
Fischen, 284
Fischerboot, 285
Fischerei, 285
Fischereifahrt, 286
Fischereifahrzeug, 285
Fischereigebiet, 285
Fischereihafen, 285
Fischereirecht, 651
Fischerknoten, 285

Fischerstek—Frachtzuschlag 984

Fischerstek, 285
Fischfang, 285
Fischgalgen, 858
Fischgrätenverband, 370
Fischgrund, 285
Fischhaken, 285
Fischkorb, 602
Fischleine, 286
Fischmehl, 286
Fischnetzgalgen, 858
Fischöl, 286
Fischplanke, 421
Fischraum, 285
Fischreep, 286, 287, 371
Fischreuse, 908
Fischschotten, 142
Fischspalter, 766
Fischstachel, 286
Fischtakel, 287
Fischtakel Hänger, 287
Fischteich, 286
Fischung, 421, 571
Fischungsplatte, 571
Fischverarbeitungsschiff, 272
Fischzug, 360
Fixe Vertauung, 521
Flabber, 290
Flach, 291
Flachbulb, 103
Flacheisen, 290
Flache Naht, 291
Flächenblitz, 718
Flächeneis, 717
Flacher Boden, 290
Flache Stelle, 729
Flachkiel, 291
Flachkopfniet, 566
Flachküste, 291
Flachs Segeltuch, 292
Flachsstoff, 292
Flachstauwerk, 292
Flachwegerung, 295
Flachwulstprofileisen, 103
Flackerlicht, 290
Flackernd Feuer, 293
Flackfeuer, 290
Flagge, 288
Flagge im Schau, 907
Flaggejolltau, 242
Flaggenfall, 736
Flaggengaffel, 518
Flaggengruss, 288
Flaggenkasten, 288
Flaggen Knebel, 289
Flaggenknopf, 499
Flaggenleine, 817
Flaggenpol, 289, 595, 773
Flaggenprüfung, 889

Flaggenrecht, 439
Flaggenschakel, 288
Flaggenstange, 289, 773
Flaggensteert, 817
Flaggenstock, 289, 598, 773
Flaggentopp, 595
Flaggentuch, 106
Flaggenwerkstatt, 288
Flaggenzoll, 289
Flaggenzuschlag, 288, 289
Flaggleineblock, 408
Flagg-Offizier, 288
Flaggstockhülsen, 289
Flämisches Auge, 292
Flammrohrkessel, 283
Flansch, 289
Flanschen, 290
Flaschenfindezettel, 86
Flaschenpost, 243
Flattern, 848
Flaue Brise, 453
Fleckhering, 422
Fledermaussegel, 48
Fleet, 292
Fleischständer, 868
Fleischtransportschiff, 503
Flensen, 292
Flick, 573
Fliegender Ballast, 721
Fliegender Bunker, 827
Fliegende Vermessung, 670
Fliegen lassen, 446
Flieger, 410
Flindersstange, 293
Flinkerndes Feuer, 688
Floss, 630
Flossboot, 450
Flossenkiel, 281
Flott, 6, 701, 900
Flottbringen, 540
Flottengeleit, 177
Flüchtiger Magnetismus, 827
Flügel, 886, 921
Flügelfläche, 67
Flügelpinne, 886
Flügelspill, 3
Flügeltank, 847
Flügelwelle, 660
Flugsand, 624
Fluidkompass, 460, 461
Flurplatte, 295
Flursente, 62, 296, 654
Flusshafen, 654
Flüssige Ladung, 460, 461
Flüssigkeitskompass, 460, 461
Flusslotse, 654
Flussmündung, 265
Flut, 295, 654, 835

Flutbare Länge, 295
Flutbarkeit, 578
Flutbecken, 910
Fluten, 295
Flutgebiet, 835
Fluthafen, 835
Flutkai, 835
Flutlinie, 372
Flutmarke, 372
Flutmesser, 836
Flutsignale, 836
Flutstrom, 295
Flutströmung, 295
Flutstundenlinie Karte, 179
Fluttor, 295
Flutwelle, 85, 835
Flutwelle Oscillation, 835
Fock, 302
Fockmast, 302
Focksegel, 302
Fock Stagsegel, 302
Focktakelage, 302
Focktakelung, 57
Forbes Logge, 299
Forcierter Zug, 300
Form Deplacement, 516
Formkoeffizienten, 459
Formplatte, 276
Formplatte Vorsteven, 276
Formschwerpunkt, 136
Formschwerpunktkurve, 191
Formstabilität, 303
Formwiderstand, 851
Fortlaufende See, 299
Fortschrittsgeschwindigkeit, 762
Föttinger Transformator, 385
Fracht, 113, 309
Frachtableilung, 310
Frachtanweisung, 310
Frachtaufschlag, 606
Frachtbrief, 64
Frachtführer, 129
Frachtgeld, 309
Frachtgeld Versicherung, 310
Frachtgut, 124
Frachtraten, 311
Frachtrechnung, 310
Frachtsatz, 311
Frachtschiff, 310
Fracht-Schiffsmakler, 464
Frachttonne, 311
Fracht- und Fahrgastschiff, 397
Frachtvertrag, 141
Frachtvorschuss, 5
Frachtzuschlag, 606

Franchise, 306
Franchise Klausel, 307
Franko Löschung, 432
Französische Bucht, 311
Französischer Knoten, 311
Frei an Bord, 308
Frei aus Schiff, 307
Freibord, 307
Freibord Besichtigung, 464
Freiborddeck, 307
Freibordhöhe, 307
Freibordmarke, 307
Freibordvertrag. 1930, 464
Freibord Zone, 307
Freideck, 905
Frei ein und aus, 308
Freie Klasse, 551
Freigebiet, 309
Freihafen, 309
Freistellungsschein, 311
Frei über Bord, 308
Frei von Beschädigung, 308
Frei von Beschleunigungsgebühr, 308
Frei von Havarie, 308
Frei von Prise und Besitz Klausel, 271
Frei von Reihenfolge, 308
Freiwache, 899
Freiwächter, 390
Freiwillige Aufstrandsetzung, 892
Freizeichnungklausel, 266
Friktionstopper, 691
Friktionswinde, 312
Frischbalje, 868
Frische Brise, 311
Frischwassererzeuger, 266
Frischwasserpumpe, 312
Front, 312
Frontbalken, 96
Frontschott, 95, 260
Froudesches Gesetz, 313
Fruchttransportschiff, 313
Frühlingspunkt, 889
Fuchjes, 833
Füchsel, 305
Füchsjes, 305
Führer, 743
Führungsblock, 442
Führungsleiste, 438
Füllen, 280
Füllholz, 281
Füllhölzer, 203, 281
Füllhölzer der Deckworp, 281
Fullplatte, 103
Fullspant, 281, 755
Füllstück, 250, 280, 281, 458

Füllung des Wasserlaufs, 457
Füllungen, 457
Füllungsbretter, 457
Fundamentbolzen, 375
Fundamentplatte, 304
Fünfmastbarke, 287
Funkapparateraum, 922
Funkbake, 627
Funkelfeuer, 623
Funkelfeuer mit Dunkelpausen, 623
Funkenspruhen, 688
Funkentelegraphisches Zeitsignal, 630
Funker, 922
Funkmessbake, 627
Funkmessempfänger, 627
Funkvavigation, 629
Funkoffizier, 629, 922
Funkortung, 629
Funkpeiler, 629
Funkpeilkompass, 628
Funkpeilstation, 628
Funkpeilung, 628
Funkraum, 629
Funksender, 627, 646
Funksicherheitszeugnis, 673
Funkstille, 630
Funkstelle, 630
Funktagebuch, 922
Funkverbot, 630
Funkverkehr, 628
Funkwache, 630
Furche, 317
Fuss, 368
Fussblock, 360, 750
Fussboden, 86
Fussbrett, 799
Fusslaschung, 368
Fusslatte, 151, 299, 799
Fussleiste, 799
Fussliek, 299
Fusspferd, 299
Fusspunkt, 527
Fussraa, 155
Fussstock, 799
Fusszapfen, 368
Füttern, 304
Futterpappe, 715

Gabel, 84
Gabelholz, 185
Gaffel, 319
Gaffelausholer, 363
Gaffel Drehreep, 575
Gaffel Gleiter, 320
Gaffelhänger, 575
Gaffel Niederholer, 275

Gaffelnock, 574
Gaffelschoner, 687
Gaffelschuh, 406, 842
Gaffelsegel, 320
Gaffeltoppsegelfall, 320
Gaffeltoppsegel Raa, 404
Gaffeltopsegelraa, 320
Gaffel Treisegel, 320
Galaboot, 42
Galerie, 10
Galgenstreber, 322
Galionsauslage, 272
Galionsbild, 280
Galionsfigur, 280
Galionsfullstuck, 272
Galionskrulle, 64
Galionsleiste, 363
Galionsreling, 363
Galiot, 322
Gallion, 50, 423
Gallionsbrett, 852
Gallionschegg, 77
Gallionsknie, 50, 323
Gallionsschegg, 428
Galvanische Wirkung, 322
Gang, 796, 801, 816
Gangplanke, 323
Gangspill, 123
Gangspillkopf, 246
Gangspill mit Handkurbelantrieb, 184
Gangspill mit Radübersetzung, 327
Gänsehals, 334
Garantie, 898
Garantiebrief, 447
Garantie-Maschinist, 341
Garn, 876, 929
Garnat, 324
Garneelenboot, 732
Garneelenkurre, 733
Garnierholz, 250
Garnierlatten, 760
Garniermatte, 127, 708
Garnierplanke, 134
Garnierung, 250
Garnreuse, 377
Garnstropp, 706
Gasboje, 325
Gasleitung, 889
Gasschweissung, 325
Gastflagge, 341
Gastrennungsapparat, 325
Gatchen, 270, 363
Gatnadel, 494
Gatnagel, 658
Gatt, 784
Gattlagel, 340, 508

Gaussische Fehler, 326
Gebauter Balken, 102
Gebauter Kiel, 734
Gebauter Mast, 481
Gebauter Ruderrahmen, 102
Gebauter Spant, 102
Gebaute Rundholz, 102
Gebläse, 71
Gebräuche der Hafen, 192
Gebräuchlicher Abzug, 192
Gebräuchlicher Nachlass, 192
Gedeckter Leichter, 208
Gedecktes Rettungsboot, 205
Geer, 886
Gefahr der Seeschiffahrt, 491
Gefahren der See, 578
Gefährliche Güter, 198
Gefährlicher Viertelkreis, 198
Gefährlicher Winkel, 198
Gefährliches Viertel, 198
Gefassung, 420
Geflanschte Kante, 289
Geflanschte Platte, 289
Geflanschtes Knieblech, 289
Gefrierladung, 313
Gefühlter Wind, 21
Gegenbrassen, 180
Gegen die Maserung, 186
Gegendruckturbine, 636
Gegendunung, 364
Gegenhalter, 231
Gegenkiel, 654, 845
Gegenkolben Motor, 553
Gegenkolben-Rudermaschine, 553
Gegen Land steuern, 775
Gegenpassat, 20
Gegenschein, 553
Gegenschraube, 175
Gegensee, 364
Gegenseitige Peilungen, 637
Gegenspantwinkel, 645
Gegenwind, 365, 526, 541
Gengenwinkel, 645
Gegisstes Besteck, 203
Gegisstes Schiffsort, 203
Gehäuse, 718
Gehrung, 514
Gei, 743
Geie, 344, 886
Geieläufer, 886
Geitau, 94, 152
Gejoggelte Plattung, 411
Gejoggeltes Spant, 411
Gekrümmter Kiel, 656
Gekühlte Ladung, 144
Geländerstütze, 632
Gelbes Fieber, 930

Geldraum, 801
Geleitklotz, 634
Geleitschiffe, 177
Geleitungsrecht, 651
Gelichtet, 26
Gemaltergang, 564
Gemeinpfandrecht, 168
Gemessene Seemeile, 502
Gemischte Gezeit, 514
Gemischte Ladung, 328
Gemischte Lüftung, 808
Gemischtes Maschinensystem, 872
Genannte Police, 529
Genau von Vorn, 363
General Distanz, 226
Generalpolice, 294
Generatorgasmaschine, 608
Genickstag, 124
Genieteter Flick, 356
Geographische Breite, 328
Geographische Länge, 471
Geographische Meile, 328
Geographisches Signal, 328
Geozentrisch, 328
Geozentrische Breite, 328
Gepäckmeister, 33
Gepäckraum, 33
Gepresste Platte, 224
Geprüfte Rettungsbootsleute, 449
Geradeaufsteigung, 650
Gerade Aufsteigung der Meridian, 650
Gerader Steven, 796
Geradeschaft-Niet, 797
Gerades Holz, 797
Gerades Ruder, 797
Gerät, 327
Gerät und Tackelage, 20
Gerbung, 823
Gerichtete Funkbake, 223
Gerichtskosten- und Arbeitslohnklausel, 806
Geripptes Blech, 647
Germallte Linie, 516
Geröllе, 722
Gesägtes Nutzholz, 478
Gesamt Distanz, 226
Gesamtzuladung, 203
Gesangsbuch, 604
Geschirr, 327
Geschlossene Klampe, 154
Geschlossener Heizraum, 154
Geschnittenes Spant, 684
Geschützbronze, 343
Geschützharpune, 343
Geschweisstes Knie, 908

Geschwindigkeit des Kielwassers, 896
Gesegelte Zeit, 254
Gesellschaftsraum, 612
Gesetzliche Zeit, 775
Gespickte Matte, 833
Gespitztes Tauende, 594
Gestade, 39
Gestirn Teleskop, 400
Gestreifte Tonne, 143
Gesundheitspass, 64
Geteertes Tauwerk, 824
Getreide, 335
Getreide Beschlag, 335
Getreideheber, 258
Getreide kubisher Inhalt, 335
Getreide Ladungsattest, 335
Getreideschott, 335
Getrockneter Fisch, 242
Getrockneter Stockfisch, 356
Gewachsener Spant, 341
Gewaltakte, 3
Gewaltige See, 605
Gewellte Platte, 179
Gewellter Schott, 179
Gewichtsbelastung, 203
Gewichtskurve, 192
Gewichtsschwerpunkt, 136
Gewitterbö, 22
Gewohnheitsrecht, 192
Gewöhnliche Beförderung, 192
Gewöhnlicher Knoten, 558
Gewöhnliche Schake, 168
Gewöhnliches Glied, 168
Gewölbe Bauart, 22
Geworbenes Gut, 679
Gezeit, 835
Gezeitenbrandung, 85
Gezeiten Diagramm, 489
Gezeitenkurve, 489
Gezeitenrechenmaschine, 836
Gezeitenstrom, 834
Gezeitentafeln, 836
Gezeitenunterschiede, 835
Gezeitenverfrühung, 606
Gezeiten Vorausberechnung, 835
Gezeitenwelle, 835, 836
Gezeitfeuer, 835
Gezeitpegel, 836
Gezeitverspätung, 429
Gezetzliche Decklinie, 778
Gezogene Platte, 876
Gien, 616
Giepen, 345, 408
Gieren, 365, 930
Gigboot, 329
Gigschlag, 329

Gillung, 180, 334, 656, 660, 811, 869
Gillungholz, 180
Gillungsbalken, 121
Gillungsheck, 180
Gillungspant, 121, 855
Gillungsplatte, 559, 869
Gissung, 202
Gitter, 336
Gitterladebaum, 436
Gittermast, 436
Glattbeplattung, 296
Glattdeck, 296
Glattdeckschiff, 296
Glätte, 750
Glätten, 272, 750
Glattenlaschung, 588
Glattes Lasch, 291
Gleichartige Ladung, 103
Gleicher Höhenkreis, 147
Gleichlastig, 266
Gleichmässig Unterbrochenes Schweissung, 139
Gleichschenkeliger Winkel, 263
Gleichzeitige Höhen, 738
Gleichzeitige Welle, 814
Gleichzeitigkeit, 814
Gleitbahn, 677, 811, 852
Gleitboot, 386
Gleitboot mit mehreren Stufen, 525
Gleitring, 343
Gleitschiene, 677, 852
Gleitschuh, 677
Gleitzeug, 343
Glippen, 377
Glockenboje, 55
Glockenförmiger Lüfter, 55
Glockengalgen, 54
Glockenpfeife, 55
Glockenstahl, 54
Glockentonne, 55
Glühkopfmotor, 707
Gnomonische Karte, 331
Gnomonische Projektion, 332
Goniometer-Peilanlage, 629
Göschstock, 404
Graben, 860
Gradbogen, 456
Gradegeteilte Parallele, 335
Graduiertes Meridiane, 335
Grad- und Strichtafel, 857
Grand Pavois a l'Anglaise, 242
Grant, 721
Grasleine, 163
Grastau, 163
Grating, 336

Grating Deckel, 336
Graupeln, 745
Greenheart, 337
Greenwicher Stundenwinkel 338
Greenwich Sternzeit, 338
Greep, 194
Greifbagger, 334
Greifeimer, 334
Greifen, 338
Greifer, 335
Greifleine, 450
Grenadierblock, 517
Grenze, 633
Griff, 351
Griffklampe, 186
Grobe Leinwand, 109
Grobe See, 660
Gross, 485
Grossboot, 470, 585
Grossbrassknie, 92
Grosse Flaggengala, 242
Grosssegel, 486
Grosse Haverei, 328
Grosser Spiegel, 391
Grosster Tiefgang, 269
Grosse Schake, 262
Grosses Glied, 262, 396, 473
Grosskreiskurs, 337
Grösste Länge, 269, 446
Grosstonnage, 339
Grummetstropp, 339
Grundangelfischerei, 337
Grunddünung, 340
Grundgeschirr, 340
Grundleine, 86
Grundleinen, 472
Grundliche Sturzsee, 337
Grundlog, 340
Grundmaterial, 570
Grundriss, 348
Grundschleppnetz, 857
Grundtakelung, 340
Grundtau, 340
Grüne Strahl, 337
Gruppenblinkfeuer, 340
Gruppen unterbrochenes Wechselfeuer, 11
Gruppenventilkasten, 226
Günstiger Wind, 273
Gurtplatte, 648
Gürtungsdeck, 799
Gürtungsplatte, 648
Gusstücke, 131
Gusstahldraht Tauwerk, 131
Gutschädigungsbrief, 447
Gütter, 333
Gut voll, 150, 333

Haager Regeln, 347
Hacke, 633, 741
Hackenblock, 732
Hackmatack, 347
Hafen, 354, 598
Hafenabgaben, 598
Hafenarbeiter, 228, 478
Hafenarzt, 365
Hafen Aufseher, 602
Hafenbarkasse, 355
Hafenbarre, 40
Hafenbecken, 45, 228
Hafenbehörde, 354, 599
Hafenbeschlagseising, 355
Hafendamm, 407, 517, 581
Hafendeck, 355
Hefenfeuer, 600
Hafenkapitän, 355
Hafenkommis, 900
Hafenmeistergebühren, 355
Hafenrisiko Police, 601
Hafenschlepper, 355
Hafensignale, 355
Hafensperre, 259
Hafenzeit, 893
Hahnenkamm, 182
Hahnepoot, 187
Hahnepot, 98
Hakenblock, 377
Hakenbolzen, 377
Hakenlaschung, 377, 816
Hakenschlag, 511
Hakentau, 377
Hakentauroller, 849
Halbdeck, 348, 621
Halbdodenwrange, 349
Halbe Back, 518
Halber Klusendeckel, 348
Halberschlag, 349
Halberschlag mit Balkenstek, 349
Halber Stek, 349
Halbe Stückpfortenklappe, 349
Halbfester Magnetismus, 804
Halbgedecktes Boot, 348
Halbklappboot, 596
Halbkreisartige Deviation, 707
Halbkreisförmiger Kompensationsmagnet, 707
Halbmast, 349
Halbmesser, 707
Halbmodell, 348
Halbrund Profleisen, 349
Halbscheibe, 349
Halbschweberuder, 706
Halbstock, 221
Halbstrick, 349
Halbtägige Gezeit, 707

Halbtidebecken, 349
Halbtidehafen, 349
Halbtür, 350
Halo, 350
Hals, 816, 832
Hals Aufholer, 817
Halsbolzen, 833
Halsgording, 833
Halsklampe, 143
Halslegel, 816
Halstalje, 817
Halteleine, 101, 521
Halten, 338, 375
Haltetau, 875
Haltwasser, 375
Hamen, 774
Hammer Keulensegel, 48
Handagelleine, 352
Handbetriebene Steuermaschine, 354
Handbieger, 60
Handelsblockade, 167
Handelsmarine, 506
Handelsschiff, 506
Handgeld, 5
Handhaben beim Schwoien, 827
Handhebel, 230
Handikap, 351
Handikapklasse, 351
Handlauf, 353
Handleine, 352, 450
Handleinefischerei, 352
Handleiste, 341, 353
Handlog, 352
Handlot, 351
Handlotleine, 352
Handnietung, 353
Handperd, 929
Handpumpe, 353
Handramme, 48
Handschliessvorrichtungstür, 327
Handschnurfischerei, 352
Handschweissung, 488
Handspake, 14, 354
Handtalje, 410, 650, 900
Handtau, 450
Hand über Hand, 353
Handuhr, 347
Hanf, 369
Hanfdrahttauwerk, 278
Hanftauwerk, 370
Hanfzopf, 339
Hängekette, 846
Hängeknie, 354
Hängekompass, 354
Hängematte, 350

Hängematte Hahnenpot, 350
Hängemattejolle, 350
Hängemattekörpertuch, 350
Hängematte Latte, 350
Hängemattensnitzel, 837
Hängemattensteert, 350
Hänger, 452, 576, 759, 929
Hängerband, 746
Hangerblock, 846
Hangerbügel, 846
Hängerkette, 929
Hangerketten, 755
Hängeruder, 880
Hängeseil, 846
Hängestropp, 746
Hängetalje, 846
Hängetür, 373
Harmattan, 356
Harmonische Komponent, 356
Harmonische Konstante, 356
Harmonische Pfeife, 144
Harpeus, 761
Harpuis, 761
Harpune, 356
Harpune Geschütz, 914
Harpuneleine, 911
Hart, 355
Hartbinsel, 833
Hartbrot, 723
Harter Wind, 515
Hartholz, 356
Harzprodukte, 530
Hasiges Wetter, 362
Haspe, 357
Haube, 82
Haufenwolke, 190
Haupt, 485
Hauptbilgeleitung, 63
Hauptbilgerohr, 62
Hauptdeck, 485
Haupt-Injektionsventil, 486
Hauptkluver, 556, 924
Hauptkompass, 497
Hauptkreis, 337
Hauptlenzrohr, 485
Hauptsegel, 925
Hauptsegeln, 588
Hauptspant, 511
Hausboot, 381
Hausflagge, 381
Havannadock, 361
Havarie, 28
Havarie Besichtigung, 197
Havariebond, 28
Havarie Klausel, 29
Havariekontrakt, 28
Havarie nach Seegebrauch, 192
Haverei, 28

Haverei Aufmachung, 29
Havereibeiträge, 328
Havarei Dispache, 28
Havereivergütung, 328
Hebe Augplatte, 452
Hebebaum, 365
Hebegeschwindigkeit, 374
Hebelarm, 651
Hebeleichter, 119
Hebemaschine, 403
Hebeprahm, 119
Hebeschraube, 403
Hebezeug, 330
Hebezylinder, 119
Heck, 7, 784, 854
Heckanker, 784, 798
Heckbalken, 854, 922
Heckbalkenknie, 745
Heckbalkenplanke, 854
Heckbalkenplatte, 854
Heckband, 189
Heckbord, 22, 818
Heckdavit, 786
Heck Dwarstau, 621
Heckkluse, 132
Heckknie, 621
Hecklicht, 786
Heckreling, 622, 818
Heckrelingslog, 818
Hecksegelkutter, 930
Hecksente, 356
Heckspant, 855
Heckspanten, 787
Heckspring, 7
Heckstütze, 734, 787
Hecktau, 787
Heckverizierung, 786
Heckverzierung, 299
Heckwelle, 788
Heckwerk, 854
Heilbuttschnur, 350
Heimatshafen, 601
Heiss, 374
Heissen, 374
Heizer, 790
Heizerlogis, 282
Heizöl, 314
Heizöltank, 314
Heizraum, 790
Heizröhrenkessel, 283
Heizrohrleitung, 365
Heliatisch, 369
Heling, 129
Heliozentrisch, 369
Hellinggerüst, 774
Hellingmast, 883
Helm, 369
Hennegat, 369

Herausliegen, 777
Herbst Aquinoctium, 28
Herd, 97
Heringsboot, 370
Herschütteln, 278
Herumbrassen, 92
Herunterreiten, 648
Herz, 365
Herzkauschen, 365
Herzstück, 764, 846
Heuernota, 5
Heultonne, 916
Hieven, 365
Hilfsbeischiff, 28
Hilfsbetriebenes Schiff, 28
Hilfskessel, 232
Hilfslohnvertrag, 679
Hilfsschiff, 28
Himmelsäquator, 264
Himmelskugel, 135
Himmelsmeridian, 135
Himmelspol, 135
Hinausfahren, 224
Hinfahren, 633
Hinten, 6
Hintenaus, 1
Hinterdeck, 6
Hintere Betingschlag, 66
Hintere Dwarsfeste, 6
Hintere Kielstütze, 741
Hintere Perpendikel, 6
Hintere Plankenenden, 6
Hinterer Seitenauflanger, 622
Hintere Seitenfeste, 622
Hinteres Klusenloch, 786
Hinteres Lot, 6
Hintergeschirr, 7
Hinterhangfahrzeug, 848
Hinterkluse, 132
Hinternetz, 47
Hinterpiek, 6
Hinterpiekband, 189, 787
Hinterradschiff, 788
Hinterschiff, 6
Hinterstefen Reitknie, 787
Hintersteven, 31, 786
Hinterstevenknie, 786
Hinterstevenschiene, 741
Hinterteil, 787
Ho, 8
Hochbehälter, 682
Hochgehender Seegang, 367
Hochgetakelter Kutter, 57
Hochheitsgewässer, 828
Hochsee-Schlepper, 545
Hochstauung, 922
Hochtakeltschuner, 58
Hochtakelung, 57

Hochtank, 211
Hoch und Trocken, 356, 371
Hochwasser, 372, 501
Hochwasserstand, 369
Hochwasservoraussage, 835
Hochwasserzeit, 839
Hochwertiger Stahl, 372
Hocke, 208
Hof, 350
Höhe, 11, 375
Höhe Bodenwrange, 210
Höhe der Gezeit, 368
Höhe im Meridian, 507
Höhe mit Zwischenzeit, 233
Höhenazimut, 11
Höhenkreis, 147, 889
Höhenparallaxe, 568
Höhen Parallel, 568
Höhenverschub, 568
Höhere Gewalt, 3
Höheres Hochwasser, 371
Hoher Spant, 210
Hoher Wasserballastkasten, 736
Hohe See, 371, 372
Hohe Spannung, 211
Hohle See, 376
Hohle Stütze, 376
Hohlfisch, 763
Hohlhering, 732
Hohlmast, 376
Hohlraumbildung, 134
Hohlrundholz, 376
Hol Aus, 473
Holen, 360
Holmeslicht, 376
Holzbekleidung, 566
Holzfender, 760
Holzlastladelinie, 838
Holznagel, 860
Holzpflock, 156
Holzpfropf, 592
Holztransportschiff, 838
Hoofdtau, 811
Hopperbagger, 378
Hörbares Signal, 758
Horizontale Intensitat Karte, 378
Horizontale Verschub, 378
Horizontalinduktion, 378
Hornbugspriet, 379
Hornklampe, 23
Hornschnecke, 914
Hosenboje, 97
Hospitalschiff, 380
Houari, 745
Houarisegel, 343, 745
Houari Takelung, 343

Hufeisenförmiger Rettungsring, 379
Hufeisensplissung, 379
Hulk, 382
Hulk mit Mastenkran, 716
Hülse, 110
Hummer, 60
Hummerkorb, 465
Hundepunt, 594
Hundewache, 510
Hundsfot, 53
Hürde, 208
Hurrikandeck, 384
Husing, 381
Hütchen, 85, 122
Hütte, 598
Hüttendeck, 598
Hütten Reling, 598
Hydraulische Nietpresse, 385
Hydraulischer Ladebaum, 384
Hydraulischer Transformator, 384, 385
Hydraulische Steuermaschine, 385
Hydrograph, 385, 386, 529
Hydrographie, 386, 529
Hydrographisches Amt, 386
Hydrographische Vermessung, 386
Hydromotor Antrieb, 407
Hygrometer, 386

Ihlen, 731
Im fahren, 880
Immer flott, 12
In Ballast, 36
In dem Wind, 399
In der Vierung, 551
In der Wendung liegen, 394
Indexfehler, 391
Indifferentes Gleichgewicht, 535
Indikatordiagramm, 392
Indizierte Pferdestärke, 392
Inducierter Magnetismus, 392
Induktionsmagnet, 827
In gutem Zustande, 775
Inholz, 306
Inholz und Fach, 306, 658
Inklination, 221, 482
Inklination Bussole, 222
Inklinationskarte, 221
Inklinationsnadel, 222
Innenkammer, 394
Innenkante der Spundung, 31
Innenkiel, 374, 393
Innensteven, 21

Innerer Klinsch, 394
Innerer Verderb, 393
Innerer Wassergang, 393
Inneres Leibholz, 393
Innere Spundungslinie, 393
In See stechen, 618
Inselschelf, 394
In Spantenstehen, 305
Instrumentalfehler, 391
Interkostal, 396
Interkostale Platte, 396
Internationale Messformel, 399
Internationales Freibordzertifikat, 399
Internationales Funkstille, 399
Internationales Signalbuch, 397
Internationales Wetterschlüssel, 397, 399
In Windstille, 52
Isherwood Bauart, 401
Isherwood Knieblechfreie Bauart, 93
Isobare, 402
Isobarische Karte, 402
Isodynamische Linie, 402
Isogonische Linie, 402
Isoklinenkarte, 402
Isoklinische, 402
Isolierlukendeckel, 592
Isolierung, 394
Isotherme, 402
Isthmus, 402

Jacht Schoner, 687
Jackstag, 56, 404
Jackstagreiter, 677
Jaegerpumpe, 800
Jageleine, 341
Jager, 37, 284, 556
Jägerbaum, 297
Jagermast, 410
Jägerstock, 297
Jakobsleiter, 405
Jalousie Tür, 745
Jigger, 410
Jiggermast, 410
Joch, 868
Jochleine, 931
Joggelpresse, 411
Joggelung, 411
Jollboot, 412
Jolle, 324, 360, 412, 915, 930
Jollenführer, 75, 458
Jollentau, 324, 915

Jolltau, 915
Judasohr, 423
Jumpen, 221
Jumpstag, 413
Jungfer, 202
Jungfernblock, 202
Jungfernfahrt, 484
Jungmann, 21, 554

Kabbelige See, 146
Kabbeln, 653
Kabbelung, 474, 653
Kabel, 114
Kabelar, 508
Kabelarkette, 508
Kabelarzeising, 537
Kabelgarn, 658
Kabelgarnknoten, 659
Kabellänge, 114, 711
Kabelschiff, 115
Kabelschlag Tauwerk, 115
Kabelstek, 362
Kabeltank, 116
Kabeltau, 114, 362
Kabeltausplissung, 492
Kabeltonne, 826
Kabeltrosse, 115
Kahn, 42
Kai, 623
Kaiabgaben, 228
Kaiarbeiter, 228, 581
Kaibesitzer, 914
Kaiempfangschein, 30, 229
Kaien, 20, 810, 863
Kaigebühren, 914
Kaigeld, 228, 623
Kaikosten, 228, 914
Kaikran, 229
Kaimeister, 914
Kaiplatz, 58
Kaischuppen, 854
Kajüte, 114
Kajütenfahrgast, 114
Kajütenjunge, 507
Kajütenluke, 83, 168
Kajütskompass, 354
Kajütspforte, 788
Kalfateisen, 118
Kalfater, 924
Kalfater Baumwolle, 118
Kalfaterfutte, 118
Kalfater Hammer, 118
Kalfaterkiste, 118
Kalfatern, 118
Kalfatfloss, 294
Kaltfront, 163
Kamel, 119

Kamm, 165, 184, 281, 904
Kammdrucklager, 379
Kammerschleuse, 466
Kammersteward, 53
Kammlager, 379
Kammzapfen, 833
Kanadier, 120
Kanalschiff, 186
Kanten, 862
Kantspant, 121
Kanu, 120
Kanu Heck, 121
Kanu mit Balancier Stange, 34
Kanu Yawl, 121
Kap, 122
Kaperbriefe, 447
Kapern, 124
Kaperschiff, 607
Kapitän, 497
Kappe, 377
Kappeil, 358
Kappnaht, 517, 661
Karabiner, 750
Kardanring, 330
Kardeel, 797
Kardinalpunkt, 124
Kargadeur, 807
Kartenhaus, 142
Kartennull, 141
Kartenzimmer, 142
Kartograph, 529
Kasko Police, 383
Kaskoversicherer, 383
Kastanienholz, 143
Kastenbalken, 91
Kastenförmiges Kiel, 248
Kastenkiel, 248
Kastenkeilschwein, 92
Kastenträger, 91
Katabatisch Wind, 416
Kattanker, 30
Kattblock, 132
Kattblocksteert, 131
Kattdavit, 132
Kattglied, 133
Katthaken, 132
Kattläufer, 132
Kattschakel, 133, 366
Kattschenkel, 132
Kattspor, 647
Katt Takel, 133
Katzenbuckel, 99
Katzenkopf, 540
Katzenpfote, 133
Katzenrücken, 99
Kaufbrief, 64
Kauffahrteischiff, 506

Kauri—Kleine Bucht

Kauri, 417
Kausche, 830
Kavielnagelring, 763
Kavitation, 134
Kehle, 832
Kehlnaht, 280
Kehlschweissung, 280
Kehlung, 182
Kehrling, 764
Keil, 420
Keillaschung, 420
Kelp, 420
Kenter-Bauart Schakel, 420
Kentergied, 573
Kentermoment, 883
Kentern, 123
Kenterpunkt, 883
Kenterwinkel, 883
Kerbe, 541, 689
Kernriss, 713
Kessel, 117
Kessellager, 672
Kesselluke, 79
Kesselmantel, 78
Kesselraum, 79
Kesselschacht, 884
Kesselstopper, 78
Kesselstuhl, 79
Kesselumbau, 78
Kesselwirkungsgrad, 78
Ketchu, 193
Ketsch, 420
Ketscher, 774
Ketshaken, 350
Kette, 897
Ketten Aufzug, 139
Kettenarm, 519
Kettenende, 711
Kettengarn, 898
Kettenhaken, 139
Kettenklau, 382
Kettenkneifer, 116
Kettenlänge, 731
Kettenmitnehmer, 918
Kettennietung, 139
Kettennuss, 915
Kettenscheibe, 918
Kettenschenkel, 151
Kettenschlinge, 139
Kettenschweissung, 139
Kettenständer, 115
Kettenstopper, 231
Kettentrommel, 918
Kettenumfang, 139
Ketten Wirbel, 813
Keuchen, 567
Kiefer, 541
Kiefernholz, 281, 541

Kieholtalje, 124
Kiel, 418
Kielablauf, 739
Kielbank, 338
Kielbruch, 99
Kielgang, 324
Kielgang Beplankung, 324
Kielhacke, 741
Kielhöhe, 419
Kielholen, 124
Kielklotz, 418
Kiellinie, 419
Kielpalle, 418
Kielraum, 61
Kielraumwasser, 63
Kielschiene, 419, 734
Kielschwein, 419
Kielschweinsohle, 648
Kielstapel, 418
Kieltunnel, 586
Kielwasser, 203, 895
Kielwegerungsgang, 457
Kielwegerungsplanke, 457
Kieselgrund, 575
Kieselstein, 575
Killen, 729
Kimm, 20, 61
Kimmbeplattung, 63
Kimmgang, 63
Kimmkiel, 62
Kimmkielschwein, 62
Kimmklotz, 62
Kimmplanken, 63
Kimmreling, 63
Kimmrelring, 419
Kimmrundung, 874
Kimmsaugung, 63
Kimmsente, 62, 654
Kimmschlitten, 503
Kimmschwert, 62
Kimmschwertyacht, 62
Kimmstapel, 62
Kimmstringer, 62
Kimmstütze, 63, 93
Kimmstutzplatte, 921
Kimmtiefe, 221
Kimmweger, 62, 144
Kimmwegerung, 62
Kimmwegerungsgang, 830
Kimmwölbung, 874
Kimpalle, 503
Kink, 422
Kinnbacksblock, 750
Kinthorn, 915
Kipp, 840
Kippbrücke, 774
Kippmoment, 883
Kissen, 80, 563

Kistluke, 123, 694
Kirksche Widerstandsformel, 422
Kittspritze, 618
Klameieisen, 362
Klameien, 379, 640
Klamei Hammer, 640
Klammenhaken, 120
Klammer, 230
Klammerbolzen, 230, 246
Klampe, 151, 357
Klappbareanker, 299
Klappbare Bootsklampe, 722
Klappbarer Mast, 163
Klappbolzen, 841
Klappboot, 163
Klappdavit, 163, 627
Klappenprahm, 378
Klapplaüfer, 109, 622, 669
Klappschute, 378
Klapptür, 373
Klar, 150
Klarbehälter, 709
Klar Bleiben, 775
Klare Ketten, 552
Klaren, 150
Klare Tage, 151
Klar fahren, 150
Klarieren, 262
Klarierung, 150, 263
Klarierung Marke, 151
Klarierungsattest, 150
Klarierungspapier, 150
Klarmachen, 150, 723
Klar passieren, 150
Klar scheren, 880
Klar stehen, 775
Klar steuern, 782
Klar Zum Wenden, 636
Klasse, 149
Klasse-Erneuerung, 578
Klassenschein, 635
Klassenzertifikat, 149
Klassifikation, 149
Klassifikation Klausel, 149
Klassifikations Zertifikat, 149
Klaue, 406, 832, 859
Klaufall, 833
Klaufallbolzen, 832
Klaulagel, 477
Klauohr, 832
Klaurack, 407
Klausurring, 75
Kleid, 155
Kleiderkiste, 748
Kleidkeule, 708
Kleidungsgut, 708
Kleine Bucht, 182, 184

Kleine Fahrt, 377
Kleine Flaggengala, 242
Kleine Haverei, 579
Kleine Langleinen, 749
Kleine Küstenfahrt, 749
Kleiner Bootsanker, 421
Kleiner Diebstahl, 581
Kleiner Spiegel, 378
Kleine Winde, 232
Klemmschraube, 149
Klimmstag, 91
Klinkbolzen, 152
Klinken, 152
Klinkerbauart, 152
Klinker Beplankung, 152
Klinkerplattung, 153
Klinkring, 152
Klinkscheibe, 658
Klippe, 152
Klipper, 153
Klipperschiff, 153
Klippersteven, 153
Klopfkeule, 486
Klosettank, 682
Klosettpumpe, 682
Klotz, 467
Klubflagge, 607
Klubholen, 156
Klumpblock, 156
Klusebacke, 361
Klusedeckel, 361
Kluseloch, 361
Klusenback, 530
Klusenband, 238, 361
Klusendeckel, 361
Klusenpforte, 308
Klusenpfropfen, 68
Klusenpolster, 361
Klusenrohr, 362
Klusenstopper, 176
Klusholz, 361
Klussack, 403
Kluver, 408
Kluver Aufholer, 410
Kluverbackstag, 409
Kluver Backstag Ausleger, 767
Kluverbaum, 408
Kluverbaumnetz, 409
Kluverdomper, 495
Kluverfock, 408
Kluverholz, 364
Kluverkopfstück, 409
Kluver Leiter, 410
Kluver Toppsegel, 410
Knagge, 753, 791
Knapper Wind, 685
Knappe See, 731

Knäuel, 354
Knebel, 841, 924
Knebelbolzen, 841
Knebelstropp, 53
Kneifen, 594
Kneifstek, 658
Kneifstopper, 172
Knick, 424, 537, 832
Knickgang, 424
Knicklinie, 424
Knickschott, 637
Knickspantboot, 887
Knie, 423
Knieblech, 93, 423
Knieholz, 185, 838
Knocke, 232
Knoten, 56, 424
Knoten Bahn, 457
Knotenpunkt, 538
Knüppeltau, 622
Knüttel, 423, 534, 791
Kochhaus, 322
Köder, 33
Koerzitivkraft, 645
Koffer, 866
Kofferdamm, 161
Kofferdeck, 867
Kofferdeckschiff, 867
Kofferkajüte, 867
Kohlenbunkerloch, 106
Kohle Electrode, 124
Kohlenfeuerung, 157
Kohlenhulk, 157
Kohlenloch, 106
Kohlenluke, 157
Kohlenpforte, 157
Kohlenschacht, 157
Kohlenschiff, 164
Kohlenschutte, 157
Kohlenschuttedeckel, 157
Kohlenstürze, 157
Kohlentrimmer, 862
Kohlenwinde, 157
Kohlenwippe, 157
Kohlenzieher, 862
Koje, 58, 106
Kolbenmaschine, 637
Kolbenmaschine mit Abdampfturbine, 872
Kollimationsachse, 457
Kollimationsfehler, 164
Kollision, 164
Kollision pro rata Klausel, 165
Kollision's Exzedentenklausel, 267
Kollisionsklausel, 165
Kollisionsmatte, 165

Kollisionsschott, 165
Koluren, 165
Kombiniertes Spantensystem, 167
Kombuse, 322
Kommandobrücke, 531
Kommodor, 167
Kompass, 491
Kompass Adjustierer, 168
Kompassalhidadenkreis, 29
Kompassäule, 170
Kompassbezug, 65, 169
Kompassbüchse, 168
Kompassdeflektor, 212
Kompassdiopter, 29
Kompassfehler, 169
Kompassgehäuse, 168, 169
Kompasshaus, 65
Kompasshause, 65
Kompasshütchen, 85
Kompasskappe, 65
Kompasskessel, 168
Kompasskreis, 778
Kompasskurs, 169
Kompassnadel, 887
Kompasspeilung, 168
Kompasspinne, 170
Kompassprüfer, 168
Kompassregulierung, 168
Kompassrose, 169
Kompass Signal, 182
Kompassständer, 65
Kompasstrich, 594
Kompass Verbesserungen, 169
Kompensationsmagnet, 171
Kompensierendes Kompasshaus, 171
Kompensierter Kompass, 171
Kompensierung des Kompass, 168
Kompositbau, 171
Kondemnation, 172
Kondenstopf, 780
Konferenz, 173
Konische Kappe, 273
Konjunktion, 173
Konnossement, 64
Konserven, 120
Konsole, 766
Konstant Steigung, 881
Konstrucktiver Totalverlust, 174
Konstruktionslänge, 446
Konstruktionsriss, 458
Konstruktionstiefe, 516
Konstruktionswasserlinien, 901
Konsul, 174

Konsular Warenrechnung, 174
Konsulatsfaktur, 174
Konterbande, 175
Kontinental Schelff, 174
Kontorflagge, 381
Kontroller, 176
Kontrolle Stelle, 176
Kontrapropeller, 175
Konvoy, 177
Konvoyierung, 177
Kopf, 363
Kopfabschneider, 363
Kopfbrett, 363
Kopf der Ruderpinne, 836
Kopflagel, 363
Kopflaschung, 716
Kopflastig, 112, 862
Kopftau, 364
Kopfzapfen, 364
Koppelkurs segeln, 856
Koppeltafel, 857
Kopseisen, 123
Korb, 45
Korkfarbe, 178
Korkfender, 178
Korkjacke, 451
Korkschwimmer, 222
Korkstein, 744
Korn, 335
Korn kubisher Inhalt, 335
Kornschott, 335
Korona, 178
Korrespondentreeder, 487, 727
Korrespondierende Geschwindigkeiten, 178
Korrespondierende Höhen, 263
Korrosion, 179
Kort Düse, 426
Kosten, 113
Kosten und Fracht, 179
Kosten Versicherung und Fracht, 179
Kourtage, 99
Kove, 182
Koveinnagel, 817
Krabbenfischer, 183
Kraftbetriebene Steuervorrichtung, 603
Krafttür, 704
Kragen, 160
Krähennest, 188
Krampe, 777
Kranbalken, 132
Kranbalksweise, 551
Krangebühren, 183
Krangeld, 183
Krangung, 367
Krangungsfehler, 368

Krangungsmagnet, 368
Krangungspendel, 153
Krangungstank, 368
Krangungsversuch, 391
Krangungswinkel, 18
Krankenraum, 380
Kräuselung, 653
Kravsack, 226
Krawel Beplankung, 130
Krebsreuse, 465
Kreisbogen, 456
Kreiselkompass, 345
Kreisfläche, 223
Kreisflächenverhaltnis des Schraubendisks, 223
Kreisförmige Ablaufbahn, 119
Kreisfunkbake, 148
Kreuzbandsel, 626
Kreuzbindsel, 187
Kreuzen, 52, 185, 856
Kreuzende Dünung, 187
Kreuzerheck, 188
Kreuzeryacht, 189
Kreuzklampe, 420
Kreuzknoten, 129, 188
Kreuzkopf, 665, 931
Kreuzmast, 410, 514
Kreuzpeilung, 185
Kreuzpoller, 188
Kreuzsee, 187
Kreuzsegel, 186
Kreuzsorrung, 626
Kreuz-Stagsegel, 513
Kreuztonne, 413
Kreuztorn, 626
Kreuzzeitige Ketten, 186
Kriegsblockade, 511
Kriegsgefahr, 898
Kriegskonterbande, 897
Kriegsmarine, 532
Kriegsrisiko, 898
Krimpender Wind, 31
Krinoline, 185
Kritische Geschwindigkeit, 185
Krücke, 189
Krulle, 692
Krummholz, 171
Krümmung, 753, 898
Kruppelwinde, 183
Kubisher Inhalt, 189
Kugelbakentonne, 331
Kugelblitz, 37
Kugelboje, 763
Kugellaterne, 331
Kugeltonne, 763
Kuhl, 895
Kühlgut, 144

Kühlmaschine, 641
Kühlraum, 394
Kühlraumladung, 640
Kühlschrank, 387
Kuhlte, 133
Kulmination, 189, 854
Künstlicher Hafen, 24
Künstlicher Zug, 300
Kunstluftung, 504
Kuntze, 624
Kupferbodig, 177
Kuperfest, 177
Kupferfestverbolzung, 177
Kupferhaut, 177, 715
Kupferhautnagel, 715
Kuppe, 424
Kuppel, 231
Kurbelwelle, 184
Kurre, 857
Kurrenfischerei, 859
Kurs, 181
Kursbeständigkeit, 783
Kursfeuer, 634
Kurskarte, 852
Kursschreiber, 181
Kurve der Breiten Metazentren, 192
Kurve der flutbaren Länge, 295
Kurve der Hebelarme, 192
Kurve der Schwimmflächen Schwerpunkte, 191
Kurz anhalten, 753
Kurzarmige Bodenwrange, 731
Kurzbalken, 348
Kurzbeständigkeit, 773
Kurze Bodenwrange, 732
Kurze Kinke, 537
Kurzer Stag, 731
Kurzer Stringerwinkel, 800
Kurzer Ton, 731
Kurzes Back, 731
Kurzes Brückenhaus, 731
Kurzes Schwert, 196
Kurze See, 731
Kurzgliedrige Kette, 154
Kurzhieven, 366
Kurzsplissung, 731
Küste, 158
Küstenfahrer, 159
Küstenfahrt, 159
Küstenfeuer, 159
Küstenfischerei, 394
Küstenfunkstelle, 159
Küstenlotse, 160
Küstenmeer, 828

Küstennebel, 695
Küstenrettungsboot, 158
Küstensaum, 836
Küstensignal, 159
Kustenstrom, 158
Küstentelegraphsignal, 706
Küstenwächter, 159
Küstenzollwachter, 160
Kutscherpeitschen, 156
Kutter, 193, 194
Kutterschlag, 194
Kutterzeug, 193

Labiles Gleichewicht, 882
Lachsfänger, 678
Lackhut, 759
Ladebaum, 214
Ladebaumgeie, 215
Ladebaumkonsole, 215
Ladebaum Löschringband, 215
Ladebaumpfosten, 682
Ladebaumstuhl, 215
Ladebereitschaftnotiz, 541
Ladeblock, 125, 215
Ladebuch, 125
Ladefähigkeit, 108, 534
Ladefrist, 464
Ladegeschirr, 126
Ladehafen, 601
Ladehaken, 126
Ladejolle, 126
Ladekühlraum, 394
Ladekühlraumschiff, 641
Ladeläufer, 126
Ladelinie Besichtigung, 464
Ladelinie-Kreis, 464
Ladeluke, 126
Lademast Saling, 557
Laden, 202
Ladeorder, 725
Ladepforte, 126, 127
Ladeplatz, 463
Laderad, 330
Laderaum, 374
Laderaume, 128
Ladereste, 545
Ladeschlitten, 125, 1.'8. 741
Ladeseil, 128
Ladestag, 768
Ladestelle, 463
Ladevermögen, 203
Ladewasserlinie, 464, 465
Ladewinde, 128
Ladezeit, 461, 464
Ladung, 124
Ladung Assekuradeur, 128
Ladungnetz, 127

Ladungsanschreiber, 820
Ladungsfähigkeit, 534
Ladungsmanifest, 488
Ladungsmatte, 127
Ladungspfandrecht, 126
Ladungsplan, 127
Ladungstragfähigkeit, 534
Ladungsverzeichnis, 99
Lage, 668
Lagel, 185, 354, 508
Lageraufseher, 793
Lagerausholer, 299
Lagergeld, 792
Lagerhälter, 337
Lagermiete, 792
Lagerpfandschein, 230
Lagune, 429
Laich, 761
Lamm, 917
Lampenkammer, 431
Lampenputzer, 431
Lampenraum, 431
Landfest, 730
Landgang, 323
Landgangtur, 343
Landkennung, 432
Landkennungs Feuer, 486
Landmarke, 433
Landpoller, 79, 142
Landspitze, 594
Landungsbrief, 604
Landungsbrücke, 433
Landungsgebühren, 433
Landungskosten, 433
Landungsplatz, 914
Landungssteg, 100
Landwade, 730
Landwind, 432
Landzunge, 363, 764
Langarmiage Bodenwrange, 470
Länge, 296, 471
Lange Brücke Schiff, 470
Lange Dünung, 472
Lange Fahrt, 302
Langefahrt Schiff, 302
Lange metazentrische Höhe, 471
Längen-Metazentrum, 471
Längenriss, 715
Langenskala, 471
Län 'enunterschied, 220
Lange Riemen, 811
Langer Ton, 608
Lange Ruder, 811
Langes Back, 470
Langes Brückenhaus, 470
Länge über alles, 269, 446

Länge zwischen den Loten, 446
Langleinen, 337, 472
Langleinenfischerei, 337
Längsablauf, 260
Längsbalken, 300
Lang Seil, 433
Längs der Küste segeln, 880
Längsnaht, 432, 697
Längsnummer, 472
Längsriegel, 357
Längsriss, 717
Längssalings, 860
Langsschiff Formschwerpunktkurve, 191
Längsschiffs, 300
Langsschiffsmagnete, 300
Längsschiffsplan, 391
Längsschnitt, 391
Längsseit anlegen, 631
Langsspantenbauart, 401
Längssplissung, 473
Längsträger des Radkastenbalkons, 766
Langsulle, 734
Lappen, 573
Lappfalbe, 67
Lappung, 138, 237
Larche, 434
Lasch, 686
Laschblech, 111
Laschen, 434, 686
Laschung, 434, 686
Lasseisen, 552
Lass Laufen, 904
Last, 435
Lastboot, 382
Lastbrechen, 95
Lastenmasstab, 20ə
Lasthaken, 126
Lasthebemagnet, 452
Lastseil, 126, 128
Lasttone, 841
Lateinischeraa, 435
Lateinische Takelung, 435
Lateinraa, 435
Lateinsegel, 435
Lateralplan, 435
Lateralschwerpunkt, 136
Lateralwiderstand, 436
Laternenbrett, 735
Laternenkasten, 735
Laternenschirm, 735
Lattengitter, 336
Lattenpegel, 836
Laubholz, 356
Laufangelleine, 865, 915
Laufbrucke, 297, 300

Laufende Gaffel, 669
Laufende Police, 294
Laufender Block, 669
Laufender Part, 670
Laufender Pfahlstek, 669
Laufender Teil, 443
Laufer, 274, 746
Laufendes Gut, 670
Laufende Tage, 669
Laufknoten, 539, 747
Lauflager, 592, 768
Laufplanke, 100, 323
Laufstag, 91, 648
Laufwelle, 396
Lavieren, 52, 592, 816
Lazarett, 441
Lazarettschiff, 380
"L" Dock, 547
Lebender Ballast, 721
Lebendiges Werk, 624
Lebendig halten, 406
Lebertran, 161
Lebhafte brise, 759
Leckage, 444
Lecksegel, 165
Lecktuch, 165
Leckverlust, 444
Ledderung, 23
Ledderungsnetz, 853
Lee, 444
Leeanker, 444
Leebord, 444
Leegierigkeit, 744
Leerer Tiefgang, 454
Leere Verdrängung, 453
Leerlinie, 455
Leesegel, 802
Leesegelfallstich, 802
Leesegelraa, 802
Leesegelspieren, 802
Leesegel Spierentalje, 84
Leeseite, 445
Leewärts, 9, 445, 880
Leewärts vorübersegeln, 905
Leeweg, 445
Legel, 185, 498
Legen, 98, 440
Legerwall, 445
Leguan, 613
Lehnbrett, 30
Leibholz, 556, 903
Leicht bewegte See, 746
Leichte Brise, 328
Leichte Nahtschweissung, 453
Leichter, 42, 454
Leichterführer, 42, 454
Leichtergeld, 454
Leichterkosten, 454

Leichterlohn, 454
Leichterrisiko, 654
Leichterschiffer, 42, 454
Leichtertransport, 454
Leichterung, 454
Leichter Wind, 453
Leichter Zug, 453
Leichtes Dunstgewölk, 692
Leichtes Lüftchen, 133
Leichtfahrzeugklausel, 183
Leichtgetreide, 455
Leichtkehlnaht, 454
Leichtkehlschweissung, 454
Leichtmatrose, 554
Leichtser Deplacement, 453
Leichtwasserlinie, 455
Leine, 457
Leinenrolle, 458
Leinentauwerk, 457
Leinen-Wurfgewehre, 732
Leiste, 48, 50
Leitbake, 633
Leitblock, 215, 360, 442, 537
Leitdamm, 407, 581
Leitender Ingenieur, 143
Leitender Maschinist, 143
Leiter, 379, 779
Leiterring, 856
Leitfeuer, 634
Leitflächenruder, 176
Leitgarn, 442
Leitkabel, 442
Leitklampe, 115
Leitlinie, 442
Leitmarke, 442
Leitrolle, 657
Leittau, 488
Leitung, 9
Leitwagen, 207
Leitwehr, 442
Lenktau, 849
Lenssen, 668, 692
Lenzen, 307, 692
Lenzleitung, 63
Lenz Pumpe, 63
Lenzpumpen, 307
Lenz- und Ballasteinrichtungsplan, 614
Leuchtfeuerabgaben, 454
Leuchtfeuerboje, 453
Leuchtfeuergeld, 454
Leuchtrakete, 737
Leuchttonne, 453
Leuchtturm, 88, 455
Leuchtturm-Tender, 455
Leuwagen, 302, 811
Lichtbogen Schweissung, 254
Lichten, 365, 907

Lichterschiff, 689
Lichtgebühren, 454
Lieferschein, 212
Lieferungsauftrag, 212
Lieferungshafen, 600
Liegegeld, 213
Liegen, 363, 648
Liegeplatz, 58, 440
Liegeplatzsignal, 59
Lieger, 732
Liegetage, 440
Liegewinkel, 18
Liegezeit, 440
Liek, 81
Liekgarn, 659
Lieknadel, 81
Lien Klausel, 448
Lige, 444
Limbus, 456
Limmerkette, 457
Linie-Konnossement, 458
Linienfrachtschiff, 127
Linien gleicher Hochwasserzeiten, 179
Linienriss, 458
Linienschiff, 457
Linksgängiger Propeller, 445
Linksgehender Propeller, 445
Linksgeschlagenes Tauwerk, 445
Lippe, 460, 461
Lippklampe, 520
Lissleine, 419, 435
Lissung, 404, 429
Litze, 797
Lloyd's Agent, 462
Lloyd's Police, 463
Lloyd's Signalstation, 463
Lochfrass, 588
Lochnaht, 592
Lochraumer, 243
Lodding, 668
Löffelartiger Bug, 767
Löffelbagger, 222
Löffelbug, 767
Löffelruder, 767
Löffeltoder, 767
Log, 467
Logbrett, 468
Logbuch, 727
Logbucheintragung, 468
Loggebreite, 436
Loggelänge, 471
Loggen, 366
Logglas, 468
Logis, 184
Logisjunge, 507
Logleine, 469

Logrechnung, 202
Log Regulator, 468
Logrolle, 469
Logscheit, 468
Logschraube, 660
Logtafel, 469
Logwerfen, 366
Los, 26
Losarbeiten, 924
Losbinden, 879
Losbrechen, 95
Löschen, 224
Löschplatz, 224
Lose, 743
Lose einholen, 820
Lose geben, 251, 744
Los Einholen, 360
Los Luggersegel, 222
Lösen, 879
Loser Hintersteven, 275
Loser Schlag, 752
Loses Bugspriet, 669
Losfieren, 744
Loskiel, 275
Losmachen, 474, 881, 879
Losnehmbares Getreideschott, 721
Losschakeln, 879
Losshafen, 601
Losshaken, 126
Lossrad, 330
Loswerfen, 131, 446
Lot, 442
Lotbarer Grund, 551
Lotblei, 442
Lotblock, 442
Lotdraht, 758
Loten, 130, 757
Loten ausrufen, 119
Lotgast, 444
Lotgast Plattform, 444
Lothpodest, 444
Lotleine, 444
Loteine Markung, 494
Lotmaschine, 757
Lotrohr, 758
Lotscheit, 804
Lotse, 581
Lotsen, 582
Lotsenbehörde, 582
Lotsenfahrzeug, 584
Lotsenfahrwasser, 582
Lotsenflagge, 583
Lotsengebühren, 582
Lotsengeld, 582
Lotsenkabel, 442
Lotsenkunst, 582
Lotsenleiter, 583

Lotsenrate, 582
Lotsenrevier, 582
Lotsensignal, 584
Lotsenstrecke, 582
Lotsentreppe, 583
Lotsenversetzschiff, 584
Lotsenzwang, 172
Lotspeise, 23
Lotung, 592, 757
Lotungslinie, 276, 457
Lotwerfen, 130, 366
Loxodrome, 647
Loxodromische Linie, 647
Loxodromisches segeln, 502
Lüften, 863
Lufterkopf, 182
Luftermündung, 182
Lüftersull, 889
Luftfänger, 919
Luftgang, 8, 9
Luftkasten, 107
Luftloch, 8
Luftspiegelung, 474, 513
Luftstein, 6
Lufttank, 247
Lufttrockenes Holz, 698
Lüftung, 888
Luftwiderstand, 8
Lüfungsfenster, 600
Lugger, 477
Lugger Grossegel, 478
Luggersegel, 478
Luggersegel Takelung, 478
Lugwinkel, 153
Luke, 357
Lukenbaum, 358
Lukenbügel, 359
Lukendavit, 358
Lukendeckel, 358
Lukeneisen, 357
Lukenendbalken, 358
Lukengrating, 335, 359
Lukenkappe, 168
Lukenlängsträger, 359
Lukenleiter, 581
Lukenprofileisen, 359
Lukenriegel, 359
Lukenrippe, 357
Lukenschalk, 357
Lukenschalkkeil, 359
Lukenschlinge, 357
Lukenstopper, 359
Lukenstringer, 467, 837
Lukenstütze, 359
Lükensüll, 157
Lukentalje, 359
Luksulle, 358
Luksullstutz, 157

Lupe, 510
Lustyacht, 928
Lut, 479
Luv abschneisen, 251
Luvballast, 721
Luvbaum, 557, 767
Luven, 477
Luvgierig, 905
Luvgierigkeit, 23, 905
Luvgierig sein, 339
Luvliek, 477
Luvruder, 905
Luv Schothorn, 905
Luvseite, 906
Luvwall, 906
Luvwärts, 29, 921
Luvwärts setzende Gezeit, 906
Luv Wind Seite, 905
Luxuskabine, 114

Maat, 579
MacIntyre Doppelboden, 480
Magnet, 481
Magnetbremse, 481
Magnetische Amplitude, 481
Magnetische Deklination, 481
Magnetische Induktion, 483
Magnetische Intensität, 483
Magnetische Karte, 481
Magnetische Kraft, 483
Magnetische Peilung, 481
Magnetische Pole, 483
Magnetischer Koeffizient, 482
Magnetischer Meridian, 483
Magnetischer Moment, 483
Magnetisches Äquator, 482
Magnetisches Eisen, 483
Magnetisches Feld, 482
Magnetische Störungen, 483
Magnetkompass, 482
Magnetnadel, 483
Magnetostriktion Echolot, 484
Mahagonyholz, 484
Maierschiffsform, 484
Maklergebühr, 99
Malershellegat, 564
Mall, 516
Mallboden, 516
Mallbreite, 516
Mallung, 516
Manganbronze, 487
Manila Hanf, 488
Manilatauwerk, 488
Mannloch, 487
Mannlochbügel, 488
Mannlochdeckel, 487
Mannlochring, 488

Mannschaft, 184
Mannschaftliste, 184
Mannschaftraum, 184
Mannschaftsabort, 696
Manntau, 450, 488
Manövrierfähigkeit, 351
Manövrierprüfung Ruderversulk, 487
Manövrierunfähiges Licht, 541
Mantel, 669
Marine, 489
Marine betreffend, 530
Marinierter Fisch, 580
Maritim, 489
Markboje, 494
Markierungsboje, 899
Marlen, 494
Marlienstek, 495
Marlleine, 494
Marlnadel, 494
Marlpfriem, 606
Marlspiker, 495
Marlspikerstek, 495
Marlstek, 495
Mars, 844
Marsrand, 847
Marsschotenblock, 620
Marssegel, 771
Marsstänge, 846
Marsstänge Hänger, 109
Martinsanker, 495
Masche, 507
Maschinenabteilung, 480
Maschinenbesichtiger, 261
Maschinenfundament, 261
Maschinengrundplatte, 53
Maschinen Inspektor, 600
Maschinenjournal, 261
Maschinenluke, 261
Maschinen Nietung, 480
Maschinennutzleistung Koeffizient, 610
Maschinenraum, 261
Maschinenraumabzug, 611
Maschinenraumhilfsmaschinen, 261
Maschinentagebuch, 261
Maschinentelegraph, 262
Maschinenumbau, 480
Maschinenvorräte, 261
Maschinen-Wirkungsgrad, 261
Maserung, 335
Massgüter, 502
Massgüterladung, 502
Mässig bewegte See, 515
Massige Brise, 515
Mässiger Fahrt, 515
Massige Scheibe, 224

Massive Fingerling, 755
Massive Kauschen, 755
Massiver Kiel, 43
Massiver Ruderrahmen, 755
Massive Schraube, 755
Massive Stütze, 755
Mass oder Gewicht, 908
Masstonne, 311
Mast, 496
Mastbacke, 143, 381
Mastband, 496, 498
Mastbezug, 497
Mastbock, 815
Mastbügel, 498
Mastducht, 499
Mastenkran, 716
Mastfisch, 499
Mastfischung, 499
Masthausung, 381
Mastkeil, 499
Mastkoker, 815
Mastkorb, 188
Mastliek, 499
Mastlochkragenkranz, 497
Mastkragen, 497
Mastkragenkranz, 497
Mastring, 868
Mastschlingen, 496
Mastspitze, 595
Mastspur, 784
Masttopp, 498
Mastung, 498
Mastwerk, 498
Mastwinde, 499
Masut, 314
Materialstärken, 685
Matrose, 677
Matrosenkiste, 696
Matrosenlogis, 697
Matte, 499
Mattfender, 500
Maulstek, 511
Mausing, 524
Mechanisch angetriebener Davit, 503
Mechanisch angetriebener Rettungsboot, 504
Mechanischer Wirkungsgrad, 558
Meer, 693
Meerbusen, 49
Meereis, 694
Meerenge, 528, 757, 797
Meeresarm, 23
Meeresfreiheit, 308
Meeresgrund, 694
Meereskunde, 545
Meeresströmung, 545

Meereswasserfarbe, 165
Meerkies, 722
Megaphon, 504
Meilenfahrt, 502
Meltau, 511
Meridian, 507
Meridian Breite, 507
Meridian Distanz, 507
Meridian Durchgang, 507
Meridian Linie, 507
Meridian Winkel, 507
Meridian Zenitdistanz, 507
Meridionaldifferenz, 507
Meridionalteile, 507
Merkatorische Projektion, 505
Merkatorkarte, 505
Messbrief, 842
Messe, 508
Messformel, 635
Messfunkreflektortonne, 627
Messing, 95, 530
Metallelectrode, 508
Metazentrische Breitenhöhe, 856
Metazentrische Evolute, 508
Metazentrische Höhe, 508
Metazentrum, 508
Meuterei, 526
Mick, 514
Mietvertrag, 212
Milchener, 653
Miltere ortsmittag, 465
Minderlieferung, 731
Mineralwolle, 512
Missweisende Peilung, 481
Missweisender Kurs, 482
Missweisung, 482
Mist, 513
Mit Backstagwind Segeln, 309
Mit beiden Bäumen abgefiert, 921
Mit dem Winde, 54, 238
Mit losem Fuss, 474
Mitreeder, 412
Mitstrom, 895
Mitstrom Koeffizient, 896
Mittag, 538
Mittagbesteck, 538
Mitte der Gezeit, 349
Mittelbreite, 510
Mittelfahrwassertonne, 273
Mittelgei, 55
Mittelgrund, 510
Mittelgrundtonne, 510
Mittelheckspant, 379
Mittelkielplatte, 135
Mittelkielschwein, 136

Mittelkluver, 510
Mittellängsschott, 136
Mittellatte, 29
Mittelliek, 648
Mittellot, 159
Mittelmast, 510
Mittelschwert, 135
Mittel Sonnensegelstutze, 510
Mittelstagsegel, 510
Mitteltau, 172
Mittelträger, 135
Mittelwache, 510
Mitternachtssonne, 511
Mittlere Greenwich Zeit, 337
Mittlere Hochwasser, 501
Mittlere höheres, 501
Mittlere Ortszeit, 465, 727
Mittlererfahrt, 159
Mittlerer Mittag, 501
Mittlerer nipptidenhub, 501
Mittlerer Sonnentag, 501
Mittlerer Springtidenhub, 501
Mittlerer Steig, 501
Mittleresniedrigwasser, 501
Mittleres Niedrigeres Niedrigwasser, 501
Mittleres Niedrigwasser Intervall, 501
Mittlere Sonne, 502
Mittleresspringniedrigwasser, 501
Mittlerer Tiefgang, 501
Mittlerer Wasserstand, 501
Mittlere Sonnenjahr, 501
Mittlere Tidenhub, 501
Mittlere Zeit, 502
Mittschiffs, 13
Mittschiffsdecklinie, 207
Mittschiffshals, 511
Mittschiffslinie, 136
Mit Vorsegel Back Gebrasst, 2
Modelltank, 515, 861
Mole, 516, 581
Molenfeuer, 600
Molenkopf, 581
Monddistanzen, 479
Mondflutintervall, 479
Mondkieker, 519
Mondneigung, 897
Mondregenbogen, 479
Mondreiter, 519
Mondtafeln, 479
Mondtag, 478
Mondumlauf, 479
Mondzyklus, 478
Monelmetall, 517
Monkireling, 518, 622
Monsun, 519

Montage, 81, 264
Moorsom Vermessungssystem, 522
Mop, 522
Morgenwache, 522
Morselampe, 522
Motorbetriebene Winde, 523
Motorboot, 523
Motor Elektrischer Antrieb, 219
Motorrettungsboot, 523
Motorschiff, 523
Motorsegler, 28
Mudderprahm, 748
Mufferdeibrigg, 688
Mulde, 866
Mündungshafen, 265
Muntzmetall, 530
Murbe Stopper, 142
Muringboje, 520
Muringketten, 339
Muring Schakel, 656
Muringstein, 421, 521
Muringswirbel, 813
Muringtau, 521
Muskeule, 167
Musterrolle, 24, 778
Musterung, 526
Mutterkompass, 497

Nach auswärts bestimmt, 558
Nach Lee setzend Ström, 445
Nachlenzleitung, 800
Nachlenzpumpe, 800
Nachmittagswache, 6
Nachrichten für Seefahrer, 541
Nachsehen, 558
Nachsehen und klaren, 880
Nachstecken, 574
Nachstrom, 895
Nachteffekt, 536
Nachtglass, 536
Nachtgleichenpunkte, 264
Nachthauslampe, 65
Nachtrettungsboje, 478
Nachtrettungsring, 478
Nachtsignal, 537
Nackte Elektrode, 42
Nadelholz, 753
Nadir, 527
Nagel, 527
Nagelband, 763
Nagelbank, 54, 585
Nagelbefestigung, 276
Näherholer, 393
Nähern, 360
Nahfahrt, 394

Nähgarn, 697
Naht, 696
Nähtaue, 703
Nahthaken, 636
Nahtloser Ladebaum, 908
Nahtloses Stahlboot, 697
Nahtspanten Beplankung, 647
Nahtstreif, 697
Nahtstreigen, 433
Nahtüberlappung, 697
Namenbrett, 528
Namenskonnossement, 796
Namenspolice, 529
Napiersches Diagramm, 529
Nasenblech, 88
Nationalflagge, 165, 262
Natürliche Luftüng, 529
Natürlicher Hafen, 529
Natürlicher Magnet, 529
Nautiker, 491, 532
Nautisch, 529
Nautische Astronomie, 529
Nautische Entfernung, 528
Nautischer Beisitzer, 25
Nautischer Tag, 529
Nautisches Instrumente, 529
Nautisches Jahrbuch, 10
Navigationsgesetze, 532
Navigationsraume, 532
Navigationszimmer, 142
Navigierbarer Halbkreis, 531
Nebel, 298
Nebelbogen, 298
Nebelgeschütz, 298
Nebelglocke, 298
Nebelgong, 298
Nebelhorn, 298
Nebelig, 298
Nebelschwaden, 298
Nebelsignal, 298
Nebengegensonne, 568
Nebenkielgang, 99
Nebenkielschwein, 740
Nebendreis, 749
Nebenmeridianbreite, 268
Nebenmeridianhöhe, 268
Nebenmond, 569
Nebensonne, 570, 807
Nebenwassergang, 393
Negativer Slip, 533
Negative Stabilitat, 533
Negligenzklausel, 533
Neigung, 221, 632
Neigungskompass, 222
Neigungswinkel, 18
Neigungswinkel des Bugspriet, 783
Nephoskop, 533

Nettoraumgehalt, 534
Netto-Tonnengehalt, 534
Netz, 286
Netzboje, 88
Netzfleet, 292
Netzgarn, 180
Netzklappe, 290
Netzknoten, 534
Netzmasche, 507
Netznadel, 507
Netzschlinge, 127
Netzwand, 460, 461
Netzwinde, 859
Neutrale Faser, 534
Nicht eingemessener Raum, 267
Nicht höher, 538
Nicht indossables, Konnossement, 796
Nichts vergeben, 541
Nickelstahl, 536
Niedergang, 168
Niedergangskappe, 168
Niedergangsluke, 429
Niedergangstreppe, 168
Niederholen, 360
Niederholer, 238
Niederlassen, 475
Niedrige Bodenwrange, 713
Niedrigeres Hochwasser, 475
Niedrigeres Niedrigwasser, 476
Niedriger Wasserstand, 369
Niedrige Wasserzeit, 839
Niedrigster beobachteter Wasserstand, 476
Niedrigstes Springniedrigwasser, 476
Niedrigwasser, 476
Niedrigwasser Gezeitennull, 476
Niedrigwassermarke, 476
Niet, 654
Nietbolzen, 152
Nietenbehälter, 655
Nietenentfernung, 587
Nietenkopfschläger, 654
Nietenträger, 655
Nietenwärmer, 365
Nieter, 654
Nietkopf, 655
Nietloch, 655
Nietschaft, 655
Nietschraube, 822
Nietstempel, 375
Nietstöckchen, 231
Nietungspresse, 655
Nietverbindung, 655

Nimbus, 537
Nippflut, 533
Nippniedrigswasser, 533
Nipptide, 533
Nipptidenhub, 533
Nitzel, 305, 791
Nockband, 215
Nockbeschlag, 215
Nockbindsel, 251, 363
Nockgording, 445
Nockhaus, 922
Nockklampe, 834
Nockohr, 832
Nockpferd, 292
Nockring, 184
Nocktakel, 929
Nominelle Pferdestärke, 538
Nominelle Steigung, 538
Nonius, 889
Nordatlantisch Triftström, 540
Norder, 541
Nordlicherfahrt, 541
Nordlicherlauf, 541
Nordlicher Polarkreis, 23
Nordostlich Durchfahrt, 540
Nordostmonsun, 540
Nord West Monsun, 541
Normalanker, 790
Normal Chronometer, 775
Normale Geschwindigkeit, 708
Normale Leistung in Pferdestärke, 708
Normaler Sprung, 775
Normalkerze, 119
Normal Kompass, 775
Normalnull, 834
Normalwiderstand, 644
Normann, 539, 540
Not, 414
Notausbesserungen, 827
Notausgang, 264, 265
Notbatterie, 259
Notbeleuchtungszentrale, 259
Not Empfanger, 259
Notfall Gruppe, 259
Notflagge, 226
Not Frequenz, 226
Notfunkstelle, 628
Nothafen, 355
Notlenzpumpe, 804
Notmast, 414
Not Periodenzahl, 226
Notruder, 414
Notschutz, 226
Notsegel, 414
Notsignal, 226
Notsignal Feuer, 226

Notstek, 356
Notsteuerapparat, 259
Nottakelage, 414
Nottalje, 644
Notzeichen, 629
Nullachse, 534
Nullspant Völligkeitsgrad, 511
Nummer, 542
Nummerflagge, 542
Nur für Totalverlust, 848
Nuss, 238
Nussplatte, 85
Nussspant, 85
Nüstergat, 457
Nutation, 542
Nutzladefähigkeit, 884
Nutzpferdestärke, 611
Nutztragfähigkeit, 311

Oben, 10
Oberbau, 203
Oberdeck, 883
Obere Kulmination, 808
Oberende einer Bodenwrange, 295
Oberer Auflanger, 847
Oberer Fallblock, 297
Obere Schlagtorn, 649
Obere Seitenteile, 847
Obere Takelage, 845
Oberfeuermeister, 442
Oberfracht, 558
Obergaffel, 518
Oberheizraum, 279
Oberheizraum Grating, 279
Oberinjektionsventil, 371
Oberkoje, 883
Oberlicht, 743
Oberlichtbezug, 743
Oberlicht Flügel, 684
Oberlichtkappe, 743
Oberlicht Schutzstangen, 743
Oberlicht Sektor, 744
Oberliek, 362
Obermarssegel, 883
Obermaschinist, 143
Obermast, 883
Obernetz Flügel, 847
Ober Offizier, 143
Oberrahmen, 262
Oberschanzkleid, 845
Oberschanzkleidreling, 845
Obersegel, 749
Obersimm, 365
Obersteward, 144
Observiertes Besteck, 602
Oberwasser, 312

Oberwerk, 203, 624, 883
Oelbrenner, 109
Oertzruder, 546
Offene Ankerplatz, 551
Offene Bodenwrange, 741
Offene Meer, 553
Offene Police, 552, 882
Offene Reede, 553
Offenes Boot, 551
Offene See, 553
Offenes Eis, 675
Offene Verholklampe, 551
Offizier, 546
Ohrholz, 423
Ohrholzspant, 423
Ohrspant, 424
Okklusion, 544
Ökonomische Geschwindigkeit, 252
Okularblende, 826
Ölabscheider, 548
Ölabscheider Leichter, 548
Ölbrenner, 547
Öldichtenietung, 549
Öldichtluke, 549
Ole, 550
Ölfeuerung, 548
Ölkleidung, 549
Ölrock, 549
Ölsack, 547
Öltankleitung, 548
Öltankschiff, 549
Ölzeug, 549
Opposition, 553
Optionsladung, 553
Orderhafen, 553
Orderkonnossement, 545
Ordnungsnummer, 727
Oregon Fichtenholz, 237
Orgelpfeife, 555
Originalfehler, 393
Orkan, 384
Orkanzentrum-Orkanauge, 893
Orlopdeck, 555
Ort, 588
Orthodrom, 555
Örtliche Ablenkung, 465
Ortszeit, 466
Öse, 474
Ösfass, 36
Oszillator, 555
Overholzheck, 855
Ozeanische Strömung, 545
Ozeanographie, 545

Pack, 389
Packeis, 561

Packetschiff, 572
Paddel, 562
Paddelboot, 120
Palinurus, 565
Pall, 573
Pallbeting, 573
Pallhieven, 365
Pallkranz, 573
Pallpfosten, 573
Pallrad, 573
Pallsetzen, 573
Pallwinden, 365
Panama Kanal Vermessung, 566
Pancakeeis, 566
Pampero, 566
Papennaht, 178
Parallaktisches Winkel, 568
Parallaxaltern, 568
Parallaxe, 568
Paralleles Mittelschiff, 771
Parallellineal, 568
Parasite Klausel, 396
Parcelladung, 569
Pardune, 31
Pariser Berechtsdeklaration, 210
Pariser Erklärung, 210
Parlamentarschiff, 129
Part, 570
Parteireeder, 412
Partikuläre Havarie, 571
Passagegeld, 571
Passagier, 571
Passagiereinrichtungen, 572
Passagier Liste, 572
Passatwinde, 852
Passtück, 122
Patent des Kapitäns, 497
Patentlog, 691
Patentlot, 757
Patentscheibe, 656
Patentscheibeblock, 573
Patentstopper, 116
Pauschalcharter, 478
Pauschalfracht, 478
Pauschalpolice, 886
Pech, 586
Pechgrapen, 587
Pechquast, 587
Pechtannenholz, 931
Pechtopf, 587
Pegelfestpunkt, 56
Pegelnull, 836
Peilboot, 810
Peildeck, 170
Peilkompass, 29
Peilrohr, 758

Peilscheibe, 576
Peilstock, 758
Peilung, 52
Penalty Klausel, 576
Penterhaken, 285
Pentern, 284
Perigaum, 577
Perihelium, 577
Periode, 578
Periodische Besichtigung, 578
Persenning, 823
Persenningleiste, 357
Persenning Nagel, 693
Persenningtuch, 823
Personen Fahrboot, 572
Pest, 100
Pfahlkompass, 595
Pfahlmast, 595, 739
Pfahlstek, 89
Pfandrecht der Bergung, 680
Pfandrecht des Lotsengeldes, 584
Pfandstall, 208
Pfanne, 566, 684
Pfannkuchen, 566
Pfeife, 916
Pfeifen, 757
Pfeifen Kontrollsystem, 917
Pferd, 299
Pferdeleine, 897
Pflichtanker, 717
Pflichtlotse, 172
Pflock, 228
Pforte, 599
Pfortenband, 564
Pfortendeckel, 600, 733, 735
Pfortendrempel, 737
Phase, 579
Phasenalter, 579
Phosphorbronze, 580
Piek, 574
Piekfall, 575
Piekohr, 574
Piekschott, 574
Piekspann, 575
Piekspant, 575
Piekstück, 787
Piekverstarkungsbalken, 567
Pier, 914
Pilger, 581
Pilzanker, 525
Pilzkopflüfter, 526
Pinasse, 585
Pinnen, 575
Pinnkompass, 856
Pipe, 585
Piratenschiff, 586
Piroge, 120

Pitchpineholz, 931
Pitot Rohr Log, 587
Pivotfenster, 552
Planke, 589
Plankenenden, 377
Plankengang, 797
Plankenstoss, 110
Plankton, 590
Plansegeln, 589
Plateau, 590
Plattbinsel, 291
Plattenabwicklungszeichnung, 719
Plattengang, 797
Plattenklemme, 590
Plattenmast, 590
Plattenmodellbock, 514
Plattenruder, 136
Plattentür, 590
Plattes Heck, 291
Plattfisch, 290
Plattform, 290, 591
Plattformdeck, 591
Plattfuss, 231
Plattgatt, 291, 772
Plattierer, 590
Plattierergang, 590
Platting, 291, 707
Plattnagel, 155
Platzfrachten, 59
Plicht, 189
Plötzlich anhalten, 753
Plötzlicher Ruck, 479
Plötzlichlaufen lassen, 446
Plumper, 377
Pneumatische Nietung, 593
Pneumatischer Gegenhalter, 406
Pocken, 749
Pockholz, 456
Pockholzstreifen, 788
Pockholzstuben, 788
Pokleine, 161, 598
Polacker Takelung, 595
Polareis, 595
Polar Front, 23, 595
Polarkreis, 595
Polar Projektion, 595
Poldistanz, 595
Poldreieck, 25
Polhöhe, 595
Poller, 66, 838
Pollerkopf, 838
Polster, 80
Polykonische Karte, 596
Polykonische Projektion, 596
Ponton, 596
Ponton Landung, 433

Porteurleine der Kattstopper, 132
Porteurleinkette, 133, 653
Portugiesisches Segel, 745
Positionslaterne, 700
Postflagge, 484
Postkammer, 485
Postsignal, 485
Postsubvention, 485
Postwimpel, 485
Pottwalöl, 763
Prahm, 42, 603
Prahmbug, 603
Prangen, 604, 799
Präzession, 604
Preien, 347, 348
Pressen, 187
Press Luftantrieb Winde, 9
Pressluft Behälter, 593
Presslufthammer, 8
Pressluftnietung, 593
Pressluft Rudermaschine, 593
Prestoff Boot, 588
Pricker, 606
Prigger, 606
Primage, 606
Prise, 124, 607
Prisengeld, 87, 608
Prisengericht, 607
Prisenhof, 607
Prisenkommando, 607
Prisenrecht, 608
Prismatische Fehler, 606
Privatschiff, 607
Privatsignal, 607
Probe der Notsteuerapparat, 259
Probefahrt, 699, 861
Probestück, 180
Profil, 40
Profile, 700
Profileisen, 40
Profilstahlstütze, 102
Progressive Probefahrten, 608
Projektionsfläche, 608
Promenadedeck, 608
Propeller, 609
Propellerabstrom, 691
Propellermutter, 611
Propellerwelle, 611
Propellerwelle Überzug, 713
Propulsionswirkungsgrad, 611
Protestflagge, 612
Proviantmeister, 144
Proviantschein, 891
Psychrometer, 612
Pulverflagge, 603
Pulverkammer, 481

Pulverkohle, 614
Pulvermagazin, 481
Pumpe, 614
Pumpen, 614
Pumpenraum, 614
Pumpensod, 457, 615
Pumpensumpf, 615
Pumpspill, 614
Punktschweissung, 767
Pünte, 616, 689
Puppblock, 740
Putting Band, 317
Puttingeisen, 139
Putting Ring, 317
Puttingsbolzen, 139
Puttingsschiene, 317
Puttingswanten, 318

Quadrant, 619
Quadrantalkugel, 619
Quadrantdavit, 619
Quadranten Kompassrose, 619
Quadrant Ruderpinne, 619
Quadratur, 619
Quarantäne, 620
Quarantäneanstalt, 441
Quarantänearzt, 365
Quarantänefahrzeug, 620
Quarantäne Flagge, 620
Quarantänegeld, 620
Quarantänehafen, 620
Quarantänesignal, 620
Quarantänestation, 620
Quarterdeck, 621
Quecksilberbarometer, 490, 506
Quenouillette, 180
Quer Ab, 1
Querablauf, 734
Querbalken, 50
Querbunker, 186
Querholzheck, 855
Querlaufende Stütze, 218
Querlaufende Wellen, 856
Querlukensull, 363
Quernummer, 856
Querschiffs, 25
Querschiffs Steuerwelle Rudermaschine, 260
Querschnitt, 511
Quersegelschiff, 771
Querspannung, 856
Querspant, 771
Querstange, 404
Querstück, 770
Querstück der Ablaufbahn, 186
Quersull, 363
Quersulle, 260

Raa, 929
Raajolle, 929
Raasegel, 771
Raatoppsegel, 232, 404
Rabatt, 10, 636
Rabatteisen, 486
Rack, 569, 868
Rackband, 868
Rackklotje, 570
Rackschlitten, 570
Racksorrung, 570
Racktau, 407, 570
Radanbau, 563
Radargerät Konsole, 627
Radgehäuse-Längsträger, 766
Radialdavit, 627
Radial veränderliche Steigung, 627
Radio-Alarm signal, 627
Radio-Anrufsignal, 628
Radio Not Frequenz, 628
Radio-Notsignal, 629
Radiosonde, 630
Radiowarte, 627
Radkasten, 562
Radkastenbalcon, 766
Radkastenbalkon, 563
Radkastengallerie, 563
Radkasten-Galleriebalken, 770
Radkastenstütze, 562
Rad mit festen Schaufeln, 627
Radschaufel, 562
Radschiff, 562
Radbandselstek, 656
Rahe, 929
Rahestropp, 622
Rahklampe, 657
Rahliek, 362, 364
Rahmenantenne, 474
Rahmenspannung, 906
Rahmenspant, 906
Rahschoner, 772
Rahsegel, 771
Rahtakelage, 771
Raketenapparat, 656
Raketenleine, 656
Rammen, 668
Rand, 252, 456
Randmaschen, 341, 706
Randplanke, 87, 489
Randplatte, 489
Randsomholz, 276
Rank, 184, 827
Rationsfass, 356
Rattenschwanz, 635
Rauchbezug, 750
Rauchbezung, 497
Räucherhering, 422

Rauchfang, 884
Rauchgassystem, 296
Rauchmelder, 750
Rauchschott, 282
Rauchsegel, 750
Raum, 374, 434
Raumahle, 636
Raumbalken, 375
Raumbalkenspannung, 375
Raumbedarf, 189, 796
Raumbunker, 375
Raumen, 888
Raumer Wind, 209, 307
Raumgebühr, 58
Rauminhalt der Verdrängung, 892
Raumleiter, 375, 581
Raumschoten, 296
Raumschotts segeln, 333
Raum segeln, 676
Raumstringer, 375
Raumstütze, 375
Raumtiefe, 214, 641
Raumwind, 443
Rebenleine, 55
Rechten Halbreis, 652
Rechtsaszension, 650
Rechtsgeschlagenes Tauwerk, 588
Rechts Hintenaus, 650
Recht so, 779
Rechtsgängiger Propeller, 650
Rechtsgehender Propeller, 650
Rechtsschlag, 650
Rechtweisende Peilung, 866
Rechtweisender Kurs, 866
Recken, 626
Reduktion der Lotung, 638
Reede, 656
Reedereiflagge, 381
Reef, 638
Reep, 658
Reepleitungs Rudermaschine, 138
Reff, 638
Reffagel, 639
Reffband, 639
Reffbandsel, 639
Reffbindsel, 639
Reffeine, 639
Reffen, 639
Reffgatt, 270
Reffjolle, 639
Reffklampe, 84
Reff Knebelsteert, 639
Reffknoten, 639
Reffknüttel, 639
Reffleine, 639

Reffseising, 639
Refftalje, 640
Refftaljenlapp, 640
Refraktion, 640
Regattanummer, 626
Regel Kompass, 775
Regelmässige Fähren, 592
Regensegel, 359
Regenzelt, 359
Regenwolke, 537
Registerhafen, 601
Registerlänge, 642
Registrierendes Thermometer, 830
Registertonne, 339
Registrierung, 642
Reibholz, 341, 663, 760
Reibungstopper, 691
Reibungswert, 312
Reibungswiderstand, 742
Reihenfolge, 873
Reihenfolge-Beladung, 464
Reihenfolge der Beladung, 464
Reihleine, 241, 404, 429
Rein, 150
Reine Charterpartie, 150
Reiner Gesundheitspass, 150
Reines Konnossement, 150
Reinigung, 336
Reinigungskette, 457
Reise, 571
Reisebefrachtung, 863
Reisegepäck, 33
Reisepolice, 893
Reissahle, 692
Reiten, 648
Reitknie, 784, 786
Relative Konterbande, 173
Relatives Geschwindigkeits-
  verhältnis, 762
Relinglog, 250
Reling Netzwerk, 105
Relingsleiste, 105
Relingsprofleisen, 105
Relingstütze, 632
Relingswinde, 718
Rennboot, 626
Rennelström, 644
Renngig, 625
Rennjacht, 626
Rennlatten, 86
Rennwert, 929
Rennzeichen, 740
Repressalien, 644
Reserve Anker, 59
Reserve Auftrieb, 644
Reservebunker, 760
Reservepinne, 260

Reserveschwimmfähigkeit, 644
Reservesteuerapparat, 259
Respekttage, 201
Rettungdrache, 450
Rettungsboje, 449
Rettungsboot Rationen, 75
Rettungsdienst, 452
Rettungsfloss, 451
Rettungsgeschütz, 459
Rettungsgürtel, 451
Rettungsrakete, 451
Rettungsring, 449
Rettungsschlepper, 680
Retungsring, 451
Reuel, 663
Reuse, 602, 856, 908
Reusel, 750
Revers, 447
Reversible Lade- und Loschzeit, 646
Revierlotse, 654
Rhumb, 647
Richtfeuer, 634
Richtige Nierlöcher, 273
Richtplatte, 56
Richtspant, 771
Richtung, 363, 860
Richtungsfeuer, 454, 634
Richtungslinie, 151
Riebahle, 636
Riemen, 543
Riemen Bandsel, 852
Riemen bei, 466, 557
Riemenblatt, 544
Riemen einlegen, 441
Riemengriff, 339
Riemen Hoch, 848
Riemen pieken, 848
Riemen Platt, 441
Riemenschaft, 474
Riff, 638
Rifflelblech, 647
Riffelplatte, 142
Rindenboot, 42
Ring, 178
Ringartiger Lukendeckelgriff, 359
Ringbolzen, 652
Ringnetz, 617
Ringplatte, 653
Rinne, 342, 903
Rinneneisen, 140
Rinnsteinwinkel, 904
Rippe, 128, 444
Rippen der Spillklampen, 809
Riss, 644
Ristorno, 636
Robbenbott, 695

Rochstasten, 778
Rogener, 653
Röhrenform Ladenbaum, 869
Röhrenpfeife, 555
Rohrflansch, 289
Rohrkoje, 585
Rohrtunnel, 586
Rojebank, 834
Rojedolle, 831
Rojegabel, 74, 543
Rojegabel Backe, 662
Rojeklampe, 841
Rojepforte, 662
Rojepfortendeckel, 733
Rojer, 544
Rollamplitude, 13
Rollangel, 410
Rolle, 640
Rollende Dünung, 658
Rollendes Torschiff, 657
Rollenmanöver, 244
Roller, 657
Rollperiode, 578
Rollstein, 663
Rollstek, 658
Rolltakel, 658
Rosenzurrung, 659
Rossbreiten, 379
Rost, 670
Rostfreies Tauwerk, 774
Rosthammer, 145
Rostkitt, 671
Rostschutzanstrich, 19
Rotangtauwerk, 636
Rote Klausel, 59
Rotierende Funkbake, 660
Rotierende Funkpeiler, 660
Rotierender, 646
Royal, 663
Royalstange, 663
Royaltopp, 663
Rücken, 648
Rückenstück, 784
Rucker, 750
Rückfracht, 391
Ruckleine, 752
Rücklieferungsanzeige, 638
Rücklieferungsklausel, 637
Rückschlagventil, 539
Rückversicherung, 643
Rückwärtsfahrt, 788
Rückwärtsgehen, 333
Rückzoll, 241
Ruder, 369, 543, 664
Ruder an, 331
Ruderarm, 664
Ruderauschlagknagge, 667
Ruderausschlag, 209

Ruderbank, 834
Ruderbarkasse, 437
Ruderblatt, 544, 664
Ruderboot, 662
Ruderbremse, 665
Ruderbrunnen, 609
Ruderdolle, 831
Ruderdrehmoment, 667
Ruderdruckkomponente, 239
Ruderer, 544
Ruderfedern, 277
Ruderfläche, 664
Rudergabel, 74, 544
Rudergabel Platte, 662
Rudergänger, 369
Rudergast, 369
Rudergrating, 914
Rudergriff, 339
Rudergrube, 667
Ruddrhacke, 31
Ruderhaken, 585
Ruderhaken Ausschnitt, 585
Ruderhaus, 915
Ruderheissring, 666
Ruderhorn, 666
Ruder in Lee, 369, 882
Ruderjoch, 931
Ruderkeil, 665
Ruderkeillager, 666
Ruderkette, 914
Ruderklampe, 544
Ruderklick, 664
Ruderknagge, 667
Ruderkoker, 667
Ruderkommando, 369
Ruderkopf, 666
Ruder Kopfloch, 369
Ruderkragen, 666
Ruderkupplung, 666
Ruderlenkstange, 239
Rudermaschine, 782
Rudermaschine mit direktem Antrieb, 223
Rudermaschine mit indirektem Antrieb, 392
Ruder mit Antriebskraft auf der Pinne, 780
Rudermoment, 666
Rudern, 613, 662
Ruder nach Luv, 369
Ruderöse, 341
Ruderpfoste, 667
Ruderpieken, 574
Ruderpinne, 667
Ruderpinne Haltetau, 783
Ruderquadrant, 667
Ruderrahmen, 666
Ruderschaft, 474

Ruderschaft Stopfbüchse, 664
Ruderschegg, 89
Ruder Schloss, 666
Ruderschlossholz, 924
Ruderschmiege, 664
Rudersektor, 667
Rudersmann, 369, 544
Ruderstange, 783
Rudersteven, 31
Ruderstopfbuchse, 667
Ruderstropp, 782
Ruderstutzen, 504
Rudertelegraph, 783
Ruderträger, 249
Rudertraglager, 665
Ruderzeiger, 369, 664
Rudertorn, 862
Ruder Tragläger, 585
Rufer, 504
Rufzeichen, 628
Ruhepause, 478
Ruhige See, 750
Rumpf, 382
Rumpf unter der Kimm, 383
Rundbrassen, 92, 360
Rundeisen, 660
Rundeisengriffe, 334
Runde Kauschen, 662
Runde Naht, 661
Runde Platting, 661
Runder Stevenlauf, 193
Rundfunksender, 148
Rundgatt, 258
Rundheck, 258
Rundholz, 760
Rundreise, 893
Rundreise Befrachtung, 661
Rundreise Vercharterung, 661
Rund Schwoien, 812
Rundsel, 662
Rundtorn, 662
Rundtorn in den Ketten, 662
Rundung, 239, 656, 660
Russischer Hanf, 670
Rüstanker, 717
Ruste, 140
Rüsteisen, 139
Rüstleine, 713
Rutenfender, 656

Sackgut, 32
Sackladung, 32
Sackleinwand, 109
Sacknetz, 33
Salondeck, 679
Salzer, 679
Salzgehalt, 678

Salzpropf, 679
Salzung, 679
Samtfrachtführer, 167
Sand, 682
Sanddüne, 238
Sandstrak, 324
Sandtopf, 682
Sanitärpumpe, 682
Sanitätspass, 64
Sargassokraut, 684
Sargasso Meer, 684
Sattel, 143
Sattelbunkerluke, 673
Sattel des Kluverbaums, 408
Sattelplatte, 183
Saugebagger, 805
Saugekasten, 805
Saugekorb, 659
Saugelüfter, 238
Sauger, 354
Saugnapf, 240
Saugzug, 392
Sceptertau, 931
Schaafhock, 487
Schablone, 827
Schachtluke, 867
Schadenbericht, 197
Schadenbesichtigung, 197
Schadenzertifikat, 196
Schadhaftes Eisenwerk, 401
Schäfchenwolken Himmel, 481
Schaftanschwellungsniet, 823
Schakel, 711
Schakelbolzen, 712
Schakwerk, 156, 161
Schakwerklaschung, 816
Schale, 285
Schalken, 48
Schalkklampe, 358
Schalkklampenwinkel, 358
Schalklatte, 357
Schalkleiste, 357
Schalldämpfer, 524
Schallempfänger, 386
Schallotung, 3
Schallsignal, 758
Schalltrichter, 378
Schallwellen Echolot, 756
Schalstück, 285, 650
Schalung, 284
Schamfielkissen, 613
Schamfielung, 138
Schamfielungsbrett, 138
Schamfielungslapp, 138
Schamfielungslatte, 138, 650, 689
Schamfielungsmatte, 138, 613

Schamfielungsplatte, 138
Schandeckel, 589
Schandeckelleiste, 717
Schandeckelwinkel, 344
Schanzkleid, 105
Schanzkleid Reling, 105
Schanzkleidstütze, 105
Schanzkleidstützen, 660
Scharf beim Wind, 154
Scharfbrassen, 92
Scharfeisen, 552
Scharfe Kimmrundung, 714
Scharfer Bug, 444
Scharfer Heck, 714
Scharfgebaut, 714
Schattendeck, 712
Schattendeckschiff, 712
Schätzer, 635
Schauer, 732
Schauerkleid, 905
Schauerleute, 206
Schauermann, 375, 478
Schauermannsknoten, 31, 896
Schaufelbagger, 222
Schaufelrad, 562
Schauloch, 879
Schaulochpflock, 879
Schaulochstöpsel, 879
Schaum, 298
Schaumwelle, 917
Schebecke, 927
Schebeckensegel, 709
Scheerbrett, 555
Scheerbrettbeschlag, 555
Scheerbretternetz, 556
Scheerenwade, 618
Scheergang, 717
Scheernetz, 556
Scheerstock, 128
Schegg, 275
Scheibe, 715
Scheibeklmape, 149
Scheibenklampe, 143
Scheibennagel, 584
Scheidemesser, 715
Scheidenagel, 792
Scheinbare Höhe, 20
Scheinbare Ortszeit, 465
Scheinbarer Horizont, 708
Scheinbarer Mittag, 20
Scheinbarer Ort, 20
Scheinbarer Ortsmittag, 465
Scheinbarer Slip, 21
Scheinbarer Wind, 21
Scheinbare Sonne, 21
Scheinbare Zeit, 21
Scheinwerfer, 698
Scheisegel, 744

Scheisegelstange, 744
Scheisegeltopp, 744
Scheitelpunkt, 889
Schelff, 718
Schellfischschnur, 347
Schellkopfniet, 750
Schenkel, 289, 445, 576
Scheren, 640, 716
Scherleine, 640
Scherstock, 300, 357
Scheuerkiel, 339
Scheuerleiste, 341, 663
Scheuerprahm, 616
Scheuerstein, 376
Schiebblindes Toppsegel, 769
Schiebebalken, 357, 721
Schiebebalken-Lager, 51, 358
Schiebeluke, 83
Schiebenetz, 618
Schieberahe, 343
Schieberkasten, 226
Schiebestänge, 745
Schiebetür, 745
Schiedsgericht Klausel, 22
Schiefe, 544
Schiemannsgarn, 770
Schiertuch, 179
Schiessleine, 865
Schiff, 722
Schiffahrtkunde, 531
Schiffahrtspool, 726
Schiffahrtsprämien, 805
Schiffahrtsrecht, 651
Schiffahrtssubvention, 805
Schiffahrttreibend, 489
Schiffbar, 531
Schiffbare Gewässer, 531
Schiffbarkeit, 531
Schiffbauholz, 728
Schiffbaukunst, 530
Schiffbäupramie, 174
Schiffbruch, 797, 925
Schiffbrüchige, 130
Schiffer, 497, 743
Schiff mit gewellter Aussenhaut, 179
Schiff mit vollem Aufbau, 171
Schiffsagent, 726
Schiffsarzt, 726
Schiffsbauer, 723
Schiffsbaumeister, 729
Schiffsbedarf, 728
Schiffsbedürfnissgelder, 223
Schiffsbergung, 680
Schiffsbesatzung, 184
Schiffsbesichtiger, 492
Schiffsbodenfarbe, 86
Schiffsbrot, 723

Schiffsdisponent, 727
Schiffsdokumente, 727
Schiffsdunst, 810
Schiffseigentümer, 724
Schiffseigner, 724
Schiffsformgütegard, 383
Schiffsführer, 497
Schiffsglocke, 54
Schiffsgruss, 288
Schiffshändler, 723
Schiffshilfsmaschinen, 28, 383
Schiffsholz, 728
Schiffsinspektor, 492
Schiffsjournal, 547
Schiffskammer, 114
Schiffskasko, 382
Schiffskörper, 382
Schiffskreisel, 346
Schiffslast, 435, 724
Schiffslaterne, 727
Schiffsleim, 491
Schiffslieferant, 723
Schiffsmagnetismus, 727
Schiffsmakler, 723
Schiffsmann, 696
Schiffsmannschaft, 184
Schiffsmaschinist, 490
Schiffsmieter, 310
Schiffsmodell, 514
Schiffsname, 727
Schiffspapiere, 727
Schiffspfandrecht, 493
Schiffsplanke, 589
Schiffsprivilegien, 493
Schiffsprofoss, 497
Schiffsräucherung, 315
Schiffsregister, 728
Schiffsstab, 728
Schiffstagebuch, 546, 727
Schiffstauverzierung, 115
Schiffstischler, 412
Schiffstrümmer, 925
Schiffsrumpf, 382
Schiffsvermessung, 502
Schiffsvorräte, 699
Schiffswache, 899
Schiffswerft, 278
Schiffszeit, 728
Schiffszertifikat, 137
Schiffszettel, 724, 725
Schiffszimmermann, 726
Schildkrötendeck, 875
Schildpatt, 143
Schillenluke, 744
Schirmanker, 525
Schlacktuch, 744
Schladden, 925
Schladding, 418

Schlafendes Knie, 85
Schlafkette, 520
Schlag, 373, 440, 445, 801, 816, 921
Schlagbalken, 48, 777
Schlagbetten, 438
Schlagen, 94, 440, 800
Schlagholz, 594
Schlagkeil, 4
Schlagmann, 801
Schlagputze, 122
Schlagriem, 801
Schlagschott, 810
Schlagseite, 460, 461, 474
Schlagständer, 245
Schlagstück, 863
Schlamm, 524, 737
Schlammeis, 749
Schlammkasten, 524
Schlange, 460, 461
Schlappgording, 862
Schlappleine, 744
Schlauch, 379
Schlechter Ankergrund, 304
Schlechter Schwairaum, 304
Schleichhandel, 175
Schleife, 422
Schleihammer, 709
Schlempknie, 784
Schlephelling, 491
Schleppangelfischerei, 865
Schleppangelleine, 865, 915
Schelppbarkasse, 849
Schleppbeting, 536
Schleppbetinge, 849
Schleppbogen, 851
Schleppdock, 747
Schleppen, 848
Schlepper, 870
Schlepperbeihilfe, 848, 849
Schlepperlaterne, 850
Schleppfischer, 857
Schleppgalgen, 851
Schleppgeschwindigkeit, 850
Schlepphaken, 849
Schleppkanal, 515
Schleppketten, 438
Schleppleine, 850, 859
Schleppleine Fischerei, 243
Schlepplohn, 848
Schleppnetz, 857
Schleppnetzfischerei, 859
Schleppollern, 849
Schlepp-Pferdestärke, 252
Schlepprinne, 515, 861
Schleppschiff, 848
Schleppsignal, 850
Schlepptau, 851, 859

Schlepptau Schackel—Schute 1006

Schlepptau Schackel, 850
Schlepptrosse, 851
Schleppwiderstand, 851
Schleppwinde, 850
Schleppzug, 848
Schleuse, 466
Schleusendock, 910
Schleusengeld, 466
Schleusenkammer, 263
Schleusenkiel, 748
Schleusenponton, 117
Schleusenschiff, 117
Schleusensignal, 467
Schleusentor, 326
Schleusenventil, 748
Schlick, 737
Schliessknie, 143, 363
Schliesskopf, 655
Schlik, 551
Schlinge, 53, 746
Schlingen, 128, 746
Schlinger, 721
Schlingerborden, 279
Schlingerkiel, 62
Schlingern, 657
Schlingerpardune, 721
Schlingerschott, 721, 810
Schlingertanks, 19
Schlippen, 747
Schlipphaken, 576, 747
Schlippschakel, 576, 747
Schlippstek, 747
Schlipp Stopper, 747
Schlipptau, 747
Schlippvorrichtung, 870
Schlitte, 183
Schlittenbalken, 746
Schlittenständer, 230, 770
Schlittenstütze, 438
Schlittenstützen Laschung, 561
Schlitznaht, 592
Schloiknie, 853
Schlossfingerling, 467
Schlossholz, 278
Schlossholzgat, 279
Schlund, 810
Schlup, 748
Schluss Datum, 155
Schlussknie, 363
Schmack, 749
Schmarting, 569
Schmelzschweissung, 317
Schmickel, 848
Schmiedestücke, 303
Schmiegebrett, 60
Schmiegen, 140
Schmiegenumfang, 742
Schmiegung, 60

Schmiegung ausser dem Winkel, 775
Schmiegung unter dem Winkel, 154
Schmiere, 802
Schmierer, 337
Schmierklampe, 84
Schmierreep, 639
Schmutzige Schiff, 223
Schmutzkasten, 524
Schnabel, 541
Schnaumast, 868
Schnauschiff, 753
Schnausegel, 762, 868
Schneckengetriebene Winde, 925
Schneesturm, 68
Schneidbrenner, 194
Schneide Eisen, 194
Schnell aufluven, 99
Schnitte, 111
Schnittholz, 478
Schnur, 752
Schnürboden, 516
Schnürbodenarbeit, 441
Schnürbodenarbeiter, 467
Schnüren, 428
Schnürleine, 286, 352, 429
Schnurloch, 270
Schnürlöcher, 429
Scholleneis, 294
Schonerbark, 772
Schonerbrigg, 98, 688
Schonersegel, 319
Schonersegelbaum, 301
Schoner Yawl, 688
Schonerzeug, 688
Schoreisen, 653
Schornstein, 773
Schornsteinabzeichen, 316
Schornsteinfarbe, 316
Schornsteinkappe, 900
Schornsteinkragen, 879
Schornsteinluke, 279
Schornsteinschacht, 884
Schornsteinstag, 750
Schornsteinumbau, 78, 279
Schot, 717
Schotenstek, 730
Schotenwide, 718
Schothorn, 151
Schothornlagel, 151
Schothornlappen, 152
Schothornring, 152
Schothornwipper, 299
Schott, 103
Schottendeck, 103
Schotteneinteilung, 803

Schotten Ladelinie, 803
Schottenmanöver, 165
Schotenpoller, 749
Schottenstellung, 803
Schottentiefgang, 803
Schottfullblech, 103
Schottfullstück, 103
Schottmann, 689
Schottraa, 155
Schottraatoppsegel, 156
Schottsulle, 103
Schott Versteifungsprofl, 104
Schraatsegel Takelung, 300
Schrabber, 691
Schragen, 334
Schräges Piekknie, 594
Schraler Wind, 685
Schrallen, 360, 685
Schratsegel, 301
Schraubbolzen, 691
Schraube, 609
Schraube mit aufgesezten Flügeln, 103
Schraubenanker, 521
Schraubenbolzen, 802
Schraubenbrunnen, 609
Schraubendiskfläche, 223
Schraubenflügel, 610
Schraubengat, 610
Schraubenklemme, 650
Schraubenkonus, 273
Schraubennabe, 610
Schraubenöffnung, 786
Schraubenpropeller, 609
Schraubenschackel, 691
Schraubenspindel-Steuervorrichtung, 692
Schraubensteigung, 586
Schraubensteven, 611
Schraubenstrom, 32
Schraubenwelle, 611
Schraubenwirkungsgrad, 610
Schraubzurring, 691
Schrecken, 142
Schreiben, 692
Schreiber, 151
Schricken, 809
Schricktau, 142
Schrottau, 569
Schrumpfung, 733
Schubbeiwert, 834
Schubblock, 730
Schubverlust, 833
Schuh, 754
Schulter, 381, 732, 791
Schulterblock, 732
Schundauslauf, 324
Schute, 42, 249, 689

Schuttladung, 103
Schuttloch, 693
Schutz, 719
Schutzdeck, 719
Schutzdeckschiff, 720
Schutzgarn, 907
Schutzkiel, 744
Schutzkleid, 230, 905
Schutzpfahl, 581
Schutzplatte, 932
Schutzring, 185
Schutzschott, 691
Schwabber, 810
Schwach bemannt, 880
Schwaien, 812
Schwairaum, 151
Schwalbennester, 117
Schwalbenschwanzplatte, 238
Schwanenhals, 334, 810
Schwanenhalsband, 334
Schwanenhals Lüfter, 810
Schwanten, 542
Schwartzfichte, 67
Schwebering, 336
Schwebe Ruder, 34
Schweinsrücken, 14
Schweissmaterial, 280
Schweissnaht, 50
Schwerer Seegang, 367
Schweres Wetter, 799
Schwergetreide, 367
Schwergut, 203, 367
Schwergutbaum, 367
Schwerkraftdavit, 336
Schwerpunkt des Treibungwiderstands, 136
Schwertkasten, 135
Schwertmatte, 813
Schwertschenkel, 135
Schwer vor Anker reiten, 648
Schwichtleine, 812
Schwichton, 750
Schwichttalje, 187
Schwichtung, 750
Schwichtungslatte, 318
Schwimmdock, 294
Schwimmend, 6, 900
Schwimmende Landung, 433
Schwimmende Portalkran, 294
Schwimmender Kran, 294
Schwimmendes Eisfeld, 294
Schwimmend Getreideheber, 294
Schwimmer, 701
Schwimmfähigkeit, 107
Schwimmflächenskala, 192
Schwimmgerät, 107
Schwimmklotz, 293

Schwimmkompass, 460, 461
Schwimmkraft, 107, 294
Schwimmlicht, 450
Schwimmnetz, 244
Schwimmweste, 451
Schwingbaum, 812
Schwingbett, 179
Schwingungsperiode, 578, 890
Schwitzwasser, 810
Schwoien, 812
Schwurmakler, 813
See, 694
Seeamt, 4
Seeäuberei, 586
Seebeute, 607
Seebrief, 573
Seebrise, 694
Seefähigkeit, 699, 905
Seefahrer, 491
Seefahrzeug, 695
Seefest zurren, 434
Seefischerei, 695
Seegang, 699
Seegefahre, 199
Seegefahren, 578
Seegefahren Klausel, 578
Seegerichtsbarkeit, 4
Seegeschwindigkeit, 708
Seegras, 420
Seegrass, 699
Seegurtel, 490
Seehafen, 698
Seehahn, 694, 699
Seehandbuch, 582
Seehandel, 694
Seehandelsrecht, 506
Seehorizont, 20
Seehundfänger, 695
Seekadett, 511
Seekanal, 723
Seekarte, 529
Seekartenzeichner, 385
Seekraut, 699
Seele, 178, 365
Seeleichter, 159
Seelöse, 698
Seemann, 696
Seemannsamt Beisitzer, 725
Seemannschaft, 696
Seemannskiste, 696
Seemannskunst, 696
Seemarke, 696
Seemaschinist, 490
Seemeile, 328, 529
Seenot, 226
Seepass, 573
Seeprotest, 612

Seeraub, 586
Seeräuber, 586
Seeräuberschiff, 586
Seerauch, 698
Seeraum, 698
Seerecht, 493
Seeschaden Berechung, 29
Seeschlepper, 695
Seeschiff, 695
Seeschwankung, 701
Seestrassenordnung, 667
Seestrom, 798
Seetang, 699, 925
Seetriftige Güter, 296
Seetüchtig, 918
Seetüchtigkeit, 695, 699
Seetüchtigkeitsattest, 700
Seeufer, 303
Seeunfähigkeit, 882
Seeunfall, 493
Seeunternehmung, 489
Seeuntüchtigkeit, 882
Seeventil, 699
Seeverkehrsrecht, 506
Seevermögen, 493
Seeversicherung, 491
Seeversicherungs Police, 491
Seewärts, 699
Seewasserkasten, 805
Seewerfen, 407
Seewurf, 407
Seezeichen, 696
Seezollgebiet, 193
Segel, 673
Segel abschlagen, 879
Segelanweisungen, 675
Segelareal, 674
Segelarn, 697
Segelboden, 676
Segelducht, 675
Segelfähigkeit, 675
Segelfahrzeug, 675
Segelhaken, 675
Segelhandbuch, 582
Segelhandschuh, 676
Segelkammer, 676
Segelkarte, 852
Segelkleid, 675
Segelkoje, 676
Segelkurs, 181
Segel kürzen, 731
Segellast, 676
Segellatte, 674
Segelleiter, 862
Segel losmachen, 474
Segelmacher, 675
Segelmacherhaken, 675
Segelmacherplatte, 676

Segelmacher Splissung—Sonnensegel 1008

Segelmacher Splissung, 676
Segel mindern, 731
Segelmoment, 517, 677
Segelnadel, 677
Segeln, 673
Segel nahen, 486
Segelnaht, 696
Segeln im grössten Kreise, 337
Segeln im Parallel, 568
Segeln in der Loxodrome, 647
Segeln nach Mittelbreite, 510
Segeln nach Vergrosserter Breite, 505
Segelösen, 270
Segelschiff, 675
Segelschwerpunkt, 136
Segel setzen, 486
Segelstell, 709
Segelstellung, 594, 675
Segeltakel, 473, 677
Segel Tillen, 713
Segeltuch, 121, 675
Segeltuchfender, 122
Segeltuchputze, 122
Segelwerkstatt, 676
Sehr grobe See, 890
Sehr hohe See, 889
Seiche, 701
Seidenraum, 737
Seil, 274, 658
Seilgehäuse, 659
Seilgeschwindigkeit, 374
Seilhülsen, 659
Seil mit doppelter Schlinge, 122
Seil und Treil, 20
Seising, 325
Seismische Welle, 701
Seite an Seite, 734
Seitenbeplattung, 735
Seitenboote, 200
Seitenbunker, 734
Seitendecklinie, 207
Seitenfenster, 600
Seitenhöhe, 516
Seiten-Kielschwein, 734
Seitenkielschwein, 740
Seitenkleid, 29, 734
Seitenkluse, 521
Seitenlampen, 735
Seitenlaternen, 735
Seitenlicht, 735
Seitenliek, 445
Seitennetz des Galions, 363
Seitenpardune, 96
Seitenrechte Dicke, 736
Seitenriss, 78
Seitenruder, 543, 622

Seitenschott, 734
Seitenschweert, 444
Seitenstringer, 736
Seitenstütze, 622
Seitentakel, 499, 576
Seitentank, 736, 922
Seitenträger, 471
Seitenwind, 52
Seitlicher Deckballasttank, 847
Seitlicher Widerstand, 436
Sektiondock, 700
Sektor, 700
Sektorfeuer, 701
Selbstaussrichtendes Boot, 704
Selbstentleerendes Boot, 704
Selbstentlerender Cockpit, 704
Selbstentzündung, 767
Selbstregieren der Hafen, 28
Selbstregistrierender Hygrometer, 386
Selbstschlussventil, 795
Selbstschmierender Block, 704
Selbststeuer, 346
Selbststeuerung, 27
Selbsttätiger Feuermelder, 282
Selbsttätiger reffender Marssegel, 704
Selbsttrimmerschiff, 705
Selbstumladungsschiff, 706
Selbstzeichnender Pegel, 27
Semaphor, 706
Semaphor Flagge, 706
Semaphorsignal, 706
Senkgeschwindigkeit, 475
Senkkopf Niete, 104
Senkrechter Bug, 796
Sente, 306, 716
Sentebene, 217
Senten im Spantenriss, 218
Sentennagel, 647
Sentenriss, 111
Settie, 709
Settie Takelung, 709
Setzbord, 899
Setzeisen, 655
Setzen, 709
Setzkopf, 655
Setzöltank, 709
Setznetz, 288
Setzweger, 764
Setzwegerplatte, 764
Sextant, 710
Sextantberichtigungen, 710
Sextantenfernrohr, 711
Shuh, 837
Sich Begeben, 797
Sicherheitsfunksignal, 629
Sicherheitslampe, 289

Sicherheitsleine, 450
Sicherheitsluke, 265
Sicherheitszeugnis, 673
Sicherheitzeichen, 629
Sichtbarer Horizont, 20
Sichtbarkeit, 891
Sichtbarkeit Bogen, 22
Sichtbarkeit Skala, 891
Sichtbarkeits Kreis, 148
Sichtweitegrenze, 478
Sickeis, 748
Sideral, 735
Sideraler Ortsmittag, 466
Siderischer Monat, 735
Siebplatte, 801
Signal, 529
Signalbuch, 161
Signalbuchflagge, 161
Signalbuchstaben, 727, 736
Signalbuchwimpel, 19, 161
Signalflagge, 736
Signallampe, 522
Signalraa, 737
Signalrakete, 737
Signalstation, 737
Simpsonsche Regel, 737
Singende Schraube, 738
Sinken, 304
Sinkfleet, 807
Sirene, 740
Sisaltauwerk, 740
Sitzer, 283, 350
Skala der Wasserlinienfläche, 192
Skiff, 626, 741
Skull, 692
Skullen, 692
Skysegel, 744
Slip, 746
Sliphaken, 849, 863
Sodalösung, 806
Sog, 805, 895
Sogziffer, 896
Sohle, 228
Sohle des Schlagbettes, 754
Solarjahr, 754
Soldatengat, 477
Solsticial Kolure, 755
Solstitialpunkte, 755
Sommerferne, 20
Sommer Solstitialpunkt, 284
Sommertank, 806
Sommer Tiefladelinie, 806
Sonnenbrenner, 125
Sonnendeck, 807
Sonnennähe, 577
Sonnensäule, 807
Sonnensegel, 29

Sonnensegel Bindseln—Stampfamplitude

Sonnensegel Bindseln, 29
Sonnensegel Jackstag, 29
Sonnensegel Querlatte, 29
Sonnensegel Seite Bindseln, 29
Sonnensegel Strecktau, 648
Sonnensegelstutz, 29
Sonnensystem, 754
Sonnentag, 754
Sonnenwende, 755
Sonnenwendepunkte, 755
Sonnenzeit, 754
Sorgketten, 665
Sorgleine, 78, 666
Sorring, 702
Sorrung, 434
Spakenscheibe, 766
Spalteisen, 766
Spaltenhering, 765
Spaltungstonne, 60, 61
Spanische Winde, 759
Spannagel, 243
Spanne, 759
Spannlaschung, 760
Spannriss, 78
Spannschraube, 873
Spant, 305
Spantarealkurve, 191
Spantbieger, 104
Spantebene, 771
Spanteneinfall, 870
Spantenplan, 692
Spantenriss, 306
Spantenskala, 305
Spantentefernung, 306
Spantflächen, 305
Spantfüllstreif, 306
Spantglühofen, 56
Spant Hinterlagstück, 306
Spantholz, 306
Spantlinien, 306
Spantmallung, 306
Spantmodul, 306
Spantschmiegung, 305
Spantwinkel, 305
Spardeck, 760
Spardeckschiff, 760
Spediteur, 303, 310
Speerreep, 363
Speicherschiff, 382
Speigat, 205, 693
Speigatrohr, 693
Speiler, 763
Speiserolle, 891
Spermöl, 763
Sperreep, 363
Sperrholz, 593
Sperrnetz, 799
Spicken, 833

Spiegel, 854
Spiegelfehler, 712
Spiegelfenster, 788
Spiegelheck, 854, 855
Spiegelhölzer, 787
Spieker, 527
Spiekernagel, 94
Spier, 577
Spiere, 83, 760
Spierenbügel, 923
Spierenbügelring, 84
Spierentonne, 581, 760
Spiker, 763
Spikerbefestigung, 763
Spikerhaut, 317
Spillbeting, 129
Spillhebel, 94
Spillklampe, 915
Spillkopf, 330, 866
Spillspake, 123
Spillspur, 684
Spinnaker, 764
Spinnakerbaum, 764
Spinnekopp, 266
Spinnkopf, 187
Spitzboje, 542
Spitze, 585, 764
Spitzetonne, 173
Spitzfüllstück, 823
Spitzkauschen, 365
Spitzkopfniete, 632
Spitztonne, 542
Splint, 302, 682
Splintbolzen, 302
Splissen, 765
Splissgang, 246
Splisshorn, 765
Splisschakel, 765
Splissung, 765
Splitflagge, 109
Splitter, 145
Splitterglied, 765
Sporn, 770
Sporn Gattchen, 770
Sponung, 625
Sponung Linie, 625
Sprachrohr, 504, 761
Sprag, 161
Spreelatte, 717
Spreit, 767
Spreizgaffel, 923
Spreizgaffel Segel, 923
Spreizgaffel Takelung, 923
Spreizlatte, 187, 716
Spreizlattende Segel, 48
Spriet, 769
Sprietkluver, 769
Sprietlatte, 716

Sprietsegel, 769
Sprietstropp, 752
Spriet Takelung, 769
Springender Bug, 290
Springflut, 85, 768
Springluke, 693
Springperd, 789
Springstag, 413, 768
Springtau, 768
Springtide, 768
Springtidenhub, 768
Springwebeleine, 717
Spritzen Prahm, 282
Spritzenprobe, 380
Spritzwasser, 767
Sprotte, 767
Spruceholz, 770
Sprühregen, 245, 767
Sprung, 716, 768
Sprungkorrektur, 178
Sprungwelle, 85
Sprut, 98
Spülbecken, 689
Spülloch, 240
Spüllwassertank, 682
Spund, 123, 336
Spundung, 625
Spürzapfen, 334
Square, 770
Stakknetz, 774
Staatsdienstschiff, 613
Stabholz, 730
Stabil, 789
Stabiles Gleichgewicht, 773
Stabilität, 773
Stabilität Anschwellung, 773
Stabilitätsgrenze, 634
Stabilitätsmoment, 517, 651
Stabilitätsmomentkurve, 192
Stag, 779
Stagblock, 365
Stagen, 618
Stagfock, 302, 303
Staggarnat, 759
Stagkant, 477
Stagliek Gattchen, 779
Stagreiter, 354
Stagsegel, 779
Stagsegelschoner, 779
Stagsegeltakelung, 779
Stagtakel, 779
Stagweise, 25
Stahlbürste, 922
Stahldrahttauwerk, 922
Stählernes Rundholz, 781
Stahlguss Ketten, 131
Stammen, 347, 348
Stampfamplitude, 13

Stampfbewegung, 587
Stampfen, 587
Stampfstag, 495
Stampfstock, 231
Stampfstock Achterholer, 495
Stampfstock Geie, 495
Stand, 461
Standgeld, 58
Standigeswind, 579
Standlinie, 602
Stange, 595, 846
Stange mit eingesetztem Schlossholz, 279
Stangengeländer, 553
Stangenreeling, 553
Stangentakelung, 656
Stängenwantblock, 740
Stängeschmiere, 749
Stängetalje, 845
Stängewanten, 846
Stängewindreep, 368, 500
Stängewindreeptakel, 847
Stapel, 747
Stapelblock, 418
Stapelkeil, 4
Stapelklotz, 418
Stapellauf, 437
Stapellaufkurven, 438
Stapellauf mit Mittelschlitte, 739
Stapellauf mit Seitenschlitten, 237
Stapelung, 69, 673
Starker Sturm, 918
Starker Wind, 373
Stassnetz, 821
Station, 622, 778
Statische Stabilität, 778
Staubregen, 245
Stauchen, 883
Stauchnagel, 152
Stauen, 795, 796
Stauer, 788
Stauerbaas, 302
Stauervize, 302
Stauhols, 99
Stauholz, 250
Staukeil, 624
Staulucken, 99
Stauraum, 796
Stauung, 796
Stauungsattest, 796
Stauungsplan, 122
Stauungsschein, 796
Stauwasser, 745
Stechkahn, 616
Steckruder, 880
Steerage, 781

Steert, 30, 31, 55, 161, 819
Steertblock, 819
Steerttalje, 819, 916
Steg, 906
Stegglied, 802
Stegkette, 802
Stegschake, 802
Stehende Bake, 288
Stehender Kluvfock, 776
Stehender Part, 776
Stehender Wind, 779
Stehendes Gut, 776
Stehendes Holz, 776
Stehendes Luggersegel, 776
Stehendes Netz, 288
Stehliek, 445
Steife Brise, 801
Steifer Wind, 515
Steifheit, 674, 789
Steifheitsballast, 789
Steifhieven, 366
Steifholen, 662
Steifigkeit unter Segel, 674
Steif vertaut, 331
Steigen und fallen, 653, 819
Steigung, 586, 783
Steigungsverhältnis, 587
Steilküste, 79
Steineichenholz, 461
Steinkoralle, 481
Stek, 56, 373
Stellage, 354, 774
Stellage Stütze, 774
Stellen, 862
Stelling, 774
Stellnetz, 288, 709
St. Elmfeuer, 677
Stemmarbeiter, 118
Stemmbretter, 299
Stemmeisen, 118
Stemmkante, 118
Stemmknüppel, 118
Stemmseite, 118
Stengevorstag, 364
Sternbüchse, 786
Sternfernrohr, 777
Sterngrössen, 484
Sternjahr, 735
Stern Ortsmittag, 466
Sterntag, 25, 735
Sternzeit, 735
Sternzeit winkel, 735
Stetige Brise, 779
Steuer, 369
Steuerapparat, 782
Steuer bekommen, 278
Steuerfähigkeit, 783
Steuerfähigkeit Probe, 487

Steuerfahrt, 782
Steuerkette, 782, 914
Steuerkompass, 782
Steuerlastig, 862
Steuerlicht, 782
Steuermacht, 783
Steuermann, 369
Steuermanns Quittung, 500
Steuermaschine, 782
Steuern, 781
Steuerplicht, 783
Steurer, 621
Steuerrad, 783
Steuerreep, 915
Steuerreep Leitrolle, 621
Steuerremen, 782
Steuerruder, 782
Steuerstand, 782
Steuerstrich, 477
Steuertafel, 216
Steuertalje, 644
Steuertelegraph, 783
Steuerung, 782
Steuervorrichtung, 782
Stevenbschlag, 238
Stevenknie, 301, 784
Stevenlauf, 301
Stevenrohr, 787
Stevenrohrbüchse, 786
Stevenrohrlager, 786
Stevenrohr Längsschiene, 788
Stevenrohrmutter, 788
Stevenrohrschlussring, 788
Stevenrohr Stopfbüchse, 788
Stevenschwert, 741
Stevens Laschung, 92
Stevensohle, 729, 741, 754
Steward, 789
Stewardess, 789
Stich, 56, 152, 373
Stickleine, 661
Stille, 478
Stiller Gürtel, 231
Stillstand des Hochwassers, 372
Stillstand des Niedrigwassers, 476
Stirnradgetriebene Winde, 770
Stockanker, 790
Stocklosanker, 790
Stockunklar, 304
Stopfbüchse, 803
Stopfbuchsenschott, 6
Stopfeisen, 144
Stoppen, 375, 792
Stopper, 209, 792
Stopperknoten, 792
Stopperstek, 792

Stopphebel, 438
Stoppring, 788
Stoss, 110
Stossblech, 111
Stossblechvernietung, 111
Stosschweissung, 111
Stossen, 799
Stosskalben, 186, 295
Stosskissen, 811
Stossklampe, 160
Stosskolben, 111
Stosslappe, 497
Stosslappen, 846
Stosslappen setzen, 815
Stosslappnadel, 816
Stossmatte, 573
Stossplatte, 111
Stosstau, 658
Stossüberlappung, 260
Stossung, 111
Stossverbindung, 111
Stossvernietung, 111
Stossverstemmung, 111
Stossverteilung, 722
Stosswade, 618
Stossweger, 148
Stosswinkel, 85
Stosszapfen, 156
Strahlenbrechung, 640
Strahlverlust, 833
Strähn, 354
Strakmallung, 717
Strand, 49, 461, 797
Strandboot, 49
Stranden, 797
Strandgut, 925
Strandhafen, 247
Strandräuber, 925
Strandsfischerei, 797
Strandtriftige Güter, 407
Strandvogt, 636, 925
Strang, 354
Strasse, 797
Strebe, 445
Strecke, 799
Strecker, 410
Strecktau, 30, 450, 648, 811
Streckungsstock, 516
Streichen, 32, 799
Streichnetz, 222
Streikklausel, 799
Strickholz, 767
Stringer, 800
Stringerpla'te, 800
Stringerwinkel, 344, 800
Strippen, 709
Strom, 798
Stromabwärts, 238

Stromanker, 798
Stromankerkette, 798
Strombetätigtes Ruder, 799
Stromgerecht, 836
Stromhafen, 265
Stromkabbelung, 836
Stromkarte, 191
Stromlinienruder, 799
Stromrichtung, 709
Stromrippling, 653
Stromschnelle, 625, 836
Stromstrecke, 636
Stromstrich, 829
Strömug, 191, 798
Stromversetzung, 242
Stromwechsel, 873
Stropp, 746, 797
Stroppen, 798
Stückgüter, 561
Stückgutladung, 328
Stufenboot, 386
Stufenweg, 10
Stuhl, 791
Stumpfbolzen, 71
Stumpfer Abfass, 791
Stumpferbramstänge, 803
Stumpfermast, 803
Stumpfertopp, 803
Stumpfe Tonne, 119, 195
Stumpfschweissung, 111
Stumpfverbolzung, 249
Stundenkreis, 147, 381
Stundenwinkel, 381
Sturm, 793, 801
Sturmbahn, 795
Sturmbesahn, 793
Sturmbö, 918
Sturmdeck, 29
Sturmdeckschiff, 29
Sturmkluver, 793
Stürmischer Wind, 312
Sturmleiter, 659
Sturmpfahl, 581
Sturmsegel, 793
Sturmsignale, 793
Sturm Stagsegel, 795
Sturm Treisegel, 795
Sturmventil, 795
Sturmwarnungssignale, 793
Sturzsee, 96, 809
Stütze, 581, 730, 774, 802
Stutzen, 504
Stützenleiter, 375
Stützplatte, 93
Stützsegel, 779
Substitutionsklausel, 805
Südäquatorialstrom, 758
Südwester, 759

Südwestmonsun, 759
Suez Kanal Vermessung, 806
Süll, 157
Süllversteifungsprofil, 157
Sullwinkel, 157
Sumner's Linie, 806
Sumner Standlinie, 806
Sumpf, 806
Sund, 757
Sunnhanf, 807
Superkargo, 807
Surfboot, 809
Surringplatte, 323
Susswassermarke, 312
Synodischer Monat, 814
Systemschwerpunkt, 136
Syzgiales Hochwasser, 372
Syzygium, 814
Syzygiumgezeit, 814

Tackbolzen, 630
Tagbogen, 226
Tagebuchkladde, 208
Tagesmark, 201
Tagestank, 196
Tagliche Drehung, 227
Täglicher Gang, 196
Täglicher Gewinn, 320
Tägliches Verlier, 474
Tägliche Tidenhub, 227
Tägliche Ungleichheit, 226
Taglicke Beschleunigung, 226
Taifun, 877
Takel, 616, 817
Takelage, 650
Takel auf Takel, 817
Takelgarn, 916
Takeln, 916
Takelung, 649, 916
Takelung mit einfachen
 Knoten, 909
Takelungskette, 613
Takelungsplan, 650
Takelwerk, 650
Takler, 649
Taklerei, 650
Taklerwerkstatt, 650
Tal, 886
Talje, 817
Taljereep, 433
Taljereepgut, 433
Taljereepkauschen, 434
Taljereepknoten, 500
Taljereepsknoten, 182
Tallymann, 820
Talweg, 829
Tangentenmethode, 821

Tankdecke—Trimmluke 1012

Tankdecke, 823
Tankfahrzeug, 822
Tankkahn, 822
Tankleichter, 822
Tankmotorschiff, 523
Tankrandplatte, 489
Tankschiff, 822
Tanktop, 823
Tannenbrett, 203
T. Antenne, 815
Tartane, 824
Tasche, 32, 593
Taschenbunker, 593
Tatsächlicher Slip, 866
Tau, 658
Tauben, 447
Taucher, 227
Tauchgrenze, 489
Tauchpumpe, 804
Tauchtiefe, 516
Taufender, 613, 658
Taukappe, 733
Taukluse, 786
Taukragen, 324
Taukranz, 231, 339
Taukranzfender, 340
Taurack, 647
Tauraumende, 188, 832
Tauschleife, 189
Taustropp, 30, 659
Taustopper, 433, 653
Tauwerkrolle, 161
Taxierte Police, 774
Teil-Bodenwrange, 570
Teildock, 700
Teilkonnossement, 212
Teiltief, 700
Teilweises Sturmdeckschiff, 570
Telegraphenboje, 826
Telemotor, 826
Teleskop, 826
Teleskopartige Stänge, 827
Tender, 827
Tenderklausel, 827
Territoriale Meerenge, 828
Territorialgewässer, 828
Teufelsklaue, 230
Themsemass, 829
Thermisches Übertragung, 829
Thermitschweissung, 829
Thunfischer, 871
Tide, 835
Tidebecken, 834
Tidehafen, 835
Tidekomponent, 834
Tidekonstante, 834
Tidenfall, 835

Tidenhub, 834, 835
Tidenkurve, 489
Tidenstieg, 835
Tief, 866
Tiefe, 210, 213, 246, 374
Tiefenkarte, 47
Tiefenlinie, 276
Tiefenmelder, 804
Tiefgang, 239
Tiefgang in der Mitte, 501
Tiefgangsanzeiger, 239
Tiefgangskala, 390
Tiefgangsmarken, 239
Tiefgangsskala, 239
Tiefgansmarken, 901
Tiefladelinie, 464, 465
Tieflot, 211
Tieflotleine, 211
Tieflotungsapparat, 297
Tiefseefischerei, 547
Tieftank, 211
Tiekholz, 825
Tierkreis, 933
Tierkreislicht, 933
Tillen, 848
Tochterkompass, 644
Ton, 67
Tönen, 757
Tonnagedeck, 842
Tonnagegeld, 844
Tonne, 107
Tonnenleger, 455
Tonnenrack, 869
Tons per Zoll Eintauchungkurve, 192
Toppen, 574
Toppenant, 452
Toppenantstalje, 452
Toppflaggen, 242
Topphänger, 498
Topplampe, 780
Topplaterne, 363, 498, 780
Topplicht, 498, 780
Toppreep, 861
Toppsegel, 320
Toppsegelraa, 769
Toppsegelschoner, 847
Toppwimpel, 529
Toppzeichen, 846
Topscgel Kopfraa, 374
Topseitentank, 847
Tor, 326
Torn, 862
Tornnehmen, 820
Torschiff, 117
Totalverlust, 848
Tote Scheibe, 249
Totes Werk, 883

Totholz, 741
Totsegeln, 302, 784
Totwasser, 203, 895
Tourenyacht, 189
T-Profil, 825
Tragbar Decksbelag, 599, 602
Tragbare Laterne, 599
Tragbügel, 868
Tragen, 241
Tragender Anker, 648
Tragesack, 694
Tragfähigkeit, 108, 203
Tragfähigkeitsskala, 225
Tragfingerling, 86
Tragflugelboot, 385
Tragkraft, 108
Tragscheibe, 585
Trajektschiff, 699
Trammelnetz, 853
Trampschiff, 853
Trampschiffahrt, 853
Transit, 854
Transithafen, 854
Transitladung, 854
Transportschakel, 336
Transportschiff, 855
Trawen, 783
Treibangel Fischerei, 243
Treibanker, 694
Treibbake, 293
Treibeis, 243
Treibend, 5
Treiber, 197, 649
Treiberbaum, 410
Treibflasche, 243
Treibfleet, 813
Treibgut, 296
Treibkraftraum, 480
Treibkrafträume, 611
Treibnetz, 244
Treibnetzfischer, 370
Treibnetzfischerei, 244
Treibsand, 624, 722
Treibungswiderstand, 436
Treideln, 852
Treidler, 373
Treisegel, 762
Trennungsplatte, 219
Trensen, 925
Trensgarn, 925
Trensing, 925
Trenungsschott, 571
Treppenstütze, 784
Triefung, 907
Triftströmung, 243
Trimm, 862
Trimmen, 862
Trimmluke, 862

Trimmoment, 517
Trimmtank, 862
Trinkwassertonne, 693
Trochoide Welle, 864
Trockendock, 246
Trockendock-Abgabe, 247
Trockenfäule, 247
Trocken gefallen, 710
Trockengrating, 338
Trockenkompass, 246
Trog, 591, 860
Troglinie, 866
Trommel, 44, 498, 640
Trompetenschnecke, 915
Trompetenstich, 716
Trapezregel, 856
Trippen, 863
Trippleine, 863
Tropisches Jahr, 865
Tropisches Niedrigwasser, 865
Tropische Tide, 865
Troposphäre, 866
Trosse, 362
Trossenklemme, 537, 923
Trossenschlag Tauwerk, 362
Trossenenspillkopf, 330
Trossenstek, 362
Trossenwinde, 362, 850
Trosskauschen, 362
Trübe Sichtigkeit, 515
Trunkdeckschiff, 867
Tulle, 50
Tunnel Brunnen, 872
Tunnelkiel, 248
Tunnel Notausgang, 871
Tunnelschraube, 872
Tunnel Spant, 871
Tunnelwellenlager, 591, 768
Turbine, 872
Turbine mit Zahnradübersetzung, 326
Turboelektrischer Antrieb, 872
Türkenbund, 873
Türkischer Knopf, 873
Türkischer Knoten, 234
Turmdeck, 874
Turmdecker, 874
Turmdeckschiff, 874
T-Wulstprofil, 825
Tyfon, 877
Typhus, 877

Überall streichen, 784
Überarbeit, 559
Überbau, 808
Überbord, 558

Überbord-Ablieferung, 559
Über Bord werfen, 407
Überbrechende Seen, 558
Überdecktrager, 2
Überfahrgeld, 571
Überfahrt, 571
Überfällig, 558
Übergehung, 721
Überhang, 558
Überhängender Bug, 153
Überholen, 558
Überkopfschweissung, 559
Überlapp, 434
Überlappung, 434
Überlappungsnietung, 434
Überlauf, 300
Überliegetage, 213
Überliegezeit, 212
Überluven, 921
Übermass in Luken, 267
Übernahmekonnossement, 637
Übernahmeschein, 229
Überschmuggler, 796
Überschreiten, 96
Überschwemmung, 304
Überseeschiff, 695
Übersegler, 852
Über Staggehen, 332, 618, 816
Überweben, 335
Übung, 244
Ufer, 49, 730, 797
Uferanweisung, 160
Uferfischerei, 730
Ufer gehörig, 461
Ufer Treibgit, 461
Ufer Treibgut, 461
Ulmenholz, 258
Ultraschallwelle Echolot, 808
Umbau, 130
Um die Betingschlagen, 66
Umdrehungsanzeiger, 646
Umdrehungsfernanzeiger, 646
Umfang, 331
Umgekehrte Ruderpinne, 645
Umgeschlagenes Tauwerk, 875
Umhüllte Elektrode, 182
Umladung, 855
Umlaufen, 721
Umlaufender Wind, 32
Umschlag, 874
Umschlagarm, 883
Umschlagblech, 419
Umschlaghafen, 281
Umschlagsgebühren, 914
Umschlagspesen, 352
Umschlag Stosslappen, 816
Umsegeln, 661, 905
Umsetzen des Stromes, 140

Umspringen, 360, 721, 888
Umspringender Wind, 360
Umsteuerschraube, 646
Unbedeutliche Garantie, 390
Unbehauener Mast, 660
Unbehauenes Holz, 660
Unbehauenes Rundholz, 660
Unbemannt Feuerschiff, 453
Unbewachtes Feuer, 879
Unbezeichnete Güter, 881
Undurchsichtiger Nebel, 213, 214
Ungedeckt, 879
Ungestümes Wetter, 799
Ungeteertes Tauwerk, 918
Ungeteertes Werg, 918
Ungetrockneter Fisch, 337
Ungleichschenkeliger Winkel, 881
Unklar, 304
Unklar Anker, 304
Unklare Ketten, 304
Unmagnetisches Schiff, 539
Unrecht, 847
Unregelmässiger Fahrer, 853
Unreiner Gesundheitspass, 304
Unterbalkweger, 148
Unterbesegelt, 879
Unterbonnett, 238
Unterbrochener Gang, 243
Unterbrochene Schweissung, 397
Unterbrochenes Feuer, 397, 545
Unterbrochenes Feuer mit Gruppenunterbrechung, 340
Unterbrochenes Funkelfeuer, 397, 545
Unterdeck, 475
Unterdeck Tonnengehalt, 880
Unter den Wind bringen, 98
Untere Kulmination, 392
Unteren Meridian, 392
Unteren Meridian Durchgang, 476
Unterer Fingerling, 86
Unteres Eselshaupt, 499
Untere Toppwant, 606
Unterfeuer, 312
Untergehen, 304
Unterheckleiste, 424
Unterkoje, 475
Unterlauf, 339
Unterliek, 299
Untermarssegel, 476
Untermast, 476
Unternehmerspfandrecht, 500

Unternetzflügel—Versuchstank 1014

Unternetzflügel, 87
Unterrand, 476
Unterraum, 374, 475
Unterscheidung, 224
Unterscheidungssignal, 736
Unterschiebung, 805
Unterschied zwischen alt und neu, 535
Unterschlag der Pardunen, 32
Unterschlagen, 316
Untersee Glocke, 805
Untersegel, 181, 880
Unterströmung, 880
Unterstützen, 731
Unterstützung, 790
Untervercharterung, 803
Unterverfrachtung, 803
Unterwant, 643
Unterwanten, 476
Unterwasserschal Apparat, 251, 259
Unterwasser Schallsignal, 804
Unterwegs sein, 880
Untiefe, 290, 713
Untiefe Watt, 729
Unverrostbarer Stahl, 774
Unverschifft, 731
Unverzollte Vorräte, 81
Unverzollte Wert, 82
Unwetter, 799
Upperwall, 906
U Profil, 140
Urlaub, 96
Ursprungsattest, 137

Variable Steigung, 391
Varladungsschein, 724
V-Bodenboot, 887
Ventilatorkappe, 889
Ventilatorsockel, 889
Veränderliche Leistungspumpe, 887
Veränderliche Steigung, 887
Veränderliche Winde, 887
Verankert, 25
Verankerungsplatte, 521
Verankerungsrecht, 651
Verbandstärken, 685
Verbesserte Hafenzeit, 178
Verbessertes Besteck, 265
Verbesserte Zeit, 178
Verbindungsbrücke, 300
Verbindungschackel, 56
Verbindungsgang, 65
Verbindungsglied, 260
Verbindungskurve, 194
Verbindungsplatte, 412

Verbindungsschackel, 412
Verbolzung, 81, 276
Verbrennungsmotor, 220, 397
Verbrennungsmotor mit Zahnradgetriebe, 327
Verdampfer, 266
Verdeckung, 544
Verderbliche Ladung, 578
Verdoppellung, 459
Verdoppeln, 233
Verdrängung, 463
Verdrängungskurve, 225
Verdrängungslänge-Koeffizient, 225
Verdrängungsschwerpunkt, 136
Verdrängungsskala, 225
Verdubeln, 238
Verdunklungsglas, 391
Vereichnis der verschiften Waren, 725
Verfahren, 292
Verfolgungsrecht, 652
Verfügung von hoher Hand, 24
Verhältnis der Tidenhub, 635
Verhinderung, 314
Verhinderungsklausel, 314
Verholboje, 360, 898
Verholen, 721, 897
Verholklampe, 115, 520
Verholklampe mit Rolle, 657
Verholkluse, 521
Verholleine, 897
Verholpoller, 79, 142
Verholspill, 330
Verholspillkopf, 330
Verholtrosse, 897
Verholungskosten, 721
Verholwinde, 898
Verjüngungsplanken, 221
Verkatten, 30
Verkenrsboot, 278
Verkehrserlaubnis, 604
Verkehrsgang, 10
Verkehrskonzern, 852
Verkehrspumpe, 901
Verkehrssignal, 852
Verkettete Kausche, 881
Verkicker, 231
Verklarung, 612
Verkleidung, 566
Verkürzungstrompete, 716
Verladen, 463, 723
Verladungsanweisung, 99
Verladungskommis, 128
Verladungspapiere, 725
Verlängerungsklausel, 175
Verlaschen, 686

Verlassene Breite, 436
Verlassene Länge, 471
Verlorener Gang, 246
Verlust, 474
Verstemmen, 118
Vermessungs Breite, 842
Vermessungsdeck, 842
Vermessungsfahrzeug, 810
Vermessungs Koeffizient, 842
Vermessungslänge, 844
Vermessungsöffnung, 844
Vermessungsregel, 635
Vermessungstiefe, 641, 844
Verminderte Bemannung, 542
Vermisst, 513
Vermuren, 519, 648
Verneinungsflagge, 533
Vernier, 889
Vernieten, 655
Vernietung, 655
Veroindungsklammer, 379
Verproviantieren, 612
Verschalken, 48
Verschanzung, 105
Verschiebung, 721
Verschiffung, 724, 855
Verschiffungsdokumente, 725
Verschleiss, 905
Verschliessende Depression, 544
Verschollen, 513
Verschub, 568
Verschütten, 764
Verschwindeflucht Punkt, 886
Versender, 173
Versenkte Ankerkluse, 16
Versenkte Hütte, 807
Versenkte Niete, 104
Versenktes Back, 807
Versenktes Gut, 429
Versenktes Mannloch, 807
Versenkung, 180
Versetzbare Stütze, 599
Versicherer, 880
Versicherung, 113
Versicherungsauszug, 182
Versicherungsmakler, 395
Versicherungsschein, 395, 746
Versicherungszertifikat, 395
Verstärkungsband, 459
Verstärkungswinkel, 789
Verstauen, 862
Versteifungsprofil, 789
Versteifungsseite, 660, 789
Verstellbarer Flügel, 3
Verstellpropeller, 3
Verstopfen, 144
Versuchstank, 514, 861

Vertauboje, 115, 867
Vertauchbare Liegetage, 646
Vertauen, 519
Vertaukluse, 521
Vertauleine, 341
Vertauschackel, 522
Vertauschenkel, 521
Vertauschraube, 521
Vertauung, 518
Vertauung Schackel, 411
Vertauungsgebühren, 519
Vertauungspfahl, 521
Vertauwirbel, 813
Verteilte Rauchfangführung, 227
Vertiefung, 241
Vertikal, 147
Vertikale Eisenmassen, 889
Vertikale Formschwerpunktkurve, 192
Vertikale Schweissung, 889
Vertikalkreis, 889
Ventilationsfenster, 600
Vertragshafen, 860
Vertragspfandrecht, 175
Vertretergebühren, 7
Verwendungszwecknummer, 185
Verwickeln, 304
Very Kunstfeuersignal, 890
Verzapfen, 238
Verzapfter Block, 522
Verzierung, 330
Verzierungsleiste, 516
Verzinkung, 322
Verzögerung, 386, 645
Viehstand, 462
Viehtransportschiff, 134
Viehtreiber, 133
Viehverschläge, 133
Viehwärter, 133
Vier arm Vertauboje, 305
Viereckige Platting, 771
Vierkant, 378, 770
Vierkant Brassen, 771
Vierkantig behauenes Holz, 734
Vierkanttoppsegel, 232
Vierkant Vertauung, 10
Vierläufer, 877
Viermastbarke, 723
Vierscheibiger Block, 305
Vierscheibiger Gien, 305
Viertelkompasstrich, 622
Viertelstrich Kompassrose, 622
Vierung, 620

Vietelkreisartige Deviation, 619
Violinblock, 473, 830
Violinen, 53
Virginisches Cedernholz, 417
Visier, 736
Visitationsrecht, 652
Visite, 892
Visitieren, 698
Volkreisteilung Kompassrose, 831
Voll, 314
Vollaufen, 810
Vollbrassen, 280
Volldecker, 315
Volldeckschiff, 315
Volle Bodenwrange, 755
Volle Fracht, 315
Volle Kehlnaht, 315
Volle Kehlschweissung, 315
Volle Ladung, 314
Voller Bug, 79
Volles Rundholz, 755
Vollgetakeltes Schiff, 315
Vollhering, 315
Völligkeitsgrad der Konstruktionswasserlinie, 901
Völligkeitsgrad der Spantflachenskala, 471
Völligkeitsgrad der Verdrängung, 69
Völligkeitsgrad des Hauptspant, 511
Vollmatrose, 2
Vollschiff, 315
Vollstauung der Deckbalken, 50
Voll und Bei, 314
Vom Land entfernt, 547
Vom Nebelgehindert, 298
Von widrigen Winden aufgehalten, 919
Vor Anker biegend, 25
Vor Anker gehen, 17
Vor Anker liegen, 648
Vor Anker reiten, 648
Vor Anker treiben, 239
Voraus, 7, 303
Vor-Bramstagsegel, 297
Vor dem Mast, 54
Vor dem Wind halsen, 905
Vor dem Wind segeln, 668
Vor den Krahn Fieren, 160
Vorderboot, 302
Vordere Dwarsfeste, 303
Vordere Plankenenden, 301
Vorderer Perpendikel, 303
Vorderes Lot, 303

Vordere Verholleine, 90
Vorderfläche, 30, 240
Vorderlicher als dwars, 54
Vorderliek, 499
Vorderschiff, 303
Vordersteven, 45, 783
Vorderteil, 363
Voreilung, 441
Vorfach, 752
Vorgebirge, 122
Vorhafen, 556
Vorhalter, 375, 655
Vorhelling, 904
Vorherrschender Wind, 605
Vorkaufsrecht, 605
Vorland, 303
Vorlastig, 112
Vorlauf, 323, 339, 556, 798
Vorläufer, 301, 302, 813
Vorlaüfige Reparaturen, 827
Vorlauf Merkzeichen, 798
Vorliek, 477
Vormast, 302
Vormittagswache, 302
Vorn, 300
Vorpiek, 302
Vorratskammer, 793
Vorratsraum, 793
Vorrichtung, 327
Vorschiff, 270
Vorschiff Bausektion, 88
Vor schleppenden Anker treiben, 156
Vorschoten, 717
Vorschriftmässig Abteilung, 168
Vorschussanweisung, 5
Vorsegel, 364
Vor-Stangestagsegel, 303
Vorsteven, 45, 783
Vorstevenplatte, 784
Vorstevenschiene, 784
Vortopp, 365
Vor Top und Takel, 8
Vor und Achter Schoner, 687
Vorwärtsdrehen, 360
Vorwärtsdringen, 784
Vorwärts Reiche, 7
V-Schweissung, 739

Waage Verhältnis, 35
Wache, 899
Wache in See, 900
Wache um Wache, 899
Wachhabender Maschinist, 25
Wachhabender Offizer, 900
Wachholderholz, 820

Wachoffizier, 900
Wachsende Steigung, 391
Wachttafel, 467
Wade, 701
Wadenetz, 49
Wadenfischer, 701
Wadenfischerei, 701
Wagenkipp, 840
Wagerung, 400
Wahre Höhe, 866
Wahrer Horizont, 635
Wahrer Ort, 866
Wahrer Wind, 866
Wahres Besteck, 866
Wahre Zeit, 866
Walboot, 911
Walfangboot, 911
Walfischbein, 911
Walfischfang, 913
Walfischfänger, 911
Walfischleine, 911
Walfischspeck, 71
Wallschiene, 663
Wolölschiff, 912
Walrat, 763
Walratöl, 763
Walreuse, 603
Walrückendeck, 875
Walverarbeitungsschiff, 912
Walzblechhintersteven, 271
Walzblechvorsteven, 26
Walzzunders, 511
Wandnetz, 330
Want, 733
Wanten nachweben, 771
Wantklampe, 650
Wantklotje, 733
Wantknoten, 733
Wantschlag-Tauwerk, 733
Wantschraube, 873
Wantstopper, 897
Wantstropp, 706
Wanttau, 733
Waren Lagerschein, 230
Warenschein, 230
Warnungsboje, 198
Warnungsfeuer, 897
Warnungsschuss, 392
Warnungssignal, 134
Warnungszeichen, 891
Warpanker, 418
Warpbalken, 854
Warpen, 418, 897
Warpklampe, 134
Warptrosse, 897
Waschbord, 487, 899
Waschbrett, 905
Waschschott, 487

Wasserablassloch, 74, 240
Wasserballast, 900
Wasserboard, 905
Wasserboot, 900
Wasserdicht, 902
Wasserdichte Bodenwrange, 902
Wasserdichte Klapptür, 373
Wasserdichte Luke, 902
Wasserdichte Nietung, 902
Wasserdichte Plattform, 902
Wasserdichter Spant, 902
Wasserdichtes Deck, 902
Wasserdichtes Schott, 902
Wasserdichte Tür, 902
Wasserdichte Unterteilung, 803
Wasserfahrzeug, 900
Wasserfass, 693
Wasserflocken, 767
Wassergang, 144, 903
Wassergangsfarbe, 85
Wasser halten, 375
Wasserhimmel, 901
Wasserhose, 901
Wasserkieker, 902
Wasserlauf, 457, 903
Wasserlaufloch, 240, 457
Wasserlaufswinkel, 904
Wasserlicht, 294, 450
Wasserlinielänge, 901
Wasserlinienriss, 348
Wasserlinienvölligkeitsgrad, 901
Wasserpassriss, 348
Wasserpforte, 308
Wasserprahme, 900
Wasserprobe, 386
Wasserrohrkessel, 903
Wassersegel, 901
Wasserstag, 77
Wasserstand, 696, 775
Wasserverdrängung, 224
Wasserwirbel, 916
Waterclerk, 72
Watt, 289
Watte, 291
Webeleine, 635
Webeleingut, 635
Webeleinsteck, 155
Webeleinstek, 901
Wechselfeuer, 11
Wechselfeuer mit Blinken, 10
Wechselfeuer mit Gruppblinken, 10
Wechselfeuer mit Gruppen, 340

Wechselseitige Versicherung, 526
Wechselstromerzeuger, 555
Wechselventilkasten, 226
Wegegeld, 841
Wegerechte Schiebetür, 378
Wegerechtschiff, 607
Wegerung, 134
Wegerungshalter, 374
Wegerungslatte, 125
Wegerungslatten, 760
Wegerungsluke, 134
Wegfieren, 744
Wegsinken, 304
Wegstauen, 796
Wegweiserbrett, 273
Wegweiser Klotje, 273
Wegweiserleine, 770
Wehen lassen, 881
Weiberknoten, 747
Weichen, 331
Weichholz, 753
Weise, 341
Weisse Bö, 918
Weisseichenholz, 918
Weisses Tauwerk, 918
Weitstehende Stütze, 918
Well, 908
Welldeck, 909
Welldeckschiff, 909
Welle, 904
Wellenbock, 713, 762, 801
Wellenbrecher, 96
Wellengefälle, 904
Wellengeschwindigkeit, 904
Wellenhose, 718
Wellenklotz, 713
Wellenlänge, 904
Wellenlinie, 904
Wellenöl, 793
Wellenperiode, 904
Wellenpferdestärke, 713
Wellenschlag, 899
Wellenschwingungsweite, 904
Wellental, 866, 904
Wellenträger, 801
Wellentunnel, 712
Wellentunnel Nische, 803
Wellenumlauf, 904
Wellenwiderstand, 904
Weltpol, 135
Wendebecken, 874
Wendekreis, 865
Wenden, 130, 332, 779
Wendepunkte des Krebses, 284
Wendepunkte des Steinbocks, 284
Wendung versagen, 513

Werfen, 365, 798
Werg, 543
Wergfass, 118
Wergzopf, 591
Werpen, 360
Wert Fracht, 5
Wertklausel, 886
Wertladung, 604
Wertzolle, 5
Wetter, 905
Wetter Anzeigesignal, 906
Wetterdeck, 905
Wetterdichtes Deck, 906
Wetterdichte Tür, 906
Wetterkunde, 509
Wetterleuchten, 718
Wettersignal Flagge, 905
Wetterskala, 906
Wettpolice, 895
Weymouthskiefer, 918
Widderpunkt, 889
Widerrufsdatum, 119
Widerrufsflagge, 637
Widersee, 880
Widerstandkurve, 191
Widerstandmodul, 515
Widerstandsschweissung, 645
Wiederholungsflagge, 644, 805
Wiedernahme, 637
Wiege, 437
Wiegegebühren, 908
Wiegegeld, 908
Wiegekosten, 908
Wientakel, 236
Wikinger Heck, 121
Wild, 918
Wildlotse, 373
Wimpel, 577
Wind, 919
Windbaum, 489
Winddruckmoment, 677
Winde, 182, 919
Winde mit Umschaltgetrieb, 645
Windenlaüfer, 128
Windenmann, 919
Windfahne, 886
Windfänger, 919
Windgerecht, 921
Windgesetze, 439
Windjammer, 919
Windmesser, 17
Windreepblock, 845
Windrose, 169, 921
Windsack, 921
Windsauger, 267
Windschutz, 719
Windstille, 119

Windstoss, 344
Windstrick, 647
Windvierung, 906
Windvierungsgalerien, 621
Windwärts, 849
Winkel, 18
Winkelbulb, 103
Winkeleisen, 18
Winkelkragen, 18, 777
Winkelkropf, 18
Winkellasche, 85
Winkellaschenprofl, 31
Winkelprofil, 18
Winkelstellung, 741
Winkflagge, 350
Winter solstitialpunkt, 284
Wintersonnenwende, 284
Wippe, 915
Wippen, 916
Wirbel, 812
Wirbelhaken, 813
Wirbelstück, 813
Wirbelsturm, 647, 847
Wirbelwiderstand, 896
Wirbelwind, 916
Wirkung des Steuers, 782
Wittling Schnur, 918
Woge, 809
Wogen, 809
Wohnraum, 2
Wohnräume für Fahrgäste, 572
Wohnschiff, 381
Wölbung, 182, 656
Wolke, 155
Wolkenlos, 155
Wolkenloser Himmel, 151
Wölken Skala, 155
Wracker, 925
Wrackgut, 214, 429
Wracktonne, 925
Wracktrümmer, 925
Wrackung, 626
Wreifholz, 760
Wricken, 693
Wrickriem, 692
Wrieckriem, 649
Wriggruder, 692
Wuhling, 661, 924
Wuhlingsgat, 323
Wuhlings Verschalung, 323
Wulstbug, 103
Wulst-Cumulus, 798
Wulstkiel, 103, 281
Wulstplatte, 103
Wulstwinkel, 103
Wurfanker, 418
Wurfgarn, 131

Wurfleine, 360
Wurfnetz, 131
Wurmstichig, 246
Wyk, 184

"X" Schweissung, 236

Yacht, 928
Yachttuch, 179
Yawl, 930

Zahlensignale, 542
Zahlleute, 820
Zahlmeister, 617
Zahnrad Gangspill, 327
Zahnradgetrieb, 327
Zahnstangengetriebener Steuerapparat, 626
Zange, 560
Zapfen, 598, 827
Zapfenlaschung, 156
Zeichen, 771
Zeigeplatte, 428
Zeigerarm, 391
Zenit, 932
Zenitdistanz, 932
Zeise, 49
Zeisen, 537
Zeising, 702
Zeisingtau, 540
Zeitazimut, 838
Zeitball, 838
Zeitbeobachtung, 839
Zeitcharter, 838
Zeitfracht, 838
Zeitgleichung, 263
Zeitsignal, 839
Zeit und Reise Police, 514
Zeitverlust Klausel, 839
Zeitversicherungspolice, 839
Zeitweilige Raparaturen, 827
Zeitwinkel, 381, 465
Zeitzone, 840
Zellartiger Doppelboden, 135
Zelt, 29
Zementmilch, 135
Zerbrechung, 95
Zerbrochene Gangreling, 244
Zerhacktes Tauwerk, 413
Zersägtes Holz, 176
Zeug, 649
Zickzachschweissung, 774
Zickzacknietung, 932
Zickzack Unterbrochene Schweissung, 774

Ziehen—Zylinderzapfen 1018

Ziehen, 241, 360
Ziehende Segeln, 588
Zimmermann's Maat, 129
Zirkummeridianhöhe, 268
Zirkumpolar, 148
Zodiakus, 933
Zoll, 193
Zollager, 82
Zollauslieferschein, 82, 193
Zollbeamten Untersuchung, 407
Zollbeamter, 193
Zollbegleitschein, 82
Zollbehörde, 192
Zollbürgschein, 193
Zolldeklarant, 193
Zolldeklaration, 64, 263
Zolleinfuhrschein, 64
Zollerlaubnisschein, 64
Zollfreischein, 725
Zollmakler, 193
Zollspeicher, 82
Zollvergütung, 241
Zonenzeit, 775, 933
Z-profil, 932
Zu Anker gehen, 17
Zuerkennungshafen, 600
Zufall der See, 493
Zufluchtshafen, 355
Zugbolzen, 709
Zugwade, 49
Zuhalten, 52
Zulässige Länge, 579
Zu leicht bemastet, 880

Zu leicht getakelt, 879
Zum kentern liegen, 50
Zum Treiben liegen, 448
Zunehmen, 184
Zunehmender Mond, 904
Zungenpfeifen Nebelhorn, 638
Zurichten, 272
Zurrbaum, 76
Zurrbroken, 76
Zurren, 702
Zurrung, 434
Zurückbrassen, 92
Zurückdrehen, 896
Zurückfahren, 618
Zurückgestellter Rabatt, 211
Zurückschlagen, 30
Zusammengesetzter Block, 102
Zusammenstoss, 164
Zusammenzeisen, 307
Zusammenzufügende Fläche, 277
Zuschärfung, 263
Zuschärfungslänge, 446
Zuschärfungswinkel, 18
Zuschlaggebühr, 809
Zusteuern, 52
Zu weit geführte Ladung, 558
Zwang durch Fürsten, 645
Zwängen, 768
Zwanglaufkessel, 300
Zwangslotse, 172
Zweibeinmast, 66, 716

Zweienderkessel, 235
Zweifelhafter Gesundheitspass, 810
Zweiklangpfeife, 144
Zweiplatterruder, 735
Zweischeibiger Block, 234
Zweiter Kluver, 556
Zweiter Maschinenassistent, 700
Zweite Wache, 510
Zweitoppsegelschoner, 486
Zwingbolzen, 926
Zwinger, 926
Zwischendeck, 781, 875
Zwischendeckbunker, 875
Zwischendeckpassagier, 782
Zwischendeckstopper, 172
Zwischendeckvermessung, 875
Zwischenhafen, 396, 600
Zwischenkardinal Strich, 396
Zwischenplatte, 396
Zwischenplatten Kielschwein, 396
Zwischenspant, 396
Zwischen Wind und Wasser, 29
Zwischen Wing und Wasser, 59
Zyklon, 195
Zylinder, 246
Zylinderkessel, 283
Zylinderkoeffizient, 471
Zylinderzapfen, 156, 238